THE EMC MASTERPIECE SERIES

Literature and the Language Arts

GRADES 6–12

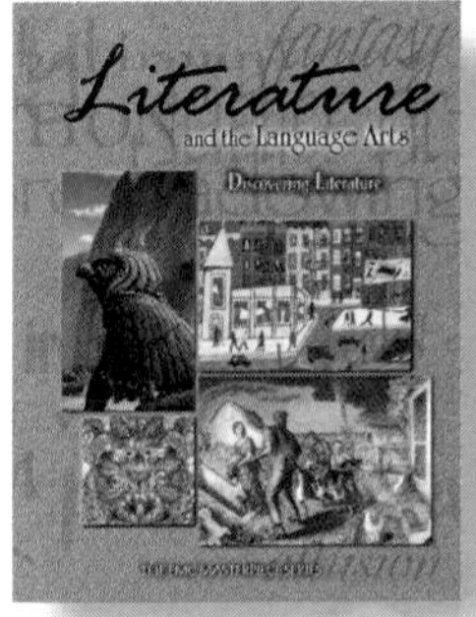

Discovering Literature
Grade 6

Exploring Literature
Grade 7

Responding to Literature
Grade 8

Experiencing Literature
Grade 9

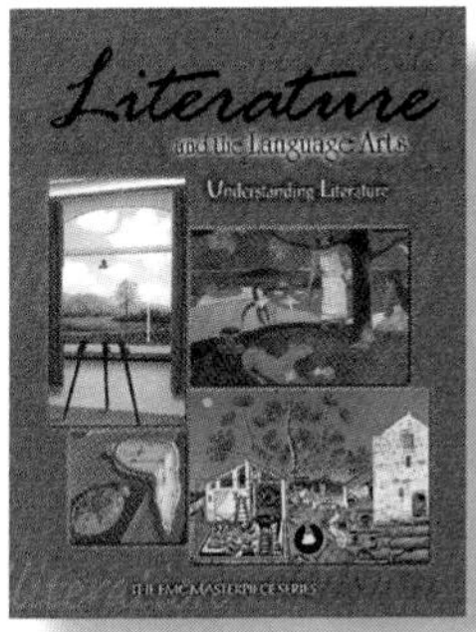

Understanding Literature
Grade 10

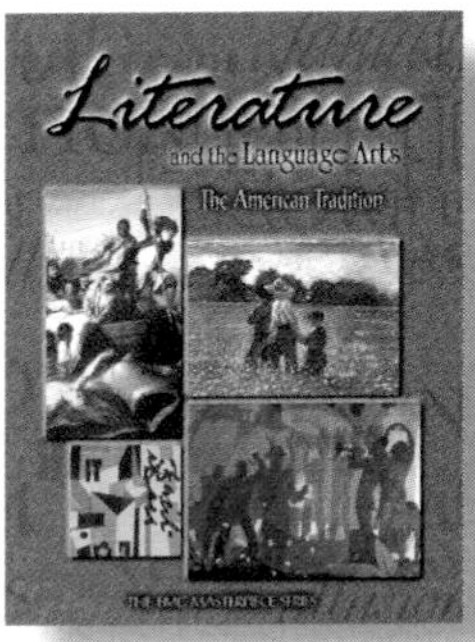

The American Tradition
Grade 11

The British Tradition
Grade 12

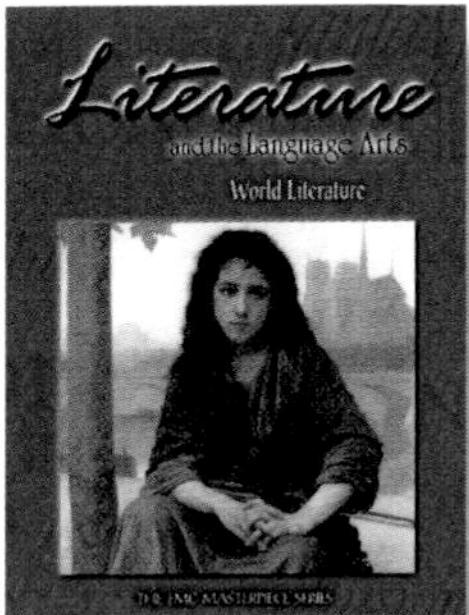

World Literature

Imagine the Possibilities...

FEATURES

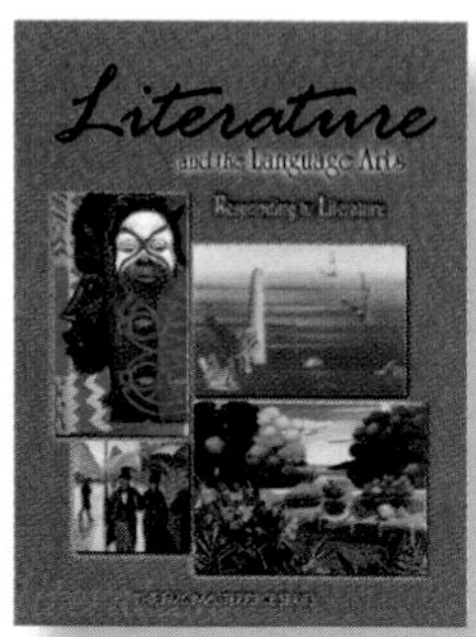

Literature
and the Language Arts

GRADES 6–12

Why Choose *The EMC Masterpiece Series*?

1. Quality of literature
2. Diversity of literature selections
3. Reading strategies that provide access for all students
4. Direct writing instruction integrated with grammar development
5. In-depth coverage of language arts skills
6. Comprehensive support materials

WORLD LITERATURE, 1st Edition

Copyright 2001

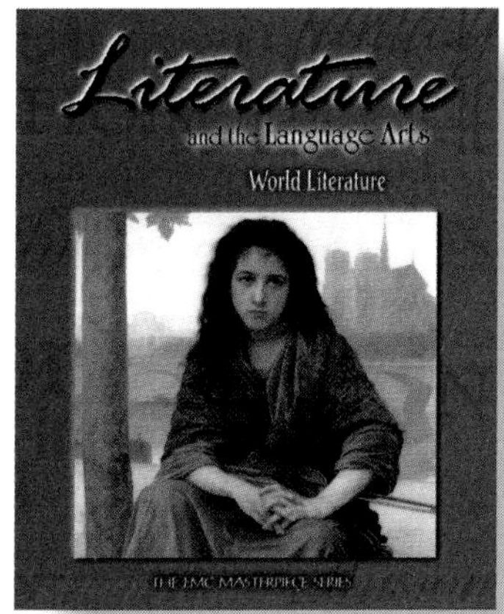

Designed to provide immediate access to diverse cultures across time and space, World Literature begins with a geographical tour hosted by students from around the world, providing insights into what it's like to live in another part of the world. The text, organized thematically, chronologically, and geographically, allows teachers to teach the way that will work best for their students.
No other series offers this approach.

WORLD LITERATURE

- Makes great literature accessible to **every** student while integrating the full range of language arts skills, eliminating the need for a separate grammar text.
- Contains a comprehensive collection of **classic literary works**, as well as compelling **contemporary and multicultural selections**.
- Emphasizes **reader response**, relating literature to student experiences while enabling the teacher to guide responses to ensure cultural transmission.
- Includes activities and projects for engaging the **multiple intelligences** and **teaching across the curriculum**.
- Contains an unequalled representation of works by **authors from various cultural backgrounds** and provides a well-rounded view of literary activity in cultural contexts from around the corner and around the world.

EXTENSIVE SUPPLEMENTARY COMPONENTS:

Annotated Teacher's Edition includes:

- Practical advice and strategies for reader-response and portfolio-based language arts instruction.
- Sample lesson cycles.
- Information on thematic and genre approaches.
- Additional resources for language arts teachers.

Annotated Teacher's Edition is available on CD-ROM for easy access to the selections.

Program Manager provides clear, simple, ready-to-use lesson plans and thorough scope and sequence charts. It offers a variety of approaches and scheduling options (including block scheduling) tailored to your classroom needs.

Teacher's Resource Kit includes:

- Program Manager
- Assessment Portfolio
- Transparency Set
- Parent and Community Involvement Handbook
- Reader's Guide and Activity Workbook
- Essential Skills Practice Books in the five language arts subject areas

Motivational multimedia components available:

- Audio Library
- Idea Generator
- Test Generator
- Electronic Library on CD-ROM
- Annotated Teacher's Edition on CD-ROM

Unique additional supplementary components:

- Easy Classics novels
- Encounters novels
- Access Edition novels and plays

World Literature

- **About the Author** gives background information on the author of the selection.
- **Reader's Journal** activities relate the literature to students' feelings and experiences.
- **About the Selection** provides a background of when and why the selection was written.
- **Connections** tie each literary work to a broader historical or thematic context to help students understand the literature they are about to read.
- **Words for Everyday Use** provide the definitions for vocabulary that is underlined in the selection.
- **Footnotes** are separated from vocabulary to provide information necessary to understand the selection.
- **Guided Reading Questions** for each selection point out key elements and encourage critical-response reading.

- In **Global Voices: A Multicultural Conversation**, international students discuss how issues such as intolerance, love, death, the environment, and cultural change are addressed in their culture.

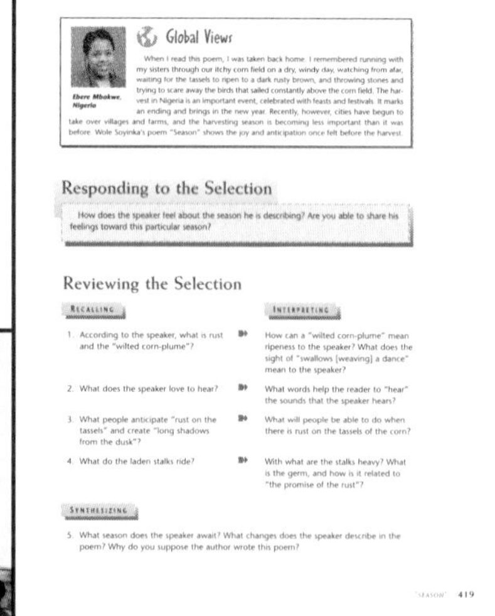

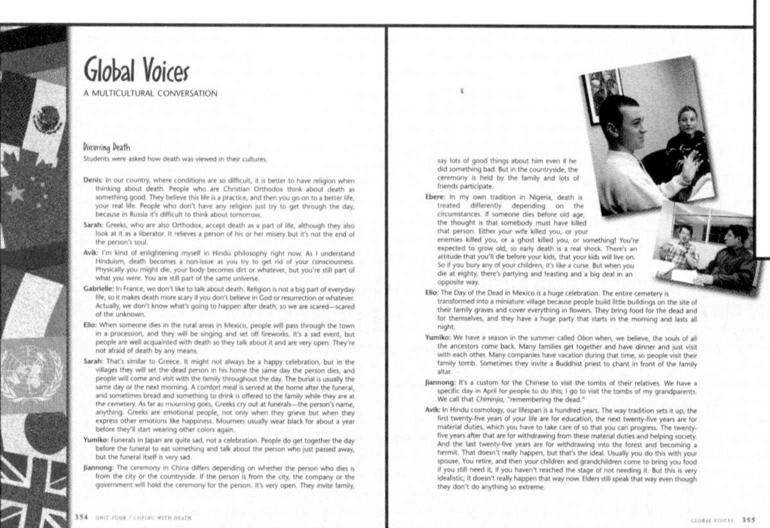

- In **Global Views**, international students respond to literature from their countries, revealing the impact it has made on them and their peers, giving your students insights into different cultures and a deeper understanding of the selection.

Introducing *The EMC Masterpiece Series*
High School Program, 2nd Edition
Copyright 2001

Six Reasons to Choose *The EMC Masterpiece Series*

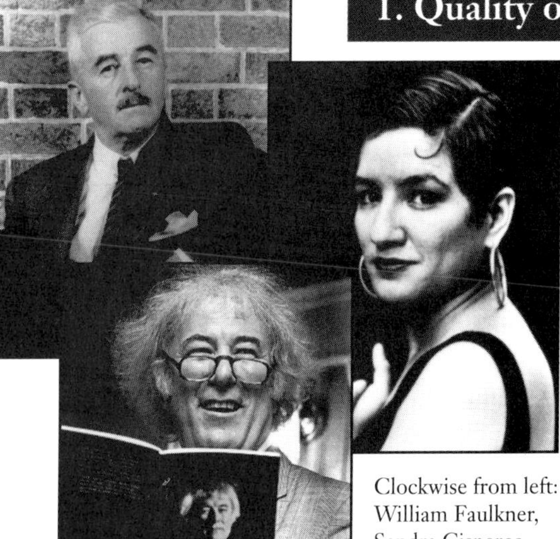

Clockwise from left: William Faulkner, Sandra Cisneros, Seamus Heaney

1. Quality of Literature

The EMC Masterpiece Series:

- Provides you and your students with **a comprehensive collection of classic literary works** as well as compelling **contemporary and multicultural selections**.

Award-Winning Authors:

- William Faulkner, "Darl" from *As I Lay Dying*
- Seamus Heaney, "Follower"
- Sandra Cisneros, "A Smart Cookie"
- Doris Lessing, "A Sunrise on the Veld"
- Eudora Welty, "A Worn Path"
- Gabriel Garcia Marquez, "A Very Old Man with Enormous Wings"

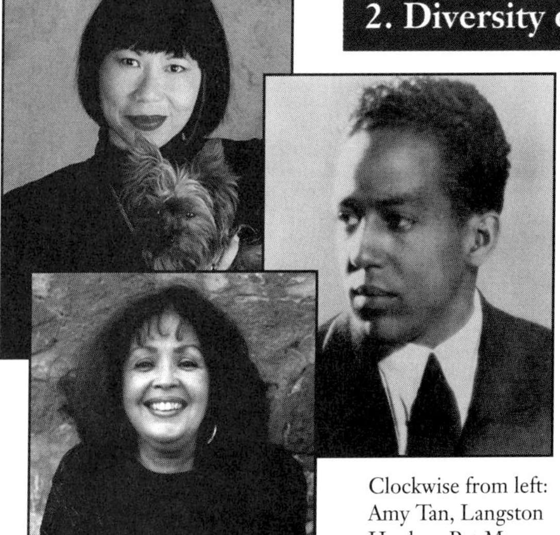

Clockwise from left: Amy Tan, Langston Hughes, Pat Mora

2. Diversity of Literature Selections

- **Expands students' imaginative abilities and sympathies** by exposing them to points of view and cultural experiences unlike their own.
- Provides selections representative of the **cultural and ethnic diversity** of our literary heritage.
- Contains an unequaled representation of works by **authors from various cultural backgrounds.**

Diversity of Literature:

- Pat Mora, "Gentle Communion"
- Langston Hughes, "Thank You, M'am"
- Amy Tan, "Rules of the Game"
- Garrett Hongo, "The Legend"
- Julia Alvarez, "A White Woman of Color"
- Li-Young Lee, "A Story"

3. Reading Strategies Provide Access for All Students

The EMC Masterpiece Series:

- Provides step-by-step study strategies to ensure the careful development of student understanding.
- Features a **reader response** emphasis that motivates students through high-interest affective and cognitive activities to relate literature to students' experiences, followed by teacher-directed activities to ensure cultural transmission.

The EMC Masterpiece Series helps students before, during, and after their reading of the selection with its **Guided Reading** program.

Before Reading

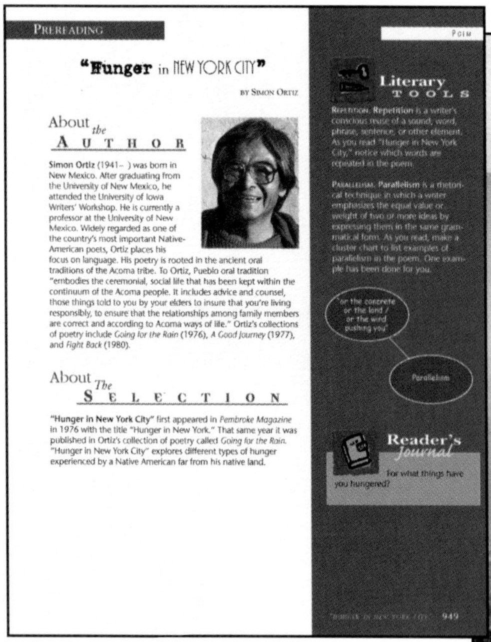

During Reading

- **About the Author** provides contextual information about the author's life and the period in which he or she lived.
- **About the Selection** provides keys to comprehension of the selection; this covers literary movements, genres, techniques, or themes, depending upon the demands of the selection and its place in literary history.
- **Literary Tools** introduces literary techniques or concepts that will help the reader under-stand the selection. The same concepts are reinforced in the Understanding Literature section of the Post-Reading materials.
- A **Graphic Organizer** or other visual literacy piece is provided for visual learners.
- **Reader's Journal** activities help create the anticipatory set by relating the literature to students' experiences.
- **Guided Reading Questions** help students gather facts about the selection that will help in their response to higher-level thinking skills.
- **Words for Everyday Use** provide pronunciations, parts of speech, definitions, and contextual sentences for vocabulary underlined in the selection.
- **Footnotes** explain obscure references, unusual usage, and terms meant to enter students' passive vocabularies.
- **Art Notes** provide historical, cultural, or artistic information about fine art.

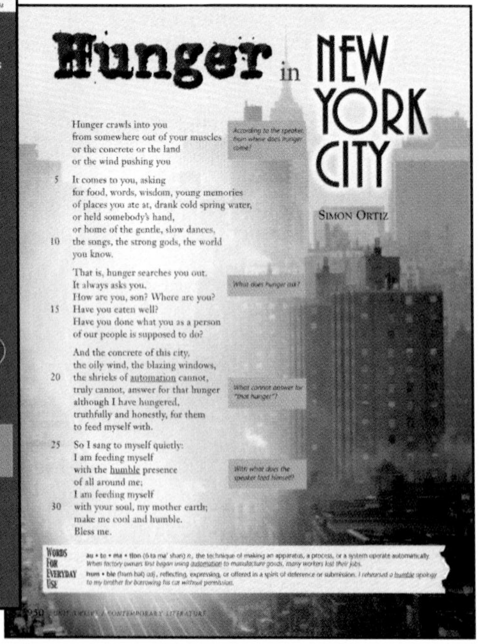

- **Respond to the Selection** activities relate the literature to students' lives.
- **Investigate, Inquire, and Imagine** questions base literature interpretation on textual evidence.
    - **Recall** questions address comprehension. **Interpret** questions use facts from the Recall question as a basis for valid interpretation.
    - **Analyze** questions ask readers to classify, compare and contrast, and identify relationships between ideas. **Synthesize** questions ask readers to integrate, restructure, predict, elaborate, and summarize.
    - **Evaluate** questions ask students to appraise, assess, critique, and justify certain aspects of a selection. **Extend** questions allow readers to try out their understanding in different situations.
    - **Perspective** questions encourage students to look for and value alternative perspectives. **Empathy** questions ask the student to demonstrate understanding of another person's worldview.
- **Understanding Literature** questions reinforce the literary concepts and techniques that were introduced on the Prereading page in the Literary Tools feature.
- **Writer's Journal** includes three quick-writing prompts that are graded as simple, moderate, and challenging.

After Reading

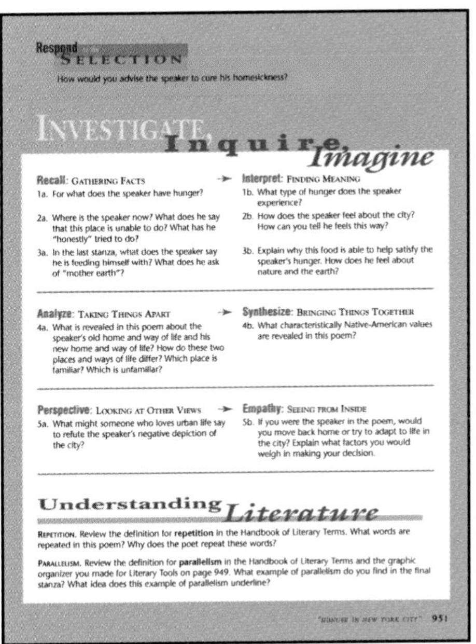

Respond to the Selection

How would you advise the speaker to cure his homesickness?

INVESTIGATE, Inquire, Imagine

Recall: Gathering Facts → **Interpret**: Finding Meaning

1a. For what does the speaker have hunger?
1b. What type of hunger does the speaker experience?

2a. Where is the speaker now? What does he say that this place is unable to do? What has he "honestly" tried to do?
2b. How does the speaker feel about the city? How can you tell he feels this way?

3a. In the last stanza, what does the speaker say he is feeding himself with? What does he ask of "mother earth"?
3b. Explain why this food is able to help satisfy the speaker's hunger. How does he feel about nature and the earth?

Analyze: Taking Things Apart → **Synthesize**: Bringing Things Together

4a. What is revealed in this poem about the speaker's old home and way of life and his new home and way of life? How do these two places and ways of life differ? Which place is familiar? Which is unfamillar?
4b. What characteristically Native-American values are revealed in this poem?

Perspective: Looking at Other Views → **Empathy**: Seeing from Inside

5a. What might someone who loves urban life say to refute the speaker's negative depiction of the city?
5b. If you were the speaker in the poem, would you move back home or try to adapt to life in the city? Explain what factors you would weigh in making your decision.

Understanding Literature

Repetition. Review the definition for **repetition** in the Handbook of Literary Terms. What words are repeated in this poem? Why does the poet repeat these words?

Parallelism. Review the definition for **parallelism** in the Handbook of Literary Terms and the graphic organizer you made for Literary Tools on page 949. What example of parallelism do you find in the final stanza? What idea does this example of parallelism underline?

951

- **Integrating the Language Arts** provides integrated activities in the following language arts areas, tying language arts instruction to the literature selection:
    - Language, Grammar, and Style
    - Speaking and Listening
    - Study and Research
    - Applied English
    - Collaborative Learning
    - Media Literacy
    - Vocabulary Development
    - Critical Thinking

4. Direct Writing Instruction Integrated with Grammar Development

The **Guided Writing Program** provides direct writing instruction for each literature unit and pairs the writing process with an **Integrated Language, Grammar, and Style** lesson. The Guided Writing lesson includes professional and student models, graphic organizers, questions that allow students to link their reading experience to the writing assignment, and an integrated grammar lesson. Additional support is provided by:

Writing Resource. This ancillary provides general and mode-specific writing rubrics, student-friendly checklists, student models for each assignment, graphic organizers, and student handouts.

EMC Masterpiece Writing: Guided Writing Interactive Software. The software provides extended lessons that deliver print content and extensions electronically.

5. In-Depth Coverage of Language Arts Skills

Language Arts Survey

The **Language Arts Survey** in *The EMC Masterpiece Series* has the most extensive language arts skills coverage of any program. The coverage of English skills is so comprehensive that an additional English skills textbook is not necessary. The Language Arts Survey sections may be taught as separate units, using the student textbook and ancillary worksheets, or may be taught in conjunction with study of the literature.

Language Arts Survey: Writing

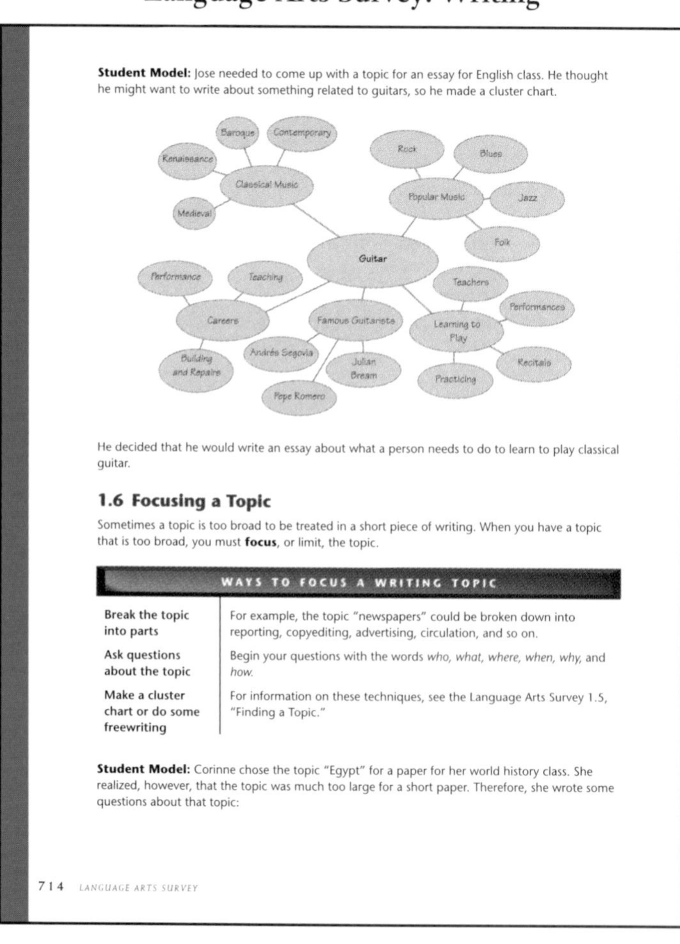

Student Model: Jose needed to come up with a topic for an essay for English class. He thought he might want to write about something related to guitars, so he made a cluster chart.

He decided that he would write an essay about what a person needs to do to learn to play classical guitar.

1.6 Focusing a Topic

Sometimes a topic is too broad to be treated in a short piece of writing. When you have a topic that is too broad, you must **focus**, or limit, the topic.

WAYS TO FOCUS A WRITING TOPIC	
Break the topic into parts	For example, the topic "newspapers" could be broken down into reporting, copyediting, advertising, circulation, and so on.
Ask questions about the topic	Begin your questions with the words *who, what, where, when, why,* and *how.*
Make a cluster chart or do some freewriting	For information on these techniques, see the Language Arts Survey 1.5, "Finding a Topic."

Student Model: Corinne chose the topic "Egypt" for a paper for her world history class. She realized, however, that the topic was much too large for a short paper. Therefore, she wrote some questions about that topic:

714 LANGUAGE ARTS SURVEY

There are six sections in the Language Arts Survey:

1. The **Reading Resource** surveys and enhances the reading process.
2. The **Writing Resource** surveys the entire process of writing. It includes computer-assisted composition and portfolio writing.
3. The **Language, Grammar, and Style Resource** surveys key concepts in grammar, usage, mechanics, spelling, vocabulary development, and language variety. Grammar, usage, and mechanics instruction focuses on editing and proofreading applications.
4. The **Speaking and Listening Resource** surveys verbal and nonverbal communication, active listening, interpersonal communication, discussion, public speaking, and oral interpretation.
5. The **Study and Research Resource** surveys thinking, reading, research, and test-taking skills, including skills for taking standardized tests.
6. The **Applied English Resource** surveys applications of English skills to the world of work.

6. Comprehensive Support Materials

Literature and the Language Arts

HIGH SCHOOL PROGRAM

Supplementary and Multimedia Components
The EMC Masterpiece Series provides a wide array of ancillary tools to offer teachers many options to help students connect with the literature.

Each level in the high school program includes the following materials:

- Pupil's Edition with Language Arts Survey
- Annotated Teacher's Edition
- Annotated Teacher's Edition on CD-ROM (with links to Language Arts Survey and ancillaries)
- Teacher's Resource Kit
  - Program Manager with Scope and Sequence / Lesson Planning Guide
  - Parent and Community Involvement Handbook
  - 12 Unit Resource Books
    - Reading Resource (Selection Worksheets and Graphic Organizers for Reader's Toolbox / Literary Tools, Post-Reading, and Understanding Literature)
    - Vocabulary SkillBuilders / Daily Oral Language Activities
    - Selection Check Tests and Selection Tests
    - Unit Tests
    - Answer Keys
    - Reading Logs
    - Research Journal
    - Language, Grammar and Style; Speaking and Listening; Study and Research; and Applied English worksheets related to unit
  - Reading Resource
  - Writing Resource
  - Language, Grammar, and Style Resource
  - Speaking and Listening Resource
  - Study and Research Resource
  - Applied English Resource
  - Assessment Resource

Additional components:

- Transparency and Visual Literacy Resource
- EMC Masterpiece Writing: Guided Writing Interactive Software
- Test Generator
- Audio Library on Audiocassette and Audio CD
- Electronic Library on CD-ROM
- Access Edition Supplemental Novels and Plays
- Assessment Manuals for Access Editions

TEACHER'S RESOURCE KIT

The Teacher's Resource Kit for each level includes the following components:

Program Manager
The Program Manager provides thorough scope and sequence charts and clear, simple, ready-to-use lesson plans. Timed activities allow for a variety of approaches and scheduling options (including block scheduling) tailored to your classroom needs.

Parent and Community Involvement Handbook
The Parent and Community Involvement Handbook, featuring an introductory letter to parents written in both Spanish and English, helps parents assist their children with their studies through study log blackline masters, parent guides, activity lists, suggested reading lists, and additional resource references.

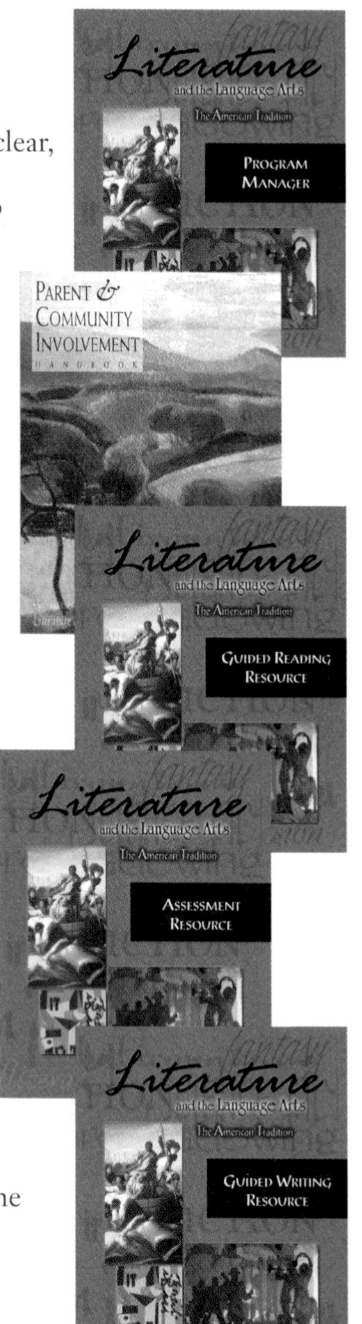

Unit Resource Books with ancillary materials for each unit:
Unit Resource Books pull together ancillary materials from a variety of sources that are used in each unit. They include the following:

- Reading Resource
- Vocabulary Skillbuilders/Daily Oral Language
- Selection Check Tests and Selection Tests
- Unit Tests
- Answer Keys
- Reading Logs
- Research Journal
- Integrated Language Arts Worksheets

Assessment Resource
The Assessment Resource provides blackline master materials for:

- Unit study guides and tests, including vocabulary worksheets
- Selection check tests and comprehensive tests
- Language arts study guides, pre-tests, and post-tests
- Worksheets and forms for portfolio assessment
- Answer keys

Resource Workbooks
The Resource workbooks contain blackline masters of exercises keyed to the Language Arts Survey sections of the student textbooks. They provide additional skill exercises in these language arts subject areas:

- Reading
- Writing
- Language, Grammar, and Style
- Speaking and Listening
- Study and Research
- Applied English

ADDITIONAL COMPONENTS FOR EACH LEVEL INCLUDE:

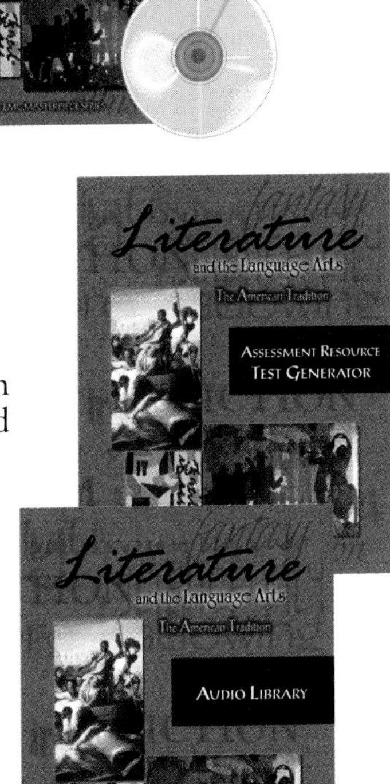

Annotated Teacher's Edition on CD-ROM

- Annotated Teacher's Edition on CD-ROM, compatible with Macintosh and Windows systems, provides easy access to the selections.
- Teachers can view on screen or print selections into a more portable form instead of carrying the textbook home to plan classes.
- Teachers can preview blackline masters from Resource workbooks and other supplemental materials via hyperlinks.

EMC Masterpiece Writing:
Guided Writing Interactive Software

The software builds on the Guided Writing and Integrated Language, Grammar, and Style lessons in the textbook. The "writer-friendly" word processor includes:

- Capacity for self-, peer, and teacher evaluation notes
- Spelling and grammar utilities
- Hypertext links providing help specific to the writing task
- Printable graphic organizers, checklists, and student handouts
- Portfolio management system for teachers
- Windows and Macintosh compatibility

Assessment Resource Test Generator

The Assessment Resource is available in electronic form, running on Windows and Macintosh formats. Teachers can generate customized true/false, multiple choice, short answer, and essay tests based on literature selections in each unit.

Audio Library on Audiocassette and Audio CD

- Includes 10 to 12 hours of audio recordings for each grade level in the program.
- Features authentic, dramatic interpretations by professional actors and academic scholars with a balance of multicultural male and female voices.
- Readings are geared toward English language and auditory learners.
- Available on audiocassette and audio compact disc.
- Accompanying Audio Library Booklet describes each performance and offers creative ideas on how to use the audio component selection in the classroom.

OTHER SUPPLEMENTARY MATERIALS

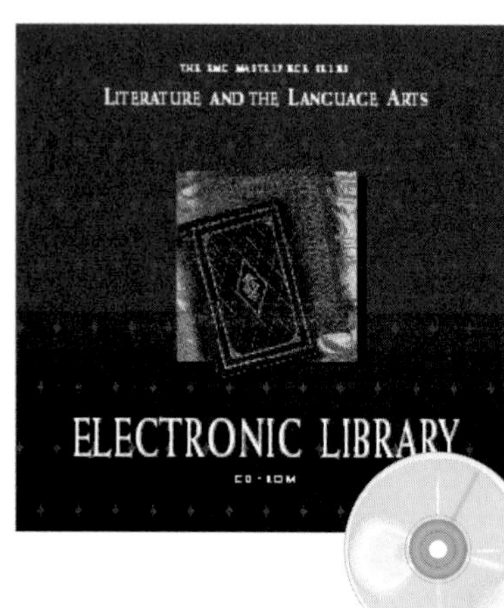

Electronic Library on CD-ROM

- Over 20,000 pages of literary classics
- Contains 120 long selections, including epic poems, novels, plays, nonfiction, and verse; as well as 194 short selections, which include poetry and excerpts.
- Can view on screen or print out individual selections instead of carrying multiple texts home to plan classes.
- Electronic Library Guide provides teaching suggestions, enrichment activities, and Guided Reading blackline masters.
- Available for Windows and Macintosh.

Access Editions

Each **Access Edition** contains the following materials:

- The complete literary work
- A historical introduction including an explanation of literary or philosophical movements relevant to the work
- A biographical introduction with a time line of the author's life
- Art, including explanatory illustrations, maps, genealogies and plot diagrams, as appropriate to the text
- Study apparatus for each chapter or section, including:
  - Guided Reading Questions
  - Words for Everyday Use entries for point-of-use vocabulary development
  - Footnotes
  - Responding to the Selection questions
  - Reviewing the Selection questions (with recalling, interpreting, and higher-level questions to assure your students a close and accessible reading of the text)
  - Understanding Literature questions
- A list of topics for creative writing, critical writing, and research projects
- A glossary of Words for Everyday Use
- A Handbook of Literary Terms

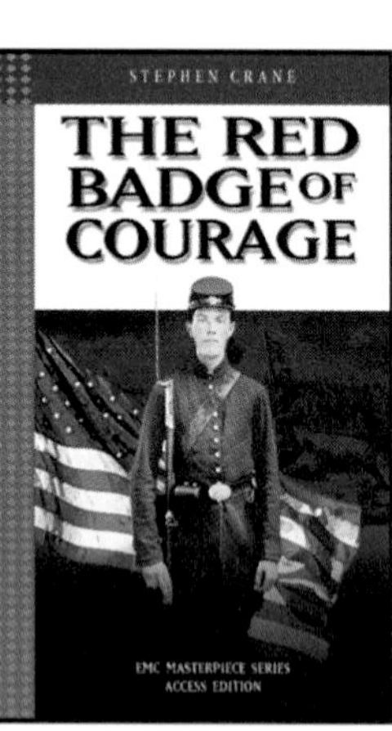

Transparency and Visual Literacy Resource

- Features colorful art transparencies and visual literacy information and activities.

Contents

Overview

Organization of the Text

Literature is the product of the culture which creates it and of the time period in which it is created. Throughout the history of world literature, common themes have emerged. This text is arranged to allow students to recognize works of literature as part of an ongoing representation of archetypal themes and to see works of literature in the context of the periods in which they were produced. The editors of this text believe that before beginning a survey of the themes and history of world literature, students should be introduced to some of the cultures that have shaped this literature in conjunction with readily accessible, high-interest selections. *Literature and the Language Arts: World Literature* has been designed to offer just such an introduction.

The text is organized into three parts:

Part One: World Literature Today: A Geographical Tour consists of a single unit that introduces the culture and literature of eight countries. Each culture is described by a student from the featured country. The student introduction is followed by a high-interest, contemporary selection from the student's country. Each selection is followed by questions designed to address reader response, recalling, interpreting, and synthsizing processes. The selections in Part One include ample reader response and teacher-assisted activities.

Part One also includes an introduction to the Language Arts Survey (see Part Four, described later on this page). Extended skills activities, integrated with the selections, introduce students to the Language Arts Survey as a resource and provide them with an overview or review of skills in the following areas: reading skills, the process of writing, research skills, speaking and listening skills, thinking skills, writing a critical essay, language skills, and creative writing.

Part Two: Themes in World Literature presents world literature using a thematic approach. (To use other approaches, see the notes on page T22 of this **Annotated Teacher's Edition**). Each of Units 2–6 begins with an introduction of various aspects of the unit's theme. The introduction is followed by an Echoes page, in which literary quotations from various periods and countries reflect the the theme of the unit. In the Table of Contents and in the Introduction to each thematic unit in this Annotated Teacher's Edition, you will find lists of **Other Selections Exploring This Theme.** These selections appear in other units of the book but may be used to explore further a given theme.

Part Three: The History of World Literature consists of six units that present significant works of world literature using a chronological approach. Each of units 7–12 begins with a historical introduction that provides background on historical events, figures, and literary movements. The introduction is followed by an Echoes page which presents quotations that reflect the spirit of the age. In the Table of Contents and in the Introduction to each historical unit in this Annotated Teacher's Edition, you will find lists of **Other Selections Exploring This Period.** These selections appear in other units of the book but may be used in conjunction with the chronological unit to provide a more comprehensive view of the period.

The selections in each unit have been chosen to meet a number of criteria:

- To provide students with engaging, stimulating reading experiences
- To provoke interesting discussions of significant themes
- To represent major writers in the world literary tradition
- To represent more fully women's contributions to the historical development of world literature
- To provide outstanding representative examples of each period
- To provide examples of the major genres of literature in each period

Each unit also teaches English vocabulary with **Words for Everyday Use** and concludes with a **Unit Review** that offers Synthesis questions for discussion or writing. Following Units 2-12 are **Selections for Additional Reading.** These selections are not accompanied by the usual teaching apparatus, for the editors and authors of this series feel that students should have some "pure" reading experiences, unburdened by exercises and exegeses. Of course, students can use these selections for research when preparing critical papers on literary movements or trends. The Selections for Additional Reading include many classics as well as many remarkable works not normally found in high school anthologies.

Part Four of this text contains four sections. **The Language Arts Survey** offers comprehensive instruction in the complete range of language arts skills. (Each lesson in the Language Arts Survey is keyed to a worksheet in one of the five Essential Skills Practice Books in the Teacher's Resource Kit.) The **Handbook of Literary Terms** defines and provides examples of literary movements and schools of thought, literary techniques, genres of literature, and common allusions. The **Glossary** collects all the Words for Everyday Use and provides both pronunciations and definitions. The text ends with indexes of titles and authors, skills, and fine art.

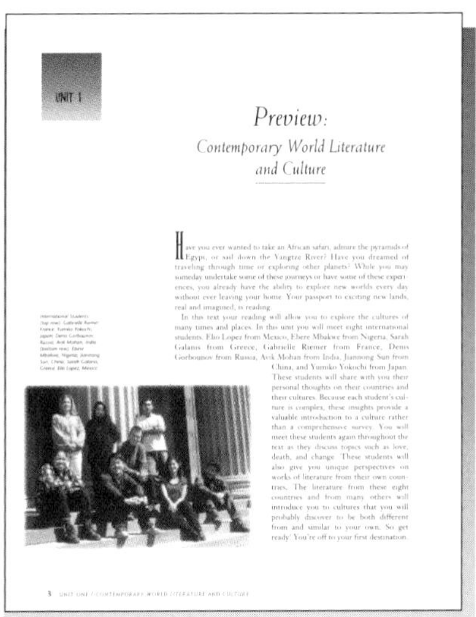

Part One: World Literature Today: A Geographical Tour introduces students to international students from eight different countries, the countries and cultures of these students, and to a contemporary work from the literature of each of these countries. This part of the text prepares students for units that follow and gives students a valuable opportunity to view eight world cultures through the eyes of native students.

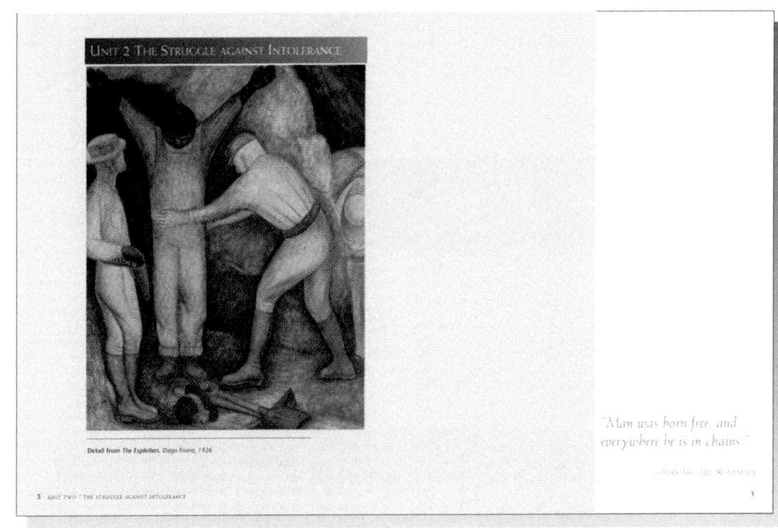

Part Two: Themes in World Literature *examines themes that reappear throughout world literature.*

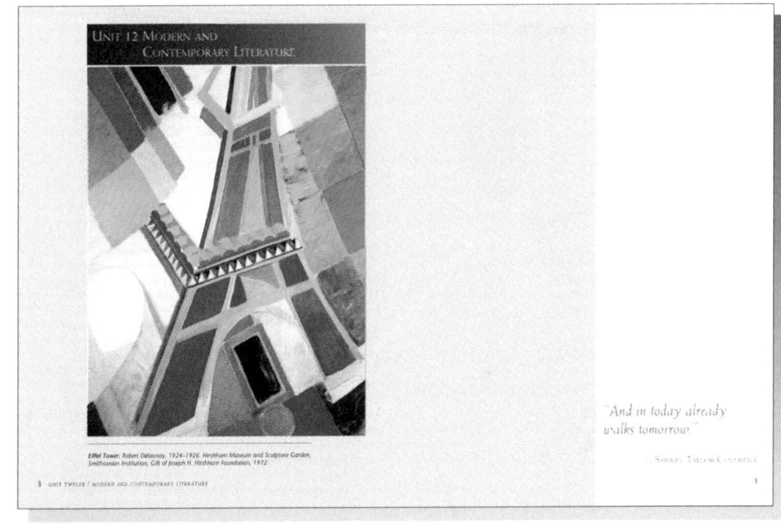

Part Three: The History of World Literature *surveys world literature from its oral roots to the present.*

Part Four *contains*

- *A comprehensive* ***Language Arts Survey***
- *A thorough* ***Handbook of Literary Terms***
- *A* ***Glossary*** *of Words for Everyday Use*
- ***Indexes*** *of Titles and Authors, Skills, and Fine Art*

THE STUDENT STRAND

Unit 1 of the Pupil's Edition introduces eight international students. The students provide an introduction to their countries and cultures in the **Passport Pages.** Students will meet these international students again throughout the book in **Global Voices**, student discussions of the ways in which world issues and themes are reflected in their cultures, and in **Global Views**, sections in which a student comments on a work of literature from his or her culture.

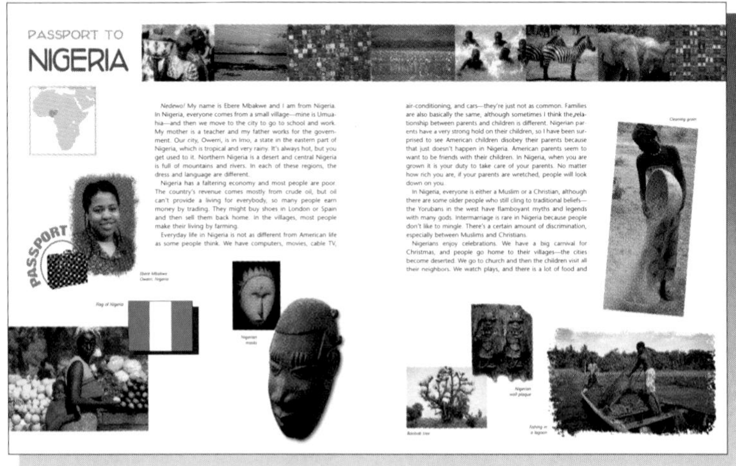

PASSPORT TO

NIGERIA

Nedewo! My name is Ebere Mbakwe and I am from Nigeria. In Nigeria, everyone comes from a small village—mine is Umuahia—and then we move to the city to go to school and work. My mother is a teacher and my father works for the government. Our city, Owerri, is in Imo, a state in the eastern part of Nigeria, which is tropical and very rainy. It's always hot, but you get used to it. Northern Nigeria is a desert and central Nigeria is full of mountains and rivers. In each of these regions, the dress and language are different.

Nigeria has a faltering economy and most people are poor. The country's revenue comes mostly from crude oil, but oil can't provide a living for everybody, so many people earn money by trading. They might buy shoes in London or Spain and then sell them back home. In the villages, most people make their living by farming.

Everyday life in Nigeria is not as different from American life as some people think. We have computers, movies, cable TV, air-conditioning, and cars—they're just not as common. Families are also basically the same, although sometimes I think the relationship between parents and children is different. Nigerian parents have a very strong hold on their children, so I have been surprised to see American children disobey their parents because that just doesn't happen in Nigeria. American parents seem to want to be friends with their children. In Nigeria, when you are grown it is your duty to take care of your parents. No matter how rich you are, if your parents are wretched, people will look down on you.

In Nigeria, everyone is either a Muslim or a Christian, although there are some older people who still cling to traditional beliefs—the Yorubans in the west have flamboyant myths and legends with many gods. Intermarriage is rare in Nigeria because people don't like to mingle. There's a certain amount of discrimination, especially between Muslims and Christians.

Nigerians enjoy celebrations. We have a big carnival for Christmas, and people go home to their villages—the cities become deserted. We go to church and then the children visit all their neighbors. We watch plays, and there is a lot of food and

Sample Passport Pages

Through pictures and the words of eight international students, students are introduced to the countries and cultures of Mexico, Nigeria, Greece, France, Russia, India, China, and Japan in the ***Passport Pages.***

Sample Global Voices Pages

In each ***Global Voices: A Multicultural Conversation,*** *international students discuss how such issues as intolerance, love, death, the environment, and cultural change are addressed in their cultures.*

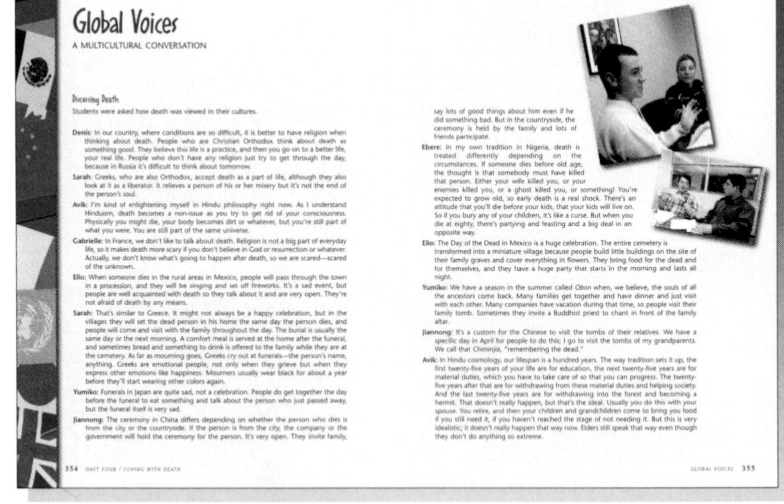

Global Voices

A MULTICULTURAL CONVERSATION

Discussing Death

Students were asked how death was viewed in their cultures.

Denis: In our country, where conditions are so difficult, it is better to have religion when thinking about death. People who are Christian Orthodox think about death as something good. They believe this life is a practice, and then you go on to a better life, your real life. People who don't have any religion just try to get through the day, because in Russia it's difficult to think about tomorrow.

Sarah: Greeks, who are also Orthodox, accept death as a part of life, although they also look at it as a liberator. It relieves a person of his or her misery but it's not the end of the person's soul.

Avik: I'm kind of enlightening myself in Hindu philosophy right now. As I understand Hinduism, death becomes a non-issue as you try to get rid of your consciousness. Physically you might die, your body becomes dirt or whatever, but you're still part of what you were. You are still part of the same universe.

Gabrielle: In France, we don't like to talk about death. Religion is not a big part of everyday life, so it makes death more scary if you don't believe in God or resurrection or whatever. Actually, we don't know what's going to happen after death, so we are scared—scared of the unknown.

Elio: When someone dies in the rural areas in Mexico, people will pass through the town in a procession, and they will be singing and set off fireworks. It's a sad event, but people are well acquainted with death so they talk about it and are very open. They're not afraid of death by any means.

Sarah: That's similar to Greece. It might not always be a happy celebration, but in the villages they will set the dead person in his home the same day the person dies, and people will come and visit with the family throughout the day. The burial is usually the same day or the next morning. A comfort meal is served at the home after the funeral, and sometimes bread and something to drink is offered to the family while they are at the cemetery. As far as mourning goes, Greeks cry out at funerals—the person's name, anything. Greeks are emotional people, not only when they grieve but when they express other emotions like happiness. Mourners usually wear black for about a year before they'll start wearing other colors again.

Yumiko: Funerals in Japan are quite sad, not a celebration. People do get together the day before the funeral to eat something and talk about the person who just passed away, but the funeral itself is very sad.

Jiannong: The ceremony in China differs depending on whether the person who dies is from the city or the countryside. If the person is from the city, the company or the government will hold the ceremony for the person. It's very open. They invite family, say lots of good things about him even if he did something bad. But in the countryside, the ceremony is held by the family and lots of friends participate.

Ebere: In my own tradition in Nigeria, death is treated differently depending on the circumstances. If someone dies before old age, the thought is that somebody must have killed that person. Either your wife killed you, or your enemies killed you, or a ghost killed you, or something! You're expected to grow old, so early death is a real shock. There's an attitude that you'll die before your kids, that your kids will live on. So if you bury any of your children, it's like a curse. But when you die at eighty, there's partying and feasting and a big deal in an opposite way.

Elio: The Day of the Dead in Mexico is a huge celebration. The entire cemetery is transformed into a miniature village because people build little buildings on the site of their family graves and cover everything in flowers. They bring food for the dead and for themselves, and they have a huge party that starts in the morning and lasts all night.

Yumiko: We have a season in the summer called *Obon* when, we believe, the souls of all the ancestors come back. Many families get together and have dinner and just visit with each other. Many companies have vacation during that time, so people visit their family tomb. Sometimes they invite a Buddhist priest to chant in front of the family altar.

Jiannong: It's a custom for the Chinese to visit the tombs of their relatives. We have a specific day in April for people to do this; I go to visit the tombs of my grandparents. We call that *Chiminjia*, "remembering the dead."

Avik: In Hindu cosmology, our lifespan is a hundred years. The way tradition sets it up, the first twenty-five years of your life are for education, the next twenty-five years are for material duties, which you have to take care of so that you can progress. The twenty-five years after that are for withdrawing from these material duties and helping society. And the last twenty-five years are for withdrawing into the forest and becoming a hermit. That doesn't really happen, but that's the ideal. Usually you do this with your spouse. You retire, and then your children and grandchildren come to bring you food if you still need it, if you haven't reached the stage of not needing it. But this is very idealistic; it doesn't really happen that way now. Elders still speak that way even though they don't do anything so extreme.

354 UNIT FOUR / COPING WITH DEATH

GLOBAL VOICES 355

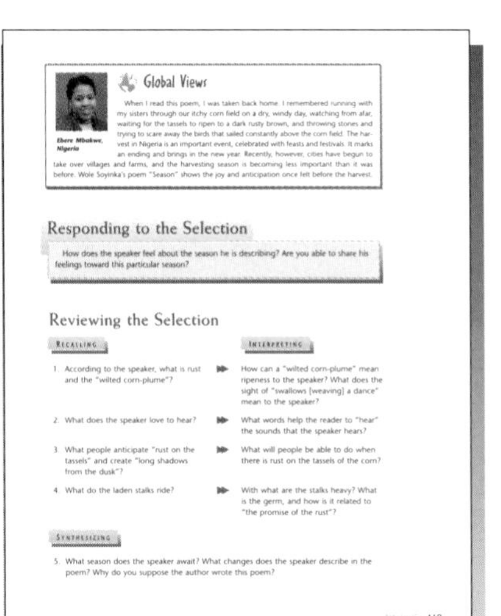

Global Views

When I read this poem, I was taken back home. I remembered running with my sisters through our itchy corn field on a dry, windy day, watching from afar, waiting for the tassels to ripen to a dark rusty brown, and throwing stones and trying to scare away the birds that sailed constantly above the corn field. The harvest in Nigeria is an important event, celebrated with feasts and festivals. It marks an ending and brings in the new year. Recently, however, cities have begun to take over villages and farms, and the harvesting season is becoming less important than it was before. Wole Soyinka's poem "Season" shows the joy and anticipation once felt before the harvest.

Ebere Mbakwe, Nigeria

Responding to the Selection

How does the speaker feel about the season he is describing? Are you able to share his feelings toward this particular season?

Reviewing the Selection

RECALLING		INTERPRETING
1. According to the speaker, what is rust and the "wilted corn-plume"?	▶▶	How can a "wilted corn-plume" mean ripeness to the speaker? What does the sight of "swallows [weaving] a dance" mean to the speaker?
2. What does the speaker love to hear?	▶▶	What words help the reader to "hear" the sounds that the speaker hears?
3. What people anticipate "rust on the tassels" and create "long shadows from the dusk"?	▶▶	What will people be able to do when there is rust on the tassels of the corn?
4. What do the laden stalks ride?	▶▶	With what are the stalks heavy? What is the germ, and how is it related to "the promise of the rust"?

SYNTHESIZING

5. What season does the speaker await? What changes does the speaker describe in the poem? Why do you suppose the author wrote this poem?

"SEASON" 419

Sample Global Views

Global Views *present a personal view from one of the international students, relating some aspect of the selection to the culture that created it. Students gain insight into a different culture and a deeper understanding of the selection.*

Lesson Design and Teaching Strategies

Literature Instruction

A typical lesson in *Literature and the Language Arts* contains materials for two phases of instruction, the Reader Response phase and the Teacher-Assisted phase.

The Reader Response Phase. Cognitive theory and common sense tell us that learning is more likely to occur when students are first provided with a context for what they are to learn. As the proverb says, a seed will grow in prepared ground. Each lesson in this book begins with a **Prereading** page that provides essential information about the author and the selection. The precise content of the entries **About the Author** and **About the Selection** varies according to the demands of the work to be read. If basic comprehension of the work requires understanding of an historical allusion, then that allusion is explained. If comprehension requires understanding of a literary technique, then that technique is described. In addition, the Prereading page provides information about the author and selection designed to arouse student interest. Each Prereading page also contains a **Connections** box which provides additional information about some person, place, event, or movement that is relevant to the author's life or to the selection. These boxes often contain cross-references to other selections, Prereading pages, or special features.

The selection page itself begins with a writing activity to be done in the student's **Reader's Journal.** The Reader's Journal activity raises a central theme from the selection and asks the student to relate that theme to his or her own life. If, for example, a selection presents

PREREADING

CHINA

"The River-Merchant's Wife: A Letter"
by Li Po, translated by Ezra Pound

About the Author

LI PO
AD 701–762

Considered one of the great poets of China, **Li Po** lived and wrote during the T'ang Dynasty (AD 618–907), a period often called the Golden Age of Chinese poetry. Li Po grew up in the Sichuan (Szechwan) province of southwestern China. As a young man, he was well educated, but he chose not to pursue a traditional career in government. Instead, Li Po decided to live as a wanderer. As he traveled, he met many people, and his poetry became popular. After serving the emperor for a short time as an imperial court poet, he worked for a rebel prince who was eventually executed for treason. Li Po was banished from the country, but this sentence was later revoked. Over the course of his life, Li Po earned a reputation for being a free spirit who loved music, friendship, and romance as well as nature and solitude. A popular legend says that he drowned when trying to embrace the reflection of the moon in the Chang (Yangtze) River.

About the Selection

"**The River-Merchant's Wife: A Letter**" is a **narrative poem**, or a poem that tells a story. The speaker of the poem is a woman from eastern China waiting for her husband, who is a river merchant on a long and potentially dangerous journey. His journey takes him up the Chang River, also called the Yangtze, the longest river in China and in all of Asia. Nearly four thousand miles long, this river runs from Tibet in western China eastward through central China before emptying into the Pacific Ocean. While the speaker, the river-merchant's wife, awaits her husband, she describes the history of their relationship—how they first met, their early married life, and the changes that have occurred in their relationship.

Ezra Pound, the translator of the poem, worked from an English prose translation of a Japanese version of the poem. That is why you will notice, by reading footnotes accompanying the selection, that Japanese names are given for Chinese villages and rivers.

CONNECTIONS: Li Po and Taoism

Li Po is closely associated with Taoism (see page 555), one of China's major philosophies. Taoists try to avoid wasting their energies on earthly distractions such as the pursuit of wealth, power, or knowledge. By ignoring these distractions, by living close to nature, and by keeping to their own thoughts, Taoists believe they are able to concentrate on the true meaning of life itself.

"THE RIVER-MERCHANT'S WIFE: A LETTER" 245

Sample Prereading Page

About the Author *provides contextual information about the author's life and the period in which he or she lived.*

About the Selection *provides keys to comprehension of the selection; this covers literary movements, genres, techniques, or themes, depending upon the demands of the selection and its place in literary history.*

Connections *provides additional information about a person, place, event, or movement that is relevant to the author or the selection.*

a character who fails to exhibit courage, the student might be asked to write about a time when he or she acted courageously or wanted to act courageously but could not. After completing this exercise, students will be thinking of courage in terms of their own lives and will be more likely, therefore, to relate personally to the selection and become emotionally invested in it. Emotional investment in the work is key to the reading of literature, and that is why the Reader's Journal activities are primarily affective in nature. Responses to these Reader's Journal activities can be made on the **Selection Worksheets** found in the ***Reader's Guide and Activity Book,*** or they can be made in the student's notebook.

Once the student begins reading the selection, he or she can then take advantage of the **Guided Reading Questions** that appear in the margins. These questions are designed to bring to the student's attention key passages in the selection and issues raised by those passages. Like a guide taking a tourist through the Roman Forum and pointing out important or interesting landmarks, these questions take the student through the selection, ensuring that the most important or interesting aspects of the selection will not be missed. (It would be wonderful if every student could have his or her own private guide to literature. These questions provide the next best thing.) The student can answer these questions on the Selection Worksheets or in his or her notebook.

After reading the selection, students can meet in small collaborative learning groups to share responses to the Reader's Journal activity and Guided Reading Questions. In these groups, students can also discuss the questions raised in the **Responding to the Selection** activity that follows the selection. Again, this is an affective-response activity, one designed to

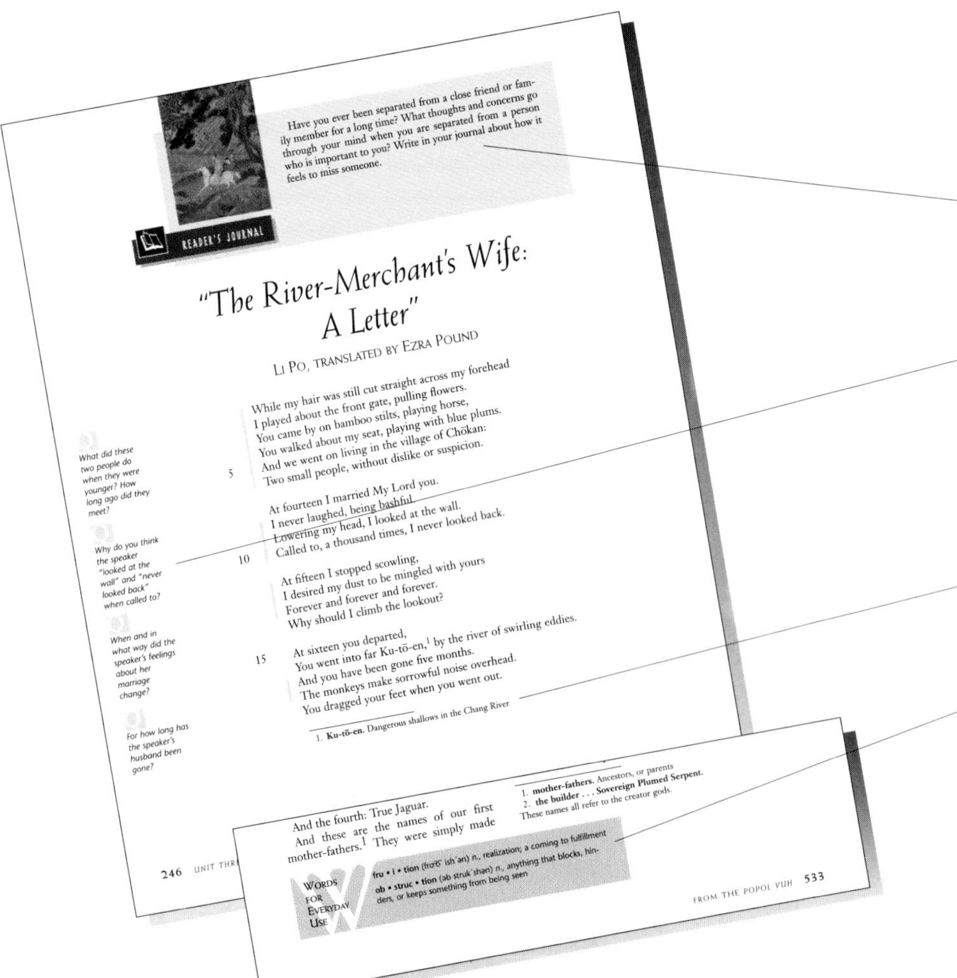

Have you ever been separated from a close friend or family member for a long time? What thoughts and concerns go through your mind when you are separated from a person who is important to you? Write in your journal about how it feels to miss someone.

READER'S JOURNAL

"The River-Merchant's Wife: A Letter"

LI PO, TRANSLATED BY EZRA POUND

While my hair was still cut straight across my forehead
I played about the front gate, pulling flowers.
You came by on bamboo stilts, playing horse,
You walked about my seat, playing with blue plums.
And we went on living in the village of Chōkan:
Two small people, without dislike or suspicion.

At fourteen I married My Lord you.
I never laughed, being bashful.
Lowering my head, I looked at the wall.
Called to, a thousand times, I never looked back.

At fifteen I stopped scowling,
I desired my dust to be mingled with yours
Forever and forever and forever.
Why should I climb the lookout?

At sixteen you departed,
You went into far Ku-tō-en,[1] by the river of swirling eddies.
And you have been gone five months.
The monkeys make sorrowful noise overhead.
You dragged your feet when you went out.

What did these two people do when they were younger? How long ago did they meet?

Why do you think the speaker "looked at the wall" and "never looked back" when called to?

When and in what way did the speaker's feelings about her marriage change?

For how long has the speaker's husband been gone?

1. **Ku-tō-en.** Dangerous shallows in the Chang River

246 UNIT THR

And the fourth: True Jaguar.
And these are the names of our first mother-fathers.[1] They were simply made

1. **mother-fathers.** Ancestors, or parents
2. **the builder . . . Sovereign Plumed Serpent.** These names all refer to the creator gods.

WORDS FOR EVERYDAY USE

fru • i • tion (frōō ish´ən) *n.,* realization; a coming to fulfillment

ob • struc • tion (ab struk´shən) *n.,* anything that blocks, hinders, or keeps something from being seen

FROM THE POPOL VUH 533

Sample Selection Page

The ***Reader's Journal*** *activity raises an important theme from the selection and connects that theme to the student's life.*

Guided Reading Questions *guide students through the selection and help them to recognize and understand important ideas and key points. The questions help all students reach a basic understanding of the selection.*

Footnotes *explain obscure references, unusual usages, and terms meant to enter students' passive vocabularies.*

Words for Everyday Use, *included in selections at point of use, define and give pronunciations for difficult terms meant to enter students' active vocabularies.*

connect the student emotionally to the literature.

These three components of the instructional apparatus, the Reader's Journal activity, the Guided Reading questions, and the Responding to the Selection activity, connect the student to the selection, guide him or her through it, and then make it possible for the student to share his or her responses with others. Together, these activities ensure that once the teacher-assisted phase of the instruction begins, the student will have a wealth of responses to share in discussions with the whole class.

Additional teaching suggestions for the Reader's Journal, Guided Reading, and Responding to the Selection activities are provided in the Annotated Teacher's Edition.

The Teacher-Assisted Phase. The **Reviewing the Selection** questions that follow the Responding to the Selection activity are designed to take the student through the selection step by step, building upon his or her responses and refining them through questions of successive complexity. These questions are organized by level of cognitive sophistication into three sections:

The **Recalling** questions ensure basic comprehension of key facts from the selection.

The **Interpreting** questions ask students to make interpretations or critical evaluations based on facts from the selection.

The **Synthesizing** questions ask students to draw together what they have gathered through recall and interpretation to make generalizations about the meaning, significance, or value of the selection. Often these questions ask the student to apply what he or she has learned from the selection to some larger context (to larger trends or themes in literature, for example, or to some larger social, cultural, ethical, or political context).

Uniquely, each Interpreting question in Reviewing the Selection is keyed by means of an arrow to a Recalling question that provides the facts on which the interpretation can be based. **This keying of interpretation to facts from the selection ensures that student responses will be based on evidence from the selection. No other text now available offers this feature.**

Because students are frequently unfamiliar with literary terminology and its applications, such terminology does not appear in the questions for Reviewing the Selection. Literary terminology and techniques are covered in the next part of the instructional apparatus, which is called **Understanding Literature.** Each Understanding Literature activity begins with a boldfaced term that names a literary movement, genre, or technique. The term is followed by its definition and by one or more questions that apply the concept to the selection. Having responded to the selection and having reviewed it in detail, the student can now learn some of the technical details about how the selection worked to achieve its effects. Students needing or desiring additional information about a term introduced in the Understanding Literature activity can refer to the discussion of that term in the **Handbook of Literary Terms** at the back of the book.

Approaches to the teacher-assisted phase of the literature instruction can vary, depending on your teaching style and the needs of your students. Some teachers will prefer to have students answer questions on Reviewing the Selection and Understanding Literature individually or in small groups and will hold afterward whole-class discussions of these questions. Others will prefer to treat these questions as prompts for whole-class, teacher-directed discussions. Another alternative, especially appropriate in advanced classes, is to assign students to conduct whole-class discussions of these questions.

Instruction in Other Language Arts Skills: An Integrated Approach

It has been shown that a student may demonstrate knowledge in a classroom but be unable to use that knowledge in "real-life" situations. Grammar, usage, mechanics, spelling, and vocabulary skills have traditionally been taught in isolation as independent skills but, just as instruction in the separate concepts of physiology does not make us healthier, neither does instruction in the abstract concepts of speech or grammar make us speak or write better (Hillocks; Braddock). Skills must be taught in ways that enable students to "transfer" them to real contexts, i.e., to use them in their lives. The transferability of knowledge is a function of meaningfulness (Prawat). Teachers can promote meaningfulness by providing (1) a wide variety of examples, (2) practice in a wide variety of contexts, (3) an explanation of the value or uses of the lesson, (4) an advance organizer at the beginning of the lesson, and (5) reviews. These five tasks have served as guideposts in the planning and writing of *Literature and the Language Arts.*

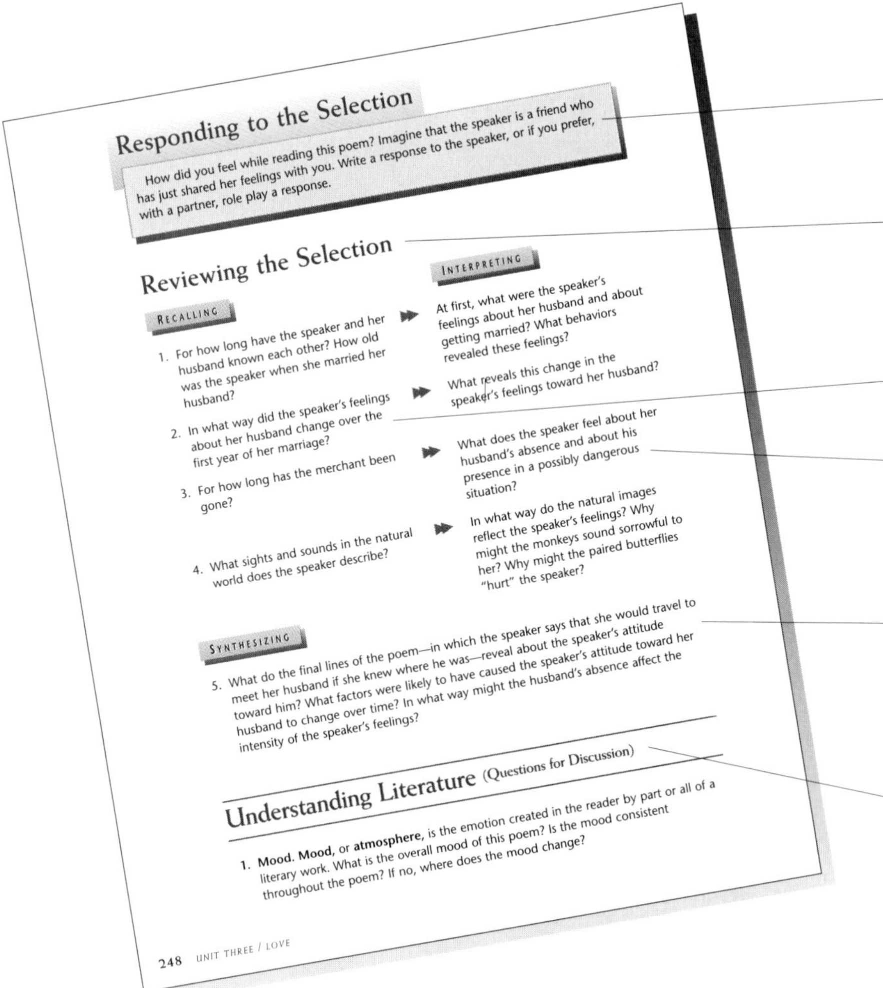

Responding to the Selection

How did you feel while reading this poem? Imagine that the speaker is a friend who has just shared her feelings with you. Write a response to the speaker, or if you prefer, with a partner, role play a response.

Reviewing the Selection

RECALLING

1. For how long have the speaker and her husband known each other? How old was the speaker when she married her husband?
2. In what way did the speaker's feelings about her husband change over the first year of her marriage?
3. For how long has the merchant been gone?
4. What sights and sounds in the natural world does the speaker describe?

INTERPRETING

At first, what were the speaker's feelings about her husband and about getting married? What behaviors revealed these feelings?

What reveals this change in the speaker's feelings toward her husband?

What does the speaker feel about her husband's absence and about his presence in a possibly dangerous situation?

In what way do the natural images reflect the speaker's feelings? Why might the monkeys sound sorrowful to her? Why might the paired butterflies "hurt" the speaker?

SYNTHESIZING

5. What do the final lines of the poem—in which the speaker says that she would travel to meet her husband if she knew where he was—reveal about the speaker's attitude toward him? What factors were likely to have caused the speaker's attitude toward her husband to change over time? In what way might the husband's absence affect the intensity of the speaker's feelings?

Understanding Literature (Questions for Discussion)

1. **Mood. Mood,** or **atmosphere,** is the emotion created in the reader by part or all of a literary work. What is the overall mood of this poem? Is the mood consistent throughout the poem? If no, where does the mood change?

248 UNIT THREE / LOVE

Sample Literary Skills Page

Responding to the Selection *is a* ***reader response*** *activity designed to elicit an affective response to the selection.*

Reviewing the Selection *takes students through the work step by step, building from their individual responses a complete interpretation of the work.*

Recalling *questions address comprehension of key facts from the selection.*

Interpreting *questions, keyed to the Recalling questions by arrows, evoke interpretations based on evidence from the selection.*

Synthesizing *questions tie together interpretations of parts of the selection and prompt students to make informed generalizations that relate the selection to larger themes or literary trends.*

Understanding Literature *questions provide selection-related study of literary movements, genres, and techniques.*

The exercises in this text are organized so that instruction in essential skills—writing, language, speaking, listening, study and research, thinking, test-taking, and applied English—develops in the context of literature appreciation activities. The study of engaging literature can provide motivation and context for teaching these practical skills.

The **Responding in Writing** activities use the selection as a springboard for creative and critical writing assignments. The lesson ends with a language lab, skills activity, or project. **Language Labs** give students practice in essential grammar, usage, and mechanics skills; explore applications of grammar skills to writing; and present key concepts related to varieties of English. **Language Arts Skills** activities provide more integrated practice in Speaking and Listening, Study and Research, or Applied English skills.

A typical skills activity asks students to read a section of the Language Arts Survey and then complete an exercise. The exercises relate to the work of literature that students have just studied. For instance, an exercise following *Oedipus the King* might teach students Greek and Latin roots by drawing words from the selection and Prereading material that include Greek roots and comparing them to their Latin equivalents. A lesson following the short story "The Fifth Story," in which the narrator is faced with a problem, asks students to use various problem-solving techniques to find solutions to such a problem.

Many lessons in the student edition end with a **Project** related to the selection. These projects extend the instruction in the lesson in ways that call upon students' multiple intelligences and may allow them to relate their reading to other curricular areas.

Many literary selections are followed or are preceded by a **Themes** or **Insights** feature which explores important literary movements and trends or historical periods and events in more

Sample Language Arts Skills Activities Page

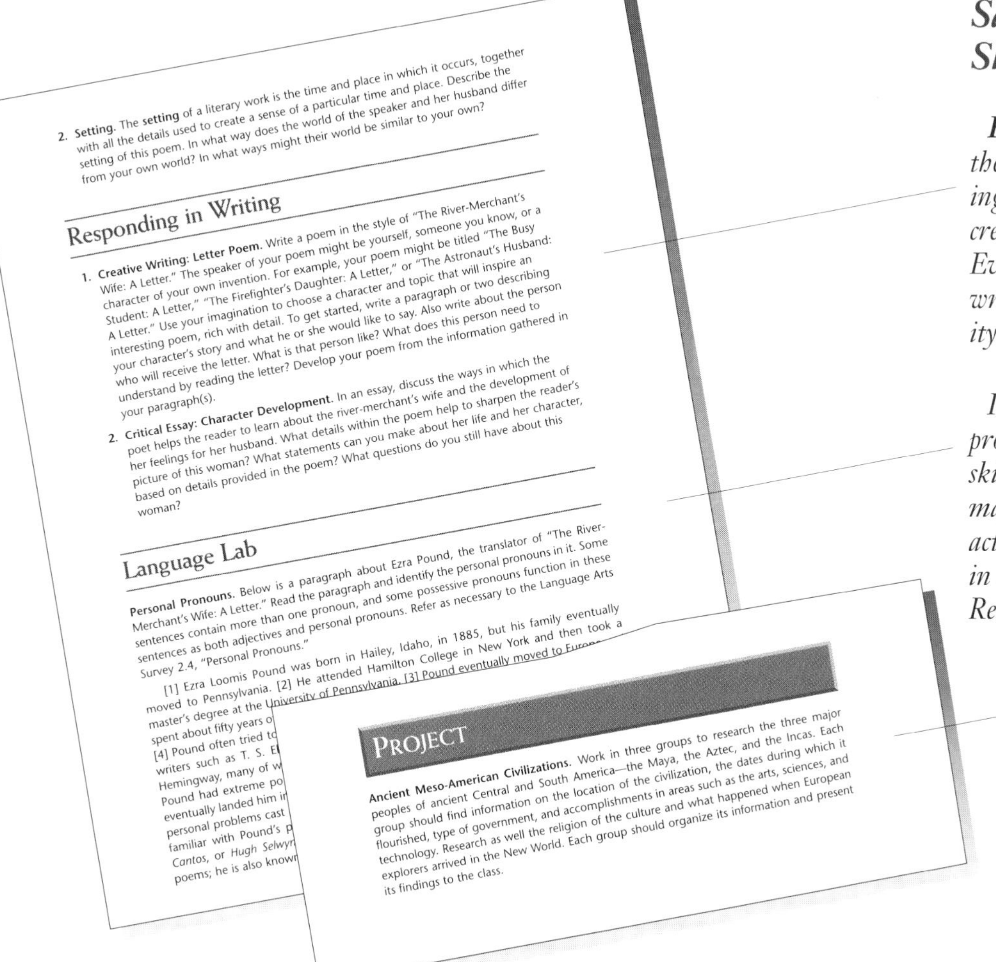

2. **Setting.** The **setting** of a literary work is the time and place in which it occurs, together with all the details used to create a sense of a particular time and place. Describe the setting of this poem. In what way does the world of the speaker and her husband differ from your own world? In what ways might their world be similar to your own?

Responding in Writing

1. **Creative Writing: Letter Poem.** Write a poem in the style of "The River-Merchant's Wife: A Letter." The speaker of your poem might be yourself, someone you know, or a character of your own invention. For example, your poem might be titled "The Busy Student: A Letter," "The Firefighter's Daughter: A Letter," or "The Astronaut's Husband: A Letter." Use your imagination to choose a character and topic that will inspire an interesting poem, rich with detail. To get started, write a paragraph or two describing your character's story and what he or she would like to say. Also write about the person who will receive the letter. What is that person like? What does this person need to understand by reading the letter? Develop your poem from the information gathered in your paragraph(s).
2. **Critical Essay: Character Development.** In an essay, discuss the ways in which the poet helps the reader to learn about the river-merchant's wife and the development of her feelings for her husband. What details within the poem help to sharpen the reader's picture of this woman? What statements can you make about her life and her character, based on details provided in the poem? What questions do you still have about this woman?

Language Lab

Personal Pronouns. Below is a paragraph about Ezra Pound, the translator of "The River-Merchant's Wife: A Letter." Read the paragraph and identify the personal pronouns in it. Some sentences contain more than one pronoun, and some possessive pronouns function in these sentences as both adjectives and personal pronouns. Refer as necessary to the Language Arts Survey 2.4, "Personal Pronouns."

[1] Ezra Loomis Pound was born in Hailey, Idaho, in 1885, but his family eventually moved to Pennsylvania. [2] He attended Hamilton College in New York and then took a master's degree at the University of Pennsylvania. [3] Pound eventually moved to Europe … spent about fifty years o… [4] Pound often tried to… writers such as T. S. El… Hemingway, many of w… Pound had extreme po… eventually landed him i… personal problems cast… familiar with Pound's p… *Cantos*, or *Hugh Selwyn*… poems; he is also known…

PROJECT

Ancient Meso-American Civilizations. Work in three groups to research the three major peoples of ancient Central and South America—the Maya, the Aztec, and the Incas. Each group should find information on the location of the civilization, the dates during which it flourished, type of government, and accomplishments in areas such as the arts, sciences, and technology. Research as well the religion of the culture and what happened when European explorers arrived in the New World. Each group should organize its information and present its findings to the class.

Responding in Writing *activities use the selection as a springboard for engaging writing assignments that require both creative and critical thinking skills. Every literary selection includes a creative writing activity and a critical essay activity.*

Integrated ***Language Lab*** *activities provide practice in essential language skills. Instead of a Language Lab, lessons may contain a* ***Language Arts Skills*** *activity that provides integrated practice in Speaking and Listening, Study and Research, or Applied English.*

Other lessons end with special ***Projects*** *that extend learning beyond immediate language arts applications to cross-curricular areas while calling upon students to use a broad range of talents and multiple intelligences.*

depth. This feature allows students to relate selections they have read to larger movements and issues.

The **Language Arts Survey** at the back of the book provides a comprehensive overview of the complete range of language arts skills. The survey is divided into five sections, as follows:

- Essential Skills: Writing
- Essential Skills: Language
- Essential Skills: Speaking and Listening
- Essential Skills: Study and Research
- Essential Skills: Applied English/ Tech Prep

Students may refer to these sections when doing writing or skills activities. Teachers wishing to give their students additional practice in any of these skills areas will find, for each lesson in the Language Arts Survey, a corresponding worksheet in one of the five **Essential Skills Practice Books** found in the Teacher's Resource Kit. Teachers wishing to present whole units related to specific skills can have students work through parts of the Language Arts Survey, doing the activities found in the Essential Skills Practice Books.

Partial Bibliography

Ausubel, D. *Educational Psychology.* 2nd ed. New York: Holt, 1978.

Braddock, R., R. Lloyd-Jones, and L. Schoer. *Research in Written Composition.* Champaign, IL: NCTE, 1963.

Bruner, J. *Toward a Theory of Instruction.* New York: Norton, 1966.

Eggen, P., and D. Kauchak. *Educational Psychology: Classroom Connections.* 2nd ed. New York: Merrill, 1994.

Eisner, E. *The Educational Imagination.* 2nd ed. New York: Macmillan, 1985.

Hillocks, G., Jr. *Research on Written Composition: New Directions for Teaching.* Urbana, IL: Natl. Conference on Research in English and ERIC/CRCS, 1986.

Prawat, R. "Promoting Access to Knowledge, Strategy, and Disposition in Students: A Research Synthesis." *Review of Educational Research* 59 (1989): 1–41.

Novak, J. D. *A Theory of Education.* Ithaca, NY: Cornell UP, 1984.

Insights

IMAGERY AND IDEOGRAPHIC WRITING

Chinese writing is ideographic, or logographic, which means that it is based on graphic symbols that represent ideas or objects. The earliest Chinese characters closely resembled the ideas or objects that they represented. With the advent of brushes and ink, the characters changed and often involved much simpler lines and shapes. About one thousand simple lines and shapes—representing concrete subjects such as man, woman, rock, or river and more abstract terms such as talk or love—form the foundation of the Chinese writing system. These basic characters are often combined to create characters that represent more complex ideas. Consider the following complex character, which represents rain:

雨

The dots within the character represent drops of rain.

雨

The lines around the dots symbolize a cloud.

雨

The line at the top of the character symbolizes heaven or sky.

雨

The "j" portion of the character, a vertical line, suggests vertical falling.

雨

The following character represents the dawn of the day:

旦

The top portion of the character represents the sun.

旦

The bottom portion of the character represents the horizon.

旦

Extended, metaphorical meanings often evolve from Chinese characters that originally referred to concrete objects. For example, the following character is a picture of a fish net:

网

Over the years, the intricate design meant to represent a net for catching fish has come to suggest the idea of gathering, or collecting.

As you have seen, a single character in Chinese such as the one for rain, is something like a brief poem, combining images to convey an idea. People who translate Chinese poetry into English often try to capture the imagistic quality of the original language by using short, concise, concrete words, as in the translation on page 246.

250 UNIT THREE / LOVE

Sample Themes/Insights Page

Themes *or* ***Insights*** *follow some selections and provide enrichment by expanding upon a theme, genre, historical period or event, or other idea relevant to the literary work. Other Themes and Insights precede selections to provide students with an overview of information that will help them to understand the selection.*

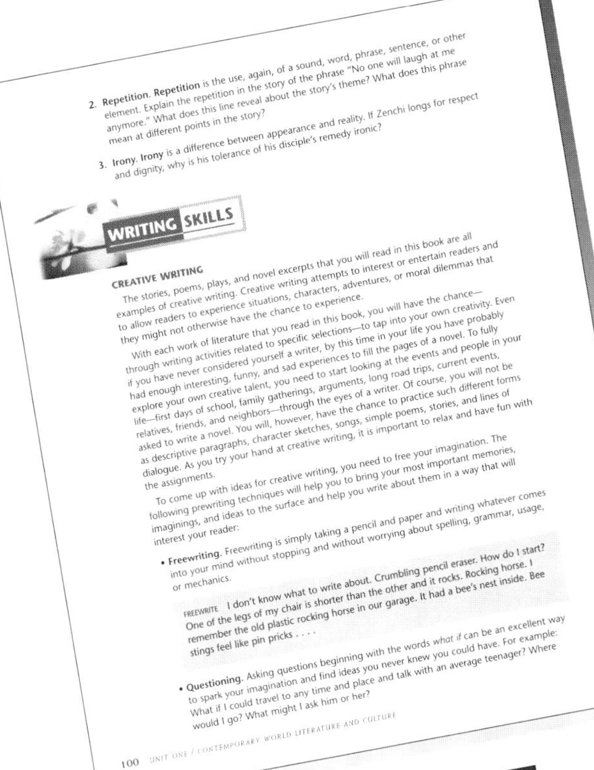

2. **Repetition. Repetition** is the use, again, of a sound, word, phrase, sentence, or other element. Explain the repetition in the story of the phrase "No one will laugh at me anymore." What does this line reveal about the story's theme? What does this phrase mean at different points in the story?
3. **Irony. Irony** is a difference between appearance and reality. If Zenchi longs for respect and dignity, why is his tolerance of his disciple's remedy ironic?

WRITING SKILLS

CREATIVE WRITING

The stories, poems, plays, and novel excerpts that you will read in this book are all examples of creative writing. Creative writing attempts to interest or entertain readers and to allow readers to experience situations, characters, adventures, or moral dilemmas that they might not otherwise have the chance to experience.

With each work of literature that you read in this book, you will have the chance—through writing activities related to specific selections—to tap into your own creativity. Even if you have never considered yourself a writer, by this time in your life you have probably had enough interesting, funny, and sad experiences to fill the pages of a novel. To fully explore your own creative talent, you need to start looking at the events and people in your life—first days of school, family gatherings, arguments, long road trips, current events, relatives, friends, and neighbors—through the eyes of a writer. Of course, you will not be asked to write a novel. You will, however, have the chance to practice such different forms as descriptive paragraphs, character sketches, songs, simple poems, stories, and lines of dialogue. As you try your hand at creative writing, it is important to relax and have fun with the assignments.

To come up with ideas for creative writing, you need to free your imagination. The following prewriting techniques will help you to bring your most important memories, imaginings, and ideas to the surface and help you write about them in a way that will interest your reader:

- **Freewriting.** Freewriting is simply taking a pencil and paper and writing whatever comes into your mind without stopping and without worrying about spelling, grammar, usage, or mechanics.

FREEWRITE I don't know what to write about. Crumbling pencil eraser. How do I start? One of the legs of my chair is shorter than the other and it rocks. Rocking horse. I remember the old plastic rocking horse in our garage. It had a bee's nest inside. Bee stings feel like pin pricks . . . .

- **Questioning.** Asking questions beginning with the words *what if* can be an excellent way to spark your imagination and find ideas you never knew you could have. For example: What if I could travel to any time and place and talk with an average teenager? Where would I go? What might I ask him or her?

100 UNIT ONE / CONTEMPORARY WORLD LITERATURE AND CULTURE

*Extended **Skills Activities** at the end of each selection in Unit 1 of the student edition are designed to introduce students to the Language Arts Survey and to introduce or review skills that will be utilized throughout the text.*

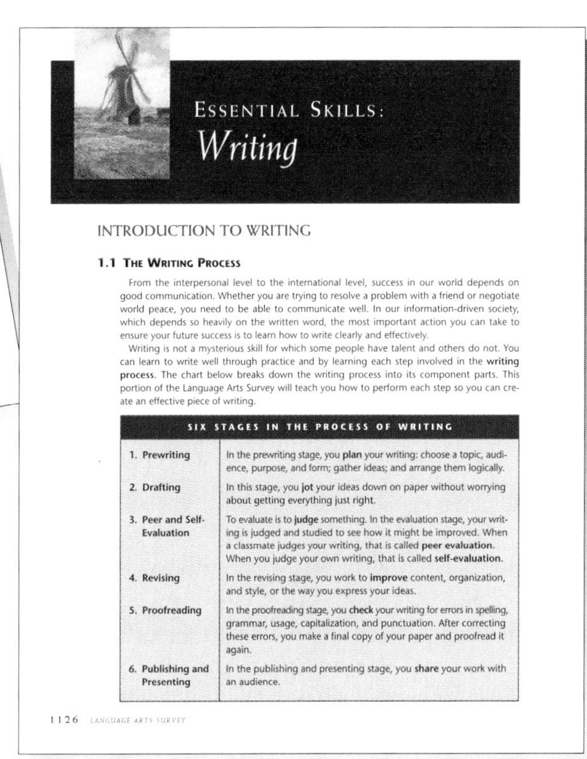

ESSENTIAL SKILLS: *Writing*

INTRODUCTION TO WRITING

1.1 The Writing Process

From the interpersonal level to the international level, success in our world depends on good communication. Whether you are trying to resolve a problem with a friend or negotiate world peace, you need to be able to communicate well. In our information-driven society, which depends so heavily on the written word, the most important action you can take to ensure your future success is to learn how to write clearly and effectively.

Writing is not a mysterious skill for which some people have talent and others do not. You can learn to write well through practice and by learning each step involved in the **writing process.** The chart below breaks down the writing process into its component parts. This portion of the Language Arts Survey will teach you how to perform each step so you can create an effective piece of writing.

SIX STAGES IN THE PROCESS OF WRITING	
1. Prewriting	In the prewriting stage, you **plan** your writing: choose a topic, audience, purpose, and form; gather ideas; and arrange them logically.
2. Drafting	In this stage, you **jot** your ideas down on paper without worrying about getting everything just right.
3. Peer and Self-Evaluation	To evaluate is to **judge** something. In the evaluation stage, your writing is judged and studied to see how it might be improved. When a classmate judges your writing, that is called **peer evaluation.** When you judge your own writing, that is called **self-evaluation.**
4. Revising	In the revising stage, you work to **improve** content, organization, and style, or the way you express your ideas.
5. Proofreading	In the proofreading stage, you **check** your writing for errors in spelling, grammar, usage, capitalization, and punctuation. After correcting these errors, you make a final copy of your paper and proofread it again.
6. Publishing and Presenting	In the publishing and presenting stage, you **share** your work with an audience.

1126 LANGUAGE ARTS SURVEY

*The **Language Arts Survey** at the end of the student edition provides a comprehensive overview of the complete range of language arts skills.*

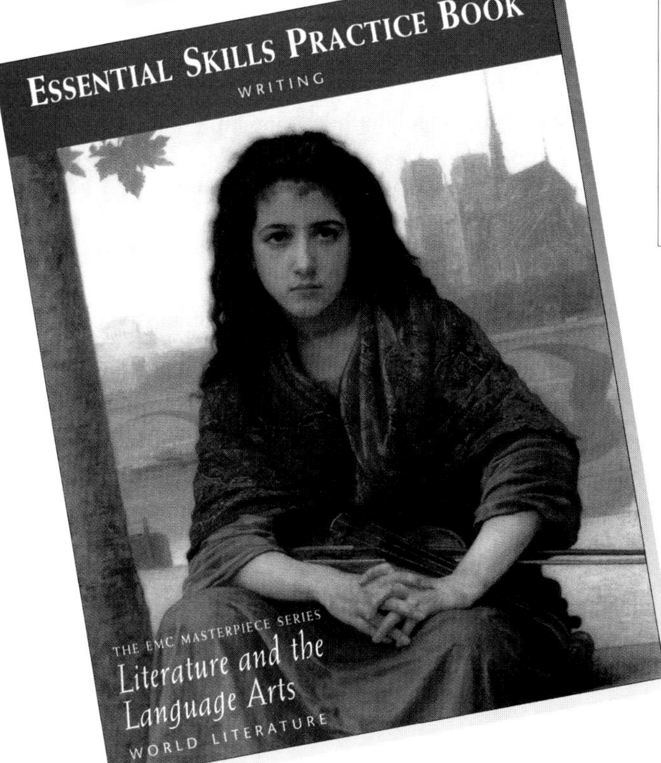

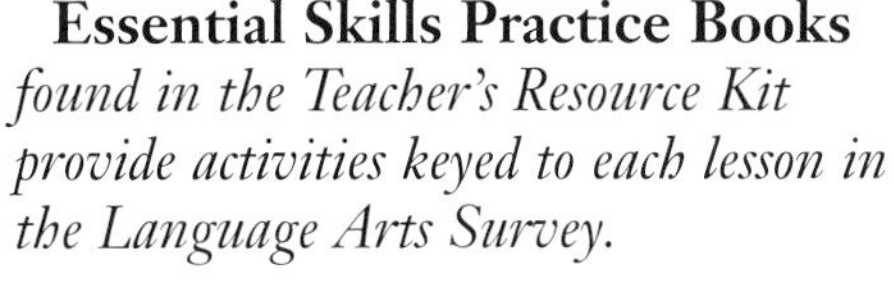

Essential Skills Practice Books *found in the Teacher's Resource Kit provide activities keyed to each lesson in the Language Arts Survey.*

Teacher's Edition Annotations

The ***Annotated Teacher's Edition*** is designed to be as "teacher-friendly" as possible. Answers for exercises are usually provided on the same pages as the exercises themselves. All items are color-coded: answers to student edition exercises are on white backgrounds, supplementary notes and activities are on yellow backgrounds, and special items, such as lists of goals, enrichment and remedial notes, and selection check test answers, use distinguishing colors.

Sample Unit Opening Pages

__Teaching the Multiple Intelligences__ lists activities from the unit that call for the exercise of students' multiple intelligences.

__Cross-curricular Connections__ lists the cross-curricular activities from the unit.

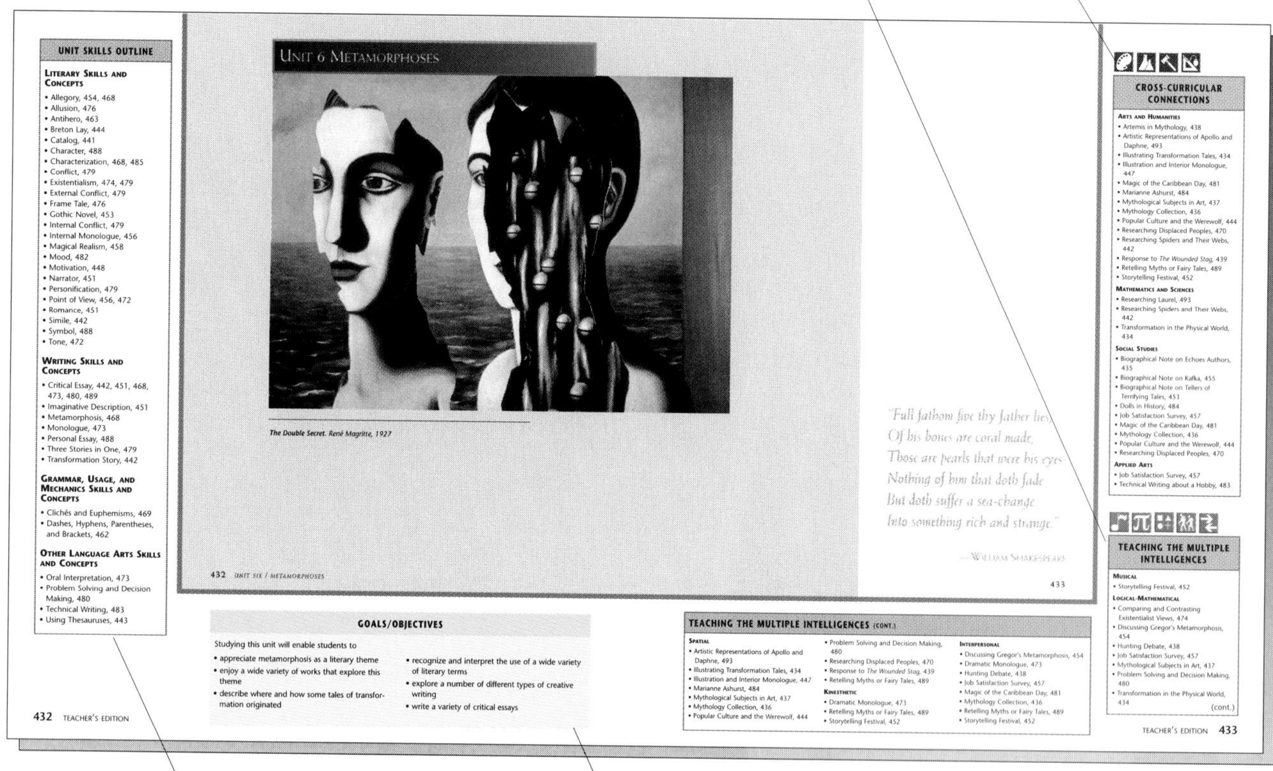

UNIT SKILLS OUTLINE

LITERARY SKILLS AND CONCEPTS
- Allegory, 454, 468
- Allusion, 476
- Antihero, 463
- Breton Lay, 444
- Catalog, 441
- Character, 488
- Characterization, 468, 485
- Conflict, 479
- Existentialism, 474, 479
- External Conflict, 479
- Frame Tale, 476
- Gothic Novel, 453
- Internal Conflict, 479
- Internal Monologue, 456
- Magical Realism, 458
- Mood, 482
- Motivation, 448
- Narrator, 451
- Personification, 479
- Point of View, 456, 472
- Romance, 451
- Simile, 442
- Symbol, 488
- Tone, 472

WRITING SKILLS AND CONCEPTS
- Critical Essay, 442, 451, 468, 473, 480, 489
- Imaginative Description, 451
- Metamorphosis, 468
- Monologue, 473
- Personal Essay, 488
- Three Stories in One, 479
- Transformation Story, 442

GRAMMAR, USAGE, AND MECHANICS SKILLS AND CONCEPTS
- Clichés and Euphemisms, 469
- Dashes, Hyphens, Parentheses, and Brackets, 462

OTHER LANGUAGE ARTS SKILLS AND CONCEPTS
- Oral Interpretation, 473
- Problem Solving and Decision Making, 480
- Technical Writing, 483
- Using Thesauruses, 443

432 TEACHER'S EDITION

UNIT 6 METAMORPHOSES

The Double Secret. René Magritte, 1927

432 UNIT SIX / METAMORPHOSES

"Full fathom five thy father lies;
Of his bones are coral made;
Those are pearls that were his eyes:
Nothing of him that doth fade
But doth suffer a sea-change
Into something rich and strange."

—WILLIAM SHAKESPEARE

433

GOALS/OBJECTIVES

Studying this unit will enable students to
- appreciate metamorphosis as a literary theme
- enjoy a wide variety of works that explore this theme
- describe where and how some tales of transformation originated
- recognize and interpret the use of a wide variety of literary terms
- explore a number of different types of creative writing
- write a variety of critical essays

CROSS-CURRICULAR CONNECTIONS

ARTS AND HUMANITIES
- Artemis in Mythology, 438
- Artistic Representations of Apollo and Daphne, 493
- Illustrating Transformation Tales, 434
- Illustration and Interior Monologue, 447
- Magic of the Caribbean Day, 481
- Marianne Ashurst, 484
- Mythological Subjects in Art, 437
- Mythology Collection, 436
- Popular Culture and the Werewolf, 444
- Researching Displaced Peoples, 470
- Researching Spiders and Their Webs, 442
- Response to *The Wounded Stag,* 439
- Retelling Myths or Fairy Tales, 489
- Storytelling Festival, 452

MATHEMATICS AND SCIENCES
- Researching Laurel, 493
- Researching Spiders and Their Webs, 442
- Transformation in the Physical World, 434

SOCIAL STUDIES
- Biographical Note on Echoes Authors, 435
- Biographical Note on Kafka, 455
- Biographical Note on Tellers of Terrifying Tales, 453
- Dolls in History, 484
- Job Satisfaction Survey, 457
- Magic of the Caribbean Day, 481
- Mythology Collection, 436
- Popular Culture and the Werewolf, 444
- Researching Displaced Peoples, 470

APPLIED ARTS
- Job Satisfaction Survey, 457
- Technical Writing about a Hobby, 483

TEACHING THE MULTIPLE INTELLIGENCES

MUSICAL
- Storytelling Festival, 452

LOGICAL-MATHEMATICAL
- Comparing and Contrasting Existentialist Views, 474
- Discussing Gregor's Metamorphosis, 454
- Hunting Debate, 438
- Job Satisfaction Survey, 457
- Mythological Subjects in Art, 437
- Problem Solving and Decision Making, 480
- Transformation in the Physical World, 434

(cont.)

TEACHING THE MULTIPLE INTELLIGENCES (CONT.)

SPATIAL
- Artistic Representations of Apollo and Daphne, 493
- Illustrating Transformation Tales, 434
- Illustration and Interior Monologue, 447
- Marianne Ashurst, 484
- Mythological Subjects in Art, 437
- Mythology Collection, 436
- Popular Culture and the Werewolf, 444
- Problem Solving and Decision Making, 480
- Researching Displaced Peoples, 470
- Response to *The Wounded Stag,* 439
- Retelling Myths or Fairy Tales, 489

KINESTHETIC
- Dramatic Monologue, 473
- Retelling Myths or Fairy Tales, 489
- Storytelling Festival, 452

INTERPERSONAL
- Discussing Gregor's Metamorphosis, 454
- Dramatic Monologue, 473
- Hunting Debate, 438
- Job Satisfaction Survey, 457
- Magic of the Caribbean Day, 481
- Mythology Collection, 436
- Retelling Myths or Fairy Tales, 489
- Storytelling Festival, 452

TEACHER'S EDITION 433

The __Unit Skills Outline__ lists the skills taught in the student edition and in additional activities in this Annotated Teacher's Edition.

A list of __Goals/Objectives__ helps you plan overall intended learning outcomes for the unit. Affective goals are consistent with the philosophy of the program and its emphasis on reader involvement. Cognitive goals encompass content, literary technique, and interpretation in historical context.

Sample Unit Review Pages

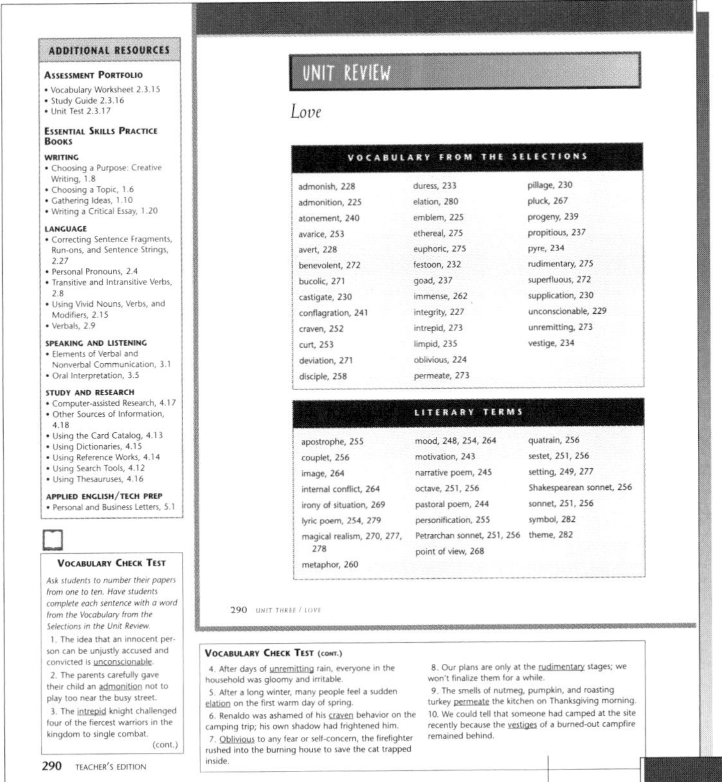

ADDITIONAL RESOURCES

Assessment Portfolio
- Vocabulary Worksheet 2.3.15
- Study Guide 2.3.16
- Unit Test 2.3.17

Essential Skills Practice Books

WRITING
- Choosing a Purpose: Creative Writing, 1.8
- Choosing a Topic, 1.6
- Gathering Ideas, 1.10
- Writing a Critical Essay, 1.20

LANGUAGE
- Correcting Sentence Fragments, Run-ons, and Sentence Strings, 2.27
- Personal Pronouns, 2.4
- Transitive and Intransitive Verbs, 2.8
- Using Vivid Nouns, Verbs, and Modifiers, 2.15
- Verbals, 2.9

SPEAKING AND LISTENING
- Elements of Verbal and Nonverbal Communication, 3.1
- Oral Interpretation, 3.5

STUDY AND RESEARCH
- Computer-assisted Research, 4.17
- Other Sources of Information, 4.18
- Using the Card Catalog, 4.13
- Using Dictionaries, 4.15
- Using Reference Works, 4.14
- Using Search Tools, 4.12
- Using Thesauruses, 4.16

APPLIED ENGLISH/TECH PREP
- Personal and Business Letters, 5.1

Vocabulary Check Test

Ask students to number their papers from one to ten. Have students complete each sentence with a word from the Vocabulary from the Selections in the Unit Review.

1. The idea that an innocent person can be unjustly accused and convicted is unconscionable.
2. The parents carefully gave their child an admonition not to play too near the busy street.
3. The intrepid knight challenged four of the fiercest warriors in the kingdom to single combat.

(cont.)

UNIT REVIEW

Love

VOCABULARY FROM THE SELECTIONS

admonish, 228	duress, 233	pillage, 230
admonition, 225	elation, 280	pluck, 267
atonement, 240	emblem, 225	progeny, 239
avarice, 253	ethereal, 275	propitious, 237
avert, 228	euphoric, 275	pyre, 234
benevolent, 272	festoon, 232	rudimentary, 275
bucolic, 271	goad, 237	superfluous, 272
castigate, 230	immense, 262	supplication, 230
conflagration, 241	integrity, 227	unconscionable, 229
craven, 252	intrepid, 273	unremitting, 273
curt, 253	limpid, 235	vestige, 234
deviation, 271	oblivious, 224	
disciple, 258	permeate, 273	

LITERARY TERMS

apostrophe, 255	mood, 248, 254, 264	quatrain, 256
couplet, 256	motivation, 243	sestet, 251, 256
image, 264	narrative poem, 245	setting, 249, 277
internal conflict, 264	octave, 251, 256	Shakespearean sonnet, 256
irony of situation, 269	pastoral poem, 244	sonnet, 251, 256
lyric poem, 254, 279	personification, 255	symbol, 282
magical realism, 270, 277, 278	Petrarchan sonnet, 251, 256	theme, 282
metaphor, 260	point of view, 268	

290 UNIT THREE / LOVE

Vocabulary Check Test (cont.)

4. After days of unremitting rain, everyone in the household was gloomy and irritable.
5. After a long winter, many people feel a sudden elation on the first warm day of spring.
6. Renaldo was ashamed of his craven behavior on the camping trip; his own shadow had frightened him.
7. Oblivious to any fear or self-concern, the firefighter rushed into the burning house to save the cat trapped inside.
8. Our plans are only at the rudimentary stages; we won't finalize them for a while.
9. The smells of nutmeg, pumpkin, and roasting turkey permeate the kitchen on Thanksgiving morning.
10. We could tell that someone had camped at the site recently because the vestiges of a burned-out campfire remained behind.

290 TEACHER'S EDITION

***Spelling Tests** use vocabulary from the selections in the unit to test students' spelling abilities.*

***Additional Resources** notes identify assessment materials for the unit and study guides and worksheets for student review and practice.*

***Vocabulary Tests** allow you to assess students' knowledge of the vocabulary from the unit. The tests also appear in the Assessment Portfolio, which is part of the Teacher's Resource Kit.*

***Synthesis Questions** extend the ideas presented throughout the unit. These questions, which are appropriate prompts for writing, research, or discussion, cover genres, themes, and historical and biographical issues and allow students to synthesize the material from the unit.*

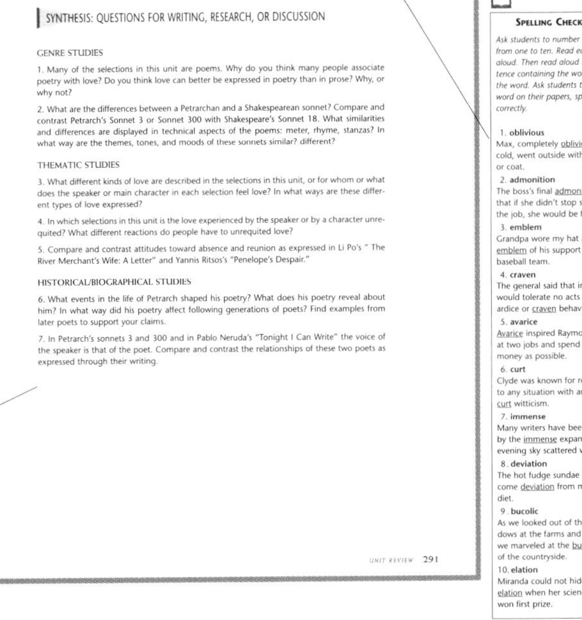

SYNTHESIS: QUESTIONS FOR WRITING, RESEARCH, OR DISCUSSION

GENRE STUDIES

1. Many of the selections in this unit are poems. Why do you think many people associate poetry with love? Do you think love can better be expressed in poetry than in prose? Why, or why not?

2. What are the differences between a Petrarchan and a Shakespearean sonnet? Compare and contrast Petrarch's Sonnet 3 or Sonnet 300 with Shakespeare's Sonnet 18. What similarities and differences are displayed in technical aspects of the poems: meter, rhyme, stanzas? In what way are the themes, tones, and moods of these sonnets similar? different?

THEMATIC STUDIES

3. What different kinds of love are described in the selections in this unit, or for whom or what does the speaker or main character in each selection feel love? In what ways are these different types of love expressed?

4. In which selections in this unit is the love experienced by the speaker or by a character unrequited? What different reactions do people have to unrequited love?

5. Compare and contrast attitudes toward absence and reunion as expressed in Li Po's " The River Merchant's Wife: A Letter" and Yannis Ritsos's "Penelope's Despair."

HISTORICAL/BIOGRAPHICAL STUDIES

6. What events in the life of Petrarch shaped his poetry? What does his poetry reveal about him? In what way did his poetry affect following generations of poets? Find examples from later poets to support your claims.

7. In Petrarch's sonnets 3 and 300 and in Pablo Neruda's "Tonight I Can Write" the voice of the speaker is that of the poet. Compare and contrast the relationships of these two poets as expressed through their writing.

UNIT REVIEW 291

Spelling Check Test

Ask students to number their papers from one to ten. Read each word aloud. Then read aloud the sentence containing the word. Repeat the word. Ask students to write the word on their papers, spelling it correctly.

1. **oblivious**
Max, completely oblivious to the cold, went outside without his hat or coat.
2. **admonition**
The boss's final admonition was that if she didn't stop sleeping on the job, she would be fired.
3. **emblem**
Grandpa wore my hat as an emblem of his support for my baseball team.
4. **craven**
The general said that in battle he would tolerate no acts of cowardice or craven behavior.
5. **avarice**
Avarice inspired Raymond to work at two jobs and spend as little money as possible.
6. **curt**
Clyde was known for responding to any situation with an ironic and curt witticism.
7. **immense**
Many writers have been inspired by the immense expanse of the evening sky scattered with stars.
8. **deviation**
The hot fudge sundae was a welcome deviation from my usual diet.
9. **bucolic**
As we looked out of the car windows at the farms and meadows, we marveled at the bucolic beauty of the countryside.
10. **elation**
Miranda could not hide her elation when her science project won first prize.

TEACHER'S EDITION 291

"The River-Merchant's Wife: A Letter"
by Li Po, translated by Ezra Pound

About the Author

LI PO
AD 701–762

Considered one of the great poets of China, **Li Po** lived and wrote during the T'ang Dynasty (AD 618–907), a period often called the Golden Age of Chinese poetry. Li Po grew up in the Sichuan (Szechwan) province of southwestern China. As a young man, he was well educated, but he chose not to pursue a traditional career in government. Instead, Li Po decided to live as a wanderer. As he traveled, he met many people, and his poetry became popular. After serving the emperor for a short time as an imperial court poet, he worked for a rebel prince who was eventually executed for treason. Li Po was banished from the country, but this sentence was later revoked. Over the course of his life, Li Po earned a reputation for being a free spirit who loved music, friendship, and romance as well as nature and solitude. A popular legend says that he drowned when trying to embrace the reflection of the moon in the Chang (Yangtze) River.

About the Selection

"The River-Merchant's Wife: A Letter" is a **narrative poem,** or a poem that tells a story. The speaker of the poem is a woman from eastern China waiting for her husband, who is a river merchant on a long and potentially dangerous journey. His journey takes him up the Chang River, also called the Yangtze, the longest river in China and in all of Asia. Nearly four thousand miles long, this river runs from Tibet in western China eastward through central China before emptying into the Pacific Ocean. While the speaker, the river-merchant's wife, awaits her husband, she describes the history of their relationship—how they first met, their early married life, and the changes that have occurred in their relationship.

Ezra Pound, the translator of the poem, worked from an English prose translation of a Japanese version of the poem. That is why you will notice, by reading footnotes accompanying the selection, that Japanese names are given for Chinese villages and rivers.

CONNECTIONS: Li Po and Taoism

Li Po is closely associated with Taoism (see page 555), one of China's major philosophies. Taoists try to avoid wasting their energies on earthly distractions such as the pursuit of wealth, power, or knowledge. By ignoring these distractions, by living close to nature, and by keeping to their own thoughts, Taoists believe they are able to concentrate on the true meaning of life itself.

"THE RIVER-MERCHANT'S WIFE: A LETTER" 245

ADDITIONAL RESOURCES

Reader's Guide
- Selection Worksheet 3.2

Assessment Portfolio
- Selection Check Test 2.3.3
- Selection Test 2.3.4

Essential Skills Practice Books
- Writing 1.8, 1.20
- Language 2.4, 2.9

PREREADING EXTENSIONS

Ezra Pound (1885–1972) founded Imagism, a literary movement that sought to recreate in poetry sensory experiences without commentary about the emotional content or meaning of those experiences. Pound's style reflects the minimalist style of traditional Chinese literature. Have groups of students research and present oral reports about the art and poetry of the T'ang Dynasty during which Li Po wrote.

Pound influenced other writers including H. D. (Hilda Doolittle), T. S. Eliot, James Joyce, William Carlos Williams, Robert Frost, Ernest Hemingway, and Marianne Moore. Students can read at least three works by one or these writers and write an analysis of the author's style.

SUPPORT FOR LEP STUDENTS

Pronunciations of Proper Nouns and Adjectives

Chō -fu-Sa (chō´ fū sä)
Chō • kan (chō´ kan)
Ki • ang (kē aŋ´)
Ku-tō -en (kū tō en´)
Li Po (lē pō)
Yang • tze (yaŋk´sē)

Additional Vocabulary

bashful—shy
scowling—frowning angrily

GOALS/OBJECTIVES

Studying this lesson will enable students to

- appreciate a narrative poem
- identify Li Po as a Chinese writer of the T'ang dynasty
- recognize mood changes
- recognize and describe a setting
- write a letter poem
- analyze character development
- identify personal pronouns
- understand and discuss the connection between imagery and ideographic writing

TEACHER'S EDITION 245

Sample Prereading Page

Additional Resources *notes identify materials from the Teacher's Resource Kit to use in teaching the selection: worksheets from the Reader's Guide and from the Essential Skills Practice Books, and selection check tests and tests from the Assessment Portfolio.*

Color-coded ***icons*** *identify at a glance* ***cross-curricular*** *activities (brown),* ***multiple intelligences*** *activities (green), and* ***SCANS*** *activities (blue). A key to these icons is provided on* *page T29* *of this Annotated Teacher's Edition.*

Prereading Extensions *provide additional prereading information or enrichment activities related to some aspect of the Prereading material.*

Support for LEP Students *provides pronunciations of proper nouns and adjectives and lists and defines potentially troublesome* ***Idioms, Colloquialisms,*** *and* ***Additional Vocabulary*** *to help you offer instruction before students encounter difficulties in reading.*

A list of ***Goals/Objectives*** *helps you plan intended learning outcomes for the selection. Affective goals are consistent with the philosophy of the program and its emphasis on reader involvement. Cognitive goals encompass content, literary technique, interpretation of the selection in historical context, and language arts skills taught in the student text.*

Sample Selection Page

Reader's Journal Notes *give suggestions for helping students relate the topic to their experience, anticipate questions or difficulties students may have, or provide additional prompts for students who have trouble starting. Special attention is given to problems that may arise from student diversity.*

Answers to Guided Reading Questions *are keyed to questions in the student edition.*

Integrated Skills Activities *provide additional exercises and activities that reinforce students' skills in language, speaking and listening, study and research, and applied English. Each activity or skill is integrated with some aspect of the selection.*

Cross-curricular Activities *are supplementary activities that involve knowledge, skills, research, and resources from disciplines other than language arts.*

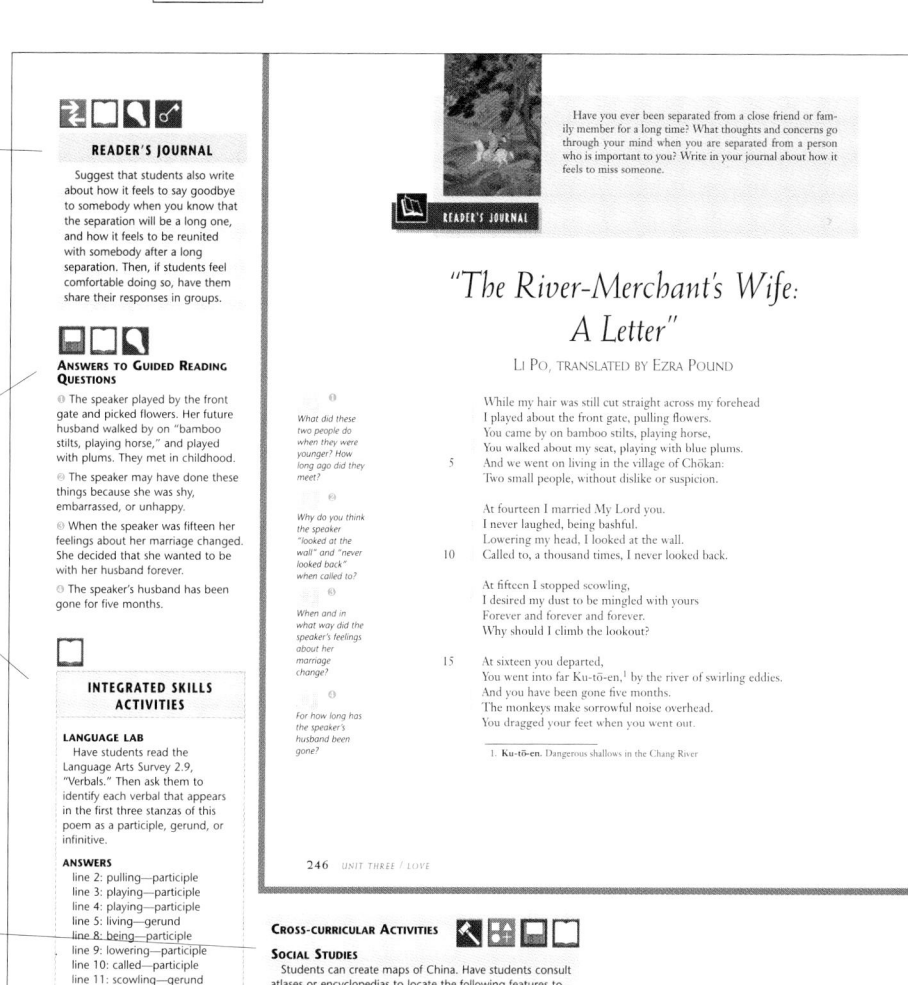

READER'S JOURNAL

Suggest that students also write about how it feels to say goodbye to somebody when you know that the separation will be a long one, and how it feels to be reunited with somebody after a long separation. Then, if students feel comfortable doing so, have them share their responses in groups.

ANSWERS TO GUIDED READING QUESTIONS

1. The speaker played by the front gate and picked flowers. Her future husband walked by on "bamboo stilts, playing horse," and played with plums. They met in childhood.
2. The speaker may have done these things because she was shy, embarrassed, or unhappy.
3. When the speaker was fifteen her feelings about her marriage changed. She decided that she wanted to be with her husband forever.
4. The speaker's husband has been gone for five months.

INTEGRATED SKILLS ACTIVITIES

LANGUAGE LAB

Have students read the Language Arts Survey 2.9, "Verbals." Then ask them to identify each verbal that appears in the first three stanzas of this poem as a participle, gerund, or infinitive.

ANSWERS

line 2: pulling—participle
line 3: playing—participle
line 4: playing—participle
line 5: living—gerund
line 8: being—participle
line 9: lowering—participle
line 10: called—participle
line 11: scowling—gerund
line 12: to be—infinitive

► Additional practice is provided in the Essential Skills Practice Book: Language 2.9.

246 TEACHER'S EDITION

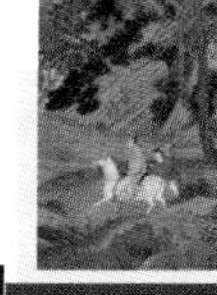

Have you ever been separated from a close friend or family member for a long time? What thoughts and concerns go through your mind when you are separated from a person who is important to you? Write in your journal about how it feels to miss someone.

READER'S JOURNAL

"The River-Merchant's Wife: A Letter"

LI PO, TRANSLATED BY EZRA POUND

1. *What did these two people do when they were younger? How long ago did they meet?*
2. *Why do you think the speaker "looked at the wall" and "never looked back" when called to?*
3. *When and in what way did the speaker's feelings about her marriage change?*
4. *For how long has the speaker's husband been gone?*

While my hair was still cut straight across my forehead
I played about the front gate, pulling flowers.
You came by on bamboo stilts, playing horse,
You walked about my seat, playing with blue plums.
And we went on living in the village of Chōkan:
Two small people, without dislike or suspicion.

At fourteen I married My Lord you.
I never laughed, being bashful.
Lowering my head, I looked at the wall.
Called to, a thousand times, I never looked back.

At fifteen I stopped scowling,
I desired my dust to be mingled with yours
Forever and forever and forever.
Why should I climb the lookout?

At sixteen you departed,
You went into far Ku-tō-en,[1] by the river of swirling eddies.
And you have been gone five months.
The monkeys make sorrowful noise overhead.
You dragged your feet when you went out.

1. **Ku-tō-en.** Dangerous shallows in the Chang River

246 UNIT THREE / LOVE

CROSS-CURRICULAR ACTIVITIES 

SOCIAL STUDIES

Students can create maps of China. Have students consult atlases or encyclopedias to locate the following features to label on their maps: the Chang (Yangtze) River, Tibet, Pacific Ocean, Szechwan province, Beijing (Peking), Yellow Sea. Ask students to identify other major regions, cities, and bodies of water in and surrounding China.

Vocabulary in Context *provides sample sentences using the target vocabulary words from Words for Everyday Use. For selections of more than one page, a list of all target vocabulary words in the selection is given in* ***Vocabulary from the Selection*** *on the first page of the selection.*

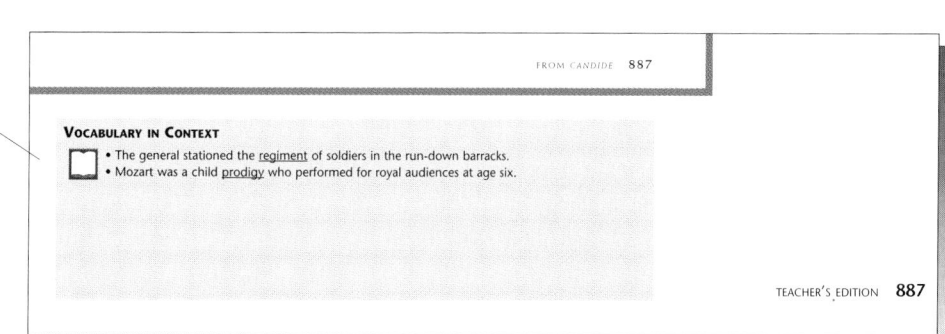

FROM CANDIDE 887

VOCABULARY IN CONTEXT

- The general stationed the <u>regiment</u> of soldiers in the run-down barracks.
- Mozart was a child <u>prodigy</u> who performed for royal audiences at age six.

TEACHER'S EDITION 887

Sample Selection Activity Page

Notes on presenting and facilitating the ***Responding to the Selection*** *assignment help you help students relate the topic to their experience, anticipate questions or difficulties students might have, or suggest alternative formats (such as large or small group discussion or role playing). These notes give special attention to concerns of diversity.*

Answers for Reviewing the Selection *give sample responses to Recalling, Interpreting, and Synthesizing questions.*

Answers to Selection Check Test *(not shown) includes the questions and an example and appears on or near the last page of each selection. You can photocopy the test from the Assessment Portfolio and distribute it, or you can present the questions orally.*

RESPONDING TO THE SELECTION

Encourage students to respond by sharing their own feelings about a lengthy separation from a loved one, by asking questions to delve into the speaker's feelings, by asking the speaker to share more memories, or by sharing a memory (imagined) about the speaker's husband.

ANSWERS FOR REVIEWING THE SELECTION

RECALLING AND INTERPRETING

1. **Recalling.** They have known each other since they were very young. The speaker was fourteen when she married her husband. **Interpreting.** At first, the speaker was shy and uncomfortable about being married. These feelings were demonstrated by her not laughing and the lowering or turning of her head when her name was called.
2. **Recalling.** The speaker learned to love her husband and became attached to him. **Interpreting.** The speaker stopped scowling and wanted her dust to be mingled with her husband's "forever and forever."
3. **Recalling.** The merchant has been gone for five months. **Interpreting.** The speaker is lonely. She misses her husband, worries about the dangers he faces, and longs for his return.
4. **Recalling.** The speaker describes the sorrowful sound of the monkeys, deep moss, the falling of autumn leaves, and paired butterflies. **Interpreting.** The monkeys sound sorrowful because the speaker feels sorrowful. The falling leaves reflect a sense of loss. The leaves and the moss also mark the passage of time. The paired butterflies painfully remind the speaker the she is not with her husband.

(cont.)

Responding to the Selection

How did you feel while reading this poem? Imagine that the speaker is a friend who has just shared her feelings with you. Write a response to the speaker, or if you prefer, with a partner, role play a response.

Reviewing the Selection

RECALLING		INTERPRETING
1. For how long have the speaker and her husband known each other? How old was the speaker when she married her husband?	▶▶	At first, what were the speaker's feelings about her husband and about getting married? What behaviors revealed these feelings?
2. In what way did the speaker's feelings about her husband change over the first year of her marriage?	▶▶	What reveals this change in the speaker's feelings toward her husband?
3. For how long has the merchant been gone?	▶▶	What does the speaker feel about her husband's absence and about his presence in a possibly dangerous situation?
4. What sights and sounds in the natural world does the speaker describe?	▶▶	In what way do the natural images reflect the speaker's feelings? Why might the monkeys sound sorrowful to her? Why might the paired butterflies "hurt" the speaker?

SYNTHESIZING

5. What do the final lines of the poem—in which the speaker says that she would travel to meet her husband if she knew where he was—reveal about the speaker's attitude toward him? What factors were likely to have caused the speaker's attitude toward her husband to change over time? In what way might the husband's absence affect the intensity of the speaker's feelings?

Understanding Literature (Questions for Discussion)

1. **Mood. Mood,** or **atmosphere,** is the emotion created in the reader by part or all of a literary work. What is the overall mood of this poem? Is the mood consistent throughout the poem? If no, where does the mood change?

248 *UNIT THREE / LOVE*

ANSWERS FOR REVIEWING THE SELECTION (CONT.)

SYNTHESIZING

Responses will vary. Possible responses are given.

5. The speaker reveals that she misses her husband greatly and that she is willing to undergo hardship herself to see him. She is also hopeful that she will be able to see her husband during this part of his trip. Over time, the speaker matured, got to know her husband better, and adapted to being married. The husband's absence may have intensified her feelings, because now that she wants to be with him she cannot be. Her feelings may follow the old adage, "Absence makes the heart grow fonder."

248 TEACHER'S EDITION

Sample Selection Activity Page

2. **Setting.** The **setting** of a literary work is the time and place in which it occurs, together with all the details used to create a sense of a particular time and place. Describe the setting of this poem. In what way does the world of the speaker and her husband differ from your own world? In what ways might their world be similar to your own?

Responding in Writing

1. **Creative Writing: Letter Poem.** Write a poem in the style of "The River-Merchant's Wife: A Letter." The speaker of your poem might be yourself, someone you know, or a character of your own invention. For example, your poem might be titled "The Busy Student: A Letter," "The Firefighter's Daughter: A Letter," or "The Astronaut's Husband: A Letter." Use your imagination to choose a character and topic that will inspire an interesting poem, rich with detail. To get started, write a paragraph or two describing your character's story and what he or she would like to say. Also write about the person who will receive the letter. What is that person like? What does this person need to understand by reading the letter? Develop your poem from the information gathered in your paragraph(s).
2. **Critical Essay: Character Development.** In an essay, discuss the ways in which the poet helps the reader to learn about the river-merchant's wife and the development of her feelings for her husband. What details within the poem help to sharpen the reader's picture of this woman? What statements can you make about her life and her character, based on details provided in the poem? What questions do you still have about this woman?

Language Lab

Personal Pronouns. Below is a paragraph about Ezra Pound, the translator of "The River-Merchant's Wife: A Letter." Read the paragraph and identify the personal pronouns in it. Some sentences contain more than one pronoun, and some possessive pronouns function in these sentences as both adjectives and personal pronouns. Refer as necessary to the Language Arts Survey 2.4, "Personal Pronouns."

[1] Ezra Loomis Pound was born in Hailey, Idaho, in 1885, but his family eventually moved to Pennsylvania. [2] He attended Hamilton College in New York and then took a master's degree at the University of Pennsylvania. [3] Pound eventually moved to Europe and spent about fifty years of his life there; it was a place in which he felt comfortable and inspired. [4] Pound often tried to assist other writers in their work. [5] He either helped or influenced writers such as T. S. Eliot, James Joyce, William Carlos Williams, Robert Frost, and Ernest Hemingway, many of whom stood by Pound when he later went through difficult times. [6] Pound had extreme political views, which got him into trouble, made him unpopular, and eventually landed him in prison. [7] We have read that there is debate about whether Pound's personal problems cast a shadow over his work. [8] Some classmates and I chose to become familiar with Pound's poetry. [9] Have you read the pieces, "Portrait d'une Femme," *The Cantos*, or *Hugh Selwyn Mauberley*? [10] These works are considered to be Pound's major poems; he is also known for translations from many languages.

"THE RIVER-MERCHANT'S WIFE: A LETTER" 249

ANSWERS FOR UNDERSTANDING LITERATURE

Responses will vary. Possible responses are given.

1. **Mood.** The poem is reminiscent and wistful, changing to lonely and sorrowful. The poem's mood is fairly consistent. In the opening lines, as the speaker refers to her past and the beginning of her relationship with her husband, the mood is sad and wistful. The mood shifts in the final few lines to a feeling of sadness and yearning.
2. **Setting.** The poem is set in a rural Chinese village, at a time when women went into arranged marriages at very young ages. It was also a time during which the river was a chief means of transportation. While these details make the speaker's world quite different from our world, students may recognize the love shared by the speaker and her husband and the feelings of sadness and helplessness that go along with missing someone and worrying for that person's safety.

ANALYTIC SCALES FOR RESPONDING IN WRITING

Grading scales for Responding in Writing appear on page 250.

ANSWERS FOR LANGUAGE LAB

1. his
2. He
3. his, it, he
4. their
5. He, he
6. him, him, him
7. We, his
8. I
9. you
10. he

▶ Additional practice is provided in the Essential Skills Practice Book: Language 2.4.

TEACHER'S EDITION 249

Answers for Understanding Literature *provides possible answers for these discussion questions.*

Analytic Scales for Responding in Writing *provide straightforward analytic criteria for evaluating student writing. Cross-references direct you to more elaborate evaluation instruments should you desire them. If, as here, the Analytic Scales do not appear on the same page as the writing assignment, a page reference is provided.*

Answers for Variable Skills *provide model answers for Language Labs, Speaking and Listening Skills, Thinking Skills, Study Skills, Research Skills, Test-taking Skills, and Applied English Skills activities. This box will often provide reference to an Essential Skills Practice Book for additional activities.*

Project Notes *provide suggestions and caveats for introducing, supporting, and monitoring student work on projects. These notes identify additional resources or persons that may be needed or useful and opportunities for enlarging or limiting the scope and duration of the project. Icons identify other cross-curricular areas involved in the project and the multiple intelligences and SCANS skills that students will use.*

PROJECT NOTES

See the evaluation form for projects, Assessment Portfolio 4.12.

Ancient Meso-American Civilizations. Students can create model cities, maps showing the areas settled by the civilization, and time lines of major events. Students may also wish to create illustrations or locate photographs of ruins or artifacts from the civilization that they are researching and use such visual aids in their presentations. Students may also wish to create a display for the library or other area about Meso-American civilizations in which they combine the visual aids from the three presentations and create written descriptions of the items for viewers.

TEACHER'S EDITION 537

Using Literature and the Language Arts *for Writing Instruction*

Recent Advances in the Theory of Writing Instruction

Let's face it. Learning to write well isn't easy. Simply mastering the conventions of spelling, grammar, usage, and mechanics takes years. Learning to write elegant, balanced sentences takes years more. Then there are all those tricks of the writer's craft—the forms or genres, the methods of organization, the rhetorical techniques and figures of speech, the modulations of tone and register, the subtleties of connotation. All these must be learned and then, in a sense, forgotten so that the writer's words flow from some deep, authentic place, from some uncommon spring, to produce a voice, a style. Little wonder it is then that Yeats should write, "there is no fine thing/Since Adam's fall but needs much laboring," or that Chaucer should remind us of the Latin adage *Ars longa; vita brevis:* "Art is long; life, short."

Given the time and effort that it takes to become even reasonably competent as a writer, it follows that no one would do so without some powerful motive. Fortunately for English teachers, children come into the world with such a motive. The child, newly arrived, cries out, trying to communicate. As children grow, they keep trying to communicate and will keep trying so long as the will to do so is not drowned in a sea of criticism.

One of the most exciting things that has happened in English education in the past few years is that a new model of writing instruction that respects the student's voice and effort has come to the fore. That model is the process and portfolio approach. Process and portfolio instruction breaks individual acts of writing and the overall business of learning to write into manageable steps, with guidance and feedback at each step. When students are given writing assignments today, they no longer have to figure out on their own how to get from the assignment to the completed piece of writing. Instead, they are trained in techniques for prewriting, drafting, evaluating their drafts by themselves and with peers, revising, and publishing. Writing portfolios and evaluation forms are used to track development of pieces of writing over time. Assessment has been expanded from simple marking of papers to include self-evaluation, peer evaluation, and a variety of approaches that avoid turning teachers into copyeditors. The result of these changes in writing instruction has been that student writing has improved dramatically in recent years.

Literature and the Language Arts contains comprehensive materials for integrated instruction in the process of writing and for management of writing portfolios. The notes that follow describe those materials and how they can be used.

Testing

Before beginning instruction in the process of writing, you may wish to have students take the Writing Skills Comprehensive Test 3.1 in the **Assessment Portfolio** contained in the Teacher's Resource Kit. This test is designed to assess students' familiarity with basic writing concepts and skills. The test may be used to assess which techniques and skills students need to focus on during the course, or it may be used at the end of the course to assess students' understanding of basic writing concepts and skills.

Introducing the Writing Process

Section 1 of the Language Arts Survey, which is called Essential Skills: Writing and begins on page 1126, surveys the entire writing process from prewriting through publishing. This section of the Survey is divided into twenty lessons. Additional practice activities for each lesson in the Language Arts Survey can be found in the Essential Skills Practice Book: Writing, in the Teacher's Resource Kit.

Teachers who wish to do so can teach the Essential Skills: Writing section of the Language Arts Survey in its entirety as a separate composition unit. Alternatively, teachers can have students refer to the writing section of the Language Arts Survey on an as-needed basis as they complete the composition assignments in the main body of the text.

Unit 1 of the student edition provides detailed instruction in the process of

writing, creative writing, and writing a critical essay. Each of these lessons introduces parts of the Language Arts Survey: Writing as a resource, provides instruction and examples, and includes an activity for students to try the skills and techniques presented in the lesson.

As students complete their first writing assignment and all subsequent writing assignments in the text, they can make use of the following general evaluation forms and checklists found in the **Assessment Portfolio:**

- Peer Evaluation and Self-evaluation Form: Process 4.1
- Peer Evaluation and Self-evaluation Form: The Writing Plan 4.2
- Peer Evaluation and Self-evaluation Form: Structure 4.3
- Peer Evaluation and Self-evaluation Form: Analytic Scale 4.4
- Peer Evaluation and Self-evaluation Form: Holistic Response 4.5
- Writing Summary Form: Student 4.6
- Comprehensive Portfolio Evaluation Form: Teacher 4.7
- Comprehensive Portfolio Evaluation Form: Student 4.8
- Revision and Proofreading Checklists 4.9

Teaching the Writing Assignments in the Text

Following every selection in Units 2–12 are activities called **Responding in Writing.** These activities use the literature selections as springboards for an enormous variety of engaging writing assignments. A glance at the Writing section of the Index of Skills on page 1329 will give you an idea of just how varied and interesting are the types of writing covered in this text. Two Responding in Writing activities are given after each selection; one is a creative writing assignment and the other is a prompt for a critical essay. You can choose to assign one or both, or you can give students the option of doing either of the two assignments.

As students complete these assignments, they can refer to relevant sections of the Essential Skills: Writing section of the Language Arts Survey. They can also make use of the many evaluation forms and checklists in the Assessment Portfolio.

The writing assignments in the text consist of prompts. Complete prewriting guidance for each writing assignment can be found on the **Selection Worksheet** that corresponds to any given selection. Selection Worksheets can be found in the **Reader's Guide and Activity Workbook** in the **Teacher's Resource Kit**.

For each writing assignment in the student edition, in this Annotated Teacher's Edition there is an **Analytic Scale for Evaluation** presenting assessment criteria for content, organization, style, and conventions of grammar, usage, mechanics, spelling, and manuscript form. The editors and authors of this text strongly suggest that these evaluation scales be given to students when they receive the initial writing prompts so that they can keep the eventual evaluation criteria in mind as they work through the writing process. These scales can also be used by students for peer evaluation and self-evaluation. Alternatively, or in addition, students can peer evaluate and self-evaluate using the evaluation forms in the Assessment Portfolio.

Process for Writing Assignments

The editors and authors recommend the sequence of activities in the chart on page T20 for each writing assignment in the main body of the text. Steps 1–11 may be repeated for each writing assignment. Then, periodically, step 12 should also be completed.

Using Writing Portfolios

The student's **Writing Portfolio** is a folder in which he or she stores drafts and finished pieces of writing. You can ask your students to keep a portfolio to enable you and the students to assess their progress over time. Portfolios show students' capabilities and progress better than any test or single writing assignment can.

You may wish to ask your students to keep **comprehensive portfolios** that contain all the writing that they do for class, along with Writing Summary Forms and/or evaluation forms for each piece of writing. Alternatively, you can ask your students to keep **selected portfolios** that contain pieces of writing chosen by the students as representative of their best work. Students should be encouraged to choose for their selected portfolios pieces that show the various skills they have developed and the various types of writing that they have done (informative, persuasive, creative, etc.).

When students place works in their portfolios, make sure that they attach their notes and drafts behind the finished works so that you will be able to see at a glance how each piece of writing was developed. Also have students attach to their works any evaluation forms they have used.

From time to time, you will want to do a comprehensive evaluation of the students' portfolios. A Comprehensive Evaluation Form: Teacher 4.7, in the Assessment Portfolio, has been provided for this purpose. You should also have each student do his or her own comprehensive evaluation using the Comprehensive Evaluation Form: Student 4.8 in the Assessment Portfolio. Once these evaluations are complete, you can meet in a conference with each student to discuss his or her progress, provide praise for work well done, and make plans for improvement in the future.

Process for Writing Assignments

1. WHOLE CLASS: Study of the literature selection in the student edition textbook, along with its corresponding instructional apparatus
2. TEACHER: Introduction of the writing prompt from the student text
3. STUDENT: Prewriting (with reference to any applicable prewriting lessons in the Essential Skills: Writing section of the Language Arts Survey, pages 1126–1146 of the student text)
4. STUDENT: Drafting (with reference to the drafting lesson in the Essential Skills: Writing section of the Language Arts Survey, page 1147 of the student text)
5. STUDENT: Sharing of draft with one or more peers
6. STUDENT and PEER(S): Evaluation of the draft and conferencing with one another and with the teacher if necessary (with reference to the Analytic Scale for Evaluation from the Annotated Teacher's Edition and/or the general evaluation forms and revision checklists 4.1–4.6 and 4.9 in the Assessment Portfolio)
7. STUDENT: Revising (with reference to the Revision and Proofreading Checklists 4.9 in the Assessment Portfolio, and to the revision section of the Essential Skills: Writing section of the Language Arts Survey on page 1148 of the student text)
8. STUDENT: Proofreading and preparation of the final manuscript (with reference to the Revising and Proofreading Checklists 4.9, in the Assessment Portfolio, and to the proofreading and manuscript preparation sections of the Essential Skills: Writing section of the Language Arts Survey, pages 1150–1151 of the student text) and completion of the Writing Summary Form 4.6 in the Assessment Portfolio
9. STUDENT and PEER(S): Publishing and/or presenting of the completed draft (with reference to the lesson on publishing and presenting in the Essential Skills: Writing section of the Language Arts Survey, page 1152 of the student text)
10. STUDENT and TEACHER: Assessment and/or conferencing with regard to the completed work
11. STUDENT: Decision as to whether to place the completed work in the student's Writing Portfolio
12. STUDENT and TEACHER: Evaluate the student's Writing Portfolio (using the Comprehensive Portfolio Evaluation Form: Teacher 4.7 and the Comprehensive Portfolio Evaluation Form: Student 4.8 in the Assessment Portfolio) and hold a teacher-student conference to discuss the evaluation and to set goals for future writing improvement.

Assessing Student Writing

(For a more complete treatment of assessment, see the introduction to the Assessment Portfolio in the Teacher's Resource Kit.)

Assessment of student writing should not have as its primary purpose meting out rewards or punishments. Instead, assessment should be seen as a development tool allowing the teacher and the student, working in collaboration, to monitor the student's progress toward achieving his or her goals.

Approaches to assessment vary. Two common approaches to assessing writing are analytic evaluation and holistic evaluation.

Analytic Evaluation. An analytic evaluation of a piece of writing begins with an analysis of the several features or qualities desired in the writing. These desired features or qualities are then used as standards or criteria against which the piece is compared. The evaluator merely goes down the list of criteria, giving the piece of writing a score for each criterion. A summary evaluation of the writing is obtained by combining these several scores.

Analytic evaluation is particularly valuable for formative evaluation. A general judgment of a student's work may be daunting, especially for students who do not do as well as they expect to do. Likewise, students who perform well, if given general comments about the writing, find in such general judgments little specific guidance telling them what they might do to write better. An analytic evaluation can show students exactly what their strengths and weaknesses are and where they should concentrate their efforts.

Analytic evaluation is valuable as a measure of either progress or achievement. To evaluate progress, you can evaluate the student's progress in each

area by comparing the current work with previous similar writing assignments. To measure raw achievement, you can compare the student's product against some imagined ideal. Of course, in either case you must make sure that your students are aware of the criteria on which they are being graded.

The Analytic Evaluation Scales provided next to the writing assignments in this Annotated Teacher's Edition provide lists of appropriate criteria for analytic evaluation, along with simple procedures for scoring. In addition, a general Writing Evaluation Form: Analytic Scale is provided as item 4.4 of the Assessment Portfolio.

Holistic Evaluation. Holistic evaluation of a piece of writing calls for an overall judgment. Holistic evaluation is most useful as a measure of achievement. It is difficult to score holistic evaluations according to a student's progress. To do a holistic evaluation, simply look over the general analytic criteria and then assign a score that reflects how well the student met those criteria taken as a whole.

Holistic evaluation takes less time than analytic evaluation and in most cases results in the same score. The saved time can be used to make encouraging written comments to the student, pointing out features of the writing that you admire and features of the writing that you would like to see improve in the student's future work. A general Writing Evaluation Form: Holistic Response is provided in the Assessment Portfolio as item 4.5.

Grading. Some teachers prefer to grade each writing assignment. Others feel that grading selected assignments chosen by the teacher and student to reflect the student's best work provides a more realistic assessment of the student's optimal capabilities. If the latter option is chosen, you may wish to provide credit for completion of assignments that are not graded.

Marking Student Papers. A student who receives from a teacher a returned paper covered with corrections in red ink is not likely to be encouraged to do more and better writing. Furthermore, such marking of student papers is enormously time consuming and discourages frequent writing practice. A more encouraging approach is to mark one or two consistent problems and to mark three or four successes in each paper or, better yet, to allow students and their peers to do such marking and then to review these evaluations in conferences. Such marking can be done in conjunction with the completion of evaluation forms and/or analytic scales.

Reports and Research Papers

Literature and the Language Arts contains complete materials for instruction in the preparation of reports and research papers. The Research Skills section of Essential Skills: Study and Research in the Language Arts Survey, pages 1228–1274 of the student text, contains a complete overview of research procedures, from using the library through documenting sources. The Synthesis questions that appear at the end of each Unit Review make excellent topics for extended reports or research papers. Further instruction on preparing longer papers can be found in the sections on outlining and drafting in Essential Skills: Writing in the Language Arts Survey, pages 1146–1147 of the student text. Of course, these sections of the Language Arts Survey are accompanied by worksheets in the corresponding Essential Skills Practice Books in the Teacher's Resource Kit.

Remedial Exercises in Specific Writing Skills

During your evaluations of students' writing, either of individual pieces or of entire portfolios, you will doubtless discover consistent areas of weakness. One student may have trouble making transitions, another may consistently use serial commas incorrectly, and another may rely too heavily on the passive voice. The Language Arts Survey in the student edition and the accompanying Essential Skills Practice Book worksheets provide ample activities for remediation of particular recurring problems. Most of the instruction and activities in the writing and language sections of the Language Arts Survey are useful for this purpose. Thus, if a student has a tendency to write sentence fragments or run-ons, you can have him or her read the Language Arts Survey 2.27, "Correcting Sentence Fragments, Run-ons, and Sentence Strings" on page 1180 of the student text. Then you can have that student do the corresponding worksheet in the Essential Skills Practice Book: Language. If a student has problems organizing his or her ideas, you can have him or her read the Language Arts Survey 1.11, "Organizing Ideas," and do the corresponding worksheet in the Essential Skills Practice Book: Writing. Thus, the Language Arts Survey and the Essential Skills Practice Books can be used to individualize your writing instruction and to target it to remediation of particular writing problems encountered by your students.

Instructional Options

Approaches to *Literature and the Language Arts*

Literature and the Language Arts contains a number of features that allow you the flexibility to organize your instruction to best suit you and your district's requirements. The following chart offers some tips for using your chosen approach to the text.

Features of the Program, by Approach

Historical Approach

- The Unit Introductions for Units 7–12 tie literary developments to influential intellectual currents and political events, providing historical contexts for the selections.
- About the Author and About the Selection prereading notes provide additional historical background and context.
- The time line at the beginning of the book provides a spatial representation of key events and developments.
- Selections from thematic units are keyed to the proper historical period in Other Selections Exploring This Period boxes in the Table of Contents for those who would like to use a historical approach.

Thematic Approach

- Units 2–6 are organized thematically and include discussion about five major themes (the struggle against intolerance, love, death, nature, and metamorphosis) by international students.
- Selections from historical units are keyed to the proper thematic unit in Other Selections Exploring This Theme boxes in the Table of Contents for those who would like to use a thematic approach.
- To examine other themes, see the Thematic Organization Chart on pages T30–T34, which classifies all the selections in the book under forty-seven major themes.
- Responding in Writing prompts following selections ask students to explore and develop their thoughts about thematic topics.
- Synthesis questions in the Unit Review help students explore thematic relations among selections.

Geographical Approach

- The home country of the author of each selection in the text is identified in the Table of Contents and on the Prereading page.
- Information about the histories and cultures of many of these countries is provided in the About the Author, About the Selection, or Connections box on the Prereading page for each selection.
- Additional cultural information is provided about the eight countries highlighted in Unit 1. Information about these countries also appears in Global Voices and Global Views features throughout the book.
- Use the Selections by Geographical Area list on pages T34–T36 to choose selections from countries or regions that you would like to study with your students.

Writing Approach

- In Unit 1, an overview is provided of the writing process, with strategies for completing a piece of creative writing and for writing a critical essay.
- The Language Arts Survey, Essential Skills: Writing following Unit 12 provides instruction in all the phases and forms of writing, editing, and proofreading.
- The Essential Skills Practice Book: Writing provides guided exercises in all the phases and forms of writing, editing, and proofreading. These worksheets are keyed to the instructional text in the Language Arts Survey.

Skills Approach

- The Language Arts Survey following Unit 12 provides instruction for the range of language arts skills and concepts, including writing, grammar, usage, mechanics, speaking and listening, study and research, thinking, and applied English.
- The Essential Skills Practice Books provide guided exercises for the range of language arts skills: writing, editing, proofreading, grammar, usage, mechanics, speaking and listening, study and research, testing, and thinking. These worksheets are coordinated with the instructional text in the Language Arts Survey.
- The Assessment Portfolio contains tests and evaluation forms for language arts skills in writing, editing, proofreading, grammar, usage, mechanics, speaking and listening, study and research, testing, and thinking (4.1–4.5). These materials are coordinated with the instructional text in the Language Arts Survey and with the worksheets in the Essential Skills Practice Books.

Teaching Strategies

Teaching to Develop Students' Multiple Intelligences and to Accommodate Diverse Learning Styles

Activities using multiple intelligences are identified by green icons. See the legend on page T29.

Use the techniques in the chart at right to teach and encourage students with diverse intellectual strengths and learning styles and to help all students use and develop the full range of their abilities.

Teaching Multiple Intelligences

- Use multiple modes of expression: e.g., read selections aloud; read questions aloud; use visual aids—charts, graphs, tables, or other graphics, art, and films; play songs; and perform demonstrations.
- Encourage students to use multiple modes of expression, including nonverbal expressions and performances such as drawing, painting, collage, sculpture, dance and choreography, acting and oral interpretation, photography, filmmaking, video production, and musicianship and singing.
- Ask students to read aloud.
- Precede written work with a related oral activity.
- Teach students to use graphic aids for understanding and for studying.
- Facilitate group work.
- Use cooperative learning.
- Allow students ample thinking time.

Teaching Students Whose Native Language Is Not English

Use the techniques in the chart at right to facilitate learning and participation for students whose native language is not English.

Teaching Students Whose Native Language Is Not English

- Ask students to read aloud.
- Precede written work with a related oral activity.
- Use cooperative learning.
- Allow ample thinking time.
- When using small groups, pair with English-proficient students.
- Provide ample opportunity for nongraded, even nonevaluated, writing in English.
- Use multiple modes of expression: e.g., read selections aloud; read questions aloud; use visual aids—charts, graphs, tables, or other graphics, art, and films; play songs; and perform demonstrations.
- Encourage students to use multiple modes of expression, including nonverbal expressions and performances such as drawing, painting, collage, sculpture, dance and choreography, acting and oral interpretation, photography, filmmaking, video production, and musicianship and singing.

Teaching Students with Diverse Cultural Backgrounds

Use the techniques in the chart at right to facilitate learning and participation for students with diverse cultural backgrounds.

Teaching Students with Diverse Cultural Backgrounds

- Encourage discussion of cultural differences; invite students to share contrasting experiences; invite them to discuss events and characters from the selections that strike them as odd. Rely on students for your cultural information; be aware that you are liable to overlook differences unless you can take a different point of view.
- Use multiple modes of expression: e.g., read selections aloud; read questions aloud; use visual aids—charts, graphs, tables, or other graphics, art, and films; play songs; and perform demonstrations.
- Encourage students to use multiple modes of expression, including nonverbal expressions and performances such as drawing, painting, collage, sculpture, dance and choreography, acting and oral interpretation, photography, filmmaking, video production, and musicianship and singing.
- Precede written work with a related oral activity.
- Use cooperative learning.
- Allow ample thinking time.
- When using small groups, pair with English-proficient students.
- Preview/explain culturally loaded terms and names.
- Discuss idioms and word origins.
- Discuss topics with universal appeal and relevance—for instance, independence versus family ties, independence versus friendship, or identity.
- Discuss literature from both an "insider" and an "outsider" perspective.

Teaching Students with Learning Disabilities

Learning disabilities are physical conditions that make it difficult to complete certain types of tasks. Students with learning disabilities are often highly intelligent but lack specific abilities; for instance, one person may lack the ability to discriminate certain sounds, while another person may be able to discriminate among sounds but be unable to remember certain auditory messages. Use the techniques in the chart at right to help students with learning disabilities succeed in your classroom.

Teaching Students with Learning Disabilities

- Discover the particular effects of each individual's disability and try to fill gaps.
- Allow ample thinking time.
- Seat students in front.
- Repeat important ideas frequently.
- Summarize and check students' bearings frequently.
- Monitor progress frequently.
- On larger projects, provide step-by-step guidance.
- Precede written work with a related oral activity.
- Use cooperative learning.
- Use multiple modes of expression: e.g., read selections aloud; read questions aloud; use visual aids—charts, graphs, tables, or other graphics, art, and films; play songs; and perform demonstrations.
- Encourage students to use multiple modes of expression, including nonverbal expressions and performances such as drawing, painting, collage, sculpture, dance and choreography, acting and oral interpretation, photography, filmmaking, video production, and musicianship and singing.

Teaching Students with Special Academic Gifts and Talents

Just as students who work below grade level may lose interest because tasks are too difficult, students with special academic gifts and talents may lose interest because they complete work quickly or because they are not sufficiently challenged.

Activities involving other curricular areas are identified by red icons. See the legend on page T29.

Teaching Students with Special Academic Gifts and Talents

- Encourage students to use multiple modes of expression, including nonverbal expressions and performances such as drawing, painting, collage, sculpture, dance and choreography, acting and oral interpretation, photography, filmmaking, video production, and musicianship and singing.
- Use cooperative learning.
- Allow ample thinking time.
- Involve students in the planning, preparation, and presentation or conduct of lessons.
- Provide or encourage extension activities once mastery is demonstrated.
- Provide or encourage self-guided activities and independent research.

> "[C]hildren come to school with misconceptions about outside ethnic groups and with a white bias. However, . . . students' racial attitudes can be modified and made more democratic and . . . the racial attitudes of young children are much more easily modified than the attitudes of older students and adults. . . . If we are to help students acquire the attitudes needed to survive in a multicultural and diverse world, we must start early. . . .
>
> "A school experience that is multicultural includes content, examples, and realistic images of diverse racial and ethnic groups. Cooperative learning activities in which students from diverse groups work to attain shared goals is also a feature of the school, as well as simulated images of ethnic groups that present them in positive and realistic ways. Also essential within such a school are adults who model the attitudes and behaviors they are trying to teach. Actions speak much louder than words."
>
> —James A. Banks
> "Multicultural Education:
> Historical Development, Dimensions, and Practice"
> *Review of Research in Education*
> 19 (1993): 37–38

Achieving Gender Equity

Sexism cannot be combatted subtly (Sadker and Sadker 123). In addition to using the techniques listed at right, make a directed effort to combat gender stereotypes and to treat all students as valued learners.

Achieving Gender Equity

Facts: Boys call out answers eight times as frequently as do girls (Sadker and Sadker 43). Boys receive more evaluative feedback—both positive and negative (Sadker, Sadker, and Klein 300; Sadker and Sadker 55).

Responses:
- Make a special effort to call on girls and to give them specific feedback, both positive and negative. (Note: If you give more than one-third of your attention to girls you may be accused of favoring girls; see Sadker and Sadker 266–267.)
- When intervening in student-student interactions, concentrate on raising girls' confidence rather than criticizing boys' behavior.

Fact: Exposure to gender-biased materials appears to increase gender stereotypes (Sadker, Sadker, and Klein 279; Sadker and Sadker 73–75, 128–135, 266).

Responses:
- Be aware of biases in literature and point them out.
- When appropriate, provide historical context for stereotyping by explaining older attitudes and practices.
- Provide direct lessons about gender stereotypes and gender-related communication styles.

Facts: Girls are more likely than boys to attribute their successes to luck and less likely than boys to attribute their successes to ability (Sadker, Sadker, and Klein 303). Girls are more likely than boys to attribute their failures to lack of ability and less likely than boys to attribute their failures to lack of effort (303). Teachers are more likely to comment on girls' appearance and the neatness of their work, and more likely to comment on the intellectual qualities of boys' work (Sadker and Sadker 57).

Responses:
- Make an effort to avoid commenting on students', especially girls', appearance.
- Make an effort to attribute all success to effort and ability.
- Make an effort to rebut forcefully students' self-deprecating comments.

Facts: Girls have lower expectations of success (Sadker, Sadker, and Klein 302) and are more likely to display signs of "learned helplessness" (303). Teachers are more likely to help boys solve their own problems, but to solve problems for girls (Sadker and Sadker 81–83).

Responses:
- Fear of being "too tough" on girls is patronizing and hinders them from developing independence and confidence. Don't be afraid to criticize girls' work and don't let them off easy (Holt; Sizer).
- Make an effort to rebut forcefully students' self-deprecating comments.

Teaching Students to Work Cooperatively

Prepare your students for work in cooperative learning groups by teaching them how to listen actively, how to participate fully in discussions, and how to give one another positive feedback. Refer students to the lessons on listening, interpersonal communication, and discussion, sections 3.2–3.3 of the Language Arts Survey.

Uses for Small Groups. Use these task and project ideas to direct the work of collaborative learning groups.

- brainstorming
- peer tutorial sessions
- learning partners for practice or review and for all stages of the writing process
- inquiry-based concept learning
- multimedia and community-based projects
- topical symposia
- panel discussions
- mock jury trials
- role playing
- dramatizations
- simulations
- reader's theater

Teaching Students to Work Cooperatively

PREPARING STUDENTS FOR SMALL GROUP WORK

Participation

- Review/preteach vocabulary and cultural concepts for nonnative speakers.
- Begin with a nongraded, fun, get-to-know-one-another activity.
- Take steps to ensure that group members know each other's names.
- Assign tasks that call on multiple intelligences.
- Ask questions that call for personal response and interpretation.
- Value interpretations that differ from your own.
- Have students determine the wording of their topics or questions.
- Don't talk too much.
- Model tentativeness and openness.
- Model courtesy and respect for all.
- Respond only holistically and orally to early drafts and initial products.
- Avoid judging early drafts; discuss ideas rather than expression.
- Discuss anonymous samples.
- Praise students for taking risks.
- Require (only) positive feedback from peers.
- Use joint grading for group work: (1) everyone in the group receives the average among the group; (2) everyone receives the lowest grade among the group; (3) a final product is graded and everyone receives that grade.

Leadership

- Ask students to conduct lessons.
- Rotate leadership assignments in groups.
- Appoint two group leaders—one to learn from the other.
- Model and give direct instruction and practice in asking questions.
- Model and give direct instruction and practice in reporting a summary.
- Model and give direct instruction and practice in involving nonparticipants.
- Model and give direct instruction and practice in restraining dominators.
- Model and give direct instruction and practice in providing positive feedback.
- Model and give direct instruction and practice in providing constructive feedback.

Listening/Discussing

- Model, explain, and encourage attentive listening, eye contact, and not interrupting.
- Give practice in paraphrasing students' words and your own.
- Ask students to identify good speaking and listening habits and skills.
- Ask students to evaluate group processes and their roles in their groups (use the form in the *Assessment Portfolio* 4.10).

FORMING GROUPS

- Groups should contain a maximum of six students for a complex task, a maximum of four otherwise.
- For peer writing groups, two may be the ideal size. Require periodically that students change partners.
- In the prewriting stage, it can be helpful to match those who share a primary language other than English.
- Working groups should contain students of varied abilities.
- Allow groups to vary their seating arrangements (suggest possibilities).

GUIDING AND MONITORING

- Give specific tasks.
- Explain criteria for success.
- Assign roles in groups, or assign groups to distribute roles.
- When assigning roles in groups, divide responsibilities to assure interdependence and cooperation. One workable division of responsibilities includes (1) a discussion leader/facilitator; (2) a recorder; (3) a reporter; (4) a materials manager.
- Specify desired behaviors (see "Preparing Students for Small Group Work," above).
- Monitor group interactions and advise when appropriate.
- Intervene to diffuse conflict and to foster collaborative skills.
- When intervening in group work, ask a question rather than giving advice directly.
- If multiple groups have the same problem, interrupt the process and clarify or reteach.

CLOSURE AND ASSESSMENT

- Ask for sharing of a product.
- Both students and teacher should assess the quality of the product. Assessment can be among the entire class or only within groups.
- Both students and teacher should assess the quality of the group processes and communication.

Planning for Conferences and Portfolio Evaluation

As a teacher you have a number of distinguishable evaluative roles as outlined in the charts at right. Of course, you will not take on all of these roles at once. Make sure that students know which role to expect *before* they receive feedback.

References

Herman, J., P. Aschbacher, and L. Winters. *A Practical Guide to Alternative Assessment.* Alexandria, VA: ASCD, 1992.

Eggen, P., and D. Kauchak. *Educational Psychology.* 2nd ed. New York: Merrill, 1994.

Gardner, H. *Frames of Mind: The Theory of Multiple Intelligences.* New York: Basic, 1985.

———. *The Unschooled Mind: How Children Think and How Schools Should Teach.* New York: Basic, 1991.

Holt, J. *How Children Learn.* New York: Putnam, 1967.

Ohrlich, D., et al. *Teaching Strategies.* 4th ed. Lexington, MA: Heath, 1994.

Sadker, M., and D. Sadker. *Failing at Fairness.* New York: Scribner's, 1993.

Sadker, M., D. Sadker, and S. Klein. "The Issue of Gender in Elementary and Secondary Education." *Review of Research in Education* 17 (1991): 269–334.

Sizer, T. *Horace's Compromise.* Boston: Houghton, 1984.

Slavin, R. *Cooperative Learning: Theory, Research, and Practice.* Englewood Cliffs, NJ: Prentice, 1990.

———. *Educational Psychology.* 3rd ed. Englewood Cliffs, NJ: Prentice, 1991.

Understanding the Roles of Evaluators

ROLE	FUNCTION
AUDIENCE	to listen to ideas, to challenge, to question, to enlarge perspective
PROOFREADER	to correct grammar, usage, and mechanics
GRADER	to judge against external, more or less objective, and more or less arbitrary standards
ADVISOR	to prod for problem soutions, to encourage, to give suggestions, to remind of objectives

ROLE	TEACHING TIPS
AUDIENCE	Act exclusively as an audience when you read and comment on drafts. Comments on drafts should avoid direct criticism and should aim at raising students' excitement about further writing and revising.
PROOFREADER	Overemphasis on proofreading and points of grammar, usage, and mechanics can drain students' interest in and enthusiasm for writing as well as their self-confidence. Use proofreading as a peer function, and allow students to learn from reading and proofreading each other's papers.
GRADER	Avoiding grading as much as possible allows both you and students to concentrate on clear and honest expression and to preserve intrinsic motivation.
ADVISOR	Because the advising function requires one-on-one interchange, you should reserve for it as much of the precious evaluation time as you can.

Conducting Conferences

- Examine the portfolio before conferencing with the student. Make sure it contains all required material, including the student's evaluations of each piece of writing (Assessment Portfolio 4.6) and of the portfolio as a whole (Assessment Portfolio 4.8).
- Evaluate the portfolio before conferencing. Complete the portfolio evaluation form (Assessment Portfolio 4.7), making special note of any discrepancies between your evaluaiton and the student's.
- Do not attempt to discuss all aspects of the portfolio or the student's class performance. Choose two or three broad, major points and one or two specific problems to focus on in the conference.
- As an alternative to conferencing, you may sometimes complete and hand to students a Portfolio Evaluation Form and additional writing evaluation forms (Assessment Portfolio 4.1–4.5). You will still need to allow time for students to respond to and ask questions about their evaluations, and to hold conferences with students who need special help or encouragement.
- To allow ample class time for conferences, you must assign sufficient work that students can do independently to keep them busy on conference days. Thus, you must establish the writing process and the peer groups early in the term.
- In addition, to allow yourself ample time to evaluate portfolios you must involve students in ongoing self- and peer evaluation.

Additional Resources for Language Arts Teachers

TEACHING LITERATURE

Applebee, A. N. *Tradition and Reform in the Teaching of English: A History.* Urbana, IL: NCTE, 1974.

Atwell, N. *In the Middle: Writing, Reading, and Learning with Adolescents.* Portsmouth, NH: Heinemann, 1987.

Beach, R., and J. Marshall. *Teaching Literature in the Secondary School.* Orlando, FL: Harcourt, 1991.

Becoming a Nation of Readers: The Report of the Commission on Reading. Washington, DC: NIE, 1984.

Buck, C., ed. *The Bloomsbury Guide to Women's Literature.* New York: Prentice, 1992.

Bushman, J., and K. Bushman. *Using Young Adult Literature in the Classroom.* New York: Macmillan, 1992.

Cooper, C. R., ed. *Researching Response to Literature and the Teaching of Literature.* Norwood, NJ: Ablex, 1988.

Farrell, E. J., and J. Squire, eds. *Transactions with Literature: A Fifty-Year Perspective.* Urbana, IL: NCTE, 1990.

Flood, J., et al., eds. *Handbook of Research on Teaching the English Language Arts.* New York: Macmillan, 1991.

Glazer, S. *Reading Comprehension: Self-monitoring Strategies That Create Independent Readers.* New York: Scholastic, 1992.

Langer, J. A., ed. *Literature Instruction: A Focus on Student Response.* Urbana, IL: NCTE, 1992.

Lee, C., and T. Gura. *Oral Interpretation.* 8th ed. Boston: Houghton, 1992.

Marzano, R. *Cultivating Thinking English and the Language Arts.* Urbana, IL: NCTE, 1991.

Newell, G. E., and R. K. Durst. *Exploring Texts: The Roles of Discussion and Writing in the Teaching and Learning of Literature.* Norwood, MA: Christopher-Gorden, 1993.

Probst, R. E. *Response and Analysis: Teaching Literature in Junior and Senior High School.* Portsmouth, NH: Boynton/Cook, 1988.

Rosenblatt, L. *Literature as Exploration.* 4th ed. New York: MLA, 1983.

———. *The Reader, the Text, the Poem: The Transactional Theory of the Literary Work.* Carbondale, IL: Southern Illinois UP, 1978.

Wagner, B. J., and M. Larson. *Situations: A Casebook of Virtual Realities for the English Teacher.* Portsmouth, NH: Boynton/Cook, 1994.

Widdowson, P., ed. *Re-reading English.* London: Routledge, 1982.

TEACHING WRITING

Bogel, F. V., and K. K. Gottschalk, eds. *Teaching Prose.* New York: Norton, 1988.

Dellinger, D. G. *Out of the Heart: How to Design Writing Assignments for High School Courses.* Berkeley, CA: Bay Area Writing Project.

Elbow, P. *Writing with Power: Techniques for Mastering the Writing Process.* New York: Oxford UP, 1981.

Flower, L. S. *Problem-Solving Strategies in Writing.* 2nd ed. Orlando, FL: Harcourt, 1985.

Fulwiler, T., ed. *The Journal Book.* Portsmouth, NH: Heinemann, 1987.

Handa, C., ed. *Computers and Community: Teaching Composition in the Twenty-First Century.* Portsmouth, NH: Boynton/Cook, 1990.

Harris, M. *Teaching One-to-One: The Writing Conference.* Urbana, IL: NCTE, 1986.

Hawisher, G. E. "Research and Recommendations for Computers and Composition." *Critical Perspectives on Computers and Composition Instruction.* Ed. G. E. Hawisher and C. L. Selfe. New York: Teacher's Coll. P, 1989: 44–69.

Irmscher, W. *Teaching Expository Writing.* New York: Holt, 1979.

Kirby, D., and T. Liner. *Inside Out: Developmental Strategies for Teaching Writing.* Upper Montclair, NJ: Boynton/Cook, 1981.

Langer, J. A., and A. N. Applebee. *How Writing Shapes Thinking: A Study of Teaching and Learning.* NCTE Research Rept. No. 22. Urbana, IL: NCTE, 1987.

Lindemann, E. *A Rhetoric for Writing Teachers.* New York: Oxford UP, 1982.

Moffett, J., and B. J. Wagner. *Student-Centered Language Arts, K–12.* 4th ed. Portsmouth, NH: Boynton/Cook, 1992.

Murray, D. *Write to Learn.* New York: Holt, 1984.

Rodrigues, D., and R. Rodrigues. *Teaching Writing with Word Processors, Grades 1–13.* Urbana, IL: NCTE, 1987.

Romano, T. *Clearing the Way: Working with Teenage Writers.* Portsmouth, NH: Heinemann, 1987.

Ross, M., D. Brackett, and A. Maxon. *Assessment and Management of Mainstreamed Hearing-Impaired Children.* Austin, TX: Pro-Ed, 1991.

Shaughnessy, M. *Errors and Expectations.* New York: Oxford UP, 1977.

Spear, K. *Sharing Writing.* Upper Montclair, NJ: Boynton/Cook, 1988.

Tate, G., and E. Corbett, eds. *The Writing Teacher's Sourcebook.* New York: Oxford UP, 1981.

Weaver, Constance. *Grammar for Teachers.* Urbana, IL: NCTE, 1979.

TEACHING GRAMMAR

Elley, W. B., et al. "The Role of Grammar in a Secondary School English Curriculum." *Research in the Teaching of English* 10 (1976): 5–21.

Hillocks, G., Jr. *Research on Written Composition.* Urbana, IL: Natl. Conference on Research in English and ERIC/CRCS, 1986.

TEACHING THINKING SKILLS

Ausubel, D. P. *Educational Psychology.* 2nd ed. New York: Holt, 1978.

Chance, P. *Thinking in the Classroom: A Survey of Programs.* New York: Teacher's Coll. P, 1986.

Costa, A. L. *Developing Minds: A Resource Book for Teaching Thinking.* Rev. ed. 2 Vols. Alexandria, VA: ASCD, 1991.

Gardner, H. *The Unschooled Mind.* New York: Basic, 1991.

Horton, S. *Thinking through Writing.* Baltimore: Johns Hopkins UP, 1982.

Lazear, D. G. *Teaching for Multiple Intelligences.* Fastback No. 342. Bloomington, IN: Phi Delta Kappa Educ. Foundation, 1992.

Nickerson, R. S., D. N. Perkins, and E. E. Smith. *The Teaching of Thinking.* Hillsdale, NJ: Erlbaum, 1985.

Novak, J. D., and D. B. Gowin. *Learning How to Learn.* New York: Cambridge UP, 1984.

Pressley, M., et al. *Cognitive Strategy Instruction That Really Improves Children's Academic Performance.* Cambridge, MA: Brookline, 1990.

Resnick, L. B. *Education and Learning to Think.* Washington, DC: Natl. Academy P, 1987.

Resnick, L. B., and L. E. Klopfer, eds. *Toward the Thinking Curriculum: Current Cognitive Research.* Alexandria, VA: ASCD, 1989.

Rogoff, B. *Apprenticeship in Thinking.* New York: Cambridge UP, 1989.

Sternberg, R. J. "How Can We Teach Intelligence?" *Educational Leadership* 42 (1984): 38–50.

Sternberg, R. J., and T. I. Lubart. "Creating Creative Minds." *Phi Delta Kappan* 72 (1991): 608–614.

Sternberg, R. J., and R. Wagner. *Practical Intelligence.* New York: Cambridge UP, 1985.

ASSESSMENT

California Assessment Program. *The California Assessment Program: A Position Paper on Testing and Instruction.* Sacramento, CA: CAP, 1990.

Cambourne, B., and J. Turbil. "Assessment in Whole-Language Classrooms: Theory into Practice." *Elementary School Journal* 90 (1991): 337–349.

García, G. E., and P. D. Pearson. "Assessment and Diversity." *Review of Research in Education* 20 (1994): 337–391.

Gronlund, N. E., and R. L. Linn. *Measurement and Evaluation in Teaching.* 6th ed. New York: Macmillan, 1990.

Herman, J. L., P. R. Aschbacher, and L. Winters. *A Practical Guide to Alternative Assessment.* Alexandria, VA: ASCD, 1992.

Johnston, P. H. *Constructive Evaluation of Literate Activity.* White Plains, NY: Longman, 1992.

Smith, M. A., and M. Ylvisaker, eds. *Teacher's Voices: Portfolios in the Classroom.* Berkeley, CA: Natl. Writing Project, 1994.

Wolf, D., et al. "To Use Their Minds Well: Investigating New Forms of Student Assessment." *Review of Research in Education* 17 (1991): 31–74.

Yancey, K. B., ed. *Portfolios in the Writing Classroom.* Urbana, IL: NCTE, 1992

TEACHING SPECIAL POPULATIONS

Banks, J., and C. M. Banks, eds. *Multicultural Education: Issues and Perspectives.* 2nd ed. Boston: Allyn, 1993.

Brooks, C., ed. *Tapping Potential: English and the Language Arts for the Black Learner.* Urbana, IL: NCTE, 1985.

Cummins, J. *Empowering Minority Students.* Sacramento, CA: CA Assoc. for Bilingual Education, 1989.

Farr, M., and H. Daniels. *Language Diversity and Writing Instruction.* New York: ERIC Clearinghouse on Urban Education/Columbia UP, 1986.

Garcia, E. E. "Language, Culture, and Education." *Review of Research in Education* 19 (1993): 51–98.

Haberman, M. "The Pedagogy of Poverty versus Good Teaching." *Phi Delta Kappan* (1991): 290–294.

Hernandez, H. *Multicultural Education: A Teacher's Guide to Content and Process.* Columbus, OH: Merrill, 1989.

Kronick, D. *New Approaches to Learning Disabilities.* Philadelphia, PA: Grune & Stratton, 1988.

Marik, R. *Special Education Students Write: Classroom Activities and Assignments.* Berkeley, CA: Bay Area Writing Project, 1982.

Shade, B. J. *Culture, Style, and the Educative Process.* Springfield, IL: Charles Thomas, 1989.

Slavin, R., N. Karweit, and N. Madden, eds. *Effective Programs for Students at Risk.* Boston: Allyn, 1989.

West, W. W. *Teaching the Gifted and Talented in the English Classroom.* Washington, DC: NEA, 1980.

GENDER ISSUES

Brown, L. M., and C. Gilligan. *Meeting at the Crossroads: Women's Psychology and Girls' Development.* Cambridge: Harvard UP, 1992.

Gilbert, P. *Gender, Literacy, and the Classroom.* Carlton South, Victoria: Austral. Reading Assn., 1989.

Sadker, M., and D. Sadker. *Failing at Fairness: How Schools Cheat Girls.* New York: Scribner's, 1994.

Sadker, M., D. Sadker, and S. Klein. "The Issue of Gender in Elementary and Secondary Education." *Review of Research in Education* 17 (1991): 269–334.

Wellesley College Center for Research on Women. *How Schools Shortchange Girls: The AAUW Report.* Washington, DC: American Assn. of Univ. Women, 1992.

TEACHING HIGH SCHOOL-AGE STUDENTS

Applebee, A. N. *The Child's Concept of Story: Ages Two to Seventeen.* Chicago: U of Chicago P, 1978.

Flavell, J. *Cognitive Development.* 2nd ed. Englewood Cliffs, NJ: Prentice, 1985.

Kohlberg, L. "Education for Justice: A Modern Statement of the Platonic View." *Five Lectures on Moral Education.* Ed. N. F. Sizer and T. R. Sizer. Cambridge: Harvard UP, 1970.

KEY TO ICONS

Cross-curriculum Icons

Arts and Humanities

Mathematics and Sciences

Social Studies

Applied Arts

Multiple Intelligence Icons

Musical Intelligence
Ability to produce and to appreciate forms of musical expression

Logical-Mathematical Intelligence
Ability to reason and to discern logical or numerical patterns

Spatial Intelligence
Ability to configure space to pose and solve problems

Kinesthetic Intelligence
Ability to use the body effectively to solve problems

Interpersonal/ Intrapersonal Intelligence
Ability to respond to the needs of others, self

SCANS Icons

Managing Resources
Identifies, organizes, plans, allocates time, money, materials, space, human resources

Interpersonal Skills
Works with others as member of team

Information Skills
Acquires, evaluates, organizes, maintains, interprets, communicates, and processes information

Systems Skills
Understands complex inter-relationships

Technology Skills
Selects, applies, and maintains appropriate technology to perform tasks and solve problems

Basic Skills
Reads, writes, performs arithmetic and mathematical operations, and listens and speaks well

Thinking Skills
Thinks creatively, makes decisions, solves problems, visualizes, knows how to learn, and reasons

Personal Qualities
Displays responsibility, self-esteem, sociability, self-management, and integrity and honesty

Thematic Organization Chart

The chart on these pages lists forty-seven common literary themes and identifies the selections in this book that deal with these themes. Choose the themes you wish to teach in your course, and use the chart to identify selections that deal with those themes.

	AGE	ALIENATION	ART AND ARTISTRY	BEAUTY	BIRTH	CONFUSION	COURAGE AND FEAR	DEATH	DISCOVERING AND LEARNING	DIVERSITY AND PLURALISM	DRAMA AND ACTING	EXILE	FAITH	FAMILY	FREEDOM	FRIENDSHIP	THE FUTURE	GIVING	GOD	GREED AND AMBITION	GROWTH/GROWING UP	HERO/HEROISM	HOME AND COUNTRY	HONESTY	HOPE	IDENTITY	IMAGINATION	INDEPENDENCE	JUSTICE	KNOWLEDGE/WISDOM	LAW AND CUSTOM	LEADERSHIP AND AUTHORITY	LOSS AND REMEMBRANCE	LOVE	NATURE	ORDER/DISORDER	PARENTS AND CHILDREN	PEACE	PRIDE AND VANITY	RELIGION	SCIENCE	STRUGGLE	TECHNOLOGY	TRUTH/REALITY	WAR	WORK	WRITING AND BOOKS
UNIT 1																																															
from *Like Water for Chocolate*, 9		●			●									●	●						●		●			●		●			●	●	●	●			●					●				●	
“Marriage Is a Private Affair,” 24									●	●		●		●									●								●	●		●			●					●					
“Poseidonians,” 37		●		●																			●			●					●		●														
from *The Bald Soprano*, 46						●					●			●												●							●			●								●			
“Conversation with an American Writer,” 58			●				●								●								●	●																							●
from *Nectar in a Sieve*, 69						●				●													●										●		●								●				
“The Street-Sweeping Show,” 80											●													●								●												●			
“The Nose,” 92		●		●																						●													●	●							
UNIT 2																																															
A Doll’s House, 110							●			●	●			●	●						●			●		●		●		●		●										●					
Requiem, 168			●				●	●					●	●	●								●		●				●				●	●			●					●					●
from *Night*, 181		●				●	●	●		●			●	●	●				●											●			●			●	●			●		●		●	●		
from *The Bluest Eye*, 189		●		●						●				●											●	●				●					●		●										
from *Kaffir Boy*, 196		●				●			●	●				●	●						●		●							●	●													●			
“By Any Other Name,” 204		●							●	●				●									●			●				●							●										
“Crazed Man in Concentration Camp,” 214		●				●		●							●																		●									●					
“The Censors,” 214							●								●								●					●	●		●											●					●
from Universal Declaration of Human Rights, 215										●					●													●	●		●	●						●									
UNIT 3																																															
from the *Aeneid*, 222								●				●										●	●										●	●					●								
“The River-Merchant’s Wife: A Letter,” 245																					●												●	●													●
Sonnet 3, “It was the morning of that blessèd day,” 251				●											●																			●													
Sonnet 300, “Great is my envy of you . . . ,” 251				●				●					●						●														●	●						●							
“Though I am Laila of the Persian romance,” 257															●											●		●		●				●	●												●
“Tonight I Can Write,” 261			●	●																					●					●			●	●	●							●					●
“Penelope’s Despair,” 266			●									●			●									●	●		●	●						●										●			
“The Little Heidelberg,” 270	●			●					●	●		●													●								●	●										●			
“Love after Love,” 279									●																	●							●	●													
from the Song of Solomon, 286				●									●						●															●	●					●							
Sonnet 75, “One day I wrote her name . . . ,” 286			●																														●	●	●												●

Selection	AGE	ALIENATION	ART AND ARTISTRY	BEAUTY	BIRTH	CONFUSION	COURAGE AND FEAR	DEATH	DISCOVERING AND LEARNING	DIVERSITY AND PLURALISM	DRAMA AND ACTING	EXILE	FAITH	FAMILY	FREEDOM	FRIENDSHIP	THE FUTURE	GIVING	GOD	GREED AND AMBITION	GROWTH/GROWING UP	HERO/HEROISM	HOME AND COUNTRY	HONESTY	HOPE	IDENTITY	IMAGINATION	INDEPENDENCE	JUSTICE	KNOWLEDGE/WISDOM	LAW AND CUSTOM	LEADERSHIP AND AUTHORITY	LOSS AND REMEMBRANCE	LOVE	NATURE	ORDER/DISORDER	PARENTS AND CHILDREN	PEACE	PRIDE AND VANITY	RELIGION	SCIENCE	STRUGGLE	TECHNOLOGY	TRUTH/REALITY	WAR	WORK	WRITING AND BOOKS
“Your love turned . . . ,” 286																										•								•	•												
from *Wuthering Heights*, 287																										•								•	•												
from *The Gardener*, 287			•																														•	•													•
“If I Forget Thee, Jerusalem,” 287																							•			•							•	•													
“Love Orange,” 287		•						•	•					•				•			•					•	•			•			•	•								•					
UNIT 4																																															
“The Weighing of the Heart of Ani,” 296								•					•											•	•				•		•									•		•					
“The Death of Socrates,” 303							•	•								•														•			•														
“Lament for His Son,” 310	•							•					•	•		•			•						•								•	•			•			•							
from *The Death of Iván Ilyich*, 314	•	•					•	•	•					•												•																•					
from *The Sound of the Mountain*, 323	•			•		•	•	•						•													•							•	•												
“Life Is Sweet at Kumansenu,” 330					•		•	•						•				•													•		•	•			•							•			
“Tuesday Siesta,” 339								•						•																			•	•			•		•								
“Rice Pudding,” 347								•						•																			•	•			•					•					
“Life is a malady . . . ,” 356								•																											•												
“David’s Lament for Jonathan,” 356								•								•																	•														
“Ode on the Death of a Favorite Cat,” 356								•																									•														
“After Death,” 357								•																									•	•													
“A Refusal to Mourn the Death by Fire of a Child in London,” 357								•																									•				•										
UNIT 5																																															
from “Hymn to the Sun,” 364													•										•									•			•	•				•							
“I Built My Cottage among the Habitations of Men,” 372												•											•												•												
“the old pond—,” 378				•																															•												
“the sound of the water jar,” 378				•																															•												
“the first snow,” 378				•																															•												
“The snow is melting,” 378				•																															•		•										
“In the summer rain,” 378				•																															•												
“In the lingering wake,” 378				•																															•												
“Song Composed in August,” 384				•											•								•											•	•	•											
“The Iguana,” 390				•				•	•											•															•												
“The Flower of Air,” 395			•																								•							•	•							•				•	•
To “Free-Spirited Fisherman,” 402			•																						•	•									•				•								•
“The Garden of Stubborn Cats,” 406		•										•								•															•							•	•				
“Season,” 417																							•												•	•											
“Of Autumn,” 421								•																								•			•												
from *Of Nature*, 427																																			•												
from *The Road from Coorain*, 427																							•												•							•				•	
UNIT 6																																															
“The Story of Actaeon,” 436				•			•	•																		•			•			•															
“The Lay of the Werewolf,” 444		•											•											•		•			•			•		•		•											
from *The Metamorphosis*, 454		•												•	•							•				•										•						•		•		•	

	AGE	ALIENATION	ART AND ARTISTRY	BEAUTY	BIRTH	CONFUSION	COURAGE AND FEAR	DEATH	DISCOVERING AND LEARNING	DIVERSITY AND PLURALISM	DRAMA AND ACTING	EXILE	FAITH	FAMILY	FREEDOM	FRIENDSHIP	THE FUTURE	GIVING	GOD	GREED AND AMBITION	GROWTH/GROWING UP	HERO/HEROISM	HOME AND COUNTRY	HONESTY	HOPE	IDENTITY	IMAGINATION	INDEPENDENCE	JUSTICE	KNOWLEDGE/WISDOM	LAW AND CUSTOM	LEADERSHIP AND AUTHORITY	LOSS AND REMEMBRANCE	LOVE	NATURE	ORDER/DISORDER	PARENTS AND CHILDREN	PEACE	PRIDE AND VANITY	RELIGION	SCIENCE	STRUGGLE	TECHNOLOGY	TRUTH/REALITY	WAR	WORK	WRITING AND BOOKS
"Lot's Wife," 470												●	●						●				●			●			●				●	●						●		●					
"The Fifth Story," 474						●		●																		●	●															●					
"The Youngest Doll," 481			●	●										●	●					●						●		●						●					●					●			
"Apollo and Daphne," 492				●																						●								●								●					
UNIT 7																																															
from *The Epic of Gilgamesh*, 502			●				●	●	●												●	●			●	●				●										●		●				●	●
from Genesis, 518					●			●				●	●						●											●	●				●	●				●		●					
from the *Popol Vuh*, 532					●				●				●																	●			●		●	●				●							
"The Five Worlds and Their Suns," 538					●			●					●					●				●														●			●	●							
from the *Tao Te Ching*, 544				●									●																	●					●	●				●		●		●			
from the *Analects*, 550									●					●		●										●				●	●	●			●		●										
"Creation Hymn," 556					●	●							●						●											●						●				●				●			
from the *Ramayana*, 560							●					●	●	●		●		●				●		●		●			●	●		●		●						●		●		●	●		
from the *Sunjata*, 575							●									●		●				●								●												●				●	
"Inanna and Ishkur," 583								●																											●	●				●					●		
from *Chuang Tzu*, 583																										●																					
"The Four Noble Truths, or the First Sermon," 583					●								●																	●					●	●				●		●					
UNIT 8																																															
from the *Iliad*, 592							●	●														●	●																●			●			●		
"But Not Everybody Wants Love," 609																										●								●													
"At Last," 609																																		●													
"It Gives Me Joy to Think," 609																																		●			●										
Fragment 144, 609			●					●																	●								●														●
"Let's Not Pretend," 609	●			●				●																		●							●						●							●	●
"Life Slips By," 609	●	●						●																																							
"I Think of Achilles," 609								●														●																				●			●		
Oedipus the King, 618					●	●			●		●	●		●	●							●				●			●	●	●	●				●	●		●			●		●			
"Pericles' Funeral Oration," 674							●	●							●			●				●	●			●		●			●		●									●			●		
from *From the Founding of the City*, Book I, 683					●			●												●		●	●			●						●							●			●					
"My life, my love, you say our love will last forever," 691																																		●													
"My woman says that she would rather wear the wedding-veil for me," 691													●											●										●													
"I hate and love," 691																																		●								●					
"You are the cause of this destruction," 691						●																												●		●											
from *The Lives of the Noble Grecians and Romans*, 696								●												●												●		●		●						●					
from *The Histories*, 710																							●												●												
UNIT 9																																															
from *The Story of the Grail*, 722		●				●	●		●				●						●		●	●				●				●										●		●		●			
from *Tristan*, 732						●																												●								●					

	AGE	ALIENATION	ART AND ARTISTRY	BEAUTY	BIRTH	CONFUSION	COURAGE AND FEAR	DEATH	DISCOVERING AND LEARNING	DIVERSITY AND PLURALISM	DRAMA AND ACTING	EXILE	FAITH	FAMILY	FREEDOM	FRIENDSHIP	THE FUTURE	GIVING	GOD	GREED AND AMBITION	GROWTH/GROWING UP	HERO/HEROISM	HOME AND COUNTRY	HONESTY	HOPE	IDENTITY	IMAGINATION	INDEPENDENCE	JUSTICE	KNOWLEDGE/WISDOM	LAW AND CUSTOM	LEADERSHIP AND AUTHORITY	LOSS AND REMEMBRANCE	LOVE	NATURE	ORDER/DISORDER	PARENTS AND CHILDREN	PEACE	PRIDE AND VANITY	RELIGION	SCIENCE	STRUGGLE	TECHNOLOGY	TRUTH/REALITY	WAR	WORK	WRITING AND BOOKS
“Lady Maria, your worth and excellence,” 742				•									•			•		•							•									•						•							
from *The Divine Comedy*, 747						•		•					•						•															•						•							
“Ballade,” 759								•					•						•			•																		•							
from *The Tale of Genji*, 765		•												•																		•		•			•		•			•					
from *The Pillow Book*, 770				•																						•				•					•	•											
The Exordium, 778													•						•																					•							
The Cataclysm, 778								•					•						•																					•							
Daylight, 778													•						•																•					•							
“The Fisherman and the Jinnee,” 784							•								•			•		•									•	•	•	•							•								
from *The Rubáiyát of Omar Khayyám*, 796								•																	•									•	•	•											
“The Man Who Fled from Azrael,” 804							•	•				•	•						•																							•		•			
“The Elephant in the Dark House,” 804						•			•																		•																	•			
from *The Song of Roland*, 809							•	•								•				•		•	•		•							•		•					•			•			•		
“I Sing of a Maiden,” 812					•								•						•															•						•							
from *The Chronicle of Contemporary Events*, 813																				•											•					•			•			•			•		
UNIT 10																																															
“Federigo’s Falcon,” 822																		•						•	•	•								•					•								
from *Orlando Furioso*, 830										•												•	•								•											•					
Sonnet 23, 847																								•										•													
from *The Ingenious Hidalgo Don Quixote de la Mancha*, 852							•									•						•			•		•																	•			
from “Of Cannibals,” 860									•	•													•							•	•																
from *Fables*, 867																		•								•			•						•							•					
from *Tartuffe*, 872														•						•			•	•							•	•							•								
from *Candide*, 884									•			•													•	•			•	•	•					•				•				•	•		
from *The Prince*, 892																				•												•															
“When You Are Very Old,” 893	•			•				•																									•	•					•								•
from *Pensées*, 893																			•											•					•	•				•	•			•			
from *An Essay on Criticism*, 894			•						•																					•					•												•
from *Natural Theology*, 895																			•											•					•	•				•	•			•			
UNIT 11																																															
“My Heart Leaps Up When I Behold,” 904				•																					•										•												
“Loreley,” 909			•	•		•		•																										•													
from *Les Misérables*, 914		•													•	•		•		•				•	•	•		•	•		•									•							
“They say that plants don’t talk . . . ,” 925																																			•												
from *Germinal*, 930												•																														•				•	
“The False Gems,” 941				•										•						•				•									•						•					•			
“The Bet,” 949		•	•	•					•			•			•					•					•			•		•						•						•		•			
from *Cyrano de Bergerac*, 958				•		•					•													•		•								•					•					•			

	AGE	ALIENATION	ART AND ARTISTRY	BEAUTY	BIRTH	CONFUSION	COURAGE AND FEAR	DEATH	DISCOVERING AND LEARNING	DIVERSITY AND PLURALISM	DRAMA AND ACTING	EXILE	FAITH	FAMILY
"The Shoes," 984						●	●	●						●
from *The Confessions*, 993									●					
"The Overcoat," 993		●												
from *Madame Bovary*, 1006				●										
UNIT 12														
"Araby," 1018		●				●			●					
from *Orlando*, 1026														
"The Guitar," 1035		●	●					●						
"And We Shall Be Steeped," 1040			●							●				
"Metonymy, or The Husband's Revenge," 1044		●												
"The Myth of Sisyphus," 1052		●						●						
"Request to a Year," 1060			●				●			●				●
"The First Sally (A) or Trurl's Electronic Bard," 1065									●					
from *Being There*, 1078		●				●								
"Snapshots of a Wedding," 1086										●				●
"Games at Twilight," 1094		●					●	●	●					●
from *The Woman Warrior*, 1104		●				●	●		●	●				●
"The Wooden Horse then said," 1112							●							
"The Book of Sand," 1118		●				●	●		●					
"A Song on the End of the World," 1120							●			●				
"Simmering," 1120							●			●				

	FREEDOM	FRIENDSHIP	THE FUTURE	GIVING	GOD	GREED AND AMBITION	GROWTH/GROWING UP	HERO/HEROISM	HOME AND COUNTRY	HONESTY	HOPE	IDENTITY	IMAGINATION	INDEPENDENCE	JUSTICE
"The Shoes," 984						●				●					
from *The Confessions*, 993												●			
"The Overcoat," 993															●
from *Madame Bovary*, 1006						●									
UNIT 12															
"Araby," 1018	●						●				●	●	●		
from *Orlando*, 1026							●					●	●		
"The Guitar," 1035															
"And We Shall Be Steeped," 1040									●		●			●	
"Metonymy, or The Husband's Revenge," 1044															●
"The Myth of Sisyphus," 1052	●							●			●				
"Request to a Year," 1060	●			●								●			
"The First Sally (A) or Trurl's Electronic Bard," 1065			●			●							●		
from *Being There*, 1078		●													
"Snapshots of a Wedding," 1086	●											●			
"Games at Twilight," 1094							●					●			
from *The Woman Warrior*, 1104	●						●	●	●			●		●	
"The Wooden Horse then said," 1112	●					●		●	●	●					●
"The Book of Sand," 1118						●									
"A Song on the End of the World," 1120	●		●									●		●	
"Simmering," 1120	●											●		●	

	KNOWLEDGE/WISDOM	LAW AND CUSTOM	LEADERSHIP AND AUTHORITY	LOSS AND REMEMBRANCE	LOVE	NATURE	ORDER/DISORDER	PARENTS AND CHILDREN	PEACE	PRIDE AND VANITY	RELIGION	SCIENCE	STRUGGLE	TECHNOLOGY	TRUTH/REALITY	WAR	WORK	WRITING AND BOOKS
"The Shoes," 984	●	●					●						●					
from *The Confessions*, 993																		●
"The Overcoat," 993															●		●	
from *Madame Bovary*, 1006				●						●								
UNIT 12																		
"Araby," 1018	●				●										●			
from *Orlando*, 1026			●		●	●	●								●			●
"The Guitar," 1035				●														
"And We Shall Be Steeped," 1040	●	●																
"Metonymy, or The Husband's Revenge," 1044					●					●					●			●
"The Myth of Sisyphus," 1052	●												●				●	
"Request to a Year," 1060	●				●			●										●
"The First Sally (A) or Trurl's Electronic Bard," 1065														●				●
from *Being There*, 1078	●		●															
"Snapshots of a Wedding," 1086		●			●			●		●								
"Games at Twilight," 1094	●							●										
from *The Woman Warrior*, 1104					●			●					●		●			
"The Wooden Horse then said," 1112		●	●															
"The Book of Sand," 1118	●						●								●			●
"A Song on the End of the World," 1120	●	●		●			●						●		●		●	●
"Simmering," 1120	●	●					●						●		●		●	●

Selections by Geographical Area

These pages list all the selections in this book, organized geographically. Choose the areas you wish to explore with your students, and use the list to identify selections that represent those places.

AFRICA

Botswana
Bessie Head
"Snapshots of a Wedding," 1086

Kenya
Isak Dinesen
"The Iguana," 390

Mali
Anonymous
from the *Sunjata*, 575

Nigeria
Chinua Achebe
"Marriage Is a Private Affair," 24

Wole Soyinka
"Season," 417

Senegal
Léopold Sédar Senghor
"And We Shall Be Steeped," 1040

Sierra Leone
Abioseh Nicol
"Life Is Sweet at Kumansenu," 330

South Africa
Mark Mathabane
from *Kaffir Boy*, 196

AUSTRALIA

Australia
Jill Ker Conway
from *The Road from Coorain*, 427

Judith Wright
"Request to a Year," 1060

CENTRAL AND SOUTH AMERICA AND THE CARIBBEAN

Argentina
Jorge Luis Borges
"The Book of Sand," 1118

Luisa Valenzuela
"The Censors," 214

Brazil
Clarice Lispector
"The Fifth Story," 474

Rachel de Queiroz
"Metonymy, or The Husband's Revenge," 1044

Chile
Isabel Allende
"The Little Heidelberg," 270

THE EMC MASTERPIECE SERIES

LITERATURE AND THE LANGUAGE ARTS

World Literature

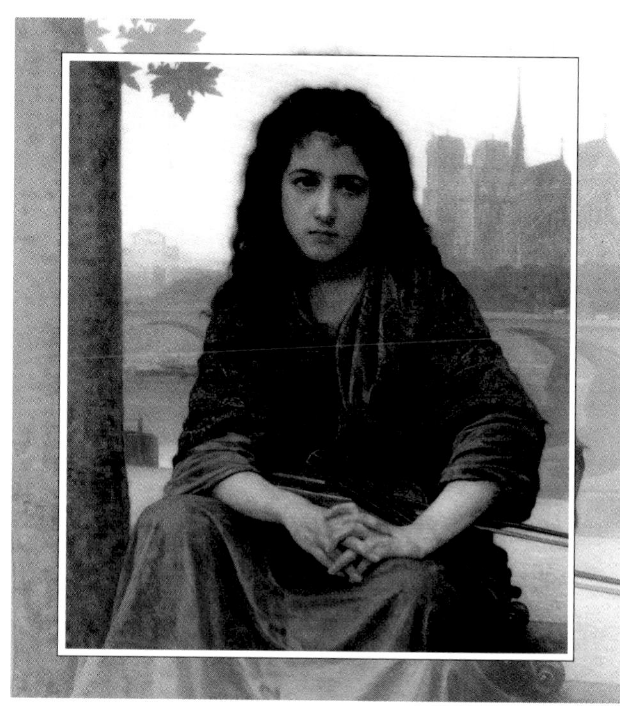

EMCParadigm Publishing
St. Paul, Minnesota

Staff Credits:

For **EMC/Paradigm Publishing,** St. Paul, Minnesota

Laurie Skiba
Editor

Shannon O'Donnell Taylor
Associate Editor

Jennifer J. Anderson
Assistant Editor

Eileen Slater
Editorial Consultant

For **Penobscot School Publishing, Inc.,** Danvers, Massachusetts

Editorial

Robert D. Shepherd
President, Executive Editor

Christina E. Kolb
Managing Editor

Kim Leahy Beaudet
Editor

Sara Hyry
Editor

Laurie Faria
Associate Editor

Sharon Salinger
Copyeditor

Marilyn Murphy Shepherd
Editorial Advisor

Design and Production

Charles Q. Bent
Production Manager

Tatiana Cicuto
Compositor

Sara Day
Art Director

Janet Stebbings
Compositor

Diane Castro
Compositor

Linda Rill
Permissions

Cover Credits

Cover Designer: C. Vern Johnson

***The Bohemian* [Detail],** 1890. William-Adolphe Bouguereau. The Minneapolis Institute of Arts.

Annotated Teacher's Edition

ISBN 0-8219-1564-9

Published by EMC/Paradigm Publishing
875 Montreal Way
St. Paul, Minnesota 55102

Printed in the United States of America
10 9 8 7 6 5 4 3 2 1
XXX 06 05 04 03 02 01 00

ISBN 0-8219-1563-0

Published by EMC/Paradigm Publishing
875 Montreal Way
St. Paul, Minnesota 55102

Printed in the United States of America
10 9 8 7 6 5 4 3 2 1 XXX 06 05 04 03 02 01 00

Acknowledgments:

Addison Wesley Longman Limited, UK.

"Love Orange," from *Summer Lightning*, by Olive Senior. Copyright © 1986 by Olive Senior. Reprinted by permission of Addison Wesley Longman Limited, UK.

Alfred A. Knopf, Inc.

Excerpt from *The Sound of the Mountain*, by Yasunari Kawabata. Copyright © 1970 by Alfred A. Knopf, Inc. Reprinted by permission of the publisher.

Excerpt from *The Road from Coorain*, by Jill Ker Conway. Copyright © 1989 by Jill Conway. Reprinted by permission of Alfred A. Knopf, Inc.

Excerpts from the *Tao Te Ching*, by Gia-fu Feng and Jane English. Copyright © 1972 by Gia-fu Feng and Jane English. Reprinted by permission of Alfred A. Knopf, Inc.

Excerpt from *The Tale of Genji* by Lady Murasaki Shikibu. Copyright © 1976 by Edward G. Seidensticker. Reprinted by permission of Alfred A. Knopf, Inc.

"The Myth of Sisyphus" from *The Myth of Sisyphus and Other Essays* by Albert Camus. Copyright 1955 by Alfred A. Knopf, Inc. Reprinted by permission of the publisher.

(continued on page 1338)

Literature and the Language Arts

Cypress Level
World Literature

Maple Level
The British Tradition

Pine Level
The American Tradition

Willow Level
Understanding Literature

Birch Level
Experiencing Literature

Consultants and Writers

Dr. Edmund J. Farrell
Emeritus Professor of English Education
University of Texas at Austin
Austin, Texas

Wole Alade
Instructor, African-American Studies
Phillips Academy
Andover, Massachusetts
Emerson College
Boston, Massachusetts

Tatiana Cicuto
Literature and Culture Consultant
Venice, Italy

Sister Kathleen Conklin
English Department Instructor
St. Genevieve High School
Panorama City, California

Roger Dick
Emeritus Instructor of English and the Humanities
Brooklyn Center High School
Brooklyn Center, Minnesota

Sofia Eleftheriadou
Literature and Culture Consultant
New Sampscunta Preveza, Greece

Martha Haynes
Lecturer, Teacher Preparation Single Subjects
Humboldt State University
Arcata, California

Kevin Houtz
Teacher of English
Lakewood High School
Lakewood, New Jersey

Sajeda Khalifa
Literature and Culture Consultant
Gandeevi, India

Marianne Kjos
Language Arts Instructor
Miami Sunset Senior High School
Dade County School District
Miami, Florida

Chi Yung Lau
Literature and Culture Consultant
Panyu, China

Ruth Ann Maury
Language Arts Department Instructor
Miami Sunset Senior High
Miami, Florida

Constance McGee
Educational Specialist
Dade County Public Schools
Miami, Florida

Atsushi Oya
Literature and Culture Consultant
Nagoya, Japan

Deborah Prato
Freelance Education Writer
Westford, Massachusetts

Eric Richey
English Department Instructor
Hialeah High School
Hialeah, Florida

Dr. Jane Shoaf
Educational Consultant
Edenton, North Carolina

Kendra Sisserson
Facilitator, Department of Education
The University of Chicago
Chicago, Illinois

James Swanson
Educational Consultant
Minneapolis, Minnesota

Jill Triplett
Special Collections Assistant
Wellesley College Library
Wellesley, Massachusetts

World Passport Student Advisory Panel
Sarah (Sotiria) Galanis, Greece
Denis Gorbounov, Russia
Elio Lopez, Mexico
Ebere Mbakwe, Nigeria
Avik Mohan, India
Gabrielle Riemer, France
Jiannong Sun, China
Yumiko Yokochi, Japan

Contents

UNIT 4 COPING WITH DEATH

"Out, out, brief candle!"

Selections for Additional Reading

Other Selections Exploring This Theme:

UNIT 5 COMMUNION WITH NATURE

"In wilderness is the preservation of the world"

Selections for Additional Reading

Other Selections Exploring This Theme:

UNIT 6 METAMORPHOSES

"A sea-change into something rich and strange"

UNIT 9 MEDIEVAL LITERATURE

"There was a knight, a most distinguished man"

Other Selections Exploring This Period:

UNIT 10 THE RENAISSANCE AND THE ENLIGHTENMENT

"I think, therefore I am"

Selections for Additional Reading

Other Selections Exploring This Period:

UNIT 11 ROMANTICISM, REALISM, AND NATURALISM

"It was the best of times, it was the worst of times"

SELECTIONS FOR ADDITIONAL READING

OTHER SELECTIONS EXPLORING THIS PERIOD:

UNIT 12 MODERN AND CONTEMPORARY LITERATURE

"And in today already walks tomorrow"

SELECTIONS FOR ADDITIONAL READING

Other Selections Exploring This Period:

Language Arts Survey

1 ESSENTIAL SKILLS: WRITING

2 ESSENTIAL SKILLS: LANGUAGE

Grammar Handbook

To the Student

Reading Literature

Have you ever become so wrapped up in a movie that when the credits started to roll and the lights came up, you felt a kind of shock? One moment you were in the world on the screen, perhaps identifying with some hero and feeling her joys and sorrows. The next moment you were back in your own world again. The art of the filmmaker transported you to another time and place.

When you read a good story, poem, or play, the same sort of transport should take place. The key to reading literature is to use your imagination to take the journey planned for you by the writer. This willingness to extend yourself imaginatively is the most important characteristic that you can have as a reader. Suppose, for example, that you read the following passage in a story:

> Three lions, a male and two females, lay sunning beside what remained of a kill—an eland, perhaps. We approached in the Range Rover. They ignored us. Chico stopped about fifty meters away, and we both took out binoculars for a closer look. The lions lay heavily, dreamily, self-satisfied. A slight breeze ruffled their fur, yellow-brown like the savannah grass in this season between the rains. It was Chico who noticed that the kill wasn't an eland at all, for attached to part of it was, unmistakably, a large black boot.

It is possible to read that passage and understand it, intellectually, without having experienced it. However, reading literature is all about having experiences. To read the passage well, you need to picture three lions, to imagine what it might be like to approach them, to see in your mind's eye the yellow grass, to feel the slight breeze, to notice the boot. If you have done that—if you have imagined the scene vividly—then it will have an impact on you. That impact will be its significance—its meaning for you.

Imagine that you have taken a journey. You have hiked up a mountainside in Peru or have wandered through the Valley of the Kings in Egypt. You have gone shopping in the Ginza district of Tokyo or have bounced in a spacesuit over the surface of the moon. After such an experience, you return home a different person. You think about the experience and what it meant to you.

A work of literature is a chance to take just such an exotic journey. Using your imagination, you take the writer's trip. You have an experience. Then you reflect on the experience that you had. You think about what you thought and felt, about what the experience meant to you. That reflection is called **reader response.**

When you sit down to read a literary work, remember that your task, at that moment, is not to prepare for a quiz or to get ready for a class discussion. Your task is to use your imagination to have the experience that the writer has prepared for you. Think of the writer as a tour guide to interesting times and places. In those times and places, you will meet fascinating people and have powerful, moving experiences, ones that will enrich your life.

Sharing Your Responses with Others

No two people are exactly alike. Because of this wonderful fact, the experience that you have when reading a particular story, poem, or play will be different from the experience had by the student who sits next to you. That's what makes discussing literature with other students interesting. You can share your experiences with others and learn from them. In this course you will have many opportunities to share responses in class discussion and in group projects.

Educating Your Imagination

You might naturally ask, at the beginning of a course such as this, what you stand to gain from it. Two answers to that question have already been suggested: First, reading literature will provide you with many fascinating imaginative experiences. Second, discussing that literature and doing group projects will provide opportunities for sharing with others. A third answer is suggested by the first two: reading literature and sharing responses with others will educate your imagination. It will train you to think and feel in new ways.

Life is short, opportunities for real-life experience are limited, and events often happen only once, without your having had the chance to practice, or even think about, how you might react to them. Reading literature is a way around all those difficulties. Through reading, you can find out what it might be like to sail around the globe, to march into battle, to fall in love, to lose a friend, to win a great prize, to live in the rain forest, to be faced with a moral problem, to confront your greatest fear, to travel backward in time or forward into the future. Writers write because they want to share interesting, valuable experiences with you, the reader. In the process of reading literary works and thinking about your own and others' responses to them, you will exercise your imagination and grow in ways that might otherwise have been impossible.

Using This Text

This text is first and foremost a literature anthology. The selections in Units 1–12 have been chosen both for their literary quality and for their interest to students like you. To assist you in understanding the selections, the writers and editors of this text have created activities that appear after the selections. These activities will also help you to develop your abilities in many language arts areas. Most of these activities ask you to refer to the section at the back of the book called the Language Arts Survey. Before doing the activity, you will read a section of the Survey, which will introduce you to some key concepts. Then you will apply what you have learned from the Survey when doing the activity.

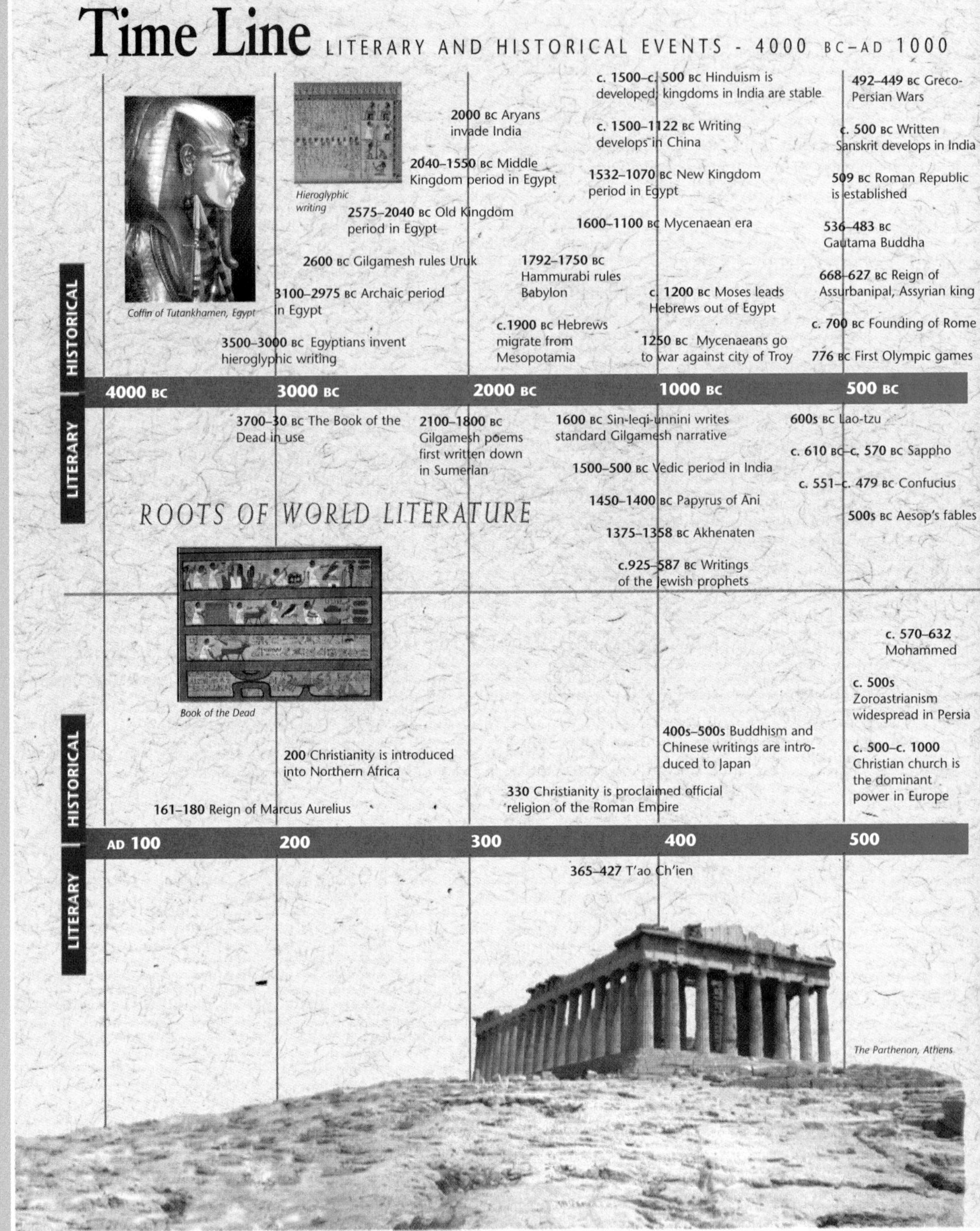
Time Line
LITERARY AND HISTORICAL EVENTS - 4000 BC–AD 1000
HISTORICAL
LITERARY
4000 BC
3000 BC
2000 BC
1000 BC
500 BC
3500–3000 BC Egyptians invent hieroglyphic writing
3100–2975 BC Archaic period in Egypt
2600 BC Gilgamesh rules Uruk
2575–2040 BC Old Kingdom period in Egypt
2040–1550 BC Middle Kingdom period in Egypt
2000 BC Aryans invade India
c.1900 BC Hebrews migrate from Mesopotamia
1792–1750 BC Hammurabi rules Babylon
1600–1100 BC Mycenaean era
1532–1070 BC New Kingdom period in Egypt
c. 1500–1122 BC Writing develops in China
c. 1500–c. 500 BC Hinduism is developed; kingdoms in India are stable
1250 BC Mycenaeans go to war against city of Troy
c. 1200 BC Moses leads Hebrews out of Egypt
776 BC First Olympic games
c. 700 BC Founding of Rome
668–627 BC Reign of Assurbanipal, Assyrian king
536–483 BC Gautama Buddha
509 BC Roman Republic is established
c. 500 BC Written Sanskrit develops in India
492–449 BC Greco-Persian Wars
3700–30 BC The Book of the Dead in use
2100–1800 BC Gilgamesh poems first written down in Sumerian
1600 BC Sin-leqi-unnini writes standard Gilgamesh narrative
1500–500 BC Vedic period in India
1450–1400 BC Papyrus of Ani
1375–1358 BC Akhenaten
c.925–587 BC Writings of the Jewish prophets
600s BC Lao-tzu
c. 610 BC–c. 570 BC Sappho
c. 551–c. 479 BC Confucius
500s BC Aesop's fables
ROOTS OF WORLD LITERATURE
AD 100
200
300
400
500
161–180 Reign of Marcus Aurelius
200 Christianity is introduced into Northern Africa
330 Christianity is proclaimed official religion of the Roman Empire
400s–500s Buddhism and Chinese writings are introduced to Japan
c. 500–c. 1000 Christian church is the dominant power in Europe
c. 500s Zoroastrianism widespread in Persia
c. 570–632 Mohammed
365–427 T'ao Ch'ien

Coffin of Tutankhamen, Egypt

Hieroglyphic writing

Book of the Dead

The Parthenon, Athens

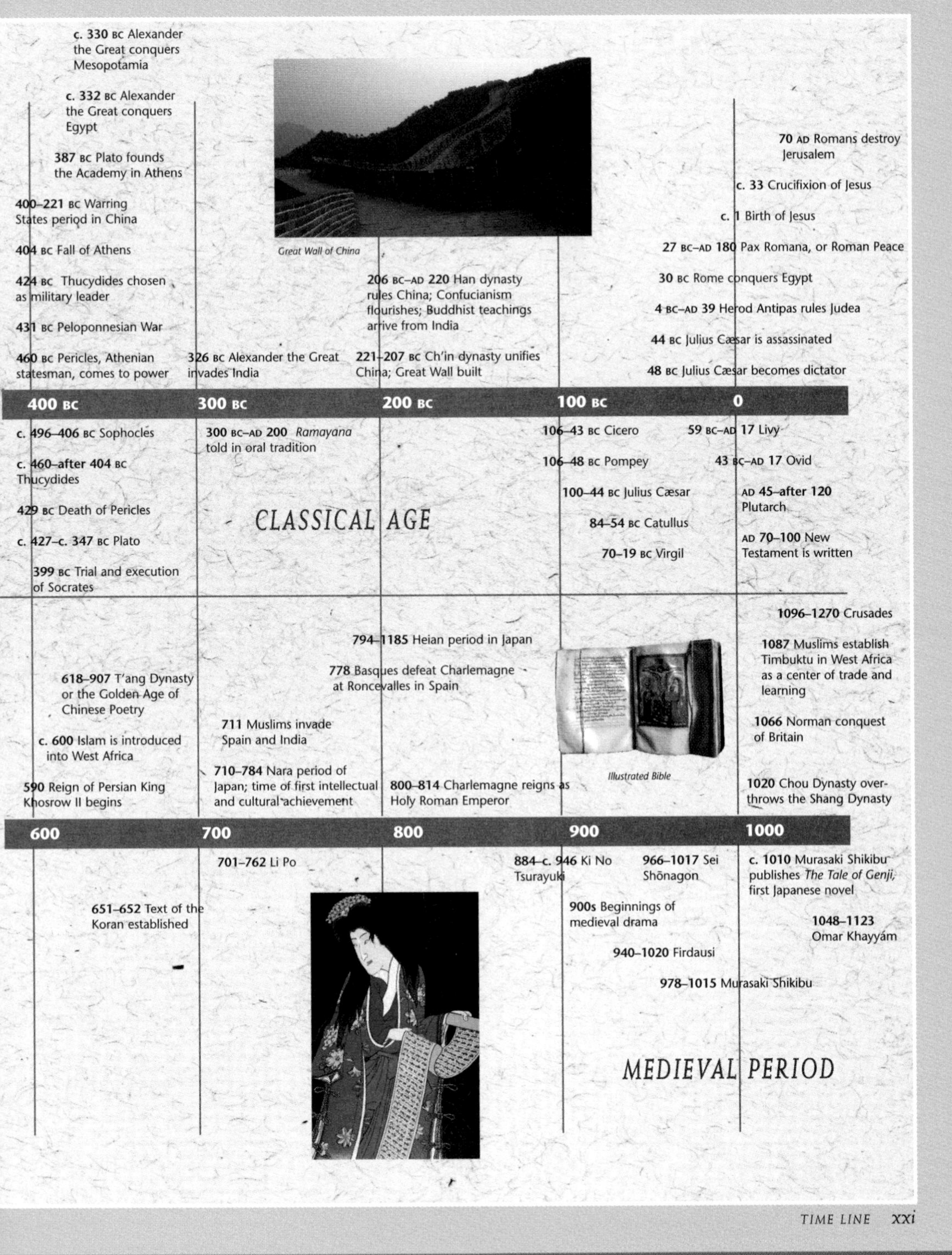

c. 330 BC Alexander the Great conquers Mesopotamia

c. 332 BC Alexander the Great conquers Egypt

387 BC Plato founds the Academy in Athens

400–221 BC Warring States period in China

404 BC Fall of Athens

424 BC Thucydides chosen as military leader

431 BC Peloponnesian War

460 BC Pericles, Athenian statesman, comes to power

326 BC Alexander the Great invades India

Great Wall of China

206 BC–AD 220 Han dynasty rules China; Confucianism flourishes; Buddhist teachings arrive from India

221–207 BC Ch'in dynasty unifies China; Great Wall built

70 AD Romans destroy Jerusalem

c. 33 Crucifixion of Jesus

c. 1 Birth of Jesus

27 BC–AD 180 Pax Romana, or Roman Peace

30 BC Rome conquers Egypt

4 BC–AD 39 Herod Antipas rules Judea

44 BC Julius Cæsar is assassinated

48 BC Julius Cæsar becomes dictator

400 BC | **300 BC** | **200 BC** | **100 BC** | **0**

c. 496–406 BC Sophocles

c. 460–after 404 BC Thucydides

429 BC Death of Pericles

c. 427–c. 347 BC Plato

399 BC Trial and execution of Socrates

300 BC–AD 200 *Ramayana* told in oral tradition

CLASSICAL AGE

106–43 BC Cicero

106–48 BC Pompey

100–44 BC Julius Cæsar

84–54 BC Catullus

70–19 BC Virgil

59 BC–AD 17 Livy

43 BC–AD 17 Ovid

AD 45–after 120 Plutarch

AD 70–100 New Testament is written

618–907 T'ang Dynasty or the Golden Age of Chinese Poetry

c. 600 Islam is introduced into West Africa

590 Reign of Persian King Khosrow II begins

711 Muslims invade Spain and India

710–784 Nara period of Japan; time of first intellectual and cultural achievement

794–1185 Heian period in Japan

778 Basques defeat Charlemagne at Roncevalles in Spain

800–814 Charlemagne reigns as Holy Roman Emperor

Illustrated Bible

1096–1270 Crusades

1087 Muslims establish Timbuktu in West Africa as a center of trade and learning

1066 Norman conquest of Britain

1020 Chou Dynasty overthrows the Shang Dynasty

600 | **700** | **800** | **900** | **1000**

651–652 Text of the Koran established

701–762 Li Po

884–c. 946 Ki No Tsurayuki

966–1017 Sei Shōnagon

900s Beginnings of medieval drama

940–1020 Firdausi

978–1015 Murasaki Shikibu

c. 1010 Murasaki Shikibu publishes *The Tale of Genji*, first Japanese novel

1048–1123 Omar Khayyám

MEDIEVAL PERIOD

Time Line LITERARY AND HISTORICAL EVENTS - AD 1100–1675

Jerusalem

HISTORICAL

1100 Feudalism begins in Japan

1187 Muslims defeat Christian crusaders and take over Jerusalem

1215 King John of England signs Magna Carta

c. 1225–1274 Thomas Aquinas

1230 Sunjata wins battle against Sumanguru

1235 Sunjata forms Mali empire

1100 · 1150 · 1200 · 1250 · 1275

LITERARY

c. 1135–c. 1190 Chrétien de Troyes

c. 1200 Marie de France

early 1200s Bieris de Romans

1207–1283 Rumi

1265–1321 Dante Alighieri

HISTORICAL

1453 Fall of Constantinople; end of Eastern Empire

c. 1454 Johann Gutenberg develops printing by movable type

1455 Gutenberg prints his first book, the Bible

1492 Columbus reaches the Americas

1495 Leonardo da Vinci paints *The Last Supper*

1502 Michelangelo finishes *David*

1517 Martin Luther challenges the Roman Catholic church

1519 Cortés conquers Mexico

1543 Nicolas Copernicus estal lishes theory tha the earth revolve around the sun

1558–1603 Reig of Elizabeth I of England

1450 · 1475 · 1500 · 1525 · 1550

LITERARY

1474–1533 Ludovico Ariosto

1525–1566 Louise Labé

1533–1592 Michel de Montaigne

1547–1616 Miguel de Cervantes

Don Quixote, Illustrated by Gustave Doré

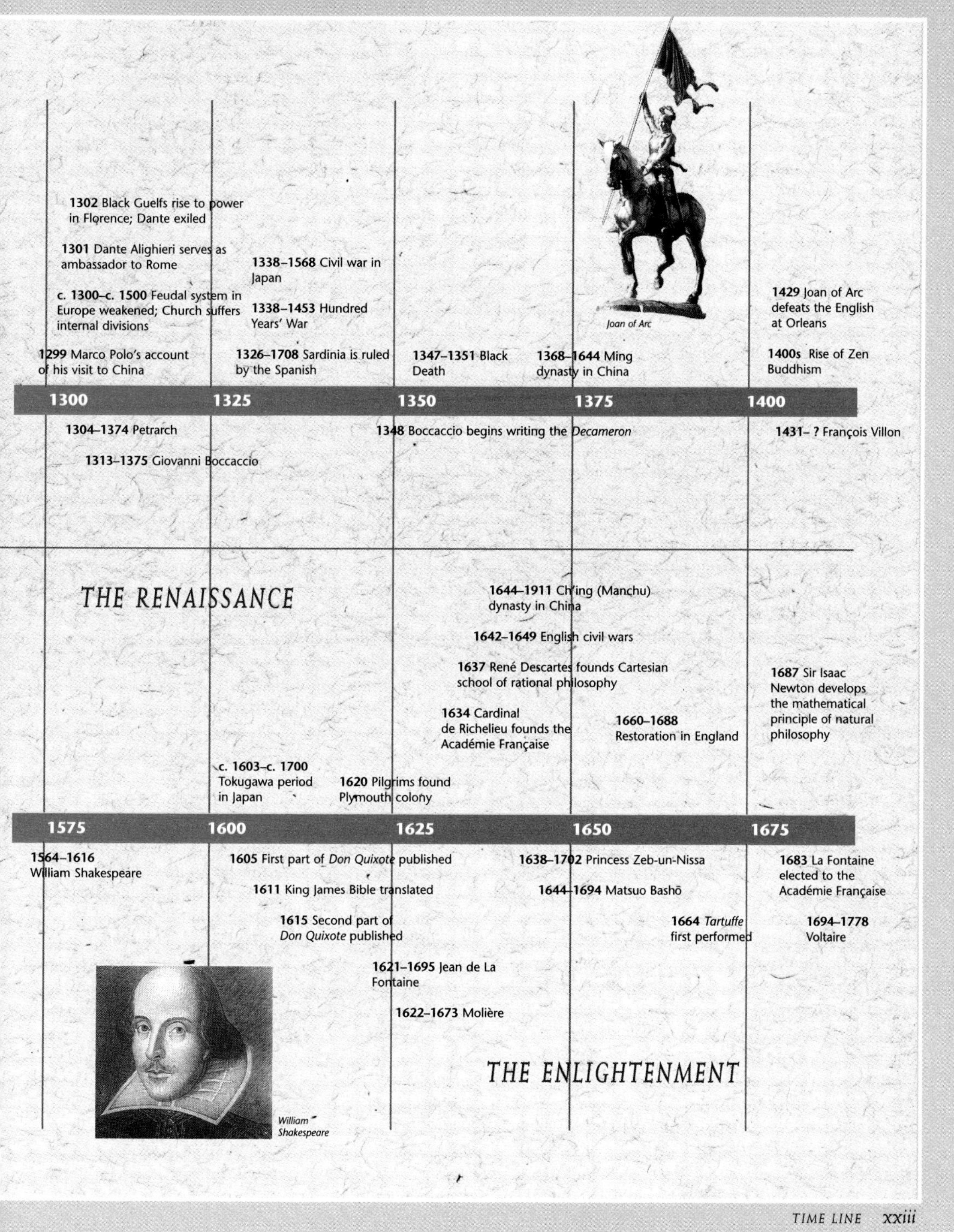
1302 Black Guelfs rise to power in Florence; Dante exiled
1301 Dante Alighieri serves as ambassador to Rome
c. 1300–c. 1500 Feudal system in Europe weakened; Church suffers internal divisions
1299 Marco Polo's account of his visit to China
1338–1568 Civil war in Japan
1338–1453 Hundred Years' War
1326–1708 Sardinia is ruled by the Spanish
1347–1351 Black Death
1368–1644 Ming dynasty in China
1429 Joan of Arc defeats the English at Orleans
1400s Rise of Zen Buddhism
1300
1325
1350
1375
1400
1304–1374 Petrarch
1313–1375 Giovanni Boccaccio
1348 Boccaccio begins writing the Decameron
1431– ? François Villon
THE RENAISSANCE
1644–1911 Ch'ing (Manchu) dynasty in China
1642–1649 English civil wars
1637 René Descartes founds Cartesian school of rational philosophy
1634 Cardinal de Richelieu founds the Académie Française
1660–1688 Restoration in England
1687 Sir Isaac Newton develops the mathematical principle of natural philosophy
c. 1603–c. 1700 Tokugawa period in Japan
1620 Pilgrims found Plymouth colony
1575
1600
1625
1650
1675
1564–1616 William Shakespeare
1605 First part of Don Quixote published
1611 King James Bible translated
1615 Second part of Don Quixote published
1621–1695 Jean de La Fontaine
1622–1673 Molière
1638–1702 Princess Zeb-un-Nissa
1644–1694 Matsuo Bashō
1664 Tartuffe first performed
1683 La Fontaine elected to the Académie Française
1694–1778 Voltaire
THE ENLIGHTENMENT

Joan of Arc

William Shakespeare

Time Line LITERARY AND HISTORICAL EVENTS - AD 1700–1993

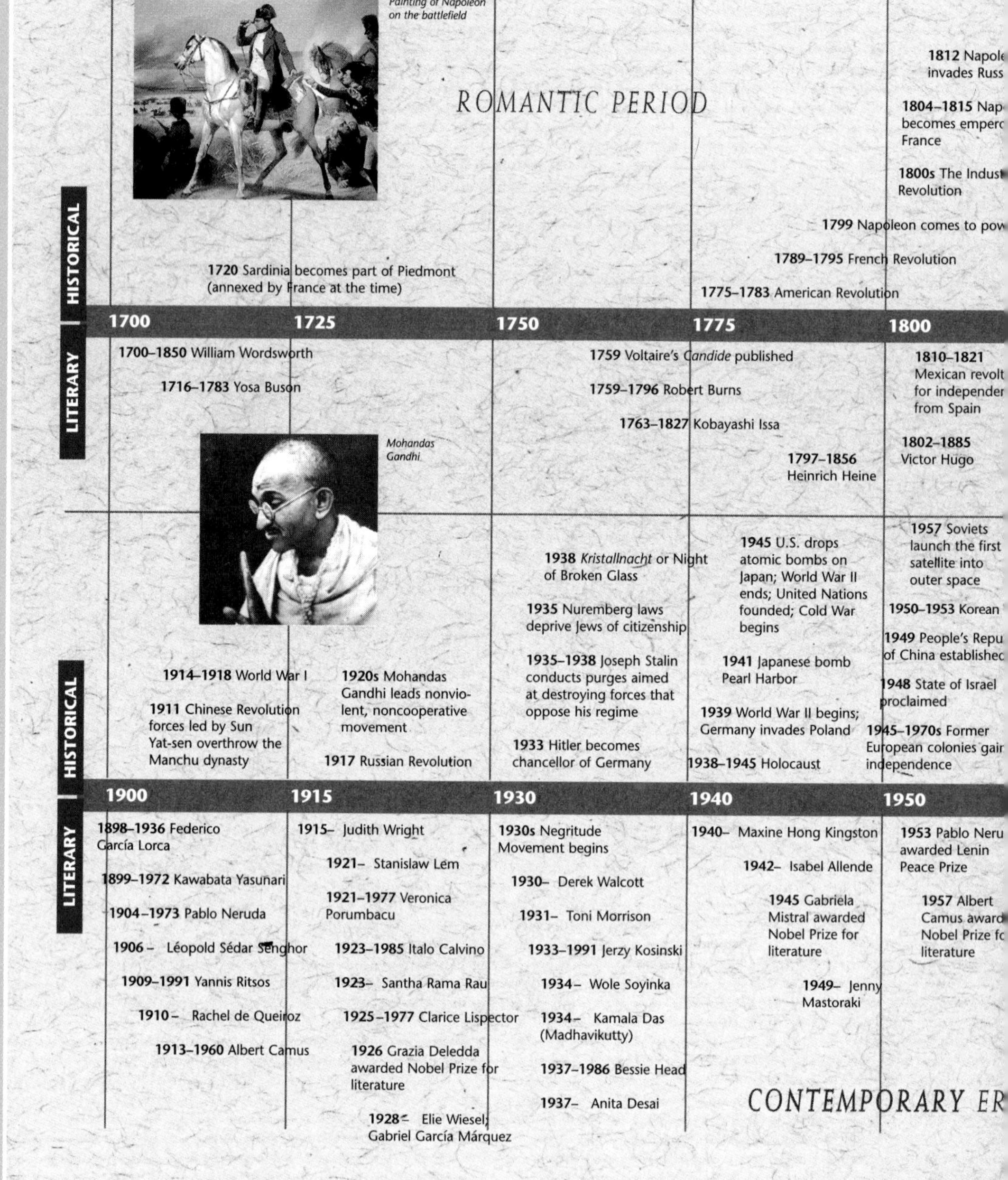

Painting of Napoleon on the battlefield
ROMANTIC PERIOD
HISTORICAL
1812 Napol
invades Russ
1804–1815 Nap
becomes emper
France
1800s The Indus
Revolution
1799 Napoleon comes to pow
1789–1795 French Revolution
1775–1783 American Revolution
1720 Sardinia becomes part of Piedmont (annexed by France at the time)
1700
1725
1750
1775
1800
LITERARY
1700–1850 William Wordsworth
1716–1783 Yosa Buson
1759 Voltaire's Candide published
1759–1796 Robert Burns
1763–1827 Kobayashi Issa
1797–1856 Heinrich Heine
1810–1821 Mexican revolt for independer from Spain
1802–1885 Victor Hugo
Mohandas Gandhi
HISTORICAL
1914–1918 World War I
1911 Chinese Revolution forces led by Sun Yat-sen overthrow the Manchu dynasty
1920s Mohandas Gandhi leads nonviolent, noncooperative movement
1917 Russian Revolution
1938 Kristallnacht or Night of Broken Glass
1935 Nuremberg laws deprive Jews of citizenship
1935–1938 Joseph Stalin conducts purges aimed at destroying forces that oppose his regime
1933 Hitler becomes chancellor of Germany
1945 U.S. drops atomic bombs on Japan; World War II ends; United Nations founded; Cold War begins
1941 Japanese bomb Pearl Harbor
1939 World War II begins; Germany invades Poland
1938–1945 Holocaust
1957 Soviets launch the first satellite into outer space
1950–1953 Korean
1949 People's Repu of China establishec
1948 State of Israel proclaimed
1945–1970s Former European colonies gair independence
1900
1915
1930
1940
1950
LITERARY
1898–1936 Federico García Lorca
1899–1972 Kawabata Yasunari
1904–1973 Pablo Neruda
1906– Léopold Sédar Senghor
1909–1991 Yannis Ritsos
1910– Rachel de Queiroz
1913–1960 Albert Camus
1915– Judith Wright
1921– Stanislaw Lem
1921–1977 Veronica Porumbacu
1923–1985 Italo Calvino
1923– Santha Rama Rau
1925–1977 Clarice Lispector
1926 Grazia Deledda awarded Nobel Prize for literature
1928– Elie Wiesel; Gabriel García Márquez
1930s Negritude Movement begins
1930– Derek Walcott
1931– Toni Morrison
1933–1991 Jerzy Kosinski
1934– Wole Soyinka
1934– Kamala Das (Madhavikutty)
1937–1986 Bessie Head
1937– Anita Desai
1940– Maxine Hong Kingston
1942– Isabel Allende
1945 Gabriela Mistral awarded Nobel Prize for literature
1949– Jenny Mastoraki
1953 Pablo Neru awarded Lenin Peace Prize
1957 Albert Camus award Nobel Prize fo literature
CONTEMPORARY ER

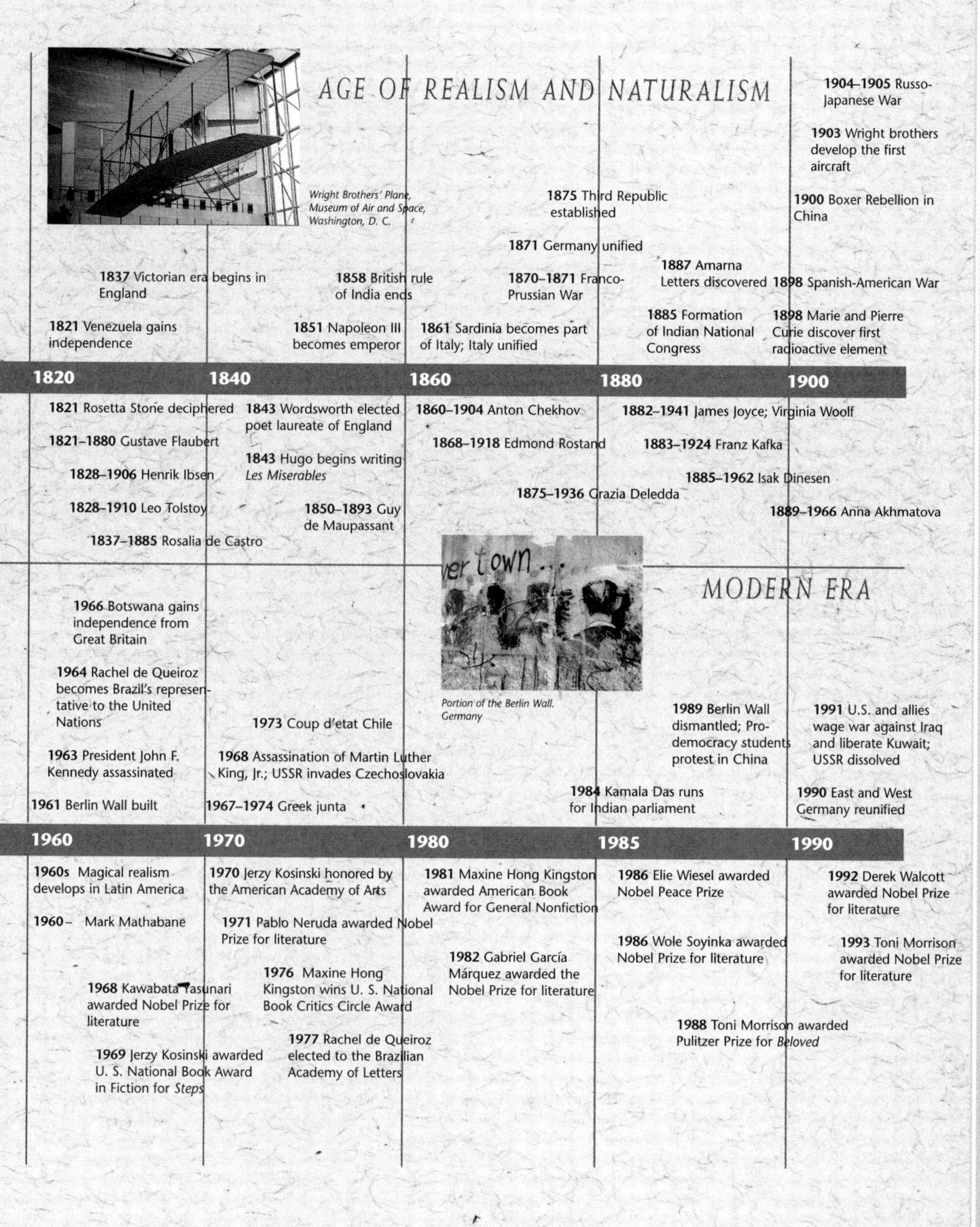

AGE OF REALISM AND NATURALISM

Wright Brothers' Plane, Museum of Air and Space, Washington, D. C.

1821 Venezuela gains independence

1837 Victorian era begins in England

1851 Napoleon III becomes emperor

1858 British rule of India ends

1861 Sardinia becomes part of Italy; Italy unified

1870–1871 Franco-Prussian War

1871 Germany unified

1875 Third Republic established

1885 Formation of Indian National Congress

1887 Amarna Letters discovered

1898 Spanish-American War

1898 Marie and Pierre Curie discover first radioactive element

1900 Boxer Rebellion in China

1903 Wright brothers develop the first aircraft

1904–1905 Russo-Japanese War

1820 | **1840** | **1860** | **1880** | **1900**

1821 Rosetta Stone deciphered

1821–1880 Gustave Flaubert

1828–1906 Henrik Ibsen

1828–1910 Leo Tolstoy

1837–1885 Rosalia de Castro

1843 Wordsworth elected poet laureate of England

1843 Hugo begins writing *Les Miserables*

1850–1893 Guy de Maupassant

1860–1904 Anton Chekhov

1868–1918 Edmond Rostand

1875–1936 Grazia Deledda

1882–1941 James Joyce; Virginia Woolf

1883–1924 Franz Kafka

1885–1962 Isak Dinesen

1889–1966 Anna Akhmatova

MODERN ERA

Portion of the Berlin Wall, Germany

1961 Berlin Wall built

1963 President John F. Kennedy assassinated

1964 Rachel de Queiroz becomes Brazil's representative to the United Nations

1966 Botswana gains independence from Great Britain

1967–1974 Greek junta

1968 Assassination of Martin Luther King, Jr.; USSR invades Czechoslovakia

1973 Coup d'etat Chile

1984 Kamala Das runs for Indian parliament

1989 Berlin Wall dismantled; Pro-democracy students protest in China

1990 East and West Germany reunified

1991 U.S. and allies wage war against Iraq and liberate Kuwait; USSR dissolved

1960 | **1970** | **1980** | **1985** | **1990**

1960s Magical realism develops in Latin America

1960– Mark Mathabane

1968 Kawabata Yasunari awarded Nobel Prize for literature

1969 Jerzy Kosinski awarded U. S. National Book Award in Fiction for *Steps*

1970 Jerzy Kosinski honored by the American Academy of Arts

1971 Pablo Neruda awarded Nobel Prize for literature

1976 Maxine Hong Kingston wins U. S. National Book Critics Circle Award

1977 Rachel de Queiroz elected to the Brazilian Academy of Letters

1981 Maxine Hong Kingston awarded American Book Award for General Nonfiction

1982 Gabriel García Márquez awarded the Nobel Prize for literature

1986 Elie Wiesel awarded Nobel Peace Prize

1986 Wole Soyinka awarded Nobel Prize for literature

1988 Toni Morrison awarded Pulitzer Prize for *Beloved*

1992 Derek Walcott awarded Nobel Prize for literature

1993 Toni Morrison awarded Nobel Prize for literature

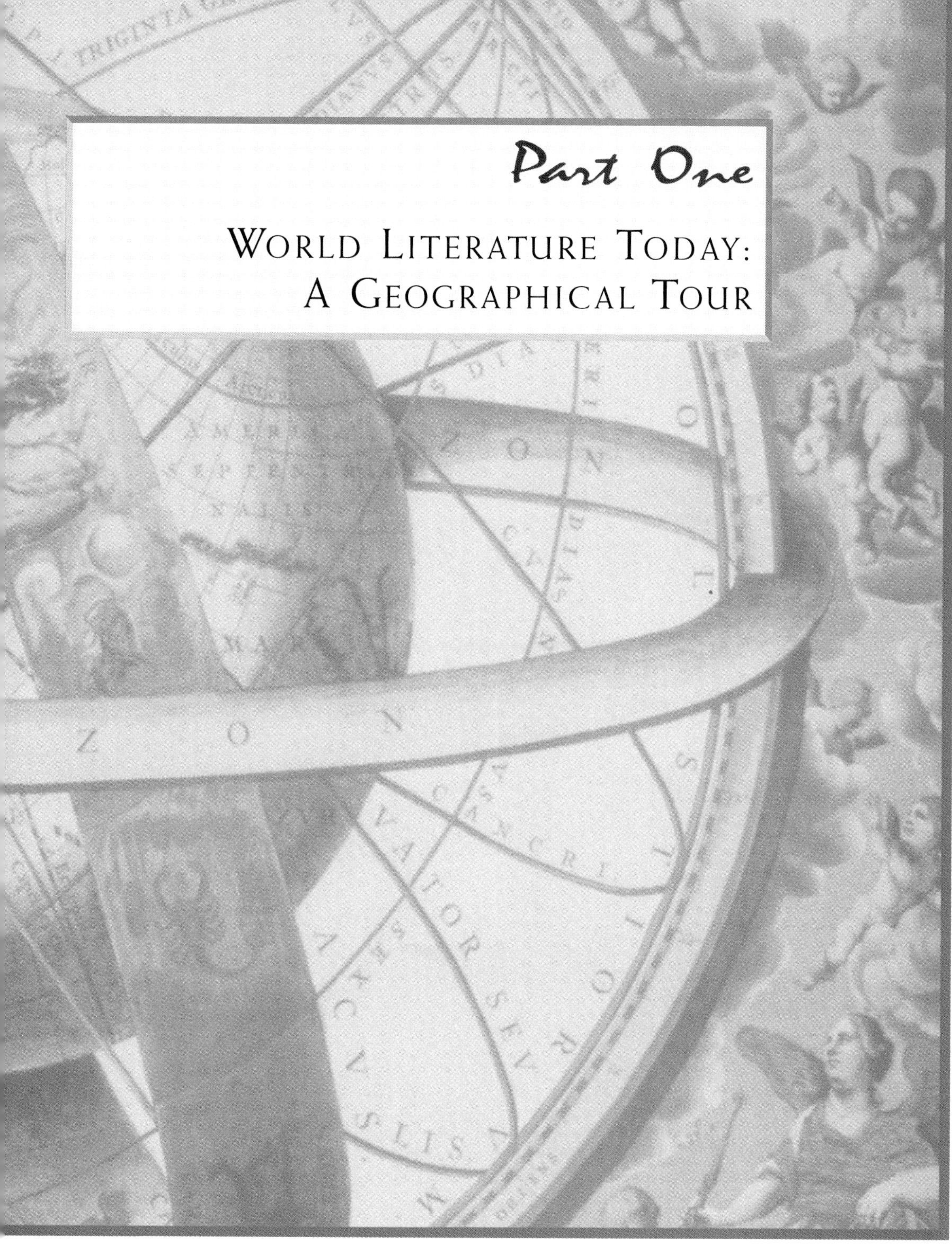

Part One

World Literature Today: A Geographical Tour

ADDITIONAL RESOURCES

In Unit 1, students will meet eight international students who describe their countries and their cultures. The ideas and opinions of these international students also appear in the features Global Voices: A Multicultural Conversation and Global Views. You may wish to remind your students that the views expressed in the Passport introductions, Global Voices, and Global Views represent one person's experiences, opinions, and interests. While they provide an introduction to another culture and an insider's point of view, they may not represent the culture as a whole. Encourage students to explore the eight cultures introduced by these international students and other cultures as well. Excellent sources include books, magazines, videos, and the Internet; literature, art, and music produced by artists of the culture; and, most importantly, people who are part of that culture.

The following list provides a reference to the student features found throughout the book.

Passport Pages

- Passport to Mexico, 5
- Passport to Nigeria, 20
- Passport to Greece, 33
- Passport to France, 42
- Passport to Russia, 54
- Passport to India, 65
- Passport to China, 76
- Passport to Japan, 88

Global Voices

- Discussing Intolerance, 212
- Discussing Love, 284
- Discussing Death, 354
- Discussing Nature, 425
- Discussing Change, 490
- Discussing the Global Village, 1116

Global Views

- Russia, Akhmatova's *Requiem*, 177
- China, Li Po's "The River-Merchant's Wife: A Letter," 247

(cont.)

ADDITIONAL RESOURCES (CONT.)

- Mexico, García Márquez's "Tuesday Siesta," 344
- Nigeria, Soyinka's "Season," 419
- India, the *Ramayana*, 572
- Greece, Sophocles's *Oedipus the King*, 671
- Japan, Sei Shōnagon's *Pillow Book*, 775
- France, Hugo's *Les Misérables*, 922

UNIT SKILLS OUTLINE

LITERARY SKILLS AND CONCEPTS

- Aim, 61
- Character, 52
- Characterization, 84
- Conflict, 30
- Description, 39
- Dialogue, 51
- Dramatic Irony, 61
- Epigraph, 39
- Existentialism, 46
- External Conflict, 30
- Image, 99
- Imagery, 96, 99
- Inciting Incident, 17
- Internal Conflict, 30
- Irony, 61, 100
- Irony of Situation, 61
- Magical Realism, 9, 17
- Motivation, 31
- One-dimensional Character, 52
- Plot, 17
- Point of View, 17, 74
- Repetition, 100
- Satire, 19, 51, 80, 85
- Stock Character, 17
- Third-person Point of View, 85
- Three-dimensional Character, 17, 52
- Tone, 39, 74
- Verbal Irony, 61

WRITING SKILLS AND CONCEPTS

- Character Sketch, 101
- Creating a Writing Plan, 32
- Creative Writing, 100
- Drafting, Evaluating, Revising, and Proofing, 75
- Finding a Topic, 75
- Gathering and Organizing Ideas, 75, 100
- Personal Letter, 32
- The Process of Writing, 31
- Writing a Critical Essay, 74

GRAMMAR USAGE AND MECHANICAL SKILLS AND CONCEPTS

- Parts of Speech, 85

OTHER LANGUAGE ARTS SKILLS AND CONCEPTS

- Active Listening and Interpersonal Communication, 53
- Bibliographies and Bibliography Cards, 41
- Documenting Sources, 41
- Elements of Verbal and Nonverbal Communication, 52
- Finding Sources, 40
- Formal Note-taking, 41
- Reading Actively, 17
- Types of Thinking, 62

CROSS-CURRICULAR CONNECTIONS

ARTS AND HUMANITIES

- Abstract Art and Vassily Kandinsky, 63
- African Textiles and Fashion, 23
- African Writers, 22
- Cathedral of Notre Dame of Paris, 43
- Celebrating Greece Day, 33
- Chinese Music, 78
- Chinese Writers, 79
- Class Cookbook, 11
- Edgar Allan Poe, 92

(cont.)

UNIT 1 CONTEMPORARY WORLD LITERATURE AND CULTURE

Improvisation VI (African). Vassily Kandinsky, 1909

GOALS/OBJECTIVES

Studying this unit will enable students to

- understand and appreciate aspects of the cultures of various countries
- enjoy works of contemporary world literature
- read actively
- understand the process of writing and use the process to write both critically and creatively about literature
- research a topic and document sources
- perform several types of thinking
- recognize the parts of speech

"My country is the world; my countrymen are all mankind."

—William Lloyd Garrison

3

CROSS-CURRICULAR CONNECTIONS (CONT.)

- Japanese Language, 94
- Japanese Religions, 88
- Kimono, 90
- The Kremlin, 57
- The Legendary Olive, 34
- The Long March, 80
- Mapping Nigeria, 20
- Mexican Revolution and Independence, 8
- Mexican Writers, 8
- Mexico City, 6
- Moscow's Attractions, 55
- The Mughals, 66
- Nigerian Government, 20
- Nonviolent Protest, 69
- Pakistan and Bangladesh, 67
- The Peloponnese, 36
- Planning a Trip to France, 42
- Pre-Columbian Civilizations in Mexico, 6
- Regional Cuisine and Traditions, 9
- Russian Nesting Doll and Other Folk Arts, 55
- Russian Revolution of 1917, 56
- Sanskrit, 65
- School in France, 45
- Slave Trade, 24

(cont.)

CROSS-CURRICULAR CONNECTIONS

(CONT. FROM PAGE 2)

- E. M. Forster, 37
- Ethnic Groups of Nigeria, 20
- Indian Films, 68
- Itinerary for a Trip to Nigeria, 21
- Japanese Culture Day, 89
- Japanese Language, 94
- The Legendary Olive, 34
- Mexican Writers, 8
- Moscow's Attractions, 55
- Music for a Film Adaptation, 13
- Planning a Trip to France, 42
- Regional Cuisine and Traditions, 9
- *The River Bridge at Uji,* 95
- Russian Nesting Doll and Other Folk Arts, 55
- Sanskrit, 65
- Theater of the Absurd, 46

Mathematics and Sciences

- Air Pollution in Mexico City, 6
- Atlantis, 36
- Class Cookbook, 11
- Crêpes with Strawberries and Cream, 44
- *Dundu Oniyeri* (Fried Yams), 22
- Economic Change in Russia, 57
- Economy of China, 76
- Ganges River, 68
- Mayan and Gregorian Calendars, 7
- Mayan Astronomy and the Equinoxes, 7
- *Pollo con mole,* 5
- Saving the Sea Turtles, 35
- Winter Olympic Games, 54

Social Studies

- The Acropolis, 35
- African Textiles and Fashion, 23
- African Writers, 22
- Air Pollution in Mexico City, 6
- Atlantis, 36
- British Rule in India, 67
- Cathedral of Notre Dame of Paris, 43
- Catherine II of Russia, 56
- Celebrating Greece Day, 33
- Changes in China, 76
- Chinese Music, 78
- Chinese Writers, 79
- Coming of Age, 90
- Cultural Views of Space, 91
- Defining *Hindu,* 66
- Delhi and Urban Growth, 65
- Discussing Censorship, 58
- Dress Codes, 88
- Early Governments of Nigeria, 23
- Economic Change in Russia, 57
- Economy of China, 76
- The Eiffel Tower, 42
- Ethnic Groups of Nigeria, 20
- French Meals, 95
- Gandhi and Nehru, 68
- Ganges River, 68
- Geography of China, 76
- Geography of India, 65
- Geography of Japan, 88
- Geography of Russia, 54
- *Glasnost* and *Perestoika,* 57
- Great Wall of China, 78
- Greek Names, 33
- Greek Orthodox Tradition, 35
- Heian Period, 91
- Holidays in India, 66
- Indian Films, 68
- Itinerary for a Trip to Nigeria, 21
- Japanese Eating Habits, 89
- Japanese Gardens, 90

(cont.)

TEACHING THE MULTIPLE INTELLIGENCES

MUSICAL

- Celebrating Greece Day, 33
- Chinese Music, 78
- Itinerary for a Trip to Nigeria, 21
- Japanese Culture Day, 89
- Music for a Film Adaptation, 13

LOGICAL-MATHEMATICAL

- Air Pollution in Mexico City, 6
- Applying Thinking Skills, 63
- Atlantis, 36
- Charting Thinking Skills, 62
- Crêpes with Strawberries and Cream, 44
- *Dundu Oniyeri* (Fried Yams), 22
- Discussing Censorship, 58
- Dress Codes, 88
- Economic Change in Russia, 57
- Economy of China, 76
- Gandhi and Nehru, 68
- Ganges River, 68
- Geography of Russia, 54
- *Gong-Bao Ji-Ding* (The King's Spicy Hot Chicken), 77
- Mayan Astronomy, 7
- Mayan and Gregorian Calendars, 7
- Nigerian Government, 20
- *Pollo con mole,* 5
- Reading Actively, 18
- Research Skills, 41
- Russian Revolution of 1917, 56
- Sanskrit, 65
- Saving the Sea Turtles, 35
- School in France, 45
- Selecting Sources, 40
- Socialized Medicine and Health Insurance, 43
- Thinking Skills, 64
- Winter Olympic Games, 54

SPATIAL

- Abstract Art and Vassily Kandinsky, 63
- African Textiles and Fashion, 23
- Atlantis, 36
- Celebrating Greece Day, 33
- Charting Thinking Skills, 62
- Cultural Views of Space, 91
- Geography of China, 76
- Geography of India, 65
- Geography of Japan, 88
- Geography of Russia, 54
- Itinerary for a Trip to Nigeria, 21
- Kimono, 90
- Mapping Nigeria, 20
- Mayan Astronomy, 7
- Mexico City, 6
- Planning a Trip to France, 42
- *The River Bridge at Uji,* 95
- Russian Nesting Doll and Other Folk Arts, 55

KINESTHETIC

- Celebrating Greece Day, 33
- Cultural Views of Space, 91
- Enacting a Scene, 53

INTERPERSONAL

- African Textiles and Fashion, 23
- Air Pollution in Mexico City, 6
- Atlantis, 36
- Chinese Music, 78
- Class Cookbook, 11
- Coming of Age, 90
- Crêpes with Strawberries and Cream, 44
- Discussing Censorship, 58
- Dress Codes, 88
- *Dundu Oniyeri* (Fried Yams), 22
- Economy of China, 76
- Enacting a Scene, 53
- Ethnic Groups of Nigeria, 20
- Gandhi and Nehru, 68
- Ganges River, 68
- Greek Recipes, 34
- Indian Films, 68
- Itinerary for a Trip to Nigeria, 21
- Japanese Culture Day, 89
- *Lassi,* 67
- Pakistan and Bangladesh, 67
- *Pollo con mole,* 5
- Saving the Sea Turtles, 35
- School in France, 45
- Selecting Sources, 40
- Socialized Medicine and Health Insurance, 43

Preview:

Contemporary World Literature and Culture

Have you ever wanted to take an African safari, admire the pyramids of Egypt, or sail down the Yangtze River? Have you dreamed of traveling through time or exploring other planets? While you may someday undertake some of these journeys or have some of these experiences, you already have the ability to explore new worlds every day without ever leaving your home. Your passport to exciting new lands, real and imagined, is reading.

In this text your reading will allow you to explore the cultures of many times and places. In this unit you will meet eight international students: Elio Lopez from Mexico, Ebere Mbakwe from Nigeria, Sarah Galanis from Greece, Gabrielle Riemer from France, Denis Gorbounov from Russia, Avik Mohan from India, Jiannong Sun from China, and Yumiko Yokochi from Japan. These students will share with you their personal thoughts on their countries and their cultures. Because each student's culture is complex, these insights provide a valuable introduction to a culture rather than a comprehensive survey. You will meet these students again throughout the text as they discuss topics such as love, death, and change. These students will also give you unique perspectives on works of literature from their own countries. The literature from these eight countries and from many others will introduce you to cultures that you will probably discover to be both different from and similar to your own. So get ready! You're off to your first destination.

International Students: (top row): Gabrielle Riemer, France; Yumiko Yokochi, Japan; Denis Gorbounov, Russia; Avik Mohan, India (bottom row): Ebere Mbakwe, Nigeria; Jiannong Sun, China; Sarah Galanis, Greece; Elio Lopez, Mexico

CROSS-CURRICULAR CONNECTIONS (CONT.)

- Soccer, 45
- Socialized Medicine and Health Insurance, 43
- Udaipur, 65
- Winter Olympic Games, 54

APPLIED ARTS

- African Textiles and Fashion, 23
- Air Pollution in Mexico City, 6
- Celebrating Greece Day, 33
- Class Cookbook, 11
- Crêpes with Strawberries and Cream, 44
- *Dundu Oniyeri* (Fried Yams), 22
- *Gong-Bao Ji-Ding* (The King's Spicy Hot Chicken), 77
- Greek Recipes, 34
- Itinerary for a Trip to Nigeria, 21
- Japanese Culture Day, 89
- Kimono, 90
- *Lassi,* 67
- Mayan Astronomy, 7
- *Pollo con mole,* 5
- Regional Cuisine and Traditions, 9
- Socialized Medicine and Health Insurance, 43
- Sushi Rice with Grilled Salmon, 89

PASSPORT TO MEXICO

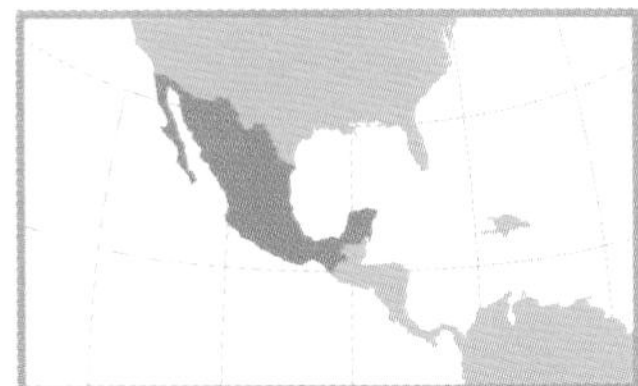

¡Hola! I am Elio Lopez. I am from a very small town in Chiapas, Mexico, in the south near Mexico's border with Guatemala. The weather is always warm there. As a child, I always liked sunny days, when we would go to the nearby creek and bathe in the cool water and chew sugar cane. The people of my town farmed sugar cane and planted groves of mangos, my favorite fruit—so sweet they were my dessert.

It may be my imagination, but as far as I can recall, it never rained in my town on Sunday. On that day, my mother always cooked a big meal for the family. She cooked great food: *chiles rellenos,* stuffed peppers, or *pollo con mole,* chicken cooked in a chocolate-based gravy. We ate almost everything with tortillas, a flat bread my mother made of cooked cornmeal baked on a grill. As my mother made them, I would eat them right off the grill. I

Elio Lopez
Soyatitán, Mexico

Flag of Mexico

Mexican sunset, Ixtapa, Pacific coast

Pyramid of the sun

Self Portrait.
Frida Kahlo, 1930

Cross-curricular Activities

Mathematics and Sciences and Applied Arts

The following is a recipe for one of Elio's favorite dishes, *pollo con mole.* You may wish to prepare this classic Mexican dish for your students or ask students to work together in groups to prepare the dish and bring it into class to share. You also might test students' math skills by asking them to calculate the amount of ingredients they would need to prepare two, three, four, or ten times the normal recipe.

Pollo Con Mole

(This simple recipe makes 2 cups of *mole* sauce, to be served on roasted chicken.)

Ingredients:

- 1 cup onion, chopped
- 1 clove garlic, minced (or more to taste)
- 2 tablespoons oil or butter
- 1/2 cup tomato sauce
- 1/4 cup raisins
- 1/4 cup smooth peanut butter
- 2 teaspoons sugar
- 1 teaspoon chili powder, or more to taste. (Try to get ground chili from the Mexican food section of your grocery store. A mild pasilla chile is good.)
- 1/4 teaspoon cinnamon
- 1/8 teaspoon ground cloves
- 1/2 ounce unsweetened chocolate (or 1 1/2 ounces Mexican chocolate, grated, if available)
- 1 1/2 cups weak chicken broth

Procedure:

1. Sauté onion and garlic in oil or butter until tender but not brown.
2. Combine onions with remaining ingredients in a blender or food processor. Blend until smooth.
3. Return to saucepan and simmer 15–20 minutes, stirring often.
4. Roast chicken according to your favorite recipe.
5. Brush *mole* sauce over chicken. Sprinkle with chopped peanuts if desired.

SUPPORT FOR LEP STUDENTS

Pronunciations of Proper Nouns and Adjectives

Car • los Fu • en • tes (kär´lōs fu en´tās)
Chi • a • pas (chē ä´päs)
Chi • chén It • zá (chē chen´ ēt sä´)
chi • les re • lle • nos (chē´lās rā yä´nōs)
El Dí • a de los Muer • tos (el dē´ä dā lōs mwer´tōs)
E • li • o Lo • pez (ā´ lē ō lō´pes)
ho • la (ō´lä)
May • a (mī´ə)
Mic • te • ca • ci • huat • l (mēk tā kä sē´wät l)
Mon • te Al • bán (mōn´tā äl bän´)
Na • huat • l (nä´wät l)
Oc • ta • vi • o Paz (ōk tä´vē ō päs)
Pa • len • que (pä leŋ´kā)
pol • lo con mo • le (poi´ō kōn mō´ lā)
Quet • zal • co • at • l (ket säl kō´ät l)
Sor Jua • na I • nés de la Cruz (sor wä´nä ē nās´ dā lä krüs)

Cross-curricular Activities

SOCIAL STUDIES

Inform students that Mexico City, the capital of Mexico, is the largest metropolitan area in the world at 1,480 square kilometers (or 3,834 square miles). With its population of 20 to 25 million people, it is also the second-largest city in the world, succeeded only by Shanghai. Mexico City is located in the Valley of Mexico and is surrounded by majestic mountains, including the legendary volcanoes of Popocatépetl and Ixtaccíhuatl. The city was built atop the ruins of the ancient Aztec capital of Tenochtitlán. Among the places to visit in Mexico City are the Palacio de Bellas Artes, a theater which boasts murals by José Clemente Orozco (1883–1949), Diego Rivera (1886–1957), and Davíd Alfaro Siquieros (1896–1974); the National Museum of Archaeology; and the National Museum of History, formerly the Castle of Chapultepec, which was home to Cortés and later to Emperor Maximilian and Empress Carlota during the French occupation of Mexico from 1864–1867.

Bring in a map of Mexico and have students locate Mexico City and other major cities in Mexico.

MATHEMATICS AND SCIENCES, SOCIAL STUDIES, AND APPLIED ARTS

Since Mexico City is so densely populated, and because it is located in a valley where smog tends to settle rather than disperse, the city has a huge problem with air pollution. Ask students to research what is being done in Mexico City to deal with the problem of air pollution. Once they have completed their research, they should form groups and come up with some solutions of their own.

Worker. *Diego Rivera, 1928*

Acapulco cliff diver

have a lot of good memories from when I was growing up. My family was very poor, and I did not have many things that American kids have, but I still had a happy childhood full of wonder.

In Mexico life is varied. Young people in the cities attend school, go to the movies, and practice sports much like in the United States, whereas in rural areas there is more poverty and young people often do not go to school because they must work to support their families. In small villages in agricultural areas, where there are no movie theaters, young people play soccer to pass the time.

Mexico is a beautiful country endowed with immense natural resources and diverse people. You probably know about salsa—yes, there is lots of salsa in Mexico, the kind you eat and also the kind you dance. Mexico has natural wonders as well, including a vast shoreline with sugar-white sand. For those who can afford it, there is a lot to do in Mexico City—many museums of art and archaeology. Also among our cultural wonders are the ruins left by the great indigenous civilizations,

The Rectory, National University

Statue of a warrior

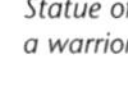

Mexican folkdance

Cultural/Historical Note

Pre-Columbian civilizations in Mexico were highly advanced. The Olmec, who between 1200 and 100 BC lived in the area which is now Tabasco and Veracruz, built one of Mexico's great civilizations. Characteristic of Olmec art are the impressive "Olmec heads," basalt sculptures of heads, some weighing over twenty tons and reaching up to forty feet in height. The Maya, who flourished in southern Mexico and Central America from 1500 BC–AD 300, left behind the great cities of Palenque, Chichén Itzá, Uxmal, and Tulum. They were masters of abstract knowledge and developed a calendar more astronomically accurate than the Gregorian calendar. They were the only people in the Americas to develop ideographic writing. (For more information on the Maya, see page 532.)

(cont.)

such as the pyramids of Palenque, Monte Albán, and Chichén Itzá.

Before the Spaniards came to Mexico, it was ruled by advanced civilizations, most prominently the Aztec and the Maya. Both peoples were highly developed in engineering, astronomy, and mathematics. The Maya, for example, invented the concept of zero, which was unknown to ancient Greek mathematicians. Today, the majority of Mexicans are of mixed Spanish and indigenous heritage.

Mexican culture, too, is a hybrid; it contains elements of both European and indigenous civilizations. The native peoples of Mexico worshipped many gods. They had gods for the rain, for the sun, and for the soil. One of the chief gods of the Aztec and the Toltec is Quetzalcoatl. The name means "serpent with feathers" in Nahuatl, the Aztec language. When the Spaniards came, they brought Catholicism and tried to make it the religion of Mexico. But instead of giving up the old ways completely, the people adapted them, and today practice a magical mix of ancient myths and Catholicism. A perfect example of this mixture is the celebration of *El Día de los Muertos*, or the Day of the Dead. Held on November 2, the Roman Catholic feast of All Souls' Day, it intermingles that Christian festival with a traditional Aztec celebration of the goddess of death, Mictecacihuatl.

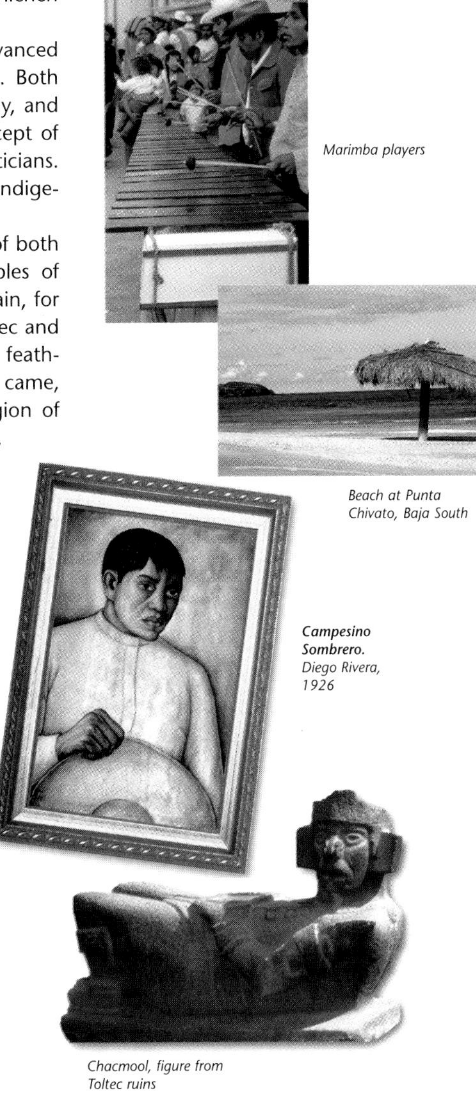

Marimba players

Beach at Punta Chivato, Baja South

Campesino Sombrero. *Diego Rivera, 1926*

Chacmool, figure from Toltec ruins

Monte Albán, Zapotec ruins

Cultural/Historical Note (cont.)

The Aztec established a powerful empire centered in the Valley of Mexico, where they founded their capital, Tenochtitlán, around 1325 AD. They were highly developed in engineering, architecture, art, math, and astronomy and had a complex social structure and an extensive trade network. The Aztec were widely feared because they sacrificed their prisoners of war to their chief god, Huitzilopochtli, who was believed to require offerings of human hearts. When Hernan Cortés arrived in Mexico in 1519, the Aztec civilization was at its height. Emperor Montezuma II mistook Cortés for a god, because according to the Aztec calendar, 1519 was the year in which the pale-skinned god Quetzalcoatl would return from the east. The Spanish kidnapped Montezuma and destroyed Tenochtitlán.

Cross-curricular Activities

MATHEMATICS AND SCIENCES AND APPLIED ARTS

The Maya were accomplished astronomers who structured their lives around the cycles of the sun, moon, and planets. Evidence of the importance of astronomy in Mayan religion and culture can be seen in El Castillo, a pyramid at Chichén Itzá built in honor of the plumed serpent god, Kukulcán. The pyramid was built with its corners precisely aligned so that on the spring, or vernal, equinox, a snakelike shadow, representing Kukulcán, appears to descend the staircase. On the autumnal equinox, the shadow-snake appears to slither back up and reclaim its position on the pyramid. The exact dates of the equinoxes vary, but they occur around March 21 and September 23.

Ask students to create models or diagrams to explain the earth's position relative to the sun on the vernal and autumnal equinoxes. For help with this project, students might want to consult an encyclopedia or an Internet source.

MATHEMATICS AND SCIENCES

The pyramid of Kukulcán was built to represent the Mayan calendar. It has 91 steps on each of its four faces, which, with the addition of the top platform, represent the 365 days of the Mayan solar year. Its nine terraced levels are each divided in two by a staircase, making 18 separate terraces which symbolize the 18 Mayan months. Finally, the 52 panels on each side of the structure stand for the 52 years in the Mayan calendar cycle. The Mayan calendar was more astronomically precise than the Gregorian calendar, the calendar we use today.

Ask students to research the Mayan and Gregorian calendars to compare the way the two calendars structure time around the cycles of the sun and moon. Students may use sources such as the encyclopedia or the Internet.

Cultural/Historical Note

Mexico was part of the Spanish empire for nearly 300 years, beginning in the early 1500s when Cortés conquered the Aztecs and established the colony of New Spain, and ending in the early 1800s with a ten-year rebellion. The revolt against Spanish rule began in the town of Dolores, just north of Mexico City. The town priest, Miguel Hidalgo y Costilla, had been secretly gathering guns and preparing a revolt when he learned that authorities had discovered his plans. There was no time to lose. At 5 A.M. on September 16, 1810, he tolled the bell of the church to wake the townspeople. He delivered a thundering speech proclaiming Mexico's independence from Spain—the *Grito de Dolores,* or Cry of Dolores. His congregation formed an army and marched on the city of Guanajuato.

Mexico had several dictators in the period following independence from Spain. In 1910, Mexicans fought a second revolution to overthrow the 31-year dictatorship of Porfirio Díaz, establish a democratic government, and write a constitution. One of the goals of this revolution was the redistribution of land, much of which was controlled by the Catholic Church and *hacendados,* or owners of large estates. Point out to students that the system of land distribution in Mexico throughout the colonial period and up to the war of 1910 was semifeudal. Indigenous people worked as serfs on estates in exchange for a place to live and credit they could use to buy food. Pancho Villa and Emiliano Zapata were among the famous revolutionary war heroes who led bands of peasants in rebellion against the rich landowners of Mexico. Ask students to write a short research paper comparing and contrasting the pre-Revolutionary system in Mexico to the feudal system of medieval Europe or medieval Japan.

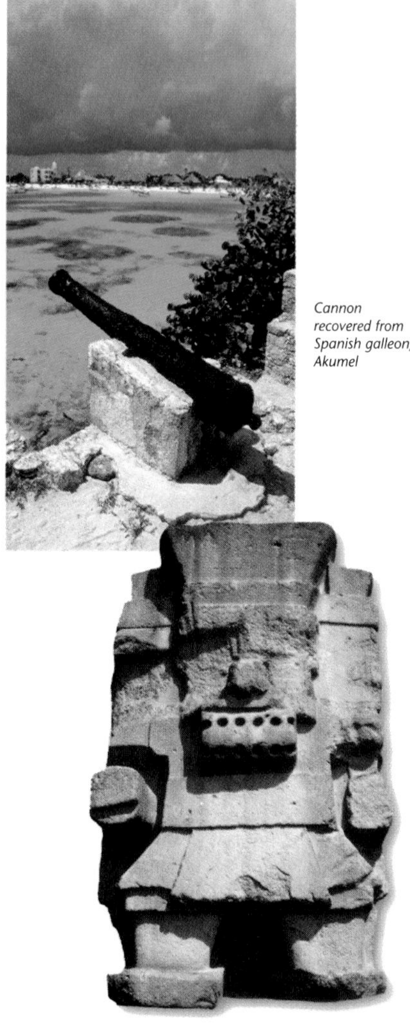

Cannon recovered from Spanish galleon, Akumel

Tlaloc, rain god

Families celebrate the Day of the Dead in the cemetery, cleaning and decorating the graves of dead relatives with a seemingly infinite number of flowers. They picnic on the graves as they await the souls of the departed. That night, nearly every house in my town has a shrine to the dead, laden with offerings of food and treats to be eaten by the returning souls. The festive atmosphere of this holiday reflects Mexicans' open attitude toward death: it is spoken of openly, not feared. As for the rest of our holidays, we celebrate most of the Catholic holidays observed in America, but the biggest celebration is that of Independence Day, September 16, which commemorates Mexico's 1810 cry for independence from Spain.

Spanish remains the official language of Mexico, although dialects of native languages are still spoken. Spanish is the language in which the poets and writers of Mexico have composed their literature. The most famous writers of Mexico are seventeenth-century poet Sor Juana Inés de la Cruz and modern writers like poet Octavio Paz, novelist and critic Carlos Fuentes, and Laura Esquivel. Contemporary Mexican writers have contributed a unique perspective to world literature. Their experimental writing captures Mexico's cultural mix of ancient Aztec and European roots, of past and present, and of myth and reality. ■

Tomb of Pacal, Palenque

Biographical Note

Sor Juana Inés de la Cruz (1651–1695) was a poet and a Catholic nun whose lyric poems are considered the greatest literature of the colonial period. She entered a convent at the age of sixteen because, as a woman, she felt it was the only way she could have the freedom to study and write. An internationally recognized literary figure, **Octavio Paz** (1914–) became, in 1990, the first Mexican writer to receive the Nobel Prize for literature. Paz has served as a diplomat in Paris, the Far East, and India. **Carlos Fuentes** (1928–) is one of Mexico's foremost contemporary novelists. The son of a Mexican diplomat, he was born in Panama and lived as a child in the United States, Chile, and Argentina. Fuentes himself served as ambassador to France and to the United Nations.

PREREADING

from *Like Water for Chocolate*
by Laura Esquivel, translated by Carol and Thomas Christensen

MEXICO

About the Author

LAURA ESQUIVEL
1950–

Soon after **Laura Esquivel** wrote the novel *Like Water for Chocolate,* she received many requests to adapt the book for film. Esquivel won multiple awards, including the Ariel Award for Best Screenplay by the Mexican Academy of Motion Pictures, for the screen adaptation she wrote. In 1993, *Like Water for Chocolate* became the highest grossing foreign film ever released in the United States.

Originally an educator of children, Esquivel later developed and wrote a television program. Her most recent novel, *La Ley del Amor,* or *The Law of Love,* features reincarnation and the intervention of good and bad angels. The novel is accompanied by Puccini arias and Mexican *danzón* numbers on CD—Esquivel intends readers to take breaks from the novel to listen to music. Shortly after the success of *Like Water for Chocolate,* Esquivel faced a painful divorce and cerebral thrombosis, a serious blood-clotting disease of the brain. Esquivel is confident that God is the "marvelous energy" that saved her. Esquivel's vivid spiritual life and her sense of different realities inform both her life and her work.

About the Selection

After studying screenwriting techniques, Laura Esquivel decided to write her conception of a perfect story: one without limits set by budget concerns or studio policy. The outcome was ***Like Water for Chocolate,*** which focuses on the traditions and responsibilities inherited by generations of Mexican women. The novel examines the everyday lives of such women around the turn of the century and expresses their frustration, love, humor, and anguish. Food preparation, recipes, and cooking play a central role in the novel; the predominance of these domestic practices suggests how few options were open to Mexican women of that time. The story is both spiritual and sensual, as Esquivel's characters move from reality into the fantastic, in a literary technique known as **magical realism** (see Insights: Magical Realism, page 278). The title, *Like Water for Chocolate,* comes from one of the recipes in the book.

CONNECTIONS: Mexican Cuisine

Like Water for Chocolate is unusual in that it is part recipe book, part novel. The recipes in the novel are traditional Mexican dishes that are linked to key moments in the life of the main character, Tita. In Mexico, corn and chiles are the staple ingredients used in most recipes. Corn is ground into meal and used to prepare the corn pancakes known as tortillas. Tortillas can be rolled around a filling of meat and baked to make enchiladas. Tostadas are tortillas fried crisp and sprinkled with chiles, beans, and cheese. Quesadillas are flour tortillas folded over a cheese filling and fried. Chiles are widely used throughout Latin American to season dishes. The tradition of hot and spicy cooking reputedly serves as a "self-cooling mechanism" in countries with hot climates. Eating the hot, spicy food is said to make one feel cooler. Even with people of colder climates, however, Mexican cuisine has become very popular.

GOALS/OBJECTIVES

Studying this lesson will enable students to

- enjoy an excerpt from a novel that focuses on the lives of turn-of-the-century Mexican women, in which the preparation of traditional Mexican recipes plays a central role
- discuss the life and work of Laura Esquivel
- define the literary terms *plot, inciting incident, point of view, magical realism, three-dimensional characters,* and *stock characters*
- practice active reading skills

ADDITIONAL RESOURCES

READER'S GUIDE

- Selection Worksheet 1.1

ASSESSMENT PORTFOLIO

- Selection Check Test 2.1.1
- Selection Test 2.1.2

ESSENTIAL SKILLS PRACTICE BOOKS

- Study and Research 4.9

PREREADING EXTENSIONS

Tell students that the cuisine of a particular country or region often reflects the traditions of its people. It can be interesting to study a country through its foods and recipes and the events and traditions associated with these foods. Ask students to get together in pairs or small groups to research the cuisine of a particular country or region other than Mexico. (See the Connections on this page.) Students should present their findings to the rest of the class. If possible, they might even want to prepare certain recipes.

SUPPORT FOR LEP STUDENTS

PRONUNCIATIONS OF PROPER NOUNS AND ADJECTIVES

Chen • cha (chān´chä)
Lau • ra Es • qui • vel (lau´rä äs´kē bāl´)
Ma • ma El • e • na (mä´mä āl ā´nä)
Na • cha (nä´chā)
Pe • dro Muz • quiz (pā´drō moos kēz´)
Ro • saur • a (rō zau´rä)
Ti • ta (tē´tä)

ADDITIONAL VOCABULARY

amid—in the middle of
archive—place where records or important materials are kept
cowering—backing down in fear
dismantled—taken apart
expanse—large, open space
subdue—calm; hold down

READER'S JOURNAL

As an alternate activity, you might ask students to write about foods that they associate with certain people, places, or occasions. Students should close their eyes and try to remember, in vivid detail, the smell and taste of the food and the people and events they associate with these foods.

ANSWERS TO GUIDED READING QUESTIONS

❶ Tita makes her entrance into the world on the kitchen table.

❷ Tita is washed into the world on a great tide of tears that floods the kitchen floor.

❸ Because of her unusual birth, Tita feels a great love for the kitchen. She spends most of her life there.

SPELLING AND VOCABULARY WORDS FROM THE SELECTION

deference ethereal

What traditions does your family practice? Describe one tradition that you would like to pass on to the family you may create one day and explain why. Describe a tradition you don't want to pass on to your future family, and explain why not.

READER'S JOURNAL

FROM

Like Water for Chocolate

LAURA ESQUIVEL, TRANSLATED BY CAROL AND THOMAS CHRISTENSEN

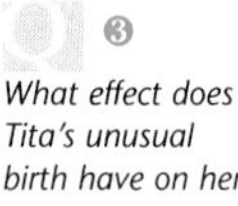

❶ *Where does Tita make her entrance into the world?*

❷ *How does Tita enter the world?*

❸ *What effect does Tita's unusual birth have on her life?*

INGREDIENTS:

1 can of sardines
1/2 chorizo sausage[1]
1 onion
oregano
1 can of chiles serranos[2]
10 hard rolls

PREPARATION:

Take care to chop the onion fine. To keep from crying when you chop it (which is so annoying!), I suggest you place a little bit on your head. The trouble with crying over an onion is that once the chopping gets you started and the tears begin to well up, the next thing you know you just can't stop. I don't know whether that's ever happened to you, but I have to confess it's happened to me, many times. Mama used to say it was because I was especially sensitive to onions, like my great-aunt, Tita.

Tita was so sensitive to onions, any time they were being chopped, they say she would just cry and cry; when she was still in my great-grandmother's belly her sobs were so loud that even Nacha, the cook, who was half-deaf, could hear them easily. Once her wailing got so violent that it brought on an early labor. And before my great-grandmother could let out a word or even a whimper, Tita made her entrance into this world, prematurely, right there on the kitchen table amid the smells of simmering noodle soup, thyme, bay leaves, and cilantro, steamed milk, garlic, and, of course, onion. Tita had no need for the usual slap on the bottom, because she was already crying as she emerged; maybe that was because she knew then that it would be her lot in life to be denied marriage. The way Nacha told it, Tita was literally washed into this world on a great tide of tears that spilled over the edge of the table and flooded across the kitchen floor.

That afternoon, when the uproar had subsided and the water had been dried up by the sun, Nacha swept up the residue the tears had left on the red stone floor. There was enough salt to fill a ten-pound sack—it was used for cooking and lasted a long time. Thanks to her unusual birth, Tita felt a deep love for the kitchen, where she spent most of her life from the day she was born.

When she was only two days old, Tita's father, my great-grandfather, died of a heart

1. ***chorizo sausage.*** Latin pork sausage highly seasoned with garlic, paprika, and other spices
2. ***chiles serranos.*** Type of hot pepper

attack and Mama Elena's milk dried up from the shock. Since there was no such thing as powdered milk in those days, and they couldn't find a wet nurse anywhere, they were in a panic to satisfy the infant's hunger. Nacha, who knew everything about cooking—and much more that doesn't enter the picture until later—offered to take charge of feeding Tita. She felt she had the best chance of "educating the innocent child's stomach," even though she had never married or had children. Though she didn't know how to read or write, when it came to cooking she knew everything there was to know. Mama Elena accepted her offer gratefully; she had enough to do between her mourning and the enormous responsibility of running the ranch—and it was the ranch that would provide her children the food and education they deserved—without having to worry about feeding a newborn baby on top of everything else.

From that day on, Tita's domain was the kitchen, where she grew vigorous and healthy on a diet of teas and thin corn gruels.[3] This explains the sixth sense Tita developed about everything concerning food. Her eating habits, for example, were attuned to the kitchen routine: in the morning, when she could smell that the beans were ready; at midday, when she sensed the water was ready for plucking the chickens; and in the afternoon, when the dinner bread was baking, Tita knew it was time for her to be fed.

Sometimes she would cry for no reason at all, like when Nacha chopped onions, but since they both knew the cause of those tears, they didn't pay them much mind. They made them a source of entertainment, so that during her childhood Tita didn't distinguish between tears of laughter and tears of sorrow. For her laughing was a form of crying.

Likewise for Tita the joy of living was wrapped up in the delights of food. It wasn't easy for a person whose knowledge of life was based on the kitchen to comprehend the outside world. That world was an endless expanse that began at the door between the kitchen and the rest of the house, whereas everything on the kitchen side of that door, on through the door leading to the patio and the kitchen and herb gardens was completely hers—it was Tita's realm.

Her sisters were just the opposite: to them, Tita's world seemed full of unknown dangers, and they were terrified of it. They felt that playing in the kitchen was foolish and dangerous. But once, Tita managed to convince them to join her in watching the dazzling display made by dancing water drops dribbled on a red hot griddle.

While Tita was singing and waving her wet hands in time, showering drops of water down on the griddle so they would "dance," Rosaura was cowering in the corner, stunned by the display. Gertrudis, on the other hand, found this game enticing, and she threw herself into it with the enthusiasm she always showed where rhythm, movement, or music were involved. Then Rosaura had tried to join them—but since she barely moistened her hands and then shook them gingerly, her efforts didn't have the desired effect. So Tita tried to move her hands closer to the griddle. Rosaura resisted, and they struggled for control until Tita became annoyed and let go, so that momentum carried Rosaura's hands onto it. Tita got a terrible spanking for that, and she was forbidden to play with her sisters in her own world. Nacha became her playmate then. Together they made up all sorts of games and activities having to do with cooking. Like the day they saw a man in the village plaza twisting long thin balloons into animal shapes, and they decided to do it with sausages. They didn't just make real animals, they also made up some of their own, creatures with the neck of a swan, the legs of a dog, the tail of a horse, and on and on.

Then there was trouble, however, when the animals had to be taken apart to fry the

3. **gruels.** Thin, easily digested porridges made by cooking meal in water or milk

❶ *Who offers to take charge of Tita's feeding? In what is this person an expert?*

❷ *What do Tita's sisters think of playing in the kitchen?*

❸ *How does Tita feel about laughter and sorrow?*

❹ *Because Tita's life is so wrapped up in the kitchen, what is difficult for her to comprehend?*

Answers to Guided Reading Questions

❶ Nacha offers to take charge of Tita's feeding. Nacha is an expert at cooking.

❷ Tita's sisters think playing in the kitchen is foolish and dangerous.

❸ Tita feels there is no difference between tears of laughter and tears of sorrow. She feels that laughing is a form of crying.

❹ It is difficult for Tita to comprehend the outside world.

Additional Questions and Activities

Encourage students to put together a class cookbook, complete with family recipes, anecdotes, and illustrations.

To begin, each student should bring in two or three family recipes or recipes that in some way have special meaning for them. The class will meet to decide which recipes from each student will be included in the book. (If you want a larger book, you might choose to use three or more from each person.) Each student should also contribute one or two original anecdotes, short stories, poems, or illustrations about cooking or about a specific recipe. Students can hold design meetings to discuss how they want to lay out their book.

To show off the recipes in the book, students might schedule a day to bring in samples of their recipes to share with other people in the school. Students can set up a table and make copies of the cookbook available.

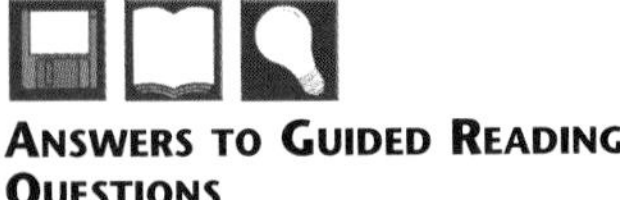

Answers to Guided Reading Questions

❶ The ingredients are for Christmas sausage rolls. Tita loves this recipe.

❷ Tita believes that smells have the power to evoke the past and bring back sounds and other smells that have "no match in the present."

Quotables

"Music, when soft voices die,
Vibrates in the memory;
Odors, when sweet violets sicken,
Live within the sense they
quicken."

—Percy Bysshe Shelley,
"To ——"

Additional Questions and Activities

Ask students to think about the poem quoted above in relation to what the narrator in *Like Water for Chocolate* says about smells and memory.

Do students agree that smells have the power to "evoke the past" by stimulating the memory? Invite students to freewrite for a few minutes about special smells and the images these smells create in their minds. Then invite students to share what they have written.

What are the ingredients that are listed at the beginning of this selection used to make? Who loves this recipe?

What power does Tita believe that smells have?

sausage. Tita refused to do it. The only time she was willing to take them apart was when the sausage was intended for the Christmas rolls she loved so much. Then she not only allowed her animals to be dismantled, she watched them fry with glee.

The sausage for the rolls must be fried over very low heat, so that it cooks thoroughly without getting too brown. When done, remove from the heat and add the sardines, which have been deboned ahead of time. Any black spots on the skin should also have been scraped off with a knife. Combine the onions, chopped chiles, and the ground oregano with the sardines. Let the mixture stand before filling the rolls.

Tita enjoyed this step enormously; while the filling was resting, it was very pleasant to savor its aroma, for smells have the power to evoke the past, bringing back sounds and even other smells that have no match in the present. Tita liked to take a deep breath and let the characteristic smoke and smell transport her through the recesses of her memory.

It was useless to try to recall the first time she had smelled one of those rolls—she couldn't, possibly because it had been before she was born. It might have been the unusual combination of sardines and sausages that had called to her and made her decide to trade the peace of ethereal existence in Mama Elena's belly for life as her daughter, in order

Words for Everyday Use

e • the • re • al (ē thir´ē əl) *adj.*, not earthly; heavenly

Vocabulary in Context

• The clouds in the sky at sunset looked mysterious and ethereal.

to enter the De la Garza family and share their delicious meals and wonderful sausage.

On Mama Elena's ranch, sausage making was a real ritual. The day before, they started peeling garlic, cleaning chiles, and grinding spices. All the women in the family had to participate: Mama Elena; her daughters, Gertrudis, Rosaura, and Tita; Nacha, the cook; and Chencha, the maid. They gathered around the dining-room table in the afternoon, and between the talking and the joking the time flew by until it started to get dark. Then Mama Elena would say:

"That's it for today."

For a good listener, it is said, a single word will suffice, so when they heard that, they all sprang into action. First they had to clear the table; then they had to assign tasks: one collected the chickens, another drew water for breakfast from the well, a third was in charge of wood for the stove. There would be no ironing, no embroidery, no sewing that day. When it was all finished, they went to their bedrooms to read, say their prayers, and go to sleep. One afternoon, before Mama Elena told them they could leave the table, Tita, who was then fifteen, announced in a trembling voice that Pedro Muzquiz would like to come and speak with her. . . .

After an endless silence during which Tita's soul shrank, Mama Elena asked:

"And why should this gentleman want to come talk to me?"

Tita's answer could barely be heard.

"I don't know."

Mama Elena threw her a look that seemed to Tita to contain all the years of repression that had flowed over the family, and said:

"If he intends to ask for your hand, tell him not to bother. He'll be wasting his time and mine too. You know perfectly well that being the youngest daughter means you have to take care of me until the day I die."

With that Mama Elena got slowly to her feet, put her glasses in her apron, and said in a tone of final command:

"That's it for today."

Tita knew that discussion was not one of the forms of communication permitted in Mama Elena's household, but even so, for the first time in her life, she intended to protest her mother's ruling.

"But in my opinion . . ."

"You don't have an opinion, and that's all I want to hear about it. For generations, not a single person in my family has ever questioned this tradition, and no daughter of mine is going to be the one to start."

Tita lowered her head, and the realization of her fate struck her as forcibly as her tears struck the table. From then on they knew, she and the table, that they could never have even the slightest voice in the unknown forces that fated Tita to bow before her mother's absurd decision, and the table to continue to receive the bitter tears that she had first shed on the day of her birth.

Still Tita did not submit. Doubts and anxieties sprang to her mind. For one thing, she wanted to know who started this family tradition. It would be nice if she could let that genius know about one little flaw in this perfect plan for taking care of women in their old age. If Tita couldn't marry and have children, who would take care of her when she got old? Was there a solution in a case like that? Or are daughters who stay home and take care of their mothers not expected to survive too long after the parent's death? And what about women who marry and can't have children, who will take care of them? And besides, she'd like to know what kind of studies had established that the youngest daughter and not the eldest is best suited to care for their mother. Had the opinion of the daughter affected by the plan ever been taken into account? If she couldn't marry, was she at least allowed to experience love? Or not even that?

Tita knew perfectly well that all these questions would have to be buried forever in the archive of questions that have no answers. In the De la Garza family, one obeyed—immediately. Ignoring Tita completely, a

1 *What is not permitted in the household? What does Mama Elena do to enforce this rule?*

2 *What does Tita do when she learns her fate? What does she realize? What does the table "realize"?*

3 *Who wants to come and speak with Mama Elena?*

4 *What has "flowed over the family"?*

5 *In Mama Elena's family, what does being the youngest daughter mean for Tita?*

Answers to Guided Reading Questions

1 Discussion is not permitted in the household. Mama Elena enforces this rule by telling Tita that she has no opinion.

2 Tita cries when she learns her fate. She realizes that she is fated to forever serve her mother and follow her orders and that there is nothing she can do about it. The table "realizes" that it will continue to receive Tita's bitter tears.

3 Pedro Muzquiz wants to come to speak with Mama Elena.

4 Years of repression have "flowed over the family."

5 In Mama Elena's family, being the youngest daughter means that she can never marry, but that she must take care of her mother until the day she dies.

Cross-curricular Activities

ARTS AND HUMANITIES

Like Water for Chocolate is a book that contains many dramatic scenes. Those involved in the adaptation of the novel to film had to choose and/or compose background music that would enhance and add to the drama of each scene. Ask students to reread the excerpt provided in this text, and then decide what kinds of music they might use for different parts of the story. Students can choose specific titles or they can simply choose to describe the type of music they might use.

Answers to Guided Reading Questions

❶ Pedro Muzquiz and his father come to speak to Mama Elena because Pedro wants to ask permission for Tita's hand in marriage.

❷ Tita sent Pedro a message telling him to abandon his attempts to marry her.

Additional Questions and Activities

Ask students to answer or discuss the following questions:

1. If you were Tita, how might you handle your role as Mama Elena's life-long caregiver? Do you think Tita is destined to have a pleasant life? Why, or why not?

2. If you were Pedro, what might you do or say upon hearing that Tita would not be allowed to marry you? Would you try to forget her, try to convince Mama Elena to change her mind, or try to convince Tita to run away with you?

3. Why do you think Tita chooses to stay with her mother, even though she realizes that her rules are unfair?

ANSWERS

Responses will vary. Possible responses are given.

1. Some students might say they would perform their tasks badly or resentfully. Tita is destined to have an unfulfilling life, made more difficult by seeing the man she loves married to her sister.

2. *Responses will vary.*

3. Students might say that in her time and place, Tita had few other choices.

❶ *Why do Pedro Muzquiz and his father appear at the house?*

❷ *What did Tita ask Pedro to do?*

very angry Mama Elena left the kitchen, and for the next week she didn't speak a single word to her.

What passed for communication between them resumed when Mama Elena, who was inspecting the clothes each of the women had been sewing, discovered that Tita's creation, which was the most perfect, had not been basted before it was sewed.

"Congratulations," she said, "your stitches are perfect—but you didn't baste[4] it, did you?"

"No," answered Tita, astonished that the sentence of silence had been revoked.

"Then go and rip it out. Baste it and sew it again and then come and show it to me. And remember that the lazy man and the stingy man end up walking their road twice."

"But that's if a person makes a mistake, and you yourself said a moment ago that my sewing was . . ."

"Are you starting up with your rebelliousness again? It's enough that you have the audacity to break the rules in your sewing."

"I'm sorry, Mami. I won't ever do it again."

With that Tita succeeded in calming Mama Elena's anger. For once she had been very careful; she had called her "Mami" in the correct tone of voice. Mama Elena felt that the word *Mama* had a disrespectful sound to it, and so, from the time they were little, she had ordered her daughters to use the word *Mami* when speaking to her. The only one who resisted, the only one who said the word without the proper deference was Tita, which had earned her plenty of slaps. But how perfectly she had said it this time! Mama Elena took comfort in the hope that she had finally managed to subdue her youngest daughter.

Unfortunately her hope was short-lived, for the very next day Pedro Muzquiz appeared at the house, his esteemed father at his side, to ask for Tita's hand in marriage. His arrival caused a huge uproar, as his visit was completely unexpected. Several days earlier Tita had sent Pedro a message via Nacha's brother asking him to abandon his suit. The brother swore he had delivered the message to Pedro, and yet, there they were, in the house. Mama Elena received them in the living room; she was extremely polite and explained why it was impossible for Tita to marry.

4. **baste.** Sew with long, loose stitches so as to keep the parts together until properly sewn; tack

Words for Everyday Use

def • er • ence (def´ər əns) *n.,* courteous regard or respect

Vocabulary in Context

• The children respected their grandparents and spoke to them with deference.

"But if you really want Pedro to get married, allow me to suggest my daughter Rosaura, who's just two years older than Tita. *She* is one hundred percent available, and ready for marriage. . . ."

At that Chencha almost dropped right onto Mama Elena the tray containing coffee and cookies, which she had carried into the living room to offer don Pascual and his son. Excusing herself, she rushed back to the kitchen, where Tita, Rosaura, and Gertrudis were waiting for her to fill them in on every detail about what was going on in the living room. She burst headlong into the room, and they all immediately stopped what they were doing, so as not to miss a word she said.

They were together in the kitchen making Christmas Rolls. As the name implies, these rolls are usually prepared around Christmas, but today they were being prepared in honor of Tita's birthday. She would soon be sixteen years old, and she wanted to celebrate with one of her favorite dishes.

"Isn't that something? Your ma talks about being ready for marriage like she was dishing up a plate of enchiladas! And the worse thing is, they're completely different! You can't just switch tacos and enchiladas like that!"

Chencha kept up this kind of running commentary as she told the others—in her own way, of course—about the scene she had just witnessed. Tita knew Chencha sometimes exaggerated and distorted things, so she held her aching heart in check. She would not accept what she had just heard. Feigning calm, she continued cutting the rolls for her sisters and Nacha to fill.

It is best to use homemade rolls. Hard rolls can easily be obtained from a bakery, but they should be small; the larger ones are unsuited for this recipe. After filling the rolls, bake for ten minutes and serve hot. For best results, leave the rolls out overnight, wrapped in a cloth, so that the grease from the sausage soaks into the bread.

When Tita was finishing wrapping the next day's rolls, Mama Elena came into the kitchen and informed them that she had agreed to Pedro's marriage—to Rosaura.

Hearing Chencha's story confirmed, Tita felt her body fill with a wintry chill: in one sharp, quick blast she was so cold and dry her cheeks burned and turned red, red as the apples beside her. That overpowering chill lasted a long time, and she could find no respite, not even when Nacha told her what she had overheard as she escorted don Pascual Muzquiz and his son to the ranch's gate. Nacha followed them, walking as quietly as she could in order to hear the conversation between father and son. Don Pascual and Pedro were walking slowly, speaking in low, controlled, angry voices.

"Why did you do that, Pedro? It will look ridiculous, your agreeing to marry Rosaura. What happened to the eternal love you swore to Tita? Aren't you going to keep that vow?"

"Of course I'll keep it. When you're told there's no way you can marry the woman you love and your only hope of being near her is to marry her sister, wouldn't you do the same?"

Nacha didn't manage to hear the answer; Pulque, the ranch dog, went running by, barking at a rabbit he mistook for a cat.

"So you intend to marry without love?"

"No, Papa, I am going to marry with a great love for Tita that will never die."

Their voices grew less and less audible, drowned out by the crackling of dried leaves beneath their feet. How strange that Nacha, who was quite hard of hearing by that time, should have claimed to have heard this conversation. Still, Tita thanked Nacha for telling her—but that did not alter the icy feelings she began to have for Pedro. It is said that the deaf can't hear but can understand. Perhaps Nacha only heard what everyone else was afraid to say. Tita could not get to sleep that night; she could not find the words for what she was feeling. How unfortunate that black holes in space had not yet been discovered, for then she might have understood the black hole in the center of her chest, infinite coldness flowing through it. ■

➊ *Whom does Mama Elena suggest that Pedro marry?*

➋ *How does Tita feel about Pedro's decision to marry Rosaura? How do you think she felt about Pedro?*

➌ *What is Pedro's reason for agreeing to marry Rosaura?*

➍ *To what does Chencha compare Mama Elena's proposal?*

➎ *What does Pedro say about his love for Tita?*

Answers to Guided Reading Questions

➊ Mama Elena suggests that Pedro marry Tita's sister Rosaura.

➋ Tita feels devastated—a "wintry chill" that she cannot shake fills her body. She loved Pedro and had believed in his love for her.

➌ Pedro's reason for agreeing to marry Rosaura is that it is his only hope of being near Tita, the one he truly loves.

➍ Chencha compares Mama Elena's proposal to "dishing up a plate of enchiladas" instead of a plate of tacos.

➎ Pedro says that his love for Tita will never die.

Selection Check Test with Answers

EX. What made Mama Elena go into early labor with Tita?
Mama Elena went into early labor because Tita was sobbing so hard in her mother's stomach from the onions that were being chopped in the kitchen.

1. When Tita was born, what was done with the salt residue from her tears?
It was swept up and used for cooking.

2. Why was Mama Elena unable to feed Tita?
Her milk had dried up from the shock of her husband's death.

3. Who came to the ranch to ask permission for Tita's hand in marriage?
Pedro Muzquiz came to the ranch, accompanied by his father.

4. What does Mama Elena suggest Pedro should do?
She suggests that Pedro marry Tita's sister Rosaura instead.

5. Why does Pedro agree to the marriage?
Pedro agrees to the marriage because he feels that it will allow him to be close to Tita.

Responding to the Selection

Students may also discuss what their opinion of Pedro would be if they were Tita.

Answers for Reviewing the Selection

RECALLING AND INTERPRETING

1. **Recalling.** Tita's crying, while still in her mother's womb, brought on early labor. She was born on the kitchen table on a "tide of tears." **Interpreting.** Tita acquires a great love of cooking, and, unlike her sisters, she spends all her time in the kitchen.

2. **Recalling.** Nacha takes charge of Tita's feeding because Mama Elena's milk has dried from the shock of her husband's death. Nacha is an expert cook. **Interpreting.** Mama Elena's decision means that she is not closely involved in the raising of her youngest daughter. Because of this, their mother/daughter relationship does not fully develop.

3. **Recalling.** Pedro wants to ask for Tita's hand in marriage. Mama Elena sees this visit as pointless because Tita cannot marry. As the youngest daughter, Tita is bound by family tradition to spend her life caring for her mother. Tita realizes that there will be no one to take care of her when she gets old. The plan is also arbitrary, requiring the youngest daughter to take care of her mother even if the oldest daughter is better suited to the job. The tradition also does not take love into account—it assumes that the youngest daughter can ignore her feelings of love. **Interpreting.** Mama Elena feels the need to enforce her power over Tita. Mama Elena seems cold, stubborn, and controlling of her daughters. Tita is a thinking person who does not merely accept things.

4. **Recalling.** Mama Elena tells Pedro that he cannot marry Tita but that he can marry Rosaura, Tita's older sister. Pedro says that being married to Rosaura will allow him to be near Tita. (cont.)

Responding to the Selection

How do you feel about Pedro's decision to marry Tita's sister Rosaura? Do you think his decision can be justified using his reasoning? Form groups to debate the issue—one group in favor of Pedro's marriage to Rosaura and the other group against it.

Reviewing the Selection

RECALLING		INTERPRETING
1. What is unusual about Tita's birth?	▶▶	In what way does Tita's birth affect her character? In what ways does it make her different from her sisters?
2. Why does Nacha offer to take charge of feeding Tita?	▶▶	What do you think about Mama Elena's decision to let Nacha take charge of Tita's feedings? What does this agreement reveal about the development of Mama Elena's and Tita's mother/daughter relationship?
3. Why does Pedro Muzquiz come to speak with Mama Elena? Why does Mama Elena say this visit is pointless? What flaws does Tita find in this family tradition?	▶▶	Why do you think Mama Elena refuses to allow Tita to break the family's tradition? What does her refusal reveal about her character? What do Tita's questions reveal about her character?
4. What does Mama Elena do when Pedro Muzquiz and his father come to speak with her? What reason does Pedro provide for agreeing to her proposal?	▶▶	What do you think motivates Mama Elena's counterproposal? How does Tita feel about this proposal and about Pedro's decision? Explain whether you believe Pedro's claims about his feelings for Tita.

SYNTHESIZING

5. What role does the recipe for Christmas rolls play in this selection? What is Tita doing when she hears about Mama Elena's proposal to Pedro? Why does the narrator continue to explain how to do this rather than dealing with Tita's emotions? What does the narrator say about the power of smell? With what will Christmas rolls forever be associated for Tita? What does cooking in general represent to Tita?

Answers for Reviewing the Selection (cont.)

Interpreting. In Mama Elena's mind, Pedro's marriage to Rosaura will end any feelings that he and Tita have for each other. She might also want to hurt Tita for showing disrespect. Tita is upset by the proposal and Pedro's decision. *Responses will vary.*

SYNTHESIZING

Responses will vary. Possible responses are given.

5. Descriptions of the making of Christmas rolls show the reader an aspect of Tita's childhood and the importance of cooking in Tita's life. Tita is wrapping the next day's rolls when she hears about Mama Elena's proposal. The narrator shows that cooking is a part of who Tita is, and is a source of comfort for her. Tita immerses herself in preparing the food to avoid thinking about what Mama Elena is saying to Pedro. The narrator says that smell conjures up memories. Tita will associate Christmas rolls with betrayal and heartbreak. For Tita, the preparation of food reflects life.

Understanding Literature (Questions for Discussion)

1. **Plot and Inciting Incident.** A **plot** is a series of events related to a central conflict, or struggle. The **inciting incident** is the event that introduces the central conflict. What is the inciting incident in *Like Water for Chocolate*? What central conflict does this incident introduce? How do you think this incident will affect the course of the story?

2. **Point of View. Point of view** is the vantage point from which a story is told. Stories are typically told from the first-person point of view, in which the narrator uses words such as *I* and *we*, or from a third-person point of view, in which the narrator uses words such as *he, she, it,* and *they* and avoids the use of *I* and *we*. In stories told in the first person, the narrator may participate in or witness the action. In those told in the third person, the narrator generally stands outside the action. From what point of view is this story told? In what way might the story be different if it were told from Mama Elena's point of view? from Tita's point of view?

3. **Magical Realism. Magical realism** is a kind of fiction that is, for the most part, realistic but that contains elements of fantasy. What elements of this story strike you as realistic? Which elements strike you as fantastic? What is the effect of the fantastic elements?

4. **Three-dimensional Characters and Stock Characters.** A **three-dimensional, full, or rounded character** is one who exhibits the complexity of traits associated with actual human beings. Tita is a three-dimensional character. What different traits does she reveal in this selection? A **stock character** is one found again and again in different literary works. Typically, stock characters are not fully developed and have a single dominating characteristic. Of what stock character in literature does Mama Elena remind you? Explain why.

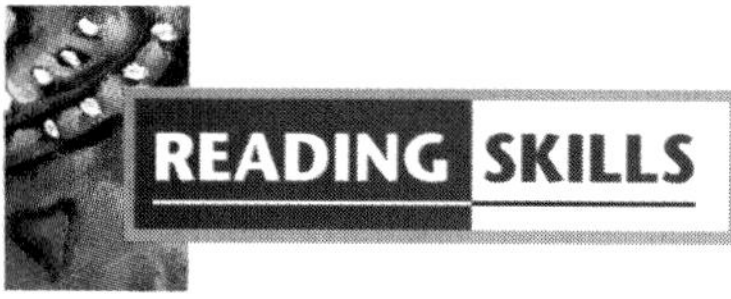

When you read the preceding selection from *Like Water for Chocolate*, did you read actively? That is, did you just skim through the selection, or did you read every word, questioning and wondering as you went? If you only skimmed the selection, you may have had trouble understanding it. While there are certainly times when you should skim—for example, when reviewing for a test material you have already read—literature is meant to be savored. It is meant to make you think, and in order for it to have this effect, you have to be an active reader. Reading actively means interacting with the text as you read. If you learn to read actively, you will find yourself enjoying your reading more as well as understanding more of what you read. The first step to active reading is keeping a journal on hand when you read so you can note questions and thoughts. Suggestions for things to consider and write about as you read appear in the Language Arts Survey.

The Language Arts Survey is a five-section handbook found at the back of your textbook. The Survey provides information about the following skills areas: writing, language, speaking

ANSWERS FOR UNDERSTANDING LITERATURE

Responses will vary. Possible responses are given.

1. Plot and Inciting Incident. The inciting incidents in *Like Water for Chocolate* are Pedro's request for Tita's hand in marriage, Mama Elena's refusal to allow Tita to get married, her offer of Rosaura, and Pedro's acceptance of this offer. These events change the direction of the story and introduce the central conflict—Tita's and Pedro's struggle with the fact that they love each other but cannot be together. Now they are to live in the same house, but Pedro will be married to someone else. Students should recognize that this story is likely to produce interesting dramatic twists.

2. Point of View. The story is told from the third-person point of view by Tita's great-niece. If it were told from Mama Elena's point of view, the story would stress Tita's disrespect for her mother, and it would focus on how Mama Elena does everything in her power to make a comfortable and secure home, adhering to the traditions of their family, receiving nothing but grief and disrespect in return. If the story were told from Tita's point of view, there would be more detail about Mama Elena's injustices and the emotions that Tita suffers as a result. Readers would also get a more vivid look into Tita's relationship with Nacha.

3. Magical Realism. The everyday activities of the household, such as cooking and sewing, are realistic. The relationships between Tita and Mama Elena and between Tita and Pedro, and the family traditions that complicate these relationships, seem realistic as well. Elements of magical realism include Tita's tears in her mother's womb, her unusual birth, the salt from Tita's tears that was used for cooking, and Tita's extreme attachment to the kitchen.

(cont.)

ANSWERS FOR UNDERSTANDING LITERATURE (CONT.)

4. Three-dimensional Characters and Stock Characters. Students might say that Tita shows that she is sensitive, romantic, smart, talented, and inquisitive. She feels love, disappointment, and anger with great intensity. She also gets herself into trouble by being too quick to challenge and irritate her mother. Mama Elena represents the cruel, domineering parent who does not understand the feelings of her child and who needs to enforce power over her household. She is harsh to an extreme, like the wicked stepmother in "Cinderella" or the wicked queen in "Snow White and the Seven Dwarfs."

▶ Additional practice of the skills taught in this lesson is provided in the Essential Skills Practice Book: Study and Research 4.9.

Answers for Skills Activities

READING SKILLS

Students should show, in their class discussion, that they understand the techniques of active reading outlined in this activity. Encourage students to take careful notes as they read the selection from "A Modest Proposal" by Jonathan Swift. You might want to gather and evaluate students' notes.

Possible responses to reading:

• Prediction based on title: In the essay, Swift is going to propose some kind of plan. His use of the word *modest* indicates that either he is not sure about his plan; his plan is a small, rather insignificant one; or that his plan is a radical one and he is being ironic.

• Questions before reading: Why is he targeting the children of poor people? What will he suggest to combat this serious problem? What is the writer's purpose?

• Author's aim (early in reading): The author's aim seems to be to address the issue of poverty in Ireland, specifically the issue of poor families with children. (cont.)

and listening, study and research, and applied English/tech prep. Throughout this textbook, you will come across references to the Survey that provide the number and title of the applicable section. You will also want to refer to the Survey to answer questions regarding these skills. Turn now to the Language Arts Survey 4.9, "Reading Actively," and read that section.

ACTIVITY

The passage you are about to read is an excerpt from an essay written by Jonathan Swift, a British writer of the Enlightenment, an eighteenth-century philosophical movement characterized by a belief in reason. Swift is the author of *Gulliver's Travels*. This essay, "A Modest Proposal," caused a furor when it was first published because many people did not read actively and misunderstood the author's intent. To avoid making the mistake many people in Swift's original audience made, employ the active reading techniques you have just reviewed. Note your predictions and questions in your journal. Use the suggestions in the margins as a starting place.

When you have read the selection, discuss your response. Refer to the notes you took while reading if necessary.

▶ Predict what the title means.

▶ Jot down any questions you have before you begin reading.

▶ Summarize what happens in each paragraph.

▶ The author's goal or aim in writing this essay is not stated explicitly. Try to infer the author's intent.

from "**A Modest Proposal**" by Jonathan Swift

FOR PREVENTING THE CHILDREN OF POOR PEOPLE IN IRELAND FROM BEING A BURDEN TO THEIR PARENTS OR COUNTRY, AND FOR MAKING THEM BENEFICIAL TO THE PUBLIC

It is a melancholy object to those who walk through this great town or travel in the country, when they see the streets, the roads, and cabin doors, crowded with beggars of the female sex, followed by three, four, or six children, all in rags and importuning every passenger for an alms. These mothers, instead of being able to work for their honest livelihood, are forced to employ all their time in strolling to beg sustenance for their helpless infants, who, as they grow up, either turn thieves for want of work, or leave their dear native country to fight for the Pretender in Spain, or sell themselves to the Barbadoes.

I think it is agreed by all parties that this prodigious number of children in the arms, or on the backs, or at the heels of their mothers, and frequently of their fathers, is in the present deplorable state of the kingdom a very great additional grievance; and therefore whoever could find out a fair, cheap, and easy method of making these children sound, useful members of the commonwealth would deserve so well of the public as to have his statue set up for a preserver of the nation.

But my intention is very far from being confined to provide only for the children of professed beggars; it is of a much greater extent, and shall take in the whole number of infants at a certain age who are born of parents in effect as little able to support them as those who demand our charity in the streets.

As to my own part, having turned my thoughts for many years upon this important subject, and maturely weighed the several schemes of other projectors, I have always found them grossly mistaken in their computation. It is true, a child just dropped from its dam may be supported by her milk for a solar year, with little other nourishment; at most not above the value of two shillings, which the mother may certainly get, or the value in scraps, by her lawful occupation of begging; and it is exactly at one year old that I propose to provide for them in such a manner as instead of being a charge upon their parents or the parish, or wanting food and raiment for the rest of their lives, they shall on the contrary contribute to the feeding, and partly to the clothing, of many thousands.

There is likewise another great advantage in my scheme, that it will prevent those voluntary abortions, and that horrid practice of women murdering their bastard children, alas, too frequent among us, sacrificing the poor innocent babes, I doubt, more to avoid the expense than the shame, which would move tears and pity in the most savage and inhuman breast.

The number of souls in this kingdom being usually reckoned one million and a half, of these I calculate there may be about two hundred thousand couples whose wives are breeders; from which number I subtract thirty thousand couples who are able to maintain their own children, although I apprehend there cannot be so many under the present distresses of the kingdom; but this being granted, there will remain an hundred and seventy thousand breeders. I again subtract fifty thousand for those women who miscarry, or whose children die by accident or disease within the year. There only remain an hundred and twenty thousand children of poor parents annually born. The question therefore is, how this number shall be reared and provided for, which, as I have already said, under the present situation of affairs, is utterly impossible by all the methods hitherto proposed. For we can neither employ them in handicraft or agriculture; we neither build houses (I mean in the country) nor cultivate land. They can very seldom pick up a livelihood by stealing till they arrive at six years old, except where they are of towardly parts; although I confess they learn the rudiments much earlier, during which time they can however be looked upon only as probationers, as I have been informed by a principal gentleman in the county of Cavan, who protested to me that he never knew above one or two instances under the ages of six, even in a part of the kingdom so renowned for the quickest proficiency in that art.

I am assured by our merchants that a boy or a girl before twelve years old is no salable commodity; and even when they come to this age they will not yield above three pounds, or three pounds and half a crown at most on the Exchange; which cannot turn to account either to the parents or the kingdom, the charge of nutriment and rags having been at least four times that value.

I shall now therefore humbly propose my own thoughts, which I hope will not be liable to the least objection.

I have been assured by a very knowing American of my acquaintance in London, that a young healthy child well nursed is at a year old a most delicious, nourishing, and wholesome food, whether stewed, roasted, baked, or boiled; and I make no doubt that it will equally serve in a fricassee or a ragout.

I do therefore humbly offer it to public consideration that of the hundred and twenty thousand children, already computed, twenty thousand may be reserved for breed, whereof only one fourth part to be males, which is more than we allow to sheep, black cattle, or swine; and my reason is that these children are seldom the fruits of marriage, a circumstance not much regarded by our savages, therefore one male will be sufficient to serve four females. That the remaining hundred thousand may at a year old be offered in sale to the persons of quality and fortune through the kingdom, always advising the mother to let them suck plentifully in the last month, so as to render them plump and fat for a good table. A child will make two dishes at an entertainment for friends; and when the family dines alone, the fore or hind quarter will make a reasonable dish, and seasoned with a little pepper or salt will be very good boiled on the fourth day, especially in winter.

I have reckoned upon a medium that a child just born will weigh twelve pounds, and in a solar year if tolerably nursed increaseth to twenty-eight pounds.

I grant this food will be somewhat dear, and therefore very proper for landlords, who, as they have already devoured most of the parents, seem to have the best title to the children. ■

◄ *What relationship do you see between the poor and the wealthy as described in this selection?*

◄ *Are the author's arguments convincing? Does he intend them to be convincing? How do you feel about what the author is saying? Why is he trying to arouse this response in you?*

◄ *What do you now think is the author's intent?*

Answers for Skills Activities (cont.)

- The relationship between the poor and the wealthy: According to this selection, the great majority of the people are poor and their living conditions are abysmal. The wealthy seem to look down with disgust on the poor, view them as an exploitable commodity, and resent them as a burden on society. Rather than feeling a need to help the poor, wealthy people seem to despise children under six who cannot work to support themselves. The wealthy also seem to assume that all poor people turn to a life of crime.
- Notes on the author's arguments: The author is trying to make a point by describing something outrageous in a mock-serious way. The writer wants readers to feel shocked, but then to think about why he is making these suggestions.
- Author's intent: The author is trying to shock wealthy people into recognizing their callous treatment of the poor.

Literary Technique

Satire

Point out to students that Swift's "A Modest Proposal" is an example of satire, meaning it is humorous writing or speech intended to point out errors, falsehoods, foibles, or failings.

SUPPORT FOR LEP STUDENTS

PRONUNCIATIONS OF PROPER NOUNS AND ADJECTIVES

Bu • chi Em • e • che • ta
(boo´chē em´ə chē´tä)

E • be • re M • bak • we
(e bâr´ā mə bä´kwā)

Ma • ri • a • ma Bâ
(mä´rē ä´mä bä)

ne • de • wo (ne dā´wō)

U • mu • a • hi • a
(oo´moo ä hā´ä)

Wo • le Soy • in • ka
(wō´lā shô yiŋ´kə)

CROSS-CURRICULAR ACTIVITIES

SOCIAL STUDIES

Have students locate Nigeria on a map. Then have them draw their own maps of Nigeria which show the major cities, rivers, and topography of the nation. So that students might visualize how large Nigeria is, ask students to compare its size in square miles to the size of of their home state.

ARTS AND HUMANITIES AND SOCIAL STUDIES

Students may be interested in learning more about the different ethnic groups of Nigeria and their long history, which archaeological evidence suggests goes back to prehistoric times. Major groups of people living in the country include the Hausa and the Fulani who live in the north, the Yoruba, who live in the southwest, and the Ibo, who live in the east. Other large ethnic groups include the Kanuri, Tiv, Edo, Nupe, Ibibio, and Ijo. Students might work in groups and use sources at the local library or on the Internet to research different aspects of one of the peoples of Nigeria, such as the language, religion, political structure, structure of families, agriculture, arts and crafts, or major cities of that people. Each group should then report their findings to the class.

PASSPORT TO NIGERIA

Nedewo! My name is Ebere Mbakwe and I am from Nigeria. In Nigeria, everyone comes from a small village—mine is Umuahia—and then we move to the city to go to school and work. My mother is a teacher and my father works for the government. Our city, Owerri, is in Imo, a state in the eastern part of Nigeria, which is tropical and very rainy. It's always hot, but you get used to it. Northern Nigeria is a desert and central Nigeria is full of mountains and rivers. In each of these regions, the dress and language are different.

Nigeria has a faltering economy and most people are poor. The country's revenue comes mostly from crude oil, but oil can't provide a living for everybody, so many people earn money by trading. They might buy shoes in London or Spain and then sell them back home. In the villages, most people make their living by farming.

Everyday life in Nigeria is not as different from American life as some people think. We have computers, movies, cable TV,

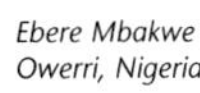
Ebere Mbakwe
Owerri, Nigeria

Flag of Nigeria

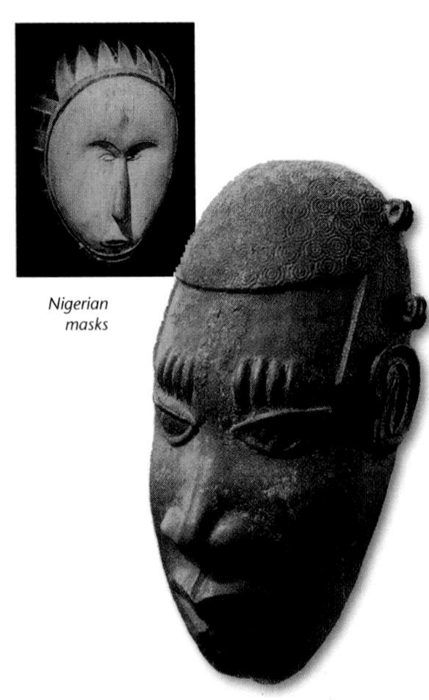
Nigerian masks

CROSS-CURRICULAR ACTIVITIES

SOCIAL STUDIES

Civil wars in Nigeria devastated the Yoruba empire of Oyo and the Muslim empire of Bornu during the 1800s, and it was during that time of weakness that the British empire's power and influence increased. Britain took over the port city of Lagos in 1861, claiming that it needed to do so to stop other European countries from continuing the slave trade there.

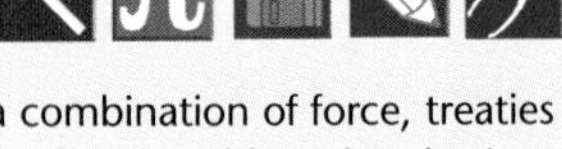

Eventually, through a combination of force, treaties with Nigerian leaders, and the wealth and authority of British companies in Africa, Britain declared Nigeria a colony in 1886. Nigeria attained independence from Britain in 1960 and became a republic in 1963. A civil war took place in 1967–1970, when the Ibo people of the east attempted to secede from Nigeria

(cont.)

air-conditioning, and cars—they're just not as common. Families are also basically the same, although sometimes I think the relationship between parents and children is different. Nigerian parents have a very strong hold on their children, so I have been surprised to see American children disobey their parents because that just doesn't happen in Nigeria. American parents seem to want to be friends with their children. In Nigeria, when you are grown it is your duty to take care of your parents. No matter how rich you are, if your parents are wretched, people will look down on you.

In Nigeria, everyone is either a Muslim or a Christian, although there are some older people who still cling to traditional beliefs—the Yorubans in the west have flamboyant myths and legends with many gods. Intermarriage is rare in Nigeria because people don't like to mingle. There's a certain amount of discrimination, especially between Muslims and Christians.

Nigerians enjoy celebrations. We have a big carnival for Christmas, and people go home to their villages—the cities become deserted. We go to church and then the children visit all their neighbors. We watch plays, and there is a lot of food and

Cleaning grain

Nigerian wall plaque

Baobab tree

Fishing in a lagoon

Cross-curricular Activities

ARTS AND HUMANITIES, SOCIAL STUDIES, AND APPLIED ARTS

Have students, working in small groups, imagine that they are to plan the itinerary for a class trip to Nigeria. Tell them that they can choose to visit any Nigerian sites that they wish, as long as they can convince other students that these places are worth visiting. To begin, students might start with Ebere's recommendations: "People should see Olumo Rock, which is very pretty. It's in a savannah in the west. Also, there is Niger Falls on the Niger River and the Yankari game reserve in the north. There is a museum in Umuahia that commemorates the war of 1967–1970. The building was a radio station during the war." Then ask students to consider the following questions: Which of these places would you be most interested in visiting? What might other students be interested in seeing? What places in Nigeria of natural, cultural, or historical importance might a tour group visit? Good resources include travel guides from the library and the Internet. When students have completed their research, they should prepare scripts introducing their tour and persuading classmates to sign up for it. When groups present their promotional pitch, they should strive to be as colorful as possible, using artwork, Nigerian music, and a prepared script. Students might also wear African dress or bring in African artifacts for visual effect. After the presentations are finished, students should vote for the tour they would most like to take.

Cross-curricular Activities (cont.)

and were opposed by the Muslims to the north. The northerners won the war and have had almost exclusive control of the government since that time. Military government has alternated with briefer periods of civilian rule. At the time Ebere wrote for this textbook, Nigeria was ruled by a military regime with General Sani Abacha as its president. General Abacha assumed power in 1994. Because Nigeria has experienced frequent shifts in power, you might want to direct students to research and report on the current political situation in Nigeria. They can do this by using current periodicals or the Internet. Key words to use in an online search include *Nigeria, Sani Abacha,* and *Nigerian government.*

Cross-curricular Activities

Mathematics and Sciences and Applied Arts

Yams are one of the staple food crops of Nigeria. Ask students to do some research on yams to find out what plant family the yam belongs to, what the plant looks like, and what soil and climate are best for growing yams. Interested students might also research the nutritional value of the yam and why it is considered such a valuable food staple. Students might then bring yams to class, or prepare an African recipe using yams, such as the one for *Dundu Oniyeri* below. You might want to play Nigerian music while students share their recipes.

Dundu Oniyeri (Fried Yams)

Yield: 8 servings

Ingredients:

- 2 pounds yams
- 1 quart and 2 tablespoons water
- 2 teaspoons salt
- 1 cup flour
- 1 teaspoon salt
- 1/2 teaspoon pepper
- 1/2 teaspoon cinnamon
- 1/2 teaspoon paprika
- 2 eggs
- Oil for frying

1. In a 2-quart saucepan, cover 2 pounds yams, peeled and cut in uniform 1/2-inch slices, with 1 quart water and 1 teaspoon salt.
2. Cook until tender and drain. Shake over heat until dry.
3. For seasoned flour, combine: 1 cup flour, 1 teaspoon salt, 1/2 teaspoon pepper, 1/2 teaspoon cinnamon, 1/2 teaspoon paprika. Dip yam slices in seasoned flour.
4. Beat 2 eggs lightly with 2 tablespoons water. Then dip flour-covered yams in egg mixture.
5. Dip slices in the flour again.
6. Deep fry in oil at 360 degrees or sauté in oil until golden brown and serve hot as a vegetable or side dish.

For more African recipes, students might consult Bea Sandler's *The African Cookbook.*

music, singing and dancing. On October 1, we celebrate Independence Day, the day we became independent from Great Britain. People go to the big stadium to watch marching bands—it is very noisy. We hold Children's Day on May 27. On this day, we celebrate children and give them a break.

Rice is our most popular food, but we also eat beef, chicken, a little fish (especially dried fish), brown beans, and maize (cooked or mashed). Yams are very important—we eat them cooked, boiled, and roasted, and we even have a special festival to celebrate them. We are not concerned about cholesterol—everything's fried. Anyway, it's so hot in Nigeria that you just sweat everything out!

Nigeria has many great writers including Chinua Achebe and Wole Soyinka, who have both won the Nobel Prize, and Buchi Emecheta. One of my favorite books by an African writer is *So Long A Letter* by Mariama Bâ. It is the story of a woman who must make a new life for herself when her husband takes a second wife. This practice, polygamy, started for economic reasons, and for many centuries it was a sign of wealth to have more than one wife. But as circumstances have changed, polygamy has become less common.

I think dating is the most unusual part of American culture. In Nigeria, we have no open dating. There is no way you're going

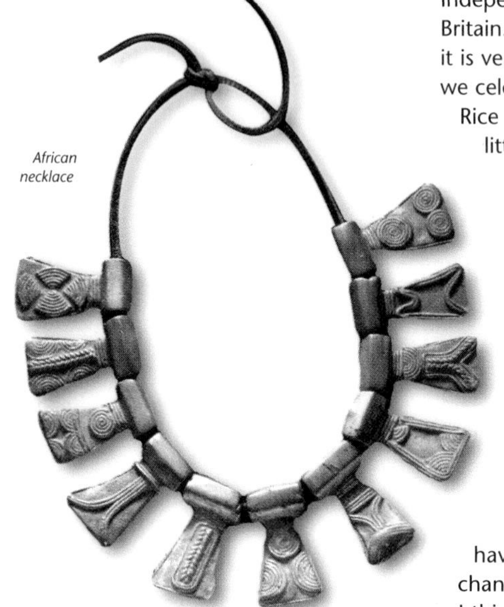

African necklace

Nigerian mask

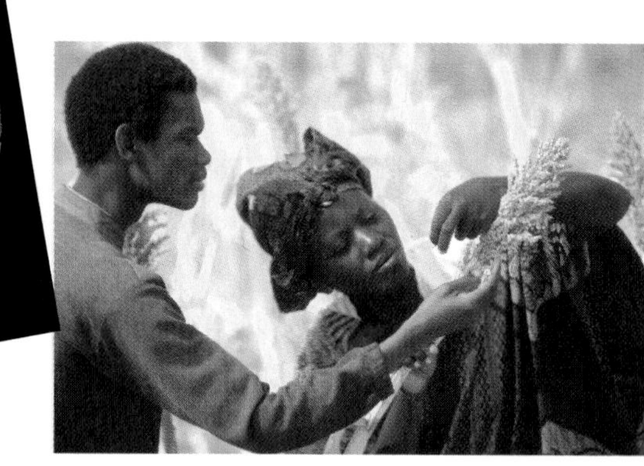

Agriculturalists inspecting sorghum grain

Biographical Note

For a biography of **Chinua Achebe**, see page 24.

For a biography of **Wole Soyinka**, see page 417.

Buchi Emecheta (1944–) is a Nigerian author who was born in Lagos but has lived most of her life in Great Britain. Although her father died when she was young, she finished her education at the Methodist Girls High School. At sixteen, she married and had five children, but she left her husband after six years. Afterward, she earned an honors degree in sociology from the University of London and began to write. Much of her fiction is autobiographical—in particular, her first book, *In the Ditch* (1972), and her second, *Second-Class Citizen* (1974). These novels tell the story of a Nigerian woman who moves to England with her student husband, who mistreats her. She finally gains the courage to leave

(cont.)

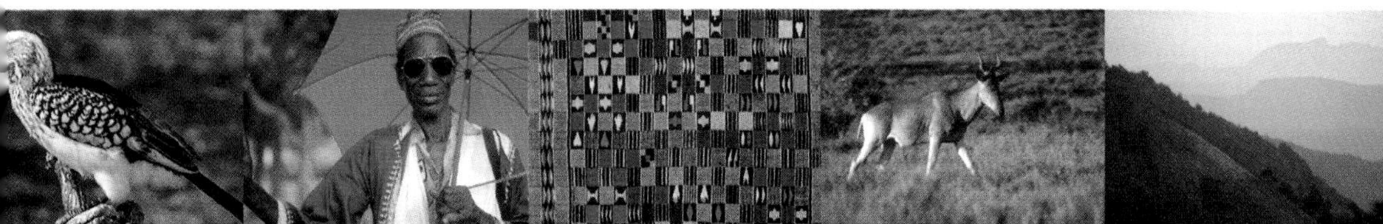

on a date if you're under twenty-four! When you finally *do* go on a date, you have to have a chaperone, like a coworker or a family member, no matter how old you are. In the United States, young men and women hang out together, but in Nigeria there is no mixing of the sexes. Most of our schools separate boys and girls, and mixing at parties is frowned upon.

Nigeria's biggest contributions to world culture are in art, literature, clothing design, and textiles. African patterns are very popular in other countries. Also, many people think that America was the first democracy, but thousands of years ago we already had democracy. There was no king, and every house spoke for itself. But more than anything, I think we communicate the attitude that it's okay to be different. Even though we have two main religions with differing ideas and over twenty languages with more than four hundred dialects, we have somehow managed to coexist quite peacefully. We are proud of our identity as a nation, but we are open to learning about other cultures and believe that different cultures can exist peacefully side by side. In Nigeria we have a saying: "Wherever something stands, something stands next to it." ■

Blackheaded Oriole

Newspaper vendor

Tailor

Biographical Note (cont.)

him, and only then is able to recognize her own worth.

Mariama Bâ (1929–1981) was a Senegalese writer, teacher, and feminist. Bâ was raised as a Muslim by her maternal grandparents. Against their wishes—and at a time when it was unusual for women in her country to become educated—she attended the École Normal (Teacher's College) in Rufusique and earned the highest exam score in 1943 for all of colonial French West Africa. Bâ's commitment to expose unfair and unequal treatment of women led her to write *So Long a Letter* (*Une Si Longue Lettre* in its original French). This novel is her best-known work, winning Bâ the 1980 Noma Award for Publishing in Africa. It has been called "the most deeply felt presentation of the female condition in African fiction."

Cultural/Historical Note

You may wish to share with students the following information after they have read Ebere's comments on democracy in Nigerian history:

The early kingdoms in Nigeria included the Sokoto caliphate in the north, which was ruled by the Muslim system of government and headed by a sultan; the Oyo Empire in the west which was ruled by a monarch, called an *Alafin;* and the Benin Empire which was also ruled by a king, or *Oba.* In contrast with these forms of government in which one individual rules, in the south-eastern part of the country, where the Ibo lived, there was no one leader. Iboland was divided into city-states that were run by tribal councils. These councils included all of the male citizens, who would meet and cast votes before any action could take place in the city.

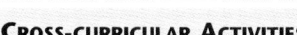

Cross-curricular Activities

ARTS AND HUMANITIES, SOCIAL STUDIES, AND APPLIED ARTS

Nigeria is known around the world for its colorful textiles and unique clothing designs. Nigerian fabrics and fashion often inspire contemporary Western fashion designers. Ebere describes the current style of dress in Nigeria in this way: "On special occasions, women usually wear wrappers and young men wear suits. The older men wear caftans and hats, and carry a staff. For everyday, boys wear jeans and T-shirts and girls wear mini-skirts, gowns, or long skirts. It is considered rude for a girl to wear pants. Many high-school kids attend boarding schools, where they wear uniforms."

Ask students to find examples of Nigerian or other African fashion as it is pictured in magazines and catalogs. Then have students discuss whether they would like to wear such clothing.

ADDITIONAL RESOURCES

READER'S GUIDE

- Selection Worksheet 1.2

ASSESSMENT PORTFOLIO

- Selection Check Test 2.1.3
- Selection Test 2.1.4

ESSENTIAL SKILLS PRACTICE BOOKS

- Writing 1.1, 1.5–1.18
- Applied English/Tech Prep 5.1

PREREADING EXTENSIONS

You might tell students that the slave trade that brought Africans to the Americas was conducted primarily on the coast of West Africa, in places like Nigeria and Cameroon. Thus, many African Americans can trace their ancestry to Nigeria and, specifically, to the Ibo people of that country.

SUPPORT FOR LEP STUDENTS

PRONUNCIATIONS OF PROPER NOUNS AND ADJECTIVES

Chin • u • a A • che • be (chēn´wä ä chā´bā)
I • bo (ē´bō)
La • gos (lā´gäs)
Nene (nā nā)
Nnae • me • ka (nī mē´kä)
O • ke • ke (ō kā kā)

ADDITIONAL VOCABULARY

commiserate—share sadness and misery
menacing—threatening
obstinately—stubbornly
opposition—state of being against something
remorse—regret, sorrow

PREREADING

"Marriage Is a Private Affair"
by Chinua Achebe

NIGERIA

About the Author

CHINUA ACHEBE
1930–

Widely acknowledged as the greatest living African novelist, **Chinua Achebe** was born in Nigeria and raised in Ogidi, an Ibo village. Educated at Government College, in Umuahia, Nigeria, and at University College in Ibadan, Nigeria, Achebe taught school before going into broadcasting. He had to leave his job as Director of External Broadcasting for Nigerian radio during a time of political upheaval that led to civil war. In 1958, he completed his first novel, *Things Fall Apart,* which was followed by *No Longer at Ease* (1960), *Arrow of God* (1964), and *A Man of the People* (1966). In 1967, Achebe started a publishing house. During the Nigerian Civil War, waged from 1967 to 1969, Achebe was a diplomat for Biafra, a short-lived African state. After the Nigerian Civil War, Achebe toured the United States, lecturing at various universities. Thereafter, he served as professor of English at the University of Nigeria and as director of two Nigerian publishing houses. He has also taught in several American universities, including the University of Massachusetts at Amherst, the University of Connecticut at Storrs, and the University of California at Los Angeles. He holds honorary doctorates from universities in Nigeria, England, Scotland, Canada, and the United States.

About the Selection

Achebe's works present the tumultuous, troubled story of Nigeria's transition from traditional to modern ways of life. **"Marriage Is a Private Affair"** deals with a conflict between traditional African customs and newer Western values. In the story, the central character's father, an Ibo man from a rural village, clings to his traditional belief that marriage should be arranged by parents. The central character acts, instead, on a shocking, modern Western notion—that marriage should be based on love.

CONNECTIONS: Nigeria's Cultural Heritage

Nigeria, a vast country on the southern coast of West Africa, takes its name from the mighty Niger river. The country covers 357,000 square miles, has a population of more than 119 million people, and contains more than 250 ethnic groups, each with its own customs, traditions, and language.

The first Europeans to come to the land that is now Nigeria were the Portuguese, who arrived in the fifteenth century and began to traffic in slaves taken first from the coast and then from the interior. The English arrived in the seventeenth century and also took part in the slave trade until it was outlawed in England in 1807. In 1886, Nigeria became a British colony. Administrators arrived to set up an English government there, along with missionaries sent to convert the people to Christianity. In 1960, Nigeria gained its indepence from Britain, but many legacies of British rule remain, including the English language (Nigeria's official language) and English laws and political structures.

Colonial rule brought to Nigeria Western technology, customs, and values that dramatically transformed the traditional lives of Nigeria's peoples. Today in the nation, Western culture exists alongside traditional cultures developed over a thousand years.

GOALS/OBJECTIVES

Studying this lesson will enable students to

- empathize with characters in conflict over traditional African customs and Western values
- discuss the life and work of Chinua Achebe
- discuss aspects of Nigerian culture
- define the literary terms *conflict* and *motivation*
- learn the steps of the writing process

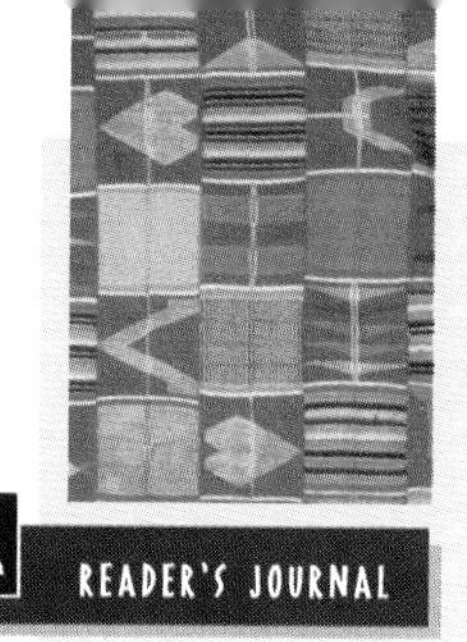

READER'S JOURNAL

For thousands of years, in most cultures around the globe, marriages were arranged by parents. Husbands and wives were chosen based on social position, wealth, family reputation, and other such criteria. Why do modern men and women typically object to arranged marriages? What might be positive aspects of arranged marriages? negative aspects? How do reasons for marrying in the modern age differ from reasons for marrying in the past? Respond to these questions in your journal.

"Marriage Is a Private Affair"

CHINUA ACHEBE

"Have you written to your dad yet?" asked Nene one afternoon as she sat with Nnaemeka in her room at 16 Kasanga Street, Lagos.[1]

"No. I've been thinking about it. I think it's better to tell him when I get home on leave!"

"But why? Your leave is such a long way off yet—six whole weeks. He should be let into our happiness now."

Nnaemeka was silent for a while and then began very slowly, as if he groped for his words: "I wish I were sure it would be happiness to him."

"Of course it must," replied Nene, a little surprised. "Why shouldn't it?"

"You have lived in Lagos all your life, and you know very little about people in remote parts of the country."

"That's what you always say. But I don't believe anybody will be so unlike other people that they will be unhappy when their sons are engaged to marry."

"Yes. They are most unhappy if the engagement is not arranged by them. In our case it's worse—you are not even an Ibo."[2]

This was said so seriously and so bluntly that Nene could not find speech immediately. In the cosmopolitan atmosphere of the city, it had always seemed to her something of a joke that a person's tribe could determine whom he married.

At last she said, "You don't really mean that he will object to your marrying me simply on that account? I had always thought you Ibos were kindly disposed to other people."

"So we are. But when it comes to marriage, well, it's not quite so simple. And this," he added, "is not peculiar to the Ibos. If your father were alive and lived in the heart of Ibibio-land,[3] he would be exactly like my father."

"I don't know. But anyway, as your father is so fond of you, I'm sure he will forgive you

Why is Nnaemeka worried about telling his father about his engagement?

1. **Lagos.** Former capital of Nigeria
2. **Ibo.** Member of a group of African people from southeastern Nigeria
3. **Ibibio-land.** An area in southeastern Nigeria

WORDS FOR EVERYDAY USE

cos • mo • pol • i • tan (käz´mə päl´ə tən) *adj.,* representative of many parts of the world

READER'S JOURNAL

As an alternative activity, you might ask students to write about how disagreements affect relationships. If you strongly disagreed with a choice made by a close family member, would you allow the disagreement to ruin your relationship, or would you say, "life is too short," and choose to care for that person despite your differences? Would it depend on the level of your discomfort with the person's choice? Explain. In what way might carrying around anger toward someone affect your life?

ANSWERS TO GUIDED READING QUESTIONS

1. He knows that the news will upset his father, who expects to arrange his son's marriage for him. He also knows his father will be upset that Nene is not an Ibo.

SPELLING AND VOCABULARY WORDS FROM THE SELECTION

cosmopolitan	parching
disconcertingly	perfunctorily
dissuasion	perplex
herbalist	theological
homily	vehemently
mutilated	

VOCABULARY IN CONTEXT

• The cosmopolitan neighborhood featured restaurants from all over the world.

Answers to Guided Reading Questions

❶ Nnaemeka says that he cannot marry Ugoye because he does not love her.

❷ Nnaemeka's father feels that love is unnecessary in marriage. He believes that the qualities that make a good wife are good character and a Christian background.

Additional Questions and Activities

Ask students to answer the following questions in writing or in a class discussion:

1. In what ways are Ugoye and Nene different?
2. What do you imagine the training Ugoye received to become a good wife might have entailed? Do you think it is important to Nnaemeka to marry someone who has been trained to be a good wife?
3. Why do you think Okeke objects to a woman teaching?
4. What jobs in today's world excluded many women in the past? Why do you think these jobs excluded women? Do you see the world changing and more careers opening to women? Why do you think it takes people a long time to open their minds to change?

Answers

Responses will vary. Possible answers are given.

1. Ugoye is a traditional Ibo woman, while Nene is a modern career woman from outside the Ibo culture.
2. Ugoye may have been trained in domestic arts and taught how to please her husband. Nnaemeka probably thinks it is more important to marry a woman with whom he is compatible and with whom he can converse.
3. A career is not part of the traditional behavior Okeke sees as desirable in a daughter-in-law.
4. *Responses will vary.*

❶ *Why does Nnaemeka say that he cannot marry Ugoye?*

❷ *What does Nnaemeka's father think about marrying for love? What qualities does he believe make a good wife?*

soon enough. Come on then, be a good boy and send him a nice, lovely letter . . ."

"It would not be wise to break the news to him by writing. A letter will bring it upon him with a shock. I'm quite sure about that."

"All right, honey, suit yourself. You know your father."

As Nnaemeka walked home that evening, he turned over in his mind different ways of overcoming his father's opposition, especially now that he had gone and found a girl for him. He had thought of showing his letter to Nene but decided on second thought not to, at least for the moment. He read it again when he got home and couldn't help smiling to himself. He remembered Ugoye quite well, an Amazon[4] of a girl who used to beat up all the boys, himself included, on the way to the stream, a complete dunce at school.

I have found a girl who will suit you admirably—Ugoye Nweke, the eldest daughter of our neighbor, Jacob Nweke. She has a proper Christian upbringing. When she stopped schooling some years ago, her father (a man of sound judgment) sent her to live in the house of a pastor where she has received all the training a wife could need. Her Sunday School teacher has told me that she reads her Bible very fluently. I hope we shall begin negotiations when you come home in December.

On the second evening of his return from Lagos, Nnaemeka sat with his father under a cassia tree. This was the old man's retreat, where he went to read his Bible when the parching December sun had set and a fresh, reviving wind blew on the leaves.

"Father," began Nnaemeka suddenly, "I have come to ask for forgiveness."

"Forgiveness? For what, my son?" he asked in amazement.

"It's about this marriage question."

"Which marriage question?"

"I can't—we must—I mean it is impossible for me to marry Nweke's daughter."

"Impossible? Why?" asked his father.

"I don't love her."

"Nobody said you did. Why should you?" he asked.

"Marriage today is different . . ."

"Look here, my son," interrupted his father, "nothing is different. What one looks for in a wife are a good character and a Christian background."

Nnaemeka saw there was no hope along the present line of argument.

"Moreover," he said, "I am engaged to marry another girl who has all of Ugoye's good qualities and who . . ."

His father did not believe his ears. "What did you say?" he asked slowly and disconcertingly.

"She is a good Christian," his son went on, "and a teacher in a Girls' School in Lagos."

"Teacher, did you say? If you consider that a qualification for a good wife, I should like to point out to you, Emeka, that no Christian woman should teach. St. Paul in his letter to the Corinthians says that women should keep silence." He rose slowly from his seat and paced forward and backward. This was his pet subject, and he condemned vehemently those church leaders who encouraged women to teach in their schools. After he had spent his emotion on a long homily, he at last came back to his son's engagement, in a seemingly milder tone.

"Whose daughter is she, anyway?"

"She is Nene Atang."

4. **Amazon.** In Greek mythology, the Amazons were a group of female warriors. The term is used to describe a tall, athletic female.

Words for Everyday Use

parch • ing (pärch´ iŋ) *adj.*, hot and drying

dis • con • cert • ing • ly (dis´kən surt´iŋ lē) *adv.*, in a manner that upsets or confuses

ve • he • ment • ly (vē´ə mənt lē) *adv.*, strongly; violently

hom • i • ly (häm´ə lē) *n.*, sermon

Vocabulary in Context

- We must water the plants that are sitting outside in the parching sun.
- Some students in the audience were disconcertingly loud while the band was trying to play.
- Sheila insisted vehemently that she she be included in our plans.
- The baby began to cry during the priest's homily.

Ashanti cloth

Nigerian door panel

"What!" All the mildness was gone again. "Did you say Neneataga? What does that mean?"

"Nene Atang from Calabar. She is the only girl I can marry." This was a very rash reply, and Nnaemeka expected the storm to burst. But it did not. His father merely walked away into his room. This was most unexpected and perplexed Nnaemeka. His father's silence was infinitely more menacing than a flood of threatening speech. That night the old man did not eat.

When he sent for Nnaemeka a day later, he applied all possible ways of dissuasion. But the young man's heart was hardened, and his father eventually gave him up as lost.

"I owe it to you, my son, as a duty to show you what is right and what is wrong. Whoever put this idea into your head might as well have cut your throat. It is Satan's work." He waved his son away.

"You will change your mind, Father, when you know Nene."

"I shall never see her," was the reply. From that night the father scarcely spoke to his son. He did not, however, cease hoping that

1 What has Nnaemeka's father decided to do?

Words for Everyday Use

per • plex (pər pleks´) *vt.,* confuse

dis • sua • sion (di swā´zhən) *n.,* persuasion against something

Answers to Guided Reading Questions

1 Nnaemeka's father has decided to never see Nene and to stop conversing with his son.

Bibliographic Note

If some students are interested in reading works by or about Chinua Achebe, you might provide them with the following selected bibliography:

Achebe, Chinua. *Anthills of the Savannah.*

———. *Arrow of God.*

———. *Hopes and Impediments: Selected Essays 1965–1987.*

———. *Morning Yet on Creation Day: Essays.*

———. and C.L. Innes. *African Short Stories.*

———. *No Longer at Ease.*

Carroll, David. *Chinua Achebe.*

Gikandi, Simon. *Reading Chinua Achebe: Language and Ideology in Fiction.* Studies in African Literature: New Series.

Moyers, Bill. Interview with Chinua Achebe. *A World of Ideas.* Ed. Betty Sue Flowers.

Vocabulary in Context

- I understood many of the math problems, but a few of them continued to perplex me.
- We tried many methods of dissuasion, but Mark insisted on spending his entire allowance on momentary whims.

Answers to Guided Reading Questions

❶ Nnaemeka's decision is particularly shocking to the villagers because according to them, never in the history of his people has someone married a person who speaks a different language.

❷ Okeke sends his son's wedding picture back to him with Nene cut out of the picture. Nene is upset by her father-in-law's actions.

❸ Okeke wants no contact with his son.

Additional Questions and Activities

Ask students to answer the following questions on paper or in group discussions:

1. Who do you think is hurt the most by Okeke's decision to give up contact with Nnaemeka? Do you think Okeke can ever be truly happy and content without his son in his life?
2. Judging from the wedding picture incident, what is Okeke's anger doing to him as a person? If you were a friend of his, what might you say to him?
3. How might you feel about the situation and your father if you were Nnaemeka? What conflicting feelings must Nnaemeka be having? How would you feel about the situation if you were Nene?

Answers

Responses will vary. Possible responses are given.

1. Okeke is hurt the most by his decision to give up his son. Students may say that it would be almost impossible to be happy after breaking off contact with a child you have raised.
2. Okeke's anger is making him a mean, petty person. A friend might tell him that forgiveness and love are the better path.
3. Nnaemeka might feel sad, frustrated, or angry, but he probably still loves his father. Nene is probably resentful.

❶ *What makes Nnaemeka's decision particularly shocking to the villagers?*

❷ *What does Okeke do to his son's wedding picture? Why? How does Nene feel about her father-in-law's reaction?*

❸ *What is Okeke's attitude toward his son?*

he would realize how serious was the danger he was heading for. Day and night he put him in his prayers.

Nnaemeka, for his own part, was very deeply affected by his father's grief. But he kept hoping that it would pass away. If it had occurred to him that never in the history of his people had a man married a woman who spoke a different tongue, he might have been less optimistic. "It has never been heard," was the verdict of an old man speaking a few weeks later. In that short sentence he spoke for all of his people. This man had come with others to commiserate with Okeke when news went round about his son's behavior. By that time the son had gone back to Lagos.

"It has never been heard," said the old man again with a sad shake of his head.

"What did Our Lord say?" asked another gentleman. "Sons shall rise against their fathers; it is there in the Holy Book."

"It is the beginning of the end," said another.

The discussion thus tending to become theological, Madubogwu, a highly practical man, brought it down once more to the ordinary level.

"Have you thought of consulting a native doctor about your son?" he asked Nnaemeka's father.

"He isn't sick," was the reply.

"What is he then? The boy's mind is diseased, and only a good herbalist can bring him back to his right senses. The medicine he requires is *Amalile*, the same that women apply with success to recapture their husbands' straying affection."

"Madubogwu is right," said another gentleman. "This thing calls for medicine."

"I shall not call in a native doctor." Nnaemeka's father was known to be obstinately ahead of his more superstitious neighbors in these matters. "I will not be another Mrs. Ochuba. If my son wants to kill himself, let him do it with his own hands. It is not for me to help him."

"But it was her fault," said Madubogwu. "She ought to have gone to an honest herbalist. She was a clever woman, nevertheless."

"She was a wicked murderess," said Jonathan, who rarely argued with his neighbors because, he often said, they were incapable of reasoning. "The medicine was prepared for her husband, it was his name they called in its preparation, and I am sure it would have been perfectly beneficial to him. It was wicked to put it into the herbalist's food and say you were only trying it out."

Six months later, Nnaemeka was showing his young wife a short letter from his father:

It amazes me that you could be so unfeeling as to send me your wedding picture. I would have sent it back. But on further thought I decided just to cut off your wife and send it back to you because I have nothing to do with her. How I wish that I had nothing to do with you either.

When Nene read through this letter and looked at the mutilated picture, her eyes filled with tears, and she began to sob.

"Don't cry, my darling," said her husband. "He is essentially good-natured and will one day look more kindly on our marriage." But years passed and that one day did not come.

For eight years, Okeke would have nothing to do with his son, Nnaemeka. Only three times (when Nnaemeka asked to come home and spend his leave) did he write to him.

"I can't have you in my house," he replied on one occasion. "It can be of no interest to me where or how you spend your leave—or your life, for that matter."

Words for Everyday Use

the • o • log • i • cal (thē ə läj´i kəl) *adj.*, based on religious doctrines

herb • al • ist (hʉr´bəl ist) *n.*, person who deals in medicinal herbs

mu • ti • lat • ed (myo͞ot ´'lāt´əd) *adj.*, damaged, especially by having a part removed

Vocabulary in Context

- You can direct any theological questions to the minister of the church.
- The herbalist prepared some tea that was supposed to ease my headache.
- I accidentally mutilated the plastic toy with the lawn mower.

The prejudice against Nnaemeka's marriage was not confined to his little village. In Lagos, especially among his people who worked there, it showed itself in a different way. Their women, when they met at their village meeting, were not hostile to Nene. Rather, they paid her such excessive deference as to make her feel she was not one of them. But as time went on, Nene gradually broke through some of this prejudice and even began to make friends among them. Slowly and grudgingly they began to admit that she kept her home much better than most of them.

The story eventually got to the little village in the heart of the Ibo country that Nnaemeka and his young wife were a most happy couple. But his father was one of the few people in the village who knew nothing about this. He always displayed so much temper whenever his son's name was mentioned that everyone avoided it in his presence. By a tremendous effort of will he had succeeded in pushing his son to the back of his mind. The strain had nearly killed him, but he had persevered, and won.

Then one day he received a letter from Nene, and in spite of himself he began to glance through it perfunctorily until all of a sudden the expression on his face changed and he began to read more carefully.

. . . Our two sons, from the day they learnt that they have a grandfather, have insisted on being taken to him. I find it impossible to tell them that you will not see them. I implore you to allow Nnaemeka to bring them home for a short time during his leave next month. I shall remain here in Lagos . . .

The old man at once felt the resolution he had built up over so many years falling in. He was telling himself that he must not give in. He tried to steel his heart against all emotional appeals. It was a reenactment of that other struggle. He leaned against a window and looked out. The sky was overcast with heavy black clouds, and a high wind began to blow, filling the air with dust and dry leaves. It was one of those rare occasions when even Nature takes a hand in a human fight. Very soon it began to rain, the first rain in the year. It came down in large, sharp drops and was accompanied by the lightning and thunder which mark a change of season. Okeke was trying hard not to think of his two grandsons. But he knew he was now fighting a losing battle. He tried to hum a favorite hymn, but the pattering of large raindrops on the roof broke up the tune. His mind immediately returned to the children. How could he shut his door against them? By a curious mental process he imagined them standing, sad and forsaken, under the harsh, angry weather—shut out from his house.

That night he hardly slept, from remorse—and a vague fear that he might die without making it up to them. ■

❶ *Over time how do people's attitudes change toward Nene?*

❷ *What has Okeke won? What has he lost?*

❸ *What does Nene ask of her father-in-law?*

Nigerian statuette

Words for Everyday Use

per • func • to • ri • ly (pər funk´tə rə lē) *adv.*, carelessly, indifferently

Answers to Guided Reading Questions

❶ Over time, people begin to treat Nene less as an outsider. She makes friends, and people admit that although Nene is not a traditional Ibo woman, she is still a very good housekeeper.

❷ Okeke has succeeded in pushing thoughts of his son to the back of his mind. He has won by standing firm in his refusal to see his son. At the same time, Okeke has lost his relationship with his son and has lost the chance to have a relationship with his son's new family.

❸ Nene asks her father-in-law to allow her sons—his grandsons—to visit him along with Nnaemeka.

Selection Check Test with Answers

EX. What are Nnaemeka and Nene planning?
They are planning to marry.

1. Why will Nnaemeka's father disapprove of his marriage to Nene?
He did not arrange the marriage and she is not Ibo.

2. What is Nnaemeka's father's reaction to news of the marriage?
He becomes upset, and when he sees he cannot dissuade Nnaemeka, he refuses to see or talk to his son.

3. What does Okeke do when Nnaemeka sends him a wedding picture?
He sends the picture back with Nene's image cut out of it.

4. What does Nene ask of Okeke in a letter?
She asks that he allow Nnaemeka to bring their children to see him.

5. In what way does the thought of his grandsons change Okeke's attitude?
He feels remorse for keeping them out of his life.

Vocabulary in Context

- The teacher returned any essays that looked as though they had been written perfunctorily.

Responding to the Selection

Do you agree with the beliefs and actions of Nnaemeka's father at the beginning of the story? in the middle? at the very end? Do you disagree with him? Do you feel understanding or compassion for him? What lesson do you think he has learned by the end of the story?

Reviewing the Selection

RECALLING / **INTERPRETING**

1. What does Nene ask Nnaemeka to do at the beginning of the story? ▶▶ Why is Nnaemeka reluctant to write to his father? Why is Nnaemeka's reluctance difficult for Nene to understand?
2. What reason does Nnaemeka give for not marrying the woman chosen by his father? What reasons does Okeke give for going through with the marriage? ▶▶ How do the values of Nnaemeka and his father differ? What characteristic of Nnaemeka's father shows that he, like his son, has been influenced by Western values?
3. What does Nnaemeka tell his father about Nene? How does his father react to this news? ▶▶ How does Nnaemeka's father feel about women teachers? Why does he feel this way? What influences might have made him feel this way?
4. What causes Okeke to change his mind? What fear does he have? ▶▶ Why is it difficult for Okeke to accept this change in his feelings?

SYNTHESIZING

5. What are the sources of Nnaemeka's father's beliefs? What source is traditional? What source is not? How does Nnaemeka's father change at the end of the story, and why?

Understanding Literature (Questions for Discussion)

1. **Conflict.** A **conflict** is a struggle between two forces in a literary work. A struggle that takes place between a character and some outside force is called an **external conflict**. What customs and values are in conflict in this story? A struggle that takes place within a character is called an **internal conflict**. What internal conflict does Nnaemeka's father experience? In what ways are the external conflict and Okeke's internal conflict resolved?

Responding to the Selection

Encourage students to think about the events of the story from the vantage point of each character in the story. They might get together in groups of three to role play—one person playing Nnaemeka, one person playing Nene, and one person playing Okeke.

Answers for Reviewing the Selection

RECALLING AND INTERPRETING

1. **Recalling.** Nene asks Nnaemeka to tell his father about their engagement. **Interpreting.** Nnaemeka knows his father will disapprove of the marriage. Nene does not understand because her father has died, and so she does not need to seek anyone's approval.

2. **Recalling.** Nnaemeka tells his father that he cannot marry the woman because he does not love her. Okeke says that he should marry her because she is Christian and comes from a good family. **Interpreting.** Nnaemeka feels that is is necessary to marry for love, while his father does not. Just as Nnaemeka's attitudes about love are Western, Okeke's Christianity reveals a Western influence.

3. **Recalling.** Nnaemeka tells his father that Nene is a good Christian and a teacher. His father says that good Christian women do not teach. **Interpreting.** Okeke feels that women should not teach because it is his religious belief that women should be silent. The influences of religion and tradition have made him feel this way.

4. **Recalling.** Nene sends a letter, asking him to allow their sons to visit. Okeke fears he will die before making up for the years of neglect. **Interpreting.** Okeke had worked hard to put thoughts of his son out of his mind. He had finally won the battle when the letter awakened his feelings of remorse. (cont.)

Answers for Reviewing the Selection (cont.)

SYNTHESIZING

Responses will vary. Possible responses are given.

5. Nnaemeka's father's beliefs come from his religion and from the Ibo traditions of many generations. His belief in arranged marriages and his ideas against marrying outside of one's cultural group come from Ibo tradition. His Christian beliefs are not part of generations of Ibo tradition. Nnaemeka's father feels remorse for having pushed his son and his son's family away. His emotional ties to Nnaemeka and to his grandsons become stronger than his ties to the rules of tradition. The change is brought on by the thought of his grandsons standing out in the rain, unwelcome in his own home. He suddenly realizes what his stubbornness has cost him and his family.

2. **Motivation**. A **motivation** is a force that moves a character to think or act in a certain way. What motivates Okeke to alienate his son, Nnaemeka? What motivates Okeke to feel remorse at the end of the story? How does his remorse change his thinking about his son's marriage?

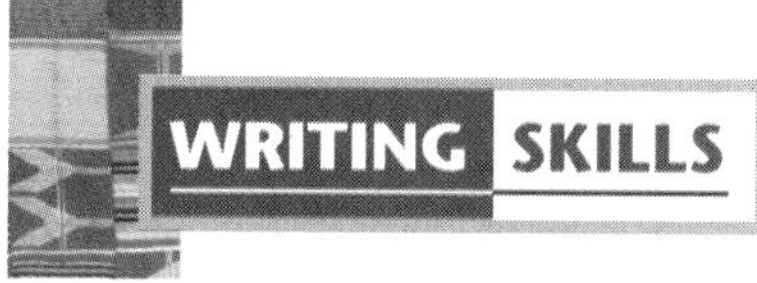

THE PROCESS OF WRITING

Writing can sometimes seem like a daunting task, whether you are writing a cover letter to a potential employer, a short story, or a critical essay. Some students look at the fine literature in their textbooks or in other sources and feel overwhelmed, wondering how they can ever hope to produce work of this quality. What students often do not realize is that writing is not so much an inherited gift as an acquired skill. Good writers spend years perfecting their craft, and most writers never just jot down a perfect poem or story—they carefully craft the poem or story over a period of time, following the stages of the process of writing. You can become a better writer by following these stages in the writing process, and by doing so, you can have the pleasure of transforming a brief moment of insight into a carefully-polished showpiece.

Throughout this textbook you will encounter a variety of writing assignments, both critical and creative. Remember that you should take each piece of writing through the following steps:

SIX STAGES IN THE PROCESS OF WRITING	
1. Prewriting	In the prewriting stage, you **plan** your writing; choose a topic, audience, purpose, and form; gather ideas; and arrange them logically.
2. Drafting	In this stage, you **jot** your ideas down on paper without worrying about getting everything just right.
3. Peer Evaluation and Self-evaluation	To evaluate is to **judge** something. In the evaluation stage, your writing is studied and judged to see how it might be improved. **Peer evaluation** occurs when a classmate judges your writing; **self-evaluation** occurs when you judge your own writing.
4. Revising	In the revising stage, you work to **improve** content, organization, and style, or the way you express your ideas based on the evaluation of your work in the previous stage.
5. Proofreading	In the proofreading stage, you **check** your writing for errors in spelling, grammar, usage, capitalization, and punctuation. After correcting these errors, you make a final copy of your paper and proofread it again.
6. Publishing and Presenting	In the publishing and presenting stage, you **share** your work with an audience.

ANSWERS FOR UNDERSTANDING LITERATURE

Responses will vary. Possible responses are given.

1. Conflict. Traditional customs and values are in conflict with modern, Western values. Nnaemeka's father wants his son to have a traditional arranged marriage, while Nnaemeka wants to marry for love. Nnaemeka's father feels forced to choose between his belief in his values and his son. It is difficult for him to keep his son out of his life and out of his mind, but he forces himself to do so because he believes his son is mocking his values. When Nnaemeka's father is told about his grandsons, he must struggle again with conflicting emotions. In the end, Okeke seems to feel that his ties to his son and his grandsons take priority over all else. He no longer wishes to keep them out of his life. He seems willing to find a way to keep both his traditions and his family.

2. Motivation. Okeke is motivated by anger and by feelings that his son is showing disrespect for both Ibo and Christian traditions. At the end of the story, Okeke is motivated to feel remorse by Nene's request that he accept his grandsons into his life. He suddenly realizes that it is wrong for his own grandsons to be unwelcome in his home. This realization pushes him to consider forgiving his son.

► Additional practice of the skills taught in this lesson is provided in the Essential Skills Practice Books: Writing 1.1, 1.5–1.18 and Applied English/Tech Prep 5.1.

In the Language Arts Survey, there are sections on Prewriting techniques (1.5–1.12), Drafting (1.13), Evaluating (1.14), Revising (1.15), Proofreading (1.16–1.17), and Publishing or Presenting Your Work (1.18). You should refer to the appropriate section if you are having difficulty with any of the stages in the writing process. Many of the writing assignments in this text will provide you with suggestions, but, ultimately, the way in which you approach the writing process is a personal decision. Writing, after all, depends upon creativity and personal expression.

Here is an example of a typical writing assignment that you might encounter in this text.

> **Creative Writing: A Personal Letter.** Imagine that you are Nnaemeka at the beginning of this story and that you have decided to write the letter that Nene is urging you to write. Write a letter to your father explaining why you cannot marry Ugoye Nweke but intend, instead, to marry Nene. Before writing, prepare the arguments that you will present in your letter. Begin by listing your reasons for marrying Nene. Then list your reasons for not marrying Ugoye. Finally, make a list of your father's reasons for wanting you to marry Ugoye, and prepare counterarguments, or rebuttals. Base your list on information provided in the story, and refer to your lists as you write. In your draft, make sure to maintain a respectful tone toward your father. Use the proper form for a personal letter. Refer to the Language Arts Survey 5.1, "Personal and Business Letters."

Imagine that you have been given this assignment. Using the chart on the previous page, list the steps you would take to complete each stage of the writing process. If you need help, refer to the Language Arts Survey: Writing. After creating your writing plan, follow each step to create the personal letter described above.

Writing Plan

Prewriting - List reasons for marrying Nene

Drafting

Answers for Skills Activities

WRITING SKILLS

Students should first create a list of the steps they plan to take, and then follow these steps to create their letters. You might want to review the list of steps each student makes and review the letters as they complete each stage.

Explain to students that learning to take these steps as they prepare a writing assignment will help their finished pieces to be thorough, well written, and free of errors, which will usually be caught in the revision and proofreading stages.

ANALYTIC SCALES FOR RESPONDING IN WRITING

Assign a score from 1 to 25 for each grading criterion below. (For more detailed evaluation, see the evaluation forms for writing, revising, and proofreading, Assessment Portfolio 4.1–4.9.)

Personal Letter

- **Content/Unity.** The personal letter is written from Nnaemeka to Okeke, and it is based on information provided in "Marriage is a Private Affair."
- **Organization/Coherence.** The letter presents reasons for marrying Nene, reasons for not marrying Ugoye, and counterarguments to Okeke's ideas about whom Nnaemeka should marry.
- **Language/Style.** The letter uses vivid and precise nouns, verbs, and modifiers and is written in the voice of Nnaemeka.
- **Conventions.** The letter avoids errors in spelling, grammar, usage, mechanics, and manuscript form.

PASSPORT TO GREECE

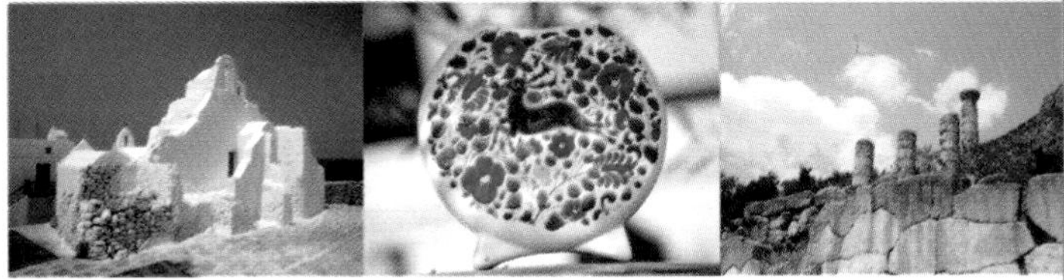

Yasu! My name is Sarah (Sotiria) Galanis, and my family is from the Peloponnesus region of Greece. I was named Sotiria after my maternal grandmother, but my friends and family call me Sarah.

In the summers we spend time in my dad's village, Prasino, and my mother's village, Hora Gortinias, which are on the Peloponnesus (the southern peninsula of Greece). My mother's village once had eight hundred people, but only two hundred remain, and most are elderly. That reflects what is happening all over Greece as people leave the villages to find work in the city. The villages grow smaller, while Athens has grown to about 4 million people out of a total population of 10 million. But even while people are in the cities, their hearts are back home. It is in their villages, not Athens, that many people build their homes, often much better than those they rent in the city. In the summer, Athens experiences a mass exodus as people close their businesses and enjoy village life once again.

Sarah Galanis
Peloponnesus,
Greece

Whitewashed buildings

Statue of Pan, Olympic Stadium, Athens

SUPPORT FOR LEP STUDENTS

Pronunciations of Proper Nouns and Adjectives

A • li • thos a • nes • ti (ä lē thōs´ ä nes´ tē)
ban • ya (bän´yə)
caf • fe • nei • on (cä´ fā nē´on)
Chri • stos a • nes • ti (krē stōs ä nes´ tē)
fri • gan • ias (frē gan yäs´)
front • is • ti • ri • o (frōn ēs tē´rē o)
Ho • ra Gor • ti • ni • as (hō rä gōr tē nē´əs)
me • si • me • ri (me zē mâ´rē)
Pe • lo • pon • ne • sus (pe lō pō´nē sus)
Pra • si • no (prä´ sē nō)
San • to • ri • ni (sän tō rē´nē)
Sa • rah Ga • la • nis (sâ´ rə gä lä´nēs)
ya • su (ya´ soo)

Cultural/Historical Note

Elements of ancient Greek culture, including names, are still part of contemporary Greek life. For example, Athena is a common name for girls, and Aristotle and Socrates are common as boys' names. Usually, children are named after their grandparents. The firstborn son is typically named after his paternal grandfather, while the oldest daughter is named after the paternal grandmother. Since Sarah is the second daughter in her family, she was named Sotiria after her mother's mother. Name days are more important to Greeks than birthdays. "If you share your name with a saint," Sarah says, "for the name day, you'll have *panegirias*, little festivals with a band and games, as part of your celebration."

Cross-curricular Activities

ARTS AND HUMANITIES, SOCIAL STUDIES, AND APPLIED ARTS

Help students host a Celebrate Greece Day, that includes Greek food and recordings of contemporary Greek music. Sarah recommends CDs by Vasilis Karas (cont.)

Cross-curricular Activities (cont.)

and Kaiti Garbi; Greek music should be available from the library or local music stores. Because Greek dance is so integral to the culture, you might invite a folk dance instructor or someone from the Greek-American community who can teach the class traditional Greek dance. Students might also create posters celebrating Greece using photographs from travel brochures and magazines.

Invite students to prepare Greek food for the celebration or to demonstrate in class how to make the recipes on page 34 or other Greek recipes; Greek cookbooks should be readily available in the public library. Students should discuss any interesting facts about the food they have prepared, including the occasion at which it might be served.

Cross-curricular Activities

APPLIED ARTS

The recipes below come from Sarah's mother, Ekaterini Galanis.

Horiatiki Salata **(Country-style Salad)**

2 cucumbers
3 tomatoes
1 medium onion
feta cheese to taste
1/2 teaspoon oregano
1/4 cup olive oil
2 tablespoons red wine vinegar
salt to taste

Slice all vegetables and put together in a bowl. Add crumbled feta cheese and remaining ingredients. Mix together. Since Greek bread is not readily available outside of Greece, serve with fresh French or Italian bread.

Tzatziki **Sauce**

2 cloves garlic
24 oz. plain yogurt*
1 cucumber, seeds removed
3 tablespoons olive oil
2 tablespoons red wine vinegar
salt and pepper to taste

1. Finely crush garlic until it forms a smooth consistency. Add a dash of salt and pepper, the oil, and the vinegar, and mix well.
2. Grate the cucumber and remove the water by squeezing it in a clean dishcloth.
3. In a separate bowl, whip the yogurt. Slowly add the garlic to the yogurt while whipping. Add grated cucumber and stir together.
4. Serve with fried eggplant, fried zucchini, chicken souvlaki (shishkabobs), or over fresh French bread.

*Note: As yogurt in Greece tends to have a thick consistency like sour cream, you may want to drain the yogurt in a cheesecloth-lined sieve in the refrigerator overnight before making the recipe.

As Sarah and her mother, Ekaterini, say, "*Kali Orexi!* Have a good appetite!"

Christian and Islamic architecture, Lindos, Rhodes

Among my favorite memories of growing up are the summers I spent in my grandparents' village. We would go every day to the *caffeneion* (coffee shop) at the edge of the village to have orange juice and a little candy bar the shop owners would give us for free. Back at my grandparents' house, we would name the chickens so our grandmother wouldn't kill them for dinner. She'd leave the ones we named alone.

In Greece, tradition is important. The well in the village, for example, used to be the only source of water. Women would line up with their buckets to get the water, which still comes from the top of the mountain. Today, people have running water going directly into their homes, but passersby still stop and drink from the well, and people water their horses there. People preserve the well and keep it painted. Every Epiphany, January 6, the priest sprinkles the well with holy water, along with everything else that is important to people: their houses, land, and animals.

School is rigorous in Greece. Students read the classical works as a regular subject and learn at least one other language, usually English. Children learn Greek myths in detail starting in second grade. In Greece, there is a lot of pressure to succeed in

Sarah Galanis with her grandfather, Angelos, and on the island of Santorini

Ancient windmills in the Cretan mountains

Cultural/Historical Note

With its rocky, arid terrain, Greece is a place where olive trees thrive. The production of olives and olive oil is a thriving industry and provides a food that is the basis of Greek cuisine. It is not uncommon to find olive trees in Greece that are hundreds or even thousands of years old.

The importance of the olive is expressed in Greek mythology. According to myth, the Greek goddess Athena created the first olive tree, while the god Poseidon used his trident to open a salt spring in the rock on which the Acropolis was later built. Legend has it that when Athena and Poseidon fought for sovereignty over Athens, the gods favored Athena, maintaining that the olive was a greater gift to humanity than salt.

school. If you slack off, you have to go to the *frontistirio,* which is an expensive afterschool tutoring program. At the end of your schooling, you take a national exam that determines which university you can attend. The most respected university is in Athens. Once you're in, the government pays for your tuition. The hardest part is just getting in.

Ninety-eight percent of the population is Greek Orthodox, so Easter is our biggest holiday. We have a midnight liturgy that goes until about 1:30 in the morning, and everyone attends. At midnight, the church is completely dark until the priest proclaims Christ's resurrection with the words, *"Christos anesti"* (Christ is risen). The people answer, *"Alithos anesti"* (Truly He is risen) and go crazy with fireworks outside and lighted candles, hugging and kissing each other. Afterwards we crack red eggs, roast lamb on a spit, and celebrate.

On a typical day, people wake up early and have coffee and maybe *friganias* (dried bread) with honey or butter. Workers return home around 2 P.M. for lunch, the first of two main meals, and *mesimeri,* the afternoon nap. During *mesimeri,* the hottest time of the day in summer, the majority of people sleep. I made

Island chapel

Restaurant on Mykonos

Switchback Road, Thera

Cultural Note

Sarah refers on page 35 to the Easter custom of cracking red eggs. Lent, the forty-day period preceding Easter, is a period of fasting and preparation for the biggest holiday of the year. Lenten activity escalates during Holy Week, the week before Easter. As part of the Easter preparations, eggs are dyed red on Holy Thursday to symbolize Christ's blood. After the midnight Resurrection Service on Holy Saturday, the Lenten fast is broken, and the first thing people eat are the *paskalina avga,* or Easter eggs. Each person cracks an egg with a relative or friend, saying "Christ is risen!" and "Truly He is risen." Sometimes, a contest is held to see who has the strongest egg: people crack their eggs point to point, then back to back. The person whose egg remains uncracked will have good luck in the year ahead.

Cultural/Historical Note

Note the picture on page 34 of Sarah Galanis in front of the Parthenon at the Acropolis, Greece's most popular tourist attraction. The Acropolis is a natural fortress, inaccessible from all sides except the west, where the entrance is located. From the earliest times, the Acropolis was both a fortress and the religious center of Athens. The principal cult was that of the goddess Athena, to whom the Greeks dedicated many temples.

Cross-curricular Activities

Mathematics and Sciences

The Greek islands of Zakynthos and Kefalonia provide some of the last loggerhead sea turtle nesting beaches in the Mediterranean. Ancient Greek texts often mention sea turtles. An ancient coin, minted on the island of Aegina, bears the image of a sea turtle.

(cont.)

Cross-curricular Activities (cont.)

Female sea turtles return to the same beaches where they were hatched to make their nests. Today, these turtles are threatened by real estate development along their nesting beaches, high tourist and fishing traffic, and pollution.

Students interested in researching protection efforts for Mediterranean sea turtles can do an Internet search or write to the Sea Turtle Protection Society of Greece, 35 Solomou Street, GR-106 82, Athens, Greece, or MEDASSET (The Mediterranean Association to Save the Sea Turtles), 1C Licavitou Street, 106 72 Athens, Greece. They might also compare and contrast efforts to protect sea turtles in Greece and along the Atlantic seaboard and Gulf of Mexico in the United States.

Cultural/Historical Note

The Peloponnesus, or Peloponnese, the southern peninsula of Greece, technically became an island with the completion of the Corinthian Canal in 1893. It is surrounded by water: the Gulf of Corinth to the north, the open Mediterranean to the south, the Ionian Sea on the west, and the Aegean Sea on the east. The name means "the island of Pelops." Pelops was the legendary grandson of Zeus and the grandfather of Agamemnon, the Greek leader in the Trojan War.

The ancient sites of Peloponnesus include Mycenae, where Agamemnon's tomb lies, and Epidaurus, with its acoustically superb theater that seats 15,000 and is one of the seven wonders of the ancient world.

Olympia, in the western Peloponnese, is the legendary sanctuary of Zeus and Hera and was the founding site in 776 BC of the Olympic Games. The Greeks calculated their chronology from this date, measuring events by the Olympiad in which they occurred.

The sacred torch, which is carried to contemporary Olympic stadiums and used to light the torch to begin the Games, still comes from Olympia. In ancient Greece, the games were always held during a Sacred Truce, during which all Greeks put aside their differences and united in the spirit of Hellenism.

Cross-curricular Activities

Mathematics and Sciences and Social Studies

Some archaeologists believe Santorini, or Thera, (pictured on pages 34, 35, and 36) is the lost island of Atlantis. The discovery this century of an entire town under one hundred and sixty feet of lava and pumice lends credibility to this theory. (cont.)

Crusader castle of Frangokastelo, Island of Crete

the mistake of calling someone once during *mesimeri* and felt pretty bad about it afterwards. People return to work around 5 P.M. and stay until 8 or 9. After they come home for the night, they eat the second meal of the day around 10 P.M., then relax and take a walk or go out for coffee. Adults usually get to sleep by midnight, although younger people sometimes don't even get ready to go out until then. Clubs and coffee shops stay open until 5 or 6 in the morning.

Greece is a land that includes over fourteen hundred islands. The sea is very important to us. Besides treasuring it as a source of livelihood, people try to go swimming every day in the summer. I love the salty water—it just feels healthy. (Some people pick gray, thumb-sized clams to cook at home; other don't wait and eat the insides while they're swimming.) At summer's end, everyone counts how many *banya* (swims) they had, tallying up how many times they went into the sea.

Of course, not only Greeks enjoy the islands. When my cousin and I went to Santorini, I was amazed to see how many people were there from other countries, especially from Scandinavia. The beautiful sea and sunny lifestyle keep attracting tourists, but I'm glad that people still look at Greece as a place of history: tourists want to see the ancient ruins, not just go to the islands. For all that Greece has contributed to civilization, people are still coming to learn from it. ■

Inside the Castle of the Knights

View from the top of Santorini's steep Caldera wall

Cross-curricular Activities (cont.)

Santorini itself is a volcano that is still active today. The caldera, or mouth of the volcano, is now filled by the sea, but is the source of what was probably the biggest volcanic eruption in history. Santorini is known for its black-sand beaches, vineyards terraced on pumice and ash, and white buildings accented by the blue Mediterranean.

Ask students to research and give presentations on one of the following topics: tourism in Santorini, theories about Atlantis, activity of the volcano of Santorini, the activity of other volcanoes, or the geology of volcanoes. Students should use appropriate visual aids, such as maps, charts, pictures, or models, in their presentations.

PREREADING

"Poseidonians"

by Constantine Cavafy, translated by Edmund Keeley and George Savidis

About the Author

CONSTANTINE CAVAFY 1863–1933

Constantine Cavafy, born Konstantínos Pétra Kaváfis, considered one of the great modern Greek poets, was born in Alexandria, Egypt, to Greek parents. His family, owners of an export business that at one time was one of the largest in Egypt, enjoyed enormous wealth until growing anti-Greek sentiment in Egypt contributed to the business's decline. Eventually the entire Greek community had to leave Egypt, and after the death of Cavafy's father, his mother was forced to take her family to live in England. It was in England that Cavafy began to develop a love for literature and language. He eventually returned to Alexandria, where he lived most of his life. The principal topics in Cavafy's work are love, politics, and art. His poetry grew popular in English-speaking nations after World War I, in part because of praise by writer E. M. Forster.

Poseidon

Treasury of the Athenians, Delphi

About the Selection

The poem you are about to read, "**Poseidonians,**" comes from a collection of Cavafy's works entitled *Passions and Ancient Days.* The poem focuses on people of Greek origin living on the shores of the Tyrrhenian Sea, the part of the Mediterranean Sea that lies between the west coast of Italy and the islands of Sardinia, Corsica, and Sicily. Hellenic culture—the culture of the ancient Greeks—began to stagnate and decline in these areas after Rome's rise to power.

Cavafy had a strong interest in Hellenic culture. Alexandria, the seaport in Egypt where Cavafy spent most of his life, was once its center. The seaport was named after Alexander the Great, a ruler of Greece in the fourth century BC, who conquered most of the ancient world. Due to Alexander the Great's conquests, Hellenism spread throughout the Mediterranean, the Middle East, and into Asia. During this time, known as the Alexandrian age, Greek culture flourished in Alexandria, influencing many people around the world. In 146 BC, when Rome conquered and overran the Greek mainland, the art, literature, architecture, and philosophies of Hellenic civilization were preserved in Alexandria, even as Hellenic culture began to decline in Greece itself.

CONNECTIONS: Poseidon

The name *Poseidonians* comes from Poseidon, who was the Greek god of the sea. According to classical mythology, Poseidon gave the horse to humanity, controlled earthquakes and storms at sea, and carried a trident, or three-pronged spear. The Romans later gave this god the name Neptune.

ADDITIONAL RESOURCES

READER'S GUIDE

- Selection Worksheet 1.3

ASSESSMENT PORTFOLIO

- Selection Check Test 2.1.5
- Selection Test 2.1.6

ESSENTIAL SKILLS PRACTICE BOOKS

- Study and Research 4.11–4.24

PREREADING EXTENSIONS

Students might be interested in learning more about E. M. Forster (1879–1970), the writer who helped to popularize the work of Cavafy in English-speaking nations.

Novelist Edward Morgan Forster was born in London, England, and devoted himself to writing at an early age. His works are rooted in the Romantic movement (see page 900), emphasizing the importance of imagination and of having a close relationship with nature.

Forster's most famous novels include *Howard's End* (1910), *A Room with a View* (1908), and *A Passage to India* (1924). He also published short stories and nonfiction.

SUPPORT FOR LEP STUDENTS

PRONUNCIATIONS OF PROPER NOUNS AND ADJECTIVES

Po • sei • don • i • ans (pō sē dōn´ē əns)
Mag • na Grae • ci • a (mag nə grē´ shē ə)
Tyrrh • en • i • ans (ti rē´ nē ənz)

ADDITIONAL VOCABULARY

barbarians—In the ancient world, a term for foreigners or non-Greeks. Today it describes a person who is savage or lacking in culture.
rites—formal, ceremonial rituals

GOALS/OBJECTIVES

Studying this lesson will enable students to

- enjoy a poem by one of the great modern poets of Greece
- discuss the life and work of Constantine Cavafy
- understand the decline of Hellenic culture on the shores of the Tyrrhenian Sea after Rome's rise to power
- define the literary terms *tone, epigraph,* and *description*
- practice research skills and the documentation of sources

READER'S JOURNAL

Students might also write about any family customs or habits that they believe can be traced back to their ancestors.

Answers to Guided Reading Questions

1 They have forgotten the Greek language. The only ancestral thing that remains to them is a Greek festival.

2 They talk about their ancient customs and speak the Greek language that many of them no longer understand.

3 The festival has a melancholy ending because they remember that they are no longer truly a part of the Hellenistic culture. The Poseidonian way of living and speaking is described as being barbaric.

Selection Check Test with Answers

EX. From where is Cavafy, author of "Poseidonians"?
Cavafy is from Greece.

1. What have the Poseidonians forgotten?
The Poseidonians have forgotten the Greek language.

2. What is the only ancestral thing that remains to them?
The only ancestral thing that remains is a Greek festival.

3. What is the tradition that takes place near the festival's end?
They tell each other about ancient Greek customs and try to speak Greek words.

4. What do they remember at this point in the festival?
They remember that they, too, are Greeks.

5. Why does the festival always have a melancholy ending?
They remember that they are no longer truly a part of the Hellenistic culture.

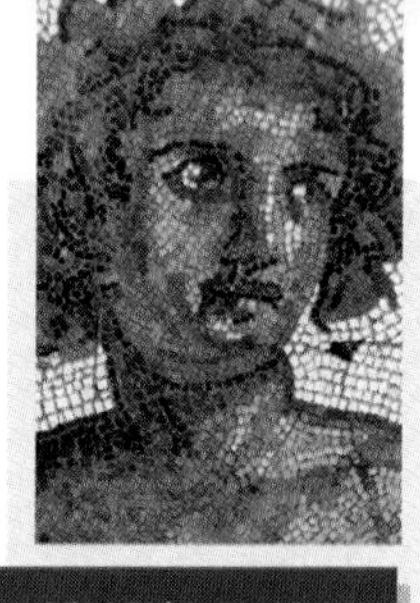

What do you know about the ancestry of your family? What interests you the most when you think about your ancestors? If you don't have specific information, try to imagine details about your ancestors based on what you know of particular countries or time periods. Write your thoughts about your ancestors in your journal.

READER'S JOURNAL

"Poseidonians"

CONSTANTINE CAVAFY, TRANSLATED BY EDMUND KEELEY AND GEORGE SAVIDIS

[We behave like] the Poseidonians in the Tyrrhenian Gulf, who, although of Greek origin, became barbarized as Tyrrhenians or Romans and changed their speech and the customs of their ancestors. But they observe one Greek festival even to this day; during this they gather together and call up from memory their ancient names and customs, and then, lamenting loudly to each other and weeping, they go away.

Athenaeus, *Deipnosophistai*, Book 14, 31A (632)

1 *What have the Poseidonians forgotten? What is the only ancestral thing that remains to them?*

2 *What do the Poseidonians do toward the festival's end?*

3 *Why does the festival always have a melancholy ending? How is the Poseidonian way of living and speaking described?*

The Poseidonians had forgotten the Greek language
after so many centuries of mingling
with Tyrrhenians, Latins, and other foreigners.
The only thing ancestral that remained to them
was a Greek festival, with beautiful rites,
with lyres[1] and flutes, contests and crowns.
And it was their habit towards the festival's end
to tell each other about their ancient customs
and once again to speak the Greek words
that hardly any of them still understood.
And so their festival always had a melancholy ending
because they remembered that they too were Greeks—
they too citizens of Magna Graecia[2] once upon a time;
but how they'd fallen, what they'd now become,
living and speaking like barbarians,
excluded—what a catastrophe!—from the Hellenic[3] way of life. ■

1. **lyres.** Small, stringed instruments
2. **Magna Graecia.** Ancient Greek colonies in southern Italy
3. **Hellenic.** Culture of ancient Greece

Words for Everyday Use

mel • an • cho • ly (mel´ən käl´ē) *adj.,* sad

ca • tas • tro • phe (kə tas´ trə fē) *n.,* disastrous end, bringing overthrow or ruin

Vocabulary in Context

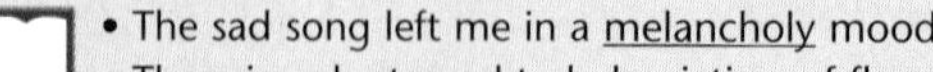

- The sad song left me in a melancholy mood.
- Theonie volunteered to help victims of floods, earthquakes, and other catastrophes.

Responding to the Selection

Today many people feel depressed after the excitement of a major holiday. Why do you think this is so? In what way is this reaction similar to or different from the "melancholy ending" to the Poseidonians' Greek festival?

Reviewing the Selection

RECALLING

INTERPRETING

1. What have the Poseidonians forgotten? What is the only ancestral thing that remains to them? What happens at the festival? ▶▶ Why might the Poseidonians have forgotten everything but this one ancient ritual? How would you characterize the speaker's attitude toward this Greek festival?

2. What traditional event takes place near the festival's end? What do the celebrants remember at this point in the festival? ▶▶ What is the reason for the melancholy ending to the festival? What has happened to the Poseidonians over the centuries?

SYNTHESIZING

3. In what way are the Poseidonians different from their ancestors? Why do they feel "excluded . . . from the Hellenic way of life," and why is this exclusion a "catastrophe" to the Poseidonians? Do you think the speaker shares the feeling that the Poseidonians' condition is catastrophic, or is the speaker being ironic? Explain. Discuss the speaker's attitude toward "the Hellenic way of life." Do you think the speaker mourns the loss of this way of life? What point might the speaker be making about the way people tend to think about their past?

Understanding Literature (Questions for Discussion)

1. **Tone. Tone** is the emotional attitude toward the reader or toward the subject implied by a literary work. Examples of the different tones that a work may have include familiar, ironic, playful, sarcastic, serious, and sincere. What is the tone of "Poseidonians"? Is the speaker positive or negative toward the Poseidonians? What specific words and phrases create this tone?

2. **Epigraph and Description.** An **epigraph** is a quotation or motto used at the beginning of the whole or part of a literary work to help establish the work's theme. The quotation Cavafy uses as an epigraph at the beginning of this poem is attributed to a Greek writer and grammarian named Athenaeus who lived around 200 AD. Why might a grammarian

RESPONDING TO THE SELECTION

Students should discuss what feelings a holiday or a festival like that of the Poseidonians might evoke in people.

ANSWERS FOR REVIEWING THE SELECTION

RECALLING AND INTERPRETING

1. **Recalling.** The Poseidonians have forgotten the Greek language. The only ancestral thing that remains to them is a Greek festival. At the festival, they take part in ancient rites, play lyres and flutes, have contests, speak the Greek language, and talk about ancient Greek customs. **Interpreting.** They are surrounded by other cultures and languages. The speaker recognizes that the Poseidonians place a great deal of importance on this festival.

2. **Recalling.** They tell each other about ancient Greek customs and try to speak Greek words even though few understand the language. They remember that they, too, are Greeks. **Interpreting.** The Poseidonians remember that they are Greek, but knowledge of their ancestors' culture has nearly died out among them.

SYNTHESIZING

Responses will vary. Possible responses are given.

3. The Poseidonians are different from their ancestors in that they do not speak the Greek language or honor ancient customs in their everyday lives. They feel excluded because they are not in touch with Hellenic culture. It is a catastrophe to them because they feel that without being able to preserve their Hellenic way of life, they have become barbarians. Responses will vary, but students should support their opinions. Some students may say that the speaker is pointing out that people tend to glorify the past and compare the present negatively to it.

ANSWERS FOR UNDERSTANDING LITERATURE

Responses will vary. Possible responses are given.

1. **Tone.** The tone of "Poseidonians" is regretful and serious. The speaker regrets their loss with the Poseidonians. The speaker may blame the Poseidonians for their loss.

2. **Epigraph and Description.** A grammarian might be inclined to view a decline in his language as a serious loss. The epigraph is somber and tragic. In the poem, Cavafy makes the feelings of the Poseidonians very human by showing them floundering as they try to honor their past. This universalizes their situation, making it understandable to every person who has felt pain in losing touch with the past.

▶ Additional practice of the skills taught in this lesson is provided in the Essential Skills Practice Book: Study and Research 4.11–4.24.

ADDITIONAL QUESTIONS AND ACTIVITIES

- If possible, allow students to make a trip to the library to view each type of source material before they begin a research project.
- As a class, discuss the advantages and disadvantages of each type of source material.
- You might want to have students practice using the different types of source materials by having them locate at least two or three interesting details about one or more of the following subjects:

Constantine Cavafy
Greek mythology
Modern Greek literature
Egypt
Hellenic art
Hellenic literature
Hellenic architecture
Hellenic philosophy
E. M. Forster

like Athenaeus have been particularly upset by the "barbarization" of the Greek language? A **description**, one of the modes of writing, portrays a character, an object, or a scene. Compare the description of the Poseidonians' festival in the epigraph from *Deipnosophistai* with the description of the same festival in Cavafy's poem. What does Cavafy add to the scene in writing his own description? What additional information might he have wanted to share with the reader by writing this poem?

RESEARCH SKILLS

Strong research skills are a tremendous asset, both in school and later in life. This textbook will help to sharpen your research skills by providing research activities related to some of the literature you will be reading. Important research skills include using research tools, finding appropriate information, taking thorough and clear notes, and documenting your sources. For a more complete treatment of these skills, turn to the Language Arts Survey 4.11–4.24, "Research Skills."

FINDING SOURCES

There are many possible sources of information. The following chart provides some of the most common sources.

COMMON SOURCES OF INFORMATION	
Reference Works	Usually, current reference works are noncirculating. Examples include atlases, encyclopedias, and almanacs.
Books	To find books on a given subject, use an online or card catalog. For information on using these tools and on finding information in libraries, refer to the Language Arts Survey 4.11, "The Classification of Library Materials," 4.12, "Using Search Tools," and 4.13, "Using the Card Catalog."
Periodicals	Magazines, newspapers, and journals are called periodicals. To locate articles in periodicals, use the *Reader's Guide to Periodic Literature,* or a database of journals. These references may be in bound form or you may find them online.
Computer-assisted Research	With a computer and a modem, you can connect to a variety of sources of information. If you, your school, or your library subscribes to an online service, you probably have access to current news, online encyclopedias, periodicals, and research services. You may also be able to use the service to connect to the Library of Congress, other libraries and museums, and the Internet. You may also have access to CD-ROM databases which work just like an online database. The difference is that you retrieve the information from a CD instead of working through a network. (cont.)

COMMON SOURCES OF INFORMATION (CONT.)	
Vertical Files	Usually housed in filing cabinets, these collections contain assorted materials including: brochures, pamphlets, maps, clippings, and photographs.
Organizations	Organizations such as local businesses, historical societies, museums, or national associations can provide information of a different sort than that found in books.
Experts	People who work in or are otherwise well-informed about the particular field or subject you are researching can provide valuable information.

DOCUMENTING SOURCES

Plagiarism is the serious crime of using someone else's words or ideas as if they were your own. To avoid plagiarizing, you must indicate to your reader when you are using the words or ideas of others. This is called documentation. A note giving the source of an idea is called a citation or a reference. It is important that you review carefully the Language Arts Survey 4.23, "Documenting Sources in Report," and 4.24, "Footnotes and Endnotes." Proper recording of sources and conscientious note-taking will help you to cite sources correctly.

BIBLIOGRAPHIES AND BIBLIOGRAPHY CARDS

A bibliography is a list of sources on a given topic. Bibliography cards provide a record of all the sources you used during your research. A bibliography may be a comprehensive list of works on your subject or it may be a list of works that you consulted or cited in your research. Various forms for bibliography entries can be found in charts featured in the Language Arts Survey 4.20, "Bibliographies and Bibliography Cards."

FORMAL NOTE-TAKING

Take formal notes when you need to quote or document your sources. Your notes will consist of quotations, paraphrases, and summaries and will allow you to identify the source of each. For the proper format of note cards and tips on formal note-taking, turn to the Language Arts Survey 4.22, "Informal and Formal Note-taking."

ACTIVITY

What different cultures make up your own background and/or the background of your family? Decide what country or culture in your family history interests you the most, then research it in the library. Try to focus your subject so you are not overwhelmed with information. For example, if you have chosen to research the country of Greece, you should narrow your focus to one topic such as Greek food, recreation, arts, government, or a particular period in its history. Use the library's various search tools to find at least four sources of information on your subject. If possible arrange to speak with a person who might know a great deal about your subject, such as a relative, a native of the country, or a representative from an organization devoted to that culture. Take notes on your subject, and prepare a bibliography of sources for people interested in learning more about the country or about your specific subject. Share a few interesting details or facts about your subject with your classmates.

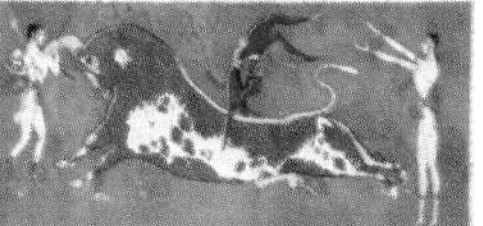

Bull-leaping fresco, Knossos, Crete

ADDITIONAL QUESTIONS AND ACTIVITIES

Because plagiarism can be such a serious problem, you might want to take extra time to be sure students understand what plagiarism is.

Using the chalkboard or other demonstration materials, show the difference between paraphrasing and documenting sources and plagiarizing.

ANSWERS FOR SKILLS ACTIVITIES

RESEARCH SKILLS

Encourage each student to begin the research activity by interviewing an older person in his or her family. General information a family member provides will help the student to focus his or her research before going to the library.

Students should try to plan before they enter the library so that they do not waste time or become overwhelmed by too much information. Before making a trip to the library, each student should be able to write a short paragraph discussing, generally, the subject area he or she plans to research. Although researchers can be open-minded about allowing a topic to evolve and change as they gather information, they also need to remain focused.

In presenting information to the rest of the class, students should feel free to use pictures, photographs, or any other visual aids.

SUPPORT FOR LEP STUDENTS

Pronunciations of Proper Nouns and Adjectives

Al • sace (al sās´)
Basque (bask)
bon • jour (bōŋ zhûr´)
Can • dide (kan dēd´)
crêpes (kreps)
E • mile Zo • la (ā mēl´ zō lä´)
Ga • bri • elle Rie • mer (gä´brē el´ re´mər)
Jean de la Fon • taine (zhän də lä fän tān´)
Les Mi • ser • a • bles (lā mē´zâr ä´blə)
Lor • raine (lô rān´)
Louvre (lo͞ov´)
Mol • ière (mōl yâr´)
Mo • na Li • sa (mō´nä lē´sä)
Tar • tuffe (tär to͞of´)
Thi • on • ville (tē´ōn vēl´)
Vic • tor Hu • go (vik´tər hyoo´gō)
Vol • taire (vōl târ´)

Cross-curricular Activities

ARTS AND HUMANITIES AND SOCIAL STUDIES

Students can use the Internet, travel books, and other sources to plan an imaginary trip to France. They could write individual itineraries or work in one of three groups, with each group researching a section of France (north, central, or southern). When students have collected enough information, they should write brief descriptions of the destinations in France to which they plan to travel and the activities they would like to try on their visit. Students might also compile a list of French words and phrases that would be helpful to a traveler. Each student or group should create a display including brochures, drawings, maps, and written itineraries.

PASSPORT TO FRANCE

Bonjour! My name is Gabrielle Riemer and I come from France. My home is in Thionville, a city of around fifteen thousand people in the northeastern part of France. The whole downtown area is restricted to pedestrians, and it is very nice to walk down the streets and shop without being worried about the cars. It's also good for the environment. Thionville is on a river, and in the summer the water is full of sailboats and water-skiers.

In the Lorraine region, where Thionville is located, there are lots of forests. This area is not flat but not too hilly either—just in between. It's very rainy and cold during the winter. Some people say that those of us who live there are grumpy because of the weather, but we are actually welcoming and kindhearted. In the South of France the climate is much warmer and sunnier, and that is why people there are considered friendlier.

The economy of France is not very good. Steel and iron production, automobile manufacturing, and telecommunication are some of our major industries, but the unemployment rate is high. Even if you go to school you might not get a job. But those who *do* work have at least five weeks of vacation per year and work thirty-nine hours per week. In France, the differences in social

Gabrielle Riemer
Thionville, France

Eiffel Tower

Poppies near Reims

Historical Note

The Eiffel Tower was designed by engineer Gustave Eiffel for the 1889 international exposition in Paris, which commemorated the centennial of the French Revolution. The monument was a (cont.)

Historical Note (cont.)

first in many ways. It was twice as tall as the dome of St. Peter's Cathedral in Rome and the Great Pyramid of Giza and was made entirely of prefabricated pieces fitted together at the site. Assembly of the fifteen thousand metal parts took more than two years. At 984 feet, the Eiffel Tower remained the tallest building in the world until the 1930 completion of the 1,048-foot Chrysler Building in New York City.

The Eiffel Tower was originally scorned by many of Paris's artistic and literary elite, who disliked its geometric structure and called it "useless and monstrous." It was almost torn down in 1909, but was spared when engineers discovered that it was an ideal platform for radio antennas. Today, the tower is accepted worldwide as a symbol of Paris.

classes are not as big as in other countries. Thanks to social laws, everyone has the benefit of health insurance, education, and unemployment pay. We pay a lot of taxes to contribute to these social policies.

Our official language is French. In Alsace, the region where I was born, people speak a German dialect, and near the border of Spain they speak "Basque," a language similar to Spanish. We have to learn at least one foreign language at school, starting in seventh grade. Usually, we learn English first.

We call our country "the country of welcome" because much of the population is originally from outside France. Most immigrants come from European countries, especially Italy and Portugal, but now many are also from the former Soviet Union. One of my best friends is from Algeria. Her parents were among the many people who came from North Africa in the 1960s to work in the steel industry. The Asian community is also well represented.

Food and meals in France are an important part of daily life. Families eat together every day, and on Sundays we invite friends or relatives to share a big lunch. We stay at the table for hours,

Grain Stacks, End of Summer.
Claude Monet, 1890

Giverny, Monet's house

Notre Dame Cathedral

Cross-curricular Activities

SOCIAL STUDIES AND APPLIED ARTS

Gabrielle says on page 43 that in France "everyone has the benefit of health insurance." Explain to students that socialized medicine is a system that provides medical and hospital care to all citizens through taxation and government regulation. Have students use the Internet or library to research different types of medical systems. They should find enough information to be able to compare and contrast at least two health-care systems found in various countries such as France, Japan, Canada, Sweden, and the United States. Then have the class form small groups and ask each group to devise an "ideal" health care system. Finally, as a class, compare the various plans, considering the benefits and drawbacks of each system.

Historical Note

The Cathedral of Notre Dame in Paris, one of the best-known examples of Gothic architecture in the world, is distinguished by its size, antiquity, and architecture. The cathedral stands upon the Île de la Cité, the small island in the Seine on which Paris was founded. The site has an interesting past: a Gallo-Roman temple of Jupiter, a Christian basilica, and a Romanesque church succeeded each other on this spot before the cathedral was erected. Construction of *Notre Dame de Paris* began in 1163 during the reign of Louis VII, and Pope Alexander III laid the cornerstone. The high altar was consecrated in 1189, but construction was not completed until the fourteenth century.

The cathedral's interior measures 427 feet by 157 feet and the ceiling soars to 115 feet. The interior is dominated by stained-glass rose windows that still hold their

(cont.)

Historical Note (cont.)

original thirteenth-century glass. The largest of these windows is on the west (front) facade and is 31 feet in diameter. According to the original design, spires were to crown the 223-foot high towers, but they were never added. The most colossal church of its generation, the cathedral is especially noted for the use of exterior supports called flying buttresses, pointed arches, and rib vaulting.

From the base of the north tower, visitors can climb to the top of the west facade and enjoy views of Paris over the cathedral's ferocious-looking gargoyles. Interested students might research various aspects of the architecture of the Cathedral of Notre Dame or they might read Victor Hugo's famous novel *The Hunchback of Notre Dame.*

Cross-curricular Activities

MATHEMATICS AND SCIENCES AND APPLIED ARTS

French high school students often stop with their friends at crêperies (crêpe shops), where they snack on dessert crêpes, or thin pancakes. Crêpes originated in Brittany in northwestern France but are now a popular dessert throughout the country.

Invite students to use the recipe below to prepare dessert crêpes at home to share with the class. Students will have to adapt the recipe to feed the number of people in the class.

Crêpes with Strawberries and Cream

Serves: 6

Ingredients:

- 1 1/2 cups milk
- 2/3 cup all-purpose flour
- 1/2 teaspoon salt
- 3 eggs
- 5 tablespoons butter, melted
- 4 tablespoons sugar
- 1 pint strawberries, thinly sliced
- 1/2 pint whipping cream
- confectioners' sugar for garnish

Procedure:

1. In medium bowl, beat milk, flour, salt, eggs, 3 tablespoons melted butter, and 1 tablespoon sugar with wire whisk until smooth. Cover and refrigerate batter for at least one hour.
2. Meanwhile, combine strawberries and 2 tablespoons sugar in a medium-sized bowl.
3. Let stand at room temperature for 20 minutes to allow sugar to dissolve and berries to marinate.
4. With pastry brush, brush bottom of nonstick, 10-inch skillet with small amount of remaining melted butter and heat pan over medium heat until hot.
5. Pour 1/4 cup batter into pan; tilt pan to evenly coat bottom and pour excess batter back into bowl. Cook for about 2 minutes or until top is set and underside is slightly browned. Using a heat-safe rubber spatula, loosen crêpe from pan.

(cont.)

Joan of Arc

talking. Bread is very popular—there is no meal without bread. We buy fresh bread and croissants every day and don't eat the leftover bread from the day before. There are many traditional dishes, depending on the region, and a lot of good desserts. My favorite dessert is *crêpes,* which are made with a pancake-like batter and served with chocolate sauce, fruit, or jam.

On the weekends many young people play sports like tennis or soccer. Soccer is very big in France. Once a week, fans go to the game to cheer for their team. On Saturday nights we go out dancing with our friends or to the movies. Sunday is usually reserved for family activities.

In France, kids start school when they are three years old. A typical day in school starts at 8:00 A.M. and ends at 4:30 or 5:00 P.M. So there is not much time to do extra-curricular activities during the week, except on Wednesdays when we have the afternoon off. School is free for everyone, even at the college and university level. People spend a lot of time with their families after work and

Soccer, a popular European sport

Versailles, palace and parterre

Cross-curricular Activities (cont.)

Flip crêpe over and cook other side for about 30 seconds.

6. Slide cooked crêpe onto waxed paper. Repeat until all batter is used, stacking crêpes between waxed paper.
7. In small bowl, beat at medium speed the whipping cream and remaining 1 tablespoon sugar until soft peaks form. Spoon cream into serving bowl.
8. Strain liquid from strawberries into small bowl with remaining melted butter, then brush strawberry liquid on crêpes. Fold each crêpe into quarters. Place strawberries in small serving bowl. Dust crêpes with confectioners' sugar, and serve with strawberries and whipped cream.

on the weekends. Usually college students live with their families, if their school is not too far from home.

The French have made many contributions to world culture in the fields of music, art, and writing. The Louvre museum in Paris is one of the largest museums in the world and holds many famous works, including the *Mona Lisa.* Jean de La Fontaine is famous for his fables, and Émile Zola wrote novels about the way people lived at the beginning of the twentieth century and how they fought for their rights. My favorite writer is Victor Hugo, a well-known poet who also wrote the novels *Les Misérables* and *The Hunchback of Notre Dame.* Other famous writers are Molière, who wrote *Tartuffe,* and Voltaire, who is best known for *Candide.* ■

Mona Lisa.
Leonardo da Vinci.
The Louvre, Paris

Arche de la Defense, Paris

The Pyramid, The Louvre, Paris

An artist's view of St. Tropez

Cultural Note

Football, or soccer, is the most popular sport in France. Nearly two million players, some amateurs, some professionals, are members of the French Football Federation. Rugby, tennis, and basketball are popular among young people, as well. Many French also enjoy individual sports, including running, swimming, skiing, horseback riding, and judo.

Since sports are not usually affiliated with schools in France, students often go to clubs to exercise and take private lessons. Communities usually offer opportunities for students to practice and compete in athletic events.

Cross-curricular Activities

Social Studies

French high school students spend up to ten hours a day at school, since classes begin as early as 8:00 A.M. and sometimes continue as late as 6:00 P.M. However, all classes do not meet every day. For example, one day a student may have six classes, and another day just two. As Gabrielle mentions on page 44, students have Wednesday afternoons off to study, play sports, or meet friends. Some classes are held on Saturday.

High school students choose a major area of study in preparation for *le baccalauréat*, the national exam which usually determines whether students may continue their studies at a university. After selecting an area of study, students take required courses and some electives that relate to their area. Unlike most students in the United States, French students may take three courses in one subject area at the same time and often study philosophy and geography.

Have students discuss the differences between French and American schools, based on the information given here and in Gabrielle's introduction.

Cultural Note

As Gabrielle says on page 43, "food and meals in France are an important part of daily life." The French love to eat well, and while nutrition is important, they also eat for pleasure.

Traditionally, the French have taken two large meals a day, but this custom is changing because people are too busy to spend extensive time preparing meals. Breakfast usually consists of a cup of coffee or hot chocolate and a slice of bread and butter or a croissant. For people who work or go to school, eating lunch in a restaurant or school cafeteria is becoming more common since they no longer have time to return home to eat. The main meal of the day was once the midday meal, but now the evening meal is more often the most substantial.

ADDITIONAL RESOURCES

READER'S GUIDE

- Selection Worksheet 1.4

ASSESSMENT PORTFOLIO

- Selection Check Test 2.1.7
- Selection Test 2.1.8

ESSENTIAL SKILLS PRACTICE BOOKS

- Speaking and Listening 3.1–3.2

PREREADING EXTENSIONS

Some students might be interested in learning more about the other playwrights who are named in the Connections box as dramatists of the theater of the absurd. **Samuel Beckett (1906–)**, a French playwright and novelist born in Ireland, is considered to be an originator of the theater of the absurd. His major works include *Waiting for Godot* (1952) and *Endgame* (1957). **Harold Pinter (1930–)** is a British dramatist and actor whose most important works include *The Birthday Party* (1958), *The Dumb Waiter* (1959), *The Homecoming* (1965), and *Betrayal* (1978). **Edward Albee (1928–)** is an American playwright, producer, and director. His masterpiece is *Who's Afraid of Virginia Woolf* (1962).

Encourage interested students to locate and read these works.

SUPPORT FOR LEP STUDENTS

PRONUNCIATIONS OF PROPER NOUNS AND ADJECTIVES

Eu • gène I • on • es • co
(yo͞o zhen´ ē ə nes´ kō)

ADDITIONAL VOCABULARY

curious—strange or unusual
plausible—possible
prolonging—lengthening, keeping something going for a long time

PREREADING

from *The Bald Soprano*
by Eugène Ionesco, translated by Donald M. Allen

FRANCE

About the Author

EUGÈNE IONESCO
1912–1994

French dramatist, critic, and political philosopher **Eugène Ionesco** was born in Slatina, Romania. As a baby, he was taken to France, where he lived until he was thirteen years old. He returned to Romania and eventually attended the University of Bucharest, earning a degree in French. After graduation, Ionesco remained in Bucharest, where he taught French and wrote poetry and literary criticism. Ionesco married in 1936 and two years later won a scholarship to work toward a doctorate in Paris. He took a job as a proofreader in Paris and decided to learn the English language. His English lessons inspired his first play, *The Bald Soprano* (1949). Although the first production of this play was a failure, Ionesco's work quickly attracted attention, and during the next five years, fourteen of his plays were produced, and two volumes of his dramatic works were published. Today Ionesco's many plays are still performed throughout the world; he is one of the most popular dramatists of the school of theater known as the theater of the absurd (see Connections below).

About the Selection

The work of Eugène Ionesco emerged from his embrace of **Existentialism**—the twentieth-century philosophical school that focused on the essential absurdity and meaninglessness of life. His dramas express, imaginatively and comically, the Existential belief. ***The Bald Soprano***, one of his most popular plays, was actually inspired by lessons Ionesco took in conversational English. He drew the heart of this play, the conversation between two middle-class British couples, from the dull, formal practice sentences in his English textbook. The excerpt that you are about to read, one of the play's most famous comic scenes, features a man and a woman who, in the course of trivial conversation, make a surprising discovery about their lives. By focusing on their dialogue, Ionesco attempts to show the difficulties of communication and the absurdity of life. He also makes fun of the melodramatic plays popular among the British middle class at the time.

CONNECTIONS: Theater of the Absurd

Eugène Ionesco helped to start and popularize what is known as the theater of the absurd. This type of twentieth-century drama, which grew out of Existentialism, presents illogical, absurd, and unrealistic scenes, characters, events, and juxtapositions in an attempt to convey the essential meaninglessness of human life. Some playwrights have also used this form to convey moral messages to the audience. Dramatists of the theater of the absurd include Samuel Beckett, Edward Albee, and Harold Pinter.

GOALS/OBJECTIVES

Studying this lesson will enable students to

- appreciate a scene from a famous comic play that attempts to show the absurdity of life
- discuss the life and work of Eugéne Ionesco
- understand the theater of the absurd
- define the literary terms *satire, dialogue*, and *character*
- practice elements of verbal and nonverbal communication, active listening, and interpersonal communication

What aspects of human nature and society, our habits, traditions, and social customs, do you find absurd? Why do these aspects of human nature or society seem particularly absurd or nonsensical to you? In your journal describe something that makes no sense to you.

READER'S JOURNAL

FROM

The Bald Soprano

EUGÈNE IONESCO, TRANSLATED BY DONALD M. ALLEN

MR. MARTIN: Excuse me, madam, but it seems to me, unless I'm mistaken, that I've met you somewhere before.

MRS. MARTIN: I, too, sir. It seems to me that I've met you somewhere before.

MR. MARTIN: Was it, by any chance, at Manchester that I caught a glimpse of you, madam?

MRS. MARTIN: That is very possible. I am originally from the city of Manchester. But I do not have a good memory, sir. I cannot say whether it was there that I caught a glimpse of you or not!

MR. MARTIN: Good God, that's curious! I, too, am originally from the city of Manchester, madam!

MRS. MARTIN: That is curious!

MR. MARTIN: Isn't that curious! Only, I, madam, I left the city of Manchester about five weeks ago.

MRS. MARTIN: That is curious! What a bizarre coincidence! I, too, sir, I left the city of Manchester about five weeks ago.

MR. MARTIN: Madam, I took the 8:30 morning train which arrives in London at 4:45.

MRS. MARTIN: That is curious! How very bizarre! And what a coincidence! I took the same train, sir, I too.

MR. MARTIN: Good Lord, how curious! Perhaps then, madam, it was on the train that I saw you?

MRS. MARTIN: It is indeed possible; that is, not unlikely. It is plausible and, after all, why not!—But I don't recall it, sir!

MR. MARTIN: I traveled second class, madam. There is no second class in England, but I always travel second class.

MRS. MARTIN: That is curious! How very bizarre! And what a coincidence! I, too, sir, I traveled second class.

MR. MARTIN: How curious that is! Perhaps we did meet in second class, my dear lady!

MRS. MARTIN: That is certainly possible, and it is not at all unlikely. But I do not

❶ *Where do Mr. Martin and Mrs. Martin believe they might have previously seen each other? What does Mrs. Martin say she lacks?*

❷ *When did both characters leave Manchester?*

WORDS FOR EVERYDAY USE

co • in • ci • dence (kō in´sə dəns) *n.*, accidental and remarkable occurrence of events or ideas at the same time

READER'S JOURNAL

Students might begin this activity by freewriting for several moments about things in the world that strike them as strange and nonsensical.

ANSWERS TO GUIDED READING QUESTIONS

❶ Mr. and Mrs. Martin believe they might have seen each other in Manchester. Mrs. Martin says that she lacks a good memory.

❷ Both Mr. and Mrs. Martin left Manchester five weeks ago on the morning train.

QUOTABLES

"Where I am, I don't know, I'll never know, in the silence you don't know, you must go on, I can't go on, I'll go on."

—Samuel Beckett
The Unnamable

VOCABULARY IN CONTEXT

- The three cousins did not expect to be at the same store buying the same items—it was a strange coincidence.

Answers to Guided Reading Questions

❶ They discover that they probably sat across from each other on the train.

❷ Mrs. Martin is surprised because she discovers that he lives at her address.

❸ Mr. Martin believes that Mrs. Martin might have asked him to put her luggage on the rack, thanked him, and given him permission to smoke.

Additional Questions and Activities

Students might find this play to be unlike anything they have ever read. You might have them read portions of the play aloud and discuss it as a class. What are their initial thoughts about these characters and their relationship?

Share with students the quotations below, and ask them to relate the quotations to what Ionesco might be trying to say or show in *The Bald Soprano.*

Quotables

"Life is full of infinite absurdities, which, strangely enough, do not even need to appear plausible, since they are true."

—Luigi Pirandello
Six Characters in Search of an Author

"People who cannot recognize a palpable absurdity are very much in the way of civilization."

—Agnes Repplier
In Pursuit of Laughter

remember very well, my dear sir!

Mr. Martin: My seat was in coach No. 8, compartment 6, my dear lady.

Mrs. Martin: How curious that is! My seat was also in coach No. 8, compartment 6, my dear sir!

Mr. Martin: How curious that is and what a bizarre coincidence! Perhaps we met in compartment 6, my dear lady?

Mrs. Martin: It is indeed possible, after all! But I do not recall it, my dear sir!

Mr. Martin: To tell the truth, my dear lady, I do not remember it either, but it is possible that we caught a glimpse of each other there, and as I think of it, it seems to me even very likely.

Mrs. Martin: Oh! truly, of course, truly, sir!

❶ *What do the Martins discover about their train trip?*

Mr. Martin: How curious it is! I had seat No. 3, next to the window, my dear lady.

Mrs. Martin: Oh, good Lord, how curious and bizarre! I had seat No. 6, next to the window, across from you, my dear sir.

Mr. Martin: Good God, how curious that is and what a coincidence! We were then seated facing each other, my dear lady! It is there that we must have seen each other!

❷ *Why is Mrs. Martin surprised when Mr. Martin describes where he lives?*

Mrs. Martin: How curious it is! It is possible, but I do not recall it, sir!

Mr. Martin: To tell the truth, my dear lady, I do not remember it either. However, it is very possible that we saw each other on that occasion.

Mrs. Martin: It is true, but I am not at all sure of it, sir.

❸ *What does Mr. Martin remember about Mrs. Martin?*

Mr. Martin: Dear madam, were you not the lady who asked me to place her suitcase in the luggage rack and who thanked me and gave me permission to smoke?

Mrs. Martin: But of course, that must have been I, sir. How curious it is, how curious it is, and what a coincidence!

Mr. Martin: How curious it is, how bizarre, what a coincidence! And well, well, it was perhaps at that moment that we came to know each other, madam?

Mrs. Martin: How curious it is and what a coincidence! It is indeed possible, my dear sir! However, I do not believe that I recall it.

Mr. Martin: Nor do I, madam. [*A moment of silence. The clock strikes twice, then once.*] Since coming to London, I have resided in Bromfield Street, my dear lady.

Mrs. Martin: How curious that is, how bizarre! I, too, since coming to London, I have resided in Bromfield Street, my dear sir.

Mr. Martin: How curious that is, well then, well then, perhaps we have seen each other in Bromfield Street, my dear lady.

Mrs. Martin: How curious that is, how bizarre! It is indeed possible, after all! But I do not recall it, my dear sir.

Mr. Martin: I reside at No. 19, my dear lady.

Mrs. Martin: How curious that is. I also reside at No. 19, my dear sir.

Mr. Martin: Well then, well then, well then, well then, perhaps we have seen each other in that house, dear lady?

Mrs. Martin: It is indeed possible but I do not recall it, dear sir.

Mr. Martin: My flat is on the fifth floor, No. 8, my dear lady.

Mrs. Martin: How curious it is, good Lord, how bizarre! And what a coincidence! I too reside on the fifth floor, in flat No. 8, dear sir!

Mr. Martin: [*musing*]: How curious it is, how curious it is, how curious it is, and what a coincidence! You know, in my bedroom there is a bed, and it is covered with a green eiderdown.[1] This room, with the bed and the green eiderdown, is at the end of the corridor between the w.c.[2] and the bookcase, dear lady!

1. **eiderdown.** Bed quilt stuffed with feathers
2. **w.c.** Water closet, or bathroom

Train in the Snow. Claude Monet, 1875

Mrs. Martin: What a coincidence, good Lord, what a coincidence! My bedroom, too, has a bed with a green eiderdown and is at the end of the corridor, between the w.c., dear sir, and the bookcase!

Mr. Martin: How bizarre, curious, strange! Then, madam, we live in the same room and we sleep in the same bed, dear lady. It is perhaps there that we have met!

Mrs. Martin: How curious it is and what a coincidence! It is indeed possible that we have met there, and perhaps even last night. But I do not recall it, dear sir!

Mr. Martin: I have a little girl, my little daughter, she lives with me, dear lady. She is two years old, she's blonde, she has a white eye and a red eye, she is very pretty, her name is Alice, dear lady.

Mrs. Martin: What a bizarre coincidence! I, too, have a little girl. She is two years old, has a white eye and a red eye, she is very pretty, and her name is Alice, too, dear sir!

Mr. Martin: [*in the same drawling, monotonous voice*]: How curious it is and what a coincidence! And bizarre! Perhaps they are the same, dear lady!

Mrs. Martin: How curious it is! It is indeed possible, dear sir. [*A rather long moment of silence. The clock strikes 29 times.*]

Mr. Martin: [*after having reflected at length, gets up slowly and, unhurriedly, moves toward Mrs. Martin, who, surprised by his solemn air, has also gotten up very quietly. Mr. Martin, in the same flat, monotonous voice, slightly singsong*]: Then, dear lady, I believe that there can be no doubt about it, we have seen

❶ *What is unusual about the clock?*

❷ *What characteristics do Mrs. Martin's daughter and Mr. Martin's daughter share?*

Answers to Guided Reading Questions

❶ The clock strikes at completely random times, and does not seem to be keeping any real time. First it strikes twice, then once, then twenty-nine times.

❷ Both daughters are two years old, have blonde hair, and have one white eye and one red eye.

Selection Check Test with Answers

EX. Who are the main characters in this excerpt from *The Bald Soprano*?
The main characters are Mr. and Mrs. Martin.

1. In what city do the Martins believe they might have met previously?
They believe they might have met in Manchester.
2. What do Mr. and Mrs. Martin realize when they tell each other where they live?
They realize that they live at the same address.
3. What does Mr. Martin deduce about their relationship?
He deduces that they are husband and wife.
4. According to Mary, why is Mr. Martin wrong?
According to Mary, Mr. Martin is wrong because he and Mrs. Martin do not actually have the same child.
5. What does Mary call herself?
Mary calls herself Sherlock Holmes.

Answers to Guided Reading Questions

❶ Mr. Martin reaches the conclusion that Mrs. Martin is his wife.

❷ Mary tells the audience that Mr. and Mrs. Martin are not really husband and wife. She reasons that Mr. Martin arrived at the wrong conclusion because, while his daughter has a white right eye and a red left eye, Mrs. Martin's daughter has a white left eye and a red right eye.

❸ Mary asks "Who is the real Donald?" and "Who is the real Elizabeth?" She then asks whether anyone is interested in prolonging the confusion. She says that her name is Sherlock Holmes.

Responding to the Selection

Ask students to form pairs or small groups to look over the dialogue. What lines do they find most humorous, strange, or illogical?

Each student should have a chance to characterize the Martins and back up the assessment he or she makes of the couple with details from the play. Does the couple, at least in an exaggerated way, remind the students of anyone they know or any characters with whom they are familiar from books, television shows, or movies, or are these characters completely unlike other people or characters?

 ❶ *What conclusion does Mr. Martin reach concerning Mrs. Martin?*

each other before and you are my own wife . . . Elizabeth, I have found you again!

[Mrs. Martin approaches Mr. Martin without haste. They embrace without expression. The clock strikes once, very loud. This striking of the clock must be so loud that it makes the audience jump. The Martins do not hear it.]

Mrs. Martin: Donald, it's you, darling!

[They sit together in the same armchair, their arms around each other, and fall asleep. The clock strikes several more times. Mary, on tiptoe, a finger to her lips, enters quietly and addresses the audience.]

❷ *What does Mary tell the audience about the Martins? What is the reasoning behind her statement?*

Mary: Elizabeth and Donald are now too happy to be able to hear me. I can therefore let you in on a secret. Elizabeth is not Elizabeth, Donald is not Donald. And here is the proof: the child that Donald spoke of is not Elizabeth's daughter, they are not the same person. Donald's daughter has one white eye and one red eye like Elizabeth's daughter. Whereas Donald's child has a white right eye and a red left eye, Elizabeth's child has a red right eye and a white left eye! Thus all of Donald's system of deduction collapses when it comes up against this last obstacle which destroys his whole theory. In spite of the extraordinary coincidences which seem to be definitive proofs, Donald and Elizabeth, not being the parents of the same child, are not Donald and Elizabeth. It is in vain[3] that he thinks he is Donald, it is in vain that she thinks she is Elizabeth. He believes in vain that she is Elizabeth. She believes in vain that he is Donald—they are sadly deceived. But who is the true Donald? Who is the true Elizabeth? Who has any interest in prolonging this confusion? I don't know. Let's not try to know. Let's leave things as they are. *[She takes several steps toward the door, then returns and says to the audience:]* My real name is Sherlock Holmes. *[She exits.]* ■

❸ *What questions does Mary ask? What does she claim is her real name?*

3. **in vain.** Futilely, uselessly

Responding to the Selection

Imagine that you overheard the conversation between Mr. Martin and Mrs. Martin. Would you interrupt them at any point to clue them in about their relationship? If so, what would you say? Based on the conversation you overheard, how would you describe the Martins to your friends?

Reviewing the Selection

RECALLING / **INTERPRETING**

1. In what city do Mr. Martin and Mrs. Martin believe they might have met? ▶▶ Why might Mr. Martin's lines and Mrs. Martin's lines be interchangeable during this discussion? How would you describe the language they use in speaking to each other?

2. What do the Martins discover about their train trip and about their homes? ▶▶ What words and phrases do the Martins repeat to describe how they feel each time another similarity in their lives is revealed? What do these repeated words reveal about the Martins as characters?

3. Review the few stage directions, or notes describing sound effects and how lines should be delivered. What word is used to describe Mr. Martin's voice? What is the one sound effect used in the scene? ▶▶ Why is the sound of Mr. Martin's voice, as prescribed by the stage directions, appropriate? Why might Ionesco have wanted random, meaningless chimes of the clock inserted throughout the Martins' conversation?

4. What does the maid, Mary, reveal about the Martins? What does she say her real name is? ▶▶ How do the Martins feel at the end of their exchange? Why do they feel this way? What destroys Donald Martin's entire theory about who he is and who Elizabeth Martin is? In what way is Mary like this famous detective?

SYNTHESIZING

5. What is unusual about Donald and Elizabeth Martin and the method they use in trying to remember each other? Why does their conversation become absurd? What role does reason play in determining meaning in the Martins' lives?

Understanding Literature (Questions for Discussion)

1. **Satire. Satire** is humorous writing or speech intended to point out errors, falsehoods, foibles, or failings. *The Bald Soprano* is considered a classic example of satire. It pokes fun at middle-class ways of life, as well as at the characters, settings, and dialogue of conventional middle-class theater. In what ways is the conversation between Mr. and Mrs. Martin an example of satire? How does Ionesco both mimic and exaggerate certain aspects of middle-class life and conventional theater?

2. **Dialogue. Dialogue** is conversation involving two or more people or characters. Plays are made up of dialogue and stage directions. As you read on the Prereading page, the

Answers for Reviewing the Selection

RECALLING AND INTERPRETING

1. **Recalling.** They believe they might have met in Manchester. **Interpreting.** They both use formal, polite language—language reserved for strangers who have just met. They both react with the same mild interest each time a new coincidence is mentioned.

2. **Recalling.** The Martins discover that they left Manchester on the same train, sat across from each other, and that they live at the same address. **Interpreting.** "That is curious," and "bizarre" are words and phrases repeated throughout the play. These repeated words indicate that both characters are dull and conventional in their behavior, although their characters and situations are strange.

3. **Recalling.** The word monotonous is used to describe Mr. Martin's voice. The striking of a clock is the one sound effect used in the scene. **Interpreting.** A monotonous tone is appropriate, since Mr. Martin is a man without originality, distinct style, or interesting things to say. The chimes are reflective of the meaninglessness and strangeness of their discussion and, by extension, the essential chaos of existence.

4. **Recalling.** Mary reveals that the Martins are not, in fact, husband and wife—that Mr. Martin was wrong in his deduction. She says that her real name is Sherlock Holmes. **Interpreting.** The Martins feel happy that they have found each other. They believe that they are husband and wife. Mr. Martin's theory is destroyed by the fact that he and Mrs. Martin's daughters, though similar, are not in fact identical. According to Mary, this means that they cannot really be husband and wife. She is "Sherlock Holmes" in the way that she tries to "crack the case" intellectually using clues.

(cont.)

Answers for Reviewing the Selection (cont.)

SYNTHESIZING

Responses will vary. Possible responses are given.

5. They happen by chance on coincidences that would normally be made irrelevant by memory. Their conversation seems absurd because the audience has leapt to the conclusion that they are husband and wife. They use deductive reasoning, albeit in a strange fashion, to come to a false conclusion. Mr. and Mrs. Martin and the maid, Mary, try to use reason to uncover the most basic information about the Martins' lives. Both the Martins' and the audience's "reasonable" assumptions that the Martins are husband and wife are contradicted, revealing that identities and relationships are far more arbitrary than reason dictates.

ANSWERS FOR UNDERSTANDING LITERATURE

Responses will vary. Possible responses are given.

1. Satire. The characters are polite and conventional in their behavior, yet what they are saying is completely banal and stupid. Their dialogue is repetitive and although their words express surprise, the characters' tone of voice is emotionless. There is no real reaction to the absurdity of their situation. The play points out what Ionesco finds shallow and meaningless in the middle-class world. The play also spoofs the conventional theatric device of having a character's identity or relationship suddenly revealed, as well as such conventions as actors portraying vivid emotions.

2. Dialogue. The language of the couple is dull, formal, and repetitive. Ionesco transformed the rehearsed, unoriginal conversations in his English-language textbook into dialogue that reflects the dull, uninspired reactions of his characters to their meaningless lives.

3. Character. The Martins are one-dimensional characters. The reader does not learn much about them, their emotions, or the details of their lives. The one-dimensional nature of the characters works well with Ionesco's ideas about the middle class and about middle-class theater. It is necessary that the characters seem uninteresting and without insight because Ionesco is interested in critiquing the middle class as well as English plays about middle-class life.

dialogue in *The Bald Soprano* is inspired, at least in part, by Ionesco's experience of studying English from a boring, formal textbook. Describe how the dialogue in the excerpt that you have read reflects Ionesco's experience with the textbook. What does the dialogue reveal about the author's feelings toward his characters and their lives?

3. **Character.** A **character** is a person who figures in the action of a literary work. A **one-dimensional character, flat character,** or **caricature** is one who exhibits a single, dominant quality. A **three-dimensional, full,** or **rounded character** is one who exhibits the complexity of traits associated with actual human beings. Are the Martins one-dimensional or three-dimensional characters? Why do you think that Ionesco chose to depict the Martins in this way?

SPEAKING AND LISTENING SKILLS

In every job, career, educational pursuit, and social situation, you will find that strong communication skills are essential. Many situations call on a person's ability to speak clearly and intelligently and to listen carefully and actively. Your work might require you to communicate with customers, manage employees, or give speeches and presentations to supervisors or clients. In a classroom, as a student or a teacher, you will need to be able to listen, ask questions, and share and discuss ideas. Throughout this textbook, you will have many opportunities to practice and strengthen your speaking and listening skills.

ELEMENTS OF VERBAL AND NONVERBAL COMMUNICATION

Communication can be verbal or nonverbal. People communicate verbally by means of words and other sounds. The chart below lists the most important elements of verbal communication.

ELEMENTS OF VERBAL COMMUNICATION	
Volume	The loudness or softness of the voice. Speak loudly enough to be heard, but not so loud as to make your audience uncomfortable.
Pitch, or intonation	The highness or lowness of the voice. Vary your pitch to give your expressions a musical quality and to communicate meaning.
Enunciation	The clearness with which syllables are spoken. Slightly exaggerate the clearness of your syllables to ensure that you are understood.
Pace	The speed with which something is said. Do not speak too slowly or too quickly.
Stress	The emphasis given to syllables, words, or phrases. Use stress to emphasize important ideas. Vary stress and pitch to avoid monotony.
Tone	The emotional quality of the speech. Suit the tone to the message.

People communicate nonverbally through eye contact, facial expressions, body language, gesture, and proximity. For descriptions of these elements, refer to the Language Arts Survey 3.1, "Elements of Verbal and Nonverbal Communication." These elements are useful in oral communication, public speaking, and oral interpretation. Elements of verbal and nonverbal communication also play a crucial role in the production of plays, such as *The Bald Soprano.* For example, you may have noticed that the stage directions call for Mr. Martin to speak in a monotone, and Mary is described as using gesture and body language (a finger raised to her lips, entering on tiptoe) to tell the audience to be silent while the Martins sleep.

ACTIVE LISTENING AND INTERPERSONAL COMMUNICATION

Interpersonal communication is communication between individuals. This is the kind of communication you use in your everyday life to share information and to establish and maintain relationships. When communicating with others, it is important to listen actively. To listen actively, you should listen for main ideas, predict, question, and interpret as you listen; take notes if you are listening to a lecture or a long monologue; and ask questions or provide other feedback. To improve your interpersonal communication, keep the following things in mind:

- Make eye contact.
- Give feedback.
- Think before you speak.
- Keep negative emotions under control by pausing, taking deep breaths, or choosing to continue the communication at another time.

As you read the excerpt from *The Bald Soprano,* you may have noted that the Martins have difficulty communicating with each other. Because neither listens actively—by posing questions or making inferences as the other speaks—it takes them an extraordinarily long time to determine the nature of their relationship. They also fail to express their emotions and so seem more like strangers than like people who have long been acquainted.

ACTIVITY

Form groups of three to enact the excerpt you have read from *The Bald Soprano.* Each person in the group should have a chance to play each of the three parts: Mr. Martin, Mrs. Martin, and Mary. (The person who plays Mary should also read stage directions and provide sound effects.) As a group, first discuss the script and identify where the characters should vary volume, pitch, pace, stress, tone, gestures, facial expressions, and body language. Then read the scene through three times, giving each person a chance to play a new part. When you have finished, discuss the quality of the readings, what each person was able to bring to each part, and which parts were most challenging. Remember to listen actively and use interpersonal communication skills in your discussion.

► Additional practice of the skills taught in this lesson is provided in the Essential Skills Practice Book: Speaking and Listening 3.1. and 3.2.

Additional Questions and Activities

You might ask students to answer the following questions:

In what situations have you found it necessary to have strong communication skills—skills in the areas of verbal and nonverbal communication, active listening, and interpersonal communication? For what situations do you think you might need these skills in the future?

Answers for Skills Activities

SPEAKING AND LISTENING SKILLS

To be successful in completing this activity, students in each group should enact the play, keeping in mind the guidelines for effective communication outlined in this lesson. Students should also be comfortable giving one another constructive criticism of their performances. You might want to walk around the room as groups read the play to hear students' rehearsals and performances and offer suggestions. Some groups might want to volunteer to perform before the entire class.

SUPPORT FOR LEP STUDENTS

PRONUNCIATIONS OF PROPER NOUNS AND ADJECTIVES

Al • ek • san • dr Push • kin (al´ ik san´dər po͞osh´ kin)
A • lek • sei Sav • ra • sov (ə lek´sā säv rä´səf)
An • na Akh • ma • to • va (ä´nä ak mä´ te vä)
An • ton Chek • hov (an tōn´ chā´ khäf)
ba • bush • ka (bä´ boosh kä´)
Bo • ris Pas • ter • nak (bō´ris pas´tər nak´)
Den • is Gor • bou • nov (den´ is gōr´bo͞o nof´)
Dr. Zhi • va • go (dok´ tər zhi vä´ gō)
Fy • o • dor Dos • toy • ev • sky (fā´ə dōr´ dos´ toi yef´ skē)
glas • nost (glaz´nust)
I • saac Lev • i • tan (ē säk´ lev´ i tän´)
Le • o Tol • stoy (le´ov tōl´stoi)
Mi • khail Gor • ba • chev (mē khīl´ gôr´ bə chôv´)
Ni • ko • lai Go • gol (nē´ kō lī´ gō´gəl)
Ni • ko • lai Rim • sky Kor • sa • kov (nē´ kō lī´ rim´ skē kôr´sə kôf)
Pa • scha (pä´skä)
pel • ma • ny (pel mā´nē)
per • e • stroi • ka (per´ i stroi´ kə)
per • o • gy (pâr ō´ gē)
Pyot • r Tchai • kov • sky (pet´ur chē käv´ skē)
sa • ra • fan (sa rä´ fän)
sdras • vi • tje (sdräs´ vē chä´)
Tri • ti • cov (trē´ tə kof´)

CROSS-CURRICULAR ACTIVITIES

SOCIAL STUDIES

Bring a map of Russia to class and have students locate major cities such as Moscow and St. Petersburg, regions such as Siberia, bodies of water such as the Volga and Dnepr Rivers; and physical features such as the Ural Mountains. Students might also locate other countries that were part of the former Soviet Union, such as the Ukraine and Georgia.

Once students identify and locate the largest cities in Russia, they should use the Internet, an (cont.)

PASSPORT TO RUSSIA

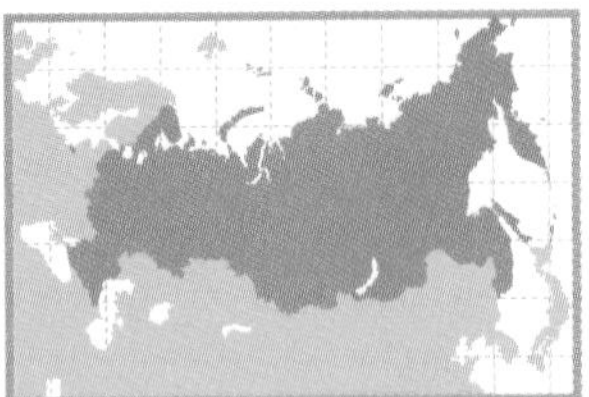

Sdrasvitje! My name is Denis Gorbounov and I am from Moscow, Russia. Many people think of Russia as a frozen country that is always cold, but we have four seasons, including a warm summer. The winter starts in October and ends in April, which gives us a lot of time to practice hockey, skiing, and figure skating. Our long winters are one reason why the Russian Olympic team is so strong in winter sports!

There are many interesting things to see and do in Moscow, which is located in the western part of Russia and is surrounded by forests and rivers. I recommend visiting Red Square because of the beautiful cathedrals, such as St. Basil's and Our Savior's. You should also see the Triticov Art Gallery, home to many beautiful icons and the most famous paintings created before the Russian Revolution of 1917. Triticov was a merchant who bought many paintings by famous Russian artists and put them on display for the people. Gorky Park is a lot like Central Park in New York. Also be sure to visit the old central districts of Moscow, which were built before the Revolution.

Denis Gorbounov
Moscow, Russia

Bolshoi Theater, Moscow

St. Basil's, Moscow

CROSS-CURRICULAR ACTIVITIES (CONT.)

encyclopedia, or an almanac to find the population of these cities and compare their size to large cities in the United States. Students might also research the climate and geography of various regions and draw parallels between regions in Russia and the United States.

MATHEMATICS AND SCIENCES

As a class, have students list the sports played in the winter Olympic games. Ask students which of these sports they like to play or like to watch, and why. Using online resources or other sources, students can research such topics as Winter Games sites, statistics, and participants. They should find statistics on Russian teams to verify or refute Denis's statement on page 54: "Our long winters are one reason why the Russian Olympic team is so strong in winter sports!"

We celebrate many of the same holidays as Americans, including New Year's Eve, birthdays, and *Pascha,* or Easter. We don't celebrate Christmas as extensively as Americans do, but we do have a Christmas tree and exchange gifts on New Year's Eve. On *Pascha* we have special cakes, decorated eggs, *perogies,* and a special service at church, where the food is blessed. Overall, Americans have more holidays than Russians, especially nonreligious holidays. We do celebrate May 9th as a day of victory over the Germans in World War II.

Typical Russian food is quite different from American food. We eat *perogies,* a pasta dish filled with different foods such as potatoes, blueberries, cherries, eggs, and meat. Another popular dish is *pelmany,* which is made with flour and water rolled into dough. Tiny pieces of dough are rolled flat, and a mixture of beef, pork, onions, and pepper is sealed inside. Then the *pelmanies* are boiled in water and onions. We also like to eat fish, pickles, tomatoes, and meat.

In the city, we wear the same types of clothing that Americans do, but in the villages you can still see women wearing the *babushka,* or grandmother, scarves. Women also wear

Eleventh-century Sveti Tskhoveli Cathedral, Miskheta

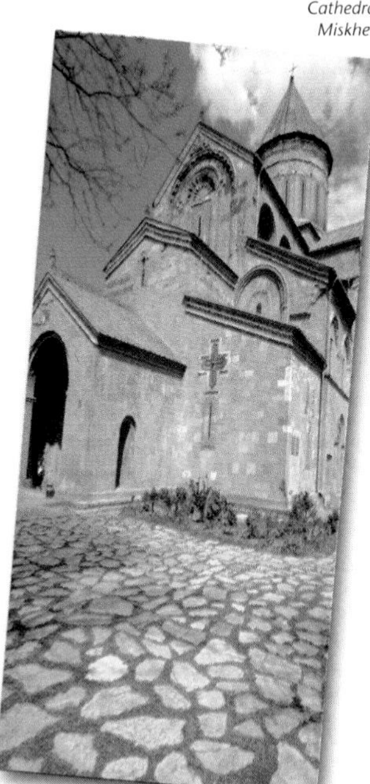

Russian nesting dolls

Heroic soldiers, Siege Monument, St. Petersburg

Cultural/Historical Note

Moscow has many fine museums to visit, including the Pushkin State Fine Arts Museum, which contains a wide selection of European works from the Renaissance onward, most of which were confiscated from private collections after the revolution. On page 54, Denis mentions the Triticov (Tretayakov) Gallery, near Gorky Park, which has the world's best collection of Russian icons and a collection of pre-revolutionary Russian art. The Central Artists' House, next to the new Triticov Gallery building, houses contemporary art. Moscow also has many literary museums, usually situated in the former homes of famous writers such as Leo Tolstoy, Aleksandr Pushkin, Fyodor Dostoyevsky, and Nikolai Gogol.

Gorky Park is the most famous of Moscow's parks and gardens, stretching approximately one mile along the Moscow River in the heart of Moscow. The park contains ornamental gardens and hosts many outdoor events, including science lectures and rock concerts. The State Art Gallery and Central House of Artists is located in the northern section of the park. In the summer, visitors can take river excursions from the park's pier, and in winter ice skaters can make use of the frozen ponds. Interested students might research Gorky Park to investigate the creation of the park and the origin of its name, as well as any significant events that took place there.

Cultural/Historical Note

The Russian *matryoshka,* or nesting, doll is traditionally a hand-crafted, hand-painted wooden set of dolls that fit one within the next. Wooden doll artists borrow their designs from the folk tales, history, and art of the Russian people.

Invite students to trace the

(cont.)

Cultural Historical Note

origins of the nesting doll, using the Internet or library. For example, one theory is that matryoshka dolls were given to infants as a sign of fertility and long life. Students should also try to find the origin of the name *matryoshka.* One possible theory is that the name comes from the Russian word for grandmother, because the largest doll in the set represents the oldest woman in the family.

Students might enjoy bringing in folk art from their own cultures. They should explain what the piece is, its folk origins, if known, and the significance it has for them. Students can display the objects, with descriptions, in the classroom.

Cross-curricular Activities

Social Studies

Encourage students to research the Russian Revolution of 1917. They should pay particular attention to the forces behind the revolution and answer the following questions: Did the revolutionaries accomplish their goals? How did the revolution tie into the events of World War I? Students might also explain the connection between the Revolution of 1917 and the Cold War.

Historical Note

Catherine II, czarina of Russia, was born on April 21, 1729, in the Baltic seaport town of Stettin, then part of German Pomerania (now Szczecin, Poland). Her father was Prince Christian Augustus of Anhalt-Zerbst and she was christened Sophia Augusta Frederica. At the age of 15, she moved to Russia to wed the heir to the throne, Peter Fedorovich, later Peter III. They married in St. Petersburg on August 21, 1745, and Sophie was christened into the Orthodox Church as Yekaterina Aleksyevna.

Her efforts to become thoroughly Russian made her popular with the politicians who opposed her eccentric husband. On June 28, 1762, with the support of the Imperial Guard, she overthrew her husband the czar and was crowned Empress of Russia in the Dormition Cathedral of the Kremlin.

Catherine's rule is regarded as one of the most prosperous periods of the Russian empire. She made vast internal political reforms, waged two successful wars against the Ottoman Empire, encouraged the colonization of Alaska, and extended Russia's borders. A voracious reader of historical and philosophical works, Catherine corresponded with some of the greatest minds in Europe, including the French

(cont.)

Historical Art Museum, Nizhny Novgorod, Russia

babushkas to church. Another traditional costume is the *sarafan,* a long, colorful dress embroidered with mosaic pictures.

School is demanding in Russia, but in our free time my friends and I like to go to the central part of Moscow to look for adventure and to go to the discos. In the winter, we like to go into the forest to walk or to make snow statues and have snowball fights. We also like to watch old Russian movies, such as the Russian version of *Dr. Zhivago.*

Russia has produced many great artists, musicians, and writers. Aleksei Savrasov and Isaac Levitan are among the most famous Russian artists. Pyotr Tchaikovsky, Nikolai Rimsky-Korsakov, and Aleksandr Borodin made significant contributions to the world of music. Our best-known writers include Anton Chekhov, Fyodor Dostoyevsky, Leo Tolstoy, Boris Pasternak, Aleksandr Pushkin, Anna Akhmatova, and Nikolai Gogol. One of my favorite stories is "The Overcoat" by Gogol, which shows the unhappy lives of Russians before the Revolution.

My country has undergone many changes since President Mikhail Gorbachev declared *glasnost* back in the 1980s. Many things such as the economy and the government are unstable

Dining Room, Catherine's Palace, Pushkin

Historical Note (cont.)

philosophers Voltaire and Diderot. Catherine died on November 6, 1796, and was buried in the Cathedral of the St. Peter and St. Paul Fortress in St. Petersburg.

Literary Note

Denis says that one of his favorite stories is "The Overcoat" by Nikolai Gogol. Have students read this story (see page 993) to gain an understanding of life in Russia before the Revolution.

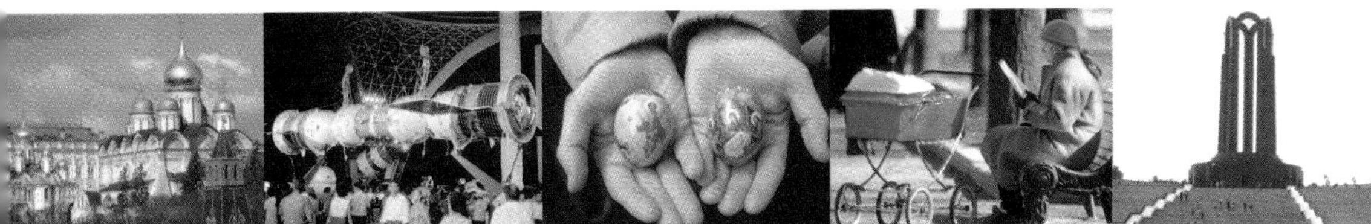

because we are really starting again from the beginning. Before its collapse in 1991, the USSR was made up of sixteen countries, whose people were required to speak Russian. Since *perestroika,* people in these countries have started to use their own languages again. Most Russians are Slavs, and the main religion is Orthodox Christianity. During Communism, practicing religion was dangerous. You could be fired from your job or kicked out of school if the authorities found out, so only elderly people practiced religion. Now a lot of young people are converting to Christianity. There are still many restrictions on personal freedom; for example, you have to have "papers" wherever you go.

In America, more people seem to have opportunities to choose what to do with their lives. In Russia, one must have money to have such choices—and not many have money. I have noticed that people smile more in America. In Russia, the faces are often sad or severe. Maybe this is because life in Russia can often be more difficult. The Russian wonders what will go wrong today, while the American seems more optimistic. ■

Danilov Monastery, Moscow

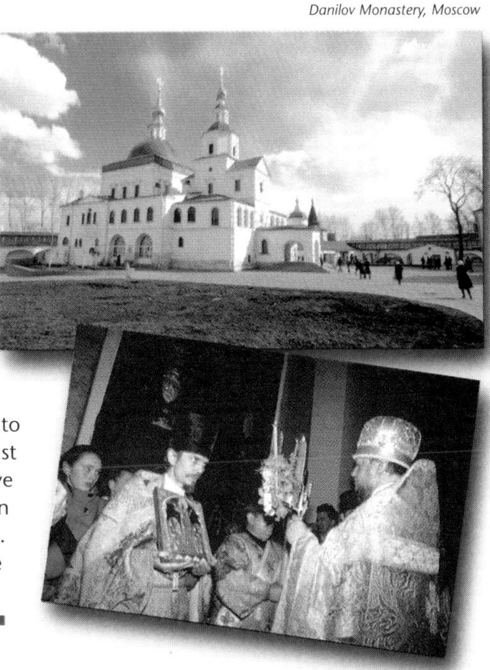

Easter celebration, Joy of All Sorrows Church, Moscow

Red Square with Kremlin and Lenin's Tomb, Moscow

Historical Note

Explain to students that the terms *glasnost,* or openness, and *perestroika,* or restructuring, were terms used by Mikhail Gorbachev to define the principles which he espoused during his years as general secretary and president. Beginning in 1985, Gorbachev strove to undo years of economic stagnation inherited from the Leonid Brezhnev era (1960–1964 and 1977–1982). Under Gorbachev, the government began to reorganize the Soviet economy and bureaucracy, and emphasized candor in discussion of social problems both internally and externally. Gorbachev won the Nobel Peace Prize in 1990 for his efforts.

Cross-curricular Activities

MATHEMATICS AND SCIENCES AND SOCIAL STUDIES

Denis notes on page 56 that his country has undergone many changes, including economic changes, since Gorbachev declared glasnost in the 1980s. Have students research some of the economic changes Russia has experienced. To start, students might research the ruble, the standard Russian currency. Using an online currency converter, students should find the exchange rate between American dollars and Russian rubles. Students should then investigate the cost of living in Russia, comparing prices for food, lodging, and clothing in Russia and America, as well as average income.

Historical Note

The Kremlin has long been the heart of Moscow, occupying ninety acres in the historic core of the city. The Moscow River lies to the south and Red Square, with Lenin's tomb, the Moscow Historical Museum, and St. Basil's Cathedral, forms the east border. The Kremlin's walls, built in the fifteenth century, are topped on each side by seven towers, including the Tower of Secrets and the Gothic and Renaissance Savior's Tower. The Kremlin was the residence of the czars until Peter the Great transferred the capital to St. Petersburg in 1712. Since 1918, when the capital was moved back to Moscow, the Kremlin has been Russia's political and administrative center. For many years, the Kremlin housed the KGB (Committee of State Security) and the notorious Lubyanka prison.

ADDITIONAL RESOURCES

READER'S GUIDE

- Selection Worksheet 1.5

ASSESSMENT PORTFOLIO

- Selection Check Test 2.1.9
- Selection Test 2.1.10

ESSENTIAL SKILLS PRACTICE BOOKS

- Study and Research 4.2

PREREADING EXTENSIONS

Invite students to hold a class discussion about government censorship, such as the kind Yevtushenko experienced from the Russian government. Why might a government feel threatened by the voices of its citizens? Is a government weakened when it allows social critics to speak, or is it weakened more when it fights desperately to keep people silent? Ask students to explain their responses.

SUPPORT FOR LEP STUDENTS

PRONUNCIATIONS OF PROPER NOUNS AND ADJECTIVES

Yev • gen • y Yev • tu • shen • ko (yiv gyā´nē yiv too´ shān´ kō)

ADDITIONAL VOCABULARY

colleagues—coworkers
descendants—offspring of a particular ancestor; generations that follow
pompous—arrogant; with an inflated opinion of oneself

PREREADING

"Conversation with an American Writer"
by Yevgeny Yevtushenko, translated by Herbert Marshall

RUSSIA

About the Author

YEVGENY YEVTUSHENKO
1933–

Yevgeny Yevtushenko, one of Russia's most acclaimed poets, has gained worldwide renown. He was graduated from the prestigious Gorki Literary Institute in Moscow. Yevtushenko first achieved fame in his homeland when he published a collection of poetry in 1955 entitled *Third Snow*. It was dangerous at that time in Russian history (soon after the death of Soviet leader Joseph Stalin) to criticize the government, but Yevtushenko did just that in his bold, honest poetry. Many of his works were censured for this reason. Nevertheless, he remained one of the Soviet Union's most notable literary figures, giving many dramatic poetry readings in Europe, Africa, and the United States.

During the 1980s, Yevtushenko began to experiment with literary forms outside of poetry. His first novel, *Wild Berries*, was a finalist for the Ritz Paris Hemingway prize in 1985, and his first feature film, *The Kindergarten,* played in the Soviet Union, England, and the United States. Yevtushenko was politically active during Mikhail Gorbachev's leadership, welcoming reforms to Soviet society. Today, Yevtushenko continues to write in a vastly changed and still-evolving Russia. His recent novel, *Don't Die Before Your Death* (1993), focuses on the changing politics in his homeland.

About the Selection

Yevtushenko has always embraced his political role as a poet by incorporating both public and personal themes in his work, as well as by speaking on current events. In "**Conversation with an American Writer**," Yevtushenko describes his frustration with his society's fear of speaking out honestly and openly. The poem was inspired by a visit to the United States, where Americans expressed their surprise that a Soviet writer could speak so honestly and openly about troubles in his homeland.

CONNECTIONS: Baby Yar

Baby Yar, (or Babiy Yar), a large ravine on the northern edge of the city of Kiev in the Ukraine, is the site of a mass grave of more than one hundred thousand victims killed by German Nazis between 1941 and 1943. While most of the victims were Russian Jews, others were Russian prisoners of war and communist government officials. As the German army retreated from the Soviet Union, the Nazis attempted to hide the evidence of the slaughter. During August and September of 1943, the bodies were hastily uncovered and burned. In 1961 Yevgeny Yevtushenko wrote a poem called "Baby Yar" in protest against plans to build a sports stadium on the site. Yevtushenko also addressed issues of Russian anti-Semitism. After Dmitry Shostakovich set the poem to music, it was performed in Moscow in 1962. Both poet and composer were reprimanded by Soviet authorities, who refused to acknowledge the primarily Jewish significance of a site where prominent Russians had been killed. To this day, the memorial that marks this site makes no mention of the Jewish dead.

GOALS/OBJECTIVES

Studying this lesson will enable students to

- appreciate a political poem related to issues of free speech
- discuss the life and work of Yevgeny Yevtushenko
- understand the role of Baby Yar, a large ravine in the Ukraine, in Russian history
- define the literary terms *aim* and *irony*
- practice thinking skills

What is an honest person? Do you consider yourself to be honest? Have you ever been in a situation in which you were afraid to tell the truth? Do you feel that you made the right decision? In your journal, record your views about honesty and dishonesty and describe an occasion when you were torn as to whether you should tell the truth.

"Conversation with an American Writer"

YEVGENY YEVTUSHENKO, TRANSLATED BY HERBERT MARSHALL

"You're a fearless young man—"
they tell me. . . .
It's not true.
I've never been fearless.
I've considered it unworthy, simply,
to sink to my colleagues' cowardice.

I didn't shake any sort of foundations.
Laughed at the false and pompous,
that's all.
Wrote—that's all.
Never wrote <u>denunciations</u>.
And tried to say
just what I thought.

Yes,
talented people I defended,
<u>branded</u> the incapable,
into literature crawling,
but did this because, in general, one has to,
and now about my fearlessness they're talking.

Oh, with feelings of bitter shame
our descendants,

1 Does the speaker consider himself "fearless"? What does the speaker consider it unworthy to do?

2 At what has the speaker laughed?

3 In what way does the speaker describe his writing?

4 Why did the speaker distinguish the "talented" from the "incapable" in his writing?

WORDS FOR EVERYDAY USE

de • nun • ci • a • tion (dē nun´sē ā´shən) *n.,* public accusation
brand (brand) *vt.,* mark with disgrace; stigmatize

READER'S JOURNAL

Students might also explore in their journals the following questions:

- Why it is often difficult for people to be honest and open about their feelings? What do people fear?
- How might it feel to live in a nation in which citizens are forbidden to express their honest opinions?

ANSWERS TO GUIDED READING QUESTIONS

1 The speaker does not consider himself to be fearless. The speaker considers it unworthy to sink to his colleagues' cowardice.

2 The speaker has laughed at the false and the pompous.

3 The speaker never wrote denunciations. He just tried to say what he thought.

4 The speaker feels that one has an obligation to distinguish the "talented" from the "incapable."

SPELLING AND VOCABULARY WORDS FROM THE SELECTION

brand
denunciation
debunk

VOCABULARY IN CONTEXT

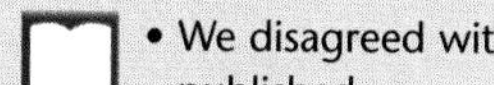

- We disagreed with the columnist and wrote a <u>denunciation</u> of his ideas, which the newspaper published.
- Do not <u>brand</u> that person a thief unless you know for sure that he is guilty.

Answers to Guided Reading Questions

❶ Our descendants will remember those strange times when simple honesty was called fearlessness.

Selection Check Test with Answers

EX. What do the people call the speaker in the selection?
They call him a fearless young man.

1. What did the speaker always try to do in his writing?
He always tried to write exactly what he thought.

2. Who did the speaker defend?
The speaker defended talented people.

3. Who did the speaker brand?
The speaker branded the incapable.

4. Why did the speaker always write the truth?
He wrote the truth because he felt he had to write the truth.

5. What will our descendants remember with "bitter shame"?
They will remember the time when simple honesty was called fearlessness.

Quotables

"Truth exists; only falsehood has to be invented."

—Georges Braque, *Pensées sur l'art*

The Soviet Union enlisted many artists to produce propaganda but did not allow individual recognition. The artist of this poster remains unknown.

❶ *What will our descendants remember?*

debunking worthlessness,
will remember
those times
so strange
when simple honesty
was called fearlessness. ■

Words for Everyday Use

de • bunk (dē buŋk´) *vt.,* expose false or exaggerated claims or pretensions

Vocabulary in Context

• The group will work to <u>debunk</u> the phony promises of that leader.

Responding to the Selection

As a class, brainstorm examples of how the speaker, as an honest critic, might evaluate current American life in such arenas as politics, the economy, social issues, the media, or the environment.

Reviewing the Selection

RECALLING / **INTERPRETING**

1. What do people call the speaker? ▶▶ Why do people feel this way about him?
2. Does the speaker agree with others' opinions of himself? ▶▶ What does the speaker consider himself to be? What is the speaker's attitude toward himself and his "fearlessness"?
3. Whom did the speaker defend? Whom did he brand? ▶▶ Why do you suppose the speaker felt the need to classify these types of people in his literature?
4. According to the speaker, what times will our descendants remember? ▶▶ Why might our descendants remember these times with "bitter shame"? How do you imagine the speaker will remember these times? Why?

SYNTHESIZING

5. In the selection, what word do others use synonymously with honesty? Why do you think the speaker discriminates between these two words?

Understanding Literature (Questions for Discussion)

1. **Aim**. A writer's **aim** is the primary purpose his or her work is meant to achieve. Works can be classified as having four broad aims: to express, to persuade, to inform, and to create a work of art. What is Yevtushenko's aim in this piece?
2. **Irony. Irony** is a difference between appearance and reality. Types of irony include the following: **dramatic irony,** in which something is known by the reader or audience but unknown to the characters; **verbal irony,** in which a statement is made that implies its opposite; and **irony of situation,** in which an event occurs that violates the expectations of the characters, the reader, or the audience. Why is this poem ironic? What type of irony does the poet employ?

ANSWERS FOR UNDERSTANDING LITERATURE

Responses will vary. Possible responses are given.

1. Aim. Yevtushenko's aim in this piece is to describe what has become of honesty in his society. Yevtushenko is trying to express and inform. He may also be trying to persuade others to return honesty to a common, not extraordinary, behavior.

2. Irony. This speaker describes with irony the fact that honesty is considered to be fearlessness. To the speaker, it is ironic that as an honest poet he is regarded as a hero. By violating the audience's ideas about honesty, the writer employs irony of situation in this poem.

RESPONDING TO THE SELECTION

You might allow students to meet in groups to discuss what the speaker of the poem might say about these areas of American life.

ANSWERS FOR REVIEWING THE SELECTION

RECALLING AND INTERPRETING

1. **Recalling.** The people call the speaker fearless. **Interpreting.** People feel the speaker is fearless because he always speaks out, laughing at the false and pompous and branding the incapable.

2. **Recalling.** The speaker does not consider himself to be fearless. **Interpreting.** The speaker considers himself to be honest. He simply writes what he thinks, refusing to hide his feelings and ideas about issues and injustices.

3. **Recalling.** The speaker defended the talented people and branded the incapable. **Interpreting.** The speaker felt that those who were talented deserved to be heard and that people should be warned about those who were "incapable."

4. **Recalling.** Descendants will remember the times when simple honesty was labeled as fearlessness. **Interpreting.** It might seem shameful that simple honesty was not expected of people, but rather viewed as extraordinary. The speaker is likely to remember these times with disappointment in the attitudes of others, but also with some satisfaction, knowing that he always stood his ground.

SYNTHESIZING

Responses will vary. Possible responses are given.

5. Fearlessness is used synonymously with honesty. The speaker feels that honesty is to be expected and that fearlessness should be reserved to describe the heroic.

► Additional practice of the skills taught in this lesson is provided in the Essential Skills Practice Book: Study and Research 4.2.

ADDITIONAL QUESTIONS AND ACTIVITIES

Ask each student to make a chart of the different thinking skills outlined in this lesson—classifying, comparing and contrasting, estimating and quantifying, analyzing, and generalizing and deducing.

Making the chart will help students to remember the different thinking skills, and the completed chart will serve as a reference tool when students must call on different types of thinking skills.

THINKING SKILLS

Throughout this textbook, you will be called upon to answer questions that will require you to use different types of thinking. You may be asked to classify works or different elements of literature, to compare and contrast two different literary works, to estimate or quantify information to support your opinion in an essay, to analyze a work of literature and to examine its parts to see how they are related to the whole of the literary work, and to make certain generalizations and deductions. Although you may not be aware of it, these are types of thinking that you probably use almost every day. These types of thinking are defined and examples of their uses in the study of literature are given below. See the Language Arts Survey 4.2, "Types of Thinking," for more information.

CLASSIFYING

To **classify** is to put into classes or categories. In the study of literature, classifying can provide a natural way of organizing a piece of writing.

EXAMPLE If you were assigned to write an essay comparing and contrasting "Conversation with an American Writer" with *Requiem*, another selection by a Russian poet in this book, you might begin by looking for similarities in both works. To do so, you might classify both works as poems written by Russians during a period of Soviet repression.

COMPARING AND CONTRASTING

To **compare** and **contrast** *A* with *B* is to examine *A* and *B* in order to describe their similarities and differences. To **compare** *A* and *B* is to describe the similarities between them. To **contrast** *A* with *B* is to describe the differences between them. Comparing and contrasting different literary writers, works, periods, forms, and techniques is essential to the study of literature.

EXAMPLE In the essay proposed for classifying, you noted that both works can be classified as poems written by Russians during a period of Soviet oppression. Upon closer examination, you might discover that the Yevtushenko poem is relatively straightforward, while the Akhmatova poem is filled with imagery and figurative language. You might also discover that the poems differ greatly in mood and tone.

ESTIMATING AND QUANTIFYING

To support your point in an argument or in a persuasive essay, you need to provide facts, and often the facts you need are numbers or **quantities. Estimating** involves finding approximate quantities.

Russian Scene. *Vassily Kandinsky, 1904*

EXAMPLE If you were writing the comparison and contrast essay previously described, you might claim that Akhmatova's tone is much bleaker than Yevtushenko's. You might support this opinion by quantifying, pointing out that Akhmatova lived from 1889 to 1966 and that the poem *Requiem* was inspired by her son's incarceration during Stalin's years of oppression; Stalin died in 1953, long before Yevtushenko (1933–) wrote many of his works. Thus, it is only natural that Akhmatova, who experienced Stalin's oppression first hand, had a bleaker world vision than Yevtushenko, who wrote during more lenient times.

ANALYZING

To **analyze** something is to break or divide it in your imagination into its parts and examine the parts and the relationships between them. You can analyze anything in many different ways.

EXAMPLE For an analysis of "Conversation with an American Writer," you might look at words, metaphors, mood, theme, tone, arguments, supporting details, genre, or purpose.

GENERALIZING AND DEDUCING

To **generalize** is to make a general or universal claim based on some particular observation. Generalizations are often false, because they make claims that are broader than what is strictly justified by the information available. A generalization is more likely to be

ART NOTE

Vassily Kandinsky (1866-1944) was a Russian abstract painter and theorist who is considered today to be the originator of abstract art.

ADDITIONAL QUESTIONS AND ACTIVITIES

As they read, ask students to think of possible future scenarios, outside of school, in which they might need the thinking skills outlined in this lesson.

Possible responses might include:

- classifying—organizing a group of people according to their strengths and interests; organizing items in a store or at a town fair
- comparing and contrasting—trying to decide on a place to live; trying to decide between two jobs or colleges
- estimating and quantifying—figuring out how many people were at a show or how many read a particular magazine
- analyzing—finding a solution to a personal problem or writing a business report
- generalizing and deducing—trying to define a moral code or deciding which candidates to elect

Answers for Skills Activities

THINKING SKILLS

1. The poem "Conversation with an American Writer" should be classified as a lyric poem.
2. Students might say that, like Yevtushenko's "Conversation with an American Writer," Cavafy's purpose in writing "Poseidonians" was to point out ironies in the situation of a particular society. Students might say that the poems differ in that "Conversation with an American Writer" is more personal, told from a first-person point of view. Cavafy's poem is told with more distance.
3. Although exact numbers will differ, students should estimate that of the hundred thousand people killed, most were Jews.
4. Students might divide the poem into tone, theme, and structure.
5. As an example of overgeneralization, students might say, based on "Conversation with an American Writer," that Yevtushenko believes that all people are liars, or that Yevtushenko has never told a single lie. A sound deduction is that Yevtushenko places value on truthfulness, or that Yevtushenko lived in Russia.

true when it is based on something more than just observation. The formation of a general rule based on reasoning—rather than on mere observation—is called a deduction. **Deducing** or inferring is coming to a logical conclusion based on facts, called premises.

EXAMPLE After reading "Conversation with an American Writer" and reading about Yevtushenko's life, you might make the generalization, "All Russian poets are politically active and write about the political climate in their country." Such an overgeneralization would prove grossly incorrect. However, by closely examining Yevtushenko's text, you might reasonably deduce that Yevtushenko is offended when honesty is considered an act of incredible bravery, citing lines 20–27 as your facts, or premises.

ACTIVITY

1. There are many different types of poetry. Poetry, for example, can be broken into three broad categories: lyric, narrative, and epic. Look up the definitions of these types of poetry in the Handbook of Literary Terms, which begins on page 1300. Then, classify "Conversation with an American Writer" as lyric, narrative, or epic poetry.

2. A writer's **aim** is the primary purpose his or her work is meant to achieve. Compare and contrast Cavafy's purpose in writing "Poseidonians" with Yevtushenko's purpose in writing "Conversation with an American Writer."

3. Through his art, Yevtushenko pointed out the atrocity of the extermination of Russian Jews at Baby Yar. How many people were killed and buried en masse there? How many of these people were Jews? How many were non-Jewish Russian prisoners of war or communist officials? (Note: If you cannot find exact numbers, you may have to estimate your response.) Possible sources include encyclopedias, online information, and books on Russian participation in World War II or on the Holocaust.

4. If you were assigned to write an analysis of "Conversation with an American Writer," into what parts could you divide the poem for examination?

5. Make at least one overgeneralization and one sound deduction about either Yevgeny Yevtushenko or "Conversation with an American Writer."

PASSPORT TO INDIA

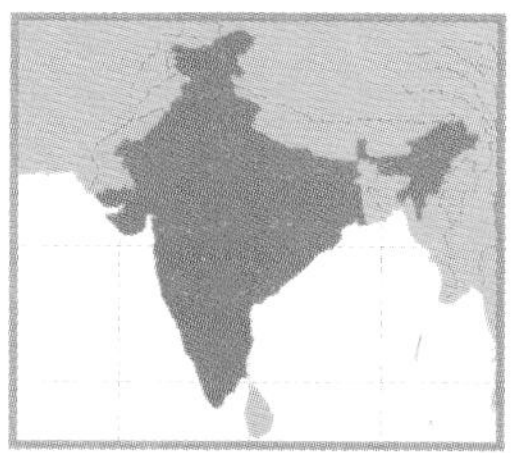

Namaskar! My name is Avik Mohan. I come from India, the land where the Indus River flows.

With its twenty-five states and five union territories, India is one-third the size of the United States with roughly three times the population. There are sixteen national languages and thousands of dialects. Hindi is the declared "link" language and English is the official language. An average Indian knows his or her "mother-tongue" (the language spoken in his or her state), a fair amount of Hindi, and passable English. Travel within India is similar to visiting many foreign lands, all in the same country.

Because my father was in the army, we moved every two to three years and I saw a lot of India. My grandparents lived in Delhi, where I spent most of my school breaks. Delhi is a city of teeming millions. It gets so hot in the summer that the tar on the roads becomes soft and people make money selling drinking water to those who have to be outside.

India has no state religion. The majority of Indians consider themselves Hindus, and Muslims are the second largest group. India also has Sikhs, Parsees, Jews, Christians, Zoroastrians, and many aboriginal religions. Until my own generation, inter-religion marriages were rare, and most occupations, except the civil services, were inherited. All this is changing rapidly. Now major

Avik Mohan
Delhi, India

Udaipur woman

Sand dunes, Thar Desert, Rajasthan

SUPPORT FOR LEP STUDENTS

Pronunciations of Proper Nouns and Adjectives

A • vik Mo • han (ä´vik mō´ hän)
Del • hi (del´ē)
Di • wa • li (di väl´ē)
Gu • lal (go͞o läl´)
gup (gup)
Hin • di (hin´dē)
Ho • li (hō´ lē)
Id (ēd)
In • dus (in´dus)
na • mas • kar (na´ mäs kär´)
Par • sees (pär´sēz)
Sikhs (sēks)
Zor • o • as • tri • ans (zôr´ō as´ trē əns)

Cross-curricular Activities

ARTS AND HUMANITIES AND SOCIAL STUDIES

Namaskar, Hindi for "hello," comes from Sanskrit, an ancient Indo-Iranian language that is the root of many languages spoken in the Middle East. Ask students to consult a chart of Indo-European languages in a dictionary or encyclopedia to find some of the other languages derived from Sanskrit.

SOCIAL STUDIES

On a map of India, have students locate the Indus and Ganges rivers, as well as Delhi, Bombay, Calcutta, and other major Indian cities. Point out features, such as the Himalayas, the tallest mountain range in the world, to the north; the Thar desert to the west; the Arabian Sea to the southwest; and the Indian Ocean to the east.

Cultural/Historical Note

Udaipur is a city in the state of Rajasthan. Built around Lake Pichola, Udaipur has been dubbed the "Venice of the East" because of its waterways. With its island palaces and plentiful water supply, Udaipur is an oasis in the midst of the desert plains of Rajasthan.

Cultural/Historical Note

The city of Delhi is comprised of Old Delhi and New Delhi. Old Delhi was largely built by Mughal invaders during the reign of the Mughal emperor Shah Jahan (1628–1658). Visitors to the city are enchanted by Old Delhi's bazaars, fragrant spice shops, and majestic temples. New Delhi is expensive, fast paced, and fairly Westernized. It was established as the capital in 1911.

Like many other large cities around the world, Delhi suffers from problems of urban growth: air pollution, traffic congestion, the growth of slums, and the movement of affluent people to outlying suburbs, which results in the segregation of socioeconomic groups and an economically poor downtown area. Students may wish to discuss problems associated with urbanization.

Cultural/Historical Note

According to Avik, there are no widely accepted guidelines to determine whether someone is a Hindu. "Caste, practicing yoga, eating a certain kind of diet, or holding the cow and the Ganges River to be sacred do not alone or in combination make one a Hindu," Avik notes, "just as denial of the above statements do not bar one from being a Hindu. A famous guru, in response to the question, 'Who is a Hindu?' once said, 'Whosoever chooses to be.'"

Cultural/Historical Note

You may wish to share more information with students about the Indian holidays Avik mentions. *Diwali* is a five-day "Festival of Lights" which commemorates the return to India of Lord Rama and his wife Sita after their victory over the demon-king of Sri Lanka, as told in Hindu scripture (see the *Ramayana,* page 560). It is celebrated with fairs in parks and dazzling fireworks displays that light up the night skies.

Id-ul-Fitr is a day of Muslim feasting and celebration held at the end of the Ramadan fast. Thousands gather for prayers on this day. *Id-ul-Zuhr* is a day for Muslims to recall the sacrifice of Ibrahim's son by feasting on mutton and sweet vermicelli and by saying prayers.

Cultural/Historical Note

The Mughals, a Muslim people from central Asia, ruled in India for more than three hundred years—beginning in 1526, when Babur and his Mughal army defeated Ibrahim, the sultan of Delhi, and ending in 1858, when the British Empire assumed complete control of the Indian subcontinent. The Mughal legacy is still apparent in (cont.)

Armenian Church, Madras, Taminadu

cities such as Bombay and Delhi are cosmopolitan in every sense of the word.

Since India is such a smorgasbord of religions, festivals are frequent and communities make them colorful in attempts to outdo each other. *Holi*, *Diwali*, and *Id* are the major Indian festivals. Even though the first two are "Hindu" festivals and Id is an "Islamic" festival, most Indians overlook these distinctions and celebrate all with gusto. My personal favorite is *Holi*, which signals the onset of spring. The focal point of *Holi* is the use of *Gulal,* a red powder which adults gently put on friends and relatives the first time they see each other during the celebration. Young people are wilder, using powders of every conceivable hue, water pistols, water balloons, and buckets of water which they throw on anyone they can catch. It usually takes a while for the colors to wash off, and it is not unusual to see people on the streets with purple, orange, or yellow faces and hair for days afterward.

The diversity of Indian culture makes Indian cuisine phenomenal. There is something to suit every palate. A common misconception is that Indian food is spicy. In India

Festival boat, Dal Lake, Srinagar, Kashmir

Amar Sagar, Jain Temple

Cultural/Historical Note (cont.)

India, especially in its architecture. Perhaps the most famous example is the Taj Mahal, a tomb built in the mid-1600s by Emperor Shah Jahan for his wife Mumtaz Mahal. This beautiful domed building, located in the city of Agra, is considered one of the seven wonders of the world.

Students might be interested in learning more about the Mughals. Ask them to research Mughal history, their rule in India, and the art, architecture, and other aspects of their culture. As an alternative, students could research other conquerors and rulers of India, such as the Aryans, the Macedonians led by Alexander the Great, the Mauryan emperors, and the Muslim armies from Ghor who established the Delhi Sultanate.

this varies; people in southern India tend to eat spicy food year round, while northern and central Indians typically eat it in the winter. Eastern Indians usually eat mild food. Most Indian meals are accompanied by cucumber, tomato, and onion salad, and homemade unflavored yogurt. These foods are eaten with the main course and serve to temper spicy foods as well. Most Indians are vegetarians and even nonvegetarians eat meat rarely.

The favorite Indian pastime is *gup,* which means "gossip." Most villages have a community banyan tree with a large circular platform constructed around it. This is where anyone with spare time participates in *gup.* Although gossip usually has a negative connotation, *gup* simply means talking about topics as diverse as politics, philosophy, business, and, of course, the latest *faux pas* a mutual acquaintance has committed.

Indian teenagers enjoy the same activities as Americans; however, they have less time and money to do so. It is virtually impossible for a teenager to get a well-paying job due to the overqualified Indian workforce and high unemployment rate. Also, the buying power of currency in India is much lower. A

Himalayan foothills

Camel driver

Udaipur, by the lake

Bronze image of Shiva

Cross-curricular Activities

APPLIED ARTS

Students might be interested in making Avik's recipe for *Lassi,* a popular summer drink in India.

Lassi

Ingredients:

- 1 cup chilled, plain, unsweetened yogurt
- 1/4 cup crushed ice
- 2–3 teaspoons sugar
- a few drops of rose water or kewra essence

Preparation:

Blend ingredients and enjoy!

If you cannot find rose water or *kewra* essence at your grocery store, look in the phone book for a specialty Indian grocery store. Almost all of them stock these items.

Cultural/Historical Note

The British takeover of India was gradual. It began with the British East India Company, a company commissioned in the early 1600s by Queen Elizabeth I to create a monopoly of trade with the Mughals. When local princes and the rivalry of the French East India Company threatened the interests of the British traders, they intervened in Indian political affairs. By the late 1700s, as Mughal power declined, the British government moved in to regulate trade and, in effect, took control of the government. India became a British colony in 1858 and remained so until 1947.

For more information on this subject, refer students to Connections: Indian Nationalism and Independence, on page 204, and Connections: The Impact of British Rule on Indian Society, on page 1094.

Cross-curricular Activities

SOCIAL STUDIES

India was partitioned in August 1947, and Pakistan, a new state, was carved out. Bangladesh seceded from Pakistan in 1971. Ask students to work in small groups to research why the state of Pakistan was created or why Bangladesh chose to become a separate nation. Some groups may wish to research the conflict over the disputed territory of Kashmir. They could consult periodicals or the Internet to investigate what is currently happening in their chosen region. Each group should present its findings on Pakistan, Bangladesh, or Kashmir to their classmates.

Cross-curricular Activities

MATHEMATICS AND SCIENCES AND SOCIAL STUDIES

For centuries, devout Hindus in India have held the Ganges River sacred. Many Hindus make pilgrimages to the holy city of Varanasi on the Ganges, and many bring their dead there to be cremated. The very poor, who cannot afford wood, often dump the bodies of loved ones directly into the river. Ironically, these practices, which are centered around Hindu reverence for the Ganges, are contributing to its pollution. Nevertheless, these activities make up only part of the problem. Ask students to form small groups and research the causes of pollution in the Ganges. What are some of the ways it is being dealt with today? Students might read about the Ganges Action Plan, an environmental plan launched in the mid-1980s, and compare its cleanup methods with those used to clean up water sources in their part of the country. As an alternative, ask them to research other pollution problems in India.

SOCIAL STUDIES

Mohandas Gandhi (1869–1948) was a great political and spiritual leader who began the independence movement in India. Jawaharlal Nehru (1889–1964) succeeded Gandhi as the leader of the Indian National Congress in 1928. He became the first prime minister of India after he proclaimed independence in August 1947. Inform students that while Nehru and Gandhi were united in their struggle to end British rule, they disagreed on what values would shape the new India. Ask students to form groups of four and to research Gandhi and Nehru in order to compare and contrast the views of the two leaders. What ideas did they share? How did their visions of the future of India differ? Which vision is closer to the India of today?

Lake Palace, former Maharajah's Palace

person working a minimum-wage job in India could buy eight sodas with a full day's wages, while an American teenager could buy the same after working only one hour. The demanding academic system also prevents the Indian student from having much spare time.

School in India is highly competitive. College entrance examinations are so taxing that most students begin preparing for them at the end of ninth grade, and students will often take a whole year off after high school to study for them. Ten- or twelve-hour study sessions are common. Less than 1 percent of those who try get into the IITs, the premier Indian Institutes of Technology. Harvard, in comparison, has an acceptance rate of over 10 percent. Parents often pressure their children to become doctors or engineers, even if they would prefer another career. This might be difficult to understand, but in our culture, individual desires are usually secondary to the expectations of the family. ■

Cattle in the streets

Mounted battalion

Traffic police

Cross-curricular Activities

ARTS AND HUMANITIES AND SOCIAL STUDIES

India has the largest film industry in the world. The South Indian film industry alone produces more films than Hollywood. The Hindi (North Indian) film industry, centered in Bombay, has been nicknamed Bollywood. According to Avik, many Indian films depict conflicts between classes (rich woman falls in love with poor man) and between loyalty and duty (policeman finds out that his brother is a criminal).

Ask students who are interested to check their local video store for Indian films with English subtitles. They could view one of these movies and write a short review of it to share with the class.

PREREADING

from *Nectar in a Sieve*
by Kamala Markandaya

INDIA

About the Author

Kamala Markandaya (1923–). Kamala Markandaya was born and educated in southern India. When she was in her late thirties she moved to England and eventually became a prolific novelist. Her early novels illustrate the political and economic struggles that India has faced. Markandaya's work also focuses on the pressures of modernization on traditional Indian society. Her titles include *Nectar in a Sieve* (1954), *The Silence of Desire* (1960), *Possession* (1963), *A Handful of Rice* (1966), *The Coffer Dams* (1969), and *The Nowhere Man* (1972). Many consider *The Golden Honeycomb* (1977), a book about Indian independence from British rule, to be her most ambitious work.

About the Selection

Nectar in a Sieve, Kamala Markandaya's first novel, opens with the following quotation by Samuel Taylor Coleridge:

> *Work without hope draws nectar in a sieve,*
> *And hope without an object cannot live.*

These words make a fitting introduction to a novel about the life of an Indian peasant woman who struggles to care for her family and to hold onto hope, even as she faces the famine and poverty that gripped India during the period of British rule. In this excerpt, the narrator tries to deal with the changes in her quiet village brought on by the opening of a large tannery. She and her friends, Kunthi, Janaki, and Kali, struggle in different ways to adapt to a new environment and to the influx of new people and cultures.

CONNECTIONS: Mohandas Gandhi

Mohandas Gandhi, who is often given the title *Mahatma,* meaning "great soul," was a spiritual teacher and a leader of India's move toward independence from British rule. Gandhi was a firm believer in passive resistance, a nonviolent type of rebellion in which people show resistance to government activities by refusing to cooperate with them. He spent several years in jail for leading this resistance movement.

Gandhi also believed strongly that all people were equal under one god, and he worked to end the caste system in India, a system which divided people into rigid social classes according to birth. Traditionally, people could never leave the classes into which they were born, nor could they associate with people outside of their own caste. Indian independence from Britain was secured by 1947, but Gandhi remained unhappy with the continuing violence between the Hindu and Muslim populations of India and often visited troubled areas in an attempt to end the hostilities. He was assassinated during a prayer vigil in 1948 by a Hindu extremist who opposed his tolerance for Muslims.

ADDITIONAL RESOURCES

READER'S GUIDE
- Selection Worksheet 1.6

ASSESSMENT PORTFOLIO
- Selection Check Test 2.1.11
- Selection Test 2.1.12

ESSENTIAL SKILLS PRACTICE BOOKS
- Writing 1.20

PREREADING EXTENSIONS

Tell students that the methods of protest used by Dr. Martin Luther King, Jr. during the American Civil Rights movement were similar to those used by Gandhi. Like Gandhi, King used nonviolent methods of opposition, including boycotts and sit-ins.

SUPPORT FOR LEP STUDENTS

PRONUNCIATIONS OF PROPER NOUNS AND ADJECTIVES

Jan • a • ki (jan´ä kē)
Ka • li (kä´ lē)
Ka • mal • a Mar • kan • day • a (ka mäl´ə mär kən dī´yə)
Kunth • i (koonth´ē)

ADDITIONAL VOCABULARY

colony—people living in a distinct group apart from others
laden—covered with, weighed down with
unfettered—unchained, unrestrained
whitewash—thin white paint

GOALS/OBJECTIVES

Studying this lesson will enable students to

- empathize with a narrator who struggles to maintain hope while facing poverty and drastic changes in her native India
- discuss the life and work of Kamala Markandaya
- discuss the life of Mohandas Gandhi
- define the literary terms *point of view* and *tone*
- study the parts of a critical essay and then write a short critical essay

READER'S JOURNAL

Suggest to students that they think about the kinds of activities available in each setting. What kinds of people would they be most likely to meet in each setting? Would they like to try one or the other for a day or a week?

Answers to Guided Reading Questions

❶ Kunthi considers the tannery to be a boon because her sons are bringing home good wages and the town is growing.

❷ The narrator prefers the quiet village life of the past. She has noticed that the village has become dirty, noisy, and filled with crime. She believes that people are more interested in money than they are in anything else.

SPELLING AND VOCABULARY WORDS FROM THE SELECTION

boon	idle
compensation	uncouth
hooligan	

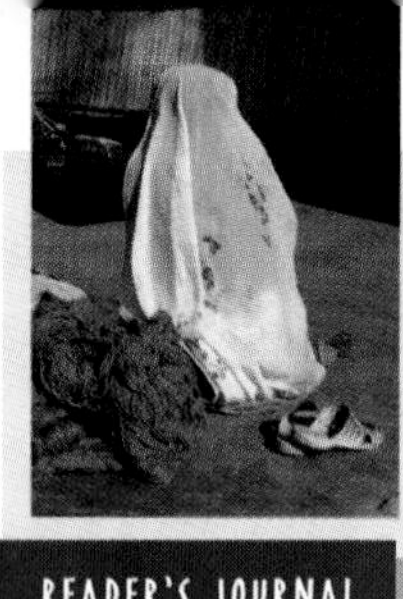

READER'S JOURNAL

What are some of the advantages of living in a busy town that attracts large businesses and new people? What are some of the advantages of living in a small village, in which people know one another and small businesses thrive? What would it be like to have to move from one to the other? In your journal, write about what you would need to do to adapt.

FROM

Nectar in a Sieve

KAMALA MARKANDAYA

❶ *Why does Kunthi find the tannery to be a "boon"?*

❷ *Does the narrator prefer the quiet village life of the past or the growing town in which she now lives? What changes has she noticed in her town?*

Kunthi's two eldest sons were among the first in the village to start work at the tannery,[1] and between them they brought home more than a man's wages.

"You see," said Kunthi. "The tannery is a boon to us. Have I not said so since it began? We are no longer a village either, but a growing town. Does it not do you good just to think of it?"

"Indeed no," said I, "for it is even as I said, and our money buys less and less. As for living in a town—if town this is—why, there is nothing I would fly from sooner if I could go back to the sweet quiet of village life. Now it is all noise and crowds everywhere, and rude young hooligans idling in the street and dirty bazaars and uncouth behaviour, and no man thinks of another but schemes only for his money."

"Words and words," said Kunthi. "Stupid words. No wonder they call us senseless peasant women; but I am not and never will be. There is no earth in my breeding."

"If there were you would be the better for it," said I wrathfully, "for then your values would be true."

Kunthi only shrugged her delicate shoulders and left us. She spent a lot of her time making unnecessary journeys into the town where, with her good looks and provocative body, she could be sure of admiration, and more, from the young men. At first the women said it and the men said they were jealous; then men too began to notice and remark on it and wonder why her husband did nothing. "Now if *I* were in his place," they said . . . but they had ordinary wives, not a woman with fire and beauty in her and the skill to use them: besides which, he was a quiet, dull man.

"Let her be," said Janaki. "She is a trollop, and is anxious only that there should be a supply of men."

Her voice held both anger and a bitter hopelessness: for a long time now her husband's

1. **tannery.** Place where animal hides are tanned, or made into leather

WORDS FOR EVERYDAY USE

boon (bo͞on) *n.* benefit
hoo • li • gan (ho͞o´li gən) *n.,* hoodlum or lawless person, especially a young one
i • dle (īd´'l) *vi.,* move aimlessly, waste time
un • couth (un ko͞oth´) *adj.,* crude

Vocabulary in Context

- A new public library will surely be a boon to the city.
- The bystanders described a young hooligan running away from the scene of the crime.
- Jan said, "Let me help you—I don't want to idle through the afternoon."
- I cringed at my sister's loud and uncouth remark.

Indian Barbers—Saharanpore. Edwin Lord Weeks, c. 1895. Josyln Art Museum, Omaha, NB

shop had been doing badly. He was unable to compete with the other bigger shopkeepers whom the easy money to be had from the tanners had drawn to the new town.

A few days after our conversation the shop finally closed down. Nobody asked: "Where do you go from here?" *They* did not say, "What is to become of us?" We waited, and one day they came to bid us farewell, carrying their possessions, with their children trailing behind, all but the eldest, whom the tannery had claimed. Then they were gone, and the shopkeepers were glad that there was less competition, and the worker who moved into their hut was pleased to have a roof over his head, and we remembered them for a while and then took up our lives again.

It was a great sprawling growth, this tannery. It grew and flourished and spread. Not a month went by but somebody's land was swallowed up, another building appeared. Day and night the tanning went on. A never-ending line of carts brought the raw material in—thousands of skins, goat, calf, lizard and snake skins—and took them away again tanned, dyed and finished. It seemed impossible that markets could be found for such quantities—or that so many animals existed—but so it was, incredibly.

① *What happens to the small shop as a result of the new tannery in town? Why are other shopkeepers glad?*

ANSWERS TO GUIDED READING QUESTIONS

① The small shop closes down, and the other shopkeepers are glad, because it means less competition for them.

QUOTABLES

"It is impossible to conduct strictly honest business. . . . What is true is that honesty is incompatible with the amassing of a large fortune."

—Mohandas Gandhi

ADDITIONAL QUESTIONS AND ACTIVITIES

Share with students the above quotation and then ask them to answer the following questions:

1. Do you think the narrator of *Nectar in a Sieve* would agree with Gandhi's statement about business and wealth? Explain your response.
2. Do you agree with all, part, or none of Gandhi's statement? Explain your response.
3. In your opinion, what are honest and wholesome ways for a business to prosper, and what are dishonest and selfish ways for a business to prosper?

ANSWERS

Responses will vary. Possible responses are given.

1. The narrator in this story prefers other values to the pursuit of wealth.
2. *Responses will vary.*
3. Students may say that business that protects the health and happiness of the public and individuals is wholesome and that business that sacrifices the well-being of others to the bottom line is selfish.

Answers to Guided Reading Questions

❶ Muslims are officials at the tannery. The Muslims live in a small colony in brick cottages with red tiled roofs.

❷ Kali's husband feels that talk of exchanging their lives for the Muslim women's lives is useless, because they are different from one another and will never be alike.

❸ The narrator feels sorry for them because they must keep themselves covered at all times and cannot feel the warm sun and breezes on their skin. Neither are they able to mix with men and work beside them. Kali does not feel sorry for them because, unlike her, they have plenty of money.

❹ The narrator does not like the closed doors or the shuttered windows of the Muslim woman's home.

Selection Check Test with Answers

EX. Does the narrator prefer a quiet village or a growing town?
The narrator prefers the quiet village of the past.

1. What changes has the narrator noticed in her town?
The village has become dirty, noisy, and filled with crime.

2. What happens to the small shop as a result of the new tannery in town?
The small shop closes down.

3. What kinds of people are officials at the tannery?
Muslims are officials at the tannery.

4. Why does the narrator feel sorry for the wives of the Muslim officials?
They are forced to keep themselves covered at all times.

5. Why does the narrator never return to the Muslim woman's home to sell vegetables?
The narrator does not like the closed doors or the shuttered windows of the woman's home.

❶ *What kinds of people are officials at the tannery? Where do some of them live?*

❷ *What talk does Kali's husband feel is useless? Why does he feel this way?*

❸ *Why does the narrator feel sorry for the wives of the Muslim officials? Why doesn't the narrator's friend, Kali, feel sorry for them as well?*

❹ *Why doesn't the narrator ever return to the Muslim woman's home to sell vegetables?*

The officials of the tannery had increased as well. Apart from the white man we had first seen—who owned the tannery and lived by himself—there were some nine or ten Muslims under him. They formed a little colony of their own, living midway between the town and open country in brick cottages with whitewashed walls and red tiled roofs. The men worked hard, some of them until late at night, the women—well, they were a queer lot, and their way of life was quite different from ours. What they did in their houses I do not know, for they employed servants to do the work; but they stayed mostly indoors, or if they went out at all they went veiled in bourkas. It was their religion, I was told: they would not appear before any man but their husband. Sometimes, when I caught sight of a figure in voluminous draperies swishing through the streets under a blazing sun, or of a face peering through a window or shutter, I felt desperately sorry for them, deprived of the ordinary pleasures of knowing warm sun and cool breeze upon their flesh, of walking out light and free, or of mixing with men and working beside them.

"They have their <u>compensations</u>," Kali said drily. "It is an easy life, with no worry for the next meal and plenty always at hand. I would gladly wear a bourka and walk veiled for the rest of my life if I, too, could be sure of such things."

"For a year perhaps," I said, "not forever. Who could endure such a filtering of sunlight and fresh air as they do?"

"You chatter like a pair of monkeys," said Kali's husband, "with less sense. What use to talk of 'exchange' and so forth. Their life is theirs and yours is yours; neither change nor exchange is possible."

Once, and once only, I actually saw one of those women, close. I was taking a few vegetables to market when I saw her beckoning me to come indoors. I did so and as soon as the door was closed the woman threw off her veil the better to select what she wanted. Her face was very pale, the bones small and fine. Her eyes were pale too, a curious light brown matching her silky hair. She took what she wanted and paid me. Her fingers, fair and slender, were laden with jewelled rings, any one of which would have fed us for a year. She smiled at me as I went out, then quickly lowered the veil again about her face. I never went there again. There was something about those closed doors and shuttered windows that struck coldly at me, used as I was to open fields and the sky and the unfettered sight of the sun. ■

Words for Everyday Use

comp • en • sa • tion (käm´pən sā´ shən) *n.,* something given to make up for a loss of something else

Vocabulary in Context

• The event was canceled, but <u>compensation</u> was offered to the people who traveled long distances to be there.

Responding to the Selection

If you lived in the narrator's village, how would you feel about the changes that are happening there? Would you consider the tannery a blessing or a curse? Explain.

Reviewing the Selection

RECALLING

INTERPRETING

1. What is Kunthi's opinion of the tannery? What is the narrator's opinion of it? ▶▶ What does the narrator's opinion of the tannery reveal about her personal values? Are money and the idea of living in a busy town important to her? Explain.

2. Why does the small shop owned by Janaki's husband close? How do other shopkeepers feel about its closing? ▶▶ In what way does the fate of her friend's small business reflect what the narrator believes is now wrong with the town?

3. Where do the Muslim officials live? What does the narrator find strange about their wives? ▶▶ Why does the narrator feel sorry for the Muslim women, despite the fact that they enjoy more money and luxuries than the narrator and her friends do? What does the narrator believe to be more important than money and luxuries?

4. When does the narrator have the opportunity to meet one of the Muslim women? What does the narrator notice about the woman's fingers? ▶▶ What is the "something" about the woman's home that strikes the narrator coldly? Do you think the narrator's negative feelings toward the tannery and the woman's obvious wealth contribute to her negative feelings toward the Muslim woman's home?

SYNTHESIZING

5. How has the tannery changed the town for the worse, in the eyes of the narrator? Why is the "sweet quiet of village life" more suitable to her?

RESPONDING TO THE SELECTION

In responding, students should think about the advantages and disadvantages of the tannery and of a busy town. Do students share the values of the story's narrator, or are their values different?

ANSWERS FOR REVIEWING THE SELECTION

RECALLING AND INTERPRETING

1. **Recalling.** Kunthi believes that the tannery is a wonderful additional to the town. The narrator dislikes the tannery. **Interpreting.** The narrator values peace, quiet, good behavior, and friendliness more than she values life in a big city.

2. **Recalling.** The small shop closes because it can no longer compete with the many other shops that opened as a result of the tannery. The other shop owners are happy that the shop closes, because they will have less competition. **Interpreting.** The narrator feels that selfishness and greed have overtaken the city. The small neighborhood store pushed out by others reflects the greed and coldness of the new town to the narrator.

3. **Recalling.** The Muslim officials live in small colonies of their own. Their wives have servants and must keep themselves covered at all times. **Interpreting.** The narrator believes that the freedom to feel the sun and breezes, and to leave one's home and work beside men is more important than money and luxuries.

4. **Recalling.** The narrator is selling vegetables when one of the Muslim women beckons to her so that she might buy some vegetables. She notices that the rings on the woman's fingers are worth enough to feed her family for a year.

(cont.)

ANSWERS FOR REVIEWING THE SELECTION (CONT.)

Interpreting. The narrator does not like that the home is dark and closed—with the closed shutters blocking the sun. She feels it represents the oppressed life that the woman must lead. Students might agree that the narrator's negative feelings toward the tannery might affect her perception of all those associated with it. She might also be reacting to the woman's wealth or to the fact that the woman's culture is unfamiliar.

SYNTHESIZING

Responses will vary. Possible responses are given.

5. The tannery has made the town dirty, loud, and greedy. She prefers to live a quiet life among family and friends and to enjoy the sun on her face. There is nothing in a large town that appeals to her.

ANSWERS FOR UNDERSTANDING LITERATURE

Responses will vary. Possible responses are given.

1. Point of View. The author of *Nectar in a Sieve* chose to write her story from the first-person point of view. Kunthi and her sons, who are employed by the tannery, would give a much different view of the tannery. They would describe it as a positive addition to the town, and they would focus on the exciting and lucrative aspects of living in a busy town. Janaki would tell a bitter and angry story of the loss of her family business. Kali, too, would be bitter, describing the obvious wealth of the officials and their wives, and how she would never enjoy such wealth.

2. Tone. The tone is sad and negative, particularly when the narrator describes the tannery, the loss of her friend's shop, and the new women in her town. Words and phrases such as "Now it is all noise and crowds everywhere, and rude, young hooligans idling in the street and dirty bazaars and uncouth behavior"; "sprawling growth" which "swallowed up" the town; and descriptions of the Muslim woman and her house all help to reveal the narrator's feelings about the changes in her town. The tone reflects the narrator's feelings of regret as her village changes.

Understanding Literature (Questions for Discussion)

1. **Point of View. Point of view** is the vantage point from which a story is told. Stories are typically written from a first-person point of view, in which the narrator uses words such as *I* and *we*, or from a third-person point of view, in which the narrator uses words such as *he, she, it,* and *they* and avoids the use of *I* and *we*. Did the author of *Nectar in a Sieve* choose to write her story using the first-person point of view or the third-person point of view? Might the descriptions of the tannery and the growing town be different if they were given by another character, such as Kunthi, Janaki, Kali, a wife of one of the tannery officials, or one of Kunthi's eldest sons? Explain your response.

2. **Tone. Tone** is the emotional attitude toward the reader or toward the subject implied by a literary work. How would you describe the tone of this excerpt from *Nectar in a Sieve,* particularly in the passages that depict the tannery and the lives of the officials and their wives? What words and phrases help the reader to determine the tone of the piece? What does the tone reveal about the narrator's feelings toward the tannery and the changes and new people associated with it?

WRITING A CRITICAL ESSAY

Each literary selection in this textbook is followed by an activity prompting you to write a critical essay. An essay, as you might already know, is a brief work of prose nonfiction. In an essay, a writer explores his or her ideas about a topic. In a critical essay, the writer analyzes some aspect of one or more literary works and offers an interpretation based on that analysis.

Most essays consist of the following parts:

- An **introduction**, often a single paragraph, should capture the reader's attention and present the subject of the essay. In most formal essays, the introduction should also present the author's main idea, or thesis.
- The **body** of the essay develops the author's main idea, or thesis, and is usually several paragraphs long. Each paragraph in the body should present a single idea that supports the thesis of the essay.
- The **conclusion**, often a single paragraph, should sum up the ideas presented in the essay and give the reader a sense of resolution.

When you are writing an essay about literature, you will follow the steps in the process of writing (see the Language Arts Survey 1.1, "The Writing Process"). The following sections show how the process relates specifically to writing a critical essay. For more detailed information, refer to the Language Arts Survey 1.20, "Writing a Critical Essay."

Finding a Topic

Your teacher may choose to assign the writing activities that follow each selection in this textbook. If you are choosing a topic on your own, refer to the chart "Ideas for Essays about Literature," in the Language Arts Survey 1.20. Once you know the main idea of your essay, put it into a sentence called a thesis statement.

Gathering and Organizing Ideas

Gather ideas and evidence from the literary work itself to support your thesis statement. You may also choose to use outside critical sources or reference works to support your thesis. Record all the ideas you gather on notecards or on notebook paper. Be sure to note the source of any material that you take from a published work, because you will need to document your sources in the final version of your paper. Then, organize your ideas for your essay into outline form. To do this, write your thesis at the top of a piece of paper and list the main points you will use to support your thesis. Under each main point, list evidence that backs up the supporting idea.

Drafting, Evaluating, Revising, and Proofing

From your outline, write a rough draft. Include your evidence from the literary work or from other sources to support the ideas that you present. This evidence can be paraphrased, summarized, or quoted directly. Use quotation marks around quotations that are less than four lines long, and run the quotation in with the rest of your writing. If the quotation is four lines long or longer, do not use quotation marks, but indent the quoted material from the left margin and single-space the quotation. Make sure that any quotations you use are relevant and form a cohesive part of your essay. Also be sure to cite a source for any direct quotations or borrowed ideas.

When your rough draft is complete, evaluate it and have a classmate evaluate your work. Make sure that the organization of your ideas is logical and that you have used enough evidence to support your ideas. Be sure that all quoted material is correct. Make your revisions, then proofread for errors in grammar, usage, spelling, capitalization, and punctuation. Make a final copy and proofread this final copy one last time.

To see a student model of an outline and an essay, turn to Language Arts Survey 1.20, "Writing a Critical Essay."

ACTIVITY

Write a short critical essay in which you analyze the narrator of *Nectar in a Sieve*. In preparing to draft your essay, first write a thesis statement about the values, beliefs, and concerns of this character. Then begin to gather ideas and evidence from the story that support your statement.

When you have gathered your ideas, organize them in an outline, following the directions above. When you have completed your outline, write a rough draft. Then evaluate your work, making sure that your essay is logical, that you have used evidence from the selection to support your ideas, and that any quotations you have used are correct. Revise your draft, proofreading for grammar, usage, spelling, capitalization, and punctuation.

ADDITIONAL QUESTIONS AND ACTIVITIES

In addition to evaluating students' final drafts using the grading scale provided below, you might want to ask them to turn in their notecards, outlines, and rough drafts for your review. Using these, you can check to see that students are following logical steps as they complete their essays. Knowing these steps will help them to complete many assignments throughout this text.

ANALYTIC SCALES FOR RESPONDING IN WRITING

Assign a score from 1 to 25 for each grading criterion below. (For more detailed evaluation, see the evaluation forms for writing, revising, and proofreading, Assessment Portfolio 4.1–4.9.)

Critical Essay

- **Content/Unity.** The essay focuses on the values, beliefs, and concerns of the narrator in *Nectar in a Sieve*.
- **Organization/Coherence.** The essay begins with an introduction that includes the thesis of the essay. The introduction is followed by supporting paragraphs with clear transitions. The essay ends with a solid conclusion.
- **Language/Style.** The essay uses vivid and precise nouns, verbs, and modifiers.
- **Conventions.** The essay avoids errors in spelling, grammar, usage, mechanics, and manuscript form.

► Additional practice is provided in the Essential Skills Practice Book: Writing 1.20.

SUPPORT FOR LEP STUDENTS

Pronunciations of Proper Nouns and Adjectives

An • hui (an hoi´)
Cao Xie • qing (chou shēr chiŋ´)
Den • pu (den po͞o´)
Du Pu (do͞o po͞o)
Huang (hwäŋ)
Ji • an • nong Sun (gē´ə nuŋ´ soon)
Ji • an • gxi (gē an´ shē)
Jin Yong (gin yōŋ)
Kong • fu (kōŋ´ fo͞o)
Li Bai (lē bī)
Lu Xun (lo͞o shēŋ)
Mao Du • n (mou do͞o´ 'n)
ni • hao (nē hou´)

Cross-curricular Activities

SOCIAL STUDIES

As an introduction, you may want to show students a map of China and have them locate Jiannong's province. They should also note some of the major cities and rivers of China and look closely at the countries that border China.

MATHEMATICS AND SCIENCES AND SOCIAL STUDIES

Students might not be familiar with the differences between a Communist economy and a capitalist economy. Ask them to consult reference sources in the library for definitions of the following concepts: Communism, capitalism, socialism, gross national product or GNP, and "Most Favored Nation Trading Status" or MFN. Interested students could expand this project by doing research on some of the economic reforms that have been taking place in China from the 1980s to the present day. They should learn about specific policies enacted by the government and answer such questions as: How and why have changes to China's basic economic structure improved the Chinese economy? In what ways have these changes also disrupted the economy and resulted in a decline in production?

PASSPORT TO CHINA

Jiannong Sun
Denpu, China

Nihao! My name is Jiannong Sun and I am from the People's Republic of China. My hometown is Denpu, located in the Jiangxi Province in the midsoutheastern part of China. The Jiangxi Province, where my family has lived for centuries, is famous for its hilly lands and small rivers. The climate there is extremely humid in the spring and summer—it often rains continuously for more than two months in the spring, becoming dry in the fall and winter. Because of this geography and climate, our major industry is agriculture and the main products are rice and oranges.

China has undergone unprecedented change since 1978, both in economics and in politics. More and more businesses are privately owned and capitalism is taking root, resulting in a strong surge in production. China is now one of the most important international trading partners in the world and America's sixth largest trading partner. I am very happy about these reforms because they

Sian Hotel

Tea cultivation, Hangzhou

Cultural/Historical Note

Jiannong notes that capitalism is taking root and that economic and political reforms are changing the lives of Chinese people. Tell students that China has undergone many changes throughout this century. After the Ch'ing Dynasty was overthrown and a republic established in 1911, the Japanese invaded China and seized the territory of Shantung early in World War I (1914–1918). Civil war broke out in China from 1945–1949, ending with the victory of the Communist party. Communist Party Chairman Mao Zedong integrated Chinese society under a People's Republic, while the exiled Guomindang leader Chiang Kai-Shek became the leader of another Chinese state on the island of Taiwan. During Mao Zedong's rule, he turned all privately held means of production over to the

(cont.)

have improved the living conditions in China. Fifteen years ago, my family only had a radio, but now we have a color TV, washing machine, refrigerator, CD player, and VCR. Also, twenty years ago no one was allowed to say anything bad about our leaders, but now you can speak out on the street and you will not get in trouble. In the small villages, the people are electing their officials, and I think this trend will extend to higher levels sooner or later.

My favorite holidays are the Spring and Mid-Autumn Festivals and the Dragon Boat Festival. The Spring Festival, which starts on February 19 and lasts up to two weeks, is the most important holiday because it celebrates our New Year, the first day of spring. It is also the greatest shopping season—just like Christmas in Western countries. We get lots of gifts and watch beautiful fireworks. During the Dragon Boat Festival, we enjoy watching the dragon-boat rowing games in all the rivers across the country, and playing the knocking-egg game, in which two children hit hard-boiled eggs together to see whose egg is

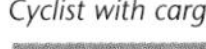

Cyclist with cargo

Panda

Courtyard, Forbidden City, Beijing

Cultural/Historical Note (cont.)

state, and initiated two great reforms, the Great Leap Forward (1958–1960), and the Cultural Revolution (1966–1976), which ended with his death. After Mao's death another series of major economic and political reforms, known as the Second Revolution, began under the direction of Deng Xiaoping, who instituted sweeping changes and established a global market economy. Deng died in 1997.

Ask students to research some of these reforms and changes in Chinese history. Some students might focus their research on the repression and intolerance exercised by the Communist government, especially during the Cultural Revolution and in the Tiananmen Square demonstrations and government crackdown on June 4, 1989.

Cross-curricular Activities

Applied Arts

Encourage students to prepare *Gong-Bao Ji-Ding*, one of Jiannong's favorite Chinese dishes. Although it is traditionally quite spicy, students can use mild dried peppers in this recipe if they prefer.

Gong-Bao Ji-Ding **(The King's Spicy Hot Chicken)**

Ingredients:
- 1/2 pound boned chicken breast
- 10 or more dried red peppers (Choose mild peppers if you don't like spicy food!)
- 2 teaspoons finely chopped fresh ginger
- 1 green onion
- 1/4 cup cashews, peanuts, or almonds
- 4 tablespoons oil

Marinade:
- 2 teaspoons cornstarch
- 2 teaspoons soy sauce
- 1 tablespoon rice wine or dry sherry
- 1 egg white
- 1/2 teaspoon salt

Seasonings:
- 2 teaspoons cornstarch
- 2 teaspoons rice wine or dry sherry
- 1–2 tablespoons soy sauce
- 1 teaspoon vinegar
- 1–2 teaspoons sugar

Procedure:

1. Cut meat into 1" pieces.
2. Make marinade by mixing ingredients in the order given, stir in chicken, and leave for at least 15 minutes.
3. Trim peppers, shake out seeds. Finely chop ginger. Slice onion into 3/4" lengths.
4. Mix seasonings in small bowl in order given.
5. Fry peppers until they start to char. Turn up the heat till peppers blacken, add chicken, reduce heat to medium.
6. Stir fry until chicken is white, then add ginger and onion. Cook for a few seconds, then add nuts and seasonings (give it a quick stir first). When sauce has thickened slightly and is glazelike, remove to serving dish and serve hot.

Cultural/Historical Note

The Great Wall of China is one of the longest structures ever built. It is about four thousand miles long, stretching over mountains and hills. Most of the Great Wall that stands today was built by the Ming dynasty in the 1400s AD as a defense against Mongol invasions. It was constructed of brick and stone entirely by hand. Although the wall was meant to provide protection against invaders, it was unable to repel major attacks. In the modern day, much repair work has been done on the Great Wall. It attracts thousands of visitors.

Cross-curricular Activities

ARTS AND HUMANITIES AND SOCIAL STUDIES

In China, music has been an important part of the culture for thousands of years and reflects Chinese philosophy and thought. In classical Chinese music, the single tone of the note was considered more important than its melody, and musicians worked to create the "perfect pitch." A famous traditional song Jiannong likes is "Two Fountains under the Moon," which was written as a solo for the Erhu fiddle. The Erhu, one of the most popular bowed instruments in the classic Chinese orchestra, is similar to the violin, but with only two strings.

If any students are familiar with Chinese music, either classical or modern, you might ask them to bring in tapes or CDs to share with the class. If not, some students might locate Chinese music either through sources on the Internet or by talking to the school audiovisual specialist. As students listen to the music, ask them to try to identify the different instruments used. Students who have had musical instruction may be able to compare the tone and musical key of classical Chinese music to that of classical Western music.

Decorative sculpture

Practicing tai chi

strongest. I enjoyed playing this game when I was a child, and it is still popular today.

Life has changed a great deal for young Chinese adults since the 1970s. Before the economic reforms, most spent their free time on housework since they were poor and had to make their own small repairs. As the Chinese economy grows, more young people are making more money and can spend more time watching TV and playing sports such as Ping-Pong and soccer. They also have more time to socialize with friends.

Most people have heard of the Great Wall of China, but my country has many other beautiful sights. One of my favorites is Mt. Huang, one of China's most spectacular mountains. Located in Anhui Province, the mountain is 120 kilometers in circumference and has 72 peaks. The highest peak, the Lotus Flower, rises more than 1,873 meters above sea level. One must climb 800 stone steps cut into an 80 degree cliff to reach the top. The second highest peak, the Heavenly Capital, has a ridge less than one meter wide. Those who make it to the summit are rewarded by the sight of ancient pines, hot springs, streams, mist, magnificent views, and a great feeling of achievement.

The Great Wall of China

Literary Note

In the first part of the twentieth century, China enjoyed a literary renaissance. During this New Literature Movement, Chinese authors borrowed techniques and ideas from Western literature. They also began to write in the modern Chinese language, which was simpler and more widely understood than the complex scholarly Chinese used in most writing. Under the Communist government, many writers were pressured to write in the style of Socialist Realism. This style was intended to promote Communism and to convey political messages; it was neither experimental nor creative.

Students may wish to read some of the literature written by one of the modern Chinese authors Jiannong mentions. Some biographical information on these authors is provided on page 79.

The greatest writers from the past are Li Bai, Du Pu, and Cao Xieqing. Today, Lu Xun, Mao Dun, and Jin Yong are popular. My favorite writers are Li Bai, Cao Xieqing, Lu Xun, and Jin Yong. I would recommend many novels, including *Dream of the Red Chamber,* a sad love story about a young boy born with a stone in his mouth and a girl without parents, and *The Eagle Hero,* an amazing tale describing how an honest but somewhat stupid young man learns *Kongfu* and beats the invaders of China. Of course, as China becomes more democratic, authors, artists, and musicians can express their ideas much more freely than before.

In China, education is less interactive than in America. For example, in China students do not raise so many questions, and the normal number of students in classrooms is larger than in American schools. I would say that because of different educational methods, young Chinese adults have better skills in mathematical calculation and reciting; however, Americans are more creative. But, along with the many reforms in China's economy and politics, the Chinese education system is changing, and these differences are becoming smaller and smaller. ■

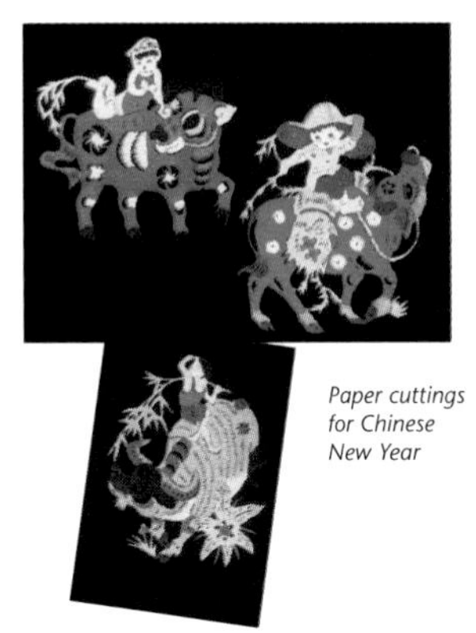

Paper cuttings for Chinese New Year

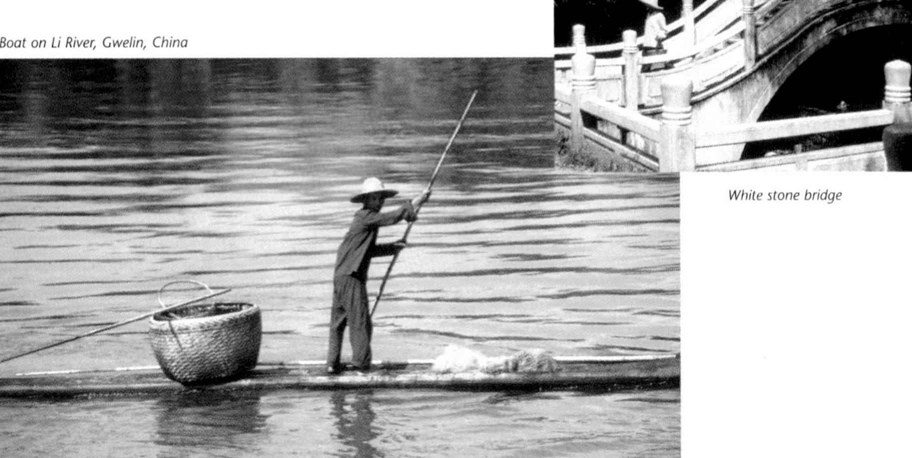

Boat on Li River, Gwelin, China

White stone bridge

BIOGRAPHICAL NOTE

Lu Xun or **Lu Hsün** (1881–1936) is often called the father of modern Chinese literature. His first story, "Diary of a Madman," is considered the first story written in modern Chinese. It was inspired in part by a story of the same title written by the Russian author Nikolai Gogol (see page 993). Lu Xun's use of a terse, satirical style and the vernacular made him popular during the Chinese literary renaissance; he was also known for his large vocabulary and for using the Chinese language colorfully. During the rule of the Guomindang, Lu Xun became increasingly opposed to the government and in 1930 helped found the League of Left Wing Writers. He supported the Communist Party but never became a member.

Mao Dun (1896–1981) also wrote during the New Literature Movement of China. In 1920, he cofounded one of its earliest literary societies, the Wenxue Yanjiu Hui (Literary Study Society), which promoted a Realist style of writing and opposed "art for art's sake." In 1930, Mao Dun joined the League of Left Wing Writers and became involved in Communist worker activities in Shanghai. After the founding of the People's Republic, he worked for the government. He returned briefly to writing and editing after the Cultural Revolution.

Jin Yong is an immensely popular modern author whose works have provided material for many martial arts movies and TV series in Hong Kong, Taiwan, China, and elsewhere. *The Eagle Hero* (or *The Eagle-Shooting Heroes*), which is the first in a trilogy of tales by Jin Yong, is set in the late Sung Dynasty, sometime during the twelfth century AD, when China was threatened by the Jurchen Chin Empire and the Mongolian Khante.

ADDITIONAL RESOURCES

Reader's Guide

- Selection Worksheet 1.7

Assessment Portfolio

- Selection Check Test 2.1.11
- Selection Test 2.1.12

Essential Skills Practice Books

- Language 2.4–2.14

PREREADING EXTENSIONS

Explain to students that Communist leader Mao Zedong, driven from southern and eastern China by Chiang Kai-shek at the end of the 1920s, led an army of workers and peasants on a long march to the northwest part of China. From there, they attacked and eventually conquered Chinese government troops. In 1949, Mao and his army gained control of China. The Long March is considered an important event in the history of Chinese Communists.

SUPPORT FOR LEP STUDENTS

Pronunciations of Proper Nouns and Adjectives

Feng Ji • cai (fəŋ´ jə kī)
Zhao (jou)

Additional Vocabulary

concealed—hidden
entourage—group of assistants
mimeographed—copied or printed on a type of machine called a mimeograph
procession—parade of people
reproachful—blaming, scolding
shrewd—clever and observant
smug—overly self-satisfied and arrogant
utilitarian—useful rather than attractive

PREREADING

"The Street-Sweeping Show"
by Feng Jicai, translated by Susan Wilff Chen

About the Author

Feng Jicai (1924–). Born in Tianjin, China, Feng Jicai pursued a career as a painter before he began writing. Forced during the Cultural Revolution to abandon art, which was considered "counter-revolutionary," Jicai turned to fiction writing. He was unable to publish anything until 1977, after the death of Mao Zedong, the Chairman of the People's Republic of China and the leader of its Communist Party. A prolific author whose work captures Chinese culture and provides insight into human nature, Feng takes advantage of his artistic gifts to depict the contemporary Chinese experience.

"The Street-Sweeping Show" is based on an actual event in which Jicai participated. The story raised controversy and, as a result, was never reprinted in any of his short story collections after its first publication in 1982. Jicai is now Vice Chairman of the Tianjin branch of the Chinese Writers' Association and Vice Chairman of the Federation of Chinese Writers and Artists. He lives in Tianjin with his wife and son.

About the Selection

In "**The Street-Sweeping Show**," Feng Jicai satirizes the way politicians often behave in front of the media, presenting a "show" for the public to inspire support. **Satire** is humorous writing or speech intended to point out errors, falsehoods, foibles, or failings. In this short story, a mayor takes part in a carefully orchestrated event designed to promote a National Cleanup Week. Feng sharply critiques the politician's actions and motivations—the mayor's media event actually accomplishes nothing substantial; the noted public figures ostensibly join the common people in a community effort but wind up pretending to clean an already clean street.

CONNECTIONS: China's Cultural Revolution

The Cultural Revolution in China (1966–1976) banned the works of most writers and artists from publication or public view. During this period, only a handful of carefully screened and scrutinized works by "acceptable" writers and artists were accessible to the public. Launched by Mao Zedong during his last decade in power, the revolution began in August of 1966. Mao shut down schools and encouraged Red Guards, groups of militant young people, to attack all institutions evidencing traditional or "bourgeois" values and to test Party officials by publicly criticizing them. He believed that these attacks would benefit both the young people and the Party cadres they attacked. The movement quickly grew, and elderly people and intellectuals were verbally and physically abused—many dying as a result. The resulting anarchy, fear, and paralysis completely disrupted the economy and the overall well-being of the culture.

GOALS/OBJECTIVES

Studying this lesson will enable students to

- read a satirical story about the actions and motivations of some politicians
- discuss the life and work of Feng Jicai
- understand the Chinese Cultural Revolution
- define the literary terms *characterization*, *third-person point of view*, and *satire*
- review language skills such as parts of speech, types of nouns, types of pronouns, verbs and verbals, adjectives, articles, adverbs, prepositions, conjunctions, and conjunctive adverbs

Think about a politician or other public figure you have seen in the media promoting a community project, organization, or event. Now, imagine what was going on behind the scenes—what the press did not cover. Write about what you envision going on behind the scenes. Do you believe that the public figure's participation was as wholehearted as it seemed? Why, or why not?

"The Street-Sweeping Show"

FENG JICAI, TRANSLATED BY SUSAN WILFF CHEN

"National Cleanup Week starts today," said Secretary Zhao, "and officials everywhere are going out to join in the street sweeping. Here's our list of participants—all top city administrators and public figures. We've just had it mimeographed over at the office for your approval."

He looked like a typical upper-echelon secretary: the collar of his well-worn, neatly pressed Mao suit was buttoned up military style; his complexion was pale; his glasses utilitarian. His gentle, deferential manner and pleasantly modulated voice concealed a shrewd, hard-driving personality.

The mayor pored over[1] the list, as if the eighty names on it were those of people selected to go abroad. From time to time he glanced thoughtfully at the high white ceiling.

"Why isn't there anyone from the Women's Federation?" he asked.

Secretary Zhao thought for a moment. "Oh, you're right—there isn't! We've got the heads of every office in the city—the Athletic Committee, the Youth League Committee, the Federation of Trade Unions, the Federation of Literary and Art Circles—even some famous university professors. The only group we forgot is the Women's Federation."

"Women are the pillars of society. How can we leave out the women's representatives?" The mayor sounded smug rather than reproachful. Only a leader could think of everything. This was where true leadership ability came into play.

Secretary Zhao was reminded of the time when the mayor had pointed out that the fish course was missing from the menu for a banquet in honor of some foreign guests.

"Add two names from the Women's Federation, and make sure you get people in positions of authority or who are proper representatives of the organization. 'International Working Women's Red Banner Pacesetters,' 'Families of Martyrs,' or 'Model Workers' would be fine." Like an elementary school teacher returning a poor homework paper to his student, the mayor handed the incomplete list back to his secretary.

1. **pored over.** Studied carefully

1 What does Secretary Zhao ask the mayor to approve?

2 Which group was accidentally left out of the Cleanup Week?

WORDS FOR EVERYDAY USE

ech • e • lon (esh´ə län´) *n.*, level of responsibility or importance in an organization

def • er • en • tial (def´ ər ən´ shəl) *adj.*, very respectful

mod • u • lat• ed (mäj´ ə lāt´ əd) *adj.*, varied in pitch or intensity, often to a lower degree

READER'S JOURNAL

You might also ask students to consider the following questions and write about them in their journals:

Do you think most people believe or trust public figures? Why, or why not? Who are the politicians and public figures that people seem to trust? Why have they earned the public trust?

ANSWERS TO GUIDED READING QUESTIONS

1 Secretary Zhao asks the mayor to approve the list of city administrators and public figures who are to participate in street sweeping for National Cleanup Week.

2 The Women's Federation was accidentally left out of the Cleanup Week.

SPELLING AND VOCABULARY WORDS FROM THE SELECTION

conspicuous
cordon
deferential
echelon
modulated
retinue

QUOTABLES

"Politics is war without bloodshed while war is politics with bloodshed."

—Mao Zedong

VOCABULARY IN CONTEXT

- To get approval for the project, Ariel had to write to the leader of the highest echelon.
- We gave her deferential treatment on her birthday.
- After the baby went to sleep, Tony's family spoke in carefully modulated voices so as not to wake him.

Answers to Guided Reading Questions

1. The mayor says that he should go to the street sweeping to set a good example.
2. Eighty-two dignitaries are sweeping the street.
3. The area is huge and the concrete pavement is already clean.
4. An old policeman gives a broom to the mayor. The mayor receives a broom that is small and neat.

Quotables

"Politicians are the same all over. They promise to build a bridge even when there is no water."

—Nikita Khrushchev

Additional Questions and Activities

1. Ask students to think about the motives behind the street-sweeping event. Are people sincerely concerned about the cleanliness of the city? Encourage students to explain their responses.

2. Ask each student to describe one present-day politician or public figure. What do students like about this person? What do students dislike about this person? What about this person seems insincere and what seems sincere?

3. Do students feel people sometimes hold public figures to standards that are too high? Why, or why not?

Answers

Responses will vary. Possible responses are given.

1. This event is for public relations purposes only. Because they have to be there for political reasons, people sweep an already clean street while the cameras roll.

2. *Responses will vary.*

3. *Responses will vary.*

"Yes, your honor, I'll do it right away. A complete list will be useful the next time something like this comes up. And I must contact everyone at once. The street sweeping is scheduled for two this afternoon in Central Square. Will you be able to go?"

"Of course. As mayor of the city, I have to set an example."

1 Why does the mayor say he will attend the event?

"The car will be at the gate for you at one-thirty. I'll go with you."

"All right," the mayor answered absent-mindedly, scratching his forehead and looking away.

Secretary Zhao hurried out.

At one-thirty that afternoon the mayor was whisked to the square in his limousine. All office workers, shop clerks, students, housewives, and retirees were out sweeping the streets, and the air was thick with dust. Secretary Zhao hastily rolled up the window. Inside the car there was only a faint, pleasant smell of gasoline and leather.

2 How many dignitaries are sweeping the square?

At the square they pulled up beside a colorful assortment of limousines. In front of them a group of top city administrators had gathered to wait for the mayor's arrival. Someone had arranged for uniformed policemen to stand guard on all sides.

3 What makes sweeping this area an unusual task?

Secretary Zhao sprang out of the limousine and opened the door for his boss. The officials in the waiting crowd stepped forward with smiling faces to greet the mayor. Everyone knew him and hoped to be the first to shake his hand.

"Good afternoon—oh, nice to see you—good afternoon—" the mayor repeated as he shook hands with each of them.

4 Who gives a broom to the mayor? What type of broom does the mayor receive?

An old policeman approached, followed by two younger ones pushing wheelbarrows full of big bamboo brooms. The old policeman selected one of the smaller, neater brooms and presented it respectfully to the mayor. When the other dignitaries had gotten their brooms, a marshal with a red armband led them all to the center of the square. Naturally the mayor walked at the head.

Groups of people had come from their workplaces to sweep the huge square. At the sight of this majestic, broom-carrying procession, with its marshal, police escort, and retinue of shutter-clicking photographers, they realized that they were in the presence of no ordinary mortals and gathered closer for a look. How extraordinary for a mayor to be sweeping the streets, thought Secretary Zhao, swelling with unconscious pride as he strutted along beside the mayor with his broom on his shoulder.

"Here we are," the marshal said when they had reached the designated spot.

All eighty-two dignitaries began to sweep.

The swelling crowd of onlookers, which was kept back by a police cordon, was buzzing with excitement:

"Look, he's the one over there."

"Which one? The one in black?"

"No. The bald fat one in blue."

"Cut the chitchat!" barked a policeman.

The square was so huge that no one knew where to sweep. The concrete pavement was clean to begin with; they pushed what little grit there was back and forth with their big brooms. The most conspicuous piece of litter was a solitary popsicle wrapper, which they all pursued like children chasing a dragonfly.

The photographers surrounded the mayor. Some got down on one knee to shoot from below, while others ran from side to side trying to get a profile. Like a cloud in a thunderstorm, the mayor was constantly illuminated by silvery flashes. Then a man in a visored cap, with a video camera, approached Secretary Zhao.

Words for Everyday Use

ret • i • nue (ret´ 'n yo͞o´) *n.,* body of assistants, followers, or servants attending a person of rank or importance

cor • don (kôr´ dən) *n.,* line or circle of police stationed around an area to guard it

con • spic • u • ous (kən spik´yo͞o es) *adj.,* attracting attention; noticeable

Vocabulary in Context

- The president never leaves his home without a retinue of bodyguards.
- The crime scene was surrounded by a cordon of police.
- I think my large, flowered hat might be too conspicuous at the ceremony.

"I'm from the TV station," he said. "Would you please ask them to line up single file so they'll look neat on camera?"

Secretary Zhao consulted with the mayor, who agreed to this request. The dignitaries formed a long line and began to wield their brooms for the camera, regardless of whether there was any dirt on the ground.

The cameraman was about to start shooting, when he stopped and ran over to the mayor.

"I'm sorry, your honor," he said, "but you're all going to have to face the other way because you've got your backs to the sun. And I'd also like the entire line to be reversed so that you're at the head."

"All right," the mayor agreed graciously, and he led his entourage, like a line of dragon dancers, in a clumsy turnaround. Once in place, everyone began sweeping again.

Pleased, the cameraman ran to the head of the line, pushed his cap up, and aimed at the mayor. "All right," he said as the camera started to whir, "swing those brooms, all together now—put your hearts into it—that's it! Chin up please, your honor. Hold it—that's fine—all right!"

He stopped the camera, shook the mayor's hand, and thanked him for helping an ordinary reporter carry out his assignment.

"Let's call it a day," the marshal said to Secretary Zhao. Then he turned to the mayor. "You have victoriously accomplished your mission," he said.

"Very good—thank you for your trouble," the mayor replied routinely, smiling and shaking hands again.

Some reporters came running up to the mayor. "Do you have any instructions, your honor?" asked a tall, thin, aggressive one.

"Nothing in particular." The mayor paused for a moment. "Everyone should pitch in to clean up our city."

The reporters scribbled his precious words in their notebooks.

The policemen brought the wheelbarrows back, and everyone returned the brooms.

Secretary Zhao replaced the mayor's for him.

It was time to go. The mayor shook hands with everyone again.

"Good-bye—good-bye—good-bye—"

The others waited until the mayor had gotten into his limousine before getting into theirs.

The mayor's limousine delivered him to his house, where his servant had drawn his bathwater and set out scented soap and fresh towels. He enjoyed a leisurely bath and emerged from the bathroom with rosy skin and clean clothes, leaving his grime and exhaustion behind him in the tub.

As he descended the stairs to eat dinner, his grandson hurriedly led him into the living room.

"Look, Granddad, you're on TV!"

There he was on the television screen, like an actor, putting on a show of sweeping the street. He turned away and gave his grandson a casual pat on the shoulder.

"It's not worth watching. Let's go have dinner." ■

❶ *What does the marshal tell the mayor?*

❷ *What "instruction" does the mayor have for the townspeople?*

❸ *How does the mayor feel about the street-sweeping show and his performance?*

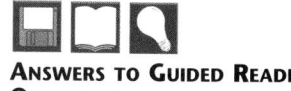

Answers to Guided Reading Questions

❶ The marshal tells the mayor that he has accomplished his mission.

❷ The mayor says that everyone should pitch in to clean up the city.

❸ He does not seem proud of the event or of his performance, since he tells his grandson that it is "not worth watching."

Selection Check Test with Answers

EX. What event is being planned for National Cleanup Week?
A group street sweeping is being planned.

1. What kinds of people will participate in the street sweeping?
Public figures, politicians, and city administrators will participate.

2. Why does the mayor of the city say he wants to participate in the event?
He says he wants to set an example.

3. Why was sweeping the square an unusual task?
It was already clean.

4. What instruction does the mayor give the people via the press?
He tells the people to pitch in to clean up their city.

5. What does the mayor tell his grandson about the event?
He tells his grandson that the event is not worth watching on television.

Responding to the Selection

Allow students to spend a few moments talking about their reactions to the story before they begin to role play. If they are unsure about the mayor's feelings toward his job, ask them to read the final paragraphs of the story aloud to each other.

Answers for Reviewing the Selection

RECALLING AND INTERPRETING

1. **Recalling.** The mayor tells Secretary Zhao that they need to invite at least two representatives from the Women's Federation. He is smug when he tells him that "women are the pillars of society." **Interpreting.** The mayor knows whom he must invite to be popular politically. The narrator means that a "true leader" knows how to please all the right people in order to be popular.

2. **Recalling.** The mayor and other top city administrators get to the street-sweeping event in Central Square by limousine. The mayor greets everyone by shaking hands and saying "Good afternoon—nice to see you—good afternoon." **Interpreting.** The mayor is treated as a celebrity—everyone rushes to shake his hand. He is probably not genuinely thrilled to see each and every person, but he knows he must act as though he is in order to be politically popular.

3. **Recalling.** The square is already clean—it does not need to be swept. The reporter has the dignitaries line up so that they will look neat on camera. **Interpreting.** The public figures are sweeping the square so that they will look good to the public. Members of the media videotape and snap pictures of the project, helping to turn the street-sweeping project into a "show" that will help the public figures to advertise themselves to the public.

(cont.)

Responding to the Selection

Imagine the mayor and his grandson are having a conversation about what it is like to be mayor. Would he encourage his grandson to go into politics? Imagine that the grandson wants to be mayor. Working in pairs, role play the dialogue between the mayor and his grandson.

Reviewing the Selection

RECALLING		INTERPRETING
1. What is the mayor's response when Secretary Zhao forgets to include someone from the Women's Federation in the event?	▶▶	What does the narrator say this reveals about the mayor's leadership abilities? Explain whether the narrator means this comment to be taken literally.
2. How do the mayor and other city administrators get to the street-sweeping in Central Square? What does the mayor say to each person he greets?	▶▶	How would you characterize the way the mayor is treated? Do you think the mayor really means these words? Why does he say them?
3. What is the condition of the square? Does it need to be swept? What does the reporter have the other dignitaries do?	▶▶	Why are these public figures sweeping the square? How do the members of the media contribute to the project?
4. What is the mayor's reaction when his grandson points out his performance on television?	▶▶	Why doesn't the mayor want his grandson to watch him? How does the mayor feel about the event? about his position?

SYNTHESIZING

5. Analyze the title of this short story. Explain whether it is appropriate, given the subject and tone of the story. What does the title "The Street-Sweeping Show" reveal about the events in the square?

Understanding Literature (Questions for Discussion)

1. **Characterization. Characterization** is the act of creating or describing a character. Writers use three major techniques to create characters: direct description, portrayal of characters' behavior, and representations of characters' internal states. When using direct description, the writer, through a speaker, a narrator, or another character, simply

Answers for Reviewing the Selection (cont.)

4. **Recalling.** The mayor tells his grandson that the event isn't worth watching. **Interpreting.** The mayor fears he might look phony to his grandson. The mayor feels that the event was a necessary part of keeping his position, but he does not seem to be proud of the way he must act.

SYNTHESIZING

Responses will vary. Possible responses are given.

5. The title is appropriate because the street-sweeping event turns into a show for the public. The "show" is built around the serious task of cleaning up the square, but it is actually a time for politicians and public leaders to show off for the cameras. Because of this, the occasion turns into something of a circus rather than a genuine event.

comments on the character. In portrayal of a character's behavior, the writer presents the actions and speech of the character, allowing the reader to draw his or her own conclusions. When using representations of internal states the writer reveals directly the character's private thoughts and emotions. Describe the mayor's character. What techniques does the author use to reveal his character?

2. **Third-person Point of View.** In a story told from the **third-person point of view**, the narrator does not take part in the action. Instead, he or she stands outside the action and tells the story using words such as *he, she, it,* and *they* and avoids the use of *I* and *we.* In what way does the use of the third-person point of view reveal the narrator's attitude toward the characters in the selection? Is the narrator sympathetic to the mayor? Secretary Zhao? How can you tell? What do you think the story would be like if it was told from the mayor's point of view? from Secretary Zhao's point of view? Describe how the story would change in each instance.

3. **Satire. Satire** is humorous writing or speech intended to point out errors, falsehoods, foibles, or failings. It is written for the purpose of reforming human behavior or human institutions. What is satirized in this short story? In what way do you imagine that the author would like to reform human behavior or institutions?

PARTS OF SPEECH REVIEW

Throughout this book, you will encounter Language Lab activities and language instruction that will sharpen your grammatical skills. Knowledge of the proper forms of written and spoken language will allow you to communicate more clearly and effectively with others. In addition, a knowledge of grammatical terms gives you a way to speak and write about literature. To illustrate, look at two passages from "The Street-Sweeping Show":

> He looked like a typical upper-echelon secretary: the collar of his well-worn, neatly pressed Mao suit was buttoned up military style; his complexion was pale; his glasses utilitarian. His gentle, deferential manner and pleasantly modulated voice concealed a shrewd, hard-driving personality.

> Secretary Zhao sprang out of the limousine and opened the door for his boss. The officials in the waiting crowd stepped forward with smiling faces to greet the mayor. Everyone knew him and hoped to be the first to shake his hand.

You can probably tell instinctively that the author has two very different intentions in these passages. In the first, the author is **describing** a character. In the second, the author is **narrating** the action of the story. What evidence could you use to support this view of these two passages? A knowledge of grammar and grammatical terms might help. Notice that the first passage makes use of more adjectives and linking verbs, while the second passage makes use of more action verbs. Thus, the first passage is more descriptive, while the second is more narrative.

Answers for Understanding Literature

Responses will vary. Possible responses are given.

1. Characterization. The mayor's actions are politically driven. He is formal, shrewd, and detail-oriented. He arrives at the event in a limousine, while his secretary hangs on his every word and request. The mayor knows what others expect from him as he greets all of the top city administrators and leads the procession of dignitaries to Central Square. He knows how he must behave in order to fulfill his role as mayor. At the end of the story, the reader learns that he also sees through some of the phoniness that surrounds his job. The reader learns about the character of the mayor primarily through description of his words and actions and through the actions of others toward him.

2. Third-person Point of View. The narrator seems to understand the absurdity of the event so he describes the scenes with cynicism. From descriptions of the procession to Central Square, the solitary popsicle wrapper everyone fights to sweep up, and the mayor's constant illumination by silvery flashes, readers can infer that the narrator probably feels some animosity and skepticism toward the mayor and his secretary. If the selection were written from the mayor's point of view, his interior thoughts as he reacts to the events of the day would be central. If the selection were written from Secretary Zhao's point of view, his actions and motivations would be central to the story.

3. Satire. The roles often played by politicians and other public figures are satirized in this selection. The writer knows that people in these positions often waste time on publicity stunts. The writer would probably like these people to spend their time doing things that are honestly worthwhile and for the public good.

▶ Additional practice of the skills taught in this lesson is provided in the Essential Skills Practice Book: Language 2.4–2.14.

Answers for Skills Activities

LANGUAGE SKILLS

ACTIVITY A

1. **literature** common, concrete
years common, concrete
2. **writing** common, concrete, collective
characters common, concrete
letters common, concrete
3. **China** proper, concrete
poetry common, concrete, collective
calligraphy common, concrete
impact common, abstract
audience common, concrete, collective
4. **bookkeepers** common, concrete
systems common, abstract
priests common, concrete
characters common, concrete
bones common, concrete
shells common, concrete
5. **Lao-tzu** proper, concrete
artist common, concrete

ACTIVITY B

1. **who** interrogative
2. **who** relative
3. **himself** intensive
4. **nothing** indefinite
5. **his** personal
6. **his** personal
7. **himself** reflexive
8. **it** personal
9. **which** relative
10. **this** demonstrative

Adjectives, linking verbs, and action verbs are some of the parts of speech. As everything that you will read, write, and discuss will be expressed through these parts of speech, it will be helpful for you to know their proper terminology. The activities below will help you to review them.

ACTIVITY A

TYPES OF NOUNS

Review the Language Arts Survey 2.3, "Types of Nouns." Then read the following sentences. On your own paper, write down the nouns in each sentence. Label each noun as common, proper, concrete, abstract, compound, or collective. Each noun will have more than one label.

EXAMPLE China has a long literary tradition.
China—proper, concrete; **tradition**—common, abstract

1. Chinese literature has existed for more than three thousand years.
2. Chinese writing uses ideographic characters, rather than phonetic letters.
3. In China, poetry, recorded in beautiful calligraphy, has a strong visual impact on its audience.
4. While bookkeepers in other cultures developed systems of writing, priests recorded the first Chinese characters on bones and tortoise shells.
5. Lao-tzu is known as the first great Chinese prose artist.

ACTIVITY B

TYPES OF PRONOUNS

Review the Language Arts Survey 2.4, "Personal Pronouns"; 2.5, "Reflexive, Intensive, and Demonstrative Pronouns"; and 2.6, "Indefinite, Interrogative, and Relative Pronouns." Read the following paragraph. Ten pronouns appear in boldface type. Identify these pronouns as personal, reflexive, intensive, demonstrative, indefinite, interrogative, or relative.

EXAMPLE Do **you** think Feng Jicai was influenced by China's literary tradition?
you—personal

Who has had the strongest impact on Chinese literary history? Most people would point to Confucius **who** was probably born in the sixth century BC. Interestingly, Confucius **himself** wrote **nothing** at all. Rather, **his** followers recorded **his** words in a collection called the *Analects.* Through this posthumous work, Confucius earned **himself** a reputation as the wisest scholar in China. **It** contained advice about moral living **which** influenced life and social interactions for many in China. **This** was truly an influential writer!

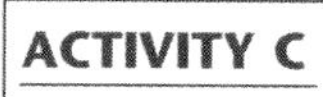

ACTIVITY C

VERBS AND VERBALS

Review the Language Arts Survey 2.7, "Types of Verbs" and 2.9, "Verbals." Then read the following sentences. On your own paper, identify the verb or verbs in each sentence, and label each verb as an action verb, a linking verb, or an auxiliary verb. Identify the verbals in each sentence, and label each as a gerund, participle, or infinitive.

EXAMPLE Translating foreign languages into Chinese is no easy task.
is—linking verb, **Translating**—gerund

1. Intrigued by newly discovered Western literature, nineteenth-century Chinese translators undertook this monumental task.
2. Reading new literary works for the first time sparked the imagination of China's writers.
3. To "westernize" Chinese literature became the goal of many writers.
4. Hoping to overhaul the literary language itself, Hu Shih called for a literature written in vernacular Chinese rather than in classical Chinese.
5. Other writers influenced Chinese literature by creating Marxist literary societies.

ACTIVITY D

ADJECTIVES, ARTICLES, ADVERBS, PREPOSITIONS, CONJUNCTIONS, AND CONJUNCTIVE ADVERBS

Review the Language Arts Survey 2.10, "Adjectives and Articles"; 2.11, "Adverbs"; 2.12, "Prepositions and Prepositional Phrases"; 2.13, "Conjunctions and Interjections"; and 2.14, "Conjunctive Adverbs." Identify the boldfaced words in the following paragraph as adjectives, proper adjectives, definite articles, indefinite articles, adverbs, prepositions, conjunctions, or conjunctive adverbs.

EXAMPLE **The** period of dynastic rule in China came to **an abrupt** end **with** the **Chinese** Revolution of 1912.
The—definite article; **an**—indefinite article; **abrupt**—adjective; **with**—preposition; **Chinese**—proper adjective

After the Chinese Revolution **in** 1912, the subjects and themes of literature produced in China became **increasingly political**; **however**, Mao Zedong's Cultural Revolution had **an even greater** impact on Chinese literature. **From** 1966 to 1977, only certain pro-Communist works were allowed to reach **the** public. Other artistic expression was prohibited. Many artists and writers kept their work private, **or** even stopped working altogether. **After** this period ended, many writers explored their **painful** memories of the years of oppression.

ANSWERS FOR SKILLS ACTIVITIES

ACTIVITY C

1. **intrigued** participle
discovered participle
undertook action verb
2. **reading** gerund
sparked action verb
3. **to "westernize"** infinitive
became linking verb
4. **hoping** gerund
to overhaul infinitive
called action verb
written participle
5. **influenced** action verb
creating gerund

ACTIVITY D

1. **in** preposition
2. **increasingly** adverb
3. **political** adjective
4. **however** conjunctive adverb
5. **an** indefinite article
6. **even** adverb
7. **greater** adjective
8. **From** preposition
9. **the** definite article
10. **or** conjunction
11. **After** preposition
12. **painful** adjective

SUPPORT FOR LEP STUDENTS

Pronunciations of Proper Nouns and Adjectives

Fu • ji (fü jē)
Ko • be (kō bā)
kon • ni • chi • wa (kō nē chē wä)
Ky • o• to (kē ōt ō)
Na • goy • a (nä goi ə)
Nik • ko (nēk ō)
sa • mu • rai (sam ə rī)
To • ky • o (tō kē ō)
Yu • mi • ko Yo • ko • chi (yü mē kō yō kō chē)

Cross-curricular Activities

SOCIAL STUDIES

Show students a map of Japan and ask them to locate the major cities, such as Tokyo, Osaka, Shikoku, Nagoya, and Kobe. Students should form groups and locate statistics about each of these cities, as well as others they select.

SOCIAL STUDIES

Yumiko notes that in most schools, students must adhere to strict dress codes. "From junior high school on, students usually wear uniforms. The length of your skirt should be within so many centimeters below your knees, and you cannot wear ribbons in your hair. Some schools do not allow students to wear a coat until November, even when it is cold! Having your ears pierced is usually against school rules. If you have earrings, you are a rebel!" Ask students to form groups and hold a debate about the question of dress codes in schools. Ask them to answer the following: Does dressing in a particular way help students to perform better in school? What problems might uniformity in dress solve? Do dress codes reinforce self-esteem, or do they restrict students' right to express themselves? You may want students to compare Yumiko's comments with Ebere's on page 23.

PASSPORT TO JAPAN

Konnichiwa! My name is Yumiko Yokochi and I am from Japan. Japan is an island country the size of California with half the population of the United States! Most of the island is mountainous, so much of the land cannot be used as residential areas. Can you imagine how crowded it is? My hometown is Nagoya, located in the central part of Japan between Tokyo and Kobe. Nagoya is the fifth biggest city in Japan, with a population of about 2.2 million.

You should feel fortunate that you are not a Japanese high school student! Japanese high school is very demanding. Many students go to cram school after regular school to get better grades and to get into a better college or university. From elementary school through high school, Japanese students attend school much longer than American students do. Japanese students attend school 240 days, or 48 weeks a year, whereas American students attend school for about 180 days, or 36 weeks. Even during summer and winter vacations, students in Japan have tons of homework to do. I remember doing most of it during the last week of the summer vacation without much sleep!

*– Yumiko Yokochi
Nagoya, Japan*

Japanese schoolboys

Bridge and cherry blossoms, Kofu

Cultural/Historical Note

Many Japanese traditions stem from Japan's religious heritage. For example, the tea ceremony is a Zen Buddhist ritual. Shinto and Buddhism are the principal religions of Japan. Only one percent of Japanese people are Christian. In addition, Chinese philosophies such as Confucianism and Taoism have deeply influenced Japanese thought. Shinto, the ancient native religion of Japan, was originally centered around the worship of *kami,* gods who were believed to reside in trees, mountains, waterfalls, and other natural objects. Buddhism came to Japan in AD 538 by way of China and Korea. Since then, variations of traditional Buddhism have developed in Japan, including Jodo, Shingon, Nicheren, and Zen. Ask students to form groups and choose one of these religions or sects to research.

Hard work in high school pays off for college students in Japan. We call college "four years of vacation." Not many Japanese college students study. The goal of a Japanese student is to get into a good university or college, which is very difficult, but once you get in, it is easy to graduate. Companies want to hire new graduates from good colleges or universities to educate them for their own corporate environment. They do not even look at college students' grades. Companies see potential in students who successfully got into a good university.

For enjoyment, Japanese high school students go to movies, play video games and sports, and go shopping. They are not allowed to drive cars, because in Japan you are allowed to get a license only when you become eighteen years old. High school students get to places by subway or bus. The Japanese subway system is very efficient. It is always on time, runs every couple of minutes, and is safe.

Comic books in Japan are very popular, even for adults. Some academic materials are available in comic book form. Sometimes

Ancient warrior dress

Bullet trains, Tokyo

Cultural/Historical Note

According to Yumiko, the diet in Japan is much healthier than in the United States. Japanese eat rice every day, even for breakfast. Japanese also eat more vegetables and less meat, in part because meat is expensive in Japan. Most people eat miso (soy bean paste) soup every day. Fast-food restaurants are becoming more popular in Japan, but the prices are much higher than in the United States. Yumiko says that studies in Japan indicate that obesity and heart disease have become more common since the introduction of Western fast-food restaurants and eating habits. Have students discuss their reactions to this information. What do they think of the claim that Western practices are causing health problems in Japan? Should more Americans emulate traditional Japanese eating patterns?

Cross-curricular Activities

ARTS AND HUMANITIES AND APPLIED ARTS

Yumiko notes that many Americans assume all sushi is raw fish, but sushi is actually the name for a variety of dishes made with sticky rice and flavored with vinegar, sugar, and salt. While some sushi dishes do contain raw fish, others are prepared with cooked fish, shrimp, or vegetables. One of Yumiko's sushi recipes follows:

Sushi Rice with Grilled Salmon

Ingredients:

- 3 cups sticky rice (don't use regular rice; it won't have the right consistency)
- 3 cups water
- 1/3 cup vinegar
- a bit less than 1/3 cup sugar
- a pinch of salt
- a filet of grilled salmon (can be found precooked in most grocery stores)
- 2 eggs
- 2 cucumbers
- dried seaweed (available at Asian food stores)

Preparation:

1. Cook the rice with water in a rice cooker.
2. Add vinegar, sugar, and salt to the cooked rice, and add flakes of the grilled salmon.
3. Fry the eggs with salt and chop them into pieces.
4. Chop the cucumbers into small pieces, and tear the seaweed by hand into small pieces.
5. Add the eggs, cucumbers, and seaweed to the rice.

Have students prepare this recipe and other Japanese dishes to share with the class. Some students might locate traditional Japanese music. Then hold a Japanese Culture Day to appreciate the music and cuisine of Japan.

Cross-curricular Activities

SOCIAL STUDIES

Yumiko mentions that in Japan, Coming of Age Day is an important day for Japanese young people. Other cultures have different ways of celebrating the beginning of adulthood. Ask students to work in groups to research coming-of-age traditions around the world, and prepare an oral report on a specific custom. Are these customs similar to any ceremonies held in the United States? What events or customs do students associate with their own "coming of age"?

SOCIAL STUDIES AND APPLIED ARTS

Although *kimono* literally means "clothes," today the word most often refers to a traditional robe. As Yumiko says on this page, Japanese men and women only wear kimonos on special occasions. Men's and boys' kimonos are made of wool and are dyed blue or dark brown. Men wear kimonos infrequently, but on *O shōgatsu* (New Year's Day), men sometimes wear kimonos to receive guests at home. Girls and women wear kimonos at coming-of-age and graduation ceremonies, wedding receptions, funeral services, and for visiting shrines on *O shōgatsu*. The appearance of women's kimonos depends on their marital status. Unmarried women wear long-sleeved, brightly colored kimonos with flower or bird designs, while married women wear black kimonos called *montsuki* that are embossed with their family crest or more subdued patterns. The most ornate kimonos are made of silk and embroidered with silver and gold thread.

Interested students can research the kimono, tracing its origins and adaptations through history. If any students have a kimono, they might bring it in to show the class. Some students might enjoy drawing pictures of their own kimono designs or sewing a doll-sized version to display in the classroom.

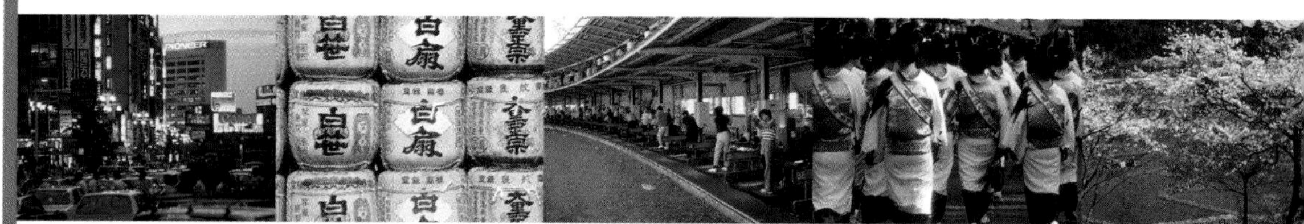

Japanese woman in traditional costume

seniors in high school read them to help study for big tests. You can learn about history, science, literature, or economics through comic books!

People in Japan usually dress in the same manner in their daily life as people do in the United States, though a little more formally—fewer jeans and sweatshirts and more skirts, slacks, blouses, and shirts. Kimonos? Only on special occasions, such as weddings, New Year's Day, and Coming of Age Day. On this day, most twenty-year-old women and men dress up, women in kimonos and men in suits, and attend a ceremony at city hall or at the local elementary school they used to attend. It is a very important day for young Japanese because it marks the day they become adults.

Some of the most popular tourist spots in Japan are Mt. Fuji, Tokyo Disneyland, and traditional towns such as Kyoto and Nikko. There are a lot of temples, shrines, and castles from centuries ago.

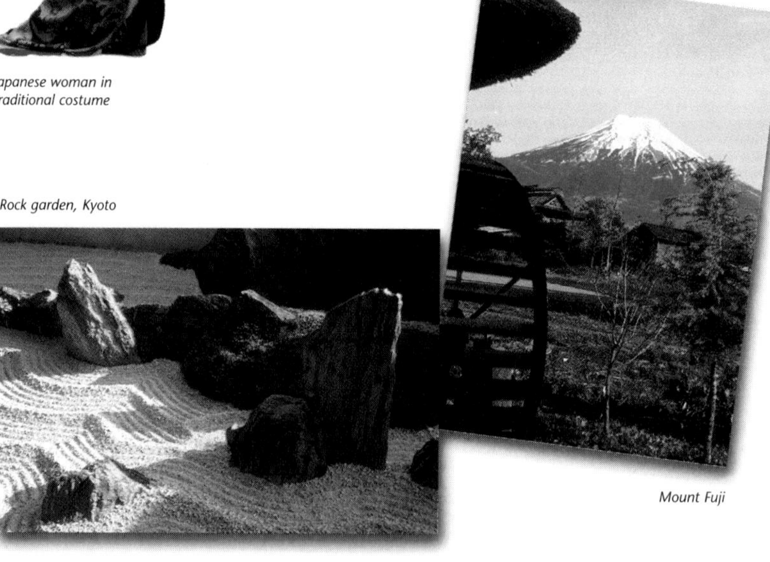

Rock garden, Kyoto

Mount Fuji

Cultural/Historical Note

Inform students that while Japanese gardens, which often feature rocks, gravel, and few plants, may look simple, gardening in Japan is a disciplined art. Gardeners carefully remove stray pine needles, hand-clip grass, and rake gravel in smooth patterns. The correct placement of stepping-stones is important, too. According to a seventeenth-century gardening guide, "There are many taboos concerning the placing of stones. It is said that if even one of them is violated . . . the place could become an abode of demons." Because gardening is so complex, shaped by Buddhist, Taoist, and Shinto traditions, training in this art once took about fifteen years. Today, although a gardener's apprenticeship rarely lasts that long, old traditions are still revered, and gardeners try to enhance rather than alter the natural landscape.

Many castles have now become museums, and you can see a lot of clothes, pictures, swords, and costumes of *samurai* from the time of feudalism.

When you meet Japanese people, you may notice that they are less talkative and look more reserved than you. We have a different value system in Japan and talking too much is not appreciated. Mature people are not supposed to talk too much but rather try to understand what others are thinking or needing without verbal messages. We value silence and space. If you look at a Japanese flower arrangement, you will notice how the space is a part of the art. There might be only a few flowers, but the space between the flowers also means something in Japanese art. There is an interesting difference in the sayings of the two countries. Here you say, "It is a squeaky wheel which gets oil," but in Japan we say, "Silence is golden," and "By your mouth you shall perish." ■

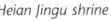

Heian Jingu shrine

Cultural/Historical Note

According to Yumiko, Japanese people "value silence and space." Ask students to consider her comment in light of what some cultural anthropologists have noted about densely populated areas such as Japan. For example, anthropologist Edward T. Hall noted that Japanese people perceive public space and private space differently than Americans do, simply because space is more limited. While more people in the United States have backyards and roomy homes or apartments to protect their privacy, Japanese people, especially those in large cities, may not have that luxury. Therefore, Japanese tend to be more respectful of each other's space when in public, and they don't behave rambunctiously when in a park or on the street. They see loud behavior in public as intruding on other people's space. Meanwhile, in the United States, more people seem to feel it is their right to behave however they wish in public spaces.

Concepts of space can affect such things as the way different cultures conduct business relations, relate to foreigners, and the way they plan their buildings and cities. (Examples in Japan include rice-paper walls and capsule hotel units.) The way people perceive space has been studied in the science of proxemics. Ask students to do further reading on this subject. Good books to consult include *The Hidden Dimension* by Edward T. Hall; *Proxemic Behavior: A Cross-Cultural Study* by O. Michael Watson; and *Spatial Representation and Behavior Across the Life Span: Theory and Application,* edited by Lynn S. Liben, Arthur H. Patterson, and Nora Newcombe.

Cultural/Historical Note

The shrine shown above was constructed during the Heian Period of Japanese history. The Heian Period (AD 794–1185) was a period of peace during which the inhabitants of Japan gained a strong sense of national identity. In the wealthy court of the emperor, the arts and literature were encouraged. The court lifestyle was extravagant, while the people who worked the land were very poor. There was widespread corruption and unrest which led to the rise of local leaders who were united near the end of the Heian period by Minamoto Yoritomo, who became the first shogun, or military dictator. For the next seven hundred years, Japan was ruled by warriors. Japanese author Murasaki Shikibu (c. 978–c. 1015) wrote about the court of Minamoto. For more about Murasaki Shikibu, see page 765.

ADDITIONAL RESOURCES

READER'S GUIDE

• Selection Worksheet 1.8

ASSESSMENT PORTFOLIO

• Selection Check Test 2.1.13
• Selection Test 2.1.14

ESSENTIAL SKILLS PRACTICE BOOKS

• Writing Skills 1.8–1.10

PREREADING EXTENSIONS

Invite students to go to the library to find some of the works of Edgar Allan Poe. Each student should copy at least two or three lines or passages that demonstrate Poe's fascination with the grotesque, with psychological horror, and with the supernatural. After they have read "The Nose," students can compare the styles of the two authors in a class discussion.

SUPPORT FOR LEP STUDENTS

PRONUNCIATIONS OF PROPER NOUNS AND ADJECTIVES

Zen • chi Na • i • gu (zen chē nä ē goo)

ADDITIONAL VOCABULARY

concoction—strange mixture
diameter—width of a circle, or something resembling a circle
dignity—pride
premeditated—planned or thought out beforehand
preoccupation—the state of being overly consumed by a particular thought
oblong—rectangular
nuisance—pest, bother
precincts—grounds surrounding a religious structure
scrutinize—study critically
tormented—seriously tortured and upset
quandary—tricky situation

PREREADING

"The Nose"
by Akutagawa Ryunosuke, translated by Takashi Kojima

JAPAN

About the Author

AKUTAGAWA RYUNOSUKE
1892–1927

Akutagawa Ryunosuke was born on a dairy farm in Tokyo. Because his mother suffered from mental illness, he was raised from infancy by his maternal grandparents. He was later adopted by an uncle, but his mother's illness troubled him and often shadowed the events of his own life. Nevertheless, as a young man, Akutagawa found success. He graduated from the prestigious Tokyo University, where he studied English. He explored Chinese and Japanese classical and modern works as well as the works of European authors such as Tolstoy, Dostoyevsky, Baudelaire, and Nietzsche. This reading shaped his writing.

Akutagawa, a versatile writer, composed short stories, plays, and poetry. His view of humanity, as reflected in his writing, grew increasingly dark, and he took his own life in 1927, shocking the literary world. A prestigious Japanese prize for young writers—the Akutagawa Prize—was named for him. This award has become distinguished and assures success to writers just beginning their careers. Akutagawa was one of the first modern Japanese writers to be read outside of Japan, and two of his stories formed the basis for the classic film *Rashomon* (1950), which was internationally acclaimed.

About the Selection

The Japanese novelist Natsume Soseki brought Akutagawa's writing before the public after reading his short story **"The Nose."** It is an imaginative story about a Buddhist priest, Zenchi Naigu, who must go through life with a most unusual nose. Zenchi wishes desperately for help in changing his situation but finds that when wishes come true, they don't always bring the results one was expecting. This theme recurs throughout Akutagawa's work. As you read, notice the colorful, almost grotesque, imagery and the dark, psychological insights for which Akutagawa is known.

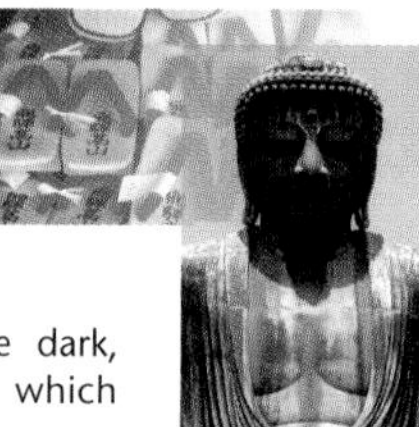

CONNECTIONS: Edgar Allan Poe's Japanese Counterpart

Because Akutagawa is best known to English readers for vividly grotesque stories about old Japan and for stories dealing with the theme of madness, he has been called the Edgar Allan Poe of Japan. Poe, the nineteenth-century American writer who pioneered the psychological horror story, wrote grotesque tales of insanity and the supernatural, including "The Tell-Tale Heart," "The Fall of the House of Usher," "The Pit and the Pendulum," and "The Black Cat." Akutagawa, like Poe, was a skilled storyteller who produced rich narratives dealing with dark themes and eccentric human behavior.

GOALS/OBJECTIVES

Studying this lesson will enable students to

• enjoy a story with colorful imagery about a priest with an unusual problem
• discuss the life and work of Akutagawa Ryunosuke
• define the literary terms *imagery, repetition,* and *irony*
• practice creative writing and techniques for gathering ideas

If you could change one part of your appearance or personality, what would it be? Why would you like to make this change? Would it be better to learn to accept yourself as you are? Why, or why not?

READER'S JOURNAL

"The Nose"

AKUTAGAWA RYUNOSUKE, TRANSLATED BY TAKASHI KOJIMA

In the town of Ike-no-O there was no one who had not heard of Zenchi Naigu's nose. Dangling from his upper lip to below his chin, five or six inches long, it was of the same thickness from end to end.

For fifty years he had been tormented at heart by the presence of his nose—from his young days as an acolyte until the time he rose to the respected office of Palace Chaplain. To others he tried to appear unconcerned about his nose, not so much because his preoccupation with such a matter was not worthy of a man whose duty it was to devote himself ardently to prayer for the advent of Paradise as because he wished to keep from the knowledge of others that he was worried over his nose. With him his apparent concern was rather a matter of pride, and his greatest dread in everyday conversation was to hear the word *nose*.

His nose was, of course, an intolerable nuisance. In the first place, he could not take his meals by himself. If he tried, the tip of his nose would reach down into the boiled rice in his bowl. So at meals he had to have one of his disciples sit opposite him and hold up the end of his nose with an oblong piece of wood about two feet long and an inch wide. This manner of taking meals was, of course, no easy matter for the priest whose nose was held up or for his disciple who held it up.

Once a page, who was acting in the place of the disciple, happened to sneeze and dropped the nose into the bowl—this incident was talked about as far as Kyoto.[1] He could accept the practical inconvenience of having a long nose, but the loss of his dignity on account of it was intolerable.

The Ike-no-O townspeople used to say that it was fortunate for the priest that he was not a layman, for surely no woman would care to be the wife of a man who had such a nose. Some went so far as to say that were it not for his nose, he might not have taken holy orders.[2]

1. **Kyoto.** City in Japan, formerly the capital
2. **holy orders.** Steps toward becoming a priest

❶ *Why had everyone in the town of Ike-no-O heard of Zenchi Naigu's nose?*

❷ *What do the townspeople say about Zenchi and his decision to become a priest?*

❸ *In what way is Zenchi's nose an intolerable nuisance?*

WORDS FOR EVERYDAY USE

ac • o • lyte (ak´ ə līt) *n.,* young religious apprentice
page (pāj) *n.,* boy servant to a person of high rank
lay • man (lā´ mən) *n.,* person who does not belong to the clergy

READER'S JOURNAL

As an alternative activity, students might write about the lengths to which some people will go to live up to some standard of beauty. Why do people do this?

ANSWERS TO GUIDED READING QUESTIONS

❶ Everyone in the town had heard of his nose because it was unusually long.

❷ People say that it was fortunate that he became a priest, because surely no woman would care for a man with such a nose.

❸ His nose is an intolerable nuisance in that it interferes with his ability to enjoy a meal.

SPELLING AND VOCABULARY WORDS FROM THE SELECTION

acolyte	ingenuity
assiduous	layman
attribute	nonchalance
caprice	page
deficient	plausible
enmity	
implicit	

VOCABULARY IN CONTEXT

- The young acolyte lit candles in the church.
- The leader's page brought him the newspaper and his appointment book.
- Many people who teach religious education classes are members of the clergy, but that teacher is a layman.

Answers to Guided Reading Questions

❶ His sole concern is to resort to every possible means to heal the wounds his pride has suffered.

❷ He looks in the mirror, studying his nose from all angles, trying to figure out ways to make his nose appear shorter.

❸ He scrutinizes the visitors to find at least one with a nose like his own.

Cultural/Historical Note

In this textbook, students will be reading other selections by Japanese authors. You might want to share with students the following facts about the Japanese language.

In Japan, the surname, or family name, is placed before a person's given name. English-speaking people will sometimes reverse Japanese names to follow the order in which names are written in English, with the given name first and the surname last. In this textbook, however, Japanese names are kept in the order in which they would be written in Japan. So, Akutagawa is this author's surname and Ryunosuke is his given name.

When speaking Japanese, pitch is directly related to meaning. The same combination of letters can have different meanings depending on how they are spoken. For example, in standard Japanese, the word *hashi* means "bridge" when it is spoken with a low pitch on *ha* and a higher pitch on *shi*. When *hashi* is spoken with a high pitch on *ha* and a low pitch on *shi*, it means "chopsticks."

Nevertheless, there are no word stress accents in Japanese as there are in English. Each syllable is spoken with even stress and rhythm; thus, in the pronunciations for Japanese words provided in this text you will note that no stress marks appear.

He did not consider that his priesthood had been a refuge which offered him any service in lightening the burden of his nose. Moreover his pride was too delicately strung for him to be influenced in the least by such a worldly eventuality as matrimony. His sole concern was to resort to every possible means to heal the wounds his pride had suffered and to repair the losses his dignity had sustained.

❶ *What is Zenchi's sole concern in his role as priest?*

He exhausted all possible means to make his nose appear shorter than it really was. When there was no one about, he would examine his nose in the mirror and look at it from various angles, taxing his ingenuity to the utmost. Just changing the reflections of his face in the mirror was not enough: prodding his cheeks, or putting his finger on the tip of his chin, he would patiently study his face in the mirror. But not once could he satisfy himself that his nose was shorter. Indeed, it often happened that the more he studied his nose the longer it seemed to be. On such occasions, he would put his mirror back into its box, sighing heavily, and sadly going back to his lectern would continue chanting the sutra to Kwannon, or the Goddess of Mercy.

❷ *What does Zenchi try to do as he looks at himself in the mirror?*

He paid close attention to other people's noses. The Temple of Ike-no-O, frequented by a large number of visitors, both priests and laymen, held Buddhist masses, receptions for visiting priests, and sermons for parishioners. The precincts of the Temple were lined with closely built cells, with a bathhouse which had heated water daily. He would closely scrutinize the visitors, patiently trying to find at least one person who might possibly have a nose like his own in order that he might ease his troubled mind. He took no notice of the rich silken attire, the ordinary hempen[3] clothes, the priests' saffron[4] hoods nor their dark sacerdotal robes,[5] all of which counted for next to nothing in his eyes. That which arrested his eyes was not the people or their attire but their noses. He could find hooked noses but none like his own. Each additional failure made his thinking darker and gloomier.

❸ *Why does Zenchi closely scrutinize the visitors at the Buddhist masses?*

While talking with others, unconsciously he would take between his fingers the tip of his dangling nose; then he would blush with shame for an act ill fitting his years and office. His misfortune had driven him to such extremes.

In his desperate attempt to find some consolation by discovering someone with a nose like his own, he delved into the voluminous Buddhist scriptures; but in all the scriptures there was not one reference to a long nose. How comforting it would have been to find, for instance, that either Mu Lien or Sha Lien[6] had a long nose.

He did find that King Liu Hsan-ti[7] of the Kingdom of Chu-han in the third century A.D. had long ears, and thought how reassuring it would have been if it had happened that the King's nose, instead of his ears, had been long.

It need hardly be said that while taking assiduous pains to seek spiritual consolation, he did try most earnestly a variety of elaborate practical measures to shorten his nose.

At one time he took a concoction with a snake-gourd[8] base. At another he bathed his nose in the urine of mice; yet with all his

3. **hempen.** Made of a heavy, rope-like fiber called hemp
4. **saffron.** Orange-yellow in color, as in the plant of the same name
5. **sacerdotal robes.** Robes worn by a priest
6. **Mu Lien or Sha Lien.** Two important disciples of Buddha
7. **King Liu Hsan-ti.** King of China mentioned in Buddhist legends
8. **snake-gourd.** Plant related to squash

Words for Everyday Use

in • ge • nu • i • ty (in´jə no͞o´ə tē) *n.*, cleverness, originality, skill
as • sid • u • ous (ə sij´o͞o əs) *adj.*, constant and careful; diligent

Vocabulary in Context

- Due to my sister's mechanical ingenuity, we were able to get the car working.
- He gives his school work consistent, assiduous effort.

The River Bridge at Uji. *Japanese; Momyama period (1568–1614). The Nelson–Atkins Museum of Art, Kansas City, MO Purchase: Nelson Trust*

persistent and unremitting efforts, he still had five to six inches of nose dangling down over his lips.

One autumn day a disciple went on a trip to Kyoto, partly on his master's business, and before his returning to Ike-no-O, his physician acquaintance happened to introduce him to the mysteries of shortening noses. The physician, who had come to Japan from China, was at that time a priest attached to the Choraku Temple.

Zenchi, with an assumed nonchalance, avoided calling for an immediate test of the remedy, and could only drop casual hints about his regret that he must cause his disciple so much bother at meals, although he eagerly waited in his heart for his disciple to persuade him to try the remedy. The disciple could not fail to see through his master's design. But his master's innermost feelings, which led him to work out such an elaborate scheme, aroused his disciple's sympathy. As Zenchi had expected, his disciple advised him to try this method with such extraordinary urgency that, according to his premeditated plan, he finally yielded to his earnest counsel.

1 *With what has the disciple become acquainted?*

Words for Everyday Use

non • cha • lance (nän´shə läns´) *n.,* state or attitude of being unconcerned

Art Note

Uji, the backdrop of the painting featured on this page, is located near the major city of Kyoto. Uji is the home of a structure called Phoenix Hall, which is considered a beautiful example of Japanese architecture and design. This structure, constructed during the Heian period (898–1185), is known for its airy spaciousness and and its beautiful setting beside a lake filled with lotus plants. A lotus is a type of water lily. Asian lotus plants are generally pink or white and they are religiously symbolic in Hinduism and Buddhism.

Answers to Guided Reading Questions

1 The disciple becomes acquainted with a method to shorten Zenchi's nose.

Bibliographic Note

If students are interested in reading more of the work of Akutagawa Ryunosuke, you can provide them with the following titles:

Hell Screen and Other Stories. Trans. W. H. H. Norman

Rashomon and Other Stories. Trans. Takashi Kojima

Japanese Short Stories. Trans. Takashi Kojima

Kappa. Trans. Geoffrey Bownas

Vocabulary in Context

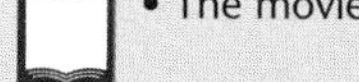

• The movie star received her award with planned nonchalance.

Answers to Guided Reading Questions

➊ The formula is as follows: boil the nose in hot water, then trample on it and torment it.

➋ Zenchi is concerned about the painful treatment, but he endures it.

➌ The treatment is a success—Zenchis nose becomes normal in size.

Literary Technique

IMAGERY

An **image** is a word or phrase that names something that can be seen, heard, touched, tasted or smelled. The images in a literary work are referred to collectively as the work's **imagery.**

Point out to students that the scene on this page, which shows Zenchi enduring a painful treatment designed to shorten his nose, features a use of grotesque imagery for which the author is well known. Ask students to find some of the strangest, most striking imagery and describe the pictures these images paint in their minds. To what senses do they appeal? Do they give the reader a good idea of what the main character is experiencing?

Additional Questions and Activities

Ask students to discuss how they feel about the fact that Zenchi is willing to put himself through such an awful treatment. Do they understand his feelings and feel bad for him, or do they think he is simply being foolish? Encourage them to explain their responses.

Q ➊ *What is the formula prescribed by the disciple?*

Q ➋ *How does Zenchi feel about the treatment prescribed by the disciple?*

Q ➌ *What is the result of this unusual "treatment"?*

The formula was a simple one: first to boil the nose in hot water, and then to let another trample on it and torment it.

At the Temple bathhouse water was kept "at the boil" daily, so his disciple brought in an iron ladle, water so hot that no one could have put a finger into it. It was feared that Zenchi's face would be scalded by steam; so they bored a hole in a wooden tray and used the tray as a lid to cover the pot so that his nose could be immersed in the boiling water.

As for his nose, no matter how long it was soaked in the scalding water, it was immune from ill effect.

"Your Reverence," the disciple said after a while, "I suppose it must be sufficiently boiled by now."

The Chaplain, with a wry smile, was thinking that no one who overheard this remark could suspect that it concerned a remedy for shortening his nose.

Heated by water and steam, his nose itched as if bitten by mosquitoes.

When the nose was withdrawn from the hole in the lid, the disciple set about trampling on that steaming object, exerting all his strength in pounding it with both his feet. Zenchi, lying on his side, and stretching his nose on the floorboards, watched his disciple's legs move up and down.

"Does it hurt, Your Reverence?" his disciple asked from time to time, looking down sympathetically on the priest's bald head.

"The physician told me to trample hard on it. Doesn't it hurt?"

Zenchi tried to shake his head by way of indicating that he was not feeling any pain, but as his nose was being trampled on he could not do this, so rolling his eyes upwards, in a tone that suggested he was offended, and with his gaze fixed on his disciple's chapped feet, he said, "No, it doesn't hurt." Although his itching nose was being trampled on, it was a comfortable rather than a painful sensation.

His nose having undergone this treatment for some time, what seemed to be grains of millet[9] began to appear, at which sight his disciple stopped trampling and said in soliloquy, "I was told to pull them out with tweezers."

The nose looked like a plucked and roasted chicken. With cheeks puffed out, though disgruntled, the priest suffered his disciple to deal with his nose as the man saw fit—although, however aware of his disciple's kindness he might have been, he did not relish his nose being treated as if it were a piece of inert matter. Like a patient undergoing an operation at the hands of a surgeon in whom he does not place implicit trust, Zenchi reluctantly watched his disciple extract, from the pores of his nose, feathers of fat curled to half an inch in diameter. The treatment finished, the disciple looked relieved and said: "Now, your Reverence, we have only to boil it once more, and it'll be all right."

Zenchi, with knit brow, submitted to the treatment meted out to him.

When his nose was taken out of the pot for the second time, it was found, to their great surprise, remarkably shorter than before and was not very different from a normal hooked nose. Stroking his greatly shortened nose, he timidly and nervously peered into the mirror which his disciple held out to him.

The nose, which previously had dangled below his chin, had miraculously dwindled, and, not protruding below his upper lip, was barely a relic of what it had once been. The red blotches which bespeckled it were probably only bruises caused by the trampling.

9. **millet.** Small pieces of grain

Words for Everyday Use

im • plic • it (im plis´it) *adj.*, complete

Vocabulary in Context

• They have implicit trust in their babysitter.

"No one will laugh at me any more," the priest thought to himself. He saw in the mirror that the face reflected there was looking into the face outside the mirror, blinking its eyes in satisfaction.

But all day long he was uneasy and feared that his nose might grow long; so whenever he had the chance, whether in chanting sutras or in eating meals, he stealthily touched his nose. However, he found his nose installed in good shape above his upper lip, without straying beyond his lower lip.

Early in the morning, at the moment of waking, he stroked the tip of his nose, and he found that it was still as short as ever. After a gap of many years he at that moment recognized the same relief he had felt when he had completed the austerities[10] required for his transcription of the lengthy Lotus Sutra of his sect.[11]

Within the course of several days, however, Zenchi had a most surprising experience. A samurai[12] who, on business, visited the Temple of Ike-no-O, looked amused as never before, and, quite incapable of uttering a word, he could but stare fixedly at the priest's nose. This was not all. The page who once had dropped Zenchi's nose into the bowl of gruel[13] happened to pass by Zenchi in the lecture hall; at first, resisting his impulse to laugh, casting down his eyes, he could not for long withhold his burst of laughter. The sextons[14] under Zenchi's supervision would listen respectfully while seated face to face with their master, but on more than one occasion they fell to chuckling as soon as he turned his back.

Zenchi at first attributed the laughter of his page and the sextons to the marked change in his features, but by and by, with his head cocked on one side, interrupting the sutra he was chanting he would mutter to himself: "The change alone does not give a plausible explanation for their laughter. Zenchi Naigu! their laughter is now different from what it was when your nose was long. If you could say that the unfamiliar nose looks more ridiculous than the familiar one, that would once and for all settle the matter. But there must be some other reason behind it; they didn't laugh heartily or irresistibly as before."

The poor amiable priest on such occasions would look up at Fugen, Goddess of Wisdom,[15] pictured on the scroll hanging close beside him, and calling to mind the long nose he had wielded until four or five days previously, he would lapse into melancholy "like one sunken low recalleth his glory of bygone days."[16] But it was to be regretted that he was deficient in judgment sufficient to find a solution to this quandary.

Man is possessed of two contradictory sentiments. Everyone will sympathize with another's misfortune. But when the other manages to pull through his misfortune, he not only thinks it safe to laugh at him to his face but also comes even to regard him with envy. In extreme cases some may feel like casting him into his former misfortune again and may even harbor some enmity, if negative, toward him.

Zenchi was at a loss to know what precisely made him forlorn, but his unhappiness was caused by nothing more than the wayward caprices of those surrounding him—the priests and laymen of Ike-no-O.

❶ *How does Zenchi feel about his new appearance?*

❷ *What concern plagues Zenchi?*

❸ *What surprises Zenchi about the reactions of those around him?*

❹ *What does the narrator say about human nature? According to the narrator, why are people now laughing at Zenchi?*

10. **austerities.** Severe rituals involving self-discipline and self-denial
11. **sect.** Religious group
12. **samurai.** Member of the military class in feudal Japan
13. **gruel.** Thin porridge
14. **sextons.** Temple officials
15. **Fugen, Goddess of Wisdom.** Spiritually superior being who sits at Buddha's side and offers human redemption
16. **"like one . . . days."** Words from Buddhist scripture

WORDS FOR EVERYDAY USE

at • trib • ute (ə trib´ yo͞ot) *vt.*, recognize as the cause of

plau • si • ble (plô´ zə bəl) *adj.*, believable, acceptable

de • fi • cient (dē fish´ ənt) *adj.*, lacking or inadequate

en • mi • ty (en´ mə tē) *n.*, anger and hostility

ca • price (kə prēs´) *n.*, sudden change in behavior

ANSWERS TO GUIDED READING QUESTIONS

❶ Zenchi is happy with his new appearance and feels that no one will laugh at him now.

❷ He is concerned that his nose might grow back to the way it was.

❸ People seem to be laughing at him and mocking him.

❹ The narrator says that, although people can sympathize with another's misfortune, when the person manages to pull through this misfortune, people will laugh or even regard the person with envy. People are laughing at Zenchi because, now that he has pulled out of his misfortune, it is safe to laugh. People might also be envious of him.

QUOTABLES

"Do not hold everything as gold that shines like gold."

—Alain De Lille
Parabolae

ADDITIONAL QUESTIONS AND ACTIVITIES

Ask students to discuss the narrator's comments about human nature, beginning "Man is possessed of two contradictory sentiments. Everyone will sympathize with another's . . ." What do these comments mean to them? Do they believe these comments to be true? Why, or why not?

VOCABULARY IN CONTEXT

- I attribute my exhaustion to not getting enough sleep at night.
- Frankly, I don't think his excuse is at all plausible.
- If you don't eat properly, you might find that your body is deficient in vitamins.
- We hope that the peace talks will calm some of the enmity between these two leaders.
- On a caprice, we decided to change our plans and take a two-hour ride to our favorite beach.

ANSWERS TO GUIDED READING QUESTIONS

❶ Zenchi hits the page with a stick because the page seems to be teasing Zenchi.

❷ Overnight, Zenchi's nose has grown back to the way it was.

❸ Zenchi is happy that his nose has returned to the way it was. He feels that nobody will laugh at him anymore.

SELECTION CHECK TEST WITH ANSWERS

EX. What is unusual about Zenchi's nose?
His nose is extremely long and dangles from his upper lip to below his chin.

1. What is Zenchi's occupation?
He is a priest.

2. Why is Zenchi's nose such a nuisance?
It affects his ability to eat and it makes him self-conscious.

3. What happens when Zenchi tries a new remedy brought to him by a disciple?
His nose gets shorter.

4. What is unusual about the reactions of people to Zenchi's new nose?
People make fun of him.

5. When Zenchi awakens at the end of the story, what has happened to his nose?
His nose has gone back to the length it was originally.

❶ *What does Zenchi do to the page? Why?*

❷ *What has happened to Zenchi's nose overnight?*

❸ *How does Zenchi feel when he realizes what has happened to his nose? Why does he feel this way?*

Day after day Zenchi, becoming more and more unhappy and vexed, would not open his mouth without speaking sharply to someone and was ever out-of-sorts until even the disciple who had administered to him the effective remedy began to backbite him, saying, "The master will be punished for his sins."

What especially enraged Zenchi was the mischief played on him by the page. One day, hearing a dog yelping wildly, he casually looked outside and found the page, with a stick about two feet long in his hand, chasing a lean and shaggy dog and shouting "Watch out there for your nose! Watch out or I'll hit your nose." Snatching the wooden stick from the page's hand, the priest struck him sharply across the face; it was the very stick which had been used to hold up Zenchi's nose.

Finally Zenchi came to feel sorry and even resentful for having had his long nose shortened.

One night after sunset it happened that the wind seeming to have arisen suddenly, the noisy tinkling of the pagoda wind bells[17] came to his cell. The cold, moreover, had so noticeably increased in severity that Zenchi could not go to sleep, try as he might; tossing and turning in his bed he became aware of an itching in his nose. Putting his hand to his nose he felt that it had become swollen as if with dropsy;[18] it seemed feverish, too.

"It was so drastically shortened that I might have caught some disease," he muttered to himself, caressing his nose as reverently as he would if he were holding the offerings of incense and flowers to be dedicated at the altar.

On the following morning Zenchi as usual awoke early, and he noticed that the garden was as bright as if it were carpeted with gold, because in the garden the ginkgo trees and horse chestnuts had overnight shed all their leaves; and the crest of the pagoda must have been encrusted with frost, for the nine copper rings of the spire were brightly shining in the still faint glimmer of the rising sun. Sitting on the veranda, the shutters already opened, he drew a deep breath, and at that same moment a certain feeling, the nature of which he had all but forgotten, came back to him.

Instinctively he put his hand to his nose, and what he touched was not the short nose that had been his the night before, but the former long nose that had dangled five or six inches over his lips; in one night, he found, his nose had grown as long as it had been previously, and this, for some reason, made him feel refreshed and as happy as he had felt in the first moments when his nose had been shortened.

"Nobody will laugh at me any more," he whispered to himself.

His long nose dangled in the autumn breeze of early morning. ■

17. **pagoda wind bells.** Wind chimes at the temple
18. **dropsy.** Type of swelling

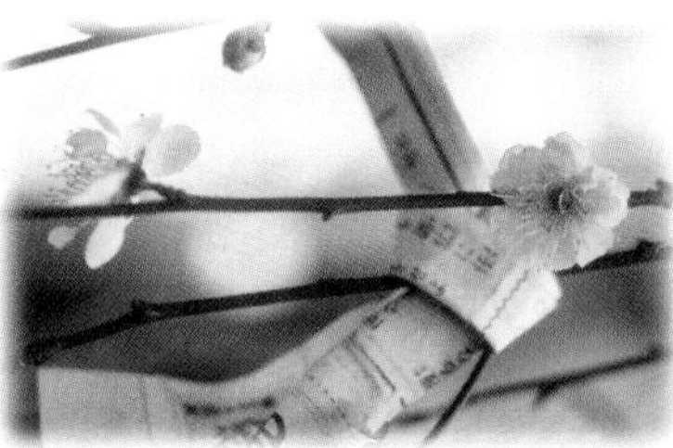

Japanese paper fortune

ANSWERS FOR REVIEWING THE SELECTION (CONT.)

4. **Recalling.** His nose has gone back to its original size. Zenchi is relieved. **Interpreting.** Zenchi wants to go back to what is normal and comfortable for himself and those around him. He has learned that going to great lengths to improve one's appearance is not always worth the effort and does not always produce expected results.

SYNTHESIZING

Responses will vary. Possible responses are given.

5. The author knows that people compare themselves to others, and that people just want to be accepted. He also knows that some people feel better about themselves in the face of another's misfortune and can feel threatened by a person's good fortune.

Responding to the Selection

If you were a disciple at Zenchi's temple, what advice would you have given him before he shrunk his nose? after?

Reviewing the Selection

RECALLING

INTERPRETING

1. Why is Zenchi's nose a nuisance? What do people say motivated his decision to become a priest? What is Zenchi's "sole concern" as a priest? ▶▶ What effect has Zenchi's nose had on his feelings of self-pride and dignity? Explain whether you think Zenchi's concerns are in keeping with his situation in life.

2. What remedy does the disciple urge Zenchi to try? What happens when Zenchi tries the remedy? ▶▶ What is the main reason for Zenchi's wanting to shorten his nose? What does he hope people will no longer do?

3. How do people react to Zenchi's shortened nose? ▶▶ To what does Zenchi attribute people's reactions to his new nose? What explanation does the narrator provide for their reactions?

4. When Zenchi awakens at the end of the story, what has happened to his new nose? What is Zenchi's reaction? ▶▶ Why does Zenchi react this way when he discovers what has happened to his nose? What has he learned by the end of the story?

SYNTHESIZING

5. What does this story reveal about the author's understanding of human nature? What does the author apparently believe motivates humans? How do you think the author feels about Zenchi in particular? humans in general?

Understanding Literature (Questions for Discussion)

1. **Imagery.** An **image** is a word or phrase that names something that can be seen, heard, touched, tasted, or smelled. The images in a literary work are referred to collectively as the work's **imagery**. Akutagawa Ryunosuke is known for his unique and grotesque, or distorted and eccentric, imagery. Cite some of the strikingly unique and grotesque images in this piece.

RESPONDING TO THE SELECTION

Students might also discuss among themselves why it is so important to Zenchi that his nose be different, and why it then becomes important to him that his nose go back to its original size.

ANSWERS FOR REVIEWING THE SELECTION

RECALLING AND INTERPRETING

1. **Recalling.** Zenchi's nose is a nuisance because it is too long. People say that he became a priest because no woman would love a man with such a long nose. Zenchi's "sole concern" is to heal the wounds his pride has suffered because of his nose. **Interpreting.** Zenchi's self-pride and dignity have suffered because of his nose. Because he has always had to deal with the problems associated with his long nose, his preoccupation with his appearance, the appearance of parishioners, and with shortening his nose is understandable.

2. **Recalling.** The disciple urges Zenchi to try a remedy that includes placing the nose in boiling water and then "trampling and tormenting" it. When Zenchi tries the remedy, his nose becomes shorter. **Interpreting.** Zenchi is hoping that he will no longer stand out as an unusual-looking person. He is hoping people will no longer laugh at him.

3. **Recalling.** People laugh at Zenchi's new nose. **Interpreting.** Zenchi attributes the laughter to the radical change in his appearance. Then he becomes concerned that the new nose is more ridiculous than the old nose. The narrator says that although people are willing to sympathize with another's misfortune, when a person manages to pull through his or her misfortune, people feel free to laugh at the person and sometimes even feel envy or anger.

(cont.)

Answers for Understanding Literature

Responses will vary. Possible responses are given.

1. Imagery. Students might name images that describe the length and awkwardness of Zenchi's nose, such as "Dangling from his upper lip to below his chin . . ," and "If he tried the tip of his nose would reach down into the boiled rice in his bowl. So at meals he had to have one of his disciples sit opposite him and hold up the end of his nose. . . ." Students might also name the images describing the measures Zenchi takes to shorten his nose, including the final, drastic remedy suggested by the disciple. For example: "The nose looked like a plucked and roasted chicken . . ," or "Zenchi reluctantly watched his disciple extract, from the pores of his nose, feathers of fat curled to half an inch in diameter."

2. Repetition. Zenchi wants to be accepted, and he does not want people to look at his nose and laugh at him. The fact that he believes that people are laughing at him is what motivates him to torture himself to get a new nose. When he is trying to get his new nose, he believes that if he changes his appearance people will stop laughing at him. By the end of the story, the reader believes that if Zenchi accepts himself and his unusual nose, people will no longer laugh at him.

3. Irony. One might expect that Zenchi would not tolerate such a degrading treatment. Someone with a great deal of self-respect would not put himself through such a treatment just to look like everyone else.

2. **Repetition. Repetition** is the use, again, of a sound, word, phrase, sentence, or other element. Explain the repetition in the story of the phrase "No one will laugh at me anymore." What does this line reveal about the story's theme? What does this phrase mean at different points in the story?

3. **Irony. Irony** is a difference between appearance and reality. If Zenchi longs for respect and dignity, why is his tolerance of his disciple's remedy ironic?

WRITING SKILLS

CREATIVE WRITING

The stories, poems, plays, and novel excerpts that you will read in this book are all examples of creative writing. Creative writing attempts to interest or entertain readers and to allow readers to experience situations, characters, adventures, or moral dilemmas that they might not otherwise have the chance to experience.

With each work of literature that you read in this book, you will have the chance—through writing activities related to specific selections—to tap into your own creativity. Even if you have never considered yourself a writer, by this time in your life you have probably had enough interesting, funny, and sad experiences to fill the pages of a novel. To fully explore your own creative talent, you need to start looking at the events and people in your life—first days of school, family gatherings, arguments, long road trips, current events, relatives, friends, and neighbors—through the eyes of a writer. Of course, you will not be asked to write a novel. You will, however, have the chance to practice such different forms as descriptive paragraphs, character sketches, songs, simple poems, stories, and lines of dialogue. As you try your hand at creative writing, it is important to relax and have fun with the assignments.

To come up with ideas for creative writing, you need to free your imagination. The following prewriting techniques will help you to bring your most important memories, imaginings, and ideas to the surface and help you write about them in a way that will interest your reader:

- **Freewriting.** Freewriting is simply taking a pencil and paper and writing whatever comes into your mind without stopping and without worrying about spelling, grammar, usage, or mechanics.

> FREEWRITE I don't know what to write about. Crumbling pencil eraser. How do I start? One of the legs of my chair is shorter than the other and it rocks. Rocking horse. I remember the old plastic rocking horse in our garage. It had a bee's nest inside. Bee stings feel like pin pricks . . . .

- **Questioning.** Asking questions beginning with the words *what if* can be an excellent way to spark your imagination and find ideas you never knew you could have. For example: What if I could travel to any time and place and talk with an average teenager? Where would I go? What might I ask him or her?

• **Clustering.** Another good way to gather ideas is to make a cluster chart. To make a cluster chart, draw a circle in the center of your paper. In it write a topic you want to explore. Draw more circles branching out from your center circle, and fill them with subtopics related to your main topic. You can then expound on your ideas by creating circles related to your subtopics. The beginning of a cluster chart is shown below.

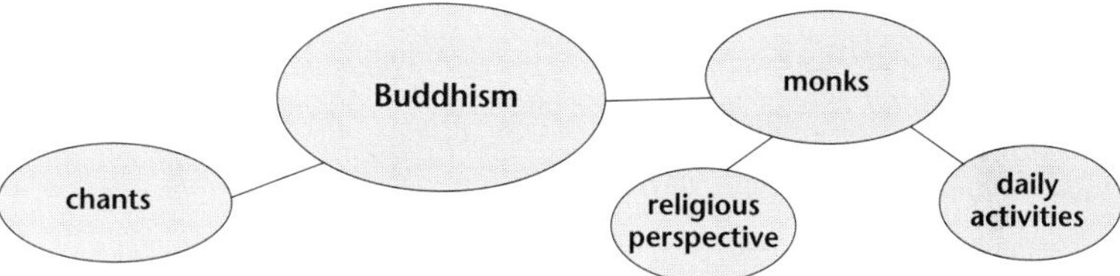

• **Sensory Detail Charts.** A sensory detail chart helps when you need to collect information about something so that you can describe it thoroughly. For example:

THE OLD MOVIE THEATER (BEFORE A SHOW STARTS)				
SIGHT	SOUND	TOUCH	TASTE	SMELL
row of seats	munching candy and popcorn	torn velvet seats	flat soda	buttered popcorn
tiny lights lining the aisle	squeaking of straws through plastic lids	sticky floors	chocolate-covered raisins	
	low talking and whispering			

• **Time Lines.** A time line is helpful if you are planning to write a story. It gives you an overview of the sequence of events during a particular time period. To make a time line, simply draw a line on a piece of paper and divide it into equal parts. Label each part with a date or a time. Then add key events at the right places along the time line. To see a sample time line, refer to the Language Arts Survey 1.10, "Gathering Ideas."

• **Story Maps.** A story map is a chart that shows the various parts of a fable, myth, tall tale, legend, short story, or other fictional work. Most story maps include setting, mood, conflict, plot, characters, and theme. To see a sample story map, turn to the Language Arts Survey 1.10, "Gathering Ideas."

ACTIVITY

Create a character who, like Zenchi Naigu and his nose, has something strange and unusual about either his or her personal appearance or his or her personality. Perhaps your character is someone who is afraid to cut his or her toenails, and so must wear special shoes; maybe your character is completely consumed by trying to find unique buttons for a button collection. You might want to base your character on a person that you know and let your imagination go from there, exaggerating this characteristic, or you might want to create a character who is completely fictional. Use one of the appropriate prewriting suggestions to help yourself get started. Your character sketch should be about one page long. Use your imagination and have fun with the assignment!

► Additional practice of the skills taught in this lesson is provided in the Essential Skills Practice Book: Writing 1.8–1.10.

ANALYTIC SCALES FOR RESPONDING IN WRITING

Assign a score from 1 to 25 for each grading criterion below. (For more detailed evaluation, see the evaluation forms for writing, revising, and proofreading, Assessment Portfolio 4.1–4.9.)

Character Sketch

• **Content/Unity.** The character in the sketch has something strange or unusual about his or her appearance or personality.
• **Organization/Coherence.** The character sketch is carefully and vividly written so that the reader understands what is unusual about its subject.
• **Language/Style.** The character sketch uses vivid and precise nouns, verbs, and modifiers.
• **Conventions.** The character sketch avoids errors in spelling, grammar, usage, mechanics, and manuscript form.

ADDITIONAL QUESTIONS AND ACTIVITIES

Students should save their prewriting activities so that you can look at them as a class and discuss which strategies helped the most in preparing their character sketches. Invite students to share their character sketches with one another.

ADDITIONAL RESOURCES

Assessment Portfolio
- Vocabulary Worksheet 2.1.15
- Study Guide 2.1.16
- Unit Test 2.1.17

Essential Skills Practice Books

WRITING
- The Process of Writing, 1.1
- Making a Writing Plan, 1.5
- Choosing a Topic, 1.6
- Choosing an Audience, 1.7
- Choosing a Purpose, 1.8
- Choosing a Form, 1.9
- Gathering Ideas, 1.10
- Organizing Ideas, 1.11
- Outlining, 1.12
- Drafting, 1.13
- Evaluating, 1.14
- Revising, 1.15
- Proofreading, 1.16
- Proper Manuscript Form, 1.17
- Publishing or Presenting Your Work, 1.18
- Writing a Critical Essay, 1.20

LANGUAGE
- Personal Pronouns, 2.4
- Reflexive, Intensive, and Demonstrative Pronouns, 2.5
- Indefinite, Interrogative, and Relative Pronouns, 2.6
- Types of Verbs, 2.7
- Transitive and Intransitive Verbs, 2.8
- Verbals, 2.9
- Adjectives and Articles, 2.10
- Adverbs, 2.11
- Prepositions and Prepositional Phrases, 2.12
- Conjunctions and Interjections, 2.13
- Conjunctive Adverbs, 2.14

SPEAKING AND LISTENING
- Elements of Verbal and Nonverbal Communication, 3.1
- Active Listening and Interpersonal Communication, 3.2

STUDY AND RESEARCH
- Types of Thinking, 4.2
- Reading Actively, 4.9
- The Classification of Library Materials, 4.11
- Using Search Tools, 4.12
- Using the Card Catalog, 4.13
- Using Reference Works, 4.14
- Using Dictionaries, 4.15
- Using Thesauruses, 4.16
- Computer-assisted Research, 4.17
- Other Sources of Information, 4.18
- Evaluating Sources, 4.19
- Bibliographies and Bibliography Cards, 4.20
- Paraphrasing and Summarizing, 4.21
- Informal and Formal Note-taking, 4.22
- Documenting Sources in a Report, 4.23
- Footnotes and Endnotes, 4.24

APPLIED ENGLISH/TECH PREP
- Personal and Business Letters, 5.1

UNIT REVIEW

Contemporary World Literature and Culture

VOCABULARY FROM THE SELECTIONS

acolyte, 93	deferential, 81	layman, 93
assiduous, 94	deficient, 97	melancholy, 38
attribute, 97	denunciation, 59	modulated, 81
boon, 70	disconcertingly, 26	mutilated, 28
brand, 59	dissuasion, 27	nonchalance, 95
caprice, 97	echelon, 81	page, 93
catastrophe, 38	enmity, 97	parching, 26
coincidence, 47	ethereal, 12	perfunctorily, 29
compensation, 72	herbalist, 28	perplex, 27
conspicuous, 82	hooligan, 70	plausible, 97
cordon, 82	homily, 26	retinue, 82
cosmopolitan, 25	idle, 70	theological, 28
debunk, 60	implicit, 96	uncouth, 70
deference, 14	ingenuity, 94	vehemently, 26

LITERARY TERMS

aim, 61	irony, 61, 100
character, 52	irony of situation, 61
characterization, 84	magical realism, 9, 17
conflict, 30	motivation, 31
description, 40	one-dimensional character, 52
dialogue, 51	plot, 17
dramatic irony, 61	point of view, 17, 74
epigraph, 39	repetition, 100
Existentialism, 46	satire, 51, 80, 85
external conflict, 30	stock character, 17
image, 99	third-person point of view, 85
imagery, 99	three-dimensional character, 17, 52
inciting incident, 17	tone, 39, 74
internal conflict, 30	verbal irony, 61

Vocabulary Check Test

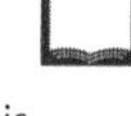

Ask students to number their papers from one to ten. Have students complete each sentence with a word from the Vocabulary from the Selections in the Unit Review.

1. Because of his usual passivity, we were surprised when Henrik vehemently refused to participate in the activity.
2. The flashy, neon sign was conspicuous and out of place in the old quarter of the town.
3. Mr. Patel caught the hooligan defacing his property with graffiti.
4. Milltown has faced many catastrophes in the past year, including floods, tornados, and widespread fires.
5. During interviews, Naomi often debunks the mystique with which celebrities surround themselves.

(cont.)

SYNTHESIS: QUESTIONS FOR WRITING, RESEARCH, OR DISCUSSION

GENRE STUDIES

1. In this unit you have encountered short stories, lyric poetry, drama, excerpts from novels, part of a satirical essay, and students' essays about their home countries. Which of these genres did you enjoy the most? Why? If there were any genres you did not enjoy, explain what you did not like about them. What similarities and differences did you note among these various genres?

2. A writer's aim is the primary purpose his or her work is meant to achieve. Identify the author's purpose underlying each selection in this unit.

THEMATIC STUDIES

3. In the excerpt from *Like Water for Chocolate,* in "Marriage Is a Private Affair," in "Poseidonians," and in the excerpt from *Nectar in a Sieve,* the main character or speaker experiences a conflict between traditional culture or ways of life and more modern ways. Explain the conflict that is encountered in each of these selections. Is it resolved, and if so, which wins out—the old ways, the new ways, or some compromise between the two?

4. In what different ways are love and romantic relationships portrayed in the following selections: *Like Water for Chocolate,* "Marriage Is a Private Affair," and *The Bald Soprano*?

HISTORICAL/BIOGRAPHICAL STUDIES

5. Choose at least three selections from the unit, and explain how the author's background, culture, or time period shaped the literary work he or she produced.

6. In what way is each student's portrayal of his or her culture similar to and different from the portrayal created by the author in the corresponding literary selection?

7. Both Yevtushenko's "Conversation with an American Writer" and Feng Jicai's "The Street-Sweeping Show" address political issues in their countries. What are these issues and what stand does each author take on this issue?

SPELLING CHECK TEST

Ask students to number their papers from one to ten. Read each word aloud. Then read aloud the sentence containing the word. Repeat the word. Ask students to write the word on their papers, spelling it correctly.

1. **ethereal**

The pattern in the sky at sunset looked mysterious and ethereal.

2. **echelon**

To get approval for the project, Ariel had to write to the leader of the highest echelon.

3. **coincidence**

The three cousins did not expect to be at the same store buying the same items—it was a strange coincidence.

4. **cosmopolitan**

The cosmopolitan neighborhood featured restaurants from all over the world.

5. **perfunctorily**

The teacher returned any essays that looked as though they had been written perfunctorily.

6. **disconcertingly**

Some students in the audience were disconcertingly loud when the band was trying to play.

7. **denunciation**

We disagreed with the columnist and wrote a denunciation of his ideas, which the newspaper published.

8. **herbalist**

The herbalist prepared some tea that was supposed to ease my headache.

9. **deferential**

We gave her deferential treatment on her birthday.

10. **melancholy**

The sad song left me in a melancholy mood.

VOCABULARY CHECK TEST (CONT.)

6. Malik's assumed nonchalance was a facade behind which his anxieties hid.

7. Halle attributes her success to hard work and determination.

8. After the accident, the car was mutilated beyond recognition.

9. Ilana's modulated voice was difficult to hear in the loud room.

10. These logic puzzles are designed to perplex anyone who tries them.

Mare Arabicum
Indicum
Tropicus
TROPICVS
AXIS
POLVS

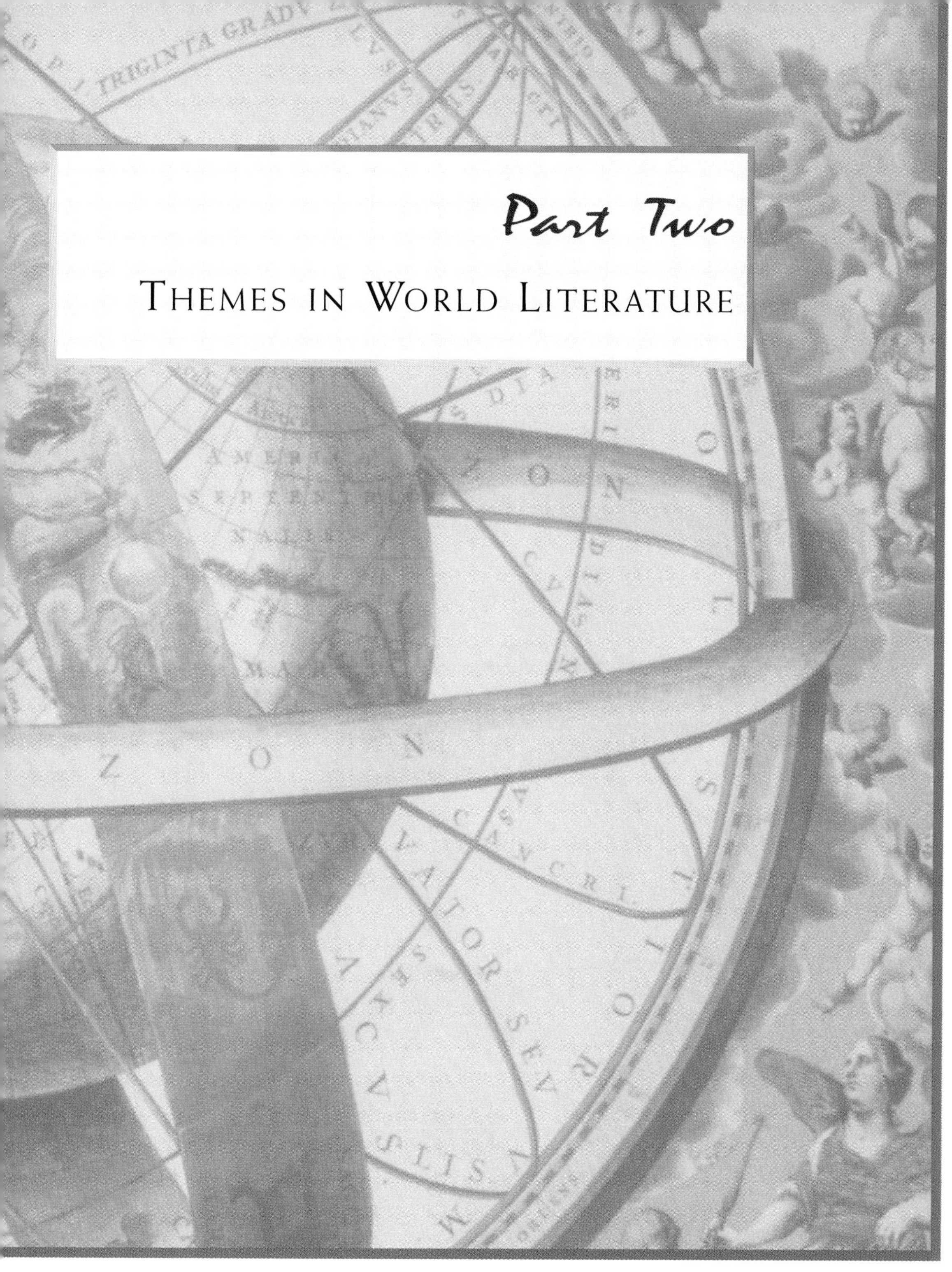

Part Two

Themes in World Literature

UNIT SKILLS OUTLINE

Literary Skills and Concepts

- Aim, 187
- Allusion, 178
- Apostrophe, 172, 179
- Archetype, 202
- Atmosphere, 132
- Autobiography, 196, 211
- Character, 132, 141, 149
- Crisis, 149
- Description, 188
- Dialogue, 112, 132, 211
- Epilogue, 176
- Foreshadowing, 188
- Image, 188
- Imagery, 188
- Mood, 132, 145
- Parody, 195
- Preface, 170
- Prologue, 170
- Realism, 110
- Requiem, 168
- Simile, 188
- Stage Directions, 165
- Suspense, 125
- Symbol, 149, 194
- Tone, 119, 202
- Verbal Irony, 166

Writing Skills and Concepts

- Children's Story, 195
- Critical Essay, 166, 179, 188, 195, 202, 211
- Dramatic Scene, 166
- Editorial, 188
- Gathering Ideas, 203
- Letter of Complaint, 202
- Personal Essay, 211
- Requiem, 179

Grammar, Usage, and Mechanics Skills and Concepts

- Capitalization, 211
- Functions of Sentences, 166
- Quotation Marks, 208
- Types of Verbs, 126

Other Language Arts Skills and Concepts

- Computer-assisted Research, 202
- Using Mnemonic Techniques, 179

Unit 2 The Struggle against Intolerance

Detail from *The Exploiters.* *Diego Rivera, 1926*

GOALS/OBJECTIVES

Studying this unit will enable students to

- empathize with characters' experiences of oppression
- recognize oppression as a worldwide problem
- have a positive experience reading drama, poetry, autobiography, and fiction
- recognize archetypes, irony, allusions, similes, symbols, images, and foreshadowing
- use mnemonic techniques
- conduct computer-assisted research
- analyze and write critically about literature

"Man was born free, and everywhere he is in chains."

—Jean-Jacques Rousseau

107

CROSS-CURRICULAR CONNECTIONS

Arts and Humanities

- Acmeism, 168
- African-American Writers, 189
- Berthe Morisot, 153
- Chopin and Women's Roles, 160
- Commemorating the Holocaust, 188
- Édouard Manet, 115
- Edvard Munch, 122
- Intolerance Art, 108
- James Sydney Ensor, 127
- Naples, 136
- Personal Names, 206
- Post-Stalinist Writing, 173
- Relating to Ibsen, 110
- Standards of Beauty, 195
- Symbolic Plants, 191
- Virginia Woolf, 167
- Writers as Social Protesters, 177

Mathematics and Sciences

- Symbolic Plants, 191
- Typhus, 174

Social Studies

- African National Congress, 203
- Anne Finch, 167
- Caste Systems in India and Japan, 212
- China's Conflict with Tibet, 213
- Commemorating the Holocaust, 188
- Communism, 173
- Concentration Camps, 182
- Elie Wiesel, 181
- Ethnic and Religious Conflicts in Nigeria, 213
- European Geography, 184
- Famous Feminists, 156, 157
- Folk Dancing, 135
- George Bernard Shaw, 116
- James Joyce, 120
- Joseph Stalin, 171
- Chopin and Women's Roles, 160
- Mary Wollstonecraft, 142
- Meaning of Aryan, 180
- Naples, 136
- Nelson Mandela, 203
- Nikita Khrushchev, 176
- Nonviolent Protest, 204
- Nuremburg Laws, 180
- Personal Names, 206
- Post-Stalinist Writing, 173
- Raoul Wallenberg, 184
- Researching the Holocaust, 184
- Researching Zapatista and NAFTA, 212
- Russian Government, 170
- Segregation, 196
- Sigmund Freud, 138
- Standards of Beauty, 195
- Suffrage, 158
- Tarantella, 135
- Virginia Woolf, 167
- Writers as Social Protesters, 177

Applied Arts

- Healthy Snacks, 114

TEACHING THE MULTIPLE INTELLIGENCES

Musical

- Folk Dancing, 135

Logical-Mathematical

- Discussing Leadership Qualities, 171
- Ethics Debate, 137
- Inferring and Predicting, 124
- Making Predictions, 146
- Nuremburg Laws, 137
- Researching Zapatista and NAFTA, 212
- Writers as Social Protesters, 177

Spatial

- Berthe Morisot, 153
- Character Chart, 123
- Édouard Manet, 115
- Edvard Munch, 122
- Intolerance Art, 108
- James Sydney Ensor, 127

Kinesthetic

- Folk Dancing, 135

(cont.)

TEACHING THE MULTIPLE INTELLIGENCES (CONT.)

Interpersonal

- African-American Writers, 189
- Are People Possessions?, 154
- Changing Attitudes, 198
- Commemorating the Holocaust, 188
- Comparing and Contrasting Nora and Mrs. Linde, 152
- Comparing Characters, 160
- Critiquing a Character, 158
- Dialogue: Nora's Problems, 139
- Discussing Forgiveness, 159
- Discussing Leadership Qualities, 171
- Discussing Wollstonecraft's Message, 143
- Dramatic Reading, 114
- Ethics Debate, 137
- Group Research, 171
- Intolerance Art, 108
- Mock Trial, 144
- Nonviolent Protest, 204
- Nuremberg Laws, 180
- Standards of Beauty, 195
- Symposium of Women Writers, 167
- Teaching Tolerance, 190
- Writers as Social Protesters, 177

Other Selections Exploring This Theme

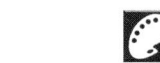

Art Note

Diego Rivera (1886–1957), creator of *Crossing Barranca*, is a twentieth-century Mexican painter well known for his murals. Considered one of modern Mexico's foremost painters, Rivera's work was inspired by native Mexican art and by his experiences in Europe. He painted large murals depicting different aspects of Mexican life, historical scenes, and social problems. The lives of peasants and farmers were of particular interest to Rivera. Rivera was married to Frida Kahlo (1907–1954), also a well-respected Mexican painter. Kahlo's work focuses on realistic, often shocking, images of women's lives and of various aspects of Mexican culture.

Cross-curricular Activities

Arts and Humanities

Ask students to work in small groups to create a work of art such as a mural, collage, sculpture, or drawing which focuses on the theme "The Struggle against Intolerance." To do this, students might research a historical or current event and then depict it in their art, or they might show a more subtle or personal example of their own struggle against intolerance.

UNIT 2

Theme:
The Struggle against Intolerance

Detail from *Crossing Barranca*. *Diego Rivera, 1929*

Around the world, throughout history, people have come into conflict because of prejudice and intolerance. As a result, individuals, groups, and whole cultures have faced discrimination, cruelty, and death. In the face of such inhumanity, the human spirit continues to prevail. People rally against oppression in strikes, protests, and boycotts. Some protest in writing. Editorials, letters of complaint, slogans on bumper stickers, billboards, or t-shirts, songs, and speeches are forms of written protest. Writers speak for the oppressed out of their own experiences or out of a belief in human rights. Poets, dramatists, and novelists use their writing to present the plight of oppressed people, or to present alternatives and ideas for social change.

In this unit, you will read about the results of intolerance: the genocide of the Holocaust, the racism in the state-sponsored system of apartheid, and the depreciation of native culture by colonists. Protagonists struggle for their rights against sexism, against the iron grip of a cruel dictator, and against prejudices that undermine identity and self-worth. Some of the people portrayed survive the inhumane treatment they face, others do not. All are deeply affected in the ways in which they define their identities and in the ways in which they view the world. As you read such accounts, you may consider the violations of human rights that you experience, see, or read about in the world today and you may wish to seek ways in which you can join the struggle against intolerance.

Additional Questions and Activities

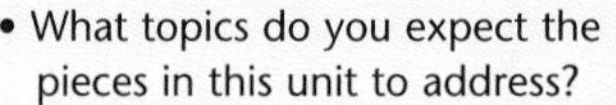

Give students a few moments to answer in writing the following questions:

- What are some examples of intolerance that you have seen in your own life?
- What examples of intolerance have you heard about in the news or read about in books or magazines?
- What topics do you expect the pieces in this unit to address?

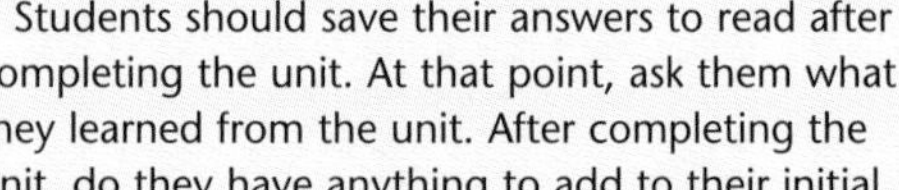

Students should save their answers to read after completing the unit. At that point, ask them what they learned from the unit. After completing the unit, do they have anything to add to their initial responses?

Echoes:

The Struggle against Intolerance

Cruelty and fear shake hands together.

—Honoré de Balzac

There is a great stir about colored men getting their rights, but not a word about the colored women; and if colored men get their rights, and not colored women theirs, you see the colored men will be masters over the women, and it will be just as bad as it was before. So I am for keeping the thing going while things are stirring; because if we wait till it is still, it will take a great while to get it going again.

—Sojourner Truth

Freedom is never voluntarily given by the oppressor; it must be demanded by the oppressed.

—Martin Luther King, Jr.

Hatred does not cease by hatred, but only by love; this is the eternal rule.

—Siddhartha Gautama, the Buddha

The function of freedom is to free someone else.

—Toni Morrison

Passive resistance is an all-sided sword; it can be used anyhow; it blesses him who uses it and him against whom it is used without drawing a drop of blood; it produces far-reaching results. It never rusts and cannot be stolen. Competition between passive resisters does not exhaust them. The sword of passive resistance does not require a scabbard and one cannot be forcibly dispossessed of it.

—Mohandas Gandhi

I am confident, of course, knowing that I shall fulfill my tasks as a writer in any circumstances, and from my grave even more successfully and incontestably than when I live. No one can bar truth's course, and for its progress I am prepared to accept even death. But perhaps repeated lessons will teach us, at least, not to arrest a writer's pen during his lifetime.

—Alexander Solzhenitsyn

Whenever we take away the liberties of those whom we hate we are opening the way to loss of liberty for those we love.

—Wendell L. Willkie

Biographical Notes

Honoré de Balzac (1799–1850) was a French writer who is considered one of the masters of the novel. He wrote a collection of nearly 80 novels and tales, called *The Human Comedy*, which is a social history of France. **Sojourner Truth** (1797–1883) was a slave in New Paltz, New York, for seventeen years. When slaves were freed in New York State, Truth moved to New York City and became involved in social and moral reform. In 1843 she began giving speaking tours. **Martin Luther King, Jr.** (1929–1968), a Civil Rights leader, minister, and orator, led protests throughout the South, advocating nonviolent civil disobedience to combat racism and bigotry. In 1964, four years before his assassination, King was awarded the Nobel Peace Prize. **Siddhartha Gautama, the Buddha,** (c. 563–c. 483 BC) is the founder of Buddhism. Siddhartha renounced the world to wander through India in poverty, searching for life's meaning. After experiencing a spiritual awakening, he devoted the rest of his life to teaching. For more information about Buddha and Buddhism, see page 583. **Toni Morrison** (1931–) is an award-winning novelist featured on page 189. **Mohandas Gandhi** (1868–1949) was a spiritual teacher in India and a believer in passive resistance, a nonviolent type of rebellion in which people show resistance to government activities by refusing to cooperate with them. For more information about Gandhi, see Connections on page 69. **Alexander Solzhenitsyn** (1918–), a Russian novelist and historian, was imprisoned for eight years for criticizing Joseph Stalin. After his release, Solzhenitsyn wrote about government repression and about the Soviet prison system, and his works were banned in the Soviet Union. For more on Stalin's Soviet Union, see page 168. **Wendell L. Willkie** (1892–1944) was an American lawyer, businessman, and politician. Willkie ran unsuccessfully for president against Franklin Delano Roosevelt in 1940.

ADDITIONAL RESOURCES

READER'S GUIDE
- Selection Worksheet 2.1

ASSESSMENT PORTFOLIO
- Selection Check Test 2.2.1
- Selection Test 2.2.2

ESSENTIAL SKILLS PRACTICE BOOKS
- Language 2.7

PREREADING EXTENSIONS

Some students might want to read examples of the work of George Bernard Shaw, James Joyce, and Sigmund Freud and then discuss why these people might have been drawn to the work of Ibsen.

SUPPORT FOR LEP STUDENTS

PRONUNCIATIONS OF PROPER NOUNS AND ADJECTIVES

Hen • rik Ib • sen (hen´rik ib´sən)
Tor • vald Hel • mer (tôr´väld hel´mər)
Mrs. Lin • de (mis´iz lin´də)
Nils Krog • stad (nils krōg´shtad)
Con • sul Sten • borg (kon´sūl shten´bôrg)

ADDITIONAL VOCABULARY

bankrupt—individual or business legally declared unable to pay debts
forged—falsified or imitated writing for the purpose of deception or fraud
macaroons—chewy cookies made chiefly of coconut, egg whites, and sugar
pander to—satisfy or encourage whims, especially unreasonable ones
pounds—basic monetary units in England
shillings—former monetary units in England
simultaneously—at the same time
spendthrift—person who spends too much money, often foolishly
steamer—ship operated by steam power
unsound—not secure

PREREADING

A Doll's House
by Henrik Ibsen, translated by Michael Meyer

About the Author

HENRIK IBSEN
1828–1906

Norwegian playwright **Henrik Ibsen** is known for introducing Realism to the stage. The son of a merchant who went bankrupt, Ibsen worked as an apprentice to a pharmacist and struggled to be accepted to the University at Christiana (now Oslo). Ibsen, however, soon left his studies to become director and playwright at the National Theater in Bergen. He later managed the Norwegian Theater in Christiana. Ibsen's plays were not immediately popular in Norway, and his theater in Christiana went bankrupt. Disappointed by the reception of his work at home, Ibsen went abroad in 1864. He spent the next twenty-seven years living in Rome, Dresden, and Munich. Although many of Ibsen's plays scandalized audiences, their realism and their depiction of middle-class characters struggling against social conventions profoundly influenced European theater. Among Ibsen's admirers were George Bernard Shaw, James Joyce, and Sigmund Freud. Ibsen returned to Norway in 1891. He continued to write until a stroke left him an invalid in 1900. He died in his home country in 1906.

George Bernard Shaw

About the Selection

Realism is the attempt to render in art an accurate portrayal of reality. When ***A Doll's House*** played to European audiences, many women recognized themselves in Nora, the play's hero. While the play was a success, audiences were scandalized by its frank portrayal of a woman questioning her traditional place in society and seeking independence. Ibsen's refusal to provide a happy ending for the drama also upset audiences. *A Doll's House* raised the controversial issue of women's rights, and the play was both condemned and praised in reviews, in public meetings, and even in Sunday sermons. During the 1880s, the play was performed in almost every country in Europe. By focusing on middle class, everyday people and their struggles against social convention, Ibsen created a new type of drama called social realism. Ibsen himself claimed that he was not so much interested in the issue of women's rights as in human rights.

James Joyce

CONNECTIONS: Tragedy and Ibsen's Social Realism

Traditionally, tragedy was drama that focused on the fall of a person of high status. It celebrated the courage and dignity of a tragic hero in the face of inevitable doom. Ibsen rejected the tragic kings of Greek and Renaissance literature and created a new type of hero to whom most audiences could easily relate—the middle-class hero. While traditional tragic heroes struggle against fate or the gods, Ibsen's heroes contend against social and political systems. Ibsen's work, however, is as serious as traditional tragedy; human frailties and political or social flaws often work together to bring about a hero's fall.

GOALS/OBJECTIVES

Studying this lesson will enable students to

- enjoy and appreciate a play that is an example of social realism; empathize with a nineteenth-century woman who is questioning her place in society
- discuss the life and work of Henrik Ibsen
- define the literary terms *character, crisis, dialogue, mood, symbol, stage directions,* and *verbal irony*
- write a dramatic scene and a critical essay
- understand the different functions of sentences

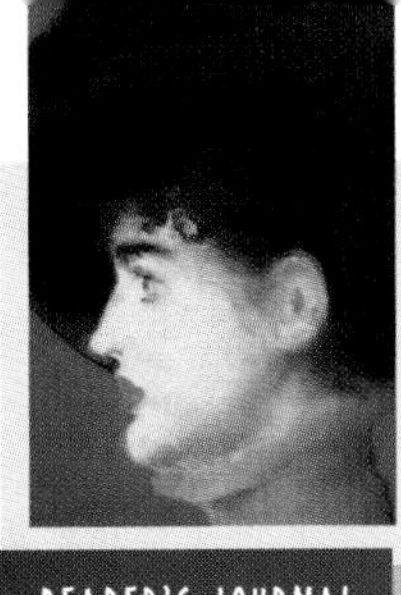

READER'S JOURNAL

In your journal, write about a time when you performed an action and overlooked the consequences of that act. For example you may have decided not to tell a friend the truth. What emotions or reasons led you to perform this action? Why were you willing to overlook the consequences of this act? If you could go back in time, would you do anything differently? Why, or why not?

A Doll's House

HENRIK IBSEN, TRANSLATED BY MICHAEL MEYER

Characters in *A Doll's House*

Torvald Helmer, a lawyer
Nora, his wife
Dr. Rank
Mrs. Linde
Nils Krogstad, also a lawyer
The Helmers' Three Small Children
Anne-Marie, their nurse
Helen, the maid
A Porter

The action takes place in the Helmers' apartment.

ACT 1

A comfortably and tastefully, but not expensively furnished room. Backstage right a door leads to the hall; backstage left, another door to HELMER*'s study. Between these two doors stands a piano. In the middle of the left-hand wall is a door, with a window downstage of it. Near the window, a round table with armchairs and a small sofa. In the right-hand wall, slightly upstage, is a door; downstage of this, against the same wall, a stove lined with porcelain tiles, with a couple of armchairs and a rocking chair in front of it. Between the stove and the side door is a small table. Engravings on the wall. A whatnot*[1] *with china and other bric-a-brac;*[2] *a small bookcase with leather-bound books. A carpet on the floor; a fire in the stove. A winter day.*

[A bell rings in the hall outside. After a moment we hear the front door being opened. NORA *enters the room, humming contentedly to herself. She is wearing outdoor clothes and carrying a lot of parcels, which she puts down on the table right. She leaves the door to the hall open; through it, we can see a* PORTER *carrying a Christmas tree and a basket. He gives these to the* MAID*, who has opened the door for them.]*

NORA. Hide that Christmas tree away, Helen. The children mustn't see it before

1 *What do you think the people who live in this house are like?*

1. **whatnot.** Set of open shelves
2. **bric-a-brac.** Small, ornamental objects; knickknacks

READER'S JOURNAL

As an alternative activity, you might ask students if they have ever found themselves in a situation in which they felt lying was necessary. Do they feel it is ever acceptable to tell a lie? Why, or why not? How did they feel when they told the lie? Did they later regret having told the lie? Why, or why not?

ANSWERS TO GUIDED READING QUESTIONS

1 Students might say that the people are wealthy and particular about their surroundings.

SPELLING AND VOCABULARY WORDS FROM THE SELECTION

ample
caprice
digression
dissemble
egocentric
impertinently
incredulously
indiscretion
patronize
pretense
punctually
scornfully
vehemently

Answers to Guided Reading Questions

❶ He calls her a skylark, a squirrel, and a squanderbird. These pet names reveal that Nora does not take herself seriously, and that she is used to having her husband treat her like a small child or a pet. The names also reveal that Torvald does not take his wife seriously. He does not think of her as an equal partner, but as someone he has to look after.

❷ Torvald feels strongly that debts ruin a household.

❸ No, Torvald does not take Nora's emotions very seriously.

Literary Technique

DIALOGUE

Dialogue is conversation involving two or more people or characters. Plays are made up of dialogue and stage directions. At this point in the play, students should be paying close attention to the dialogue between Torvald and Nora, since their relationship is key to the play. What do students learn about their relationship by reading what the two characters say to each other and the manner in which they speak to each other? Ask students to notice the pet names Torvald uses when addressing Nora, and the way in which he always seems to scold her. What lines do students feel are particularly revealing about their relationship?

I've decorated it this evening. (*to the* PORTER, *taking out her purse*) How much?

PORTER. A shilling.

NORA. Here's ten shillings. No, keep it.

[*The* PORTER *touches his cap and goes.* NORA *closes the door. She continues to laugh happily to herself as she removes her coat, etc. She takes from her pocket a bag containing macaroons and eats a couple. Then she tiptoes across and listens at her husband's door.*]

NORA. Yes, he's here. (*starts humming again as she goes over to the table, right.*)

❶ *What pet names does Torvald Helmer have for his wife? What do these pet names reveal about Nora? about Torvald?*

HELMER (*from his room*). Is that my skylark twittering out there?

NORA (*opening some of the parcels*). It is!

HELMER. Is that my squirrel rustling?

NORA. Yes!

HELMER. When did my squirrel come home?

NORA. Just now. (*pops the bag of macaroons in her pocket and wipes her mouth*) Come out here, Torvald, and see what I've bought.

❷ *How does Torvald feel about borrowing money?*

HELMER. You mustn't disturb me!

[*Short pause; then he opens the door and looks in, his pen in his hand.*]

❸ *Does Torvald take Nora's emotions seriously?*

HELMER. Bought, did you say? All that? Has my little squanderbird been overspending again?

NORA. Oh, Torvald, surely we can let ourselves go a little this year! It's the first Christmas we don't have to scrape.

HELMER. Well, you know, we can't afford to be extravagant.

NORA. Oh yes, Torvald, we can be a little extravagant now. Can't we? Just a tiny bit? You've got a big salary now, and you're going to make lots and lots of money.

HELMER. Next year, yes. But my new salary doesn't start till April.

NORA. Pooh; we can borrow till then.

HELMER. Nora! (*goes over to her and takes her playfully by the ear*) What a little spendthrift you are! Suppose I were to borrow fifty pounds today, and you spent it all over Christmas, and then on New Year's Eve a tile fell off a roof onto my head—

NORA (*puts her hand over his mouth*). Oh, Torvald! Don't say such dreadful things!

HELMER. Yes, but suppose something like that did happen? What then?

NORA. If anything as frightful as that happened, it wouldn't make much difference whether I was in debt or not.

HELMER. But what about the people I'd borrowed from?

NORA. Them? Who cares about them? They're strangers.

HELMER. Oh, Nora, Nora, how like a woman! No, but seriously, Nora, you know how I feel about this. No debts! Never borrow! A home that is founded on debts and borrowing can never be a place of freedom and beauty. We two have stuck it out bravely up to now; and we shall continue to do so for the few weeks that remain.

NORA (*goes over towards the stove*). Very well, Torvald. As you say.

HELMER (*follows her*). Now, now! My little songbird mustn't droop her wings. What's this? Is little squirrel sulking? (*takes out his purse*) Nora; guess what I've got here!

NORA (*turns quickly*). Money!

HELMER. Look. (*hands her some bank notes*) I know how these small expenses crop up at Christmas.

NORA (*counts them*). One—two—three—four. Oh, thank you, Torvald, thank you! I should be able to manage with this.

HELMER. You'll have to.

NORA. Yes, yes, of course I will. But come over here, I want to show you everything I've bought. And so cheap! Look, here are new clothes for Ivar—and a sword. And a horse and a trumpet for Bob. And a doll and a cradle for Emmy—they're nothing much, but she'll pull them apart in a few days. And some bits of material and handkerchiefs for the maids. Old Annie-Marie ought to have had something better, really.

HELMER. And what's in that parcel?

NORA (*cries*). No, Torvald, you mustn't see that before this evening!

HELMER. Very well. But now, tell me, my little spendthrift, what do you want for Christmas?

NORA. Me? Oh, pooh, I don't want anything.

HELMER. Oh yes, you do. Now tell me, what within reason would you most like?

NORA. No, I really don't know. Oh, yes—Torvald—!

HELMER. Well?

NORA (*plays with his coat buttons; not looking at him*). If you really want to give me something, you could—you could—

HELMER. Come on, out with it.

NORA (*quickly*). You could give me money, Torvald. Only as much as you feel you can afford: then later I'll buy something with it.

HELMER. But, Nora—

NORA. Oh yes, Torvald dear, please! Please! Then I'll wrap up the notes in pretty gold paper and hang them on the Christmas tree. Wouldn't that be fun?

HELMER. What's the name of that little bird that can never keep any money?

NORA. Yes, yes, squanderbird; I know. But let's do as I say, Torvald; then I'll have time to think about what I need most. Isn't that the best way? Mm?

HELMER (*smiles*). To be sure it would be, if you could keep what I give you and really buy yourself something with it. But you'll spend it on all sorts of useless things for the house, and then I'll have to put my hand in my pocket again.

NORA. Oh, but Torvald—

HELMER. You can't deny it, Nora dear. (*puts his arm around her waist*) The squanderbird's a pretty little creature, but she gets through an awful lot of money. It's incredible what an expensive pet she is for a man to keep.

> ❶ *What is Torvald saying about Nora? To what is he comparing her?*

NORA. For shame! How can you say such a thing? I save every penny I can.

HELMER (*laughs*). That's quite true. Every penny you can. But you can't.

NORA (*hums and smiles, quietly gleeful*). Hm. If you only knew how many expenses we larks and squirrels have, Torvald.

HELMER. You're a funny little creature. Just like your father used to be. Always on the lookout for some way to get money, but as soon as you have any it just runs through your fingers and you never know where it's gone. Well, I suppose I must take you as you are. It's in your blood. Yes, yes, yes, these things are hereditary, Nora.

NORA. Oh, I wish I'd inherited more of Papa's qualities.

> ❷ *What is Nora eager to have for Christmas?*

HELMER. And I wouldn't wish my darling little songbird to be any different from what she is. By the way, that reminds me. You look awfully—how shall I put it?—awfully guilty today.

NORA. Do I?

HELMER. Yes, you do. Look me in the eyes.

NORA (*looks at him*). Well?

HELMER (*wags his finger*). Has my little sweet tooth been indulging herself in town today, by any chance?

> ❸ *About what is Torvald concerned?*

NORA. No, how can you think such a thing?

HELMER. Not a tiny little digression into a pastry shop?

WORDS FOR EVERYDAY USE

di • gres • sion (dī gresh´ən) *n.,* departure from main path, subject, or idea

ANSWERS TO GUIDED READING QUESTIONS

❶ Torvald is saying that Nora is pretty but that she spends too much money. He is comparing her to a pet.

❷ Nora is eager to have money for Christmas.

❸ Torvald is concerned that Nora has been eating sweets.

ADDITIONAL QUESTIONS AND ACTIVITIES

Ask students to answer the following questions:

1. Why do you think Nora seems to want money so badly?
2. Do you think she truly is a "squanderbird," or do you think it is possible that Torvald is being unfair to her?
3. Do you think the two have a truly open relationship? Why, or why not?

ANSWERS

Responses will vary.

1. Some students might feel that Nora has a valid reason for needing money—a reason that she cannot share with Torvald.
2. Some students might feel that she is a spendthrift.
3. Students should realize, even at this early stage in the play, that the relationship between Nora and Torvald is quite shallow—that they do not seem particularly close. It is possible that Nora does not tell her husband everything.

VOCABULARY IN CONTEXT

- Our discussion of the weather in English class was a brief digression.

Answers to Guided Reading Questions

❶ Nora is lying to Torvald; she has eaten some macaroons. Students may say that Torvald is treating Nora like a child rather than an adult.

❷ They are happy that Torvald will be making more money so that they won't have to struggle.

Additional Questions and Activities

Invite students to form pairs to read aloud the opening scene between Nora and Torvald. One student in each pair should assume the role of Nora, and one student should assume the role of Torvald. Students should pay close attention to stage directions so that they know how each of their lines should be read. Give each pair plenty of time to read through the scene and discuss it. How did they feel playing these characters?

Cross Curricular Connections

APPLIED ARTS

One of the things Torvald belittles Nora for is her indulgence of her sweet tooth. Ask students to list some of their favorite snacks and rate each snack for nutritional value. Then have students brainstorm a list of healthy snacks. Students can prepare various treats from their list and have a tasting party.

NORA. No, Torvald, I promise—

HELMER. Not just a wee jam tart?

NORA. Certainly not.

❶ *Is Nora telling Torvald the truth? What do you think about the way Torvald is questioning Nora?*

HELMER. Not a little nibble at a macaroon?

NORA. No, Torvald—I promise you, honestly—!

HELMER. There, there. I was only joking.

NORA (*goes over to the table, right*). You know I could never act against your wishes.

HELMER. Of course not. And you've given me your word—(*goes over to her*) Well, my beloved Nora, you keep your little Christmas secrets to yourself. They'll be revealed this evening, I've no doubt, once the Christmas tree has been lit.

NORA. Have you remembered to invite Dr. Rank?

HELMER. No. But there's no need; he knows he'll be dining with us. Anyway, I'll ask him when he comes this morning. I've ordered some good wine. Oh, Nora, you can't imagine how I'm looking forward to this evening.

NORA. So am I. And, Torvald, how the children will love it!

❷ *What are Nora and Torvald happy about?*

HELMER. Yes, it's a wonderful thing to know that one's position is assured and that one has an ample income. Don't you agree? It's good to know that, isn't it?

NORA. Yes, it's almost like a miracle.

HELMER. Do you remember last Christmas? For three whole weeks you shut yourself away every evening to make flowers for the Christmas tree, and all those other things you were going to surprise us with. Ugh, it was the most boring time I've ever had in my life.

NORA. I didn't find it boring.

HELMER (*smiles*). But it all came to nothing in the end, didn't it?

NORA. Oh, are you going to bring that up again? How could I help the cat getting in and tearing everything to bits?

HELMER. No, my poor little Nora, of course you couldn't. You simply wanted to make us happy, and that's all that matters. But it's good that those hard times are past.

NORA. Yes, it's wonderful.

HELMER. I don't have to sit by myself and be bored. And you don't have to tire your pretty eyes and your delicate little hands—

NORA (*claps her hands*). No, Torvald, that's true, isn't it? I don't have to any longer! Oh, it's really all just like a miracle. (*takes his arm*) Now I'm going to tell you what I thought we might do, Torvald. As soon as Christmas is over—

[*A bell rings in the hall.*]

Oh, there's the doorbell. (*tidies up one or two things in the room*) Someone's coming. What a bore.

HELMER. I'm not at home to any visitors. Remember!

MAID (*in the doorway*). A lady's called, madam. A stranger.

NORA. Well, ask her to come in.

MAID. And the doctor's here too, sir.

HELMER. Has he gone to my room?

MAID. Yes, sir.

[HELMER *goes into his room. The* MAID *shows in* MRS. LINDE, *who is dressed in traveling clothes; then closes the door.*]

WORDS FOR EVERYDAY USE

am • ple (am´pəl) *adj.,* more than enough; abundant

Vocabulary in Context

• My friend and I were given ample time to complete our project.

Mrs. Linde (*shyly and a little hesitantly*). Good morning, Nora.

Nora (*uncertainly*). Good morning—

Mrs. Linde. I don't suppose you recognize me.

Nora. No, I'm afraid I—Yes, wait a minute—surely—I—(*exclaims*) Why, Christine! Is it really you?

Mrs. Linde. Yes, it's me.

Nora. Christine! And I didn't recognize you! But how could I—? (*more quietly*) How you've changed, Christine!

Mrs. Linde. Yes, I know. It's been nine years—nearly ten—

Nora. Is it so long? Yes, it must be. Oh, these last eight years have been such a happy time for me! So you've come to town? All that way in winter! How brave of you!

Mrs. Linde. I arrived by the steamer this morning.

Nora. Yes, of course, to enjoy yourself over Christmas. Oh, how splendid! We'll have to celebrate! But take off your coat. You're not cold, are you? (*helps her off with it*) There! Now let's sit down here by the stove and be comfortable. No, you take the armchair. I'll sit here in the rocking chair. (*clasps* Mrs. Linde's *hands*) Yes, now you look like your old self. Just at first I—you've got a little paler, though, Christine. And perhaps a bit thinner.

Mrs. Linde. And older, Nora. Much, much older.

Nora. Yes, perhaps a little older. Just a tiny bit. Not much (*checks herself suddenly and says earnestly*) Oh, but how thoughtless of me to sit here and chatter away like this! Dear, sweet Christine, can you forgive me?

Mrs. Linde. What do you mean, Nora?

Irma Brunner. Édouard Manet, 1880

Nora (*quietly*). Poor Christine, you've become a widow.

Mrs. Linde. Yes. Three years ago.

Nora. I know, I know—I read it in the papers. Oh, Christine, I meant to write to you so often, honestly. But I always put it off, and something else always cropped up.

Mrs. Linde. I understand, Nora dear.

Nora. No, Christine, it was beastly of me. Oh, my poor darling, what you've gone through! And he didn't leave you anything?

Mrs. Linde. No.

Nora. No children, either?

Mrs. Linde. No.

Nora. Nothing at all, then?

Mrs. Linde. Not even a feeling of loss or sorrow.

Nora (*looks incredulously at her*). But, Christine, how is that possible?

❶ *Why does Nora ask Christine Linde to forgive her?*

❷ *What is Christine saying about her deceased husband?*

Words for Everyday Use

in • cred • u • lous • ly (in krej´oo ləs lē) *adv.,* with disbelief; skeptically

Answers to Guided Reading Questions

❶ Nora asks Christine to forgive her because she has been chattering and has forgotten to ask Christine about her husband's death.

❷ Christine is saying that she didn't love her husband and is not sad about his death.

Art Note

Édouard Manet (1832–1883) was a French painter of the nineteenth century. Manet's work was influenced by Spanish painters Diego de Velázquez and Francisco de Goya. Velázquez was a seventeenth-century painter known for his portraits of members of the court, and Goya was a painter of the late eighteenth and early nineteenth centuries known for his paintings and etchings that depict wartime horrors. Manet's later work was influenced by Japanese printmakers.

The art establishment of Manet's time found his subject matter, style, and technical innovations to be shocking and offensive. As a result, Manet elicited outrage and hostility from art critics and the public alike throughout his career. Manet's style, although despised at the time, profoundly influenced Impressionism, a style of painting that attempts to capture the artist's or viewer's fleeting emotional impression of a scene. This style is usually characterized by indistinct outlines, attention to light, and many small brushstrokes of unexpected color.

Manet's major works include *Luncheon on the Grass* (1863), *Olympia* (1863), *The Fife Player* (1866), and *The Balcony* (1869). These paintings are on display in the Louvre, Paris's most famous art museum.

Vocabulary in Context

• Rolanda stared at her brother incredulously when he said that he wanted to try skydiving.

Answers to Guided Reading Questions

❶ Nora says she is going to avoid being selfish by listening to what Christine has to say, but instead she begins talking about herself.

❷ Torvald worked so hard he became ill, so Torvald and Nora had to spend a year in Italy while he recuperated.

❸ Christine says that Nora hasn't grown up—she's still a spendthrift.

Biographical Note

Irish playwright and critic George Bernard Shaw (1856–1950) was not only a great admirer of the work of Ibsen, he was responsible in part for drawing audiences to Ibsen's work by his favorable reviews.

Shaw was born into a working-class family and experienced poverty throughout his youth. He tried in early adulthood to become a novelist and failed miserably. Eventually he took up journalism and wrote book and theater reviews for London periodicals.

Not until middle age did Shaw begin writing his own plays, which were received more successfully than his fiction. At the time, most British plays were characterized by fairly simple plots and overly romantic characters. Shaw's plays were much more complex and challenged the social morals and political attitudes of late nineteenth-century England. Since his plays were controversial, they were not as popular in England as they were in the rest of Europe. His great range as a writer enabled him to express his political views in highly effective tragedies and comedies. *Pygmalion* is considered one of Shaw's finest satires. In 1925 Shaw won the Nobel Prize for literature.

Mrs. Linde (*smiles sadly and strokes* Nora's *hair*). Oh, these things happen, Nora.

Nora. All alone. How dreadful that must be for you. I've three lovely children. I'm afraid you can't see them now, because they're out with Nanny. But you must tell me everything—

Mrs. Linde. No, no, no. I want to hear about you.

❶ *What does Nora say she is going to do? What does she do instead?*

Nora. No, you start. I'm not going to be selfish today, I'm just going to think about you. Oh, but there's one thing I *must* tell you. Have you heard of the wonderful luck we've just had?

Mrs. Linde. No. What?

❷ *What happened to Torvald?*

Nora. Would you believe it—my husband's just been made vice-president of the bank!

Mrs. Linde. Your husband? Oh, how lucky—!

Nora. Yes, isn't it? Being a lawyer is so uncertain, you know, especially if one isn't prepared to touch any case that isn't—well—quite nice. And of course Torvald's been very firm about that—and I'm absolutely with him. Oh, you can imagine how happy we are! He's joining the bank in the new year, and he'll be getting a big salary, and lots of percentages too. From now on we'll be able to live quite differently—we'll be able to do whatever we want. Oh, Christine, it's such a relief! I feel so happy! Well, I mean, it's lovely to have heaps of money and not to have to worry about anything. Don't you think?

Mrs. Linde. It must be lovely to have enough to cover one's needs, anyway.

Nora. Not just our needs! We're going to have heaps and heaps of money!

❸ *What does Christine say about Nora?*

Mrs. Linde (*smiles*). Nora, Nora, haven't you grown up yet? When we were at school you were a terrible little spendthrift.

Nora (*laughs quietly*). Yes, Torvald still says that. (*wags her finger*) But "Nora, Nora" isn't as silly as you think. Oh, we've been in no position for me to waste money. We've both had to work.

Mrs. Linde. You too?

Nora. Yes, little things—fancywork, crocheting, embroidery and so forth. (*casually*) And other things, too. I suppose you know Torvald left the Ministry when we got married? There were no prospects of promotion in his department, and of course he needed more money. But the first year he overworked himself dreadfully. He had to take on all sorts of extra jobs, and worked day and night. But it was too much for him, and he became frightfully ill. The doctors said he'd have to go to a warmer climate.

Mrs. Linde. Yes, you spent a whole year in Italy didn't you?

Nora. Yes. It wasn't easy for me to get away, you know. I'd just had Ivar. But, of course, we had to do it. Oh, it was a marvelous trip! And it saved Torvald's life. But it cost an awful lot of money, Christine.

Mrs. Linde. I can imagine.

Nora. Two hundred and fifty pounds. That's a lot of money, you know.

Mrs. Linde. How lucky you had it.

Nora. Well, actually, we got it from my father.

Mrs. Linde. Oh, I see. Didn't he die just about that time?

Nora. Yes, Christine, just about then. Wasn't it dreadful, I couldn't go and look after him. I was expecting little Ivar any day. And then I had my poor Torvald to care for—we really didn't think he'd live. Dear, kind Papa! I never saw him again, Christine. Oh, it's the saddest thing that's happened to me since I got married.

Mrs. Linde. I know you were very fond of him. But you went to Italy—?

Nora. Yes. Well, we had the money, you see, and the doctors said we mustn't delay. So we went the month after Papa died.

Mrs. Linde. And your husband came back completely cured?

Nora. Fit as a fiddle!

MRS. LINDE. But—the doctor?

NORA. How do you mean?

MRS. LINDE. I thought the maid said that the gentleman who arrived with me was the doctor.

NORA. Oh yes, that's Dr. Rank, but he doesn't come because anyone's ill. He's our best friend, and he looks us up at least once every day. No, Torvald hasn't had a moment's illness since we went away. And the children are fit and healthy and so am I. (*jumps up and claps her hands*) Oh, God, oh God, Christine, isn't it a wonderful thing to be alive and happy! Oh, but how beastly of me! I'm only talking about myself. (*sits on a footstool and rests her arms on* MRS. LINDE'*s knee*) Oh, please don't be angry with me! Tell me, is it really true you didn't love your husband? Why did you marry him, then?

MRS. LINDE. Well, my mother was still alive; and she was helpless and bedridden. And I had my two little brothers to take care of. I didn't feel I could say no.

NORA. Yes, well, perhaps you're right. He was rich then, was he?

MRS. LINDE. Quite comfortably off, I believe. But his business was unsound, you see, Nora. When he died it went bankrupt and there was nothing left.

NORA. What did you do?

MRS. LINDE. Well, I had to try to make ends meet somehow, so I started a little shop, and a little school, and anything else I could turn my hand to. These last three years have been just one endless slog[3] for me, without a moment's rest. But now it's over, Nora. My poor dead mother doesn't need me any more; she's passed away. And the boys don't need me either; they've got jobs now and can look after themselves.

NORA. How relieved you must feel—

MRS. LINDE. No, Nora. Just unspeakably empty. No one to live for any more. (*gets up restlessly*) That's why I couldn't bear to stay out there any longer, cut off from the world. I thought it'd be easier to find some work here that will exercise and occupy my mind. If only I could get a regular job—office work of some kind—

NORA. Oh but, Christine, that's dreadfully exhausting; and you look practically finished already. It'd be much better for you if you could go away somewhere.

MRS. LINDE (*goes over to the window*). I have no papa to pay for my holidays, Nora.

NORA (*gets up*). Oh, please don't be angry with me.

MRS. LINDE. My dear Nora, it's I who should ask you not to be angry. That's the worst thing about this kind of situation—it makes one so bitter. One has no one to work for; and yet one has to be continually sponging for jobs. One has to live; and so one becomes completely egocentric. When you told me about this luck you've just had with Torvald's new job—can you imagine?—I was happy not so much on your account, as on my own.

NORA. How do you mean? Oh, I understand. You mean Torvald might be able to do something for you?

MRS. LINDE. Yes, I was thinking that.

NORA. He will too, Christine. Just you leave it to me. I'll lead up to it so delicately, so delicately; I'll get him in the right mood. Oh, Christine, I do so want to help you.

MRS. LINDE. It's sweet of you to bother so much about me, Nora. Especially since you know so little of the worries and hardships of life.

3. **slog.** Toil

❶ *Why does Christine respond this way to Nora?*

❷ *What does Christine want from Nora?*

❸ *What have the last few years been like for Christine? How does this compare with what Nora has revealed of her life?*

WORDS FOR EVERYDAY USE

e • go • cen • tric (ē´gō sen´ trik) *adj.*, self-centered

ANSWERS TO GUIDED READING QUESTIONS

❶ Christine responds this way to Nora because she believes Nora to be silly, well-off, and incapable of understanding a serious situation.

❷ Christine wants Nora to convince Torvald to give her a job.

❸ Christine has struggled to support her family on her own, so they have been difficult years. Students may say that Christine's life seems much more difficult and serious than Nora's life.

QUOTABLES

"Though society is founded on intolerance, all improvement is founded on tolerance."

—George Bernard Shaw, *Saint Joan*

"The secret of being miserable is to have leisure to bother about whether you are happy or not. The cure for it is occupation."

—George Bernard Shaw, *Parents and Children*

VOCABULARY IN CONTEXT

• The egocentric young man felt that he should always be the center of attention.

Answers to Guided Reading Questions

❶ Christine has said that Nora is a child who has never experienced worry or hardship.

❷ Nora found the money needed to take the trip which saved Torvald's life. Students may predict that she borrowed the money without Torvald's consent.

❸ A wife can't borrow money without her husband's consent. Nora implies that she borrowed money without Torvald's approval.

Additional Questions and Activities

Ask students the following questions:

Why does Mrs. Linde call Nora a child? What seems to bother Mrs. Linde about Nora? Ask students if they have ever felt envious of certain friends. Have they ever felt misunderstood by certain friends?

ANSWERS

Responses will vary.

Mrs. Linde calls Nora a child because she thinks Nora lives a carefree life. Mrs. Linde is bothered by the fact that Nora seems to know nothing of hardship, unlike herself. By responding to the last questions, the students will be putting themselves in the place of both Nora and Mrs. Linde.

 ❶ *What has Christine said that upsets Nora?*

NORA. I? You say I know little of—?

MRS. LINDE (*smiles*). Well, good heavens—those bits of fancywork of yours—well, really! You're a child, Nora.

NORA (*tosses her head and walks across the room*). You shouldn't say that so patronizingly.

MRS. LINDE. Oh?

❷ *What is Nora happy and proud of doing? How do you think she got the money?*

NORA. You're like the rest. You all think I'm incapable of getting down to anything serious—

MRS. LINDE. My dear—

NORA. You think I've never had any worries like the rest of you.

MRS. LINDE. Nora dear, you've just told me about all your difficulties—

NORA. Pooh—that! (*quietly*) I haven't told you about the big thing.

MRS. LINDE. What big thing? What do you mean?

NORA. You patronize me, Christine; but you shouldn't. You're proud that you've worked so long and so hard for your mother.

MRS. LINDE. I don't patronize anyone, Nora. But you're right—I am both proud and happy that I was able to make my mother's last months on earth comparatively easy.

NORA. And you're also proud at what you've done for your brothers.

MRS. LINDE. I think I have a right to be.

 ❸ *What can't a woman do without her husband's consent? What does Nora imply?*

NORA. I think so, too. But let me tell you something, Christine. I, too, have done something to be proud and happy about.

MRS. LINDE. I don't doubt it. But—how do you mean?

NORA. Speak quietly! Suppose Torvald should hear! He mustn't, at any price—no one must know, Christine—no one but you.

MRS. LINDE. But what is this?

NORA. Come over here. (*pulls her down onto the sofa beside her*) Yes, Christine—I, too, have done something to be happy and proud about. It was I who saved Torvald's life.

MRS. LINDE. Saved his—? How did you save it?

NORA. I told you about our trip to Italy. Torvald couldn't have lived if he hadn't managed to get down there—

MRS. LINDE. Yes, well—your father provided the money—

NORA (*smiles*). So Torvald and everyone else thinks. But—

MRS. LINDE. Yes?

NORA. Papa didn't give us a penny. It was I who found the money.

MRS. LINDE. You? All of it?

NORA. Two hundred and fifty pounds. What do you say to that?

MRS. LINDE. But, Nora, how could you? Did you win a lottery or something?

NORA (*scornfully*). Lottery? (*sniffs*) What would there be to be proud of in that?

MRS. LINDE. But where did you get it from, then?

NORA (*hums and smiles secretively*). Hm; tra-la-la-la!

MRS. LINDE. You couldn't have borrowed it.

NORA. Oh? Why not?

MRS. LINDE. Well, a wife can't borrow money without her husband's consent.

NORA (*tosses her head*). Ah, but when a wife has a little business sense, and knows how to be clever—

MRS. LINDE. But Nora, I simply don't understand—

Words for Everyday Use

pa • tron • ize (pa´trən īz´) *vt.,* be kind or helpful, but in a snobby manner, as if dealing with an inferior

scorn • ful • ly (skôrn´ fəl lē) *adv.,* with disdain or contempt

Vocabulary in Context

- The older student seemed to patronize me when I asked for help.
- The police officer scornfully questioned the dangerous criminal.

The Travelling Companions.
Augustus Egg

NORA. You don't have to. No one has said I borrowed the money. I could have got it in some other way. (*throws herself back on the sofa*) I could have got it from an admirer. When a girl's as pretty as I am—

MRS. LINDE. Nora, you're crazy!

NORA. You're dying of curiosity now, aren't you, Christine?

MRS. LINDE. Nora dear, you haven't done anything foolish?

NORA (*sits up again*). Is it foolish to save one's husband's life?

MRS. LINDE. I think it's foolish if without his knowledge you—

NORA. But the whole point was that he mustn't know! Great heavens, don't you see? He hadn't to know how dangerously ill he was. It was me they told that his life was in danger and that only going to a warm climate could save him. Do you suppose I didn't try to think of other ways of getting him down there? I told him how wonderful it would be for me to go abroad like other young wives; I cried and prayed; I asked him to remember my condition, and said he ought to be nice and tender to me; and then I suggested he might quite easily borrow the money. But then he got almost angry with me, Christine. He said I was frivolous, and that it was his duty as a husband not to pander to my moods and caprices—I think that's what he called them. Well, well, I thought, you've got to be saved somehow. And then I thought of a way—

❶ *When did Torvald become "almost angry" with Nora?*

MRS. LINDE. But didn't your husband find out from your father that the money hadn't come from him?

❷ *Why did Nora have to borrow money without Torvald knowing?*

NORA. No, never. Papa died just then. I'd thought of letting him into the plot and asking him not to tell. But since he was so ill!—And as things turned out, it didn't become necessary.

WORDS FOR EVERYDAY USE

ca • price (kə prēs´) *n.,* sudden, impulsive change in the way one thinks or acts; whim

ANSWERS TO GUIDED READING QUESTIONS

❶ Torvald became "almost angry" with Nora when she suggested that he borrow money for the trip.

❷ Torvald could not know how ill he was and that only a change in climate could save his life, so Nora needed to raise money in secret.

LITERARY TECHNIQUE

TONE

Tone is the emotional attitude toward the reader or toward the subject implied by a literary work. Examples of different tones that a work may have include familiar, playful, enthusiastic, excited, sarcastic, or sincere. The narrator, speaker, or writer may project the tone of all or part of a work. A character may also project a particular tone. Have students reread the scene in which Nora describes her loan scheme to Mrs. Linde. Ask students to identify Nora's tone as she describes the scheme. What does this tone reveal about how she feels about what she has done? How has the action made her feel about herself?

ANSWERS

Students should notice that Nora's tone is one of excitement and pride. She is obviously excited about what she has done. At this point in the play, the action has filled her with pride and made her feel worthwhile.

VOCABULARY IN CONTEXT

- One Saturday, on a caprice, we decided to ride our bikes to the amusement park and ride the large roller coaster.

Answers to Guided Reading Questions

❶ Nora says that Torvald is too proud to know that he owes his life to Nora and that such knowledge would wreck their relationship.

❷ Nora thought that working to earn money was tiring but fun and exciting, adding that it almost made her feel like a man.

❸ Nora says that she will tell him when she grows older and Torvald does not find her so pretty.

Biographical Note

James Joyce (1882–1941), another great admirer of Ibsen's work, was born in Dublin, Ireland. Like Ibsen's, Joyce's work incited controversy when it first appeared before the public. His great experimental novels *Ulysses* and *Finnegan's Wake* were denounced as obscure, nonsensical, and even obscene. Critics defended Joyce's innovative methods and eventually other writers began to imitate his style, called stream-of-consciousness writing. This type of writing attempts to render the flow of feelings, thoughts, and impressions that occur within the minds of characters.

Quotables

"The artist, like the God of the creation, remains within or behind or beyond or above his handiwork, invisible, refined out of existence, indifferent, paring his fingernails."

—James Joyce
Portrait of the Artist as a Young Man

❶ According to Nora, why can't she tell Torvald about the money she borrowed?

❷ How does Nora feel about working to earn money?

❸ When does Nora say she will tell Torvald about what she has done?

Mrs. Linde. And you've never told your husband about this?

Nora. For heaven's sake, no! What an idea! He's frightfully strict about such matters. And besides—he's so proud of being a man—it'd be so painful and humiliating for him to know that he owed anything to me. It'd completely wreck our relationship. This life we have built together would no longer exist.

Mrs. Linde. Will you never tell him?

Nora (*thoughtfully, half-smiling*). Yes—sometime, perhaps. Years from now, when I'm no longer pretty. You mustn't laugh! I mean, of course, when Torvald no longer loves me as he does now; when it no longer amuses him to see me dance and dress up and play the fool for him. Then it might be useful to have something up my sleeve. (*breaks off*) Stupid, stupid, stupid! That time will never come. Well, what do you think of my big secret, Christine? I'm not completely useless, am I? Mind you, all this has caused me a frightful lot of worry. It hasn't been easy for me to meet my obligations punctually. In case you don't know, in the world of business there are things called quarterly installments and interest, and they're a terrible problem to cope with. So I've had to scrape a little here and save a little there, as best I can. I haven't been able to save much on the housekeeping money, because Torvald likes to live well; and I couldn't let the children go short of clothes—I couldn't take anything out of what he gives me for them. The poor little angels!

Mrs. Linde. So you've had to stint yourself, my poor Nora?

Nora. Of course. Well, after all, it was my problem. Whenever Torvald gave me money to buy myself new clothes, I never used more than half of it; and I always bought what was cheapest and plainest. Thank heaven anything suits me, so that Torvald's never noticed. But it made me a bit sad sometimes, because it's lovely to wear pretty clothes. Don't you think?

Mrs. Linde. Indeed it is.

Nora. And then I've found one or two other sources of income. Last winter I managed to get a lot of copying to do. So I shut myself away and wrote every evening, late into the night. Oh, I often got so tired, so tired. But it was great fun, though, sitting there working and earning money. It was almost like being a man.

Mrs. Linde. But how much have you managed to pay off like this?

Nora. Well, I can't say exactly. It's awfully difficult to keep an exact check on these kind of transactions. I only know I've paid everything I've managed to scrape together. Sometimes I really didn't know where to turn. (*smiles*) Then I'd sit here and imagine some rich old gentleman had fallen in love with me—

Mrs. Linde. What! What gentleman?

Nora. Silly! And that now he'd died and when they opened his will it said in big letters: "Everything I possess is to be paid forthwith to my beloved Mrs. Nora Helmer in cash."

Mrs. Linde. But, Nora dear, who was this gentleman?

Nora. Great heavens, don't you understand? There wasn't any old gentleman; he was just something I used to dream up as I sat here evening after evening wondering how on earth I could raise some money. But

Words for Everyday Use

punc • tu • al • ly (puŋk´ cho͞o əl lē) *adv.*, promptly, on time

Vocabulary in Context

• You must arrive at the movie theater punctually if you expect to get a good seat.

what does it matter? The old bore can stay imaginary as far as I'm concerned, because now I don't have to worry any longer! (*jumps up*) Oh, Christine, isn't it wonderful? I don't have to worry any more! No more troubles! I can play all day with the children, I can fill the house with pretty things, just the way Torvald likes. And, Christine, it'll soon be spring, and the air'll be fresh and the skies blue—and then perhaps we'll be able to take a little trip somewhere. I shall be able to see the sea again. Oh, yes, yes, it's a wonderful thing to be alive and happy!

[*The bell rings in the hall.*]

MRS. LINDE (*gets up*). You've a visitor. Perhaps I'd better go.

NORA. No, stay. It won't be for me. It's someone for Torvald—

MAID (*in the doorway*). Excuse me, madam, a gentleman's called who says he wants to speak to the master. But I didn't know—seeing as the doctor's with him—

NORA. Who is this gentleman?

KROGSTAD (*in the doorway*). It's me, Mrs. Helmer.

[MRS. LINDE *starts, composes herself and turns away to the window.*]

NORA (*takes a step towards him and whispers tensely*). You? What is it? What do you want to talk to my husband about?

KROGSTAD. Business—you might call it. I hold a minor post in the bank, and I hear your husband is to become our new chief—

NORA. Oh—then it isn't—?

KROGSTAD. Pure business, Mrs. Helmer. Nothing more.

NORA. Well, you'll find him in his study.

[*Nods indifferently as she closes the hall door behind him. Then she walks across the room and sees to the stove.*]

MRS. LINDE. Nora, who was that man?

NORA. A lawyer called Krogstad.

MRS. LINDE. It was him, then.

NORA. Do you know that man?

MRS. LINDE. I used to know him—some years ago. He was a solicitor's[4] clerk in our town, for a while.

NORA. Yes, of course, so he was.

MRS. LINDE. How he's changed!

NORA. He was very unhappily married, I believe.

MRS. LINDE. Is he a widower now?

NORA. Yes, with a lot of children. Ah, now it's alight.

[*She closes the door of the stove and moves the rocking chair a little to one side.*]

MRS. LINDE. He does—various things now, I hear?

NORA. Does he? It's quite possible—I really don't know. But don't let's talk about business. It's so boring.

[DR. RANK *enters from* HELMER*'s study.*]

DR. RANK (*still in the doorway*). No, no, my dear chap, don't see me out. I'll go and have a word with your wife. (*closes the door and notices* MRS. LINDE) Oh, I beg your pardon. I seem to be *de trop*[5] here, too.

NORA. Not in the least. (*introduces them*) Dr. Rank. Mrs. Linde.

RANK. Ah! A name I have often heard in this house. I believe I passed you on the stairs as I came up.

MRS. LINDE. Yes. Stairs tire me. I have to take them slowly.

RANK. Oh, have you hurt yourself?

MRS. LINDE. No, I'm just a little run down.

RANK. Ah, is that all? Then I take it you've come to town to cure yourself by a round of parties?

4. **solicitor's.** Lawyer's
5. ***de trop.*** French phrase meaning "in the way"

❶ *How does Christine seem to feel about Krogstad?*

❷ *How does Nora seem to feel about Krogstad?*

ANSWERS TO GUIDED READING QUESTIONS

❶ Christine seems very curious about and interested in Krogstad.

❷ Nora seems to fear and detest Krogstad.

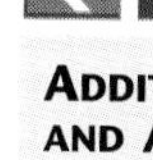

ADDITIONAL QUESTIONS AND ACTIVITIES

What is Nora's mood as she tells Mrs. Linde that her loan will soon be paid? What happens to Nora's mood when Krogstad arrives? What do you think is the reason for this change?

ANSWERS

Responses will vary.

Nora is excited and relieved as she tells Mrs. Linde about the loan being paid off soon. Her mood becomes tense and cold when Krogstad enters the room. Students might guess that Nora and Krogstad have met before under unpleasant circumstances, or that Krogstad knows something about Nora that she does not want Torvald to know.

Answers to Guided Reading Questions

1 Nora is amused to think that her husband will be Krogstad's boss.

2 Dr. Rank describes Krogstad as "crippled" and "morally twisted."

3 Students might say that Nora is feeling reckless and full of nervous energy.

Cross-curricular Activities

Art and Humanities

Edvard Munch (1863–1944) was a gifted painter and printmaker from Ibsen's native Norway. Munch is not only considered his country's greatest artist, but he also played an important role in the development of German expressionism. Expressionism is an artistic style that departs from the conventions of realism and attempts to show true inner experiences by distorting rather than exactly representing natural images. Munch's work often portrayed such themes as misery, sickness, and death. *The Scream*, probably his most familiar painting, is typical of Munch's work in the way it shows anguish and fear.

Students complete one or all of the following activities:

- Learn more about Edvard Munch and other Expressionist painters. Go to libraries and museums to find examples of Expressionist works of art.
- Write an essay comparing and contrasting three paintings of three different styles—Impressionist, Expressionist, and Realist.
- Create an original work of art in the expressionist style of Edvard Munch. You might also create two other paintings of the same subject—one in the Expressionist style and one in the Realist style.

Mrs. Linde. I have come here to find work.

Rank. Is that an approved remedy for being run down?

Mrs. Linde. One has to live, Doctor.

Rank. Yes, people do seem to regard it as a necessity.

Nora. Oh, really, Dr. Rank. I bet you want to stay alive.

Rank. You bet I do. However wretched I sometimes feel, I still want to go on being tortured for as long as possible. It's the same with all my patients; and with people who are morally sick, too. There's a moral cripple in with Helmer at this very moment—

1 *What amuses Nora?*

Mrs. Linde (*softly*). Oh!

Nora. Whom do you mean?

Rank. Oh, a lawyer fellow called Krogstad—you wouldn't know him. He's crippled all right, morally twisted. But even he started off by announcing, as though it were a matter of enormous importance, that he had to live.

2 *In what way does Dr. Rank describe Krogstad?*

Nora. Oh? What did he want to talk to Torvald about?

3 *How would you characterize Nora's mood?*

Rank. I haven't the faintest idea. All I heard was something about the bank.

Nora. I didn't know that Krog—that this man Krogstad had any connection with the bank.

Rank. Yes, he's got some kind of job down there. (*to* Mrs. Linde) I wonder if in your part of the world you too have a species of creature that spends its time fussing around trying to smell out moral corruption? And when they find a case they give him some nice, comfortable position so that they can keep a good watch on him. The healthy ones just have to lump it.

Mrs. Linde. But surely it's the sick who need care most?

Rank (*shrugs his shoulders*). Well, there we have it. It's that attitude that's turning human society into a hospital.

[Nora, *lost in her own thoughts, laughs half to herself and claps her hands.*]

Rank. Why are you laughing? Do you really know what society is?

Nora. What do I care about society? I think it's a bore. I was laughing at something else—something frightfully funny. Tell me, Dr. Rank—will everyone who works at the bank come under Torvald now?

Rank. Do you find that particularly funny?

Nora (*smiles and hums*). Never you mind! Never you mind! (*walks around the room*) Yes, I find it very amusing to think that we—I mean, Torvald—has obtained so much influence over so many people. (*takes the paper bag from her pocket*) Dr. Rank, would you like a small macaroon?

Rank. Macaroons! I say! I thought they were forbidden here.

Nora. Yes, well, these are some Christine gave me.

Mrs. Linde. What? I—?

Nora. All right, all right, don't get frightened. You weren't to know Torvald had forbidden them. He's afraid they'll ruin my teeth. But, dash it—for once—! Don't you agree, Dr. Rank? Here! (*pops a macaroon into his mouth*) You, too, Christine. And I'll have one, too. Just a little one. Two at the most. (*begins to walk round again*) Yes, now I feel really, really happy. Now there's just one thing in the world I'd really love to do.

Rank. Oh? And what is that?

Nora. Just something I'd love to say to Torvald.

Rank. Well, why don't you say it?

Nora. No, I daren't. It's too dreadful.

Mrs. Linde. Dreadful?

Rank. Well then, you'd better not. But you can say it to us. What is it you'd so love to say to Torvald?

Nora. I've the most extraordinary longing to say: "Bloody hell!"

RANK. Are you mad?

MRS. LINDE. My dear Nora—!

RANK. Say it. Here he is.

NORA (*hiding the bag of macaroons*). Ssh! Ssh!

[HELMER, *with his overcoat on his arm and his hat in his hand, enters from his study.*]

NORA (*goes to meet him*). Well, Torvald dear, did you get rid of him?

HELMER. Yes, he's just gone.

NORA. May I introduce you—? This is Christine. She's just arrived in town.

HELMER. Christine—? Forgive me, but I don't think—

NORA. Mrs. Linde, Torvald dear. Christine Linde.

HELMER. Ah. A childhood friend of my wife's, I presume?

MRS. LINDE. Yes, we knew each other in earlier days.

NORA. And imagine, now she's traveled all this way to talk to you.

HELMER. Oh?

MRS. LINDE. Well, I didn't really—

NORA. You see, Christine's frightfully good at office work, and she's mad to come under some really clever man who can teach her even more than she knows already—

HELMER. Very sensible, madam.

NORA. So when she heard you'd become head of the bank—it was in her local paper—she came here as quickly as she could and—Torvald, you will, won't you? Do a little something to help Christine? For my sake?

HELMER. Well, that shouldn't be impossible. You are a widow, I take it, Mrs. Linde?

MRS. LINDE. Yes.

HELMER. And you have experience of office work?

MRS. LINDE. Yes, quite a bit.

HELMER. Well, then, it's quite likely I may be able to find some job for you—

NORA (*claps her hands*). You see, you see!

HELMER. You've come at a lucky moment, Mrs. Linde.

MRS. LINDE. Oh, how can I ever thank you—?

HELMER. There's absolutely no need. (*puts on his overcoat*) But now I'm afraid I must ask you to excuse me—

RANK. Wait. I'll come with you.

[*He gets his fur coat from the hall and warms it at the stove.*]

NORA. Don't be long, Torvald dear.

HELMER. I'll only be an hour.

NORA. Are you going, too, Christine?

MRS. LINDE (*puts on her outdoor clothes*). Yes, I must start to look round for a room.

HELMER. Then perhaps we can walk part of the way together.

NORA (*helps her*). It's such a nuisance we're so cramped here—I'm afraid we can't offer to—

MRS. LINDE. Oh, I wouldn't dream of it. Goodbye, Nora dear, and thanks for everything.

NORA. *Au revoir.* You'll be coming back this evening, of course. And you too, Dr. Rank. What? If you're well enough? Of course you'll be well enough. Wrap up warmly, though.

[*They go out, talking, into the hall.* CHILDREN'S *voices are heard from the stairs.*]

NORA. Here they are! Here they are!

[*She runs out and opens the door. The* NURSE, ANNE-MARIE, *enters with the* CHILDREN.]

NORA. Come in, come in! (*stoops down and kisses them*) Oh, my sweet darlings—! Look at them, Christine! Aren't they beautiful?

RANK. Don't stand here chattering in this draft!

HELMER. Come, Mrs. Linde. This is for mothers only.

❶ *In what way do Nora's and Torvald's reactions to the children differ?*

ANSWERS TO GUIDED READING QUESTIONS

❶ Nora is openly affectionate toward the children and is eager to show them off to Christine, but Torvald brings Christine and Dr. Rank away, indicating that he cares less about the children than their mother does.

ADDITIONAL QUESTIONS AND ACTIVITIES

You might ask students to make a chart of the different characters in the play so far. In the chart, they should list the name of each character and then make notes about each character's personality.

ANSWERS TO GUIDED READING QUESTIONS

❶ Nora seems frightened; she cries out and jumps.

❷ Krogstad seems to be implying that he has the power to ruin things for Nora.

ADDITIONAL QUESTIONS AND ACTIVITIES

Ask students to think about what Krogstad might want from Nora. What do students predict will happen between the two, and why?

ANSWERS

Responses will vary.

[DR. RANK, HELMER, *and* MRS. LINDE *go down the stairs. The* NURSE *brings the* CHILDREN *into the room.* NORA *follows, and closes the door to the hall.*]

❶ *What is Nora's reaction to Krogstad's arrival?*

NORA. How well you look! What red cheeks you've got! Like apples and roses!

[*The* CHILDREN *answer her inaudibly as she talks to them.*]

NORA. Have you had fun? That's splendid. You gave Emmy and Bob a ride on the sledge? What, both together? I say! What a clever boy you are, Ivar! Oh, let me hold her for a moment, Anne-Marie! My sweet little baby doll! (*takes the* SMALLEST CHILD *from the* NURSE *and dances with her*) Yes, yes, mummy will dance with Bob, too. What? Have you been throwing snowballs? Oh, I wish I'd been there! No, don't—I'll undress them myself, Anne-Marie. No, please let me; it's such fun. Go inside and warm yourself; you look frozen. There's some hot coffee on the stove.

[*The* NURSE *goes into the room on the left.* NORA *takes off the* CHILDREN*'s outdoor clothes and throws them anywhere while they all chatter simultaneously.*]

NORA. What? A big dog ran after you? But he didn't bite you? No, dogs don't bite lovely little baby dolls. Leave those parcels alone, Ivar. What's in them? Ah, wouldn't you like to know! No, no; it's nothing nice. Come on, let's play a game. What shall we play? Hide-and-seek? Yes, let's play hide-and-seek. Bob shall hide first. You want me to? All right, let me hide first.

❷ *Why does Krogstad's remark seem threatening?*

[NORA *and the* CHILDREN *play around the room and in the adjacent room to the right, laughing and shouting. At length* NORA *hides under the table. The* CHILDREN *rush in, look, but cannot find her. Then they hear her half-stifled laughter, run to the table, lift up the cloth and see her. Great excitement. She crawls out as though to frighten them. Further excitement. Meanwhile, there has been a knock on the door leading from the hall, but no one has noticed it. Now the door is half opened and* KROGSTAD *enters. He waits for a moment; the game continues.*]

KROGSTAD. Excuse me, Mrs. Helmer—

NORA (*turns with a stifled cry and half jumps up*). Oh! What do you want?

KROGSTAD. I beg your pardon—the front door was ajar. Someone must have forgotten to close it.

NORA (*gets up*). My husband is not at home, Mr. Krogstad.

KROGSTAD. I know.

NORA. Well, what do you want here, then?

KROGSTAD. A word with you.

NORA. With—? (*to the* CHILDREN, *quietly*) Go inside to Anne-Marie. What? No, the strange gentleman won't do anything to hurt mummy. When he's gone we'll start playing again.

[*She takes the* CHILDREN *into the room on the left and closes the door behind them.*]

NORA (*uneasy, tense*). You want to speak to me?

KROGSTAD. Yes.

NORA. Today? But it's not the first of the month yet.

KROGSTAD. No, it is Christmas Eve. Whether or not you have a merry Christmas depends on you.

NORA. What do you want? I can't give you anything today—

KROGSTAD. We won't talk about that for the present. There's something else. You have a moment to spare?

NORA. Oh, yes. Yes, I suppose so—though—

KROGSTAD. Good. I was sitting in the café down below and I saw your husband cross the street—

NORA. Yes.

KROGSTAD. With a lady.

NORA. Well?

KROGSTAD. Might I be so bold as to ask; was not that lady a Mrs. Linde?

NORA. Yes.

KROGSTAD. Recently arrived in town?

NORA. Yes, today.

KROGSTAD. She is a good friend of yours, is she not?

NORA. Yes, she is. But I don't see—

KROGSTAD. I used to know her, too, once.

NORA. I know.

KROGSTAD. Oh? You've discovered that. Yes, I thought you would. Well then, may I ask you a straight question: is Mrs. Linde to be employed at the bank?

NORA. How dare you presume to cross-examine me, Mr. Krogstad? You, one of my husband's employees? But since you ask, you shall have an answer. Yes, Mrs. Linde is to be employed by the bank. And I arranged it, Mr. Krogstad. Now you know.

KROGSTAD. I guessed right, then.

NORA (*walks up and down the room*). Oh, one has a little influence, you know. Just because one's a woman it doesn't necessarily mean that—When one is in a humble position, Mr. Krogstad, one should think twice before offending someone who—hm—!

KROGSTAD. —who has influence?

NORA. Precisely.

KROGSTAD (*changes his tone*). Mrs. Helmer, will you have the kindness to use your influence on my behalf?

NORA. What? What do you mean?

KROGSTAD. Will you be so good as to see that I keep my humble position at the bank?

NORA. What do you mean? Who is thinking of removing you from your position?

KROGSTAD. Oh, you don't need to play the innocent with me. I realize it can't be very pleasant for your friend to risk bumping into me. And now I also realize whom I have to thank for being hounded out like this.

NORA. But I assure you—

KROGSTAD. Look, let's not beat about the bush. There's still time, and I'd advise you to use your influence to stop it.

NORA. But, Mr. Krogstad, I have no influence!

KROGSTAD. Oh? I thought you just said—

NORA. But I didn't mean it like that! I? How on earth could you imagine that I would have any influence over my husband?

KROGSTAD. Oh, I've known your husband since we were students together. I imagine he has his weaknesses like other married men.

NORA. If you speak impertinently of my husband, I shall show you the door.

KROGSTAD. You're a bold woman, Mrs. Helmer.

NORA. I'm not afraid of you any longer. Once the new year is in, I'll soon be rid of you.

KROGSTAD (*more controlled*). Now listen to me, Mrs. Helmer. If I'm forced to, I shall fight for my little job at the bank as I would fight for my life.

NORA. So it sounds.

KROGSTAD. It isn't just the money—that's the last thing I care about. There's something else. Well, you might as well know. It's like this, you see. You know of course, as everyone else does, that some years ago I committed an indiscretion.

❶ *In whom is Krogstad interested?*

❷ *What does Krogstad ask of Nora? Whom does he blame for his dismissal? Why?*

WORDS FOR EVERYDAY USE

im • per • ti • nent • ly (im purt´'n ənt lē) *adv.*, insolently, impudently, not showing the proper respect

in • dis • cre • tion (in´di skresh´ən) *n.*, unwise or immoral act or remark

ANSWERS TO GUIDED READING QUESTIONS

❶ Krogstad is interested in Christine Linde.

❷ Krogstad asks Nora to convince her husband to allow Krogstad to keep his job. Krogstad blames Nora because he thinks she asked Torvald to fire him.

LITERARY TECHNIQUE

SUSPENSE

Suspense is a feeling of expectation, anxiousness, or curiosity created by questions raised in the mind of a reader or viewer. Ask students to notice the suspense generated by the conversation between Nora and Krogstad. What does Ibsen do to create this suspense? What questions does the scene raise in students' minds?

VOCABULARY IN CONTEXT

- Maggie was punished for speaking impertinently to members of her family.
- Telling her friend about her sister's secret was an indiscretion.

Answers to Guided Reading Questions

❶ Krogstad had hoped that the job in the bank would bring respectability to him and his family.

❷ Nora borrowed the money from Krogstad.

❸ Nora's father was supposed to sign an I.O.U. for security.

INTEGRATED SKILLS ACTIVITIES

LANGUAGE SKILLS

Ask students to review the Language Arts Survey 2.7, "Types of Verbs." Then have them make three columns and label them "action," "linking," and "auxilliary." Students should go through *A Doll's House* and find five examples of action verbs, five examples of linking verbs, and five examples of auxiliary verbs to enter in each column.

►For additional practice, see the Essential Skills Practice Book: Language 2.7.

❶ *Why is Krogstad's job so important to him?*

❷ *From whom did Nora borrow the money?*

❸ *What was one of the conditions of the loan?*

NORA. I think I did hear something—

KROGSTAD. It never came into court; but from that day, every opening was barred to me. So I turned my hand to the kind of business you know about. I had to do something; and I don't think I was one of the worst. But now I want to give up all that. My sons are growing up: for their sake, I must try to regain what respectability I can. This job in the bank was the first step on the ladder. And now your husband wants to kick me off that ladder back into the dirt.

NORA. But, my dear Mr. Krogstad, it simply isn't in my power to help you.

KROGSTAD. You say that because you don't want to help me. But I have the means to make you.

NORA. You don't mean you'd tell my husband that I owe you money?

KROGSTAD. And if I did?

NORA. That'd be a filthy trick! (*almost in tears*) This secret that is my pride and my joy—that he should hear about it in such a filthy, beastly way—hear about it from you! It'd involve me in the most dreadful unpleasantness—

KROGSTAD. Only—unpleasantness?

NORA (*vehemently*). All right, do it! You'll be the one who'll suffer. It'll show my husband the kind of man you are, and then you'll never keep your job.

KROGSTAD. I asked you whether it was merely domestic unpleasantness you were afraid of.

NORA. If my husband hears about it, he will of course immediately pay you whatever is owing. And then we shall have nothing more to do with you.

KROGSTAD (*takes a step closer*). Listen, Mrs. Helmer. Either you've a bad memory or else you know very little about financial transactions. I had better enlighten you.

NORA. What do you mean?

KROGSTAD. When your husband was ill, you came to me to borrow two hundred and fifty pounds.

NORA. I didn't know anyone else.

KROGSTAD. I promised to find that sum for you—

NORA. And you did find it.

KROGSTAD. I promised to find that sum for you on certain conditions. You were so worried about your husband's illness and so keen to get the money to take him abroad that I don't think you bothered much about the details. So it won't be out of place if I refresh your memory. Well—I promised to get you the money in exchange for an I.O.U., which I drew up.

NORA. Yes, and which I signed.

KROGSTAD. Exactly. But then I added a few lines naming your father as security for the debt. This paragraph was to be signed by your father.

NORA. Was to be? He did sign it.

KROGSTAD. I left the date blank for your father to fill in when he signed this paper. You remember, Mrs. Helmer?

NORA. Yes, I think so—

KROGSTAD. Then I gave you back this I.O.U. for you to post to your father. Is that not correct?

NORA. Yes.

KROGSTAD. And of course you posted it at once; for within five or six days you brought

WORDS FOR EVERYDAY USE

ve • he • ment • ly (vē´ə mənt lē) *adv.*, passionately, fervently

Vocabulary in Context

• Lucy vehemently denies denting the fender on her mother's car.

it along to me with your father's signature on it. Whereupon I handed you the money.

NORA. Yes, well. Haven't I repaid the installments as agreed?

KROGSTAD. Mm—yes, more or less. But to return to what we are speaking about—that was a difficult time for you just then, wasn't it, Mrs. Helmer?

NORA. Yes, it was.

KROGSTAD. Your father was very ill, if I am not mistaken.

NORA. He was dying.

KROGSTAD. He did in fact die shortly afterwards?

NORA. Yes.

KROGSTAD. Tell me, Mrs. Helmer, do you by any chance remember the date of your father's death? The day of the month, I mean.

NORA. Papa died on the twenty-ninth of September.

KROGSTAD. Quite correct; I took the trouble to confirm it. And that leaves me with a curious little problem—(*takes out a paper*)—which I simply cannot solve.

NORA. Problem? I don't see—

KROGSTAD. The problem, Mrs. Helmer, is that your father signed this paper three days after his death.

NORA. What? I don't understand—

KROGSTAD. Your father died on the twenty-ninth of September. But look at this. Here your father has dated his signature the second of October. Isn't that a curious little problem, Mrs. Helmer?

[NORA *is silent.*]

KROGSTAD. Can you suggest any explanation?

[*She remains silent.*]

KROGSTAD. And there's another curious thing. The words "second of October" and the year are written in a hand which is not your father's, but which I seem to know.

Dejected Lady. *James Sydney Ensor, 1881*

Well, there's a simple explanation to that. Your father could have forgotten to write in the date when he signed, and someone else could have added it before the news came of his death. There's nothing criminal about that. It's the signature itself I'm wondering about. It *is* genuine, I suppose, Mrs. Helmer? It was your father who wrote his name here?

NORA (*after a short silence, throws back her head and looks defiantly at him*). No, it was not. It was I who wrote Papa's name there.

KROGSTAD. Look, Mrs. Helmer, do you realize this is a dangerous admission?

NORA. Why? You'll get your money.

KROGSTAD. May I ask you a question? Why didn't you send this paper to your father?

1 *What crime has Nora committed?*

ANSWERS TO GUIDED READING QUESTIONS

1 Nora has committed forgery.

ART NOTE

James Sydney Ensor (1860–1949) was a Belgian painter and etcher who is often considered to be the father of expressionism. Some of his works depict realistic interiors and panoramic scenes. Other examples of his work depict mystical fantasies containing strong, bizarre imagery. Some of his paintings, particularly those with religious themes, were regarded as scandalous. It is said that Ensor paved the way for surrealism, an artistic movement of the early twentieth century that attempts to show imaginative dreams and visions.

ADDITIONAL QUESTIONS AND ACTIVITIES

Do you feel that Nora's crime is really evil, given the circumstances? Why, or why not?

ANSWERS

Responses will vary.

Students might feel that Nora had no choice and that, at the time she committed the crime, she felt that she was protecting the people she loved.

Answers to Guided Reading Questions

❶ Krogstad says that forgery was the same crime that ruined his reputation.

❷ Nora believes that her crime was good and selfless because she was protecting her father and her husband. She claims that the law is "stupid" not to consider a person's motivations.

Additional Questions and Activities

Ask students to respond to the following questions either in writing or in a class discussion:

1. Do you agree with Nora that her crime was justified?
2. What motivates Krogstad's actions?

ANSWERS

Responses will vary.

1. Students are likely to understand Nora's feelings of desperation.
2. They might also understand why Krogstad feels desperate enough to threaten Nora.

NORA. I couldn't. Papa was very ill. If I'd asked him to sign this, I'd have had to tell him what the money was for. But I couldn't have told him in his condition that my husband's life was in danger. I couldn't have done that!

KROGSTAD. Then you would have been wiser to have given up your idea of a holiday.

NORA. But I couldn't! It was to save my husband's life. I couldn't put it off.

KROGSTAD. But didn't it occur to you that you were being dishonest towards me?

NORA. I couldn't bother about that. I didn't care about you. I hated you because of all the beastly difficulties you'd put in my way when you knew how dangerously ill my husband was.

❶ *What does Krogstad say about Nora's crime?*

KROGSTAD. Mrs. Helmer, you evidently don't appreciate exactly what you have done. But I can assure you that it is no bigger nor worse a crime than the one I once committed and thereby ruined my whole social position.

NORA. You? Do you expect me to believe that you would have taken a risk like that to save your wife's life?

❷ *What attitude does Nora take toward the law and her crime in front of Krogstad?*

KROGSTAD. The law does not concern itself with motives.

NORA. Then the law must be very stupid.

KROGSTAD. Stupid or not, if I show this paper to the police, you will be judged according to it.

NORA. I don't believe that. Hasn't a daughter the right to shield her father from worry and anxiety when he's old and dying? Hasn't a wife the right to save her husband's life? I don't know much about the law, but there must be something somewhere that says that such things are allowed. You ought to know that, you're meant to be a lawyer, aren't you? You can't be a very good lawyer, Mr. Krogstad.

KROGSTAD. Possibly not. But business, the kind of business we two have been transacting—I think you'll admit I understand something about that? Good. Do as you please. But I tell you this. If I get thrown into the gutter for a second time, I shall take you with me.

[*He bows and goes out through the hall.*]

NORA (*stands for a moment in thought, then tosses her head*). What nonsense! He's trying to frighten me! I'm not that stupid. (*busies herself gathering together the children's clothes; then she suddenly stops.*) But—? No, it's impossible. I did it for love, didn't I?

CHILDREN (*in the doorway, left*). Mummy, the strange gentleman has gone out into the street.

NORA. Yes, yes, I know. But don't talk to anyone about the strange gentleman. You hear? Not even to Daddy.

CHILDREN. No, Mummy. Will you play with us again now?

NORA. No, no. Not now.

CHILDREN. Oh but, Mummy, you promised!

NORA. I know, but I can't just now. Go back to the nursery. I've a lot to do. Go away, my darlings, go away.

[*She pushes them gently into the other room, and closes the door behind them. She sits on the sofa, takes up her embroidery, stitches for a few moments, but soon stops.*]

NORA. No! (*throws the embroidery aside, gets up, goes to the door leading to the hall and calls*) Helen! Bring in the Christmas tree! (*She goes to the table on the left and opens the drawer in it; then pauses again.*) No, but it's utterly impossible!

MAID (*enters with the tree*). Where shall I put it, madam?

NORA. There, in the middle of the room.

MAID. Will you be wanting anything else?

NORA. No, thank you. I have everything I need.

[*The* MAID *puts down the tree and goes out.*]

Nora (*busy decorating the tree*). Now—candles here—and flowers here. That loathsome man! Nonsense, nonsense, there's nothing to be frightened about. The Christmas tree must be beautiful. I'll do everything that you like, Torvald. I'll sing for you, dance for you—

[Helmer, *with a bundle of papers under his arm, enters.*]

Nora. Oh—are you back already?

Helmer. Yes. Has anyone been here?

Nora. Here? No.

Helmer. That's strange. I saw Krogstad come out of the front door.

Nora. Did you? Oh yes, that's quite right—Krogstad was here for a few minutes.

Helmer. Nora, I can tell from your face, he has been here and asked you to put in a good word for him.

Nora. Yes.

Helmer. And you were to pretend you were doing it of your own accord? You weren't going to tell me he'd been here? He asked you to do that too, didn't he?

Nora. Yes, Torvald. But—

Helmer. Nora, Nora! And you were ready to enter into such a conspiracy? Talking to a man like that, and making him promises—and then, on top of it all, to tell me an untruth!

Nora. An untruth?

Helmer. Didn't you say no one had been here? (*wags his finger*) My little songbird must never do that again. A songbird must have a clean beak to sing with. Otherwise she'll start twittering out of tune. (*puts his arm around her waist*) Isn't that the way we want things? Yes, of course it is. (*lets go of her*) So let's hear no more about that. (*sits down in front of the stove*) Ah, how cozy and peaceful it is here! (*glances for a few moments at his papers*)

Nora (*busy with the tree; after a short silence*). Torvald.

Helmer. Yes.

Nora. I'm terribly looking forward to that fancy-dress ball at the Stenborgs on Boxing Day.[6]

Helmer. And I'm terribly curious to see what you're going to surprise me with.

Nora. Oh, it's so maddening.

Helmer. What is?

Nora. I can't think of anything to wear. It all seems so stupid and meaningless.

Helmer. So my little Nora has come to that conclusion, has she?

Nora (*behind his chair, resting her arms on its back*). Are you very busy, Torvald?

Helmer. Oh—

Nora. What are those papers?

Helmer. Just something to do with the bank.

Nora. Already?

Helmer. I persuaded the trustees to give me authority to make certain immediate changes in the staff and organization. I want to have everything straight by the new year.

Nora. Then that's why this poor man Krogstad—

Helmer. Hm.

Nora (*still leaning over his chair, slowly strokes the back of his head*). If you hadn't been so busy, I was going to ask you an enormous favor. Torvald.

Helmer. Well, tell me. What was it to be?

Nora. You know I trust your taste more than anyone's. I'm so anxious to look really beautiful at the fancy-dress ball. Torvald, couldn't you help me to decide what I shall go as, and what kind of costume I ought to wear?

Helmer. Aha! So little Miss Independent's in trouble and needs a man to rescue her, does she?

Nora. Yes, Torvald. I can't get anywhere without your help.

6. **Boxing Day.** December 26 holiday named after the custom of giving gift boxes to employees

❶ *How does Nora feel about her conversation with Krogstad? Why is she concerned that her home appear beautiful and that she appear happy?*

❷ *How does Torvald feel about Krogstad? about Nora's agreeing to intercede on Krogstad's behalf?*

Answers to Guided Reading Questions

❶ Nora is frightened and nervous. She is desperately trying to keep up appearances so that Torvald will not suspect that anything is wrong.

❷ Torvald dislikes Krogstad. He thinks that it is wrong of Nora to speak to Krogstad and even worse for her to agree to intercede on his behalf.

Bibliographic Note

Ibsen, generally considered the father of modern drama, has created many characters who, like Nora, are at odds with society's strict and arbitrary rules. Students might enjoy reading or performing any of the following Ibsen dramas to complement their reading of *A Doll's House*:

Peer Gynt (1867)

Ghosts (1881)

An Enemy of the People (1883)

The Wild Duck (1884)

Hedda Gabler (1891)

ANSWERS TO GUIDED READING QUESTIONS

❶ By finding out what Torvald thinks of Krogstad's crime, Nora hopes to discover what Torvald's reaction would be if her own crime were to become known.

SELECTION CHECK TEST WITH ANSWERS

EX. At what time of year does act 1 take place?
Act 1 takes place at Christmastime.

1. What does Nora want for Christmas?
Nora asks for money for Christmas.

2. What does Christine Linde want from Torvald?
Christine Linde wants a job from Torvald.

3. What did Nora do to save Torvald's life?
Nora borrowed the money for a trip to Italy when her husband was in poor health.

4. What does Krogstad want Nora to do?
Krogstad wants Nora to convince Torvald to let him keep his job.

5. Of what crime is Nora guilty?
She is guilty of forgery.

Pretty Penny. *Edward Hopper, 1939*

HELMER. Well, well, I'll give the matter thought. We'll find something.

NORA. Oh, how kind of you! (*goes back to the tree; pauses*) How pretty these red flowers look! But, tell me, is it so dreadful, this thing that Krogstad's done?

❶ *Why does Nora ask Torvald these questions?*

HELMER. He forged someone else's name. Have you any idea what that means?

NORA. Mightn't he have been forced to do it by some emergency?

HELMER. He probably just didn't think—that's what usually happens. I'm not so heartless as to condemn a man for an isolated action.

NORA. No, Torvald, of course not!

HELMER. Men often succeed in reestablishing themselves if they admit their crime and take their punishment.

NORA. Punishment?

HELMER. But Krogstad didn't do that. He chose to try and trick his way out of it. And that's what has morally destroyed him.

NORA. You think that would—?

HELMER. Just think how a man with that load on his conscience must always be lying and cheating and dissembling—how he must wear a mask even in the presence of those who are dearest to him, even his own wife and children! Yes, the children. That's the worst danger, Nora.

NORA. Why?

HELMER. Because an atmosphere of lies contaminates and poisons every corner of the home. Every breath that the children draw in such a house contains the germs of evil.

NORA (*comes closer behind him*). Do you really believe that?

HELMER. Oh, my dear, I've come across it so often in my work at the bar. Nearly all young criminals are the children of mothers who are constitutional liars.

NORA. Why do you say mothers?

HELMER. It's usually the mother— though of course the father can have the same influence. Every lawyer knows that only too well. And yet this fellow Krogstad has been sitting at home all these years poisoning his children with his lies and pretenses. That's why I say that, morally speaking, he is dead. (*stretches out his hand towards her*) So my pretty little Nora must promise me not to plead his case. Your hand on it. Come, come, what's this? Give me your hand. There. That's settled, now. I assure you it'd be quite impossible for me to work in the same building as him. I literally feel physically ill in the presence of a man like that.

WORDS FOR EVERYDAY USE

dis • sem • ble (di sem´bəl) *vt.,* disguise, conceal under false appearance

pre • tense (prē tens´) *n.,* false claim or show

VOCABULARY IN CONTEXT

- We know that he will probably dissemble when testifying in order to escape punishment.
- The thief got into the house on the pretense that he was a traveling salesman.

NORA (*draws her hand from his and goes over to the other side of the Christmas tree*). How hot it is in here! And I've so much to do.

HELMER (*gets up and gathers his papers*). Yes, and I must try to get some of this read before dinner. I'll think about your costume, too. And I may even have something up my sleeve to hang in gold paper on the Christmas tree. (*lays his hand on her head*) My precious little songbird!

[*He goes into his study and closes the door.*]

NORA (*softly, after a pause*). It's nonsense. It must be. It's impossible. It *must* be impossible!

NURSE (*in the doorway, left*). The children are asking if they can come in to Mummy.

NORA. No, no, no—don't let them in. You stay with them, Anne-Marie.

NURSE. Very good, madam. (*closes the door*)

NORA (*pale with fear*). Corrupt my little children—! Poison my home! (*short pause; she throws back her head*) It isn't true! It *couldn't* be true!

1 *What does Nora tell herself about what Torvald has said? What does she tell Anne-Marie to do with the children?*

Responding to the Selection

Do you think Torvald and Nora have a good relationship by today's standards? Why, or why not? If you could give both Torvald and Nora some advice about their relationship, what would you say?

Reviewing the Selection

RECALLING		INTERPRETING
1. What does Torvald accuse Nora of being? What does she want for a Christmas present?	▶▶	Is Nora really what Torvald claims? Why, or why not? Why does she want this gift for Christmas?
2. Why does Mrs. Linde come to visit Nora?	▶▶	What does Mrs. Linde think of Nora at first? Why does Nora feel that she has to disprove this opinion?
3. Why does Krogstad come to visit Nora? What crime have both he and Nora committed?	▶▶	Why did Nora commit this crime? How does Nora pretend to feel about this crime in front of Krogstad? How does she really feel?
4. What does Torvald say is the worst thing about Krogstad's crime?	▶▶	Why does Nora tell the nurse not to let the children in to see her?

ANSWERS TO GUIDED READING QUESTIONS

1 Nora tells herself that what Torvald has said about her crime and its effect on the children must be nonsense. She tells Anne-Marie not to let the children in to see her.

RESPONDING TO THE SELECTION

It might help students to freewrite first about what makes a good and a bad relationship by today's standards.

ANSWERS FOR REVIEWING THE SELECTION

RECALLING AND INTERPRETING

1. **Recalling.** Torvald accuses Nora of being a spendthrift. She wants money for a Christmas present. **Interpreting.** No, Nora is not a spendthrift; she has been forced to scrimp and save to pay back Krogstad. She wants money for Christmas so she can use it to pay back Krogstad.

2. **Recalling.** Mrs. Linde wants Nora to convince Torvald to give her a job. **Interpreting.** Mrs. Linde thinks that Nora has never grown up—that she is a spoiled child who has never known hardship. Nora is constantly patronized at home, so she resents her childhood friend patronizing her. Because Nora has known worry, she is eager to unburden herself to a friend.

3. **Recalling.** Krogstad visits Nora to blackmail her; Krogstad threatens to tell her husband about the money she has borrowed from him unless she convinces her husband to let Krogstad keep his job. Nora and Krogstad have both committed forgery; she signed her father's name as security for her loan.

(cont.)

ANSWERS FOR REVIEWING THE SELECTION (CONT.)

Interpreting. Nora committed this crime because she couldn't bear to tell her father about her husband's illness when her father himself was so sick and she felt she had to do something to save her husband's life. Nora pretends to feel that her crime was justified and that both her husband and the law will accept her motivation as an excuse. She really feels fearful and agitated; she doubts whether either her husband or the law will understand what led her to commit forgery.

4. **Recalling.** Torvald says that because Krogstad tried to escape punishment for his crime, his house is full of evil lies that will contaminate his children. **Interpreting.** Nora is worried that Torvald might be right, so she doesn't want to contaminate the children with her "evil" presence.

ANSWERS FOR REVIEWING THE SELECTION (CONT.)

SYNTHESIZING

Responses will vary. Possible responses are given.

5. Students might say that Nora is pretending to be happy because she is interested in maintaining appearances and is afraid to reveal her inner anxiety. Nora is really very anxious and worried. Students might cite the passage in which Nora is so full of nervous energy that she longs to eat macaroons and say something "dreadful" to Torvald and the passage in which Nora tells herself "there's nothing to be frightened about. The Christmas tree must be beautiful. I'll do everything you like, Torvald. I'll sing for you, dance for you—."

ANSWERS FOR UNDERSTANDING LITERATURE

Responses will vary. Possible responses are given.

1. **Character and Dialogue.** Torvald does not take Nora very seriously as a person, nor does he respect her. His nicknames for Nora such as "squirrel," "skylark," and "songbird" reveal that he thinks of Nora as a little, amusing pet. He also speaks to her as if she were a child, always lecturing and scolding her. Nora is not as simple and dependent as she seems. She is proud of having been resourceful enough to save the life of her husband, and she has a strong code of ethics based upon her love for him; she believes love to be more important than honesty or obeying the law.

2. **Mood.** The mood at the beginning of the act is one of happiness and joy. By the end of the act, the mood is one of anxiety, tension, and suspense.

SYNTHESIZING

5. Nora tells both Torvald and Christine that she is terribly happy. Is she really happy? If she is not happy, how is she feeling? Find passages that support your conclusion.

Understanding Literature (Questions for Discussion)

1. **Character and Dialogue.** A **character** is a person (or sometimes an animal) who figures in the action of a literary work. **Dialogue** is conversation involving two or more people or characters. Dialogue in a drama serves to establish characters, to reveal relationships, to move the plot forward, and to create mood. In this drama, almost everything the reader or the audience learns about Nora's character is revealed through dialogue. Examine Torvald's dialogue, paying close attention to the way he speaks to Nora. What does this dialogue reveal about Torvald's attitude toward Nora? Then, look at Nora's dialogue. What is different about the way she speaks to Torvald and Christine? What does this difference reveal about Nora? Is she really as simple and dependent as she seems? Explain.

2. **Mood. Mood,** or **atmosphere,** is the emotion created in the reader by part or all of a literary work. What is the mood at the beginning of act 1? In what way has the mood changed by the end of act 1?

How do you feel about keeping secrets? Do they make you nervous? excited? Have you ever had something you wanted kept secret revealed? How did the revelation make you feel? Have you ever revealed something that somebody else wished to keep secret? What were the ramifications of your actions?

READER'S JOURNAL

ACT 2

The same room. In the corner by the piano the Christmas tree stands, stripped and disheveled, *its candles burned to their sockets.* NORA'S *outdoor clothes lie on the sofa. She is alone in the room, walking restlessly to-and-fro. At length she stops by the sofa and picks up her coat.*

NORA (*drops the coat again*). There's someone coming! (*goes to the door and listens*) No, it's no one. Of course—no one'll come today, it's Christmas Day. Nor tomorrow. But perhaps—! (*opens the door and looks out*) No. Nothing in the letter box. Quite empty. (*walks across the room*) Silly, silly. Of course he won't do anything. It couldn't happen. It isn't possible. Why, I've three small children.

[*The* NURSE, *carrying a large cardboard box, enters from the room on the left.*]

NURSE. I found those fancy dress clothes at last, madam.

NORA. Thank you. Put them on the table.

NURSE (*does so*). They're all rumpled up.

NORA. Oh, I wish I could tear them into a million pieces!

NURSE. Why, madam! They'll be all right. Just a little patience.

NORA. Yes, of course. I'll go and get Mrs. Linde to help me.

NURSE. What, out again? In this dreadful weather? You'll catch a chill, madam.

NORA. Well, that wouldn't be the worst. How are the children?

NURSE. Playing with their Christmas presents, poor little dears. But—

NORA. Are they still asking to see me?

NURSE. They're so used to having their mummy with them.

NORA. Yes, but, Anne-Marie, from now on I shan't be able to spend so much time with them.

NURSE. Well, children get used to anything in time.

NORA. Do you think so? Do you think they'd forget their mother if she went away from them—forever?

NURSE. Mercy's sake, madam! Forever!

NORA. Tell me, Anne-Marie—I've so often wondered. How could you bear to give your child away—to strangers?

NURSE. But I had to when I came to nurse my little Miss Nora.

NORA. Do you mean you wanted to?

1 *Why does Nora say she won't be able to spend time with her children? Why does she ask these questions about her children?*

WORDS FOR EVERYDAY USE

di • shev • eled (di shev´əld) *adj.,* disarranged and untidy, tousled, rumpled

ADDITIONAL RESOURCES

READER'S GUIDE

- Selection Worksheet 2.2

ASSESSMENT PORTFOLIO

- Selection Check Test 2.2.3
- Selection Test 2.2.4

READER'S JOURNAL

You might give students time to freewrite about the different kinds of secrets people keep. What kinds of secrets are most fun to keep, and what kinds of secrets are most stressful to keep?

ANSWERS TO GUIDED READING QUESTIONS

1 Nora is afraid that her crime makes her unfit to take care of her children. She may be wondering how her children will cope if she has to go away to escape scandal.

SUPPORT FOR LEP STUDENTS

PRONUNCIATIONS OF PROPER NOUNS AND ADJECTIVES

Ne • a • pol • i • tan (nē ə pol´ət'n)

ADDITIONAL VOCABULARY

atone—make amends
laughingstock—object of jokes and ridicule
pampered—overindulged
petty—minor, unimportant
pretext—front; false reason
retribution—punishment or reward for something done
rogue—mischievous person
tactless—without skill in dealing with people or situations
unassailable—unable to be attacked or defeated
vindictiveness—vengefulness, spite

VOCABULARY IN CONTEXT

- After his long nap, the toddler looked sleepy and disheveled.

ANSWERS TO GUIDED READING QUESTIONS

1 Nora doesn't dare to go out because she is afraid that Krogstad will come to the house and reveal everything to Torvald.

2 Dr. Rank has spinal tuberculosis.

SPELLING AND VOCABULARY WORDS FROM THE SELECTION

amicably
depraved
disheveled
obloquy
obstinate

QUOTABLES

On solving problems:

"Everything has two handles, one by which it may be borne, the other by which it may not."

—Epictetus
Encheiridion

NURSE. When I had the chance of such a good job? A poor girl what's got into trouble can't afford to pick and choose. That good-for-nothing didn't lift a finger.

NORA. But your daughter must have completely forgotten you.

NURSE. Oh no, indeed she hasn't. She's written to me twice, once when she got confirmed and then again when she got married.

NORA (*hugs her*). Dear old Anne-Marie, you were a good mother to me.

NURSE. Poor little Miss Nora, you never had any mother but me.

NORA. And if my little ones had no one else, I know you would—no, silly, silly, silly! (*opens the cardboard box*) Go back to them, Anne-Marie. Now I must—! Tomorrow you'll see how pretty I shall look.

NURSE. Why, there'll be no one at the ball as beautiful as my Miss Nora.

[*She goes into the room, left.*]

1 *Why doesn't Nora dare to go out?*

2 *What is wrong with Dr. Rank?*

NORA (*begins to unpack the clothes from the box, but soon throws them down again*). Oh, if only I dared go out! If I could be sure no one would come and nothing would happen while I was away! Stupid, stupid! No one will come. I just mustn't think about it. Brush this muff. Pretty gloves, pretty gloves! Don't think about it, don't think about it! One, two, three, four, five, six—(*cries*) Ah—they're coming—!

[*She begins to run towards the door, but stops uncertainly.* MRS. LINDE *enters from the hall, where she has been taking off her outdoor clothes.*]

NORA. Oh, it's you, Christine. There's no one else outside, is there? Oh, I'm so glad you've come.

MRS. LINDE. I hear you were at my room asking for me.

NORA. Yes, I just happened to be passing. I want to ask you to help me with something. Let's sit down here on the sofa. Look at this. There's going to be a fancy-dress ball tomorrow night upstairs at Consul Stenborg's, and Torvald wants me to go as a Neapolitan fisher-girl and dance the tarantella.[1] I learned it in Capri.

MRS. LINDE. I say, are you going to give a performance?

NORA. Yes, Torvald says I should. Look, here's the dress. Torvald had it made for me in Italy—but now it's all so torn, I don't know—

MRS. LINDE. Oh, we'll soon put that right—the stitching's just come away. Needle and thread? Ah, here we are.

NORA. You're being awfully sweet.

MRS. LINDE (*sews*). So you're going to dress up tomorrow, Nora? I must pop over for a moment to see how you look. Oh, but I've completely forgotten to thank you for that nice evening yesterday.

NORA (*gets up and walks across the room*). Oh, I didn't think it was as nice as usual. You ought to have come to town a little earlier, Christine. . . . Yes, Torvald understands how to make a home look attractive.

MRS. LINDE. I'm sure you do, too. You're not your father's daughter for nothing. But, tell me—is Dr. Rank always in such low spirits as he was yesterday?

NORA. No, last night it was very noticeable. But he's got a terrible disease—he's got spinal tuberculosis, poor man. His father was a frightful creature who kept mistresses and so on. As a result Dr. Rank has been sickly ever since he was a child—you understand—

MRS. LINDE (*puts down her sewing*). But, my dear Nora, how on earth did you get to know about such things?

NORA (*walks about the room*). Oh, don't be silly, Christine—when one has three children, one comes into contact with women who—

1. **tarantella.** Fast, whirling southern Italian dance

Still Life in an Interior. Paul Gauguin, 1885

well, who know about medical matters, and they tell one a thing or two.

MRS. LINDE (*sews again; a short silence*). Does Dr. Rank visit you every day?

NORA. Yes, every day. He's Torvald's oldest friend, and a good friend to me too. Dr. Rank's almost one of the family.

MRS. LINDE. But, tell me—is he quite sincere? I mean, doesn't he rather say the sort of thing he thinks people want to hear?

NORA. No, quite the contrary. What gave you that idea?

MRS. LINDE. When you introduced me to him yesterday, he said he'd often heard my name mentioned here. But later I noticed your husband had no idea who I was. So how could Dr. Rank—

NORA. Yes, that's quite right, Christine. You see, Torvald's so hopelessly in love with me that he wants to have me all to himself—those were his very words. When we were first married, he got quite jealous if I as much as mentioned any of my old friends back home. So naturally, I stopped talking about them. But I often chat with Dr. Rank about that kind of thing. He enjoys it, you see.

MRS. LINDE. Now listen, Nora. In many ways you're still a child; I'm a bit older than you and have a little more experience of the world. There's something I want to say to you. You ought to give up this business with Dr. Rank.

NORA. What business?

MRS. LINDE. Well, everything. Last night you were speaking about this rich admirer of yours who was going to give you money—

NORA. Yes, and who doesn't exist—unfortunately. But what's that got to do with—?

MRS. LINDE. Is Dr. Rank rich?

NORA. Yes.

MRS. LINDE. And he has no dependents?

NORA. No, no one. But—

MRS. LINDE. And he comes here to see you every day?

1 *In what way does Nora's relationship with Dr. Rank differ from her relationship with Torvald?*

ANSWERS TO GUIDED READING QUESTIONS

1 Nora feels more free to chat openly with Dr. Rank than she does with her husband.

CULTURAL NOTE

The tarantella is an Italian folk dance performed by a circle of couples around a center couple. Tambourines emphasize its variable tempo.

People have handed down folk dances such as the tarantella from generation to generation, and the dances have come to reflect the temperament and environment of the people who perform them. The sword, morris, and other country dances of England are lively but dignified. They require precision, agility, and endurance. Skilled footwork is needed for Ireland's reel, jig, and hornpipe. The Highland fling, sword dance, reel, and schottische of Scotland incorporate vigorous kicking and a driving beat. The cossack dance of Russia is both wild and dignified, and the polonaise of Poland is stately. Poland's rustic dances are lively, with much jumping. The bolero, fandango, and seguidilla of Spain are spirited and picturesque, and the schuhplatteltanz of Bavaria has a lively beat that is marked by the dancers' clapping hands.

CROSS-CURRICULAR ACTIVITIES

ARTS AND HUMANITIES

Ask students to form small groups to research folk dances from different parts of the world. Each group should focus on one region or country. Each group should find a folk dance, learn its history, and then try to perform it for the rest of the class.

Answers to Guided Reading Questions

❶ She thinks that Dr. Rank has loaned Nora the money.

❷ Nora is thinking about talking to Dr. Rank about her difficulties.

Cross-curricular Activities

SOCIAL STUDIES

Nora and Torvald spent time in the Neapolitan area of Italy, or the area around the city of Naples. Ask students to go to the library to research this city. Students should look into the history of the city, what it is like today, and what it was like when Nora and Torvald would have been there.

As a variation, you might assign the study of different aspects of the city to different groups of students. For example, students can research the area's history, food, arts and leisure, and geography. Groups should share their findings with one another.

❶ *What does Mrs. Linde think about Nora's relationship with Dr. Rank?*

❷ *What is Nora thinking about doing?*

Nora. Yes, I've told you.

Mrs. Linde. But how dare a man of his education be so forward?

Nora. What on earth are you talking about?

Mrs. Linde. Oh, stop pretending, Nora. Do you think I haven't guessed who it was who lent you that two hundred pounds?

Nora. Are you out of your mind? How could you imagine such a thing? A friend, someone who comes here every day! Why, that'd be an impossible situation!

Mrs. Linde. Then it really wasn't him?

Nora. No, of course not. I've never for a moment dreamed of—anyway, he hadn't any money to lend then. He didn't come into that till later.

Mrs. Linde. Well, I think that was a lucky thing for you, Nora dear.

Nora. No, I could never have dreamed of asking Dr. Rank—Though I'm sure that if ever I did ask him—

Mrs. Linde. But of course you won't.

Nora. Of course not. I can't imagine that it should ever become necessary. But I'm perfectly sure that if I did speak to Dr. Rank—

Mrs. Linde. Behind your husband's back?

Nora. I've got to get out of this other business—and *that's* been going on behind his back. I've *got* to get out of it.

Mrs. Linde. Yes, well, that's what I told you yesterday. But—

Nora (*walking up and down*). It's much easier for a man to arrange these things than a woman—

Mrs. Linde. One's own husband, yes.

Nora. Oh, bosh. (*stops walking*) When you've completely repaid a debt, you get your I.O.U. back, don't you?

Mrs. Linde. Yes, of course.

Nora. And you can tear it into a thousand pieces and burn the filthy, beastly thing!

Mrs. Linde (*looks hard at her, puts down her sewing and gets up slowly*). Nora, you're hiding something from me.

Nora. Can you see that?

Mrs. Linde. Something has happened since yesterday morning. Nora, what is it?

Nora (*goes towards her*). Christine! (*listens*) Ssh! There's Torvald. Would you mind going into the nursery for a few minutes? Torvald can't bear to see sewing around. Anne-Marie'll help you.

Mrs. Linde (*gathers some of her things together*). Very well. But I shan't leave this house until we've talked this matter out.

[*She goes into the nursery, left. As she does so,* Helmer *enters from the hall.*]

Nora (*runs to meet him*). Oh, Torvald dear, I've been so longing for you to come back!

Helmer. Was that the dressmaker?

Nora. No, it was Christine. She's helping me mend my costume. I'm going to look rather splendid in that.

Helmer. Yes, that was quite a bright idea of mine, wasn't it?

Nora. Wonderful! But wasn't it nice of me to give in to you?

Helmer (*takes her chin in his hand*). Nice—to give in to your husband? All right, little silly, I know you didn't mean it like that. But I won't disturb you. I expect you'll be wanting to try it on.

Nora. Are you going to work now?

Helmer. Yes. (*shows her a bundle of papers*) Look at these. I've been down to the bank—(*turns to go into his study*)

Nora. Torvald.

Helmer (*stops*). Yes.

Nora. If little squirrel asked you really prettily to grant her a wish—

Helmer. Well?

Nora. Would you grant it to her?

HELMER. First I should naturally have to know what it was.

NORA. Squirrel would do lots of pretty tricks for you if you granted her wish.

HELMER. Out with it, then.

NORA. Your little skylark would sing in every room—

HELMER. My little skylark does that already.

NORA. I'd turn myself into a little fairy and dance for you in the moonlight, Torvald.

HELMER. Nora, it isn't that business you were talking about this morning?

NORA (*comes closer*). Yes, Torvald—oh, please! I beg of you!

HELMER. Have you really the nerve to bring that up again?

NORA. Yes, Torvald, yes, you must do as I ask! You must let Krogstad keep his place at the bank!

HELMER. My dear Nora, his is the job I'm giving to Mrs. Linde.

NORA. Yes, that's terribly sweet of you. But you can get rid of one of the other clerks instead of Krogstad.

HELMER. Really, you're being incredibly obstinate. Just because you thoughtlessly promised to put in a word for him, you expect me to—

NORA. No, it isn't that, Helmer. It's for your own sake. That man writes for the most beastly newspapers—you said so yourself. He could do you tremendous harm. I'm so dreadfully frightened of him—

HELMER. Oh, I understand. Memories of the past. That's what's frightening you.

NORA. What do you mean?

HELMER. You're thinking of your father, aren't you?

NORA. Yes, yes. Of course. Just think what those dreadful men wrote in the papers about Papa! The most frightful slanders. I really believe it would have lost him his job if the Ministry hadn't sent you down to investigate, and you hadn't been so kind and helpful to him.

HELMER. But, my dear little Nora, there's a considerable difference between your father and me. Your father was not a man of unassailable reputation. But I am. And I hope to remain so all my life.

❶ *What kind of a person does Torvald claim to be? What does he think of himself?*

NORA. But no one knows what spiteful people may not dig up. We could be so peaceful and happy now, Torvald—we could be free from every worry—you and I and the children. Oh, please, Torvald, please—!

HELMER. The very fact of your pleading his cause makes it impossible for me to keep him. Everyone at the bank already knows that I intend to dismiss Krogstad. If the rumor got about that the new vice-president had allowed his wife to persuade him to change his mind—

❷ *According to Torvald, why does Nora's request make it impossible for him to keep Krogstad?*

NORA. Well, what then?

HELMER. Oh, nothing, nothing. As long as my little Miss Obstinate gets her way—! Do you expect me to make a laughingstock of myself before my entire staff—give people the idea that I am open to outside influence? Believe me, I'd soon feel the consequences! Besides—there's something else that makes it impossible for Krogstad to remain in the bank while I am its manager.

NORA. What is that?

HELMER. I might conceivably have allowed myself to ignore his moral obloquies—

WORDS FOR EVERYDAY USE

ob • sti • nate (äb´stə nət) *adj.*, stubborn; not yielding to reason or plea

ob • lo • quy (äb´lə kwē) *n.*, ill repute; disgrace

ANSWERS TO GUIDED READING QUESTIONS

❶ Torvald claims to be a person of "unassailable reputation." Torvald thinks of himself as being admired for his morals and ethics.

❷ Torvald says that he wouldn't want everyone to think of him as the kind of person who is influenced by his wife.

ADDITIONAL QUESTIONS AND ACTIVITIES

Students can form teams and debate whether Torvald is an ethical person. The following questions may help them as they prepare for the debate.

Do you think Torvald's morals and ethics are impressive by his society's standards? Why, or why not? Does Torvald strike you as a moral and ethical person? Why, or why not? What do you think is Torvald's idea of a truly moral or ethical person? Who, so far, do you think is the most ethical person in the play? Explain your response.

ANSWERS

Responses will vary.

Students may say that Torvald's morals and ethics are based on a rigid adherence to rules. His superiority rests heavily on what others think of him. His rejection of Krogstad has something to do with wanting to distance himself from Krogstad's display of their schoolyard friendship. He is petty. His idea of a truly moral person is one who has a perfect reputation. Students may say that Nora, Dr. Rank, or Mrs. Linde is the most ethical person thus far in the play.

VOCABULARY IN CONTEXT

- We felt that Jackson was obstinate not to give in to our reasonable request.
- Their rowdy behavior at the town meeting was a terrible obloquy.

Answers to Guided Reading Questions

❶ Torvald used to be friends with Krogstad and he now regrets the friendship, so he is annoyed whenever Krogstad reveals to others that they are on familiar terms.

❷ Nora thinks that Torvald is being petty. Most students will agree with Nora.

❸ Torvald says that he has the strength and courage to bear any burden for both of them. Nora interprets this to mean that Torvald is strong and courageous enough to take the blame for her crime and to shield her from accusation.

Biographical Note

Another great admirer of Ibsen's work was the Austrian physician Sigmund Freud (1856–1939). Freud believed that psychological problems could be traced to repressed childhood experiences, and that dreams often provide clues about a person's concerns. Freud is the founder of psychoanalysis, also referred to as analysis, a method of treating psychological problems in which a trained mental health professional helps a patient discover and then confront the cause of the problem, which might be buried deep in the psyche.

Quotables

"The voice of the intellect is a soft one, but it does not rest until it has gained a hearing."

—Sigmund Freud, *The Future of an Illusion*

❶ *What is Torvald's real reason for wanting to dismiss Krogstad?*

❷ *What does Nora think of Torvald's reasoning? Do you agree with her?*

❸ *What does Torvald say about himself? In what way does Nora interpret this remark?*

Nora. Yes, Torvald, surely?

Helmer. And I hear he's quite efficient at his job. But we—well, we were school friends. It was one of those friendships that one enters into overhastily and so often comes to regret later in life. I might as well confess the truth. We—well, we're on Christian name terms. And the tactless idiot makes no attempt to conceal it when other people are present. On the contrary, he thinks it gives him the right to be familiar with me. He shows off the whole time, with "Torvald this" and "Torvald that." I can tell you, I find it damned annoying. If he stayed, he'd make my position intolerable.

Nora. Torvald, you can't mean this seriously.

Helmer. Oh? And why not?

Nora. But it's so petty.

Helmer. What did you say? Petty? You think *I* am petty?

Nora. No, Torvald dear, of course you're not. That's just why—

Helmer. Don't quibble! You call my motives petty. Then I must be petty too. Petty! I see. Well, I've had enough of this. (*goes to the door and calls into the hall*) Helen!

Nora. What are you going to do?

Helmer (*searching among his papers*). I'm going to settle this matter once and for all.

[*The* Maid *enters.*]

Helmer. Take this letter downstairs at once. Find a messenger and see that he delivers it. Immediately! The address is on the envelope. Here's the money.

Maid. Very good, sir. (*goes out with the letter*)

Helmer (*putting his papers in order*). There now, little Miss Obstinate.

Nora (*tensely*). Torvald—what was in that letter?

Helmer. Krogstad's dismissal.

Nora. Call her back, Torvald! There's still time. Oh, Torvald, call her back! Do it for my sake—for your own sake—for the children! Do you hear me, Torvald? Please do it! You don't realize what this may do to us all!

Helmer. Too late.

Nora. Yes. Too late.

Helmer. My dear Nora, I forgive you this anxiety. Though it is a bit of an insult to me. Oh, but it is! Isn't it an insult to imply that I should be frightened by the vindictiveness of a depraved hack journalist? But I forgive you, because it so charmingly testifies to the love you bear me. (*takes her in his arms*) Which is as it should be, my own dearest Nora. Let what will happen, happen. When the real crisis comes, you will not find me lacking in strength or courage. I am man enough to bear the burden for us both.

Nora (*fearfully*). What do you mean?

Helmer. The whole burden, I say—

Nora (*calmly*). I shall never let you do that.

Helmer. Very well. We shall share it, Nora—as man and wife. And that's as it should be. (*caresses her*) Are you happy now? There, there, there; don't look at me with those frightened little eyes. You're simply imagining things. You go ahead now and do your tarantella, and get some practice on that tambourine. I'll sit in my study and close the door. Then I won't hear anything, and you can make all the noise you want. (*turns in the doorway*) When Dr. Rank comes, tell him where to find me. (*He nods to her, goes into his room with his papers and closes the door.*)

Words for Everyday Use

de • praved (dē prāvd´) *adj.,* morally bad, corrupt, perverted

Vocabulary in Context

- Some of the images in that writer's novel seem shocking and depraved.

NORA (*desperate with anxiety, stands as though transfixed, and whispers*). He said he'd do it. He will do it. He will do it, and nothing'll stop him. No, never that. I'd rather anything. There must be some escape—Some way out—!

[*The bell rings in the hall.*]

NORA. Dr. Rank—! Anything but that! Anything, I don't care—!

[*She passes her hand across her face, composes herself, walks across and opens the door to the hall.* DR. RANK *is standing there, hanging up his fur coat. During the following scene it begins to grow dark.*]

NORA. Good evening, Dr. Rank. I recognized your ring. But you mustn't go in to Torvald yet. I think he's busy.

RANK. And— you?

NORA (*as he enters the room and she closes the door behind him*). Oh, you know very well I've always time to talk to you.

RANK. Thank you. I shall avail myself of that privilege as long as I can.

NORA. What do you mean by that? As long as you *can?*

RANK. Yes. Does that frighten you?

NORA. Well, it's rather a curious expression. Is something going to happen?

RANK. Something I've been expecting to happen for a long time. But I didn't think it would happen quite so soon.

NORA (*seizes his arm*). What is it? Dr. Rank, you must tell me!

RANK (*sits down by the stove*). I'm on the way out. And there's nothing to be done about it.

NORA (*sighs with relief*). Oh, it's you—?

RANK. Who else? No, it's no good lying to oneself. I am the most wretched of all my patients, Mrs. Helmer. These last few days I've been going through the books of this poor body of mine, and I find I am bankrupt. Within a month I may be rotting up there in the churchyard.

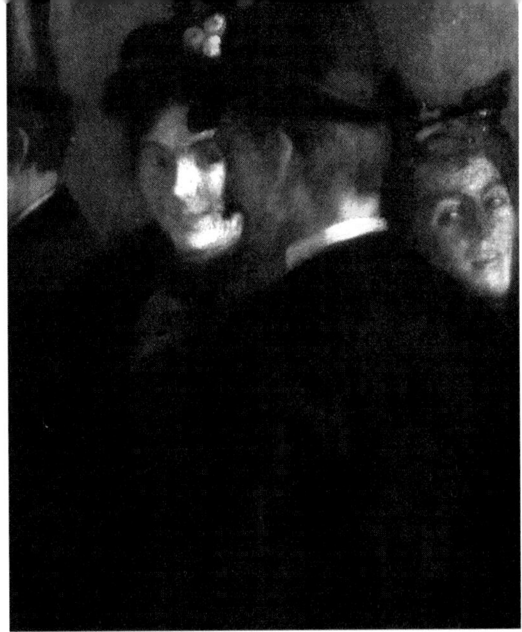

Theater Foyer. Louis Anquentin, 1892

NORA. Ugh, what a nasty way to talk!

RANK. The facts aren't exactly nice. But the worst is that there's so much else that's nasty that's got to come first. I've only one more test to make. When that's done I'll have a pretty accurate idea of when the final disintegration is likely to begin. I want to ask you a favor. Helmer's a sensitive chap, and I know how he hates anything ugly. I don't want him to visit me when I'm in hospital—

NORA. Oh but, Dr. Rank—

RANK. I don't want him there. On any pretext. I shan't have him allowed in. As soon as I know the worst, I'll send you my visiting card with a black cross on it, and then you'll know that the final filthy process has begun.

NORA. Really, you're being quite impossible this evening. And I did hope you'd be in a good mood.

① *What is wrong with Dr. Rank? Why doesn't he want anyone to see him? What will he do to notify the Helmers of his condition?*

ANSWERS TO GUIDED READING QUESTIONS

① Dr. Rank knows that he will probably be dead in less than a month. He doesn't want anyone to be disturbed by having to watch him get weaker and sicker. He will send the Helmers a visiting card with a black cross on it when "the final filthy process has begun."

ADDITIONAL QUESTIONS AND ACTIVITIES

Ask each student to imagine that he or she has been hired to sit with Nora and analyze the troubles she is having with her life and with Torvald. Ask students to write dialogues between themselves and Nora. In these dialogues, they should ask Nora specific questions about her childhood and her adult life and then write her responses based on what they know of her life and her character. When the dialogue is complete, students should make notes about what Nora might do to solve her current problems or to raise the courage to confront Torvald with her secret.

Answers to Guided Reading Questions

❶ Nora says that Dr. Rank should imagine tomorrow that she is dancing just for him. Nora seems to feel very fond of and close to Dr. Rank.

Additional Questions and Activities

Ask students to describe why they think Nora feels so close to and comfortable with Dr. Rank.

ANSWERS

Responses will vary. Possible responses are given.

Students might say that Dr. Rank allows Nora to talk about herself and does not try to constrain her. He also seems to enjoy her company.

❶ *What does Nora say Dr. Rank should imagine? How does Nora feel about Dr. Rank?*

RANK. With death on my hands? And all this to atone for someone else's sin? Is there justice in that? And in every single family, in one way or another, the same merciless law of retribution is at work—

NORA (*holds her hands to her ears*). Nonsense! Cheer up! Laugh!

RANK. Yes, you're right. Laughter's all the damned thing's fit for. My poor innocent spine must pay for the fun my father had as a gay young lieutenant.

NORA (*at the table, left*). You mean he was too fond of asparagus and *foie gras?*[2]

RANK. Yes; and truffles too.

NORA. Yes, of course, truffles, yes. And oysters too, I suppose?

RANK. Yes, oysters, oysters. Of course.

NORA. And all that port and champagne to wash them down. It's too sad that all those lovely things should affect one's spine.

RANK. Especially a poor spine that never got any pleasure out of them.

NORA. Oh yes, that's the saddest thing of all.

RANK (*looks searchingly at her*). Hm—

NORA (*after a moment*). Why did you smile?

RANK. No, it was you who laughed.

NORA. No, it was you who smiled, Dr. Rank!

RANK (*gets up*). You're a worse little rogue than I thought.

NORA. Oh, I'm full of stupid tricks today.

RANK. So it seems.

NORA (*puts both her hands on his shoulders*). Dear, dear Dr. Rank, you mustn't die and leave Torvald and me.

RANK. Oh, you'll soon get over it. Once one is gone, one is soon forgotten.

NORA (*looks at him anxiously*). Do you believe that?

RANK. One finds replacements, and then—

NORA. Who will find a replacement?

RANK. You and Helmer both will, when I am gone. You seem to have made a start already, haven't you? What was this Mrs. Linde doing here yesterday evening?

NORA. Aha! But surely you can't be jealous of poor Christine?

RANK. Indeed I am. She will be my successor in this house. When I have moved on, this lady will—

NORA. Ssh—don't speak so loud! She's in there!

RANK. Today again? You see!

NORA. She's only come to mend my dress. Good heavens, how unreasonable you are! (*sits on the sofa*) Be nice now, Dr. Rank. Tomorrow you'll see how beautifully I shall dance; and you must imagine that I'm doing it just for you. And for Torvald, of course; obviously. (*takes some things out of the box*) Dr. Rank, sit down here and I'll show you something.

RANK (*sits*). What's this?

NORA. Look here! Look!

RANK. Silk stockings!

NORA. Flesh-colored. Aren't they beautiful? It's very dark in here now, of course, but tomorrow—! No, no, no; only the soles. Oh well, I suppose you can look a bit higher if you want to.

RANK. Hm—

NORA. Why are you looking so critical? Don't you think they'll fit me?

RANK. I can't really give you a qualified opinion on that.

NORA. (*looks at him for a moment*). Shame on you! (*flicks him on the ear with the stockings*) Take that. (*puts them back in the box*)

RANK. What other wonders are to be revealed to me?

2. ***foie gras.*** Pâté, or spread, made from goose liver

NORA. I shan't show you anything else. You're being naughty.

[*She hums a little and looks among the things in the box.*]

RANK (*after a short silence*). When I sit here like this being so intimate with you, I can't think—I cannot imagine what would have become of me if I had never entered this house.

NORA (*smiles*). Yes, I think you enjoy being with us, don't you?

RANK (*more quietly, looking into the middle distance*). And now to have to leave it all—

NORA. Nonsense. You're not leaving us.

RANK (*as before*). And not to be able to leave even the most wretched token of gratitude behind; hardly even a passing sense of loss; only an empty place, to be filled by the next comer.

NORA. Suppose I were to ask you to—? No—

RANK. To do what?

NORA. To give me proof of your friendship—

RANK. Yes, yes?

NORA. No, I mean—to do me a very great service—

RANK. Would you really for once grant me that happiness?

NORA. But you've no idea what it is.

RANK. Very well, tell me, then.

NORA. No, but, Dr. Rank, I can't. It's far too much—I want your help and advice, and I want you to do something for me.

RANK. The more the better. I've no idea what it can be. But tell me. You do trust me, don't you?

NORA. Oh, yes, more than anyone. You're my best and truest friend. Otherwise I couldn't tell you. Well then, Dr. Rank—there's something you must help me to prevent. You know how much Torvald loves me—he'd never hesitate for an instant to lay down his life for me—

RANK (*leans over towards her*). Nora—do you think he is the only one—?

NORA (*with a slight start*). What do you mean?

RANK. Who would gladly lay down his life for you?

NORA (*sadly*). Oh, I see.

RANK. I swore to myself I would let you know that before I go. I shall never have a better opportunity. . . . Well, Nora, now you know that. And now you also know that you can trust me as you can trust nobody else.

NORA (*rises; calmly and quietly*). Let me pass, please.

RANK (*makes room for her but remains seated*). Nora—

NORA (*in the doorway to the hall*). Helen, bring the lamp. (*goes over to the stove*) Oh, dear Dr. Rank, this was really horrid of you.

RANK (*gets up*). That I have loved you as deeply as anyone else has? Was that horrid of me?

NORA. No—but that you should go and tell me. That was quite unnecessary—

RANK. What do you mean? Did you know, then—?

[*The* MAID *enters with the lamp, puts it on the table and goes out.*]

RANK. Nora—Mrs. Helmer—I am asking you, did you know this?

NORA. Oh, what do I know, what did I know, what didn't I know—I really can't say. How could you be so stupid, Dr. Rank? Everything was so nice.

RANK. Well, at any rate now you know that I am ready to serve you, body and soul. So—please continue.

NORA (*looks at him*). After this?

RANK. Please tell me what it is.

NORA. I can't possibly tell you now.

❶ *How does Dr. Rank feel about Nora?*

❷ *How does Dr. Rank feel about helping and advising Nora?*

❸ *Did Nora know that Dr. Rank felt this way? Why won't she let him help her?*

Answers to Guided Reading Questions

❶ Dr. Rank loves Nora and would lay down his life for her.

❷ Dr. Rank would be honored and happy to help and advise Nora.

❸ Nora may have thought that Dr. Rank felt this way about her but the feelings had never been articulated. Once his love for her is out in the open, she feels it would be improper to accept his help.

Literary Technique

Character

A **character** is a person who figures in the action of a literary work. Ask each student to describe on paper the character of Dr. Rank. What kind of person is he? What evidence from the play can they find to back up their descriptions?

Answers to Guided Reading Questions

❶ Dr. Rank thought that Nora loved him as much as she loved Torvald and wished that she could be with him instead.

❷ Nora compares her love for Torvald to her love for her father.

Historical Note

A Doll's House is a feminist play in that it examines Nora, her relationships with her father and her husband, and her place in society. Nora, in the beginning of the play, is a character reduced to a dependent state, much like that of a child. She is this way due to her upbringing and the continual condescending treatment by her husband.

English writer Mary Wollstonecraft (1759–1797) is widely recognized as one of the first great feminist writers and thinkers. Her famous work *Vindication of the Rights of Woman* examines the lives of women at the time in which she wrote. She believed that continual denial of power and opportunities robbed women of self-sufficiency and made them weak and docile. She argued that society kept women of the time from becoming fully human. Share with students the following excerpt from this essay:

"If then women are not a swarm of ephemeron triflers, why should they be kept in ignorance under the specious name of innocence? Men complain, and with reason, of the follies and caprices of our sex, when they do not keenly satirize our headstrong passions and groveling vices.—Behold, I should answer, the natural effect of ignorance! The mind will ever be unstable that has only prejudices to rest on, and the current will run with destructive fury when there are no barriers to break its force. Women are told

(cont.)

RANK. Yes, yes! You mustn't punish me like this. Let me be allowed to do what I can for you.

NORA. You can't do anything for me now. Anyway, I don't need any help. It was only my imagination—you'll see. Yes, really. Honestly. (*sits in the rocking chair, looks at him and smiles*) Well, upon my word you are a fine gentleman, Dr. Rank. Aren't you ashamed of yourself, now that the lamp's been lit?

RANK. Frankly, no. But perhaps I ought to say—*adieu?*

NORA. Of course not. You will naturally continue to visit us as before. You know quite well how Torvald depends on your company.

RANK. Yes, but you?

NORA. Oh, I always think it's enormous fun having you here.

❶ *What did Dr. Rank think about Nora?*

RANK. That was what misled me. You're a riddle to me, you know. I'd often felt you'd just as soon be with me as with Helmer.

NORA. Well, you see, there are some people whom one loves, and others whom it's almost more fun to be with.

RANK. Oh yes, there's some truth in that.

❷ *To what does Nora compare her love for Torvald?*

NORA. When I was at home, of course I loved Papa best. But I always used to think it was terribly amusing to go down and talk to the servants; because they never told me what I ought to do; and they were such fun to listen to.

RANK. I see. So I've taken their place?

NORA (*jumps up and runs over to him*). Oh, dear, sweet Dr. Rank, I didn't mean that at all. But I'm sure you understand—I feel the same about Torvald as I did about Papa.

MAID (*enters from the hall*). Excuse me, madam. (*whispers to her and hands her a visiting card*)

NORA (*glances at the card*). Oh! (*puts it quickly in her pocket*)

RANK. Anything wrong?

NORA. No, no, nothing at all. It's just something that—it's my new dress.

RANK. What? But your costume is lying over there.

NORA. Oh—that, yes—but there's another—I ordered it specially—Torvald mustn't know—

RANK. Ah, so that's your big secret?

NORA. Yes, yes. Go in and talk to him—he's in his study—keep him talking for a bit—

RANK. Don't worry. He won't get away from me. (*goes into* HELMER*'s study*)

NORA (*to the* MAID). Is he waiting in the kitchen?

MAID. Yes, madam, he came up the back way—

NORA. But didn't you tell him I had a visitor?

MAID. Yes, but he wouldn't go.

NORA. Wouldn't go?

MAID. No, madam, not until he'd spoken with you.

NORA. Very well, show him in; but quietly. Helen, you mustn't tell anyone about this. It's a surprise for my husband.

MAID. Very good, madam. I understand. (*goes*)

NORA. It's happening. It's happening after all. No, no, no, it can't happen, it mustn't happen.

[*She walks across and bolts the door of* HELMER*'s study. The* MAID *opens the door from the hall to admit* KROGSTAD, *and closes it behind him. He is wearing an overcoat, heavy boots and a fur cap.*]

NORA (*goes towards him*). Speak quietly. My husband's at home.

KROGSTAD. Let him hear.

NORA. What do you want from me?

KROGSTAD. Information.

NORA. Hurry up, then. What is it?

Historical Note (cont.)

from their infancy, and taught by the example of their mothers, that a little knowledge of human weakness, justly turned cunning, softness of temper, *outward* obedience, and a scrupulous attention to a puerile kind of propriety will obtain for them the protection of man; and should they be beautiful, everything else is needless, for, at least, twenty years of their lives."

KROGSTAD. I suppose you know I've been given the sack.

NORA. I couldn't stop it, Mr. Krogstad. I did my best for you, but it didn't help.

KROGSTAD. Does your husband love you so little? He knows what I can do to you, and yet he dares to—

NORA. Surely you don't imagine I told him?

KROGSTAD. No, I didn't really think you had. It wouldn't have been like my old friend Torvald Helmer to show that much courage—

NORA. Mr. Krogstad, I'll trouble you to speak respectfully of my husband.

KROGSTAD. Don't worry, I'll show him all the respect he deserves. But since you're so anxious to keep this matter hushed up, I presume you're better informed than you were yesterday of the gravity of what you've done?

NORA. I've learned more than you could ever teach me.

KROGSTAD. Yes, a bad lawyer like me—

NORA. What do you want from me?

KROGSTAD. I just wanted to see how things were with you, Mrs. Helmer. I've been thinking about you all day. Even duns[3] and hack journalists have hearts, you know.

NORA. Show some heart, then. Think of my little children.

KROGSTAD. Have you and your husband thought of mine? Well, let's forget that. I just wanted to tell you, you don't need to take this business too seriously. I'm not going to take any action, for the present.

NORA. Oh, no—you won't, will you? I knew it.

Interior, Rue Carcel. Paul Gauguin, 1881

KROGSTAD. It can all be settled quite amicably. There's no need for it to become public. We'll keep it among the three of us.

❶ *What does Krogstad say he plans to do with his knowledge of Nora's crime?*

NORA. My husband must never know about this.

KROGSTAD. How can you stop him? Can you pay the balance of what you owe me?

NORA. Not immediately.

KROGSTAD. Have you any means of raising the money during the next few days?

NORA. None that I would care to use.

KROGSTAD. Well, it wouldn't have helped anyway. However much money you offered me now I wouldn't give you back that paper.

NORA. What are you going to do with it?

3. **duns.** People who ask insistently or repeatedly for payment

WORDS FOR EVERYDAY USE

am • i • ca • bly (am´i kə blē) *adv.,* with friendliness or good will

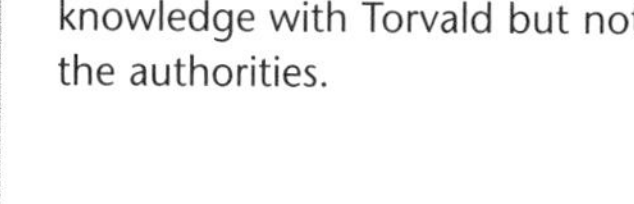

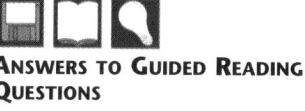

ANSWERS TO GUIDED READING QUESTIONS

❶ Krogstad plans to share this knowledge with Torvald but not with the authorities.

ADDITIONAL QUESTIONS AND ACTIVITIES

Ask students to relate Mary Wollstonecraft's message (see the Historical Note on page 142) to the character of Nora. Invite students who wish to do so to find the complete copy of *Vindication of the Rights of Woman* in the library and read it. Afterwards, they should discuss the ideas Wollstonecraft advocates or report on them to the rest of the class.

VOCABULARY IN CONTEXT

• After a pleasant afternoon during which they settled their differences, Natasha and Gabrielle parted amicably.

Answers to Guided Reading Questions

❶ Krogstad wants to blackmail Torvald into giving him an important job from which he imagines he will soon rise to running the bank himself.

❷ Nora has been thinking of drowning herself. The thought of Krogstad blackmailing her husband and taking his job makes her determined to stop Krogstad any way she can.

Quotables

"No man chooses evil because it is evil; he only mistakes it for happiness, the good he seeks."

—Mary Wollstonecraft

Additional Questions and Activities

Have students hold classroom trials of Nora and of Krogstad. In the trials, students should examine the crimes of each character—Nora's forgery and Krogstad's blackmail—and decide how each character should be punished. In deciding the case, students should look closely at all the issues and ask themselves the following questions:

Was there malice surrounding the commission of the crime? What was each character's motive? Who has been most hurt by each crime?

Encourage students to decide on creative punishments for each crime.

 ❶ *What does Krogstad want to blackmail Torvald into doing?*

Krogstad. Just keep it. No one else need ever hear about it. So in case you were thinking of doing anything desperate—

Nora. I am.

Krogstad. Such as running away—

Nora. I am.

Krogstad. Or anything more desperate—

Nora. How did you know?

Krogstad. —just give up the idea.

Nora. How did you know?

❷ *What has Nora been thinking of doing? Why does she say that she has the courage now?*

Krogstad. Most of us think of that at first. I did. But I hadn't the courage—

Nora (*dully*). Neither have I.

Krogstad (*relieved*). It's true, isn't it? You haven't the courage, either?

Nora. No. I haven't. I haven't.

Krogstad. It'd be a stupid thing to do anyway. Once the first little domestic explosion is over . . . I've got a letter in my pocket here addressed to your husband—

Nora. Telling him everything?

Krogstad. As delicately as possible.

Nora (*quickly*). He must never see that letter. Tear it up. I'll find the money somehow—

Krogstad. I'm sorry, Mrs. Helmer. I thought I'd explained—

Nora. Oh, I don't mean the money I owe you. Let me know how much you want from my husband, and I'll find it for you.

Krogstad. I'm not asking your husband for money.

Nora. What do you want, then?

Krogstad. I'll tell you. I want to get on my feet again, Mrs. Helmer. I want to get to the top. And your husband's going to help me. For eighteen months now my record's been clean. I've been in hard straits all that time: I was content to fight my way back inch by inch. Now I've been chucked back into the mud, and I'm not going to be satisfied with just getting back my job. I'm going to get to the top, I tell you. I'm going to get back into the bank, and it's going to be higher up. Your husband's going to create a new job for me—

Nora. He'll never do that!

Krogstad. Oh yes, he will. I know him. He won't dare to risk a scandal. And once I'm in there with him, you'll see! Within a year I'll be his right-hand man. It'll be Nils Krogstad who'll be running that bank, not Torvald Helmer!

Nora. That will never happen.

Krogstad. Are you thinking of—?

Nora. Now I *have* the courage.

Krogstad. Oh, you can't frighten me. A pampered little pretty like you—

Nora. You'll see! You'll see!

Krogstad. Under the ice? Down in the cold, black water? And then, in the spring, to float up again, ugly, unrecognizable, hairless—?

Nora. You can't frighten me.

Krogstad. And you can't frighten me. People don't do such things, Mrs. Helmer. And anyway, what'd be the use? I've got him in my pocket.

Nora. But afterwards? When I'm no longer—?

Krogstad. Have you forgotten that then your reputation will be in my hands?

[*She looks at him speechlessly.*]

Krogstad. Well, I've warned you. Don't do anything silly. When Helmer's read my letter, he'll get in touch with me. And remember, it's your husband who has forced me to act like this. And for that I'll never forgive him. Goodbye, Mrs. Helmer. (*He goes out through the hall.*)

Nora (*runs to the hall door, opens it a few inches and listens*). He's going. He's not going to give him the letter. Oh, no, no, it couldn't possibly happen. (*opens the door, a little wider*) What's he doing? Standing outside the front door. He's not going downstairs. Is he changing his mind? Yes, he —!

[*A letter falls into the letter box.* KROGSTAD*'s footsteps die away down the stairs.*]

NORA (*with a stifled cry, runs across the room towards the table by the sofa; a pause*). In the letter box. (*steals timidly over towards the hall door*) There it is! Oh, Torvald, Torvald! Now we're lost!

MRS. LINDE (*enters from the nursery with* NORA*'s costume*). Well, I've done the best I can. Shall we see how it looks—?

NORA (*whispers hoarsely*). Christine, come here.

MRS. LINDE (*throws the dress on the sofa*). What's wrong with you? You look as though you'd seen a ghost!

NORA. Come here. Do you see that letter? There—look—through the glass of the letter box.

MRS. LINDE. Yes, yes, I see it.

NORA. That letter's from Krogstad—

MRS. LINDE. Nora! It was Krogstad who lent you the money!

NORA. Yes. And now Torvald's going to discover everything.

MRS. LINDE. Oh, believe me, Nora, it'll be best for you both.

NORA. You don't know what's happened. I've committed a forgery—

MRS. LINDE. But, for heaven's sake—!

NORA. Christine, all I want is for you to be my witness.

MRS. LINDE. What do you mean? Witness what?

NORA. If I should go out of my mind—and it might easily happen—

MRS. LINDE. Nora!

NORA. Or if anything else should happen to me—so that I wasn't here any longer—

MRS. LINDE. Nora, Nora, you don't know what you're saying!

NORA. If anyone should try to take the blame, and say it was all his fault—you understand—?

MRS. LINDE. Yes, yes—but how can you think—?

NORA. Then you must testify that it isn't true, Christine. I'm not mad—I know exactly what I'm saying—and I'm telling you, no one else knows anything about this. I did it entirely on my own. Remember that.

MRS. LINDE. All right. But I simply don't understand—

NORA. Oh, how could you understand? A—miracle—is about to happen.

MRS. LINDE. Miracle?

NORA. Yes. A miracle. But it's so frightening, Christine. It mustn't happen, not for anything in the world.

MRS. LINDE. I'll go over and talk to Krogstad.

NORA. Don't go near him. He'll only do something to hurt you.

MRS. LINDE. Once upon a time he'd have done anything for my sake.

NORA. He?

MRS. LINDE. Where does he live?

NORA. Oh, how should I know—? Oh yes, wait a moment—! (*feels in her pocket*) Here's his card. But the letter, the letter—!

HELMER (*from his study, knocks on the door*). Nora!

NORA (*cries in alarm*). What is it?

HELMER. Now, now, don't get alarmed. We're not coming in—you've closed the door. Are you trying on your costume?

NORA. Yes, yes—I'm trying on my costume. I'm going to look so pretty for you, Torvald.

MRS. LINDE (*who has been reading the card*). Why, he lives just round the corner.

1 *What does Nora ask Christine to do?*

2 *What does Krogstad drop in the letter box?*

3 *What does Nora say is about to happen? What does Nora say about this thing?*

4 *What does Christine say about Krogstad?*

ANSWERS TO GUIDED READING QUESTIONS

1 Nora asks Christine to tell people that Nora acted alone if Torvald tries to take the blame for her crime.

2 Krogstad drops a letter in the letter box telling Torvald about Nora's crime.

3 Nora says that a miracle is about to happen. Nora says that the miracle must not happen, "not for anything in the world."

4 Christine says that he once would have done anything for her sake.

LITERARY TECHNIQUE

MOOD

Mood, or **atmosphere**, is the emotion created in the reader by all or part of a literary work. Ask students to notice how the mood of the scene becomes tense at this point. Point out to students that they as readers can understand the tension of the scene, even without the benefit of seeing and hearing actors. The reader feels the tension in this scene as Nora begins speaking in loud, short, unfinished exclamations and the characters move about the stage, each pursuing a separate agenda.

Answers to Guided Reading Questions

❶ Nora pretends that she cannot remember the tarantella and that she desperately needs Torvald's help.

Additional Questions and Activities

Ask students to predict, based on what they know of his character, how Torvald would react if he learned Nora's secret. Is it likely that he would be understanding? Why, or why not? What concerns might he have?

ANSWERS

Responses will vary.

Students should base their predictions on concrete details about Torvald's character that are revealed in the play.

NORA. Yes; but it's no use. There's nothing to be done now. The letter's lying there in the box.

MRS. LINDE. And your husband has the key?

NORA. Yes, he always keeps it.

MRS. LINDE. Krogstad must ask him to send the letter back unread. He must find some excuse—

NORA. But Torvald always opens the box at just about this time—

MRS. LINDE. You must stop him. Go in and keep him talking. I'll be back as quickly as I can.

[*She hurries out through the hall.*]

NORA (*goes over to* HELMER*'s door, opens it and peeps in*). Torvald!

HELMER (*offstage*). Well, may a man enter his own drawing room again? Come on, Rank, now we'll see what—(*in the doorway*) But what's this?

❶ *What does Nora do to keep Torvald from opening the letter box?*

NORA. What, Torvald dear?

HELMER. Rank's been preparing me for some great transformation scene.

RANK (*in the doorway*). So I understood. But I seem to have been mistaken.

NORA. Yes, no one's to be allowed to see me before tomorrow night.

HELMER. But, my dear Nora, you look quite worn out. Have you been practicing too hard?

NORA. No, I haven't practiced at all yet.

HELMER. Well, you must.

NORA. Yes, Torvald, I must, I know. But I can't get anywhere without your help. I've completely forgotten everything.

HELMER. Oh, we'll soon put that to rights.

NORA. Yes, help me, Torvald. Promise me you will? Oh, I'm so nervous. All those people—! You must forget everything except me this evening. You mustn't think of business—I won't even let you touch a pen. Promise me, Torvald?

HELMER. I promise. This evening I shall think of nothing but you—my poor, helpless little darling. Oh, there's just one thing I must see to—(*goes towards the hall door*)

NORA. What do you want out there?

HELMER. I'm only going to see if any letters have come.

NORA. No, Torvald, no!

HELMER. Why what's the matter?

NORA. Torvald, I beg you. There's nothing there.

HELMER. Well, I'll just make sure.

[*He moves towards the door.* NORA *runs to the piano and plays the first bars of the* Tarantella.]

HELMER (*at the door, turns*). Aha!

NORA. I can't dance tomorrow if I don't practice with you now.

HELMER (*goes over to her*). Are you really so frightened, Nora dear?

NORA. Yes, terribly frightened. Let me start practicing now, at once—we've still time before dinner. Oh, do sit down and play for me, Torvald dear. Correct me, lead me, the way you always do.

HELMER. Very well, my dear, if you wish it.

[*He sits down at the piano.* NORA *seizes the tambourine and a long multicolored shawl from the cardboard box, wraps the shawl hastily around her, then takes a quick leap into the center of the room and cries:*]

NORA. Play for me! I want to dance!

HELMER *plays and* NORA *dances.* DR. RANK *stands behind* HELMER *at the piano and watches her.*]

HELMER (*as he plays*). Slower, slower!

NORA. I can't!

HELMER. Not so violently, Nora.

Nora. I must!

Helmer (*stops playing*). No, no, this won't do at all.

Nora (*laughs and swings her tambourine*). Isn't that what I told you?

Rank. Let me play for her.

Helmer (*gets up*). Yes, would you? Then it'll be easier for me to show her.

[Rank *sits down at the piano and plays.* Nora *dances more and more wildly.* Helmer *has stationed himself by the stove and tries repeatedly to correct her, but she seems not to hear him. Her hair works loose and falls over her shoulders; she ignores it and continues to dance.* Mrs. Linde *enters.*]

Mrs. Linde (*stands in the doorway as though tongue-tied*). Ah—!

Nora (*as she dances*). Oh, Christine, we're having such fun!

Helmer. But, Nora darling, you're dancing as if your life depended on it.

Nora. It does.

Helmer. Rank, stop it! This is sheer lunacy. Stop it, I say!

[Rank *ceases playing.* Nora *suddenly stops dancing.*]

Helmer (*goes over to her*). I'd never have believed it. You've forgotten everything I taught you.

Nora (*throws away the tambourine*). You see!

Helmer. I'll have to show you every step.

Nora. You see how much I need you! You must show me every step of the way. Right to the end of the dance. Promise me you will, Torvald?

Helmer. Never fear. I will.

Nora. You mustn't think about anything but me—today or tomorrow. Don't open any letters—don't even open the letter box—

Helmer. Aha, you're still worried about that fellow—

Dance at Bougival. *Pierre Auguste Renoir, 1892*

1 *What does Torvald say about Nora's dancing? In what way is he right?*

Answers to Guided Reading Questions

1 Torvald says that Nora is dancing as if her life depended on it. Nora is dancing to distract Torvald from the letter that will ruin, or possibly end, her life.

Quotables

"Women have served all these centuries as looking glasses possessing the magic and delicious power of reflecting the figure of man at twice its natural size."

—Virginia Woolf
A Room of One's Own

Additional Questions and Activities

Ask students to answer the following questions:

What options do you think Nora has? What do you think Nora should do—continue to hide the money issue from Torvald or tell him the truth? What do you think she will do, and why?

ANSWERS

Responses will vary.

Students might recognize that a good relationship is based on honesty, and therefore Nora should tell Torvald the truth. They will probably understand, however, that Nora and Torvald do not have a very open and honest relationship, so Nora might not be able to tell the truth.

Answers to Guided Reading Questions

❶ Torvald can tell that there is a letter from Krogstad in the letter box. Nora asks Torvald not to let anything "ugly" come between them until after the dance. Dr. Rank senses that something is wrong, so, because of his love for Nora, he tries to convince Torvald to obey her wishes.

❷ She feels she has only a short time to live before she must commit suicide.

Responding to the Selection

You might have students form pairs to brainstorm different solutions to Nora's problem. Ask them to discuss why they do or do not sympathize with her.

Selection Check Test with Answers

EX. Who does Christine Linde think loaned Nora the money?
Christine thinks that Dr. Rank loaned Nora the money.

1. Whom does Nora plan to ask for help and advice?
Nora plans to ask Dr. Rank for help and advice.

2. What relationship used to exist between Torvald and Krogstad?
They used to be friends.

3. What does Torvald do when Nora calls his reasons for firing Krogstad petty?
Torvald sends Krogstad his dismissal.

4. What is about to happen to Dr. Rank?
Dr. Rank is about to die.

5. What does Krogstad want to do with Nora's I.O.U.?
Krogstad wants to keep the I.O.U. to blackmail Torvald into advancing his career.

❶ *What can Torvald tell from Nora's behavior? What does Nora ask of Torvald? Why does Dr. Rank try to convince Torvald?*

❷ *Why do you think Nora is determined to behave wildly and with abandon?*

NORA. Oh, yes, yes, him too.

HELMER. Nora, I can tell from the way you're behaving, there's a letter from him already lying there.

NORA. I don't know. I think so. But you mustn't read it now. I don't want anything ugly to come between us till it's all over.

RANK (*quietly to* HELMER). Better give her her way.

HELMER (*puts his arm round her*). My child shall have her way. But tomorrow night, when your dance is over—

NORA. Then you will be free.

MAID (*appears in the doorway, right*). Dinner is served, madam.

NORA. Put out some champagne, Helen.

MAID. Very good, madam. (*goes*)

HELMER. I say! What's this, a banquet?

NORA. We'll drink champagne until dawn! (*calls*) And, Helen! Put out some macaroons! Lots of macaroons—for once!

HELMER (*takes her hands in his*). Now, now, now. Don't get so excited. Where's my little songbird, the one I know?

NORA. All right. Go and sit down—and you, too, Dr. Rank. I'll be with you in a minute. Christine, you must help me put my hair up.

RANK (*quietly, as they go*). There's nothing wrong, is there? I mean, she isn't—er—expecting—?

HELMER. Good heavens no, my dear chap. She just gets scared like a child sometimes—I told you before—

[*They go out, right.*]

NORA. Well?

MRS. LINDE. He's left town.

NORA. I saw it from your face.

MRS. LINDE. He'll be back tomorrow evening. I left a note for him.

NORA. You needn't have bothered. You can't stop anything now. Anyway, it's wonderful really, in a way—sitting here and waiting for the miracle to happen.

MRS. LINDE. Waiting for what?

NORA. Oh, you wouldn't understand. Go in and join them. I'll be with you in a moment.

[MRS. LINDE *goes into the dining room.*]

NORA (*stands for a moment as though collecting herself. Then she looks at her watch*). Five o'clock. Seven hours till midnight. Then another twenty-four hours till midnight tomorrow. And then the tarantella will be finished. Twenty-four and seven? Thirty-one hours to live.

HELMER (*appears in the doorway, right*). What's happened to my little songbird?

NORA (*runs to him with her arms wide*). Your songbird is here!

Responding to the Selection

Do you sympathize with Nora's situation? Why, or why not? What would you do if you were in her position?

Reviewing the Selection

RECALLING / **INTERPRETING**

1. What does Nora ask Torvald to do? What reasons does Torvald give for not doing this? ▶▶ What do Torvald's reasons for refusing to do what Nora asks reveal about his character?

2. What does Torvald say that he can do "when the real crisis comes"? ▶▶ To what crisis is Torvald referring? In what way does Nora interpret Torvald's statement?

3. From whom does Christine think that Nora borrowed the money? How does Dr. Rank feel about Nora? ▶▶ Why won't Nora accept Dr. Rank's help and advice?

4. What does Krogstad want from Torvald? What does he leave behind at the Helmers' home? What does Christine offer to do to help Nora? ▶▶ What relationship do you think exists between Christine Linde and Krogstad? In what way do Krogstad's threats affect Nora's state of mind? In what way does the letter affect her emotionally?

SYNTHESIZING

5. To Dr. Rank, Nora says, "When I was at home, of course I loved Papa best. . . . I feel the same about Torvald as I did about Papa." In what way is Nora's and Torvald's relationship like that of daughter and father? In what ways is Nora encouraged to behave in a childish and silly manner? How might she behave if people treated her more seriously? In what ways does Nora encourage Torvald's paternal treatment of her? Why might she do so?

Understanding Literature (Questions for Discussion)

1. **Crisis.** In the plot of a story or drama, the **crisis** is that point in the development of the conflict at which a decisive event occurs that causes the main character's situation to become better or worse. What crisis occurs for Nora in act 2? In what way do you think this crisis will affect her?

2. **Symbol.** A **symbol** is a thing that stands for or represents both itself and something else. Of what does the letter in the letter box become a symbol?

3. **Character.** A **character** is a person (or sometimes an animal) who figures in the action of a literary work. Character can also refer to the qualities attributed to a person in life or in a literary work. Nora seems to think that Torvald is strong and loyal enough to take the blame for her crime because of his love for her. Do you agree with Nora's assessment of Torvald's character? Why, or why not?

ANSWERS FOR REVIEWING THE SELECTION

RECALLING AND INTERPRETING

1. **Recalling.** Nora asks Torvald to let Krogstad keep his job at the bank. Torvald says that he cannot do this because he is afraid people will think that his wife influences him and because Krogstad annoys him by talking familiarly to him. **Interpreting.** Torvald reveals himself to be egotistical and petty.

2. **Recalling.** Torvald says that when the real crisis comes, he will have the strength and courage to bear the burden for both Nora and himself. **Interpreting.** Torvald means that he is strong enough to deal with any slander Krogstad writes about him. Nora interprets Torvald's statement to mean that he would be strong enough to take the blame for her crime.

3. **Recalling.** Christine thinks that Nora borrowed the money from Dr. Rank. Dr. Rank loves Nora. **Interpreting.** Once Dr. Rank declares his love for her, Nora feels that it would be improper to ask him for help.

4. **Recalling.** Krogstad wants to blackmail Torvald into creating a higher position for him at the bank. He leaves behind a letter to Torvald. Christine offers to talk to Krogstad. **Interpreting.** Students might say that Krogstad may once have been in love with Christine. Nora is so desperate to escape that she considers drowning herself. After the letter is put in the letter box, Nora becomes almost hysterical.

SYNTHESIZING

Responses will vary. Possible responses are given.

5. Torvald lectures Nora as if she understands little of life and calls her by pet names. Like a child, Nora begs and performs tricks to get what she wants from Torvald. She might be more straightforward if she was rewarded for honesty and strength. Nora manipulates Torvald by acting more frivolous than she is and by indulging his appetite for her tricks. She does this because it is the only way she knows of getting what she wants.

ANSWERS FOR UNDERSTANDING LITERATURE

Responses will vary. Possible responses are given.

1. **Crisis.** The crisis in act 2 occurs when Krogstad tells Nora his plans to blackmail them and then puts his letter to her husband in the letter box. Some students may say that this crisis will affect Nora for the worse because her husband will discover her forgery, while other students may say that her situation may become better because at least everything will be out in the open.

2. **Symbol.** The letter becomes a symbol of Nora's crime and of the lack of honest communication in the Helmer household.

3. **Character.** Students may disagree and point to Torvald's pettiness and egotism as evidence against the likelihood that he would do anything to endanger his reputation.

ADDITIONAL RESOURCES

Reader's Guide

- Selection Worksheet 2.3

Assessment Portfolio

- Selection Check Test 2.2.5
- Selection Test 2.2.6

Essential Skills Practice Books

- Writing 1.8, 1.20
- Language 2.16

READER'S JOURNAL

As an alternative activity, you might ask students to write about the qualities that they most admire and respect in people and the qualities that they least admire and respect in people.

Answers to Guided Reading Questions

1 Christine and Krogstad used to be involved in a romantic relationship. Christine broke off her relationship with Krogstad to marry someone who would be better able to support her family.

SUPPORT FOR LEP STUDENTS

Additional Vocabulary

contemplate—think carefully about something
evasion—an avoiding of questions or responsibilities
exhilarated—feeling thrilled and in high spirits
henceforth—from this point on
hypocrite—person who pretends to be something he or she is not
hysterical—emotionally out of control
initiative—the act of starting something or making the first move
masquerade—a party at which costumes are worn
melodramatic—so overly emotional as to seem put on or insincere
scruples—feelings of uneasiness when something seems wrong, unethical, or immoral

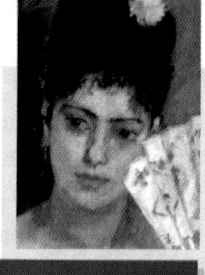

READER'S JOURNAL

In your journal, write about a time when you became disillusioned with someone or something. What happened to make you lose your belief in this person or thing? In what way did this experience change you?

ACT 3

The same room. The table which was formerly by the sofa has been moved into the center of the room; the chairs surround it as before. A lamp is burning on the table. The door to the hall stands open. Dance music can be heard from the floor above. MRS. LINDE *is seated at the table, absentmindedly glancing through a book. She is trying to read, but seems unable to keep her mind on it. More than once she turns and listens anxiously towards the front door.*

MRS. LINDE (*looks at her watch*). Not here yet. There's not much time left. Please God he hasn't—! (*listens again*) Ah, here he is.

1 *What relationship used to exist between Christine and Krogstad? What happened to end this relationship?*

[*Goes out into the hall and cautiously opens the front door. Footsteps can be heard softly ascending the stairs.*]

MRS. LINDE (*whispers*). Come in. There's no one here.

KROGSTAD (*in the doorway*). I found a note from you at my lodgings. What does this mean?

MRS. LINDE. I must speak with you.

KROGSTAD. Oh? And must our conversation take place in this house?

MRS. LINDE. We couldn't meet at my place; my room has no separate entrance. Come in. We're quite alone. The maid's asleep, and the Helmers are at the dance upstairs.

KROGSTAD (*comes into the room*). Well, well! So the Helmers are dancing this evening? Are they indeed?

MRS. LINDE. Yes, why not?

KROGSTAD. True enough. Why not?

MRS. LINDE. Well, Krogstad. You and I must have a talk together.

KROGSTAD. Have we two anything further to discuss?

MRS. LINDE. We have a great deal to discuss.

KROGSTAD. I wasn't aware of it.

MRS. LINDE. That's because you've never really understood me.

KROGSTAD. Was there anything to understand? It's the old story, isn't it—a woman chucking a man because something better turns up?

MRS. LINDE. Do you really think I'm so utterly heartless? You think it was easy for me to give you up?

KROGSTAD. Wasn't it?

MRS. LINDE. Oh, Nils, did you really believe that?

KROGSTAD. Then why did you write to me the way you did?

MRS. LINDE. I had to. Since I had to break with you, I thought it my duty to destroy all the feelings you had for me.

KROGSTAD (*clenches his fists*). So that was it. And you did this for money!

MRS. LINDE. You mustn't forget I had a helpless mother to take care of, and two little brothers. We couldn't wait for you, Nils. It would have been so long before you'd have had enough to support us.

Krogstad. Maybe. But you had no right to cast me off for someone else.

Mrs. Linde. Perhaps not. I've often asked myself that.

Krogstad (*more quietly*). When I lost you, it was just as though all solid ground had been swept from under my feet. Look at me. Now I'm a shipwrecked man, clinging to a spar.[1]

Mrs. Linde. Help may be near at hand.

Krogstad. It was near. But then you came, and stood between it and me.

Mrs. Linde. I didn't know, Nils. No one told me till today that this job I'd found was yours.

Krogstad. I believe you, since you say so. But now you know, won't you give it up?

Mrs. Linde. No—because it wouldn't help you even if I did.

Krogstad. Wouldn't it? I'd do it all the same.

Mrs. Linde. I've learned to look at things practically. Life and poverty have taught me that.

Krogstad. And life has taught me to distrust fine words.

Mrs. Linde. Then it has taught you a useful lesson. But surely you still believe in actions?

Krogstad. What do you mean?

Mrs. Linde. You said you were like a shipwrecked man clinging to a spar.

Krogstad. I have good reason to say it.

Mrs. Linde. I'm in the same position as you. No one to care about, no one to care for.

Krogstad. You made your own choice.

Mrs. Linde. I had no choice—then.

Krogstad. Well?

Mrs. Linde. Nils, suppose we two shipwrecked souls could join hands?

Krogstad. What are you saying?

Mrs. Linde. Castaways have a better chance of survival together than on their own.

Krogstad. Christine!

Mrs. Linde. Why do you suppose I came to this town?

Krogstad. You mean—you came because of me?

Mrs. Linde. I must work if I'm to find life worth living. I've always worked, for as long as I can remember. It's been the greatest joy of my life—my only joy. But now I'm alone in the world, and I feel so dreadfully lost and empty. There's no joy in working just for oneself. Oh, Nils, give me something—someone—to work for.

❶ *Why did Christine come to town? What does she need to make life worth living?*

Krogstad. I don't believe all that. You're just being hysterical and romantic. You want to find an excuse for self-sacrifice.

Mrs. Linde. Have you ever known me to be hysterical?

Krogstad. You mean you really—? Is it possible? Tell me—you know all about my past?

Mrs. Linde. Yes.

Krogstad. And you know what people think of me here?

Mrs. Linde. You said just now that with me you might have become a different person.

Krogstad. I know I could have.

Mrs. Linde. Couldn't it still happen?

Krogstad. Christine—do you really mean this? Yes—you do—I see it in your face. Have you really the courage—?

Mrs. Linde. I need someone to be a mother to; and your children need a mother. And you and I need each other. I believe in you, Nils. I am afraid of nothing—with you.

Krogstad (*clasps her hands*). Thank you, Christine—thank you! Now I shall make

❷ *What is Christine suggesting?*

1. **spar.** Pole or mast that supports or extends the sail of a ship

Answers to Guided Reading Questions

❶ Christine came to town to look for Krogstad. She needs someone and something to work for to make life worth living.

❷ Christine is suggesting that she and Krogstad get back together.

SPELLING AND VOCABULARY WORDS FROM THE SELECTION

aesthetically	clandestine
aloof	dissolution
apparition	infallible
capricious	sordid

Quotables

"There are days when solitude is a heady wine that intoxicates you with freedom, others when it is a bitter tonic, and still others when it is a poison that makes you beat your head against the wall."

—Colette

Answers to Guided Reading Questions

❶ Krogstad is suspicious that Christine is simply trying to win him over to save Nora.

❷ Christine says that Nora's secret must be revealed so that she and Torvald can come to an understanding; therefore, Krogstad should not demand his letter back.

Additional Questions and Activities

Ask students to answer the following questions about Mrs. Linde:

In what way is her life different from Nora's life? In what way is her life similar to Nora's life?

ANSWERS

Responses will vary.

Students are likely to say that Mrs. Linde has been lonely and isolated. She has been forced to be independent and to take care of herself and her family. Nora, on the surface, seems to have everything Mrs. Linde does not. Nora, however, is also lonely in her own way. She, too, had to shoulder the burden of caring for her family when Torvald was ill. She had to take it upon herself to borrow the money to get him to Italy. Both women have sold themselves "for the sake of others," Mrs. Linde by marrying for money and Nora by committing forgery to get it.

the world believe in me as you do! Oh—but I'd forgotten—

Mrs. Linde (*listens*). Ssh! The tarantella! Go quickly, go!

Krogstad. Why? What is it?

Mrs. Linde. You hear that dance? As soon as it's finished, they'll be coming down.

Krogstad. All right, I'll go. It's no good, Christine. I'd forgotten—you don't know what I've just done to the Helmers.

Mrs. Linde. Yes, Nils. I know.

Krogstad. And yet you'd still have the courage to—?

Mrs. Linde. I know what despair can drive a man like you to.

Krogstad. Oh, if only I could undo this!

Mrs. Linde. You can. Your letter is still lying in the box.

Krogstad. Are you sure?

Mrs. Linde. Quite sure. But—

❶ *What is Krogstad suspicious that Christine is doing?*

Krogstad (*looks searchingly at her*). Is that why you're doing this? You want to save your friend at any price? Tell me the truth. Is that the reason?

Mrs. Linde. Nils, a woman who has sold herself once for the sake of others doesn't make the same mistake again.

Krogstad. I shall demand my letter back.

❷ *Why does Christine tell Krogstad that he should not ask for the letter back?*

Mrs. Linde. No, no.

Krogstad. Of course I shall. I shall stay here till Helmer comes down. I'll tell him he must give me back my letter—I'll say it was only to do with my dismissal, and that I don't want him to read it—

Mrs. Linde. No, Nils, you mustn't ask for that letter back.

Krogstad. But—tell me—wasn't that the real reason you asked me to come here?

Mrs. Linde. Yes—at first, when I was frightened. But a day has passed since then, and in that time I've seen incredible things happen in this house. Helmer must know the truth. This unhappy secret of Nora's must be revealed. They must come to a full understanding. There must be an end of all these shiftings and evasions.

Krogstad. Very well. If you're prepared to risk it. But one thing I can do—and at once—

Mrs. Linde (*listens*). Hurry! Go, go! The dance is over. We aren't safe here another moment.

Krogstad. I'll wait for you downstairs.

Mrs. Linde. Yes, do. You can see me home.

Krogstad. I've never been so happy in my life before!

[*He goes out through the front door. The door leading from the room into the hall remains open.*]

Mrs. Linde (*tidies the room a little and gets her hat and coat*). What a change! Oh, what a change! Someone to work for—to live for! A home to bring joy into! I won't let this chance of happiness slip through my fingers. Oh, why don't they come? (*listens*) Ah, here they are. I must get my coat on.

[*She takes her hat and coat.* Helmer*'s and* Nora*'s voices become audible outside. A key is turned in the lock and* Helmer *leads* Nora *almost forcibly into the hall. She is dressed in an Italian costume with a large black shawl. He is in evening dress, with a black coat.*]

Nora (*still in the doorway, resisting him*). No, no, no—not in here! I want to go back upstairs. I don't want to leave so early.

Helmer. But my dearest Nora—

Nora. Oh, please, Torvald, please! Just another hour!

Helmer. Not another minute, Nora, my sweet. You know what we agreed. Come along, now. Into the drawing room. You'll catch cold if you stay out here.

[*He leads her, despite her efforts to resist him, gently into the room.*]

MRS. LINDE. Good evening.

NORA. Christine!

HELMER. Oh, hullo, Mrs. Linde. You still here?

MRS. LINDE. Please forgive me. I did so want to see Nora in her costume.

NORA. Have you been sitting here waiting for me?

MRS. LINDE. Yes. I got here too late, I'm afraid. You'd already gone up. And I felt I really couldn't go home without seeing you.

HELMER (*takes off* NORA'S *shawl*). Well, take a good look at her. She's worth looking at, don't you think? Isn't she beautiful, Mrs. Linde?

MRS. LINDE. Oh, yes, indeed—

HELMER. Isn't she unbelievably beautiful? Everyone at the party said so. But dreadfully stubborn she is, bless her pretty little heart. What's to be done about that? Would you believe it, I practically had to use force to get her away!

NORA. Oh, Torvald, you're going to regret not letting me stay—just half an hour longer.

HELMER. Hear that, Mrs. Linde? She dances her tarantella—makes a roaring success—and very well deserved—though possibly a trifle too realistic—more so than was aesthetically necessary, strictly speaking. But never mind that. Main thing is—she had a success—roaring success. Was I going to let her stay on after that and spoil the impression? No, thank you! I took my beautiful little Capri signorina—my capricious little Capricienne, what?—under my arm—a swift round of the ballroom, a curtsy to the company, and, as they say in novels, the beautiful apparition disappeared! An exit should always be dramatic, Mrs. Linde. But unfortunately that's just what I can't get Nora to realize. I say, it's hot in here. (*throws his cloak on a chair and opens the door to his study*) What's this? It's dark in here. Ah, yes, of course—excuse me. (*goes in and lights a couple of candles*)

At the Ball. *Berthe Morisot, 1875*

NORA (*whispers softly, breathlessly*). Well?

MRS. LINDE (*quietly*). I've spoken to him.

NORA. Yes?

MRS. LINDE. Nora—you must tell your husband everything.

1 *In what way does Christine disappoint Nora's hopes?*

WORDS FOR EVERYDAY USE	
	aes • thet • i • cal • ly (es thet´i kal ē) *adv.,* relating to beauty
	ca • pri • cious (kə prish´ əs) *adj.,* erratic, flighty, tending to change abruptly
	ap • pa • ri • tion (ap´ə rish´ən) *n.,* anything that appears unexpectedly or in an extraordinary way

ANSWERS TO GUIDED READING QUESTIONS

1 Christine tells Nora that she must tell her husband everything.

ART NOTE

Berthe Morisot (1841–1895) was a French impressionist painter and printmaker who was a close friend, sister-in-law, and pupil of Édouard Manet (see page 115). Morisot's paintings, which frequently pictured members of her family, include such titles as *The Artist's Sister, Mme. Pontillon, Seated on the Grass* and *The Artist's Sister Edma and Their Mother.* During her lifetime, Morisot actually outsold such well-known painters as Monet, Renoir, and Sisley.

ADDITIONAL QUESTIONS AND ACTIVITIES

Invite students to discuss why Mrs. Linde urges Nora to tell Torvald everything. Why might it be better for Nora to share her secret?

ANSWERS

Responses will vary.

Students are likely to say that Nora would feel better if everything were out in the open.

VOCABULARY IN CONTEXT

- The design for the new building is not practical, but it is aesthetically pleasing.
- Martin's capricious nature was fun at times but annoying when he ignored his responsibilities.
- Jonah's long-lost friend appeared like an apparition before him.

Answers to Guided Reading Questions

❶ Torvald says that Christine should take up embroidery because it is prettier than knitting. Students may say that Torvald is being intrusive and bossy.

❷ Torvald says that Nora is "talking just like a real big human being." He is implying that she is the opposite—something less than a human being.

❸ Torvald calls Nora his "most treasured possession."

Additional Questions and Activities

Ask students to discuss, aloud or in writing, the fact that Torvald calls Nora his "most treasured possession." Ask them to address the following questions:

What kinds of things do you consider possessions? Is it wrong to view one's spouse, children, or friends as possessions? Why, or why not? How would you feel if someone considered you a possession? If a person feels that he or she owns you, what kind of relationship are you likely to have with this person? Would the person respect you as an equal?

ANSWERS

Responses will vary.

Students might say that their possessions consist of clothing, books, photographs, souvenirs, and other inanimate objects. Many students will agree that it is wrong to think of people as possessions, and that they themselves would not like to be "owned." A relationship in which one person feels he or she owns the other is not likely to be based on respect.

Nora (*dully*). I knew it.

Mrs. Linde. You have nothing to fear from Krogstad. But you must tell him.

Nora. I shan't tell him anything.

Mrs. Linde. Then the letter will.

Nora. Thank you, Christine. Now I know what I must do. Ssh!

Helmer (*returns*). Well, Mrs. Linde, finished admiring her?

Mrs. Linde. Yes. Now I must say good night.

Helmer. Oh, already? Does this knitting belong to you?

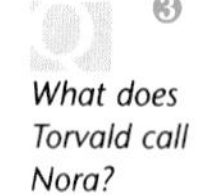

❶ *What advice does Torvald give to Christine? What do you think of his giving this advice?*

❷ *What does Torvald say Nora is doing? What is he implying about her?*

❸ *What does Torvald call Nora?*

Mrs. Linde (*takes it*). Thank you, yes. I nearly forgot it.

Helmer. You knit, then?

Mrs. Linde. Why, yes.

Helmer. Know what? You ought to take up embroidery.

Mrs. Linde. Oh? Why?

Helmer. It's much prettier. Watch me, now. You hold the embroidery in your left hand, like this, and then you take the needle in your right hand and go in and out in a slow, easy movement—like this. I am right, aren't I?

Mrs. Linde. Yes, I'm sure—

Helmer. But knitting, now—that's an ugly business—can't help it. Look—arms all huddled up—great clumsy needles going up and down—I say that really was a magnificent champagne they served us.

Mrs. Linde. Well, good night, Nora. And stop being stubborn! Remember!

Helmer. Quite right, Mrs. Linde!

Mrs. Linde. Good night, Mr. Helmer.

Helmer (*accompanies her to the door*). Good night, good night! I hope you'll manage to get home all right? I'd gladly—but you haven't far to go, have you? Good night, good night.

[*She goes. He closes the door behind her and returns.*]

Helmer. Well, we've got rid of her at last. Dreadful bore that woman is!

Nora. Aren't you very tired, Torvald?

Helmer. No, not in the least.

Nora. Aren't you sleepy?

Helmer. Not a bit. On the contrary, I feel extraordinarily exhilarated. But what about you? Yes, you look very sleepy and tired.

Nora. Yes, I am very tired. Soon I shall sleep.

Helmer. You see, you see! How right I was not to let you stay longer!

Nora. Oh, you're always right, whatever you do.

Helmer (*kisses her on the forehead*). Now my little songbird's talking just like a real big human being. I say, did you notice how cheerful Rank was this evening?

Nora. Oh? Was he? I didn't have a chance to speak with him.

Helmer. I hardly did. But I haven't seen him in such a jolly mood for ages. (*looks at her for a moment, then comes closer*) I say, it's nice to get back to one's home again, and be all alone with you. Upon my word, you're a distractingly beautiful young woman.

Nora. Don't look at me like that, Torvald!

Helmer. What, not look at my most treasured possession? At all this wonderful beauty that's mine, mine alone, all mine.

Nora (*goes round to the other side of the table*). You mustn't talk to me like that tonight.

Helmer (*follows her*). You've still the tarantella in your blood, I see. And that makes you even more desirable. Listen! Now the other guests are beginning to go. (*more quietly*) Nora—soon the whole house will be absolutely quiet.

NORA. Yes, I hope so.

HELMER. Yes, my beloved Nora, of course you do! You know—when I'm out with you among other people like we were tonight, do you know why I say so little to you, why I keep so aloof from you, and just throw you an occasional glance? Do you know why I do that? It's because I pretend to myself that you're my secret mistress, my clandestine little sweetheart, and that nobody knows there's anything at all between us.

NORA. Oh, yes, yes, yes—I know you never think of anything but me.

HELMER. And then when we're about to go, and I wrap the shawl round your lovely young shoulders, over this wonderful curve of your neck—then I pretend to myself that you are my young bride, that we've just come from the wedding, that I'm taking you to my house for the first time—that, for the first time, I am alone with you—quite alone with you, as you stand there young and trembling and beautiful. All evening I've had no eyes for anyone but you. When I saw you dance the tarantella, like a huntress, a temptress, my blood grew hot, I couldn't stand it any longer! That was why I seized you and dragged you down here with me—

NORA. Leave me, Torvald! Get away from me! I don't want all this.

HELMER. What? Now, Nora, you're joking with me. Don't want, don't want—? Aren't I your husband?

[*There is a knock on the front door.*]

NORA (*starts*). What was that?

HELMER (*goes towards the hall*). Who is it?

DR. RANK (*outside*). It's me. May I come in for a moment?

HELMER (*quietly, annoyed*). Oh, what does he want now? (*calls*) Wait a moment. (*walks over and opens the door*) Well! Nice of you not to go by without looking in.

RANK. I thought I heard your voice, so I felt I had to say good-bye. (*His eyes travel swiftly around the room.*) Ah, yes—these dear rooms, how well I know them. What a happy, peaceful home you two have.

HELMER. You seemed to be having a pretty happy time yourself upstairs.

RANK. Indeed I did. Why not? Why shouldn't one make the most of this world? As much as one can, and for as long as one can. The wine was excellent—

HELMER. Especially the champagne.

RANK. You noticed that, too? It's almost incredible how much I managed to get down.

NORA. Torvald drank a lot of champagne, too, this evening.

RANK. Oh?

NORA. Yes. It always makes him merry afterwards.

RANK. Well, why shouldn't a man have a merry evening after a well-spent day?

HELMER. Well-spent? Oh, I don't know that I can claim that.

RANK (*slaps him across the back*). I can, though, my dear fellow!

NORA. Yes, of course, Dr. Rank—you've been carrying out a scientific experiment today, haven't you?

RANK. Exactly.

HELMER. Scientific experiment! Those are big words for my little Nora to use!

NORA. And may I congratulate you on the finding?

❶ *Is Torvald happy to see his "dearest friend"? How do you know?*

❷ *What experiment does Nora know Dr. Rank has been carrying out?*

WORDS FOR EVERYDAY USE

a • loof (ə lo͞of´) *adv.,* at a distance, removed

clan • des • tine (klan des´tin) *adj.,* kept secret or hidden; furtive

ANSWERS TO GUIDED READING QUESTIONS

❶ Torvald is not happy to see Dr. Rank. His asides, sarcastic speech, and the stage directions show this.

❷ Nora knows that Dr. Rank has been testing to determine when he will begin to die.

ADDITIONAL QUESTIONS AND ACTIVITIES

How does Nora feel about Torvald's affectionate overtures on this evening? Why does she feel this way?

ANSWERS

Responses will vary.

Nora's guilt over the secret is making her irritable and unable to relax.

VOCABULARY IN CONTEXT

- Tinker, my dog, is friendly but Cleopatra, my cat, keeps herself aloof.
- My cat slinks about in a clandestine manner, trying to steal food.

Answers to Guided Reading Questions

❶ Nora tells Dr. Rank to sleep well as a way of wishing him the best as she knows he will soon die. She asks him to wish her the same because her life as she knows it is also coming to an end.

❷ Dr. Rank means that he will be invisible at the next masquerade because he will be dead by then.

Historical Note

Below is a list of some notable people who worked for or who wrote about women's rights and woman's place in different societies:

Susan B. Anthony (1820–1906). Leader of women's suffrage movement in U.S.

Simone de Beauvoir (1908–1986). French philosopher and writer

Clementina Black (1855?–1923). American social reformer and writer

Catherine Booth (1829–1890). Evangelist and writer; born in Ashbourne, England; joint founder of the Salvation Army with her husband

Judy Chicago (1939–). American artist

Kate Chopin (1851–1904). American writer

Marcia Freedman (1938–). Politician born in Newark, N.J; founder of the modern Israeli women's movement in 1972

Betty Friedan (1921–). American feminist

Margaret Fuller (1810–1850). American writer and lecturer

Germaine Greer (1939–). Australian feminist and writer

Charlotte Perkins Gilman (1860–1935). American feminist and writer

Ho Hsiang-ning (1879–1972). Revolutionary Chinese feminist

(cont.)

Rank. You may indeed.

Nora. It was good then?

Rank. The best possible finding—both for the doctor and the patient. Certainty.

Nora (*quickly*). Certainty?

Rank. Absolute certainty. So aren't I entitled to have a merry evening after that?

Nora. Yes, Dr. Rank. You were quite right to.

Helmer. I agree. Provided you don't have to regret it tomorrow.

Rank. Well, you never get anything in this life without paying for it.

Nora. Dr. Rank—you like masquerades, don't you?

❶ *Why does Nora tell Dr. Rank to sleep well? Why does she ask him to wish her the same?*

Rank. Yes, if the disguises are sufficiently amusing.

Nora. Tell me. What shall we two wear at the next masquerade?

Helmer. You little gadabout![2] Are you thinking about the next one already?

Rank. We two? Yes, I'll tell you. You must go as the Spirit of Happiness—

Helmer. You try to think of a costume that'll convey that.

Rank. Your wife need only appear as her normal, everyday self—

Helmer. Quite right! Well said! But what are you going to be? Have you decided that?

Rank. Yes, my dear friend. I have decided that.

Helmer. Well?

❷ *What does Dr. Rank mean by this statement?*

Rank. At the next masquerade, I shall be invisible.

Helmer. Well, that's a funny idea.

Rank. There's a big, black hat—haven't you heard of the invisible hat? Once it's over your head, no one can see you any more.

Helmer (*represses a smile*). Ah yes, of course.

Rank. But I'm forgetting what I came for. Helmer, give me a cigar. One of your black Havanas.

Helmer. With the greatest pleasure. (*offers him the box*)

Rank (*takes one and cuts off the tip*). Thank you.

Nora (*strikes a match*). Let me give you a light.

Rank. Thank you. (*She holds out the match for him. He lights his cigar.*) And now—goodbye.

Helmer. Goodbye, my dear chap, goodbye.

Nora. Sleep well, Dr. Rank.

Rank. Thank you for that kind wish.

Nora. Wish me the same.

Rank. You? Very well—since you ask. Sleep well. And thank you for the light. (*He nods to them both and goes.*)

Helmer (*quietly*). He's been drinking too much.

Nora (*abstractedly*). Perhaps.

[Helmer *takes his bunch of keys from his pocket and goes out into the hall.*]

Nora. Torvald, what do you want out there?

Helmer. I must empty the letter box. It's absolutely full. There'll be no room for the newspapers in the morning.

Nora. Are you going to work tonight?

Helmer. You know very well I'm not. Hullo, what's this? Someone's been at the lock.

Nora. At the lock—

Helmer. Yes, I'm sure of it. Who on earth—? Surely not one of the maids? Here's a broken hairpin. Nora, it's yours—

2. **gadabout.** Restless seeker of fun

Additional Questions and Activities

Ask each student to research in the library or on the Internet one of the women listed on pages 156–157. Some students might choose to research another feminist or woman writer of their own choosing. When gathering information, they should keep in mind the following questions:

Who was this person? Where was she born? What was her background? What did she contribute, in a small or large way, to the women's movement or to changes in the role of women in society?

When students have finished their research, you might invite them to share their findings with one another.

NORA (*quickly*). Then it must have been the children.

HELMER. Well, you'll have to break them of that habit. Hm, hm. Ah, that's done it. (*takes out the contents of the box and calls into the kitchen*) Helen! Helen! Put out the light on the staircase. (*comes back into the drawing room and closes the door to the hall*)

HELMER (*with the letters in his hand*). Look at this! You see how they've piled up? (*glances through them*) What on earth's this?

NORA (*at the window*). The letter! Oh no, Torvald, no!

HELMER. Two visiting cards—from Rank.

NORA. From Dr. Rank?

HELMER (*looks at them*). Peter Rank, M.D. They were on top. He must have dropped them in as he left.

NORA. Has he written anything on them?

HELMER. There's a black cross above his name. Rather gruesome, isn't it? It looks just as though he was announcing his death.

NORA. He is.

HELMER. What? Do you know something? Has he told you anything?

NORA. Yes. When these cards come, it means he's said goodbye to us. He wants to shut himself up in his house and die.

HELMER. Ah, poor fellow. I knew I wouldn't be seeing him for much longer. But so soon—! And now he's going to slink away and hide like a wounded beast.

NORA. When the time comes, it's best to go silently. Don't you think so, Torvald?

HELMER (*walks up and down*). He was so much a part of our life. I can't realize that he's gone. His suffering and loneliness seemed to provide a kind of dark background to the happy sunlight of our marriage. Well, perhaps it's best this way. For him, anyway. (*stops walking*) And perhaps for us too, Nora. Now we have only each other. (*embraces her*) Oh, my beloved wife—I feel as though I could never hold you close enough. Do you know, Nora, often I wish some terrible danger might threaten you, so that I could offer my life and my blood, everything, for your sake.

Madeleine Bernard. Paul Gauguin, 1888

❶ *Who do you think feels worse about Dr. Rank's approaching death? Who was the better friend to Dr. Rank?*

❷ *What does Torvald say he wishes for?*

NORA (*tears herself loose and says in a clear, firm voice*). Read your letters now, Torvald.

HELMER. No, no. Not tonight. Tonight I want to be with you, my darling wife—

NORA. When your friend is about to die—?

HELMER. You're right. This news has upset us both. An ugliness has come between us; thoughts of death and dissolution. We must try to forget them. Until

WORDS FOR EVERYDAY USE

dis • so • lu • tion (dis´ə lo͞o´ shən) *n.,* dissolving or being dissolved; death

ANSWERS TO GUIDED READING QUESTIONS

❶ Nora seems to feel worse about Dr. Rank's approaching death, while Torvald says, "perhaps it's best this way." Nora was a better, more sympathetic and caring friend to Dr. Rank.

❷ Torvald says that he wishes some terrible danger would threaten Nora so he could sacrifice everything for her sake.

HISTORICAL NOTE (CONT.)

Emily Murphy (1886–1933). Lawyer and writer. Campaigned against rural poverty and for women's suffrage

Emmeline Pankhurst (1858–1928). Suffragist; formed the Women's Social and Political Union

Josephine Ruffin (1842–1924). Society leader; born in Boston; active worker for African-American rights

George Sand (1804–1876). French novelist. Her unconventional life was symbolized by the male attire she adopted to protest the unequal treatment accorded to women.

Elizabeth Cady Stanton (1815–1902). American reformer and feminist

Gloria Steinem (1934–). American writer and editor

Mary Wollstonecraft (1759–1797). British radical thinker and writer

Virginia Woolf (1882–1941). British writer and speaker

VOCABULARY IN CONTEXT

• The dissolution of a close relationship is always sad.

Answers to Guided Reading Questions

❶ Nora is beginning to understand that Torvald is not the person she thought he was—that he is unable to understand why she committed the forgery and is too weak to support and protect her.

❷ Nora is contemplating killing herself. She would be deserting her children and Helmer.

❸ Torvald is most concerned for himself. Torvald asks Nora what good it would do him is she were "gone from this world."

❹ He tells her not to make silly excuses and to stop being theatrical.

Historical Note

Suffrage is a term meaning "the right to vote." In the United States, a suffragist was a person who participated in the movement to win voting rights for women. This fight for women's suffrage was organized in the nineteenth century. Arguments against women's suffrage included the notion that women were incapable of rational decisions and that women would vote as their husbands or fathers told them to, giving some men more votes than others. Wyoming, which was not yet a state, was the first place to grant woman's suffrage in 1869. It was not until 1920 that the Nineteenth Amendment to the Constitution was ratified and guaranteed a woman's right to vote.

---

then—you go to your room; I shall go to mine.

NORA (*throws her arms round his neck*). Good night, Torvald! Good night!

HELMER (*kisses her on the forehead*). Good night, my darling little songbird. Sleep well, Nora. I'll go and read my letters.

> ❶ *What is Nora beginning to understand?*

[*He goes into the study with the letters in his hand, and closes the door.*]

> ❷ *What is Nora contemplating? Why would this be a terrible thing to do to the others around her?*

NORA (*wild-eyed, fumbles around, seizes* HELMER*'s cloak, throws it round herself and whispers quickly, hoarsely*). Never see him again. Never. Never. Never. (*throws the shawl over her head*) Never see the children again. Them, too. Never. Never. Oh—the icy black water! Oh—that bottomless—that—! Oh, if only it were all over! Now he's got it—he's reading it. Oh no, no! Not yet! Goodbye, Torvald! Goodbye, my darlings!

[*She turns to run into the hall. As she does so,* HELMER *throws open his door and stands there with an open letter in his hand.*]

HELMER. Nora!

NORA (*shrieks*). Ah—!

HELMER. What is this? Do you know what is in this letter?

NORA. Yes, I know. Let me go! Let me go!

> ❸ *For whom is Torvald most concerned? What does Torvald say when Nora promises that he will be free when she is "gone from this world"?*

HELMER (*holding her back*). Go? Where?

NORA (*tries to tear herself loose*). You mustn't try to save me, Torvald!

HELMER (*staggers back*). Is it true? Is it true, what he writes? Oh, my God! No, no—it's impossible, it can't be true!

NORA. It *is* true. I've loved you more than anything else in the world.

> ❹ *In what way does Torvald respond when Nora tells him how much she loved him and how she does not want him to suffer for her sake?*

HELMER. Oh, don't try to make silly excuses.

NORA (*takes a step towards him*). Torvald—

HELMER. Wretched woman! What have you done?

NORA. Let me go! You're not going to suffer for my sake. I won't let you!

HELMER. Stop being theatrical. (*locks the front door*) You're going to stay here and explain yourself. Do you understand what you've done? Answer me! Do you understand?

NORA (*looks unflinchingly at him and, her expression growing colder, says*). Yes. Now I am beginning to understand.

HELMER (*walking round the room*). Oh, what a dreadful awakening! For eight whole years—she who was my joy and pride—a hypocrite, a liar—worse, worse—a criminal! Oh, the hideousness of it! Shame on you, shame!

[NORA *is silent and stares unblinkingly at him.*]

HELMER (*stops in front of her*). I ought to have guessed that something of this sort would happen. I should have foreseen it. All your father's recklessness and instability—be quiet!—I repeat, all your father's recklessness and instability he has handed on to you! No religion, no morals, no sense of duty! Oh, how I have been punished for closing my eyes to his faults! I did it for your sake. And now you reward me like this.

NORA. Yes. Like this.

HELMER. Now you have destroyed all my happiness. You have ruined my whole future. Oh, it's too dreadful to contemplate! I am in the power of a man who is completely without scruples. He can do what he likes with me, demand what he pleases, order me to do anything—I dare not disobey him. I am condemned to humiliation and ruin simply for the weakness of a woman.

NORA. When I am gone from this world, you will be free.

HELMER. Oh, don't be melodramatic. Your father was always ready with that kind of remark. How would it help me if you were "gone from this world," as you put it? It wouldn't assist me in the slightest. He can still make all the facts public; and if he does,

Additional Questions and Activities

Ask students to critique the way in which Torvald is handling the situation with Nora presented on pages 158–159. Are they surprised by his actions? Why, or why not? If students were in his place, what would they do?

ANSWERS

Responses will vary.

Students will probably be critical of Torvald's selfishness, rigidity, and quick rejection of Nora. Many will likely say they expected him to react poorly. Students may say they would respect Nora's reasons for doing as she did or that they would stand by a loved one no matter what.

I may quite easily be suspected of having been an accomplice in your crime. People may think that I was behind it—that it was I who encouraged you! And for all this I have to thank you, you whom I have carried on my hands through all the years of our marriage! Now do you realize what you've done to me?

NORA (*coldly calm*). Yes.

HELMER. It's so unbelievable I can hardly credit it. But we must try to find some way out. Take off that shawl. Take it off, I say! I must try to buy him off somehow. This thing must be hushed up at any price. As regards our relationship—we must appear to be living together just as before. Only *appear*, of course. You will therefore continue to reside here. That is understood. But the children shall be taken out of your hands. I dare no longer entrust them to you. Oh, to have to say this to the woman I once loved so dearly—and whom I still—! Well, all that must be finished. Henceforth there can be no question of happiness, we must merely strive to save what shreds and tatters—

[*The front door bell rings.* HELMER *starts.*]

HELMER. What can that be? At this hour? Surely not—? He wouldn't—? Hide yourself, Nora. Say you're ill.

[NORA *does not move.* HELMER *goes to the door of the room and opens it. The* MAID *is standing half-dressed in the hall.*]

MAID. A letter for madam.

HELMER. Give it me. (*seizes the letter and shuts the door*) Yes, it's from him. You're not having it. I'll read this myself.

NORA. Read it.

HELMER (*by the lamp*). I hardly dare to. This may mean the end for us both. No. I must know. (*tears open the letter hastily; reads a few lines; looks at a piece of paper which is enclosed with it; utters a cry of joy*) Nora! (*She looks at him questioningly*) Nora! No—I must read it once more. Yes, yes, it's true! I am saved! Nora, I am saved!

NORA. What about me?

HELMER. You too, of course. We're both saved, you and I. Look! He's returning your I.O.U. He writes that he is sorry for what has happened—a happy accident has changed his life—oh, what does it matter what he writes? We are saved, Nora! No one can harm you now. Oh, Nora, Nora—no, first let me destroy this filthy thing. Let me see—! (*glances at the I.O.U.*) No, I don't want to look at it. I shall merely regard the whole business as a dream. (*He tears the I.O.U. and both letters into pieces, throws them into the stove and watches them burn.*) There. Now they're destroyed. He wrote that ever since Christmas Eve you've been—oh, these must have been three dreadful days for you, Nora.

NORA. Yes. It's been a hard fight.

HELMER. It must have been terrible—seeing no way out except—no, we'll forget the whole <u>sordid</u> business. We'll just be happy and go on telling ourselves over and over again: "It's over! It's over!" Listen to me, Nora. You don't seem to realize. It's over! Why are you looking so pale? Ah, my poor little Nora, I understand. You can't believe that I have forgiven you. But I have, Nora. I swear it to you. I have forgiven you everything. I know that what you did you did for your love of me.

NORA. That is true.

❶ *What does Torvald think of what Nora has been through?*

❷ *What plans does Torvald make for the future?*

❸ *In what way does Torvald change his plans after reading the second letter?*

WORDS FOR EVERYDAY USE

sor • did (sôr´did) *adj.*, dirty; ignoble

ANSWERS TO GUIDED READING QUESTIONS

❶ Torvald only thinks of what Nora has been through once he realizes that his reputation has been saved.

❷ Torvald says that they must keep up the appearance of living together but that the children will be taken away from Nora, that he will not love Nora anymore, and that they will never be happy together again.

❸ Torvald forgives Nora and seems to think that their life together will go on exactly the way it did before this incident.

ADDITIONAL QUESTIONS AND ACTIVITIES

Ask students if they believe that Nora should forgive Torvald and continue with him as if nothing has happened. Ask them to explain their responses. In their opinion, what kind of person is Torvald?

ANSWERS

Responses will vary.

Students are likely to notice that Torvald's love for Nora does not run deep; he is more concerned with keeping up appearances. For this reason, they might feel that Nora should not go back to living as she did before. Some students might feel more sympathy for Torvald than others.

VOCABULARY IN CONTEXT

• The movie star's life was not as <u>sordid</u> as the media made it out to be.

Answers to Guided Reading Questions

❶ Torvald says that he will shield and protect Nora. Most students will say that Nora probably doesn't believe this anymore.

❷ Nora finds it unusual that she and Torvald have never talked seriously together.

❸ Torvald says that forgiveness makes a wife her husband's property in a double sense, as a wife and as a child.

Literary Note

Kate Chopin (1851–1904) is an American writer whose works have a strong feminist message. Like *A Doll's House,* Chopin's novel *The Awakening* scandalized her contemporaries because it challenges the traditional woman's role by showing the intellectual and emotional development of a young woman and her rebellion against her husband's authority.

Additional Questions and Activities

Ask students to read *The Awakening* and compare the novel's main character to Nora and her character's relationship with her husband to Nora's with Torvald.

Helmer. You have loved me as a wife should love her husband. It was simply that in your inexperience you chose the wrong means. But do you think I love you any the less because you don't know how to act on your own initiative? No, no. Just lean on me. I shall counsel you. I shall guide you. I would not be a true man if your feminine helplessness did not make you doubly attractive in my eyes. You mustn't mind the hard words I said to you in those first dreadful moments when my whole world seemed to be tumbling about my ears. I have forgiven you, Nora. I swear it to you; I have forgiven you.

Nora. Thank you for your forgiveness. (*She goes out through the door, right.*)

Helmer. No, don't go—(*looks in*) What are you doing there?

Nora (*offstage*). Taking off my fancy dress.

❶ *What does Torvald say he will do? Do you think Nora believes him?*

Helmer (*by the open door*). Yes, do that. Try to calm yourself and get your balance again, my frightened little songbird. Don't be afraid. I have broad wings to shield you. (*begins to walk around near the door*) How lovely and peaceful this little home of ours is, Nora. You are safe here; I shall watch over you like a hunted dove which I have snatched unharmed from the claws of the falcon. Your wildly beating little heart shall find peace with me. It will happen, Nora; it will take time; but it will happen, believe me. Tomorrow all this will seem quite different. Soon everything will be as it was before. I shall no longer need to remind you that I have forgiven you; your own heart will tell you that it is true. Do you really think I could ever bring myself to disown you, or even to reproach you? Ah, Nora, you don't understand what goes on in a husband's heart. There is something indescribably wonderful and satisfying for a husband in knowing that he has forgiven his wife—forgiven her unreservedly, from the bottom of his heart. It means that she has become his property in a double sense; he has, as it were, brought her into the world anew; she is now not only his wife but also his child. From now on that is what you shall be to me, my poor, helpless, bewildered little creature. Never be frightened of anything again, Nora. Just open your heart to me. I shall be both your will and your conscience. What's this? Not in bed? Have you changed?

❷ *What does Nora find unusual?*

❸ *What does Torvald say about forgiveness?*

Nora (*in her everyday dress*). Yes, Torvald. I've changed.

Helmer. But why now—so late—?

Nora. I shall not sleep tonight.

Helmer. But, my dear Nora—

Nora (*looks at her watch*). It isn't that late. Sit down there, Torvald. You and I have a lot to talk about.

[*She sits down on one side of the table.*]

Helmer. Nora, what does this mean? You look quite drawn—

Nora. Sit down. It's going to take a long time. I've a lot to say to you.

Helmer (*sits down on the other side of the table*). You alarm me, Nora. I don't understand you.

Nora. No, that's just it. You don't understand me. And I've never understood you—until this evening. No, don't interrupt me. Just listen to what I have to say. You and I have got to face facts, Torvald.

Helmer. What do you mean by that?

Nora (*after a short silence*). Doesn't anything strike you about the way we're sitting here?

Helmer. What?

Nora. We've been married for eight years. Does it occur to you that this is the first time we two, you and I, man and wife, have ever had a serious talk together?

Helmer. Serious? What do you mean, serious?

Nora. In eight whole years—no, longer—ever since we first met—we have never exchanged a serious word on a serious subject.

HELMER. Did you expect me to drag you into all my worries—worries you couldn't possibly have helped me with?

NORA. I'm not talking about worries. I'm simply saying that we have never sat down seriously to try to get to the bottom of anything.

HELMER. But, my dear Nora, what on earth has that got to do with you?

NORA. That's just the point. You have never understood me. A great wrong has been done to me, Torvald. First by Papa, and then by you.

HELMER. What? But we two have loved you more than anyone in the world!

NORA (*shakes her head*). You have never loved me. You just thought it was fun to be in love with me.

HELMER. Nora, what kind of a way is this to talk?

NORA. It's the truth, Torvald. When I lived with Papa, he used to tell me what he thought about everything, so that I never had any opinions but his. And if I did have any of my own, I kept them quiet, because he wouldn't have liked them. He called me his little doll, and he played with me just the way I played with my dolls. Then I came here to live in your house—

HELMER. What kind of a way is that to describe our marriage?

NORA (*undisturbed*). I mean, then I passed from Papa's hands into yours. You arranged everything the way you wanted it, so that I simply took over your taste in everything—or pretended I did—I don't really know—I think it was a little of both—first one and then the other. Now I look back on it, it's as if I've been living here like a pauper, from hand to mouth. I performed tricks for you, and you gave me food and drink. But that was how you wanted it. You and Papa have done me a great wrong. It's your fault that I have done nothing with my life.

HELMER. Nora, how can you be so unreasonable and ungrateful? Haven't you been happy here?

NORA. No; never. I used to think I was. But I haven't ever been happy.

HELMER. Not—not happy?

NORA. No. I've just had fun. You've always been very kind to me. But our home has never been anything but a playroom. I've been your doll-wife, just as I used to be Papa's doll-child. And the children have been my dolls. I used to think it was fun when you came in and played with me, just as they think it's fun when I go in and play games with them. That's all our marriage has been, Torvald.

HELMER. There may be a little truth in what you say, though you exaggerate and romanticize. But from now on it'll be different. Playtime is over. Now the time has come for education.

NORA. Whose education? Mine or the children's?

HELMER. Both yours and the children's, my dearest Nora.

NORA. Oh Torvald, you're not the man to educate me into being the right wife for you.

HELMER. How can you say that?

NORA. And what about me? Am I fit to educate the children?

HELMER. Nora!

NORA. Didn't you say yourself a few minutes ago that you dare not leave them in my charge?

HELMER. In a moment of excitement. Surely you don't think I meant it seriously?

NORA. Yes. You were perfectly right. I'm not fitted to educate them. There's something else I must do first. I must educate myself. And you can't help me with that. It's something I must do by myself. That's why I'm leaving you.

HELMER (*jumps up*). What did you say?

❶ *What does Nora say about their house?*

❷ *What does Nora say has been done to her? According to Nora, how did her father and her husband feel about her?*

❸ *What does Nora say about Torvald?*

❹ *Why didn't Nora ever show her father that she had opinions? What did Nora's father call her? In what way does she describe her marriage to Torvald?*

❺ *What does Nora say she must do?*

Answers to Guided Reading Questions

❶ Nora says that their house is a playroom where she is the doll-wife just as she used to be the doll-child for her father.

❷ Nora says that a great wrong has been done to her, first by her father and then by Torvald. She says her father and her husband never loved her but just thought it was fun to be in love with her.

❸ Nora says that Torvald is not qualified to educate her.

❹ Nora never showed her opinions to her father because he wouldn't have liked them. Nora's father called her his little doll. She describes her marriage as passing from her father's hands to Torvald's.

❺ Nora says she must educate herself on her own and so must leave Torvald.

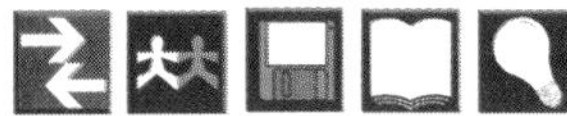

Additional Questions and Activities

Ask students to answer the following questions:

1. In what way do the quotations on this page apply to Nora's situation?
2. What has Nora learned about herself and the people around her?

ANSWERS

Responses will vary.

1. Nora has set herself the goal of learning about herself and discovering her own opinions.
2. Students should realize that Nora has reached a turning point in her life—for the first time she sees herself and others around her clearly. She has to start trusting her own judgments. Nora realizes that she has been used and underappreciated by her father and husband.

Quotables

"Trust thyself: every heart vibrates to that iron string."

—Ralph Waldo Emerson
Essays, "Self-Reliance"

"He who knows others is learned;
He who knows himself is wise."

—Lao-tzu
Tao-te Ching

Answers to Guided Reading Questions

❶ Nora doesn't believe anymore that she is first and foremost a wife and mother. She believes that she is first and foremost a human being.

❷ To Nora, her duty toward herself is as sacred as the duty she owes her husband and to her children.

❸ Torvald is content to live with the rules of society and Nora is not. She is interested in seeking some kind of truth, while Torvald would like to remain in their safe, artificial world.

ANALYTIC SCALES FOR RESPONDING IN WRITING

(SEE PAGE 166.)

Assign a score from 1 to 25 for each grading criterion below. (For more detailed evaluation, see the evaluation forms for writing, revising, and proofreading, Assessment Portfolio 4.1–4.9.)

Dramatic Scene

- **Content/Unity.** The scene features two characters, dialogue, and stage directions.
- **Organization/Coherence.** The personal qualities of characters in the scene are revealed through dialogue and stage directions.
- **Language/Style.** The scene uses dialogue that sounds realistic and vivid stage directions.
- **Conventions.** The scene avoids errors in spelling, grammar, usage, mechanics (excluding errors that are part of a particular character's dialect), and manuscript form.

▶ Additional practice is provided in the Essential Skills Practice Book: Writing 1.8.

❶ *What doesn't Nora believe anymore? What does she believe?*

❷ *What duty is, to Nora, as sacred as the duty she owes to her husband and to her children?*

❸ *In what way do Nora and Torvald differ? Which character do you most respect, and why?*

NORA. I must stand on my own feet if I am to find out the truth about myself and about life. So I can't go on living here with you any longer.

HELMER. Nora, Nora!

NORA. I'm leaving you now, at once. Christine will put me up for tonight—

HELMER. You're out of your mind! You can't do this! I forbid you!

NORA. It's no use your trying to forbid me any more. I shall take with me nothing but what is mine. I don't want anything from you, now or ever.

HELMER. What kind of madness is this?

NORA. Tomorrow I shall go home—I mean, to where I was born. It'll be easiest for me to find some kind of a job there.

HELMER. But you're blind! You've no experience of the world—

NORA. I must try to get some, Torvald.

HELMER. But to leave your home, your husband, your children! Have you thought what people will say?

NORA. I can't help that. I only know that I must do this.

HELMER. But this is monstrous! Can you neglect your most sacred duties?

NORA. What do you call my most sacred duties?

HELMER. Do I have to tell you? Your duties towards your husband, and your children.

NORA. I have another duty which is equally sacred.

HELMER. You have not. What on earth could that be?

NORA. My duty towards myself.

HELMER. First and foremost you are a wife and mother.

NORA. I don't believe that any longer. I believe that I am first and foremost a human being, like you—or anyway, that I must try to become one. I know most people think as you do, Torvald, and I know there's something of the sort to be found in books. But I'm no longer prepared to accept what people say and what's written in books. I must think things out for myself, and try to find my own answer.

HELMER. Do you need to ask where your duty lies in your own home? Haven't you an <u>infallible</u> guide in such matters—your religion?

NORA. Oh, Torvald, I don't really know what religion means.

HELMER. What are you saying?

NORA. I only know what Pastor Hansen told me when I went to confirmation. He explained that religion meant this and that. When I get away from all this and can think things out on my own, that's one of the questions I want to look into. I want to find out whether what Pastor Hansen said was right—or anyway, whether it is right for me.

HELMER. But it's unheard of for so young a woman to behave like this! If religion cannot guide you, let me at least appeal to your conscience. I presume you have some moral feelings left? Or—perhaps you haven't? Well, answer me.

NORA. Oh, Torvald, that isn't an easy question to answer. I simply don't know. I don't know where I am in these matters. I only know that these things mean something quite different to me from what they do to you. I've learned now that certain laws are different from what I'd imagined them

Words for Everyday Use

in • fal • li • ble (in fal′ə bəl) *adj.,* reliable, not likely to fail, sure

Vocabulary in Context

- The Olympic swimmer was <u>infallible</u>—she never lost a race.

to be; but I can't accept that such laws can be right. Has a woman really not the right to spare her dying father pain, or save her husband's life? I can't believe that.

HELMER. You're talking like a child. You don't understand how society works.

NORA. No, I don't. But now I intend to learn. I must try to satisfy myself which is right, society or I.

HELMER. Nora, you're ill. You're feverish. I almost believe you're out of your mind.

NORA. I've never felt so sane and sure in my life.

HELMER. You feel sure that it is right to leave your husband and your children?

NORA. Yes. I do.

HELMER. Then there is only one possible explanation.

NORA. What?

HELMER. That you don't love me any longer.

NORA. No, that's exactly it.

HELMER. Nora! How can you say this to me?

NORA. Oh, Torvald, it hurts me terribly to have to say it, because you've always been so kind to me. But I can't help it. I don't love you any longer.

HELMER (*controlling his emotions with difficulty*). And you feel quite sure about this, too?

NORA. Yes, absolutely sure. That's why I can't go on living here any longer.

HELMER. Can you also explain why I have lost your love?

NORA. Yes, I can. It happened this evening, when the miracle failed to happen. It was then that I realized you weren't the man I'd thought you to be.

HELMER. Explain more clearly. I don't understand you.

NORA. I've waited so patiently, for eight whole years—well, good heavens, I'm not such a fool as to suppose that miracles occur every day. Then this dreadful thing happened to me, and then I *knew*: "Now the miracle will take place!" When Krogstad's letter was lying out there, it never occurred to me for a moment that you would let that man trample over you. I *knew* that you would say to him: "Publish the facts to the world!" And when he had done this—

HELMER. Yes, what then? When I'd exposed my wife's name to shame and scandal—

NORA. Then I was certain that you would step forward and take all the blame on yourself, and say: "I am the one who is guilty!"

HELMER. Nora!

NORA. You're thinking I wouldn't have accepted such a sacrifice from you? No, of course I wouldn't! But what would my word have counted for against yours? That was the miracle I was hoping for, and dreading. And it was to prevent it happening that I wanted to end my life.

HELMER. Nora, I would gladly work for you night and day, and endure sorrow and hardship for your sake. But no man can be expected to sacrifice his honor, even for the person he loves.

NORA. Millions of women have done it.

HELMER. Oh, you think and talk like a stupid child.

NORA. That may be. But you neither think nor talk like the man I could share my life with. Once you'd got over your fright—and you weren't frightened of what might threaten me, but only of what threatened you—once the danger was past, then as far as you were concerned it was exactly as though nothing had happened. I was your little songbird just as before—your doll whom henceforth you would take particular care to protect from the world because she was so weak and fragile. (*gets up*) Torvald, in that moment I realized that for eight years I had been living here with a complete stranger, and had borne him three children—!

❶ *What was the "miracle" Nora had hoped for?*

❷ *What makes Nora so certain of her position at this point in the play? What has she learned about the beliefs of her husband and of the society around her?*

❸ *What does Torvald say about this "miracle"? What does Nora point out?*

❹ *Why has Torvald lost Nora's love?*

ANSWERS TO GUIDED READING QUESTIONS

❶ Nora hoped that Torvald would stand up to Krogstad, telling him to publish the facts to the world and that he would then take the blame for the crime to protect Nora.

❷ She finally realizes that she is her own person and can question the rules of society. She realizes that she does not respect her husband or some of society's rules. She trusts her own judgments.

❸ Torvald says that he could never sacrifice his honor, even for the person he loves. Nora points out that millions of women sacrifice themselves for the people they love.

❹ When Torvald chose respectability over Nora, she realized he was not the man she thought he was and this destroyed her love.

ANALYTIC SCALES FOR RESPONDING IN WRITING

(SEE PAGE 166.)

Assign a score from 1 to 25 for each grading criterion below. (For more detailed evaluation, see the evaluation forms for writing, revising, and proofreading, Assessment Portfolio 4.1–4.9.)

Critical Essay

- **Content/Unity.** The essay analyzes the moral codes of Torvald and Nora.
- **Organization/Coherence.** The essay includes an introduction that states the thesis of the essay, supporting paragraphs, and a conclusion.
- **Language/Style.** The essay uses vivid and precise nouns, verbs, and modifiers.

ADDITIONAL QUESTIONS AND ACTIVITIES

Ask students to answer the following questions in a class discussion:

Do you agree with Nora's decision to leave Torvald? With her ideas about duty? Why does she feel that leaving is the only choice she has? What would you do if you were Nora? Do you sympathize at all with Torvald?

ANSWERS

Responses will vary.

Students might recognize that Nora feels she can never educate herself and find true happiness while she is trapped in her life with Torvald and that she owes it to herself and to her family to be a whole person. Students might also sympathize with Torvald, for whom this is a devastating shock.

ANSWERS TO GUIDED READING QUESTIONS

1 Nora says that she is no longer Torvald's wife. She says that losing her may help Torvald to change for the better. She must leave because he is a stranger to her.

2 Nora doesn't believe in miracles anymore.

3 The "miracle of miracles" would be if both Nora and Torvald change so much that their life together could be called a marriage.

ADDITIONAL QUESTIONS AND ACTIVITIES

Ask students the following questions:

What does Nora mean when she says that "millions of women" have sacrificed their honor? What inequities does she see between her world and her husband's world?

ANSWERS

Responses will vary.

In Nora's experience, women must constantly sacrifice themselves for their families. She sees that her husband can be who he wants to be at any given moment, but that she must fit into a particular mold. If she does not fit into this mold, she is considered selfish or childish.

SELECTION CHECK TEST WITH ANSWERS

EX. Who used to be in love with Christine?
Krogstad used to be in love with Christine.

1. Who persuades Krogstad not to ask for his letter back?
Christine persuades Krogstad not to ask for his letter back.

2. What does Dr. Rank come by to do?
Dr. Rank comes by to say goodbye to Nora and Torvald.

3. After Torvald reads the first letter, what does he say about Nora and the children?

(cont.)

Oh, I can't bear to think of it! I could tear myself to pieces!

HELMER (*sadly*). I see it, I see it. A gulf has indeed opened between us. Oh, but Nora—couldn't it be bridged?

1 *What does Nora say about her relationship to Torvald? Why must she leave?*

NORA. As I am now, I am no wife for you.

HELMER. I have the strength to change.

NORA. Perhaps—if your doll is taken from you.

HELMER. But to be parted—to be parted from you! No, no, Nora. I can't conceive of it happening!

NORA (*goes into the room, right*). All the more necessary that it should happen.

[*She comes back with her outdoor things and a small traveling bag, which she puts down on a chair by the table.*]

HELMER. Nora, Nora, not now! Wait till tomorrow!

NORA (*puts on her coat*). I can't spend the night in a strange man's house.

HELMER. But can't we live here as brother and sister, then—?

NORA (*fastens her hat*). You know quite well it wouldn't last. (*puts on her shawl*) Goodbye, Torvald. I don't want to see the children. I know they're in better hands than mine. As I am now, I can be nothing to them.

2 *What doesn't Nora believe in anymore?*

HELMER. But some time, Nora—some time—?

NORA. How can I tell? I've no idea what will happen to me.

HELMER. But you are my wife, both as you are and as you will be.

3 *What is the "miracle of miracles"?*

NORA. Listen, Torvald. When a wife leaves her husband's house, as I'm doing now, I'm told that according to the law he is freed of any obligations towards her. In any case, I release you from any such obligations. You mustn't feel bound to me in any way however small, just as I shall not feel bound to you. We must both be quite free. Here is your ring back. Give me mine.

HELMER. That too?

NORA. That too.

HELMER. Here it is.

NORA. Good. Well, now it's over. I'll leave the keys here. The servants know about everything to do with the house—much better than I do. Tomorrow, when I have left town, Christine will come to pack the things I brought here from home. I'll have them sent on after me.

HELMER. This is the end, then! Nora, will you never think of me any more?

NORA. Yes, of course. I shall often think of you and the children and this house.

HELMER. May I write to you, Nora?

NORA. No. Never. You mustn't do that.

HELMER. But at least you must let me send you—

NORA. Nothing. Nothing.

HELMER. But if you should need help—?

NORA. I tell you, no. I don't accept things from strangers.

HELMER. Nora—can I never be anything but a stranger to you?

NORA (*picks up her bag*). Oh, Torvald! Then the miracle of miracles would have to happen.

HELMER. The miracle of miracles!

NORA. You and I would both have to change so much that—oh, Torvald, I don't believe in miracles any longer.

HELMER. But I want to believe in them. Tell me. We should have to change so much that—!

NORA. That life together between us two could become a marriage. Goodbye.

[*She goes out through the hall.*]

HELMER (*sinks down on a chair by the door and buries his face in his hands*). Nora! Nora! (*looks round and gets up*) Empty! She's gone! (*a hope strikes him*) The miracle of miracles—?

[*The street door is slammed shut downstairs.*] ■

SELECTION CHECK TEST WITH ANSWERS (CONT.)

Torvald says that the children must be taken out of Nora's care.

4. What does the second letter from Krogstad say?
The letter says that Krogstad is sorry and that he is returning the I.O.U. because a happy accident changed his life.

5. What important decision does Nora make at the end of the play?
She decides to leave Torvald.

Responding to the Selection

What do you think of Nora's decision to leave? Is it the right decision? If you were in her position, would you stay or would you go? Why?

Reviewing the Selection

RECALLING		INTERPRETING
1. What relationship existed in the past between Christine and Krogstad? What does Christine suggest that they do?	▶▶	Why does Christine dissuade Krogstad from demanding his letter back from Torvald? What effect might this decision have on her friendship with Nora?
2. What does Torvald say he wishes would happen to Nora? What is Torvald's reaction when he reads the first letter from Krogstad?	▶▶	In what way is Torvald proved a hypocrite?
3. What is Torvald's reaction when he reads the second letter from Krogstad?	▶▶	Why does Nora's manner toward Torvald change once Torvald condemns her actions? Why does Torvald's attitude toward Nora change after reading the second letter? Why doesn't Nora gratefully accept Torvald's forgiveness?
4. What does Nora say about living in her father's home and in Torvald's home? What does Nora say her most important duty is? What is she "first and foremost"?	▶▶	What is the "great wrong" that has been done to Nora? Why does Nora leave Torvald and her children?

SYNTHESIZING

5. Discuss whether the title *A Doll's House* is appropriate to the play. Consider and discuss both character and plot development in light of the title. Would you suggest another title for the play? If so, what?

Understanding Literature (Questions for Discussion)

1. **Stage Directions. Stage directions** are notes included in a play in addition to the dialogue for the purpose of describing how something should be performed on stage. At the very end of the play, Nora says that she and Torvald must remain apart until the "miracle of miracles" occurs—they both change so much that their life together

ANSWERS FOR REVIEWING THE SELECTION

RECALLING AND INTERPRETING

1. **Recalling.** Christine and Krogstad were once romantically involved. Christine suggests that they start a new life together.
Interpreting. Christine dissuades Krogstad from demanding the letter back because she says that the Helmers can come to an understanding only if the truth comes out. This decision might destroy their friendship.

2. **Recalling.** Torvald says that he wishes a terrible danger would threaten Nora so that he could offer everything for her sake. Torvald rants and raves about his ruined reputation and says that Nora has ruined his life, that he will never love her again, and that the children must be taken from her.
Interpreting. Torvald's imagined rescue of Nora is shown to be hypocritical when an actual danger is revealed; he thinks only of himself and does not try to protect Nora at all.

3. **Recalling.** Torvald is relieved that he is saved and tells Nora that he has forgiven her.
Interpreting. Nora realizes that Torvald is not the person she thought he was and that he cares only for his reputation. Once Torvald realizes that his reputation is protected, he wants to forget the whole scandal and return to his life with Nora. Nora doesn't gratefully accept Torvald's forgiveness because she saw how quick he was to turn against her.

4. **Recalling.** Nora says that in both her father's home and in Torvald's she adopted the men's opinions because she knew they wouldn't like her own; neither man loved her as a person but as a doll. Nora says her most important duty is to herself. She says that "first and foremost" she is a human being. (cont.)

ANSWERS FOR REVIEWING THE SELECTION (CONT.)

Interpreting. Both her father and her husband have encouraged Nora to become silly, opinionless, and dependent. Students may say that Nora leaves Torvald and her children to discover who she is, to grow as a person, and to develop into an independent and self-sufficient human being.

SYNTHESIZING

Responses will vary. Possible responses are given.

5. *A Doll's House* is an appropriate title because it refers to the way Nora has been made into a silly, dependent doll, or plaything, first in her father's home and then in Torvald's. The title indicates that the "happiness" at the play's beginning was not true happiness, just as Torvald's household was not a real household but a doll's house in which they pretended to have a happy marriage.

ANSWERS FOR UNDERSTANDING LITERATURE

Responses will vary. Possible responses are given.

1. Stage Directions. Torvald expresses hope that such a miracle might occur. The mood is one of negation and grim finality. Nora's slamming the door makes Torvald's hopeful mood seem ill-founded and unrealistic.

2. Verbal Irony. Nora seems to be saying that she understands the gravity of her crime. She is really saying that she is beginning to understand that Torvald is not the person she once thought him to be. Nora seems to be agreeing that she has changed into every-day clothes; however, she is really indicating that she herself has changed.

ANALYTIC SCALES FOR RESPONDING IN WRITING

Grading scales for Responding in Writing appear on pages 162, 163.

ANSWERS FOR LANGUAGE LAB

1. declarative
2. imperative
3. interrogative
4. declarative
5. exclamatory

► Additional practice is provided in the Essential Skills Practice Book: Language 2.16.

could become a marriage. What attitude toward this "miracle" does Torvald express in his final line in the drama? What is the mood of the stage direction that follows this line? What impact does this stage direction have on Torvald's words?

2. **Verbal Irony. Verbal irony** is a difference between appearance and reality in which a statement is made that implies its opposite. After Torvald reads the first letter, he demands that Nora explain herself and asks if she understands what she has done. Nora responds coldly, "Yes. Now I am beginning to understand." What does she seem to be saying? What is she really saying? When Torvald notes that Nora has not changed into her nightgown but into everyday clothes, he asks her "Have you changed?" Nora responds, "Yes, Torvald. I've changed." In what way is Nora's response an example of verbal irony? What two levels of meaning are present in her statement?

Responding in Writing

1. **Creative Writing: Dramatic Scene.** Write a two-page scene using dialogue and stage directions in which two characters reveal their personal qualities. Such qualities can be shown by what they say to each other, what they say about others, the words and tones that they use, and how they appear and act.

2. **Critical Essay: Personal Codes of Ethics.** Torvald and Nora have very different codes of ethics. Write an essay in which you analyze which character is the more ethical or moral person. You should first examine what each of these characters considers ethical or morally correct. Then consider the following questions: Which character seems to be more ethical at the beginning of the play? Which characters seems to be more ethical at the play's end? Which character is more concerned with outer respectability? Which character is more concerned with inner respectability? Why does Torvald condemn Nora? Why does Nora become disillusioned with Torvald? After you have thought about all these questions, present your thesis in an introductory paragraph; expand upon and support your thesis with evidence from the text in following paragraphs; and come to a conclusion in a final paragraph.

Language Lab

The Functions of Sentences. Read the Language Arts Survey 2.16, "The Functions of Sentences." Then classify the sentences below as declarative, imperative, interrogative, or exclamatory.

1. Monomoy Theater is presenting my favorite play, *A Doll's House.*
2. Pay attention to the lesson that this play teaches.
3. Has Torvald fallen into a trap?
4. Yes, he sacrifices personal integrity for social responsibility.
5. That Torvald is a fool!

Themes

Women—Rights and Writers

Edna St. Vincent Millay

Women have long faced more difficulties than men in becoming well-known writers. Throughout much of European history, women's educations were inferior to those men received. When a well-educated woman turned to writing, she was often condemned for being "unladylike." Often, early European women writers wrote about the prejudices women faced and the obstacles they encountered. In 1717, Anne Finch wrote:

> Alas! a woman that attempts the pen
> Such an intruder on the rights of men,
> Such a presumptuous creature is esteemed,
> The fault can by no virtue be redeemed.
> They tell us we mistake our sex and way;
> Good breeding, fashion, dancing, dressing, play
> Are the accomplishments we should desire;
> To write, or read, or think, or to enquire
> Would cloud our beauty, and exhaust our time,
> And interrupt the conquests of our prime; . . .

Women, however, were not content to amuse themselves solely with fashion and dancing, and an increasing number of men and women believed that women should receive equal education and encouragement to write. One early supporter of women and their accomplishments, the Renaissance Italian writer Ludovico Ariosto wrote:

> Women in ancient times have wondrous things
> Performed in arms and in the sacred arts.
> Their deeds, their works, their fair imaginings
> Resound in glory in all minds and hearts. . . .
>
> And truly women have excelled indeed
> In every art to which they set their hand,
> And any who to history pay heed
> Their fame will find diffused in every land.
> If in some ages they do not succeed,
> Their renaissance is not for ever banned.
> Envy their merits has perhaps concealed
> Or unawareness left them unrevealed.

From the end of the eighteenth century to the nineteenth century, more and more writers, both men and women, called out for women's rights. Mary Wollstonecraft argued in *A Vindication of the Rights of Woman* that inequalities reduced women to the dependent state of children and kept women from achieving their full potential. John Mill asserted in *The Subjection of Women* that women should be treated as equals under the law, and Henrik Ibsen's *A Doll's House* encouraged women to view their role in society in a new light.

In the twentieth century, women writers have indeed experienced the "renaissance" Ariosto foretold more than four hundred and eighty years ago. Writers such as Virginia Woolf and Edna St. Vincent Millay gained reputations both as brilliant writers and as strong, independent women. In her sonnet "Oh, oh, you will be sorry for that word!" Millay describes a relationship very similar to that which Ibsen portrayed in *A Doll's House*. In Millay's poem a female speaker's intellectual pursuits are belittled by her mate, who expects her to be pretty, well-dressed, and intellectually vacant.

> Oh, oh, you will be sorry for that word!
> Give back my book and take my kiss instead.
> Was it my enemy or my friend I heard,
> "What a big book for such a little head!"
> Come, I will show you my newest hat,
> And you may watch me purse my mouth and prink!
> Oh, I shall love you still, and all of that.
> I never again shall tell you what I think.
> I shall be sweet and crafty, soft and sly;
> You will not catch me reading any more:
> I shall be called a wife to pattern by;
> And some day when you knock and push the door,
> Some sane day, not too bright and not too stormy,
> I shall be gone, and you may whistle for me.

Although they have gained many opportunities in the twentieth century, women writers continue to struggle to be taken seriously and to be viewed as the equals of male writers.

Biographical Note

Anne Finch, Countess of Winchelsea (1661–1720) circulated her poetry in manuscript form before publishing a book in 1713. Her reluctance to display her literary talents was due to the often hostile treatment of women writers in her day. Wealthy and well-educated, Anne served as a member of the royal court of King James and married Heneage Finch, another member of the court. When King James was exiled in the late 1680s, Anne, Heneage, and her family retreated into political exile until Heneage's cousin, the Earl of Winchelsea, died, leaving him an elegant estate. This estate created a retreat from a world that Anne found very limiting. There, she became more open about her poetry and wrote many poems celebrating rural life. Today, her work is difficult to find, but those works that have survived have been admired by such writers and critics as William Wordsworth and Virginia Woolf.

Literary Note

Virginia Woolf's important book *A Room of One's Own* eloquently describes the plight of intelligent and creative women who for centuries were unable to employ their writing talents or enjoy education, influence, fame, or even control over their own lives. Woolf writes about how women were denied a voice in the literary world. Woolf also questions what would have happened if Shakespeare had had a sister—one as talented and imaginative as her brother. In what way would her society have treated her attempts to write plays? Woolf is convinced that there have been many "suppressed poets" and "mute and inglorious Jane Austen(s)" who were too busy cooking, cleaning, and raising families to follow their own ambitions as writers.

Additional Questions and Activities

Ask students to plan a symposium of women writers. Each person from the class should choose one writer from any era and then use the library or the Internet to research this person thoroughly. After each person has completed his or her research, have students organize the symposium. Explain to students that a symposium is a conference, meeting, or social gathering where ideas are exchanged or a particular subject is discussed. Plan with the class a list of topics related to women's writing, to educational and career opportunities for women, and to the ways the world is changing in these areas. Then plan to have each person attend the symposium as the writer he or she has researched. Each "writer" should introduce herself and describe what she has written and why she has decided to attend the symposium.

ADDITIONAL RESOURCES

READER'S GUIDE

- Selection Worksheet 2.2

ASSESSMENT PORTFOLIO

- Selection Check Test 2.2.7
- Selection Test 2.2.8

ESSENTIAL SKILLS PRACTICE BOOKS

- Writing 1.8, 1.20
- Study and Research 4.3

PREREADING EXTENSIONS

As the biography on this page states, Anna Akhmatova and her husband Nikolai Gumilyov were leaders of the Russian Acmeism movement. Osip Mandelstam was another important poet of this movement. Some students might be interested in reading poetry by Gumilyov and Mandelstam and comparing it to the work of Akhmatova.

SUPPORT FOR LEP STUDENTS

PRONUNCIATIONS OF PROPER NOUNS AND ADJECTIVES

Anna Akh • ma • to • va (ä´nə äk mät´ə vä)
Len • in • grad (len´in grad)
Mary Mag • da • lene (mer´ē mag´də lən)
Yez • hov (yezh´əv)

ADDITIONAL VOCABULARY

ardent—enthusiastic
comprehend—understand
consolation—comfort
lofty—noble
meager—not adequate; of small amount or inferior quality
momentous—important
poplar—type of tree
ravine—hollow in the earth's surface, usually caused by running water
regiments—large, rigidly organized groups of people
stupor—a dullness of the senses
submissive—without resistance
woe—sorrow

PREREADING

Requiem
by Anna Akhmatova, translated by Judith Hemschemeyer

RUSSIA

About the Author

ANNA AKHMATOVA
1889–1966

Anna Andreyevna Gorenko was born into an aristocratic family in Bolshoy Fontan and raised mainly in Tsarsko Selo. She took **Anna Akhmatova** as a pseudonym. In 1910, Akhmatova married Nikolai Gumilyov. They traveled to Paris where they met many artists and writers. On their return, they started a Poets' Guild that served as the core of the Acmeism movement, which rejected Russian Symbolism and valued clarity and concreteness. Akhmatova's first collection of poetry, *Evening,* was published in 1912.

The Revolution of 1917 and the ensuing civil war caused many Russians to flee, but Akhmatova refused to leave her homeland. Gumilyov was shot by the Bolsheviks in 1921. During the Stalin regime, Akhmatova was persecuted and kept from publishing her poetry. The authorities arrested her son, Lev, several times, trying to torture Akhmatova through her son's imprisonment. After Stalin's death, she was reinstated to the Writers' Union and began aiding younger writers, including Joseph Brodsky. She was awarded the Taormina Poetry Prize and an honorary degree from Oxford University. Akhmatova died in 1966, having lived to see her son freed from prison.

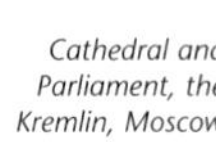
Cathedral and Parliament, the Kremlin, Moscow

About the Selection

A **requiem** is a song or service for the dead. In ***Requiem,*** Akhmatova writes about Stalin's Great Purge (see Connections, below) and its effects on a personal and societal level. The earliest poems in *Requiem* were inspired by the arrest of her son, Lev, in 1935. She explores her own fears and grief, but she also expresses the collective suffering and terror of the Russian people.

In the opening poems of this cycle, Akhmatova sets a scene of collective waiting and agonizing; women wait in line hoping to see loved ones who are imprisoned. In the core poems of *Requiem,* Akhmatova chronicles the emotions of a mother who fears for her son. In the Epilogues, she returns again to the collective loss.

Writing *Requiem* was a dangerous act, so Akhmatova and a friend memorized each part of the poem as it was composed. Akhmatova did not put *Requiem* on paper until after the death of Stalin in 1953. *Requiem* was published in Munich in 1963. It was not published in the Soviet Union until 1987.

CONNECTIONS: Stalin's Great Purge

From 1935 to 1938, Joseph Stalin, dictator of Russia, conducted a number of purges aimed at destroying forces that opposed or criticized his regime. Many of Stalin's foes were tried, convicted, and executed. Millions of other "enemies of the people" were thrown into prison camps. Many people involved in the arts, academia, law, and diplomacy were persecuted and arrested at this time. The Great Purge is the historical backdrop to Akhmatova's *Requiem.*

GOALS/OBJECTIVES

Studying this lesson will enable students to

- empathize with a speaker and a group of people who experience persecution during the era of Stalin's Great Purge
- discuss the political climate of Russia between the years 1935 and 1938
- discuss the life and work of Anna Akhmatova
- define the literary terms *allusion* and *apostrophe*
- write a requiem and an essay that contains biographical criticism
- practice mnemonic techniques

Have you ever been separated from somebody whom you love? Have you ever feared for the safety of a close friend or family member? Think about a time when you experienced one or both of these situations. In your journal, write about the situation and the feelings you had.

READER'S JOURNAL

Requiem

1935–1940

ANNA AKHMATOVA, TRANSLATED BY JUDITH HEMSCHEMEYER

No, not under the vault of alien skies,
And not under the shelter of alien wings—
I was with my people then,
There, where my people, unfortunately, were.

1961

❶ *Where was the speaker during the time to which she refers? How does she feel about this place?*

INSTEAD OF A PREFACE

In the terrible years of the Yezhov terror,[1] I spent seventeen months in the prison lines of Leningrad. Once someone "recognized" me. Then a woman with bluish lips standing behind me, who, of course, had never heard me called by name before, woke up from the stupor to which everyone had succumbed and whispered in my ear (everyone spoke in whispers there):

"Can you describe this?"

And I answered: "Yes, I can."

Then something that looked like a smile passed over what had once been her face.

❷ *What does the woman want the speaker to do?*

April 1, 1957
Leningrad

DEDICATION

Mountains bow down to this grief,
Mighty rivers cease to flow,
But the prison gates hold firm,

1. **Yezhov terror.** Nikolai Yezhov was the head of the secret police. Between 1937 and 1938 he ordered mass arrests.

WORDS FOR EVERYDAY USE

vault (vôlt) *n.,* arched space
al • ien (āl´ yən) *adj.,* foreign, strange
suc • cumb (sə kum´) *vi.,* give way to, yield

READER'S JOURNAL

As an alternative activity, you might ask students to imagine what it would be like to live in a society that tries to silence opinions or beliefs that do not match those of people in power. In what ways would their own society be different if people were not allowed to express and discuss a variety of opinions? Have they ever been in a situation in which they felt their ideas or beliefs were not welcome? How did this feel?

ANSWERS TO GUIDED READING QUESTIONS

❶ The speaker was with her people in her native land. She felt that it was an unfortunate place to be, but that it was necessary for her to be there.

❷ The woman wants the speaker to describe their situation to others.

SPELLING AND VOCABULARY WORDS FROM THE SELECTION

alien	luxuriate
appendage	mantle
askew	minion
censer	succumb
confiscate	supplicate
cuneiform	tempestuous
diabolical	vault
impending	

VOCABULARY IN CONTEXT

- We walked through the vault created by bending tree branches.
- When Jason got off the train, the alien city made him feel lost and unwelcome.
- Gina finished the marathon, refusing to succumb to her feelings of exhaustion.

Answers to Guided Reading Questions

❶ The women do not share the luxury of enjoying things such as sunsets or fresh breezes because they are suffering as they wait outside of a prison.

❷ The dead were happy because they were at rest.

Literary Technique

Preface and Prologue

A **preface** is a statement made at the beginning of a literary work, often by way of introduction. A **prologue** is an introduction to a literary work, often one that sets the scene and introduces the conflict or the main characters.

Ask students to describe the section of the poem called "Instead of a Preface." Why do students think she gives the section this title? Then ask students to describe the section of the poem called the "Prologue." What scene does the author set? What characters are introduced?

Historical Note

Akhmatova lived through the 1917–1918 Russian Revolution, which was prompted by Russian losses and setbacks in World War I. During the revolution, the czar, or emperor, of Russia was overthrown and the Bolsheviks, a Communist party led by revolutionary Vladimir Ilyich Lenin, was brought to power. The Bolsheviks seized the Russian government and merged with Ukrainian, Belorussian, and Transcaucasian republics to form the USSR. Lenin was honored in the Soviet Union as the founder of the modern Soviet state. Joseph Stalin succeeded Lenin. Both leaders believed that the Soviet Union would never be completely secure until the entire world was Communist.

 ❶

What experiences do the women not share with other people? Why are these experiences not part of the lives of the waiting women?

And behind them are the "prisoners' burrows"
And mortal woe.
For someone a fresh breeze blows,
For someone the sunset luxuriates—
We wouldn't know, we are those who everywhere
Hear only the rasp of the hateful key
And the soldiers' heavy tread.
We rose as if for an early service,
Trudged through the savaged capital
And met there, more lifeless than the dead;
The sun is lower and the Neva[2] mistier,
But hope keeps singing from afar.
The verdict . . . And her tears gush forth,
Already she is cut off from the rest,
As if they painfully wrenched life from her heart,
As if they brutally knocked her flat,
But she goes on . . . Staggering . . . Alone . . .
Where now are my chance friends
Of those two diabolical years?
What do they imagine is in Siberia's storms,
What appears to them dimly in the circle of the moon?
I am sending my farewell greeting to them.

March 1940

❷

Who was glad during this time? Why were these people happy?

PROLOGUE

That was when the ones who smiled
Were the dead, glad to be at rest.
And like a useless appendage, Leningrad
Swung from its prisons.
And when, senseless from torment,
Regiments of convicts marched,
And the short songs of farewell
Were sung by locomotive whistles.
The stars of death stood above us
And innocent Russia writhed
Under bloody boots
And under the tires of the Black Marias.[3]

2. **Neva.** Large river that runs through Leningrad
3. **Black Marias.** Police vans used to take prisoners away

Words for Everyday Use

lux • u • ri • ate (lug zhōōr´ē āt´) *vi.*, take great pleasure
di • a • bol • i • cal (dī´ə bäl´i kəl) *adj.*, wicked or cruel
ap • pend • age (ə pen´dij) *n.*, branch or limb of a plant or animal

Vocabulary in Context

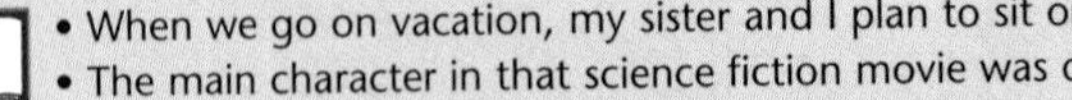

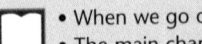

- When we go on vacation, my sister and I plan to sit on the beach and luxuriate in the warm sun.
- The main character in that science fiction movie was destructive and diabolical.
- A tail is a useful appendage; a cat uses it for balance.

Joseph Stalin. Bolshevik poster

I

They led you away at dawn,
I followed you, like a mourner,
In the dark front room the children were crying,
By the icon[4] shelf the candle was dying.
On your lips was the icon's chill.
The deathly sweat on your brow . . . Unforgettable!—
I will be like the wives of the Streltsy,
Howling under the Kremlin[5] towers.

1935

➊ *Whom does the speaker say she will be like? In what way will she be like them?*

II

Quietly flows the quiet Don,[6]
Yellow moon slips into a home.

4. **icon.** Small religious figure or painting
5. **Streltsy . . . Kremlin.** The Streltsy were troops organized by Ivan the Terrible around 1550. They rebelled and were killed by Peter the Great in 1698. The pleas of their wives and mothers went unheeded as the troops were executed by the tower of the Kremlin. The Kremlin is a citadel in Moscow that houses government offices.
6. **Don.** Russian river often referred to in folk songs

Answers to Guided Reading Questions

➊ The speaker says that she will be like the wives of the Streltsy in the way that she mourns and protests the killing of her loved ones.

Historical Note

Stalin, whose name is an alias that comes from the Russian word *stal*, meaning "steel," has gone down in history as one of the most ruthless dictators of modern times. Nearly 500,000 people were executed, imprisoned, or forced into labor camps on his orders. His secret police, organized to root out "political criminals," or those people who did not agree with him, later became known in the Soviet Union as the KGB.

Additional Questions and Activities

You might discuss with students the following questions: Why might some leaders feel a need to silence any opinions or beliefs that are different from their own? What does this need say about the character of such a leader and his or her ability to lead people? Do you respect a leader like this? Why, or why not? Why do you think ruthless or cruel leaders are allowed to gain power in certain societies?

Answers

Responses will vary.

Additional Questions and Activities

You might ask students to work in pairs or small groups to research other oppressive societies in which specific groups of people were denied, or are still being denied, their civil rights. When students have gathered their information, they should prepare presentations to share with the rest of the class. If students are in need of ideas, you might share the following list of research possibilities:

- Nazi Germany
- Serbian forces in Bosnia
- Khmer Rouge in Cambodia
- England, Ireland, and the Potato Famine
- South Africa and Apartheid
- United States during the slave era or during the time of Jim Crow laws

Answers to Guided Reading Questions

❶ The woman's husband has been killed, and her son is in prison.

❷ The speaker does not believe that she can endure the pain and suffering to which she is subjected.

❸ The speaker's childhood was free and easy. It is in sharp contrast with the grim suffering of her adult life as she waits, sorrowfully, outside of prison.

❹ The speaker has cried out and pleaded with the authorities for the release of her son. The speaker fears that her son will be killed.

Literary Technique

APOSTROPHE

An **apostrophe** is a rhetorical technique in which an object or person is directly addressed. Ask students to reread sections IV and V for two different examples of apostrophe. In section IV, the speaker directly addresses herself. In section V, the speaker directly addresses her son.

INTEGRATED SKILLS ACTIVITIES

LANGUAGE LAB

Explain to students that precise and colorful nouns, verbs, and modifiers—adjectives and adverbs—help to make writing come alive for a reader. Ask students to reread sections of *Requiem*, writing down the best examples of vivid nouns, verbs, adjectives, and adverbs they can find. Ask them how these specific words add to the overall effect of the poem. Then ask students to rewrite some of the lines, leaving out vivid adjectives and adverbs. How does the absence of a particular modifier change the meaning of a sentence?

He slips in with cap askew,
He sees a shadow, yellow moon.

❶ *Why is the woman alone?*

This woman is ill,
This woman is alone,

Husband in the grave, son in prison,
Say a prayer for me.

III

❷ *What is the speaker's reaction in this stanza?*

No, it is not I, it is somebody else who is suffering.
I would not have been able to bear what happened,
Let them shroud it in black,
And let them carry off the lanterns . . .
Night.

1940

IV

❸ *What was the speaker's childhood like? In what way do the events of her adult life contrast with her childhood?*

You should have been shown, you mocker,
Minion of all your friends,
Gay little sinner of Tsarskoye Selo,[7]
What would happen in your life—
How three-hundredth in line, with a parcel,
You would stand by the Kresty[8] prison,

Your tempestuous tears
Burning through the New Year's ice.
Over there the prison poplar bends,
And there's no sound—and over there how many
Innocent lives are ending now . . .

V

❹ *What has the speaker done since her son was arrested? What does the speaker fear will happen?*

For seventeen months I've been crying out,
Calling you home.
I flung myself at the hangman's feet,[9]
You are my son and my horror.
Everything is confused forever,
And it's not clear to me
Who is a beast now, who is a man,
And how long before the execution.

7. **Tsarskoye Selo.** Village near St. Petersburg where Akhmatova spent her childhood
8. **Kresty.** Meaning "cross," because of its shape
9. **I flung . . . feet.** Akhmatova wrote to Stalin to beg for her son's release.

Words for Everyday Use

a • skew (ə skyo͞o) *adv.,* to one side, crooked
min • ion (min´yən) *n.,* favorite; servile follower
tem • pes • tu • ous (tem pes´cho͞o əs) *adj.,* violent, stormy

Vocabulary in Context

- One of the pictures on the wall is askew.
- People call that man a spineless minion of the brutal king.
- We were forced to cancel our afternoon picnic plans because of the tempestuous weather.

And there are only dusty flowers,
And the chinking of the censer, and tracks
From somewhere to nowhere.
And staring me straight in the eyes,
And threatening impending death,
Is an enormous star.

1939

VI

The light weeks will take flight,
I won't comprehend what happened.
Just as the white nights
Stared at you, dear son, in prison

So they are staring again,
With the burning eyes of a hawk,
Talking about your lofty cross,
And about death.

1939

❶ *What does the speaker say that she is unable to comprehend?*

VII

THE SENTENCE

And the stone word fell
On my still-living breast.
Never mind, I was ready.
I will manage somehow.

Today I have so much to do:
I must kill memory once and for all,
I must turn my soul to stone,
I must learn to live again—

Unless . . . Summer's ardent rustling
Is like a festival outside my window.
For a long time I've foreseen this
Brilliant day, deserted house.

June 22, 1939
Fountain House

❷ *How does the speaker react to the sentence? What must the speaker do?*

VIII

TO DEATH

You will come in any case—so why not now?
I am waiting for you—I can't stand much more.

❸ *Why does the speaker invite death?*

WORDS FOR EVERYDAY USE

cen • ser (sen´sər) *n.,* container in which incense is burned
im • pend • ing (im pend´iŋ) *adj.,* threatening; about to happen

ANSWERS TO GUIDED READING QUESTIONS

❶ The speaker says that she is unable to comprehend what has happened—that her son is imprisoned and awaiting death.

❷ The speaker says that she was ready for the sentence and that she will manage. She says she must kill her memory and turn her soul to stone so that she might go on living.

❸ The speaker invites death now because she cannot stand much more pain and grief.

LITERARY NOTE

After the death of Stalin in 1953, Russian writers began to have more artistic freedom. Some works were published that, had they come out during the Stalin years, would have meant prison, torture, or death for the writers. The Soviet Union then went into another conservative period, but finally artistic freedom again returned with Mikhail Gorbachev's presidency in the late 1980s.

Popular themes of post-Stalinist writing included life in Siberian prison camps, the Russian Revolution and its aftermath, the horrors of the Stalin years, the lives of rural peasants, and World War II.

CROSS-CURRICULAR ACTIVITIES

SOCIAL STUDIES

Explain to students that in a communist society, the economy is controlled by a central government that places emphasis on the needs of the state as a whole rather than on individuals. Some students might be interested in doing research on this topic and then contrasting the communist system with the capitalist. Students might also want to learn more about the fall of communism and the Soviet Union with the election of Boris Yeltsin.

VOCABULARY IN CONTEXT

- The priest chanted and swung his censer, diffusing the fragrant incense throughout the church.
- The community prepared emergency shelters when it received news of the impending storm.

Answers to Guided Reading Questions

1. Death might come with the burst of a gas shell, like a gangster with a length of pipe, in the form of an infectious disease, or with the appearance of the secret police.

Additional Questions and Activities

Ask students to answer the following questions:

How is the speaker feeling as she talks about the different ways in which death might come? Why does she feel this way?

ANSWERS

Responses will vary.

Students are likely to say that the speaker is depressed and unwilling to fight any longer. She feels this way because her emotional pain has worn her down.

Cross-curricular Activities

MATHEMATICS AND SCIENCES

Typhus is a group of related diseases caused by bacteria of the Rickettsiaceae family, and it is considered one of history's most devastating epidemic diseases. The disease is transmitted by lice, fleas, or ticks, and it spreads quickly in areas with poor sanitation. People with typhus are afflicted with headaches, chills, fever, pains, toxic substances in the blood, and rashes. The disease can also cause cardiac failure. Typhus began to occur less often in the twentieth century as living conditions and sanitation improved. A vaccine for the disease was discovered in the 1940s.

Ask students to work in small groups to research other plagues or epidemics that have stricken different parts of the world at different times. Describe the circumstances surrounding specific diseases. Are they still a threat?

La Jeune Bonne (The Servant Girl). *Amedeo Modigliani, circa 1918. Albright-Knox Art Gallery, Buffalo, NY*

I've put out the light and opened the door
For you, so simple and miraculous.
So come in any form you please,
Burst in as a gas shell
Or, like a gangster, steal in with a length of pipe,
Or poison me with typhus[10] fumes.
Or be that fairy tale you've dreamed up,
So sickeningly familiar to everyone—
In which I glimpse the top of a pale blue cap[11]
And the house attendant white with fear.
Now it doesn't matter anymore. The Yenisey[12] swirls,
The North Star shines.
And the final horror dims
The blue luster of beloved eyes.

1 *In what ways might death come?*

August 19, 1939
Fountain House

10. **typhus.** Infectious disease
11. **pale blue cap.** Worn by the NKVD, or secret police
12. **Yenisey.** River in Siberia along which there are many prison camps

IX

Now madness half shadows
My soul with its wing,
And makes it drunk with fiery wine
And beckons toward the black ravine.

And I've finally realized
That I must give in,
Overhearing myself
Raving as if it were somebody else.

And it does not allow me to take
Anything of mine with me
(No matter how I plead with it,
No matter how I supplicate):

Not the terrible eyes of my son—
Suffering turned to stone,
Not the day of the terror,
Not the hour I met with him in prison,

Not the sweet coolness of his hands,
Not the trembling shadow of the lindens,
Not the far-off, fragile sound—
Of the final words of consolation.

May 4, 1940
Fountain House

1

What effect has the strain and sorrow had on the speaker?

X

CRUCIFIXION

"Do not weep for Me, Mother,
I am in the grave."

1

A choir of angels sang the praises of that momentous hour,
And the heavens dissolved in fire.
To his Father He said: "Why hast Thou forsaken me!"[13]
And to his Mother: "Oh, do not weep for Me. . ."[14]

1940
Fountain House

---

13. **To his Father . . . me!"** Reference to Jesus' last words
14. **"Oh . . . Me. . ."** In this line from a Russian Orthodox prayer that ends "when you look upon the grave," Jesus comforts Mary with the promise of his resurrection.

WORDS FOR EVERYDAY USE

sup • pli • cate (sup´lə kāt´) *vt.*, ask for humbly and earnestly

VOCABULARY IN CONTEXT

- My brother and I will supplicate forgiveness from our parents for breaking our curfew.

ANSWERS TO GUIDED READING QUESTIONS

1 The speaker has gone mad.

ANALYTIC SCALES FOR RESPONDING IN WRITING

(SEE PAGE 179.)

Assign a score from 1 to 25 for each grading criterion below. (For more detailed evaluation, see the evaluation forms for writing, revising, and proofreading, Assessment Portfolio 4.1–4.9.)

1. Requiem

- **Content/Unity.** The requiem focuses on a person, place, or thing lost to the writer.
- **Organization/Coherence.** The requiem describes the lost person, place, or thing and why he, she, or it was special, and then expresses what effect this person, place, or thing had on the writer and the rest of the world.
- **Language/Style.** The requiem uses vivid and precise nouns, verbs, and modifiers.
- **Conventions.** The requiem avoids errors in spelling, grammar, usage, mechanics, and manuscript form.

► Additional practice is provided in the Essential Skills Practice Book: Writing 1.8.

2. Critical Essay

- **Content/Unity.** The essay analyzes the biographical aspects of *Requiem.*
- **Organization/Coherence.** The essay begins with an introduction that includes the essay's thesis, followed by supporting paragraphs with clear transitions and a solid conclusion.
- **Language/Style.** The essay uses vivid and precise nouns, verbs, and modifiers.
- **Conventions.** The essay avoids errors in spelling, grammar, usage, mechanics, and manuscript form.

► Additional practice is provided in the Essential Skills Practice Book: Writing 1.20.

ANSWERS TO GUIDED READING QUESTIONS

❶ The speaker refers to Mary, the mother of Christ.

❷ The speaker recognizes that her experience is not unique, that many other people shared similar suffering and sorrow.

❸ The poem serves as a memorial to those who stood by the prison door, those who waited and suffered with her.

LITERARY TECHNIQUE

EPILOGUE

An **epilogue** is a concluding section or statement, often one that comments on or draws conclusions from the work as a whole. Ask students to reread Epilogues I and II in *Requiem.* Then ask them to explain what the author accomplishes with these sections.

BIOGRAPHICAL NOTE

Nikita Khrushchev succeeded Joseph Stalin as the sole dictator of Russia within a few years after Stalin's death on March 5, 1953, and stayed in this position until 1964. Stalin had been dictator for twenty-nine years, but Khrushchev led a "de-Stalinization" campaign to remove Stalin's influence from Soviet society. Unlike Stalin, Khrushchev believed in an idea known as "peaceful coexistence," which meant that communist nations and capitalist nations should be able to live and compete in peace. Khrushchev believed that the communists would ultimately prevail because of economic and political strength. Within the Soviet Union, Khrushchev was severe in his suppression of resistance.

2

Mary Magdalene[15] beat her breast and sobbed,
The beloved disciple turned to stone,
But where the silent Mother stood, there
No one glanced and no one would have dared.

❶ *To what mother does the speaker refer?*

1943
Tashkent

EPILOGUE I

I learned how faces fall,
How terror darts from under eyelids,
How suffering traces lines
Of stiff cuneiform on cheeks,
How locks of ashen-blonde or black
Turn silver suddenly,
Smiles fade on submissive lips
And fear trembles in a dry laugh.
And I pray not for myself alone,
But for all those who stood there with me
In cruel cold, and in July's heat,
At that blind, red wall.

❷ *What does the speaker recognize about her experience?*

EPILOGUE II

Once more the day of remembrance[16] draws near.
I see, I hear, I feel you:

The one they almost had to drag at the end,
And the one who tramps her native land no more,

And the one who, tossing her beautiful head,
Said: "Coming here's like coming home."

I'd like to name them all by name,
But the list has been confiscated and is nowhere to be found.

I have woven a wide mantle for them
From their meager, overheard words.

I will remember them always and everywhere,
I will never forget them no matter what comes.

❸ *What purpose does this poem serve, according to the speaker?*

15. **Mary Magdalene.** Reformed woman who became a follower of Jesus
16. **day of remembrance.** Russian Orthodox memorial service held on the anniversary of a death

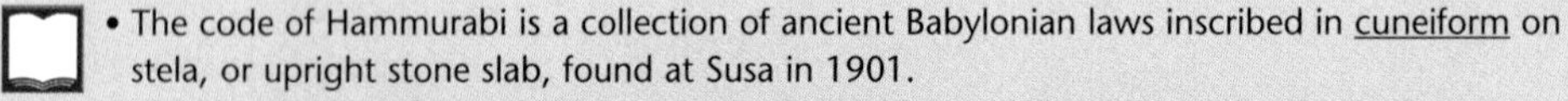

cu • ne • i • form (kyo͞o nē´ə fôrm´) *n.,* wedge-shaped characters from ancient Middle Eastern inscriptions
con • fis • cate (kän´fis kāt´) *vt.,* seize or take away by authority
man • tle (man´təl) *n.,* anything that cloaks or covers

VOCABULARY IN CONTEXT

- The code of Hammurabi is a collection of ancient Babylonian laws inscribed in cuneiform on a stela, or upright stone slab, found at Susa in 1901.
- I know ushers might confiscate my homemade popcorn when I go to the movie theater.
- The tree branches form a mantle of protection from the sun.

And if they gag my exhausted mouth
Through which a hundred million scream,

Then may the people remember me
On the eve of my remembrance day.

And if ever in this country
They decide to erect a monument to me,

I consent to that honor
Under these conditions—that it stand

Neither by the sea, where I was born:
My last tie with the sea is broken,

Nor in the tsar's garden near the cherished pine stump,
Where an inconsolable shade looks for me,

But here, where I stood for three hundred hours,
And where they never unbolted the doors for me.

This, lest in blissful death
I forget the rumbling of the Black Marias,

Forget how that detested door slammed shut
And an old woman howled like a wounded animal.

And may the melting snow stream like tears
From my motionless lids of bronze,

And a prison dove coo in the distance,
And the ships of the Neva sail calmly on.

March 1940 ■

➊ *Where does the poet want to be remembered? Why do you think she chooses this place?*

➋ *What mood is expressed in the last few lines of the poem?*

Denis Gorbounov, Russia

I admire Anna Akhmatova because she was brave enough to show in her writing what was going on in the Soviet Union at a time when speaking out could land you in jail or a concentration camp in Siberia. We never read Akhmatova's work in school; I came upon it on my own by accident. During Communism we didn't know anything about her or her poetry, but after the government changed, many people began reading her work, and she has become very popular.

I can't say that her work describes our country today because we have a completely different life now. Much of our culture now comes from Europe and the West: music, fast food, magazines, television, and movies, but Akhmatova provides a good representation of a part of our past. She won't let us forget what went on for many years in Russia.

Answers to Guided Reading Questions

➊ The speaker wants to be remembered standing by the prison. She spent so much time by the prison, waiting. A monument in this place would serve as a reminder of the suffering she, and so many others, endured.

➋ The mood expressed in the last few lines of the poem is one of extreme sadness but also one of calm.

Selection Check Test with Answers

EX. During what years do the events described in *Requiem* take place?
The events take place between 1935 and 1940.

1. Where do the women stand in line?
They stand in line outside of the prison.

2. Who does the speaker say she will be like?
She will be like the wives of the Streltsy.

3. What escape does the speaker wish from her suffering?
She wishes for death.

4. What three people who witness the crucifixion of Jesus are mentioned?
Mary Magdalene, his mother, and the beloved disciple are mentioned.

5. Why does the speaker not "name them all by name"?
The list has been confiscated and lost.

Additional Questions and Activities

Denis says that Anna Akhmatova's writings "won't let us forget what went on for many years in Russia." As a class, have students think of other writers who have protested issues or governments through their work. How were these people treated? What impact did their work have on the world, either at the time they were writing, or later, as in the case of Akhmatova? Invite students to imagine that they are a writer or poet living under persecution in any time or place in history. What would they want to write about? Have students write a poem, story, or essay about this issue. Students could also choose to write about persecution that has occurred in their own lives.

Responding to the Selection

Ask students to form pairs and read their favorite poems from this poetic cycle aloud to each other. The pair can discuss what they find most moving and powerful about the sections and what emotions these sections evoke.

Answers for Reviewing the Selection

RECALLING AND INTERPRETING

1. **Recalling.** *Requiem* is set during the period of Stalin's Great Purges, from 1935 to 1940. The speaker shares the fear caused by mass arrests and the possibility of a death sentence for loved ones. **Interpreting.** The speaker feels strongly about being in her homeland despite the danger and sorrow she has suffered there. She feels that the events are horrifying, and that the only people who are happy are the dead because they are at rest.

2. **Recalling.** The speaker's childhood was pleasant and carefree. Standing in line outside of a prison, hoping her son will not be executed, and fighting for his release have had a profound effect upon her adult life. **Interpreting.** The speaker's childhood might suggest the innocence of Russia before the Revolution, civil war, and Stalin's purges.

3. **Recalling.** The speaker faces despair, struggle, disassociation, numbness, a wish for death, and madness. She refers to Mary, the mother of Jesus. **Interpreting.** "Do not weep for Me, Mother,/I am in the grave," are the words of comfort spoken to Mary. The speaker, like many Russian mothers and like Mary, loses her son unjustly. The mothers are stunned by their losses and struggle with their grief.

(cont.)

Responding to the Selection

Which poem from this poetic cycle did you find most powerful or moving? What emotions did this section of *Requiem* evoke in you? Which images were particularly powerful, and why?

Reviewing the Selection

Recalling / Interpreting

1. During what historical period is *Requiem* set? What experience did the speaker share with many people? ▶▶ How does the speaker feel about her homeland? about the events that are taking place?

2. What evidence can you find describing what the speaker's childhood was like? What events seem to have had a profound effect on her adult life? ▶▶ In what way might the speaker's childhood be symbolic of Russia during a period earlier than the one described in the poem?

3. What different stages does the speaker go through as she faces the imprisonment and death sentence of her son? To what other mother does the speaker refer in Poem X? ▶▶ What words of comfort are offered to the mother in Poem X? In what way is this mother like the speaker?

4. In Epilogue II, what does the speaker say she would like to do? What has she done? ▶▶ In what way is *Requiem* a monument to all of those who were killed?

Synthesizing

5. What role do writers play in social criticism? What are some other examples of writing done to effect social change?

Understanding Literature (Questions for Discussion)

1. **Allusion.** An **allusion** is a rhetorical technique in which reference is made to a person, event, object, or work from history or literature. In *Requiem,* Akhmatova makes many allusions. In poem I, to what historical event does Akhmatova allude? In what way is the event like her own situation? In poem II, what allusion does Akhmatova make? What is the significance of this thing? When paired with the folk song style of this poem, what effect does this allusion have? What allusions are made in stanza 1 of poem X? In what way are these allusions related to the speaker's situation?

Answers for Reviewing the Selection (cont.)

4. **Recalling.** The speaker says she would like to name every mother who waited for an imprisoned child. She has "woven a wide mantle for them" from their own words as she overheard them, and she continues to remember them. **Interpreting.** *Requiem* serves as a reminder of those who were killed although their names have been lost. It testifies to the dedication and suffering of the loved ones who waited for news of the imprisoned.

SYNTHESIZING

Responses will vary. Possible responses are given.

5. Students may say that writers do play an important role in social criticism. They might cite many examples from works in this unit or other works they have read. They might also point to the fact that Stalin feared writers and other artists because of criticism they might present of his regime.

2. **Apostrophe.** An **apostrophe** is a rhetorical technique in which an object or a person is directly addressed. What is addressed in poem VIII? Why? What suggestions does the speaker make to the thing she addresses?

Responding in Writing

1. **Creative Writing: Requiem.** A requiem is a dirgelike song, chant, or poem. Write a requiem for someone or something that has been lost to you. You might write your requiem in response to death, such as a requiem for a loved one who has passed away or for the lives lost in a local or national disaster, or you might write about another loss such as a forest destroyed by developers, innocence that you have lost through experience, or a lost friendship. Do a focused freewrite in which you consider these questions: What words describe the lost person, place, or thing? What qualities made the person, place, or thing special? What effect did the person, place, or thing have on you? What effect did he, she, or it have on others or on the world? How do you feel without the person, place, or thing? Then use the images and emotions that you gathered in your freewrite as you compose your requiem.

2. **Critical Essay: Biographical Criticism.** Biographical criticism attempts to account for elements of literary works by relating them to events in the lives of their authors. Reread the information about Akhmatova in About the Author and About the Selection. Do some research to learn more about Akhmatova's life. Then write an essay in which you analyze the biographical aspects of *Requiem*. Consider the following questions: How does Akhmatova feel about her country, its people, and its political situation? What is the significance of the dates on which she wrote particular poems within this cycle? What specific events in her life shaped each poem? What personal emotions does Akhmatova express through these poems? In what way does she act as a voice for others? Why did Akhmatova go to great risk to write *Requiem*? You may wish to focus on three or four poems from this cycle, but you should also address the effect of *Requiem* as a whole and its relation to Akhmatova's life.

Thinking Skills

Using Mnemonic Techniques. Anna Akhmatova had to commit her poetry to memory because it was dangerous to be found with written copies of her work. When memorizing something like a poem, it is often easiest to repeat a small part, such as a line or a stanza until you know it, and then do the same for the next small part. For other types of information, repetition is a poor way of memorizing. Read the Language Arts Survey 4.3, "Using Mnemonic Techniques." Then find the names of Russian or Soviet rulers from the 1950s through the 1990s. Devise a mnemonic to help you remember their names in order.

ANALYTIC SCALES FOR RESPONDING IN WRITING

Grading scales for Responding in Writing appear on page 175.

ANSWERS FOR SKILLS ACTIVITIES

THINKING SKILLS

Students should develop a mnemonic to help them remember these Soviet and Russian leaders:
Joseph Stalin 1924–1953
Georgy Malenkov 1953
Nikita Khrushchev 1953–1964
Leonid Brezhnev 1964–1982
Yury Andropov 1982–1984
Konstantin Chernenko 1984–1985
Mikhail Gorbachev 1985–1991
Boris Yeltsin 1991–

► Additional practice is provided in the Essential Skills Practice Book: Study and Research 4.3.

ANSWERS FOR UNDERSTANDING LITERATURE

Responses will vary. Possible responses are given.

1. Allusion. In Poem I, Akhmatova refers to the killing of the Streltsy by Peter the Great in 1698. The wives and mothers of the Streltsy watched as their husbands and sons were executed. Akhmatova and many other women wait and protest the imprisonment and possible execution of their husbands and sons. In Poem II, Akhmatova alludes to the Don river. The Don appears often in folk songs. Paired with the folk song style of the poem, Poem II has a softer, songlike effect. The mood is sad; the tone is calmer than that of the previous poem. In stanza 1 of Poem X, Akhmatova alludes to the death of Jesus on the cross. She specifically alludes to his last words and to a line from a Russian Orthodox prayer.

(cont.)

ANSWERS FOR UNDERSTANDING LITERATURE (CONT.)

Responses will vary. Possible responses are given.

2. Apostrophe. The speaker addresses death. The speaker asks death to come now, because she feels that she can no longer go on living. She suggests different ways in which death might come for her.

CULTURAL/HISTORICAL NOTE

Aryan, a term made notorious by the Nazis, was originally used to describe prehistoric, warlike, nomadic tribes who, it is believed, migrated into Europe and India from southern Russia, Asia Minor, and Mesopotamia around 1500 BC. These people, speakers of ancient Indo-European languages, are believed to be the distant ancestors of Anglo-Saxon, Celtic, Latin, Greek, Hindu, and Persian peoples.

According to anthropologists, *Aryan* is not a valid term for describing any cultures, societies, or language groups that exist today or that have existed in the recent past. The Nazis, however, appropriated this term and used it freely in their racist, anti-Jewish propaganda. They idealized the Aryan conquest of Europe, claimed that Germans were close descendants of the Aryans, and tried to spread the idea that Jews were of an entirely different, inferior race. According to inaccurate Nazi propaganda, a true "Aryan," was a member of the "white race" and usually tall and blond. Nazis believed that people fitting this description were part of a "master race" that should take over the world.

ADDITIONAL QUESTIONS AND ACTIVITIES

Ask students to refer to the Nuremberg Laws and to the other human rights abuses that led up to Hitler's "final solution." Then ask them to discuss the following questions: Why might Hitler have wanted to establish a societal structure that separated Jews from other German citizens? Why might this earlier separation have made it easier for some German citizens to dehumanize Jews and later to go along with Hitler's extermination plans?

ANSWERS

Responses will vary.

People who are segregated from the community at large are easier to treat as less than human. Once people are seen as different and are deprived of human rights, it is easier to escalate their mistreatment.

Insights

THE HOLOCAUST

Between 1933 and 1945, Jews and other minorities were persecuted and systematically killed by the Nazis. This dark period is known as the **Holocaust**. Persecution of the Jews in Germany began shortly after Adolf Hitler became chancellor in January of 1933. Hitler believed in the supremacy of the Aryan race. In his view, Jews were parasites who leeched off and threatened the "master race." Under his rule, laws and regulations prevented Jews from attending universities and from owning businesses or property. In 1935, the Nuremberg laws deprived Jews of their citizenship and banned them from marrying other Germans. Jewish synagogues were destroyed in the *Kristallnacht* pogrom, or Night of the Broken Glass, in 1938. By 1939, Jews were stripped of almost all rights and had been forced into ghettos. By 1941, all Jews over the age of six were forced to wear yellow Stars-of-David. Anti-Jewish laws were soon passed in other countries such as Italy, Austria, Czechoslovakia, and Hungary.

Part of Hitler's plan to conquer the world included wiping out the entire Jewish population. For a time, Jews and others in conquered towns were rounded up, shot, and buried in mass graves, or were forced onto a truck or train into which gas was pumped, killing them on their way to a mass burial site. Because the Nazis found these methods inefficient and such methods raised public uneasiness, the Nazis sought other means to solve the "Jewish problem." In 1942, at the Wannsee Conference, the "final solution" to the Jewish problem was discussed—Jews would be forced into camps in Eastern Europe, where they would be "dealt with accordingly." In the camps many were selected to be exterminated immediately, often by poison gas in areas designed to look like mass showers. Others would be forced into slave labor until they died or were selected for extermination. Over six million Jewish people and another five million Europeans including Gypsies, Poles, and Slavs were systematically killed during the Holocaust.

Some people survived the concentration camps, and others were able to escape the camps entirely. In some cases, Jews were hidden, provided with false papers, or helped to safer countries by courageous individual or group efforts. For example, Swedish businessman and diplomat Raoul Wallenberg used his position as a neutral Swedish citizen to help about one hundred thousand Hungarian Jews escape being sent to Nazi death camps. Oskar Schindler was able to save fifteen hundred Jews whom he employed in his factories. When eight thousand Danish Jews were to be deported, the Danish people organized food, money, and boats to transport them to the safety of Sweden. While some Jews were able to leave their homes for safer places, many more were unable to leave, as many countries would not accept them or severely limited the number of immigrants they would allow to cross their borders. Overall, public outcry in reaction to the plight of the Jews and other victims was very limited. Too little was done too late to save the more than ten million victims of the Nazi death camps. The testimonies of survivors and various Holocaust memorials remind us of the nightmare that became a reality and force us to remember that we must remain vigilant and active against intolerance and prejudice.

Archive Photos/Leo Baeck Institute

Adolf Hitler, September 23, 1933

PREREADING

from *Night*
by Elie Wiesel, translated by Stella Rodway

ROMANIA

About the Author

ELIE WIESEL
1928–

Elie Wiesel was born in the village of Sighet, Romania. There, in a Hasidic community, he lived and was educated until 1944 when all the Jews of the town were deported to the Nazi death camp at Auschwitz. Wiesel and his father were later moved to Buchenwald, where his father was killed. Wiesel survived the concentration camps, but his parents and younger sister did not. He was later reunited with his two older sisters.

After the war, he moved to France, where he studied at the Sorbonne and wrote for French and Israeli newspapers. During this time, he was encouraged to "bear witness" to the atrocities of the Holocaust that he had seen and experienced. In 1956, Wiesel moved to the United States, where he has taught at universities and served as chairman of the United States Holocaust Memorial Council. Wiesel was awarded the Nobel Peace Prize in 1986.

About the Selection

Night recounts the horror of the Holocaust as Wiesel experienced it. (For more information about the Holocaust, see page 180.) It is considered one of the most powerful accounts of the Holocaust ever written. As in many of his writings and actions, Wiesel's purpose in writing *Night* was to keep the memory of the Holocaust alive to serve as a reminder of the outrage against humanity that had occurred. In his Nobel Prize acceptance speech, Wiesel said, "I have tried to fight those who would forget. Because if we forget, we are guilty, we are accomplices." Wiesel first wrote his account in Yiddish. The eight-hundred page Yiddish version was cut down to one hundred pages and translated into French. In 1960, *Night* was translated into English.

German troops

CONNECTIONS: The Nobel Peace Prize

Elie Wiesel won the Nobel Peace Prize in 1986 in recognition for his continued work in the field of human rights. His unending efforts to keep the memory of the Holocaust alive are only one stand that Wiesel has taken. Wiesel has also fought against violence and oppression of peoples around the globe. In accepting his Nobel Prize, he explained that he had vowed never to be silent when humans were suffering. He chooses to take a stand on issues of human rights because "neutrality helps the oppressor, never the victim. Silence encourages the tormentor, never the tormented."

ADDITIONAL RESOURCES

READER'S GUIDE
- Selection Worksheet 2.3

ASSESSMENT PORTFOLIO
- Selection Check Test 2.2.9
- Selection Test 2.2.10

ESSENTIAL SKILLS PRACTICE BOOKS
- Writing 1.8, 1.20

PREREADING EXTENSIONS

Elie Wiesel grew up in a Hasidic Jewish community. If some students are familiar with Hasidism, ask them to share their information or beliefs with the rest of the class. If your students are unfamiliar, invite them to research Hasidism using resources at the library.

SUPPORT FOR LEP STUDENTS

PRONUNCIATIONS OF PROPER NOUNS AND ADJECTIVES

Ausch • witz (oush´vitz)
Bir • ken • au (bēr´ kən ou)
Czecho • slo • vak (chek´ə slō´ väk)
Hun • ga • ry (huŋ´gər ē)
Kas • chau (kaz´chou)
Ma • dame Schäch • ter (mə däm´ shäk´tər)
El • ie Wie • sel (el´ ē vē zel´)

ADDITIONAL VOCABULARY

bade—past tense of bid
barometer—something that measures or shows change
barracks—large, plain buildings for housing soldiers or prisoners
hermetically—made to be airtight
lieutenant—military officer ranking below a captain
monotonous—unchanging
pious—showing extreme moral or religious devotion
provisions—supplies

GOALS/OBJECTIVES

Studying this lesson will enable students to

- empathize with a narrator's feelings of denial, disbelief, fear, and horror as he and his family are transported to a Nazi concentration camp
- become familiar with the life and work of Elie Wiesel
- define the literary terms *aim, description, simile, foreshadowing, image*, and *imagery*
- write an editorial or speech and a critical essay
- learn about and commemorate the Holocaust as a class through art and presentations

READER'S JOURNAL

You might also turn students' attention to Wiesel's statement that "neutrality helps the oppressor, never the victim. Silence encourages the tormentor, never the tormented." What does this statement mean to students as they think about the Holocaust and other instances of human rights abuses?

ANSWERS TO GUIDED READING QUESTIONS

➊ The people did not know what to expect about their futures, but they feared that tomorrow might be worse than the present situation.

SPELLING AND VOCABULARY WORDS FROM THE SELECTION

abominable abyss

HISTORICAL NOTE

Of an estimated 8.3 million Jews living in Europe after 1939, about 6 million were killed during the Holocaust. It was said of the concentration camps that "Death seemed to guard all exits."

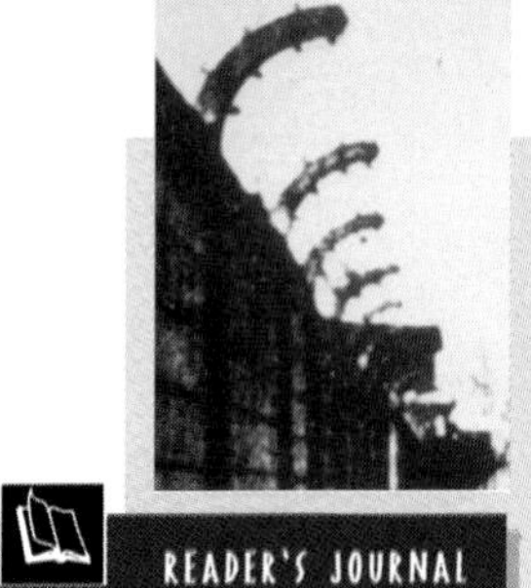

READER'S JOURNAL

Elie Wiesel has said that "if we forget [the Holocaust], we are guilty, we are accomplices." What do you think he means by this statement? Why is it so important for people to remember the Holocaust? In your journal, write your thoughts about the Holocaust and why it should be remembered.

FROM

Night

ELIE WIESEL, TRANSLATED BY STELLA RODWAY

[Editor's note: In the beginning of Night, *all foreigners are expelled from the village of Sighet and are transported away by cattle trains. Those on the trains are subsequently killed. One person manages to escape and to return to the village. Though he tells everyone he meets of the atrocities he saw, nobody believes him. The next year, German soldiers appear in Sighet. At first the situation does not seem to be bad. Then two ghettos are established where Jews are forced to live, and finally, deportation begins. Jews are forced into cattle cars not knowing where they are being taken.]*

What expectations do the people on the train have about their future?

We still had a few provisions left. But we never ate enough to satisfy our hunger. To save was our rule; to save up for tomorrow. Tomorrow might be worse.

The train stopped at Kaschau, a little town on the Czechoslovak frontier. We realized then that we were not going to stay in Hungary. Our eyes were opened, but too late.

The door of the car slid open. A German officer, accompanied by a Hungarian lieutenant-interpreter, came up and introduced himself.

"From this moment, you come under the authority of the German army. Those of you who still have gold, silver, or watches in your possession must give them up now. Anyone who is later found to have kept anything will be shot on the spot. Secondly, anyone who feels ill may go to the hospital car. That's all."

The Hungarian lieutenant went among us with a basket and collected the last possessions from those who no longer wished to taste the bitterness of terror.

"There are eighty of you in this wagon," added the German officer. "If anyone is missing, you'll all be shot, like dogs. . . ."

They disappeared. The doors were closed. We were caught in a trap, right up to our necks. The doors were nailed up; the way back was finally cut off. The world was a cattle wagon hermetically sealed.

We had a woman with us named Madame Schächter. She was about fifty; her ten-year-old son was with her, crouched in a corner. Her husband and two eldest sons had been deported with the first transport by mistake. The separation had completely broken her.

I knew her well. A quiet woman with tense, burning eyes, she had often been to our house. Her husband, who was a pious man, spent his days and nights in study, and

QUOTABLES

"Suffering, in Jewish tradition, confers no privileges. It all depends on what one makes of that suffering. It is possible to suffer and despair an entire lifetime and still not give up the art of laughter."

—Elie Wiesel

it was she who worked to support the family.

Madame Schächter had gone out of her mind. On the first day of the journey she had already begun to moan and to keep asking why she had been separated from her family. As time went on, her cries grew hysterical.

On the third night, while we slept, some of us sitting one against the other and some standing, a piercing cry split the silence:

"Fire! I can see a fire! I can see a fire!"

There was a moment's panic. Who was it who had cried out? It was Madame Schächter. Standing in the middle of the wagon, in the pale light from the windows, she looked like a withered tree in a cornfield. She pointed her arm toward the window, screaming:

"Look! Look at it! Fire! A terrible fire! Mercy! *Oh, that fire!*"

Some of the men pressed up against the bars. There was nothing there; only the darkness.

The shock of this terrible awakening stayed with us for a long time. We still trembled from it. With every groan of the wheels on the rail, we felt that an abyss was about to open beneath our bodies. Powerless to still our own anguish, we tried to console ourselves:

"She's mad, poor soul. . . ."

Someone had put a damp cloth on her brow, to calm her, but still her screams went on:

"Fire! Fire!"

Her little boy was crying, hanging onto her skirt, trying to take hold of her hands. "It's all right, Mummy! There's nothing there. . . . Sit down. . . ." This shook me even more than his mother's screams had done.

Some women tried to calm her. "You'll find your husband and your sons again . . . in a few days. . . ."

She continued to scream, breathless, her voice broken by sobs. "Jews, listen to me! I can see a fire! There are huge flames! It is a furnace!"

It was as though she were possessed by an evil spirit which spoke from the depths of her being.

We tried to explain it away, more to calm ourselves and to recover our own breath than to comfort her. "She must be very thirsty, poor thing! That's why she keeps talking about a fire devouring her."

But it was in vain. Our terror was about to burst the sides of the train. Our nerves were at breaking point. Our flesh was creeping. It was as though madness were taking possession of us all. We could stand it no longer. Some of the young men forced her to sit down, tied her up, and put a gag in her mouth.

Silence again. The little boy sat down by his mother, crying. I had begun to breathe normally again. We could hear the wheels churning out that monotonous rhythm of a train traveling through the night. We could begin to doze, to rest, to dream. . . .

An hour or two went by like this. Then another scream took our breath away. The woman had broken loose from her bonds and was crying out more loudly than ever:

"Look at the fire! Flames, flames everywhere. . . ."

Once more the young men tied her up and gagged her. They even struck her. People encouraged them:

"Make her be quiet! She's mad! Shut her up! She's not the only one. She can keep her mouth shut. . . ."

❶ *What additional information does Madame Schächter give about her vision?*

❷ *What does Madame Schächter say she sees? Do the other people see what she sees?*

❸ *How do the other people on the train react to Madame Schächter's cries?*

Words for Everyday Use

a • byss (ə bis´) *n.,* bottomless gulf or pit

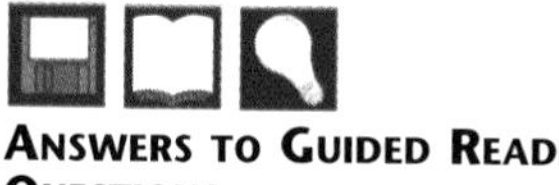

Answers to Guided Reading Questions

❶ Madame Schächter says that the flames are a huge furnace.

❷ Madame Schächter says that she sees a fire. Nobody else sees the flames.

❸ The other people beat Madame Schächter and gag her to keep her from shouting.

Bibliographic Note

Students who are interested in reading more materials related to the Holocaust might look for some of the following selections:

Fiction

Arrick, Fran. *Chernowitz.*

Horgan, Dorothy. *The Edge of War.*

Orlev, Uri. *Island on Bird Street.*

Samuels, Gertrude. *Mottele: A Partisan Odyssey.*

Nonfiction

Frank, Anne. *The Diary of a Young Girl.*

Gies, Miep. *Anne Frank Remembered.*

Hyams, Joseph. *A Field of Buttercups.*

Joffo, Joseph. *A Bag of Marbles.* Translated from the French by Martin Sokolenski.

Kuper, Jack. *Child of the Holocaust.*

Steenmeijer, Anneke (in collaboration with Otto Frank). *A Tribute to Anne Frank.*

Werstein, Irving. *The Uprising of the Warsaw Ghetto.*

Vocabulary in Context

• Lee lost his hat when it fell into the deep abyss of the well.

Answers to Guided Reading Questions

❶ The train stops at Auschwitz. The people hear that it is a labor camp, conditions are good, families will not be split up, and that older people and invalids will work in the fields while the younger people toil in factories.

Historical Note

Swedish businessman/diplomat Raoul Wallenberg used his position as a neutral Swedish citizen to help about one hundred thousand Hungarian Jews escape deportation to Nazi death camps. For his selfless work he was granted honorary United States' citizenship—the only foreigner other than Winston Churchill to be so honored.

Cross-curricular Activities

Social Studies

- Ask students to investigate how European geography changed under the Nazis. In addition to Holland, what other countries did Germany invade? Have students draw or trace maps of Europe before and after the Nazi takeover and label the differences.
- Have students explore other aspects of the Holocaust. What groups besides Jews were persecuted? Why? How was the founding of the state of Israel related to the Holocaust? Why was the creation of Israel significant to Jews throughout the world? Students might want to look at some specific works about the Holocaust, such as *The War Against the Jews*, by Lucy Dawidowicz.

Archive Photos

Auschwitz

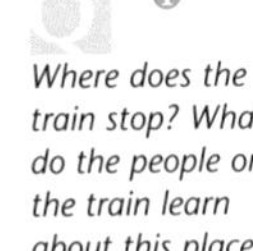

❶ *Where does the train stop? What do the people on the train learn about this place?*

They struck her several times on the head—blows that might have killed her. Her little boy clung to her; he did not cry out; he did not say a word. He was not even weeping now.

An endless night. Toward dawn, Madame Schächter calmed down. Crouched in her corner, her bewildered gaze scouring the emptiness, she could no longer see us.

She stayed like that all through the day, dumb, absent, isolated among us. As soon as night fell, she began to scream: "There's a fire over there!" She would point at a spot in space, always the same one. They were tired of hitting her. The heat, the thirst, the pestilential stench, the suffocating lack of air—these were as nothing compared with these screams which tore us to shreds. A few days more and we should all have started to scream too.

But we had reached a station. Those who were next to the windows told us its name: "Auschwitz."[1]

No one had ever heard that name.

The train did not start up again. The afternoon passed slowly. Then the wagon doors slid open. Two men were allowed to get down to fetch water.

When they came back, they told us that, in exchange for a gold watch, they had discovered that this was the last stop. We would be getting out here. There was a labor camp. Conditions were good. Families would not be split up. Only the young people would go to work in the factories. The old men and invalids would be kept occupied in the fields.

The barometer of confidence soared. Here was a sudden release from the terrors of the previous nights. We gave thanks to God.

Madame Schächter stayed in her corner, wilted, dumb, indifferent to the general confidence. Her little boy stroked her hand.

1. **Auschwitz.** Concentration camp in southern Poland notorious as a center of extermination

Historical Note

Anne Frank was a Jewish teenager who is today known all over the world for her diary. Her diary describes the two years she, her family, and another family spent in hiding, trying to avoid capture by the Nazis. The group was eventually discovered by Hitler's secret police, and Anne Frank, her mother, and her sister died of disease in Nazi camps. Frank's *Diary of a Young Girl* was published by her father, Otto Frank, the only member of the family to survive. Since then, Anne Frank's writings have been published in many languages, helping to inspire courage around the world.

As dusk fell, darkness gathered inside the wagon. We started to eat our last provisions. At ten in the evening, everyone was looking for a convenient position in which to sleep for a while, and soon we were all asleep. Suddenly:

"The fire! The furnace! Look, over there!"

Waking with a start, we rushed to the window. Yet again we had believed her, even if only for a moment. But there was nothing outside save the darkness of night. With shame in our souls, we went back to our places, gnawed by fear, in spite of ourselves. As she continued to scream, they began to hit her again, and it was with the greatest difficulty that they silenced her.

The man in charge of our wagon called a German officer who was walking about on the platform, and asked him if Madame Schächter could be taken to the hospital car.

"You must be patient," the German replied. "She'll be taken there soon."

Toward eleven o'clock, the train began to move. We pressed against the windows. The convoy was moving slowly. A quarter of an hour later, it slowed down again. Through the windows we could see barbed wire; we realized that this must be the camp.

We had forgotten the existence of Madame Schächter. Suddenly, we heard terrible screams:

"Jews, look! Look through the window! Flames! Look!"

And as the train stopped, we saw this time that flames were gushing out of a tall chimney into the black sky.

Madame Schächter was silent herself. Once more she had become dumb, indifferent, absent, and had gone back to her corner.

We looked at the flames in the darkness. There was an abominable odor floating in the air. Suddenly, our doors opened. Some odd-looking characters, dressed in striped shirts and black trousers leapt into the wagon. They held electric torches and truncheons.[2] They began to strike out to right and left, shouting:

"Everybody get out! Everyone out of the wagon! Quickly!"

We jumped out. I threw a last glance toward Madame Schächter. Her little boy was holding her hand.

In front of us flames. In the air that smell of burning flesh. It must have been about midnight. We had arrived—at Birkenau, reception center for Auschwitz.

◆ ◆ ◆

[Editor's note: At Auschwitz, the people of Sighet are stripped of their possessions, and men are sent in one direction and women in another. The narrator will never see his mother and his younger sister again. The narrator and his father manage to stay together. The chimney and flames are pointed out to them, and they are told that they are going to meet their death in the crematorium. As he marches, uncertain of his fate, the narrator watches in disbelief as others are killed in the flames.]

I pinched my face. Was I still alive? Was I awake? I could not believe it. How could it be possible for them to burn people, children, and for the world to keep silent? No, none of this could be true. It was a nightmare. . . . Soon I should wake with a start, my heart pounding, and find myself

2. **truncheons.** Short, thick clubs

❶ *What does Madame Schächter scream as the train stops? What do the other people on the train finally see?*

Words for Everyday Use

a • bom • i • na • ble (ə bäm´ə nə bəl) *adj.,* extremely disagreeable

Answers to Guided Reading Questions

❶ Madame Schächter screams again about the fires. The people on the train finally see the flames of a giant chimney.

ANALYTIC SCALES FOR WRITING SKILLS

(SEE PAGE 188.)

Assign a score from 1 to 25 for each grading criterion below. (For more detailed evaluation, see the evaluation forms for writing, revising, and proofreading, Assessment Portfolio 4.1–4.9.)

1. Editorial or Speech

- **Content/Unity.** The editorial or speech focuses on an injustice against humanity and presents clear and logical ideas for change.
- **Organization/Coherence.** The speech or editorial is clearly organized, with a beginning, a middle, and an end.
- **Language/Style.** The speech or editorial uses vivid and precise nouns, verbs, and modifiers.
- **Conventions.** The speech or editorial avoids errors in spelling, grammar, usage, mechanics, and manuscript form.

► For additional practice, see Essential Skills Practice Book: Writing 1.8.

2. Critical Essay

- **Content/Unity.** The essay identifies difficulties that the narrator and others have in believing in an event and discusses the reasons for this disbelief. The essay also analyzes the narrator's view of humanity and how this view changes.
- **Organization/Coherence.** The essay presents original ideas that are backed up by specific examples from the selection.
- **Language/Style.** The essay uses vivid and precise nouns, verbs, and modifiers.
- **Conventions.** The essay avoids errors in spelling, grammar, usage, mechanics, and manuscript form.

► For additional practice, see Essential Skills Practice Book: Writing 1.20

Vocabulary in Context

- I left the theater because the violence in the movie was abominable to me.

Answers to Guided Reading Questions

❶ The narrator believes that people cannot be burned—that humanity would never tolerate it. His father believes that today anything is possible—that humanity does not care about them.

❷ The narrator and his father now know that Madame Schächter's screams on the train were more than the rantings of a woman torn by grief and despair. Her screams predicted what is now their reality.

❸ The first night in the camp is unforgettable to the narrator. It turned his life into one long, cursed night.

Selection Check Test with Answers

EX. What did Madam Schächter claim to see?
She claimed she saw a fire.

1. What had caused Madame Schächter to go out of her mind?
She had been separated from her husband and two oldest sons.

2. At what station did the train finally stop?
It stopped at Auschwitz.

3. When is the narrator separated from his mother and his sister?
He is separated from them as they get off the train and the men and boys are separated from the women and girls.

4. What do the people begin to recite?
They begin to recite the Kaddish, the prayer for the dead.

5. What happened to the narrator's life on the first night in camp?
His life was turned into one long night that he can never forget.

Archive Photos

German troops

back in the bedroom of my childhood, among my books. . . .

My father's voice drew me from my thoughts:

"It's a shame . . . a shame that you couldn't have gone with your mother. . . . I saw several boys of your age going with their mothers. . . ."

His voice was terribly sad. I realized that he did not want to see what they were going to do to me. He did not want to see the burning of his only son.

What does the narrator believe cannot happen to people? Why does his father disagree?

My forehead was bathed in cold sweat. But I told him that I did not believe that they could burn people in our age, that humanity would never tolerate it. . . .

"Humanity? Humanity is not concerned with us. Today anything is allowed. Anything is possible, even these crematories. . . ."

His voice was choking.

❷ *What do the narrator and his father now know about Madame Schächter?*

What effect does the first night in camp have on the narrator?

"Father," I said, "if that is so, I don't want to wait here. I'm going to run to the electric wire. That would be better than slow agony in the flames."

He did not answer. He was weeping. His body was shaken convulsively. Around us, everyone was weeping. Someone began to recite the Kaddish, the prayer for the dead. I do not know if it has ever happened before, in the long history of the Jews, that people have ever recited the prayer for the dead for themselves.

"*Yitgadal veyitkadach shmé raba.* . . . May His Name be blessed and magnified. . . ." whispered my father.

For the first time, I felt revolt rise up in me. Why should I bless His name? The Eternal, Lord of the Universe, the All-Powerful and Terrible, was silent. What had I to thank Him for?

We continued our march. We were gradually drawing closer to the ditch, from which an infernal heat was rising. Still twenty steps to go. If I wanted to bring about my own death, this was the moment. Our line had now only fifteen paces to cover. I bit my lips so that my father would not hear my teeth chattering. Ten steps still. Eight. Seven. We marched slowly on, as though following a hearse at our own funeral. Four steps more. Three steps. There it was now, right in front of us, the pit and its flames. I gathered all that was left of my strength, so that I could break from the ranks and throw myself upon the barbed wire. In the depths of my heart, I bade farewell to my father, to the whole universe; and, in spite of myself, the words formed themselves and issued in a whisper from my lips: *Yitgadal veyitkadach shmé raba.* . . . May His name be blessed and magnified. . . . My heart was bursting. The moment had come. I was face to face with the Angel of Death. . . .

No. Two steps from the pit we were ordered to turn to the left and made to go into a barracks.

I pressed my father's hand. He said:

"Do you remember Madame Schächter, in the train?"

Never shall I forget that night, the first night in camp, which has turned my life into one long night, seven times cursed and seven times sealed. Never shall I forget that smoke. Never shall I forget the little faces of the children, whose bodies I saw turned into wreaths of smoke beneath a silent blue sky. ■

Quotables

"The book [*Night*] was about my anger with God, not my disbelief. I quarrel with God. But after I quarrel, I pray."

—Elie Wiesel

Responding to the Selection

What words or images made the greatest impression on you? With your classmates, discuss the effect this selection had on you.

Reviewing the Selection

RECALLING / **INTERPRETING**

1. What does Madame Schächter see from the train? What do others on the train do in response to her cries? ▶▶ Why do you think the people on the train responded in this way to Madame Schächter's cries?
2. Where does the train stop? What do the people know about this place? What do the men who go for water learn about this place? ▶▶ How do the people feel about stopping at this place? Why do they feel this way?
3. What does the narrator have trouble believing is happening? ▶▶ Why does the narrator have trouble believing the events that are occurring around him? In what way do the thoughts of the narrator's father differ from the narrator's thoughts?
4. What do people begin to recite? What is strange about their recitation? ▶▶ What do the people believe about their fate?

SYNTHESIZING

5. What effect does the narrator's first night in camp have on him? In what way is this effect related to Wiesel's beliefs about bearing witness to the Holocaust?

Understanding Literature (Questions for Discussion)

1. **Aim.** A writer's **aim** is the primary purpose that his or her work is meant to achieve. Some general purposes that people have for writing include to express themselves, to persuade, to inform, and to create works of literary art. What aim or aims do you think Wiesel had when writing *Night*? Explain your response.

RESPONDING TO THE SELECTION

Ask students to write down the words and images that most affected them. Then ask them to form pairs or groups of three to discuss what they've written and their feelings about the selection.

ANSWERS FOR REVIEWING THE SELECTION

RECALLING AND INTERPRETING

1. **Recalling.** Madame Schächter sees flames and a great furnace. Other people on the train strike her and gag her.

Interpreting. The others on the train think Madame Schächter is mad. They are frightened by their situation and her cries are increasing their fear. Tempers are rising because they are in close quarters, without food or water. They may feel powerless over their situation, so making Madame Schächter quiet may make them feel that they can control something. They may fear that they will be punished if her cries are not quieted.

2. **Recalling.** The train stops at Auschwitz. The people have not heard of this place. They learn that it is a labor camp, conditions are good, families will not be split up, and that older people and invalids will work in the fields while the younger people toil in factories.

Interpreting. The people are relieved, because this place seems to be a fairly safe place.

3. **Recalling.** The narrator has trouble believing that people can get away with burning other people—that humanity would allow this.

Interpreting. The events that are occurring are so shocking and appalling that they seem impossible. The narrator's father is much more experienced and cynical than his son. He feels that "today anything is allowed."

(cont.)

ANSWERS FOR REVIEWING THE SELECTION (CONT.)

4. **Recalling.** The people begin to recite the prayer for the dead for themselves. The narrator has never seen people recite the prayer for the dead for themselves.

Interpreting. The people believe that they are about to die.

SYNTHESIZING

Responses will vary. Possible responses are given.

5. The narrator's first night in camp is burned into his memory. The narrator says he can never forget what happened on that night. Wiesel feels it is important for everyone to remember such horrors as those described in *Night*, as a memorial for those who died and as a reminder that such atrocities must never happen again.

Answers for Understanding Literature

Responses will vary. Possible responses are given.

1. Aim. *Night* aims to inform people about the horrors of the Holocaust. It is also a work of literary art.

2. Description and Simile. Madame Schächter is described as a quiet woman of about fifty with tense, burning eyes. She appears mad as she moans and cries out that she sees a fire. "She looked like a withered tree in a cornfield" is the simile used. She is like a withered tree in that she seems to have lost vitality. She may appear wrinkled, frail, and gray. She is like the withered tree in the cornfield because she is alone and out of place. She stands up, while the others try to blend in and stay in line to avoid trouble.

3. Foreshadowing. Madame Schächter has visions of a terrible fire and then of a furnace. She shouts out to others on the train car, asking them to see the flames, and they try to quiet her. Her shouts, however, make everyone in the car uneasy and add an element of tension to the selection. The people on the car do not want to believe that her vision might reflect events to come. The reader, too, is left wondering what meaning the woman's shouts might have in relation to the fate of the prisoners.

4. Image and Imagery. The desperate shouts of Madame Schächter, the barbed wire fences of the camp, the groups of people walking toward the frightening ditch reciting the Kaddish, and, finally, the flames shooting from a tall chimney into the black sky, are all images that make a lasting impression on the narrator.

Analytic Scale for Writing Skills

Grading scales for Responding in Writing appear on page 185.

2. **Description and Simile.** A **description** portrays a character, an object, or a scene. A **simile** is a comparison using *like* or *as.* What words and phrases are used to describe Madame Schächter? What simile does Wiesel use to describe her? In what way is she like the item to which she is compared?
3. **Foreshadowing. Foreshadowing** is the act of presenting materials that hint at events to occur later in a story. Explain Madame Schächter's vision, its effect, and its function in this selection.
4. **Image and Imagery.** An **image** is a word or phrase that names something that can be seen, heard, touched, tasted, or smelled. The images in a literary work are referred to, collectively, as the work's **imagery**. Which sensory experiences, or images, produce the most lasting and emotional memories for the narrator? for you?

Responding in Writing

1. **Creative Writing: Editorial or Speech.** Elie Wiesel has said, "Silence encourages the tormentor, never the tormented." With this in mind, choose an injustice against humanity about which you feel strongly. What do you want people to know about this injustice? What can people do to fight it? Write an editorial or speech about this injustice, one in which you denounce the actions or policies that cause human suffering and present ideas for change.
2. **Critical Essay: Analyzing the Narrator's Reactions.** At two points in this selection, the narrator and other people are filled with disbelief about their fates. Previously, they had been warned by a survivor of an earlier exile that people were being tortured and killed *en masse*, yet they failed to believe him. Identify the experiences or occurrences in this selection in which the narrator and others have difficulty believing. Discuss why they may have been filled with disbelief about the situation. What underlying beliefs did the narrator have about humanity? In what way are these beliefs related to his disbelief in the situation he faces? Do his feelings about humanity change? Explain.

Project

Commemorating the Holocaust. Holocaust Day is observed on April 15. As a class, observe your own Holocaust Day. Invite others from your community to take part in your observation of this event. Your commemoration might include sharing information about the Holocaust, speaking with survivors, or sharing published accounts of survivors' experiences. You may also wish to prepare works such as writing, sculpture, drawings or paintings, music, or theatrical performances as ways of sharing responses to what you have learned about the Holocaust. You may also wish to share information about current violations of human rights or to form a group at school that informs others about such abuses and offers suggestions about fighting injustice.

Project Notes

See the evaluation form for projects, Assessment Portfolio 4.12.

Commemorating the Holocaust. Ask students to hold a brainstorming session in which they gather ideas for their observation of Holocaust Day. Be sure that each student has a chance to contribute ideas for the event. When students have a general plan for the commemoration, they might want to divide tasks according to their interests and abilities. For example, students who are interested in theater or the arts might focus on this area. Other students might be in charge of doing library or Internet research, and others might be interested in doing interviews or arranging guest speakers.

PREREADING

from *The Bluest Eye*
by Toni Morrison

About the Author

TONI MORRISON
1931–

Toni Morrison was born Chloe Anthony Wofford in Lorain, Ohio. She grew up during the Great Depression and was educated at Howard University and at Cornell University, where she met her former husband, Harold Morrison. To support her two sons, Morrison worked as an editor at Random House, where she edited books written by Muhammad Ali, Angela Davis, and Toni Cade Bambara. She also taught classes at many colleges and universities. Morrison's novels, including *The Bluest Eye, Sula, The Song of Solomon, Tar Baby, Beloved,* and *Jazz,* explore issues central to the African-American female experience. Her work is renowned for its lyrical beauty and its power. She frequently uses elements of magical realism in her writing without sacrificing the realism and authenticity of her characters' experiences and voices. Morrison received a Pulitzer Prize in 1988 for *Beloved* and a Nobel Prize for literature in 1993.

About the Selection

The Bluest Eye is a starkly realistic and symbolically rich novel that reveals the difficulty of growing up as an African-American female in a racist society. The novel tells the tragic story of a young African-American girl named Pecola Breedlove, who is destroyed by the racism, poverty, and violence that surround and engulf her. In the following selection from the novel, Morrison reveals some of the ways in which Pecola's surroundings eat away at her sense of dignity and self-worth. Confronted with a narrow "white" standard of physical beauty, Pecola finds that her physical characteristics do not meet this ideal and believes that she is ugly. She desperately longs for blue eyes, believing that if she is conventionally pretty the suffering she experiences will end. Pecola's longing for blue eyes becomes a powerful and recurring symbol. Morrison also interweaves strands of children's literature throughout the novel, further emphasizing the difference between "white" ideals of childhood and Pecola's reality.

CONNECTIONS: Standards of Beauty

The physical characteristics that are considered beautiful vary greatly in different cultures, places, and historical periods. In the United States during the first part of the twentieth century, many girls longed to look like the child star Shirley Temple who was popular in films of the 1930s. Shirley Temple had curly fair hair, blue eyes, and dimpled cheeks. Narrow standards of beauty, such as the blond-haired, blue-eyed ideal, often emotionally scar people who do not match these standards. Today, more and more people are recognizing that beauty transcends hair or eye color, racial or cultural background, size, and age.

ADDITIONAL RESOURCES

READER'S GUIDE

- Selection Worksheet 2.4

ASSESSMENT PORTFOLIO

- Selection Check Test 4.2.7
- Selection Test 4.2.8

ESSENTIAL SKILLS PRACTICE BOOKS

- Writing 1.8, 1.20
- Study and Research 4.17

PREREADING EXTENSIONS

Some students might be interested in reading *The Bluest Eye* in its entirety or reading other works by Toni Morrison. You might also encourage them to read fiction and poetry by other acclaimed African-American women writers such as Alice Walker, Maya Angelou, Toni Cade Bambara, Mari Evans, Nikki Giovanni, and Gwendolyn Brooks. Students can find a novel, story collection, or poetry to read and present to the rest of the class.

SUPPORT FOR LEP STUDENTS

PRONUNCIATIONS OF PROPER NOUNS AND ADJECTIVES

Ma • rie Ap • pol • on • aire (mə rē´ ə päl´ə ner)
Pe • co • la Breed • love (pə kō´ la brēd´luv)
Miss Dun • ion (mis dun´ yən)
Ya • co • bow • ski (yä kub ou´ skē)

ADDITIONAL VOCABULARY

imperceptibly—unable to be detected
in earshot—within hearing distance
precaution—care taken to avoid danger
static—unchanging
vacuum—emptiness because of the absence of something

GOALS/OBJECTIVES

Studying this lesson will enable students to

- understand an African-American narrator's painful struggle with her self-image while living in a racist society
- describe Toni Morrison's literary accomplishments
- define the literary terms *parody* and *symbol*
- write a children's story and a critical essay which compares and contrasts the effects of racism
- work in small groups to research the standards of beauty that exist now or in the past in different cultures

READER'S JOURNAL

As an alternative activity, you might ask students to write about the reasons that people sometimes mistreat those whose appearance or lifestyle is different from their own. Have they ever witnessed this firsthand or felt that they themselves were the target of prejudice? How did witnessing such treatment or being the target of such treatment make them feel?

ANSWERS TO GUIDED READING QUESTIONS

1. Pecola wishes that she would disappear.

2. Pecola feels that she is ugly. She attributes her terrible family life and the way people treat her at school to her ugliness.

SPELLING AND VOCABULARY WORDS FROM THE SELECTION

assertion	inanimate
buffet	peal
conviction	petulant
despised	retina
ebb	rivulet
endurable	sundries
fervently	surfeit
flux	surge
hone	

VOCABULARY IN CONTEXT

- During the hurricane, giant waves will surge and cause damage to beachfront homes.
- The despised company continues to pollute the town's water supply.

READER'S JOURNAL

If you could change one of your characteristics, either a physical characteristic or a personality trait, which one would you change? Why? In what way do you think that this change would affect your life?

FROM

The Bluest Eye

TONI MORRISON

[Editor's note: Pecola Breedlove's home life is filled with poverty and violence. Pecola's mother, Mrs. Breedlove, and her father, Cholly, often have violent arguments. Pecola's brother Sammy often runs away to escape these arguments. Just before the following selection begins, Mrs. Breedlove and Cholly have had another terrible fight.]

Letting herself breathe easy now, Pecola covered her head with the quilt. The sick feeling, which she had tried to prevent by holding in her stomach, came quickly in spite of her precaution. There surged in her the desire to heave, but as always, she knew she would not.

"Please, God," she whispered into the palm of her hand. "Please make me disappear." She squeezed her eyes shut. Little parts of her body faded away. Now slowly, now with a rush. Slowly again. Her fingers went, one by one; then her arms disappeared all the way to the elbow. Her feet now. Yes, that was good. The legs all at once. It was hardest above the thighs. She had to be real still and pull. Her stomach would not go. But finally it, too, went away. Then her chest, her neck. The face was hard, too. Almost done, almost. Only her tight, tight eyes were left. They were always left.

Try as she might, she could never get her eyes to disappear. So what was the point? They were everything. Everything was there, in them. All of those pictures, all of those faces. She had long ago given up the idea of running away to see new pictures, new faces, as Sammy had so often done. He never took her, and he never thought about his going ahead of time, so it was never planned. It wouldn't have worked anyway. As long as she looked the way she did, as long as she was ugly, she would have to stay with these people. Somehow she belonged to them. Long hours she sat looking in the mirror, trying to discover the secret of the ugliness, the ugliness that made her ignored or despised at school, by teachers and

1 *What does Pecola wish would happen?*

2 *How does Pecola feel about herself? What effect does she think her physical characteristics have on her life?*

WORDS FOR EVERYDAY USE

surge (surj) *vi.,* have a heavy, violent swelling motion

de • spised (di spīz´d) *adj.,* looked down on; hated

ADDITIONAL QUESTIONS AND ACTIVITIES

Children are especially sensitive to differences in others. This is why teasing and ridicule among groups of children is so common. If people are taught when they are young that differences in others are to be valued, not ridiculed, then they have a better chance of growing up to be tolerant adults. If you could spend an afternoon with Pecola Breedlove's peers, what might you try to teach them about tolerance and respect? What different methods would you use to try to change the attitudes of these children? With a partner, create a lesson plan that attempts to teach tolerance to children. When you have completed your plan, present it to the rest of the class for critique.

classmates alike. She was the only member of her class who sat alone at a double desk. The first letter of her last name forced her to sit in the front of the room always. But what about Marie Appolonaire? Marie was in front of her, but she shared a desk with Luke Angelino. Her teachers had always treated her this way. They tried never to glance at her, and called on her only when everyone was required to respond. She also knew that when one of the girls at school wanted to be particularly insulting to a boy, or wanted to get an immediate response from him, she could say, "Bobby loves Pecola Breedlove! Bobby loves Pecola Breedlove!" and never fail to get peals of laughter from those in earshot, and mock anger from the accused.

It had occurred to Pecola some time ago that if her eyes, those eyes that held the pictures, and knew the sights—if those eyes of hers were different, that is to say, beautiful, she herself would be different. Her teeth were good, and at least her nose was not big and flat like some of those who were thought so cute. If she looked different, beautiful, maybe Cholly would be different, and Mrs. Breedlove too. Maybe they'd say, "Why, look at pretty-eyed Pecola. We mustn't do bad things in front of those pretty eyes."

Pretty eyes. Pretty blue eyes. Big blue pretty eyes.
Run, Jip, run. Jip runs, Alice runs. Alice has blue eyes.
Jerry has blue eyes. Jerry runs. Alice runs. They run
with their blue eyes. Four blue eyes. Four pretty
blue eyes. Blue-sky eyes. Blue—like Mrs. Forrest's
blue blouse eyes. Morning-glory-blue-eyes.
Alice-and-Jerry-blue-storybook-eyes.

Each night, without fail, she prayed for blue eyes. Fervently, for a year she had prayed. Although somewhat discouraged, she was not without hope. To have something as wonderful as that happen would take a long, long time.

Thrown, in this way, into the binding conviction that only a miracle could relieve her, she would never know her beauty. She would see only what there was to see: the eyes of other people.

She walks down Garden Avenue to a small grocery store which sells penny candy. Three pennies are in her shoe—slipping back and forth between the sock and the inner sole. With each step she feels the painful press of the coins against her foot. A sweet, endurable, even cherished irritation, full of promise and delicate security. There is plenty of time to consider what to buy. Now, however, she moves down an avenue gently buffeted by the familiar and therefore loved images. The dandelions at the base of the telephone pole. Why, she wonders, do people call them weeds? She thought they were pretty. But grownups say, "Miss Dunion keeps her yard so nice. Not a dandelion anywhere." Hunkie women in black babushkas[1] go into the fields with baskets to pull them up. But they do not want the yellow heads—only the jagged leaves. They make dandelion soup. Dandelion wine. Nobody loves the head of a dandelion. Maybe because they are so many, strong, and soon.

There was the sidewalk crack shaped like a Y, and the other one that lifted the concrete up from the dirt floor. Frequently her sloughing step had made her trip over that one. Skates would go well over this sidewalk—old it was, and smooth; it made the

1. **babushkas.** Scarves worn over the heads of women or girls and tied under the chin

❶ *What has Pecola prayed for every night for a year?*

❷ *According to the narrator, what effect does Pecola's wish have on her life?*

❸ *In what way does Pecola think her life would be different if she had pretty eyes?*

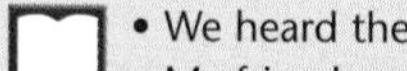

Words for Everyday Use

peal (pēl) *n.,* loud, prolonged sound
fer • vent • ly (fur´vənt lē) *adv.,* intensely
con • vic • tion (kən vik´shən) *n.,* strong belief
en • dur • a • ble (en do͞or´ə bəl) *adj.* bearable
buf • fet (buf´it) *vt.,* hit, strike

Answers to Guided Reading Questions

❶ Pecola has prayed for blue eyes every night for a year.

❷ The narrator says that because Pecola believes that only blue eyes can relieve her suffering, she will never know her own beauty.

❸ Pecola thinks her parents would behave more kindly if she had pretty eyes.

Cross-curricular Activities

Arts and Humanities and Mathematics and Sciences

Throughout this selection, Pecola refers to dandelions as plants that have special meaning for her. The dandelions become an important element in the story because they reflect both the feelings of rejection Pecola experiences and Pecola's own beauty, of which she has only a vague notion. Have students research different types of flowers, plants, and trees and find one that reflects something in their lives or their personalities. Make notes about its physical characteristics, where it grows, and what moisture and sunlight it needs in order to grow. Students might also make notes about the popular view of this particular flower, plant, or tree. Encourage them to write a description that expresses why this flower, plant, or tree has special meaning.

Vocabulary in Context

- We heard the peal of the school bell and rushed to our lockers.
- My friend and I worked fervently for many days on our important presentation.
- His conviction was that all children deserve a good education.
- The weather this month was warm and uncomfortable but endurable.
- We heard the tapping of the raindrops as they began to buffet our car.

Answers to Guided Reading Questions

1 Mr. Yacobowski is unable to see Pecola as a person.

ANALYTIC SCALES FOR WRITING SKILLS

(SEE PAGE 195.)

Assign a score from 1 to 25 for each grading criterion below. (For more detailed evaluation, see the evaluation forms for writing, revising, and proofreading, Assessment Portfolio 4.1–4.9.)

1. Children's Story

- **Content/Unity.** The story includes characters of different cultural, social, and economic backgrounds and centers around a conflict based on these differences.
- **Organization/Coherence.** The story features a clear conflict and a character who resolves the conflict in a believable and interesting way.
- **Language/Style.** The story uses simple language that is appropriate for young children.
- **Conventions.** The story avoids errors in spelling, grammar, usage, mechanics, and manuscript form.

▶ For additional practice, see Essential Skills Practice Book: Writing 1.8.

2. Critical Essay

- **Content/Unity.** The critical essay compares and contrasts the effects of the two types of racism presented in *Kaffir Boy* and *The Bluest Eye*.
- **Organization/Coherence.** The essay presents a thesis in an introductory paragraph, supports this thesis with evidence from both texts, and comes to a conclusion in a final paragraph.
- **Language/Style.** The essay uses vivid and precise nouns, verbs, and modifiers.
- **Conventions.** The essay avoids errors in spelling, grammar, usage, mechanics, and manuscript form.

▶ For additional practice, see Essential Skills Practice Book: Writing 1.20.

***Gwendolyn.** John Sloan, 1918. National Museum of American Art, Smithsonian Institution, Gift of Mrs. John Sloan/Art Resource, NY*

wheels glide evenly, with a mild whirr. The newly paved walks were bumpy and uncomfortable, and the sound of skate wheels on new walks was grating.

These and other inanimate things she saw and experienced. They were real to her. She knew them. They were the codes and touchstones of the world, capable of translation and possession. She owned the crack that made her stumble; she owned the clumps of dandelions whose white heads, last fall, she had blown away; whose yellow heads, this fall, she peered into. And owning them made her part of the world, and the world a part of her.

She climbs four wooden steps to the door of Yacobowski's Fresh Veg. Meat and Sundries Store. A bell tinkles as she opens it. Standing before the counter, she looks at the array of candies. All Mary Janes, she decides. Three for a penny. The resistant sweetness that breaks open at last to deliver peanut butter—the oil and salt which complement the sweet pull of caramel. A peal of anticipation unsettles her stomach.

1 *What is Mr. Yacobowski unable to do?*

She pulls off her shoe and takes out the three pennies. The gray head of Mr. Yacobowski looms up over the counter. He urges his eyes out of his thoughts to encounter her. Blue eyes. Blear-dropped. Slowly, like Indian summer moving imperceptibly toward fall, he looks toward her. Somewhere between retina and object, between vision and view, his eyes draw back, hesitate, and hover. At some fixed point in time and space he senses that he need not waste the effort of a glance. He does not see her, because for him there is nothing to see. How can a fifty-two-year-old white immigrant storekeeper with the taste of potatoes

Words for Everyday Use

in • an • i • mate (in an´ ə mit) *adj.,* not living
sun • dries (sun´ drēz) *n.,* minor items
ret • i • na (ret´´n ə) *n.,* innermost coat lining the interior of the eyeball

Vocabulary in Context

- Luckily, only dishes, knickknacks, and other inanimate objects were harmed during the earthquake.
- We weaved through the aisles of the market, which were packed with food and sundries.
- The chart showed the different parts of the human eye, including the cornea, the iris, and the retina.

and beer in his mouth, his mind honed on the doe-eyed Virgin Mary, his sensibilities blunted by a permanent awareness of loss, *see* a little black girl? Nothing in his life even suggested that the feat was possible, not to say desirable or necessary.

"Yeah?"

She looks up at him and sees the vacuum where curiosity ought to lodge. And something more. The total absence of human recognition—the glazed separateness. She does not know what keeps his glance suspended. Perhaps because he is grown, or a man, and she a little girl. But she has seen interest, disgust, even anger in grown male eyes. Yet this vacuum is not new to her. It has an edge; somewhere in the bottom lid is the distaste. She has seen it lurking in the eyes of all white people.

So. The distaste must be for her, her blackness. All things in her are flux and anticipation. But her blackness is static and dread. And it is the blackness that accounts for, that creates, the vacuum edged with distaste in white eyes.

She points her finger at the Mary Janes—a little black shaft of finger, its tip pressed on the display window. The quietly inoffensive assertion of a black child's attempt to communicate with a white adult.

"Them." The word is more sigh than sense.

"What? These? These?" Phlegm and impatience mingle in his voice.

She shakes her head, her fingertip fixed on the spot which, in her view, at any rate, identifies the Mary Janes. He cannot see her view—the angle of his vision, the slant of her finger, makes it incomprehensible to him. His lumpy red hand plops around in the glass casing like the agitated head of a chicken outraged by the loss of its body.

"Christ. Kantcha talk?"

His fingers brush the Mary Janes.

She nods.

"Well, why'nt you say so? One? How many?"

Pecola unfolds her fist, showing the three pennies. He scoots three Mary Janes toward her—three yellow rectangles in each packet. She holds the money toward him. He hesitates, not wanting to touch her hand. She does not know how to move the finger of her right hand from the display counter or how to get the coins out of her left hand. Finally he reaches over and takes the pennies from her hand. His nails graze her damp palm.

Outside, Pecola feels the inexplicable shame ebb.

Dandelions. A dart of affection leaps out from her to them. But they do not look at her and do not send love back. She thinks, "They *are* ugly. They *are* weeds." Preoccupied with that revelation, she trips on the sidewalk crack. Anger stirs and wakes in her; it opens its mouth, and like a hot-mouthed puppy, laps up the dredges of her shame.

Anger is better. There is a sense of being in anger. A reality and presence. An awareness of worth. It is a lovely surging. Her thoughts fall back to Mr. Yacobowski's eyes, his phlegmy voice. The anger will not hold; the puppy is too easily surfeited. Its thirst too quickly quenched, it sleeps. The shame wells up again, its muddy rivulets seeping into her eyes. What to do before the tears come. She remembers the Mary Janes.

Each pale yellow wrapper has a picture on it. A picture of little Mary Jane, for whom the candy is named. Smiling white face. Blond hair in gentle disarray, blue eyes looking at her out of a world of clean comfort. The eyes are petulant, mischievous. To Pecola they are simply pretty. She eats the candy, and its sweetness is good. To eat the candy is somehow to eat the eyes, eat Mary Jane. Love Mary Jane. Be Mary Jane. ■

❶ *What emotions is Pecola feeling? What does she think about the dandelions now?*

❷ *What does Pecola realize about Mr. Yacobowski's gaze?*

❸ *What is anger better than? Why?*

❹ *Why does Pecola love to eat Mary Janes?*

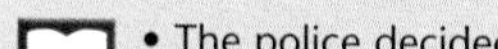

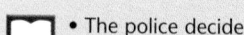

WORDS FOR EVERYDAY USE

hone (hōn´) *vi.,* focus
flux (fluks) *n.,* continuous movement or change
as • ser • tion (a sur´shən) *n.,* positive statement
ebb (eb) *vi.,* flow back out, recede
sur • feit (sur´fit) *vi.,* overindulge; fill to excess
riv • u • let (riv´yoo lit) *n.,* little stream, brook
pet • u • lant (pech´ə lənt) *adj.,* impatient or irritable

Answers to Guided Reading Questions

❶ Pecola is feeling shame and anger. She decides that dandelions are ugly weeds after all.

❷ Mr. Yacobowski's gaze contains distaste for her blackness.

❸ Anger is better than the hopeless shame that makes Pecola feel as though she does not exist at all. Pecola feels that there is a "sense of being" in anger. It is an awareness of a her worth as a human being.

❹ Pecola loves to eat Mary Janes because she feels that somehow they allow her to consume and be blue-eyed Mary Jane.

Selection Check Test with Answers

EX. What part of her body can't Pecola imagine away?
Pecola can't imagine away her eyes.

1. What is Pecola the only member of her class to do?
Pecola is the only member of her class to sit alone at a double desk.

2. What has Pecola prayed for every day for a year?
She has prayed for blue eyes.

3. For what does Pecola go to the grocery store?
Pecola goes to the grocery store to buy Mary Janes.

4. What is Mr. Yacobowski unable to see?
He is unable to see Pecola.

5. What type of flower does Pecola decide is an ugly weed?
Pecola decides that dandelions are ugly weeds.

Vocabulary in Context

- The police decided to hone in on the suspicious-looking black van.
- Jean lost her job last month, and since then her life has been in a state of flux.
- The students' protest was an assertion of their rights as citizens of the community.
- We sat on the deck and watched the ebb and flow of the tide.
- The elaborate buffet should surfeit everyone's hunger.
- Our feet were cold and damp from crossing the many rivulets in the forest.
- The petulant child threw a temper tantrum in the grocery store.

RESPONDING TO THE SELECTION

You might ask students to form pairs and take turns role playing conversations between themselves and one of Pecola's teachers or Mr. Yacobowski. One student can play the role of the teacher or Mr. Yacobowski while the other plays himself or herself.

ANSWERS FOR REVIEWING THE SELECTION

RECALLING AND INTERPRETING

1. **Recalling.** Pecola prays to God and asks Him to make her disappear. She tries to imagine parts of her body fading away. **Interpreting.** Pecola is terribly frightened by her parents' arguments and feels insignificant and worthless, so she longs to simply disappear to escape from her troubles.

2. **Recalling.** Pecola thinks that she is ugly. She thinks that blue eyes would make her beautiful. **Interpreting.** A white standard of beauty has damaged Pecola's self-esteem and has convinced her that she is ugly and that only blue eyes can make her life better. Pecola believes that her parents might behave better if she had blue eyes.

3. **Recalling.** Pecola goes to Mr. Yacobowski's store to buy candy—three Mary Janes. Pecola points to the display window to indicate what she wants. Mr. Yacobowski is rude to Pecola. **Interpreting.** Mr. Yacobowski is unable to "see" Pecola as a person because of his racism; he only feels distaste for her blackness. Pecola is frightened of and shamed by Mr. Yacobowski. She is too ashamed to move.

4. **Recalling.** Pecola thinks that dandelions are pretty and she wonders why nobody loves them and thinks that it is because "they are so many, strong, and soon." After she leaves the store, Pecola decides that they are ugly weeds. **Interpreting.** Pecola feels relatively happy and secure because (cont.)

Responding to the Selection

Imagine that you are Pecola's friend. What advice would you give her about her life? What would you say if you had an opportunity to speak to her teachers? to Mr. Yacobowski?

Reviewing the Selection

RECALLING		INTERPRETING
1. What does Pecola pray for at the beginning of the selection? What does she try to imagine?	▶▶	Why do you think Pecola prays for and tries to imagine this thing happening?
2. What does Pecola think about the way she looks? What does she think would make her beautiful?	▶▶	In what way has a white standard of beauty affected the way that Pecola feels about herself? In what way does Pecola think "pretty" eyes would make her life different?
3. Why does Pecola go to Yacobowski's store? What does she do to indicate what she wants? In what way does Mr. Yacobowski treat Pecola?	▶▶	Why is Mr. Yacobowski unable to "see" Pecola? How does she feel about Mr. Yacobowski? Why is she unable to move her right hand to give him the coins held in her left hand?
4. What does Pecola think about dandelions before she arrives at the store? What does she think about dandelions after she leaves the store?	▶▶	How does Pecola feel before she arrives at the store? after she leaves? Why? Why does her attitude toward dandelions change?

SYNTHESIZING

5. Racism is the belief in the inferiority of a group of people based on genetic, observable physical features. In what way has racism affected Pecola Breedlove? In what way has it damaged how she feels about herself? In what way has it affected how she interacts with others?

Understanding Literature (Questions for Discussion)

1. **Symbol.** A **symbol** is a thing that stands for or represents both itself and something else. What do Mary Janes represent to Pecola? What do blue eyes represent to Pecola? What do blue eyes symbolize in this selection? What do dandelions symbolize in this selection?

ANSWERS FOR REVIEWING THE SELECTION (CONT.)

she is going down a familiar street to buy her favorite candy. After she leaves, Pecola feels ashamed because of the way Mr. Yacobowski treats her. Pecola starts to entertain her own opinions about beauty, but once she has been shamed she accepts the standard view of beauty.

SYNTHESIZING

Responses will vary. Possible responses are given.

5. Racism has destroyed Pecola's sense of self-worth. Because she cannot meet the white standard of beauty, Pecola believes that she is ugly and that her ugliness causes others to despise her. She feels ashamed and wishes that she would disappear. Racism has made it difficult for Pecola to talk to and interact with others, particularly whites because she senses their distaste.

2. **Parody.** A **parody** is a literary work that imitates another work for humorous, often satirical, purposes. On page 191, Morrison parodies typical young children's literature. What flaws or failings in this literature is Morrison trying to point out?

Responding in Writing

1. **Creative Writing: Children's Story.** Throughout *The Bluest Eye,* Morrison parodies children's literature that presents an overly idealistic view of the world and that only focuses on white children. Write a children's story that includes racial and cultural diversity and characters of different social and economic backgrounds. Choose a situation in which one of your characters faces a conflict based on difference. Your story should show your character resolving the conflict himself or herself. Focus on a problem or issue and how it affects your character. Keep your audience in mind and use simple language. You may wish to illustrate your story and share it with a younger student.

2. **Critical Essay: Comparing and Contrasting Effects of Racism.** Read the selection from Mark Mathabane's *Kaffir Boy* on page 196. Then write an essay in which you compare and contrast the effects of racism, manifested in the system of apartheid, on South African blacks as presented in *Kaffir Boy* with the effects of a more subtle sort of racism on African Americans as presented in *The Bluest Eye.* Begin by creating a Venn diagram like the one below and listing ways in which apartheid and its effects on Mathabane are similar to or different from racism and its effects on Pecola Breedlove. Present your thesis in an introductory paragraph; support your thesis with evidence from both texts in following paragraphs; and come to a conclusion in a final paragraph.

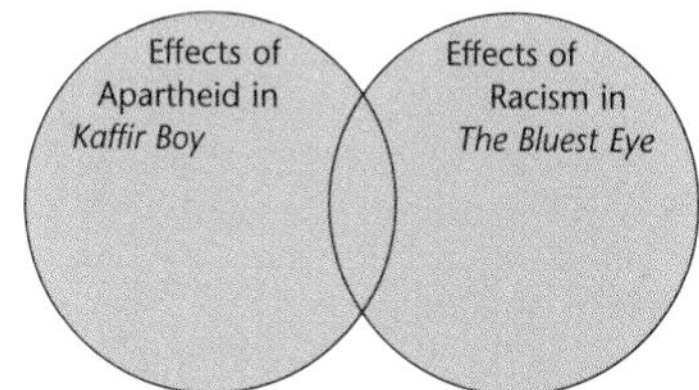

Project

Researching Standards of Beauty. Work in small groups to research the standards of beauty that exist in different cultures and time periods. For example, one group might research the standard of beauty idealized during the European Renaissance or during Europe's Baroque period. Other groups might research standards of beauty in India, China, Japan, or in some of the many African cultures. Bring in photographs, sketches, or pictures from magazines showing the physical characteristics that are considered beautiful in the culture and historical period you researched. Then use a world map and your images to create a collage showing the many different ideals of beauty around the world.

Answers for Understanding Literature

Responses will vary. Possible responses are given.

1. **Symbol.** Mary Janes represent the attainment of beauty to Pecola. Blue eyes represent beauty, happiness, and goodness to Pecola. In this selection, blue eyes symbolize the negative impact of a white standard of beauty on a young African-American female. Dandelions are a symbol of African-American beauty—Pecola finds these flowers beautiful and wonders why nobody admires and loves them, but she too decides they are ugly when Mr. Yacobowski's scorn makes her feel ashamed and angry about who she is.

2. **Parody.** Morrison is trying to point out that many young children's books present overly idealized and vapid views of family life and that many of them focus exclusively on white children, their families, and activities.

Analytic Scales for Writing Skills

Grading scales for Responding in Writing appear on page 192.

Project Notes

See the evaluation form for projects, Assessment Portfolio 4.12.

Researching Standards of Beauty. Allow students adequate time to conduct their research in small groups. Remind them of the different resources available to them at the library such as books, encyclopedias, and magazines. Remind students that they can create their own original drawings to use in the class collage.

To create the class collage, you can use a poster-size map from a bookstore or ask the students to trace or draw freehand a map on a large sheet of paper.

ADDITIONAL RESOURCES

READER'S GUIDE

- Selection Worksheet 2.5

ASSESSMENT PORTFOLIO

- Selection Check Test 2.2.13
- Selection Test 2.2.14

ESSENTIAL SKILLS PRACTICE BOOKS

- Writing 1.8, 1.10, 1.20
- Study and Research 4.17
- Applied English/Tech Prep 5.1

PREREADING EXTENSIONS

Ask students to research racial segregation in the United States and the people and events that led to the dissolution of segregation laws. Each student should focus on one aspect of this era in United States history. Possible topics include Jim Crow laws, Rosa Parks and the Montgomery Bus Boycott, the formation of the NAACP, Thurgood Marshall, Brown vs. Board of Education, Governor George Wallace and the University of Alabama, Martin Luther King, Jr., and the Civil Rights Act of 1964. Students should share their information with the rest of the class.

SUPPORT FOR LEP STUDENTS

PRONUNCIATIONS OF PROPER NOUNS AND ADJECTIVES

Kaf • fir (kaf´ər)
Mer • ce • des Benz (mer sā´dēz benz´)
Pre • tor • i • a (prē tôr´ē ə)
Rolls Royce (rols´ rois´)

ADDITIONAL VOCABULARY

grovelling—extremely humble
recesses—hollow places
stupor—mental dullness
trodden—walked
venom—hatred, ill will

PREREADING

from *Kaffir Boy*
by Mark Mathabane

About the Author

MARK MATHABANE
1960–

Mark Mathabane grew up in a shack in Alexandra, a ghetto on the outskirts of Johannesburg. Mathabane and his siblings slept on a piece of cardboard under the kitchen table, and his family often suffered from hunger. Education was not free for blacks in South Africa, and Mathabane's mother, who believed that education was the only way to succeed, struggled to send him to a tribal school where blacks were compelled to study in their native Bantu languages. Believing that learning English was a "key" that would "unlock doors," Mathabane improved his English by reading books forbidden in his school. Inspired by outspoken African-American tennis player Arthur Ashe, Mathabane took up tennis and won a scholarship to a university in the United States. When he realized that he would not become a professional tennis player, Mathabane began to write his autobiography. *Kaffir Boy* was published in 1986. Mathabane works today as a writer and lecturer. Many of his family members remain in South Africa.

About the Selection

Kaffir Boy is an **autobiography,** or story of a person's life written by that person. It tells of a young man who grew up under apartheid in South Africa, a country composed of many different peoples. In addition to the many native African peoples, South Africa is home to people of mixed heritage; to Asians; and to whites, including Afrikaners (or descendants of Dutch, French, and German settlers) and people of English descent. Although whites compose only a sixth of the population, they controlled South Africa's government until recently. *Apartheid* is an Afrikaans word meaning "apartness." In practice, apartheid is a policy of racial segregation and political and economic discrimination against nonwhites. Under this system, nonwhites were forced to live in separate regions and were allowed to perform only the most menial jobs. Native Africans also received inferior educations. Because they were deprived of citizenship, they were not allowed to participate in their country's government. The word *Kaffir* is an Arabic term meaning "infidel," an insulting term that white South Africans often used when referring to blacks. (For more information on apartheid, see Insights: Apartheid, page 203.)

CONNECTIONS: Segregation at Home and Abroad: The Montgomery Bus Boycott

During the first half of the nineteenth century, many laws that segregated and discriminated against African Americans existed in the United States. On December 1, 1955, a woman named Rosa Parks challenged one of these laws when she refused to give up her seat on a segregated bus to a white person. Mrs. Parks was arrested, but her act of defiance sparked a successful boycott of the Montgomery buses led by Civil Rights leader Martin Luther King, Jr. In the following selection, the narrator also faces arrest when he mistakenly boards a "whites only" bus in South Africa.

GOALS/OBJECTIVES

Studying this lesson will enable students to

- experience a young black narrator's confrontation with the cold reality of apartheid
- describe the life and accomplishments of Mark Mathabane
- discuss apartheid in South Africa
- define the literary terms *tone* and *archetype*
- write a fictional letter of complaint and write a critical essay that analyzes a character
- conduct computer-assisted research on a specific topic

READER'S JOURNAL

Imagine that you live in a place and time in which you are discriminated against based on whether or not you have dimples. For example, if you don't have dimples, you are deprived of certain freedoms and economic and political opportunities. (If you do have dimples, imagine that it is your group instead that is experiencing this oppression.) Then respond to the following questions: How would you feel about yourself and your dimples or lack thereof? How would you feel about your oppressors? What would you think of the laws that limited opportunities or created opportunities, depending on your dimples?

FROM

Kaffir Boy

MARK MATHABANE

After a dozen or so trips to the white world, I began to feel somewhat comfortable amid the sea of white faces. There were still remnants of my childhood dread of white people somewhere in the recesses of my mind, but nothing major happened to rekindle it. On the contrary, the Smiths' kind treatment of me each time I visited them, though in most ways paternalistic, did much to alleviate that fear, and I began to naively assume that maybe white people weren't all that bad after all.

But one day something happened to cause me to think twice before declaring white terror more the fantasy of movies than the reality of day-to-day living.

It was a Saturday, and Granny took me along to her other gardening job in Pretoria, the capital of apartheid, because she needed help. Thinking that this was another way of getting books, I eagerly accompanied her. We spent the day doing the usual: raking leaves, pruning bushes, watering flowers and weeding the lawn. I washed cars, swept driveways and polished the *baas*'s[1] shoes. At four, dead tired, we left for the bus stop about a mile away.

As we waited for the bus to Alexandra, Granny untied a rag from her waist, in which she kept money, and said, "Wait here, child, I'm going to the store across the street to get some change. These black drivers may leave us if we don't have the proper change. Be on the lookout for the bus. If it comes while I'm still away, kindly ask the driver to wait. Don't wander away from here or you'll end up in trouble."

I understood well what she meant by "trouble." It being a sunny Saturday afternoon, white people milled all over the place—walking in and out of boutiques, in and out of flowershops, in and out of hotels, in and out of department stores, in and out of Mercedes Benzes, Rolls-Royces and other expensive cars, in and out of tennis courts, in and out of houses and flats, and in but never out of my consciousness.

1. ***baas's.*** Boss's

❶ Of what did the narrator have a childhood dread?

❷ Why did the narrator begin to assume that white people were not so bad? What word does he use to qualify the Smiths' kindness?

❸ What does the narrator's grandmother mean by "trouble"?

WORDS FOR EVERYDAY USE

rem • nant (rem´nənt) *n.*, what is left over; small, remaining part

pa • ter • nal • is • tic (pə tʉr´nəl is´tik) *adj.*, fatherly in a condescending manner

al • le • vi • ate (ə lē´vē āt´) *vt.*, reduce or decrease

READER'S JOURNAL

If some students have experienced prejudice and felt excluded because of race, gender, religion, lifestyle, or appearance, ask them to describe their experiences in their journals. How did this mistreatment make them feel?

ANSWERS TO GUIDED READING QUESTIONS

❶ The narrator had a childhood dread of white people.

❷ The narrator began to feel differently about white people because the Smiths were kind to him. The narrator qualifies the Smiths' kindness with the word paternalistic.

❸ The narrator's grandmother means that the narrator should keep out of the way of white people or he might get in trouble.

SPELLING AND VOCABULARY WORDS FROM THE SELECTION

affirm
alleviate
appease
contritely
disembark
fusillade
paternalistic
pervasiveness
remnant
segregation
tirade
vigorously

VOCABULARY IN CONTEXT

- The empty bottle of sunscreen was the last remnant of my vacation at the beach.
- Jody disliked it when her brother acted bossy and paternalistic toward her.
- Exercising daily helps Vanessa to alleviate her feelings of stress.

Answers to Guided Reading Questions

❶ Granny takes the blame for the narrator's mistake in a groveling tone of voice. The bus driver says that he could have the narrator and his grandmother arrested.

❷ The narrator mistakenly got on a "white" bus. The bus driver is angry and rude and he further humiliates the narrator.

❸ The situation seems particularly unreal to the narrator because he never knew that white people rode buses since he sees so many cars.

❹ The narrator's grandmother says that the narrator is deranged and unable to learn. She wipes the steps that he has trodden upon with her dress.

Additional Questions and Activities

Inform students that although the laws of apartheid have now been repealed in South Africa, it remains difficult to change racial stereotypes and hostility held by people like the bus driver in this selection. If you were on the bus when the narrator was being mistreated by the driver, what might you have done? Do you think you could have done anything to change the man's mind at that moment? Why, or why not? What kinds of things might be done to change these attitudes over time?

Quotables

"Children's talent to endure stems from their ignorance of alternatives."

—Maya Angelou

❶ *What does Granny say to the bus driver? In what tone of voice must she say it? What does the bus driver say that he could do?*

❷ *What mistake has the narrator made? In what way does the bus driver react to the narrator's mistake?*

❸ *What makes the situation seem particularly unreal to the narrator?*

❹ *What does the narrator's grandmother say about him? What does she do that horrifies the narrator?*

Granny hobbled across the street. Exhausted by the day's work, I sat on the bundle of newspapers, took out a comic book from my knapsack and buried my face in it. I had been reading for some time when I heard a bus screech to a halt not too far from where I sat. Dropping the comic book, I rushed to the door, so I could tell the driver to wait for Granny, who was waving vigorously at me from across the street, yelling something I couldn't quite make out. Lifting my head up as I came up the steps, I saw that I was in a "white" bus. I froze. My presence on the bus so startled several white old ladies who were about to disembark that they fled to the back.

"*Vootsek*, off this bus, Kaffir!" thundered the red-necked white driver. "Don't you see this is a white bus!"

Realising the tragic mistake I had committed, I tried to fly off the bus, but I could not. I thought I was in some kind of nightmare, and the fact that I had thought white people never rode buses because of all the cars they had made everything the more unreal.

But reality came in the venom the white bus driver was spitting as he reached for the side door to come after me. "I said get off the bloody bus, Kaffir!" I shut my eyes. I felt a pair of cold hands clutch my neck and yank me off the bus. I tumbled down the steps and landed on the concrete pavement. I must have prayed a million times.

Thinking that anytime I would be kicked in the face by the white bus driver, I started begging for mercy.

"Sorry, *mei baas*," I whimpered. "Sorry, *mei baas*. Me make big mistake. Forgive me, *mei baas*. This Kaffir did not know bus for white people."

All this time my eyes were shut.

Suddenly I heard, "He's my pickaninny,[2] *baas*. I'm at fault." It was Granny's voice. I opened my eyes to find her standing behind me, facing the white bus driver, who was in front of me. Apparently it was she who had jerked me off the bus.

"He's harmless, *mei baas*," Granny went on in the most grovelling of voices. "He no cause *lo* trouble. Me to blame, me, *baas*. Me left him alone."

"Never mind who's to blame," the white driver said hotly, "why do you let him get into the wrong buses! You know I could have you both arrested for it!"

"He no know, *mei baas*. He no know. He only *kind* [child]."

"What do you mean he doesn't know," the white bus driver returned. "Don't you teach Kaffir children anything about the laws?"

"He can't learn, *mei baas*," Granny said dramatically. "*Lo* pickaninny *lo mal* [The pickaninny is deranged, my lord]," Granny gestured with her hands to indicate that mine was not a normal insanity. She then shoved me aside, and to my moral horror, began wiping with her dress the steps where I had trodden. This appeased the white bus driver, for after unleashing a tirade of how stupid and uncivilized black people were, he returned to the bus and drove off. Granny dragged me—I was in some sort of stupor—by the neck back to the black bus stop.

"What do you mean climbing into white people's buses, heh?" She shook with rage. "Do you want to get us killed?"

"I didn't know it was the white people's bus," I said contritely.

"You black liar," Granny exploded. "What do you mean you didn't know? Haven't you got eyes to see?"

2. **pickaninny.** Derogatory term for a black child

Words for Everyday Use

vig • or • ous • ly (vig´ ər əs lē) *adv.*, with energy and force

dis • em • bark (dis´im bärk´) *vi.*, leave a means of transportation

ap • pease (ə pēz´) *vt.*, satisfy by giving into the demands of

ti • rade (tī´rād´) *n.*, long speech, especially one that is critical or angry

con • trite • ly (kən trīt´lē) *adv.*, apologetically

Vocabulary in Context

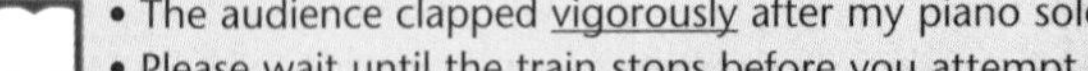

- The audience clapped vigorously after my piano solo.
- Please wait until the train stops before you attempt to disembark.
- A bottle of juice and a toy might appease the crying baby for several moments.
- The customer went into an angry tirade about the store's rising prices.
- "I didn't mean to step on your foot," Josh said contritely.

Courtesy of Archive Photo

"Granny, I swear I didn't know. I had never seen white people riding buses before, so when I heard this bus coming, I thought it was ours."

"Don't lie to me." She shook a finger in my face. "Can't you tell a black bus when you see one! Are you colour-blind? Or have you really gone mad! It must be all those books you're always reading!"

"I promise it won't happen again."

"If that's how you're going to behave each time you're among white people," Granny continued her verbal fusillade, "then this is the last trip you'll make with me. You know that had that white bus driver not been kind, we would now be in Number Four,[3] you know that?"

"But Granny, I only stood on the steps," I said. "I would have understood had I sat on any seat."

"Shut up, you black imp," Granny screamed. "Shut up before I make you! You're always doing things you shouldn't be doing! That's your nature and you know it! You can get away with your bad behaviour in Alexandra, among black people, but not here! This is the white world!"

I remained silent, wondering whether I had underestimated the enormity of my crime of standing on the steps of a white bus. Were the poor white passengers going to die as a result?

➊ *What does the narrator wonder?*

3. **Number Four.** Prison for nonwhite South Africans

Words for Everyday Use

fu • sil • lade (fyo͞o´sə lād´) *n.*, rapid fire or attack

Vocabulary in Context

• The soldiers could hear the fusillade of enemy missiles all day and all night.

Answers to Guided Reading Questions

➊ The narrator wonders if he has underestimated the seriousness of his actions and if the white passengers will die as a result of his actions.

Analytic Scales for Writing Skills

(SEE PAGE 202.)

Assign a score from 1 to 25 for each grading criterion below. (For more detailed evaluation, see the evaluation forms for writing, revising, and proofreading, Assessment Portfolio 4.1–4.9.)

1. Letter of Complaint

- **Content/Unity.** The letter complains about the humiliating experience of the narrator and his grandmother in *Kaffir Boy* and then demands that the bus company change its policy.
- **Organization/Coherence.** The letter first describes the writer's complaints about the bus company's policy of segregation and then explains why this policy needs to change.
- **Language/Style.** The letter uses language that sounds clear, firm, and professional in tone.
- **Conventions.** The letter avoids errors in spelling, grammar, usage, and mechanics, and it follows proper business letter form.

▶For additional practice, see Essential Skills Practice Books: Writing 1.8 and Applied English/Tech Prep 5.1.

2. Critical Essay

- **Content/Unity.** The essay analyzes the character and attitudes of Granny as they are revealed in the selection from *Kaffir Boy*.
- **Organization/Coherence.** The essay begins with a thesis paragraph, supports this thesis with evidence and quotations from the selection, and then contains a conclusion in the final paragraph.
- **Language/Style.** The essay uses clear and vivid language.
- **Conventions.** The essay avoids errors in spelling, grammar, usage, mechanics, and manuscript form.

▶For additional practice, see Essential Skills Practice Books: Writing 1.20.

Answers to Guided Reading Questions

❶ Granny says that what the narrator did was a serious crime in the eyes of the white people who control South Africa. She says that apartheid means whites and nonwhites have always been apart and will always be apart.

❷ She says that she has never seen a nonwhite use the white phone booth and that a nonwhite would not use a white phone booth even if it were a matter of life and death.

❸ The narrator knows his grandmother can't read, so he wonders how she functions normally in a world ruled by signs. The narrator's consciousness is awakened to signs of racial segregation everywhere he goes.

Selection Check Test with Answers

EX. Where does Granny take the narrator?
Granny takes the narrator to her gardening job in Pretoria.

1. Why does Granny leave the narrator?
She leaves the narrator to get change for the bus.
2. What does the narrator do while waiting for the bus?
The narrator reads a comic book while waiting for the bus.
3. What is the narrator worried the driver of the white bus will do?
The narrator is worried that the driver of the white bus will kick him in the face.
4. What does Granny do to the steps of the bus?
She wipes them with her dress.
5. To what is the narrator's consciousness awakened?
His consciousness is awakened to the pervasiveness of "petty apartheid."

❶
What reason does Granny give the narrator for her outburst? What does she say apartheid *means?*

❷
What does Granny say about the phone booths?

❸
Why does the narrator wonder how his grandmother functions normally? To what is the narrator's consciousness awakened?

After a long pause, during which she calmed down, Granny said, "Forgive me for the outburst, child, but what you did was no small thing in the eyes of white people and the law. There's something you ought to know about how things are in this country, something your Mama I see has not told you yet. Black and white people live apart—very much apart—that, you already know. What you may not know is that they've always been apart, and will always be apart—that's what apartheid means. White people want it that way, and they've created all sorts of laws and have the guns to keep it that way.

"We live in our world," she continued, after taking a pinch of snuff and loading it under her tongue, "and white people live in their world. We're their servants, they're our masters. Our people fought hard to change things, but each time the white man always won. He has all the guns. Maybe another generation of black people will come which will defeat the white man, despite his many guns. But for now, he says how things should be, and we have to obey. Do you see those two things over there?" Granny pointed across the street.

"Yes, Granny, they're phone boxes."

"That's right," she affirmed. "But they are not just phone boxes. One is a *black* phone box, the other a *white* phone box. Don't forget that. And for as long as I've been working for white people, and God knows I've been working for them for centuries, I've never seen a black person in his right mind go into the wrong one. It might be a matter of life and death, and still he wouldn't. Even blind people know which is which."

"Which one is for black people, Granny?" I asked, somewhat confused, for the two phone booths were exactly the same in all respects—colour, size and shape.

"I don't know which is which," Granny groped for words, "but there's always a sign on each door, to tell which race is allowed to use which phone."

As she said this, it struck me that she could not read, like millions of other blacks who worked for whites. How did they function normally in a world totally ruled by signs?

Thus my consciousness was awakened to the pervasiveness of "petty apartheid," and everywhere I went in the white world, I was met by visible and invisible guards of racial segregation. ■

Words for Everyday Use

af • firm (ə furm´) *vt.,* say positively

per • va • sive • ness (pər vā´siv nəs) *n.,* penetration throughout

seg • re • ga • tion (seg´rə gā´shən) *n.,* policy of compelling people of different racial groups to live separately from each other

Vocabulary in Context

- I can affirm that Dennis was at swim team practice last night.
- Dr. Wong was impressed by the pervasiveness of positive thinking in the hospital ward.
- We read about the court case that put an end to school segregation in the United States.

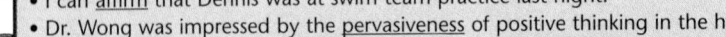

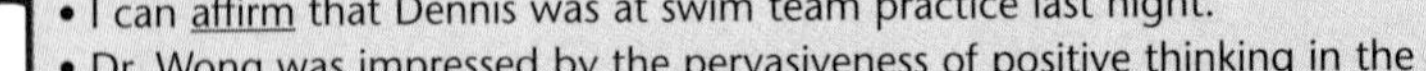

Responding to the Selection

Imagine that you are a friend of the narrator in this selection. What advice would you give him after his grandmother tells him how apartheid works? Would you advise him to follow the rules of apartheid? Would you advise him to organize nonviolent protests against apartheid, or would you tell him to do something else? Discuss your advice to the narrator with your classmates.

Reviewing the Selection

RECALLING		INTERPRETING
1. Of what does the narrator say he still had remnants? Despite this, how was he beginning to feel about "the white world"?	▶▶	Why was the narrator beginning to feel this way? Why does the narrator say that his feelings were "naive"?
2. What is the narrator doing when the bus pulls up? What does the narrator see in the bus? What does the narrator say to the bus driver?	▶▶	Why does the narrator freeze when he gets on the bus? Why does the experience seem unreal, like a nightmare, to him?
3. What does the narrator's grandmother say about him when she is apologizing to the bus driver? What does she do that disturbs the narrator?	▶▶	How might the narrator feel when he hears his grandmother talk about him in this way? How does he feel when he sees his grandmother's actions? Why? What is the grandmother feeling as she scolds her grandson? Do you think that she believes in the stereotypes that some white South Africans have of black people? Why, or why not?
4. What does the narrator's grandmother explain to him about South Africa?	▶▶	In what way is the narrator changed by what he learns?

SYNTHESIZING

5. In what way does the narrator portray South Africa during the late 1960s and early 1970s? Discuss the concept of apartheid and whether you see evidence of similar intolerance in your life or in the society in which you live.

RESPONDING TO THE SELECTION

Ask students to weigh the pros and cons of each response to the rules of apartheid.

ANSWERS FOR REVIEWING THE SELECTION

RECALLING AND INTERPRETING

1. **Recalling.** The narrator says that he still had remnants of his childhood dread of white people. He was beginning to feel comfortable among the white people. **Interpreting.** The narrator was beginning to feel this way because nothing terrible happened to rekindle his fear, and the Smiths, a white family, are kind to him. The narrator means that something happened that proved that he should not feel content or comfortable around white people.

2. **Recalling.** The narrator is reading a comic book when he hears the bus pull up. The narrator sees that he is in a white bus and that his presence is frightening the old ladies. The narrator apologizes to the bus driver and begs for his forgiveness. **Interpreting.** The narrator freezes because he is startled; he has been absorbed in his reading and is alarmed and frightened to find he has mistakenly boarded a "white" bus. The experience seems unreal to the narrator because he thought that all white people had cars so that they never had to ride the bus.

3. **Recalling.** The narrator's grandmother says that the narrator is deranged. She wipes the steps of the bus where the narrator has stepped. **Interpreting.** The narrator might feel confused, angry, and upset. The narrator might feel outraged and ashamed to see his grandmother debase herself in this way.

4. **Recalling.** She tells the narrator that apartheid means that black and white people always have been and always will be

(cont.)

ANSWERS FOR REVIEWING THE SELECTION (CONT.)

apart, and that black people must follow segregation rules. She also says that their people have fought to change things but that they have always lost. **Interpreting.** The narrator is awakened to "petty apartheid" and now sees signs of racial segregation everywhere he goes. The narrator has lost his innocence about the relationship between the races.

SYNTHESIZING

Responses will vary. Possible responses are given.

5. The narrator portrays South Africa during this period as a place of intolerance and segregation in which blacks are humiliated and oppressed. Students might cite as examples of intolerant societies Nazi Germany, Serbian forces in Bosnia, the Khmer Rouge in Cambodia, or the conflicts in Europe between Catholics and Protestants.

Understanding Literature (Questions for Discussion)

1. **Tone. Tone** is the emotional attitude toward the reader or toward the subject implied by a literary work. What is the tone of this selection? What words and phrases reveal this tone?

2. **Archetype.** An **archetype** is an inherited, often unconscious ancestral memory or motif that recurs throughout history and literature. Stories about a fall from a state of innocence to a state of experience, or new awareness, have recurred throughout world literature for thousands of years, from the story of Adam and Eve eating the apple and other early stories to the fiction and nonfiction of today. In what way does the narrator of this selection experience the archetypal fall from a state of innocence to a state of experience, or new awareness? What effect does his new knowledge have on him?

Responding in Writing

1. **Creative Writing: Letter of Complaint.** The narrator of this selection did not have the freedom to speak out and defend himself during his confrontation with the bus driver. Write a letter to the bus company complaining about the way the narrator and his grandmother were treated by the driver. You might suggest that the bus company change its policy of segregating buses. You also might tell the bus company that you plan to organize a petition, protest, march, or boycott if their policy is not reversed.

2. **Critical Essay: Analyzing Character.** Write a brief essay in which you analyze the character of Granny as it is revealed in this selection. You should analyze what Granny's reaction to the encounter with the bus driver reveals about her attitude toward apartheid. Does Granny accept the role defined for her by society or not? Does she hope for change in society? State a thesis in an initial paragraph; support your thesis with evidence and quotations from the selection in paragraphs that follow; and come to a conclusion in a final paragraph.

Research Skills

Computer-assisted Research. Use a computer to find information on people who have struggled against apartheid. Read the Language Arts Survey 4.17, "Computer-assisted Research." Then, use the computers in your classroom, library, or school computer lab to search encyclopedias and other resources on CD-ROM, the Internet, and online services for information on one of the following people: Nelson Mandela, Steven Biko, Donald Woods, Nadine Gordimer, or Desmond Tutu. You should find at least three different sources of information, then write a brief paragraph based on information from each source. In each paragraph, include where and how you found the information as well as a brief description of what this resource revealed about the person you chose.

Answers for Understanding Literature

Responses will vary. Possible responses are given.

1. Tone. Students may say that the tone is resentful, indignant, horrified, angry, or sad. Students may identify the following words and phrases: "I began to naively assume that maybe white people weren't all that bad"; "white people milled . . . in but never out of my consciousness"; "tragic mistake"; "nightmare"; "Thinking that anytime I would be kicked in the face by the white bus driver"; "To my moral horror"; and "wondering whether I had underestimated the enormity of my crime . . . Were the poor white passengers going to die as a result?"

2. Archetype. The narrator of this selection was beginning to believe that white people were not all bad and that the racial situation in his country was tolerable. The narrator loses this innocent view of the world when he is humiliated by a white bus driver and his grandmother then tells him how the racial situation in his country really is.

Analytic Scales for Writing Skills

Grading scales for Responding in Writing appear on page 199.

Answers for Skills Activities

RESEARCH SKILLS

When students have finished their research, ask them to discuss their experience and compare it with going to a library to conduct research. Which method do they prefer, and why?

▶ For additional practice, see the Essential Skills Practice Book: Study and Research 4.17.

Insights

Apartheid

Nelson Mandela

Throughout much of the twentieth century, the relationship between whites and nonwhites in South Africa has been dominated by a policy of racial segregation and discrimination known as apartheid. While segregation was legal in South Africa in the first half of the twentieth century, this practice gained strength and first became known by the name *apartheid* in 1950, when the Group Areas Act and South Africa's Population Registration Act were passed by a government that represented the views of the white minority of the country. Under the Group Areas Act, areas in which each race could live and work were mapped out, and it became illegal for nonwhites to live, run businesses, or own land in areas designated for whites. This act and the Land Acts that followed gave the white minority control of more than 80 percent of the land in South Africa. The Population Registration Act required that all South Africans be registered at birth as belonging to one of four races: white, colored (people of mixed race ancestry), Asian, or Bantu (black Africans). All nonwhites had to carry passes documenting their background and needed proper authorization to be in restricted "white" areas. Nonwhites whose passes were not in order were often jailed for long periods of time.

Although all nonwhites had to deal with the humiliation of segregation, separate educations, and job restrictions, black South Africans had to face further oppression. Laws passed between 1951 and 1970 made all black Africans citizens of different tribal homelands even if they had never lived in the tribal homelands. These laws forbade black Africans to vote or otherwise to participate in the government of South Africa. While education was free and compulsory for whites, coloreds, and Asians, all Bantu schools charged tuition and required students to buy uniforms and books. These schools were terribly run down and short-staffed, and their curricula focused on tribal issues.

Black South Africans often protested or rebelled against this unjust system, and such attempts often ended in bloodshed. Nelson Mandela, a leader of the African National Congress, struggled against apartheid and received a term of life imprisonment in 1964. In Soweto in 1976, students who protested being forced to learn Afrikaans, the language of their Dutch-descended oppressors, were attacked with guns and tear gas. Mark Mathabane joined in the Soweto riots, which lasted for several weeks and claimed the lives of hundreds of people, including many school children. Violent protests increased to the extent that the government declared a state of emergency throughout most of the 1980s.

In addition to internal conflict, South Africa faced international censure. Many nations were outraged by the practice of apartheid in South Africa, and Great Britain and the United States issued economic sanctions against South Africa in 1985. Frederick W. de Klerk became President of South Africa in 1989 and began to loosen some of apartheid's restrictions. Nelson Mandela's release from prison, which had become a rallying point for those opposed to apartheid, was ordered by de Klerk in 1990. Mandela became president of the African National Congress in 1991. Under the influence of Mandela and de Klerk, segregation laws and regulations requiring race registration at birth were repealed. In 1994, South Africa held its first multiracial election, resulting in the election of Nelson Mandela as president.

Historical Note

The African National Congress (ANC), founded in 1912, is the oldest black political organization in South Africa. The radical organization became well known for its opposition to apartheid, and it was actually banned by the white minority government of South Africa in 1960. Despite the fact that the ANC was outlawed, it remained a powerful force behind mass resistance to apartheid throughout the 1970s and the 1980s. The ban on the group was finally lifted in 1990 as part of a series of steps made by the government to end apartheid and reach some kind of compromise with South African blacks. The ANC is now made up of both black and white South Africans.

Biographical Note

Nelson Mandela was born on July 19, 1918, near Umtata, Transkei. He was supposed to succeed his father as chief of the Tembu tribe, but he renounced this right because he wanted to pursue a political career. Mandela studied law, and in 1944 he joined the African National Congress, helping to found the group's influential Youth League. He received his first jail sentence, which was suspended, in 1952 for his work on the ANC's Defiance against Unjust Laws Campaign. Even after Mandela received his life sentence in 1964 for sabotage and conspiracy against the white government, he remained the acknowledged leader of the ANC. In 1993, three years after his release from prison, Mandela received the Nobel Peace Prize. He shared the award with F. W. de Klerk.

Additional Questions and Activities

Have students form small groups to make creative time lines that show the history of South Africa including its most recent radical political changes. Allow students time to go to the library in small groups to research dates and events not described on this page. Once they have gathered their data, they can plan how their time line will look. You might refer students to the Language Arts Survey 1.10, "Gathering Ideas," which features a section on preparing time lines. Students might want to insert corresponding pictures, drawings, or photographs with certain dates.

►For additional practice, see the Essential Skills Practice Book: Writing 1.10.

ADDITIONAL RESOURCES

READER'S GUIDE

- Selection Worksheet 2.6

ASSESSMENT PORTFOLIO

- Selection Check Test 2.2.11
- Selection Test 2.2.12

ESSENTIAL SKILLS PRACTICE BOOKS

- Writing 1.8, 1.10, 1.20
- Language 2.52, 2.55

PREREADING EXTENSIONS

Inform students that a major figure involved in winning India its independence from Great Britain was Mohandas Gandhi (1869–1948), also called Mahatma, which means "great-souled." Gandhi's doctrine of nonviolent protest against British rule led to his repeated imprisonment but won him international esteem. He began negotiations for Indian independence with Great Britain in 1947 but was assassinated in 1948. Today, he is often considered the father of India. Encourage students to work in groups to research Gandhi's life or the lives of other historical figures who either supported nonviolent protest or were imprisoned for struggling against injustice. Possible figures to research include Henry David Thoreau, Martin Luther King, Jr., or Nelson Mandela.

SUPPORT FOR LEP STUDENTS

PRONUNCIATIONS OF PROPER NOUNS AND ADJECTIVES

Krish • na (krish´nə)
Na • li • ni (nə lē´nē)
Pre • mil • a (prə mil´ə)
San • tha Ra • ma Rau (sän´ thə rä´mə rou)
Zor • in • a • bad (zōr in´ ə bad)

PREREADING

"By Any Other Name" from *Gifts of Passage* by Santha Rama Rau

INDIA

About the Author

SANTHA RAMA RAU 1923–

Santha Rama Rau was born in Madras, India. As a child, she lived in India and spent much of her time at the home of her grandmother, who followed Hindu traditions. Her father was a diplomat, and when she was six, he was sent to England, where her family lived for many years. On returning to India, Rama Rau realized that she had become distanced from her native culture. Her book *Home to India* is about her experience of returning to her native land.

Rama Rau has also lived in South Africa; in Japan, where she met her husband, an American writer; and in the United States, where she studied at Wellesley College and later lived in New York. Despite some initial disapproval from her family, Rama Rau decided on a writing career. Her first book was published in 1945. Her works include travel books, fiction, and memoirs.

About the Selection

For many years, beginning in 1858, the British ruled India. During this time, the government instituted sweeping changes in law, property distribution, and education. Learning English became important to people who wished to prosper under the British system. The beliefs and traditions of the two cultures differed greatly. In matters as important as religion and social organization, as well as in the simpler issues of dress, food, and daily habits, British practices and Indian practices diverged. Over time, aspects of both societies were combined, although British culture dominated.

"By Any Other Name" recounts an incident from Santha Rama Rau's childhood. In describing her experiences at a British school in India, she illuminates the conflict and cultural differences between the British and the Indians. The essay also explores the idea of identity. "By Any Other Name" was first published in *The New Yorker* and also appears in Rama Rau's autobiography, ***Gifts of Passage.***

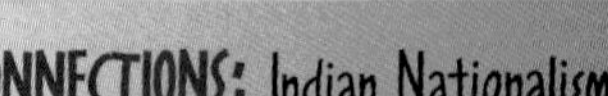

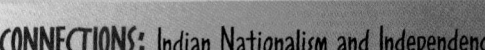

Santha Rama Rau witnessed the independence of her country in 1947. Since 1818, when the British East India Company took control of the country, India had been under British rule and influence. The British government itself took control of India in 1858. The Indian nationalist movement began with the formation of the Indian National Congress in 1885. In the 1920s, Mohandas Gandhi began a nonviolent, non-cooperation movement. In 1919 and 1935, India obtained limited powers of self-government, but full independence was not achieved until 1947.

GOALS/OBJECTIVES

Studying this lesson will enable students to

- relate to an autobiographical story about intolerance and prejudice
- explain why British influence remains in India
- define *autobiography* and *dialogue* and recognize these types of writing in their reading
- write a personal essay about a childhood incident
- write a critical essay about names and identity
- identify errors in the capitalization of names of persons, occupations, and family members

How do you identify yourself? To what groups or classifications do you belong? Have you ever been treated unfairly because of one of these classifications? Classifications might include gender, age, race, ability, financial status, or physical characteristics. Write about an experience you have had with discrimination.

READER'S JOURNAL

"By Any Other Name"

SANTHA RAMA RAU

At the Anglo-Indian day school in Zorinabad[1] to which my sister and I were sent when she was eight and I was five and a half, they changed our names. On the first day of school, a hot, windless morning of a north Indian September, we stood in the headmistress's study and she said, "Now you're the *new* girls. What are your names?"

My sister answered for us. "I am Premila, and she"—nodding in my direction—"is Santha."

The headmistress had been in India, I suppose, fifteen years or so, but she still smiled her helpless inability to cope with Indian names. Her rimless half-glasses glittered, and the precarious bun on the top of her head trembled as she shook her head. "Oh, my dears, those are much too hard for me. Suppose we give you pretty English names. Wouldn't that be more jolly? Let's see, now—Pamela for you, I think." She shrugged in a baffled way at my sister. "That's as close as I can get. And for *you*," she said to me, "how about Cynthia? Isn't that nice?"

My sister was always less easily intimidated than I was, and while she kept a stubborn silence, I said, "Thank you," in a very tiny voice.

We had been sent to that school because my father, among his responsibilities as an officer of the civil service, had a tour of duty to perform in the villages around that steamy little provincial town, where he had his headquarters at that time. He used to make his shorter inspection tours on horseback, and a week before, in the stale heat of a typically postmonsoon[2] day, we had waved good-by to him and a little procession—an assistant, a secretary, two bearers, and the man to look after the bedding rolls and luggage. They rode away through our large garden, still bright green from the rains, and we turned back into the twilight of the house

1. **Zorinabad.** City in India
2. **postmonsoon.** After a tropical storm

❶ *Why does the headmistress say she makes the change that she does? What is the real reason she makes this change?*

WORDS FOR EVERYDAY USE

pre • car • i • ous (prē ker´ē əs) *adj.*, uncertain, insecure
in • tim • i • date (in tim´ə dāt´) *vt.*, make afraid
pro • vin • cial (prō vin´ shəl) *adj.*, of or like rural country

READER'S JOURNAL

If students cannot remember a time when someone discriminated against them or find such memories too painful to write about, students may write about stereotypes and why they are limiting. They may also write about people they know who have transcended the classifications others have placed on them.

ANSWERS TO GUIDED READING QUESTIONS

❶ The headmistress says that she changes the girls' names because English names are "more jolly." The real reason she makes this change is that she is unwilling or unable to learn foreign names, even though she has lived abroad for fifteen years.

SPELLING AND VOCABULARY WORDS FROM THE SELECTION

abruptly	rigid
accordance	sedately
incomprehensible	siesta
insular	solemn
intimidate	tepid
palpitate	valid
peevishness	veranda
precarious	wizened
provincial	

VOCABULARY IN CONTEXT

- The vase teetered on its precarious perch at the edge of the table.
- An unfriendly teacher can intimidate a new student.
- The new student was surprised by the provincial attitudes held by the school in this small village.

Answers to Guided Reading Questions

❶ The Indian children dress differently and they have to sit at the back of the room.

❷ The narrator's mother had refused to send her children to a British school until this point because she felt the British were insular. She had been educating her children at home until her health gave out.

❸ The name change made the narrator feel as though she had a second identity in which she was not very interested and for which she felt no responsibility.

Cross-curricular Activities

SOCIAL STUDIES

Encourage students to work in small groups to discover personal names common in different countries around the world. After doing some research and reading, each group should try to list at least five male names and five female names common in their chosen country, along with the meanings of the names.

ARTS AND HUMANITIES

After completing the activity above, encourage each student to choose a name from any group's list and to imagine that a teacher, employer, or family member insists upon calling him or her by this new name instead of his or her given name. Then have students complete one of the following assignments:

- Write a journal entry explaining your situation and your feelings about being given this name.
- Write a poem about your new name and what it means to you.
- Write a story, either humorous or serious, about the results of being renamed.
- Represent your feelings about your old name and your new name visually in some medium, such as a drawing, painting, collage, or sculpture.

❶ *In what way are the Indian children different from the British children?*

❷ *Why had the narrator's mother refused to send her children to a British school until this point? What happened to change her mind?*

❸ *What effect did the name change have on the narrator?*

and the sound of fans whispering in every room.

Up to then, my mother had refused to send Premila to school in the British-run establishments of that time, because, she used to say, "you can bury a dog's tail for seven years and it still comes out curly, and you can take a Britisher away from his home for a lifetime and he still remains insular." The examinations and degrees from entirely Indian schools were not, in those days, considered valid. In my case, the question had never come up, and probably never would have come up if Mother's extraordinary good health had not broken down. For the first time in my life, she was not able to continue the lessons she had been giving us every morning. So our Hindi books were put away, the stories of the Lord Krishna[3] as a little boy were left in mid-air, and we were sent to the Anglo-Indian school.

That first day at school is still, when I think of it, a remarkable one. At that age, if one's name is changed, one develops a curious form of dual personality. I remember having a certain detached and disbelieving concern in the actions of "Cynthia," but certainly no responsibility. Accordingly, I followed the thin, erect back of the headmistress down the veranda to my classroom feeling, at most, a passing interest in what was going to happen to me in this strange, new atmosphere of School.

The building was Indian in design, with wide verandas opening onto a central courtyard, but Indian verandas are usually whitewashed, with stone floors. These, in the tradition of British schools, were painted dark brown and had matting on the floors. It gave a feeling of extra intensity to the heat.

I suppose there were about a dozen Indian children in the school—which contained perhaps forty children in all—and four of them were in my class. They were all sitting at the back of the room, and I went to join them. I sat next to a small, solemn girl who didn't smile at me. She had long, glossy-black braids and wore a cotton dress, but she still kept on her Indian jewelry—a gold chain around her neck, thin gold bracelets, and tiny ruby studs in her ears. Like most Indian children, she had a rim of black kohl[4] around her eyes. The cotton dress should have looked strange, but all I could think of was that I should ask my mother if I couldn't wear a dress to school, too, instead of my Indian clothes.

I can't remember too much about the proceedings in class that day, except for the beginning. The teacher pointed to me and asked me to stand up. "Now, dear, tell the class your name."

I said nothing.

"Come along," she said, frowning slightly. "What's your name, dear?"

"I don't know," I said, finally.

The English children in the front of the class—there were about eight or ten of them—giggled and twisted around in their chairs to look at me. I sat down quickly and opened my eyes very wide, hoping in that way to dry them off. The little girl with the braids put out her hand and very lightly touched my arm. She still didn't smile.

Most of that morning I was rather bored. I looked briefly at the children's drawings pinned to the wall, and then concentrated on a lizard clinging to the ledge of the high, barred window behind the teacher's head. Occasionally it would shoot out its long yellow tongue for a fly, and then it would rest, with its eyes closed and its belly palpitating,

3. **Lord Krisha.** Hindu god, a human incarnation of Vishnu
4. **kohl.** Black powder used as eye makeup

Words for Everyday Use

in • su • lar (in´sə lər) *adj.*, isolated
val •id (val´id) *adj.*, binding under law
ve • ran • da (və ran´ də) *n.*, open porch, usually roofed, along the outside of a building
sol • emn (säl´əm) *adj.*, serious, quiet
pal • pi • tate (pal´pə tāt´) *vi.*, beat rapidly, flutter

Vocabulary in Context

- Natural boundaries, such as oceans, rivers, and mountains, can protect a group of people from outside invaders, but such boundaries can also keep a group insular.
- To drive, one needs a valid driver's license.
- It was a scorching afternoon and too hot to stay in the house, so she sat in the shade of the veranda, hoping to catch a breeze.
- Just before the exam, the schoolchildren cast aside their customary smiles and put on a solemn appearance.
- His heart began to palpitate rapidly with anxiety before he took the test.

as though it were swallowing several times quickly. The lessons were mostly concerned with reading and writing and simple numbers—things that my mother had already taught me—and I paid very little attention. The teacher wrote on the easel blackboard words like "bat" and "cat," which seemed babyish to me; only "apple" was new and incomprehensible.

When it was time for the lunch recess, I followed the girl with braids out onto the veranda. There the children from the other classes were assembled. I saw Premila at once and ran over to her, as she had charge of our lunchbox. The children were all opening packages and sitting down to eat sandwiches. Premila and I were the only ones who had Indian food—thin wheat chapatties,[5] some vegetable curry, and a bottle of buttermilk. Premila thrust half of it into my hand and whispered fiercely that I should go and sit with my class, because that was what the others seemed to be doing.

The enormous black eyes of the little Indian girl from my class looked at my food longingly, so I offered her some. But she only shook her head and plowed her way solemnly through her sandwiches.

I was very sleepy after lunch, because at home we always took a siesta. It was usually a pleasant time of day, with the bedroom darkened against the harsh afternoon sun, the drifting off into sleep with the sound of Mother's voice reading a story in one's mind, and, finally, the shrill, fussy voice of the ayah[6] waking one for tea.

At school, we rested for a short time on low, folding cots on the veranda, and then we were expected to play games. During the hot part of the afternoon we played indoors, and after the shadows had begun to lengthen and the slight breeze of the evening had come up we moved outside to the wide courtyard.

I had never really grasped the system of competitive games. At home, whenever we played tag or guessing games, I was always allowed to "win"— "because," Mother used to tell Premila, "she is the youngest, and we have to allow for that." I had often heard her say it, and it seemed quite reasonable to me, but the result was that I had no clear idea of what "winning" meant.

When we played twos-and-threes that afternoon at school, in accordance with my training, I let one of the small English boys catch me, but was naturally rather puzzled when the other children did not return the courtesy. I ran about for what seemed like hours without ever catching anyone, until it was time for school to close. Much later I learned that my attitude was called "not being a good sport," and I stopped allowing myself to be caught, but it was not for years that I really learned the spirit of the thing.

When I saw our car come up to the school gate, I broke away from my classmates and rushed toward it yelling, "Ayah! Ayah!" It seemed like an eternity since I had seen her that morning—a wizened, affectionate figure in her white cotton sari,[7] giving me dozens of urgent and useless instructions on how to be a good girl at school. Premila followed more sedately, and she told me on the way home never to do that again in front of the other children.

When we got home we went straight to Mother's high, white room to have tea with

5. **chapatties.** Indian flat bread
6. **ayah.** Indian nursemaid
7. **sari.** Long piece of cloth traditionally worn as the principal outer garment by Hindu women

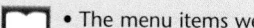

Why doesn't the narrator understand the meaning of winning? What difficulty does this cause her?

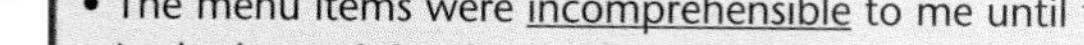

Words for Everyday Use

in • com • pre • hen • si • ble (in´ käm´prē hen´sə bəl) *adj.*, not understandable

si • es • ta (sē es´tə) *n.*, brief nap or rest taken after the noon meal

ac • cord • ance (ə kôrd´ ´ns) *n.*, agreement

wiz • ened (wiz´ənd) *adj.*, dried up, shriveled

se • date • ly (si dāt´lē) *adv.*, calmly, quietly

Answers to Guided Reading Questions

The narrator has always been allowed to win because she was the youngest. She gets a reputation as a bad sport for following the example she has been taught.

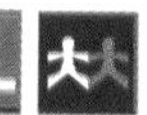

Additional Questions and Activities

Encourage students to discuss the following questions: In what ways does the English school create prejudice against traditional Indian customs? What does the narrator wish to do after seeing the way her classmates are dressed? Why is the narrator unable to respond when asked to state her name? Why might a word like *apple* be totally incomprehensible to the narrator? How are the lunches that Premila and the narrator bring different from the lunches of other students? Why won't the Indian girl share the narrator's food even though she looks at it "longingly"? Why might a school such as the narrator's have a damaging effect on its students' identities? If you were in the narrator's position, would you try to "fit in" with the English way of life promoted at the school, even if it meant giving up some of your traditions?

ANSWERS

Responses will vary.

Students may say that the school encourages students to model English behavior and abandon Indian traditions. The narrator wishes to abandon Indian clothes and wear a cotton dress. She has been given a new English name and is unsure which name the teacher wants to know. Apples aren't native to India, so the narrator would be unfamilar with this fruit. Premila and the narrator have traditional Indian food, and the other children have sandwiches. The girl may be afraid of seeming different from the rest of the children. The school is encouraging students to reject a part of their own heritage.

Vocabulary in Context

- The menu items were incomprehensible to me until the waiter explained them.
- In the heat of the day, Indian children slept, taking a pleasant siesta.
- Many American civil rights leaders, including Martin Luther King, Jr., were in accordance with Mohandas Gandhi's system of nonviolent protest.
- After working many years in his fields, the farmer's face was wizened by the wind and sun.
- While I always wriggle in my seat, my sister sits sedately.

INTEGRATED SKILLS ACTIVITIES

LANGUAGE LAB

Quotation marks are used to enclose a direct quotation, or a person's exact words. They are not used to enclose an indirect quotation, or a reworded version of a person's words. Identify an example of each on this page of "By Any Other Name." Then rewrite the following sentences, punctuating and capitalizing both direct and indirect quotations correctly.

1. My mother asked me "whether I enjoyed my first day of school."
2. I said it was confusing, Mom. What does *apple* mean?
3. Premila told Mom that "She had a test next week."
4. I wanted to know "What a test was."
5. Premila said you won't have to worry about tests for several more years.

ANSWERS

1. My mother asked me whether I enjoyed my first day of school.
2. I said, "It was confusing, Mom. What does *apple* mean?"
3. Premila told Mom that she had a test next week.
4. I wanted to know what a test was.
5. Premila said, "You won't have to worry about tests for several more years."

► Additional practice is provided in the Essential Skills Practice Book: Language 2.52.

her, and I immediately climbed onto the bed and bounced gently up and down on the springs. Mother asked how we had liked our first day in school. I was so pleased to be home and to have left that peculiar Cynthia behind that I had nothing whatever to say about school, except to ask what "apple" meant. But Premila told Mother about the classes, and added that in her class they had weekly tests to see if they had learned their lessons well.

I asked, "What's a test?"

Premila said, "You're too small to have them. You won't have them in your class for donkey's years." She had learned the expression that day and was using it for the first time. We all laughed enormously at her wit. She also told Mother, in an aside, that we should take sandwiches to school the next day. Not, she said, that *she* minded. But they would be simpler for me to handle.

That whole lovely evening I didn't think about school at all. I sprinted barefoot across the lawns with my favorite playmate, the cook's son, to the stream at the end of the garden. We quarreled in our usual way, waded in the <u>tepid</u> water under the lime trees, and waited for the night to bring out the smell of the jasmine. I listened with fascination to his stories of ghosts and demons, until I was too frightened to cross the garden alone in the semidarkness. The ayah found me, shouted at the cook's son, scolded me, hurried me in to supper—it was an entirely usual, wonderful evening.

It was a week later, the day of Premila's first test, that our lives changed rather

WORDS FOR EVERYDAY USE

tep • id (tep´id) *adj.,* lukewarm

VOCABULARY IN CONTEXT

- The surface water of even the iciest ponds becomes <u>tepid</u> after a few months in the sun.

abruptly. I was sitting at the back of my class, in my usual inattentive way, only half listening to the teacher. I had started a rather guarded friendship with the girl with the braids, whose name turned out to be Nalini (Nancy, in school). The three other Indian children were already fast friends. Even at that age it was apparent to all of us that friendship with the English or Anglo-Indian children was out of the question. Occasionally, during the class, my new friend and I would draw pictures and show them to each other secretly.

The door opened sharply and Premila marched in. At first, the teacher smiled at her in a kindly and encouraging way and said, "Now, you're little Cynthia's sister?"

Premila didn't even look at her. She stood with her feet planted firmly apart and her shoulders rigid, and addressed herself directly to me. "Get up," she said. "We're going home."

I didn't know what had happened, but I was aware that it was a crisis of some sort. I rose obediently and started to walk toward my sister.

"Bring your pencils and your notebook," she said.

I went back for them, and together we left the room. The teacher started to say something just as Premila closed the door, but we didn't wait to hear what it was.

In complete silence we left the school grounds and started to walk home. Then I asked Premila what the matter was. All she would say was "We're going home for good."

It was a very tiring walk for a child of five and a half, and I dragged along behind Premila with my pencils growing sticky in my hand. I can still remember looking at the dusty hedges, and the tangles of thorns in the ditches by the side of the road, smelling the faint fragrance from the eucalyptus trees and wondering whether we would ever reach home. Occasionally a horse-drawn tonga[8] passed us, and the women, in their pink or green silks, stared at Premila and me trudging along on the side of the road. A few coolies[9] and a line of women carrying baskets of vegetables on their heads smiled at us. But it was nearing the hottest time of day, and the road was almost deserted. I walked more and more slowly, and shouted to Premila, from time to time, "Wait for me!" with increasing peevishness. She spoke to me only once, and that was to tell me to carry my notebook on my head, because of the sun.

When we got to our house the ayah was just taking a tray of lunch into Mother's room. She immediately started a long, worried questioning about what are you children doing back here at this hour of the day.

Mother looked very startled and very concerned, and asked Premila what had happened.

Premila said, "We had our test today, and She made me and the other Indians sit at the back of the room, with a desk between each one."

Mother said, "Why was that, darling?"

"She said it was because Indians cheat," Premila added. "So I don't think we should go back to that school."

Mother looked very distant, and was silent a long time. At last she said, "Of course not, darling." She sounded displeased.

We all shared the curry she was having for lunch, and afterward I was sent off to the beautifully familiar bedroom for my siesta. I could hear Mother and Premila talking through the open door.

8. **tonga.** Two-wheeled carriage of India
9. **coolies.** Unskilled native laborers

➊ *What causes Premila to leave the school?*

Words for Everyday Use

a • brupt • ly (ə brupt´lē) *adv.*, suddenly, unexpectedly
rig • id (rij´id) *adj.*, stiff and hard
pee • vish • ness (pēv´ish nəs) *n.*, impatience; crossness

Answers to Guided Reading Questions

➊ Premila leaves the school because of prejudice: the teacher says that Indians cheat.

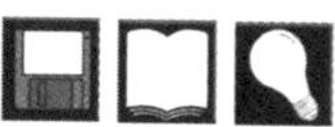

Selection Check Test with Answers

EX. What name was the narrator given on her first day at school?
She was given the name Cynthia.

1. Why did the teacher give Santha and Premila new names?
She could not pronounce the Indian names.

2. What new word did Santha learn at school?
She learned the word *apple*.

3. With whom did Santha play in the evening after school?
She played with the cook's son.

4. Why didn't Santha do well at games at school?
She did not understand what winning or competition meant because she had always been allowed to win at home.

5. What does Premila's teacher say about Indians?
She says that Indians cheat.

Answers for Language Lab
(See page 211.)

1. During her childhood, Santha Rama Rau spent a lot of time at her grandmother's house.
2. She remembers that one of her uncles knew how to drive a car.
3. When she went to school, the headmistress changed her name to Cynthia.
4. When the car arrived to bring her home, she shouted, "I missed you, Ayah!"
5. Her father was the Deputy High Commissioner for India.

▶ Additional practice is provided in the Essential Skills Practice Book: Language 2.55.

Vocabulary in Context

- Just as suddenly as the tropical rain storm began, the rain clouds abruptly parted and the sun shone through.
- The cat's posture was tense and rigid as it watched the neighbor's dog pass.
- Ravi's peevishness increased as the slow-moving lunch line inched forward.

Answers to Guided Reading Questions

❶ She was indifferent to the unpleasant incident in the school because it happened to the uninteresting girl called Cynthia.

Responding to the Selection

Students may also wish to discuss why the narrator remembers this incident so vividly and the effect it may have had on her in later years.

Answers for Reviewing the Selection

RECALLING AND INTERPRETING

1. **Recalling.** The narrator and her sister have their names changed by the headmistress. The narrator feels that the entity known as Cynthia is not really related to her in any way. **Interpreting.** This change demonstrates that the British had difficulty with Indian words and customs. The British seem to lack respect for Indian people and customs.

2. **Recalling.** Santha notices that the other Indian children are wearing cotton dresses instead of Indian attire. She also notes that they eat sandwiches instead of Indian food. **Interpreting.** Santha wishes she were more like the other children. She wants to ask her mother if she can wear a dress to school.

3. **Recalling.** Santha runs to her ayah, shouting. In the evening she plays outside with the cook's son and does not think about school at all. It is a normal evening for her. **Interpreting.** Santha does not like school. It disrupts the normal patterns of her life. She also feels removed from school because she is known as Cynthia there.

4. **Recalling.** Premila leaves the school because the teacher makes the Indian students sit at the back

(cont.)

What was the narrator's attitude toward this incident? Why did she feel this way?

Mother said, "Do you suppose she understood all that?"

Premila said, "I shouldn't think so. She's a baby."

Mother said, "Well, I hope it won't bother her."

Of course, they were both wrong. I understood it perfectly, and I remember it all very clearly. But I put it happily away, because it had all happened to a girl called Cynthia, and I never was really particularly interested in her. ■

Responding to the Selection

What do you think about Premila's decision to leave the school? Do you think that doing so was a good way to handle the problem? How would you have reacted had you been in her place? Discuss these questions in small groups, or role play situations in which you explore different ways in which Premila could have responded.

Reviewing the Selection

Recalling / **Interpreting**

1. What happens to the narrator and her sister on the first day of school? What effect does this change have on the narrator? ▶▶ What does this change demonstrate about relations between the British in India and the Indians?

2. What differences does Santha note between herself and the other Indian children at the school? ▶▶ How does Santha feel about the differences between herself and the other Indian children?

3. What does Santha do at the end of the school day? What does she do in the evening? ▶▶ How does Santha feel about school? Why does she feel this way?

4. What reason does Premila give for leaving the school and not returning? ▶▶ Is Santha bothered by this incident? How do you know?

Synthesizing

5. What does this essay reveal about the relationship between British culture and Indian culture during Rama Rau's childhood?

Answers for Reviewing the Selection (cont.)

of the room with desks between them, saying she must do this because Indians cheat. **Interpreting.** Santha says that she is not bothered by this incident because it happened to a girl named Cynthia. The incident did make an impression upon Santha, however, as shown by her inclusion of it in her autobiography.

SYNTHESIZING

Responses will vary. Possible responses are given.

5. The relationship between Indians and British is strained when it exists at all. Examples of this include the mother's unwillingness to send her children to a British school, the British names forced upon Santha and Premila, the separate seating of Indian and British students, the fact that a friendship between a British child and an Indian child is inconceivable, and by the teacher's comment that Indians cheat.

Understanding Literature (Questions for Discussion)

1. **Autobiography.** An **autobiography** is the story of a person's life, written by that person. What part of Rama Rau's life is described in this section of her autobiography? What do you learn about Rama Rau's life beyond the incident at school?
2. **Dialogue. Dialogue** is conversation involving two or more people or characters. What information does the dialogue at the end of the selection between Premila and her mother reveal? What do you know about the relationship between Premila and Santha, based on their conversations with each other?

Responding in Writing

1. **Creative Writing: Personal Essay.** In "By Any Other Name," Rama Rau describes an incident from her childhood that made an impression on her and illuminated something about her life. Choose an incident from your own childhood that has special meaning to you. You may wish to freewrite first to gather possible ideas. Then, write a short personal essay describing the event and its impact on your life. When writing a personal essay, you should use the first-person point of view to convey a direct experience, use direct quotation and dialogue, and create images that reveal a sense of time, place, events, and people.
2. **Critical Essay: "What's in a Name?"** The title of Rama Rau's work, "By Any Other Name," is an allusion to a line from Shakespeare's *The Tragedy of Romeo and Juliet* (act II, scene ii): "What's in a name? That which we call a rose/By any other name would smell as sweet." Write an essay in which you answer the question, "What's in a name?" Is a name an important part of your identity? Do you have different identities attached to different names? For example, does your given name mean something different to you than your nickname? State the kind of impact a name has on a person. Then compare and contrast your attitude with that of Rama Rau. Use examples from your own life and from the selection to support your responses.

Language Lab

Capitalization. When referring to somebody by name, his or her name should be capitalized. Other forms of address or ways of referring to people have different rules for capitalization. Read the Language Arts Survey 2.55, "Names, Titles of Persons, Occupations, and Family Relationships." Then, on your own paper, rewrite the following sentences, correcting any errors in capitalization. If a sentence has no errors, write *Correct.*

1. During her childhood, Santha rama rau spent a lot of time at her Grandmother's house.
2. She remembers that one of her Uncles knew how to drive a car.
3. When she went to school, the Headmistress changed her name to cynthia.
4. When the car arrived to bring her home, she shouted, "I missed you, ayah!"
5. Her father was the deputy high commissioner for India.

ANALYTIC SCALES FOR RESPONDING IN WRITING

Assign a score from 1 to 25 for each grading criterion below. (For more detailed evaluation, see the evaluation forms for writing, revising, and proofreading, Assessment Portfolio 4.1–4.9.)

1. Personal Essay

- **Content/Unity.** The personal essay describes an event from the writer's childhood.
- **Organization/Coherence.** The personal essay relates events in the first-person point of view in a sensible order.
- **Language/Style.** The personal essay uses vivid and precise nouns, verbs, and modifiers.
- **Conventions.** The personal essay avoids errors in spelling, grammar, usage, mechanics, and manuscript form.

► Additional practice is provided in the Essential Skills Practice Book: Writing 1.8, 1.10.

2. Critical Essay

- **Content/Unity.** The essay examines names as a part of identity.
- **Organization/Coherence.** The essay contains an introduction, a body, and a conclusion and is sensibly ordered.
- **Language/Style.** The essay uses vivid and precise nouns, verbs, and modifiers.
- **Conventions.** The essay avoids errors in spelling, grammar, usage, mechanics, and manuscript form.

► Additional practice is provided in the Essential Skills Practice Book: Writing 1.20.

ANSWERS FOR UNDERSTANDING LITERATURE

Responses will vary. Possible responses are given.

1. Autobiography. Rama Rau describes an incident from her childhood. This extract from her autobiography reveals that she enjoyed playing with the cook's son outside in the evenings and that she enjoyed scary stories. She was used to a siesta in the afternoon during which time she rested in her cool, quiet room and her mother read her a story. She was attached to her ayah. She was less bold than her sister.

2. Dialogue. Premila reveals why she left school. She tells her mother that her teacher has said that Indians cheat. Her mother agrees that she should not return to the school and wonders whether Santha has understood the situation. Premila is protective of Santha.

ANSWERS FOR LANGUAGE LAB

Answers for Language Lab appear on page 209.

Cross-curricular Activities

SOCIAL STUDIES

Students may be interested in learning more about the uprising of Zapatista rebels in Chiapas, Mexico. The Zapatistas, who took their name from the revolutionary war hero Emiliano Zapata, took over San Cristóbal de las Casas, the largest city in the state of Chiapas, on January 1, 1994. They were protesting the signing of NAFTA, the North American Free Trade Agreement, which they believed would increase unemployment in Mexico and worsen the poverty of the mostly indigenous peasant farmers of southern Mexico. The Zapatistas also demanded land, food, housing, education, and health care from the government. Interested students can research the Zapatista movement or NAFTA by consulting newspaper and magazine articles in the library or by doing online research. Have students present their findings in an oral report, or have students discuss their findings in small groups.

Historical Note

Tibet is a vast country in the southwest of China. Surrounded by mountain ranges and situated mostly on a plateau with an average altitude of 16,000 feet, Tibet is often called "the roof of the world." In 1951, China began a forcible occupation of Tibet, which led to an uprising in the Tibetan capital of Lhasa. Thousands were killed; the head of state and religious leader of Tibet, the Dalai Lama, fled to India in exile. Thousands more Tibetans joined in the exodus. Although Tibet is presently still under Chinese rule, there is a movement to reinstate the Dalai Lama as official leader and reestablish Tibet as an independent country.

Global Voices

A MULTICULTURAL CONVERSATION

Discussing Intolerance

Students were asked to discuss intolerance in their countries.

Jiannong: In China we have fifty-six different peoples. The majority are Han—that is the ethnic group I belong to—but there are many minority groups like the Tibetans and the Zhuang. During our reform in the 1980s, the government started a policy to provide benefits for some minorities. They get tax cuts to open businesses and priority admission to college. They can have as many children as they want, while the majority are only allowed one child per family. There is a lot of conflict over this.

Elio: In Mexico we don't have such a variety of ethnic groups. The great majority of Mexicans, even the elite, are of mixed race. What matters is class and economic status. Basically, if you have the money, you can do just about anything, but if you're poor, you're at a big disadvantage. You don't have the same rights that you can buy with money. The situation in Mexico right now is basically the haves against the have-nots. Developers and ranchers come in and buy the land from the farmers, force them off the land. That's why there have been uprisings in Chiapas, the state I'm from.

Ebere: In northern Nigeria, most people are Muslim, and in the east and west, they are Christian, like me. We don't have anything in common—the language, clothing, food, religion—everything is different. Everyone knows that Christians and Muslims don't intermarry; they don't give each other jobs; they just don't mix. And there are riots and bombings between the two regions. We're trying to get together, but it's going to take a while. The only time we're like one happy family is during soccer games, or during the Olympics. Then we are "Nigeria together!"

Denis: In Russia, religious intolerance was enforced by the Communist government, which outlawed all religion. My family is Russian Orthodox, but during Communism, my parents could not practice their faith for fear they would lose their jobs. My grandparents could practice because they were retired and had nothing the government could take away. Now with the collapse of the U.S.S.R., things have changed. We have some political problems with people from Georgia and Armenia; because of wars there, they come into Russia, and many people don't like them. We have a mix of people from all sixteen countries of the former U.S.S.R. but not many people from foreign countries.

Gabrielle: France is called the country of welcome because we have many immigrants from Europe and Africa, but ironically, it's becoming a problem. During the 1930s the economy was good, and the French government invited the North Africans to come and work in industry. Now the economy is bad, and there are no more jobs for these people.

Sarah: Greeks, too, are known for their hospitality, or *filoxenia.* Greeks love to entertain and will offer food and drinks to someone they've just met. *Filoxenia* has been portrayed in our literature since Homer's *Odyssey*. But when it comes to tourists, attitudes are

Cultural/Historical Note

Northern Nigeria, historically the home of the Fulani and Hausa peoples, is predominantly Muslim. In the southeast, the majority of people are Ibo and practice Christianity. In the southwest, most people are Yoruba. Most Yoruba are also Christian, but many still practice a traditional Yoruba religion with its pantheon of gods, or *orisha.* The tension that exists today among these three groups stems from a history of division and conflict.

The years following Nigeria's independence from Britain, which took place in 1960, were characterized by particularly fierce conflicts. Three main political parties, one based in the north, one supported by the Ibo in the east, and one supported by the Yoruba, emerged to compete for the leadership of the free Nigeria. After several hotly contested elections, Ibo army officers staged a short-lived coup in 1966. This takeover (cont.)

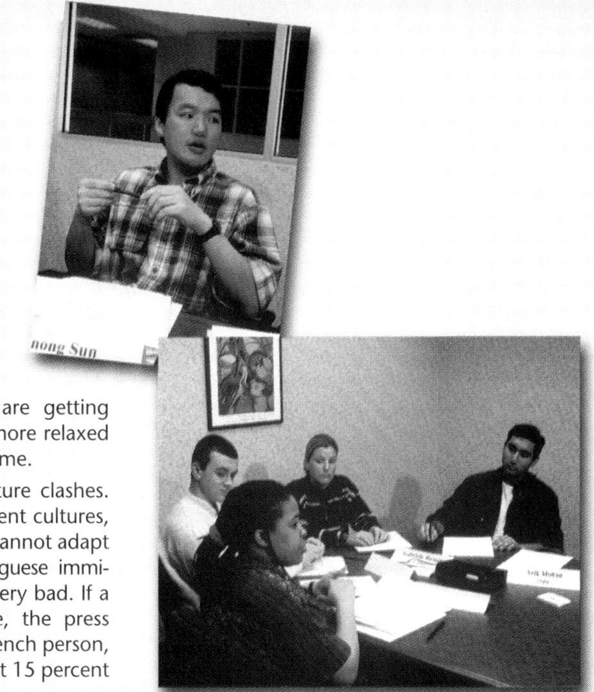

different. Tourism is what makes money for Greece, but as tourists are becoming more demanding, Greek attitudes toward them are getting worse. It may be that the Greeks, with their more relaxed lifestyles, are experiencing stress for the first time.

Gabrielle: A lot of times stress is caused by culture clashes. North Africans coming into France have different cultures, different religions, different clothes, and they cannot adapt to French culture as well as Italian and Portuguese immigrants, for example. I think racism is getting very bad. If a North African commits a crime or violence, the press makes a bigger deal about it than if it was a French person, and now the Nazi party is getting big. They got 15 percent of the vote in the presidential election.

Sarah: In Greece, there is discrimination against the Albanians and Turkish immigrants who come looking for jobs. The Turks have been coming for a long time now so we've adopted a lot of their customs—dances, foods, clothing. A lot of Greeks don't like that; to them, these customs are not Greek. Gypsies have lived in Greece for hundreds of years, and even now they're looked down upon.

Yumiko: In Japan, Korean immigrants suffer discrimination. They have difficulty getting into schools or getting jobs, and I think it's so unfair. They live in Japan and they speak Japanese fluently. There is a lot of other discrimination. In Japan there used to be a class system, and the lowest class, the *burakumin*, was considered untouchable. They did jobs that were considered dirty, like making leather goods or dealing with dead people, and were called "not-human." Although today they are considered normal people, they are still discriminated against. People don't want their children to marry the *burakumin*; they don't want to hire them. Also, there are the indigenous people, the Ainu, who are discriminated against. But most of these issues are not talked about—it's all kept underwater.

Avik: In India, too, there is discrimination on the basis of caste. Many people refuse to sit on the same bus or work in the same office as a person of a lower caste. Caste lines are breaking down slowly, but for a long time they were so rigid that you could not break out of them. Your caste determined what occupation you could have; there was no way to move up in the hierarchy.

Elio: In Mexico, to get out of poverty you have to fight and scrape for everything. Or, you have to know people. The education system is great, but it's just not accessible. If you are an extremely gifted student, you can go to any university; tuition is free. But the problem is that if you are very poor, the chances for you to develop as a gifted student are few. Instead of studying, you may have to work to support your family. ■

Cultural/Historical Note

Students may be interested in learning more about the caste systems in India and Japan. The five major castes in the Hindu caste system are *brahmins, kshatriyas, vaishyas, shudras,* and *panchamas.* The ordering represents their hierarchical standing in society. Traditionally, the *brahmins* are concerned with intellectual and religious activities. The *kshatriyas* are supposed to engage in politics and warfare. The *vaishyas* comprise the merchant class, and the *shudras* are consigned to tasks such as manufacturing leather, cleaning, and so forth. The lowest caste was comprised of the untouchables, or *panchamas,* who were supposed to perform the most menial tasks. In the past in India, segregation between the castes was rigid. Although attitudes are changing in India and untouchability was declared illegal in 1949, these prejudices run deep.

What might be called a caste system in Japanese history began under the Tokugawa shogunate of 1603–1867, a centralized feudal state led by a dictator called a shogun. Society was rigidly divided under the Tokugawa: the aristocracy included the *daimyo,* or barons, and the *samurai,* or warrior class; the peasants, artisans, and merchants constituted the other social classes. The lowest class on this scale was the *burakumin,* who were called *senmin* (despised citizens), *hinin* (non-people), or *eta* (Chinese for "much filth"). Much of the prejudice against the *burakumin*, many of whom worked with leather or as butchers, arose from a Buddhist belief that handling dead things was dirty. The Tokugawa may also have encouraged prejudice against the *burakumin* in order to decrease resistance among the other classes. Although today in Japan there is no official caste system, the *burakumin* still suffer much discrimination.

Cultural/Historical Note (cont.)

provoked a massacre of Ibo living in the north; the Ibo leader was ousted and killed by Hausa army officers. Following this fiasco, the east decided to secede from Nigeria and created the state of Biafra in 1967. However, the Ibo secession from Nigeria triggered a long, painful civil war, which ended in 1970 with the surrender of the separatists and a return to a united Nigeria.

"Crazed Man in Concentration Camp"

ABOUT THE AUTHOR

Ágnes Gergely (1933–) was born in Budapest, Hungary. She attended the University of Budapest and spent six months at the University of Iowa's International Writing Program. Gergely has published four books of poetry, three novels, and numerous translations. She has worked as a teacher, radio producer, feature editor at a literary weekly, and editor of a publishing house in Budapest.

ABOUT THE SELECTION

In the twentieth century, millions of political dissidents and members of unwanted religious or ethnic groups have been confined to concentration camps, where they have been annihilated, abused, or exploited in the name of national security or racial purity. **"Crazed Man in Concentration Camp"** expresses the horror of the concentration camp by focusing on the pain of one man. In this poem, a man tries desperately to hold on to the last piece of his former life and identity as he is marched to his death in a concentration camp.

"The Censors"

ABOUT THE AUTHOR

Born in Buenos Aires, Argentina, **Luisa Valenzuela** (1938–) began her writing career when, at age fifteen, she landed a job as a journalist for the magazine *Quince abriles*.

In 1969, Valenzuela took part in a University of Iowa writing workshop on a Fulbright scholarship. Since then, she has worked as writer-in-residence at Columbia University and at the Center for Inter-American Relations, and she has conducted many writing workshops.

The author of numerous novels and short stories, Valenzuela is one of Latin America's most famous fiction writers. Most of her works have been translated into English.

SELECTIONS FOR ADDITIONAL READING

HUNGARY

"Crazed Man in Concentration Camp"

by Ágnes Gergely, translated by Edwin Morgan

All through the march, besides bag and blanket
he carried in his hands two packages of empty boxes,
and when the company halted for a couple of minutes
he laid the two packages of empty boxes neatly at each side,
being careful not to damage or break either of them,
the parcels were of
ornamental boxes
dovetailed[1] by sizes each to each
and tied together with packing-cord,
the top box with a picture on it.
When the truck was about to start, the sergeant
shouted something in sergeant's language,
they sprang up suddenly,
and one of the boxes rolled down to the wheel,
the smallest one, the one with the picture:
"It's fallen," he said and made to go after it,
but the truck moved off
and his companions held his hands
while his hands held the two packages of boxes
and his tears trailed down his jacket.
"It's fallen," he said that evening in the queue[2]—
and it meant nothing to him to be shot dead.

ARGENTINA

"The Censors"

by Luisa Valenzuela, translated by David Unger

Poor Juan! One day they caught him with his guard down before he could even realize that what he had taken as a stroke of luck was really one of fate's dirty tricks. These things happen the minute you're careless and you let down your guard, as one often does. Juancito let happiness—a feeling you can't trust—get the better of him when he received from a confidential source Mariana's new address in Paris and he knew that she hadn't forgotten him. Without thinking twice, he sat down at his table and wrote her a letter. *The* letter that keeps his mind off his job during the day and won't let him sleep at night (what had he scrawled, what had he put on that sheet of paper he sent to Mariana?).

Juan knows there won't be a problem with the letter's contents, that it's irreproachable, harmless. But what about the rest? He knows that they examine, sniff, feel, and read between the lines of each and every letter, and check its tiniest comma and most accidental stain. He knows that all letters pass from hand to hand and go through all sorts of tests in the huge censorship[3] offices and that, in the end, very few continue on their way. Usually it takes months, even years, if there aren't any snags; all this time the freedom, maybe even the life, of both sender and receiver is in jeopardy. And that's why Juan's so down in the dumps: thinking that something might happen to Mariana because of his letters. Of all people, Mariana, who must finally feel safe there where she always dreamed she'd live. But he knows that the Censor's Secret Command operates all over the world and cashes in on the discount in air rates; there's nothing to stop them from going as far as that hidden Paris neighborhood, kidnapping Mariana, and returning to their cozy homes, certain of having fulfilled their noble mission.

Well, you've got to beat them to the punch, do what everyone tries to do: sabotage the machinery, throw sand in its gears, get to the bottom of the problem so as to stop it.

This was Juan's sound plan when he, like many others, applied for a censor's job—not because he had a calling or needed a job: no, he applied simply to intercept his own letter, a consoling but unoriginal idea. He was hired immediately, for each day more and more censors are needed and no one would bother to check on his references.

Ulterior motives couldn't be overlooked by the Censorship Division, but they needn't be too strict with those who applied. They knew how hard it would be for those poor guys to find the letter they wanted and even if they did, what's a letter or two when the new censor would snap up so many others? That's how Juan managed to join the Post Office's Censorship Division, with a certain goal in mind.

1. **dovetailed.** Composed of wedge-shaped parts that fit into corresponding cutout parts to form interlocking joints
2. **queue.** Line
3. **censorship.** Official act of examining writing to remove what is considered offensive or inappropriate

ADDITIONAL QUESTIONS AND ACTIVITIES

Ask students to answer on paper or in a group discussion the following questions about "Crazed Man in Concentration Camp":

- Where is the man going? What is he holding?
- How do you know that the items he holds are important to him?
- What happens to one of the items? Why is this item particularly important to him?
- How does he feel at the end of the poem? Why does he feel this way?
- In what ways is "Crazed Man in Concentration Camp" a poem about loss?

The building had a festive air on the outside which contrasted with its inner staidness. Little by little, Juan was absorbed by his job and he felt at peace since he was doing everything he could to get his letter for Mariana. He didn't even worry when, in his first month, he was sent to Section K where envelopes are very carefully screened for explosives.

It's true that on the third day, a fellow worker had his right hand blown off by a letter, but the division chief claimed it was sheer negligence on the victim's part. Juan and the other employees were allowed to go back to their work, albeit feeling less secure. After work, one of them tried to organize a strike to demand higher wages for unhealthy work, but Juan didn't join in; after thinking it over, he reported him to his superiors and thus got promoted.

You don't form a habit by doing something once, he told himself as he left his boss's office. And when he was transferred to Section J, where letters are carefully checked for poison dust, he felt he had climbed a rung in the ladder.

By working hard, he quickly reached Section E where the work was more interesting, for he could now read and analyze the letters' contents. Here he could even hope to get hold of his letter which, judging by the time that had elapsed, had gone through the other sections and was probably floating around in this one.

Soon his work became so absorbing that his noble mission blurred in his mind. Day after day he crossed out whole paragraphs in red ink, pitilessly chucking many letters into the censored basket. These were horrible days when he was shocked by the subtle and conniving ways employed by people to pass on subversive messages; his instincts were so sharp that he found behind a simple "the weather's unsettled" or "prices continue to soar" the wavering hand of someone secretly scheming to overthrow the Government.

His zeal brought him swift promotion. We don't know if this made him happy. Very few letters reached him in Section B—only a handful passed the other hurdles—so he read them over and over again, passed them under a magnifying glass, searched for microprint with an electronic microscope, and tuned his sense of smell so that he was beat by the time he made it home. He'd barely manage to warm up his soup, eat some fruit, and fall into bed, satisfied with having done his duty. Only his darling mother worried, but she couldn't get him back on the right road. She'd say, though it wasn't always true: Lola called, she's at the bar with the girls, they miss you, they're waiting for you. Or else she'd leave a bottle of red wine on the table. But Juan wouldn't overdo it: any distraction could make him lose his edge and the perfect censor had to be alert, keen, attentive, and sharp to nab cheats. He had a truly patriotic task, both self-denying and uplifting.

His basket for censored letters became the best fed as well as the most cunning basket in the whole Censorship Division. He was about to congratulate himself for having finally discovered his true mission, when his letter to Mariana reached his hands. Naturally, he censored it without regret. And just as naturally, he couldn't stop them from executing him the following morning, another victim of his devotion to his work. ■

from Universal Declaration of Human Rights

Article 1

All human beings are born free and equal in dignity and rights. They are endowed with reason and conscience and should act towards one another in a spirit of brotherhood.

Article 2

Everyone is entitled to all the rights and freedoms set forth in this Declaration, without distinction of any kind, such as race, colour, sex, language, religion, political or other opinion, national or social origin, property, birth or other status.

Furthermore, no distinction shall be made on the basis of the political, jurisdictional or international status of the country or territory to which a person belongs, whether it be independent, trust, non-self-governing or under any other limitation of sovereignty.

Article 3

Everyone has the right to life, liberty and the security of person.

Article 4

No one shall be held in slavery or servitude; slavery and the slave trade shall be prohibited in all their forms.

Article 5

No one shall be subjected to torture or to cruel, inhuman or degrading treatment or punishment.

Article 6

Everyone has the right to recognition everywhere as a person before the law.

Article 19

Everyone has the right to freedom of opinion and expression; this right includes freedom to hold opinions without interference and to seek, receive and impart information and ideas through any media and regardless of frontiers. ■

About the Selection

"The Censors" shows the effects of an oppressive political environment. Luisa Valenzuela is known for her ability to capture in her stories, with shocking realism, the terror and political chaos that plagued her native Argentina.

In 1976, the military took over Argentina and General Jorge Rafael Videla assumed the presidency. During the civil war that followed, called the "dirty war," thousands of leftists and other political opponents were killed or imprisoned. Often those who were regarded as dangerous by the military leadership simply disappeared. The Argentine government was criticized at home and by other countries for civil rights violations.

From Universal Declaration of Human Rights

About the Selection

The United Nations, an international organization that includes about 160 member nations, was established immediately after World War II for the purpose of maintaining international peace and security and to encourage nations to work together to solve problems.

The General Assembly of the United Nations attempts to guide international policies and finances. The United Nations's Security Council tries to control crises and keep peace throughout the world. The United Nations also includes a World Court and works with several independent agencies in areas of health, education, science, and child welfare throughout the world. The governing treaty of the United Nations was drawn up in 1945 in San Francisco. The headquarters have been located in New York City since 1946.

The Universal Declaration of Human Rights, drawn up by the General Assembly, reflects the beliefs of the members of the United Nations, and, as it states, is supposed to set a standard for all people and all nations.

Additional Questions and Activities

Ask each student to choose and write about one human right from the list of universal human rights. As they write they might want to keep some of the following questions in mind:

- Why does this human right seem especially important or have particular meaning?
- Have you ever seen a violation of this right firsthand, or heard or read about a violation of this right?
- Why is it important to make an official declaration of human rights?

ADDITIONAL RESOURCES

Assessment Portfolio
- Vocabulary Worksheet 2.2.17
- Study Guide 2.2.18
- Unit Test 2.2.19

Essential Skills Practice Books

WRITING
- Choosing a Purpose, 1.8
- Gathering Ideas, 1.10
- Writing a Critical Essay, 1.20

LANGUAGE
- Types of Verbs, 2.7
- Other Uses of Quotation Marks, 2.52
- Capitalization: Names, Titles of Persons, Occupations, and Family Relationships, 2.55

STUDY AND RESEARCH
- Computer-assisted Research, 4.17

APPLIED ENGLISH/TECH PREP
- Personal and Business Letters, 5.1

Vocabulary Check Test

Ask students to number their papers from one to ten. Have students complete each sentence with a word from the Vocabulary from the Selections in the Unit Review.

1. We never go to that restaurant because the food there is abominable.
2. We were happy to meet each other, so we shook hands vigorously.
3. The gossip columnists were hoping that the actor had a sordid past.
4. Margie always arrives late, but Lynne always arrives punctually.
5. The surface water of even the iciest pond becomes tepid after a few months in the sun.
6. The practice of segregation prevented black children and white children from attending the same schools.
7. The soldiers held a clandestine meeting so that they could (cont.)

UNIT REVIEW

The Struggle against Intolerance

VOCABULARY FROM THE SELECTIONS

abominable, 185
abruptly, 209
abyss, 183
accordance, 207
aesthetically, 153
affirm, 200
alien, 169
alleviate, 197
aloof, 155
amicably, 143
ample, 114
apparition, 153
appease, 198
appendage, 170
askew, 172
assertion, 193
buffet, 191
caprice, 119
capricious, 153
censer, 173
clandestine, 155
confiscate, 176
contritely, 198
conviction, 191
cuneiform, 176
depraved, 138
despised, 190
diabolical, 170
digression, 113
disembark, 198
disheveled, 133
dissemble, 130
dissolution, 157
ebb, 193
egocentric, 117
endurable, 191
fervently, 191
flux, 193
fusillade, 199
hone, 193
impending, 173
impertinently, 125
inanimate, 192
incomprehensible, 207
incredulously, 115
indiscretion, 125
infallible, 162
insular, 206
intimidate, 205
luxuriate, 170
mantle, 176
minion, 172
obloquy, 137
obstinate, 137
palpitate, 206
paternalistic, 197
patronize, 118
peal, 191
peevishness, 209
pervasiveness, 200
petulant, 193
precarious, 205
pretense, 130
provincial, 205
punctually, 120
remnant, 197
retina, 192
rigid, 209
rivulet, 193
scornfully, 118
sedately, 207
segregation, 200
siesta, 207
solemn, 206
sordid, 159
succumb, 169
sundries, 192
supplicate, 175
surfeit, 193
surge, 190
tempestuous, 172
tepid, 208
tirade, 198
valid, 206
vault, 169
vehemently, 126
veranda, 206
vigorously, 198
wizened, 207

Vocabulary Check Test (cont.)

secretly plan their next move.

8. The bully tried to intimidate younger students into giving him their lunch money.
9. We sat on the deck and watched the ebb and flow of the ocean tide.
10. On a wild caprice, we took a ride in a hot-air balloon.

LITERARY TERMS

aim, 187	description, 188	requiem, 168
allusion, 178	dialogue,132, 211	simile, 188
apostrophe, 179	foreshadowing, 188	stage directions, 165
archetype, 202	image, 188	symbol, 149, 194
atmosphere, 132	imagery, 188	tone, 202
autobiography, 196, 211	mood, 132	verbal irony, 166
character, 132, 149	parody, 195	
crisis, 149	realism, 110	

SYNTHESIS: QUESTIONS FOR WRITING, RESEARCH, OR DISCUSSION

GENRE STUDIES

1. Define *autobiography*. Which selections in this unit would you classify as autobiographical? Explain what you believe each author's aim, or purpose, was in writing his or her autobiography.

THEMATIC STUDIES

2. Many of the selections in this unit feature young people who gain knowledge of oppression, prejudice, or intolerance. Focusing upon *A Doll's House, Night, Kaffir Boy,* and "By Any Other Name," describe what the main characters were like before they gained this knowledge. Discuss what they are like afterwards. In what way did this knowledge change them?

3. The narrators of many of these selections take on the roles of witnesses for their cultures and what their cultures have suffered. Which narrators would you classify as "witnesses"? Why do you think each narrator felt the need to serve as a witness for his or her culture?

4. In what way do the narrators or main characters in each of these selections react to oppression and discrimination? What inner resources allow them to survive their experiences?

5. Compare and contrast the ways in which oppression, discrimination, or intolerance affects the identities of the main characters or narrators in *A Doll's House, Night, Kaffir Boy, The Bluest Eye,* and "By Any Other Name." Do their experiences of oppression become an essential part of their identities? Why, or why not?

HISTORICAL/BIOGRAPHICAL STUDIES

6. Which selections feature cultures in conflict? What groups of people are in conflict? Is one group the oppressor and the other the oppressed? Do some research to discover the ways in which these conflicts were resolved or are currently being resolved.

7. Through research, identify current abuses of human rights. Who is being oppressed? How is this group's plight being portrayed to the rest of the world? How are people reacting to this oppression?

SPELLING CHECK TEST

Ask students to number their papers from one to ten. Read each word aloud. Then read aloud the sentence containing the word. Repeat the word. Ask students to write the word on their papers, spelling it correctly.

1. **succumb**
Gina finished the marathon, refusing to succumb to her feelings of exhaustion.
2. **aloof**
The aloof group of students barely spoke to anyone.
3. **luxuriate**
When we go on vacation, my sister and I plan to sit on the beach and luxuriate in the warm sun.
4. **aesthetically**
The design for the new building is not practical, but it is aesthetically pleasing.
5. **disheveled**
After his long nap, the toddler looked sleepy and disheveled.
6. **abyss**
Lee lost his hat when it fell into the deep abyss of the well.
7. **obstinate**
We felt that Jackson was being obstinate in not giving in to our reasonable request.
8. **amicably**
After a pleasant afternoon, during which they settled their differences, Natasha and Gabrielle parted amicably.
9. **alleviate**
Exercising daily helps Vanessa to alleviate her feelings of stress.
10. **surge**
During the hurricane, giant waves will surge and cause damage to beachfront homes.

UNIT SKILLS OUTLINE

Literary Skills and Concepts

- Apostrophe, 255
- Characterization, 230
- Image, 264
- Internal Conflict, 264
- Irony of Situation, 269
- Lyric Poem, 254
- Magical Realism, 270, 277
- Metaphor, 260
- Mood, 235, 248, 254, 264
- Motivation, 243
- Narrative Poem, 245
- Octave, 251
- Pastoral Poem, 233, 244
- Personification, 238, 255
- Petrarchan Sonnet, 251
- Point of View, 268
- Sestet, 251
- Setting, 249, 277
- Sonnet, 251
- Symbol, 282
- Theme, 282

Writing Skills and Concepts

- Critical Essay, 244, 249, 255, 260, 265, 269, 277, 283
- Description, 277
- "Feast on Your Life" Poem, 283
- Journal Entries, 244
- Letter Poem, 249
- Lyric Poem, 255
- Mood Paragraph or Poem, 265
- Point of View Experiment, 269
- "Though I am . . ." Poem, 260

Grammar, Usage, and Mechanics Skills and Concepts

- Personal Pronouns, 249
- Sentence Fragments and Run-ons, 255
- Transitive and Intransitive Verbs, 283
- Using Vivid Language, 265
- Verbals, 246

Other Language Arts Skills and Concepts

- Oral Interpretation, 263
- Personal and Business Letters, 277
- Research Skills: Researching Heroes, 269
- Using Elements of Verbal Communication, 260
- Writing Personal Letters, 228

Unit 3 Love

Alfred Sisley. *Pierre Auguste Renoir, 1868*

GOALS/OBJECTIVES

Studying this unit will enable students to

- appreciate love as a theme recurring throughout world literature
- identify a number of important world authors who explore love in their work
- describe and identify the characteristics of sonnets
- define and identify examples of magical realism
- use selections that explore love as prompts for creative writing projects
- write a number of critical essays on literary works that explore love as a theme

"The heart has its reasons of which reason knows nothing."

—Blaise Pascal

219

CROSS-CURRICULAR CONNECTIONS

Arts and Humanities

- Balcony Scene from *Romeo and Juliet*, 285
- Epic Poetry and Lyric Poetry, 279
- "Epigram on Milton," 234
- Imagism and Ezra Pound, 245
- Love in Literature and Movies, 285
- Mapping Aeneas's Journey, 224
- Persian Empire Research, 257
- Representations of Love Stories, 273
- Researching Heroes, 269
- Roman Empire Project, 222
- South America Research, 270
- T'ang and Ming Dynasty Art, 247
- Vincent van Gogh, 220

Mathematics and Sciences

- Gender Roles in Marriage, 284

Social Studies

- Arranged Marriages vs. Romantic Love, 284
- Biographical Notes on Echoes Authors, 221
- Cultural Differences in Displaying Affection, 285
- "Epigram on Milton," 234
- Gender Roles in Marriage, 284
- Germany and the Caribbean Research, 272
- Hellenistic Poetry, 231
- High School Dating, 285
- Horace, 232
- Isabel Allende, 273
- *La Araucana*, 261
- Love in Literature and Movies, 285
- Mapping Aeneas's Journey, 224
- Mapping China, 246
- Mercury and Hermes, 225
- Persian Empire Research, 257
- Pygmalion, 227
- Researching Heroes, 269
- Roman Empire Project, 222
- South America Research, 270
- Trojan War, 236

TEACHING THE MULTIPLE INTELLIGENCES

Musical

- Comparing and Contrasting Types of Music, 272
- Love in Literature and Movies, 285

Logical-Mathematical

- Analyzing Poetry, 245
- Arranged Marriages vs. Romantic Love, 284
- Gender Roles in Marriage, 284
- Germany and the Caribbean Research, 272
- High School Dating, 285

(cont.)

TEACHING THE MULTIPLE INTELLIGENCES (CONT.)

- Recalling Verses, 247
- Searching for Pertrarchan Conventions, 251

Spatial

- Illustrating Personified Nature Images, 238
- Mapping Aeneas's Journey, 224
- Mapping China, 246
- Persian Empire Research, 257
- Representations of Love Stories, 273
- South America Research, 270
- T'ang and Ming Dynasty Art, 247
- Vincent van Gogh, 220

Kinesthetic

- Balcony Scene from *Romeo and Juliet*, 285
- Oral Interpretation, 263
- Representations of Love Stories, 273
- Retelling a Story from the *Odyssey*, 266
- South America Research, 270

Other Selections Exploring This Theme

Art Note

Vincent van Gogh (1853–1890), was a nineteenth-century Dutch painter whose work, virtually unknown in his lifetime, became quite influential after his death. Van Gogh is considered the first of the great modern Expressionist painters. Many of van Gogh's most striking, expressive paintings were produced in the twenty-nine months before he committed suicide. Three of his most famous works are *The Potato Eaters* (1885), *The Night Café* (1888), and *Starry Night* (1889). He also painted a number of self-portraits.

UNIT 3

Theme:
Love

Detail from *Two Lovers*. *Vincent van Gogh, 1888*

People have expressed their feelings and ideas about love in art and literature for centuries in almost every culture. Artists have painted pictures, created sculptures, and written poems, stories, plays, and songs about the different kinds of love that exist. Through these different mediums, people have expressed ideas about love between family members, romantic love, self-love, love of country, and religious love. Despite the human fascination with this subject, real love remains mysterious, powerful, and difficult to control, explain, or truly express. People will forever try to explore this subject through art and literature.

This unit presents literature that explores different types of love. You will read an ancient Roman epic that pits romantic love against a leader's love for his people and his sense of duty. You will see the ways in which thwarted love and misdirected passion can cause pain and destruction. You will read a poem about love that has grown between a husband and wife who married while very young and the loneliness the wife experiences as she waits for her husband to return from a long journey. You will read selections that deal with the pain of unrequited love, the lack of courage to pursue a relationship, and the loss of a loved individual to death. You will also read a poem that offers a message of self-love in the face of rejection. All of these selections will help you to examine the different faces of this powerful and always interesting human emotion.

Teaching the Multiple Intelligences (cont.)

Interpersonal

- Arranged Marriages vs. Romantic Love, 284
- Balcony Scene from *Romeo and Juliet*, 285
- Comparing and Contrasting Types of Music, 272
- Cultural Differences in Displaying Affection, 285
- Discussing "Whoso List to Hunt," 256
- Epic Poetry and Lyric Poetry, 279
- Gender Roles in Marriage, 284
- Germany and the Caribbean Research, 272
- High School Dating, 285
- Illustrating Personified Nature Images, 238
- Imagism and Ezra Pound, 245
- Mapping Aeneas's Journey, 224
- Oral Interpretation, 263
- Persian Empire Research, 257
- Recalling Verses, 247
- Researching Heroes, 269
- Retelling a Story from the *Odyssey*, 266
- Searching for Petrarchan Conventions, 251
- South America Research, 270

Echoes:

Love

O lyric Love, half angel and half bird
And all a wonder and a wild desire.

—Robert Browning

Whoso loves believes the impossible.

—Elizabeth Barrett Browning

Love does not consist in gazing at each other but in looking together in the same direction.

—Antoine de Saint-Exupéry

Love many things, for therein lies the true strength, and whosoever loves much performs much, and can accomplish much, and what is done in love is well done.

—Vincent van Gogh

If you'd be loved, be worthy to be loved.

—Ovid

A new commandment I give unto you, That ye love one another; as I have loved you, that ye also love one another.

—from the King James Bible (John 13:34)

Love is like a mousetrap—you go in when you wish, but you don't come out when you like.

—Spanish proverb

I wanted to escape from love but didn't know how.

—Ding Ling

Love consists in this, that two Solitudes protect and touch and greet each other.

—Rainer Maria Rilke

'Tis better to have loved and lost
Than never to have loved at all.

—Alfred, Lord Tennyson

Love conquers all things: let us too give in to Love.

—Virgil

Before you love, learn to run through snow, leaving no footprints.

—Turkish proverb

Additional Questions and Activities

Ask students to do a focused freewrite for several minutes about the subject of love. As they write, they might want to keep the following questions in mind:

1. What are the different types of love that they personally have felt or experienced? What effect has love had on them?
2. What have been some of their favorite depictions of love in books, movies, songs, or other works of art? What made these depictions stand out for them?
3. What images in nature remind them of love? Why do they make this connection?

Biographical Notes

Robert Browning (1812–1889) was an English poet known primarily for his dramatic monologues, or poems that represent the speech of one character. Browning was skilled at capturing realistic speech and the psychological states of characters.

Elizabeth Barrett Browning (1806–1861) was one of England's best-known female poets. She is most often associated with the love poetry she wrote for her husband, Robert Browning. At the time during which she wrote, however, she was respected as a scholarly poet whose large body of work examined moral and political issues.

Antoine de Saint-Exupéry (1900–1944) was a French author and aviator who is best known for his classic fable, *The Little Prince* (1943). He was lost in action during World War II.

For information about **Vincent van Gogh**, turn to page 220.

For information about **Ovid**, turn to page 436.

For information about the **King James Bible**, turn to page 286.

Ding Ling (1904–1986) was one of China's most popular twentieth-century authors. She introduced a new kind of Chinese heroine, independent and passionate, and also wrote novels of social realism.

Rainer Maria Rilke (1875–1926) was a German poet considered by many to be one of the most important lyric poets of the twentieth century. His poetry has been translated into many languages.

Alfred, Lord Tennyson (1809–1892) achieved great fame as a poet in England. His work often dealt with patriotic themes and subjects from medieval romance.

For information about **Virgil**, turn to page 222.

ADDITIONAL RESOURCES

READER'S GUIDE

- Selection Worksheet 3.1

ASSESSMENT PORTFOLIO

- Selection Check Test 2.3.1
- Selection Test 2.3.2

ESSENTIAL SKILLS PRACTICE BOOKS

- Writing 1.8, 1.20
- Applied English/Tech Prep 5.1

PREREADING EXTENSIONS

Some students might be interested in learning more about the fall of the Roman Republic and the emergence of the Roman Empire. Give them time to go to the library to conduct research, and then ask them to complete a paper or a creative project on some aspect of the Roman Republic or the Roman Empire.

SUPPORT FOR LEP STUDENTS

PRONUNCIATIONS OF PROPER NOUNS AND ADJECTIVES

Aus • o • ni • a (ô sō´nē ä)
Bac • chan • të (bə kan´tē)
Bacch • us (bak´əs)
Carth • age (cär´ thij)
Dar • dan • us (där´dən əs)
Phoe • ni • cian (fō nēsh´ən)
Sych • ae • us (sə kī´əs)
Teu • cri • ans (tu´ crē əns)
Tyr • i • an (tir´ē ən)

ADDITIONAL VOCABULARY

alighting—perching after flight
bereft—left in a state of loneliness or sadness
consequence—result of an action
desolate—deserted; wretched
dissolution—a breaking up
impassioned—full of strong feeling
indignity—embarrassment
traversed—moved along or across
two-faced—deceitful, insincere

PREREADING

from the *Aeneid*
by Virgil (Publius Vergilius Maro), translated by Robert Fitzgerald

 ROME

About the Author

VIRGIL
70-19 BC

Publius Vergilius Maro, known to readers as **Virgil**, is considered the greatest and most influential Roman poet who ever lived. Virgil was born on a farm in the village of Andes, near Mantua. His family was prosperous and sent Virgil to schools in Cremona, Milan, and Rome to study rhetoric and philosophy. Virgil studied the works of the Greek poets, and his earliest poems were pastoral, focusing on nature and agriculture. The most famous of these are the *Eclogues* and *Georgics*. The *Aeneid* was the last, as well as the most famous, of Virgil's works. This piece reflects the exciting period in which Virgil lived.

About the Selection

The epic poem the ***Aeneid*** is a masterpiece that combines historical fact with legend and myth. Virgil wrote this epic to glorify the fall of the Roman Republic and the beginning of the Roman Empire (see Connections below). As he describes the travels and adventures of the Trojan hero Aeneas, Virgil infuses the founding of this empire with noble emotions. The action takes place after the end of the Trojan War, a legendary war fought in ancient times between forces from mainland Greece and defenders of the city of Troy. The Greeks eventually conquered Troy and drove the Trojans from their homeland. When the *Aeneid* begins, Aeneas and his companions have been traveling the Mediterranean area for seven years in search of a new homeland. Their journey has been troubled, mainly because Juno, queen of the gods, resents the Trojans' destiny as a great people who will found the powerful Roman Empire and overtake Carthage, her city in North Africa. After Aeneas's ships are wrecked off the African coast near Carthage, Aeneas meets and falls in love with Dido, the city's queen. The stormy relationship between Aeneas and Dido is the subject of this excerpt from book 4 of the *Aeneid*.

CONNECTIONS: The Roman Empire

Rome, which according to legend was founded in 753 BC, was at first ruled by kings. Then the Roman Republic was established, governed by two elected consuls and a senate. This system weakened, and the Roman Empire began to emerge, headed first by Julius Cæsar and then by Augustus, the first emperor. The entire Western world was eventually ruled by the Roman Empire, which enjoyed centuries of peace known as the *Pax Romana*, or the Roman Peace. The *Pax Romana* lasted from 27 BC to AD 180.

GOALS/OBJECTIVES

Studying this lesson will enable students to

- enjoy and appreciate an epic masterpiece that combines historical fact with legend
- discuss the life and work of Virgil
- define the literary terms *motivation* and *pastoral poem*
- write a journal entry for a character in the *Aeneid*
- write a critical essay that analyzes the character of Queen Dido
- study and create artistic representations of Greek and Roman gods

What happens to a relationship when the people involved find that they have completely different goals and values? Do you think people should follow their hearts and stay involved at all costs or stay true to their individual goals? Is it possible to do both? Explain your response. You may use examples from your own life or from books and movies.

FROM THE

Aeneid

VIRGIL, TRANSLATED BY ROBERT FITZGERALD

Characters in the *Aeneid*

Aeneas (i nē´əs), son of Anchisës and Venus, goddess of love; leader of the Trojans after the destruction of Troy

Anchisës (an kī´sēz´), deceased father of Aeneas

Apollo (ə päl´ō), god of music, poetry, prophecy, and medicine. The voice of Apollo's oracle told Aeneas to travel to Italy, the land of the Trojans' ancestors.

Ascanius (as kā´nē əs), also called Iulus (yoo´ lus), son of Aeneas and Creusa, Aeneas's former wife who was lost in the flight from Troy. He represents the future of the Trojans.

Diana (dī an´ə), goddess of the Moon and hunting

Dido (dī´dō), Queen of Carthage who loves Aeneas

Eumenides (yōō men´i dēz), goddesses who punish crimes; also called the Avenging Ones or Furies

Hecate (hek´ ə tē), goddess of the Moon, Earth, and the world of the dead

Juno ((jōō ´nō), wife of Jupiter; enemy of Trojans. She causes trouble for Aeneas on his journey because she knows he is destined to overthrow Carthage.

Jupiter (jōō ´pit ər), also known as Jove (jōv), king of the gods and the most powerful of the gods

Mercury (mur´kyoo rē), messenger of the gods who commands Aeneas to leave Dido

Priam (prī´əm), king of Troy during the Trojan War

Pygmalion (pig māl´ē ən), Dido's brother, who killed Dido's husband and paid Dido to leave her homeland. She left and built Carthage.

READER'S JOURNAL

As an alternative activity, you might ask students to describe a time when they felt deserted or hurt by someone. Who was the person who left them feeling deserted? What emotions did they experience? Were their thoughts and feelings surrounding the situation rational, or were they unreasonable?

SPELLING AND VOCABULARY WORDS FROM THE SELECTION

admonish, admonition, avert, atonement, castigate, conflagration, duress, emblem, festoon, goad, integrity, limpid, oblivious, pillage, progeny, propitious, pyre, supplication, unconscionable, vestige

QUOTABLES

"Whatever it be, every fortune is to be overcome by bearing it."

—Virgil
Aeneid

"Time speeds away irretrievably."

—Virgil
Georgics

Answers to Guided Reading Questions

❶ Mercury finds Aeneas supervising the building of houses and towers.

❷ Mercury accuses Aeneas of being oblivious to the needs of his country and to future generations.

Cross-curricular Activities

Arts and Humanities and Social Studies

Students might want to work in pairs or small groups to create original maps showing the journey of Aeneas. Encourage students to list all the places to which Aeneas and his men travel. They can then use the library or online resources to find these places.

Students should try to make their maps vivid and interesting to view. They can use paints on a large piece of posterboard or white paper; they can make detailed illustrations of scenes from the story; or they can use glue and various everyday items to make the maps three-dimensional. Students can display their maps in the classroom or in the library.

Additional Questions and Activities

Ask students to guess what Aeneas's reaction to Mercury's visit and reprimand might be. Do they think Aeneas will want to leave? Why is Aeneas so easily distracted?

From Book 4
The Passion of Queen Dido

[Editor's note: Dido, the queen of Carthage, and Aeneas fall in love. This happens with the help of the goddess Juno, who hopes that Aeneas will be distracted from his journey to Italy, and with the assistance of the goddess Venus, Aeneas's mother, who wants her son to be happy. Queen Dido, also referred to as Elissa, begins to view their relationship as a marriage. When the following excerpt begins, Jupiter, father of the gods, has learned of this love affair and is not happy that Aeneas has stopped in Carthage. Jupiter is concerned that Aeneas has forgotten his responsibilities to his country and to future generations. Jupiter sends his messenger Mercury to speak to Aeneas.]

❶ *What does Mercury find Aeneas doing?*

❷ *To what does Mercury accuse Aeneas of being oblivious?*

Alighting tiptoe
On the first hutments,[1] there he[2] found Aeneas
Laying foundations for new towers and homes.
He noted well the swordhilt[3] the man wore,
Adorned with yellow jasper;[4] and the cloak
Aglow with Tyrian dye[5] upon his shoulders—
Gifts of the wealthy queen, who had inwoven
Gold thread in the fabric. Mercury
Took him to task at once:
"Is it for you
To lay the stones for Carthage's high walls,
Tame husband that you are, and build their city?
Oblivious of your own world, your own kingdom!
From bright Olympus[6] he[7] that rules the gods
And turns the earth and heaven by his power—
He and no other sent me to you, told me
To bring this message on the running winds:
What have you in mind? What hope, wasting your days
In Libya?[8] If future history's glories
Do not affect you, if you will not strive
For your own honor, think of Ascanius,
Think of the expectations of your heir,
Iulus, to whom the Italian realm, the land
Of Rome, are due."

1. **hutments.** Hut or group of huts, as in an army camp
2. **he.** Mercury, messenger of the gods
3. **swordhilt.** Handle of a sword
4. **jasper.** Type of quartz that is usually yellow, red, or brown
5. **Tyrian dye.** Purple dye made from the glands of snails and used to color cloth
6. **Olympus.** Home of the gods
7. **he.** Jupiter, father of the gods and the most powerful among them
8. **Libya.** In ancient Greek and Roman times, the name of an area in North Africa, west of Egypt. Now it is a country in North Africa.

Words for Everyday Use

ob • liv • i • ous (ə bliv´ē əs) *adj.,* forgetful or unmindful

Vocabulary in Context

- Max, completely oblivious to the cold, went outside without his hat or coat.

And Mercury, as he spoke,
Departed from the visual field of mortals
To a great distance, ebbed in subtle air.
Amazed, and shocked to the bottom of his soul
By what his eyes had seen, Aeneas felt
His hackles rise, his voice choke in his throat.
As the sharp <u>admonition</u> and command
From heaven had shaken him awake, he now
Burned only to be gone, to leave that land
Of the sweet life behind. What can he do? How tell
The impassioned queen and hope to win her over?
What opening shall he choose? This way and that
He let his mind dart, testing alternatives,
Running through every one. And as he pondered
This seemed the better tactic: he called in
Mnestheus, Sergestus and stalwart Serestus,[9]
Telling them:
"Get the fleet ready for sea,
But quietly, and collect the men on shore.
Lay in ship stores and gear."
As to the cause
For a change of plan, they were to keep it secret,
Seeing the excellent Dido had no notion,
No warning that such love could be cut short;
He would himself look for the right occasion,
The easiest time to speak, the way to do it.
The Trojans to a man gladly obeyed.

The queen, for her part, felt some plot afoot
Quite soon—for who deceives a woman in love?
She caught wind of a change, being in fear
Of what had seemed her safety. Evil Rumor,
Shameless as before, brought word to her
In her distracted state of ships being rigged
In trim for sailing. Furious, at her wits' end,
She traversed the whole city, all aflame
With rage, like a Bacchantë[10] driven wild
By <u>emblems</u> shaken, when the mountain revels
Of the odd year possess her, when the cry
Of Bacchus[11] rises and Cithaeron[12] calls

1 *What must Aeneas tell Queen Dido?*

2 *What are Aeneas's men to keep secret? Why does Aeneas want them to keep this secret?*

3 *What does Dido find out on her own? What is her reaction to the information?*

9. **Mnestheus, Sergestus, and . . . Serestus.** The crew working with Aeneas
10. **Bacchantë.** Worshiper of Bacchus, the god of wine and revelry
11. **Bacchus.** God of wine and revelry
12. **Cithaeron.** Mountain in Greece near Thebes, sacred to Bacchus

Words for Everyday Use

ad • mo • ni • tion (ad´mə nish´ən) *n.,* warning; reprimand
em • blem (em´bləm) *n.,* visible symbol

Answers to Guided Reading Questions

❶ Aeneas must tell Queen Dido that he must leave to fulfill his duties.

❷ Aeneas's men are told to keep their departure a secret. He knows his departure will anger and hurt Queen Dido.

❸ Dido finds out on her own that Aeneas is leaving. She is furious.

Literary Note

Mercury, who is the Roman version of the Greek god Hermes, was not only the messenger of the gods but also the god of mischief. He was said to be a beautiful youth with winged sandals and a winged cap. He carried a magic wand, the caduceus, with two serpents twined around it.

Additional Questions and Activities

Judging from Aeneas's reaction to Mercury's words, how does he feel about leaving Dido and Carthage? What does he seem to dread most about leaving?

ANSWERS

Responses will vary.

Aeneas is not happy to leave. He would like to stay with Dido in this comfortable place. He dreads most telling the queen that he must leave.

Vocabulary in Context

- The boss's final <u>admonition</u> to Harriet was that if she didn't stop sleeping on the job, she would be fired.
- Grandpa wore my hat as an <u>emblem</u> of his support for my baseball team.

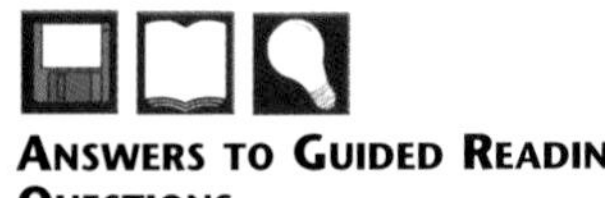

Answers to Guided Reading Questions

① Dido tries to compel Aeneas to stay by reminding him of his pledges, making him feel guilty, and warning him of the winter seas.

Additional Questions and Activities

How does Queen Dido show her desperation to have Aeneas stay? How seriously does she take their relationship?

ANSWERS

Responses will vary.

She tells him that he must not leave in such stormy seas. She takes their relationship quite seriously. She considers it a marriage.

***Roman Temple.** Canaletto Bellotto (Bernardo Bellotto)*

All through the shouting night. Thus it turned out
She was the first to speak and charge Aeneas:

① *What does Dido do to try to get Aeneas to stay with her?*

"You even hoped to keep me in the dark
As to this outrage, did you, two-faced man,
And slip away in silence? Can our love
Not hold you, can the pledge we gave not hold you,
Can Dido not, now sure to die in pain?
Even in winter weather must you toil
With ships, and fret to launch against high winds
For the open sea? Oh, heartless!
Tell me now,
If you were not in search of alien lands
And new strange homes, if ancient Troy remained,
Would ships put out for Troy on these big seas?
Do you go to get away from me? I beg you,
By these tears, by your own right hand, since I
Have left my wretched self nothing but that—
Yes, by the marriage that we entered on,
If ever I did well and you were grateful
Or found some sweetness in a gift from me,
Have pity now on a declining house!

Put this plan by, I beg you, if a prayer
Is not yet out of place.
Because of you, Libyans and nomad kings
Detest me, my own Tyrians[13] are hostile;
Because of you, I lost my integrity
And that admired name by which alone
I made my way once toward the stars.
To whom
Do you abandon me, a dying woman,
Guest that you are—the only name now left
From that of husband? Why do I live on?
Shall I, until my brother Pygmalion comes
To pull my walls down? Or the Gaetulan
Iarbas leads me captive? If at least
There were a child by you for me to care for,
A little one to play in my courtyard
And give me back Aeneas, in spite of all,
I should not feel so utterly defeated,
Utterly bereft."
She ended there.
The man by Jove's command held fast his eyes
And fought down the emotion in his heart.
At length he answered:
"As for myself, be sure
I never shall deny all you can say,
Your majesty, of what you meant to me.
Never will the memory of Elissa[14]
Stale for me, while I can still remember
My own life, and the spirit rules my body.
As to the event, a few words. Do not think
I meant to be deceitful and slip away.
I never held the torches of a bridegroom,
Never entered upon the pact of marriage.
If Fate permitted me to spend my days
By my own lights, and make the best of things
According to my wishes, first of all
I should look after Troy and the loved relics
Left me of my people. Priam's great hall
Should stand again; I should have restored the tower
Of Pergamum[15] for Trojans in defeat.

❶ *Why does Dido believe that Aeneas should take pity on her? What has happened as a result of their relationship?*

❷ *Is Aeneas happy to be going? Is he leaving of his own free will?*

13. **Tyrians.** People from Dido's former homeland of Phoenicia
14. **Elissa.** One of Dido's names
15. **Pergamum.** Ancient Greek kingdom, later a Roman province

Words for Everyday Use

in • teg • ri • ty (in teg´rə tē) *n.*, quality or state of being honest or sincere

Answers to Guided Reading Questions

❶ Dido believes that Aeneas should pity the state she is in. As a result of their relationship, she feels she has lost her integrity as queen, that other kings are hostile, and that her own people are unhappy with her.

❷ Aeneas is not happy to be leaving Dido and upsetting her. He is not going of his own free will—the gods have ordered him to go.

Literary Note

As students read in the character chart on page 223, Pygmalion was Queen Dido's brother. He was also king of Cyprus and a sculptor. Pygmalion is the subject of a popular myth in which he carves the statue of a girl from a block of snow-white ivory. The statue was more beautiful than any woman who had ever lived, and Pygmalion loved the statue so much that it seemed to him nearly alive. He dressed it and adorned it with jewelry and ribbons.

On the holiday of Venus, the goddess of love and beauty, Pygmalion made an offering to Venus. He almost asked that his statue be made into his wife but changed his mind. He simply asked for a wife like his statue. Venus heard his prayer and the true wish behind it. After offering his prayer, Pygmalion returned to his statue, only to find its cold limbs flushed with color, moving gracefully. The statue had come to life! Venus had taken his wish seriously and smiled on the couple from above.

Invite students to read the original version of this story in Ovid's *Metamorphoses*. They might especially enjoy Edith Hamilton's translation of Ovid's tale in her book *Mythology*.

Vocabulary in Context

• Yolanda would never cheat—she has too much integrity.

Answers to Guided Reading Questions

❶ Aeneas is going to Italy. He feels that Dido, who loves her own land, should understand his need to find a home for his people.

❷ The gods have ordered him to go.

Quotables

"Do your duty, and leave the rest to the gods."

—Pierre Corneille
Horace

INTEGRATED SKILLS ACTIVITIES

APPLIED ENGLISH/TECH PREP

Aeneas and Queen Dido are at odds over Aeneas's decision to leave. Ask students to write two personal letters—one from Dido to Aeneas, and one from Aeneas to Dido. Each letter should express the feelings and wishes of its writer. Encourage students to concentrate on what Dido and Aeneas are truly thinking and feeling at this point of decision-making in the poem.

The letters should be persuasive—each character wants the other to understand his or her point of view.

Before students begin, they might want to review the Language Arts Survey 5.1, "Personal and Business Letters."

► For additional practice, see Essential Skills Practice Book: Applied English/Tech Prep 5.1.

❶ *Where exactly is Aeneas going? Why does he believe that Dido should understand what motivates him to leave?*

But now it is the rich Italian land
Apollo tells me I must make for: Italy,
Named by his oracles. There is my love;
There is my country. If, as a Phoenician,[16]
You are so given to the charms of Carthage,
Libyan city that it is, then tell me,
Why begrudge the Teucrians[17] new lands
For homesteads in Ausonia? Are we not
Entitled, too, to look for realms abroad?
Night never veils the earth in damp and darkness,
Fiery stars never ascend the east,
But in my dreams my father's troubled ghost
Admonishes and frightens me. Then, too,
Each night thoughts come of young Ascanius,
My dear boy wronged, defrauded of his kingdom,
Hesperian lands of destiny. And now
The gods' interpreter, sent by Jove himself—
I swear it by your head and mine—has brought
Commands down through the racing winds! I say
With my own eyes in full daylight I saw him
Entering the building! With my very ears
I drank his message in! So please, no more
Of these appeals that set us both afire.
I sail for Italy not of my own free will."

❷ *Why is Aeneas's trip "not of [his] own free will"?*

During all this she had been watching him
With face averted, looking him up and down
In silence, and she burst out raging now:

"No goddess[18] was your mother. Dardanus[19]
Was not the founder of your family.
Liar and cheat! Some rough Caucasian cliff
Begot you on flint. Hyrcanian tigresses
Tendered their teats to you. Why should I palter?
Why still hold back for more indignity?
Sigh, did he, while I wept? Or look at me?

16. **Phoenician.** Person of Phoenicia, an ancient region at the east end of the Mediterranean which included the city of Carthage. Queen Dido is Phoenician.
17. **Teucrians.** Trojans
18. **goddess.** Venus is Aeneas's mother, but Dido, in her rage, tells Aeneas that this is not so.
19. **Dardanus.** Ancestor of the house of Priam, founder of Troy

Words for Everyday Use

ad • mon • ish (ad män´ish) *vt.,* caution against or scold mildly
a • vert (ə vʉrt´) *vt.,* turn away from

Vocabulary in Context

- I needed to admonish the toddler for dumping his cereal on the floor.
- Paloma needed to avert her eyes from the sunset in order to concentrate on her studies.

Or yield a tear, or pity her who loved him?
What shall I say first, with so much to say?
The time is past when either supreme Juno
Or the Saturnian[20] father viewed these things
With justice. Faith can never be secure.
I took the man in, thrown up on this coast
In dire need, and in my madness then
Contrived a place for him in my domain,
Rescued his lost fleet, saved his shipmates' lives.
Oh, I am swept away burning by furies!
Now the prophet Apollo, now his oracles,
Now the gods' interpreter, if you please,
Sent down by Jove himself, brings through the air
His formidable commands! What fit employment
For heaven's high powers! What anxieties
To plague serene immortals! I shall not
Detain you or dispute your story. Go,
Go after Italy on the sailing winds,
Look for your kingdom, cross the deepsea swell!
If divine justice counts for anything,
I hope and pray that on some grinding reef
Midway at sea you'll drink your punishment
And call and call on Dido's name!
From far away I shall come after you
With my black fires, and when cold death has parted
Body from soul I shall be everywhere
A shade to haunt you! You will pay for this,
Unconscionable! I shall hear! The news will reach me
Even among the lowest of the dead!"

At this abruptly she broke off and ran
In sickness from his sight and the light of day,
Leaving him at a loss, alarmed, and mute
With all he meant to say. The maids in waiting
Caught her as she swooned and carried her
To bed in her marble chamber.
Duty-bound,
Aeneas, though he struggled with desire
To calm and comfort her in all her pain,
To speak to her and turn her mind from grief,

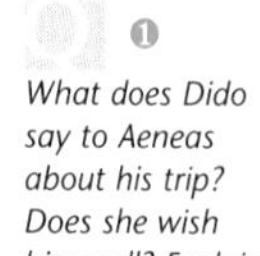

❶ *What does Dido say to Aeneas about his trip? Does she wish him well? Explain.*

❷ *How does Aeneas feel about leaving Dido when she is so upset?*

20. **Saturnian.** Of the Roman god Saturn, who ruled during the Golden Age, an age of innocence and prosperity, until his son Jupiter dethroned him

Words for Everyday Use

un • con • scion • a • ble (un kän´shən ə bəl) *adj.*, not fair or just

Answers to Guided Reading Questions

❶ Dido is furious with Aeneas and with the gods because of his trip. She does not wish Aeneas well—in fact, she wishes destruction on him and his fleet.

❷ Aeneas is not happy about leaving Dido when she is so upset, but he knows that he must.

Additional Questions and Activities

Ask students to answer the following questions:

Why does Dido wish misfortune on Aeneas and his fleet, even though she loves him? What emotions are behind her harsh statements? Have you ever felt so hurt by someone you love that your feelings of hurt turned to feelings of anger? Explain.

ANSWERS

Responses will vary.

Dido is frustrated and angry. Feelings of hurt, abandonment, and anger are behind the harsh statements. Encourage students to relate their own feelings to those that Dido is feeling.

Vocabulary in Context

- Blaming the young child for his own mistake was completely unconscionable.

Answers to Guided Reading Questions

❶ The narrator asks to what painful extremes Love will not go to torture hearts. Dido is going to "[humble] her pride" by sending her sister to speak to Aeneas.

Additional Questions and Activities

Why do students think Dido decides to humble herself?

ANSWERS

Responses will vary.

Students might say that Dido has reached another stage of desperation and is trying to do everything she can to get Aeneas to stay.

Literary Technique

CHARACTERIZATION

Characterization is the use of literary techniques to create a character. Writers use three major techniques to create characters: direct description, portrayal of characters' behavior, and representation of characters' inner states. Ask students to discuss Queen Dido and Aeneas as characters thus far in the selection. Students should notice that, because Aeneas is being directed by the gods to take his role as a fearless leader who cannot be distracted, Dido seems to be a much more complex character. The reader is shown the ups and downs of her emotions, and the feelings she has for Aeneas. Students should also realize that, because Aeneas was afraid to approach her with news of his departure, it is clear that she is a strong and volatile character.

And though he sighed his heart out, shaken still
With love of her, yet took the course heaven gave him
And went back to the fleet. Then with a will
The Teucrians fell to work and launched the ships
Along the whole shore: slick with tar each hull
Took to the water. Eager to get away,
The sailors brought oar-boughs out of the woods
With leaves still on, and oaken logs unhewn.
Now you could see them issuing from the town
To the water's edge in streams, as when, aware
Of winter, ants will pillage a mound of spelt[21]
To store it in their granary; over fields
The black battalion moves, and through the grass
On a narrow trail they carry off the spoil;
Some put their shoulders to the enormous weight
Of a trundled grain, while some pull stragglers in
And castigate delay; their to-and-fro
Of labor makes the whole track come alive.
At that sight, what were your emotions, Dido?
Sighing how deeply, looking out and down
From your high tower on the seething shore
Where all the harbor filled before your eyes
With bustle and shouts! Unconscionable Love,
To what extremes will you not drive our hearts!
She now felt driven to weep again, again
To move him, if she could, by supplication,
Humbling her pride before her love—to leave
Nothing untried, not to die needlessly.

 ❶

What question does the narrator ask about love? In what way is Dido going to humble her pride?

"Anna, you see the arc of waterfront
All in commotion: they come crowding in
From everywhere. Spread canvas calls for wind,
The happy crews have garlanded the stems.
If I could brace myself for this great sorrow,
Sister, I can endure it, too. One favor,
Even so, you may perform for me.
Since that deserter chose you for his friend
And trusted you, even with private thoughts,
Since you alone know when he may be reached,
Go, intercede with our proud enemy.

21. **spelt.** Primitive species of wheat, now seldom cultivated

Words for Everyday Use

pil • lage (pil´ij) *vt.*, rob; take as booty or loot

cas • ti • gate (kas´ti gāt´) *vt.*, punish or rebuke severely

sup • pli • ca • tion (sup´lə kā´shən) *n.*, humble request or prayer

Vocabulary in Context

- Pirates used to pillage the ships that they attacked.
- The judge will castigate the group for its terrible act of vandalism.
- Her daily supplication was for good weather and good health.

Map of the Roman Empire. *Icon, 1851*

Remind him that I took no oath at Aulis
With Danaans to destroy the Trojan race;
I sent no ship to Pergamum. Never did I
Profane his father Anchisës' dust and shade.
Why will he not allow my prayers to fall
On his unpitying ears? Where is he racing?
Let him bestow one last gift on his mistress:
This, to await fair winds and easier flight.
Now I no longer plead the bond he broke
Of our old marriage, nor do I ask that he
Should live without his dear love, Latium,
Or yield his kingdom. Time is all I beg,
Mere time, a respite and a breathing space
For madness to subside in, while my fortune
Teaches me how to take defeat and grieve.
Pity your sister. This is the end, this favor—
To be repaid with interest when I die."

She pleaded in such terms, and such, in tears,
Her sorrowing sister brought him, time and again.

➊ *What does Dido ask her sister Anna to say to Aeneas? What happens when Anna goes to Aeneas?*

Answers to Guided Reading Questions

➊ Dido instructs her sister, Anna, to tell Aeneas that, although Dido accepts that he must leave, she asks that he wait for calmer winds. When Anna goes to Aeneas, she relays her sister's message.

Historical Note

Hellenistic poetry, or poetry reflective of the Greek culture after the death of Alexander the Great in 323 BC, influenced such Roman poets as Virgil and Ovid. The chief Greek poets of this period were Theocritus, Callimachus, and Apollonius of Rhodes.

Theocritus, who lived from about 310–250 BC, was the originator of pastoral poetry. This type of poetry idealizes rural life. The poem *Harvest Home* is considered the best of his rural farm poetry. He also wrote plays set in the country, minor epics, and lyric poetry about various subjects. The pastoral style Theocritus established was the style Virgil followed in his well-known work *Eclogues*.

Callimachus, who lived at the same time as Theocritus, wrote a famous work called *Aetia*, an elegy in four books. The poem explains the legendary origins of customs, festivals, and names. This lengthy piece served as a model for Ovid's work.

Apollonius of Rhodes, born about 295 BC, was a pupil of Callimachus. He wrote an epic called *Argonautica* about the mythical hero Jason who with his shipmates sought a golden fleece. This piece strongly influenced Virgil's writing in the *Aeneid*.

Answers to Guided Reading Questions

❶ Aeneas is not moved by Dido's request. He does not change his plans.

❷ Dido prays for death, and begins to plan her own death.

❸ Dido hears the voice and words of her husband. She has nightmares about being hunted down by Aeneas and going on a frightening journey.

Quotables

"Anger is a brief madness."

—Horace, *Epistles*

Biographical Note

Horace (65 BC–8 BC) was the greatest lyric poet of Rome during the reign of Emperor Augustus. His surviving writings include 121 lyric poems and 41 verse essays. His major works are *Odes*, *Epodes*, *Secular Hymn*, *Epistles*, *Satires*, and *Ars Poetica* (Art of Poetry). Much of his writing is devoted to praising Augustus and the changes the emperor made in the Roman state.

❶ *Is Aeneas moved by Dido's request? Does he change his plans?*

But no tears moved him, no one's voice would he
Attend to tractably. The fates opposed it;
God's will blocked the man's once kindly ears.
And just as when the north winds from the Alps
This way and that contend among themselves
To tear away an oaktree hale with age,
The wind and tree cry, and the buffeted trunk
Showers high foliage to earth, but holds
On bedrock, for the roots go down as far
Into the underworld as cresting boughs
Go up in heaven's air: just so this captain,
Buffeted by a gale of pleas
This way and that way, dinned all the day long,
Felt their moving power in his great heart,
And yet his will stood fast; tears fell in vain.

❷ *For what does Dido pray after she is sure Aeneas will leave? What act does she plan to perform?*

On Dido in her desolation now
Terror grew at her fate. She prayed for death,
Being heartsick at the mere sight of heaven.
That she more surely would perform the act
And leave the daylight, now she saw before her
A thing one shudders to recall: on altars
Fuming with incense where she placed her gifts,
The holy water blackened, the spilt wine
Turned into blood and mire. Of this she spoke
To no one, not to her sister even. Then, too,
Within the palace was a marble shrine
Devoted to her onetime lord, a place
She held in wondrous honor, all festooned
With snowy fleeces and green festive boughs.
From this she now thought voices could be heard
And words could be made out, her husband's words,
Calling her, when midnight hushed the earth;
And lonely on the rooftops the night owl
Seemed to lament, in melancholy notes,
Prolonged to a doleful cry. And then, besides,
The riddling words of seers in ancient days,
Foreboding sayings, made her thrill with fear.
In nightmare, fevered, she was hunted down
By pitiless Aeneas, and she seemed
Deserted always, uncompanioned always,
On a long journey, looking for her Tyrians
In desolate landscapes—

❸ *What voices does Dido hear? About what does she have nightmares?*

Words for Everyday Use

fes • toon (fes to͞on´) *vt.*, adorn or hang with a wreath or garland of flowers

Vocabulary in Context

• After we festoon the room with decorations, we will really be in the mood for a celebration.

as Pentheus gone mad
Sees the oncoming Eumenidës and sees
A double sun and double Thebes appear,
Or as when, hounded on the stage, Orestës[22]
Runs from a mother armed with burning brands,
With serpents hellish black,
And in the doorway squat the Avenging Ones.

So broken in mind by suffering, Dido caught
Her fatal madness and resolved to die.
She pondered time and means, then visiting
Her mournful sister, covered up her plan
With a calm look, a clear and hopeful brow.

"Sister, be glad for me! I've found a way
To bring him back or free me of desire.
Near to the Ocean boundary, near sundown,
The Aethiops' farthest territory lies,
Where giant Atlas[23] turns the sphere of heaven
Studded with burning stars. From there
A priestess of Massylian stock has come;
She had been pointed out to me: custodian
Of that shrine named for daughters of the west,
Hesperidës;[24] and it is she who fed
The dragon, guarding well the holy boughs
With honey dripping slow and drowsy poppy.
Chanting her spells she undertakes to free
What hearts she wills, but to inflict on others
Duress of sad desires; to arrest
The flow of rivers, make the stars move backward,
Call up the spirits of deep Night. You'll see
Earth shift and rumble underfoot and ash trees
Walk down mountainsides. Dearest, I swear
Before the gods and by your own sweet self,
It is against my will that I resort
For weaponry to magic powers. In secret

➊ *To what type of ritual does Dido turn in her desperation?*

22. **Orestës.** Character in classical mythology who takes revenge on his mother for the murder of his father by killing her
23. **Atlas.** Titan who carries the world and the heavens on his shoulders
24. **Hesperidës.** Daughters of Atlas who guard golden apples from the Tree of Life

Words for Everyday Use

du • ress (do͞o res´) *n.*, compulsion; use of force or threats

Answers to Guided Reading Questions

➊ Dido chants spells and resorts to "magic powers."

Literary Technique

PASTORAL POEM

A **pastoral poem** is verse that deals with idealized rural life. You might want to turn students' attention to the rich description in this part of the poem, including "Near to the Ocean boundary, near sundown . . . With honey dripping slow and drowsy poppy," and "The flow of rivers, make the stars move backward,/Call up the spirits of deep Night. You'll see/Earth shift and rumble underfoot and ash trees/Walk down mountainsides."

Additional Questions and Activities

Ask each student to write two or three lines of pastoral verse. Students can write about a favorite place in the country, in a park, or can simply look out the window and focus on some small detail that catches their attention. Students should try more to capture a scene in rich, vivid detail than to make their lines fall into rhyme and meter.

Vocabulary in Context

• Extreme mental duress drove the leader from office.

Answers to Guided Reading Questions

❶ She asks her sister to build a pyre. She says that she plans to burn Aeneas's weapons, his clothing, and their bed.

❷ Anna believes that this ritual—burning items that remind Dido of Aeneas—will help her sister. She is unable to see the extent of her sister's madness.

Literary Note

In his poem "Epigram on Milton," English literary figure John Dryden reveals the influence Greek and Roman literature had on his work.

An **epigram** is a short, often witty, saying or poem. In this epigram, Dryden praises English poet John Milton, comparing him to the ancient Greek poet Homer and the ancient Roman poet Virgil. John Milton is the author of the famous twelve-book epic *Paradise Lost.*

"Epigram on Milton"
by John Dryden

Three poets, in three different ages born
Greece, Italy, and England did adorn.
The first in loftiness of thought surpassed,
The next in majesty, in both the last:
The force of Nature could no further go;
To make a third, she joined the former two.

The Fountain.
Hubert Robert

❶ *What does Dido ask her sister to build? What does she tell her sister she plans to do?*

Build up a pyre in the inner court
Under the open sky, and place upon it
The arms that faithless man left in my chamber,
All his clothing, and the marriage bed
On which I came to grief—solace for me
To annihilate all vestige of the man,
Vile as he is: my priestess shows me this."

❷ *Why does Anna build the pyre? What is Anna's mistake?*

While she was speaking, cheek and brow grew pale.
But Anna could not think her sister cloaked
A suicide in these unheard-of rites;
She failed to see how great her madness was
And feared no consequence more grave
Than at Sychaeus'[25] death. So, as commanded,

25. **Sychaeus'.** Dido's first husband who was murdered by her brother Pygmalion

Words for Everyday Use

pyre (pīr) *n.,* pile, especially of wood, on which a dead body is burned in a funeral rite

ves • tige (ves´tij) *n.,* trace; mark or sign of something that once existed but now has passed away

Vocabulary in Context

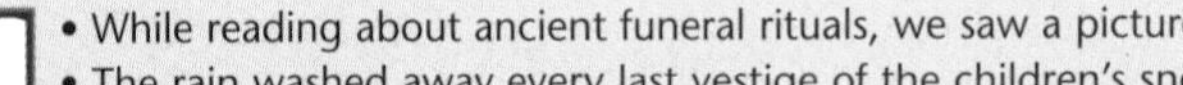

- While reading about ancient funeral rituals, we saw a picture of a burning pyre.
- The rain washed away every last vestige of the children's snow fort.

She made the preparations. For her part,
The queen, seeing the pyre in her inmost court
Erected huge with pitch-pine and sawn ilex,
Hung all the place under the sky with wreaths
And crowned it with funereal cypress boughs.
On the pyre's top she put a sword he left
With clothing, and an effigy[26] on a couch,
Her mind fixed now ahead on what would come.
Around the pyre stood altars, and the priestess,
Hair unbound, called in a voice of thunder
Upon three hundred gods, on Erebus,[27]
On Chaos, and on triple Hecatë,
Three-faced Diana. Then she sprinkled drops
Purportedly from the fountain of Avernus.[28]
Rare herbs were brought out, reaped at the new moon
By scythes of bronze, and juicy with a milk
Of dusky venom; then the rare love-charm
Or caul[29] torn from the brow of a birthing foal
And snatched away before the mother found it.
Dido herself with consecrated grain
In her pure hands, as she went near the altars,
Freed one foot from sandal straps, let fall
Her dress ungirdled, and, now sworn to death,
Called on the gods and stars that knew her fate.
She prayed then to whatever power may care
In comprehending justice for the grief
Of lovers bound unequally by love.

The night had come, and weary in every land
Men's bodies took the boon of peaceful sleep.
The woods and the wild seas had quieted
At that hour when the stars are in mid-course
And every field is still; cattle and birds
With vivid wings that haunt the limpid lakes
Or nest in thickets in the country places
All were asleep under the silent night.
Not, though, the agonized Phoenician queen:

❶ *To whom does Dido call out? For what does she want justice?*

26. **effigy.** Likeness; often, a crude representation of a person
27. **Erebus.** Dark place under the earth where the dead pass on their way to Hades, the underworld and home of the dead
28. **Avernus.** Small lake in an extinct volcano in Italy. It was believed to be near the entrance to Hades.
29. **caul.** Membrane enclosing a fetus, sometimes enveloping the head of a child at birth; saving it after a birth was thought to bring good luck.

Words for Everyday Use

lim • pid (lim´pid) *adj.,* perfectly clear; transparent

Answers to Guided Reading Questions

❶ Dido calls out to the gods. She wants justice for her suffering and humiliation.

Literary Technique

MOOD

Mood, or **atmosphere**, is the emotion created in the reader by all or part of a literary work. Ask students to notice the poem's change in mood now that Queen Dido has had time to absorb the idea of Aeneas's departure. Ask them to notice how her "madness" has moved away from fury and toward hopelessness and depression. She is now resigned to her belief that she must die—she feels she has nothing for which to live but thinks dying could be a wonderful type of revenge. Ask students to compare this section of the poem to the section in which Dido first discovers what she perceives as Aeneas's betrayal.

Quotables

"Revenge, at first though sweet,
Bitter ere long back on itself recoils."

—John Milton
Paradise Lost

Vocabulary in Context

• We dangled our legs in the calm, limpid pond.

Answers to Guided Reading Questions

❶ Her strong feelings of love and anger prevent her from sleeping.

❷ She feels that she cannot turn to her old suitors for company, since she has treated them with disdain in the past. She knows that she cannot "trail the Ilian ships . . . like a slave." She feels that there is no end to her loneliness.

❸ Aeneas can sleep because he has become completely engaged in his mission. He is a warrior now, fulfilling his duty, and nothing else is on his mind.

Literary Note

You might want to refer students to the selection from the *Iliad*, page 592, or give them the following brief synopsis of the myth of the Trojan War after they have finished this selection:

Paris, son of the king of Troy, earned the favor of Aphrodite, goddess of love, by judging her the most beautiful of all the goddesses of Olympus. Aphrodite rewarded Paris by promising him the fairest woman on Earth for his wife. Helen was the prize, and although she was already married to Menelaus, King of Sparta, she went to Troy with Paris. Menelaus summoned the kings of Greece to help him get his wife back, and a ten-year war between the Greeks and the Trojans followed. The Greek heroes, including skillful warriors Achilles and Odysseus, greatly outnumbered the Trojans, but Troy was protected by high, thick walls that prevented the Greeks from entering the city. Finally, the Greeks conceived a plan to capture Troy: They built a huge wooden horse and left it on the shore. Then they sailed away, though only far enough to be out of sight.

Thinking they had caused the Greeks to flee in defeat, the

(cont.)

❶ *Why can't Dido sleep?*

She never slackened into sleep and never
Allowed the tranquil night to rest
Upon her eyelids or within her heart.
Her pain redoubled; love came on again,
Devouring her, and on her bed she tossed
In a great surge of anger.
So awake,
She pressed these questions, musing to herself:

❷ *Why does Dido feel her situation is hopeless?*

"Look now, what can I do? Turn once again
To the old suitors, only to be laughed at—
Begging a marriage with Numidians[30]
Whom I disdained so often? Then what? Trail
The Ilian[31] ships and follow like a slave
Commands of Trojans? Seeing them so agreeable,
In view of past assistance and relief,
So thoughtful their unshaken gratitude?
Suppose I wished it, who permits or takes
Aboard their proud ships one they so dislike?
Poor lost soul, do you not yet grasp or feel
The treachery of the line of Laömedon?[32]
What then? Am I to go alone, companion
Of the exultant sailors in their flight?
Or shall I set out in their wake, with Tyrians,
With all my crew close at my side, and send
The men I barely tore away from Tyre
To sea again, making them hoist their sails
To more sea-winds? No: die as you deserve,
Give pain quietus[33] with a steel blade.
Sister,
You are the one who gave way to my tears
In the beginning, burdened a mad queen
With sufferings, and thrust me on my enemy.
It was not given me to lead my life
Without new passion, innocently, the way
Wild creatures live, and not to touch these depths.
The vow I took to the ashes of Sychaeus
Was not kept."
So she broke out afresh
In bitter mourning. On his high stern deck
Aeneas, now quite certain of departure,
Everything ready, took the boon of sleep.
In dream the figure of the god returned
With looks reproachful as before: he seemed
Again to warn him, being like Mercury

❸ *Why can Aeneas sleep while Dido cannot?*

30. **Numidians.** People of Numidia, a country in ancient northern Africa
31. **Ilian.** Trojan
32. **Laömedon.** Founder of Troy
33. **quietus.** Discharge or release

Literary Note (cont.)

Trojans triumphantly pulled the horse into their city as a trophy. The horse, however, was filled with Greek soldiers who slipped out at night and opened the gates of Troy. Greek warriors stormed into the city, setting fire to it and killing its inhabitants. The city was destroyed, and Helen was brought back to Sparta. One Trojan prince, Aeneas, escaped and traveled to Italy, where he helped to found Rome.

In every way, in voice, in golden hair,
And in the bloom of youth.
"Son of the goddess,
Sleep away this crisis, can you still?
Do you not see the dangers growing round you,
Madman, from now on? Can you not hear
The offshore westwind blow? The woman hatches
Plots and drastic actions in her heart,
Resolved on death now, whipping herself on
To heights of anger. Will you not be gone
In flight, while flight is still within your power?
Soon you will see the offing[34] boil with ships
And glare with torches; soon again
The waterfront will be alive with fires,
If Dawn comes while you linger in this country.
Ha! Come, break the spell! Woman's a thing
Forever fitful and forever changing."

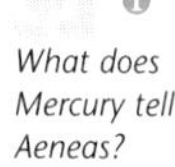

1 *What does Mercury tell Aeneas?*

At this he merged into the darkness. Then
As the abrupt phantom filled him with fear,
Aeneas broke from sleep and roused his crewmen:
"Up, turn out now! Oarsmen, take your thwarts!
Shake out sail! Look here, for the second time
A god from heaven's high air is goading me
To hasten our break away, to cut the cables.
Holy one, whatever god you are,
We go with you, we act on your command
Most happily! Be near, graciously help us,
Make the stars in heaven propitious ones!"

2 *What does Aeneas do in response to Mercury's advice and comment?*

He pulled his sword aflash out of its sheath
And struck at the stem hawser.[35] All the men
Were gripped by his excitement to be gone,
And hauled and hustled. Ships cast off their moorings,
And an array of hulls hid inshore water
As oarsmen churned up foam and swept to sea.

Soon early Dawn, quitting the saffron bed

34. **offing.** Distant part of the sea visible from the shore
35. **stem hawser.** Large rope attached to the prow of the ship and used for mooring

Words for Everyday Use

goad (gōd) *vt.*, prod into action; urge on

pro • pi • tious (prō pi´shəs) *adj.*, favorable

Answers to Guided Reading Questions

1 Mercury tells Aeneas that he is in danger because of Dido's wrath. Mercury says that Dido is planning drastic action against Aeneas and his fleet, and that he must leave as quickly as possible.

2 Aeneas orders his crew to set sail in the middle of the night.

Additional Questions and Activities

Why does Aeneas leave after talking to Mercury? What has happened to his feelings for Dido?

ANSWERS

Responses will vary.

Aeneas now has only one mission—to get to Italy. His feelings of romance have been replaced by his devotion to his people and his need to fulfill his duty.

Vocabulary in Context

- We will goad our mother into entering that race because we know she will win.
- Because of the propitious weather, we were able to picnic all day and into the evening.

Answers to Guided Reading Questions

❶ Dido feels that Aeneas has mocked her and her kingdom by leaving.

❷ She wishes that she had gone into his camp with torches and killed everyone, including herself.

Literary Technique

PERSONIFICATION

Personification is a figure of speech in which something not human is described as if it were human. Point out to students the appearance of "Dawn" in lines 459–460. Dawn's job is to "cast new light on earth" each morning. Ask students to discuss this image of morning. How do they imagine Dawn looks? Does this figure of speech give them a clear picture of morning light?

Additional Questions and Activities

Ask students to create an example of personification, like the image of Dawn, to illustrate a regular occurrence in nature such as thunder, lightning, rain, sunset, snow, wind, or earthquake. What kind of figure with human-like qualities might be behind such occurrences? Have students start by making quick sketches or cartoons. Students can then describe their personified nature image in a paragraph or poem. Invite them to share their work with one another.

Of old Tithonus,[36] cast new light on earth,
And as air grew transparent, from her tower
The queen caught sight of ships on the seaward reach
With sails full and the wind astern. She knew
The waterfront now empty, bare of oarsmen.
Beating her lovely breast three times, four times,
And tearing her golden hair,
"O Jupiter,"
She said, "will this man go, will he have mocked
My kingdom, stranger that he was and is?
Will they not snatch up arms and follow him
From every quarter of the town? and dockhands
Tear our ships from moorings? On! Be quick
With torches! Give out arms! Unship the oars!
What am I saying? Where am I? What madness
Takes me out of myself? Dido, poor soul,
Your evil doing has come home to you.
Then was the right time, when you offered him
A royal scepter. See the good faith and honor
Of one they say bears with him everywhere
The hearthgods of his country! One who bore
His father, spent with age, upon his shoulders!
Could I not then have torn him limb from limb
And flung the pieces on the sea? His company,
Even Ascanius could I not have minced
And served up to his father at a feast?
The luck of battle might have been in doubt—
So let it have been! Whom had I to fear,
Being sure to die? I could have carried torches
Into his camp, filled passage ways with flame,
Annihilated father and son and followers
And given my own life on top of all!
O Sun, scanning with flame all works of earth,
And thou, O Juno, witness and go-between
Of my long miseries; and Hecatë,
Screeched for at night at crossroads in the cities;
And thou, avenging Furies,[37] and all gods
On whom Elissa dying may call: take notice,
Overshadow this hell with your high power,
As I deserve, and hear my prayer!
If by necessity that impious wretch

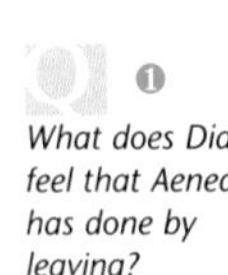

❶ *What does Dido feel that Aeneas has done by leaving?*

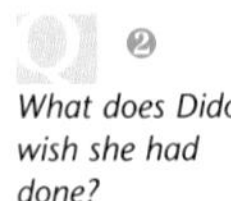

❷ *What does Dido wish she had done?*

36. **Dawn . . . old Tithonus.** The goddess of dawn, Eos in Greek mythology and Aurora in Roman mythology, obtains immortality for her love, Tithonus. She neglects, however, to obtain eternal youth for him, so he lives forever but shrivels up into a grasshopper. These lines mean that it is morning—Dawn leaves her love's side to cast light on the earth.

37. **Furies.** Three female spirits with hair made of snakes. The Furies punish unavenged crimes.

Temple of Athena, Paestum

Must find his haven and come safe to land,
If so Jove's destinies require, and this,
His end in view, must stand, yet all the same
When hard beset in war by a brave people,
Forced to go outside his boundaries
And torn from Iulus, let him beg assistance,
Let him see the unmerited deaths of those
Around and with him, and accepting peace
On unjust terms, let him not, even so,
Enjoy his kingdom or the life he longs for,
But fall in battle before his time and lie
Unburied on the sand! This I implore,
This is my last cry, as my last blood flows.
Then, O my Tyrians, besiege with hate
His progeny and all his race to come:
Make this your offering to my dust. No love,
No pact must be between our peoples; No,
But rise up from my bones, avenging spirit!
Harry[38] with fire and sword the Dardan countrymen
Now, or hereafter, at whatever time
The strength will be afforded. Coast with coast
In conflict, I implore, and sea with sea,
And arms with arms: may they contend in war,
Themselves and all the children of their children!"

❶ *What vow does Dido make about Aeneas and his people?*

38. **Harry.** Raid, pillage, or plunder

WORDS FOR EVERYDAY USE

prog • e • ny (präj´ə nē) *n.,* offspring; descendants

ANSWERS TO GUIDED READING QUESTIONS

❶ Dido forever curses relations between the Trojans and the Carthaginians.

ADDITIONAL QUESTIONS AND ACTIVITIES

Ask students to answer the following questions in writing or in oral discussion:

1. With which character in this epic do you most sympathize? Why?

2. Do you think Aeneas is a hero, or is he merely doing what he was told to do? Do you think he handled the situation with Queen Dido appropriately? Why, or why not?

ANSWERS

Responses will vary.

Students should back up their responses to these questions with concrete details from the selection.

VOCABULARY IN CONTEXT

• Dwayne plans to leave his successful business to his progeny.

Answers to Guided Reading Questions

➊ Dido's death by suicide is the "enormous thing afoot."

➋ Dido says that she led a happy life until Aeneas arrived in Carthage. She wishes that Aeneas had never come into her life. Dido plans to kill herself. She wants her death to bring a bad omen and misfortune to Aeneas.

Analytic Scales for Responding in Writing

(See page 244.)

Assign a score from 1 to 25 for each grading criterion below. (For more detailed evaluation, see the evaluation forms for writing, revising, and proofreading, Assessment Portfolio 4.1–4.9.)

1. Journal Entries

- **Content/Unity.** The journal entry expresses the feelings of one character in the *Aeneid.*
- **Organization/Coherence.** The journal entry uses details from the poem and creative assumptions based on what the writer knows of the character and his or her situation.
- **Language/Style.** The journal entry uses vivid and precise nouns, verbs, and modifiers.
- **Conventions.** The journal entry avoids errors in spelling, grammar, usage, mechanics, and manuscript form.

▶ Additional practice is provided in the Essential Skills Practice Book: Writing 1.8.

Now she took thought of one way or another,
At the first chance, to end her hated life,
And briefly spoke to Barcë, who had been
Sychaeus' nurse; her own an urn of ash
Long held in her ancient fatherland.
"Dear nurse,
Tell Sister Anna to come here, and have her
Quickly bedew herself with running water
Before she brings our victims for atonement.
Let her come that way. And you, too, put on
Pure wool around your brows. I have a mind
To carry out that rite to Stygian Jove
That I have readied here, and put an end
To my distress, committing to the flames
The pyre of that miserable Dardan."

At this with an old woman's eagerness
Barcë hurried away. And Dido's heart
Beat wildly at the enormous thing afoot.
She rolled her bloodshot eyes, her quivering cheeks
Were flecked with red as her sick pallor grew
Before her coming death. Into the court
She burst her way, then at her passion's height
She climbed the pyre and bared the Dardan sword—
A gift desired once, for no such need.
Her eyes now on the Trojan clothing there
And the familiar bed, she paused a little,
Weeping a little, mindful, then lay down
And spoke her last words:
"Remnants dear to me
While god and fate allowed it, take this breath
And give me respite from these agonies.
I lived my life out to the very end
And passed the stages Fortune had appointed.
Now my tall shade goes to the under world.
I built a famous town, saw my great walls,
Avenged my husband, made my hostile brother
Pay for his crime. Happy, alas, too happy,
If only the Dardanian keels had never
Beached on our coast." And here she kissed the bed.
"I die unavenged," she said, "but let me die.
This way, this way, a blessed relief to go

➊ *What is "the enormous thing afoot"?*

➋ *What does Dido say about her life? What does she wish never happened? What does Dido plan to do, and what effect does she want this action to have on Aeneas?*

Words for Everyday Use

a • tone • ment (ə tōn´mənt) *n.,* satisfactory payment for an offense or injury

Vocabulary in Context

- Proper atonement for the crime would be decided by the judge.

Into the undergloom. Let the cold Trojan,
Far at sea, drink in this <u>conflagration</u>
And take with him the omen of my death!"

Amid these words her household people saw her
Crumpled over the steel blade, and the blade
Aflush with red blood, drenched her hands. A scream
Pierced the high chambers. Now through the shocked city
Rumor went rioting, as wails and sobs
With women's outcry echoed in the palace
And heaven's high air gave back the beating din,
As though all Carthage or old Tyre fell
To storming enemies, and, out of hand,
Flames billowed on the roofs of men and gods.
Her sister heard and trembling, faint with terror,
Lacerating her face, beating her breast,
Ran through the crowd to call the dying queen:

"It came to this, then, sister? You deceived me?
The pyre meant this, altars and fires meant this?
What shall I mourn first, being abandoned? Did you
Scorn your sister's company in death?
You should have called me out to the same fate!
The same blade's edge and hurt, at the same hour,
Should have taken us off. With my own hands
Had I to build this pyre, and had I to call
Upon our country's gods, that in the end
With you placed on it there, O heartless one,
I should be absent? You have put to death
Yourself and me, the people and the fathers
Bred in Sidon, and your own new city.
Give me fresh water, let me bathe her wound
And catch upon my lips any last breath
Hovering over hers."
Now she had climbed
The topmost steps and took her dying sister
Into her arms to cherish, with a sob,
Using her dress to stanch the dark blood flow.
But Dido trying to lift her heavy eyes
Fainted again. Her chest-wound whistled air.
Three times she struggled up on one elbow

1 *Why does Dido's sister Anna feel deceived? For what does she wish?*

Words for Everyday Use

con • fla • gra • tion (kän´flə grā´shən) *n.*, great and destructive fire

Answers to Guided Reading Questions

1 Dido's sister feels that she was tricked into helping her sister kill herself. She now wishes for death as well.

ANALYTIC SCALES FOR RESPONDING IN WRITING

(SEE PAGE 244.)

2. Critical Essay

- **Content/Unity.** The essay analyzes the downfall of Queen Dido by answering questions about when her spiral into madness begins, why it begins, and why it becomes so destructive.
- **Organization/Coherence.** The essay begins with a thesis stated in the introductory paragraph. The introductory paragraph is followed by paragraphs which use concrete details to support the thesis and then a conclusion about Dido's downfall in a final paragraph.
- **Language/Style.** The essay uses vivid and precise nouns, verbs, and modifiers.
- **Conventions.** The essay avoids errors in spelling, grammar, usage, mechanics, and manuscript form.

► Additional practice is provided in the Essential Skills Practice Book: Writing 1.20.

Vocabulary in Context

- The firefighters tried to control the <u>conflagration</u> that overcame the building.

Answers to Guided Reading Questions

➊ Juno takes pity on Dido because of the long, difficult suffering Dido has endured. She sends Iris down from Olympus to set Dido's soul free.

Selection Check Test with Answers

EX. With whom has Queen Dido fallen in love?
Queen Dido has fallen in love with Aeneas.

1. What does Mercury tell Aeneas that he must do?
Mercury tells Aeneas that he must leave Dido and continue his journey.

2. Where is Aeneas supposed to go?
Aeneas is supposed to go to Italy.

3. What is Dido's reaction to the news that Aeneas must leave?
She becomes enraged.

4. What does Dido ask her sister to build?
She asks her sister to build a pyre.

5. What is Dido planning to do?
She is planning to kill herself on the pyre.

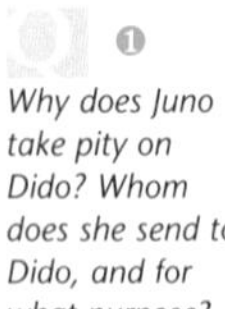

➊ *Why does Juno take pity on Dido? Whom does she send to Dido, and for what purpose?*

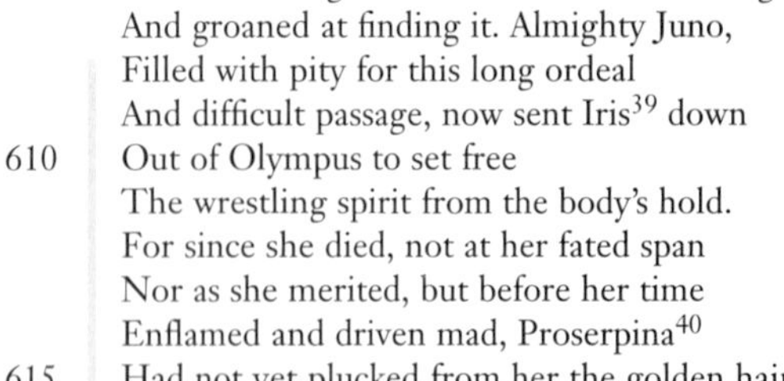

And each time fell back on the bed. Her gaze
Went wavering as she looked for heaven's light
And groaned at finding it. Almighty Juno,
Filled with pity for this long ordeal
And difficult passage, now sent Iris[39] down
Out of Olympus to set free
The wrestling spirit from the body's hold.
For since she died, not at her fated span
Nor as she merited, but before her time
Enflamed and driven mad, Proserpina[40]
Had not yet plucked from her the golden hair,
Delivering her to Orcus of the Styx.[41]
So humid Iris through bright heaven flew
On saffron-yellow wings, and in her train
A thousand hues shimmered before the sun.
At Dido's head she came to rest.
"This token
Sacred to Dis[42] I bear away as bidden
And free you from your body."
Saying this,
She cut a lock of hair. Along with it
Her body's warmth fell into dissolution,
And out into the winds her life withdrew. ■

---

39. **Iris.** Goddess of the rainbow and a messenger
40. **Proserpina.** Wife of Pluto, ruler of the underworld. In Greek mythology Pluto is called Hades and Proserpina is Persephone, who guided spirits to Hades.
41. **Orcus of the Styx.** *Orcus*—the underworld; *Styx*—river encircling the underworld
42. **Dis.** Another name for Pluto, god of the underworld

Responding to the Selection

How do you feel about the relationship between Aeneas and Queen Dido? Do you sympathize more with Dido or with Aeneas? Explain your response.

Reviewing the Selection

Recalling

1. Why does Mercury speak to Aeneas at the beginning of the selection? What is Aeneas's response to his meeting with Mercury?
2. How does Queen Dido find out that Aeneas is leaving her? Of what does she accuse him?
3. How does Aeneas respond to Queen Dido's plea that he stay or postpone his trip? What does the queen plan to do to herself when she realizes that he will not stay? What does Aeneas do when Mercury tells him of Queen Dido's plans?
4. What does Queen Dido ask her sister Anna to build for her? What does Dido tell Anna she is doing? What is she actually doing?

Interpreting

1. In what way has Aeneas been neglecting his duties? How does he feel about approaching Queen Dido with his change of plans?
2. In what way does Queen Dido's view of their relationship differ from Aeneas's view? In what way are their priorities different?
3. Why does Aeneas react the way he does to Queen Dido's pleas for him to stay and to the information given to him by Mercury? What pressures influence his actions?
4. In what way does Dido turn her rage inward? In what way does she turn it outward?

Synthesizing

5. Who is responsible for the downfall of Queen Dido—Aeneas, Anna, the gods, or Queen Dido herself? What options did Dido have other than the path she chose? What options did Aeneas have? Was choice available to either of them, or were they fated to respond as they did? Explain your response.

Understanding Literature (Questions for Discussion)

1. **Motivation.** A **motivation** is a force that moves a character to think, feel, or behave in a certain way. What is Aeneas's motivation as he makes his decision to leave Queen Dido? What is the motivation behind Queen Dido's behavior after Aeneas leaves? Support your responses with details from the text.

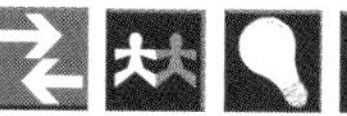

Responding to the Selection

Students might get together in pairs to make notes about and discuss their first impressions of Dido, Aeneas, and their situation.

Answers for Reviewing the Selection

RECALLING AND INTERPRETING

1. **Recalling.** Mercury speaks to Aeneas because he is angry with Aeneas for wasting time with Dido when he is supposed to sail to Italy and honor his responsibilities to his country. Aeneas does not want to leave Dido, but he knows he must. **Interpreting.** Aeneas has become sidetracked by becoming involved with Dido. When he is with her, he no longer wants to sail to Italy and fulfill his duty. He agonizes over informing Dido of his change of plans.

2. **Recalling.** Queen Dido senses change and finds out that Aeneas's fleet is being prepared for sailing. She accuses him of trying to slip away quietly, without telling her. **Interpreting.** Queen Dido views their relationship as a sacred marriage that should take priority over all other things, and Aeneas feels that his responsibilities to his people are more important. Dido wants to preserve their connection, despite her own responsibilities and Aeneas's desire to be a true leader.

3. **Recalling.** Aeneas ignores Queen Dido's pleas for him to stay or postpone his trip. Queen Dido plans to kill herself. When Mercury tells him of her violent plots, Aeneas realizes he might be in danger of an attack and sets sail immediately. **Interpreting.** Aeneas knows he must no longer allow himself to be distracted from his journey. The pressures of the gods and of his responsibilities weigh on him.

4. Queen Dido asks her sister Anna to build a pyre for her. Dido tells Anna that she plans to burn the weapons, bed, and (cont.)

Answers for Reviewing the Selection (cont.)

clothing of Aeneas. She is actually planning her own death. **Interpreting.** Dido turns her rage inward by harming herself. She turns her rage outward by wishing harm on Aeneas.

SYNTHESIZING

Responses will vary. Possible responses are given.

5. Some students might think Aeneas is responsible because he hurt and humiliated Dido and broke his promises to her. Some might say that the gods are to blame because they are insensitive to the feelings of both Dido and Aeneas. Others might say that Dido herself is responsible because she cannot accept the reality of her situation. Some may say Aeneas had no options other than to do as the gods directed. Dido could have chosen to continue in her role as queen.

ANSWERS FOR UNDERSTANDING LITERATURE

Responses will vary. Possible responses are given.

1. Motivation. Aeneas is motivated by the gods and by his wish to take care of his country and future generations. Aeneas might have been perfectly happy to stay with Dido and experiences great anguish at leaving her. He knows, however, that he must follow the wishes of the gods. Once Aeneas reclaims his position as leader, he is again driven by his wish to fulfill his obligations.

Queen Dido is motivated by hurt feelings, anger, and finally, madness. The relationship is important to her, and she is outraged that Aeneas would think of leaving her, especially in a secretive way. When Dido realizes that her desperate pleas mean nothing to him, her rage and hurt feelings escalate.

2. Pastoral Poem. Responses will vary, but students might describe the scene in which Dido chants spells, the passages that describe Dawn casting light on the Earth, or the passage that describes the stars and the peaceful silence of night in contrast to Dido's anguish and desire for revenge.

ANALYTIC SCALES FOR RESPONDING IN WRITING

Grading scales for Responding in Writing appear on pages 240, 241.

2. **Pastoral Poem.** A **pastoral poem,** from the Latin *pastor,* meaning "shepherd," is verse that deals with idealized rural life. Virgil is considered one of the first great writers of pastoral poetry. Although his earlier work is more pastoral than the *Aeneid,* book 4 of the *Aeneid* contains some examples of his skill in describing rural life. Find two or three lines or passages in which Virgil shows his ability to describe nature in a vivid and magical way.

Responding in Writing

1. **Creative Writing: Journal Entries.** Pick one character from book 4 of the *Aeneid.* Then write a journal entry for that character in which you express the character's feelings about the events in the section you have read. You may choose to write an entry for Queen Dido or Aeneas, or you may choose to focus on Dido's sister, Anna, or one of the gods. Before you write your piece, try to place yourself in this character's position—try to understand what your character is thinking and feeling. Use details from the poem as the basis for your character's journal entry, but also use your imagination to make assumptions based on what you know about your character and his or her situation.

2. **Critical Essay: The Madness of Queen Dido.** In a critical essay, analyze the downfall of Queen Dido. Before you begin writing, consider the following questions: What critical moment in the excerpt starts Dido's downward spiral into madness and toward her ultimate destruction? Why was it impossible for her to change Aeneas's mind about their relationship? In what way is her inability to accept his change of plans destructive to herself and to others? How does Virgil show her emotional state becoming worse and worse? Once you have formulated a thesis, state it clearly in an introductory paragraph; use concrete details from the selection to support your thesis in following paragraphs; and state some conclusion about Dido's downfall in a final paragraph.

PROJECT

Greek and Roman Gods. As you have read, the interactions and tensions between gods and humans inspire much of classical Greek and Roman literature. As a class, generate a list of Greek gods and their Roman counterparts. You can generate this list from books at the library and from encyclopedias. When you have generated a large enough list, split into small groups. Each group should focus on two or three immortal characters from Greek and Roman mythology whom group members find particularly interesting. (You may also choose to complete this project individually, rather than in collaborative groups.) Write descriptions of these gods and then create artistic representations of them. You might draw or paint pictures; make sculptures, models, or mobiles; or create some type of collage or scrapbook that is representative of a particular god. You might also choose to write a poem or riddle about the god or make a board game featuring trivia questions about these gods and goddesses. Present your information and your works of art and literature to the rest of the class.

PROJECT NOTES

See the evaluation form for projects, Assessment Portfolio 4.12.

Greek and Roman Gods. You might have the class try to remember as many Greek and Roman gods as they can before going to the library. Students might know some names already. The following is a list of the most well-known Greek gods and their Roman counterparts (Roman gods are in boldface): Aphrodite, **Venus**; Ares, **Mars**; Artemis, **Diana**; Athena, **Minerva**; Demeter, **Ceres**; Dionysus, **Bacchus**; Hades, **Pluto**; Hephaestus, **Vulcan**; Hera, **Juno**; Hermes, **Mercury**; Hestia, **Vesta**; Persephone, **Proserpina**; Poseidon, **Neptune**; Zeus, **Jupiter (Jove).**

PREREADING

"The River-Merchant's Wife: A Letter"
by Li Po, translated by Ezra Pound

About the Author

LI PO
AD 701–762

Considered one of the great poets of China, **Li Po** lived and wrote during the T'ang Dynasty (AD 618–907), a period often called the Golden Age of Chinese poetry. Li Po grew up in the Sichuan (Szechwan) province of southwestern China. As a young man, he was well educated, but he chose not to pursue a traditional career in government. Instead, Li Po decided to live as a wanderer. As he traveled, he met many people, and his poetry became popular. After serving the emperor for a short time as an imperial court poet, he worked for a rebel prince who was eventually executed for treason. Li Po was banished from the country, but this sentence was later revoked. Over the course of his life, Li Po earned a reputation for being a free spirit who loved music, friendship, and romance as well as nature and solitude. A popular legend says that he drowned when trying to embrace the reflection of the moon in the Chang (Yangtze) River.

About the Selection

"The River-Merchant's Wife: A Letter" is a **narrative poem,** or a poem that tells a story. The speaker of the poem is a woman from eastern China waiting for her husband, who is a river merchant on a long and potentially dangerous journey. His journey takes him up the Chang River, also called the Yangtze, the longest river in China and in all of Asia. Nearly four thousand miles long, this river runs from Tibet in western China eastward through central China before emptying into the Pacific Ocean. While the speaker, the river-merchant's wife, awaits her husband, she describes the history of their relationship—how they first met, their early married life, and the changes that have occurred in their relationship.

Ezra Pound, the translator of the poem, worked from an English prose translation of a Japanese version of the poem. That is why you will notice, by reading footnotes accompanying the selection, that Japanese names are given for Chinese villages and rivers.

CONNECTIONS: Li Po and Taoism

Li Po is closely associated with Taoism (see page 555), one of China's major philosophies. Taoists try to avoid wasting their energies on earthly distractions such as the pursuit of wealth, power, or knowledge. By ignoring these distractions, by living close to nature, and by keeping to their own thoughts, Taoists believe they are able to concentrate on the true meaning of life itself.

GOALS/OBJECTIVES

Studying this lesson will enable students to

- appreciate a narrative poem
- identify Li Po as a Chinese writer of the T'ang dynasty
- recognize mood changes
- recognize and describe a setting
- write a letter poem
- analyze character development
- identify personal pronouns
- understand and discuss the connection between imagery and ideographic writing

ADDITIONAL RESOURCES

Reader's Guide
- Selection Worksheet 3.2

Assessment Portfolio
- Selection Check Test 2.3.3
- Selection Test 2.3.4

Essential Skills Practice Books
- Writing 1.8, 1.20
- Language 2.4, 2.9

PREREADING EXTENSIONS

Ezra Pound (1885–1972) founded Imagism, a literary movement that sought to recreate in poetry sensory experiences without commentary about the emotional content or meaning of those experiences. Pound's style reflects the minimalist style of traditional Chinese literature. Have groups of students research and present oral reports about the art and poetry of the T'ang Dynasty during which Li Po wrote.

Pound influenced other writers including H. D. (Hilda Doolittle), T. S. Eliot, James Joyce, William Carlos Williams, Robert Frost, Ernest Hemingway, and Marianne Moore. Students can read at least three works by one or these writers and write an analysis of the author's style.

SUPPORT FOR LEP STUDENTS

Pronunciations of Proper Nouns and Adjectives

Chō -fu-Sa (chō´ fū sä)
Chō • kan (chō´ kan)
Ki • ang (kē aŋ´)
Ku-tō -en (kū tō en´)
Li Po (lē pō)
Yang • tze (yaŋk´ sē)

Additional Vocabulary

bashful—shy
scowling—frowning angrily

READER'S JOURNAL

Suggest that students also write about how it feels to say goodbye to somebody when you know that the separation will be a long one, and how it feels to be reunited with somebody after a long separation. Then, if students feel comfortable doing so, have them share their responses in groups.

ANSWERS TO GUIDED READING QUESTIONS

➊ The speaker played by the front gate and picked flowers. Her future husband walked by on "bamboo stilts, playing horse," and played with plums. They met in childhood.

➋ The speaker may have done these things because she was shy, embarrassed, or unhappy.

➌ When the speaker was fifteen her feelings about her marriage changed. She decided that she wanted to be with her husband forever.

➍ The speaker's husband has been gone for five months.

INTEGRATED SKILLS ACTIVITIES

LANGUAGE

Have students read the Language Arts Survey 2.9, "Verbals." Then ask them to identify each verbal that appears in the first three stanzas of this poem as a participle, gerund, or infinitive.

ANSWERS

line 2: pulling—participle
line 3: playing—participle
line 4: playing—participle
line 5: living—gerund
line 8: being—participle
line 9: lowering—participle
line 10: called—participle
line 11: scowling—gerund
line 12: to be—infinitive

► Additional practice is provided in the Essential Skills Practice Book: Language 2.9.

Have you ever been separated from a close friend or family member for a long time? What thoughts and concerns go through your mind when you are separated from a person who is important to you? Write in your journal about how it feels to miss someone.

READER'S JOURNAL

"The River-Merchant's Wife: A Letter"

LI PO, TRANSLATED BY EZRA POUND

➊ *What did these two people do when they were younger? How long ago did they meet?*

➋ *Why do you think the speaker "looked at the wall" and "never looked back" when called to?*

➌ *When and in what way did the speaker's feelings about her marriage change?*

➍ *For how long has the speaker's husband been gone?*

While my hair was still cut straight across my forehead
I played about the front gate, pulling flowers.
You came by on bamboo stilts, playing horse,
You walked about my seat, playing with blue plums.
And we went on living in the village of Chōkan:
Two small people, without dislike or suspicion.

At fourteen I married My Lord you.
I never laughed, being bashful.
Lowering my head, I looked at the wall.
Called to, a thousand times, I never looked back.

At fifteen I stopped scowling,
I desired my dust to be mingled with yours
Forever and forever and forever.
Why should I climb the lookout?

At sixteen you departed,
You went into far Ku-tō-en,[1] by the river of swirling eddies.
And you have been gone five months.
The monkeys make sorrowful noise overhead.
You dragged your feet when you went out.

1. **Ku-tō-en.** Dangerous shallows in the Chang River

CROSS-CURRICULAR ACTIVITIES

SOCIAL STUDIES

Students can create maps of China. Have students consult atlases or encyclopedias to locate the following features to label on their maps: the Chang (Yangtze) River, Tibet, Pacific Ocean, Szechwan province, Beijing (Peking), Yellow Sea. Ask students to identify other major regions, cities, and bodies of water in and surrounding China.

Saying Farewell at Hsü-yang. (Hsun-yang sung-pieh). Ch'iu Ying, Ming Dynasty, 1368–1644. The Nelson-Atkins Museum of Art, Kansas City, MO (Purchase: Nelson: Trust)

By the gate now, the moss is grown, the different mosses,
Too deep to clear them away!
The leaves fall early this autumn, in wind.
The paired butterflies are already yellow with August
Over the grass in the West garden;
They hurt me. I grow older.
If you are coming down through the narrows of the river Kiang,[2]
Please let me know beforehand,
And I will come out to meet you
As far as Chō-fu-Sa.[3] ■

❶ *Why is the moss at the gate now overgrown? Of what does this moss become a symbol?*

❷ *What will the speaker do if she hears that her husband is coming along the river Kiang?*

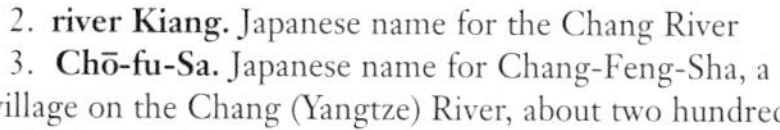

2. **river Kiang.** Japanese name for the Chang River
3. **Chō-fu-Sa.** Japanese name for Chang-Feng-Sha, a village on the Chang (Yangtze) River, about two hundred miles from Chōkan

Jiannong Sun, China

Global Views

Li Po was one of the most famous poets in China, and the hundreds of poems he wrote are in the treasure house of Chinese literature. One of his poems I like best is "Pondering at Silent Night," which I memorized when I was five:

The silver moon lights my bed,
like a layer of silent frost.
Overhead the springtime moon—
all around me, memories of my home.

Just two sentences, which are like a simple line drawing in traditional Chinese brush style, express all the nostalgic feeling from the ancient time to the present. This exquisite description of sentiment deeply moves me, especially since I have the same homesickness after leaving both my parents and my home country.

Art Note

During the Ming dynasty, independent creation and personal style was highly valued. Have students research the arts of the Ming dynasty to observe the characteristics of the different art forms. Small groups might focus on various visual or performance arts such as painting, sculpture, dance, and music.

Answers to Guided Reading Questions

❶ The moss is overgrown because it has not been worn by passing feet. The moss that was worn away when the husband dragged his feet has grown back. Its increasing depth signifies the length of his absence.

❷ The speaker will go to meet her husband at Chō -fu-Sa.

Selection Check Test with Answers

EX. Who is the speaker in "The River-Merchant's Wife: A Letter"?
The speaker is the river-merchant's wife.

1. When and where did the speaker and her husband first meet?
The speaker and her husband met as children in their village.

2. What were the speaker's first feelings about getting married?
She was nervous, bashful, and unhappy.

3. What feelings did the speaker have toward her husband when she was fifteen?
She began to love him and wanted to be with him forever.

4. For how long has the speaker's husband been gone?
He has been gone five months.

5. What are the speaker's feelings about her husband's absence?
The speaker is sad and lonely. She wishes that he would return.

Additional Questions and Activities

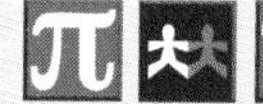

Jiannong says that the poems of Li Po are in the "treasure house of Chinese literature." As a class, discuss the following questions: Have you ever had to memorize a poem, or part of a poem? Can you still recite any of the verses from memory? Have you ever memorized a poem on your own? What poem did you choose, and why?

Next, have students brainstorm famous poets and poems that they would place in a "treasure house" of literature. Ask students to explain why they chose their selections. You could also ask students to name examples of poetry that they see in their everyday lives, such as song lyrics and greeting cards.

Responding to the Selection

Encourage students to respond by sharing their own feelings about a lengthy separation from a loved one, by asking questions to delve into the speaker's feelings, by asking the speaker to share more memories, or by sharing a memory (imagined) about the speaker's husband.

Answers for Reviewing the Selection

RECALLING AND INTERPRETING

1. **Recalling.** They have known each other since they were very young. The speaker was fourteen when she married her husband. **Interpreting.** At first, the speaker was shy and uncomfortable about being married. These feelings were demonstrated by her not laughing and the lowering or turning of her head when her name was called.
2. **Recalling.** The speaker learned to love her husband and became attached to him. **Interpreting.** The speaker stopped scowling and wanted her dust to be mingled "forever and forever" with her husband's.
3. **Recalling.** The merchant has been gone for five months. **Interpreting.** The speaker is lonely. She misses her husband, worries about the dangers he faces, and longs for his return.
4. **Recalling.** The speaker describes the sorrowful sound of the monkeys, deep moss, the falling of autumn leaves, and paired butterflies. **Interpreting.** The monkeys sound sorrowful because the speaker feels sorrowful. The falling leaves reflect a sense of loss. The leaves and the moss also mark the passage of time. The paired butterflies painfully remind the speaker that she is not with her husband.

(cont.)

Responding to the Selection

How did you feel while reading this poem? Imagine that the speaker is a friend who has just shared her feelings with you. Write a response to the speaker, or if you prefer, with a partner, role play a response.

Reviewing the Selection

RECALLING / **INTERPRETING**

1. For how long have the speaker and her husband known each other? How old was the speaker when she married her husband? ▶▶ At first, what were the speaker's feelings about her husband and about getting married? What behaviors revealed these feelings?
2. In what way did the speaker's feelings about her husband change over the first year of her marriage? ▶▶ What reveals this change in the speaker's feelings toward her husband?
3. For how long has the merchant been gone? ▶▶ What does the speaker feel about her husband's absence and about his presence in a possibly dangerous situation?
4. What sights and sounds in the natural world does the speaker describe? ▶▶ In what way do the natural images reflect the speaker's feelings? Why might the monkeys sound sorrowful to her? Why might the paired butterflies "hurt" the speaker?

SYNTHESIZING

5. What do the final lines of the poem—in which the speaker says that she would travel to meet her husband if she knew where he was—reveal about the speaker's attitude toward him? What factors were likely to have caused the speaker's attitude toward her husband to change over time? In what way might the husband's absence affect the intensity of the speaker's feelings?

Understanding Literature (Questions for Discussion)

1. **Mood. Mood,** or **atmosphere,** is the emotion created in the reader by part or all of a literary work. What is the overall mood of this poem? Is the mood consistent throughout the poem? If no, where does the mood change?

Answers for Reviewing the Selection (cont.)

SYNTHESIZING

Responses will vary. Possible responses are given.

5. The speaker reveals that she misses her husband greatly and that she is willing to undergo hardship herself to see him. She is also hopeful that she will be able to see her husband during this part of his trip. Over time, the speaker matured, got to know her husband better, and adapted to being married. The husband's absence may have intensified her feelings, because now that she wants to be with him she cannot be. Her feelings may follow the old adage, "Absence makes the heart grow fonder."

2. **Setting.** The **setting** of a literary work is the time and place in which it occurs, together with all the details used to create a sense of a particular time and place. Describe the setting of this poem. In what way does the world of the speaker and her husband differ from your own world? In what ways might their world be similar to your own?

Responding in Writing

1. **Creative Writing: Letter Poem.** Write a poem in the style of "The River-Merchant's Wife: A Letter." The speaker of your poem might be yourself, someone you know, or a character of your own invention. For example, your poem might be titled "The Busy Student: A Letter," "The Firefighter's Daughter: A Letter," or "The Astronaut's Husband: A Letter." Use your imagination to choose a character and topic that will inspire an interesting poem, rich with detail. To get started, write a paragraph or two describing your character's story and what he or she would like to say. Also write about the person who will receive the letter. What is that person like? What does this person need to understand by reading the letter? Develop your poem from the information gathered in your paragraph(s).
2. **Critical Essay: Character Development.** In an essay, discuss the ways in which the poet helps the reader to learn about the river-merchant's wife and the development of her feelings for her husband. What details within the poem help to sharpen the reader's picture of this woman? What statements can you make about her life and her character, based on details provided in the poem? What questions do you still have about this woman?

Language Lab

Personal Pronouns. Below is a paragraph about Ezra Pound, the translator of "The River-Merchant's Wife: A Letter." Read the paragraph and identify the personal pronouns in it. Some sentences contain more than one pronoun, and some possessive pronouns function in these sentences as both adjectives and personal pronouns. Refer as necessary to the Language Arts Survey 2.4, "Personal Pronouns."

[1] Ezra Loomis Pound was born in Hailey, Idaho, in 1885, but his family eventually moved to Pennsylvania. [2] He attended Hamilton College in New York and then took a master's degree at the University of Pennsylvania. [3] Pound eventually moved to Europe and spent about fifty years of his life there; it was a place in which he felt comfortable and inspired. [4] Pound often tried to assist other writers in their work. [5] He either helped or influenced writers such as T. S. Eliot, James Joyce, William Carlos Williams, Robert Frost, and Ernest Hemingway, many of whom stood by Pound when he later went through difficult times. [6] Pound had extreme political views, which got him into trouble, made him unpopular, and eventually landed him in prison. [7] We have read that there is debate about whether Pound's personal problems cast a shadow over his work. [8] Some classmates and I chose to become familiar with Pound's poetry. [9] Have you read the pieces, "Portrait d'une Femme," *The Cantos*, or *Hugh Selwyn Mauberley*? [10] These works are considered to be Pound's major poems; he is also known for translations from many languages.

Answers for Understanding Literature

Responses will vary. Possible responses are given.

1. **Mood.** The poem is reminiscent and wistful, changing to lonely and sorrowful. The poem's mood is fairly consistent. In the opening lines, as the speaker refers to her past and the beginning of her relationship with her husband, the mood is sad and wistful. The mood shifts in the final few lines to a feeling of sadness and yearning.
2. **Setting.** The poem is set in a rural Chinese village, at a time when women went into arranged marriages at very young ages. It was also a time during which the river was a chief means of transportation. While these details make the speaker's world quite different from our world, students may recognize the love shared by the speaker and her husband and the feelings of sadness and helplessness that go along with missing someone and worrying for that person's safety.

Analytic Scales for Responding in Writing

Grading scales for Responding in Writing appear on page 250.

Answers for Language Lab

1. his
2. He
3. his, it, he
4. their
5. He, he
6. him, him, him
7. We, his
8. I
9. you
10. he

▶Additional practice is provided in the Essential Skills Practice Book: Language 2.4.

ANALYTIC SCALES FOR RESPONDING IN WRITING

Assign a score from 1 to 25 for each grading criterion below. (For more detailed evaluation, see the evaluation forms for writing, revising, and proofreading, Assessment Portfolio 4.1–4.9.)

1. Letter Poem

- **Content/Unity.** The letter poem presents the story and emotions of the speaker.
- **Organization/Coherence.** The letter poem relates one story or event and the emotions related to it. The letter poem is arranged in a logical order and is written in verse.
- **Language/Style.** The letter poem uses vivid and precise nouns, verbs, and modifiers.
- **Conventions.** The letter poem avoids errors in spelling, grammar, usage, mechanics, and manuscript form.

▶ Additional practice is provided in the Essential Skills Practice Book: Writing 1.8.

2. Critical Essay

- **Content/Unity.** The essay presents conclusions the reader has drawn about the speaker and uses evidence from the poem to support such conclusions.
- **Organization/Coherence.** The essay begins with an introduction that includes the thesis of the essay. The introduction is followed by supporting paragraphs with clear transitions. The essay ends with a solid conclusion.
- **Language/Style.** The essay uses vivid and precise nouns, verbs, and modifiers.
- **Conventions.** The essay avoids errors in spelling, grammar, usage, mechanics, and manuscript form.

▶ Additional practice is provided in the Essential Skills Practice Book: Writing 1.20.

Insights

Imagery and Ideographic Writing

Chinese writing is ideographic, or logographic, which means that it is based on graphic symbols that represent ideas or objects. The earliest Chinese characters closely resembled the ideas or objects that they represented. With the advent of brushes and ink, the characters changed and often involved much simpler lines and shapes. About one thousand simple lines and shapes—representing concrete subjects such as man, woman, rock, or river and more abstract terms such as talk or love—form the foundation of the Chinese writing system. These basic characters are often combined to create characters that represent more complex ideas. Consider the following complex character, which represents rain:

The dots within the character represent drops of rain.

The lines around the dots symbolize a cloud.

The line at the top of the character symbolizes heaven or sky.

The "j" portion of the character, a vertical line, suggests vertical falling.

The following character represents the dawn of the day:

The top portion of the character represents the sun.

The bottom portion of the character represents the horizon.

Extended, metaphorical meanings often evolve from Chinese characters that originally referred to concrete objects. For example, the following character is a picture of a fish net:

Over the years, the intricate design meant to represent a net for catching fish has come to suggest the idea of gathering, or collecting.

As you have seen, a single character in Chinese such as the one for rain, is something like a brief poem, combining images to convey an idea. People who translate Chinese poetry into English often try to capture the imagistic quality of the original language by using short, concise, concrete words, as in the translation on page 246.

Additional Questions and Activities

After examining the characters for the words *rain, dawn,* and *gathering,* have students create their own ideographs for the words *river, sadness,* and *sunset.* Students may wish to create symbols for other words as well. Ask students to share their creations with the class, providing an explanation if necessary of the parts of their ideographs.

PREREADING

from the *Canzoniere*
Sonnet 3, translated by Joseph Auslander
Sonnet 300, translated by Edwin Morgan
by Petrarch (Francesco Petrarca)

ITALY

About the Author

PETRARCH
1304–1374

Known in English-speaking countries as **Petrarch**, **Francesco Petrarca** is often considered to be the father of the European tradition of lyric poetry. Petrarch was born in Arezzo, Tuscany, now part of Italy, in 1304. In 1312, he and his family moved to Avignon, France, where he received his early education. In 1316, his father sent him to study law in Montpellier, France. Although Petrarch returned to Bologna, Italy, in 1320 to continue to study law, he was becoming increasingly interested in literature. After his father died in 1326, Petrarch returned to Avignon. There he met a woman named Laura, for whom he developed a deep, unrequited love that inspired his great vernacular Italian sonnets and other poems. In later years, Petrarch made a name for himself as a classical scholar and as a poet, and both Paris and Rome invited him to be crowned poet laureate. Petrarch spent the last years of his life living in Italy, writing works with a religious focus.

About the Selection

The following two poems are sonnets. A **sonnet** is a fourteen-line poem, usually in iambic pentameter, that follows one of a number of different rhyme schemes. Petrarch perfected and made popular the Italian sonnet, also known as the Petrarchan sonnet. The **Petrarchan sonnet** has two parts: an **octave**, which is an eight-line stanza, and a **sestet**, which is a six-line stanza. The rhyme scheme of the octave is *abbaabba*. The rhyme scheme of the sestet is generally *cdecde, cdcdcd,* or *cdedce.* Because these selections are poetic translations from the original Italian, rhyme schemes may vary from those typical of Petrarchan sonnets.

The following sonnets are from the ***Canzoniere***, a collection of poems about Petrarch's feelings for Laura. This collection of poems is divided into works written during Laura's life and those written after she died of the plague. **Sonnet 3** describes the day Petrarch first sees Laura and falls in love with her. This love is difficult for him from the start because it is unrequited, or not returned. **Sonnet 300** expresses his feelings of sadness after Laura's death.

CONNECTIONS: Petrarchan Conventions

Petrarch's sonnets shaped the way in which many people have written and talked about love. Numerous poets followed Petrarch in creating poems addressed to an idealized, distant beloved. Such poets also frequently used Petrarchan imagery, describing the beloved as having golden hair, eyes like the sun or like stars, skin like ivory or snow, cheeks like roses, and movements like a goddess or an angel. For more information on Petrarchan ideals, see Insights: The Petrarchan Ideal, page 851.

GOALS/OBJECTIVES

Studying this lesson will enable students to

- have a positive experience reading Petrarchan sonnets
- explain the characteristics of a Petrarchan sonnet
- define *lyric poem, mood, personification,* and *apostrophe* and identify and interpret these when they encounter them in their reading
- write a lyric poem about a particular person
- write a critical essay about pain and loss
- correct sentence fragments and run-ons

ADDITIONAL RESOURCES

READER'S GUIDE
- Selection Worksheet 3.3

ASSESSMENT PORTFOLIO
- Selection Check Test 2.3.5
- Selection Test 2.3.6

ESSENTIAL SKILLS PRACTICE BOOKS
- Writing 1.6, 1.8, 1.10, 1.20
- Language 2.27

PREREADING EXTENSIONS

To help students understand Petrarch's influence on the way we talk about love, encourage them to bring in popular song lyrics, contemporary poems, or greeting cards that take love as a central theme. Then, after students have read Connections: Petrarchan Conventions on this page and Insights: The Petrarchan Ideal (page 851), encourage them to work in groups to analyze a number of the song lyrics, poems, or cards. Ask each group to note any similarities they discover. Which of the contemporary examples seem to express Petrarchan ideals or conventions?

SUPPORT FOR LEP STUDENTS

PRONUNCIATIONS OF PROPER NOUNS AND ADJECTIVES

A • vi • gnon (ä vē nyōn´)
Bo • lo • gna (bə lōn´yə)
Mont • pel • lier (mōn pəl yā´)
Fran • ces • co Pe • trar • ca (frän chā´ skə pā trar´kə)
Pet • rarch (pe´ trärk)

ADDITIONAL VOCABULARY

shaft—stalk (of an arrow)
sheaf—bundle (of arrows)
snare—trap
strife—struggle; conflict
sway—influence or force; rule

IDIOM

biding-place—residence, dwelling

READER'S JOURNAL

Inform students that they need not discuss romantic love and admiration if they are not comfortable doing so. They may prefer to write about their feelings of love for a family member or friend, or to explore their admiration for an acquaintance or a public figure of the past or present.

ANSWERS TO GUIDED READING QUESTIONS

1 The speaker addresses his beloved. The speaker falls captive to her beauty, especially the beauty of her eyes.

2 The speaker finds his cue in "man's most tragic play," that is, unrequited love.

3 The speaker was not prepared but "ambush[ed]" and "surprise[d]" by love. He feels only pain and anguish because he cannot be with her. The lady is unresponsive—she does not love the speaker.

SPELLING AND VOCABULARY WORDS FROM THE SELECTION

avarice
curt
craven

READER'S JOURNAL

Describe a person for whom you have felt great love or admiration. What is special about this person? Did you ever have to face the thought of not having this person in your life? If yes, explain your experience. If no, try to imagine what life would be like without this person.

Sonnet 3

PETRARCH, TRANSLATED BY JOSEPH AUSLANDER

1 *Whom does the speaker address in this poem? To what does the speaker fall captive on this day?*

2 *Where does the speaker find his cue?*

3 *Was the speaker prepared for love? Is he comfortable with these feelings? What is the response of the lady with whom he has fallen in love?*

It was the morning of that blessèd day
Whereon the Sun in pity veiled his glare
For the Lord's agony, that, unaware,
I fell a captive, Lady, to the sway

Of your swift eyes: that seemed no time to stay
The strokes of Love: I stepped into the snare
Secure, with no suspicion: then, and there
I found my cue[1] in man's most tragic play.

Love caught me naked to his shaft, his sheaf,
The entrance for his ambush and surprise
Against the heart wide open through the eyes,

The constant gale and fountain of my grief:
How craven so to strike me stricken so,
Yet from you fully armed conceal his bow! ■

1. **cue.** Bit of dialogue, action, or music that is a signal for an actor's entrance or speech

WORDS FOR EVERYDAY USE

cra • ven (krā′vən) *adj.*, cowardly, afraid

VOCABULARY IN CONTEXT

• The general said that in battle he would tolerate no acts of cowardice or craven behavior.

Villa Malta, Rome. *Sanford Robinson Gifford, 1879. National Museum of American Art, Washington, DC/Art Resource, NY*

Sonnet 300

PETRARCH, TRANSLATED BY EDWIN MORGAN

Great is my envy of you, earth, in your greed
Folding her in invisible embrace,
Denying me the look of the sweet face
Where I found peace from all my strife at need!
Great is my envy of heaven which can lead
And lock within itself in avarice
That spirit from its lovely biding-place
And leave so many others here to bleed!

Great is my envy of those souls whose reward
Is the gentle heaven of her company,
Which I so fiercely sought beneath these skies!

Great is my envy of death whose curt hard sword
Carried her whom I called my life away;
Me he disdains, and mocks me from her eyes! ■

❶ *Whom or what is the speaker addressing in this poem?*

❷ *Why is the speaker envious? What or who was taken from him?*

❸ *What do earth, heaven, souls in heaven, and death have to do with the speaker's loss? What does he envy?*

WORDS FOR EVERYDAY USE

av • a • rice (av´ə ris) *n.,* greed

curt (kʉrt) *adj.,* short; brief to the point of rudeness

ANSWERS TO GUIDED READING QUESTIONS

❶ The speaker is addressing the earth which has claimed his beloved since her death.

❷ The speaker is envious of heaven because it has taken his beloved's spirit away from him.

❸ The speaker feels that they have taken Laura from him, and that they are now enjoying her presence. The speaker is envious of the earth, of death, and of the souls in heaven.

SELECTION CHECK TEST WITH ANSWERS

EX: What emotion do both Sonnet 3 and Sonnet 300 address?

Both sonnets address feelings of love.

1. Whom does Petrarch address in Sonnet 3?

Petrarch addresses a woman that he loves.

2. To what does the speaker in Sonnet 3 fall captive?

The speaker in Sonnet 3 falls captive to the beauty of the woman's eyes.

3. For what was the speaker in Sonnet 3 not prepared?

The speaker was not prepared for feelings of love.

4. In Sonnet 300, what has happened to the subject of the poem?

The subject of the poem has died.

5. Of what or whom is the speaker envious?

The speaker is envious of death, the earth, and the souls in heaven.

VOCABULARY IN CONTEXT

- Avarice inspired Raymond to work at two jobs and spend as little money as possible.
- Clyde was known for responding to any situation with an ironic and curt witticism.

Responding to the Selection

Students might also work in pairs to role play a conversation between Petrarch and Laura, bearing in mind that while Petrarch was smitten, Laura never returned his love.

Answers for Reviewing the Selection

RECALLING AND INTERPRETING

1. **Recalling.** The speaker says that the sun became dim in pity for the Lord's agony, that is, it was Good Friday, the day Jesus was crucified. The speaker falls captive to the woman's beautiful eyes. **Interpreting.** The speaker falls in love. These feelings of love cause him pain and anguish.

2. **Recalling.** The speaker says he steps into love that will bring him nothing but sorrow. He feels this is a mistake because his beloved cannot return his love. Love wields a bow and arrow. **Interpreting.** He is not prepared for love. His experience is not positive because his love is not returned. "Man's most tragic play" is probably unrequited love.

3. **Recalling.** The speaker addresses death and the earth in Sonnet 300. The speaker is being denied the life of his beloved. **Interpreting.** The female subject of the poem, Laura, has died. This is revealed through images of her within the earth and in heaven. The speaker loves her and misses her presence and her beauty.

4. **Recalling.** The speaker feels envious of the earth, of heaven, of death, and of the souls in heaven because they now have Laura. **Interpreting.** Each reminds him that Laura is no longer with him.

SYNTHESIZING

Responses will vary. Possible responses are given.

5. In Sonnet 3, the speaker's feelings of love are painful because these feelings are not returned. In Sonnet 300, the speaker's feelings of love are tragic and difficult because the object of his love has died.

Responding to the Selection

Suppose the speaker had written his feelings in a journal, rather than in the form of two sonnets. What might he have entered in his journal about the feelings expressed in the poems? Write a journal entry expressing Petrarch's feelings, or discuss what Petrarch might write in such an entry.

Reviewing the Selection

Recalling		Interpreting
1. In Sonnet 3, what does the speaker say about the sun on "that blessèd day"? To what does the speaker fall captive?	▶▶	What exactly happens on the "morning of that blessèd day"? What feelings does the speaker experience?
2. In Sonnet 3, into what does the speaker say he steps? Why does he feel this a mistake? According to the speaker, what weapons does love wield?	▶▶	Is the speaker prepared for love? Is his experience positive? What might "man's most tragic play" be? Explain.
3. Whom does the speaker address in Sonnet 300? What is the speaker being denied?	▶▶	What has happened to the female subject of Sonnet 300? How is this revealed? What are the speaker's feelings toward this woman, and why does he miss her?
4. What different things in Sonnet 300 cause the speaker to feel envy?	▶▶	In what way does each target of the speaker's envy contribute to his suffering?

Synthesizing

5. Describe the feelings of love expressed in both poems. What is tragic and difficult about the love expressed in each sonnet?

Understanding Literature (Questions for Discussion)

1. **Lyric Poem.** A **lyric poem** is a highly musical verse that expresses the emotions of a speaker. Petrarch is often considered the father of English lyric verse because of the way he popularized the form. In what ways are the sonnets you have just read lyric poems?

2. **Mood. Mood**, or **atmosphere**, is the emotion created in the reader by part or all of a literary work. What is the mood of each of the sonnets you have read? What are some words, phrases, and images that create these moods?

Answers for Understanding Literature

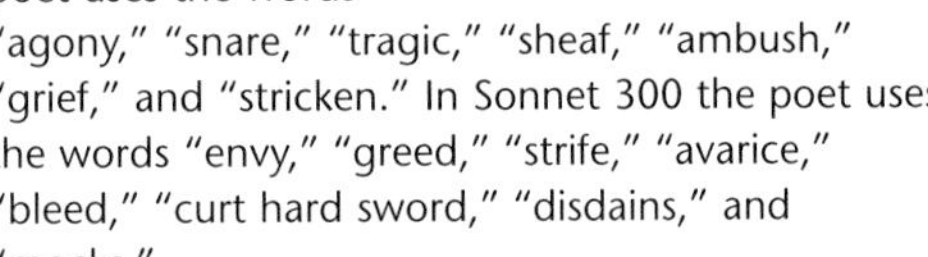

Responses will vary. Possible responses are given.

1. **Lyric Poem.** Both sonnets are musical in their rhyme and meter. The sonnets are highly personal and expressive of intense feelings.

2. **Mood.** Both sonnets are sad and yearning. They both express the speaker's mental anguish—in the first, of unrequited love, and in the second, of despair over the beloved's death. In Sonnet 3, the poet uses the words "agony," "snare," "tragic," "sheaf," "ambush," "grief," and "stricken." In Sonnet 300 the poet uses the words "envy," "greed," "strife," "avarice," "bleed," "curt hard sword," "disdains," and "mocks."

3. **Personification and Apostrophe.** The speaker's reference to love in the third stanza of

(cont.)

3. **Personification and Apostrophe. Personification** is a figure of speech in which an idea, animal, or thing is described as if it were a person. **Apostrophe** is a rhetorical technique in which an object or person is directly addressed. Name an example of personification in stanza 3 of Sonnet 3. What is personified in Sonnet 300? Describe Petrarch's use of apostrophe in Sonnet 300.

Responding in Writing

1. **Creative Writing: Lyric Poem.** Write your own lyric poem in the tradition of Petrarch. Your poem should express your feelings about a person in your life. To begin, first brainstorm possible subjects. You might also refer to your response to the Reader's Journal activity. Then choose one person as the subject of your poem. As you write your poem, try to use vivid words and phrases so that your reader understands your feelings toward your subject.
2. **Critical Essay: Images of Pain and Loss.** Both sonnets that you have read talk about the tragic twists love can take. In Sonnet 3, the speaker expresses pain over unrequited love. In Sonnet 300, the speaker expresses sadness over the loss of a love. Write a critical essay in which you discuss the images—words or phrases that can be seen, heard, touched, tasted, or smelled—that Petrarch uses in each poem to express pain, loss, and frustration. You may write about both sonnets, or you may choose to focus closely on one of the sonnets.

Language Lab

Sentence Fragments and Run-ons. Rewrite the following paragraph, correcting any sentence fragments and run-ons by adding words and/or punctuation. For more information about sentence fragments and run-ons, turn to the Language Arts Survey 2.27, "Correcting Sentence Fragments, Run-ons, and Sentence Strings."

[1] The movement known as Humanism. Came out of the European Renaissance. [2] The word *renaissance* means, literally, a "rebirth," the word is used to refer to a period between the fifteenth and early seventeenth centuries. [3] During this period. A rebirth of interest in Greek and Roman classics. [4] Aristotle, one of the Greek philosophers who influenced Renaissance thought. [5] Aristotle believed in pursuing happiness he believed happiness came from intellectual and moral pursuits. [6] He believed that government had a responsibility. To encourage happiness among citizens. [7] He felt that human happiness on earth was attainable he knew, though, that not everyone would be able to find true happiness. [8] His ideas were different from the medieval view. Of human happiness. [9] It was the medieval belief that earthly happiness was not important. That life after death was important. [10] The ideas of Aristotle and other Greek and Roman philosophers gained popularity these ideas shaped the Renaissance.

ANALYTIC SCALES FOR RESPONDING IN WRITING

Assign a score from 1 to 25 for each grading criterion below. (For more detailed evaluation, see the evaluation forms for writing, revising, and proofreading, Assessment Portfolio 4.1–4.9.)

1. Lyric Poem

- **Content/Unity.** The lyric poem expresses the writer's feelings about a person in his or her life.
- **Organization/Coherence.** The poem presents the writer's feelings and adds details in a logical order.
- **Language/Style.** The poem uses vivid and precise nouns, verbs, and modifiers.
- **Conventions.** The poem avoids errors in spelling, grammar, usage, mechanics, and manuscript form.

▶ Additional practice is provided in the Essential Skills Practice Book: Writing 1.6, 1.8, and 1.10.

2. Critical Essay

- **Content/Unity.** The essay discusses the images Petrarch uses to express his pain and loss.
- **Organization/Coherence.** The essay contains an introduction, a body that presents main points in a sensible order, and a conclusion.
- **Language/Style.** The essay uses vivid and precise nouns, verbs, and modifiers.
- **Conventions.** The essay avoids errors in spelling, grammar, usage, mechanics, and manuscript form.

▶ Additional practice is provided in the Essential Skills Practice Book: Writing 1.20.

ANSWERS FOR UNDERSTANDING LITERATURE (CONT.)

Sonnet 3 is an example of personification. Death and earth are both personified in Sonnet 300. The speaker also addresses earth and death directly, which is an example of apostrophe.

ANSWERS FOR LANGUAGE LAB

Answers for Language Lab appear on page 256.

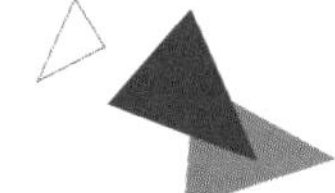

The Form of the Sonnet

The **sonnet**, a fourteen-line poem, usually in iambic pentameter, that follows one of a number of different rhyme schemes, was extremely popular in Renaissance Italy, Spain, Portugal, France, Germany, and England. There are two prominent types of sonnets—the Italian, or Petrarchan sonnet, and the English, Elizabethan, or Shakespearean sonnet.

The **Italian**, or **Petrarchan sonnet** is divided into the following two parts, or stanzas: an octave and a sestet. An **octave** is an eight-line stanza. A **sestet** is a six-line stanza. The rhyme scheme of the octave is usually *abbaabba*, and the rhyme scheme of the sestet is generally *cdecde*, *cdcdcd*, or *cdedce*. Petrarch perfected and made popular the form of the Italian sonnet with his *Canzoniere*, so this particular form of the sonnet came to be named for him. Two sonnets from Petrarch's *Canzoniere* appear on pages 252 and 253. Many writers, including sixteenth-century English writer Sir Thomas Wyatt, were influenced by Petrarch's style. Wyatt introduced the Petrarchan sonnet to England with poems such as the following, called "Whoso List to Hunt."

> Whoso list to hunt, I know where is an hind,[1]
> But as for me, alas, I may no more.
> The vain travail hath wearied me so sore
> I am of them that farthest cometh behind.
> Yet may I, by no means, my wearied mind
> Draw from the deer, but as she fleeth afore,
> Fainting I follow. I leave off therefore,
> Since in a net I seek to hold the wind.
> Who list her hunt, I put him out of doubt,
> As well as I, may spend his time in vain.
> And graven with diamonds in letters plain
> There is written, her fair neck round about,
> "*Noli me tangere*,[2] for Cæsar's I am,
> And wild for to hold, though I seem tame."

In the sonnet cycle *Astrophil and Stella*, English writer Sir Philip Sidney also used sonnet conventions popularized by Petrarch. Wyatt and Sidney also deal with the subject matter of most Petrarchan sonnets: unrequited love.

The **English**, **Elizabethan**, or **Shakespearean sonnet** is divided into the following four parts, or stanzas: three **quatrains**, which are four-line stanzas, and a final two-line stanza called a **couplet**. The rhyme scheme of such a sonnet is typically *abab cdcd efef gg*, and the verse's meter is iambic pentameter. Often, the three quatrains build upon a theme, and the final couplet gives the conclusion and highlights the meaning of the poem. Shakespeare was a master of the Elizabethan sonnet, which was a popular form in England at the time that he was writing. Because his 154 numbered sonnets were so revered, the form came to be named for him. Read *Sonnet 18*, one of Shakespeare's most popular sonnets, paying close attention to the poem's structure:

> Shall I compare thee to a summer's day?
> Thou art more lovely and more temperate:
> Rough winds do shake the darling buds of May,
> And summer's lease hath all too short a date:
> Sometime too hot the eye of heaven shines
> And often is his gold complection dimmed;
> And every fair from fair sometimes declines,
> By chance or nature's changing course untrimmed;
> But thy eternal summer shall not fade,
> Nor lose possession of that fair thou ow'st,
> Nor shall death brag thou wander'st in his shade,
> When in eternal lines to time thou grow'st:
> So long as men can breathe, or eyes can see,
> So long lives this, and this gives life to thee.

Other notable writers who used the sonnet form include Dante, Edmund Spenser, John Keats, Elizabeth Barrett Browning, George Meredith, Edna St. Vincent Millay, and W. H. Auden. For an example of a modern sonnet see Millay's "Oh, oh, you will be sorry for that word!" on page 167.

1. **hind.** Deer
2. ***Noli me tangere.*** Touch me not

Answers for Language Lab

[1] The movement known as Humanism came out of the European Renaissance. [2] The word *renaissance* means, literally, a "rebirth." The word is used to refer to a period between the fifteenth and early seventeenth centuries. [3] During this period, there was a rebirth of interest in Greek and Roman classics. [4] Aristotle was one of the Greek philosophers who influenced Renaissance thought. [5] Aristotle believed in pursuing happiness. He believed happiness came from intellectual and moral pursuits. [6] He believed that government had a responsibility to encourage happiness among citizens. [7] He felt that human happiness on earth was attainable. He knew, though, that not everyone would be able to find true happiness. [8] His ideas were different from the medieval view of human happiness. [9] It was the medieval belief that earthly happiness was not important, but that life after death was important. [10] The ideas of Aristotle and other Greek and Roman philosophers gained popularity. These ideas shaped the Renaissance.

▶ Additional practice is provided in the Essential Skills Practice Book: Language 2.27.

Additional Questions and Activities

Ask students the following questions about "Whoso List to Hunt":

1. For what is the speaker hunting?
2. How has the hunt progressed? How is the speaker feeling?
3. Why might the hind be unattainable for other pursuers as well?

Ask students the following questions about Sonnet 18:

4. What is the speaker's opening question? How is it answered?
5. What does the speaker say "shall not fade" in the beloved? Why?

(cont.)

Additional Questions and Activities (cont.)

Answers

1. On a literal level, the speaker is hunting a deer. The poet uses this deer hunt as a metaphor for a man pursuing an unattainable woman.
2. The hunt has been long and exhausting. The speaker is resigned to failure but is wiser for his experience.
3. The hind belongs to Cæsar and may not be touched by anyone else.
4. "Shall I compare thee to a summer's day?" is the question. The response is an extended comparison of the two.
5. The beloved's "eternal summer," or beauty, shall not fade because the speaker has immortalized it in his poem.

PREREADING

"Though I am Laila of the Persian romance"
by Princess Zeb-un-Nissa, translated by Willis Barnstone

INDIA

About the Author

Princess Zeb-un-Nissa (1638–1702). Princess Zeb-un-Nissa, who wrote in Persian, was a supporter of the arts and education, serving as a patron of poets and scholars. She was also dedicated to her religion. Princess Zeb-un-Nissa was later imprisoned by her father, most likely because she took her brother's side when he led a rebellion.

About the Selection

"**Though I am Laila of the Persian romance**" is a **lyric poem**, meaning it is highly musical verse that expresses the emotions of its speaker. The speaker describes her feelings about love and her inability to pursue a particular love relationship because of her humility and reserve. Because of the intense feelings she experiences, she calls herself an expert in things of love. She even teaches the nightingale, a bird known for its beautiful song during mating and nesting season, about matters of the heart. This bird sings day and night to mark its territory, which is often quite small. Interestingly enough, the bird's beautiful song is in sharp contrast with its drab feathers. The speaker of the poem draws connections between herself and this plain bird which, within the confines of a small world, sings beautiful love songs.

Raiphut Palace, Rajasthan

Thar Desert, Rajasthan

CONNECTIONS: The Persian Empire

The Persian empire was an ancient empire in western Asia. The oldest Persian writing is found in ancient inscriptions, but the first major literary works are the scriptures of Zoroaster, a religious teacher and prophet of ancient Persia, and the writings of the last dynasty of native rulers to reign (c. AD 224-640) in Persia before the Arab conquest.

The Arab invasion of the seventh century made Arabic the primary literary language and the beliefs of Islam the dominant literary theme. Many important works of Arabic literature are by Persians, whose language eventually came back as the literary language in the ninth century. The centuries that followed were important in the development of classical Persian literature. The great poet Firdausi (see page 310) wrote a national epic called the *Book of Kings*, and Omar Khayyám wrote the well-known *Rubáiyát* (see page796). Other great writers of the thirteenth century included the poets of Sufism, Farid Ad-Din Attar, Rumi (see page 804), and Saadi. In the fourteenth century, a poet named Hafiz wrote many skillful lyrics. Also during this period, great prose such as tales, fables, allegories, histories, and philosophical and scientific works flourished.

One of the most famous Persian, Indian, and Arabian achievements is a collection of folktales called both *Arabian Nights* and *The Thousand and One Nights* (see page 784). Though many of the tales are set in India, their individual origins are unknown. The present form of the collection is thought to be from Persia or an Arabic-speaking country.

ADDITIONAL RESOURCES

READER'S GUIDE
- Selection Worksheet 3.4

ASSESSMENT PORTFOLIO
- Selection Check Test 2.3.7
- Selection Test 2.3.8

ESSENTIAL SKILLS PRACTICE BOOKS
- Writing 1.8, 1.20
- Speaking and Listening 3.1

PREREADING EXTENSIONS

Students can conduct additional research on the Persian Empire. As a class, students should form research teams and create a plan to gather information about the following: geography, government, relationships with other countries or kingdoms, religion, and the arts. Some students may want to focus on the rise of the empire while others examine its downfall.

The country once known as Persia is now Iran. As an alternate activity, students may wish to research some of the previous topics in relation to Iran.

SUPPORT FOR LEP STUDENTS

PRONUNCIATIONS OF PROPER NOUNS AND ADJECTIVES

Lai • la (lā´lə)
Maj • nun (mäj´nun)
Zeb-un-Nissa (zeb´ə nis´ə)

ADDITIONAL VOCABULARY

ferocious—fierce, cruel
modesty—decency and moderation

GOALS/OBJECTIVES

Studying this lesson will enable students to

- have a positive experience reading a love poem
- define *lyric poetry*
- recognize the themes of love and longing
- define *image*
- identify images
- define *metaphor*
- identify and explain a metaphor
- write a lyric poem
- write a critical essay about imagery
- use elements of verbal communication

READER'S JOURNAL

Suggest that students consider images from various media such as movies, television, and music for common or accepted images of romantic love. As an extension of this activity, have students brainstorm common and individual images for love other than romantic love.

ANSWERS TO GUIDED READING QUESTIONS

❶ The speaker says she is Laila of the Persian romance. Her heart is like ferocious Majnun.

❷ The speaker wants to go to the desert. Modesty chains her feet.

❸ The speaker is an expert on love.

SELECTION CHECK TEST WITH ANSWERS

EX. Who wrote "Though I am Laila of the Persian Romance"?
The poem was written by Princess Zeb-un-Nissa.

1. Like whom does the speaker love?
She loves like ferocious Majnun.

2. Where does she want to go?
She wants to go to the desert.

3. What chains her feet?
Modesty chains her feet.

4. What came to the garden?
A nightingale came to the garden.

5. In what area is the speaker an expert?
The speaker is an expert on love.

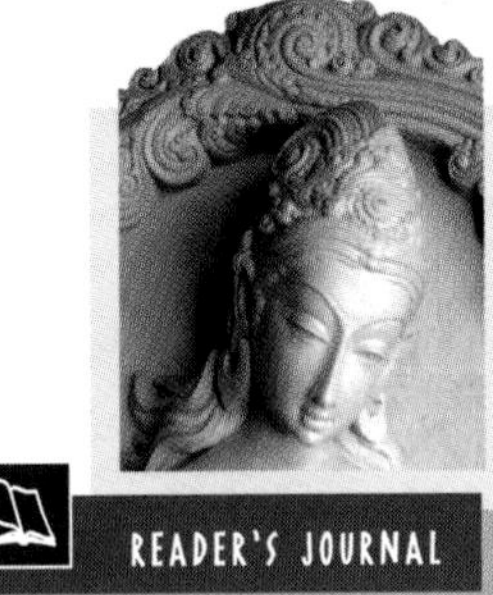

READER'S JOURNAL

When you think of the word *love*, what are some images—words that name things that can be seen, heard, touched, tasted, or smelled—that come to mind? List images commonly associated with romantic love. Identify some unique images of your own that express or describe romantic love.

"Though I am Laila of the Persian romance"

PRINCESS ZEB-UN-NISSA, TRANSLATED BY WILLIS BARNSTONE

Though I am Laila of the Persian romance,
my heart loves like ferocious Majnun.
I want to go to the desert
but modesty is chains on my feet.
A nightingale came to the flower garden
because she was my pupil.
I am an expert in things of love.
Even the moth is my disciple. ■

❶ *Who is the speaker? What is her heart like?*

❷ *Where does the speaker want to go? What chains her feet?*

❸ *In what is the speaker an expert?*

WORDS FOR EVERYDAY USE

dis • ci • ple (di sī´pəl) *n.*, pupil or follower of any teacher or school of religion, learning, or art

VOCABULARY IN CONTEXT

• The disciples listened eagerly as Buddha gave the sermon of the four noble truths.

Responding to the Selection

What is the speaker of the poem like? What adjectives might you use to describe her feelings about herself and about love? Explain your choices.

Reviewing the Selection

RECALLING / **INTERPRETING**

1. Who does the speaker say she is? What word does she use to describe her love? ▶▶ What might a "ferocious" heart be like? What feelings does this speaker have?
2. Where does the speaker want to go? What does the speaker say about modesty? ▶▶ Why might the speaker want to go to this place? What might this place represent? In what way can modesty be like chains on the feet?
3. Who comes to the speaker's flower garden? ▶▶ Think about what you have read about nightingales on the Prereading page. What might the speaker and the nightingale have in common? What might she have taught the nightingale?
4. In what is the speaker an expert? Who is the speaker's disciple? ▶▶ In what way is this speaker connected with nature?

SYNTHESIZING

5. Why does the speaker call herself an expert in things of love? Does her claim seem justified? Explain. What feelings does the speaker have? Why does she have trouble truly expressing these feelings?

RESPONDING TO THE SELECTION

Students might compare the speaker to the speaker of another love poem or to another literary character who speaks about love.

ANSWERS FOR REVIEWING THE SELECTION

RECALLING AND INTERPRETING

1. **Recalling.** The speaker says she is Laila of the Persian romance. Her love is ferocious. **Interpreting.** A ferocious heart is passionate and determined in love. The speaker's love is strong and powerful.

2. **Recalling.** The speaker wants to go to the desert, but modesty restricts her. **Interpreting.** She might want to go to the desert to meet her beloved. Modesty keeps the speaker from acting upon her feelings.

3. **Recalling.** A nightingale comes to the garden. **Interpreting.** Although both the speaker and the nightingale are modest in appearance, they are strong of heart and intention. She might have instructed the nightingale in the things of love.

4. **Recalling.** The speaker is an expert on love. The moth is her disciple. **Interpreting.** The speaker teaches love to everything in the natural world.

SYNTHESIZING

Responses will vary. Possible responses are given.

5. The speaker considers herself an expert because of the depth of her feelings. She supports her claim by calling herself Laila of the Persian romance and by noting that the nightingale and the moth take lessons in love from her. She is very much in love and has passionate feelings. Her trouble in expressing feelings may be caused by society's restraints which call on her to be modest and passive.

Answers for Understanding Literature

Responses will vary. Possible responses are given.

Metaphor. The speaker refers to modesty as chains. Chains restrain a person from moving freely, as modesty restrains the speaker from freely expressing her love.

ANALYTIC SCALES FOR RESPONDING IN WRITING

Assign a score from 1 to 25 for each grading criterion below. (For more detailed evaluation, see the evaluation forms for writing, revising, and proofreading, Assessment Portfolio 4.1–4.9.)

1. "Though I am . . ." Poem

- **Content/Unity.** The poem begins "Though I am . . ." and describes an aspect of the student's life or personality.
- **Organization/Coherence.** The poem reflects one aspect of the student in depth.
- **Language/Style.** The poem uses vivid and precise language.
- **Conventions.** The poem avoids errors in spelling, grammar, usage, mechanics, and manuscript form.

▶ Additional practice is provided in the Essential Skills Practice Book: Writing 1.8.

2. Critical Essay

- **Content/Unity.** The essay presents similarities and differences between two works.
- **Organization/Coherence.** The essay begins with an introduction, followed by supporting paragraphs with clear transitions, and ends with a solid conclusion.
- **Language/Style.** The essay uses vivid and precise language.
- **Conventions.** The essay avoids errors in spelling, grammar, usage, mechanics, and form.

▶ Additional practice is provided in the Essential Skills Practice Book: Writing 1.20.

Understanding Literature (Questions for Discussion)

Metaphor. A **metaphor** is a figure of speech in which one thing is spoken or written about as if it were another. In line 4, what does the speaker compare indirectly to chains? What would chains do to a person's ability to move freely? What is the speaker saying about herself?

Responding in Writing

1. **Creative Writing: "Though I am . . . " Poem.** Write a poem that begins the same way Princess Zeb-un-Nissa's poem begins. Focus on something about your personality or your life that is not widely known but that you are willing to share with others. For example, a class clown who wants people to realize that he or she has deep and serious emotions might write, "Though life is a circus and I am a clown, my mask hides the face of grief." Before you begin, brainstorm a list of your personality traits. Think of colorful and interesting images or metaphors that you might use in your poem.
2. **Critical Essay: Comparison and Contrast.** Write an essay in which you compare and contrast Zeb-un-Nissa's experiences with and feelings about love to those of the speaker in "The River-Merchant's Wife: A Letter" or those of the speaker in one of Petrarch's sonnets. In what way is the situation of the two speakers similar? In what way is it different? Also compare the reactions of each speaker to his or her own situation. Create a Venn diagram to compare the two speakers. (See the Language Arts Survey 1.10, "Gathering Ideas," for more information.) Then, develop a thesis, state the thesis clearly in your introduction, support your thesis in the body of your essay, and come to a conclusion in your final paragraph.

Speaking and Listening Skills

Using Elements of Verbal Communication. Consult the Language Arts Survey 3.1, "Elements of Verbal and Nonverbal Communication." Mark the poem about yourself that you wrote for the Creative Writing activity above to show where you might increase or decrease volume or pace, vary pitch, and use especially clear enunciation. Place a letter or letters from the following key above each word. Then get into groups of three and read the poems aloud to one another.

l = loud	l = low pitch	e = enunciate	t = tone
s = soft	h = high pitch	r = rapid	sl = slow

Answers for Skills Activities

SPEAKING AND LISTENING SKILLS

Students should use volume, pitch, enunciation, pace, and a varied tone effectively when reading their poems. Ask students to critique each other's work based on each of these criteria.

▶ Additional practice is provided in the Essential Skills Practice Book: Speaking and Listening 3.1.

"Tonight I Can Write"
by Pablo Neruda, translated by W. S. Merwin

CHILE

About the Author

PABLO NERUDA
1904–1973

Born Neftalí Ricardo Reyes Basoalto in Parral, Chile, **Pablo Neruda** is known internationally as a poet and diplomat who was dedicated to social reform. He was awarded the Lenin Peace Prize in 1953 and the Nobel Prize for literature in 1971. Neruda began writing as a teenager and published his first book of poems, *Crepusculario,* in 1923. The next year he published another book, *Twenty Love Poems and a Song of Despair.* Neruda became interested in politics early in his life, first serving in government in 1927 as a representative of Chile in South Asia. From 1933 to 1934 he was Chilean consul in Buenos Aires, Argentina. Then he traveled to Spain, where he served through the early part of the Spanish Civil War. He returned to Chile and served as a senator for three years but was forced into hiding during political turmoil. Neruda later served as Chilean ambassador to France. He continued to travel and publish books of poetry throughout his life. His other books include *Residence on Earth* (1933); *General Song,* an epic poem; and *One Hundred Love Sonnets* (1959).

About the Selection

The following selection comes from a group of twenty poems that Neruda wrote as he grieved about the end of a relationship with a woman he had deeply loved. In the early poems of this series, he studies the relationship, trying to remember what he loved about the woman. In **"Tonight I Can Write,"** the last of the twenty poems, Neruda faces the painful reality of the loss of the woman he loves.

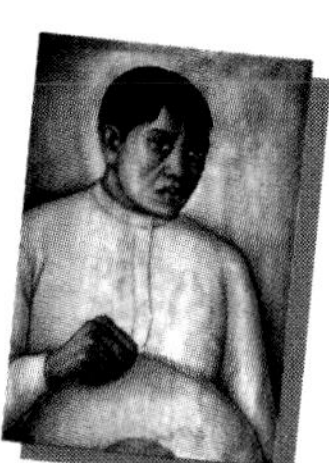
Campesino Sombrero.
Diego Rivera, 1926

CONNECTIONS: Chilean Arts

Chile, Pablo Neruda's birthplace, is a beautiful country with a rich heritage of literature, art, music, and theater. In fact, Chile stands out as having one of the richest cultural traditions in Latin America. Chileans have been particularly accomplished as poets. One famous poetic work inspired by Chile is *La Araucana,* written during the Renaissance by Alonso de Ercilla y Zúñiga. Many people consider this work to be the most important epic poem written in the Spanish language. An important native Chilean poet is Gabriela Mistral (see page 395), who won the Nobel Prize for literature in 1945. Fiction writer Isabel Allende (see page 270) is one of Chile's leading contemporary writers. Chile's artistic achievements extend to other areas, and the country's capital of Santiago is home to the Palace of Fine Arts, the National Library, the National Ballet, and many orchestras and theaters.

GOALS/OBJECTIVES

Studying this lesson will enable students to

- appreciate the speaker's feelings of love and loss
- define *mood, image,* and *internal conflict* and identify these elements in literary works that they read
- write a paragraph or poem that establishes a definite mood using imagery
- write a critical essay about internal conflict
- distinguish between dull and vivid language
- edit sentences to make the language more vivid

ADDITIONAL RESOURCES

READER'S GUIDE

- Selection Worksheet 3.5

ASSESSMENT PORTFOLIO

- Selection Check Test 2.3.9
- Selection Test 2.3.10

ESSENTIAL SKILLS PRACTICE BOOKS

- Writing 1.8, 1.20
- Language 2.15
- Speaking and Listening 3.5

PREREADING EXTENSIONS

Inform students that *La Araucana,* the poem mentioned in Connections: Chilean Arts on this page, is the first epic poem written about the Americas. Its author, Alonso de Ercilla y Zúñiga, was a Spanish soldier and student of literature who ventured to Chile in 1555. There, he took part in the Spanish wars against the Araucanians, a Native American group who successfully resisted the Spanish, and later the Chileans, for 350 years. The poet was sympathetic to the Araucanian cause (although he was in Chile to oppose it) and admired the fierceness of their resistance. Encourage students to research the Araucanians or other Native American groups indigenous to Chile, such as the Chincha, the Quechua, and the Inca.

SUPPORT FOR LEP STUDENTS

PRONUNCIATIONS OF PROPER NOUNS AND ADJECTIVES

Nef • ta • lí Ri • car • do Rey • es Ba • so • al • to (nef tä lē´ rē kär´dō rā´yās bä sō äl´tō)
Bue • nos Ai • res (bwā´nōs ī´rās)
Chi • le (chē´lā)
Chil • e • an (chē lā´ən)
A • lon • so de Er • cil • la y Zú • ñi • ga (ä lōn´sō ther sēl yä ē sū´nyē gä)
Pa • blo Ne • ru • da (pä´blō nā ro͞o´thä)

READER'S JOURNAL

If students are having trouble with this assignment, you might ask them to list images they associate with any other strong emotion they have felt, such as happiness, anger, fear, or jealousy.

ANSWERS TO GUIDED READING QUESTIONS

❶ The speaker might write the saddest verse. His example is: "The night is starry/and the stars are blue and shiver in the distance."

❷ The woman once loved the speaker. He loved her "great still eyes."

❸ The night seems even more immense to the speaker without his beloved. He compares his verse falling on the soul to dew falling upon a pasture.

ANSWERS FOR LANGUAGE LAB

(SEE PAGE 265.)

Responses will vary. Possible responses are given.

1. Admirers of verse are enchanted when they read Pablo Neruda's melodic lines.
2. Neruda's poems can seem as bleak and stark as a hillside in February.
3. He won renown for depicting his native Chile in his verse.
4. He also writes to illuminate the world's ills.
5. We sat under the towering oak, reading Neruda's poetry.
6. The golden afternoon sun warmed the earth.
7. One poem described an inky night scattered with stars.
8. The poem's speaker mourned the loss of someone he had loved.
9. He was stricken by the points of fire that seemed to dance in her eyes.
10. Although he knew they would meet no more, her fragile face still haunted him.

► Additional practice is given in Essential Skills Practice Book: Language 2.15.

Think about the last time you felt sad and lonely. Then freewrite images—words that name things that can be seen, heard, touched, tasted, or smelled—that remind you of these feelings. For example, you might list things like an abandoned building; a dark, empty street; or the call of a bird.

"Tonight I Can Write"

PABLO NERUDA, TRANSLATED BY W. S. MERWIN

❶ *What type of verse might the speaker write tonight? What example of such verses does he give?*

❷ *Did the woman the speaker describes ever love him? What is one feature that he loved about her?*

❸ *According to the speaker, what is the night like without his beloved? To what does he compare his verse?*

Tonight I can write the saddest lines.

Write, for example, "The night is starry
and the stars are blue and shiver in the distance."

The night wind revolves in the sky and sings.

Tonight I can write the saddest lines.
I loved her, and sometimes she loved me too.

Through nights like this one I held her in my arms.
I kissed her again and again under the endless sky.

She loved me, sometimes I loved her too.
How could one not have loved her great still eyes.

Tonight I can write the saddest lines.
To think that I do not have her. To feel that I have lost her.

To hear the immense night, still more immense without her.
And the verse falls to the soul like dew to the pasture.

What does it matter that my love could not keep her.
The night is starry and she is not with me.

WORDS FOR EVERYDAY USE

im • mense (im mens´) *adj.,* limitless; very large

VOCABULARY IN CONTEXT

• Many writers have been inspired by the immense expanse of the evening sky scattered with stars.

Three Women [Detail]. *Jan Toorop, 1885*

This is all. In the distance someone is singing. In the distance.
My soul is not satisfied that it has lost her.

My sight tries to find her as though to bring her closer
My heart looks for her, and she is not with me.

The same night whitening the same trees.
We, of that time, are no longer the same.

I no longer love her, that's certain, but how I loved her.
My voice tried to find the wind to touch her hearing.

Another's. She will be another's. As she was before my kisses.
Her voice, her bright body. Her infinite eyes.

I no longer love her, that's certain, but maybe I love her.
Love is so short, forgetting is so long.

Because through nights like this I held her in my arms
my soul is not satisfied that it has lost her.

Though this be the last pain that she makes me suffer
and these the last verses that I write for her. ■

1 *What does the speaker hear in the distance? How does he feel about having lost this woman?*

2 *What does the speaker say about the woman's current situation?*

3 *What is important about the pain the speaker feels and the verses that he writes tonight?*

Answers to Guided Reading Questions

1 The speaker hears someone singing. He cannot accept that he has lost this woman.

2 The speaker says that the woman will be with someone else.

3 The speaker says that this is the last time he will feel this pain and that he will write no more verses for her.

Selection Check Test with Answers

EX. What does the speaker say he can do tonight?
The speaker says that he can write the saddest lines.

1. What example of a sad line does the speaker provide?
"The night is starry/ and the stars are blue and shiver in the distance."

2. What relationship once existed between the woman and the speaker?
The two were once in love.

3. What does the speaker hear in the distance?
The speaker hears someone singing.

4. What claim does the speaker make about his love for this woman?
The speaker claims that he no longer loves her.

5. What does the speaker reveal about the poem in the final line?
He says that this is the last poem he will write for her.

Integrated Skills Activities

Speaking and Listening

Encourage students to form small groups and to prepare choral readings of this poem. Refer students to the Language Arts Survey 3.5, "Oral Interpretation," for more instruction.

► Additional practice is provided in the Essential Skills Practice Book: Speaking and Listening 3.5.

Responding to the Selection

Students may feel more comfortable discussing their reactions to the poem in small groups. Remind students that they can discuss lines that moved them as well as elements of the poem that did not move them, as long as they back up their opinions with evidence.

Answers for Reviewing the Selection

RECALLING AND INTERPRETING

1. **Recalling.** The speaker says he can write the saddest lines. **Interpreting.** The speaker seems to be feeling melancholy, contemplative, and lonely.

2. **Recalling.** The speaker remembers that he was once with a woman he loved on such nights. He remembers her "great still eyes." **Interpreting.** The speaker is saddened because their relationship ended and his "love could not keep her." The night seems more immense and he is more lonely now that he has lost her.

3. **Recalling.** The speaker describes the immense starry night and someone singing in the distance. **Interpreting.** The largeness of the night may remind the speaker of his insignificance and loneliness. The person singing in the distance may remind the speaker that his loved one is now distant from him as well.

4. **Recalling.** She is lost to the speaker—he speculates that she will be another's. The speaker says he no longer loves her because "We, of that time, are no longer the same." **Interpreting.** He declares that he does not love her because he knows that they will never be reunited and he feels that he should give up his love. At the same time, he is having difficulty forgetting his love for this woman.

SYNTHESIZING

Responses will vary. Possible responses are given.

5. Students' responses will vary widely but should be supported.

Responding to the Selection

How does this poem make you feel? Cite a line from the poem that you find especially vivid and heartfelt and tell why you find it so.

Reviewing the Selection

RECALLING		INTERPRETING
1. What does the speaker say he can write tonight?	▶▶	How does the speaker seem to be feeling?
2. What does the speaker remember about a woman he loved? What is one feature in particular that he keeps remembering?	▶▶	What thoughts are causing the speaker's sadness? Why are these thoughts sad for him?
3. What does the speaker describe about his surroundings? What does he hear in the distance?	▶▶	Which sights and sounds reflect the speaker's loneliness?
4. Where is the woman that the speaker loves? Why can he not permit himself to love her?	▶▶	Why does the speaker continue to declare that he does not love the woman when he continues to show that he still does love her?

SYNTHESIZING

5. Imagine that you are the woman about whom Neruda writes. How would you feel upon reading or hearing these words? Would it change your mind about him and your relationship? Why, or why not?

Understanding Literature (Questions for Discussion)

1. **Mood and Image. Mood,** or **atmosphere,** is the emotion created in the reader by part or all of a literary work. As you have read in the Reader's Journal activity, an **image** is a word or phrase that names something that can be seen, heard, touched, tasted, or smelled. What is the mood of this poem? Is the mood consistent throughout the poem? Name specific images that help to create this mood or these moods.

2. **Internal Conflict.** An **internal conflict** is a struggle that takes place within a character. Describe the internal conflict of the speaker of this poem. Although he is aware of the reality of his situation, what struggle goes on in his mind? Does the speaker finally accept the reality of his situation? Explain.

Answers for Understanding Literature

Responses will vary. Possible responses are given.

1. **Mood and Image.** Students may say the mood is a consistent one of melancholy and longing. Students should note the images of the starry, immense night and the distant singer.

2. **Internal Conflict.** The speaker is trying to cast aside his old love for a woman but is having difficulty because he remembers their love so vividly. He claims that he no longer loves her, but then is forced to admit that he probably does still love her. He also looks for her with his sight and his heart and hopes that his voice will reach her wherever she is, although he knows that she is lost to him forever and probably will fall in love with someone else. *Responses will vary.*

Responding in Writing

1. **Creative Writing: Mood Paragraph or Poem.** Write a paragraph or a short poem in which you try to establish a specific mood. Think about the images used by Neruda to establish mood in his poem. Then choose a particular mood—sadness, happiness, excitement, or anger—and try to create this mood in a poem or paragraph using specific images. You might choose to write your piece using the images that you named in the Reader's Journal activity.

2. **Critical Essay: Conflict.** Based on your answers to Understanding Literature, question 2, write a critical essay in which you describe the central conflict of this poem. Support your statement about the poem's conflict by naming specific words, phrases, and images from the poem. Think about the struggle and pain in the mind of the speaker, and then think about the ways in which the words of the poem make this struggle clear to the reader.

Language Lab

Using Vivid Language. Read the sentences below, then rewrite them using words and phrases that are more specific and vivid. Use your imagination as you try to create sentences that are lively and exciting. For more information, consult the Language Arts Survey 2.15, "Using Vivid Nouns, Adjectives, and Modifiers."

EXAMPLE That nice poem was interesting and made me feel sad.
That blues poem still sings its melancholy song to me in the dark.

1. Poetry students like the work of Pablo Neruda.
2. Neruda's poems are often sad.
3. He was famous for writing about Chile and its outdoors.
4. He also writes to point out things that are bad and unfair in the world.
5. We sat by some big trees and read some of his poems.
6. The sun was out and it was a nice day.
7. One poem we read was about a night that was very dark and had stars.
8. The man in the poem was unhappy and felt alone without a woman whom he had loved a lot.
9. He thought her eyes were pretty.
10. He knew their relationship was over, but her face was hard to forget.

ANALYTIC SCALES FOR RESPONDING IN WRITING

Assign a score from 1 to 25 for each grading criterion below. (For more detailed evaluation, see the evaluation forms for writing, revising, and proofreading, Assessment Portfolio 4.1–4.9.)

1. Mood Paragraph or Poem

- **Content/Unity.** The paragraph or poem establishes a specific mood using images.
- **Organization/Coherence.** The paragraph or poem should be arranged in a logical order.
- **Language/Style.** The paragraph or poem uses vivid and precise nouns, verbs, and modifiers.
- **Conventions.** The paragraph or poem avoids errors in spelling, grammar, usage, mechanics, and manuscript form.

► Additional practice is provided in the Essential Skills Practice Book: Writing 1.8.

2. Critical Essay

- **Content/Unity.** The essay explains the poem's central conflict and the way that this conflict is developed.
- **Organization/Coherence.** The essay should begin with an introduction that includes the thesis of the essay. The introduction should be followed by supporting paragraphs with clear transitions. The essay should end with a solid conclusion.
- **Language/Style.** The essay uses vivid and precise nouns, verbs, and modifiers.
- **Conventions.** The essay avoids errors in spelling, grammar, usage, mechanics, and manuscript form.

► Additional practice is provided in the Essential Skills Practice Book: Writing 1.20.

ANSWERS FOR LANGUAGE LAB

Answers for Language Lab appear on page 262.

ADDITIONAL RESOURCES

READER'S GUIDE

- Selection Worksheet 3.6

ASSESSMENT PORTFOLIO

- Selection Check Test 2.3.11
- Selection Test 2.3.12

ESSENTIAL SKILLS PRACTICE BOOKS

- Writing 1.8, 1.20
- Speaking and Listening 3.1–3.4
- Study and Research 4.12–4.18

PREREADING EXTENSIONS

Assign pairs of students excerpts from the *Odyssey* to read. Each pair should then write a summary of their excerpt and present a brief retelling of the excerpt to the class. For help in preparing their oral retellings, refer students to the Language Arts Survey 3.1, "Elements of Verbal and Nonverbal Communication," and 3.4, "Public Speaking."

SUPPORT FOR LEP STUDENTS

PRONUNCIATIONS OF PROPER NOUNS AND ADJECTIVES

O • dys • se • us (ō dis´ ē əs)
Pe • nel • o • pe (pə nel´ ō pē)
Yan • nis Rit • sos (yä´nēs rēt´sōs)
Tel • e • ma • chus (tə lem´ ə kəs)

ADDITIONAL VOCABULARY

cunning—slyness; craftiness
hearth—fireside; fireplace

PREREADING

"Penelope's Despair"
by Yannis Ritsos, translated by Edmund Keeley

GREECE

About the Author

Yannis Ritsos (1909–1991). Yannos Ritsos was one of Greece's best known modern poets. His earlier poems reflect his knowledge of the works of ancient Greece and Rome, while his later works deal more with personal issues and his own life experiences. Active politically, Ritsos endured exile and house arrest for opposing the Greek junta, military leaders who governed Greece from 1967 to 1974.

About the Selection

"Penelope's Despair" is based on characters in classical Greek and Roman mythology. According to legend, Penelope is the wife of Odysseus, King of Ithaca, who was called Ulysses by the Romans. Odysseus is separated from his wife and their son, Telemachus, for twenty years as he fights in the ten-year Trojan War and wanders for ten years afterward, trying to sail home from Troy to Ithaca. Penelope remains true to her husband while he is gone, despite constant harassment by men wanting to marry her. Hoping that her husband is not dead, Penelope puts her suitors off by telling them that she will marry as soon as she finishes weaving a shroud for Odysseus's father. Every night, however, she unravels what she has woven during the day. After many years, Penelope's situation becomes intolerable and her faith in her husband's return begins to wane. She decides to choose a new husband from among the suitors, despite predictions by a soothsayer (or fortune teller) and dreams sent by the goddess Athena, promising her husband's return. Eventually, Odysseus does return, disguised as a beggar. Penelope shows him hospitality, unaware that he is her husband. She tells the beggar that she is going to choose a suitor—that she will marry the man who can shoot an arrow through the holes in a row of twelve axes, a feat she has seen Odysseus accomplish. The beggar tells her that her husband will return before the contest is over, but she does not believe him. On the day of the contest, the disguised Odysseus is reluctantly given a chance to shoot the arrow through the axes. He does so, reveals his identity, and kills Penelope's suitors one by one. Then Penelope and Odysseus are reunited.

CONNECTIONS: Ancient References in Modern Literature

Many contemporary Greek writers draw upon the rich history and literary tradition of their country. Ritsos's "Penelope's Despair" refers to the legend of Odysseus which is told by Homer in the epic poem the *Odyssey.* Contemporary Greek poet Jenny Mastoraki (see page 1112) also alludes to ancient times, specifically to the legendary Trojan War, in "The Wooden Horse then said." Other poets, such as C. P. Cavafy (see page 37) and Nobel Prize winner Odysseus Elytis, also frequently allude in their writing to the history and literature of ancient Greece.

GOALS/OBJECTIVES

Studying this lesson will enable students to

- appreciate an ironic treatment of a classical subject—Odysseus's return to Ithaca
- identify Odysseus and Penelope as figures in classical mythology
- identify point of view and irony of situation in works that they read
- write a creative experiment with point of view
- write a critical essay about Penelope's character
- research heroic figures and present their findings

When was the last time you felt disappointed or let down? Did an exciting or happy event end too soon? Did a person, place, or occasion fail to meet your expectations? In your journal, describe the experience and your emotional responses to the experience.

READER'S JOURNAL

"Penelope's Despair"

YANNIS RITSOS, TRANSLATED BY EDMUND KEELEY

It wasn't that she didn't recognize him in the light from the hearth; it wasn't
the beggar's rags, the disguise—no. The signs were clear:
the scar on his knee, the <u>pluck</u>, the cunning in his eye. Frightened,
her back against the wall, she searched for an excuse,
a little time, so she wouldn't have to answer,
give herself away. Was it for him, then, that she'd used up twenty years,
twenty years of waiting and dreaming, for this miserable
blood-soaked, white-bearded man? She collapsed voiceless into a chair,
studied the slaughtered suitors on the floor as though seeing
her own desires dead there. And she said "Welcome" to him,
hearing her voice sound foreign, distant. In the corner, her loom
covered the ceiling with a trellis[1] of shadows; and all the birds she'd woven
with bright red thread in green foliage, now,
this night of the return, suddenly turned ashen and black,
flying low on the level sky of her final enduring. ■

❶ *What type of disguise is Odysseus, the subject of the poem, wearing? Why is Penelope able to recognize him despite this?*

❷ *What question does Penelope ask herself?*

❸ *Who lies dead on the floor? What of Penelope lies dead on the floor as well?*

❹ *What does Penelope say to Odysseus? How does her voice sound?*

1. **trellis.** Archway

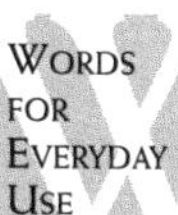
WORDS FOR EVERYDAY USE

pluck (pluk) *n.*, courage; strength to bear misfortune or pain

VOCABULARY IN CONTEXT

- Ivan showed remarkable <u>pluck</u> when he gathered his courage to stand in for the play's star at the last moment.

READER'S JOURNAL

As an alternate activity, the student can imagine that he or she is older and that his or her romantic partner has had to leave for twenty years. Would he or she await the loved one's return or move on with his or her life? Explain.

ANSWERS TO GUIDED READING QUESTIONS

❶ Odysseus is wearing beggar's rags. Penelope is still able to recognize him because of the scar on his knee, his pluck, and the cunning in his eye.

❷ Penelope asks herself if it was really for him that she has used up twenty years, waiting and dreaming.

❸ Suitors lie dead on the floor. Penelope's own desires are dead on the floor as well.

❹ Penelope says "Welcome" to him, but her voice sounds foreign and distant.

SELECTION CHECK TEST WITH ANSWERS

EX: Who is Penelope's husband?
Penelope's husband is Odysseus.

1. What kind of disguise is Odysseus wearing when he returns from war?
He is wearing beggar's rags.
2. What does Penelope recognize about Odysseus?
She recognizes the scar on his knee, his pluck, and the cunning in his eye.
3. What does Odysseus do to Penelope's suitors?
He kills them.
4. About what does Penelope wonder when she sees Odysseus?
She wonders if this is really the man for whom she waited twenty years.
5. What happens to the birds in Penelope's weaving?
They change color from red and green to black and ashen.

Responding to the Selection

Have students work in pairs to role play a conversation between Penelope and her friend. Tell students to take a turn playing each role.

Answers for Reviewing the Selection

RECALLING AND INTERPRETING

1. **Recalling.** Penelope's husband is dressed in beggar's rags. She recognizes the scar on his knee, his pluck, and the cunning in his eye. **Interpreting.** Penelope is disappointed and questions her love for her husband.

2. **Recalling.** Penelope has been waiting for and dreaming of her husband's return, and she has fought off many suitors. **Interpreting.** Penelope wonders whether she should have spent so many years waiting for this "miserable/blood-soaked, white-bearded man."

3. **Recalling.** Penelope's suitors are dead on the floor, killed by Odysseus. **Interpreting.** What she has been waiting for and dreaming about for twenty years has happened, but she finds that she no longer has strong feelings for her husband. The possibility of love with the husband she remembers is gone.

4. **Recalling.** A loom, holding Penelope's weaving, sits in the corner. It covers the ceiling with shadows. Her woven birds have changed from red and green to ashen and black. **Interpreting.** The birds, woven as Penelope waited for the return of her husband, represented hope. When her husband returns and she is disappointed, the birds no longer represent hope but a kind of unhappiness and tarnished dreams.

SYNTHESIZING

Responses will vary. Possible responses are given.

5. "Penelope's Despair" is that

(cont.)

Responding to the Selection

Suppose you were one of Penelope's close friends. What might she say to you about the night of Odysseus's return? How might she now feel about the time she spent waiting for him?

Reviewing the Selection

Recalling		Interpreting
1. What type of disguise is Odysseus, Penelope's husband, wearing? What distinguishing features help her to recognize him?	▶▶	What are Penelope's initial feelings on seeing her husband after so many years?
2. What has Penelope been doing for the last twenty years?	▶▶	What thoughts show that Penelope expected to feel differently upon her husband's return? What type of words does she use to describe him?
3. Where are Penelope's suitors? What has happened to them?	▶▶	Why does Penelope see her own desires as "dead there" on the floor? What possibilities no longer exist for her life?
4. What sits in the corner? With what does it cover the ceiling? In what way have her woven birds changed?	▶▶	What is significant about the change in the birds? In what way do the birds reflect what has happened to Penelope's hopes and dreams?

Synthesizing

5. What is "Penelope's Despair"? What is her "final enduring"?

Understanding Literature (Questions for Discussion)

1. **Point of View. Point of view** is the vantage point from which a story is told. Refer to the Handbook of Literary Terms for explanation of the different points of view. From whose point of view is "Penelope's Despair" told? In what way might the poem be different if it were told from the point of view of Odysseus or of one of the suitors? What unique perspective do Penelope's personal feelings bring to the event described in this poem?

Answers for Reviewing the Selection (cont.)

she waited, wasting twenty years of her life, for her husband to return. When he finally returns, she is still unhappy. In fact, her unhappiness is more intense because she no longer has anything for which to hope. Her "final enduring" is, after twenty years of waiting, a life with a man whom she neither knows or loves.

Answers for Skills Activities

RESEARCH SKILLS

Each group should report on a different mythical hero. Refer students to Insights: The Hero and the Quest on page 516 as a starting place.

▶ Additional practice is provided in the Essential Skills Practice Book: Study and Research 4.12–4.18.

2. **Irony of Situation. Irony of situation** is a type of irony in which an event occurs that violates the expectations of the characters, the reader, or the audience. What is ironic about the situation described in "Penelope's Despair"? How might you expect Penelope to feel and react when she is reunited with her husband after twenty years? What is her actual reaction?

Responding in Writing

1. **Creative Writing: Point of View Experiment.** Think about one of your favorite poems, plays, or stories. From whose point of view is the piece told? Think about how different the piece would be if it were told from another character's point of view. Rewrite the poem or a scene from the play or story using another character's point of view. Before writing, consider these questions: What unique feelings and ideas would this character bring to the piece? How might this character's perspective change the story or poem?

2. **Critical Essay: Penelope.** Based on what you have learned from the Prereading section on page 266 and from the poem "Penelope's Despair," write a critical essay in which you examine the character of Penelope. Does her twenty-year wait for Odysseus make her strong and virtuous or foolish and pitiful? Why might she be experiencing unexpected feelings on Odysseus's return?

Research Skills

Researching Heroes. Review the Language Arts Survey 4.12–4.18, "Research Skills." Then, working in small groups, go to the library to find more information on a mythical hero such as Odysseus. What works of art have been created based on this character and his or her experiences? What works of literature have been inspired by this character and his or her experiences? Each group should present its findings to the class. Then, as a class, discuss why these characters have been so influential. What are people able to learn about other cultures from the myths of these heroes?

ANSWERS FOR UNDERSTANDING LITERATURE

Responses will vary. Possible responses are given.

1. Point of View. "Penelope's Despair" is told from the point of view of Penelope. Odysseus might feel excitement on returning home and anger at the number of suitors who were calling on his wife. He might expect her to feel happy to see him. The suitors would probably describe the return of Odysseus with fear and disappointment.

2. Irony of Situation. It is ironic that Penelope feels disappointed after waiting so long for her husband to return. The reader might expect Penelope to feel happiness, excitement, or relief on seeing her husband. Instead, she wonders if she should have waited for him.

ANALYTIC SCALES FOR RESPONDING IN WRITING

Assign a score from 1 to 25 for each grading criterion below. (For more detailed evaluation, see the evaluation forms for writing, revising, and proofreading, Assessment Portfolio 4.1–4.9.)

1. Point of View Experiment

- **Content/Unity.** The writing explores a poem, play, or story from a different point of view.
- **Organization/Coherence.** The writing follows a logical order.
- **Language/Style.** The writing uses vivid and precise nouns, verbs, and modifiers.
- **Conventions.** The writing avoids errors in spelling, grammar, usage, mechanics, and manuscript form.

► Additional practice is provided in the Essential Skills Practice Book: Writing 1.8.

(cont.)

ANALYTIC SCALES FOR RESPONDING IN WRITING (CONT.)

2. Critical Essay

- **Content/Unity.** The essay examines Penelope's character.
- **Organization/Coherence.** The essay begins with an introduction that includes the thesis of the essay. The introduction is followed by supporting paragraphs with clear transitions. The essay ends with a solid conclusion.
- **Language/Style.** The essay uses vivid and precise nouns, verbs, and modifiers.
- **Conventions.** The essay avoids errors in spelling, grammar, usage, mechanics, and manuscript form.

► Additional practice is provided in the Essential Skills Practice Book: Writing 1.20.

ADDITIONAL RESOURCES

READER'S GUIDE

- Selection Worksheet 3.7

ASSESSMENT PORTFOLIO

- Selection Check Test 2.3.13
- Selection Test 2.3.14

ESSENTIAL SKILLS PRACTICE BOOKS

- Writing 1.8, 1.20
- Applied English/Tech Prep 5.1

PREREADING EXTENSIONS

Students can work in three groups to research the geography, history, arts, and attractions of Peru, where Isabel Allende was born; Chile, where she grew up; and Venezuela, the country to which she fled. If you would like students to work in smaller groups, suggest that some groups research other South American countries, including Argentina, Bolivia, Brazil, Colombia, Ecuador, French Guyana, Guyana, Paraguay, Suriname, and Uruguay. Resources include the Internet and other online services, books and periodicals, travel agents, and tourism boards. Have students create skits, posters, maps, or travelogues about the country they researched.

SUPPORT FOR LEP STUDENTS

PRONUNCIATIONS OF PROPER NOUNS AND ADJECTIVES

Is • a • bel Al • len • de (ē sä bel´ ī yen´dā)
Hei • del • berg (hī´dəl berg)
***ni* • *ña* E • lo • í • sa** (nē´nyä ā lō ē´sä)
An • da • lu • si • a (an´də lo͞o´zhe)

ADDITIONAL VOCABULARY

formidable—impressive; causing fear
invigorating—energizing
intuition—understanding without reasoning

PREREADING

"The Little Heidelberg"
by Isabel Allende, translated by Margaret Sayers Peden

CHILE

About the Author

Isabel Allende (1942–). Born in Peru, Isabel Allende grew up in Santiago, Chile. The niece and goddaughter of Chile's former democratic president Salvador Allende, she was forced to flee the country and live in Caracas, Venezuela, after her uncle was killed in a coup in 1973. Allende worked as a journalist for many years before beginning to write fiction in 1981. Her first published novel, *The House of the Spirits*, was a widely acclaimed bestseller and was later made into a film. Allende's other works include the novels *Of Love and Shadows*, *Eva Luna*, and *Paula*, as well as the short story collection *The Stories of Eva Luna*. Allende, a fan of Colombian novelist Gabriel García Márquez, combines elements of realism and fantasy with political ideas in her novels. She is considered to be one of the most notable contemporary Latin American writers and the first South American woman novelist to break sexist literary barriers and become widely read. Allende now makes her home in the San Francisco area of California.

About the Selection

"**The Little Heidelberg**" is taken from Isabel Allende's short story collection, *The Stories of Eva Luna*. Eva Luna, a character who first appeared in Allende's novel *Eva Luna*, is a strong woman who has a brilliant gift for storytelling. In the prologue of the short story collection, her romantic partner, who also appeared in the novel, asks her to tell him a story that she has never told anyone before. This request serves as a frame—or storytelling device that encompasses other stories—for the tales in the collection.

Set in the Caribbean in a tavern called The Little Heidelberg, the story unfolds in a world of **magical realism** (see Insights: Magical Realism, page 278), a combination of realism and fantasy. Heidelberg is a busy town in Germany, and the aptly named tavern looks and sounds as though it were plucked right out of western Europe. Filled with tourists and European immigrants, The Little Heidelberg is a unique setting for a story about a strange and special relationship between two of the tavern's patrons.

CONNECTIONS: Venezuela

Venezuela, the country to which Isabel Allende fled in 1973, serves as the backdrop for some of her fiction. Because this beautiful country, a part of Spain until 1821, has rich oil deposits, it enjoys the highest per capita income in South America. Venezuela has welcomed many European immigrants; in fact, 21 percent of its population is of European descent.

GOALS/OBJECTIVES

Studying this lesson will enable students to

- enjoy a magical realist story about love
- recognize Isabel Allende as a notable, contemporary Latin American author
- define *magical realism*
- identify elements of magical realism
- describe the setting of the story
- write a description
- analyze elements of reality and fantasy
- write a personal letter
- write a business letter

Describe an interesting or unusual place that you have seen or visited. When did you see or visit this place? What is most special about it, the actual place or the people whom you saw or met there? In your journal, write a letter to a friend in which you describe this place in detail.

READER'S JOURNAL

"The Little Heidelberg"

ISABEL ALLENDE, TRANSLATED BY MARGARET SAYERS PEDEN

El Capitán and the woman *niña* Eloísa had danced together so many years that they had achieved perfection. Each could sense the other's next movement, divine the exact instant of the next turn, interpret the most subtle hand pressure or deviation of a foot. They had not missed a step once in forty years; they moved with the precision of a couple used to making love and sleeping in a close embrace. This was what made it so difficult to believe that they had never exchanged a single word.

The Little Heidelberg is a tavern a certain distance from the capital and located on a hill surrounded by banana groves; there, besides good music and invigorating air, they offer a unique aphrodisiac stew made heady with a combination of spices, too heavy for the fiery climate of the region but in perfect harmony with the traditions that activate the proprietor *don* Rupert. Before the oil crisis, when there was still an illusion of plenty and fruits were imported from other latitudes, the specialty of the house had been apple strudel, but now that nothing is left from the petroleum but a mountain of indestructible refuse and a memory of better times, they make the strudel with guavas and with mangoes. The tables, arranged in a large circle that leaves an open space in the middle for dancing, are covered with green-and-white-checked cloths, and the walls display bucolic scenes of country life in the Alps: shepherdesses with golden braids, strapping youths, and immaculate bovines. The musicians—dressed in lederhosen,[1] woolen knee socks, Tyrolean suspenders, and felt hats that with the sweat of years have lost their dash and from a distance resemble greenish wigs—sit on a platform crowned by a stuffed eagle that according to *don* Rupert sprouts new feathers from time to time. One plays the accordion, another the saxophone, and the third, through some feat of agility involving all his extremities, simultaneously manipulates bass drum, snares, and top hat. The accordion player is a master of his instrument, and he also sings in a warm

1. **lederhosen.** Short leather pants worn with suspenders by men and boys in the Alps

1. *Why was it difficult to believe that El Capitán and niña Eloísa had never spoken a single word?*

2. *What clothing do the musicians wear?*

3. *Where is The Little Heidelberg located? What food is served there?*

WORDS FOR EVERYDAY USE

de • vi • a • tion (dē´vē ā´shən) *n.,* sharp divergence from normal behavior

bu • col • ic (byo͞o käl´ik) *adj.,* pastoral; of country life or farms; rustic

READER'S JOURNAL

Students may wish to bring to class photos, drawings, or mementos of the special place they wrote about in their journals. Students can share these items in small groups as they discuss their descriptions.

ANSWERS TO GUIDED READING QUESTIONS

1. El Capitán and *niña* Eloísa had danced together for many years and had achieved perfection as dance partners. They moved with the precision of a couple that has a close relationship.

2. The musicians wear lederhosen, woolen knee socks, Tyrolean suspenders, and felt hats.

3. The Little Heidelberg is located a certain distance from the capital, on a hill surrounded by banana groves. The tavern serves a unique, spicy aphrodisiac stew and strudel made with guavas and mangoes.

SPELLING AND VOCABULARY WORDS FROM THE SELECTION

benevolent	intrepid
bucolic	permeate
deviation	rudimentary
ethereal	superfluous
euphoric	unremitting

VOCABULARY IN CONTEXT

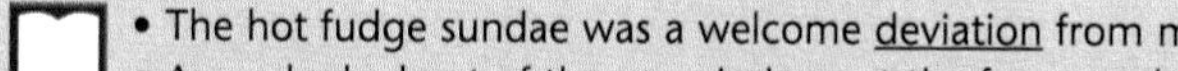

- The hot fudge sundae was a welcome deviation from my usual diet.
- As we looked out of the car windows at the farms and meadows, we marveled at the bucolic beauty of the countryside.

Answers to Guided Reading Questions

❶ The median age of women at the tavern is nearly seventy. Their age does not diminish "the sensuality stirred by the tenor."

❷ Teenagers usually come to the tavern to make fun of the older people, but they are usually frightened away by the drummer and the saxophonist.

❸ The musicians play polkas, mazurkas, waltzes, and European folk dances. This music seems slightly out of place because the tavern is located in the Caribbean, not on the shores of the Rhine.

❹ The tavern's clientele include European émigrés who were escaping poverty or war, businessmen, farmers, and tradesman—"a pleasant and uncomplicated group of people who may not always have been so," but who have mellowed with age.

Additional Questions and Activities

Have students find and listen to recordings of German polkas, mazurkas, waltzes, and European folk dances. Have them listen to Caribbean music as well. Ask them to compare and contrast the two types of music.

Cross-curricular Activities

Social Studies

Have students work in two groups to research Germany, the country where The Little Heidelberg might be expected to fit, and the Caribbean, the place where The Little Heidelberg is actually located. Each group can present information about climate, terrain, major products, and cultural aspects of the region they researched. Students can then compare and contrast the two regions.

❶ *What is the median age of the women at the tavern? What does their age not diminish?*

❷ *What do the teenagers do when they visit the tavern? Why do they leave?*

❸ *What do the musicians play? Why does this music seem out of place?*

❹ *Who are the people that make up the tavern's clientele?*

tenor voice that vaguely suggests Andalusia.[2] Despite his foolish Swiss publican's garb, he is the favorite of the female faithful, and several of these *señoras* secretly nurture the fantasy of being trapped with him in some mortal adventure—a landslide, say, or bombing—in which they would happily draw their last breath folded in the strong arms capable of tearing such heartrending sobs from the accordion. The fact that the median age of these ladies is nearly seventy does not diminish the sensuality stirred by the tenor; it merely adds the gentle breath of death to their enchantment. The orchestra begins playing shortly after sunset and ends at midnight, except on Saturdays and Sundays, when the place is filled with tourists and the trio must keep playing until near dawn when the last customer leaves. They play only polkas, mazurkas, waltzes, and European folk dances, as if instead of being firmly established in the Caribbean, The Little Heidelberg were located on the shores of the Rhine.[3]

Doña Burgel, *don* Rupert's wife, reigns in the kitchen, a formidable matron whom few know because she spends her days amid stewpots and mounds of vegetables; lost in the task of preparing foreign dishes with local ingredients. It was she who invented the strudel with tropical fruits, and the aphrodisiac stew capable of restoring dash to the most disheartened. The landlords' two daughters wait on the tables, a pair of sturdy women smelling of cinnamon, clove, vanilla, and lemon, along with a few local girls, all with rosy cheeks. The clientele is composed of European emigrés who reached these shores escaping poverty or some war or other, businessmen, farmers, and tradesmen, a pleasant and uncomplicated group of people who may not always have been so but who with the passing of time have eased into the benevolent courtesy of healthy old people. The men wear bow ties and jackets, but as the exertion of the dancing and abundance of beer warms their souls, they shed superfluous garments and end up in their shirt-sleeves. The women wear bright colors in antiquated styles, as if their dresses have been rescued from bridal trunks brought with them from their homeland. From time to time a gang of aggressive teenagers stops by; their presence is preceded by the thundering roar of motorcycles and the rattle of boots, keys, and chains, and they come with the sole purpose of making fun of the old people, but the event never goes any further than a skirmish, because the drummer and the saxophonist are prepared to roll up their sleeves and restore order.

On Saturdays, about nine, when all present have enjoyed their servings of the aphrodisiac stew and abandoned themselves to the pleasure of the dance, La Mexicana arrives and sits alone. She is a provocative fiftyish woman with the body of a galleon—proud bow, rounded keel, ample stern, and face like a carved figurehead—who displays a mature but still firm décolletage[4] and a flower over one ear. She is not, of course, the only woman dressed like a flamenco dancer, but on her it looks more natural than on ladies with white hair and resigned waistlines who do not even speak proper Spanish. La Mexicana dancing the polka is a ship adrift on a storm-tossed sea, but to the rhythm of the waltz she seems to breast calm waters. This is how El Capitán sometimes espies her in his dreams, and awakens with the nearly forgotten restiveness of adolescence. They

2. **Andalusia.** Region of southern Spain on the Mediterranean and the Atlantic

3. **Rhine.** River in western Europe flowing from east Switzerland north through Germany, then west through the Netherlands into the North Sea

4. **décolletage.** Neckline or top of a dress cut low so as to bare the neck and shoulders

Words for Everyday Use

be • nev • o • lent (bə nev´ə lənt) *adj.*, kindly

su • per • flu • ous (sə pur´flo͞o əs) *adj.*, unnecessary

Vocabulary in Context

- The benevolent stranger helped André find his way back to his hotel in the foreign city.
- Maria wore a slicker, boots, and cap, making her umbrella superfluous.

say that this captain sailed with a Nordic line whose name no one could decipher. He was an expert on old ships and sea lanes, but all that knowledge lay buried in the depths of his mind, with no possible application in a land where the sea is a placid aquarium of green, crystalline waters unsuited to the intrepid vessels of the North Sea. El Capitán is a leafless tree, a tall, lean man with straight back and still firm neck muscles, a relic clothed in a gold-buttoned jacket and the tragic aura of retired sailors. No one has ever heard a word of Spanish from his lips, nor any other recognizable language. Thirty years ago *don* Rupert argued that El Capitán must be Finnish because of the icy color of his eyes and the unremitting justice of his gaze; as no one could contradict him everyone came to accept his opinion. Anyway, language is secondary at The Little Heidelberg, for no one comes there to talk.

A few of the standard rules of conduct have been modified for the comfort and convenience of all. Anyone can go onto the dance floor alone, or invite someone from another table; if they wish to, the women can take the initiative and ask the men. This is a fair solution for unaccompanied widows. No one asks La Mexicana to dance because it is understood that she considers it offensive; the men must wait, trembling with anticipation, until she makes the request. She deposits her cigarette in the ashtray, uncrosses the daunting columns of her legs, tugs at her bodice, marches toward the chosen one, and stops before him without a glance. She changes partners with every dance, but always reserves at least four numbers for El Capitán. He places a firm helmsman's hand at her waist and pilots her about the floor without allowing his years to curtail his inspiration.

The oldest client of The Little Heidelberg, one who in half a century has never missed a Saturday, is *niña* Eloísa, a tiny lady, meek and gentle, with rice-paper skin and a corona of baby-fine hair. She has earned a living for so many years making bonbons in her kitchen that she is permeated with the scent of chocolate, and always smells of birthday parties. Despite her age, she has retained some of her girlish mannerisms and she still has the strength to spend the entire evening whirling around the dance floor without disturbing a curl of her topknot or skipping a heartbeat. She came to this country at the turn of the century from a village in the south of Russia, accompanied by her mother, who was then a raving beauty. They lived together for years, making their chocolates, completely indifferent to the rigors of the climate, the century, or loneliness, without husbands, family, or major alarms, their sole diversion The Little Heidelberg every weekend. When her mother died, *niña* Eloísa came alone. *Don* Rupert always received her at the door with great deference and showed her to her table as the orchestra welcomed her with the first chords of her favorite waltz. At some tables, mugs of beer were raised to greet her, because she was the oldest person there and undoubtedly the most beloved. She was shy; she had never dared invite a man to dance, but in all those years she had never needed to do so; everyone considered it a privilege to take her hand, place his arm—delicately, so as not to break a crystal bone—about her waist, and lead her to the dance floor. She was a graceful dancer and, besides, she had that sweet fragrance that recalled to any who smelled it his happiest childhood memories.

El Capitán always sat alone, and always at the same table; he drank in moderation and

1 Who is the oldest client of The Little Heidelberg? What has she spent her life doing?

2 When did niña Eloísa come to the village?

3 How important is language and conversation at The Little Heidelberg?

4 What are the rules of the dance floor? What is understood about the woman called La Mexicana?

5 How do people at The Little Heidelberg feel about niña Eloísa?

WORDS FOR EVERYDAY USE

in • trep • id (in trep´id) *adj.,* not afraid, bold, fearless

un • re • mit • ting (un ri mit´iŋ) *adj.,* persistent

per • me • ate (pʉr´mē āt´) *vt.,* penetrate or spread through

VOCABULARY IN CONTEXT

- The intrepid travelers relished the adventure of the uncharted course.
- Myron was disconcerted by Lykesha's unremitting stare.
- As the bread baked, a warm odor permeated the whole house.

ANSWERS TO GUIDED READING QUESTIONS

1 The oldest client of The Little Heidelberg is *niña* Eloísa. She has spent many years of her life making chocolate bonbons.

2 *Niña* Eloísa came to the village at the turn of the century from a village in the south of Russia.

3 Language and conversation is not important at The Little Heidelberg—no one comes to the tavern to talk.

4 Anyone can go onto the dance floor alone or invite someone from another table. Women who wish can ask men to dance. The woman called La Mexicana considers it offensive to be asked to dance—men must wait for her to select a dance partner.

5 People at The Little Heidelberg admire *niña* Eloísa's dancing ability. She reminds people of their happiest childhood memories.

CROSS-CURRICULAR ACTIVITIES

ARTS AND HUMANITIES

At The Little Heidelberg, "language is secondary." Discuss with students means of nonverbal communication. Interested students can prepare representations or interpretations of love stories using dance or mime instead of words. After students have performed, discuss which elements were effective and why.

BIOGRAPHICAL NOTE

Isabel Allende comes from a line of storytellers. She uses her writing to share her stories with many people, trying to reflect the voice of the "little people" not the "winners." *The House of the Spirits* grew out of her feelings of nostalgia after leaving Chile; *Of Love and Shadows* arose from her anger and sense of powerlessness; and *The Stories of Eva Luna* reflects her pleasure in "being a woman and telling stories."

Answers to Guided Reading Questions

① El Capitán is drawn to the Scandinavian tourist couple who visit the tavern one December Saturday.

ANALYTIC SCALES FOR RESPONDING IN WRITING

(SEE PAGE 277.)

Assign a score from 1 to 25 for each grading criterion below. (For more detailed evaluation, see the evaluation forms for writing, revising, and proofreading, Assessment Portfolio 4.1–4.9.)

1. Description

- **Content/Unity.** The description is detailed and includes sensory details.
- **Organization/Coherence.** The description is arranged in a logical order.
- **Language/Style.** The description uses vivid and precise nouns, verbs, and modifiers.
- **Conventions.** The description avoids errors in spelling, grammar, usage, mechanics, and manuscript form.

► Additional practice is provided in the Essential Skills Practice Book: Writing 1.8.

2. Critical Essay

- **Content/Unity.** The essay analyzes the use of fantasy and reality in the story.
- **Organization/Coherence.** The essay begins with an introduction that includes a thesis. The introduction is followed by supporting paragraphs with clear transitions. The essay has a solid conclusion.
- **Language/Style.** The essay uses vivid and precise nouns, verbs, and modifiers.
- **Conventions.** The essay avoids errors in spelling, grammar, usage, mechanics, and manuscript form.

► Additional practice is provided in the Essential Skills Practice Book: Writing 1.20.

Cafe at Arles. *Paul Gauguin, 1888*

Q ① *Who is particularly drawn to the Scandinavian tourist couple that visits the tavern one December Saturday?*

showed no enthusiasm for *doña* Burgel's aphrodisiac stew. He tapped his toe in time with the music, and when *niña* Eloísa was unengaged he would invite her to dance, stopping smartly before her with a discreet click of his heels and a slight bow. They never spoke, they merely looked at each other and smiled between the gallops, skips, and obliques[5] of some old-time dance.

One December Saturday less humid than others, a tourist couple came into The Little Heidelberg. These were not the disciplined Japanese they had been seeing recently but tall Scandinavians with tanned skin and pale eyes; they took a table and watched the dancers with fascination. They were merry and noisy; they clinked their mugs of beer, laughed heartily, and chatted in loud voices. The strangers' words reached the ears of El Capitán at his table and, from a long way away, from another time and another world, came the sound of his own language, as whole and fresh as if it had just been invented, words he had not heard for several decades but retained intact in his memory. An unfamiliar expression softened the features of this ancient mariner and he wavered several minutes between the absolute reserve in which he felt comfortable and the almost forgotten delight of losing himself in conversation. Finally he rose and walked toward the

5. **obliques.** Changes of direction

strangers. Behind the bar, *don* Rupert observed El Capitán as he leaned forward slightly, hands clasped behind his back, and spoke to the new arrivals. Soon the other customers, the waitresses, and the musicians realized that the man was speaking for the first time since they had known him, and they, too, fell silent in order to hear him better. He had a voice like a great grandfather, reedy and deliberate, but he uttered every phrase with clear determination. When he had poured out the contents of his heart, the room was so silent that *doña* Burgel hurried from the kitchen to find out whether someone had died. Finally, after a long pause, one of the tourists emerged from his astonishment, summoned *don* Rupert, and asked him in rudimentary English to help translate the capitain's words. The Nordic couple followed the elderly seaman to the table where *niña* Eloísa sat, and *don* Rupert trailed along, removing his apron on the way, with the intuition that a solemn event was about to occur. El Capitán spoke a few words in his language, one of the strangers translated it into English, and *don* Rupert, his ears pink and his mustache trembling, repeated it in his hind-to-fore Spanish.

"Niña Eloísa, asks El Capitán will you marry him."

The fragile old lady sat there, her eyes round with surprise and her mouth hidden behind her batiste handkerchief, while all waited, holding their breath, until she was able to find her voice.

"Don't you think this is a little sudden?" she whispered.

Her words were repeated by the tavernkeeper and then the tourist, and the answer traveled the same route in reverse.

"El Capitán says he has waited forty years to ask you, and that he could not wait until again comes someone who speaks his language. He says please to do him the favor of answering now."

"All right," *niña* Eloísa whispered faintly, and it was not necessary to translate her answer because every one understood.

A euphoric *don* Rupert threw his arms in the air and announced the engagement; El Capitán kissed the cheeks of his fiancée, the tourists shook everyone's hand, the musicians struck up a ringing triumphal march, and the guests formed a circle around the couple. The women wiped away tears, the men offered sentimental toasts, *don* Rupert sat down at the bar and buried his head in his arms, shaken with emotion, while *doña* Burgel and her two daughters uncorked bottles of their best rum. The trio began to play *The Blue Danube* waltz and the dance floor emptied.

El Capitán took the hand of the gentle lady he had wordlessly loved for so many years and walked with her to the center of the room, where they began to dance with the grace of two herons in their courtship dance. El Capitán held *niña* Eloísa in his arms with the same loving care with which in his youth he had caught the wind in the sails of an ethereal sailing ship, gliding with her around the floor as if they were skimming the calm waves of a bay, while he told her in the language of blizzards and forests all the things his heart had held silent until that moment. Dancing, dancing, El Capitán felt as if time were flowing backward, as if they were growing younger, as if with every step they were happier and lighter on their feet. Turn after turn, the chords of the music grew more vibrant, their feet more rapid, her waist more slender, the weight of her tiny hand fainter in his, her presence less substantial. El Capitán danced on as *niña* Eloísa turned to lace, to froth, to mist, until she was but a shadow, then, finally, nothing but air,

❶ *What is the reaction of the regulars at the tavern to the couple's news?*

❷ *What does El Capitán ask niña Eloísa? What is her first response? What does she finally say?*

❸ *What happens to niña Eloísa as she dances with El Capitán?*

Words for Everyday Use

ru • di • men • ta • ry (ro͞o´də men´tər ē) *adj.,* incompletely or imperfectly developed; basic

eu • phor • ic (yo͞o fôr´ik) *adj.,* happy; in high spirits

e • the • re • al (ē thir´ē əl) *adj.,* not earthly; heavenly

Answers to Guided Reading Questions

❶ People cry and celebrate when they hear the good news.

❷ El Capitán asks *niña* Eloísa to marry him. She first comments on the suddenness of his question but then agrees to marry him.

❸ *Niña* Eloísa turns to lace, to froth, and then to mist. She then turns into a shadow, and then to nothing but air and a faint aroma of chocolate.

Selection Check Test with Answers

EX. Where is the tavern The Little Heidelberg located?
The tavern is located in the Caribbean.

1. What is unusual about the relationship between El Capitán and *niña* Eloísa?
The two have achieved perfection as dancing partners but have never spoken.

2. What kind of music does the band play?
The band plays waltzes.

3. What scent does *niña* Eloísa emit?
She smells of chocolate.

4. What question does El Capitán ask *niña* Eloísa?
He asks *niña* Eloísa if she will marry him.

5. What happens to *niña* Eloísa?
She disappears.

Vocabulary in Context

- Six months ago Leo spoke only rudimentary English; now he is a fluent speaker.
- The players were euphoric after winning the state championship.
- The music was ethereal, like a choir of angels.

Answers to Guided Reading Questions

❶ The musicians continue to play the special waltz because they realize that if they stop, El Capitán's memory of *niña* Eloísa will disappear forever. La Mexicana moves toward El Capitán to dance with him.

Responding to the Selection

Ask students if they would like to frequent a place like The Little Heidelberg. They might also compare the atmosphere and clientele of The Little Heidelberg with that of one of their favorite clubs.

Answers for Reviewing the Selection

RECALLING AND INTERPRETING

1. **Recalling.** El Capitán and *niña* Eloísa have been dancing for many years. They seem to sense the other's next movement and have not once missed a step in forty years. **Interpreting.** Although El Capitán and *niña* Eloísa are perfect dance partners and seem perfectly in tune with each other, they have never exchanged a single word.

2. **Recalling.** The Little Heidelberg is on a hill surrounded by banana groves. It serves a spicy aphrodisiac stew and guava and mango strudel. Its clientele are businessmen, farmers, tradesmen, and emigrés who left Europe to escape poverty or war. **Interpreting.** The Little Heidelberg seems out of place—it is located in the Caribbean but it seems to belong in Germany. The club has rules for the dance floor that everyone observes.

3. **Recalling.** Anyone can dance or invite another to dance. No one dares ask La Mexicana to dance. *Niña* Eloísa is the oldest client. **Interpreting.** El Capitán is (cont.)

❶ *Why do the musicians continue to play the special waltz? What does La Mexicana do?*

and he found himself whirling, whirling, with empty arms, his only companion a faint aroma of chocolate.

The tenor indicated to the musicians that they should continue playing the same waltz, because he realized that with the last note the captain would wake from his reverie and the memory of *niña* Eloísa would disappear forever. Deeply moved, the elderly customers of The Little Heidelberg sat motionless in their chairs until finally La Mexicana, her arrogance transformed into affection and tenderness, stood and walked quietly toward the trembling hands of El Capitán, to dance with him. ■

Responding to the Selection

What do you think of The Little Heidelberg tavern and its clientele? What was your impression of El Capitán and his relationship with *niña* Eloísa?

Reviewing the Selection

Recalling		Interpreting
1. For how long have El Capitán and *niña* Eloísa been dancing? In what way have they "achieved perfection" in their dance?	▶▶	What is unusual about the relationship between El Capitán and *niña* Eloísa?
2. Where is The Little Heidelberg located? What types of food are served there? What people go there?	▶▶	In what way is The Little Heidelberg an unusual world all its own?
3. What are the rules of dancing at The Little Heidelberg? Whom does no one ask to dance? Who is the oldest client of The Little Heidelberg?	▶▶	What are the defining, or most imposing, characteristics of El Capitán, La Mexicana, and *niña* Eloísa?
4. Why does El Capitán approach the Scandinavian tourists? What does he ask *niña* Eloísa? What is her response?	▶▶	Why does the presence of the Scandinavian tourists "soften the features" of El Capitán? How does *niña* Eloísa feel about the question asked of her? How do the others in the tavern feel about her response?

Synthesizing

5. What happens to *niña* Eloísa? What is the importance of the waltz? How do you think El Capitán feels as he dances with *niña* Eloísa and finds himself "whirling with empty arms"? What view of love is portrayed in this story, particularly in its ending?

Answers for Reviewing the Selection (cont.)

a silent former sea captain. He lives to dance and be with *niña* Eloísa. La Mexicana is a quiet but assertive woman who likes to choose her own dance partners. *Niña* Eloísa, a kind older woman, is the perfect dance partner for El Capitán. She makes people have sweet memories of childhood.

4. **Recalling.** El Capitán wants the Scandinavian tourists to help him ask *niña* Eloísa to marry him. She finally says yes. **Interpreting.** El Capitán is moved by hearing his own language. *Niña* Eloísa is surprised by the suddenness of El Capitán's question. The others in the tavern become sentimental.

SYNTHESIZING

Responses will vary. Possible responses are given.

5. *Niña* Eloísa disappears, remaining a precious memory to El Capitán until the dance ends. The waltz is important because it shows El Capitán's (cont.)

Understanding Literature (Questions for Discussion)

1. **Setting.** The **setting** of a literary work is the time and place in which it occurs, together with all the details used to create a sense of a particular time and place. What are the most interesting details about the setting of this story? Name some words and phrases that give the reader a strong sense of the place in which this story is set.

2. **Magical Realism. Magical realism** is a kind of fiction that is for the most part realistic but that contains elements of fantasy. For more information, see Insights: Magical Realism, page 278. Why might "The Little Heidelberg" be considered an example of magical realism? What are the realistic elements of the story? What are the fantastic elements of the story? Did you enjoy the fantastic elements of the story? Why, or why not?

Responding in Writing

1. **Creative Writing: Description.** Isabel Allende creates a unique world in her story "The Little Heidelberg." Invent your own unique place. For example, you might decide to create a café, a pizza house, a pastry shop, a toy store, a bookstore, or a daycare center. Begin by thinking about the unique qualities of your place and its people. What is hanging on the walls? Is there music playing in the background? What are the smells and sounds of your place? What do people wear? What do they talk about? Then write a detailed description of your place, describing some of the people who regularly inhabit your place.

2. **Critical Essay: Reality and Fantasy.** Write a critical essay in which you answer the following questions: In what way does Allende weave reality and fantasy together in her story "The Little Heidelberg"? What is the effect of this intermingling of fantasy and reality? Support your responses with concrete details from the story.

Applied English/Tech Prep Skills

Personal and Business Letters. Review the Language Arts Survey 5.1, "Personal and Business Letters." Then practice writing both a personal letter and a business letter by completing the following exercises:

- Pretend that you are a tourist visiting The Little Heidelberg. Using the standard form for a personal letter, write home to a friend or family member describing your impressions of the tavern. What did you eat? Whom did you meet? What did the place look like? How were people dressed? You should use details from the story, but you may also use your imagination to create details based on what you know about the place.
- Pretend that you want to start your own version of The Little Heidelberg in your own city or town. Using the proper form for a business letter, write a letter to a potential investor explaining why this business would be a success and stating the exact amount of money that you would need and the purposes for which it will be used.

Answers for Understanding Literature

Responses will vary. Possible responses are given.

1. Setting. Students might describe the location, the food, and the clientele of The Little Heidelberg as interesting and vivid. Although the tavern has a German atmosphere, it is located in the Caribbean. Foods such as aphrodisiac stew and guava and mango strudel are served, and one can hear the musicians continually playing waltzes. Most people in the tavern know each other and sit and dance without speaking.

2. Magical Realism. Realistic elements of the story include the music and dancing. The food and location of the tavern are somewhat real and somewhat fantastic. The author includes concrete, realistic details such as the teenagers attempting to enter the tavern, the lack of apples for the strudel, and realistic-sounding backgrounds of the clientele. The most basic elements of The Little Heidelberg could actually exist. The unusual relationship between El Capitán and *niña* Eloisa and her disappearance during the waltz are two fantastic elements in the story.

Analytic Scales for Responding in Writing

Grading scales for Responding in Writing appear on page 274.

Answers for Skills Activities

APPLIED ENGLISH/TECH PREP

Students should demonstrate a knowledge of the forms of both a personal letter and a business letter. The personal letter should include descriptive details from the story, although it may include other details from the student's imagination. The business letter should be clear and specific.

► Additional practice is provided in the Essential Skills Practice Book: Applied English/Tech Prep 5.1.

Answers for Reviewing the Selection (cont.)

feelings for *niña* Eloísa. While he is dancing, he is focusing on her and oblivious to his surroundings; when the dance ends he will face the emptiness of being without *niña* Eloísa. The story shows that love is literally intangible and cannot be grasped. El Capitán tries to hold onto his love by holding his beloved but is left empty-handed. The story also shows that love can transform the person in love and create a separate world for those in love.

BIBLIOGRAPHIC NOTE

Students interested in magical realism may wish to read the following novels or short story collections.

Allende, Isabel. *The House of the Spirits.*

——. *Of Love and Shadows.*

——. *The Stories of Eva Luna.*

Borges, Jorge Luis. *A Universal History of Infamy.*

Carpentier, Alejo. *The Kingdom of this World.*

Colchie, Thomas, ed. *A Hammock Beneath the Mangoes: Stories from Latin America.*

Correas de Zapata, Celia, ed. *Short Stories by Latin American Women: The Magic and the Real.*

Esquivel, Laura. *Like Water for Chocolate.*

Ferré, Rosario. *The Youngest Doll and Other Stories.*

García Márquez, Gabriel. *One Hundred Years of Solitude.*

——. *Love in the Time of Cholera.*

——. *Leaf Storm.*

——. *Innocent Erendira and Other Stories.*

Hogan, Linda. *Mean Spirit.*

Solomon, Barbara H., ed. *Other Voices, Other Vistas: Short Stories from Africa, China, India, Japan, and Latin America.*

LITERARY NOTE

Once when asked to define *magical realism,* Isabel Allende said, "I think it's just an awareness of how complicated and weird life is. Not only on our continent, but everywhere. And to be able to talk about it in a casual way—because *life* is casual. . . . In Europe and the United States, there's a tendency to deny and ignore everything that people can't control. . . . You have no explanation for these things so they're banished. . . . Maybe, because Latin Americans can control so little we are more tolerant, more open to them."

Insights

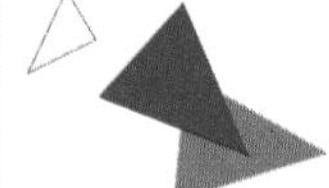

MAGICAL REALISM

Magical realism is a writing style that mingles realistic events and characters with elements of fantasy and myth, creating a unique world that is both familiar and dreamlike. In magical realist tales, the fantastic elements themselves are treated as though they are relatively normal and ordinary. Isabel Allende's "The Little Heidelberg" is a striking example of magical realism. The term *magical realism* is most often used to describe the works of certain Latin American authors of the twentieth century, such as Gabriel García Márquez, whose epic masterpiece is *One Hundred Years of Solitude;* Miguel Ángel Asturias; Julio Cortázar; and Carlos Fuentes. Read the following passage from a Márquez magical realist short story called "Eyes of a Blue Dog." The characters are everyday people holding a normal conversation, yet they are people visiting each other in a dream.

> "It's already dawning," I said without looking at her. "When it struck two I was awake and that was a long time back." I went to the door. When I had the knob in my hand, I heard her voice again, the same, invariable. "Don't open the door," she said. "The hallway is full of difficult dreams." And I asked her: "How do you know?" And she told me: "Because I was there a moment ago and I had to come back when I discovered I was sleeping on my heart." I had the door half opened. I moved it a little and a cold, thin, breeze brought me the fresh smell of vegetable earth, damp fields. She spoke again. I gave the turn, still moving the door, mounted on silent hinges, and I told her: "I don't think there's any hallway outside here. I'm getting the smell of country." And she, a little distant, told me: "I know that better than you. What's happening is there's a woman outside dreaming about the country." She crossed her arms over the flame. She continued speaking: "It's that woman who always wanted to have a house in the country and was never able to leave the city." I remember having seen the woman in some previous dream, but I knew, with the door ajar now, that within half an hour I would have to go down for breakfast. And I said: "In any case, I have to leave here in order to wake up."

Trinity. Planetts, 1929

In this book, you have already found or will soon encounter magical realism in the works of Latin American writers such as Laura Esquivel (see page 9), Gabriel García Márquez (see page 395), and Clarice Lispector (see page 474).

Other examples of magical realism include novels and short stories by Italian writer Italo Calvino (see page 406). African-American authors Toni Morrison (see About the Author, page 189) and Alice Walker make use of magical realism in their writing in works like Morrison's *Beloved* and Alice Walker's *The Temple of My Familiar.*

PREREADING

"Love after Love"
by Derek Walcott

ST. LUCIA

About the Author

DEREK WALCOTT
1930–

Winner of the 1992 Nobel Prize for literature, poet and playwright **Derek Walcott** began his writing career when he was a teenager, and by the age of nineteen he had published twenty-five poems. Walcott and his twin brother, Roderick, were born on January 23, 1930, on the the Caribbean island of St. Lucia. Walcott graduated from St. Mary's College in St. Lucia and then went on to attend the University of the West Indies in Jamaica. After graduating, Walcott taught at schools in St. Lucia, Grenada, and Jamaica. He then moved to Trinidad, where he wrote articles and essays for newspapers and journals. Since the 1950s he has lived and taught at universities in Boston, New York, New Jersey, and Connecticut, but he continues to spend part of each year in the West Indies. Walcott has written several book-length poems and numerous plays.

About the Selection

The following poem, **"Love after Love,"** is taken from Walcott's *Collected Poems 1948–1984*. It is a poem that deals with the subject of rediscovering and learning to love one's inner self. Critics have said that Walcott's poetry combines the English tradition of **lyric poetry**—that is, highly musical verse that expresses the emotions of the speaker—with the scenery, attitudes, and sounds of the Caribbean and urban America.

CONNECTIONS: The Tradition of the Epic

Derek Walcott's literary interests have always included such traditional forms as the epic. An **epic** is a long story involving heroes and gods, often told in verse, that provides a portrait of the legends, beliefs, values, laws, arts, and ways of life of a people. Famous epic poems include Virgil's *Aeneid* (see page 222), Homer's *Odyssey* and *Iliad* (see page 592), and Dante's *The Divine Comedy* (see page 747). Walcott's epic poem *Omeros* (1990), which examines the past and present of St. Lucia and the Caribbean, echoes the *Iliad* and the *Odyssey* and received special mention from the Nobel Prize judges. Walcott has also written a Jamaican historical epic play, *Drums and Colours* (1958), and a poem titled "Map of the New World" about the writing of Homer's *Odyssey*. This poem is featured in *Collected Poems 1948–1984*.

ADDITIONAL RESOURCES

READER'S GUIDE

- Selection Worksheet 3.7

ASSESSMENT PORTFOLIO

- Selection Check Test 2.3.13
- Selection Test 2.3.14

ESSENTIAL SKILLS PRACTICE BOOKS

- Writing 1.8, 1.20
- Language 2.8

PREREADING EXTENSIONS

Ask students to go to the library to find good examples of epic poetry and of lyric poetry. Each student should find one example of each type of poem, make a copy of the poems, and bring them to class. (Students need not copy entire epic poems. They may bring in excerpts.) Students should read the poems aloud and then discuss what they like or dislike about each poem that is shared. Ask students to discuss which type of poetry they enjoy most, and why.

SUPPORT FOR LEP STUDENTS

PRONUNCIATIONS OF PROPER NOUNS AND ADJECTIVES

Der • ek Wal • cott (der´ik wəl cät)

ADDITIONAL VOCABULARY

image—reflection

GOALS/OBJECTIVES

Studying this lesson will enable students to

- appreciate a poem that emphasizes self-love and self-respect
- describe the life and literary accomplishments of Derek Walcott
- define the literary terms *symbol* and *theme*
- write an encouraging "feast on your life" poem
- write a critical essay that analyzes a poem's symbolism
- practice identifying transitive and intransitive verbs

READER'S JOURNAL

You might also ask students to write about a time when they felt alone or rejected and had to look within themselves to boost their spirits. Was this easy to do? Why, or why not? What thoughts or activities help them to feel good about themselves?

Answers to Guided Reading Questions

❶ The time will come when "you will greet yourself" with elation as you arrive at your own door or see yourself in a mirror.

❷ Your heart must be given back to itself. The subject of the poem must learn to love again the stranger who is his or her self.

❸ Love letters, photographs, and desperate notes to others should be discarded. The subject's own image should be peeled from the mirror.

SPELLING AND VOCABULARY WORDS FROM THE SELECTION

elation

Additional Questions and Activities

Invite students to write a description of a specific time or incident when they felt most proud of themselves or of a particular place or activity that helps them to relax and feel most in tune with themselves.

READER'S JOURNAL

What do you like most about yourself? In your journal, record as many positive aspects of yourself as you can. Why is it important to remind oneself of these things from time to time?

"Love after Love"

DEREK WALCOTT

❶ *According to the speaker, what time will come? Who will be greeted at the door?*

❷ *What does the speaker say must be given back to "itself"? According to the speaker, whom should the subject of the poem learn to love again?*

❸ *What items should be discarded? What should be peeled from the mirror?*

The time will come
when, with elation,
you will greet yourself arriving
at your own door, in your own mirror,
and each will smile at the other's welcome,

and say, sit here. Eat.
You will love again the stranger who was your self.
Give wine. Give bread. Give back your heart
to itself, to the stranger who has loved you

all your life, whom you ignored
for another, who knows you by heart.
Take down the love letters from the bookshelf,

the photographs, the desperate notes,
peel your own image from the mirror.
Sit. Feast on your life. ■

WORDS FOR EVERYDAY USE

e • la • tion (ē lā´shən) *n.,* feeling of joy or pride, high spirits

Vocabulary in Context

• Miranda could not hide her elation when her science project won first prize.

Flower Garden and Bungalow, Bermuda. *Winslow Homer, 1899, pencil and watercolor, 13 5/8 x 20 1/2 in. Amelia B. Lazarus Fund, 1910, the Metropolitan Museum of Art, New York, NY*

Responding to the Selection

"Sit. Feast on your life." What does this line from Walcott's poem mean to you? Discuss with your classmates why this poem might be encouraging to someone who is experiencing rejection or a difficult relationship with another person.

Responding to the Selection

You might invite students to form pairs or small groups to discuss the poem. Among fewer classmates, students might feel more comfortable openly discussing how the poem affected them.

Selection Check Test with Answers

EX. Who wrote the poem "Love after Love?"
Derek Walcott wrote the poem "Love after Love."

1. According to the speaker, what time will come?
The time will come when the subject of the poem will greet himself or herself at his or her own door.

2. In what way will the subject of the poem treat himself or herself?
The subject of the poem will welcome himself or herself.

3. What should the subject of the poem give back to himself or herself?
The subject of the poem should give back his or her heart.

4. What should the subject of the poem take down from the bookshelf?
The subject of the poem should take down love letters, photographs, and desperate notes.

5. On what should the subject feast?
The subject should feast on his or her life.

Quotables

"Resolve to be thyself; and know that he,
Who finds himself, loses his misery!"

—Matthew Arnold, "Self-Dependence"

ANSWERS FOR REVIEWING THE SELECTION

RECALLING AND INTERPRETING

1. **Recalling.** According to the speaker, the subject of the poem will greet himself or herself. **Interpreting.** The speaker wants the subject of the poem to welcome and treat with kindness himself or herself. The subject will feel happy.

2. **Recalling.** The speaker wants the subject of the poem to give himself or herself wine and bread. **Interpreting.** The subject of the poem has probably been treating himself or herself harshly. The speaker would like this person to treat himself or herself more kindly and lovingly.

3. **Recalling.** The subject's heart must be returned to itself. The subject of the poem has ignored himself or herself. **Interpreting.** The subject might have been more concerned about winning the love and respect of others than winning the love and respect of himself or herself. Students might say that a person's true self can become lost if he or she spends too much time trying to win the love and approval of others, or if he or she mistreats himself or herself.

4. **Recalling.** The speaker wants love letters, photographs, and desperate notes taken down from the bookshelf. The speaker wants the subject of the poem to peel his or her own image from the mirror. **Interpreting.** The items represent rejection. The subject of the poem seems to have been rejected or caught in a draining relationship that kept him or her from being in touch with his or her own feelings and emotions. The mirror represents a return to self-love.

SYNTHESIZING

Responses will vary. Possible responses are given.

5. The speaker of the poem is encouraging self-love. The subject must start respecting his or her own feelings and treating himself or herself with kindness.

Reviewing the Selection

RECALLING / INTERPRETING

1. According to the speaker, whom will the subject of the poem greet and invite to "sit here. Eat"? ▶▶ Whom does the speaker want the subject of the poem to welcome and treat with kindness? How will the subject of the poem feel when this happens?

2. What does the speaker want the subject of the poem to give to himself or herself? ▶▶ How do you think the subject of the poem has been treating himself or herself lately? What sort of change does the speaker recommend?

3. What, according to the speaker, should happen to the subject's heart? Who has been ignored? ▶▶ Why might the subject's heart be unfamiliar to him or her? Why might the subject's self be a stranger? In what situations might somebody's true self be lost?

4. What does the speaker want taken down from the bookshelf? What should be peeled from the mirror? ▶▶ What do the items that the speaker wants removed represent? What situation has the subject of the poem experienced? What positive change might peeling this image from the mirror represent?

SYNTHESIZING

5. What type of love is the speaker in this poem encouraging? What must the subject of the poem do to attain this love?

Understanding Literature (Questions for Discussion)

1. **Theme.** A **theme** is a central idea in a literary work. Explain the poem's title, "Love after Love." What type of love is being discussed in the poem? What is the central idea of the poem?

2. **Symbol.** A **symbol** is a thing that stands for or represents both itself and something else. What do the symbols in this poem—the mirror, food and eating, love letters, photographs, and desperate notes—represent? How do these items relate to the poem's theme? In what way do they make the poem vivid and interesting for the reader?

ANSWERS FOR UNDERSTANDING LITERATURE

Responses will vary. Possible responses are given.

1. **Theme.** The title of the poem reflects the situation presented in the poem—a person has been rejected by a romantic partner and must learn to love himself or herself again. The theme of this poem is self-love.

2. **Symbol.** The mirror is symbolic of the subject's need to turn away from what others might see and look within himself or herself. Food and wine are symbolic of the way in which the subject must begin caring for his or her own needs. The items on the bookshelf are symbolic of the failed relationship and the subject's attempts to win the approval and love of another, regardless of the cost to his or her self-esteem. All of these items represent the path from rejection to self-love.

Responding in Writing

1. **Creative Writing: "Feast on Your Life" Poem.** Imagine that a friend or family member is having a difficult time. Write a poem that focuses on this person's special qualities and encourages the person to feel good about himself or herself. You might also write such a poem to yourself. Before you begin, freewrite about the subject of your poem. Try to use vivid, descriptive words as you write.

2. **Critical Essay: Symbolism.** Think about the ideas raised in Understanding Literature, question 2. Then write a critical essay in which you discuss the following idea: The speaker of the poem wants the subject of the poem to turn inward and nurture his or her self rather than look for empty gratification outside the self. What symbols in the poem support this idea? In what way does each symbol make the poem's theme more vivid for the reader?

Language Lab

Transitive and Intransitive Verbs. Below are ten sentences that refer to the poem "Love after Love." Review the sentences, then tell whether the boldfaced verbs are transitive or intransitive. If the verb is transitive, identify the verb's direct object. For more information about transitive and intransitive verbs, consult the Language Arts Survey 2.8, "Transitive and Intransitive Verbs."

EXAMPLE Derek Walcott **wrote** that poem.
wrote, transitive; poem, direct object

1. The speaker says that you should **greet** yourself.
2. Smile to yourself and then **eat**.
3. Learn to **love** this stranger who is yourself.
4. Why did you **become** a stranger?
5. **Welcome** yourself back.
6. "Know your heart," **says** the speaker.
7. **Return** your heart to yourself.
8. The speaker says please **sit**. Feast on your life.
9. **Understand** your own life.
10. The speaker of the poem **encourages** "love after love."

ANALYTIC SCALES FOR RESPONDING IN WRITING

Assign a score from 1 to 25 for each grading criterion below. (For more detailed evaluation, see the evaluation forms for writing, revising, and proofreading, Assessment Portfolio 4.1–4.9.)

1. "Feast on Your Life" Poem

- **Content/Unity.** The poem encourages a person who is having a difficult time by describing the person's special qualities.
- **Organization/Coherence.** The poem introduces a subject and then focuses in great detail on the good and interesting qualities of that subject.
- **Language/Style.** The poem uses vivid and precise nouns, verbs, and modifiers.
- **Conventions.** The poem avoids errors in spelling, grammar, usage, mechanics, and manuscript form.

► Additional practice is provided in the Essential Skills Practice Book: Writing 1.8.

2. Critical Essay

- **Content/Unity.** The essay analyzes the symbols in "Love after Love" and the way in which they support the poem's main idea.
- **Organization/Coherence.** The essay begins with an introduction that includes the thesis of the essay. The introduction is followed by supporting paragraphs with clear transitions. The essay ends with a solid conclusion.
- **Language/Style.** The essay uses vivid and precise nouns, verbs, and modifiers.
- **Conventions.** The essay avoids errors in spelling, grammar, usage, mechanics, and manuscript form.

► Additional practice is provided in the Essential Skills Practice Book: Writing 1.20.

Answers for Language Lab

1. **greet,** transitive; **yourself,** direct object
2. **eat,** intransitive
3. **love,** transitive; **stranger,** direct object
4. **become,** transitive; **stranger,** direct object
5. **Welcome,** transitive; **yourself,** direct object
6. **says,** transitive; **know your heart,** direct object
7. **Return,** transitive; **heart,** direct object
8. **sit,** intransitive
9. **Understand,** transitive; **life,** direct object
10. **encourages,** transitive; **"love after love,"** direct object

Cross-curricular Activities

MATHEMATICS AND SCIENCES AND SOCIAL STUDIES

In addition to comments made in this Global Voices discussion, Avik notes that one reason for the low rate of divorce in India might be attributed to different attitudes in Indian culture about the roles of men and women. In India, women and men have complementary but very separate and distinct roles that govern their relationships and make them more interdependent.

Ask students to form pairs, one male student to every female student where possible, and make a list of traditionally "feminine" tasks and traditionally "masculine" tasks. These tasks should include household duties and other activities associated with everyday life in a marriage. Then ask students to discuss whether they would feel limited if they had to stick to one list or the other. Are there tasks that they think are done better by men or women? Are there any biological factors that dictate the roles a man or woman should assume? Can gender roles be useful in making a relationship work, or do students think that these roles are no longer valid in today's society? Extend the exploration of these issues by having interested students research the biology or psychology of gender to support or clarify their views.

SOCIAL STUDIES

Ask students if they have heard the expression "Love conquers all." Explain that the fairy tales and love stories of Western culture convey the message that once two people fall in love, something magical happens and they live "happily ever after." Love is supposed to melt away a couple's differences and solve all their problems. Do students think this romantic attitude is unrealistic, or do they see some truth in it?

Avik says that in India arranged marriages work well and are less likely to end in divorce than marriages in places like the United States where marriages (cont.)

Global Voices

A MULTICULTURAL CONVERSATION

Discussing Love

Students were asked to comment on how love, dating, and marriage are viewed in their countries.

Yumiko: A lot of Japanese students go on dates in high school, or even in junior high school. They usually go to movies or coffee shops.

Gabrielle: French high school students go out in groups—it's not very formal, but there is usually no one-on-one dating.

Sarah: In Greece, it's more important to have your own *parea* than to date just one person. Your *parea* is your group of friends, the people you share everything with. Forming your *parea* starts early, but people of all ages have their special group.

Jiannong: Dating is forbidden in high school in China—definitely forbidden. If people find out you are dating, you are in big trouble. When we were Communist, most marriages were arranged by families or even by the government. Even in college, undergraduates were not encouraged to date. Now you can date in college, although kissing is forbidden in some areas.

Yumiko: Oh, Japanese people don't kiss in public at all. It's very private.

Elio: It's okay to be demonstrative in Mexico.

Ebere: Well, dating is definitely not acceptable in Nigeria. Boys and girls just do not mix. But when it comes to marriage, you can pretty much choose whom you want to marry. If you say to your parents, "I met this person and I want to marry him," your relatives will go and ask questions about him. And then, if they find that he's okay, you can get married.

Sarah: Arranged marriages still happen in Greece, but they're pretty rare.

Elio: In rural Mexico, courtship is still an interesting system. You see a lot of "Romeo and Juliet at the balcony" scenes. The man visits the woman at her house and she comes to the door or window and they talk for hours. Or a man will serenade his beloved with a mariachi band. He'll come in the middle of the night, wake up the parents—wake up the whole neighborhood. If she turns on the light, that means he's in, but otherwise . . .

Avik: In India, there's a separation between the ideal of romantic love and real life. All the books and movies represent people falling in love in these romantic and tragic ways. They'll read the books and watch the movies and be touched by them, but when it comes to real life, it's usually the arranged marriage that works.

Gabrielle: I don't think French people are very romantic, either, actually. Probably our culture or literature makes everyone think that we are.

Avik: The surprising thing is, I don't see very many marriage problems in India, as opposed to countries that have this ideal of love where you fall in love at first sight, get married, and then have no problems.

Cross-curricular Activities (cont.)

are based on romantic love. Inform students that in the arranged marriage system in India, young people go out on chaperoned dates with people their parents select for them. Point out that this system helps young people understand that a strong marriage is based on similar values and a similar background, not on feelings of romantic love that might not last.

Divide students into two groups and have them debate which is better: the arranged marriage system or marriage based on romantic love.

Yumiko: Most people in Japan choose their partners by themselves. But if you're too busy working or have no place to meet someone, when you reach a certain age your neighbors and relatives will start bringing you resumes and pictures of people with compatible backgrounds.

Denis: In the past in Russia people with lots of money would decide, "Okay, our children will be husband and wife when they are older." Or maybe a family had a good friend who was not married or his wife died and—even if he was seventy years old and she was fourteen—they would give their daughter to him for a lot of money. Now, you just find a girl, and if you love her you get married.

Jiannong: Most of the urban people can choose for themselves now, too. Everything's changing in China because of our reforms.

Elio: One thing that's still popular in the rural areas is to steal your wife. If the parents won't give their permission, the couple will decide to run away. The man comes with his horse, the woman hops on, and they ride off. We love that stuff—it's been immortalized in lots of songs. Then, of course, about a week later, they have to face the parents and get married for real.

Sarah: Is divorce accepted in your countries?

Avik: Divorce is pretty rare in India. But unfortunately, these people are kind of ostracized. If a person is divorced, then it's very hard to get married again. So it might be fears like this that are really preventing people from separation rather than the fact that their marriage was arranged.

Gabrielle: In France you marry the one you love, so you should be happy. But after a few years, sometimes you have problems. In my grandparents' generation, there were no divorces. I think it's because women stayed home and took care of the kids. They couldn't earn their own money, so they had to stay with their husbands even if they didn't love them any more. But now, women work and have degrees, so they don't need a man to support them, and that's why there is divorce.

Ebere: In Nigeria, once you are married you don't get divorced; that's the rule. The attitude is that you don't have any right to. And if a woman doesn't want to be married to her husband anymore, she packs her things and goes to her parents' house. The marriage is over, but they don't go to court. And you don't get remarried because if you're a divorced woman, people will gossip.

Avik: I think that from the Western perspective, happiness in a marriage means something very different in India, and maybe in other countries as well. In India, happiness in marriage comes from the success of your children and the happiness of your relatives. In the West, happiness seems to start with the individual and then go outwards.

Cross-curricular Activities

ARTS AND HUMANITIES

In the discussion, Elio refers to the balcony scene in Shakespeare's play *Romeo and Juliet* (Act II, scene ii). The dialogue from this scene is often repeated and alluded to in popular culture. What phrases can students recall from this scene without referring to a copy of the play? Why do they think the balcony scene is so well known? Give students a copy of this scene and ask them to work in pairs to enact it for the class.

ARTS AND HUMANITIES AND SOCIAL STUDIES

Ask students to brainstorm a list of plays, novels, movies, or songs that deal with the theme of romantic love. Then ask each student to choose one work and discuss its treatment of love in an essay. What attitude toward love does the work display? Is this attitude realistic? Does it provide a good model to follow in real life?

SOCIAL STUDIES

In Greece, high school students place more emphasis on having a group of friends than on having a steady boyfriend or girlfriend. In China and Nigeria, high school dating is not acceptable because young people are expected to be concerned with their studies and with making friends of the same sex. Ask students whether these points of view make sense to them. They should list the pros and cons of dating in high school and then write a personal essay or hold a discussion explaining their views on the subject.

Cross-curricular Activities

SOCIAL STUDIES

Share the quotation from Nathaniel Hawthorne on this page with students. Point out that while showing affection occurs in every culture, the way it is displayed often varies. Ask students to research the different ways in which people display affection around the world. Each student might choose a culture to research. They might answer such questions as: Is kissing in public acceptable in this culture? Do friends often hold hands in public? Do men in this culture hug each other? How do people greet each other when they meet for the first time?

Quotables

"Caresses, expressions of one sort or another, are necessary to the life of the affections as leaves are to the life of a tree. If they are wholly restrained, love will die at the roots."

—Nathaniel Hawthorne

King James Bible

About the Selection

The Bible is the sacred book of the Christian religion. It includes the Old Testament, which is identical with the Holy Scriptures of Judaism, and the New Testament, which begins with the birth of Jesus. According to Christians, the prophecies of the Old Testament are fulfilled in Jesus, the son of God, whose life and mission on earth is described in the New Testament.

The first of the great translators of the Bible into English, William Tyndale, (1494–1536), was imprisoned and put to death by authorities who believed the word of God should be directly accessible only to the clergy, who read Latin. Eventually, Biblical translations met with official approval. The King James Bible, or Authorized Version, appeared in 1611 and was the work of fifty-four scholars appointed by the king.

The Song of Solomon is a collection of poems and fragments of verses about love that is found in the Bible's Old Testament. These verses are attributed to King Solomon, the successor and son of King David of Israel.

Sonnet 75 from *Amoretti*

About the Author

Edmund Spenser (1552–1599) has been called the greatest nondramatic poet of the Elizabethan era. Born in London to a family of meager means, he attended Merchant Taylor's School and Cambridge University.

Spenser went to Ireland as aide to Lord Grey of Wilton, the Lord Deputy of Ireland, and tried unsuccessfully for the rest of his life to return to England.

Staunchly nationalistic and Protestant, he wrote an apology for British colonial repression of the Irish titled *A View of the Present State of Ireland*. On his death, Spenser was buried in the Poet's Corner of Westminster Abbey. (cont.)

Selections for Additional Reading

Israel and Judea

from the Song of Solomon
from the King James Bible

CHAPTER 2

I am the rose of Sharon, and the lily of the valleys.
2 As the lily among thorns, so is my love among the
daughters.
3 As the apple tree among the trees of the wood, so is
my beloved among the sons. I sat down under his shadow
with great delight, and his fruit was sweet to my taste.
4 He brought me to the banqueting house, and his
banner over me was love.
5 Stay me with flagons, comfort me with apples: for I
am sick of love.
6 His left hand is under my head, and his right hand
doth embrace me.
7 I charge you, O ye daughters of Jerusalem, by the
roes[1], and by the hinds[2] of the field, that ye stir not up,
nor awake my love, till he please.
8 The voice of my beloved! behold, he cometh
leaping upon the mountains, skipping upon the hills.
9 My beloved is like a roe or a young hart: behold, he
standeth behind our wall, he looketh forth at the
windows, shewing himself through the lattice.
10 My beloved spake, and said unto me, Rise up, my
love, my fair one, and come away.
11 For, lo, the winter is past, the rain is over and gone;
12 The flowers appear on the earth; the time of the
singing of birds is come, and the voice of the turtle is
heard in our land;
13 The fig tree putteth forth her green figs, and the
vines with the tender grape give a good smell. Arise, my
love, my fair one, and come away.
14 O my dove, that art in the clefts of the rock, in the secret
places of the stairs, let me see thy countenance, let me hear thy
voice; for sweet is thy voice, and thy countenance is comely.
15 Take us the foxes, the little foxes, that spoil the vines:
for our vines have tender grapes.
16 My beloved is mine, and I am his: he feedeth among
the lilies.
17 Until the day break, and the shadows flee away, turn,
my beloved, and be thou like a roe or a young hart upon the
mountains of Bether. ■

Great Britain

Sonnet 75
from *Amoretti*
by Edmund Spenser

One day I wrote her name upon the strand,[3]
But came the waves and washèd it away:
Agayne I wrote it with a second hand,
But came the tyde, and made my paynes his pray.[4]
"Vayne man," sayd she, "that doest in vaine assay,[5]
A mortall thing so to immortalize,
For I my selve shall lyke to this decay,
And eek[6] my name bee wypèd out lykewize."
"Not so," quod I, "let baser things devize,
To dy in dust, but you shall live by fame:
My verse your vertues rare shall eternize,
And in the heavens wryte your glorious name.
Where whenas death shall all the world subdew,
Our love shall live, and later life renew." ■

Persia

"Your love turned . . ."
by Empress Nur Jahan,
translated by Willis Barnstone

Your love turned my body
into water.
My eye-paint dripped into the eyes
of foamy water.
Morning wind in the garden
opens blossoms.
The key to my locked spirit is
your laughing mouth. ■

---

1. **roes.** Small and graceful European and Asiatic deer
2. **hinds.** Female red deer
3. **strand.** Beach
4. **pray.** Prey
5. **assay.** Attempt
6. **eek.** Also

Sonnet 75 (cont.)

About the Selection

Sonnet 75, written in iambic pentameter with a rhyme scheme *abab bcbc bdbd ee*, is neither Elizabethan nor Petrarchan in form. (See Insights: The Form of the Sonnet, page 256). The sonnet addresses the theme of immortality through literature. Although the subject of the poem is mortal, she and the speaker's love for her will live on in the poetry the speaker writes about her.

GREAT BRITAIN

from *Wuthering Heights*
by Emily Brontë

"What were the use of my creation if I were entirely contained here? My great miseries in this world have been Heathcliff's miseries, and I watched and felt each from the beginning; my great thought in living is himself. If all else perished, and *he* remained, I should still continue to be; and, if all else remained, and he were annihilated, the Universe would turn to a mighty stranger. I should not seem a part of it. My love for Linton is like the foliage in the woods. Time will change it, I'm well aware, as winter changes the trees—my love for Heathcliff resembles the eternal rocks beneath—a source of little visible delight, but necessary. Nelly, I *am* Heathcliff—he's always, always in my mind—not as a pleasure, any more than I am always a pleasure to myself—but, as my own being—so, don't talk of our separation again." ■

INDIA

from *The Gardener*
by Rabindranath Tagore

XXXVIII

My love, once upon a time your poet launched a great epic[1] in his mind.

Alas, I was not careful, and it struck your ringing anklets and came to grief.

It broke up into scraps of songs and lay scattered at your feet.

All my cargo of the stories of old wars was tossed by the laughing waves and soaked in tears and sank.

You must make this loss good to me, my love.

If my claims to immortal fame after death are shattered, make me immortal while I live.

And I will not mourn for my loss nor blame you. ■

ISRAEL

"If I Forget Thee, Jerusalem"
by Yehuda Amichai,
translated by Assia Gutmann

If I forget thee, Jerusalem,
Then let my right be forgotten.
Let my right be forgotten, and my left remember.
Let my left remember, and your right close
And your mouth open near the gate.

I shall remember Jerusalem
And forget the forest—my love will remember,
Will open her hair, will close my window,
Will forget my right,
Will forget my left.

If the west wind does not come
I'll never forgive the walls,
Or the sea, or myself.

Should my right forget,
My left shall forgive,
I shall forget all water,
I shall forget my mother.

If I forget thee, Jerusalem,
Let my blood be forgotten.
I shall touch your forehead,
Forget my own,
My voice change
For the second and last time
To the most terrible of voices—
Or silence. ■

JAMAICA

"Love Orange"
by Olive Senior

Work out your own salvation with fear and trembling.
Philippians

Somewhere between the repetition of Sunday School lessons and the broken doll which the lady sent me one

1. **epic.** Long narrative poem or story

FROM *WUTHERING HEIGHTS*

ABOUT THE AUTHOR

Emily Brontë (1818–1848), was born and raised in the Yorkshire district of northern England. Brontë was a passionate and talented person, although she was also quiet and reserved and left few records of her personal life. In 1841, Emily and her sister Charlotte traveled to Brussels, Belgium, to study languages and school management. They were hoping to establish a school for girls in England. After the death of one of their aunts, however, the sisters returned home. Emily never went back to Belgium, and in fact, never left her homeland again. In 1845, Emily, Charlotte, and another sister, Anne, published a book of poetry. The book, which was published under the pseudonyms Currer Bell, Ellis Bell, and Acton Bell, was unsuccessful at the time; however the work is now looked at with new respect, mainly because of Emily's poetry. She published her only novel and greatest literary achievement, *Wuthering Heights*, two years later.

ABOUT THE SELECTION

Wuthering Heights is a romantic novel set in the bleak moorland countryside of Emily's home district of Yorkshire. Heathcliff is the proprietor of Wuthering Heights, the house he was adopted into as an orphaned gypsy boy. The story relates the ill-fated romance and marriages of Heathcliff and Catherine Earnshaw, his childhood companion and beloved. *Wuthering Heights* is ranked among the greatest novels of English literature.

In this excerpt, Catherine Earnshaw describes the depth of her feelings for Heathcliff and contrasts these feelings with her feelings for Edgar Linton, the man she marries.

ADDITIONAL QUESTIONS AND ACTIVITIES

Ask students to respond orally or in writing to the following questions and topics:

- Christians interpret the Song of Solomon as expressing the love of Jesus for his followers. Other people interpret the verses as expressing romantic love. Do both interpretations make sense to you? Which interpretation do you prefer? Why?
- According to Spenser's poem, Sonnet 75 of the *Amoretti*, of what importance is literature to human beings?
- In *Wuthering Heights*, what similes, or comparisons using like or as, does the speaker use to contrast her love for Linton with her love for Heathcliff?

"Your love turned . . ."

About the Author

Empress Nur Jahan (?–1645). Mihr-un-Ni-sā, known as Nur Jahan (Light of the World) or Nur Mahal (Light of the Palace), was born into poverty and was abandoned as a child. Nevertheless, she married Jahāngir, a powerful Emperor of India.

About the Selection

"Your love turned . . ." is a lyric poem, meaning it is highly musical verse that expresses the emotions of its speaker. The speaker of this poem expresses feelings of love through striking images.

from *The Gardener*

About the Author

Rabindranath Tagore (1861–1941) was a writer and philosopher born in Calcutta, India. Tagore began to write early in his life, publishing in 1890 a collection of verse, *Manasi*, which marked the maturing of his genius. The next year, Tagore moved to Shilaidah and Saiyadpur, where he wrote several collections of verse, stories, and two plays. He won the Nobel Prize for literature in 1913 for his collection *Gitanjali* ("Song Offering"). In his country, Tagore is widely known for his lyrics and songs about nature, love, and childhood. Also a gifted composer, Tagore set hundreds of poems to music. English translations of Tagore's work include *The Crescent Moon*, *One Hundred Poems of Kabir*, *The Gardener*, *Red Oleanders*, and *Fireflies*. His *Collected Poems and Plays* was published in 1936 and again in 1976.

About the Selection

In *The Gardener*, Tagore expresses how strong feelings of love make the speaker vulnerable. He compares the speaker's feelings to a cargo ship that is "tossed by the laughing waves."

Christmas I lost what it was to be happy. But I didn't know it then even though in dreams I would lie with my face broken like the doll's in the pink tissue of a shoebox coffin. For I was at the age where no one asked me for commitment and I had a phrase which I used like a talisman.[1] When strangers came or lightning flashed, I would lie in the dust under my grandfather's vast bed and hug the dog, whispering "our worlds wait outside" and be happy.

Once I set out to find the worlds outside, the horizon was wide and the rim of the far mountains beckoned. I was happy when they found me in time for bed and a warm supper, for the skies, I discovered, were the same shade of China blue as the one intact eye of the doll. "Experience can wait," I whispered to the dog, "death too."

I knew all about death then because in dreams I had been there. I also knew a great deal about love. Love, I thought, was like an orange, a fixed and sharply defined amount, limited, finite. Each person had this amount of love to distribute as he may. If one had many people to love then the segments for each person would be smaller and eventually love, like patience, would be exhausted. That is why I preferred to live with my grandparents then since they had fewer people to love than my parents and so my portion of their love-orange would be larger.

My own love-orange I jealously guarded. Whenever I thought of love I could feel it in my hand, large and round and brightly coloured, intact and spotless. I had moments of indecision when I wanted to distribute the orange but each time I would grow afraid of the audacity of such commitment. Sometimes, in a moment of rare passion, I would extend the orange to the dog or my grandmother but would quickly withdraw my hand each time. For without looking I would feel in its place the doll crawling into my hand and nestling there and I would run into the garden and be sick. I would see its face as it lay in the pink tissue of a shoebox tied with ribbons beside the stocking hanging on the bedpost and I would clutch my orange tighter, thinking that I had better save it for the day when occasions like this would arise again and I would need the entire orange to overcome the feelings which arose each time I thought of the doll.

I could not let my grandmother know about my being sick because she never understood about the doll. For years I had dreamed of exchanging homemade dolls with button eyes and ink faces for a plaster doll with blue eyes and limbs that moved. All that December I haunted my grandmother's clothes closet until beneath the dresses I discovered the box smelling faintly of camphor[2] and without looking I knew that it came from Miss Evangeline's toy shop and that it would therefore be a marvel. But the doll beside the Christmas stocking, huge in a billowing dress and petticoats, had half a face and a finger missing. "It can be mended," my grandmother said, "I can make it as good as new. 'Why throw away a good thing?' Miss Evangeline said as she gave it to me."

But I could no longer hear I could no longer see for the one China blue eye and the missing finger that obscured my vision. And after that I never opened a box again and I never waited up for Christmas. And although I buried the box beneath the allamanda tree the doll rose up again and again, in my throat, like a sickness to be got rid of from the body, and I felt as if I too were half a person who could lay down in the shoebox and sleep forever. But on awakening from these moments, I could find safely clutched in my hands the orange, conjured up from some deep part of myself, and I would hug the dog saying "our worlds wait outside."

That summer I saw more clearly the worlds that awaited. It was filled with many deaths that seemed to tie all the strands of my life together and which bore some oblique[3] relationship to both the orange and the doll.

The first to die was a friend of my grandparents who lived nearby. I sometimes played with her grandchildren at her house when I was allowed to, but each time she had appeared only as a phantom, come on the scene silently, her feet shod in cotton stockings rolled down to her ankles, thrust into a pair of her son's broken down slippers. In all the years I had known her I had never heard her say anything but whisper softly; her whole presence was a whisper. She seemed to appear from the cracks of the house, the ceiling, anywhere, she made so little noise in her coming, this tiny, delicate, slightly absurd old woman who lived for us only in the secret and mysterious prison of the aged.

When she died it meant nothing to me, I could think then only of my death which I saw nightly in dreams but I could not conceive of her in the flesh, to miss her or to weep tears.

The funeral that afternoon was 5.00 p.m. on a hot summer's day. My grandmother dressed me all in white and I trailed down the road behind her, my corseted and whaleboned[4] grandmother lumbering from side to side in a black romaine dress now shiny in the sunlight, bobbing over her head a huge black umbrella. My grandfather stepped high in shiny black shoes and a shiny black suit ahead of her. Bringing up the rear, I skipped lightly on the gravel, clutching in my hand a new, shiny, bright and bouncy red rubber ball. For me, the funeral, any occasion

1. **talisman.** Anything thought to have magic power or charm
2. **camphor.** Substance, with a strong characteristic odor, derived from the camphor tree and used to protect fabric from moths
3. **oblique.** Indirect, not straightforward
4. **corseted and whaleboned.** Wearing a tight, fitted undergarment reinforced by whalebone

Additional Questions and Activities

Ask students to write about or discuss their responses to the following questions and topics:

- What different kinds of love are expressed in "Your love turned . . ." and in the verses from *The Gardener*? How do you think you would feel if you were the person the speaker of each poem is addressing? In what way might you respond?
- What images in "Your love turned . . ." and in the verses from *The Gardener* stand out to you? Why?

to get out of the house was a holiday, like breaking suddenly from a dark tunnel into the sunlight where gardens of butterflies waited.

They had dug a grave in the red clay by the side of the road. The house was filled with people. I followed my grandparents and the dead woman's children into the room where they had laid her out, unsmiling, her nostrils stuffed with cotton. I stood in the shadows where no one saw me, filled with the smell of something I had never felt before, like a smell rising from the earth itself which no sunlight, no butterflies, no sweetness could combat. "Miss Aggie, Miss Aggie," I said silently to the dead old woman and suddenly I knew that if I gave her my orange to take into the unknown with her it would be safe, a secret between me and one who could return no more. I gripped the red ball tightly in my hands and it became transformed into the rough texture of an orange; I tasted it on my tongue, smelled the fragrance. As my grandmother knelt to pray I crept forward and gently placed between Miss Aggie's closed hands the love-orange, smiled because we knew each other and nothing would be able to touch either of us. But as I crept away my grandmother lifted her head from her hands and gasped when she saw the ball. She swiftly retrieved it while the others still prayed and hid it in her voluminous skirt. But when she sent me home, in anger, on the way the love-orange appeared comforting in my hand, and I went into the empty house and crept under my grandfather's bed and dreamt of worlds outside.

The next time I saw with greater clarity the vastness of this world outside. I was asked to visit some new neighbours and read to their son. He was very old, I thought, and he sat in the sunshine all day, his head covered with a calico skull cap. He couldn't see very clearly and my grandmother said he had a brain tumour and would perhaps die. Nevertheless I read to him and worried about all the knowledge that would be lost if he did not live. For every morning he would take down from a shelf a huge Atlas and together we would travel the cities of the world to which he had been. I was very happy and the names of these cities secretly rolled off my tongue all day. I wanted very much to give him my orange but held back. I was not yet sure if he were a whole person, if he would not recover and need me less and so the whole orange would be wasted. So I did not tell him about it. And then he went off with his parents to England, for an operation, my grandmother said, and he came back only as ashes held on the plane by his mother. When I went to the church this time there was no coffin, only his mother holding this tiny box which was so like the shoe box of the doll that I was sure there was some connection which I could not grasp but I thought, if they bury this box then the broken doll cannot rise again.

But the doll rose up one more time because soon my grandmother lay dying. My mother had taken me away when she fell too ill and brought me back to my grandmother's house, even darker and more silent now, this one last time. I went into the room where she lay and she held out a weak hand to me, she couldn't speak so she followed me with her eyes and I couldn't bear it. "Grandma," I said quickly, searching for something to say, something that would save her, "Grandma, you can have my whole orange," and I placed it in the bed beside her hand. But she kept on dying and I knew then that the orange had no potency, that love could not create miracles. "Orange," my grandmother spoke for the last time trying to make connections that she did not see, "orange . . . . ?" and my mother took me out of the room as my grandmother died. "At least," my mother said, "at least you could have told her that you loved her, she waited for it."

"But . . ." I started to say and bit my tongue, for nobody, not then or ever could understand about the orange. And in leaving my grandmother's house, the dark tunnel of my childhood, I slammed the car door hard on my fingers and as my hand closed over the breaking bones, felt nothing. ■

"If I Forget Thee, Jerusalem"

ABOUT THE AUTHOR

Yehuda Amichai (1924–) has become one of the most significant poets writing in Hebrew in the twentieth century. Amichai is part of an important generation of Israeli poets that includes Leah Goldberg, Hayyim Guri, Nathan Zach, David Avidan, and Daliah Ravikovitz.

ABOUT THE SELECTION

"If I Forget Thee, Jerusalem" is a poem that deals with the theme of loyalty to and love of an important place. Jerusalem is the capital and largest city in Israel. After David, king of Israel, captured Jerusalem (c. 1000 BC) and his successor, Solomon, built the Temple there, Jerusalem became the spiritual and political capital of Judaism. Jerusalem is also a holy city for Christians and Muslims.

"Love Orange"

ABOUT THE AUTHOR

Olive Senior is a writer from Jamaica, an island country in the Caribbean. Black slaves were once treated as property in Jamaica, which has since become a multiracial society enjoying social and political harmony. Many captivating folk tales have come out of Jamaica.

ABOUT THE SELECTION

"Love Orange" addresses the themes of love and death from the point of view of a young girl. The young speaker tries to make sense of difficult experiences, but she misunderstands and is misunderstood by people around her and becomes confused and sad.

Additional Questions and Activities

Ask students to write about or discuss their responses to the following questions or topics:

- What does Jersalem mean to the speaker in "If I Forget Thee, Jerusalem"? What does the speaker of the poem want not to do?
- Explain the significance of the orange and the doll in "Love Orange."
- When you think of love, what images come to mind? Which of these images would be recognized by other people as images of love, and which images are personal, related mainly to your own experiences?

ADDITIONAL RESOURCES

Assessment Portfolio
- Vocabulary Worksheet 2.3.15
- Study Guide 2.3.16
- Unit Test 2.3.17

Essential Skills Practice Books

WRITING
- Choosing a Purpose: Creative Writing, 1.8
- Choosing a Topic, 1.6
- Gathering Ideas, 1.10
- Writing a Critical Essay, 1.20

LANGUAGE
- Correcting Sentence Fragments, Run-ons, and Sentence Strings, 2.27
- Personal Pronouns, 2.4
- Transitive and Intransitive Verbs, 2.8
- Using Vivid Nouns, Verbs, and Modifiers, 2.15
- Verbals, 2.9

SPEAKING AND LISTENING
- Elements of Verbal and Nonverbal Communication, 3.1
- Oral Interpretation, 3.5

STUDY AND RESEARCH
- Computer-assisted Research, 4.17
- Other Sources of Information, 4.18
- Using the Card Catalog, 4.13
- Using Dictionaries, 4.15
- Using Reference Works, 4.14
- Using Search Tools, 4.12
- Using Thesauruses, 4.16

APPLIED ENGLISH/TECH PREP
- Personal and Business Letters, 5.1

Vocabulary Check Test

Ask students to number their papers from one to ten. Have students complete each sentence with a word from the Vocabulary from the Selections in the Unit Review.

1. The idea that an innocent person can be unjustly accused and convicted is unconscionable.
2. The parents carefully gave their child an admonition not to play too near the busy street.
3. The intrepid knight challenged four of the fiercest warriors in the kingdom to single combat.

(cont.)

UNIT REVIEW

Love

VOCABULARY FROM THE SELECTIONS

admonish, 228	duress, 233	pillage, 230
admonition, 225	elation, 280	pluck, 267
atonement, 240	emblem, 225	progeny, 239
avarice, 253	ethereal, 275	propitious, 237
avert, 228	euphoric, 275	pyre, 234
benevolent, 272	festoon, 232	rudimentary, 275
bucolic, 271	goad, 237	superfluous, 272
castigate, 230	immense, 262	supplication, 230
conflagration, 241	integrity, 227	unconscionable, 229
craven, 252	intrepid, 273	unremitting, 273
curt, 253	limpid, 235	vestige, 234
deviation, 271	oblivious, 224	
disciple, 258	permeate, 273	

LITERARY TERMS

apostrophe, 255	mood, 248, 254, 264	quatrain, 256
couplet, 256	motivation, 243	sestet, 251, 256
image, 264	narrative poem, 245	setting, 249, 277
internal conflict, 264	octave, 251, 256	Shakespearean sonnet, 256
irony of situation, 269	pastoral poem, 244	sonnet, 251, 256
lyric poem, 254, 279	personification, 255	symbol, 282
magical realism, 270, 277, 278	Petrarchan sonnet, 251, 256	theme, 282
metaphor, 260	point of view, 268	

Vocabulary Check Test (cont.)

4. After days of unremitting rain, everyone in the household was gloomy and irritable.
5. After a long winter, many people feel a sudden elation on the first warm day of spring.
6. Renaldo was ashamed of his craven behavior on the camping trip; his own shadow had frightened him.
7. Oblivious to any fear or self-concern, the firefighter rushed into the burning house to save the cat trapped inside.
8. Our plans are only at the rudimentary stages; we won't finalize them for a while.
9. The smells of nutmeg, pumpkin, and roasting turkey permeate the kitchen on Thanksgiving morning.
10. We could tell that someone had camped at the site recently because the vestiges of a burned-out campfire remained behind.

SYNTHESIS: QUESTIONS FOR WRITING, RESEARCH, OR DISCUSSION

GENRE STUDIES

1. Many of the selections in this unit are poems. Why do you think many people associate poetry with love? Do you think love can better be expressed in poetry than in prose? Why, or why not?

2. What are the differences between a Petrarchan and a Shakespearean sonnet? Compare and contrast Petrarch's Sonnet 3 or Sonnet 300 with Shakespeare's Sonnet 18. What similarities and differences are displayed in technical aspects of the poems: meter, rhyme, stanzas? In what way are the themes, tones, and moods of these sonnets similar? different?

THEMATIC STUDIES

3. What different kinds of love are described in the selections in this unit, or for whom or what does the speaker or main character in each selection feel love? In what ways are these different types of love expressed?

4. In which selections in this unit is the love experienced by the speaker or by a character unrequited? What different reactions do people have to unrequited love?

5. Compare and contrast attitudes toward absence and reunion as expressed in Li Po's " The River Merchant's Wife: A Letter" and Yannis Ritsos's "Penelope's Despair."

HISTORICAL/BIOGRAPHICAL STUDIES

6. What events in the life of Petrarch shaped his poetry? What does his poetry reveal about him? In what way did his poetry affect following generations of poets? Find examples from later poets to support your claims.

7. In Petrarch's sonnets 3 and 300 and in Pablo Neruda's "Tonight I Can Write" the voice of the speaker is that of the poet. Compare and contrast the relationships of these two poets as expressed through their writing.

SPELLING CHECK TEST

Ask students to number their papers from one to ten. Read each word aloud. Then read aloud the sentence containing the word. Repeat the word. Ask students to write the word on their papers, spelling it correctly.

1. **oblivious**
Max, completely oblivious to the cold, went outside without his hat or coat.

2. **admonition**
The boss's final admonition was that if she didn't stop sleeping on the job, she would be fired.

3. **emblem**
Grandpa wore my hat as an emblem of his support for my baseball team.

4. **craven**
The general said that in battle he would tolerate no acts of cowardice or craven behavior.

5. **avarice**
Avarice inspired Raymond to work at two jobs and spend as little money as possible.

6. **curt**
Clyde was known for responding to any situation with an ironic and curt witticism.

7. **immense**
Many writers have been inspired by the immense expanse of the evening sky scattered with stars.

8. **deviation**
The hot fudge sundae was a welcome deviation from my usual diet.

9. **bucolic**
As we looked out of the car windows at the farms and meadows, we marveled at the bucolic beauty of the countryside.

10. **elation**
Miranda could not hide her elation when her science project won first prize.

UNIT SKILLS OUTLINE

Literary Skills and Concepts

- Apostrophe, 312
- Apposition, 300
- Character, 352
- Characterization, 352
- Conventional Symbol, 328
- Couplet, 310
- Dialogue, 309
- Drama, 300
- Foreshadowing, 337
- Hymn, 300
- Idiosyncratic Symbol, 328
- Image, 328
- Magical Realism, 339
- Metaphor, 312
- Mood, 321, 338
- Nonfiction, 300
- Psychological Fiction, 321
- Setting, 338, 346
- Suspense, 337
- Symbol, 328
- Theme, 321, 338

Writing Skills and Concepts

- Character Sketch, 301
- Critical Essay, 301, 309, 313, 322, 329, 338, 346, 352
- Description, 346
- Eulogy, 352
- Dialogue, 309
- Memorial, 322
- Sharing a Ritual, Tradition, or Belief, 338
- Symbols, 328
- Sympathy Card, 313

Grammar, Usage, and Mechanics Skills and Concepts

- Proofreading for Errors in Capitalization, 353
- Proofreading for Errors in Quotation Marks, 309
- Reducing Wordiness, 322
- Using End Marks, 313
- Using Vivid Nouns, Verbs, and Modifiers, 329

Other Language Arts Skills and Concepts

- Finding Career Information, 301, 349
- Researching Author and Nation, 338

Unit 4 Coping with Death

Burial of St. Lucy. *Caravaggio (Michelangelo Merisi)*

GOALS/OBJECTIVES

Studying this unit will enable students to

- appreciate literature that explores coping with death as a theme
- identify a number of world authors who explore death in their work
- describe different rituals associated with death
- recognize and interpret the use of a number of literary techniques in their reading
- write in a variety of creative forms
- write a variety of critical essays

"Out, out, brief candle!"

—William Shakespeare

293

CROSS-CURRICULAR CONNECTIONS

Arts and Humanities
- Anthology of Latin American Writing, 346
- The Book of the Dead, 299
- Critique of Contemporary Indian Writing, 347
- David's *The Death of Socrates*, 305
- *1812 Overture*, 317
- European Modernism, 325
- Funeral Music, 355
- Frida Kahlo, 341
- Group Art, 294
- Honoring Ancestors, 355
- Literature Review, 323
- Myths about Osiris, 296
- Orozco and Fresco Painting, 294
- Potemkin Villages, 314
- Presentations on Funeral Customs, 354
- Psychology of Mourning, 354
- Sutton Hoo Research, 302

Mathematics and Sciences
- Indian Recipes, 348
- Psychology of Mourning, 354

Social Studies
- Death Penalty Debate, 303
- Death Rituals and Monuments, 302
- *1812 Overture*, 317
- History of Egyptian Hieroglyphics, 298
- Honoring Ancestors, 355
- Mapping the Middle East, 310
- Marcus Garvey, 330
- Politics and García Márquez, 339
- Potemkin Villages, 314
- Presentations on Funeral Customs, 354
- Sutton Hoo Research, 302
- A Traditional Practice, 331
- Traditional and Western Beliefs, 334

Applied Arts
- Anthology of Latin American Writing, 346
- Indian Recipes, 348
- Medicine and Healing, 318

TEACHING THE MULTIPLE INTELLIGENCES

Musical
- *1812 Overture*, 317
- Funeral Music, 355

Logical-Mathematical
- Charting a Life, 355
- Classifying Attitudes about Death, 354
- Death Penalty Debate, 303

(cont.)

TEACHING THE MULTIPLE INTELLIGENCES (CONT.)

- Discussing Religious Differences, 342
- Medicine and Healing, 318

Spatial
- Anthology of Latin American Writing, 346
- The Book of the Dead, 299
- Charting a Life, 355
- Classifying Attitudes about Death, 354
- David's *The Death of Socrates*, 305
- Frida Kahlo, 341
- Group Art, 294
- Honoring Ancestors, 355
- Mapping the Middle East, 310
- Orozco and Fresco Painting, 294
- Potemkin Villages, 314
- Presentations on Funeral Customs, 354

Kinesthetic
- Presentations on Funeral Customs, 354

(cont.)

Other Selections Exploring This Theme:

Anonymous
from Gilgamesh, page 502
Federico García Lorca
"The Guitar," page 1035
from the Koran, page 778
Sappho
"Let's Not Pretend," page 609
"Life Slips By," page 609
Thucydides
"Pericles' Funeral Oration," 674
François Villon
"Ballade," page 759
Virgil
from the *Aeneid,* page 222
Elie Wiesel
from *Night,* page 181

Art Note

José Clemente Orozco (1883–1949) was a Mexican painter who is today considered the greatest fresco painter of the twentieth century. Fresco is the art of painting with watercolor on wet plaster. As a young man, Orozco joined a group of Mexican artists who sought to reject European domination of art and to create works that addressed Mexican themes and life. For a time, his plan to execute large murals on government buildings was put aside because of civil war. During this war, Orozco witnessed much horror and suffering. This experience may have shaped his painting, as it is known for being strongly political, sometimes grotesque, and often anguished.

Cross-curricular Activities

ARTS AND HUMANITIES

Encourage students who are interested in art to create, alone or in small groups, a work of art, such as a painting, collage, sculpture, or mural, that addresses death as a theme.

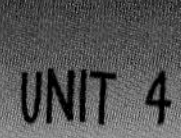

UNIT 4

Theme:
Coping with Death

The Cemetery. *José Clemente Orozco, 1931*

Death is an inevitable part of life. Since our earliest days, humankind has struggled to explain, overcome, and accept it. Even the most ancient civilizations developed elaborate funeral rituals and undertook massive tasks, such as the erection of pyramids in Egypt and Latin America, in an effort to control and explain the uncontrollable and inexplicable fact of death. Contemplation of mortality inspired some of the earliest literature, and death continues to be an important theme for contemporary writers. Writers throughout the ages have approached this subject in different ways: some have found consolation in their faith and in the afterlife, some have struggled against death, some have vowed to live life to the fullest before death overtakes them, some have been drawn to death's mysterious nature, and some have striven to accept and make peace with death. As long as death remains a part of life, people will be drawn to this topic.

This unit is composed of selections from many places and times, pieces that present a spectrum of possible attitudes toward death. You will read ancient Egyptian ritual prayers designed to ensure the safe passage of the dead into the afterlife, as well as an account of how an ancient Greek philosopher faced his death sentence. You will discover how three parents—one in an epic poem of ancient Persia, one in a short story from modern South America, and one in a short story from modern Sierra Leone—cope with the death of a child. In addition, you will read a short story from India that shows how children react to a parent's death. You will also encounter characters who confront their own death—characters who face in different ways their own mortality.

TEACHING THE MULTIPLE INTELLIGENCES (CONT.)

Interpersonal
- Anthology of Latin American Writing, 346
- Charting a Life, 355
- Classifying Attitudes about Death, 354
- Critique of Contemporary Indian Writing, 347
- Death Penalty Debate, 303
- Discussing García Márquez's Attitude toward the Poor, 341
- Discussing Religious Differences, 342
- Discussing Socratic Ideas, 305
- Group Art, 294
- Honoring Ancestors, 355
- Identifying Stages of Accepting Death, 316
- Marcus Garvey, 330
- Mapping the Middle East, 310
- Medicine and Healing, 318
- Politics and García Márquez, 339
- Presentations on Funeral Customs, 354
- Sutton Hoo Research, 302

Echoes:

Coping with Death

Death be not proud, though some have called thee
Mighty and dreadful, for thou art not so,
For those whom thou think'st thou dost overthrow,
Die not, poor death, nor yet canst thou kill me.

—John Donne
from *Holy Sonnets*

Death, I have seen your blank,
Lonely features, I carried myself
Away from them like a strange child
Who vaguely resembled me.

—Bella Akhmadulina

Winter is on my head, but eternal spring is in my heart. The nearer I approach the end the plainer I hear around me the immortal symphonies of the worlds which invite me.

—Victor Hugo

Do not go gentle into that good night,
Old age should burn and rage at close of day;
Rage, rage, against the dying of the light.

—Dylan Thomas

Death is a black camel, which kneels at the gates of all.

—Abd-al-Qādir

It is certain that to most men the preparation for death has been a greater torment than the suffering of it.

—Michel de Montaigne

O death, where is thy sting? O grave, where is thy victory?

—from the King James Bible
(I Corinthians 15:55)

When I am dead, my dearest, sing no sad songs for me.

—Christina Rossetti

Pale death, with impartial step, knocks at the hut of the poor and the towers of kings.

—Horace

I have lived, and I have run the course which fortune allotted me; and now my shade shall descend illustrious to the grave.

—Virgil
from the *Aeneid*

Forget not death, O man! For thou may be of one thing certain—he forgets not thee.

—Persian saying

Biographical Note

John Donne (1572–1631) was an English writer born into a Roman Catholic family at a time when strong anti-Catholic feelings in England prohibited him from following many of the usual paths to success. At twenty-six, he won a position as secretary to one of Queen Elizabeth I's officials, but he was fired and imprisoned for secretly marrying Anne More against her father's wishes. In 1614, he joined the Anglican Church and soon became a priest and a great preacher. His poetry, published after his death, came to be known as Metaphysical poetry and influenced many writers. This quotation, among Donne's most famous lines, is from **Holy Sonnet 10**, one of his later, religious poems.

Bella Akhmadulina (1937–) is a renowned Russian poet, whose first book of poetry *String*, published in 1962, was criticized by the Soviet government. For a time, she was married to another great Russian poet—Yevgeny Yevtushenko (see page 58).

For a biography of **Victor Hugo** (1802–1885), see page 914.

For a biography of **Dylan Thomas** (1914–1953), see page 357.

Abd-al-Qādir (1807–1883) was an Algerian leader who founded the modern state of Algeria.

For a biography of **Michel de Montaigne** (1533–1592), see page 860.

I Corinthians is the seventh book in the New Testament. It is the text of a letter St. Paul, a missionary of the early Christian church, wrote to a Christian community at Corinth, probably around AD 53–54.

For a biography of **Christina Rossetti** (1830–1894), see page 357.

Horace (65–8 BC) was a Latin lyric poet and satirist who lived under the reign of the emperor Augustus. His father was a freed

(cont.)

Additional Questions and Activities

Ask students to freewrite on the following questions:

1. What feelings do you have regarding your own death? the death of others?
2. How should people face the death of a loved one?
3. What do you think of the way death is portrayed in the popular media?

Biographical Note (cont.)

slave who provided his son with the best possible education. Horace joined Brutus's army after the murder of Julius Cæsar. Among Horace's satirical works are ten poems called the *Satires* and a collection called the *Epodes*. He is also renowned for the lyric poetry of his *Odes*.

For a biography of **Virgil** (70–19 BC), see page 222.

ADDITIONAL RESOURCES

READER'S GUIDE

- Selection Worksheet 4.1

ASSESSMENT PORTFOLIO

- Selection Check Test 2.4.1
- Selection Test 2.4.2

ESSENTIAL SKILLS PRACTICE BOOKS

- Writing 1.8, 1.20
- Applied English/Tech Prep 5.2

PREREADING EXTENSIONS

Students who are intrigued by ancient Egypt may wish to know more about Osiris. Inform them that according to myth, the god Osiris was formerly king of Egypt. His jealous brother, Seth, tricked him into entering a chest, then sent the chest adrift on the Nile, leaving Osiris to drown. Osiris's wife, Isis, rescued his body, but Seth took Osiris's body, tore it into fourteen pieces, and scattered them over the earth. Isis found and buried the pieces; Horus, Isis and Osiris's son, sought revenge on Seth; and Osiris was resurrected as king of the dead. Encourage interested students to locate and read Plutarch's account of the Osiris myth.

SUPPORT FOR LEP STUDENTS

PRONUNCIATIONS OF PROPER NOUNS AND ADJECTIVES

Am • mit (a´mit)
A • ni (a´nē)
A • nu • bis (ə no͞o´bis)
Ma' • at (ma´ət)
O • si • ris (ō sī´ris)
Thoth (thōth)

IDIOM

borne testimony on his behalf—given evidence or proof to support him

ADDITIONAL VOCABULARY

verily—truly

PREREADING

"The Weighing of the Heart of Ani" from The Book of the Dead

Anonymous, translated by Sir Wallis Budge

EGYPT

About the Selection

The Book of the Dead refers to an enormous collection of funerary texts written by Egyptian scribes to guide the dead through the underworld. This title was given to the texts uncovered in the early part of the nineteenth century by Egyptologists who did not yet know the contents of these texts. Grave robbers referred to papyrus scrolls found in tombs as *Kitâb al-Mayyitun,* or "book of the dead [men]," so early Egyptologists mistakenly believed that the grave robbers were referring to a single work. Later scholars discovered that the Book of the Dead is composed of many collections of spells, hymns, prayers, and magical words that have been found on papyrus, painted on coffins, and engraved in the stone of pyramid chambers.

The Egyptians' myths about the god Osiris shaped their beliefs about the afterlife and their funerary practices. They believed that Osiris had been horribly murdered but resurrected as king of the underworld. This myth was appealing to Egyptians, who longed to survive death and enjoy the afterlife themselves. It was the priests of Osiris who first established the practice of embalming and preserving corpses for burial in secure, hidden tombs. The Egyptians identified with the god Osiris so strongly that funerary texts often refer to dead people as Osiris. Osiris was either unable or unwilling to make the passage to the next world an easy one. The Egyptians believed that the road from the human world to the afterlife was filled with many dangers and evil powers that threatened even the gods. Thoth, a god who represented divine intelligence, created and wrote down spells and magical words to protect the gods from these dangers. Hoping to invoke Thoth's aid, Egyptian priests followed his example and composed funerary texts of spells, hymns, prayers, and magical words designed to ensure safe passage through the underworld.

One of the longest and most beautiful Egyptian funerary texts is the Papyrus of Ani. The text was composed sometime between 1450 and 1400 BC for a royal scribe named Ani who held an important official position as chancellor of the ecclesiastical revenues of all the temples in Thebes and Abydos. The hieroglyphic text is accompanied by colorful pictures that illustrate Ani's journey through the underworld. The following selection includes the Egyptian hieroglyphics as well as the English translation.

CONNECTIONS: The Judgment of the Dead

The selection from the Papyrus of Ani that follows contains passages relating to a crucial moment in the passage of the deceased through the underworld—the weighing of the heart. The Egyptians believed that this event in the judgment hall of Osiris determined the fate of the deceased. The heart of the deceased, the symbol of his or her conscience, was weighed against an ostrich feather that symbolized Ma'at, the goddess of order, truth, justice, and righteousness. The jackal-headed god Anubis examined the scale, and Thoth recorded the result of the weighing. The heart could be neither too light nor too heavy. If the heart of the deceased and the feather of Ma'at were balanced, the deceased passed on to eternal blessedness. Those who failed this test were eaten by a terrifying monster named Amam or Am-mit, which means "the devourer" or "the eater of the dead." In the following selection, Ani addresses his heart and recites a prayer that no harm come to him during the weighing. This prayer, one of the oldest in the world, remained a part of The Book of the Dead from about 3700 BC to about 30 BC.

GOALS/OBJECTIVES

Studying this lesson will enable students to

- appreciate ancient Egyptian prayers and hymns for the dead
- describe ancient Egyptian beliefs about the final judgment of the dead
- define *drama, nonfiction, hymn,* and *apposition* and identify these in their reading
- write a character sketch
- write a critical essay on Egyptian religion
- find and evaluate career information

In your journal, write about a time when your character was judged by others. Why were you judged? What did others have to say about your character? Did you think the judgment was fair? Why, or why not? Explain how you felt about the results of this judgment.

"The Weighing of the Heart of Ani"

ANONYMOUS, TRANSLATED BY SIR WALLIS BUDGE

TEXTS RELATING TO THE WEIGHING OF THE HEART OF ANI

1. 2. 3. 4. 5. 6. 7. 8. 9. 10. 11. 12.

I. The Names of the Gods of the Great Company: 1. Ra Harmakhis, the Great God in his boat. 2. Temu. 3. Shu. 4. Tefnut. 5. Keb. 6. Nut, the Lady of Heaven. 7. Isis. 8. Nephthys. 9. Horus, the Great God. 10. Hathor, Lady of Amentet. 11. Hu. 12. Sa.[1]

II. The Prayer of Ani: My heart, my mother; my heart, my mother! My heart whereby I came into being! May nought stand up to oppose me at [my] judgment, may there be no opposition to me in the presence of the Chiefs (Tchatchau);[2] may there be no parting of thee from me in the presence of him that keepeth the Balance! Thou art my Ka,[3] which dwelleth in my body; the god Khnemu[4] who knitteth together and strengtheneth my limbs. Mayest thou come forth into the place of happiness whither we go. May the Sheniu officials,[5] who make the conditions of the lives of men, not cause my name to stink, and may no lies be spoken against me in the presence of the God. [Let it be satisfactory unto us, and let the Listener god be favourable unto us, and let there be joy of

❶ *What is being evaluated at this judgment?*

❷ *What does the speaker mean by "May the Sheniu officials . . . not cause my name to stink"?*

1. **The Names of the Gods . . . Sa.** Egyptians believed that knowing the names of all the gods was essential to their safe passage through the underworld. These twelve gods listed above sat as judges before the deceased's offerings during the weighing of the heart.
2. **Chiefs (Tchatchau).** Twelve gods who help administer the kingdom of Osiris, serving as taskmasters
3. **Ka.** Vital force; detached part of a personality—it was born with a person, accompanied that person through life, and then left the body, one of many parts of the person to journey to the underworld.
4. **Khnemu.** Ram-headed god considered to be one of the creators of the universe
5. **Sheniu officials.** Another set of gods who help administer the kingdom of Osiris

WORDS FOR EVERYDAY USE

nought (nôt) *n.*, nothing

READER'S JOURNAL

As an alternative activity, you might ask students to describe their beliefs about what happens to a person's soul or essence after death.

ANSWERS TO GUIDED READING QUESTIONS

❶ The speaker's heart, or his conscience and character, are being evaluated.

❷ The speaker means that he hopes the Sheniu officials will not tarnish his reputation or deprive him of a good name.

SPELLING AND VOCABULARY WORDS FROM THE SELECTION

abiding	prevail
nought	utter

LITERARY NOTE

To capture the formal nature and the importance of The Book of the Dead, the translator has chosen to use highly formal and archaic English. The archaic language may cause some students difficulty initially. Point out that *thou, thy,* and *ye* are all forms of the pronoun *you* and that a *th* often appears at the end of certain verbs but does not change their meaning. For example, *dwelleth* means "dwells," *hath* means "has." Tell students that translation involves trying to capture the spirit and mood of a piece of writing, as well as its literal meaning. Encourage students to discuss what the translator's choices in language convey about the spirit and mood of The Book of the Dead.

VOCABULARY IN CONTEXT

- The grave robber found his way into the pharaoh's tomb, but because it had been plundered long ago he found nought but dust.

Answers to Guided Reading Questions

❶ The result of this judgment is that Ani has been found righteous.

❷ Those who do evil are devoured by Am-mit.

Cultural/Historical Note

Inform students that, as they may have observed from the hieroglyphics recreated here, the ancient Egyptians wrote in pictorial symbols. Ancient Egyptians used both these hieroglyphics and demotic (a cursive form of hieroglyphics) for many thousands of years, until late in the Roman period. Then, when Christianity gained popularity in Egypt in the fourth century AD, most Egyptians affiliated themselves with the Coptic Church, a branch of Christianity, which developed the Coptic language. This language was descended from the ancient Egyptian language, but it was written using Greek characters and a few new characters. Coptic served as Egypt's everyday language and its religious language until the country was invaded by Arabs (AD 639) who spread the Islamic religion and the Arabic language. By the twelfth century, the Coptic language had been completely replaced by Arabic.

As hieroglyphic writing had been abandoned for so many centuries, scholars were unable to decipher the inscriptions they found on ancient Egyptian ruins and on papyrus scrolls. Then, in 1799, a Frenchman discovered the famed Rosetta stone (named for Rashīd, the town in Egypt where it was found), which contained the same inscription in hieroglyphics, demotic, and ancient Greek. After the stone was acquired by the British Museum, nineteenth-century scholars used it to decipher Egyptian hieroglyphics, and translators, including Sir Wallis Budge, curator of Egyptian and Assyrian antiquities at the British Museum, rendered the lost works of Egypt into English.

heart (to us) at the weighing of words. Let not that which is false be uttered against me before the Great God, the Lord of Amentet.[6] Verily, how great shalt thou be when thou risest in triumph.]

III. The Speech of Thoth: Thoth, the judge of right and truth of the Great Company of the Gods who are in the presence of Osiris, saith: Hear ye this judgment. The heart of Osiris[7] hath in very truth been weighed, and his Heart-soul hath borne testimony on his behalf; his heart hath been found right by the trial in the Great Balance. There hath not been found any wickedness in him; he hath not wasted (or stolen) the offerings which have been made in the temples; he hath not committed any evil act; and he hath not set his mouth in motion with words of evil whilst he was upon earth.

❶ *What is the finding of this judgment?*

❷ *What punishment do those who do evil receive?*

IV. Speech of the Dweller in the Embalmment Chamber (*i.e.*, Anubis): Pay good heed, O righteous Judge to the Balance to support [the testimony] thereof. Variant: Pay good heed (or, turn thy face) to the weighing in the Balance of the heart of the Osiris, the singing-woman of Amen, Anhai, whose word is truth, and place thou her heart in the seat of truth in the presence of the Great God.

V. The Speech of the Gods: The Great Company of the Gods say to Thoth who dwelleth in Khemenu[8] (Hermopolis): That which cometh forth from thy mouth shall be declared true. The Osiris the scribe Ani, whose word is true, is holy and righteous. He hath not committed any sin, and he hath done no evil against us. The devourer Ām-mit shall not be permitted to prevail over him. Meat offerings and admittance into the presence of the god Osiris shall be granted unto him, together with an abiding habitation in the Field of Offerings (Sekhet-hetepet),[9] as unto the Followers of Horus.[10]

6. **Amentet.** Name of cemeteries on the western bank of the Nile; originally, the place where the sun set
7. **Osiris.** Thoth is referring to the deceased Ani as Osiris.
8. **Khemenu.** City of the eight great cosmic gods—Nu, Nut, Hehu, Hehut, Kekui, Kekuit, Kerh, and Kerhet
9. **Field of Offerings (Sekhet-hetepet).** Place of peace and plenty where the dead live
10. **Followers of Horus.** Beings who served as body-guards to Horus

ut • ter (ut´ər) *vt.,* produce, speak, or express audibly

pre • vail (prē vāl´) *vi.,* gain the advantage or mastery

a • bid • ing (ə bid´iŋ) *adj.,* continuing without change; enduring; lasting

Vocabulary in Context

- Each morning at sunrise, an Egyptian priest would utter a prayer to Ra, god of the sun.
- Egyptian pharaohs hoped to prevail over death by building enormous pyramids and lavish tombs.
- The pyramids have proved an abiding monument to the architectural skill of the ancient Egyptians.

VI. The Speech of Horus to Osiris[11] in Introducing Ani to Him: Horus, the son of Isis, saith: I have come to thee, O Un-Nefer,[12] and I have brought unto thee the Osiris Ani. His heart is righteous, and it hath come forth from the Balance; it hath not sinned against any god or any goddess. Thoth hath weighed it according to the decree pronounced unto him by the Company of the Gods, and it is most true and righteous. Grant thou that cakes and ale may be given unto him, and let him appear in the presence of the god Osiris, and let him be like unto the Followers of Horus for ever and ever.

VII. The Speech of Ani: And the Osiris Ani saith: Behold. I am in thy presence, O Lord of Amentet. There is no sin in my body. I have not spoken that which is not true knowingly, nor have I done anything with a false heart. Grant thou that I may be like unto those favoured ones who are in thy following, and that I may be an Osiris greatly favoured of the beautiful god, and beloved of the Lord of the Two Lands (*i.e.,* the king of Egypt), I who am a veritable royal scribe[13] who loveth thee, Ani, whose word is true before the god Osiris.

Scene from The Book of the Dead

VIII. Description of the Beast Ām-mit: Her forepart is like that of a crocodile, the middle of her body is like that of a lion, her hind quarters are like those of a hippopotamus. ■

11. **Osiris.** Horus is speaking to Osiris, god of the underworld, not Ani as Osiris.
12. **Un-Nefer.** One of Osiris's names used mainly when Osiris is serving as god and judge of the dead
13. **veritable royal scribe.** Scribe who really practiced his profession, as opposed to one who enjoyed the honorary rank of royal scribe—a title which was often bestowed on people of high birth and rank

 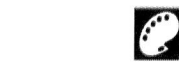

ART NOTE

The Book of the Dead is illuminated with many pictures of the journey of the dead to the afterlife. This picture from the Papyrus of Ani shows a few of the twelve gods who sit in judgment above the central scene. Here, Anubis is in the process of weighing Ani's heart against the feather of Ma'at. The art to the left of the Reader's Journal activity on page 297 shows the monster Ām-mit waiting to devour Ani should he fail.

SELECTION CHECK TEST WITH ANSWERS

EX. To what trial does this selection relate?

This selection relates to the weighing of Ani's heart.

1. Name at least two of the gods of the "Great Company."

Students may name any two of the following: Ra Harmakhis, Temu, Shu, Tefnut, Keb, Nut, Isis, Nephthys, Horus, Hathor, Hu, or Sa.

2. To whom or what does Ani address his prayer?

Ani addresses his prayer to his heart.

3. Which god first announces the results of Ani's judgment?

Thoth first announces the results of Ani's judgment.

4. What do the gods say shall not be permitted to prevail over Ani?

The gods say that the devourer Am-mit shall not be permitted to prevail over Ani.

5. What does Am-mit look like?

Am-mit has the forepart of a crocodile, the middle of a lion, and the hind quarters of a hippopotamus.

CULTURAL/HISTORICAL NOTE

Inform students that during the Old Kingdom (2575–2040 BC) Egyptians believed that only the pharaoh became Osiris, gaining eternal life after death. By the Middle Kingdom (1532–1070 BC), Egyptians believed that even the *ka,* or soul, of commoners could enjoy eternal life.

Responding to the Selection

Some students may have trouble relating to the Egyptian conception of the afterlife. Remind students that not every culture accepts the same view of death and the afterlife. Encourage them to read Insights: Death Rituals on page 302.

Answers for Reviewing the Selection

RECALLING AND INTERPRETING

1. **Recalling.** Ani addresses his heart. He prays that no one opposes him at his judgment, that he is not parted from his heart, that his reputation is not tarnished, that no lies are spoken against him, and that he receives a favorable judgment. **Interpreting.** The Egyptians believed that the heart represented a person's conscience or character. Ani might pray to his heart because he hopes it will not fail him when it is weighed.
2. **Recalling.** Ani's heart is weighed in the "Great Balance." He passes this test. **Interpreting.** Passing the test reveals that Ani is righteous, honest, and just.
3. **Recalling.** Ani is called "Osiris," "the Osiris the scribe Ani," and "Osiris Ani." **Interpreting.** Egyptians may have given the name Osiris to the dead in hopes that, like Osiris, the dead would be resurrected and experience eternal life.
4. **Recalling.** Ani says that there is no sin in his body, that he has not knowingly lied or "done anything with a false heart," that he loves Osiris, and that he is a "veritable royal scribe." **Interpreting.** Egyptians may have believed that reassuring Osiris of one's honesty, righteousness, and worship might further ensure smooth passage into the next world.

(cont.)

Responding to the Selection

What do you think of the Egyptian passage to the afterlife as it is portrayed in this selection? If you were in Ani's position, what would you say to convince the gods to spare you from Ām-mit?

Reviewing the Selection

Recalling		Interpreting
1. Whom does Ani address? For what does he pray?	▶▶	What did the Egyptians believe the heart represented? Why does Ani address his prayer to his heart?
2. What judgment does Ani undergo? Does he pass or fail this test?	▶▶	What does the outcome of the trial reveal about Ani's character?
3. By what names, other than his own, is Ani called in this selection?	▶▶	Why did the Egyptians call those in Ani's position by such names?
4. What does Ani say about himself to Osiris after the judgment?	▶▶	Why was this final speech after the judgment part of the Egyptian guide to the underworld?

Synthesizing

5. What qualities and characteristics seem to have been valued in Egyptian society during Ani's time? Why might these qualities and characteristics have been considered important?

Understanding Literature (Questions for Discussion)

1. **Drama, Nonfiction, and Hymn.** A **drama** is a story told through characters played by actors. The script of a drama typically consists of characters' names, dialogue spoken by the characters, and stage directions. **Nonfiction** is writing about real events. One type of nonfiction writing provides instructions, or directions. A **hymn** is a song or verse of praise, often religious. In what ways is this selection like a drama? In what ways is it like a set of instructions, or directions? In what way is it like a hymn? In what way do you think Egyptians viewed this writing? Be sure to support your answer.
2. **Apposition.** An **apposition** is a grammatical form in which a thing is renamed, in a word, phrase, or clause. The Egyptians believed that they needed to know certain

Answers for Reviewing the Selection (cont.)

SYNTHESIZING

Responses will vary. Possible responses are given.

5. Honesty, righteousness, scrupulousness, and obedience to the gods seem to have been valued. *Responses will vary.* Students might say that all of these values may have been necessary for the ancient culture to survive or flourish.

Answers for Skills Activities

APPLIED ENGLISH/TECH PREP SKILLS

To evaluate the essays, refer to the Evaluation Forms in the Assessment Portfolio 2.2–2.4.

words and names to pass on to Osiris's kingdom. Thus, their writing is often filled with appositions, or renamings such as "my heart, my mother!" Find at least three other examples of apposition in the selection from The Book of the Dead.

Responding in Writing

1. **Creative Writing: Character Sketch.** Write a character sketch in which you create a modern character who must soon face the gods and monsters described in the selection and undergo the weighing of the heart. Use your imagination to describe details about your character's life, as well as your character's personality traits, inner emotions, and physical characteristics. Hint at the outcome of this test based on your character's traits, mannerisms, and flaws. If you have time, you might want to write a rough scene which describes your character actually going through with the test.

2. **Critical Essay: Egyptian Religion.** Choose one of the following prompts and write a one- to two-page essay. Be sure to include an introductory paragraph in which you state your thesis, or main idea; supporting paragraphs in which you prove your thesis; and a conclusion:

   a. Was the Egyptian view of the afterlife optimistic and hopeful or negative and gloomy?

   b. What was the Egyptian view of the relationship between humanity and the gods? Were the gods remote, awe-inspiring, and relatively uninvolved in human affairs? Were the gods immediate and close to mortals, humanlike, and relatively involved in human affairs? In what ways could humans aspire to become more godlike, from an ancient Egyptian point of view?

   c. Research the Egyptian concept of the soul. What function did the following parts of an individual serve: *ka, ba, khaibit, khu,* and *sekhem?* In what ways were these parts of an individual similar to one another? In what ways were they different?

Applied English/Tech Prep Skills

Finding Career Information. In the selection from The Book of the Dead, Ani's career and some of his professional duties are described. As a royal scribe, Ani was a professional who copied manuscripts. He also oversaw church revenues, as is evident from the line "he hath not wasted (or stolen) the offerings which have been made in the temples." Think about a career that you might be interested in practicing. You may wish to focus on a career in Egyptology by examining the careers of archaeologists, translators, or museum curators, or you may wish to choose something completely unrelated. Then read the Language Arts Survey 5.2, "Finding Career Information." Locate an individual who practices your chosen career. You might locate such an individual by talking to family and friends, by searching the Internet, by looking through newspapers and periodicals, and for many professions, simply by browsing through the phone book. Correspond with or talk to this person to find out more about his or her career. Prior research about this career will help you to formulate questions and best draw upon the experience of the person with whom you communicate. Finally, write a short essay on what you have learned about this career, evaluating whether this career would be right for you.

ANALYTIC SCALES FOR RESPONDING IN WRITING

Assign a score from 1 to 25 for each grading criterion below. (For more detailed evaluation, see the evaluation forms for writing, revising, and proofreading, Assessment Portfolio 4.1–4.9.)

1. Character Sketch

- **Content/Unity.** The character sketch portrays a character about to undergo the weighing of the heart and hints at an outcome.
- **Organization/Coherence.** The character sketch presents details in a sensible order.
- **Language/Style.** The character sketch uses vivid and precise nouns, verbs, and modifiers.
- **Conventions.** The character sketch avoids errors in spelling, grammar, usage, mechanics, and manuscript form.

▶ Additional practice is provided in the Essential Skills Practice Book: Writing 1.8.

2. Critical Essay

- **Content/Unity.** The essay presents the writer's view on one of the three given topics.
- **Organization/Coherence.** The essay begins with an introduction that includes the thesis of the essay. The introduction is followed by supporting paragraphs with clear transitions. The essay ends with a solid conclusion.
- **Language/Style.** The essay uses vivid and precise nouns, verbs, and modifiers.
- **Conventions.** The essay avoids errors in spelling, grammar, usage, mechanics, and manuscript form.

▶ Additional practice is provided in the Essential Skills Practice Book: Writing 1.20.

Answers for Understanding Literature

Responses will vary. Possible responses are given.

1. **Drama, Nonfiction, and Hymn.** The selection is like a drama in that it is composed of dialogue spoken by characters. The selection is like a set of instructions in that it provides the magical names and prayers necessary to pass through the underworld. The selection is like a hymn in that it is religious in nature and offers praise. Students may say that the Egyptians viewed this writing as a set of instructions and as a hymn, because it had both practical and religious significance to them.

2. **Apposition.** Students may find the following examples: "the Great God, the Lord of Amentet"; "Thoth, the judge of right and truth of the Great Company of the Gods"; and "the Osiris the scribe."

CULTURAL/HISTORICAL NOTE

You may wish to share the death rituals and monuments of other cultures with students. Worth mentioning are the following:

- The Taj Mahal, often considered one of the most beautiful buildings in the world, is a mausoleum in India. Built by emperor Shah Jahan in memory of his wife Arjumand Banu Baygam, it took twenty-two years to build and the project employed more than twenty thousand workers every day.
- In the Hindu tradition, bodies are cremated. The deceased is carried to a pyre in a funeral procession led by a mourner carrying a piece of burning wood. After cremation, mourners scatter the ashes in sacred rivers. For a time, the widow of the deceased was expected to throw herself on the funeral pyre.
- Ancient Roman funeral processions involved a parade of the death masks of the ancestors of the deceased. The body was later cremated except for one finger, which was buried.

CROSS-CURRICULAR ACTIVITIES

ARTS AND HUMANITIES AND SOCIAL STUDIES

Inform students that burials of entire ships have been found in two parts of the world—Sweden and East Suffolk, Great Britain. In 1939, the tomb of a seventh-century king was discovered on top of a cliff in Sutton Hoo in Suffolk. A ship with a hut built to enclose a coffin and a treasure trove of fine burial goods were discovered. Encourage students to work in pairs to learn more about this burial at Sutton Hoo. Invite each pair to choose a treasure or two from the burial to research, to bring in photographs of these treasures, and to share with their classmates what they have learned about them.

Insights

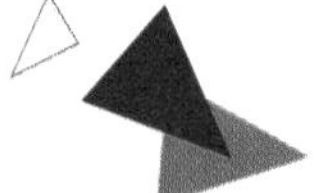

DEATH RITUALS

In almost every culture, people have created ceremonies and rituals to prepare for and memorialize death. Many of these ceremonies and rituals are thousands of years old. Funeral traditions created to prepare the dying or deceased for the afterworld often focus upon the preparation and removal of the body. Other traditions are part of the mourning process, designed to help the people who survive the deceased. These rituals are often related to a culture's beliefs about what happens to a person after death.

Few cultures have been as obsessed with death and the afterlife as the ancient Egyptians. Egyptian pharaohs began the construction of their enormous tombs many years before their deaths. The Book of the Dead illuminates many beliefs the ancient Egyptians held about death. The hope for a favorable judgment that would allow the dead to continue on in the afterlife led to the creation of series of prayers and incantations. Mummification was important to preserve the person's body for the next life. Perhaps the best-known collection of funerary objects from Egypt came from the tomb of King Tutankhamen. When his tomb was discovered intact in 1922, it contained his mummy in a nest of three coffins, the innermost one made of gold. His head was covered with a funerary mask, and jewelry and amulets decorated the body which was surrounded by gold-covered shrines, furniture, clothes, weapons, and many other items.

Ancient Egyptians were not the only people to surround their dead with items that were beloved by them in this world or that might be necessary in the afterworld. Archaeologists discovered many such treasures in the great burial site of the emperor Shih Huang-ti of the Ch'in dynasty in China, in 1974. Excavations have revealed an army of more than six thousand terra-cotta soldiers and horses prepared for battle and facing east, the direction from which the emperor's adversaries came. Of the life-sized figures, no two are alike, suggesting that they may have been modeled on actual people. Chariots, bridles, jade objects, and weapons were also found surrounding the burial chamber. Excavators of the twenty-square-mile site continue to unearth more figures and objects that were included in the burial complex.

Traditions used to mark the death of common people often differ from the death rituals for powerful leaders. Some practices, however, including providing the dead with items that they will need for their post-death journey, are not restricted to people of high status. Preparation for a burial in Mexican tradition includes displaying the body in a dignified manner with offerings to take on the journey to the next world. Such offerings include food and drink and items needed for such necessary tasks as planting or creating fire. The dead are also remembered by families on November 2, the Day of the Dead. Useful objects and food are delivered to the dead after burial. Families bring food and flowers to be placed on the grave. The living then picnic on the food. Bread and candy are commonly made in the shapes of skeletons and skulls, as symbols of the holiday.

Current death rituals in the United States most commonly include viewing the embalmed body before burial, or cremation and sprinkling of the ashes in a place meaningful to the deceased.

PREREADING

"The Death of Socrates"
from *Phaedo*
by Plato, translated by Hugh Tredennick and Harold Tarrant

About the Author

PLATO
c. 427 BC–c. 347 BC

Plato was the second of the three most renowned philosophers of ancient Greece. The first was his teacher, Socrates, and the third was Plato's student, Aristotle. Plato came from an aristocratic family long involved in Athenian politics. Plato's political ambitions waned soon after meeting Socrates, who became not only a teacher but a friend. When Socrates was put to death in 399 BC for allegedly corrupting the youth of Athens and "neglecting the gods whom the city worships" and for "the practice of religious novelties," Plato became sickened by Athenian politics and decided that the only just state would be one in which political power rests with philosophers—his ideal leader being a "philosopher-king." Plato described his vision of an ideal state in *The Republic.* He also wrote about Socrates's trial, final days, and death in a series of works that included *Euthyphro,* the *Apology, Crito,* and *Phaedo.* After Socrates's death, Plato and many other of Socrates's followers fled from Athens to Megara. Plato traveled for a time but returned to Athens and founded, in 387 BC, a philosophic and scientific school called the Academy.

About the Selection

Plato's ***Phaedo*** portrays Socrates on his last day, as he awaits his execution by poisonous hemlock. In *Phaedo,* the narrator, Phaedo of Elis, one of Socrates's students, tells his friend Echecrates about Socrates's final hours. Plato was not present at Socrates's death and wrote *Phaedo* many years afterward. The *Phaedo* presents an idealized and personalized version of Socrates as a man who continually urges others to "know themselves" and to examine their own beliefs, one who is touched with divine knowledge, who is confident about the existence of an afterlife, and who would choose to die rather than renounce his life's work.

Plato wrote most of his philosophical works in the form of dialogues, in which a few characters enter into discussion and debate with the principal speaker, Socrates. This literary form reflects the profound impact Socrates's teaching methods—engaging others in dialogue—had upon Plato.

Corinthian columns

CONNECTIONS: The Socratic Method

Socrates's method of teaching was very unusual. Filthy and shabbily clothed, he would wander the streets of Athens questioning people about their beliefs in such things as virtue and truth, pretending to be ignorant himself. Whenever a person made a moral claim that Socrates would not accept, he would ask more questions, introducing new ideas or claims seemingly related to the person's original idea. Socrates would then show how all these ideas were inconsistent with the person's original claim, thereby demonstrating problems with the other person's point of view. This method of instruction was so effective that it is still used today to teach law, philosophy, and logic.

GOALS/OBJECTIVES

Studying this lesson will enable students to

- have a positive experience with a classical work
- identify Plato as a Greek philosopher and writer
- recognize Socrates's contributions to Western culture
- define *dialogue*
- write a dialogue
- evaluate fictional and nonfictional elements of a literary work
- proofread for errors in quotation mark usage

ADDITIONAL RESOURCES

READER'S GUIDE
- Selection Worksheet 4.2

ASSESSMENT PORTFOLIO
- Selection Check Test 2.4.3
- Selection Test 2.4.4

ESSENTIAL SKILLS PRACTICE BOOKS
- Writing 1.8, 1.20
- Language 2.52

PREREADING EXTENSIONS

Students can read the section from Plato's *Apology* in which Socrates defends himself against the charges brought against him by Meletus and in which he reacts to being found guilty. Ask students to pay particular attention to the passage in which Socrates responds to Meletus's suggestion of the death penalty. Have students discuss or debate their feelings about the death penalty.

SUPPORT FOR LEP STUDENTS

PRONUNCIATIONS OF PROPER NOUNS AND ADJECTIVES

As • cle • pi • us (as klē´pe əs)
A • pol • lo • dor • us (ə pol ə dô´rəs)
Cri • to (krī´tō)
Da • vid (dä vēd´)
Ech • e • cra • tes (ek ē´krə tēz)
Phae • do (fē´dō)
Pla • to (plā´tō)
Soc • ra • tes (säk´rə tēz)
Xan • thip • pe (zan tip´ē)

ADDITIONAL VOCABULARY

calamity—disaster
console—comfort
discordant—not harmonious
magistrate—officer of the law
marshalling—directing, arranging
tremor—a trembling or shaking

READER'S JOURNAL

As an alternative activity, students may wish to write about something that they learned from a dying person. Students may wish to focus on ways in which such lessons have affected their lives or ways in which their beliefs about an afterlife affect their personal philosophies about life and death.

ANSWERS TO GUIDED READING QUESTIONS

1 Socrates tells his followers that he will be pleased if they look after themselves.

2 Socrates asks his followers to assure Crito that when he is dead he will have left his body, and therefore Crito should not be upset if he sees Socrates's body being burned.

3 Socrates says that his followers can bury him any way they wish if they can catch him and he doesn't slip through their fingers.

SPELLING AND VOCABULARY WORDS FROM THE SELECTION

fervently libation

ADDITIONAL QUESTIONS AND ACTIVITIES

Based on their reading of "The Death of Socrates" and what they learned about Socrates on the Prereading page, ask students to write a eulogy for Socrates which describes his accomplishments, his values, and the course he wished his followers to take after his death.

As an alternate assignment, ask students to think about a person who has taught them something. Students can write a thank-you note to this person explaining what they have learned and how it has helped them.

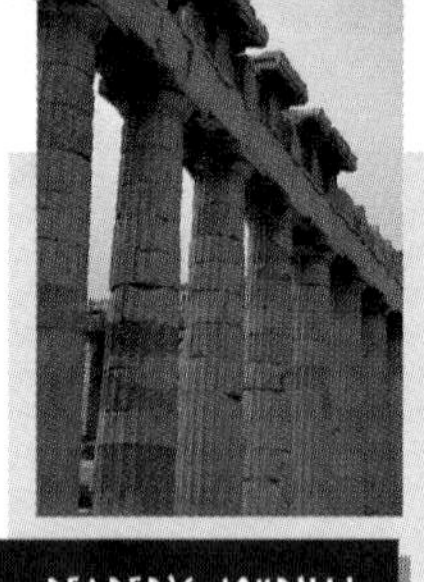

READER'S JOURNAL

Imagine that you knew that you would die within a few hours. What instructions or advice would you give to your family or friends as the time of your death approached? In what way might they best honor your memory?

"The Death of Socrates"

PLATO, TRANSLATED BY HUGH TREDENNICK AND HAROLD TARRANT

When he had finished speaking, Crito said, 'Very well, Socrates. But have you no directions for the others or myself about your children or anything else? What can we do to please you best?'

'Nothing new, Crito,' said Socrates; 'just what I am always telling you. If you look after your own selves, whatever you do will please me and mine and you too, even if you don't agree with me now. On the other hand, if you neglect yourselves and fail in life to follow the track that we have spoken of both now and in the past, however fervently you agree with me now, it will do no good at all.'

> 1 What can Socrates's followers do to please him?
>
> 2 What assurance does Socrates ask his followers to give Crito?
>
> 3 What does Socrates say about being buried after his death?

'We shall be keen to do as you say,' said Crito. 'But how shall we bury you?'

'Any way you like,' replied Socrates, 'that is, if you can catch me and I don't slip through your fingers.' He laughed gently as he spoke, and turning to us went on: 'I can't persuade Crito that I am this Socrates here who is talking to you now and marshalling all the arguments; he thinks that I am the corpse whom he will see presently lying dead; and he asks how he is to bury me! As for my long and elaborate explanation that when I have drunk the poison I shall remain with you no longer, but depart to a world of happiness that belongs to the blessed, my words seem to be wasted on him though I console both you and myself. You must give an assurance to Crito for me—the opposite of the one which he gave to the court which tried me. He undertook that I should stay; but you must assure him that when I am dead I shall not stay, but depart and be gone. That will help Crito to bear it more easily, and keep him from being distressed on my account when he sees my body being burned or buried, as if something dreadful were happening to me, or from saying at the funeral that it is Socrates whom he is laying out or carrying to the grave or burying. Believe me, my dear friend Crito: misstatements are not

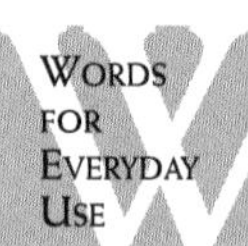

WORDS FOR EVERYDAY USE

fer • vent • ly (fʉr′vənt lē) *adv.,* passionately, with intensity

VOCABULARY IN CONTEXT

• Lia hoped fervently that she might one day go to Greece.

The Death of Socrates. *Jacques-Louis David, 1787. The Metropolitan Museum of Art, Catharine Lorillard Wolfe Collection, Wolfe Fund, 1931.*

merely jarring in their immediate context; they also have a bad effect upon the soul. No, you must keep up your spirits and say that it is only my body that you are burying; and you can bury it as you please, in whatever way you think is most proper.'

With these words he got up and went into another room to bathe; and Crito went after him, but told us to wait. So we waited, discussing and reviewing what had been said, or else dwelling upon the greatness of the calamity which had befallen us; for we felt just as though we were losing a father and should be orphans for the rest of our lives. Meanwhile, when Socrates had taken his bath, his children were brought to see him—he had two little sons and one big boy—and the women of his household you know—arrived. He talked to them in Crito's presence and gave them directions about carrying out his wishes; then he told the women and children to go away, and came back himself to join us.

It was now nearly sunset, because he had spent a long time inside. He came and sat down, fresh from the bath, and he had only been talking for a few minutes when the prison officer came in, and walked up to him. 'Socrates,' he said, 'at any rate I shall not have to find fault with you, as I do with others, for getting angry with me and cursing when I tell them to drink the poison—carrying out the magistrates' orders. I have come to know during this time that you are the noblest and the gentlest and the bravest of all the men that have ever come here, and now especially I am sure that you are not angry with me, but with them; because you know who are responsible. So now—you know what I have come to say—goodbye,

❶ *How do Socrates's followers feel about losing him?*

❷ *What does the prison officer say about Socrates? Of what is the prison officer sure?*

ART NOTE

Jacques-Louis David (1748–1825) was one of the most prominent French artists of his time. David was a major proponent of the Neoclassical movement. Neoclassical art is inspired by the art of ancient Greece and Rome and is characterized by harmony, clarity, restraint, and idealism. A Neoclassical ideal in literature emerged also at this time (refer students to Unit 10).

David painted *The Death of Socrates* in 1788. The painting applies a classical style to a classical subject. Ask students to compare David's interpretation of Socrates's death with Plato's. Note Socrates's wife, Xanthippe, being led away. What emotions does Socrates display? the jailkeeper? the other figures? How does the artist show these emotions? What effect do you think David intended this painting to have?

ANSWERS TO GUIDED READING QUESTIONS

❶ Socrates's followers feel as if they will be losing their own father.

❷ The prison officer says that Socrates is the most gentle and brave man who has ever come there. He is sure that Socrates is not angry with him because he knows that Socrates doesn't blame him for his punishment.

QUOTABLES

"Man is a prisoner who has no right to open the door of his prison and run away. . . . A man should wait, and not take his own life until God summons him."

—Socrates

"Mankind censures injustice, fearing that they may be the victims of it and not because they shrink from committing it."

—Plato

ADDITIONAL QUESTIONS AND ACTIVITIES

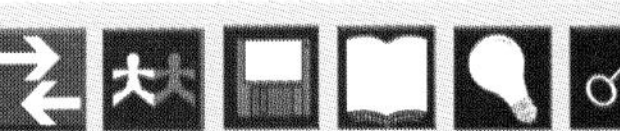

Discuss with students the two quotations on this page.

- The first is from *Phaedo.* Ask students whether they agree with Socrates's statement. Does the idea seem in keeping with the attitude toward death expressed in the selection they just read?
- The second quotation is from Plato's *Republic.* Ask students whether they agree or disagree with this statement, and why. Have them apply the quotation to current injustices they see in the world.

Answers to Guided Reading Questions

❶ Socrates thinks that the prison officer is a charming and kind man with whom he has enjoyed discussions.

❷ The narrator weeps, not for Socrates, but for himself and his own loss of a friend.

❸ Socrates feels that he would be ridiculous if he clung to life "when it has no more to offer."

❹ Socrates reproaches his friends for their tears and tells them that they are behaving like women and disturbing the "reverent silence" that should accompany one's end.

Selection Check Test with Answers

EX. Where does this selection take place?
It takes place in an Athenian prison.

1. What can Socrates's followers do to please him?
They can please him by looking after themselves.

2. About what does Socrates tell Crito he should not worry?
Socrates tells Crito that he should not worry about how Socrates is buried.

3. Whom does Socrates find to be a "charming person"?
Socrates finds the prison officer to be a charming person.

4. What does Socrates refuse to put off?
Socrates refuses to put off drinking the poison.

5. What do Socrates's followers do when he drinks the poison?
Socrates's followers weep.

and try to bear what must be as easily as you can.' As he spoke he burst into tears, and turning round, began to go away.

❶ *What does Socrates think of his captor, the prison officer?*

Socrates looked up at him and said, 'Goodbye to you, too; we will do as you say.' Then addressing us he went on, 'What a charming person! All the time I have been here he has visited me, and sometimes had discussions with me, and shown me the greatest kindness; and how generous of him now to shed tears at my departure! But come, Crito, let us do as he says. Someone had better bring in the poison, if it is ready prepared; if not, tell the man to prepare it.'

'But surely, Socrates,' said Crito, 'the sun is still upon the mountains; it has not yet gone down. Besides, I know that in other cases people have dinner and enjoy their wine, and sometimes the company of those whom they love, long after they receive the warning; and only drink the poison quite late at night. Please don't hurry; there is still plenty of time.'

❷ *Why does the narrator weep?*

❸ *Why doesn't Socrates want to wait until evening to drink the poison?*

'It is natural that these people whom you speak of should act in that way, Crito,' said Socrates, 'because they think that they gain by it. And it is also natural that I should not; because I believe that I should gain nothing by drinking the poison a little later—I should only make myself ridiculous in my own eyes if I clung to life and hugged it when it has no more to offer. Come, do as I say and don't make difficulties.'

❹ *What is Socrates's reaction to his friends' tears?*

At this Crito made a sign to his slave, who was standing nearby. The slave went out and after spending a considerable time returned with the man who was to administer the poison; he was carrying it ready prepared in a cup. When Socrates saw him he said, 'Well, my good fellow, you understand these things; what ought I to do?'

'Just drink it,' he said, 'and then walk about until you feel a weight in your legs, and then lie down. Then it will act of its own accord.'

As he spoke he handed the cup to Socrates, who received it quite cheerfully, Echecrates,[1] without a tremor, without any change of colour or expression, and said, looking up bull-like from under his brows with his usual steady gaze, 'What do you say about pouring a libation from this drink? Is it permitted, or not?'

'We only prepare what we regard as the normal dose, Socrates,' he replied.

'I see,' said Socrates. 'But I suppose I am allowed, or rather bound, to pray the gods that my removal from this world to the other may be prosperous. This is my prayer, then; and I hope that it may be granted.' With these words, quite calmly and with no sign of distaste, he drained the cup in one draught.

Up till this time most of us had been fairly successful in keeping back our tears; but when we saw that he was drinking, that he had actually drunk it, we could do so no longer; in spite of myself the tears came pouring out, so that I covered my face and wept broken-heartedly—not for him, but for my own calamity in losing such a friend. Crito had given up even before me, and had gone out when he could not restrain his tears. But Apollodorus, who had never stopped crying even before, now broke out into such a storm of passionate weeping that he made everyone in the room break down, except Socrates himself, who said: 'Really, my friends, what a way to behave! Why, that was my main reason for sending away the women, to prevent this sort of discordant

1. **Echecrates.** Phaedo, the narrator of this work, is telling a man named Echecrates about Socrates's final days. Here, Phaedo addresses Echecrates directly.

Words for Everyday Use

li • ba • tion (lī bā´shən) *n.,* ritual of pouring wine or oil as a sacrifice to a god

Vocabulary in Context

- At the ancient temple, Dmitri poured the water from his canteen as a libation to the gods.

behaviour; because I am told that one should make one's end in a reverent silence. Calm yourselves and be brave.'

This made us feel ashamed, and we controlled our tears. Socrates walked about, and presently, saying that his legs were heavy, lay down on his back—that was what the man recommended. The man (he was the same one who had administered the poison) kept his hand upon Socrates, and after a little while examined his feet and legs; then pinched his foot hard and asked if he felt it. Socrates said no. Then he did the same to his legs; and moving gradually upwards in this way let us see that he was getting cold and numb. Presently he felt him again and said that when it reached the heart, Socrates would be gone.

The coldness was spreading about as far as his waist when Socrates uncovered his face—for he had covered it up—and said (they were his last words): 'Crito, we ought to offer a cock to Asclepius.[2] See to it, and don't forget.'

'No, it shall be done,' said Crito. 'Are you sure that there is nothing else?'

Socrates made no reply to this question, but after a little while he stirred; and when the man uncovered him, his eyes were fixed. When Crito saw this, he closed the mouth and eyes.

This, Echecrates, was the end of our comrade, who was, we may fairly say, of all those whom we knew in our time the bravest and also the wisest and the most just. ■

2. **Asclepius.** God of healing

❶ *In what way does the narrator sum up Socrates's character?*

Treasury of Athenians, Delphi

ANSWERS TO GUIDED READING QUESTIONS

❶ The narrator says that Socrates is the wisest, bravest, most just man of his time.

ANALYTIC SCALES FOR RESPONDING IN WRITING

(SEE PAGE 309.)

Assign a score from 1 to 25 for each grading criterion below. (For more detailed evaluation, see the evaluation forms for writing, revising, and proofreading, Assessment Portfolio 4.1–4.9.)

1. Dialogue

- **Content/Unity.** The dialogue presents a conversation between a living character and one who has returned from the dead.
- **Organization/Coherence.** The dialogue flows naturally.
- **Language/Style.** The dialogue uses vivid and precise nouns, verbs, and modifiers.
- **Conventions.** The dialogue avoids errors in spelling, grammar, usage, mechanics, and manuscript form.

▶ Additional practice is provided in the Essential Skills Practice Book: Writing 1.8.

2. Critical Essay

- **Content/Unity.** The essay presents opinions and supporting material about fictional and nonfictional aspects of the selection.
- **Organization/Coherence.** The essay begins with an introduction that includes a thesis. The introduction is followed by supporting paragraphs with clear transitions. The essay ends with a solid conclusion.
- **Language/Style.** The essay uses vivid and precise language.
- **Conventions.** The essay avoids errors in spelling, grammar, usage, mechanics, and manuscript form.

▶ Additional practice is provided in the Essential Skills Practice Book: Writing 1.20.

Responding to the Selection

In discussing these questions, students may also wish to discuss what it means to "die with dignity."

Answers for Reviewing the Selection

RECALLING AND INTERPRETING

1. **Recalling.** Socrates says that Crito should not be concerned with burying Socrates's body because he will have already departed from that body. **Interpreting.** Socrates believes that once he is dead the essential part of him, his soul, will have left his body to "depart to a world of happiness that belongs to the blessed." Socrates is unconcerned with his physical remains because he believes in an afterlife and in the existence of the human soul.

2. **Recalling.** The prison officer tells Socrates to bear his punishment as easily as he can, says he is "the noblest and the gentlest and the bravest of all the men that have ever come here," and then bursts into tears. Socrates likes the prison officer, finding him to be charming, kind, and a good conversationalist. **Interpreting.** It is surprising that a condemned man and the person who holds him captive could become friends. The prison officer's strong feelings reveal that Socrates had a magnetic personality and a noble, wise, and just manner.

3. **Recalling.** Socrates says that he would find himself to be ridiculous if he clung to life "when it has no more to offer." Socrates receives the poison "cheerfully" and drinks it down all at once. **Interpreting.** Socrates's manner of meeting his death reveals that he has great self-control, determination, and confidence that he will be passing on to a better world.

4. **Recalling.** Socrates's followers begin weeping. Socrates says that they are behaving badly and should calm themselves (cont.)

Responding to the Selection

What do you think of the way in which Socrates approaches and meets his death? If you were in his position, would you hope to emulate his attitudes and actions, or would you want to behave differently? Explain.

Reviewing the Selection

Recalling		Interpreting
1. According to Socrates, why shouldn't Crito worry about how Socrates is to be buried?	▶▶	Describe Socrates's beliefs about what happens after a person dies. In what way are Socrates's beliefs about the afterlife and his lack of concern with his own burial related?
2. What is the prison officer's reaction to Socrates's impending death? What attitude does Socrates express toward the prison officer?	▶▶	What makes the relationship between the prison officer and Socrates surprising? What do the prison officer's feelings reveal about Socrates's character?
3. What explanation does Socrates give for his unwillingness to wait longer before drinking the poison? In what manner does Socrates receive and drink the poison?	▶▶	What does Socrates's way of meeting his death reveal about his character? What does it reveal about his beliefs concerning an afterlife?
4. What do Socrates's followers do after they see that he has drunk the poison? What objections does Socrates raise to his followers' actions? Why did Socrates send away the women?	▶▶	How do Socrates's followers feel about losing him? In what way has Socrates been more than a teacher to them? What does Socrates's objective in sending away the women reveal about ancient Greek attitudes toward women?

Synthesizing

5. In what way does acceptance of death differ for a person who is dying and for people who love the person who is dying? Why might this situation be easier for the person who is dying?

Answers for Reviewing the Selection (cont.)

because "one should make one's end in a reverent silence." He sent away the women to prevent such "discordant behavior." **Interpreting.** His followers are broken-hearted and will be lost without him. Socrates has been a father figure and a close friend to them. Women seem to have been neither respected nor treated as equals.

SYNTHESIZING

Responses will vary. Possible responses are given.

5. The person who is dying is losing his or her own life and may face the fear of the unknown. The people who know the dying person must come to terms with life without their loved one. In some cases a person's beliefs about what happens after death may make acceptance of death easier for a dying person than for the people who will miss him or her.

Understanding Literature (Questions for Discussion)

Dialogue. Dialogue is conversation between two or more people or characters. **Dialogue** is also used to describe a type of literary composition in which characters debate or discuss an idea. What might Plato have hoped to achieve by writing this dialogue? Why might presenting Socrates's dialogue with his followers be an effective means of portraying his character? What ideas are discussed and debated in this dialogue?

Responding in Writing

1. **Creative Writing: Dialogue.** Write a dialogue in which you are the main character, communicating with someone who has died and returned to your world for a brief visit. You may hold this discussion with a fictional character of your own creation, with a character from a story that you have read, or with a real historical figure. You might want to include the following questions in your dialogue: What has his or her experience after death been like? What kind of life did this person lead on earth? Did the person's life on earth affect his or her experience after death? What is one thing this person might want to change about his or her life? How did the person die? What was it like passing from life into death? Use your imagination to think of interesting responses to your questions. You may also wish to include narration with your dialogue as Plato does.

2. **Critical Essay: Evaluating Fictional and Nonfictional Elements.** Plato was not present at Socrates's death, but probably wrote this selection about twenty years later, using accounts given by Plato's companions. Obviously, Plato's work cannot exactly portray the scene that took place just before Socrates's death. Write an essay in which you evaluate which elements of this selection seem like nonfiction to you and which elements seem like Plato's own invention. Make sure that your essay has an introduction, supporting paragraphs, and a conclusion.

Language Lab

Proofreading for Errors in Quotation Marks. In a dialogue, quotation marks and line breaks help to indicate where each speaker's words begin and end. Review the Language Arts Survey 2.52, "Other Uses of Quotation Marks." Then, rewrite the paragraph below, using quotation marks and line breaks to indicate when the speaker changes.

> Which of Socrates's writings most influenced Plato? I asked Ms. Terashima. Actually, she said, Socrates didn't produce any writing. Curious to learn more, I asked, How could his philosophy have been so influential throughout Western history if he never wrote anything? Plato and other students of Socrates presented their view of Socrates and his ideas in their own writing, she said.

Answers for Understanding Literature

Responses will vary. Possible responses are given.

Dialogue. Presenting Socrates's dialogue with his followers allows the reader to see how he interacted with others. It also portrays his beliefs more vividly and directly. Some ideas that are discussed and debated are why one should not weep over the physical remains of a person, the immortality of the soul, and the proper way to approach and meet death.

Analytic Scales for Responding in Writing

Grading scales for Responding in Writing appear on page 307.

Answers for Language Lab

"Which of Socrates's writings most influenced Plato?" I asked Ms. Terashima.

"Actually," she said, "Socrates didn't produce any writing."

Curious to learn more, I asked, "How could his philosophy have been so influential throughout Western history if he never wrote anything?"

"Plato and other students of Socrates presented their view of Socrates and his ideas in their own writing," she said.

ADDITIONAL RESOURCES

READER'S GUIDE

- Selection Worksheet 4.3

ASSESSMENT PORTFOLIO

- Selection Check Test 2.4.5
- Selection Test 2.4.6

ESSENTIAL SKILLS PRACTICE BOOKS

- Writing 1.8, 1.20
- Language 2.46

PREREADING EXTENSIONS

Encourage small groups of students to create their own maps. Some groups might make maps of the Middle East today, while others might create a map of the Islamic empire in the tenth century (such a map would include southern Spain, northern India, North Africa, Arabia, Syria, Anatolia, Iran, central Asia, and the Indus Valley). Tell students to strive to make their maps both visually appealing and accurate. Group members might then use their maps to quiz each other on place names.

SUPPORT FOR LEP STUDENTS

PRONUNCIATIONS OF PROPER NOUNS AND ADJECTIVES

Fir • dau • si (fər dau´sē)
Mah • mud (mä mo͞od´)
A • bu Ol Qa • sem Man • sur (a bo͞o´ol ka sem´ man so͞or´)
Shah • na • ma (shä´nə mä´)
Se • pah • bad Shah • re • yar (se pä bad´ shä´rā yär´)

ADDITIONAL VOCABULARY

perchance—maybe
striving—trying very hard to gain

PREREADING

"Lament for His Son"
from the *Shah-nama*
by Firdausi, translated by Reuben Levy

About the Author

Firdausi (932–1025). Abu Ol-Qasem Mansur, who took the pen name Firdausi, meaning "From Paradise," was born in the Persian city of Tus, in what is now Iran, about two centuries after the Arabs conquered Persia and converted the people to the Islamic religion. Despite this conquest, the sultans who ruled during Firdausi's lifetime encouraged the preservation of the Persian language and culture. From another poet, Firdausi inherited the enormous task of compiling the history of Persia into a national epic. He devoted thirty-five years of his life to recording Persian history from the mythical beginning of time through the beginning of the reign of the Persian King Khosrow II in AD 590. While this "history" was full of myths and legends from Persia's oral tradition, these stories were regarded as historical fact in Firdausi's day. Firdausi's completed work, the *Shah-nama,* or *Book of Kings,* was an epic poem composed of more than 60,000 couplets.

According to legend, when Firdausi went to Sultan Mahmud to collect payment for his work, the sultan gave Firdausi less than half of the reward he had been promised. Disgusted and bitter, Firdausi gave the money to the attendants at a bathhouse and fled to the court of Persian Prince Sepahbad Shahreyar. There, Firdausi wrote a satire about the sultan and offered to dedicate the *Shah-nama* to the prince instead. The savvy prince paid Firdausi handsomely for the work, bought the satire and removed it from the poem, and convinced Firdausi to retain the dedication to Sultan Mahmud.

About the Selection

Persians consider Firdausi to be their greatest poet. Just as studying the King James Bible and Shakespeare is considered to be an essential part of a Western education, every educated Iranian is familiar with and has read at least part of the ***Shah-nama.*** Firdausi made a conscious effort when writing this epic to avoid the use of the Arabic words and phrases that were rapidly entering the Persian language, so this work is considered to be the epitome of "pure" Persian poetry. Firdausi wrote this epic in **couplets,** or pairs of rhyming lines that express a complete thought. The selection that you are about to read is a prose translation of a portion of the *Shah-nama* in which a speaker laments the death of his son.

CONNECTIONS: The *Shah-nama:* A Different Type of Epic

Many of the epics that you will read in this text, such as *The Epic of Gilgamesh* (see page 502), the *Ramayana* (see page 560), the *Iliad* (see page 592), and the *Aeneid* (see page 222), center on a particular hero and a particular historical moment. These epics also include a cast of gods who interact with the mortal characters. Unlike these epics, the *Shah-nama* recounts hundreds of years of history, relates many different stories, and features many heroes. In addition, it is a monotheistic epic, although it focuses more on members of the court than it does on Allah.

GOALS/OBJECTIVES

Studying this lesson will enable students to

- identify with the speaker's feelings about the loss of his son
- explain Firdausi's status among Persian poets
- define *apostrophe* and *metaphor* and explain the use of these techniques in works that they read
- design and write a sympathy card
- write a persuasive critical essay
- use end marks correctly

Why is it especially sad when a person dies young, before he or she has lived a full life? What experiences and opportunities might someone who dies young miss? In your journal, explain your feelings about untimely death.

READER'S JOURNAL

"Lament for His Son"

FIRDAUSI, TRANSLATED BY REUBEN LEVY

My years have passed sixty and five and no purpose now would be served for me by striving after wealth. Perhaps I should take my own counsel and give a thought to the death of my son. It was my turn to have gone, but it was the younger man who departed and in my agony for him I am a body without a soul. I hasten about dreaming that perchance I may find him; and if I find him I will hasten to him with reproaches, telling him that it was my turn to go and demanding why he has gone, robbing me of hope and tranquillity. He had ever been one to take me by the hand when distresses came and now he has taken a path far from his old fellow-wayfarer. Have you perchance found younger companions on the way, since you have so swiftly gone ahead of me? When this young man reached the age of thirty-seven, the world no longer went according to his liking. He has gone and what remains is my grief and sorrow for him; he has steeped my heart and eyes in blood.

Now that he is departed, going towards the light, he would surely choose out a place for his father? Long is the time that has passed over me and none of my fellow-wayfarers have returned. Surely he awaits me and is angry at my tarrying? May the All-possessor keep your spirit ever in brightness! May wisdom ever be the shield that guards your soul. ■

❶ *What does the speaker say it was his turn to do? What happened instead? What does the speaker say he has become without his son?*

❷ *What does the speaker believe his son has done in the afterlife? Why does the speaker believe his son is angry with him?*

WORDS FOR EVERYDAY USE

way • far • er (wā´fer´ər) *n.,* person who travels, especially on foot

tar • ry (tar´ē) *vi.,* delay, linger, be tardy

READER'S JOURNAL

If students are having difficulty writing on this topic, ask them to write instead about a family member with whom they are particularly close. Why do they value this family member?

ANSWERS TO GUIDED READING QUESTIONS

❶ The speaker says that it was his turn to "go" or die. His son died. The speaker says that he has become "a body without a soul."

❷ The speaker believes that his son has chosen a place in the "light" for him. The speaker believes that his son is angry with him because he has tarried on earth and has not yet joined his son.

SELECTION CHECK TEST WITH ANSWERS

EX. Whose death is the speaker lamenting?

The speaker is lamenting the death of his son.

1. How old is the speaker of this selection?

The speaker is older than sixty-five.

2. What does the speaker dream will happen?

The speaker dreams that he will find his son.

3. What does the speaker plan to do when he finds his son?

The speaker plans to reproach his son and ask him why he has gone.

4. What happened when the son reached thirty-seven?

The son no longer liked the way the world "went."

5. According to the speaker, why might his son be angry with him?

The son might be angry with the speaker for tarrying on earth.

VOCABULARY IN CONTEXT

- In the narrow streets of the ancient city, wayfarers had to stand against the wall to allow horse-drawn carts or automobiles to pass.
- In the evening, the gates of the desert oasis were closed to all outsiders, so if residents tarried outside after dark, they had to spend a night without shelter in the desert.

Responding to the Selection

You might also ask students to discuss, based on this selection, what they think of the speaker's son. What type of person does he seem to be?

Answers for Reviewing the Selection

RECALLING AND INTERPRETING

1. **Recalling.** The speaker is thinking about his son's death because he is more than sixty-five and worldly goals no longer hold any attraction. The speaker says that it was his turn to "go." The speaker wants to reproach his son for dying before his father. **Interpreting.** The speaker feels as if he has lost his soul. The speaker is particularly troubled because his son died so young. Many students will suggest that the speaker would take his son's place if he could.

2. **Recalling.** The speaker says that his son "had ever been one to take me by the hand when distresses came." The speaker wonders if his son has found younger companions. He hopes that his son has chosen a place for him in the afterlife and that he awaits him there. **Interpreting.** The father's speculations about the son finding comforting new companions and remembering his father seem appropriate because the son was always compassionate. The speaker poses so many questions because he is unsure whether he and his son will ever be reunited. He is expressing hope, rather than confidence.

SYNTHESIZING

Responses will vary. Possible responses are given.

3. The speaker is still trying to understand and accept his son's death and has not yet been able to resolve his feelings of loss. The speaker's faith allows him to feel confident that the All-Possessor is protecting his son's soul, but he still experiences anxiety about whether he and his son will be reunited.

Responding to the Selection

With your classmates, discuss whether the speaker in this selection evokes your sympathy. Do you think he deals with his grief well? Explain why or why not.

Reviewing the Selection

RECALLING		INTERPRETING
1. According to the speaker, why does he "give a thought" to his son's death? According to the speaker, whose "turn" was it to "go"? With what does the speaker wish to reproach his son?	▶▶	How does the speaker feel about the death of his son? Why is the speaker particularly troubled by this death? Do you think the speaker would take his son's place if he could? Explain.
2. What does the speaker say his son was like when he was alive? What does the speaker wonder? What does he hope?	▶▶	Why, given the description of the son's actions when he was alive, might the father's depiction of his son in the afterlife be appropriate? Why do you think the speaker poses so many unanswered questions in the latter part of this lament?

SYNTHESIZING

3. In what way would you describe the speaker's attitude toward his son's death? Has the speaker accepted his son's death, or has he been unable to do so? In what way does the speaker's faith comfort him? Does his faith completely reassure him? Explain why or why not. Compare your journal entry about your thoughts on untimely death with the attitude the speaker expresses in the poem. Is your attitude similar to or different from that of the speaker?

Understanding Literature (Questions for Discussion)

1. **Apostrophe.** An **apostrophe** is a rhetorical technique in which an object or person is directly addressed. Throughout most of this lament, the speaker refers to his son in the third person, using words such as *he* and *him.* At what points in the lament does the speaker use apostrophe, addressing his son directly as *you*? Why do you think the speaker directly addresses his son in these places? What effect does this use of apostrophe have on the reader?

2. **Metaphor.** A **metaphor** is a figure of speech in which one thing is spoken or written about as if it were another. This figure of speech invites the reader to make a

Answers for Understanding Literature

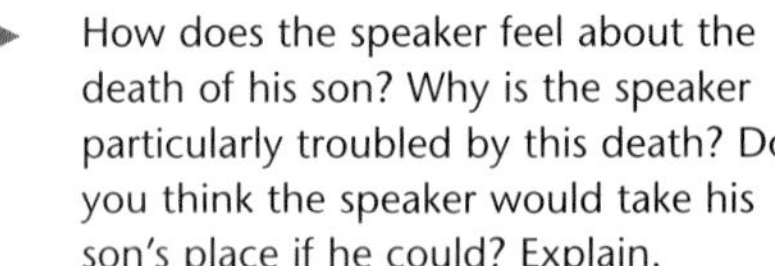

Responses will vary. Possible responses are given.

1. **Apostrophe.** The speaker uses apostrophe in the last two sentences, when he offers a prayer for his son, as well as when he asks his son if he has found younger companions. The speaker addresses his son directly in these places because he is looking for answers and because he is hoping that his prayer will be effective and that his son will be protected. The use of the more personal "you" affirms the speaker's belief that his son's soul still exists in the afterlife. It makes his hope more poignant.

2. **Metaphor.** The speaker is inviting the reader to compare life to a journey. The father felt close to his son, as if they were traveling together through life.

comparison between the two things. The speaker refers to his son as if he were a "fellow-wayfarer." To what is the speaker inviting the reader to compare life? What does the use of this metaphor reveal about the father's relationship with his son?

Responding in Writing

1. **Creative Writing: Sympathy Card.** In our culture, it is customary to send a card expressing sympathy to the family of a person who has died. Imagine that you are a friend of the speaker's family. Design and write a sympathy card for the speaker of "Lament for His Son" in which you console him for his loss. When you are designing the image for the front of the card, make sure that it is appropriate for the occasion. For example, you might draw a stand of weeping willows by a tranquil river. Your message on the inside of the card can be either prose or verse, but it should express your sympathy with the speaker's situation. You may also wish to offer the speaker your emotional support or some words of advice. Remember that when writing about a loss such as the one experienced by the speaker, a few well-phrased sentences can be more comforting and meaningful than many sentences.

2. **Critical Essay: Persuading the Speaker of "Lament for His Son."** The speaker of this selection seems eager to follow his son into the afterlife. Write an essay in which you explain whether you think it is best for the speaker to focus on the afterlife or whether it is better for him to try to enjoy what remains of his present life. Provide reasons or examples from your own life or from the lives of others to support your point of view. When writing, imagine that your essay will be read by the speaker of "Lament for His Son," so try to make your essay as persuasive as possible. Appeal to the emotions of the speaker to state your case convincingly.

Language Lab

Using End Marks. Throughout this selection, the writer poses many questions that could also be read as declarative sentences, such as "Surely he awaits me and is angry at my tarrying?" End marks like the question mark in the above sentence are useful tools for showing the purpose of a sentence. Review the Language Arts Survey 2.46, "Using End Marks." Then, on your own paper, rewrite the sentences below, using the correct end marks to punctuate them.

1. Ben Jonson was an English poet and playwright who also wrote epitaphs on the death of his children
2. I can't believe you haven't read him
3. Are you familiar with this famous line from "On My First Son": "Here doth lie Ben Jonson his best piece of poetry"
4. Ben Jonson began his "Epitaph on Elizabeth, L. H." with the question, "Would thou hear what man can say in a little"
5. My teacher said, "Ben Jonson outlived and buried two of his children, a son and a daughter. How awful for him"

ANALYTIC SCALES FOR RESPONDING IN WRITING

Assign a score from 1 to 25 for each grading criterion below. (For more detailed evaluation, see the evaluation forms for writing, revising, and proofreading, Assessment Portfolio 4.1–4.9.)

1. Sympathy Card

- **Content/Unity.** The card offers sympathy to the speaker of the poem and has an appropriate cover.
- **Organization/Coherence.** The message in the card is written in a sensible order.
- **Language/Style.** The card uses vivid and precise nouns, verbs, and modifiers.
- **Conventions.** The card avoids errors in spelling, grammar, usage, mechanics, and manuscript form.

▶ Additional practice is provided in the Essential Skills Practice Book: Writing 1.8.

2. Critical Essay

- **Content/Unity.** The essay should attempt to persuade the speaker to adopt a particular attitude.
- **Organization/Coherence.** The essay should begin with an introduction that includes the thesis of the essay. The introduction should be followed by supporting paragraphs with clear transitions. The essay should end with a solid conclusion.
- **Language/Style.** The essay uses vivid and precise nouns, verbs, and modifiers.
- **Conventions.** The essay avoids errors in spelling, grammar, usage, mechanics, and manuscript form.

▶ Additional practice is provided in the Essential Skills Practice Book: Writing 1.20.

ANSWERS FOR LANGUAGE LAB

1. Ben Jonson was an English poet and playwright who also wrote epitaphs on the death of his children.
2. I can't believe you haven't read him!
3. Are you familiar with this famous line from "On My First Son": "Here doth lie Ben Jonson his best piece of poetry"?
4. Ben Jonson began his "Epitaph on Elizabeth, L. H." with the question, "Would thou hear what man can say in a little?"
5. My teacher said, "Ben Jonson outlived and buried two of his children, a son and a daughter. How awful for him!"

ADDITIONAL RESOURCES

READER'S GUIDE

- Selection Worksheet 4.4

ASSESSMENT PORTFOLIO

- Selection Check Test 2.4.7
- Selection Test 2.4.8

ESSENTIAL SKILLS PRACTICE BOOKS

- Writing 1.8, 1.20
- Language 2.26

PREREADING EXTENSIONS

Students can research the lives of serfs in Russia. Ask them to discover the meaning of the term *Potemkin villages.* (The term refers to any facade that covers up an undesirable condition, named after the fake villages Grigory Aleksandrovich Potemkin allegedly erected to hide the unhappy, squalid lives of Russian serfs from Catherine II, who was touring southern Russia.) Students might make models of such villages showing a positive front and a realistic behind-the-scenes view of serf life.

SUPPORT FOR LEP STUDENTS

PRONUNCIATIONS OF PROPER NOUNS AND ADJECTIVES

I • ván Il • yich (i vän´ il yēch´)
I • ván • o • vich (i vän´ əv yich´)
Ge • rá • sim (gyi räs´yim)
Go • lo • vin (go lōv´vin)
Leo Tol • stoy (lē´ō təl stoi´)
Mi • khá • il Mi • kháy • lo • vich (myik ə´ēl myi kil´əv yich)
Pra • skóv • ya Fë • dor • ov • na (prä skov´yä fā dor´əv nə)
She • bek (shəb´ək)

ADDITIONAL VOCABULARY

acutely—intensely
indubitably—without a doubt
obscure—not easily understood
sledge—sled, sleigh

PREREADING

from *The Death of Iván Ilyich*

by Leo Tolstoy, translated by Louisa Maude and Aylmer Maude

RUSSIA

About the Author

LEO TOLSTOY
1828–1910

Leo Tolstoy, a Russian writer and philosopher, is considered to be one of the world's greatest novelists. He wrote close to one hundred volumes of stories, plays, diaries, essays, and novels, including *War and Peace* and *Anna Karenina.* Tolstoy was born into a wealthy family. Both of his parents died by the time he was nine years old, and he was raised by relatives. As an adult, Tolstoy was a landowner and enjoyed literary success. As he aged, Tolstoy became interested in leading a simple, moral life and gave away many of his worldly possessions. Tolstoy often opposed the Russian government, which censored many of his works. His worldwide fame and his loyal followers, however, protected him from harm.

About the Selection

The Death of Iván Ilyich is considered the masterpiece of Tolstoy's later period. Tolstoy wrote the novella, or short novel, after publishing his most famous novels when he was undergoing a spiritual rebirth. His concerns during this period—the evils of worldly wealth and conformity—are reflected in this tale of Iván Ilyich, a man whose life "had been most simple and most ordinary and therefore most terrible."

Iván Ilyich is a Russian judge who devotes his life to achieving order and a measure of financial success. He marries and sets up a proper home—moves necessary to advance his career—but alienates his family by devoting himself to work and card games. On the job, he is the perfect bureaucrat, never becoming personally involved nor questioning the system in which he works.

Beneath the orderly, polished surface of Iván's life of conformity, material wealth, and artificial relationships, something is terribly wrong. This problem emerges in the form of a fatal illness. The selection you are about to read, book 4 of the story, describes the onset of the terrible disease and the reactions of the people in Iván's life. Iván Ilyich is confronted with the harsh reality of his failed relationships and the meaningless activities filling his life.

CONNECTIONS: Serfdom in Russia

In medieval Europe, many peasant farmers and their families were bound to work particular plots of land owned by a lord. These people, called serfs, had to give a large proportion of the grain from this land to their lord and could not move, marry, or change occupation without the lord's permission. While the system of serfdom died out in the fourteenth century in western Europe, it lasted much longer in eastern Europe. Russian serfs were not freed until 1861. Although himself a landowner, Tolstoy was concerned with the plight of Russian peasantry and started a school for peasant children during the 1850s.

GOALS/OBJECTIVES

Studying this lesson will enable students to

- empathize with Iván Ilyich
- recognize Leo Tolstoy as a great Russian novelist
- define *psychological fiction, mood,* and *theme*
- analyze a literary work and explain why it is characterized as psychological fiction
- describe a mood
- explain how mood is related to theme
- write a memorial
- write a critical essay
- edit sentences to reduce wordiness

What is a meaningful life? What is a superficial life? What is a strong, genuine relationship? What is an artificial, shallow relationship? Can the pursuit of superficial goals and relationships be destructive to an individual and to society? Explain your answer.

READER'S JOURNAL

FROM

The Death of Iván Ilyich

LEO TOLSTOY, TRANSLATED BY LOUISA MAUDE AND AYLMER MAUDE

BOOK IV

They were all in good health. It could not be called ill health if Iván Ilyich sometimes said that he had a queer taste in his mouth and felt some discomfort in his left side.

But this discomfort increased and, though not exactly painful, grew into a sense of pressure in his side accompanied by ill humour. And his irritability became worse and worse and began to mar the agreeable, easy, and correct life that had established itself in the Golovin family. Quarrels between husband and wife became more and more frequent, and soon the ease and amenity disappeared and even the decorum was barely maintained. Scenes again became frequent, and very few of those islets remained on which husband and wife could meet without an explosion. Praskóvya Fëdorovna now had good reason to say that her husband's temper was trying. With characteristic exaggeration she said he had always had a dreadful temper, and that it had needed all her good nature to put up with it for twenty years. It was true that now the quarrels were started by him. His bursts of temper always came just before dinner, often just as he began to eat his soup. Sometimes he noticed that a plate or dish was chipped, or the food was not right, or his son put his elbow on the table, or his daughter's hair was not done as he liked it, and for all this he blamed Praskóvya Fëdorovna. At first she retorted and said disagreeable things to him, but once or twice he fell into such a rage at the beginning of dinner that she realized it was due to some physical derangement brought on by taking food, and so she restrained herself and did not answer, but only hurried to get the dinner over. She regarded this self-restraint as highly praiseworthy. Having come to the conclusion that her husband had a dreadful temper and made her life miserable, she began to feel sorry for herself, and the more she pitied

❶ *When do Iván Ilyich's bursts of temper occur? To what does his wife, Praskóvya Fëdorovna, attribute these bursts of temper?*

❷ *What accompanies the pressure in Iván Ilyich's side? How does the mood in his home change as a result of this discomfort?*

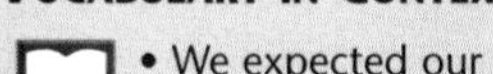

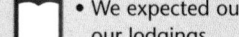

WORDS FOR EVERYDAY USE

a • men • i • ty (ə men′ə tē) *n.,* pleasant quality, attractiveness

de • cor • um (di kō′rəm) *n.,* propriety and good taste in behavior

re • tort (ri tôrt′) *vi.,* reply or respond rudely or insultingly

READER'S JOURNAL

You might suggest that students choose to focus their response on one of the questions posed in the Reader's Journal activity, or they might answer two questions, showing a contrast between a meaningful and a superficial life or between a genuine and a shallow relationship. After writing in their journals, students can discuss their responses in small groups.

ANSWERS TO GUIDED READING QUESTIONS

❶ The bursts of temper occur at dinner. Praskóvya Fëdorovna attributes these bursts of temper to some physical derangement brought on by food.

❷ Ill humor accompanies the pain in his side. He becomes irritable and quarrels with his wife become more frequent.

SPELLING AND VOCABULARY WORDS FROM THE SELECTION

amenity	indulgently
decorum	jocularity
despondent	retort
disconsolately	savoir-faire
exasperation	supposition
gaily	vexation
implicitly	vivacity
incessant	

VOCABULARY IN CONTEXT

- We expected our stay in Russia to be grim, but we were pleasantly surprised by the amenity of our lodgings.
- Hoping to make a good impression on our hosts, we acted with reserve and decorum.
- "I'm strong enough to carry it all," retorted Jean-Luc after Noreen suggested that he pack more lightly.

Answers to Guided Reading Questions

❶ His wife wishes for his death. She is unhappy because, in the event of Ivan's death, she would be without his salary.

❷ Iván concludes that his problem is serious. He pities himself and is bitter toward the doctor. He asks the doctor if his problem is dangerous.

❸ The doctor's behavior reminds Iván of his own behavior when he, as a judge, is dealing with criminals.

Additional Questions and Activities

Students might read Elisabeth Kübler-Ross's *On Death and Dying* to learn about the five stages a person undergoes when facing death: denial, anger, bargaining, grief, acceptance. They can then try to identify the stage that describes Iván's state in this selection, or they might read all of *The Death of Iván Ilyich* and classify his attitude, according to these stages, throughout the story.

Quotables

"If the will of every man were free, that is if every man could act as he chose, the whole of history would be a tissue of disconnected accidents."

—Leo Tolstoy
War and Peace

❶ *For what does Iván's wife wish? Why does she consider herself dreadfully unhappy?*

❷ *What does Iván conclude from the doctor's explanation of his problem? How does this conclusion make him feel? What does he ask the doctor?*

❸ *Of what does the doctor's behavior remind Iván?*

herself the more she hated her husband. She began to wish he would die; yet she did not want him to die because then his salary would cease. And this irritated her against him still more. She considered herself dreadfully unhappy just because not even his death could save her, and though she concealed her exasperation, that hidden exasperation of hers increased his irritation also.

After one scene in which Iván Ilyich had been particularly unfair and after which he had said in explanation that he certainly was irritable but that it was due to his not being well, she said that if he was ill it should be attended to, and insisted on his going to see a celebrated doctor.

He went. Everything took place as he had expected and as it always does. There was the usual waiting and the important air assumed by the doctor, with which he was so familiar (resembling that which he himself assumed in court), and the sounding and listening, and the questions which called for answers that were foregone conclusions and were evidently unnecessary, and the look of importance which implied that "if only you put yourself in our hands we will arrange everything—we know indubitably how it has to be done, always in the same way for everybody alike." It was all just as it was in the law courts. The doctor put on just the same air towards him as he himself put on towards an accused person.

The doctor said that so-and-so indicated that there was so-and-so inside the patient, but if the investigation of so-and-so did not confirm this, then he must assume that and that. If he assumed that and that, then . . . and so on. To Iván Ilyich only one question was important: was his case serious or not? But the doctor ignored that inappropriate question. From his point of view it was not the one under consideration, the real question was to decide between a floating kidney, chronic catarrh, or appendicitis. It was not a question of Iván Ilyich's life or death, but one between a floating kidney and appendicitis. And that question the doctor solved brilliantly, as it seemed to Iván Ilyich, in favour of the appendix, with the reservation that should an examination of the urine give fresh indications that matter would be reconsidered. All this was just what Iván Ilyich had himself brilliantly accomplished a thousand times in dealing with men on trial. The doctor summed up just as brilliantly, looking over his spectacles triumphantly and even gaily at the accused. From the doctor's summing up Iván Ilyich concluded that things were bad, but that for the doctor, and perhaps for everybody else, it was a matter of indifference, though for him it was bad. And this conclusion struck him painfully, arousing in him a great feeling of pity for himself and of bitterness towards the doctor's indifference to a matter of such importance.

He said nothing of this, but rose, placed the doctor's fee on the table, and remarked with a sigh: "We sick people probably often put inappropriate questions. But tell me, in general, is this complaint dangerous or not?. . ."

The doctor looked at him sternly over his spectacles with one eye, as if to say: "Prisoner, if you will not keep to the questions put to you, I shall be obliged to have you removed from the court."

"I have already told you what I consider necessary and proper. The analysis may show something more." And the doctor bowed.

Iván Ilyich went out slowly, seated himself disconsolately in his sledge, and drove home. All the way home he was going over what the

Words for Everyday Use

ex • as • per • a • tion (eg zas´ pər ā´ shən) *n.*, great irritation or annoyance

gai • ly (gā´ lē) *adv.*, happily, merrily

dis • con • so • late • ly (dis kän´ sə lit lē) *adv.*, so unhappily that nothing will comfort; cheerlessly

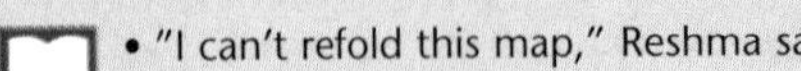

Vocabulary in Context

- "I can't refold this map," Reshma said in exasperation as she crumpled it into a ball.
- Victor whistled gaily as he set off on his vacation.
- Tonya sobbed disconsolately when she heard that Iván was dying.

doctor had said, trying to translate those complicated, obscure, scientific phrases into plain language and find in them answer to the question: "Is my condition bad? Is it very bad? Or is there as yet nothing much wrong?" And it seemed to him that the meaning of what the doctor had said was it was very bad. Everything in the streets seemed depressing. The cabmen, the houses, the passers-by, and the shops, were dismal. His ache, this dull gnawing ache that never ceased for a moment, seemed to have acquired a new and more serious significance from the doctor's dubious remarks. Iván Ilyich now watched it with a new and oppressive feeling.

He reached home and began to tell his wife about it. She listened, but in the middle of his account his daughter came in with her hat on, ready to go out with her mother. She sat down reluctantly to listen to this tedious story, but could not stand it long, and her mother too did not hear him to the end.

"Well, I am very glad," she said. "Mind now to take your medicine regularly. Give me the prescription and I'll send Gerásim to the chemist's." And she went to get ready to go out.

While she was in the room Iván Ilyich had hardly taken time to breathe, but he sighed deeply when she left it.

"Well," he thought, "perhaps it isn't so bad after all."

He began taking his medicine and following the doctor's directions, which had been altered after the examination of the urine. But then it happened that there was a contradiction between the indications drawn from the examination of the urine and the symptoms that showed themselves. It turned out that what was happening differed from what the doctor had told him, and that he had either forgotten, or blundered, or hidden something from him. He could not, however, be blamed for that, and Iván Ilyich still obeyed his orders <u>implicitly</u> and at first derived some comfort from doing so.

From the time of his visit to the doctor, Iván Ilyich's chief occupation was the exact fulfilment of the doctor's instructions regarding hygiene and the taking of medicine, and the observation of his pain and his excretions. His chief interests came to be people's ailments and people's health. When sickness, deaths, or recoveries were mentioned in his presence, especially when the illness resembled his own, he listened with agitation which he tried to hide, asked questions, and applied what he heard to his own case.

The pain did not grow less, but Iván Ilyich made efforts to force himself to think that he was better. And he could do this so long as nothing agitated him. But as soon as he had any unpleasantness with his wife, any lack of success in his official work, or held bad cards at bridge, he was at once acutely sensible of his disease. He had formerly borne such mischances, hoping soon to adjust what was wrong, to master it and attain success, or make a grand slam. But now every mischance upset him and plunged him into despair. He would say to himself, "There now, just as I was beginning to get better and the medicine had begun to take effect comes this accursed misfortune, or unpleasantness . . ." And he was furious with the mishap, or with the people who were causing the unpleasantness and killing him, for he felt that this fury was killing him but could not restrain it. One would have thought that it should have been clear to him that this exasperation with circumstances and people aggravated his illness, and that he ought therefore to ignore unpleasant occurrences. But he drew the

❶ *What becomes the focus of Iván's life? What does he do when he hears people talk about illness?*

❷ *How do the things he sees in the streets seem to Iván as he drives home? Why has his ache acquired new significance?*

❸ *What are the attitudes of his wife and daughter as Iván describes his meeting with the doctor?*

❹ *What three things continually interfere with Iván's efforts to force himself to feel better?*

Words for Everyday Use

im • plic • it • ly (im plis´ it lē) *adv.*, without reservation or doubt, absolutely

Vocabulary in Context

- The rules <u>implicitly</u> stated that nobody was to disturb the judge when she was in her chambers.

Answers to Guided Reading Questions

❶ Illness and following the doctor's instructions become the focus of Iván's life. He listens when people speak about illness, always trying to compare the illness being discussed to his own situation.

❷ Everything seems depressing. His ache has acquired new significance because of the doctor's remarks.

❸ His wife and his daughter seem indifferent to his problem.

❹ Whenever he has a fight with his wife, a lack of success in his work, or holds bad cards in his bridge game, he is reminded of his illness and of feeling bad.

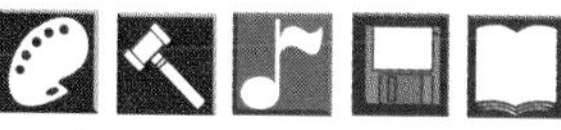

Cultural/Historical Note

Like *The Death of Iván Ilyich,* Tolstoy's *War and Peace* explores the struggle to find the meaning of life. *War and Peace* is a historical novel that tells the story of several Russian families during Napoleon's invasion of Russia in September of 1812.

As relations soured between Napoleon and Russian Czar Alexander, Napoleon gathered his forces in Poland in the spring of 1812. As his armies advanced, the Russians retreated, adopting a scorched earth policy. Napoleon's armies did not approach Moscow until September. On September 7, a brutal but indecisive battle was fought at Borodino. Although Napoleon entered Moscow a week later, he was forced to retreat due to a lack of food and shelter for his troops. Napoleon lost two-thirds of his army during this disastrous invasion.

You might play for students Tchaikovsky's *1812 Overture,* which was inspired by the Battle of Borodino, and ask them to write a description of the mood and sounds of the battle based on this musical work.

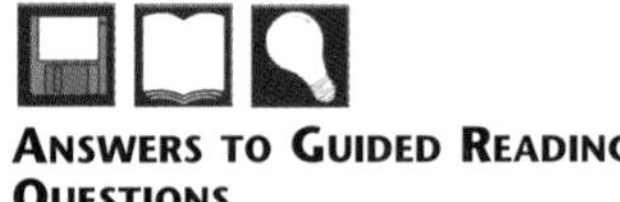

Answers to Guided Reading Questions

1 Seeing doctors seems to make his condition worse because they remind him of its seriousness.

2 That the world goes on as usual despite his illness torments Iván.

3 Iván fears that his mind has weakened when he almost takes an acquaintance's advice about a miracle cure.

4 Iván's wife says that sometimes Ivan does as he should do, taking his medicine and sleeping regular hours, and other days he does not do the things he should. She believes that Iván does not take proper care of himself.

Cross-curricular Activities

APPLIED ARTS

Iván consults a number of medical specialists. Ask students to research aspects of medicine and healing today including homeopathy, acupuncture, faith healers, the role of specialists and generalists, and the impact of HMOs. Students may find other issues related to the field of health that they may wish to research. Have students discuss the results of their research in small groups.

1 *What seems to make Iván's condition worse? Why?*

2 *What torments Iván more than anything else?*

3 *What incident causes Iván to fear that his mind has weakened?*

4 *What does Iván's wife say about his behavior and his ability to care for himself?*

very opposite conclusion: he said that he needed peace, and he watched for everything that might disturb it and became irritable at the slightest infringement of it. His condition was rendered worse by the fact that he read medical books and consulted doctors. The progress of his disease was so gradual that he could deceive himself when comparing one day with another—the difference was so slight. But when he consulted the doctors it seemed to him that he was getting worse, and even very rapidly. Yet despite this he was continually consulting them.

That month he went to see another celebrity, who told him almost the same as the first had done but put his questions rather differently, and the interview with this celebrity only increased Iván Ilyich's doubts and fears. A friend of a friend of his, a very good doctor, diagnosed his illness again quite differently from the others, and though he predicted recovery, his questions and <u>suppositions</u> bewildered Iván Ilyich still more and increased his doubts. A homeopathist diagnosed the disease in yet another way, and prescribed medicine which Iván Ilyich took secretly for a week. But after a week, not feeling any improvement and having lost confidence both in the former doctor's treatment and in this one's, he became still more <u>despondent</u>. One day a lady acquaintance mentioned a cure effected by a wonder-working icon.[1] Iván Ilyich caught himself listening attentively and beginning to believe that it had occurred. This incident alarmed him. "Has my mind really weakened to such an extent?" he asked himself. "Nonsense! It's all rubbish. I mustn't give way to nervous fears but having chosen a doctor must keep strictly to his treatment. That is what I will do. Now it's all settled. I won't think about it, but will follow the treatment seriously till summer, and then we shall see. From now there must be no more of this wavering!" This was easy to say but impossible to carry out. The pain in his side oppressed him and seemed to grow worse and more <u>incessant</u>, while the taste in his mouth grew stranger and stranger. It seemed to him that his breath had a disgusting smell, and he was conscious of a loss of appetite and strength. There was no deceiving himself: something terrible, new, and more important than anything before in his life, was taking place within him of which he alone was aware. Those about him did not understand or would not understand it, but thought everything in the world was going on as usual. That tormented Iván Ilyich more than anything. He saw that his household, especially his wife and daughter who were in a perfect whirl of visiting, did not understand anything of it and were annoyed that he was so depressed and so exacting, as if he were to blame for it. Though they tried to disguise it he saw that he was an obstacle in their path, and that his wife had adopted a definite line in regard to his illness and kept to it regardless of anything he said or did. Her attitude was this: "You know," she would say to her friends, "Iván Ilyich can't do as other people do, and keep to the treatment prescribed for him. One day he'll take his drops and keep strictly to his diet and go to bed in good time, but the next day unless I watch him he'll suddenly forget his medicine, eat sturgeon—which is forbidden—and sit up playing cards till one o'clock in the morning."

"Oh, come, when was that?" Iván Ilyich would ask in <u>vexation</u>. "Only once at Peter Ivánovich's."

1. **icon.** Religious image

Words for Everyday Use

sup • po • si • tion (sup´ə zish´ən) *n.*, something supposed; assumption

de • spond • ent (di spän´dənt) *adj.*, dejected, without courage or hope

in • ces • sant (in ses´ənt) *adj.*, never ceasing, constant

vex • a • tion (veks ā´shən) *n.*, state of disturbance, annoyance, irritation

Vocabulary in Context

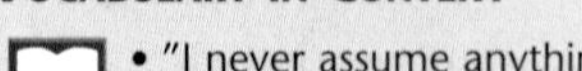

- "I never assume anything," said Trent after Luisa's <u>supposition</u> had been proven wrong.
- After receiving his first rejection letter, Roger became <u>despondent</u> and swore he would never write again.
- Only by hanging up the phone was Janis able to find relief from Merle's <u>incessant</u> chatter.
- Frida's grimace and irritated tone of voice showed her <u>vexation</u>.

"And yesterday with Shebek."

"Well, even if I hadn't stayed up, this pain would have kept me awake."

"Be that as it may you'll never get well like that, but will always make us wretched."

Praskóvya Fëdorovna's attitude to Iván Ilyich's illness, as she expressed it both to others and to him, was that it was his own fault and was another of the annoyances he caused her. Iván Ilyich felt that this opinion escaped her involuntarily—but that did not make it easier for him.

At the law courts too, Iván Ilyich noticed, or thought he noticed, a strange attitude towards himself. It sometimes seemed to him that people were watching him inquisitively as a man whose place might soon be vacant. Then again, his friends would suddenly begin to chaff[2] him in a friendly way about his low spirits, as if the awful, horrible, and unheard-of thing that was going on within him, incessantly gnawing at him and irresistibly drawing him away, was a very agreeable subject for jests. Schwartz in particular irritated him by his jocularity, vivacity, and *savoir-faire*, which reminded him of what he himself had been ten years ago.

❶ *What is Praskóvya Fëdorovna's attitude toward Iván's illness?*

❷ *What does Iván notice about his treatment by friends and colleagues?*

2. **chaff.** Tease in a good-natured way

Words for Everyday Use

joc • u • lar • i • ty (jäk´ yo͞o lar´ə tē) *n.,* state of being full of jokes and fun

vi • vac • i • ty (vī vas´ə tē) *n.,* liveliness

sa • voir • faire (sav´wär fer´) *n.,* ready knowledge of what to do or say

Answers to Guided Reading Questions

❶ Praskóvya Fëdorovna's attitude toward Iván's illness is that it is his fault and something he is doing to annoy her.

❷ Iván notices that friends and colleagues are treating him in an artificial, overly-friendly way, teasing him and joking about his illness. Some also seem to be eyeing his job.

Selection Check Test with Answers

EX. With whom does Iván Ilyich live?
Iván Ilyich lives with his wife and daughter.

1. What is happening to Iván Ilyich's health?
His health is deteriorating.

2. What is happening to Iván's relationship with his wife?
They are quarreling all the time and becoming irritable with each other.

3. For what does Iván's wife wish?
She wishes for his death.

4. Of what does his doctor's behavior remind Iván?
The doctor's behavior reminds Iván of himself when he is at work.

5. What does Iván begin to realize about his life and its effect on others?
Iván begins to realize that his life is poisoned and that it is poisoning those around him.

Vocabulary in Context

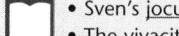

- Sven's jocularity gave a light-hearted air to the usually staid meeting.
- The vivacity of the speaker kept us all enthralled even though we had expected her lecture on the history of birdhouses to be dull.
- Her savoir-faire has helped Ayesha out of many trying and difficult situations.

Answers to Guided Reading Questions

1 Normally a grand slam in his card game would make Iván feel happy, but in light of his illness it seems unimportant.

2 Iván realizes that his life is poisoned and is poisoning the lives of others.

3 He is forced to live all alone on the brink of an abyss, with no one who understands or pities him.

Responding to the Selection

Ask students if they have ever felt that they were "on the brink of an abyss, with no one who understood or pitied [them]." When? What might they do to help somebody who felt this way?

Answers for Understanding Literature

Responses will vary. Possible responses are given.

1. Psychological Fiction. The story presents the subjective experience of Iván Ilyich and provides the reader with a detailed description of his mental anguish and his questioning of the value of his life.

2. Mood and Theme. The mood presented by this writing is one of sadness, frustration, and irritability. The following passages contribute to the creation of this mood: "And his irritability became worse and worse and began to mar the agreeable, easy, and correct life that had established itself"; "this conclusion struck him painfully, arousing in him a great feeling of pity for himself and of bitterness towards the doctor's indifference"; "every mischance plunged him into despair"; and "Those about him did not understand or would not understand it. . . . That tormented Iván Ilyich more than anything." This mood is heightened in such scenes as those between Iván and his wife, at the doctor's office, or playing cards.

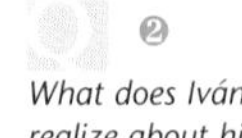

1 *What ought to have made Iván feel jolly and lively? Why doesn't it?*

2 *What does Iván realize about his life?*

3 *Where is Iván forced to live? What is he forced to live without?*

Friends came to make up a set and they sat down to cards. They dealt, bending the new cards to soften them, and he sorted the diamonds in his hand and found he had seven. His partner said "No trumps" and supported him with two diamonds. What more could be wished for? It ought to be jolly and lively. They would make a grand slam. But suddenly Iván Ilyich was conscious of that gnawing pain, that taste in his mouth, and it seemed ridiculous that in such circumstances he should be pleased to make a grand slam.

He looked at his partner Mikháil Mikháylovich, who rapped the table with his strong hand and instead of snatching up the tricks pushed the cards courteously and indulgently towards Iván Ilyich that he might have the pleasure of gathering them up without the trouble of stretching out his hand for them. "Does he think I am too weak to stretch out my arm?" thought Iván Ilyich, and forgetting what he was doing he over-trumped his partner, missing the grand slam by three tricks. And what was most awful of all was that he saw how upset Mikháil Mikháylovich was about it but did not himself care. And it was dreadful to realize why he did not care.

They all saw that he was suffering, and said: "We can stop if you are tired. Take a rest." Lie down? No, he was not at all tired, and he finished the rubber. All were gloomy and silent. Iván Ilyich felt that he had diffused this gloom over them and could not dispel it. They had supper and went away, and Iván Ilyich was left alone with the consciousness that his life was poisoned and was poisoning the lives of others, and that this poison did not weaken but penetrated more and more deeply into his whole being.

With this consciousness, and with physical pain besides the terror, he must go to bed, often to lie awake the greater part of the night. Next morning he had to get up again, dress, go to the law courts, speak, and write; or if he did not go out, spend at home those twenty-four hours a day each of which was a torture. And he had to live thus all alone on the brink of an abyss, with no one who understood or pitied him. ■

Responding to the Selection

"And he had to live thus all alone on the brink of an abyss, with no one who understood or pitied him." Do you think this statement reflects Iván Ilyich's situation? Why, or why not? How do you feel toward Iván Ilyich? How do you feel about the people in his life?

Words for Everyday Use

in • dul • gent • ly (in dul´ jent lē) *adv.,* leniently, with an attempt to gratify or humor

Vocabulary in Context

• The babysitter indulgently read Pierre another story before sending him to bed.

Reviewing the Selection

RECALLING / **INTERPRETING**

1. What is happening to Iván Ilyich? How does his condition affect his mood and his relationship with his wife? For what does his wife wish? ▶▶ Is Praskóvya Fëdorovna, Iván Ilyich's wife, more concerned about herself or her husband's condition? How might you characterize her relationship with Iván?

2. What are the doctor's responses to Iván's questions concerning the seriousness of his condition? Of what does the doctor's attitude remind Iván? ▶▶ How does Iván's meeting with the doctor leave him feeling? What kind of attitude does the doctor assume in dealing with Iván? In what way is Iván's position as judge similar to the doctor's position?

3. What does Iván notice about his wife's attitude toward his illness? What does he notice about how he is treated by colleagues and friends? ▶▶ Why is Iván bothered by the attitudes of his friends? Does Iván have many close and genuine relationships in his life? Explain using evidence from the text.

4. What does Iván begin to realize about his life and its effect on others? ▶▶ To what kind of poison does Iván refer? In what way might his life be poisoned?

SYNTHESIZING

5. What circumstances of Iván's life make dealing with his fatal illness intolerable? How does his illness, and the feelings of loneliness brought on by his illness, make him feel about his life? What do these feelings make him realize about his family, his friends, and the way he has lived his life? After reading this story, how might you advise those not ill to behave toward a person who is ill?

Understanding Literature (Questions for Discussion)

1. **Psychological Fiction. Psychological fiction** is fiction that emphasizes the interior, subjective experiences of its characters, and especially such fiction when it deals with emotional and mental disturbance or anguish. In what way is *The Death of Iván Ilyich* a good example of psychological fiction? Whose subjective experience is being emphasized? What is causing his mental anguish?

2. **Mood and Theme. Mood,** or **atmosphere,** is the emotion created in a reader by part or all of a literary work. What is the mood of this section of *The Death of Iván Ilyich*? A **theme** is a central idea in a literary work. Why is this mood appropriate for the theme of this selection? What words and phrases help to create this mood? Which specific scenes evoke this mood?

Answers for Reviewing the Selection

RECALLING AND INTERPRETING

1. **Recalling.** Iván is becoming sick. His illness is characterized by discomfort in his left side and a bad taste in his mouth. This condition affects his mood by making him irritable. He and his wife quarrel constantly and she often wishes that he would die. **Interpreting.** Praskóvya Fëdorovna seems more concerned about her own discomfort and the inconveniences of her husband's illness and inevitable death. There is not a great deal of love and affection between them—their marriage seems cold and based on practical matters.

2. **Recalling.** The doctor is aloof and continually dodges Iván's questions. The doctor's attitude reminds Iván of his own attitude when he deals with people at work. **Interpreting.** Iván's meeting with the doctor leaves him feeling pity for himself and bitterness toward the doctor. The doctor is cold and businesslike. Iván feels that he shows the same lack of compassion toward people in his courtroom as the doctor is showing him as a patient.

3. **Recalling.** Iván notices that his wife seems to blame him for the illness and is more concerned with how it is affecting her life, that some colleagues are looking out for themselves by noticing that his job might soon be vacant, and that his friends treat him with superficial kindness and try to make light of his condition. **Interpreting.** Iván realizes that his friends do not understand how he feels. He does not have many close personal relationships. His friends do not take his illness or his feelings about it seriously.

4. **Recalling.** Iván begins to realize that his life is poisoned and that it seems to be poisoning everyone around him. **Interpreting.** The poison is the illness that is taking over Iván's body and affecting the moods of

(cont.)

Answers for Reviewing the Selection (cont.)

everyone around him. He is starting to feel dissatisfied with his life, which is full of people who do not understand nor care about him.

SYNTHESIZING

Responses will vary. Possible responses are given.

5. Iván does not have a great deal of support from people around him, and this makes dealing with his illness harder. He feels frustrated because he has reached the point where he cannot function as he has done, so he is forced to think more about his life and relationships. Thinking about his life brings feelings of emptiness. People should be compassionate and understanding of people who are ill.

ANALYTIC SCALES FOR RESPONDING IN WRITING

Assign a score from 1 to 25 for each grading criterion below. (For more detailed evaluation, see the evaluation forms for writing, revising, and proofreading, Assessment Portfolio 4.1–4.9.)

1. Memorial

- **Content/Unity.** The memorial presents the writer's ideas about a well-lived life.
- **Organization/Coherence.** The memorial is arranged in a logical order and uses transitions to connect ideas.
- **Language/Style.** The memorial uses vivid and precise nouns, verbs, and modifiers.
- **Conventions.** The memorial avoids errors in spelling, grammar, usage, mechanics, and manuscript form.

▶ Additional practice is provided in the Essential Skills Practice Book: Writing 1.8.

2. Critical Essay

- **Content/Unity.** The essay centers on the reader's perception of the given quotation and uses information and examples from the selection to support the reader's ideas.
- **Organization/Coherence.** The essay begins with an introduction that includes a thesis. The introduction is followed by supporting paragraphs with clear transitions. The essay ends with a solid conclusion.
- **Language/Style.** The essay uses vivid and precise nouns, verbs, and modifiers.
- **Conventions.** The essay avoids errors in spelling, grammar, usage, mechanics, and manuscript form.

▶ Additional practice is provided in the Essential Skills Practice Book: Writing 1.20.

Responding in Writing

1. **Creative Writing: Memorial.** As Iván Ilyich reaches the final days of his life, he begins to wonder if his life has been worthwhile. What do you believe makes a life worthwhile? Write a memorial for a person, real or fictional, who has lived his or her life well. In the memorial, point out what has made his or her life worthwhile and why this life might be held up as a model for others.

2. **Critical Essay: The Life of Iván Ilyich.** Book 2 of *The Death of Iván Ilyich* opens, "Iván Ilyich's life had been most simple and most ordinary and therefore most terrible." Write a short essay in which you explain this line based on what you have learned about Iván Ilyich from the Prereading page and from this excerpt from *The Death of Iván Ilyich*. As you plan your essay, think about the following questions: What does Iván do for a living? What kinds of things had he valued most in his life before his illness? What kind of relationship does he have with his wife and family? Does he have many close friends? How do people feel about Iván's illness? Why do they have these feelings? In your essay, examine why the words *ordinary* and *terrible* seem to describe the life of Iván Ilyich.

Language Lab

Reducing Wordiness. Review the Language Arts Survey 2.26, "Reducing Wordiness." Then rewrite the sentences in the following paragraph, reducing their wordiness.

EXAMPLE Later in his life, when he became older, Tolstoy became a highly religious man and focused more on religion.
Later in his life, Tolstoy became a highly religious man.

[1] Tolstoy, who had been born to a wealthy family, had always been wealthy and had a great deal of money, land, and personal wealth. [2] When he converted to Christianity in 1876 and became religious he decided to adopt an attitude in which he would renounce all worldly wealth. [3] In keeping with his religious beliefs, which were strong beliefs, he sold his land, donated his money, and began dressing as a peasant. [4] It was his opinion, an opinion in which he firmly believed, that people in the world became too distracted by worldly symbols of power and prestige such as money and land ownership and that people should should adopt new attitudes where wealth was concerned. [5] He devoted the rest of his life until his death to his moral convictions, and works such as *The Death of Iván Ilyich*, which he wrote at that time in his life, reflect these moral convictions.

ANSWERS FOR LANGUAGE LAB

Responses will vary. Possible responses are given.

[1] Tolstoy, who had been born to a wealthy family, had a great deal of money and land. [2] When he converted to Christianity in 1876, he decided to renounce all worldly wealth. [3] In keeping with his strong religious beliefs, he sold his land, donated his money, and began dressing as a peasant. [4] He believed that people became too distracted by worldly symbols of power and prestige and that they should adopt new attitudes about wealth. [5] He devoted the rest of his life to his moral convictions, and works such as *The Death of Iván Ilyich* reflect these moral convictions.

▶ Additional practice is provided in the Essential Skills Practice Book: Language 2.26.

PREREADING

from *The Sound of the Mountain*
by Kawabata Yasunari, translated by Edward M. Seidensticker

JAPAN

About the Author

KAWABATA YASUNARI
1899–1972

Kawabata Yasunari's writing combines an appreciation for beauty with a preoccupation with death. Kawabata described his childhood as a time in which he became "an expert in funerals." His parents died when he was three, his grandmother when he was seven, his only sister when he was nine, and his grandfather when he was fifteen. Kawabata spent a lonely adolescence living in school dormitories. As a student at Tokyo University, he joined others to form a group of writers who called themselves "Neosensualists;" they were influenced by European modernism and believed that literature should be purely artistic rather than propagandistic. Kawabata was also influenced by traditional Japanese literary forms. In fact, his novels and short stories have often been called haiku-like, and the fact that his writing is without strict form has been attributed to the influence of a type of linked verse popular in fifteenth century Japan called *renga,* in which verses were connected by imagery rather than by elements of plot. In 1968, Kawabata became the first Japanese and the second Asian writer to be awarded the Nobel Prize for literature. He committed suicide in 1972, soon after the death of his friend and fellow writer Mishima Yukio.

About the Selection

The Sound of the Mountain is a novel Kawabata wrote soon after the defeat of Japan in World War II. This novel displays Kawabata's concern with death as well as his propensity to link decay and emptiness with beauty. The novel is set in post-war Japan and deals with the lives of the Ogata family, focusing upon the thoughts and feelings of Shingo, the head of the household. In addition to portraying Shingo's fear of aging and death, the novel also depicts the way relationships and family life were changing in post-war Japan. Japan was rapidly becoming Westernized, and traditional ways of life were changing—the generations of a family no longer lived together, youth lost some of their respect for their elders, divorce became more common, and women were gradually claiming more independence. Ogata Shingo sees beauty and harmony in the old ways of life and struggles to understand and find meaning and beauty in his changing society.

CONNECTIONS: The Japanese Novel

The novel as a genre arose independently in the East and the West, first in Japan, in the eleventh century, and later in Europe, in the seventeenth. The first Japanese novel was Murasaki Shikibu's *The Tale of Genji* (c. 1010; see page 765), which inspired many imitators during the Heian period (AD 794–1185) and throughout later periods of Japanese history. The early Tokugawa period (1603–c. 1770) also produced a great novelist—Ihara Saikaku. After Western literature was introduced to Japan in the late nineteenth century, creative Japanese novelists flourished. In addition to Kawabata, some of the many renowned modern Japanese novelists include Akutagawa Ryunosuke (see page 92), Tanizaki Jun'ichiro, Mishima Yukio, and 1994 Nobel Prize winner Ōe Kenzaburō.

GOALS/OBJECTIVES

Studying this lesson will enable students to

- enjoy the imagery in the selection and understand the feelings of the central character
- identify *images* and *symbols* in writing
- distinguish between conventional and idiosyncratic symbols
- write sentences using conventional and idiosyncratic symbols
- write a critical essay analyzing influences in Kawabata's work
- use vivid nouns, verbs, and modifiers

ADDITIONAL RESOURCES

READER'S GUIDE
- Selection Worksheet 4.5

ASSESSMENT PORTFOLIO
- Selection Check Test 2.4.9
- Selection Test 2.4.10

ESSENTIAL SKILLS PRACTICE BOOKS
- Writing 1.8, 1.20
- Language 2.15

PREREADING EXTENSIONS

Encourage interested students to read and write a review of a short story or a novel by any one of the following Japanese writers: Natsume Soseki, Kawabata Yasunari, Mishima Yukio, Akutagawa Ryunosuke, or Tanizaki Jun'ichiro. In their reviews, students might mention how the works they have chosen compare with this except from *The Sound of the Mountain.* You may wish to review a number of works for content and theme and then choose a body of works from which students might make their selections.

SUPPORT FOR LEP STUDENTS

PRONUNCIATIONS OF PROPER NOUNS AND ADJECTIVES

Ka • wa • ba • ta Ya • su • na • ri (kä wä bä tä yä so͞o nä rē)
Mi • shi • ma Yu •ki • o (mi shē mä yo͞o kē ō)
O • ga • ta Shin • go (ō gä tä shēŋ gō)
Shu • i • chi (sho͞o ē chē)
Ya • su • ko (yä so͞o kō)

ADDITIONAL VOCABULARY

furrowed—wrinkled
locusts—large grasshoppers
robust—strong, hardy, full of vigor
veranda—open porch, usually roofed, along the outside of a building

READER'S JOURNAL

As an alternative activity, you might ask students to write about a time when they had to struggle to remember something, such as information for a test or the names of classmates at a new school. How did they feel about this experience? Why did they feel this way?

Answers to Guided Reading Questions

❶ Ogata Shingo would appear sad to a stranger. Shuichi realizes that his father is thinking and is trying to remember something. Shuichi gives "little thought" to the matter because his father is often trying to remember something.

❷ Shingo is trying to remember the name of the maid who has left and how long ago she left. He says he can remember nothing about her. Shuichi believes that his father is exaggerating how little he can remember.

SPELLING AND VOCABULARY WORDS FROM THE SELECTION

diminutive	provincial
futile	

Biographical Note

Kawabata traveled throughout Manchuria, a region in northeast China, during World War II, thus avoiding getting involved in the war. Indeed, Mishima Yukio called Kawabata "the eternal traveler." Traveling, distance, and a sense of estrangement all play central roles in Kawabata's work.

READER'S JOURNAL

Do you enjoy lingering over your memories, or do you focus more on the present and the future? How would you feel if your memory grew dim and you were unable to recall clear images from the past? In your journal, explain whether a loss of memory would affect your life profoundly, or whether this loss would have little effect in your life.

FROM

The Sound of the Mountain

KAWABATA YASUNARI, TRANSLATED BY EDWARD M. SEIDENSTICKER

❶ *How would Ogata Shingo appear to a stranger? What does Shuichi realize Shingo is doing? Why does Shuichi give "little thought" to what is happening?*

❷ *What is Shingo trying to remember? What does he say he is unable to do? What does Shuichi think of his father's claim?*

CHAPTER 1

Ogata Shingo, his brow slightly furrowed, his lips slightly parted, wore an air of thought. Perhaps to a stranger it would not have appeared so. It might have seemed rather that something had saddened him.

His son Shuichi knew what was happening. It happened so frequently that he gave it little thought.

Indeed, more was apparent to him than the simple fact that his father was thinking. He knew that his father was trying to remember something.

Shingo took off his hat and, absently holding it in his right hand, set it on his knee. Shuichi put it on the rack above them.

"Let me see. What was it, I wonder?" At such times Shingo found speech difficult. "What was the name of the maid that left the other day?"

"You mean Kayo?"

"Kayo. That was it. And when was it that she left?"

"Last Thursday. That would make it five days ago."

"Five days ago? Just five days ago she quit, and I can't remember anything about her."

To Shuichi his father's performance seemed a trifle exaggerated.

"That Kayo—I think it must have been two or three days before she quit. When I went out for a walk I had a blister on my foot, and I said I thought I had picked up ringworm. 'Footsore,' she said. I liked that. It had a gentle, old-fashioned ring to it. I liked it very much. But now that I think about it I'm sure she said I had a boot sore. There was something wrong with the way she said it. Say 'footsore.'"

"Footsore."

"And now say 'boot sore.'"

"Boot sore."

"I thought so. Her accent was wrong."

Of provincial origins, Shingo was never very confident about standard Tokyo pronunciation. Shuichi had grown up in Tokyo.

WORDS FOR EVERYDAY USE

pro • vin • cial (prō vin´ shəl) *adj.*, having the ways, speech, attitudes of a certain province, especially a rural one; countrified; rustic

Vocabulary in Context

- People who live in provincial regions often live a more traditional lifestyle than those who live in fast-paced urban centers.

"It had a very pleasant sound to it, very gentle and elegant, when I thought she said 'footsore.' She was there in the hallway. And now it occurs to me what she really said, and I can't even think of her name. I can't remember her clothes or her face. I imagine she was with us six months or so?"

"Something of the sort." Used to these problems, Shuichi offered his father no sympathy.

Shingo was accustomed enough to them himself, and yet he felt a twinge of something like fear. However hard he tried to remember the girl, he could not summon her up. There were times when such futile searchings were leavened[1] by sentimentality.

So it was now. It had seemed to him that Kayo, leaning slightly forward there in the hallway, was consoling him for being footsore.

She had been with them six months, and he could call up only the memory of that single word. He felt that a life was being lost.

FROM CHAPTER 2

Yasuko, Shingo's wife, was sixty-three, a year older than he.

They had a son, a daughter, and two grandchildren, daughters of the girl, Fusako.

Yasuko was young for her age. One would not have taken her to be older than her husband. Not that Shingo himself seemed particularly old. They seemed natural together, he just enough older than she to make them a most ordinary couple. Though diminutive, she was in robust health.

Yasuko was no beauty. In their younger years she had looked older than he, and had disliked being seen in public with him.

Shingo could not have said at what age she had begun to look the younger of the two. Probably it had been somewhere toward their mid-fifties. Women generally age faster than men, but in their case the reverse had been true.

The year before, the year he had entered his second cycle of sixty years, Shingo had spat up blood—from his lungs, it had seemed. He had not had a medical examination, however, and presently the affliction had gone away. It had not come back.

Nor had it meant that he grew suddenly older. His skin had seemed firmer since, and in the two weeks or so that he had been in bed the color of his eyes and lips had improved.

Shingo had not detected symptoms of tuberculosis in himself, and to spit blood at his age gave him the darkest forebodings. Partly because of them he refused to be examined. To Shuichi such behavior was no more than the stubborn refusal of the aged to face facts. Shingo was not able to agree.

Yasuko was a good sleeper. Sometimes, in the middle of the night, Shingo would be tempted to blame her snoring for having awakened him. She had snored, it seemed, as a girl of fifteen or sixteen, and her parents had been at great pains to correct the habit; it had stopped when she married. Then, when she passed fifty, it had begun again.

When she snored Shingo would twist her nose in an effort to stop her. If the twisting had no effect, he would take her by the throat and shake her. On nights when he was not in good spirits he would be repelled by the sight of the aged flesh with which he had lived for so long.

Tonight he was not in good spirits. Turning on the light, he looked at her profile and took her by the throat. She was a little sweaty.

1. **leavened.** Tempered; mingled with

❶ *Why doesn't Shuichi feel sympathy for his father? How does Shingo feel when he cannot remember the girl?*

❷ *How does Shingo feel about this symptom—spitting blood? Why won't he see a doctor? What does Shuichi think of his father's behavior?*

❸ *What habit did Shingo's wife, Yasuko, have when she was younger? When does she resume this habit?*

WORDS FOR EVERYDAY USE

fu • tile (fyo͞o t´ l) *adj.,* useless; vain; hopeless

di • min • u • tive (də min´ yo͞o tiv) *adj.,* much smaller than ordinary or average

ANSWERS TO GUIDED READING QUESTIONS

❶ Shuichi doesn't feel sympathy for his father because he is used to his father's bouts of memory loss. Shingo is a little afraid, but he also enjoys the "sentimentality" of his struggles to remember trivial details. He also feels that "a life was being lost" when he is unable to remember Kayo, the maid.

❷ Shingo sees the symptom as a troubling sign. He won't see a doctor because he is afraid that there may be something wrong with him. Shuichi thinks that his father is stubbornly refusing to face facts about his health.

❸ Yasuko snored when she was a girl. She resumed snoring once she passed fifty years of age.

LITERARY NOTE

Kawabata was influenced by European Modernism. Inform students that three important Modernist movements were Imagism, Symbolism, and Surrealism. Imagism was a movement that attempted to free poetry of the poet's explicit comments about feeling or meaning. An Imagist poem does not tell the reader how to feel about the image but relies on the image itself to create emotion in the reader. Symbolists revolted against Realism, relying on suggestion rather than direct description and portraying material or spiritual truths through symbols. They also focused on the musical properties of language. Surrealists strove to heighten human awareness by juxtaposing seemingly unrelated images. They made use of apparent contradictions and startling images in their writing. Encourage students to discuss what elements of these three movements they find in Kawabata's work.

VOCABULARY IN CONTEXT

- Shingo knew it was futile to hope to live forever.
- The diminutive child was the smallest in the class picture—most of her classmates loomed over her like giants.

Answers to Guided Reading Questions

❶ Shingo is saddened that he only touches his wife to keep her from snoring.

❷ Autumn insects are singing even though it is still August.

Selection Check Test with Answers

EX. Who is Shuichi?

Shuichi is Ogata Shingo's son.

1. Who is Kayo?

Kayo is Shingo's former maid who left five days ago.

2. What does Shingo remember about Kayo?

Shingo remembers that he had a blister on his foot and that Kayo called it a "footsore."

3. What did Yasuko begin to do when she turned fifty?

Yasuko began to snore again.

4. What sings outside Shingo's window?

Locusts sing outside his window.

5. What strange sound does Shingo hear?

He hears the sound of the mountain.

Mount Fuji in Clear Weather. *(Art from Edo Japan) Musées Royaux D'art et D'histoire*

❶ *What saddens Shingo?*

Only when she snored did he reach out to touch her. The fact seemed to him infinitely saddening.

He took up a magazine lying at his pillow. Then, the room being sultry, he got up, opened a shutter, and sat down beside it.

The moon was bright.

One of his daughter-in-law's dresses was hanging outside, unpleasantly gray. Perhaps she had forgotten to take in her laundry, or perhaps she had left a sweat-soaked garment to take the dew of night.

❷ *What is happening too early in the season?*

A screeching of insects came from the garden. There were locusts on the trunk of the cherry tree to the left. He had not known that locusts could make such a rasping sound; but locusts indeed they were.

He wondered if locusts might sometimes be troubled with nightmares.

A locust flew in and lit on the skirt of the mosquito net. It made no sound as he picked it up.

"A mute." It would not be one of the locusts he had heard at the tree.

Lest it fly back in, attracted by the light, he threw it with all his strength toward the top of the tree. He felt nothing against his hand as he released it.

Gripping the shutter, he looked toward the tree. He could not tell whether the locust had lodged there or flown on. There was a vast depth to the moonlit night, stretching far on either side.

Though August had only begun, autumn insects were already singing.

He thought he could detect a dripping of dew from leaf to leaf.

Then he heard the sound of the mountain.

Answers for Reviewing the Selection (cont.)

mountain disturbs Shingo because he is not sure of its source and feels that it is a signal that death is coming.

SYNTHESIZING

Responses will vary. Possible responses are given.

5. Shingo is saddened by the aging process and is struck with fear by the thought of his own mortality. *Responses will vary.*

It was a windless night. The moon was near full, but in the moist, sultry air the fringe of trees that outlined the mountain was blurred. They were motionless, however.

Not a leaf on the fern by the veranda was stirring.

In these mountain recesses of Kamakura[2] the sea could sometimes be heard at night. Shingo wondered if he might have heard the sound of the sea. But no—it was the mountain.

It was like wind, far away, but with a depth like a rumbling of the earth. Thinking that it might be in himself, a ringing in his ears, Shingo shook his head.

The sound stopped, and he was suddenly afraid. A chill passed over him, as if he had been notified that death was approaching. He wanted to question himself, calmly and deliberately, to ask whether it had been the sound of the wind, the sound of the sea, or a sound in his ears. But he had heard no such sound, he was sure. He had heard the mountain. ■

2. **Kamakura.** Historical site, resort, and residential district on the Pacific Ocean, enclosed on three sides by hills lying south of Tokyo

❶ *How does Shingo feel when he hears this sound?*

❷ *What does the mountain sound like?*

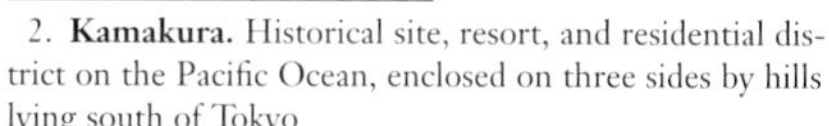

Responding to the Selection

Do you feel sympathy for Shingo? If you were in Shuichi's position, would you feel and behave as he does, or would you feel and act differently toward your father? Discuss your response with your classmates.

Reviewing the Selection

Recalling

1. What is Shingo trying to remember about Kayo, the maid? What does Shingo look like when he is trying to remember something? What does Shingo remember about Kayo? In what way is even this memory proved incorrect?

Interpreting

How does Shingo feel about these "futile searchings" through his memory? What pleases Shingo about his one memory of Kayo? What does this reveal about his character?

Recalling

2. What does Shuichi think of his father's "performance"? What is Shuichi's reaction to his father's "problems"? To what does Shuichi attribute his father's unwillingness to see a doctor?

Interpreting

In what way would you characterize Shuichi's attitude toward his father? What do you think is the reason why Shingo refuses to see a doctor? What does Shuichi's attitude toward his father reveal about Shuichi as a character?

Answers to Guided Reading Questions

❶ Shingo feels as if he has been notified that death is approaching.

❷ The mountain sounds far away like wind but has a depth like the rumbling of the earth. Shingo also thinks the sound may be a ringing in his ears.

Responding to the Selection

Remind students that they can take any position on Shingo's character and Shuichi's actions as long as they support their opinions with evidence from the text.

Answers for Reviewing the Selection

RECALLING AND INTERPRETING

1. **Recalling.** Shingo is trying to remember Kayo's name and when she left his family's employment. Shingo looks as if something has saddened him. Shingo remembers that when he discovered he had a blister, Kayo called it a "footsore." Shingo realizes that Kayo had actually said "boot sore." **Interpreting.** Shingo is alarmed, feeling "a twinge of something like fear," but he also enjoys the sentimentality of his searches to remember. He feels that Kayo's very life is being lost when he is unable to remember her. Shingo is pleased by the gentle, elegant, and "old-fashioned ring" to the word *footsore.* Shingo is essentially an "old-fashioned" person.

2. **Recalling.** Shuichi thinks that his father's "performance"—his struggle to remember Kayo—is "a trifle exaggerated." Shuichi is used to these "problems," so he does not offer his father any sympathy. Shuichi attributes his father's unwillingness to "the stubborn refusal of the aged to face facts." **Interpreting.** Shuichi is unsympathetic and cold to his father. (cont.)

Answers for Reviewing the Selection (cont.)

Students may say that Shingo is afraid to see a doctor because he is worried that the doctor will discover that something is wrong with him. Shuichi's attitude toward his father reveals that he lacks compassion and is self-interested.

3. **Recalling.** Yasuko began snoring again once she passed fifty. Shingo is saddened by this fact. **Interpreting.** Shingo might be saddened because he may think their lack of touching indicates a growing distance between them. Shingo and Yasuko have become less intimate and more distant as they have grown older.

4. **Recalling.** Shingo hears locusts singing and the "sound of the mountain," a distant but deep rumble. **Interpreting.** Shingo is disturbed by the locusts because they are autumn insects and they are singing in August, signifying death before its time. The sound of the (cont.)

Answers for Understanding Literature

Responses will vary. Possible responses are given.

Image and Symbol. Students may note the following conventional symbols of death: Shingo's forgetting Kayo as a symbol of the loss of life, autumn insects singing in August as a symbol of time passing and the later years of life, and night as a symbol of death. Forgetting, autumn, and night have long been associated with death. Kawabata may be indicating that death is a natural and inevitable part of life that should not be feared as something horrible but accepted as another one of life's many facets.

Answers for Language Lab

Responses will vary. Possible responses are given.

1. ancient tradition
2. aesthetic beauty
3. elegant but austere
4. construct; diminutive; stoop
5. displays; serves; delicious; brews

▶ Additional practice is provided in the Essential Skills Practice Book: Writing 2.15.

Recalling

3. When did Yasuko pick up her girlhood habit of snoring again? What does Shingo think about the fact that he only reaches out to touch Yasuko when she snores?

Interpreting

▶▶ Why might Shingo feel this way? What does this detail indicate about how Shingo and Yasuko's relationship is changing?

4. What two things does Shingo hear outside his window?

▶▶ Why do these two sounds disturb Shingo?

Synthesizing

5. Describe Shingo's attitude toward growing older and facing death. What do you think of Shingo as a character? What do you think of his relationships with family members? How might they relate to his attitudes about his impending death? Do you think that he ridiculously exaggerates situations, or do you think that he is merely contemplative and sensitive? In what way does Shingo's personality color his interpretation of the sound of the mountain? Explain your responses.

Understanding Literature (Questions for Discussion)

Image and Symbol. An **image** is a word or phrase that names something that can be seen, heard, touched, tasted, or smelled. A **symbol** is a thing that stands for or represents both itself and something else. Writers use two types of symbols—conventional, and personal or idiosyncratic. A **conventional symbol** is one with traditional, widely recognized associations, such as doves for peace. A **personal** or **idiosyncratic symbol** is one that assumes its secondary meaning because of the special use to which it is put by a writer. In this selection, Kawabata's images of the natural world are symbols of death and mortality. Kawabata creates a personal or idiosyncratic symbol of death in the image of the sound of the mountain. What conventional symbols of death and mortality appear in this selection? Why do you think Kawabata chooses to link death with beautiful images from the natural world? What may he be trying to indicate about death?

Responding in Writing

1. **Creative Writing: Symbols.** This selection from *The Sound of the Mountain* contains several symbols of human mortality and death, both conventional and personal, or idiosyncratic. Try creating your own symbols of human mortality and death, and use these symbols in a sentence or two. Try to come up with at least five conventional

symbols and at least two or three personal or idiosyncratic symbols. To begin, you might work as a class to list conventional symbols for death on the board. (A good starting place for a list of these conventional symbols would be the Handbook of Literary Terms, under the entry *symbol.*) Choose five symbols from this list that you would like to work with, and then freewrite about the images these symbols create in your mind. For example, if you have chosen to use the conventional symbol of eternal sleep for death, you might write, "Wearing satin slippers, eternal sleep silently crept past the 'Do Not Disturb' sign on the door to steal her away." It will be more difficult to come up with your own symbols, so spend some time using your imagination to think of unusual things that you associate with the word *death.* For example, you may remember seeing a mouse caught in a mouse trap when you were younger, so you might write, "The steel spring snaps shut on the victim, enchanted with the scent of life, a smell like overripe cheese, before he can even squeak." Save your symbols in your writing portfolio, so you can make use of them in a poem, personal essay, or story.

2. **Critical Essay: Analyzing the Influence of Japanese Poetry.** Kawabata is known as an author who was inspired by both modernist European literature and traditional Japanese literature. Read the work of the Japanese tanka and haiku poets on page 378. Then, write a three- or four-paragraph essay in which you explain the way in which you believe Kawabata was influenced by traditional Japanese poetry. In the first paragraph, you should clearly state your thesis, explaining the influence Japanese poetry may have had upon Kawabata's work. In a supporting paragraph or two, support your thesis by providing examples from Kawabata's work and the work of the Japanese tanka and haiku poets. Explain the ways in which the examples you have chosen are similar. Finally, come to a conclusion in a final paragraph.

Language Lab

Using Vivid Nouns, Verbs, and Modifiers. In writing such as Kawabata's that relies heavily on imagery, it is essential to use vivid nouns, verbs, and modifiers. Read the Language Arts Survey 2.15, "Using Vivid Nouns, Verbs, and Modifiers." The sentences below discuss a traditional part of Japanese life—the tea ceremony. Dull nouns, modifiers, and verbs appear in bold type. On your own paper, replace these words with more vivid words or phrases.

1. *Chado*, or the tea ceremony, is an **old thing** in Japanese culture.
2. The ceremony is seen as a way of introducing **prettiness** into everyday routine.
3. The tea house or room, or *cha-shitsu,* is **nice but very plain.**
4. The Japanese **make** tea rooms with **small** doors so that a person has to **bend** to enter.
5. A host **shows** the tea utensils, **gives** the guests **good** sweets, then **makes** and serves the tea.

ANALYTIC SCALES FOR RESPONDING IN WRITING

Assign a score from 1 to 25 for each grading criterion below. (For more detailed evaluation, see the evaluation forms for writing, revising, and proofreading, Assessment Portfolio 4.1–4.9.)

1. Symbols

- **Content/Unity.** The writer has come up with at least five conventional symbols and two or three idiosyncratic symbols for death and used them in sentences.
- **Organization/Coherence.** Each sentence is written in a sensible order.
- **Language/Style.** The symbols make use of vivid and precise nouns, verbs, and modifiers.
- **Conventions.** The symbols are written without errors in spelling, grammar, usage, mechanics, and manuscript form.

► Additional practice is provided in the Essential Skills Practice Book: Writing 1.8.

2. Critical Essay

- **Content/Unity.** The essay analyzes the influence of traditional Japanese poetry on Kawabata's work.
- **Organization/Coherence.** The essay begins with an introduction that includes the thesis of the essay. The introduction is followed by supporting paragraphs with clear transitions. The essay ends with a solid conclusion.
- **Language/Style.** The essay uses vivid and precise nouns, verbs, and modifiers.
- **Conventions.** The essay avoids errors in spelling, grammar, usage, mechanics, and manuscript form.

► Additional practice is provided in the Essential Skills Practice Book: Writing 1.20.

ADDITIONAL RESOURCES

READER'S GUIDE
- Selection Worksheet 4.6

ASSESSMENT PORTFOLIO
- Selection Check Test 2.4.11
- Selection Test 2.4.12

ESSENTIAL SKILLS PRACTICE BOOKS
- Writing 1.8, 1.10, 1.20
- Study and Research 4.12–4.18

PREREADING EXTENSIONS

Point out to students that African nations like Sierra Leone and Liberia, which are home to a small population of the descendants of freed slaves, have continued to attract people of African descent even after the abolition of slavery. Have students research and hold a discussion on Marcus Garvey (1887–1940), a Jamaican black leader who had an estimated following of two million and who advocated creating the first black-governed nation in Africa. What do students think of Garvey and his views? Encourage students to listen to each other respectfully as this topic has the potential to raise strong feelings in some students.

SUPPORT FOR LEP STUDENTS

PRONUNCIATIONS OF PROPER NOUNS AND ADJECTIVES

A • si (ä sē´)
Bo • la (bō´lä)
Ku • man • se • nu (ko͞o man sā´no͞o)
Me • ji (mā´jē)
A • bi • o • seh Ni • col (ä bē ō´sə nə kōl´)
Si • er • ra Le • one (sē er´ə lē ōn´)

ADDITIONAL VOCABULARY

gabardine—cloth twilled on one side with a fine diagonal weave
tapioca—starch; granular substance made from the root of the cassava plant

PREREADING

"Life Is Sweet at Kumansenu"
by Abioseh Nicol

About the Author

ABIOSEH NICOL
1924–

Born Davidson Nicol in Freetown, Sierra Leone, **Abioseh Nicol** has made valuable contributions in fields as diverse as literature, health, science, education, and public service. As a young man he won a scholarship to study medicine at the University of London. He later became the first black African to receive a fellowship at Cambridge University. While studying in England, he noted that most books about Africans were written by Europeans and were often flawed or negative in their portrayals of native Africans. Nicol began writing his own fiction, hoping to present a more accurate portrait of Africa. Today, Nicol's best-known story collection is *The Truly Married Woman and Other Stories*, published in 1965. He is regarded as one of Africa's best short story writers.

After teaching medicine in England and winning fame for his research into the structure of insulin, a hormone used in treating diabetes, Nicol returned to Sierra Leone to serve as principal of Fourah Bay College and vice-chancellor of the University of Sierra Leone. He also was appointed an ambassador to the United Nations and has worked with the Red Cross, the World Health Organization, and many important West African committees.

About the Selection

Abioseh Nicol has long felt that the true spirit of Africa lived in its countryside and rural villages, where he sets most of his stories. The story you are about to read, "**Life Is Sweet at Kumansenu**," takes place in a rural village and focuses on an old West African belief that the restless spirit of a child who has died can return to his or her mother's womb to be born again. In this situation, the mother marks the body of the dead child and checks to see if the mark appears on the next child she bears. The reappearance of the mark means that the new baby is in fact the dead child, reborn. According to tradition, the mother can break the cycle only if she follows special burial customs. "Life Is Sweet at Kumansenu," which tells the story of a woman named Bola, her son Meji, and her granddaughter Asi, presents a unique and moving view of this ancient tribal belief.

CONNECTIONS: Freetown, Sierra Leone

Sierra Leone is a West African nation bordered by the Atlantic Ocean and the countries of Guinea and Liberia. Today, the population is composed of a number of different ethnic groups, the most prominent of these being the Mende and the Temne. The country's capital and largest city, Freetown, was founded in 1792 by about eleven hundred freed slaves from Nova Scotia, Canada. This new colony was controlled by a private company until Britain took it over in 1808. During the next fifty years, about fifty thousand liberated slaves settled in Freetown. Under British rule, the descendants of these liberated slaves, called Creoles, were largely kept from participating in government. Sierra Leone won its independence in 1961, and today Creoles, although they are in the minority, play an active role in the modern city of Freetown.

GOALS/OBJECTIVES

Studying this lesson will enable students to

- empathize with Bola's feelings about her son
- define *foreshadowing, suspense, setting, mood,* and *theme*
- identify elements of foreshadowing and suspense in a short story
- identify the major theme of a literary work
- write a prose piece that shares a ritual or a belief
- write a critical essay on foreshadowing and suspense
- research a topic online or in the library

READER'S JOURNAL

Describe a situation in which you followed your own instincts instead of the advice or opinions of others. Why did you do this? Did everything work out for the best? Why, or why not?

"Life Is Sweet at Kumansenu"

ABIOSEH NICOL

The sea and the wet sand to one side of it; green tropical forest on the other; above it, the slow, tumbling clouds. The clean round blinding disc of sun and the blue sky covered and surrounded the small African village, Kumansenu.

A few square mud houses with roofs like helmets were here thatched, and there covered with corrugated zinc, where the prosperity of cocoa or trading had touched the head of the family.

The widow Bola stirred her palm-oil stew and thought of nothing in particular. She chewed a kola nut[1] rhythmically with her strong toothless jaws, and soon unconsciously she was chewing in rhythm with the skipping of Asi, her granddaughter. She looked idly at Asi, as the seven-year-old brought the twisted palmleaf rope smartly over her head and jumped over it, counting in English each time the rope struck the ground and churned up a little red dust. Bola herself did not understand English well, but she could easily count up to twenty in English, for market purposes. Asi shouted six and then said nine, ten. Bola called out that after six came seven. And I should know, she sighed. Although now she was old and her womb and breasts were withered, there was a time when she bore children regularly every two years. Six times she had borne a boy child and six times they had died. Some had swollen up and with weak plaintive cries had faded away. Others had shuddered in sudden convulsions, with burning skins, and had rolled up their eyes and died. They had all died; or rather he had died, Bola thought; because she knew it was one child all the time whose spirit had crept up restlessly into her womb to be born and mock her. The sixth time, Musa, the village magician whom time had now transformed into a respectable Muslim, had advised her and her husband to break the bones of the quiet little corpse and

1 *Where is this story set? What kinds of houses are in the village?*

2 *How many of Bola's infant sons died?*

3 *What does Bola believe about the deaths? On the birth and death of her sixth child, what did the village magician advise Bola to do? Did Bola follow his advice?*

1. **kola nut.** Seed of the kola tree, which is native to Africa. The nuts contain caffeine and produce a mild stimulating effect when chewed.

WORDS FOR EVERYDAY USE

cor • ru • gat • ed (kôr´ə gāt id) *adj.,* shaped into ridges for added strength

plain • tive (plān´tiv) *adj.,* sad

con • vul • sion (kən vul´shən) *n.,* violent spasm

VOCABULARY IN CONTEXT

- The children built a playhouse from a corrugated cardboard refrigerator box.
- The cat, caught high up in the branches of the oak tree, mewed plaintive cries for help.
- If treated with medication, people who have epilepsy can avoid convulsions and seizures.

READER'S JOURNAL

You might also ask students to write about times when it is important to consider the advice of others.

ANSWERS TO GUIDED READING QUESTIONS

1 The story is set in the small village of Kumansenu. The village has square mud houses with roofs like helmets that are thatched or covered with corrugated zinc.

2 Six of Bola's infant sons died.

3 Bola feels that she gave birth to the same child six times. On the death of the sixth child, Musa, the village magician, told Bola to mangle the corpse so that the child could not come back to torment them. Bola did not follow this advice.

SPELLING AND VOCABULARY WORDS FROM THE SELECTION

convulsion	provision
corrugated	sash
crestfallen	surreptitiously
discomfiture	threshold
irrelevantly	veranda
plaintive	

CULTURAL/HISTORICAL NOTE

Some students may find the description of the traditional practice Musa advises disturbing. Explain that the practice results from the belief that deaths of children are caused by evil spirits who are born as human infants but die soon after birth to torment the parents. Point out to students that possible Western explanations for Bola's many dead children include poor prenatal care, poor nutrition, and unsanitary delivery conditions, as people in traditional societies often have inadequate medical care.

Answers to Guided Reading Questions

❶ Bola notices a mark on the body of her seventh child similar to the mark she had made on the dead body of her sixth child. The seventh child, named Meji, actually lives and grows to manhood.

❷ Meji leaves his daughter Asi with Bola so that Bola might have someone to run errands and do chores, as well as someone to love.

❸ He tells her that he wants to rest and would prefer that nobody know of his presence.

❹ Meji says that the villagers will know soon enough and that the three should enjoy each other's company while they can because "Life is too short."

Analytic Scales for Responding in Writing

(See page 338.)

Assign a score from 1 to 25 for each grading criterion below. (For more detailed evaluation, see the evaluation forms for writing, revising, and proofreading, Assessment Portfolio 4.1–4.9.)

1. Sharing a Ritual, Tradition, or Belief

- **Content/Unity.** The descriptive piece shares a unique ritual, tradition, or belief.
- **Organization/Coherence.** The descriptive piece relates the details of this tradition in a sensible order.
- **Language/Style.** The descriptive piece uses vivid and precise nouns, verbs, and modifiers.
- **Conventions.** The descriptive piece avoids errors in spelling, grammar, usage, mechanics, and manuscript form.

► Additional practice is provided in the Essential Skills Practice Book: Writing 1.8, 1.10.

❶ *What does Bola notice on the body of her seventh child? What becomes of this child? What is his name?*

❷ *Why does Meji leave his daughter Asi with Bola?*

❸ *What does Meji say to Bola when he hears that she wants to tell the neighbors about his visit?*

❹ *What reason does Meji give for this secrecy?*

mangle it so that it could not come back to torment them alive again. But she had held on to the child and refused to let them mutilate it. Secretly, she had marked it with a sharp pointed stick at the left buttock before it was wrapped in a mat and taken away. When at the seventh time she had borne a son and the purification ceremonies had taken place, she had turned it surreptitiously to see whether the mark was there. It was. She showed it to the old woman who was the midwife and asked her what it was, and she had forced herself to believe that it was an accidental scratch made while the child was being scrubbed with herbs to remove placental blood. But this child had stayed. Meji, he had been called. And he was now thirty years of age and a second-class clerk in government offices in a town ninety miles away. Asi, his daughter, had been left with her to do the things an old woman wanted a small child for: to run and take messages to the neighbors, to fetch a cup of water from the earthenware pot in the kitchen, to sleep with her, and to be fondled.

She threw the washed and squeezed cassava leaves[2] into the red boiling stew, putting in a finger's pinch of salt, and then went indoors, carefully stepping over the threshold to look for the dried red pepper. She found it and then dropped it, leaning against the wall with a little cry. He turned round from the window and looked at her with a twisted half smile of love and sadness. In his short-sleeved, open-necked white shirt and gray gabardine trousers, gold-plated wrist watch and brown suede shoes, he looked like the picture in African magazines of a handsome clerk who would get to the top because he ate the correct food or regularly took the correct laxative, which was being advertised. His skin was grayish brown and he had a large red handkerchief tied round his neck.

"Meji, God be praised," Bola cried. "You gave me quite a turn. My heart is weak and I can no longer take surprises. When did you come? How did you come? By lorry,[3] by fishing boat? And how did you come into the house? The front door was locked. There are so many thieves nowadays. I'm so glad to see you, so glad," she mumbled and wept, leaning against his breast.

Meji's voice was hoarse, and he said, "I'm glad to see you, too, mother," rubbing her back affectionately.

Asi ran in and cried "Papa, Papa," and was rewarded with a lift and a hug.

"Never mind how I came, mother," Meji said, laughing, "I'm here, and that's all that matters."

"We must make a feast, we must have a big feast. I must tell the neighbors at once. Asi, run this very minute to Mr. Addai, the catechist,[4] and tell him your papa is home. Then to Mamie Gbera to ask her for extra provisions, and to Pa Babole for drummers and musicians . . ."

"Stop," said Meji, raising his hand. "This is all quite unnecessary. I don't want to see anyone, no one at all. I wish to rest quietly and completely. No one is to know I'm here."

Bola looked very crestfallen. She was so proud of Meji and wanted to show him off. The village would never forgive her for concealing such an important visitor. Meji must have sensed this because he held her shoulder comfortingly and said, "They will know soon enough. Let us enjoy one another, all three of us, this time. Life is too short."

2. **cassava leaves.** Leaves of a tropical plant that grows edible roots. The roots are used in making bread and tapioca.
3. **lorry.** Truck
4. **catechist.** Person who teaches catechism. A catechism is a handbook of questions and answers for teaching the principles of a religion.

Words for Everyday Use

sur • rep • ti • tious • ly (sur´əp tish´əs lē) *adv.*, secretly
thresh • old (thresh´ōld´) *n.*, entrance
pro • vi • sion (prō vizh´ən) *n.*, stock of food or supplies
crest • fall • en (krest´fôl´ən) *adj.*, sad; humbled

Vocabulary in Context

- In "Life Is Sweet at Kumansenu," Meji surreptitiously throws the food his mother cooks for him out his bedroom window.
- Many people believe it is good luck for a groom to carry his bride over the threshold of their front door after they are married.
- For our camping trip, we bought essential provisions, such as sleeping bags, backpacks, and sturdy hiking shoes.
- We knew from Giovanni's crestfallen expression that he hadn't done as well on the test as he had hoped.

African textile

African bronze mask

Bola turned to Asi, picked up the packet of pepper and told her to go and drop a little into the boiling pot outside, taking care not to go too near the fire or play with it. After the child had gone, Bola said to her son, "Are you in trouble? Is it the police?"

He shook his head, "No," he said. "It's just that I like returning to you. There will always be this bond of love and affection between us, and I don't wish to share it with others. It is our private affair and that is why I've left my daughter with you." He ended up irrelevantly, "Girls somehow seem to stay with relations longer."

"And don't I know it," said Bola. "But you look pale," she continued, "and you keep scraping your throat. Are you ill?" she laid her hand on his brow. "And you're cold, too."

"It's the cold wet wind," he said, a little harshly. "I'll go and rest now if you can open and dust my room for me. I'm feeling very tired. Very tired indeed. I've traveled very far today and it has not been an easy journey."

"Of course, my son, of course," Bola replied, bustling away hurriedly but happily.

Meji slept all afternoon till evening, and his mother brought his food to his room and, later, took the empty basins away. Then he slept again till morning.

The next day, Saturday, was a busy one, and after further promising Meji that she would tell no one he was about, Bola went off to

1 *What worry does Bola have about Meji's visit? What is Meji's response?*

2 *What does Bola notice about Meji?*

Words for Everyday Use

ir • rel • e • vant • ly (ir rel´ə vənt´lē) *adv.*, without importance

Answers to Guided Reading Questions

1 Bola worries that Meji might be in trouble. Meji explains that he simply enjoys being with his mother and does not wish to share their time with others.

2 Bola notices that Meji is pale, that he keeps scraping his throat, and that he is cold.

Analytic Scales for Responding in Writing

(See page 338.)

Assign a score from 1 to 25 for each grading criterion below. (For more detailed evaluation, see the evaluation forms for writing, revising, and proofreading, Assessment Portfolio 4.1–4.9.)

2. Critical Essay

- **Content/Unity.** The essay defines *foreshadowing* and *suspense* and outlines Nicol's use of these techniques.
- **Organization/Coherence.** The essay begins with an introduction that includes the thesis of the essay. The introduction is followed by supporting paragraphs with clear transitions. The essay ends with a solid conclusion.
- **Language/Style.** The essay uses vivid and precise nouns, verbs, and modifiers.
- **Conventions.** The essay avoids errors in spelling, grammar, usage, mechanics, and manuscript form.

► Additional practice is provided in the Essential Skills Practice Book: Writing 1.20.

Vocabulary in Context

- Ramon was marked down several points in the debate finals because he had been unable to stay on topic and had even closed his argument irrelevantly.

Answers to Guided Reading Questions

❶ Meji takes Asi on a long walk through a deserted path and up into the hills.

❷ Bola brings Meji to her husband's grave so that he might know that his son is a successful, grown man.

❸ Asi notices that Meji does not have a shadow. She also notices that his watch is stopped at twelve o'clock and that he always wears a scarf.

❹ Meji says that he has never felt closer to his father than he does when visiting his grave.

❺ Bola notices that her son has not been eating, but has been throwing food away outside his window. She tells him that there is a smell of decay in his room.

Cultural/Historical Note

Point out that in traditional African cultures that have been influenced by the West, sometimes traditional beliefs exist alongside Western beliefs. For example, Kumansenu is home to such a traditional figure as Musa the magician as well as to Mr. Addai, the catechist who teaches the principles of Christianity. Encourage students to discuss characters or elements of setting that appear to belong to a traditional society and elements that seem to belong to a more Western society. What do students think it would be like to live in a society that embraced traditional ways of thought alongside Western ways?

❶ *Where does Meji take Asi while Bola goes to market?*

❷ *Why does Bola want to bring Meji to his father's grave? What does she want her husband to know about their son?*

❸ *What does Asi notice about Meji's shadow? What does she notice about his watch and his neck?*

❹ *What does Meji say about his father?*

❺ *What does Bola notice outside her son's window? What does she say?*

market. Meji took Asi for a long walk through a deserted path and up into the hills. She was delighted. They climbed high until they could see the village below in front of them, and the sea in the distance, and the boats with their wide white sails. Soon the sun had passed its zenith and was half way towards the west. Asi had eaten all the food, the dried fish and the flat tapioca pancakes and the oranges. Her father said he wasn't hungry, and this had made the day perfect for Asi, who had chattered, eaten, and then played with her father's fountain pen and other things from his pocket. They soon left for home because he had promised that they would be back before dark; he had carried her down some steep boulders and she had held on to his shoulders because he had said his neck hurt so and she must not touch it. She had said, "Papa, I can see behind you and you haven't got a shadow. Why?"

He had then turned her round facing the sun. Since she was getting drowsy, she had started asking questions and her father had joked with her and humored her. "Papa, why has your watch stopped at twelve o'clock?"

"Because the world ends at noon." Asi had chuckled at that. "Papa, why do you wear a scarf always round your neck?" "Because my head will fall off if I don't." She had laughed out loud at that. But soon she had fallen asleep as he bore her homewards.

Just before nightfall, with his mother dressed in her best, they had all three, at her urgent request, gone to his father's grave, taking a secret route and avoiding the main village. It was a small cemetery, not more than twenty years or so old, started when the Rural Health Department had insisted that no more burials were to take place in the backyard of households. Bola took a bottle of wine and a glass and four split halves of kola, each a half sphere, two red and two white. They reached the graveside and she poured some wine into the glass. Then she spoke to her dead husband softly and caressingly. She had brought his son to see him, she said. This son whom God had given success, to the confusion and <u>discomfiture</u> of their enemies. Here he was, a man with a pensionable clerk's job and not a poor farmer, a fisherman, or a simple mechanic.

All the years of their married life, people had said she was a witch because her children had died young. But this boy of theirs had shown that she was a good woman. Let her husband answer her now, to show that he was listening. She threw the four kola nuts up into the air and they fell on to the grave. Three fell with the flat face upwards and one with its flat face downwards. She picked them up again and conversed with him once more and threw the kola nuts up again. But still there was an odd one or sometimes two.

They did not fall with all four faces up, or with all four faces down, to show that he was listening and was pleased. She spoke endearingly, she cajoled, she spoke severely. But all to no avail. She then asked Meji to perform. He crouched by the graveside and whispered. Then he threw the kola nuts and they rolled a little, Bola following them eagerly with her sharp old eyes. They all ended up face downwards. Meji emptied the glass of wine on the grave and then said that he felt nearer his father at that moment than he had ever done before in his life.

It was sundown, and they all three went back silently home in the short twilight. That night, going outside the house towards her son's window, she had found, to her sick disappointment, that he had been throwing all the cooked food away out there. She did not mention this when she went to say good night, but she did sniff and say that there was a smell of decay in the room. Meji said that

Words for Everyday Use

dis • com • fi • ture (dis kum´fi chər) *n.,* frustration

Quotables

"Wherever something stands, something stands next to it."

—African proverb

Vocabulary in Context

- To the <u>discomfiture</u> of many Americans at the time, the Soviets launched the first satellite, Sputnik I, in 1957.

he thought there was a dead rat up in the rafters, and he would clear it away after she had gone to bed.

That night it rained heavily, and sheet lightning turned the darkness into brief silver daylight for one or two seconds at a time. Then the darkness again and the rain. Bola woke soon after midnight and thought she could hear knocking. She went to Meji's room to ask him to open the door, but he wasn't there. She thought he had gone out for a while and had been locked out by mistake. She opened the door quickly, holding an oil lamp upwards. He stood on the veranda, curiously unwet, and refused to come in.

"I have to go away," he said hoarsely, coughing.

"Do come in," she said.

"No," he said, "I have to go, but I wanted to thank you for giving me a chance."

"What nonsense is this?" she said. "Come in out of the rain."

"I did not think I should leave without thanking you."

The rain fell hard, the door creaked, and the wind whistled.

"Life is sweet, mother dear, goodbye, and thank you."

He turned round and started running.

There was a sudden diffuse flash of silent lightning and she saw that the yard was empty. She went back heavily and fell into a restless sleep. Before she slept she said to herself that she must see Mr. Addai next morning, Sunday, or better still, Monday, and tell him about all this, in case Meji was in trouble. She hoped Meji would not be annoyed. He was such a good son.

But it was Mr. Addai who came instead, on Sunday afternoon, quiet and grave, and met Bola sitting on an old stool in the veranda, dressing Asi's hair in tight thin plaits.

Mr. Addai sat down and, looking away, he said, "The Lord giveth and the Lord taketh away." Soon half the village were sitting round the veranda and in the yard.

"But I tell you, he was here on Friday and left Sunday morning," Bola said. "He couldn't have died on Friday."

Bola had just recovered from a fainting fit after being told of her son's death in town. His wife, Asi's mother, had come with the news, bringing some of his property. She said Meji had died instantly at noon on Friday and had been buried on Saturday at sundown. They would have brought him to Kumansenu for burial. He had always wished that. But they could not do so in time as bodies did not last more than a day in the hot season, and there were no lorries available for hire.

"He was here, he was here," Bola said, rubbing her forehead and weeping.

Asi sat by quietly. Mr. Addai said comfortingly, "Hush, hush, he couldn't have been, because no one in the village saw him."

"He said we were to tell no one," Bola said.

The crowd smiled above Bola's head and shook their heads. "Poor woman," someone said, "she is beside herself with grief."

"He died on Friday," Mrs. Meji repeated, crying. "He was in the office and he pulled up the window to look out and call the messenger. Then the sash broke. The window fell, broke his neck, and the sharp edge almost cut his head off; they say he died at once."

"My papa had a scarf around his neck," Asi shouted suddenly.

"Hush," said the crowd.

Mrs. Meji dipped her hand into her bosom and produced a small gold locket and put it round Asi's neck, to quiet her.

❶ *What does Mr. Addai come to tell Bola? Why doesn't Bola believe him?*

❷ *What does Meji tell his mother as he stands on the veranda, "curiously unwet"?*

❸ *What is the crowd's opinion about Bola's claim that she had just seen her son? How did Meji die? What does Asi shout out about her father?*

WORDS FOR EVERYDAY USE

ve • ran • da (və ran´də) *n.*, open porch outside of a building

sash (sash) *n.*, frame holding glass of a window

Answers to Guided Reading Questions

❶ Mr. Addai comes to tell Bola that Meji died on the Friday before. Bola does not believe him because that's the day Meji visited her.

❷ Meji thanks his mother for giving him a chance but tells her that he must go.

❸ The crowd believes that Bola did not really see Meji, but that she is simply beside herself with grief. A window fell on Meji's neck and broke it, nearly cutting his head off. Asi shouts that her father had a scarf around his neck.

Selection Check Test with Answers

EX: What happened to Bola's first six children?

Bola's first six children all died.

1. What advice, given by Musa, the village magician, does Bola choose to ignore on the death of her sixth child?

Musa, the village magician, told Bola to mangle the corpse so that the child could not come back to torment them.

2. Who is Asi and where does she live?

Asi is the daughter of Meji, Bola's seventh child. She lives with Bola.

3. Why do Bola, Asi, and Meji visit a graveyard?

Bola brings Meji to her husband's grave so that he might know that his son is a successful, grown man.

4. What does Bola notice about the food she prepares for Meji?

She notices that he does not eat it.

5. Why, according to Bola, is Musa unable to understand Bola's appreciation of her son's life?

According to Bola, he cannot understand because he is a man.

Vocabulary in Context

- After their Dalmatian got sprayed by a skunk, the Marshalls no longer let the dog sleep on the couch but had it sleep outside on the veranda.
- On the first day of spring, Wole threw open the sash of his window to listen to the sparrows and feel the cool morning breeze.

Answers to Guided Reading Questions

❶ Asi's mother gives her a locket her father had planned to give her. She tries to remember how he told her to open it. Mrs. Meji angrily tells Asi that she could never have seen the locket.

❷ Musa the magician tells Bola that she should have followed his advice and mangled the body of her sixth child.

❸ According to Bola, Meji came back to thank her before he left for good. She is glad that she did not destroy the body of the child and allowed Meji to live for several years, that she chose instead to give Meji another chance at life. She does not expect Musa to understand why she did so because he is "only a man."

Responding to the Selection

Students might also discuss what this story reveals about differences in the roles of women and men in the society described. What tensions between the sexes seem to exist?

Answers for Reviewing the Selection

RECALLING AND INTERPRETING

1. **Recalling.** Bola's first six children died in infancy. She was told to mangle the body of her sixth child. Bola's fortune seems to change with the birth of her seventh child, because the child survives to become a successful adult. **Interpreting.** *Responses will vary.* Students might say that she keeps the body intact out of love for her child or that her instincts tell her not to destroy it. The deaths depress Bola and seem to make her feel like a failure.

2. **Recalling.** Meji tells his mother that he wants to spend his time only with her. Asi notices that her father does not have a shadow, that his watch is stopped (cont.)

 ❶

What does Asi's mother give her? What does Asi try to remember? What does Mrs. Meji angrily tell the child?

 ❷

What does Musa the magician tell Bola she should have done thirty-one years ago?

 ❸

According to Bola, why did her son come back? About what is she glad? Why doesn't she expect Musa to understand?

"Your papa had this made last week for your Christmas present. You may as well have it now."

Asi played with it and pulled it this way and that.

"Be careful, child," Mr. Addai said, "it is your father's last gift."

"I was trying to remember how he showed me yesterday to open it," Asi said.

"You have never seen it before," Mrs. Meji said, sharply, trembling with fear mingled with anger.

She took the locket and tried to open it.

"Let me have it," said the village goldsmith, and he tried whispering magic words of incantation. Then he said, defeated, "It must be poor quality gold; it has rusted. I need tools to open it."

"I remember now," Asi said in the flat complacent voice of childhood.

The crowd gathered round quietly and the setting sun glinted on the soft red African gold of the dangling trinket. The goldsmith handed the locket over to Asi and asked in a loud whisper, "How did he open it?"

"Like so," Asi said and pressed a secret catch. It flew open and she spelled out gravely the word inside, "A-S-I."

The silence continued.

"His neck, poor boy," Bola said a little wildly. "This is why he could not eat the lovely meals I cooked for him."

Mr. Addai announced a service of intercession after vespers[5] that evening. The crowd began to leave quietly.

Musa, the magician, was one of the last to leave. He was now very old and bent. In times of grave calamity, it was known that even Mr. Addai did not raise objection to his being consulted.

He bent over further and whispered in Bola's ear. "You should have had his bones broken and mangled thirty-one years ago when he went for the sixth time and then he would not have come back to mock you all these years by pretending to be alive. I told you so. But you women are naughty and stubborn."

Bola stood up, her black face held high, her eyes terrible with maternal rage and pride.

"I am glad I did not," she said, "and that is why he came back specially to thank me before he went for good."

She clutched Asi to her. "I am glad I gave him the opportunity to come back, for life is sweet. I do not expect you to understand why I did so. After all, you are only a man." ■

5. **vespers.** Evening prayers

Responding to the Selection

If you were in Bola's position, would you wish that you had never had a seventh son to die young and leave you in grief, or would you be happy to have been able to enjoy him during his brief life? Explain your reasoning.

Answers for Reviewing the Selection (cont.)

at twelve o'clock, and that he wears a scarf around his neck at all times. Meji says that the world ends at noon and that his head would fall off without the scarf. Bola learns that he does not eat the meals but throws them out the window. **Interpreting.** Bola and Asi wonder about Meji's sudden visit; his wish to avoid neighbors and a feast; his scarf; his stopped watch; his tired, pale appearance; the fact that he does not have a shadow; and the fact that he does not eat. The reader learns that he is making this final visit to his mother as a spirit, as he was killed in a terrible accident. A window breaks his neck, which explains why he wears a scarf and cannot eat. The fact that he is dead explains why he has a pale, ghostly appearance. It is possible that he cannot be seen by people other than Bola (cont.)

Reviewing the Selection

RECALLING | INTERPRETING

1. What happened to Bola's first six children? What was she told to do with the body of her sixth child? In what way did Bola's fortune seem to change with the birth of her seventh child?

   ▶▶ What do you think kept Bola from following the Musa's advice after her sixth child died? What effect do the repeated deaths seem to have on Bola and her opinion of herself?

2. What reason does Meji give for not wanting to visit with neighbors? What does Asi notice about her father's shadow, his watch, and his neck when the two go for their walk? How does Meji respond? What does Bola learn later that night about the meals she prepared for Meji?

   ▶▶ Which of Meji's actions raise questions in the minds of Bola and Asi? In what ways are these questions answered later in the story?

3. What does Meji want to tell Bola before he goes away? What does Mr. Addai tell Bola the next day? Why does Bola refuse to believe him? What does Asi do that proves she met with her father?

   ▶▶ Why do you think Meji tells his mother these things? Why do people in the crowd smile and shake their heads when Bola talks of Meji's visit? What do you think is the reason for the crowd's quiet reaction to Asi and the locket?

4. What does Musa tell Bola she should have done thirty-one years ago? What is Bola's response?

   ▶▶ Why is Bola glad she did not take Musa's advice thirty-one years ago? Why do you think Bola clutches Asi as she tells Musa that "life is sweet"?

SYNTHESIZING

5. Why did Meji return to Bola? Why does Bola suddenly realize that "life is sweet"? What effect do you believe this visit will have on Bola's life? What does Bola believe that Musa does not understand because he is a man? Why does she believe that being male might prevent him from understanding this? In what way did Bola change the course of her life by following her own instincts? Explain.

Understanding Literature (Questions for Discussion)

1. **Foreshadowing and Suspense. Foreshadowing** is the act of presenting materials that hint at events to occur later in a story. **Suspense** is a feeling of expectation, anxiousness, or curiosity created by questions raised in the mind of a reader or viewer. Foreshadowing and suspense are related, in that the materials that hint at events that are to occur later in the story often raise questions in a reader's mind and create feelings of expectation and curiosity. In "Life Is Sweet at Kumansenu," what clues provided in the opening pages of the story create suspense and foreshadow the story's ending? Were you surprised by the ending? Why, or why not?

ANSWERS FOR REVIEWING THE SELECTION (CONT.)

and Asi, which explains why he does not want to visit with neighbors.

3. **Recalling.** Meji wants to thank Bola for giving him a chance. Mr. Addai tells Bola that Meji is dead. Bola refuses to believe him because he came to visit her on the day he supposedly died. Asi tells the crowd that her father showed her how to open the locket. She then proceeds to open it when nobody else can. **Interpreting.** Meji may wish to assure her that she did the right thing by following her instincts rather than Musa's advice. The crowd believes that Bola is nearly mad with grief. The crowd is obviously stunned that Asi is able to open the locket. They seem to be confused and wonder if there is perhaps more to the story.

4. **Recalling.** Musa tells Bola that she should have mangled the dead body of her sixth child. Bola says that she is happy she did not, "for life is sweet." **Interpreting.** Bola knows that Meji's life was worthwhile and that he changed her life for the best. Asi is one joyful result of Meji's time on earth. He knew he would not be staying, but he wanted Bola to have a child who would be company for her.

SYNTHESIZING

Responses will vary. Possible responses are given.

5. Meji returned to his mother to thank her for allowing him to live. Bola realizes that "life is sweet" because she knows her son loved her, that his life was worthwhile, and that she did the right thing thirty-one years ago. *Responses will vary.* Musa does not understand the love Bola has for her son and the instincts that told her to spare her son's life. Musa could never find himself in exactly her situation. Bola followed her own instincts instead of tribal rules and as a result, she had the opportunity to raise Meji and a granddaughter.

ANSWERS FOR UNDERSTANDING LITERATURE

Responses will vary. Possible responses are given.

1. **Foreshadowing and Suspense.** The following clues hint at the story's ending: Meji shows up unexpectedly and does not wish to see anyone but Bola and Asi; he cannot eat and always wears a scarf; he does not cast a shadow; and his watch is stopped. Also, when the three are at the grave, Meji is the only one who seems to be able to communicate with the father, and he says that he feels closer to his father than he ever did before.

2. **Setting and Mood.** When Meji and Asi are going for a walk, the setting is a deserted path and a high hill from which they can view the entire village and the sea below. The mood of this scene is peaceful and happy. When Bola, Meji, and

(cont.)

2. **Setting and Mood.** The **setting** of a literary work is the time and place in which it occurs, together with all the details used to create a sense of a particular time and place. The **mood**, or **atmosphere**, is the emotion created in the reader by part or all of a literary work. In some of the story's most important moments, the author's description of setting influences mood. Think about the following scenes: Meji and Asi going for a walk; Bola, Meji, and Asi at the graveyard; and Meji standing on the veranda thanking his mother. What are some of the concrete words and phrases that describe setting in each of these scenes? What are the different moods expressed by these scenes? In what ways does description of setting influence the moods of these scenes?

3. **Theme.** A **theme** is a central idea in a literary work. Judging from the story's title and the final lines of the story, what would you identify as the major theme of "Life Is Sweet at Kumansenu"? What values are emphasized in the story?

Responding in Writing

1. **Creative Writing: Sharing a Ritual, Tradition, or Belief.** In "Life Is Sweet at Kumansenu," Nicol captures with vividly descriptive language some of the rituals and beliefs of Bola and the people in her community. Write a descriptive piece that you can share with your classmates about a ritual, tradition, or belief that is unique to your own family or community. You might write about a superstitious habit your grandfather taught you, your family's tradition of planting a new tree each year, or a holiday or religious ritual. First, try to settle on an idea by freewriting for several minutes. Remember, you can focus on something small and simple if it is important to you and potentially interesting to a reader. Once you have an idea, try to capture and share with the reader this tradition or belief using vivid details and descriptive language.

2. **Critical Essay: Foreshadowing and Suspense.** Write a critical essay in which you define the terms *foreshadowing* and *suspense,* and then outline Nicol's use of these techniques in "Life Is Sweet at Kumansenu." Go through the story and name each example of foreshadowing, identify the effect the foreshadowing produces in the reader, and explain to what event or information presented later in the story this clue is related. You may also wish to speculate whether this story would have been as effective without the use of foreshadowing.

Research Skills

Researching Author and Nation. Review the Language Arts Survey 4.12–4.18. Then, using resources available through online services or the library, look up the following names and places associated with Abioseh Nicol or Sierra Leone. Write two or three lines about each name or place.

Temne	Captain Valentine Strasser	Red Cross
Mende	Cambridge University	World Health Organization
Liberia	insulin	
Krio	United Nations	

Answers for Understanding Literature (cont.)

Asi are at the graveyard, the setting is a dark, rural cemetery. The mood is tense but becomes peaceful when Meji feels he finally communicates with his father. When Meji stands on the porch thanking his mother, the setting is a dark night with heavy rain; lightning occasionally lights the darkness. There is an ominous, scary mood to this scene. There is also some sadness and confusion.

3. Theme. Students might feel that the theme of the story is specifically stated when Bola says "I am glad I gave him the opportunity to come back, for life is sweet. I do not expect you to understand why I did so. After all, you are only a man." In this phrase is the message that Bola did the right thing, despite the fact that it went against tradition. She also states that there is no way that Musa, a man, could understand the bond she has with her child. This is also where she acknowledges that a potentially negative situation was turned into something positive.

Analytic Scales for Responding in Writing

Grading scales for Responding in Writing appear on pages 332, 333.

Answers for Skills Activities

RESEARCH SKILLS

1. The Temne are a farming people who live in Sierra Leone.
2. The Mende are another group native to Sierra Leone.
3. Liberia is Africa's oldest republic and, like Freetown, was intended to be the home of freed slaves.
4. Krio is a mixture of English and several indigenous languages of West Africa. Although English is the official language of Sierra Leone, Krio is spoken by many people.
5. Captain Valentine Strasser served as president of Sierra Leone, from 1992 to 1996. His presidency followed a period of military rule after Major General Joseph Saidu was overthrown.

(cont.)

Answers for Skills Activities (cont.)

6. Abioseh Nicol was the first black African to attend Cambridge University in England. This university dates back to the thirteenth century.
7. Insulin is a pancreatic hormone that regulates levels of sugar in the blood. Abioseh won awards for his research into insulin's structure.
8. The United Nations is composed of 160 nations and guides world policies and finances. Abioseh Nicol was an ambassador to the United Nations.
9. Nicol has worked with the Red Cross, an organization founded under the terms of the Geneva Convention to care for the injured, sick, and homeless during war.
10. Nicol was a member of the World Health Organization, which exists to promote high health standards.

PREREADING

"Tuesday Siesta"
by Gabriel García Márquez, translated by S. J. Bernstein

COLOMBIA

About the Author

GABRIEL GARCÍA MÁRQUEZ
1928–

Gabriel García Márquez was born in Aracataca, Colombia. He studied at Bogotá University, then left for Cartagena, where he began his career in journalism. Two years later, he went to Europe on assignment as a newspaper reporter. He spent many years away from Colombia. In *Leaf Storm,* his first book, García Márquez introduced the imaginary town of Macondo, the setting for many of his later works, including his epic masterpiece *One Hundred Years of Solitude.* Other notable works by García Márquez include *No One Writes to the Colonel and Other Stories, Chronicle of a Death Foretold, Love in the Time of Cholera, The General in His Labyrinth,* and *Strange Pilgrims.* In 1982, García Márquez was awarded the Nobel Prize for literature. Now recognized as one of the world's greatest living writers, García Márquez resides in Mexico City, Mexico.

About the Selection

Gabriel García Márquez is known as a pioneer of **magical realism**, a kind of fiction that is for the most part realistic but that contains elements of fantasy. His work successfully blends comedy, myth, fantasy, and satire. In "**Tuesday Siesta**," he tells the story of a woman and her daughter who journey to a cemetery in an unusual town under uncomfortable circumstances. This story displays García Márquez's talent for vivid description and for giving his stories moments of magic and intensity.

CONNECTIONS: Gabriel García Márquez and Simón Bolívar

In 1989, Gabriel García Márquez wrote *The General in His Labyrinth,* a novel based on the last years of Venezuelan revolutionary leader Simón Bolívar. Bolívar is responsible for fighting Spanish troops for the independence of countries in northern South America. People in the countries of Venezuela, Colombia, Panama, Ecuador, Peru, and Bolivia—the country named in his honor—think of Bolívar as their liberator. A writer, revolutionary general, and politician, Bolívar is known to many as the George Washington of South America. At the peak of his power, he was the president of Gran Colombia (now Panama, Venezuela, Colombia, and Ecuador); Peru and Bolivia. In this capacity he liberated slaves and urged the American republics in South America to form a union. Opposition to this union became strong, however, and his final years were bitter and difficult.

GOALS/OBJECTIVES

Studying this lesson will enable students to

- appreciate a short story by one of the most renowned writers of Latin America
- briefly explain the significance of Simón Bolívar
- define *setting* and analyze the impact of setting on a work of fiction
- write a description of a fictional village or town
- write a critical essay analyzing how imagery contributes to the mood of a literary work
- create an anthology of Latin American writing

ADDITIONAL RESOURCES

READER'S GUIDE
- Selection Worksheet 4.7

ASSESSMENT PORTFOLIO
- Selection Check Test 2.4.13
- Selection Test 2.4.14

ESSENTIAL SKILLS PRACTICE BOOKS
- Writing 1.8, 1.10, 1.20

PREREADING EXTENSIONS

García Márquez is also known for his controversial political beliefs. A friend of Fidel Castro, he has been so outspoken against "rightist" regimes that he has at times had difficulty obtaining a visa to enter the United States. In 1975, he said that he wouldn't write any more books until Chile's leader, Augusto Pinochet, was deposed. Encourage students to work in groups to research the United States' often troubled relationship with Cuba and its leader or what Chile was like under Pinochet's regime.

SUPPORT FOR LEP STUDENTS

PRONUNCIATIONS OF PROPER NOUNS AND ADJECTIVES

Ar • a • ca • ta • ca (ar´ä kä tä´ kä)
Si • món Bo • lí • var (se mōn´ bō lē´vär)
Bo • go • tá (bō´gə tä)
Car • ta • ge • na (kär tə hā´nə)
Ga • bri • el Gar • cí • a Már • quez (gäb rē el´ gär sē´a mär´kās)

ADDITIONAL VOCABULARY

intervals—gaps between two things
scrutinized—looked at very carefully
siesta—nap taken at midday in hot climates
symmetrical—showing similarity of form on either side of a dividing line

READER'S JOURNAL

Some students may find writing about being an outsider too painful, so you might suggest the following alternate activity: Imagine that in the future one of your children does not live up to your hopes or expectations. Describe such an imaginary situation and explain how you would handle it. Explain whether your feelings for your child would change in any way.

ANSWERS TO GUIDED READING QUESTIONS

1 The mother and her daughter wear severe and poor mourning clothes.

2 Oxcarts full of bananas could be seen on the narrow road. The train is traveling at about eleven in the morning.

SPELLING AND VOCABULARY WORDS FROM THE SELECTION

cassock
interminable
inscrutable

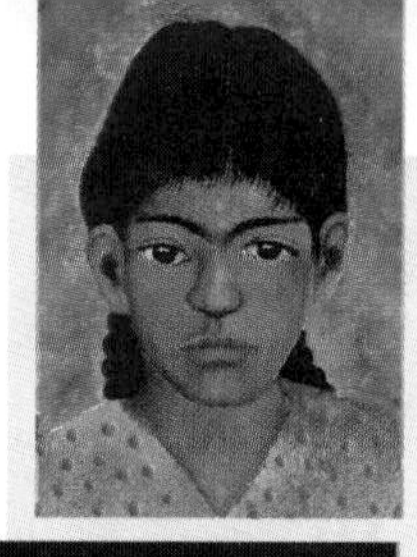

Describe a situation in which you felt like an outsider. Why did you feel this way? Why did you feel unwelcome or uncomfortable in your surroundings? What effect did these feelings have on your behavior? In your journal, explain how you felt in that situation.

"Tuesday Siesta"

GABRIEL GARCÍA MÁRQUEZ, TRANSLATED BY S. J. BERNSTEIN

1 *What do the mother and her daughter wear?*

2 *What could be seen on the narrow road? At what time of day is the train traveling?*

The train emerged from the quivering tunnel of sandy rocks, began to cross the symmetrical, interminable banana plantations, and the air became humid and they couldn't feel the sea breeze any more. A stifling blast of smoke came in the car window. On the narrow road parallel to the railway there were oxcarts loaded with green bunches of bananas. Beyond the road, in uncultivated spaces set at odd intervals there were offices with electric fans, red-brick buildings, and residences with chairs and little white tables on the terraces among dusty palm trees and rosebushes. It was eleven in the morning, and the heat had not yet begun.

"You'd better close the window," the woman said. "Your hair will get full of soot."

The girl tried to, but the shade wouldn't move because of the rust.

They were the only passengers in the lone third-class car. Since the smoke of the locomotive kept coming through the window, the girl left her seat and put down the only things they had with them: a plastic sack with some things to eat and a bouquet of flowers wrapped in newspaper. She sat on the opposite seat, away from the window, facing her mother. They were both in severe and poor mourning clothes.

The girl was twelve years old, and it was the first time she'd ever been on a train. The woman seemed too old to be her mother, because of the blue veins on her eyelids and her small, soft, and shapeless body, in a dress cut like a cassock. She was riding with her spinal column braced firmly against the back of the seat, and held a peeling patent-leather handbag in her lap with both hands. She bore the conscientious serenity of someone accustomed to poverty.

By twelve the heat had begun. The train stopped for ten minutes to take on water at a station where there was no town. Outside, in the mysterious silence of the plantations, the shadows seemed clean. But the still air inside

WORDS FOR EVERYDAY USE

in • ter • mi • na • ble (in tur′mi nə bəl) *adj.,* without end, lasting forever

cas • sock (kas′ək) *n.,* long, close-fitting vestment, generally black, worn by clergy

VOCABULARY IN CONTEXT

- On a hot day, an hour spent in a train without air conditioning can seem interminable.
- The minister wore his cassock only for services; on other days, he wore ordinary clothes.

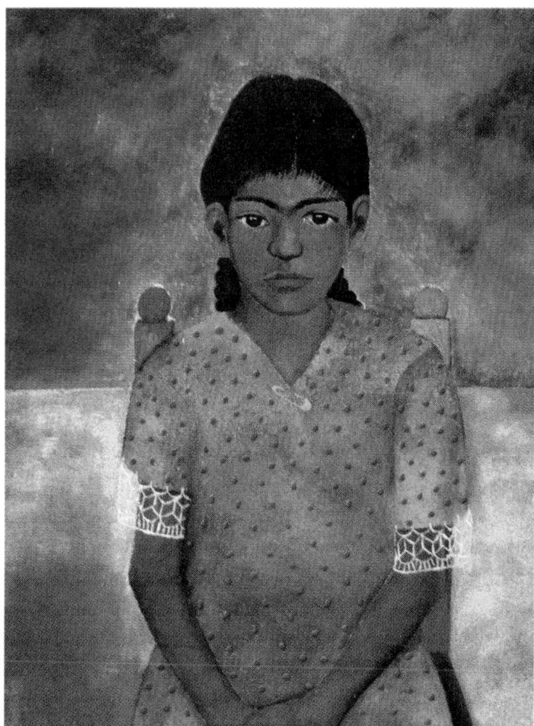

Portrait of Virginia.
Frida Kahlo, 1929

the car smelled like untanned leather. The train did not pick up speed. It stopped at two identical towns with wooden houses painted bright colors. The woman's head nodded and she sank into sleep. The girl took off her shoes. Then she went to the washroom to put the bouquet of flowers in some water.

When she came back to her seat, her mother was waiting to eat. She gave her a piece of cheese, half a corn-meal pancake, and a cookie, and took an equal portion out of the plastic sack for herself. While they ate, the train crossed an iron bridge very slowly and passed a town just like the ones before, except that in this one there was a crowd in the plaza. A band was playing a lively tune under the oppressive sun. At the other side of town the plantations ended in a plain which was cracked from the drought.

The woman stopped eating.

"Put on your shoes," she said.

The girl looked outside. She saw nothing but the deserted plain, where the train began to pick up speed again, but she put the last piece of cookie into the sack and quickly put on her shoes. The woman gave her a comb.

"Comb your hair," she said.

The train whistle began to blow while the girl was combing her hair. The woman dried the sweat from her neck and wiped the oil from her face with her fingers. When the girl stopped combing, the train was passing the outlying houses of a town larger but sadder than the earlier ones.

"If you feel like doing anything, do it now," said the woman. "Later, don't take a drink anywhere even if you're dying of thirst. Above all, no crying."

The girl nodded her head. A dry, burning wind came in the window, together with the

❶ *Why does the girl go to the washroom? What does she do just before she goes to the washroom?*

❷ *What does the woman tell her daughter she must not do once they reach their destination?*

Art Note

Frida Kahlo (1907–1954) was a Mexican painter known for her brightly colored self-portraits. Her painting style has been compared to the Primitivist work of artists such as Gaugin, as well as to the work of Surrealists. Kahlo learned to paint while recuperating from a near-fatal bus accident. She later married another well-known Mexican artist—Diego Rivera.

Answers to Guided Reading Questions

❶ The girl goes to the washroom to put her flowers in some water. Before she goes to the washroom, she takes off her shoes.

❷ The woman tells her daughter that she must not cry or drink water.

Additional Questions and Activities

Inform students that García Márquez's political sympathies lie with the poor and the oppressed. Ask students to discuss what attitude, if any, García Márquez reveals toward the poor in this short story. Tell them to cite phrases from the selection that reveal the author's attitude toward the poor as evidence for their opinions.

ANSWERS

Students should note that García Márquez seems to sympathize with, respect, and admire the poor. They might cite lines such as the following: "She bore the conscientious serenity of someone accustomed to poverty"; "She stared at him with quiet self-control, and the Father blushed"; and the last two paragraphs of the story.

Answers to Guided Reading Questions

❶ The girl wraps her flowers in newspaper. When she stares at her mother, her mother returns a pleasant expression.

❷ The mother and daughter step off the train at about two o'clock when the town is having a siesta.

❸ The priest wants them to come back later because he had just begun a nap. They can't come back later because they will miss their train.

❹ The girl and her mother immediately go to the priest's house.

Literary Note

Point out to students that the woman's dead son, Carlos Centeno, is the only major character in the story who is named. The rest of the characters are referred to as "the woman," "the girl," or "the priest." Encourage students to discuss possible reasons why García Márquez chose to provide a name only for the dead son. Tell them that there is no right or wrong answer to this question, as long as they support their opinions.

❶ *In what does the girl wrap her flowers? What happens when she stares at her mother?*

❷ *At what time of day do the mother and daughter step off the train? What is going on in the town?*

❸ *Why does the priest want the mother and daughter to come back later? Why are they unable to do that?*

❹ *Where do the girl and her mother immediately go?*

locomotive's whistle and the clatter of the old cars. The woman folded the plastic bag with the rest of the food and put it in the handbag. For a moment a complete picture of the town, on that bright August Tuesday, shone in the window. The girl wrapped the flowers in the soaking-wet newspapers, moved a little farther away from the window, and stared at her mother. She received a pleasant expression in return. The train began to whistle and slowed down. A moment later it stopped.

There was no one at the station. On the other side of the street, on the sidewalk shaded by the almond trees, only the pool hall was open. The town was floating in the heat. The woman and the girl got off the train and crossed the abandoned station—the tiles split apart by the grass growing up between—and over to the shady side of the street.

It was almost two. At that hour, weighted down by drowsiness, the town was taking a siesta. The stores, the town offices, the public school were closed at eleven, and didn't reopen until a little before four, when the train went back. Only the hotel across from the station, with its bar and pool hall, and the telegraph office at one side of the plaza stayed open. The houses, most of them built on the banana company's model, had their doors locked from inside and their blinds drawn. In some of them it was so hot that the residents ate lunch in the patio. Others leaned a chair against the wall, in the shade of the almond trees, and took their siesta right out in the street.

Keeping to the protective shade of the almond trees, the woman and the girl entered the town without disturbing the siesta. They went directly to the parish house. The woman scratched the metal grating on the door with her fingernail, waited a moment, and scratched again. An electric fan was humming inside. They did not hear the steps. They hardly heard the slight creaking of a door, and immediately a cautious voice, right next to the metal grating: "Who is it?" The woman tried to see through the grating.

"I need the priest," she said.

"He's sleeping now."

"It's an emergency," the woman insisted.

Her voice showed a calm determination.

The door was opened a little way, noiselessly, and a plump, older woman appeared, with very pale skin and hair the color of iron. Her eyes seemed too small behind her thick eyeglasses.

"Come in," she said, and opened the door all the way.

They entered a room permeated with an old smell of flowers. The woman of the house led them to a wooden bench and signaled them to sit down. The girl did so, but her mother remained standing, absentmindedly, with both hands clutching the handbag. No noise could be heard above the electric fan.

The woman of the house reappeared at the door at the far end of the room. "He says you should come back after three," she said in a very low voice. "He just lay down five minutes ago."

"The train leaves at three-thirty," said the woman.

It was a brief and self-assured reply, but her voice remained pleasant, full of undertones. The woman of the house smiled for the first time.

"All right," she said.

When the far door closed again, the woman sat down next to her daughter. The narrow waiting room was poor, neat, and clean. On the other side of the wooden railing which divided the room, there was a worktable, a plain one with an oilcloth cover, and on top of the table a primitive typewriter next to a vase of flowers. The parish records were beyond. You could see that it was an office kept in order by a spinster.

The far door opened and this time the priest appeared, cleaning his glasses with a handkerchief. Only when he put them on was it evident that he was the brother of the woman who had opened the door.

Additional Questions and Activities

In his review on page 344, Elio says that as the Latin American and Spanish cultures "violently came together," the natives held on to their own religion while incorporating elements of Catholicism. If students have parents or grandparents who come from different religious backgrounds or if they have friends with religions different from their own, invite them to discuss the following: How did your family merge the different religions? Did they experience conflict? a broader understanding of each background? For example, if one parent is Jewish and the other is Christian, do you observe both Hanukkah and Christmas? Do religious issues affect your friendships? Why, or why not? Finally, students can discuss the value of being open to other religions, and what they might learn from them.

"How can I help you?" he asked.

"The keys to the cemetery," said the woman.

The girl was seated with the flowers in her lap and her feet crossed under the bench. The priest looked at her, then looked at the woman, and then through the wire mesh of the window at the bright, cloudless sky.

"In this heat," he said. "You could have waited until the sun went down."

The woman moved her head silently. The priest crossed to the other side of the railing, took out of the cabinet a notebook covered in oilcloth, a wooden penholder, and an inkwell, and sat down at the table. There was more than enough hair on his hands to account for what was missing on his head.

"Which grave are you going to visit?" he asked.

"Carlos Centeno's," said the woman.

"Who?"

"Carlos Centeno," the woman repeated.

The priest still did not understand.

"He's the thief who was killed here last week," said the woman in the same tone of voice. "I am his mother."

The priest scrutinized her. She stared at him with quiet self-control, and the Father blushed. He lowered his head and began to write. As he filled the page, he asked the woman to identify herself; and she replied unhesitatingly, with precise details, as if she were reading them. The Father began to sweat. The girl unhooked the buckle of her left shoe, slipped her heel out of it, and rested it on the bench rail. She did the same with the right one.

It had all started the Monday of the previous week, at three in the morning, a few blocks from there. Rebecca, a lonely widow who lived in a house full of odds and ends, heard above the sound of the drizzling rain someone trying to force the front door from the outside. She got up, rummaged around in her closet for an ancient revolver that no one had fired since the days of Colonel Aureliano Buendía, and went into the living room without turning on the lights. Orienting herself not so much by the noise at the lock as by a terror developed in her by twenty-eight years of loneliness, she fixed in her imagination not only the spot where the door was but also the exact height of the lock. She clutched the weapon with both hands, closed her eyes, and squeezed the trigger. It was the first time in her life that she had fired a gun. Immediately after the explosion, she could hear nothing except the murmur of the drizzle on the galvanized roof. Then she heard a little metallic bump on the cement porch, and a very low voice, pleasant but terribly exhausted: "Ah, Mother." The man they found dead in front of the house in the morning, his nose blown to bits, wore a flannel shirt with colored stripes, everyday pants with a rope for a belt, and was barefoot. No one in town knew him.

"So his name was Carlos Centeno," murmured the Father when he finished writing.

"Centeno Ayala," said the woman. "He was my only boy."

The priest went back to the cabinet. Two big rusty keys hung on the inside of the door; the girl imagined, as her mother had when she was a girl and as the priest himself must have imagined at some time, that they were Saint Peter's keys. He took them down, put them on the open notebook on the railing, and pointed with his forefinger to a place on the page he had just written, looking at the woman.

"Sign here."

The woman scribbled her name, holding the handbag under her arm. The girl picked up the flowers, came to the railing shuffling her feet, and watched her mother attentively.

The priest sighed.

"Didn't you ever try to get him on the right track?"

The woman answered when she finished signing.

"He was a very good man."

The priest looked first at the woman and then at the girl, and realized with a kind of pious amazement that they were not about to cry. The woman continued in the same tone:

❶ *What do they need from the priest? Why does he feel that they should wait?*

❷ *What had Carlos's last words been? What had he been wearing?*

❸ *Whose grave do they want to visit? How is the deceased known to the priest?*

❹ *Who killed Carlos? Why?*

❺ *What kind of man does Carlos's mother feel he was?*

Answers to Guided Reading Questions

❶ They need keys to the cemetery, but the priest feels that they should wait until nightfall, when it isn't as hot.

❷ He said "Ah, Mother." He wore a flannel shirt with colored stripes, everyday pants with a rope for a belt, and no shoes.

❸ They want to visit the grave of Carlos Centeno, the woman's son. He had been a thief and had been killed the week before.

❹ A woman named Rebecca killed Carlos because he had been trying to break into her house.

❺ Carlos's mother feels he was a good man.

ANALYTIC SCALES FOR RESPONDING IN WRITING

(See page 346.)

Assign a score from 1 to 25 for each grading criterion below. (For more detailed evaluation, see the evaluation forms for writing, revising, and proofreading, Assessment Portfolio 4.1–4.9.)

1. Description

- **Content/Unity.** The description is of an imaginary village or town.
- **Organization/Coherence.** The description should include details in a logical order.
- **Language/Style.** The description uses vivid and precise nouns, verbs, and modifiers.
- **Conventions.** The description avoids errors in spelling, grammar, usage, mechanics, and manuscript form.

► Additional practice is provided in the Essential Skills Practice Book: Writing 1.8, 1.10.

(cont.)

ANALYTIC SCALES FOR RESPONDING IN WRITING (CONT.)

2. Critical Essay

- **Content/Unity.** The essay explains how the story's imagery contributes to its mood.
- **Organization/Coherence.** The essay begins with an introduction that includes the thesis of the essay. The introduction is followed by supporting paragraphs with clear transitions. The essay ends with a solid conclusion.
- **Language/Style.** The essay uses vivid and precise nouns, verbs, and modifiers.
- **Conventions.** The essay avoids errors in spelling, grammar, usage, mechanics, and manuscript form.

► Additional practice is provided in the Essential Skills Practice Book: Writing 1.20.

Answers to Guided Reading Questions

❶ She had taught Carlos never to steal food from people. On Saturday nights he used to box for money.

❷ People notice the two and are staring through the windows.

❸ A group of children is gathered.

Selection Check Test with Answers

EX: At what time of day is the train traveling?

The train is traveling at 11:00 A.M.

1. What do the mother and daughter wear?

The mother and daughter wear mourning clothes.

2. What is the town doing when the mother and daughter step off the train?

The town is in the middle of a siesta.

3. Where do the mother and daughter go when they get off the train?

They go to the priest's house.

4. What does the mother want from the priest?

She wants keys to the cemetery.

5. What was the woman's son doing when he was killed?

He was killed while robbing someone's home.

Responding to the Selection

Students might enjoy working in groups of three to role play a scene, as they imagine it, in the Centeno home. They may wish to choose a time when the son has come home from boxing, or the day he decided to become a thief.

What was one of the rules Carlos was taught by his mother? What did he do on Saturday nights before he became a thief?

Why do the priest and his sister want the woman and her daughter to wait before they leave?

Who is gathered outside the priest's house?

"I told him never to steal anything that anyone needed to eat, and he minded me. On the other hand, before, when he used to box, he used to spend three days in bed, exhausted from being punched."

"All his teeth had to be pulled out," interrupted the girl.

"That's right," the woman agreed. "Every mouthful I ate those days tasted of the beatings my son got on Saturday nights."

"God's will is inscrutable," said the Father.

But he said it without much conviction, partly because experience had made him a little skeptical and partly because of the heat. He suggested that they cover their heads to guard against sunstroke. Yawning, and now almost completely asleep, he gave them instructions about how to find Carlos Centeno's grave. When they came back, they didn't have to knock. They should put the key under the door; and in the same place, if they could, they should put an offering for the Church. The woman listened to his directions with great attention, but thanked him without smiling.

The Father had noticed that there was someone looking inside, his nose pressed against the metal grating, even before he opened the door to the street. Outside was a group of children. When the door was opened wide, the children scattered. Ordinarily, at that hour there was no one in the street. Now there were not only children. There were groups of people under the almond trees. The Father scanned the street swimming in the heat and then he understood. Softly, he closed the door again.

"Wait a moment," he said without looking at the woman.

His sister appeared at the far door with a black jacket over her nightshirt and her hair down over her shoulders. She looked silently at the Father.

"What was it?" he asked.

"The people have noticed," murmured his sister.

"You'd better go out by the door to the patio," said the Father.

"It's the same there," said his sister. "Everybody is at the windows."

The woman seemed not to have understood until then. She tried to look into the street through the metal grating. Then she took the bouquet of flowers from the girl and began to move toward the door. The girl followed her.

"Wait until the sun goes down," said the Father.

"You'll melt," said his sister, motionless at the back of the room. "Wait and I'll lend you a parasol."

"Thank you," replied the woman. "We're all right this way."

She took the girl by the hand and went into the street. ■

Elio Lopez, Mexico

Global Views

García Márquez's story reminds me of the small town in which I grew up. I vividly recall walking down the street in midafternoon, when the heat sent everyone into the shade of their houses, and feeling that I was in a ghost town. Magical realism works in García Márquez's stories because in Latin America, magic is part of reality. Before the Spanish *conquistadores* came, bringing Catholicism, the Latin American peoples believed in many gods. As the two cultures violently came together, the native people did not forget their old religions. Instead, they combined the rigid European forms with the magic of their ancestors.

Words for Everyday Use

in • scru • ta • ble (in skro͞ot′ə bəl) *adj.,* not easily understood

Vocabulary in Context

• Until the Rosetta stone allowed people to decipher the writing of the ancient Egyptians, scholars found Egyptian hieroglyphics to be inscrutable.

Responding to the Selection

With your classmates, discuss whether the mother in this story is an admirable character. Be sure to explain why you feel as you do about this character.

Reviewing the Selection

Recalling / Interpreting

1. From where does the train emerge, and across what does it travel? Why does the mother tell the young girl to close the window? What does the girl carry with her? What are she and her mother wearing?
   ▶▶ What can you tell about the financial circumstances of the woman and the girl? What emotions are they experiencing on this trip? What details help you to draw your conclusions?

2. Why does the girl go to the washroom? What orders does the woman give to her daughter when her daughter returns from the washroom?
   ▶▶ Why might the woman be concerned about her daughter's appearance? Why might she want her daughter to refrain from crying? What sort of uncomfortable weather are the two passengers experiencing?

3. What is going on in the town when the woman and her daughter leave the train? Where do the woman and her daughter immediately go? What do they ask of the priest?
   ▶▶ How do the priest and his sister treat the woman and daughter? What is their home like? Why do they advise the mother and daughter to wait until after sundown? Why does the mother refuse to wait?

4. What has happened to Carlos Centeno? What does the priest ask about the woman's son? What does she say about her son's character, and about what he used to do on Saturday nights?
   ▶▶ How does the mother feel about her son and what happened to him? Why have his experiences with boxing affected her so strongly? Why did the mother not mind Carlos's stealing? Why are there no tears?

Synthesizing

5. Why do the woman and her daughter take the train ride? Why do people in the town stare at them? What role does the weather—the oppressive heat—play in this story?

Answers for Reviewing the Selection

RECALLING AND INTERPRETING

1. **Recalling.** The train emerges from a tunnel and travels across banana plantations. The mother tells the young girl to close the window to avoid getting soot in her hair. The girl carries with her a plastic sack of food and a bouquet of flowers. They are both wearing "severe and poor" mourning clothes. **Interpreting.** They are most likely poor, judging from their seats on the train, their lunch, and their clothes. Their mood is one of sadness, judging from the mourning clothes and the lack of conversation.

2. **Recalling.** The girl goes to the washroom to water her flowers. Her mother tells her to put on her shoes, comb her hair, and not to drink water or cry when they arrive at their destination. **Interpreting.** The woman's pride might be behind her concern for her daughter's appearance and her desire to refrain from showing emotions. They are experiencing hot, uncomfortable weather.

3. **Recalling.** The townspeople are taking their siesta. The woman and her daughter go to the priest's house looking for a key to the cemetery. **Interpreting.** They are treated with kindness but with caution. Their house is extremely neat and tidy. They advise them to wait because the sun is so intensely hot. The mother fears that she will miss the return train.

4. **Recalling.** Carlos Centeno is shot as a thief. The priest asks if she ever tried to set her son on the right path. She tells the priest that her son was a good man and that he used to box and get beat up on Saturday nights. **Interpreting.** She feels sadness because she believes her son is a good person who had unfortunate circumstances. She would think about his pain whenever she ate the food his boxing paid for. She

(cont.)

Answers for Reviewing the Selection (cont.)

felt that stealing, as long as no one got hurt, was a better profession than boxing. The woman doesn't cry because she was proud of her son and doesn't want others to think she regretted his actions.

SYNTHESIZING

Responses will vary. Possible responses are given.

5. The woman and the girl take the train ride because they need to visit the cemetery where the woman's son lies. The people in the town stare at them because they are outsiders and have interfered with the siesta. The heat is reflective of the oppressive, uncomfortable mood in the story.

ANSWERS FOR UNDERSTANDING LITERATURE

Responses will vary. Possible responses are given.

Setting. The town is described as being sad, quiet, drowsy, and in the midst of miserably hot weather. They travel across dry plains that are cracked with drought. The houses in the village they visit are all alike—built according to the banana companies' model—and are locked from the inside. This setting is important because it reflects the oppressive, uncomfortable mood of the story. The weather interferes with how everyone in the town functions.

ANALYTIC SCALES FOR RESPONDING IN WRITING

Grading scales for Responding in Writing appear on page 343.

Understanding Literature (Questions for Discussion)

Setting. The **setting** of a literary work is the time and place in which it occurs, together with all the details used to create a sense of a particular time and place. Describe the setting of the story "Tuesday Siesta." What are the dominating features of the areas through which the mother and daughter travel? Why is setting so important in this story? In what ways does the setting reflect death?

Responding in Writing

1. **Creative Writing: Description.** García Márquez is known for his creation of a fictional Colombian village called Macondo. In his masterpiece *One Hundred Years of Solitude* he details the history of this village and its founders. Try creating your own fictional village or town. This exercise will help you to use your imagination and to practice your descriptive writing skills, and your finished description might also be helpful if someday you would like to build a short story around it. First spend some time freewriting, trying to come up with interesting ideas for possible villages or towns. As you write, think about the following questions: What will your village or town look like? Who will inhabit this place? Is it set in modern times or is it set in the past? Is the village or town quiet or rowdy? Who are its founders? When you have settled on specific details, begin to weave them into a one- to two-page description.

2. **Critical Essay: Imagery and Mood.** An image is a word or phrase that names something that can be seen, heard, touched, tasted, or smelled. The images in a literary work are referred to collectively as the work's imagery. Mood is the emotion created in a reader by all or part of a literary work. In a short essay, describe the mood of "Tuesday Siesta." Then describe how certain repeated images work together to create this mood. Use specific examples from the selection.

PROJECT

Anthology of Latin American Writing. As a class, put together an anthology of your favorite poetry and prose from Latin America. Each student should be responsible for researching and finding at least two selections. You might also include illustrations and brief histories and descriptions of the countries featured in your anthology. Try to include writers from a variety of countries, and divide the tasks necessary to create your anthology evenly among everyone in the class. When your anthology is finished, you might want to design a cover and make it available to other students at your school or local library. Below is a list of countries that you should research in your search for interesting writers.

Argentina	Brazil	Costa Rica	Guatemala	Nicaragua	Peru
Belize	Chile	Ecuador	Honduras	Panama	Uruguay
Bolivia	Colombia	El Salvador	Mexico	Paraguay	Venezuela

PROJECT NOTES

See the evaluation form for projects, Assessment Portfolio 4.12.

Anthology of Latin American Writing. After each student has found two selections, you might have groups divide up the remaining tasks. Have one group write brief histories and descriptions, another provide illustrations, another typeset the anthology, another proofread the text, and so on. You may wish to make several photocopies of the anthology so each student can have one.

PREREADING

"Rice Pudding"
by Kamala Das (Madhavikutty)

INDIA

About the Author

Kamala Das (1934–). Kamala Das writes in both English and Malayalam, a language spoken in southwest India. She uses her given name when she writes in English and the pseudonym **Madhavikutty,** her maternal grandmother's name, when she writes in Malayalam. Das's love of writing was fostered by her mother, the poet Nalapat, the scholar and poet Balamani Amma, and her great-uncle Nalapat Narayana Menon.

Das was born in Malabar, in the south of India, and grew up in Calcutta with her five brothers. She was educated by governesses and tutors. Following Nair tradition, she was married at fifteen to her uncle K. Madhava Das. They moved to Bombay and had three sons. In 1984, Das ran as an independent candidate for parliament, standing against the corruption and hypocrisy of public officials. Although her campaign received positive press coverage, it was unsuccessful. Das's first collection of short stories, *Walls,* was published in 1955. She has published other collections of stories, several collections of poetry, a novel, and an autobiography.

About the Selection

Das originally wrote **"Rice Pudding"** in Malayalam, using her pen name Madhavikutty, and published it under the title "Neipayasam." She later translated the story into English.

The theme of "Rice Pudding" is death, a recurrent theme in her works. The story deals with the impact of a sudden death on a family. Madhavikutty focuses on the ways in which a death can shatter the complacency of daily life and explores the differences in the ways that adults and children perceive and understand death. She portrays the beginning stages of mourning and the changing emotions that accompany the loss of a loved one.

CONNECTIONS: Grieving

The death of a loved one often creates a sense of emptiness and abandonment. Sadness, anger, denial, and acceptance are all part of the grieving process. Children react to death differently, depending on their stage of development. Many children do not understand the permanence of death; therefore the grieving process is often different for them than it is for adults. The grieving process is highly personal. Some people show many outward signs of grief, while others withdraw into themselves. Grieving takes time. While the initial shock, sadness, or anger related to a death may pass, later experiences, emotions, or memories may trigger new stages of grief.

GOALS/OBJECTIVES

Studying this lesson will enable students to

- enjoy a bittersweet story about death
- identify Kamala Das (Madhavikutty) as a contemporary Indian author
- define *character* and *characterization*
- identify the three main means of characterization
- describe a character and identify the elements of characterization used to create that character
- write a eulogy
- create and use a Venn diagram to organize ideas
- write a comparison and contrast essay

ADDITIONAL RESOURCES

READER'S GUIDE

- Selection Worksheet 4.8

ASSESSMENT PORTFOLIO

- Selection Check Test 2.4.15
- Selection Test 2.4.16

ESSENTIAL SKILLS PRACTICE BOOKS

- Writing 1.8, 1.20
- Language 2.55
- Applied English/Tech Prep 5.2

PREREADING EXTENSIONS

Students can research and report on the lives and works of other contemporary Indian writers including Anita Desai, Kamala Markandaya, Mahasweta Devi, Ruth Prawer Jhabvala, R. K. Narayan, Khushwant Singh, and Santha Rama Rau. Students can prepare critiques of one or more works by the author they choose and share them with other students.

SUPPORT FOR LEP STUDENTS

PRONUNCIATIONS OF PROPER NOUNS AND ADJECTIVES

Am • ma (ä´mä)
Ba • lan (ba län´)
Ka • ma • la Das (kä mä´lä däs)
Mad • ha • vi • kut • ty (mad há´və ko͝ot´ tē)
Ra • jan (rä´ jän)
Un • ni (o͞on´ ē)

ADDITIONAL VOCABULARY

comprehend—understand
condolences—sympathies
frugal—economical

READER'S JOURNAL

Suggest that students also make notes or write questions about things that they cannot remember. After students have written, they can work in pairs or small groups to discuss their responses. Be sensitive to the emotions of students who have lost a parent or other family member.

ANSWERS TO GUIDED READING QUESTIONS

❶ The narrator calls the man Daddy. The name is appropriate because that is what his children call him and it is his children who understand the importance of the man.

❷ The man remembers his wife saying, "Have you forgotten that today is Monday?" He repeats the words because they are the last words he remembers his wife saying.

SPELLING AND VOCABULARY WORDS FROM THE SELECTION

vessel

CROSS-CURRICULAR ACTIVITIES

MATHEMATICS AND SCIENCES AND APPLIED ARTS

Students can find recipes for rice pudding, chapatis, or other Indian dishes. Then students can prepare these dishes for the class to sample.

Students should read the recipe to find out how many it feeds. Working with recipes is a good way to practice fractions. Have students figure how much of each ingredient they would need to feed the class, one hundred people, or three people.

Choose one member of your family. Think about your interaction with this person yesterday. Write as much as you can remember about what this person looked like, what he or she was doing, and what he or she said. Try to remember details of the person's appearance, voice, and exact words. How did you feel while you were with this person?

READER'S JOURNAL

"Rice Pudding"

MADHAVIKUTTY

❶ *What does the narrator choose to call the man? Why is this name appropriate?*

Let us call him Daddy, the man who returned home at night after giving his wife a frugal cremation and, later, expressed his gratitude to his colleagues for their words of comfort, for after all he was called Daddy by the three children who were the only ones who knew his exact value and importance.

Seated on the bus, among total strangers, he tried to relive each moment of that accursed day. The morning had begun for him with her voice calling out to the boys. "How can you lie like this wrapped up in blankets? Have you forgotten that today is Monday?"

After waking Unni, the eldest, she had walked into the kitchen, wearing a white sari.[1] Afterwards she had brought him a large mug of coffee. Then what had happened? Had she said anything memorable, anything significant? However much he tried, he could recollect nothing that she had said afterwards.

❷ *What words does the man remember? Why does he repeat these words?*

"Have you forgotten that today is Monday?"

Only that sentence remained stuck in his thoughts. He repeated it in silence, chanting it with reverence as though it were a mantra.[2] He felt that his loss would become unbearable if he were to lose that sentence.

In the morning he had taken the boys to their school as usual. She had given each a lunch packed into a flat aluminum box. There was a smudge of yellow, probably a touch of turmeric,[3] on her cheek.

Once he reached the office he had stopped thinking of her. He had married her after a courtship of two years, against the wishes of his wealthy parents. And yet, not for a moment had he regretted his decision. There had been the usual quota of minor disasters. Children's illnesses, unpaid bills, promotions denied . . . but she had never displayed dissatisfaction or unhappiness. Gradually, she had lost interest in her own appearance. She laughed rarely. But the neighbors still thought her a pretty woman. He had been proud of her complexion.

They had loved each other. Their children had given them delightful moments. They talked of making Unni an engineer, for was he not always trying to take things apart to see if he could put them together again? Balan, the second, would probably make a good doctor, being so gentle and compassionate.

1. **sari.** Principal outer garment of a Hindu woman, consisting of a long piece of cloth wrapped around the body, forming a skirt and shawl
2. **mantra.** Hymn or portion of text in Hinduism, often repeated as an incantation
3. **turmeric.** Yellow, aromatic seasoning

Once he nursed a wounded bird back to health, feeding it with an eye dropper. And five-year-old Rajan, brave even when the lights failed, would make a fine soldier. Oh yes, together they had dreamt of a bright, happy future.

They were living in a tenement on a street where only the lower middle classes lived. She had not hung a curtain on the bedroom window, fearing that such sophistication might offend the poorer people who were her neighbors. But on the windowsill she had kept a potted rose which refused to bloom though she watered it every morning. In the kitchen she had hung her ladles and serving spoons on the yellow walls. Each day she had scrubbed her brass utensils with tamarind[4] and made them shine like gold. She used to sit on a wooden seat near the stove while making the chapatis[5] for their supper. When he got off the bus his knee hurt a little. Would it turn into arthritis? he wondered. He thought of his sons, now without a mother, and all of a sudden tears welled up in his eyes. The tears embarrassed him. He walked towards his house, wiping his face with the back of his hand. He had never used a handkerchief in his life.

Would they be sleeping, the boys, his and hers? Would they have eaten something? They were too young to comprehend death. When he had lifted her lifeless form into the taxi, Unni had stood watching in silence. Only the youngest had cried, but that because he was told he could not ride in the taxi.

No, they would not know death's merciless ways. For that matter, had he foreseen this? Had he guessed that she would, one evening, without a warning, collapse while sweeping and lie there dead and free? Yes, she had released herself from the bondage of her responsibility. He envied her her freedom. Now he was saddled with the young children . . .

He recollected how shaken he was when he spotted her lying near the broom with her mouth half-open, her pale limbs flung out in absolute disarray. He had covered her legs first. Then he had placed his ear next to her breast to find out if she breathed. He had not heard heartbeats, although he could hear his own, thumping like breakers in his other ear. Was she dead? he had asked himself. At the hospital, the doctor said that she had been dead for two hours.

At that moment, blinded by an irrational hate, he cursed the woman who had been his wife. How could she have done this to him? How would he bathe the children? How would he cook their lunches and send them to school? How would he be able to nurse them back to health when they fell ill? No, it was not possible for him to bring them up alone. My wife is dead, he said to himself. It did not sound convincing. "As my wife has suddenly died of a heart attack, I request that you grant me a week's leave to put things in order." He would be justified in asking for leave. His wife was not merely ill, she was dead.

The boss might even call him to his air-conditioned cabin to offer condolences. "I am so sorry to hear of your wife's untimely demise . . . I wish I could do something to help you, perhaps a raise, or would you take a loan from our emergency fund . . . ?"

Well, so much for the boss's sorrow. He had not known the dead young woman. He had not ever seen her grace, her long tresses, her milk-white complexion.

His loss was terrifying. He had lost the beauty of existence.

As soon as he entered the house, the youngest rushed out of the bedroom to embrace him.

"Why didn't you bring Amma with you?" he asked angrily.

"Why didn't Amma return with you?" asked Unni.

How could the ten-year-old have forgotten everything so fast? How could he have imagined that the lifeless form carried away in the taxi would revive in an hour's time and

4. **tamarind.** Substance from a tropical tree of the same name

5. **chapatis.** Flat, thin, unleavened breads of India

❶ *What emotion suddenly overcomes the man? Why does he curse his wife?*

❷ *What happens when the man thinks of his sons? How does the man feel about his reaction?*

❸ *How does the man view his wife's death? How does he feel about his responsibilities?*

❹ *What questions do the man's sons ask when he returns home? Why is he surprised by these questions?*

Answers to Guided Reading Questions

❶ The man is overcome with hatred. He curses his wife for leaving him alone to take care of the children.

❷ The man begins to cry. He is embarrassed by his tears.

❸ He sees her death as an escape from the routine and responsibilities of life. He feels weighed down by his responsibilities.

❹ The sons ask where their mother is and why the father did not bring her home. The man is surprised that the older son does not comprehend that his mother has died.

INTEGRATED SKILLS ACTIVITIES

APPLIED ENGLISH/TECH PREP

In "Rice Pudding," the parents had made plans for their children's future careers based on their skills and interests. Have students evaluate their own skills and interests and identify five careers in which they might be interested. Refer them to the Language Arts Survey 5.2, "Finding Career Information." Using the information provided, have them research one of these careers in depth. Then students with similar interests can work together in small groups to describe the career they researched and explain why they think they would or would not be interested in that career.

► Additional practice is provided in the Essential Skills Practice Book: Applied English/Tech Prep 5.2.

Answers to Guided Reading Questions

1 The father thinks that perhaps it is wrong to eat food touched by death. No, the children do not understand what has happened to their mother.

Responding to the Selection

Students may wish to discuss what they did to comfort someone who had lost a loved one. Ask students if their actions would apply to the situation described in the story.

Selection Check Test with Answers

EX. What does the narrator call the man whose wife has died?
The narrator calls the man Daddy.

1. On what day of the week did the woman die?
The woman died on a Monday.

2. How many children did the couple have?
They had three children.

3. Why is the man angry at his wife?
He is angry at her for leaving him alone with the responsibility for the family.

4. What do the man's children ask him when he returns?
They ask where their mother is and why she did not return with him.

5. What do the children eat for dinner?
They eat the meal, including the rice pudding, that their mother made before she died.

1 *Why does the father offer to make new food for his sons? Do the children understand what has happened to their mother?*

travel home? He felt angry and exasperated. He entered the dark kitchen and switched on the light.

"Balan has fallen asleep," said Unni.

"Let him sleep. I shall feed you."

He removed the lids of the vessels placed neatly on the ledge and peered inside each of them.

She had cooked a full supper for her family before dying. There were chapatis, some rice, and *dal* [lentils]. The curds were set in a crystal bowl. In another bowl he found some *payasam*, the kind she made each Sunday for her children, cooking rice mixed with ghee and jaggery.[6]

Perhaps it would be wrong to eat food touched by death, he thought.

"This food is cold. I can make some hot, savory *upma* for you," he said, smiling at the boys.

"No, Daddy, we'll eat the payasam Amma made for us," said the children.

Eating the payasam, the youngest licked his middle finger and said, "Our Amma cooks the best payasam, this is wonderful . . ."

"Yes, she's the best cook in the world," Unni smiled. ■

6. **ghee and jaggery.** Clarified butter and dark palm sugar

Words for Everyday Use

ves • sel (ves´əl) *n.*, container such as a vase, bowl, or pot

Vocabulary in Context

- When the roof sprung a leak, we collected any vessels—bowls, pans, soup tureens, and old cans—we could find to catch the dripping water.

Responding to the Selection

Imagine that you are a friend of this family. What would you do to help the father deal with his sons? What might you do to comfort them and help them to understand? Discuss possible responses with your classmates.

Reviewing the Selection

RECALLING		INTERPRETING
1. What does the narrator choose to call the man who has lost his wife? What is the man able to recall about his wife's last day? What can't he remember?	▶▶	What does this name tell you about the character? What is significant about the day on which the man's wife died? What does this suggest about many relationships? about our view of death?
2. What feelings does the man have toward his wife during the course of the day?	▶▶	What causes these changes in emotion? What fears and worries does the man have?
3. What do the youngest and oldest child ask the father when he returns? What is the middle child doing?	▶▶	Why is the man surprised by these questions? What does the children's reaction show about their understanding of death?
4. What does the man do for his children? What had the mother done before she died?	▶▶	Why do the children choose to eat the food their mother made? What might the man think and feel when he hears his children's conversation about the meal?

SYNTHESIZING

5. In what way is the woman's death connected with mundane issues in the man's life? In what way are these everyday details related to deeper emotions?

ANSWERS FOR REVIEWING THE SELECTION

RECALLING AND INTERPRETING

1. **Recalling.** The narrator chooses to call the man Daddy. The man remembers that his wife brought him coffee; said, "Have you forgotten that today is Monday?"; and had a smudge of yellow on her face as she handed lunches to their sons. He cannot remember anything else that she said or did. **Interpreting.** The name tells you that the man's family is a central part of his life, that his identity lies in being a father. Nothing is significant, the day unfolds like many others. The insignificance of the day of her death suggests that people often take one another for granted. It also suggests that while we try to make sense of death, it can happen on any day without warning or sense.

2. **Recalling.** The man is longing and anxious, sad, angry, and resigned. **Interpreting.** The changes occur as the man struggles to comprehend that his wife has died. He anxiously tries to recall her last morning as a way of making sense of her death and of remembering her life. He is angry when he thinks of his situation. He is afraid of being saddled with responsibility without her to help him.

3. **Recalling.** The youngest child asks where their mother is. The oldest child asks why the father did not bring their mother back. The middle child is sleeping. **Interpreting.** The man is surprised that the oldest son does not realize that his mother is dead and will not return. The children do not seem to understand the concept of death and certainly have not accepted the finality of death.

4. **Recalling.** The man feeds the children. The mother had cooked a full meal. **Interpreting.** The mother's meal is normal to the children. They do not share their father's superstitions about death. The man might further realize that (cont.)

ANSWERS FOR REVIEWING THE SELECTION (CONT.)

his children do not understand what has happened to their mother. He may be saddened by this realization or he might be angered by his new responsibilities.

SYNTHESIZING

Responses will vary. Possible responses are given.

5. The man worries about the things he must do, such as talking to his boss, putting affairs in order, and taking care of his children. Thinking of other things allows him to avoid facing his pain. His concerns about feeding, clothing, and otherwise caring for his children lead to a resentment of his wife for leaving him and suggest that his family's well-being is important to him. He may be afraid of failing his children without the help of his wife. These feelings are all related to the sudden void in his life.

Answers for Understanding Literature

Responses will vary. Possible responses are given.

Character and Characterization. The woman who has died was beautiful and considerate. She took care of her family and tended her house. Through direct description, the reader knows that the woman laughed rarely and paid little attention to her appearance, but was considered pretty. The woman did not hang a curtain for fear of offending her neighbors but kept a rose plant, which indicates that she valued beauty but still remained sensitive to her neighbors' feelings. She enjoyed beauty in her life. That she scrubbed her brass utensils everyday and made them shine shows that she took pride in her home. That she had cooked a meal for her family just before dying shows that her work for her family was central to her life.

Answers for Language Lab

1. The children in this story call their father Daddy; their mother has died.
2. The youngest son is Rajan; his older brother is Unni.
3. Kamala Das's mother was also a writer.
4. One of Ms. Das's influences was her great-uncle.
5. She married her uncle K. Madhava Das.

▶ Additional practice is provided in the Essential Skills Practice Book: Language 2.55.

Understanding Literature (Questions for Discussion)

Character and Characterization. A **character** is a person who figures in the action of a literary work. **Characterization** is the use of literary techniques to create a character. Writers use three major techniques to create characters: direct description, portrayal of characters' behavior, and representations of characters' internal states. When using direct description, the writer, through a narrator or another character, simply comments on the character, telling the reader about such matters as the character's appearance, habits, dress, background, personality, motivations, and so on. When using portrayal of a character's behavior, the writer presents the actions and speech of the character, allowing the reader to draw his or her own conclusions from what the character says or does. Describe the woman who has died. Identify examples of direct description and of portrayal of characters' behavior, and explain what you know about the woman based on these details.

Responding in Writing

1. **Creative Writing: Eulogy.** A eulogy is a formal speech praising somebody who has recently died. Write a eulogy for the character who has died in "Rice Pudding." Consider what kind of person she was, what she valued, what she did, and the impact she had on the lives of others. You may wish to refer to the details you gathered and the description you wrote for the Understanding Literature exercise. Your speech should praise the woman and reflect upon the effect her death has had on the people she left behind.

2. **Critical Essay: Comparing and Contrasting Attitudes toward Death.** What attitude toward death is expressed in "Rice Pudding"? Choose any other selection in this unit. What attitude toward death is expressed in that selection? Write an essay in which you compare and contrast the two attitudes. In a thesis statement, identify each attitude and state which author's presentation you find more convincing. Then use examples from each selection to support your response. Before you begin writing, you might organize your ideas using a Venn diagram, such as the one shown below. For more information on Venn diagrams, see the Language Arts Survey 1.10, "Gathering Ideas."

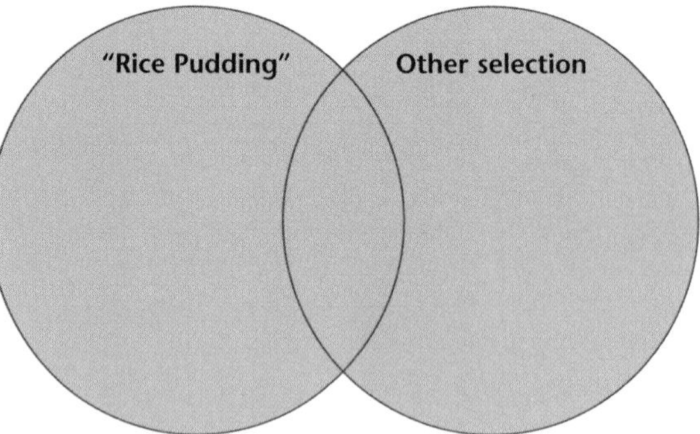

Language Lab

Proofreading for Errors in Capitalization. Read the Language Arts Survey 2.55, "Names, Titles of Persons, Occupations, and Family Relationships." Then, on your own paper, rewrite the sentences below correcting any errors in capitalization.

1. The children in this story call their Father daddy; their Mother has died.
2. The youngest Son is Rajan; his older Brother is Unni.
3. Kamala Das's Mother was also a Writer.
4. One of ms. Das's influences was her Great-uncle.
5. She married her uncle K. madhava das.

Humayun's Tomb. *Delhi, India.*

ANALYTIC SCALES FOR RESPONDING IN WRITING

Assign a score from 1 to 25 for each grading criterion below. (For more detailed evaluation, see the evaluation forms for writing, revising, and proofreading, Assessment Portfolio 4.1–4.9.)

1. Eulogy

- **Content/Unity.** The eulogy honors the character who has died in "Rice Pudding." The eulogy refers to characteristics described in or inferred from the text.
- **Organization/Coherence.** The eulogy is arranged in a logical order.
- **Language/Style.** The eulogy uses vivid and precise nouns, verbs, and modifiers.
- **Conventions.** The eulogy avoids errors in spelling, grammar, usage, mechanics, and manuscript form.

▶ Additional practice is provided in the Essential Skills Practice Book: Writing 1.8.

2. Critical Essay

- **Content/Unity.** The essay compares and contrasts the attitudes presented toward death in "Rice Pudding" and in another selection.
- **Organization/Coherence.** The essay begins with an introduction that includes a thesis. The introduction is followed by supporting paragraphs with clear transitions. The essay ends with a solid conclusion. The essay is presented in a logical order such as comparison-and-contrast order.
- **Language/Style.** The essay uses vivid and precise nouns, verbs, and modifiers.
- **Conventions.** The essay avoids errors in spelling, grammar, usage, mechanics, and manuscript form.

▶ Additional practice is provided in the Essential Skills Practice Book: Writing 1.20.

Cross-curricular Activities

ARTS AND HUMANITIES AND SOCIAL STUDIES

Have students form nine groups and research mourning rituals and funeral or burial customs of the eight countries represented in the Global Voices discussion (China, France, Greece, India, Japan, Mexico, Nigeria, and Russia), as well as those of the United States. Students should explore the following questions: How did funeral customs originate? How has the country's climate, geography, and religious or philosophical understandings of death shaped these customs? Encourage students to use the Internet and library resources to conduct their research, to prepare visual materials, and to present their findings to the class.

Additional Questions and Activities

After students have read the differing ideas about death in the Global Voices discussion, instruct them to classify each World Passport student's attitudes, using a chart like the one described below.

Title your chart "Attitudes about Death." Then list the names Avik, Denis, Ebere, Elio, Gabrielle, Jiannong, Sarah, Yumiko, and your own name down the left-hand side of the chart. Next, write the following categories across the top of the chart: fearful, non-issue, positive, sad occasion, religious view, other (specify). Check off the appropriate attitude for each student, including yourself.

Students can explore their own attitudes further in an essay, addressing these questions: Which views expressed in the discussion are most like my own? most unlike my views? Which attitudes do I find most interesting? Why? What ideas about death had I not considered before reading this discussion?

Global Voices

A MULTICULTURAL CONVERSATION

Discussing Death

Students were asked how death was viewed in their cultures.

Denis: In our country, where conditions are so difficult, it is better to have religion when thinking about death. People who are Christian Orthodox think about death as something good. They believe this life is a practice, and then you go on to a better life, your real life. People who don't have any religion just try to get through the day, because in Russia it's difficult to think about tomorrow.

Sarah: Greeks, who are also Orthodox, accept death as a part of life, although they also look at it as a liberator. It relieves a person of his or her misery but it's not the end of the person's soul.

Avik: I'm kind of enlightening myself in Hindu philosophy right now. As I understand Hinduism, death becomes a non-issue as you try to get rid of your consciousness. Physically you might die, your body becomes dirt or whatever, but you're still part of what you were. You are still part of the same universe.

Gabrielle: In France, we don't like to talk about death. Religion is not a big part of everyday life, so it makes death more scary if you don't believe in God or resurrection or whatever. Actually, we don't know what's going to happen after death, so we are scared—scared of the unknown.

Elio: When someone dies in the rural areas in Mexico, people will pass through the town in a procession, and they will be singing and set off fireworks. It's a sad event, but people are well acquainted with death so they talk about it and are very open. They're not afraid of death by any means.

Sarah: That's similar to Greece. It might not always be a happy celebration, but in the villages they will set the dead person in his home the same day the person dies, and people will come and visit with the family throughout the day. The burial is usually the same day or the next morning. A comfort meal is served at the home after the funeral, and sometimes bread and something to drink is offered to the family while they are at the cemetery. As far as mourning goes, Greeks cry out at funerals—the person's name, anything. Greeks are emotional people, not only when they grieve but when they express other emotions like happiness. Mourners usually wear black for about a year before they'll start wearing other colors again.

Yumiko: Funerals in Japan are quite sad, not a celebration. People do get together the day before the funeral to eat something and talk about the person who just passed away, but the funeral itself is very sad.

Jiannong: The ceremony in China differs depending on whether the person who dies is from the city or the countryside. If the person is from the city, the company or the government will hold the ceremony for the person. It's very open. They invite family,

Cross-curricular Activities

ARTS AND HUMANITIES AND MATHEMATICS AND SCIENCES

Sarah describes Greek people as emotional, often crying out at funerals and expressing their state of mourning visibly by wearing black for a year after a person's death. Have students research the psychology of the grieving process. What do studies suggest about an emotionally demonstrative approach to mourning, rather than a subdued one? Which approach is healthier, and why? Students might also explore recommended ways to grieve or cope with death or write a brief journal entry on how they grieved the death of a family member, friend, or pet.

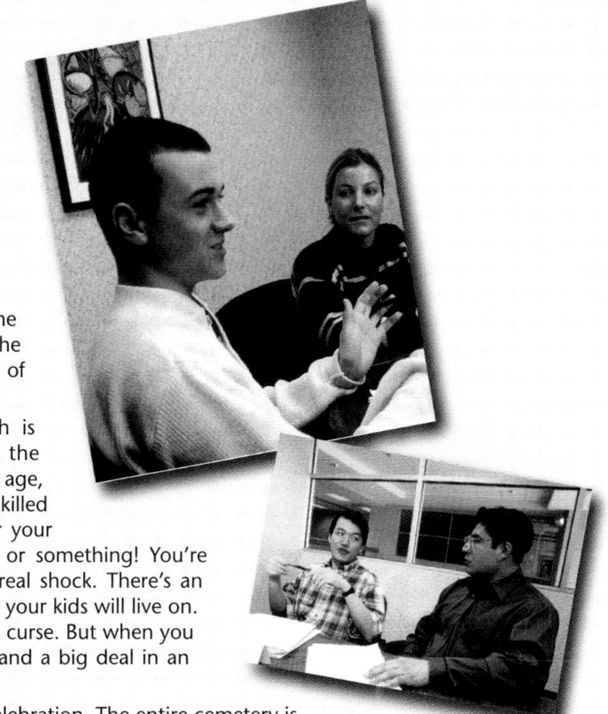

say lots of good things about him even if he did something bad. But in the countryside, the ceremony is held by the family and lots of friends participate.

Ebere: In my own tradition in Nigeria, death is treated differently depending on the circumstances. If someone dies before old age, the thought is that somebody must have killed that person. Either your wife killed you, or your enemies killed you, or a ghost killed you, or something! You're expected to grow old, so early death is a real shock. There's an attitude that you'll die before your kids, that your kids will live on. So if you bury any of your children, it's like a curse. But when you die at eighty, there's partying and feasting and a big deal in an opposite way.

Elio: The Day of the Dead in Mexico is a huge celebration. The entire cemetery is transformed into a miniature village because people build little buildings on the site of their family graves and cover everything in flowers. They bring food for the dead and for themselves, and they have a huge party that starts in the morning and lasts all night.

Yumiko: We have a season in the summer called *Obon* when, we believe, the souls of all the ancestors come back. Many families get together and have dinner and just visit with each other. Many companies have vacation during that time, so people visit their family tomb. Sometimes they invite a Buddhist priest to chant in front of the family altar.

Jiannong: It's a custom for the Chinese to visit the tombs of their relatives. We have a specific day in April for people to do this; I go to visit the tombs of my grandparents. We call that *Chiminjia*, "remembering the dead."

Avik: In Hindu cosmology, our lifespan is a hundred years. The way tradition sets it up, the first twenty-five years of your life are for education, the next twenty-five years are for material duties, which you have to take care of so that you can progress. The twenty-five years after that are for withdrawing from these material duties and helping society. And the last twenty-five years are for withdrawing into the forest and becoming a hermit. That doesn't really happen, but that's the ideal. Usually you do this with your spouse. You retire, and then your children and grandchildren come to bring you food if you still need it, if you haven't reached the stage of not needing it. But this is very idealistic; it doesn't really happen that way now. Elders still speak that way even though they don't do anything so extreme.

Additional Questions and Activities

Avik says on page 355 that a person's lifespan, according to Hindu cosmology, is one hundred years. Ask students to imagine that they each have been given a lifespan of one hundred years and that they can determine which parts of that lifespan they can apportion to certain tasks. Would they use the twenty-five-year segments for education, career and material duties, helping others, and contemplation that Avik outlined? If not, how would they divide their own lives? Have them diagram their lifespans using a circle chart (pie chart). For more information, consult the Language Arts Survey 4.10, "Reading Charts and Graphs."

Cross-curricular Activities

ARTS AND HUMANITIES

Have the class form groups of three or four students, and assign them to research and play for the class different types of funeral music. Music might include Mexican songs like those Elio mentions in this discussion, New Orleans funeral jazz, and gospel hymns. What music might be part of a Russian or Greek Orthodox funeral liturgy? a Chinese or Japanese funeral? What types of music are played at funerals in the United States? If students need help, an audiovisual specialist in the school or public library should be able to assist them; students might also use the Internet or other online resources using key words such as "funeral music" to focus their search. Once students have listened to funeral music from several cultures, ask them what each type of music expresses about death.

ARTS AND HUMANITIES AND SOCIAL STUDIES

In what ways are deceased family members or ancestors in the cultures discussed on these pages given respect? In what ways do we honor deceased family members in the United States? After discussing these questions as a class, have each student prepare a small display, scrapbook, or photo collage honoring a family member who has died. Students might want to learn about a relative who may have been previously unknown to them; at the same time, they should choose someone about whom information is readily available. Encourage students to involve their families in this project through interviews and to share the results with them when the project is completed. Refer students to the Language Arts Survey 1.10, "Gathering Ideas," and 3.2, "Active Listening and Interpersonal Communication" for information on the interviewing process.

"Life is a malady . . ."

ABOUT THE AUTHOR

Abu'l-Ala al-Ma'arri (973–1057) was a poet born in Ma'arratu, near Aleppo. Although he was blinded at four as a result of smallpox, he devoted himself to becoming a student and a scholar. He was an unusual poet for his culture and time in that he displayed skepticism about Islam.

ABOUT THE SELECTION

"Life is a malady . . ." displays the pessimism that led al-Ma'arri to become a recluse and to reject human company.

"David's Lament for Jonathan"

ABOUT THE AUTHOR

Pierre Abélard (1079–1142) was a French philosopher and poet. While teaching in Paris, he was hired by the canon of the Paris cathedral to teach his niece. Her name was Héloïse, and the two fell in love and secretly married. Héloïse's uncle was enraged. Héloïse fled to a convent and the canon had Abélard emasculated. Abélard joined a monastery and Héloïse became a nun. Abélard's theological writings were very controversial—he often was arrested or had to flee his monastic communities. Eventually he became the abbot of a foundation of nuns founded by Héloïse. On his death, his body was given to Héloïse. They are buried side by side in a Parisian cemetery.

ABOUT THE SELECTION

In **"David's Lament for Jonathan,"** David, the famed king of Israel, laments the death in battle of his friend.

"Ode on the Death of a Favorite Cat"

ABOUT THE AUTHOR

Thomas Gray (1716–1771) was a British poet and a scholar of Old Norse and Welsh literature. One of the early Romantic poets, he is most celebrated for his "Elegy Written in a Country Churchyard."

(cont.)

SELECTIONS FOR ADDITIONAL READING

SYRIA

"Life is a malady . . ."
by Abu'l-Ala al-Ma'arri,
translated by R. A. Nicholson

Life is a malady whose one medicine is death. . . .
All come to die, alike the householder and
  wanderer.
The earth seeketh, even as we, its livelihood day
  by day
Apportioned; it eats and drinks of human flesh
  and blood. . . .
Meseemeth the crescent moon, that shines in
  the firmament[1]
Is death's curved spear, its point well sharpened,
And splendor of breaking day a sabre
  unsheathed by the Dawn. ■

FRANCE

"David's Lament for Jonathan"
by Pierre Abélard, translated by F. J. Raby

If I might lie in one same grave with thee,
  Happily would I die,
Since of all gifts that earthly love can give
  No greater boon know I.
That I should live when thou art cold and dead
  Would be unceasing death;
Nor in my wraith would half a soul suffice
  To life, or half a breath.

I let the harp lie still.
  Would that I might
So still my tears and plaints!
  My hands are sore with striking,
Sore my throat
  With grief. My spirit faints. ■

GREAT BRITAIN

"Ode on the Death of a Favorite Cat"
DROWNED IN A TUB OF GOLDFISHES[2]
by Thomas Gray

'Twas on a lofty vase's side,
Where China's gayest art had dyed
  The azure flowers that blow;[3]
Demurest of the tabby kind,
The pensive Selima reclined,
  Gazed on the lake below.

Her conscious tail her joy declared;
The fair round face, the snowy beard,
  The velvet of her paws,
Her coat, that with the tortoise vies,
Her ears of jet, and emerald eyes,
  She saw; and purred applause.

Still had she gazed; but 'midst the tide
Two angel forms were seen to glide,
  The genii of the stream:
Their scaly armor's Tyrian[4] hue
Through richest purple to the view
  Betrayed a golden gleam.

The hapless nymph with wonder saw:
A whisker first and then a claw,
  With many an ardent wish,
She stretched in vain to reach the prize:
What female heart can gold despise?
  What cat's averse to fish?

Presumptuous maid! with looks intent
Again she stretched, again she bent,

1. **firmament.** Heavens
2. **Cat . . . Goldfishes.** Horace Walpole asked Gray to write a memorial for his drowned cat, Selima.
3. **blow.** Bloom
4. **Tyrian.** Purple

"Ode on the Death of a Favorite Cat" (cont.)

ABOUT THE SELECTION

Inform students that an **ode** is a lofty lyric poem written on a serious theme. **Ode on the Death of a Favorite Cat"** is a mock ode, or one that uses the same elevated language to describe a more commonplace subject—here, the death of a cat. Gray wrote this ode for his close friend Horace Walpole (1717–1797), who was also a writer. In his time, Walpole was best known for composing the first Gothic novel, *The Castle of Otranto.*

Nor knew the gulf between.
(Malignant Fate sat by and smiled)
The slippery verge her feet beguiled,
She tumbled headlong in.

Eight times emerging from the flood
She mewed to every watery god,
Some speedy aid to send.
No dolphin came, no nereid stirred:
Nor cruel Tom, nor Susan heard.
A favorite has no friend!

From hence, ye beauties, undeceived,
Know one false step is ne'er retrieved,
And be with caution bold.
Not all that tempts your wandering eyes
And heedless hearts is lawful prize;
Nor all that glisters gold. ■

GREAT BRITAIN

"After Death"

by Christina Rossetti

The curtains were half drawn, the floor was swept
And strewn with rushes, rosemary and may[1]
Lay thick upon the bed on which I lay,
Where thro' the lattice ivy-shadows crept.
He leaned above me, thinking that I slept
And could not hear him; but I heard him say:
"Poor child, poor child:" and as he turned away
Came a deep silence, and I knew he wept.
He did not touch the shroud, or raise the fold
That hid my face, or take my hand in his,
Or ruffle the smooth pillows for my head:
He did not love me living; but once dead
He pitied me; and very sweet it is
To know he still is warm tho' I am cold. ■

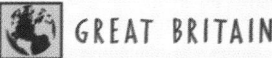

GREAT BRITAIN

"A Refusal to Mourn the Death, By Fire, of a Child in London"

by Dylan Thomas

Never until the mankind making
Bird beast and flower
Fathering and all humbling darkness
Tells with silence the last light breaking
And the still hour
Is come of the sea tumbling in harness

And I must enter again the round
Zion[2] of the water bead
And the synagogue of the ear of corn
Shall I let pray the shadow of a sound
Or sow my salt seed
In the least valley of sackcloth[3] to mourn

The majesty and burning of the child's death.
I shall not murder
The mankind of her going with a grave truth
Nor blaspheme down the stations of the breath
With any further
Elegy of innocence and youth.

Deep with the first dead lies London's daughter,
Robed in the long friends,
The grains beyond age, the dark veins of her mother,
Secret by the unmourning water
Of the riding Thames.[4]
After the first death, there is no other. ■

1. **may**. Green, flowering branches
2. **Zion.** Heaven; the heavenly city
3. **sackcloth.** Rough cloth worn as a symbol of mourning
4. **Thames.** The Thames River, which runs through London

"After Death"

ABOUT THE AUTHOR

Christina Rossetti (1830–1894) was born in Great Britain, the daughter of an exiled Italian poet and politician. She and her siblings, Maria, Dante, and William, began to write and paint when they were children. A deeply religious person, Rossetti became involved in a contemporary movement to restore elements of Catholicism to Anglican religious services, although her commitment to the Anglican Church was strong. Her first book of poetry, *Goblin Market and Other Poems,* published in 1862, was an immediate success.

ABOUT THE SELECTION

"After Death" is a poem written from the point of view of a dead woman, unloved in life yet pitied in death.

"A Refusal to Mourn the Death, By Fire, of a Child in London"

ABOUT THE AUTHOR

Born in Wales, **Dylan Thomas** (1914–1953) achieved fame both as a poet and a personality during his brief life. He published his first book of poems when he was only twenty years old and then moved to London, where he worked for the BBC and also wrote stories and plays. Thomas gave many public readings in a rich, Welsh-accented voice that captivated audiences. These readings made him quite popular, even among people who ordinarily did not appreciate poetry.

ABOUT THE SELECTION

"A Refusal to Mourn the Death, By Fire, of a Child in London" reveals a unique attitude toward death, a subject Thomas also considers in his famous poem "Do Not Go Gentle into That Good Night."

ADDITIONAL RESOURCES

Assessment Portfolio

- Vocabulary Worksheet 2.4.17
- Study Guide 2.4.18
- Unit Test 2.4.19

Essential Skills Practice Books

WRITING

- Choosing a Purpose: Creative Writing, 1.8
- Gathering Ideas, 1.10
- Writing a Critical Essay, 1.20

LANGUAGE

- Names, Titles of Persons, Occupations, and Family Relationships, 2.55
- Other Uses of Quotation Marks, 2.52
- Reducing Wordiness, 2.26
- Using End Marks, 2.46
- Using Vivid Nouns, Verbs, and Modifiers, 2.15

STUDY AND RESEARCH

- Computer-assisted Research, 4.17
- Other Sources of Information, 4.18
- Using the Card Catalog, 4.13
- Using Dictionaries, 4.15
- Using Reference Works, 4.14
- Using Search Tools, 4.12
- Using Thesauruses, 4.16

APPLIED ENGLISH/TECH PREP

- Finding Career Information, 5.2

Vocabulary Check Test

Ask students to number their papers from one to ten. Have students complete each sentence with a word from the Vocabulary from the Unit in the Unit Review.

1. Just when Jed felt that it was futile to continue the game any longer, his teammate scored a point.
2. Edgar found the question to be so silly that no retort was necessary.
3. Sven was so avaricious and money hungry that he found those who contribute to charity to be inscrutable. (cont.)

UNIT REVIEW

Coping with Death

VOCABULARY FROM THE SELECTIONS

abiding, 298	gaily, 316	retort, 315
amenity, 315	implicitly, 317	sash, 335
cassock, 340	incessant, 318	savoir-faire, 319
convulsion, 331	indulgently, 320	supposition, 318
corrugated, 331	inscrutable, 344	surreptitiously, 332
crestfallen, 332	interminable, 340	tarry, 311
decorum, 315	irrelevantly, 333	threshold, 332
despondent, 318	jocularity, 319	utter, 298
diminutive, 325	libation, 306	veranda, 335
discomfiture, 334	nought, 297	vessel, 350
disconsolately, 316	plaintive, 331	vexation, 318
exasperation, 316	prevail, 298	vivacity, 319
fervently, 304	provincial, 324	wayfarer, 311
futile, 325	provision, 332	

LITERARY TERMS

apostrophe, 312	drama, 300	nonfiction, 300
apposition, 300	foreshadowing, 337	personal symbol, 328
atmosphere, 321, 338	hymn, 300	psychological fiction, 321
character, 352	idiosyncratic symbol, 328	setting, 338, 346
characterization, 352	image, 328	suspense, 337
conventional symbol, 328	magical realism, 339	symbol, 328
couplet, 310	metaphor, 312	theme, 321, 338
dialogue, 309	mood, 321, 338	

Vocabulary Check Test (cont.)

4. Jana decided to give the lacrosse game her all, hoping that her team would prevail in the end.
5. Theresa's concentration was disturbed by her brother's incessant chatter.
6. Meg looked disconsolately through the window at the pouring rain that had destroyed all her hopes for a sunny Fourth of July barbeque.
7. We told him that if he did not follow us quickly, without tarrying, he would lose his way in the mazelike city.
8. Nicole longed for curly hair and found her straight locks an endless vexation.
9. Lyle hoped fervently to be given the lead in the school musical.
10. Raymond indulgently fed his cat nothing but fresh fish and turkey.

SYNTHESIS: QUESTIONS FOR WRITING, RESEARCH, OR DISCUSSION

GENRE STUDIES

1. Two common forms of literature that treat the theme of death include the prayer and the lament. Examine the examples of each of these literary forms in this unit, including the excerpt from The Book of the Dead and "Lament for His Son." Identify the aim, or primary purpose, that the work is meant to achieve, of both of these works. What different responses to death do these aims reflect?

THEMATIC STUDIES

2. In the excerpt from *The Death of Iván Ilyich* and the excerpt from *The Sound of the Mountain* what different reactions do the main characters have to their own mortality? Why do you think their reactions differ?

3. What visions of the afterlife are presented in the selection from The Book of the Dead, "The Death of Socrates," and "Lament for His Son"? What do the narrators or speakers of these selections believe the afterlife is like? What qualities or deeds do they think ensure acceptance into this place?

4. Compare and contrast the responses to the death of a child shown in "Tuesday Siesta" and "Life Is Sweet at Kumansenu." How do others or outsiders perceive the reactions or behavior of the grieving parents?

5. Compare and contrast the children's reaction to death in "Rice Pudding" to the adults' reactions to death in the selections in this unit. What is revealed about children's perceptions of death and about adults' perceptions of death?

HISTORICAL/BIOGRAPHICAL STUDIES

6. What does the selection from the Book of the Dead reveal about Egyptian funeral rites, Egyptian attitudes toward death, and about Egyptian religion? What does "The Death of Socrates" reveal about ancient Greek culture, including the value of friends, marriage, and family; the system of justice, and beliefs in an afterlife?

SPELLING CHECK TEST

Ask students to number their papers from one to ten. Read each word aloud. Then read aloud the sentence containing the word. Repeat the word. Ask students to write the word on their papers, spelling it correctly.

1. **interminable**
On a hot day, an hour spent in a train without air conditioning can seem interminable.

2. **amenity**
We expected our stay in Russia to be grim, but we were pleasantly surprised by the amenity of our lodgings.

3. **decorum**
Hoping to make a good impression on our hosts, we acted with reserve and decorum.

4. **exasperation**
"I can't refold this map," Reshma said in exasperation as she crumpled it into a ball.

5. **discomfiture**
To the discomfiture of many Americans at the time, the Soviets launched the first satellite, Sputnik I, in 1957.

6. **threshold**
Many people believe it is good luck for a groom to carry his bride over the threshold of their front door after they are married.

7. **vivacity**
The vivacity of the speaker kept us all enthralled even though we had expected her lecture on the history of birdhouses to be dull.

8. **plaintive**
The cat, which was caught high up in the branches of the oak tree, mewed plaintive cries for help.

9. **surreptitiously**
In "Life Is Sweet at Kuman-senu," Meji surreptitiously throws the food his mother cooks for him out his bedroom window.

10. **irrelevantly**
Ramon was marked down several points in the debate finals because he had been unable to stay on topic and had even closed his argument irrelevantly.

UNIT SKILLS OUTLINE

Literary Skills and Concepts

- Aim, 382
- Allegory, 400
- Anecdote, 393
- Apposition, 370
- Dialect, 389
- Eclogue, 376
- Extended Metaphor, 423
- Haiku, 379
- Hymn, 370
- Idyll, 376
- Image, 379, 420
- Imagery, 401
- Irony, 420
- Magical Realism, 406, 411, 415
- Metaphor, 369
- Mood, 401
- Muses, 395
- Parallelism, 370
- Pastoral Poem, 374
- Personification, 404, 428
- Point of View, 415
- Psalm, 370
- Repetition, 370
- Romanticism, 389
- Simile, 393
- Symbol, 405
- Tanka, 379
- Theme, 372, 415
- Tone, 382, 423

Writing Skills and Concepts

- Anecdote, 394
- Anticipation Poem, 420
- Critical Essay, 369, 375, 383, 389, 394, 401, 405, 416, 420, 424
- Description, 416
- Haiku and Tanka, 383
- Images of Nature and Mood, 401
- Hymn, 369
- Love Song, 389
- Pastoral Piece, 375
- Season Poem, 424
- Song Lyrics, 405

Grammar, Usage, and Mechanics Skills and Concepts

- Dialects of English, 389
- Proofreading for Errors in Capitalization, 416
- Reflexive, Intensive, and Demonstrative Pronouns, 383
- Types of Verbs, 375

Other Language Arts Skills and Concepts

- Active Listening and Interpersonal Communication, 401
- Comparing and Contrasting, 424

Unit 5 Communion with Nature

The Kirifuri Waterfall at Mount Kurokami, Shimozuke Province. *Katsushika Hokusa, circa 1831, Edo period (1615–1867). The Nelson-Atkins Museum of Art, Kansas City, MO (Purchase: Nelson Trust)*

GOALS/OBJECTIVES

Studying this unit will enable students to

- appreciate communion with nature as a literary theme
- enjoy poetry and prose that celebrate the natural environment
- describe the characteristics of hymns, psalms, and pastoral poetry
- practice creative writing in a number of different literary forms
- write a variety of critical essays

"In wilderness is the preservation of the world."

—Henry David Thoreau

361

TEACHING THE MULTIPLE INTELLIGENCES

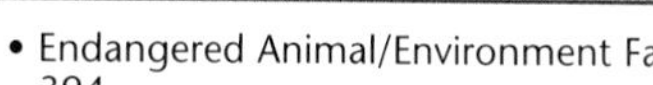

Musical
- A Closer Look at Song Lyrics, 405
- Listening to Hymns and Psalms, 370
- Memorizing and Reciting Burns's Poetry, 384

Logical-Mathematical
- Comparing and Contrasting Leaders, 424
- Discussing Violence, 425
- Effects of Colonization, 425
- Endangered Animal/Environment Fair, 394
- Environmental Summit, 426
- Researching Environmental Issues and Solutions, 426
- Town Meeting, 417

Spatial
- Celebrating Gauguin, 362
- Endangered Animal/Environment Fair, 394
- Places of Worship, 425
- Researching Environmental Issues and Solutions, 426

Kinesthetic
- Conversing about Nature, 401
- Endangered Animal/Environment Fair, 394

(cont.)

CROSS-CURRICULAR CONNECTIONS

Arts and Humanities
- Appreciating Christopher Marlowe, 377
- The Art, Architecture, and Letters of Amarna, 369
- Biographical Notes on Echoes Authors, 363
- Cats in the Arts, 406
- Celebrating Gauguin, 362
- A Closer Look at Song Lyrics, 405
- Comparing and Contrasting Leaders, 424
- Comparing and Contrasting Romantic Poetry and Japanese Poetry, 379
- Folk Tale Collections, 410
- Ki no Tsurayuki, 380
- The Life and Art of Paul Gauguin, 362
- Listening to Hymns and Psalms, 370
- Memorizing and Reciting Burns's Poetry, 384
- Places of Worship, 425
- Presenting Mistral's Poetry, 395
- Su Tung-p'o, 402
- Viewing Egyptian Art, 364

Mathematics and Sciences
- Agricultural Research, 417
- Endangered Animal/Environment Fair, 394
- Environmental Summit, 426
- Environmentalist Research, 363
- Preserving the Natural World, 390
- Researching Environmental Issues and Solutions, 426
- Researching Types of Plants, 376

Social Studies
- Agricultural Research, 417
- The Art, Architecture, and Letters of Amarna, 369
- The Babylonian Captivity, 371
- Biographical Notes on Echoes Authors, 363
- The Black Plague, 408
- China during T'ao Ch'ien's Life, 372
- Comparing and Contrasting Leaders, 424
- Discussing Violence, 425
- Effects of Colonization, 425
- Endangered Animal/Environment Fair, 394
- Environmental Summit, 426
- Folk Tale Collections, 410
- Ki no Tsurayuki, 380
- The Life and Art of Paul Gauguin, 362
- Modern-Day Romania, 421
- Places of Worship, 425
- Planning a Harvest Festival, 420
- Preserving the Natural World, 390
- Researching Environmental Issues and Solutions, 426
- Su Tung-p'o, 402
- Viewing Egyptian Art, 364

Applied Arts
- Endangered Animal/Environment Fair, 394
- Environmental Summit, 426
- Researching Environmental Issues and Solutions, 426

(cont.)

Other Selections Exploring This Theme

Rosalia de Castro
"They say that plants don't talk," page 925
Kawabata Yasunari
from *The Sound of the Mountain*, page 323
Jean de La Fontaine
from *Fables*, page 867
Stanislaw Lem
"The First Sally (A) or Trurl's Electronic Bard," page 1065

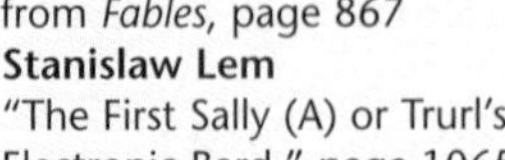

Art Note

Paul Gauguin (1848–1903) worked as a stockbroker in Paris and painted on Sundays. A collector of Impressionist paintings, Gauguin took every opportunity to take part in Impressionist exhibitions.

Gauguin eventually left his family and his job and moved to Brittany. He left for Tahiti in 1891, spending the rest of his life in the South Sea Islands. Gauguin's last years were filled with struggle, including poverty, illness, and problems with Tahitian authorities.

The majority of Gauguin's earlier work can be classified as Impressionist. Later, however, his rejection of Western civilization led him to settle in Tahiti and adopt a Primitivist style, depicting the simplicity of everyday life among a sensual, nontechnological people. His work has deeply influenced twentieth-century art.

Cross-curricular Activities

Students might want to try one of the following activities:

- Go to a library or museum to find examples of the work of Gaugin. Then freewrite about his style. What is unique about the way in which he renders the natural world in his paintings?
- Create a painting in the style of Gaugin. Share your work with the rest of the class.

UNIT 5

Theme:
Communion with Nature

Nafea Faa. Paul Gauguin, 1892

If you walk into any art museum, read song lyrics and poetry of different ages, or examine the religions and philosophies of cultures all over the world, you will understand that the beauty and power of nature has long been for people a source of wonder and mystery. The natural world has also encouraged human creativity and the search for inner peace.

In this unit, you will read pieces with different perspectives on nature. You will read an ancient Egyptian hymn in praise of the sun and a poem about turning to nature to find peace within a busy world. Japanese haiku and tanka poems will invite you to notice simple but striking images in nature, and a Scottish song lyric will help you to associate natural images with feelings of love and romance. You will read about the tragedy of animal abuse and the problems of urbanization, and you will see humankind's dependence on the natural world expressed in poems that anticipate the harvest and turn to nature for comfort during difficult times. Works of art and literature that take nature as their theme explore questions about the natural world and attempt to capture its beauty and celebrate the gifts of this bountiful planet.

TEACHING THE MULTIPLE INTELLIGENCES (CONT.)

Interpersonal
- Appreciating Christopher Marlowe, 377
- The Art, Architecture, and Letters of Amarna, 369
- A Closer Look at Song Lyrics. 405
- Comparing and Contrasting Leaders, 424
- Conversing about Nature, 401
- Discussing Violence, 425
- Effects of Colonization, 425
- Endangered Animal/Environment Fair, 394
- Environmental Summit, 426
- Environmentalist Research, 363
- Listening to Hymns and Psalms, 370
- Modern-Day Romania, 421
- Planning a Harvest Festival, 420
- Presenting Mistral's Poetry, 395
- Preserving the Natural World, 390
- Researching Types of Plants, 376
- Town Meeting, 417

Echoes:

Communion with Nature

Know you the land where the lemon-trees bloom? In the dark foliage the gold oranges glow; a soft wind hovers from the sky, the myrtle is still and the laurel stands tall—do you know it well? There, there, I would go, O my beloved, with thee!

—Johann Wolfgang von Goethe

Nature is a temple whose living colonnades
Breath forth a mystic speech in fitful sighs;
Man wanders among symbols in those glades
Where all things watch him with familiar eyes.

—Charles Baudelaire

Over increasingly large areas of the United States, spring now comes unheralded by the return of the birds, and the early mornings are strangely silent where once they were filled with the beauty of bird song.

—Rachel Carson

When we depend less on industrially produced consumer goods, we can live in quiet places. Our bodies become vigorous; we discover the serenity of living with the rhythms of the earth. We cease oppressing one another.

—Alicia Bay Laurel

I have learned
To look on nature, not as in the hour
Of thoughtless youth; but hearing often-times
The still, sad music of humanity,
Nor harsh nor grating, though of ample power
To chasten and subdue. And I have felt
A presence that disturbs me with the joy
Of elevated thoughts; a sense sublime
Of something far more deeply interfused,
Whose dwelling is the light of setting suns,
And the round ocean and the living air,
And the blue sky, and in the mind of man.

—William Wordsworth

We abuse land because we regard it as a commodity belonging to us. When we see land as a community to which we belong, we may begin to use it with love and respect.

—Aldo Leopold

Only people who live on cement streets and carpeted floors can ever forget the inherent drama in nature and, by mere habits of city living, become nature-blind.

—Lin Yutang

A man should wander about treating all creatures as he himself would be treated.

—Sutra-Kritange Sutra

Biographical Notes

Johann Wolfgang von Goethe (1749–1832) was a German poet and dramatist who greatly influenced European literature, especially with his celebrated work *Faust*.

Charles Baudelaire (1821–1867) was a French poet and essayist whose poetry is known for its morbid yet beautiful and evocative language. His most famous collection of poems is *Les Fleurs du mal* (*Flowers of Evil.*)

Rachel Carson (1907–1964) developed a deep interest in wildlife when she was a child. In her long career as a biologist, Carson worked for the U.S. Bureau of Fisheries and the U.S. Fish and Wildlife Service. She won the National Book Award for *The Sea Around Us*. Her book *Silent Spring* awakened the world to the dangers of environmental pollution.

Alicia Bay Laurel (1949–) is an American naturalist, writer, and illustrator.

William Wordsworth (1770–1850) is said to have influenced English poetry more than any other writer after William Shakespeare. For information on Wordsworth, see page 904.

Aldo Leopold (1887–1948) graduated from Yale Forestry School, became supervisor of the Carson National Forest in New Mexico, taught at the University of Wisconsin, and helped found the Wilderness Society. Throughout his career as a conservationist, Leopold urged a responsible land ethic, confronting issues of economic and industrial expansion and wasteful land use.

Lin Yutang (1895–1976) was born in China but moved to the United States in about 1928. Lin wrote many volumes on China, including *My Country and My People*. He also wrote several novels and translated and edited many works.

(cont.)

Additional Questions and Activities

Students can try one of the following activities:

• Choose a favorite song, poem, story, essay, painting, or photograph that celebrates nature. Why does this work appeal to you?

• Research a famous environmentalist or a writer or painter whose works focus on nature. Write a paper or prepare a presentation and share your work with your class.

Biographical Notes (cont.)

Sutra-Kritange Sutra. Part of the main body of the classical literature of India, Sutras contain principles, rules, and statements of truth written in the final stages of the Vedic period in India (c. 500–c. 200 BC).

ADDITIONAL RESOURCES

READER'S GUIDE

- Selection Worksheet 5.1

ASSESSMENT PORTFOLIO

- Selection Check Test 2.5.1
- Selection Test 2.5.2

ESSENTIAL SKILLS PRACTICE BOOKS

- Writing 1.8, 1.20

PREREADING EXTENSIONS

You might ask students to go to a library, a bookstore, or, if possible, an art museum to find and view examples of Egyptian art from the period of Akhenaten. If students will be doing their research in a library, suggest that they look for pictures in encyclopedias or art history books. After students have seen examples of Egyptian art from this period, ask them to write a brief essay describing their impressions of the art. If you have the time and materials, students might enjoy completing their own art projects, imitating the style of this period.

SUPPORT FOR LEP STUDENTS

PRONUNCIATIONS OF PROPER NOUNS AND ADJECTIVES

Akh • en • at • en (äk ə nat´'n)

ADDITIONAL VOCABULARY

bedazzling—confusing because brilliant
exalted—raised high in honor
majestic—grand
perceive—observe and understand

PREREADING

from "Hymn to the Sun"
by Akhenaten, translated by John L. Foster

EGYPT

About the Author

Akhenaten (1375–1358 BC). Although he began his reign as a pharaoh named Amenhotep IV, the ninth pharaoh of the eighteenth Egyptian dynasty is best known as Akhenaten, or "He Who Serves Aten," a name he chose for himself. Aten was a sun god who was represented as a thin, flat circle, or disk, resembling the sun. Akhenaten claimed to be the son of Aten, and he and his wife Nefertiti worshiped Aten as the "sole god," developing an early and short-lived form of monotheism—the belief that there is only one god. Soon after he ascended the throne, the pharaoh abandoned the temples to the old sun god Ra, or Re, and built new temples to Aten. Akhenaten also moved his capital from Thebes to Amarna, which he renamed Akhetaten, or "The Place of Aten's Effective Power." Unlike the old temples, the new temples of Aten were open to the sunlight. The new religion itself was less austere than the old and took shape as an ecstatic form of nature worship that focused on the sun's life-giving power. Akhenaten had the names of other gods and occasionally even the plural phrase *the gods* hacked from inscriptions in many monuments. Akhenaten's new monotheistic religion did not spread to the Egyptian people. Soon after his death, the Egyptian people returned to worshipping their old gods, and priests reclaimed their power. Ironically, just as Akhenaten tried to obliterate the names of Amon, Ra, and the other gods, those who came after him tried to obliterate both the name *Akhenaten* and all references to Aten worship.

About the Selection

Akhenaten's **"Hymn to the Sun"** was found on the wall of a royal scribe's tomb. In this hymn, Akhenaten praises the sun disk as the giver of all life. Sun worship was an ancient tradition in Egypt, whose citizens had long associated the rising of the sun with life and the setting of the sun with death, believing that the sun god Ra traveled at night to the underworld, the realm of the dead. It was also traditional for a pharaoh to view himself as the son of a sun god; most pharaohs, however, claimed to be descended from Ra. What was new and unusual about Akhenaten's hymn was that it identified Aten as the "one God" who has many different incarnations, thus introducing a form of monotheism. In the hymn, Akhenaten also describes himself as an intermediary between Aten and the Egyptian people.

CONNECTIONS: Egyptian Art During Akhenaten's Reign

The radical nature of Akhenaten's reign is apparent in the art of the period, which is more realistic than the art of preceding periods. Akhenaten is presented with all his bodily flaws in scenes depicting his everyday life with his wife and daughters. The sun god, Aten, is depicted realistically as a thin, flat circle, while both before and after Akhenaten's reign, the sun god is depicted as a crowned man, as a falcon or other animal, or as a combination of man and animal.

GOALS/OBJECTIVES

Studying this lesson will enable students to

- appreciate an ancient Egyptian hymn in praise of the sun
- discuss Akhenaten, the ninth pharaoh of the eighteenth Egyptian dynasty, and the period in which he lived
- discuss ancient Egyptian art
- define the literary term *metaphor*
- write a hymn and a critical essay
- complete a project on the art, architecture, and letters of Amarna

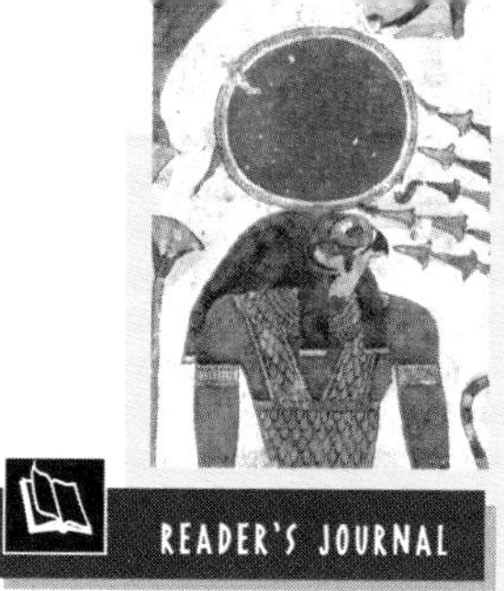

Imagine that you know no scientific explanation for the rising and the setting of the sun. What might you think the sun is? How might you explain its rising and setting? Where might you think the sun goes when it sets?

READER'S JOURNAL

FROM

"Hymn to the Sun"

AKHENATEN, TRANSLATED BY JOHN L. FOSTER

I

When in splendor you first took your throne
high in the <u>precinct</u> of heaven,
O living God,
life truly began!
Now from eastern horizon risen and streaming
you have flooded the world with your beauty.
You are majestic, awesome, bedazzling, exalted,
overlord over all earth,
yet your rays, they touch lightly, <u>compass</u> the lands
to the limits of all your creation.
There in the Sun, you reach to the farthest of those
you would gather in for your Son,[1]
whom you love;
Though you are far, your light is wide upon earth;
and you shine in the faces of all
who turn to follow your journeying.

II

When you sink to rest below western horizon
earth lies in darkness like death,

1. **Son.** Akhenaten is referring to himself as the son of Aten, the sun-disk.

1 According to the speaker, when did life begin?

2 How far does the sun reach? What do you think Akhenaten means by this statement?

WORDS FOR EVERYDAY USE

pre • cinct (prē´ siŋkt´) *n.,* any limited area; boundary

com • pass (kum´ ps) *vt.,* go around, make a circuit; reach successfully

READER'S JOURNAL

As an alternate activity, you might ask students to explain another act or event in nature, such as an earthquake, thunderstorm, or the growth of flowers and trees. They should imagine that they know of no scientific explanations for the act or event.

ANSWERS TO GUIDED READING QUESTIONS

1 According to the speaker, life began when the "living God" took his throne high in heaven.

2 The sun reaches "to the farthest of those / you would gather in for your Son." Akhenaten means that the sun shines over all the lands and peoples whom Aten, the sun-disk, wishes to make part of the Egyptian empire.

SPELLING AND VOCABULARY WORDS FROM THE SELECTION

compass
incarnation
precinct

VOCABULARY IN CONTEXT

- In which <u>precinct</u> of the city does your aunt work as a police officer?
- My brother and I will start in the harbor, then <u>compass</u> the vast ocean in our boat.

Answers to Guided Reading Questions

➊ According to the speaker, after the sun goes down, lions come out of their caves, snakes bite, darkness muffles all sound, and the sun disk Aten, "he who created all things," lies in a tomb.

➋ According to the speaker there is only one god, Aten, who has many possible incarnations.

ANALYTIC SCALES FOR RESPONDING IN WRITING

(SEE PAGE 369.)

Assign a score from 1 to 25 for each grading criterion below. (For more detailed evaluation, see the evaluation forms for writing, revising, and proofreading, Assessment Portfolio 4.1–4.9.)

1. Hymn

- **Content/Unity.** The hymn focuses on an aspect of the natural world that the writer particularly appreciates and admires.
- **Organization/Coherence.** The hymn praises its subject and ends enthusiastically and joyfully.
- **Language/Style.** The hymn uses vivid and precise nouns, verbs, and modifiers.
- **Conventions.** The hymn avoids errors in spelling, grammar, usage, mechanics, and manuscript form.

▶ Additional practice is provided in the Essential Skills Practice Book: Writing 1.8.

➊ *What happens after the sun goes down, according to the speaker?*

Sleepers are still in bedchambers, heads veiled,
eye cannot spy a companion;
All their goods could be stolen away,
heads heavy there, and they never knowing!
Lions come out from the deeps of their caves,
snakes bite and sting;
Darkness muffles, and earth is silent:
he who created all things lies low in his tomb.

III

Earth-dawning mounts the horizon,
glows in the sun-disk as day:
You drive away darkness, offer your arrows of shining
and the Two Lands[2] are lively with morningsong.
Sun's children awaken and stand,
for you, golden light, have upraised the sleepers;
Bathed are their bodies, who dress in clean linen,
their arms held high to praise your Return.
Across the face of the earth
they go to their crafts and professions.

◆ ◆ ◆

XI

➋ *According to the speaker, how many gods are there?*

You are the one God,
shining forth from your possible incarnations
as Aten, the Living Sun,
Revealed like a king in glory, risen in light,
now distant, now bending nearby.
You create the numberless things of this world
from yourself, who are One alone—
cities, towns, fields, the roadway, the River,[3]
And each eye looks back and beholds you
to learn from the day's light perfection.
O God, you are in the Sun-disk of Day.
Over-Seer of all creation
—your legacy
passed on to all who shall ever be;
For you fashioned their sight, who perceive your universe,
that they praise with one voice
all your labors.

2. **Two Lands.** Upper and lower Egypt
3. **River.** Nile River

Words for Everyday Use

in • car • na • tion (in kär nā´ shen) *n.,* any person or animal serving as the embodiment of a god or spirit

Vocabulary in Context

- Many people believe that this generous man is the incarnation of kindness and goodness.

Painted stele of Lady Taperet: Taperet before Re-Harakhte.
Lower Egypt (Libya), 22nd dynasty, 950–730 BC.
Louvre, Paris, France.
Giraudon/Art Resource, NY

XII

And you are in my heart;
there is no other who truly knows you
but for your son, Akhenaten.
May you make him wise with your inmost counsels,
wise with your power,
that earth may aspire to your godhead,[4]
its creatures fine as the day you made them.
Once you rose into shining, they lived;
when you sink to rest, they shall die.
For it is you who are Time itself,
the span of the world;
life is by means of you.
Eyes are filled with Beauty
until you go to your rest;
All work is laid aside
as you sink down the western horizon.
Then, Shine reborn! Rise splendidly!
my Lord, let life thrive for the King!
For I have kept pace with your every footstep
since you first measured ground for the world.
Lift up the creatures of earth for your Son
who came forth from your Body of Fire! ■

❶ *What does Akhenaten ask of Aten?*

❷ *To what does the speaker compare the sun-disk?*

4. **godhead.** Godhood, divinity

Answers to Guided Reading Questions

❶ Akhenaten asks that Aten make him wise with his counsels and power.

❷ The speaker compares the sun-disk to "Time itself."

ANALYTIC SCALES FOR RESPONDING IN WRITING

(SEE PAGE 369.)

Assign a score from 1 to 25 for each grading criterion below. (For more detailed evaluation, see the evaluation forms for writing, revising, and proofreading, Assessment Portfolio 4.1–4.9.)

2. Critical Essay

- **Content/Unity.** The essay focuses on the question of whether the sun in "Hymn to the Sun," is presented as a life-giving force or as a personified god who rules the universe as a king would.
- **Organization/Coherence.** The essay begins with an introduction that includes the thesis of the essay. The introduction is followed by supporting paragraphs with clear transitions. The essay ends with a solid conclusion.
- **Language/Style.** The essay uses vivid and precise nouns, verbs, and modifiers.
- **Conventions.** The essay avoids errors in spelling, grammar, usage, mechanics, and manuscript form.

► Additional practice is provided in the Essential Skills Practice Book: Writing 1.20.

Additional Questions and Activities

Ask students to review About the Selection on the Prereading page, which describes Akhenaten's hymn as unusual because it identifies Aten as the "one God." Therefore, this poem can be seen as an expression of monotheism.

Ask students to look up the words *monotheism*, the belief and worship of one god, and *polytheism*, the belief and worship of many gods. Then as a class, discuss different religions with which students are familiar. Ask them if the religions they mention are monotheistic or polytheistic.

As an extra research project, you might ask students to find specific examples of each type of religion, both monotheistic and polytheistic, in the library.

RESPONDING TO THE SELECTION

Ask students to form pairs to role play the conversation between themselves and Akhenaten. Students may take turns playing Akhenaten.

ANSWERS FOR REVIEWING THE SELECTION

RECALLING AND INTERPRETING

1. **Recalling.** According to the speaker, after the sun sets the "earth lies in darkness like death," people sleep in dark chambers, lions come out of their caves, snakes bite, darkness muffles all sound, and "he who created all things" lies in a tomb. The speaker compares darkness and night to death and to tombs. **Interpreting.** The speaker uses such images to express that night is a time of sadness, despair, and gloom.

2. **Recalling.** The speaker calls the Egyptians "Sun's children." The Egyptians awaken, bathe, dress in clean linen, stand in the sun, and hold their arms high to praise the sun's return. **Interpreting.** Egyptians may have viewed the sun as a god and as creator of all things because the sun is the most noticeable feature of the Egyptian environment and the Egyptians realized that growing crops and experiencing life itself would be impossible without the sun.

3. **Recalling.** The speaker describes Aten as the "one God, shining forth from your possible incarnations," as "the Living Sun," as a "king in glory," as the creator of "the numberless things of this world," as "One alone," as "Sun-disk of Day," and as "Over-Seer of all creation." No gods exist other than Aten, according to the speaker. **Interpreting.** Some Egyptians may have been shocked; others may have accepted this description of Aten, under the assumption that their traditional gods were part of the "possible incarnations" of Aten.

4. **Recalling.** Only Akhenaten truly knows Aten. Akhenaten claims to be the son of Aten. Akhenaten claims to have come forth from Aten's "Body of Fire." **Interpreting.** People would be more likely (cont.)

Responding to the Selection

If you could go back in time to speak with Akhenaten, what questions would you ask him about his religion, Aten worship? What information might you share with him about the sun? What do you think Akhenaten's reaction might be?

Reviewing the Selection

RECALLING / INTERPRETING

1. According to the speaker, what happens to the earth after the sun sets? To what does the speaker compare darkness and night? ▶▶ How does the speaker feel about the time between sunset and sunrise? How is this feeling communicated in the poem?

2. In stanza 3, what does the speaker call the Egyptian people? What do the Egyptians do at dawn to praise the sun? ▶▶ Why might the Egyptians have viewed the sun as a god and creator of all things? In what way is the sun responsible for life, and how might the Egyptians have observed this?

3. In stanza 11, in what way does the speaker describe Aten? According to the speaker, how many gods exist other than Aten? ▶▶ In what way might Egyptians, who worshiped many gods and who believed that Atum, Ra (or Re), or Ptah created the world, have reacted to this description of Aten?

4. Who is the only person who "truly knows" Aten? In what way is this person related to Aten? From what does the speaker claim to have come forth? ▶▶ Why might claiming close kinship to and knowledge of a god have given a pharaoh more power?

SYNTHESIZING

5. Scholars have long debated the extent to which Akhenaten's religion was monotheistic. Based upon this hymn, to what extent do you believe that his religion was monotheistic? Does Akhenaten see Aten only as the one god of Egypt or as the one god of the whole world? The Egyptian people had long worshiped the pharaoh as the divine son of Ra or Re and as the incarnation of Horus. Explain whether you think the Egyptians would have been likely to worship Akhenaten as divine, given that he claimed to be the son of a god. Why do you think Akhenaten's religion failed to catch on? In other words, why might the Egyptians reject Akhenaten's religion in favor of their former, polytheistic beliefs?

ANSWERS FOR REVIEWING THE SELECTION (CONT.)

to obey a pharaoh who was semi-divine and who was the only person who could understand a god's will.

SYNTHESIZING

Responses will vary. Possible responses are given.

5. Some students may say that Akhenaten's personal religion seems monotheistic, as expressed in the hymn. Akhenaten seems to think that people in other lands also share the life-giving glory of Aten. By claiming that he was the son of Aten, Akhenaten was following Egyptian tradition and practically ensuring that he too would be worshiped as a god alongside Aten. Students might say the new religion didn't succeed because people were more comfortable with their earlier traditions. Also, they may have found it hard to accept monotheism with Aten as the sole god when Akhenaten was also claiming divinity.

Understanding Literature (Questions for Discussion)

Metaphor. A **metaphor** is a figure of speech in which one thing is spoken or written about as if it were another. Throughout this hymn, the sun is described as if it were a unit of measure. Identify lines in which the sun is described in this way. Why do you think the poet may have chosen this metaphor for the sun?

Responding in Writing

1. Creative Writing: Hymn. A hymn is a song or verse of praise (see Insights: Hymns and Psalms, page 370). Think of an aspect of the natural world that you particularly appreciate or admire and write a hymn in praise of this thing. Try to end your hymn as enthusiastically and joyfully as Akhenaten ended his. Although you may wish to experiment with rhyme and meter, remember that you can also write a free-verse hymn if you wish.

2. Critical Essay: Personification. Personification is a figure of speech in which an idea, animal, or thing is described as if it were a person. It has been said that "the Egyptians might—and did—personify almost anything." Akhenaten's religion was a departure from typical sun worship in that Akhenaten did not worship the sun as an animal, person, or combination of animal and human, but worshipped the sun as a thin, flat circle. While Akhenaten includes more realistic images of the sun disk in this hymn, he also personifies the sun. Write a critical essay focusing upon the following question: In "Hymn to the Sun," is the sun presented more as a life-giving force or as a personified god who rules the universe as a king would?

Project

The Art, Architecture, and Letters of Amarna. Because Akhenaten chose to build his capital city of Akhetaten on a new site, and because the city was deserted after Akhenaten's death, the ruins and tombs of Akhetaten in present-day Tell el-Amarna offer archaeologists a unique view of an ancient Egyptian city. In addition, the discovery of the Amarna Letters, three hundred records found in 1887, provided valuable information about Egypt's role as an international power during Akhenaten's reign. The art of Akhetaten evoked interest because it marked a departure from the typically idealized, static, and formal art of earlier periods. The unconventional naturalistic style that characterized art in Akhetaten has come to be known as the Amarna style.

Working in small groups, choose one of the following elements of the city to research: the physical layout of Akhetaten (also spelled Akhetaton), the Great Temple of the Aten (or Aton), depictions of Akhenaten's physical features, major artistic finds such as the portrait bust of Nefertiti and depictions of Akhenaten and his family, Akhenaten's family tomb, depictions of Tutankhamen (the Amarna style influenced the art of Akhenaten's follower), or the Amarna Letters. Possible sources of information on these topics include libraries, museums, and the Internet. Each group should then present its findings to the class. Try to find photographs, illustrations, or slides to make your presentation more vivid and appealing.

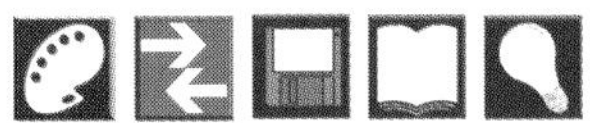

Answers for Understanding Literature

Responses will vary. Possible responses are given.

Metaphor. The sun is described as if it were a unit of measure in the following lines: "your rays . . . compass the lands to the limits of all your creation"; "it is you who are Time itself, / the span of the world"; and "For I have kept pace with your every footstep / since you first measured ground for the world." The poet may have described the sun in this way because, as creator of the world, Aten would know the measure of the world in both distance and time. Also, the poet may have believed that, as the sun provides life for the planet, the sun determines the lifespan of its inhabitants.

Analytic Scales for Responding in Writing

Grading scales for Responding in Writing appear on pages 366, 367.

Selection Check Test with Answers

EX. To whom is this hymn addressed?
It is addressed to the sun.

1. What happened when the sun took its throne high in heaven?
When the sun took its throne, "life truly began."

2. What animals are active after the sun sets?
Lions and snakes are active.

3. What do the "Sun's children" do when the sun rises?
They awaken and stand.

4. What does the speaker say Aten, the sun-disk, created?
The speaker says that Aten created "the numberless things of the world."

5. According to the speaker, who "truly knows" Aten, the sun-disk?
Akhenaten is the only one who truly knows Aten.

Project Notes

See the evaluation form for projects, Assessment Portfolio 4.12.

The Art, Architecture, and Letters of Amarna. After each group has chosen a different element of the city to research, encourage students to get together in their groups and hold planning meetings. During their meetings, they can decide where they should go to conduct their research and how they might present their findings to the rest of the class. You might also encourage students to divide up certain tasks among themselves, such as parts of the research process and the gathering of materials for the presentation. Students should write out their plans on paper.

ADDITIONAL QUESTIONS AND ACTIVITIES

Ask students to answer the following questions:

1. With what items is Inanna "clothed"?

2. What aspects of the hymn to Inanna do you find most striking? Why? Do you think she is powerful? Why, or why not?

ANSWERS

Responses will vary.

1. The heavens are a crown on the head of Inanna, the earth is sandals on her feet, a holy robe is wrapped around her body, and a holy scepter is in her hand.

2. Responses will vary, but students should refer to concrete details from the selection in their responses.

CROSS-CURRICULAR ACTIVITIES

ARTS AND HUMANITIES

Ask students to go a library, music store, or bookstore to find hymns and psalms that have been set to music. Students who sing or play musical instruments might want to perform some of these hymns and psalms for the rest of the class.

Students may also try setting "Hymn to the Sun" or some of the hymns and psalms on these pages to music of their own.

HYMNS AND PSALMS

A **hymn** is a song or verse of praise, often religious. Hymns of praise were common in the ancient Near East, with Egyptian and Mesopotamian hymns often praising elements of the natural world. As both the Egyptians and the Mesopotamians worshiped certain aspects of the natural world as gods, these hymns are religious and many are both reverent and celebratory in tone. Part of an ancient Mesopotamian hymn to the goddess Inanna appears below. Just as "Hymn to the Sun" praised the many different aspects of the solar disk, this hymn celebrates different aspects of Inanna, goddess of the storehouse, love, war, and the morning and evening stars.

My father gave me the heavens,
he gave me the earth,
I am Inanna!
Kingship he gave me,
queenship he gave me,
waging of battle he gave me,
the attack he gave me,
the floodstorm he gave me,
the hurricane he gave me!
He crowned my head with the heavens,
He sandaled my feet with the earth,
He wrapped my body with a holy robe.
He placed a holy scepter in my hand.
The gods are sparrows—I am a falcon;
the Anunnaki trod along—I am a splendid wild cow;
I am father Enlil's splendid wild cow,
his splendid wild cow leading the way!

Egyptian and Mesopotamian hymns of praise undoubtedly influenced the Jewish writers of the **psalms**—lyrical hymns of praise, request, or thanksgiving. If you look closely at the hymn above, you will notice that it relies heavily on repetition, parallelism, and apposition. The 150 psalms in the Book of Psalms in the Bible also make use of these three literary techniques, as demonstrated below.

Repetition is the use, again, of a sound, word, phrase, sentence, or other element.

Sing praises to God, sing praises: sing
praises unto our King, sing praises.
—from Psalm 47

Parallelism is a rhetorical technique in which a writer emphasizes the equal value or weight of two or more ideas by expressing them in the same grammatical form.

The Lord is my light and my salvation;
whom shall I fear? the Lord is the strength
of my life; of whom shall I be afraid?
—from Psalm 27

An **apposition** is a grammatical form in which a thing is renamed in a different word, phrase, or clause.

The Lord is my rock, and my fortress, and
my deliverer; my God, my strength, in
whom I will trust; my buckler, and the horn
of my salvation, and my high tower.
—from Psalm 18

The psalms below have very different subjects and tones. The speaker in Psalm 23 expresses a confident yet grateful contentment in being protected by God. The speaker in Psalm 137 at first expresses sorrow and then an angry and bitter desire for vengeance. Like "Hymn to the Sun" and the Mesopotamian hymn to Inanna, both psalms use natural imagery.

Psalm 23
A Psalm of David

The Lord is my shepherd; I shall not want.

2 He maketh me to lie down in green pastures: he leadeth me beside the still waters.

3 He restoreth my soul: he leadeth me in the paths of righteousness for his name's sake.

4 Yea, though I walk through the valley of the shadow of death, I will fear no evil: for thou art with me; thy rod and thy staff they comfort me.

5 Thou preparest a table before me in the presence of mine enemies: thou anointest my head

ADDITIONAL QUESTIONS AND ACTIVITIES

Ask students to answer the following questions:

What is the tone of the first four verses of Psalm 137? What seems particularly cruel to the speaker about his captivity? Why do you believe the speaker chose to describe this request?

ANSWERS

Responses will vary. Possible responses are given.

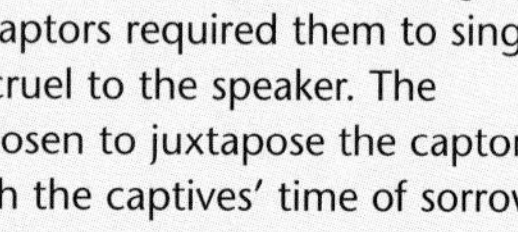

The tone of verses 1–4 is one of grief and longing for home. That the captors required them to sing seemed particularly cruel to the speaker. The speaker may have chosen to juxtapose the captors' request for mirth with the captives' time of sorrow in order to emphasize the extreme nature of his people's grief. The request also further emphasizes the captors' cruelty.

with oil;[1] my cup runneth over.
6 Surely goodness and mercy shall follow me all the days of my life: and I will dwell in the house of the Lord for ever.

Psalm 137

By the rivers of Babylon, there we sat down, yea, we wept, when we remembered Zion.[2]
2 We hanged our harps upon the willows in the midst thereof.
3 For there they that carried us away captive required of us a song; and they that wasted us required of us mirth, saying, Sing us one of the songs of Zion.
4 How shall we sing the Lord's song in a strange land?
5 If I forget thee, O Jerusalem, let my right hand forget her cunning.
6 If I do not remember thee, let my tongue cleave[3] to the roof of my mouth; if I prefer not Jerusalem above my chief joy.
7 Remember, O Lord, the children of Edom[4] in the day of Jerusalem; who said, Rase[5] it; rase it, even to the foundation thereof.
8 O daughter of Babylon, who art to be destroyed; happy shall he be, that rewardeth thee as thou has served us.
9 Happy shall he be, that taketh and dasheth thy little ones against the stones.

1. **anointest . . . oil.** Ceremonial pouring of oil on a person's head; a symbol of blessing and hospitality
2. **Zion.** Hill in Jerusalem where the Temple was built; another name for Israel, having the connotation of an idealized Jewish homeland
3. **cleave.** Adhere, cling
4. **Edom.** Ancient kingdom in Southwest Asia, south of the Dead Sea
5. **Rase.** Archaic spelling of *raze*, meaning to tear down completely

Jerusalem

HISTORICAL NOTE

Many of the psalms of the Bible are attributed to King David, who united the kingdom of Israel and who ruled from about 1000 to 962 BC. He was succeeded by his son Solomon, after whose death the kingdom was divided into Israel in the north and Judah in the south. Unfortunately located between the competing empires of Egypt and Assyria, Israel was crushed by the Assyrians in about 722 BC. Judah survived a while longer but eventually fell to the Babylonians under King Nebuchadnezzar II in about 587 BC. The Babylonians destroyed Solomon's Temple in Jerusalem and took many Jews back to Babylonia as slaves.

Psalm 137 describes the experience of one Jewish writer in the Babylonian captivity. In about 536 BC, the Persian leader Cyrus the Great conquered Babylonia and allowed the Jews to return home and rebuild the Temple.

ADDITIONAL QUESTIONS AND ACTIVITIES

Ask students to answer the following questions:

What is the tone, or the emotional attitude, of the speaker in Psalm 23? For what life experience might this psalm prove most comforting? Why?

ANSWERS

Responses will vary. Possible responses are given.

The tone is one of peace and calm. The speaker seems to feel safe and comforted by the idea that God will take care of him. A person who is near death or who has a loved one near death might find this psalm most comforting because it promises God's care and that he or she will "dwell in the house of the Lord forever."

ADDITIONAL RESOURCES

READER'S GUIDE
- Selection Worksheet 5.2

ASSESSMENT PORTFOLIO
- Selection Check Test 2.5.3
- Selection Test 2.5.4

ESSENTIAL SKILLS PRACTICE BOOKS
- Writing 1.8, 1.20
- Language 2.7

PREREADING EXTENSIONS

Ask students to go to the library to find more facts about the period of China in which T'ao Ch'ien lived, AD 365–427. They should take notes and write a brief description of the information they find.

SUPPORT FOR LEP STUDENTS

PRONUNCIATIONS OF PROPER NOUNS AND ADJECTIVES

T'ao Ch'ien (tau´ chē en´)

ADDITIONAL VOCABULARY

habitations—homes; living areas
solitude—state of being completely alone
dusk—time of day during which the sun is setting; the end of the day

PREREADING

"I Built My Cottage among the Habitations of Men"
by T'ao Ch'ien, translated by Liu Wu-chi

CHINA

About the Author

T'ao Ch'ien (AD **365–427**). T'ao Ch'ien was born into a family of relatively high social standing, although his immediate family suffered some financial hardships. As an adult, he worked as a minor public official in several different positions. T'ao Ch'ien was always unhappy in these jobs, however, and felt that he was sacrificing too much of his freedom and individuality for work he did not find interesting and for people whom he did not respect. T'ao Ch'ien wanted to lead a natural life; he highly regarded farming communities. He eventually left public life and spent his last twenty-two years concentrating on family, farming, and writing. T'ao Ch'ien's poetry, as well as his prose, has come to be recognized as some of the greatest writing of his age.

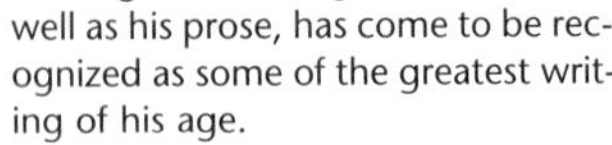

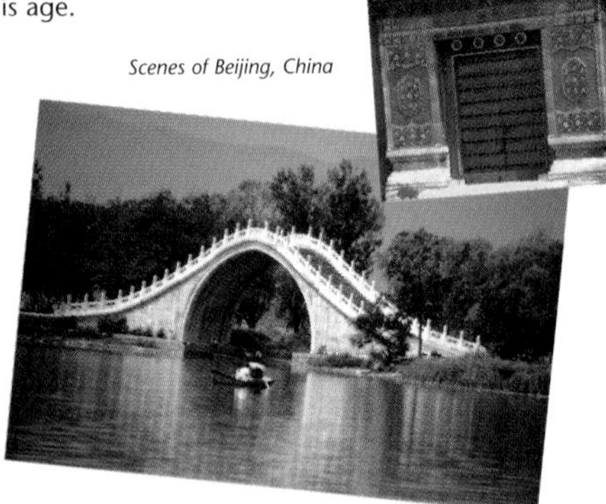

Scenes of Beijing, China

About the Selection

A **theme** is a central idea in a literary work. Scholars say that the themes in T'ao Ch'ien's writings often reflect aspects of both Taoism and Confucianism. As expressed in the *Tao Te Ching* (see page 544), Taoism encourages simplicity, quiet reflection, appreciation for nature, and retreat from the complications of the world. As expressed in the *Analects* (see page 550), Confucianism emphasizes community, family responsibility, and the idea that one has a duty to teach and reform society rather than isolate oneself from it. In **"I Built My Cottage among the Habitations of Men,"** the influence of Taoism is apparent in T'ao Ch'ien's vivid descriptions of nature and his emphasis on seeking solitude and keeping one's heart at a distance from the clamor of the outside world. The speaker of this poem, however, chooses to build a cottage among the habitations of other people. This suggests the influence of Confucianism since community is obviously important to the speaker. The speaker in this poem shares the idea that a person can live peacefully and thoughtfully within a busy community.

CONNECTIONS: Period of Disunity in China

T'ao Ch'ien lived during troubled times. Foreign invaders had conquered northern China and established their own states, leaving the country divided and without a centralized government for three and a half centuries. This period of political unrest influenced T'ao Ch'ien's writing, in which he often reflects on how to live peacefully and simply in a confused and complicated world.

GOALS/OBJECTIVES

Studying this lesson will enable students to

- enjoy a descriptive poem that encourages simplicity and quiet reflection in a chaotic world
- discuss the life of T'ao Ch'ien, as well as his work and the historical period in China during which he lived
- define *pastoral poem*
- write an original pastoral piece and a critical essay about imagery and theme in "I Built My Cottage among the Habitations of Men"
- review types of verbs and identify them in sentences

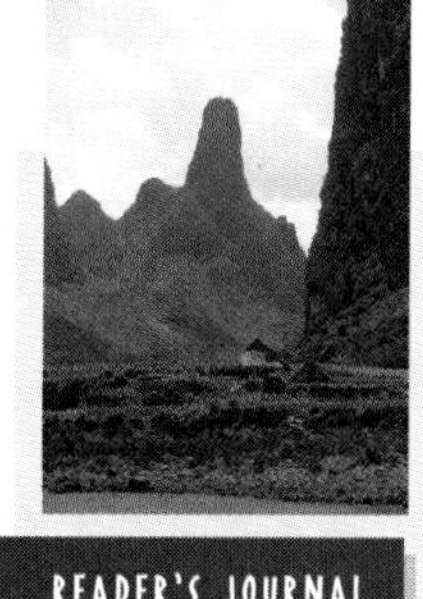

What do you do when you need to escape from the world and relax? What is the place or activity that refreshes you and helps you to think more clearly? Describe this special place or activity. Why might it be important for people to have such places and activities?

READER'S JOURNAL

"I Built My Cottage among the Habitations of Men"

T'AO CH'IEN, TRANSLATED BY LIU WU-CHI

I built my cottage among the habitations of men,
And yet there is no clamor of carriages and horses.
You ask: "Sir, how can this be done?"
"A heart that is distant creates its own solitude."
I pluck chrysanthemums[1] under the eastern hedge,
Then gaze afar towards the southern hills.
The mountain air is fresh at the dusk of day;
The flying birds in flocks return.
In these things there lies a deep meaning;
I want to tell it, but have forgotten the words. ■

1. **chrysanthemums.** Plants that bloom in late summer and fall

❶ *Why is it puzzling that the speaker does not hear the "clamor of carriages and horses"? Why doesn't the speaker hear these noises?*

❷ *In what things does the speaker find "deep meaning"? Why are these things important to the speaker?*

WORDS FOR EVERYDAY USE

clam • or (klaˊmər) *n.,* long, loud noise

READER'S JOURNAL

Encourage students to freewrite about the place or activity that refreshes them in times of stress.

ANSWERS TO GUIDED READING QUESTIONS

❶ It is puzzling that the speaker does not hear the "clamor of carriages and horses" because he lives among other people. The speaker does not hear the noises because he is able to create his own solitude.

❷ The speaker finds deep meaning in chrysanthemums under the eastern hedge, the southern hills, fresh mountain air, and birds in flocks. These aspects of nature provide the speaker with peaceful solitude.

SELECTION CHECK TEST WITH ANSWERS

EX. Where did the speaker build a cottage?
The speaker built a cottage "among the habitations of men."

1. What doesn't the speaker hear?
The speaker doesn't hear the "clamor of carriages and horses."

2. According to the speaker, what does a distant heart create?
According to the speaker, a distant heart creates its own solitude.

3. What does the speaker do when he is in search of solitude?
The speaker observes nature.

4. According to the speaker, in what lies deep meaning?
In the natural world there is deep meaning.

5. Why does the speaker not describe the deep meaning?
The speaker has forgotten the words to describe the deep meaning.

VOCABULARY IN CONTEXT

• Everyone in the dining room could hear the clamor of the falling pots and pans.

Responding to the Selection

Students might want to get together in pairs to compare their responses to the poem.

Answers for Reviewing the Selection

RECALLING AND INTERPRETING

1. **Recalling.** He built a cottage among the habitations of other men. **Interpreting.** It is puzzling that the speaker lives among other people, yet does not hear the "clamor of carriages and horses."
2. **Recalling.** There is no "clamor of carriages and horses" because he is able to create his own solitude. **Interpreting.** The speaker values solitude greatly.
3. **Recalling.** The speaker describes plucking chrysanthemums and gazing out toward the southern hills. He observes that the mountain air is fresh and that the flying birds return in flocks. **Interpreting.** All of these activities and observations involve the natural world. The speaker is able to distance himself from the busy world by concentrating on nature.
4. **Recalling.** The speaker finds deep meaning in nature. **Interpreting.** In the beauty and tranquility of nature, the speaker has found a way to live happily and peacefully. The meaning the speaker finds in nature transcends human communication and thought.

SYNTHESIZING

Responses will vary. Possible responses are given.

5. The speaker can enjoy being part of a community because he knows that he can distance himself from the commotion of the busy world when the need arises. The speaker believes that a distant heart is a positive trait. A person with a distant heart can step back and create his or her own solitude.

Responding to the Selection

Which do you prefer, quiet solitude or activity and company, or do you welcome each at different times? Are you similar to or different from the speaker of this poem?

Reviewing the Selection

Recalling / Interpreting

1. Where did the speaker build a cottage? ▶▶ What is puzzling or unusual about the situation presented in the opening lines of the poem?
2. According to the speaker, why is there no "clamor of carriages and horses" where he lives? ▶▶ Based on the speaker's thoughts in the poem, how does he value solitude?
3. What activities and observations does the speaker describe in lines 5 through 8? ▶▶ What do the activities and observations described in lines 5 through 8 have in common? In what way might they be related to having a "distant" heart?
4. According to the speaker, in what lies "deep meaning"? ▶▶ What do you believe is the deep meaning that the speaker finds? Given the Taoist belief that the Tao—or the "Way"—is above simple human expression, explain the last line of the poem.

Synthesizing

5. Why might the speaker choose to "live among the habitations of men" despite his strong feelings about solitude and being close to nature? According to this poem, is having a "distant heart" a positive trait? Why, or why not?

Understanding Literature (Questions for Discussion)

Pastoral Poem. A **pastoral poem,** from the Latin *pastor,* meaning "shepherd," is a verse that deals with idealized rural life. In what way does "I Built My Cottage among the Habitations of Men" fit the definition of a pastoral poem? Give specific examples of the way in which the poem idealizes rural life. What aspects of rural life have special meaning to the speaker of the poem?

Answers for Understanding Literature

Responses will vary. Possible responses are given.

Pastoral Poem. "I Built My Cottage among the Habitations of Men" fits the definition of a pastoral poem because it is filled with vivid, idealized descriptions of rural life. Images of plucking chrysanthemums, southern hills, fresh mountain air at the dusk of day, and flying birds in flocks give the poem its rural, pastoral flavor. Rural life has special meaning to the speaker of the poem because he turns his attention to the natural world when he wants to feel peaceful and enjoy moments of solitude. The speaker maintains that the appreciation of rural life is the key to staying content in a busy world.

Responding in Writing

1. **Creative Writing: Pastoral Piece.** Write a pastoral poem, prose poem, or essay about your favorite place. In keeping with a true pastoral perspective, idealize your special place and try to capture the most interesting details of this place as you write. Allow your reader to see the place through your eyes. Although traditional pastoral verse almost always focuses on the beauty of nature, feel free to write about your favorite place if it is in the city or the suburbs.

2. **Critical Essay: Imagery and Theme.** The imagery of a poem is made up of all its words and phrases for things that can be seen, heard, touched, tasted, or smelled. A poet chooses images for a poem carefully and deliberately. Write a short essay describing how the imagery of "I Built My Cottage among the Habitations of Men" develops the poem's theme.

Language Lab

Types of Verbs. The sentences below describe the story "The Peach-Blossom Fountain," one of T'ao Ch'ien's most famous prose pieces. Review the Language Arts Survey 2.7, "Types of Verbs." Write the following sentences on your own paper. Then, underline the verbs in the sentences. Tell whether they are action verbs, linking verbs, or auxiliary verbs. Many of these sentences contain more than one verb.

EX. Utopia stories are stories about ideal societies. **are, linking verb**
T'ao Ch'ien wrote "The Peach-Blossom Fountain," a type of utopia story. **wrote, action verb**

1. In "The Peach-Blossom Fountain," a fisherman is sailing along an unfamiliar river.
2. He approaches a grove of peach trees in full bloom, and the trees smell wonderful.
3. The fisherman travels until a strange cave appears just beyond the grove of peach trees.
4. The fisherman feels that he should enter the mysterious cave.
5. Strangely enough, the fisherman discovers a lovely community just past the cave entrance.
6. The community seems strange but advanced and beautiful, and friendly inhabitants invite him to a feast.
7. The fisherman eats delicious food and shares stories about political troubles in China with the people.
8. The people mourn; their own ancestors had left China many years earlier.
9. The ancestors started new, trouble-free lives in the strange place; they removed themselves from human pain and suffering.
10. The fisherman eventually departs; he can never find the wonderful community again.

ANALYTIC SCALES FOR RESPONDING IN WRITING

Assign a score from 1 to 25 for each grading criterion below. (For more detailed evaluation, see the evaluation forms for writing, revising, and proofreading, Assessment Portfolio 4.1–4.9.)

1. Pastoral Piece

- **Content/Unity.** The pastoral piece idealizes the writer's favorite place.
- **Organization/Coherence.** The pastoral piece is a poem or essay that captures interesting details about the place and allows the reader to see the place through the eyes of the writer.
- **Language/Style.** The pastoral piece uses vivid and precise nouns, verbs, and modifiers.
- **Conventions.** The pastoral piece avoids errors in spelling, grammar, usage, mechanics, and manuscript form.

▶ Additional practice is provided in the Essential Skills Practice Book: Writing 1.8.

2. Critical Essay

- **Content/Unity.** The essay describes how the imagery of the poem develops the poem's theme.
- **Organization/Coherence.** The essay begins with an introduction that includes the thesis of the essay. The introduction is followed by paragraphs which describe specific examples of imagery developing the poem's theme. The essay then ends with a solid conclusion.
- **Language/Style.** The essay uses vivid and precise nouns, verbs, and modifiers.
- **Conventions.** The essay avoids errors in spelling, grammar, usage, mechanics, and manuscript form.

▶ Additional practice is provided in the Essential Skills Practice Book: Writing 1.20.

ANSWERS FOR LANGUAGE LAB

1. is, auxiliary verb; sailing, main verb
2. approaches, action verb; smell, linking verb
3. travels, action verb; appears, linking verb
4. feels, linking verb; should, auxiliary verb; enter, action verb
5. discovers, action verb
6. seems, linking verb; invite, action verb
7. eats, action verb; shares, action verb
8. mourn, action verb; had, auxiliary verb; left, action verb
9. started, action verb; removed, action verb
10. departs, action verb; can, auxiliary verb; find, action verb

▶ Additional practice is provided in the Essential Skills Practice Book: Language 2.7.

Additional Questions and Activities

Ask students to answer the following questions:

1. Who is being addressed in the excerpt from one of Virgil's eclogues?
2. What "native dowries" does the earth bring? Why might these things be needed?
3. From what evils in nature will the subject of the poem be protected?
4. In Sir Philip Sidney's poem, where did Astrophel and Stella meet? How do they seem to feel about each other?

ANSWERS

1. A child or infant is being addressed in this poem.
2. The earth brings the wandering ivy with flowers and other plants, and goats with "swelling udders." These things are needed because they are attractive and nourishing.
3. The child will be protected from mighty lions, the serpent's sting, and poisonous herbs.
4. Astrophel and Stella meet in a shady grove filled with songbirds and flowers. They are happy and "blessed" to be together.

Cross-curricular Activities

MATHEMATICS AND SCIENCES

Virgil refers to specific types of plants in the excerpt students read from his *Eclogues*. Some students might be interested in working together to research these plants—ivy, colocasia, acanthus—and find out what they look like and where they are found.

Insights

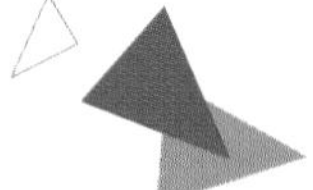

The Pastoral Tradition

The pastoral literary tradition can include verse, fiction, and drama that deals with simple, idealized country life. The word *pastoral* comes from the Latin word *pastor*, which means "shepherd." In traditional pastoral writing, a shepherd often represents idealized rural life, and the purity and simplicity of rural life is described as a desirable alternative to the corruption of city life or politics. An early example of pastoral verse is Psalm 23 from the Bible's Old Testament, of which the lines below are a part (see page 370 for the psalm in its entirety).

The Lord is my shepherd, I shall not want.
He maketh me to lie down in green pastures:
he leadeth me beside still waters.

When people refer to the pastoral tradition, they are most commonly referring to English pastoral poetry, which is derived from Greek and Roman pastoral verse. The origins of this form can be found in such works as the *Idylls* of Greek writer Theocritus and the *Eclogues* of Roman writer Virgil. An **idyll** is a short poem or work of prose that describes a peaceful rural scene. An **eclogue** is a type of pastoral poem that usually consists of a dialogue between two shepherds and attempts to reflect the feelings surrounding a simple rural life. The following is an example of pastoral verse from one of Virgil's eclogues:

To thee—sweet child—the Earth brings native dowries,
The wandering ivy, with fair bacchar's flowers,
And colocasia, sprung from Egypt's ground,
With smiling leaves of green acanthus crown'd;
The goats their swelling udders home shall bear,
The droves no more shall mighty lions fear:
For thee, Thy cradle, pleasing flowers shall bring;
Imperious Death shall blunt the serpent's sting;
No herbs shall with deceitful poison flow,
And sweet amomum ev'ry where shall grow.

—Virgil, from *Eclogue IV*

Orchard in Spring. *Loiseau, 1899*

Pastoral verse became popular during the European Renaissance, with the work of Italian writers such as Dante, Petrarch, and Boccaccio, and English writers such as Sir Philip Sidney, Edmund Spenser, William Shakespeare, and Christopher Marlowe. Edmund Spencer made use of the eclogue format Virgil practiced, writing twelve well known eclogues entitled the *Shepheardes Calender*. The following are examples of pastoral verse from the Renaissance:

In a grove most rich of shade,
Where birds wanton musique made,
May, then young, his pyed weeds showing,
New perfum'd, with flowers fresh growing,
Astrophel with Stella sweete,
Did for mutuall comfort meete,
Both within themselves oppressed,
But each in the other blessed . . .

—Sir Philip Sidney, from *Astrophel and Stella*

Monet's Garden. *Claude Monet, 1900*

Come live with me and be my love,
And we will all the pleasures prove
That valleys, groves, hills, and fields,
Woods, or steepy mountain yields.

—Christopher Marlowe, from "The Passionate Shepherd to His Love"

That time of year thou mayst in me behold
When yellow leaves, or none, or few, do hang
Upon those boughs which shake against the cold,
Bare ruined choirs, where late the sweet birds sang.

—William Shakespeare, from Sonnet 73

Works that can be described as pastoral have appeared in almost every culture. Pastoral writing often emerges from a society when its people grow resentful of a changing, complicated world and search for a life that is simple, beautiful, and free. The writing of many Chinese writers such as T'ao Ch'ien is pastoral in the way that it focuses on the beauty and simplicity of nature and treats nature as an important refuge from a complicated world.

Literary Note

Below is the classic pastoral poem "The Passionate Shepherd to His Love" by Christopher Marlowe in its entirety. You might read it aloud to students and then encourage them to locate and read "The Nymph's Reply to the Shepherd," Sir Walter Raleigh's response to the Marlowe poem.

Come live with me and be my love,
And we will all the pleasures prove
That valleys, groves, hills, and fields,
Woods, or steepy mountain yields.

And we will sit upon the rocks,
Seeing the shepherds feed their flocks,
By shallow rivers to whose falls
Melodious birds sing madrigals.

And I will make thee beds of roses
And a thousand fragrant posies,
A cap of flowers, and a kirtle
Embroidered all with leaves of myrtle;

A gown made of the finest wool
Which from our pretty lambs we pull;
Fair lined slippers for the cold,
With buckles of the purest gold;

A belt of straw and ivy buds,
With coral clasps and amber studs:
And if these pleasures may thee move,
Come live with me, and be my love.

The shepherds' swains shall dance and sing
For thy delight each May morning;
If these delights thy mind may move,
Then live with me and be my love.

Students might also be interested in located and reading more of Shakespeare's sonnets.

Additional Questions and Activities

Ask students to complete the following questions or activities:

1. What does the speaker in Marlowe's poem want the person to whom he addresses his words to do? With what pleasures does he try to entice this person?

2. What time of year is Shakespeare describing? What images best indicate the time of year?

3. Why might pastoral poetry offer comfort to people in times of stress? Why does nature seem peaceful?

4. In the poems you've just read, which lines do you enjoy most? Which lines seem most pastoral? Explain.

ADDITIONAL RESOURCES

READER'S GUIDE

- Selection Worksheet 5.3

ASSESSMENT PORTFOLIO

- Selection Check Test 2.5.5
- Selection Test 2.5.6

ESSENTIAL SKILLS PRACTICE BOOKS

- Writing 1.8, 1.20
- Language 2.5

SUPPORT FOR LEP STUDENTS

PRONUNCIATIONS OF PROPER NOUNS AND ADJECTIVES

Mat • su • o Ba • shō (mät so͞o ō bä shō)
Ko • ba • ya • shi Is • sa (kō bä yäsh ē ēs sä)
Yo • sa Bu • son (yō sä bo͞o sōn)
Ki no Tsur • a • yu • ki (kē nō tso͞or ä yo͞o kē)

ADDITIONAL VOCABULARY

daffodil—flower, usually yellow
wake—trail left behind a moving object, usually in water

PREREADING

Haiku and Tanka

JAPAN

About the Authors

Matsuo Bashō (1644–1694). Bashō was the pen name of Matsuo Munefusa, considered the greatest of the Japanese haiku poets. Bashō became interested in poetry when he was still a youth, but for several years he put poetry aside so that he could serve a local lord. After the death of this lord, Bashō finally decided to pursue a literary career, and he moved to the city of Edo, today known as Tokyo. There, Bashō worked as a poet and critic and was active in Edo's literary circle. Later, influenced by Zen philosophy, he was drawn to a simple, reclusive life. In 1684, Bashō began a series of travels that would fill most of the rest of his life. His travel journals, written in verse and prose, have become classics of Japanese literature. Books describing his various journeys include *Journal of Weather-Beaten Skeleton*, *Notes in My Knapsack*, and *The Narrow Road to the Deep North and Other Travel Sketches*, long considered Bashō's masterpiece.

Kobayashi Issa (1763–1827). Issa is known as a skilled poet whose work can be both humorous and cynical. Issa was born Kobayashi Yatarō to a farming family. When Issa was a teenager, his father hired him out as an apprentice and sent him to the city of Edo. In Edo, Issa studied haiku under a man named Chikua and published his poems in the anthologies of Chikua's group. Issa eventually returned to his family's home to help nurse his sick father. After his father died, Issa married and settled in his father's house. He suffered a difficult period during which three children and his wife died. In addition to hundreds of poems, Issa wrote two prose pieces about the death of his father and the deaths of his children—*A Journal of My Father's Last Days* and *A Year of My Life.*

Yosa Buson (1716–1783). Buson was a masterful haiku poet as well as a skilled painter. In fact, people often say that his poems are like paintings in their visual intensity. Buson left home at the age of twenty to study painting and poetry in the city of Edo. During this period, he published thirty-six poems in anthologies and became a part of the literary and artistic circle of Edo. After a dear teacher and mentor died, Buson spent the next ten years wandering, training himself as a poet and painter, and retracing the journeys of Bashō. At the age of thirty-six, Buson traveled to Kyoto where he married and resided for the rest of his life. By the age of fifty-five he was a leader of the poets of Kyoto and making a comfortable living as a painter. He eventually published three books of poetry, *Light from the Snow*, *Around Here,* and *A Crow at Dawn.*

Ki no Tsurayuki (c. 884–c. 946). Tsurayuki was one of the greatest of the Japanese tanka poets and a writer of literary criticism that influenced court poets for many years. Tsurayuki compiled a famous collection of Japanese writings.

GOALS/OBJECTIVES

Studying this lesson will enable students to

- enjoy haiku and tanka poems which describe vivid scenes in nature
- discuss the lives and work of Matsuo Bashō, Kobayashi Issa, Yosa Buson, and Ki no Tsurayuki
- define *tone* and *aim*
- discuss tanka and haiku forms
- write an original haiku and an original tanka
- write a critical essay about imagery and emotion
- review and identify in sentences reflexive, intensive, and demonstrative pronouns

About the Selections

A **haiku** is a traditional Japanese three-line poem containing seventeen syllables—five syllables in the first line, seven in the second, and five again in the third. A **tanka** is a traditional Japanese five-line poem containing five syllables in the first line, seven in the second, five in the third, seven in the fourth and seven in the fifth. A haiku or a tanka will usually present one or more **images**—words that describe things that can be seen, touched, tasted, heard, or smelled—in an attempt to capture a single, passing moment. These poems are typically short and simple. Their purpose is to suggest a particular mood or to give the reader a glimpse of a scene. The reader then must make connections and "complete" the poem by using his or her own imagination to fill in the scene that the poem suggests. Images in haiku and tanka poems are usually of the natural world. The selections that follow include examples of five traditional haiku poems—**"the old pond— ,"** **"the sound of a water jar,"** **"the first snow,"** all by Matsuo Bashō; **"The snow is melting,"** by Kobayashi Issa; and **"In the summer rain"** by Yosa Buson. There appears, as well, one traditional tanka—**"In the lingering wake"** by Ki no Tsurayuki. Because these selections are translated into English from the original Japanese, the syllable counts will vary.

CONNECTIONS: Romanticism

Romanticism (see Unit 11) was a movement in literature, music, and painting in the late eighteenth and early nineteenth centuries. This movement, a reaction against Neoclassicism (see Unit 10), celebrated nature over civilization and valued human emotion and imagination over reason. Important literary figures associated with this movement are German authors Johann Wolfgang von Goethe and Friedrich von Schiller; French author Victor Hugo; English poets William Wordsworth, Samuel Taylor Coleridge, William Blake, Lord Byron, John Keats, and Percy Bysshe Shelley; British prose writers Mary Shelley and Ann Radcliffe; and American writers such as Ralph Waldo Emerson.

Matsuo Bashō and other haiku and tanka poets lived and wrote in Japan more than one hundred years before the Romantic movement began in Europe, and explore the same themes of harmony between humans and nature, the need for people to retreat from the damaging influences of the civilized world, and the need to become reacquainted with the true self through nature.

Lord Byron, one English Romantic poet, wrote a book entitled *Childe Harold's Pilgrimage* that is similar to Bashō's *The Narrow Road to the Deep North and Other Travel Sketches*. Both books were written as the poets traveled extensively and communed with nature. The following is a brief excerpt from "She Walks in Beauty," a piece from *Childe Harold's Pilgrimage*:

She walks in Beauty, like the night
  Of cloudless climes and starry skies;
And all that's best of dark and bright
  Meet in her aspect and her eyes;
Thus mellow'd to the tender light
  Which heaven to gaudy day denies.

PREREADING EXTENSIONS

Ask students to locate a work of literature written by someone associated with the Romantic movement of the late eighteenth and early nineteenth centuries such as Johann Wolfgang von Goethe, Friedrich von Schiller, Victor Hugo, William Wordsworth, Samuel Taylor Coleridge, William Blake, Lord Byron, John Keats, Percy Bysshe Shelley, Mary Wollstonecraft Shelley, Ann Radcliffe, or Ralph Waldo Emerson. Then ask students to compare and contrast this piece with some of the haiku and tanka poems featured in this lesson, either in a short paper or in a class or group discussion.

SPELLING AND VOCABULARY WORDS FROM THE SELECTION

wavelet

ADDITIONAL QUESTIONS AND ACTIVITIES

Writers of the Romantic movement celebrated nature over civilization and human emotion over reason. Ask students to think about these ideas for several minutes and then to freewrite about what these ideas mean to them. Do students consider themselves "romantics"? Why, or why not? If not, what would they consider themselves?

READER'S JOURNAL

Remind students that they do not need to be in a rural area to appreciate nature. In fact, students who live in cities or busy suburbs have their own unique perspective on nature. Ask students to find images that are truly unique to their own environment or to places they have traveled.

ANSWERS TO GUIDED READING QUESTIONS

❶ The frog creates water's sound by jumping in the water.

❷ The speaker hears a jar crack.

❸ The speaker notices that it is just enough snow to bend the daffodil leaves.

LITERARY NOTE

Ki no Tsurayuki, writer of the tanka "In the lingering wake" on page 381, was a chief compiler of a famous collection of Japanese writings known as the "Kokin-shu," which consists of more than 1100 poems, divided into 20 books arranged according to topics such as nature, the seasons, travel, love, congratulations, and mourning. Tsurayuki influenced Japanese literature with this collection and with a travel diary, an account of his travels from Tosa, where he had worked as a governor, to his home in Kyoto. This diary broke tradition because Tsurayuki wrote it in Japanese, while most male writers of his time were writing in Chinese. For further information on female writers during this period, refer students to the Connections feature on page 770. This book was also one of the earliest examples of a literary diary, a genre that became popular among Japanese writers.

READER'S JOURNAL

In your journal describe some favorite scenes from nature. For example, you might write about the sky just before a heavy rain shower, a ladybug climbing a blade of grass, a moth on a lampshade, or a flower beginning to wilt. You may either write down images from memory, or spend some time outside observing the natural world before you write.

Haiku and Tanka

"the old pond—"

MATSUO BASHŌ, TRANSLATED BY MAKOTO UEDA

❶ *What noise is created by the frog?*

the old pond—
a frog jumps in,
water's sound ■

"the sound of a water jar"

MATSUO BASHŌ, TRANSLATED BY MAKOTO UEDA

❷ *What does the speaker hear during the icy night?*

the sound of a water jar
cracking on this icy night
as I lie awake ■

"the first snow"

MATSUO BASHŌ, TRANSLATED BY MAKOTO UEDA

❸ *What does the speaker notice about the first snow?*

the first snow
just enough to bend
the daffodil leaves ■

"The snow is melting"

KOBAYASHI ISSA, TRANSLATED BY ROBERT HASS

The snow is melting
and the village is flooded
with children. ■

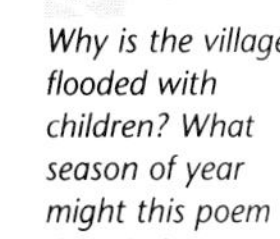

Why is the village flooded with children? What season of year might this poem describe?

"In the summer rain"

YOSA BUSON, TRANSLATED BY ROBERT HASS

In the summer rain
the path
has disappeared. ■

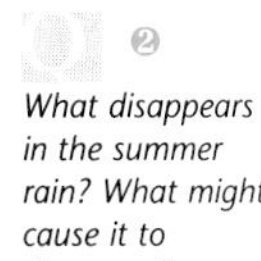

What disappears in the summer rain? What might cause it to disappear?

"In the lingering wake"

KI NO TSURAYUKI, TRANSLATED BY HELEN CRAIG MCCULLOUGH

In the lingering wake
of the breeze that has scattered
the cherry tree's bloom,
petal wavelets go dancing
across the waterless sky. ■

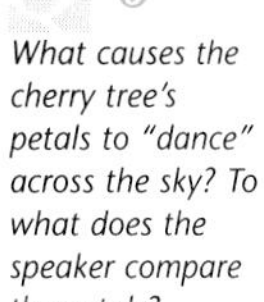

What causes the cherry tree's petals to "dance" across the sky? To what does the speaker compare the petals?

WORDS FOR EVERYDAY USE

wave • let (wāv´lit) *n.,* little wave, ripple

ANSWERS TO GUIDED READING QUESTIONS

❶ The snow has melted and the village is flooded with children, who have perhaps come out to play. The poem is probably describing the beginning of spring.

❷ The path disappears in the summer rain. The water probably turns the path to mud.

❸ The breeze cause the petals to "dance" across the sky. The speaker compares the petals to "wavelets."

SELECTION CHECK TEST WITH ANSWERS

EX. How many lines are in a haiku poem?
Three lines are in a haiku poem.

1. What noise is created by the frog?
The frog creates a splashing noise by jumping into a pond.
2. What does the speaker hear during the icy night?
The speaker hears a jar break.
3. What does the speaker notice about the first snow?
The speaker notices that there is just enough snow to bend the leaves of a daffodil.
4. Why is the village flooded with children?
The village is flooded with children because the snow has melted.
5. What disappears in the summer rain?
The path disappears in the summer rain.

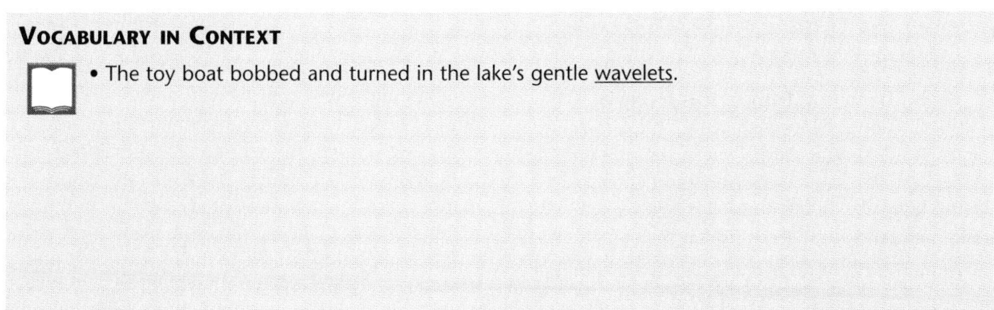

VOCABULARY IN CONTEXT

• The toy boat bobbed and turned in the lake's gentle wavelets.

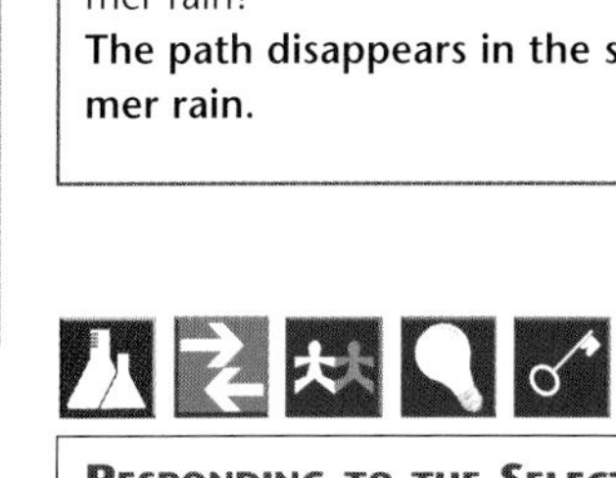

RESPONDING TO THE SELECTION

Ask students to discuss which images they can truly hear or see. Can they relate any of these images to things they have seen in their own lives?

Answers for Reviewing the Selection

RECALLING AND INTERPRETING

1. **Recalling.** The frog jumps into the water and creates a splash. The jar breaks because it is cold outside. **Interpreting.** The reader is asked to imagine how the sound of splashing water might interrupt the silence of the woods, or how the sound of cracking pottery would interrupt the still, icy night. In both poems, noise erupts in a relatively silent, still environment.

2. **Recalling.** Only a light snow falls. **Interpreting.** Bashō carefully creates the image of the light snow barely bending the leaves of a plant.

3. **Recalling.** Children flood the village as the snow melts. **Interpreting.** When the reader reads the word *flooded,* he or she imagines the melted snow and also of the crowd of children running through the village. The weather is probably becoming warmer, pleasant, and more inviting.

4. **Recalling.** The path disappears in the summer rain. The breeze causes petal wavelets to go dancing. **Interpreting.** Students might say that they imagine mud, wet leaves, the sound of rain falling on grass and leaves, and thunder and lightning when they think of a summer rainstorm. The petals and sky in Ki no Tsurayuki's poem are being compared to small waves in a vast ocean. The sky might be described as "waterless" because although it may be the color of the ocean, it is dry.

SYNTHESIZING

Responses will vary. Possible responses are given.

5. Students might say that the poems appeal to the senses of hearing, touching, and seeing. They might say that the frog jumping into the water or the glass breaking in the cold night are images that evoke loneliness; that the Issa poem about children flooding the village evokes happiness and excitement; and that the Bashō poem about the first snow evokes wonder.

Responding to the Selection

What images from the poems you have just read do you find unique and interesting? Why do you enjoy them?

Reviewing the Selection

RECALLING		INTERPRETING
1. In Bashō's poem "the old pond—," what action takes place? In "the sound of a water jar," why does the water jar break?	▶▶	In what way does Bashō use sound in "the old pond—" and in "the sound of a water jar"? Describe how both poems express a feeling of solitude.
2. In Bashō's poem "the first snow," how much snow falls?	▶▶	What image does Bashō carefully create to show the reader how much snow has fallen?
3. In Issa's poem "The snow is melting," what floods the village as the snow melts?	▶▶	What two images does the word *flooded* bring to mind in the context of Issa's poem? What circumstances surrounding the melting of the snow would cause the village to become "flooded"?
4. In Buson's poem "In the summer rain," what disappears in the summer rain? In Ki no Tsurayuki's poem "In the lingering wake," what causes petal wavelets to go dancing?	▶▶	What sounds and sights come to mind as you picture the summer rain falling on the ground? To what are the petals in Ki no Tsurayuki's poem being compared? Why might the sky be described as "waterless"?

SYNTHESIZING

5. To what senses do the different poems appeal? What emotions, such as loneliness, excitement, wonder, or sadness, do specific images in the poems evoke?

Understanding Literature (Questions for Discussion)

1. **Tone. Tone** is the emotional attitude toward the reader or toward the subject implied by a literary work. Different tones that a work might have include familiar, ironic, playful, sarcastic, serious, or sad. How would you describe the tone of Bashō's "the sound of a water jar"? What feelings might the speaker have about the icy night and his solitude? Compare this poem's tone with the tone of Issa's "The snow is melting" and the tone of Tsurayuki's "In the lingering wake."

Answers for Understanding Literature

Responses will vary. Possible responses are given.

1. **Tone.** The tone of Bashō's "the sound of a water jar" is one of lonely stillness. The speaker might be cold and feeling alone in the quiet night. Both Issa's "The snow is melting" and Tsurayuki's "In the lingering wake" evoke lighter tones of excitement and wonder.

2. **Aim.** The clear aim of most haikus and tankas is to capture an interesting moment in time as a camera would. The writers want the reader to notice the smallest, most vivid moments in nature. The success of these authors can be measured by how vividly the reader can experience the moment depicted.

2. **Aim.** A writer's **aim** is the primary purpose that his or her work is meant to achieve. What seems to be the aim of each haiku and tanka that you have read? What do you think the writers of these types of poems want readers to experience? Have these authors successfully fulfilled their aim? Why, or why not?

Responding in Writing

1. **Creative Writing: Haiku and Tanka.** Try to write one original haiku and one original tanka. Using the notes you made in the Reader's Journal activity as a starting point, focus on images that are simple but striking. Then, construct your poems using traditional haiku/tanka forms. (See the About the Selection on page 379 for descriptions of the proper syllable counts and numbers of lines.) Experiment with tone. One of your pieces might be dark and serious, while the other might be light or humorous. Be prepared to share your results with classmates.

2. **Critical Essay: Imagery and Emotion.** A haiku usually presents one or more images in an attempt to capture a moment of reflection. Write an essay in which you discuss the imagery of several haiku poems and the emotions that these images create for readers.

Language Lab

Reflexive, Intensive, and Demonstrative Pronouns. It is important to make correct use of pronouns in your own writing. Turn to the Language Arts Survey 2.5, "Reflexive, Intensive, and Demonstrative Pronouns." After you have reviewed the lesson and the examples provided, read the sentences below, identifying the reflexive, intensive, or demonstrative pronouns. Hint: Some sentences have more than one reflexive, intensive, or demonstrative pronoun.

EX. Bashō himself is considered the master of the Haiku.
himself, intensive

1. These are the poems that people call tankas; those are the poems that people call haiku.
2. After reading the book, I told myself that I could try writing poetry.
3. Do you see? That is the beautiful pine tree referred to by Bashō.
4. Gabrielle surprised herself by writing a poem that everyone enjoyed.
5. Look at this book called *The Essential Haiku.*
6. My sister prefers Buson, but I myself enjoy the wit of Issa.
7. Now that is a clever image!
8. We fooled ourselves into thinking that haiku are easy to write because they are brief.
9. Showing the human experience—that is Bashō's specialty.
10. Some prefer capturing city scenes in poetry; they themselves seem to prefer rural scenes.

ANALYTIC SCALES FOR RESPONDING IN WRITING

Assign a score from 1 to 25 for each grading criterion below. (For more detailed evaluation, see the evaluation forms for writing, revising, and proofreading, Assessment Portfolio 4.1–4.9.)

1. Haiku and Tanka

- **Content/Unity.** The poems focus on images that are simple but striking.
- **Organization/Coherence.** The poems are constructed using traditional haiku/tanka forms.
- **Language/Style.** The poems use vivid and precise nouns, verbs, and modifiers.
- **Conventions.** The poems avoid errors in spelling, grammar, usage, mechanics, and manuscript form.

▶ Additional practice is provided in the Essential Skills Practice Book: Writing 1.8.

2. Critical Essay

- **Content/Unity.** The essay focuses on the imagery of several haiku poems and the emotions that these images evoke in readers.
- **Organization/Coherence.** The essay begins with an introduction that includes the thesis of the essay. The introduction is followed by supporting paragraphs that present specific images from the haiku poems and the emotions these images evoke. The essay ends with a solid conclusion.
- **Language/Style.** The essay uses vivid and precise nouns, verbs, and modifiers.
- **Conventions.** The essay avoids errors in spelling, grammar, usage, mechanics, and manuscript form.

▶ Additional practice is provided in the Essential Skills Practice Book: Writing 1.20.

ANSWERS FOR LANGUAGE LAB

1. These, demonstrative; those, demonstrative
2. myself, reflexive
3. that, demonstrative
4. herself, reflexive
5. this, demonstrative
6. myself, intensive
7. that, demonstrative
8. ourselves, reflexive
9. that, demonstrative
10. themselves, intensive

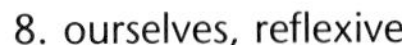

▶ Additional practice is provided in the Essential Skills Practice Book: Language 2.5.

ADDITIONAL RESOURCES

READER'S GUIDE

- Selection Worksheet 5.4

ASSESSMENT PORTFOLIO

- Selection Check Test 2.5.7
- Selection Test 2.5.8

ESSENTIAL SKILLS PRACTICE BOOKS

- Writing 1.8, 1.20
- Language 2.70

PREREADING EXTENSIONS

Have students, in pairs, locate, memorize, and take turns reciting a Robert Burns poem that is written in dialect. Encourage students to explore the musical elements of the poem and to practice reading the dialect accurately. Give students time to rehearse and then invite them to perform for the class. Some favorite Burns poems that students might consider are "Auld Lang Syne," "John Anderson, My Jo," "To a Mouse," and "A Red, Red, Rose."

SUPPORT FOR LEP STUDENTS

ADDITIONAL VOCABULARY

dominion—place over which one has the power to rule
ev'ning's—evening's
ev'ry—every
fells—rocky hills
flutt'ring—fluttering
gladsome—happy, content
murd'ring—murdering
muse—think about
o'er—over
o'erhangs—overhangs
rove—roam, travel
slaught'ring—slaughtering
thro'—through
tyrannic—harsh, cruel, brutal

PREREADING

"Song Composed in August"
by Robert Burns

About the Author

ROBERT BURNS
1759–1796

Considered the national poet of Scotland, **Robert Burns** had a natural gift for poetry. Burns, largely self-educated, was the son of an unsuccessful farmer who valued books and learning but who died and left his young sons with responsibility for the family farm. Burns began writing poetry at the age of fifteen and by the age of twenty-seven had become famous among intellectuals. During his lifetime, he wrote hundreds of songs about love, work, friendship, patriotism, and the nobility of common men and women. Something of a social rebel, he was criticized for his radical lifestyle. Burns, who eventually married and began working as a tax inspector, was extremely patriotic and passionate about Scotland. During his last years he worked hard to preserve his country's music in published form. Although he often needed money, he would take no financial compensation for his work on volumes of Scottish lyrics. He continued to work on the Scottish anthologies until he died at the age of thirty-seven.

About the Selection

The poetic style employed by Robert Burns directly follows Scottish folkloric and literary traditions. "**Song Composed in August**," like most of his best work, is written in Scots, his native dialect. It was unusual during Burns's lifetime for a poet to write in the informal language of everyday people, but Burns avoided the formal, restrained language of other poets in almost everything he wrote. "Song Composed in August" deals with one of the poet's favorite topics: love, romance, and courtship. The poem also captures vivid images of the season and the countryside. In fact, Burns was one of the earliest poets of the Romantic movement, which emphasized nature and human emotion. (See Unit 11 and Connections: Romanticism, page 379.) As you read "Song Composed in August," try to notice the musical qualities of the meter and rhyme.

Haystacks

CONNECTIONS: The Languages of Scotland

People living in Northern Scotland, known as the Highlanders, are of Celtic descent. About ninety thousand of them still speak Gaelic, an ancient Celtic language. People living in southern and central Scotland, called the Lowlanders, speak English with a Scots dialect, the dialect Robert Burns features in "Song Composed in August."

GOALS/OBJECTIVES

Studying this lesson will enable students to

- appreciate a musical love poem written in Scottish dialect by one of the earliest Romantic poets
- discuss the life, work, and dialect of Robert Burns
- define the terms *dialect* and *Romanticism*
- write a love song using descriptive language
- write an essay that examines how Robert Burns uses nature imagery in his work
- recognize different dialects of English

Think about the different kinds of love songs that you have heard. What aspects of nature are often associated with love and romance in these songs and poems? What aspects of nature remind you of love and romance?

"Song Composed in August"

BY ROBERT BURNS

Now westlin winds, and slaught'ring guns
Bring Autumn's pleasant weather;
And the moorcock springs, on whirring wings,
Amang the blooming heather:
Now waving grain, wide o'er the plain,
Delights the weary farmer;
And the moon shines bright, when I rove at night,
To muse upon my charmer.

The partridge loves the fruitful fells;
The plover loves the mountains;
The woodcock haunts the lonely dells;
The soaring hern the fountains:
Thro' lofty groves, the cushat roves,
The path of man to shun it;
The hazel bush o'erhangs the thrush,
The spreading thorn the linnet.[1]

Thus ev'ry kind their pleasure find,
The savage and the tender;
Some social join, and leagues combine;
Some solitary wander;
Avaunt, away! the cruel sway,
Tyrannic man's dominion;
The sportsman's joy, the murd'ring cry,
The flutt'ring, gory pinion![2]

❶ *At what time of day is the speaker traveling? Whom is the speaker going to see?*

❷ *According to the narrator, who is able to find pleasure?*

1. **partridge . . . linnet.** The partridge, plover, woodcock, hern, cushat, thrush, and linnet are all species of birds.
2. **pinion.** Bird's wing

READER'S JOURNAL

Ask students to analyze why particular elements of nature seem related to romantic love.

Students may also focus on details of one image of love and nature that is particularly striking or moving to them.

ANSWERS TO GUIDED READING QUESTIONS

❶ The speaker is traveling at night. The speaker is going to see his "charmer," someone he loves.

❷ Both the "savage and the tender" are able to find pleasure.

SPELLING AND VOCABULARY WORDS FROM THE SELECTION

vernal

QUOTABLES

"O my luve's like a red, red rose,
That's newly sprung in June:
O my luve's like the melodie
That's sweetly play'd in tune."

—Robert Burns
"A Red, Red Rose"

ANALYTIC SCALES FOR RESPONDING IN WRITING
(SEE PAGE 389.)

Assign a score from 1 to 25 for each grading criterion below. (For more detailed evaluation, see the evaluation forms for writing, revising, and proofreading, Assessment Portfolio 4.1–4.9.)

1. Love Song

- **Content/Unity.** The love song is descriptive and focuses on a person, place, thing, activity, or food that the writer loves.
- **Organization/Coherence.** The love song adopts a specific tone as it introduces a subject and then expresses the writer's feelings about the subject using concrete details.
- **Language/Style.** The love song uses vivid and precise nouns, verbs, and modifiers.
- **Conventions.** The love song avoids errors in spelling, grammar, usage, mechanics, and manuscript form.

▶ Additional practice is provided in the Essential Skills Practice Book: Writing 1.8.

2. Critical Essay

- **Content/Unity.** The essay examines Robert Burns's use of nature imagery to express the speaker's feelings of love.
- **Organization/Coherence.** The essay begins with an introduction that describes the speaker's feelings for his subject and the way in which Burns reflects the speaker's feelings with images of nature. The introduction is followed by supporting paragraphs that explore specific images. The essay ends with a solid conclusion.
- **Language/Style.** The essay uses vivid and precise nouns, verbs, and modifiers.
- **Conventions.** The essay avoids errors in spelling, grammar, usage, mechanics, and manuscript form.

▶ Additional practice is provided in the Essential Skills Practice Book: Writing 1.20.

Walking in Park. *Slavicek, 1897*

But Peggy dear, the ev'ning's clear,
Thick flies the skimming swallow;
The sky is blue, the fields in view,
All fading-green and yellow:
Come let us stray our gladsome way,
And view the charms of nature;
The rustling corn, the fruited thorn,
And ev'ry happy creature.

We'll gently walk, and sweetly talk,
Till the silent moon shine clearly;
I'll grasp thy waist, and fondly prest,
Swear how I love thee dearly:
Not vernal show'rs to budding flow'rs,
Not autumn to the farmer,
So dear can be, as thou to me,
My fair, my lovely charmer! ■

❶ *What does the speaker want to do? What things does the speaker say cannot possibly be as dear as his "lovely charmer" is to him?*

WORDS FOR EVERYDAY USE

ver • nal (vurn´ əl) *adj.*, of the spring

VOCABULARY IN CONTEXT

- The warm weather and the vernal flowers put James in a good mood as he walked to school one April morning.

ANSWERS TO GUIDED READING QUESTIONS

❶ The speaker wants to walk gently and talk sweetly with his beloved until the moon shines. He also wants to grasp her waist and swear how much he loves her. Vernal showers to budding flowers or autumn to a farmer cannot possibly be as dear as his "lovely charmer" is to him.

RESPONDING TO THE SELECTION

Each partner should have a chance both to read and to listen to part of the poem.

SELECTION CHECK TEST WITH ANSWERS

EX. At what time of day is the speaker in "Song Composed in August" traveling?
The speaker is traveling at night.

1. Where is the speaker going?
The speaker is going to visit his "charmer," or his beloved.

2. What particular type of animal does the speaker notice as he walks?
He notices birds.

3. What are both the savage and the tender able to find in nature?
Both the savage and the tender are able to find pleasure.

4. Where does the speaker want to take Peggy?
The speaker wants to take Peggy for a walk.

5. What does the speaker want to tell Peggy?
The speaker wants to tell Peggy that he loves her.

Answers for Reviewing the Selection

RECALLING AND INTERPRETING

1. **Recalling.** The speaker talks about autumn's winds and pleasant weather, the blooming heather, the waving grain that delights the weary farmer, and the brightly shining moon. **Interpreting.** The speaker is feeling happy, peaceful, and carefree. The speaker uses images that are upbeat and positive. He uses the word "charmer" to describe the person he is going to see, so the reader knows that he is fond of this person.
2. **Recalling.** Students need only choose two of the following: the partridge in the fruitful fells, the plover in the mountains, the woodcock in the lonely dells, the soaring hern in the fountains, the cushat roving to shun the path of man, the thrush in the hazel bush, and the linnet in the spreading thorn. **Interpreting.** The speaker is on his way to a place that he loves, so he is relating his own contentedness to his observations about the birds.
3. **Recalling.** Both the "savage and the tender" can find their pleasure in nature. **Interpreting.** The speaker mentions the savage and the tender, those who experience nature socially, others who experience it alone, and those who experience nature as they dominate it or sport in it. Although they may differ, they are able to find what pleases them just as he does. He also contrasts the abuse and disruption of the natural world with his appreciation of it.
4. **Recalling.** The speaker wants to take Peggy to view the "charms of nature." They will gently walk until nightfall and then he will tell her that he loves her dearly. **Interpreting.** Flowers need rain showers in order to bloom, and a farmer's livelihood depends on the autumn harvest. His love and need for Peggy are equally important.

(cont.)

Responding to the Selection

Form pairs and read the song aloud to one another. Why is it important to hear this piece aloud? What words and phrases stand out to you as you listen to the poem?

Reviewing the Selection

RECALLING		INTERPRETING
1. In the first stanza, what observations does the speaker make about the time of year? What does he notice as he travels at night? Who is he going to see?	▶▶	How does the speaker feel as he travels? What words and phrases help the reader determine how the speaker is feeling about himself, the person he is going to see, and the world around him?
2. Name two of the animals that Burns mentions in the second stanza. Where does he say one can find these animals?	▶▶	Why does the speaker mention different animals and the place each loves to be? In what way does this reference relate to this speaker's destination?
3. What can both the "savage and the tender" find?	▶▶	What different types of people does the speaker mention in stanza three? Why does he mention these people? How does he relate their ability to find the particular things that please them to his own situation?
4. Where does the speaker want to take Peggy? What does he want to tell her?	▶▶	Why does the speaker mention "vernal show'rs to budding flow'rs" and the importance of "autumn to the farmer"? Why are these appropriate things by which to measure how dear Peggy is to him?

SYNTHESIZING

5. What emotions does the speaker express in this poem? In what way does Burns's environment influence his verse? How might these images be different if Burns lived in a city?

Answers for Reviewing the Selection (cont.)

SYNTHESIZING

Responses will vary. Possible responses are given.

5. The speaker expresses the emotions of love and happiness. Burns's verse is inspired by his surroundings, and he relates his feelings to the natural world. If Burns lived in the city, he might not know the same intimate details about nature. He might use images reflective of city life rather than images of birds, harvests, and moonlight to make his point.

Understanding Literature (Questions for Discussion)

1. **Dialect.** A **dialect** is a version of a language spoken by the people of a particular place, time, or social group. Provide examples of dialect in this poem. What words or phrases from your own language or dialect might you use in place of these words? Does the poet's use of dialect add any particular mood or flavor to this poem? Explain.
2. **Romanticism. Romanticism** was a literary and artistic movement of the eighteenth and nineteenth centuries. For more information on this movement, see the Handbook of Literary Terms or the Unit 11 introduction. In what way does Burns comment upon social class by writing in dialect? In what way does he contrast the works of man and nature in this poem? In what way does the poem promote emotion over reason? In what way does the poem associate nature with emotion (in particular, the emotion of love)?

Responding in Writing

1. **Creative Writing: Love Song.** Write a love song, using descriptive language and concrete details, to express your feelings. Adopt any tone you like—your love song may be serious, sincere, whimsical, humorous, or sarcastic. You may write about love of a person, place, thing, activity, or food. Freewrite about your subject before you begin writing so that you have plenty of vivid details with which to work. You can choose to create your own rhythm and melody, or you can write your song to the tune of an existing song. You may choose to work in pairs to complete this assignment.
2. **Critical Essay: Nature Imagery and Love.** Write an essay in which you examine how Robert Burns uses nature imagery to express the speaker's feelings of love. In your essay, answer the following questions: How does the speaker feel about his subject? What images of nature directly reflect his feelings of love?

Language Lab

Dialects of English. Review the Language Arts Survey 2.70, "Dialects of English." Then read the following lines from another well-known poem by Robert Burns, "Auld Lang Syne," which is often sung during New Year's Eve celebrations. Rewrite the lines, replacing examples of dialect with words from standard English or words from your own dialect.

1. Should auld acquaintance be forgot/And never brought to min'?
2. We'll tak a cup o' kindness yet/For auld lang syne.
3. But we've wandered mony a wary foot,/Sin' auld lang syne.
4. But seas between us braid hae roared,/Sin' auld lang syne.
5. And there's a hand, my trusty fiere,/And gie's a hand o' thine;

Answers for Understanding Literature

Responses will vary. Possible responses are given.

1. Dialect. Examples of dialect include the following words and phrases: *slaught'ring,* which might be replaced with *slaughtering; amang,* which might be replaced with *among; o'er,* which might be replaced with *over; Thro',* which might be replaced with *through; o'erhangs,* which might be replaced with *overhangs; ev'ry,* which might be replaced with *every; murd'ring,* which might be replaced with *murdering; flutt'ring,* which might be replaced with *fluttering;* and *flow'rs,* which might be replaced with *flowers.* Students might say that the dialect gives the poem a light, informal mood and a genuine Scottish flavor.

2. Romanticism. Burns, unlike many of his contemporaries, chose to write in the informal language of everyday people. By doing this, he is saying that the enjoyment of poetry should not be limited to the upper classes. The everyday person has valuable thoughts and experiences that can inspire poetry, and the everyday person should be able to read and enjoy poetry that is not written in formal, restrained language.
In "Song Composed in August," Burns contrasts the beauty and tranquility of being part of nature with the harsh brutality of the hunter and his gun. The poem promotes emotion over reason and associates nature with the emotions of love and happiness in the way that it shows the speaker being swept away by beauty and love as he walks through the night and admires the wildlife, the trees, plants, flowers, and the moon.

Answers for Language Lab

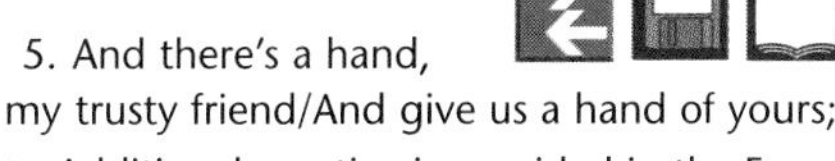

1. Should old acquaintances be forgotten/And never brought to mind?
2. We'll take a cup of kindness yet/For old times gone by.
3. But we've wandered many a weary foot,/Since old times gone by.
4. But broad seas between us have roared/Since old times gone by.
5. And there's a hand, my trusty friend/And give us a hand of yours;

► Additional practice is provided in the Essential Skills Practice Book: Language 2.70.

ANALYTIC SCALES FOR RESPONDING IN WRITING

Grading scales for Responding in Writing appear on page 386.

ADDITIONAL RESOURCES

READER'S GUIDE

- Selection Worksheet 5.5

ASSESSMENT PORTFOLIO

- Selection Check Test 4.5.9
- Selection Test 4.5.10

ESSENTIAL SKILLS PRACTICE BOOKS

- Writing 1.8, 1.20

PREREADING EXTENSIONS

As students read in Connections, many species of animals in Kenya risked extinction, so game management plans were put into effect to restrict hunting.

Hold a class discussion about measures that have been taken, or that should be taken, in students' opinions, to preserve the natural world. For example, students might describe recycling plans, hunting restrictions, waste management, and clean-up efforts in parks or on highways. Do students believe these measures are worthwhile? Why, or why not?

SUPPORT FOR LEP STUDENTS

PRONUNCIATIONS OF PROPER NOUNS AND ADJECTIVES

Is • ak Din • e • sen (ē´säk dē´nə sən)

ADDITIONAL VOCABULARY

pulsating—throbbing
radiated—sent out

PREREADING

"The Iguana" from *Out of Africa* by Isak Dinesen

KENYA

About the Author

ISAK DINESEN 1885–1962

Born in 1885 in Denmark, Karen Dinesen wrote under the pen name **Isak Dinesen.** She studied in Denmark and in Switzerland, where she began painting. In 1914, Dinesen married Baron Bror Blixen and moved to British East Africa, where she and her husband started a coffee plantation. She and her husband divorced in 1921, and Dinesen stayed in Africa and continued to run the plantation despite fires, droughts, and poor harvests. After losing the plantation, she returned to her mother's house in Denmark and devoted herself to writing. Dinesen also wrote about her native Denmark and penned several story collections, including *Seven Gothic Tales* and *Winter's Tales.* Having faced illness for many years, she died of malnutrition in 1962.

About the Selection

Dinesen's experiences in Africa are the source of her most famous work, ***Out of Africa,*** published in 1937 and later made into a movie. This memoir is rich in imagery and description of the terrain and wildlife of British East Africa, now Kenya. Dinesen expresses her admiration for the native people she lives among and for a way of life that she sees changing. In "**The Iguana,**" a selection from *Out of Africa,* Dinesen describes an experience with one of the interesting creatures that she encounters in the Ngong Hills of Kenya.

CONNECTIONS: Kenyan Wildlife

Eastern Africa is known for its abundance of wildlife. When Europeans began to colonize Africa in the nineteenth century, hunting expeditions became very popular. Game in Africa seemed limitless and was hunted indiscriminately. As a result, many species were killed off entirely or were in danger of becoming extinct. Around the beginning of the twentieth century, game management plans were put into effect to restrict hunting. Many animals can now be seen in protected areas, such as Mount Kenya National Park. Kenya especially is renowned for its wildlife, including lions, leopards, wild dogs, elephants, buffaloes, rhinoceroses, zebras, antelopes, gazelles, hippopotamuses, and crocodiles. Mount Kenya National Park covers areas of forest and sparse vegetation high (above 10,800 feet) on Mount Kenya.

GOALS/OBJECTIVES

Studying this lesson will enable students to

- empathize with a character who learns an important lesson about respecting the natural world
- discuss the life and work of Isak Dinesen, and discuss Kenyan wildlife
- define the literary terms *anecdote* and *simile*
- write an anecdote based on personal experience
- analyze the theme of a story in a critical essay
- organize an endangered animal/environment fair for the school or community that includes colorful and informative displays

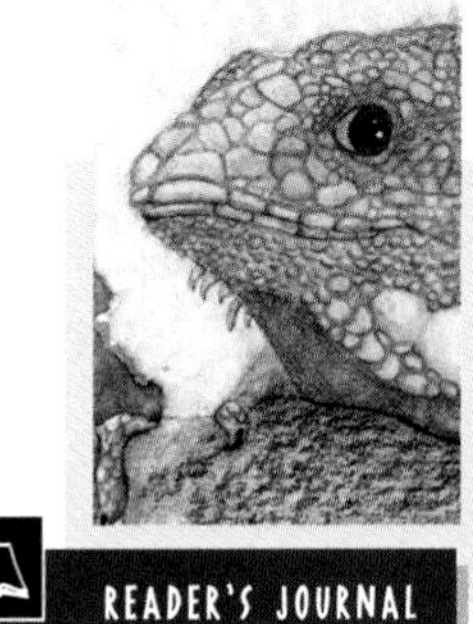

Have you ever admired something so much that you just had to possess it? What was it that you admired? How did you feel once you had this thing? Did possessing it change your perception of this thing in any way? Respond to these questions in your journal.

READER'S JOURNAL

"The Iguana"

Isak Dinesen

In the Reserve[1] I have sometimes come upon the Iguana, the big lizards, as they were sunning themselves upon a flat stone in a river-bed. They are not pretty in shape, but nothing can be imagined more beautiful than their coloring. They shine like a heap of precious stones or like a pane cut out of an old church window. When, as you approach, they swish away, there is a flash of azure, green and purple over the stones, the color seems to be standing behind them in the air, like a comet's luminous tail.

Once I shot an Iguana. I thought that I should be able to make some pretty things from his skin. A strange thing happened then, that I have never afterwards forgotten. As I went up to him, where he was lying dead upon his stone, and actually while I was walking the few steps, he faded and grew pale, all color died out of him as in one long sigh, and by the time that I touched him he was gray and dull like a lump of concrete. It was the live impetuous blood pulsating within the animal, which had radiated out all that glow and splendor. Now that the flame was put out, and the soul had flown, the Iguana was as dead as a sandbag.

Often since I have, in some sort, shot an Iguana, and I have remembered the one of the Reserve. Up at Meru[2] I saw a young native girl with a bracelet on, a leather strap two inches wide, and embroidered all over with very small turquoise-colored beads which varied a little in color and played in green, light blue and ultramarine. It was an extraordinarily live thing; it seemed to draw breath on her arm, so that I wanted it for myself, and made Farah[3] buy it from her. No sooner had it come upon my own arm than it gave up the ghost. It was nothing now, a

1. **Reserve.** Animal reservation in the Ngong Hills in Kenya
2. **Meru.** Mountain in Tanzania
3. **Farah.** Dinesen's servant

❶ *What is noticeable or unique about the iguana? To what does Dinesen compare this characteristic?*

❷ *What did Dinesen buy at Meru? What change seemed to occur to this item once she possessed it?*

❸ *Why did Dinesen hunt the iguana? What happened after she shot it?*

Words for Everyday Use

az • ure (azh´ər) *adj.*, blue

lu • mi • nous (lo͞o ´mə nəs) *adj.*, bright, shining, giving off light

im • pet • u • ous (im pech´o͞o əs) *adj.*, moving with great force

READER'S JOURNAL

As an alternative activity, you might ask students to describe the ways in which they've seen people abuse and mistreat the natural world. Ask why people feel that they can simply take or use whatever they want. What do students feel might happen when people fail to respect animals and natural environments?

Answers to Guided Reading Questions

❶ The coloring of the iguana is beautiful. Dinesen compares this coloring to a heap of precious stones or to a pane from a church window.

❷ Dinesen bought a bracelet. The bracelet lost its beauty and became small and cheap.

❸ Dinesen hunted the iguana because she thought that she would be able to make something pretty with the skin. After she shot it, the color faded out of it as it died, until it was only a gray lump.

Spelling and Vocabulary Words from the Selection

azure	luminous
impetuous	quick

Vocabulary in Context

- The red kite was strikingly beautiful against the azure sky and the white clouds.
- It was late at night when we finally entered the large, luminous city.
- Impetuous winds blew shingles from many rooftops.

Answers to Guided Reading Questions

➊ Dinesen suggests that others not shoot the iguana.

Selection Check Test with Answers

EX. What kind of animal is featured in this selection?
An iguana is featured in this selection.

1. Why did Dinesen shoot an iguana?
She shot it because she thought that she could make something pretty with its skin.

2. What change did the iguana undergo after being shot?
The iguana died and, as it did so, it lost its color.

3. What did Dinesen buy in Meru?
She bought a bracelet.

4. What did Dinesen see in the Zoological Museum that reminded her of the iguana?
She saw a colorful deep-water fish.

5. What advice does Dinesen give to the settlers of East Africa?
She advises them not to shoot the iguana.

Quotables

"Like winds and sunsets, wild things were taken for granted until progress began to do away with them. Now we face the question whether a still higher "standard of living" is worth its cost in things natural, wild, and free."

—Aldo Leopold

small, cheap, purchased article of finery. It had been the play of colors, the duet between the turquoise and the "nègre"—that quick, sweet, brownish black, like peat and black pottery, of the native's skin—that had created the life of the bracelet.

In the Zoological Museum of Pietermaritzburg,[4] I have seen, in a stuffed deep-water fish in a showcase, the same combination of coloring, which there had survived death; it made me wonder what life can well be like, on the bottom of the sea, to send up something so live and airy. I stood in Meru and looked at my pale hand and at the dead bracelet; it was as if an injustice had been done to a noble thing, as if truth had been suppressed. So sad did it seem that I remembered the saying of the hero in a book that I had read as a child: "I have conquered them all, but I am standing amongst graves."

In a foreign country and with foreign species of life one should take measures to find out whether things will be keeping their value when dead. To the settlers of East Africa I give the advice: "For the sake of your own eyes and heart, shoot not the Iguana." ■

4. **Pietermaritzburg.** South African city

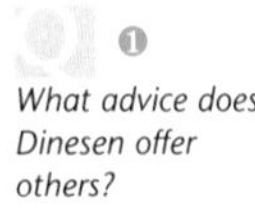

➊ *What advice does Dinesen offer others?*

Words for Everyday Use

quick (kwik) *adj.,* living, alive

Vocabulary in Context

- The quick, green branches of the evergreen trees were covered with snow.

Responding to the Selection

In this selection, Dinesen remembers a quote she had read as a child, "I have conquered them all, but I am standing amongst graves." What does this quote mean to you? Describe a time when you felt this way about a situation.

Reviewing the Selection

RECALLING | **INTERPRETING**

1. Why did Dinesen shoot an iguana? What happened to the iguana after she shot it? ▶▶ How did Dinesen feel about shooting the iguana?
2. What did Dinesen see on a girl in Meru? ▶▶ Why did Dinesen's feelings about this item change after she owned it?
3. What did Dinesen see in the Zoological Museum of Pietermaritzburg? What saying did Dinesen recall while at the museum? ▶▶ In what way was the object like the iguana? It what way did it differ from the iguana? What emotional connection did Dinesen have with this saying?
4. What advice does Dinesen give? ▶▶ Why does she give this advice?

SYNTHESIZING

5. What broader meaning might Dinesen have had in mind when she wrote, "One should take measures to find out whether things will be keeping their value when dead"?

Understanding Literature (Questions for Discussion)

1. **Simile**. A **simile** is a comparison using *like* or *as*. What similes does Dinesen use to describe the colors of the iguana when it is alive? What similes does she use to describe the iguana after she has shot it?
2. **Anecdote**. An **anecdote** is a brief story, usually with a specific point or moral. What three anecdotes does Dinesen share in "The Iguana"? What specific point do the anecdotes together make?

RESPONDING TO THE SELECTION

Give students time to themselves to freewrite responses to this quote. They might then want to discuss their responses in small groups.

ANSWERS FOR REVIEWING THE SELECTION

RECALLING AND INTERPRETING

1. **Recalling.** Dinesen shot the iguana because she thought that she would be able to make something pretty with the skin. The iguana lost its color as it died. **Interpreting.** Dinesen regretted what she did as she watched the creature lose its glory.

2. **Recalling.** Dinesen saw a bracelet that she greatly admired. **Interpreting.** The bracelet lost its beauty when Dinesen saw it on her own pale arm. Part of its charm was in the way it looked on the dark skin of the girl.

3. **Recalling.** Dinesen saw a stuffed deep-water fish of amazing colors. She recalls the saying, "I have conquered them all, but I am standing amongst graves." **Interpreting.** The fish shared the astounding colors of the iguana, but the fish's colors had been preserved although it was dead. Dinesen feels that although she has possession of beautiful things, her victory is empty because of the loss involved in her conquering.

4. **Recalling.** Dinesen advises people to find out whether things will keep their value when dead and not to shoot the iguana. **Interpreting.** Dinesen gives this advice based on her own experience of trying to capture the beauty of a living thing and destroying it in the process.

SYNTHESIZING

Responses will vary. Possible responses are given.

5. Dinesen might mean that people should think about their actions before destroying living things, habitats, or ways of life.

ANSWERS FOR UNDERSTANDING LITERATURE

Responses will vary. Possible responses are given.

1. **Simile.** Dinesen says that the colors of the living iguana shine like a heap of precious stones or like a pane cut out of an old church window. She says that when the iguana moves, the colors linger like a comet's tail. After she killed the iguana, it turned gray and dull like a lump of concrete.

2. **Anecdote.** Dinesen shares anecdotes about killing the iguana for its pretty skin, only to watch its beauty fade; buying the bracelet in Meru, only to find that part of its beauty came from its wearer; and seeing the stuffed, colorful fish. The three anecdotes make the point that there is beauty in living things that should be appreciated. Even when such beauty can be preserved in death, there is a sense of loss.

ANALYTIC SCALES FOR RESPONDING IN WRITING

Assign a score from 1 to 25 for each grading criterion below. (For more detailed evaluation, see the evaluation forms for writing, revising, and proofreading, Assessment Portfolio 4.1–4.9.)

1. Anecdote

- **Content/Unity.** The anecdote is based on the writer's personal experience and makes a point about a subject or issue.
- **Organization/Coherence.** The anecdote is brief and conveys a specific message.
- **Language/Style.** The anecdote uses vivid and precise nouns, verbs, and modifiers.
- **Conventions.** The anecdote avoids errors in spelling, grammar, usage, mechanics, and manuscript form.

▶ Additional practice is provided in the Essential Skills Practice Book: Writing 1.8.

2. Critical Essay

- **Content/Unity.** The essay identifies the theme of "The Iguana" and explains how each anecdote Dinesen relates supports this theme.
- **Organization/Coherence.** The essay begins with an introduction that states the theme of "The Iguana." The introduction is followed by paragraphs that describe how the anecdotes in the story support the theme and that provide specific examples from the story to prove this idea. The essay ends with a solid conclusion.
- **Language/Style.** The essay uses vivid and precise nouns, verbs, and modifiers.
- **Conventions.** The essay avoids errors in spelling, grammar, usage, mechanics, and manuscript form.

▶ Additional practice is provided in the Essential Skills Practice Book: Writing 1.20.

Responding in Writing

1. **Creative Writing: Anecdote**. Think about a point that you would like to get across to others. You may wish to make a statement about respecting others, caring about the environment, or understanding differences. Think about experiences you have had, actions you have witnessed, or stories you have heard about somebody doing one of these things. Use such an experience to create an anecdote. Remember that an anecdote is a very brief story that will convey a specific message. Share your anecdote with some of your classmates, or make a class anecdote book.

2. **Critical Essay: Analyzing Theme**. A theme is a central idea in a literary work. First identify the theme of "The Iguana." Then describe each anecdote Dinesen relates, and explain how each anecdote supports this theme. Is one anecdote more powerful than the others? Might one of the anecdotes stand on its own to make Dinesen's point, or are the anecdotes dependent upon one another to make the point? Explain. Refer to the text for examples to support your responses.

PROJECT

Endangered Animal/Environment Fair. As a class, organize an "Endangered Animal/Environment Fair" to raise student and community awareness of environmental issues. Your fair should be a fun event which includes colorful and creative displays about endangered animal species and other threats to the environment. First, hold a class meeting in which you discuss the details of the event. Decide where it will be held, and what kinds of information and exhibits you might present. Appropriate locations might include your school cafeteria or gymnasium, your school or local library, or, if weather permits, outside on school grounds, in a public park, or at a school sporting event.

During your class meeting, form groups of three or four. Each group should be in charge of creating one exhibit. Once you form your groups, use online sources, CD-ROM encyclopedias, and other resources to research possible topics. There should be no need for duplicate displays—there are plenty of environmental issues on which you can focus. One group might focus its entire display on one endangered animal, one group might focus on polluted water and its effect on marine animals, and another group might focus on an animal that has already become extinct and the factors that led to its extinction. Along with informational displays, you might want to design pamphlets or prepare refreshments to go with your displays. Try to make your event as interesting and enjoyable as possible, and try to hold it at a time that is convenient for many different people. Advertise the event using posters, flyers, local media, and your school public address system.

PROJECT NOTES

See the evaluation form for projects, Assessment Portfolio 4.12.

Endangered Animal/Environment Fair. Your class's fair may be as simple or elaborate as time and resources permit. Even if the students create simple projects and displays on environmental issues, they would most likely enjoy inviting people from outside the class to view their hard work. Remind students that they may contact specific environmental organizations for information on their topics and for membership information. They might want to provide people with this membership information at the fair.

PREREADING

"The Flower of Air"
by Gabriela Mistral, translated by Doris Dana

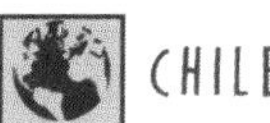 CHILE

About the Author

GABRIELA MISTRAL
1889–1957

Born Lucila Godoy Alcayaga in Vicuña, Chile, **Gabriela Mistral** renamed herself after the archangel Gabriel and the mistral—a cold, dry, wind that blows over the coast of France. Mistral's first poems became public in 1914, while she was a schoolteacher in Chile. For these poems, she won Chile's national prize for poetry. After this achievement, Mistral produced many other works, publishing in 1917 alone about fifty stories and poems. Mistral also worked as a diplomat and collaborated with the Mexican minister of education to create an education reform program for rural areas. In 1945, Mistral received the Nobel Prize for literature. Her lyric works include *Sonnets of Death* (1914), *Desolación* (1922), *Tala* (1938), and *Lagar* (1954).

About the Selection

Gabriela Mistral's poetry often focuses on the important struggles in human life such as birth and death. The poem you are about to read, **"The Flower of Air,"** tells of a different kind of struggle—the effort to find the inspiration and courage to put words on paper and create poetry. In fact, Mistral first called this poem "The Adventure," referring to her adventure with poetry. To illustrate her "adventure," she tells a simple allegory, or a story in which each element symbolizes, or represents, something else. By describing a woman in a meadow who demands that the speaker bring her flowers, Mistral relates her own efforts to find and nurture her poetic inspiration, or muse. In ancient Greek and Roman myth, the **Muses** were beautiful goddesses believed to provide the inspiration for the arts and sciences. Later, writers used the idea of the muse to explain the mystery of literary inspiration.

CONNECTIONS: Gabriel the Archangel

The archangel Gabriel, whose name Gabriela Mistral adopted, figures in the traditions of Christians, Jews, and Muslims. In the Bible, Gabriel is an angel of the highest rank who serves as heavenly messenger and as a trumpeter of the Last Judgment. In the Old Testament, he is sent by God to save the Hebrew prophet Daniel from being devoured in a lion's den. In the New Testament, Gabriel is sent to the Virgin Mary to announce that she is to give birth to Jesus. In the tradition of Islam, Gabriel reveals the Koran (see page 778) to Mohammed, acting as the angel of truth.

ADDITIONAL RESOURCES

READER'S GUIDE

- Selection Worksheet 5.6

ASSESSMENT PORTFOLIO

- Selection Check Test 2.5.11
- Selection Test 2.5.12

ESSENTIAL SKILLS PRACTICE BOOKS

- Writing 1.8, 1.20
- Speaking and Listening 3.2

PREREADING EXTENSIONS

Encourage students to locate some of Mistral's other lyric works. Students can work individually or in pairs to choose a poem to present to the rest of the class. Each student can recite a poem, explain why he or she chose the poem, and then explain why it is similar to or different from other works by Mistral.

SUPPORT FOR LEP STUDENTS

PRONUNCIATIONS OF PROPER NOUNS AND ADJECTIVES

El • e • o • nor • a (el ē ō nôr´ə)
Li • gei • a (lī gē´ə)
Me • de • a (mə dē´ə)

ADDITIONAL VOCABULARY

crevice—deep crack
governing—ruling over
reaping—gathering
straightway—without stopping, right away
tribute—something done in honor of something or someone
vague—unclear

GOALS/OBJECTIVES

Studying this lesson will enable students to

- empathize with a writer trying to find and nurture poetic inspiration
- discuss the life and work of Gabriela Mistral
- define *allegory*, *mood*, and *imagery*
- write a descriptive piece that evokes a particular mood
- write a critical essay which analyzes the title of a poem
- practice active listening and interpersonal communication skills

READER'S JOURNAL

As an alternate activity, you might ask students who enjoy writing, painting, or any other art form to describe how it feels to try to perfect their art. Do they ever feel blocked when they sit down to write? Do they ever feel frustration when practicing a musical instrument or trying to depict a scene with paints or drawing pencil? How does it feel to complete a work of art and be satisfied with it? What different emotions do they experience as the artistic process progresses?

SPELLING AND VOCABULARY WORDS FROM THE SELECTION

burden	deluge
crag	somnambulant

ANSWERS TO GUIDED READING QUESTIONS

❶ The woman stands in the middle of the meadow. She governs all who pass or address her.

❷ The speaker covers the woman with the white flowers. The woman next asks for red flowers.

Describe a time when you struggled to accomplish, change, or perfect something. How did it feel to face the struggle? Did you get the results you wanted, or were you disappointed? Explain your responses.

READER'S JOURNAL

"The Flower of Air"

GABRIELA MISTRAL, TRANSLATED BY DORIS DANA

❶ *Where does the woman stand? What does she do there?*

I met her, not by chance,
standing in the middle of the meadow,
governing all who passed,
all who addressed her.

She said to me: "Climb the mountain—
I never leave the meadow.
Cut me flowers white
as snows, crisp and tender."

I climbed the mountain
and searched where flowers whiten
among the rocks,
half sleeping, half waking.

❷ *What does the speaker do with the white flowers? What does the woman ask the speaker to bring her next?*

When I came down with my burden
I found her in the middle of the meadow.
Like a crazy one, I covered her
with a deluge of lilies.

She never glanced at their whiteness.
She said to me: "Now bring me
red flowers, only the red.
I cannot leave the meadow."

WORDS FOR EVERYDAY USE

bur • den (burd´'n) *n.*, anything which is carried; load
del • uge (del´yo͞oj´) *n.*, great flood; overwhelming abundance

VOCABULARY IN CONTEXT

- That package is an enormous burden to carry on the train.
- The bottom fell out of the bucket and a deluge of water poured out.

I clambered up crags with deer
and searched for flowers of madness,
those that grow red and appear
to live and die of redness.

When I came down, I offered them
in trembling tribute;
she became red as water bloodied
by the wounded deer.

She gazed at me, half dreaming,
and said: "Go climb again and bring me
the yellow, only the yellow.
I never leave the meadow."

I went straightway to the mountain
and searched for clustered flowers,
color of sun, color of saffron,[1]
newly born, already eternal.

When I returned, I found her still standing
in the middle of the meadow.
I showered her with sun-burst blossoms
till she was golden as the threshing floor.

And once again, crazy with gold,
she said: "Go up, my servant,
and cut flowers that have no color,
not saffron, not burnished red.

"Bring me flowers that I love,
remembering Eleonora and Ligeia,[2]
flowers color of dream, color of dreaming.
I am the woman of the meadow."

1 *What happens when the speaker offers the woman the red flowers?*

2 *To what things does the speaker compare the yellow of the flowers? Is the woman finally satisfied with the yellow flowers?*

3 *With what does the woman associate the flowers of no color?*

1. **saffron.** Orange-yellow seasoning made from the stigmas of the crocus
2. **Eleonora and Ligeia.** Characters from works by Edgar Allan Poe; both characters are beautiful women who die soon after marriage.

Words for Everyday Use

crag (krag) *n.*, steep, rugged rock that rises above other rocks

Answers to Guided Reading Questions

1 The woman turns as red as a bloodied stream.

2 The speaker compares the yellow flowers to sun, saffron, gold, and a threshing floor. The woman is not satisfied and makes another request.

3 The woman associates flowers of no color with Eleonora, Ligeia, and dreams.

Quotables

"A poet is a nightingale, who sits in darkness and sings to cheer its own solitude with sweet sounds."

—Percy Bysshe Shelley
A Defense of Poetry

Analytic Scales for Responding in Writing

(See page 401.)

Assign a score from 1 to 25 for each grading criterion below. (For more detailed evaluation, see the evaluation forms for writing, revising, and proofreading, Assessment Portfolio 4.1–4.9.)

1. Images of Nature and Mood

- **Content/Unity.** The description presents a scene in nature that evokes a particular mood.
- **Organization/Coherence.** The writer describes images using concrete details that convey a strong mood.
- **Language/Style.** The description uses vivid and precise nouns, verbs, and modifiers.
- **Conventions.** The description avoids errors in spelling, grammar, usage, mechanics, and manuscript form.

▶ Additional practice is provided in the Essential Skills Practice Book: Writing 1.8.

Vocabulary in Context

- Television ads often place cars on rocky crags, silhouetted against a western sky.

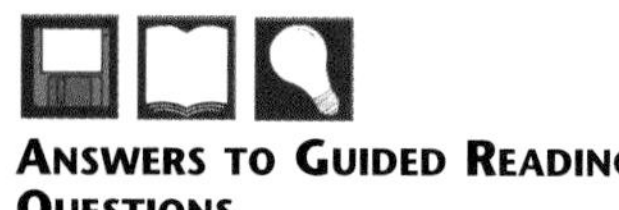

Answers to Guided Reading Questions

➊ The speaker gets the flowers without color from the soft air.

ANALYTIC SCALES FOR RESPONDING IN WRITING

(SEE PAGE 401.)

Assign a score from 1 to 25 for each grading criterion below. (For more detailed evaluation, see the evaluation forms for writing, revising, and proofreading, Assessment Portfolio 4.1–4.9.)

2. Critical Essay

- **Content/Unity.** The essay explains the meaning of the title of the poem "The Flower of Air," and the meaning of the title "The Adventure," the earlier title.
- **Organization/Coherence.** The essay begins with an introduction that includes the thesis of the essay. The introduction is followed by supporting paragraphs with clear transitions. The essay ends with a solid conclusion.
- **Language/Style.** The essay uses vivid and precise nouns, verbs, and modifiers.
- **Conventions.** The essay avoids errors in spelling, grammar, usage, mechanics, and manuscript form.

▶ Additional practice is provided in the Essential Skills Practice Book: Writing 1.20.

Valle de México. *José Maria Velasco. Courtesy of Smithsonian Institution Travelling Exhibition Service, Washington, DC*

I approached the mountain
now black as Medea,[3]
with not a crevice of brightness,
vague and clear as a cavern.[4]

Those flowers did not grow on branches
or open among rocks.
I cut them from the soft air;
I cut them with gentle shears.

➊ *Where does the speaker get the flowers without color?*

I cut as if I the cutter
walked blind.
I cut from one air and another
as if air were my forest.

3. **Medea.** Sorceress from Greek mythology who falls in love with Jason and helps him to get the Golden Fleece of a miraculous flying ram. Later, when he deserts her to marry another woman, she kills the children they had together.
4. **cavern.** Cave

When I came down from the mountain
and went in search of my queen,
I found her now walking,
no longer white or violent red.

Somnambulant, she was leaving,
abandoning the meadow,
and I followed her, following
through pastures and poplar groves.

Burdened thus with so many flowers,
shoulders, hands, garlanded with air,
from the air ever cutting more flowers,
I went reaping a harvest of air.

She goes before me, faceless,
leaving no footprint,
and I follow her, still follow
through dense clusters of fog,

bearing colorless flowers,
not white or burnished red,
until my release at the farthest limit
when my time dissolves . . . ■

❶ *What is the woman doing when the speaker comes down the mountain?*

❷ *What does the speaker do when the woman walks away?*

❸ *Until when will the speaker follow the woman?*

Responding to the Selection

Would you encourage the speaker to continue to struggle to please and follow the woman? Why, or why not? What do you think is the speaker's reward for continuing the struggle?

Words for Everyday Use

som • nam • bu • lant (säm nam´ byo͞o lant) *adj.*, sleepwalking; in a trance

Vocabulary in Context

• We guided the somnambulant child back to his bed.

Answers to Guided Reading Questions

❶ The woman is leaving the meadow.

❷ The speaker follows the woman.

❸ The speaker will follow the woman "until [her] release at the farthest limit."

Responding to the Selection

If students find the poem challenging, encourage them to review the information provided in About the Selection on page 395.

Selection Check Test with Answers

EX. Where does the woman stand?
The woman stands in the middle of the meadow.

1. What does the woman tell the speaker to do?
The woman tells the speaker to climb the mountain and bring back flowers for her.

2. Is the woman satisfied with the flowers the speaker brings to her?
No, the woman is not satisfied.

3. From where do flowers the "color of dream" need to be cut?
Flowers the "color of dream" need to be cut from air.

4. When the speaker comes down from the mountain, what is the woman doing?
The woman is leaving the meadow.

5. With what is the speaker burdened at the end of the poem?
The speaker is burdened with too many flowers.

Reviewing the Selection

RECALLING / **INTERPRETING**

1. Where does the speaker find the woman in the poem? What does the woman tell the speaker to do? What does the speaker do in response? ▶▶ How do you know that the woman is important to the speaker? How do you know that she has power over the speaker?

2. Is the woman satisfied when she gets the red flowers? What does the speaker do with the yellow blossoms that he or she finds? Is the woman satisfied with those? ▶▶ To what part of the writing process might you compare the speaker's struggle to find flowers of just the right color? What does a poet have to perfect as he or she works on a poem?

3. What flowers does the woman of the meadow say she loves? Where does the speaker have to go to find these flowers? From where are they cut? ▶▶ Why might the mountain that the speaker approaches be dark and "vague . . . as a cavern"? How might the speaker be feeling at this point in the struggle, since he or she has been unable so far to find the right flowers, or, in the larger sense, the right words for the poem? How are the flowers he or she finally finds different from the ones previously found?

4. Where is the woman when the speaker finally finds the flowers without color? With what is the speaker burdened? What harvest does the speaker reap? ▶▶ Knowing what you know about Mistral's theme, why is it so important to the speaker to follow the woman even when it becomes almost impossible? In what way might the speaker have reached a point at which it is impossible to give up the struggle?

SYNTHESIZING

5. What draws the speaker to the woman in the poem? What does the woman represent? What is the "flower of air" to this speaker? How does the adventure the poem's speaker experiences compare to the struggle to write a poem?

Understanding Literature (Questions for Discussion)

1. **Allegory.** An **allegory** is a work in which each element symbolizes, or represents, something else. Discuss this poem as an allegory. What do you think individual characters, objects, places, and actions represent? Why might the author have chosen a natural setting—one that includes meadows, mountains, pastures, flowers, and trees—as the setting for her allegory? Why are these things often associated with poetry and creativity?

ANSWERS FOR REVIEWING THE SELECTION

RECALLING AND INTERPRETING

1. **Recalling.** The speaker finds the woman in the poem standing in the middle of the meadow. The woman tells the speaker of the poem to climb the mountain and cut crisp and tender flowers for her because she never leaves the meadow. The speaker obeys the woman's wishes. **Interpreting.** The speaker goes to great trouble to find the flowers for the woman, and the speaker observes that the woman is "governing all who [pass]."

2. **Recalling.** The woman is not satisfied with the red flowers. The speaker then follows the woman's order to gather yellow flowers. The woman is not satisfied with those. **Interpreting.** The speaker's struggle to find flowers of just the right color might be compared to a poet's struggle for the perfect words or images to express his or her meaning. The poet constantly has to perfect the language of the poem.

3. **Recalling.** The woman of the meadow says that she loves flowers that are the color of "dreaming." To find these flowers, the speaker must go to the mountain and cut them from the "soft air." **Interpreting.** The speaker might be feeling frustrated and hopeless. The flowers he or she finally finds are not of the earth, but of the air. They are special and more mysterious.

4. **Recalling.** The speaker finds the woman walking, almost in her sleep, abandoning the meadow. The speaker is burdened with too many flowers. The speaker reaps a harvest of air. **Interpreting.** The woman seems to be the speaker's source of inspiration. It is important to the speaker to choose the right flowers, or choose the right words for the poem. The speaker has invested so much time and emotional energy into perfecting her work that she cannot give up this struggle. (cont.)

ANSWERS FOR REVIEWING THE SELECTION (CONT.)

SYNTHESIZING

Responses will vary. Possible responses are given.

5. The speaker is drawn to the woman's power and to the woman's advice about what flowers to gather. The woman represents the speaker's artistic inspiration. The flower of air is the woman's poetry. The adventure the speaker of the poem experiences is similar to the writing of a poem in that the speaker, like the poet, struggles to nurture inspiration. Also, the speaker, like a poet, must work hard to complete her task successfully, and she becomes discouraged at times because she feels that she is fighting a losing battle. The speaker searches for the right flowers, just as the poet struggles to find the right words and images to best express his or her meaning.

2. **Mood and Imagery. Mood**, or **atmosphere**, is the emotion created in the reader by part or all of a literary work. An **image** is a word or phrase that names something that can be seen, heard, touched, tasted, or smelled. The images in a literary work are referred to, collectively, as the work's **imagery**. Describe the mood of this poem and the ways in which the poem's imagery contributes to its mood. What specific images relate directly to a particular mood? What does the mood of the poem say about the speaker's feelings regarding his or her struggle?

Responding in Writing

1. **Creative Writing: Images of Nature and Mood.** Write a one-page description of a scene in nature that evokes a particular mood or atmosphere. For example, what images in nature would you describe to create a peaceful mood? What images would you describe to create a frightening atmosphere? Before you put anything on paper, imagine yourself outside in the woods, in your backyard, in the city park, or in some other place you have visited. What are some of the images that come to mind? When you have a familiar scene in mind, begin to freewrite. Use the information you gather as the basis for your description. Remember that the images of nature that you use do not have to be beautiful ones. What you choose to include in your description depends on the mood you are trying to create.

2. **Critical Essay: Titles.** Imagine that you need to explain to someone why Gabriela Mistral originally wanted to call this poem "The Adventure." Write a short essay in which you explain the reference of the title "The Adventure." Describe what the poem is about, and how this title reflects the poem's theme. Then explain the title "The Flower of Air." To what does this title refer, and how does it reflect the poem's theme?

Speaking and Listening Skills

Active Listening and Interpersonal Communication. Review the Language Arts Survey 3.2, "Active Listening and Interpersonal Communication," and engage in a conversation with another student about a memorable experience you have had with nature. You might tell a story about the time lightning struck your house, or you might share a camping experience. You might talk about planting flowers at the city park, or about the first time you were stung by a bee. After one of you has related an experience, reverse roles. As you speak and listen, apply the techniques of interpersonal communication that you have learned. Remember to do the following:

- Make eye contact
- Keep your body stance relaxed and open
- Give feedback
- Think before you speak
- Keep your emotions under control

Answers for Understanding Literature

Responses will vary. Possible responses are given.

1. **Allegory.** Students are likely to say that "The Flower of Air" is an allegory for writing a poem. The woman of the meadow represents poetic inspiration, while the speaker represents the poet. The flowers are words and images, and the speaker's action of bringing different flowers to the woman, only to have them be the wrong color, represents the poet's continual struggle to perfect the language in his or her work. The "flower of air" that the speaker continually seeks is the completed poem. A natural setting is appropriate for an allegory about the creative process because it is alive and bursting with colors. Meadows, mountains, pastures, flowers, and trees are often associated with poetry and creativity because they conjure images of life, growth, natural beauty, and freedom.

2. **Mood and Imagery.** The mood of this poem is serious, sincere, and thoughtful. It also has moments of sadness and frustration. The images of the speaker searching over and over for flowers that will please the woman in the meadow, as well as the nervousness and anticipation the speaker experiences as she repeatedly gives the woman the flowers, contribute to the poem's feeling of seriousness and sincerity. When the speaker fails to please the woman and searches on a "mountain/now black as Medea,/with not a crevice of brightness," the reader finds sadness and frustration. The speaker's change in mood reflects the changing emotions surrounding the struggle to write a good poem—a struggle the speaker takes seriously.

Answers for Skills Activities

SPEAKING AND LISTENING SKILLS

Give students time to think about what they might discuss when it is their turn to speak.

As students engage in their conversations, you might walk around the room listening and observing. Be sure students have grasped most of the basic techniques of interpersonal communication. Students can also critique themselves.

Analytic Scales for Responding in Writing

Grading scales for Responding in Writing appear on pages 397, 398.

ADDITIONAL RESOURCES

READER'S GUIDE

- Selection Worksheet 5.7

ASSESSMENT PORTFOLIO

- Selection Check Test 2.5.13
- Selection Test 2.5.14

ESSENTIAL SKILLS PRACTICE BOOKS

- Writing 1.8, 1.20

PREREADING EXTENSIONS

You might want to tell students that another important poet of the Sung Dynasty was Su Tung-p'o, often considered the foremost poet of the era. Interested students might try to find examples of his work at a library or bookstore.

You might also point out that during the era of the Sung Dynasty, popular prose and verse written in the vernacular, or the native language or dialect of common people, began to appear and become popular.

SUPPORT FOR LEP STUDENTS

PRONUNCIATIONS OF PROPER NOUNS AND ADJECTIVES

Li • Ch'ing • chao (lē chiŋ´ jau´)
P'eng (p'eŋ)

ADDITIONAL VOCABULARY

billowing—large and swelling
immortal—lasting forever

PREREADING

To "Free-Spirited Fisherman"
by Li Ch'ing-chao, translated by Stephen Owen

About the Author

Li Ch'ing-chao (AD 1084–c. 1151). One of China's finest female poets, as well as one of the greatest writers of traditional song lyrics, Li Ch'ing-chao was born during the Sung Dynasty into a family of writers, scholars, and government officials. She studied the arts and classical literature as she grew up. It was highly unusual in the time during which she lived for a woman to receive such an education or to be encouraged to share her writing publicly. Li Ch'ing-chao, however, was outspoken and confident, and her poetry began to attract attention and to earn respect when she was as young as seventeen years old.

Li Ch'ing-chao was married at the age of eighteen to Chao Te-fu, a man who shared her love of literature and writing. Over the course of their marriage, the two gathered one of the largest collections of books and antiques in China. Life began to change dramatically for the couple in 1126 and 1127, when the Sung Dynasty began to collapse. Foreign invaders from the north invaded the capital, captured the Sung emperor, and took over the northern part of China. Li Ch'ing-chao and her husband were forced to move south. Their collection of books and antiques was scattered and destroyed, and shortly after they escaped the north, Chao Te-fu died of illness. Li Ch'ing-chao's last years were difficult due to the combination of the death of her husband, her displacement, and the loss of the books and antiques that she loved so much.

About the Selection

Li Ch'ing-chao's song lyrics were part of a long tradition in China of setting poetic works to popular music. The poem that you are about to read was sung to a tune called "Free-Spirited Fisherman." (Thus the poem is referred to as **To "Free-Spirited Fisherman."**) Li Ch'ing-chao's particular style uses allusion and description to create a hopeful and mystical mood, or atmosphere, and to rouse feelings in the reader or listener.

CONNECTIONS: Allusions in Li Ch'ing-chao's Writing

An **allusion** is a reference to a person, event, object, or work from history or literature. In this piece, Li Ch'ing-chao makes two allusions. The P'eng, mentioned in line 15, is a large mythical bird that appears in the *Chuang-tzu* (fourth century BC), a treatise on Taoist philosophy written by the Chinese philosopher whose name gives the work its title (see page 583). The *Chuang-tzu* taught that wise people accept the changes and inconsistencies of life without challenging them, and that true enlightenment involves freeing oneself of tradition and personal goals, which are merely earthly distractions. In the *Chuang-tzu,* the P'eng rises ninety thousand miles in a whirlwind in order to fly to the southern ocean, and his greatness is not understood or appreciated by smaller creatures. Li Ch'ing-chao also alludes to the Three Immortal Isles, which are believed to be inhabited by people who live forever. In Taoist philosophy, it is believed that ignoring earthly distractions and concentrating on the true Tao, or "way" through nature, helps one to live a longer life. The longer the life, the more saintly a person becomes. Immortality is the final goal.

GOALS/OBJECTIVES

Studying this lesson will enable students to

- enjoy traditional song lyrics by one of China's finest early poets
- discuss the life and work of Li Ch'ing-chao
- define the literary terms *personification* and *symbol*
- write original song lyrics
- write a critical essay examining originality and cliché in popular song
- research song lyrics from different eras

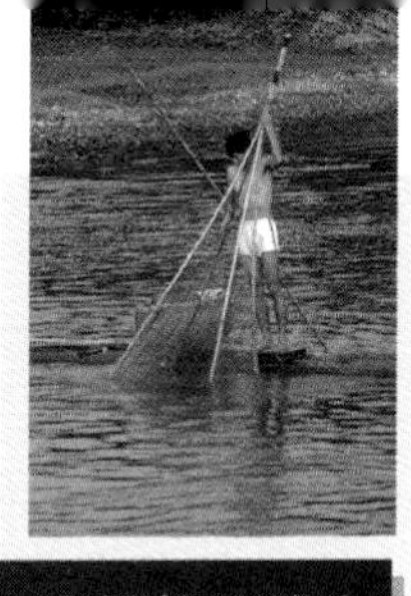

What in your life makes you most proud? What in your life makes you least proud? In your journal respond to these questions and explain why your feelings are positive or negative toward each thing.

To "Free-Spirited Fisherman"

LI CH'ING-CHAO, TRANSLATED BY STEPHEN OWEN

Billowing clouds touch the sky and reach
 the early morning fog,
the river of stars is ready to set,
 a thousand sails dance.
My dreaming soul moves in a daze
 to where the high god dwells—
I hear Heaven speak,
asking with deep concern
 where I am going now.

And I reply that my road is long,
 and, alas, twilight draws on;
I have worked at my poems and in vain have achieved
 bold lines that cause surprise.
Into strong winds ninety thousand miles
 upward the P'eng[1] now flies.
May that wind never stop,
may it blow this tiny boat away
 to the Three Immortal Isles.[2] ■

1. **P'eng.** Huge mythical bird that rises in a whirlwind
2. **Three Immortal Isles.** Mythical islands in the eastern sea, believed to be inhabited by immortals

❶ *What word does the speaker use to describe his or her soul? What question does Heaven ask of the speaker?*

❷ *What is the speaker's opinion about his or her poetry?*

❸ *Where does the speaker hope the tiny boat will go?*

WORDS FOR EVERYDAY USE

a • las (ə las´) *interj.,* exclamation of worry or sorrow

READER'S JOURNAL

Encourage students to think about and describe why they are prouder of some things than other things. What does this say about their values and character?

ANSWERS TO GUIDED READING QUESTIONS

❶ The speaker uses the word *dreaming* to describe the soul. Heaven asks where the speaker is going now.

❷ The speaker feels that the poems were written in vain.

❸ The speaker hopes the tiny boat will go to the Three Immortal Isles.

SELECTION CHECK TEST WITH ANSWERS

EX. To what song was this Li Ch'ing-chao poem usually sung?
The Li Ch'ing-chao poem was usually sung to the song "Free-Spirited Fisherman."

1. In what way does the speaker's "dreaming soul" move?
The speaker's dreaming soul moves in a daze.

2. What question is posed to the speaker, and by whom?
Heaven asks where the speaker is going.

3. What activity does the speaker feel has been in vain?
The speaker feels that writing poems has been in vain.

4. Into what does the bird P'eng fly?
P'eng flies into strong winds.

5. Where does the speaker want to go?
The speaker wants to go to the Three Immortal Isles.

VOCABULARY IN CONTEXT

• The weather announcer said, "Alas, winter is not over yet."

Responding to the Selection

Ask students if they feel that writing great poetry or songs can serve an important purpose in peoples' lives. Students might want to form pairs to answer and debate these questions.

Answers for Reviewing the Selection

RECALLING AND INTERPRETING

1. **Recalling.** The speaker describes the setting with words and phrases such as "billowing clouds," "early morning fog," and "river of stars." The speaker's soul is described as "dreaming" and moving in a daze. **Interpreting.** The speaker is feeling lost and disoriented. The reader knows this because the speaker is described as being in a daze and in a dream-like state.

2. **Recalling.** The speaker hears Heaven speak. Heaven asks where the speaker is going. The speaker replies by saying "my road is long, alas, twilight draws on." **Interpreting.** Heaven feels deep concern that the speaker is misguided and not on the right spiritual path. The speaker feels he or she has a long way to go spiritually.

3. **Recalling.** The speaker has worked at writing poems that are bold and fresh. **Interpreting.** The speaker no longer feels that one can learn all the answers by writing poetry. The speaker is more concerned with spiritual growth.

4. **Recalling.** P'eng flies into strong winds "ninety thousand miles upward." **Interpreting.** The bird symbolizes the greatness and mystery of spiritual experience.

SYNTHESIZING

Responses will vary. Possible responses are given.

5. The islands stand for the immortality that one reaches through spiritual knowledge. The speaker is on a spiritual journey.

Responding to the Selection

How do you feel about the ability to write great poems or songs? How does the speaker feel about having this ability? Explain whether you share the speaker's feelings.

Reviewing the Selection

RECALLING		INTERPRETING
1. What words and phrases does the speaker use to describe the setting, or the time and place in which the poem occurs? What words are used to describe the speaker's soul and the way in which it moves?	▶▶	What is the speaker's state of mind in the opening lines of the poem? How do you know?
2. Whom does the speaker hear? What is being asked of the speaker? What is the speaker's reply?	▶▶	Why is the question asked of the speaker "with deep concern"? How does the speaker feel about the road on which he or she has been?
3. At what has the speaker worked? Has the speaker been good at this work?	▶▶	Why might the speaker feel that this work was done in vain? What might be more important to the speaker than literary accomplishments?
4. Where does the P'eng fly?	▶▶	As you read earlier, small creatures can not fully understand the greatness of the P'eng. What does this bird and the blindness to the bird's greatness have to do with the speaker and her journey toward understanding?

SYNTHESIZING

5. What are the Three Immortal Isles, and why might this speaker want to go to them? What kind of journey is the speaker undertaking?

Understanding Literature (Questions for Discussion)

1. **Personification. Personification** is a figure of speech in which an idea, animal, or thing is described as if it were a person. What examples of personification can you find in this poem? What qualities of the natural world are described by personification?

Answers for Understanding Literature

Responses will vary. Possible responses are given.

1. **Personification.** Descriptions of clouds touching the sky and reaching the early morning fog and of Heaven questioning the speaker are examples of personification. Students might say that the poet uses these figures of speech to make the setting more vivid and alive to the reader. Students might also say that these figures of speech give a more lively and spirited picture of the world surrounding the speaker.

2. **Symbol.** The speaker moves along a long road, the tiny boat journeys to the Immortal Isles, and the P'eng, which might symbolize spiritual truth, travels upward. These are all spiritual journeys.

2. **Symbol.** A **symbol** is a thing that stands for or represents both itself and something else. Describe the two types of journeys in this piece, the symbolic journey and the speaker's actual journey. Also explain what the P'eng might symbolize.

Responding in Writing

1. **Creative Writing: Song Lyrics.** Try writing your own song about a topic, issue, or idea that is important to you. You might also write your song about an important person in your life. Use vivid, descriptive words and phrases to establish a specific mood. Make the reader understand why the topic, issue, or idea is important to you or to the speaker in your song lyrics. Your song need not be any longer than the piece you read by Li Ch'ing-chao. Aim to create a short piece that is interesting and moving to a reader or listener.

2. **Critical Essay: Originality and Cliché in Popular Song.** A cliché is a tired, overused expression. Some popular songs are weakened by the use of clichés. Others, however, are original and interesting. Choose some popular songs that you think of as clichéd and some that you think of as interesting and original. Write an essay in which you contrast these songs and suggest originality as one important criterion for judging songs and songwriters.

Project

A Closer Look at Song Lyrics. Song lyrics often express a great deal about the people writing them and about the specific time period in which they are written. Through the years, lyrics have been written about relationships, religion, politics, and specific people, places, and events. What are your favorite song lyrics? What period in history is most musically interesting to you? Working in pairs or in groups of three, write or discuss answers to these questions.

First brainstorm a list of songs that you currently enjoy or that you enjoyed when you were younger. Pick some songs that are currently popular and some that are older, and list songs about a variety of subjects. After you have brainstormed, you might also go to the library to research lyrics from other countries or periods in history. Finalize your list, settling on three or four interesting and diverse choices. Then prepare a presentation for your class. As a group you will want to share the lyrics with the rest of the class and explain why you find them interesting. Your group might choose to find recordings of the songs (You can usually rent or borrow tapes or CDs from your local library) or simply write out the lyrics on posterboard so that the class can read them. If you are musically inclined, you might choose to perform the pieces yourself. Lyrics to many popular songs can be found in music stores. After you have shared the song lyrics with the class, discuss with your classmates whether the lyrics were interesting and evocative.

ANALYTIC SCALES FOR RESPONDING IN WRITING

Assign a score from 1 to 25 for each grading criterion below. (For more detailed evaluation, see the evaluation forms for writing, revising, and proofreading, Assessment Portfolio 4.1–4.9.)

1. Song Lyrics

- **Content/Unity.** The song lyrics are about a specific topic, issue, or idea important to the writer.
- **Organization/Coherence.** The song lyrics describe the specific topic, issue, or idea and show the reader or listener why it is important to the speaker or the writer.
- **Language/Style.** The lyrics use vivid and precise nouns, verbs, and modifiers.
- **Conventions.** The lyrics avoid errors in spelling, grammar, usage, mechanics, and manuscript form.

▶ Additional practice is provided in the Essential Skills Practice Book: Writing 1.8.

2. Critical Essay

- **Content/Unity.** The essay contrasts originality and cliché in popular songs.
- **Organization/Coherence.** The essay begins with an introduction that includes the thesis of the essay. The introduction is followed by supporting paragraphs that present examples of both clichéd and original song lyrics. The essay ends with a solid conclusion.
- **Language/Style.** The essay uses vivid and precise nouns, verbs, and modifiers.
- **Conventions.** The essay avoids errors in spelling, grammar, usage, mechanics, and manuscript form.

▶ Additional practice is provided in the Essential Skills Practice Book: Writing 1.20.

PROJECT NOTES

See the evaluation form for projects, Assessment Portfolio 4.12.

A Closer Look at Song Lyrics. Encourage students to look closely at popular songs from different eras and then discuss how the topics of song lyrics have changed through the years. Students might ask themselves the following questions: Which songs seem to deal with light, less serious subjects? Which songs deal with social activism, philosophies, or other, more serious matters? Do students think songwriting can and should be used to teach or make changes in people's attitudes?

ADDITIONAL RESOURCES

Reader's Guide

- Selection Worksheet 5.7

Assessment Portfolio

- Selection Check Test 2.5.15
- Selection Test 2.5.16

Essential Skills Practice Books

- Writing 1.8, 1.20
- Language 2.54–2.61

PREREADING EXTENSIONS

Ask each student to locate a poem, story, painting, or song that gives an interesting view of or perspective on cats or other animals. Students should describe or present what they find to the rest of the class.

SUPPORT FOR LEP STUDENTS

Pronunciations of Proper Nouns and Adjectives

Mar • co • val • do (mär´ kō val´ do)
Mar • che • sa (mär kā´ zə)

Additional Vocabulary

brandishing—shaking or showing in a threatening manner
demolition—destruction
distinction—that which makes something different or special
domestic—having to do with home; animal that has been tamed
mortar—cement mixture or plaster used to hold bricks or stones together
plateau—level area
riveted—held or fastened
scrutinized—studied critically
sphinxes—ancient Egyptian statues, typically with the bodies of lions and the heads of women
stucco—plastic material used to make walls
surveillance—careful watch
taut—tight

PREREADING

"The Garden of Stubborn Cats"
by Italo Calvino, translated by William Weaver

About the Author

ITALO CALVINO
1923–1985

Italo Calvino grew up in San Remo, Italy, on the Italian Riviera. Both his parents were botanists, and his father was a curator of local botanical gardens. Although his parents encouraged him to follow in their footsteps and pursue a career in science, he found himself attracted to writing and literature. During World War II, Calvino fought against Fascist control of Italy and the Nazi occupation. His experiences in war inspired his first novel, *The Path to the Nest of Spiders*, and three short story collections, *Adam, One Afternoon*, and *Entering the War*. Immediately after the war ended, Calvino moved to the city of Turin, where he studied literature. After graduation, he worked in publishing and wrote essays and criticism. Calvino edited a large collection of folk tales, work which was greatly praised. He had always been interested in the themes and characters of fables and folktales, and much of his own fiction reflects this interest. His writing is recognized for its imaginative and humorous qualities, and for combining realistic and fanciful elements with scientific and philosophical ideas. His works include *The Nonexistent Knight and The Cloven Viscount*, *Cosmicomics*, *The Watcher and Other Stories*, *Invisible Cities*, *The Castle of Crossed Destinies*, and *Italian Folktales*.

About the Selection

"**The Garden of Stubborn Cats**" is an example of **magical realism.** (See Insights: Magical Realism, page 278.) The story has realistic elements, yet it also uses elements of fantasy to create a world that is familiar but dreamlike. "The Garden of Stubborn Cats" reflects Calvino's fascination with the tensions between characters and their environments. In this fairytale-like story, Calvino shows the growth of a city and resistance to this growth by a society of powerful cats that wants to preserve its garden, the only bit of nature left in a city of concrete and tall buildings. This story explores the disadvantages of urban growth, including the way in which it can smother the natural world.

CONNECTIONS: Cats in the Arts

The cat is a subject that has fascinated artists and writers for centuries. Some of the earliest artistic representations of the cat were ancient Egyptian sculptures and drawings of the cat goddess Bastet. Japanese artists were especially skilled in portraying the cat. Their drawings were so realistic that people hung them in homes and temples believing that they would keep mice and rats away. Such European artists as Leonardo da Vinci, William Hogarth, and Pablo Picasso portrayed cats. The personality and grace of the cat has inspired countless writers, including T. S. Eliot, Mark Twain, Ursula K. LeGuin, and Rudyard Kipling. Fables and folk tales about cats appear in most cultures. For example, versions of the story "Puss in Boots" exist in almost every language.

GOALS/OBJECTIVES

Studying this lesson will enable students to

- read a story, an example of magical realism, that explores the clash between urban growth and the natural world
- discuss the life and work of Italo Calvino
- define the literary terms *magical realism, point of view,* and *theme*
- write a description of an imaginary place
- write an essay about a poem's imagery and theme
- proofread for errors in capitalization

List some different ways in which civilization interferes with nature. When have you noticed this happening? What steps can people take to protect the natural world? What are the possible consequences if the natural world is not protected?

READER'S JOURNAL

"The Garden of Stubborn Cats"

ITALO CALVINO, TRANSLATED BY WILLIAM WEAVER

The city of cats and the city of men exist one inside the other, but they are not the same city. Few cats recall the time when there was no distinction: the streets and squares of men were also streets and squares of cats, and the lawns, courtyards, balconies, and fountains: you lived in a broad and various space. But for several generations now domestic felines have been prisoners of an uninhabitable city: the streets are uninterruptedly overrun by the mortal traffic of cat-crushing automobiles; in every square foot of terrain where once a garden extended or a vacant lot or the ruins of an old demolition, now condominiums loom up, welfare housing, brand-new skyscrapers; every entrance is crammed with parked cars; the courtyards, one by one, have been roofed by reinforced concrete and transformed into garages or movie houses or storerooms or workshops. And where a rolling plateau of low roofs once extended, copings,[1] terraces, water tanks, balconies, skylights, corrugated-iron sheds, now one general superstructure rises wherever structures can rise; the intermediate differences in height, between the low ground of the street and the supernal heaven of the penthouses, disappear; the cat of a recent litter seeks in vain the itinerary of its fathers, the point from which to make the soft leap from balustrade[2] to cornice[3] to drainpipe, or for the quick climb on the roof-tiles.

But in this vertical city, in this compressed city where all voids tend to fill up and every block of cement tends to mingle with other blocks of cement, a kind of counter-city opens, a negative city that consists of empty slices between wall and wall, of the minimal distances ordained by the building regulations between two constructions, between the rear of one construction and the rear of the next; it is a city of cavities, wells, air conduits,[4] driveways, inner yards, accesses

1. **copings.** Top layer of a masonry wall, sloped to carry off water
2. **balustrade.** Railing held up by small posts
3. **cornice.** Horizontal molding along the top of a wall or building
4. **conduits.** Pipes or channels for conveying fluid or gas

❶ *What two cities are being discussed?*

❷ *What do few cats recall? Of what have domestic cats been prisoners for several generations?*

❸ *What does the city look like? What still scurries through a "network of dry canals on a planet of stucco and tar"?*

WORDS FOR EVERYDAY USE

su • per • nal (sə pʉrn´əl) *adj.*, divine
i • tin • er • ar • y (ī tin´ər er´ē) *n.*, record of a journey
or • dain (ôr dān´) *vt.*, predetermine; establish

READER'S JOURNAL

You might ask students to focus specifically on people and animals. In what ways do humans tend to interfere with the peaceful existence of certain animals? What might people do to change this? Do students believe that humans should have the right to do whatever they please with the natural environment of animals? Why, or why not? Should humans be more respectful of animals? Why, or why not?

ANSWERS TO GUIDED READING QUESTIONS

❶ The "city of cats" and the "city of men" are the two cities being discussed.

❷ Few cats recall the time when their was no distinction between the city of cats and the city of men. Domestic cats have been prisoners of an uninhabitable city.

❸ The city is tall and overcrowded with buildings, homes, and driveways, and it is covered in concrete and stucco. An ancient cat population still scurries through a "network of dry canals on a planet of stucco and tar."

SPELLING AND VOCABULARY WORDS FROM THE SELECTION

altruistic	pate
aviary	practicable
futile	protégé
indigence	squalid
itinerary	supernal
ordain	

VOCABULARY IN CONTEXT

- The people listened carefully in church as the supernal words were repeated.
- Wayne kept a careful itinerary when he traveled across the country.
- The committee decided to ordain that all town playgrounds be closed at sundown.

Answers to Guided Reading Questions

➊ He believes that the cats have a world of their own which is not revealed to him. He believes that he is not yet permitted to know of the secret world of the cats.

➋ He had made friends with a well-fed tabby cat. He would share an afternoon stroll with the cat.

➌ Marcovaldo had begun to look at places through the eyes of a cat.

➍ The tabby leads Marcovaldo to discover the Biarritz Restaurant. He sees a luxurious hall, silver dishes held by waiters wearing white gloves, parquet floors, potted palms, tablecloths, crystal, and buckets of champagne. Everything is upside-down because Marcovaldo looks at the reversed reflection of the room in the tilted pane.

Historical Note

In 1347, the black plague first struck Europe in the Italian city of Messina. By the year 1351, one-third of Europe's population had died of the plague. The plague was carried by rats infested with infected fleas. Cats might have limited the spread of the disease by killing the rats. At the time, however, there were few cats in Europe because of superstitions about cats. People believed them to be evil, and many cats were killed. Ironically, attempts to prevent misfortune indirectly contributed to the overpopulation of infected rats that spread the plague.

➊ *How does Marcovaldo explain the sudden disappearance of the cats? What is he not yet permitted to do?*

➋ *With whom had Marcovaldo made friends? What would he do on his lunch break?*

➌ *In what way had Marcovaldo begun looking at places?*

➍ *What does the tabby lead Marcovaldo to discover? What does he see? Why is everything upside-down?*

to basements, like a network of dry canals on a planet of stucco and tar, and it is through this network, grazing the walls, that the ancient cat population still scurries.

On occasion, to pass the time, Marcovaldo would follow a cat. It was during the work-break, between noon and three, when all the personnel except Marcovaldo went home to eat, and he—who brought his lunch in his bag—laid his place among the packing-cases in the warehouse, chewed his snack, smoked a half-cigar, and wandered around, alone and idle, waiting for work to resume. In those hours, a cat that peeped in at a window was always welcome company, and a guide for new explorations. He had made friends with a tabby, well fed, a blue ribbon around its neck, surely living with some well-to-do family. This tabby shared with Marcovaldo the habit of an afternoon stroll right after lunch; and naturally a friendship sprang up.

Following his tabby friend, Marcovaldo had started looking at places as if through the round eyes of a cat and even if these places were the usual environs of his firm he saw them in a different light, as settings for cattish stories, with connections practicable only by light, velvety paws. Though from the outside the neighborhood seemed poor in cats, every day on his rounds Marcovaldo made the acquaintance of some new face, and a miau, a hiss, a stiffening of fur on an arched back was enough for him to sense ties and intrigues and rivalries among them. At those moments he thought he had already penetrated the secrecy of the felines' society: and then he felt himself scrutinized by pupils that became slits, under the surveillance of the antennae of taut whiskers, and all the cats around him sat impassive as sphinxes, the pink triangles of their noses convergent on the black triangles of their lips, and the only things that moved were the tips of the ears, with a vibrant jerk like radar. They reached the end of a narrow passage, between squalid blank walls; and, looking around, Marcovaldo saw that the cats that had led him this far had vanished, all of them together, no telling in which direction, even his tabby friend, and they had left him alone. Their realm had territories, ceremonies, customs that it was not yet granted to him to discover.

On the other hand, from the cat city there opened unsuspected peepholes onto the city of men: and one day the same tabby led him to discover the great Biarritz Restaurant.

Anyone wishing to see the Biarritz Restaurant had only to assume the posture of a cat, that is, proceed on all fours. Cat and man, in this fashion, walked around a kind of dome, at whose foot some low, rectangular little windows opened. Following the tabby's example, Marcovaldo looked down. They were transoms[5] through which the luxurious hall received air and light. To the sound of gypsy violins, partridges and quails swirled by on silver dishes balanced by the white-gloved fingers of waiters in tailcoats. Or, more precisely, above the partridges and quails the dishes whirled, and above the dishes the white gloves, and poised on the waiters' patent-leather shoes, the gleaming parquet[6] floor, from which hung dwarf potted palms and tablecloths and crystal and buckets like bells with the champagne bottle for their clapper: everything was turned upside-down because Marcovaldo, for fear of being seen, wouldn't stick his head inside the window and confined himself to looking

5. **transoms.** Small windows directly over a door
6. **parquet.** Wood floor decorated with geometric designs

Words for Everyday Use

prac • ti • ca • ble (prak´ti kə bəl) *adj.,* possible
squal • id (skwäl´id) *adj.,* foul or unclean

Vocabulary in Context

- It is not practicable to paint the entire house in one weekend.
- The restaurant was closed by the Board of Health because of its squalid conditions.

Un chat couche, allongé de gauche à droit. *Théophile Alexandre Steinlen. Courtesy, Museum of Fine Arts, Boston. Bequest of W. G. Russell Allen*

at the reversed reflection of the room in the tilted pane.

But it was not so much the windows of the dining-room as those of the kitchens that interested the cat: looking through the former you saw, distant and somehow transfigured, what in the kitchens presented itself—quite concrete and within paw's reach—as a plucked bird or a fresh fish. And it was toward the kitchens, in fact, that the tabby wanted to lead Marcovaldo, either through a gesture of altruistic friendship or else because it counted on the man's help for one of its raids. Marcovaldo, however, was reluctant to leave his belvedere[7] over the main room: first as he was fascinated by the luxury of the place, and then because something down there had riveted his attention. To such an extent that, overcoming his fear of being seen, he kept peeking in, with his head in the transom.

In the midst of the room, directly under that pane, there was a little glass fish tank, a kind of aquarium, where some fat trout were swimming. A special customer approached, a man with a shiny bald pate, black suit, black

1 What catches Marcovaldo's attention in the main room?

7. **belvedere.** Open roofed gallery in an upper story

Words for Everyday Use

al • tru • is • tic (al´tro͞o is´tik) *adj.*, unselfish

pate (pāt) *n.*, head

Answers to Guided Reading Questions

1 A little glass fish tank in which fat trout are swimming catches Marcovaldo's attention.

Quotables

"When she walked . . . she stretched out long and thin like a little tiger, and held her head high to look over the grass as if she were threading the jungle."

—Sarah Orne Jewett

Additional Questions and Activities

Ask students to answer the following questions:

1. What, according to the author, might be the cat's reasons for wanting to show Marcovaldo the restaurant's kitchens?
2. What type of personality does the author give the cat? Why might the author have chosen to use cats as the focus of his story? What is the stereotypical image of a cat's personality?
3. Do you as a reader find the cat to be a sympathetic character? Why, or why not?

ANSWERS

Responses will vary.

1. The author says that the cat's decision to show Marcovaldo the kitchens might be an honest gesture of friendship or it might be the cat's attempt to enlist Marcovaldo's help in a raid on the kitchen.
2. Students might say that the cat is intelligent, sneaky, and independent. People often think of cats as being sneaky and independent.
3. *Responses will vary.*

Vocabulary in Context

- The governor's visits to local hospitals were not entirely altruistic—he thought the visits might help his campaign for reelection.
- The man placed a felt hat on his pate.

Answers to Guided Reading Questions

❶ Marcovaldo follows the cat to an overgrown, decaying garden full of cats and a small, abandoned building. Marcovaldo realizes that he has reached the cats' secret realm.

❷ The cat watches Marcovaldo fish in the restaurant's fish tank. The cat steals the trout Marcovaldo catches.

Bibliographic Note

Many people have enjoyed the Italian folk tales that Italo Calvino compiled. Folk tales, which are stories that have been passed by word of mouth from generation to generation, can provide interesting historical and cultural details about a particular country. Below are some famous collections of folk tales from all over the world that students might be interested in locating and reading:

Abrahams, R. D. *Afro-American Folktales* (Pantheon, 1985)

Afanasyev, Alexander, ed. *Russian Folk Tales* (Shambhala, 1980)

Ainsworth, C. H. *Polish-American Folktales* (Clyde Press, 1977)

Booss, Claire, ed. *Scandinavian Folk and Fairy Tales* (Outlet, 1984)

Botkin, B. A. *Treasury of American Folklore* (Crown, 1989)

Briggs, Catherine. *British Folktales* (Pantheon, 1980)

Chin, Y. C. and others, eds. *Traditional Chinese Folktales* (M. E. Sharpe, 1989)

Chodzko, A. B. *Fairy Tales of the Slav Peasants and Herdsmen* (Kraus, repr. of 1986 ed.)

Colum, Padraic, ed. *Treasury of Irish Folklore*, rev. ed. (Crown, 1969)

Courlander, Harold. *Treasury of African Folklore* (Crown, 1974)

Delarue, Paul. *The Borzoi Book of French Folk Tales* (Ayer, 1980, repr. of 1956 ed.)

(cont.)

beard. An old waiter in tailcoat followed him, carrying a little net as if he were going to catch butterflies. The gentleman in black looked at the trout with a grave, intent air; then he raised one hand and with a slow, solemn gesture singled out a fish. The waiter dipped the net into the tank, pursued the appointed trout, captured it, headed for the kitchens, holding out in front of him, like a lance, the net in which the fish wriggled. The gentleman in black, solemn as a magistrate who has handed down a capital sentence, went to take his seat and wait for the return of the trout, sautéed "à la meunière."[8]

If I found a way to drop a line from up here and make one of those trout bite, Marcovaldo thought, I couldn't be accused of theft; at worst, of fishing in an unauthorized place. And ignoring the miaus that called him toward the kitchens, he went to collect his fishing tackle.

Nobody in the crowded dining room of the Biarritz saw the long, fine line, armed with hook and bait, as it slowly dropped into the tank. The fish saw the bait, and flung themselves on it. In the fray one trout managed to bite the worm: and immediately it began to rise, rise, emerge from the water, a silvery flash, it darted up high, over the laid tables and the trolleys of hors d'oeuvres, over the blue flames of the crêpes Suzette, until it vanished into the heavens of the transom.

Marcovaldo had yanked the rod with the brisk snap of the expert fisherman, so the fish landed behind his back. The trout had barely touched the ground when the cat sprang. What little life the trout still had was lost between the tabby's teeth. Marcovaldo, who had abandoned his line at that moment to run and grab the fish, saw it snatched from under his nose, hook and all. He was quick to put one foot on the rod, but the snatch had been so strong that the rod was all the man had left, while the tabby ran off with the fish, pulling the line after it. Treacherous kitty! It had vanished.

But this time it wouldn't escape him: there was that long line trailing after him and showing the way he had taken. Though he had lost sight of the cat, Marcovaldo followed the end of the line: there it was, running along a wall; it climbed a parapet, wound through a doorway, was swallowed up by a basement . . . Marcovaldo, venturing into more and more cattish places, climbed roofs, straddled railings, always managed to catch a glimpse—perhaps only a second before it disappeared— of that moving trace that indicated a thief's path.

Now the line played out down a sidewalk, in the midst of the traffic, and Marcovaldo, running after it, almost managed to grab it. He flung himself down on his belly: there, he grabbed it! He managed to seize one end of the line before it slipped between the bars of a gate.

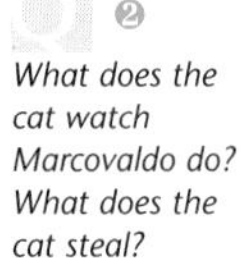

To where does Marcovaldo follow the cat? What does Marcovaldo realize that almost makes him forget his fish?

❷ *What does the cat watch Marcovaldo do? What does the cat steal?*

Beyond a half-rusted gate and two bits of wall buried under climbing plants, there was a little rank garden, with a small, abandoned-looking building at the far end of it. A carpet of dry leaves covered the path, and dry leaves lay everywhere under the boughs of the two plane-trees, forming actually some little mounds in the yard. A layer of leaves was yellowing in the green water of a pool. Enormous buildings rose all around, skyscrapers with thousands of windows, like so many eyes trained disapprovingly on that little square patch with two trees, a few tiles, and all those yellow leaves, surviving right in the middle of an area of great traffic.

And in this garden, perched on the capitals and balustrades, lying on the dry leaves of the flowerbeds, climbing on the trunks of the trees or on the drainpipes, motionless on their four paws, their tails making a question-mark, seated to wash their faces, there were tiger cats, black cats, white cats, calico cats, tabbies, angoras, Persians, house cats and stray cats, perfumed cats and mangy cats. Marcovaldo realized he had finally reached the heart of the cats' realm, their secret island. And, in his emotion, he almost forgot his fish.

8. **à la meunière.** Fish cooked in a flour batter topped with lemon and parsley; French recipe

Bibliographic Note (cont.)

Eichhorn, D. M. ed. *Joys of Jewish Folklore* (Jonathan David, 1981)

El-Shamy, H. M. ed. *Folktales of Egypt* (University of Chicago Press, 1982)

Gupta, Rupa. *Tales from Indian Classics* (Auromere, 1981)

Jacobs, Joseph. *Celtic Fairy Tales* (Dover, 1968)

Jain, N. P. *Folktales of Mexico* (Apt, 1987)

Ozaki, Y. T., ed. *Japanese Fairy Tales* (Gordon, 1977)

Ratcliff, Ruth. *Scottish Folk Tales* (State Mutual, 1977)

It had remained, that fish, hanging by the line from the branch of a tree, out of reach of the cats' leaps; it must have dropped from its kidnapper's mouth at some clumsy movement, perhaps as it was defended from the others, or perhaps displayed as an extraordinary prize. The line had got tangled, and Marcovaldo, tug as he would, couldn't manage to yank it loose. A furious battle had meanwhile been joined among the cats, to reach that unreachable fish, or rather, to win the right to try and reach it. Each wanted to prevent the others from leaping: they hurled themselves on one another, they tangled in midair, they rolled around clutching each other, and finally a general war broke out in a whirl of dry, crackling leaves.

After many futile yanks, Marcovaldo now felt the line was free, but he took care not to pull it: the trout would have fallen right in the midst of that infuriated scrimmage of felines.

It was at this moment that, from the top of the walls of the gardens, a strange rain began to fall: fish-bones, heads, tails, even bits of lung and lights. Immediately the cats' attention was distracted from the suspended trout and they flung themselves on the new delicacies. To Marcovaldo, this seemed the right moment to pull the line and regain his fish. But, before he had time to act, from a blind of the little villa, two yellow, skinny hands darted out: one was brandishing scissors; the other, a frying pan. The hand with the scissors was raised above the trout, the hand with the frying pan was thrust under it. The scissors cut the line, the trout fell into the pan; hands, scissors and pan withdrew, the blind closed: all in the space of a second. Marcovaldo was totally bewildered.

"Are you also a cat lover?" A voice at his back made him turn round. He was surrounded by little old women, some of them ancient, wearing old fashioned hats on their heads; others, younger, but, with the look of spinsters; and all were carrying in their hands or their bags packages of leftover meat or fish, and some even had little pans of milk. "Will you help me throw this package over the fence, for those poor creatures?"

All the ladies, cat lovers, gathered at this hour around the garden of dry leaves to take the food to their protégés.

"Can you tell me why they are all here, these cats?" Marcovaldo inquired.

"Where else could they go? This garden is all they have left! Cats come here from other neighborhoods, too, from miles and miles around . . ."

"And birds, as well," another lady added. "They're forced to live by the hundreds and hundreds on these few trees . . ."

"And the frogs, they're all in that pool, and at night they never stop croaking . . . You can hear them even on the eighth floor of the buildings around here."

"Who does this villa belong to anyway?" Marcovaldo asked. Now, outside the gate, there weren't just the cat-loving ladies but also other people: the man from the gas pump opposite, the apprentices from a mechanic's shop, the postman, the grocer, some passers-by. And none of them, men and women, had to be asked twice: all wanted to have their say, as always when a mysterious and controversial subject comes up.

"It belongs to a Marchesa.[9] She lives there, but you never see her . . ."

"She's been offered millions and millions, by developers, for this little patch of land, but she won't sell . . ."

9. **Marchesa.** Italian noblewoman

❶ *Why, according to the women, are the cats and other animals in the garden?*

❷ *What distracts the cats away from the fish? What happens just when Marcovaldo tries to recover his fish?*

❸ *Who owns the villa? Who wants to buy the villa?*

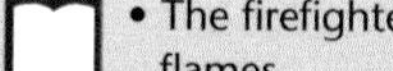

Words for Everyday Use

fu • tile (fyo͞ot´'l) *adj.*, useless

pro • té • gé (prōt´ə zhā) *n.*, person guided or helped by another

Answers to Guided Reading Questions

❶ According to the women, the cats and other animals are in the garden because it is the only place they have left in the overdeveloped city.

❷ A "strange rain" of fish-bones, heads, tails, and bits of fish distracts the cats' attention. Just as Marcovaldo tries to recover his fish, two skinny hands dart out with a pair of scissors and a frying pan and steal the fish.

❸ The Marchesa owns the village. Developers want to buy the land.

Additional Questions and Activities

Ask students to write two brief descriptions of the same garden. The first description should make the garden seem like the most beautiful place on earth. The second description should make the garden seem like an ugly, miserable place. Tell students that they can change readers' perceptions of the same place by carefully choosing specific, vivid images.

Literary Technique

MAGICAL REALISM

You might want to direct students to the parts of the story that are examples of **magical realism,** a kind of fiction that is for the most part realistic but that contains elements of fantasy. You might want to point out the way in which Calvino's magical realist style comes through in this section of the story. The details about the city seem realistic, but the relationship between Marcovaldo and the cat, the image of Marcovaldo fishing in a restaurant fish tank, the struggle with the cat over the fish, and the strange garden are all magical details.

Vocabulary in Context

- The firefighters tried to save the burning building, but their attempts were futile against the large flames.
- The young writer became the famous poet's protégé.

Answers to Guided Reading Questions

① Some believe that she is an "old miser," never feeding the cats properly. Some say that she is a saint in the way that she cares for the cats.

ANALYTIC SCALES FOR RESPONDING IN WRITING
(SEE PAGE 416.)

Assign a score from 1 to 25 for each grading criterion below. (For more detailed evaluation, see the evaluation forms for writing, revising, and proofreading, Assessment Portfolio 4.1–4.9.)

1. Description

- **Content/Unity.** The one-page description is about an imaginary place.
- **Organization/Coherence.** The description portrays vivid details of the imaginary place, and includes the appearance of the place, who lives there, and why the place exists.
- **Language/Style.** The description uses vivid and precise nouns, verbs, and modifiers.
- **Conventions.** The description avoids errors in spelling, grammar, usage, mechanics, and manuscript form.

▶ Additional practice is provided in the Essential Skills Practice Book: Writing 1.8.

Additional Questions and Activities

Ask students to discuss the portrayals of the townspeople. In what way are the people's reactions to the issue of the cats and the gossip surrounding the Marchesa's strange behavior realistic? With which people might students side?

Precious Paisley. *Susan Y. West*

"What would she do with millions, an old woman all alone in the world? She wants to hold on to her house, even if it's falling to pieces, rather than be forced to move . . ."

"It's the only undeveloped bit of land in the downtown area . . . Its value goes up every year . . . They've made her offers—"

"Offers! That's not all. Threats, intimidation, persecution . . . You don't know the half of it! Those contractors!"

"But she holds out. She's held out for years . . ."

① *What differing opinions are held about the Marchesa?*

"She's a saint. Without her, where would those poor animals go?"

"A lot she cares about the animals, the old miser! Have you ever seen her give them anything to eat?"

"How can she feed the cats when she doesn't have food for herself? She's the last descendant of a ruined family!"

"She hates cats! I've seen her chasing them and hitting them with an umbrella!"

"Because they were tearing up her flowerbeds!"

"What flowerbeds? I've never seen anything in this garden but a great crop of weeds!"

Marcovaldo realized that with regard to the old Marchesa opinions were sharply divided: some saw her as an angelic being, others as an egoist and a miser.

"It's the same with the birds; she never gives them a crumb!"

"She gives them hospitality. Isn't that plenty?"

"Like she gives the mosquitoes, you mean. They all come from here, from that pool. In the summertime the mosquitoes eat us alive, and it's all the fault of that Marchesa!"

"And the mice? This villa is a mine of mice. Under the dead leaves they have their burrows, and at night they come out . . ."

"As far as the mice go, the cats take care of them . . ."

"Oh, you and your cats! If we had to rely on them . . ."

"Why? Have you got something to say against cats?"

Here the discussion degenerated into a general quarrel.

"The authorities should do something: confiscate the villa!" one man cried.

"What gives them the right?" another protested.

"In a modern neighborhood like ours, a mouse-nest like this . . . it should be forbidden . . ."

"Why, I picked my apartment precisely because it overlooked this little bit of green . . ."

"Green, hell! Think of the fine skyscraper they could build here!"

Marcovaldo would have liked to add something of his own, but he couldn't get a word in. Finally, all in one breath, he exclaimed: "The Marchesa stole a trout from me!"

The unexpected news supplied fresh ammunition to the old woman's enemies, but her defenders exploited it as proof of the <u>indigence</u> to which the unfortunate noblewoman was reduced. Both sides agreed that Marcovaldo should go and knock at her door to demand an explanation.

It wasn't clear whether the gate was locked or unlocked; in any case, it opened, after a push, with a mournful creak. Marcovaldo picked his way among the leaves and cats, climbed the steps to the porch, knocked hard at the entrance.

At a window (the very one where the frying pan had appeared), the blind was raised slightly and in one corner a round, pale blue eye was seen, and a clump of hair dyed an undefinable color, and a dry skinny hand. A voice was heard, asking: "Who is it? Who's at the door?" the words accompanied by a cloud smelling of fried oil.

"It's me, Marchesa. The trout man," Marcovaldo explained. "I don't mean to trouble you. I only wanted to tell you, in case you didn't know, that the trout was stolen from me, by that cat, and I'm the one who caught it. In fact the line . . ."

"Those cats! It's always those cats . . ." the Marchesa said, from behind the shutter, with a shrill, somewhat nasal voice. "All my troubles come from the cats! Nobody knows what I go through! Prisoner night and day of those horrid beasts! And with all the refuse people throw over the walls, to spite me!"

"But my trout . . ."

"Your trout! What am I supposed to know about your trout!" The Marchesa's voice became almost a scream, as if she wanted to drown out the sizzle of oil in the pan, which came through the window along with the aroma of fried fish. "How can I make sense of anything, with all the stuff that rains into my house?"

"I understand, but did you take the trout or didn't you?"

"When I think of all the damage I suffer because of the cats! Ah, fine state of affairs! I'm not responsible for anything! I can't tell you what I've lost! Thanks to those cats, who've occupied house and garden for years! My life at the mercy of those animals! Go and find the owners! Make them pay damages! Damages? A whole life destroyed! A prisoner here, unable to move a step!"

"Excuse me for asking: but who's forcing you to stay?"

From the crack in the blind there appeared sometimes a round, pale blue eye, sometimes a mouth with two protruding teeth; for a moment the whole face was visible, and to Marcovaldo it seemed, bewilderingly, the face of a cat.

"They keep me prisoner, they do, those cats! Oh, I'd be glad to leave! What wouldn't I give for a little apartment all my own, in a

❶ *What are the different opinions about the Marchesa's property?*

❷ *What is the Marchesa doing with Marcovaldo's trout? Does she admit to taking the trout?*

WORDS FOR EVERYDAY USE	**in • di • gence** (inˊdi jəns) *n.,* condition of being poor or in poverty

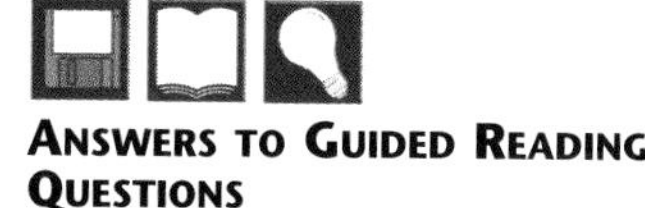

ANSWERS TO GUIDED READING QUESTIONS

❶ Some people believe that contractors should confiscate the property because it is dirty and ugly, while others believe contractors should leave it alone, since it is the only bit of green in the entire city.

❷ The Marchesa is cooking the trout. She does not admit to taking the fish.

ANALYTIC SCALES FOR RESPONDING IN WRITING

(SEE PAGE 416.)

Assign a score from 1 to 25 for each grading criterion below. (For more detailed evaluation, see the evaluation forms for writing, revising, and proofreading, Assessment Portfolio 4.1–4.9.)

2. Critical Essay

- **Content/Unity.** The essay focuses on the story's theme and the ways in which the story's images illustrate this theme.
- **Organization/Coherence.** The essay begins with an introduction that includes the thesis of the essay. The introduction is followed by supporting paragraphs that give supporting details from the story and answer questions about the author's view of urban growth. The essay ends with a solid conclusion.
- **Language/Style.** The essay uses vivid and precise nouns, verbs, and modifiers.
- **Conventions.** The essay avoids errors in spelling, grammar, usage, mechanics, and manuscript form.

► Additional practice is provided in the Essential Skills Practice Book: Writing 1.20.

VOCABULARY IN CONTEXT

- The king was blind to the terrible <u>indigence</u> of many of his subjects.

Answers to Guided Reading Questions

➊ The cats follow her, block her path, and trip her. According to her, they are afraid that she will sell her lot.

➋ As soon as the Marchesa dies, contractors take over the property and begin developing it. Cats walk on planks and spill buckets of mortar, drop bricks, fight in piles of sand, and hiss at workers. Birds make nests in the trestles, and frogs croak and hop in the buckets of water.

Selection Check Test with Answers

EX. What two cities are discussed in "The Garden of Stubborn Cats"?
The city of cats and the city of people are discussed in the story.

1. In what way has the city changed over the years?
The city has become overdeveloped.

2. With whom does Marcovaldo begin spending time?
Marcovaldo begins spending time with a large tabby cat.

3. What happens to the fish Marcovaldo steals from the restaurant?
The tabby cat steals the fish that Marcovaldo steals from the restaurant.

4. To where does the cat lead Marcovaldo?
The cat leads Marcovaldo to an old, decaying garden.

5. Why, after the Marchesa dies, do contractors have trouble developing the land?
The animals get in the way of the work as a type of protest.

➊ *What do the cats do to keep the Marchesa from leaving? Why, according to her, do they want to keep her from leaving?*

➋ *What happens to the garden as soon as the Marchesa dies? What do the cats and other animals do to protest?*

nice clean modern building! But I can't go out . . . They follow me, they block my path, they trip me up!" The voice became a whisper, as if to confide a secret. "They're afraid I'll sell the lot . . . They won't leave me . . . won't allow me . . . When the builders come to offer me a contract, you should see them, those cats! They get in the way, pull out their claws; they even chased a lawyer off! Once I had the contract right here, I was about to sign it, and they dived in through the window, knocked over the inkwell, tore up all the pages . . ."

All of a sudden Marcovaldo remembered the time, the shipping department, the boss. He tiptoed off over the dried leaves, as the voice continued to come through the slats of the blind, enfolded in that cloud apparently from the oil of a frying pan. "They even scratched me . . . I still have the scar . . . All alone here at the mercy of these demons . . ."

Winter came. A blossoming of white flakes decked the branches and capitals and the cats' tails. Under the snow, the dry leaves dissolved into mush. The cats were rarely seen, the cat lovers even less; the packages of fish-bones were consigned only to cats who came to the door. Nobody, for quite a while, had seen anything of the Marchesa. No smoke came now from the chimneypot of the villa.

One snowy day, the garden was again full of cats, who had returned as if it were spring, and they were miauing as if on a moonlight night. The neighbors realized that something had happened: they went and knocked at the Marchesa's door. She didn't answer: she was dead.

In the spring, instead of the garden, there was a huge building site that a contractor had set up. The steam shovels dug down to great depths to make room for the foundations, cement poured into the iron armatures,[10] a very high crane passed beams to the workmen who were making the scaffoldings. But how could they get on with their work? Cats walked along all the planks, they made bricks fall and upset buckets of mortar, they fought in the midst of the piles of sand. When you started to raise an armature, you found a cat perched on top of it, hissing fiercely. More treacherous pusses climbed onto the masons' backs as if to purr, and there was no getting rid of them. And the birds continued making their nests in all the trestles, the cab of the crane looked like an <u>aviary</u> . . . And you couldn't dip up a bucket of water that wasn't full of frogs, croaking and hopping . . . ■

10. **armatures.** Frameworks for supporting building materials

Responding to the Selection

If you were the official spokesperson for the stubborn cats, what would you say to explain the cats' feelings about the city and their garden? Would you have been happy to keep the garden if you were the Marchesa?

Words for Everyday Use

a • vi • ar • y (ā′vē er′ē) *n.,* large cage or building for keeping birds

Vocabulary in Context

• The parrot <u>aviary</u> was Monique's favorite exhibit at the wildlife center in her town.

Reviewing the Selection

RECALLING

INTERPRETING

1. Of what have domestic felines been "prisoners" for several generations? What has replaced gardens, rolling plateaus, and low roofs?
   ▶▶ Why are cats "prisoners"? What changes have occurred to their world? What has caused these changes?
2. What does Marcovaldo do on his lunch break? What catches his interest at the Biarritz Restaurant?
   ▶▶ In what way do Marcovaldo's perceptions change when he begins to look at places "as if through the round eyes of a cat"? What interests Marcovaldo about the cats?
3. What happens to Marcovaldo's fish? Who owns the villa and garden that he finds? Why, according to passers-by, will the owner not sell the property?
   ▶▶ What do the animals and the Marchesa have in common? How does the Marchesa feel about her property?
4. What happens to the villa when the Marchesa dies? Why do construction workers have a difficult time at the villa?
   ▶▶ What are the animals trying to protect? How much power do the animals have? What do you predict will happen after the end of the story?

SYNTHESIZING

5. In what ways are both the Marchesa and the cats victims of their environments? In what ways does the world become "uninhabitable" for them? On what kind of growth and change is the author commenting? In what ways are both people and animals victims of this growth and change?

Understanding Literature (Questions for Discussion)

1. **Theme.** A **theme** is a central idea in a literary work. What is the theme of "The Garden of Stubborn Cats"? In what way does the description of setting in the opening paragraphs of the story contribute to the story's theme? In what way does the conversation among the Marchesa's neighbors contribute to the story's theme?
2. **Point of View. Point of view** is the vantage point from which a story is told. Calvino switches from third-person point of view (he, she, it) to second-person point of view (you) at the end of the story. Why might he have chosen to do this? What effect might his use of the word *you* at the end of the story have on a reader?
3. **Magical Realism. Magical realism** is a kind of fiction that is for the most part realistic but that contains elements of fantasy. Discuss why this story is an example of magical realism. What are the story's realistic elements? What are the story's elements of fantasy? How do the realistic and fantastic elements of the story work together to shape the author's theme?

RESPONDING TO THE SELECTION

Students might also attempt to explain the position of the contractors. What distracts them from feeling sad about the loss of the city's last garden? What might be done to show them the value of maintaining some of the natural world?

ANSWERS FOR REVIEWING THE SELECTION

RECALLING AND INTERPRETING

1. **Recalling.** Domestic felines have been prisoners of an uninhabitable city. Condominiums, skyscrapers, movie houses, and concrete garages have replaced gardens and low roofs. **Interpreting.** Cats are prisoners because they have no place to roam freely and they have to be careful about the possibility of being hit by a car. The city has become overdeveloped. There is no place for animals. The continual development of the city has caused problems.

2. **Recalling.** Marcovaldo takes strolls with a fat tabby cat who leads him to a restaurant. A large fish tank catches Marcovaldo's eye. **Interpreting.** Marcovaldo begins to see the invisible city of cats who live an undercover existence. The exciting, hidden life of a cat interests Marcovaldo.

3. **Recalling.** The cat steals Marcovaldo's fish. The Marchesa owns the garden and the villa. Some people say that she is simply a grouchy old miser who will not let go of her house out of spite, and others say that she is trying to preserve the only undeveloped bit of land for herself and for the animals. **Interpreting.** Both the Marchesa and the cats are displaced and are suffering in a world that is changing too rapidly. The Marchesa says that she would like to get rid of the property, but the animals will not allow it.

4. **Recalling.** The villa is torn down and a building site (cont.)

ANSWERS FOR REVIEWING THE SELECTION (CONT.)

is constructed on the property. The cats disrupt the workers by jumping on them, hissing at them, and overturning materials. Birds nest in the structure and frogs live in the water. **Interpreting.** The animals are trying to protect the last piece of the city that is theirs. The animals have limited power; they can annoy or temporarily slow down the workers but cannot stop the work. *Responses will vary.*

SYNTHESIZING

Responses will vary. Possible responses are given.

5. The Marchesa and the cats find it difficult to prosper in the modern city. The Marchesa claims to be a prisoner of the cats and the cats are confined to the narrow spaces between buildings. The author is commenting on the problems of urbanization. People and animals both need green spaces to thrive.

ANSWERS FOR UNDERSTANDING LITERATURE

Responses will vary. Possible responses are given.

1. Theme. The theme of "The Garden of Stubborn Cats" is the negative effects of urbanization on people and animals. The description of the setting in the beginning of the story shows the reader the ways in which the changes in the city have destroyed the natural world and displaced animals. The conversation among Marchesa's neighbors is an example of the ongoing debate about progress and development versus preserving the natural environment.

2. Point of View. The change in point of view personalizes the story, placing the reader in the action. The reader might be better able to imagine that the story could occur in his or her own community.

3. Magical Realism. The details about the city, the garden, and the debate between the neighbors are realistic for the most part. The secret world of the cats and the other animals, and the different ways in which the cats take control of their destiny, seems more fantastic and magical. The reader is drawn into the story by realistic details with which he or she can identify, and then is moved by the magical world of the animals and the strange garden. Because the cats are given humanlike qualities and free will, the reader is better able to empathize with them.

ANALYTIC SCALES FOR RESPONDING IN WRITING

Grading scales for Responding in Writing appear on pages 412, 413.

Responding in Writing

1. **Creative Writing: Description.** Invent an unusual, almost magical, imaginary place like the garden of stubborn cats. What does your imaginary place look like? Who lives there? Why does this place exist? Write a one-page description of your place. Use imagery, precise nouns, vibrant verbs, and carefully chosen modifiers to make your description vivid to the reader.
2. **Critical Essay: Imagery and Theme.** A story's imagery is all of its words or phrases for things that can be seen, heard, touched, tasted, or smelled. Write an essay in which you discuss the theme of the story, and then describe some of the images that best illustrate the central idea of the story. As you plan your essay, consider the following questions. What is the author's view of the growth of cities and its effect on the natural world? What images of urban growth help the author to express these views?

Language Lab

Proofreading for Errors in Capitalization. Rewrite the following sentences, changing lowercase letters to capital letters wherever necessary. If a sentence is correct, write *Correct.* Before completing this exercise, consult the Language Arts Survey 2.54–2.61, "Proofreading for Errors in Capitalization."

EX. We read calvino's "The garden of stubborn cats" in english class.
We read Calvino's "The Garden of Stubborn Cats" in English class.

1. I saw a presentation about cats by professor Jane Moore at the centerville natural history museum.
2. She told us that the domestic cat is thought to have evolved from the african wild cat.
3. Ancient egyptians first used cats to control vermin in their grain supply.
4. The cat was revered as a hunter, and it became known as an incarnation of the goddess bastet.
5. Domestic cats spread across europe when phoenician traders took tame felines to italy.
6. Cats even traveled on the *mayflower* with the pilgrims.
7. In the middle ages, cats experienced some persecution when it was thought that they represented evil.
8. By the eighteenth century, cats had become popular all over the world as pets.
9. We have an orange tiger cat and a black cat, and our neighbors have a white persian cat and a gray siamese cat.
10. Raul said that many people adopt their cats from silver paws pet store or from the local chapter of the animal rescue league.

ANSWERS FOR LANGUAGE LAB

1. I saw a presentation about cats by Professor Jane Moore at the Centerville Natural History Museum.
2. She told us that the domestic cat is thought to have evolved from the African wild cat.
3. Ancient Egyptians first used cats to control vermin in their grain supply.
4. The cat was revered as a hunter, and it became known as an incarnation of the goddess Bastet.
5. Domestic cats spread across Europe when Phoenician traders took tame felines to Italy.
6. Cats even traveled on the Mayflower with the Pilgrims.
7. In the Middle Ages, cats experienced some persecution when it was thought that they represented evil.
8. *Correct.*
9. We have an orange tiger cat and a black cat, and our neighbors have a white Persian cat and a grey Siamese cat.
10. Raul said that many people adopt their cats from Silver Paws Pet Store or from the local chapter of the Animal Rescue League.

PREREADING

"Season"
by Wole Soyinka

NIGERIA

About the Author

WOLE SOYINKA
1934–

Nigerian poet, playwright, and novelist **Wole Soyinka** was born Akinwande Oluwole Soyinka in Abeokuta, Nigeria, on July 13, 1934. He attended Government College and University College in Ibadan but graduated from the University of Leeds in England in 1958. He returned to Nigeria and founded a national theater called the 1960 Masks, and from 1960 to 1964 he was coeditor of the literary journal *Black Orpheus*. Soyinka has been a fighter for Nigerian democracy and has been jailed and exiled several times for his political activism. In 1986 he was awarded the Nobel Prize for literature, and in 1994 he was forced to flee his homeland after opposing military rule. Soyinka's works include the plays *The Invention, A Dance of the Forests,* and *A Play of Giants*; the novel *The Interpreters*; and the autobiography *Ake: Years of Childhood.* He has also published several volumes of poetry.

About the Selection

Harvesting crops is important because it provides food; consequently, many cultures around the world celebrate harvest time. **"Season"** is a poem about the anticipation people feel at this important time of year. The speaker in the poem focuses on waiting for a corn crop. Soyinka uses **imagery** (language that names something that can be seen, heard, touched, tasted, or smelled) related to the corn to portray this expectation.

CONNECTIONS: The Growth of Corn

If you have ever eaten corn on the cob, you probably recognize some parts of the corn plant: the cob, the kernels, the cornsilk, and the husks, or leaves. Knowing some other parts of the corn plant and understanding the growth cycle of corn will help you to understand "Season." Corn stalks grow as tall as twenty feet high. At the top of this stem is a tassel or plume which produces the male flowers of the plant. Lower on the stem the spikes that develop into ears of corn grow. Cornsilk grows from germs on the spikes called ovules. If the cornsilk is fertilized by pollen, it produces a seed or kernel. When the flower parts of the plant develop, farmers say that the corn is "tasseling out." As corn ripens, the ends of the tassels begin to change color darkening from a golden yellow to a dark rust.

GOALS/OBJECTIVES

Studying this lesson will enable students to

- enjoy a poem that describes the anticipation and excitement of harvest season
- discuss the life and work of Wole Soyinka
- define the literary terms *image* and *irony*
- write a poem that deals with waiting and anticipation
- write an essay that examines the relationship between people and their environment
- plan a harvest festival based on the harvest celebrations of different cultures

ADDITIONAL RESOURCES

READER'S GUIDE
- Selection Worksheet 5.9

ASSESSMENT PORTFOLIO
- Selection Check Test 2.5.17
- Selection Test 2.5.18

ESSENTIAL SKILLS PRACTICE BOOKS
- Writing 1.8, 1.20

PREREADING EXTENSIONS

Have students research on other aspects of farming and agriculture in different time periods and parts of the world. Each student can research a particular aspect of farming and agriculture, and then present his or her findings to the rest of the class.

SUPPORT FOR LEP STUDENTS

PRONUNCIATIONS OF PROPER NOUNS AND ADJECTIVES

Wol • e Soy • in • ka (wō´ lā shô yiŋ´ kə)

ADDITIONAL VOCABULARY

corn-plume—silky tuft at the end of an ear of corn
laden—loaded

ADDITIONAL QUESTIONS AND ACTIVITIES

On page 419, Ebere says that life in Nigeria is changing because "cities have begun to take over villages and farms." Ask students if they have experienced similar changes in their communities, and how they felt about these changes. Have students imagine that they live in a small town that is being developed. Hold a "town meeting" with one side representing the developers, who want to create jobs and boost the economy, and the other side representing interests that want to protect the land.

READER'S JOURNAL

Ask students to close their eyes and imagine themselves outside during their favorite season. What do they hear and smell?

Answers to Guided Reading Questions

❶ The speaker associates rust and the "wilted corn-plume" with ripeness. To the speaker, pollen is mating-time, when swallows "Weave a dance / Of feathered arrows."

❷ The speaker loves to hear the wind and the "rasps in the field," where corn leaves "pierce like bamboo slivers."

❸ The harvesters await the promise of the rust.

SPELLING AND VOCABULARY WORDS FROM THE SELECTION

rasp	spliced

Selection Check Test with Answers

EX. What is rust to the speaker?
Rust is ripeness.

1. What is the sight of pollen to the speaker?
Pollen means mating-time to the speaker.

2. At what time of year does "Season" take place?
"Season" takes place at harvest time.

3. What do the harvesters love to hear?
They love to hear the wind and the rustle of the corn leaves.

4. What do the harvesters await?
They await the promise of the rust.

5. What will they do when the wait is over?
They will gather the corn crop.

READER'S JOURNAL

Describe your favorite season. Why do you enjoy this time of the year? What are some images—sights, sounds, and smells—that come to mind when you think about this particular period of time?

"Season"

WOLE SOYINKA

 ❶ *What does the speaker associate with ripeness? What does the speaker associate with pollen?*

 ❷ *What does the speaker love to hear?*

❸ *Who awaits the promise of the rust?*

Rust is ripeness, rust
And the wilted corn-plume;
Pollen is mating-time when swallows
Weave a dance
Of feathered arrows
Thread cornstalks in winged
Streaks of light. And, we loved to hear
Spliced phrases of the wind, to hear
Rasps in the field, where corn leaves
Pierce like bamboo slivers.

Now, garnerers[1] we,
Awaiting rust on tassels, draw
Long shadows from the dusk, wreathe
Dry thatch in woodsmoke. Laden stalks
Ride the germ's decay—we await
The promise of the rust. ■

1. **garnerers.** Gatherers, as in gatherers of crops

WORDS FOR EVERYDAY USE

spliced (splīsd´) *adj.,* joined or united by weaving together
rasp (räsp) *n.,* rough, grating sound

Vocabulary in Context

- The spliced pieces of string did not hold together, and the sign fell.
- We heard the rasp of chains dragging against concrete and knew that a frightening scene of the movie was about to take place.

Ebere Mbakwe, Nigeria

Global Views

When I read this poem, I was taken back home. I remembered running with my sisters through our itchy corn field on a dry, windy day, watching from afar, waiting for the tassels to ripen to a dark rusty brown, and throwing stones and trying to scare away the birds that sailed constantly above the corn field. The harvest in Nigeria is an important event, celebrated with feasts and festivals. It marks an ending and brings in the new year. Recently, however, cities have begun to take over villages and farms, and the harvesting season is becoming less important than it was before. Wole Soyinka's poem "Season" shows the joy and anticipation once felt before the harvest.

Responding to the Selection

How does the speaker feel about the season he is describing? Are you able to share his feelings toward this particular season?

Reviewing the Selection

Recalling		Interpreting
1. According to the speaker, what is rust and the "wilted corn-plume"?	▶▶	How can a "wilted corn-plume" mean ripeness to the speaker? What does the sight of "swallows [weaving] a dance" mean to the speaker?
2. What does the speaker love to hear?	▶▶	What words help the reader to "hear" the sounds that the speaker hears?
3. What people anticipate "rust on the tassels" and create "long shadows from the dusk"?	▶▶	What will people be able to do when there is rust on the tassels of the corn?
4. What do the laden stalks ride?	▶▶	With what are the stalks heavy? What is the germ, and how is it related to "the promise of the rust"?

Synthesizing

5. What season does the speaker await? What changes does the speaker describe in the poem? Why do you suppose the author wrote this poem?

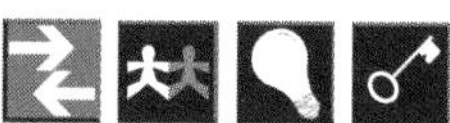

Responding to the Selection

Ask students to think about why the season is so important to the speaker.

Answers for Reviewing the Selection

RECALLING AND INTERPRETING

1. **Recalling.** According to the speaker, the rust and the wilted corn-plume are signs of "ripeness." **Interpreting.** The "wilted corn-plume" means the corn is nearly ripe, and ready to be harvested. The dance of the swallows means mating season to the speaker.

2. **Recalling.** The speaker loves to hear the wind and the rustling corn leaves. **Interpreting.** Words and phrases such as "spliced phrases" of wind and "rasps" help the reader to hear what the speaker hears.

3. **Recalling.** The harvesters anticipate "rust on tassels" and create "long shadows from the dusk." **Interpreting.** The people will be able to harvest the corn.

4. **Recalling.** The laden stalks "ride the germ's decay." **Interpreting.** The stalks are heavy with ripe corn. The germ is part of the corn plant, and its decay leads to the darkening of the tassels of the corn to the color of rust.

SYNTHESIZING

Responses will vary. Possible responses are given.

5. The speaker awaits harvest season. The speaker describes the changes in the environment at harvest time—the changes in animal and human behavior, and the changes in the corn plants. The author probably wrote this poem to share with readers the connectedness of humans and nature, and the excitement of harvest time. The speaker probably also wanted to show people's dependence on the natural world.

Answers for Understanding Literature

Responses will vary. Possible responses are given.

1. **Image.** Students might name the color of rust, the wilted corn-plumes, and the dancing swallows—striking images that appeal to sight; spliced phrases of wind and rasps in the field are images appealing to sound; and dry thatch in woodsmoke could be related to smell and taste.

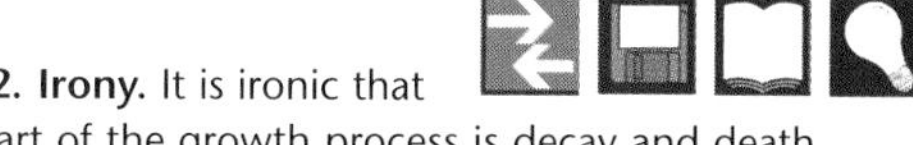

2. **Irony.** It is ironic that part of the growth process is decay and death.

ANALYTIC SCALES FOR RESPONDING IN WRITING

Assign a score from 1 to 25 for each grading criterion below. (For more detailed evaluation, see the evaluation forms for writing, revising, and proofreading, Assessment Portfolio 4.1–4.9.)

1. Anticipation Poem

- **Content/Unity.** The poem deals with the feelings that accompany waiting and anticipation.
- **Organization/Coherence.** The poem captures the feeling of anticipation with concrete details about the sights and sounds of the environment of the speaker.
- **Language/Style.** The poem uses vivid and precise nouns, verbs, and modifiers.
- **Conventions.** The poem avoids errors in spelling, grammar, usage, mechanics, and manuscript form.

▶ Additional practice is provided in the Essential Skills Practice Book: Writing 1.8.

2. Critical Essay

- **Content/Unity.** The essay examines the relationship between people and nature, as presented in the poem "Season."
- **Organization/Coherence.** The poem begins with an introduction that states a thesis about the relationship between people and nature. The introduction is followed by supporting paragraphs and a strong conclusion.
- **Language/Style.** The essay uses vivid and precise nouns, verbs, and modifiers.
- **Conventions.** The essay avoids errors in spelling, grammar, usage, mechanics, and manuscript form.

▶ Additional practice is provided in the Essential Skills Practice Book: Writing 1.20.

Understanding Literature (Questions for Discussion)

1. **Image.** An **image** is a word or phrase that describes something that can be seen, heard, touched, tasted, or smelled. The images presented in this poem appeal to a variety of these senses. Describe some of the most striking images in the poem. Which images appeal to the reader's sense of sight? Which images appeal to the reader's sense of sound, taste, or smell? Use your imagination as you allow the language of the poem to conjure pictures and memories in your mind.

2. **Irony. Irony** is the difference between appearance and reality. What changes in the environment is the speaker describing? What is ironic about phrases describing "wilted corn plumes" and a germ's "decay"?

Responding in Writing

1. **Creative Writing: Anticipation Poem.** Write a poem that, like "Season," deals with waiting and anticipation. Your poem might describe waiting for a change in season, waiting for a day to end, waiting for a cake to finish baking, or waiting for something to begin. In "Season," Soyinka captures the feeling of anticipation by describing the waiting harvesters and the sights and sounds of the environment as they await "the promise of the rust." Try to follow this technique as you capture feelings of anticipation in your own poem.

2. **Critical Essay: Humans and Nature.** Imagine that you have been asked to write an essay to be read at an Earth Day celebration. In your essay, examine the critical relationship between people and their environment. Describe this relationship as it is presented in "Season." In what way does this poem show the respect the speaker has for nature as a result of this relationship?

PROJECT

Planning a Harvest Festival. As a class, plan a Harvest Festival. Spend time at the library researching harvest celebrations of different cultures, particularly traditional African harvest festivals. Discuss these festivals and decide what you would like to do for your own festival. Your class might decide to base its festival closely on the traditions of another culture, or you might decide to use the research as a springboard from which to plan something completely original. If you have a large class, you might decide to break the class into committees. Plan food, decorations, entertainment, and anything else that would make your festival interesting.

PROJECT NOTES

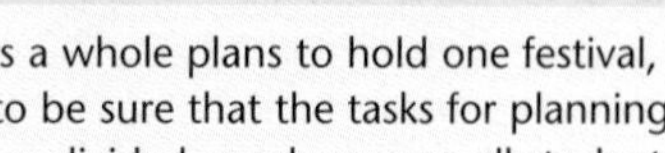

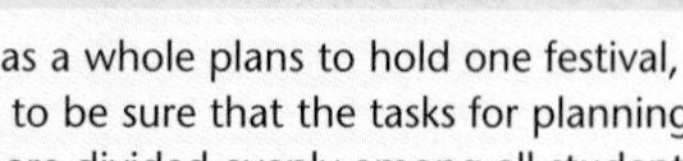

See the evaluation form for projects, Assessment Portfolio 4.12.

Planning a Harvest Festival. You might also ask the class to form small groups and have each group research a different festival from a different country or culture. Each group can plan its own "mini-festival" for the rest of the class.

If the class as a whole plans to hold one festival, it might help to be sure that the tasks for planning the festival are divided evenly among all students, according to their interests.

PREREADING

"Of Autumn"
by Veronica Porumbacu, translated by W. B. and Matei Calinescu

About the Author

Veronica Porumbacu (1921–1977). Born in Romania, Porumbacu attended the University of Bucharest. She spent a great deal of time translating poetry, concentrating on poetry by women, and eventually editing an anthology of the work of women poets from around the world. Porumbacu's own books of poetry include *Dreams of Old Dokia* (1947); *Poems, Retrospective Selection* (1962); and *Circle* (1971). Porumbacu died in March 1977 in an earthquake.

About the Selection

In her poem "**Of Autumn**," Veronica Porumbacu shares a unique interpretation of the change in seasons from summer to fall. When presenting a picture of an autumn night, Porumbacu does not simply describe the drop in temperature and the changes in the leaves. She tells a dramatic story that presents this season in a new light. In the poem, Porumbacu makes an allusion to King Herod, ruler of Judea from 37 to 4 BC. Although Herod is credited with increasing the prosperity of his land, he is known primarily for his cruel, tyrannical behavior in the later years of his life. Just before his death, he ordered the ruthless slaying of every male infant in the town of Bethlehem because he had heard that a child had been born there who was to be the "king of the Jews."

CONNECTIONS: Romania

The brutality expressed in the poem "Of Autumn" reflects the tumultuous Romanian political climate that existed during Porumbacu's lifetime. The World War II era was a time of change and tremendous suffering in Romania. In 1941, the country took part in a German invasion of the Soviet Union where about 350,000 soldiers were killed. Although Romania had a monarch, King Michael, General Ion Antonescu, who had German support, ran the country. When the Soviet Army entered Romania in 1944, King Michael arrested Antonescu and pledged to support the Soviet Union against Germany.

Following World War II in 1947, local Communists, with the support of the Soviet Union, seized control of the Romanian government. Forcing King Michael to abdicate, they established the Romanian People's Republic. One man, Nicolae Ceausescu, steadily gained power within the party and became its leader in 1965. Ceausescu was a cruel dictator who maintained a rigid Communist government. His ruthless efforts to foster the growth of industry in Romania plunged the country into poverty. He also brutally suppressed the country's ethnic minorities as well as anyone who dared speak out against him or his government. Ceausescu was overthrown in 1989.

ADDITIONAL RESOURCES

READER'S GUIDE

- Selection Worksheet 5.10

ASSESSMENT PORTFOLIO

- Selection Check Test 2.5.19
- Selection Test 2.5.20

ESSENTIAL SKILLS PRACTICE BOOKS

- Writing 1.8, 1.20
- Thinking Skills 4.2

PREREADING EXTENSIONS

Students might want to learn more about the country of Romania and what has changed since Nicolae Ceausescu was overthrown in 1989. Encourage students to use encyclopedias, books, magazines, newspapers, and the Internet to research modern-day Romania.

SUPPORT FOR LEP STUDENTS

PRONUNCIATIONS OF PROPER NOUNS AND ADJECTIVES

Ve • ron • i • ca Por • um • ba • cu (və rän´i kə pôr əm bä´ k o͞o)

ADDITIONAL VOCABULARY

massacred—savagely mass murdered

GOALS/OBJECTIVES

Studying this lesson will enable students to

- appreciate a powerful poem which uses an extended metaphor
- discuss the life and work of Veronica Porumbacu
- define the literary terms *extended metaphor* and *tone*
- write a poem about a season
- write a critical essay about creating tone in poetry
- practice comparing and contrasting two or more topics

READER'S JOURNAL

Ask students to write about the positive aspects and negative aspects of each season.

ANSWERS TO GUIDED READING QUESTIONS

❶ Summer was killed in the street. The wind could be heard yelling in the garden.

❷ Blood drips from the ivy on the walls. "King Herod of the Autumn" massacred hundreds of leaves.

SELECTION CHECK TEST WITH ANSWERS

EX. When was there a murder?
There was a murder in the night.

1. Who or what was killed?
Summer was killed.
2. What could be heard in the garden?
The wind could be heard yelling in the garden.
3. What do the trees stop doing?
The trees stop talking.
4. What drips from the ivy on the walls?
Blood drips from the ivy on the walls.
5. Who is responsible for the massacre?
King Herod of the Autumn is responsible for the massacre.

Think of some of your favorite details of each of the four seasons—winter, spring, summer, and fall. What events or details are commonly associated with each season? What are some less commonly observed details that are perhaps unique to your perspective?

READER'S JOURNAL

"Of Autumn"

VERONICA PORUMBACU, TRANSLATED BY W. B. AND MATEI CALINESCU

❶ *What happened to Summer? What could be heard in the garden?*

❷ *What drips from the ivy on the walls? Who is responsible for the massacre of the leaves?*

In the night there was murder in the street.
Summer was killed.
At the window you could hear the wind yelling
in the garden.

The trees stopped talking.
Blood drips from the ivy on the walls.
King Herod[1] of the Autumn massacred hundreds
of leaves with his words. ■

1. **King Herod.** Idumaean king of Judea (37–4 BC); called Herod the Great

Autumn.
Werenskiold, 1891

Responding to the Selection

Have you ever viewed autumn from this perspective? How does this poem make you feel about this season? What might have caused the poet to generate these images of autumn?

Reviewing the Selection

RECALLING		INTERPRETING
1. What happened to Summer? What could be heard in the garden?	▶▶	Is the speaker describing an actual murder? What kind of change is occurring? What might the "yell" of the wind be like?
2. How did the trees react to the incident?	▶▶	How does a tree "talk"? What might cause the tree to be silent?
3. What drips from the ivy?	▶▶	What has actually happened to the ivy?
4. What did "King Herod of the Autumn" do?	▶▶	Why does the speaker make reference to King Herod?

SYNTHESIZING

5. How does this speaker feel about autumn? Why might the speaker have chosen such violent images to convey these feelings?

Understanding Literature (Questions for Discussion)

1. **Tone. Tone** is the emotional attitude toward the reader or toward the subject implied by a literary work. Examples of the different tones that a work may have include familiar, ironic, playful, sarcastic, serious, and sincere. What is the tone of "Of Autumn"? What specific words and phrases help to create this tone?

2. **Extended Metaphor.** An **extended metaphor** is a point-by-point presentation of one thing as though it were another. The reader is invited to associate a particular thing being described with something that is quite different from it. What two things are being compared in "Of Autumn"? In what way is the metaphor extended throughout the poem?

RESPONDING TO THE SELECTION

Remind students to think about the information given to them in the Prereading section on page 421.

ANSWERS FOR REVIEWING THE SELECTION

RECALLING AND INTERPRETING

1. **Recalling.** Summer was murdered one night. **Interpreting.** The speaker is actually describing the change of seasons from summer to autumn. A strong wind might blow loudly.

2. **Recalling.** The trees stopped talking. **Interpreting.** The wind blowing through a tree's leaves might be heard as "talking." Losing its leaves in autumn would cause the tree to be silent.

3. **Recalling.** Blood drips from the ivy. **Interpreting.** The ivy leaves turn red because of the change in season.

4. **Recalling.** "King Herod of the Autumn" massacred hundreds of leaves. **Interpreting.** The speaker makes reference to King Herod because he was a cruel, tyrannical leader who ordered the murders of many people.

SYNTHESIZING

Responses will vary. Possible responses are given.

5. The speaker does not like autumn. It is described in the poem as a vicious, murderous, season. The poet is talking about autumn but is actually referring to the brutality of King Herod of Judea and the brutality she saw in her own country of Romania under the leadership of Nicolae Ceausescu. The violent images reflect the violence in Romania at the time in which the poet was writing.

ANSWERS FOR UNDERSTANDING LITERATURE

Responses will vary. Possible responses are given.

1. **Tone.** The tone of this poem is dark and violent, as if the speaker is reporting horrible, frightening news. Words and phrases such as "summer was killed," "the wind yelling," "blood drips from the ivy," and "massacred" create this tone.

2. **Extended Metaphor.** The writer is comparing the coming of autumn to the massacres carried out by King Herod, ruler of Judea from 37 to 4 BC. The speaker describes the changes of autumn throughout the poem as murder, blood, and the silencing of trees. The speaker makes the change of season sound like a massacre by a brutal dictator.

ANALYTIC SCALES FOR RESPONDING IN WRITING

Assign a score from 1 to 25 for each grading criterion below. (For more detailed evaluation, see the evaluation forms for writing, revising, and proofreading, Assessment Portfolio 4.1–4.9.)

1. Season Poem

- **Content/Unity.** The poem features an extended metaphor about one of the four seasons.
- **Organization/Coherence.** The writer uses concrete details to create a metaphor that gets the reader to look at a particular season in a new and original way.
- **Language/Style.** The poem uses vivid and precise nouns, verbs, and modifiers.
- **Conventions.** The poem avoids errors in spelling, grammar, usage, mechanics, and manuscript form.

► Additional practice is provided in the Essential Skills Practice Book: Writing 1.8.

2. Critical Essay

- **Content/Unity.** The essay defines *tone* and discusses the tone in the poem "Of Autumn."
- **Organization/Coherence.** The essay begins with an introduction that includes the thesis of the essay. The introduction is followed by supporting paragraphs with clear transitions and ends with a solid conclusion.
- **Language/Style.** The essay uses vivid and precise nouns, verbs, and modifiers.
- **Conventions.** The essay avoids errors in spelling, grammar, usage, mechanics, and manuscript form.

► Additional practice is provided in the Essential Skills Practice Book: Writing 1.20.

Responding in Writing

1. **Creative Writing: Season Poem.** Write a poem about one of the four seasons, using an extended metaphor in the style of Veronica Porumbacu's "Of Autumn." To what might you compare your season? How might you get a reader to view this season in a completely new and original way? Before you begin, review the notes you made in the Reader's Journal. You might also freewrite again, focusing on the details of one season.

2. **Critical Essay: Tone.** Imagine that you are writing an essay that you will be presenting to a group of poetry students. You are trying to teach the students about creating tone in poetry. In your essay, first define tone. Then discuss the tone of "Of Autumn." What emotions are evoked in the reader by the poem? What words or phrases does the poet use to evoke these emotions?

Thinking Skills

Comparing and Contrasting. Review the Language Arts Survey 4.2, "Types of Thinking," paying special attention to the information on comparing and contrasting. Prepare for one of the topics below. Then have a group discussion in which you compare and contrast two or more things.

- Compare and contrast "Of Autumn" with another poem or poems about autumn or about changing seasons.
- Compare and contrast King Herod, Nicolae Ceausescu, Adolph Hitler, Mohandas Gandhi, Martin Luther King, Jr., and another leader of your choice.

Archive Photos/Popperfoto

ANSWERS FOR SKILLS ACTIVITIES

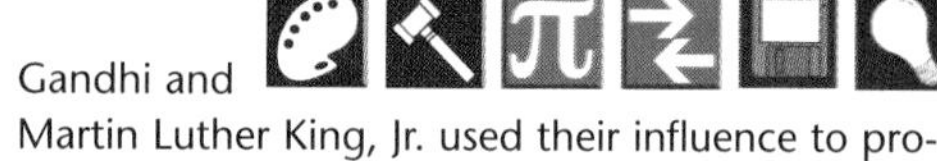

THINKING SKILLS

- Suggest that students look at the work of some of the English Romantic poets. They might also compare this poem to "Season" on page 418.
- Students should recognize that all the people listed had power, but that King Herod, Nicolae Ceausescu, and Adolph Hitler abused their power and used it to hurt people, and that Mohandas Gandhi and Martin Luther King, Jr. used their influence to promote peace and tolerance among people.

Global Voices

A MULTICULTURAL CONVERSATION

Discussing Nature

Students were asked to discuss whether protecting the environment is important in their countries and how nature is regarded.

Yumiko: Traditionally, I think Japanese people have tried to harmonize with nature rather than destroy it. For example, at our shrines we try to plant trees or make a pond to create a natural setting, so when you go into a shrine, you feel an awesome, supernatural feeling from nature and not from the building itself.

Elio: In the village where I lived as a kid in southern Mexico, the older men would tell of a time when there was a forest all around the town, but all that was left was one little area where you could see the way it used to be. Everything else had been taken over for agriculture. I think the problem was that there was such a vast amount of natural resources that people took it for granted.

Ebere: In the past in Nigeria, when a child was born a tree was planted in his or her name. We also had holy forests that you couldn't touch. When the British came and wanted to build railroads and cities, they just cut down all the trees, so there aren't many forests and holy sites anymore.

Avik: Trees are given religious significance in India too. If villagers don't want certain trees to be cut down by the government, they'll put a flower garland around the tree and start worshipping it. Religion is a very touchy subject in India, so as soon as you attach religion to something, no one messes with it.

Denis: In Russia, many people still live close to nature in places like Siberia, but in big cities like Moscow or St. Petersburg, people are spending a lot of money to buy land far from the city so they can go there during the summer for peace and quiet.

Sarah: That happens in the big cities in Greece too. Also, a lot of people leave cities in the summer for health reasons because there's so much air pollution. The government is trying to control the problem by allowing only a certain number of cars into the city each day.

Elio: Mexico City has a big air pollution problem too, which is not hard to believe since it is the biggest metropolitan area in the world. The rest of the country is still quite clean, although trash is getting to be a problem because there's not much control of it. Most villages have outdoor dumps and some still burn their trash, but like in the big cities, they're having to change things.

Jiannong: In Communist China, people would just put garbage outside their door. Now, we have garbage collectors, and the situation in big cities, especially in Shanghai and Beijing, is becoming better.

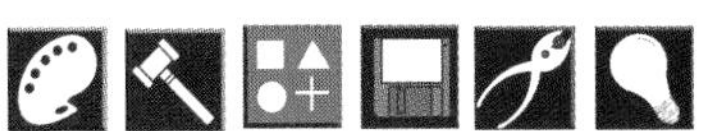

Cross-curricular Activities

ARTS AND HUMANITIES AND SOCIAL STUDIES

As Yumiko states, the Japanese people traditionally have created shrines in natural settings designed to capture the essence of nature. Generally, a Shinto shrine is a simple, unpainted wooden building. Shinto, an ancient native religion of Japan, is still practiced today in a form modified by the influence of Buddhism and Confucianism. In its present form, Shinto is not so much a religion as a set of traditional rituals and customs involving pilgrimages to famous shrines and celebrating popular festivals. Shintoists believe that shrines are the homes of the *kami*, or spirits, and therefore serve as a center for spiritual life.

Have students name different types of places where people worship, such as cathedrals, churches, synagogues, and shrines. Using the Internet, books, and magazines, students should find examples of religious structures from the eight countries discussed in this conversation. For example, students might bring in pictures of Buddhist temples in China or cathedrals in France. Have students research and discuss the significance of the style of the different structures.

Additional Questions and Activities

Have students discuss Ebere's statement: "When the British came and wanted to build railroads and cities, they just cut down all the trees, so there aren't many forests and holy sites anymore." Students might further investigate the colonization of Nigeria or colonization throughout history. Have students discuss the reasons for colonialism and the effect that colonization had on the people and land in the conquered areas.

Quotables

"Strictly speaking, no activity and no industry is possible without a certain amount of violence, no matter how little. Even the very process of living is impossible without a certain amount of violence. What we have to do is to minimize it to the greatest extent possible."

—Mohandas Gandhi

Additional Questions and Activities

Read the quotation by Mohandas Gandhi. Have students discuss the following: To what kind of violence might Gandhi be referring? Do you agree that no activity or industry is possible without "a certain amount of violence"? What are some ways to minimize this type of violence?

Cross-curricular Activities

MATHEMATICS AND SCIENCES, SOCIAL STUDIES, AND APPLIED ARTS

- Have students list the environmental issues that are discussed in this conversation, including deforestation, air pollution, waste management, and recycling. Which of these issues are important in the United States as well? What additional issues, if any, does the United States face? Using the Internet or other resources, students should find information about these environmental problems and about what various countries are doing to solve the problems. Students might also build models or demonstrate workable solutions to problems. For example, students might create a display showing how plastics are recycled.
- Hold a summit to discuss global environmental issues. Divide the class into small groups to gather information on the current environmental situation in the eight countries represented by the World Passport students: China, France, Greece, India, Japan, Mexico, Nigeria, and Russia. (You might want to have one group represent the United States as well.) As representatives of their country, students must look out for the best interest of their nation while keeping the global picture in mind. Students should research and be prepared to discuss each nation's political system, population, main industries, natural resources, and social systems. Students should include maps, charts, and other visual aids in their plans. Each group should present a topic: for example, the group representing China might speak about population control, while the Mexico group might discuss air pollution. Students should also seek resolutions for problematic issues.

Yumiko: I've heard that Japanese people consume much less energy in a day than people in the United States. But at the same time, many people in Japan are not very aware of environmental issues. We consume less, but not many people recycle.

Gabrielle: We have containers in which you can put your glasses or newspaper for recycling, but you have to drive there, so nobody does it because it's too much work.

Denis: We don't have any recycling, either.

Ebere: Neither do we.

Denis: We just put everything in one garbage container.

Avik: To me it seems like recycling is this big American myth. "I'll get rid of my guilt by recycling." But it takes resources to recycle stuff and most of it ends up in stacks somewhere because there isn't a market for recycled goods. In developing countries, the trash you produce is usually pretty organic, so you don't really need to recycle most of it. And in India, these guys come around on bicycles, and they yell at the top of their voices—

Ebere: Bottles!

Avik: Yeah, they yell *"Kabadiwalah!"*

Ebere: Exactly the same thing in Nigeria.

Avik: They buy tin cans or whatever you want to sell. And then they'll do something with the stuff, like make paper bags out of newspapers.

Ebere: Or they'll wash the bottles and use them to sell something else. That's the kind of recycling we have too. At least you know they're not dumping it somewhere.

Yumiko: I think it's important to educate everyone about the environment, because it comes back to all of us.

Sarah: I agree that a lack of education is a big part of the problem, but I also think the government needs to regulate pollution controls.

Elio: In Mexico, we used the resources and thought they would never go away. But as the country has grown, people have realized that they need to educate the population and replenish the resources by doing things like planting trees.

Additional Questions and Activities

Have students discuss Avik's comment that "recycling is this big American myth." Do students agree or disagree with this statement? Do they or their families recycle? Why, or why not? Does the school recycle? What recycling procedure, if any, is implemented in your community? If students do not recycle in their home or school, they can create a plan for recycling.

Have students research the recycling process and how materials are re-used. What are some ways to improve the current recycling process? Students can also brainstorm new products that could be developed by using recycled materials or products that would biodegrade after use.

SELECTIONS FOR ADDITIONAL READING

GERMANY

from "Of Nature"
by Johann Wolfgang von Goethe,
translated by Paul Carus

Nature! By her we are surrounded and encompassed—unable to step out of her, and unable to enter deeper into her. She receives us, unsolicited and unwarned, into the circle of her dance, and hurries along with us, till we are exhausted, and drop out of her arms. . . .

She creates ever new forms; what now is, was never before; what was, comes not again; all is new, and yet always the old. . . .

She seems to have contrived everything for individuality, but cares nothing for individuals. She is ever building, ever destroying, and her workshop is inaccessible . . .

She has thought, and is constantly meditating; not as a man, but as nature. She has an all-embracing mind of her own; no one can penetrate it. . . .

She lets every child tinker with her, every fool pass judgment on her; thousands stumble over her and see nothing; she has her joy in all. . . .

She is kindly. I praise her with all her works. She is wise and quiet. One can tear no explanation from her, extort from her no gift which she gives not of her own free will. . . .

She has placed me here, she will lead me away. I trust myself to her. She may do as she likes with me. She will not hate her work. ■

AUSTRALIA

from *The Road from Coorain*
by Jill Ker Conway

The Western Plains of New South Wales[1] are grasslands. Their vast expanse flows for many hundreds of miles beyond the Lachlan and Murrumbidgee rivers until the desert takes over and sweeps inland to the dead heart of the continent. In a good season, if the eyes are turned to the earth on those plains, they see a tapestry of delicate life—not the luxuriant design of a book of hours by any means, but a tapestry nonetheless, designed by a spare modern artist. What grows there hugs the earth firmly with its extended system of roots above which the plant life is delicate but determined. After rain there is an explosion of growth. Nut-flavored green grass puts up the thinnest of green spears. Wild grains appear, grains which develop bleached gold ears as they ripen. Purple desert peas weave through the green and gold, and bright yellow bachelor's buttons cover acres at a time, like fields planted with mustard. Closest to the earth is trefoil clover, whose tiny, vivid green leaves and bright flowers creep along the ground in spring, to be replaced by a harvest of seed-filled burrs in autumn—burrs which store within them the energy of the sun as concentrated protein. At the edges of pans of clay, where the topsoil has eroded, live waxy succulents bearing bright pink and purple blooms, spreading like splashes of paint dropped in widening circles on the earth.

Above the plants that creep across the ground are the bushes, which grow wherever an indentation in the earth, scarcely visible to the eye, allows for the concentration of more moisture from the dew and the reluctant rain. There is the ever-present round mound of prickly weed, which begins its life a strong acid green with hints of yellow, and then is burnt by the sun or the frost to a pale whitish yellow. As it ages, its root system weakens so that on windy days the wind will pick it out of the earth and roll it slowly and majestically about like whirling suns in a Van Gogh painting. Where the soil contains limestone, stronger bushes grow, sometimes two to three feet high, with the delicate narrow-leaved foliage of arid climates, bluish green and dusty grey in color, perfectly adapted to resist the drying sun. Where the soil is less porous and water will lie for a while after rain, comes the annual saltbush, a miraculous silvery-grey plant which stores its own water in small balloonlike round leaves and thrives long after the rains have vanished. Its sterner perennial cousin, which resembles sagebrush, rises on woody branches and rides out the strongest wind.

Very occasionally, where a submerged watercourse rises a little nearer the surface of the earth, a group of eucalyptus trees will cluster. Worn and gnarled by wind and lack of moisture, they rise up on the horizon so

1. **New South Wales.** State in southeast Australia

FROM "OF NATURE"

ABOUT THE AUTHOR

Johann Wolfgang von Goethe (1749–1832) was a poet and dramatist born in Frankfurt, Germany. Goethe grew up during a time of great political change in Germany due to the Seven Years' War, fought from 1756 to 1763. He was tutored at home and began to develop his interest in literature as a young boy. He wrote his first plays for a small puppet theater.

When Goethe was sixteen he became a law student at the University of Leipzig. He was awarded a doctor of laws degree in 1771, but when he returned to Frankfurt to practice law he was immediately drawn to a career in writing. Goethe's standing among German writers is comparable to Shakespeare's standing among English writers.

ABOUT THE SELECTION

This selection from Goethe's poem "Of Nature" presents an interesting perspective on the power and beauty of nature and shows Goethe's skill as a poet.

LITERARY TECHNIQUE

PERSONIFICATION

Personification is a figure of speech in which something not human is described as if it were human. Ask students to notice Goethe's use of personification as he describes nature, and to identify the character traits Goethe attributes to nature. Why do they think he wrote about nature in this way?

You might ask students to compare Goethe's view of nature with their own views of nature. If they had to assign character traits to nature, what traits would they choose?

FROM *THE ROAD FROM COORAIN*

ABOUT THE AUTHOR

Jill Ker Conway (1934–), an educator, feminist, and historian, was born in Australia. She eventually moved to the United States and served as the President of Smith College in Northampton, Massachusetts, from 1975 to 1985. Ker Conway is known for her autobiographical pieces *True North* and *The Road from Coorain.*

ABOUT THE SELECTION

This selection from *The Road from Coorain,* Ker Conway's well-respected autobiographical book, describes the Western Plains of New South Wales, an area in southeast Australia. Ker Conway first describes in careful detail the area's physical environment, the area's interesting wildlife, and the climate. She then describes some of the earliest human settlers in the area.

dramatically they appear like an assemblage of local deities. Because heat and mirages make them float in the air, they seem from the distance like surfers endlessly riding the plains above a silvery wave. The ocean they ride is blue-grey, silver, green, yellow, scarlet, and bleached gold, highlighting the red clay tones of the earth to provide a rich palette illuminated by brilliant sunshine, or on grey days a subdued blending of tones like those observed on a calm sea.

The creatures that inhabit this earth carry its colors in their feathers, fur, or scales. Among its largest denizens are emus, six-foot-high flightless birds with dun-gray feathers and tiny wings, and kangaroos. Kangaroos, like emus, are silent creatures, two to eight feet tall, and ranging in color from the gentlest dove-gray to a rich red-brown. Both species blend with their native earth so well that one can be almost upon them before recognizing the familiar shape. The fur of the wild dogs has the familiar yellow of the sunbaked clay, and the reptiles, snakes and goannas, look like the earth in shadow. All tread on the fragile habitat with padded paws and claws which leave the roots of grass intact.

On the plains, the earth meets the sky in a sharp black line so regular that it seems as though drawn by a creator interested more in geometry than the hills and valleys of the Old Testament. Human purposes are dwarfed by such a blank horizon. When we see it from an island in a vast ocean we know we are resting in shelter. On the plains, the horizon is always with us and there is no retreating from it. Its blankness travels with our every step and waits for us at every point of the compass. Because we have very few reference points on the spare earth, we seem to creep over it, one tiny point of consciousness between the empty earth and the overarching sky. Because of the flatness, contrasts are in a strange scale. A scarlet sunset will highlight grey-yellow tussocks of grass as though they were trees. Thunderclouds will mount thousands of feet above one stunted tree in the foreground. A horseback rider on the horizon will seem to rise up and emerge from the clouds. While the patterns of the earth are in small scale, akin to complex needlepoint on a vast tapestry, the sky is all drama. Cumulus clouds pile up over the center of vast continental spaces, and the wind moves them at dramatic pace along the horizon or over our heads. The ever-present red dust of a dry earth hangs in the air and turns all the colors from yellow through orange and red to purple on and off as the clouds bend and refract the light. Sunrise and sunset make up in drama for the fact that there are so few songbirds in that part of the bush. At sunrise, great shafts of gold precede the baroque sunburst. At sunset, the cumulus ranges through the shades of a Turner seascape before the sun dives below the earth leaving no afterglow, but at the horizon, tongues of fire.

Except for the bush canary and the magpie, the birds of this firmament court without the songs of the northern forest. Most are parrots, with the vivid colors and rasping sounds of the species. At sunset, rosella parrots, a glorious rosy pink, will settle on trees and appear to turn them scarlet. Magpies, large black and white birds, with a call close to song, mark the sunrise, but the rest of the day is the preserve of the crows, and the whistle of the hawk and the golden eagle. The most startling sound is the ribald laughter of the kookaburra, a species of kingfisher, whose call resembles demonic laughter. It is hard to imagine a kookaburra feeding St. Jerome or accompanying St. Francis. They belong to a physical and spiritual landscape which is outside the imagination of the Christian West.

The primal force of the sun shapes the environment. With the wind and the sand it bakes and cleanses all signs of decay. There is no cleansing by water. The rivers flow beneath the earth, and rain falls too rarely. In the recurring cycles of drought the sand and dust flow like water, and like the floods of other climates they engulf all that lies in their path. Painters find it hard to capture the shimmer of that warm red earth dancing in the brilliant light, and to record at the same time the subtle greens and greys of the plants and trees. Europeans were puzzled by the climate and vegetation, because the native eucalyptus trees were not deciduous. The physical blast of the sun in hot dry summers brought plants to dormancy. Slow growth followed in autumn, and a burst of vigorous growth after the brief winter rainy season. Summer was a time of endurance for all forms of life as moisture ebbed away and the earth was scorched. Winter days were like summer in a northern climate, and spring meant the onset of unbroken sunshine. On the plains, several winters might go by without a rainy season, and every twenty years or so the rain might vanish for a decade at a time. When that happened, the sun was needed to cleanse the bones of dead creatures, for the death toll was immense.

The oldest known humans on the continent left their bones on the western plains. Nomadic peoples hunted over the land as long as forty thousand years ago. They and their progeny left behind the blackened stones of ovens, and the hollowed flat pieces of granite they carried from great distances to grind the native nardoo grain. Their way of life persisted until white settlers came by bullock wagon, one hundred and thirty years ago, to take possession of the land. They came to graze their flocks of sharphooved sheep and cattle, hoping to make the land yield wealth. Other great inland grasslands in Argentina, South Africa, or North America were settled by pastoralists and ranchers who used forced labor: Indian peons, Bantus, or West African slaves. On Australia's great plains there were no settled native people to enslave. The settlers moved onto the plains long after the abandonment of transportation from Great

Britain, the last form of forced labor available in the Antipodes. As a result, the way of life that grew up for white settlers was unique.

A man could buy the government leasehold for hundreds of thousands of acres of grassland at a modest price if he settled the land and undertook to develop it. Others, beyond the reach of government scrutiny, simply squatted with their flocks on likely looking land. The scale of each holding was beyond European dreams of avarice. Each settler could look out to the vacant horizon knowing that all he saw was his. To graze the unfenced land required a population of sheepherders, or, as they came to be called, boundary riders. A settler would need twelve to fifteen hands for his several hundred thousand acres, but most would live out on the "run" (sheep run) at least a day's ride from the main settlement. The hands were solitary males, a freewheeling rural proletariat, antisocial, and unconcerned with comfort or the domestic pleasures. Their leisure went in drink and gambling, and their days in a routine of lonely and backbreaking work. The main house would be spare and simple also, its roof of iron and its walls of timber laboriously transported from the coast. The garden would be primitive and the boss's recreations would be little different from his hands'. If he shared his life with a wife and children, they lived marginally on the edge of his world of male activity. There was no rain for orchards, no water for vegetable gardens, and no society for entertaining. Women worked over wood stoves in 100 degree heat and heated water for laundry over an open fire. There was little room for the culinary arts, because everyone's diet was mutton and unleavened bread, strong black tea, and spirits. The ratio of women to men was as distorted in this wave of settlement as anywhere in the settlement of the New World. ■

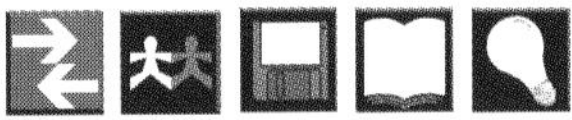

Additional Questions and Activities

You might have students complete one of the following activities:

- Write a descriptive piece about the area in which you grew up. You can describe your backyard, a town or community, or a special place in which you spent a great deal of time. Students should try to write in the style of Jill Ker Conway, using as many vivid, unique details as possible.
- Research the terrain, the wildlife, the climate, and some of the early history of the area in which you live. Write a descriptive essay similar in style to the selection you've just read by Jill Ker Conway.

ADDITIONAL RESOURCES

Assessment Portfolio

- Vocabulary Worksheet 2.5.21
- Study Guide 2.5.22
- Unit Test 2.5.23

Essential Skills Practice Books

WRITING

- Choosing a Purpose: Creative Writing, 1.8
- Writing a Critical Essay, 1.20

LANGUAGE

- Astronomical Terms, Time, Days, Months, Years, Holidays, and Periods, 2.54
- Dialects of English, 2.70
- Directions, Regions, Place Names, Organizations, Institutions, Brand and Trade Names, Buildings, Structures, and Vehicles, 2.56
- First Words, Interjections, and the Pronoun *I*, 2.57
- Names, Titles of Persons, Occupations, and Family Relationships, 2.55
- Poetry, Outlines, and Letters, 2.60
- Quotations and Sacred Names, 2.59
- Reflexive, Intensive, and Demonstrative Pronouns, 2.5
- School Subjects, Classes, Grades, and Awards, 2.61
- Titles of Works of Art, Literature, and Music, 2.58
- Types of Verbs, 2.7

SPEAKING AND LISTENING

- Active Listening and Interpersonal Communication, 3.2

STUDY AND RESEARCH

- Types of Thinking, 4.2

UNIT REVIEW

Communion with Nature

VOCABULARY FROM THE SELECTIONS

LITERARY TERMS

Vocabulary Check Test

Ask students to number their papers from one to ten. Have students complete each sentence with a word from the Vocabulary from the Selections in the Unit Review.

1. Because it was election time, we questioned whether the candidate's motives for donating to the charity were purely altruistic.
2. The trash-filled alley was so squalid, it made Skip cringe.
3. The aviary was filled with exotic birds from many lands.
4. Alice knew her efforts to fix her CD player were futile, but she still kept trying.
5. The ruler ordained that his subjects could practice any religion they wished.

(cont.)

SYNTHESIS: QUESTIONS FOR WRITING, RESEARCH, OR DISCUSSION

GENRE STUDIES

1. What is a hymn? What is a psalm? Compare and contrast the apparent purpose and tone, as well as the imagery, of Akhenaten's "Hymn to the Sun" with Psalm 23 or Psalm 137 found in Insights: Hymns and Psalms.

2. Define pastoral verse. Identify selections from this unit that could be classified as pastoral verse. Use examples from each selection to explain why the selection is an example of pastoral verse.

3. What are the characteristics of a haiku? In what way does a haiku differ from a tanka? Why is the use of imagery so important in both of these forms?

THEMATIC STUDIES

4. Compare and contrast the strong images of the haiku and tanka poems that you have read with images in other selections in this unit.

5. What contrast between nature and human construction is made in T'ao Ch'ien's "I Built My Cottage among the Habitations of Men" and Italo Calvino's "The Garden of Stubborn Cats"? Compare the attitudes toward nature expressed in these selections.

6. A change of seasons is described in the following works: Robert Burns's "Song Composed in August," Wole Soyinka's "Season," Veronica Porumbacu's "Of Autumn," and Alexander Pushkin's "Autumn." Compare and contrast the imagery used in two or more of these poems. In what way does the imagery of each poem seem to relate to the speaker's feelings about the season?

HISTORICAL/BIOGRAPHICAL STUDIES

7. Both *Out of Africa,* written about Kenya by Isak Dinesen, and *The Road from Coorain,* written about Australia by Jill Ker Conway, are memoirs, a form of autobiographical writing. In what way did the natural worlds in which these women lived affect their lives? Give examples from the selections to support your response.

SPELLING CHECK TEST

Ask students to number their papers from one to ten. Read each word aloud. Then read aloud the sentence containing the word. Repeat the word. Ask students to write the word on their papers, spelling it correctly.

1. **precinct**
In which precinct of the city does your aunt work as a police officer?
2. **incarnation**
Many people believe that this generous man is the incarnation of kindness and goodness.
3. **clamor**
Everyone in the dining room could hear the clamor of the falling pots and pans.
4. **azure**
The red kite was strikingly beautiful against the azure sky and the white clouds.
5. **impetuous**
Impetuous winds blew shingles from many rooftops.
6. **deluge**
The bottom fell out of the cup and a deluge of water poured out.
7. **somnambulant**
We guided the somnambulant child back to his bed.
8. **supernal**
The people listened carefully in church as the supernal words were repeated.
9. **practicable**
It is not practicable to paint the entire house in one weekend.
10. **protégé**
The young writer became the famous poet's protégé.

VOCABULARY CHECK TEST (CONT.)

6. The rock climber decided to make her way up that high crag near the top of the mountain.
7. Shana listed the places she toured in her itinerary.
8. The small child's burden was too heavy for him to carry.
9. The night was completely dark except for a luminous crescent of moon.
10. Homer wore a hat as often as he could to cover his bald pate.

UNIT SKILLS OUTLINE

Literary Skills and Concepts

- Allegory, 454, 468
- Allusion, 476
- Antihero, 463
- Breton Lay, 444
- Catalog, 441
- Character, 488
- Characterization, 468, 485
- Conflict, 479
- Existentialism, 474, 479
- External Conflict, 479
- Frame Tale, 476
- Gothic Novel, 453
- Internal Conflict, 479
- Internal Monologue, 456
- Magical Realism, 458
- Mood, 482
- Motivation, 448
- Narrator, 451
- Personification, 479
- Point of View, 456, 472
- Romance, 451
- Simile, 442
- Symbol, 488
- Tone, 472

Writing Skills and Concepts

- Critical Essay, 442, 451, 468, 473, 480, 489
- Imaginative Description, 451
- Metamorphosis, 468
- Monologue, 473
- Personal Essay, 488
- Three Stories in One, 479
- Transformation Story, 442

Grammar, Usage, and Mechanics Skills and Concepts

- Clichés and Euphemisms, 469
- Dashes, Hyphens, Parentheses, and Brackets, 462

Other Language Arts Skills and Concepts

- Oral Interpretation, 473
- Problem Solving and Decision Making, 480
- Technical Writing, 483
- Using Thesauruses, 443

Unit 6 Metamorphoses

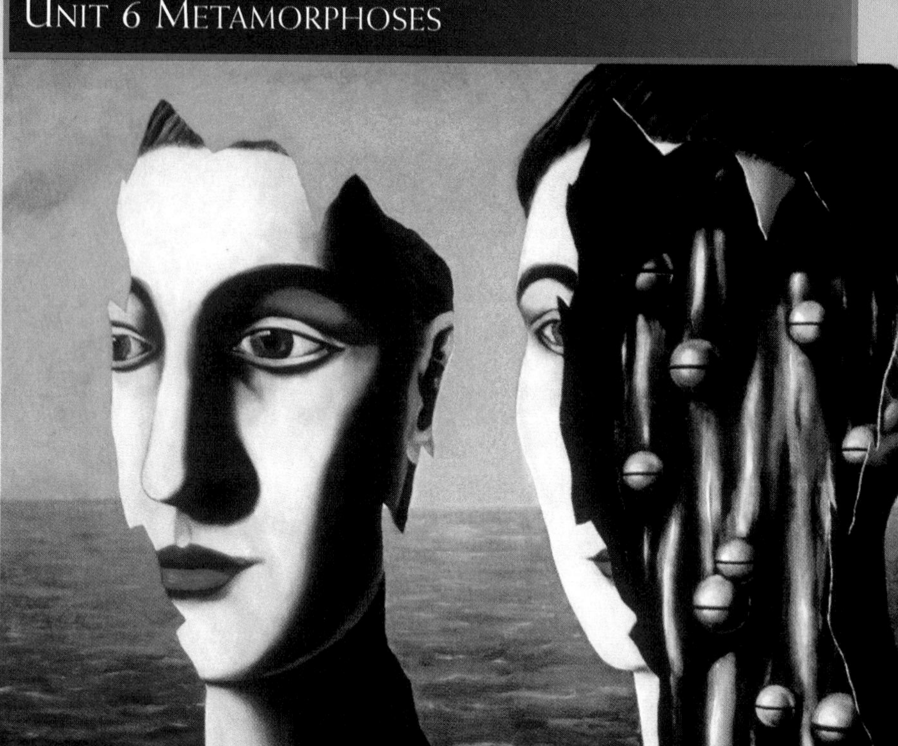

The Double Secret. *René Magritte, 1927*

GOALS/OBJECTIVES

Studying this unit will enable students to

- appreciate metamorphosis as a literary theme
- enjoy a wide variety of works that explore this theme
- describe where and how some tales of transformation originated
- recognize and interpret the use of a wide variety of literary terms
- explore a number of different types of creative writing
- write a variety of critical essays

"Full fathom five thy father lies;
Of his bones are coral made;
Those are pearls that were his eyes:
Nothing of him that doth fade
But doth suffer a sea-change
Into something rich and strange."

—William Shakespeare

433

CROSS-CURRICULAR CONNECTIONS

Arts and Humanities
- Artemis in Mythology, 438
- Artistic Representations of Apollo and Daphne, 493
- Changes that Affect Our Lives, 490
- Collages of Change, 490
- Illustrating Transformation Tales, 434
- Illustration and Interior Monologue, 447
- Magic of the Caribbean Day, 481
- Marianne Ashurst, 484
- Mythological Subjects in Art, 437
- Mythology Collection, 436
- Popular Culture and the Werewolf, 444
- Researching Displaced Peoples, 470
- Researching Spiders and Their Webs, 442
- Response to *The Wounded Stag,* 439
- Retelling Myths or Fairy Tales, 489
- Storytelling Festival, 452

Mathematics and Sciences
- Changes that Affect Our Lives, 490
- Researching Laurel, 493
- Researching Spiders and Their Webs, 442
- Transformation in the Physical World, 434

Social Studies
- Biographical Note on Echoes Authors, 435
- Biographical Note on Kafka, 455
- Biographical Note on Tellers of Terrifying Tales, 453
- "Brain Drain," 491
- Changes that Affect Our Lives, 490
- Collages of Change, 490
- Dolls in History, 484
- Effecting a Plan of Action, 491
- Job Satisfaction Survey, 457
- Magic of the Caribbean Day, 481
- Mythology Collection, 436
- Popular Culture and the Werewolf, 444
- Projecting the Future, 490
- Researching Displaced Peoples, 470

Applied Arts
- Effecting a Plan of Action, 491
- Job Satisfaction Survey, 457
- Technical Writing about a Hobby, 483

TEACHING THE MULTIPLE INTELLIGENCES

Musical
- Collages of Change, 490
- Storytelling Festival, 452

Logical-Mathematical
- "Brain Drain," 491
- Changes that Affect Our Lives, 490
- Comparing and Contrasting Existentialist Views, 474
- Discussing Gregor's Metamorphosis, 454
- Effecting a Plan of Action, 491
- Hunting Debate, 438
- Job Satisfaction Survey, 457
- Mythological Subjects in Art, 437
- Problem Solving and Decision Making, 480
- Projecting the Future, 490
- Transformation in the Physical World, 434

(cont.)

TEACHING THE MULTIPLE INTELLIGENCES (cont.)

Spatial
- Artistic Representations of Apollo and Daphne, 493
- Collages of Change, 490
- Illustrating Transformation Tales, 434
- Illustration and Interior Monologue, 447
- Marianne Ashurst, 484
- Mythological Subjects in Art, 437
- Mythology Collection, 436
- Popular Culture and the Werewolf, 444
- Problem Solving and Decision Making, 480
- Researching Displaced Peoples, 470
- Response to *The Wounded Stag,* 439
- Retelling Myths or Fairy Tales, 489

Kinesthetic
- Dramatic Monologue, 473
- Retelling Myths or Fairy Tales, 489
- Storytelling Festival, 452

Interpersonal
- "Brain Drain," 491
- Changes that Affect Our Lives, 490
- Collages of Change, 490
- Discussing Gregor's Metamorphosis, 454
- Dramatic Monologue, 473
- Effecting a Plan of Action, 491
- Hunting Debate, 438
- Job Satisfaction Survey, 457
- Magic of the Caribbean Day, 481
- Mythology Collection, 436
- Retelling Myths or Fairy Tales, 489
- Storytelling Festival, 452

Theme:

Metamorphoses

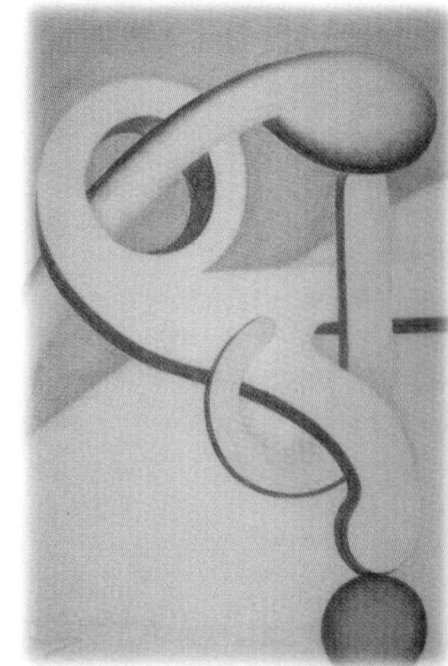

Composition. Niebla, 1936

A metamorphosis is a transformation—any sort of change in shape, substance, or structure. The idea of transformation is basic to most works of literature. In novels, short stories, and poems you will often find characters dealing with experiences or conflicts that change them in profound ways. Through these experiences, characters end up with transformed views of themselves, of other people, and of the world around them. In some works the transformations that occur are quite literal. In tales of fantasy, mythology, or magical realism, you can read about characters or places that magically change form. In realistic fiction, you can read about characters who change their looks or surroundings in dramatic ways.

In this unit, you will have the chance to enjoy works of literature that deal with dramatic transformations of the most literal kind. Imagine that after years of uneventful life, you wake up one morning transformed into a giant insect. Imagine that you are a handsome baron by day who at night becomes a vicious, human-eating werewolf lurking in a dark forest. These are the experiences of two characters who appear in this unit, and you will have the chance to see the results of their frightening transformations. You will also read a poem that reflects on a Biblical story in which a woman disobeys God and, as a result, becomes a pillar of salt. You will become acquainted with the magical metamorphoses of classical Greek and Roman mythology, and you will read a story in which a woman transforms the simple act of exterminating pesky cockroaches into an elaborate series of meditations. No two works in this unit are exactly alike, but all are vivid and often strange tales of metamorphosis that will capture your imagination.

Other Selections Exploring This Theme

Cross-curricular Activities

ARTS AND HUMANITIES

As students read the introduction, they will get a glimpse of the stories they are about to read. Ask students to make some predictions or to think creatively about the information they are given about the selections in this unit. Have them create illustrations for one or more of the selections from the unit as they imagine it will be from the brief description on page 434. If, after reading the selection, the student does not feel that his or her illustration relates well to the selection, ask him or her to write a story, poem, or other literary work that more closely matches his or her original ideas about the theme or topic.

MATHEMATICS AND SCIENCES

Ask students interested in science to discuss transformation in the natural or physical world. For example, a student could demonstrate or explain a science experiment in which adding an element or compound to another substance produces a change in color, form, or some other aspect of the materials, or a student could show the stages of transformation from a tadpole to a full-grown frog. Students should use visual aids to present their information to the class.

Additional Questions and Activities

This unit is devoted to changes in form, changes that are often quite literal. As students read the selections in this unit, and as they contemplate the quotations on page 435, you may wish to have them keep in mind other types of transformation, such as the metamorphosis from child to adult, the change from a naive person to an experienced person, or the transformation from an ugly character to a beautiful one, either physically or spiritually. Ask students to think about major changes in their lives or about the transformations that they have seen in the people around them. Students can write about or discuss life-changing experiences.

Echoes:

Metamorphoses

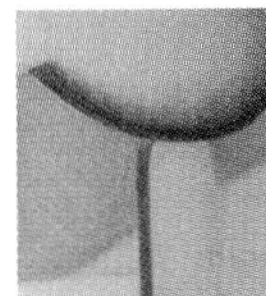

My intention is to tell of bodies changed
To different forms; the gods, who made the
changes,
Will help me—or I hope so—with a poem
That runs from the world's beginning to our
own days.

—Ovid
from *The Metamorphoses*

"I am a man upon the land,
And I am a silkie in the sea;
And when I'm far away from land,
My dwelling is in Shule Skerrie."

—Anonymous Scottish Ballad

O God! that men should put an enemy in their mouths to steal away their brains; that we should, with joy, pleasance, revel, and applause, transform ourselves into beasts.

—William Shakespeare
from *The Tragedy of Othello, the Moor of Venice*

How should we be able to forget those ancient myths that are at the beginning of all peoples, the myths about dragons that at the last moment turn into princesses. Perhaps all the dragons of our lives are princesses who are only waiting to see us once beautiful and brave.

—Rainer Maria Rilke
from *Letters to a Young Poet*

All things must change
To something new, to something strange.

—Henry Wadsworth Longfellow

Everything is in a state of metamorphosis. Thou thyself art in everlasting change and in corruption to correspond; so is the whole universe.

—Marcus Aurelius

I have risen up out of the *seshett* chamber, like the golden hawk which cometh forth from his egg. I fly, I alight (or, flutter in the air) like a hawk with a back of seven cubits, and the wings of which are like unto the mother-of-emerald of the South.

—from "The Chapter of Changing into a Hawk of Gold" from *The Book of the Dead*

The lump on his forehead had grown longer; he was staring fixedly at me, apparently without seeing me. Or, rather, he must have seen me quite clearly, for he charged at me with his head lowered. . . .

"You are a rhinoceros!" I cried.

"I'll trample on you! I'll trample on you!" I made out these words as I dashed toward the door.

—Eugène Ionesco
from "Rhinoceros"

Biographical Note

Ovid (43 BC–AD 17) was an ancient Greek poet. A biography of Ovid appears on page 436.

William Shakespeare (1564–1616) is one of the best-known authors of the English language. He is famous for such plays as *Romeo and Juliet, Macbeth, Hamlet,* and *King Lear.* He also wrote many sonnets, and the Shakespearian sonnet bears his name for the rhyme scheme and stanza form he used.

Rainer Maria Rilke (1875–1926) was a German poet considered by many to be one of the most important lyric poets of the twentieth century. Rilke's correspondence is also praised for its literary value.

Henry Wadsworth Longfellow (1807–1882) was one of the popular "Fireside Poets," a group of American poets that included Ralph Waldo Emerson, John Greenleaf Whittier, James Russell Lowell, and Oliver Wendell Holmes. The group took its name from the popular evening entertainment of reading by the fireside. Longfellow was born in Maine. He studied at Bowdoin College and in Europe. After his death, a bust of Longfellow was installed in the Poet's Corner of Westminster Abbey, making him the only American poet to be so honored.

Marcus Aurelius (121–180) ruled as Roman emperor from 161 to 180. He was also a Stoic philosopher.

The Book of the Dead is a collection of funerary writings from ancient Egypt. For more information, see page 296.

Eugène Ionesco (1912–) is a French playwright who was born in Romania. For a biography of Ionesco, see page 46.

ADDITIONAL RESOURCES

READER'S GUIDE

- Selection Worksheet 6.1

ASSESSMENT PORTFOLIO

- Selection Check Test 2.6.1
- Selection Test 2.6.2

ESSENTIAL SKILLS PRACTICE BOOKS

- Writing 1.8, 1.20
- Study and Research 4.16

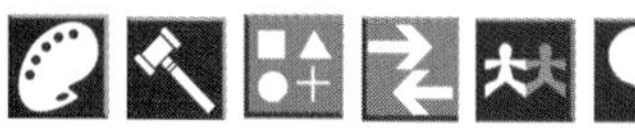

PREREADING EXTENSIONS

Ask students to choose other stories from Ovid's *Metamorphoses* or from another source of Greek and Roman myths, such as Edith Hamilton's *Mythology.* Then students can work as a group to create a collection of mythology for younger children. Each student should write a simple version of the story that he or she read. Students can illustrate the stories, make a chart of the gods and mortals included in the book, create a table of contents, and design a cover. After compiling the book, students should share it with a class of younger students.

SUPPORT FOR LEP STUDENTS

PRONUNCIATIONS OF PROPER NOUNS AND ADJECTIVES

Ac • tae • on (ak tē´ in)
Cro • ca • le (krō kā´ lē)
Gar • ga • phie (gar´ga fē)
Ne • phe • le (nef´ ə lē)
Ov • id (äv´ id)
Phy • a • le (fī´ ə lē)
Pse • cas (sē´ kas)
Rha • nis (rän´ nis)

ADDITIONAL VOCABULARY

cypress—type of tree
grotto—cave
lacerate—tear jaggedly
mute—silent, without words
vengeance—desire for revenge

PREREADING

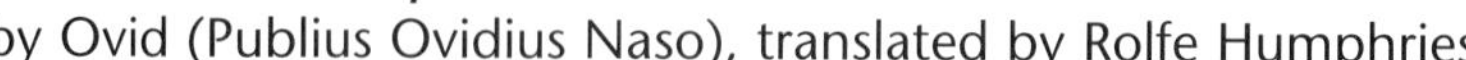

"The Story of Actaeon"
from *Metamorphoses*
by Ovid (Publius Ovidius Naso), translated by Rolfe Humphries

ROME

About the Author

Ovid (43 BC–AD 17). **Publius Ovidius Naso** is better known to many readers as **Ovid.** He was born in Sulmo, east of Rome, to a well-to-do family that was able to send him to Athens to finish his education. Originally destined for a law career, he soon turned to poetry and gained some success with a series of love poems, *Amores,* around 15 BC. Ovid's early work contained a casual and witty treatment of love and marriage, and it is as a love poet that he was principally known from his own time until the Renaissance. Ovid's fortunes turned drastically in AD 8, when he was banished from Rome by Emperor Augustus for an offense that remains unknown. He was sent to live in Tomis, part of modern-day Romania, then a remote outpost of the Roman Empire. There Ovid spent the rest of his life, at times depressed and despondent, while his wife vainly pleaded his case in Rome. Ovid's years in exile were still productive, for he continued to write poetry. His interest in love as a poetic theme decreased, and during this time he wrote *Metamorphoses,* generally considered to be his greatest work.

Colosseum, Rome, Italy

About the Selection

"The Story of Actaeon" comes from Ovid's ***Metamorphoses,*** a work whose title means "changing forms." *Metamorphoses* is a vast compendium of the myths of classical Greece and Rome, many of which deal with miraculous transformations. In one of these myths, for example, Midas's daughter is turned to gold. In another, the weaver Arachne is transformed into a spider.

The following myth focuses upon Actaeon, a hunter who was the son of the god Aristaeus and of Autonoë, daughter of Cadmus, the legendary founder of Thebes. In "The Story of Actaeon," Actaeon angers the goddess Diana, who transforms him into a stag. In some versions of this story, Actaeon angers Diana by claiming to be a better hunter than she, but Ovid provides a different motivation.

CONNECTIONS: Diana and Artemis

The Roman goddess Diana, known to the Greeks as Artemis, was goddess of the moon and of hunting. She made her home in the woodlands and was known both as a protector of animals and as a hunter. In visual renderings of Diana, she often appears with a hunting bow and quiver or with a crescent moon, often in her hair. Because of her chastity, Diana was also the patron of virgins. Many other stories about Diana appear in Ovid's *Metamorphoses.*

GOALS/OBJECTIVES

Studying this lesson will enable students to

- appreciate a myth about transformation
- identify Ovid as an ancient Roman writer
- recognize attributes of the goddess Diana, or Artemis
- identify and analyze a catalog
- define *simile*
- identify and understand similes
- write a transformation story
- write an essay of biographical criticism
- use a thesaurus

READER'S JOURNAL

If you could be something else, such as an animal or a tree, what would you be? In your journal, describe what you think it would be like to be this thing. Include some of the benefits and drawbacks that you imagine would be part of the experience.

"The Story of Actaeon"

OVID, TRANSLATED BY ROLFE HUMPHRIES

[Editor's note: Before telling the story of Actaeon, Ovid discusses the life of his grandfather, Cadmus. Ovid describes how Cadmus founded the city of Thebes and ends that story with the tantalizing phrase, "But always, always,/A man must wait the final day, and no man/Should ever be called happy before burial." Ovid then relates the tale of Cadmus's grandson, Actaeon.]

One of these grandsons was the lad Actaeon,
First cause of Cadmus' sorrow. On his forehead
Horns sprouted, and his hound-dogs came to drink
The blood of their young master. In the story
You will find Actaeon guiltless; put the blame
On luck, not crime: what crime is there in error?

There was a mountain, on whose slopes had fallen
The blood of many kinds of game: high noon,
Short shadows, and Actaeon, at ease and friendly
Telling his company: "Our nets and spears
Drip with the blood of our successful hunting.
To-day has brought us luck enough; to-morrow
We try again. The Sun-god, hot and burning,
Is halfway up his course. Give up the labor,
Bring home the nets." And they obeyed his orders.

There was a valley there, all dark and shaded
With pine and cypress sacred to Diana.
Gargaphie, its name was, and it held
Deep in its inner shade a secret grotto
Made by no art, unless you think of Nature
As being an artist. Out of rock and tufa[1]

1 *What happens to Actaeon? Does the narrator believe that Actaeon deserves his fate?*

2 *Where does Diana go to relax after hunting?*

1. **tufa.** Type of porous stone

READER'S JOURNAL

Students might use this assignment to experiment with point of view by writing from the point of view of the alternate identity. Students can describe the positive and negative aspects of life in this form without identifying the form. Then students can read their descriptions to other students who can try to guess which object or creature is speaking.

ANSWERS TO GUIDED READING QUESTIONS

1 Actaeon sprouted horns and was killed by his own hounds. The narrator blames bad luck rather than Actaeon for his fate.

2 Diana went to her grotto in Gargaphie to relax.

LITERARY NOTE

In Greek mythology, Cadmus was the son of Agenor, the king of Phoenicia. Cadmus tried unsuccessfully to find his sister Europa after she was abducted by Zeus. Following the order of the oracle at Delphi, Cadmus followed a cow until she lay down. At that spot, he founded the city of Thebes. Legend also credits Cadmus with bringing the alphabet to Greece.

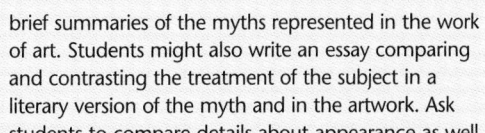

CROSS-CURRICULAR ACTIVITIES

ARTS AND HUMANITIES

Mythological subjects have been widely painted and represented in sculpture. Ask students to find examples of works of art based on myths of Diana, or her Greek counterpart Artemis, or other Greek or Roman gods. Students can compile a list of names to use in their search. Ask students to write or present brief summaries of the myths represented in the work of art. Students might also write an essay comparing and contrasting the treatment of the subject in a literary version of the myth and in the artwork. Ask students to compare details about appearance as well as the mood and theme presented in each work.

Answers to Guided Reading Questions

❶ Actaeon wanders into Diana's grotto by mistake.

❷ Diana is embarrassed. She splashes Actaeon with water and tells him to tell others that he has seen her naked if he can.

❸ He sprouts horns on his forehead, his neck stretches out, his ears become long and pointed, his arms and hands become legs and feet, and his skin becomes a dappled hide. In short, he becomes a stag.

Literary Note

Many love stories involving Artemis's nymphs appear in mythology. These stories were originally told of Artemis herself, but, after Homer, Artemis became associated with chastity. According to myth, the chaste Artemis asked her father, Zeus, to allow her never to marry. For a literary allusion to this myth, have students read the lyric poem "But Not Everybody Wants Love" by Sappho on page 610. Ask students if the image of Artemis they find in Sappho's poem matches the image of Diana in Ovid's work.

INTEGRATED SKILLS ACTIVITIES

Speaking and Listening Skills

Have students hold a debate about hunting. Suggest the following proposition: Hunting, while necessary in the past, is no longer necessary and should be banned. Have students form two teams and research their team's position before entering into the debate.

She had formed an archway, where the shining water
Made slender watery sound, and soon subsided
Into a pool, and grassy banks around it.
The goddess of the woods, when tired from hunting,
Came here to bathe her limbs in the cool crystal.
She gave her armor-bearer spear and quiver[2]
And loosened bow; another's arm received
The robe, laid off; two nymphs[3] unbound her sandals,
And one, Crocale, defter than the others,
Knotted the flowing hair; others brought water,
Psecas, Phyale, Nephele, and Rhanis,
Pouring it out from good-sized urns, as always.
But look! While she was bathing there, all naked,
Actaeon came, with no more thought of hunting
Till the next day, wandering, far from certain,
Through unfamiliar woodland till he entered
Diana's grove, as fate seemed bound to have it.
And when he entered the cool dripping grotto,
The nymphs, all naked, saw him, saw a man,
And beat their breasts and screamed, and all together
Gathered around their goddess, tried to hide her
With their own bodies, but she stood above them,
Taller by head and shoulders. As the clouds
Grow red at sunset, as the daybreak reddens,
Diana blushed at being seen, and turned
Aside a little from her close companions,
Looked quickly for her arrows, found no weapon
Except the water, but scooped up a handful
And flung it in the young man's face, and over
The young man's hair. Those drops had vengeance in them.
She told him so: "Tell people you have seen me,
Diana, naked! Tell them if you can!"
She said no more, but on the sprinkled forehead
Horns of the long-lived stag began to sprout,
The neck stretched out, the ears were long and pointed,
The arms were legs, the hands were feet, the skin
A dappled hide, and the hunter's heart was fearful.
Away in flight he goes, and, going, marvels
At his own speed, and finally sees, reflected,
His features in a quiet pool. "Alas!"
He tries to say, but has no words. He groans,
The only speech he has, and the tears run down

❶ *Where does Actaeon go by mistake?*

❷ *How does Diana feel because Actaeon has seen her? What does she do to him?*

❸ *What changes occur in Actaeon's form?*

2. **quiver.** Case for holding arrows
3. **nymphs.** Young and beautiful minor nature goddesses

The Wounded Stag. *Ralph Albert Blakelock, circa 1880. The Hirshhorn Museum and Sculpture Garden, Smithsonian Institution, Gift of Joseph H. Hirshhorn, 1966.*

Photo: John Tennant

Cheeks that are not his own. There is one thing only
Left him, his former mind. What should he do?
Where should he go—back to the royal palace
Or find some place of refuge in the forest?
Fear argues against one, and shame the other.
And while he hesitates, he sees his hounds,
Blackfoot, Trailchaser, Hungry, Hurricane,
Gazelle and Mountain-Ranger, Spot and Sylvan,
Swift Wingfoot, Glen, wolf-sired, and the bitch Harpy
With her two pups, half-grown, ranging beside her,
Tigress, another bitch, Hunter, and Lanky,
Chop-jaws, and Soot, and Wolf, with the white marking
On his black muzzle, Mountaineer, and Power,
The Killer, Whirlwind, Whitey, Blackskin, Grabber,
And others it would take too long to mention,
Arcadian[4] hounds, and Cretan-bred, and Spartan.
The whole pack, with the lust of blood upon them,
Come baying over cliffs and crags[5] and ledges

 1

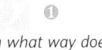

In what way does Actaeon remain unchanged? What choices does he think he has? Why doesn't he like either choice?

4. **Arcadian.** Of Arcadia, region of central Greece
5. **crags.** Steep, rugged rocks

ART NOTE

Have students look at Ralph Albert Blakelock's *The Wounded Stag.* Have students respond to the painting in one of the following ways: writing an interior monologue from the point of view of the deer, writing an editorial or speech for or against hunting based on the image, or writing a description of the scene depicted in the painting.

ANSWERS TO GUIDED READING QUESTIONS

1 Actaeon can still think like a human. He can go to the royal palace or to the forest. He is too afraid and proud to choose either option.

QUOTABLES

"Let us be Diana's foresters, gentlemen of the shade, minions of the moon."

—William Shakespeare

ADDITIONAL QUESTIONS AND ACTIVITIES

As noted in the Connections on page 436 and reflected in the quotation above, the moon is often given as one of Diana's attributes. Ask students to research other symbols used to represent various gods and goddesses of ancient Greece and Rome. Knowledge of such symbols is useful in interpreting the literature and art of various periods.

Answers to Guided Reading Questions

❶ His "old companions" now hunt and pursue him.

❷ Actaeon's companions urge the dogs on. They shout for Actaeon and call him lazy. Actaeon turns his head to plead for mercy in the only way he can.

❸ Actaeon is killed by his own dogs.

Selection Check Test with Answers

EX. Who is Actaeon's grandfather?
Cadmus is Actaeon's grandfather.

1. What goddess does Actaeon accidentally see?
He accidentally sees Diana.

2. Where was the goddess when Actaeon saw her?
She was in a private grotto.

3. Into what kind of animal is Actaeon transformed?
He is transformed into a stag.

4. What do Actaeon's companions want him to see?
They want him to see the stag they have at bay.

5. What ultimately happens to Actaeon?
He is killed by his own hunting dogs.

❶ *In what new way do Actaeon's "old companions" behave toward him?*

❷ *What do Actaeon's companions do? In what way does Actaeon respond to his companions?*

❸ *What is Actaeon's fate?*

Where no trail runs: Actaeon, once pursuer
Over this very ground, is now pursued,
Fleeing his old companions. He would cry
"I am Actaeon: recognize your master!"
But the words fail, and nobody could hear him
So full the air of baying. First of all
The Killer fastens on him, then the Grabber,
Then Mountaineer gets hold of him by a shoulder.
These three had started last, but beat the others
By a short-cut through the mountains. So they run him
To stand at bay[6] until the whole pack gathers
And all together nip and slash and fasten
Till there is no more room for wounds. He groans,
Making a sound not human, but a sound
No stag could utter either, and the ridges
Are filled with that heart-breaking kind of moaning.
Actaeon goes to his knees, like a man praying,
Faces them all in silence, with his eyes
In mute appeal, having no arms to plead with,
To stretch to them for mercy. His companions,
The other hunting lads, urge on the pack
With shouts as they did always, and not knowing
What has become of him, they call *Actaeon*!
Actaeon! each one louder than the others,
As if they thought him miles away. He answers,
Hearing his name, by turning his head toward them,
And hears them growl and grumble at his absence,
Calling him lazy, missing the good show
Of quarry[7] brought to bay. Absence, for certain,
He would prefer, but he is there; and surely
He would rather see and hear the dogs than feel them.
They circle him, dash in, and nip, and mangle
And lacerate and tear their prey, not master,
No master whom they know, only a deer.
And so he died, and so Diana's anger
Was satisfied at last. ■

6. **stand at bay.** Situation of a hunted animal forced to turn and fight
7. **quarry.** Animal being hunted

Responding to the Selection

The narrator says, "You will find Actaeon guiltless; put the blame/On luck, not crime: what crime is there in error?" Do you, as the narrator expects, find Actaeon guiltless? Do you think that he deserved his fate? How do you feel toward Actaeon? How do you feel toward Diana?

Reviewing the Selection

RECALLING		INTERPRETING
1. What is Actaeon's occupation? Where does he find himself? What does he see?	▶▶	Should Actaeon be blamed for what he sees? Why, or why not?
2. What does Diana do when she sees Actaeon?	▶▶	What personal qualities does Diana's reaction suggest?
3. What physical change does Actaeon undergo? In what way is he still human?	▶▶	Why might the human characteristic remaining to Actaeon make the change he has undergone more difficult for him to accept?
4. In what way has Actaeon's position changed because of his physical change? Why are his companions excited?	▶▶	In what way might Actaeon's feelings about hunting have changed? Do you think he would continue to hunt if he were turned back into a human? How might his companions feel if they knew where their missing companion was?

SYNTHESIZING

5. What feelings prompted Diana to treat Actaeon in this way? Do you think the punishment fit the crime in this case? In what way do Diana's actions reflect her role as goddess of hunting, protector of animals, and patron of virgins?

Understanding Literature (Questions for Discussion)

1. **Catalog.** A **catalog** is a list of people or things. "The Story of Actaeon" includes a catalog of the names of Actaeon's dogs. What do the names tell you about the dogs? In what way do the names make Actaeon's situation seem more bleak?

Responding to the Selection

Students might also discuss a time when they were punished more harshly than they thought they deserved or a time when they wanted to punish somebody for a wrong, major or minor, done to them.

Answers for Reviewing the Selection

RECALLING AND INTERPRETING

1. **Recalling.** Actaeon is a hunter. He wanders into Diana's grotto and sees her naked. **Interpreting.** Actaeon did not set out to see Diana; he happened upon her by chance, so he should not be blamed for what he saw.

2. **Recalling.** Diana blushes, looks for her arrows, and, not finding them, splashes Actaeon with water. **Interpreting.** Diana's actions suggest her modesty and perhaps a quick temper.

3. **Recalling.** Actaeon takes on the form of a stag. He is able to think and feel like a human. **Interpreting.** Maintaining his mental capacity allows Actaeon to be aware of the life that he has lost and to understand the danger he is in.

4. **Recalling.** Actaeon is now the hunted rather than the hunter. His companions are excited to have a magnificent stag at bay. **Interpreting.** Actaeon may have gone from love of hunting to a fear or hatred of hunting. *Responses will vary.* His companions might feel horrified that they urged the dogs to attack him.

SYNTHESIZING

Responses will vary. Possible responses are given.

5. Diana was embarrassed and angry. Students may or may not agree that the punishment fit the crime. Students should give reasons for their responses. As a hunter, Diana knew what effect being turned into an animal would have on Actaeon; she did not protect him as she sometimes did animals, and she reacted strongly to the threat to her chastity.

Answers for Understanding Literature

Responses will vary. Possible responses are given.

1. Catalog. The names describe the dogs and their attributes. They reflect the dogs' viciousness, thus presenting Actaeon's situation as very dangerous and grim.

2. Simile. Diana blushed "As the clouds/Grow red at sunset, as the daybreak reddens." These natural elements and Diana's complexion take on a growing, rosy glow.

Answers for Skills Activities

RESEARCH SKILLS

Responses will vary. Possible responses are given.

Students may suggest the following words as alternatives to *change: alter, modify, adapt, adjust, transform.* Students may suggest the following words as alternatives to *hunt: chase, gun, scent, poach, course.*

1. account, tale, yarn
2. proclaimed, swore, announced
3. fault, defect, weakness
4. beat, bash, bludgeon
5. wrath, rage, fury
6. tiny, miniature, insignificant
7. kept on, persisted in, remained
8. exceptional, fine, admirable

Cross-curricular Activities

ARTS AND HUMANITIES AND MATHEMATICS AND SCIENCES

Students can research species of spiders and the kinds of webs they create. Students can also find other tales or myths about spiders. Ask students to draw some conclusions about attitudes toward spiders based on their research.

2. **Simile.** A **simile** is a comparison using *like* or *as*. What simile is used to describe Diana's embarrassment? In what way is her physical appearance similar to these natural phenomena?

Responding in Writing

1. **Creative Writing: Transformation Story.** In many stories from the folklore tradition, a character is changed into another form. You may have read a fairy tale in which a prince is turned into a frog or a myth in which a person is transformed into a flower. In many cases, the transformation occurs because the character angers a magical being or powerful god, as in "The Story of Actaeon." Create your own story in which a character is changed into another form as a punishment. First identify a powerful being who can make a character undergo such a transformation. Then think about what might make this being angry enough to change the form of your character. Choose carefully the animal or object into which the person is transformed. You might consider an animal or object that emphasizes one of your character's negative qualities. For example, a greedy person might be turned into a bag of money, or a beautiful but vain girl who taunts the less lovely might be turned into a toad. You might consider having the transformation itself lead to a greater punishment, as in the case of Actaeon. What might your character do after being transformed? What might happen to your character in his or her new form? Write a brief story in which you explore these suggestions and questions.

2. **Critical Essay: Biographical Criticism.** At the beginning of this story, the narrator predicts what the reader will think about Actaeon's guilt and punishment. While the narrator's voice may represent the voice of a fictional character, it might also represent the author's voice. If "The Story of Actaeon" is read with the assumption that the narrator's voice is Ovid's, what do we learn about Ovid? In what way is his life reflected in this work? Write a critical essay in which you analyze the story, taking into account Ovid's experiences and his position in life at the time when he wrote the *Metamorphoses.* Begin by researching the life and works of Ovid. You may wish to consider the message the story conveys about power and punishment. Then write a thesis that presents a relationship between Ovid's life and the tone and message of "The Story of Actaeon." Support your thesis with information about Ovid's life and with passages from the text.

Research Skills

Using Thesauruses. In the last few lines of "The Story of Actaeon," the dogs "nip," "mangle," "lacerate," and "tear their prey." While all these words and phrases indicate that the dogs are biting and destroying Actaeon, their exact meanings vary. To find words with similar meanings, use a thesaurus. For advice on using one, see the Language Arts Survey 4.16, "Using Thesauruses." A thesaurus, a book that groups words with similar meanings, is a handy reference tool when you want to replace an overused word in your writing or when you are looking for a more precise way to say something. For example, in a thesaurus under the entry *walk* you might find the words *stroll, shuffle,* and *march.* Each of these words means "to walk," but in a different way. Try using a thesaurus to find five words with similar meanings to the words *change* and *hunt.* Then use this resource to find words to replace the underlined words in the sentences below.

1. Another story about transformation is the story of Arachne.
2. Arachne was a weaver who said that her skill outshone that of the goddess Minerva.
3. Neither Minerva nor Envy could find a flaw in Arachne's work.
4. Angered, Minerva began to hit Arachne with the shuttle of the loom, until Arachne hanged herself with the torn weaving.
5. Minerva's anger turned to pity; she told Arachne to live on but to hang always.
6. Arachne's hair, nose, and ears fell off; her head and body shrank until she was small.
7. Her fingers remained and continued spinning.
8. That is why the spider is such a good weaver.

ANALYTIC SCALES FOR RESPONDING IN WRITING

Assign a score from 1 to 25 for each grading criterion below. (For more detailed evaluation, see the evaluation forms for writing, revising, and proofreading, Assessment Portfolio 4.1–4.9.)

1. Transformation Story

- **Content/Unity.** The transformation story is about a single punishment involving a transformation.
- **Organization/Coherence.** The story shows a transformation and the effects of the transformation. The events of the story should be arranged in a logical order.
- **Language/Style.** The story uses vivid and precise nouns, verbs, and modifiers.
- **Conventions.** The story avoids errors in spelling, grammar, usage, mechanics, and manuscript form.

► Additional practice is provided in the Essential Skills Practice Book: Writing 1.8.

2. Critical Essay

- **Content/Unity.** The essay presents conclusions the student has drawn about the speaker and Ovid's life. The essay uses examples from the text and information about Ovid's life to support the writer's analysis.
- **Organization/Coherence.** The essay begins with an introduction that includes the thesis of the essay. The introduction is followed by supporting paragraphs with clear transitions. The essay ends with a solid conclusion.
- **Language/Style.** The essay uses vivid and precise nouns, verbs, and modifiers.
- **Conventions.** The essay avoids errors in spelling, grammar, usage, mechanics, and manuscript form.

► Additional practice is provided in the Essential Skills Practice Book: Writing 1.20.

ADDITIONAL RESOURCES

READER'S GUIDE
- Selection Worksheet 6.2

ASSESSMENT PORTFOLIO
- Selection Check Test 2.6.3
- Selection Test 2.6.4

ESSENTIAL SKILLS PRACTICE BOOKS
- Writing 1.8, 1.20
- Speaking and Listening 3.5

PREREADING EXTENSIONS

Students may enjoy discussing popular literature and films about werewolves. Encourage a discussion of this topic to help students explore their conceptions of werewolves. After they have read "The Lay of the Werewolf," have them discuss how the portrayal of werewolves in this tale is similar to or different from the portrayals they have seen in other works.

SUPPORT FOR LEP STUDENTS

PRONUNCIATIONS OF PROPER NOUNS AND ADJECTIVES

Bis • cla • va • ret (bis klá′ və rā)
Brit • ta • ny (brit′ ə nē)
Gar • wal (gâr′ wal)
Ma • rie de France (mä rē′ də fräŋs)
Nor • man (nôr′mən)

ADDITIONAL VOCABULARY

abode—stayed, dwelt
aught—anything at all
comely—handsome
devour—eat
frank—open and honest
jesting—joking, playful
semblance—appearance
vain—useless

PREREADING

"The Lay of the Werewolf"
by Marie de France, translated by Eugene Mason

FRANCE

About the Author

Marie de France (c. 1200). Marie de France was a French poet who had considerable influence on English writers, having spent most of her life at the English court. Some scholars believe she was the half-sister of Henry II, who was king of England from 1133 to 1189. Marie de France perfected the **Breton lay**, a brief medieval romance in the form of a narrative poem or song, and she is probably responsible for its introduction in England. Many of Marie de France's lays had Celtic themes and included characters and story lines from the legends of King Arthur and his Knights of the Round Table.

About the Selection

"The Lay of the Werewolf" is one of the fifteen Breton lays known to be written by Marie de France. It tells the story of a baron of Brittany, France, who is forced to live a double life—as an esteemed knight and as a fearsome werewolf who lurks in the forest. This lay deals with the theme of metamorphosis while also treating themes of betrayal, friendship, and loyalty.

Werewolves, men who are magically transformed into wolf-like creatures at night, have been popular figures of superstition throughout the ages. Folklore concerning werewolves has been found on almost every continent of the world since the days of ancient Greece and Rome. Tigers, lions, bears, or hyenas replace wolves in these tales in countries where wolves are not commonly found. According to most legends, werewolves prowl at night, usually when the moon is full, and devour humans. Usually these creatures cannot be killed with ordinary weapons, and they are believed to turn into vampires after death.

CONNECTIONS: Storytelling through Song

Lays were originally written to be sung. The singing and reciting of ballads, romances, and other narratives with musical accompaniment was very popular in Europe during the Middle Ages. Traveling British minstrels sang lays, poems, and stories about ancestors, warriors, great battles, romance, marriage, and harvest. These entertainers resemble the wandering singer-storytellers called *skalds* of the Viking period (the eighth to tenth centuries in Scandinavia); the *minnesingers* of twelfth to fourteenth century Germany; and the *troubadours* who sang of love and chivalry in northern Spain, southern France, and Italy from the eleventh through the thirteenth century.

GOALS/OBJECTIVES

Studying this lesson will enable students to

- enjoy reading a transformation story
- recognize Marie de France as a writer of lays and medieval romances
- define *Breton lay* and *romance*
- identify elements of romance in the selection
- identify narration and explain its purpose
- use a sensory detail chart
- write a description
- analyze the themes of loyalty and betrayal
- prepare and participate in a storytelling festival

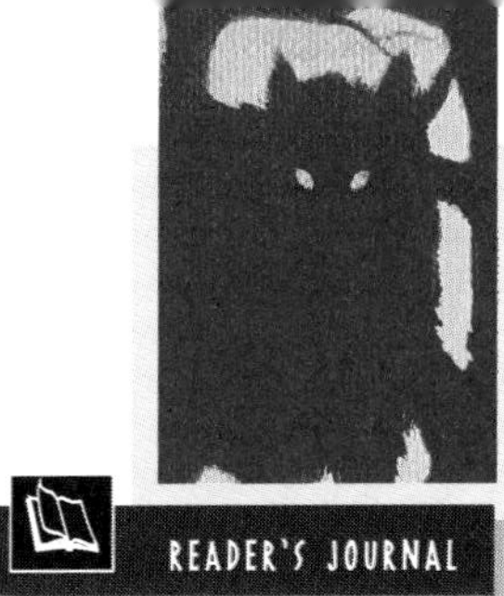

READER'S JOURNAL

What were some favorite legends that you heard through stories, poems, or songs as you grew up? What purposes did these tales serve? What elements of these legends or lessons did you find most interesting?

"The Lay of the Werewolf"

MARIE DE FRANCE, TRANSLATED BY EUGENE MASON

Amongst the tales I tell you once again, I would not forget the Lay of the Werewolf. Such beasts as he are known in every land. Bisclavaret he is named in Brittany; whilst the Norman calls him Garwal.

It is a certain thing, and within the knowledge of all, that many a christened man has suffered this change, and ran wild in woods, as a Werewolf. The Werewolf is a fearsome beast. He lurks within the thick forest, mad and horrible to see. All the evil that he may, he does. He goeth to and fro, about the solitary place, seeking man, in order to devour him. Hearken, now, to the adventure of the Werewolf, that I have to tell.

In Brittany there dwelt a baron who was marvellously esteemed of all his fellows. He was a stout knight, and a comely, and a man of office and repute. Right private was he to the mind of his lord, and dear to the counsel of his neighbors. This baron was wedded to a very worthy dame, right fair to see, and sweet of semblance. All his love was set on her, and all her love was given again to him. One only grief had this lady. For three whole days in every week her lord was absent from her side. She knew not where he went, nor on what errand. Neither did any of his house know the business which called him forth.

On a day when this lord was come again to his house, altogether joyous and content, the lady took him to task, right sweetly, in this fashion,

"Husband," said she, "and fair, sweet friend, I have a certain thing to pray of you. Right willingly would I receive this gift, but I fear to anger you in the asking. It is better for me to have an empty hand, than to gain hard words."

When the lord heard this matter, he took the lady in his arms, very tenderly, and kissed her.

"Wife," he answered, "ask what you will. What would you have, for it is yours already?"

"By my faith," said the lady, "soon shall I be whole. Husband, right long and wearisome are the days you spend away from your home. I rise from my bed in the morning, sick at heart, I know not why. So fearful am I, lest you do aught to your loss, that I may not find any comfort. Very quickly shall I die for reason of my dread. Tell me now, where you go, and on what business! How may the knowledge of one who loves so closely, bring you to harm?"

"Wife," made answer the lord, "nothing but evil can come if I tell you this secret. For the mercy of God do not require it of me.

1 *What are the different names for the werewolf? What do werewolves do?*

2 *What kind of life does the baron lead? To whom is he married? What is his wife's only grief?*

READER'S JOURNAL

Students might discuss fairy tales, fables, tall tales, or other legends. They may also wish to draw upon modern urban legends. Discussing variations of some of the stories they have heard may help students to understand how myths, legends, and other materials are altered as they spread through the oral tradition. Remind students that there is no correct version of such tales. Ask them why such stories are so popular and what they think their purposes are.

ANSWERS TO GUIDED READING QUESTIONS

1 The werewolf is called Bisclavaret in Brittany and Garwal by the Normans. Werewolves run wild in the forest, seeking people to devour.

2 The baron is a handsome knight, and he is held in high esteem by his neighbors. He is married to an attractive, "worthy" woman. His wife's only grief is that her husband is absent from her side for three whole days of every week.

SPELLING AND VOCABULARY WORDS FROM THE SELECTION

abase	malice
assail	sanguine
covet	succor
fawn	tribulation
importunity	visage

Answers to Guided Reading Questions

❶ The baron does not want to tell his wife his secret because he believes nothing but evil will come of it. His wife convinces him to tell her that he becomes Bisclavaret by pleading and giving him "tender" looks and speech.

❷ His wife begins to feel afraid of her husband. She contacts a knight who had at one time wanted her love. She tells him that she will not deny him her love any longer. She betrays her husband by telling the other knight where to steal his clothing so that her husband will be unable to return as a man.

❸ If the man's clothing is taken while he is a werewolf, he cannot turn back into a man. His wife convinces him to tell her where his lair is by telling him that she loves him and by making him feel guilty for mistrusting her.

Additional Questions and Activities

As students to contemplate the saying "Clothes make the man [or person]." What meaning does this saying have in the context of the story? What meaning might it have in contemporary life? Have students discuss the role of apparel in the way we are perceived by others.

Answers

Responses will vary.

In this story, clothes literally make the man, changing the knight from a werewolf to a human being again. People often judge the interests, character, and social status of a person by what he or she wears. Students may say that clothes are related to individuality. Remind students to be polite and focus on the question, not on individuals, and be careful that the discussion does not become too personal.

Why is the baron unwilling to reveal his secret? How does his wife convince him to disclose the secret? What is the secret?

How does the wife begin to feel about her husband? Whom does she contact? How does she betray her husband?

Why does the baron believe that he can never tell the location of his lair, where he leaves his clothing? What does his wife say to convince him to tell her?

If you but knew, you would withdraw yourself from my love, and I should be lost indeed."

When the lady heard this, she was persuaded that her baron sought to put her by with jesting words. Therefore she prayed and required him the more urgently, with tender looks and speech, till he was overborne, and told her all the story, hiding naught.

"Wife, I become Bisclavaret. I enter in the forest, and live on prey and roots, within the thickest of the wood."

After she had learned his secret, she prayed and entreated the more as to whether he ran in his raiment,[1] or went spoiled of vesture.[2]

"Wife," said he, "I go naked as a beast."

"Tell me, for hope of grace, what you do with your clothing?"

"Fair wife, that will I never. If I should lose my raiment, or even be marked as I quit my vesture, then a Werewolf I must go for all the days of my life. Never again should I become man, save in that hour my clothing were given back to me. For this reason never will I show my lair."[3]

"Husband," replied the lady to him. "I love you better than all the world. The less cause have you for doubting my faith, or hiding any tittle from me. What savor is here of friendship? How have I made forfeit of your love; for what sin do you mistrust my honor? Open now your heart, and tell what is good to be known."

So at the end, outwearied and overborne by her importunity, he could no longer refrain, but told her all.

"Wife," said he, "within this wood, a little from the path, there is a hidden way, and at the end thereof an ancient chapel, where oftentimes I have bewailed my lot. Near by is a great hollow stone, concealed by a bush, and there is the secret place where I hide my raiment, till I would return to my own home."

On hearing this marvel the lady became sanguine of visage, because of her exceeding fear. She dared no longer to lie at his side, and turned over in her mind, this way and that, how best she could get her from him. Now there was a certain knight of those parts, who, for a great while, had sought and required this lady for her love. This knight had spent long years in her service, but little enough had he got thereby, not even fair words, or a promise. To him the dame wrote a letter, and meeting, made her purpose plain.

"Fair friend," said she, "be happy. That which you have coveted so long a time, I will grant without delay. Never again will I deny your suit. My heart, and all I have to give, are yours, so take me now as love and dame."

Right sweetly the knight thanked her for her grace, and pledged her faith and fealty.[4] When she had confirmed him by an oath, then she told him all this business of her lord—why he went, and what he became, and of his ravening[5] within the wood. So she showed him of the chapel, and of the hollow stone, and of how to spoil the Werewolf of his vesture. Thus, by the kiss of his wife, was Bisclavaret betrayed. Often enough had he ravished his prey in desolate places, but from this journey he never returned. His kinsfolk and acquaintance came together to ask of his tidings, when this absence was noised abroad. Many a man, on many a day, searched the woodland, but none might find him, nor learn where Bisclavaret was gone.

The lady was wedded to the knight who had cherished her for so long a space. More than a year had passed since Bisclavaret

1. **raiment.** Clothing, or coverings
2. **spoiled of vesture.** Unclothed
3. **lair.** Bed or resting place of a wild animal
4. **fealty.** Loyalty, fidelity
5. **ravening.** Greedily searching for prey

Words for Everyday Use

im • por • tu • ni • ty (im´pôr to͞on´ i tē) *n.,* persistence in requesting or demanding

san • guine (saŋ´ gwin) *adj.,* reddish, ruddy

vis • age (viz´ ij) *n.,* face

cov • et (kuv´it) *vi.,* long for with envy

Vocabulary in Context

- Salima was determined not to give in until her demands had been met, and her importunity finally paid off.
- Just before Nelson fainted, his normally sanguine complexion turned pale.
- Among the smiling faces there was a single glum visage.
- "The grass is always greener in somebody else's yard," chides Lacey to a friend who tends to covet anything somebody else owns.

disappeared. Then it chanced that the King would hunt in that selfsame wood where the Werewolf lurked. When the hounds were unleashed they ran this way and that, and swiftly came upon his scent. At the view the huntsman winded on his horn, and the whole pack were at his heels. They followed him from morn to eve, till he was torn and bleeding, and was all adread lest they should pull him down. Now the King was very close to the quarry, and when Bisclavaret looked upon his master, he ran to him for pity and for grace. He took the stirrup within his paws, and fawned upon the prince's foot. The King was very fearful at this sight, but presently he called his courtiers to his aid.

"Lords," cried he, "hasten hither, and see this marvellous thing. Here is a beast who has the sense of man. He abases himself before his foe, and cries for mercy, although he cannot speak. Beat off the hounds, and let no man do him harm. We will hunt no more today, but return to our own place, with the wonderful quarry we have taken."

The King turned him about, and rode to his hall, Bisclavaret following at his side.

1 *What order does the king give to his men and their hounds regarding the beast? Why?*

WORDS FOR EVERYDAY USE

fawn (fôn) *vi.,* act servilely, cringe

a • base (ə bās´) *vt.,* humble, humiliate

Vocabulary in Context

- Easily impressed by titles, Basil fawned over the guest who introduced himself as Lord Maybury.
- Sybil refused to abase herself for any guest, no matter how mighty he thought he was.

Answers to Guided Reading Questions

1 The king orders the men and the hounds to stop attacking the werewolf because he recognizes that the beast has the "sense of man."

Cross-curricular Activities

Arts and Humanities

Have students study the illustration on page 447. Notice the eyes of the werewolf peering out of the woods. Ask students to write an interior monologue from the point of view of the werewolf. Students can also create their own illustrations for "The Lay of the Werewolf."

Additional Questions and Activities

Ask students to read carefully the scene on pages 446–447 in which Bisclavaret is chased by the king and his hunting dogs. Then have them read or review the scene in Ovid's "The Story of Actaeon" in which Actaeon is hunted by his own dogs. Ask them to compare and contrast these two scenes, noting mood, suspense, and outcome.

Literary Note

Suggest that students read Themes: Chivalry and Courtly Love (see page 720) for more information on the two codes that are associated with medieval romances. Students may benefit from comparing "The Lay of the Werewolf" to other medieval romances. Refer them to the selections from Chrétien de Troyes's *The Story of the Grail* (page 722), Gottfried von Strassburg's *Tristan* (page 732), and *The Song of Roland* (page 809).

Answers to Guided Reading Questions

1. The king treats Bisclavaret well, feeding him and allowing him to live in the castle. The king is proud of Bisclavaret.

2. The former wife of Bisclavaret visits the king, who is staying in a lodge in her part of the country, to speak to him and give him a present. Bisclavaret reacts with fury and attacks the lady.

3. Bisclavaret attacks the knight. The household assumes that the knight has in some way mistreated Bisclavaret.

Literary Technique

Motivation

A **motivation** is a force that moves a character to think, feel, or behave in a certain way. What motivates Bisclavaret to attack his former wife?

Answers

Bisclavaret might be motivated by anger or malice toward his wife. He may also be motivated by a desire to make her tell the truth about his condition.

1 How does the king treat Bisclavaret?

2 Why does the former wife of Bisclavaret visit the King? What is Bisclavaret's reaction when she arrives?

3 How does Bisclavaret react to the knight who had taken his wife? What does the household assume from Bisclavaret's actions?

Very near to his master the Werewolf went, like any dog, and had no care to seek again the wood. When the King had brought him safely to his own castle, he rejoiced greatly, for the beast was fair and strong, no mightier had any man seen. Much pride had the King in his marvellous beast. He held him so dear, that he bade all those who wished for his love, to cross the Wolf in naught, neither to strike him with a rod, but ever to see that he was richly fed and kennelled warm. This commandment the Court observed willingly. So all the day the Wolf sported with the lords, and at night he lay within the chamber of the King. There was not a man who did not make much of the beast, so frank was he and debonair.[6] None had reason to do him wrong, for ever was he about his master, and for his part did evil to none. Every day were these two companions together, and all perceived that the King loved him as his friend.

Hearken now to that which chanced.

The King held a high Court, and bade his great vassals and barons, and all the lords of his venery[7] to the feast. Never was there a goodlier feast, nor one set forth with sweeter show and pomp. Amongst those who were bidden, came that same knight who had the wife of Bisclavaret for dame. He came to the castle, richly gowned, with a fair company, but little he deemed whom he would find so near. Bisclavaret marked his foe the moment he stood within the hall. He ran towards him, and seized him with his fangs, in the King's very presence, and to the view of all. Doubtless he would have done him much mischief, had not the King called and chidden him, and threatened him with a rod. Once, and twice, again, the Wolf set upon the knight in the very light of day. All men marvelled at his malice, for sweet and serviceable was the beast, and to that hour had shown hatred of none. With one consent the household deemed that this deed was done with full reason, and that the Wolf had suffered at the knight's hand some bitter wrong. Right wary of his foe was the knight until the feast had ended, and all the barons had taken farewell of their lord, and departed, each to his own house. With these, amongst the very first, went that lord whom Bisclavaret so fiercely had assailed. Small was the wonder that he was glad to go.

No long while after this adventure it came to pass that the courteous King would hunt in that forest where Bisclavaret was found. With the prince came his wolf, and a fair company. Now at nightfall the King abode within a certain lodge of that country, and this was known of that dame who before was the wife of Bisclavaret. In the morning the lady clothed her in her most dainty apparel, and hastened to the lodge, since she desired to speak with the King, and to offer him a rich present. When the lady entered in the chamber, neither man nor leash might restrain the fury of the Wolf. He became as a mad dog in his hatred and malice. Breaking from his bonds he sprang at the lady's face, and bit the nose from her visage. From every side men ran to the succor of the dame. They beat off the wolf from his prey, and for a little would have cut him in pieces with their swords. But a certain wise counsellor said to the King,

"Sire, hearken now to me. This beast is always with you, and there is not one of us all who has not known him for long. He goes in and out amongst us, nor has molested any man, neither done wrong or felony to any, save only to this dame, one only time as we have seen. He has done evil

6. **debonair.** Pleasant and friendly in a cheerful way
7. **venery.** Hunting party

Words for Everyday Use

mal • ice (mal´is) *n.*, active ill will
as • sail (ə sāl´) *vi.*, attack physically, assault
suc • cor (suk´ər) *n.*, help, aid, relief

Vocabulary in Context

- Gordy often plays playful pranks, but his last joke was committed with malice and intent to injure.
- After she assailed a neighbor, Nina realized that she needed to learn to control her anger.
- The volunteers' efforts provided succor to the people who had lost their homes in the fire.

to this lady, and to that knight, who is now the husband of the dame. Sire, she was once the wife of that lord who was so close and private to your heart, but who went, and none might find where he had gone. Now, therefore, put the dame in a sure place, and question her straitly,[8] so that she may tell—if perchance she knows thereof—for what reason this Beast holds her in such mortal hate. For many a strange deed has chanced, as well we know, in this marvellous land of Brittany."

The King listened to these words, and deemed the counsel good. He laid hands upon the knight, and put the dame in surety[9] in another place. He caused them to be questioned right straitly, so that their torment was very grievous. At the end, partly because of her distress, and partly by reason of her exceeding fear, the lady's lips were loosed, and she told her tale. She showed them of the betrayal of her lord, and how his raiment was stolen from the hollow stone. Since then she knew not where he went, nor what had befallen him, for he had never come again to his own land. Only, in her heart, well she deemed and was persuaded, that Bisclavaret was he.

Straightway the King demanded the vesture of his baron, whether this were to the wish of the lady, or whether it were against her wish. When the raiment was brought him, he caused it to be spread before Bisclavaret, but the Wolf made as though he had not seen. Then that cunning and crafty counsellor took the King apart, that he might give him a fresh rede.[10]

"Sire," said he, "you do not wisely, nor well, to set this raiment before Bisclavaret, in the sight of all. In shame and much tribulation must he lay aside the beast, and again become man. Carry your wolf within your most secret chamber, and put his vestment therein. Then close the door upon him, and leave him alone for a space. So we shall see presently whether the ravening beast may indeed return to human shape."

The King carried the Wolf to his chamber, and shut the doors upon him fast. He delayed for a brief while, and taking two lords of his fellowship with him, came again to the room. Entering therein, all three, softly together, they found the knight sleeping in the King's bed, like a little child. The King ran swiftly to the bed and taking his friend in his arms, embraced and kissed him fondly, above a hundred times. When man's speech returned once more, he told him of his adventure. Then the King restored to his friend the fief[11] that was stolen from him, and gave such rich gifts, moreover, as I cannot tell. As for the wife who had betrayed Bisclavaret, he bade her avoid his country, and chased her from the realm. So she went forth, she and her second lord together, to seek a more abiding city, and were no more seen.

The adventure that you have heard is no vain fable. Verily and indeed it chanced as I have said. The Lay of the Werewolf, truly, was written that it should ever be borne in mind. ■

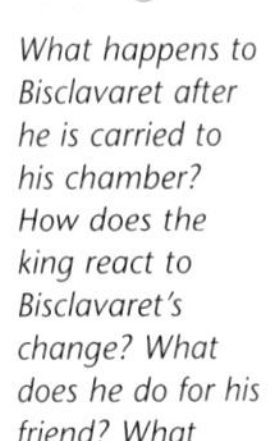

1 *What happens to Bisclavaret after he is carried to his chamber? How does the king react to Bisclavaret's change? What does he do for his friend? What happens to Bisclavaret's former wife and her second lord?*

2 *What does Bisclavaret's former wife tell the people who are questioning her? After hearing the woman's tale, what does the king demand?*

8. **straitly.** Strictly
9. **surety.** In a secure place
10. **rede.** Advice
11. **fief.** Under feudalism, heritable land held from a lord in return for service. In the story, the land is granted by the king to the knight, who can then rent it to others who work the land.

Words for Everyday Use

trib • u • la • tion (trib´ yo͞o lā´shən) *n.,* great misery or distress

Answers to Guided Reading Questions

1 Bisclavaret turns back into the baron. The king cries because he is so happy to see his friend. The king returns to the baron the land that had been stolen from him and gives him gifts. Bisclavaret's former wife and her second lord are ordered to leave the city. They are never heard from again.

2 Bisclavaret's former wife tells the people the truth about what she has done to her husband, and that she believes Bisclavaret must be her husband. The king demands that the baron's clothes be placed on Bisclavaret.

Selection Check Test with Answers

EX. What is the baron's secret?
His secret is that he is a werewolf.

1. Why does the baron believe he should keep the truth about being a werewolf from his wife?
He believes he must keep his situation secret because if it got out it would bring nothing but evil.

2. What does the knight's wife decide to do to her husband?
The knight's wife becomes frightened and decides to betray her husband by getting another knight to take his clothing.

3. What does the king decide to do when he sees Bisclavaret?
The king decides to take the werewolf in and treat him well.

4. How does Bisclavaret treat his former wife and her new knight?
Bisclavaret tries to attack them both.

5. What does the King decide to ask the former wife?
The king decides to question the wife to find out if she knows why Bisclavaret might be attacking them.

Vocabulary in Context

• Bianca is able to get through difficult times by believing that after tribulation comes great joy.

Responding to the Selection

Students might imagine that the fate of the wife has not been sealed. They can hold a mock trial to decide her case.

Answers for Reviewing the Selection

RECALLING AND INTERPRETING

1. **Recalling.** He believes he must keep his situation secret because if it got out it would bring nothing but evil. He decides the lair must also be kept a secret because if someone ever discovered it and took his clothing, he would never be able to go back to being a knight. **Interpreting.** The knight's wife tries to manipulate him with guilt about not trusting her and not understanding her love for him. The knight might be feeling cautious or he might secretly feel that he cannot trust his wife.

2. **Recalling.** The knight's wife becomes frightened and decides to betray her husband by getting another knight to take his clothing. **Interpreting.** Bisclavaret's wife seems to be selfish and cruel, and her love does not appear to be genuine. If she really loved him, she would not have betrayed him.

3. **Recalling.** The king calls off his men and dogs and takes the werewolf in and treats him well. **Interpreting.** The king is a kind person. He sees something human in the werewolf and takes great pride in having the beast around.

4. **Recalling.** Bisclavaret tries to attack both of them. The wife reveals that she thinks the werewolf is her former husband and that she had had a knight take his clothes. **Interpreting.** She might be feeling fear, guilt, and curiosity. The king's faith in Bisclavaret allowed him to blame the wife and her new knight, rather than Bisclavaret. This belief in the werewolf prompts him to question the wife and learn the truth.

(cont.)

Responding to the Selection

Why do you think the wife turned against the baron so quickly? Was she justified in her actions? Was the punishment received by the wife and her new husband appropriate? Why, or why not?

Reviewing the Selection

RECALLING		INTERPRETING
1. Why does the baron believe that he should keep the truth about being a werewolf from his wife? Why does he believe that he should keep the location of his lair a secret?	▶▶	What tactics does the baron's wife use to get her questions answered? Why might the baron be inclined to keep these secrets?
2. What does the baron's wife decide to do after learning her husband's secrets? Why does she make this decision?	▶▶	What kind of person is Bisclavaret's wife? Was the love she claimed to have for her husband genuine? Explain.
3. What does the king do when he sees Bisclavaret? How does he treat the creature?	▶▶	What kind of person is the king? Why does he treat Bisclavaret the way he does?
4. How does Bisclavaret treat his former wife and her new knight? What does his former wife reveal?	▶▶	How might Bisclavaret's former wife be feeling as she is questioned? In what way has the king's faith in Bisclavaret corrected Bisclavaret's terrible situation?

SYNTHESIZING

5. What does the narrator say at the end of the story that indicates there is a lesson to be learned from "The Lay of the Werewolf"? What might this lesson be? Support your response with details from the story.

Answers for Reviewing the Selection (cont.)

SYNTHESIZING

Responses will vary. Possible responses are given.

5. The narrator tells the reader that "The Lay of the Werewolf" should never leave people's minds. Students might say that this tale teaches lessons about honesty, trust, betrayal, and loyalty. Students can support these answers by describing the outcome of the story and the consequences of people's actions.

▶ Ask students how this lesson might apply to their own lives. In what situations have they had to make choices about loyalty and honesty or betrayal?

Understanding Literature (Questions for Discussion)

1. **Romance.** A **romance** is a type of medieval literature that tells highly imaginative stories of the adventures and loves of knights. What elements in "The Lay of the Werewolf" indicate that the story is a romance?

2. **Narrator.** A **narrator** is one who tells a story. "The Lay of the Werewolf" is a story framed by a narrative voice outside of the action of the story. What part of the selection is the actual lay? What part is the outside narration? What information does this narration give that would be absent if the lay started at the line on page 445 "In Brittany there dwelt a baron . . ." and ended with " . . . and were no more seen" on page 449. Based on what you have learned about the way narrative songs such as "The Lay of the Werewolf" were presented to audiences, why might the story be framed in this way?

Responding in Writing

1. **Creative Writing: Imaginative Description.** How do you think the baron behaved when he assumed his werewolf state in the wood? In what way do you imagine the baron's transformation from a nobleman to a werewolf, or the reverse transformation, unfolded? Write an imaginative description of the baron's transformation, his behavior in the wood, or both. Before you begin, you might create a sensory detail chart like the one below to help you capture vivid images of the werewolf's transformation and/or behavior.

THE TRANSFORMATION OF BISCLAVARET				
Sight	Hearing	Touch	Taste	Smell
Fangs begin to protrude from the baron's lips	snarling	teeth sharp as razor blades		

2. **Critical Essay: Betrayal and Loyalty.** Write a short essay in which you analyze the themes of betrayal and loyalty as treated in "The Lay of the Werewolf." First make a statement about what you think this piece says about betrayal and loyalty. Then support your statement with examples from the story. In putting together your essay, think about specific characters, their actions, the reasons for their actions, and the consequences of their actions.

ANALYTIC SCALES FOR RESPONDING IN WRITING

Assign a score from 1 to 25 for each grading criterion below. (For more detailed evaluation, see the evaluation forms for writing, revising, and proofreading, Assessment Portfolio 4.1–4.9.)

1. Imaginative Description

- **Content/Unity.** The description includes sensory details to create images of transformation.
- **Organization/Coherence.** The description of the transformation is presented in a logical order, such as chronological order.
- **Language/Style.** The description uses vivid and precise nouns, verbs, and modifiers.
- **Conventions.** The description avoids errors in spelling, grammar, usage, mechanics, and manuscript form.

► Additional practice is provided in the Essential Skills Practice Book: Writing 1.8.

2. Critical Essay

- **Content/Unity.** The essay offers analysis of the themes of betrayal and loyalty in the selection.
- **Organization/Coherence.** The essay begins with an introduction that includes a thesis. The introduction is followed by supporting paragraphs with clear transitions. The essay ends with a solid conclusion.
- **Language/Style.** The essay uses vivid and precise nouns, verbs, and modifiers.
- **Conventions.** The essay avoids errors in spelling, grammar, usage, mechanics, and manuscript form.

► Additional practice is provided in the Essential Skills Practice Book: Writing 1.20.

Answers for Understanding Literature

Responses will vary. Possible responses are given.

1. Romance. This story is an imaginative tale that focuses on the adventures of a knight. The relationships between the knight and his wife and the knight and the king are explored. The story also deals with the theme of loyalty and trust, ideals expected of knights.

2. Narrator. The two opening paragraphs and the final paragraphs are narration. The opening paragraphs provide the reader with background about werewolves and the closing paragraph reminds the reader not to forget the lesson taught by this lay. Students might understand that the lay is framed in this way because the piece was written to be recited or sung by a real narrator.

Bibliographic Note

Refer students interested in Marie de France or in medieval lives and writings to the following sources.

Ariès, Philippe, and George Duby, ed. *A History of a Private Life: Revelations of the Medieval World.* Trans. Arthur Golhammer. 1988.

Durant, Will. *The Age of Faith. 1950.* Vol. 4 of *The Story of Civilization.* 11 vols. 1935–75.

Marie de France. *The Lais of Marie de France.* Trans. Glyn S. Burgess and Keith Busby. 1986.

Moriarity, Catherine, ed. *The Voice of the Middle Ages in Personal Letters, 1100–1500.* 1989.

Power, Eileen. *Medieval People.* 1963.

Thiébeaux, Marcelle. *The Writings of Medieval Women: An Anthology.* 1994.

Tuchman, Barbara. *A Distant Mirror.* 1978.

Literary Note

For more information on troubadours, refer students to the Connections that accompanies Bieris de Romans's "Lady Maria, your worth and excellence" on page 742.

Project

Storytelling Festival. As a class, plan a storytelling festival. Attend the festival transformed into a traveling British minstrel, a Scandinavian skald, a German minnesinger, or a troubadour. Research and put together your costume; it need not be elaborate. You need only one item made of cloth, paper, or cardboard to represent something that would have been worn by a medieval storyteller. Most important is that everyone participate in character by reading or reciting from memory an original narrative song, a selection by a medieval author, or one from any era that deals with themes of metamorphosis, betrayal, or loyalty. If possible, invite people from outside your classroom to attend your festival. You might choose to serve refreshments and design programs for your storytelling festival. If possible, videotape your performances. Give this recording to the library or audiovisual center so that others may view it.

PROJECT NOTES

See the evaluation form for projects, Assessment Portfolio 4.12.

Storytelling Festival. Students may wish to present their performances to younger children. Remind students that whoever their audience is, they need to speak clearly and use elements of verbal and nonverbal communication to support their presentations. Refer them to the Language Arts Survey 3.5, "Oral Interpretation" for more information.

▶ Additional practice is provided in the Essential Skills Practice Book: Speaking and Listening 3.5.

Themes

Terrifying Tales of Transformation

Tales about humans who undergo transformation into terrifying, otherworldly creatures such as werewolves or vampires first arose in the oral tradition. The werewolf appears in the legends of many cultures, although in certain places the human is transformed into another creature such as a bear, tiger, or hyena. Some storytellers attribute to the werewolf the ability to change shape at will, but others portray the transformation as occurring only on the night of a full moon. Werewolves were believed to eat animals, other human beings, or corpses. A werewolf craze afflicted France in the sixteenth century. Not only were there many reported sightings of these man/wolves, but many people supposed to be werewolves were convicted and executed.

Tales about vampires were not only common throughout much of medieval Europe and Asia but were also accepted as fact rather than fiction. The legend was most common and most fully developed among the Slavic peoples of eastern Europe, who believed that vampires were the spirits of the "unclean" dead, or those who had died without having expiated their sins. These spirits supposedly walked the earth at night, feeding upon human blood. Those who had been bitten by vampires were doomed to die and become vampires. The belief in vampires in Slavic countries can be traced to a pre-Christian form of religion, ancestor worship. While certain dead ancestors were revered, others, particularly young women who died before marriage, were feared. Because they were believed to have missed out on the richness of life, they were thought to return to life to claim some of its joy, and, in the process, endanger the living. Reports of vampires reached a peak in Hungary in the early part of the eighteenth century.

While belief in these terrifying transformations was largely rooted out by scientists and other rationalists, vampires, werewolves, and other such horrifying creatures found a new foothold in literature, film, and the popular imagination. **The Gothic novel**, or **Gothic romance**, popular in the late eighteenth and nineteenth centuries, is a long story combining elements of horror, suspense, mystery, and magic. One of the most popular Gothic romances of all times is *Dracula*, Bram Stoker's vampire tale published in 1897. Other Gothic romances that feature terrifying transformations include Mary Shelley's *Frankenstein* (1818) and Robert Louis Stevenson's *The Strange Case of Dr. Jekyll and Mr. Hyde* (1886). Stoker's *Dracula* has inspired dozens of vampire movies in the twentieth century. Werewolf movies and film versions of *Frankenstein* and *Jekyll and Hyde* have also abounded.

Today, vampires are again enjoying popularity in contemporary literature, most notably in the work of novelist Anne Rice, and people still share horror stories about such creatures through the oral tradition, in midnight yarns and ghost stories. The enduring popularity of figures such as the vampire and the werewolf illustrates the allure of terrifying transformations for people of many cultures and eras. Not only do such stories thrill the reader, viewer, or listener, but they also help us to examine, safely, our fears about human nature. They examine such questions as why some humans "transform" themselves into dangers to society, whether human nature is so changeable or insubstantial that humans can revert to a base or animal-like state, and whether we ourselves will have an experience or undergo a transformation that will alter our identity.

Biographical Note

Bram Stoker (1847–1912) was born in Dublin. After a sickly childhood, he became a star athlete at the University of Dublin. He was a drama critic and civil servant for many years. During the later years of his life he began writing fiction. His best-known work is *Dracula*.

Mary Wollstonecraft Shelley (1797–1851) was the daughter of writer William Godwin and Mary Wollstonecraft, a women's rights activist. She eloped and married the poet Percy Bysshe Shelley. During a rainy summer, the Shelleys spent time with friends, reading ghost stories and having storytelling contests of their own. It was during this time that Mary Shelley created *Frankenstein, or the Modern Prometheus*.

Robert Louis Stevenson (1850–1894) was born in Edinburgh, Scotland. He studied law, but chose instead to be a writer. At age twenty-three he developed a respiratory illness that he battled for the rest of his life. He traveled extensively and lived in California for a time with his wife. His works include *Treasure Island, Kidnapped,* and *The Strange Case of Dr. Jekyll and Mr. Hyde.*

Additional Questions and Activities

- Many films have been made of the stories of Dracula, Frankenstein, and Dr. Jekyll and Mr. Hyde. Students can choose one or more of these movies to watch and review.
- Ask students to discuss ways in which people can transform themselves without actually changing shape.

ADDITIONAL RESOURCES

READER'S GUIDE

- Selection Worksheet 6.3

ASSESSMENT PORTFOLIO

- Selection Check Test 2.6.5
- Selection Test 2.6.6

ESSENTIAL SKILLS PRACTICE BOOKS

- Writing 1.8, 1.10, 1.20
- Language 2.49, 2.72

PREREADING EXTENSIONS

Encourage interested students to read the rest of *The Metamorphosis.* Then have them discuss in small groups the effect that Gregor Samsa's metamorphosis has upon the rest of his family. In what ways does it transform them as well? You might also encourage students to debate whether they would define Gregor's fate as tragic. Tell them to be sure to provide support for their opinions.

SUPPORT FOR LEP STUDENTS

PRONUNCIATIONS OF PROPER NOUNS AND ADJECTIVES

Czech • o • slo • va • ki • a (chek'ə slō vä´ kē ə)
Franz Kaf • ka (fränts käf´kə)
Prague (präg)
Gre • gor Sam • sa (grā´gor zäm´za)

ADDITIONAL VOCABULARY

gilt—overlaid with a substance like gold
indisposition—slight illness
melancholy—gloomy
omission—failure to do as one should
reverberating—echoing

PREREADING

from *The Metamorphosis*
by Franz Kafka, translated by Willa and Edwin Muir

About the Author

FRANZ KAFKA
1883–1924

Franz Kafka, a novelist and short-story writer who spoke and wrote in German, is known for his visionary and imaginative fiction. He was born into a middle-class Jewish family in Prague, Bohemia, an area now in the Czech Republic. Kafka eventually studied literature and then law at the University of Prague, where he received his doctorate in 1906. He worked for a short time as a legal apprentice but then took a job in an insurance company, remaining there until he was forced to retire because of illness. Although he was a conscientious worker who was continually promoted to positions of responsibility at the insurance company, the routine, stress, and long hours on the job often kept him from the activity that was most important to him—writing. After working at the office all day, Kafka wrote at night. During his lifetime, he published five short volumes of prose. Just before his death from tuberculosis, Kafka wrote a note to his friend, novelist Max Brod, asking that all his papers and manuscripts be burned. His friend chose to disregard this request and instead had many of Kafka's works published in the late 1920s. Among those published were the three novels that would help to establish Kafka's reputation as a great writer—*Amerika*, *The Trial*, and *The Castle*. His works disappeared in Germany during the Nazi period, but by then they had been translated and were being read in cities in France, Great Britain, and the United States.

About the Selection

Franz Kafka's work is characterized by themes of guilt, alienation, and the average person's search for personal salvation. ***The Metamorphosis*** is one of the most widely read works of the twentieth century. In this classic **allegory**, or work in which each element symbolizes something else, Kafka explores the burden of the working class—those who must devote themselves to long hours of work just to support themselves and their families. Through his character Gregor Samsa, Kafka shows how destructive a life of work in a dehumanized, industrial society can be. The reader sees how Gregor Samsa has, quite literally, sacrificed his humanness for a life of thankless work. In this excerpt, Gregor awakens in a new body that simply will not allow him to make his train and fulfill his "all-important" obligations for another day.

CONNECTIONS: Austro-Hungarian Empire

When Kafka was born in 1883, Prague was the capital of a province of the Austro-Hungarian Empire. This empire fell apart in 1918, and the country of Czechoslovakia emerged from its ruins. As a German-speaking Jew, Kafka suddenly found himself displaced—part of a newly unpopular minority group living in the Czech-speaking land. This situation contributed to the feelings of anxiety and alienation that filled his life and inspired much of his work.

GOALS/OBJECTIVES

Studying this lesson will enable students to

- appreciate a classic work of Modernist fiction
- define *allegory* and identify what the elements in an allegory symbolize
- define *characterization* and explain the techniques writers use to create a character
- write an imaginative description about undergoing a transformation
- write a critical essay on the causes of Gregor Samsa's transformation
- revise clichés and euphemisms in writing

Do you think sometimes that you work too hard or too little? Do you think your family members work too hard? How important should work be in one's life? How important should fun and relaxation be? What are some ways in which one can try to balance each?

READER'S JOURNAL

FROM

The Metamorphosis

FRANZ KAFKA, TRANSLATED BY WILLA AND EDWIN MUIR

As Gregor Samsa awoke one morning from uneasy dreams he found himself transformed in his bed into a gigantic insect. He was lying on his hard, as it were armor-plated, back and when he lifted his head a little he could see his domelike brown belly divided into stiff arched segments on top of which the bed quilt could hardly keep in position and was about to slide off completely. His numerous legs, which were pitifully thin compared to the rest of his bulk, waved helplessly before his eyes.

What has happened to me? he thought. It was no dream. His room, a regular human bedroom, only rather too small, lay quiet between the four familiar walls. Above the table on which a collection of cloth samples was unpacked and spread out—Samsa was a commercial traveler—hung the picture which he had recently cut out of an illustrated magazine and put into a pretty gilt frame. It showed a lady, with a fur cap on and a fur stole,[1] sitting upright and holding out to the spectator a huge fur muff into which the whole of her forearm had vanished!

Gregor's eyes turned next to the window, and the overcast sky—one could hear raindrops beating on the window gutter—made him quite melancholy. What about sleeping a little longer and forgetting all this nonsense, he thought, but it could not be done, for he was accustomed to sleep on his right side and in his present condition he could not turn himself over. However violently he forced himself toward his right side he always rolled onto his back again. He tried it at least a hundred times, shutting his eyes to keep from seeing his struggling legs, and only desisted when he began to feel in his side a faint dull ache he had never experienced before.

Oh God, he thought, what an exhausting job I've picked on! Traveling about day in, day out. It's much more irritating work than doing the actual business in the office, and

1. **stole.** Woman's long scarf of cloth or fur worn around the shoulders

❶ *Why is this morning unusual for Gregor Samsa?*

❷ *What does Gregor do for a living?*

WORDS FOR EVERYDAY USE

de • sist (di sist´) *v.,* stop

VOCABULARY IN CONTEXT

- So many fallen leaves covered the lawn that Ryan longed to desist in his hopeless efforts to rake them all.

READER'S JOURNAL

As an alternative activity, students might write about how they feel about insects, particularly cockroaches. Ask them why they believe so many people loathe and fear insects.

ANSWERS TO GUIDED READING QUESTIONS

❶ Gregor Samsa awakens as an insect.

❷ He is a traveling salesperson.

SPELLING AND VOCABULARY WORDS FROM THE SELECTION

amiably	injunction
arbitrary	laden
brusque	malingerer
composure	obstinate
desist	plaintive
discernable	precursor
divine	presentiment
entreaty	prudent
equilibrium	repose
heedless	reproach
imminent	superfluous
impede	supposition
incapacitate	unassailable

BIOGRAPHICAL NOTE

You might point out to students that there are some similarities between Franz Kafka and his hero Gregor Samsa. Kafka's father pressured him to enter the business world even though he was interested in literature. Although he eventually became an efficient senior executive at an insurance company, Kafka resented his job. Kafka's attitude toward the working world is made clear in his description of Gregor's work. Like Gregor, Kafka also lived with his parents most of his life.

Answers to Guided Reading Questions

❶ Gregor dislikes his long hours and constant travel.

❷ Gregor must keep his job because he has to support his family and keep them out of debt.

❸ Gregor panics when he realizes that he missed his train. He fears he will have a confrontation with his chief, or supervisor.

Literary Technique

INTERNAL MONOLOGUE AND POINT OF VIEW

Inform students that an **internal monologue** presents the private sensations, thoughts, and emotions of a character. The reader is allowed to step inside the character's mind and overhear his or her thoughts. Which characters' internal states will be revealed in a work of fiction depends on the point of view of the work. **Point of view** is the vantage point from which a story is told. (Refer students to the Handbook of Literary Terms for more information on point of view.) Ask students the following questions: From what point of view is this story told? Identify the internal monologue that appears on this page. Whose private thoughts are presented? What interrupts this character's flow of thoughts? What does the character's flow of thoughts reveal about this character?

ANSWERS

This story is told from the third-person point of view. The narrator is limited to revealing the internal thoughts of Gregor Samsa. The internal monologue begins after Gregor tried to scratch an itch and ends when he hears a "cautious tap" on his door. Gregor is too preoccupied with work to consider fully his transformation into an insect.

❶ *What does Gregor dislike about his job?*

❷ *Why must Gregor keep his job, even though he despises it?*

❸ *What panics Gregor most about the situation? What does he fear his boss will do?*

on top of that there's the trouble of constant traveling, of worrying about train connections, the bed and irregular meals, casual acquaintances that are always new and never become intimate friends. The devil take it all! He felt a slight itching up on his belly; slowly pushed himself on his back nearer to the top of the bed so that he could lift his head more easily; identified the itching place which was surrounded by many small white spots the nature of which he could not understand and made to touch it with a leg, but drew the leg back immediately, for the contact made a cold shiver run through him.

He slid down again into his former position. This getting up early, he thought, makes one quite stupid. A man needs his sleep. Other commercials[2] live like harem women. For instance, when I come back to the hotel of a morning to write up the orders I've got, these others are only sitting down to the breakfast. Let me just try that with my chief; I'd be sacked[3] on the spot. Anyhow, that might be quite a good thing for me, who can tell? If I didn't have to hold my hand because of my parents I'd have given notice long ago, I'd have gone to the chief and told him exactly what I think of him. That would knock him endways from his desk! It's a queer way of doing, too, this sitting on high at a desk and talking down to employees, especially when they have to come quite near because the chief is hard of hearing. Well, there's still hope; once I've saved enough money to pay back my parents' debts to him—that should take another five or six years—I'll do it without fail. I'll cut myself completely loose then. For the moment, though, I'd better get up, since my train goes at five.

He looked at the alarm clock ticking on the chest. Heavenly Father! he thought. It was half-past six o'clock and the hands were quickly moving on, it was even past the half-hour, it was getting on toward a quarter to seven. Had the alarm clock not gone off? From the bed one could see that it had been properly set for four o'clock; of course it must have gone off. Yes, but was it possible to sleep quietly through that ear-splitting noise? Well, he had not slept quietly, yet apparently all the more soundly for that. But what was he to do now? The next train went at seven o'clock; to catch that he would need to hurry like mad and his samples weren't even packed up, and he himself wasn't feeling particularly fresh and active. And even if he did catch the train he wouldn't avoid a row[4] with the chief, since the firm's porter would have been waiting for the five o'clock train and would have long since reported his failure to turn up. The porter was a creature of the chief's, spineless and stupid. Well, supposing he were to say he was sick? But that would be most unpleasant and would look suspicious, since during his five years' employment he had not been ill once. The chief himself would he sure to come with the sick-insurance doctor, would reproach his parents with their son's laziness, and would cut all excuses short by referring to the insurance doctor, who of course regarded all mankind as perfectly healthy malingerers. And would he be so far wrong on this occasion? Gregor really felt quite well, apart from a drowsiness that was utterly superfluous after such a long sleep, and he was even unusually hungry.

As all this was running through his mind at top speed without his being able to decide to leave his bed—the alarm clock had just struck

2. **commercials.** Salespeople
3. **sacked.** Dismissed from employment; fired
4. **row.** An unpleasant confrontation; argument

Words for Everyday Use

re • proach (ri prōch´) *v.,* severely criticize; blame

ma • lin • ger • er (mə ling´gər ər) *n.,* one who pretends to be ill to evade work

su • per • flu • ous (so͞o ´pûr´ flo͞o əs) *adj.,* unnecessary

Vocabulary in Context

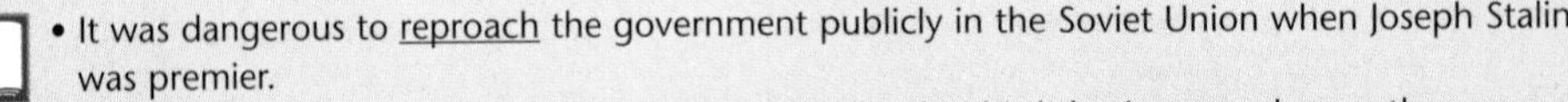

- It was dangerous to reproach the government publicly in the Soviet Union when Joseph Stalin was premier.
- When Nikita pretended to be too sick for school for the third day in a row, her mother accused her of being a malingerer.
- Many ascetics, or people who live lives of strict self-denial and contemplation, reject what they see as the superfluous complications of the modern world.

a quarter to seven—there came a cautious tap at the door behind the head of his bed. "Gregor," said a voice—it was his mother's—"it's a quarter to seven. Hadn't you a train to catch?" That gentle voice! Gregor had a shock as he heard his own voice answering hers, unmistakably his own voice, it was true, but with a persistent horrible twittering squeak behind it like an undertone, which left the words in their clear shape only for the first moment and then rose up reverberating around them to destroy their sense, so that one could not be sure one had heard them rightly. Gregor wanted to answer at length and explain everything, but in the circumstances he confined himself to saying: "Yes, yes, thank you, Mother, I'm getting up now." The wooden door between them must have kept the change in his voice from being noticeable outside, for his mother contented herself with this statement and shuffled away. Yet this brief exchange of words had made the other members of the family aware that Gregor was still in the house, as they had not expected, and at one of the side doors his father was already knocking, gently, yet with his fist. "Gregor, Gregor," he called, "What's the matter with you?" And after a little while he called again in a deeper voice: "Gregor! Gregor!" At the other side door his sister was saying in a low, plaintive tone: "Gregor? Aren't you well? Are you needing anything?" He answered them both at once: "I'm just ready," and did his best to make his voice sound as normal as possible by enunciating the words very clearly and leaving long pauses between them. So his father went back to his breakfast, but his sister whispered: "Gregor, open the door, do." However, he was not thinking of opening the door, and felt thankful for the prudent habit he had acquired in traveling of locking all doors during the night, even at home.

His immediate intention was to get up quietly without being disturbed, to put on his clothes and above all eat his breakfast, and only then consider what else was to be done, since in bed, he was well aware, his meditations would come to no sensible conclusion. He remembered that often enough

1 *Why does Gregor feel he must get out of bed?*

Words for Everyday Use

plain • tive (plān´tiv) *adj.*, mournful; sad

pru • dent (pro͞od´ nt) *adj.*, cautiously wise

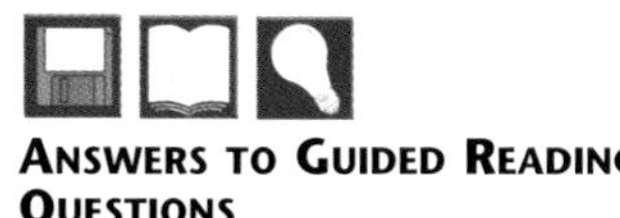

Answers to Guided Reading Questions

1 Gregor feels he must get up in order to know what to do next.

Cross-curricular Activities

SOCIAL STUDIES AND APPLIED ARTS

Gregor Samsa is extremely dissatisfied with his job and Kafka seems to imply that this situation applies to many workers. Give students the following project to see to what extent Gregor's feelings are similar to those of workers in contemporary society: Working as a class, create a job-satisfaction survey. Include on the survey questions such as the following: What is your profession? How many hours a week do you work? What do you like best and least about your job? Also, ask those you survey to rate their satisfaction with their professions on a scale of one to ten. Students should then work in small groups to distribute their surveys to as wide a number of workers as possible. When results come in, analyze them. On the whole, how satisfied are people with their jobs? How many hours do most people work? What professions demand the most hours of work? Do people in certain fields seem to be more satisfied with their jobs than others? Do the findings support or refute the attitude toward work and workers that Kafka portrays in this selection? You may want to finish the discussion on the survey results by asking students how these results affect them. What are their own career goals and attitudes toward work?

Vocabulary in Context

- The first plaintive notes the pianist played brought tears to the audience's eyes.
- People came from distant cities to visit the philosopher because of his prudent advice.

Answers to Guided Reading Questions

❶ Gregor expects that once he gets up, the morning's "delusions" will "gradually fall away."

❷ Gregor has trouble controlling his insect legs, he cannot move the lower part of his body, and he cannot get off his back.

Literary Technique

MAGICAL REALISM

Inform students that **magical realism** is a kind of fiction that is for the most part realistic but that contains elements of fantasy. Kafka is known for combining the prosaic, or everyday, world with fantastic or nightmarish events in his writing. Although Kafka's work was not classified as magical realism, it had a profound impact on such magical realist writers as Gabriel García Márquez. Encourage students to identify and discuss elements of prosaic realism and nightmarish fantasy in this excerpt from *The Metamorphosis.* What is the effect Kafka achieves by combining the everyday world with the fantastic?

ANSWERS

Responses will vary. Possible responses are given.

Students might note that the transformation itself is an example of nightmarish fantasy. The other details in the story—the setting, Gregor's working life, the description of how he manages to get out of bed, his family's reaction, and the chief's reaction are all prosaic and realistic. Perhaps most prosaic of all is Gregor's reaction or lack of reaction to his condition. He tries to treat this fantastic occurrence as if it were an everyday event. Students might say that the combination of realism and fantasy makes Gregor's situation both more humorous and more pathetic.

 ❶

What does Gregor expect will happen when he gets out of bed?

 ❷

Why is getting out of bed a difficult maneuver for him?

in bed he had felt small aches and pains, probably caused by awkward postures, which had proved purely imaginary once he got up, and he looked forward eagerly to seeing this morning's delusions gradually fall away. That the change in his voice was nothing but the precursor of a severe chill, a standing ailment of commercial travelers, he had not the least possible doubt.

To get rid of the quilt was quite easy; he had only to inflate himself a little and it fell off by itself. But the next move was difficult, especially because he was so uncommonly broad. He would have needed arms and hands to hoist himself up; instead he had only the numerous little legs which never stopped waving in all directions and which he could not control in the least. When he tried to bend one of them it was the first to stretch itself straight; and did he succeed at last in making it do what he wanted, all the other legs meanwhile waved the more wildly in a high degree of unpleasant agitation. "But what's the use of lying idle in bed," said Gregor to himself.

He thought that he might get out of bed with the lower part of his body first, but this lower part, which he had not yet seen and of which he could form no clear conception, proved too difficult to move; it shifted so slowly; and when finally, almost wild with annoyance, he gathered his forces together and thrust out recklessly, he had miscalculated the direction and bumped heavily against the lower end of the bed, and the stinging pain he felt informed him that precisely this lower part of his body was at the moment probably the most sensitive.

So he tried to get the top part of himself out first, and cautiously moved his head toward the edge of the bed. That proved easy enough, and despite its breadth and mass the bulk of his body at last slowly followed the movement of his head. Still, when he finally got his head free over the edge of the bed he felt too scared to go on advancing, for after all if he let himself fall in this way it would take a miracle to keep his head from being injured. And at all costs he must not lose consciousness now, precisely now; he would rather stay in bed.

But when after a repetition of the same efforts he lay in his former position again, sighing, and watched his little legs struggling against each other more wildly than ever, if that were possible, and saw no way of bringing any order into this arbitrary confusion, he told himself again that it was impossible to stay in bed and that the most sensible course was to risk everything for the smallest hope of getting away from it. At the same time he did not forget to remind himself occasionally that cool reflection, the coolest possible, was much better than desperate resolves. In such moments he focused his eyes as sharply as possible on the window, but, unfortunately, the prospect of the morning fog, which muffled even the other side of the narrow street, brought him little encouragement and comfort. "Seven o'clock already," he said to himself when the alarm clock chimed again, "seven o'clock already and still such a thick fog." And for a little while he lay quiet, breathing lightly, as if perhaps expecting such complete repose to restore all things to real and normal condition.

But then he said to himself: "Before it strikes a quarter past seven I must be quite out of this bed, without fail. Anyhow, by that time someone will have come from the office to ask for me, since it opens before seven." And he set himself to rocking his whole body at once in a regular rhythm, with the idea of swinging it out of the bed. If he tipped himself out in

Words for Everyday Use

pre • cur • sor (prē kûr´sər) *n.,* that which comes before; harbinger

ar • bi • trar • y (är´bə trer´ē) *adj.,* not fixed by rules, but left to one's judgment or choice

re • pose (ri pōz´) *n.,* rest or sleep

Vocabulary in Context

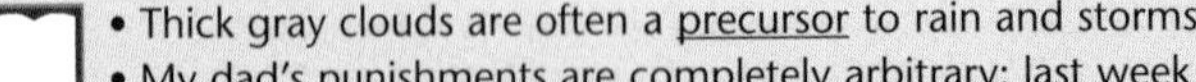

- Thick gray clouds are often a precursor to rain and storms.
- My dad's punishments are completely arbitrary; last week he grounded me for coming home one minute after curfew, but yesterday he just smiled and shook his head.
- Yolanda likes nothing better than a refreshing repose in her hammock between the two old oak trees.

that way he could keep his head from injury by lifting it at an acute angle when he fell. His back seemed to be hard and was not likely to suffer from a fall on the carpet. His biggest worry was the loud crash he would not be able to help making, which would probably cause anxiety, if not terror, behind all the doors. Still, he must take the risk.

When he was already half out of the bed—the new method was more a game than an effort, for he needed only to hitch himself across by rocking to and fro—it struck him how simple it would be if he could get help. Two strong people—he thought of his father and the servant girl—would be amply sufficient; they would only have to thrust their arms under his convex back, lever him out of the bed, bend down with their burden, and then be patient enough to let him turn himself right over onto the floor, where it was to be hoped his legs would then find their proper function. Well, ignoring the fact that the doors were all locked, ought he really to call for help? In spite of his misery he could not suppress a smile at the very idea of it.

He had got so far that he could barely keep his <u>equilibrium</u> when he rocked himself strongly, and he would have to nerve himself very soon for the final decision since in five minutes' time it would be quarter past seven—when the front doorbell rang. "That's someone from the office," he said to himself, and grew almost rigid, while his little legs only jigged about all the faster. For a moment everything stayed quiet. "They're not going to open the door," said Gregor to himself, catching at some kind of irrational hope. But then of course the servant girl went as usual to the door with her heavy tread and opened it. Gregor needed only to hear the first good morning of the visitor to know immediately who it was—the chief clerk himself. What a fate, to be condemned to work for a firm where the smallest omission at once gave rise to the gravest suspicion! Were all employees in a body nothing but scoundrels, was there not among them one single loyal devoted man who, had he wasted only an hour or so of the firm's time in a morning, was so tormented by conscience as to be driven out of his mind and actually incapable of leaving his bed? Wouldn't it really have been sufficient to send an apprentice to inquire—if any inquiry were necessary at all—did the chief clerk himself have to come and thus indicate to the entire family, an innocent family, that this suspicious circumstance could be investigated by no one less versed in affairs than himself? And more through the agitation caused by these reflections than through any act of will Gregor swung himself out of bed with all his strength. There was a loud thump, but it was not really a crash. His fall was broken to some extent by the carpet, his back, too, was less stiff than he thought, and so there was merely a dull thud, not so very startling. Only he had not lifted his head carefully enough and had hit it; he turned it and rubbed it on the carpet in pain and irritation.

"That was something falling down in there," said the chief clerk in the next room to the left. Gregor tried to suppose to himself that something like what had happened to him today might someday happen to the chief clerk; one really could not deny that it was possible. But as if in <u>brusque</u> reply to this <u>supposition</u> the chief clerk took a couple of firm steps in the next-door room and his patent leather boots cracked. From the right-hand room his sister was whispering to inform him of the situation: "Gregor, the chief clerk's here." "I know," muttered

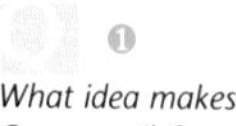

❶ *What idea makes Gregor smile?*

❷ *Who is the visitor? What does Gregor lament about the firm? Why does he feel their response to his absence is unreasonable? What does he believe is happening to him?*

WORDS FOR EVERYDAY USE

e • qui • lib • ri • um (ē´kwə lib´rē əm) *n.*, proper steadiness, balance of the body

brusque (brusk) *adj.*, abrupt

sup • pos • i • tion (sup´ə zish´ən) *n.*, assumption

ANSWERS TO GUIDED READING QUESTIONS

❶ The idea of his father and the servant girl helping him to move makes him smile.

❷ The chief clerk visits. Gregor laments that his firm does not appreciate his hard work. He has never missed a day of work, so he feels their response is unreasonable. Gregor thinks that he is so tormented about being late that he is going mad and is unable to leave his bed.

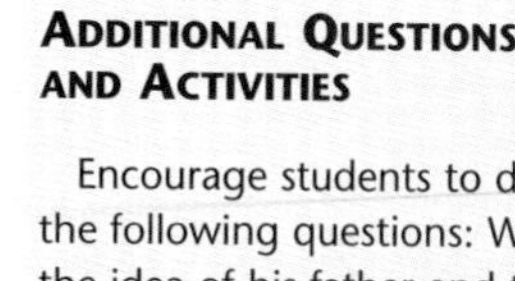

ADDITIONAL QUESTIONS AND ACTIVITIES

Encourage students to discuss the following questions: Why does the idea of his father and the servant girl helping him out of bed make Gregor smile? What attitude is he taking toward his condition? What does this reveal about his mental state? Gregor wonders if it is possible that he is "so tormented by conscience as to be driven out of his mind and actually incapable of leaving his bed." What does Gregor realize about himself? Do you think that this is a possible explanation for the events in this story? Why, or why not?

ANSWERS

Responses will vary.

Gregor smiles because he feels that his helplessness is ridiculous. He seems to find his situation uncomfortable, preposterous, and almost humorous in an ironic way. He seems focused only on his overriding need to get to work and is not in touch with the "reality" of his situation. Gregor realizes that he is so overworked that it is possible that he has gone mad. *Responses will vary but should be supported with reasons and evidence from the selection.*

VOCABULARY IN CONTEXT

- It took Joshua several days to gain his <u>equilibrium</u> on the ship during high seas.
- Mrs. Pruitt's <u>brusque</u> manner of speaking made Chelsea feel unwelcome as a guest.
- Clive strove to prove his <u>supposition</u> about the molecule through meticulous research.

Answers to Guided Reading Questions

❶ His sister might be sobbing because she believes that Gregor surely will be fired and the family will be unable to pay their debt.

❷ The chief clerk wants to know why Gregor did not make his train. Gregor's mother tells the chief that Gregor must be sick, or he would never miss work.

❸ The chief clerk criticizes Gregor for not being dependable.

Quotables

"You are free and that is why you are lost."

"Every revolution evaporates and leaves behind only the slime of a new bureaucracy."

"In the fight between you and the world, back the world."

"The meaning of life is that it stops."

"What is written is merely the dregs of experience."

"There will be no proof that I ever was a writer."

—Franz Kafka

Additional Questions and Activities

Read students the above quotations or write them on the board. Then ask students, based on these quotations and on students' reading of *The Metamorphosis,* to discuss Kafka's worldview. What type of person do they imagine Kafka to have been? In what way is their view of the world similar to or different from Kafka's?

Gregor to himself; but he didn't dare to make his voice loud enough for his sister to hear it.

"Gregor," said his father now from the left-hand room, "the chief clerk has come and wants to know why you didn't catch the early train. We don't know what to say to him. Besides, he wants to talk to you in person. So open the door, please. He will be good enough to excuse the untidiness of your room." "Good morning, Mr. Samsa," the chief clerk was calling amiably meanwhile. "He's not well," said his mother to the visitor, while his father was still speaking through the door, "he's not well, sir, believe me. What else would make him miss a train! The boy thinks about nothing but his work. It makes me almost cross the way he never goes out in the evenings; he's been here the last eight days and has stayed at home every single evening. He just sits there quietly at the table reading a newspaper or looking through railway timetables. The only amusement he gets is doing fretwork.[5] For instance, he spent two or three evenings cutting out a little picture frame; you would be surprised to see how pretty it is; it's hanging in his room; you'll see it in a minute when Gregor opens the door. I must say I'm glad you've come, sir; we should never have got him to unlock the door by ourselves; he's so obstinate; and I'm sure he's unwell, though he wouldn't have it to be so this morning." "I'm just coming," said Gregor slowly and carefully, not moving an inch for fear of losing one word of the conversation. "I can't think of any other explanation, madame," said the chief clerk, "I hope it's nothing serious. Although on the other hand I must say that we men of business—fortunately or unfortunately—very often simply have to ignore any slight indisposition, since business must be attended to." "Well, can the chief clerk come in now?" asked Gregor's father impatiently, again knocking on the door. "No," said Gregor. In the left-hand room a painful silence followed this refusal, in the right-hand room his sister began to sob.

❶ *According to Gregor, why might his sister be sobbing?*

❷ *Why does the chief clerk want to speak with Gregor? What does Gregor's mother tell the chief in defense of Gregor?*

❸ *For what does the chief clerk criticize Gregor?*

Why didn't his sister join the others? She was probably newly out of bed and hadn't even begun to put on her clothes yet. Well, why was she crying? Because he wouldn't get up and let the chief clerk in, because he was in danger of losing his job, and because the chief would begin dunning[6] his parents again for the old debts? Surely these were things one didn't need to worry about for the present. Gregor was still at home and not in the least thinking of deserting the family. At the moment, true, he was lying on the carpet and no one who knew the condition he was in could seriously expect him to admit the chief clerk. But for such a small discourtesy, which could plausibly be explained away somehow later on, Gregor could hardly be dismissed on the spot. And it seemed to Gregor that it would be much more sensible to leave him in peace for the present than to trouble him with tears and entreaties. Still, of course, their uncertainty bewildered them all and excused their behavior.

"Mr. Samsa," the chief clerk called now in a louder voice, "what's the matter with you? Here you are, barricading yourself in your room, giving only 'yes' and 'no' for answers, causing your parents a lot of unnecessary trouble and neglecting—I mention this only in passing—neglecting your business duties in an incredible fashion. I am speaking here in the name of your parents and of your chief, and I beg you quite seriously to give me an immediate and precise explanation. You amaze me, you amaze me. I thought you were a quiet, dependable person, and now all

5. **fretwork.** Decorative carving
6. **dunning.** Demanding payment for debt

Words for Everyday Use

a • mi • a • bly (ā´mē ə blē) *adv.,* in a friendly manner; agreeably

ob • sti • nate (ob´stə nit) *adj.,* stubborn

en • treat • y (en trē´tē) *n.,* earnest plea

Vocabulary in Context

- Gretchen was well liked because she always spoke so amiably to everyone.
- Zachary was known for being obstinate; he never changed his mind on an issue, no matter how much evidence there was to the contrary.
- The ruthless knight paid no heed to his foe's entreaty for mercy.

at once you seem bent on making a disgraceful exhibition of yourself. The chief did hint to me early this morning a possible explanation for your disappearance—with reference to the cash payments that were entrusted to you recently—but I almost pledged my solemn word of honor that this could not be so. But now that I see how incredibly obstinate you are, I no longer have the slightest desire to take your part at all. And your position in the firm is not so unassailable. I came with the intention of telling you all this in private, but since you are wasting my time so needlessly I don't see why your parents shouldn't hear it too. For some time past your work has been most unsatisfactory; this is not the season of the year for a business boom, of course, we admit that, but a season of the year for doing no business at all, that does not exist, Mr. Samsa, must not exist."

"But, sir," cried Gregor, beside himself and in his agitation forgetting everything else, "I'm just going to open the door this very minute. A slight illness, an attack of giddiness, has kept me from getting up. I'm still lying in bed. But I feel all right again. I'm getting out of bed now. Just give me a moment or two longer! I'm not quite so well as I thought. But I'm all right, really. How a thing like that can suddenly strike one down! Only last night I was quite well, my parents can tell you, or rather I did have a slight presentiment. I must have showed some sign of it. Why didn't I report it at the office! But one always thinks that an indisposition can be got over without staying in the house. Oh sir, do spare my parents! All that you're reproaching me with now has no foundation; no one has ever said a word to me about it. Perhaps you haven't looked at the last orders I sent in. Anyhow, I can still catch the eight o'clock train, I'm much the better for my few hours' rest. Don't let me detain you here, sir; I'll be attending to business very soon, and do be good enough to tell the chief so and to make my excuses to him!"

And while all this was tumbling out pell-mell[7] and Gregor hardly knew what he was saying, he had reached the chest quite easily, perhaps because of the practice he had had in bed, and was now trying to lever himself upright by means of it. He meant actually to open the door, actually to show himself and speak to the chief clerk; he was eager to find out what the others, after all their insistence, would say at the sight of him. If they were horrified then the responsibility was no longer his and he could stay quiet. But if they took it calmly, then he had no reason either to be upset, and could really get to the station for the eight o'clock train if he hurried. At first he slipped down a few times from the polished surface of the chest, but at length with a last heave he stood upright; he paid no more attention to the pains in the lower part of his body, however they smarted. Then he let himself fall against the back of a nearby chair, and clung with his little legs to the edges of it. That brought him into control of himself again and he stopped speaking, for now he could listen to what the chief clerk was saying.

"Did you understand a word of it?" the chief clerk was asking; "surely he can't be trying to make fools of us?" "Oh dear," cried his mother, in tears, "perhaps he's terribly ill and we're tormenting him. Grete! Grete!" she called out then. "Yes Mother?" called his sister from the other side. They were calling to each other across Gregor's room. "You must go this minute for the doctor. Gregor is ill. Go for the doctor, quick. Did you hear

7. **pell-mell.** In a jumbled, confused manner

① What did the chief hint might be a possible explanation for Gregor's disappearance? What, according to the clerk, does not exist in the business world?

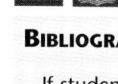

② What does the clerk notice about Gregor's voice? What begins to concern his mother?

WORDS FOR EVERYDAY USE	
	un • as • sail • a • ble (uńə sāl´ə bəl) *adj.*, that which cannot be attacked
	pre • sen • ti • ment (prē zent´ə mənt) *n.*, a sense that something unfortunate is about to happen

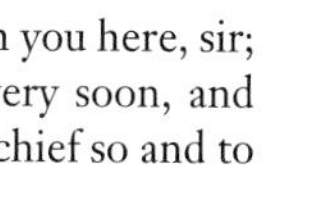
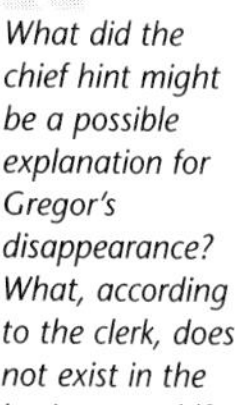
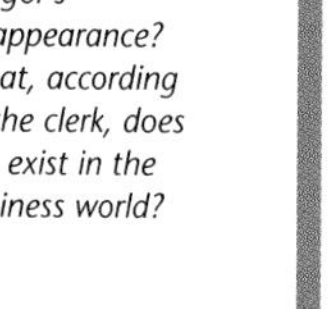

ANSWERS TO GUIDED READING QUESTIONS

① The chief hints that perhaps Gregor has stolen from the company. According to the chief, "a season of the year for not doing business" does not exist in the business world.

② The clerk notices that Gregor's voice sounds strange. His mother becomes concerned that he is truly ill.

BIBLIOGRAPHIC NOTE

If students enjoy this excerpt from *The Metamorphosis*, you might encourage them to read Kafka's short story "The Hunger Artist." The story appears in the collection below.

Kafka, Franz. "The Hunger Artist" from *The Metamorphosis, The Penal Colony, and Other Stories.*

VOCABULARY IN CONTEXT

- Because the castle was built on top of a cliff and was surrounded by sturdy walls, it was virtually unassailable.
- The fortune-teller had a presentiment of doom so he tried to warn Cæsar to take caution.

INTEGRATED SKILLS ACTIVITIES

LANGUAGE LAB

Point out to students that Kafka uses dashes on page 462 to mark abrupt breaks in thought. Have them review the Language Arts Survey 2.49, "Dashes, Hyphens, Parentheses, and Brackets," and then rewrite the sentences below correctly.

1. I have a complete collection of Kafka's works in my bookshelf it is a three volume set with blue covers.
2. In Kafka's well known novel *The Trial,* a man named Joseph K. is arrested.
3. He is convicted now here is the nightmarish part of the story! but never can discover why.
4. Overcome with confusion, Joseph consults a priest, who mean spiritedly tells him that he will never receive the justice he seeks his protestations of innocence are a sign of his guilt.

ANSWERS

1. I have a complete collection of Kafka's works in my bookshelf (it is a three-volume set with blue covers).
2. In Kafka's well-known novel *The Trial,* a man named Joseph K. is arrested.
3. He is convicted—now here is the nightmarish part of the story!—but never can discover why.
4. Overcome with confusion, Joseph consults a priest, who mean-spiritedly tells him that he will never receive the justice he seeks—his protestations of innocence are a sign of his guilt.

▶ Additional practice is provided in the Essential Skills Practice Book: Language 2.49.

how he was speaking?" "That was no human voice," said the chief clerk in a voice noticeably low beside the shrillness of the mother's. "Anna! Anna!" his father was calling through the hall to the kitchen, clapping his hands, "get a locksmith at once!" And the two girls were already running through the hall with a swish of skirts—how could his sister have got dressed so quickly?—and were tearing the front door open. There was no sound of its closing again; they had evidently left it open, as one does in houses where some great misfortune has happened.

But Gregor was now much calmer. The words he uttered were no longer understandable, apparently, although they seemed clear enough to him, even clearer than before, perhaps because his ear had grown accustomed to the sound of them. Yet at any rate people now believed that something was wrong with him, and were ready to help him. The positive certainty with which these first measures had been taken comforted him. He felt himself drawn once more into the human circle and hoped for great and remarkable results from both the doctor and the locksmith, without really distinguishing precisely between them. To make his voice as clear as possible for the decisive conversation that was now <u>imminent</u> he coughed a little, as quietly as he could, of course, since this noise too might not sound like a human cough for all he was able to judge. In the next room meanwhile there was complete silence. Perhaps his parents were sitting at the table with the chief clerk, whispering, perhaps they were all leaning against the door and listening.

Slowly Gregor pushed the chair toward the door, then let go of it, caught hold of the door for support—the soles at the end of his little legs were somewhat sticky—and rested against it for a moment after his efforts. Then he set himself to turning the key in the lock with his mouth. It seemed, unhappily, that he hadn't really any teeth—what could he grip the key with?—but on the other hand his jaws were certainly very strong; with their help he did manage to set the key in motion, <u>heedless</u> of the fact that he was undoubtedly damaging them somewhere, since a brown

WORDS FOR EVERYDAY USE

im • mi • nent (im´ə nənt) *adj.,* likely to happen; impending

heed • less (hēd´lis) *adj.,* careless; unmindful

VOCABULARY IN CONTEXT

- Even though the volcano rumbled and smoke seeped out, the residents of the town remained in their homes, unwilling or unable to believe that they were in <u>imminent</u> danger.
- If you plan to scale Mount Everest, it is better to be well prepared and cautious than filled with <u>heedless</u> enthusiasm.

fluid issued from his mouth, flowed over the key, and dripped on the floor. "Just listen to that," said the chief clerk next door; "he's turning the key." That was a great encouragement to Gregor; but they should all have shouted encouragement to him, his father and mother too: "Go on, Gregor," they should have called out, "keep going, hold on to that key!" And in the belief that they were all following his efforts intently, he clenched his jaws recklessly on the key with all the force at his command. As the turning of the key progressed he circled around the lock, holding on now only with his mouth, pushing on the key, as required, or pulling it down again with all the weight of his body. The louder click of the finally yielding lock literally quickened Gregor. With a deep breath of relief he said to himself: "So I didn't need the locksmith," and laid his head on the handle to open the door wide.

Since he had to pull the door toward him, he was still invisible when it was really wide open. He had to edge himself slowly around the near half of the double door, and to do it very carefully if he was not to fall plump upon his back just on the threshold. He was still carrying out this difficult maneuver, with no time to observe anything else, when he heard the chief clerk utter a loud "Oh!"—it sounded like a gust of wind—and now he could see the man, standing as he was nearest to the door, clapping one hand before his open mouth and slowly backing away as if driven by some invisible steady pressure. His mother—in spite of the chief clerk's being there her hair was still undone and sticking up in all directions—first clasped her hands and looked at his father, then took two steps toward Gregor and fell on the floor among her outspread skirts, her face quite hidden on her breast. His father knotted his fist with a fierce expression on his face as if he meant to knock Gregor back into room, then looked uncertainly around the living room, covered his eyes with his hands, and wept till his great chest heaved.

Gregor did not go now into the living room, but leaned against the inside of the firmly shut wing of the door, so that only half his body was visible and his head above it bending sideways to look at the others. The light had meanwhile strengthened; on the other side of the street one could see clearly a section of the endlessly long, dark gray building opposite—it was a hospital—abruptly punctuated by its row of regular windows; the rain was still falling, but only in large singly <u>discernible</u> and literally singly splashing drops. The breakfast dishes were set out on the table lavishly, for breakfast was the most important meal of the day to Gregor's father, who lingered it out for hours over various newspapers. Right opposite Gregor on the wall hung a photograph of himself in military service, as a lieutenant, hand on sword, a carefree smile on his face, inviting one to respect his uniform and military bearing. The door leading to the hall was open, and one could see that the front door stood open too, showing the landing beyond and the beginning of the stairs going down.

"Well," said Gregor, knowing perfectly that he was the only one who had retained any <u>composure</u>, "I'll put my clothes on at once, pack up my samples, and start off. Will you only let me go? You see, sir, I'm not obstinate, and I'm willing to work; traveling is a hard life, but I couldn't live without it. Where are you going, sir? To the office? Yes? Will you give a true account of all this? One can be temporarily <u>incapacitated</u>, but that's just the moment for remembering former services and bearing in mind that later on,

1 *What is Gregor finally able to do? How?*

2 *In contrast to how Gregor usually spends his mornings, how does Gregor's father spend his mornings?*

3 *What is the clerk's and the family's first reaction when Gregor opens the door?*

4 *What does Gregor tell the clerk about his temporary "incapacity" and his loyalty? What kind of employee does he promise to be? What does he ask the clerk to understand about the life of a traveler?*

Words for Everyday Use

dis • cern • i • ble (di zurn´ə bəl) *adj.,* recognizable
com • po • sure (kəm pō´zher) *n,* calmness of mind or manner
in • ca • pac • i • tate (in´kə pas´ə tāt´) *vt.,* make incapable of normal activity

Answers to Guided Reading Questions

1 Gregor is finally able to open the door with his mouth.

2 Gregor's father spends his mornings at the breakfast table reading newspapers.

3 Everyone is shocked by Gregor's appearance.

4 Gregor tells the clerk that his problem is temporary and that it will never occur again. He tells the clerk that traveling is a hard life and that people who work such hours are bound to have off days.

Literary Technique

ANTIHERO

Inform students that an **antihero** is a central character who lacks many of the qualities traditionally associated with heroes. An antihero is a modern and ironic interpretation of the traditional hero in earlier literature. Encourage students to explain whether they would classify Gregor Samsa as an antihero. Why, or why not? If students believe Gregor is an antihero, encourage them to discuss why Kafka chose to create an antihero as the central figure for this story rather than a more traditionally heroic central character.

Vocabulary in Context

- Heidi thought she recognized her cousin, but from such a distance his features were not <u>discernible</u>.
- Miranda is calm—no matter what disaster strikes, she always maintains her <u>composure</u>.
- In many adventure movies, a suave hero manages to <u>incapacitate</u> an explosive device in the nick of time.

Answers to Guided Reading Questions

1 If the clerk leaves, he will fire Gregor.

2 The chief clerk is horrified and frightened. His lips are parted in surprise, his shoulder twitches, and he steals toward the door.

ANALYTIC SCALES FOR RESPONDING IN WRITING

(SEE PAGE 468.)

Assign a score from 1 to 25 for each grading criterion below. (For more detailed evaluation, see the evaluation forms for writing, revising, and proofreading, Assessment Portfolio 4.1–4.9.)

1. Metamorphosis

- **Content/Unity.** The writing describes the narrator undergoing a metamorphosis and trying to leave his or her room.
- **Organization/Coherence.** The description relates details appropriate to the metamorphosed form in a sensible order.
- **Language/Style.** The metamorphosis uses vivid and precise nouns, verbs, and modifiers.
- **Conventions.** The metamorphosis avoids errors in spelling, grammar, usage, mechanics, and manuscript form.

▶ Additional practice is provided in the Essential Skills Practice Book: Writing 1.8, 1.10.

(cont.)

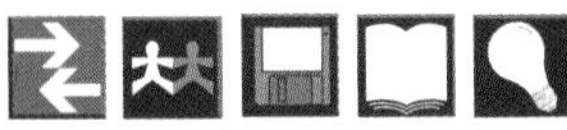

Additional Questions and Activities

After they have read pages 465–466, encourage students to discuss why Gregor's father reacts as he does to Gregor's condition. Why is he so angry and exasperated with Gregor when the transformation is not Gregor's fault?

when the incapacity has been got over, one will certainly work with all the more industry and concentration. I'm loyally bound to serve the chief, you know that very well. Besides, I have to provide for my parents and my sister. I'm in great difficulties, but I'll get out of them again. Don't make things any worse for me than they are. Stand up for me in the firm. Travelers are not popular there, I know. People think they earn sacks of money and just have a good time. A prejudice there's no particular reason for revising. But you, sir, have a more comprehensive view of affairs than the rest of the staff, yes, let me tell you in confidence, a more comprehensive view than the chief himself, who, being the owner, lets his judgment easily be swayed against one of his employees. And you know very well that the traveler, who is never seen in the office almost the whole year around, can so easily fall a victim to gossip and ill luck and unfounded complaints, which he mostly knows nothing about, except when he comes back exhausted from his rounds, and only then suffers in person from their evil consequences, which he can no longer trace back to the original causes. Sir, sir, don't go away without a word to me to show that you think me in the right at least to some extent!"

1 Why, according to Gregor, must the chief clerk not be allowed to leave?

But at Gregor's very first words the chief clerk had already backed away and only stared at him with parted lips over one twitching shoulder. And while Gregor was speaking he did not stand still one moment but stole away toward the door, without taking his eyes off Gregor, yet only an inch at a time, as if obeying some secret injunction to leave the room. He was already at the hall, and the suddenness with which he took his last step out of the living room would have made one believe he had burned the sole of his foot. Once in the hall he stretched his right arm before him toward the staircase, as if some supernatural power were waiting there to deliver him.

2 How does the chief clerk feel when he sees Gregor? How can you tell?

Gregor perceived that the chief clerk must on no account be allowed to go away in this frame of mind if his position in the firm were not to be endangered to the utmost. His parents did not understand this so well; they had convinced themselves in the course of years that Gregor was settled for life in this firm, and besides they were so preoccupied with their immediate troubles that all foresight had forsaken them. Yet Gregor had this foresight. The chief clerk must be detained, soothed, persuaded, and finally won over; the whole future of Gregor and his family depended on it! If only his sister had been there! She was intelligent; she had begun to cry while Gregor was still lying quietly on his back. And no doubt the chief clerk, so partial to ladies, would have been guided by her; she would have shut the door of the flat and in the hall talked him out of his horror. But she was not there, and Gregor would have to handle the situation himself. And without remembering that he was still unaware what power of movement he possessed, without even remembering that his words in all possibility, indeed in all likelihood, would again be unintelligible, he let go the wing of the door, pushed himself through the opening, started to walk toward the chief clerk, who was already ridiculously clinging with both hands to the railing on the landing; but immediately, as he was feeling for a support, he fell down with a little cry upon all his numerous legs. Hardly was he down when he experienced for the first time this morning a sense of physical comfort; his legs had firm ground under them; they were completely obedient, as he noted

Words for Everyday Use

in • junc • tion (in juŋk´shən) *n.,* command

Vocabulary in Context

- The brutal leader warned that if anyone disobeyed his injunction the punishment would be death.

with joy; they even strove to carry him forward in whatever direction he chose; and he was inclined to believe that a final relief from all his sufferings was at hand. But in the same moment as he found himself on the floor, rocking with suppressed eagerness to move, not far from his mother, indeed just in front of her, she, who had seemed so completely crushed, sprang all at once to her feet, her arms and fingers outspread, cried: "Help, for God's sake, help!" bent her head down as if to see Gregor better, yet on the contrary kept backing senselessly away; had quite forgotten that the laden table stood behind her; sat upon it hastily, as if in absence of mind, when she bumped into it; and seemed altogether unaware that the big coffeepot beside her was upset and pouring coffee in a flood over the carpet.

"Mother, Mother," said Gregor in a low voice, and looked up at her. The chief clerk, for the moment, had quite slipped from his mind; instead, he could not resist snapping his jaws together at the sight of the streaming coffee. That made his mother scream again, she fled from the table and fell into the arms of his father, who hastened to catch her. But Gregor had now no time to spare for his parents; the chief clerk was already on the stairs; with his chin on the banisters he was taking one last backward look. Gregor made a spring, to be as sure as possible of overtaking him; the chief clerk must have divined his intention, for he leaped down several steps and vanished; he was still yelling "Ugh!" and it echoed through the whole staircase.

Unfortunately, the flight of the chief clerk seemed completely to upset Gregor's father, who had remained relatively calm until now, for instead of running after the man himself, or at least not hindering Gregor in his pursuit, he seized in his right hand the walking stick that the chief clerk had left behind on a chair, together with a hat and greatcoat, snatched in his left hand a large newspaper from the table, and began stamping his feet and flourishing the stick and the newspaper to drive Gregor back into his room. No entreaty of Gregor's availed, indeed no entreaty was even understood, however humbly he bent his head his father only stamped on the floor the more loudly. Behind his father his mother had torn open a window, despite the cold weather, and was leaning far out of it with her face in her hands. A strong draught set in from the street to the staircase, the window curtains blew in, the newspapers on the table fluttered, stray pages whisked over the floor. Pitilessly Gregor's father drove him back, hissing and crying "Shoo!" like a savage. But Gregor was quite unpracticed in walking backwards, it really was a slow business. If he only had a chance to turn around he could get back to his room at once, but he was afraid of exasperating his father by the slowness of such a rotation and at any moment the stick in his father's hand might hit him a fatal blow on the back or on the head. In the end, however, nothing else was left for him to do since to his horror he observed that in moving backwards he could not even control the direction he took; and so, keeping an anxious eye on his father all the time over his shoulder, he began to turn around as quickly as he could, which was in reality very slowly. Perhaps

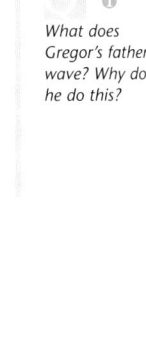

❶ *What does Gregor's father wave? Why does he do this?*

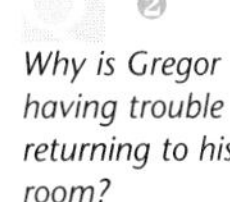

❷ *Why is Gregor having trouble returning to his room?*

❸ *Do you think the chief clerk recognizes the creature he sees as Gregor? Explain.*

WORDS FOR EVERYDAY USE

lad • en (lād´'n) *adj.,* densely loaded; full

di • vine (də vīn´) *vt.,* to guess by intuition

VOCABULARY IN CONTEXT

- The brunch table was laden with every type of dish and delicacy one could desire.
- Tara said smugly, "Only a mind reader would be able to divine your muddled intentions."

ANSWERS TO GUIDED READING QUESTIONS

❶ Gregor's father begins waving a stick and a newspaper at Gregor to drive him back into his room.

❷ Gregor is having trouble returning to his room because he is not used to walking backward on so many legs and he is afraid his father will get impatient if he tries to turn around.

❸ *Responses will vary.* Students might say that the chief clerk probably thinks of Gregor as a hideous monster.

ANALYTIC SCALES FOR RESPONDING IN WRITING (CONT.)

Assign a score from 1 to 25 for each grading criterion below. (For more detailed evaluation, see the evaluation forms for writing, revising, and proofreading, Assessment Portfolio 4.1–4.9.)

2. Critical Essay

- **Content/Unity.** The essay explains how Gregor's role in the world leads to his metamorphosis.
- **Organization/Coherence.** The essay begins with an introduction that includes the thesis of the essay. The introduction is followed by supporting paragraphs with clear transitions. The essay ends with a solid conclusion.
- **Language/Style.** The essay uses vivid and precise nouns, verbs, and modifiers.
- **Conventions.** The essay avoids errors in spelling, grammar, usage, mechanics, and manuscript form.

▶ Additional practice is provided in the Essential Skills Practice Book: Writing 1.20.

Answers to Guided Reading Questions

① Gregor's father pushes him roughly through the door. The words "at last" indicate that Gregor seems relieved that the morning's commotion has come to an end.

Selection Check Test with Answers

EX: Into what is Gregor Samsa transformed one morning?

He is transformed into an insect.

1. Why does Gregor decide that he must get out of bed?

He decides that he must go to work or he'll be fired.

2. What does Gregor do for a living?

He is a traveling salesperson.

3. Why does Gregor have to work so hard?

Gregor must work hard because his family is in debt.

4. How does Gregor feel about his job?

He dislikes his job intensely.

5. What people knock on Gregor's bedroom door?

Gregor's family and his boss, the chief clerk, knock on his door.

his father noted his good intentions, for he did not interfere except every now and then to help him in the maneuver from a distance with the point of the stick. If only he would have stopped making that unbearable hissing noise! It made Gregor quite lose his head. He had turned almost completely around when the hissing noise so distracted him that he even turned a little the wrong way again. But when at last his head was fortunately right in front of the doorway, it appeared that his body was too broad simply to get through the opening. His father, of course, in his present mood was far from thinking of such a thing as opening the other half of the door, to let Gregor have enough space. He had merely the fixed idea of driving Gregor back into his room as quickly as possible. He would never have suffered Gregor to make the circumstantial preparations for standing up on end and perhaps slipping his way through the door. Maybe he was now making more noise than ever to urge Gregor forward, as if no obstacle impeded him; to Gregor, anyhow, the noise in his rear sounded no longer like the voice of one single father; this was really no joke, and Gregor thrust himself—come what might—into the doorway. One side of his body rose up, he was tilted at an angle in the doorway, his flank was quite bruised, horrid blotches stained the white door, soon he was stuck fast and, left to himself, could not have moved at all, his legs on one side fluttered trembling in the air, those on the other were crushed painfully to the floor—when from behind his father gave him a strong push which was literally a deliverance and he flew far into the room, bleeding freely. The door was slammed behind him with the stick, and then at last there was silence. ■

Q ① *What finally helps Gregor through the door? How does it feel to Gregor to be back in his room?*

Words for Everyday Use

im • pede (im pēd´) *vt.,* bar or hinder the progress of

Vocabulary in Context

• Herds of goats crossing the narrow mountain road sometimes impede motorists.

Responding to the Selection

If you were a physician, to what would you attribute Gregor's physical condition? If you were a psychiatrist, what would you have to say about Gregor's mental state? What might you say to his family and the chief clerk about their treatment of Gregor?

Reviewing the Selection

Recalling / Interpreting

1. Into what does Gregor find himself transformed one morning? What does he look like? ▶▶ What are Gregor's initial thoughts about his unusual condition? How is he feeling as he hears the raindrops beating on the window gutter?

2. What does Gregor do for a living? What circumstances of his life force him to work so hard? ▶▶ How does Gregor feel about his job? Why does he feel this way? Why does Gregor only daydream and not plan seriously to leave his job? For whom does he feel responsible? What does this reveal about his character?

3. What does Gregor say to himself when he finally notices the time? When was his alarm to have gone off? How does Gregor expect to be treated by his employer? ▶▶ Although Gregor awakens to find himself in a strange and frightening situation, what is the only thing that sends him into a panic? In what way is his reaction both humorous and sad? Does it seem that Gregor deserves the treatment he expects from his employer? Why, or why not?

4. Who comes to the house to check on Gregor? What excuses do Gregor's family members make for him? ▶▶ What kind of person is the chief clerk? What drives Gregor to open his door—concern about himself and his condition, or concern about his family and job? How do the others react to Gregor's appearance when he finally emerges?

Synthesizing

5. Describe the life in which Gregor Samsa has been trapped. How have his job and his attitude toward his work affected his energy level and his self-respect? In what way might his unusual physical condition reflect his feelings of exhaustion and despair over what he has failed to accomplish? Given that insects are industrious creatures who often labor together in colonies, why is Gregor's transformation particularly significant? What might the author be suggesting about the modern world?

RESPONDING TO THE SELECTION

Students might enjoy working in pairs to role play a conversation between Gregor and a counselor, psychologist, or psychiatrist.

ANSWERS FOR REVIEWING THE SELECTION

RECALLING AND INTERPRETING

1. **Recalling.** Gregor finds himself transformed into an insect. He has an armor-plated back; a domelike, segmented brown belly; and numerous thin legs. **Interpreting.** Gregor wonders what has happened to him but then decides to sleep longer to forget "this nonsense." The rain makes him feel melancholy.

2. **Recalling.** Gregor is a traveling salesperson. The chief at Gregor's workplace is demanding and Gregor's parents owe him money, so Gregor is trying to pay off his parents' debt. **Interpreting.** Gregor loathes his job because it consumes all his time, he must always travel, and he dislikes the strict chief. He only daydreams about leaving his job because he knows he has to work to repay his parents' debts. He feels responsible for his parents. Gregor is loyal and conscientious.

3. **Recalling.** Gregor says "heavenly Father" when he realizes that he has overslept. He wonders if his alarm clock went off and whether he could say he is sick. His alarm was set to go off at four o'clock. He expects to be severely reprimanded. **Interpreting.** Gregor is sent into a panic only when he realizes that he has overslept and will probably miss his train. His reaction is humorous because he is disturbed by the prospect of being late, and not by having been transformed into an insect. His reaction is sad because it shows how much he has been forced to focus only on his work. Gregor seems conscientious and hard-working, so he probably does not deserve the treatment he receives. (cont.)

ANSWERS FOR REVIEWING THE SELECTION (CONT.)

4. **Recalling.** The chief clerk comes to check on Gregor. His family says that he must be sick because he is of such a hard-working nature that he otherwise never would miss work. **Interpreting.** The chief clerk seems obsessed with work and is unforgiving of any lapse in his employees. Gregor opens the door because he is worried about his family and job. They react with shock and horror.

SYNTHESIZING

Responses will vary. Possible responses are given.

5. Gregor is trapped in a cycle of endless, unrewarding work. He is exhausted and has lost his self-respect, so he will never stand up for himself. He has been transformed into a body that will not permit him to work, reflecting his exhaustion and despair. The transformation may represent (cont.)

Answers for Reviewing the Selection (cont.)

a complete physical and emotional breakdown. Gregor is a relatively insignificant worker with little interest outside work and he has been transformed into another mindless working creature, viewed as vermin by others. The author may be suggesting that the modern world has transformed working people into mindless drones.

Answers for Understanding Literature

Responses will vary. Possible responses are given.

1. **Allegory.** Gregor's emotional and physical breaking point is represented by his transformation into a form that will not allow him to work but at the same time represents the mindless work to which he has been subjected. It might represent a mental breakdown. His parents' debts and his browbeating employer have led to his downfall. The chief clerk represents the harsh employer.
2. **Characterization.** Gregor Samsa is a hardworking character who has lost all his hopes and dreams and can focus only on work. Students should find at least one example of each characterization technique. "As Gregor awoke . . . he found himself transformed in his bed into a gigantic insect," is an example of direct description. "He looked at the alarm clock ticking on the chest," is an example of portrayal of a character's behavior. "What has happened to me? he thought" is an example of representation of characters' internal states. The chief clerk is a bullying, unforgiving character. Kafka creates the clerk by portrayal of his behavior and by direct description. *Examples will vary.*

ANALYTIC SCALES FOR RESPONDING IN WRITING

Grading scales for Responding in Writing appear on pages 464–465.

Understanding Literature (Questions for Discussion)

1. **Allegory.** An **allegory** is a work in which each element symbolizes, or represents, something else. Much has been written about the allegorical qualities of *The Metamorphosis.* Gregor's plight is said to symbolize that of many working people who must spend every waking hour in the service of others. According to Kafka, people who continually sacrifice their personal lives and their own needs to unceasing labor will inevitably reach a breaking point. How has Kafka illustrated Gregor's breaking point in a creative and unusual way? What might Gregor's condition represent? What people and circumstances have specifically led to Gregor's downfall? If Gregor represents the working-class man or woman, whom does the chief clerk represent?
2. **Characterization. Characterization** is the use of literary techniques to create a character. Writers use three major techniques to create characters: direct description, portrayal of characters' behavior, and representations of characters' internal states. See the entry on *characterization* in the Handbook of Literary Terms for more information. What kind of character is Gregor Samsa? Find examples of each method of characterization. What does each example show about Gregor? What kind of character is the chief clerk? What methods of characterization does Kafka use to illustrate this character? Support your responses with specific examples from the story.

Responding in Writing

1. **Creative Writing: Metamorphosis.** Through careful description, Kafka is able to show the reader how one character reacts to finding himself in a radically altered physical form. He includes many passages of description that show how difficult it is for Gregor to move in his new body; he must think carefully even about such simple actions as getting out of bed and opening a door. Write a descriptive piece in which you awaken to a similar experience. What would happen if you found yourself one day in the body of a giraffe? a cat? a snake? Think carefully about the logistical problems you would face as you attempted to get out of bed and leave your room. How might others react to you? Would they be frightened? What thoughts would be going through your mind as you tried to get used to this new body? Choose the "form" you would like to take, and then spend time freewriting about the details of this form and about your emotions upon inhabiting it. Try to come up with images that are truly vivid and unique and that will give your reader a sense of how you are feeling.
2. **Critical Essay: The Role of Gregor Samsa.** In a short essay, describe Gregor Samsa's role in his world and how this role leads to his metamorphosis. To get started, consider the following questions: How much of Gregor's life is devoted to work? How seriously does he take this work? Does Gregor work for himself, or for the good of others? How much gratitude does Gregor enjoy from his family? How much respect does Gregor get from the people with whom he works? Support your statements with concrete details from the story.

Language Lab

Clichés and Euphemisms. Review the Language Arts Survey 2.72, "Clichés and Euphemisms." Then, on your own paper, complete the following exercises.

Exercise A. Complete each sentence by filling in the blanks with a cliché.

EX. The popularity of Kafka's *Metamorphosis* has **spread like wildfire** over the years.

1. Gregor Samsa is exhausted because he works like a ______________. (He works hard.)
2. On the most unusual morning of his life, it is raining ______________. (It is raining hard.)
3. He has the ______________ (He feels sad) already, and the rain doesn't help.
4. Gregor has overslept, and he is worried because his boss is as tough as ______________. (His boss is severe.)
5. Gregor's body is awkward and uncomfortable, but his mind is sharp as a ______________. (His mind is very alert.)

Exercise B. Each sentence below contains a cliché in bold-faced type. Rewrite each sentence, replacing the cliché with a more direct or vivid word or phrase.

EX. When Gregor's mother realized that her son had turned into an insect, she **turned as white as a ghost**.

When Gregor's mother realized that her son had turned into an insect, she grew pale.

1. One can hardly expect Gregor's family to be **as happy as clams** with Gregor's transformation.
2. After all, most people **aren't crazy about** insects.
3. When many people see an insect, they crush it until the poor thing is **as flat as a pancake**.
4. Others use pesticides, hoping that all creeping, flying insects will soon be **as dead as doornails**.
5. Gregor, however, might advise others to try **walking a mile in the** insect's **shoes** before senselessly killing it.

Exercise C. For each word or phrase, write a more direct term, using a thesaurus as needed.

EX. well-to-do: **wealthy**

1. passed away
2. offender
3. refuse receptacle
4. restroom
5. embellish a story

Answers for Language Lab

EXERCISE A

1. dog
2. cats and dogs
3. blues
4. nails
5. pin

EXERCISE B

1. One can hardly expect Gregor's family to be pleased with Gregor's transformation.
2. After all, most people aren't fond of insects.
3. When many people see an insect, they crush it until the poor thing is squashed and oozing.
4. Others use pesticides, hoping that all creeping, flying insects will soon be eliminated.
5. Gregor, however, might advise others to empathize with the insect before senselessly killing it.

EXERCISE C

1. died
2. criminal
3. garbage can
4. toilet
5. lie

▶ Additional practice is provided in the Essential Skills Practice Book: Language 2.72.

ADDITIONAL RESOURCES

READER'S GUIDE

- Selection Worksheet 6.4

ASSESSMENT PORTFOLIO

- Selection Check Test 2.6.7
- Selection Test 2.6.8

ESSENTIAL SKILLS PRACTICE BOOKS

- Writing 1.8, 1.20
- Speaking and Listening 3.5

PREREADING EXTENSIONS

Have students work in groups to research peoples who have been displaced from their homelands. Students might choose ancient or contemporary groups as their subjects. Students can map migration routes and explain why the group left their homeland. If any students in your class had been forced to leave their homelands before coming to the United States, they may wish to share their experiences. Ask students to illustrate posters about such displacement.

SUPPORT FOR LEP STUDENTS

PRONUNCIATIONS OF PROPER NOUNS AND ADJECTIVES

Akh • ma • to • va (ak mä´ tə və)
Go • mor • rah (gə môr´ə)
Sod • om (säd´əm)

ADDITIONAL VOCABULARY

hulking—large and heavy; bulky and clumsy
welded—seared; melded by heat

PREREADING

"Lot's Wife"
by Anna Akhmatova, translated by Richard Wilbur

RUSSIA

About the Author

A biography of **Anna Akhmatova** appears on page 168.

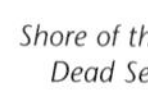
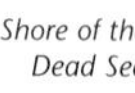

Shore of the Dead Sea

About the Selection

The poem you are about to read, **"Lot's Wife,"** is based on the story of Lot, which is found in Genesis, the first book of the Bible's Old Testament. Lot lived in the city of Sodom, which along with the city of Gomorrah, bordered the Dead Sea. Because their inhabitants lived decadent, wicked lives, Sodom and Gomorrah were targeted for destruction by God. Fire from heaven destroyed these cities and most people in them because the inhabitants failed to obey and respect God. Lot was warned of the coming destruction and was given a chance to flee with his family. His wife, however, disobeying God's orders, looked back at the city and was turned into a pillar of salt. The passages below are from the Old Testament version of the story.

> And when the morning arose, then the angels hastened Lot, saying, Arise, take thy wife, and thy two daughters, which are here; lest thou be consumed in the iniquity of the city. . . .
>
> And it came to pass, when they had brought them forth abroad, that he said, Escape for thy life; look not behind thee, neither stay thou in all the plain; escape to the mountain, lest thou be consumed. . . .
>
> Then the Lord rained upon Sodom and upon Gomorrah brimstone and fire from the Lord out of heaven;
>
> And he overthrew those cities, and all the plain, and all the inhabitants of the cities, and that which grew upon the ground.
>
> But his wife looked back from behind him, and she became a pillar of salt.
>
> —Genesis 19:15–26

Anna Akhmatova's poem "Lot's Wife" tells this same story from a different perspective. Her poem takes a closer look at Lot's wife and the experience of suddenly having to leave one's home. Akhmatova carefully takes one brief moment in the original story and opens from it a whole world based on the complicated emotions of one person. This poem, part of a short poetry cycle titled *Biblical Verses*, was later added to her book *Anno Domini.*

CONNECTIONS: Akhmatova's Soviet Union

Akhmatova may identify so well with Lot's wife because she herself experienced the pain of being forced to abandon her home. During a large portion of Akhmatova's adult life, the Soviet Union was under the cruel leadership of Joseph Stalin. Stalin's reign was characterized by brutal repression of all opposition, government management of economic life, and the end of private ownership. To enforce his policies and strengthen his own power, Stalin executed many officials and ordinary citizens who were accused of disloyalty. In this political climate, Akhmatova was often silenced as a poet. In 1946, she was expelled from the country, and her son was arrested. After Stalin's death in 1953, her son was released and her property returned. In "Lot's Wife," Akhmatova reveals her understanding of the importance of home and the pain of homelessness and upheaval.

GOALS/OBJECTIVES

Studying this lesson will enable students to

- empathize with the feelings of Lot's wife
- recognize Anna Akhmatova as a Russian poet
- define *point of view* and *tone*
- identify the point of view and explain how it differs from the story of Lot in the Book of Genesis
- identify the tone of the poem
- write a monologue
- identify the motivation of a character and support such motivation in an essay
- prepare and present an oral interpretation

READER'S JOURNAL

How would you feel if you were forced to leave your home? Have you ever had to leave a place that was filled with happy memories and feelings of security for you? If yes, describe these feelings. If no, write about what you imagine these feelings would be like.

"Lot's Wife"

ANNA AKHMATOVA, TRANSLATED BY RICHARD WILBUR

The just man followed then his angel guide
Where he strode on the black highway, hulking and bright;
But a wild grief in his wife's bosom cried,
Look back, it is not too late for a last sight

Of the red towers of your native Sodom, the square
Where once you sang, the gardens you shall mourn,
And the tall house with empty windows where
You loved your husband and your babes were born.

She turned, and looking on the bitter view
Her eyes were welded shut by mortal pain;
Into transparent salt her body grew,
And her quick feet were rooted in the plain.

Who would waste tears upon her? Is she not
The least of our losses, this unhappy wife?
Yet in my heart she will not be forgot
Who, for a single glance, gave up her life. ■

1 *Whom did Lot follow? What did his wife's grief for her lost home tell her to do?*

2 *What happened to Lot's wife when she looked back?*

3 *Why will this woman "not be forgot"? For what did she give up her life?*

READER'S JOURNAL

If students have difficulty writing about their feelings about leaving a place, they may wish to focus on the place itself and record some of their memories. After students have written in their journals, they can discuss their responses in groups.

ANSWERS TO GUIDED READING QUESTIONS

1 The just man, Lot, followed his angel guide. His wife's grief caused her to look back.

2 Her eyes were welded shut by mortal pain, and she turned into salt and her feet were "rooted in the plain."

3 This woman will "not be forgot" because she gave up her life for a single glance back at her home.

SELECTION CHECK TEST WITH ANSWERS

EX. Who is leaving Sodom?
Lot and his wife are leaving Sodom.

1. Whom does Lot follow?
Lot follows his angel guide.

2. What causes Lot's wife to look back at Sodom?
Grief causes her to look back.

3. What memories does she have of Sodom?
She has memories of singing in the square and of giving birth to her children in her home.

4. What happens when Lot's wife looks back at Sodom?
Lot's wife's eyes are welded shut by mortal pain, and she turns to salt.

5. Why will the speaker of the poem not forget Lot's wife?
The speaker of the poem will not forget Lot's wife because she gave up her life to look back at her home.

RESPONDING TO THE SELECTION

Students may also wish to write about or discuss the metaphorical idea of "not looking back," or not worrying about past decisions.

ANSWERS FOR REVIEWING THE SELECTION

RECALLING AND INTERPRETING

1. **Recalling.** The just man, Lot, followed his angel guide. **Interpreting.** Lot is called the "just" man. He is considered honorable, unlike the citizens of Sodom who were seen as sinful and wicked.

2. **Recalling.** Lot's wife remembers singing in the square of Sodom. She also remembers loving her husband in her home and her children being born in her home. **Interpreting.** Lot's wife considers Sodom her home because she has raised her family there and has had many good memories there. *Responses will vary.*

3. **Recalling.** Lot's wife takes one last look at Sodom and turns into salt. **Interpreting.** Lot's wife defies these warnings because it is impossible to surrender all the things that were so meaningful to her.

4. **Recalling.** Lot's wife gave up her life for one last glance at her home. **Interpreting.** The poem stresses that emotional ties to home can be strong and compelling. The poem suggests that for home and country one might give up his or her life.

SYNTHESIZING

Responses will vary. Possible responses are given.

5. Lot's wife may go unnoticed because in the original story her feelings and motivations are not explored. Her destruction seems almost minor compared with the mass destruction of Sodom and Gomorrah. The speaker of the poem feels empathy and respect for her.

Responding to the Selection

Why do you suppose Lot's wife looked back? If you were Lot's wife, might you have done the same thing that she did? Why, or why not?

Reviewing the Selection

RECALLING		INTERPRETING
1. Who did Lot, the "just man," follow?	▶▶	In what way did Lot differ from many of the people of Sodom?
2. What memories does Lot's wife have of the square in Sodom? of her home?	▶▶	How does Lot's wife feel about Sodom? Why might she feel that way despite the conditions in the city that are causing its destruction?
3. What does Lot's wife do? What happens to her as a result?	▶▶	Why does Lot's wife defy the warnings she has been given?
4. What did Lot's wife give up? Why did she do so?	▶▶	What does this poem say about loyalty and ties to one's home?

SYNTHESIZING

5. Why might Lot's wife seem unimportant to some people? Why, especially in the original version of the story, might her plight go unnoticed? How does the speaker of this poem feel about her?

Understanding Literature (Questions for Discussion)

1. **Point of View. Point of view** is the vantage point from which a story is told. Refer to the definition of *point of view* in the Handbook of Literary Terms. Is this poem told from the first person, the second person, or the third person point of view, or from a combination of these? Explain. Who tells most of the story? Whose thoughts and feelings are emphasized? In what way is this version of the story of Lot different from the version that appears in the Old Testament? What fresh perspective does this poem give?

2. **Tone. Tone** is the emotional attitude toward the reader or toward the subject implied by a literary work. What seems to be the speaker's attitude toward Lot's wife, the subject of this poem? Does the speaker seem sympathetic or judgmental? Explain your choice.

ANSWERS FOR UNDERSTANDING LITERATURE

Responses will vary. Possible responses are given.

1. Point of View. Throughout most of the poem, this story is told in the first person, from the point of view of a speaker. In lines 4–8, the speaker relays the words of the wild grief that speaks to the woman. In stanza 4, the speaker addresses the audience rhetorically, asking, "Who would waste tears upon her?" The speaker's response that Lot's wife will not be forgotten confirms his or her identification with Lot's wife. This poem focuses on the feelings of Lot's wife, while the original focuses on the experience of Lot. The poem gives Lot's wife's perspective on how difficult it is to abandon the past.

2. Tone. The speaker feels sympathetic toward the subject of the poem. He or she seems to

(cont.)

Responding in Writing

1. **Creative Writing: Monologue.** A monologue presents the speech of a single character. It is an opportunity for one character to present his or her feelings and ideas uninterrupted. Think about stories and poems that you have read since you were a child. From one of these stories or poems, choose a minor character, a person or animal, whose point of view is not available or immediately obvious. Use your imagination to write a monologue for this character, in which you give the character a chance to voice his or her opinions. For example, you might explore the point of view of the grandmother or the wolf in "Little Red Riding Hood," one of Cinderella's stepsisters' point of view, or the point of view of the giant in "Jack and the Beanstalk." To begin, spend some time freewriting about your character. What feelings does this character have toward the actors and the actions in the story or poem? Decide what you want your character to say and how you want him or her to say it.

2. **Critical Essay: The Motivation of Lot's Wife.** A motivation is a force that moves a character to think, feel, or behave in a certain way. In a short essay, explain what motivates Lot's wife to turn and look back at Sodom even though she knows she is forbidden to do so. What is Lot's wife feeling? What is she remembering? In your essay, you might also describe the speaker's feelings toward Lot's wife. Is the speaker sympathetic to the woman's motives? Why, or why not? Support your statements with details from the poem.

Speaking and Listening Skills

Oral Interpretation. Oral interpretation is the process of presenting a dramatic reading of a literary work or group of works. The presentation should be dramatic enough to convey to the audience a sense of the particular qualities of the work. For more information about oral interpretation, turn to the Language Arts Survey 3.5, "Oral Interpretation." Then complete the following activity:

- Write an introduction to the monologue you wrote as a creative writing activity. Your introduction should explain who the character is and why you chose to write about this character.
- With a partner, practice reading your introduction and monologue. You and your partner should listen carefully to each other and then offer tips and constructive criticism. Help your partner to make his or her presentation the strongest it can be, using the guidelines for oral interpretation presented in the Language Arts Survey.
- When every person in the class has rehearsed thoroughly, each person should present his or her monologue to the entire class.

ANALYTIC SCALES FOR RESPONDING IN WRITING

Assign a score from 1 to 25 for each grading criterion below. (For more detailed evaluation, see the evaluation forms for writing, revising, and proofreading, Assessment Portfolio 4.1–4.9.)

1. Monologue

- **Content/Unity.** The monologue presents the emotions of a minor character from a well-known story or poem.
- **Organization/Coherence.** The monologue flows naturally and is arranged in a logical order.
- **Language/Style.** The monologue uses vivid and precise nouns, verbs, and modifiers.
- **Conventions.** The monologue avoids errors in spelling, grammar, usage, mechanics, and manuscript form.

▶ Additional practice is provided in the Essential Skills Practice Book: Writing 1.8.

2. Critical Essay

- **Content/Unity.** The essay presents opinions and supporting material about the motivation of Lot's wife.
- **Organization/Coherence.** The essay begins with an introduction that includes a thesis. The introduction is followed by supporting paragraphs with clear transitions. The essay ends with a solid conclusion.
- **Language/Style.** The essay uses vivid and precise nouns, verbs, and modifiers.
- **Conventions.** The essay avoids errors in spelling, grammar, usage, mechanics, and manuscript form.

▶ Additional practice is provided in the Essential Skills Practice Book: Writing 1.20.

ANSWERS FOR UNDERSTANDING LITERATURE (CONT.)

understand what Lot's wife is going through, and why the experience would affect her emotionally. The speaker recognizes Lot's wife's grief by refusing to forget this woman and her loyalty.

ANSWERS FOR SKILLS ACTIVITIES

SPEAKING AND LISTENING SKILLS

Oral interpretations should utilize elements of verbal and nonverbal communication such as appropriate volume, tone, pace, gestures, and facial expressions. Students should look for these elements as they rehearse with a partner.

▶ For assessment, see Assessment Portfolio 4.11, "Public Speaking Evaluation Form."

"The Fifth Story"
by Clarice Lispector, translated by Giovanni Pontiero

BRAZIL

About the Author

CLARICE LISPECTOR 1925-1977

Clarice Lispector (1925–1977). Clarice Lispector is considered to be one of the most important Brazilian writers of the twentieth century. Born in 1925 in the Ukraine, then a part of the Soviet Union, Lispector moved to Brazil with her parents when she was an infant. Her father was a farm laborer, and the family was poor. An avid reader as a child, Lispector decided early in her life that she wanted to be a writer. She sent her writing to a Brazilian company that published work written by children, but her manuscripts were rejected. Discouraged, Lispector put writing aside for a long time, deciding to become a lawyer. After earning a law degree, Lispector eventually determined that a career in law was not for her and returned to writing, working for a newspaper. She also wrote essays, novels, short stories, and children's literature. Lispector's works are best known in Latin America and Europe because English translations of her writing are not always readily available.

About the Selection

Clarice Lispector's writing examines the often painful struggles of individuals as they try to make sense of their lives in an absurd world. Lispector's writing was influenced by **Existentialism**, a philosophy that explores what its supporters view as the essential absurdity and meaninglessness of life. Existentialists believe that humans find themselves alive and aware without any essential, defining direction. Any choices that a person makes in order to define himself or herself are made freely, and therefore absurdly—one may as well make one choice as another. Some Existentialists see freedom of will as a terrific burden. They believe that choice causes anguish to a thinking person who instinctively feels that life should be meaningful but intellectually knows it not to be.

Lispector illustrates this struggle in **"The Fifth Story,"** a short story about a woman trying to purge her home of cockroaches. This seemingly simple problem becomes a great moral struggle for the narrator, and the story leaves the reader wondering what the protagonist's struggle has accomplished.

CONNECTIONS: The Cockroach

The cockroach is an insect found and despised all over the world. Cockroach species vary in size and shape, but most are brown or black in color and have broad, flat bodies and long, powerful legs. These insects like warm, dark areas, and the shape of their bodies allows them to crawl in narrow cracks and along pipes. Cockroaches hide in the daytime and come out at night to feed on food, paper, clothing, books, and other dead insects. Difficult to control, they have been found in houses, apartments, ships, trains, airplanes, and office buildings. Cockroaches are among the oldest living insects. Scientists have found fossil cockroaches from 320 million years ago that resemble species of today. Scientists speculate that cockroaches would be one of the species adaptable enough to survive a nuclear holocaust.

ADDITIONAL RESOURCES

READER'S GUIDE
- Selection Worksheet 6.5

ASSESSMENT PORTFOLIO
- Selection Check Test 2.6.9
- Selection Test 2.6.10

ESSENTIAL SKILLS PRACTICE BOOKS
- Writing 1.8, 1.20
- Study and Research 4.1

PREREADING EXTENSIONS

You might ask interested students to write an essay comparing and contrasting the way Lispector's Existentialist views shaped "The Fifth Story" with the way Existentialist views are presented in either Eugène Ionesco's *The Bald Soprano* or Albert Camus's "The Myth of Sisyphus." Students might begin their essays by referring to the definition of Existentialism in the Handbook of Literary Terms. Students might then create Venn diagrams and note similarities and differences in the ways the two authors express Existentialist beliefs. For more information on Venn diagrams, refer students to the Language Arts Survey 1.10, "Gathering Ideas."

SUPPORT FOR LEP STUDENTS

PRONUNCIATIONS OF PROPER NOUNS AND ADJECTIVES

Clar • ice Lis • pec • tor (klä rēs´ li spek´ tər)
U • kraine (yo͞o krān´)

ADDITIONAL VOCABULARY

constitute—make up
loathing—intense dislike or disgust
organic—natural, bodily
reproach—blame

GOALS/OBJECTIVES

Studying this lesson will enable students to
- enjoy an unusual work of short fiction
- differentiate between and identify internal and external conflicts
- define *personification* and recognize the use of this technique in works that they read
- define *Existentialism* and recognize the influence of this movement in a literary work
- describe a situation with three distinct attitudes
- write a critical essay on the narrator's attitudes
- use problem-solving and decision-making skills

In your journal, describe some decisions that have been easy for you to make and some that have required careful thought. Provide reasons why the latter are more difficult than the former.

READER'S JOURNAL

"The Fifth Story"

CLARICE LISPECTOR, TRANSLATED BY GIOVANNI PONTIERO

This story could be called "The Statues." Another possible title would be "The Killing." Or even "How to Kill Cockroaches." So I shall tell at least three stories, all of them true, because none of the three will contradict the others. Although they constitute one story, they could become a thousand and one, were I to be granted a thousand and one nights.

The first story, "How To Kill Cockroaches," begins like this: I was complaining about the cockroaches. A woman heard me complain. She gave me a recipe for killing them. I was to mix together equal quantities of sugar, flour and gypsum.[1] The flour and sugar would attract the cockroaches, the gypsum would dry up their insides. I followed her advice. The cockroaches died.

The next story is really the first, and it is called "The Killing." It begins like this: I was complaining about the cockroaches. A woman heard me complain. The recipe follows. And then the killing takes place. The truth is that I had only complained in abstract terms about the cockroaches, for they were not even mine: they belonged to the ground floor and climbed up the pipes in the building into our apartment. It was only when I prepared the mixture that they also became mine. On our behalf, therefore, I began to measure and weigh ingredients with greater concentration. A vague loathing had taken possession of me, a sense of outrage. By day, the cockroaches were invisible and no one would believe in the evil secret which eroded such a tranquil household. But if the cockroaches, like evil secrets, slept by day, there I was preparing their nightly poison. Meticulous, eager, I prepared the elixir of prolonged death. An angry fear and my own evil secret guided me. Now I coldly wanted one thing only: to kill every cockroach in existence. Cockroaches climb up the pipes while weary people sleep. And now the recipe was ready, looking so white. As if I were dealing

1. **gypsum.** Natural substance used for making plaster of Paris

① *What are the different story titles the narrator considers? At least how many stories does the narrator say will be told?*

② *How does the narrator begin to feel about the cockroaches? What "guides" the narrator as she prepares the poison?*

③ *What is the recipe for killing cockroaches? What did the mixture do to the creatures?*

WORDS FOR EVERYDAY USE

me • tic • u • lous (mə tik´yo͞o ləs) *adj.*, extremely or excessively careful about details

e • lix • ir (ē liks´ir) *n.*, supposed remedy for all ailments

READER'S JOURNAL

Some students might prefer to describe in detail one decision that required considerable thought rather than generalize about many decisions they have made.

ANSWERS TO GUIDED READING QUESTIONS

① The writer considers "The Statues," "The Killing," and "How to Kill Cockroaches." At least three stories make up the one story that is to be told.

② The narrator begins to feel rage and loathing toward the cockroaches. Angry fear and the narrator's own evil secret (her desire to kill the pests) "guide" the narrator as she prepares the poison.

③ The recipe is equal quantities of sugar, flour, and gypsum. The mixture will attract the creatures and then dry up their insides.

SPELLING AND VOCABULARY WORDS FROM THE SELECTION

avidity	meticulous
depraved	mummify
elixir	scullery
gratuitous	somnambulant
infestation	

VOCABULARY IN CONTEXT

- Jamie was so meticulous that I could not find anything out of place in his tidy room.
- Hundreds of years ago, people believed that this spring water was an elixir that could cure any illness or wound.

Answers to Guided Reading Questions

❶ The poison kills the insects, drying them up. The narrator sees their dried, statue-like bodies in the morning.

Literary Technique

ALLUSION AND FRAME TALE

Inform students that an **allusion** is a rhetorical technique in which reference is made to a person, event, object, or work from history or literature. A **frame tale** is a story that itself provides a vehicle for the telling of other stories. Ask students the following questions: What allusion does the author make in the first paragraph of this selection? Why is this reference appropriate, given the nature of Lispector's story? In what ways is "The Fifth Story" similar to a frame tale?

ANSWERS

The author alludes to *The Thousand and One Nights.* This reference is appropriate because, like Shahrazad, the narrator of "The Fifth Story" tells a number of stories that "constitute" one story and says that she could tell a thousand and one stories if she had as many nights. "The Fifth Story" is like a frame tale in that it sets up a vehicle or framework for the telling of stories on a given subject or theme.

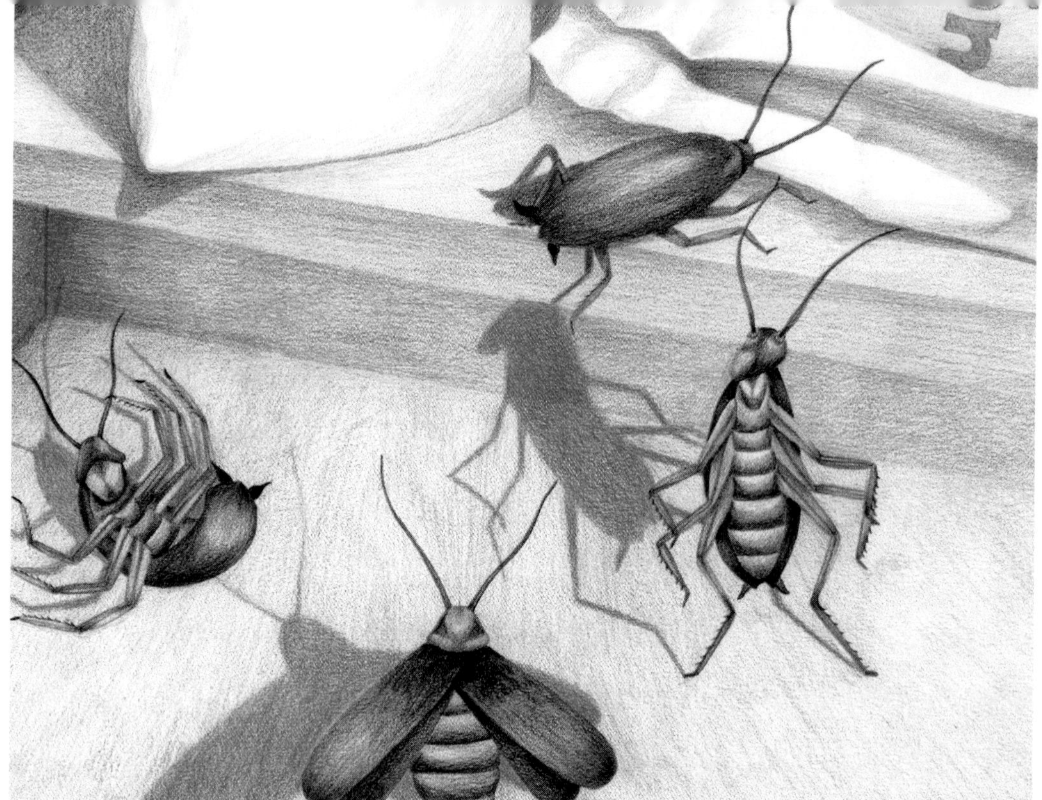

❶ *What has the poison done to the cockroaches? What does the narrator see when she awakens?*

with cockroaches as cunning as myself, I carefully spread the powder until it looked like part of the surface dust. From my bed, in the silence of the apartment, I imagined them climbing up one by one into the kitchen where darkness slept, a solitary towel alert on the clothesline. I awoke hours later, startled at having overslept. It was beginning to grow light. I walked across the kitchen. There they lay on the floor of the scullery, huge and brittle. During the night I had killed them. On our behalf, it was beginning to grow light. On a nearby hill, a cockerel[2] crowed.

The third story which now begins is called "The Statues." It begins by saying that I had been complaining about the cockroaches. Then the same woman appears on the scene. And so it goes on to the point where I awake as it is beginning to grow light, and I awake still feeling sleepy and I walk across the kitchen. Even more sleepy is the scullery floor with its tiled perspective. And in the shadows of dawn, there is a purplish hue which distances everything; at my feet, I perceive patches of light and shade, scores of rigid statues scattered everywhere. The cockroaches that have hardened from core to

2. **cockerel.** Young rooster

Words for Everyday Use

scul • ler • y (skul´ər ē) *n.,* room adjoining the kitchen

Vocabulary in Context

- We kept all our extra dry goods, such as flour, sugar, and canned or dried foods, in the scullery rather than in the kitchen itself.

shell. Some are lying upside down. Others arrested in the midst of some movement that will never be completed. In the mouths of some of the cockroaches, there are traces of white powder. I am the first to observe the dawn breaking over Pompei.[3] I know what this night has been, I know about the orgy in the dark. In some, the gypsum has hardened as slowly as in some organic process, and the cockroaches, with ever more tortuous movements, have greedily intensified the night's pleasures, trying to escape from their insides. Until they turn to stone, in innocent terror and with such, but *such* an expression of pained reproach. Others—suddenly assailed by their own core, without even having perceived that their inner form was turning to stone!—these are suddenly crystallized, just like a word arrested on someone's lips: I love . . . The cockroaches, invoking the name of love in vain, sang on a summer's night. While the cockroach over there, the one with the brown antennae smeared with white, must have realized too late that it had become mummified precisely because it did not know how to use things with the gratuitous grace of the *in vain:* "It is just that I looked too closely inside myself! It is just that I looked too closely inside . . ." From my frigid height as a human being, I watch the destruction of a world. Dawn breaks. Here and there, the parched antennae of dead cockroaches quiver in the breeze. The cockerel from the previous story crows.

The fourth story opens a new era in the household. The story begins as usual: I was complaining about the cockroaches. It goes on up to the point when I see the statues in plaster of Paris. Inevitably dead. I look toward the pipes where this same night an infestation will reappear, swarming slowly upwards in Indian file. Should I renew the lethal sugar every night? like someone who no longer sleeps without the avidity of some rite. And should I take myself somnambulant out to the terrace early each morning? in my craving to encounter the statues which my perspiring night has erected. I trembled with a depraved pleasure at the vision of my double existence as a witch. I also trembled at the sight of that hardening gypsum, the depravity of existence which would shatter my internal form.

The grim moment of choosing between two paths, which I thought would separate, convinced me that any choice would mean sacrificing either myself or my soul. I chose. And today I secretly carry a plaque of virtue in my heart: "This house has been disinfected."

The fifth story is called "Leibnitz and the Transcendence of Love in Polynesia." It begins like this: I was complaining about the cockroaches. ■

3. **Pompei.** Usually spelled Pompeii; ancient city destroyed by a sudden volcanic eruption that mummified the inhabitants in the midst of daily activity

❶ *To what does the narrator compare the cockroaches? What does the narrator imagine the cockroaches thinking and doing just before they die?*

❷ *What choice does the narrator feel she has? What choice does she end up making?*

❸ *What does the narrator say she watches from her "frigid height as a human being"?*

Words for Everyday Use

mum • mi • fy (mum´ə fī´) *vt.,* turn into a mummy

gra • tu • i • tous (grə to͞o´i təs) *adj.,* without cause or justification

in • fes • ta • tion (in´fes ta´tion) *n.,* swarm of harmful or bothersome things

a • vid • i • ty (ə vid´ə tē) *n.,* greedy desire or craving

som • nam • bu • lant (säm nam´byo͞o lant) *adj.,* sleepwalking

de • praved (dē prāv´d) *adj.,* morally bad, corrupt

Answers to Guided Reading Questions

❶ The narrator compares the solidified cockroaches to "a word arrested on someone's lips: I love. . . ." The narrator imagines them singing and invoking the name of love in vain; she imagines one cockroach blaming its mummification on looking too closely inside itself.

❷ The narrator feels she must decide whether she is going to continue to poison the insects. She decides to give up her fight against the cockroaches.

❸ The narrator watches the destruction of a world from her "frigid height as a human being."

Selection Check Test with Answers

EX: At least how many stories make up the one story that is to be told?

At least three stories make up the one story that is to be told.

1 In the first story, what advice does the narrator follow?

The narrator makes the poison recipe and kills the cockroaches.

2. What has the poison done to the cockroaches?

The poison has killed the insects by drying them up.

3. In the second story, how does the narrator begin to feel about the cockroaches?

The narrator begins to feel rage and loathing.

4. How does the narrator begin to feel about the cockroaches in the third story, when she finds them dead?

The narrator begins to feel remorse. She feels as though the cockroaches are victims.

5. What choice does the narrator face?

She must decide if she is going to continue killing the cockroaches.

Vocabulary in Context

- In certain hot, dry regions, the remains of people and animals have been found in excellent condition, mummified by their natural environment.
- A common criticism of popular films is that they contain gratuitous violence.
- Every summer, Carla's house was invaded by an infestation of black ants seeking food.
- Herman had such a sweet tooth that his avidity for desserts knew no bounds.
- Jonathan's father is somnambulant in the morning before his first cup of coffee.
- One of the charges brought against the ancient Greek philosopher Socrates was that his depraved teachings corrupted the morals of Athenian youths.

Responding to the Selection

Can you identify with the narrator's continually changing feelings about the action of ridding her apartment of cockroaches? Why, or why not? What other stories might be possible for her?

Reviewing the Selection

RECALLING / **INTERPRETING**

1. What are the basic events of the narrator's first story, "How To Kill Cockroaches"? ▶▶ In "How to Kill Cockroaches," does the narrator express any feelings toward the cockroaches, or does she simply report facts? Explain.

2. In the story "The Killing," what one wish drives the narrator as she mixes the poison? ▶▶ What feelings are introduced into the action of killing cockroaches in "The Killing"? Why does the narrator begin to have these feelings? How is this story different from the first story?

3. In "The Statues," when the narrator gets up in the morning, what does she see on her floor? What does she imagine about the cockroaches? ▶▶ What feelings does the narrator express toward the cockroaches in "The Statues"? Why does she feel this way? In what way has her perception of these creatures changed from her perception of them in "The Killing"?

4. What decision does the narrator make in the fourth story? What, from that day forward, does the narrator carry in her heart? ▶▶ What struggle surrounding the killing of cockroaches takes place within the narrator? What does the narrator believe is the result of her decision?

SYNTHESIZING

5. Why do you think the narrator introduces a fourth and a fifth story in addition to the first three? Why does she transform a simple situation into a large, complicated problem? Is the narrator truly better off for having spent so much time thinking about the cockroaches, or is she held captive by her thoughts? What might this story be saying about the human impulse to continually analyze and find meaning in every action? Explain.

RESPONDING TO THE SELECTION

You might also ask students: If you were in the narrator's position, would you turn killing the cockroaches into a moral dilemma, or would you poison them without remorse? Explain.

ANSWERS FOR REVIEWING THE SELECTION

RECALLING AND INTERPRETING

1. **Recalling.** The narrator complains of cockroaches; a woman gives her a recipe for killing them; she follows the woman's advice; and the cockroaches die. **Interpreting.** In "How to Kill Cockroaches," the narrator simply reports facts. She expresses no feeling toward the cockroaches.

2. **Recalling.** The narrator wishes to kill every cockroach in existence. **Interpreting.** The narrator begins to feel rage toward the cockroaches. She thinks of them as a secret evil that emerges as people sleep. This story is different from the first story because of the anger that is shown. The cockroaches are not simply a nuisance but evil beings whose presence the narrator takes personally.

3. **Recalling.** The narrator sees the dead cockroaches in the morning. They are frozen, like little statues. She imagines that they suffer as they die, that they are suddenly frozen like words of love on a person's lips, and that one believed he died because he looked too closely inside himself. **Interpreting.** The narrator begins to feel remorse. She no longer views the cockroaches as the aggressors but as victims.

4. **Recalling.** The narrator decides to give up her fight against the cockroaches. She carries a plaque of virtue in her heart. **Interpreting.** The narrator must decide if she is going to allow this struggle against cockroaches to take over her life. She doesn't know if she should continue to destroy them or let go of the fight. Once she decides to stop her war against the (cont.)

ANSWERS FOR REVIEWING THE SELECTION (CONT.)

insects, she feels that she has been "disinfected" of the moral struggle that was causing her anguish.

SYNTHESIZING

Responses will vary. Possible responses are given.

5. The narrator is showing how her struggle with the cockroaches could go on forever. The narrator believes that her actions against the cockroaches have large moral implications. Students will most likely say that the struggle was uncalled for, since her actions against the cockroaches will not have much of an impact on the world. Students might say that the story is using this woman's struggle as an extreme example of how humans believe their existence has more importance and impact on the world than it actually does.

Understanding Literature (Questions for Discussion)

1. **Conflict.** A **conflict** is a struggle between two forces in a literary work. A struggle between a character and some outside force is called an **external conflict**. A struggle that takes place within a character is called an **internal conflict**. What is the external conflict in "The Fifth Story"? What is the internal conflict? Which of these conflicts seems more dramatic? Explain your response.

2. **Personification. Personification** is a figure of speech in which an idea, animal, or thing is described as if it were a person. What human qualities does the narrator attribute to the cockroaches? In what way does the narrator's personification of the cockroaches affect her feelings toward them?

3. **Existentialism. Existentialism** is a twentieth-century philosophical school that assumes the essential absurdity and meaninglessness of life. Existentialists believe that any choices that a person makes in order to define himself or herself are made freely, but because there is no essential meaning, no one "right" choice is possible. Existentialists believe that despite the meaninglessness of individual choice, one is still forced to choose, and these decisions determine the fate of the individual, for better or for worse. Free will is therefore seen by the Existentialist as a terrific burden, one causing anguish to the thinking person, who longs for meaningful, not absurd, choice. In what way does "The Fifth Story" focus upon this idea of absurd choice and the mental anguish free will causes the thinking person? The title of the narrator's final story "Leibnitz and the Transcendence of Love in Polynesia" is decidedly absurd. The narrator is attempting to connect seemingly unrelated subjects such as Leibnitz, a German philosopher and mathematician; love; Polynesia; and cockroaches. In what way is this title more evidence of a thinking person's futile attempt to find meaning in an absurd world? In other words, how can this title be seen as the narrator's attempt to create meaning where there is none? Do you agree with existential beliefs about life? Why, or why not?

Responding in Writing

1. **Creative Writing: Three Stories in One.** In "The Fifth Story," Lispector creates from one situation—ridding her apartment of cockroaches—a number of different stories. She manages to do this by changing her attitude in each story from indifferent, to angry, to remorseful. Try to imitate this technique by choosing a simple situation, such as exchanging an item at the store, painting a mailbox, or dusting furniture. Then describe this situation in three different ways, with three distinct attitudes. First, describe the situation using the nonemotional language of a factual news report. Then, use your imagination to decide what conflicts and emotions could possibly arise in the situation. Do you start to feel remorseful about abandoning an item at the store? Do you feel excitement with each stroke of the paint brush, as if you are improving your life? Do you start to feel hatred toward dust? Don't worry about sounding absurd. Try to have fun with your descriptions.

ANSWERS FOR UNDERSTANDING LITERATURE

Responses will vary. Possible responses are given.

1. Conflict. The external conflict in "The Fifth Story" is the struggle between the narrator and the cockroaches. The internal conflict in "The Fifth Story" is the struggle that takes place in the mind of the narrator. The internal conflict might seem more dramatic since the narrator turns what might be a simple problem into a large moral struggle.

2. Personification. The narrator attributes to the cockroaches "innocent terror," reproach, the ability to invoke the name of love, and the ability to examine their own thoughts and feelings. Once she sees the cockroaches as possessing human qualities she begins to feel remorse for them.

3. Existentialism. The narrator turns the extermination of pesky insects into a critical dilemma. She is searching for meaning in something about which some people would not think twice. Cockroaches have been around for millions of years despite the fact that people are continually trying to purge them from their homes. Her actions, poisoning cockroaches, simply do not have the larger implications that she believes they have. The title of her final story is another example of trying to find meaning in something that does not necessarily have meaning. The connection between the philosopher and mathematician Leibnitz, love, and Polynesia, is not apparent. The narrator might be again trying to focus on something that she believes, falsely, to have large moral implications. *Responses will vary.*

ANALYTIC SCALES FOR RESPONDING IN WRITING

Assign a score from 1 to 25 for each grading criterion below. (For more detailed evaluation, see the evaluation forms for writing, revising, and proofreading, Assessment Portfolio 4.1–4.9.)

1. Three Stories in One

- **Content/Unity.** The writing describes the same situation with three distinct attitudes.
- **Organization/Coherence.** Each of the three descriptions presents details in a logical order.
- **Language/Style.** The three descriptions use vivid and precise nouns, verbs, and modifiers.
- **Conventions.** The three descriptions avoid errors in spelling, grammar, usage, mechanics, and manuscript form.

► Additional practice is provided in the Essential Skills Practice Book: Writing 1.8.

2. Critical Essay

- **Content/Unity.** The essay describes the different stages of the narrator's metamorphosis.
- **Organization/Coherence.** The essay begins with an introduction that includes the thesis of the essay. The introduction is followed by supporting paragraphs with clear transitions. The essay ends with a solid conclusion.
- **Language/Style.** The essay uses vivid and precise nouns, verbs, and modifiers.
- **Conventions.** The essay avoids errors in spelling, grammar, usage, mechanics, and manuscript form.

► Additional practice is provided in the Essential Skills Practice Book: Writing 1.20.

2. **Critical Essay: The Language of Transformation.** In this piece, the narrator appears to be transformed by her experience with the cockroaches. Write a short essay in which you describe the different stages of the narrator's metamorphosis. What is her initial attitude toward the cockroaches? How does this attitude change? What words and phrases show this change in her attitude? Support your thesis with examples from the story.

Thinking Skills

Problem Solving and Decision Making. In "The Fifth Story," the narrator has a problem that she must solve, and she has trouble deciding how to deal with this problem. Review the Language Arts Survey 4.1, "Problem Solving and Decision Making." Then try to solve the narrator's problem using the various problem-solving frameworks and strategies outlined there. Use your imagination and have fun trying to think of creative ways to control the insect population in the narrator's apartment. Maybe you will use poison or traps, or maybe you will simply devise a way for humans and cockroaches to live peacefully with one another. Remember, however, that many poisons contaminate food and air, that traps only affect a small proportion of the geometrically expanding insect population, and that the narrator may be unwilling or unable to simply abandon her insect-filled apartment for a new one. Use any two of the following strategies:

A. Create a general problem-solving framework using the following four steps: understand the problem, devise a course of action, take the action, evaluate the results.

B. Represent the situation by drawing a diagram or picture or by constructing a model. Your diagram or picture might show where in the apartment the cockroaches are, from where they seem to be coming, where you must place your poison or trap, or where you will establish a place for the cockroaches to live.

C. Write a means-ends analysis. Compare what you know now about the current situation with the situation that will exist when the problem is solved.

D. Divide and conquer. Divide the problem into parts, and then solve each part.

E. Work backward. Decide what the ideal situation would be, and then decide what you might do to create that ideal situation.

ANSWERS FOR SKILLS ACTIVITIES

THINKING SKILLS

Students' solutions and strategies will vary widely. Make sure that they follow the conditions outlined—that they don't involve poisons that contaminate food or air, that they don't involve traps to eliminate a small percentage of the population, and that the plan doesn't involve the narrator abandoning her apartment for a new one.

► Additional practice is provided in the Essential Skills Practice Book: Study and Research 4.1.

PREREADING

"The Youngest Doll"
by Rosario Ferré, translated by Diana Vélez

About the Author

ROSARIO FERRÉ
1942–

Rosario Ferré was born in Ponce, Puerto Rico. Her father was politically active and served as governor of Puerto Rico from 1968 to 1972. Throughout most of Ferré's early life, her mother mourned the untimely death of her brother, Rosario's uncle. To escape from this atmosphere of sadness, Ferré began reading fairly tales voraciously. About reading Ferré says, "[it] helped reconcile me with my own destiny." Reading led her to forgive both herself and her mother, and sparked her interest in writing. In school, she studied English, French, Spanish, and Latin American literature, earning a bachelor's degree from Manhattanville College, a master's degree from the University of Puerto Rico, and a doctoral degree from the University of Maryland. In addition to writing short stories, poetry, a novel, and feminist reinterpretations of myths, Ferré has also founded and edited a literary magazine and written a newspaper column. Like other Latin American writers, Ferré uses magical realism to play with notions of what is real and what is fantasy. She approaches writing with a feminist interpretation of reality and fantasy, and she distinguishes herself from other recent Latin American magical realist writers, saying she would like to be thought of as an "independent writer" and a "chronicler" of Puerto Rico.

About the Selection

"**The Youngest Doll,**" written in 1970, was Ferré's first published story. Since then, the story has appeared in a collection of Ferré's poetry and short stories, *Pandora's Papers* (1976), and in an English collection, *The Youngest Doll and Other Stories* (1990). The story is set in Puerto Rico at the beginning of the twentieth century—a time when the aristocratic way of life enjoyed by a few powerful families who controlled plantations was declining, and a new class of wealthy businessmen was rising. Like many of Ferré's stories, "The Youngest Doll" reveals the author's disdain for the bourgeois class in Puerto Rico. Ferré exposes the hypocrisy of the middle-class, which sought to display its new-found wealth, was indifferent to the poverty and sufferings of others, and harbored prejudices of class, race, and sex. Ferré frequently uses dolls in her writing as a symbol of the way in which the bourgeois class thwarts girls' potential and limits them to a subordinate position as "doll-women" later in life. In this nightmarish story, Ferré depicts members of the new bourgeoisie feeding upon the former wealth and prestige of Puerto Rico's "aristocrats."

CONNECTIONS: History of the Plantation Economy in Puerto Rico

During the nineteenth century Puerto Rico, then a Spanish colony, developed a plantation economy based on sugar cane, tobacco, and coffee. In such an economy, a few families grow wealthy from cash crops by exploiting the labor of many impoverished workers. Puerto Rico was ceded to the United States in 1898, after the Spanish-American War. Its economy remained largely unchanged until foreign investors developed manufacturing industries on the island, beginning in the 1940s. A new class of industrialists and professionals gained wealth as more and more workers left plantation life and flocked to the cities.

GOALS/OBJECTIVES

Studying this lesson will enable students to

- enjoy a magical realist short story
- briefly explain the economic and social situation in Puerto Rico at the turn of the twentieth century
- identify symbols and what they represent in works that they read
- define *doppelgänger* and identify this type of character in literary works
- write a personal essay with vivid imagery
- write a critical essay analyzing mood
- retell a myth or fairy tale

ADDITIONAL RESOURCES

READER'S GUIDE

- Selection Worksheet 6.6

ASSESSMENT PORTFOLIO

- Selection Check Test 2.6.11
- Selection Test 2.6.12

ESSENTIAL SKILLS PRACTICE BOOKS

- Writing 1.8, 1.20
- Applied English/Tech Prep 5.5

PREREADING EXTENSIONS

Asked about the relationship between the reality of her native Puerto Rico and the fantasy world she creates in her writing, Ferré said, "Puerto Rico, like all the countries of the Caribbean is a nation where fantastic reality, the world of magic, is ever present. . . . It is a reality that is very palpable in our environment, and this is why there are no great differences between fantasy and reality." Encourage students to work in small groups to explore the "magic" of the Caribbean. Some groups may research the history of different islands, the art forms created there, Caribbean religions such as *Santería*, or local celebrations such as Carnival. Then hold a "Magic of the Caribbean Day," in which groups give presentations on their findings.

SUPPORT FOR LEP STUDENTS

PRONUNCIATIONS OF PROPER NOUNS AND ADJECTIVES

Ro • sa • ri • o Fer • ré (rō sä´ rē ō fer ā´)

ADDITIONAL VOCABULARY

exuberant—full of life; characterized by good health and high spirits
nimbly—moving quickly and lightly
ulcer—open sore
vanity—excessive pride, self-conceit

READER'S JOURNAL

As an alternative activity, you might ask students to write about what they think an ideal relationship between husband and wife entails in this day and age. Then ask them to write about what they imagine many marriages were like in the past. In what way does this image compare with their ideal?

ANSWERS TO GUIDED READING QUESTIONS

❶ The aunt no longer felt beautiful, so she refused to see suitors and devoted herself to her sister's children.

❷ A prawn has bitten the aunt and worked its way into her leg to live.

❸ The family has lost nearly all its money. Their former wealth is described as breaking apart like the crumbling dining-room chandelier.

SPELLING AND VOCABULARY WORDS FROM THE SELECTION

exorbitant	ostentatious
furtively	reverberation
impassive	squeamishly
nestle	

LITERARY TECHNIQUE

MOOD

Mood, or **atmosphere,** is the emotion created in the reader by part or all of a literary work. Ask students to identify the dominant mood in the first paragraph of this short story. At what point in the paragraph does the mood change?

ANSWERS

The mood is peaceful and dreamlike. It changes once the aunt is bitten by the prawn.

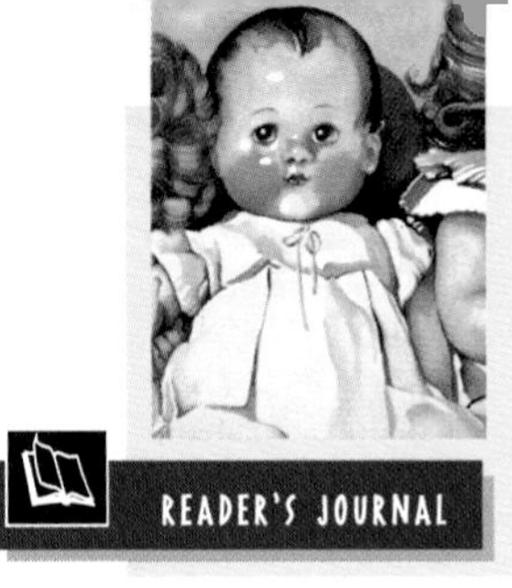

READER'S JOURNAL

Have you ever been in a situation in which you were judged, not on your personal characteristics or on any quality you could control, but on circumstances beyond your influence, such as your heritage, sex, or family background? What happened? What did it feel like to be unable to control the way in which you were perceived? In what way did this situation affect your behavior during that particular moment?

"The Youngest Doll"

ROSARIO FERRÉ, TRANSLATED BY DIANA VÉLEZ

Early in the morning the maiden aunt took her rocking chair out onto the porch facing the cane fields, as she always did whenever she woke up with the urge to make a doll. As a young woman, she had often bathed in the river, but one day when the heavy rains had fed the dragontail current, she had a soft feeling of melting snow in the marrow of her bones. With her head nestled among the black rocks' reverberations, she could hear the slamming of salty foam on the beach rolled up with the sound of waves, and she suddenly thought that her hair had poured out to sea at last. At that very moment, she felt a sharp bite in her calf. Screaming, she was pulled out of the water and, writhing in pain, was taken home on a stretcher.

❶ *In what way did the incident with the prawn change the aunt's life?*

❷ *What has happened to the aunt?*

❸ *What is the financial situation of this family? To what is their wealthy past compared?*

The doctor who examined her assured her it was nothing, that she had probably been bitten by an angry river prawn.[1] But days passed and the scab wouldn't heal. A month later the doctor concluded that the prawn had worked its way into the soft flesh of her calf and had nestled there to grow. He prescribed a mustard plaster so that the heat would force it out. The aunt spent a whole week with her leg covered with mustard from thigh to ankle, but when the treatment was over, they found that the ulcer had grown even larger and that it was covered with a slimy, stonelike substance that couldn't be removed without endangering the whole leg. She then resigned herself to living with the prawn permanently curled up in her calf.

She had been very beautiful, but the prawn hidden under the long, gauzy folds of her skirt stripped her of all vanity. She locked herself up in her house, refusing to see any suitors. At first she devoted herself entirely to bringing up her sister's children, dragging her enormous leg around the house quite nimbly. In those days, the family was nearly ruined; they lived surrounded by a past that was breaking up around them with the same impassive musicality with which the dining

1. **prawn.** Large shrimp, or a creature that lives in water and has a hard outer shell, many legs for swimming, and antennae

WORDS FOR EVERYDAY USE

nes • tle (nes´əl) *vi.,* settle down comfortably and snugly

re • ver • be • ra • tion (ri vʉr´bə rā´shən) *n.,* echo and re-echo; multiple reflections of sound waves

im • pas • sive (im pas´iv) *adj.,* not feeling or showing emotion; placid; calm

VOCABULARY IN CONTEXT

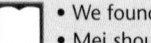

- We found the missing kitten nestled comfortably in a basket of laundry just taken from the dryer.
- Mei shouted in the canyon and heard her voice's reverberation off the canyon walls.
- Byet was expecting bad news, so when it arrived, her face remained impassive.

room chandelier crumbled on the frayed linen cloth of the dining room table. Her nieces adored her. She would comb their hair, bathe and feed them, and when she read them stories, they would sit around her and furtively lift the starched ruffle of her skirt so as to sniff the aroma of ripe sweetsop[2] that oozed from her leg when it was at rest.

As the girls grew up, the aunt devoted herself to making dolls for them to play with. At first they were just plain dolls, with cotton stuffing from the gourd tree and stray buttons sewn on for eyes. As time passed, though, she began to refine her craft, gaining the respect and admiration of the whole family. The birth of a doll was always cause for a ritual celebration, which explains why it never occurred to the aunt to sell them for profit, even when the girls had grown up and the family was beginning to fall into need. The aunt had continued to increase the size of the dolls so that their height and other measurements conformed to those of each of the girls. There were nine of them, and the aunt made one doll for each per year, so it became necessary to set aside a room for the dolls alone. When the eldest turned eighteen, there were one hundred and twenty-six dolls of all ages in the room. Opening the door gave the impression of entering a dovecote[3] or the ballroom in the Czarina's[4] palace or a warehouse in which someone had spread out a row of tobacco leaves to dry. But the aunt did not enter the room for any of these pleasures. Instead, she would unlatch the door and gently pick up each doll, murmuring a lullaby as she rocked it: "This is how you were when you were a year old, this is you at two, and like this at three," measuring out each year of their lives against the hollow they left in her arms.

The day the eldest had turned ten, the aunt sat down in her rocking chair facing the cane fields and never got up again. She would rock away entire days on the porch, watching the patterns of rain shift in the cane fields, coming out of her stupor only when the doctor paid a visit or whenever she awoke with the desire to make a doll. Then she would call out so that everyone in the house would come and help her. On that day, one could see the hired help making repeated trips to town like cheerful Inca messengers, bringing wax, porcelain clay, lace, needles, spools of thread of every color. While these preparations were taking place, the aunt would call the niece she had dreamt about the night before into her room and take her measurements. Then she would make a wax mask of the child's face, covering it with plaster on both sides, like a living face wrapped in two dead ones. She would draw out an endless flaxen thread of melted wax through a pinpoint on its chin. The porcelain of the hands and face was always translucent; it had an ivory tint to it that formed a great contrast with the curdled whiteness of the bisque faces. For the body, the aunt would send out to the garden for twenty glossy gourds. She would hold them in one hand, and with an expert twist of her knife, would slice them up against the railing of the balcony, so that the sun and breeze would dry out the cottony *guano* brains. After a few days, she would scrape off the dried fluff with a teaspoon and, with infinite patience, feed it into the doll's mouth.

The only items the aunt would agree to use that were not made by her were the glass

2. **sweetsop.** Green, fast-ripening, tropical fruit with sweet pulp and black seeds

3. **dovecote.** Small house or box with compartments for nesting pigeons

4. **Czarina's.** Referring to the wife of a czar, or emperor of Russia

❶ *What does the aunt spend all day doing? When are the only times she will wake from her stupor?*

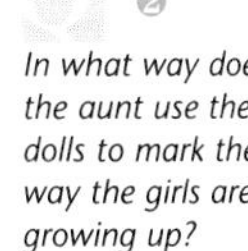

❷ *In what way does the aunt use the dolls to mark the way the girls are growing up?*

Words for Everyday Use

fur • tive • ly (fur´tiv lē) *adv.,* in a sneaky or stealthy manner

Answers to Guided Reading Questions

❶ The aunt spends all day rocking in her chair on the porch. She will only wake from her stupor to see the doctor or to make another doll.

❷ The aunt makes one doll for each girl every year, making the doll to the girl's exact measurements.

INTEGRATED SKILLS ACTIVITIES

APPLIED ENGLISH/TECH PREP SKILLS

Inform students that on this page, the author describes the materials the aunt uses to create the dolls as well as how she creates them. Then give students the following assignment: Think of one of your hobbies or something you know how to do. Then write a set of instructions explaining how to do this thing. For example, you may wish to explain how to make a favorite recipe, how to build a birdhouse, how to play a computer game, or how to use a certain Web browser. Refer to the Language Arts Survey 5.5, "Technical Writing," for help in documenting your chosen procedure.

▶ Additional practice is provided in the Essential Skills Practice Book: Writing 5.5.

Additional Questions and Activities

Encourage students to discuss whether the aunt treats the dolls as objects or as if they were the daughters themselves. You may wish to draw their attention to the aunt rocking and singing lullabies to the dolls and to the way she stuffs each doll by feeding a cottony substance through its mouth with a teaspoon.

Vocabulary in Context

• The thief crept furtively down the dark alleyway.

ART NOTE

Marianne Ashurst (1945–) is an American artist whose work is an example of Realism, a movement that seeks to render in art an accurate portrayal of reality. ***Baby Dolls*** is a watercolor. Encourage students to discuss whether this image matches their own mental picture of the dolls in the story. Some students may enjoy using watercolors or another medium to create their own depictions, either realistic or fantastic, of the dolls in Ferré's story.

ANSWERS TO GUIDED READING QUESTIONS

1. The aunt puts the dolls' glass eyes in the stream so that they will "learn to recognize the slightest stirrings of the prawns' antennae."

2. The aunt gives the daughter her last doll. She tells the groom that the doll is a sentimental, old-fashioned ornament.

CULTURAL/HISTORICAL NOTE

Dolls are perhaps the oldest toy in human history. Egyptian and Babylonian dolls created between 3000 and 2000 BC have been discovered. Inform students that while they may think of dolls as just one of the toys they have outgrown long ago, not all cultures viewed dolls as playthings. Some, including the Aztecs, Egyptians, Greeks, and Romans, may have found religious significance in the dolls and buried them in graves with the dead. The Japanese hold doll festivals for both boys and girls. In Syria, a doll hung in the window means that a girl in the household is of marriageable age.

Baby Dolls. *Marianne Ashurst*

1 *Why does the aunt put the dolls' glass eyes in the stream?*

2 *What does the aunt do when one of the daughters gets married? What does she tell the groom?*

eyeballs. They were mailed to her from Europe in all colors, but the aunt considered them useless until she had left them submerged at the bottom of the stream for a few days, so that they could learn to recognize the slightest stirring of the prawns' antennae. Only then would she carefully rinse them in ammonia water and place them, glossy as gems and nestled in a bed of cotton, at the bottom of one of her Dutch cookie tins. The dolls were always dressed in the same way, even though the girls were growing up. She would dress the younger ones in Swiss embroidery and the older ones in silk *guipure*[5] and on each of their heads she would tie the same bow, wide and white and trembling like the breast of a dove.

The girls began to marry and leave home. On their wedding day, the aunt would give each of them their last doll, kissing them on the forehead and telling them with a smile, "Here is your Easter Sunday." She would reassure the grooms by explaining to them that the doll was merely a sentimental ornament, of the kind that people used to place on the lid of grand pianos in the old days. From the porch, the aunt would watch the girls walk down the staircase for the last time. They would carry a modest checkered cardboard suitcase in one hand, the other hand slipped around the waist of the exuberant doll made in their image and likeness, still wearing the same old-fashioned kid slippers and gloves, and with Valenciennes[6] bloomers barely showing under their snowy, embroidered skirts. But the hands and faces of these new dolls looked less transparent than those

5. ***guipure.*** Type of lace
6. **Valenciennes.** Type of lace with a floral pattern on a diamond-shaped mesh

of the old: they had the consistency of skim milk. This difference concealed a more subtle one: the wedding doll was never stuffed with cotton but filled with honey.

All the older girls had married and only the youngest was left at home when the doctor paid his monthly visit to the aunt, bringing along his son, who had just returned from studying medicine up north. The young man lifted the starched ruffle of the aunt's skirt and looked intently at the huge, swollen ulcer which oozed from the tip of its greenish scales. He pulled out his stethoscope and listened to her carefully. The aunt thought he was listening for the breathing of the prawn to see if it was still alive, and she fondly lifted his hand and placed it on the spot where he could feel the constant movement of the creature's antennae. The young man released the ruffle and looked fixedly at his father. "You could have cured this from the start," he told him. "That's true," his father answered, "but I just wanted you to come and see the prawn that has been paying for your education these twenty years."

From then on it was the young doctor who visited the old aunt every month. His interest in the youngest was evident from the start, so the aunt was able to begin her last doll in plenty of time. He would always show up wearing a pair of brightly polished shoes, a starched collar, and an ostentatious tiepin of extravagantly poor taste. After examining the aunt, he would sit in the parlor, lean his paper silhouette against the oval frame of the chair and, each time, hand the youngest an identical bouquet of purple forget-me-nots. She would offer him ginger cookies, taking the bouquet squeamishly with the tips of her fingers, as if she were handling a sea urchin turned inside out. She made up her mind to marry him because she was intrigued by his sleepy profile and also because she was deathly curious to see what the dolphin flesh was like.

On her wedding day, as she was about to leave the house, the youngest was surprised to find that the doll her aunt had given her as a wedding present was warm. As she slipped her arm around its waist, she looked at it curiously, but she quickly forgot about it, so amazed was she at the excellence of its craft. The doll's face and hands were made of the most delicate Mikado porcelain. In the doll's half-open and slightly sad smile she recognized her full set of baby teeth. There was also another notable detail: the aunt had embedded her diamond eardrops inside the doll's pupils.

The young doctor took her off to live in town, in a square house that made one think of a cement block. Each day he made her sit out on the balcony, so that passersby would be sure to see that he had married into high society. Motionless inside her cubicle of heat, the youngest began to suspect that it wasn't only her husband's silhouette that was made of paper, but his soul as well. Her suspicions were soon confirmed. One day, he pried out the doll's eyes with the tip of his scalpel and pawned them for a fancy gold pocket watch with a long embossed chain. From then on the doll remained seated on the lid of the grand piano, but with her gaze modestly lowered.

A few months later, the doctor noticed the doll was missing from her usual place and asked the youngest what she'd done with it. A sisterhood of pious ladies had offered him a healthy sum for the porcelain hands and face, which they thought would be perfect for the image of the Veronica in the next Lenten procession.[7]

7. **the Veronica . . . procession.** The Veronica is the image of Jesus' face that appeared on the handkerchief or veil Saint Veronica used to wipe Jesus' bleeding face; the Lenten procession is a ritual occurring during Lent, a period of penitence and fasting that Christians observe between Ash Wednesday and Easter.

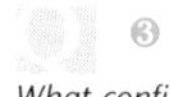

❶ *How does the young doctor treat his wife? What does she begin to suspect?*

❷ *What does the doctor's son realize about the prawn in the aunt's leg? What explanation does the doctor provide for his actions?*

❸ *What confirms the youngest daughter's suspicions?*

❹ *Why does the doctor want to know where the doll is?*

WORDS FOR EVERYDAY USE

os • ten • ta • tious (äs´tən tā´shəs) *adj.,* pretentious; showy

squeam • ish • ly (skwēm´ish lē) *adv.,* in a prudish, excessively fastidious, oversensitive, or dainty manner

Answers to Guided Reading Questions

❶ The young doctor makes his wife sit on the balcony so that passers-by will know that he has married into "high society." She begins to suspect that her husband's soul is made of paper, just like a silhouette.

❷ The doctor's son realizes that the doctor could have cured the aunt from the start. The doctor explains that he didn't cure the aunt but merely "treated" her periodically to get the money to pay for his son's education.

❸ The youngest daughter's suspicions are confirmed when her husband pries the diamonds from the doll's eyes to pawn them for a fancy pocket watch.

❹ The doctor wants to know where the doll is so that he can sell its porcelain hands and face.

Literary Technique

CHARACTERIZATION

Characterization is the use of literary techniques to create a character. Writers use three major techniques to create characters: direct description, in which a speaker, a narrator, or another character simply comments on the character; portrayal of character's behavior, in which the writer presents the actions or speech of a character, allowing the reader to draw his or her own conclusions; and representations of character's internal states, in which the writer reveals directly the character's private thoughts and emotions. Ask students which methods Ferré uses to create the character of the young doctor. What method does she avoid, and why? In what way would students describe this character?

ANSWERS

Ferré uses direct description and portrayal of behavior but not representation of internal states. She may avoid exploring the young doctor's internal state to create suspense or to let the reader discover what the doctor is really like on his or her own. *Responses will vary.*

Vocabulary in Context

- The pious parish priest lived a simple life and disapproved of the extravagant and ostentatious lifestyle that some of the landed gentry lived.
- When the scientist handed Rick a test tube containing a mysterious green ooze, Rick handled it squeamishly.

Answers to Guided Reading Questions

❶ Visitors note a strange scent like "oozing sweetsop." They feel an urge to rub their hands together as though they were paws.

❷ The youngest daughter now sits motionless in her rocking chair on the balcony with lowered eyelids. Her presence as a "genuine member of the extinct sugar aristocracy" has made her husband into a millionaire.

❸ The youngest daughter is now called "the doll." The antennae of prawns come from her eyes. The youngest daughter has been transformed into an eyeless doll full of prawns.

Selection Check Test with Answers

EX. What does the aunt have an urge to do one day?

She has an urge to bathe in a stream.

1. What happens to the aunt there?

A prawn bites her leg and works its way into her flesh.

2. What does the aunt make for her nieces each year?

She makes them each a doll.

3. To whom does the doctor show the aunt's leg?

He shows it to his son.

4. Whom does the youngest daughter marry?

She marries the doctor's son who is himself a doctor.

5. What does the younger doctor observe when he sees his wife sleeping?

He sees her eyelids open and prawns' antennae coming from her eyes.

❶ *What do visitors notice about the youngest daughter? What do the visitors feel an urge to do?*

❷ *What does the youngest daughter now do? What effect has her presence had on her husband's business?*

❸ *What word is used to describe the youngest daughter? What comes from her eyes? Into what has the youngest daughter been transformed?*

The youngest answered that the ants had at last discovered the doll was filled with honey and, streaming over the piano, had devoured it in a single night. "Since its hands and face were of Mikado porcelain," she said, "they must have thought they were made of sugar and at this very moment they are most likely wearing down their teeth, gnawing furiously at its fingers and eyelids in some underground burrow." That night the doctor dug up all the ground around the house, to no avail.

As the years passed, the doctor became a millionaire. He had slowly acquired the whole town as his clientele, people who didn't mind paying exorbitant fees in order to see a genuine member of the extinct sugar cane aristocracy up close. The youngest went on sitting in her rocking chair on the balcony, motionless in her muslin[8] and lace, and always with lowered eyelids. Whenever her husband's patients, draped with necklaces and feathers and carrying elaborate canes, would seat themselves beside her, shaking their self-satisfied rolls of flesh with a jingling of coins, they would notice a strange scent that would involuntarily remind them of a slowly oozing sweetsop. They would then feel an uncomfortable urge to rub their hands together as though they were paws.

There was only one thing missing from the doctor's otherwise perfect happiness. He noticed that although he was aging, the youngest still kept that same firm, porcelained skin she had had when he would call on her at the big house on the plantation. One night he decided to go into her bedroom to watch her as she slept. He noticed that her chest wasn't moving. He gently placed his stethoscope over her heart and heard a distant swish of water. Then the doll lifted her eyelids, and out of the empty sockets of her eyes came the frenzied antennae of all those prawns. ■

8. **muslin.** Strong, sheer cotton cloth of plain weave

Words for Everyday Use

ex • or • bi • tant (eg zor´bi tənt) *adj.,* going beyond what is reasonable, just, proper, or usual

Vocabulary in Context

• The owners of my favorite writer's childhood home charged such an exorbitant fee to tour the place that I could not afford to make a visit.

Responding to the Selection

What is your reaction to this story? What images from this story particularly surprised or shocked you? If you were asked to review this story for a classmate, what would you say?

Reviewing the Selection

RECALLING / **INTERPRETING**

1. What event alters the aunt's life? To what does she devote herself after this accident? Describe the financial situation of this family. ▸▸ Why is the aunt's accident particularly gruesome? Explain how the aunt's life would have been different after the accident if she had been a laborer on the plantation rather than one of the plantation's former "aristocrats." In what way is the aunt's condition similar to the family's situation?

2. What does the aunt spend most of her time doing? When does she wake from her stupor? What does she do to the dolls' eyes and faces? What does she give each of the daughters when they get married? ▸▸ Why do you think the aunt makes the dolls? Why do you think the aunt does this unusual thing to the dolls' eyes? Why do you think the aunt has to reassure the grooms that the doll is just a "sentimental ornament"?

3. What does the old doctor's son note when he examines the aunt's leg? ▸▸ Why didn't the old doctor do anything about this situation? In what way are the old doctor and the young doctor like the prawn?

4. What does the youngest daughter begin to suspect soon after she marries the young doctor? What does he do to confirm her suspicions? What does the youngest daughter spend all her time doing toward the end of the story? What does the young doctor find at the end of the story? ▸▸ In what way is the young doctor's treatment of the doll similar to the way he treats his wife? In what way has the youngest daughter become like her aunt? Explain what has happened to the youngest daughter at the end of this story.

RESPONDING TO THE SELECTION

As an alternate activity, students might work in pairs to role play a discussion between the youngest daughter and her husband in which they try to work out their differences.

ANSWERS FOR REVIEWING THE SELECTION

RECALLING AND INTERPRETING

1. **Recalling.** The aunt is bitten in the leg by a prawn which works its way into her leg to live in her flesh. The aunt devotes herself to her sister's children. The family was once considered the aristocracy of a sugar cane plantation, but the family is now ruined financially. **Interpreting.** The aunt's accident is particularly gruesome because the prawn is still living, embedded in her flesh, oozing "the aroma of ripe sweetsop." The aunt probably wouldn't have had the luxury of simply doting on her sister's children and rocking on the porch, but would probably have had to work to support herself regardless of her injury. The aunt's leg is slowly festering, just as the family's fortune and social position is slowly rotting away. The prawn is feeding upon the aunt, just as the family fed off the labor of the plantation workers.

2. **Recalling.** The aunt spends most of her time rocking on the porch. She only wakes from her stupor to see the doctor or to make a doll. She makes the dolls' faces from a porcelain mask of each daughter's face. She puts the dolls' eyes in the stream. She gives each daughter her last doll. **Interpreting.** The aunt probably wants to make exact duplicates of the girls so she can remember them at all the stages in their lives; she may also hope that, while she cannot always look after the girls, she will be able to continue to look after the dolls. The aunt might want to make (cont.)

ANSWERS FOR REVIEWING THE SELECTION (CONT.)

the dolls and the girls they represent more wary of prawns than she was. The dolls are probably a little uncanny in appearance and might alarm the grooms.

3. **Recalling.** The old doctor's son notes that his father could have cured the aunt's wound from the start. **Interpreting.** The old doctor didn't cure the aunt so he could collect money for regular visits and put his son through college and medical school. The old doctor and the young doctor have been feeding off the aunt, draining away her former wealth, just as the prawn is feeding off the aunt's flesh.

4. **Recalling.** The youngest daughter begins to suspect that her husband's soul is made of paper, or that he is a shallow person of insubstantial character. He pries the doll's diamond eyes (cont.)

Answers for Reviewing the Selection (cont.)

from its head to pawn them for a fancy pocket watch and tries to sell the doll's porcelain hands and face. The youngest daughter spends all her time sitting motionless in her rocking chair on the balcony, eyelids lowered. The doctor goes into his wife's room to watch her sleep, and then "the doll" lifts her eyelids to reveal the antennae of prawn. **Interpreting.** The young doctor uses his wife's social prominence to earn admiration and money just as he uses the eyes of the doll (and plans to use its hands and face) to get money. The youngest daughter spends all her time in a rocking chair, just as her aunt did before her. Some students may say that the youngest daughter has been transformed into the doll because her husband treats her like a mere ornament. Others may suggest that the wife may have escaped her husband, leaving the doll in her place, which the husband fails to notice until the story's end.

SYNTHESIZING

Responses will vary. Possible responses are given.

5. Students may say that the author is suggesting that this male-dominated society stifles women's potential, limiting them to doll-like ornamental roles within a household. The husband views the youngest daughter more as a sentimental ornament of a bygone time than as a person. Students may say that the author does not name her characters to reinforce the idea that the daughters are ornaments, not known except in a superficial way. They may also note that not naming the daughters or the dolls makes them more interchangeable, less like individuals with distinct personalities.

SYNTHESIZING

5. In what way does the author use the dolls in this story to comment upon the role of women in the society she is describing? When formulating your response, think about the similarity of the dolls to the daughters and about the aunt's description of the dolls as "sentimental ornaments." Why can the youngest daughter also be described as a "sentimental ornament"? What do you think is significant about the fact that none of the characters in this story are given personal names?

Understanding Literature (Questions for Discussion)

1. **Symbol.** A **symbol** is a thing that stands for or represents both itself and something else. What might the prawns symbolize? What other symbols do you recognize in this story and what do these symbols represent?

2. **Character.** A **character** is a person (or sometimes an animal) who figures in the action of a literary work. Many writers have used the device of the doppelgänger, creating a double for a character. In legend, a doppelgänger is a ghostly double, or exact replica, of an individual. In traditional tales, one who met his or her double would soon die. In literature, doppelgängers serve to point out similarities between characters or to emphasize certain characteristics or personality traits. In "The Youngest Doll," dolls serve as doppelgängers, or doubles, for the daughters. This is especially true of the youngest daughter and her wedding doll. Explain what other characters in this story have doubles. Why can these groups of characters be considered doubles?

Responding in Writing

1. **Creative Writing: Personal Essay.** The youngest daughter in the story you have just read is viewed as an object by those around her—so much so that, at the story's end, she is seemingly transformed into a doll full of prawns. Write a personal essay, from one to two pages long, about a time in your life when a situation you were in was so difficult that it left you feeling a little less than human. Describe your situation and then describe the object or animal you felt like in the situation. Ferré's transformation scene is particularly vivid because she includes such powerful, memorable imagery as the smell of "slowly oozing sweetsop" and the "frenzied antennae" of the prawns. Include vivid imagery in your personal essay, particularly when you describe your emotional transformation. For example, you might remember a time when you were grounded and unable to attend an event important to you. You might describe this situation and then write something like, "Trapped, pacing the walls of my cell, I became a hamster locked in a metal cage." You might include vivid imagery such as in the following:

Answers for Understanding Literature

Responses will vary. Possible responses are given.

1. **Symbol.** The prawns may symbolize the way the sugar cane aristocracy preyed upon laborers as well as the way the new middle class professionals were preying on others for status and for financial gain. They may also symbolize corruption or stagnation.

2. **Character.** The aunt and the youngest daughter can be considered doubles because they both end up sitting motionless in rocking chairs because of parasites preying upon them. The father and son—the elder and the younger doctor—can also be considered doubles because they both use women to gain a material advantage in the world.

"Yearning to breathe free, I gnawed and rattled at the grimy bars of my cage, using my little, yellow rodent teeth." If you are having trouble choosing an experience to write about, refer to the writing you did in the Reader's Journal activity.

2. **Critical Essay: Analyzing Mood.** Mood, or atmosphere, is the emotion created in the reader by part or all of a literary work. Write a brief critical essay identifying the mood of this story, and then interpret the techniques the author used to create this particular mood. In your thesis, definitively state the mood of the story and the major ways in which this mood was created. In the body of your essay, refer to specific passages to support and expand on your thesis. Come to a conclusion in a final paragraph.

Project

Retelling Myths or Fairy Tales. Rosario Ferré has made a significant contribution to literature by retelling myths in her own way. Working in small groups, choose a fairy tale or myth with which you are familiar and retell it, changing certain characters, settings, or events to reflect your own personal interests and ideas. For example, you and a friend might wish to retell "The Little Mermaid" so that the mermaid regains her speech in time to tell the prince exactly what she thinks of him for marrying that silly princess whom he mistakenly believed saved his life. You might wish to retell Utnapishtim's flood story (see page 508) in such a way that Utnapishtim outsmarts the gods by wringing up all the flood water with a special mop he saw advertised on late-night television. You and your group might put your retelling on paper, illustrate a series of panels depicting your tale, or enact it in a skit. Regardless of format, each group should present its retelling to the class.

ANALYTIC SCALES FOR RESPONDING IN WRITING

Assign a score from 1 to 25 for each grading criterion below. (For more detailed evaluation, see the evaluation forms for writing, revising, and proofreading, Assessment Portfolio 4.1–4.9.)

1. **Personal Essay**

- **Content/Unity.** The personal essay describes a time when the speaker felt as if he or she were something else.
- **Organization/Coherence.** The personal essay relates one situation and describes the animal or object the writer felt like. The personal essay is arranged in a logical order.
- **Language/Style.** The personal essay uses vivid and precise nouns, verbs, and modifiers.
- **Conventions.** The personal essay avoids errors in spelling, grammar, usage, mechanics, and manuscript form.

▶ Additional practice is provided in the Essential Skills Practice Book: Writing 1.8.

2. **Critical Essay**

- **Content/Unity.** The essay identifies the mood of the story and explains how this mood was created.
- **Organization/Coherence.** The essay begins with an introduction that includes the thesis of the essay. The introduction is followed by supporting paragraphs with clear transitions. The essay ends with a solid conclusion.
- **Language/Style.** The essay uses vivid and precise nouns, verbs, and modifiers.
- **Conventions.** The essay avoids errors in spelling, grammar, usage, mechanics, and manuscript form.

▶ Additional practice is provided in the Essential Skills Practice Book: Writing 1.20.

PROJECT NOTES

See the evaluation form for projects, Assessment Portfolio 4.12.

Retelling Myths or Fairy Tales. Tell students that each group member should have a clearly defined role or roles. For example, students might decide to involve all group members in choosing a myth or tale, in brainstorming ways in which to retell it, or in enacting the retelling as a skit. One or two students might be in charge of writing down the retelling in rough form. Another pair of students might then be in charge of creating illustrations or serving as skit directors.

Cross-curricular Activities

ARTS AND HUMANITIES AND SOCIAL STUDIES

In this discussion, the World Passport students talk about political changes that have impacted their lives. Gabrielle, for example, speaks of nationwide protests that prompted a better educational system, and Denis discusses a new political system that allows him the freedom to practice his religion. Direct students to work in small groups to make visual and audio collages of political events that have affected their lives. Visual collages might include drawings, magazine clippings, photographs, and newspaper headlines, artfully arranged. Audio collages might include recordings of famous speeches, news broadcasts, contemporary music, and interviews of family members or others who participated in or witnessed an event. Have half the group assemble a visual collage, with the other half creating an audio collage; students might also coordinate their projects to create an audio-visual collage. Students might present their work to parents during parents' night or another school event.

MATHEMATICS AND SCIENCES AND SOCIAL STUDIES

Yumiko and Ebere state that changes that occurred in their lifetimes and in their parents' lifetimes have allowed them access to an education previously denied to women. Ask students to list changes in their lives that have occurred because of events that happened during their own lives or during the lives of their parents or grandparents. Then have students focus on one item on their list and research the historical or scientific developments that led to these changes. For example, if someone has faced a time of economic depression or prosperity, what events created these conditions? If someone has experienced serious illness, in what

(cont.)

Global Voices

A MULTICULTURAL CONVERSATION

Discussing Change

Just as the characters throughout this unit experience physical transformations, international students have experienced many transformations in their cultures and countries. Students were asked how these changes have affected their lives.

Avik: After Indian independence from Britain, Prime Minister Nehru decided that India should have a strong industrial base. With its well-qualified workforce and cheap labor, India is now a major contender in the global marketplace.

Jiannong: China experienced massive economic reforms in the 1980s, started by our economic architect Deng Xiaoping. Basically he eliminated the components of Communism and slowly shifted to the style of the Western market economy. I saw the benefits in very big ways in my family, in myself, in my high school. Before the reform, I never wore new clothes; everything I wore was from my brother or other relatives, but now everything has changed. Everybody has new things—new clothing, new Walkmans, new TVs. It's amazing.

Sarah: Greece experienced a big change in 1974 when it escaped dictatorship and moved into full-fledged democracy. We've joined the European Union and cities like Athens and Thessaloniki are showing more of a European influence; you can see it in the fashions and stores. You can also see progress in road improvement. When I was younger, it took eight hours to drive from Athens to my mom's village. Now it takes three. And these days even my mom's village has TV.

Gabrielle: Change in France tends to come about through people protesting. Any time people don't agree with a new law or the way the government runs the country, they go out into the streets and strike. In May 1968, there was a big protest that lasted more than a month and ended with the resignation of the president. It started with students asking for a free and more equal education for everyone. Then the whole country got involved. After a few weeks France seemed as if it were in a war: there was no more gas, no food in the grocery stores, no mail, no services; everybody had stopped working. This protest changed the way people think; they became more liberal and women gained more rights. At the same time, religion lost a lot of its power over the people.

Denis: After Communism ended in Russia, going to church actually became popular. Before, it was dangerous to practice religion because someone might report you. Now the churches are crowded. Fifty percent of the people in the churches are younger than twenty-five.

Yumiko: Changes in Japan were dramatic after World War II, when the economy changed and women's rights began to emerge. When my dad was born, women didn't have equal rights. My mother was born right after equal rights were enacted in the law, but she was still not allowed to do many things. For example, my mom

Cross-curricular Activities (cont.)

ways have medical discoveries affected that person's health?

SOCIAL STUDIES

Have students summarize the kinds of change Elio, Ebere, Gabrielle, and Yumiko would like to see occur in their countries. Then ask students to write a short essay on changes they would like to see in their own communities or country in the next five to ten years. The essays should include specific changes that must occur to realize these hopes. For example, if a student hopes for a reduction in crime, he or she should also consider conditions necessary for this change to occur, such as better education, less poverty, and revised legislation.

was not allowed to eat eggs when she was a child; they were only for the boys in her family. My parents found it difficult to accept the idea of my going to college. They wanted me to get married and become a mother while I was still young, but they see how well I am doing and how happy I am in school. So now they realize that this must be right for me.

Ebere: Luckily, many significant changes happened in Nigeria before I was born. Thirty years ago, it was unusual for a woman to go beyond high school. Parents didn't send their daughters to the university no matter how smart they were. If not for this change, I wouldn't be able to go to college.

Elio: There is a trend towards valuing education more in Mexico as well. Kids in rural areas are learning that there's a world out there, they want to learn more. That's changing the culture. One of Mexico's big goals is a better educational system. There needs to be change, not in what is taught but in access to education. Mexico needs a rush of educated people to contribute to the society. These people could better the country, strengthen the base for a stronger economy and culture.

Ebere: That's what we need in Nigeria, too. In the future, the first change I expect to see is a return to civilian rule—a return to democracy and central government. I would also like to see us catch up in technological advances. Teachers and lecturers are not paid well, and this has caused a "brain drain," since most of the best teachers and professors have left the country to teach where they are compensated better. I think education and leadership are the top issues that Nigeria must address.

Gabrielle: Right now the economy in France is not very good. People are still working for change, but the government has no solutions. I hope the European Union will make a difference. The idea is to gather the European countries together as a unique union with a strong and powerful economy. The EU now has sixteen countries working together, but people are afraid to lose their national identity and the rights they have achieved in their own country, so change is slow. Still, it will be great if it works.

Elio: I hope that, for Mexico, there will be some major changes in the government. Groups like the Zapatistas are bringing attention to problems that the government previously pushed aside. The international media is going into Mexico and other developing countries and is forcing the government to take action.

Yumiko: I hope Japan becomes more open to new ideas and people from other countries. My friends from other countries who have lived in Japan tell me we still have the mind-set of the closed-door period. Japanese people might like the material goods from other countries, but they don't always know how to interact with the people. Beyond that, I hope that women's status become more equal and that there's more integration between people from different backgrounds. That kind of change would be positive.

Quotables

"Few will have the greatness to bend history itself; but each of us can work to change a small portion of events, and in the total of all those actions will be written the history of this generation."

—Robert F. Kennedy

Cross-curricular Activities

SOCIAL STUDIES AND APPLIED ARTS

Read or display on the board the above quotation by Robert Kennedy and discuss it with students. Then ask them to think of concrete ways that people they have learned about in the news are working together to solve problems. Next, have students list problems at school or in their community that they would like to see addressed. After listing several items, ask students to select one problem and brainstorm possible actions that they can contribute to its solution. Working in small groups or as an entire class, students should outline and write a plan of action and present it to the student council, school principal, board of education, or city council. The project can be ongoing, with appointed students tracking on a weekly basis the progress of their plan. Students might chronicle in a scrapbook or journal their steps toward change. Others might prepare news releases for the local media inviting other community members to become involved in their plan, or to announce the success of their project.

SOCIAL STUDIES

Elio talks about the need in Mexico for "a rush of educated people," and Ebere discusses the problem of "brain drain"— the phenomenon of well-educated Nigerians leaving the country to contribute their talents elsewhere. Discuss with students the importance of education to a culture and how various companies, communities, (cont.)

Cross-curricular Activities (cont.)

and even entire countries deal with the challenge of retaining human resources. Students can then research this issue via the Internet or library reference materials. A search on the Internet with the key words "brain drain" should provide a substantial number of entries for students to explore.

"Apollo and Daphne"

About the Author

A biography of **Ovid** appears on page 436.

About the Selection

"Apollo and Daphne" is another tale of transformation from *Metamorphoses.* (For more information about *Metamorphoses,* see page 436.) Apollo is the Greek and Roman god of music, poetry, prophecy, and medicine who exemplifies youth and beauty. Struck by Cupid's arrow, he falls in love with Daphne. Unfortunately, Cupid has used his art to drive love out of Daphne's heart, and the nymph is changed into a laurel tree to escape Apollo's advances.

Literary Note

- According to Greek myth, the Python guarded Delphi, believed to be the center of the earth. Apollo killed the Python and is often given the epithet Pythios in honor of this feat. Apollo established his oracle at Delphi (for more information, refer to Connections: The Oracle at Delphi, page 619). For other works involving Apollo, refer students to the selection from the *Iliad* (page 592) and *Oedipus the King* (page 618) in which Apollo's oracle at Delphi is consulted.
- Daphne refers to Diana's request to remain a virgin. Refer students to Sappho's "But Not Everybody Wants Love" (page 610) which deals with Diana's (Artemis's) request.

SELECTIONS FOR ADDITIONAL READING

ROME

"Apollo and Daphne"

from *Metamorphoses*
by Ovid (Publius Ovidius Naso),
translated by Rolfe Humphries

Now the first girl Apollo[1] loved was Daphne,
Whose father was the river-god Peneus,
And this was no blind chance, but Cupid's[2] malice.
Apollo, with pride and glory still upon him
Over the Python[3] slain, saw Cupid bending
His tight-strung little bow. "O silly youngster,"
He said, "What are you doing with such weapons?
Those are for grown-ups! The bow is for my shoulders;
I never fail in wounding beast or mortal,
And not so long ago I slew the Python
With countless darts; his bloated body covered
Acre on endless acre, and I slew him!
The torch, my boy, is enough for you to play with,
To get the love-fires burning. Do not meddle
With honors that are mine!" And Cupid answered:
"Your bow shoots everything, Apollo—maybe—
But mine will fix you! You are far above
All creatures living, and by just that distance
Your glory less than mine." He shook his wings,
Soared high, came down to the shadows of Parnassus,[4]
Drew from his quiver different kinds of arrows,
One causing love, golden and sharp and gleaming,
The other blunt, and tipped with lead, and serving
To drive all love away, and this blunt arrow
He used on Daphne, but he fired the other,
The sharp and golden shaft, piercing Apollo
Through bones, through marrow, and at once he loved
And she at once fled from the name of lover,
Rejoicing in the woodland hiding places
And spoils of beasts which she had taken captive,
A rival of Diana, virgin goddess.
She had many suitors, but she scorned them all;
Wanting no part of any man, she travelled
The pathless groves, and had no care whatever
For husband, love, or marriage. Her father often
Said, "Daughter, give me a son-in-law!" and "Daughter,
Give me some grandsons!" But the marriage torches
Were something hateful, criminal, to Daphne,
So she would blush, and put her arms around him,
And coax him: "Let me be a virgin always;
Diana's father said she might. Dear father!
Dear father—please!" He yielded, but her beauty
Kept arguing against her prayer. Apollo
Loves at first sight; he wants to marry Daphne,
He hopes for what he wants—all wishful thinking!—
Is fooled by his own oracles.[5] As stubble
Burns when the grain is harvested, as hedges
Catch fire from torches that a passer-by
Has brought too near, or left behind in the morning,
So the god burned, with all his heart, and burning
Nourished that futile love of his by hoping.
He sees the long hair hanging down her neck
Uncared for, says, "But what if it were combed?"
He gazes at her eyes—they shine like stars!
He gazes at her lips, and knows that gazing
Is not enough. He marvels at her fingers,
Her hands, her wrists, her arms, bare to the shoulder,
And what he does not see he thinks is better.
But still she flees him, swifter than the wind,
And when he calls she does not even listen:
"Don't run away, dear nymph![6] Daughter of Peneus,
Don't run away! I am no enemy,
Only your follower: don't run away!
The lamb flees from the wolf, the deer the lion,
The dove, on trembling wing, flees from the eagle.
All creatures flee their foes. But I, who follow,
Am not a foe at all. Love makes me follow,
Unhappy fellow that I am, and fearful
You may fall down, perhaps, or have the briars[7]

1. **Apollo.** God of music, poetry, prophecy, and medicine
2. **Cupid.** God of Love
3. **Python.** Enormous serpent lurking in cave of Mount Parnassus
4. **Parnassus.** Mountain in central Greece—sacred in ancient times
5. **oracles.** Divine prophecies
6. **nymph.** Young and beautiful minor nature goddess
7. **briars.** Prickly, thorny bushes

Make scratches on those lovely legs, unworthy
To be hurt so, and I would be the reason.
The ground is rough here. Run a little slower,
And I will run, I promise, a little slower.
Or wait a minute: be a little curious
Just who it is you charm. I am no shepherd,
No mountain-dweller, I am not a ploughboy,[1]
Uncouth and stinking of cattle. You foolish girl,
You don't know who it is you run away from,
That must be why you run. I am lord of Delphi[2]
And Tenedos[3] and Claros and Patara.
Jove is my father. I am the revealer
Of present, past and future; through my power
The lyre[4] and song make harmony; my arrow
Is sure in aim—there is only one arrow surer,
The one that wounds my heart. The power of healing
Is my discovery; I am called the Healer
Through all the world: all herbs are subject to me.
Alas for me, love is incurable
With any herb; the arts which cure the others
Do me, their lord, no good!"
He would have said
Much more than this, but Daphne, frightened, left him
With many words unsaid, and she was lovely
Even in flight, her limbs bare in the wind,
Her garments fluttering, and her soft hair streaming,
More beautiful than ever. But Apollo,
Too young a god to waste his time in coaxing,
Came following fast. When a hound starts a rabbit
In an open field, one runs for game, one safety,
He has her, or thinks he has, and she is doubtful
Whether she's caught or not, so close the margin,
So ran the god and girl, one swift in hope,
The other in terror, but he ran more swiftly,
Borne on the wings of love, gave her no rest,
Shadowed her shoulder, breathed on her streaming hair.
Her strength was gone, worn out by the long effort
Of the long flight; she was deathly pale, and seeing
The river of her father, cried "O help me,
If there is any power in the rivers,
Change and destroy the body which has given
Too much delight!" And hardly had she finished,
When her limbs grew numb and heavy, her soft breasts
Were closed with delicate bark, her hair was leaves,
Her arms were branches, and her speedy feet
Rooted and held, and her head became a tree top,
Everything gone except her grace, her shining.
Apollo loved her still. He placed his hand
Where he had hoped and felt the heart still beating
Under the bark; and he embraced the branches
As if they still were limbs, and kissed the wood,
And the wood shrank from his kisses, and the god
Exclaimed: "Since you can never be my bride,
My tree at least you shall be! Let the laurel
Adorn, henceforth, my hair, my lyre, my quiver:
Let Roman victors, in the long procession,
Wear laurel wreaths for triumph and ovation.
Beside Augustus'[5] portals let the laurel
Guard and watch over the oak, and as my head
Is always youthful, let the laurel always
Be green and shining!" He said no more. The laurel,
Stirring, seemed to consent, to be saying *Yes.* ■

1. **ploughboy.** One who plows; country boy
2. **Delphi.** Town in ancient Phocis, seat of famous oracle
3. **Tenedos.** Base of the Greek fleet in the Trojan war
4. **lyre.** Small, stringed instrument used in ancient Greece
5. **Augustus'.** Belonging to the first Roman Emperor

Additional Questions and Activities

Apollo is the god of music, poetry, prophecy, and medicine. Ask students to find lines in the selection that refer to his patronage of these arts.

ANSWERS

In lines 81–90 Apollo refers to his powers as the revealer of present, past, and future; to the harmony of his lyre and song, and to his powers as the Healer.

Literary Note

For another selection in which outside powers inspire love or lack of love between two people, refer to the selection from *Tristan* on page 732.

Cross-curricular Activities

ARTS AND HUMANITIES

Have students look for works of art representing the story of "Apollo and Daphne" or have them create their own representation of the story.

SCIENCE

If possible, bring in laurel branches to show to your class. If laurel is not available, have students find pictures of this evergreen tree. Students might also research the laurel to discover its uses, characteristics, location, and ideal growing conditions.

ADDITIONAL RESOURCES

ASSESSMENT PORTFOLIO

- Vocabulary Worksheet 2.6.13
- Study Guide 2.6.14
- Unit Test 2.6.15

ESSENTIAL SKILLS PRACTICE BOOKS

WRITING
- Choosing a Purpose: Creative Writing, 1.8
- Gathering Ideas, 1.10
- Writing a Critical Essay, 1.20

LANGUAGE
- Clichés and Euphemisms, 2.72
- Dashes, Hyphens, Parentheses, and Brackets, 2.49

SPEAKING AND LISTENING
- Oral Interpretation, 3.5

STUDY AND RESEARCH
- Problem Solving and Decision Making, 4.1
- Using Thesauruses, 4.16

APPLIED ENGLISH/TECH PREP
- Technical Writing, 5.5

VOCABULARY CHECK TEST

Ask students to number their papers from one to ten. Have students complete each sentence with a word from the Vocabulary from the Unit in the Unit Review.

1. It was hard to tell what Julie was really feeling because her expression remained impassive.
2. The eagle's nest on top of that bleak cliff is virtually unassailable by any would-be predators.
3. Jim furtively hid his sister's birthday present just as she came in the door.
4. The ice and snow will impede our progress up the mountain.
5. She had gone without sleep for so long that she walked about in a somnambulant state.
6. The lifeguard warned his swimming students that it was not prudent to swim in areas with swift currents or undertows.
7. To win the election, Mabel made many heedless campaign promises that she could not deliver.

(cont.)

UNIT REVIEW

Metamorphoses

VOCABULARY FROM THE SELECTIONS

abase, 447	gratuitous, 477	precursor, 458
amiably, 460	heedless, 462	presentiment, 461
arbitrary, 458	imminent, 462	prudent, 457
assail, 448	impassive, 482	repose, 458
avidity, 477	impede, 466	reproach, 456
brusque, 459	importunity, 446	reverberation, 482
composure, 463	incapacitate, 463	sanguine, 446
covet, 446	infestation, 477	scullery, 476
depraved, 477	injunction, 464	somnambulant, 477
desist, 455	laden, 465	squeamishly, 485
discernible, 463	malice, 448	succor, 448
divine, 465	malingerer, 456	superfluous, 456
elixir, 475	meticulous, 475	supposition, 459
entreaty, 460	mummify, 477	tribulation, 449
equilibrium, 459	nestle, 482	unassailable, 461
exorbitant, 486	obstinate, 460	visage, 446
fawn, 447	ostentatious, 485	
furtively, 483	plaintive, 457	

LITERARY TERMS

allegory, 454, 468	Existentialism, 474, 479	point of view, 472
Breton lay, 444	external conflict, 479	romance, 451
catalog, 441	Gothic novel, 453	simile, 442
character, 488	internal conflict, 479	symbol, 488
characterization, 468	narrator, 451	tone, 472
conflict, 479	personification, 479	

VOCABULARY CHECK TEST (CONT.)

8. Michelle was a meticulous painter who paid close attention to all the details.
9. Jack's top hat and coat and tails looked rather ostentatious at the small family gathering.
10. Elena was such an obstinate person that you could never get her to listen to reason once her mind was set.

SYNTHESIS: QUESTIONS FOR WRITING, RESEARCH, OR DISCUSSION

GENRE STUDIES

1. Compare and contrast the prose pieces in this unit. What are the distinct styles of each piece? In what unique way does each piece deal with a type of transformation or metamorphosis? How are the pieces similar? How are they different? Comment on the structure, the role of the narrator, and the tone in each story.

2. Compare and contrast the way transformations were treated in classical literature (the stories from Ovid's *Metamorphoses*) and in medieval literature ("The Lay of the Werewolf") with the way transformations are treated in modern literature, such as Kafka's *The Metamorphosis*, Lispector's "The Fifth Story," and Ferré's "The Youngest Doll." What differentiates modern treatments of this plot element from the more ancient treatments?

THEMATIC STUDIES

3. What different types of metamorphoses are described in selections in this unit? What is the impetus for each metamorphosis? What effect do the transformations have on the lives of people in the selections? Focus your response on three selections in the unit.

4. Which metamorphoses in this unit are the results of punishment? What crimes were committed? What are the punishments for, or consequences of, these acts? Who punishes the characters, and why?

5. Compare the character of Gregor Samsa with the narrator of Clarice Lispector's "The Fifth Story." What internal conflicts does each character experience? What transformations occur as a result of these internal conflicts?

HISTORICAL/BIOGRAPHICAL STUDIES

6. Compare the two selections from Ovid's *Metamorphoses*—"The Story of Actaeon" and "Apollo and Daphne." What do these pieces have in common? What miraculous transformations occur in each selection? How do both pieces treat the mythology of classical Greece and Rome?

7. Both Franz Kafka and Anna Akhmatova experienced political change during their lives that left them feeling displaced and alienated. How did these experiences influence their works presented in this unit? Explain the social and political conditions that may have inspired Ferré to write "The Youngest Doll."

8. Which selections in this unit are based on characters or legends with which readers might already be familiar? What elements make the versions of these legends and characters that appear in this unit unique?

SPELLING CHECK TEST

Ask students to number their papers from one to ten. Read each word aloud. Then read aloud the sentence containing the word. Repeat the word. Ask students to write the word on their papers, spelling it correctly.

1. **importunity**

Salima was determined not to give in until her demands had been met, and her importunity finally paid off.

2. **sanguine**

Just before Nelson fainted, his normally sanguine complexion turned pale.

3. **succor**

The volunteer efforts provided succor to the people who had lost their homes in the fire.

4. **brusque**

Mrs. Pruitt's brusque manner of speaking made Chelsea feel unwelcome as a guest.

5. **imminent**

Even though the volcano rumbled and smoke seeped out, the residents of the town remained in their homes, unwilling to believe they were in imminent danger.

6. **discernible**

Heidi thought she recognized her cousin, but from such a distance his features were not discernible.

7. **elixir**

Hundreds of years ago, people believed that this spring water was an elixir that could cure any illness or wound.

8. **gratuitous**

A common criticism of popular films is that they contain gratuitous violence.

9. **impassive**

Byet was expecting bad news, so when it arrived her face remained impassive.

10. **exorbitant**

The owners of my favorite writer's childhood home charged such an exorbitant fee to tour the place that I could not afford to make a visit.

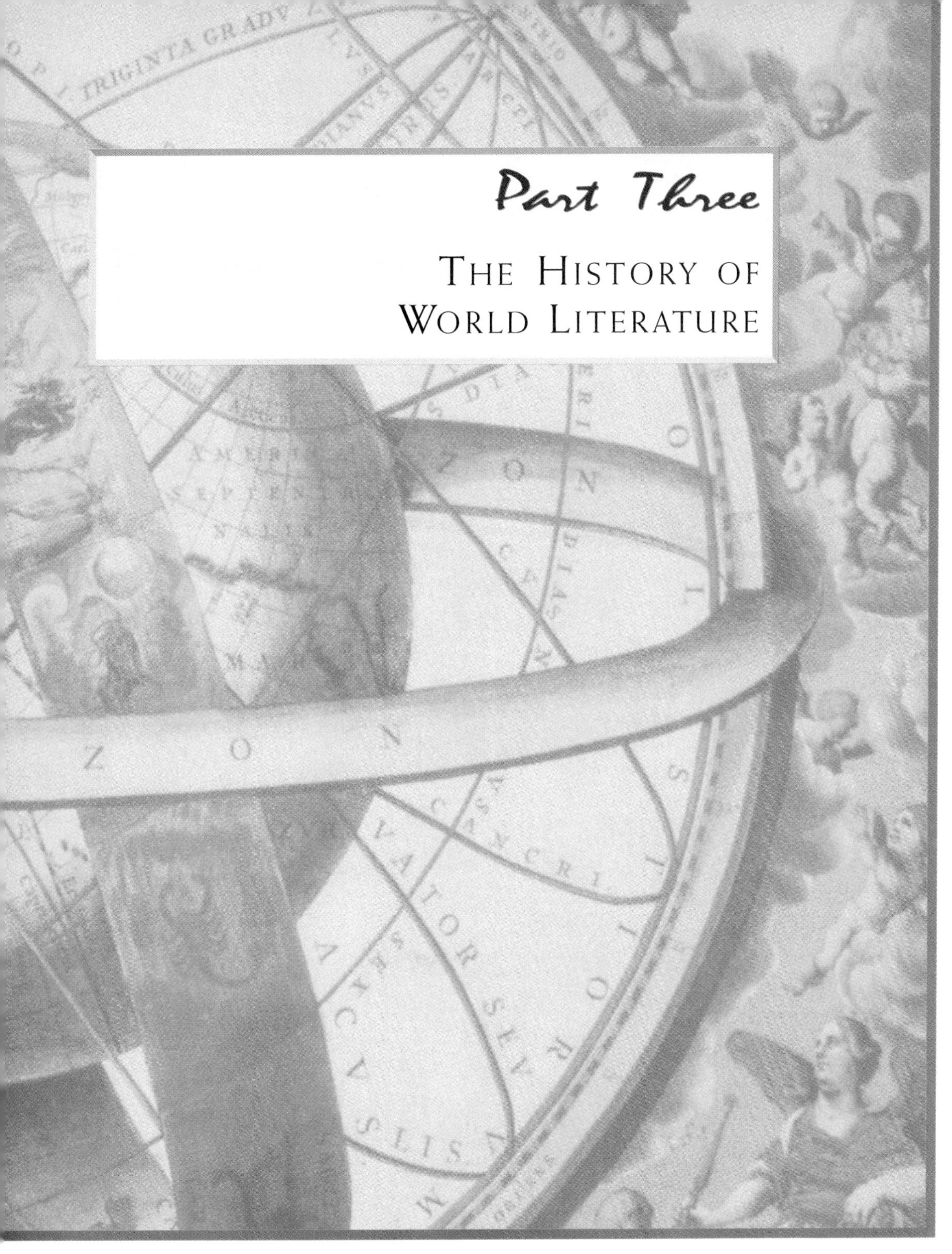

Part Three

The History of World Literature

UNIT SKILLS OUTLINE

Literary Skills and Concepts

- Allegory, 573
- Analects, 550
- Antihero, 516
- Aphorism, 554
- Archetype, 516, 524, 530, 542
- Conflict, 514
- Epic, 502, 516, 560, 573, 581
- Epic Hero, 516
- External Conflict, 514
- Foreshadowing, 514
- Hero, 516
- Heroic Epic, 516
- Hubris, 506
- Hymn, 556
- Internal Conflict, 514
- Irony, 514
- Irony of Situation, 514
- Motif, 509
- Myth, 536, 573
- Paradox, 549
- Parallelism, 510, 530, 536, 548
- Repetition, 510, 581
- Rhetorical Question, 559
- Theme, 554
- Tragic Flaw, 516
- Tragic Hero, 516

Writing Skills and Concepts

- Aphorisms, 554
- Character Sketch, 582
- Critical Essay, 515, 530, 537, 543, 549, 554, 559, 574, 582
- Description, 537, 574
- Descriptive Paragraph, 559
- Heroic Quest, 514
- Journal Entry, 530
- Paradoxical Scene, 549
- Praise Poem, 543

Grammar, Usage, and Mechanics Skills and Concepts

- Functions of Sentences, 527
- Transitive and Intransitive Verbs, 549
- Types of Nouns, 531

Other Language Arts Skills and Concepts

- Bibliographies and Bibliography Cards, 511
- Documenting Sources in a Report, 511
- Oral Interpretation, 582
- Types of Thinking, 543
- Writing Resumes and Cover Letters, 554

Unit 7 Roots of World Literature

Autumn Effect at Argenteuil. *Claude Monet, 1873*

GOALS/OBJECTIVES

Studying this unit will enable students to

- gain an overall understanding of the oral tradition
- have a positive experience reading the myths and epics of several ancient cultures
- understand how religion, culture, and human experience shaped ancient literature
- recognize archetypes, myths, epics, heroes, and irony
- analyze and write critically about literature
- understand some of the important types of thinking
- write resumes and cover letters

"The past is but the beginning of a beginning, and all that is and has been is but the twilight of the dawn."

—H. G. Wells

CROSS-CURRICULAR CONNECTIONS

TEACHING THE MULTIPLE INTELLIGENCES

(cont.)

TEACHING THE MULTIPLE INTELLIGENCES (CONT.)

Other Selections Exploring This Period

Akhenaten
from "Hymn to the Sun," page 296

Anonymous
from *The Book of the Dead*, page 364

Cross-curricular Activities

ARTS AND HUMANITIES, SOCIAL STUDIES, AND APPLIED ARTS

The cultures represented in this unit create a diverse and interesting group. Before beginning the study of this unit, students might research the cultures represented: the Mesopotamians, the Israelites and Judeans, the Maya, the Aztecs, the ancient Chinese, the ancient Indians, and the ancient peoples of Mali. Have students work in groups to research and prepare an introduction to each culture to be presented before the literature of each culture is studied.

Each presentation should include a map, time line of important events, and illustrations or photographs of important people, monuments, works of art, inventions, or other items. Students should describe major accomplishments of the cultures they research, including achievements in the areas of art and architecture, language and literature, agriculture, mathematics, science, medicine, technology, philosophy, and government. Students should also describe the major historical figures and events that shaped the civilization, as well as the religious beliefs of the people. They might also demonstrate inventions or display models of agricultural methods to the class. While the selections in this unit can be read as a group to show some of the major themes, issues, and ideas that link different cultures, the historical and cultural background provided by student presentations will give students a broader context in which to look at each work as a product of the culture that created it.

Students may also be interested

(cont.)

UNIT 7

Preview:
Roots of World Literature

Jain Temple, Jaiselmer, India

Literature began for all cultures as an oral tradition. Long before they developed written forms of communication, people told stories to one another. The earliest stories stemmed from people's questions about the world around them and their attempts to make sense of their observations and experiences. How did the world begin? How did human beings come to be? What is our relationship to the world around us? Why are we here? How should we live our lives? Why are suffering, pain, and death a part of human life? Questions such as these shaped some of the earliest forms of literature—myths and epics. A myth is a story that explains objects or events in the natural world as resulting from the action of a supernatural force or entity, usually a god. An epic is a long story involving heroes and gods that provides a portrait of an entire culture. Like myths, epics answer questions about the world and the human condition. Myths and epics not only explore universal human questions but also reveal the values and beliefs of the cultures that created them. The myths and epics of ancient cultures, some of them thousands of years old, still intrigue readers today, allowing each succeeding generation to see that it is not alone, that people of other times and cultures have pondered the same questions that concern us. No matter what our personal beliefs may be, we can enrich our own views by examining how others have viewed the world.

In this unit, you will read examples of the earliest literature of several ancient cultures, including those of Mesopotamia, Israel and Judea, Mesoamerica, China, India, and Mali. These cultures were scattered around the globe and flourished at different times over a time span of more than four thousand years. Despite differences of time and place, you will find many similarities in these works that form the roots of world literature. You will find some of the ideas that have shaped not only our literature but also our society today.

Cross-curricular Activities (cont.)

to explore other early cultures such as the ancient Egyptians, the Incas, the Assyrians, the Hittites, or the Phoenicians. Students might present their findings by writing an analysis of the interactions between two or more of these cultures or by writing a comparison and contrast essay about the views toward some topic such as religion or death as expressed by two or more of these cultures.

Echoes:

Roots of World Literature

Arteries I will knot
and bring bones into being.
I will create *Lullu,* "man" be his name,
I will form *Lullu,* man.
Let *him* be burdened with the toil of the gods,
that they may breathe freely.

—from the *Enuma elish*
(Mesopotamian creation myth)

Now therefore, if ye will obey my voice indeed, and keep my covenant, then ye shall be a peculiar treasure unto me above all people; for all the earth is mine: And ye shall be unto me a kingdom of priests, and an holy nation.

—from the King James Bible
(Exodus 19:5–6)

With shield flowers, with eagle-trophy flowers, the princes are rejoicing in their bravery, adorned with necklaces of pine flowers. Songs of beauty, flowers of beauty, glorify their blood-and-shoulder toil. They who have accepted flood and blaze become our Black Mountain friends, with whom we rise warlike on the great road. Offer your shield, stand up, you eagle jaguar!

—from "Song Admonishing Those Who Seek No Honor in War," from the Cantares Mexicanos
(Aztec song)

When you are content to be simply yourself
and don't compare or compete,
everybody will respect you.

—Lao-tzu
from the *Tao Te Ching*

There are three concerns above all—injure no creature; tell the truth as much as it may be told; be free from anger when you are not in danger.

—from the *Mahabharata* (Indian epic poem)

One man believes he is a slayer, another believes he is the slain. Both are ignorant; there is neither slayer nor slain. You were never born; you will never die. You have never changed; you can never change. Unborn, eternal, immutable, immemorial, you do not die when the body dies. Realizing that which is indestructible, eternal, unborn, and unchanging, how can you slay or cause another to slay?

—from the Bhagavad Gita (Hindu religious text)

You would call me a bard. To my own people, I am a royal griot, the historian of my village in Mali, the teacher and adviser of my king. I am the living memory of our nation's past and a master of my ancient art. Just as my father has taught me what, in his time, he learned from his father, so I will teach these time-honored tales of the Keita people to my son in the form that I have learned them. It is speaking of the past, and not reading about it in books, that enables you, my listeners, to feel its life.

—from the *Sunjata*
(epic of the Mande-speaking people)

BIOGRAPHICAL/HISTORICAL NOTE

The ***Enuma elish*** is a Babylonian creation myth. Two versions of this epic have been found, one that uses the Babylonian god Marduk, and another that uses the Assyrian god Ashur, signifying that the myth was important to the Assyrians as well as the Babylonians. The *Enuma elish* was dramatized as part of the Babylonian New Year festival, which focused on renewing and symbolically recreating the order of the universe.

For information about the **King James Bible** see page 518.

The **Cantares Mexicanos,** or Songs of the Aztecs, is the main source of Aztec poetry that has survived. Written in Nahuatl, or Aztec, the songs are difficult to render faithfully because of figurative language, metaphoric passages, and kennings, or imaginative compound nouns. Although recorded after the Spanish Conquest of 1521, the Cantares is a native document that exerts less influence from Christian missionaries than many other sources of the period.

Lao-tzu (c. sixth century BC) was the founder of Taoism. For a biography of Lao-tzu, see page 544.

The ***Mahabharata*** is the longest poem ever written. Traditionally ascribed to a poet named Vyasa, whose name in Sanskrit means "the arranger," the Mahabharata probably originated around 500 BC, was expanded over many centuries by countless poets, and took its final massive form in the fourth century AD.

The poem tells the story of the rivalry between two related warring families, the Pandavas and the Kurus. In the poem, the Pandava king engages in a game of dice with the Kurus. The Kurus, using loaded dice, win the game and, as a result, take over the Pandava kingdom for twelve years. At the end of this time, the Kurus refuse to relinquish the kingdom, and the Pandavas declare war. A great battle ensues, several hundred million warriors on both sides are (cont.)

BIOGRAPHICAL/HISTORICAL NOTE (CONT.)

slain, and the Pandavas emerge victorious.

The **Bhagavad Gita,** or Song of the Lord, is contained within the Mahabharata. It is against the backdrop of the war previously described that the Bhagavad Gita, a digression into law, philosophy, sermons, and doctrine, appears. The Gita raises the question of dharma, or duty, and reconciles this concept with the philosophy of renunciation of the world. The Gita states that, although one must act in the world, it is necessary to cultivate detachment from the fruits of one's actions, for it is attachment, not action, that prevents one from achieving salvation.

For more information about the ***Sunjata,*** see page 575.

ADDITIONAL RESOURCES

READER'S GUIDE

- Selection Worksheet 7.1

ASSESSMENT PORTFOLIO

- Selection Check Test 2.7.1
- Selection Test 2.7.2

ESSENTIAL SKILLS PRACTICE BOOKS

- Writing 1.8, 1.20
- Study and Research 4.20, 4.23

PREREADING EXTENSIONS

A reading of the Mesopotamian creation myth the *Enuma elish* might enhance students' readings of this selection. The *Enuma elish* describes many of the Mesopotamian gods, their domains, and their relation to other gods. The Mesopotamians believed in many gods, the most powerful of which met in an assembly to discuss various issues and to decide upon their course of action. Early Mesopotamian government was modeled on the assembly of the gods, so an understanding of this system would help students to understand Mesopotamian society.

SUPPORT FOR LEP STUDENTS

PRONUNCIATIONS OF PROPER NOUNS AND ADJECTIVES

A • nun • na • ki (ə nun´na kē)
E • an • na (ə an´na)
Shur • ru • pak (sho͞or ro͞o´pak)
Ur • uk (o͞or uk´)
Ur • sha • na • bi (o͞or sha´na bē)

ADDITIONAL VOCABULARY

engraved—carved or cut words
lamented—mourned
livid—brightly colored
slew—killed
torrents—violent stream; flood
wrathful—angry

PREREADING

from *The Epic of Gilgamesh*

Anonymous, translated by N. K. Sanders

About the Selection

An **epic** is a long story, often told in verse, involving heroes and gods. Grand in length and scope, an epic provides a portrait of an entire culture—of the legends, beliefs, values, laws, arts, and ways of life of a people. An epic poem of unrivaled antiquity, ***The Epic of Gilgamesh*** relates the odyssey of Gilgamesh, King of Uruk, who struggles against death, hoping to attain eternal life. Gilgamesh, mentioned in the Sumerian list of kings as having reigned sometime after the great flood, probably ruled around the year 2600 BC in the city of Uruk, located in the southern part of Mesopotamia on the Euphrates River. People first settled in Uruk around 5000 BC. At the time of Gilgamesh's rule, its residents wrote in the Sumerian language and primarily worshiped the god Anu and the goddess Inanna, later called Ishtar by the Akkadians.

Tales and legends about Gilgamesh were probably circulated through the oral tradition as early as 2500 BC. The kings of the Third Dynasty of Ur considered themselves to be descendants of Gilgamesh and so preserved some of the oral tales about Gilgamesh in writing; these first poems were written in the Sumerian language between 2100 and 1800 BC. According to Mesopotamian tradition, a priest named Sîn-leqi-unninni assembled the many different tales and poems about Gilgamesh into a cohesive narrative around 1600 BC. From Sîn-leqi-unninni's work, a standard Babylonian version of *The Epic of Gilgamesh* evolved and was widely known throughout the Middle East. The fullest version of the epic that has been found to date was located in Nineveh at the library of the Assyrian king Assurbanipal, who ruled from 668 to 627 BC. This version of the epic, which has become our standard version, was written in the Akkadian language on twelve clay tablets, some of which were damaged by Persian invaders. The epic was never translated into later alphabets, so for a time the great epic of the Mesopotamians was forgotten. When a young Assyriologist named George Smith deciphered some of the inscriptions on Assurbanipal's clay tablets and presented his findings to the Biblical Archeological Society in 1872, scholars were astounded by the resemblance between the story of Noah and the flood and the earlier story of Utnapishtim and the flood in the Gilgamesh epic.

CONNECTIONS: The Mesopotamian Worldview and *The Epic of Gilgamesh*

The worldview of any culture is shaped by that culture's geography. The Sumerian, Akkadian, and Babylonian civilizations developed between two unpredictable rivers—the Tigris and the Euphrates—in a harsh climate. Flooding and drought were common, and invaders often attacked the developing city-states. *The Epic of Gilgamesh* reflects the pessimistic outlook of the ancient Mesopotamians. Gilgamesh's search for eternal life is doomed to failure from its outset, and his struggle is often portrayed ironically. Nevertheless, in the process of searching fruitlessly for eternal life, Gilgamesh gains knowledge and mature understanding. When Gilgamesh returns to Uruk, bitter with the hard-won knowledge that death is the lot of all humans, he points out the walls he has built and engraves his story on a stone. He has realized that humans can attain a limited form of immortality through their works and through their writing. Back among the walls that he built and abandoned to search for immortality, Gilgamesh realizes that lost youth cannot be restored and that these very walls and the tale he tells represent, according to Mesopotamian thought, the only form of immortality that humans can achieve.

GOALS/OBJECTIVES

Studying this lesson will enable students to

- have a positive experience reading an epic
- recognize the story of Gilgamesh as a Mesopotamian epic
- define *conflict, foreshadowing,* and *irony*
- identify examples of irony and foreshadowing
- write a story about a heroic quest
- write a critical essay
- create visual representations of characters and events from their reading
- cite heroic qualities and elements of heroic stories

In your journal respond to the following questions: Do you think that people should be able to live forever? If you had the opportunity to drink from the fountain of youth and live forever would you take it? Why, or why not? What might be the advantages and disadvantages of living for hundreds or thousands of years?

READER'S JOURNAL

FROM

The Epic of Gilgamesh

ANONYMOUS, TRANSLATED BY N. K. SANDARS

Characters in *The Epic of Gilgamesh*

Adad (ā´dad), god of rain and thunderstorms

Anu (ä´no͞o), god of the sky and the heavens; father of the gods

Ea (ā´ä), also known as **Enki** (en´kē), god of the drinkable waters, fertility, and artists and artisans; usually a god who acts favorably toward humans

Enkidu (eŋ´kē do͞o), Gilgamesh's friend; a wild man whom the gods created of clay

Enlil (en lil´), god of the storm and the wind as both a life-giving and a destructive force

Gilgamesh (gil´gə mesh´), hero of the epic and king of Uruk

Humbaba (hum bä´bə), giant whom Enlil appointed to guard the cedar forest and who is killed by Enkidu and Gilgamesh

Irkalla (ir kä´lə), also known as **Ereshkigal** (er esh kē´gäl), goddess and queen of the underworld; sister to Ishtar and Shamash

Ishtar (ish´tär), also known as **Inanna** (i nä´nä), goddess of the storehouse, love, war, and the morning and the evening star; sometimes called the Queen of Heaven

Nergal (nʉr´gäl), husband of Irkalla or Ereshkigal; god of the underworld

Ninurta (ni nʉr´tə), god of the plow, war, thunder, lightning, hail, and heavy rain

Shamash (shä´mäsh), also known as **Utu** (o͞o´ to͞o), god of the sun, justice, and law; brother of Ishtar

Utnapishtim (o͝ot nə pēsh´təm), survivor of a flood sent by the gods to destroy humanity; granted immortality; Gilgamesh's ancestor and a former king of Shurrupak

READER'S JOURNAL

Students can make pro and con charts about the benefits and disadvantages of living forever. After students have responded to these questions in their journals, have them discuss or debate the issue.

SPELLING AND VOCABULARY WORDS FROM THE SELECTION

abomination	level
allot	libation
babel	pestilence
clamor	precinct
consign	stupor
deluge	teem
endow	

LITERARY NOTE

To help students understand this selection from *The Epic of Gilgamesh,* you may wish to share the following synopsis with students before they read the selection.

In the beginning of the epic, Gilgamesh has a typical hero's view of mortality—he hopes for a glorious death in battle, but otherwise thinks of death very little. With the death of his friend and companion Enkidu, however, Gilgamesh is confronted by the reality of death. Gilgamesh becomes obsessed with death and decides to seek his ancestor Utnapishtim, who had gained eternal life, to learn the secret of immortality. What Utnapishtim tells Gilgamesh ends his hope. His initial failure is followed by further defeat. Utnapishtim invites Gilgamesh to struggle against Sleep, symbolic of death, and Gilgamesh immediately loses this contest. As Gilgamesh is departing, dejected and defeated,

(cont.)

LITERARY NOTE (CONT.)

Utnapishtim's wife suggests that Utnapishtim give Gilgamesh some reward for his struggles. Utnapishtim tells Gilgamesh about a thorny underwater plant that can restore lost youth. Gilgamesh finds this plant and almost immediately loses it after carelessly leaving it on shore while bathing. A snake seizes the plant and sheds its old skin, becoming young again.

Answers to Guided Reading Questions

1 According to the narrator, Gilgamesh engraved the "whole story" in stone.

2 The gods give Gilgamesh a perfect body, perfect beauty, and courage. They also make him two-thirds god and one-third man.

3 Enkidu dreams that the assembly of gods meet and decide that Enkidu must die because Gilgamesh and Enkidu killed Humbaba and the Bull of Heaven. Enkidu reveals by his behavior that he believes that this dream will come to pass.

Cultural/Historical Note

Goddesses held a precarious position in the ancient Near East. As Mesopotamian religions became increasingly patriarchal, anxiety about the role of female gods emerged in Mesopotamian mythology. The female fertility figure is often seen as a violent goddess of war, death, and lamentation, revealing an inherent anxiety in the ancient consciousness that the mother, the bringer of life and fertility, may turn violent, denying her fertile gifts and plunging the land into sterility and destruction. The authors of the existing remnants of ancient Near Eastern literature resolved these fears by increasingly focusing on the life-affirming aspect of the goddess and de-emphasizing her darker associations with violence and death. The powerful fertility figure is not subdued totally in the myths of Mesopotamia and Canaan; rather, she is absorbed into the male-dominated pantheon. The goddess's magical power over life and death is made less threatening by surrounding her with more powerful, stable, and benign male figures. (cont.)

1 *According to the narrator, who originally wrote The Epic of Gilgamesh?*

2 *In what ways is Gilgamesh unlike an ordinary mortal?*

3 *What does Enkidu dream? Why does Anu say that Enkidu must die? Does Enkidu believe that this dream will come to pass, or does he believe this dream is just an idle imagining, or does he believe it will come to pass?*

PROLOGUE

I will proclaim to the world the deeds of Gilgamesh. This was the man to whom all things were known; this was the king who knew the countries of the world. He was wise, he saw mysteries and knew secret things, he brought us a tale of the days before the flood. He went on a long journey, was weary, worn-out with labour, returning he rested, he engraved on a stone the whole story.

When the gods created Gilgamesh they gave him a perfect body. Shamash the glorious sun endowed him with beauty, Adad the god of the storm endowed him with courage, the great gods made his beauty perfect, surpassing all others, terrifying like a great wild bull. Two thirds they made him god and one third man.

In Uruk he built walls, a great rampart,[1] and the temple of blessed Eanna[2] for the god of the firmament Anu, and for Ishtar the goddess of love. Look at it still today: the outer wall where the cornice[3] runs, it shines with the brilliance of copper; and the inner wall, it has no equal. Touch the threshold, it is ancient. Approach Eanna the dwelling of Ishtar, our lady of love and war, the like of which no latter-day king, no man alive can equal. Climb upon the wall of Uruk; walk along it, I say; regard the foundation terrace[4] and examine the masonry: is it not burnt brick and good? The seven sages[5] laid the foundations.

◆ ◆ ◆

[Editor's note: Gilgamesh arrogantly drives the people of Uruk too hard, oppressing even the weak. The people of Uruk pray to the gods for relief, and the gods grant the people's prayers by creating Enkidu. Enkidu is a wild man, covered with hair, but he is tamed by a priestess who encourages him to strive against Gilgamesh. Gilgamesh and Enkidu have a furious and prolonged wrestling match but emerge from the contest the best of friends. Gilgamesh and Enkidu set off on an adventure to kill a giant monster named Humbaba whom the god Enlil has appointed to guard a great cedar forest. Even though Humbaba begs for his life and is favored by the great god Enlil, Gilgamesh and Enkidu kill him and cut down the trees in the forest, incurring Enlil's anger. Ishtar then falls in love with Gilgamesh and asks him to marry her, but the arrogant Gilgamesh insults the goddess, telling her that she is never faithful to those whom she loves. Enraged, Ishtar asks her father Anu to make the Bull of Heaven to destroy Gilgamesh and Enkidu. Gilgamesh and Enkidu kill the Bull of Heaven, and Enkidu throws the thighbone of the Bull in Ishtar's face, a terrible sign of disrespect. The heroes celebrate their victory and then rest for the night.]

THE DEATH OF ENKIDU

When the daylight came Enkidu got up and cried to Gilgamesh, "O my brother, such a dream I had last night. Anu, Enlil, Ea and heavenly Shamash took counsel together, and Anu said to Enlil, 'Because they have killed the Bull of Heaven, and because they have killed Humbaba who guarded the Cedar Mountain one of the two must die.' Then glorious Shamash answered the hero Enlil, 'It was by your command they killed the Bull of Heaven, and killed Humbaba, and must Enkidu die although

1. **rampart.** Embankment of earth
2. **Eanna.** Sacred area where temples were built in Uruk
3. **cornice.** Horizontal molding along the top of a wall or building
4. **terrace.** Raised, flat platform with sloping sides
5. **seven sages.** Legendary wise men who founded the seven oldest cities in Mesopotamia

Words for Everyday Use

en • dow (en dou´) *vt.,* provide with some talent or quality

Vocabulary in Context

- Yasmin would endow the main character in her story with the qualities that she wished for herself—patience and grace.

Gilgamesh. *Syrio-Hittite stele. ET Archive, London/Superstock*

innocent?' Enlil flung round in rage at glorious Shamash, 'You dare to say this, you who went about with them every day like one of themselves!'"

So Enkidu lay stretched out before Gilgamesh; his tears ran down in streams and he said to Gilgamesh, "O my brother, so dear as you are to me, brother, yet they will take me from you." Again he said, "I must sit down on the threshold of the dead and never again will I see my dear brother with my eyes."

[*Editor's note: Enkidu's dream proves well-founded, as he immediately falls sick. Not long after his first dream, Enkidu relates another dream to Gilgamesh.*]

As Enkidu slept alone in his sickness, in bitterness of spirit he poured out his heart to his friend. "It was I who cut down the cedar, I who levelled the forest, I who slew Humbaba and now see what has become of me. Listen, my friend, this is the dream I dreamed last night. The heavens roared, and earth rumbled back an answer; between them stood I before an awful being, the sombre-faced man-bird; he had directed on me his purpose. His was a vampire face, his foot was a lion's foot, his hand was an eagle's talon. He fell on me and his claws were in my hair, he held me fast and I smothered; then he transformed me so that my arms became wings covered with feathers. He

1 *How does Enkidu feel about the fact that he must die?*

Words for Everyday Use

lev • el (lev´əl) *vt.,* knock to the ground, demolish, lay low

Answers to Guided Reading Questions

1 Enkidu is bitter about the fact that he must die and regrets that he will never see his "dear brother"—Gilgamesh—again.

Cultural/Historical Note (cont.)

In the Gilgamesh epic, the goddess figure is surrounded by more powerful male figures. That the primary source of Ishtar's strength—her fertility—is ridiculed in this story indicates that male gods and heroes have begun to overshadow the female fertility figures. Ishtar asks Gilgamesh to be her beloved, offering him riches, crops, animals, and an exalted position. He, however, scorns her, and Anu seems to agree that Inanna has incurred this derision. Even Inanna's dreaded power, her ability to raise the dead to eat the living, is not enough to avenge her. She sets loose the Bull of Heaven, denying fertility to the land for seven years, but even when she casts aside her role of fertility goddess and becomes the goddess of war and destruction, Inanna again is derided. Gilgamesh and Enkidu slay the bull and cast its thigh in her face. Fertility and war are two powers that Inanna loses, and she is left in the epic mourning for the Bull of Heaven, a less-powerful goddess of lamentation only, foiled by a mere mortal.

Vocabulary in Context

- The city plans to level these buildings to make room for a new park.

Answers to Guided Reading Questions

❶ In his dream, the "awful being" brings Enkidu to the palace of Irkalla, the realm of death from which no one returns.

❷ The underworld is dark, and the dead have only dust and clay for their food. Great kings and rulers share this wretched state with common people, and their "crowns" are "put away for ever."

❸ Enkidu is shamed that he dies of sickness. He had hoped to die gloriously in battle.

❹ Students may say that it seems that Gilgamesh has gone mad with grief.

Literary Note

Hubris is wanton insolence or arrogance resulting from exessive pride. In ancient literature, a human hero often commits an act of hubris, thereby offending the gods who punish the hero and send the hero's fate on a downward spiral.

Gilgamesh and Enkidu commit acts of hubris by killing monsters created by the gods. Gilgamesh commits an enormous act of hubris by insulting the goddess Ishtar, or Inanna. Enkidu's death and Gilgamesh's painful and ultimately unsuccessful journey can be seen as punishment for the heroes' acts of hubris.

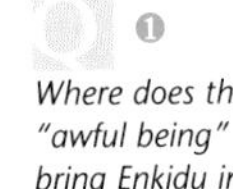

❶ *Where does the "awful being" bring Enkidu in his dream?*

❷ *What is the underworld like? In what way is death an equalizing force?*

❸ *What shames Enkidu about his death? How had he hoped to die?*

❹ *In what way would you characterize Gilgamesh's reaction to Enkidu's death?*

turned his stare towards me, and he led me away to the palace of Irkalla, the Queen of Darkness,[6] to the house from which none who enters ever returns, down the road from which there is no coming back.

"There is the house whose people sit in darkness; dust is their food and clay their meat. They are clothed like birds with wings for covering, they see no light, they sit in darkness. I entered the house of dust and I saw the kings of the earth, their crowns put away for ever; rulers and princes, all those who once wore kingly crowns and ruled the world in the days of old. They who had stood in the place of the gods like Anu and Enlil, stood now like servants to fetch baked meats in the house of dust, to carry cooked meat and cold water from the water-skin. In the house of dust which I entered were high priests and acolytes,[7] priests of the incantation[8] and of ecstasy; there were servers of the temple, and there was Etana, that king of Kish whom the eagle carried to heaven in the days of old. I saw also Samuqan, god of cattle, and there was Ereshkigal the Queen of the Underworld; and Belit-Sheri squatted in front of her, she who is recorder of the gods and keeps the book of death. She held a tablet from which she read. She raised her head, she saw me and spoke: 'Who has brought this one here?' Then I awoke like a man drained of blood who wanders alone in a waste of rushes;[9] like one whom the bailiff[10] has seized and his heart pounds with terror."

[*Editor's note: Gilgamesh says that Enkidu's dream is ominous and prays to the gods to spare his friend.*]

This day on which Enkidu dreamed came to an end and he lay stricken with sickness. One whole day he lay on his bed and his suffering increased. He said to Gilgamesh, the friend on whose account he had left the wilderness, "Once I ran for you, for the water of life, and I now have nothing." A second day he lay on his bed and Gilgamesh watched over him but the sickness increased. A third day he lay on his bed, he called out to Gilgamesh, rousing him up. Now he was weak and his eyes were blind with weeping. Ten days he lay and his suffering increased, eleven and twelve days he lay on his bed of pain. Then he called to Gilgamesh, "My friend, the great goddess[11] cursed me and I must die in shame. I shall not die like a man fallen in battle; I feared to fall, but happy is the man who falls in the battle, for I must die in shame." And Gilgamesh wept over Enkidu.

[*Editor's note: Enkidu dies. At dawn, Gilgamesh gives a long address to the counselors of Uruk mourning Enkidu's death.*]

He touched his heart but it did not beat, nor did he lift his eyes again. When Gilgamesh touched his heart it did not beat. So Gilgamesh laid a veil, as one veils the bride, over his friend. He began to rage like a lion, like a lioness robbed of her whelps.[12] This way and that he paced round the bed, he tore out his hair and strewed it around. He dragged off his splendid robes and flung them down as though they were abominations.

In the first light of dawn Gilgamesh cried out, "I made you rest on a royal bed, you reclined on a couch at my left hand, the princes of the earth kissed your feet. I will cause all the people of Uruk to weep over

6. **Irkalla, the Queen of Darkness.** Also called Ereshkigal, queen of the underworld
7. **acolytes.** Attendants, followers, helpers
8. **incantation.** Chanting of magical words or formulas
9. **rushes.** Plants that grow in wet, swampy places
10. **bailiff.** Court officer or law officer, sheriff
11. **great goddess.** Ishtar
12. **whelps.** Young lions

Words for Everyday Use

a • bom • i • na • tion (ə bäm´ə nā´ shən) *n.,* anything hateful and disgusting

Vocabulary in Context

• That monstrosity of a building has been an abomination since the day it was constructed.

you and raise the dirge[13] of the dead. The joyful people will stoop with sorrow; and when you have gone to the earth I will let my hair grow long for your sake, I will wander through the wilderness in the skin of a lion." The next day also, in the first light, Gilgamesh lamented; seven days and seven nights he wept for Enkidu, until the worm fastened on him. Only then he gave him up to the earth, for the Anunnaki, the judges,[14] had seized him.

Then Gilgamesh issued a proclamation through the land, he summoned them all, the coppersmiths, the goldsmiths, the stone-workers, and commanded them, "Make a statue of my friend." The statue was fashioned with a great weight of lapis lazuli[15] for the breast and of gold for the body. A table of hard-wood was set out, and on it a bowl of carnelian[16] filled with honey, and a bowl of lapis lazuli filled with butter. These he exposed and offered to the Sun; and weeping he went away.

♦ ♦ ♦

THE SEARCH FOR EVERLASTING LIFE

Bitterly Gilgamesh wept for his friend Enkidu; he wandered over the wilderness as a hunter, he roamed over the plains; in his bitterness he cried, "How can I rest, how can I be at peace? Despair is in my heart. What my brother is now, that shall I be when I am dead. Because I am afraid of death I will go as best I can to find Utnapishtim whom they call the Faraway, for he has entered the assembly of the gods." So Gilgamesh travelled over the wilderness, he wandered over the grasslands, a long journey, in search of Utnapishtim, whom the gods took after the deluge; and they set him to live in the land of Dilmun,[17] in the garden of the sun; and to him alone of men they gave everlasting life.

[Editor's note: Gilgamesh sets out on a long journey to find Utnapishtim. He travels through a pass in the Mashu mountains which guard the rising and the setting of the Sun, journeys through terrible and absolute darkness, and reaches the garden of the gods. There both Shamash and a goddess named Siduri tell Gilgamesh that his quest is hopeless, that he will never find immortal life. Despite their advice, Gilgamesh goes on, driven by his desperate fear of death and grief for the loss of Enkidu. Finally, Gilgamesh reaches a great ocean, referred to as the waters of death, and is ferried across by Urshanabi. Urshanabi brings Gilgamesh to Utnapishtim's residence in Dilmun. Gilgamesh tells Utnapishtim about the death of Enkidu and about his long quest. Gilgamesh then asks Utnapishtim how he can attain eternal life.]

"O, father Utnapishtim, you who have entered the assembly of the gods, I wish to question you concerning the living and the dead, how shall I find the life for which I am searching?"

Utnapishtim said, "There is no permanence. Do we build a house to stand for ever, do we seal a contract to hold for all time? Do brothers divide an inheritance to keep for ever, does the flood-time of rivers endure? It is only the nymph of the dragon-fly who sheds her larva and sees the sun in his glory. From the days of old there is no permanence. The sleeping and the dead, how alike they are, they are like a painted death. What is there between the master and the servant when both have fulfilled their doom? When the Anunnaki, the judges, come together, and Mammetun the

13. **dirge.** Funeral hymn, lament
14. **Anunnaki, the judges.** Gods who serve Ereshkigal and judge the dead in the underworld
15. **lapis lazuli.** Azure-blue semiprecious stone
16. **carnelian.** Red variety of quartz
17. **Dilmun.** Sumerian paradise

① *What makes Gilgamesh finally give up Enkidu to the earth?*

② *What does Utnapishtim's answer mean?*

③ *Why can't Gilgamesh rest? What does he hope to do?*

WORDS FOR EVERYDAY USE

del • uge (del´yo͞oj´) *n.,* great flood

ANSWERS TO GUIDED READING QUESTIONS

① The fact that Enkidu's body eventually begins to decay forces Gilgamesh to accept that he can do nothing about Enkidu's death and to give him "up to the earth."

② Utnapishtim's answer means that Gilgamesh, in searching for eternal life, is searching for a permanence that is impossible.

③ Gilgamesh can't rest because he is obsessed with death and his own mortality. He hopes to find Utnapishtim, who has gained immortality, and to perhaps learn how to gain eternal life from him.

ADDITIONAL QUESTIONS AND ACTIVITIES

In considering what it would be like to be granted everlasting life, students may enjoy reading some works on the theme of immortality, such as Mary Shelley's short story "The Mortal Immortal." After reading one or more works on this theme, students can use the following prompts to generate discussion or they can respond to them in a written essay.

- Describe the attitude toward immortality in the work or works that you read.
- Compare and contrast the attitudes from the works of literature with your own feelings.
- Does your idea of an afterlife affect your feelings about immortality? Explain.

VOCABULARY IN CONTEXT

- The roads were flooded by the sudden deluge, and people paddled down Main Street in canoes.

ANSWERS TO GUIDED READING QUESTIONS

❶ Gilgamesh is surprised that Utnapishtim appears ordinary and is relaxing rather than preparing for battle. Gilgamesh expected that Utnapishtim would somehow appear immortal.

❷ Ea tells Utnapishtim to say that because Enlil is angry with him, he is going to the Gulf to live with Ea, but that Enlil is pleased with the city-dwellers and is going to rain down "abundance" upon them. Ea tells Utnapishtim to lie because Ea is unable to save all of the city-dwellers from Enlil's anger.

❸ The gods wanted to exterminate humankind because people were making too much noise and disturbing the gods' sleep. Ea warns Utnapishtim because of an "oath."

❹ Ea tells Utnapishtim to tear down his house, to build a boat, and to take into the boat "the seed of all living creatures."

LITERARY NOTE

The story that Utnapishtim relates about the flood and the way in which he achieved immortality crushes Gilgamesh's hopes. Sumerian scholar Thorkild Jacobsen wrote about Utnapishtim's story, "It is the story of a unique event which will never recur, not a secret recipe or set of instructions for others to follow. It has no relevance for Gilgamesh and his situation, and so destroys utterly all basis for the hope that drove him on his quest."

mother of destinies, together they decree the fates of men. Life and death they allot but the day of death they do not disclose."

❶ *What surprises Gilgamesh about Utnapishtim? Why does this surprise him?*

Then Gilgamesh said to Utnapishtim the Faraway, "I look at you now, Utnapishtim, and your appearance is no different from mine; there is nothing strange in your features. I thought I should find you like a hero prepared for battle, but you lie here taking your ease on your back. Tell me truly, how was it that you came to enter the company of the gods, and to possess everlasting life?" Utnapishtim said to Gilgamesh, "I will reveal to you a mystery, I will tell you a secret of the gods."

♦ ♦ ♦

THE STORY OF THE FLOOD

❷ *What does Ea tell Utnapishtim to say to the people of Shurrupak? Why does Ea tell Utnapishtim to lie?*

"You know the city Shurrupak, it stands on the banks of Euphrates?[18] That city grew old and the gods that were in it were old. There was Anu, lord of the firmament,[19] their father, and warrior Enlil their counsellor, Ninurta the helper, and Ennugi watcher over canals; and with them also was Ea. In those days the world teemed, the people multiplied, the world bellowed like a wild bull, and the great god was aroused by the clamour. Enlil heard the clamour and he said to the gods in council, 'The uproar of mankind is intolerable and sleep is no longer possible by reason of the babel.' So the gods agreed to exterminate mankind. Enlil did this, but Ea because of his oath warned me in a dream. He whispered their words to my house of reeds, 'Reed-house, reed-house! Wall, O wall, hearken reed-house, wall reflect; O man of Shurrupak, son of Ubara-Tutu; tear down your house and build a boat, abandon possessions and look for life, despise worldly goods and save your soul alive. Tear down your house, I say, and build a boat. These are the measurements of the barque[20] as you shall build her: let her beam equal her length, let her deck be roofed like the vault that covers the abyss; then take up into the boat the seed of all living creatures.'

❸ *Why do the gods want to exterminate humankind? Who warns Utnapishtim and why?*

❹ *What does Ea tell Utnapishtim to do?*

"When I had understood I said to my lord, 'Behold what you have commanded I will honour and perform, but how shall I answer the people, the city, the elders?' Then Ea opened his mouth and said to me, his servant, 'Tell them this: I have learnt that Enlil is wrathful against me, I dare no longer walk in his land nor live in his city; I will go down to the Gulf to dwell with Ea my lord. But on you he will rain down abundance, rare fish and shy wild-fowl, a rich harvest-tide. In the evening the rider of the storm[21] will bring you wheat in torrents.'

"In the first light of dawn all my household gathered round me, the children brought pitch and the men whatever was necessary. On the fifth day I laid the keel[22] and the ribs, then I made fast the planking. The ground-space was one acre, each side of the deck measured one hundred and twenty cubits,[23] making a square. I built six decks below, seven in all, I divided them into nine sections with bulkheads[24] between. I drove in wedges where needed, I saw to the punt-poles,[25] and laid in supplies. The carriers brought oil in baskets, I

18. **Euphrates.** River that flows from Turkey southward through Syria and Iraq to join the Tigris River; one of the two most important rivers in the Mesopotamian region
19. **firmament.** Sky, viewed poetically as an arch
20. **barque.** Boat
21. **the rider of the storm.** Enlil
22. **keel.** Chief timber running the entire length of the bottom of the boat and supporting the frame
23. **cubits.** Ancient units of measurement; each one about twenty inches
24. **bulkheads.** Upright partitions separating parts of a ship
25. **punt-poles.** Poles used to push and maneuver a boat in shallow water

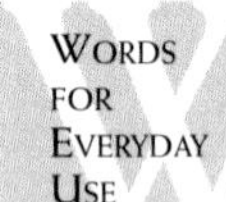

WORDS FOR EVERYDAY USE

al • lot (ə lät´) *vt.,* give or assign as one's share
teem (tēm) *vi.,* be full; abound; swarm
clam • or (klam´ər) *n.,* loud outcry; uproar (*clamour* is the British spelling of this word)
ba • bel (bab´əl) *n.,* confusion of sounds or voices

VOCABULARY IN CONTEXT

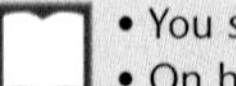

- You should allot no more than twenty minutes for the first part of the test.
- On hot summer days, the beaches teem with people.
- The clamor of sirens woke Nevil and alerted him that something was amiss.
- The babel of the crowd in the theater died down as the lights were dimmed.

poured pitch into the furnace and asphalt and oil; more oil was consumed in caulking, and more again the master of the boat took into his stores. I slaughtered bullocks for the people and every day I killed sheep. I gave the shipwrights wine to drink as though it were river water, raw wine and red wine and oil and white wine. There was feasting then as there is at the time of the New Year's festival; I myself anointed my head. On the eleventh day the boat was complete.

"Then was the launching full of difficulty; there was shifting of ballast[26] above and below till two thirds was submerged. I loaded into her all that I had of gold and of living things, my family, my kin, the beast of the field both wild and tame, and all the craftsmen. I sent them on board, for the time that Shamash had ordained was already fulfilled when he said, 'In the evening, when the rider of the storm sends down the destroying rain, enter the boat and batten her down.'[27] The time was fulfilled, the evening came, the rider of the storm sent down the rain. I looked out at the weather and it was terrible, so I too boarded the boat and battened her down. All was now complete, the battening and the caulking; so I handed the tiller to Puzur-Amurri the steersman, with the navigation and the care of the whole boat.

"With the first light of dawn a black cloud came from the horizon; it thundered within where Adad, lord of the storm was riding. In front over hill and plain Shullat and Hanish, heralds of the storm, led on. Then the gods of the abyss rose up; Nergal pulled out the dams of the nether waters, Ninurta the war-lord threw down the dykes, and the seven judges of hell, the Annunaki, raised their torches, lighting the land with their livid flame. A stupor of despair went up to heaven when the god of the storm turned daylight to darkness, when he smashed the land like a cup. One whole day the tempest raged, gathering fury as it went, it poured over the people like the tides of battle; a man could not see his brother nor the people be seen from heaven. Even the gods were terrified at the flood, they fled to the highest heaven, the firmament of Anu; they crouched against the walls, cowering like curs. Then Ishtar the sweet-voiced Queen of Heaven cried out like a woman in travail:[28] 'Alas the days of old are turned to dust because I commanded evil; why did I command this evil in the council of all the gods? I commanded wars to destroy the

Persian bull, from the Ishtar Gate, Istanbul

1 *In what way do the gods react to the flood? What does Ishtar regret?*

26. **ballast.** Anything heavy carried in a ship to give stability

27. **batten her down.** Seal or reinforce the hatches of a boat or ship

28. **travail.** Labor; intense pain

WORDS FOR EVERYDAY USE

stu • por (stoo͞′pər) *n.,* state in which the mind and senses are dulled, as from shock

ANSWERS TO GUIDED READING QUESTIONS

1 Even the gods are afraid of the flood. Ishtar regrets calling out in the assembly of gods for the destruction of humanity.

LITERARY TECHNIQUE

MOTIF

A **motif** is any element that recurs in one or more works of literature or art. The flood story is a motif in world literature, with the story of Noah in the Bible one of the most well-known stories that uses this motif. Ancient India, China, Greece, and Meso-America also have flood stories as part of their literary traditions.

Have students research these and other flood stories. After students have read some of these stories, they can discuss the similarities and differences between them. Ask students to hypothesize why flood stories were common among many ancient peoples.

VOCABULARY IN CONTEXT

• In an exhausted stupor, Finney was unable to focus on his work.

Answers to Guided Reading Questions

❶ The world is covered by a calm ocean. It is silent, and all of humanity has perished or "turned to clay."

❷ Ea says that Enlil has punished all of humanity too harshly and has failed to "lay upon the sinner his sin," or to punish only those who require punishment.

❸ Utnapishtim makes a sacrifice and pours out a libation to the gods. Utnapishtim compares the gods to flies gathering about the sacrifice. No, this is not a flattering comparison.

Literary Technique

PARALLELISM AND REPETITION

Inform students that two of the most common literary techniques found in Mesopotamian literature are parallelism and repetition. **Parallelism** is a rhetorical technique in which a writer emphasizes the equal value or weight of two or more ideas by expressing them in the same grammatical form. **Repetition** is the use, again, of a sound, word, phrase, sentence, or other element. Ask students to identify examples of parallelism and repetition on this page.

ANSWERS

Ea's words chastising Enlil use parallelism. "Lay upon the transgressor his transgression" is presented in the same form as "Lay upon the sinner his sin." This is followed by a list of things that Ea thinks would have been better than the flood. The list is presented in parallel form. The phrase "Rather than the flood" is repeated.

people, but are they not my people, for I brought them forth? Now like the spawn of fish they float in the ocean.' The great gods of heaven and of hell wept, they covered their mouths.

"For six days and six nights the winds blew, torrent and tempest and flood overwhelmed the world, tempest and flood raged together like warring hosts. When the seventh day dawned the storm from the south subsided, the sea grew calm, the flood was stilled; I looked at the face of the world and there was silence, all mankind was turned to clay. The surface of the sea stretched as flat as a roof-top; I opened a hatch and the light fell on my face. Then I bowed low, I sat down and I wept, the tears streamed down my face, for on every side was the waste of water. I looked for land in vain, for fourteen leagues distant there appeared a mountain, and there the boat grounded; on the mountain of Nisir the boat held fast, she held fast and did not budge. One day she held, and a second day on the mountain of Nisir she held fast and did not budge. A third day, and a fourth day she held fast on the mountain and did not budge; a fifth day and a sixth day she held fast on the mountain. When the seventh day dawned I loosed a dove and let her go. She flew away, but finding no resting-place she returned. Then I loosed a swallow, and she flew away but finding no resting-place she returned. I loosed a raven, she saw that the waters had retreated, she ate, she flew around, she cawed, and she did not come back. Then I threw everything open to the four winds, I made a sacrifice and poured out a <u>libation</u> on the mountain top. Seven and again seven cauldrons I set up on their stands, I heaped up wood and cane and cedar and myrtle. When the gods smelled the sweet savour, they gathered like flies over the sacrifice. Then, at last, Ishtar also came, she lifted her necklace with the jewels of heaven that once Anu had made to please her. 'O you gods here present, by the lapis lazuli round my neck I shall remember these days as I remember the jewels of my throat; these last days I shall not forget. Let all the gods gather round the sacrifice, except Enlil. He shall not approach this offering, for without reflection he brought the flood; he <u>consigned</u> my people to destruction."

❶ *What has happened to the world?*

❷ *According to Ea, why was Enlil's punishment "senseless"?*

❸ *What does Utnapishtim do when he sees that the waters have retreated? To what does Utnapishtim compare the gods? Is this a flattering comparison?*

"When Enlil had come, when he saw the boat, he was wrath and swelled with anger at the gods, the host of heaven, 'Has any of these mortals escaped? Not one was to have survived the destruction.' Then the god of the wells and canals Ninurta opened his mouth and said to the warrior Enlil, 'Who is there of the gods that can devise without Ea? It is Ea, alone who knows all things.' Then Ea opened his mouth and spoke to warrior Enlil, 'Wisest of gods, hero Enlil, how could you so senselessly bring down the flood?

Lay upon the sinner his sin,
Lay upon the transgressor his
    transgression,
Punish him a little when he breaks loose,
Do not drive him too hard or he perishes;
Would that a lion had ravaged mankind
Rather than the flood,
Would that a wolf had ravaged mankind
Rather than the flood,
Would that famine had wasted the world
Rather than the flood,
Would that <u>pestilence</u> had wasted
    mankind
Rather than the flood.

It was not I that revealed the secret of the gods; the wise man learned it in a dream. Now take your counsel what shall be done with him.'

Words for Everyday Use

li • ba • tion (lī bā´shən) *n.,* ritual pouring out of wine or oil upon the ground as a sacrifice to a god

con • sign (kən sīn´) *vt.,* hand over; give up or deliver

pes • ti • lence (pes´tə ləns) *n.,* any deadly infectious disease

Vocabulary in Context

- As part of the ritual, the people poured a <u>libation</u> in honor of the gods.
- The whole class was <u>consigned</u> to detention for talking too much.
- The outbreak of cholera could turn into an epidemic if we don't get this <u>pestilence</u> under control.

"Then Enlil went up into the boat, he took me by the hand and my wife and made us enter the boat and kneel down on either side, he standing between us. He touched our foreheads to bless us saying, 'In time past Utnapishtim was a mortal man; henceforth he and his wife shall live in the distance at the mouth of the rivers.' Thus it was that the gods took me and placed me here to live in the distance, at the mouth of the rivers."

♦ ♦ ♦

THE RETURN

Utnapishtim said, "As for you, Gilgamesh, who will assemble the gods for your sake, so that you may find that life for which you are searching? But if you wish, come and put it to the test: only prevail against sleep for six days and seven nights." But while Gilgamesh sat there resting on his haunches, a mist of sleep like soft wool teased from the fleece drifted over him, and Utnapishtim said to his wife, "Look at him now, the strong man who would have everlasting life, even now the mists of sleep are drifting over him." His wife replied, "Touch the man to wake him, so that he may return to his own land in peace, going back through the gate by which he came." Utnapishtim said to his wife, "All men are deceivers, even you he will attempt to deceive; therefore bake loaves of bread, each day one loaf, and put it beside his head; and make a mark on the wall to number the days he has slept."

So she baked loaves of bread, each day one loaf, and put it beside his head, and she marked on the walls the days that he slept; and there came a day when the first loaf was hard, the second loaf was like leather, the third was soggy, the crust of the fourth had mould, the fifth was mildewed, the sixth was fresh, and the seventh was still on the embers. Then Utnapishtim touched him and he woke. Gilgamesh said to Utnapishtim the Faraway, "I hardly slept when you touched and roused me." But Utnapishtim said, "Count these loaves and learn how many days you slept, for your first is hard, your second like leather, your third is soggy, the crust of your fourth has mould, your fifth is mildewed, your sixth is fresh and your seventh was still over the glowing embers when I touched and woke you." Gilgamesh said, "What shall I do, O Utnapishtim, where shall I go? Already the thief in the night has hold of my limbs, death inhabits my room; wherever my foot rests, there I find death."

Then Utnapishtim spoke to Urshanabi the ferryman: "Woe to you Urshanabi, now and for ever more you have become hateful to this harbourage; it is not for you, nor for you are the crossings of this sea. Go now, banished from the shore. But this man before whom you walked, bringing him here, whose body is covered with foulness and the grace of whose limbs has been spoiled by wild skins, take him to the washing-place. There he shall wash his long hair clean as snow in the water, he shall throw off his skins and let the sea carry them away, and the beauty of his body shall be shown, the fillet[29] on his forehead shall be renewed, and he shall be given clothes to cover his nakedness. Till he reaches his own city and his journey is accomplished, these clothes will show no sign of age, they will wear like a new garment." So Urshanabi took Gilgamesh and led him to the washing-place, he washed his long hair as clean as snow in the water, he threw off his skins, which the sea carried away, and showed the beauty of his body. He renewed the fillet on his forehead, and to cover his nakedness gave him clothes which would show no sign of age, but would wear like a new garment til he reached his own city, and his journey was accomplished.

Then Gilgamesh and Urshanabi launched the boat on to the water and boarded it, and

29. **fillet.** Narrow band worn around the head to keep the hair in place

❶ *What is the first thing that Gilgamesh says when he awakens? In what way does this prove true Utnapishtim's belief about humanity?*

❷ *What does Enlil do in response to Ea's criticism of his actions?*

❸ *What does Utnapishtim ask Gilgamesh? What contest does Utnapishtim suggest to Gilgamesh? What does Gilgamesh do immediately?*

❹ *What does Utnapishtim say about humans? What does he tell his wife to do? Why?*

ANSWERS TO GUIDED READING QUESTIONS

❶ Gilgamesh says that he had hardly fallen asleep before Utnapishtim woke him. The fact that with his waking words Gilgamesh tries to deceive Utnapishtim proves true Utnapishtim's belief that all humans are deceivers.

❷ Enlil gives up his anger that all of humanity has not been destroyed and blesses Utnapishtim and his wife, making them immortal.

❸ Utnapishtim asks Gilgamesh who will assemble the gods for him so that he can attain eternal life. Utnapishtim suggests that Gilgamesh try to "prevail against sleep for six days and seven nights." Gilgamesh falls asleep immediately.

❹ Utnapishtim says that "all men are deceivers." He tells his wife to bake loaves of bread and to mark the wall each day that Gilgamesh sleeps. Utnapishtim wants to be able to prove indisputably to Gilgamesh that he has lost the contest against sleep.

INTEGRATED SKILLS ACTIVITIES

STUDY AND RESEARCH

Point out to students that Utnapishtim uses bread and marks on the wall to document the time that Gilgamesh sleeps. Tell them that documentation plays an important role in many areas. Remind students that in research, it is important to document their sources to give credit to other writers and researchers. Review with students proper documentation of sources in a report and the form for entries in a bibliography (see the Language Arts Survey 4.20, "Bibliographies and Bibliography Cards," and 4.23, "Documenting Sources in a Report." Have students write a research paper on one of the topics presented in the Unit Review on page 585 or on one of the following topics:

(cont.)

INTEGRATED SKILLS ACTIVITIES (CONT.)

- the influence of geography on Mesopotamian religion
- a comparative study of the religions of Akkad, Assyria, Babylonia, and Sumer
- study of Gilgamesh as a legendary hero and as a real ruler
- analysis of the decline of Mesopotamian civilizations

Students may also chose a topic of their own to research. Students should pay special attention to documenting their sources correctly.

▶ Additional practice is provided in the Essential Skills Practice Book: Study and Research 4.20 and 4.23.

Answers to Guided Reading Questions

❶ A snake snatches away the plant, which Gilgamesh has carelessly left on shore. The story explains why snakes can shed their old skin.

❷ Utnapishtim gives Gilgamesh information about the plant that can restore lost youth.

❸ Gilgamesh gains a type of immortality through his works—the story of his adventures that he engraves—which will live on after his death.

Selection Check Test with Answers

EX. Who is Enkidu?
Enkidu is the wild man created by the gods in response to the people of Uruk's prayers; he is Gilgamesh's friend and companion.

1. What happens to Enkidu after he and Gilgamesh kill Humbaba and the Bull of Heaven?
By the gods' decision, Enkidu falls sick and dies.

2. Who does Gilgamesh decide to find?
Gilgamesh decides to find his ancestor Utnapishtim, who was granted eternal life.

3. What disaster did Utnapishtim and his wife survive?
They survived a terrible flood that destroyed the rest of humanity.

4. What contest does Utnapishtim offer Gilgamesh?
Utnapishtim challenges Gilgamesh to prevail against sleep for six days and seven nights.

5. What does Gilgamesh find underwater and what happens to this thing?
Gilgamesh finds a thorny plant that can renew youth, but a snake takes it from him and eats it.

❶ *What happens to the plant? What occurrence in the natural world does this story explain?*

❷ *What does Utnapishtim "give" Gilgamesh for a gift?*

❸ *In what way does Gilgamesh achieve a limited type of immortality?*

they made ready to sail away; but the wife of Utnapishtim the Faraway said to him, "Gilgamesh came here wearied out, he is worn out; what will you give him to carry him back to his own country?" So Utnapishtim spoke, and Gilgamesh took a pole and brought the boat in to the bank. "Gilgamesh, you came here a man wearied out, you have worn yourself out; what shall I give you to carry you back to your own country? Gilgamesh, I shall reveal a secret thing, it is a mystery of the gods that I am telling you. There is a plant that grows under the water, it has a prickle like a thorn, like a rose; it will wound your hands, but if you succeed in taking it, then your hands will hold that which restores his lost youth to a man."

When Gilgamesh heard this he opened the sluices[30] so that a sweet-water current might carry him out to the deepest channel; he tied heavy stones to his feet and they dragged him down to the water-bed. There he saw the plant growing; although it pricked him he took it in his hands; then he cut the heavy stones from his feet, and the sea carried him and threw him on to the shore. Gilgamesh said to Urshanabi the ferryman, "Come here, and see this marvellous plant. By its virtue a man may win back all his former strength. I will take it to Uruk of the strong walls; there I will give it to the old men to eat. Its name shall be 'The Old Men Are Young Again'; and at last I shall eat it myself and have back all my lost youth." So Gilgamesh returned by the gate through which he had come, Gilgamesh and Urshanabi went together. They travelled their twenty leagues and then they broke their fast; after thirty leagues they stopped for the night.

Gilgamesh saw a well of cool water and he went down and bathed; but deep in the pool there was lying a serpent, and the serpent sensed the sweetness of the flower. It rose out of the water and snatched it away, and immediately it sloughed[31] its skin and returned to the well. Then Gilgamesh sat down and wept, the tears ran down his face, and he took the hand of Urshanabi, "O Urshanabi, was it for this that I toiled with my hands, is it for this I have wrung out my heart's blood? For myself I have gained nothing; not I, but the beast of the earth has joy of it now. Already the stream has carried it twenty leagues back to the channels where I found it. I found a sign and now I have lost it. Let us leave the boat on the bank and go."

After twenty leagues they broke their fast, after thirty leagues they stopped for the night; in three days they had walked as much as a journey of a month and fifteen days. When the journey was accomplished they arrived at Uruk, the strong-walled city. Gilgamesh spoke to him, to Urshanabi the ferryman, "Urshanabi, climb up on to the wall of Uruk, inspect its foundation terrace, and examine well the brickwork; see if it is not of burnt bricks; and did not the seven wise men lay these foundations? One third of the whole is city, one third is garden, and one third is field, with the precinct of the goddess Ishtar. These parts and the precinct are all Uruk."

This too was the work of Gilgamesh, the king, who knew the countries of the world. He was wise, he saw mysteries and knew secret things, he brought us a tale of the days before the flood. He went a long journey, was weary, worn out with labour, and returning engraved on a stone the whole story. ■

30. **sluices.** Gates or valves used to regulate the flow of water

31. **sloughed.** Shed

Words for Everyday Use

pre • cinct (prē´siŋkt´) *n.*, grounds surrounding an area; enclosure between buildings, walls, etc.

Vocabulary in Context

• No Trespassing signs are posted at the edge of the precinct of the recluse's home.

Responding to the Selection

What does the word *hero* mean to you? Did Gilgamesh seem heroic to you? Why, or why not? Discuss with your classmates why you would or would not classify Gilgamesh as a hero.

Reviewing the Selection

RECALLING	INTERPRETING
1. What do the gods decide about Enkidu? What does Enkidu dream the underworld is like? What happens to Enkidu?	How does Enkidu feel about what is happening to him? Why does he find it shameful? How would you characterize Gilgamesh's reaction to what happens to Enkidu?
2. According to Utnapishtim, how did he receive eternal life?	In what way do you interpret Utnapishtim's question to Gilgamesh, "As for you, Gilgamesh, who will assemble the gods for your sake, so that you may find that life for which you are searching?" What is Utnapishtim implying to Gilgamesh about his quest?
3. What chance does Utnapishtim offer Gilgamesh? What does Gilgamesh do immediately? What happens to the plant that Gilgamesh takes?	In what way does Utnapishtim's gift of the plant seem like an afterthought? What might Utnapishtim's attitude toward telling Gilgamesh about the plant signify? How does Gilgamesh feel about his repeated failures to attain immortality?
4. What does Gilgamesh tell Urshanabi to do on his return to Uruk? What does the narrator say about Uruk? about Gilgamesh's actions upon his return?	Why does Gilgamesh tell Urshanabi to do this thing? Why does Gilgamesh perform this action upon his return? What has Gilgamesh realized about the nature of immortality and the meaning of his quest?

RESPONDING TO THE SELECTION

Students' opinions about Gilgamesh may vary based on their personal definitions of *hero*. Ask students first to agree on several qualities of a hero.

ANSWERS FOR REVIEWING THE SELECTION

RECALLING AND INTERPRETING

1. **Recalling.** The gods decide that Enkidu must die because he and Gilgamesh killed the Bull of Heaven and Humbaba. Enkidu dreams that the underworld is a place of darkness and dust in which crowns are "put away for ever." Enkidu falls sick and dies. **Interpreting.** Enkidu feels bitter and ashamed that he is to be leveled by death just as he leveled the great cedar forest. He finds it shameful that he is dying in sickness rather than dying gloriously in battle. Gilgamesh becomes like a madman in his grief over Enkidu's death.

2. **Recalling.** According to Utnapishtim, he and his wife were the survivors of a terrible flood that destroyed all of humanity; once the god Enlil realized that he had punished humanity too harshly, Enlil blessed Utnapishtim and his wife with immortality. **Interpreting.** Students may say that Utnapishtim is telling Gilgamesh that the event that led to Utnapishtim's immortality will never be repeated. Utnapishtim is telling Gilgamesh that his quest will be fruitless.

3. **Recalling.** Utnapishtim offers Gilgamesh a contest against sleep. Gilgamesh falls asleep immediately. Gilgamesh leaves the plant to bathe and a serpent snatches the plant away, shedding its skin. **Interpreting.** Utnapishtim's information about the plant seems like an afterthought because he only tells Gilgamesh about the plant at his wife's prompting, when Gilgamesh is already leaving. Utnapishtim may realize that Gilgamesh's (cont.)

ANSWERS FOR REVIEWING THE SELECTION (CONT.)

search is futile and knows that Gilgamesh will lose the plant and eternal life. If so, he might want to avoid giving Gilgamesh this final disappointment. Gilgamesh is terribly dismayed and disappointed and is bitter that all his work has done only the snake good.

4. **Recalling.** Gilgamesh tells Urshanabi to climb up and examine the walls of the city. The narrator says of Uruk, "This too was the work of Gilgamesh." The narrator says that Gilgamesh was weary but that he engraved the whole story on a stone. **Interpreting.** Gilgamesh both shows Urshanabi the walls he built and writes down his story because he knows that it is only through the existence of his works that he can attain a limited form of immortality.

(cont.)

Answers for Reviewing the Selection (cont.)

SYNTHESIZING

Responses will vary. Possible responses are given.

5. The Mesopotamian gods are moody and unpredictable, sometimes helping humanity and sometimes punishing them harshly. Like humans, they can be argumentative, vengeful, fearful, and kind, and they change their minds as often as humans do. The interaction between the gods is like that of humans, as the gods bicker and argue among themselves. They have power over human destinies, but their wills can sometimes be averted; they behave unpredictably toward human beings.

Answers for Understanding Literature

Responses will vary. Possible responses are given.

1. **Irony.** Utnapishtim's telling of the flood story is ironic because it does not reveal how to obtain eternal life but reveals that Utnapishtim's achieving immortality is an event that will not be repeated, contradicting the expectations of Gilgamesh and the reader. Gilgamesh's contest with sleep is ironic because Gilgamesh falls asleep immediately, sleeps for several days, and lies about having fallen asleep as Utnapishtim predicted. This event contradicts the expectations of both Gilgamesh and the reader. The fact that a snake eats the plant is ironic because all Gilgamesh's work has benefited only the snake, contradicting Gilgamesh's expectations and those of the audience.

2. **Conflict.** The external conflict is between Gilgamesh and death or human mortality. The internal conflict is Gilgamesh's struggle to put aside his fear of death and to grow up and accept death as an inevitable part of life.

(cont.)

Synthesizing

5. In what way is the assembly of Mesopotamian gods portrayed in this epic? What human qualities do the gods possess? In what way do the gods interact with each other? with humans?

Understanding Literature (Questions for Discussion)

1. **Irony. Irony** is a difference between appearance and reality. An event that contradicts the expectations of the characters, the reader, or the audience of a literary work is an example of **irony of situation.** Gilgamesh's quest for immortality is filled with many examples of irony of situation. Why is Utnapishtim's tale of the flood an ironic response to Gilgamesh's desire to learn how eternal life can be obtained? What makes Gilgamesh's contest with sleep ironic? Why is what happens to the youth-restoring plant ironic?
2. **Conflict.** A **conflict** is a struggle between two or more forces in a literary work. A struggle that takes place between a character and some outside force is called an **external conflict**. A struggle that takes place within a character is called an **internal conflict**. What is the external conflict in this epic? What internal conflict does Gilgamesh experience?
3. **Foreshadowing. Foreshadowing** is the act of presenting materials that hint at events to occur later in a story. What passages in *The Epic of Gilgamesh* hint at Gilgamesh's ultimate failure to attain eternal life for humanity?

Responding in Writing

1. **Creative Writing: Heroic Quest.** Write your own story about a hero who goes on a quest, an adventurous journey in search of something. First, freewrite about your hero, focusing on the following questions: Is your hero male or female? Is your hero a historical figure, a figure from popular culture or literature, or your own imaginative creation? What heroic qualities does your hero possess? What does he or she look like? How does he or she sound? What does your hero value? For what might your hero undertake a quest? Then, review the Language Arts Survey 1.10, "Gathering Ideas," and make a story map in which you outline your story's plot. Refer to your freewriting and your story map when writing the first draft of your heroic quest.

Answers for Understanding Literature (cont.)

3. **Foreshadowing.** Shamashand Siduri warn Gilgamesh that he will fail. Utnapishtim says that death is part of human life and asks Gilgamesh who will assemble the gods to grant him eternal life. Gilgamesh falls asleep immediately in his contest with death, and his sleep is measured by the extent to which bread decays. Utnapishtim tells Gilgamesh about the plant as an afterthought, and Gilgamesh quickly loses the plant to a snake.

2. **Critical Essay: Growing Up—The Quest.** In this epic, Gilgamesh undertakes a quest to gain eternal life for humanity. Although he fails to achieve his objective, he does grow and change as a character along the way. Write an essay in which you explain what Gilgamesh has gained while on his quest for eternal life. Before you begin writing, think about the following questions: What is Gilgamesh like at the beginning of the epic? What is he like at the epic's end? What does Gilgamesh lose on his quest? What does he gain? Why might it sometimes be necessary to lose something in order to gain something? Is what Gilgamesh gains worth its cost? Freewrite your answers to these questions. Then, refer to your freewriting when developing a thesis. State your thesis clearly in an introductory paragraph, support it with evidence from the text in following paragraphs, and come to a conclusion in a final paragraph.

PROJECT

Mural. *The Epic of Gilgamesh* is a visually appealing story. Work together as a class to create a mural depicting different scenes from Gilgamesh's adventures. You may wish to create the mural on large sheets of paper taped to the wall. First, divide the story of Gilgamesh into a number of key scenes that would be fun to illustrate. Then form small groups, each group illustrating one scene. Next, each group should do some research to discover if the characters they will be depicting are represented in Mesopotamian art. Use any pictures and photos of Mesopotamian art as springboards for your imagination. Plan out your scene on sketch paper before drawing or painting the final mural.

Persian lion, from the Ishtar Gate, Istanbul

PROJECT NOTES

See the evaluation form for projects, Assessment Portfolio 4.12.

Mural. Since panels of the mural will be created by different groups, students may wish to make some decisions as a class regarding style and content of the mural. Also, if characters appear in more than one scene of the mural, groups may wish to collaborate to establish an image of the character that will be consistent throughout the mural.

If space for the mural is limited, students might work in groups to create page-size illustrations for various parts of the Gilgamesh story.

ART NOTE

The Babylonian Lion from the Processional Way is one of sixty figures of lions carved in relief on brick that lined the approach to Ishtar's Gate, the entrance to the temple complex, in Babylon around 575 BC. Lions were sacred to the goddess Ishtar.

ANALYTIC SCALES FOR RESPONDING IN WRITING

Assign a score from 1 to 25 for each grading criterion below. (For more detailed evaluation, see the evaluation forms for writing, revising, and proofreading, Assessment Portfolio 4.1–4.9.)

1. Heroic Quest

- **Content/Unity.** The heroic quest is presented in a story about a hero who goes in search of something.
- **Organization/Coherence.** The heroic quest is arranged in a logical order, such as chronological order.
- **Language/Style.** The heroic quest uses vivid and precise nouns, verbs, and modifiers.
- **Conventions.** The heroic quest avoids errors in spelling, grammar, usage, mechanics, and manuscript form.

► Additional practice is provided in the Essential Skills Practice Book: Writing 1.8.

2. Critical Essay

- **Content/Unity.** The essay analyzes the effects of Gilgamesh's journey on his character.
- **Organization/Coherence.** The essay introduces a thesis and uses evidence from the text to support it.
- **Language/Style.** The essay uses vivid and precise language.
- **Conventions.** The essay avoids errors in spelling, grammar, usage, mechanics, and manuscript form.

► Additional practice is provided in the Essential Skills Practice Book: Writing 1.20.

Additional Questions and Activities

Have students brainstorm a list of contemporary heroes. Such heroes may be represented in popular media such as films or comic books, or they may be actual people. After students have constructed their list, ask them what qualities of the figures on the list make them heroes. Have students create their own heroes who possess many of the qualities they have attributed to heroes.

Literary Technique

Students should be familiar with the following literary terms for additional reading of works about heroes.

ANTIHERO

An **antihero** is a central character who lacks many of the qualities traditionally associated with heroes. An antihero may be lacking in beauty, courage, grace, intelligence, or moral scruples. Antiheroes are common figures in modern fiction and drama.

ARCHETYPE

An **archetype** is an inherited, often unconscious, ancestral memory or motif that recurs throughout history and literature. The story of the journey in which someone sets out on a path, experiences adventures, and emerges wiser may be considered archetypal. Archetypal themes and motifs often occur in heroic literature.

EPIC AND HEROIC EPIC

An **epic** is a long story, often told in verse, involving heroes and gods. Grand in length and scope, an epic provides a portrait of an entire culture, of the legends, beliefs, values, laws, arts, and ways of life of a people. A **heroic epic** is an epic that has a main purpose of telling the life story of a great hero. (cont.)

Themes

The Hero and the Quest

Don Quixote. Gustave Doré

The Hero

You may have seen action films or read contemporary fantasy or science fiction novels in which characters who possess incredible strength, savvy, or courage set out on adventures and overcome seemingly impossible odds to achieve a particular goal. When you see such a film or read such a novel, you are experiencing one modern interpretation of a very ancient literary archetype. Epic, or mythic, heroes who undertake quests have appeared in world literature for thousands of years.

Heroes of epics and myths represent the ideals of the cultures that create them. In early literature, the hero is often part divine and has both an unusual birth and a remarkable childhood. A hero may be either a religious or secular leader, or some other person of high status. The hero usually has remarkable abilities, such as magical power, superhuman strength, or great courage and dignity. As the finest example of his or her society's values, the hero possesses a glory conferred by the poets and storytellers of a culture.

The Heroic Quest

Stories about heroes usually contain some of the following elements. Initially, the hero may experience a **fall** from a state of innocence to a state of experience. In other words, the hero gains an awareness that the world is not perfect and that evil, suffering, and death exist. The hero then typically undertakes a **task,** or a test to prove himself or herself. This task can involve conquering a monster or a foe, finding a treasure, or proving his or her mental or physical prowess. Sometimes the hero has a companion in his or her early adventures. The companion is often the hero's **double,** or **alter ego.** The Greek term for the double, *therápon,* literally "ritual substitute," reveals that the hero's double often dies before the hero, almost as a scapegoat. The death of the double sometimes foreshadows the eventual death of the hero. By successfully completing the task or tasks, the hero proves himself or herself worthy of taking on a **quest,** or **journey.** During a quest, a hero searches for something material or for something immaterial, such as knowledge or wisdom. Often, the hero searches for insight or a treasure that will make it possible for humanity to return to the state of innocence or perfection that existed before the fall. The journey taken to attain this knowledge or treasure can be either literal or metaphorical. The climax of the quest or journey often involves a descent into the underworld, into death itself, or simply into human despair. Heroes experience many moral difficulties as well as physical challenges while on quests. For example, there may be temptations that will lead the hero off his or her path, or the hero's flaws may hinder him or her in attaining his or her goal. Sometimes, the plot of a heroic epic contains a final part, what the Greeks called a *nóstos,* or a homecoming.

Gilgamesh as an Epic Hero

In many ways Gilgamesh's journey presents perfectly the archetype of the epic hero and the quest. Gilgamesh's quest is unusual, however, because it is full of ironic failures and because Gilgamesh falls short of attaining his goal, gaining knowledge instead of eternal life. In this respect, Gilgamesh foreshadows another modern interpretation of the hero—the **antihero,** or the ironic hero. Antiheroes lack many of the qualities traditionally associated with heroes and often reject, or fail at, the heroic quest.

Literary Technique (cont.)

HERO, EPIC HERO, AND TRAGIC HERO

A **hero** is a character whose actions are inspiring and courageous. An **epic hero** represents the ideals of the culture that creates it. A **tragic hero** is a character of high status who possesses noble qualities but who also has a tragic flaw. In much contemporary literature, the term *hero* often refers to any main character.

TRAGIC FLAW

A **tragic flaw** is a personal weakness that brings about the fall of a character in a tragedy, or a story about the fall of a person of high status.

The Many Faces of Heroes

As you read world literature, you will encounter the heroes of many different cultures, and each hero will reveal something about the values of his or her culture. In this unit, you will discover, in addition to Gilgamesh of the ancient Near East, Rama of India and Sunjata, hero of the Mande-speaking people of Mali. In other units, traditional epic heroes include the Roman Aeneas in Unit 3, Achilles of Greece in Unit 8, the medieval Tristan and Perceval in Unit 9, and the female knight Bradamante in Unit 10. Also appearing in Unit 10 is Miguel de Cervantes's famous mock hero Don Quixote, whose actions parody and parallel the actions of more traditional heroes. During your reading of world literature, you might look for modern interpretations of heroes. Gregor Samsa in Kafka's *The Metamorphosis* is a dramatic, but highly imaginative, example of an anti-hero. In *Night,* Elie Wiesel's autobiographical account of surviving German concentration camps, the writer himself emerges as a hero of epic proportion, and his real-life story contains many of the plot elements typical of the epic. Reading about the heroes of different cultures is not unlike being able to time-travel to another land as it once existed. The past comes alive, and you are given the opportunity to observe the thoughts, feelings, and values of a people who lived in another place at another time.

Saint George and the Dragon. *Paolo Uccello, c. 1440*

ART NOTE

Paolo Uccello (1397–1475) was a Florentine painter whose work represented aspects of both the Gothic and Renaissance styles. By age ten, he was apprenticed in the studio of sculptor Lorenzo Ghiberti. In 1415 Uccello joined the Arte dei Medici e degli Speziali, or the artists' guild. He created frescoes, mosaics, and paintings. Uccello is recognized for his careful studies in perspective. His famous works include *The Creation of the Animals, The Creation of Adam, The Creation of Eve, The Fall, The Rout of San Romano, The Flood,* and two versions of *Saint George and the Dragon.*

CROSS-CURRICULAR ACTIVITIES

ARTS AND HUMANITIES

Ask students to add to the list of heroes from world literature. For example, they might add Odysseus and King Arthur. Then have them research various depictions of these heroes in art. Ask students to analyze one of these works of art, answering the following questions: Is the hero depicted as a high or mighty being? Does the portrayal of the hero show human emotions? What qualities of the hero does the artist capture? What is the hero doing? What is happening around the hero? What is the hero's reaction to his or her surroundings?

Students can also work in groups to create a collage of their own depictions of heroes from literature, movies, and real life. Have students create captions as part of the collage explaining why each figure has been included.

QUOTABLES

"A hero is no braver than an ordinary man, but he is brave five minutes longer."

—Ralph Waldo Emerson

ADDITIONAL RESOURCES

READER'S GUIDE

- Selection Worksheet 7.2

ASSESSMENT PORTFOLIO

- Selection Check Test 2.7.3
- Selection Test 2.7.4

ESSENTIAL SKILLS PRACTICE BOOKS

- Writing 1.8, 1.20
- Language 2.3

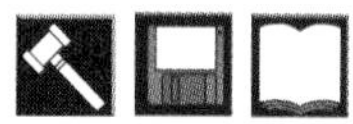

PREREADING EXTENSIONS

Inform students that the Hebrew people, like many others in the Fertile Crescent, were initially nomadic. As wanderers they came into contact with many different peoples of the ancient Near East, and the Bible provides a record of many of these encounters. According to the Bible, Abraham led his people from Ur, a city in ancient Sumer, into Canaan. Canaan is not as fertile as the area around the Tigris and Euphrates or the Nile; the area is subject to periods of drought and famine. A drought and famine may have led the Hebrew people to migrate to Egypt. Roughly about the same time, another group of people called the Hyksos conquered Egypt. Some scholars speculate that the Hebrews and the Hyksos were in close contact and that the Hyksos made it possible for the Hebrews to gain status in Egypt, a country that did not look kindly upon outsiders. Some scholars point to the Biblical story of Joseph's success in the Egyptian court as possible proof that the Hebrews may have come to Egypt when the Hyksos were in command.

Encourage interested students to read other chapters in Genesis in which the Hebrews encounter other peoples of the Near East. Possible chapters include Genesis 12, 13, 26, 37, 39–47.

PREREADING

from Genesis
from the King James Bible

About the Selection

For thousands of years, the **Bible** has influenced the literature, art, music, and the ways of life of people from the Near East and Europe. No other single work has played such a significant role in the development of Western civilization. Three great world religions—Judaism, Christianity, and Islam—have developed from the moral and religious tenets expressed in the Bible. The word *Bible* comes from the Greek word *biblia,* meaning "books," indicating that the Bible is not a single book but actually a collection of many books that were composed during many different time periods and that feature many different types of writing. The Jewish Bible consists of twenty-four books. Christians call the Jewish Bible the Old Testament and recognize another twenty-seven books called the New Testament.

The books that make up the Jewish Bible are divided into three parts. The first, the Torah, or Pentateuch, presents the history of the Hebrew people and their laws. The Torah is composed of five books, **Genesis**, Exodus, Leviticus, Numbers, and Deuteronomy. The second division is the Nev'im, or Prophets. The Nev'im continues the story of Israel and its kings and contains histories and writings of such famous prophets as Isaiah, Jeremiah, and Ezekiel. The third division, the Ketuvim, or Writings, contains many different types of books, including lyrical hymns of praise (Psalms), wisdom literature (Proverbs), drama (the Book of Job), and a biographical tale similar to a short story (the Book of Ruth).

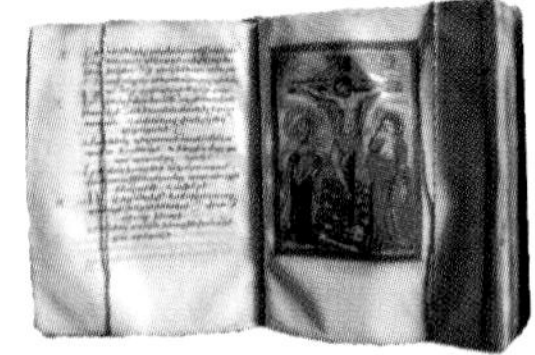

The Torah is traditionally attributed to Moses. Nineteenth-century Biblical scholars, however, noted stylistic and thematic differences throughout the Bible and came to believe that several different writers composed, or transcribed from the oral tradition, many different texts that were later compiled into the Torah as it now exists. The different historical perspectives of these writers influenced their work, providing the modern reader with an opportunity to gain a richer understanding of the early Hebrew people's view of God, the world around them, and the relationship between God and humanity. The following selection is taken from the King James Bible, the best-selling book of all time, which was translated by a group of scholars in 1611. The poetry and prose of this translation have had a profound effect on Western literature and thought.

CONNECTIONS: The Hebrew Covenant with God

In Genesis, God makes a covenant, or solemn agreement, with Noah and his family that He will never again destroy the earth. To the Hebrews, God was not a remote force but rather an active presence in everyday life, and the covenant was the symbol of God's concern with the Hebrew people. The concept of a covenant with God is further developed in Exodus. According to this covenant, the Hebrews became God's chosen people in return for their faith and obedience. The covenant thus signified an intense, dynamic relationship between the Hebrew people and God.

GOALS/OBJECTIVES

Studying this lesson will enable students to

- appreciate an excerpt from Genesis
- briefly explain the Hebrew covenant with God
- define *parallelism* and recognize it as an important literary technique in the Bible
- define *archetype* and recognize archetypes in literary works
- write a journal entry from a character's viewpoint
- write a critical essay comparing and contrasting the Mesopotamian and Biblical flood stories
- identify types of nouns

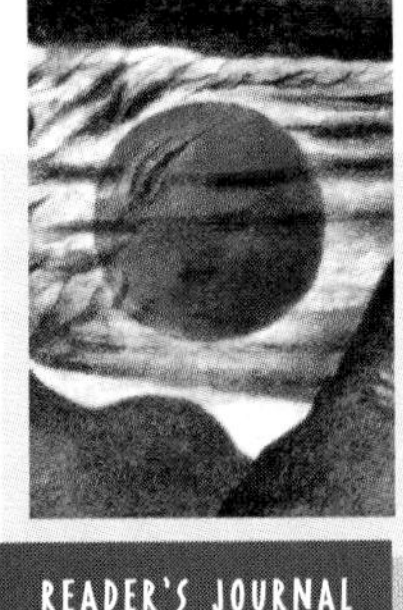

READER'S JOURNAL

Describe your idea of paradise. What would it be like to live there? How would you feel upon being forced to leave?

FROM

Genesis

CHAPTER 1

In the beginning God created the heaven and the earth.

2 And the earth was without form, and void; and darkness was upon the face of the deep. And the spirit of God moved upon the face of the waters.

3 And God said, Let there be light: and there was light.

4 And God saw the light, that it was good: and God divided the light from the darkness.

5 And God called the light Day, and the darkness he called Night. And the evening and the morning were the first day.

6 And God said, Let there be a firmament in the midst of the waters, and let it divide the waters from the waters.

7 And God made the firmament, and divided the waters which were under the firmament from the waters which were above the firmament: and it was so.

8 And God called the firmament Heaven. And the evening and the morning were the second day.

9 And God said, Let the waters under the heaven be gathered together unto one place, and let the dry land appear: and it was so.

10 And God called the dry land Earth; and the gathering together of the waters called he Seas: and God saw that it was good.

11 And God said, Let the earth bring forth grass, the herb yielding seed, and the fruit tree yielding fruit after his kind, whose seed is in itself, upon the earth: and it was so.

12 And the earth brought forth grass, and herb yielding seed after his kind, and the tree yielding fruit, whose seed was in itself, after his kind: and God saw that it was good.

13 And the evening and the morning were the third day.

14 And God said, Let there be lights in the firmament of the heaven to divide the day from the night; and let them be for signs, and for seasons, and for days, and years:

15 And let them be for lights in the firmament of the heaven to give light upon the earth: and it was so.

❶ *What is the earth like before the beginning of creation?*

❷ *In what way does God create light?*

WORDS FOR EVERYDAY USE

fir • ma • ment (furm´ə mənt) *n.*, sky, viewed poetically as a solid arch or vault

READER'S JOURNAL

As an alternate activity, encourage students to imagine surviving a disaster so terrible that most of life on earth is destroyed. How would they feel about having survived? thankful? guilty? How would they feel about the destruction of all they have known?

ANSWERS TO GUIDED READING QUESTIONS

❶ The earth is a dark, watery void without form.

❷ God creates light through His word, or His command, "Let there be light."

SPELLING AND VOCABULARY WORDS FROM THE SELECTION

abate	firmament
assuage	perpetual
beguile	prevail
countenance	replenish
dominion	token
enmity	vagabond

SUPPORT FOR LEP STUDENTS

ADDITIONAL VOCABULARY

fowl—birds
subdue—conquer

ARCHAIC TERMS

compasseth—goes around

VOCABULARY IN CONTEXT

• While the shepherd lay on his back in the field, watching clouds stream across the firmament, his flock wandered away.

Answers to Guided Reading Questions

❶ Fish, fowl, whales, and other water creatures are created first. These life forms are created by both the word of God and the water, which brings forth creatures "abundantly."

❷ Humans are created as male and female in God's image. God blesses the humans, telling them to be fruitful, to multiply, to replenish and to subdue the earth, and to rule over the creatures of the earth.

Cultural/Historical Note

You may wish to point out to students that, while in Genesis 2 God creates man by forming him from dust and breathing life into him and creates woman from the rib of man, in Genesis 1 God creates man and woman the same way that He creates light, heaven, and land—through His word alone. The ancient Hebrews thus revealed their belief in the power of words, a belief also echoed in the New Testament in John 1:1, "In the beginning was the Word, and the Word was with God, and the Word was God." Inform students that the Egyptian creation myth from Memphis, the capital city in Egypt during the period of the First Dynasty (c. 2925–c. 2775 BC), also reveals a belief in the creative power of words. You might ask students to discuss the quotation on page 521.

16 And God made two great lights; the greater light to rule the day, and the lesser light to rule the night: he made the stars also.

17 And God set them in the firmament of the heaven to give light upon the earth,

18 And to rule over the day and over the night, and to divide the light from the darkness: and God saw that it was good.

19 And the evening and the morning were the fourth day.

❶ *What life forms are created first? In what way are these life forms created?*

20 And God said, Let the waters bring forth abundantly the moving creature that hath life, and fowl that may fly above the earth in the open firmament of heaven.

21 And God created great whales, and every living creature that moveth, which the waters brought forth abundantly, after their kind, and every winged fowl after his kind: and God saw that it was good.

22 And God blessed them, saying, Be fruitful, and multiply, and fill the waters in the seas, and let fowl multiply in the earth.

23 And the evening and the morning were the fifth day.

24 And God said, Let the earth bring forth the living creature after his kind, cattle, and creeping thing, and beast of the earth after his kind: and it was so.

25 And God made the beast of the earth after his kind, and cattle after their kind, and every thing that creepeth upon the earth after his kind: and God saw that it was good.

❷ *In what way are humans created? What blessing does God give to humans?*

26 And God said, Let us make man in our image, after our likeness: and let them have dominion over the fish of the sea, and over the fowl of the air, and over the cattle, and over all the earth, and over every creeping thing that creepeth upon the earth.

27 So God created man in his own image, in the image of God created he him; male and female created he them.

28 And God blessed them, and God said unto them, Be fruitful, and multiply, and replenish the earth, and subdue it: and have dominion over the fish of the sea, and over the fowl of the air, and over every living thing that moveth upon the earth.

29 And God said, Behold, I have given you every herb bearing seed, which is upon the face of all the earth, and every tree, in the which is the fruit of a tree yielding seed; to you it shall be for meat.

30 And to every beast of the earth, and to every fowl of the air, and to every thing that creepeth upon the earth, wherein there is life, I have given every green herb for meat: and it was so.

31 And God saw every thing that he had made, and, behold, it was very good. And the evening and the morning were the sixth day.

CHAPTER 2

1 Thus the heavens and the earth were finished, and all the host of them.

2 And on the seventh day God ended his work which he had made; and he rested on the seventh day from all his work which he had made.

3 And God blessed the seventh day, and sanctified it: because that in it he had rested from all his work which God created and made.

4 These are the generations of the heavens and of the earth when they were created, in the day that the LORD God made the earth and the heavens,

5 And every plant of the field before it was in the earth, and every herb of the field before it grew: for the LORD God had not caused it to rain upon the earth and there was not a man to till the ground.

Words for Everyday Use

do • min • ion (də min´yən) *n.,* rule or power to rule; sovereign authority

re • plen • ish (ri plen´ish) *vt.,* make full or complete again; repeople

Vocabulary in Context

- The forest ranger considered the part of the preserve he supervised to be his dominion.
- We sold everything so quickly at the school's bake sale that we had to send someone out for more baked goods to replenish our supply.

Elohim Creating Adam. William Blake. Tate Gallery, London, Great Britain. Art Resource, NY

6 But there went up a mist from the earth, and watered the whole face of the ground.
7 And the LORD God formed man of the dust of the ground, and breathed into his nostrils the breath of life; and man became a living soul.
8 And the LORD God planted a garden eastward in Eden; and there he put the man whom he had formed.
9 And out of the ground made the LORD God to grow every tree that is pleasant to the sight, and good for food; the tree of life also in the midst of the garden, and the tree of knowledge of good and evil.
10 And a river went out of Eden to water the garden; and from thence it was parted, and became into four heads.
11 The name of the first is Pi´-sŏn: that is it which compasseth the whole land of Hăv´-i-läh, where there is gold;
12 And the gold of that land is good: There is bdellium[1] and the onyx stone.
13 And the name of the second river is Gi´-hŏn: the same is it that compasseth the whole land of Ē-thi-ō´-pi-ă.[2]
14 And the name of the third river is Hid´-dĕ-kĕl: that is it which goeth toward the east of Assyria. And the fourth river Éù-phrā´-tēs.[3]
15 And the LORD God took the man, and put him into the garden of Eden to dress it[4] and to keep it.
16 And the LORD God commanded the man, saying, Of every tree of the garden thou mayest freely eat:
17 But of the tree of the knowledge of good and evil, thou shalt not eat of it: for in the day that thou eatest thereof thou shalt surely die.

❶ *In what way is man created?*

❷ *What does God cause to grow in Eden?*

❸ *What are God's instructions to the man?*

1. **bdellium.** Jewel interpreted as being a deep red garnet, a crystal, or a pearl
2. **Ē-thi-ō´-pi-ă.** Ancient kingdom in northeast Africa where the countries of Sudan and North Ethiopia are now located
3. **Assyria . . . Éù-phrā´-tēs.** *Assyria*—ancient empire in southwest Asia; *Euphrates*—river that flows through Turkey southward through Syria and Iraq and joins with the Tigris River
4. **dress it.** Tend it

Answers to Guided Reading Questions

❶ God creates man by shaping him of dust and by breathing into his nostrils.

❷ In Eden, God causes beautiful, fruit-bearing trees; the tree of life; and the tree of knowledge of good and evil to grow.

❸ God instructs the man that he may eat from every tree except from the tree of knowledge of good and evil, and says that the man will die if he eats this fruit.

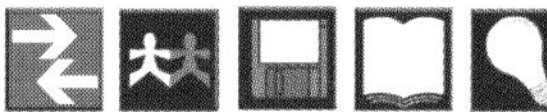

Additional Questions and Activities

You might encourage students to discuss what different sides of God Genesis 1 and Genesis 2 reveal. In what different ways are humans portrayed in these two chapters? What does each chapter reveal about the relationship between humans and God?

ANSWERS

Responses will vary.

In the first creation story, humans seem more godlike, as they are created in God's image, and they are given dominion over the earth. God seems to be a remote, benevolent, omnipotent force. In the second creation story, God seems less remote and more personally involved in the creation, as He is described as shaping Adam of dust and breathing into his nostrils. In this story, God gives Adam the power to name all the creatures He has created, but man is put in Eden not to "subdue" or to "have dominion" but to "dress it and keep it," or to work as a groundskeeper. God also commands Adam never to eat of the fruit of the tree of knowledge of good and evil. Humans seem to have less power in this creation story, and God is both more demanding and more personally involved with humans' fates.

Quotables

"There came into being as the heart and there came into being as the tongue something in the form of Atum. The mighty Great One is Ptah, who transmitted life to all gods, as well as to their *ka*'s, through this heart. . . . The sight of the eyes, the hearing of the ears, and the smelling the air by the nose, they report to the heart. It is this which causes every completed concept to come forth, and it is the tongue which announces what the heart thinks. . . . Indeed, all the divine order really came into being through what the heart thought and the tongue commanded."

—from the Memphite creation myth

Answers to Guided Reading Questions

❶ After eating the fruit of the tree, Adam and Even know shame and guilt for the first time.

❷ The serpent is subtle in that he cleverly awakens Eve's curiosity about the fruit of the tree by asking her a series of questions that encourage her to doubt God's instructions.

Cultural/Historical Note

You may wish to share with students the following background on the Hebrews after their arrival in Egypt: Some time after the Hebrew people's arrival in Egypt, the Hyksos were overthrown and the Hebrew people were enslaved, but they kept their religion and did not adopt that of the Egyptians. Moses, a religious leader, led the Hebrew people out of Egypt and back toward Canaan, which they called the Promised Land. The journey through the desert took forty years. In that time the Hebrew faith was strengthened by two events—Moses receiving God's commandments on top of Mount Sinai and the development of a Covenant, or agreement with God, that God would make the Hebrews His chosen people in return for their obedience and trust.

The Hebrew people fought hard to establish themselves in Canaan, which already had a thriving culture of its own. Eventually, they were successful in founding their own land, called Israel. Israel became a major power in the region during the reign of its first king, Saul (1020–1005 BC). David, who followed Saul, was perhaps the greatest of Israel's kings. He united the twelve tribes of Israel and established a capital at Jerusalem. David is popularly known for his battle against Goliath and for writing many beautiful psalms. David was followed by King Solomon. After

(cont.)

18 And the LORD God said, It is not good that the man should be alone; I will make him an help meet[5] for him.

19 And out of the ground the LORD God formed every beast of the field, and every fowl of the air; and brought them unto Adam to see what he would call them: and whatsoever Adam called every living creature, that was the name thereof.

20 And Adam gave names to all cattle, and to the fowl of the air, and to every beast of the field; but for Adam there was not found an help meet for him.

❶ *What effect does tasting the fruit from the tree of knowledge of good and evil have on Adam and Eve?*

21 And the LORD God caused a deep sleep to fall upon Adam, and he slept: and he took one of his ribs, and closed up the flesh instead thereof;

22 And the rib, which the LORD God had taken from man, made he a woman, and brought her unto the man.

23 And Adam said, This is now bone of my bones, and flesh of my flesh: she shall be called Woman, because she was taken out of Man.

24 Therefore shall a man leave his father and his mother, and shall cleave unto his wife: and they shall be one flesh.

25 And they were both naked, the man and his wife, and were not ashamed.

CHAPTER 3

1 Now the serpent was more subtil[6] than any beast of the field which the LORD God had made. And he said unto the woman, Yea, hath God said, Ye shall not eat of every tree of the garden?

❷ *In what way is the serpent subtle?*

2 And the woman said unto the serpent, We may eat of the fruit of the trees of the garden:

3 But of the fruit of the tree which is in the midst of the garden, God hath said, Ye shall not eat of it, neither shall ye touch it, lest ye die.

4 And the serpent said unto the woman, Ye shall not surely die:

5 For God doth know that in the day ye eat thereof, then your eyes shall be opened, and ye shall be as gods, knowing good and evil.

6 And when the woman saw that the tree was good for food, and that it was pleasant to the eyes, and a tree to be desired to make one wise, she took of the fruit thereof, and did eat, and gave also unto her husband with her; and he did eat.

7 And the eyes of them both were opened, and they knew that they were naked; and they sewed fig leaves together, and make themselves aprons.

8 And they heard the voice of the LORD God walking in the garden in the cool of the day and Adam and his wife hid themselves from the presence of the LORD God amongst the trees of the garden.

9 And the LORD God called unto Adam, and said unto him, Where art thou?

10 And he said, I heard thy voice in the garden, and I was afraid, because I was naked; and I hid myself.

11 And he said, Who told thee that thou wast naked? Hast thou eaten of the tree, whereof I commanded thee that thou shouldest not eat?

12 And the man said, The woman whom thou gavest to be with me, she gave me of the tree, and I did eat.

13 And the LORD God said unto the woman, What is this that thou hast done? And the woman said, The serpent beguiled me, and I did eat.

5. **help meet.** Appropriate helper
6. **subtil.** Archaic spelling of *subtle*, meaning clever, crafty, or sly

Words for Everyday Use

be • guile (bē gīl´) *vt.*, deceive; mislead by cheating or tricking

Vocabulary in Context

- No one would suspect that man to be a traitor because he could beguile us all with his friendly and loyal manner.

14 And the LORD God said unto the serpent, Because thou hast done this, thou art cursed above all cattle, and above every beast of the field; upon thy belly shalt thou go, and dust shalt thou eat all the days of thy life:

15 And I will put enmity between thee and the woman, and between thy seed[7] and her seed; it shall bruise thy head, and thou shalt bruise his heel.

16 Unto the woman he said, I will greatly multiply thy sorrow and thy conception; in sorrow thou shalt bring forth children; and thy desire shall be to thy husband, and he shall rule over thee.

17 And unto Adam he said, Because thou hast hearkened unto[8] the voice of thy wife, and hast eaten of the tree, of which I commanded thee, saying, Thou shalt not eat of it: Cursed is the ground for thy sake; in sorrow shalt thou eat of it all the days of thy life;

18 Thorns also and thistles shall it bring forth to thee; and thou shalt eat the herb of the field;

19 In the sweat of thy face shalt thou eat bread, till thou return unto the ground; for out of it wast thou taken: for dust thou art, and unto dust shalt thou return.

20 And Adam called his wife's name Eve; because she was the mother of all living.

21 Unto Adam also and to his wife did the LORD God make coats of skins, and clothed them.

22 And the LORD God said, Behold, the man is become as one of us, to know good and evil: and now, lest he put forth his hand, and take also of the tree of life, and eat, and live for ever:

23 Therefore the LORD God sent him forth from the garden of Eden, to till[9] the ground from whence he was taken.

24 So he drove out the man; and he placed at the east of the garden of Eden Chĕr´-ū-bims,[10] and a flaming sword which turned every way, to keep the way of the tree of life.

FROM CHAPTER 4

1 And Adam knew Eve his wife; and she conceived, and bare Cain, and said, I have gotten a man from the LORD.

2 And she again bare his brother Abel. And Abel was a keeper of sheep, but Cain was a tiller of the ground.

3 And in process of time it came to pass, that Cain brought of the fruit of the ground an offering unto the LORD.

4 And Abel, he also brought of the firstlings[11] of his flock and of the fat thereof. And the LORD had respect unto Abel and to his offering:

5 But unto Cain and to his offering he had not respect. And Cain was very wroth,[12] and his countenance fell.

6 And the LORD said unto Cain, Why art thou wroth? and why is thy countenance fallen?

7 If thou doest well, shalt thou not be accepted? and if thou doest not well, sin lieth at the door. And unto thee shall be his desire, and thou shalt rule over him.

8 And Cain talked with Abel his brother: and it came to pass, when they were in the

1 *In what different ways do Cain and Abel make their livelihoods?*

2 *What effect does Adam and Eve's fall have on the future of humankind?*

3 *How does Cain feel toward Abel and why?*

4 *Why does God expel Adam and Eve from Eden?*

7. **seed.** Descendants
8. **hearkened unto.** Listened carefully to; heeded
9. **till.** Work land to raise crops
10. **Cherubims.** Archaic spelling of plural *cherubim*, meaning winged heavenly beings that support the throne of God or act as guardian spirits
11. **firstlings.** First offspring of an animal
12. **wroth.** Angry, wrathful

WORDS FOR EVERYDAY USE

en • mi • ty (en´mə tē) *n.*, bitter attitude or feelings of an enemy or of mutual enemies

coun • te • nance (koun´tə nəns) *n.*, look on a person's face that shows one's nature or feelings

ANSWERS TO GUIDED READING QUESTIONS

1 Cain is a farmer and Abel is a shepherd.

2 Because of Adam and Eve's fall, humans have to work hard to grow the food they need to survive, and they are doomed to die, or return to dust.

3 Cain feels jealous of and resentful toward Abel because the Lord respects and accepts Abel's offering and does not respect or accept Cain's offering.

4 God is concerned that Adam and Eve will eat of the tree of life, gain immortality, and become godlike.

CULTURAL/HISTORICAL NOTE (CONT.)

Solomon's death in 925 BC, the kingdom split in two, mostly because of financial disagreements. Judah kept its capital at Jerusalem in the south, and Israel established Samaria as its capital in the north.

Both Judah and Israel lay in the path of many mighty empires, and both nations were weaker than they had been when they were united under David. Assyria conquered Israel in 722. The Babylonians conquered Judah in 586 and destroyed the temple at Jerusalem. Once again, the Israelites were enslaved. This time they were brought away from their homeland into Babylon. It was not until 539 that Cyrus, a Persian ruler, allowed the Israelites to return to their homeland and rebuild their temple at Jerusalem. Despite enslavement and the destruction of their seat of worship, the Israelites remained faithful to their beliefs and did not adopt the religions of those who conquered and surrounded them. Their extraordinary faith made them unique and one of the most steadfast peoples in the area of the Fertile Crescent.

VOCABULARY IN CONTEXT

- The enmity between the two rivals drove them to scheme and plot against each other.
- As soon as we saw Fiori's joyful countenance, we knew that he had the part he wanted in the school play.

Answers to Guided Reading Questions

❶ Noah is spared from the flood because he "found grace in the eyes of the Lord" and because he is "a just man and perfect in his generations."

❷ Because Cain spilled his brother's blood upon the earth, he can no longer farm the land, and he is condemned to be an eternal wanderer or outcast.

❸ God tells Noah to make an ark of gopher wood and to cover it with pitch.

❹ God repents making humans because of their wickedness.

Literary Technique

ARCHETYPE

Inform students that an **archetype** is an inherited, often unconscious ancestral memory or motif that recurs throughout history or literature. The outcast or outsider is an archetypal character who appears in literature from many cultures. In Western literature, Cain is perhaps the most widely known example of this archetypal character. Ask students the following questions: How does Cain feel about his punishment—becoming an outcast? What does he fear will happen to him? Why does the Lord put a mark upon Cain? What does this archetypal story reveal about ancient Hebrew beliefs?

ANSWERS

Cain feels that his punishment is greater than he can bear. He fears he will be killed. God seems to feel that being condemned to wander the earth is enough of a punishment for Cain and sets His mark upon Cain so that others will know not to kill him. The story reveals an early Hebrew taboo against fratricide.

❶ *Why is Noah spared from the flood?*

❷ *What is Cain's punishment for spilling his brother's blood?*

❸ *What does God tell Noah to do?*

❹ *Why does God repent making humans?*

field, that Cain rose up against Abel his brother, and slew[11] him.

9 And the LORD said unto Cain, Where is Abel thy brother? And he said, I know not: Am I my brother's keeper?

10 And he said, What hast thou done? the voice of thy brother's blood crieth unto me from the ground.

11 And now art thou cursed from the earth, which hath opened her mouth to receive thy brother's blood from thy hand;

12 When thou tillest the ground, it shall not henceforth yield unto thee her strength; a fugitive and a <u>vagabond</u> shalt thou be in the earth.

13 And Cain said unto the LORD, My punishment is greater than I can bear.

14 Behold, thou hast driven me out this day from the face of the earth; and from thy face shall I be hid; and I shall be a fugitive and a vagabond in the earth; and it shall come to pass that every one that findeth me shall slay me.

15 And the LORD said unto him, Therefore whosoever slayeth Cain, vengeance shall be taken on him sevenfold. And the LORD set a mark upon Cain, lest any finding him should kill him.

16 And Cain went out from the presence of the LORD, and dwelt in the land of Nod, on the east of Eden.

FROM CHAPTER 6

5 And God saw that the wickedness of man was great in the earth, and that every imagination of the thoughts of his heart was only evil continually.

6 And it repented the Lord that he had made man on the earth, and it grieved him at his heart.

7 And the Lord said, I will destroy man whom I have created from the face of the earth; both man, and beast, and the creeping thing, and the fowls of the air; for it repenteth me that I have made them.

8 But Noah found grace in the eyes of the Lord.

9 These are the generations of Noah: Noah was a just man and perfect in his generations, and Noah walked with God.

10 And Noah begat three sons, Shem, Ham, and Jā´-phĕth.

11 The earth also was corrupt before God, and the earth was filled with violence.

12 And God looked upon the earth, and, behold, it was corrupt; for all flesh had corrupted his way upon the earth.

13 And God said unto Noah, The end of all flesh is come before me; for the earth is filled with violence through them; and, behold, I will destroy them with the earth.

14 Make thee an ark of gō´-phĕr wood; rooms shalt thou make in the ark; and shalt pitch it within and without with pitch.[14]

15 And this is the fashion which thou shalt make it of: The length of the ark shall be three hundred cubits,[15] the breadth of it fifty cubits, and the height of it thirty cubits.

16 A window shalt thou make to the ark, and in a cubit shalt thou finish it above; and the door of the ark shalt thou set in the side thereof; with lower, second, and third stories shalt thou make it.

17 And, behold, I, even I, do bring a flood of waters upon the earth, to destroy all flesh, wherein is the breath of life, from

13. **slew.** Killed
14. **pitch . . . pitch.** Waterproof with a black, sticky substance
15. **cubits.** Ancient units of measurement; each one about twenty inches

Words for Everyday Use

vag • a • bond (vag´ə band´) *n.*, person who wanders from place to place

Vocabulary in Context

- The soldier enjoyed traveling so much that even after the service he remained a <u>vagabond</u>, constantly traveling.

Photo: John Webb

The Body of Abel Found by Adam and Eve. *William Blake. Tate Gallery, London, Great Britain. Art Resource, NY*

under heaven; and every thing that is in the earth shall die.

18 But with thee will I establish my covenant; and thou shalt come into the ark, thou, and thy sons, and thy wife, and thy sons' wives with thee.

19 And of every living thing of all flesh, two of every sort shalt thou bring into the ark, to keep them alive with thee; they shall be male and female.

20 Of fowls after their kind, and of cattle after their kind, of every creeping thing of the earth after his kind, two of every sort shall come unto thee, to keep them alive.

21 And take thou unto thee of all food that is eaten, and thou shalt gather it to thee; and it shall be food for thee, and for them.

22 Thus did Noah; according to all that God commanded him, so did he.

CHAPTER 7

1 And the Lord said unto Noah, Come thou and all thy house into the ark; for thee have I seen righteous before me in this generation.

2 Of every clean[16] beast thou shalt take to thee by sevens, the male and his female: and of beasts that are not clean by two, the male and his female.

3 Of fowls also of the air by sevens, the male and the female; to keep seed alive upon the face of all the earth.

4 For yet seven days, and I will cause it to rain upon the earth forty days and forty nights; and every living substance that I have made will I destroy from off the face of the earth.

➊ *What does God ask Noah to bring with him? Why does God ask Noah to bring these things?*

➋ *When will God send the flood? How long will the flood last? What is the purpose of the flood?*

16. **clean.** Fit for food

ANSWERS TO GUIDED READING QUESTIONS

➊ God asks Noah to bring two of every sort of creature into the ark, saying, "They shall be male and female." God asks Noah to bring these animals so that each species of living things will survive the flood.

➋ God will send the flood in seven days. It will rain for forty days and forty nights. The purpose of the flood is to destroy every living thing God has created from the face of the earth.

QUOTABLES

"No man but I can bear my evil doom."

—Sophocles
Oedipus the King

LITERARY NOTE

Have students review Aristotle's definition of tragedy on page 617. Point out that, although a tragic hero's flaw leads to his downfall, a tragic hero must remain great. Often this involves rising above one's fate by accepting it, as in the above lines from *Oedipus.* Have students compare and contrast Oedipus's attitude toward his fate, revealed above, with Cain's attitude. Encourage students to write a short scene in which a character expresses either Cain's or Oedipus's attitude toward his or her fate.

Answers to Guided Reading Questions

❶ The flood covers the tops of mountains, and all creatures that need air to breathe die.

Additional Questions and Activities

Point out to students that Genesis 1 expresses a belief found in many cultures—that a sort of primeval, watery chaos existed before creation: "And the earth was without form, and void; and darkness was upon the face of the deep. And the spirit of God moved upon the face of the waters." Encourage students to discuss the significance of God's destroying his creation by flood. To what state does the world return?

ANSWERS

Responses will vary.

The flood reveals God's determination to destroy His creation completely. Students may say that God is essentially undoing the creation by causing the flood. He is returning the world to the state of watery chaos that existed before the creation.

Cultural/Historical Note

You may wish to point out to the students that the Hebrew people practiced monotheism, unlike all the other cultures of the area that practiced polytheism. This revolutionary change in religious thought is perhaps the greatest contribution of the Hebrews to the history of human civilization.

5 And Noah did according unto all that the Lord commanded him.

6 And Noah was six hundred years old when the flood of waters was upon the earth.

7 And Noah went in, and his sons, and his wife, and his sons' wives with him, into the ark, because of the waters of the flood.

Q ❶ *What effect does the flood have on the earth?*

8 Of clean beasts, and of beasts that are not clean, and of fowls, and of every thing that creepeth upon the earth,

9 There went in two and two unto Noah into the ark, the male and the female, as God had commanded Noah.

10 And it came to pass after seven days, that the waters of the flood were upon the earth.

11 In the six hundredth year of Noah's life, in the second month, the seventeenth day of the month, the same day were all the fountains of the great deep broken up, and the windows of heaven were opened.

12 And the rain was upon the earth forty days and forty nights.

13 In the selfsame day entered Noah, and Shem, and Ham, and Jā´-phĕth, the sons of Noah, and Noah's wife, and the three wives of his sons with them, into the ark;

14 They, and every beast after his kind, and all the cattle after their kind, and every creeping thing that creepeth upon the earth after his kind, and every fowl after his kind, every bird of every sort.

15 And they went in unto Noah into the ark, two and two of all flesh, wherein is the breath of life.

16 And they that went in, went in male and female of all flesh, as God had commanded him: and the Lord shut him in.

17 And the flood was forty days upon the earth; and the waters increased, and bare up the ark, and it was lift up above the earth.

18 And the waters prevailed, and were increased greatly upon the earth; and the ark went upon the face of the waters.

19 And the waters prevailed exceedingly upon the earth; and all the high hills, that were under the whole heaven, were covered.

20 Fifteen cubits upward did the waters prevail; and the mountains were covered.

21 And all flesh died that moved upon the earth, both of fowl, and of cattle, and of beast, and of every creeping thing that creepeth upon the earth, and every man:

22 All in whose nostrils was the breath of life, of all that was in the dry land, died.

23 And every living substance was destroyed which was upon the face of the ground, both man, cattle, and the creeping things, and the fowl of the heaven; and they were destroyed from the earth: and Noah only remained alive, and they that were with him in the ark.

24 And the waters prevailed upon the earth an hundred and fifty days.

CHAPTER 8

1 And God remembered Noah, and every living thing, and all the cattle that was with him in the ark: and God made a wind to pass over the earth, and the water assuaged;

2 The fountains also of the deep and the windows of heaven were stopped, and the rain from heaven was restrained;

3 And the waters returned from off the earth continually: and after the end of the hundred and fifty days the waters were abated.

4 And the ark rested in the seventh month, on the seventeenth day of the month, upon the mountains of Ăr´-ă-răt.[17]

17. **Ăr´-ă-răt.** Mountain in eastern Turkey

pre • vail (prē vāl´) *vi.,* become stronger
as • suage (ə swāj´) *vt.,* calm
a • bate (ə bāt´) *vi.,* make less in amount

Vocabulary in Context

- Thanks to his speed and agility, Chris would always prevail over his fencing opponent, winning first place in the competition.
- It is too dangerous to go sailing in these high winds; we will have to wait until they assuage.
- Over time, Chelsea's fear of heights gradually abated until she could look out from the top of a skyscraper and only feel the smallest twinge of unease.

5 And the waters decreased continually until the tenth month: in the tenth month, on the first day of the month, were the tops of the mountains seen.

6 And it came to pass at the end of forty days, that Noah opened the window of the ark which he had made:

7 And he sent forth a raven, which went forth to and fro, until the waters were dried up from off the earth.

8 Also he sent forth a dove from him, to see if the waters were abated from off the face of the ground;

9 But the dove found no rest for the sole of her foot, and she returned unto him into the ark, for the waters were on the face of the whole earth: then he put forth his hand, and took her, and pulled her in unto him into the ark.

10 And he stayed yet other seven days; and again he sent forth the dove out of the ark;

11 And the dove came in to him in the evening; and, lo, in her mouth was an olive leaf plucked off: so Noah knew that the waters were abated from off the earth.

12 And he stayed yet other seven days; and sent forth the dove; which returned not again unto him any more.

13 And it came to pass in the six hundredth and first year, in the first month, the first day of the month, the waters were dried up from off the earth: and Noah removed the covering of the ark, and looked, and, behold, the face of the ground was dry.

14 And in the second month, on the seven and twentieth day of the month, was the earth dried.

15 And God spake unto Noah, saying,

16 Go forth of the ark, thou, and thy wife, and thy sons, and thy sons' wives with thee.

17 Bring forth with thee every living thing that is with thee, of all flesh, both of fowl, and of cattle, and of every creeping thing that creepeth upon the earth; that they may breed abundantly in the earth, and be fruitful, and multiply upon the earth.

18 And Noah went forth, and his sons, and his wife, and his sons' wives with him:

19 Every beast, every creeping thing, and every fowl, and whatsoever creepeth upon the earth, after their kinds, went forth out of the ark.

20 And Noah builded an altar unto the Lord; and took of every clean beast, and of every clean fowl, and offered burnt offerings on the altar.

21 And the Lord smelled a sweet savour; and the Lord said in his heart, I will not again curse the ground any more for man's sake; for the imagination of man's heart is evil from his youth; neither will I again smite[18] any more every thing living, as I have done.

22 While the earth remaineth, seedtime and harvest, and cold and heat, and summer and winter, and day and night shall not cease.

FROM CHAPTER 9

1 And God blessed Noah and his sons, and said unto them, Be fruitful, and multiply, and replenish the earth.

2 And the fear of you and the dread of you shall be upon every beast of the earth, and upon every fowl of the air, upon all that moveth upon the earth, and upon all the fishes of the sea; into your hand are they delivered.

3 Every moving thing that liveth shall be meat for you; even as the green herb have I given you all things.

4 But flesh with the life thereof, which is the blood thereof, shall ye not eat.

5 And surely your blood of your lives will I require; at the hand of every beast will I require it, and at the hand of man; at the hand of every man's brother will I require the life of man.

6 Whoso sheddeth man's blood, by man shall his blood be shed: for in the image of God made he man.

18. **smite.** Destroy, kill

(1) *For how long was the earth covered by the waters?*

(2) *What is the first thing that Noah does once he is upon dry land?*

(3) *What does the Lord decide in His heart? Why does He make this decision?*

(4) *What sign reveals that the waters have abated?*

Answers to Guided Reading Questions

(1) The earth was covered by water until the tenth month.

(2) Noah builds an altar and burns sacrifices to the Lord.

(3) The Lord decides that He will never again destroy every living thing on earth. Students may say that the Lord comes to this decision because of Noah's faith and goodness or because He realizes that humans' hearts are inevitably "evil from . . . [their] youth."

(4) The olive leaf in the dove's beak is a sign that the waters have abated.

INTEGRATED SKILLS ACTIVITIES

LANGUAGE

Have students read the Language Arts Survey 2.16, "The Functions of Sentences." Then have students identify each of the following sentences as declarative, imperative, interrogative, or exclamatory.

1. In the beginning God created the heaven and the earth.
2. Let there be light.
3. Ye shall not eat of every tree of the garden?
4. Hast thou eaten of the tree, whereof I commanded thee that thou shouldest not eat?
5. Cain went out from the presence of the Lord, and dwelt in the land of Nod, on the east of Eden.
6. Make thee an ark of gopher wood.

ANSWERS

1. declarative
2. imperative
3. interrogative
4. interrogative
5. declarative
6. imperative

► Additional practice is provided in the Essential Skills Practice Book: Writing 1.8.

Answers to Guided Reading Questions

❶ God's covenant with Noah is that He will never send another flood to destroy the earth.

Selection Check Test with Answers

ex. What is the first book of the Jewish Bible?

Genesis is the first book of the Jewish Bible.

1. In the first account of creation, what are the first and last things God creates?

God creates light first and humans last.

2. In the second account of creation, how are Adam and Eve created?

God shapes Adam of dust and breathes into his nostrils, giving him life, while Eve is created from Adam's rib.

3. Of what tree does God forbid Adam and Eve to eat the fruit?

God forbids Adam and Eve to eat the fruit of the tree of knowledge of good and evil.

4. What occupations do Cain and Abel practice?

Cain is a farmer, and Abel is a shepherd.

5. What does God do when he observes the wickedness of the earth?

God repents having created humans and decides to destroy His creation by flood.

7 And you, be ye fruitful, and multiply; bring forth abundantly in the earth, and multiply therein.

8 And God spake unto Noah, and to his sons with him, saying,

9 And I, behold, I establish my covenant with you, and with your seed after you;

10 And with every living creature that is with you, of the fowl, of the cattle, and of every beast of the earth with you; from all that go out of the ark, to every beast of the earth.

❶ *What is God's covenant with Noah?*

11 And I will establish my covenant with you; neither shall all flesh be cut off any more by the waters of a flood; neither shall there any more be a flood to destroy the earth.

12 And God said, This is the token of the covenant which I make between me and you and every living creature that is with you, for perpetual generations:

13 I do set my bow[19] in the cloud, and it shall be a token of a covenant between me and the earth.

14 And it shall come to pass, when I bring a cloud over the earth, that the bow shall be seen in the cloud:

15 And I will remember my covenant, which is between me and you and every living creature of all flesh; and the waters shall no more become a flood to destroy all flesh.

16 And the bow shall be in the cloud; and I will look upon it, that I may remember the everlasting covenant between God and every living creature of all flesh that is upon the earth.

17 And God said unto Noah, This is a token of the covenant, which I have established between me and all flesh that is upon the earth.

18 And the sons of Noah, that went forth of the ark, were Shem, and Ham, and Jā´phĕth: and Ham is the father of Canaan.

19 These are the three sons of Noah: and of them was the whole earth overspread. ■

19. **bow.** Rainbow

Words for Everyday Use

to • ken (tō´kən) *n.,* symbol

per • pet • u • al (pər pech´ o͞o əl) *adj.,* lasting forever

Vocabulary in Context

- The university awarded Mrs. Bernstein an honorary doctorate as a token of their esteem for her tireless efforts to end intolerance.
- Rita was unable to concentrate because her two younger sisters interrupted her with perpetual questions and complaints.

Responding to the Selection

Which Biblical story, the creation or the flood, evoked the strongest emotional reaction in you? Discuss your reaction to this story with your classmates. Do you think this story produced the same reaction in an ancient Hebrew audience? Why, or why not?

Reviewing the Selection

Recalling		Interpreting
1. Over what does God give humans dominion in Genesis 1? In what way does the creation of humans differ in Genesis 1 and Genesis 2?	▶▶	What attitude toward humanity is expressed in each of the creation stories? What attitude toward women is expressed in each of the stories? Is this attitude similar to or different from attitudes toward women reflected in our culture?
2. What command is disobeyed by Adam and Eve? What consequences does this disobedience have both for Adam and Eve and for generations to come?	▶▶	Why does Eve succumb to the serpent's temptation? In what way do Adam and Eve change after they violate God's command? For what problems or hardships in the world does this story provide an explanation?
3. What crime does Cain commit? What punishment does Cain receive?	▶▶	Why does Cain commit this crime? Why does Cain say that his punishment is greater than he can bear?
4. Describe the humans that God destroys. In what way is Noah different from these humans? What warning and instructions does God give Noah?	▶▶	In what way does the flood bring both destruction and rebirth? In what way does God's attitude toward His creation change throughout this story?

Synthesizing

5. What parts of these selections from Genesis reflect the Hebrew belief in a personal God, intimately concerned with human affairs?

Responding to the Selection

As an alternate activity, students might discuss which Biblical characters they found most appealing and least appealing.

Answers for Reviewing the Selection

RECALLING AND INTERPRETING

1. **Recalling.** God gives humans dominion over the other creatures of earth. In Genesis 1, God makes man and woman at the same time in His own image. Their creation is the final event in the creation. In Genesis 2, man is created from the dust and God's breath. God creates the trees in Eden and has Adam name all the animals before creating Eve from Adam's rib. **Interpreting.** In both stories, the creation of humans is portrayed as the pinnacle of, or most important event in, the creation. Students may say that in the first creation story women seem equal to men because they are created at the same time, while in the second creation story women are portrayed as being inferior to men because Eve is created later from Adam's rib as a "help meet." *Responses will vary.*

2. **Recalling.** Adam and Eve eat the fruit of the tree of knowledge of good and evil. The serpent is cursed and enmity exists between the serpent and women, women experience pain and suffering in childbirth, humans have to labor long hours to farm the land, humans die and return to dust, humans developed shame about their bodies, and humans are driven out of Eden. **Interpreting.** Eve is tempted by the serpent's claim that the result of eating the fruit is not death but becoming "as gods, knowing good and evil." Adam and Eve know that they are naked for the first time and feel shame and guilt. This story provides an explanation for human death, suffering, pain, and labor.

(cont.)

Answers for Reviewing the Selection (cont.)

3. **Recalling.** Cain kills his brother Abel. Cain can no longer till the ground and is condemned to be a "fugitive and vagabond." **Interpreting.** Cain is angry and jealous because God does not respect his offering but respects Abel's offering. Cain says that he cannot bear his punishment because he has lost his livelihood, is condemned to wander, and believes that everyone will try to kill him.

4. **Recalling.** The humans that God destroys are wicked and have evil imaginations, and the earth is corrupt and violent. Unlike the other humans, Noah finds "grace in the eyes of the Lord" because he is "a just man and perfect in his generations." God tells Noah that He is planning to destroy the earth, and He commands Noah to build an ark and to take at least two of every living creature aboard the ark.

(cont.)

Understanding Literature (Questions for Discussion)

1. **Parallelism. Parallelism** is a rhetorical technique in which a writer emphasizes the equal value or weight of two or more ideas by expressing them in the same grammatical form. Parallelism is an important literary technique in the Bible, creating rhythmical patterns in both prose and verse passages. The following passage from Ecclesiastes 3:2 provides an example.

   A time to be born,
   and a time to die;
   a time to plant, and
   a time to pluck up that
   which is planted;

   Find some examples of parallelism in either of the creation stories in Genesis. In what way might the use of parallelism contribute to the theme of God creating order from disorder in the creation stories?

2. **Archetype.** An **archetype** is an inherited, often unconscious ancestral memory or motif that recurs throughout history and literature. The Book of Genesis is filled with literary archetypes that have recurred throughout both Western and non-Western literature. Among the most common of these archetypes are the idea of a watery chaos preceding the creation of the present world and the idea of a human experiencing a "fall" from an innocent state to a more worldly, corrupt state. Identify other archetypes from Genesis that recur throughout history or literature.

Responding in Writing

1. **Creative Writing: Journal Entry.** Imagine that you are one of the following characters: Adam or Eve after their expulsion from the Garden of Eden, Cain after he receives his punishment, or Noah either immediately before or immediately after the flood. After you have chosen a point of view that you find particularly interesting, try to imagine what the reactions of this person might have been to his or her situation. Then, write a journal entry in which you record your thoughts and feelings from this person's point of view.

2. **Critical Essay: Comparison and Contrast.** Write a comparison and contrast essay on the similarities and differences in the Biblical account of Noah and the Flood and the Mesopotamian account of a great flood in *The Epic of Gilgamesh* on page 508. When contrasting the two selections, focus on the different reasons God and the Mesopotamian gods have for causing the floods, the different fates of Noah and Utnapishtim, and the different contexts in which the flood stories are told. Explain your thesis in an introductory paragraph. In subsequent paragraphs, support your thesis with examples from the texts. Then, come to a conclusion in a final paragraph.

Answers for Reviewing the Selection (cont.)

Interpreting. The flood is a symbol of destruction because it is God's method of destroying "all in whose nostrils was the breath of life." It is a symbol of rebirth because it cleanses the world of wickedness so that a new generation of humans, descendants of the just Noah and his family, can thrive. Initially, God repents having created man and is determined to destroy His creation. By the story's end, however, God makes a covenant, or promise, to never again cause a flood to destroy the earth, His creation.

SYNTHESIZING

Responses will vary. Possible responses are given.

5. God seems closely involved and concerned with humankind in the second creation story and in the story of the fall. In the story of Cain and Abel, although God punishes Cain, He is concerned with being just and with protecting Cain from harm. In the story of Noah and the flood, God is concerned with human behavior, almost undoing all of his creation, but then He makes a covenant with the remaining humans to protect His creation. God's punishments for wicked behavior show that God is concerned that humans obey His will and behave in an upright manner. God's punishments vary in severity from the terrible flood and the expulsion from Eden to Cain's punishment to wander the earth, showing that God judges different human situations differently.

Answers for Understanding Literature

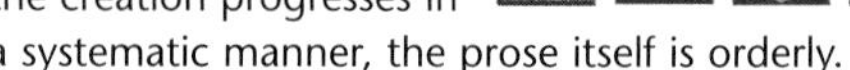

Responses will vary. Possible responses are given.

1. **Parallelism.** Students may note the following examples of parallelism: "And God said, Let there be"; "and God saw that it was good"; "And the evening and the morning were the [nth] day"; and "Be fruitful, and multiply." The use of parallelism provides an organizational and stylistic scheme that reflects the orderly nature of the creation. Just as the creation progresses in a systematic manner, the prose itself is orderly.

2. **Archetype.** Students may identify the following archetypes: a flood that destroys the world, light as civilization and goodness, the temptation, snakes as a symbol of earth and as a symbol of evil, death and rebirth, the outcast, the human desire for knowledge as a form of power.

Language Lab

Types of Nouns. Although the King James Bible makes use of language that sounds archaic to a modern reader, you were probably able to understand much of this language partly because of your innate knowledge of the parts of speech. For example, even though you may have been unfamiliar with the term *firmament,* you probably could figure out that it is a common noun, referring to the heavens. Review the Language Arts Survey 2.3, "Types of Nouns." Read the sentences below about the escape of the Hebrew people from Egypt. Identify the nouns in each sentence, and write whether each noun is common or proper, and concrete or abstract. Also indicate if the noun is a compound or a collective noun.

1. Moses led the Hebrews out of slavery in Egypt.
2. The escaping slaves were pursued by a group of Egyptians on chariots and on horseback.
3. Moses stretched out a hand, parted the Red Sea, and led the people across.
4. This miracle, however, did not shake the confidence of the horsemen who followed them.
5. Foolishly following the children of Israel, the Egyptians were swallowed up by the sea.

The Creation (detail). *Michelangelo*

ANALYTIC SCALES FOR RESPONDING IN WRITING

Assign a score from 1 to 25 for each grading criterion below. (For more detailed evaluation, see the evaluation forms for writing, revising, and proofreading, Assessment Portfolio 4.1–4.9.)

1. Journal Entry

- **Content/Unity.** The journal entry expresses the thoughts and feelings of either Adam or Eve after their expulsion, Cain after he receives his punishment, or Noah either before or after the flood.
- **Organization/Coherence.** The journal entry reveals the thoughts and feelings of the chosen subject in a sensible order.
- **Language/Style.** The journal entry uses vivid and precise nouns, verbs, and modifiers.
- **Conventions.** The journal entry avoids errors in spelling, grammar, usage, mechanics, and manuscript form.

▶ Additional practice is provided in the Essential Skills Practice Book: Writing 1.8.

2. Critical Essay

- **Content/Unity.** The essay compares and contrasts the Mesopotamian and the Biblical accounts of a great flood.
- **Organization/Coherence.** The essay begins with an introduction that includes the thesis of the essay. The introduction is followed by supporting paragraphs with clear transitions. The essay ends with a solid conclusion.
- **Language/Style.** The essay uses vivid and precise nouns, verbs, and modifiers.
- **Conventions.** The essay avoids errors in spelling, grammar, usage, mechanics, and manuscript form.

▶ Additional practice is provided in the Essential Skills Practice Book: Writing 1.20.

ANSWERS FOR LANGUAGE LAB

1. Moses—proper, concrete; Hebrews—proper, concrete; slavery—common, abstract; Egypt, proper, concrete
2. slaves—common, concrete; group—common, concrete, collective; Egyptians—proper, concrete; chariots—common, concrete; horseback—common, concrete, compound
3. Moses—proper, concrete; hand—common, concrete; Red Sea—proper, concrete; people—common, concrete, collective
4. miracle,—common, abstract; confidence—common, abstract; horsemen—common, concrete, compound
5. children—common, concrete; Israel—proper, concrete; Egyptians—proper, concrete; sea—common, concrete

▶ Additional practice is provided in the Essential Skills Practice Book: Language 2.3.

ADDITIONAL RESOURCES

READER'S GUIDE

- Selection Worksheet 7.3

ASSESSMENT PORTFOLIO

- Selection Check Test 2.7.5
- Selection Test 2.7.6

ESSENTIAL SKILLS PRACTICE BOOKS

- Writing 1.8, 1.20

PREREADING EXTENSIONS

Ask students to research other myths about creation. Have them try to identify common themes in creation myths. Students might also discuss how the geography, climate, and natural resources and phenomena of the area of different civilizations affected their mythologies.

Students should be able to find many versions of various creation myths. The following sources may be helpful as they begin their research.

- Bonnefoy, Yves, comp. *American, African, and Old European Mythologies.*
- Campbell, Joseph. *The Masks of God.*
- Campbell, Joseph, with Bill Moyers. *The Power of Myth.*
- Rosenberg, Donna. *World Mythologies.*
- Sproul, Barbara C. *Primal Myths.*

SUPPORT FOR LEP STUDENTS

PRONUNCIATIONS OF PROPER NOUNS AND ADJECTIVES

Ma • hu • cu • tah (mä hä co͞o´tä)
Po • pol Vuh (pō pōl´vä)
Qui • ché (kē chā´)

ADDITIONAL VOCABULARY

intense—very strong
triumph—joy or celebration of victory

PREREADING

from the *Popol Vuh*

Anonymous, translated by Dennis Tedlock

MAYA

About the Selection

The ***Popol Vuh,*** the sacred epic of the Quiché Maya, is an elegant, sophisticated work often compared to the *Odyssey* of Greece. The Quiché are a group of Maya from the western highlands of Guatemala. The Maya reached great intellectual and artistic heights as a civilization, developing a form of hieroglyphic writing, working with gold and other precious metals, and building great stone palaces and stepped pyramids. Mayan astronomy and mathematics were refined and intellectually advanced. Mayan astronomers predicted solar eclipses, created tables charting the movements of Venus and the Moon, calculated the solar year accurately, and created a complex calendar using two concurrently running cycles of 260 and 365 days.

Mayan astronomers were also priests, so the religion of the Mayan people was closely tied to their calendar. The Maya believed that a number of worlds had been created and destroyed before the present world came into being. The *Popol Vuh* describes how the people of each world were destroyed for failing to pay reverence to the gods. The pinnacle of this creation story is the first dawn; when the sun first rose upon the present world, it hardened the previously fluid earth, making life as the Maya knew it possible. The Maya worshipped the Sun and the Moon as gods, along with an assortment of other deities, including rain gods, a death god, a war god, and Kukulcan, or the Feathered Serpent, a god who was later worshipped by the Aztecs as Quetzalcoatl. The Maya thought that the favor of the gods had to be insured with sacrifices of flowers, jade, agricultural products, and animals. Even human captives were sacrificed to the gods to insure fertility. The Maya believed that just as past worlds had been destroyed, this present world too was doomed to come to the end of its cycle. Time and cycles were so important to Mayan religion that time itself was considered a deity, as were different time periods. In addition to revealing the Mayan fascination with cycles of time, the *Popol Vuh* also reveals the Mayan love of numbers. Characters and gods are frequently paired, and sometimes it is difficult to tell whether the writer is renaming a character or god or is introducing a new character or god. This pattern of pairing, tripling, or quadrupling phrases gives the *Popol Vuh* a formal quality akin to the Hebrew Old Testament, with its poetic technique of parallel restatement.

Temple of the Jaguars, Chichén Itzá, Mexico

CONNECTIONS: The Fall of the Maya

The highly developed culture of the Maya flourished from about AD 250–900. Then the time of Mayan glory came to an abrupt and inexplicable end. Large lowland cities were left vacant, and although cities on the highland of the Yucatan peninsula continued to thrive for a while, by the sixteenth century, the time the Spanish arrived in the Americas, the Maya were living and farming in small villages, all their great cities abandoned to the encroaching jungle. The Quiché Maya were conquered by Pedro de Alvarado in 1524. Believing that native creeds were sinful, the Spanish destroyed many Mayan codices, or documents written on bark paper. Later, Spanish missionaries taught the Latin alphabet to Mayan students, who transliterated their myths from surviving records and oral tradition. These transliterations were translated into Spanish. The *Popol Vuh* is one such work, recorded anonymously between 1554 and 1558 in the Mayan language using Latin letters. Toward the end of the seventeenth century, Father Francisco Ximénez, a parish priest living in Guatemala, translated the *Popol Vuh* into Spanish. Since that time, the manuscript written in Mayan has been lost, but the Spanish translation was rediscovered in the 1850s.

GOALS/OBJECTIVES

Studying this lesson will enable students to

- have a positive experience reading a creation myth
- identify the *Popol Vuh* as the sacred epic of the Quiché Maya
- define *myth* and *parallelism*
- identify examples of parallelism
- write a description
- compare and contrast two works
- research an ancient civilization
- prepare and present a group presentation

Think about the questions you have about the existence of the world around you. Choose one question and write a possible explanation for it.

READER'S JOURNAL

FROM THE

Popol Vuh

ANONYMOUS, TRANSLATED BY DENNIS TEDLOCK

[*Editor's note: The creator gods separate the earth from the waters and create animals, birds, and snakes. Finding that these creatures are unable to sing their praises, the creator gods decide to create humans. First, the creator gods try to make humans of mud. The humans made of mud are limp, weak, and mindless, so the creator gods destroy these people. Then, the creator gods try to carve humans from wood. The wooden humans have neither souls nor minds, and they pay no attention to the creator gods, so they too are destroyed, although some are transformed into monkeys. Finally, a fox, a coyote, a parrot, and a crow bring the creator gods corn, and the gods create four men from corn meal. These four are the ancestors of the Quiché Maya people.*]

These are the names of the first people who were made and modeled.

This is the first person: Jaguar Quitze.

And now the second: Jaguar Night.

And now the third: Mahucutah.

And the fourth: True Jaguar.

And these are the names of our first mother-fathers.[1] They were simply made and modeled, it is said; they had no mother and no father. We have named the men by themselves. No woman gave birth to them, nor were they begotten by the builder, sculptor, Bearer, Begetter. By sacrifice alone, by genius alone they were made, they were modeled by the Maker, Modeler, Bearer, Begetter, Sovereign Plumed Serpent.[2] And when they came to fruition, they came out human:

They talked and they made words.
They looked and they listened.
They walked, they worked.

They were good people, handsome, with looks of the male kind. Thoughts came into existence and they gazed; their vision came all at once. Perfectly they saw, perfectly they knew everything under the sky, whenever they looked. The moment they turned around and looked around in the sky, on the earth, everything was seen without any obstruction. They didn't have to walk

1 *What could the four new people do?*

2 *In what way were the four "truly gifted"?*

1. **mother-fathers.** Ancestors, or parents
2. **the builder . . . Sovereign Plumed Serpent.** These names all refer to the creator gods.

WORDS FOR EVERYDAY USE

fru • i • tion (frōō ish´ən) *n.*, realization; a coming to fulfillment

ob • struc • tion (əb struk´shən) *n.*, anything that blocks, hinders, or keeps something from being seen

VOCABULARY IN CONTEXT

- Seeing her novel on the shelves of the bookstore, Mitali felt that her dreams of being a writer had come to fruition.
- Gavin was gasping for air until the obstruction was knocked out of his windpipe.

READER'S JOURNAL

Encourage students to be creative and imaginative in their journal writing. They may wish to create a more polished myth by doing additional work with the ideas that they freewrite about in their journals.

ANSWERS TO GUIDED READING QUESTIONS

1 The four new people could talk, make words, look, listen, walk, and work.

2 The four were "truly gifted" because they could see and understand everything "perfectly."

SPELLING AND VOCABULARY WORDS FROM THE SELECTION

fruition	penitent
mar	proliferate
obstruction	

CROSS-CURRICULAR ACTIVITIES

SOCIAL STUDIES

Chichén Itzá is a ruined city of the ancient Maya. It is located in what is now Mexico. The city is located in an arid area watered only by large wells at the site. The wells give the city part of its name: *Chi,* Mayan for "mouths," and *chén,* Mayan for "wells." The word *Itzá* in the city name comes from the particular group of Maya who eventually settled there.

Ask students to research the history of Chichén Itzá. In so doing, students should look at Mayan architecture, political structure, and opposition from other peoples. Students can also research the archaeological excavation of Chichén Itzá.

Answers to Guided Reading Questions

❶ The creators mar their creations by weakening their eyesight and, hence, their understanding.

❷ The creator gods are worried that the new people will become as great as gods because of their great understanding.

Selection Check Test with Answers

EX. What people created the epic the *Popol Vuh*?
The Quiché Maya created the *Popol Vuh*.

1. What did the first four people look like?
They were "handsome, with looks of the male kind."

2. For what do the first four people give thanks?
They give thanks for being made and modeled.

3. In what way are the first four people marred?
Their vision and understanding is weakened.

4. What happens to the first four men when the first four women are created?
The first four men become wider awake and happy at heart again.

5. At what event do the first people rejoice?
They rejoice at the first sunrise.

around before they could see what was under the sky; they just stayed where they were.

As they looked, their knowledge became intense. Their sight passed through trees, through rocks, through lakes, through seas, through mountains, through plains. Jaguar Quitze, Jaguar Night, Mahucutah, and True Jaguar were truly gifted people.

And then they were asked by the builder and mason:[3]

"What do you know about your being? Don't you look, don't you listen? Isn't your speech good, and your walk? So you must look, to see out under the sky. Don't you see the mountain-plain clearly? So try it," they were told.

And then they saw everything under the sky perfectly. After that, they thanked the Maker, Modeler:

"Truly now,
double thanks, triple thanks
that we've been formed, we've been given
our mouths, our faces,
we speak, we listen,
we wonder, we move,
our knowledge is good, we've understood
what is far and near,
and we've seen what is great and small
under the sky, on the earth.
Thanks to you we've been formed,
we've come to be made and modeled,
our grandmother, our grandfather,"

❶ *In what way do the creators mar their creations?*

they said when they gave thanks for having been made and modeled. They understood everything perfectly, they sighted the four sides, the four corners in the sky, on the earth, and this didn't sound good to the builder and sculptor:

"What our works and designs have said is no good:

'We have understood everything, great and small,' they say." And so the Bearer, Begetter took back their knowledge:

❷ *About what are the creator gods worried?*

"What should we do with them now? Their vision should at least reach nearby, they should see at least a small part of the face of the earth, but what they're saying isn't good. Aren't they merely 'works' and 'designs' in their very names? Yet they'll become as great as gods, unless they procreate, proliferate at the sowing, the dawning, unless they increase."

"Let it be this way: now we'll take them apart just a little, that's what we need. What we've found out isn't good. Their deeds would become equal to ours, just because their knowledge reaches so far. They see everything," so said

the Heart of Sky, Hurricane,
Newborn Thunderbolt, Raw Thunderbolt,
Sovereign Plumed Serpent,
Bearer, Begetter,
Xpiyacoc, Xmucane,
Maker, Modeler,[4]

as they are called. And when they changed the nature of their works, their designs, it was enough that the eyes[5] be marred by the Heart of Sky. They were blinded as the face of a mirror is breathed upon. Their eyes were weakened. Now it was only when they looked nearby that things were clear.

And such was the loss of the means of understanding, along with the means of knowing everything, by the four humans. The root was implanted.

And such was the making, modeling of our first grandfather, our father, by the Heart of Sky, Heart of Earth.

And then their wives and women came into being. Again, the same gods thought of it. It was as if they were asleep when they

3. **the builder and the mason.** Creator god or gods
4. **the Heart . . . Modeler.** Creator gods
5. **the eyes.** The eyes of their creations—Jaguar Quitze, Jaguar Night, Mahucutah, and True Jaguar

Words for Everyday Use

pro • lif • er • ate (prō lif´ər āt´) *vi.,* multiply rapidly; increase profusely

mar (mär) *vt.,* injure or damage so as to make imperfect

Vocabulary in Context

- Mosquitoes proliferate in this swampy area.
- Mitch's absence today marred his otherwise perfect attendance record.

received them, truly beautiful women were there with Jaguar Quitze, Jaguar Night, Mahucutah, and True Jaguar. With their women there they became wider awake. Right away they were happy at heart again, because of their wives.

Celebrated Seahouse is the name of the wife of Jaguar Quitze.

Prawn House is the name of the wife of Jaguar Night.

Hummingbird House is the name of the wife of Mahucutah.

Macaw House is the name of the wife of True Jaguar.

So these are the names of their wives, who became ladies of rank, giving birth to the people of the tribes, small and great.

♦ ♦ ♦

And here is the dawning and showing of the sun, moon, and stars.[6] And Jaguar Quitze, Jaguar Night, Mahucutah, and True Jaguar were overjoyed when they saw the daybringer.[7] It came up first. It looked brilliant when it came up, since it was ahead of the sun.

After that they unwrapped their copal incense,[8] which came from the east, and there was triumph in their hearts when they unwrapped it. They gave their heartfelt thanks with three kinds at once:

Mixtam Copal is the name of the copal brought by Jaguar Quitze.

Cauiztan Copal, next, is the name of the copal brought by Jaguar Night.

Godly Copal, as the next one is called, was brought by Mahucutah.

The three of them had their copal, and this is what they burned as they incensed the direction of the rising sun. They were crying sweetly as they shook their burning copal, the precious copal.

After that they cried because they had yet to see and yet to witness the birth of the sun.

Ruins of Monte Alban, near Oaxaca, Mexico

And then, when the sun came up, the animals, small and great, were happy. They all came up from the rivers and canyons; they waited on all the mountain peaks. Together they looked toward the place where the sun came out.

So then the puma[9] and jaguar cried out, but the first to cry out was a bird, the parrot by name. All the animals were truly happy. The eagle, the white vulture, small birds, great birds spread their wings, and the penitents and sacrificers knelt down. ■

6. **dawning . . . stars.** The Maya believed that prior to this first dawning, the world was in darkness or was lit by other, inferior suns.

7. **daybringer.** Morning star

8. **copal incense.** Incense made from the resin of a tropical tree

9. **puma.** Cougar

❶ *Why were the new people crying?*

WORDS FOR EVERYDAY USE

pen • i • tent (pen´i tənt) *n.,* person who is truly sorry for having sinned or done wrong

ANSWERS TO GUIDED READING QUESTIONS

❶ The new people were crying because they "had yet to see and yet to witness the birth of the sun."

ANALYTIC SCALES FOR RESPONDING IN WRITING

(SEE PAGE 537.)

Assign a score from 1 to 25 for each grading criterion below. (For more detailed evaluation, see the evaluation forms for writing, revising, and proofreading, Assessment Portfolio 4.1–4.9.)

1. Description

- **Content/Unity.** The description portrays the land of a past time.
- **Organization/Coherence.** The description is presented in a logical order, such as part by part order.
- **Language/Style.** The description uses vivid and precise nouns, verbs, and modifiers.
- **Conventions.** The description avoids errors in spelling, grammar, usage, mechanics, and manuscript form.

▶ Additional practice is provided in the Essential Skills Practice Book: Writing 1.8.

2. Critical Essay

- **Content/Unity.** The essay explains the similarities and differences between a Biblical story and a story in the *Popol Vuh.*
- **Organization/Coherence.** The essay presents a thesis in its introduction. The thesis is supported in following paragraphs. The essay ends with a solid conclusion.
- **Language/Style.** The essay uses vivid and precise language.
- **Conventions.** The essay avoids errors in spelling, grammar, usage, mechanics, and manuscript form.

▶ Additional practice is provided in the Essential Skills Practice Book: Writing 1.20.

VOCABULARY IN CONTEXT

- Jorge is penitent, but Karl shows no sign of remorse for his role in the catastrophe.

Responding to the Selection

Students may wish to share other creation myths that they know as they discuss their response to the selection from the *Popol Vuh.*

Answers for Reviewing the Selection

RECALLING AND INTERPRETING

1. **Recalling.** Jaguar Quitze, Jaguar Night, Mahucutah, and True Jaguar can see and understand everything in the world "perfectly." They thank their creators for making them and tell their creators that they are able to speak, listen, wonder, move, and understand. **Interpreting.** The first men are thankful and respectful toward their creators, but they do not look on them as higher beings.
2. **Recalling.** The creator gods mar the eyes of their creations so that they can only see nearby things clearly. **Interpreting.** The gods lessen the ability of their creations because they are worried that their creations will become as great as gods. Because the gods marred the sight of these first four people, people in the present world are unable to see and understand everything in the world and possess only limited knowledge.
3. **Recalling.** The wives of the first men came into being next. The first men became wider awake and happy at heart. **Interpreting.** The gods seem pleased that their beautiful new creations make their first creations "happy at heart." They may also be pleased because the women give birth to "the people of the tribes."
4. **Recalling.** The first sunrise is celebrated by the four men and their wives. **Interpreting.** The sunrise may have been the climax of the creation myth because it symbolizes the dawning of life in this world. (cont.)

Responding to the Selection

What ideas or beliefs expressed in this myth seemed strange or unfamiliar to you? Which of your beliefs might seem strange to a person from the ancient Mayan culture?

Reviewing the Selection

RECALLING		INTERPRETING
1. What ability do Jaguar Quitze, Jaguar Night, Mahucutah, and True Jaguar have when they first come into existence? What do they say to their creators?	▶▶	What attitude do the first men have toward their creators?
2. What do the creator gods do to lessen the ability of the first men?	▶▶	Why do the gods lessen the ability of their creations? In what way did this act of the gods affect the present world?
3. Who comes into being next? What effect did these people have on the first men?	▶▶	Why were the creators pleased with the effect of their new creations?
4. What important event do the first four men and their wives celebrate?	▶▶	Why might this event have been the climax of the creation myth?

SYNTHESIZING

5. This creation myth focuses on the sun and ancestors. In your own words, describe the beliefs that the Maya held about the sun and about their ancestors.

Understanding Literature (Questions for Discussion)

1. **Myth.** A **myth** is a story that explains objects or events in the natural world as resulting from the action of some supernatural force or entity, most often a god. What event does this myth explain? What human abilities does it explain?
2. **Parallelism. Parallelism** is a rhetorical technique in which a writer emphasizes the equal value or weight of two or more ideas by expressing them in the same grammatical form. For an example of parallelism, refer to the Handbook of Literary Terms. Find examples of parallelism in the selection. Does the use of parallelism make the writing seem formal or informal? Explain.

Answers for Reviewing the Selection (cont.)

SYNTHESIZING

Responses will vary. Possible responses are given.

5. The Maya seem to have worshiped the sun and to have associated the sunrise with life and renewal. The Maya believed that their ancestors were beautiful, gifted people of astonishing ability. They also believed that the superior vision and understanding of their ancestors was taken away from them by the jealous gods.

Responding in Writing

1. **Creative Writing: Description.** A description portrays a character, an object, or a scene. Imagine what the world was like long ago when your distant ancestors lived. Describe your idea of the land in which your distant ancestors lived. You may also wish to describe your own environment and compare and contrast the two worlds.

2. **Critical Essay: Comparison and Contrast.** Write a comparison and contrast essay on the similarities and differences between God's decision to expel Adam and Eve from the Garden of Eden in Genesis and the creator gods' decision to "take . . . apart just a little" the first four men in the *Popol Vuh.* Focus on the role knowledge plays in the fall of both sets of characters, the reason for God's and the creator gods' decisions, and the effect of this fall on future generations. Bear in mind that the *Popol Vuh* was written down after the Maya had contact with Christian missionaries and that it may show some Biblical influence.

Project

Ancient Meso-American Civilizations. Work in three groups to research the three major peoples of ancient Central and South America—the Maya, the Aztec, and the Inca. Each group should find information on the location of the civilization, the dates during which it flourished, type of government, and accomplishments in areas such as the arts, sciences, and technology. Research as well the religion of the culture and what happened when European explorers arrived in the New World. Each group should organize its information and present its findings to the class.

PROJECT NOTES

See the evaluation form for projects, Assessment Portfolio 4.12.

Ancient Meso-American Civilizations. Students can create model cities, maps showing the areas settled by the civilization, and time lines of major events. Students may also wish to create illustrations or locate photographs of ruins or artifacts from the civilization that they are researching and use such visual aids in their presentations. Students may also wish to create a display for the library or other area about Meso-American civilizations in which they combine the visual aids from the three presentations and create written descriptions of the items for viewers.

Answers for Understanding Literature

Responses will vary. Possible responses are given.

1. **Myth.** This myth explains the creation of human beings and the dawning of life. The myth also explains the limitations of human knowledge and understanding.

2. **Parallelism.** Examples of parallelism include "They talked and they made words. / They looked and they listened" and "Perfectly they saw, perfectly they knew." The use of parallelism makes the writing seem more formal, as if it has been carefully crafted in a certain rhetorical and poetical style.

Analytic Scales for Responding in Writing

Grading scales for Responding in Writing appear on page 535.

ADDITIONAL RESOURCES

Reader's Guide

- Selection Worksheet 7.4

Assessment Portfolio

- Selection Check Test 2.7.7
- Selection Test 2.7.8

Essential Skills Practice Books

- Writing 1.8, 1.20
- Study and Research 4.2

PREREADING EXTENSIONS

Inform students that according to Aztec tradition, their original home was a place called Aztlán, or "place of the herons," probably located in northern Mexico. Huitzilopochtli, a hummingbird god, god of war, and the patron god of the Aztecs, ordered the Aztecs to leave their homeland, and they began to migrate southward, probably in the twelfth century AD. The Aztecs believed that while their ancestors were on their journey Huitzilopochtli gave them a new name, calling them "Mexica," from which comes the name later given to the nation of Mexico. During their migration, the Aztecs encountered the Toltec people and gained knowledge of Toltec culture calendar (which the Toltecs may have learned from the Maya). The Aztecs were so impressed by the Toltecs that they said that the Toltecs grew giant ears of corn and cotton in colors. The first Aztec ruler even claimed descent from Quetzalcoatl, the god and founder of the Toltecs.

SUPPORT FOR LEP STUDENTS

Pronunciations of Proper Nouns and Adjectives

Na • huat • l (nä hwät´l)
Na • naut • zin (nä not´zin)
Quet • zal • co • at • l (ket säl´ kō ät´l)
Ten • och • tit • lán (tā nôch´tēt län´)

PREREADING

"The Five Worlds and Their Suns"
Anonymous, retold by Donna Rosenberg

AZTEC

About the Selection

The Aztec creation myth **"The Five Worlds and Their Suns"** reveals the Aztecs to be inheritors of many Mayan beliefs and traditions. In the swampy land around Lake Texcoco, the Aztecs developed superior agricultural techniques, freeing them to develop architecture, the arts, and literature. The Aztecs never reached the intellectual height of the Maya but were known for being fierce warriors. Not long after establishing their capital of Tenochtitlán, site of present-day Mexico City, at Lake Texcoco, the Aztecs waged war against their neighbors and conquered them. In the fifteenth century, the Aztec empire may have contained between five and six million people. Tenochtitlán, spread over five square miles and populated by more than 140,000 people, was far larger than any Spanish city of the time.

The Aztec religion grew by assimilation of other cultures' beliefs and traditions. In addition to worshiping Huitzilopochtli, god of war, and Quetzalcoatl, the Feathered Serpent, the Aztecs also worshiped Tonatiuh, god of the sun, and Tlaloc, god of rain. The Aztecs believed that a number of worlds, or "suns," had been created and destroyed before the present universe was created. The first sun was destroyed by jaguars, the guise of a creator god; the second sun was destroyed by Quetzalcoatl in the form of a wind god; the third sun was destroyed by fire, or Tlaloc as god of thunder and lightning; and the fourth sun was destroyed by a great flood. The Aztecs called themselves "People of the Sun," believing that they were the chosen people of the fifth world, or sun. The Aztecs were terrified that the sun would stop on its daily journey and burn up the Earth. In the Aztec worldview, humans played only a small part and existed only to serve the gods who kept the sun and the universe in motion. They believed that the sun required blood and human hearts to continue on its journey through the sky, so Aztec religion laid a heavy emphasis on sacrifice. Indeed, many of the Aztec wars were waged to acquire new victims to be sacrificed to the gods. The Aztec priests practiced bloodletting and offered their own blood to the gods. "The Five Worlds and Their Suns" reveals the Aztec preoccupation with sacrifice as well as Aztec beliefs about the sun.

Overview of Pyramid of the Moon and Pyramid of the Sun

CONNECTIONS: When Cultures Collide: Spanish Influences on Native Literature

The Aztecs came into contact with the Spanish while their empire was still developing and flourishing. Spaniards under Hernán Cortés entered Tenochtitlán in 1519, captured the Aztec emperor Montezuma II, and defeated the Aztec decisively in 1521. The Spanish were aided in their conquest by neighboring groups who had suffered under Aztec rule. Considering native beliefs to be sinful, the Spanish destroyed most Aztec literature. Luckily, Spanish missionaries also encouraged the Aztecs to write in their own language, Nahuatl, using Latin letters, so some older documents and works from the oral tradition were preserved. "The Five Worlds and Their Suns" was written in Nahuatl sometime in the sixteenth century. "The Five Worlds and Their Suns" may reflect some Western influence, since it was recorded after contact with the Spanish. Thus, it is difficult to determine if certain elements of the story, such as a couple surviving the great flood, were originally part of Aztec mythology or were introduced after missionaries had converted the Aztecs to Christianity.

GOALS/OBJECTIVES

Studying this lesson will enable students to

- enjoy an Aztec myth
- briefly explain Aztec religious views
- explain the effect contact with the Spanish had upon Aztec literature
- define *archetype* and recognize archetypes in a literary work
- write a praise poem
- write a critical essay comparing "The Five Worlds and Their Suns" and the *Popol Vuh*
- apply different types of thinking to problems

In your journal, write about a time in your life when you had to make a sacrifice. Maybe you had to give up something you enjoyed to help someone else, or perhaps you had to sacrifice a short-term desire to achieve a long-term goal. Was it difficult to make this sacrifice? How did you feel about doing so?

READER'S JOURNAL

"The Five Worlds and Their Suns"

ANONYMOUS, RETOLD BY DONNA ROSENBERG

Five worlds were created, each with its own sun, each following upon the death of the preceding one. The first world was illuminated by the sun of earth. The people of this first world acted improperly, so the gods punished them by causing jaguars to feast upon their flesh. No one survived, and their sun died along with them.

The second world was illuminated by the sun of air. Its people acted without wisdom, so hurricane winds descended upon the earth, and the people were punished by being turned into apes. Their sun died when they became animals.

The third world was illuminated by the sun of the rain of fire. Its people acted without respect and reverence for the gods, refusing to sacrifice to them, so they were punished by earthquakes, volcanic eruptions of fiery ash, and other forms of flaming death. Their sun burned along with them.

The fourth world was illuminated by the sun of water. The great god Quetzalcoatl[1] created a race of human beings from ash. The people were very greedy, so they were punished by a great flood. Their sun drowned when most of the people were transformed into fish.

The Supreme Being tried to save one human couple from the deluge. His voice came to them and said, "Find a mighty tree, make a hole in the trunk large enough to hide in, and take refuge there until the flood waters recede. You will survive if you master your greed and eat only one corncob each."

The husband and wife eagerly obeyed the instructions of the Supreme Being. They found a great tree, took refuge in it, and survived the flood.

When the waters had receded, they looked upon a strange world. Fish lay twitching on the ground where animals once had roamed. "Why should we gnaw on a corncob when fish are so plentiful?" they asked one another.

They proceeded to break off dry twigs from their tree, make a fire, and roast one of the fish. The gods smelled the savory smoke

1. **Quetzalcoatl.** Aztec god who took the form of a feathered serpent and who was considered the patron of priests, the god of death and resurrection, and the inventor of the calendar and of books

1 *Under what condition will the human couple survive the flood?*

2 *What explanation is offered for the origin of apes?*

3 *Why do the gods become enraged with the couple?*

4 *What flaw did people of the fourth world have?*

WORDS FOR EVERYDAY USE

del • uge (del´ yo͞oj´) *n.,* great flood

sa • vor • y (sā´vər ē) *adj.,* pleasing to the taste or smell

READER'S JOURNAL

As an alternate activity, students might write about whether they have observed people doing things only to impress others. What do they think about such people and their actions?

ANSWERS TO GUIDED READING QUESTIONS

1 The human couple will survive the flood if they master their greed and eat only one corncob each.

2 Apes are the descendants of people of the second world who acted without wisdom.

3 The gods become enraged with the couple because they disobey the instructions of the gods and behave in a greedy manner.

4 The people of the fourth world were greedy.

ADDITIONAL QUESTIONS AND ACTIVITIES

Ask students to discuss the following questions: What suns illuminate the third and fourth worlds? Why are the punishments meted out in these worlds appropriate, given their suns? What reason might the gods have had, other than testing the couple's obedience, for telling them only to eat one corncob?

ANSWERS

The third sun is the sun of the rain of fire, and the fourth is the sun of water. The people of the third world meet flaming forms of death, and the people of the fourth world experience a flood. Their punishments seem to be derived from their suns. The people of the fourth world are transformed into fish that lie flopping on land after the flood, and the gods may have wanted to prevent the couple from eating their former companions.

VOCABULARY IN CONTEXT

- Many early cultures have stories about a great deluge, or flood.
- On Thanksgiving afternoon, Trevor's kitchen was filled with the savory scents of turkey roasting and pumpkin pie baking.

Answers to Guided Reading Questions

❶ The other gods ignore and despise Nanautzin. The gods promise Nanautzin that if he helps to bring forth a fifth world they will value him.

❷ The offerings of the two gods differ in that the wealthy god's offerings present a "mighty show," and that the offerings of Nanautzin seem meager in comparison.

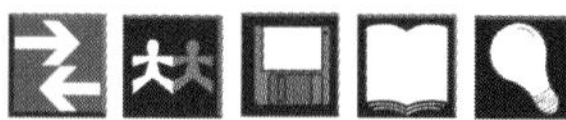

Additional Questions and Activities

- Students who are interested in the flood stories in this unit may wish to read the ancient Greek myth in which Deucalion and Pyrrha survive a flood.
- Encourage students to hold a discussion in which they compare and contrast the flood stories in *The Epic of Gilgamesh,* Genesis, and "The Five Worlds and Their Suns." In what ways is the Aztec story similar to and different from these two Near Eastern stories?

ANSWERS

Responses will vary.

Students should note that in the Aztec tale, as in the others, people are punished by the flood for disturbing divine figures. While the Mesopotamians are punished merely for being noisy, the Aztecs are punished for greed and lack of obedience, which is closer to the Biblical story in which humans are punished for being sinful. One major difference is that while Noah and his wife and Utnapishtim and his wife survive the flood and live afterward in harmony with gods, the Aztec couple survive the flood only to be transformed into dogs for their disobedience. Another difference is the Aztec couple take refuge in a tree trunk, not an ark, and that they do not take two of each species of animal with them.

and became enraged at the greed and disobedience of this couple. They descended upon them in wrath and cut off part of their heads, giving them brains the size of animals'. Then they transformed them into dogs.

Before the gods created the fifth world, our own world, they gathered together in the darkness to choose who would illuminate it by creating the fifth sun, the sun of four movements. This sun would combine within it the earlier four elements of earth, air, fire, and water. One wealthy god, lavishly dressed in shining feathers of the hummingbird and in jewels of turquoise and gold, volunteered—thinking more about the praise he would receive than about what the deed would entail.

"One will not be enough for this great deed," the gods said. "We need a second volunteer." Each god remained silent. Finally the gods asked, "Will you help us, Nanautzin?"

Nanautzin looked up in surprise. Never before had he been worthy of their attention. He knew that the other gods despised him because he was misshapen, ugly, covered with disgusting-looking sores, and dressed in plain clothing made from woven reeds.

> Q ❶ *How do the other gods feel about Nanautzin? What do the gods promise Nanautzin?*

"If you will help us bring forth a fifth world, we will truly value you!" they said.

"If you wish it, I will do it," Nanautzin replied.

The two gods spent the next four days purifying themselves for the sacrifice. Then they approached the blazing fire upon the stone altar with their best gifts. The customary offerings were hay, dead branches, cactus needles, and bloody thorns. However, the wealthy god made a mighty show as he offered nuggets of gold, rich feathers, and gems. Nanautzin's offering seemed scanty as he placed in the fire three bundles of three green reeds, hay, the scabs from his sores, and thorns covered with his own blood.

> Q ❷ *In what way do the offerings of the wealthy god and of Nanautzin differ?*

Atlantean carving, fifteen feet high

All of the gods then built a towering pyramid of stone, made a bonfire on top of it, and let it burn for four nights while they too

Words for Everyday Use

lav • ish • ly (lav´ish lē) *adv.,* extravagantly; in a generous, abundant, or liberal manner

cus • tom • ar • y (kus´tə mer´ē) *adj.,* usual

Vocabulary in Context

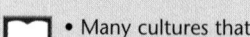

- Many cultures that consider hospitality a sacred obligation entertain their guests as lavishly as possible.
- In most cultures, thanking someone who has given you a gift or help is customary.

Pyramid of the Sun at Teotihuacan Ruins, near Mexico City

purified themselves. Finally they said to the wealthy god, "We are ready. Now perform the deed that you said you would do. Light up the world."

"How do you expect me to do this?" the wealthy god asked.

"You must leap into the center of the flames!" the gods replied.

The wealthy god's heart filled with terror, but he was ashamed to go back on his word. Four times he gingerly approached the flaming bonfire, and four times he retreated in the face of the terrifying flames and the great heat. "I know I volunteered, but I just cannot do this," he admitted in shame.

"Then, Nanautzin, it is your turn to perform this great deed," the gods said.

So Nanautzin forced courage into his heart and jumped into the flames. As the fire burned away his life, his blazing clothing lighted up the sky and gave life to the sun. The wealthy, cowardly god felt that he had no choice but to follow Nanautzin's brave example, so he too gathered the courage to sacrifice his life and he cast himself into the flames. But because Nanautzin had courageously led the way, from that time forth it was he who was honored among the gods. Many even say that Nanautzin was a form of the great god Quetzalcoatl. ■

1 *In what way does the behavior of the two gods differ?*

Words for Everyday Use

gin • ger • ly (jin´ jər´lē) *adv.*, carefully or cautiously

Answers to Guided Reading Questions

1 While the wealthy god is cowardly, Nanautzin is courageous.

Selection Check Test with Answers

EX. In the Aztec myth, how many worlds are created?
Five worlds are created.

1. By what sun was the fourth world illuminated, and by what are the people of the fourth world punished for their greed?
The fourth world is illuminated by the sun of water, and its people are punished for their greed by a great flood.

2. Why do the gods punish the people who survive the flood by turning them into dogs?
The gods punish them because the people are too greedy and disobedient to follow the gods' instructions to only eat one corncob each.

3. Who is the first god who volunteers to help illuminate the fifth sun?
The first god is a wealthy and lavishly dressed god.

4. Who is the other volunteer? How do the gods feel about this god, and why?
The other volunteer is Nanautzin. The other gods despise him because he is misshapen and ugly.

5. What happens when the two gods prepare to jump in the bonfire to illuminate the sun?
The wealthy god is too afraid to jump in, so Nanautzin does and illuminates the sun, and then the wealthy god follows.

Vocabulary in Context

• The striped cat stepped gingerly around the puddle.

Responding to the Selection

Students might also discuss what they think of the Aztec gods. Do they seem forgiving or very strict? What do the gods seem to value?

Answers for Reviewing the Selection

RECALLING AND INTERPRETING

1. **Recalling.** The people of the first three worlds are destroyed because they act without wisdom and do not show the gods the proper respect. **Interpreting.** The people of the first three worlds are proud, selfish, unwise, disrespectful, and ungrateful.

2. **Recalling.** The people of the fourth world are greedy and are punished by a great flood during which they are transformed into fish. The couple is punished by being transformed into dogs. **Interpreting.** The couple is punished because they disobeyed the gods and greedily ate fish instead of only one corncob as they were ordered. The Aztecs believed that it was very important to respect and obey the gods. They valued gratitude, selflessness, and generosity.

3. **Recalling.** Two gods must sacrifice themselves in flame to create the sun of the fifth world. **Interpreting.** This tale might have reminded people of their duty to the gods because it both describes what happens to people who forget their duty and describes the sacrifices that the gods have made for the people of this world.

4. **Recalling.** Nanautzin is honored among the gods for lighting up the world. **Interpreting.** It is surprising that Nanautzin is honored by the others because they used to despise him because of his appearance. He performed this deed both because he was naturally courageous and to gain honor.

(cont.)

Responding to the Selection

Do you admire Nanautzin? Why, or why not? What is your opinion of the wealthy god? Explain.

Reviewing the Selection

Recalling		Interpreting
1. In "The Five Worlds and Their Suns," what happens to the people of the first three worlds? Why?	▶▶	What characteristics do the people of the first three worlds display?
2. What happened to the people of the fourth world? What happened to the couple who were almost saved by the Supreme Being?	▶▶	Why was the couple punished? What do the fates of the first four worlds suggest about Aztec values?
3. What action is necessary to create the sun of the fifth world?	▶▶	Why might this tale have served as a reminder to people that it was necessary for them to worship and offer sacrifices to the gods?
4. Who is honored among the gods for what he did to light up the world?	▶▶	Why is it surprising that this god is honored by the others? Why did he perform this feat?

Synthesizing

5. The myth focuses on the sun and on ancestors. In your own words, describe the beliefs that the Aztec held about the sun and about their ancestors.

Understanding Literature (Questions for Discussion)

Archetype. An **archetype** is an inherited, often unconscious ancestral memory or motif that recurs throughout history and literature. Many cultures, including the Hindu, Greek, Irish, Navajo, Mayan, and Aztec, have expressed the archetypal belief that a number of worlds were created and either abandoned or destroyed before this one. Cultures that share this archetype frequently also believe in a "golden age," or a period in which humans were happy, prosperous, and innocent. What other archetypes, or common mythological motifs, do you recognize in this selection?

Answers for Reviewing the Selection (cont.)

SYNTHESIZING

Responses will vary. Possible responses are given.

5. The Aztec believed that four inferior suns existed before the present sun, which was created by the sacrifice of two gods. The Aztec also seem to have worshiped the sun. They believed that previous groups of people failed to pay honor to the gods and so were destroyed.

Responding in Writing

1. **Creative Writing: Praise Poem.** Nanautzin made a great sacrifice to create the sun for the fifth world. Think about a sacrifice, either large or small, that somebody has made to benefit you in some way. Write a poem of praise in honor of this person.

2. **Critical Essay: Comparison and Contrast.** Write an essay comparing and contrasting "The Five Worlds and Their Suns" with the selection from the *Popol Vuh,* focusing on the view of humans and humanity presented in each myth. You may wish to consider the way in which the relationship between humans and their environment and/or the gods is depicted in each myth. Try to determine which culture had the more optimistic view of humanity and which culture had the more pessimistic view. Present your thesis, or main idea, in an introductory paragraph; support your argument in the following paragraphs; and summarize your argument, drawing some conclusion from it, in a final paragraph.

Thinking Skills

Types of Thinking. Different tasks in life require you to think in different ways. Some important types of thinking include classifying, comparing and contrasting, estimating and quantifying, analyzing, generalizing, and deducing. Read about these different types of thinking in the Language Arts Survey 4.2, "Types of Thinking." Then read the descriptions of different tasks below and identify what type of thinking each task requires. Create a plan for carrying out one of these tasks.

1. You need to support an idea in an essay by figuring out approximately how many native people lived in Meso-America just before the arrival of the Spanish.
2. You are asked to come to a conclusion about the Aztec empire based on some facts that you have learned in history class.
3. Your task is to examine the similarities and differences between Mayan literature and Aztec literature.
4. You need to determine what genre of literature a piece of Mayan writing best fits.
5. You need to examine the different elements, or parts, of Aztec society.

ANALYTIC SCALES FOR RESPONDING IN WRITING

Assign a score from 1 to 25 for each grading criterion below. (For more detailed evaluation, see the evaluation forms for writing, revising, and proofreading, Assessment Portfolio 4.1–4.9.)

1. Praise Poem

- **Content/Unity.** The poem praises someone who has made a sacrifice for the writer.
- **Organization/Coherence.** The praise poem expresses ideas in a sensible order.
- **Language/Style.** The praise poem uses vivid and precise nouns, verbs, and modifiers.
- **Conventions.** The praise poem avoids errors in spelling, grammar, usage, mechanics, and manuscript form.

▶ Additional practice is provided in the Essential Skills Practice Book: Writing 1.8.

2. Critical Essay

- **Content/Unity.** The essay compares and contrasts the view of humans presented in "The Five Worlds and Their Suns" and the *Popol Vuh.*
- **Organization/Coherence.** The essay begins with an introduction that includes the thesis of the essay. The introduction is followed by supporting paragraphs with clear transitions. The essay ends with a solid conclusion.
- **Language/Style.** The essay uses vivid and precise nouns, verbs, and modifiers.
- **Conventions.** The essay avoids errors in spelling, grammar, usage, mechanics, and manuscript form.

▶ Additional practice is provided in the Essential Skills Practice Book: Writing 1.20.

ANSWERS FOR UNDERSTANDING LITERATURE

Responses will vary. Possible responses are given.

Archetype. Students may mention the following archetypes: a great flood with a human couple being spared, an outcast proving his or her worth, and gods punishing their creations.

ANSWERS FOR SKILLS ACTIVITIES

THINKING SKILLS

1. estimating and quantifying
2. deducing
3. comparing and contrasting
4. classifying
5. analyzing

▶ Additional practice is provided in the Essential Skills Practice Book: Study and Research 4.2.

ADDITIONAL RESOURCES

READER'S GUIDE

- Selection Worksheet 7.5

ASSESSMENT PORTFOLIO

- Selection Check Test 2.7.9
- Selection Test 2.7.10

ESSENTIAL SKILLS PRACTICE BOOKS

- Writing 1.8, 1.20

PREREADING EXTENSIONS

Taoism is one of the three dominant Chinese philosophical schools, along with Buddhism and Confucianism. Have students research the three philosophies and identify the main tenets of each. While students should use other sources, they might begin their research by reading the selection by Siddhartha Gautama, the Buddha, on page 583 and the information about Confucianism and the selection by Confucius on pages 550 and 551. Have students discuss their findings.

SUPPORT FOR LEP STUDENTS

PRONUNCIATIONS OF PROPER NOUNS AND ADJECTIVES

Lao-tzu (lou so͞o´)
Tao • Te • Ching (dou dā ching´)

ADDITIONAL VOCABULARY

eternal—everlasting
cease—end

PREREADING

from the *Tao Te Ching*
by Lao-tzu, translated by Gia-fu Feng and Jane English

About the Author

Lao-tzu (circa sixth century BC). Lao-tzu, the mysterious founder of the Chinese philosophy of Taoism, wrote the first version of the fundamental text of Taoist philosophy, the *Tao Te Ching*. Like many other elusive historical figures, Lao-tzu has become a subject for legend. One legend says that he was in his mother's womb for many years before his birth and then was born a wise, elderly, white-haired man. Another legend says that Lao-tzu became disturbed by the political turmoil of his day and concerned about what he saw as the decay of society, so he decided to ride into the desert to seek solitude and to be closer to nature. On his way, a gatekeeper who recognized Lao-tzu as a wise person stopped him. The gatekeeper told Lao-tzu that he would not be allowed to pass unless he put his teachings into writing so that the society he was abandoning would have something from which to learn. The legend tells us that Lao-tzu agreed to do this and proceeded to write the *Tao Te Ching*.

About the Selection

The title ***Tao Te Ching*** can be translated as *The Way (or Path) and Its Power (or Virtue)*. The word *Tao,* meaning "way," refers to the way of nature. Taoists reject what they believe to be the artificial life of the city, which involves vain desire for luxuries and prestige. They seek to find a simple, peaceful life in harmony with the natural world. A Taoist rejects law in favor of custom, learning in favor of wisdom, and the hurried pace of civilized life in favor of the easy pace of life in the countryside. To the Taoist, the accomplishments of civilization are entrapments. They are not part of the orderly, calm process of nature and do not make people wiser or happier. According to the *Tao te Ching*, the Tao is the reality that lies behind all the manifestations of the natural world. The Tao cannot be known directly but can be experienced by observing nature. Taoists view nature as involving balanced, complementary forces, the yin and the yang of traditional Chinese philosophy. A wise person, according to Taoism, does not struggle or desire but rather cultivates a serene detachment, accepting what comes with desireless calm.

CONNECTIONS: Taoism and the Back-to-Nature Movement

In the 1960s, many young people in America and Europe, sickened by such excesses of civilization as warfare, nuclear weapons, and environmental pollution, embraced Taoist ideas as part of the so-called back-to-nature movement. These people hoped to achieve serenity by following Taoist ideals. Like traditional Taoists, they sought to simplify life, to live close to nature, and to avoid earthly distractions such as the pursuit of wealth, power, or knowledge.

GOALS/OBJECTIVES

Studying this lesson will enable students to

- have a pleasant experience reading a work by a Taoist philosopher
- identify Lao-tzu as a Chinese philosopher and the founder of Taoism
- define *parallelism* and *paradox*
- identify examples of parallelism and paradox
- write a paradoxical scene
- apply aspects of Taoism to their own lives
- distinguish between transitive and intransitive verbs and identify direct objects

READER'S JOURNAL

Answer the following question in your journal: Do you believe that people have become too caught up in earthly distractions, such as money, cars, clothing, television, and careers? Explain, drawing from examples you see in your own life and the lives of others.

FROM THE

Tao Te Ching

LAO-TZU, TRANSLATED BY GIA-FU FENG AND JANE ENGLISH

ONE

The Tao that can be told is not the eternal Tao.
The name that can be named is not the eternal name.
The nameless is the beginning of heaven and earth.
The named is the mother of ten thousand things.
Ever desireless, one can see the mystery.
Ever desiring, one sees the manifestations.
These two spring from the same source but differ in name;
this appears as darkness.
Darkness within darkness.
The gate to all mystery.

❶ *What is not the eternal Tao? What is the beginning of heaven and earth?*

❷ *Why might one need to be "desireless" to understand the mystery?*

TWO

Under heaven all can see beauty as beauty only because there is ugliness.
All can know good as good only because there is evil.
Therefore having and not having arise together.
Difficult and easy complement each other.
Long and short contrast each other;

❸ *Why is one able to see beauty as beauty? Why is one able to know good?*

WORDS FOR EVERYDAY USE

man • i • fes • ta • tion (man´ə fes tā´shən) *n.,* concrete form in which something reveals itself

com • ple • ment (käm´plə mənt´) *vt.,* differ but balance and complete

READER'S JOURNAL

As an alternate activity, ask students if they think people should or should not try to change the world. Students should explain why they feel the way they do and provide examples, anecdotes, or other information to support their opinions.

ANSWERS TO GUIDED READING QUESTIONS

❶ The Tao that can be told is not the eternal Tao. The nameless is the beginning of heaven and earth.

❷ One might need to be "desireless" because one must be free of distractions in order to understand the mystery.

❸ One is able to see beauty as beauty because of ugliness. One is able to know good because there is evil.

SPELLING AND VOCABULARY WORDS FROM THE SELECTION

competent	manifestation
complacency	sage
complement	strive
harmonize	

QUOTABLES

"To remain whole, be twisted!

To become straight, let yourself be bent.

To become full, be hollow.

Be Tattered, that you may be renewed."

—Lao-tzu

VOCABULARY IN CONTEXT

- Maura's accusations are a manifestation of her fears of being found guilty herself.
- The sweet and spicy flavors in this dish complement each other.

Answers to Guided Reading Questions

❶ Lao-tzu describes the world as being balanced, with opposites—difficult and easy, long and short, high and low, voice and sound, and front and back—complementing one another.

❷ The highest good is like water because water gives life but does not strive to do so, and because it flows in places men reject.

❸ When in action, one should be aware of the time and the season.

❹ According to Lao-tzu, if you try to change the universe, you will ruin it, and if you try to hold the universe, you will lose it.

Selection Check Test with Answers

EX. Who spread the word of the Tao Te Ching?
Lao-tzu spread the word of the Tao Te Ching.

1. What is not the eternal Tao?
The spoken Tao is not the eternal Tao.

2. Why is one able to see beauty as beauty?
One is able to see beauty as beauty because of ugliness.

3. What is like the highest good because it gives life but does not strive?
Water is like the highest good.

4. When in action, of what should one be aware?
One should be aware of the time and the season.

5. What happens when one tries to hold or change the universe?
When one tries to hold or change the universe, it can be ruined or lost.

❶ *In what way is the universe perfectly balanced, according to Lao-tzu?*

High and low rest upon each other;
Voice and sound harmonize each other;
Front and back follow one another.

Therefore the sage goes about doing nothing, teaching no-talking.
The ten thousand things rise and fall without cease,
Creating, yet not possessing,
Working, yet not taking credit.
Work is done, then forgotten.
Therefore it lasts forever.

EIGHT

❷ *Why is the highest good like water?*

The highest good is like water.
Water gives life to the ten thousand things and does not strive.
It flows in places men reject and so is like the Tao.

In dwelling, be close to the land.
In meditation, go deep in the heart.
In dealing with others, be gentle and kind.
In speech, be true.
In ruling, be just.
In daily life, be competent.
In action, be aware of the time and the season.

❸ *When in action, of what should one be aware?*

No fight: No blame.

TWENTY-NINE

Do you think you can take over the universe and improve it?
I do not believe it can be done.

The universe is sacred.
You cannot improve it.
If you try to change it, you will ruin it.
If you try to hold it, you will lose it.

❹ *What will happen if one tries to change or to hold the universe?*

Words for Everyday Use

har • mon • ize (här´mə nīz´) *vi.,* work together in an orderly way

sage (sāj) *n.,* wise teacher; experienced person, respected for having good judgment

strive (strīv) *vi.,* make great efforts; try very hard

com • pe • tent (käm´pə tənt) *adj.,* capable

Vocabulary in Context

- The two groups were able to harmonize and work together on the project.
- "What is the meaning of life?" the young man asked the sage.
- The sage advised him to strive for perfection but not for recognition.
- Although Shira questions Vic's skills, he is very competent at his job.

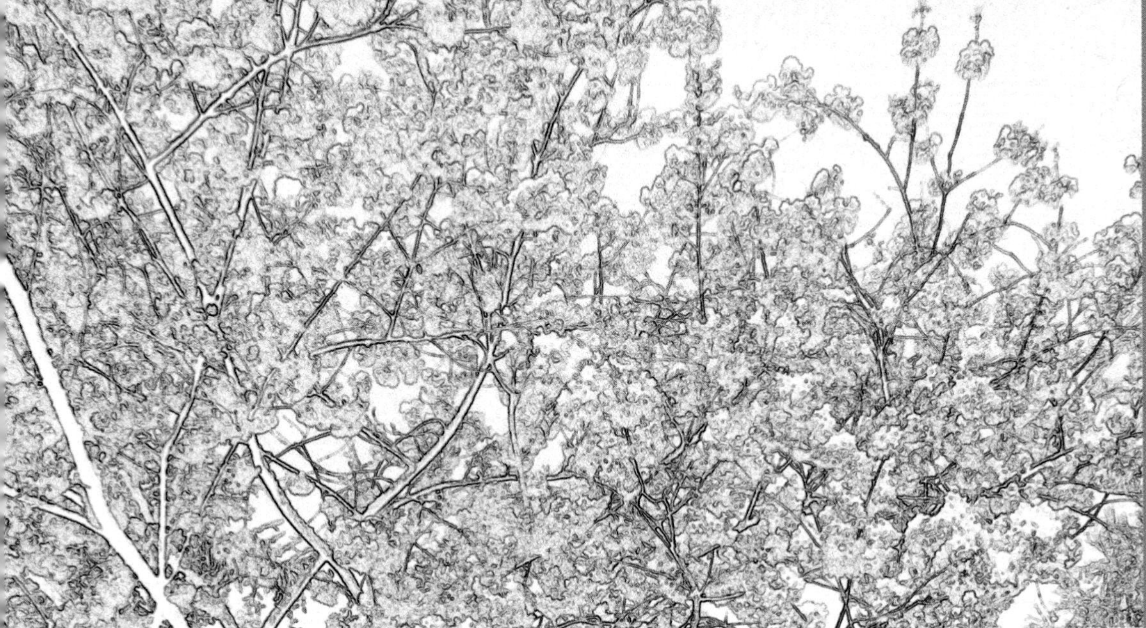

So sometimes things are ahead and sometimes they are behind;
Sometimes breathing is hard, sometimes it comes easily;
Sometimes there is strength and sometimes weakness;
Sometimes one is up and sometimes down.

Therefore the sage avoids extremes, excesses, and complacency. ■

Responding to the Selection

What do you consider most interesting about the teachings of Lao-tzu? If you were to meet Lao-tzu, what might you ask him or tell him about his work?

WORDS FOR EVERYDAY USE

com • pla • cen • cy (käm plā´sən sē) *n.*, being too self-satisfied or smug

RESPONDING TO THE SELECTION

Students might choose one section of the selection on which to focus their impressions. For example, students might explain how the ideas expressed in a certain section apply to their lives or why they agree or disagree with Lao-tzu's ideas. Responses to these questions will help students to complete the critical essay activity of Responding in Writing.

ANALYTIC SCALES FOR RESPONDING IN WRITING

(SEE PAGE 549.)

Assign a score from 1 to 25 for each grading criterion below. (For more detailed evaluation, see the evaluation forms for writing, revising, and proofreading, Assessment Portfolio 4.1–4.9.)

1. Paradoxical Scene

- **Content/Unity.** The writing describes an event that is seemingly contradictory in some way.
- **Organization/Coherence.** The scene is organized logically.
- **Language/Style.** The scene uses vivid and precise language.
- **Conventions.** The scene avoids errors in spelling, grammar, usage, mechanics, and manuscript form.

▶ Additional practice is provided in the Essential Skills Practice Book: Writing 1.8.

2. Critical Essay

- **Content/Unity.** The essay presents the writer's opinion about one part of Lao-tzu's teachings.
- **Organization/Coherence.** The essay presents a thesis that is supported throughout the essay with specific examples.
- **Language/Style.** The essay uses vivid and precise language.
- **Conventions.** The essay avoids errors in spelling, grammar, usage, mechanics, and manuscript form.

▶ Additional practice is provided in the Essential Skills Practice Book: Writing 1.20.

VOCABULARY IN CONTEXT

- Instead of falling into complacency, you should always strive to improve yourself.

ANSWERS FOR REVIEWING THE SELECTION

RECALLING AND INTERPRETING

1. **Recalling.** The eternal Tao cannot be told or named. If one is desireless, one will see the mystery. **Interpreting.** Lao-tzu tries to convey the elusive nature of the Tao by repeating the fact that the true Tao cannot be named or spoken, and that one must reach another level of spirituality to know the true Tao. Earthly desires for possessions or power might keep people from seeing beneath the surface of things.

2. **Recalling.** According to Lao-tzu, people see beauty as beauty because of ugliness, and people see good as good because of evil. **Interpreting.** Lao-tzu is teaching that the universe is perfectly balanced, and that opposites or seemingly contradictory things complement one another in an important way. Lao-tzu does not believe that people should tamper with the universe in any way, because it would upset the balance.

3. **Recalling.** Water is like the highest good because it gives life but does not strive to do so, and because it, like the Tao, flows in places that men reject. Lao-tzu mentions the following qualities: being gentle, kind, truthful, just, and competent. **Interpreting.** Lao-tzu would not respect an overly aggressive person who pursued a career at all costs. Lao-tzu would believe that this person is too preoccupied with earthly distractions and is not practicing kindness and gentleness. Lao-tzu believes that neither fighting nor blaming solves problems. Fighting and blame should be avoided in attempts to maintain balance.

4. **Recalling.** Lao-tzu believes that the universe will be ruined or lost if is held or changed. **Interpreting.** People must accept that the universe is complex, perfectly balanced, and beyond human comprehension. Humans must accept that sometimes

(cont.)

Reviewing the Selection

RECALLING / **INTERPRETING**

1. What cannot be told or named? If one is "desireless," what will one see? ▶▶ In section 1, how does Lao-tzu convey the elusive nature of the Tao? According to Lao-tzu, what keeps people from being able to see beneath the surface into the essence of things?

2. According to section 2, why do people see beauty as beauty? Why do they see good as good? ▶▶ What advice do you think Lao-tzu might give to someone who is experiencing bad times? What purpose, according to Lao-tzu, is served by evil and ugliness? Does Lao-tzu feel that people should attempt to do away with ugliness or otherwise interfere with the balance of the universe? Why, or why not?

3. According to section 8, how is the highest good like water? In section 8, Lao-tzu names a variety of situations. What qualities does he believe that people should exhibit in each of these situations? ▶▶ Would Lao-tzu respect someone who was aggressive and constantly striving for success and recognition? Why, or why not? What do you believe Lao-tzu means by "No fight: No blame"?

4. According to section 29, what will happen if one tries to improve, change, or hold the universe? ▶▶ What must one learn to accept about the balance of the universe?

SYNTHESIZING

5. According to Lao-tzu's beliefs, what desires, mistakes, or misunderstandings keep people from knowing the eternal Tao and thus unlocking the gate to all mystery? How should one live in order to come closer to understanding the mystery?

Understanding Literature (Questions for Discussion)

1. **Parallelism. Parallelism** is a rhetorical technique in which a writer emphasizes the equal value or weight of two or more ideas by expressing them in the same grammatical form. What examples of parallelism can you find in the *Tao Te Ching*? In each case, what is similar about the ideas being expressed in parallel form?

ANSWERS FOR REVIEWING THE SELECTION (CONT.)

things will be hard, sometimes they will be easy, and that sometimes there is strength and sometimes there is weakness. Everything has a purpose.

SYNTHESIZING

Responses will vary. Possible responses are given.

5. According to Lao-tzu, people often mistakenly believe that they can change the universe and do away with certain aspects of it. People also allow themselves to be too caught up in earthly distractions and desires. People who are gentle, kind, just, and without desire for earthly distractions can become closer to understanding the mystery. People must learn that they cannot control the universe, and that the universe has its own balance.

2. **Paradox.** A **paradox** is a seemingly contradictory statement, idea, or event. The following quotation from Oscar Wilde's *Lady Windermere's Fan* is an example of paradox: "In this world there are only two tragedies. One is not getting what one wants, and the other is getting it." What examples of paradox can you find in the *Tao Te Ching*? How does Lao-tzu feel about the common human desire to know and understand things? Why might a person with his opinions embrace paradoxes?

Responding in Writing

1. **Creative Writing: Paradoxical Scene.** Lao-tzu makes use of paradox in the *Tao Te Ching*. Write your own brief scene in which you explore this technique. For example, you might write about a character who tries very hard and fails but then succeeds after giving up, or you might show how a character gains something mentally, emotionally, or spiritually while losing something materially. Before you begin writing, you might review the definition of *paradox* in the Handbook of Literary Terms and freewrite about paradoxical situations.

2. **Critical Essay: Applying Taoism.** Which of Lao-tzu's teachings did you find helpful and possibly applicable to your own life? Were there any of Lao-tzu's ideas with which you did not agree? Choose one teaching from the *Tao Te Ching* and write a brief essay in which you praise or criticize this teaching. Use specific examples to support your acceptance or rejection of this teaching.

Language Lab

Transitive and Intransitive Verbs. Verbs that must have direct objects are transitive verbs. Verbs that do not need direct objects are intransitive verbs. For more information and for examples, consult the Language Arts Survey 2.8, "Transitive and Intransitive Verbs." Below are ten sentences from the *Tao Te Ching*. Review the sentences. Then tell whether the boldfaced verbs are transitive or intransitive. If a verb is transitive, identify the verb's direct object.

1. Water **flows** in places men reject and so is like the Tao.
2. Ever desireless, one can **see** the mystery.
3. Long and short **contrast** each other.
4. The hard and strong will **fall**. The soft and weak will overcome.
5. Lao-tzu says that the Tao alone **nourishes**.
6. **See** simplicity in the complicated.
7. **Achieve** greatness in little things.
8. Mercy is the means by which heaven **saves** and guards.
9. **Cultivate** virtue in yourself, and virtue will be real.
10. **Achieve** results, but not through violence.

Answers for Understanding Literature

Responses will vary. Possible responses are given.

1. **Parallelism.** In part 1, lines 5 and 6 use parallelism to emphasize how opposite states—being always desireless and desiring—work together and "spring from the same source." In part 2, lines 10 and 11 use parallelism to show two examples of something that can be seen only because its opposite exists and to emphasize the necessity of balance in the universe. In part 8, lines 27–33, the parallel structure is used to explain how one should act in various situations. In section 29, lines 39–40 are parallel. The parallel structure emphasizes the idea that it is equally important not to try to change or to hold the world.

2. **Paradox.** Lao-tzu makes long lists of items that contradict one another—long and short, high and low, front and back, creating but not possessing, working but not taking credit. Lao-tzu feels that the common human desire to know things is understandable but will never be completely satisfied. He believes that because life is full of contradictions, paradoxes help a person contemplate the mysteries of existence. Paradoxes are therefore something he embraces. Through the use of these paradoxes, Lao-tzu is trying to show the delicate balance of the universe and the way everything fits together.

Analytic Scales for Responding in Writing

Grading scales for Responding in Writing appear on page 547.

Answers for Language Lab

1. *flows,* intransitive
2. *see,* transitive; *mystery,* direct object
3. *contrast,* transitive; *each other,* direct object
4. *fall,* intransitive
5. *nourishes,* intransitive
6. *See,* transitive; *simplicity,* direct object
7. *Achieve,* transitive; *greatness,* direct object
8. *saves,* intransitive
9. *Cultivate,* transitive; ***virtue,*** direct object
10. *Achieve,* transitive; ***results,*** direct object

ADDITIONAL RESOURCES

READER'S GUIDE

- Selection Worksheet 7.6

ASSESSMENT PORTFOLIO

- Selection Check Test 2.7.11
- Selection Test 2.7.12

ESSENTIAL SKILLS PRACTICE BOOKS

- Writing 1.8, 1.10, 1.20
- Applied English/Tech Prep 5.3

PREREADING EXTENSIONS

You might share with students the following additional biographical information: Confucius continually searched for a ruler who might consider his traditional moral code. He also hoped to find an important position in government for himself so that he might have a more direct hand in reforming society. Confucius believed that learning should lead people to public service. Confucius did eventually serve time as a government official, but he then returned to teaching a small group of his followers in his home state.

Encourage students to brainstorm a list of ways that they, too, might make a difference in society through public service.

SUPPORT FOR LEP STUDENTS

PRONUNCIATIONS OF PROPER NOUNS AND ADJECTIVES

Con • fu • cius (kən fyo͞o′shəs)
K'ung Fu • tzu (ko͝oŋ′ fo͞o′dzu′)

ADDITIONAL VOCABULARY

diligent—persevering and careful in work; industrious
fleeting—passing swiftly; not lasting
honeyed—flattering
legitimately—lawfully

PREREADING

from the *Analects*
by Confucius (K'ung Fu-tzu), translated by Xin Guanjie

CHINA

About the Author

CONFUCIUS
c. 551–c. 479 BC

Confucius is the Latinized name of **K'ung Fu-tzu**, the most famous teacher and philosopher in Chinese history. Confucius was born to a poor family of noble ancestry. When Confucius was twenty-two, he opened a school for young men. He welcomed students who were able to pay him as well as students who could not pay but who had a talent for learning. Confucius taught his students moral conduct and spirituality in an age of great political unrest and greed. He was concerned that government leaders had discarded personal ethics so they could seek power and wealth. Confucius believed that political leaders needed to set high moral standards for themselves so that they might serve as models for others. Since his death, Confucius has at times been revered as a god. Temples in his honor were erected in each county in China. Confucius, however, never claimed to be more than a man, a teacher, and a "transmitter" of ancient ideas about the moral order of the universe.

About the Selection

Analects are collections of passages from the works of one or more authors. The following excerpts are from what is perhaps the most famous example of such a collection—***Lun Yu***, or the ***Analects*** of Confucius. Confucius himself left behind no writings. The *Analects* is a collection of his sayings, teachings, and dialogues gathered by the disciples of Confucius after his death. The ideals and teachings of Confucius presented in this collection have guided and influenced the Chinese people for more than two thousand years. In the *Analects*, Confucius addresses politics, literature, philosophy, art, education, moral issues, and the cultivation of inherent human goodness. Confucius believed that each person has a true self that is marked by kindness, unselfishness, and honor. According to Confucius, nurturing the true self is the key to social harmony. The *Analects* encourages people to seek moral education and to develop in themselves respect for others, particularly parents and elders; a sense of loyalty, social responsibility, duty, and justice; and a commitment to family and community.

CONNECTIONS: Structured Social Order: Confucianism and Feudalism

Under Confucianism, an individual owes his or her loyalty and obedience to the patriarch of the family. Similarly, the emperor is seen as the head of an even larger family and so is due the honor and complete obedience of his subjects. Medieval European society was organized along a very similar principle known as feudalism. In a feudal society, each person is bound by a system of loyalties to some person higher on the social hierarchy. For more information, see Themes: Society and the Individual on page 555.

GOALS/OBJECTIVES

Studying this lesson will enable students to

- enjoy some of Confucius's analects
- briefly explain what analects are
- define *aphorism* and identify these in speech and literature
- write their own aphorisms
- define *theme* and recognize major themes in a literary work
- write a critical essay comparing and contrasting Lao-tzu's and Confucius's ideas
- write a resume and a cover letter

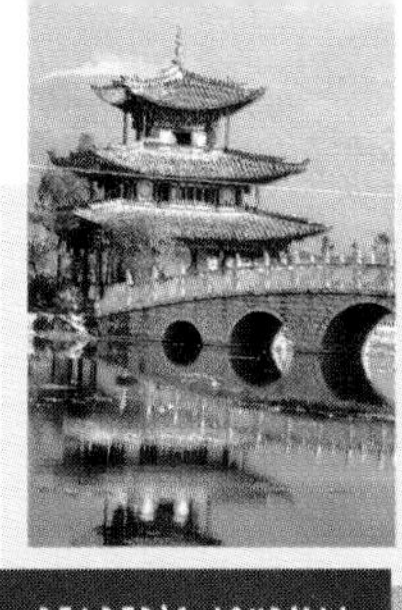

In your opinion, what makes a person wise? In your journal, answer the above question, and then list two or three people whom you consider to be wise. These people can be teachers, religious leaders, family members, or friends. Explain why you consider these people to be wise.

READER'S JOURNAL

FROM THE

Analects

CONFUCIUS, TRANSLATED BY XIN GUANJIE

Confucius said, "A man who speaks with honeyed words and pretends to be kind cannot be benevolent."

◆ ◆ ◆

Zeng Zi (a disciple of Confucius') said, "Every day I examine myself once and again: Have I tried my utmost to help others? Have I been honest to my friends? Have I diligently reviewed the instructions from the Master?"

◆ ◆ ◆

Confucius said, "At home, a young man should be dutiful towards his parents; going outside, he should be respectful towards his elders; he should be cautious in deeds and trustworthy in words; he should love everyone yet make close friends only with those of benevolence. If he has any more energy to spare, let him devote it to books."

◆ ◆ ◆

Confucius said, "Don't worry about being misunderstood but about understanding others."

◆ ◆ ◆

Ji Kangzi (Jisun Fei, then a minister of Lu[1]) asked, "What can I do to make the people respect and be loyal to their superiors and try their best in service?" Confucius said, "Be upright in their presence, and they will hold you in respect; be filial and benevolent, and they will be loyal to you; use the righteous and instruct the unqualified, and they will try their best in service."

◆ ◆ ◆

Confucius said, "Flattery, false amiability and obsequiousness, these Zuo Qiuming (a historian of Lu) found shameful. So do I. To be friendly towards some one while concealing one's hostility, this Zuo Qiuming found shameful. So do I."

1. **Lu.** Vassal state of Ancient China and the birthplace of Confucius

1 *What is more important than being understood?*

2 *What does the disciple of Confucius ask himself every day? Who is the "Master" to whom the disciple Zeng Zi refers?*

3 *According to Confucius, in what way should a young man treat his parents? his elders?*

WORDS FOR EVERYDAY USE

be • nev • o • lent (bə nev´ə lənt) *adj.*, good, charitable

dil • i • gent • ly (dil´ə jənt lē) *adv.*, carefully and steadily

fil • i • al (fil´ē əl) *adj.*, showing respect to a parent or superior

am • i • a • bil • i • ty (ā´mē ə bil´ə tē) *n.*, good nature; friendliness

ob • se • qui • ous • ness (əb sē´kwē əs nes) *n.*, overwillingness to please others

READER'S JOURNAL

You might also ask students to write about what the word *wisdom* means to them. How is wisdom different from intelligence?

ANSWERS TO GUIDED READING QUESTIONS

1 Understanding others is more important than being understood.

2 The disciple asks himself if he has tried his utmost to help others, if he has been honest to his friends, and if he has reviewed the instructions from the Master. The "Master" is Confucius.

3 A young man should be dutiful toward his parents and respectful toward his elders.

SPELLING AND VOCABULARY WORDS FROM THE SELECTION

amiability	filial
benevolent	innate
diligently	obsequiousness

QUOTABLES

"The strength of a nation is derived from the integrity of its homes."

—Confucius

"The superior man understands what is right; the inferior man understands what will sell."

—Confucius

VOCABULARY IN CONTEXT

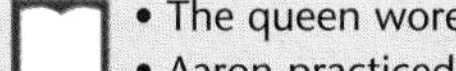

- The queen wore a benevolent expression that revealed her natural goodness.
- Aaron practiced the piano diligently because he hoped to earn a scholarship to a music school.
- Because filial ties are strong in China, adults often have their parents live with them and consider them respected family advisors.
- Because Lynne expected the transition to a new school to be difficult, the amiability of her new classmates surprised her.
- The king's favorite courtier was renowned for his obsequiousness; he would say only what he thought would most please the king.

Answers to Guided Reading Questions

❶ Confucius learns to follow the merits of another person, and to pick out a person's shortcomings so that he may overcome his own.

❷ Confucius would say that he is a man who can be so diligent that he forgets his meals, so happy that he forgets his worries, and who is unaware of approaching old age.

Selection Check Test with Answers

EX: In what country did Confucianism originate?

Confucianism originated in China.

1. What does Confucius believe about a man who pretends to be kind?

Confucius believes that a man who pretends to be kind cannot be benevolent.

2. According to Confucius, in what way should a young man treat his parents?

A young man should be dutiful toward his parents.

3. What is more important than being understood?

Understanding others is more important than being understood.

4. What are Confucius's feelings toward ill-gotten wealth and rank?

Confucius feels that ill-gotten wealth and rank are "just like fleeting clouds."

5. Why does Confucius learn from another person's merits, as well as his shortcomings?

Confucius learns to follow the merits of another person, and to pick out a person's shortcomings so that he may overcome his own.

Confucius (c. 551–479 BC). Ink rubbing from a Chinese stele, 1734. The Granger Collection, NY

◆ ◆ ◆

Confucius said, "I would pursue wealth so long as it could be obtained legitimately, even by being a common cart driver. If wealth could not be obtained legitimately, I would rather follow my own preferences."

◆ ◆ ◆

Confucius said, "There is happiness in eating coarse food, drinking cold water and sleeping on the floor. Ill-gotten wealth and rank are just like fleeting clouds to me."

◆ ◆ ◆

The Duke of Ye asked Zi Lu about Confucius, Zi Lu failed to give a reply. Confucius said to him afterwards, "Why did you not say something like this. He is the sort of person who can be so diligent that he forgets his meals, so happy that he forgets his worries and is even unaware of approaching old age."

◆ ◆ ◆

Confucius said, "When walking in the company of other men, there must be one I can learn something from. I shall pick out his merits to follow and his shortcomings for reference to overcome my own."

◆ ◆ ◆

Confucius said, "I am not one of those who pretend to understand what they do not. I suggest that one should listen to different views and choose the sound one to follow, see different things and keep them in mind. Knowledge obtained in this way is reliable, though not as good as <u>innate</u> knowledge." ■

❶ *Why does Confucius learn from another person's merits, as well as from his or her shortcomings?*

❷ *What would Confucius say to describe himself to a stranger?*

Words for Everyday Use

in • nate (in´nāt´) *adj.*, existing naturally rather than acquired

Vocabulary in Context

• Wisdom is not an <u>innate</u> quality; it comes not with birth but only with experience.

Responding to the Selection

Which two teachings did you find most interesting and applicable to your own life? Why did these teachings appeal to you?

Reviewing the Selection

RECALLING / **INTERPRETING**

1. What does Confucius say about a "man who speaks with honeyed words and pretends to be kind?" What does Zeng Zi, a disciple, frequently ask himself? ▶▶ In what situations might a person "speak with honeyed words and pretend to be kind"? Why is a person who behaves in this way in conflict with the teachings of Confucius as described by Zeng Zi?

2. According to Confucius, what are a young man's duties at home and in the outside world? If he has energy to spare after he fulfills these duties, what must he do? According to Confucius, what is more important than being understood? ▶▶ How much value does Confucius place on human relationships? How do you know?

3. According to Confucius, what can leaders do to encourage people to show respect and loyalty? What does Confucius say about wealth and how it must be obtained? ▶▶ Why might eating coarse food, drinking cold water, and sleeping on the floor bring happiness? In what ways are Confucius's opinions on leadership and wealth in conflict with the actions of many leaders and wealthy people throughout history?

4. What does Confucius say about the way in which he lives his life? What does his happiness help him to forget? When Confucius is walking in the company of other men, what does he seek? ▶▶ How valuable is learning and knowledge to Confucius? In what way does Confucius learn from other people?

SYNTHESIZING

5. What do these passages reveal about Confucius's attitude toward honesty and truth? What do these passages reveal about Confucius's attitude toward power, wealth, and human relationships? How does his attitude compare and contrast with contemporary American views?

RESPONDING TO THE SELECTION

Students might also discuss what qualities make a person moral. Do they think Confucius would agree with their definition of a moral person? Why, or why not?

ANSWERS FOR REVIEWING THE SELECTION

RECALLING AND INTERPRETING

1. **Recalling.** Confucius says that such a man cannot be benevolent. Zeng Zi, a disciple, frequently asks himself if he has tried his utmost to help others, if he has been honest to his friends, and if he has reviewed the instructions from the Master. **Interpreting.** *Responses will vary.* According to Zeng Zi, honesty is important when one is following the teachings of Confucius.

2. **Recalling.** According to Confucius, a young man must be dutiful toward parents, be respectful toward elders, be cautious and trustworthy, and love everyone yet only make close friends of those with benevolence. If he has energy to spare after he fulfills these duties, he can study books. According to Confucius, understanding others is more important than being understood. **Interpreting.** Confucius greatly values human relationships. His messages about honesty and having respect for people reveal his ideas about the importance of good relationships.

3. **Recalling.** According to Confucius, leaders must be upright in the presence of people, be filial and benevolent, and be righteous. Confucius believes that wealth must be obtained legitimately. **Interpreting.**These things can bring happiness if they are obtained honestly. Confucius's opinions conflict with the actions of many people who have obtained their power and wealth dishonestly. (cont.)

ANSWERS FOR REVIEWING THE SELECTION (CONT.)

4. **Recalling.** Confucius lived his life by working hard and living so happily that he forgot his worries. When Confucius was walking in the company of other men, he sought at least one man from whom he could learn. **Interpreting.** Learning and knowledge are valuable activities to Confucius. Confucius learns from people's merits and shortcomings. He follows the merits of others and examines the shortcomings of others to master his own.

SYNTHESIZING

Responses will vary. Possible responses are given.

5. Confucius values honesty and being true to one's own nature. Confucius was against leaders who abuse power and fail to set a good examples, and people who gain wealth through inappropriate means. Of major importance was the idea that one must make a constant effort to understand and respect other people.

Answers for Understanding Literature

Responses will vary. Possible responses are given.

1. Aphorism. Students should be able to name brief passages from the *Analects* that address certain points. Students might name any sayings and aphorisms that they had heard in their lives. They might say that aphorisms appeal to people because they are short, simple, and they get right to the point. Because they are short, they stay in people's minds and can be jotted onto pieces of paper. This is an advantage over longer works.

2. Theme. Students should be able to name honesty, leadership, understanding, and knowledge as some of the major themes of Confucius's teachings. All of these themes can be supported with examples from the selection.

Answers for Skills Activities

APPLIED ENGLISH/TECH PREP SKILLS

Students' resumes should be honest and contain all the essential parts indicated in the Language Arts Survey 5.3, "Resumes and Cover Letters." Students' cover letters should be persuasive and concise. They should also follow the proper form for business letters as outlined in the Language Arts Survey 5.2, "Personal and Business Letters."

▶ Additional practice is provided in the Essential Skills Practice Book: Applied English/Tech Prep 5.3.

Understanding Literature (Questions for Discussion)

1. **Aphorism.** An **aphorism** is a short saying or pointed statement. What are some of your favorite aphorisms in these excerpts from the *Analects*? What are some other aphorisms that you have heard in your life? Why might aphorisms, more than longer statements, be an effective way of sharing and remembering important ideas or rules?

2. **Theme.** A **theme** is a central idea in a literary work. After reading the brief excerpts from the *Analects*, can you name some of the major themes of the teachings of Confucius? Support your response with examples from the excerpts.

Responding in Writing

1. **Creative Writing: Aphorisms.** Create your own aphorisms that express your ideas about life. Through interesting but concise sayings, address rules of conduct or share truths as you see them about life, politics, leadership, and relationships. You might also share interesting observations that you have made about people. To begin, review your responses to the questions in the Reader's Journal activity.

2. **Critical Essay: Comparison and Contrast.** You have read about the beliefs of Confucius and excerpts from the *Analects*. If you have not already done so, read about the beliefs of Lao-tzu and excerpts from the *Tao Te Ching* (see pages 544–547). Write a brief essay in which you compare and contrast the ideas of the two great Chinese philosophers. To begin, create a Venn diagram listing similarities and differences between the beliefs of the two men. For more information on Venn diagrams, see the Language Arts Survey 1.10, "Gathering Ideas." Then begin the first draft of your essay, using passages from the *Tao Te Ching* and the *Analects* to support your points.

Applied English/Tech Prep Skills

Writing Resumes and Cover Letters. Confucius was a man who was sure of himself and his purpose in the world, and who was constantly in search of ways to learn and to improve himself. As you become older, jobs, volunteer positions, and other activities can help you to grow as a person and to figure out your own purpose in the world. A well-written resume and cover letter can open doors to these unique opportunities. Consult the Language Arts Survey 5.3, "Writing Resumes and Cover Letters." Then, imagine that you are applying for a special job or volunteer position. Prepare a resume and a cover letter in which you state your objective, list your accomplishments and activities, and show why you are the best person for the job. Be honest but confident and assertive as you prepare your materials. Finally, share your resume and cover letter with a small group of classmates.

Themes

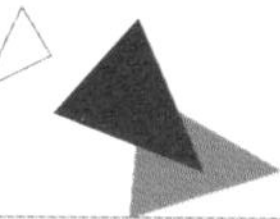

Society and the Individual

Cultures throughout history and across the globe have adopted different views of the individual's role in society. Some cultures have viewed society as a highly structured system, in which people are born into certain stations and must live and work within the confines of these stations in order to keep the society running correctly. Other societies have encouraged an individual's retreat from the world and a strong connection with nature, spirituality, or the self. These trends have been reflected in literature throughout the ages.

Confucianism, which encouraged a return to community commitment and structure, was China's state teaching from the beginning of the Han Dynasty in 202 BC to the end of the imperial period in AD 1911. Confucius was disturbed by constant warfare among the states; he felt that most of his society's problems occurred because people forgot their stations in life and rulers lost their drive to be virtuous. Confucius advocated a return to proper social order, which he considered crucial to having social harmony. He defined five important relationships: between ruler and ruled, between husband and wife, between parents and children, between older and younger brothers, and between friends. He believed that in these relationships, the "inferior" person must show complete obedience to the "superior" person. In turn, the "superior" person must treat the "inferior" person with kindness and fairness.

In contrast to the structured world of Confucius, Taoists advocated a total retreat from structured society and a return to nature. Lao-tzu and the followers of his *Tao Te Ching* believed that getting too caught up in society interfered with one's ability to understand the true meaning of life. This meaning was only attainable by those who turned away from structured society, cleared their minds, and focused on nature. Through the years Taoism and Confucianism took turns being the popular philosophical choice among the people of China.

During Europe's Middle Ages, people lived under a highly structured system called feudalism. This was a social system of rights and obligations that was based on land ownership. In feudal states the king owned all land, of which he granted pieces to members of the nobility, called barons, in exchange for service, loyalty, armies, and tax money. In turn the barons often gave land to lesser nobles in exchange for services. At the bottom of the social order was a class of bondsmen known as peasants, or serfs, who worked the land. In this feudal system, each person was bound by a system of loyalties to a person higher on the social hierarchy. The code of proper conduct for knights and other members of the nobility during the feudal period was known as chivalry. According to this code, a knight was to be loyal to his lord or lady and always display such virtues as bravery, courage, courtesy, and honesty. Just as in the world of Confucius, this society emphasized social order and the idea that people must fulfill their specific obligations to society in order to maintain social harmony.

Much later in European history, during the eighteenth and nineteenth centuries, a literary and artistic movement known as Romanticism developed which had more in common with Taoist beliefs than Confucian ideals. In this movement, emotion was valued over reason, and the individual was valued over society as a whole. People turned to nature and wildness and away from human works, and they came to appreciate country more than cities and towns. In addition to these changes, people valued common people over aristocrats and sought freedom from authority. Just as in Taoist movement, this movement encouraged a turning away from societal structure and an appreciation of the spirit of the individual and his or her relationship to the natural world.

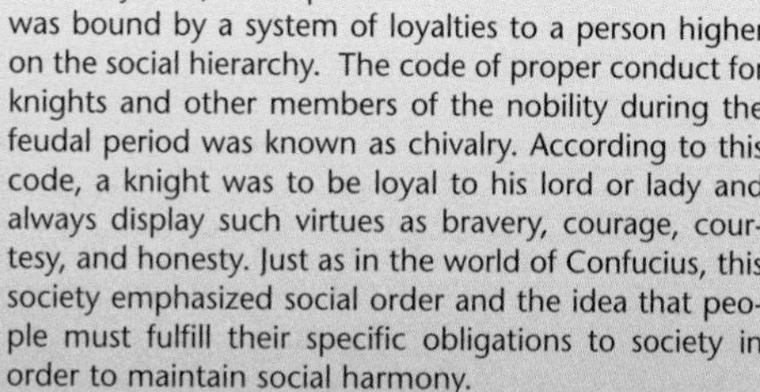

ANALYTIC SCALES FOR RESPONDING IN WRITING

Assign a score from 1 to 25 for each grading criterion below. (For more detailed evaluation, see the evaluation forms for writing, revising, and proofreading, Assessment Portfolio 4.1–4.9.)

1. Aphorisms

- **Content/Unity.** The writing consists of aphorisms that address rules of conduct or truths.
- **Organization/Coherence.** Each aphorism expresses one sensible idea.
- **Language/Style.** The aphorisms use vivid and precise nouns, verbs, and modifiers.
- **Conventions.** The aphorisms avoid errors in spelling, grammar, usage, mechanics, and manuscript form.

▶ Additional practice is provided in the Essential Skills Practice Book: Writing 1.8.

2. Critical Essay

- **Content/Unity.** The essay compares and contrasts Confucius's ideas with Lao-tzu's ideas.
- **Organization/Coherence.** The essay begins with an introduction that includes the thesis of the essay. The introduction is followed by supporting paragraphs with clear transitions. The essay ends with a solid conclusion.
- **Language/Style.** The essay uses vivid and precise nouns, verbs, and modifiers.
- **Conventions.** The essay avoids errors in spelling, grammar, usage, mechanics, and manuscript form.

▶ Additional practice is provided in the Essential Skills Practice Book: Writing 1.10, 1.20.

ADDITIONAL RESOURCES

READER'S GUIDE

- Selection Worksheet 7.7

ASSESSMENT PORTFOLIO

- Selection Check Test 2.7.13
- Selection Test 2.7.14

ESSENTIAL SKILLS PRACTICE BOOKS

- Writing 1.8, 1.10, 1.20

PREREADING EXTENSIONS

"The Creation Hymn" is one of the most famous of all the hymns in the Vedas. It is also one of the most difficult to interpret. You may wish to explain that Hindu theologians have debated the meaning of this hymn for millennia. What can be determined for certain is the subject of the hymn. It deals with an ancient philosophical and theological question: Was there a beginning of all things? Suppose that we assume that there was a beginning. Then we might naturally ask, did anything exist before the beginning? If we answer no, then we are faced with the paradox of something arising from nothing. If we answer yes, then we have contradicted ourselves, for there could not have been a something that existed before anything existed. The medieval Catholic theologian Saint Thomas Aquinas (c. 1225–1274) argued on these grounds that there must be a God, or prime mover—a being who is eternal, who did not have a beginning but was Himself the beginning of everything else. Aquinas believed that he had shown by means of this prime mover argument that disbelief in an eternal god was logically absurd. "The Creation Hymn" does not take the argument that far. Instead, it suggests that perhaps the beginning of things is unknowable, given that before the beginning of all things, nothing existed to know anything.

PREREADING

INDIA

"Creation Hymn" from the Rig Veda

translated by Wendy Doniger O'Flaherty

About the Selection

The Sanskrit word *veda* means "knowledge." The Vedas, or Books of Knowledge, are the earliest of the sacred Hindu religious texts and are among the oldest known human records. The Vedas originated among the Aryan peoples who invaded India sometime around 2000 BC. These poetic texts, which include hymns, myths, prayers, rituals, and charms, were not originally written down. Instead, they were composed, recited, and taught orally. The written texts as we know them are anthologies of works created over many thousands of years. Some parts of the Vedas probably originated before the Aryan invasion and so provide information about one of the earliest of human cultures.

The Aryan invaders of India worshiped many gods, who were personifications of elements in nature. These gods included Indra, the warrior king, god of rain and thunder; Agni, the king as law-giver, god of fire; Usas, the goddess of dawn; and countless others. The oldest of the Vedas, the Rig Veda, is a collection of hymns praising natural objects—the sky, the sun, the earth, the rain, and so on—all viewed as gods. Over half of the hymns are devoted to Indra, the god of rain and thunder, who is paralleled by Zeus and Thor, respectively, in Greek and Norse mythology.

Hindu god Shiva

Over time, the Indian descendants of the Aryans developed a variety of monotheism, or belief in one god. Hindus continued to worship many gods but saw these as manifestations, or parts of, the one god Brahma, the ultimate reality behind all things in the universe. In Hindu belief, Brahma is identical with the Atman, or soul, within each person. Other major gods, in addition to Brahma, the creator of the universe, are Vishnu, the Preserver, and Shiva, the Destroyer. The identity of the Atman with Brahma is the primary concern of the philosophical portions of the Vedas known as the Upanishads.

"Creation Hymn" comes from the **Rig Veda,** one of the four surviving Vedas. It is a **hymn,** or song or verse of praise, often religious, like those of other early cultures—the hymns of Mesopotamia and Egypt and the psalms of Israel and Judea. (For more information on songs or verse of praise, see Insights: Hymns and Psalms, page 370.) "Creation Hymn" raises an ancient puzzle about creation: If there was nothing in the beginning, how did something come of it? If the creation was an action, how did this action occur without an actor?

CONNECTIONS: Common Ancestors: India and Europe

The Aryans spoke dialects of Sanskrit, a language that shares a common ancestor with other members of the Indo-European language group, such as Persian, Greek, Latin, German, English, and Norse. The many similarities between Aryan religious beliefs and Greek and Norse myths also suggest a common ancestor. In ancient times a single Aryan people, living on the shores of the Caspian Sea and speaking a Proto-Indo-European language, probably traveled to Europe and to India, carrying with them variants of their language and their religion, variants which developed into the languages and religions of the Hindu, Persian, Greek, Roman, and Germanic peoples. Study of the Vedas thus gives us glimpses into the prehistory of the beliefs of much of the Western world.

GOALS/OBJECTIVES

Studying this lesson will enable students to

- appreciate the questions raised in the "Creation Hymn"
- briefly explain why India and Europe have a common ancestor
- define *rhetorical question* and identify these in their reading
- write a descriptive paragraph
- write a critical essay comparing and contrasting mythologies
- explore Indian music

Think of a time when you had a question about the world that remained unanswered. Maybe you wondered what our planet looked like long ago, or perhaps you wondered what you would discover if you could dive to the bottom of the deepest ocean. Write about your questions in your journal.

"Creation Hymn"

TRANSLATED BY WENDY DONIGER O'FLAHERTY

1 There was neither non-existence nor existence then; there was neither the realm of space nor the sky which is beyond. What stirred? Where? In whose protection? Was there water, bottomlessly deep?[1]

2 There was neither death nor immortality[2] then. There was no distinguishing sign of night nor of day. That one[3] breathed, windless, by its own impulse.[4] Other than that there was nothing beyond.

3 Darkness was hidden by darkness in the beginning; with no distinguishing sign, all this was water. The life force that was covered with emptiness, that one arose through the power of heat.

4 Desire came upon that one in the beginning; that was the first seed of mind.[5] Poets[6] seeking in their heart with wisdom found the bond of existence in non-existence.

5 Their cord was extended across. Was there below? Was there above? There were seed-placers; there were powers. There was impulse breath; there was giving-forth above.

6 Who really knows? Who will here proclaim it? Whence was it produced? Whence is this creation? The gods came afterwards, with the creation of this universe. Who then knows whence it has arisen?[7]

7 Whence this creation has arisen—perhaps it formed itself, or perhaps it did not—the one who looks down on it, in the highest heaven, only he knows—or perhaps he does not know. ■

1. **water . . . deep.** Many ancient peoples perceived of the heavens as a firmament separating waters above from waters below.
2. **neither death nor immortality.** That is, before the beginning of time, there were neither beings who could die (such as humans) nor immortal beings (such as gods).
3. **That one.** The second verse suggests a partial answer to the question posed in the first. There was a "one"; however, the questions about the nature of this "one" remain unanswered.
4. **breathed, windless . . . impulse.** Many ancient peoples identified the soul with the wind and the breath. The verse may be saying that the one who stirred at the beginning was self-sufficient and self-animated, not animated by the wind (or soul), as later creatures were.
5. **Desire . . . mind.** The Sanskrit word for desire, *kama*, also means love. The verse explains the origin of mind as the desire that led the "one" to bring forth the creation.
6. **Poets.** The Sanskrit word *kavi*, here translated as "poet," also meant "sage" or "wise person."
7. **Who really knows? . . . whence it has arisen?** The verse suggests that even the gods, who came afterward, do not know how creation came about.

❶ *Does the speaker in this hymn know the answers to his or her questions? Does anyone know, according to the speaker?*

READER'S JOURNAL

Encourage students to share their unanswered questions in small groups to determine what unanswered questions are common among the students.

ANSWERS TO GUIDED READING QUESTIONS

❶ The speaker believes that neither he or she nor anyone else knows the answers to these questions.

SUPPORT FOR LEP STUDENTS

PRONUNCIATIONS OF PROPER NOUNS AND ADJECTIVES

Rig Ve • da (rig vā´da)

ADDITIONAL VOCABULARY

realm—region; sphere; area
whence—from what place

SELECTION CHECK TEST WITH ANSWERS

EX. What does the speaker say about space and the sky before the creation?
The speaker says that neither space nor the sky existed.

1. What "deep" thing does the speaker wonder about the existence of before the creation?
The speaker wonders if "water, bottomlessly deep" existed.

2. What hid darkness in the beginning?
Darkness hid darkness in the beginning.

3. What being came into existence in the beginning?
A being the speaker calls "that one" came into existence.

(cont.)

SELECTION CHECK TEST WITH ANSWERS (CONT.)

4. What came "afterwards, with the creation of this universe"?
The gods came afterwards with the creation of this universe.

5. Who is the only being who might know "whence this creation has arisen"?
The "one who looks down on it, in the highest heaven" may or may not know.

RESPONDING TO THE SELECTION

Tell students that they are free to express their true feelings about whether they are interested in such questions, even if they are not, as long as they explain why.

ANSWERS FOR REVIEWING THE SELECTION

RECALLING AND INTERPRETING

1. **Recalling.** Existence, nonexistence, space, and sky were nonentities. **Interpreting.** The speaker is thinking about how nothing existed, so he or she wonders what happened to make things exist.

2. **Recalling.** Death, immortality, night, and day did not exist. "That one" breathed "windless, by its own impulse." **Interpreting.** "That one" seems strange because this is a being whose nature the speaker is not able to explain or even comprehend.

3. **Recalling.** The speaker says that the gods were not present at the creation but were one of its results. **Interpreting.** The speaker seems to view the gods as less powerful or knowledgeable than "that one."

4. **Recalling.** The "one who looks down on it" from "the highest heaven" might know whence the creation has arisen. **Interpreting.** According to the Creation hymn, the mystery of "[w]hence this creation has arisen" might be unknowable by any person or god.

SYNTHESIZING

Responses will vary. Possible responses are given.

5. The hymn suggests that the early Aryans worshiped many gods (were polytheistic), that they believed that there was one powerful and supernatural creator, and that the mysteries of creation could not be explained or understood by mere mortals or even the gods.

Responding to the Selection

What do you think about the questions posed in "The Creation Hymn"? Do questions such as these interest you? Why, or why not?

Reviewing the Selection

RECALLING / **INTERPRETING**

1. According to the first verse, what was the world like before the creation? ▶▶ Why might thinking about the world before the creation raise in the speaker's mind the questions posed in verse 1?

2. According to verse 2, what did not exist before the creation? In what way did "that one" breathe? ▶▶ What makes "that one" seem unusual or strange?

3. In verse 6, what does the speaker say about the gods? ▶▶ In what way does the speaker seem to view the gods?

4. According to the last verse of the "Creation Hymn," who might know how the creation arose? ▶▶ What mystery, according to "The Creation Hymn," might be unknowable by any person or god?

SYNTHESIZING

5. What can you deduce about the nature of early Aryan religion from this Vedic hymn?

Understanding Literature (Questions for Discussion)

Rhetorical Question. A **rhetorical question** is one asked for effect but not meant to be answered because the answer is clear from context. This selection poses many questions. Are the answers implied, or are some questions left unanswered? Would you classify the questions posed in the selection as rhetorical? Why, or why not?

ANSWERS FOR UNDERSTANDING LITERATURE

Responses will vary. Possible responses are given.

Rhetorical Question. Some of the questions are left unanswered. Students may classify the questions as rhetorical because they are meant to be questions that even the gods cannot answer.

Responding in Writing

1. **Creative Writing: Descriptive Paragraph.** Using details from "The Creation Hymn" as well as your own imagination, write a paragraph describing the world before the creation as an ancient Aryan might have perceived it. To begin, you might create a sensory detail chart. (See the Language Arts Survey 1.10, "Gathering Ideas," for more information on sensory detail charts.)

2. **Critical Essay: Comparative Mythology.** Reread the About the Selection on page 556. Then, do some research in the library to learn more about Indra, Zeus, and Thor. Write a brief essay in which you compare these three gods from the mythologies of ancient India, Greece, and Scandinavia, pointing out the similarities among them that suggest that the myths of all three peoples had a common origin.

PROJECT

Indian Music. The hymns in the Vedas were originally chanted or sung. They represent a part of the magnificent musical tradition of India. Working with your classmates, do some research on traditional Indian music and musical instruments. Devote one day in class to discussing and to playing examples of Indian traditional music. Use the following notes as a starting place for your research:

> Traditional Indian music differs from Western music in many respects. First, Western music is based on a twelve-note scale, whereas Indian music is based on a twenty-two note scale. Thus Indian music recognizes different standard pitches than Western music does, a fact that gives Indian music an odd sound to the uninitiated Western ear. Second, traditional Indian music makes use of instruments not commonly found in the west, such as the sitar, the tambura, and the tablas. Third, while Western music places emphasis on chords and counterpoint, Indian music places its emphasis on melody and rhythm. Fourth, unlike Western classical music, traditional Indian music, like Western jazz, is largely improvisational. In a typical performance, a small ensemble of Indian musicians improvises on one of thirty-six traditional melodic themes, known as ragas. (Strictly speaking, there are only six ragas, each of which has, in addition, five modifications called *ragini*).

ANALYTIC SCALES FOR RESPONDING IN WRITING

Assign a score from 1 to 25 for each grading criterion below. (For more detailed evaluation, see the evaluation forms for writing, revising, and proofreading, Assessment Portfolio 4.1–4.9.)

1. Descriptive Paragraph

- **Content/Unity.** The description describes the world before the creation as an ancient Aryan might have perceived it.
- **Organization/Coherence.** The description presents details in a sensible order.
- **Language/Style.** The description uses vivid and precise nouns, verbs, and modifiers.
- **Conventions.** The description avoids errors in spelling, grammar, usage, mechanics, and manuscript form.

► Additional practice is provided in the Essential Skills Practice Book: Writing 1.8, 1.10.

2. Critical Essay

- **Content/Unity.** The essay compares and contrasts myths about Indra, Zeus, and Thor.
- **Organization/Coherence.** The essay begins with an introduction that includes the thesis of the essay. The introduction is followed by supporting paragraphs with clear transitions. The essay ends with a solid conclusion.
- **Language/Style.** The essay uses vivid and precise nouns, verbs, and modifiers.
- **Conventions.** The essay avoids errors in spelling, grammar, usage, mechanics, and manuscript form.

► Additional practice is provided in the Essential Skills Practice Book: Writing 1.20.

PROJECT NOTES

See the evaluation form for projects, Assessment Portfolio 4.12.

Indian Music. Some students may wish to research the influence that Indian music has had in the West. You might point out that several musicians in the 1960s and 1970s played music that had been inspired by Indian music.

ADDITIONAL RESOURCES

READER'S GUIDE

- Selection Worksheet 7.8

ASSESSMENT PORTFOLIO

- Selection Check Test 2.7.15
- Selection Test 2.7.16

ESSENTIAL SKILLS PRACTICE BOOKS

- Writing 1.8, 1.10, 1.20

PREREADING EXTENSIONS

You may wish to share with students the following background information on the Indian Heroic Age, the time when the *Ramayana* and the *Mahabharata* were composed. The Heroic Age of India, between 1000 and 500 BC, was a period of warfare among rival Aryan clans. (The Aryans were a group of people from the north who migrated into India between 2000 and 1400 BC, settling in the Indus Valley region. These people became the dominant civilization soon after their arrival.) Also during this time, under the guidance of the Brahmins, the Hindu religion developed its mature form, expressed in sacred works such as the later Vedas, the Upanishads, and the Bhagavad Gita. Toward the end of the Heroic Age, two new religions sprang up in India as offshoots of Hinduism. Buddhism, founded by Siddhartha Gautama, the Buddha, promised relief from suffering through renunciation of desire and stressed living a moderate life that avoided extremes. Jainism, founded by Vardhamana Mahavira, stressed total nonviolence and renunciation of worldly pleasures and pursuits.

PREREADING

from the *Ramayana*
by Valmiki, retold by William Buck

About the Author

Valmiki. The Hindu epic poem known as the *Ramayana,* or *Rama's Way,* is traditionally said to be the work of India's first poet, Valmiki. Little is known about Valmiki except what is told about him in the *Ramayana,* in which he figures as one of the characters. In this work, Valmiki becomes unhappy because of the lack of friendliness and hope in the world and retires to a life as a forest-dwelling ascetic. He sits in meditation for thousands of years, during which time a great anthill is built around him. He finally decides to leave the anthill when he hears the voice of Narada, the god of music, telling him to leave the anthill to care for Prince Rama's wife, Sita, who has been banished to the forest because of false rumors spread about her in Rama's kingdom. Like the Greek epic poet Homer, to whom the *Iliad* and the *Odyssey* are attributed, Valmiki, if he existed at all, was probably a poet who compiled materials that already existed in the oral tradition.

About the Selection

An **epic** is a long work, often told in verse, that tells the story of a hero or god and that is comprehensive enough to give a portrait of an entire culture. The ***Ramayana,*** one of the two great epics of ancient India, was composed in the oral tradition, probably between 300 BC and AD 200. In its more than twenty-five thousand verses, the *Ramayana* tells the story of the life and deeds of Rama, a warrior hero who saves the world from the ravages of demons called Rakshasas. Rama was thought to be an incarnation of Vishnu, the god associated with dharma, or duty. For thousands of years Rama has provided Hindus with a model of perfect conduct as a son, brother, friend, husband, ruler, and warrior. Rama's mate, Sita, has served for centuries as the Hindu model of the perfect companion—one who is patient, obedient, faithful, loving, and willing to bear misfortune with humility and grace. While the *Ramayana* was originally written in verse, the following selection is from a prose retelling of this epic.

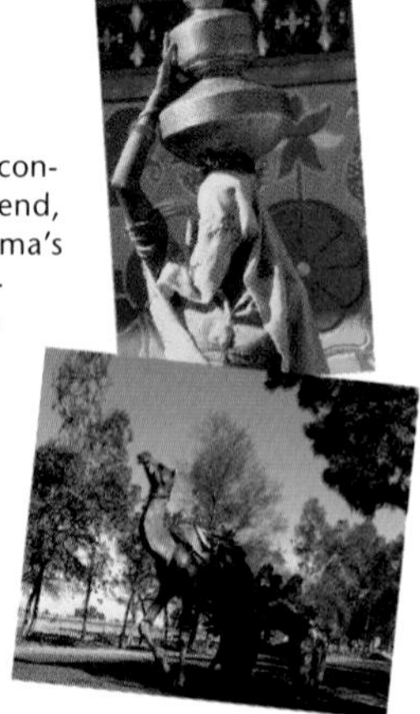

CONNECTIONS: Greek and Indian Epic Poetry

The two epic poems of ancient India, the *Mahabharata* and the *Ramayana,* closely parallel the two great epics of ancient Greece, the *Iliad* and the *Odyssey.* Both the *Mahabharata* and the *Iliad* are war stories. Each tells of a great battle between related peoples. Both the *Ramayana* and the *Odyssey* tell stories of the adventures of individual heroes, Rama and Odysseus.

GOALS/OBJECTIVES

Studying this lesson will enable students to

- have a positive experience reading a selection from an Indian epic
- explain what this epic reveals about the beliefs and values of Indians during the Heroic Age
- define *myth* and identify elements of myth in literature
- define *allegory* and interpret an allegory
- write a description of an imaginary creature
- write a critical essay analyzing allegorical elements
- retell a scene from the *Ramayana*

READER'S JOURNAL

Who are your own heroes? What qualities do you most admire in these people? Write responses to these questions in your journal.

FROM THE

Ramayana

VALMIKI, RETOLD BY WILLIAM BUCK

THE FIRST POEM

[Editor's note: After Narada, the god of music, awakens him from his thousand-year meditation, the poet Valmiki finds the exiled Sita by a riverbank and resolves to take care of her. Valmiki helps Sita to raise her children by Rama. Though exiled by her husband because of false rumors, Sita nonetheless remains loyal to him and teaches her sons about their father's heroic life. The following passage appears just after Valmiki meets Sita.]

Valmiki went alone to the clear Ganga[1] waterside and bathed. He washed away the anthill dust and peeled grey bark from a tree and made new fresh clothes.

Then he sat back resting against a stone. He watched two small white waterbirds in a tree nearby. The male bird was singing to his mate when before Valmiki's eyes an arrow hit him, and the little bird fell from the limb. He thrashed on the ground an instant and then lay dead, and blood drops stained his feathers.

Heartbroken the dead bird's mate cried—
Your long feathers! Your tuneful songs!

A bird-hunter came from the forest holding a bow. Valmiki's heart was pounding and he cursed the killer—

You will find no rest for the long years of Eternity,
For you killed a bird in love and unsuspecting.

One look at Valmiki and the hunter ran for his life, but fever already burned in his blood; he died that day. Valmiki turned back to his hermitage thinking, "This is truly how I remember the ways of the world." Then he thought, "Those words I cursed him with make a verse, and that verse could be sung to music."

For days the words ran through Valmiki's mind. Whatever he seemed to be doing he was really thinking of his verse. On the fourth day after Sita's rescue, Lord Brahma[2] the creator of the worlds appeared in Valmiki's new retreat. He looked like an old man with red skin and white hair, with four arms, with four faces around one head, holding in his hands a ladle and a rosary,[3] a waterpot and a holy book.

Valmiki greeted Brahma, "Sit by me," and taking water from a pitcher he washed Brahma's feet, and gave him other water to

1. **Ganga.** River Ganges, considered sacred by Hindus
2. **Lord Brahma.** Supreme god in the Hindu religion
3. **rosary.** Prayer beads

❶ *How does Valmiki respond to the killing of the bird? What happens to the hunter as a result?*

READER'S JOURNAL

As an alternate activity, students might write about what qualities make the ultimate villain. If they had to imagine a terrible villain who would threaten the earth, what would this villain be like?

ANSWERS TO GUIDED READING QUESTIONS

❶ Valmiki curses the killer of the bird. The killer runs away but dies of a fever that same day.

SPELLING AND VOCABULARY WORDS FROM THE SELECTION

boon	rend
dowry	resonant
embellish	saffron
illumined	spectral
parasol	summit
pavilion	supple

SUPPORT FOR LEP STUDENTS

PRONUNCIATIONS OF PROPER NOUNS AND ADJECTIVES

Brah • ma (brä´mə)
Ha • nu • man (hän´o͞o män´)
Na • ra • ya • na (nä rä yä´nə)
Ra • ma • ya • na (rä mä yä´ nə)
Ra • va • na (rä vä´ nə)
Si • ta (sē´ tə)
Val • mi • ki (val mē´ kē)
Vish • nu (vish´ no͞o)

ADDITIONAL VOCABULARY

bestial—like a beast; brutal
disdain—contempt or scorn
embellished—adorned
perilous—dangerous
wantonly—in a playful or frolicsome manner

Answers to Guided Reading Questions

❶ Ravana makes destructive raids, captures and eats heavenly creatures, devours men, and steals fair maidens.

❷ Pity, love, and compassion for a tiny bird gave birth to the world's first verse. Brahma asks Valmiki to tell Rama's story in verse.

❸ Ravana kills the messenger and has him roasted to be eaten.

Cultural/Historical Note

So that students will better understand the religious principles behind the *Ramayana,* you might share the following description of Hinduism with them:

The primary religion of India, Hinduism, developed out of the Vedic religion of the Aryans. The Aryans were polytheistic, or worshipers of many gods, and they generally absorbed into their pantheon, or group of gods, the deities of the peoples whom they conquered. Gradually, they began to view all these gods as manifestations of a single god, Brahma, the Creator, whose dream is the created universe. According to Hinduism, there have been many such dreams, each representing a cycle, or *Kalpa,* that lasts for 4,320,000,000 years. During each *Kalpa,* the universe is sustained by Vishnu, the Preserver, until it is brought to an end by Shiva, the Destroyer. Both Vishnu and Shiva are viewed as aspects of Brahma. Although Brahma is the supreme god, most Hindus are devotees either of Vishnu or of Shiva.

Vishnu is believed to be the joyful, creative force that sustains the world. Associated with Vishnu is the law of dharma, a term difficult to translate into English but connoting not only the cosmic regulatory law that binds the universe together but also the moral law to be followed by gods

(cont.)

❶ *What evil deeds does Ravana do?*

❷ *According to Brahma, what gave birth to the world's first verse? What does Brahma ask Valmiki to do?*

❸ *How does Ravana violate the Hindu law of hospitality toward guests and the universal rule of proper conduct toward a messenger, emissary, or diplomat?*

drink. But after that, even sitting there with the Grandfather of all the Universe watching him, still Valmiki remembered only the two waterbirds and thought to himself, "What a crime! There was not one bite of meat on that little bird! What use is a world run all wrong without a grain of mercy in it?"

Those thoughts were as clear to Brahma as if Valmiki had been shouting in his ear. Brahma said, "So, by a river, the world's first verse has been born from pity, and love and compassion for a tiny bird has made you a poet. Use your discovery to tell Rama's story, and your verses will defeat Time."

THE BIRTH OF RAVANA

[*Editor's note: As Valmiki holds water cupped in his hands, Brahma causes the story of Rama's life to be shown in this water. Following Brahma's command, Valmiki composes an epic poem about Rama's deeds, the* Ramayana. *The poem relates the struggle between Prince Rama and a tribe of evil demons, the Rakshasas, of the kingdom of Lanka (modern-day Sri Lanka). The following passage describes the birth of Ravana, the ruler of the Rakshasas.*]

Vishrava[4] took her [Kaikasi] for his second wife, and when she gave birth it was to four Rakshasas, three sons and a daughter. First-born was Ravana. Ravana had ten hideous heads and twenty arms; he was blacker than a heap of soot and fit to horrify the Universe; he had two fangs curving up from each mouth and coppery lips and twenty red eyes. When he was born every dog in the world howled as loud as he could and chased his tail madly turning left in circles.

THE WICKEDNESS OF RAVANA

[*Editor's note: From Brahma, Ravana has won a promise that he will be invincible to death at the hands of any god, devil, demon, or serpent. With this assurance of immortality, Ravana and his fellow Rakshasas embark on a campaign of terror.*]

They would make many raids into the Himalya hills[5] and there like the Wind they broke down trees and tore the orchards and pavilions set along the paths to heaven. Gandharvas[6] and Apsarasas[7] visiting on Earth were captured and eaten, men were devoured, Ravana stole fair maidens of every race for his warriors in Lanka; and then refugees ran to Vaishravana[8] on Mount Kailasa.

Vaishravana sent a Yaksha to see Ravana in Lanka. The Yaksha said, "The noble Treasure King hears of your bestial attacks on the innocent and asks you to remember right and wrong and not to dishonor your family. He tells you—*Stop, brother, for I live near heaven and I hear the gods wish for your destruction and seek ways to kill you.*"

Ravana smiled. "My jewel-bellied brother!" He drew a sword and killed the Yaksha. He sent him to the kitchen to be roasted and served, and his bones made into broth.

VISHNU AGREES TO BE BORN INTO THE WORLD

[*Editor's note: In his pride and wanton impiety, Ravana attacks and destroys the kingdom of Indra, the rain god who rules over the created world. Indra goes to visit Vishnu, the Preserver god.*]

4. **Vishrava.** Father of Ravana
5. **Himalya hills.** Himalaya Mountains, a mountain system extending along the India-Tibet border and containing the tallest mountains on Earth
6. **Gandharvas.** Heavenly musicians or fairies
7. **Apsarasas.** Heavenly damsels
8. **Vaishravana.** Ravana's half-brother, one of the race of sprites or fairies called the Yakshas, made by Brahma into the Lord of Wealth and Treasure

Words for Everyday Use

pa • vil • ion (pə vil´yən) *n.,* large tent or building, partly open, once used by royalty and now typically used at fairs and other outdoor entertainments

Vocabulary in Context

- The king ordered that a pavilion be raised in the meadow to serve as a place to feast during the summer celebration.

Indra went to Narayana, the Lord Vishnu,[9] the Soul of the Universe. Narayana sat watching Indra approach. Indra pressed together his hands, touched his brow, and bent his head low to Narayana's feet. "Searcher of Hearts, I bow to you, *namas.*[10] I have still faith in the Good Law of Dharma."[11] Indra looked up past Narayana's wide dark chest crossed by a neckchain of sapphires, up into the great god's joyful black eyes wide as lotus petals.

Narayana in his yellow saffron summer robes smiled down at Indra. "Yes, a good enough fight," said Narayana. "No fear, Lord of Gods."

"How shall we bring down Ravana?" asked Indra. "Because of Brahma's boon is the Demon King strong, and for no other cause of his own. Help me, you are my only refuge, there is no other for me. *I will gather my storms again and attack Lanka, give me your permission to fight Ravana once more!*"

"Never!" said Narayana. "Don't you understand that Brahma's words are always true? Do not falsify the three spheres of life. I would not have let you fight in the first place, though you were right to resist and Ravana was wrong. Ravana asked Brahma—*Let me be unslayable by every creature of Heaven and of the underworlds.* And Brahma promised—*So be it.* That boon is unbreakable, yet will I cause Ravana's death. That is the truth. Only ask me. . . ."

"Ah," said Indra, "from disdain Ravana did not mention men or animals, and took no safeguard against them. He eats men; they are his food and why should he fear them? Lord, on Earth life resembles Hell again. We need you again. Look at us, see us, and bless us. For the good of all the worlds, Lord Narayana, accept birth as a man."

"I already have."

Waves of happiness washed over Indra. "Dark blue Narayana clad in yellow, become four. Put aside the shell trumpet, the razor-edged chakra,[12] the lotus and mace you hold in your four hands. Empty your dark hands; descend into the borrowed and fanciful world of men, desperate and glittering. Become Dasaratha's[13] four sons born of blood and seed. Take your Goddess Lakshmi and let her be your mortal wife."

"We will go down," said Narayana.

"Lord, kill him, kill Ravana forever. I hate that proud and pampered Rakshasa. Favor me and curse him; give to Death his faces torn apart; dry away our fear as the Sun dries morning dew."

"I will," said Narayana.

SHIVA'S BOW

[*Editor's note: Vishnu is born into the world as four mortals, sons of Dasaratha, the king of Ayodhya. The oldest of these sons and heir to the throne is Rama. As a young man, Prince Rama goes with his brother Lakshmana and a sage named Viswamitra to visit Janaka, the king of Mithila. On this visit he meets Sita, a child of the earth whose name in Sanskrit means*

9. **Narayana, the Lord Vishnu.** Narayana, or Vishnu, is the second member of the Hindu trinity. The supreme god, Brahma, is seen by Hindus as having three parts: Brahma, the creator of the universe; Vishnu, the preserver of the universe; and Shiva, the destroyer of the universe.
10. ***namas.*** Sanskrit word meaning "names." This is probably a reference to the idea that all creatures (and thus all names) are part of Vishnu, who is part of Brahma.
11. **Dharma.** Righteousness, duty, and virtue. One of the aims of Hindu life is to live according to dharma, the moral law of the universe. Vishnu, as the Preserver, regulates dharma. (Rama, Vishnu's incarnation in the world, is seen as the embodiment of dharma and thus as a model of correct behavior.)
12. **chakra.** Discus, a round, sharp-edged weapon
13. **Dasaratha.** King of Ayodhya, later the father of Rama

❶ *What universal law is embodied in the person of the god Vishnu?*

❷ *What physical characteristics show Vishnu to be more than an ordinary being?*

❸ *Why does Vishnu refuse to permit Indra to wage war again on Ravana?*

❹ *What does Indra ask Vishnu to do?*

WORDS FOR EVERYDAY USE

saf • fron (saf´rən) *adj.*, orange-yellow

boon (bo͞on) *n.*, favor granted, gift, or request

ANSWERS TO GUIDED READING QUESTIONS

❶ The law of dharma, or duty, is embodied in the god Vishnu.

❷ Vishnu is dark blue and has four hands.

❸ Vishnu refuses to let Indra fight Ravana because Brahma has granted Ravana a boon that he cannot be killed by any creature of Heaven or the underworlds.

❹ Indra asks Vishnu to accept birth as a mortal in order to conquer Ravana.

CULTURAL/HISTORICAL NOTE (CONT.)

and mortals. Often the term is translated simply as "duty." Because of his role in preserving the creation, Vishnu is believed by Hindus to take human form in times of great evil or need. Rama, in the *Ramayana,* and Krishna, in the Bhagavad Gita, are both incarnations, or avatars, of Vishnu, and both are worshiped by millions of Hindus.

Shiva, sometimes portrayed as an ascetic, or holy person who lives in poverty, is believed to be the universal force of destruction, death, and decay at work in the universe. The worship of Shiva is therefore a recognition of the impermanence of all things. This impermanence is symbolized by the dance of Shiva, often depicted in statues of the god. Shiva is also associated with the regenerative, reproductive forces at work in the world. According to the Hindus, the end of the current cycle of the universe is overdue, but Shiva so loves the world that he hesitates to destroy it.

Just as Hindus believe that the universe goes through cycles of death and rebirth, so they believe that every individual goes through similar cycles, being born again and again in a process known as reincarnation. In the Hindu faith, a person's future state depends upon

(cont.)

VOCABULARY IN CONTEXT

- Alicia wore a saffron-colored dress as golden as the morning sun.
- The knight requested that his king allow him the honor of trying to rescue the captive treasure as a boon.

ART NOTE

Encourage students to discuss if this representation of Ravana matches their imaginations. Some students may wish to create their own depictions of Ravana.

ANSWERS TO GUIDED READING QUESTIONS

1 They want to see the bow that Shiva gave to King Janaka. Whoever can bend the bow will receive both it and the hand in marriage of the king's daughter Sita.

CULTURAL/HISTORICAL NOTE (CONT.)

the law of karma, which ensures that creatures will reap what they sow. Living a good life by following one's dharma builds positive karma and brings about positive results in one's future life or lives. Living a wicked life builds negative karma, with consequent negative results.

Hindus think of every creature as containing a soul, the Atman, which is identical to or coexistent with Brahma. A creature that follows its dharma will be reborn in a higher state. A creature that does not will be reborn in a lower state. Thus a person who lives virtuously might be reborn into a higher caste, and a person who lives wickedly might be reborn into a lower caste or even into an animal. Because Hindus believe that animals have souls, many abstain from eating meat and treat all life with reverence. Especially venerated among the Hindus are cattle and elephants.

The ultimate goal of the Hindu is to pass, in the course of many lives, through progressively higher states of being and eventually to win release, or *moksha*, at which point the person escapes the cycle of rebirth and rejoins Brahma.

Ravana. *Courtesy of the Freer Gallery of Art, Smithsonian Institution, Washington, D.C.; 07.271–297V—Indian Manuscript; late 16th century; Mughal; Akbar school; Persian translation of "Ramayana" of Valmiki; 130 miniatures in opaque colors and gold; 27.5 x 15.2 cm. (10 7/8 x 6") average leaf size*

"furrow." Rama demonstrates his godlike strength by bending and breaking a bow that once belonged to Shiva, the Destroyer.]

Soon they saw Mithila, a city of castles and spires, and they found King Janaka coming to meet them. He brought cool water to Viswamitra. "Blessed are we, brahmana.[14] Obliged and well-favored are we with your visit. But why have you led young warriors by this back trail to my city?"

"These are the Ayodhya princes Rama and Lakshmana," said Viswamitra. "They are eager to see your bow."

> 1 *What do Rama and Lakshmana want to see? Who will receive the bow and under what circumstances?*

"Long since did Shiva give me that heavenly bow," said the King. "To bend Shiva's Bow is the dowry of my daughter Sita, whose mother is Prithivi, the goddess Earth."

Rama asked, "How could that be, Majesty?"

Janaka answered, "Rama, this land, this kingdom, all this wide world under the curving blue sky belongs to Mother Earth and to no one else. Only in a flight of the mind, only in a dream is all this worldly land called a kingdom. Fourteen years ago I was plowing in a clearing beyond the city, when turning back I found her lying in the

14. **brahmana.** Holy man

WORDS FOR EVERYDAY USE

dow • ry (dou´rē) *n.,* property that a woman brings to her husband on marriage, provided by the bride's family

VOCABULARY IN CONTEXT

- In cultures where marriages are not arranged and people marry for love rather than for economic concerns, the practice of a bride bringing a dowry to her husband has gradually died out.

furrow I had just made; I found Sita. As a golden-skinned baby she rose from her mother Earth and sat throwing handfuls of dust over her feet. I consider her a treasure well-found, well-revealed. She is a delight for my fields and hills. And Sita is beautiful, a girl more lovely than any garden, half divine and unmarried."

Rama said, "We are curious to see the strength of your bow."

King Janaka called an order, and five strong men with great difficulty brought Shiva's Bow out from its own house in Mithila, drawing it along on an eight-wheeled cart, that held the bow protected within a long iron case covered with flowers.

"You must understand," said Janaka, "that Sita has the final consent. Others have come; none could even lift this bow. I passed them by, I have used this jewel of a bow as my raft to cross the sea of fourteen years. Now you have come. It is sad for me, but it is time for her to marry, and I am a poor man about to spend his last coin."

Janaka's minister came and said, "Here it is, Majesty, show it if you think it worth showing."

Janaka said, "Rama, open the box."

Rama raised the lid. Sandalwood dust and incense ash fell off from it in a powdery cloud. Rama looked and thought, "This bow is beyond men. But playfully first let me just touch it." He touched it. "Perhaps I can try to hold it. . . ."

All the Videha men had come out of the city and were watching. Rama balanced the bow and lifted it. He strung it. Then he drew it so strongly that it broke in two above the grip, with a noise so loud that everyone watching fell down, except Rama and Lakshmana, Viswamitra and King Janaka.

Janaka shook his head. "Who would have believed?" He helped his minister to rise. "Ask Sita."

The minister rubbed his ears. "She has seen him from her high window and touched him with her eyes and fallen in love with him already."

RAMA'S WAY

[*Editor's note: Rama and Sita live happily together in Ayodhya for twelve years, and Rama proves himself to be the noblest of men.*]

Little by little Dasaratha turned over the work of the kingdom to Rama.

Rama's nature was quiet and free. He didn't give good advice and tell others what he thought best and show them their mistakes. He knew when to save and when to spend. He could judge men finely and keep his own counsel. He could read hearts. He knew his own faults better than the failings of others. He could speak well and reason in a chain of eloquent words. Half a benefit was more to him than a hundred injuries. Bad accidents never happened near him. He could speak every language and was an expert archer who shot golden arrows; and he didn't believe that what he preferred from himself was always best for everyone else.

Rama was kind and courteous and never ill. To harsh words he returned no blame. He was warmhearted and generous and a real friend to all. He tried living right and found it easier than he'd thought. He collected the King's taxes so that over half the people didn't really mind paying him. He was a remarkable prince and every Kosala[15] loved him except for five or six fools. He was hospitable and he spoke first to every guest in welcome words. He was a quiet strong man; he could bend iron in his hands or fix a bird's broken wing. He would not scold the whole world nor take to task the universe, and so his pleasure and his anger never went for nothing.

15. **Kosala.** People of the kingdom of Ayodhya

❶ *What unusual circumstances are involved in Sita's birth?*

❷ *What has happened to Sita?*

❸ *Is Rama one to remember injuries and to hold grudges? How does Rama show that he respects individual differences?*

❹ *What does Rama find surprisingly easy? Why might this be easy for him?*

❺ *What abilities show Rama to be both strong and gentle? Under what circumstances, according to the* Ramayana, *does a person's anger "go for nothing"?*

Answers to Guided Reading Questions

❶ Sita was found lying in a furrow King Janaka had made in the earth with a plow.

❷ Sita has seen Rama from her window and fallen in love with him.

❸ Rama does not remember injuries or hold grudges. Rama does not believe that what he prefers is also best for everyone else.

❹ Rama finds "living right" surprisingly easy. This might be easy for him because he is such a noble, courteous, and generous character. It also might be easy for him because he is the incarnation of the god Vishnu.

❺ Rama can both bend iron and fix a bird's broken wing. A person's anger "goes for nothing," or is futile, when he or she tries to find fault with the whole world or with the universe.

Literary Note

To make this epic clearer to students, you may wish to reinforce the idea that Rama is a human incarnation of Vishnu, and Sita, Rama's wife, is the incarnation of Vishnu's immortal companion, the goddess Lakshmi. Both, however, are manifestations of Brahma.

ANSWERS TO GUIDED READING QUESTIONS

1 Ravana wears the disguise of an elderly holy man—he has a single lock of white hair, a parasol and sandals, a bamboo staff with a waterjar, and he begs for food in the manner of holy men.

CULTURAL/HISTORICAL NOTE

Students may wonder why Sita is courteous to her guest when he speaks to her so strangely. Inform students that in the Hindu religion, as among the ancient Greeks, hospitality to guests is considered a high moral duty. Since, according to Hinduism, every person contains within himself or herself the divine Atman, the soul of the universe, every human guest should be treated as a visiting deity.

[Editor's note: Rashly, Dasaratha has agreed to grant two wishes to one of his wives, Rama's evil stepmother. This wife asks the king to banish Rama and to make her own son, Bharata, heir to the throne of Ayodhya. Rama shows his lack of pride and obedience toward his father by graciously accepting banishment. After Dasaratha's death, Bharata does not want to assume the throne, but Rama insists that their father's command be respected. Bharata agrees to hold the throne in trust for Rama for fourteen years. Rama goes to the Dandaka Forest to live with Sita and his brother Lakshmana. There Rama comes into conflict with the evil Rashakas and kills many of them. Ravana plots his revenge. He sends a demon disguised as a golden deer to the Dandaka Forest. Rama goes after the deer, leaving Lakshmana and Sita behind.]

Lakshmana . . . drew a circle around Sita on the ground, with the tip of his bow.

"Do not step out of this circle and do not cross this line," said Lakshmana. "Let these trees witness that I have done right!"

Sita was paying no attention. Lakshmana thrust out his lower lip in anger. He took his quiver and entered the edge of the forest, bent low a bit, went under a branch and was out of sight.

1 *What disguise does Ravana use?*

The Rakshasa King Ravana watched him go. Then Ravana came boldly across the clearing toward Rama's house covered with the disguise of an old holy man, like a treacherous deep well covered and hidden by tall grass. Sita saw him coming and dried her eyes.

Ravana looked like a man. He wore soft red silk. There was one lock of white hair left long on his shaven head. He held a parasol and wore sandals, and he carried resting over his left shoulder a long triple bamboo staff with a waterjar slung on it. Ravana came and stood silently by Sita's house, as holy men do when begging their daily food. There was no sign of Lakshmana or Rama. All around them there was only the forest land of green and brown.

Sita stepped over Lakshmana's line and said, "Worshipful brahmana, be our guest. Sit, take some water, wash and I will bring food."

Ravana hummed—*I walk the sweet Earth, Lord; I see you have made beautiful creatures, Lord; how fine and true, Oh Lord of Love.*

He spoke very fair. "How do you come to live here alone, my girl, in perilous Dandaka Land?" He stood looking at her. "By the Book, fair are your jewels."

"I am Sita. These jewels were presents. Don't fear demons, for my husband Rama will be back soon."

"Ah," said Ravana, "his name can't be Rama, he must be Kama![16] You are Rati the wife of Love, wantonly hiding in the forest." He smiled like a father. "Oh, you timid girl, of slender waist and tapering thighs! You've had a lovers' quarrel with Kama. You belong in a palace. I can see you like jewels and luxury!"

"Brahmana, sit down and what can I give you? I am Sita, a mortal woman and my husband is the Ayodhya King. These jewels were gifts from Anasuya[17] and this necklace came from Guha.[18] Tell me your name and family."

"Beautiful," said Ravana. "I am the Rakshasa King Ravana. I rule the universe. Come to me, Sita. I will take you to Lanka

16. **Kama.** Hindu god of love
17. **Anasuya.** Wife of a saint who befriended Rama and Sita
18. **Guha.** Hunter king who befriended Rama and Sita

WORDS FOR EVERYDAY USE

par • a • sol (par´ə sol´) *n.,* lightweight umbrella used to provide shade from the sun

VOCABULARY IN CONTEXT

- Before the twentieth century, it was the Western ideal for women to be very fair of complexion, so most fashionable ladies would never even consider walking outdoors without a parasol.

with her engines and weapons, and I will put you over all my other Queens."

Sita laughed. "Garuda[19] mating with a goose? A firefly courting the Sun?"

"Seek me! Cross the ocean with me!"

"A gnat trying to suck up a bowl of butter! Can you swim?"

"Don't play around with *me*!"

"I won't, don't worry," said Sita.

"You will have five thousand serving maids."

"Never." Sita looked again at the quiet forest and could see no one.

Woman, I am Ravana feared by the Gods! Ravana clapped his hands and his disguise fell away. He was tall as a tree. He had ten dark faces and twenty dark arms, and twenty red eyes red-rimmed like fire. He had yellow up-pointing fangs. He licked his lips with sharp tongues. He wore golden armor, long heavy gold earrings swaying, gold bracelets, gold armbands, ten golden crowns set with golden pearls, gold belt-chains crashing and gold rings all over his fingers. Fragrant white flower-garlands went over his shoulders and around his ten necks.

Ravana had a long ivory bow hanging down along one shoulder, its back rich with pearls, and by his hip he had a supple sword, of blue steel in a blue case. And on his back he had a long quiver formed of human skins stretched over a frame of men's bones, and the outside of that quiver was painted with demon faces drawn in blood, and those spectral faces moved of themselves; they were grim or laughing at will, changing as though alive, following with their eyes. The quiver held fifty tall blue-black arrows of solid iron, vaned with thin iron blades.

Ravana shook his heads and rattled his crowns and looked down at Sita. Seeing that evil one revealed, the leaves did not flutter. The trees of Dandaka did not move. No breath of wind dared stir about in the woods. The fast-streaming Godavari river slackened her speed from fright. The glorious Sun, who every day looks down upon our world, this time dimmed his light from the sadness of what he saw.

"I will have you!" said Ravana. "Princess Sita, you are half divine, why mingle more with men? Rule every world with me. Sita, I stand in space and I pick up Earth in my hand. I close the Moon within my fingers and put the Sun in my pocket, and arrest the aimless planets.[20] You will forget Rama with me!"

Ravana bent down, a black mountain come to life. Sita knelt near his feet hiding her face, clinging to a tree. Sita wore a clear yellow robe and Anasuya's ornaments and Guha's necklace. Her skin was golden, she was like sunlight in among the trees, and Ravana reached for her. In one left hand he held her long dark hair. He caught her legs in two of his right arms and lifted her, and his demon chariot came to meet him through the air.

HANUMAN'S LEAP

[Editor's note: Rama and Lakshmana look for Sita to no avail. They form an alliance with the

19. **Garuda.** Great swan, the king of birds, ridden by Vishnu

20. **aimless planets.** The word *planet* comes from a Greek word meaning "wanderer." The ancient Indians were great astronomers and saw that from our vantage point on Earth, the planets appear not to follow a regular course about the sky but rather to wander about. We now know that this appearance is due to the concentric orbits of the Earth and the other planets.

❶ *How does Sita respond to Ravana's flattery and promises?*

❷ *Why does Ravana suddenly become angry and show his true form?*

❸ *What happens to Sita?*

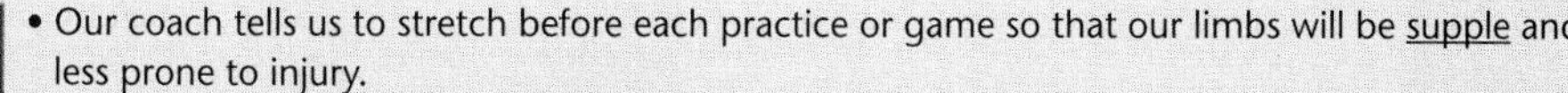
WORDS FOR EVERYDAY USE

sup • ple (sup´əl) *adj.*, easily bent or twisted; flexible

spec • tral (spek´trəl) *adj.*, ghostlike

ANSWERS TO GUIDED READING QUESTIONS

❶ Sita scornfully refuses and rejects Ravana's flattery and promises.

❷ Ravana suddenly becomes angry and reveals his true form because Sita has scornfully refused to become his queen; he may hope that his appearance and identity will frighten her into submitting.

❸ Ravana carries Sita away.

CULTURAL/HISTORICAL NOTE

Some students may be upset by the subservient portrayal of Sita. As noted on the Prereading page, Sita serves as the Hindu model of the ideal wife during this time period—completely loyal, obedient, and submissive. If students are interested in learning more about the role of women in Hindu society, you might inform them that women in early Aryan society had substantial freedoms. They could join in public ceremonies, study, and remarry on the deaths of their husbands. Over time, however, the status of women changed. Beginning in the Heroic Age, women were denied access to study, and Hindus began practicing *purdah,* the forced seclusion of women, and *suttee,* wherein a widow was expected to throw herself on the funeral pyre of her deceased husband. Polygamy, the practice of marrying more than one woman, was common. All of these practices continued into the twentieth century but are disappearing as India becomes more and more modernized.

VOCABULARY IN CONTEXT

- Our coach tells us to stretch before each practice or game so that our limbs will be supple and less prone to injury.
- For our Halloween party, we bought a CD that played spooky sounds, such as rattling chains, bloodcurdling screams, and spectral howls.

Answers to Guided Reading Questions

❶ Hanuman kills Sinhika by making himself small, flying down her throat, and crushing her heart.

❷ Hanuman's leap over the sea was the greatest leap ever taken.

Cross-curricular Activities

MATHEMATICS AND SCIENCES

In this selection, monkeys, wildcats, and birds are mentioned. Some students might enjoy working together to create reports on animal life in India. Some groups may wish to create reports of animals found in different regions, while others may wish to focus on specific species to create more in-depth reports on animals such as the Indian elephant or the tiger. Some groups might focus on endangered species and what is being done to protect them. Have these efforts been successful? Each group should present their report to the class, as well as bring in photos of the animals they are describing.

SOCIAL STUDIES

Encourage interested students to choose a period in Indian history to research as independent projects. You might share the following information about certain periods to spark student interest:

- **Indus Valley Civilization.** In 1924, archaeologist R. D. Banerji discovered the remains of a vast brick city in northeastern India called Mohenjo-daro. Surprisingly, the city proved to be five thousand years old, making it one of the oldest ever unearthed. Mohenjo-daro was a capital city of the ancient Indus Valley Civilization, which flourished on the fertile banks of the Indus River between 3000 and 1500 BC. Excited by this find, archaeologists proceeded to uncover more than seventy other villages and another great city, Harappa, all part of the same culture. (cont.)

monkey king Hanuman. The monkeys discover that Ravana has taken Sita across the ocean to Lanka, and Hanuman resolves to jump across to the land of the demon king.]

In his mind[21] Hanuman had already crossed the sea and entered the demon city. He climbed one of the Malaya hills to get firm ground under his feet. . . . Hanuman neared the summit. His feet squeezed water from the hill. Rivers tumbled down, rock-slides rolled, bright fresh-broken veins of gold sparkled, tigers ran off and birds flew away. The tree spirits fled, and in their dens the wildcats yelled in a frightful chorus, like the cry of the mountain himself through the voice of all his animals.

❶ *How does Hanuman kill the demon Sinhika?*

Hanuman stood on the hilltop. He held his breath and sucked in his stomach. He frisked his tail and raised it a little at the end. He bent his knees and swung back his arms, and on one finger gleamed Rama's gold ring. Then without pausing to think he drew in his neck, laid back his ears and jumped.

❷ *What is exceptional about Hanuman's leap?*

It was grand! It was the greatest leap ever taken. The speed of Hanuman's jump pulled blossoms and flowers into the air after him and they fell like little stars on the waving treetops. The animals on the beach had never seen such a thing; they cheered Hanuman, then the air burned from his passage, and red clouds flamed over the sky and Hanuman was far out of sight of land. . . .

In the strong sea-currents that lay twenty leagues[22] off Lanka lived the old Rakshasi Sinhika. She saw Hanuman flying and said, "This is the strangest bird I've seen in eight hundred years!" She swam to the surface and seized his shadow, and in the air Hanuman felt himself being dragged down and held back.

Sinhika stood on the water holding Hanuman's shadow in her claws and looking at him with tiny red eyes. She opened her ugly mouth and bared her yellow scaly teeth, and started to pull at his shadow.

"Watch out!" said Hanuman. "Beware, I am on Rama's service, and his kingdom is all the world. . . ."

She pulled him closer. "You can never escape me!"

"Oh yes, I will if I want to!"

She saw how large Hanuman was and opened her mouth wide as a cave with a long tongue. But Hanuman became quickly small as a thumb and flew down her throat like a tiny hurricane. He crushed her heart with his sharp fingernails, turned, and darted up out from her ear. Sinhika threw her arms about and collapsed on the sea. Her blood burst and spread through the water, and the fish came quickly to eat her.

Then Hanuman regained his jumping size and flew on in the sky, where birds fly and rainbows gleam, where heroes ride in bright chariots drawn by miraculous lions, where the smoke of fires rises and the rains and winds live. He went on through the pure sky embellished by planets and stars and luminous saints and by the holy Sun and Moon, the support and glorious canopy of this live world, the sky made and well made by Lord Brahma long ago.

The green hills of Lanka Island rose from the horizon. Hanuman saw the shoreline of warm white sand and scattered stones and water pools, and behind that

21. **In his mind.** According to Hindu thought, the created world is an illusion. The only reality is the Atman/Brahma. Therefore, much Hindu literature contains references to the power of mind or spirit over matter.
22. **leagues.** Nautical measurements equal to about three miles

sum • mit (sum´it) *n.,* the top, as of a mountain

em • bel • lish (em bel´ish) *vt.,* decorate or adorn

Vocabulary in Context

- Reaching the summit of Mt. Everest is a feat accomplished only by the most skillful and experienced mountain climbers.
- They will embellish the silver box with a gold *fleur-de-lis,* the coat of arms of the French royal family.

The Death of Ravana. *Courtesy of the Freer Gallery of Art, Smithsonian Institution, Washington, D.C.; 07.270–297V—Indian Manuscript; late 16th century; Mughal; Akbar school; Persian translation of "Ramayana" of Valmiki; 130 miniatures in opaque colors and gold; 27.5 x 15.2 cm. (10 7/8 x 6") average leaf size*

many tall swaying palms, and plane trees, and forests of aloes. He saw rivers meet the sea, and saw where pearls and cowrie shells and fine corals had been spread to dry. He flew inland, over stacks of gold and silver from the demon mines that lay blazing in the sunlight, and then he saw the City.

THE DEATH OF RAVANA

[*Editor's note: The monkeys build a great bridge across the ocean to Lanka. A great battle ensues, pitting Ravana and the Rakshasas against Rama and the monkeys led by Hanuman.*]

Rama and Ravana dueled with arrows. One after another, Rama broke the bows out of Ravana's hands until ninety-nine were gone and only one remained. The Demon King shot arrows long and short, thick and thin, quick and slow, from close range or far away; but Rama's armor was hard and impenetrable, he was unharmed and many arrows melted away when he saw them come.

Ravana seized his mace[23] of iron set with lapis stones and embellished with gold, hung with iron-mouthed bells and entwined with red blossoms, for years daily washed with blood and now smoking and straining to strike, an eight-sided mace which would return from flight into the thrower's hands.

Ravana drove to attack. He gripped the iron handle with four hands and swung as the chariots met. It was too soon and the blow fell on the charioteer and not Rama, but Matali knocked that mace hard aside with his bronze fist.

➊ *What magical power does Ravana's mace have?*

23. **mace.** Battle hammer or club

Answers to Guided Reading Questions

➊ After being thrown, Ravana's mace will always return to the thrower's hands.

Cross-curricular Activities (cont.)

- **Mauryan Dynasty.** In 327 BC, Alexander the Great invaded India and established a short-lived Macedonian client state ruled by the conquered king, Porus. Shortly thereafter, Chandragupta Maurya ousted the Macedonians and established the Mauryan Dynasty, the most powerful in the world at that time. Chandragupta's reign was widely hailed as an age of plenty and justice among the Indian people.
- **Gupta Dynasty.** In the first century AD, the Kushans of central Asia captured most of northwestern India. In northeastern India, however, Chandragupta I, born in 322 AD, founded the Gupta Dynasty. His successors conquered much of India and ruled over it for two centuries. Considered by many to be the golden age of Indian history, the Gupta Dynasty was characterized by peace, prosperity, trade with distant lands, religious freedom, and a great flourishing of the arts of literature, philosophy, architecture, sculpture, and painting.
- **Muslim Conquest.** Beginning in 664 AD, India's Muslim neighbors began a series of raids that eventually resulted in the subjugation of India to Muslim rule. The Muslims, followers of the religion of Islam, had a strong militaristic tradition based upon belief in their duty to conquer infidels, or nonbelievers, and convert them to their faith. India was both well and poorly defended due to its native philosophies of withdrawal, asceticism, and nonviolence.

Answers to Guided Reading Questions

1. Matali saves Rama's life by placing himself in the path of Ravana's mace so that it will miss Rama.

Cultural/Historical Note

Inform students that during the time when the *Ramayana* takes place, a rigid caste system was in effect in India. This caste system came into being not long after the arrival of the Aryan invaders. Initially, the highest class, or caste, of Aryan society were the Kshatriyas, the rulers and warriors. Below these on the social hierarchy were the Brahmins, or priests; the Vaisyas, or merchants and freemen; the Shudras, or workers; and the Pariahs, or Outcasts. The Shudras and the Pariahs were descendants of the native, non-Aryan peoples of India. Over time, as the Vedic religion of the Aryans developed into Hinduism, the Brahmins gained power, challenging and overcoming the supremacy of the Kshatriyas. Caste membership became more and more rigid, regulated by laws prohibiting intermarriage. One of the oldest lawbooks in the world, the ancient Indian Code of Manu, describes in great detail the duties and regulations governing the members of each caste. Only in recent years has India begun to break away from the rigid caste system observed for thousands of years.

Then Ravana drew apart and stopped. He whirled his mace in a circle rising and dipping his heads; and the mace moaned—*Woe . . . Woe . . . Woe—*

The mace went faster and faster. Matali drove to deceive Ravana's aim and Rama reached for Indra's weapons-racks. He took a spear, held it in one hand slapped it with the palm of his other hand and threw it. That great dart went at Ravana resonant and vibrating with sound, with a noise like the thunder of a rockslide, a loud falling noise like a cliff falling, the dark world falling, Ravana falling. . . .

And the Demon Lord let go his mace; it sped, and Rama stood in its way. Ravana's chariot turned to run.

Rama's spear broke Ravana's flagpole; the cloth-of-gold war-flag fell. Rama broke the ten arrows of the Rakshasa Empire, and when he did, the running demon car lost its rattle and clatter and its wheels turned on in mournful silence. The flag of Lanka lay in the dust.

1 How does the charioteer Matali save Rama's life?

Matali couldn't outdrive Ravana's mace, but he dropped his reins and stood up himself in its path; and it glanced off his broad chest and knocked him violently from the car, and went by Rama deflected just enough to miss him.

Rama wept and bit his lip. The mace turned to go back to Ravana, but Rama threw himself from the chariot and seized it. He knelt and broke it like a stick over his thigh—*Good Fortune to you!*—once, into two pieces—*Peace to you!*—and twice, into four. Deep red blood ran over his green skin.

The four pieces of the mace kept pulling back to Ravana, and Rama cried—*Would you?*—and hurled them at the Demon King. Ravana quickly turned aside; and as he had spurned them, the four angry chunks of iron tore into Earth and vanished noisily underground.

Matali lay on his back unconscious. His heavenly armor was torn, and his ten horses stood still, their faces near his, looking down at him. A flood of sorrow filled Rama's heart to see him hurt. Rama touched him and untied his breastplate, and said, "Here indeed your loyalty has had unjust reward!"

Matali revived from Rama's touch. He looked up and saw Rama bending over him, saw his horses raise their heads, and following their look saw Ravana's chariot coming again, but moving strangely slow. By some chance he yet lived, and he felt the life flow back into his body.

Rama brought water from Indra's chariot, and some cloth that he began to rip apart for binding Matali's wide wounds. The silver car was stricken and dented. The horses pawed at the ground with their front feet. "Majesty," said Matali, "I'll be well, there's time enough for that later."

Rama said, "Good. It's fast nearing dawn, but drink just a little." Then after Matali drank, Rama sipped water three times. "Lie still, I don't need the car now." Rama took up his every-colored bow, and there stood Rama the great archer, Rama the good bowman, the friend of every man.

He was all fiery to see. Wild little flames came from his skin, his green eyes gleamed, then swift as thought Rama shot his arrows. He broke off one wheel of Ravana's chariot and it tipped over and left the Demon King also standing on the ground, holding his last bow and a sword, facing him; and the white horses ran away with the broken car.

Rama opened a long bamboo case at his belt and took out the brass-bladed grass

Words for Everyday Use

res • o • nant (rez´ə nənt) *adj.,* full of echoing sound

Vocabulary in Context

- The area around the waterfall was resonant with the sound of churning water.

Udipur, Lake Palace, former maharajah's palace

arrow given to him by Agastya,[24] and notched it on his bowstring. That arrow could rend walls and gateways of stone; it breathed and sighed. Rama pulled his bow. He took three aiming steps backwards and held his breath.

Ravana took on the brilliant form of Indra the King of Heaven. He was glorious and gracious, all illumined; he could scarcely be looked at, and a halo of radiance and energy danced around him. Rama was dazed by Ravana's false figure. He could not bear to shoot at such a divine form, at such fair beauty.

Matali the Charioteer was watching. He could be enchanted by no beauty but a fair woman's. He raised himself painfully on one arm and called out to Rama—*Strike, Strike, That's not my Master.*

That was then the destined time and true setting of Ravana's death. Rama thought—*I must believe it! Oh kill him!*—

Rama shot. The bowstring rang out, all over the Universe. That arrow first broke the sword and bow Ravana raised to ward it, then it hit Ravana's breast and struck through his heart, stealing his life, and never stopped, but came out from his back and entered the Earth.

 1 *How does Ravana die?*

2 *What shape does Ravana assume? Why does Rama hesitate?*

LORD RAMA

[*Editor's note: After Ravana's death, Rama learns that he is an incarnation of Vishnu. This fact is revealed to Rama by the Rakshasa Suka, carrying a message from Ravana, the dead demon king.*]

Lord Narayana, you are the witness, you make the Moon walk in brightness and the stars vanish in the daylight.

Dear Rama, Lord of the Worlds—Think and remember, how you promised Indra to

24. **Agastya.** Forest-dwelling saint who befriended Rama and gave him a bow and arrow

Words for Everyday Use

rend (rend) *vt.,* tear

il • lu • mined (i lo͞o ´mənd) *adj.,* lighted up

Answers to Guided Reading Questions

1 Rama shoots an arrow that breaks Ravana's sword, hits his breast, and pierces his heart, killing him.

2 Ravana assumes the shape of Indra the King of Heaven. Rama feels that he should not shoot such a divine form.

Quotables

"The world is the wheel of God, turning round

And round with all living creatures upon its rim.

The world is the river of God,

Flowing from him and flowing back to him.

On this ever-revolving wheel of being

The individual self goes round and round

Through life after life, believing itself

To be a separate creature, until

It sees its identity with the Lord of Love

And attains immortality in the indivisible whole."

—from the Shvetashvatara Upanishad

Additional Questions and Activities

Encourage students to discuss the quotation above from a Hindu religious text. Ask them to compare and contrast the message in this quotation with the message presented at the end of this excerpt from the *Ramayana.*

Vocabulary in Context

- The old gowns we found upstairs in the attic were so ancient and delicate that we were afraid the slightest touch might rend the tissue-like fabric.
- At night the city put on a festive appearance with illumined neon signs in every shop window.

Answers to Guided Reading Questions

❶ Ravana always knew that Rama was an incarnation of Narayana, or Vishnu, and that he had to die at the hands of a mortal to be again made a part of Vishnu.

Selection Check Test with Answers

EX. Who is the poet who helped Sita and told Rama's story?
The poet is Valmiki.

1. Who is the evil ruler of the Rakshasas?
Ravana is the evil ruler of the Rakshasas.

2. What does Indra ask Narayana, the Lord Vishnu to do?
Indra asks Vishnu to accept birth as a man in order to kill the demon king Ravana.

3. Whose bow is Rama able to draw, and whom does he marry?
Rama is able to draw Shiva's bow, and he marries Sita.

4. What happens to Sita when she is alone in the forest?
Ravana meets her disguised as a holy man, then kidnaps her.

5. Whom did Ravana know Rama truly was?
Ravana knew that Rama was truly Vishnu.

Responding to the Selection

As an alternate activity, you might ask students to discuss their thoughts about Ravana. Did their feelings about Ravana change over the course of this story, and if so, how?

kill me forever. Nothing is forever except yourself. Except dying at your hand, how else could I make you take me into your own Self?

❶ *What did Ravana know about Rama all along?*

I was only a Rakshasa, and you were very hard to approach. Yet seeking wisdom I learned many things. You do not know who you are again. I knew it all along, but even still you do not know. Nothing you do ever fails, one glance of yours and people sing again the good old songs.

I took no protection against men. You go everywhere, and know every thing that ever has or ever will be done. How was I careless? I was nowhere careless! Oh Narayana, Lo, I looked, I marveled—Men are mines, Men are precious mines. Oh Rama, did you think that dark was bad?

You see whatever happens and you support all creatures. I saw that heaven was impermanent and Hell itself did not endure; I discovered that the time of every life is one day full; and I found how all creatures that are separate from you are ever and again reborn, over and over, always changing. I do not love things that come and go and slip away with Time, and Time himself I hate. I warned him when we first met that I took him for my enemy, I told him so.

Best of Men, there are many kinds of Love, and I never hurt her. I kept Lakshmi to lure you here. I offered you my life and you accepted it.

You are Narayana who moves on the waters. You flow through us all. You are Rama and Sita born out of Earth and Ravana the Demon King, you are Hanuman like the wind, you are Lakshmana like a mirror, you are Indrajit and Indra, you are the Poet and the Players and the Play. ■

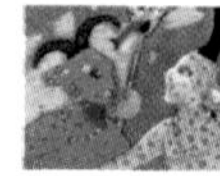

Global Views

Avik Mohan, India

Present-day India is a far cry from Valmiki's India in the material sense. Spiritually, however, they are very much the same. The traditional values presented in the *Ramayana* are instilled in every child in the form of bedside stories and are depicted in popular culture in movies and soap operas. My grandmother, for instance, narrated stories at meals and bedtime. If a moral issue needed clarifying, a section of one of the epics—Rama's hospitality, for example—was put forward and analyzed. Thus, the essence of the *Ramayana*, as the actions of Rama, Sita, Laxman, and even Ravan to some extent, exemplified it, still live on in India. Most Indians can relate to the mental turmoil these demigods experience in the *Ramayana.* Beyond merely empathizing with them, however, people have the chance to transcend their own situation as they attempt to emulate these ideals.

Additional Questions and Activities

In his review, Avik says that "if a moral issue needed clarifying, a section of one of the epics . . . was put forward and analyzed." Ask students to discuss the following: How are moral lessons taught to children in America? Responses will vary, but students might include the following as examples: children's television programs that teach about issues such as cooperation and telling the truth, fables and stories with a moral, movies with clear definitions of good versus evil, or religious instruction. Ask students which method, or methods, they think are most effective, and why.

Responding to the Selection

Does Rama fit your idea of a hero? Why, or why not?

Reviewing the Selection

RECALLING		INTERPRETING
1. In response to what action does Valmiki compose his first verse?	➤➤	How does the *Ramayana* explain the origins of poetry?
2. What does Indra request of Vishnu?	➤➤	Why must Vishnu take human form in order to defeat Ravana?
3. How does Rama respond to banishment by his father?	➤➤	In what way does Rama reveal his devotion to dharma, or duty?
4. What does Rama learn after Ravana's death and from whom?	➤➤	How can Rama be all the things that Ravana says he is—Rama, Sita, Ravana, Hanuman, Lakshmana, Indrajit, Indra, the Poet, the Players, and the Play?

SYNTHESIZING

5. What might Ravana mean by his question, "Oh Rama, did you think dark was bad?" How does Hindu theology differ from Western thinking in its conception of the ultimate source of good and evil?

Understanding Literature (Questions for Discussion)

1. **Epic.** An **epic** is a long story, often told in verse, involving heroes and gods. Grand in length and scope, an epic provides a portrait of an entire culture, of the legends, beliefs, values, laws, arts, and ways of life of a people. What qualities make Rama heroic? In what ways does he embody the value placed by Hindus on dharma, or devotion to duty?

2. **Myth.** A **myth** is a story that explains objects or events in the natural world as resulting from the action of some supernatural force or entity, most often a god. In the *Ramayana,* what role does the god Brahma play in the introduction of poetry into the world? What role does Brahma play in the introduction of evil, personified as Ravana, into the world? What role does the god Vishnu play in the destruction of this evil?

Answers for Reviewing the Selection

RECALLING AND INTERPRETING

1. **Recalling.** Valmiki composes his first verse while cursing a hunter who has killed a little bird that was singing to its mate. **Interpreting.** According to the *Ramayana,* poetry was born from the emotions of love, pity, and compassion.

2. **Recalling.** Indra requests that Vishnu accept birth as a man to destroy Ravana. **Interpreting.** Vishnu must take human form to defeat Ravana because Ravana won a boon from Brahma that prevents him from being killed by any creature of Heaven or the underworlds. Only an earthly mortal can slay him.

3. **Recalling.** Rama is obedient and gracefully accepts his banishment. **Interpreting.** Rama reveals his devotion to duty by obeying his father without question.

4. **Recalling.** Rama learns from a letter sent by Ravana that he is an incarnation of Narayana, the Lord Vishnu. **Interpreting.** Rama can be all these things because every human contains a soul that is identical to Brahma. Every person is a manifestation of the divine soul of the universe.

SYNTHESIZING

Responses will vary. Possible responses are given.

5. Ravana means that both darkness and light are part of Brahma the Creator, hence one is no better or worse than the other. Students may say that Christians see good and evil as a dichotomy—all evil comes from the devil, and all good comes from God. The Hindus seem to see both good and evil as essential parts of the divine.

Answers for Understanding Literature

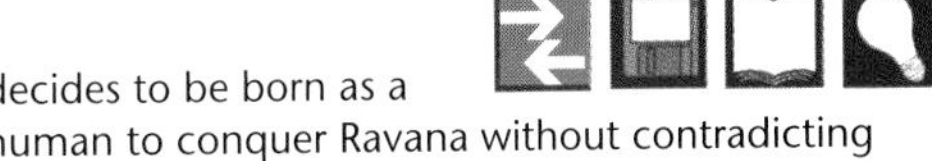

Responses will vary. Possible responses are given.

1. **Epic.** Rama's strength, kindness, courtesy, and forgiving nature make him heroic. He willingly obeys his father's order that he be banished, showing duty toward his elders.

2. **Myth.** Brahma encourages Valmiki to write the story of Rama in verse. Brahma the Creator is responsible for the creation of evil as personified by Ravana and even grants Ravana a boon. Vishnu decides to be born as a human to conquer Ravana without contradicting Brahma's boon to Ravana.

3. **Allegory.** Ravana appears as Indra, the King of Heaven. He learns that he is an incarnation of Vishnu and that all things are a part of the soul of the universe. Evil is an illusion because it too is part of the soul of the universe. It indicates that by following dharma one sees the ultimate reality behind all things.

ANALYTIC SCALES FOR RESPONDING IN WRITING

Assign a score from 1 to 25 for each grading criterion below. (For more detailed evaluation, see the evaluation forms for writing, revising, and proofreading, Assessment Portfolio 4.1–4.9.)

1. Description

- **Content/Unity.** The description portrays the unusual appearance of a new opponent for Rama.
- **Organization/Coherence.** The description presents details about this opponent in a sensible order.
- **Language/Style.** The description uses vivid and precise nouns, verbs, and modifiers.
- **Conventions.** The description avoids errors in spelling, grammar, usage, mechanics, and manuscript form.

▶ Additional practice is provided in the Essential Skills Practice Book: Writing 1.8, 1.10.

2. Critical Essay

- **Content/Unity.** The essay defines the term *allegory* and applies it to an analysis of the *Ramayana.*
- **Organization/Coherence.** The essay begins with an introduction that includes the thesis of the essay. The introduction is followed by supporting paragraphs with clear transitions. The essay ends with a solid conclusion.
- **Language/Style.** The essay uses vivid and precise nouns, verbs, and modifiers.
- **Conventions.** The essay avoids errors in spelling, grammar, usage, mechanics, and manuscript form.

▶ Additional practice is provided in the Essential Skills Practice Book: Writing 1.20.

3. **Allegory.** An **allegory** is a work in which each element symbolizes, or represents, something else. Remember that according to Hinduism, the world is an illusion (Sanskrit *maya*). According to Hindu belief, once one pierces the illusion, one sees the reality that underlies all things. That reality is the all-pervading soul of the universe. In what way does Ravana reveal himself to be a master of illusion just before Rama shoots him? After Rama pierces this illusion with an arrow, what does he learn? In what sense, according to this poem, is evil (and all the suffering that it brings) actually an illusion? What might the *Ramayana* be saying about the relationship between courage and devotion to duty (dharma) on the one hand and piercing the veil of illusion on the other?

Responding in Writing

1. **Creative Writing: Description.** Many of the characters in the *Ramayana* have highly unusual appearances. Ravana, for example, is described as having ten heads, twenty arms, twenty red eyes, and two fangs in each mouth. Imagine a new opponent to challenge Rama. Create a sensory detail chart to collect details about your imaginary character's appearance and actions. (For more information on sensory detail charts, see the Language Arts Survey 1.10, "Gathering Ideas.") Then write a brief but detailed description of this new character whom you have dreamed up to challenge Rama.

2. **Critical Essay: Allegory.** Write a brief essay in which you define the term *allegory* and then apply it to an analysis of the *Ramayana.* In your analysis, recall that Rama is a human who embodies the concept of dharma—faithful, dutiful adherence to moral law. Ravana embodies the illusions of this world—pride, envy, covetousness, greed, gluttony, blasphemy, and so on. Explain how the battle with Ravana might be read as a description of the path that humans must follow in order to overcome illusion, escape rebirth, and rejoin god. (Hindus believe in incarnation and hold as their goal the achievement of a state called nirvana, in which the chain of rebirth is broken and the soul is reunited with Brahma.)

PROJECT

A Retelling. The stories from the *Ramayana* have been retold countless times in many ways. Choose a scene from the *Ramayana* to retell and a format in which to retell it. You might retell the scene as a script for a play, television program, or film. You might retell it in sign language or, if you speak and write another language, in a translation. You also might retell it through pictures or art—in a musical composition, in a slide show, in drawings, in staged photographs, in cartoons, in a diorama, or even in clay figurines or models. Use your imagination to come up with a unique method for retelling the scene, and share your retelling with your classmates.

PROJECT NOTES

See the evaluation form for projects, Assessment Portfolio 4.12.

A Retelling. If students have difficulty coming up with ideas for retellings on their own, you might have students work in groups of four or five, so they can brainstorm ideas together. You might encourage each group to share their retelling with another classroom or a younger group of students.

PREREADING

from the *Sunjata*
Anonymous, retold by Donna Rosenberg

 MALI

About the Selection

The ***Sunjata*** is the epic of the Mande-speaking people of West Africa. Between AD 500 and 1700, a number of empires flourished in this region of West Africa. One group of Mande people, the Malinke, established a kingdom in Kangaba, on the Upper Niger River, before 1000. This kingdom came to be known as Mali, after the Malinke people. During this period, the empire of Ghana was the major power in West Africa, but by 1200 its power was beginning to wane. In 1230, a king of Mali named Sunjata revolted against rule by Ghana and won a decisive battle against Sumanguru, a chief who had declared himself the ruler of Ghana. By 1235, Sunjata had taken over what remained of ancient Ghana and had formed an even greater empire. Composed in the oral tradition, the *Sunjata* focuses on the rise to power and the adventures of this historical king.

Among the Mande, there is a class of professional bards known as *dyeli, belein-tigui,* or by the more common French term *griot. Griots* have an important role in Mande society; according to the *Sunjata,* they even advised kings. They are expected to be able to recite epics such as the *Sunjata* from memory and to use their poetic skills to refine their tales. This version of the *Sunjata* was initially told by a *griot* from Guinea named Mamudu Kuyate.

The *Sunjata* reveals that the Mande-speaking people believed that a person's destiny is predetermined. Throughout the epic, the griot repeatedly offers this comment:

Guétéma Village, Mali

> Poor [character's name]! People are so impatient and blind about life! They cannot understand God's mysterious ways, nor do they realize that one's destiny cannot be changed. Each event adds its thread to the tapestry of one's life, and those who try to separate themselves from their destiny only succeed in furthering that which they would destroy!

The words and actions of many characters in this epic are shaped by resignation toward the inexorability of fate.

The *Sunjata* presents Sunjata as both historical figure and cultural hero. While the *Sunjata* presents some historical figures and events, such as Sunjata's battle against Sumanguru, the epic is also filled with magic and shape-shifting. As a cultural hero, Sunjata embodies many of the qualities considered virtues among the Mande. Most prominent among Sunjata's virtues are his generosity, hospitality, strength, intelligence, courage, loyalty, and respect for his parents and his elders.

CONNECTIONS: The Hero and the Task

In this selection from the *Sunjata,* Sunjata undertakes a task, or test to prove himself. Sunjata's task is to kill the beast that has been ravaging the land of the Mande people. Often in epics and other forms of heroic literature, a hero must successfully complete such a task before setting out on further adventures. For example, in *The Epic of Gilgamesh* in this unit, Gilgamesh kills Humbaba and the Bull of Heaven to prove himself before he undertakes his search for eternal life.

GOALS/OBJECTIVES

Studying this lesson will enable students to

- enjoy an excerpt from an epic describing how a hero completes a task
- briefly explain who the historical Sunjata was and what he did
- explain what an epic reveals about a culture
- identify repetition in a literary work
- write a character sketch for a hero
- write a critical essay analyzing the view of fate and free will in the *Sunjata*
- prepare an oral interpretation

ADDITIONAL RESOURCES

READER'S GUIDE
- Selection Worksheet 7.9

ASSESSMENT PORTFOLIO
- Selection Check Test 2.7.17
- Selection Test 2.7.18

ESSENTIAL SKILLS PRACTICE BOOKS
- Writing 1.8, 1.20
- Speaking and Listening 3.1, 3.5

PREREADING EXTENSIONS

You might encourage students to read sections of the rest of the *Sunjata* and then to prepare summaries of their sections to share with the class. Students might read the version of the story as it appears in Donna Rosenberg's *World Mythology* anthology. Students who are very interested in the story of Mali's epic hero might read a small section of a more "literal" version of the epic as told by Fa-Digi Sisoko and translated by John William Johnson. It appears under the title *The Epic of Son-Jara: A West African Tradition.* Students might then work together to create a large mural on paper showing scenes from the *Sunjata* epic.

SUPPORT FOR LEP STUDENTS

PRONUNCIATIONS OF PROPER NOUNS AND ADJECTIVES

Man • de (män dā´)
Ni • a • ni (nē ä´nē)
Sun • ja • ta (so͞on jä´tə)

ADDITIONAL VOCABULARY

chaff—unusable part of wheat or other grain
mortally—fatally; in a manner that causes death
reap—gather

READER'S JOURNAL

You might encourage students to hold a debate on whether fate or free will plays the greater role in human life. Tell students to be sure to support their opinions with reasons and examples.

Answers to Guided Reading Questions

1. The beast possesses a magical power that turns away all weapons and gives it the strength to kill any man.

2. Sunjata wants to kill the beast to prove to the people of Niani that he is the rightful king of Keita and Manding.

SPELLING AND VOCABULARY WORDS FROM THE SELECTION

ravage

Quotables

"Sundiata Keita is the King Arthur and the George Washington of Mali. He was a warrior-king who united a weak and scattered people, and, under his benevolent leadership, ushered in a glorious period of peace and prosperity."

—Patricia and Frederick McKissack

READER'S JOURNAL

Do you believe in fate or destiny? Have you ever felt that something occurred because it was destined to be? If so, describe this occurrence as well as what led you to feel that the occurrence was predetermined. If not, explain why you do not believe in fate or destiny.

FROM THE

Sunjata

ANONYMOUS, RETOLD BY DONNA ROSENBERG

[Editor's note: Sunjata is born, son of Nare Maghan Kon Fatta, king of Keita and Manding, or Mali, and Sogolon Kedju, a woman of great magic also called the Buffalo Woman. It is predicted that Sunjata will become the greatest of Mali's kings. Nonetheless, the boy seems an unlikely future hero because he is lame and cannot walk. The old king's first wife seizes power after her husband dies, proclaims her own son as king, and forces Sogolon Kedju and Sunjata to live in a small hut, subjecting them to constant humiliation. With the help of a golden staff, Sunjata walks and soon becomes the strongest man in the village. Sunjata and his mother gain acceptance throughout the kingdom, and Sunjata is sent to the court in Niani to be educated.]

It came to pass at this time that a strange animal began to ravage the crops that grew in Niani. The kingdom of Manding was known for its hunters, and they were quick to take this opportunity to show off their courage and skill. Coming from far and wide in the kingdom, one group of hunters after another arrived in Niani and set out to kill the beast.

One week passed, and they had no success. Two weeks passed, and they had no success. Three weeks passed, and they had no success. Four weeks passed, and still they had no success.

Group after group showed the greatest courage and skill, but they were all powerless against this beast. It possessed a magic that would turn away any weapon and a strength that would kill any man. The most skillful hunter who sent forth the sharpest arrow would find himself charged and mortally wounded by the beast that he had attempted to kill. Therefore, by the end of a month, the greatest hunters had decided that they could do nothing more and had returned to their own villages.

Sunjata was much younger than they, but he knew that he was not only a skillful hunter but a sorcerer as well. He said to his mother, "If I am able to kill the beast that is too powerful for all the hunters of Manding,

1 *What special powers does the beast possess?*

2 *Why does Sunjata want to kill the beast?*

WORDS FOR EVERYDAY USE

rav • age (rav´ij) *vt.,* destroy violently; ruin

Vocabulary in Context

• In their greed for new territory and riches, colonial explorers set out to ravage many areas along the African coast.

maybe it will prove to the people of Niani that the Lion of Manding[1] is their true king and the one who should be ruling our kingdom!"

"This is, indeed, just the task for you, my son!" Sogolon Kedju replied. "I know that your father found it necessary to kill a young man who attempted to take over our kingdom. I also know that the mother of that youth is as powerful a sorceress as I am, and that she turns herself into this beast and destroys our crops in order to punish our people for her son's death. If you wish to kill the beast, you will first have to conquer it in its human form.

"Therefore, Sunjata," she continued, "in addition to your food, I will give you a gold coin that I have been saving for you and two white kola nuts. Put them into your hunter's bag, and gather twenty-five cows from the royal herd. When the sun begins its morning journey, take these with you into the forest, and what will be, will come!"

So it came to pass that Sunjata set out on his first heroic adventure. He had traveled far enough into the forest for the sun to have completed half its journey, when he realized that he was hungry enough to stop and have something to eat. Just then, he saw a blind man at the side of the path.

"Can I do anything for you, old man?" he asked.

"Would you please give me something to chew?" he replied. "My teeth hurt with hunger! The few hunters who have passed by here have had hearts of stone and have hurried on their way."

"I just have enough food for my lunch, but I also have two white kola nuts, a gold coin that my mother saved for me, and this herd of twenty-five cows," Sunjata replied. "You are welcome to take whatever you need. Some will satisfy you now; some will satisfy you later."

"I do not want the only food that you have with you, and I do not want the gold coin that your mother saved for you," the old man replied. "But I would be pleased to have your two kola nuts to chew."

Sunjata took the nuts from his hunter's bag and handed them to the old man, who immediately put them into his pocket.

Then, the old man said, "You are a good prince, Sunjaṭa, for offering me what you have. And because you have been so generous, may it come to pass that you reap as fine a harvest from these seeds of kindness as you have sown.

"I know that you are searching for the strange beast that is ravaging Niani. But are you aware of your great danger? The sharpest arrow sent forth by the most skillful hunter will not make its mark, and those who would bring death, find death instead!

"However, if you would still pursue this beast," he continued, "your kindness to me will bring you good fortune. You will do what the most powerful and skillful hunters in your kingdom have been unable to do. You will conquer the beast, and it will spare your life."

He then concluded by saying, "In order to succeed, you must follow this path to the next village. It is not near, but it is not too far, either! When the sun begins to return to its home, you will come upon its walls. Then, you must look for an old woman. She will be working in the field, using a broken calabash[2] to remove the chaff from her grain, and on the ground beside her will be a stack of wood. You must give her the gold coin that your mother saved for you, and you must manage to get her to let you stay in her house with her. If you succeed, what will be, will come!"

Sunjata continued on his way. As the old man had said, he came to the walled village and the old woman just as the sun was beginning to return to its home.

1 *Who is the beast? How does Sogolon Kedju say it can be killed?*

2 *How does Sunjata treat the old man? What does the old man say Sunjata will reap?*

1. **Lion of Manding.** Title referring to Sunjata. The name *Sunjata* means "our lion."
2. **calabash.** Dried, hollow shell of a gourd, used as a bowl

Answers to Guided Reading Questions

1 The beast is the mother of a youth who had been killed by Sunjata's father. Sogolon Kedju says that the beast can be killed if it is conquered in its human form.

2 Sunjata behaves kindly and generously toward the old man. The old man says that Sunjata will reap good fortune because of his kindness.

Cultural/Historical Note

You may wish to share with students that the famed city of Timbuktu, long regarded as the most inaccessible place on earth, is located in Mali. Originally a meeting place for nomads, or wandering peoples, in the Sahara Desert, Timbuktu was no more than a well next to a sand dune around the year AD 1000. Its name is said to have come from *tim,* which means "place," and *Buktu,* the name of a slave girl. A city was founded there in about AD 1100, when nomad tents were replaced by straw huts. Later the city became an important commercial center and an Islamic stronghold. Today, the best way to get there is still by camel.

Cross-curricular Activities

MATHEMATICS AND SCIENCES AND SOCIAL STUDIES

Encourage students to prepare reports on the location, size, conditions, and ecosystems existing in some of the world's deserts. Students may wish to focus on the harsh conditions and the creatures and groups of people that survive these conditions. Possible choices include the Sahara, the Gobi, the Kakahari, the Libyan, the Mojave, the Rub al Khali, the Syrian, or any other desert students are interested in researching.

Literary Note

You may wish to avoid confusion by pointing out to students that there are many variant spellings of this great hero and king of the Mande people. Among them are Sunjata Keita, Sundiata, Sogolon-Djata, and Son-Jara.

Answers to Guided Reading Questions

➊ Students may say that Sunjata conceals his identity because he does not yet know the identity of the woman (she may, in fact, be the mother of the youth who was killed by Sunjata's father) and wishes to conceal the purpose of his quest from her.

Cultural/Historical Note

The *Sunjata* shows Islamic influence, mentioning Allah throughout. Inform students that Mali has long been a cultural meeting place because it is crossed by major trading routes. These trading routes also allowed the Islam religion to spread quickly throughout the region, mostly through Muslim traders. Muslim merchants came to Ghana as early as the ninth century AD, and by the fourteenth century, kings of Mali were converting to Islam and most of the *griots* in West Africa would have been familiar with the Koran. The *Sunjata* includes both Islamic and local beliefs and customs, indicating that Islam was probably practiced alongside the older, native religion. Changing aspects of a culture, such as the mixture of Islamic and native beliefs, are often incorporated into works in the oral tradition.

Ashanti stool. Ghana

When Sunjata approached her, the woman saw him and stopped working. She then bent down to pick up her wood and appeared to be ready to return to her home. Sunjata took the gold coin from his hunter's bag, dropped it into her calabash, and said, "Here, old woman, take this coin, and may it make your life a little easier!"

The old woman stared at him and asked, "Who are you, and why are you here?"

Q ➊ *Why do you think Sunjata conceals his identity?*

Sunjata decided that it was best to conceal his identity, so he created both a name and a task. "I have come to sell my cows at your village market," he replied, "but I have arrived so late that I need a place to spend the night. May I stay with you?"

"My hut is too small, and I have no one to wait on you," she replied. "It is all I can do, at my age, to take care of myself!"

"Do not worry, old woman," Sunjata replied. "No hut is too small for my needs, and it is I who will take care of you!"

So it came to pass that Sunjata stayed the night with the old woman. When the sun began its morning journey, he killed one of his cows and gave the old woman its meat. He then spent the day at the village market, where he sold the cows that he could sell. At the end of the first day, he had sold three cows, and he spent the night with the old woman. At the end of the second day, he had sold three more cows, and he spent the night with the old woman. At the end of the third day, he had sold three more cows, and he spent the night with the old woman. So it came to pass for five more days and four more nights that each day he sold three more cows, and each night he spent with the old woman.

When Sunjata returned from the village market at the end of the eighth day, he had sold the last of his cows. The old woman met him at the entrance to her hut, and, again, asked him his name. Sunjata repeated the name that he had first given her.

"You are not giving me your real name because you want to kill me!" the old woman exclaimed. "I know who you are! You are Mari Djata, the son of the Lion, King Nare Maghan Kon Fatta, and the Buffalo Woman, Sogolon Kedju.[3]

"I also know that you are here because you want to kill the strange beast that is ravaging Niani's crops," she continued. "Because you have been kind and generous to me, you will do what the most powerful and skillful hunters have been unable to do. You will conquer the beast, and it will spare your life.

"But in order to succeed," she added, "you must listen carefully to my directions and follow them without fail. Take this rice, this charcoal, and this egg, and return to your village. When the sun has returned to its home for the second time, take your bow and a good supply of arrows, take the hunters of Niani who have the courage to accompany you, and go into the forest until you reach the three lakes of Manding. Tell

3. **Mari Djata . . . Sogolon Kedju.** Mari Djata is another of Sunjata's names. Sunjata's father, King Nare Maghan Kon Fatta, was called the Lion. His mother, Sogolon Kedju, is called the Buffalo Woman.

the hunters to climb into the trees, for, when I arrive, I will kill any hunter I find.

"While you are waiting for me, the sun will be asleep," the old woman continued. "But you will see a beast with six horns approach the lakes from the east in order to drink its fill. Do not lift your bow, for I will not be that beast. You have nothing to fear. After it roars three times, it will wander away.

"The sun will still be asleep, but you will then see a beast with twelve horns approach the lakes from the east in order to drink its fill. Do not lift your bow, for I will not be that beast. Again, you will have nothing to fear. After it roars six times, it will wander away."

She continued, "Just as the sun is about to begin its morning journey, you will feel the earth shake under your feet, and you will hear the forest rustle as if an army of warriors is marching through it. Then, you will see a great beast with eighteen horns, and with an eye in the middle of its forehead, approach the lakes from the east in order to drink its fill.

"After it roars nine times, you must lift your bow, for I will be that beast! You must send forth your arrows while I drink from the first lake, but you have nothing to fear. You must send forth your arrows while I drink from the second lake, but, still, you have nothing to fear. However, if you do not stop me from drinking from the third lake, I will kill you!" she exclaimed.

"I will confront you between the second lake and the third lake. You will now be in great danger! When I lower my head with my great horns, I will rush toward you. You must be prepared for my attack, and you must resist the urge to run. Instead, you must stand your ground and throw my rice on the earth between us. The land on which it falls will become a thick web of bamboo.

"Once I have struggled through this patch of bamboo, you will again be in great danger!" she exclaimed. "I will again lower my head with my great horns and rush toward you. Again, you must be prepared for my attack, and again you must resist the urge to run. Instead, you must stand your ground and, now, you must throw my charcoal on the earth between us. The land on which it falls will burn with a raging fire. I will walk into this fire, take its flames into my mouth, and blow them toward you. But, once again, you must stand your ground and resist the urge to run.

"Once I have struggled through this patch of fire, you will again be in great danger!" she exclaimed. "I will again lower my head with my great horns and rush toward you. Again, you must be prepared for my attack, and again you must resist the urge to run. Instead, you must stand your ground and, now, you must throw my egg on the earth between us. The land on which it falls will become a great river. I will walk into this river, but I will be unable to struggle through its strong currents. It is here that I will die, and once I am dead, the river waters will disappear. Command the hunters of Manding to descend from their trees and bury me in a secret place.

Ashanti carved wood. Ghana

1 *What does the old woman reveal? What does she tell Sunjata he must do?*

2 *How will the beast die? What role is Sunjata to play in this death?*

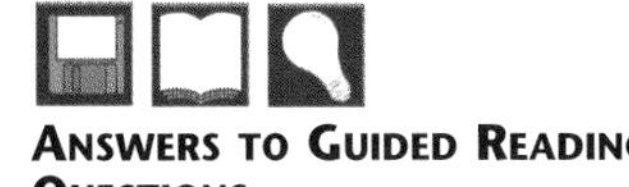

Answers to Guided Reading Questions

1 The old woman reveals that she is the beast. She tells Sunjata that he must kill her before she drinks from the third lake or she will kill him.

2 The beast will die in the swift currents of a river created by the old woman's egg. Sunjata is to throw the egg on the ground when the beast (the old woman) approaches him the third time, and the egg will change the land into a great river.

Literary Note

You may wish to point out to students that Sunjata's characteristics and adventures parallel those of the heroes of many other civilizations. Like Hercules of Greece, Sunjata has an unusual childhood. Like Odysseus of Greece and Rama of India, Sunjata undergoes a period of exile. Like the Roman Aeneas, Sunjata founds a nation. Like the medieval Perceval, Sunjata is close to his mother and carefully follows her advice, and like countless heroes, including the Greek Theseus and the Mesopotamian Gilgamesh, Sunjata proves his heroism on his first adventure by defeating a monster.

Interested students might wish to hold a discussion in which they compare and contrast Sunjata to other heroes they have encountered in their reading, such as Gilgamesh (see page 502), Rama (see page 560), Aeneas (see page 222), Achilles (see page 592), or Perceval (see page 722).

Selection Check Test with Answers

EX. Where does this part of the epic take place?

This part of the epic takes place in Niani.

1. What is ravaging the crops in Niani?

A beast is ravaging the crops.

2. What does Sunjata decide to do about the beast?

Sunjata decides to go on an adventure to kill the beast.

3. What does Sunjata give to the old man?

Sunjata gives the old man two kola nuts.

4. What does the beast look like?

The beast has eighteen horns and an eye in the middle of its forehead.

5. Who is the beast who ravages the crops?

The beast who ravages the crops is really the old woman whose son was killed by Sunjata's father.

Responding to the Selection

Students should note that the woman's decision to tell Sunjata how to kill her is not very realistic. If students have trouble explaining why realism may not have been a priority in this epic, you might encourage them to brainstorm a list of possible reasons for the creation of this epic.

"If you remember my advice," she concluded, "all will go well with you. I know, because I am the strange beast that is ravaging the crops that grow in Niani! Your father is responsible for the death of my son. However, I am now satisfied that I have punished the people of Niani enough for his deed."

Each event came to pass just as the old woman had said it would. The rice, the charcoal, and the egg worked their magic; the beast charged angrily through the bamboo and the raging fire; it died in the strong currents of the river; and the hunters of Niani buried it in a hollow tree. ■

Ape mask. Mali

Responding to the Selection

Did the events described in the *Sunjata* seem realistic to you? Why, or why not? What did you think of the old woman's decision to tell Sunjata how to kill her? Did this seem realistic? Why, or why not? Discuss with your classmates why realism may not have been a priority in this epic.

Reviewing the Selection

RECALLING / **INTERPRETING**

1. In what way is the beast that is destroying the crops in Niani unusual? ▶▶ Why does Sunjata wish to kill the beast?
2. Who does Sogolon Kedju say this beast really is? ▶▶ How does Sogolon Kedju know the true identity of the beast?
3. Who is the first person whom Sunjata meets on his adventure? What does Sunjata do for this person? ▶▶ Why does this person reward Sunjata?
4. Who is the second person whom Sunjata meets on his adventure? What does Sunjata do for this person? In what way does this person reward Sunjata? ▶▶ What makes this reward so unusual?

SYNTHESIZING

5. In the *Sunjata,* the old woman says that the reason she tells Sunjata how to defeat the beast is because "I am now satisfied that I have punished the people of Niani enough for his [Sunjata's father's] deed." Two other possible reasons for her advice are that she is rewarding Sunjata for his generosity and that she understands that it is her personal destiny to be defeated by Sunjata. Why do you think the old woman decides to help Sunjata? Does she help Sunjata for one of the reasons stated above, for a combination of these reasons, or for a different reason altogether? Support your response with evidence from both the text and the About the Selection feature on page 575.

Understanding Literature (Questions for Discussion)

1. **Epic.** An **epic** is a long story, often told in verse, involving heroes and gods. Grand in length and scope, an epic provides a portrait of an entire culture, of the legends, beliefs, values, laws, arts, and ways of life of a people. Think about what this selection from the epic of *Sunjata* reveals about the Mande. Answer these questions: What did the Mande do to make their living? What types of weapons did they use? How did they think people should behave toward those who are less fortunate? What personal qualities did they value? What were their beliefs about the supernatural?

2. **Repetition. Repetition** is the use, again, of a sound, word, phrase, or other element. There are many repeated phrases throughout the *Sunjata,* including "may it come to pass that you reap as fine a harvest from these seeds of kindness as you have sown" and "what will be, will come!" Elements of plot are also repeated. In what way does repetition affect the plot of this selection? What events or occurrences are repeated? Why do you think that the griot chose to use repetition in this way?

Answers for Reviewing the Selection

RECALLING AND INTERPRETING

1. **Recalling.** The beast is unusual because it possesses the magical power to turn away all weapons and the strength to kill any man. **Interpreting.** Sunjata wants to kill the beast to prove to the people of Niani that he is the rightful king.

2. **Recalling.** Sogolon Kedju says that the beast is a sorceress whose son was killed by Sunjata's father and that this sorceress destroys the crops to revenge herself upon "our people." **Interpreting.** Sogolon Kedju may know the identity of the beast because she herself is a powerful sorceress.

3. **Recalling.** Sunjata meets a blind man. Sunjata offers the man anything he has and then gives the man his kola nuts. **Interpreting.** The man rewards Sunjata by telling Sunjata what he must do to succeed in his quest. He rewards Sunjata because Sunjata has behaved generously.

4. **Recalling.** Sunjata meets an old woman. Sunjata gives the woman a coin, offers to take care of her, and gives her the meat of one of his cows. The old woman rewards Sunjata by revealing that she is the beast, telling him how to conquer her, and giving him the means to conquer her. **Interpreting.** This reward is unusual because the old woman is sacrificing herself for Sunjata's glory.

SYNTHESIZING

Responses will vary. Possible responses are given.

5. Responses will vary, but students should support their reasoning with evidence from the text and from About the Selection on page 575.

Answers for Understanding Literature

Responses will vary. Possible responses are given.

1. **Epic.** The Mande made their living by farming and hunting. The Mande used bows and arrows. They believed that people (cont.)

Answers for Understanding Literature (cont.)

should behave kindly and generously to the less fortunate. Generosity, kindness, hospitality, courage, wisdom, and strength were valued. The Mande believed in divining the future, in magical objects, and in shape-shifting.

2. **Repetition.** Sunjata's encounter with an older man in need, his generosity, and the advice he receives as a reward is repeated in a similar encounter with the older woman. The griot may have been trying to emphasize that kind, generous behavior is rewarded. Students may also note that the old woman describes the appearance of three beasts and the course of action Sunjata should take when he meets each beast. The griot may have used repetition in this scene to heighten the suspense. Also, repetition helped storytellers to remember their stories.

ANALYTIC SCALES FOR RESPONDING IN WRITING

Assign a score from 1 to 25 for each grading criterion below. (For more detailed evaluation, see the evaluation forms for writing, revising, and proofreading, Assessment Portfolio 4.1–4.9.)

1. Character Sketch

- **Content/Unity.** The character sketch describes a hero from literature, history, or real life.
- **Organization/Coherence.** The character sketch presents details about the hero in a sensible order.
- **Language/Style.** The character sketch uses vivid and precise nouns, verbs, and modifiers.
- **Conventions.** The character sketch avoids errors in spelling, grammar, usage, mechanics, and manuscript form.

► Additional practice is provided in the Essential Skills Practice Book: Writing 1.8.

2. Critical Essay

- **Content/Unity.** The essay discusses the view of fate and free will presented in the *Sunjata.*
- **Organization/Coherence.** The essay begins with an introduction that includes the thesis of the essay. The introduction is followed by supporting paragraphs with clear transitions. The essay ends with a solid conclusion.
- **Language/Style.** The essay uses vivid and precise nouns, verbs, and modifiers.
- **Conventions.** The essay avoids errors in spelling, grammar, usage, mechanics, and manuscript form.

► Additional practice is provided in the Essential Skills Practice Book: Writing 1.20.

Responding in Writing

1. **Creative Writing: Character Sketch.** Write a character sketch describing a hero from literature, from history, or from real life. First, choose someone about whom you would like to write. Then, think about the qualities that make this person admirable. Next, think about your character's appearance and mannerisms. What does your hero wear? What does his or her voice sound like? In what manner does he or she speak? Finally, think about your hero's deeds. What actions make this person remarkable? After you have formed a clear mental picture of your hero, write a character sketch in which you imagine this person being interviewed about his or her life. Use concrete details to create a vivid sketch of your character.

2. **Critical Essay: Fate and Free Will.** Throughout the *Sunjata,* the phrase "what will be, will come" is repeated. Write an essay in which you discuss the view of fate that is presented in the *Sunjata.* In the first paragraph, identify the Mande attitude toward fate, and explain what you think the phrase "what will be, will come" means. Then, in following paragraphs, discuss the extent to which characters have control over their personal destinies in the *Sunjata* and how they react to their fate. Consider the following questions: To what extent are the events that occur in the characters' lives the result of fate? What impact does the belief in predestination have on the actions of the characters? Would the outcome of this adventure have been different if Sunjata had been able to separate himself from his destiny and behave differently, or did Sunjata's character determine his actions and, hence, his fate? Draw some conclusions in a final paragraph.

Speaking and Listening Skills

Oral Interpretation. Both verbal and nonverbal communication skills are very important to a *griot.* The *griot* varies elements of verbal communication, such as volume, pace, stress, and tone, and elements of nonverbal communication, such as eye contact, facial expressions, and gestures, to engage an audience's attention and imagination. Work in a small group to retell a story from the oral tradition. First, choose a work from the oral tradition by looking through this book or by doing research in the library or on the Internet. Next, divide up the story among the members of your group, with each member receiving a section of the story to be performed in front of the class. Read the Language Arts Survey 3.1, "Elements of Verbal and Nonverbal Communication." On a copy of your selection, mark places where you might vary pace, volume, or tone, or where you might use facial expressions or gestures. Then practice your section of the story in front of a mirror, trying to make your presentation as intriguing as possible. Use both verbal and nonverbal communication to make your part of the story come alive for your audience. As a group, practice putting the parts of your story together. Assess each others' performances and provide suggestions for improving them. Finally, as a group, present your retelling of the story to your class as a whole.

ANSWERS FOR SKILLS ACTIVITIES

SPEAKING AND LISTENING SKILLS

You may evaluate students' performances using either of the following methods:

- Assign students a score from 1 to 9 for each of the following elements: volume, pitch, enunciation, pace, stress, tone, eye contact, facial expressions, body language, gestures, and proximity.
- Have students rate their classmates' performances in each of the above elements of communication. Have students discuss ways in which performances might have been improved.

► Additional practice is provided in the Essential Skills Practice Book: Speaking and Listening 3.1, 3.5.

SELECTIONS FOR ADDITIONAL READING

"Inanna and Ishkur"

by Enheduanna, translated by Kenneth Rexroth and Ikuko Atsumi and adapted by Willis and Aliki Barnstone

You strike everything down in battle.
O my lady, on your wings
you hack away the land and charge disguised
as a charging storm,
roar as a roaring storm,
thunder and keep thundering, and snort
with evil winds.
Your feet are filled with restlessness.

On your harp of sighs
I hear your dirge.[1] ■

from *Chuang Tzu*

by Chuang Chou, translated by Burton Watson

Once Chuang Chou dreamt he was a butterfly, a butterfly flitting and fluttering around, happy with himself and doing as he pleased. He didn't know he was Chuang Chou. Suddenly he woke up and there he was, solid and unmistakable Chuang Chou. But he didn't know if he was Chuang Chou who had dreamt he was a butterfly, or a butterfly dreaming he was Chuang Chou. Between Chuang Chou and a butterfly there must be *some* distinction! This is called the Transformation of Things. ■

"The Four Noble Truths, or The First Sermon"

by Siddhartha Gautama, the Buddha, edited by Léon Freer and C. A. F. Rhys Davids

Thus I have heard. Once the Lord[2] was at Varanasi,[3] at the deer park called Isipatana. There he addressed the five monks:[4]

There are two ends not to be served by a wanderer. What are these two? The pursuit of desires and the pleasure which springs from desire, which is base, common, leading to rebirth, ignoble, and unprofitable; and the pursuit of pain and hardship, which is grievous, ignoble, and unprofitable. The Middle Way of the Tathagata[5] avoids both these ends. It is enlightened, it brings clear vision, it makes for wisdom and leads to peace, insight, enlightenment, and Nirvana. What is the Middle Way? . . . It is the Noble Eightfold Path—Right Views, Right Resolve, Right Speech, Right Conduct, Right Livelihood, Right Effort, Right Mindfulness, and Right Concentration. This is the Middle Way. . . .

And this is the Noble Truth of Sorrow. Birth is sorrow, age is sorrow, disease is sorrow; death is sorrow, contact with the unpleasant is sorrow, separation from the pleasant is sorrow, every wish unfulfilled is sorrow—in short all the five components of individuality are sorrow.

And this is the Noble Truth of the Arising of Sorrow. It arises from craving, which leads to rebirth, which brings delight and passion and seeks pleasure now here, now there—the craving for sensual pleasure, the craving for continued life, the craving for power.

And this is the Noble Truth of the Stopping of Sorrow. It is the complete stopping of that craving, so that no passion remains, leaving it, being emancipated from it, being released from it, giving no place to it.

And this is the Noble Truth of the Way which Leads to the Stopping of Sorrow. It is the Noble Eightfold Path—Right Views, Right Resolve, Right Speech, Right Conduct, Right Livelihood, Right Effort, Right Mindfulness, and Right Concentration. ■

1. **dirge.** Funeral hymn; lament
2. **the Lord.** Reference, in this context, to the Buddha
3. **Varanasi.** City in Northeast India, on the Ganges River, formerly known as Benares
4. **the five monks.** Five former associates, ascetics who had turned from Siddhartha when he renounced the ascetic life
5. **Tathagata.** One of the names traditionally given to the Buddha, meaning "he who has attained [enlightenment]"

"INANNA AND ISHKUR"

ABOUT THE AUTHOR

Enheduanna (born c. 2300 BC), the daughter of King Sargon of Agade, or Akkad, who established the world's first empire, was a princess and a moon priestess. She is the earliest writer whose name has survived along with her work.

ABOUT THE SELECTION

"Inanna and Ishkur" is one of many poems by Enheduanna in which she speaks to Inanna, the Sumerian goddess of love and war.

FROM *CHUANG TZU*

ABOUT THE AUTHOR

Chuang Chou (1783–1859) was an extremely significant interpreter of Taoism. His teachings influenced Chinese Buddhism, landscape painting, and poetry.

ABOUT THE SELECTION

Many scholars consider ***Chuang Tzu*** to be a more definitive and comprehensive treatment of Taoism than the *Tao te Ching.* Although Chuang Chou drew heavily from Lao-tzu's teachings, he presented a broader view. For more information on Taoism, see page 544.

"THE FOUR NOBLE TRUTHS, OR THE FIRST SERMON"

ABOUT THE AUTHOR

Siddhartha Gautama, the Buddha (c. 563–c. 483 BC), was born to a wealthy family. After seeing an elderly man, a sick man, and a dead man in the streets outside his palace, Siddhartha realized that he, too, would eventually grow old and die, be reborn and grow old and die again in a seemingly endless cycle of meaningless suffering. Troubled by this idea, he decided to leave his wealth and his family to become a spiritual seeker. After unsuccessfully living as an ascetic, he turned to meditation under a bodhi tree. There, according to Orthodox Buddhist belief, he attained enlightenment. His followers thereafter would call him the Buddha, which means "the enlightened one."

(cont.)

ABOUT THE AUTHORS AND SELECTIONS (CONT.)

ABOUT THE SELECTION

According to **"The Four Noble Truths, or The First Sermon,"** all life is suffering, and suffering is caused by unfulfilled desire. Therefore, by ridding oneself of all desires, one can also rid oneself of suffering and experience complete joy, or bliss. Renouncing desires, the Buddha taught, enables one to reach a state of perfection called nirvana. According to one school of Buddhist thought, when a person reaches nirvana, his or her individual self is annihilated. To Buddhists, the very idea of the existence of individuals is an illusion to be overcome. Once a person sees through this illusion, he or she escapes from the otherwise endless cycle of rebirth and suffering.

ADDITIONAL RESOURCES

Assessment Portfolio

- Vocabulary Worksheet 2.7.19
- Study Guide 2.7.20
- Unit Test 2.7.21

Essential Skills Practice Books

WRITING
- Choosing a Purpose, 1.8
- Gathering Ideas, 1.10
- Writing a Critical Essay, 1.20

LANGUAGE
- Types of Nouns, 2.3

SPEAKING AND LISTENING
- Elements of Verbal and Nonverbal Communication, 3.1
- Oral Interpretation, 3.5

STUDY AND RESEARCH
- Types of Thinking, 4.2
- Bibliographies and Bibliography Cards, 4.20
- Documenting Sources in a Report, 4.23

APPLIED ENGLISH/TECH PREP
- Writing Resumes and Cover Letters, 5.3

Vocabulary Check Test

Ask students to number their papers from one to ten. Have students complete each sentence with a word from the Vocabulary from the Selections in the Unit Review.

1. Susan is penitent for taking her mother's favorite hat without permission.
2. All that rain caused a deluge in the center of town.
3. I sent them a flower arrangement as a token of my appreciation for all of their hard work.
4. We knew as soon as we saw Gretchen's cheerless countenance that she had received the bad news.
5. My brother was a real vagabond when he backpacked across Europe for almost a year.
6. The spring rains would replenish the dry earth and make it fertile again.

(cont.)

UNIT REVIEW

Roots of World Literature

VOCABULARY FROM THE SELECTIONS

abate, 526	embellish, 568	perpetual, 528
abomination, 506	endow, 504	pestilence, 510
allot, 508	enmity, 523	precinct, 512
amiability, 551	filial, 551	prevail, 526
assuage, 526	firmament, 519	proliferate, 534
babel, 508	fruition, 533	ravage, 576
beguile, 522	gingerly, 541	rend, 571
benevolent, 551	harmonize, 546	replenish, 520
boon, 563	illumined, 571	resonant, 570
clamor, 508	innate, 552	saffron, 563
competent, 546	lavishly, 540	sage, 546
complacency, 547	level, 505	savory, 539
complement, 545	libation, 510	spectral, 567
consign, 510	manifestation, 545	strive, 546
countenance, 523	mar, 534	stupor, 509
customary, 540	obsequiousness, 551	summit, 568
deluge, 507, 539	obstruction, 533	supple, 567
diligently, 551	parasol, 566	teem, 508
dominion, 520	pavilion, 562	token, 528
dowry, 564	penitent, 535	vagabond, 524

LITERARY TERMS

allegory, 573	hymn, 556
analects, 550	internal conflict, 514
antihero, 516	irony, 514
aphorism, 554	irony of situation, 514
archetype, 530, 542	myth, 536, 573
conflict, 514	paradox, 549
epic, 502, 560, 573, 581	parallelism, 530, 536, 548
external conflict, 514	repetition, 581
foreshadowing, 514	rhetorical question, 559
hero, 516	theme, 554

Vocabulary Check Test (cont.)

7. Stephanie gingerly placed the bowl of cereal back on the tray to avoid spilling it.
8. Determined to win an award, Jonathan worked diligently to perfect his science project.
9. Even though my parents are completely different, people say that they really complement each other.
10. It is important to constantly strive to achieve one's highest goals and aspirations.

SYNTHESIS: QUESTIONS FOR WRITING, RESEARCH, OR DISCUSSION

GENRE STUDIES

1. What is a heroic epic? What works in this unit would you classify as heroic epics? In what ways do the heroes of these epics meet the ideals of their cultures? What cultural values are revealed in these heroic epics?

2. An oral tradition is a work, a motif, an idea, or a custom that is passed by word-of-mouth from generation to generation. Read about the oral tradition in the Handbook of Literary Terms. Choose two or three selections from this unit that were transmitted in this way. What elements of oral transmission do they display?

THEMATIC STUDIES

3. Explore the theme of the journey or the quest in *The Epic of Gilgamesh,* the *Ramayana,* and the *Sunjata.* What is the result of each hero's journey or quest? Does the hero change over the course of his quest? If so, in what way?

4. Explore the theme of the fall from a state of innocence, or a state of perfection, to a state of experience or worldliness, or a lesser state, in the selections from Genesis and the selection from the *Popol Vuh.* In what way is the gods' decision to mar their creations' abilities in the *Popol Vuh* similar to God's decision to expel Adam and Eve from the garden of Eden?

5. Many writers have been influenced by the works of Lao-tzu and Confucius. Both philosophers address the question "What is the individual's role in the universe?" What are Lao-tzu's and Confucius's ideas concerning a person's role in the universe and what one must do in order to find the true meaning of life? Compare and contrast these ideas to those expressed by Siddhartha Gautama, the Buddha, in "The Four Noble Truths, or The First Sermon," which is found in Selections for Additional Reading.

6. Compare and contrast the great flood described in *The Epic of Gilgamesh,* the selections from Genesis, and "The Five Worlds and Their Suns." Compare and contrast the way in which snakes bring evil to humanity in *The Epic of Gilgamesh* and in the selections from Genesis.

7. Compare and contrast the use of images of light and sunlight as symbols of life and order and the use of images of darkness as symbols of chaos and disorder in the following selections: *The Epic of Gilgamesh,* the selections from Genesis, the selection from the *Popol Vuh*, and "The Five Worlds and Their Suns."

HISTORICAL/BIOGRAPHICAL STUDIES

8. Compare and contrast the worldviews of two of the great cultures of the ancient Near East—Mesopotamia and Israel. What ideas seem to have been shared between these cultures? What ideas and concepts are specific to a given culture? In what way do you think the geography of these cultures helped to shape their worldviews?

9. Both Gilgamesh and Sunjata are mythical heroes who were based on actual historical figures. Do some research to learn more about these leaders and the people they ruled. What kinds of rulers were they? What difficulties were faced by these early cultures?

SPELLING CHECK TEST

Ask students to number their papers from one to ten. Read each word aloud. Then read aloud the sentence containing the word. Repeat the word. Ask students to write the word on their papers, spelling it correctly.

1. **endow**
Yasmin would endow her main character with the qualities that she wished for herself—patience and grace.

2. **teem**
On hot summer days, the beaches teem with people.

3. **beguile**
No one would suspect that man to be a traitor because of the way he could beguile us all with his friendly and loyal manner.

4. **enmity**
The enmity between the two rivals drove them to scheme and plot against each other.

5. **prevail**
Thanks to his speed and agility, Chris would always prevail over his fencing opponent, winning first place in every competition.

6. **perpetual**
Rita was unable to concentrate because her two younger sisters interrupted her with perpetual questions and complaints.

7. **complacency**
Instead of falling into complacency, you should always strive to improve yourself.

8. **obsequiousness**
The king's favorite courtier was renowned for his obsequiousness; he would say only what he thought would most please the king.

9. **pavilion**
The king ordered that a pavilion be raised in the meadow to serve as a place to feast during the summer celebration.

10. **illumined**
At night the city put on a festive appearance with illumined neon signs in every shop window.

UNIT SKILLS OUTLINE

LITERARY SKILLS AND CONCEPTS

- Aim, 682
- Allusion, 614, 707
- Anecdote, 707
- Antistrophe, 617, 627
- Apostrophe, 694
- Apposition, 627
- Archetype, 689
- Comedy, 617
- Convention, 617, 672
- Description, 607
- *Deus Ex Machina*, 616
- Dramatic Irony, 651
- Epic, 592, 607
- Epithet, 594
- Foreshadowing, 605, 635, 707
- Homeric Simile, 599
- *In Medias Res,* 593
- Irony, 603, 651
- Irony of Situation, 603
- Metaphor, 614, 651
- Mode, 682
- Motivation, 607
- Myth, 689
- Nonfiction, 689
- Paradox, 651, 694
- Pathetic Fallacy, 707
- Personification, 611
- Plot, 660
- Simile, 599, 614, 651
- Speaker, 610
- Strophe, 617, 627
- Style, 607
- Theme, 614, 682
- Tone, 610
- Tragedy, 617, 673
- Tragic Flaw, 592, 617, 673
- Tragic Hero, 592

WRITING SKILLS AND CONCEPTS

- Choosing a Topic, 664
- Critical Essay, 608, 615, 673, 682, 690, 695, 707
- Description, 707
- Dialogue, 673
- Founding Story, 690
- Fragments, 614
- Gathering Ideas, 601
- Lyric Poem, 695
- Parody, 608
- Song or Speech of Praise, 682

GRAMMAR, USAGE, AND MECHANICS SKILLS AND CONCEPTS

- Expanding and Combining Sentences, 695
- Greek and Latin Roots, 673
- Varying Sentence Openings, Length, and Structure, 686

OTHER LANGUAGE ARTS SKILLS AND CONCEPTS

- Active Listening and Interpersonal Communication, 690
- Bibliographies and Bibliography Cards, 664
- Distinguishing Fact and Opinion, 708
- Elements of Verbal and Nonverbal Communication, 648
- Finding Career Information, 644
- Oral Interpretation, 608, 709
- Paraphrasing and Summarizing, 620

UNIT 8 CLASSICAL LITERATURE

Sick Bacchus. *Caravaggio (Michelangelo Merisi)*

GOALS/OBJECTIVES

Studying this unit will enable students to

- gain an overall understanding of classical literature
- have a positive experience reading literature and poetry from the cultures of ancient Greece and Rome
- understand how classical culture has influenced the development of Western thought
- recognize allusions, dramatic irony, and personification
- briefly explain the characteristics of Greek drama
- analyze and write critically about literature
- distinguish between fact and opinion

> "To the glory that was
> Greece,
> And the grandeur that was
> Rome."
>
> —Edgar Allan Poe

587

CROSS-CURRICULAR CONNECTIONS

Arts and Humanities
- Achilles and Odysseus, 601
- Achilles as Hero, 595
- Activities on Plutarch, 696
- Agamemnon's Story, 596
- Aging Process, 611
- Comparing Athena and Ares, 685
- Contributions from Classical Greece, 588
- Doric Columns, 646
- Foster's Translation of Livy, 686
- The Founding of Troy, 592
- Greek Gods, 598
- Herodotus and Thucydides, 676
- Illustrating Fragments, 615
- Oral Interpretation, 608
- Researching the History and Geography of Greece, 618
- Shakespeare and Classical Sources, 709

Mathematics and Sciences
- Contributions from Classical Greece, 588
- Earthquakes in and History of Lesbos, 609
- Greek Gods, 598
- Reporting on the Crocodile, 710
- Researching Wolves, 685
- Ruins of Troy, 604

Social Studies
- Activities on Plutarch, 696
- Aristotle, 617
- Athenian Tragic Dramatists, 628
- Biographical Notes on Echoes Authors, 590
- Cæsar and Catullus, 691
- Cleopatra VII, 704
- Comparing Athena and Ares, 685
- Contributions from Classical Greece, 588
- Corinth, 647
- Cultural Influence of Greece, 589
- The Dorians, 646
- Earthquakes in and History of Lesbos, 609
- The Fates, 626
- Foretelling the Future, 621
- Founding of Troy, 592
- Freud and the Oedipus Complex, 636
- Gettysburg Address and Pericles's Funeral Oration, 674
- Gnaeus Pompey, 700
- Greek Gods in Oedipus, 623
- Greek Theory of Hope, 670
- Herodotus and Thucydides, 676
- Julius Cæsar, 698
- Mark Anthony, 703
- The Mycenaean Age, 602
- Oral History, 682
- Peloponnesian War, 677
- The Phoenix, 711
- Plutarch's View of Fortune, 702
- Political Assassinations, 701
- Researching the History and Geography of Greece, 618
- Researching the Punic War, 683
- River Lethe, 605
- Roman Empire, 589
- Ruins of Troy, 604
- Sigmund Freud and Psychoanalysis, 637
- The Sphinx, 625
- Theater in Athens, 616

Applied Arts
- Career Information, 644
- Comparing and Contrasting Types of Stages, 616
- Contributions from Classical Greece, 588

TEACHING THE MULTIPLE INTELLIGENCES

Musical
- Aging Process, 611
- Elements of Verbal and Nonverbal Communication, 648
- Illustrating Fragments, 615

Logical-Mathematical
- Achilles and Odysseus, 601
- Achilles as Hero, 595
- Activities on Plutarch, 696
- Aristotle's Definition of Tragedy, 624
- Comparing and Contrasting Types of Stages, 616
- Comparing Athena and Ares, 685
- Conflicts of Achilles and Hector, 600
- Contributions from Classical Greece, 588
- Debating Violence in the Media, 617
- Distinguishing Fact and Opinion, 708
- Earthquakes in and History of Lesbos, 609
- Gettysburg Address and Pericles's Funeral Oration, 674
- Greek Gods, 598
- Oral History, 682
- Paraphrasing and Summarizing, 620
- Reporting on the Crocodile, 710
- Researching the History and Geography of Greece, 618

(cont.)

TEACHING THE MULTIPLE INTELLIGENCES (cont.)

- Research Skills, 664
- Riddles, 634
- Ruins of Troy, 604
- Superstitions, 671

Spatial
- Activities on Plutarch, 696
- Aging Process, 611
- Greek Gods, 598
- Oral Interpretation, 709
- Paraphrasing and Summarizing, 620
- Researching the History and Geography of Greece, 618
- Roman Empire, 589

Kinesthetic
- Active Listening and Interpersonal Communication, 690
- Activities on Plutarch, 696
- Comparing and Contrasting Types of Stages, 616
- Elements of Verbal and Nonverbal Communication, 648
- Finding Career Information, 644
- Oral History, 682
- Oral Interpretation, 608, 709

Interpersonal
- Achilles and Odysseus, 601
- Active Listening and Interpersonal Communication, 690
- Activities on Plutarch, 696
- Aristotle's Definition of Tragedy, 624
- Choosing an Epigraph, 591
- Comparing and Contrasting Types of Stages, 616
- Comparing Athena and Ares, 685
- Conflicts of Achilles and Hector, 600
- Debating Violence in the Media, 617
- Discussing Truth, 633
- Earthquakes in and History of Lesbos, 609
- Elements of Verbal and Nonverbal Communication, 648
- Illustrating Fragments, 615
- Oral History, 682
- Oral Interpretation, 608, 709
- Plot Diagrams, 661
- Political Assassinations, 701
- Reporting on the Crocodile, 710
- Researching the Punic War, 683
- Ruins of Troy, 604

Other Selections Exploring This Period

Ovid
from *Metamorphoses,* pages 436, 492
Plato
"The Death of Socrates," page 303
Virgil
from the *Aeneid,* page 222

Cultural/Historical Note

The people of classical Greece made contributions to the world in many areas. The following list outlines some of their accomplishments. These subjects serve only as an introduction to Greek culture. Students might choose topics from this list to research further.

- **Art and Architecture.** The Greeks are known for beautiful pottery including black figure ware and red figure ware. They also created idealized statues, busts, and reliefs of gods, goddesses, and important people. Greek architecture, which often included graceful columns, had a profound effect on later architecture. Students might research specific works of Greek art or architecture, or they might research the effects of Greek art and architecture on works of later periods.
- **History.** Herodotus and Thucydides are highly regarded for their work recording Greek history. Students can compare and contrast the style of these two writers, or they can research a specific event from Greek history using one of their works as a source.
- **Language.** Thousands of words in the English language, such as *sophisticated, democracy,* and *telephone,* are derived from Greek. Have students identify other words derived from the Greek language and create a word game using them.
- **Mathematics.** Euclid,

(cont.)

UNIT 8

Preview:

Classical Literature

*Detail from **The School of Athens**, Raphael, c. 1510. Stanza della Segnatura, Vatican Museum*

Classical culture, the culture of ancient Greece and Rome, has influenced the development of Western thought for many centuries. In ancient times, Greece gave rise to a series of civilizations that had profound impact on world history, literature, art, and architecture. Rome is often viewed as an ideal civilization because the enormous and powerful Roman Empire survived for centuries and produced innovations in engineering, art, law, and government. The drive to excel and to leave a mark upon the world led the Greeks and Romans to create new literary genres, forms, and techniques and to write literature of such quality that its equal would not be found in the West for many hundreds of years.

The first of the great Greek civilizations emerged on the island of Crete around 6000 BC. By 2000 BC, this Minoan civilization dominated the eastern Mediterranean and prospered, developing tools, warships, and systems of writing. The Minoans were eventually overrun by a much more aggressive civilization from the city of Mycenae in southern Greece. The Mycenaean era, also known as the Heroic Age, lasted roughly from 1600 to 1100 BC. In 1250 BC, Mycenaean Greeks went to war against the city of Troy, known as Ilium to the Romans, in Asia Minor. The story of this war was told hundreds of years later in an epic poem, the *Iliad,* attributed to the Greek poet Homer. By 1150 BC, most Mycenaean towns had been destroyed, and by 1000 BC, groups such as Achaeans, Aeolians, Ionians, and Dorians had settled in the region that is now modern Greece. During Greece's Dark Ages, lasting from about 1100 to 800 BC, standards of living declined, and the system of writing used by the Mycenaeans was forgotten. The Dark Ages were followed by the Archaic period, from 800 to 500 BC. During this time, the first Olympic Games were held, art flourished, and a new Greek alphabet was developed. The Greeks of this time also developed a tradition of oral literature performed by professional poets known as bards. The

Cultural/Historical Note (cont.)

Pythagoras, and Archimedes are recognized for their work in the areas of mathematics and physics. Have interested students explain some of the major contributions of these people and explain how they affect the work of mathematicians and scientists today.

- **Medicine.** Today, doctors take the Hippocratic oath, a pledge to follow a code of medical ethics. The oath takes its name from Hippocrates, who founded a medical school. Ask students to find a copy of the Hippocratic oath and discuss its application in medicine today.
- **Philosophy.** Influential Greek philosophers include Socrates, Plato, Aristotle, Diogenes, and Zeno. Ask students to contemplate some of the concerns of the major branches of philosophy and discuss their ideas in small groups. Questions for discussion

(cont.)

most famous of these bards was Homer, who is traditionally credited with composing a series of hymns and two great epic poems, the *Iliad*, based on the Trojan war, and the *Odyssey*, which told the tale of the wanderings and return of the war hero Odysseus from the Trojan War to his home state.

During the sixth century BC, the Ionians, who lived in Greek states in Asia Minor, fell under the rule of the expanding Persian Empire. This began a series of conflicts known as the Persian Wars. Greek success in these wars paved the way for Greece's Golden Age. In 508 BC, Cleisthenes introduced a new system of government—democracy—to Athens, one of the largest city-states. Under this system, a council was elected each year to make laws and run the state. All male citizens had the right to vote on proposals put forth by the council. From 479 to 431 BC, Athens prospered and art, philosophy, theater, literature, and trade flourished. Important people of this period included the three great philosophers Socrates, Plato, and Aristotle; playwrights Aeschylus, Sophocles, Euripides, and Aristophanes; historians Herodotus and Thucydides; political leader Pericles; and lyric poet Sappho. Drama was particularly important to Athenians, and plays evolved from rituals that celebrated harvests and military victories and often reflected religious and political issues. Playwrights usually based their plays on ancient myths and heroic tales. People were actually paid to stop work and attend theater performances, because it was believed that theater helped people to deal with political and religious problems.

The people of Sparta, a militaristic rival city-state, began to see prosperous Athens as a threat. The Golden Age ended with the Peloponnesian War, a twenty-seven year conflict between Athens and Sparta. Although Athens eventually lost the war to Sparta, Athenian thought remained influential in Greece. In the years following the end of the Peloponnesian War, Alexander the Great, king of the Greek nation of Macedonia, conquered a territory that stretched from Greece to India. Alexander spread the Greek culture and language throughout the territory over which he reigned, even founding a great center of Hellenic, or Greek, knowledge in Egypt called Alexandria. Many aspects of Greek culture, including mythology, art, and philosophy, were later adopted by the Romans.

According to tradition, the city of Rome was founded in the center of the Italian peninsula by native Italic peoples in 753 BC. Around this time, the area was settled by a variety of other groups competing for power, including the Etruscans, some Greek colonists on the southern coast and on the island of Sicily, and the Phoenicians on the northern shore of Africa, just across the Mediterranean. One legend about the founding of Rome says that Aeneas, an ancient Trojan prince, fled from his destroyed city to the Italian peninsula and married the daughter of a native king. The most well-known version of the story of Aeneas is the *Aeneid*, told by the Roman poet Virgil (70–19 BC). Many generations later, according to legend, one of Aeneas's descendants gave birth to twins, Romulus and Remus, by Mars, the god of war. The legend tells

Ancient Greek gold earrings, 300 BC.
British Museum

Cross-curricular Activities

SOCIAL STUDIES

At its height, the Roman Empire extended across much of Europe and parts of Asia and Africa. Have students map the extent of the Empire. Then have students choose different areas to research. Each student should choose some interaction between Romans and other peoples, vestiges of Roman civilization in locations outside of Italy, or some other aspect of the expansion of the Empire to research. A few possible topics include the Emperor Hadrian and Hadrian's wall in Great Britain, Boadicea and her battle against the Romans, Roman ruins in Sicily, or the decline of the Roman Empire. Have students use maps, illustrations, or other visual aids when presenting their research in an oral or written report.

Cultural/Historical Note

The Romans drew heavily upon the culture of the Greeks. For many years, the Romans read and conducted foreign policy in Greek. They also had a great deal of contact with Greek art, literature, and religion. Many of the Roman gods correspond to Greek gods. For example, Jove, or Jupiter, the god of the sky, corresponds to the Greek Zeus, while Neptune, the god of the sea, corresponds to the Greek Poseidon. Roman lyric poets and philosophers also borrowed much from the works of the Greeks who came before them.

Cultural/Historical Note (cont.)

might include the following: What is the good life? Under what circumstances is an argument valid? invalid? true? false? Is there a difference between the world of appearances and the underlying realities? What is beauty? Can knowledge come from pure thought or does it always depend upon sensory experience?

- **Politics.** Democracy flourished in Athens under Pericles. Students might write a biography of this leader. A useful starting point for their research might be Pericles's funeral oration, as recorded by Thucydides (see page 674), which provides an insight into his view of democracy.

In addition to the areas listed above, the Greeks contributed to our literary tradition. The selections in this unit will provide a valuable introduction to Greek literature.

Biographical Note

Aeschylus (525–456 BC) was the earliest of the three great Athenian tragic playwrights. More information about Aeschylus appears on page 628 of this Annotated Teacher's Edition.

Sophocles (c. 496–406 BC) was another of the three great tragic dramatists of classical literature. A biography of Sophocles appears on page 618.

Herodotus (c. 485–c. 425 BC) was a Greek historian. He is often called the Father of History. His *Histories* (see page 710) focused on the wars fought between Greece and Persia from 499 to 479 BC. The work provides accounts and descriptions of the wars and tells the story of the growth of the Persian Empire including its geography, history, and social organizations.

Socrates (c. 470–399 BC) was an Athenian philosopher and teacher. His teachings directed young men to analyze human character and the conduct of life, especially of their own lives. Authorities of Athens charged Socrates with impiety, corruption of the young, neglect of the gods whom the city worshiped, and the practice of religious novelties. He was sentenced to death. An account of his death appears in Plato's *Phaedo* (see page 303).

Plato (c. 427–c. 347 BC) was one of the most renowned philosophers of ancient Greece. A biography of Plato appears on page 303.

Aristotle (384–322 BC) was a Greek philosopher, scientist, and researcher. He is considered one of the greatest intellectuals of ancient Greece, the other being Plato. Aristotle attended the Athenian Academy of Plato for twenty years. After Plato's death, Aristotle spent twelve years traveling. During this time, he established two of his own academies at Assus and Mytilene. From 343 or 342, he tutored the young Alexander of Macedon, who would

(cont.)

Remains of Augustus's Forum. *Rome, Italy*

how the twins were abandoned, raised by a she-wolf, and later returned to the place of their birth to found the city of Rome.

For the first few centuries of its existence, Rome was ruled by Etruscan kings, but by 509 BC, the people of Rome had established a republic ruled by aristocrats called patricians. Over the years, the general public, called plebeians, gained more and more political power and eventually won the right to veto any patrician-sponsored bill not in their best interest and to have laws put in writing. In the early days of the Roman Republic, Rome expanded its territory and tried to defeat warlike neighboring tribes. After years of difficult battles, the Roman Empire eventually spread over Spain, North Africa, Egypt, Syria, Asia Minor, Greece, Gaul, and Britain.

With new territories and a large population, Rome began to experience problems within its own boundaries. While powerful military leaders continued to try to extend the empire, hoping to win powerful positions in government, people back in Rome were fighting for those same positions within the government. This set the stage for powerful and violent rivalries that helped to end the Republic, begin a civil war, and bring about a return to monarchy. It was during this time that such people as Julius Cæsar, Mark Antony, and Octavian, later called Augustus, experienced the struggles, successes, and defeats Plutarch described in *The Lives of the Noble Grecians and Romans.*

Throughout this time of danger and political upheaval, Roman culture, particularly Roman literature, flourished. Roman writers and scholars had thorough training in Greek culture and often felt overshadowed by the work of Greek writers and scholars. Working with the Greek ideas and styles that they loved and had mastered, they strove at the same time to find their own original voices. In the last years of the Republic, writers such as poets Catullus and Virgil succeeded in doing this. Catullus used Greek meters and stanza forms with original Latin lyrics. Virgil based his *Aeneid* on the work of Homer, but incorporated Roman history, his own personal vision of divine destiny, and the idea of having to play, against one's will, the role of hero. Other important names of this period include the poet Ovid, historians Titus Livius and Tacitus, and orator and philosopher Cicero. Because Latin was the second language of priests, lawyers, scholars, and scientists until the nineteenth century, Roman literature had a profound impact on later European civilization. Every student learned Latin, so the works of Latin writers were read, enjoyed, and respected by every educated European (despite the fact the early Romans were considered pagans by Christian Europeans). Like any literature that has lasted for centuries, the literature of Classical Rome explores universal human themes such as love, friendship, ambition, loyalty, and fear.

Biographical Note (cont.)

become known as Alexander the Great. Returning to Athens in 335, he established the Lyceum, which became the rival of the Academy. His philosophy has had an enormous effect on Western thought.

Horace (65–8 BC) was a Latin poet and satirist known for his odes. He wrote on the themes of love, friendship, philosophy, and poetry. His poetry was very popular during the Renaissance and had a powerful influence on poetry into the nineteenth century.

Plutarch (AD 45–after 120) is most famous for a series of biographies called *The Lives of the Noble Grecians and Romans.* For additional biographical information about Plutarch and a selection from his work, turn to page 696.

(cont.)

Echoes:

Classical Literature

By suffering comes wisdom.

—Aeschylus
Agamemnon

Wonders are many, and none is more wonderful than man.

—Sophocles
Antigone

Call no man happy till you know the nature of his death; he is at best but fortunate.

—Herodotus

The unexamined life is not worth living.

—Socrates
Plato's *Apology*

Beauty of style and harmony and grace and good rhythm depend on simplicity.

—Plato
The Republic

If liberty and equality, as is thought by some, are chiefly to be found in democracy, they will be best attained when all persons alike share in government to the utmost.

—Aristotle
Politics

For mortal daring nothing is too high.
In our blind folly we storm heaven itself.

—Horace

Alexander wept when he heard from Anaxarchus that there was an infinite number of worlds; and his friends asking him if any accident had befallen him, he returns this answer: "Do you not think it a matter worthy of lamentation that when there is such a vast multitude of them, we have not yet conquered one?"

—Plutarch
On the Tranquility of the Mind

Veni, vidi, vici. (I came, I saw, I conquered.)

—Julius Cæsar

To plunder, to slaughter, to steal, these things they misname empire; and where they make a wilderness, they call it peace.

—Tacitus

I sing of warfare and a man at war
From the sea-coast of Troy in early days
He came to Italy by destiny,
To our Lavinian western shore,
A fugitive, this captain, buffeted
Cruelly on land as on the sea.

—Virgil
the *Aeneid*

Biographical Note (cont.)

Julius Cæsar (c. 100–44 BC) was born into a noble Roman family. One of the ablest leaders the world has known, Cæsar bore a name that became forever synonymous with power and leadership. The Russian word *czar,* the German *kaiser,* and the Arabic *qaysar,* meaning "king" or "ruler," are all variations on his name. The month of July is also named after him.

For additional information about Cæsar, see the selection about him in Plutarch's *Lives of the Noble Grecians and Romans,* on page 696.

Tacitus (AD c. 56–c. 120) was a great Roman historian and orator. His works include *Germania,* which describes the German tribes, and *Histories* and *Annals,* which discuss different periods in the history of the Roman Empire. Tacitus's works are studied for their historical value and for their literary merit.

Virgil (70–19 BC) is considered the greatest and most influential Roman poet who ever lived. His masterpiece is the epic poem the *Aeneid.* For more information about Virgil and his work, see page 222.

Additional Questions and Activities

Ask students to choose one of the quotations on page 591 as an epigraph for an essay, poem, or short story that they will write. Remind students that an epigraph is a quotation or motto used at the beginning of a literary work that usually helps to establish the theme of the work. Students can critique one another's writing.

ADDITIONAL RESOURCES

READER'S GUIDE

- Selection Worksheet 8.1

ASSESSMENT PORTFOLIO

- Selection Check Test 2.8.1
- Selection Test 2.8.2

ESSENTIAL SKILLS PRACTICE BOOKS

- Writing 1.8, 1.20
- Speaking and Listening 3.5

PREREADING EXTENSIONS

You may wish to share as background with students the myths about the founding of Troy. According to legend, Dardanus, son of Zeus and a nymph named Electra, was king in the region of Troy, located in northwestern Anatolia (in modern-day Turkey) near the entrance to the Hellespont, the ancient name for the Dardanelles, the strait that divides European Turkey from Asiatic Turkey. (In the *Iliad,* the Trojans are often called *Dardanians* after Dardanus.) Dardanus's son Erichthonius had a son named Tros, who gave his name to future generations of Trojans. Tros had three sons: Ilus, Assaracus, and Ganymede, whom Zeus carried away to be his cup bearer. Ilus founded the city of Troy, also known as Ilium, after a spotted cow pointed out the location. His son Laomedon succeeded him and hired Apollo and Poseidon to build the city's walls. Laomedon later refused to pay the gods, so Poseidon sent a sea monster to attack the city. Laomedon offered his own daughter Hesione to the monster, but Heracles saved her. Laomedon then refused to give Heracles some horses he had promised, so Heracles attacked Troy and killed Laomedon and all his sons, except for Priam, who was king of Troy, during the time depicted in the *Iliad.*

PREREADING

from the *Iliad*
by Homer, translated by Robert Fagles

About the Author

Homer. In ancient Greece, before the development of writing, oral poets created long poems that told stories of heroic adventures. These poems, partly memorized and partly improvised, were written down long after their creation. According to tradition, the greatest of the oral poets, or bards, of ancient Greece was Homer. Nothing is known of the historical Homer. According to legend, however, he was blind and came from Ionia in Asia Minor (site of modern-day Turkey). Homer is attributed with the composition of the two greatest epic poems of ancient Greece, the *Iliad* and the *Odyssey*, which probably date from the seventh or eighth century BC and which served as prototypes for later epic poetry.

About the Selection

An **epic** is a long story, often told in verse, involving heroes and gods. One of the oldest and greatest of all epic poems is the ***Iliad***. This poem tells the story of the Greek, or Achaean, hero Achilles and his role in the Trojan War. The epic portrays the relationship between gods and mortals as well as the roles both play in destiny. The *Iliad*'s epic style and its descriptions of the adventures of a war hero and his responsibilities to his nation have inspired countless imitators, including the later Roman poet Virgil (see page 222).

In classical mythology, the Trojan War was a devastating struggle between the Greeks, or Achaeans, and the Trojans. The struggle began when a Trojan prince, Paris, kidnapped Helen of Troy, considered the most beautiful woman in the world, who was both the daughter of Zeus and the wife of Greek King Menelaus. Greeks sailed to Troy to recover Helen, and fighting between the Greeks and the Trojans endured for ten years. The Greeks finally achieved victory through the ruse of the Trojan horse (see About the Selection for "The Wooden Horse then said," page 1113).

The *Iliad* focuses on the development of the character of Achilles, the son of Peleus, a Greek king, and Thetis, a sea goddess. An example of an epic hero, Achilles, like other epic heroes such as Gilgamesh (see page 502), can be viewed as an early example of the tragic hero. A **tragic hero** is a character of high status who possesses noble qualities but who also has a **tragic flaw**, or personal weakness, that brings about a fall. Achilles's tragic flaw is his destructive anger. According to legend, when Achilles was an infant, his mother held him by one heel and dipped him in the River Styx to make him immortal, but the heel by which she held him remained vulnerable. This was the only spot in which Achilles was able to receive a mortal wound. From this legend comes the phrase "Achilles's heel," which refers to the one weak or vulnerable spot in a person's character. The phrase "the wrath of Achilles," also occasionally heard, refers to the destructive temper of this hero. Besides relating the adventures of Achilles, the *Iliad* examines Greek ideals of heroism, honor, and revenge; narrates the events of the Trojan War; and presents vivid portraits of characters in classical mythology.

Bust of Homer
SEF/Art Resource, New York

GOALS/OBJECTIVES

Studying this lesson will enable students to

- interpret and appreciate an excerpt from the *Iliad*
- briefly explain the background of the *Iliad*
- define *motivation, description, style,* and *tragic flaw,* and identify these elements in a literary work
- identify the characteristics of an *epic* and explain what an epic reveals about a society
- write a parody of a Homeric battle scene
- write a critical essay explaining what Achilles reveals about ancient Greek values
- prepare an oral interpretation

CONNECTIONS: Paris and the Beginning and End of the Trojan War

When composing the *Iliad,* Homer chose to focus on the role that Achilles played in the Trojan War. Although Homer develops numerous subplots involving other heroes, the spotlight remains on the epic's primary hero—Achilles, who was considered the best of the Achaeans. Tales of the Trojan War were popular, however, and were told in many other works. Homer excluded both the beginning of the Trojan War and its end in retelling this epic struggle between the Greeks and the Trojans. At the root and the resolution of the Trojan War stands Paris, a Trojan prince. Although his role in the *Iliad* is relatively minor, he is a figure of central importance.

Paris was the son of King Priam and Queen Hecuba of Troy. Just before his birth, Hecuba had a terrible nightmare that she gave birth to a flaming torch. This dream was interpreted to mean that Paris, if he lived, would cause the destruction of Troy. Soon after his birth, Paris's parents ordered that he be left to die on a mountain, but he was rescued and raised by a shepherd.

Meanwhile, the Greek gods were experiencing troubles of their own. Eris, goddess of discord, was not invited to the wedding of the sea goddess Thetis and the hero Peleus. Angry, Eris appeared at the festivities and threw a golden apple at the feet of the gods, announcing that it was "for the fairest."

Hera, Athena, and Aphrodite all desired the apple, but Zeus refused to choose the fairest and put an end to their arguments. Instead, he ordered Hermes, the messenger god, to bring the apple to Paris on Mount Ida and to let him award the apple as he wished. Hera promised to give Paris wealth and power in return for the apple. Athena promised wisdom and might in war. Aphrodite promised him Helen, the most beautiful woman in the world. Paris accepted Aphrodite's bribe, making Hera and Athena bitter enemies of the Trojans. Paris later took Helen away from her husband, Menelaus, bringing her to Troy, thus setting in motion both the Trojan War and the eventual destruction of Troy.

After the point where Homer ends the *Iliad,* legend holds that Paris shot an arrow into Achilles's one weak spot, his heel, and the greatest of the Achaeans fell and died. The Greek hero Ajax rescued Achilles's body, but the Greeks decided to award Achilles's armor to Odysseus (who figures in the *Iliad* and is the subject of Homer's *Odyssey*) rather than Ajax. Enraged and ashamed, Ajax went mad. Paris was eventually killed by the archer Philoctetes, who carried the bow of the hero Heracles (Hercules).

SUPPORT FOR LEP STUDENTS

Pronunciations of Proper Nouns and Adjectives

A • chae • an (ə kē´ən)
Ho • mer (hō´mər)
Il • i • ad (il´ē əd)

Additional Vocabulary

bluff—putting up a bold, false front in order to trick someone
brace—make ready for an impact, shock, etc.
brazen—like brass in color or quality
burnished—polished
citadel—fortress
courses—pursues
defiled—made filthy or dirty; profaned
fawning—servile; cringing; flattering
glens—narrow, secluded valleys
gluts—feeds or fills to excess
gutted—destroyed the interior of
harried—tormented or worried
marshals—directs or manages
maul—injure by beating or tearing
quarry—anything being hunted or pursued
seething—boiling
staking— risking
supple—able to bend and move easily
winging—causing to fly or speed, as on wings

Literary Technique

IN MEDIAS RES

In medias res is a Latin term meaning, "in the midst of things." Authors who use this technique begin telling a story in the middle of the action and fill in background information through flashbacks and summaries. You may wish to point out that one reason that Homer omits the story about the roots of the Trojan War described in the *Iliad* is because Homer begins his poem *in medias res,* knowing that his audience would have been familiar with both that story and the (cont.)

Literary Technique (cont.)

rest of the material he is retelling. The convention of beginning a story *in medias res* captures an audience's attention by immediately plunging them into crucial events and key actions.

READER'S JOURNAL

As an alternate activity, you may ask students either to imagine the most terrifying enemy possible and describe this imaginary person, or to write about what the word *ruthless* means to them.

SPELLING AND VOCABULARY WORDS FROM THE SELECTION

brandish	scourge
career	straits
grovel	tempered
implore	tripod
recourse	whetted
rend	wrought

LITERARY TECHNIQUE

EPITHET

Inform students that an **epithet** is a word or phrase used to describe a characteristic of a person, place, or thing. For example, Achilles is often described as "swift-footed Achilles," "Achilles the runner," "Achilles the racer," "godlike Achilles," or "brilliant Achilles," and Hector is often called "Hector breaker of horses." Many stock epithets appear in the *Iliad,* partly because this epic was composed and heard through the oral tradition. These epithets that often appear with or instead of a character's name helped both the audience to follow the narrative and the poet to improvise the story. They were standard patterns of words that would have been easy for the poet to memorize.

You might have students list all the epithets they find for characters in this selection. Encourage them to discuss what each epithet reveals about the personal qualities of each character. In what way does the author intend for us to view this character?

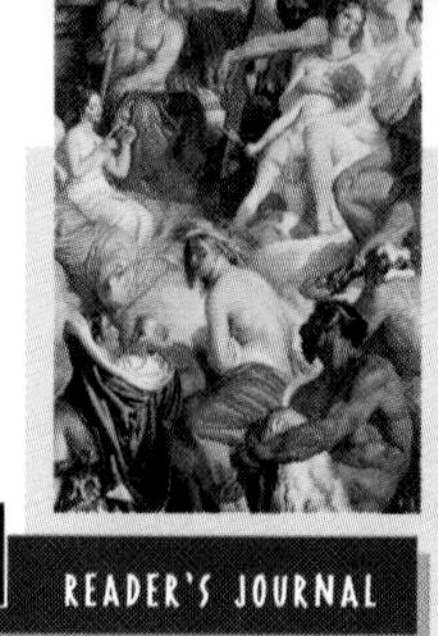

What images does the word *revenge* bring to your mind? What emotions do you think a person seeking revenge feels? Is vengeance always the best way to deal with people who have wronged you? Why, or why not?

READER'S JOURNAL

FROM THE

Iliad

HOMER, TRANSLATED BY ROBERT FAGLES

Characters in the *Iliad*

MORTALS

Achilles (ə kil´ēz´), Achaean warrior and the hero of the *Iliad.* His actions and development as a character are the focus of the epic.

Agamemnon (ag´ə mem´nän´), Achaean commander-in-chief whose disagreement and rivalry with Achilles place the Achaeans at risk of losing the war to the Trojans

Hector (hek´tər), Trojan war leader. He becomes the object of Achilles's anger when he kills Achilles's friend Patroclus.

Menelaus (me ne lā´əs), Achaean soldier and king, brother of Agamemnon, and husband of Helen, for whom the Trojan War is fought

Patroclus (pə trō´kləs), close and loyal friend of Achilles. His death at the hands of Hector fills Achilles with rage.

Priam (prī´əm), king of Troy and the father of Hector

GODS

Apollo (ə pä´ lō), god of music, poetry, wisdom, light, and truth. He is often referred to as Phoebus Apollo. Phoebus means "shining," and in later myths he was often called the god of the sun. Apollo fights on the side of the Trojans.

Ares (er´ēz´), cruel god of war who delights in slaughter. His companions are Discord, Strife, Terror, and Panic.

Athena (ə thē´nə), goddess of wisdom who aids the Achaeans. She is also referred to as Pallas Athena.

Hera (hir´ə), queen of the gods and the wife of Zeus. She is the enemy of the Trojans and wants to see them defeated.

Thetis (thēt´is), a Nereid, or sea goddess, and the mother of Achilles. She helps Achilles in his disagreement with Agamemnon.

Zeus (zo͞os), king of the gods. He holds ultimate authority over the actions and interventions of the gods in mortal affairs. He remains fairly neutral throughout the Trojan war.

FROM BOOK 22
THE DEATH OF HECTOR

[Editor's note: At the beginning of the Iliad, Agamemnon, the Achaean war leader, and Achilles have an argument which results in Agamemnon claiming Achilles's war prize as his own. Enraged by Agamemnon's arrogance, Achilles vows never to aid the Achaeans in the battle against the Trojans. He warns that some day the Achaeans will need his aid and that then Agamemnon will regret his deeds. True to Achilles's prediction, the Trojans, led by the mighty Hector, defeat the Achaeans in one battle after another. Finally, Achilles's best friend and constant companion, Patroclus, begs him to aid the Achaeans. Achilles relents long enough to allow Patroclus to fight in Achilles's armor, an action by which Patroclus hopes to shake the confidence of the Trojans. Patroclus, however, dies in the ensuing battle, with Hector dealing his death blow. Hector then removes Achilles's armor from Patroclus's body and claims it for his own. Achilles, overwhelmed by grief when he learns of Patroclus's death, decides to end his disagreement with Agamemnon and to avenge himself upon Hector. Just before this selection begins, Hector stands alone outside Troy's gates as Achilles approaches. Hector's parents, King Priam and Queen Hecuba, beg Hector to return inside the gates, but to no avail.]

So they wept, the two of them crying out
to their dear son, both pleading time and again
but they could not shake the fixed resolve of Hector.
No, he waited Achilles, coming on, gigantic in power.
As a snake in the hills, guarding his hole, awaits a man—
bloated with poison, deadly hatred seething inside him,
glances flashing fire as he coils round his lair . . .
so Hector, nursing his quenchless fury, gave no ground,

Mask of Agamemnon. *Athens Museum, Athens, Greece. Silvio Fiore/Superstock*

LITERARY NOTE

Before students read the selection from the *Iliad,* you might encourage them to read or reread Themes: The Hero and the Quest, on page 516. Point out that the path of the hero is something that Achilles chose. When Achilles was a boy, his father Peleus heard an oracle reveal that Achilles would die fighting at Troy. To avoid this fate, Peleus sent his son to a distant court and had him dressed as a girl and kept among the women of the court. When Achilles refuses to fight for the Achaeans after his argument with Agamemnon, he is aware of the two possible paths ahead of him—if he avoids fighting in the Trojan War he will live a long, insignificant, and unremembered life, but if he fights, he will die young but be remembered always as a great hero. Thus, once Achilles decides to take up arms again, he has also decided to seek everlasting fame and an early death. Point out that the Greek term for lasting glory and fame after death conferred by the poets is *kléos.* The ancient Greeks placed great value on *kléos,* and Achilles's inevitable decision, as a hero, to pursue *kléos* rather than longevity is part of what makes him an early example of a tragic hero.

You may also wish to point out that in this epic Patroclus is Achilles's *therápon,* or ritual substitute. Like Gilgamesh and Enkidu, the two are constant companions and best friends. Just as Enkidu's death foreshadows Gilgamesh's own eventual death and sparks his journey, Patroclus's death compels Achilles to join in the fight against the Trojans, which he realizes will hasten his own death.

Encourage students to discuss how Achilles is similar to or different from other heroes they have encountered in their reading.

Answers to Guided Reading Questions

❶ Hector feels that he must fight Achilles because Achilles destroyed his army. Because he decided to risk his forces against Achilles, he feels he will have to enter Troy in shame if he does not fight Achilles to the death. He does not want to face the men and women of Troy.

❷ Hector is tempted to end the fighting by telling Achilles he will give Helen and all the treasure of Troy back to the Achaeans.

❸ Hector realizes that Achilles will not listen to reason and will not show him any mercy. He believes Achilles would kill him right away if he tried to parley.

Literary Note

You may wish to share with students the Greek legends about what happened to Agamemnon, king of Mycenae and commander of the Greek forces, immediately before and after the war. Agamemnon was married to Clytemnestra, and together they had four children, Orestes, Iphigeneia, Electra, and Chrysothemis. When Agamemnon assembled the fleet to venture to Troy to wage war, he incurred the wrath of Artemis, who controlled the winds so that Agamemnon and his fleet could not set sail. To appease Artemis, Agamemnon sacrificed his own daughter, Iphigeneia. This action deeply horrified Clytemnestra. While Agamemnon was away, Clytemnestra fell in love with a man named Aegisthus, and together they plotted against Agamemnon. When Agamemnon returned to Greece, he brought with him one of King Priam's daughters, Cassandra. She had been doomed by the god Apollo to speak prophecies no one would believe. Clytemnestra gives Agamemnon a royal welcome, but Cassandra predicts that both she

(cont.)

leaning his burnished shield against a jutting wall,
but harried still, he probed his own brave heart:
"No way out. If I slip inside the gates and walls,
Polydamas will be first to heap disgrace on me—
he was the one who urged me to lead our Trojans
back to Ilium[1] just last night, the disastrous night
Achilles rose in arms like a god. But did I give way?
Not at all. And how much better it would have been!
Now my army's ruined, thanks to my own reckless pride.
I would die of shame to face the men of Troy
and the Trojan women trailing their long robes . . .
Someone less of a man than I will say, 'Our Hector—
staking all on his own strength, he destroyed his army!'
So they will mutter. So now, better by far for me
to stand up to Achilles, kill him, come home alive
or die at his hands in glory out before the walls.
But wait—what if I put down my studded shield
and heavy helmet, prop my spear on the rampart
and go forth, just as I am, to meet Achilles,
noble Prince Achilles . . .
why, I could promise to give back Helen,[2] yes,
and all her treasures with her, all those riches
Paris once hauled home to Troy in the hollow ships—
and they were the cause of all our endless fighting—
Yes, yes, return it all to the sons of Atreus now
to haul away, and then, at the same time, divide
the rest with all the Argives, all the city holds,
and then I'd take an oath for the Trojan royal council
that we will hide nothing! Share and share alike the hoards
our handsome citadel stores within its depths and—
Why debate, my friend? Why thrash things out?
I must not go and <u>implore</u> him. He'll show no mercy,
no respect for me, my rights—he'll cut me down
straight off—stripped of defenses like a woman
once I have loosed the armor off my body.
No way to parley[3] with that man—not now—
not from behind some oak or rock to whisper,
like a boy and a young girl, lovers' secrets —
a boy and girl might whisper to each other . . .

❶ *Why does Hector feel that he must fight Achilles? Why does he feel shame? Whom does he not want to face unless he challenges Achilles alone?*

❷ *What is Hector tempted to do?*

❸ *Why does Hector decide not to try to reason with Achilles? What does he believe would happen if he tried to do this?*

1. **Ilium.** Another name for Troy
2. **Helen.** Wife of Menelaus. It was her removal to Troy by Hector's brother Paris that began the war.
3. **parley.** Have a conference or discussion, especially with an enemy

Words for Everyday Use

im • plore (im plôr´) *vt.,* beg

Vocabulary in Context

- To <u>implore</u> forgiveness from Achilles was a useless task; his heart was hardened after Patroclus's death.

Better to clash in battle, now, at once—
see which fighter Zeus awards the glory!"
So he wavered,
waiting there, but Achilles was closing on him now
like the god of war, the fighter's helmet flashing,
over his right shoulder shaking the Pelian ash spear,
that terror, and the bronze around his body flared
like a raging fire or the rising, blazing sun.
Hector looked up, saw him, started to tremble,
nerve gone, he could hold his ground no longer,
he left the gates behind and away he fled in fear—
and Achilles went for him, fast, sure of his speed
as the wild mountain hawk, the quickest thing on wings,
launching smoothly, swooping down on a cringing dove
and the dove flits out from under, the hawk screaming
over the quarry, plunging over and over, his fury
driving him down to beak and tear his kill—
so Achilles flew at him, breakneck on in fury
with Hector fleeing along the walls of Troy,
fast as his legs would go. On and on they raced,
passing the lookout point, passing the wild fig tree
tossed by the wind, always out from under the ramparts
down the wagon trail they <u>careered</u> until they reached
the clear running springs where whirling Scamander[4]
rises up from its double wellsprings bubbling strong—
and one runs hot and the steam goes up around it,
drifting thick as if fire burned at its core
but the other even in summer gushes cold
as hail or freezing snow or water chilled to ice . . .
And here, close to the springs, lie washing-pools
scooped out in the hollow rocks and broad and smooth
where the wives of Troy and all their lovely daughters
would wash their glistening robes in the old days,
the days of peace before the sons of Achaea came . . .
Past these they raced, one escaping, one in pursuit
and the one who fled was great but the one pursuing
greater, even greater—their pace mounting in speed
since both men strove, not for a sacrificial beast
or oxhide trophy, prizes runners fight for, no,
they raced for the life of Hector breaker of horses.
Like powerful stallions sweeping round the post for trophies,

❶ *What does Hector do when he sees Achilles approaching? What does Achilles do? To what is this encounter compared?*

4. **Scamander.** River god and chief river on the Trojan plain. The gods called the same river Xanthus.

Words for Everyday Use

ca • reer (kər rir´) *vi.,* rush

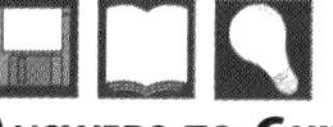

Answers to Guided Reading Questions

❶ Hector starts to tremble and then flees when Achilles approaches. Achilles chases him. This encounter is compared to a wild mountain hawk flying after a cringing dove.

Literary Note (cont.)

and Agamemnon will be killed. Of course her prediction goes unheeded, and Clytemnestra and Aegisthus kill Agamemnon as he bathes and then kill Cassandra as well. Fearing her son will avenge his father's death, Clytemnestra sends Orestes away. When he returns many years later, both he and his sister Electra still desire revenge. To test his mother, Orestes comes to her in disguise and tells her that her only son has died. When he detects that she seems secretly joyful, Orestes kills Aegisthus and Clytemnestra. This bloody tale about the house of Atreus was the subject of the playwright Aeschylus's trilogy *Oresteia,* and both Sophocles and Euripides wrote tragedies on this subject. Ironically, although Agamemnon risked his life in battle, his life is most in danger when he returns home. The violence that would erupt in his family is already foreshadowed when he sacrifices his own daughter to set sail for the Trojan War.

Vocabulary in Context

• The driver would <u>career</u> his chariot around corners so quickly that it would almost tip over.

Quotables

"For so much suffering,
I tell you, someone plots revenge."

—Aeschylus

(Cassandra's words in *Agamemnon* from the *Oresteia*)

Answers to Guided Reading Questions

❶ Zeus feels grief for Hector because Hector made many sacrifices to Zeus. The gods must decide if Hector is to live or die.

❷ Athena says that if Zeus spares Hector, the gods will never again praise Zeus.

Cross-curricular Activities

MATHEMATICS AND SCIENCES AND ARTS AND HUMANITIES

Inform students that the Greek gods are, essentially, personified elements of nature. As such, they reveal qualities that may seem more human than godlike to a modern audience. For example, the gods argue with each other, and the immortals are as concerned with praise and reputation as the mortal Greek heroes. The Greeks also believed that the gods took an active interest in the human world—the gods take sides in the Trojan War and even affect the outcome of certain events. Based on what students learn of the Greek gods on this and following pages, encourage them to complete one of the following activities.

- Zeus, king of the gods, is also the god of lightning and thunder. Many cultures, including the Hindus and the Norse, have viewed thunder and lightning as the actions of a god. Interested students may prepare written reports on the scientific causes of the natural phemonena of lightning and thunder.
- Students might write journal entries describing their thoughts about the Greek gods, or they might write a brief, humorous scene in which the gods seem more human than godlike.
- Some students may enjoy creating artistic representations of the gods described in this section of the *Iliad*. What do the gods in council look like? How does Athena appear as she interacts with Achilles?

galloping full stretch with some fine prize at stake,
a tripod, say, or woman offered up at funeral games
for some brave hero fallen—so the two of them
whirled three times around the city of Priam,
sprinting at top speed while all the gods gazed down
and the father of men and gods broke forth among them now:
"Unbearable—a man I love, hunted round his own city walls
and right before my eyes. My heart grieves for Hector.
Hector who burned so many oxen in my honor, rich cuts
now on the rugged crests of Ida, now on Ilium's heights.
But now, look, brilliant Achilles courses him round
the city of Priam in all his savage, lethal speed.
Come, you immortals, think this through. Decide.
Either we pluck the man from death and save his life
or strike him down at last, here at Achilles' hands—
for all his fighting heart."
But immortal Athena,
her gray eyes wide, protested strongly: "Father!
Lord of the lightning, king of the black cloud,
what are you saying? A man, a mere mortal,
his doom sealed long ago? You'd set him free
from all the pains of death?
Do as you please—
but none of the deathless gods will ever praise you."

❶ Why does Zeus feel grief for Hector? What must the gods decide?

❷ How does Athena say the other gods will respond if Zeus spares Hector?

And Zeus who marshals the thunderheads replied,
"Courage, Athena, third-born of the gods, dear child.
Nothing I said was meant in earnest, trust me,
I mean you all the good will in the world. Go.
Do as your own impulse bids you. Hold back no more."

So he launched Athena already poised for action—
down the goddess swept from Olympus' craggy peaks.

And swift Achilles kept on coursing Hector, nonstop
as a hound in the mountains starts a fawn from its lair,
hunting him down the gorges, down the narrow glens
and the fawn goes to ground, hiding deep in brush
but the hound comes racing fast, nosing him out
until he lands his kill. So Hector could never throw
Achilles off his trail, the swift racer Achilles—
time and again he'd make a dash for the Dardan Gates,

Words for Everyday Use

tri • pod (trī´päd) *n.*, three-legged caldron, or large kettle

Vocabulary in Context

- A *chüeh* is a bronze tripod, or vessel with three legs, that was used in sacrificial rites during the Shang period in China.

trying to rush beneath the rock-built ramparts, hoping
men on the heights might save him, somehow, raining spears
but time and again Achilles would intercept him quickly,
heading him off, forcing him out across the plain
and always sprinting along the city side himself—
endless as in a dream . . .
when a man can't catch another fleeing on ahead
and he can never escape nor his rival overtake him—
so the one could never run the other down in his speed
nor the other spring away. And how could Hector have fled
the fates of death so long? How unless one last time,
one final time Apollo had swept in close beside him,
driving strength in his legs and knees to race the wind?
And brilliant Achilles shook his head at the armies,
never letting them hurl their sharp spears at Hector—
someone might snatch the glory, Achilles come in second.
But once they reached the springs for the fourth time,
then Father Zeus held out his sacred golden scales:
in them he placed two fates of death that lays men low—
one for Achilles, one for Hector breaker of horses—
and gripping the beam mid-haft the Father raised it high
and down went Hector's day of doom, dragging him down
to the strong House of Death—and god Apollo left him.
Athena rushed to Achilles, her bright eyes gleaming,
standing shoulder-to-shoulder, winging orders now:
"At last our hopes run high, my brilliant Achilles—
Father Zeus must love you—
we'll sweep great glory back to Achaea's fleet,
we'll kill this Hector, mad as he is for battle!
No way for him to escape us now, no longer—
not even if Phoebus the distant deadly Archer
goes through torments, pleading for Hector's life,
groveling over and over before our storming Father Zeus.
But you, you hold your ground and catch your breath
while I run Hector down and persuade the man
to fight you face-to-face."
So Athena commanded
and he obeyed, rejoicing at heart—Achilles stopped,
leaning against his ashen spearshaft barbed in bronze.
And Athena left him there, caught up with Hector at once,
and taking the build and vibrant voice of Deiphobus[5]
stood shoulder-to-shoulder with him, winging orders:

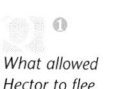

❶ *What allowed Hector to flee from death for so long?*

❷ *What happens when Zeus takes out the sacred golden scales? What does Athena promise Achilles? What must she persuade Hector to do?*

5. **Deiphobus.** Son of Priam

WORDS FOR EVERYDAY USE

grov • el (gruv´əl) *vi.,* lie prone or crawl in a prostrate position; behave humbly or abjectly, as before authority

ANSWERS TO GUIDED READING QUESTIONS

❶ Hector fled from death for so long because Apollo gave him strength.

❷ Zeus weighs Hector's fate against Achilles's fate and finds that it is to be Hector's day of doom. Athena promises Achilles that they will kill Hector. She must persuade Hector to fight Achilles face-to-face.

LITERARY TECHNIQUE

HOMERIC SIMILE

A **simile** is a comparison using *like* or *as.* **Homeric** similes, or extended similes of two to twenty lines, appear throughout the *Iliad* and other epics and contribute to the epic's high style. Homeric similes typically have an *as . . . so* construction. Ask students the following questions: What Homeric simile does Homer use to describe Hector's attempt to flee Achilles in lines 129–134? What two things are being compared? In what ways are these two things alike?

ANSWERS

Homer says that Hector's "always sprinting along the city side himself" is "endless as in a dream." Homer is comparing Hector's experience of being pursued to a dream. This experience may very well seem like a nightmare to Hector because it is so frightening and it seems that the chase will have no end.

ADDITIONAL QUESTIONS AND ACTIVITIES

Ask students the following questions: What does Zeus do to decide the fate of these two men? What does Athena say to Achilles after this judgment? Are her words true, or was the decision a matter of chance?

(cont.)

VOCABULARY IN CONTEXT

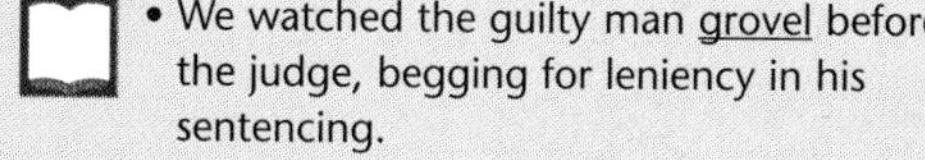

• We watched the guilty man grovel before the judge, begging for leniency in his sentencing.

ADDITIONAL QUESTIONS AND ACTIVITIES (CONT.)

ANSWERS

Zeus weighs the men's fates against each other in a golden scale. Athena says that Zeus must love Achilles. This is not strictly true because the judgment was the result of chance, not favor.

Answers to Guided Reading Questions

❶ Athena pretends to be Hector's brother Deiphobus coming to his aid.

❷ Hector swears that if he kills Achilles he will treat the body honorably and return it to his companions.

❸ Achilles says Hector's actions are so unforgivable that there can be no pact between them. He compares himself and Hector to "men and lions—/wolves and lambs [that] can enjoy no meeting of the minds."

Additional Questions and Activities

Encourage students to debate whether this fight between Achilles and Hector is fair. Tell them to support their opinions with evidence from the text.

Students might also, either in group discussion or in a piece of critical writing, compare and contrast Achilles, great hero of the Achaeans, and Hector, great hero of the Trojans. In their discussion or writing, students may wish to consider which hero is presented as more "human" and which is presented as "godlike," or as a force of nature.

Another possible topic for an essay would be to compare the conflict between Achilles and Hector and its end result to the conflict between Aeneas and Dido in the *Aeneid* (see page 222), between the city and the cats in "The Garden of the Stubborn Cats" (see page 406), between the cockroaches and the narrator in "The Fifth Story" (see page 474), or between Cain and Abel in Genesis (see page 518).

"Dear brother, how brutally swift Achilles hunts you—
Come, let us stand our ground together—beat him back."

"Deiphobus!"—Hector, his helmet flashing, called out to her—
"dearest of all my brothers, all these warring years,
of all the sons that Priam and Hecuba produced!
Now I'm determined to praise you all the more,
you who dared—seeing me in these straits—
to venture out from the walls, all for *my* sake,
while the others stay inside and cling to safety."

Q ❶ *How does Athena try to deceive Hector into fighting Achilles "face-to-face"?*

The goddess answered quickly, her eyes blazing,
"True, dear brother—how your father and mother both
implored me, time and again, clutching my knees,
and the comrades round me begging me to stay!
Such was the fear that broke them, man for man,
but the heart within me broke with grief for you.
Now headlong on and fight! No letup, no lance spared!
So now, now we'll *see* if Achilles kills us both
and hauls our bloody armor back to the beaked ships
or he goes down in pain beneath your spear."

Athena luring him on with all her immortal cunning—
and now, at last, as the two came closing for the kill
it was tall Hector, helmet flashing, who led off:
"No more running from you in fear, Achilles!
Not as before. Three times I fled around
the great city of Priam—I lacked courage then
to stand your onslaught. Now my spirit stirs me
to meet you face-to-face. Now kill or be killed!
Come, we'll swear to the gods, the highest witnesses—
the gods will oversee our binding pacts. I swear
I will never mutilate you—merciless as you are—
if Zeus allows me to last it out and tear your life away.
But once I've stripped your glorious armor, Achilles,
I will give your body back to your loyal comrades.
Swear you'll do the same."
A swift dark glance
and the headstrong runner answered, "Hector, stop!
You unforgivable, you . . . don't talk to me of pacts.
There are no binding oaths between men and lions—
wolves and lambs can enjoy no meeting of the minds—

Q ❷ *What does Hector swear?*

Q ❸ *Why won't Achilles swear the same oath? To what does he compare himself and Hector?*

Words for Everyday Use

straits (strātz) *n.,* difficulty, distress

Vocabulary in Context

- When Adam's car skidded off the road into a snowbank and his tires only dug him deeper into the icy drift, he knew he would require help to free himself from these straits.

Fresco of the Iliad. *Sabatelli*
Scala/Art Resource, New York

they are all bent on hating each other to the death.
So with you and me. No love between us. No truce
till one or the other falls and gluts with blood
Ares who hacks at men behind his rawhide shield.
Come, call up whatever courage you can muster.
Life or death—now prove yourself a spearman,
a daring man of war! No more escape for you—
Athena will kill you with my spear in just a moment.
Now you'll pay at a stroke for all my comrades' grief,
all you killed in the fury of your spear!"
With that,
shaft poised, he hurled and his spear's long shadow flew
but seeing it coming glorious Hector ducked away,
crouching down, watching the bronze tip fly past
and stab the earth—but Athena snatched it up
and passed it back to Achilles
and Hector the gallant captain never saw her.
He sounded out a challenge to Peleus' princely son:
"You missed, look—the great godlike Achilles!
So you knew nothing at all from Zeus about my death—

 ❶

What happens when Achilles throws a spear at Hector? What does Athena do?

Answers to Guided Reading Questions

❶ Achilles misses Hector with the spear, but Athena rushes to grab it and give it back to Achilles.

Literary Note

Achilles and Odysseus are the two greatest heroes of ancient Greece, yet they are more different than alike. For example, while in the *Iliad* Achilles dies in a foreign land and is denied a *nóstos,* or homecoming, the entire focus of the *Odyssey* is Odysseus's *nóstos.* Achilles is known for courage and skill in battle, as befits the *Iliad,* while the main quality that helps Odysseus on his journey is his cleverness. Achilles's enemies are neither good nor evil, but are well-rounded, complex, and sympathetic characters. Odysseus's enemies in the *Odyssey* tend to be outright villains. If students have read the *Odyssey* or have read portions of the epic, you might encourage them to complete one of the following activities:

- Students might hold a group discussion in which they examine the similarities and differences between Achilles and Odysseus and list these similar and dissimilar qualities in a simple graphic organizer, such as a Venn diagram. (See the Language Arts Survey 1.10, "Gathering Ideas.")
- Interested students might write a critical essay comparing and contrasting these two heroes and analyzing what their similarities and differences reveal about Greek values. (See the Language Arts Survey 1.20, "Writing a Critical Essay.")
- Students may enjoy writing a humorous scene featuring one or both heroes in which students exaggerate certain elements of their character or characters.

Answers to Guided Reading Questions

❶ Hector says that Achilles's death would make the war much easier for the Trojans because Achilles has been their "greatest scourge."

❷ Hector realizes that Athena has tricked him when he calls out for Deiphobus for a lance and the man has disappeared. He realizes that Deiphobus was never really there. He refuses to give in and goes to meet his doom with glory. He pulls out his sharpened sword, swinging it at Achilles.

Cultural/Historical Note

Inform students that the heroes described in the *Iliad* would have been the leaders and kings of Greece's Mycenaean age. During this period, many different cities, each with their own governments, flourished. Among them were Agamemnon's Mycenae; Thebes, where Oedipus was one of the legendary kings; Pylos, where the ancient hero Nestor was king; Menelaus's Sparta; and Tiryns. The bronze age cultures in these cities developed a form of writing known as Linear B, and many of them accumulated great wealth. If the Trojan War actually did take place around 1250 BC, when the heroes of the Trojan War returned home, they returned to a changing land. Ironically, although the Greeks returned as victors, having plunged Troy into chaos, they soon struggled to hold their own civilization together. Perhaps because the leaders of these city-states were gone for so long, civil unrest was becoming more of a problem. Toward the end of the thirteenth century, many of the palaces of the Mycenaean age were burned and leveled, and people fled the cities. Different scholars have speculated that drought, famine, epidemics, unrest, or bands of invaders may have been responsible for the weakening of the Mycenaean cities and the abandonment (cont.)

and yet how sure you were! All bluff, cunning with words,
that's all you are—trying to make me fear you,
lose my nerve, forget my fighting strength.
Well, you'll never plant your lance in my back
as I flee *you* in fear—plunge it through my chest
as I come charging in, if a god gives you the chance!
But now it's for you to dodge *my* brazen spear—
I wish you'd bury it in your body to the hilt.
How much lighter the war would be for Trojans then
if you, their greatest scourge, were dead and gone!"

❶ *According to Hector, what would Achilles's death mean for the Trojans?*

Shaft poised, he hurled and his spear's long shadow flew
and it struck Achilles' shield—a dead-center hit—
but off and away it glanced and Hector seethed,
his hurtling spear, his whole arm's power poured
in a wasted shot. He stood there, cast down . . .
he had no spear in reserve. So Hector shouted out
to Deiphobus bearing his white shield—with a ringing shout
he called for a heavy lance—
but the man was nowhere near him,
vanished—
yes and Hector knew the truth in his heart
and the fighter cried aloud, "My time has come!
At last the gods have called me down to death.
I thought he was at my side, the hero Deiphobus—
he's safe inside the walls, Athena's tricked me blind.
And now death, grim death is looming up beside me,
no longer far away. No way to escape it now. This,
this was their pleasure after all, sealed long ago—
Zeus and the son of Zeus, the distant deadly Archer—
though often before now they rushed to my defense.
So now I meet my doom. Well let me die—
but not without struggle, not without glory, no,
in some great clash of arms that even men to come
will hear of down the years!"
And on that resolve
he drew the whetted sword that hung at his side,
tempered, massive, and gathering all his force
he swooped like a soaring eagle
launching down from the dark clouds to earth
to snatch some helpless lamb or trembling hare.
So Hector swooped now, swinging his whetted sword

❷ *When does Hector realize that Athena had tricked him? What is his attitude toward his inevitable death? What does he do in his attempt to die with glory?*

Words for Everyday Use

scourge (skurj) *n.*, means of inflicting severe punishment, suffering, or vengeance

whet • ted (hwet´əd) *adj.*, sharpened

tem • per • ed (tem´pərd) *adj.*, brought to proper texture, hardness, and strength

Vocabulary in Context

- The Black Death was a scourge upon medieval Europe, claiming millions of lives.
- The burly young hero whetted his sword against the stone to prepare for battle.
- Before metal is tempered, it can shatter with a single blow.

and Achilles charged too, bursting with rage, barbaric,
guarding his chest with the well-wrought blazoned shield,
head tossing his gleaming helmet, four horns strong
and the golden plumes shook that the god of fire
drove in bristling thick along its ridge.
Bright as that star amid the stars in the night sky,
star of the evening, brightest star that rides the heavens,
so fire flared from the sharp point of the spear Achilles
brandished high in his right hand, bent on Hector's death,
scanning his splendid body—where to pierce it best?
The rest of his flesh seemed all encased in armor,
burnished, brazen—*Achilles'* armor that Hector stripped
from strong Patroclus when he killed him—true,
but one spot lay exposed,
where collarbones lift the neckbone off the shoulders,
the open throat, where the end of life comes quickest—*there*
as Hector charged in fury brilliant Achilles drove his spear
and the point went stabbing clean through the tender neck
but the heavy bronze weapon failed to slash the windpipe—
Hector could still gasp out some words, some last reply . . .
he crashed in the dust—
godlike Achilles gloried over him:
"Hector—surely you thought when you stripped Patroclus' armor
that you, you would be safe! Never a fear of me—
far from the fighting as I was—you fool!
Left behind there, down by the beaked ships
his great avenger waited, a greater man by far—
that man was I, and I smashed your strength! And you—
the dogs and birds will maul you, shame your corpse
while Achaeans bury my dear friend in glory!"

Struggling for breath, Hector, his helmet flashing,
said, "I beg you, beg you by your life, your parents—
don't let the dogs devour me by the Argive ships!
Wait, take the princely ransom of bronze and gold,
the gifts my father and noble mother will give you—
but give my body to friends to carry home again,
so Trojan men and Trojan women can do me honor
with fitting rites of fire once I am dead."

Staring grimly, the proud runner Achilles answered,
"Beg no more, you fawning dog—begging me by my parents!

❶ *Whose armor is Hector wearing? What vulnerability does Achilles detect?*

❷ *What does Achilles say to taunt Hector?*

❸ *What does Hector fear might happen to his body after he is dead? What last request does he make of Achilles?*

Words for Everyday Use

wrought (rôt) *adj.,* shaped and designed

bran • dish (bran´dish) *vt.,* wave, shake, or exhibit in a menacing or challenging way

Vocabulary in Context

- Hephaestus could hammer swords and tools of iron at his forge, but he could also create intricately wrought ornaments of silver and gold.
- The Viking warrior was particularly terrifying in appearance when he brandished his battle axe.

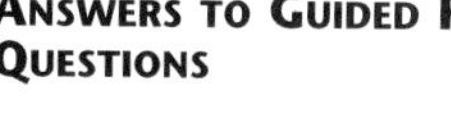

Answers to Guided Reading Questions

❶ Hector is wearing Achilles's armor, which he won after he killed Patroclus, as Patroclus wore it. Achilles sees a place near Hector's throat that the armor leaves exposed.

❷ Achilles says that Hector thought he would be safe wearing the armor he stripped from Patroclus, but now dogs and birds will tear at his body.

❸ Hector fears that his body will be destroyed and that he will not get a proper burial. He requests that Achilles accept a ransom for his body and return it to the Trojans.

Cultural/Historical Note (cont.)

or destruction of many of them. With the fall of the cities, standards of living declined, writing was forgotten, and chaos emerged. New peoples, including the Dorians, migrated into Greece. In short, the Heroic Age had come to an end, and the Greek Dark Ages emerged (1100–900 BC). Nevertheless, it was during these Dark Ages that poets of the oral tradition, such as Homer, composed and told tales about the noble exploits of a race of heroes from the bygone Mycenaean age.

Literary Technique

Irony of Situation

Irony is a difference between appearance and reality. **Irony of situation** occurs when an event violates the expectations of the characters, the reader, or the audience. Encourage students to discuss why Achilles's finding a weakness in the armor that Hector wears is an example of irony of situation.

Answers

The situation is ironic because Hector's armor was originally Achilles's, and so Hector may have used the same weak spot to kill Achilles if he had not taken the armor from Patroclus's body.

Answers to Guided Reading Questions

❶ Achilles is not sympathetic, and he promises Hector that dogs and birds will devour his body.

Selection Check Test with Answers

EX. Who begs Hector to come back inside Troy's gates?
Hector's parents beg him to come back inside Troy's gates.

1. Whom does Hector consider giving back to the Achaeans?
Hector considers giving Helen back to the Achaeans.

2. Who helps Achilles in his face-to-face confrontation with Hector?
Athena helps Achilles.

3. What is the end result of the conflict between Achilles and Hector?
Achilles kills Hector.

4. What does Achilles remember about Patroclus?
He remembers that Patroclus has not yet been buried.

5. What does Achilles do as his final outrage upon Hector's body?
Achilles lashes Hector's body by the ankles to his chariot and drives it around, dragging Hector's head in the dust.

Cross-curricular Activities

Mathematics and Science and Social Studies

Inform students that in 1822, Charles McLaren identified a mound called Hissarlik as the site of Homeric Troy. Since that time the city has been excavated and a number of different ruins found, although scholars still debate which level of the city would correspond to the Troy the Achaeans destroyed. Interested students might work together to prepare reports on the archaeological discoveries of Heinrich Schliemann and Wilhelm Dörpfeld at the ruins of Troy.

Achilles dragging Hector. *c. 520 BC. Attic; attributed to the Antiope Group. William Francis Warden Fund. Museum of Fine Arts, Boston*

Would to god my rage, my fury would drive me now
to hack your flesh away and eat you raw—
such agonies you have caused me! Ransom?
No man alive could keep the dog-packs off you
not if they haul in ten, twenty times that ransom
and pile it here before me and promise fortunes more—
no, not even if Dardan Priam should offer to weigh out
your bulk in gold! Not even then will your noble mother
lay you on your deathbed, mourn the son she bore . . .
The dogs and birds will rend you—blood and bone!"

Q ❶ *Is Achilles sympathetic to Hector's request? According to Achilles, what will happen to Hector's body?*

At the point of death, Hector, his helmet flashing,
said, "I know you well—I see my fate before me.
Never a chance that I could win you over . . .
Iron inside your chest, that heart of yours.

Words for Everyday Use

rend (rend) *vt.*, tear, pull, or rip with violence

Vocabulary in Context

- If you walk through that patch of thorns and briars, I guarantee you will rend your new pants beyond recognition.

But now beware, or my curse will draw god's wrath
upon your head, that day when Paris and lord Apollo—
for all your fighting heart—destroy you at the Scaean Gates!"

Death cut him short. The end closed in around him.
Flying free of his limbs
his soul went winging down to the House of Death,
wailing his fate, leaving his manhood far behind,
his young and supple strength. But brilliant Achilles
taunted Hector's body, dead as he was, "Die, die!
For my own death, I'll meet it freely—whenever Zeus
and the other deathless gods would like to bring it on!"

With that he wrenched his bronze spear from the corpse,
laid it aside and ripped the bloody armor off the back.
And the other sons of Achaea, running up around him,
crowded closer, all of them gazing wonder-struck
at the build and marvelous, lithe beauty of Hector.
And not a man came forward who did not stab his body,
glancing toward a comrade, laughing: "Ah, look here—
how much softer he is to handle now, this Hector,
than when he gutted our ships with roaring fire!"

Standing over him, so they'd gloat and stab his body.
But once he had stripped the corpse the proud runner Achilles
took his stand in the midst of all the Argive troops
and urged them on with a flight of winging orders.
"Friends—lords of the Argives, O my captains!
Now that the gods have let me kill this man
who caused us agonies, loss on crushing loss—
more than the rest of all their men combined—
come, let us ring their walls in armor, test them,
see what recourse the Trojans still may have in mind.
Will they abandon the city heights with this man fallen?
Or brace for a last, dying stand though Hector's gone?
But wait—what am I saying? Why this deep debate?
Down by the ships a body lies unwept, unburied—
Patroclus . . . I will never forget him,
not as long as I'm still among the living
and my springing knees will lift and drive me on.
Though the dead forget their dead in the House of Death,
I will remember, even there, my dear companion.
Now,

1 *Of what does Hector warn Achilles?*

2 *What attitude does Achilles express toward his own death?*

3 *What do Achilles and his men do to Hector's body?*

4 *What does Achilles wonder about the Trojans? What does he then remember about Patroclus? What does he vow?*

WORDS FOR EVERYDAY USE

re • course (rē´kôrs´) *n.,* something to which one turns for safety or help

VOCABULARY IN CONTEXT

- The troops were so badly outnumbered by their enemy that their only recourse was to flee the battle.

ANSWERS TO GUIDED READING QUESTIONS

1 He warns Achilles that Paris and Apollo will destroy him at the Scaean Gates.

2 Achilles says that he will meet his death whenever the gods desire; he seems to care little about his own eventual death.

3 Achilles and his men strip Hector of his armor and take turns stabbing his body.

4 Achilles wonders if the Trojans will now give up or if they will make a last stand against the Achaeans. He remembers that Patroclus lies unburied. He vows that he will never forget Patroclus even after his own death.

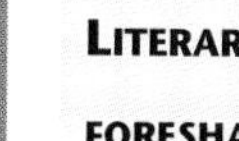

LITERARY TECHNIQUE

FORESHADOWING

Foreshadowing is the act of presenting materials that hint at events to occur later in a story. Ask students to discuss what example of foreshadowing they find in lines 313–325. Why do students believe Achilles doesn't feel more strongly about the event foreshadowed? What does he care about more than this event?

ANSWERS

Achilles's own death is foreshadowed. Hector says that Paris will kill Achilles at the Scaean Gates with Apollo's help. Students may say that Achilles would rather die young with glory than live without glory and without avenging his friend. He cares about honor and revenge.

CULTURAL/HISTORICAL NOTE

Point out that when Achilles mentions the dead forgetting their dead, he is referring to the River Lethe, which was believed to pass through Hades, the underworld. When the dead drank from the river, they forgot their mortal lives.

ANSWERS TO GUIDED READING QUESTIONS

❶ Achilles lashes Hector's body to his chariot by the ankles and then drives around, dragging Hector's head in the dust.

RESPONDING TO THE SELECTION

Encourage students to try to understand each character's point of view, but encourage them to discuss with whom they believe the author intended the audience to sympathize.

ANSWERS FOR REVIEWING THE SELECTION

RECALLING AND INTERPRETING

1. **Recalling.** He considers offering to give Helen back to Menelaus and sharing all the Trojan wealth with the Achaeans in the hope that these actions would put an end to the war. **Interpreting.** Hector knows that Achilles would never accept this bribe. He knows that Achilles is merciless and will kill him right away if he tries to bargain with him.
2. **Recalling.** Zeus allows Athena to talk him out of sparing Hector, and he also allows her to enter the battle on Achilles's side. Athena assists Achilles by tricking Hector into thinking she is another Trojan warrior come to help him fight against Achilles. **Interpreting.** Hector's fatal mistake is allowing himself to be tricked by Athena into facing Achilles in single combat. He believed that with the aid of his brother, Deiphobus, he stood a chance against Achilles in battle.
3. **Recalling.** According to Achilles, dogs and birds will maul the body of Hector as he buries his friend Patroclus in glory. Hector begs Achilles to treat his body with respect and to return it to the people of Troy. (cont.)

come, you sons of Achaea, raise a song of triumph!
Down to the ships we march and bear this corpse on high—
we have won ourselves great glory. We have brought
magnificent Hector down, that man the Trojans
glorified in their city like a god!"
So he triumphed
and now he was bent on outrage, on shaming noble Hector.
Piercing the tendons, ankle to heel behind both feet,
he knotted straps of rawhide through them both,
lashed them to his chariot, left the head to drag
and mounting the car, hoisting the famous arms aboard,
he whipped his team to a run and breakneck on they flew,
holding nothing back. And a thick cloud of dust rose up
from the man they dragged, his dark hair swirling round
that head so handsome once, all tumbled low in the dust—
since Zeus had given him over to his enemies now
to be defiled in the land of his own fathers. ■

❶ *What "outrage" upon Hector's dead body does Achilles commit?*

Responding to the Selection

How would Achilles describe Hector and his actions? How would Hector's parents and the people of Troy describe Achilles? For whom do you feel the most sympathy and understanding?

Reviewing the Selection

RECALLING		INTERPRETING
1. What actions does Hector consider as he waits for Achilles?	▶▶	Why doesn't Hector do either of these things? What does he know about Achilles's character?
2. What does Zeus allow Athena to do? In what way does she assist Achilles?	▶▶	What is Hector's fatal mistake? Why does he make it?
3. According to Achilles, what will happen to the body of Hector as he buries his friend in glory? What does Hector beg of Achilles?	▶▶	Why do you think that simply defeating Hector is not enough for Achilles? Why is his possession of the body an added victory?

ANSWERS FOR REVIEWING THE SELECTION (CONT.)

Interpreting. Defeating Hector is not enough because Achilles is so angry he does not want Hector to die in glory or be honorably buried. He must shame Hector by dragging his body around.

4. **Recalling.** The Achaeans do not attack the Trojans immediately because Achilles remembers that he has left Patroclus's body unburied. Achilles vows that he will never again forget Patroclus, even after his own death. **Interpreting.** Achilles wants to honor Patroclus's body and to savagely dishonor Hector's body. Achilles remembers Patroclus's body while mutilating the body of Hector. It is ironic that Achilles remembers the body of a friend he loved while mutilating the body of an enemy he hated.

(cont.)

4. Why don't the Achaeans attack Troy as Achilles has suggested? What does Achilles vow?

Compare and contrast Achilles's attitude toward Patroclus's body and toward Hector's body. What is significant about the moment when Achilles remembers Patroclus?

SYNTHESIZING

5. Do you think Achilles has found peace in his victory? Do you think that his revenge has gone too far? Explain your response. Why do you think Achilles's anger is so intense, even with his vengeance complete?

Understanding Literature (Questions for Discussion)

1. **Motivation.** A **motivation** is a force that moves a character to think, feel, or behave in a certain way. What is the motivation behind Achilles's return to battle? What is the motivation behind Hector's desire to stand up to the most feared Achaean warrior?

2. **Description.** A **description**, one of the modes of writing, portrays a character, an object, or a scene. In lines 4–7, as Achilles comes upon the city of Troy, prepared to attack Hector, he is described in great detail. What words and phrases describe Achilles? What does this description reveal about Achilles's character?

3. **Style. Style** is the manner in which something is said or written. Traditionally, critics and scholars have referred to three levels of style: high style, for formal occasions or subjects; middle style, for ordinary occasions or subjects; and low style, for extremely informal occasions or subjects. A writer's style depends on many things, including his or her own diction (the words a writer chooses), selection of grammatical structures (simple versus complex sentences, for example), and preference for abstract or concrete words. Identify the style of this epic. Then find examples of diction and grammatical structures that contribute to this style. What other elements of this selection contribute to this style?

4. **Epic.** An **epic** is a long story, often told in verse, involving heroes and gods. Grand in length and scope, an epic provides a portrait of an entire culture, of the legends, beliefs, values, laws, arts, and ways of life of a people. An epic hero, such as Achilles, represents the ideals of the culture that creates him or her. For more information on epic heroes, see Themes: The Hero and the Quest, page 516. Throughout the *Iliad*, Achilles is called "the best of the Achaeans," the epitome of his culture's heroic ideal. Based on this selection, explain whether you find this view of Achilles surprising. Do you consider him heroic? Many readers of Greek literature have noted that Greek heroes are extreme in their actions and attitudes. They constantly strive for excellence, honor, and lasting fame. In doing so, these heroes sometimes develop *hubris*, or excessive pride, which leads them to act recklessly, without thinking of the consequences of their extreme acts. Explain whether you would describe Achilles as extreme. For what does he strive? Does he achieve these things? Explain whether Achilles exhibits *hubris*.

ANSWERS FOR REVIEWING THE SELECTION (CONT.)

SYNTHESIZING

Responses will vary. Possible responses are given.

5. Students may say that it seems that Achilles has not found peace in his victory but is still mad with grief for his friend Patroclus and filled with anger at Hector for killing him. Students may say that the mistreatment of Hector's body by Achilles is a horrific display of revenge that has gone too far. Achilles's anger is probably intensified by his grief for Patroclus.

ANSWERS FOR UNDERSTANDING LITERATURE

Responses will vary. Possible responses are given.

1. Motivation. The motivation behind Achilles's return to battle is the thought of destroying the man who killed his close friend. Hector is ashamed to return and face the Trojans because he risked an army against the Achaeans and Achilles destroyed this army. He also wishes to destroy Achilles, the "scourge" of the Trojans.

2. Description. Achilles is described as "gigantic in power," and as a "snake," "bloated with poison, deadly hatred seething inside him, / glances flashing fire as he coils round his lair." Achilles is so full of rage and hate that he is like a superhuman or a deadly beast. He is a very angry and dangerous person.

3. Style. The epic is written in high style. Students' examples will vary widely, but students should note that Homer's diction is elevated and the grammatical structures are formal. Students might point out that the subject matter—a great war between two peoples—contributes to the high style, as well as the inclusion of gods as characters. In addition, the use of figurative language helps to create the high style of the selection.

(cont.)

ANSWERS FOR UNDERSTANDING LITERATURE (CONT.)

4. Epic. Some students may initially find Achilles a surprising hero because he seems bloodthirsty and cruel. Achilles is definitely an extreme character—his grief for Patroclus is extreme, his rage with Hector is extreme, and the form his vengeance takes is extreme. He strives for honor and to be the best warrior. He also strives to honor his friendship with Patroclus. Students might say that Achilles does achieve these things but that he does display *hubris*—especially in his proud refusal to accept Hector's plea to treat his body with honor.

ANALYTIC SCALES FOR RESPONDING IN WRITING

Assign a score from 1 to 25 for each grading criterion below. (For more detailed evaluation, see the evaluation forms for writing, revising, and proofreading, Assessment Portfolio 4.1–4.9.)

1. Parody

- **Content/Unity.** The parody pokes fun at a Homeric battle scene by describing an everyday conflict in a lofty manner.
- **Organization/Coherence.** The parody presents details in a sensible order.
- **Language/Style.** The parody uses vivid and precise nouns, verbs, and modifiers.
- **Conventions.** The parody avoids errors in spelling, grammar, usage, mechanics, and manuscript form.

► Additional practice is provided in the Essential Skills Practice Book: Writing 1.8.

2. Critical Essay

- **Content/Unity.** The essay explains what the choice of Achilles as a model for the epic hero reveals about the values of the ancient Greeks.
- **Organization/Coherence.** The essay begins with an introduction that includes the thesis of the essay. The introduction is followed by supporting paragraphs with clear transitions. The essay ends with a solid conclusion.
- **Language/Style.** The essay uses vivid and precise nouns, verbs, and modifiers.
- **Conventions.** The essay avoids errors in spelling, grammar, usage, mechanics, and manuscript form.

► Additional practice is provided in the Essential Skills Practice Book: Writing 1.20.

Responding in Writing

1. **Creative Writing: Parody.** The language used to describe the battle between Achilles and Hector is filled with formal but vivid descriptions of the two warriors, and the warriors' speeches, threatening and pleading with each other, are rendered in detail. Write a parody of this battle scene by choosing a very ordinary, everyday conflict and writing about it while trying to emulate the Homeric style. Your parody need not be long; one or two pages will be sufficient. For example, you might begin by deciding to write about the struggle between two kindergarten children for possession during play time of a toy telephone that makes barnyard animal noises. Then exaggerate this struggle by describing it in inflated terms, using Homeric imagery, such as in the following:

   > "Timmy, swift as a leaping tiger, pounced upon the barnyard animal phone, brandishing it between his mighty fists. His eyes shooting fire, his tiny plaid shirt gleaming brightly, he swung the phone above his head and shouted to his grasping foe: 'Unhand me, you insupportable villain. Never shall you possess the magnificent and wondrous barnyard animal phone! Never!'"

2. **Critical Essay: The Epic Hero.** An epic is a long story, often told in verse, involving heroes and gods. A heroic epic is an epic that has as its main purpose the telling of a great hero's life story. The ancient Greeks viewed Achilles as "the best of the Achaeans," and the perfect embodiment of a hero. Write an essay in which you formulate and support a thesis in response to the following question: What does the choice of Achilles as the perfect model for a hero reveal about the values of the ancient Greeks? (For more information on epic heroes, refer to Themes: The Hero and the Quest, page 516.) You may wish to freewrite your ideas on the following questions as a starting point: What does Homer want the reader to understand about the character of Achilles the hero, and about his dealings with such characters as Agamemnon, Patroclus, and Hector? What does this epic say about the hero's role? In formulating your thesis, you may wish to consider your responses to the fourth Understanding Literature question.

Speaking and Listening Skills

Oral Interpretation. The great epics of classical Greece and Rome were meant to be sung or read aloud to an audience. Review the Language Arts Survey 3.5, "Oral Interpretation." Then, as a class, plan to hold dramatic readings of passages from the *Iliad*, the *Odyssey*, or the *Aeneid*. Every member of the class should choose a passage that he or she finds interesting. Form small groups and rehearse the recital of your chosen excerpts. Each student should introduce his or her selection briefly and then read it or recite it from memory, paying close attention to the guidelines for oral interpretation. In your small groups, offer constructive criticism. Then hold a class reading during which all students present their oral interpretations.

ANSWERS FOR SKILLS ACTIVITIES

SPEAKING AND LISTENING SKILLS

You may wish to give students examples of constructive criticism and nonconstructive criticism so that students will make the distinction while working in groups. Tell students that when offering criticism they should focus on a fellow student's *work,* not on the student himself or herself.

► Additional practice is provided in the Essential Skills Practice Book: Speaking and Listening 3.5.

PREREADING

Lyric Poems
by Sappho, translated by Paul Roche

GREECE

About the Author

SAPPHO
C. 610 BC–C. 570 BC

Sappho is one of the greatest lyric poets of ancient Greece. She was born and spent most of her life on the Greek island of Lesbos, off the coast of present-day Turkey, which she left only when political turbulence banished her and other aristocrats to Sicily. Sappho married, raised a daughter named Cleïs, and spent most of her time in the society of a group of upper-class women. While some speculate that these women were priestesses dedicated to Aphrodite, others believe that they were simply admirers and apprentices who devoted themselves to Sappho's poetry and to musical study. Sappho's lyric poetry was greatly admired in her own day, and her fame won her both praise and criticism. Awed by the beauty of her poetry, Plato called her the tenth Muse. Greek dramatists, however, parodied her on stage in their comedies, perhaps leading to the condemnation her work received in later centuries. According to one legend, Sappho's life ended when she threw herself off a cliff into the sea after a boatman named Phaon refused to return her love. Others say that she died of old age, cared for by her daughter Cleïs.

Sappho was a prolific writer—centuries after her death scholars at the library in Alexandria organized more than five hundred of her poems into nine volumes. Most of her works were destroyed during the Medieval Period when the Bishop of Constantinople ordered all copies of her work burned. Sappho's work lived on in fragments quoted in the works of other authors. Only a very few entire poems remained. Archaeological digs in Egypt in the late nineteenth century revealed more Sapphic fragments on papyrus that had been used to stuff mummified crocodiles.

About the Selection

Sappho's poetry was meant to be sung to the accompaniment of a stringed instrument called the lyre. Our term *lyric*, meaning "musical" or "songlike," is derived from the name of this instrument. Unlike many poets of her time who concerned themselves with political themes, Sappho explored intensely personal themes in her poetry. She described the love, friendships, and enmities that arose among a highly cultured society of women. The poems and fragments that you are about to read will give you a glimpse into Sappho's society, which placed great emphasis on love in all its forms—romantic love, love of friends, and love of family. You will see the Greek emphasis on achieving fame that lasts after death. You will also gain insight into Sappho as a person who valued beauty and society and feared aging and loneliness.

CONNECTIONS: A Society Apart: The Status of Young Women in Ancient Greece

In ancient Greece, women and men lived very separate lives. While a man could go about in public places, a woman of the upper-class was raised in the seclusion of her father's *gynaeceum*, or women's quarters, where she was taught domestic arts as well as singing, dancing, music, and sometimes reading and writing. Unmarried women had to appear in public properly veiled and attended and were not allowed to stand in the windows of their fathers' homes. This seclusion led to the development of very strong female friendships, but these often ended when a woman left her father's home to marry.

GOALS/OBJECTIVES

Studying this lesson will enable students to

- enjoy Sappho's fragments and poems
- briefly explain how young women lived in ancient Greece
- identify the tenors and vehicles of different similes and metaphors
- identify allusions and themes in poetry
- write creative fragments of poetry
- write an essay comparing and contrasting Homeric and Sapphic values
- illustrate Sapphic fragments

ADDITIONAL RESOURCES

READER'S GUIDE
- Selection Worksheet 8.2

ASSESSMENT PORTFOLIO
- Selection Check Test 2.8.3
- Selection Test 2.8.4

ESSENTIAL SKILLS PRACTICE BOOKS
- Writing 1.8, 1.10, 1.20

PREREADING EXTENSIONS

Encourage interested students to complete one of the following projects, either alone or in small groups:

- Lesbos is a volcanic island that has been the site of many earthquakes. Research the effects of one of the earthquakes upon the island. Speculate why so many earthquakes occur on this island.
- Many different nations have claimed Lesbos throughout history. Write a brief report on the many nations with which Lesbos has been associated. Explain why so many nations have been interested in controlling the island.
- During Byzantine times, the empress Irene was exiled to Lesbos. Like Sappho herself, Irene was a strong and unusual woman for her culture and time period. Write a brief report on the life of Empress Irene.

SUPPORT FOR LEP STUDENTS

PRONUNCIATIONS OF PROPER NOUNS AND ADJECTIVES

Cle • ïs (clē´is)
Sap • pho (saf´ō)

ADDITIONAL VOCABULARY

assent—in consent or agreement
delude—mislead; deceive; trick
exquisite—beautiful
renown—great fame or reputation

READER'S JOURNAL

Students may wish to hold a class discussion on how important fame after death really is. What achievements or parts of life do they consider more important?

Answers to Guided Reading Questions

❶ The goddess Artemis does not want love.

❷ The speaker compares her feelings to a torch flaring in her heart.

❸ The speaker and the person whom she addresses were parted, but the person she addresses has returned to the speaker.

SPELLING AND VOCABULARY WORDS FROM THE SELECTION

oblivion toil

Literary Technique

SPEAKER AND TONE

The **speaker** is the character who speaks in, or narrates, a poem—the voice assumed by the writer. **Tone** is the emotional attitude toward a reader or toward the subject implied by a literary work. Encourage students to identify the tone with which the speaker approaches the subject in each of these poems or poetic fragments. Students might then discuss their different ideas about the tones represented in these poems.

READER'S JOURNAL

Do you ever hope that your name will live on long after your death? What might you do to make future generations remember you? For example, you might decide to effect political change or to create a revolutionary new style of music. In your journal, write down your thoughts about what you might do to be remembered. Then answer the following questions: How important is it to you to be remembered after your death? Why is it so important, or why isn't it important to you?

Lyric Poems

SAPPHO, TRANSLATED BY PAUL ROCHE

"But not Everybody Wants Love"

❶ *Who does not want love?*

Young Artemis[1] swore a great oath:
"A virgin forever I shall be,
Pure on the peaks of the mountains.
Father, for my sake, agree."
And the Father of the Blessed Immortals
Nodded assent. On Olympus
She is known to the gods as Deer-shooter,
Goddess of wilderness: title
Great in renown. And the god
Who never comes near her is Love.

"At Last"

❷ *To what does the speaker compare her feelings for the person addressed?*

❸ *What has happened between the speaker and the person whom she addresses?*

You have come
and you did well to come
I pined for you.
And now you have put a torch to my heart
a flare of love—
O bless you and bless you and bless you:
you are back . . .
we were parted

1. **Artemis.** Goddess of the moon, wild animals, and hunting

"It Gives Me Joy to Think"

I have a pretty little girl
lovely as a golden flower;
Cleïs, whom I so adore
I would not take all Lydia
Nor Lesbos (even lovelier)
in exchange for her

Why wouldn't the speaker take all of these lands in exchange for Cleïs?

144

Many have been cheated by oblivion
But by good judges
None:
And afterwards, I say,
I shall be remembered
Certainly by some

What does the speaker believe will keep her name from "oblivion"?

"Let's Not Pretend"

No, Children, do not delude me.
You mock the good gifts of the Muses[2]
When you say: "Dear Sappho we'll crown you,
Resonant player,
First on the clear sweet lyre. . . ."[3]
Do you not see how I alter:
My skin with its aging,
My black hair gone white,
My legs scarcely carrying
Me, who went dancing
More neatly than fawns once
(Neatest of creatures)?
No, no one can cure it; keep beauty from going,
And I cannot help it.
God himself cannot do what cannot be done.
So age follows after and catches
Everything living.

Why doesn't Sappho wish to be crowned as the best player of the lyre?

2. **Muses.** Nine goddesses who preside over literature, arts, and sciences
3. **lyre.** Small stringed instrument used in ancient Greece

Words for Everyday Use

ob • liv • i • on (ə bliv´ē ən) *n.,* condition or fact of being forgotten

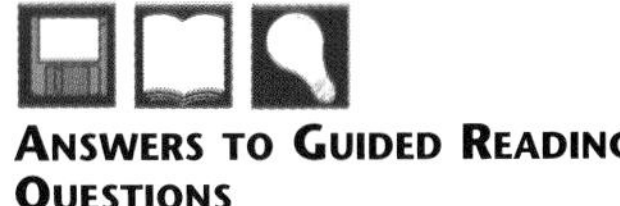

Answers to Guided Reading Questions

❶ The speaker would not take all of these lands in exchange for Cleïs because the speaker loves her so much.

❷ The speaker believes that "good judges" will remember her work and name.

❸ Sappho does not want to be crowned for her lyre-playing because she feels that she is growing old and that her beauty is waning.

Cross-curricular Activities

Arts and Humanities

Point out that in "Let's Not Pretend," Sappho expresses negative feelings toward the aging process. Encourage students to create works of art that express their own feelings about the aging process. Students may express negative feelings, if they desire, but you should try to get them to see the positive side of growing older as well. Students might write poems or short stories; deliver speeches; create paintings, sculptures, murals, or collages; or compose and/or perform musical compositions.

Literary Technique

Personification

Personification is a figure of speech in which an idea, animal, or thing is described as if it were a person. What is personified in "Let's Not Pretend," near the end of page 611? What human quality is attributed to this thing? What attitude does this example of personification reveal that the speaker has toward this thing?

Answers

Age is personified as being able to follow after and catch things. The speaker fears aging almost as if it were a stalker or predator.

Vocabulary in Context

- Although the king erected a large stone monument in his honor, after a thousand years the monument had been broken into stones, and even the king's name had faded into oblivion.

Answers to Guided Reading Questions

❶ Sappho knows that she must "waste away." She enjoys "exquisite" things—glitter, sunlight, and love.

❷ Sappho refuses to creep away and die in the dark. She says that she will go on living, loving and loved, with the people whom she addresses.

❸ The speaker says that Achilles is dead and lies in the earth. The speaker says that the sons of Atreus brought suffering to pass.

Selection Check Test with Answers

EX. Who was Cleïs?

Cleïs was Sappho's daughter.

1. Who does not want love?

Artemis does not want love.

2. For what wouldn't the speaker take all of Lydia and Lesbos in exchange?

The speaker would not take all of Lydia and Lesbos in exchange for her daughter, Cleïs.

3. Who could not save Tithonus from the "grasp of old age"?

Eos, or Dawn, could not save her beloved Tithonus from old age.

4. In "Life Slips By," what is already gone? What is passing?

The moon and the Pleiades have gone. Time is passing.

5. What did the sons of Atreus cause?

They caused suffering.

Even rosy-armed Eos, the Dawn,
Who ushers in morning to the ends of the earth,
Could not save from the grasp of old age
Her lover immortal Tithonus.
And I too, I know, must waste away.
Yet for me—listen well
My delight is the exquisite.
Yes, for me,
Glitter and sunlight and love
Are one society.
So I shall not go creeping away
To die in the dark:
I shall go on living with you,
Loving and loved.

 ❶ *What does Sappho know? What does she enjoy?*

❷ *What does she refuse to do? What does she say she will do?*

"Life Slips By"

The moon has gone
The Pleiades[4] gone
In dead of night
Time passes on
I lie alone

"I Think of Achilles"

He lies
in the black earth at last
at the end of his toils.
Oh what suffering was brought to pass
by the sons of Atreus![5] ■

❸ *What does the speaker say has become of Achilles? What does she say about Atreus's sons?*

4. **Pleiades.** Seven daughters of Atlas and Pleione, placed by Zeus in the sky and turned to stars
5. **Atreus.** King of Mycenae and father of Agamemnon and Menelaus; Menelaus was the husband of Helen of Troy. A Trojan named Paris kidnapped Helen so Menelaus and Agamemnon gathered the Argive forces to attack Troy, beginning the Trojan war.

Words for Everyday Use

toil (toil) *n.*, labor; hard work

Vocabulary in Context

- The hot noonday sun and the stinging insects made Lois's toil of weeding the garden seem even more difficult.

Responding to the Selection

Is Sappho a person that you would like to have known? Explain why, or why not. Which of her qualities do you find admirable? disagreeable?

Reviewing the Selection

Recalling		Interpreting
1. Who never comes near Artemis? What effect does the end of separation from the beloved have on the speaker of "At Last"? For whom does the speaker express love in "It Gives Me Joy to Think"? What wouldn't the speaker do?	▶▶	What attitude do you think the speaker has toward Artemis? After looking at "At Last" and "It Gives Me Joy to Think," do you believe the speaker of these poems would ever make the decision Artemis made? In what ways are the speaker's ways of expressing her love in "At Last" and "It Gives Me Joy to Think" different? In what ways are they similar?
2. According to Fragment 144, by what have people been cheated? By what haven't people been cheated? What does the speaker say will happen "afterwards"?	▶▶	To what is the speaker referring when she speaks of "oblivion" and "afterwards"? Why will the speaker be remembered? What is the speaker implying about her work?
3. In "Let's Not Pretend," what does the speaker note is happening to her? What does the speaker say she will continue to do? What does the speaker note about time in "Life Slips By"? Who is with the speaker?	▶▶	In "Let's Not Pretend," what doesn't the speaker want the "Children" she addresses to pretend? In what sense does the speaker hope to live on? Why do you think the translator titled "Life Slips By" as he did? What mood does this poem express?
4. In "I Think of Achilles," where is Achilles? What brought his toils to an end? What does the speaker say about the sons of Atreus?	▶▶	What attitude does the speaker express toward the great heroes of the Trojan War?

Responding to the Selection

You might also ask students to imagine what Sappho might have said to Artemis had she been given a chance to talk to her about her decision to avoid love. Students might then role play this conversation.

Answers for Reviewing the Selection

RECALLING AND INTERPRETING

1. **Recalling.** The god of love never comes near Artemis. The speaker says her heart burns with love like a torch, and the speaker blesses the person she addresses for returning. The speaker expresses love for her daughter. The speaker wouldn't take all of Lydia and Lesbos in exchange for her daughter. **Interpreting.** The speaker may feel sorry for Artemis who will never know love. Students may say that the speaker would never have made the same decision as Artemis because the speaker values love highly. Other students may say that the speaker respects Artemis and understands her decision. The speaker expresses her love for the friend from whom she was parted in terms of gratitude and passion. The speaker expresses her love for her daughter in terms of protectiveness and glowing admiration. The speaker's love for these two people is similar in that it is expressed proudly and in that this powerful emotion completely fills and transforms the speaker.

2. **Recalling.** People have been cheated by oblivion. People have not been cheated by good judges. The speaker says that she will "certainly" be remembered by some. **Interpreting.** The speaker is referring to death and the way in which one's name becomes forgotten after one's death. Students may say that the speaker believes that she will be remembered by "good judges" of poetry. The speaker is implying that she has produced

(cont.)

Answers for Reviewing the Selection (cont.)

good work that is worthy of being remembered.

3. **Recalling.** The speaker notes that she is growing older and that her beauty is fading. The speaker says that she will continue living on with the people whom she addresses. The speaker notes that time is passing on. The speaker is alone. **Interpreting.** The speaker does not want these "Children" to pretend that she is as young and talented as she was in her youth. She feels that she is growing old and that her companions are flattering her by pretending not to notice the way in which she has changed. The speaker hopes to live on through what remains of her beauty—her poetry. The translator may have been trying to capture the loneliness and desperation of the poem in his title. The poem expresses loneliness and a longing for the past.

(cont.)

SYNTHESIZING

5. If you gave Sappho the following list of eight achievements that can be won in life, in what order of importance do you think she would rank them: fame after death, friendship and hospitality, honor in war, love, physical strength, power, pride, and wealth? Refer to the selections to explain why you chose to order the achievements in this way.

Understanding Literature (Questions for Discussion)

1. **Simile and Metaphor.** A **simile** is a comparison using *like* or *as.* A **metaphor** is a figure of speech in which one thing is spoken or written about as if it were another. This figure of speech invites the reader to make a comparison between the two things. Similes and metaphors are analyzed by division into two parts, the tenor (or subject being described), and the vehicle (or object used for comparison). For example, in the simile "your locks are like the snow," the tenor is "locks of hair" and the vehicle is "snow." What simile does the author use in "It Gives Me Joy to Think"? What are the tenor and vehicle of this simile? In what way are the two things similar? What metaphor does the author use in "At Last"? What are the tenor and vehicle in this metaphor? In what way are the things being compared similar?
2. **Allusion.** An **allusion** is a rhetorical technique in which reference is made to a person, event, object, or work from history or literature. To what mythological characters does the poet allude in "Let's Not Pretend"? Why do you think the author makes this allusion? To what events does the author allude in "I Think of Achilles"? What purpose does the author serve by making this allusion?
3. **Theme.** A **theme** is a central idea in a literary work. In many ancient Greek works, including the *Iliad,* characters struggle to achieve lasting fame after death. The Greek term for this fame is *kléos,* which means "glory conferred by the poets." Which of Sappho's poems explore this theme? What does her attitude toward *kléos* seem to be? Why do you think Sappho found this to be an important theme?

Responding in Writing

1. **Creative Writing: Fragments.** Although all we have left of many of Sappho's poems is a line or two, people have been dazzled by the beauty of these fragments for hundreds of years. Try your hand at writing your own poetic fragments. These fragments do not have to express entire ideas but might capture an image in a unique way, create a surprising metaphor or simile, or simply make use of words you find irresistibly beautiful. For example, you might write, "The crisp, cucumber grass" or "Toxic red sunsets." Try to write at least ten poetic fragments, being as imaginative as possible.

ANSWERS FOR REVIEWING THE SELECTION (CONT.)

4. **Recalling.** Achilles lies in the earth. His death brought his toils to an end. The speaker says that the sons of Atreus created much suffering. **Interpreting.** The speaker seems to find the suffering, death, and warfare caused by these heroes to be wasteful and pointless.

SYNTHESIZING

Responses will vary. Possible responses are given.

5. Students' lists may vary, but students should recognize that Sappho probably would have found love, friendship, and fame after death far more important than physical strength, pride, and honor in war.

ANSWERS FOR UNDERSTANDING LITERATURE

Responses will vary. Possible responses are given.

1. **Simile and Metaphor.** The author compares the little girl to a golden flower. The tenor of the simile is the girl, and the vehicle is the golden flower. The two are similar because of their loveliness. The speaker describes her love as if it were a torch that the person addressed has caused to flare in her heart. The tenor is love, and the vehicle is a flaring torch. The two are similar because both love and a burning torch are bright, powerful, and consuming.
2. **Allusion.** The author alludes to the Dawn's, Eos's, beloved Tithonus, who was granted immortality but not eternal youth and so wasted away with old age. The author makes this allusion to show that sometimes even the immortals cannot stop the aging process. The author alludes to the Trojan War. The author makes this allusion to point out that such wars cause suffering and death.

(cont.)

ANSWERS FOR UNDERSTANDING LITERATURE (CONT.)

3. **Theme.** Fragment 144 and "Let's Not Pretend" explore this theme. Sappho seems to want to achieve this sort of lasting fame after death and hopes to continue to spread beauty long after her own beauty has faded to dust. *Responses will vary.*

You might share your fragments with each other as a class. Save your fragments in your writing portfolio. You might choose to make use of them in other writing assignments, either as a springboard for ideas or as images in a complete poem.

2. **Critical Essay: Comparing and Contrasting Values.** As you have read in the Connections feature on the Prereading page, men and women lived separate and different lives in ancient Greece. Thus, it is not surprising that male writers and female writers expressed different values. Write an essay comparing and contrasting the values expressed in Homer's *Iliad* (see page 592) with the values expressed in Sappho's fragments and poems. Before writing, review the excerpts from both works, and review your answers to the Synthesizing questions above. Then make a Venn diagram (see the Language Arts Survey 1.10, "Gathering Ideas") like the one below, listing different values and shared values. In your introductory paragraph, formulate a thesis that states how Homeric values were similar to and different from Sappho's values. In the paragraphs that follow, support your thesis with evidence from both texts. In your final paragraph, speculate why men valued certain things more than women, why women valued certain things more than men, and why men and women shared certain values.

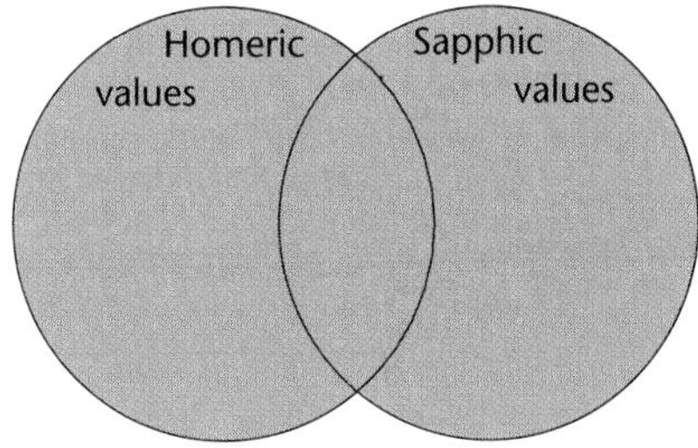

PROJECT

Illustrating Fragments. Sappho's fragments create vivid images in the reader's imagination. Working individually or in small groups, illustrate one or more of Sappho's poetic fragments. In addition to illustrating the fragments in this textbook, you might wish to go to the library to find more Sapphic fragments to illustrate. Your class can then create an illustrated anthology of these fragments to share with each other, to show to other classes, or to put in the school library.

ANALYTIC SCALES FOR RESPONDING IN WRITING

Assign a score from 1 to 25 for each grading criterion below. (For more detailed evaluation, see the evaluation forms for writing, revising, and proofreading, Assessment Portfolio 4.1–4.9.)

1. Fragments

- **Content/Unity.** The writing consists of at least ten poetic fragments.
- **Organization/Coherence.** Each fragment is written in a sensible order.
- **Language/Style.** The fragments use vivid and precise nouns, verbs, and modifiers.
- **Conventions.** The fragments avoid errors in spelling, grammar, usage, mechanics, and manuscript form.

▶ Additional practice is provided in the Essential Skills Practice Book: Writing 1.8.

2. Critical Essay

- **Content/Unity.** The essay compares and contrasts Homeric and Sapphic values.
- **Organization/Coherence.** The essay begins with an introduction that includes the thesis of the essay. The introduction is followed by supporting paragraphs with clear transitions. The essay ends with a solid conclusion.
- **Language/Style.** The essay uses vivid and precise nouns, verbs, and modifiers.
- **Conventions.** The essay avoids errors in spelling, grammar, usage, mechanics, and manuscript form.

▶ Additional practice is provided in the Essential Skills Practice Book: Writing 1.10, 1.20.

PROJECT NOTES

See the evaluation form for projects, Assessment Portfolio 4.12.

Illustrating Fragments. You might encourage students to create illustrations for other lyric poems they enjoy and to include these illustrations and poems in the anthology. You might also expand this project by asking students to create other works of visual art to represent the poetry, such as sculptures, models, murals, and collages. Students who have a strong interest in music might compose or locate and play for the class examples of music to which the fragments might be set.

Cultural/Historical Note

In Athens, during three-day festivals in honor of Dionysus, plays were performed from early morning until late at night. On each day, five plays were presented, four (three tragedies and a satyr play) by a single playwright. The fifth play was a comedy by a different playwright. Usually, the playwright not only wrote the scripts but also directed the actors, planned the music and the dancing of the chorus, and performed one of the leading roles. At the end of the three days, judges awarded first-, second-, and third-place prizes.

Literary Note

The Greek word for actor, *hypokrites,* means, literally, an "answerer"—someone who answers the chorus. From this word comes our English word *hypocrite,* for a false person, or impersonator.

Cross-curricular Activities

APPLIED ARTS

Encourage groups of students to research the similarities and differences among amphitheaters, or arena stages, used by the ancient Greeks; thrust stages used during the Renaissance; and proscenium or picture stages, commonly used in the nineteenth and twentieth centuries. Each group should then make a model of one of these three types of stages. Models may be as sophisticated as skills will allow, from simple cardboard constructions to elaborate scale replicas made of wood.

Insights

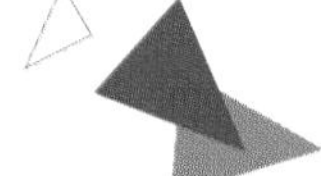

Greek Drama

The Birth of Drama in the West

One of the greatest contributions that ancient Greece made to Western culture was the invention of drama. In the West, as in other parts of the world, drama grew out of ritual religious performances. In early Greece, festivals honoring Dionysus, the god of the vine and revelry, included performances by **choruses,** or troupes of dancers who would chant and sing. According to legend, in the early sixth century BC, a chorus leader named **Thespis** separated himself from the chorus and gave himself individual lines. This innovation made possible dramatic interaction between the chorus and the lone actor, and thus drama was born. To this day, actors are sometimes called **thespians.** The first great Athenian playwright, **Aeschylus** (525–456 BC), introduced a second actor into his scenes. A younger playwright, **Sophocles** (496–406 BC), soon introduced a third actor, and in this way Greek drama reached its mature form. Aeschylus and Sophocles, along with **Euripides** (484–406 BC) and **Aristophanes** (450–388 BC), achieved a level of dramatic artistry not rivaled until many centuries after their demise.

Greek Theaters, Scenery, and Costumes

The audience of a Greek play sat in an amphitheater, open to the sky, with tiered, stone seats arranged in a semicircle around a central area called the **orchestra,** where the chorus performed. Behind the orchestra was a wooden building called the ***skene,*** from which we get our modern word *scene.* The *skene* served as part of the set, representing a temple, a shrine, a cave, or a home. Actors performed on top of the *skene* or in the area in front of it, the **proscenium.** Painted backgrounds on the *skene* provided scenery. In addition, on either side of the proscenium were prism-shaped columns called ***periaktoi*** that were painted with scenery and that could be revolved to change the scene. On top of the *skene* was the ***mechane,*** a device for raising and lowering gods onto the stage. In some plays a god would be lowered onto the stage to set affairs in order at the end of a play. To this day, an overly simplistic ending to a drama is known as a ***deus ex machina,*** or "god from the machine."

Greek theaters seated as many as fifteen thousand people, so elaborate measures had to be taken to make sure that everyone in the audience could see and hear the action. The actors wore expensive costumes and large masks fitted with small brass megaphones for projecting their voices. They also wore padding, headpieces, and platform shoes to increase their size. Because of the masks, actors did not depend on facial expressions as they do today but rather communicated feelings by means of gestures, body movements, and tones of voice.

Types of Greek Theater

The Greeks also created the major types, or genres, of theater—tragedy, comedy, and farce. Plays were an integral part of many festivals, and on a given festival day, an ancient Greek audience would see three tragedies and a satyr play by a single playwright, followed by a comedy by a different playwright. Hence, tragedies were usually written in a cycle of three.

Aristotle Contemplating the Bust of Homer. Rembrandt

The best definition we have of Greek **tragedy** was written by the philosopher and critic

Greek theater, Athens

Aristotle in a work called the ***Poetics.*** Greek tragedy depicts the downfall of a character of high status who is neither completely good nor completely evil. The hero's fall is brought about by some flaw in his or her character, known as a **tragic flaw.** Aristotle's term for the tragic flaw, *hamartia,* has also been translated as "an error in judgment." One of the most commonly presented tragic flaws is that of ***hubris,*** or excessive pride. Aristotle believed that witnessing the downfall of a basically good but flawed individual, not unlike ourselves, would evoke the emotions of pity and fear in the audience (pity for the suffering the hero experiences and fear for ourselves—that we could be in the hero's situation). Aristotle stated that the emotions of pity and fear bring about "the catharsis of such emotions," meaning that in watching a tragedy the viewer experiences a sort of emotional cleansing or release.

Classical Greek **comedies** often contained humorous satires of public figures or of types of people, and this humorous side of the classical comedy prefigured our current use of the word *comedy* to refer to any funny enactment. **Satyr plays** were wild, humorous romps dealing with ludicrous situations and characters. The name of this type of play comes from the characters, who were dressed as satyrs, creatures half human and half goat. Satyr plays were the first examples of the modern theatrical form known as **farce,** in which ludicrous, improbable, funny situations are the norm.

Conventions of Greek Drama

Every type of literature has its **conventions,** or characteristics that most works of that type share. The use of masks, costumes, scenery, music, and choral dancing are some of the conventions of Greek drama. Also, although plots often deal with cataclysmic events, violent actions, according to Greek convention, took place off stage and were reported to the actors and the audience rather than witnessed. Typically, a Greek drama alternated between scenes with actors and ***paradoi,*** scenes in which the chorus danced and sang commentaries on the action of the drama. A *parados* was itself divided into alternating parts, the **strophe** and the **antistrophe.** (During the strophe, the chorus sang and turned from stage right to stage left. During the antistrophe, the chorus sang in answer to the previous strophe and returned from stage left to stage right.)

Another convention of Greek drama was its observance of the **three unities of action, space, and time.** According to Greek poetic theory, a play should present a unified action (that is, events all related to the working out of a central conflict or struggle). This action should all occur in a single place and at a single time, usually in the course of one day. In the words of Aristotle, a well-made play is a unified "imitation of an action" and has a definite "beginning, middle, and end."

INTEGRATED SKILLS ACTIVITIES

SPEAKING AND LISTENING SKILLS

After discussing with students the convention of Greek drama involving violence, have students discuss the following question: What might an ancient Greek think about the violence in a modern movie?

Students can then hold a debate about violence on television and in movies. Students might choose to focus their debate on one of the following topics: the effects on society of violence in popular media, whether there should be bans or warnings about graphic or gratuitous violence, or whether art mirrors life or vice versa. Students may also use a different focus of their choice. Students should work in two teams to research the subject and argue their position.

QUOTABLES

"In practical matters the end is not mere speculative knowledge of what is to be done, but rather the doing of it. It is not enough to know about Virtue, then, but we must endeavor to possess it, and to use it, or to take any other steps that may make us good."

—Aristotle

ADDITIONAL RESOURCES

READER'S GUIDE

- Selection Worksheet 8.3

ASSESSMENT PORTFOLIO

- Selection Check Test 2.8.5
- Selection Test 2.8.6

ESSENTIAL SKILLS PRACTICE BOOKS

- Speaking and Listening 3.1
- Study and Research 4.21
- Applied English/Tech Prep 5.2

PREREADING EXTENSIONS

Have students research the history and geography of ancient Greece by completing one or more of the following activities individually or in groups:

- Create a map of ancient Greece including the following places: Athens, Colonus, Corinth, Crete, Delphi, Doris, Macedonia, Peloponnesus, Sparta, Thebes, and Thrace.
- Compare and contrast the cultures of Sparta and Athens.
- Make a time line of events in Greek history including but not limited to the following: the first Olympic games, the birth and death of Sophocles, the birth and death of Pericles, the beginning and end of the Persian Wars, the beginning and end of the Peloponnesian War, the Battle of Salamis, and the Battle of Thermopylae.
- Present in comic book or picture book form the events of the Battle of Salamis, including the events leading up to the battle.
- Read or view a performance of a play by Sophocles other than *Oedipus the King*. Write a review of the work or the performance.

PREREADING

Oedipus the King
by Sophocles, translated by David Grene

About the Author

SOPHOCLES
c. 496 BC– 406 BC

Classical literature produced three great tragic dramatists—Aeschylus, **Sophocles**, and Euripides. Sophocles's work is perhaps the most familiar to a modern audience. Born in Colonus, near Athens, during Athens's rise to power, Sophocles died shortly before the fall of the city to Sparta in the Peloponnesian War. His father, a rich armor-maker, provided an excellent education for his son, who excelled at dancing, lyre playing, and wrestling. When he was sixteen, Sophocles was chosen to lead a celebratory procession to mark the Athenian victory in the Battle of Salamis.

Best known as a playwright, Sophocles also served Athens as a treasurer and as a military commander under Pericles (see page 674). At age twenty-eight, he merited distinction in theater by defeating Aeschylus and winning his first dramatic competition. This victory was for Sophocles the beginning of a successful career as a dramatist. He wrote more than 120 plays that were entered into competition. Of these plays, twenty-four won first place, and the rest came in second. Only seven of Sophocles's plays have survived in complete form: *Ajax, The Women of Trachis, Antigone, Oedipus the King, Electra, Philoctetes,* and *Oedipus at Colonus,* which was produced after his death in 406 BC. Sophocles is credited with many innovations in theater, including adding an additional actor, enlarging the chorus, using some types of scenery, and introducing the *mechane.*

About the Selection

Oedipus the King is part of a trilogy called the Theban plays which also includes *Antigone* and *Oedipus at Colonus*. Unlike many ancient Greek trilogies, the Theban plays were not written for a single festival. Instead, they were composed over the course of more than thirty years. Written sometime after 430 BC, *Oedipus the King* was the second of these three plays to be produced; however, if the plays were arranged chronologically according to their action, it would be the first in the cycle. The play begins in the city of Thebes, which is struggling against a plague—a scenario that Athenians knew well, having experienced a deadly plague in 430 BC.

Because the story of Oedipus was an important part of the Greek oral tradition, Greek audiences were very familiar with the events Sophocles portrayed. In brief, the story goes thus: The city of Thebes was founded by Cadmus, who angered the god Apollo. In retaliation, Apollo placed a curse upon the city. According to Apollo's oracle, the son of King Laius and Queen Jocasta would kill his father and marry his mother. When King Laius and Queen Jocasta's son was born, his ankles were pierced and bound together (Oedipus's name, which means literally "swollen foot," came from this traumatic injury) and a servant carried him to Mount Cithaeron where he was to be abandoned. The servant, however, took pity on the child and delivered him to a shepherd, who in turn delivered the boy to King Polybus of Corinth.

As he grew, Oedipus heard taunts and rumors that he was not the true son of Polybus, so he consulted the oracle at Delphi. Before he received an answer, a priestess drove him away, claiming that he would kill his father and wed his mother. Determined never to fulfill this prophesy, Oedipus left Corinth. One day, on a road in central Greece, he lost his temper and killed a man and his servants. This man was King Laius, Oedipus's father, so Oedipus unknowingly fulfilled the first part of the prophecy. He continued on to Thebes, which was being terrorized by the Sphinx, a monster that devoured anyone who could not solve her riddle: What walks on four legs in the morning, two legs in the afternoon, and three legs in the evening? Oedipus's answer, *man*, was correct because humans crawl on all fours as children, walk upright during the middle years of their life, and walk with the aid of a cane in old age.

GOALS/OBJECTIVES

Studying this lesson will enable students to

- appreciate and interpret a Greek tragedy
- identify Sophocles as a great Greek tragedian
- recognize and explain irony, paradoxes, metaphors, and similes
- recognize conventions of Greek drama
- identify a tragic flaw
- write a dialogue
- analyze the meaning of blindness and sight in *Oedipus*
- recognize Greek and Latin roots

Photo: Scala/Art Resource, New York

Detail of Oedipus and the Sphinx

By foiling the Sphinx, Oedipus saved the city of Thebes and won the hand of Queen Jocasta, which had been offered as a reward by her brother, Creon. By marrying Jocasta, Oedipus fulfilled the second part of the prophecy. Oedipus had ruled for almost twenty years and had four children with Jocasta when a plague struck Thebes. It was a plague of infertility, indicating that someone had polluted the kingdom. Creon reported from the oracle of Apollo that the plague would not end until the person who murdered their late king, Laius, was found and banished from the city. Ironically, Oedipus committed himself to finding the murderer. Sophocles begins his story in the plague-stricken city of Thebes as Oedipus awaits the return of Creon.

CONNECTIONS: The Oracle at Delphi

Greeks and people from other lands traveled to Delphi to receive advice or answers from the god Apollo. The Greeks believed that Delphi, located on Mount Parnassus, was first sacred to Gaea, the earth goddess. According to legend, Delphi was discovered to be the navel, or center, of the world after Zeus released two eagles from opposite ends of the earth and they met at Delphi. The spot was supposedly guarded by Python, a terrible serpent, until the god Apollo slew the beast. In honor of this feat he was called the Pythian, and his priestess was known as the Pythia. On the spot where Python was slain, Apollo established his oracle. Requests from leaders about matters of state, questions about new enterprises and personal matters, such as whether to marry or move, were some of the issues put before Apollo. The Greeks believed that the god responded through his priestess once she had reached a certain frenzied state. They also believed that Apollo knew everything and always spoke the truth, though he sometimes gave his responses in riddles or cryptic language. Delphi attracted many visitors, from as early as 750 BC until AD 390 when the sanctuary was closed by Emperor Theodosius, a follower of the new Christian religion.

SPELLING AND VOCABULARY WORDS FROM THE SELECTION

balk
calumny
compulsion
conjecture
contrivance
countenance
despotic
expiation
induce
infamy
insolence
invoke
knave
obstinacy
pestilence
rankle
suborn
surfeit
vexation

SUPPORT FOR LEP STUDENTS

Pronunciations of Proper Nouns and Adjectives

Bac • chic (bak´ik)
Cad • mus (kad´məs)
Cith • aer • on (sith´ər on)
Lai • us (lā´əs)
Lox • i • as (läks´ē əs)
Ly • ce • an (lī sē´ən)
Men • oe • ce • us (men´ō sē´əs)
Par • nas • sus (pär nas´əs)
Phoe • bus (fē´bəs)
Po • ly • bus (pō lē´bus)
Thebes (thēbz)
Thra • ci • an (thrā´shən)
Zeus (zo͞os)

Additional Vocabulary

blight—anything that destroys or prevents growth
chide—scold
lamentation—expression of sorrow or distress
omen—sign of something to come
ordinance—authoritative decree or fate
perishes—dies
prow—front end of a ship or boat
quack—person who pretends to have skills that he or she does not have
rite—ritual, ceremony
roused—awakened
scheme—plan, plot
sluggard—lazy
vexes—upsets

READER'S JOURNAL

Students might also write about a time when they hid the truth from somebody else. Ask them to consider the following questions: Did they conceal the truth to spare the other person discomfort? Did they hide the truth to save themselves trouble or punishment? Did they hide the truth for a different reason? Explain.

INTEGRATED SKILLS ACTIVITIES

RESEARCH SKILLS

Discuss with students the difference between summarizing and paraphrasing. You may wish to refer them to the Language Arts Survey 4.21, "Paraphrasing and Summarizing" for more information. Explain that the story of Oedipus as it appears on the Prereading pages is a summary. To make sure that students understand the story before they begin reading the play, have them paraphrase the summary of the Oedipus story. For further clarification, students can also diagram the relationships between Oedipus, Creon, Jocasta, Laius, Antigone, and Ismene.

▶ Additional practice is provided in the Essential Skills Practice Book: Study and Research 4.21.

READER'S JOURNAL

Do think it is always best to know the truth? Consider a time when you wanted to know the truth about something and others warned you that it would be best if you did not know. What happened as a result of your push to learn the truth? Write about such an incident in your journal.

Oedipus the King

SOPHOCLES, TRANSLATED BY DAVID GRENE

Characters in *Oedipus the King*

Oedipus (ed´ə pəs), king of Thebes

Jocasta (jō kas´ta), wife and mother of Oedipus

Creon (krē´on), Jocasta's brother and Oedipus's brother-in-law and uncle

Teiresias (tə rē´sē əs), blind seer, or prophet

Priest

First Messenger from Corinth

Second Messenger from inside the palace

Herdsman

Chorus made up of citizens of Thebes

Antigone (an tig'ə nē), daughter of Oedipus and Jocasta

Ismene (is mā´ nē), daughter of Oedipus and Jocasta

Scene: In front of the palace of Oedipus *at Thebes. To the right of the stage near the altar stands the* Priest *with a crowd of children.* Oedipus *emerges from the central door.*

Oedipus. Children, young sons and daughters of old Cadmus,[1]
why do you sit here with your suppliant crowns?[2]
The town is heavy with a mingled burden
of sounds and smells, of groans and hymns and incense;
I did not think it fit that I should hear
of this from messengers but came myself,—
I Oedipus whom all men call the Great.

He turns to the Priest.

You're old and they are young; come, speak for them.
What do you fear or want, that you sit here
suppliant? Indeed I'm willing to give all
that you may need; I would be very hard
should I not pity suppliants like these.

Priest. O ruler of my country, Oedipus,
you see our company around the altar;
you see our ages; some of us, like these,
who cannot yet fly far, and some of us
heavy with age; these children are the chosen
among the young, and I the priest of Zeus.[3]
Within the marketplace sit others crowned
with suppliant garlands, at the double shrine
of Pallas[4] and the temple where Ismenus
gives oracles by fire.[5] King, you yourself
have seen our city reeling like a wreck
already; it can scarcely lift its prow
out of the depths, out of the bloody surf.
A blight is on the fruitful plants of the earth,
A blight is on the cattle in the fields,
a blight is on our women that no children
are born to them; a God that carries fire,
a deadly pestilence, is on our town,

1. **Cadmus.** Founder of Thebes
2. **suppliant crowns.** Wreaths woven and worn by people requesting something of the gods
3. **Zeus.** Chief god in Greek mythology
4. **double shrine of Pallas.** Two temples of Athene, goddess of wisdom
5. **temple . . . fire.** At the temple of Apollo near the river Ismenus, priests foretold the future based on patterns in ashes.

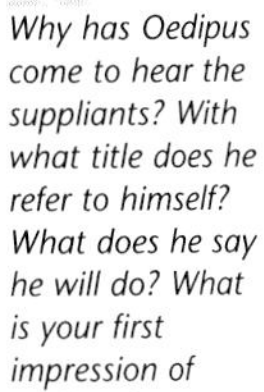

Why has Oedipus come to hear the suppliants? With what title does he refer to himself? What does he say he will do? What is your first impression of Oedipus?

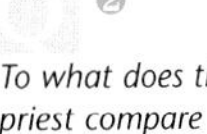

To what does the priest compare the troubles that face Thebes? What is happening in Thebes?

Words for Everyday Use

pes • ti • lence (pes´tə ləns) *n.,* fatally contagious or infectious disease

Answers to Guided Reading Questions

❶ Oedipus thinks that he should hear about the needs of his people directly. He refers to himself as "the Great," a name he says everyone gives him. He says he will give the suppliants whatever they need. Responses will vary. Students may say that Oedipus seems to be a leader who cares for the needs of his people and who is accessible to his people. They might also say that Oedipus seems very proud or cocky.

❷ The priest compares the troubles to a sinking ship. The plants and livestock of Thebes are dying; many people are dying.

Cultural/Historical Note

Throughout history, people have tried to predict or foretell the future. The oracle's use of the ashes is one such method. Other methods include gazing into crystal balls, reading the patterns in tea leaves, analyzing the lines on the palm of the hand, studying the stars and other celestial bodies, and reading special cards. Students are probably familiar with horoscopes, psychics, and palmreaders. Explain that prophecies were taken very seriously by the Greeks. Students can discuss their own feelings about the ability of people to predict the future. You may also wish to discuss the idea of self-fulfilling prophecy, or something that is brought about because it is expected.

Vocabulary in Context

- Without medical supplies, the population of the city will be decimated by the pestilence.

Answers to Guided Reading Questions

❶ Oedipus, without help from the people but with the help of the gods, saved the Thebans from the horrible killing of the Sphinx. They hope that he will again be able to save them.

❷ Oedipus says that he is touched by sorrow, not only for himself but for each person who seeks his help and for the city as a whole.

Quotables

"The ship of state—the gods once more,

After much rocking on the stormy surge,

Set her on an even keel."

—Sophocles
from *Antigone*

Literary Note

Point out to students that Sophocles uses imagery related to a ship to describe the state of Thebes several times in the Priest's speech, which begins on page 621. He refers to "our city reeling like a wreck" that "can scarcely lift its prow out of the depths" (lines 23–25). Later he says that an empty ship is nothing (lines 64–65).

strikes us and spares not, and the house of Cadmus
is emptied of its people while black Death
grows rich in groaning and in lamentation.
We have not come as suppliants to this altar
because we thought of you as of a God,
but rather judging you the first of men
in all the chances of this life and when
we mortals have to do with more than man.
You came and by your coming saved our city,
freed us from tribute which we paid of old
to the Sphinx,[6] cruel singer. This you did
in virtue of no knowledge we could give you,
in virtue of no teaching; it was God
that aided you, men say, and you are held
with God's assistance to have saved our lives.
Now Oedipus, Greatest in all men's eyes,
here falling at your feet we all entreat you,
find us some strength for rescue.
Perhaps you'll hear a wise word from some God,
perhaps you will learn something from a man
(for I have seen that for the skilled of practice
the outcome of their counsels live the most).
Noblest of men, go, and raise up our city,
go,—and give heed. For now this land of ours
calls you its savior since you saved it once.
So, let us never speak about your reign
as of a time when first our feet were set
secure on high, but later fell to ruin.
Raise up our city, save it and raise it up.
Once you have brought us luck with happy omen;
be no less now in fortune.
If you will rule this land, as now you rule it,
better to rule it full of men than empty.
For neither tower nor ship is anything
when empty, and none live in it together.

❶ *Why do the people of Thebes turn to Oedipus to help them with their current problem?*

Oedipus. I pity you, children. You have come full of longing,
but I have known the story before you told it
only too well. I know you are all sick,
yet there is not one of you, sick though you are,
that is as sick as I myself.
Your several sorrows each have single scope
and touch but one of you. My spirit groans
for city and myself and you at once.
You have not roused me like a man from sleep;

❷ *In what way does Oedipus's sorrow differ from the sorrow the people of Thebes experience?*

6. **Sphinx.** Monster that killed Thebans who could not solve her riddle. When Oedipus solved the riddle, the outraged Sphinx destroyed herself.

know that I have given many tears to this,
gone many ways wandering in thought,
but as I thought I found only one remedy
and that I took. I sent Menoeceus' son
Creon, Jocasta's brother, to Apollo,
to his Pythian temple,
that he might learn there by what act or word
I could save this city. As I count the days,
it vexes me what ails him; he is gone
far longer than he needed for the journey.
But when he comes, then, may I prove a villain,
if I shall not do all the God commands.

1 What has Oedipus done to discover the cause of the plague that threatens Thebes?

PRIEST. Thanks for your gracious words. Your servants here
signal that Creon is this moment coming.

OEDIPUS. His face is bright. O holy Lord Apollo,
so grant that his news too may be bright for us
and bring us safety.

PRIEST. It is happy news,
I think, for else his head would not be crowned
with sprigs of fruitful laurel.[7]

OEDIPUS. We will know soon,
he's within hail. Lord Creon, my good brother,
what is the word you bring us from the God?

CREON *enters.*

CREON. A good word,—for things hard to bear themselves
if in the final issue all is well
I count complete good fortune.

OEDIPUS. What do you mean?
What you have said so far
leaves me uncertain whether to trust or fear.

CREON. If you will hear my news before these others
I am ready to speak, or else to go within.

OEDIPUS. Speak it to all;
the grief I bear, I bear it more for these
than for my own heart.

CREON. I will tell you, then,
what I heard from the God.
King Phoebus[8] in plain words commanded us
to drive out a pollution from our land,
pollution grown ingrained within the land;
drive it out, said the God, not cherish it,
till it's past cure.

2 What news does Creon bring back from the oracle? Why is it difficult to carry out the god's demand?

7. **laurel.** A type of evergreen, laurel symbolized victory or honor. A crown of laurel signified good news.
8. **King Phoebus.** Apollo

Answers to Guided Reading Questions

1 Oedipus has sent Creon, the brother of his wife, to Apollo's Pythian temple to ask for advice or guidance.

2 Creon says that the murderers of Laius must be found and punished by execution or banishment if Thebes is to be freed from the plague. Laius's murder happened many years ago, and little is known about it.

Cultural/Historical Note

Inform or remind students of the following information about some of the Greek gods referred to in *Oedipus*.

- **Apollo** was the god of music, poetry, wisdom, light, and truth. Often, especially in later myths, he was called Phoebus Apollo. *Phoebus* means "shining," and in these later myths, Apollo was often called the god of the sun. He was associated with the laurel tree, whose leaves were used to crown great poets and heroes. His sacred animals were the dolphin and the crow.
- **Artemis,** sister of Apollo, was the goddess of the woods, the moon, and the hunt. A protector of chastity and of youth, she was often pictured carrying a bow and arrow and wearing the moon in her hair. She was associated with the cypress tree and with wild animals including boars and deer.
- **Athene,** or **Athena,** was the goddess of wisdom, justice, war, civilization, and peace. She sprang from the head of her father Zeus. She was called "tamer of the horses" and was the patron of cities and of handicrafts such as spinning and weaving. She often carried the shield and thunderbolt of Zeus and was described as "gray-eyed." She was associated with the olive tree and the owl.

(cont.)

Cultural/Historical Note (cont.)

- **Dionysus** was the god of revelry and of the vine. He was often pictured as a handsome youth with grape leaves and vines in his hair and pan pipes in his hands. His worshippers, the fierce female maenads, honored him with ecstatic, frenzied, and often brutal rituals.
- **Zeus** was the leader of the Olympian gods, the god of the sky and of thunder. He carried a thunderbolt, wore a breastplate called the aegis, and was associated with the oak tree and the eagle. His palace was on Mount Olympus.

Answers to Guided Reading Questions

❶ The man refers to many robbers. Oedipus refers to a single robber.

Quotables

"Tragedy . . . is an imitation of an action that is serious, complete, and of a certain magnitude; in language embellished with each kind of artistic ornament . . . in the form of action, not of narrative; through pity and fear effecting the proper purgation of these emotions."

—Aristotle
from the *Poetics*

Additional Questions and Activities

Share with students Aristotle's definition of tragedy (see above). As they read, ask them to keep this definition in mind. When they have finished reading *Oedipus the King*, ask them to analyze the drama as a tragedy, according to Aristotle's definition. In other words, have them explain why the play meets or does not meet the criteria for tragedy set forth by Aristotle.

OEDIPUS. What is the rite
of purification? How shall it be done?

CREON. By banishing a man, or expiation
of blood by blood, since it is murder guilt
which holds our city in this destroying storm.

OEDIPUS. Who is this man whose fate the God pronounces?

CREON. My Lord, before you piloted the state we had a king called Laius.

OEDIPUS. I know of him by hearsay. I have not seen him.

CREON. The God commanded clearly: let some one
punish with force this dead man's murderers.

OEDIPUS. Where are they in the world? Where would a trace
of this old crime be found? It would be hard
to guess where.

CREON. The clue is in this land;
that which is sought is found;
the unheeded thing escapes:
so said the God.

OEDIPUS. Was it at home,
or in the country that death came upon him,
or in another country travelling?

CREON. He went, he said himself, upon an embassy,[9]
but never returned when he set out from home.

OEDIPUS. Was there no messenger, no fellow traveller
who knew what happened? Such a one might tell
something of use.

CREON. They were all killed save one. He fled in terror
and he could tell us nothing in clear terms
of what he knew, nothing, but one thing only.

OEDIPUS. What was it?
If we could even find a slim beginning
in which to hope, we might discover much.

CREON. This man said that the robbers they encountered
were many and the hands that did the murder
were many; it was no man's single power.

 ❶

What did the only survivor from Laius's party say about the slaying of the king? How do Oedipus's words differ from this man's account?

---

9. **embassy.** Important mission

Words for Everyday Use

ex • pi • a • tion (eks´pē ā´shən) *n.*, act of atonement or reconciliation

Vocabulary in Context

• Ulysses used prayer as expiation for his sins.

OEDIPUS. How could a robber dare a deed like this
were he not helped with money from the city,
money and treachery?

CREON. That indeed was thought.
But Laius was dead and in our trouble
there was none to help.

OEDIPUS. What trouble was so great to hinder you
inquiring out the murder of your king?

CREON. The riddling Sphinx induced us to neglect
mysterious crimes and rather seek solution
of troubles at our feet.

OEDIPUS. I will bring this to light again. King Phoebus
fittingly took this care about the dead,
and you too fittingly.
And justly you will see in me an ally,
a champion of my country and the God.
For when I drive pollution from the land
I will not serve a distant friend's advantage,
but act in my own interest. Whoever
he was that killed the king may readily
wish to dispatch me with his murderous hand;
so helping the dead king I help myself.

Come, children, take your suppliant boughs and go;
up from the altars now. Call the assembly
and let it meet upon the understanding
that I'll do everything. God will decide
whether we prosper or remain in sorrow.

PRIEST. Rise, children—it was this we came to seek,
which of himself the king now offers us.
May Phoebus who gave us the oracle
come to our rescue and stay the plague.

Exeunt all but the CHORUS.

CHORUS.

Strophe

What is the sweet spoken word of God from the shrine of Pytho[10]
rich in gold

10. **Pytho.** From *Python,* the serpent that once guarded the spot, another name for Delphi

① Why is Oedipus intent upon finding the killer?

WORDS FOR EVERYDAY USE

in • duce (in do͞os´) *vt.,* persuade; lead on to some action, condition, or belief

ANSWERS TO GUIDED READING QUESTIONS

① Oedipus, aside from wanting to free his city from the plague, recognizes that a man who has once killed a king might do so again, therefore it is in Oedipus's best interest to catch the killer.

CULTURAL/HISTORICAL NOTE

The sphinx is a prominent creature in both Egyptian and Greek mythology and art. The sphinx has the head of a human and the body of a lion. The most famous image of the sphinx in art is the Great Sphinx at Giza, which was created as a partial portrait of King Khafre of Egypt (c. 2575–2465 BC). After this period, as stories about the sphinx spread to Mesopotamia and later to Greece, wings were added to the lion's body. Scholars believe that myths about and depictions of the sphinx first appeared in Greece around 1600 BC but disappeared for roughly 400 years. In later depictions, the Greek sphinx was normally female and wore a long, tiered wig. The confrontation between Oedipus and the sphinx was widely depicted on vases.

VOCABULARY IN CONTEXT

- Imogene's clownlike antics never failed to induce a wave a laughter from her friends.

Answers to Guided Reading Questions

❶ Fear is expressed. The oracle's words suggest that the situation is not pleasant in Thebes. The idea of reopening old troubles may be frightening.

❷ The second antistrophe acts as a reminder of the dead and dying, and requests deliverance from the plague.

Cultural/Historical Note

In Greek mythology, the Fates are three goddesses who determine the length of a person's life and how much misery or suffering he or she will experience. Beginning in the eighth century BC with Hesiod, the Fates have been depicted as three elderly female spinners of human destiny. In later writings specific tasks are attributed to each of the Fates: Clotho spins the thread of human life, Lachesis dispenses the thread, and Atropos cuts the thread and ends the life. Some writers combine the idea of the Fates into a single Fate.

The concept of fate, as opposed to free will, plays a major role in this drama. The ancient Greeks believed that each person has a fate or destiny assigned to him or her. They believed that it was useless to try to avoid one's fate and that it was best to accept it with dignity. Oedipus tries to avoid his fate but is unable to do so.

 ❶

What emotion is expressed in the first strophe? Why might the words of the oracle have aroused such feelings?

❷

Summarize the second antistrophe. What does the Chorus ask of Athene?

that has come to glorious Thebes?
I am stretched on the rack of doubt, and terror and trembling hold
my heart, O Delian Healer,[11] and I worship full of fears
for what doom you will bring to pass, new or renewed in the revolving years.
Speak to me, immortal voice,
child of golden Hope.

Antistrophe

First I call on you, Athene, deathless daughter of Zeus,
and Artemis, Earth Upholder,
who sits in the midst of the marketplace in the throne which men call Fame,
and Phoebus, the Far Shooter, three averters of Fate,[12]
come to us now, if ever before, when ruin rushed upon the state,
you drove destruction's flame away
out of our land.

Strophe

Our sorrows defy number;
all the ship's timbers are rotten;
taking of thought is no spear for the driving away of the plague.
There are no growing children in this famous land;
there are no women bearing the pangs of childbirth.
You may see them one with another, like birds swift on the wing,
quicker than fire unmastered,
speeding away to the coast of the Western God.[13]

Antistrophe

In the unnumbered deaths
of its people the city dies;
those children that are born lie dead on the naked earth
unpitied, spreading contagion of death; and grey haired mothers and wives
everywhere stand at the altar's edge, suppliant, moaning;
the hymn to the healing God rings out but with it the wailing voices are blended.
From these our sufferings grant us, O golden Daughter of Zeus,[14]
glad-faced deliverance.

Strophe

There is no clash of brazen shields but our fight is with the War God,[15]
a War God ringed with the cries of men, a savage God who burns us;
grant that he turn in racing course backwards out of our country's bounds
to the great palace of Amphitrite[16] or where the waves of the Thracian sea

---

11. **Delian Healer.** Apollo, born on the island of Delos, could cause and cure plagues and was popularly called the Healer.
12. **Athene . . . averters of Fate.** Athene, Artemis, and Apollo, three gods to whom the chorus prays for protection from death
13. **Western God.** Death
14. **golden Daughter of Zeus.** Athene
15. **War God.** Ares
16. **Amphitrite.** Sea goddess, wife of Poseidon, god of the sea

Temple of Zeus, Athens

deny the stranger safe anchorage.
Whatsoever escapes the night
at last the light of day revisits;
so smite the War God, Father Zeus,
beneath your thunderbolt,
for you are the Lord of the lightning, the lightning that carries fire.

Antistrophe

And your unconquered arrow shafts, winged by the golden corded bow,
Lycean King,[17] I beg to be at our side for help;
and the gleaming torches of Artemis with which she scours the Lycean hills,
and I call on the God with the turban of gold, who gave his name to this country of ours,
the Bacchic God with the wind flushed face,
Evian One,[18] who travel
with the Maenad company,[19]
combat the God that burns us
with your torch of pine;
for the God that is our enemy is a God unhonored among the Gods.

---

17. **Lycean King.** From the title *Lykios*, meaning god of light; refers to Apollo
18. **God with the turban . . . Evian One.** References to Dionysus, god of the vine and revelry who comes from the east and wears a turban, has a rosy complexion, and is addressed by his followers with the cry "evoi"
19. **Maenad company.** Female followers of Dionysus

Literary Technique

Strophe* and *Antistrophe

Remind students that the ***strophe*** and ***antistrophe*** are parts of the *paradoi,* or scenes in which the chorus dances and sings commentary on the action of the play. The antistrophe is a reply to the strophe.

Apposition

An **apposition** is a grammatical form in which a thing is renamed in a different word, phrase, or clause. Point out, or have students identify, the apposition on page 627 in which the phrases "the Bacchic God with the wind flushed face," "Evian One," and "who travel with the Maenad company," refer back to "God with the turban of gold," a reference to Dionysus.

ANSWERS TO GUIDED READING QUESTIONS

➊ Oedipus demands that any Theban who knows anything of Laius's killer report what he or she knows.

➋ Oedipus demands that the killer be cast out of the city. The killer is not to be welcomed by anyone of the city, and will be cursed to "wear out" the rest of his or her life in misery. The audience knows that Oedipus is the killer whom he himself is seeking.

BIOGRAPHICAL NOTE

Sophocles was one of three great Athenian tragic dramatists. The others were Aeschylus and Euripides.

Aeschylus (525–456 BC) was the earliest of the three. His innovations include adding a second actor (traditionally, there had been only one actor in Greek theater performances) and making the dialogue more important than the choral parts in his plays. Seven of his works survive, including the *Oresteia* trilogy, which consists of *Agamemnon, The Libation Bearers,* and *The Furies.* The trilogy tells the story of how Agamemnon was murdered by his wife and later avenged by his son. Aeschylus's other works are *Persians, Seven against Thebes, Suppliants,* and *Prometheus Bound.*

Euripides (480–406 BC) was the youngest of these three dramatists. Although Euripides was the least successful of the three during his lifetime, a greater number of his plays have survived. He is especially noted for his sympathetic portrayal of ordinary people, especially women. His works include *Medea, Hippolytus, Electra, Trojan Women, Ion, Iphigenia at Aulis,* and *Bacchants.*

OEDIPUS *returns.*

OEDIPUS. For what you ask me—if you will hear my words,
and hearing welcome them and fight the plague,
you will find strength and lightening of your load.

Hark to me; what I say to you, I say
as one that is a stranger to the story
as stranger to the deed. For I would not
be far upon the track if I alone
were tracing it without a clue. But now,
since after all was finished, I became
a citizen among you, citizens—
now I proclaim to all the men of Thebes:
who so among you knows the murderer
by whose hand Laius, son of Labdacus,
died—I command him to tell everything
to me,—yes, though he fears himself to take the blame
on his own head; for bitter punishment
he shall have none, but leave this land unharmed.
Or if he knows the murderer, another,
a foreigner, still let him speak the truth.
For I will pay him and be grateful, too.
But if you shall keep silence, if perhaps
some one of you, to shield a guilty friend,
or for his own sake shall reject my words—
hear what I shall do then:
I forbid that man, whoever he be, my land,
my land where I hold sovereignty[20] and throne;
and I forbid any to welcome him
or cry him greeting or make him a sharer
in sacrifice or offering to the Gods,
or give him water for his hands to wash.
I command all to drive him from their homes,
since he is our pollution, as the oracle
of Pytho's God[21] proclaimed him now to me.
So I stand forth a champion of the God
and of the man who died.
Upon the murderer I invoke this curse—

➊ *What demand does Oedipus make of the citizens of Thebes?*

➋ *What punishment and curse does Oedipus prescribe for Laius's killer? What does the audience know about the killer that Oedipus does not know?*

20. **sovereignty.** Complete authority
21. **Pytho's God.** Apollo, who killed Python

WORDS FOR EVERYDAY USE

in • voke (in vōk´) *vt.,* call on; summon

VOCABULARY IN CONTEXT

• In times of trouble, he would invoke the gods to come to his aid.

whether he is one man and all unknown,
or one of many—may he wear out his life
in misery to miserable doom!
If with my knowledge he lives at my hearth
I pray that I myself may feel my curse.
On you I lay my charge to fulfill all this
for me, for the God, and for this land of ours
destroyed and blighted, by the God forsaken.

Even were this no matter of God's ordinance
it would not fit you so to leave it lie,
unpurified, since a good man is dead
and one that was a king. Search it out.
Since I am now the holder of his office,
and have his bed and wife that once was his,
and had his line not been unfortunate
we would have common children—(fortune leaped
upon his head)—because of all these things,
I fight in his defense as for my father,
and I shall try all means to take the murderer
of Laius the son of Labdacus
the son of Polydorus and before him
of Cadmus and before him of Agenor.
Those who do not obey me, may the Gods
grant no crops springing from the ground they plough
nor children to their women! May a fate
like this, or one still worse than this consume them!
For you whom these words please, the other Thebans,
may Justice as your ally and all the Gods
live with you, blessing you now and for ever!

❶ *What two things that once belonged to Laius now belong to Oedipus? With what intensity will Oedipus search for the killer of Laius?*

CHORUS. As you have held me to my oath, I speak:
I neither killed the king nor can declare
the killer; but since Phoebus set the quest
it is his part to tell who the man is.

OEDIPUS. Right; but to put compulsion on the Gods
against their will—no man can do that.

CHORUS. May I then say what I think second best?

OEDIPUS. If there's a third best, too, spare not to tell it.

CHORUS. I know that what the Lord Teiresias
sees, is most often what the Lord Apollo
sees. If you should inquire of this from him
you might find out most clearly.

❷ *Why doesn't Oedipus want to ask Apollo's oracle about the killer's identity?*

❸ *Why does the Chorus suggest consulting Teiresias? How does Oedipus respond?*

WORDS FOR EVERYDAY USE

com • pul • sion (kəm pul´shən) *n.,* compelling, driving force

Answers to Guided Reading Questions

❶ Oedipus now has Laius's position and is married to Laius's former wife. Oedipus says he will search for the killer of Laius as he would if the murdered were his own father.

❷ Oedipus claims that nobody can compel the gods to do something they do not want to do.

❸ The Chorus says that Teiresias usually sees what Apollo sees and he may very well be able to help Oedipus. Oedipus replies that he has already called for Teiresias.

Quotables

"Destiny
Waiteth alike for them that men call free
And them by others mastered."

—Aeschylus
from *The Furies*

"I think that Fortune watcheth o'er our lives,
Surer than we. But well said: he who strives
Will find his gods strive for him equally."

—Euripides
from *Electra*

Vocabulary in Context

• Liam claims that he could not control the compulsion to break into song during the movie.

Answers to Guided Reading Questions

❶ Oedipus urges Teiresias to do whatever he can to save himself and the city by sharing any information he has or can obtain about Laius's killer.

❷ Wisdom is terrible when it does not help the person who is wise. Teiresias regrets that he knows Laius's killer and that he has come to face Oedipus's questions.

Literary Note

Aeschylus's *Prometheus Bound* serves as a fine example of Greek tragedy. In this drama, the Titan Prometheus helps human beings by bringing them fire and by teaching them useful arts such as writing and building. In his pride, Prometheus ignores the warnings of Zeus, who does not want human beings to have such power, and as a result, Zeus condemns Prometheus to be chained to a rock and tortured. Some common themes that appear not only in *Prometheus Bound* but throughout Greek tragedy are justice and injustice, the relationship between power and knowledge, and the struggle to exert one's free will while caught in the web of fate. Usually, Greek tragedy pits the hero against one or more gods, and the hero's downfall in such a case is inevitable, a matter of fate in which the hero's character, or personality, becomes his or her destiny.

Oedipus. Even in this my actions have not been sluggard.
On Creon's word I have sent two messengers
and why the prophet is not here already
I have been wondering.

Chorus. His skill apart
there is besides only an old faint story.

Oedipus. What is it?
I look at every story.

Chorus. It was said
that he was killed by certain wayfarers.

Oedipus. I heard that, too, but no one saw the killer.

Chorus. Yet if he has a share of fear at all,
his courage will not stand firm, hearing your curse.

Oedipus. The man who in the doing did not shrink
will fear no word.

Chorus. Here comes his prosecutor:
led by your men the godly prophet comes
in whom alone of mankind truth is native.

Enter Teiresias, *led by a little boy.*

Oedipus. Teiresias, you are versed in everything,
things teachable and things not to be spoken,
things of the heaven and earth-creeping things.
You have no eyes but in your mind you know
with what a plague our city is afflicted.
My lord, in you alone we find a champion,
in you alone one that can rescue us.
Perhaps you have not heard the messengers,
but Phoebus sent in answer to our sending
an oracle declaring that our freedom
from this disease would only come when we
should learn the names of those who killed King Laius,
and kill them or expel from our country.
Do not begrudge us oracles from birds,[22]
or any other way of prophecy
within your skill; save yourself and the city,
save me; redeem the debt of our pollution
that lies on us because of this dead man.
We are in your hands; pains are most nobly taken
to help another when you have means and power.

Teiresias. Alas, how terrible is wisdom when

Q ❶ *What plea does Oedipus make to Teiresias?*

Q ❷ *When is wisdom "terrible"? What does Teiresias regret?*

22. **oracles from birds.** Birds were commonly used to foretell the future.

it brings no profit to the man that's wise!
This I knew well, but had forgotten it,
else I would not have come here.

OEDIPUS. What is this?
How sad you are now you have come!

TEIRESIAS. Let me
go home. It will be easiest for us both
to bear our several destinies to the end
if you will follow my advice.

OEDIPUS. You'd rob us
of this your gift of prophecy? You talk
as one who had no care for law nor love
for Thebes who reared you.

TEIRESIAS. Yes, but I see that even your own words
miss the mark; therefore I must fear for mine.

OEDIPUS. For God's sake if you know of anything,
do not turn from us; all of us kneel to you,
all of us here, your suppliants.

TEIRESIAS. All of you here know nothing. I will not
bring to the light of day my troubles, mine—
rather than call them yours.

OEDIPUS. What do you mean?
You know of something but refuse to speak.
Would you betray us and destroy the city?

TEIRESIAS. I will not bring this pain upon us both,
neither on you nor on myself. Why is it
you question me and waste your labor? I
will tell you nothing.

OEDIPUS. You would provoke a stone! Tell us, you villain,
tell us, and do not stand there quietly
unmoved and balking at the issue.

TEIRESIAS. You blame my temper but you do not see
your own that lives within you; it is me
you chide.

OEDIPUS. Who would not feel his temper rise
at words like these with which you shame our city?

TEIRESIAS. Of themselves things will come, although I hide them
and breathe no word of them.

1 *Why is Teiresias unwilling to share what he knows with Oedipus? Do you think Oedipus would believe Teiresias if the seer told all that he knew?*

WORDS FOR EVERYDAY USE

balk (bôk´) *vi.,* obstinately refuse to move or act

ANSWERS TO GUIDED READING QUESTIONS

1 Teiresias knows that Oedipus is the killer and that such a revelation will bring terrible suffering. Oedipus would probably find Teiresias's story difficult to believe.

QUOTABLES

"The men that stood for office, noted for acknowledged worth

And for manly deeds of honor, and for honorable birth;

Train'd in exercise and art, in sacred dances and in song,

All are ousted and supplanted by a base ignoble throng."

—Aristophanes
from *Frogs*

LITERARY NOTE

While Aeschylus, Sophocles, and Euripides were the foremost Greek tragedy writers, **Aristophanes** (c. 450–c. 388 BC) was the greatest Greek comic playwright. Little is known about the life of Aristophanes. He is believed to have written about forty plays, though only eleven still remain. They are *Acharnians, Knights, Clouds, Wasps, Peace, Birds, Lysistrata, Women at the Thesmophoria, Frogs, Women at the Ecclesia,* and *Wealth.* His works often satirized Athenian society, philosophical fads, and the foreign policy of Athens during the Peloponnesian War.

VOCABULARY IN CONTEXT

- Ivar openly discussed his ideas, but he balked when I asked him to share his thoughts on my radio show.

Answers to Guided Reading Questions

1 Oedipus accuses Teiresias of having been part of the plot to kill Laius. He may think that Teiresias was involved because of his unwillingness to talk or he may be trying to goad Teiresias into revealing what he knows.

2 Teiresias says that Oedipus is the murderer of King Laius. Oedipus says that Teiresias is a liar and will be punished if he makes such accusations again.

Quotables

"At times truth may not seem probable."

—Nicolas Boileau-Despréaux

"Truth is mighty and will prevail."

—Thomas Brooks

"Our minds possess by nature an insatiable desire to know the truth."

—Cicero

"For truth is unwelcome, however divine."

—William Cowper

"All truths are not meant to be told."

—George Herbert

"The truth shall make you free."

—John 7:32

Oedipus. Since they will come
tell them to me.

Teiresias. I will say nothing further.
Against this answer let your temper rage
as wildly as you will.

1 Of what does Oedipus accuse Teiresias? Why does he make this accusation?

Oedipus. Indeed I am
so angry I shall not hold back a jot
of what I think. For I would have you know
I think you were complotter[23] of the deed
and doer of the deed save in so far
as for the actual killing. Had you had eyes
I would have said alone you murdered him.

Teiresias. Yes? Then I warn you faithfully to keep
the letter of your proclamation and
from this day forth to speak no word of greeting
to these nor me; you are the land's pollution.

Oedipus. How shamelessly you started up this taunt!
How do you think you will escape?

Teiresias. I have.
I have escaped; the truth is what I cherish
and that's my strength.

Oedipus. And who has taught you truth?
Not your profession surely!

Teiresias. You have taught me,
for you have made me speak against my will.

Oedipus. Speak what? Tell me again that I may learn it better.

Teiresias. Did you not understand before or would you
provoke me into speaking?

Oedipus. I did not grasp it,
not so to call it known. Say it again.

2 What does Teiresias reveal? How does Oedipus react?

Teiresias. I say you are the murderer of the king
whose murderer you seek.

Oedipus. Not twice you shall
say calumnies like this and stay unpunished.

Teiresias. Shall I say more to tempt your anger more?

23. **complotter.** One who plots with another

Words for Everyday Use

ca • lum • ny (kal´əm nē) *n.,* false and malicious statement meant to hurt someone's reputation

Vocabulary in Context

• The calumny spread by her opponent in the dirty campaign damaged Deirdre's reputation.

Oedipus and Teiresias. *Photo courtesy of Lyric Stage Company*

OEDIPUS. As much as you desire; it will be said
in vain.

TEIRESIAS. I say that with those you love best
you live in foulest shame unconsciously
and do not see where you are in calamity.

OEDIPUS. Do you imagine you can always talk
like this, and live to laugh at it hereafter?

TEIRESIAS. Yes, if the truth has anything of strength.

OEDIPUS. It has, but not for you; it has no strength
for you because you are blind in mind and ears
as well as in your eyes.

TEIRESIAS. You are a poor wretch
to taunt me with the very insults which
every one soon will heap upon yourself.

OEDIPUS. Your life is one long night so that you cannot
hurt me or any other who sees the light.

TEIRESIAS. It is not fate that I should be your ruin,
Apollo is enough; it is his care
to work this out.

OEDIPUS. Was this your own design
or Creon's?

TEIRESIAS. Creon is no hurt to you,
but you are to yourself.

❶ *What does Oedipus say about Teiresias's blindness? Who does Oedipus really describe?*

❷ *What prediction does Teiresias make?*

❸ *Whom does Oedipus now blame? Explain Teiresias's warning.*

ANSWERS TO GUIDED READING QUESTIONS

❶ Oedipus says that Teiresias is unable to hear or think clearly, that he is blind to the truth. Oedipus, in refusing to hear Teiresias or to understand the truth, is describing himself.

❷ Teiresias predicts that soon everyone will know that Oedipus is the one who has been blind. He also hints that Oedipus will soon be literally sightless.

❸ Oedipus lays blame on Creon. Teiresias says that Oedipus should fear himself because in his blindness to the truth, Oedipus is unknowingly seeking to condemn and punish himself.

ADDITIONAL QUESTIONS AND ACTIVITIES

In the dialogue on pages 632 and 633, Teiresias refers several times to the truth. He says that he cherishes the truth and believes the the strength of the truth will save him from Oedipus's wrath. Share the ideas about truth expressed in the Quotables box on page 632. Ask students which of these sentiments apply to *Oedipus*. Students should explain their responses. Then have students explain which of the quotations expresses their own feelings about truth. Ask them to create their own aphorisms about truth.

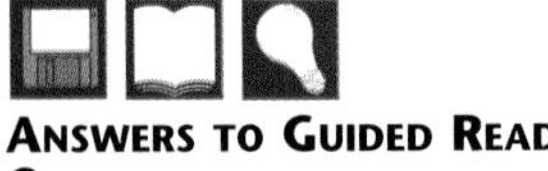

Answers to Guided Reading Questions

1. Oedipus points out that he saved the city from the Sphinx while Teiresias was unable to do anything.

2. The Chorus feels that both Teiresias and Oedipus have spoken in anger. They remind the two men that their anger will not solve the problems of Thebes.

3. Oedipus does not see the truth about his situation—that he has killed his father and has married his mother. He does not realize that he will soon be literally blind.

Additional Questions and Activities

Oedipus refers with pride to his accomplishment in solving the riddle of the sphinx. Solving riddles and other puzzles involves creative and logical thinking. Have students try to answer the following riddles:

1. I have no wings, but they say I fly. Every second I'm passing by. You cannot see me though you try. You cannot stop me, for you see, I march on eternally.
2. I have an eye but cannot see. I'm of no use unless something trails me.
3. I follow you everywhere. Where you go I do not care. In certain lights I disappear. I weigh nothing; I'm thinner than air.

Students may wish to try other mental puzzles. Suggest that they find books of logic puzzles, riddles, or brain teasers in the library. They might also try to create their own puzzles to share with other students.

Answers

1. Time
2. Needle
3. Shadow

Oedipus. Wealth, sovereignty and skill outmatching skill
for the <u>contrivance</u> of an envied life!
Great store of jealousy fill your treasury chests,
if my friend Creon, friend from the first and loyal,
thus secretly attacks me, secretly
desires to drive me out and secretly
<u>suborns</u> this juggling, trick devising quack,
this wily beggar who has only eyes
for his own gains, but blindness in his skill.
For, tell me, where have you seen clear, Teiresias,
with your prophetic eyes? When the dark singer,
the sphinx, was in your country, did you speak
word of deliverance to its citizens?
And yet the riddle's answer was not the province
of a chance comer. It was a prophet's task
and plainly you had no such gift of prophecy
from birds nor otherwise from any God
to glean a word of knowledge. But I came,
Oedipus, who knew nothing, and I stopped her.
I solved the riddle by my wit alone.
Mine was no knowledge got from birds. And now
you would expel me,
because you think that you will find a place
by Creon's throne. I think you will be sorry,
both you and your accomplice, for your plot
to drive me out. And did I not regard you
as an old man, some suffering would have taught you
that what was in your heart was treason.

1 What excuse does Oedipus use to discount Teiresias's abilities?

Chorus. We look at this man's words and yours, my king,
and we find both have spoken them in anger.
We need no angry words but only thought
how we may best hit the God's meaning for us.

2 How does the Chorus feel about the exchange between Oedipus and Teiresias? With what are they concerned?

Teiresias. If you are king, at least I have the right
no less to speak in my defense against you.
Of that much I am master. I am no slave
of yours, but Loxias', and so I shall not
enroll myself with Creon for my patron.
Since you have taunted me with being blind,
here is my word for you.
You have your eyes but see not where you are
in sin, nor where you live, nor whom you live with.

3 In what way is Oedipus blind? In what way will Oedipus's situation become similar to Teiresias's?

Words for Everyday Use

con • tri • vance (kən tri´vəns) *n.,* act of devising, scheming, or planning

sub • orn (sə bôrn´) *vt.,* induce or instigate to do something illegal, especially to commit perjury

Vocabulary in Context

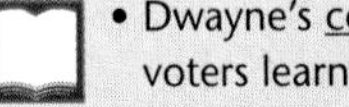

- Dwayne's <u>contrivance</u> to ruin his opponent's chances by a smear campaign backfired when the voters learned of his deception.
- Threatening Lucas with bodily harm, the criminal's lackey <u>suborned</u> him to keep him from testifying against the accused.

Do you know who your parents are? Unknowing
you are an enemy to kith and kin
in death, beneath the earth, and in this life.
A deadly footed, double striking curse,
from father and mother both, shall drive you forth
out of this land, with darkness on your eyes,
that now have such straight vision. Shall there be
a place will not be harbor to your cries,
a corner of Cithaeron[24] will not ring
in echo to your cries, soon, soon,—
when you shall learn the secret of your marriage,
which steered you to a haven in this house,—
haven no haven, after lucky voyage?
And of the multitude of other evils
establishing a grim equality
between you and your children, you know nothing.
So, muddy with contempt my words and Creon's!
Misery shall grind no man as it will you.

OEDIPUS. Is it endurable that I should hear
such words from him? Go and a curse go with you!
Quick, home with you! Out of my house at once!

TEIRESIAS. I would not have come either had you not called me.

OEDIPUS. I did not know then you would talk like a fool—
or it would have been long before I called you.

TEIRESIAS. I am a fool then, as it seems to you—
but to the parents who have bred you, wise.

OEDIPUS. What parents? Stop! Who are they of all the world?

TEIRESIAS. This day will show your birth and will destroy you.

OEDIPUS. How needlessly your riddles darken everything.

TEIRESIAS. But it's in riddle answering you are strongest.

OEDIPUS. Yes. Taunt me where you will find me great.

TEIRESIAS. It is this very luck that has destroyed you.

OEDIPUS. I do not care, if it has saved this city.

TEIRESIAS. Well, I will go. Come, boy, lead me away.

OEDIPUS. Yes, lead him off. So long as you are here,
you'll be a stumbling block and a vexation;
once gone, you will not trouble me again.

24. **Cithaeron.** Mountain on which the infant Oedipus was abandoned

1 *What, according to Teiresias, will happen within the day? Why should Oedipus understand the situation? What role does luck play in his destiny?*

WORDS FOR EVERYDAY USE

vex • a • tion (veks ā´shən) *n.*, cause of annoyance or distress

ANSWERS TO GUIDED READING QUESTIONS

1 Teiresias says that within the day Oedipus's parents will be revealed and the truth will destroy him. Oedipus should be able to figure out the situation because his special skill is in solving riddles or problems. While Oedipus is lucky that he can solve riddles, this time it would be better if he were not so good at solving riddles. His luck will destroy him.

LITERARY NOTE

Teiresias refers to "a grim equality" between Oedipus and his children, referring to the fact that Oedipus and his children have the same mother, Jocasta.

LITERARY TECHNIQUE

FORESHADOWING

Foreshadowing is the act of presenting materials that hint at events to occur later in a story. In lines 485–499, Teiresias foreshadows the revelation that Jocasta is Oedipus's mother as well as his wife, and that he will take his own sight and become blind.

VOCABULARY IN CONTEXT

• The directions were easy to follow, but the vexation of heavy traffic made the trip difficult.

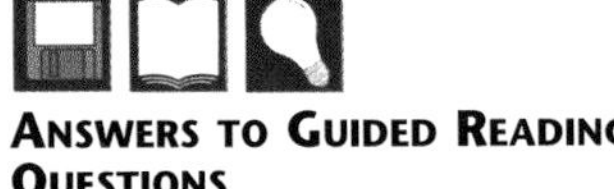

Answers to Guided Reading Questions

❶ Teiresias means that the truth about Oedipus's parents, Laius and Jocasta, who were both Thebans, will be revealed. He is predicting that Oedipus will blind himself.

❷ As an infant, Oedipus's feet were bound with a spike, leaving permanent damage. While he may need to run "with a stronger foot than Pegasus," he is unable to do so.

Cross-curricular Activities

SOCIAL STUDIES

Sigmund Freud introduced the concept of the Oedipus complex in his 1899 work *Interpretation of Dreams.* The term refers to a person's desire for sexual relations with the parent of the opposite sex and a sense of rivalry with the parent of the same sex. (Originally the term was used only for this condition in a male, while the term *Electra complex* was used for the condition in females. Now the term *Oedipus complex* is generally used in reference to both males and females.) The term takes its name, of course, from the legend of Oedipus who killed his father and married his mother. Freud attributed this complex to children between the ages of three and five. This stage usually ends when the child represses his or her sexual instincts and identifies with the parent of the same sex.

Interested students can read from Freud's works or from the works of Anna Freud, daughter of Sigmund and a highly respected psychoanalyst in her own right.

TEIRESIAS. I have said
what I came here to say not fearing your
countenance: there is no way you can hurt me.
I tell you, king, this man, this murderer
(whom you have long declared you are in search of,
indicting him in threatening proclamation
as murderer of Laius)—he is here.
In name he is a stranger among citizens
but soon he will be shown to be a citizen
true native Theban, and he'll have no joy
of the discovery: blindness for sight
and beggary for riches his exchange,
he shall go journeying to a foreign country
tapping his way before him with a stick.
He shall be proved father and brother both
to his own children in his house; to her
that gave him birth, a son and husband both;
a fellow sower in his father's bed
with that same father that he murdered.
Go within, reckon that out, and if you find me
mistaken, say I have no skill in prophecy.

Exit separately TEIRESIAS *and* OEDIPUS.

❶ *What does Teiresias mean when he says that Oedipus will be shown to be a "true native Theban"? Why does he say that Oedipus will go "tapping his way before him with a stick"?*

CHORUS.

Strophe
Who is the man proclaimed
by Delphi's prophetic rock
as the bloody handed murderer,
the doer of deeds that none dare name?
Now is the time for him to run
with a stronger foot
than Pegasus[25]
for the child of Zeus leaps in arms upon him
with fire and the lightning bolt,
and terribly close on his heels
are the Fates that never miss.

Antistrophe
Lately from snowy Parnassus
clearly the voice flashed forth,
bidding each Theban track him down,

❷ *Oedipus's name means "swollen foot." What significance might Oedipus's name and history have upon the Chorus's statement, "Now is the time for him to run with a stronger foot than Pegasus"?*

25. **Pegasus.** Winged horse

WORDS FOR EVERYDAY USE
coun • te • nance (koun´tə nəns) *n.,* facial expression

Vocabulary in Context

• By Duleeka's sympathetic countenance, I could tell that she was moved by the touching story.

the unknown murderer.
In the savage forests he lurks and in
the caverns like
the mountain bull.
He is sad and lonely, and lonely his feet
that carry him far from the navel of earth;[26]
but its prophecies, ever living,
flutter around his head.

Strophe

The augur[27] has spread confusion,
terrible confusion;
I do not approve what was said
nor can I deny it.
I do not know what to say;
I am in a flutter of foreboding;
I never heard in the present
nor past of a quarrel between
the sons of Labdacus and Polybus,
that I might bring as proof
in attacking the popular fame
of Oedipus, seeking
to take vengeance for undiscovered
death in the line of Labdacus.

Antistrophe

Truly Zeus and Apollo are wise
and in human things all knowing;
but amongst men there is no
distinct judgment, between the prophet
and me—which of us is right.
One man may pass another in wisdom
but I would never agree
with those that find fault with the king
till I should see the word
proved right beyond doubt. For once
in visible form the Sphinx
came on him and all of us
saw his wisdom and in that test
he saved the city. So he will not be condemned by my mind.

Enter CREON.

CREON. Citizens, I have come because I heard
deadly words spread about me, that the king
accuses me. I cannot take that from him.
If he believes that in these present troubles
he has been wronged by me in word or deed

26. **navel of the earth.** Refers to Delphi, which was considered the center of the earth
27. **augur.** Prophet, here Teiresias

❶ *What is the Chorus's reaction to Teiresias's words?*

❷ *How do the Thebans, as represented by the Chorus, regard their king?*

Answers to Guided Reading Questions

❶ The Chorus blames Teiresias for spreading confusion. The Chorus does not approve or deny what Teiresias has said.

❷ The people of Thebes still remember how Oedipus saved them, and they are unwilling to condemn him until the accusations are proved to be true.

Biographical Note

Sigmund Freud (1856–1939) founded psychoanalysis and the Freudian theory of psychology. Freud studied at the University of Vienna and the General Hospital of Vienna. Beginning in Paris in 1885, French neurologist Jean-Martin Charcot had a major impact on Freud's work. It was during work with Charcot on patients diagnosed as hysterics that Freud began to believe in the concept of mental disorders with purely psychological causes. Freud first presented his method of psychoanalysis by free association in his 1895 work *Studies in Hysteria,* a collaboration with physician Josef Breuer. Freud delved deeper into the layers of the mind. In 1899 he published *The Interpretation of Dreams,* and in 1905 he published his study *Three Essays on the Theory of Sexuality,* which introduces his ideas about infant sexuality and enlarges upon the concept of the Oedipus complex. His other works include *Totem and Taboo* and *Civilization and Its Discontents.*

Answers to Guided Reading Questions

❶ Oedipus accuses Creon of trying to steal the crown. Oedipus has no evidence; he is lashing out at Creon because of his own fears.

❷ Creon accuses Oedipus of lacking wisdom and of failing to see the facts. *Responses will vary.*

Additional Questions and Activities

Oedipus accuses Creon, and Creon says that he does "not want to live with the burden of such a scandal" upon him. Oedipus's words may have arisen out of anger at Teiresias's words, or fear of being thought guilty himself, but whatever their reason, Oedipus's words have a negative effect on the opinion people have of Creon. Discuss with your students the idea of defamation and the terms *libel* and *slander.* Explain that *libel* refers to written or printed words or images produced with the intent to injure somebody's reputation. The word *slander* refers to verbal statements of the same kind. Ask students to think about and discuss how they would feel if their reputation were wrongly tarnished. What impact might libel or slander have on a person's life?

I do not want to live on with the burden
of such a scandal on me. The report
injures me doubly and most vitally—
for I'll be called a traitor to my city
and traitor also to my friends and you.

Chorus. Perhaps it was a sudden gust of anger
that forced that insult from him, and no judgment.

Creon. But did he say that it was in compliance
with schemes of mine that the seer told him lies?

Chorus. Yes, he said that, but why, I do not know.

Creon. Were his eyes straight in his head? Was his mind right
when he accused me in this fashion?

Chorus. I do not know; I have no eyes to see
what princes do. Here comes the king himself.

Enter Oedipus.

❶ *Of what does Oedipus accuse Creon? Does Oedipus have any evidence to prove these accusations?*

Oedipus. You, sir, how is it you come here? Have you so much
brazen-faced daring that you venture in
my house although you are manifestly
the murderer of that man, and though you tried,
openly, highway robbery of my crown?
For God's sake, tell me what you saw in me,
what cowardice or what stupidity,
that made you lay a plot like this against me?
Did you imagine I should not observe
the crafty scheme that stole upon me or
seeing it, take no means to counter it?
Was it not stupid of you to make the attempt,
to try to hunt down royal power without
the people at your back or friends? For only
with the people at your back or money can
the hunt end in the capture of a crown.

Creon. Do you know what you're doing? Will you listen
to words to answer yours, and then pass judgment?

Oedipus. You're quick to speak, but I am slow to grasp you,
for I have found you dangerous,—and my foe.

Creon. First of all hear what I shall say to that.

Oedipus. At least don't tell me that you are not guilty.

❷ *What does Creon accuse Oedipus of lacking? Do you agree with him?*

Creon. If you think obstinacy without wisdom
a valuable possession, you are wrong.

Words for Everyday Use

ob • sti • na • cy (äb´stə nə sē) *n.,* stubbornness; unreasonable determination to have one's way

Vocabulary in Context

• Tyrone knew that he was wrong, but his obstinacy would not let him give up the argument.

OEDIPUS. And you are wrong if you believe that one,
a criminal, will not be punished only
because he is my kinsman.

CREON. This is but just—
but tell me, then, of what offense I'm guilty?

OEDIPUS. Did you or did you not urge me to send
to this prophetic mumbler?

CREON. I did indeed,
and I shall stand by what I told you.

OEDIPUS. How long ago is it since Laius . . .

CREON. What about Laius? I don't understand.

OEDIPUS. Vanished—died—was murdered?

CREON. It is long,
a long, long time to reckon.

OEDIPUS. Was this prophet
in the profession then?

CREON. He was, and honored
as highly as he is today.

OEDIPUS. At that time did he say a word about me?

CREON. Never, at least when I was near him.

OEDIPUS. You never made a search for the dead man?

CREON. We searched, indeed, but never learned of anything.

OEDIPUS. Why did our wise old friend not say this then?

CREON. I don't know; and when I know nothing, I
usually hold my tongue.

OEDIPUS. You know this much,
and can declare this much if you are loyal.

CREON. What is it? If I know, I'll not deny it.

OEDIPUS. That he would not have said that I killed Laius
had he not met you first.

CREON. You know yourself
whether he said this, but I demand that I
should hear as much from you as you from me.

OEDIPUS. Then hear,—I'll not be proved a murderer.

CREON. Well, then. You're married to my sister.

OEDIPUS. Yes,
that I am not disposed to deny.

CREON. You rule
this country giving her an equal share
in the government?

❶ *Why is Oedipus following this line of questioning?*

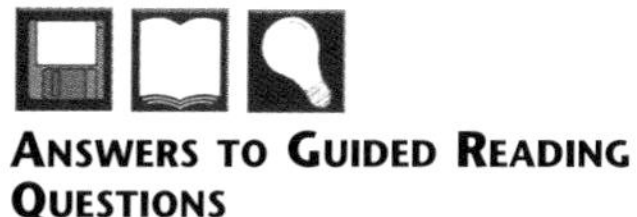

ANSWERS TO GUIDED READING QUESTIONS

❶ Oedipus, by questioning Teiresias's past account of the murder, is trying to show that Teiresias has only blamed Oedipus at Creon's prompting.

Answers to Guided Reading Questions

❶ Creon explains that he does not want to be king, because he already has all the benefits of being king without the fear or danger the position entails.

❷ Creon suggests that Oedipus consult the oracle at Delphi. Creon claims that if he is found to be guilty of conspiring with Teiresias he should be killed. He puts a terrible sentence upon his own head. By putting forth a sentence for the killer of Laius, Oedipus has unknowingly done the same. Ironically, Creon appears to be guilty to Oedipus although he is innocent, while Oedipus appears to be innocent yet is actually guilty.

Oedipus. Yes, everything she wants
she has from me.

Creon. And I, as thirdsman[28] to you,
am rated as the equal of you two?

Oedipus. Yes, and it's there you've proved yourself false friend.

Creon. Not if you will reflect on it as I do.
Consider, first, if you think any one
would choose to rule and fear rather than rule
and sleep untroubled by a fear if power
were equal in both cases. I, at least,
I was not born with such a frantic yearning
to be a king—but to do what kings do.
And so it is with every one who has learned
wisdom and self-control. As it stands now,
the prizes are all mine—and without fear.
But if I were the king myself, I must
do much that went against the grain.
How should despotic rule seem sweeter to me
than painless power and an assured authority?
I am not so besotted yet that I
want other honours than those that come with profit.
Now every man's my pleasure; every man greets me;
now those who are your suitors fawn on me,—
success for them depends upon my favour.
Why should I let all this go to win that?
My mind would not be traitor if it's wise;
I am no treason lover, of my nature,
nor would I ever dare to join a plot.
Prove what I say. Go to the oracle
at Pytho and inquire about the answers,
if they are as I told you. For the rest,
if you discover I laid any plot
together with the seer, kill me, I say,
not only by your vote but by my own.
But do not charge me on obscure opinion
without some proof to back it. It's not just
lightly to count your knaves as honest men,
nor honest men as knaves. To throw away
an honest friend is, as it were, to throw

❶ Explain the argument Creon uses to show that he is not trying to take Oedipus's position as king.

❷ What does Creon suggest that Oedipus do to prove that he is telling the truth? In what way is the punishment that Creon suggests for himself similar to the punishment Oedipus suggests for the killer of Laius? What about each man's situation makes his claim different?

28. **thirdsman.** Third in line

Words for Everyday Use

des • pot • ic (des pät´ik) *adj.,* autocratic; tyrannical; absolute

knave (nāv) *n.,* dishonest or deceitful person

Vocabulary in Context

- The tyrant was overthrown only to be replaced by an equally despotic leader.
- My neighbor puts on a facade of honesty, but he is a knave at heart.

your life away, which a man loves the best.
In time you will know all with certainty;
time is the only test of honest men,
one day is space enough to know a rogue.

CHORUS. His words are wise, king, if one fears to fall.
Those who are quick of temper are not safe.

OEDIPUS. When he that plots against me secretly
moves quickly, I must quickly counterplot.
If I wait taking no decisive measure
his business will be done, and mine be spoiled.

CREON. What do you want to do then? Banish me?

OEDIPUS. No, certainly; kill you, not banish you.

CREON. I do not think that you've your wits about you.

OEDIPUS. For my own interests, yes.

CREON. But for mine, too,
you should think equally.

OEDIPUS. You are a rogue.

CREON. Suppose you do not understand?

OEDIPUS. But yet
I must be ruler.

CREON. Not if you rule badly.

OEDIPUS. O, city, city!

CREON. I too have some share
in the city; it is not yours alone.

CHORUS. Stop, my lords! Here—and in the nick of time
I see Jocasta coming from the house;
with her help lay the quarrel that now stirs you.

Enter JOCASTA.

JOCASTA. For shame! Why have you raised this foolish squabbling
brawl? Are you not ashamed to air your private
griefs when the country's sick? Go in, you, Oedipus,
and you, too, Creon, into the house. Don't magnify
your nothing troubles.

CREON. Sister, Oedipus,
your husband, thinks he has the right to do
terrible wrongs—he has but to choose between
two terrors: banishing or killing me.

OEDIPUS. He's right, Jocasta; for I find him plotting
with knavish tricks against my person.

CREON. That God may never bless me! May I die
accursed, if I have been guilty of
one tittle of the charge you bring against me!

❶ *Why does Oedipus insist that he must kill Creon? What objection does Creon make?*

ANSWERS TO GUIDED READING QUESTIONS

❶ Oedipus insists that killing Creon is part of being a leader. Creon says that Oedipus should not be a ruler if he rules badly.

ADDITIONAL QUESTIONS AND ACTIVITIES

Ask students to look at lines 710–717 and then to answer the following questions:

1. Why does Creon urge Oedipus to take time to make his decision?
2. To what aspect of Oedipus does he appeal?
3. What does this passage say about the things that Creon values?

ANSWERS

1. Creon urges Oedipus to wait so that he may gain more information and calm his temper rather than make a rash decision.
2. Creon appeals to Oedipus's reason and sense of duty to a friend.
3. Creon values honesty, friendship, and time-proven worth.

Answers to Guided Reading Questions

❶ The Chorus advises Oedipus to spare Creon. *Responses will vary.* Students may say that Oedipus will not spare Creon in his efforts to save himself. Others may say that Oedipus will see the truth and spare an innocent man.

❷ The Chorus claims that killing Creon will only add more troubles to those that the country is already facing. Oedipus spares Creon out of pity for the Chorus or the citizens of Thebes.

❸ Creon says that Oedipus sulks and has a dangerous temper. He also claims that Oedipus is the one who suffers the most from his own bad temperment.

Additional Questions and Activities

Jocasta chides Oedipus and Creon for squabbling in public while matters of state are unsettled. Ask students to discuss the role of personal lives and relationships in the public perception of leaders today. In their discussion, students might address the following questions: Do public figures have a right to privacy? Are private matters related to a person's ability to perform his or her public duties? What effect do decisions or actions in a leader's private life have on people's perceptions of him or her? Ask students to cite examples to support their opinions.

Jocasta. I beg you, Oedipus, trust him in this,
spare him for the sake of this his oath to God,
for my sake, and the sake of those who stand here.

What does the Chorus advise Oedipus to do? Do you think Oedipus will follow the advice of the Chorus?

Chorus. Be gracious, be merciful,
we beg of you.

Oedipus. In what would you have me yield?

Chorus. He has been no silly child in the past.
He is strong in his oath now.
Spare him.

Oedipus. Do you know what you ask?

Chorus. Yes.

Oedipus. Tell me then.

Chorus. He has been your friend before all men's eyes; do not cast him
away dishonoured on an obscure conjecture.

Oedipus. I would have you know that this request of yours
really requests my death or banishment.

❷ *What reason does the Chorus offer Oedipus for sparing Creon? Why does Oedipus spare him?*

Chorus. May the Sun God,[29] king of Gods, forbid! May I die without
God's blessing, without friends' help, if I had any such thought.
But my spirit is broken by my unhappiness for my wasting
country; and this would but add troubles amongst ourselves to the
other troubles.

Oedipus. Well, let him go then—if I must die ten times for it,
or be sent out dishonoured into exile.
It is your lips that prayed for him I pitied,
not his; wherever he is, I shall hate him.

❸ *What does Creon say about Oedipus's nature?*

Creon. I see you sulk in yielding and you're dangerous
when you are out of temper; natures like yours
are justly heaviest for themselves to bear.

Oedipus. Leave me alone! Take yourself off, I tell you.

Creon. I'll go, you have not known me, but they have,
and they have known my innocence.

Exit.

Chorus. Won't you take him inside, lady?

Jocasta. Yes, when I've found out what was the matter.

Chorus. There was some misconceived suspicion of a story, and on the
other side the sting of injustice.

---

29. **Sun God.** Apollo

Words for Everyday Use

con • jec • ture (kən jec´chər) *n.,* guess; prediction made with incomplete evidence

Vocabulary in Context

- Until we have more evidence, we well not be able to verify whether or not Gwenyth's conjecture is correct.

Oedipus and Jocasta. Photo courtesy of Lyric Stage Company

JOCASTA. So, on both sides?

CHORUS. Yes.

JOCASTA. What was the story?

CHORUS. I think it best, in the interests of the country, to leave it where it ended.

OEDIPUS. You see where you have ended, straight of judgment
although you are, by softening my anger.

CHORUS. Sir, I have said before and I say again—be sure that I would have been proved a madman, bankrupt in sane council, if I should put you away, you who steered the country I love safely when she was crazed with troubles. God grant that now, too, you may prove a fortunate guide for us.

JOCASTA. Tell me, my lord, I beg of you, what was it
that roused your anger so?

OEDIPUS. Yes, I will tell you.
I honour you more than I honour them.
It was Creon and the plots he laid against me.

JOCASTA. Tell me—if you can clearly tell the quarrel—

ADDITIONAL QUESTIONS AND ACTIVITIES

Ask students the following questions:

1. What opinion does Creon hold about Oedipus's disposition? Why does he feel this way?
2. At this point in the drama, how do the people of Thebes, represented by the Chorus, feel about Oedipus?

ANSWERS

1. Creon thinks that Oedipus has a sulking, quick-tempered disposition. He thinks this type of disposition is dangerous. He notices that Oedipus yields to the pleas to spare Creon, but he does so grudgingly, without quitting his anger.
2. At this point, the Chorus still backs Oedipus. They respect him for his past leadership and hope that he will be able to lead them out of their latest troubles.

Answers to Guided Reading Questions

❶ Jocasta claims that prophecies are useless. She bases her beliefs on the prophecy that her son by Laius would kill Laius, a prophecy she believes was never carried out. *Responses will vary.*

❷ Oedipus asks Jocasta about Laius's murder because he needs more details. When Jocasta says that Laius was killed at the crossroads, Oedipus thinks of the man he killed at a crossroads.

INTEGRATED SKILLS ACTIVITIES

APPLIED ENGLISH

Have students use the idea of finding and punishing a murderer to explore career options. First have students brainstorm a list of professionals who might be involved if the Oedipus case were an open murder case today. (Some possible responses are detective, lawyer, judge, reporter, talk show host, etc.) Have students choose one of these professions and do some research about the schooling or training needed to enter the field, skills needed, and what a person in the field actually does. Information on careers is provided in the Language Arts Survey 5.2, "Finding Career Information." Students can share their findings by imagining they are working in their chosen profession and are involved in the Oedipus case. They can write a description of or prepare a skit showing their role in the process.

► Additional practice is provided in the Essential Skills Practice Book: Applied English/Tech Prep 5.2.

❶ *How does Jocasta feel about prophecies? What incident does she use to support her claim? How do you think Oedipus feels upon hearing her story?*

❷ *Why does Oedipus question Jocasta about Laius's murder? What do you think is on Oedipus's mind?*

OEDIPUS. Creon says
that I'm the murderer of Laius.

JOCASTA. Of his own knowledge or on information?

OEDIPUS. He sent this rascal prophet to me, since
he keeps his own mouth clean of any guilt.

JOCASTA. Do not concern yourself about this matter;
listen to me and learn that human beings
have no part in the craft of prophecy.
Of that I'll show you a short proof.
There was an oracle once that came to Laius,—
I will not say that it was Phoebus' own,
but it was from his servants—and it told him
that it was fate that he should die a victim
at the hands of his own son, a son to be born
of Laius and me. But, see now, he,
the king, was killed by foreign highway robbers
at a place where three roads meet—so goes the story;
and for the son—before three days were out
after his birth King Laius pierced his ankles
and by the hands of others cast him forth
upon a pathless hillside. So Apollo
failed to fulfill his oracle to the son,
that he should kill his father, and to Laius
also proved false in that the thing he feared,
death at his son's hands, never came to pass.
So clear in this case were the oracles,
so clear and false. Give them no heed, I say;
what God discovers need of, easily
he shows to us himself.

OEDIPUS. O dear Jocasta,
as I hear this from you, there comes upon me
a wandering of the soul—I could run mad.

JOCASTA. What trouble is it, that you turn again
and speak like this?

OEDIPUS. I thought I heard you say
that Laius was killed at a crossroads.

JOCASTA. Yes, that was how the story went and still
that word goes round.

OEDIPUS. Where is this place, Jocasta,
where he was murdered?

JOCASTA. Phocis is the country
and the road splits there, one of two roads from Delphi,
another comes from Daulia.

OEDIPUS. How long ago is this?

JOCASTA. The news came to the city just before

you became king and all men's eyes looked to you.
What is it, Oedipus, that's in your mind?

OEDIPUS. What have you designed, O Zeus, to do with me?

JOCASTA. What is the thought that troubles your heart?

OEDIPUS. Don't ask me yet—tell me of Laius—
How did he look? How old or young was he?

JOCASTA. He was a tall man and his hair was grizzled
already—nearly white—and in his form
not unlike you.

OEDIPUS. O God, I think I have
called curses on myself in ignorance.

JOCASTA. What do you mean? I am terrified
when I look at you.

OEDIPUS. I have a deadly fear
that the old seer had eyes. You'll show me more
if you can tell me one more thing.

❶ What does Oedipus fear?

JOCASTA. I will.
I'm frightened,—but if I can understand,
I'll tell you all you ask.

OEDIPUS. How was his company?
Had he few with him when he went this journey,
or many servants, as would suit a prince?

JOCASTA. In all there were but five, and among them
a herald;[30] and one carriage for the king.

OEDIPUS. It's plain—it's plain—who was it told you this?

JOCASTA. The only servant that escaped safe home.

OEDIPUS. Is he at home now?

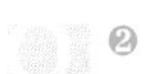

JOCASTA. No, when he came home again
and saw you king and Laius was dead,
he came to me and touched my hand and begged
that I should send him to the fields to be
my shepherd and so he might see the city
as far off as he might. So I
sent him away. He was an honest man,
as slaves go, and was worthy of far more
than what he asked of me.

❷ Why do you think the servant asked to be sent away from the city when he returned?

OEDIPUS. O, how I wish that he could come back quickly!

JOCASTA. He can. Why is your heart so set on this?

OEDIPUS. O dear Jocasta, I am full of fears
that I have spoken far too much; and therefore
I wish to see this shepherd.

30. **herald.** Person who carries messages and proclamations

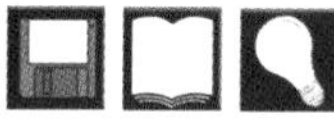

ANSWERS TO GUIDED READING QUESTIONS

❶ He fears that Teiresias might have been right. He is learning more that points to him as the killer.

❷ The servant had witnessed Oedipus's murder of Laius and was probably afraid Oedipus would have him killed.

Answers to Guided Reading Questions

❶ Oedipus is taunted for being a bastard and wants to learn the truth about his parentage. He learns that he is to lie with his mother and kill his father.

❷ Oedipus flees to avoid his fate. In trying to run away from what has been predicted, he encounters Laius, slays him and continues on to Thebes where the rest of the prophecy is fulfilled.

Cultural/Historical Note

The Dorians, Greek peoples who took their name from the city of Doris in central Greece, are considered the conquerors of the Peloponnesus (c. 1100 BC). According to legend, the sons of Hercules were driven out of the Peloponnesus. They took refuge in Doris, and many years later led the Dorian people in a successful invasion of the Peloponnesus. The historical origins of the Dorians is unclear, but scholars believe that they originated in northern and northwestern Greece before moving into the southern part of Greece. The migration of the Dorians spread as far as Sicily, northern Africa, and the Crimean Peninsula in the Black Sea.

The Doric culture was not highly advanced, but they did make significant contributions in literature and in architecture. In literature, the Dorians introduced the use of choral lyrics in Greek tragedy. In architecture, their innovations are known as the Doric order. This simple, restrained order is defined by its columns. A Doric column has a slightly tapered, fluted shaft, generally without a base. The capital is simple while the entablature includes a frieze with alternating triglyphs and receding panels. You may wish to show students a diagram of a Doric column and explain the architectural terms: shaft, base, capital, entablature, frieze, and triglyphs.

Jocasta. He will come;
but, Oedipus, I think I'm worthy too
to know what it is that disquiets you.

Oedipus. It shall not be kept from you, since my mind
has gone so far with its forebodings. Whom
should I confide in rather than you, who is there
of more importance to me who have passed
through such a fortune?
Polybus was my father, king of Corinth,
and Merope, the Dorian, my mother.[31]
I was held greatest of the citizens
in Corinth till a curious chance befell me
as I shall tell you—curious, indeed,
but hardly worth the store I set upon it.
There was a dinner and at it a man,
a drunken man, accused me in his drink
of being bastard. I was furious
but held my temper under for that day.
Next day I went and taxed my parents with it;
they took the insult very ill from him,
the drunken fellow who had uttered it.
So I was comforted for their part, but
still this thing rankled always, for the story
crept about widely. And I went at last
to Pytho, though my parents did not know.
But Phoebus sent me home again unhonoured
in what I came to learn, but he foretold
other and desperate horrors to befall me,
that I was fated to lie with my mother,
and show to daylight an accursed breed
which men would not endure, and I was doomed
to be murderer of the father that begot me.
When I heard this I fled, and in the days
that followed I would measure from the stars
the whereabouts of Corinth—yes, I fled
to somewhere where I should not see fulfilled
the infamies told in that dreadful oracle.
And as I journeyed I came to the place

❶ *What prompted Oedipus to seek the truth about his parentage? What does he learn instead?*

❷ *What does Oedipus do to try to avoid his fate? In what way does his attempt to flee his fate contribute to his fulfilling the prophesy?*

31. **Polybus . . . mother.** Oedipus was raised by Polybus, king of Corinth, a city west of Athens, and Merope, a native of Doris. Dorians were one of the four main peoples of ancient Greece.

Words for Everyday Use

ran • kle (raŋ´kəl) *vt.,* cause to have long-lasting anger, rancor, or resentment

in • fa • my (in´fə mē) *n.,* disgraceful or dishonorable act

Vocabulary in Context

- Carmen's nasty remark still rankles Miranda.
- Benedict Arnold is linked with the infamy of treason.

where, as you say, this king met with his death.
Jocasta, I will tell you the whole truth.
When I was near the branching of the crossroads,
going on foot, I was encountered by
a herald and a carriage with a man in it,
just as you tell me. He that led the way
and the old man himself wanted to thrust me
out of the road by force. I became angry
and struck the coachman who was pushing me.
When the old man saw this he watched his moment,
and as I passed he struck me from his carriage,
full on the head with his two pointed goad.[32]
But he was paid in full and presently
my stick had struck him backwards from the car
and he rolled out of it. And then I killed them
all. If it happened there was any tie
of kinship twixt this man and Laius,
who is then now more miserable than I,
what man on earth so hated by the Gods,
since neither citizen nor foreigner
may welcome me at home or even greet me,
but drive me out of doors? And it is I,
I and no other have so cursed myself.
And I pollute the bed of him I killed
by the hands that killed him. Was I not born evil?
Am I not utterly unclean? I had to fly
and in my banishment not even see
my kindred nor set foot in my own country,
or otherwise my fate was to be yoked
in marriage with my mother and kill my father,
Polybus who begot me and had reared me.
Would not one rightly judge and say that on me
these things were sent by some malignant God?
O no, no, no—O holy majesty
of God on high, may I not see that day!
May I be gone out of men's sight before
I see the deadly taint of this disaster
come upon me.

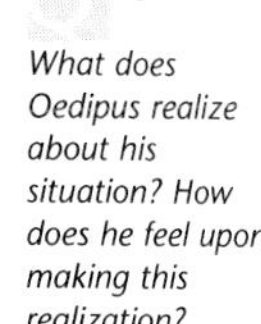

What does Oedipus realize about his situation? How does he feel upon making this realization?

Chorus. Sir, we too fear these things. But until you see this man face to face and hear his story, hope.

Oedipus. Yes, I have just this much of hope—to wait until the herdsman comes.

Jocasta. And when he comes, what do you want with him?

Oedipus. I'll tell you; if I find that his story is the same as yours, I at least will be clear of this guilt.

32. **goad.** Pointed stick used to herd animals

Answers to Guided Reading Questions

① Oedipus realizes that he is the murderer of Laius. He thinks that he was born evil. He is distraught at what he has done and at what must now happen to him.

Historical Note

Corinth is the name of both an ancient and modern Greek city. The modern city is located three miles northeast of the remains of the ancient city of Corinth which lies west of Athens. Located on the Isthmus of Corinth, which separates the Peloponnesus from central Greece, Corinth commanded a position of strategic and commercial importance. The expansion of the Corinthian power led to colonies in Corcyra (now Corfu) and Syracuse (still a city in Sicily) which put Corinth in a powerful trading position in the western Mediterranean.

ANSWERS TO GUIDED READING QUESTIONS

❶ Oedipus wants to know if the shepherd spoke of robbers or of a single robber.

❷ The Chorus hopes to be found "pious in word and deed." They are horrified by the details that have been revealed and they hope that they may be free of the corruption that is being revealed in Oedipus.

INTEGRATED SKILLS ACTIVITIES

SPEAKING AND LISTENING SKILLS

Because of the Chorus, the play lends itself nicely to a group reading. Choose a scene with both dialogue between characters and insight from the Chorus. Assign students to the various parts. Have one group of students read the *strophe* and another group read the *antistrophe.* Refer students to the Language Arts Survey 3.1, "Elements of Verbal and Nonverbal Communication" for advice on using these elements in their dramatic readings.

▶ Additional practice is provided in the Essential Skills Practice Book: Speaking and Listening 3.1.

 ❶

What detail of the shepherd's story does Oedipus want to clarify?

JOCASTA. Why what so particularly did you learn from my story?

OEDIPUS. You said that he spoke of highway *robbers* who killed Laius. Now if he uses the same number, it was not I who killed him. One man cannot be the same as many. But if he speaks of a man travelling alone, then clearly the burden of the guilt inclines toward me.

JOCASTA. Be sure, at least, that this was how he told the story. He cannot unsay it now, for every one in the city heard it—not I alone. But, Oedipus, even if he diverges from what he said then, he shall never prove that the murder of Laius squares rightly with the prophecy—for Loxias[33] declared that the king should be killed by his own son. And that poor creature did not kill him surely,—for he died himself first. So as far as prophecy goes, henceforward I shall not look to the right hand or the left.

OEDIPUS. Right. But yet, send some one for the peasant to bring him here; do not neglect it.

JOCASTA. I will send quickly. Now let me go indoors. I will do nothing except what pleases you.

Exeunt.

CHORUS.

❷

For what does the Chorus hope? What may have prompted the Chorus to express this hope?

Strophe

May destiny ever find me
pious in word and deed
prescribed by the laws that live on high:
laws begotten in the clear air of heaven,
whose only father is Olympus;
no mortal nature brought them to birth,
no forgetfulness shall lull them to sleep;
for God is great in them and grows not old.

Antistrophe

Insolence breeds the tyrant, insolence
if it is glutted with a surfeit, unseasonable, unprofitable,
climbs to the rooftop and plunges
sheer down to the ruin that must be,
and there its feet are no service.
But I pray that the God may never
abolish the eager ambition that profits the state.
For I shall never cease to hold the God as our protector.

Strophe

If a man walks with haughtiness

33. **Loxias.** Apollo

WORDS FOR EVERYDAY USE

in • so • lence (in´sə ləns) *n.,* impudence; bold disrespect
sur • feit (sʉr´fit) *n.,* excess; too great an amount or supply

VOCABULARY IN CONTEXT

- The student was given detention for her insolence after talking back to the principal.
- After the drought, a sudden surfeit of water flooded the town.

of hand or word and gives no heed
to Justice and the shrines of Gods
despises—may an evil doom
smite him for his ill-starred pride of heart!—
if he reaps gains without justice
and will not hold from impiety
and his fingers itch for untouchable things.
When such things are done, what man shall contrive
to shield his soul from the shafts of the God?
When such deeds are held in honour,
why should I honour the Gods in the dance?

Antistrophe
No longer to the holy place,
to the navel of earth I'll go
to worship, nor to Abae
nor to Olympia,
unless the oracles are proved to fit,
for all men's hands to point at.
O Zeus, if you are rightly called
the sovereign lord, all-mastering,
let this not escape you nor your ever-living power!
The oracles concerning Laius
are old and dim and men regard them not.
Apollo is nowhere clear in honour; God's service perishes.

❶ *How does the Chorus feel about the gods? about prophecies?*

Statue of Apollo, Pompeii

Answers to Guided Reading Questions

❶ The chorus says that they will no longer worship at many of the shrines, nor will they trust the prophecies.

Selection Check Test with Answers

EX. Of what is Oedipus king?
Oedipus is King of Thebes.

1. Where had Oedipus sent Creon?
He had sent Creon to Apollo's Pythian temple.

2. What deed allowed Oedipus to become king?
He saved Thebes by solving the riddle of the Sphinx.

3. What must be done to save Thebes from the plague?
The murderer of King Laius must be found and punished.

4. Who is Teiresias?
Teiresias is a blind prophet. He identifies Oedipus as the murderer.

5. Why had Oedipus left Corinth?
Oedipus had left his native Corinth to avoid fulfilling the prophecy that he would kill his father and marry his mother.

Responding to the Selection

Suggest that students make some predictions about the second part of the play based on their opinions of Oedipus at this point in the drama.

You may also have students discuss the qualities they admire in a leader and whether or not they see these qualities in national, state, or local government officials.

Answers for Reviewing the Selection

RECALLING AND INTERPRETING

1. **Recalling.** Thebes is facing a terrible plague. Oedipus has sent Creon to Apollo's Pythian temple to learn what they must do to rid the city of the plague. Oedipus wants to find the killer to save Thebes and to protect himself. **Interpreting.** Oedipus's desire to save the city makes him admirable. His determination to learn the truth to save himself despite the danger that learning the truth seems to bring makes him pitiable.

2. **Recalling.** The killer was not sought because at the time of Laius's murder the Sphinx was tormenting Thebes and everyone was preoccupied with trying to rid the city of that scourge. Oedipus plans to curse the killer and to ban him from the city. **Interpreting.** If Oedipus knew the truth, he might set a more lenient punishment and proceed with less zeal.

3. **Recalling.** Jocasta tells Oedipus not to worry about the oracle because she has known prophecies that have not come true. Oedipus is alarmed by the detail that Laius was killed at a crossroads. **Interpreting.** Jocasta supports her belief by telling of the prophecy that Laius would die by his own son's hands, which she believes to be false, since she thinks that their only son died as a baby and that Laius was killed by highway robbers at a crossroads. (cont.)

Responding to the Selection

What do you think of Oedipus as a leader? Which of his actions or words have most strongly affected your opinion of him? Has that opinion changed over the course of part 1?

Reviewing the Selection

Recalling / Interpreting

1. What problem faces the city of Thebes at the beginning of the play? What has Oedipus done to solve the problem? What two reasons does Oedipus have for searching out and punishing Laius's killer? ▶▶ What effect does each of these two reasons have on your perception of Oedipus?

2. Why was Laius's killer never sought? What does Oedipus plan to do regarding this killer? ▶▶ How might Oedipus proceed if he knew the truth about his past?

3. What does Jocasta say about prophecies? What details from her story alarm Oedipus? ▶▶ Why is Jocasta so confident that the prophecies cannot be trusted? Why are these details so alarming to Oedipus?

4. What prophecy had Oedipus learned before coming to Thebes? What did he do as a result of this prophecy? Why does Oedipus call for the herdsman? What does he hope the herdsman's story will do? ▶▶ How much of what is happening to Oedipus do you believe is the result of fate? How much of what is happening to Oedipus do you see as the result of his own free will?

Synthesizing

5. What role does the Chorus play in this scene? Why is the Chorus important? What relationship does Oedipus seem to have with the Chorus? What does this relationship reveal about Oedipus as a king? about the Chorus?

Answers for Reviewing the Selection (cont.)

Oedipus is alarmed by this detail because he had killed some men at a crossroads. He is starting to realize that he could be the killer.

4. **Recalling.** Oedipus had been told that he was destined to kill his father and wed his mother. He fled from Corinth. He calls for the herdsman to learn the details of the murder of Laius. He hopes that the herdsman's story will contain something that will clear him of the murder. **Interpreting.** *Responses will vary.* Students' reactions may be based on their own beliefs in fate or free will. Discuss with students the attitudes toward fate held by the ancient Greeks to help students achieve a better understanding of Oedipus's reaction to his situation.

(cont.)

Understanding Literature (Questions for Discussion)

1. **Irony and Dramatic Irony. Irony** is a difference between appearance and reality. **Dramatic irony** occurs when something is known by the reader or audience but unknown to the characters. What does the audience know about Laius's killer that Oedipus does not know? Identify several statements made by Oedipus that are ironic.

2. **Paradox.** A **paradox** is a seemingly contradictory statement, idea, or event. Teiresias is a called a "blind seer." In what way is this a contradictory idea? In what way is Teiresias blind? In what way can he see? What does he mean when he says to Oedipus, "You have your eyes but see not where you are in sin, nor where you live, nor whom you live with"? Why is Oedipus the one who is blind?

3. **Metaphor and Simile.** A **metaphor** is a figure of speech in which one thing is written or spoken about as if it were another. A **simile** is a comparison using *like* or *as.* In his first speech, the priest compares the city of Thebes to a reeling wreck of a ship. In what way are the two things similar? Identify the metaphor he uses to continue this comparison. Are the comparisons appropriate and effective? Explain.

Columns in olive grove, Olympus

Answers for Understanding Literature

Responses will vary. Possible responses are given.

1. **Irony and Dramatic Irony.** The audience knows that Oedipus is Laius's killer. Students may point to many statements in which Oedipus heaps curses upon the killer and eagerly seeks to learn the identity of the killer, such as "I forbid any to welcome him [the murderer] or cry him greeting or make him a sharer in sacrifice or offering to the Gods, or give him water for his hands to wash. I command all to drive him from their homes, since he is our pollution" (lines 257–262). Students might also refer to the passage in which Oedipus accuses Teiresias of being not only physically blind but blind to the truth as well.

2. **Paradox.** Teiresias is deprived of the sense of sight. He can, however, see the future and can sense the truth of a situation. Oedipus has the sense of sight, but he does not see his own situation. Oedipus is blind to the fact that the prophecy about his life has been fulfilled.

3. **Metaphor and Simile.** Both the ship and Thebes are failing, causing a great loss of human life. The priest continues the comparison by saying that "it can scarcely lift its prow out of the depths, out of the bloody surf," meaning that the city hardly has the strength to continue to exist.

Answers for Reviewing the Selection (cont.)

SYNTHESIZING

Responses will vary. Possible responses are given.

5. The Chorus serves as the collective voice of the people of Thebes. The Chorus builds tension by commenting upon what has happened and hinting at what will happen. Oedipus often responds to the emotions expressed by the Chorus, and the Chorus offers warnings and forebodings to their king. Oedipus also appeals to the Chorus to support him as king and to denounce Creon. Oedipus hopes that popular support from the citizens, represented by the Chorus, will help in this time of trial.

ADDITIONAL RESOURCES

READER'S GUIDE

- Selection Worksheet 8.4

ASSESSMENT PORTFOLIO

- Selection Check Test 2.8.7
- Selection Test 2.8.8

ESSENTIAL SKILLS PRACTICE BOOKS

- Writing 1.6, 1.8, 1.20
- Language 2.66
- Study and Research 4.20

SUPPORT FOR LEP STUDENTS

PRONUNCIATIONS OF PROPER NOUNS AND ADJECTIVES

Cith • aer • on (sith´ər on)
Cyl • lene (sil lēn´)
Lox • i • as (läks´ē əs)
Po • ly • bus (po lē´bəs)

ADDITIONAL VOCABULARY

brooches—ornamental pins
festered—decayed
foreknow—know beforehand; predict
savager—more cruel
thrice—three times
treachery—deceit, treason

ANSWERS TO GUIDED READING QUESTIONS

❶ Jocasta carries garlands as an offering to Apollo. She asks him to free them from the curse.

READER'S JOURNAL

Do you believe in fate or destiny, or do you think people have the ability to determine the course of their own lives? In your journal write about fate and free will using examples from your own life or from the lives of others to support your opinions.

Enter JOCASTA, *carrying garlands.*

❶ *Why is Jocasta carrying garlands? What does she request of Apollo?*

JOCASTA. Princes of the land, I have had the thought to go
to the Gods' temples, bringing in my hand
garlands and gifts of incense, as you see.
For Oedipus excites himself too much
at every sort of trouble, not conjecturing,
like a man of sense, what will be from what was,
but he is always at the speaker's mercy,
when he speaks terrors. I can do no good
by my advice, and so I came as suppliant
to you, Lycaean Apollo, who are nearest.
These are the symbols of my prayer and this
my prayer: grant us escape free of the curse.
Now when we look to him we are all afraid;
he's pilot of our ship and he is frightened.

Enter MESSENGER.

MESSENGER. Might I learn from you, sirs, where is the house of Oedipus? Or best of all, if you know, where is the king himself?

CHORUS. This is his house and he is within doors. This lady is his wife and mother of his children.

MESSENGER. God bless you, lady, and God bless your household! God bless Oedipus' noble wife!

WORDS FOR EVERYDAY USE

con • jec • ture (kən jec´chər) *vt.,* predict from incomplete evidence

VOCABULARY IN CONTEXT

- Jocelyn conjectured that Marcel would like the peanut butter cookies before she knew he was allergic to peanuts.

JOCASTA. God bless you, sir, for your kind greeting! What do you want of us that you have come here? What have you to tell us?

MESSENGER. Good news, lady. Good for your house and for your husband.

JOCASTA. What is your news? Who sent you to us?

MESSENGER. I come from Corinth and the news I bring will give you pleasure. Perhaps a little pain too.

JOCASTA. What is this news of double meaning?

MESSENGER. The people of the Isthmus[1] will choose Oedipus to be their king. That is the rumour there.

JOCASTA. But isn't their king still old Polybus?

MESSENGER. No. He is in his grave. Death has got him.

JOCASTA. Is that the truth? Is Oedipus' father dead?

MESSENGER. May I die myself if it be otherwise!

JOCASTA. [*To a servant.*] Be quick and run to the King with the news! O oracles of the Gods, where are you now? It was from this man Oedipus fled, lest he should be his murderer! And now he is dead, in the course of nature, and not killed by Oedipus.

Enter OEDIPUS.

OEDIPUS. Dearest Jocasta, why have you sent for me?

JOCASTA. Listen to this man and when you hear reflect what is the outcome of the holy oracles of the Gods.

OEDIPUS. Who is he? What is his message for me?

JOCASTA. He is from Corinth and he tells us that your father Polybus is dead and gone.

OEDIPUS. What's this you say, sir? Tell me yourself.

MESSENGER. Since this is the first matter you want clearly told: Polybus has gone down to death. You may be sure of it.

OEDIPUS. By treachery or sickness?

MESSENGER. A small thing will put old bodies asleep.

OEDIPUS. So he died of sickness, it seems,—poor old man!

MESSENGER. Yes, and of age—the long years he had measured.

OEDIPUS. Ha! Ha! O dear Jocasta, why should one look to the Pythian hearth?[2] Why should one look to the birds screaming overhead? They prophesied that I should kill my father! But he's dead,

1. **people of the Isthmus.** Refers to the people of Corinth
2. **Pythian hearth.** Oracle of Delphi

What news does the messenger bring? Why does he think it will be good news to Oedipus? Why does Jocasta also believe it to be good news?

How does Oedipus feel about oracles and prophecies?

READER'S JOURNAL

After students have written in their journals, have them compare their ideas in informal discussions. Students may also wish to consider what effect their beliefs have on their decision-making process and sense of personal responsibility.

ANSWERS TO GUIDED READING QUESTIONS

1. The messenger says that Polybus, Oedipus's father, is dead. He thinks it will be good news to Oedipus, who will now become king of Corinth. To Jocasta it is good news because it will end Oedipus's fears of the prophecy that he will kill his father.

2. He thinks they are useless, since he has seemingly avoided his prophesied fate.

SPELLING AND VOCABULARY WORDS FROM THE SELECTION

conjecture	lineage
dirge	purge
fettered	reverence
imprecation	suffice
infamously	vilely

Answers to Guided Reading Questions

1 Oedipus still fears the part of the prophecy regarding his mother. Jocasta advises him to live lightly, unthinkingly. The advice does not seem sound since many pieces of information, including Teiresias's speech, have pointed at Oedipus as the killer.

Literary Note

The legendary roots of the Oedipus story can be found in the folk traditions of Albania, Finland, Cyprus, and Greece. The story has inspired many writers, including Seneca, Pierre Corneille, John Dryden, and Voltaire. (Quotations from some of these writers appear on page 655 of this annotated teacher's edition.) In the twentieth century, the story has been presented by Igor Stravinsky in his oratorio *Oedipus Rex,* by André Gide in *Oedipe,* and by Jean Cocteau in *La Machine Infernale.* Students may enjoy reading another version of the Oedipus story and comparing Sophocles's version of the story to its treatment in a contemporary work.

1 *Why isn't Oedipus completely comforted by the news of his father's death? What advice does Jocasta give him? Do you think this is sound advice?*

and hidden deep in earth, and I stand here
who never laid a hand on spear against him,—
unless perhaps he died of longing for me,
and thus I am his murderer. But they,
the oracles, as they stand—he's taken them
away with him, they're dead as he himself is,
and worthless.

Jocasta. That I told you before now.

Oedipus. You did, but I was misled by my fear.

Jocasta. Then lay no more of them to heart, not one.

Oedipus. But surely I must fear my mother's bed?

Jocasta. Why should man fear since chance is all in all
for him, and he can clearly foreknow nothing?
Best to live lightly, as one can, unthinkingly.
As to your mother's marriage bed,—don't fear it.
Before this, in dreams too, as well as oracles,
many a man has lain with his own mother.
But he to whom such things are nothing bears
his life most easily.

Oedipus. All that you say would be said perfectly
if she were dead; but since she lives I must
still fear, although you talk so well, Jocasta.

Jocasta. Still in your father's death there's light of
comfort?

Oedipus. Great light of comfort; but I fear the living.

Messenger. Who is the woman that makes you afraid?

Oedipus. Merope, old man, Polybus' wife.

Messenger. What about her frightens the queen and you?

Oedipus. A terrible oracle, stranger, from the Gods.

Messenger. Can it be told? Or does the sacred law
forbid another to have knowledge of it?

Oedipus. O no! Once on a time Loxias said
that I should lie with my own mother and
take on my hands the blood of my own father.
And so for these long years I've lived away
from Corinth; it has been to my great happiness;
but yet it's sweet to see the face of parents.

Messenger. This was the fear which drove you out of Corinth?

Oedipus. Old man, I did not wish to kill my father.

Messenger. Why should I not free you from this fear, sir,
since I have come to you in all goodwill?

Oedipus. You would not find me thankless if you did.

MESSENGER. Why, it was just for this I brought the news,—
to earn your thanks when you had come safe home.

OEDIPUS. No, I will never come near my parents.

MESSENGER. Son,
it's very plain you don't know what you're doing.

OEDIPUS. What do you mean, old man? For God's sake, tell me.

MESSENGER. If your homecoming is checked by fears like these.

OEDIPUS. Yes, I'm afraid that Phoebus may prove right.

MESSENGER. The murder and the incest?

OEDIPUS. Yes, old man;
that is my constant terror.

MESSENGER. Do you know
that all your fears are empty?

OEDIPUS. How is that,
if they are father and mother and I their son?

MESSENGER. Because Polybus was no kin to you in blood.

OEDIPUS. What, was not Polybus my father?

MESSENGER. No more than I but just so much.

OEDIPUS. How can
my father be my father as much as one
that's nothing to me?

MESSENGER. Neither he nor I
begat you.

OEDIPUS. Why then did he call me son?

MESSENGER. A gift he took you from these hands of mine.

OEDIPUS. Did he love so much what he took from another's hand?

MESSENGER. His childlessness before persuaded him.

OEDIPUS. Was I a child you bought or found when I
was given to him?

MESSENGER. On Cithaeron's slopes
in the twisting thickets you were found.

OEDIPUS. And why
were you a traveler in those parts?

MESSENGER. I was
in charge of mountain flocks.

OEDIPUS. You were a shepherd?
A hireling vagrant?[3]

MESSENGER. Yes, but at least at that time
the man that saved your life, son.

3. **hireling vagrant.** Wanderer who works at odd jobs

① *Why, according to the messenger, are Oedipus's fears empty? What new fears might Oedipus experience in light of this information?*

Answers to Guided Reading Questions

① Oedipus's fears of going near his parents were empty because, as the messenger tells Oedipus, Polybus and Merope were not his real parents. Oedipus may become afraid when he realizes that he does not know who his birth parents are and is unable to avoid them. He may begin to wonder whether Teiresias spoke the truth.

Quotables

"Many have reached their fate while dreading fate . . . No one becomes guilty by fate."

—Seneca
from *Oedipus*

"Of no distemper, of no blast he died,
But fell like autumn fruit that mellow'd long—
Even wonder'd at, because he dropp'd no sooner.
Fate seem'd to wind him up fourscore years,
Yet freshly ran he on ten winters more;
Till like a clock worn out with eating time,
The wheels of weary life at last stood still."

—John Dryden
from *Oedipus*

"Virtue debases itself in justifying itself."

—Voltaire
from *Oedipe*

Answers to Guided Reading Questions

❶ Oedipus does not understand how the messenger knows about his ankles, nor why it is related to the story of his parentage. The messenger had found Oedipus as a baby on Mount Cithaeron with his tendons pierced and his feet fettered.

❷ Jocasta knows what the shepherd will say, and she wants to keep the truth from being known.

Literary Note

The plays that complete the trilogy of which *Oedipus the King* is part are *Oedipus at Colonus* and *Antigone.* In the chronology of the story of Oedipus, *Oedipus at Colonus* follows *Oedipus the King.* After being sent out from the city of Thebes, Oedipus wanders in exile for many years, cared for by his daughters Antigone and Ismene. He is granted refuge at Colonus near Athens by Theseus, king of Athens. Oedipus's son Polyneices is intent on attacking Thebes, but Oedipus will have no part of the attack and curses his son and his plan. At his strange death, he is swallowed into the earth where he becomes a defending force for Colonus.

Antigone was the first of these three plays to be written and produced, but the action of the drama follows that of *Oedipus at Colonus.* Polyneices has been killed in his attack on Thebes, and Creon decrees that his body is not to be buried. Antigone, despite the death penalty attached to anyone found disobeying this order, chooses to bury her brother. Caught in her defiance, Antigone is sentenced to die. By the time Teiresias convinces Creon to spare Antigone, she has taken her own life. Creon's son, Haemon, kills himself for love of Antigone, and

(cont.)

❶ *Why is Oedipus surprised when the messenger mentions his pained ankles? How does the messenger know of Oedipus's ailment?*

Oedipus. What ailed me when you took me in your arms?

Messenger. In that your ankles should be witnesses.

Oedipus. Why do you speak of that old pain?

Messenger. I loosed you;
the tendons of your feet were pierced and <u>fettered</u>,—

Oedipus. My swaddling clothes brought me a rare disgrace.

Messenger. So that from this you're called your present name.[4]

Oedipus. Was this my father's doing or my mother's?
For God's sake, tell me.

Messenger. I don't know, but he
who gave you to me has more knowledge than I.

Oedipus. You yourself did not find me then? You took me
from someone else?

Messenger. Yes, from another shepherd.

Oedipus. Who was he? Do you know him well enough to tell?

Messenger. He was called Laius' man.

Oedipus. You mean the king who reigned here in the old days?

Messenger. Yes, he was that man's shepherd.

Oedipus: Is he alive
still, so that I could see him?

Messenger. You who live here
would know that best.

Oedipus. Do any of you here
know of this shepherd whom he speaks about
in town or in the fields? Tell me. It's time
that this was found out once for all.

Chorus. I think he is none other than the peasant
whom you have sought to see already; but
Jocasta here can tell us best of that.

Oedipus. Jocasta, do you know about this man
whom we have sent for? Is he the man he mentions?

❷ *Why does Jocasta try to dismiss the messenger's story?*

Jocasta. Why ask of whom he spoke? Don't give it heed;
nor try to keep in mind what has been said.
It will be wasted labour.

---

4. **present name.** Refers to Oedipus's name which means "swollen foot"

Words for Everyday Use

fet • tered (fet´ərd) *adj.,* shackled or chained by the feet

Vocabulary in Context

- The escaped prisoner was quickly captured because he could not move very quickly on his <u>fettered</u> feet.

Oedipus and Jocasta. *Photo courtesy of Lyric Stage Company*

Oedipus. With such clues
I could not fail to bring my birth to light.

Jocasta. I beg you—do not hunt this out—I beg you,
if you have any care for your own life.
What I am suffering is enough.

Oedipus. Keep up
your heart, Jocasta. Though I'm proved a slave,
thrice slave, and though my mother is thrice slave,
you'll not be shown to be of lowly lineage.

Jocasta. O be persuaded by me, I entreat you;
do not do this.

Oedipus. I will not be persuaded to let be
the chance of finding out the whole thing clearly.

Jocasta. It is because I wish you well that I
give you this counsel—and it's the best counsel.

Oedipus. Then the best counsel vexes me, and has
for some while since.

Jocasta. O Oedipus, God help you!
God keep you from the knowledge of who you are!

❶ *Why does Jocasta want to put an end to Oedipus's search? Has Oedipus realized what Jocasta knows?*

❷ *Why doesn't Oedipus follow Jocasta's advice? What does this reveal about Oedipus's character? Do you agree that Jocasta's advice is the "best counsel"?*

Words for Everyday Use

lin • e • age (lin ´ē ij) *n.*, ancestry, family line

Answers to Guided Reading Questions

❶ Jocasta knows what will be revealed if Oedipus continues with his search and is afraid of the truth coming out. Oedipus thinks that Jocasta is concerned that he will discover that he is of low lineage.

❷ Oedipus insists upon learning the whole truth. In this quest, Oedipus reveals that he is determined, stubborn, and adamant about following a course he has set. *Responses will vary.* Students may say that Jocasta's counsel is the best because Oedipus will be devastated when he learns the truth. Others may say that Jocasta's counsel is not the best because it is necessary for the truth to come out.

Literary Note (cont.)

Creon's wife, Eurydice, kills herself when she learns of her son's death. Creon is left desolate. The drama addresses the conflict between civic and personal responsibility.

Like the story of Oedipus, the story of Antigone, Oedipus's daughter, has had an impact on other writers. Polish poet Czeslaw Milosz used the classical characters and their situation to reflect on the suffering of Hungarians during and after World War II. Jean Anouilh's *Antigone* comments on the situation in France during the German occupation.

Vocabulary in Context

- Gladys made a family tree to record her lineage.

Answers to Guided Reading Questions

❶ Jocasta is thrust into despair and agony by Oedipus's decision. She has run away so she will not have to witness the revelation of the truth. She is going to kill herself, as warned by her words that "unhappy Oedipus" is the last thing she will ever call her husband.

❷ Oedipus thinks that Jocasta is ashamed of his low birth.

❸ Oedipus claims he is a child of Fortune.

Additional Questions and Activities

Ask students to think of other stories in which a child is supposed to be killed or abandoned but instead is raised by people other than his or her parents, and stories in which a child's true parents are unknown for a time. Ask students what purpose such situations have in a story. For what effect are they used?

ANSWERS

Responses will vary.

Students might mention the fairy tale of Snow White and the Seven Dwarfs, the legends of King Arthur, or the myth of Romulus and Remus. Such stories provide tension between characters who are unknowingly related to each other, resulting in dramatic irony. Often times such stories provide for the archetypal motif of the person of humble status who is transformed into a person of powerful status.

❶ *How does Jocasta feel about Oedipus's decision to continue his quest for the truth? Why has she run away?*

❷ *What explanation does Oedipus provide for Jocasta's reaction?*

❸ *Whom does Oedipus claim as his mother?*

Oedipus. Here, some one, go and fetch the shepherd for me;
and let her find her joy in her rich family!

Jocasta. O Oedipus, unhappy Oedipus!
that is all I can call you, and the last thing
that I shall ever call you.

Exit.

Chorus. Why has the queen gone, Oedipus, in wild
grief rushing from us? I am afraid that trouble
will break out of this silence.

Oedipus. Break out what will! I at least shall be
willing to see my ancestry, though humble.
Perhaps she is ashamed of my low birth,
for she has all a woman's high-flown pride.
But I account myself a child of Fortune,
beneficent Fortune, and I shall not be
dishonored. She's the mother from whom I spring;
the months, my brothers, marked me, now as small,
and now again as mighty. Such is my breeding,
and I shall never prove so false to it,
as not to find the secret of my birth.

Chorus.

Strophe

If I am a prophet and wise of heart
you shall not fail, Cithaeron,
by the limitless sky, you shall not!—
to know at tomorrow's full moon
that Oedipus honours you,
as native to him and mother and nurse at once;
and that you are honoured in dancing by us, as finding favor in sight of our king.
Apollo, to whom we cry, find these things pleasing!

Antistrophe

Who was it bore you, child? One of
the long-lived nymphs[5] who lay with Pan[6]—
the father who treads the hills?
Or was she a bride of Loxias, your mother? The grassy slopes
are all of them dear to him. Or perhaps Cyllene's king,[7]
or the Bacchants' God that lives on the tops
of the hills received you a gift from some
one of the Helicon Nymphs, with whom he mostly plays?

Enter an old man, led by Oedipus' *servants.*

Oedipus. If some one like myself who never met him
may make a guess,—I think this is the herdsman,

5. **nymphs.** Minor female divinities
6. **Pan.** Shepherd god of the mountains
7. **Cyllene's king.** Hermes, the messenger god

whom we were seeking. His old age is consonant
with the other. And besides, the men who bring him
I recognize as my own servants. You
perhaps may better me in knowledge since
you've seen the man before.

CHORUS. You can be sure
I recognize him. For if Laius
had ever an honest shepherd, this was he.

What does the Chorus say about the herdsman's character?

OEDIPUS. You, sir, from Corinth, I must ask you first,
is this the man you spoke of?

MESSENGER. This is he
before your eyes.

OEDIPUS. Old man, look here at me
and tell me what I ask you. Were you ever
a servant of King Laius?

HERDSMAN. I was,—
no slave he bought but reared in his own house.

OEDIPUS. What did you do as work? How did you live?

HERDSMAN. Most of my life was spent among the flocks.

OEDIPUS. In what part of the country did you live?

HERDSMAN. Cithaeron and the places near to it.

OEDIPUS. And somewhere there perhaps you knew this man?

HERDSMAN. What was his occupation? Who?

OEDIPUS. This man here,
have you had any dealings with him?

HERDSMAN. No—
not such that I can quickly call to mind.

MESSENGER. That is no wonder, master. But I'll make him remember what he does not know. For I know, that he well knows the country of Cithaeron, how he with two flocks, I with one kept company for three years—each year half a year—from spring till autumn time and then when winter came I drove my flocks to our fold home again and he to Laius' steadings. Well—am I right or not in what I said we did?

HERDSMAN. You're right—although it's a long time ago.

How does the herdsman feel when questioned about the child he found? Why do you think he feels this way?

MESSENGER. Do you remember giving me a child
to bring up as my foster child?

HERDSMAN. What's this?
Why do you ask this question?

MESSENGER. Look old man,
here he is—here's the man who was that child!

HERDSMAN. Death take you! Won't you hold your tongue?

OEDIPUS. No, no,

Answers to Guided Reading Questions

1. The Chorus says that the shepherd is honest.

2. He is upset by the questioning and urges his questioners not to discuss the subject. He may be worried that he will be punished for not following orders to kill the child, or he may realize the damage this truth could cause.

Answers to Guided Reading Questions

❶ Oedipus threatens to torture the herdsman. He is motivated by his desire to know the truth. He may also be motivated by fear.

❷ The herdsman realizes the impact of what he has done. He is afraid to tell Oedipus what happened.

Literary Technique

PLOT

A **plot** is a series of events related to a central conflict, or struggle. A typical plot involves the introduction of a conflict, its development, and its eventual resolution. The following terms are used to describe the elements of plot:

- The **exposition,** or **introduction,** sets the tone or mood, introduces the characters and the setting, and provides background information.
- The **inciting incident** is the event that introduces the central conflict.
- The **rising action,** or **complication,** develops the conflict to a high point of intensity.
- The **climax** is the high point of interest or suspense in the plot.
- The **crisis,** or **turning point,** often the same event as the climax, is the point in the plot where something decisive happens to determine the future course of events and the eventual working out of the conflict.
- The **falling action** is all of the events that follow the climax.
- The **resolution** is the point at which the central conflict is ended, or resolved.
- The **dénouement** is any material that follows the resolution and that ties up loose ends.
- The **catastrophe,** in tragedy, is the event that marks the ultimate tragic fall of the central character. Often this event is the character's death.

do not find fault with him, old man. Your words
are more at fault than his.

Herdsman. O best of masters,
how do I give offense?

Oedipus. When you refuse
to speak about the child of whom he asks you.

Herdsman. He speaks out of his ignorance, without meaning.

❶ *What does Oedipus threaten to do? What prompts him to make these threats?*

Oedipus. If you'll not talk to gratify me, you
will talk with pain to urge you.

Herdsman. O please, sir,
don't hurt an old man, sir.

Oedipus. (*To the servants.*) Here, one of you,
twist his hands behind him.

Herdsman. Why, God help me, why?
What do you want to know?

❷ *Why does the herdsman wish that he had died the day he gave the child to the messenger?*

Oedipus. You gave a child
to him,—the child he asked you of?

Herdsman. I did.
I wish I'd died the day I did.

Oedipus. You will
unless you tell me truly.

Herdsman. And I'll die
far worse if I should tell you.

Oedipus. This fellow
is bent on more delays, as it would seem.

Herdsman. O no, no! I have told you that I gave it.

Oedipus. Where did you get this child from? Was it your own or
did you get it from another?

Herdsman. Not
my own at all; I had it from some one.

Oedipus. One of these citizens? or from what house?

Herdsman. O master, please—I beg you, master, please
don't ask me more.

Oedipus. You're a dead man if I
ask you again.

Herdsman. It was one of the children
of Laius.

Oedipus. A slave? Or born in wedlock?

Herdsman. O God, I am on the brink of frightful speech.

Oedipus. And I of frightful hearing. But I must hear.

Herdsman. The child was called his child; but she within, your wife would tell you best how all this was.

OEDIPUS. *She* gave it to you?

HERDSMAN. Yes, she did, my lord.

OEDIPUS. To do what with it?

HERDSMAN. Make away with it.

OEDIPUS. She was so hard—its mother?

HERDSMAN. Aye, through fear
of evil oracles.

OEDIPUS. Which?

HERDSMAN. They said that he
should kill his parents.

OEDIPUS. How was it that you
gave it away to this old man?

HERDSMAN. O master,
I pitied it, and thought that I could send it
off to another country and this man
was from another country. But he saved it
for the most terrible troubles. If you are
the man he says you are, you're bred to misery.

OEDIPUS. O, O, O, they will all come,
all come out clearly! Light of the sun, let me
look upon you no more after today!
I who first saw the light bred of a match
accursed, and accursed in my living
with them I lived with, cursed in my killing.

Exeunt all but the CHORUS.

CHORUS.

Strophe

O generations of men, how I
count you as equal with those who live
not at all!
What man, what man on earth wins more
of happiness than a seeming
and after that turning away?
Oedipus, you are my pattern of this,
Oedipus, you and your fate!
Luckless Oedipus, whom of all men
I envy not at all.

Antistrophe

In as much as he shot his bolt
beyond the others and won the prize
of happiness complete—
O Zeus—and killed and reduced to nought

❶ *Why had Jocasta given the child to the herdsman?*

❷ *What was the herdsman supposed to do with the child? What did he do with the boy instead? Why didn't he follow orders?*

❸ *To what event does the Chorus refer?*

Answers to Guided Reading Questions

❶ Jocasta told the herdsman to get rid of the child because she feared the prophecy that he was to kill his parents.

❷ He was supposed to kill the child or leave him to die. Instead he gave the child to another shepherd to raise. He did not follow the orders he was given because he took pity on the helpless child. He regrets what he has done because the child has grown to face a terrible fate.

❸ The Chorus refers to Oedipus's feat of saving Thebes from the Sphinx.

Additional Questions and Activities

After reviewing with your students the parts of a plot (see Literary Technique, page 660), have them diagram the plot of *Oedipus the King* to this point in the story indicating the events that mark each element of the plot. As they continue to read the play, have students fill in additional elements on their plot diagrams. This activity will provide valuable review of the part of the play already read as well as creating a vehicle for analyzing and taking notes on the conclusion of the play.

Answers to Guided Reading Questions

❶ They regret that they ever knew Oedipus. They are sorrowful for his fate.

the hooked taloned maid of the riddling speech,[8]
standing a tower against death for my land:
hence he was called my king and hence
was honoured the highest of all
honours; and hence he ruled
in the great city of Thebes.

Strophe

But now whose tale is more miserable?
Who is there lives with a savager fate?
Whose troubles so reverse his life as his?

O Oedipus, the famous prince
for whom a great haven
the same both as father and son
sufficed for generation,
how, O how, have the furrows ploughed
by your father endured to bear you, poor wretch,
and hold their peace so long?

Antistrophe

Time who sees all has found you out
against your will; judges your marriage accursed,
begetter and begot at one in it.

❶ *How does the Chorus feel about Oedipus now?*

O child of Laius,
would I had never seen you.
I weep for you and cry
a dirge of lamentation.

To speak directly, I drew my breath
from you at the first and so now I lull
my mouth to sleep with your name.

Enter a Second Messenger.

Second Messenger. O Princes always honoured by our country,
what deeds you'll hear of and what horrors see,
what grief you'll feel, if you are true born Thebans
care for the house of Labdacus's sons.
Phasis nor Ister[9] cannot purge this house,
I think, with all their streams, such things
it hides, such evils shortly will bring forth
into the light, whether they will or not;

8. **hooked . . . speech.** The Sphinx
9. **Phasis nor Ister.** Refers to two rivers that flow into the Black Sea

Words for Everyday Use

suf • fice (sə fīs´) *vi.,* be enough; be sufficient or adequate
dirge (durj) *n.,* slow, sad song or poem expressing grief or mourning
purge (pərj) *vt.,* cleanse of guilt, sin, or ceremonial defilement

Vocabulary in Context

- One gallon of milk is not enough, but two should suffice.
- As the funeral procession wound its way to the cemetery, the sorrowful dirge sung by the mourners could be heard for miles.
- The contaminated objects were burned in a ceremony to purge the community of evil.

Oedipus threatening the herdsman.
Photo courtesy of Lyric Stage Company

and troubles hurt the most
when they prove self-inflicted.

CHORUS. What we had known before did not fall short
of bitter groanings' worth; what's more to tell?

SECOND MESSENGER. Shortest to hear and tell—our glorious queen
Jocasta is dead.

CHORUS. Unhappy woman! How?

SECOND MESSENGER. By her own hand. The worst of what was done
you cannot know. You did not see the sight.
Yet in so far as I remember it
you'll hear the end of our unlucky queen.
When she came raging into the house she went
straight to her marriage bed, tearing her hair
with both her hands, and crying upon Laius
long dead—Do you remember, Laius,
that night long past which bred a child for us
to send you to your death and leave
a mother making children with her son?
And then she groaned and cursed the bed in which
she brought forth husband by her husband, children
by her own child, an infamous double bond.
How after that she died I do not know,—
for Oedipus distracted us from seeing.

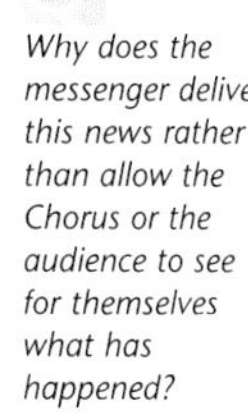

Why does the messenger deliver this news rather than allow the Chorus or the audience to see for themselves what has happened?

ANSWERS TO GUIDED READING QUESTIONS

❶ According to Greek dramatic conventions, violence should take place offstage; therefore, such actions were usually relayed to the audience and characters by another character. During the production of this play, it is also simpler to have the messenger relay the news than to change sets to go within the palace where Jocasta took her life.

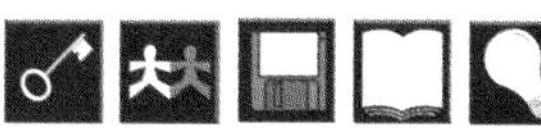

ADDITIONAL QUESTIONS AND ACTIVITIES

Ask students the following questions:

1. What, according to the messenger, does Jocasta say as she enters the house?
2. What does she curse?
3. Why is the messenger unable to say how she died?

ANSWERS

1. The messenger reports that Jocasta spoke to Laius as she entered the house, saying, "Do you remember, Laius, that night long past which bred a child for us to send you to your death and leave a mother making children with her son?"
2. She curses "the bed in which she brought forth husband by her husband, children by her own child."
3. The messenger cannot report how she died because Oedipus entered and distracted him.

Answers to Guided Reading Questions

1 Oedipus strikes his eyes with brooches, thus blinding himself.

INTEGRATED SKILLS ACTIVITIES

RESEARCH SKILLS

Remind students that when writing critically about literature, it is often necessary or useful to consult sources other than the literary subject. For example, it may be useful to access biographical information about the author, historical information about the period in which the work was written or set, or critical analyses of the work.

Have students use the library and online sources to find information about *Oedipus the King,* Sophocles, Greek history during the time that Sophocles wrote, and to find critical works about Sophocles's plays. If students have read another work by Sophocles or a work by another author based on the Oedipus or Antigone stories, they may wish to research information on that work and author instead. Students should locate at least five sources. Have students prepare a bibliography card for each source. Refer them to the Language Arts Survey, 4.20, "Bibliographies and Bibliography Cards," for the proper form. Students should also evaluate the source and identify the kind of information it contains and the kind of paper for which it would provide appropriate information.

You might also have students use the sources they find to write a critical essay on the play. A critical essay topic is provided on page 673; however, this drama also offers a good opportunity for students to choose and narrow a topic on their own. Refer students to the Language Arts Survey 1.6, "Choosing a Topic," and 1.20, "Writing a Critical Essay."

(cont.)

He burst upon us shouting and we looked
to him as he paced frantically around,
begging us always: Give me a sword, I say,
to find this wife no wife, this mother's womb,
this field of double sowing whence I sprang
and where I sowed my children! As he raved
some god showed him the way—none of us there.
Bellowing terribly and led by some
invisible guide he rushed on the two doors,—
wrenching the hollow bolts out of their sockets,
he charged inside. There, there, we saw his wife
hanging, the twisted rope around her neck.
When he saw her, he cried out fearfully
and cut the dangling noose. Then, as she lay,
poor woman, on the ground, what happened after,
was terrible to see. He tore the brooches—
the gold chased brooches fastening her robe—
away from her and lifting them up high
dashed them on his own eyeballs, shrieking out
such things as: they will never see the crime
I have committed or had done upon me!
Dark eyes, now in the days to come look on
forbidden faces, do not recognize
those whom you long for—with such imprecations
he struck his eyes again and yet again
with the brooches. And the bleeding eyeballs gushed
and stained his beard—no sluggish oozing drops
but a black rain and bloody hail poured down.

1 *What harm does Oedipus inflict upon himself?*

So it has broken—and not on one head
but troubles mixed for husband and for wife.
The fortune of the days gone by was true
good fortune—but today groans and destruction
and death and shame—of all ills can be named
not one is missing.

CHORUS. Is he now in any ease from pain?

SECOND MESSENGER. He shouts
for some one to unbar the doors and show him
to all the men of Thebes, his father's killer,
his mother's—no I cannot say the word,
it is unholy—for he'll cast himself,
out of the land, he says, and not remain

WORDS FOR EVERYDAY USE

im • pre • ca • tion (im´pri kā´shən) *n.,* act of invoking evil or cursing

Vocabulary in Context

• Karina feared the evil that would come of the imprecations Helvi made in anger.

to bring a curse upon his house, the curse
he called upon it in his proclamation. But
he wants for strength, aye, and some one to guide him;
his sickness is too great to bear. You, too,
will be shown that. The bolts are opening.
Soon you will see a sight to waken pity
even in the horror of it.

Enter the blinded OEDIPUS.

CHORUS. This is a terrible sight for men to see!
I never found a worse!
Poor wretch, what madness came upon you!
What evil spirit leaped upon your life
to your ill-luck—a leap beyond man's strength!
Indeed I pity you, but I cannot
look at you, though there's much I want to ask
and much to learn and much to see.
I shudder at the sight of you.

❶ *How does the Chorus feel as Oedipus is led back into their sight?*

OEDIPUS. O, O,
where am I going? Where is my voice
borne on the wind to and fro?
Spirit, how far have you sprung?

CHORUS. To a terrible place whereof men's ears
may not hear, nor their eyes behold it.

OEDIPUS. Darkness!
Horror of darkness enfolding, resistless, unspeakable visitant sped by
an ill wind in haste!
madness and stabbing pain and memory
of evil deeds I have done!

CHORUS. In such misfortunes it's no wonder
if double weighs the burden of your grief.

OEDIPUS. My friend,
you are the only one steadfast, the only one that attends on me;
you still stay nursing the blind man.
your care is not unnoticed. I can know
your voice, although this darkness is my world.

CHORUS. Doer of dreadful deeds, how did you dare
so far to do despite to your own eyes?
what spirit urged you to it?

OEDIPUS. It was Apollo, friends, Apollo,
that brought this bitter bitterness, my sorrows to completion.
But the hand that struck me
was none but my own.
Why should I see
whose vision showed me nothing sweet to see?

❷ *Whom does Oedipus blame for this bitter situation? Whom does he blame for his present condition?*

CHORUS. These things are as you say.

ANSWERS TO GUIDED READING QUESTIONS

❶ The Chorus feels pity for Oedipus, but they are also horrified by him.

❷ Oedipus blames Apollo for his current sorrow, but he takes upon himself the responsibility for striking himself blind.

INTEGRATED SKILLS ACTIVITIES (CONT.)

Encourage students to choose an aspect of the work that interests them. Essays should refer to other information students have found, but ultimately they should present the students' own analyses.

► Additional practice is provided in the Essential Skills Practice Books: Writing 1.6 and 1.20 and Study and Research 4.20.

Answers to Guided Reading Questions

❶ Oedipus says that he is greatly miserable and the most cursed person on earth; if he had been allowed to die as a child, he would have spared family and friends much misery. He wishes to be taken to an out-of-the-way place.

❷ The Chorus thinks Oedipus would have been better off if he had killed himself, because now he must live a life of misery. *Responses will vary.*

❸ Oedipus feels the punishment of sightlessness is appropriate because he cannot look upon what he has done to his father, his mother, his children, and his city and people.

Oedipus. What can I see to love?
What greeting can touch my ears with joy?
Take me away, and haste—to a place out of the way!
Take me away, my friends, the greatly miserable,
the most accursed, whom God too hates
above all men on earth!

❶ *What does Oedipus say about himself? For what does he wish?*

Chorus. Unhappy in your mind and your misfortune,
would I had never known you!

Oedipus. Curse on the man who took
the cruel bonds from off my legs, as I lay in the field.
He stole me from death and saved me,
no kindly service.
Had I died then
I would not be so burdensome to friends.

Chorus. I, too, could have wished it had been so.
Oedipus. Then I would not have come
to kill my father and marry my mother infamously.
Now I am godless and child of impurity,
begetter in the same seed that created my wretched self.
If there is any ill worse than ill,
that is the lot of Oedipus.

Chorus. I cannot say your remedy was good;
you would be better dead than blind and living.

❷ *What does the Chorus think Oedipus should have done rather than blinding himself? Why does it think he should have done this? Do you agree with the Chorus? Why, or why not?*

Oedipus. What I have done here was best done—don't tell me
otherwise, do not give me further counsel.
I do not know with what eyes I could look
upon my father when I die and go
under the earth, nor yet my wretched mother—
those two to whom I have done things deserving
worse punishment than hanging. Would the sight
of children, bred as mine are, gladden me?
No, not these eyes, never. And my city,
its towers and sacred places of the Gods,
of these I robbed my miserable self
when I commanded all to drive *him* out,
the criminal since proved by God impure
and of the race of Laius.
To this guilt I bore witness against myself—
with what eyes shall I look upon my people?
No. If there were a means to choke the fountain

❸ *Why does Oedipus feel that the punishment he has inflicted upon himself is appropriate?*

Words for Everyday Use

in • fa • mous • ly (in′fə məs lē) *adv.*, notoriously; disgracefully; scandalously

Vocabulary in Context

• In the 1920s, Al Capone infamously terrorized Chicago with his powerful crime syndicate.

of hearing I would not have stayed my hand
from locking up my miserable carcass,
seeing and hearing nothing; it is sweet
to keep our thoughts out of the range of hurt.

Cithaeron, why did you receive me? why
having received me did you not kill me straight?
And so I had not shown to men my birth.

O Polybus and Corinth and the house,
the old house that I used to call my father's—
what fairness you were nurse to, and what foulness
festered beneath! Now I am found to be
a sinner and a son of sinners. Crossroads,
and hidden glade, oak and the narrow way
at the crossroads, that drank my father's blood
offered you by my hands, do you remember
still what I did as you looked on, and what
I did when I came here? O marriage, marriage!
you bred me and again when you had bred
bred children of your child and showed to men
brides, wives and mothers and the foulest deeds
that can be in this world of ours.

Come—it's unfit to say what is unfit
to do.—I beg of you in God's name hide me
somewhere outside your country, yes, or kill me
or throw me into the sea, to be forever
out of your sight. Approach and deign to touch me
for all my wretchedness, and do not fear.
No man but I can bear my evil doom.

Why, according to Oedipus, shouldn't the Chorus fear to touch him? What has Oedipus recognized about himself?

Chorus. Here Creon comes in fit time to perform
or give advice in what you ask of us.
Creon is left sole ruler in your stead.

Oedipus. Creon! Creon! What shall I say to him?
How can I justly hope that he will trust me?
In what is past I have been proved towards him
an utter liar.

Enter Creon.

Creon. Oedipus, I've come
not so that I might laugh at you nor taunt you
with evil of the past. But if you still
are without shame before the face of men
reverence at least the flame that gives all life,

Words for Everyday Use

rev • er • ence (rev´ər əns) *vt.,* treat with great respect, love, and awe, as for something sacred

Answers to Guided Reading Questions

Oedipus says that people should not fear to touch him because he is the only person who can bear his evil doom. He recognizes that he has not escaped his fate, that the prophecy he has long feared has caught up with him.

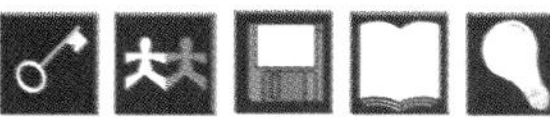

Additional Questions and Activities

Students can discuss whether they agree with the Chorus that Oedipus would be better off "dead than blind and living" or if they agree with Oedipus that his self-inflicted affliction was the best option. Point out that Oedipus's blinding was a painful torture that he inflicted on himself. Also point out that progressive attitudes and technology to help people who are blind were not available to Oedipus, as they would be today. Encourage students to recognize that blindness is not a fate worse than death.

Vocabulary in Context

• Vinny knelt in reverence at the entrance to the shrine.

Answers to Guided Reading Questions

➊ Oedipus may make this request because he wants to save Thebes from plague and further curses that might spring from his presence. He may also feel that he should be punished further. Creon does not act immediately upon Oedipus's request because he is waiting to hear the will of the god.

Selection Check Test with Answers

EX. What news does the messenger bring?
He brings news that Polybus is dead and Oedipus will be named king of Corinth.

1. Why is Oedipus gladdened by the news of Polybus's death?
He no longer has to worry about killing his father.

2. What does the messenger tell Oedipus about his father?
He says that Polybus was not Oedipus's father.

3. From whom did the herdsman receive orders to abandon Oedipus on Mount Cithaeron?
He received orders from Jocasta.

4. What does Oedipus do when he finally realizes the prophecy has been fulfilled?
He gouges his eyes with pins from Jocasta's clothes.

5. Who does Oedipus ask Creon to care for?
He asks Creon to care for his daughters Antigone and Ismene.

our Lord the Sun, and do not show unveiled
to him pollution such that neither land
nor holy rain nor light of day can welcome.

(To a servant.)
Be quick and take him in. It is most decent
that only kin should see and hear the troubles
of kin.

Oedipus. I beg you, since you've torn me from
my dreadful expectations and have come
in a most noble spirit to a man
that has used you vilely—do a thing for me.
I shall speak for your own good, not for my own.

Creon. What do you need that you would ask of me?

➊ *What does Oedipus ask Creon to do? Why does he make this request? Why does Creon hesitate to act upon Oedipus's request?*

Oedipus. Drive me from here with all the speed you can
to where I may not hear a human voice.

Creon. Be sure, I would have done this had not I
wished first of all to learn from the God the course
of action I should follow.

Oedipus. But his word
has been quite clear to let the parricide,[10]
the sinner, die.

Creon. Yes, that indeed was said.
But in the present need we had best discover
what we should do.

Oedipus. And will you ask about
a man so wretched?

Creon. Now even you will trust
the God.

Oedipus. So. I command you—and will beseech you—
to her that lies inside that house give burial
as you would have it; she is yours and rightly
you will perform the rites for her. For me—
never let this my father's city have me
living a dweller in it. Leave me live
in the mountains where Cithaeron is, that's called
my mountain, which my mother and my father
while they were living would have made my tomb.
So I may die by their decree who sought

10. **parricide.** Murderer of one's father

Words for Everyday Use

vile • ly (vil´lē) *adv.,* sinfully, wickedly

Vocabulary in Context

• The cruel dictator treated his people vilely, with no concern for what was right.

indeed to kill me. Yet I know this much:
no sickness and no other thing will kill me.
I would not have been saved from death if not
for some strange evil fate. Well, let my fate
go where it will.
Creon, you need not care
about my sons; they're men and so wherever
they are, they will not lack a livelihood.
But my two girls—so sad and pitiful—
whose table never stood apart from mine,
and everything I touched they always shared—
O Creon, have a thought for them! And most
I wish that you might suffer me to touch them
and sorrow with them.

Enter ANTIGONE *and* ISMENE, OEDIPUS' *two daughters.*

O my lord! O true noble Creon! Can I
really be touching them, as when I saw?
What shall I say?
Yes, I can hear them sobbing—my two darlings!
and Creon has had pity and has sent me
what I loved most?
Am I right?

CREON. You're right: it was I gave you this
because I knew from old days how you loved them
as I see now.

OEDIPUS. God bless you for it, Creon,
and may God guard you better on your road
than he did me!
O children,
where are you? Come here, come to my hands,
a brother's hands which turned your father's eyes,
those bright eyes you knew once, to what you see,
a father seeing nothing, knowing nothing,
begetting you from his own source of life.
I weep for you—I cannot see your faces—
I weep when I think of the bitterness
there will be in your lives, how you must live
before the world. At what assemblages
of citizens will you make one? to what
gay company will you go and not come home
in tears instead of sharing in the holiday?
And when you're ripe for marriage, who will he be,
the man who'll risk to take such infamy
as shall cling to my children, to bring hurt
on them and those that marry with them? What
curse is not there? "Your father killed his father
and sowed the seed where he had sprung himself

1 *What does Oedipus know about himself? For what does he believe he has been preserved? What attitude does he express toward fate now?*

2 *About whom does Oedipus worry?*

3 *What does Oedipus fear will happen to his daughters? What does he ask Creon to do?*

ANSWERS TO GUIDED READING QUESTIONS

1 Oedipus knows that he cannot be killed by sickness or other means. He believes that he has been saved from death for some evil fate. He holds the attitude that his fate can take him where it will.

2 Oedipus worries about his daughters, Antigone and Ismene.

3 Oedipus worries that his daughters will be outcasts and that they will never marry. He asks Creon to keep his children from suffering his fate of wandering homeless and despised.

ANALYTIC SCALES FOR RESPONDING IN WRITING
(SEE PAGE 673)

Assign a score from 1 to 25 for each grading criterion below. (For more detailed evaluation, see the evaluation forms for writing, revising, and proofreading, Assessment Portfolio 4.1–4.9.)

1. Dialogue

- **Content/Unity.** The dialogue addresses questions and answers about Oedipus and his situation.
- **Organization/Coherence.** The dialogue flows naturally.
- **Language/Style.** The dialogue uses vivid and precise nouns, verbs, and modifiers.
- **Conventions.** The dialogue avoids errors in spelling, grammar, usage, mechanics, and manuscript form.

▶ Additional practice is provided in the Essential Skills Practice Book: Writing 1.8.

2. Critical Essay

- **Content/Unity.** The essay analyzes imagery of blindness and sight in *Oedipus.*
- **Organization/Coherence.** The essay presents a thesis that is supported in subsequent paragraphs. The essay ends with a solid conclusion.

(cont.)

ANALYTIC SCALES FOR RESPONDING IN WRITING (CONT.)

- **Language/Style.** The essay uses vivid and precise language.
- **Conventions.** The essay avoids errors in spelling, grammar, usage, mechanics, and manuscript form.

▶ Additional practice is provided in the Essential Skills Practice Book: Writing 1.20.

CULTURAL/HISTORICAL NOTE

In addition to her comments in the Global Views box on page 671, Sarah Galanis notes that although Greeks tend to be superstitious and always trying to read their future, there is also a great deal of hope in their culture. She says, "Fate does play a big role in Greek lives, but at the same time, the Orthodox religion focuses a lot on hope, so Greeks pretty much take life as it comes."

and begot you out of the womb that held him."
These insults you will hear. Then who will marry you?
No one, my children; clearly you are doomed
to waste away in barrenness unmarried.
Son of Menoeceus,[11] since you are all the father
left these two girls, and we, their parents, both
are dead to them—do not allow them wander
like beggars, poor and husbandless.
They are of your own blood.
And do not make them equal with myself
in wretchedness; for you can see them now
so young, so utterly alone, save for you only.
Touch my hand, noble Creon, and say yes.
If you were older, children, and were wiser,
there's much advice I'd give you. But as it is,
let this be what you pray: give me a life
wherever there is opportunity
to live, and better life than was my father's.

CREON. Your tears have had enough of scope; now go within the house.

OEDIPUS. I must obey, though bitter of heart.

CREON. In season, all is good.

OEDIPUS. Do you know on what conditions I obey?

CREON. You tell me them,
and I shall know them when I hear.

OEDIPUS. That you shall send me out
to live away from Thebes.

CREON. That gift you must ask of the God.

OEDIPUS. But I'm now hated by the Gods.

CREON. So quickly you'll obtain your prayer.

OEDIPUS. You consent then?

CREON. What I do not mean, I do not use to say.

OEDIPUS. Now lead me away from here.

CREON. Let go the children, then, and come.

OEDIPUS. Do not take them from me.

CREON. Do not seek to be master in everything,
for the things you mastered did not follow you throughout your life.

11. **Son of Menoeceus.** Creon

Chorus. (*As* Creon *and* Oedipus *go out.*) You that live in my
ancestral Thebes, behold this Oedipus,—
him who knew the famous riddles and was a man most masterful;
not a citizen who did not look with envy on his lot—
see him now and see the breakers of misfortune sallow him!
Look upon that last day always. Count no mortal happy till
he has passed the final limit of his life secure from pain. ■

What does the final speech of the Chorus suggest about life?

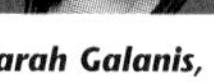

Sarah Galanis, Greece

Global Views

Contemporary Greeks don't look at fate exactly as it's portrayed in *Oedipus the King*, but they do believe that certain things are predetermined for you. *Ti na kanome* is a saying everybody uses; it means, "What can we do?" You might say it at a funeral or when something happens that you can't control. Some people try to protect themselves from the evil eye, a source of bad luck. Older people in the villages often pin a glass bead that looks like a blue eye to a baby's t-shirt for protection against *matiasis*—the curse of the evil eye. Some people, especially in my generation, say they don't believe in these superstitions. But the idea of fate has been part of our culture for so long that it can be difficult to ignore.

Responding to the Selection

By the end of the selection do you sympathize with Oedipus, or do you think he is to blame for the trouble and pain he suffers? Explain your response.

Answers to Guided Reading Questions

➊ The Chorus's speech suggests that although life may seem happy and good, misery may come. A life cannot be judged until death.

Responding to the Selection

Students may have feelings of both sympathy and blame for Oedipus. They may also express other feelings about this character. In any case, students should explain why they feel as they do, using examples if possible to support their opinions.

Additional Questions and Activities

Ask students to read the quotation from Herodotus in the Echoes on page 591. Have them compare the idea presented by Herodotus to the idea presented by Creon in lines 1727–1728. What understanding of life and death do the two views present? Do these ideas agree with students' own ideas about life and death? Students should explain their responses.

Additional Questions and Activities

Sarah discusses superstition in her review. Ask students the following questions: Do you have any superstitions? For example, do you toss salt over your shoulder, stay out of the path of black cats, or avoid walking under a ladder? Do you say "gesundheit" or "bless you" when someone sneezes? Ask students to name as many superstitions as they can. How did they learn these superstitions? Interested students can research various superstitions to discover how they originated and share this information with the class.

Reviewing the Selection

RECALLING / **INTERPRETING**

1. What news does the messenger bring? What effect does the messenger expect this news to have on Oedipus? What is Oedipus's first reaction to the news? Why does his mood change? ▶▶ Does Oedipus believe in prophecies? Is his fear warranted? Explain.

2. What does the messenger reveal to ease Oedipus's fears? How does Jocasta react to Oedipus's questions about what the messenger discloses? ▶▶ Why does Jocasta rush away? Does Oedipus understand the truth of his parentage yet? How do you know?

3. What role did the herdsman play in Oedipus's past? ▶▶ How does the herdsman feel about answering Oedipus's questions? How does he feel about his actions toward the young Oedipus? Why does he feel this way?

4. What does Jocasta do when the truth is revealed? What does Oedipus do when he finally discovers the truth? On whom does he place blame for his condition? ▶▶ Does Oedipus accept responsibility for his fate? Explain. What are his feelings toward the gods and prophecies at the end of the play? Have they changed over the course of the tragedy?

SYNTHESIZING

5. Oedipus is warned many times throughout the play to leave things alone and not to pry into the past. Although warned against the truth, he continues to seek it. Why does Oedipus ignore all of the advice he is given and continue to seek to find the truth? What traits does he exhibit in this search? Do you admire him or find him foolish for continuing? Explain.

Understanding Literature (Questions for Discussion)

1. **Convention.** A **convention** is an unrealistic element in a literary work that is accepted by readers or viewers because the element is traditional. Review the conventions of Greek drama explained in Insights: Greek Drama (see page 616). Explain how the conventions of unity are followed in the play. What dramatic convention did the ancient Greeks have regarding violence? How does Sophocles maintain this convention when dealing with Jocasta's hanging and Oedipus's self-mutilation?

Answers for Reviewing the Selection

RECALLING AND INTERPRETING

1. **Recalling.** The messenger brings the news that Polybus is dead. The messenger expects his news to make Oedipus a bit sad over the death of his father but mainly happy that he will become king of Corinth. Oedipus is first happy to hear that his father is dead, because he had feared the prophecy that said he would kill his father. His feelings change when he realizes that he could still fulfill part of the prophecy. **Interpreting.** Oedipus does believe in prophecies, although he says that he need not think of them. He continues to be frightened of fulfilling the evil deeds foretold. If he believes in prophecies, his fear is still warranted, but if he looks at his father's death as proof of the inconsequence of prophecies, his fear is unfounded.

2. **Recalling.** The messenger reveals that Polybus was not Oedipus's father. Jocasta asks Oedipus to ignore or forget what the messenger has said. **Interpreting.** Jocasta, horrified by the truth, does not want to witness what happens when it is revealed. Oedipus does not yet know of his parentage. He thinks that Jocasta is worried that he is of low birth.

3. **Recalling.** The herdsman had found Oedipus on Mount Cythaeron and had given him to the messenger, a fellow herdsman at the time, to raise. **Interpreting.** The herdsman does not wish to reveal the truth to Oedipus. He wishes he had not saved Oedipus's life, because he sees what a terrible tragedy has befallen Oedipus.

4. **Recalling.** Jocasta hangs herself. Oedipus gouges his eyes, blinding himself. Oedipus says that Apollo is to blame for the actions that were prophesied, but he takes responsibility for the physical harm that he has inflicted upon himself. **Interpreting.** Oedipus finally accepts his (cont.)

Answers for Reviewing the Selection (cont.)

fate. He believes in prophecies when he sees that he has not avoided them. His fear of the prophecies throughout the play suggests that, despite some doubts, he has believed in them all along.

SYNTHESIZING

Responses will vary. Possible responses are given.

5. Oedipus wants to learn the truth about Laius's killers to save Thebes and to protect himself. As he looks into this mystery, the question of his own identity is raised. He is stubbornly determined to learn the truth about his past, perhaps to be able to further avoid the prophecy. At the beginning of the play, he exhibits concern for his people. Throughout the play, he exhibits stubbornness, pride, and courage in the face of information against which he has been warned.

2. **Tragedy and Tragic Flaw.** A **tragedy** is a drama that tells the story of the fall of a person of high status. It celebrates the courage and dignity of a tragic hero in the face of inevitable doom. Sometimes that doom is made inevitable by a tragic flaw. A **tragic flaw** is a personal weakness that brings about the fall of a character in a tragedy. What is Oedipus's tragic flaw? In what way was his doom caused by fate, or forces beyond his control? In what way did he contribute to his own downfall? Find examples from the latter part of the play in which Oedipus faces his downfall with courage and dignity. To what extent does Oedipus remain great despite his downfall?

Responding in Writing

1. **Creative Writing: Dialogue.** Imagine that Oedipus were a current leader. Think about the scandal that would follow the revelation that he killed his father and married his mother. Imagine that you are interviewing Oedipus for a prime time television show. To what questions would you want answers? What feelings about Oedipus would you want to inspire in your audience? You might choose to be sympathetic, accusatory, or contemptuous of him. Write a set of questions that reflect your opinion of Oedipus in tone and content. Then trade questions with a partner, imagine you are Oedipus and write Oedipus's answers to the questions. Feel free to invent details and words, but stay true to the story told in the play. Do you think Oedipus would be contrite, proud, angry? What motivation would he have for appearing on the show? Consider these questions before formulating your responses.

2. **Critical Essay: Blindness and Sight in *Oedipus the King*.** Throughout *Oedipus the King,* there is much discussion of blindness and sight. Consider the way in which the blind Teiresias can see or the way in which Oedipus is blind to his identity and the truth of his situation. Write an essay in which you discuss Oedipus's blindness before he gouged his own eyes and whether his later self-inflicted punishment is appropriate. Find examples throughout the play of language related to sight, eyes, or blindness. You might begin by looking at Oedipus's and Teiresias's speeches in lines 395–490. Use such examples to support your statements about Oedipus.

Language Lab

Greek and Latin Roots. Many English words are based on ancient Greek and Latin. For example the word *telephone* comes from the Greek root *tele-,* meaning "far away," and *phone,* meaning "voice." Other Greek prefixes include *dys-* for bad, *hypo-* for under, and *dia-* for through. Some prefixes from Latin include *mal-* for bad, *sup-* for under, and *trans-* for through. For more examples, see the Language Arts Survey 2.66, "Greek and Latin Roots." Using these roots, try to determine the meanings of the following words.

1. hypothermia
2. monorail
3. unicycle
4. diameter
5. suppress
6. dynasty
7. hypocrite
8. triumvirate
9. patriarchy
10. malediction

Answers for Understanding Literature

Responses will vary. Possible responses are given.

1. Convention. Although the play discusses events that took place many years ago, all of the action takes place within one day. The action occurs in one place, and all of the action is related to Oedipus's central conflict. One convention of ancient Greek drama called for violent actions to take place offstage and be described to the characters and the audience. Jocasta's hanging and Oedipus's self-mutilation are not shown. Instead, a messenger relates the information.

2. Tragedy and Tragic Flaw. Oedipus's tragic flaw is his hubris, or excessive pride. The gods had prophesized that Oedipus would kill his father and marry his mother. Oedipus, though he tried, could not avoid this fate. His insistence upon learning the truth about the killer of Laius, despite warnings not to proceed in such a search, led to his downfall. Oedipus shows dignity in asking of the shepherd that the matter might be settled "once for all." He faces his fate with dignity when he asks Creon to spare his daughters from being exiled or outcast like himself. Oedipus remains great in finally accepting his fate, conceding to leave, and in looking after his family.

Answers for Language Lab

1. *hypo* (under) + *thermia* (heat) = subnormal temperature
2. mono (one) + rail = single-railed track
3. *uni* (one) + *cycle* (circle/wheel) = one-wheeled vehicle
4. *dia* (through) + *meter* (measure) = length of line through center of a circle
5. *sub* (under) + *press* (strike) = put down by force
6. *dyna* (power) + *sty* = ruling family

(cont.)

Analytic Scales for Responding in Writing

Grading scales for Responding in Writing appear on page 669.

Answers for Language Lab (cont.)

7. *hypo* (under) + *crite* (decide or judge) = an actor = insincere person
8. *trium* (plural three) + *virum* (men) = government by three people
9. *patria* (father) + *arches* (to rule) = government or rule by males
10. *male* (bad) + *diction* (say) = curse or slander

▶ Additional practice is provided in the Essential Skills Practice Book: Language 2.66.

ADDITIONAL RESOURCES

READER'S GUIDE
• Selection Worksheet 8.4

ASSESSMENT PORTFOLIO
• Selection Check Test 2.8.7
• Selection Test 2.8.8

ESSENTIAL SKILLS PRACTICE BOOKS
• Writing 1.8, 1.20

PREREADING EXTENSIONS

Comparison can be made between Pericles's funeral oration and Abraham Lincoln's Gettysburg Address, which was delivered at the dedication of a national cemetery during the Civil War. Have students read the Gettysburg Address and write an essay comparing the two. Students might note that the occasion for the two speeches was similar and that both Pericles and Lincoln try to heal the wounds of war and ease the sorrow of loss by calling upon the glory of the cause for which the dead sacrificed their lives. They both encourage a nation to continue on in war by reminding them of the benefits their nation offers them and of the debt they owe the dead.

SUPPORT FOR LEP STUDENTS

PRONUNCIATIONS OF PROPER NOUNS AND ADJECTIVES

Pel • o • pon • ne • sian (pel´ə pə nē´zhən)
Per • i • cles (per´i klēz´)
Thu • cyd • i • des (tho͞o sid´i dēz´)

ADDITIONAL VOCABULARY

engage—enter into conflict with
exploits—bold deeds
hazarded—attempted or ventured
liberality—generosity
obscurity—condition of not being well known

PREREADING

"Pericles' Funeral Oration"
from *History of the Peloponnesian War*
by Thucydides, translated by Rex Warner

About the Author

THUCYDIDES
C. 460 BC–AFTER 404 BC

While Greek historian Herodotus (see page 710) is often called the Father of History, the Greek historian **Thucydides** originated a systematic approach to the study of history. Based on his writings, historians estimate that Thucydides must have been born sometime around 460 BC. Thucydides was an Athenian who owned land in Thrace. He suffered but survived the great plague that struck Athens between 430 and 429. In 424, he was chosen as a *strategos,* or military leader. He lost the city of Amphipolis to the Spartans and was subsequently tried and exiled. Thucydides regarded his exile as a chance to devote himself to a history of the Peloponnesian War, a conflict between Athens and Sparta which began in 431. Thucydides's narrative begins shortly before the start of the war and analyzes the events that led up to it. With the fall of Athens in 404 and the transfer of power from Athens to Sparta, Thucydides's exile was ended. He probably died in the violence of the turbulent times following the war.

About the Selection

In ***History of the Peloponnesian War,*** Thucydides set out to write an account of a war which he believed would be an influential and decisive conflict between two states at the height of their power—Athens and Sparta. Working with his own observations and those of other eyewitnesses, Thucydides organized a chronology to construct a full narrative complete with analysis of personalities, the technical aspects of war, and policies of state. Thucydides's history ends more than six years before the end of the war, perhaps due to his untimely death. The accuracy of his work is supported in part by other records.

Included in the *History* are several speeches that reveal the character of the speaker and the attitudes of the warring states. Thucydides said of the speeches that he did not always remember the exact words; instead, he tried to keep "as closely as possible to the general sense of the words that were actually used, to make the speakers say what, in [his] opinion, was called for by each situation." **"Pericles' Funeral Oration,"** given at the Athenian burial of their war dead in 430, is an eloquent celebration of democracy.

Temple of Apollo, Delphi

CONNECTIONS: Pericles

Thucydides greatly admired Pericles, an Athenian statesman. Pericles was a central force in the development of Athenian democracy and in making Athens a political and cultural center. Pericles came to power in 460 BC, and although public opinion turned against him in his later years, he remained influential until his death in 429. The period in which he lived and in which Athenian culture and democracy flourished is often called the Periclean Age or the Golden Age of Athens.

GOALS/OBJECTIVES

Studying this lesson will enable students to

• have a positive experience reading a work celebrating Athenian democracy
• briefly explain who Pericles was
• define *aim* and *mode,* and recognize argumentation as a literary mode
• identify the major theme in a literary work
• write a song or speech of praise
• write a critical essay comparing and contrasting Athenian and American democracy
• gather oral history

READER'S JOURNAL

What does the word *democracy* mean to you? In your journal, define *democracy* and write about the benefits you perceive in your own life that come of living in a democracy. What do you think are the responsibilities of the citizens of a democracy? In what way does the democracy of the United States differ from an ideal democracy?

"Pericles' Funeral Oration"

THUCYDIDES, TRANSLATED BY REX WARNER

In the same winter the Athenians, following their annual custom, gave a public funeral for those who had been the first to die in the war. These funerals are held in the following way: two days before the ceremony the bones of the fallen are brought and put in a tent which has been erected, and people make whatever offerings they wish to their own dead. Then there is a funeral procession in which coffins of cypress wood are carried on wagons. There is one coffin for each tribe, which contains the bones of members of that tribe. One empty bier[1] is decorated and carried in the procession: this is for the missing, whose bodies could not be recovered. Everyone who wishes to, both citizens and foreigners, can join in the procession, and the women who are related to the dead are there to make their laments at the tomb. The bones are laid in the public burial-place, which is in the most beautiful quarter outside the city walls. Here the Athenians always bury those who have fallen in war. The only exception is those who died at Marathon,[2] who, because their achievement was considered absolutely outstanding, were buried on the battlefield itself.

When the bones have been laid in the earth, a man chosen by the city for his intellectual gifts and for his general reputation makes an appropriate speech in praise of the dead, and after the speech all depart. This is the procedure at these burials, and all through the war, when the time came to do so, the Athenians followed this ancient custom. Now, at the burial of those who were the first to fall in the war, Pericles, the son of Xanthippus,[3] was chosen to make the speech. When the moment arrived, he came forward from the tomb and, standing on a high platform, so that he might be heard by as many people as possible in the crowd, he spoke as follows:

1 *What happens before the funeral procession? What is the significance of the empty coffin? Who takes part in the procession? Where are the dead buried? What does the funeral custom suggest about Athenian attitudes toward their war dead?*

1. **bier.** Platform on which a coffin or corpse is placed
2. **Marathon.** Ancient Greek village in east Attica where a small group of Athenians defeated a mighty Persian army under Darius I
3. **Xanthippus.** Athenian general who fought in the war against Persia. He belonged to one of the noblest families in Athens.

WORDS FOR EVERYDAY USE

la • ment (lə ment´) *n.,* mourning, wailing

READER'S JOURNAL

As an alternate activity, you might ask students to write about veterans and war heroes they know personally or have learned about in history or social studies classes. Why is it important to honor veterans and war heroes? In what ways might veterans and war heroes be honored?

ANSWERS TO GUIDED READING QUESTIONS

1 Before the funeral procession the bones of the war dead are displayed so that people can make offerings if they wish. Any citizen or foreigner can participate. The dead are buried in the most beautiful part of the city. The custom suggests that the Athenians respect and honor their war dead.

SPELLING AND VOCABULARY WORDS FROM THE SELECTION

commiserate	oration
consummation	toil
incredulous	versatility
lament	

QUOTABLES

"My work is not a piece of writing designed to meet the taste of an immediate public, but was done to last for ever."

—Thucydides

VOCABULARY IN CONTEXT

• In Islamic countries, professional mourners are hired for funerals to make laments.

Answers to Guided Reading Questions

1 Pericles does not believe speeches are a proper or adequate way to honor the heroism of the dead. He thinks the actions of the living in the valiant continuation of battle best honor the dead.

2 Pericles proposes to discuss the spirit of Athens in the face of trials and then to speak in praise of the dead.

3 Athens is a democracy because the power is in the hands of the whole people. Pericles says that everyone is equal before the law and that the abilities of a man are most important when choosing a public figure. Poverty should not keep a person from serving in politics.

Literary Note

Refer students to the selection by Herodotus on page 710, or ask them to browse his *Histories* for comparison with Thucydides. The tone and sources of these two early historians differ greatly. Herodotus was a storyteller, who included mythical elements in his history and often recorded popular belief whether or not he had evidence to support it. He claimed, "It is my principle, that I ought to repeat what is said; but I am not bound always to believe it." Thucydides, on the other hand, prided himself on searching for the truth of an incident among the many stories people might tell and on leaving popular misconceptions and mythical elements out of his records.

Q 1 *What problems does Pericles perceive in the tradition of funeral oration? How does Pericles think the dead should be honored?*

"Many of those who have spoken here in the past have praised the institution of this speech at the close of our ceremony. It seemed to them a mark of honor to our soldiers who have fallen in war that a speech should be made over them. I do not agree. These men have shown themselves valiant in action, and it would be enough, I think, for their glories to be proclaimed in action, as you have just seen it done at this funeral organized by the state. Our belief in the courage and manliness of so many should not be hazarded on the goodness or badness of one man's speech. Then it is not easy to speak with a proper sense of balance, when a man's listeners find it difficult to believe in the truth of what one is saying. The man who knows the facts and loves the dead may well think that an oration tells less than what he knows and what he would like to hear: others who do not know so much may feel envy for the dead, and think the orator over-praises them, when he speaks of exploits that are beyond their own capacities. Praise of other people is tolerable only up to a certain point, the point where one still believes that one could do oneself some of the things one is hearing about. Once you get beyond this point, you will find people becoming jealous and incredulous. However, the fact is that this institution was set up and approved by our forefathers, and it is my duty to follow the tradition and do my best to meet the wishes and the expectations of every one of you.

Q 2 *What does Pericles propose to do in his speech?*

"I shall begin by speaking about our ancestors, since it is only right and proper on such an occasion to pay them the honor of recalling what they did. In this land of ours there have always been the same people living from generation to generation up till now, and they, by their courage and their virtues, have handed it on to us, a free country. They certainly deserve our praise. Even more so do our fathers deserve it. For to the inheritance they had received they added all the empire we have now, and it was not without blood and toil that they handed it down to us of the present generation. And then we ourselves, assembled here today, who are mostly in the prime of life, have, in most directions, added to the power of our empire and have organized our state in such a way that it is perfectly well able to look after itself both in peace and in war.

"I have no wish to make a long speech on subjects familiar to you all: so I shall say nothing about the warlike deeds by which we acquired our power or the battles in which we or our fathers gallantly resisted our enemies, Greek or foreign. What I want to do is, in the first place, to discuss the spirit in which we faced our trials and also our constitution and the way of life which has made us great. After that I shall speak in praise of the dead, believing that this kind of speech is not inappropriate to the present occasion, and that this whole assembly, of citizens and foreigners, may listen to it with advantage.

Q 3 *Why is Athenian government called a democracy? What qualities are important in legal decisions and in the choosing of public officials?*

"Let me say that our system of government does not copy the institutions of our neighbors. It is more the case of our being a model to others, than of our imitating anyone else. Our constitution is called a democracy because power is in the hands not of a minority but of the whole people. When it is a question of settling private disputes, everyone is equal before the law; when it is a question of putting one person before another in positions of public responsibility, what counts is not membership of a particular class, but the actual ability which the man possesses. No one, so long as he has it in him to be of service to the state, is kept in political obscurity because of poverty. And, just as

Words for Everyday Use

o • ra • tion (ō rā´shən) *n.*, formal public speech

in • cred • u • lous (in krej´oo ləs) *adj.*, unwilling or unable to believe

toil (toil) *n.*, labor; hard work

Vocabulary in Context

- President Abraham Lincoln gave an oration to honor the soldiers who died in the battle at Gettysburg, Pennsylvania.
- We could see the scientist did not agree with her colleague's theory by the incredulous expression on her face.
- Plowing the field under the hot afternoon sun was difficult toil for the team of oxen.

our political life is free and open, so is our day-to-day life in our relations with each other. We do not get into a state with our next-door neighbor if he enjoys himself in his own way, nor do we give him the kind of black looks which, though they do no real harm, still do hurt people's feelings. We are free and tolerant in our private lives; but in public affairs we keep to the law. This is because it commands our deep respect.

"We give our obedience to those whom we put in positions of authority, and we obey the laws themselves, especially those which are for the protection of the oppressed, and those unwritten laws which it is an acknowledged shame to break.

"And here is another point. When our work is over, we are in a position to enjoy all kinds of recreation for our spirits. There are various kinds of contests and sacrifices regularly throughout the year; in our own homes we find a beauty and a good taste which delight us every day and which drive away our cares. Then the greatness of our city brings it about that all the good things from all over the world flow in to us, so that to us it seems just as natural to enjoy foreign goods as our own local products.

"Then there is a great difference between us and our opponents, in our attitude toward military security. Here are some examples: Our city is open to the world, and we have no periodical deportations in order to prevent people observing or finding out secrets which might be of military advantage to the enemy. This is because we rely, not on secret weapons, but on our own real courage and loyalty. There is a difference, too, in our educational systems. The Spartans,[4] from their earliest boyhood, are submitted to the most laborious training in courage; we pass our lives without all these restrictions, and yet are just as ready to face the same dangers as they are. Here is proof of this: When the Spartans invade our land, they do not come by themselves, but bring all their allies with them; whereas we, when we launch an attack abroad, do the job by ourselves, and, though

Greece

fighting on foreign soil, do not often fail to defeat opponents who are fighting for their own hearths and homes. As a matter of fact none of our enemies has ever yet been confronted with our total strength, because we have to divide our attention between our navy and the many missions on which our troops are sent on land. Yet, if our enemies engage a detachment[5] of our forces and defeat it, they give themselves credit for having thrown back our entire army; or, if they lose, they claim that they were beaten by us in full strength. There are certain advantages, I think, in our way of meeting danger voluntarily, with an easy mind, instead of with a laborious training, with natural rather than with state-induced courage. We do not have to spend our time practicing to meet sufferings which are still in the future; and when they are actually upon us we show ourselves just as brave as these others who are always in strict training. This is one point in which, I think, our city deserves to be admired. There are also others:

❶ *What connection does Athens have to the rest of the world? What aspect of Athens does Pericles praise in this part of his speech?*

❷ *In what ways does Athens differ from Sparta?*

4. **Spartans.** People of ancient Sparta, military rival of Athens

5. **engage a detachment.** Enter into conflict with only a portion of the entire military force

Answers to Guided Reading Questions

❶ "Good things" from all over the world have been brought to Athens to be enjoyed by the people. According to Pericles, Athens serves as a model of government and cultural greatness to the rest of the world.

❷ Athens does not deport people for fear of having political secrets disclosed. Spartans rely on a strictly disciplined method of upbringing to raise fine warriors. Athenians do not share the Spartan restrictions, but they succeed in battle. The Athenians often fight without allies unlike the Spartans.

Cultural/Historical Note

The Peloponnesian War, which Thucydides took as the subject of his life work, was fought between Athens and Sparta, the two leading city-states of ancient Greece, and involved almost all of the Greek states. The war began in 431 BC and ended with the defeat of Athens in 404 BC. The Spartans had a stronger army, but the Athenians had the dominant navy.

The war that began in 431 was preceded by a war between Athens and Sparta that is often referred to as the First Peloponnesian War, which ended with the Thirty Years' Treaty in 445 BC. When Athens sided with Corcyra in Corinth, fighting began, and the Athenians took action that violated the peace treaty. The Spartans accused Athens of aggression, Athens refused to back down, and the tenuous peace dissolved into war. The fighting can be divided into two distinct periods separated by a six-year truce. During the first ten years of fighting, Pericles encouraged the Athenians to depend upon their navy. A plague that struck Athens killed many soldiers and civilians and wounded morale, but the Athenians (cont.)

Cultural/Historical Note (cont.)

managed to repulse Spartan offensives. In the later part of this period, the Athenians took the attack position. In 421, the Peace of Nicias began. It ended in 415 when Athens attacked Sicily. It was in Sicily that Athens suffered decisive defeat of both its army and navy. The Athenian navy was defeated in 405 BC and the war ended in 404 BC.

Answers to Guided Reading Questions

❶ Pericles thinks that Athens is "an education to Greece." Athens proves its greatness through its power, which, according to Pericles, stems from the kindness and generosity of the people, as well as the fact that each person is his or her own "rightful lord." He thinks that future ages will wonder at Athens the way current generations do.

❷ Individuals have the responsibility to be as interested in the well-being of the state as they are in their own affairs. Decisions of policy should be submitted to the people for proper discussion.

ANALYTIC SCALES FOR RESPONDING IN WRITING

(SEE PAGE 682.)

Assign a score from 1 to 25 for each grading criterion below. (For more detailed evaluation, see the evaluation forms for writing, revising, and proofreading, Assessment Portfolio 4.1–4.9.)

1. Song or Speech of Praise

- **Content/Unity.** The song or speech praises democracy.
- **Organization/Coherence.** The song or speech first defines democracy and then explains its benefits. Ideas are presented in a sensible order.
- **Language/Style.** The song or speech uses vivid and precise nouns, verbs, and modifiers.
- **Conventions.** The song or speech avoids errors in spelling, grammar, usage, mechanics, and manuscript form.

▶ Additional practice is provided in the Essential Skills Practice Book: Writing 1.8.

What effect does Pericles think Athens has on the rest of Greece? In what way does Athens prove its greatness? How does Pericles think future ages will view Athens?

What responsibility does an individual have in a democracy? How should decisions of policy be made?

"Our love of what is beautiful does not lead to extravagance; our love of the things of the mind does not make us soft. We regard wealth as something to be properly used, rather than as something to boast about. As for poverty, no one need be ashamed to admit it: the real shame is in not taking practical measures to escape from it. Here each individual is interested not only in his own affairs but in the affairs of the state as well: even those who are mostly occupied with their own business are extremely well informed on general politics—this is a peculiarity of ours: we do not say that a man who takes no interest in politics is a man who minds his own business; we say that he has no business here at all. We Athenians, in our own persons, take our decisions on policy or submit them to proper discussions: for we do not think that there is an incompatibility between words and deeds; the worst thing is to rush into action before the consequences have been properly debated. And this is another point where we differ from other people. We are capable at the same time of taking risks and of estimating them beforehand. Others are brave out of ignorance; and, when they stop to think, they begin to fear. But the man who can most truly be accounted brave is he who best knows the meaning of what is sweet in life and of what is terrible, and then goes out undeterred to meet what is to come.

"Again, in questions of general good feeling there is a great contrast between us and most other people. We make friends by doing good to others, not by receiving good from them. This makes our friendship all the more reliable, since we want to keep alive the gratitude of those who are in our debt by showing continued good will to them: whereas the feelings of one who owes us something lack the same enthusiasm, since he knows that, when he repays our kindness, it will be more like paying back a debt than giving something spontaneously. We are unique in this. When we do kindnesses to others, we do not do them out of any calculations of profit or loss: we do them without afterthought, relying on our free liberality. Taking everything together then, I declare that our city is an education to Greece, and I declare that in my opinion each single one of our citizens, in all the manifold aspects of life, is able to show himself the rightful lord and owner of his own person, and do this, moreover, with exceptional grace and exceptional versatility. And to show that this is no empty boasting for the present occasion, but real tangible fact, you have only to consider the power which our city possesses and which has been won by those very qualities which I have mentioned. Athens, alone of the states we know, comes to her testing time in a greatness that surpasses what was imagined of her. In her case, and in her case alone, no invading enemy is ashamed at being defeated, and no subject can complain of being governed by people unfit for their responsibilities. Mighty indeed are the marks and monuments of our empire which we have left. Future ages will wonder at us, as the present age wonders at us now. We do not need the praises of a Homer,[6] or of anyone else whose words may delight us for the moment, but whose estimation of facts will fall short of what is really true. For our adventurous spirit has forced an entry into every sea and into every land; and everywhere we have left behind us everlasting memorials of good done to our friends or suffering inflicted on our enemies.

6. **Homer.** Greek epic poet of eighth century BC

Words for Everyday Use

ver • sa • til • i • ty (vʉr´sə til´ə tē) *n.,* competence or skill in many things

Vocabulary in Context

- During the Renaissance, the ideal person displayed great versatility—he or she had many different skills and areas of expertise.

"This, then, is the kind of city for which these men, who could not bear the thought of losing her, nobly fought and nobly died. It is only natural that every one of us who survives them should be willing to undergo hardships in her service. And it was for this reason that I have spoken at such length about our city, because I wanted to make it clear that for us there is more at stake than there is for others who lack our advantages; also I wanted my words of praise for the dead to be set in the bright light of evidence. And now the most important of these words has been spoken. I have sung the praises of our city; but it was the courage and gallantry of these men, and of people like them, which made her splendid. Nor would you find it true in the case of many of the Greeks, as it is true of them, that no words can do more than justice to their deeds.

"To me it seems that the consummation which has overtaken these men shows us the meaning of manliness in its first revelation and in its final proof. Some of them, no doubt, had their faults; but what we ought to remember first is their gallant conduct against the enemy in defense of their native land. They have blotted out evil with good, and done more service to the commonwealth than they ever did harm in their private lives. No one of these men weakened because he wanted to go on enjoying his wealth: no one put off the awful day in the hope that he might live to escape his poverty and grow rich. More to be desired than such things, they chose to check the enemy's pride. This, to them, was a risk most glorious, and they accepted it, willing to strike down the enemy and relinquish everything else. As for success or failure, they left that in the doubtful hands of Hope, and when the reality of battle was before their faces, they put their trust in their own selves. In the fighting, they thought it more honorable to stand their ground and suffer death than to give in and save their lives. So they fled from the reproaches of men, abiding with life and limb the brunt of battle; and, in a small moment of time, the climax of their lives, a culmination of glory, not of fear, were swept away from us.

"So and such they were, these men—worthy of their city. We who remain behind may hope to be spared their fate, but must resolve to keep the same daring spirit against the foe. It is not simply a question of estimating the advantages in theory. I could tell you a long story (and you know it as well as I do) about what is to be gained by beating the enemy back. What I would prefer is that you should fix your eyes every day on the greatness of Athens as she really is, and should fall in love with her. When you realize her greatness, then reflect that what made her great was men with a spirit of adventure, men who knew their duty, men who were ashamed to fall below a certain standard. If they ever failed in an enterprise, they made up their minds that at any rate the city should not find their courage lacking to her, and they gave to her the best contribution that they could. They gave her their lives, to her and to all of us, and for their own selves they won praises that never grow old, the most splendid of sepulchers[7]—not the sepulcher in which their bodies are laid, but where their glory remains eternal in men's minds, always there on the right occasion to stir others to speech or to action. For famous men have the whole earth as their memorial: it is not only the inscriptions on their graves in their own country that mark them out; no, in for-

7. **sepulchers.** Vaults for burial, graves

❶ *Why has Pericles sung the praises of Athens? In what way does he relate his words to the dead?*

❷ *What does Pericles want his audience to do?*

❸ *What virtues of the dead does Pericles praise? What does Pericles say about the faults of the dead?*

WORDS FOR EVERYDAY USE

con • sum • ma • tion (kän´sə mā shen) *n.,* completeness; fulfillment

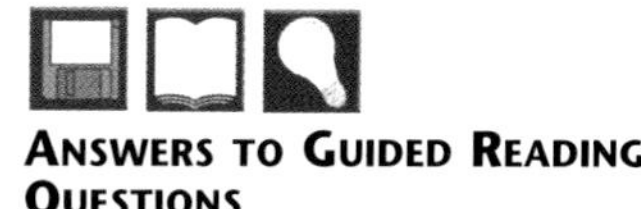

ANSWERS TO GUIDED READING QUESTIONS

❶ Pericles has sung the praises of Athens to give context to his praise for the dead and to show why Athenians have a lot at stake in the war in which their soldiers have died. The dead fought for the glory of Athens, which Pericles has just praised.

❷ Pericles wants his audience to look upon Athens and fall in love with the city.

❸ Pericles praises them for not weakening in the face of suffering and pain and for trusting in themselves. He says that the faults of the dead are overshadowed by the glory they have achieved.

ANALYTIC SCALES FOR RESPONDING IN WRITING

(SEE PAGE 682.)

2. Critical Essay

- **Content/Unity.** The essay compares and contrasts American and Athenian democracy.
- **Organization/Coherence.** The essay begins with an introduction that includes the thesis of the essay. The introduction is followed by supporting paragraphs with clear transitions. The essay ends with a solid conclusion.
- **Language/Style.** The essay uses vivid and precise nouns, verbs, and modifiers.
- **Conventions.** The essay avoids errors in spelling, grammar, usage, mechanics, and manuscript form.

▶ Additional practice is provided in the Essential Skills Practice Book: Writing 1.20.

VOCABULARY IN CONTEXT

- As the consummation to their study of Greek literature, the group planned to take a trip to Greece.

Answers to Guided Reading Questions

❶ Happiness depends upon freedom. People must be courageous and not relax their efforts to maintain their freedom.

❷ Their futures will be difficult because it will be hard to live up to the reputation of their dead fathers and brothers. The reputation of the dead goes untarnished by the jealousies that can affect the living.

❸ Pericles reminds the parents that the sons they have lost have been lost in honor to the cause of freedom, which will ensure happiness for themselves and others.

❹ Pericles says that the glory of women is to be least talked about by men. Pericles does not see women as important. His words also suggest that women have no role in the public life of the state.

Selection Check Test with Answers

EX. On what occasion does Pericles give this address?

He gives this address at the annual public funeral for the war dead.

1. How, according to Pericles, should those people slain in war be honored?

They should be honored through actions, not words.

2. What kind of government is Athens?

Athens is a democracy.

3. Who are the opponents to whom Pericles contrasts Athenians?

Pericles speaks of the Spartans.

4. What opinion does Pericles think people will have of Athens in the future?

He thinks that people will wonder at the greatness of Athens.

5. Upon what does happiness depend?

Happiness depends upon being free.

❶ *On what does happiness depend? In what way are people responsible for their own happiness?*

❷ *Why will the future be difficult for the sons and brothers of the dead? What does Pericles say about the reputation of the dead?*

❸ *In what way does Pericles try to comfort the parents of those who have died?*

❹ *What words does Pericles direct at the women in the audience? What does this suggest about his attitude toward women and the role of women in Athenian society?*

eign lands also, not in any visible form but in people's hearts, their memory abides and grows. It is for you to try to be like them. Make up your minds that happiness depends on being free, and freedom depends on being courageous. Let there be no relaxation in face of the perils of the war. The people who have most excuse for despising death are not the wretched and unfortunate, who have no hope of doing well for themselves, but those who run the risk of a complete reversal in their lives, and who would feel the difference most intensely, if things went wrong for them. Any intelligent man would find a humiliation caused by his own slackness more painful to bear than death, when death comes to him unperceived, in battle, and in the confidence of his patriotism.

"For these reasons I shall not commiserate with those parents of the dead, who are present here. Instead I shall try to comfort them. They are well aware that they have grown up in a world where there are many changes and chances. But this is a good fortune—for men to end their lives with honor, as these have done, and for you honorably to lament them: their life was set to a measure where death and happiness went hand in hand. I know that it is difficult to convince you of this. When you see other people happy you will often be reminded of what used to make you happy too. One does not feel sad at not having some good thing which is outside one's experience: real grief is felt at the loss of something which one is used to. All the same, those of you who are of the right age must bear up and take comfort in the thought of having more children. In your own homes these new children will prevent you from brooding over those who are no more, and they will be a help to the city, too, both in filling the empty places, and in assuring her security. For it is impossible for a man to put forward fair and honest views about our affairs if he has not, like everyone else, children whose lives may be at stake. As for those of you who are now too old to have children, I would ask you to count as gain the greater part of your life, in which you have been happy, and remember that what remains is not long, and let your hearts be lifted up at the thought of the fair fame of the dead. One's sense of honor is the only thing that does not grow old, and the last pleasure, when one is worn out with age, is not, as the poet said, making money, but having the respect of one's fellow men.

"As for those of you here who are sons or brothers of the dead, I can see a hard struggle in front of you. Everyone always speaks well of the dead, and, even if you rise to the greatest heights of heroism, it will be a hard thing for you to get the reputation of having come near, let alone equaled, their standard. When one is alive, one is always liable to the jealousy of one's competitors, but when one is out of the way, the honor one receives is sincere and unchallenged.

"Perhaps I should say a word or two on the duties of women to those among you who are now widowed. I can say all I have to say in a short word of advice. Your great glory is not to be inferior to what God has made you, and the greatest glory of a woman is to be least talked about by men, whether they are praising you or criticizing you. I have now, as the law demanded, said what I had to say. For the time being our offerings to the dead have been made, and for the future their children will be supported at the public expense by the city, until they come of age. This is the crown and prize which she offers, both to the dead and to their children, for the ideals which they have faced. Where the rewards of valor are the greatest, there you will find also the best and brightest spirits among people. And now, when you have mourned for your dear ones, you must depart." ■

Words for Everyday Use

com • mis • er • ate (kə miz´ər āt) *vt.,* feel pity for

Vocabulary in Context

- When Jill saw the devastation the flood left in its wake, she commiserated with the townspeople and contacted a relief organization to see how she could help.

Responding to the Selection

Pericles says, "Make up your minds that happiness depends on being free, and freedom depends on being courageous." Do you agree or disagree with this statement? What kinds of courage do you think members of a democracy need to display during war time? in times of peace? Discuss these questions with your classmates.

Reviewing the Selection

Recalling

1. What events mark the public funeral of the war dead?
2. What reservations does Pericles have about giving a funeral oration? What does he say he will do in his speech?
3. What differences between Athens and Sparta does Pericles note?
4. What words of comfort does Pericles offer to the parents of those who died in battle? What advice does he offer? What does he say to the sons and brothers of the slain?

Interpreting

1. What does the Athenian funeral custom suggest about the attitude of the Athenians toward their war dead?
2. In what way are the matters about which Pericles proposes to speak related to the dead whom he has been called upon to honor?
3. What military advantages might each state have? Why does Pericles declare Athens to be "an education to Greece"?
4. How would Pericles define *heroism*? How have these dead soldiers demonstrated heroism, as Pericles defines it?

Synthesizing

5. Pericles says, "Mighty indeed are the marks and monuments of our empire which we have left. Future ages will wonder at us, as the present age wonders at us now." Do you think Pericles's prediction about the way future generations will view Athens has come to pass? Explain. In what ways are your feelings about our own society similar to or different from Pericles's feelings for Athens?

Responding to the Selection

Encourage students to discuss ways in which their lives would be different if they lacked certain freedoms.

Answers for Reviewing the Selection

RECALLING AND INTERPRETING

1. **Recalling.** The bodies are placed in a tent so that families might make offerings. Then there is a funeral procession that includes a coffin for each tribe and an empty bier as a reminder of the bodies that could not be recovered. The dead are buried in the beautiful public burial area outside the city walls. Then a man admired for his reputation and intellect is chosen to give a speech. **Interpreting.** The Athenians respect their war dead and show it by choosing for the burial site a place of honor and beauty and by creating a ritual in which anyone can participate and that calls upon a respected member of the community to dedicate the ceremonies.

2. **Recalling.** Pericles does not feel that words can do justice to the actions of those who have died in war. He says he will speak about the glory of Athens and then in praise of the dead. **Interpreting.** The greatness of Athens is the cause of the efforts of the dead, and their glory lies in the fact that they died in defense of their state.

3. **Recalling.** Pericles says that Athenians do not follow the restrictions of education and upbringing that the Spartans follow and that they usually rely on their own forces, while Spartans rely on allies. **Interpreting.** The Spartans might have better-trained soldiers since their style of living is centered on military training. The Athenians may be more appreciative of their way of life and the freedoms it offers and thus more dedicated to fighting to preserve it. (cont.)

Answers for Reviewing the Selection (cont.)

4. **Recalling.** Pericles reminds the parents that their sons died for the glory of Athens. He advises parents who can to have more children to ease their sorrow. He warns the sons and brothers of the slain that their futures will be difficult because it will be hard to equal the reputation of the slain. **Interpreting.** Pericles might define *heroism* as maintaining courage, not backing down in the face of a foe, relying on oneself, and fighting for freedom even to the death. *Responses will vary.*

SYNTHESIZING

Responses will vary. Possible responses are given.

5. Students might suggest that Pericles's prophecy has come to pass, citing evidence such as the appreciation of the Classical age and the ideals of Athenian democracy that have shaped the government of the United States.

Answers for Understanding Literature

Responses will vary. Possible responses are given.

1. Aim and Mode. Pericles's aim is to persuade the Athenians to honor their dead by continuing to fight for the glory of their state. He outlines the meaning of democracy, reminds the Athenians of the many areas in which Athens flourishes, points out the ways in which Athens is superior to its rival Sparta, and suggests that action is the best way to honor the dead.

2. Theme. Pericles focuses on the glory and wonders of Athens. Pericles appeals to the pride and patriotism of the Athenians by describing the greatness of their state. He claims the freedom Athens offers is happiness. He uses these reasons to encourage the continued efforts of the Athenians in the war that has killed their soldiers.

Analytic Scales for Responding in Writing

Grading scales for Responding in Writing appear on pages 678, 679.

Understanding Literature (Questions for Discussion)

1. **Aim and Mode.** A writer's **aim** is the primary purpose that his or her work is meant to achieve. The aim of Pericles's speech is to persuade. A **mode** is a form of writing. **Argumentation,** one of the modes of writing, presents reasons or arguments for accepting a position or for adopting a course of action. What course of action does Pericles try to persuade the Athenians to accept? What reasons or arguments does he present?
2. **Theme.** A **theme** is a central idea in a literary work. What is the major theme of Pericles's funeral oration? In what way is this theme related to Pericles's aim?

Responding in Writing

1. **Creative Writing: Song or Speech of Praise.** "Pericles' Funeral Oration" offers eloquent praise of democracy. Write a song or speech in which you praise democracy. First, try to define *democracy* and gather ideas about the benefits you receive and the responsibilities you face as a citizen of a democracy. You may wish to refer to your response to the Reader's Journal activity. Then, use these ideas to support a statement praising democracy.
2. **Critical Essay: Comparing and Contrasting Democracies.** In what ways do you think American democracy is similar to to Athenian democracy? Do you think, as Pericles says of the government of Athens, that the United States serves as a model to other nations? If Pericles's statements about the responsibilities and benefits of a democracy were applied to the United States would you agree with them? Is Pericles's portrait of Athens realistic? Consider these questions before drafting your essay. In a thesis statement, identify your opinion of the democracy in ancient Athens and in the contemporary United States. Support your argument by referring to the text and to current events in American politics. In a final paragraph, draw some conclusions about democracy and its practice in two different places and times.

Project

Oral History. In the introduction to *The History of the Peloponnesian War,* Thucydides claims that the truth is not easy to discover for "different eye-witnesses give different accounts of the same events, speaking out of partiality for one side or the other or else from imperfect memories." As an experiment in oral history, try to gather the "truth" about an incident of local history. Work in small groups to learn about different events. Each group should choose an event from recent history in your community. Any members of your group who witnessed this event should record their memories of the event. Then, interview other members of your community to try to gather details about the event. Based on your findings, try to give an account of the event and explain the impact of the event on your community and the feelings it evoked in the members of your community.

Project Notes

See the evaluation form for projects, Assessment Portfolio 4.12.

Oral History. You may wish to advise students in the type of community events they choose to investigate. For example, students should not try to gather the "truth" about a local crime or any other dangerous situation. Possible events for students to explore include natural phenomena or disasters, parades or public ceremonies, speeches, and so on.

PREREADING

from *From the Founding of the City, Book I*
by Livy (Titus Livius), translated by B. O. Foster

ROME

About the Author

Titus Livius (59 BC–AD 17). Titus Livius, better known as **Livy,** achieved fame as one of the greatest Roman historians in his own lifetime, and his work continued to influence historical writers for centuries. Livy grew up in a wealthy family in the rich city of Patavium (modern-day Padua in northern Italy) during the time of Julius Cæsar's rise to power. Unlike the people of Rome who lived in lavish but corrupt splendor, the people of Patavium lived more simply and were famed for their strict morality. Livy would later apply these morals to his writing. He was unable to follow the path of most educated Romans and study abroad in Greece because of the civil wars that followed Cæsar's death, but he did study rhetoric and philosophy at home.

By 31 BC, Livy was living in Rome. By 29 BC, he had decided to write a history of Rome from its very beginning to the present day. This enormous undertaking required its author to write at least three books a year. He was tempted for a time to abandon this daunting task, but Livy was truly fascinated by history. In the end he completed his life's work, writing a complete history of Rome that filled 142 books. Unlike many historians of his day, Livy was not active in Rome's politics nor did he associate with famed writers such as Virgil or Ovid. Livy did become close to the emperor Augustus and approved of the emperor's religious and moral reforms.

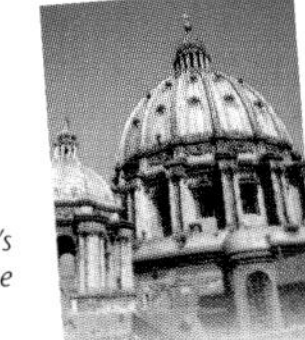

Dome, St. Peter's Basilica, Rome

About the Selection

Histories were popular in Rome; Romans were interested in and proud of their past. Among Rome's many historians were Sallust, Tacitus, the elder Cato, and Julius Cæsar himself. A complete history of Rome was not unique in itself. Livy's innovation lay in trying to understand history by examining the character of historical figures. In fact, he is known to sacrifice accuracy to focus on character. Livy's overriding message seems to have been inspired by the attitudes of his place of birth—it was high moral ground that made Rome great but morality was steadily declining.

Livy referred to his work as ***Ab Urbe Condita,*** or ***"From the Founding of the City."*** Of the 142 original books, only books 1 through 10 and 21 through 45 remain. The following excerpt is from Livy's first book. It describes Rome's legendary founding.

Temple of Antonius and Faustina, Palatine, Rome

CONNECTIONS: Founding Myths

In many cultures around the world, people develop myths about how their city or culture was founded. Often these myths dignify the culture or city by drawing links to a heroic age or a god. As you may have already read in the *Aeneid* (see page 222), the Romans believed that Aeneas led the defeated Trojans to Italy to found a colony that would later become Rome. In this selection, Mars, god of war, is linked to Rome's founders. The god chosen by a people as the patron or founder of their city reveals much about the values of a particular culture.

GOALS/OBJECTIVES

Studying this lesson will enable students to

- appreciate the founding legend of Rome
- briefly explain Livy's approach to history
- define *archetype* and recognize archetypes in literature
- distinguish between nonfiction and myth
- write a founding story
- write a critical essay analyzing a founding story
- listen actively and use interpersonal communication skills

ADDITIONAL RESOURCES

READER'S GUIDE
- Selection Worksheet 8.5

ASSESSMENT PORTFOLIO
- Selection Check Test 2.8.9
- Selection Test 2.8.10

ESSENTIAL SKILLS PRACTICE BOOKS
- Writing 1.8, 1.10, 1.20
- Language 2.23
- Speaking and Listening 3.2

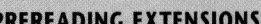

PREREADING EXTENSIONS

Ten of the remaining books in Livy's history (Books 21–30) describe the Second Punic War. Inform students that the Punic Wars were a series of struggles between the Roman Republic and the Carthaginian Empire. Encourage students to work in small groups to research and present oral reports on the Punic War. Groups may choose to focus on either of the three wars, Carthaginian culture and society, the destruction of Masinissa, or major figures in the wars such as Hannibal Barca, Publius Scipio the Elder, or Scipio the Younger.

SUPPORT FOR LEP STUDENTS

PRONUNCIATIONS OF PROPER NOUNS AND ADJECTIVES

Ca • to (cā´tō)
Li • vy (li´vē)
Nu • mi • tor (no͞o´mi tər)
Re • mus (rē´məs)
Rhe • a Sil • vi • a (rē´ə sil´vē ə)
Rom • u • lus (räm´yo͞o ləs)
Sal • lust (səl lust´)
Ta • ci • tus (tas´i təs)

ADDITIONAL VOCABULARY

consecrate—make or declare as sacred
slew—killed

READER'S JOURNAL

Students may also wish to work in teams to debate their views about the duties of historians. Tell students to be sure to provide reasons for their opinions.

Answers to Guided Reading Questions

❶ The author says he will not affirm or refute the poetic legends about Rome's founding because it is the right of ancient cities to "mingle divine things with human" to add dignity.

❷ The Romans claim the god Mars as their father and father of their founder. The author says that the Roman people should be allowed to claim Mars as their father in this way because of the military glory of Rome. The author says that the nations of the earth should submit to this claim just as they have submitted to rule by Rome.

SPELLING AND VOCABULARY WORDS FROM THE SELECTION

affray	slake
augury	throng
pillage	

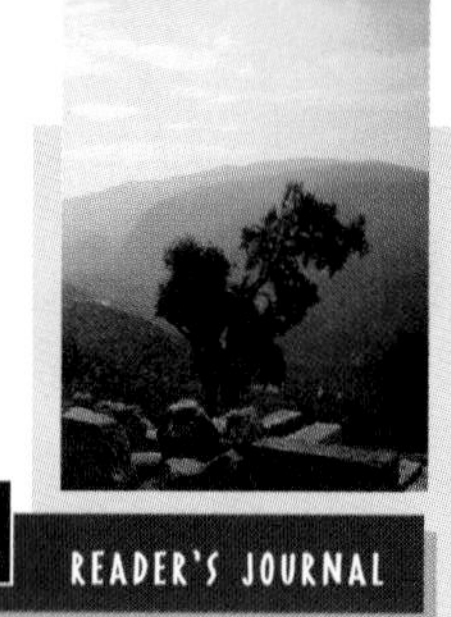

Do you think a historian should relate nothing but the facts in a history, or should the historian also describe the legends of the people? Does a historian have a duty to separate fact from fiction for his or her readers? In your journal, write your opinion of what a historian should and should not do when writing a history.

READER'S JOURNAL

FROM

From the Founding of the City, Book I

LIVY, TRANSLATED BY B. O. FOSTER

❶ *Why won't the author affirm or refute legends about Rome's founding?*

❷ *Whom do the Romans claim as their father and the father of their founder? What is the author's attitude toward this claim? According to the author, how should "the nations of the earth" respond to this claim?*

[Editor's note: The Trojan leader Aeneas, son of Anchises and the goddess Venus, and Aeneas's followers journey to the Italian peninsula. Once there, Aeneas and the Trojans experience conflict with the native people of that region, who are subjects of a king named Latinus. Aeneas eventually marries Latinus's daughter, Lavinia, and founds a town called Lavinium. Aeneas and Lavinia have a son named Ascanius. Neighboring kingdoms attack both the Trojans and the subjects of Latinus, so Aeneas unites the two peoples, calling them all Latins, and the Latin troops are victorious over their enemies. Aeneas, however, dies in battle, and Lavinia becomes regent of the kingdom until Ascanius can claim the throne. Once king, Ascanius founds the city called Alba Longa. The reigns of Lavinia and Ascanius are peaceful. A long line of kings, descended from Ascanius, follows. Just before the following selection begins, a king named Proca gives the kingdom to his elder son, Numitor. After his father's death, the younger son, Amulius, drives out Numitor and takes over the kingdom. Amulius kills Numitor's sons and makes his daughter, Rhea Silvia, into a vestal virgin who can never marry. The vestal virgins are virgin priestesses who serve Vesta, goddess of the hearth.]

Such traditions as belong to the time before the city was founded, or rather was presently to be founded, and are rather adorned with poetic legends than based upon trustworthy historical proofs, I purpose neither to affirm nor to refute. It is the privilege of antiquity to mingle divine things with human, and so to add dignity to the beginnings of cities; and if any people ought to be allowed to consecrate their origins and refer them to a divine source, so great is the military glory of the Roman People that when they profess that their Father and the Father of their Founder was none other than Mars,[1] the nations of the earth may well submit to this also with as good a grace as they submit to Rome's dominion.

◆ ◆ ◆

IV. But the Fates were resolved, as I suppose, upon the founding of this great City, and the beginning of the mightiest of empires, next after that of Heaven. The

1. **Mars.** Roman god of war, identified with the Greek god Ares. Mars was named as the father of Romulus and Remus by Rhea Silvia.

Vestal [Rhea Silvia] was ravished, and having given birth to twin sons, named Mars as the father of her doubtful offspring, whether actually so believing, or because it seemed less wrong if a god were the author of her fault. But neither gods nor men protected the mother herself or her babes from the king's cruelty; the priestess he ordered to be manacled and cast into prison, the children to be committed to the river. It happened by singular good fortune that the Tiber[2] having spread beyond its banks into stagnant pools afforded nowhere any access to the regular channel of the river, and the men who brought the twins were led to hope that being infants they might be drowned, no matter how sluggish the stream. So they made shift to discharge the king's command, by exposing the babes at the nearest point of the overflow, where the fig-tree Ruminalis—formerly, they say, called Romularis—now stands. In those days this was a wild and uninhabited region. The story persists that when the floating basket in which the children had been exposed was left high and dry by the receding water, a she-wolf, coming down out of the surrounding hills to slake her thirst, turned her steps towards the cry of the infants, and with her teats gave them suck so gently, that the keeper of the royal flock found her licking them with her tongue. Tradition assigns to this man the name of Faustulus, and adds that he carried the twins to his hut and gave them to his wife Larentia to rear. Some think that Larentia, having been free with her favors, had got the name of she-wolf among the shepherds, and that this gave rise to this marvellous story. The boys, thus born and reared, had no sooner attained to youth than they began—yet without neglecting the farmstead or the flocks—to range the glades of the mountains for game. Having in this way gained both strength and resolution, they would now not only face wild beasts, but would attack robbers laden with their spoils, and divide up what they took from them among the shepherds, with whom they shared their toils and pranks, while their band of young men grew larger every day.

V. They say that the Palatine was even then the scene of the merry festival of the Lupercalia[3] which we have today, and that the hill was named Pallantium, from Pallanteum, an Arcadian city, and then Palatium. There Evander, an Arcadian of that stock, who had held the place many ages before the time of which I am writing, is said to have established the yearly rite, derived from Arcadia, that youths should run naked about in playful sport, doing honor to Lycaean Pan, whom the Romans afterwards called Inuus. When the young men were occupied in this celebration, the rite being generally known, some robbers who had been angered by the loss of their plunder laid an ambush for them, and although Romulus successfully defended himself, captured Remus[4] and delivered up their prisoner to King Amulius, even lodging a complaint against him. The main charge was that the brothers made raids on the lands of Numitor, and pillaged them, with a band of young fellows which they had got together, like an invading enemy. So Remus was given up to Numitor to be punished. From the very beginning Faustulus had entertained the suspicion that they were children of the royal blood that he was bringing up in his house; for he was aware both that infants had

1 What does King Amulius do to Rhea Silvia and her twin sons?

2 Who discovers the twins and takes care of them?

3 What do the robbers do to the twins?

4 What had Faustulus always suspected? What does Faustulus do?

2. **Tiber.** River in central Italy
3. **Lupercalia.** Roman festival held on February 15, in honor of Lupereus, a pastoral god
4. **Romulus . . . Remus.** Romulus and Remus are the names of the twins.

Words for Everyday Use

slake (slāk) *vt.,* satisfy or make less intense
pil • lage (pil´ij) *vt.,* rob violently; plunder

Answers to Guided Reading Questions

1. King Amulius throws Rhea Silvia into prison and orders that her children be thrown into the river.
2. A female wolf discovers the twins and takes care of them.
3. The robbers ambush the twins and capture Remus. They deliver him to King Amulius, saying that Remus was raiding Numitor's lands, so Amulius turns Remus over to Numitor to be punished.
4. Faustulus always suspected that Romulus and Remus might be Rhea Silvia's children and of royal blood. Faustulus tells Romulus of his suspicions about his parentage.

Cross-curricular Activities

Arts and Humanities and Social Studies

Encourage students to explore the differences between ancient Athens and ancient Rome by comparing the attributes of the gods associated with each city. Inform them that Athena, the patron goddess of Athens, was associated with wisdom, justice, civilization, handicrafts, and skill in war. The Romans, who appropriated many of their gods, including Mars, from the Greeks, claimed Mars as the father of the founders of Rome; the Greeks called him Ares and thought of him as the bloodthirsty god of war, discord, strife, terror, and panic. Encourage students to share myths and legends about Athena and Mars. Although both are associated with war, in what way are these associations different? What do these gods reveal about the difference in values revered in ancient Athens and ancient Rome?

Mathematics and Sciences

Many societies have generated stories in which human beings are raised or accepted by wolves, perhaps because of the close kinship in wolf packs. Interested students may prepare reports on wolves and their social organization.

Vocabulary in Context

- The athlete took a long drink of cool water to slake her thirst.
- The Vandals, a Germanic people, invaded Italy and captured and pillaged Rome in AD 455.

Answers to Guided Reading Questions

❶ Romulus kills King Amulius.

❷ Numitor wonders if Remus might be one of his lost grandsons.

❸ Numitor informs a council of Amulius's crimes and the identities of Romulus and Remus. He declares himself responsible for Amulius's death. Romulus and Remus hail their grandfather as king.

Literary Note

Inform students that Foster's translation of Livy's work is very literal. He has preserved the extremely long sentences that are characteristic of Latin prose.

INTEGRATED SKILLS ACTIVITIES

LANGUAGE LAB

As this is a very literal translation, the language may seem foreign or awkward to some students. Encourage students to read the Language Arts Survey 2.23, "Varying Sentence Openings, Length, and Structure." Students might then choose a paragraph and rewrite it in their own words, trying to retain the same meaning. They might, for example, divide long independent clauses linked by semicolons into separate sentences or replace Latinate words with their more common Anglo-Saxon equivalents.

▶ Additional practice is provided in the Essential Skills Practice Book: Language 2.23.

She-Wolf of the Capitol. *Musei Capitolini, Rome. The totem of Rome, this statue depicts the she-wolf raising the abandoned infants Romulus and Remus.*

❶ *What happens to King Amulius?*

❷ *What does Numitor wonder about Remus?*

❸ *What do Numitor, Romulus, and Remus do to regain Numitor's throne?*

been exposed by order of the king, and that the time when he had himself taken up the children exactly coincided with that event. But he had been unwilling that the matter should be disclosed prematurely, until opportunity offered or necessity compelled. Necessity came first; accordingly, driven by fear, he revealed the facts to Romulus. It chanced that Numitor too, having Remus in custody, and hearing that the brothers were twins, had been reminded, upon considering their age and their far from servile nature, of his grandsons. The inquiries he made led him to the same conclusion, so that he was almost ready to acknowledge Remus. Thus on every hand the toils were woven about the king. Romulus did not assemble his company of youths—for he was not equal to open violence—but commanded his shepherds to come to the palace at an appointed time, some by one way, some by another, and so made his attack upon the king; while from the house of Numitor came Remus, with another party which he had got together, to help his brother. So Romulus slew the king.

VI. At the beginning of the fray Numitor exclaimed that an enemy had invaded the city and attacked the palace, and drew off the active men of the place to serve as an armed garrison for the defense of the citadel; and when he saw the young men approaching, after they had dispatched the king, to congratulate him, he at once summoned a council, and laid before it his brother's crimes against himself, the parentage of his grandsons, and how they had been born, reared, and recognized. He then announced the tyrant's death, and declared himself to be responsible for it. The brothers advanced with their band through the midst of the crowd, and hailed their grandfather king, whereupon such a shout of assent arose from the entire throng as confirmed the new monarch's title and authority.

The Alban state being thus made over to Numitor, Romulus and Remus were seized with the desire to found a city in the region where they had been exposed and brought up. And in fact the population of Albans and Latins was too large; besides, there were the shepherds. All together, their numbers might easily lead men to hope that Alba would be small, and Lavinium small, compared with the city which they should build. These considerations were interrupted by the curse of their grandsires, the greed of kingly power, and by a shameful quarrel which grew out of it, upon an occasion innocent enough. Since the brothers were twins, and respect for their age could not determine between them, it was agreed that the gods who had those places in their protection should choose by augury who should give the new city its name, who should govern it when built. Romulus took the Palatine for his augural quarter, Remus the Aventine.

VII. Remus is said to have been the first to receive an augury, from the flight of six vultures. The omen had been already reported when twice that number appeared to Romulus. Thereupon each was saluted king by his own followers, the one party laying claim to the honour from priority, the other from the number of the birds. They then engaged in a battle of words and, angry taunts leading to bloodshed, Remus was struck down in the affray. The commoner story is that Remus leaped over the new walls in mockery of his brother, whereupon Romulus in great anger slew him, and in menacing wise added these words withal, "So perish whoever else shall leap over my walls!" Thus Romulus acquired sole power, and the city, thus founded, was called by its founder's name. ■

❶ *What did Romulus and Remus want to do in their home region? What prevented them from doing so?*

❷ *What causes the conflict between Romulus and Remus?*

Roman relief. *Vatican Museum, Rome, Italy*

Words for Everyday Use

throng (thrông) *n.,* crowd; great number of people

au • gu • ry (ô´gyōō rē) *n.,* divination from omens

af • fray (ə frā´) *n.,* attack; alarm

Answers to Guided Reading Questions

❶ Romulus and Remus wished to found a city in their home region. Their plans are interrupted by "the curse of their grandsires, the greed of kingly power, and by a shameful quarrel" between the brothers.

❷ Remus believes that he should rule and name the city because he had an augury of six vultures first, and Romulus believes that he should rule and name the city because he saw a greater number of vultures.

Selection Check Test with Answers

EX. What city is founded by Romulus?

Rome is founded by Romulus.

1. Who did the mother of the twins say was their father?

The mother of the twins said that Mars was their father.

2. What did King Amulius do to the twins?

King Amulius had them put in a basket and cast into the river.

3. Who found the twins and nursed them?

A female wolf found the twins and nursed them.

4. Who became king after Romulus killed Amulius?

The twins' grandfather Numitor became king.

5. What happened to Remus as a result of the twins' disagreement?

Remus was killed by Romulus as a result of the twins' disagreement.

Vocabulary in Context

- When the film star left her limousine, she was surrounded by a throng of enthusiastic fans.
- Ancient peoples have interpreted everything from the flights of birds to the size of an animal's liver as auguries of future events.
- The Roman general led an affray against their ancient enemies—the Sabines.

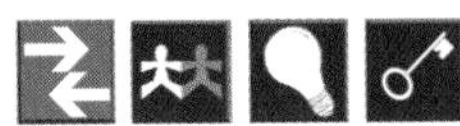

Responding to the Selection

As an alternate activity, you might encourage students to discuss what they think of Romulus and Remus and to explain whether they are admirable figures.

Answers for Reviewing the Selection

RECALLING AND INTERPRETING

1. **Recalling.** The author intends to neither affirm nor refute these legends but to relate them. The author says that the Roman people should be allowed to claim divine origins for their city because of their great "military glory." **Interpreting.** The author seems to be very patriotic and proud of Rome, but he seems to look down on other nations and assumes that Rome will conquer them all.

2. **Recalling.** Rhea Silvia names the god Mars as the father of her twins. King Amulius imprisons Rhea Silvia and has the twins put into a basket and cast into the Tiber River. **Interpreting.** King Amulius treats Rhea Silvia and her twins in this way to protect his wrongly seized kingship from legitimate heirs to the throne. The author finds Rhea Silvia's claim that Mars is the father of the twins "doubtful" and says that she claims Mars as the father "because it seemed less wrong if a god were the author of her fault." Students may say the author expresses this attitude because he finds Rhea Silvia's pregnancy to be morally wrong; others may say the author is amused by the explanation. The author claimed that he would neither affirm nor refute poetic legends, but he does refute the legend that Mars is the father of Rhea Silvia's children.

3. **Recalling.** A female wolf saves the twins and nurses them. Bandits ambush the twins, capture Remus, and deliver him to King Amulius, saying that he raided Numitor's lands, so Amulius delivers Remus to Numitor for punishment. The twins lead an attack against King Amulius, slay him, and proclaim their grandfather Numitor as the rightful king.

(cont.)

Responding to the Selection

What makes this history different from other histories you have read? What makes it similar to other histories you have read? Do you agree with the author that "It is the privilege of antiquity to mingle divine things with human, and so to add dignity to the beginnings of cities"?

Reviewing the Selection

RECALLING	INTERPRETING
1. What does the author intend to do with the legends of the founding of Rome? According to the author, why should the Roman people be allowed to claim divine origins for their city?	In what way would you describe the author's attitude toward his nation? toward other nations?
2. Who does Rhea Silvia name as the father of her twins? What does King Amulius do to Rhea Silvia and the twins?	Why does King Amulius treat Rhea Silvia and the twins in this way? What attitude does the author express toward Rhea Silvia's claim? Why do you think he expresses this attitude? Are Livy's comments consistent with the attitude he earlier says he will take toward "poetic legends" that are not "based upon trustworthy historical proofs"? Explain.
3. Who or what saves the twins, Romulus and Remus, from the river? What happens to put Remus in contact with his grandfather Numitor? What do the twins do for Numitor? What does Numitor do for the twins?	What does this legend about the rescue of the twins reveal about their characters? Why does Numitor suspect that Remus is his grandson? What motivates Romulus and Remus to aid their grandfather?
4. After the twins decide to build a city, how do they decide who will rule and name the city? What causes their disagreement? What ends this disagreement?	What feelings motivate the twins during their argument? What does this disagreement reveal about the twins' characters? Explain whether or not you would classify Romulus as a heroic founder.

Answers for Reviewing the Selection (cont.)

Numitor reveals the regal parentage of the twins. **Interpreting.** The wolf may have nurtured the twins because she realized they were special. The twins' contact with the wolf may symbolize the developments of their warlike and ferocious natures. Numitor suspects that Remus is his grandson because he is a twin of the right age and because he has a "far from servile nature." *Responses will vary.*

4. **Recalling.** The twins decide that the ruler of the city will be chosen by augury or omen. Remus sees the first augury, a flight of six vultures, but Romulus sees a flight of twelve vultures, so the brothers disagree as to who is the rightful ruler of the city. The disagreement is ended when Romulus kills Remus. **Interpreting.** The twins are motivated by ambition. The twins value power more than love of family. Students may say that the fact that Romulus kills his own brother prevents him from being a hero.

(cont.)

5. What do you think this legend about the founding of Rome reveals about the character and values of the Roman people? What does the fact that Mars is described as the father of the founder of Rome reveal about Roman values? What do the violence and bloodshed in this legend reveal about the Romans? In many cultures, fratricide is perceived as a horrific crime that places an unremovable stigma upon the murderer. For example, in Genesis, Cain is exiled and marked for the crime of killing Abel. What, if any, attitude is expressed toward Romulus's killing of Remus?

Understanding Literature (Questions for Discussion)

1. **Archetype.** An **archetype** is an inherited, often unconscious, ancestral memory or motif that recurs throughout history or literature. In literature about cultural heroes, the hero is often described as having been a foundling (an infant, of unknown parents, who has been found abandoned). Often, the infant is noble or the child of people of high status. Several cultures have described a future leader being cast into a river in a basket. For example, you may be familiar with the story of Moses in the Bible. The child is then raised by surrogate parents who may or may not know the child's true identity. There are usually indications that the foundling is someone special when he or she is still a child. Eventually the hero's true identity is revealed, both to himself or herself and to others, and the hero claims his or her rightful position in society. Why do you think this is such a popular archetype? To what desires and fears in people does it appeal?

2. **Nonfiction and Myth. Nonfiction** is writing about real events. A **myth** is a story that explains objects or events in the natural world as resulting from the action of some supernatural force or entity, most often a god. Which elements of this selection seemed like nonfiction to you? Which elements of this selection seemed like myth? Use a simple graphic organizer like the one below to record your responses.

NONFICTION	MYTH

Answers for Reviewing the Selection (cont.)

SYNTHESIZING

Responses will vary. Possible responses are given.

5. Students may say that the legend reveals that the Romans were warlike, violent, and eager to gain political power. The fact that Mars is so closely linked with the city reveals that the Romans valued skill in warfare. The amount of violence and bloodshed reveals that Romans had long been a warlike people who fought against neighboring kingdoms. Romulus's murder of Remus is treated very matter-of-factly, indicating that his crime was not viewed as harshly as Cain's.

Answers for Understanding Literature

Responses will vary. Possible responses are given.

1. **Archetype.** Students may say that the foundling archetype appeals to a child's fear or hope that his parents aren't really his parents, that he or she has been "adopted" and is really of much greater status. Such an archetype may give people hope that one day their real worth will be revealed and they will gain a better position in society.

2. **Nonfiction and Myth.** Students may say that the descriptions of conflicts and battles seem like nonfiction, and the mythical elements include the depiction of Mars as the father of the twins and the she-wolf rescuing and nursing the twins.

ANALYTIC SCALES FOR RESPONDING IN WRITING

Assign a score from 1 to 25 for each grading criterion below. (For more detailed evaluation, see the evaluation forms for writing, revising, and proofreading, Assessment Portfolio 4.1–4.9.)

1. Founding Story

- **Content/Unity.** The founding story presents either a nonfiction account of or an imaginative legend about the founding of the the writer's country.
- **Organization/Coherence.** The founding story presents details in a logical order.
- **Language/Style.** The founding story uses vivid and precise nouns, verbs, and modifiers.
- **Conventions.** The founding story avoids errors in spelling, grammar, usage, mechanics, and manuscript form.

► Additional practice is provided in the Essential Skills Practice Book: Writing 1.8, 1.10.

2. Critical Essay

- **Content/Unity.** The essay explains what the legend of the founding of Rome reveals about the ancient Romans.
- **Organization/Coherence.** The essay begins with an introduction that includes the thesis of the essay. The introduction is followed by supporting paragraphs with clear transitions. The essay ends with a solid conclusion.
- **Language/Style.** The essay uses vivid and precise nouns, verbs, and modifiers.
- **Conventions.** The essay avoids errors in spelling, grammar, usage, mechanics, and manuscript form.

► Additional practice is provided in the Essential Skills Practice Book: Writing 1.20.

Responding in Writing

1. **Creative Writing: Founding Story.** Write a brief, one- or two-page children's story about the founding of your own country. You might choose to research and use your knowledge of history to make a nonfiction account of your country's founding, or you might use your imagination to make a creative legend about your country's founding. For example, you might write about how the United States was founded after George Washington won the American Revolution by cutting down a cherry tree so tall that it landed upon the king of England. After you have brainstormed a few ideas for your founding story, choose the one in which you are most interested. Then, review the Language Arts Survey 1.10, "Gathering Ideas," for instructions on how to create a story map. Refer to your story map when drafting your story. If possible, share your founding stories with a younger audience.

2. **Critical Essay: Analyzing a Founding Story.** Write an essay in which you explain what the story of the founding of Rome reveals about the ancient Romans. As a starting point, think about your responses to the Synthesizing questions. Then review the selection carefully, keeping a list of particularly revealing passages. Refer to this list of passages when you are looking for evidence to support your thesis in your essay. Make sure that your essay has an introductory paragraph that states your thesis clearly, three or four supporting paragraphs, and a final paragraph that provides a conclusion to your essay.

Speaking and Listening Skills

Active Listening and Interpersonal Communication. Conflicts such as the disagreement between Romulus and Remus are often the result of poor communication skills. Review the Language Arts Survey 3.2, "Active Listening and Interpersonal Communication." Then, work with a partner to role play the argument that might have taken place between Romulus and Remus. Next, role play a second conversation, this time applying the rules for effective communication contained in the Language Arts Survey. In this second conversation, try to have the brothers come to some agreement.

ANSWERS FOR SKILLS ACTIVITIES

SPEAKING AND LISTENING SKILLS

Inform students that in the second conversation they should make eye contact, provide feedback as they are listening, think before speaking, and try to keep their emotions under control. They should avoid these techniques in the first conversation.

► Additional practice is provided in the Essential Skills Practice Book: Speaking and Listening 3.2.

PREREADING

Selected Poems
by Gaius Valerius Catullus, translated by Horace Gregory

ROME

About the Author

CATULLUS
84 BC–54 BC

Gaius Valerius Catullus, widely held to be the greatest of the Latin lyric poets, was born in Verona in northern Italy but lived in Rome among such illustrious contemporaries as Cicero, Pompey, and Julius Cæsar. During his brief life, Catullus witnessed civil war in Rome that led, finally, to the overthrow of the Republic and the establishment of the Empire under Cæsar Augustus. Although references to Catullus's life appear in the writings of his contemporaries and later authors, much of what we know about him is taken from his poetry. Of the surviving 116 poems attributed to him, 25 deal with the speaker's disastrous love affair with a woman, probably Clodia, a member of a well-known Roman family who was often connected with scandal. Catullus addressed her as Lesbia after the Greek island of Lesbos, home of the poet Sappho whose love poetry influenced Catullus's work. Catullus may have also wanted to hide Clodia's identity as she was married to a powerful Roman politician. Other poems by Catullus make caustic, contemptuous commentary on public figures. Catullus is noted for his innovative use of meter and form.

About the Selection

Although Catullus's writings cover a wide range of themes and forms, he is best known for his poetry of love and hate. The twenty-five poems addressed to Lesbia show the rise and fall of his relationship with Clodia. "**My life, my love, you say our love will last forever**" and "**My woman says that she would rather wear the wedding-veil for me**" express the heights of the speaker's love. "**I hate and love**" presents the mixed emotions that develop as the relationship takes a new turn, and "**You are the cause of this destruction**" shows the speaker plunged into despair when his relationship ends but his feelings of love remain.

CONNECTIONS: Catullus's Contemporaries

Among the notable Romans of Catullus's time were Cicero, Pompey, and Julius Cæsar. Cicero (106 BC–43 BC), a statesman, scholar, and writer, was known as a great orator. Pompey (106 BC–48 BC), was a respected general of the Roman Republic. He was one of a ruling triumvirate with Cæsar and Crassus, and later became an opponent to Cæsar. Julius Cæsar (100 BC–44 BC), dictator of the Roman Empire from 49 to 44 BC, was assassinated by a conspiracy of senators (see Plutarch's *The Lives of the Noble Grecians and Romans*, page 696).

GOALS/OBJECTIVES

Studying this lesson will enable students to

- appreciate Catullus's lyric poetry
- briefly explain what inspired much of Catullus's lyric poetry
- define *apostrophe* and *paradox*, and recognize examples of apostrophe and paradox in lyric poetry
- write a lyric poem that expresses strong feelings about a person, place, or thing
- write a critical essay comparing and contrasting one of Catullus's poems to song lyrics
- expand and combine sentences

ADDITIONAL RESOURCES

READER'S GUIDE

- Selection Worksheet 8.6

ASSESSMENT PORTFOLIO

- Selection Check Test 2.8.13
- Selection Test 2.8.14

ESSENTIAL SKILLS PRACTICE BOOKS

- Writing 1.8, 1.20
- Language 2.20–2.22

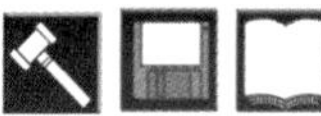

PREREADING EXTENSIONS

Inform students that Verona, where Catullus was born, was then a part of Cisalpine Gaul. According to Roman biographer Seutonius, Catullus's father may have been Julius Cæsar's host while Cæsar governed Gaul, and Cæsar and Catullus's father became good friends. Despite this family friendship, Catullus ridiculed Cæsar in his writing, and Cæsar found the remarks to be damaging. Nevertheless, when Catullus apologized, Cæsar immediately responded with an invitation to his home. Point out that Cæsar was known for forgiving his enemies. You may wish to refer students to Plutarch's account of Cæsar on page 696.

SUPPORT FOR LEP STUDENTS

PRONUNCIATIONS OF PROPER NOUNS AND ADJECTIVES

Ca • tul • lus (kə tul´əs)
Ci • cer • o (sis´ər ō´)
Clo • di • a (clō´dē ə)
Pom • pey (päm´pē)

ADDITIONAL VOCABULARY

constancy—faithfulness
convert—transform; change
discern—perceive or recognize
inviolate—kept sacred or unbroken

READER'S JOURNAL

If students have not yet experienced the end of a relationship or a relationship that has changed greatly over time, or if students are not comfortable describing such a relationship, they may describe their feelings about any current relationship.

Answers to Guided Reading Questions

❶ The speaker expects his love to last forever.

❷ The speaker says that a woman's words to a ravenous lover should be "written upon the wind / and engraved in rapid waters." The speaker thinks women say what their lovers want to hear and therefore should not be trusted.

Answers for Language Lab

(See page 695.)

Responses will vary. Possible responses are given.

1. Catullus was a Roman lyric poet.
2. Several of his poems were about love for a woman he called Lesbia.
3. The name *Lesbia* is probably a reference to the island of Lesbos where Sappho lived.
4. Catullus greatly admired the work of Sappho.
5. Catullus expresses love and hate in his poems.

▶ Additional practice is provided in the Essential Skills Practice Book: Language 2.20–2.22.

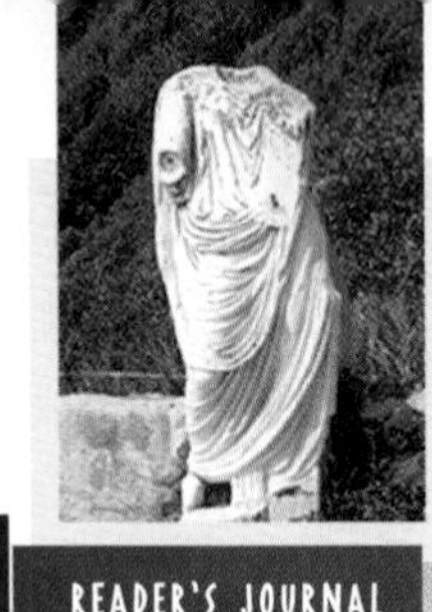

READER'S JOURNAL

Think about a relationship in your life that changed over time. Write about what this relationship was like in its early stages, its middle stages, and its end stages. What feelings did you have toward the other person at each of these times? How did you express these feelings?

Selected Poems

Catullus, translated by Horace Gregory

❶ *How long does the speaker expect his love to last?*

5

My life, my love, you say our love will last forever;
O gods remember
her pledge, convert the words of her <u>avowal</u> into prophecy.
Now let her blood speak, let sincerity govern each syllable fallen
from her lips, so that the long years of our lives shall be
a contract of true love inviolate
against time itself, a symbol of eternity.

❷ *What does the speaker say about a woman's words? What does he mean?*

7

My woman says that she would rather wear the wedding-veil for me
than anyone: even if Jupiter[1] himself came storming after her;
that's what she says, but when a woman talks to a hungry,
ravenous lover, her words should be written upon the wind
and engraved in rapid waters.

1. **Jupiter.** Chief Roman god

Words for Everyday Use

a • vow • al (ə vou´ əl) *n.,* open acknowledgment or declaration

Vocabulary in Context

• The Roman emperor's <u>avowal</u> revealed that he intended to send troops into Gaul.

Detail from ***Birth of Venus.*** *Sandro Botticelli, c. 1482*

10

I hate and love
    And if you ask me why,
I have no answer, but I discern,
can feel, my senses rooted in eternal torture.

❶ *How does the speaker feel? What do you imagine the cause of these feelings to be?*

11

You are the cause of this destruction, Lesbia,
that has fallen upon my mind;
this mind that has ruined itself
by fatal constancy.
And now it cannot rise from its own misery
to wish that you become
best of women, nor can it fail
to love you even though all is lost and you destroy
all hope. ■

❷ *Whom does the speaker blame for his misery? How does the speaker feel about this person?*

Responding to the Selection

Imagine that you are Lesbia, whom these poems address. How would you feel when you read each poem? Imagine how you might respond to Catullus. Write a response to each poem in the form of a letter or a poem, or role play with a partner a series of discussions between Catullus and Lesbia at each stage of their relationship.

Answers to Guided Reading Questions

❶ The speaker feels both love and hate. The speaker cannot explain these feelings, but students may say that his relationship has probably ended or is experiencing problems.

❷ The speaker blames Lesbia. The speaker cannot help loving Lesbia despite his belief that she is the cause of his pain.

Selection Check Test with Answers

EX. Where was Catullus born?
He was born in Verona.

1. What name does Catullus give the subject of his love poems?
He gives her the name *Lesbia.*

2. Of what does Catullus want their love to be a symbol?
He wants their love to be a symbol of eternity.

3. What does the woman say about marrying Catullus?
She says that she would rather marry him than anybody including Jupiter.

4. In what are the speaker's senses rooted?
They are rooted in eternal torture.

5. In the last poem, what has fallen upon the speaker's mind?
Destruction has fallen upon the speaker's mind.

Responding to the Selection

As an alternate activity, encourage students to discuss in small groups whether they empathize more with Catullus or with his beloved.

Answers for Reviewing the Selection

RECALLING AND INTERPRETING

1. **Recalling.** She says the love between them will last forever. The speaker would like their love to be a symbol of eternity. **Interpreting.** Poem 5 represents the early stages of the relationship when everything seems wonderful and hopeful. The speaker is full of love and affection for her.

2. **Recalling.** She would reject anybody, including Jupiter. The speaker says that a woman's words should be "written upon the wind / and engraved in rapid waters." **Interpreting.** The speaker does not believe her, although he would like to believe her. He thinks that she is just saying what he wants to hear and that the feelings she expresses are fleeting.

3. **Recalling.** The speaker feels both love and hate toward his beloved. **Interpreting.** The speaker continues to feel love for her for many reasons, but some of her actions may have angered him and led to his hatred of her.

4. **Recalling.** The speaker's mind has been plunged into misery and destruction. The speaker blames his beloved Lesbia. **Interpreting.** The relationship between the speaker and his beloved has ended bitterly, but the speaker has not gotten over the relationship and still feels strongly about her. She has probably moved on with her life and does not continue to love the speaker. She might be scornful of him or annoyed by his persistence.

SYNTHESIZING

Responses will vary. Possible responses are given.

5. The relationship begins with hope and excitement. The two see no fault in one another. The relationship progresses to a point where the speaker does not trust Lesbia, and they are no longer as happy as at the beginning. The speaker loves Lesbia throughout the poems, though in some of the poems his feelings of love

(cont.)

Reviewing the Selection

RECALLING / **INTERPRETING**

1. In poem 5, how long does the speaker's beloved say that love between the two of them will last? Of what would the speaker like their love to be a symbol? ▶▶ What point in the relationship between the speaker and his beloved does poem 5 represent? What does the speaker feel for her at this time?

2. Whom would the speaker's beloved reject as a suitor in favor of the speaker? What does he say should be done with the words a woman speaks to her beloved? ▶▶ Does the speaker believe his beloved? How do you know?

3. How does the speaker feel in poem 10? ▶▶ Why might the speaker feel both of these emotions?

4. In poem 11, what has happened to the speaker? Whom does he blame for his current condition? ▶▶ Describe the relationship between the speaker and his beloved as expressed in poem 11. How does the speaker feel about his relationship with her at this point? How do you think she feels about the speaker at this point?

SYNTHESIZING

5. Based on these four poems, describe the course of the relationship between Clodia, or Lesbia, and the speaker. What differences in the speaker's feelings can you note in each poem? What similarities in the speaker's feelings can you see? What feelings and ideas about her or about their relationship might the speaker present in his next poem?

Understanding Literature (Questions for Discussion)

1. **Apostrophe.** An **apostrophe** is a rhetorical technique in which an object or person is directly addressed. The speaker addresses his beloved directly in poems 5 and 11. What does he call her when he addresses her in poem 5? What does this suggest about his feelings for her? Who else does the speaker address in poem 5? Why?

2. **Paradox.** A **paradox** is a seemingly contradictory statement, idea, or event. Why is the first line of poem 10, "I hate and love," a paradox? Try to explain the line as a noncontradictory idea. Identify other times when one might feel conflicting emotions.

Answers for Reviewing the Selection (cont.)

are matched with hatred, anger, or distrust. Poems 10 and 11 are especially similar in the strong positive and negative feelings they express toward Lesbia. The next poem might express a feeling of regret over their ended relationship, without the angry, bitter tones of poems 10 and 11. The speaker might also heighten his anger and hatred toward Lesbia and continue to belie these feelings with talk of his love.

Answers for Language Lab

Answers for Language Lab appear on page 692.

Responding in Writing

1. **Creative Writing: Lyric Poem.** A lyric poem is a highly musical verse that expresses the emotions of a speaker. In poem 10, Catullus expresses feelings of love and hate. Both are very strong emotions. Choose a person, place, or thing for which you have intense feelings, either positive or negative. Freewrite about your subject and those aspects that inspire your feelings. Have your emotions about this person, place, or thing changed over time? If so, you may wish to write about this change as well. Then, write a lyric poem that expresses these feelings. Your poem may be very brief, but it should express powerful emotions. You do not have to use meter or a rhyme scheme—simply try to express your feelings in a number of lines. You might begin by stating your emotions as Catullus does in poem 10 and then elaborating on this statement, or you might try to show how you feel without stating your feelings directly.
2. **Critical Essay: Comparison and Contrast.** Poets and songwriters throughout the ages have continued to find love to be a compelling theme. Think about a song that discusses love. Write an essay in which you compare and contrast the song lyrics to one of the poems by Catullus. Consider the following questions when examining both the song lyrics and the poem by Catullus: Who is the speaker? What is the speaker's attitude toward his or her beloved? Do the speaker's feelings change over the course of the song or poem? Do they express a change of feelings from an earlier stage of the relationship? What effect has this relationship had on the speaker's life? Begin your essay by expressing an opinion about the different ways Catullus's ancient lyric and the recent song treat love. Then support this opinion with references to both works. You may wish to include a copy of the song lyrics you chose for people who are unfamiliar with the work.

Language Lab

Expanding and Combining Sentences. You can make your writing more interesting by varying the types of sentences you use. One way to change the structure of your sentences is to expand them by adding modifiers, prepositional phrases, appositives, predicates, or subordinate clauses. You can also combine sentences to create compound, complex, or compound-complex sentences, thus avoiding repetition and choppiness. See the Language Arts Survey 2.20–2.22, "Expanding and Combining Sentences." Then, combine the sentences in each numbered item below. If there is only one sentence, expand the sentence using one of the methods listed above. Use a variety of techniques to expand or combine the sentences.

1. Catullus was a Roman poet. He wrote lyric poetry.
2. Several of his poems were about love. The subject of his love was a woman he called Lesbia.
3. The name *Lesbia* is probably a reference to the island of Lesbos. Sappho lived on the island Lesbos.
4. Catullus admired the work of Sappho.
5. Catullus expresses love in his poems. Catullus also expresses hate.

ANSWERS FOR UNDERSTANDING LITERATURE

Responses will vary. Possible responses are given.

1. Apostrophe. In poem 5, Catullus calls Lesbia his life and his love. This suggests that his feelings for her are so strong that she has become his life itself. He also addresses the gods to witness her words and to make their love a symbol of eternity.

2. Paradox. The first line of poem 10 is a paradox because love and hate seem to be contradictory emotions. While the speaker might have an overall feeling of love for Lesbia, he might also hate her or be angry with her for saying or doing certain things. Another time of conflicting emotions might be an occasion of great happiness and sorrow, such as a graduation, which is a celebratory event but also often brings feelings of sadness about the end of a period in one's life and separation from friends.

ANALYTIC SCALES FOR RESPONDING IN WRITING

Assign a score from 1 to 25 for each grading criterion below. (For more detailed evaluation, see the evaluation forms for writing, revising, and proofreading, Assessment Portfolio 4.1–4.9.)

1. Lyric Poem

- **Content/Unity.** The lyric poem expresses strong feelings, either positive or negative, about a chosen subject.
- **Organization/Coherence.** The lyric poem presents details in a sensible order.
- **Language/Style.** The lyric poem uses vivid and precise nouns, verbs, and modifiers.
- **Conventions.** The lyric poem avoids errors in spelling, grammar, usage, mechanics, and manuscript form. (cont.)

ANALYTIC SCALES FOR RESPONDING IN WRITING (CONT.)

▶ Additional practice is provided in the Essential Skills Practice Book: Writing 1.8.

2. Critical Essay

- **Content/Unity.** The essay compares and contrasts one of Catullus's poems with love lyrics.
- **Organization/Coherence.** The essay begins with an introduction that includes the thesis of the essay. The introduction is followed by supporting paragraphs with clear transitions. The essay ends with a solid conclusion.
- **Language/Style.** The essay uses vivid and precise nouns, verbs, and modifiers.
- **Conventions.** The essay avoids errors in spelling, grammar, usage, mechanics, and manuscript form.

▶ Additional practice is provided in the Essential Skills Practice Book: Writing 1.20.

ADDITIONAL RESOURCES

Reader's Guide

- Selection Worksheet 8.7

Assessment Portfolio

- Selection Check Test 2.8.13
- Selection Test 2.8.14

Essential Skills Practice Books

- Writing 1.8, 1.10, 1.20
- Speaking and Listening 3.5
- Study and Research 4.5

PREREADING EXTENSIONS

Interested students might complete one of the following activities:

- Students who have read either *The Tragedy of Julius Cæsar* or *The Tragedy of Antony and Cleopatra,* or who are comfortable enough with reading Shakespeare to examine one of these works might write a critical essay exploring the way Shakespeare used Plutarch's work as a source in one of these plays. How much did Shakespeare borrow? What details did he alter, and why?
- Other students might enjoy writing a chapter of a biography by interviewing someone they know or by doing some research on a historical, literary, entertainment, or sports figure.
- Artistically inclined students might draw or paint one of the scenes Plutarch describes, such as the scene of Cleopatra on her barge.
- Students might work in groups to dramatize, produce, and enact any of the scenes Plutarch describes in this section of *The Lives.*

PREREADING

from *The Lives of the Noble Grecians and Romans*
by Plutarch, translated by John Dryden

About the Author

Plutarch (AD **45–after** AD **120**). Plutarch was born in Chaeronea, Boeotia, a region of Greece. A student of mathematics and philosophy, a founder of a school of philosophy, and a statesman in Chaeronea, Plutarch also traveled widely. At Delphi, he became a priest of Apollo, and in Athens, he held citizenship. He visited Egypt and spent time in Rome, where he met Roman emperors Trajan and Hadrian, lectured on philosophy, received Roman citizenship, and was awarded the rank of consul. Plutarch is most famous for his series of biographies, or stories of people's lives, entitled *The Lives of the Noble Grecians and Romans,* or *Parallel Lives.* His surviving biographies have had an enormous impact on Western writing and thought. Plutarch also wrote the *Moralia,* a number of essays and dialogues on ethical, political, religious, and literary topics. His writing inspired enormous respect in his own time, and when Byzantine scholars introduced Italian scholars to his works in the fifteenth century, Plutarch became the most popular of Greek authors during the European Renaissance.

About the Selection

Plutarch published his biographies of Greek and Roman heroes in pairs, including with each pair an essay comparing and contrasting the heroes. He hoped that these biographies would increase mutual respect between Greeks and Romans. Many years of scholarly investigation were invested in ***The Lives of the Noble Grecians and Romans***, particularly in the Roman biographies, as Plutarch's Latin was imperfect. Despite his intensive research, Plutarch did not see his biographies as history but as moral portraits that would delight and instruct. Plutarch's *Lives* is made up of anecdotes and the author's comments on ethical matters. Plutarch himself saw fortune as a wheel, which brings humans to the zenith of their fortunes but then turns and leads them to their downfall. The following selections deal with the demise of Roman leader Julius Cæsar and the character traits that would lead to the ruin of another Roman—Mark Antony.

Julius Cæsar

CONNECTIONS: Plutarch and Renaissance and Enlightenment Writers

Plutarch wrote *The Lives of the Noble Grecians and Romans* in Greek, but Renaissance scholars soon translated his writings into Latin, Italian, French, and English. A large number of Renaissance writers were influenced by Plutarch's work, including Michel de Montaigne, whose essays were shaped by Plutarch's methods of revealing character, and Shakespeare, who used Plutarch's *Lives* as a source for several of his plays, including *The Tragedy of Julius Cæsar* and *The Tragedy of Antony and Cleopatra.* Plutarch continued to influence writers throughout the Enlightenment. This translation was edited by one of the foremost English poets of that period—John Dryden.

GOALS/OBJECTIVES

Studying this lesson will enable students to

- have a positive experience reading the work of one of the world's most famous biographers
- briefly explain Plutarch's influence on the Renaissance
- define *foreshadowing, pathetic fallacy, allusion,* and *anecdote* and recognize these techniques in literature
- write a character description
- write a critical essay comparing biography and history
- distinguish between fact and opinion

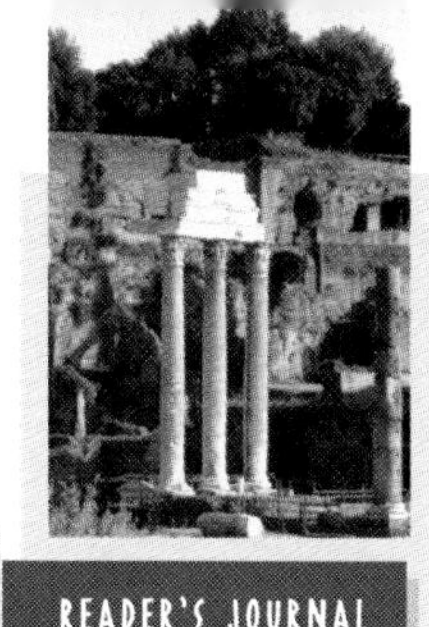

READER'S JOURNAL

Have you ever offered flattery to get something you wanted? Have you ever been flattered? Of what benefit is flattery? What problems might flattery cause?

FROM

The Lives of the Noble Grecians and Romans

PLUTARCH, TRANSLATED BY JOHN DRYDEN

FROM CÆSAR

[Editor's note: Plutarch describes how Julius Cæsar's desire to become king of Rome was awakening "mortal hatred" in his enemies, who supported the Roman Republic. Just before this selection begins, Mark Antony offers Cæsar a crown at a Roman festival called the Lupercalia, and a few people who have been planted in the audience for the purpose raise a shout of approval. When Cæsar refuses this crown, he is applauded. Mark Antony offers and Cæsar refuses the crown twice. After this festival, Cæsar's statues are found crowned. Two Romans named Flavius and Marullus pull off the crowns and arrest those who shouted to make Cæsar a king. The people commend Flavius and Marullus, calling them by the name of Brutus, as Brutus was involved in ending kingship in Rome and strengthening the Roman Republic.]

This made the multitude turn their thoughts to Marcus Brutus, who, by his father's side, was thought to be descended from that first Brutus, and by his mother's side from the Servilii, another noble family, being besides nephew and son-in-law to Cato.[1] But the honours and favours he had received from Cæsar took off the edge from the desires he might himself have felt for overthrowing the new monarchy. For he had not only been pardoned himself after Pompey's defeat at Pharsalia,[2] and had procured the same grace for many of his friends, but was one in whom Cæsar had a particular confidence. He had at that time the most honourable prætorship[3] for the year, and was

❶ *Why isn't Brutus eager to overthrow Cæsar? What relationship exists between the two?*

1. **Cato.** Roman statesman
2. **Pharsalia.** District in ancient Thessaly
3. **prætorship.** Office of magistrate in ancient Rome

WORDS FOR EVERYDAY USE

pro • cure (prō kyo͞or´) *vt.,* obtain

READER'S JOURNAL

As an alternate activity, you might ask students to write their thoughts about overthrowing a leader. Are there times when such a revolt is necessary, or is it always wrong? Encourage them to cite examples they know from history in their responses.

ANSWERS TO GUIDED READING QUESTIONS

❶ Brutus is not eager to overthrow Cæsar because Cæsar has shown him forgiveness and has given him many honors. The two seem to like and respect each other, and Cæsar has "confidence" in Brutus.

SPELLING AND VOCABULARY WORDS FROM THE SELECTION

adjourn	juncture
adroitness	mirth
countenance	pinnacle
dexterous	preternatural
diadem	procure
dormant	raillery
inauspicious	soothsayer
intimate	thither
invidious	

SUPPORT FOR LEP STUDENTS

PRONUNCIATIONS OF PROPER NOUNS AND ADJECTIVES

Ar • te • mi • dor • us (är´tə mə dor´əs)
Boe • o • ti • a (bē ō´shə)
Cni • di • an (ni´dē ən)
Plu • tarch (plo͞o´tärk´)

ADDITIONAL VOCABULARY

brands—burning sticks
prodigies—extraordinary happenings, thought to indicate good or evil fortune
scoffingly—in a mocking or scornful manner

VOCABULARY IN CONTEXT

• During World War II, it was difficult for average American citizens to procure meat, clothing, machinery, and other items due to shortages caused by the war.

Answers to Guided Reading Questions

➊ The soothsayer tells Cæsar to prepare for some danger on the Ides of March. Cæsar confidently ridicules the soothsayer on this date, pointing out that the fateful day has come. The soothsayer tells Cæsar that the day has not yet passed, indicating that there is still time for something to occur.

➋ They think that Brutus is the only or most proper person to effect this change. They leave papers in the night near his chair urging him to action, and Cassius, who has a private grudge against Cæsar, "work[s] him yet further."

➌ Lights are seen in the heavens, noises are heard at night, birds perch in the forum. Men are seen burning and fighting, flame issues from a soldier's hand but he is not burned, and a sacrificed animal is discovered to have no heart.

Biographical Note

Julius Cæsar was born on the twelfth or thirteenth of July, sometime around the year 100 BC, into a noble Roman family. One of the ablest leaders the world has known, Cæsar bore a name that became forever synonymous with power and leadership. The Russian word *czar,* the German *kaiser,* and the Arabic *qaysar,* meaning "king" or "ruler," are all variations on his name. The month of July is also named after him.

As a young man, Cæsar left Rome to travel to the Greek city of Rhodes, where he intended to study oratory. On the way, he was captured by pirates, who released him after he raised a large ransom. Cæsar retaliated by raising a private naval force, capturing the pirates, and crucifying them. Over the following years, he moved steadily up the political ladder in Rome, holding a number of important positions, culminating in his election to the post of consul in 59 BC.

(cont.)

➊ *What warning does the soothsayer give Cæsar? What is Cæsar's attitude toward this warning? What is the soothsayer's response to Cæsar's "raillery"?*

➋ *Why do those who want to prevent Cæsar from becoming king want Brutus to join their cause? What do they do to achieve this goal?*

➌ *What strange omens indicate that something "unavoidable" is about to happen?*

named for the consulship[4] four years after, being preferred before Cassius, his competitor. Upon the question as to the choice, Cæsar, it is related, said that Cassius had the fairer pretensions, but that he could not pass by Brutus. Nor would he afterwards listen to some who spoke against Brutus, when the conspiracy against him was already afoot, but laying his hand on his body, said to the informers, "Brutus will wait for this skin of mine," intimating that he was worthy to bear rule on account of his virtue, but would not be base and ungrateful to gain it. Those who desired a change, and looked on him as the only, or at least the most proper, person to effect it, did not venture to speak with him; but in the nighttime laid papers about his chair of state, where he used to sit and determine causes, with such sentences in them as, "You are asleep, Brutus," "You are no longer Brutus." Cassius, when he perceived his ambition a little raised upon this, was more instant than before to work him yet further, having himself a private grudge against Cæsar for some reasons that we have mentioned in the Life of Brutus. Nor was Cæsar without suspicions of him, and said once to his friends, "What do you think Cassius is aiming at? I don't like him, he looks so pale." And when it was told him that Antony and Dolabella were in a plot against him, he said he did not fear such fat, luxurious men, but rather the pale, lean fellows, meaning Cassius and Brutus.

Fate, however, is to all appearance more unavoidable than unexpected. For many strange prodigies and apparitions are said to have been observed shortly before this event. As to the lights in the heavens, the noises heard in the night, and the wild birds which perched in the forum, these are not perhaps worth taking notice of in so great a case as this. Strabo, the philosopher, tells us that a number of men were seen, looking as if they were heated through with fire, contending with each other; that a quantity of flame issued from the hand of a soldier's servant, so that they who saw it thought he must be burnt, but that after all he had no hurt. As Cæsar was sacrificing, the victim's heart was missing, a very bad omen, because no living creature can subsist without a heart. One finds it also related by many that a soothsayer bade him prepare for some great danger on the Ides of March.[5] When this day was come, Cæsar, as he went to the senate, met this soothsayer, and said to him by way of raillery, "The Ides of March are come," who answered him calmly, "Yes, they are come, but they are not past." The day before his assassination he supped with Marcus Lepidus; and as he was signing some letters according to his custom, as he reclined at table, there arose a question what sort of death was the best. At which he immediately, before any one could speak, said, "A sudden one."

After this, as he was in bed with his wife, all the doors and windows of the house flew open together; he was startled at the noise, and the light which broke into the room, and sat up in his bed, where by the moonshine he perceived Calpurnia fast asleep, but heard her utter in her dream some indistinct words and inarticulate groans. She fancied at that time she was weeping over Cæsar, and holding him butchered in her arms. Others say this was not her dream, but that she dreamed that a pinnacle, which the senate, as Livy relates, had ordered to be raised on Cæsar's house by way of ornament and grandeur, was tumbling down, which was the occasion of

4. **consulship.** Position of either of the two magistrates of the ancient Roman Republic

5. **Ides of March.** Fifteenth day of March

Words for Everyday Use

in • ti • mate (in´ tə māt´) *vt.,* hint, make known indirectly or subtly

sooth • say • er (sōōth´sā ər) *n.,* person who professes to foretell the future

rail • ler • y (rāl´ər ē) *n.,* good-natured ridicule

pin • na • cle (pin´ə kəl) *n.,* small turret or spire

Vocabulary in Context

- The defense witness intimated that she knew the defendant was innocent, but she could not substantiate her claim.
- Soothsayers' future predictions and warnings were taken very seriously by the people of ancient Greece and Rome.
- The schoolchildren did not mean to insult the new boy with their good-natured raillery; instead they sought to make him feel included with their joking and teasing.
- The king's emblem waved from the castle's highest pinnacle.

her tears and ejaculations. When it was day, she begged of Cæsar, if it were possible, not to stir out, but to adjourn the senate to another time; and if he slighted her dreams, that she would be pleased to consult his fate by sacrifices and other kinds of divination. Nor was he himself without some suspicion and fears; for he never before discovered any womanish superstition in Calpurnia, whom he now saw in such great alarm. Upon the report which the priests made to him, that they had killed several sacrifices, and still found them inauspicious, he resolved to send Antony to dismiss the senate.

In this juncture, Decimus Brutus, surnamed Albinus, one whom Caesar had such confidence in that he made him his second heir, who nevertheless was engaged in the conspiracy with the other Brutus and Cassius, fearing lest if Cæsar should put off the senate to another day, the business might get wind, spoke scoffingly and in mockery of the diviners, and blamed Cæsar for giving the senate so fair an occasion of saying he had put a slight upon them, for that they were met upon his summons, and were ready to vote unanimously that he should be declared king of all the provinces out of Italy, and might wear a diadem in any other place but Italy, by sea or land. If any one should be sent to tell them they might break up for the present, and meet again when Calpurnia should chance to have better dreams, what would his enemies say? Or who would with any patience hear his friends, if they should presume to defend his government as not arbitrary and tyrannical? But if he was possessed so far as to think this day unfortunate, yet it were more decent to go himself to the senate, and to adjourn it in his own person. Brutus, as he spoke these words, took Cæsar by the hand, and conducted him forth. He was not gone far from the door, when a servant of some other person's made towards him, but not being able to come up to him, on the account of the crowd of those who pressed about him, he made his way into the house, and committed himself to Calpurnia, begging of her to secure him till Cæsar returned, because he had matters of great importance to communicate to him.

Artemidorus, a Cnidian, a teacher of Greek logic, and by that means so far acquainted with Brutus and his friends as to have got into the secret, brought Cæsar in a small written memorial the heads of what he had to depose. He had observed that Cæsar, as he received any papers, presently gave them to the servants who attended on him; and therefore came as near to him as he could, and said, "Read this, Cæsar, alone, and quickly, for it contains matter of great importance which nearly concerns you." Cæsar received it, and tried several times to read it, but was still hindered by the crowd of those who came to speak to him. However, he kept it in his hand by itself till he came into the senate. Some say it was another who gave Cæsar this note, and that Artemidorus could not get to him, being all along kept off by the crowd.

All these things might happen by chance. But the place which was destined for the scene of this murder, in which the senate met that day, was the same in which Pompey's statue stood, and was one of the edifices which Pompey[6] had raised and dedicated with his theatre to the use of the public, plainly showing that there was something of a supernatural influence which guided the action and ordered it to that par-

6. **Pompey.** Pompey was a Roman general who ruled along with Cæsar as a member of the First Triumvirate, but he later became Cæsar's opponent and was defeated by him.

1 *Who tries to warn Cæsar of the plot against him? Why is the warning ineffectual?*

2 *How does Decimus Brutus lure Cæsar to the senate?*

3 *What does the narrator see as evidence of some "supernatural influence" over Cæsar's fate?*

Words for Everyday Use

ad • journ (ə jurn´) *vt.,* put off or suspend until a future time

in • aus • pi • cious (in ôs´pish əs´) *adj.,* ill-omened; unlucky

junc • ture (juŋk´chər) *n.,* particular or critical moment in the development of events

di • a • dem (dī´ə dem´) *n.,* crown

Answers to Guided Reading Questions

1 Artemidorus tries to warn Cæsar of the plot by passing him a note. The crowd of people speaking to him prevents Cæsar from reading the note.

2 Decimus Brutus speaks "scoffingly and in mockery" of the evil portents and tells Cæsar that his ambition will today be realized—the senate was ready to crown him king.

3 The narrator sees the fact that the scene of the murder is near a statue of Cæsar's old enemy Pompey as evidence that some "supernatural influence" was at work.

Biographical Note (cont.)

Between 58 and 50 BC, Cæsar conducted a series of brilliant military campaigns that won for Rome all of Gaul (modern-day France) and that extended Roman power as far north as Britain. Members of the nobility, known as patricians, in Rome came to fear Cæsar because he commanded a large army made up of fiercely loyal troops and because he was much loved by the plebeians of the city. The patricians of the senate, fearing that Cæsar would make himself king and overthrow the republic, voted on January 1, 49 BC, to have Cæsar lay down his command. Cæsar refused and instead led his troops across the Rubicon, a small river between Gaul and Italy, and entered Rome. In doing so, he flouted a time-honored tradition of the Roman Republic—it was forbidden for generals to enter the city at the head of an army. This tradition was maintained to prevent precisely what followed Cæsar's crossing of the Rubicon—civil war. In the civil war, Cæsar defeated the forces of his former ally, the Roman general Pompey. He then returned to Rome and assumed the title of dictator. This selection begins not long after Cæsar assumed this title.

Vocabulary in Context

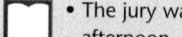

- The jury was overwhelmed with facts and details, so the judge adjourned the court for the afternoon.
- We took the dark clouds brooding above the field as an inauspicious omen that the baseball game would be rained out.
- The would-be governor's political advisor told him that at this juncture in his career it would be prudent to focus on environmental issues.
- The queen wore a diadem of intricately wrought gold upon her head.

Answers to Guided Reading Questions

❶ Cæsar had been fighting and resisting the blows, but when he sees Brutus's dagger drawn against him, he covers his face with his robe and lets himself fall.

❷ Antony is loyal to Cæsar. One of the conspirators delays him outside with a long conversation.

❸ Cæsar falls at the base of the statue of Pompey. The narrator says that it seems as if Pompey himself presided over the murder to gain revenge on his former adversary.

❹ Brutus tries to provide a reason for the killing, but the senate runs out and informs the people of Cæsar's death.

Cultural/Historical Note

So that students can better see why Plutarch describes Pompey's statue as presiding over Cæsar's death, you might give them the following information: Gnaeus Pompey (106–48 BC) was a great general and statesman of the Roman Republic. Like Cæsar, he had many military victories abroad, and the Senate gave him three triumphs (the most prestigious honor granted to a triumphant general) in Rome. Pompey, Crassus, and Cæsar later formed the first triumvirate to share power in Rome. Pompey even married Cæsar's daughter, Julia. Soon after Julia's death in 54, Pompey began using his power to turn the Roman senate against Cæsar. The senate declared war between Pompey and Cæsar on January 7, 49. On January 11, Cæsar crossed the Rubicon.

Pompey's strategy was to abandon Rome to Cæsar and to beat him at sea and with his forces in the East. Nevertheless, Cæsar soon defeated Pompey decisively in Pharsalus in 48. Pompey fled to to seek the aid of Egyptian leader Ptolemy XIII, who had given him help in the past. Hoping to side with the victory, Ptolemy treacherously invited Pompey aboard one of his small boats. As Pompey was just about to step to shore, he was killed.

 ❶ *What is Cæsar's reaction when he discovers that Brutus has turned against him?*

 ❷ *Who is loyal to Cæsar? What do the conspirators do to keep this person from interfering?*

 ❸ *Where does Cæsar fall? What does the narrator say about this scene?*

❹ *What happens after Cæsar is killed?*

ticular place. Cassius, just before the act, is said to have looked towards Pompey's statue, and silently implored his assistance, though he had been inclined to the doctrines of Epicurus.[7] But this occasion, and the instant danger, carried him away out of all his reasonings, and filled him for the time with a sort of inspiration. As for Antony, who was firm to Cæsar, and a strong man, Brutus Albinus kept him outside the house, and delayed him with a long conversation contrived on purpose. When Cæsar entered, the senate stood up to show their respect to him, and of Brutus's confederates, some came about his chair and stood behind it, others met him, pretending to add their petitions to those of Tillius Cimber, in behalf of his brother, who was in exile; and they followed him with their joint applications till he came to his seat. When he was sat down, he refused to comply with their requests, and upon their urging him further began to reproach them severely for their importunities, when Tillius, laying hold of his robe with both his hands, pulled it down from his neck, which was the signal for the assault. Casca gave him the first cut in the neck, which was not mortal nor dangerous, as coming from one who at the beginning of such a bold action was probably very much disturbed; Cæsar immediately turned about, and laid his hand upon the dagger and kept hold of it. And both of them at the same time cried out, he that received the blow, in Latin, "Vile Casca, what does this mean?" and he that gave it, in Greek to his brother, "Brother, help!" Upon this first onset, those who were not privy to the design were astonished, and their horror and amazement at what they saw were so great that they durst not fly nor assist Cæsar, nor so much as speak a word. But those who came prepared for the business enclosed him on every side, with their naked daggers in their hands. Which way soever he turned he met with blows, and saw their swords levelled at his face and eyes, and was encompassed like a wild beast in the toils[8] on every side. For it had been agreed they should each of them make a thrust at him, and flesh themselves with his blood; for which reason Brutus also gave him one stab in the groin. Some say that he fought and resisted all the rest, shifting his body to avoid the blows, and calling out for help, but that when he saw Brutus's sword drawn, he covered his face with his robe and submitted, letting himself fall, whether it were by chance or that he was pushed in that direction by his murderers, at the foot of the pedestal on which Pompey's statue stood, and which was thus wetted with his blood. So that Pompey himself seemed to have presided, as it were, over the revenge done upon his adversary, who lay here at his feet, and breathed out his soul through his multitude of wounds, for they say he received three-and-twenty. And the conspirators themselves were many of them wounded by each other, whilst they all levelled their blows at the same person.

When Cæsar was despatched, Brutus stood forth to give a reason for what they had done, but the senate would not hear him, but flew out of doors in all haste, and filled the people with so much alarm and distraction, that some shut up their houses, others left their counters and shops. All ran one way or the other, some to the place to see the sad spectacle, others back again after they had seen it. Antony and Lepidus, Cæsar's most faithful friends, got off privately, and hid themselves in some friends' houses. Brutus and his followers, being yet hot from the deed, marched in a body from the senate-house to the capitol with their drawn swords, not like persons who thought of escaping, but with an air of confidence and assurance, and as they went along, called to the people to resume their liberty, and invited the company of any more distinguished people whom they met. And some of these joined the procession and went up along with them, as if they also had been of the conspiracy,

7. **Epicurus.** Greek philosopher who founded a school of ethical philosophy

8. **toils.** Nets or webs

Roman Forum and the Palatine Hill. Rome, Italy

and could claim a share in the honour of what had been done. As, for example, Caius Octavius and Lentulus Spinther, who suffered afterwards for their vanity, being taken off by Antony and the young Cæsar, and lost the honour they desired, as well as their lives, which it cost them, since no one believed they had any share in the action. For neither did those who punished them profess to revenge the fact, but the ill-will. The day after, Brutus with the rest came down from the capitol and made a speech to the people, who listened without expressing either any pleasure or resentment, but showed by their silence that they pitied Cæsar and respected Brutus. The senate passed acts of oblivion[9] for what was past, and took measures to reconcile all parties. They ordered that Cæsar should be worshipped as a divinity, and nothing, even of the slightest consequence, should be revoked which he had enacted during his government. At the same time they gave Brutus and his followers the command of provinces, and other considerable posts. So that all the people now thought things were well settled, and brought to the happiest adjustment.

But when Cæsar's will was opened, and it was found that he had left a considerable legacy to each one of the Roman citizens, and when his body was seen carried through the marketplace all mangled with wounds, the multitude could no longer contain themselves within the bounds of tranquility and order, but heaped together a pile of benches, bars, and tables, which they placed the corpse on, and setting fire to it, burnt it on them. Then they took brands from the pile

9. **acts of oblivion.** Official overlooking of offenses; pardon

❶ *How do people react to Cæsar's murder after hearing Brutus's speech?*

❷ *What changes the way the people of Rome feel about the murder? What attitude does the populace adopt toward the conspirators?*

Answers to Guided Reading Questions

❶ The people pity Cæsar but remain silent to show respect for Brutus.

❷ The people begin to feel differently about the murder when they discover that Cæsar left money to each Roman citizen in his will and when they see his body all mangled with wounds. The populace adopts an angry attitude toward the conspirators, deciding to burn their houses and to tear the men to pieces.

Cross-curricular Activities

SOCIAL STUDIES

In this selection, chaos breaks out after the assassination of a political leader. Encourage students to work in small groups to research other infamous political assassinations in history. Each group should then report the basic facts (if known) about the case, explain what the leader stood for, speculate why the leader was assassinated, and explain what happened as a result of the assassination. Possible subjects include American presidents Abraham Lincoln, James Abram Garfield, William McKinley, and John F. Kennedy; presidential candidate Robert F. Kennedy; American Civil Rights leaders Martin Luther King, Jr., and Malcolm X; Louisiana governor and U.S. senator Huey Long; leader of the Indian nationalist movement Mohandas Gandhi; Indian prime minister Indira Gandhi; Egyptian president Anwar el-Sadat; Russian revolutionist Leon Trotsky; Benigno Aquino, Jr., opposition political leader in the Philippines; and Mexican rebel leader General Francisco "Pancho" Villa.

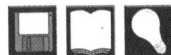

Answers to Guided Reading Questions

1. The narrator says that as a result of Cæsar's death, a comet appeared for seven nights and then disappeared, the sun dimmed and gave off little heat, the air dampened, and fruits rotted on the tree.

2. The appearance of a phantom shows that the murder was not pleasing to the gods.

3. Cæsar pursued empire and power. The narrator says that Cæsar achieved the goal of ruling a powerful empire but did not live to enjoy his triumph, having raised too

Quotables

"Anyone who is prosperous may by the turn of fortune's wheel become most wretched before evening."

—Ammianus Marcellinus

"Whatever fortune has raised to a height, she has raised only to cast down."

—Seneca

"I find my zenith doth depend upon
A most auspicious star; whose influence
If now I court not, but omit, my fortunes
Will ever after droop."

—William Shakespeare
The Tempest

Cultural/Historical Note

Plutarch's belief that fortune was a wheel that brought humans to their zenith but then quickly turned and brought them to their nadir was popular not only in the Classical world but in the Medieval period and the Renaissance as well. Encourage students to discuss this concept of fate in relation to Julius Cæsar's life story. In what way would this view of fate explain Cæsar's murder?

and ran some to fire the houses of the conspirators, others up and down the city, to find out the men and tear them to pieces, but met, however, with none of them, they having taken effectual care to secure themselves.

1 *What events in the natural world does the narrator say were the result of Cæsar's murder?*

One Cinna, a friend of Cæsar's, chanced the night before to have an odd dream. He fancied that Cæsar invited him to supper, and that upon his refusal to go with him, Cæsar took him by the hand and forced him, though he hung back. Upon hearing the report that Cæsar's body was burning in the marketplace, he got up and went thither, out of respect to his memory, though his dream gave him some ill apprehensions, and though he was suffering from a fever. One of the crowd who saw him there asked another who that was, and having learned his name, told it to his neighbour. It presently passed for a certainty that he was one of Cæsar's murderers, as, indeed, there was another Cinna, a conspirator, and they, taking this to be the man, immediately seized him and tore him limb from limb upon the spot.

2 *What shows that Brutus's part in the murder was not pleasing to the gods?*

Brutus and Cassius, frightened at this, within a few days retired out of the city. What they afterwards did and suffered, and how they died, is written in the Life of Brutus. Cæsar died in his fifty-sixth year, not having survived Pompey above four years. That empire and power which he had pursued through the whole course of his life with so much hazard, he did at last with much difficulty compass, but reaped no other fruits from it than the empty name and invidious glory. But the great genius which attended him through his lifetime even after his death remained as the avenger of his murder, pursuing through every sea and land all those who were concerned in it, and suffering none to escape, but reaching all who in any sort or kind were either actually engaged in the fact, or by their counsels any way promoted it.

3 *What had Cæsar pursued throughout his life? What were the results of the pursuit?*

The most remarkable of mere human coincidences was that which befell Cassius, who, when he was defeated at Philippi, killed himself with the same dagger which he had made use of against Cæsar. The most signal preternatural appearances were the great comet, which shone very bright for seven nights after Cæsar's death, and then disappeared, and the dimness of the sun, whose orb continued pale and dull for the whole of that year, never showing its ordinary radiance at its rising, and giving but a weak and feeble heat. The air consequently was damp and gross for want of stronger rays to open and rarefy it. The fruits, for that reason, never properly ripened, and began to wither and fall off for want of heat before they were fully formed. But above all, the phantom which appeared to Brutus showed the murder was not pleasing to the gods. The story of it is this.

Brutus, being to pass his army from Abydos[10] to the continent on the other side, laid himself down one night, as he used to do, in his tent, and was not asleep, but thinking of his affairs, and what events he might expect. For he is related to have been the least inclined to sleep of all men who have commanded armies, and to have had the greatest natural capacity for continuing awake, and employing himself without need of rest. He thought he heard a noise at the door of his tent, and looking that way, by the light of his lamp, which was almost out, saw a terrible figure, like that of a man, but of unusual stature and severe countenance. He was somewhat frightened at first, but seeing

10. **Abydos.** Ancient city in Asia Minor, on the Hellespont, a strait now known as the Dardanelles that separates European and Asiatic Turkey

Words for Everyday Use

thith • er (thith´ər) *adv.*, to or toward that place

in • vid • i • ous (in vid´ē əs) *adj.*, giving offense; exciting envy

pre • ter • nat • u • ral (prēt´ər nach´ər əl) *adj.*, abnormal; supernatural

coun • te • nance (koun´tə nəns) *n.*, facial expression

Vocabulary in Context

- Once the firefighters learned the location of the blazing factory, they hurried thither.
- Owen found Marla's obviously expensive gown and piles of jewelry to be an invidious and ostentatious reminder of her newfound wealth.
- Tony enjoyed watching television shows about preternatural events and unexplained phenomena, such as UFOs and ghosts.
- Wanda's wan countenance revealed that she had been ill and unable to sleep.

it neither did nor spoke anything to him, only stood silently by his bedside, he asked who it was. The spectre answered him, "Thy evil genius, Brutus, thou shalt see me at Philippi." Brutus answered courageously, "Well, I shall see you," and immediately the appearance vanished. When the time was come, he drew up his army near Philippi against Antony and Cæsar, and in the first battle won the day, routed the enemy, and plundered Cæsar's camp. The night before the second battle, the same phantom appeared to him again, but spoke not a word. He presently understood his destiny was at hand, and exposed himself to all the danger of the battle. Yet he did not die in the fight, but seeing his men defeated, got up to the top of a rock, and there presenting his sword to his naked breast, and assisted, as they say, by a friend, who helped him to give the thrust, met his death.

FROM ANTONY

[Editor's note: Mark Antony is the loyal supporter of Julius Cæsar who thrice offered him a crown during the Lupercalia. After Julius Cæsar's death, a power struggle breaks out between those loyal to Cæsar, including Mark Antony and Cæsar's grand-nephew Gaius Julius Cæsar Octavianus, later called Augustus, and the conspirators, including Marcus Brutus and Cassius. Cæsar and Antony are ultimately victorious. Together Cæsar, Antony, and a Roman named Lepidus form a triumvirate to rule Rome. Antony, who is known as a lover of luxury, travels through Greece into Asia, where he enjoys the wealth, beauty, and pleasures of the Asian land and its peoples.]

Such being his temper, the last and crowning mischief that could befall him came in the love of Cleopatra, to awaken and kindle

Antony and Cleopatra. *G. Lerouisse. Petershof Museum. SuperStock*

to fury passions that as yet lay still and dormant in his nature, and to stifle and finally corrupt any elements that yet made resistance in him of goodness and a sound judgment. He fell into the snare thus. When making preparation for the Parthian[11] war, he sent to command her to make her personal appearance in Cilicia, to answer an accusation, that she had given great assistance, in the late wars, to Cassius. Dellius, who was sent on this message, had no sooner seen her face, and remarked her adroitness and subtlety in speech, but he felt convinced that

❶ *Why does Antony command Cleopatra to appear before him?*

❷ *What effect does the narrator say Antony's love for Cleopatra had upon him?*

11. **Parthian.** Of the ancient country in southwest Asia, southeast of the Caspian Sea

WORDS FOR EVERYDAY USE

dor • mant (dôr´mənt) *adj.,* inoperative; inactive

a • droit • ness (ə droit´nəs) *n.,* clever skill; resourcefulness

ANSWERS TO GUIDED READING QUESTIONS

❶ Antony commands Cleopatra to appear before him to answer the accusation that she aided Cassius in the recent civil wars.

❷ The narrator says that Antony's love for Cleopatra stifles and corrupts his goodness and sound judgment.

QUOTABLES

"Let Rome in Tiber melt, and the wide arch
Of the rang'd empire fall! Here is my space."

—William Shakespeare
The Tragedy of Antony and Cleopatra

(Mark Antony on Rome while in Egypt and in love with Cleopatra)

BIOGRAPHICAL NOTE

Mark Antony (82–30 BC) sided with Julius Cæsar in the civil war that broke out between Cæsar and Pompey in 49 BC. After Cæsar's death, Antony, Octavian (later the Emperor Augustus), and Marcus Lepidus formed the second triumvirate and engaged in a civil war against Brutus and Cassius. The triumvirate defeated the conspirators and divided up Rome's empire. In 41, Antony went to the east where he questioned Cleopatra about her aid to Cassius; he ended up spending the winter with her in Alexandria. Although Antony returned to Rome and later married Octavian's sister, tensions between the two leaders increased, and Antony returned to Cleopatra. After Antony divorced Octavian's sister, Octavian declared war against Cleopatra and soon defeated Antony's and Egypt's forces in a naval battle. Octavian followed the two to Egypt, and when Antony and Cleopatra found they could not resist the Roman forces, they both committed suicide.

VOCABULARY IN CONTEXT

- In the winter, the dormant land leaves farmers free to make equipment repairs.
- The diplomat was renowned for her adroitness in resolving conflicts between different groups of people.

Answers to Guided Reading Questions

❶ Cleopatra is sure of impressing Antony because Cæsar and Pompey fell in love with her when she was younger and more ignorant, but now she is at the height of both her beauty and intellect.

❷ Cleopatra is not so much physically beautiful as a charming and bewitching conversationalist.

❸ Cleopatra, dressed as Venus, goddess of love, sails leisurely up the river in a decorated barge.

❹ Unlike other rulers, she knows so many languages she hardly ever requires an interpreter.

❺ The multitude is told that Venus (Cleopatra) is coming to feast with Bacchus (Antony) for the good of Asia.

Biographical Note

Cleopatra VII (69–30 BC) was the last ruler of the Macedonian dynasty in Egypt. After Egypt was conquered by Alexander the Great, Alexander's general Ptolemy I became king of Egypt in 305 BC, thus establishing a long line of Macedonian rulers in Egypt. Egypt was essentially ruled by foreigners, which explains why Plutarch considered it unusual that Cleopatra had bothered to learn Egyptian.

Cleopatra was an ambitious ruler who sought to bring Egypt back to the glory it knew under the first Ptolemaic rulers. Realizing that Rome was the dominant world power, she decided to use Rome's power to gain more for her country, at first captivating and winning influence with Julius Cæsar. When he was assassinated, she was actually in Rome, having entertained lavishly and been given many honors by Cæsar. After his death, she turned to Antony as the heir of Cæsar's power because his nephew Octavian was young and known to be sickly. After her death, Egypt fell under Roman control.

❶ *Why is Cleopatra so sure of herself?*

❷ *What makes Cleopatra so attractive?*

❸ *What does Cleopatra do "in mockery" of Antony's urgent summons?*

❹ *What evidence is there of Cleopatra's linguistic ability?*

❺ *What message is sent to the multitude?*

Antony would not so much as think of giving any molestation to a woman like this; on the contrary, she would be the first in favor with him. So he set himself at once to pay his court to the Egyptian, and gave her his advice, "to go," in the Homeric[12] style, to Cilicia, "in her best attire," and bade her fear nothing from Antony, the gentlest and kindest of soldiers. She had some faith in the words of Dellius, but more in her own attractions; which, having formerly recommended her to Cæsar and the young Cnæus Pompey, she did not doubt might yet prove more successful with Antony. Their acquaintance was with her when a girl, young and ignorant of the world, but she was to meet Antony in the time of life when women's beauty is most splendid, and their intellects are in full maturity. She made great preparation for her journey, of money, gifts, and ornaments of value, such as so wealthy a kingdom might afford, but she brought with her her surest hopes in her own magic arts and charms.

She received several letters, both from Antony and from his friends, to summon her, but she took no account of these orders; and at last, as if in mockery of them, she came sailing up the river Cydnus, in a barge with gilded stern and outspread sails of purple, while oars of silver beat time to the music of flutes and fifes and harps. She herself lay all along under a canopy of cloth of gold, dressed as Venus in a picture; and beautiful young boys, like painted Cupids, stood on each side to fan her. Her maids were dressed like sea nymphs and graces, some steering at the rudder, some working at the ropes. The perfumes diffused themselves from the vessel to the shore, which was covered with multitudes, part following the galley up the river on either bank, part running out of the city to see the sight. The market-place was quite emptied, and Antony at last was left alone sitting upon the tribunal; while the word went through all the multitude, that Venus was come to feast with Bacchus, for the common good of Asia. On her arrival, Antony sent to invite her to supper. She thought it fitter he should come to her; so, willing to show his good-humour and courtesy, he complied, and went. He found the preparations to receive him magnificent beyond expression, but nothing so admirable as the great number of lights; for on a sudden there was let down altogether so great a number of branches with lights in them so ingeniously disposed, some in squares, and some in circles, that the whole thing was a spectacle that has seldom been equalled for beauty.

The next day, Antony invited her to supper, and was very desirous to outdo her as well in magnificence as contrivance; but he found he was altogether beaten in both, and was so well convinced of it that he was himself the first to jest and mock at his poverty of wit and his rustic awkwardness.

She, perceiving that his raillery was broad and gross, and savored more of the soldier than the courtier, rejoined in the same taste, and fell into it at once, without any sort of reluctance or reserve. For her actual beauty, it is said, was not in itself so remarkable that none could be compared with her, or that no one could see her without being struck by it, but the contact of her presence, if you lived with her, was irresistible; the attraction of her person, joining with the charm of her conversation, and the character that attended all she said or did, was something bewitching. It was a pleasure merely to hear the sound of her voice, with which, like an instrument of many strings, she could pass from one language to another; so that there were few of the barbarian nations that she answered by an interpreter; to most of them she spoke herself, as to the Æthiopians, Troglodytes, Hebrews, Arabians, Syrians, Medes, Parthians, and many others, whose language she had learnt; which was all the more surprising because most of the kings, her predecessors, scarcely gave themselves the trouble to acquire the Egyptian tongue, and several of them quite abandoned the Macedonian.

12. **Homeric.** Characteristic of the poet Homer, his poems, or the Greek civilization that they describe

Quotables

"Give me mine angle; we'll to the river: there—
My music playing far off—I will betray
Tawny-finn'd fishes; my bended hook shall pierce
Their slimy jaws; and, as I draw them up,
I'll think every one an Antony,
And say, 'Ah, ha!' you're caught."

—William Shakespeare
The Tragedy of Antony and Cleopatra
(Cleopatra's words soon after Antony sees her as Venus on her barge)

♦ ♦ ♦

To return to Cleopatra; Plato admits four sorts of flattery, but she had a thousand. Were Antony serious or disposed to mirth, she had at any moment some new delight or charm to meet his wishes; at every turn she was upon him, and let him escape her neither by day nor by night. She played at dice with him, drank with him, hunted with him; and when he exercised in arms, she was there to see. At night she would go rambling with him to disturb and torment people at their doors and windows, dressed like a servant-woman, for Antony also went in servant's disguise, and from these expeditions he often came home very scurvily[13] answered, and sometimes even beaten severely, though most people guessed who it was. However, the Alexandrians[14] in general liked it all well enough, and joined good-humouredly and kindly in his frolic and play, saying they were much obliged to Antony for acting his tragic parts at Rome, and keeping his comedy for them. It would be trifling without end to be particular in his follies, but his fishing must not be forgotten. He went out one day to angle with Cleopatra, and, being so unfortunate as to catch nothing in the presence of his mistress, he gave secret orders to the fishermen to dive under water, and put fishes that had been already taken upon his hooks; and these he drew so fast that the Egyptian perceived it. But, feigning great admiration, she told everybody how dexterous Antony was, and invited them next day to come and see him again. So, when a number of them had come on board the fishing-boats, as soon as he had let down his hook, one of her servants was beforehand with his divers, and fixed upon his hook a salted fish from Pontus.[15] Antony, feeling his line give, drew up the prey, and when, as may be imagined, great laughter ensued, "Leave," said Cleopatra, "the fishing-rod, general, to us poor sovereigns of Pharos and Canopus; your game is cities, provinces, and kingdoms." ■

13. **scurvily.** In a low, vile, or contemptible way
14. **Alexandrians.** Hellenistic or late Hellenic people whose culture flourished in Alexandria, Egypt
15. **Pontus.** Ancient kingdom in northeast Asia Minor

1 *What does Antony do to impress Cleopatra?*

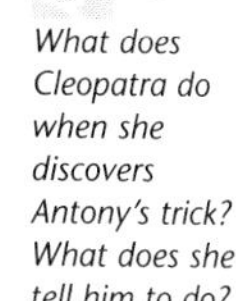

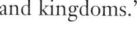

2 *What does Cleopatra do when she discovers Antony's trick? What does she tell him to do?*

WORDS FOR EVERYDAY USE

mirth (murth) *n.,* pleasure, joy

dex • ter • ous (deks´tər əs) *adj.,* having or showing skill in use of hands or body

Answers to Guided Reading Questions

1 Antony has fishermen dive under water and place fish upon his fishhook.

2 Cleopatra has her own divers place a salted fish upon Antony's hook. Cleopatra tells him to leave fishing to Asian monarchs as he should be concerned with "cities, provinces, and kingdoms."

Selection Check Test with Answers

EX. Who convinces Brutus to join the conspirators?

Cassius convinces Brutus to join the conspirators.

1. Who warns Cæsar about the Ides of March?

A soothsayer warns Cæsar about the Ides of March.

2. What do the conspirators do to Cæsar?

The conspirators stab Cæsar to death.

3. Where does Cæsar fall?

Cæsar falls at the base of Pompey's statue.

4. What queen does Mark Antony encounter in Asia?

Antony encounters Cleopatra of Egypt.

5. What does Antony do to impress this queen when they are fishing?

Antony has fishermen dive underwater to place fish upon his hook.

Vocabulary in Context

- Alex had always enjoyed the mirth and festivity of the holiday season.
- With one dexterous leap, the dancer left the ground to soar gracefully before coming back to earth.

RESPONDING TO THE SELECTION

Encourage students to discuss which of these historical figures they would be most interested in meeting.

ANSWERS FOR REVIEWING THE SELECTION

RECALLING AND INTERPRETING

1. **Recalling.** Brutus feels loyal to Cæsar because Cæsar has pardoned, befriended, and bestowed honors upon him. The conspirators leave notes in his chair during the night inciting him to action, and Cassius "work[s]" upon Brutus's ambition. Cæsar desperately tries to avoid the blows of the daggers, but when he sees that Brutus has turned against him, he covers his face and submits to the blows. Cæsar falls at the base of the statue of Pompey, his former adversary. **Interpreting.** Students may say that Cæsar submits to his fate when he realizes that even his close friend Brutus has turned against him. Students may say that Plutarch sees evidence of "supernatural influence" in the fact that Cæsar is murdered near Pompey's statue. He seems to be indicating that Cæsar's downfall is in retribution for Pompey's downfall.

2. **Recalling.** The narrator says that this silence indicates that the people pity Cæsar but respect Brutus. The senate orders that Cæsar should be worshiped as a divinity and that Brutus and the conspirators should hold important governmental posts. The crowd hears Cæsar's generous will and see his wounded body. The crowd mistakes Cinna for a conspirator by the same name and tears him limb from limb. **Interpreting.** The crowd is characterized as fickle and violent. Students may say that the crowd's gratitude and pity for Cæsar was stronger than their respect for Brutus.

(cont.)

Responding to the Selection

Explain why you did or did not sympathize with Julius Cæsar. Can you justify Brutus's motivations for his actions? Why, or why not? Whom do you find more interesting, Antony or Cleopatra? Why? Discuss these questions in small groups.

Reviewing the Selection

RECALLING		INTERPRETING
1. What prevents Brutus from being eager to overthrow Cæsar? What do the conspirators do to get Brutus to join them? What does Cæsar do when he sees Brutus's sword drawn against him? Where does Cæsar fall?	▶▶	Why do you think Cæsar reacts in this way when he sees Brutus's sword drawn against him? Explain whether Plutarch views Cæsar's death more as the result of chance or of "supernatural influence."
2. What does the narrator say the crowd's silence after Brutus's speech reveals about how the people feel about Cæsar and Brutus? What does the senate order? What happens to make the crowd turn against Brutus and the conspirators? What happens to Cæsar's friend Cinna?	▶▶	How would you describe the people of Rome as Plutarch portrays them? How might you explain their behavior?
3. What does Brutus see before the battle of Philippi? What does he do after he survives the battle?	▶▶	What do the apparition and Brutus's actions reveal about his state of mind? How do you think Brutus feels about having killed Cæsar?
4. What does the narrator say Cleopatra does to Antony's nature? What does Cleopatra do to impress and flatter him?	▶▶	Why do you think a person like Cleopatra would have this sort of effect on Antony? What flaws exist in his character?

SYNTHESIZING

5. What motivates Cleopatra to woo Antony? Do you think she truly loves him, or does she have some other motive? In what way is Cleopatra's reason for wooing Antony similar to Brutus's reason for killing Cæsar?

ANSWERS FOR REVIEWING THE SELECTION (CONT.)

3. **Recalling.** Brutus sees a phantom that warns him that it will see him at Philippi. Brutus kills himself with the assistance of a friend. **Interpreting.** Brutus is probably overwhelmed with guilt. Brutus probably feels guilty and reproaches himself for killing Cæsar.

4. **Recalling.** The narrator says that Cleopatra stifles and corrupts Antony's goodness and his sound judgment. Cleopatra appears on the barge as Venus, throws sumptuous dinners, and flatters Antony by saying that he should leave fishing to lesser monarchs and concentrate on his "game" of "cities, provinces, and kingdoms." **Interpreting.** Antony already is proud and enjoys luxurious living, so someone who flatters and indulges him might have a corrupting influence upon his character.

(cont.)

Understanding Literature (Questions for Discussion)

1. **Foreshadowing and Pathetic Fallacy. Foreshadowing** is the act of presenting materials that hint at events to occur later in a story. The **pathetic fallacy** is the tendency to attribute human emotions to nonhuman things, particularly to things in the natural world. What supernatural events occur that foreshadow Cæsar's murder? What disturbances in the natural world occur as the result of Cæsar's death in this selection? Might attributing disturbances in the natural world to a ruler's death be an example of the pathetic fallacy? Explain.

2. **Allusion.** An **allusion** is a rhetorical technique in which reference is made to a person, event, object, or work from history or literature. To what gods from classical mythology does Plutarch allude when describing Antony and Cleopatra? Is this description appropriate? Why, or why not?

3. **Anecdote.** An **anecdote** is a brief story, usually with a specific point or moral. What is the specific point or moral of the anecdote about Antony's fishing with Cleopatra?

Responding in Writing

1. **Creative Writing: Description.** Plutarch's description of Cleopatra and the barge in which she sails up the river Cydnus is one of the most famous descriptions in classical literature. Write a brief (no more than one page) description of a character. The character you describe may be someone famous from history or literature, someone you know such as a friend or family member, or someone you have imagined. After you have chosen a character you would like to describe, review the Language Arts Survey 1.10, "Gathering Ideas," for information on creating sensory detail charts. Then create a sensory detail chart for your character. Refer to this chart when writing your description.

2. **Critical Essay: Analyzing Forms of Literature.** This selection is excerpted from two different biographies. A biography is the story of a person's life, told by someone other than that person. A history, such as Livy's *From the Founding of the City,* is an account of what has happened in the life or development of a people, country, or institution, usually in chronological order with an analysis and explanation. Write an essay in which you compare and contrast history and biography. Before writing your essay, consider carefully the following questions: In what way do biographies, such as those you have just read, differ from a history? In what way is the aim or goal of a biographer different from the aim or goal of a historian? In what way is the aim of a biographer similar to that of a historian? What can a biography reveal about the history of a people, country, or institution? Be sure to state your thesis clearly in an introductory paragraph; support your thesis in following paragraphs using examples from the text; and come to a conclusion in a final paragraph.

Answers for Reviewing the Selection (cont.)

SYNTHESIZING

Responses will vary. Possible responses are given.

5. Students may say that Cleopatra is looking out for the best interests of her country by wooing Antony and gaining his favor. Students may say that Cleopatra's ambition, at least initially, is political. Cleopatra woos Antony to protect Egypt, and Brutus kills Cæsar to protect the republican form of government. In other words, they are both politically motivated.

Answers for Understanding Literature

Responses will vary. Possible responses are given.

1. **Foreshadowing and Pathetic Fallacy.** Students may list any or all of the following: Cæsar says he fears "pale, lean fellows" such as Cassius and Brutus, lights appear in the heavens, noises are heard at night, wild birds perch in the forum, men who appear as if they were heated through with fire fight, an animal Cæsar sacrifices lacks a heart, a soothsayer warns Cæsar about the Ides of March, and Calpurnia has ominous dreams. A comet shines for seven days after Cæsar's death and then disappears, the sun is dim and feeble for an entire year, the air is damp, and fruit never ripens but rots on the tree. By attributing natural disturbances to a ruler's death, one is assuming that nature is capable of noticing and responding in sorrow to a human's death.

2. **Allusion.** Antony is described as Bacchus, and Cleopatra is described as Venus. These descriptions are appropriate because like the goddess of love, Cleopatra is able to influence men through her own beauty and their adoration, and Antony, like Bacchus, god of revelry, enjoys luxury and pleasure.

3. **Anecdote.** Students may say that the point or moral is that Antony is being corrupted by Cleopatra's flattery and his own desire to please her.

Analytic Scales for Responding in Writing

Grading scales for Responding in Writing appear on page 708.

ANALYTIC SCALES FOR RESPONDING IN WRITING

(SEE PAGE 707.)

Assign a score from 1 to 25 for each grading criterion below. (For more detailed evaluation, see the evaluation forms for writing, revising, and proofreading, Assessment Portfolio 4.1–4.9.)

1. Description

- **Content/Unity.** The description vividly portrays a character.
- **Organization/Coherence.** The description presents details about the character in a sensible order.
- **Language/Style.** The description uses vivid and precise nouns, verbs, and modifiers.
- **Conventions.** The description avoids errors in spelling, grammar, usage, mechanics, and manuscript form.

▶ Additional practice is provided in the Essential Skills Practice Book: Writing 1.8, 1.10.

2. Critical Essay

- **Content/Unity.** The essay compares and contrasts history and biography as literary forms.
- **Organization/Coherence.** The essay begins with an introduction that includes the thesis of the essay. The introduction is followed by supporting paragraphs with clear transitions. The essay ends with a solid conclusion.
- **Language/Style.** The essay uses vivid and precise nouns, verbs, and modifiers.
- **Conventions.** The essay avoids errors in spelling, grammar, usage, mechanics, and manuscript form.

▶ Additional practice is provided in the Essential Skills Practice Book: Writing 1.20.

Thinking Skills

Distinguishing Fact and Opinion. A fact is a statement that, at least in principle, could be proved by direct observation. Every statement of fact is either true or false. An opinion is a statement that expresses not a fact about the world but rather the speaker's or writer's attitude or desire. Three common types of opinions are statements of value, statements of policy, and certain types of predictions. A statement of value expresses an attitude toward something, using judgmental words such as *beautiful, dishonest,* or *worthless.* A statement of policy tells not what is but what someone believes should be, using words such as *should, ought not,* or *must.* A prediction makes a statement about the future. Review the Language Arts Survey 4.5, "Distinguishing Fact and Opinion," to learn more about facts and opinions. Then read the sentences below. On your own paper, indicate whether each statement is a fact or an opinion. If the statement is an opinion, state whether it is a statement of value, statement of policy, or prediction.

1. Mammals, birds, and reptiles cannot live without a heart.
2. Trying to predict the future by reading omens is silly and pointless.
3. Cæsar should have read the letter Artemidorus passed to him.
4. Mark Antony was defeated by Octavian, later known as Augustus.
5. One day, all biographies will be written in emulation of Plutarch's *Lives.*

Cæsar Augustus

ANSWERS FOR SKILLS ACTIVITIES

THINKING SKILLS

1. fact
2. opinion; statement of value
3. opinion; statement of policy
4. fact
5. opinion; prediction

▶ Additional practice is provided in the Essential Skills Practice Book: Study and Research 4.5.

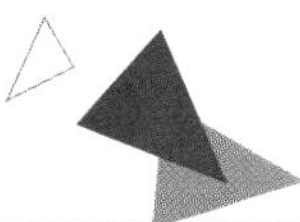

The Renaissance: The Classics Revisited

The European Renaissance spanned the fifteenth to the early seventeenth centuries and was marked by renewed interest in classical literature, the literature of ancient Greece and Rome. As you have read on the Prereading page of this selection, Plutarch was the most popular Greek author of the Renaissance. Few Renaissance writers owe a greater debt to Plutarch than the greatest English dramatist of the period—William Shakespeare. Although Shakespeare did know some Greek, he probably used an English translation of Plutarch's *Lives* made by Sir Thomas North in 1579. If you have already read Shakespeare's *The Tragedy of Julius Cæsar,* you probably noticed similarities between this play and Plutarch's account of Cæsar's life. Shakespeare also used Plutarch as a source for his *Tragedy of Coriolanus* and *The Tragedy of Antony and Cleopatra.* To get a sense of how indebted Shakespeare was to Plutarch's work, compare Plutarch's description of Cleopatra on her barge to the following passage from Shakespeare's *The Tragedy of Antony and Cleopatra.*

ENOBARBUS. I will tell you.
The barge she sat in, like a burnish'd throne,
Burnt on the water. The poop[1] was beaten gold,
Purple the sails, and so perfumed that
The winds were love-sick with them; the oars were silver,
Which to the tune of flutes kept stroke, and made
The water which they beat to follow faster,
As amorous of their strokes. For her own person,
It beggar'd all description: she did lie
In her pavilion—cloth of gold, of tissue—
O'er-picturing that Venus where we see
The fancy outwork nature. On each side her
Stood pretty dimpled boys, like smiling Cupids,
With divers-color'd fans, whose wind did seem
To glow the delicate cheeks which they did cool,
And what they undid did.

AGRIPPA. O, rare for Antony!

ENOBARBUS. Her gentlewomen, like the Nereides,
So many mermaids, tendered her i' th' eyes,
And made their bends adornings. At the helm
A seeming mermaid steers; the silken tackle
Swell with the touches of those flower-soft hands,
That yarely frame the office. From the barge
A strange invisible perfume hits the sense
Of the adjacent wharfs. The city cast
Her people out upon her; and Antony
Enthron'd i' th' market-place, did sit alone,
Whistling to th' air, which, but for vacancy,
Had gone to gaze on Cleopatra too,
And made a gap in nature.

AGRIPPA. Rare Egyptian!

ENOBARBUS. Upon her landing, Antony sent to her,
Invited her to supper. She replied,
It should be better he became her guest;
Which she entreated. Our courteous Antony,
Whom ne'er the word of "No" woman heard speak,
Being barber'd ten times o'er, goes to the feast;
And for his ordinary pays his heart
For what his eyes eat only.

1. **poop.** Raised deck at the stern of a sailing ship

Additional Questions and Activities

Encourage students to list words and phrases from Plutarch's description of Cleopatra's arrival on page 704 that Shakespeare used in this dramatic scene.

Literary Note

You may wish to point out to students that Shakespeare was not showing a lack of originality or imagination by relying on classical sources. Play writing in Shakespeare's day was not so much a matter of inventing a subject and characters previously unknown to the stage as it was a process of adapting, alluding to, and drawing inspiration from both classical and contemporary sources. One of Shakespeare's virtues as a writer was his ability to use the work of classical and contemporary writers in imaginative and, as some enthusiasts believe, even more engaging ways. Educated members of Shakespeare's audience would have recognized the allusion to Plutarch in the scene from *Antony and Cleopatra* presented on this page.

Integrated Skills Activities

Speaking and Listening

You may wish to use this opportunity to encourage students to memorize and present an oral interpretation of a Shakespearean speech. Students may choose Enobrabus's speech beginning with the line, "The barge she sat in . . . ," and ending with the line, "And what they undid did." They may also choose any other Shakespearean speech of reasonable length that they find engaging. If students need help in preparing an oral interpretation, refer them to the Language Arts Survey 3.5, "Oral Interpretation."

▶ Additional practice is provided in the Essential Skills Practice Book: Speaking and Listening 3.5.

FROM *THE HISTORIES*

ABOUT THE AUTHOR

Herodotus (c. 484 – c. 420 BC), the first historian of the Western world, was born in Halicarnassus, a Greek city in southwest Asia, which at that time was under Persian rule. It is believed that he later traveled to Athens where he met Sophocles and then moved to Thurii, a Greek colony in Italy. Herodotus loved to travel, and throughout his life he visited much of the Persian Empire, Egypt, Libya, Syria, Babylonia, Lydia, Macedonia, and a portion of the Black Sea.

ABOUT THE SELECTION

The Histories, the work that won Herodotus the name "the father of history," is a narrative history of the war between Greece and the Persian Empire (499– 479 BC). In addition to describing this military conflict itself, the work also describes the Persian Empire, its structure and its growth. Herodotus is renowned for his love of story-telling, and he inserted many interesting stories, speeches, dialogues, and descriptions into his narrative history. His extensive travel experiences gave him skill in describing the customs and history of other lands; these experiences also made him tolerant of and openminded about other cultures. In this selection, Herodotus describes the wildlife of Egypt, both the real and the legendary.

SELECTION FOR ADDITIONAL READING

GREECE

from *The Histories*

by Herodotus, translated by Aubrey de Sélincourt

There are not a great many wild animals in Egypt, in spite of the fact that it borders on Libya. Such as there are—both wild and tame—are without exception held to be sacred. To explain the reason for this, I should have to enter into a discussion of religious principles which is a subject I particularly wish to avoid—any slight mention I have already made of such matters having been forced upon me by the needs of my story. But, reasons apart, how they actually behave towards animals I will proceed to describe. The various sorts have guardians appointed for them, sometimes men, sometimes women, who are responsible for feeding them; and the office of guardian is handed down from father to son. Their manner, in the various cities, of performing vows is as follows: praying to the god to whom the particular creature, whichever it may be, is sacred, they shave the heads of their children—sometimes completely, sometimes only half or a third part—and after weighing the hair in a pair of scales, give an equal weight of silver to the animals' keeper, who then cuts up fish (the animals' usual food) to an equivalent value and gives it to them to eat. Anyone who deliberately kills one of these animals, is punished with death; should one be killed accidentally, the penalty is whatever the priests choose to impose; but for killing an ibis[1] or a hawk, whether deliberately or not, the penalty is inevitably death.

The number, already large, of domestic animals would have been greatly increased, were it not for an odd thing that happens to the cats. The females, when they have kittens, avoid the toms; but the toms, thus deprived of their satisfaction, get over the difficulty very ingeniously, for they either openly seize, or secretly steal, the kittens and kill them—but without eating them—and the result is that the females, deprived of their kittens and wanting more (for their maternal instinct is very strong), go off to look for mates again. What happens when a house catches fire is most extraordinary; nobody takes the least trouble to put it out, for it is only the cats that matter; everyone stands in a row, a little distance from his neighbour, trying to protect the cats, who nevertheless slip through the line, or jump over it, and hurl themselves into the flames. This causes the Egyptians deep distress. All the inmates of a house where a cat has died a natural death shave their eyebrows, and when a dog dies they shave the whole body including the head. Cats which have died are taken to Bubastis, where they are embalmed and buried in sacred receptacles; dogs are buried, also in sacred burial-places, in the towns where they belong. Weasels are buried in the same way as dogs; field-mice and hawks are taken to Buto, ibises to Hermopolis. Bears, which are scarce, and wolves (which in Egypt are not much bigger than jackals) are buried wherever they happen to be found lying dead.

The following is an account of the crocodile. During the four winter months it takes no food. It is a four-footed, amphibious creature, lays and hatches its eggs on land, where it spends the greater part of the day, and stays all night in the river, where the water is warmer than in the night-air and the dew. The difference in size between the young and the full-grown crocodile is greater than in any other known creature; for a crocodile's egg is hardly bigger than a goose's, and the young when hatched is small in proportion, yet it grows to a size of some twenty-three feet long or even more. It has eyes like a pig's but great fang-like teeth in proportion to its body, and is the only animal to have no tongue and a stationary lower jaw; for when it eats it brings the upper jaw down upon the under. It has powerful claws and a scaly hide, which on its back is impenetrable. It cannot see under water, though on land its sight is remarkably quick. One result of its spending so much time in the water is that the inside of its mouth gets covered with leeches. Other animals avoid the crocodile, as do all birds too with one exception—the sandpiper, or Egyptian plover:[2] this bird is of service to the crocodile and lives, in consequence, in the greatest amity with him; for when the crocodile comes ashore and lies with his mouth wide open (which he generally does facing towards the west), the bird hops in and swallows the leeches. The crocodile enjoys this, and never, in consequence, hurts the bird. Some Egyptians reverence the crocodile as a sacred beast; others do not, but treat it as an enemy. The strongest belief in its sanctity is to be found in Thebes and round about Lake Moeris; in these

1. **ibis.** Any of several large wading birds
2. **plover.** Any of a worldwide family of shorebirds

CROSS-CURRICULAR ACTIVITIES 

MATHEMATICS AND SCIENCES

Encourage students to work together to prepare reports on the crocodile, its appearance, and its habits. Students might then compare and contrast what they have learned about crocodiles with Herodotus's report of these creatures to discover how accurate his description is.

places they keep one particular crocodile, which they tame, putting rings made of glass or gold into its ears and bracelets round its front feet, and giving it special food and ceremonial offerings. In fact, while these creatures are alive they treat them with every kindness, and, when they die, embalm them and bury them in sacred tombs. On the other hand, in the neighbourhood of Elephantine crocodiles are not considered sacred animals at all, but are eaten. In the Egyptian language these creatures are called *champsae*. The name crocodile—or 'lizard'—was given them by the Ionians, who saw they resembled the lizards commonly found on stone walls in their own country.

Of the numerous different ways of catching crocodiles I will describe the one which seems to me the most interesting. They bait a hook with a chine of pork and let it float out into midstream, and at the same time, standing on the bank, take a live pig and beat it. The crocodile, hearing its squeals, makes a rush towards it, encounters the bait, gulps it down, and is hauled out of the water. The first thing the huntsman does when he has got the beast on land is to plaster its eyes with mud; this done, it is dispatched easily enough—but without this precaution it will give a lot of trouble.

The hippopotamus is held sacred in the district of Papremis, but not elsewhere. This animal has four legs, cloven hoofs like an ox, a snub nose, a horse's mane and tail, conspicuous tusks, a voice like a horse's neigh, and is about the size of a very large ox. Its hide is so thick and tough that when dried it can be made into spear-shafts. Otters, too, are found in the Nile; they, and the fish called lepidotus, and eels are all considered sacred to the Nile, as is also the bird known as the foxgoose. Another sacred bird is the phoenix; I have not seen a phoenix myself, except in paintings, for it is very rare and visits the country (so at least they say at Heliopolis) only at intervals of 500 years, on the occasion of the death of the parent-bird. To judge by the paintings, its plumage is partly golden, partly red, and in shape and size it is exactly like an eagle. There is a story about the phoenix; it brings its parent in a lump of myrrh[3] all the way from Arabia and buries the body in the temple of the Sun. To perform this feat, the bird first shapes some myrrh into a sort of egg as big as it finds, by testing, that it can carry; then it hollows the lump out, puts its father inside and smears some more myrrh over the hole. The egg-shaped lump is then just of the same weight as it was originally. Finally it is carried by the bird to the temple of the Sun in Egypt. Such, at least, is the story. ■

3. **myrrh.** Fragrant, bitter-tasting gum resin used in making incense and perfume

CULTURAL/HISTORICAL NOTE

Inform students that the phoenix is a legendary bird that was associated with sun worship. Supposedly, only one phoenix lived at a time. At the end of its 500-year life cycle, it built a nest of rich spices and aromatic wood, set it on fire, and immolated itself. It was believed that a new phoenix sprang from the flames that had consumed the old. The new phoenix then placed the ashes of the old phoenix, its "father," in an egg of myrrh and brought the ashes to the temple of Ra, or Re, in Heliopolis. Because of this legend, the phoenix became associated with immortality. The Romans later used the phoenix as a symbol of their unending empire.

ADDITIONAL QUESTIONS AND ACTIVITIES

Encourage students to discuss whether Herodotus describes the phoenix as if it were a mythological creature or a real creature. If he realizes it is a mythological creature, why does he describe it along with real Egyptian animals?

QUOTABLES

"You may have noticed how the thunderbolt of Heaven chastises the insolence of more enormous animals, whilst it passes over without injury the weak and insignificant: before these weapons of the gods you must have seen how the proudest palaces and the loftiest trees fall and perish."

—Herodotus

ADDITIONAL RESOURCES

Assessment Portfolio

- Vocabulary Worksheet 2.8.17
- Study Guide 2.8.18
- Unit Test 2.8.19

Essential Skills Practice Books

WRITING

- Choosing a Topic,1.6
- Choosing a Purpose, 1.8
- Gathering Ideas, 1.10
- Writing a Critical Essay, 1.20

LANGUAGE

- Expanding Sentences, 2.20
- Combining Sentences Using Words and Phrases, 2.21
- Combining Sentences Using Clauses, 2.22
- Varying Sentence Openings, Length, and Structure, 2.23
- Greek and Latin Roots, 2.66

SPEAKING AND LISTENING

- Elements of Verbal and Nonverbal Communication, 3.1
- Active Listening and Interpersonal Communication, 3.2
- Oral Interpretation, 3.5

STUDY AND RESEARCH

- Distinguishing Fact and Opinion, 4.5
- Bibliographies and Bibliography Cards, 4.20
- Paraphrasing and Summarizing, 4.21

APPLIED ENGLISH/TECH PREP

- Finding Career Information, 5.2

UNIT REVIEW

Classical Literature

VOCABULARY FROM THE SELECTIONS

adjourn, 699
adroitness, 703
affray, 687
augury, 687
avowal, 692
balk, 631
brandish, 603
calumny, 632
career, 597
commiserate, 680
compulsion, 629
conjecture, 642, 652
consummation, 679
contrivance, 634
countenance, 636, 702
despotic, 641
dexterous, 705
diadem, 699
dirge, 662
dormant, 703
expiation, 624
fettered, 656
grovel, 599
implore, 596
imprecation, 664
inauspicious, 699
incredulous, 676
induce, 625
infamously, 666
infamy, 646
insolence, 648
intimate, 698
invidious, 702
invoke, 628
juncture, 699
knave, 641
lament, 675
lineage, 657
mirth, 705
oblivion, 611
obstinacy, 638
oration, 676
pestilence, 621
pillage, 685
pinnacle, 698
preternatural, 702
procure, 697
purge, 662
raillery, 698
rankle, 646
recourse, 605
rend, 604
reverence, 667
scourge, 602
slake, 685
soothsayer, 698
straits, 600
suborn, 634
suffice, 662
surfeit, 648
tempered, 602
thither, 702
throng, 687
toil, 612, 676
tripod, 598
versatility, 678
vexation, 635
vilely, 668
whetted, 602
wrought, 603

Vocabulary Check Test

Ask students to number their papers from one to ten. Have students complete each sentence with a word from the Vocabulary from the Selections in the Unit Review.

1. We watched the guilty man grovel before the judge, begging for leniency in his sentencing.
2. Although the king erected a large stone monument in his own honor, after a thousand years the monument had been broken into stones, and even the king's name had faded into oblivion.
3. Ulysses used prayer as expiation for his sins.
4. Liam claims that he could not control the compulsion to break into song during the movie.
5. One gallon of milk is not enough, but two should suffice.
6. We could tell the scientist did not agree

(cont.)

LITERARY TERMS

aim, 682
allusion, 614, 707
anecdote, 707
apostrophe, 694
archetype, 689
argumentation, 682
comedy, 617
convention, 617, 672
description, 607
dramatic irony, 651
epic, 592, 607
foreshadowing, 707
irony, 651
metaphor, 614, 651
mode, 682
motivation, 607
myth, 689
nonfiction, 689
paradox, 651, 694
pathetic fallacy, 707
simile, 614, 651
style, 607
theme, 614, 682
tragedy, 617, 673
tragic flaw, 592, 617, 673
tragic hero, 592

SYNTHESIS: QUESTIONS FOR WRITING, RESEARCH, OR DISCUSSION

GENRE STUDIES

1. What is a history? What is a biography? In what ways do the two forms differ? In what ways are the two forms similar? What aspects of the histories and biographies in this unit surprise you? Why do these aspects seem unconventional in works of nonfiction?

2. What is an epic? What is a tragedy? In what way do the heroes of an epic and of a tragedy differ? In what way are they similar? Use examples from the *Iliad* and from *Oedipus the King* to support your responses.

THEMATIC STUDIES

3. Both Sappho and Catullus wrote several lyrics about love. Compare and contrast the poems by Catullus and these love poems by Sappho: "But Not Everybody Wants Love," "At Last," or "It Gives Me Joy to Think." Who is the speaker in each poem? What kinds of love are explored? What attitudes toward love are expressed in these poems?

4. What attitude toward death and remembrance is presented in the following works: Homer's *Iliad*, and Sappho's "Let's Not Pretend," Fragment 144, and "Life Slips By."

HISTORICAL/BIOGRAPHICAL STUDIES

5. Based on what you have read about Julius Cæsar and Mark Antony, which man do you most admire? Which do you find most interesting? Why? What questions do you have about each of these men? Use other sources on the lives of Julius Cæsar and Mark Antony to try to find answers to your questions.

6. What values, customs, and beliefs of the ancient Greeks can you deduce from the Greek selections in this unit? What values, customs, and beliefs of the ancient Romans can you infer from the Roman selections in this unit? Compare and contrast the two cultures.

SPELLING CHECK TEST

Ask students to number their papers from one to ten. Read each word aloud. Then read aloud the sentence containing the word. Repeat the word. Ask students to write the word on their papers, spelling it correctly.

1. **suffice**
   Melanie said that two gallons of water would suffice, but I brought three just in case.
2. **dirge**
   The dirge playing from the woman's stereo put us all in a sad and gloomy mood.
3. **vexation**
   The directions were easy to follow, but the vexation of heavy traffic made the trip difficult.
4. **throng**
   No one could believe the great throng of people at the shopping center this afternoon.
5. **countenance**
   Gerald's gloomy countenance told us that he had heard the bad news.
6. **induced**
   Induced by the salesperson to buy more than I had originally planned, I had to return all of the unwanted items.
7. **conjecture**
   Based on the weather pattern thus far, Jessie made a conjecture that we will have a long winter.
8. **grovelled**
   Stephanie grovelled to the stage manager to let her come back to the show.
9. **tripod**
   My sister made a tripod for her new camera out of three wooden chair legs.
10. **implore**
    I implore you to give me just two minutes of your time to let me say what I have been wanting to tell you.

VOCABULARY CHECK TEST (CONT.)

with her colleague's theory by the incredulous expression on her face.

7. Plowing the field under a hot afternoon sun was difficult toil for the team of oxen.

8. When the film star left her limousine, she was surrounded by a throng of enthusiastic fans.

9. The Roman emperor's avowal revealed that he intended to send troops into Gaul.

10. During World War II, it was difficult for average American citizens to procure meat, clothing, machinery, and other items due to shortages caused by the war.

UNIT SKILLS OUTLINE

Literary Skills and Concepts

- Allegory, 747
- Ambiguity, 728
- Anecdotes, 770
- Apostrophe, 763
- Apposition, 735
- *Bildungsroman,* 724
- Canto, 747
- Catalog, 745
- Chivalry, 720, 731, 740
- Courtly Love, 721, 740, 746
- Description, 731
- Epigram, 796
- Epitaph, 759
- Exposition, 769
- Frame Tale, 784, 788, 793, 795
- Hero, 811
- Image, 783
- Imagery, 763
- Irony of Situation, 807
- Journal, 776
- Medieval Romance, 732
- Metaphor, 735, 740
- Mood, 800
- Motif, 757
- Parallelism, 781
- Point of View, 763
- Psychological Fiction, 765
- Realism, 763
- Refrain, 763
- Repetition, 782
- Simile, 758, 800
- Symbol, 730
- Theme, 793, 800, 808
- Tone, 768, 776, 783

Writing Skills and Concepts

- Advice Column, 731
- Continuation, 741
- Critical Essay, 731, 741, 758, 764, 769, 777, 783, 794, 801, 808
- Epitaph, 763
- Frame Tale, 794
- Guide, 783
- Introduction, 769
- Journey Tale, 758
- Lyric Poem, 746
- Parable, 808
- Pillow Book, 777
- Recipe for Paradise, 801

Grammar, Usage, and Mechanics Skills and Concepts

- Combining Sentences Using Words and Phrases, 769
- Correcting Errors in Verb Usage, 794
- Editing for Punctuation Errors, 808
- Reducing Wordiness, 741
- Using Commas, 758

Other Language Arts Skills and Concepts

- Making and Testing Hypotheses, 777
- Oral Interpretation, 746
- Problem Solving and Decision Making, 801
- Public Speaking, 772
- Reading Skills, 734

Unit 9 Medieval Literature

Detail from the book of hours, the ***Très Riches Heures du duc de Berry****. The Limbourg brothers, 1416*

714 *UNIT NINE / MEDIEVAL LITERATURE*

GOALS/OBJECTIVES

Studying this unit will enable students to

- interpret and appreciate medieval literature
- briefly explain social, literary, and historical developments during the Medieval Period in Europe, Japan, and Arabia and Persia
- identify and explain the characteristics of medieval romances and elements of the romantic tradition, such as courtly love and chivalry
- explain the characteristics of a frame tale
- write both critically and creatively in response to medieval literature

"There was a Knight, a most distinguished man,
Who from the day on which he first began
To ride abroad had followed chivalry,
Truth, honor, generousness and courtesy."

—Geoffrey Chaucer

715

CROSS-CURRICULAR CONNECTIONS

Arts and Humanities

- Arthurian Legend, 731
- Burne-Jones's Medieval Subjects, 724
- Classical Allusions in Dante's Work, 753
- Dante's Admirers and Critics, 749
- Dante's Inferno, 751
- Depicting a Genie, 790
- Elihu Vedder, 790
- Exploring Asian Art, 717
- Exploring *The Thousand and One Nights,* 784
- Female Troubadours, 742
- John William Waterhouse's *Destiny,* 736
- Mapping Skills, 810
- Medieval "Scholarly" Writing in Japan and Europe, 765
- Oral Interpretation, 746
- Paul Cézanne, 761
- Representing the Afterlife, 748
- Robin Hood, 759
- Shahrazad in the Arts, 785
- Significance of the Number Three, 747
- *The Story of the Grail* Presentations, 729
- Sufist Parables, 804
- Tapestries, 729
- The Tristan and Isolde Story, 732
- Virtues and Vices, 760
- William Blake's Visual Art, 752

Mathematics and Sciences

- Death as a Biological Process, 796

Social Studies

- The Bible's Translators, 802
- Biographical Notes on Echoes Authors, 719
- Books in the Medieval Period, 717
- Chivalry and the Church, 723
- The Crusades, 720
- Feminist Movements, 774
- The Five Pillars of Islam, 718
- The History of Romantic Love, 721
- Japanese History, 717
- Laws and Punishments, 764
- Mapping Skills, 810
- Medieval "Scholarly" Writing in Japan and Europe, 765
- Researching the Guelfs and the Ghibellines, 755
- Researching Islam, 718
- Researching the Lives of Medieval Peasants, 716
- Researching Mecca, 778
- Rosaries, 773
- Shintoism and Buddhism, 773
- Significance of the Lance, 725
- Significance of the Number Three, 747
- *Song of Roland*—Legend and History, 809
- Sufist Parables, 804
- Vassalage, 716

Applied Arts

- Arthurian Legend, 731

TEACHING THE MULTIPLE INTELLIGENCES

Musical

- Female Troubadours, 742
- Oral Interpretation, 746
- Representing the Afterlife, 748
- Shahrazad in the Arts, 785
- The Tristan and Isolde Story, 732

Logical-Mathematical

- Feminist Movements, 774
- Death as a Biological Process, 796
- Contemporary Quests, 722
- Problem Solving and Decision Making, 801

Spatial

- Burne-Jones's Medieval Subjects, 724
- Depicting a Genie, 790
- Elihu Vedder, 790
- Exploring Asian Art, 717
- Exploring *The Thousand and One Nights,* 784

(cont.)

UNIT 9

Preview:

Medieval Literature

Detail from the ***Très Riches Heures***

The decline of Roman control over Europe in the fifth century marks the beginning of what is known as the Medieval Period, also called the Middle Ages. Germanic tribes moving throughout northern Europe spread a system called vassalage, in which one lord swore allegiance to a greater one in return for privileges or property. Vassalage soon developed into a system that historians call feudalism. As the chaos from the fall of the Roman Empire began to settle, leaders gradually began to establish delineated nations, and feudalism took a firm hold of Europe. In feudal states, all land and all people ultimately belonged to the king, who granted large tracts of land to members of the nobility. The nobles, in exchange, were bound to be loyal to the king, to raise armies to fight in his battles, and to pay taxes to support his court. In turn, these nobles granted land to lesser nobles and required service and support from them. At the very bottom of this social order was a class of bondsmen, known as peasants, serfs, or villeins, who lived on the nobles' land. The lot of the serfs was generally miserable. They were the property of their feudal lords and could not leave the land or even marry without permission. They lived on meager diets, suffered terribly from disease, and worked very hard only to turn over much of what they produced to support the lord's household.

Religion played an important role in the structured feudal society of Europe. While Germanic tribes practiced pagan religions, they gradually converted to Christianity. Early medieval literature shows that Christian belief coexisted alongside pagan belief. After a few centuries, however, most people in Europe were Christian and looked to Rome for guidance. As the pope in Rome sent emissaries throughout Europe, a group of highly literate clergy developed. The clergy not only led people in worship but also served as the scholars of the period, keeping and

OTHER SELECTIONS EXPLORING THIS PERIOD

Firdausi
"Lament for His Son," page 310

Ki no Tsurayuki
"In the lingering wake," page 378

Li Po
"The River-Merchant's Wife: A Letter," page 245

Marie de France
"The Lay of the Werewolf," page 444

CULTURAL/HISTORICAL NOTE

Point out that the organization of medieval society depended on vassalage—the loyalty or obligation that a lesser member of the society owed to a higher member in exchange for favors granted. For example, a knight might be granted property by a great lord—a duke, an earl, or a king. That knight would then owe obligations of loyalty to the lord. This loyalty would be demonstrated through a public act of homage.

CROSS-CURRICULAR ACTIVITIES

SOCIAL STUDIES

Inform students that the nobility and upper classes viewed the peasant classes with hostility and disdain, especially since peasants sometimes revolted. The nobility's attitude toward the peasant class, or villeins, has carried over to the modern use of the word *villain.* Encourage students to work in groups to research what life was like for this scorned class of individuals. Possible research topics include: standards of living for serfs, the legal status of serfs, the Peasant's Revolt led by Wat Tyler, how and why the serf system died out in Western Europe, why it lingered in Eastern Europe and Russia, and the end of serfdom in Russia.

TEACHING THE MULTIPLE INTELLIGENCES (CONT.)

- Female Troubadours, 742
- John William Waterhouse's *Destiny,* 736
- Laws and Punishments, 764
- Mapping Skills, 810
- Paul Cézanne, 761
- Representing the Afterlife, 748
- Shahrazad in the Arts, 785
- *The Story of the Grail* Presentations, 729
- Tapestries, 729
- The Tristan and Isolde Story, 732
- William Blake's Visual Art, 752

KINESTHETIC

- Arthurian Legend, 731
- Shahrazad in the Arts, 785
- *The Story of the Grail* Presentations, 729

INTERPERSONAL

- Arthurian Legend, 731
- Contemporary Quests, 722
- Death as a Biological Process, 796

(cont.)

copying books in monasteries. While many of these works were in Latin, monks did transcribe and preserve some popular, vernacular examples of literature that existed primarily through the oral tradition.

Detail from the ***Très Riches Heures***

Feudalism did not develop in medieval Europe alone. The rise of Confucianism in China, with its focus on the loyalties owed by one social class to another, led to the development of a Chinese state that might be considered feudal. Feudalism also took root in Japan beginning around AD 1100, although it originated hundreds of years earlier, and lasted well into the nineteenth century. Social classes were divided much as they were in medieval Europe—there was a class of aristocratic lords, known as *daimyo*, and their ladies; a class of warriors, known as *samurai*, who owed allegiance to a particular daimyo; a class of Buddhist monks and nuns who served as scholars, much as Christian clergy served as scholars in Europe; and a class of commoners, including both freemen and serfs, or slaves. Like the knights of Europe, the samurai followed a strict code of conduct that emphasized honor and loyalty, and, as in Europe, lords or daimyo often quarreled with one another, so feudal Japan was also often at war.

While medieval Europeans never came into contact with their feudal counterparts in Japan, they did interact with one of the most powerful civilizations of this period—the Muslim civilization of Persia and Arabia. In the early eighth century, feudal Europe was faced with a challenge. Muslims, called Moors by the Europeans, had spread their religion and way of life throughout the Middle East and Africa and now sought to establish a stronghold in Europe. The Muslims practiced Islam, a religion whose central scripture is the Koran, which contains revelations received by Mohammed. Unlike medieval Christians, who believed that all other religions were heretical, Muslims believed that Jewish and Christian scriptures were also divine. They also believed, however, that Islam was the one perfect religion, and they aimed to spread the word of Islam. Muslims swept into Spain, rapidly conquering much of that country, though Christians resisted the Moorish influence and struggled to expel these invaders or to at least keep the Muslim influence from spreading.

Once the Muslim threat had been contained in Europe, the church sponsored a series of Crusades, or holy wars which sent Europeans to

Cultural/Historical Note

Inform students that during the Medieval Period, books were copied by hand—a painstaking task. While monks preserved a large number of books in monasteries, many books were destroyed during wars, when invading troops would sack and burn whole towns. Point out, for example, that all the major Old English elegies exist only in one original tenth-century book called the Exeter Book. The epic *Beowulf* also is found only in one damaged manuscript from the period. Thus, much of the literature of the Medieval Period has undoubtedly been lost. The wealth of literature that does exist is largely the result of the dedication of learned clergy.

Cross-curricular Activities

ARTS AND HUMANITIES

Students may enjoy visiting a Japanese garden or an Asian art exhibit. Suggest that students research traditional Japanese art forms, such as painting, flower arranging, sculpture, No theater, or Kabuki theater. They can present their findings to the class.

SOCIAL STUDIES

Encourage students to write research reports on one of the following aspects of Japanese history: the Yamato culture; politics, court life, or major events during the Heian period; the civil war between the Taira and the Minamoto; the development of feudalism in Japan; the development of the shogunate; the Mongol invasions; and the end of feudalism in Japan.

TEACHING THE MULTIPLE INTELLIGENCES (CONT.)

CULTURAL/HISTORICAL NOTE

Inform students that all Muslims are expected to practice the Five Pillars of Islam. These five pillars are to recite a profession of faith at least once in one's lifetime, to observe the five daily prayers, to pay a charitable tax for the poor, to observe the fast from sunrise to sunset during the entire month of Ramadan, and to make the pilgrimage to Mecca.

CROSS-CURRICULAR ACTIVITIES

SOCIAL STUDIES

Interested students might work in small groups to prepare a report on the differences between the two main sects of Islam—Sunni and Shiite. Other students may research the "golden age" of Islam under the Abbasid dynasty, or Genghis Khan and the effects of the Mongol invasion in Persia.

Detail of illuminated manuscript page from the ***Très Riches Heures***

the Middle East to recapture Jerusalem from the Muslims. From the eleventh to the thirteenth century, Christians from all over Europe participated in the Crusades, bringing back with them Persian and Arabic stories and scholarship. Of considerable influence on the Crusaders was Persian love poetry with its many portraits of idealized women. This poetry influenced the development, beginning in the twelfth century, of passionate devotion to the Virgin Mary, mother of Jesus, who was portrayed in popular and religious literature as the ideal of perfect womanhood.

The Crusades and devotion to the Virgin Mary contributed to the evolution of the unique literature known as romance, which portrayed the standards of knightly conduct known as chivalry. Medieval romances were stories of adventure. They dealt with the exploits of knights and with the love that inspired these heroics. Typically, a romance would present a series of loosely connected adventures, each a trial or test of the knight's virtues, that were often undertaken to rescue or win the favor of a fair lady who was represented in idealized terms. The idealization of the woman, and of the knight's faithful service, formed the core of the code of behavior known as courtly love.

In addition to producing the love poetry that so influenced medieval Christians, Persian and Arabic writers of that time experimented with many other types of writing. Devotion to Islam led many writers to religious commentaries, while other writers composed works offering moral advice. Like medieval Europeans, the people of Arabia and Persia told adventure tales featuring heroes. Persian and Arabic scholarship was much more advanced than that of medieval Europe; indeed, Arabians and Persians preserved many Greek and Latin works that tribes of vandals and certain zealous Christians had destroyed in Europe soon after the fall of the Roman Empire. Following the Crusades, a flood of knowledge—Arabic as well as classical Greek and Roman—was opened to medieval scholars. This return to classical learning was one of the primary forces behind the European Renaissance.

Echoes:

Medieval Literature

Therefore the man wise in his heart considers carefully this wall-place and this dark life, remembers the multitude of deadly combats long ago, and speaks these words: Where has the horse gone? Where the young warrior? Where is the giver of treasure? What has become of the feasting seats? Where are the joys of the hall? Alas, the bright cup! Alas, the mailed warrior! Alas, the prince's glory! How that time has gone, vanished beneath the night's cover, just as if it never had been!

—Anonymous
from "The Wanderer"

O long, long may their ladies sit,
Wi' their fans into their hand,
Or e'er they see Sir Patrick Spens
Come sailing to the land.

O long, long may their ladies stand,
Wi' their gold combs in their hair,
Waiting for their own dear lords,
For they'll see them no more.

—Anonymous
from "Sir Patrick Spens"

Yet some men say in many parts of England that King Arthur is not dead, but had by the will of Our Lord Jesu into another place; and men say that he shall come again, and he shall win the holy cross. I will not say that it shall be so, but rather I will say, here in this world he changed his life. But many men say that there is written upon his tomb this verse:

HIC IACET ARTHURUS, REX QUONDAM REXQUE FUTURUS.[1]

—Sir Thomas Malory
from *Le Morte d'Arthur*

Love thrives on inextinguishable pain,
Which tears the soul, then knits the threads
again.
A mote of love exceeds all bounds; it gives
The vital essence to whatever lives.
But where love thrives, there pain is always
found;
Angels alone escape this weary round—

—Faridoddin Attar
from *The Conference of the Birds*

Disloyalty is a warrior's shame. We will accompany His Majesty until we die, whether the destination be inside or outside of Japan—whether it be Silla, Paekche, Koguryō, Bohai, the farthest reaches of the clouds, or the farthest reaches of the sea.

—Anonymous
from *The Tale of the Heike*

1. **Hic . . . Futurus.** Latin for "Here lies Arthur, the once and future king."

Biographical/Literary Note

"The Wanderer" is an anonymous Old English elegy found in the tenth-century Exeter Book (see note on page 717). In this poem an exile describes his sorrows and yearnings to be with his old companions.

"Sir Patrick Spens" is one of the most famous of anonymous English folk ballads. It was passed through the oral tradition and tells of a shipwreck of a Scottish knight and his men, a story that may be based on an actual thirteenth-century tragedy.

Very little is known about **Sir Thomas Malory** (c. 1405–1471). Although he seems to have led a quiet life in his younger years, he began having trouble with the law in 1451. By some accounts, Malory spent most of his life after 1451 in prison, where he completed the manuscript for ***Le Morte d'Arthur*** around 1469. Malory's prose romance was greatly influenced by the Arthurian romances of thirteenth-century France. Although he wrote *Le Morte d'Arthur* toward the end of the Medieval Period when romance literature had declined in popularity, Malory's book is the most complete retelling of Arthurian legend.

Faridoddin Attar (1145–1221) was a Persian writer and pharmacist born in Iran. He lived in Nishapur and probably died when the invading Mongol army slaughtered the entire population of Nishapur in 1221. He is greatly respected as one of the Sufi (or mystical) poets.

The Tale of the Heike is an anonymous Japanese epic prose tale that was probably passed through the oral tradition by chanters, much like the *Iliad* or the *Odyssey.* The most widely known version was written down in 1371. Its subject is the *samurai* and the civil war and power struggles of the late twelfth century in Japan.

CULTURAL/HISTORICAL NOTE

Inform students that the concept of chivalry was strengthened by the series of European military expeditions known as the Crusades. The Crusades inspired knights to form different orders of chivalry that were originally intended to protect those making pilgrimages to the Holy Land. If students are unfamiliar with the Crusades, you might encourage them to research this series of expeditions, or you might give them the following synopsis:

The Crusades took place between 1095 and 1270. The Byzantine Empire was threatened by the Turks, so the Byzantine emperor requested the aid of Pope Urban II. (The Byzantine Empire was a Christian empire and the eastern half of the Roman Empire. It survived many centuries after the western half of the Roman Empire had fallen into separate feudal kingdoms.) In 1095, the pope called for a Christian army to recapture the Holy Land, thus beginning the First Crusade. The First Crusaders seized Jerusalem and killed all its Muslim and Jewish residents, then established several "crusader states" in the region.

A powerful Muslim ruler captured a city ruled by the Crusaders in 1144, so the current pope called for a Second Crusade. Muslim forces crushed the Second Crusaders and recaptured Jerusalem. The Third Crusade set out in 1189 in an attempt to recapture Jerusalem. While this Crusade failed in that endeavor, Richard I (or Richard the Lion-Hearted) made a treaty so that European Christians might make pilgrimages to the holy sites in the East.

The Fourth Crusade was called against Egypt in 1198. Instead, the Crusaders attacked Constantinople, the capital of the Byzantine Empire, which had requested the Crusaders' aid one hundred years earlier—thus severing any alliance between the Byzantine and the Latin churches.

(cont.)

Themes

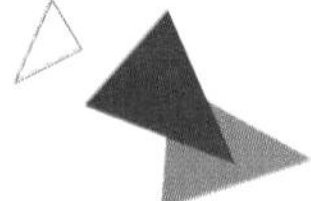

CHIVALRY AND COURTLY LOVE

*Detail from the **Très Riches Heures***

Knighthood

The knight was an important member of medieval society. Becoming a knight was a long and difficult process open only to the sons of aristocrats. Around age seven, a knight-to-be entered as a page into the service of a lord. Within seven years, at age fourteen, he became a squire. During this time, he served his lord, strengthened himself, and learned to handle weapons. After seven years of apprenticeship, at the age of twenty-one, he was inducted into knighthood and given armor, a horse, a helmet, and a lance. Knights often participated in tournaments to showcase and test their bravery and skill. They were expected to be completely loyal to their lords, to protect all women, and to show courtesy to other knights.

The Chivalric Code

The code of conduct of the medieval knight is called **chivalry.** The word *chivalry,* from the French word for horse, *cheval,* reflects the knights' reliance on the horse in battle, because heavy armor made movement on the ground difficult. According to the code of chivalry, a knight was to be a loyal servant to his lord or lady and a perfect exemplar of such virtues as bravery, courage, courtesy, honesty, faith, and gentleness. Of course, actual knights may not have lived up to the code, but many medieval romances portray this ideal. In such romances, a knight faces a series of adventures testing the chivalric virtues, either in the form of trials or quests. The most famous quest was the search for the Holy Grail. Often, the knight performed trials to win the favor of a lady who was represented in idealized terms. The code

CULTURAL/HISTORICAL NOTE (CONT.)

The next crusade, begun in 1212, was the Children's Crusade. Tens of thousands of children set out to conquer the Holy Land through love, not force. Thousands of these children were lost on their journey, and many more were sold into slavery by avaricious merchants. The Fifth Crusade, the last ordered by the pope, ended in a truce with Egypt around 1219. In the Sixth Crusade the German Emperor Frederick II won a treaty returning Jerusalem to the Europeans from 1229 to 1239. After Jerusalem returned to Muslim control, King Louis IX of France launched two unsuccessful Crusades, the Seventh and the Eighth, in which Louis and most of the Crusaders died of disease. Although Crusades continued from time to time, the impetus to continue the struggle had largely died out by the end of the thirteenth century.

of behavior governing the relationship between an idealized lady and her faithful knight formed the core of the art of courtly love.

Courtly Love

Courtly love is a code of romantic love celebrated in songs and romances of the Medieval Period. According to this code, the lover knows himself or herself to be truly in love if he or she is overcome by extreme, transforming emotion. The female lover is often portrayed in ideal and unrealistic terms. She usually requires that her partner prove his love through a series of tasks. The male lover is led sometimes to heights of gentleness, courtesy, and heroism to prove his worth to his lady. Courtly love was one of the primary themes of medieval romances. The twelfth-century French writer André le Chapelain, also known as Andreas Capellanus, presented a thorough exposition of the ideals of this type of love in *The Art of Courtly Love.* He codified these ideals into the following rules:

1. Marriage is no real excuse for not loving.
2. He who is not jealous cannot love.
3. No one can be bound by a double love.
4. It is well known that love is always increasing or decreasing.
5. That which a lover takes against the will of his beloved has no relish.
6. Boys do not love until they arrive at the age of maturity.
7. When one lover dies, a widowhood of two years is required of the survivor.
8. No one should be deprived of love without the very best of reasons.
9. No one can love unless he is impelled by the persuasion of love.
10. Love is always a stranger in the home of avarice.
11. It is not proper to love any woman whom one would be ashamed to seek to marry.
12. A true lover does not desire to embrace in love anyone except his beloved.
13. When made public, love rarely endures.
14. The easy attainment of love makes it of little value; difficulty of attainment makes it prized.
15. Every lover regularly turns pale in the presence of his beloved.
16. When a lover suddenly catches sight of his beloved, his heart palpitates.
17. A new love puts to flight an old one.
18. Good character alone makes any man worthy of love.
19. If love diminishes, it quickly fails and rarely revives.
20. A man in love is always apprehensive.
21. Real jealousy always increases the feeling of love.
22. Jealousy, and therefore love, are increased when one suspects his beloved.

Detail from the ***Très Riches Heures***

23. He whom the thought of love vexes, eats and sleeps very little.
24. Every act of a lover ends in the thought of his beloved.
25. A true lover considers nothing good except what he thinks will please his beloved.
26. Love can deny nothing to love.
27. A lover can never have enough of the solaces of his beloved.
28. A slight presumption causes a lover to suspect his beloved.
29. A man who is vexed by too much passion usually does not love.
30. A true lover is constantly and without intermission possessed by the thought of his beloved.
31. Nothing forbids one woman being loved by two men or one man by two women.

These ideals are the core of the theme of courtly love presented in medieval romances such as Gottfried von Strassburg's *Tristan* (see page 732) and the lays, or songs, of Marie de France (see page 444).

Cultural/Historical Note

Inform students that before the notion of courtly love was developed in southern France in the eleventh century, the concept of romantic love that most Westerners hold as an ideal was essentially nonexistent. In the Medieval Period and beyond, marriages were usually the result of economic necessities or, for the nobility, political alliances.

Poets drew the ideal of courtly love partly from the cult of adoration of the Virgin Mary and partly from Ovid's depiction of love in *Ars amatoria,* or *The Art of Love.* Point out that the sort of relationship idealized under the code of courtly love was extramarital, as love and marriage were rarely associated, but it was also hardly ever physical. (Nevertheless, the medieval church strictly condemned adultery, viewing courtly love as idolatrous and, often, as treasonous. Many morally minded writers condemned the courtly love in the romances they told.) The relationship between a lady and her admirer was close to that of a lord and his vassal. The admirer was supposed to worship and respect his lady, obeying her whims just as he would the commands of his lord.

After the code of courtly love spread throughout Europe, largely through the influence of Eleanor of Aquitaine and her daughter, Marie de Champagne, it revolutionized the way people thought of love and marriage. Eventually it was transformed into the notion of a courtship ritual leading to a marriage based on love.

Literary Note

Students might be familiar with the story of the love between Lancelot and Guinevere—one example of a relationship epitomizing courtly love. If students are unfamiliar with this story, you might share it with them either in sections of Sir Thomas Malory's *Le Mort d'Arthur* or in the earlier Chrétien de Troyes's *Lancelot,* a courtly romance written at the request of Marie de Champagne.

ADDITIONAL RESOURCES

READER'S GUIDE

- Selection Worksheet 9.1

ASSESSMENT PORTFOLIO

- Selection Check Test 2.9.1
- Selection Test 2.9.2

ESSENTIAL SKILLS PRACTICE BOOKS

- Writing 1.8, 1.20

PREREADING EXTENSIONS

Ask students to brainstorm a list of quests that a contemporary hero might undertake. Students can work in groups to create a plot outline of a contemporary quest and the difficulties a hero might face.

SUPPORT FOR LEP STUDENTS

PRONUNCIATIONS OF PROPER NOUNS AND ADJECTIVES

Chré • ti • en de Troyes (krā tyan də trwå´)
Ga • wain (gə wān´)
Per • ce • val (pʉr´si vəl)

ADDITIONAL VOCABULARY

fast—firmly; fixedly
league—unit of linear measure varying in different times and different countries, sometimes equal to three miles
pommel—knob on the end of the hilt of a sword
scabbard—sheath or case to hold the blade of a sword

PREREADING

from *The Story of the Grail*
by Chrétien de Troyes, translated by William W. Kibler

About the Author

Chrétien de Troyes (c.1135–c.1190). Little is known about Chrétien de Troyes, who probably was born and lived in Troyes in the eastern Champagne region of France. A large part of his career was spent at the court of Marie de Champagne, the daughter of Eleanor of Aquitaine. (Eleanor of Aquitaine was the queen of both Louis VII of France and Henry II of England, and she was one of the most powerful women in twelfth-century Europe. She was a great patron to writers of the courtly love tradition and writers of medieval romances.) Based on his writings, Chrétien seems to have been well educated and familiar with Latin, Provençal, and Breton culture. Many of his romances are based on Breton folklore. Some of Chrétien's work, such as his version of the Tristan and Isolde story, have been lost, but stories including those of Lancelot, Perceval, and Yvain survive. Many writers have copied and adapted the works of Chrétien, who is credited with contributing to Arthurian legend the first mention of Camelot, the affair of Guinevere and Lancelot, and the first descriptions of the adventure of the Grail.

About the Selection

The Story of the Grail contained in Chrétien de Troyes's collection of Arthurian legends is incomplete, but the portion that exists deals with the quest of two knights, Perceval and Gawain, to find the Grail. In this romance, Chrétien contrasts Perceval's naive simplicity and religious dedication with Gawain's worldliness. In the beginning of the story, Perceval, a simple and inexperienced Welshman, wants to become a knight and so sets out for King Arthur's court. Before he leaves, his mother explains that his father, a knight, had been wounded by a lance. She advises Perceval against displeasing women, to assist any lady who needs his help, and never to refuse a kiss, a ring, or a purse offered him by a lady. She also tells him to learn the names of those he meets, to keep company with gentlemen, and to worship the Lord. Perceval, a character so innocent about the ways of the world that he doesn't even know his own name, tries to follow her instructions, but his actions show him to be uncouth. At the court of King Arthur, he wins the armor of a knight and sets off for adventure. He encounters a gentleman named Gornemant who instructs him in the ways of knighthood and suggests that he speak little to avoid being thought a fool. After leaving Gornemant, Perceval aids the people of a besieged village, winning the heart and hand of a lady named Blancheflor. Following this adventure, he sets off to visit his mother. It is at this point in the story that the selection begins. Here, Perceval encounters the Grail for the first time.

CONNECTIONS: The Quest for the Grail

The Grail is a symbol of perfection that has its roots in Celtic legend and symbolizes the search for God. According to Christian tradition, the Grail is the cup from which Jesus drank at the Last Supper. According to legend, Joseph of Arimathea or his descendants brought the Grail to England. One legend claims that Joseph hid the Grail near a spring in Glastonbury, England; the spring runs red because the Grail contained Jesus' blood. Many medieval romances tell stories of searches, or quests, undertaken to find the Grail. In some romances, Perceval is the knight who attains the Grail. In Thomas Malory's *Le Morte d'Arthur,* Galahad, Perceval, and Bors attain the Grail.

GOALS/OBJECTIVES

Studying this lesson will enable students to

- appreciate an excerpt from one of the most renowned medieval romances
- briefly explain the significance of the Quest for the Grail
- identify symbols and descriptions
- explain the concept of chivalry and interpret the way it is applied in a literary work
- write an advice column
- write a critical essay analyzing character
- research Arthurian legend

Have you ever seen something strange, interesting, or wondrous that you did not understand? Did you ask questions to try to gain an understanding? Did you learn about it in another way? Describe this thing or event, and explain what you know about its significance.

FROM

The Story of the Grail

CHRÉTIEN DE TROYES, TRANSLATED BY WILLIAM W. KIBLER

He continued on his way all day without meeting a living soul, neither man nor woman, who could direct him on his travels. And he prayed unceasingly to Almighty God, the heavenly Father, to permit him to find his mother alive and healthy, if it were His will. And this prayer lasted until he reached a river carving its way down a hillside. He looked at the deep and rushing waters and dared not attempt to cross.

'Ah! Almighty God,' he said, 'if I could cross this river I feel sure I'd find my mother if she's still alive.'

So he rode along the bank until he neared a large boulder sitting in the water and blocking his path. Then he caught sight of a boat drifting downriver with two men in it. He stopped and waited, thinking they would eventually come as far as where he was. But they both stopped in midstream and stayed perfectly still, for they were anchored fast. The man in front was fishing with a line, baiting his hook with a little fish, somewhat larger than a minnow.

The knight, not knowing what to do or how to cross, greeted them and inquired: 'Tell me, my lords, if there is a ford[1] or bridge across this river.'

And the one who was fishing replied: 'Not at all, brother, upon my word; nor is there a boat, I assure you, larger than the one we're in, which would not hold five men. There's no way to get a horse across, for there's no ferry, bridge, or ford for twenty leagues upstream or down.'

'Then tell me, in God's name, where I can find lodgings.'

And he replied: 'You'll need that and more, I believe. I'll give you lodging tonight. Go up through that cleft cut into the rock, and when you reach the top you'll see in a valley before you a house where I live, near the river and woods.'

The young knight climbed until he reached the top of the hill; and when he was at the top he looked all around him and saw only sky and earth, and said: 'What have I come for?

1. **ford.** Shallow place in a stream or river where one can cross

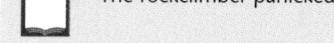

① *What does Perceval want to know from the fishermen and what do they tell him?*

② *What does Perceval first see after following the fisherman's directions?*

WORDS FOR EVERYDAY USE

cleft (kleft) *n.*, crack, crevice

VOCABULARY IN CONTEXT

• The rockclimber panicked when her foot became caught in a cleft in the rock face.

READER'S JOURNAL

As an alternative activity, you might ask students to write about a quest or journey they have undertaken or would like to take. Point out that the quest can be to visit a place, to gain something material such as a fortune, or to gain something immaterial such as wisdom, happiness, or truth.

ANSWERS TO GUIDED READING QUESTIONS

① Perceval wants to know if there is a bridge, boat, or place to ford the river. The fishermen tell him there is no way to cross the river.

② Perceval sees only sky and earth.

SPELLING AND VOCABULARY WORDS FROM THE SELECTION

admonishment	salutation
cleft	temper
don	uncouth
ordain	

CULTURAL/HISTORICAL NOTE

Point out that, according to medieval thought, chivalry and the teachings of the church were closely related. A knight was expected to be the loyal servant of not only his earthly lord but also of the Lord, or God. Tell students to bear in mind as they read this selection that by displaying perfect chivalry, a knight was showing himself to be a loyal Christian and that only the purest and most virtuous of all knights would be allowed to attain the Grail. Ask students to consider what Perceval's actions reveal not only about his knighthood but about his spiritual development. Is Perceval faithful enough to attain the Grail? At what point in the story does he seem spiritually closer to doing so?

ART NOTE

Sir Edward Coley Burne-Jones (1833–1898), one of the foremost painters of late-nineteenth-century England, produced vivid, romantic paintings, often on medieval subjects and themes. In addition to this tapestry depicting a scene from the Grail legend, Burne-Jones painted such works as *Merlin and Nemue* and *The Beguiling of Merlin.* A follower of the painter and poet Dante Gabriel Rossetti, Burne-Jones is associated with Rossetti's Pre-Raphaelite Brotherhood, which sought to return painting to an imagined purity that existed in the late Medieval Period and the early days of the Italian Renaissance. He created many designs for the famous *Kelmscott Chaucer* published by his friend and fellow artist William Morris. He also contributed to the decorative arts, creating stained glass, reliefs, and decorations for musical instruments.

Answers to Guided Reading Questions

❶ A tower and great hall appear to Perceval. He praises the fisherman when he sees the lodging that had been described to him.

Literary Technique

BILDUNGSROMAN

A ***Bildungsroman*** is a novel that tells the story of the growth or development of a person from youth to adulthood. Inform students that although the *Bildungsroman* is a form of literature that emerged many centuries after the medieval romance flourished, this romance shares some similarities with the *Bildungsroman.* In *The Story of the Grail,* Perceval grows and changes from an uncouth and ignorant young man to a chivalrous and faithful knight.

Quest for the Holy Grail. *Sir Edward Burne-Jones. Tapestry woven by Morris & Company, Birmingham City Museum and Art Gallery. Bridgeman Art Library/Art Resource, NY*

❶ *What appears to Perceval? In what way does Perceval's opinion of the fisherman change?*

Deceit and trickery! May God bring shame today on him who sent me here. He sent me on a wild goose chase when he told me I'd see a house when I came up here! Fisherman, you did me great dishonour when you told me this, if you said it out of malice!'

Then, in a valley before him, he caught sight of the top of a tower. From there to Beirut[2] you could not find a finer or better situated one. It was square in construction, of dark stone, with two turrets flanking it. The hall was in front of the keep,[3] and the galleries in front of the hall. The youth headed down in that direction, exclaiming now that the man who had sent him there had guided him well. And so he praised the fisherman and no longer called him deceitful, disloyal, or lying, since now he had found lodgings. He rode towards the gate, before which he discovered a lowered drawbridge. He crossed over the bridge and four squires hastened towards him: two of them helped him remove his armour, the third took charge of his horse and gave it hay and oats, while the fourth robed him in a fresh, new mantle[4] of scarlet. Then they took him towards the galleries, which I assure you were more splendid than any that could be sought out or seen from here to Limoges.[5] The youth waited in the galleries until the lord of the castle sent two squires there to summon him, and he accompanied them into the great hall, which was square in shape—as long as it was wide.

In the middle of the hall he saw a handsome nobleman with graying hair seated upon a bed. His head was covered by a cap of sable[6]—black as mulberry, with a purple peak—and his robe was of the same material. He was leaning on his elbow before a very large fire of dry logs, blazing brightly between four columns. Four hundred men could easily sit around that fire, and each would have a comfortable spot. A tall, thick, broad, brass chimney was supported by those strong columns. The two squires who

2. **Beirut.** Today, the capital of Lebanon
3. **keep.** Stronghold, fort, or castle
4. **mantle.** Loose, sleeveless cloak or cape
5. **Limoges.** City in France
6. **sable.** Dark type of fur

were escorting his guest came before their lord, flanking him on either side.

When the lord saw him approaching he greeted him at once, saying: 'Friend, don't be offended if I don't rise to greet you, for it is not easy for me to do so.'

'In God's name, sire' he replied, 'say no more, for I am not at all offended, as God gives me health and happiness.'

To do his guest honour, the gentleman rose as much as he was able, and said: 'Friend, come over here and don't be frightened of me; sit down confidently at my side, for so I command you.' The youth sat down beside him and the nobleman continued: 'Friend, where did you come from today?'

'Sire,' he said, 'this morning I left Biaurepaire, so the place is called.'

'So help me God,' said the nobleman, 'you've ridden a great distance today. You must have set off this morning before the watchman sounded the dawn.'

'No,' said the youth, 'I assure you that the hour of prime[7] had already been sounded.'

As they were conversing in this way, a squire entered by the door. He was carrying a sword hanging by straps from his neck; he handed it to the noble lord, who unsheathed it halfway so that it could clearly be seen where it had been made, for it was engraved upon the blade. He also saw that it was made of such good steel that it could not be broken except in one singularly perilous circumstance known only to him who had forged and tempered it.

The squire who had brought it said: 'Sire, your niece, the beautiful maiden with the blonde tresses, sent you this gift; you can never have beheld a finer sword, in its length and weight, than this one here. You may bestow it upon whomsoever you choose; but my lady would be most pleased if it were given to someone who would use it well, for the man who forged it made only three and he will die before being able to make another sword after this one.'

Immediately, the lord invested the stranger among them with the sword by placing its straps, a great treasure in themselves, over his shoulders. The sword's pommel was of gold, the finest in Arabia or Greece; its scabbard was the work of a Venetian goldsmith. The lord gave it to him in all its splendour and said: 'Good brother, this sword was ordained and destined for you, and I am eager for you to have it. Put it on now and draw it.'

He thanked him and strapped it on loosely, then drew it shining from its scabbard; after he had held it for a moment he replaced it in its scabbard. I assure you it was magnificent at his side and even better in his grip, and it was obvious that in time of need he would wield it bravely. Behind him he saw squires standing around the blazing fire: he caught sight of the one in charge of his armour and handed him the sword to keep. Then he sat down again beside the lord, who paid him every honour. Within that hall the light from the burning candles was as bright as could be found in any castle.

As they were speaking of one thing and another, a squire came forth from a chamber carrying a white lance by the middle of its shaft; he passed between the fire and those seated upon the bed. Everyone in the hall saw the white lance with its white point from whose tip there issued a drop of blood, and this red drop flowed down to the squire's hand. The youth who had come there that night observed this marvel but refrained from asking how it came about, for he recalled the admonishment given by the gentleman who had knighted him, who

7. **prime.** First of the canonical hours, usually sunrise or 6 A.M.

❶ *What greeting does the lord of the castle offer Perceval? What is the lord unable to do?*

❷ *What is impressive about the sword the squire brings into the room? What does the squire say the lord may do with this sword?*

❸ *What does Perceval notice about the lance that is carried through the room? Why doesn't he ask about this strange occurrence?*

WORDS FOR EVERYDAY USE

tem • per (tem´pər) *vt.,* bring to proper texture, consistency, or hardness

or • dain (ôr dān´) *vi.,* predetermine, predestine

ad • mon • ish • ment (ad män´ish mənt) *n.,* warning

ANSWERS TO GUIDED READING QUESTIONS

❶ The gentleman addresses Perceval as "friend," apologizes for not rising, and asks Perceval to sit near him. The lord is unable to stand unaided.

❷ The sword is made of fine steel that cannot be broken except in a way known only to the man who forged it. It is of fine length and weight and is meant to be given to someone who will use it well. The lord bestows this sword upon Perceval.

❸ Perceval notices that a drop of blood issues from the tip of the lance. He does not ask about this occurrence because he had been counseled not to ask so many questions for fear of being thought uncouth.

CULTURAL/HISTORICAL NOTE

If you have a number of Christian students in your class, encourage them to explain the significance of the lance that drips blood. If you do not have students who can explain the significance of the lance Perceval sees, tell them that the lance that drips blood refers to the one used to pierce Jesus' side during the crucifixion.

QUOTABLES

"But when they came to Jesus, and saw that he was dead already, they brake not his legs:

But one of the soldiers with a spear pierced his side, and forthwith came there out blood and water."

—John 19:33–34

VOCABULARY IN CONTEXT

- Part of the blacksmith's art was knowing how to temper the iron until it reached a perfect state.
- Stephen, the French shepherd boy who led the Children's Crusade, believed that he was ordained to win the Holy Land from the Muslims through love rather than force.
- The young prince was filled with foolish boldness, so he ignored his tutor's admonishment not to attempt swordplay until he was better instructed in the art.

Answers to Guided Reading Questions

1. The maiden carries a grail.

2. Perceval would like to know who is served from the Grail. He does not ask because he remembers Gornemant's advice about asking too many questions. The narrator comments that at times it is just as wrong to speak too little as it is to speak too much.

3. The Grail is carried past them several times, and Perceval sees it completely uncovered. He resolves to ask one of the squires about it before he leaves.

ANALYTIC SCALES FOR RESPONDING IN WRITING

(SEE PAGE 731.)

Assign a score from 1 to 25 for each grading criterion below. (For more detailed evaluation, see the evaluation forms for writing, revising, and proofreading, Assessment Portfolio 4.1–4.9.)

1. Advice Column

- **Content/Unity.** The advice column contains a letter from Perceval explaining his predicament and an appropriate response.
- **Organization/Coherence.** Perceval's letter is followed by a response. Both letters are written in a sensible order.
- **Language/Style.** The advice column uses vivid and precise nouns, verbs, and modifiers.
- **Conventions.** The advice column avoids errors in spelling, grammar, usage, mechanics, and manuscript form.

▶ Additional practice is provided in the Essential Skills Practice Book: Writing 1.8.

taught and instructed him not to talk too much; he was afraid that if he asked they would consider him uncouth, and therefore he did not ask.

Then two other squires entered holding in their hands candelabra[8] of pure gold, crafted with enamel inlays. The young men carrying the candelabra were extremely handsome. In each of the candelabra there were at least ten candles burning. A maiden accompanying the two young men was carrying a grail with her two hands; she was beautiful, noble, and richly attired. After she had entered the hall carrying the grail the room was so brightly illumined that the candles lost their brilliance like stars and the moon when the sun rises. After her came another maiden, carrying a silver carving platter. The grail, which was introduced first, was of fine pure gold. Set in the grail were precious stones of many kinds, the best and costliest to be found in earth or sea: the grail's stones were finer than any others in the world, without any doubt. The grail passed by like the lance; they passed in front of the bed and into another chamber. The young knight watched them pass by but did not dare ask who was served from the grail, for in his heart he always held the wise gentleman's advice. Yet I fear that this may be to his misfortune, for I have heard it said that at times it is just as wrong to keep too silent as to talk too much. Whether for good or for ill he did not ask or inquire anything of them.

1. What does the maiden carry through the room?

2. What would Perceval like to ask about the Grail? Why does he refrain from asking? What comment does the narrator make about Perceval's silence?

3. What happens while Perceval and the lord are eating? Why does Perceval keep silent? What does he resolve to do?

The lord of the castle ordered his squire to bring water and to prepare the tablecloths. Those whose duty it was did these things as they were accustomed. The lord and his young guest washed their hands in warm water, and two squires carried in a broad ivory table: as the story relates, it was entirely made of a single piece. They held it a moment before their lord and the youth, until two other squires came bearing two trestles.[9] The wood of the supports had two excellent qualities: the trestles would last for ever since they were of ebony, a wood that no one need fear would ever rot or burn, for ebony will do neither. The table was placed upon these supports, with the tablecloth over it. What could I say about the cloth? No pope, cardinal, or papal legate ever ate off one so white.

The first course was a haunch of venison cooked in its fat with hot pepper. They were not short of clear, strong wine, which could be drunk easily from golden goblets. Before them a squire carved the haunch of peppered venison, which he had brought within his reach upon its silver carving platter, and he placed the pieces before them on whole loaves of flat bread. Meanwhile the grail passed again in front of them, and again the youth did not ask who was served from the grail. He held back because the gentleman had so gently admonished him not to talk too much, and he kept this warning constantly to heart. But he kept more silent than he should have, because with each course that was served he saw the grail pass by completely uncovered before him. But he did not learn who was served from it, though he wanted to know; he said to himself that he would be sure to ask one of the court squires before he left there, but would wait until he was taking leave of the lord and all the rest of his household in the morning. So the question was put off, and he set his mind to drinking and eating. The wine and food were delicious and agreeable, and were served at table in generous portions. The

8. **candelabra.** Large, branched candlestick holders
9. **trestles.** Wooden structures used for support

Words for Everyday Use

un • couth (un ko͞oth´) *adj.,* uncultured, crude

Vocabulary in Context

- Knights usually scorned members of the peasantry, considering their behavior to be uncouth.

meal was excellent and good: the nobleman was served that evening with food fit for a king, count or emperor, and the young knight with him.

After the meal the two stayed a long while in conversation. As squires were preparing the beds, baskets of all the finest fruits were served them: dates, figs and nutmeg, cloves and pomegranates, and electuaries for dessert, with Alexandrian gingerbread, pliris and arcoticum, resontif and stomaticum.[10] Afterwards they drank many a drink, sweet wine without honey or pepper, good mulberry wine, and clear syrup.

The youth was astonished by all this, for he had never experienced anything like it; and the nobleman said to him: 'Friend, now it is time for bed. Don't be offended if I leave you and go into my own chambers to sleep; and whenever you are ready you may lie down out here. I have no strength in my body and will have to be carried.'

Four strong and nimble servants promptly came out from a chamber, seized by its four corners the coverlet that was spread over the bed on which the nobleman was lying, and carried it to where they were ordered. Other squires remained with the youth to serve him, and saw to his every need. When he requested, they removed his shoes and clothing and bedded him down in fine, white, linen sheets.

And he slept until morning, when dawn had broken and the household was awake. But he saw no one there when he looked around and so he had to get up alone, although it bothered him to do so. Seeing he had no choice he arose, for there was nothing else to do, and pulled on his shoes without help; then he went to <u>don</u> his armour, which he found at the head of the dais,[11] where it had been left for him. After having armed himself fully, he approached the doors of chambers he had observed open the night before; but his steps were wasted, for he found them tightly closed. He shouted and knocked for a long while: no one opened them or gave a word in reply. After having shouted a long while, he tried the door to the great hall; finding it open, he went down the steps, where he discovered his horse saddled and saw his lance and shield leaning against the wall. He mounted and rode all around, but he found none of the servants and saw no squire or serving boy. So he went straight to the gate and found the drawbridge lowered; it had been left like that so that nothing might prevent him from traversing it unimpeded whenever he came there. When he found the bridge lowered, he thought that perhaps the squires had gone into the forest to check the traps and snares. He made up his mind to set off at once in pursuit, to see whether any of them would explain to him why the lance bled (if it were possible for him to know) and tell him to where the grail was carried.

Then he rode off through the gate, but before he had crossed the bridge he felt it drawing up under the hooves of his horse; but the horse made a great leap, and if he had not done so both horse and rider would have come to grief. The youth turned around to see what had happened and saw that the drawbridge had been raised; he shouted out, but no one answered.

'Say there,' he said, 'whoever raised the bridge, speak to me! Where are you that I can't see you? Come forward where I can see you and ask you about something I want to know.'

❶ *What does Perceval set out to find? What happens when Perceval is leaving the castle?*

❷ *What is surprising about the household to which Perceval awakes in the morning?*

10. **electuaries . . . stomaticum.** A list of exotic delicacies; the unusual names of these delicacies vary in different manuscripts.

11. **dais.** Platform raised above the flood at one end of the hall or room, as for a throne

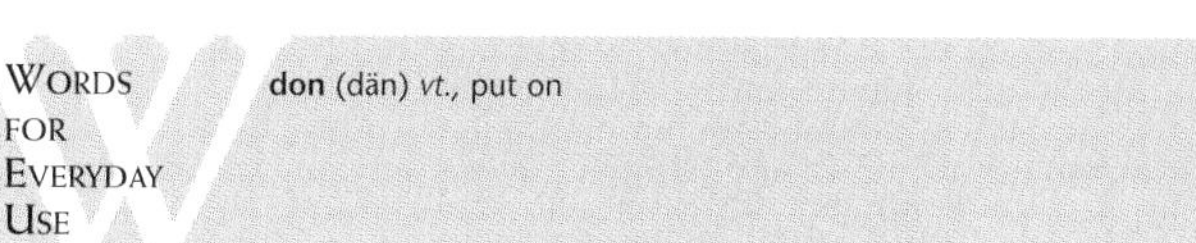

Words for Everyday Use

don (dän) *vt.,* put on

Answers to Guided Reading Questions

❶ Perceval sets off to find the squires to ask them about the lance and the Grail. The drawbridge suddenly raises as Perceval is crossing it on horseback.

❷ There are no servants to aid him. The building seems to be deserted.

ANALYTIC SCALES FOR RESPONDING IN WRITING

(SEE PAGE 731.)

2. Critical Essay

- **Content/Unity.** The essay analyzes Perceval's character and the way in which it affects his quest.
- **Organization/Coherence.** The essay begins with an introduction that includes the thesis of the essay. The introduction is followed by supporting paragraphs with clear transitions. The essay ends with a solid conclusion.
- **Language/Style.** The essay uses vivid and precise nouns, verbs, and modifiers.
- **Conventions.** The essay avoids errors in spelling, grammar, usage, mechanics, and manuscript form.

▶ Additional practice is provided in the Essential Skills Practice Book: Writing 1.20.

Vocabulary in Context

- The knight was in too much of a hurry to <u>don</u> his heavy armor before setting off to rescue the imprisoned damsel.

Answers to Guided Reading Questions

1. The maiden explains that the Fisher King had been struck through the thighs with a javelin. He fishes to ease his pain and to relax, thus earning the name of the Fisher King.

2. The lady is surprised to see Perceval looking so fresh because there is no lodging in the direction from which he came for more than twenty-five leagues.

Quotables

"And Jesus, walking by the sea of Galilee, saw two brethren, Simon called Peter, and Andrew his brother, casting a net into the sea: for they were fishers.

And he saith unto them, Follow me, and I will make you fishers of men."

—Matthew 4:18–19

Literary Technique

Ambiguity

An **ambiguity** is a statement that has a double meaning or a meaning that cannot be clearly resolved. Inform students that much of this section of *The Story of the Grail* is intentionally ambiguous. Chrétien hopes to make the reader share in Perceval's confusion, which represents all mortals' confusion and ignorance when compared to divine wisdom. Point out, for example, that Perceval's mother tells him that his father was wounded by a lance. The Fisher King thus may represent Perceval's long-lost father. However, as Christ was also wounded with a lance and because he referred to his followers and himself as "fishers of men," the Fisher King may also represent Perceval's heavenly father, or he may represent a Jesus-figure. Encourage students to discuss how they interpret the Fisher King.

But he made a fool of himself shouting like this, for no one would reply. Then he headed for the forest and found a path on which he discovered fresh hoofprints of horses that recently had passed by.

'This makes me think,' he said to himself, 'that those I'm seeking passed this way.'

He rode swiftly through the forest following the tracks as far as they went, until he saw by chance beneath an oak tree a maiden crying, weeping, and lamenting, as though she were a woman in great distress. 'Wretched me!' she exclaimed. 'I was born in an evil hour! Cursed be the hour I was begotten and the day I was born, for I've never before been made so miserable by anything! So help me God, I shouldn't have to hold my dead lover in my arms; it would have been far better if he were alive and I were dead! Why did Death, which tortures me, take his soul instead of mine? When I behold lying dead the one I most love what is life to me? With him dead, indeed I have no interest in my life or body. So come, Death, and take my soul and let it be a servant and companion to his, if he'll deign to accept it.'

1 What does the maiden explain to Perceval about the Fisher King?

Her grief was caused by a knight she held in her arms, whose head had been cut off. The youth, after catching sight of her, rode right up to where she sat. As he came before her he greeted her and she, with head still lowered and without ceasing her lament, returned his salutation.

And the youth asked her: 'My lady, who has slain this knight lying in your lap?'

2 Why is the lady surprised by the appearance of Perceval?

'Good sir,' said the maiden, 'a knight killed him just this morning. But your appearing here is truly remarkable: as God is my witness, they say that one could ride for twenty-five leagues in the direction from which you have come without finding a good, honest, and proper lodging place. Yet your horse's belly is so full and his coat so shining that he couldn't appear more satisfied or his coat smoother had he been washed and combed and given a bed of hay and oats. And it appears to me that you yourself have had a comfortable and restful night.'

'Upon my word,' he said, 'I was as comfortable as I could possibly be, and it's only right that it should show. If you were to shout out loudly from this spot, it could easily be heard at the place where I slept last night. You must not know this country well or have travelled through all of it, for without a doubt I had the best lodgings I've ever enjoyed.'

'Ah, my lord! Did you sleep then in the castle of the noble Fisher King?'

'Maiden, by our Lord and Saviour, I don't know if he is a fisherman or a king, but he is most noble and courteous. All I can tell you is that late last night I came upon two men, sitting in a boat rowing slowly along. One of the men was rowing while the other was fishing with a hook, and this latter showed me the way to his house last night and gave me lodging.'

And the maiden said: 'Good sir, I can assure you that he is a king, but he was wounded and maimed in the course of a battle so that he can no longer manage on his own, for he was struck by a javelin through both thighs and is still in so much pain that he cannot ride a horse. Whenever he wants to relax or to go out to enjoy himself, he has himself put in a boat and goes fishing with a hook: this is why he's called the Fisher King. And he relaxes in this way because he cannot tolerate the pain of any other diversion: he cannot hunt for flesh or fowl, but he has hunters, archers, and gamesmen who hunt his forests for him. That is why he likes to stay in this hidden retreat, for there's no retreat in the world more suited to his needs, and he has had a mansion built that is worthy of a noble king.'

Words for Everyday Use

sal • u • ta • tion (sal´yo͞o tā´shən) *n.*, act of greeting or welcoming

Vocabulary in Context

• The king's cheerful salutation made the knight immediately feel welcome in the hall.

'My lady,' he said, 'what you say is true, upon my word, for I was in awe last night as soon as I was brought before him. I kept back a little distance from him, and he told me to be seated beside him and not to consider him too proud for not rising to greet me, since he didn't have the means or strength. And I went to sit beside him.'

'Indeed he did you a great honour by having you sit beside him. And as you were sitting beside him, tell me whether you saw the lance with the tip that bleeds, though it has neither blood nor veins.'

'Yes, upon my word, I did see it!'

'And did you ask why it bled?'

'I never spoke a word.'

'So help me God, let me tell you then that you have done ill. And did you see the grail?'

'Quite clearly.'

'Who carried it?'

'A maiden.'

'Where did she come from?'

'From a chamber.'

'And where did she go?'

'She entered another chamber.'

'Did anyone precede the grail?'

'Yes.'

'Who?'

'Only two squires.'

'And what were they holding in their hands?'

'Candelabra full of candles.'

'And who came after the grail?'

'Another maiden.'

'What was she holding?'

'A small silver carving platter.'

'Did you ask the people where they were going in this manner?'

'No question came from my mouth.'

'So help me God, now it's even worse! What is your name, friend?'

And the youth, who did not know his name, guessed and said he was called Perceval the Welshman. But although he did not know if that were true or not, he spoke the truth without knowing it. And when the damsel heard him, she stood up before him and said as in anger: 'Your name is changed, fair friend!'

The Quest for the Holy Grail. Tapestry. Birmingham City Museums, Birmingham, Great Britain. Bridgeman Art Library/Art Resource, NY

'To what?'

'Perceval the wretched! Ah, unlucky Perceval, how unfortunate you were when you failed to ask all this, because you would have brought great succour[12] to the good king who is maimed: he would have totally regained the use of his limbs and ruled his lands, and much good would have come of it! But understand this now: much suffering will befall you and others. And understand, too, that it came upon you because you sinned against your mother, who has died of grief on your account. I know you better than you do me, for you do not know who I am. I was raised with you for many years in your mother's house; I am your first cousin and you are mine. Your failure to have asked what is done with the grail and where it is carried is just as painful to me as your mother's death or the death of this knight whom I loved and held dear, who called me his dearest friend and loved me like a good and faithful knight.' ■

1 *Why is Perceval's failure to question the wondrous things he observed such a wretched thing? What does Perceval learn about his mother?*

2 *About what does the youth have to guess? Why is this lack of knowledge unusual?*

12. **succour.** Aid, help, relief

ART NOTE

Tapestries are luxurious woven fabrics used to cover furniture, walls, or floors. To make a tapestry a weaver and a designer must work closely together, and the final design emerges only after arduous work by the weaver. Tapestries flourished as an art form during the Medieval Period but began declining soon after the Renaissance. They found renewed favor in nineteenth-century England, particularly among Pre-Raphaelite artists such as Burne-Jones.

ANSWERS TO GUIDED READING QUESTIONS

1 By asking about the lance and the Grail, Perceval could have freed the Fisher King from his misery. He learns that his mother has died of grief because of him.

2 The youth has to guess his name. Such complete ignorance is highly unusual.

SELECTION CHECK TEST WITH ANSWERS

EX. Who does Perceval ask for lodging?
He asks a fisherman.

1. What does the lord of the house ask Perceval to forgive?
He asks Perceval to forgive him for not rising.

2. What does the lord give to Perceval?
He gives him a mighty sword.

3. What unusual thing does Perceval notice about the lance?
The lance drips with blood.

4. Why does Perceval refrain from asking about the lance and the Grail?
He remembers the advice he has been given and is afraid of being thought a fool.

5. What does the maiden he encounters in the woods call Perceval?
She calls him Perceval the wretched.

ADDITIONAL QUESTIONS AND ACTIVITIES

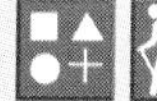

Divide the rest of Chrétien's *The Story of the Grail* into sections for groups of students to read. Each group should then present an oral report on their assigned section to the rest of the class. The group should present a brief summary and a visual representation of part of their section, or they might choose to enact it as a drama. If students' presentations are given in the order the story follows, the class will then gain a good sense of *The Story of the Grail* as a whole.

RESPONDING TO THE SELECTION

The narrator of this selection says, "At times it is just as wrong to keep too silent as to talk too much." As an alternate activity, encourage students to discuss this statement, giving examples of when it is wrong to keep silent and when it is wrong to talk too much.

ANSWERS FOR REVIEWING THE SELECTION

RECALLING AND INTERPRETING

1. **Recalling.** Perceval asks for a way to cross the river; barring that, he asks for lodging. The man in the boat gives him directions to his house. Perceval at first sees only land and sky; then he sees a tower. **Interpreting.** The house appears suddenly and is located in what seems to be an uninhabited area.

2. **Recalling.** The lance drips blood. Perceval remembers the advice he had been given about asking too many questions and remains silent. **Interpreting.** *Responses will vary.* Perceval is carrying the advice too far by not asking any questions when the situation demands it.

3. **Recalling.** Perceval wants to know who is being served from the Grail. He plans to ask one of the squires in the morning. **Interpreting.** Perceval does not want to be thought stupid, so he plans to ask one of the squires rather than posing his question in front of the whole assembled party. Despite his curiosity, Perceval is trying to follow the advice he has been given.

4. **Recalling.** Perceval is unable to ask his question because the house is deserted. He learns that he should have asked the questions, since in doing so he would have freed the Fisher King. **Interpreting.** The maiden reveals

(cont.)

Responding to the Selection

Upon hearing what the maiden has to say, how would you feel if you were Perceval? What do you think Perceval will do in response to this news?

Reviewing the Selection

RECALLING		INTERPRETING
1. What does Perceval ask of the men in the boat? Where does the man in the boat tell him to go? What does Perceval see after following the man's directions?	▶▶	What is strange about the house to which the man directs Perceval?
2. What is unusual about the lance that is carried through the room? Why doesn't Perceval ask any questions about this lance?	▶▶	Do you think Perceval is right to contain his curiosity? Explain.
3. What question does Perceval have about the Grail? How does he plan to have his question answered?	▶▶	Why does Perceval wait to ask his question? Is his plan in accordance with the advice he has been given?
4. Why was Perceval unable to ask his question about the Grail the next morning? What does he learn from the crying maiden about his experience at the home of the Fisher King?	▶▶	Why is it necessary to the story for Perceval to encounter the maiden in the wood? The maiden calls him Perceval the wretched for his failure to help the king. Do you think this failure is his fault? Explain.

SYNTHESIZING

5. Describe the perfect knight. What knightly qualities does Perceval possess? In what ways is he atypical of the perfect knight?

Understanding Literature (Questions for Discussion)

1. **Symbol.** A **symbol** is a thing that stands for or represents both itself and something else. What does the Grail represent? Of what importance is Perceval's failure to ask about the Grail and the lance? What might Perceval's failure to ask the right questions symbolize? Of what might Perceval's quest for the Grail be a symbol?

ANSWERS FOR REVIEWING THE SELECTION (CONT.)

to Perceval the importance of the events of the previous night. Students may say that Perceval is to blame for not trusting his instincts or for misinterpreting the advice he has been given. Others may say that Perceval was following a celebrated code of behavior and should therefore not be blamed for keeping silent.

SYNTHESIZING

Responses will vary. Possible responses are given.

5. The perfect knight is brave, courageous, courteous, honest, faithful, and gentle. He is loyal to his liege lord or lady. Perceval has acquired the outfit of a knight, and he is honest and brave. He is not polished and often does not display the manners of a knight.

2. **Description.** A **description**, one of the modes of writing, portrays a character, an object, or a scene. Descriptions make use of sensory details—words and phrases that describe how things look, sound, smell, taste, or feel. What details are used in the descriptions of the Grail procession and the meal served at the Fisher King's home?

3. **Chivalry. Chivalry** was the code of conduct of the medieval knight. The word derives from the French *cheval,* for "horse," indicating the importance of this animal to the knight who typically traveled and fought on horseback. According to this code, a knight was to be a loyal servant to his lord or lady and a perfect exemplar of such virtues as bravery, courage, courtesy, honesty, faith, and gentleness. Does the Fisher King embody the code of chivalry? Explain why, or why not. In what way does Perceval fail the code of chivalry in this episode? What qualities does he show he is lacking? What is the significance of the drawbridge raising upon Perceval's horse? Why might Perceval's knighthood be questioned or threatened? What is the significance of his failure to help the Fisher King?

Responding in Writing

1. **Creative Writing: Advice Column**. Perceval has been following advice from his mother and from Gornemant. Write a letter from Perceval to an advice columnist in which he explains the advice he has been given, his attempts to follow it in the case of the Grail, and the unhappy outcome of this matter. Conclude by asking what he should do now. Then write a response suggesting what Perceval might do to mend the matter at hand and counseling him on applying advice to different situations.

2. **Critical Essay: Analyzing Character**. One of the defining characteristics of Perceval is his exaggerated uncouthness or naiveté. Write an essay in which you discuss Perceval's character and how it affects his quest. In your essay, first describe Perceval's character using the text to support your description. Then discuss the impact of Perceval's character upon the search for the Grail. In what way might his character allow him to succeed in his quest? In what way might it hinder him?

Project

Arthurian Legend. Chrétien de Troyes's Arthurian romances are only one of the many versions of the Arthurian tales written over the ages. Find other sources of these tales, such as Thomas Malory's *Le Morte d'Arthur;* Alfred, Lord Tennyson's *The Idylls of the King;* T. H. White's *The Once and Future King;* and Marion Zimmer Bradley's *The Mists of Avalon.* You may choose to search specifically for stories about Perceval or the quest for the Grail, or you may choose to explore the adventures of other knights. There are also many modern versions of the Grail legend; you might choose to research how this legend continues to be retold. Work in small groups to prepare a presentation or display of the Arthurian tales you have read. You might adapt one tale for a dramatic presentation, or you might write your own Arthurian adventure.

Answers for Understanding Literature

Responses will vary. Possible responses are given.

1. Symbol. The Grail symbolizes Jesus's death and the attainment of perfection. Perceval's asking about the Grail would signify his understanding that the Grail is important without understanding completely the mysteries it contains. His failure to ask these questions suggests that he is not firm in his readiness to seek the Grail. The search for the Grail might represent a spiritual journey to become the perfect Christian.

2. Description. The hall is very bright; the lance is white. The red blood runs down the squire's hand. The candelabra carried by the handsome squires are of pure gold. The maiden carrying the Grail is beautiful, noble, and richly attired. She overshadows the brilliance of the candles as the sun overshadows the light of the moon and stars. The Grail is pure gold set with many costly, fine stones. The table is broad and made of a single piece of ivory with ebony supports. The meal consists of peppery venison, clear, strong wine, and flat bread.

3. Chivalry. The Fisher King embodies chivalry because he is a man of faith and he is courteous and hospitable to his guests. Perceval reveals that he does not yet have enough faith to attain the Grail, and he fails to be courageous enough to pose the questions that would heal the Fisher King. The drawbridge raising shows that Perceval's knighthood is being questioned, since without a horse he cannot be considered a knight. Perceval is not yet a perfect knight—he has much to learn about chivalry.

Project Notes

See the evaluation form for projects, Assessment Portfolio 4.12.

Arthurian Legend. As an alternate activity, you may choose to give students different episodes or figures from Arthurian legend to research. For example, groups might research any of the following topics: Arthur's birth, how Arthur was crowned king, the story of Tristan and Isolde, the marriage of Arthur and Guinevere, the love of Lancelot and Guinevere, the attainment of the Grail, the final battle with Mordred, the death of Arthur, or any of the other numerous stories considered part of Arthurian legend.

Analytic Scales for Responding in Writing

Grading scales for Responding in Writing appear on pages 726 and 727.

ADDITIONAL RESOURCES

READER'S GUIDE

- Selection Worksheet 9.2

ASSESSMENT PORTFOLIO

- Selection Check Test 2.9.3
- Selection Test 2.9.4

ESSENTIAL SKILLS PRACTICE BOOKS

- Writing 1.8, 1.20
- Language 2.26

PREREADING EXTENSIONS

Have students research other versions of the Tristan and Isolde story. Some suggestions of other versions of the story appear in the Connections box on page 732. Another source is the lays of Marie de France. Before students begin their research, they should note that Tristan is sometimes called Tristram, and Isolde is sometimes called Iseut or Isolt. Students might seek other literary versions of the story, musical compositions, or works of visual art. Have students discuss the differences in the works they study.

SUPPORT FOR LEP STUDENTS

PRONUNCIATIONS OF PROPER NOUNS AND ADJECTIVES

Bran • gane (bran gān´)
Gott • fried von Strass • burg (got´frēd von stras´bu̵rg)
Gur • mun (gu̵r´mən)
I • sol • de (i sōl´də)
Tris • tan (tris´tən)

ADDITIONAL VOCABULARY

endowed—provided with some quality
nuptial—having to do with a wedding or marriage
procured—obtained, gotten
prudent—wise
purged—cleansed, emptied
succumbing—giving in to something

PREREADING

from *Tristan*

by Gottfried von Strassburg, translated by A. T. Hatto

About the Author

Gottfried von Strassburg (c. 1210). Little is known about German medieval poet Gottfried von Strassburg. Although the dates of his birth and death are uncertain, he probably wrote *Tristan* around 1210. Most likely, Gottfried was not a member of the nobility but lived among the upper classes in the city of Strassburg. His writing reveals that he had been well educated, probably in monastic schools, and that he read widely in German, French, and Latin. *Tristan* also indicates that Gottfried had once been deeply in love and that he enjoyed hunting and music. Although Gottfried never finished *Tristan,* he tells the traditional tale of Tristan and Isolde's love so masterfully and with such poetic skill that he is considered one of the greatest of medieval German poets.

About the Selection

Tristan is both an epic poem and an example of a **medieval romance**, or a story about the adventures of knights and the love between a knight and a lady. The romance centers on the love between a hero named Tristan and a queen named Isolde, who is married to Tristan's uncle, King Mark. Stories about Tristan and Isolde were originally part of Celtic legend. They later became part of the French romantic tradition, and from there the story spread to Germany. Gottfried's source for the poem was the work of a twelfth-century poet named Thomas who was from either Brittany or Great Britain. Conveniently, the surviving fragment of Thomas's work begins where Gottfried's telling of the story leaves off.

Originally, the story of Tristan and Isolde was a crude tale of violence, adultery, and betrayal, and romancers took a very moralistic and disapproving tone with the subject matter. Thomas took a less disapproving tone than most; however, Gottfried completely transformed the tale into an eloquent story of the way in which true courtly love can transcend conventional ethics. Gottfried intended his story to serve as an example for courtiers of perfect and loyal love. While Gottfried wrote *Tristan* in short rhyming couplets, the following selection is a prose translation.

CONNECTIONS: The Popularity of Tristan and Isolde's Story

The story of Tristan and Isolde's forbidden love inspired countless storytellers in the Medieval Period. This story, however, has intrigued a number of more contemporary artists. The German composer Richard Wagner created the opera *Tristan und Isolde,* first performed in 1865, based on Gottfried's telling of the tale. The British poet Alfred, Lord Tennyson also retold this story, basing his verse on Sir Thomas Malory's *Le Morte d'Arthur.* Matthew Arnold is another British poet who was intrigued by the tale, publishing his poem "Tristan and Iseult" in 1852.

GOALS/OBJECTIVES

Studying this lesson will enable students to

- interpret and appreciate a medieval romance
- recognize Gottfried von Strassburg's version as one of many stories of Tristan and Isolde
- define *courtly love, chivalry,* and *metaphor*
- identify and understand a metaphor
- recognize the role of courtly love and chivalry in the selection
- write a continuation
- analyze the portrayal of love in the selection
- edit sentences to reduce wordiness

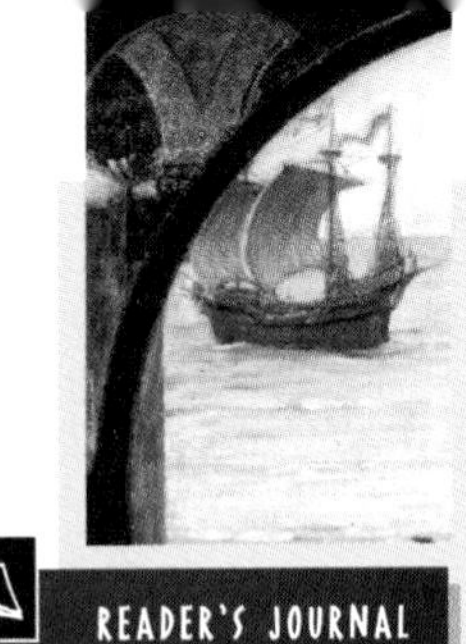

READER'S JOURNAL

Write in your journal about a time when you felt an emotion so strong that you could not control or hide it. What was this emotion, and why did you think you had to control or hide it? What happened when you finally revealed your feelings?

FROM

Tristan

GOTTFRIED VON STRASSBURG, TRANSLATED BY A. T. HATTO

[Editor's note: Tristan, the hero of the romance, is the nephew of Mark, king of England and Cornwall. Gurmun, king of Ireland, sends his brother-in-law, an Irish duke named Morold, to demand money from King Mark. Tristan challenges Morold to combat and kills him, but in the battle he receives a terrible, festering wound that doctors cannot cure. Tristan has heard that Morold's sister, Queen Isolde of Ireland, is a great healer, so he sails to Ireland. Disguised as a court minstrel named Tantris, Tristan meets and is cured by Queen Isolde. He meets her beautiful daughter, also named Isolde, and becomes her tutor. When he returns to England, Tristan tells his uncle Mark about young Isolde. King Mark decides to marry her, so Tristan returns to Ireland to gain the princess as Mark's bride. A dragon has been plaguing the Irish countryside, and King Gurmun has declared that whoever slays the dragon will be allowed to marry the princess. Tristan slays the dragon and cuts off its tongue; however, the tongue of the dragon emits fumes that leave Tristan in a death-like stupor. Meanwhile, a cowardly steward who is in love with Isolde finds the dead dragon, cuts off its head, and attempts to claim the princess as his bride. The two Isoldes find Tristan and the dragon's tongue, and once again, the elder Isolde heals Tristan. Working together, Gurmun, Tristan, and the two Isoldes shame the steward into agreeing to a duel in the near future with Tristan. When young Isolde discovers that the person she knows as Tantris is really Tristan, killer of her uncle Morold, she decides to slay him in his bath. Through her mother's intercession and her own "tender womanliness," Isolde is unable to kill Tristan. Tristan declares that he has come to arrange the princess's marriage to powerful King Mark. By showing the dragon's tongue, Tristan proves to all the Irish nobles that it was he who killed the dragon, and the steward tells Tristan to arm himself for battle. The cowardly steward, however, is too afraid to fight Tristan and drops all claims to Princess Isolde.]

READER'S JOURNAL

Ask students if they think that people have a responsibility to control their emotions. Are there ways of expressing emotion that are inappropriate? If so, what are they? Are these emotions inappropriate at all times or only in certain situations? Students can also discuss unconventional ways of expressing certain emotions.

SPELLING AND VOCABULARY WORDS FROM THE SELECTION

abiding	limpid
assail	pang
burgeon	rapaciously
console	ratify
covertly	stipulate
enmity	variance
guile	vassal
jubilation	vial

LITERARY NOTE

For many centuries, marriages in Western countries were based on political or economic value rather than on love. It is not strange that Isolde is being married to Mark of England although she has never met him. Point out that throughout literature women of high status—queens and princesses—were often offered as prizes. For example, Oedipus's marriage to Jocasta was a reward for freeing Thebes from the plague of the Sphinx. Ask students to discuss this practice. What does such a practice suggest about a given culture's attitudes toward women and marriage?

Answers to Guided Reading Questions

❶ The elder Isolde is brewing a powerful love potion.

❷ The elder Isolde tells Brangane to take the potion and to give it to Isolde and Mark once they have been married. She warns Brangane to make sure that no one else drinks the potion.

❸ Isolde hates Tristan.

INTEGRATED SKILLS ACTIVITIES

READING SKILLS

In addition to answering the Guided Reading Questions and the Responding to the Selection questions, responding to the following prompts will help students to read this selection actively:

- Predict what will happen as a result of the love potion Isolde gives to Brangane.
- Write down your feelings toward the two Isoldes and toward Tristan at this point in the story.
- Describe the relationship between Queen Isolde and Brangane and identify material in the story that supports your beliefs.
- Summarize what has happened so far in the selection.

As you read, continue to predict and see if your predictions are correct. If your feelings toward the main characters change, note when, how, and why they changed. Note other relationships among the characters and describe them. Continue to summarize various parts of the story. Refer to these notes, if necessary, when you discuss the selection with your classmates or as you prepare to write about this selection.

❶ *What is the elder Isolde doing?*

❷ *What does the elder Isolde tell Brangane to do? About what does she warn her?*

❸ *How does Isolde feel about Tristan?*

When this affair had been concluded the King announced to the knights and barons, the companions of the realm, throughout the Palace that the man before them was Tristan. He informed them, in the terms which he had heard, why Tristan had come to Ireland and how the latter had promised to give him guarantees in all the points which he, Gurmun, had stipulated, jointly with Mark's grandees.[1]

The Irish court was glad to hear this news. The great lords declared that it was fitting and proper to make peace; for long-drawn enmity between them, as time went on, brought nothing but loss. The King now requested Tristan to ratify the agreement, as he had promised him, and Tristan duly did so. He and all his sovereign's vassals swore that Isolde should have Cornwall for her nuptial dower,[2] and be mistress of all England. Hereupon Gurmun solemnly surrendered Isolde into the hands of Tristan her enemy. I say 'enemy' for this reason: she hated him now as before.

Tristan laid his hand upon Isolde: 'Sire,' he said, 'lord of Ireland, we ask you, my lady and I, for her sake and for mine, to deliver up to her any knights or pages that were surrendered to this land as tribute from Cornwall and England; for it is only right and just that they should be in my lady's charge, now that she is Queen of their country.'

'With pleasure,' said the King, 'it shall be done. It has our royal approval that they should all depart with you!' This gave pleasure to many.

Tristan then ordered a ship to be procured in addition to his own, to be reserved for Isolde and himself and any others he might choose. And when it had been supplied, he made ready for the voyage. Wherever any of the exiles were traced, up and down the land, at court or in the country, they were sent for at once.

While Tristan and his compatriots[3] were making ready, Isolde,[4] the prudent Queen, was brewing in a vial a love-drink so subtly devised and prepared, and endowed with such powers, that with whomever any man drank it he had to love her above all things, whether he wished it or no, and she love him alone. They would share one death and one life, one sorrow and one joy.

The wise lady took this philtre[5] and said softly to Brangane: 'Brangane, dear niece, do not let it depress you, but you must go away with my daughter. Frame your thoughts to that, and listen to what I say. Take this flask with its draught,[6] have it in your keeping and guard it above all your possessions. See to it that absolutely no one gets to hear of it. Take care that nobody drinks any! When Isolde and Mark have been united in love, make it your strict concern to pour out this liquor as wine for them, and see that they drink it all between them. Beware lest anyone share with them—this stands to reason—and do not drink with them yourself. This brew is a love-philtre! Bear it well in mind! I most dearly and urgently commend Isolde to your care. The better part of my life is bound up with her. Remember that she and I are in your hands, by all your hopes of Paradise! Need I say more?'

1. **grandees.** Men of high rank
2. **nuptial dower.** Usually property that a woman brings to her husband upon her wedding; in this case, a gift from the king to his bride
3. **compatriots.** Fellow countrymen
4. **Isolde.** Both the queen of Ireland and her daughter who is to be married to King Mark in England are named Isolde. Here, referring to the queen of Ireland
5. **philtre.** Potion thought to arouse love
6. **draught.** Portion of liquid for drinking

Words for Everyday Use

stip • u • late (stip´ yo͞o lāt´) *vt.*, include specifically in the terms of an agreement
en • mi • ty (en´mə tē) *n.*, bitter attitude toward an enemy; hostility
rat • i • fy (rat´ ə fī´) *vt.*, approve or confirm
vas • sal (vas´əl) *n.*, person who held land and owed loyalty and military service to a lord
vi • al (vī´əl) *n.*, small vessel or bottle, usually of glass, for containing liquids

Vocabulary in Context

- The lease stipulates that the tenant cannot have pets in the apartment.
- Freed of enmity, the opposing sides formed a partnership.
- Delaware was the first state to ratify the United States Constitution.
- Before the battle, the vassal renewed his pledge of loyalty to his lord.
- Trying to determine the mysterious contents of the vial, Priya ran a series of tests on the odorless green liquid.

'Dearest lady,' answered Brangane, 'if you both wish it, I shall gladly accompany her and watch over her honour and all her affairs, as well as ever I can.'

Tristan and all his men took their leave, in one place and another. They left Wexford with jubilation. And now, out of love for Isolde, the King and Queen and the whole court followed him down to the harbour. The girl he never dreamt would be his love, his abiding anguish of heart, radiant, exquisite Isolde, was the whole time weeping beside him. Her mother and father passed the brief hour with much lamenting. Many eyes began to redden and fill with tears. Isolde brought distress to many hearts, for to many she was a source of secret pain. They wept unceasingly for their eyes' delight, Isolde. There was universal weeping. Many hearts and many eyes wept there together, both openly and in secret.

And now that Isolde and Isolde, the Sun and her Dawn, and the fair Full Moon, Brangane, had to take their leave, the One from the Two, sorrow and grief were much in evidence. That faithful alliance was severed with many a pang. Isolde kissed the pair of them many, many times.

When the Cornishmen and the ladies' Irish attendants had embarked and said good-bye, Tristan was last to go on board. The dazzling young Queen,[7] the Flower of Ireland, walked hand in hand with him, very sad and dejected. They bowed towards the shore and invoked God's blessing on the land and on its people. Then they put to sea, and, as they got under way, began to sing the anthem 'We sail in God's name' with high, clear voices, and they sang it once again as they sped onward on their course.

Now Tristan had arranged for a private cabin to be given to the ladies for their comfort during the voyage. The Queen occupied it with her ladies-in-waiting and no others were admitted, with the occasional exception of Tristan. He sometimes went in to console the Queen as she sat weeping. She wept and she lamented amid her tears that she was leaving her homeland, whose people she knew, and all her friends in this fashion, and was sailing away with strangers, she neither knew whither nor how. And so Tristan would console her as tenderly as he could. Always when he came and found her sorrowing he took her in his arms gently and quietly and in no other way than a liege[8] might hand his lady. The loyal man hoped to comfort the girl in her distress. But whenever he put his arm round her, fair Isolde recalled her uncle's death.

'Enough, Captain,' she said. 'Keep your distance, take your arm away! What a tiresome man you are! Why do you keep on touching me ?'

'But, lovely woman, am I offending you?'

'You are—because I hate you!'

'But why, dear lady?' he asked.

'You killed my uncle!'

'But that has been put by.'

'Nevertheless I detest you, since but for you I should not have a care in the world. You and you alone have saddled me with all this trouble, with your trickery and deceit. What spite has sent you here from Cornwall to my harm? You have won me by guile from those who brought me up, and are taking me I do not know where! I have no idea what fate I have been sold into, nor what is going to become of me!'

'No, lovely Isolde, you must take heart! You had much rather be a great Queen in a strange land than humble and obscure at

7. **Queen.** Here refers to the younger Isolde

8. **liege.** One bound to give service

❶ *Why is Isolde upset?*

❷ *How does Tristan treat Isolde?*

❸ *Why do many people weep at Isolde's departure?*

❹ *Why does Isolde hate Tristan?*

❺ *According to Tristan, why should Isolde be eager to marry Mark?*

Words for Everyday Use

ju • bi • la • tion (jo͞o´bə lā´shən) *n.*, happy celebration

a • bid • ing (ə bīd´iŋ) *adj.*, continuing without change; enduring; lasting

pang (paŋ) *n.*, sudden pain, sharp and brief

con • sole (kən sōl´) *vt.*, help to feel less sad or disappointed

guile (gīl) *n.*, slyness and cunning in dealing with others

Answers to Guided Reading Questions

❶ Isolde is upset because she is leaving her homeland and her friends.

❷ Tristan treats Isolde kindly and respectfully.

❸ Many people weep, some secretly and some openly, because they love Isolde.

❹ Isolde hates Tristan because he killed her uncle.

❺ Tristan says that Isolde should be eager to gain wealth and fame as a great queen although she must go to a strange land.

Literary Technique

Apposition and Metaphor

An **apposition** is a grammatical form in which a thing is renamed in a different word, phrase, or clause. Ask students to find an example of apposition on page 735 in which the two Isoldes and Brangane are renamed. This apposition is also a metaphor. A **metaphor** is a figure of speech in which one thing is spoken or written about as if it were another. Ask students to explain how the relationship of the elder Isolde, Isolde, and Brangane is expressed through this metaphor.

Answers

The third paragraph on this page contains apposition. Isolde and Isolde are referred to as "the Sun and her Dawn," and Brangane is "the fair Full Moon." The passage refers to the parting of Brangane and the younger Isolde from the older Isolde, comparing it to the parting of the sun from the dawn and the moon.

Vocabulary in Context

- The crowd surged onto the field in jubilation after the winning touchdown was scored.
- Austin assured Carrie that his abiding love for her would never change.
- Mishele felt a pang of regret about missing the party, but she knew that she had been working too hard to miss the competition.
- Boris was devastated when he lost the election and would not be consoled.
- I would rather work with a straightforward, honest person than one who uses guile to trick me.

Art Note

John William Waterhouse (1849–1917) began his career painting in the classical mode but developed a Romantic style in his later years. His works were influenced by those of Dante Gabriel Rossetti and other members of the Pre-Raphaelite Brotherhood. The Pre-Raphaelites attempted to restore painting to an imagined purity that existed in the late Middle Ages and early Renaissance. They often treated medieval subjects in a highly romantic manner tinged with mysticism. Waterhouse's other famous subjects include the Lady of Shalott and the *Odyssey*.

Destiny was painted for an auction to raise money for the Artists' War Fund to support British soldiers in the Boer War. In the Boer War (1899–1902), the British defeated the Boers, or descendants of Dutch colonists in South Africa.

Ask students to comment upon *Destiny* as an illustration for this selection from *Tristan*. Is it appropriate and consistent with the selection? Why, or why not? Interested students may create their own illustrations for this selection.

Answers to Guided Reading Questions

❶ Isolde says that she would prefer less wealth and ease of mind to the great worry and trouble connected to great wealth.

Destiny. *J William Waterhouse, 1900. Towneley Hall Art Gallery and Museum, Manchester, Great Britain. Bridgeman Art Library/Art Resource, NY*

home. Honour and ease abroad, and shame in your father's kingdom have a very different flavour!'

❶ *What circumstances does Isolde say she would prefer?*

'Take my word for it, Captain Tristan,' answered the girl, 'whatever you say, I would prefer indifferent circumstances with ease of mind and affection, to worry and trouble allied with great wealth!'

'You are right there,' replied Tristan, 'yet where you can have wealth together with mental ease, these two blessings run better as a team than either runs alone. But tell me, suppose things had come to the point where you would have had no alternative but to marry the Steward, how would it have been then? I am sure you would have been glad of my help. So is this the way you thank me for coming to your aid and saving you from him?'

'You will have to wait a long time before I thank you, for, even if you saved me from him, you have since so bewildered me with trouble that I would rather have married the Steward than set out on this voyage with you. However worthless he is, he would mend his ways, if he were for any time with me. From this, Heaven knows, I would then have seen that he loved me.'

'I don't believe a word of it,' answered Tristan. 'It demands great effort for anybody to act worthily against his own nature—no one believes that the leopard can change his spots. Lovely woman, do not be downcast. I shall soon give you a king for your lord in whom you will find a good and happy life, wealth, noble excellence and honour for the rest of your days!'

Meanwhile the ships sped on their course. They both had a favourable wind and were making good headway. But the fair company, Isolde and her train, were unused to such hard going in wind and water. Quite soon they were in rare distress. Their Captain, Tristan, gave orders to put to shore and lie idle for a while. When they had made land and anchored in a haven, most of those on board went ashore for exercise. But Tristan went without delay to see his radiant lady and pass the time of day with her. And when he had sat down beside her and they were discussing various matters of mutual interest he called for something to drink.

Now, apart from the Queen, there was nobody in the cabin but some very young ladies-in-waiting. 'Look,' said one of them, 'here is some wine in this little bottle.' No, it held no wine, much as it resembled it. It was their lasting sorrow, their never-ending anguish, of which at last they died! But the child was not to know that. She rose and went at once to where the draught had been hidden in its vial. She handed it to Tristan, their Captain, and he handed it to Isolde. She drank after long reluctance, then returned it to Tristan, and he drank, and they both of them thought it was wine. At that moment in came Brangane, recognized the flask, and saw only too well what was afoot. She was so shocked and startled that it robbed her of her strength and she turned as pale as death. With a heart that had died within her she went and seized that cursed, fatal flask, bore it off and flung it into the wild and raging sea!

'Alas, poor me,' cried Brangane, 'alas that ever I was born! Wretch that I am, how I have ruined my honour and trust! May God show everlasting pity that I ever came on this journey and that death failed to snatch me, when I was sent on this ill-starred voyage with Isolde! Ah, Tristan and Isolde, this draught will be your death!'

Now when the maid and the man, Isolde and Tristan, had drunk the draught, in an instant that arch-disturber of tranquillity was there, Love, waylayer[9] of all hearts, and she had stolen in! Before they were aware of it she had planted her victorious standard[10] in their two hearts and bowed them beneath her yoke. They who were two and divided now became one and united. No longer were they at variance: Isolde's hatred was gone. Love, the reconciler, had purged their hearts of enmity, and so joined them in affection that each was to the other as limpid as a mirror. They shared a single heart. Her anguish was his pain: his pain her anguish. The two were one both in joy and in sorrow, yet they hid their feelings from each other. This was

9. **waylayer.** Person who lies in wait for someone to attack or ambush

10. **standard.** Flag or banner

1 *What does Brangane realize about what has just occurred? How does she feel about this occurrence?*

2 *Why does the captain bring the boat to shore?*

3 *What effect does the potion have on Tristan and Isolde?*

4 *What does the lady-in-waiting give to Tristan and Isolde?*

Words for Everyday Use

var • i • ance (ver´ē əns) *n.,* disagreement; quarrel

lim • pid (lim´pid) *adj.,* perfectly clear; transparent

Answers to Guided Reading Questions

1 Brangane realizes that Tristan and Isolde have just drunk the love potion and that this drink will be their ruin. She feels that she is at fault and that she has betrayed her "honour and trust."

2 The captain brings the boat to shore to give Isolde and her companions a rest from their voyage.

3 The potion causes them to fall in love and to become emotionally joined as one.

4 The lady-in-waiting thinks she is giving wine to Tristan and Isolde, but she really serves them the love potion.

Additional Questions and Activities

Students might compare the story of the love potion in *Tristan* to another story of external forces interfering with love. Suggest that they read or reread Ovid's "Apollo and Daphne" (page 492) and the selection from Virgil's *Aeneid* (page 222). Students may also identify other stories in which a god, potion, or other magical or powerful force does something to affect the love of characters in the work. Have students identify similarities and differences between the following aspects of the stories: the being who interferes, the means of interference, the reason and intent for the interference, and the results of the interference.

Vocabulary in Context

- After the successful mediation, the two sides were no longer at variance.
- Runoff from the heavy rains turned the once limpid pools into muddy ponds.

Answers to Guided Reading Questions

① Love and honor make Tristan try to hide his love for Isolde.

② Isolde can only think about love and Tristan.

③ Modesty makes Isolde try to hide her love for Tristan.

Selection Check Test with Answers

EX. How does Isolde feel about Tristan at the beginning of the selection?
She hates him.

1. Who gives the love potion to Brangane?
The elder Isolde gives the love potion to Brangane.

2. For whom is the love potion intended?
The love potion is intended for Isolde and Mark.

3. Why does Isolde hate Tristan?
She hates Tristan because he killed her uncle.

4. What does Brangane do when she realizes that Tristan and Isolde have drunk the love potion?
She throws the flask into the ocean and laments her own loss of honor and the problems that Tristan and Isolde will now face.

5. Why doesn't Tristan feel free to love Isolde?
He does not feel free to love her because of his honor and his loyalty to Mark.

① *What feelings make Tristan try to hide his love for Isolde?*

② *What are the only things Isolde can think about?*

③ *What feelings make Isolde try to hide her love for Tristan?*

from doubt and shame. She was ashamed, as he was. She went in doubt of him, as he of her. However blindly the craving in their hearts was centred on one desire, their anxiety was how to begin. This masked their desire from each other.

When Tristan felt the stirrings of love he at once remembered loyalty and honour, and strove to turn away. 'No, leave it, Tristan,' he was continually thinking to himself, 'pull yourself together, do not take any notice of it.' But his heart was impelled towards her. He was striving against his own wishes, desiring against his desire. He was drawn now in one direction, now in another. Captive that he was, he tried all that he knew in the snare, over and over again, and long maintained his efforts.

The loyal man was afflicted by a double pain: when he looked at her face and sweet Love began to wound his heart and soul with her, he bethought himself of Honour, and it retrieved him. But this in turn was the sign for Love, his liege[11] lady, whom his father had served before him, to assail him anew, and once more he had to submit. Honour and Loyalty harassed him powerfully, but Love harassed him more. Love tormented him to an extreme, she made him suffer more than did Honour and Loyalty combined. His heart smiled upon Isolde, but he turned his eyes away: yet his greatest grief was when he failed to see her. As is the way of captives, he fixed his mind on escape and how he might elude her, and returned many times to this thought: 'Turn one way, or another! Change this desire! Love and like elsewhere!' But the noose was always there. He took his heart and soul and searched them for some change: but there was nothing there but Love—and Isolde.

And so it fared with her. Finding this life unbearable, she, too, made ceaseless efforts. When she recognized the lime[12] that bewitching Love had spread and saw that she was deep in it, she endeavoured to reach dry ground, she strove to be out and away. But the lime kept clinging to her and drew her back and down. The lovely woman fought back with might and main,[13] but stuck fast at every step. She was succumbing against her will. She made desperate attempts on many sides, she twisted and turned with hands and feet and immersed them ever deeper in the blind sweetness of Love, and of the man. Her limed senses failed to discover any path, bridge, or track that would advance them half a step, half a foot, without Love being there too. Whatever Isolde thought, whatever came uppermost in her mind, there was nothing there, of one sort or another, but Love, and Tristan.

This was all below the surface, for her heart and her eyes were at variance—Modesty chased her eyes away, Love drew her heart towards him. That warring company, a Maid and a Man, Love and Modesty, brought her into great confusion; for the Maid wanted the Man, yet she turned her eyes away: Modesty wanted Love, but told no one of her wishes. But what was the good of that? A Maid and her Modesty are by common consent so fleeting a thing, so short-lived a blossoming, they do not long resist. Thus Isolde gave up her struggle and accepted her situation. Without further delay the vanquished

11. **liege.** Lord or sovereign; someone who must be served loyally
12. **lime.** Birdlime—sticky substance spread on twigs to catch birds
13. **with might and main.** With physical strength, force, or power

Words for Everyday Use

as • sail (ə sāl´) *vt.,* attack

Vocabulary in Context

• The odor of ammonia assailed my senses, causing my eyes to sting and my nose to run.

girl resigned herself body and soul to Love and to the man.

Isolde glanced at him now and again and watched him covertly, her bright eyes and her heart were now in full accord. Secretly and lovingly her heart and eyes darted at the man rapaciously, while the man gave back her looks with tender passion. Since Love would not release him, he too began to give ground. Whenever there was a suitable occasion the man and the maid came together to feast each other's eyes. These lovers seemed to each other fairer than before—such is Love's law, such is the way with affection. It is so this year, it was so last year and it will remain so among all lovers as long as Love endures, that while their affection is growing and bringing forth blossom and increase of all lovable things, they please each other more than ever they did when it first began to burgeon. Love that bears increase makes lovers fairer than at first. This is the seed of Love, from which it never dies.

Love seems fairer than before and so Love's rule endures. Were Love to seem the same as before, Love's rule would soon wither away. ■

What effect does the author say love will always have on people?

Responding to the Selection

"Love seems fairer than before and so Love's rule endures. Were Love to seem the same as before, Love's rule would soon wither away." Explain in your own words the meaning of this moral. Do you agree or disagree with this sentiment? Discuss your response with your classmates.

Reviewing the Selection

Recalling		Interpreting
1. How does Isolde feel about going to Cornwall? about Tristan?	►►	Why does she feel this way? Is it likely that her feelings toward Tristan will change? Why, or why not?
2. What does Queen Isolde give to Brangane? What instructions does she give with this item?	►►	Why does Isolde give this thing to Brangane? What danger does this item pose?

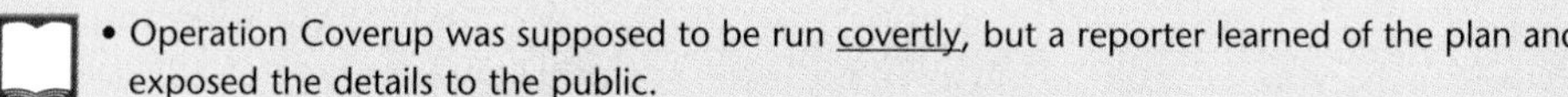

Words for Everyday Use

co • vert • ly (kuv´ərt lē) *adv.,* secretly
ra • pa • cious • ly (rə pā´shəs lē) *adv.,* greedily
bur • geon (bʉr´jən) *vi.,* put forth buds; sprout; flourish

Answers to Guided Reading Questions

The author says that burgeoning love will always make a couple appear fairer to each other than they did before.

Responding to the Selection

Students should consider the unique feelings that each new relationship creates. Students might rewrite the moral to reflect the way they see love.

Answers for Reviewing the Selection

RECALLING AND INTERPRETING

1. **Recalling.** Isolde is not happy about leaving her home to go to Cornwall. She hates Tristan. **Interpreting.** Isolde would rather stay at home than go to another place where she could be more powerful and well known. She hates Tristan because he killed her uncle. It seems unlikely that her feelings toward Tristan will change because she feels so strongly and the reason for her hatred can never be erased.

2. **Recalling.** Queen Isolde gives Brangane a love potion and tells her to keep it a secret and to allow no one but Isolde and Mark to drink it. **Interpreting.** Isolde gives this potion to Brangane so that Isolde and Mark will fall in love with each other, allowing them to have a marriage that has both political benefits and affection. The potion is dangerous because it could fall into the wrong hands and have an undesired effect.

(cont.)

Vocabulary in Context

- Operation Coverup was supposed to be run covertly, but a reporter learned of the plan and exposed the details to the public.
- As soon as the slop was poured, the pigs ate rapaciously until it was gone.
- It seems that both flowers and love burgeon in the spring.

Answers for Reviewing the Selection (cont.)

3. **Recalling.** The sea voyage makes Isolde ill. The lady-in-waiting gives Isolde and Tristan what she thinks is some wine. When Brangane sees what has happened, she flings the flask into the sea and begins to lament having been born. **Interpreting.** Tristan and Isolde fall in love with each other. Isolde's hatred for Tristan melts away and turns to love. While the cause of the change of emotion, the love potion, may be unrealistic, students might argue that both love and hate are emotions of passion and that such a change might easily occur. They might also say that Tristan's treatment of Isolde during the voyage may have won her over. Others might argue that the change of emotion is unrealistic.

4. **Recalling.** Isolde is torn by her love for Tristan and her modesty. Tristan is torn between his love and devotion to Isolde and his honor and devotion to his lord, Mark. **Interpreting.** Isolde and Tristan are bound by the codes of courtly love and chivalry, which constrict their actions and cause a conflict of desire and duty.

SYNTHESIZING

Responses will vary. Possible responses are given.

5. Tristan and Isolde begin to live solely for each other. They must break the code of honor—courtly love—that has defined their lives. The selection suggests that love

3. What effect does the sea voyage have on Isolde? What does the lady-in-waiting give to Isolde and Tristan? What does Brangane do when she sees what the lady-in-waiting has given them? ▶▶ What happens as a result of the mishap with the bottle that Queen Isolde had given Brangane? In what way are Isolde's feelings toward Tristan changed? Is this change realistic?

4. What conflicting emotions do Isolde and Tristan experience? ▶▶ Why are Isolde and Tristan unable to express their feelings for one another?

Synthesizing

5. In what way does love transform or change Tristan and Isolde? What traditional values does their love force them to reject? What conclusion do you think Gottfried von Strassburg means for his readers to draw about love?

Understanding Literature (Questions for Discussion)

1. **Courtly Love and Chivalry. Courtly love** is a code of romantic love celebrated in songs and romances of the Medieval Period. According to this code, the lover knows himself or herself to be truly in love if he or she is overcome by extreme, transforming emotion. Some of the rules of courtly love Andreas Capellanus wrote are "Marriage is no real excuse for not loving" and "No one should be deprived of love without the very best of reasons." **Chivalry** was the code of conduct of the medieval knight. According to the code of chivalry, a knight was to be a loyal servant to his lord or lady and a perfect exemplar of such virtues as bravery, courage, courtesy, honesty, faith, and gentleness. In what way do these two codes of conduct conflict in Tristan's life? Which code of conduct wins out in his struggle? What does this episode say about the nature of love?

2. **Metaphor.** A **metaphor** is a figure of speech in which one thing is spoken or written about as if it were another. This figure of speech invites the reader to make a comparison between the two things. Look at the paragraph beginning "And so it fared with her" on page 738. To what is the reader encouraged to compare love? To what is the reader encouraged to compare Isolde? Explain whether this is an appropriate metaphor.

Answers for Understanding Literature

Responses will vary. Possible responses are given.

1. **Courtly Love and Chivalry.** Tristan is torn between his duty to be loyal and true to his lord, Mark, and his desire and love for Isolde. According to the rules of courtly love, marriage (or betrothal) should not hinder true love, yet Isolde is promised to Mark, Tristan's lord. Forced to be true to either Isolde or to Mark, Tristan chooses Isolde. The episode suggests that love is stronger than honor or loyalty, or at least stronger than the rules that govern such ideals.

2. **Metaphor.** Isolde's struggle against love is compared to a bird struggling to get out of birdlime, a sticky substance used to catch birds. The metaphor is appropriate because Isolde, like a bird, is being trapped. She cannot escape love no matter how hard she struggles.

Responding in Writing

1. **Creative Writing: Continuation.** What do you think will happen when Tristan and Isolde reach Cornwall and Isolde is to be married to Mark? Write a continuation of this selection in which you present what might happen next. Your continuation may present either what you would like to happen or what you think will happen; it may have a happy or an unhappy ending. You may wish to resolve the conflict in your continuation, or you may wish to present a scene in which the conflict changes, grows, or takes another turn. Before you write your continuation, do some freewriting on the following questions: Will anyone discover that Tristan and Isolde drank the love potion? Will the elder Isolde who concocted the love potion be able to intercede? Will Tristan and Isolde give up their love for each other? If not, will Mark discover their love?

2. **Critical Essay: Modern or Medieval Ideas on Love.** Some modern critics of *Tristan* have suggested that Tristan and Isolde were in fact in love before drinking the love potion. Others claim that such a view takes into account modern ideas about the psychology of love and that Gottfried's intent was for the love potion to be the true cause of their love. You might also consider how the potion might be a metaphor for the "magic" quality of love—the unexplainable urge to love one person over others. Given Tristan's actions and speeches toward Isolde, what reasons might she have for falling in love with him? Write a critical essay in which you defend one of these interpretations. State your thesis in an opening paragraph. Then support your thesis with a discussion of medieval and modern views of love as well as with examples from the text. Come to a conclusion in a final paragraph.

Language Lab

Reducing Wordiness. Carefully constructed sentences contain no unnecessary words or repeated ideas. Wordiness can be reduced by combining sentences to eliminate repetition. Read the Language Arts Survey 2.26, "Reducing Wordiness." Then, rewrite the following paragraph on your own paper, editing sentences as necessary to reduce wordiness.

Richard Wagner was born in 1813. Wagner, who wrote music, was a German composer. A playwright, he also wrote dramas. Richard Wagner drew heavily upon the German Romantic tradition in the musical dramatic works that he wrote. Influenced by wonderful French and Italian opera, which had profound effects on him, he wrote the words and also the music for grand operas. The great work, Wagner's masterpiece, *Tristan and Isolde,* which is based on the legend of Tristan and Isolde as told by Gottfried von Strassburg in *Tristan,* is one of his later masterpieces. Wagner, as an important opera writer himself, greatly influenced in a profound way many future writers of opera.

ANALYTIC SCALES FOR RESPONDING IN WRITING

Assign a score from 1 to 25 for each grading criterion below. (For more detailed evaluation, see the evaluation forms for writing, revising, and proofreading, Assessment Portfolio 4.1–4.9.)

1. Continuation

- **Content/Unity.** The continuation presents a possible resolution of the conflict introduced in the selection, or the continuation presents further development of the existing conflict.
- **Organization/Coherence.** The continuation is arranged in a logical order such as chronological order.
- **Language/Style.** The continuation uses vivid and precise nouns, verbs, and modifiers.
- **Conventions.** The continuation avoids errors in spelling, grammar, usage, mechanics, and manuscript form.

▶ Additional practice is provided in the Essential Skills Practice Book: Writing 1.8.

2. Critical Essay

- **Content/Unity.** The essay analyzes the love between Tristan and Isolde and classifies it as modern or medieval.
- **Organization/Coherence.** The essay begins with an introduction that includes a thesis. The introduction is followed by supporting paragraphs with clear transitions. The essay ends with a solid conclusion.
- **Language/Style.** The essay uses vivid and precise nouns, verbs, and modifiers.
- **Conventions.** The essay avoids errors in spelling, grammar, usage, mechanics, and manuscript form.

▶ Additional practice is provided in the Essential Skills Practice Book: Writing 1.20.

ANSWERS FOR LANGUAGE LAB

Responses will vary. Possible responses are given.

Richard Wagner, a German composer and playwright, was born in 1813. He drew heavily upon the German Romantic tradition and was influenced by Italian and French opera. Wagner conveys both of these influences in his masterpiece *Tristan and Isolde.* Wagner's operatic style greatly influenced future opera writers.

▶ Additional practice is provided in the Essential Skills Practice Book: Language 2.26.

ADDITIONAL RESOURCES

READER'S GUIDE

- Selection Worksheet 9.3

ASSESSMENT PORTFOLIO

- Selection Check Test 2.9.5
- Selection Test 2.9.6

ESSENTIAL SKILLS PRACTICE BOOKS

- Writing 1.8, 1.20
- Speaking and Listening 3.5

PREREADING EXTENSIONS

If students are interested in other female troubadours, they might research the following women: Tibors, Lombarda, Almuc de Castelnou, Iseut de Capio, Alaisina, Iselda, Carenza, Gormonda, Azalais de Porcairuagues, and the Countess of Dia. Many of these women are not widely known. Two fine sources of information are *The Writings of Medieval Women,* translated by Marcelle Thiébaux, and *A History of Their Own: Women in Europe from Prehistory to the Present,* Volume I, by Bonnie S. Anderson and Judith P. Zinsser.

SUPPORT FOR LEP STUDENTS

PRONUNCIATIONS OF PROPER NOUNS AND ADJECTIVES

Bi • er • is de Ro • mans (bē är´is də rō mənz´)

ADDITIONAL VOCABULARY

amorous—loving; affectionate
derived—received
exquisite—of highest quality

PREREADING

"Lady Maria, your worth and excellence"
by Bieris de Romans, translated by Marcelle Thiébaux

FRANCE

About the Author

Bieris de Romans (early thirteenth century). Little is known about Bieris de Romans, beyond the fact that she was one of the *trobairitz,* or female troubadours, who flourished during the Medieval Period. The troubadour is traditionally thought of as male, and the works of at least four hundred male troubadours are known. Nevertheless, the works of at least twenty female troubadours have also been passed down to us. Like many of the *trobairitz,* Bieris was probably of the aristocracy and well educated. The *trobairitz* addressed love and desire as openly as their male counterparts did.

About the Selection

Beginning in the twelfth century, the influence of Persian love poetry led to the development of passionate devotional poems to the Virgin Mary, mother of Jesus, who was portrayed in both popular and religious literature as the ideal of perfect womanhood. **"Lady Maria, your worth and excellence"** is one such poem. In it, the speaker praises the Virgin Mary and pleads with her for help. It is common in these poems for the speaker to address Mary, or Maria, as a courtly lover would his or her beloved. The poem can also be read on two levels, as a devotional poem to Mary or as a secular, or nonreligious, love lyric. In other words, the poem is intentionally ambiguous, inviting two possible readings.

Angel Band. *Italy*

CONNECTIONS: The Troubadour

Troubadours flourished in southern France, northern Spain, and northern Italy from the late eleventh century to the late thirteenth century. They were lyric poets whose name derived from the Provençal word *trobar,* meaning "to find" or "to invent," referring to the way the troubadours invented their lyrics. Poetic forms used by the troubadour included the *canso,* or love song; the *tenso,* or debate; the *partimen* or *joc parti,* an intellectual debate; the *sirventes,* or satirical song; the *alba,* or conversation between a couple about parting at dawn; the *pastorela,* or exchange between a knight and a female shepherd; and the *planh,* or lament. Many of the lyrics of the troubadours were set to music.

GOALS/OBJECTIVES

Studying this lesson will enable students to

- enjoy a love poem
- define *catalog* and *courtly love*
- identify and explain the effect of a catalog
- explain how the selection reflects the code of courtly love
- write a lyric poem
- compare the devotion to Mary movement and the development of courtly love, and analyze elements of these movements in the selection
- prepare and present an oral interpretation

Think of a time when you had to request something important from someone. Describe your request. What did you do to try to convince the person to grant your request? Did you compliment the person? offer a rationale? beg? Was your request granted? Write about what you did to make the person take your request seriously.

READER'S JOURNAL

"Lady Maria, your worth and excellence"

BIERIS DE ROMANS, TRANSLATED BY MARCELLE THIÉBAUX

Lady Maria, your worth and excellence,
joy, understanding, and exquisite beauty,
the warmth of your welcome, your excellence and honor,
your elegant conversation and charming company,
your gentle face and amiable gaiety,
your gentle gaze and amorous mien—
all these things are yours, without deviousness.
And these things have drawn my truant heart to you.

For this reason I plead with you—if true love pleases you—
and my joyfulness and sweet submission
could elicit from you the succor that I need,
then give me, lovely woman, if it's pleasing to you,
the gift in which I have most joy and hope.
For in you I have fixed my heart and desire,
and from you I have derived all my happiness,
and from you—so many times—my painful yearning.

❶ *What draws the speaker to Lady Maria?*

❷ *What does the speaker ask of Lady Maria?*

WORDS FOR EVERYDAY USE

a • mi • a • ble (ā′mē ə bəl) *adj.*, good-natured
mien (mēn) *n.*, manner, bearing
tru • ant (tro͞o′ənt) *adj.*, straying
suc • cor (suk′ər) *n.*, help, aid

READER'S JOURNAL

Students might role play situations in which one person is making a request and the other is deciding whether or not to grant it. Have students brainstorm a list of situations. Suggest the following to get them started: a student requesting an extension on an assignment, a child asking a parent to buy a toy. Students can then write about or discuss methods that they think are effective when making a request and those that they find to be ineffective.

ANSWERS TO GUIDED READING QUESTIONS

❶ The speaker is drawn to Lady Maria's worth, excellence, joy, understanding, beauty, warmth, and honor. The speaker also respects Lady Maria's elegant conversation, charming company, gentle face and gaze, gaiety, and loving manner.

❷ The speaker asks Lady Maria for succor and for the gift in which the speaker has "most joy and hope."

SPELLING AND VOCABULARY WORDS FROM THE SELECTION

amiable	succor
mien	truant

VOCABULARY IN CONTEXT

- Rahmun is well liked for his amiable disposition.
- Charis's proud mien is often mistaken for snobbery.
- Hearing my name brought me out of my daydream and returned my truant mind to the class discussion.
- The good Samaritan stopped to offer succor to the motorist with a flat tire.

ANSWERS TO GUIDED READING QUESTIONS

❶ Lady Maria would not suffer the anguish of being betrayed.

SELECTION CHECK TEST WITH ANSWERS

EX. Who is addressed in this poem?
Lady Maria is addressed.

1. Name three things that the speaker praises in Lady Maria.
The speaker praises Lady Maria's worth, excellence, joy, understanding, beauty, warmth, gaiety, honor, elegant conversation, charming company, gentle face and gaze, and loving manner.
2. What have these qualities drawn to Lady Maria from the speaker?
These qualities have drawn the speaker's truant heart.
3. What does the speaker offer to win succor?
The speaker offers joyfulness and sweet submission.
4. What has the speaker fixed in Lady Maria?
The speaker has fixed his or her heart and desire.
5. What reason does the speaker give for accepting him or her rather than another suitor?
The speaker suggests that another suitor might betray Lady Maria.

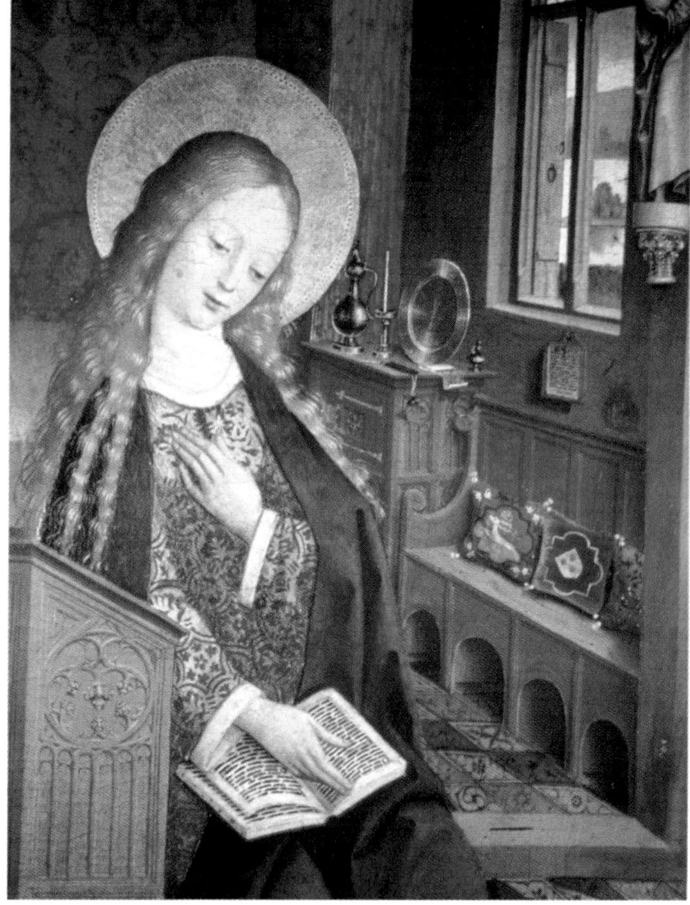

Virgin Mary with Book–Annunciation. *Italy*

And since your beauty and worth enhance you
above all women, so that no other is superior,
I plead with you—please! It would bring you honor,
too, not to love some suitor who'd betray you.

Glorious lady, woman, enhanced by worth, joy,
and gracious speech, my verses go to you.
For in you are gaiety and happiness,
and every good that one demands of a lady. ■

❶ *Why would loving the speaker benefit Lady Maria?*

ANSWERS FOR SKILLS ACTIVITIES (SEE PAGE 746.)

SPEAKING AND LISTENING SKILLS

As students begin their searches, you might suggest the lays of Marie de France (either a verse translation or a prose translation) or one of the many medieval ballads. If students choose a musical piece, they may choose to sing their selection. Students may also set a lyrical piece to music. If students wish to sing, they should still follow the guidelines for oral interpretations.

► Additional practice is provided in the Essential Skills Practice Book: Speaking and Listening 3.5.

Responding to the Selection

How would you feel if such a poem were addressed to you? What response would you give the speaker?

Reviewing the Selection

RECALLING / **INTERPRETING**

1. What draws the speaker to Lady Maria? ▶▶ Why might the speaker begin by praising Lady Maria in this way?
2. What does the speaker ask of Lady Maria? ▶▶ Why might the speaker be asking this of Lady Maria?
3. What reason does the speaker give Lady Maria for not choosing another as her beloved? ▶▶ What is the speaker implying about his or her love?
4. Why does the speaker address verses to Lady Maria? In the last stanza, what opinion does the speaker express about her? ▶▶ What influences may have caused the speaker to develop this opinion of Lady Maria?

SYNTHESIZING

5. Why might the speaker have written about his or her devotion to the Virgin Mary in worldly terms? How do you feel about the way in which the speaker writes about the Virgin Mary? Does this manner of address make the speaker's devotion seem more powerful? Explain why or why not. Discuss why elements of courtly love might have been used to express religious devotion. Draw a conclusion based on evidence in this poem concerning possible experiences the speaker has had with love relationships.

Understanding Literature (Questions for Discussion)

1. **Catalog.** A **catalog** is a list of people or things. Which of Maria's qualities are presented in the catalog in the first stanza of this poem? What effect does the speaker wish to achieve by presenting this catalog?

RESPONDING TO THE SELECTION

If students have difficulty responding to this question, suggest that they think of a time when somebody made a heartfelt plea to them. What effect did the way in which the plea was presented have on them? What effect did it have on their response? How did they respond? What, if anything, might have made them respond differently to the plea? Students can write in their journals or discuss their responses in groups.

ANSWERS FOR REVIEWING THE SELECTION

RECALLING AND INTERPRETING

1. **Recalling.** The speaker is drawn to Lady Maria by qualities such as her worth, understanding, beauty, warmth, honor, charm, gaiety, and gentleness. **Interpreting.** The speaker might begin by praising her to put Lady Maria in the mood to grant the speaker's request.

2. **Recalling.** The speaker asks Lady Maria to grant him or her succor. **Interpreting.** The speaker may ask this of Lady Maria because she can grant love to ease the speaker's longing, or the speaker may address Mary as Lady Maria because she is able to intercede for all people.

3. **Recalling.** Another person might betray Lady Maria. **Interpreting.** The speaker implies that his or her love is true and would never hurt Lady Maria.

4. **Recalling.** The speaker's verses go to Lady Maria because she possesses "gaiety, happiness, and every good that one demands of a lady." **Interpreting.** The evolving devotion to Mary may have led to the speaker's feelings. The speaker might also be basing such idealization on other literature of the period, which created many idealized female characters.

(cont.)

ANSWERS FOR REVIEWING THE SELECTION (CONT.)

SYNTHESIZING

Responses will vary. Possible responses are given.

5. Worldly terms of romantic love are understandable to many people and became a more concrete way of referring to a mystical devotion. Students may say that worldly terms are more accessible to people and are therefore more powerful. Others may say that comparing a religious experience to a worldly one takes away from the wonder or the power of the religious experience. In devotions to Mary, the mortal tries to please the Virgin Mary as a male courtly lover would try to please a lady. She, like a female courtly lover, is an ideal woman and has the power to grant or deny the wishes of those who appeal to her.

ANALYTIC SCALES FOR RESPONDING IN WRITING

Assign a score from 1 to 25 for each grading criterion below. (For more detailed evaluation, see the evaluation forms for writing, revising, and proofreading, Assessment Portfolio 4.1–4.9.)

1. Lyric Poem

- **Content/Unity.** The lyric poem expresses the feelings of the speaker and presents a supplication or request.
- **Organization/Coherence.** The poem presents the request in a logical manner.
- **Language/Style.** The poem uses vivid and precise language.
- **Conventions.** The poem avoids errors in spelling, grammar, usage, mechanics, and manuscript form.

▶ Additional practice is provided in the Essential Skills Practice Book: Writing 1.8.

2. Critical Essay

- **Content/Unity.** The essay compares the development of the devotion to Mary and the code of courtly love, and explains how both movements are represented in the poem.
- **Organization/Coherence.** The essay begins with an introduction that includes a thesis. Subsequent paragraphs support the thesis. The essay ends with a solid conclusion.
- **Language/Style.** The essay uses vivid and precise language.
- **Conventions.** The essay avoids errors in spelling, grammar, usage, mechanics, and manuscript form.

▶ Additional practice is provided in the Essential Skills Practice Book: Writing 1.20.

Answers for Skills Activities

Answers for Skills Activities appear on page 744.

2. **Courtly Love. Courtly love** is a code of romantic love celebrated in songs and romances of the Medieval Period. According to this code, the lover knows himself or herself to be truly in love if he or she is overcome by extreme, transforming emotion. The female lover is often portrayed in ideal and unrealistic terms. She usually requires that the male lover prove his love through a series of tasks. The male lover is led sometimes to the depths of despair and sometimes to the heights of courtesy and heroism to prove his worth to his lady. In what ways does this poem reflect the code of courtly love?

Responding in Writing

1. **Creative Writing: Lyric Poem.** Write a lyric poem of supplication or request. You may wish to think about an actual request that you have made or that you would like to make. Freewrite to come up with reasons why your request should be granted and ways in which you might praise the recipient of your request. You might also refer to your response to the Reader's Journal activity. Try to model your poem after "Lady Maria, your worth and excellence" by praising the recipient of your request before presenting your request.

2. **Critical Essay: Devotion to Mary and the Development of Courtly Love.** The development of courtly love grew out of the flourishing movement of devotion to the Virgin Mary. What did Mary represent? In what way did she become symbolic of the courtly lady? In what way were the two movements similar? Discuss how the lyric poem "Lady Maria, your worth and excellence" expresses both of these codes. Use examples from the poem to support your ideas.

Speaking and Listening Skills

Oral Interpretation. During the time that the troubadour flourished, verses were recited, or often sung, at court. Use the library to find other love poetry from the Medieval Period or from other time periods. Then choose one poem and prepare an oral interpretation. For advice on preparing an oral interpretation, refer to the Language Arts Survey 3.5, "Oral Interpretation." Present the poem to your class. After each interpretation, discuss with other students how the poem reflects or deviates from the ideals of the courtly love tradition. For more information on courtly love, see the introduction to this unit or the Handbook of Literary Terms.

Answers for Understanding Literature

Responses will vary. Possible responses are given.

1. Catalog. The speaker catalogs Lady Maria's worth, understanding, beauty, warmth, honor, charm, gaiety, and gentleness. By presenting this catalog of qualities, the speaker hopes to make Lady Maria more open to his or her request.

2. Courtly Love. This poem reflects the idealization and veneration of women that were part of the code of courtly love. It also reflects other elements of courtly love, such as the anguish of the lover who is trying to prove his worth, and the importance of courtesy, honor, and gentleness.

PREREADING

from *The Divine Comedy*
by Dante Alighieri, translated by John Ciardi

ITALY

About the Author

DANTE
1265–1321

Dante is considered Italy's greatest poet and one of the masters of western literature. He was born in Florence, Italy, just before the Renaissance, Europe's period of literary and artistic rebirth. As a young boy, Dante met a woman named Beatrice and fell in love with her. Dante loved her from a distance throughout his adult life, and she inspired many of his later poems. *The Divine Comedy* is in fact a memorial to Beatrice, who appears in the poem as the poet's guide through Heaven.

As a leader of the political party called the White Guelfs, Dante rose to a high government position in Florence and served as ambassador to the Pope in Rome in 1301. In 1302, the Black Guelfs, a rival political party, rose to power in Florence, and Dante and others of his party were sent into exile from Florence. He wandered throughout Italy but finally settled in Ravenna, where he stayed until his death. Dante composed *The Divine Comedy*, a poem in one hundred cantos, while living in exile. A **canto** is a section or part of a long poem. His works also include *The New Life* (La *vita nuova*), c.1292, a meditation on the nature of love. Dante made literary history by writing in his native Italian rather than in Latin.

About the Selection

Dante's poetic masterpiece, ***The Divine Comedy***, tells the story of his imaginary epic journey through Hell (*Inferno*), Purgatory (*Purgatorio*), and Heaven (*Paradiso*). Dante has strayed from the straight and narrow path and must make this journey so that he can recognize his errors and save his soul. The *Inferno*, or Hell, is the place for condemned souls. It is entered via a funnel-shaped opening in the earth that stretches from the earth's surface toward its center. Dante begins his journey by traveling through the nine different levels, or circles, of Hell. He witnesses the fates of the different ranks of sinners and sees how each is punished in the afterlife. *Purgatorio*, or Purgatory, is located on a mountain rising out of the ocean. This is the place for purification—where minor sins can be purged from the soul through confession and punishment. *Paradiso*, or Heaven, like *Inferno*, is made up of nine levels, or circles. To get to Heaven, souls travel through a hierarchy of planets and stars. The Roman poet Virgil (see page 222) guides Dante through the *Inferno* and *Purgatorio,* but because Virgil was not a Christian he is unable to guide Dante through *Paradiso*. There, Beatrice takes over as guide. *The Divine Comedy* is an elaborately constructed **allegory**, or a work in which each element symbolizes, or represents, something else. Dante himself represents the noble soul of humankind, Virgil represents human reason, and Beatrice, Dante's guide through *Paradiso*, represents divine love, or the love of God. In canto 1 of this work, Dante explains his reasons for undertaking his journey and embarks with Virgil for the *Inferno*. In canto 31, Dante meets Beatrice in *Paradiso,* purges himself of sin, and experiences divine love.

CONNECTIONS: Medieval Beliefs about God and the Afterlife

The Divine Comedy directly reflects ideas held by Christians in the Middle Ages and the early Renaissance. People viewed the universe as a highly structured, changeless place ordered by God. Souls entered eternal Paradise, or Heaven, only by recognizing and purging their sins, and by having faith in God. Descriptions of Hell and Purgatory were popular subjects for theologians of the time.

ADDITIONAL RESOURCES

READER'S GUIDE
- Selection Worksheet 9.4

ASSESSMENT PORTFOLIO
- Selection Check Test 2.9.7
- Selection Test 2.9.8

ESSENTIAL SKILLS PRACTICE BOOKS
- Writing 1.8, 1.20
- Language 2.47

PREREADING EXTENSIONS

Point out to students that the number three figures prominently in Dante's work. *The Divine Comedy* is divided into three sections (*Inferno, Purgatorio,* and *Paradiso*), but it is also part of a trilogy of works (the other two are *Vita nuova* and *Convivo*). The cantos in *The Divine Comedy* are written in *terza rima,* a three-line stanza. The number three figures so often in this work because medieval writers associated it with the Holy Trinity. If you have Catholic students in your class, ask them to explain the concept of the Holy Trinity to the others, or you might have the class read about it.

SUPPORT FOR LEP STUDENTS

PRONUNCIATIONS OF PROPER NOUNS AND ADJECTIVES

Dan • te A • li • ghie • ri (dän´tā ä lē gē´ ye´ rē)
Guelf (gelf)

ADDITIONAL VOCABULARY

equinoctial—referring to either of the equinoxes, or times when the sun crosses the equator; here meaning the vernal equinox, or March 21
incontinence—lewdness; lack of self-restraint
threescore—sixty; a score is twenty

READER'S JOURNAL

Before students begin to write, you may wish to point out that this activity is *not* an invitation for them to focus on stereotypes, prejudices, or other intolerant views. Encourage students to be thoughtful of others' feelings both when writing their journal essays and in discussion.

SPELLING AND VOCABULARY WORDS FROM THE SELECTION

allurement	enticement
arduous	gaunt
attrition	lamentation
avarice	piteous
commemoration	rank
discourse	ravening
eloquence	repentance
	tremulous

Cross-curricular Activities

ARTS AND HUMANITIES

Encourage students to create drawings, paintings, or models of the way they envision either Heaven or Hell. Students may draw their depictions from the Bible or from classical works of art, or they may rely on their own imaginations to create highly personal depictions. Other students may wish to find music that they believe captures the essence of either Heaven or Hell and share this music with their classmates.

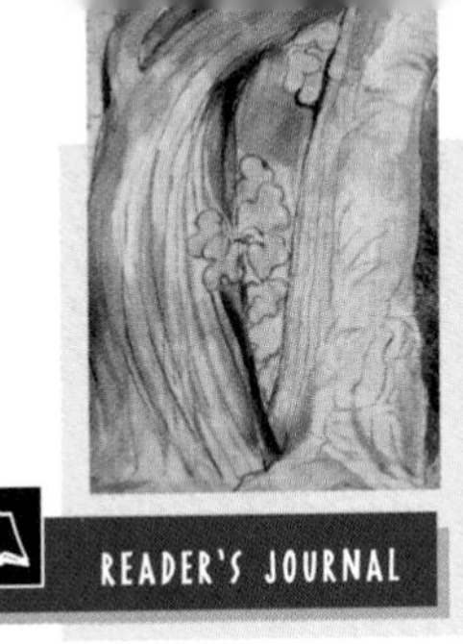

READER'S JOURNAL

What people, places, and things do you associate with the words *good* and *virtuous*? What people, places, and things come to mind when you think about the words *evil* and *immoral*? What representations of good and evil have you seen in books, movies, and television? List at least three representations of good and three representations of evil. Then pick the best one from each category to discuss in class.

FROM

The Divine Comedy

DANTE, TRANSLATED BY JOHN CIARDI

CANTO I
THE DARK WOOD OF ERROR

Midway in his allotted threescore years and ten, Dante comes to himself with a start and realizes that he has strayed from the True Way into the Dark Wood of Error (Worldliness). As soon as he has realized his loss, Dante lifts his eyes and sees the first light of the sunrise (the Sun is the Symbol of Divine Illumination) lighting the shoulders of a little hill (the Mount of Joy). It is the Easter Season, the time of resurrection, and the sun is in its equinoctial rebirth. This juxtaposition of joyous symbols fills Dante with hope and he sets out at once to climb directly up the Mount of Joy, but almost immediately his way is blocked by the Three Beasts of Worldliness: the Leopard of Malice and Fraud, the Lion of Violence and Ambition, and the She-Wolf of Incontinence. These beasts, and especially the She-Wolf, drive him back despairing into the darkness of error. But just as all seems lost, a figure appears to him. It is the shade of Virgil, Dante's symbol of Human Reason.

Virgil explains that he has been sent to lead Dante from error. There can, however, be no direct ascent past the beasts: the man who would escape them must go a longer and harder way. First he must descend through Hell (the Recognition of Sin), then he must ascend through Purgatory (the Renunciation of Sin), and only then may he reach the pinnacle of joy and come to the Light of God. Virgil offers to guide Dante, but only as far as Human Reason can go. Another guide (Beatrice, symbol of Divine Love) must take over for the final ascent, for Human Reason is self-limited. Dante submits himself joyously to Virgil's guidance and they move off.

Midway in our life's journey, I went astray
from the straight road and woke to find myself
alone in a dark wood. How shall I say
what wood that was! I never saw so drear,
so rank, so arduous a wilderness!
Its very memory gives a shape to fear.
Death could scarce be more bitter than that place!
But since it came to good, I will recount
all that I found revealed there by God's grace.
How I came to it I cannot rightly say,
so drugged and loose with sleep had I become
when I first wandered there from the True Way.
But at the far end of that valley of evil
whose maze had sapped my very heart with fear,
I found myself before a little hill
and lifted up my eyes. Its shoulders glowed
already with the sweet rays of that planet
whose virtue leads men straight on every road,
and the shining strengthened me against the fright
whose agony had wracked the lake of my heart
through all the terrors of that piteous night.
Just as a swimmer, who with his last breath
flounders ashore from perilous seas, might turn
to memorize the wide water of his death—
so did I turn, my soul still fugitive
from death's surviving image, to stare down
that pass that none had ever left alive.
And there I lay to rest from my heart's race
till calm and breath returned to me. Then rose
and pushed up that dead slope at such a pace
each footfall rose above the last. And lo!
almost at the beginning of the rise
I faced a spotted Leopard, all tremor and flow
and gaudy pelt. And it would not pass, but stood
so blocking my every turn that time and again
I was on the verge of turning back to the wood.
This fell at the first widening of the dawn
as the sun was climbing Aries[1] with those stars
that rode with him to light the new creation.
Thus the holy hour and the sweet season

1. **Aries.** Northern constellation between Pisces and Taurus

❶ *Where does Dante find himself? What is the place like? How does it make him feel?*

❷ *From where did Dante wander to this place?*

❸ *With what did the shoulders of the little hill glow? How does this sight make Dante feel? What does he turn to do?*

❹ *What creature blocks Dante's way?*

WORDS FOR EVERYDAY USE

rank (raŋk) *adj.,* growing vigorously and coarsely

ar • du • ous (är´jo͞o´əs) *adj.,* difficult, burdensome

pit • e • ous (pit´ē əs) *adj.,* arousing or deserving pity or compassion

ANSWERS TO GUIDED READING QUESTIONS

❶ Dante finds himself alone in a dark wood. The place is dark, dreary, and arduous, and it makes him feel frightened.

❷ Dante wandered to this place from the "True Way."

❸ The shoulders of the little hill glowed "with the sweet rays of that planet / whose virtue leads men straight on every road." This sight makes Dante feel more brave. He turns to "stare down / that pass that none had ever left alive."

❹ A spotted leopard blocks him.

LITERARY NOTE

Although today Dante is often considered Italy's greatest poet, his contemporaries had mixed reactions to his work. Giovanni Boccaccio (see page 822) admired his immediate predecessor Dante, produced many writings on his work, and devoted his later years to giving public readings, with commentary, of *The Divine Comedy.* Petrarch, however (see page 251), did not share Boccaccio's enthusiasm for Dante. Although Petrarch wrote the work for which he is remembered today—the *Canzoniere*—in his native Italian, he was a classicist who believed it was vulgar to write in the vernacular. Despite Petrarch's dislike of Dante's work, the two share many similarities. Dante loved Beatrice, who died at a young age, from afar. He later transformed her into a symbol of spiritual purity in *The Divine Comedy,* renouncing his physical love for her. Similarly, Petrarch loved Laura from afar; she died young, and Petrarch later decided his love for Laura detracted from his love of God. He then described in the *Canzoniere* the transition from his "error," his physical love for Laura, to his love for and trust in God.

VOCABULARY IN CONTEXT

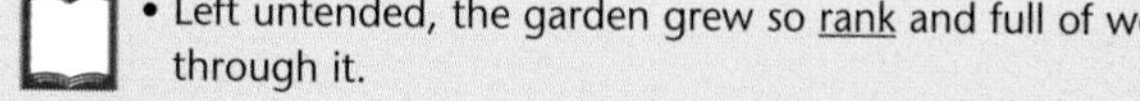

- Left untended, the garden grew so rank and full of weeds that it was impossible to walk through it.
- Giselle set out on her journey with a heavy heart, for the road ahead of her was long and arduous.
- The child we cast as the lonely orphan in the school play won the role because his piteous expression could move any audience to tears.

Answers to Guided Reading Questions

❶ Dante encounters a lion and a she-wolf. They both appear hungry and eager to devour him.

❷ The beasts drive Dante back into the sunless wood.

❸ The poet Virgil stands before him. He is familiar with this figure, having loved his verses.

Quotables

"I am the way into the city of woe.
I am the way to a forsaken people.
I am the way to the eternal sorrow.
Sacred justice moved my architect.
I was raised here by divine omnipotence,
Primordial love and ultimate intellect.
Only those elements time cannot wear
Were made before me, and beyond time I stand.
Abandon all hope ye who enter here."

—Dante

Additional Questions and Activities

Inform students that the quotation above is the inscription that Dante describes on the Gate of Hell through which he and Virgil must pass. Encourage students to discuss what they think of this inscription and to explain whether it is appropriate. What emotions might it evoke in one of the damned who must pass through to remain in Hell forever?

❶ *What other beasts does Dante encounter What is terrifying about these creatures?*

❷ *Where do the beasts drive Dante?*

❸ *Who appears before Dante? Why is Dante familiar with this figure?*

of commemoration did much to arm my fear
of that bright murderous beast with their good omen.
Yet not so much but that I shook with dread
at sight of a great Lion that broke upon me
raging with hunger, its enormous head
held high as if to strike a mortal terror
into the very air. And down his track,
a She-Wolf drove upon me, a starved horror
ravening and wasted beyond all belief.
She seemed a rack for avarice, gaunt and craving.
Oh many the souls she has brought to endless grief!
She brought such heaviness upon my spirit
at sight of her savagery and desperation,
I died from every hope of that high summit.
And like a miser—eager in acquisition
but desperate in self-reproach when Fortune's wheel
turns to the hour of his loss—all tears and attrition
I wavered back; and still the beast pursued,
forcing herself against me bit by bit
till I slid back into the sunless wood.
And as I fell to my soul's ruin, a presence
gathered before me on the discolored air,
the figure of one who seemed hoarse from long silence.
At sight of him in that friendless waste I cried:
"Have pity on me, whatever thing you are,
whether shade or living man." And it replied:
"Not man, though man I once was, and my blood
was Lombard, both my parents Mantuan.
I was born, though late, *sub Julio*,[2] and bred
in Rome under Augustus in the noon
of the false and lying gods. I was a poet
and sang of old Anchises' noble son[3]
who came to Rome after the burning of Troy.
But you—why do *you* return to these distresses
instead of climbing that shining Mount of Joy
which is the seat and first cause of man's bliss?"
"And are you then that Virgil and that fountain
of purest speech?" My voice grew tremulous:
"Glory and light of poets! now may that zeal
and love's apprenticeship that I poured out

2. ***sub Julio.*** During the rule of Julius Cæsar
3. **Anchises' noble son.** Aeneas, the forefather of the Roman people and hero of Virgil's *Aeneid*

Words for Everyday Use

com • mem • o • ra • tion (kə mem´ə rā´shən) *n.,* celebration in remembrance
rav • en • ing (rav´ən iŋ) *adj.,* greedily searching
av • a • rice (av´ə ris) *n.,* too great a desire for wealth; greediness
gaunt (gônt) *adj.,* thin and bony, haggard
at • tri • tion (ə trish´ən) *n.,* act or process of wearing away or weakening
trem • u • lous (trem´yo͞o ləs) *adj.,* trembling, quivering; fearful, timid

Vocabulary in Context

- In certain cultures, people hold commemorations to honor the saints after whom they have been named.
- The ravening vultures eyed the plains, seeking dead or dying creatures.
- We all felt that Chad's relentless avarice for wealth and power would be his downfall.
- When the gray cat first arrived on our doorstep, it was gaunt and bony, but now it is sleek and lean.
- The attrition caused by wind and sand had worn a hollow in the stone.
- Just before the wren attempted her first flight, she appeared tremulous, her feathers shaking warily.

on your heroic verses serve me well!
For you are my true master and first author,
the sole maker from whom I drew the breath
of that sweet style whose measures have brought me honor.
See there, immortal sage, the beast I flee.
For my soul's salvation, I beg you, guard me from her,
for she has struck a mortal tremor through me."
And he replied, seeing my soul in tears:
"He must go by another way who would escape
this wilderness, for that mad beast that fleers[4]
before you there, suffers no man to pass.
She tracks down all, kills all, and knows no glut,
but, feeding, she grows hungrier than she was.
She mates with any beast, and will mate with more
before the Greyhound comes to hunt her down.
He will not feed on lands nor loot, but honor
and love and wisdom will make straight his way.
He will rise between Feltro and Feltro, and in him
shall be the resurrection and new day
of that sad Italy for which Nisus died,
and Turnus, and Euryalus, and the maid Camilla.
He shall hunt her through every nation of sick pride
till she is driven back forever to Hell
whence Envy first released her on the world.
Therefore, for your own good, I think it well
you follow me and I will be your guide
and lead you forth through an eternal place.
There you shall see the ancient spirits tried
in endless pain, and hear their lamentation
as each bemoans the second death of souls.[5]
Next you shall see upon a burning mountain
souls in fire and yet content in fire,
knowing that whensoever it may be
they yet will mount into the blessed choir.
To which, if it is still your wish to climb,
a worthier spirit shall be sent to guide you.
With her shall I leave you, for the King of Time,
who reigns on high, forbids me to come there
since, living, I rebelled against his law.[6]

4. **fleers.** Snickers; jeers
5. **second death of souls.** Damnation in Hell
6. **rebelled . . . law.** In Virgil's time, Romans did not worship the Christian God; hence, Virgil is forbidden to enter Heaven.

❶ *Why can't Dante travel past the beasts? Which way must he go?*

❷ *Why is Virgil unable to accompany Dante for his entire journey?*

Words for Everyday Use

lam • en • ta • tion (lam´ən tā´shən) *n.*, expression of grief or sorrow, especially through weeping or wailing

Answers to Guided Reading Questions

❶ Dante can't travel past the beasts because they will eat him. He must follow Virgil as he guides him forth through an eternal place.

❷ Virgil must be replaced by a "worthier spirit." He cannot complete the journey with Dante because during his lifetime he was a pagan and rebelled against God's law.

Literary Note

Inform students that Dante saw the Inferno, or Hell, as a funnel with nine different levels or circles. The worst sinners are condemned to the lowest level. On the first level, Limbo, are virtuous pagans and unbaptized children, people who took no side in the struggle between God and the Devil. Lower levels are reserved for the lustful, the gluttonous, the avaricious, the wrathful, the violent, the fraudulent, and the deceitful. The lowest level of Hell is reserved for traitors to kin, homeland, guests, and benefactors. Dante populated Hell with many of his personal enemies. Other inhabitants of Hell with whom students may be familiar include Dido, Cleopatra, Helen, Achilles, Paris, and Tristan, whose circle is reserved for those who have loved unlawfully. Judas Iscariot, Brutus, and Cassius appear in the ninth circle reserved for traitors, with Satan himself, whose treason lay in denying the love of God.

Vocabulary in Context

- When they heard that the king had been killed in battle, the courtiers began a loud and wailing lamentation.

Art Note

William Blake (1757–1827) was a British Romantic poet and artist who earned a living by giving drawing lessons, illustrating books, and engraving. Blake's paintings, drawings, and engravings were highly unusual for their time period, stressing line over color and filled with dramatically posed figures. Unlike many painters of his day, Blake believed that art should be drawn from the imagination rather than nature. Much of Blake's art depicts Biblical scenes or scenes from Milton and Dante.

Answers to Guided Reading Questions

① Dante is willing to be led through Peter's gate and through the "sad halls of Hell."

Photo: John Web

Dante and Virgil Penetrating the Forest. *William Blake, 1824–1827. Tate Gallery, London, Great Britain. Art Resource, NY*

① *Where does Dante say he is willing to be led?*

He rules the waters and the land and air
and there holds court, his city and his throne.
Oh blessed are they he chooses!" And I to him:
"Poet, by that God to you unknown,
lead me this way. Beyond this present ill
and worse to dread, lead me to Peter's gate[7]
and be my guide through the sad halls of Hell."
And he then: "Follow." And he moved ahead
in silence, and I followed where he led.

7. **Peter's gate.** Gate by which one enters Purgatory

CANTO XXXI

THE EARTHLY PARADISE LETHE; BEATRICE, MATILDA

Beatrice continues her reprimand, forcing Dante to confess his faults until he swoons with grief and pain at the thought of his sin. He wakes to find himself in Lethe,[8] held in the arms of Matilda, who leads him to the other side of the stream and there immerses him that he may drink the waters that wipe out all memory of sin.

Matilda then leads him to the Four Cardinal Virtues,[9] who dance about him and lead him before the Griffon[10] where he may look into the eyes of Beatrice. In them Dante sees, in a first Beatific Vision, the radiant reflection of the Griffon, who appears now in his human and now in his godly stature.

The Three Theological Virtues[11] now approach and beg that Dante may behold the smile of Beatrice. Beatrice removes her veil, and in a Second Beatific Vision, Dante beholds the splendor of the unveiled shining of Divine Love.

"You, there, who stand upon the other side—"
(turning to me now, who had thought the edge
of her discourse was sharp, the point) she cried
without pause in her flow of eloquence,
"Speak up! Speak up! Is it true? To such a charge
your own confession must give evidence."
I stood as if my spirit had turned numb:
the organ of my speech moved, but my voice
died in my throat before a word could come.
Briefly she paused, then cried impatiently:
"What are you thinking? Speak up, for the waters[12]
have yet to purge sin from your memory."
Confusion joined to terror forced a broken
"yes" from my throat, so weak that only one
who read my lips would know that I had spoken.
As an arbalest[13] will snap when string and bow
are drawn too tight by the bowman, and the bolt
will strike the target a diminished blow—
so did I shatter, strengthless and unstrung,
under her charge, pouring out floods of tears,
while my voice died in me on the way to my tongue.
And she: "Filled as you were with the desire
I taught you for That Good beyond which nothing

1 *What does Beatrice demand that Dante do?*

8. **Lethe.** In Greek and Roman mythology, the river of forgetfulness flowing through Hades, the afterworld
9. **the Four Cardinal Virtues.** Justice, Prudence, Fortitude, and Temperance
10. **the Griffon.** Mythical monster with the body and hind legs of a lion and the head, wings, and claws of an eagle
11. **The Three Theological Virtues.** Faith, Hope, and Charity
12. **the waters.** The river Lethe
13. **arbalest.** Medieval crossbow

WORDS FOR EVERYDAY USE

dis • course (dis´kôrs) *n.*, communication of ideas and information

el • o • quence (el´ə kwəns) *n.*, speech or writing that is vivid, forceful, and persuasive

ANSWERS TO GUIDED READING QUESTIONS

1 Beatrice demands that Dante confess his faults.

LITERARY NOTE

Dante read classical literature, the literature of Greece and Rome, widely. Thus, elements from Greek and Roman mythology have worked their way into Dante's conception of the afterlife. For example, Charon, the boatman who ferries the dead across the River Styx into Hades in Greek mythology, appears in canto III to ferry the damned across the River Acheron into Hell. Lethe, a river in Dante's Paradise, was the river of forgetfulness flowing through Hades in Greek and Roman mythology, and the Griffon is also a creature from Greek and Roman mythology.

VOCABULARY IN CONTEXT

- Everyone enjoyed listening to Laura's discourse because she was bubbling over with whimsical notions and unusual ideas.
- The candidate impressed the audience, not with new ideas or insights, but with sheer eloquence—he was a born public speaker.

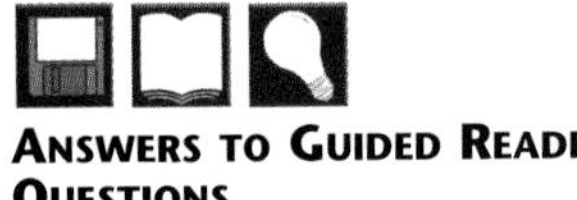

Answers to Guided Reading Questions

❶ Dante mistakenly treasured false pleasures and enticements.

❷ It is important for Dante to face his sins so that he might learn from them and become stronger. He feels guilt, grief, and pain.

❸ His love of mortal things has been useless. Beatrice says he should have turned away from mortal things and focused on the spiritual.

Additional Questions and Activities

If there are students in your class who have gone to Confession (Penance), you might ask them to explain to the rest of the class their thoughts on this experience. You might also ask students to write a two- or three-page story in which confession plays a major role.

❶ *What things did Dante mistakenly treasure?*

❷ *Why is it important for Dante to speak of and understand his sins? How does Dante feel after he confesses his sins?*

❸ *What has Dante gained from his love of mortal things? What does Beatrice say he should have learned?*

exists on earth to which man may aspire,
what yawning moats or what stretched chain-lengths[14] lay
across your path to force you to abandon
all hope of pressing further on your way?
What increase or allurement seemed to show
in the brows of others that you walked before them
as a lover walks below his lady's window?"
My breath dragged from me in a bitter sigh;
I barely found a voice to answer with;
my lips had trouble forming a reply.
In tears I said: "The things of the world's day,
false pleasures and enticements, turned my steps
as soon as you had ceased to light my way."
And she: "Had you been silent, or denied
what you confess, your guilt would still be known
to Him from Whom no guilt may hope to hide.
But here, before our court, when souls upbraid
themselves for their own guilt in true remorse,
the grindstone is turned back against the blade.
In any case that you may know your crime
truly and with true shame and so be stronger
against the Siren's song[15] another time,
control your tears and listen with your soul
to learn how my departure from the flesh
ought to have spurred you to the higher goal.
Nothing in Art or Nature could call forth
such joy from you, as sight of that fair body
which clothed me once and now sifts back to earth.
And if my dying turned that highest pleasure
to very dust, what joy could still remain
in mortal things for you to seek and treasure?
At the first blow you took from such vain things
your every thought should have been raised to follow
my flight above decay. Nor should your wings
have been weighed down by any joy below—
love of a maid, or any other fleeting
and useless thing—to wait a second blow.
The fledgling waits a second shaft, a third;
but nets are spread and the arrow sped in vain

14. **yawning moats . . . chain lengths.** Defensive military measure used to obstruct enemy movement

15. **Siren's song.** Song of a mythological creature who lured sailors to their deaths by singing

Words for Everyday Use

al • lure • ment (ə lo͞or´mənt) *n.,* something tempting or fascinating

en • tice • ment (en tīs´mənt) *n.,* something that attracts by offering hope, reward, or pleasure

Vocabulary in Context

- The cool, shimmering swimming hole was an allurement no child could resist on a scorching afternoon.
- When Jeremiah lost his wallet, he offered a reward, no questions asked, as an enticement for its return.

in sight or hearing of the full-grown bird."
As a scolded child, tongue tied for shame, will stand
and recognize his fault, and weep for it
bowing his head to a just reprimand
so did I stand. And she said: "If to hear me
grieves you, now raise your beard and let your eyes
show you a greater cause for misery."
The blast that blows from Libya's hot sand,
or the Alpine gale, overcomes less resistance
uprooting oaks than I, at her command,
overcame then in lifting up my face;
for when she had referred to it as my "beard"
I sensed too well the venom of her phrase.
When I had raised my eyes with so much pain,
I saw those Primal Beings, now at rest,
who had strewn blossoms round her thick as rain;
and with my tear-blurred and uncertain vision
I saw Her turned to face that beast[16] which is
one person in two natures without division.
Even veiled and across the river from me
her face outshone its first-self[17] by as much
as she outshone all mortals formerly.
And the thorns of my repentance pricked me so
that all the use and substance of the world
I most had loved, now most appeared my foe.
Such guilty recognition gnawed my heart
I swooned for pain; and what I then became
she best knows who most gave me cause to smart.
When I returned to consciousness at last
I found the lady who had walked alone
bent over me. "Hold fast!" she said, "Hold fast!"
She had drawn me into the stream up to my throat,
and pulling me behind her, she sped on
over the water, light as any boat.
Nearing the sacred bank, I heard her say
in tones so sweet I cannot call them back,
much less describe them here: *"Asperges me."*[18]
Then the sweet lady took my head between
her open arms, and embracing me, she dipped me
and made me drink the waters that make clean.

Whom does Dante find when he returns to consciousness? What does she make him do, and why?

16. **beast.** The Griffon
17. **first-self.** Beatrice's mortal self
18. ***"Asperges me."*** "Purge me."

Words for Everyday Use

re • pent • ance (ri pen´təns) *n.*, feeling of sorrow for wrongdoing, remorse

Answers to Guided Reading Questions

❶ Dante finds Matilda, "the lady who had walked alone." She leads him to the other side of the stream, immerses him, and makes him drink the waters that wipe out all memories of sin.

Cross-curricular Activities

SOCIAL STUDIES

Dante belonged to a political party known as the White Guelfs. Encourage students to work in small groups to research the conflict between the Black and White Guelfs and the Black and White Ghibellines. They may prepare either written or oral reports on their findings. You might also encourage students to read the excerpt from Dino Compagni's *Chronicle of Contemporary Events,* which deals with the roots of this conflict and appears on page 813.

Vocabulary in Context

- The priest told the condemned criminal that he should express his repentance for his crimes and ask for divine forgiveness.

Answers to Guided Reading Questions

❶ They dance before him and lead him before the Griffon, where he may look into the eyes of Beatrice. There he will see a joyous light that will instruct him.

❷ Dante looks into Beatrice's eyes and sees the Griffin shining in them.

❸ Dante cannot put his feelings into words when he sees Beatrice's smile.

Selection Check Test with Answers

EX: Where does Dante find himself?

Dante finds himself in a dark wood.

1. Why can't Dante leave the dark wood?

Three beasts block his way.

2. What figure appears before Dante to guide him out of the wood?

The figure of the poet Virgil appears before Dante.

3. What does Beatrice force Dante to do?

Beatrice forces Dante to confront his sins.

4. To where does Matilda lead Dante?

She leads Dante to a stream that will cleanse him of all memory of sin.

5. What does Dante see when he looks into the smile of Beatrice?

He sees Divine Love.

❶ *What are the Four Maidens, appearing as nymphs, supposed to be doing for Dante?*

Then raising me in my new purity
  she led me to the dance of the Four Maidens;[19]
  each raised an arm and so joined hands above me.
"Here we are nymphs; stars are we in the skies.
  Ere Beatrice went to earth we were ordained
  her handmaids. We will lead you to her eyes;
but that your own may see what joyous light
  shines in them, yonder Three, who see more deeply,
  will sharpen and instruct your mortal sight."
Thus they sang, then led me to the Griffon.
  Behind him, Beatrice waited. And when I stood
  at the Griffon's breast, they said in unison:

❷ *Where must Dante look first? What does he see?*

"Look deep, look well, however your eyes may smart.
  We have led you now before those emeralds[20]
  from which Love shot his arrows through your heart."
A thousand burning passions, every one
  hotter than any flame, held my eyes fixed
  to the lucent eyes she held fixed on the Griffon.
Like sunlight in a glass the twofold creature
  shone from the deep reflection of her eyes,
  now in the one, now in the other nature.
Judge, reader, if I found it passing strange
  to see the thing unaltered in itself
  yet in its image working change on change.
And while my soul in wonder and delight
  was savoring that food which in itself
  both satisfies and quickens appetite,
the other Three, whose bearing made it clear
  they were of higher rank, came toward me dancing
  to the measure of their own angelic air.
"Turn, Beatrice, oh turn the eyes of grace,"
  was their refrain, "upon your faithful one
  who comes so far to look upon your face.
Grant us this favor of your grace: reveal
  your mouth to him, and let his eyes behold
  the Second Beauty,[21] which your veils conceal."

❸ *What effect does Beatrice's smile have on Dante?*

O splendor of the eternal living light!
  who that has drunk deep of Parnassus'[22] waters,
  or grown pale in the shadow of its height,
would not, still, feel his burdened genius fail
  attempting to describe in any tongue
  how you appeared when you put by your veil
in that free air open to heaven and earth
whose harmony is your shining shadowed forth! ■

19. **Four Maidens.** Four cardinal virtues
20. **emeralds.** Beatrice's eyes
21. **Second Beauty.** Beatrice's smile
22. **Parnassus'.** Belonging to a mountain believed sacred to Apollo and the Muses; symbolizes poetic activity

Responding to the Selection

In what way is your image of the afterlife similar to or different from Dante's? Explain.

Reviewing the Selection

RECALLING / INTERPRETING

1. In canto 1 of *Inferno*, where does Dante find himself? What prevents him from leaving this place? ▶▶ How does Dante feel when he finds himself "astray"? Why has he strayed into this place?

2. In canto 1, what figure appears to Dante? What is the figure there to help Dante do? Why does Dante recognize the figure? Why is this figure unable to guide Dante for the entire journey? ▶▶ What is the purpose of Dante's journey? Why is the role of the figure who appears before him important?

3. In canto 31, what is Dante forced to confess? Who orders him to make this confession? ▶▶ Why is Dante forced to make a confession? How does Dante feel as he makes his confession? Why does he feel this way?

4. What does Dante see as he looks into Beatrice's eyes and at her smile? ▶▶ What quality does Dante experience through his vision of Beatrice's eyes and smile? What has he had to do to earn this experience?

SYNTHESIZING

5. Why is Dante, the speaker, forced on his imaginary journey? What in his own life must he examine? What will happen if he successfully completes his journey?

Understanding Literature (Questions for Discussion)

1. **Motif.** A **motif** is any element that recurs in one or more works of literature or art. One common motif in medieval literature is that of the spiritual journey. A character who is lost or in a state of moral confusion undertakes a journey during which he or she has a transformative experience. What is the journey that the main character, Dante, undertakes in *The Divine Comedy*? What leads him to undertake this journey? In what way does this journey represent the journey that all people, according to the medieval Christian view, must undertake? What is the culmination of Dante's journey? What realization, or epiphany, occurs at this culminating moment?

RESPONDING TO THE SELECTION

Students should discuss their ideas in small groups. Remind students to be respectful of the ideas of others regarding the afterlife.

ANSWERS FOR REVIEWING THE SELECTION

RECALLING AND INTERPRETING

1. **Recalling.** Dante finds himself in a dark and frightening wood. Three beasts prevent him from leaving this place. **Interpreting.** Dante feels frightened. He has strayed from the word of God.

2. **Recalling.** The figure of Virgil appears to Dante. Virgil is there to help the speaker out of the wood and away from error. Dante recognizes Virgil because he has read his poetry. Virgil cannot guide Dante through Heaven because VIrgil was a pagan who never experienced Christian grace. **Interpreting.** Dante's journey is from earthly attachments to spiritual truth. Virgil is a fellow epic poet, who wrote about a descent to the underworld, and whom Dante hopes to equal in this work.

3. **Recalling.** Dante is forced to confess his sins. Beatrice orders him to make this confession. **Interpreting.** Dante must be free of sin to experience Divine Love and to enter Heaven. Dante feels guilt, grief, and pain as he makes his confession because he is ashamed of his mistakes.

4. **Recalling.** Dante sees Divine Love as he looks into Beatrice's eyes and at her smile. **Interpreting.** These visions represent God's Divine Love. He has had to travel through Hell and Purgatory and cleansed himself of sin.

SYNTHESIZING

Responses will vary. Possible responses are given.

5. Dante, because of his earthly sins, cannot go directly to God. He is forced to examine the error of his ways, renounce these ways, and successfully complete his journey, to experience divine love.

ANSWERS FOR UNDERSTANDING LITERATURE

Responses will vary. Possible responses are given.

1. **Motif.** Dante journeys through Hell, Purgatory, and Heaven. He realizes he has strayed from the true path into the dark wood of error. According to the medieval Christian view, all people must undertake a journey to reach salvation. Dante experiences Divine Love in the culmination of his journey.
Responses will vary.

2. **Simile.** Dante's attempt to escape the dark wood is compared to the attempt of a swimmer to "flounder" ashore from perilous seas. Dante is feeling helpless and hopeless. In lines 16–20, Dante compares himself to an arbalest, a medieval crossbow, because he feels he is being "drawn too tight" by Beatrice, who is causing him much pain by forcing him to acknowledge his sins.

ANALYTIC SCALES FOR RESPONDING IN WRITING

Assign a score from 1 to 25 for each grading criterion below. (For more detailed evaluation, see the evaluation forms for writing, revising, and proofreading, Assessment Portfolio 4.1–4.9.)

1. A Journey Tale

- **Content/Unity.** The journey tale describes a character's quest to learn something about himself or herself.
- **Organization/Coherence.** The journey tale presents details in a sensible order.
- **Language/Style.** The journey tale uses vivid and precise nouns, verbs, and modifiers.
- **Conventions.** The journey tale avoids errors in spelling, grammar, usage, mechanics, and manuscript form.

▶ Additional practice is provided in the Essential Skills Practice Book: Writing 1.8.

2. Critical Essay

- **Content/Unity.** The essay discusses the allegorical characters in *The Divine Comedy.*
- **Organization/Coherence.** The essay begins with an introduction that includes the thesis of the essay. The introduction is followed by supporting paragraphs with clear transitions. The essay ends with a solid conclusion.
- **Language/Style.** The essay uses vivid and precise nouns, verbs, and modifiers.
- **Conventions.** The essay avoids errors in spelling, grammar, usage, mechanics, and manuscript form.

▶ Additional practice is provided in the Essential Skills Practice Book: Writing 1.20.

2. **Simile.** A **simile** is a comparison using *like* or *as.* Lines 22–25 of canto 1 contain an extended, or Homeric simile. What two things are being compared in this simile? In what way does this simile show vividly how Dante is feeling at that moment? The section from canto 31 of *Purgatorio* also contains a long simile intended to give the reader a vivid picture of how Dante is feeling. In lines 16–20, what similarity does Dante point out between himself and an arbalest, or medieval crossbow?

Responding in Writing

1. **Creative Writing: Journey Tale.** Many literary works have focused on characters who undertake journeys to learn more about themselves. Gilgamesh (see page 202) was one of the earliest heroes to undertake such a journey; later works describing such a journey include *Catcher in the Rye, Adventures of Huckleberry Finn,* and *Heart of Darkness.* In *The Divine Comedy,* the speaker goes on an imaginary journey through the afterlife to learn how to overcome earthly distractions and live a better life. Plan a journey tale of your own in which a character is on a quest to learn something about himself or herself. Make a map of this journey, and write a few paragraphs describing the journey. These paragraphs should describe the path the character will take, obstacles that he or she must overcome along the way, details about the setting, and the character's ultimate goal. Your character can be real or fictional, and the journey can seem realistic or have elements of fantasy.

2. **Critical Essay: Allegory.** The allegory of *The Divine Comedy* adds to the brilliance and timelessness of the epic poem. In a short essay, discuss the following allegorical characters: Dante, the speaker, as humankind; Virgil, the speaker's guide, as human reason; the leopard as malice and fraud; the lion as violence and ambition; the she-wolf as incontinence, or lack of restraint; and Beatrice as divine love, or the love of God. You may choose to write briefly about each of these figures, or you may choose to focus more thoroughly on two or three of them. In your essay, discuss the relationship of each part of the allegory to the overall goal of the main character.

Language Lab

Using Commas. Review the Language Arts Survey 2.47, "Using Commas." Then add commas as they are needed in the following sentences.

EX. Yes I would enjoy reading more about angels.

Yes, I would enjoy reading more about angels.

1. The word *angel* comes from the Greek word *angelos* meaning "messenger."
2. Angels figure in Western religions such as Judaism Christianity and Islam.
3. Angels a class of beings between God and humankind are believed to perform services for God.
4. People believe that angels can serve as guides protect humans and deliver messages to humans from God.
5. In *The Divine Comedy* Dante's greatest work angels appear both as messengers and as guardians.

ANSWERS FOR LANGUAGE LAB

1. The word *angel* comes from the Greek word *angelos,* meaning "messenger."
2. Angels figure in Western religions, such as Judaism, Christianity, and Islam.
3. Angels, a class of beings between God and humankind, are believed to perform services for God.
4. People believe that angels can serve as guides, protect humans, and deliver messages to humans from God.
5. In *The Divine Comedy,* Dante's greatest work, angels appear both as messengers and as guardians.

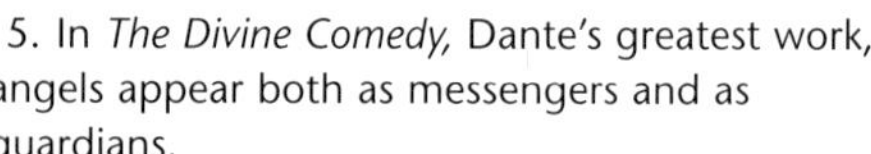
▶ Additional practice is provided in the Essential Skills Practice Book: Language 2.47.

PREREADING

"Ballade"
by François Villon, translated by Galway Kinnell

FRANCE

About the Author

FRANÇOIS VILLON
1431–?

François Villon is the pen name of François Montcorbier, a man known as much for his disreputable life as for the lyric poetry that made him one of France's greatest medieval poets. Villon was born in Paris and educated at the Sorbonne, where he received a master's degree in 1452. Three years later, he killed a man with a sword in a tavern-room brawl but received a royal pardon on grounds of self-defense. Soon afterward he was involved in a theft, left Paris, and stayed for a time at the court of Charles d'Orléans, who was both a poet and a patron of other poets. Villon was imprisoned at Meung-sur-Loire in 1461 but was released in a general amnesty declared later that year. He then returned to Paris, where he was unable to avoid further difficulties for long. Villon was arrested for robbery in 1462 and was condemned to be hanged and strangled to death; however, in 1463, this death sentence was commuted to banishment from Paris. From the time of his exile, Villon's history remains unknown.

About the Selection

Villon wrote **"Ballade"** while awaiting his death sentence in Paris. The poem is starkly realistic and ghastly in its depiction of a group of men hanged upon a scaffold, their decaying bodies swaying in the wind. The poem asserts a kinship between these criminals and the rest of humanity and makes a poignant appeal to God's mercy. The original title for this ballad was either "Ballade des pendus," meaning "Ballad of the Hanged," or "L'Epitaphe Villon," meaning "Villon's Epitaph." Given his situation at the time he wrote this poem, Villon undoubtedly intended "Ballade" as his own **epitaph** (a verse written to be used on a tomb or to commemorate one who has died). Many of Villon's works reflect the medieval preoccupation with and fear of death. Longing for times gone by, for a past inhabited by great men and women is another recurring theme in Villon's work as is regret for his own misspent youth. Villon expresses some of this regret in the warning he provides in "Ballade."

CONNECTIONS: Epitaphs

People have long been concerned with their final words—the words that appear on their tombs. In the West, the ancient Greeks began the tradition of epitaphs, later followed by the Romans, whose epitaphs frequently warned against disturbing the tomb. The writing of epitaphs had become a profession by the sixteenth century, and such poets as Ben Jonson, John Milton, and Alexander Pope are known for writing fine epitaphs for others. Examples of epitaphs appear on page 763. While most epitaphs are serious in tone, others are wryly humorous or witty.

GOALS/OBJECTIVES

Studying this lesson will enable students to

- have positive experiences reading a poem written from an unusual point of view
- briefly explain what an epitaph is
- identify the point of view of a literary work
- identify and explain the use of apostrophe, refrain, realism, and imagery in a poem
- write an epitaph
- write a critical essay explaining whether "Ballade" expresses typical medieval attitudes about death

ADDITIONAL RESOURCES

READER'S GUIDE
- Selection Worksheet 9.5

ASSESSMENT PORTFOLIO
- Selection Check Test 2.9.9
- Selection Test 2.9.10

ESSENTIAL SKILLS PRACTICE BOOKS
- Writing 1.8, 1.20

PREREADING EXTENSIONS

Inform students that, while Villon was a disreputable figure who wrote during the Medieval Period, at the same time another disreputable figure was being celebrated in the popular ballads of the day—Robin Hood. Some people believe that Robin Hood was an actual historical figure who lived sometime during the thirteenth century. In the Robin Hood ballads that were composed as early as the fourteenth century, he is presented as a rebel who struggles against the local sheriff, robs the rich, kills only in self-defense, and chivalrously protects women and the poor. While the knights of romantic legend were the heroes of the nobility, Robin Hood was a hero of the common people. His legends represent a form of social protest against authority figures and hunting restrictions. Encourage students to locate and read ballads about Robin Hood.

SUPPORT FOR LEP STUDENTS

PRONUNCIATIONS OF PROPER NOUNS AND ADJECTIVES

Charles d'Or • lé • ans (chärlz dôr´lā ənz)

Meung • sur • Loire (mʉng ser lwär´)

Fran • çois Vil • lon (frän swä´ vē yōn´)

ADDITIONAL VOCABULARY

magpie—type of bird that noisily chatters

READER'S JOURNAL

As an alternative activity, you might ask students to write about a time in their lives when they showed someone mercy or forgiveness or witnessed someone else displaying these qualities.

Answers to Guided Reading Questions

❶ The speakers say that humans should pity them to gain God's mercy. The speakers call living humans their "brothers."

❷ The speakers are dead because they are described as already decayed. The speakers ask the living not to joke about their plight but to pray that God will absolve all humans.

❸ Jesus' mercy keeps the speakers from "hellfire."

Cultural/Historical Note

Medieval theologians enumerated seven cardinal virtues—prudence, temperance, justice, fortitude, faith, hope, and love—and seven deadly sins—pride, avarice, lechery, anger, gluttony, envy, and sloth. Much of medieval literature provides illustrations of, or warnings about, these virtues and vices. Ask students the following questions: Of what deadly sin(s) are the speakers guilty? What virtues do they advocate in others?

ANSWERS

The speakers are guilty of loving flesh too well, so they may be guilty of avarice, lechery, sloth and/or gluttony. They advocate justice, faith, hope, and love.

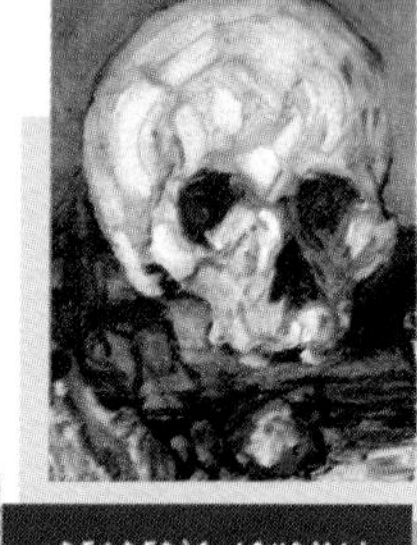

Imagine that you have been sentenced to death. What would you think about? Would you worry about the pain of your execution? about what others would think of you? about your condition in the afterlife? Would you accept the sentence with resignation, or would you be angry and struggle against it? In your journal, write about what you would want to express to others if you received such a sentence.

"Ballade"

FRANÇOIS VILLON, TRANSLATED BY GALWAY KINNELL

❶ *According to the speakers, why should living human beings pity the speakers? What do the speakers call the living human beings?*

❷ *What is the condition of the speakers? How can you tell the speakers are dead? What do the speakers ask of the living?*

❸ *What keeps the speakers from "hellfire"?*

Brother humans who live on after us
Don't let your hearts harden against us
For if you have pity on wretches like us
More likely God will show mercy to you
You see us five, six, hanging here

As for the flesh we loved too well
A while ago it was eaten and has rotted away
And we the bones turn to ashes and dust
Let no one make us the butt[1] of jokes
But pray God that he absolve us all.

Don't be insulted that we call you
Brothers, even if it was by Justice
We were put to death, for you understand
Not every person has the same good sense
Speak up for us, since we can't ourselves

Before the son of the virgin Mary
That his mercy toward us shall keep flowing
Which is what keeps us from hellfire
We are dead, may no one taunt us
But pray God that he absolve us all.

1. **butt.** Object of ridicule or criticism

WORDS FOR EVERYDAY USE

ab • solve (ab zälv´) *vt.,* pronounce free from guilt or blame

Vocabulary in Context

- His confessor told him to pray to absolve himself from the sin of excessive pride.

Skull. Paul Cézanne, 1865

The rain has rinsed and washed us
The sun dried us and turned us black
Magpies and ravens have pecked out our eyes
And plucked our beards and eyebrows
Never ever can we stand still

Now here, now there, as the wind shifts
At its whim it keeps swinging us
Pocked[2] by birds worse than a sewing thimble
Therefore don't join in our brotherhood
But pray God that he absolve us all.

Prince Jesus, master over all
Don't let us fall into hell's dominion
We've nothing to do or settle down there
Men, there's nothing here to laugh at
But pray God that he absolve us all. ■

2. **pocked.** Marked; disfigured

❶ *What do the speakers warn others not to do? Why shouldn't others do this?*

❷ *According to the speakers, why shouldn't they "fall into hell's dominion"?*

ART NOTE

Paul Cézanne (1839–1906) was a French Post-Impressionist painter who had a profound effect on the development of modern painting. He is known for painting landscapes, portraits, and still lifes such as *Skull,* often dark and violent in appearance.

ANSWERS TO GUIDED READING QUESTIONS

❶ The speakers warn others not to join in the brotherhood of the hanged because the hanged are scarred by scavengers and sway endlessly in the wind.

❷ The speakers claim to be people who do not deserve to be sent to "hell's dominion." They say they have "nothing to do or settle down there."

SELECTION CHECK TEST WITH ANSWERS

EX. What do the speakers call other humans?

They call other humans their brothers.

1. Who are the speakers in this poem?

The speakers are five or six men who have died by hanging.

2. What did the speakers love too well?

They loved flesh too well.

3. What keeps the speakers from "hellfire"?

The mercy of the son of the Virgin Mary keeps the speakers from "hellfire."

4. What have birds done to the speakers?

Birds have pecked out their eyes, beards, and eyebrows.

5. What does the wind do to the speakers?

The wind keeps swinging them at its whim.

Responding to the Selection

Some students may prefer to write a response to the speakers. Others might work in pairs to role play a conversation.

Answers for Reviewing the Selection

RECALLING AND INTERPRETING

1. **Recalling.** The speakers call other human beings "brothers." **Interpreting.** The speakers are trying to point out that both the hanged men and the reader share kinship as members of the human race. This is a good tactic because it causes the reader to identify with the speakers and be more sympathetic toward their plight.
2. **Recalling.** The speakers admit that they loved flesh, or worldly things, too well. Their flesh has now rotted away. The speakers ask others not to joke about or make light of their plight. **Interpreting.** The speakers are admitting that they loved worldly things too well and were put to death by "Justice." The speakers say that they do not have the same "good sense" as others, including the reader. This excuse is designed to flatter the reader and make him or her more sympathetic.
3. **Recalling.** They ask their fellow humans to take pity on them and "pray God that he absolve us all." The speakers want other humans to speak up to Jesus for them. The speakers say that God must absolve all human beings of their sins. **Interpreting.** The speakers seem to regret their past sins. They are hoping to attain salvation. The speakers are trying to make the reader identify with them by pointing out that they, too, will one day need God's absolution.
4. **Recalling.** The speakers have been washed in the rain and dried and blackened in the sun. Birds have pecked out the eyes, beards, and eyebrows of the men. The wind keeps swinging them from (cont.)

Responding to the Selection

How would you feel if you encountered the speakers as they are described in this poem? What would your attitude toward them be? Imagine that you then hear the speakers' plea. Would this plea change your attitude toward the speakers? If so, in what way? If not, why not?

Reviewing the Selection

Recalling		Interpreting
1. What do the speakers call other humans?	▶▶	What are the speakers trying to point out? Why might it be a good tactic for the speakers to address the reader in this way?
2. What do the speakers admit they "loved too well"? What do they say has happened to this thing? What do they ask others not to do?	▶▶	In what way are the speakers admitting their guilt? What excuse do they have for their crimes? What effect is this excuse designed to have upon the reader?
3. What do the speakers ask their fellow humans to do? To whom do the speakers want other humans to "speak up"? What do they say God must do for all?	▶▶	How do the speakers feel about their past sins? What are they hoping to attain? In what way are they trying to make the reader identify with them?
4. What has weather done to the speakers? What have birds done to them? What does the wind do to them? What warning do the speakers offer the reader?	▶▶	What effect are lines 21–30 designed to have upon the reader? In what way do these lines further emphasize line 34, "Men, there's nothing here to laugh at"?

Synthesizing

5. Why do you think the hanged men are concerned that people might laugh at their bodies? In what way is laughing at a person who has been hanged to death similar to judging him or her? Why, according to the speakers, is it wrong to judge the hanged men? What attitude should people take toward those condemned to death, according to this poem? How are those condemned to death similar to the rest of humanity?

Answers for Reviewing the Selection (cont.)

their scaffold. The speakers warn the reader not to join their "brotherhood." **Interpreting.** These lines are meant to horrify the reader and make death seem like something horrible that should be pitied and feared, not ridiculed.

SYNTHESIZING

Responses will vary. Possible responses are given.

5. The speakers fear that people will think their fate is deserved and find their end amusing. Laughing at a hanged person means that you have judged that person guilty and unworthy of pity or mercy. According to the speakers, one should not judge others because all human beings are one day judged by God. The speakers believe that others should be compassionate and understanding toward those condemned to death.

Understanding Literature (Questions for Discussion)

1. **Point of View and Apostrophe. Point of view** is the vantage point from which a story is told. Some common points of view are the first-person point of view, in which the narrator uses words such as *I* and *we,* and the third-person point of view, in which the narrator uses words such as *he, she, it,* and *they* and avoids the use of *I* and *we.* An **apostrophe** is a rhetorical technique in which an object or person is directly addressed. From what point of view is this poem written? What makes this point of view unusual? Would this poem be as successful if it were told from another point of view? Why or why not? Whom do the speakers directly address? Why do the speakers directly address these people?

2. **Refrain.** A **refrain** is a line or group of lines repeated in a poem or song. Many ballads contain refrains. What refrain is repeated throughout this ballad? Why do you think the author chose to use this line as the refrain?

3. **Realism and Imagery. Realism** is the attempt to render in art an accurate portrayal of reality. An **image** is a word or phrase that names something that can be seen, heard, touched, tasted, or smelled. To what senses do the images in this poem appeal? What words would you use to characterize this poem's imagery? What graphic details contribute to the central image of this poem? Why might the author have decided to use Realism in depicting these images?

Responding in Writing

1. **Creative Writing: Epitaph.** An epitaph is an inscription or verse written to be used on a tomb or written in commemoration of someone who has died. Write your own epitaph, either in verse like Villon's or in prose. Keep in mind that, unlike Villon's example, many epitaphs are brief—not more than a few lines—and that while some are serious in tone, others are wryly humorous or witty. To begin, you might think about how you want people to remember you when you die and what message you would wish to pass on to the living. For further inspiration, you might also look to examples of epitaphs such as those below.

William Butler Yeats's epitaph:

Cast a cold eye
On life, on death.
Horseman, pass by!

William Shakespeare's epitaph:

Good friend for Jesus sake forbeare,
To digg the dust enclosed heare!
Blest be the man that spares thes stones
And curst be he that moves my bones.

from Ben Jonson's "Epitaph on Elizabeth L.H.":

Underneath this stone doth lie
As much beauty as could die,
Which in life did harbor give
To more virtue than doth live.

John Gay's epitaph:

Life's a jest, and all things show it;
I thought so once, and now I know it.

Answers for Understanding Literature

Responses will vary. Possible responses are given.

1. Point of View and Apostrophe. This poem is written from the first-person point of view. This point of view is unusual because the speakers are men who have been hanged to death. The speakers directly address the living. The speakers hope to change the attitude of others toward those who have been condemned to death.

2. Refrain. The refrain is the line "But pray God that he absolve us all." The author used this line as his refrain both because it is a plea for mercy and because it emphasizes that all people will be judged one day, so people should not judge others.

3. Realism and Imagery. The images appeal to the reader's sense of sight. The poem's imagery is gruesome and horrifying. The author may have been striving to make the condition of his subjects more shocking through the use of Realism, hoping that readers would sympathize with his subjects when confronted with the horror of their reality.

ANALYTIC SCALES FOR RESPONDING IN WRITING

Assign a score from 1 to 25 for each grading criterion below. (For more detailed evaluation, see the evaluation forms for writing, revising, and proofreading, Assessment Portfolio 4.1–4.9.)

1. Epitaph

- **Content/Unity.** The epitaph expresses the way the writer wishes to be remembered or offers a message to the living.
- **Organization/Coherence.** The epitaph is written in a sensible order.
- **Language/Style.** The epitaph uses vivid and precise nouns, verbs, and modifiers.
- **Conventions.** The epitaph avoids errors in spelling, grammar, usage, mechanics, and manuscript form.

▶ Additional practice is provided in the Essential Skills Practice Book: Writing 1.8.

2. Critical Essay

- **Content/Unity.** The essay explains whether "Ballade" expresses typical medieval attitudes toward death.
- **Organization/Coherence.** The essay begins with an introduction that includes the thesis of the essay. The introduction is followed by supporting paragraphs with clear transitions. The essay ends with a solid conclusion.
- **Language/Style.** The essay uses vivid and precise nouns, verbs, and modifiers.
- **Conventions.** The essay avoids errors in spelling, grammar, usage, mechanics, and manuscript form.

▶ Additional practice is provided in the Essential Skills Practice Book: Writing 1.20.

2. **Critical Essay: Medieval Attitudes toward Death.** In the Medieval Period, people were faced with many reminders of death. Lifespans were shorter during the fourteenth century and the bubonic plague killed about one-third of the population of Europe. Both religious and secular literature commonly made use of the *memento mori,* or "reminder of death" theme, in which death is portrayed as something that comes soon and without warning. Therefore, this kind of work reminds, people must focus on and prepare themselves for the life hereafter. Another common theme was that of *contemptu mundi,* or "contempt for the world," in which wealth, beauty, social position, and other worldly concerns are seen as fleeting vanities because all a person can bring to the grave are good deeds, which are weighed on Judgment Day. Write a critical essay in which you explain whether "Ballade" does or does not express typical medieval attitudes toward death. Develop an opinion on this topic, and state your thesis in an introductory paragraph. Support your thesis with a discussion of the *memento mori* and *contemptu mundi* themes as well as with evidence from "Ballade." Come to a conclusion in a final paragraph.

PROJECT

Laws and Punishments. Laws and punishments in medieval Europe were much harsher than those most European countries practice today. For example, François Villon was sentenced to death by hanging and strangulation for robbery. In small groups, research the codes of law and punishment practiced in different time periods and places. Your group may wish to research the codes practiced in medieval Europe, in modern-day Iran, in feudal Japan, or among the Sioux. After choosing a place and time and conducting research, each group should present its findings in an oral report to the class. You might map the similarities and differences among the law codes of different times and places by presenting them in a chart such as the following:

COUNTRIES & TIME PERIODS	CRIMES		
	Stealing	Murder	Adultery
Medieval Europe			
Feudal Japan			
Modern-day France			

PROJECT NOTES

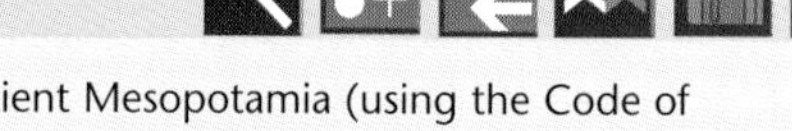

See the evaluation form for projects, Assessment Portfolio 4.12.

Laws and Punishments. If students have difficulty finding information on laws and punishments, you might ask them to compare and contrast the code of law of the ancient Israelites (using the Old Testament as their source), the code of law in ancient Mesopotamia (using the Code of Hammurabi), and the code of law in the contemporary United States.

PREREADING

from *The Tale of Genji*
by Murasaki Shikibu, translated by Edward G. Seidensticker

JAPAN

About the Author

Murasaki Shikibu (978-1015). Often referred to as Lady Murasaki, **Murasaki Shikibu** was born around the year 978 AD in Kyoto, Japan. Her real name is unknown, as it was often the practice to leave unrecorded the names of "well-born" women. It is believed that she was called Murasaki after the heroine in her novel *The Tale of Genji.* The details of her life are sketchy, but it is generally agreed that she was a highly educated, talented woman. Her father was a minor government official who allegedly worried that his brilliant daughter's talents would be wasted because she was not a man. After her husband's death in 1001, Murasaki considered devoting her life to religious service but instead served as an attendant to the empress Joto Mon'in. Murasaki's beautiful verses became popular in the court, where she was surrounded by painters, dancers, and poets. Her most popular works are *The Tale of Genji,* which chronicles the loves and adventures of Prince Genji, and her diary. By the time Murasaki died around 1015, she was one of the most celebrated prose writers of her era.

About the Selection

Murasaki Shikibu's ***The Tale of Genji*** is a long and complex epic describing the court life of Heian Japan (794–1185) while telling the story of Genji, the sensitive and talented son of a Japanese emperor. This novel, completed in the eleventh century, is considered to be the first full novel ever written and an early example of **psychological fiction**, or fiction that emphasizes the interior, subjective experiences of its characters. The opening paragraphs of *The Tale of Genji* take place in the distant past and introduce readers to Genji's mother and to his father, the emperor. This selection describes the birth of Prince Genji.

CONNECTIONS: Scroll Painting

Scroll painting was an early art form practiced by both the Chinese and the Japanese. These scrolls were typically created in ink or watercolor on thin silk or soft paper and mounted on paper or silk. While Chinese artists usually painted landscapes on their scrolls, Japanese artists created narrative scrolls, which combined images and words to tell stories. Long, horizontal, narrative scroll paintings called *emakimono* were produced in Japan in the twelfth and thirteenth centuries. A scroll telling *The Tale of Genji* in words and pictures is one of the earliest examples of this form. Scrolls depicting people's lives and fictional tales were popular during Japan's Middle Ages.

GOALS/OBJECTIVES

Studying this lesson will enable students to

- enjoy an excerpt about court life from a work often considered to be the world's first novel
- define *tone* and identify the tone in literary works
- explain the purpose of an exposition and identify what an exposition reveals
- write an introduction to a fantasy or science fiction novel or for a computer game
- write a critical essay on court life in two different cultures
- combine sentences using words and phrases

ADDITIONAL RESOURCES

READER'S GUIDE
- Selection Worksheet 9.6

ASSESSMENT PORTFOLIO
- Selection Check Test 2.9.11
- Selection Test 2.9.12

ESSENTIAL SKILLS PRACTICE BOOKS
- Writing 1.8, 1.20
- Language 2.21

PREREADING EXTENSIONS

You may wish to point out to students the following similarity between feudal Europe and Japan: Just as medieval European scholars wrote in Latin, medieval Japanese writers wrote mainly in Japanese using Chinese characters or, for formal writing, in the Chinese language. (Medieval Europeans admired classical Greek and Roman scholarship, much as the Japanese admired Chinese scholarship.) Opportunities for education were as limited for medieval Japanese women as they were for women in medieval Europe, so most Japanese women wrote in *kana,* an alphabetic representation of the Japanese language, just as many European women writers wrote in the vernacular.

SUPPORT FOR LEP STUDENTS

PRONUNCIATIONS OF PROPER NOUNS AND ADJECTIVES

Gen • ji (jen jē)
Ky • o • to (kē ō tō)
Mu • ra • sa • ki Shi • ki • bu (mʉ ra sa kē shē kē bo͞o)

ADDITIONAL VOCABULARY

lineage—ancestry; family
upstart—person who has recently come into wealth and power, especially one who behaves in an overconfident, aggressive manner

READER'S JOURNAL

As an alternate activity, you might point out to students that palaces have long been places of rivalries, power struggles, and intrigues. Have students write their thoughts in their journals about why palaces are hotbeds of these types of conflicts.

ANSWERS TO GUIDED READING QUESTIONS

1 Other women resent the woman who is Genji's mother because the emperor adores her despite the fact that she is of a lower social class.

ANSWERS FOR LANGUAGE LAB

(SEE PAGE 769.)

Responses will vary. Possible responses are given.

1. Today the novel, which developed much later than did poetry or drama, is one of the most popular literary forms.
2. Epics, dramas, and essays all appeared long before the novel did.
3. *The Tale of Genji* is the oldest full novel of the Far East.
4. One of the first novels of the Western World is Cervantes's *Don Quixote,* published in two parts in 1605 and 1615.
5. Marco and I like poems and short stories, but we really love novels.

▶ Additional practice is provided in the Essential Skills Practice Book: Language 2.21.

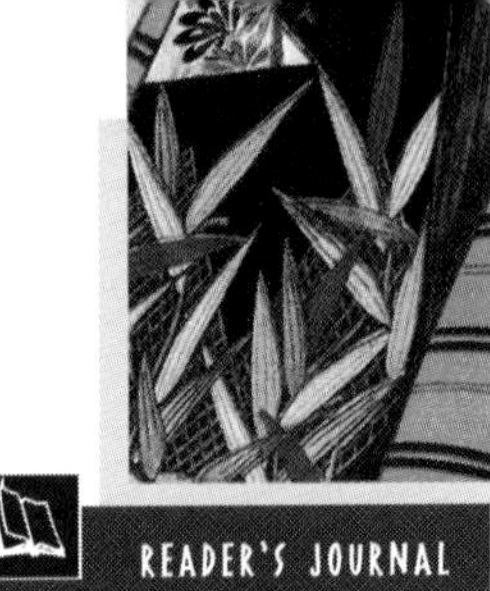

READER'S JOURNAL

What images come to mind when you think about royal courts, emperors, and princes? What people, places, and events do you expect to find in a romantic adventure novel about a royal court and a popular prince?

FROM

The Tale of Genji

MURASAKI SHIKIBU, TRANSLATED BY EDWARD G. SEIDENSTICKER

CHAPTER ONE
THE PAULOWNIA COURT

In a certain reign there was a lady not of the first rank whom the emperor loved more than any of the others. The grand ladies with high ambitions thought her a <u>presumptuous</u> upstart, and lesser ladies were still more resentful. Everything she did offended someone. Probably aware of what was happening, she fell seriously ill and came to spend more time at home than at court. The emperor's pity and affection quite passed bounds. No longer caring what his ladies and courtiers might say, he behaved as if intent upon stirring gossip.

1 *Why were the "grand ladies" resentful of the woman, Genji's mother? What feelings did the emperor have for this woman?*

His court looked with very great misgiving upon what seemed a reckless <u>infatuation</u>. In China just such an unreasoning passion had been the undoing of an emperor and had spread turmoil through the land. As the resentment grew, the example of Yang Kuei-fei was the one most frequently cited against the lady.

She survived despite her troubles, with the help of an unprecedented bounty of love. Her father, a grand councillor, was no longer living. Her mother, an old-fashioned lady of good lineage, was determined that matters be no different for her than for ladies who with paternal support were making careers at court. The mother was attentive to the smallest detail of etiquette and deportment. Yet there was a limit to what she could do. The sad fact was that the girl was without strong backing, and each time a new incident arose she was next to defenseless.

It may have been because of a bond in a former life that she bore the emperor a beautiful son, a jewel beyond compare. The emperor was in a fever of impatience to see the child, still with the mother's family; and

WORDS FOR EVERYDAY USE

pre • sump • tu • ous (prē zump´cho͞o əs) *adj.,* too bold or forward; showing overconfidence

in • fat • u • a • tion (in fach´o͞o ā´shən) *n.,* love

VOCABULARY IN CONTEXT

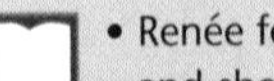

- Renée found her dinner guest's behavior <u>presumptuous</u>—he criticized her taste in everything, and she had only just met him.
- The farmer felt that his <u>infatuation</u> with the emperor's daughter would only lead him to misery, for surely the emperor would scoff at the idea of a princess marrying a mere commoner.

Lady Fujitsubo Watching Prince Genji in Moonlight. *Hiroshige, Ando Tokitaro. 1797–1858. Japanese Private Collection. Bridgeman Art Library, London/Superstock*

when, on the earliest day possible, he was brought to the court, he did indeed prove to be the most marvelous babe. The emperor's eldest son was the grandson of the Minister of the Right. The world assumed that with this powerful support he would one day be named crown prince; but the new child was far more beautiful. On public occasions the emperor continued to favor his eldest son. The new child was a private treasure, so to speak, on which to lavish uninhibited affection. ■

❶ *In what way was the woman's new child a "private treasure"?*

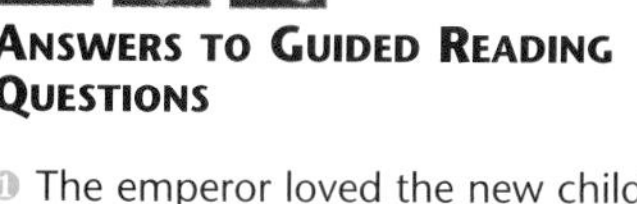

Answers to Guided Reading Questions

❶ The emperor loved the new child and privately favored him above his other children.

Selection Check Test with Answers

EX: Who is Genji's father?
Genji's father is the emperor.

1. Why is the emperor's love for Genji's mother shocking to people?
She is of a lower social standing.
2. What was Genji's mother taught by her mother?
She was taught rules of etiquette.
3. How do the other women of the court feel about Genji's mother?
They dislike her and treat her with disdain.
4. Who is expected to be the crown prince?
The emperor's first son is expected to be crown prince.
5. How does the emperor feel about Genji?
The emperor favors Genji.

RESPONDING TO THE SELECTION

In considering their thoughts about the world described in the selection, students might write journal entries, they might engage in discussion as a class, or they might draw pictures of the way they imagine the ladies of the Paulownia Court.

ANSWERS FOR REVIEWING THE SELECTION

RECALLING AND INTERPRETING

1. **Recalling.** People do not like the woman because the emperor adores her despite the fact that she is young and not of the appropriate social rank. **Interpreting.** People in her society place a great deal of emphasis on social rank.

2. **Recalling.** Her mother helps her to survive by being strong and guiding her in the ways of high society. **Interpreting.** Her mother is strong in her determination, but her influence is limited without the support of her husband and others. Social position, beauty, and etiquette seem to have been most valued in women of this period.

3. **Recalling.** The woman's baby is described as "beautiful," "a jewel beyond compare," "marvelous," and a "private treasure" for the emperor. **Interpreting.** The emperor was fascinated by and drawn to the woman's baby. Students might say the emperor feels this way simply because the child is very beautiful, or because the emperor is so much in love with the mother that he loves her child, too.

4. **Recalling.** The world assumed that the emperor's oldest son would be named crown prince. **Interpreting.** The emperor favors his oldest son publicly and his new son privately, because favoring his new son is not socially acceptable.

(cont.)

Responding to the Selection

What are your feelings about the world in which Genji's mother lives, as described in the opening of *The Tale of Genji*? Would you want to live in such a world? Why, or why not?

Reviewing the Selection

RECALLING / **INTERPRETING**

1. Why do people resent the woman whom the emperor loves and look unfavorably on the fact that the emperor loves her? ▶▶ What do the negativity and prejudice that the woman faces say about how people in her society regard social rank?

2. What helps the woman to survive despite her troubles? ▶▶ Why was there a limit to what the woman's mother could do? What qualities and abilities were most valued in women at this time?

3. What words are used to describe the woman's baby? ▶▶ How did the emperor feel about the baby? Why do you think he felt this way?

4. What did the world assume about the emperor's oldest son? ▶▶ Why do you think the emperor favored his oldest son publicly and his new son privately?

SYNTHESIZING

5. After reading the excerpt from *The Tale of Genji,* what statements can you make about the emperor and his power? What statements can you make about the role of women in this society?

Understanding Literature (Questions for Discussion)

1. **Tone. Tone** is the emotional attitude toward the reader or toward the subject implied by a literary work. Examples of different tones that a work may have include familiar, playful, sad, sarcastic, spiteful, or sincere. Describe the tone of the opening paragraphs of *The Tale of Genji.* What tone does the narrator take toward the woman?

ANSWERS FOR REVIEWING THE SELECTION (CONT.)

SYNTHESIZING

Responses will vary. Possible responses are given.

5. Although the emperor was a highly respected man with a great deal of power, his power seems restricted by the prevailing opinions of the courtiers. Women were restricted by their social rank which determined how they could prosper and succeed in the world. For many women, survival and personal success rested solely on marrying well.

ANSWERS FOR LANGUAGE LAB

Answers for Language Lab appear on page 766.

2. **Exposition.** In a plot, the **exposition,** or **introduction,** is that part of a narrative that provides background information, often about the characters, setting, or conflict. What characters are introduced in this excerpt from the exposition of *The Tale of Genji*? What do you learn about the setting? What conflict do you think might emerge based on this brief introduction?

Responding in Writing

1. **Creative Writing: Introduction.** This selection is an introduction to *The Tale of Genji*. Try writing your own introduction for a fantasy or science fiction novel or for a computer game. Brainstorm ideas for your novel or game. Choose your favorite idea and write two or three paragraphs of introduction for it. Your paragraphs should introduce some important details about the time and place of the action in your novel or game, and perhaps about the major characters involved.

2. **Critical Essay: Court Life.** What does the excerpt that you read from *The Tale of Genji* tell you about court life and about the roles of men and women in society at the time of Genji's birth? Compare and contrast courtly life in Heian Japan as presented in this selection with the courtly life of medieval Europe as expressed in the excerpts from *The Story of the Grail* (see page 722) or *Tristan* (page 732) or the courtly life of medieval Persia as expressed in "The Fisherman and the Jinnee" (page 784). Write a critical essay in which you make one or two judgments about these societies and support your judgments with details from the excerpts.

Language Lab

Combining Sentences Using Words and Phrases. Writers, whether of novels or of business letters, should be comfortable with methods of editing sentences to make them smooth and interesting. Review Language Arts Survey 2.21, "Combining Sentences Using Words and Phrases." Then combine the following sets of sentences by inserting a word or phrase from one sentence into the other, or by using a comma and a conjunction such as *and, but, or, so,* and *yet.*

EX. We read a novel called *The Tale of Genji.* The novel was excellent.
We read an excellent novel called *The Tale of Genji.*

1. Today the novel is one of the most popular literary forms. The form developed much later than did poetry or drama.
2. The epic appeared long before the novel did. Drama appeared long before the novel did. Essays appeared long before the novel did.
3. *The Tale of Genji* is a novel of the Far East. It is the oldest full novel of the Far East.
4. One of the novels of the Western world is *Don Quixote* by Cervantes. It is one of the first novels of the Western world. It was published in two parts in 1605 and 1615.
5. Marco and I like poems and short stories. We really love novels.

Answers for Understanding Literature

Responses will vary. Possible responses are given.

1. **Tone.** The tone of the opening paragraphs from *The Tale of Genji* is serious and matter-of-fact—no names are given and events are described briefly, point by point. The narrator seems to have a more sympathetic tone toward the plight of Genji's mother.
2. **Exposition.** Genji, Genji's mother, the emperor, and members of the court are introduced. The setting is a royal court where a woman of low social class and her son are favored by the emperor. The situation introduces conflict that might develop between Genji's mother and other women in the court, between the emperor's son and Gengi, and between the emperor and his court.

Analytic Scales for Responding in Writing

Assign a score from 1 to 25 for each grading criterion below. (For more detailed evaluation, see the evaluation forms for writing, revising, and proofreading, Assessment Portfolio 4.1–4.9.)

1. Introduction

- **Content/Unity.** The introduction presents important background about a novel or game.
- **Organization/Coherence.** The introduction presents background information in a sensible order.
- **Language/Style.** The introduction uses vivid and precise nouns, verbs, and modifiers.
- **Conventions.** The introduction avoids errors in spelling, grammar, usage, mechanics, and manuscript form.

(cont.)

Analytic Scales for Responding in Writing (cont.)

► Additional practice is provided in the Essential Skills Practice Book: Writing 1.8.

2. Critical Essay

- **Content/Unity.** The essay presents and supports judgments about court life in two different cultures.
- **Organization/Coherence.** The essay presents a thesis in the introduction, supports it in subsequent paragraphs, and has a solid conclusion.
- **Language/Style.** The essay uses vivid and precise nouns, verbs, and modifiers.
- **Conventions.** The essay avoids errors in spelling, grammar, usage, mechanics, and manuscript form.

► Additional practice is provided in the Essential Skills Practice Book: Writing 1.20.

ADDITIONAL RESOURCES

READER'S GUIDE

- Selection Worksheet 9.7

ASSESSMENT PORTFOLIO

- Selection Check Test 2.9.13
- Selection Test 2.9.14

ESSENTIAL SKILLS PRACTICE BOOKS

- Writing 1.8, 1.20
- Speaking and Listening 3.4
- Study and Research 4.4

PREREADING EXTENSIONS

Inform students that Murasaki Shikibu and Sei Shōnagon were contemporaries, but it seems that while they were acquainted with each other, they were not close. Read to students Murasaki's comments on Sei Shōnagon that appear on the following page, or copy this quotation on the board. Then have students read the insights of Yumiko Yokochi, a contemporary Japanese student, on Sei Shōnagon (see page 775). Ask students to discuss what these comments reveal about Sei Shōnagon. How was she different from her contemporaries? What does Murasaki object to in her character? What does Yumiko admire in her character? What risks might a woman have faced by daring to be different in feudal Japan?

SUPPORT FOR LEP STUDENTS

PRONUNCIATIONS OF PROPER NOUNS AND ADJECTIVES

Hei • an (hā an)
Sei Shō • na • gon (sā shō nä gōn)

ADDITIONAL VOCABULARY

brazen—shameless
exalted—elevated in status, dignity, or power
gesticulate—make or use gestures

PREREADING

from *The Pillow Book*
by Sei Shōnagon, translated by Ivan Morris

JAPAN

About the Author

Sei Shōnagon (966–1017). Sei Shōnagon was the daughter of a minor public official who was also a scholar and a poet. It is believed that sometime around 990, she traveled to Kyoto, where she served in the royal court as a lady-in-waiting to the empress Sadako. Her *Pillow Book* chronicles many of her experiences during ten years in court service. Few details are known about Sei Shōnagon's life, but *The Pillow Book* provides readers with insight into her personality. She shows herself to be complex, intelligent, educated, and full of scathing wit. Sei Shōnagon has at times been criticized for her lack of respect for lower classes, her judgmental nature, and her anger toward men. Despite these criticisms, many believe that the pages of *The Pillow Book* contain some of the most beautiful, evocative language ever written.

About the Selection

The Pillow Book is a unique diary that, like *The Tale of Genji*, chronicles court life in Heian Japan (see Connections below). More importantly, this interesting work allows the reader a glimpse into the mind of Sei Shōnagon, a highly skilled, clever, and cynical writer and observer of human nature. The diary is full of descriptions of people and places; **anecdotes**, or brief stories with specific points or morals; and 164 lists. The writer lists everything: things that please her, things she hates, and things she finds elegant. People still speculate on the origin of the name *The Pillow Book*. Some say it refers to the wooden pillows of Sei Shōnagon's day, which had drawers for storing letters or journals. Others say that it simply comes from something Sei Shōnagon once said: that she would rather make her manuscript into a pillow than have others read it.

Gold Pavilion. *Kyoto, Japan*

CONNECTIONS: Heian Prose Writing

Both *The Tale of Genji* and *The Pillow Book* are considered among the finest and most important examples of prose writing from the Heian period of Japan (AD 794–1185). Most boys of the Heian court were trained to write in Chinese, a language that was considered too difficult and sophisticated for women. Educated women such as Murasaki Shikibu and Sei Shōnagon wrote in "low Japanese." This worked to their advantage, however, since more people were actually able to read and enjoy works written in Japanese.

GOALS/OBJECTIVES

Studying this lesson will enable students to

- enjoy some entries from Sei Shōnagon's unique diary
- define *journal* and explain what insights into the author's personality diaries and journals can give
- identify different tones within a literary work
- write a creative "Pillow Book" of lists
- write a critical essay analyzing Sei Shōnagon's character
- make and test hypotheses

READER'S JOURNAL

Take a few moments to record in your journal your thoughts about something that happened to you today or about particular people you have dealt with recently. Then think about how writing in a journal helps to clarify your thoughts and feelings. In what ways do you find writing in a journal to be a useful or interesting activity?

FROM

The Pillow Book

SEI SHŌNAGON, TRANSLATED BY IVAN MORRIS

IN SPRING IT IS THE DAWN

In spring it is the dawn that is most beautiful. As the light creeps over the hills, their outlines are dyed a faint red and wisps of purplish cloud trail over them.

In summer the nights. Not only when the moon shines, but on dark nights too, as the fireflies flit to and fro, and even when it rains, how beautiful it is!

In autumn the evenings, when the flittering sun sinks close to the edge of the hills and the crows fly back to their nests in threes and fours and twos; more charming still is a file of wild geese, like specks in the distant sky. When the sun has set, one's heart is moved by the sound of the wind and the hum of the insects.

In winter the early mornings. It is beautiful indeed when snow has fallen during the night, but splendid too when the ground is white with frost; or even when there is no snow or frost, but it is simply very cold and the attendants hurry from room to room stirring up the fires and bringing charcoal, how well this fits the season's mood! But as noon approaches and the cold wears off, no one bothers to keep the braziers[1] alight, and soon nothing remains but piles of white ashes.

1 What time of day does Sei Shōnagon enjoy most during each season of the year?

WHEN I MAKE MYSELF IMAGINE

When I make myself imagine what it is like to be one of those women who live at home, faithfully serving their husbands—women who have not a single exciting prospect in life yet who believe that they are perfectly happy—I am filled with scorn. Often they are of quite good birth, yet have had no opportunity to find out what the world is like. I wish they could live for a while in our society, even if it should mean taking service as Attendants, so that they might come to know the delights it has to offer.

2 What type of woman fills Sei Shōnagon with scorn? What does she feel these women should do differently?

I cannot bear men who believe that women serving in the Palace are bound to be frivolous and wicked. Yet I suppose their prejudice is understandable. After all, women at Court

1. **braziers.** Metal pans or bowls that hold burning coals or charcoal

WORDS FOR EVERYDAY USE

friv • o • lous (friv′ə ləs) *adj.*, not properly serious or sensible

READER'S JOURNAL

As an alternate activity, you might ask students to jot down a list of things they find either hateful or pleasing.

ANSWERS TO GUIDED READING QUESTIONS

1 In spring she enjoys the dawn, in summer she enjoys the nights, in autumn she enjoys the evenings, and in winter she enjoys the early mornings.

2 Sei Shōnagon scorns women who live to do nothing but serve their husbands. She feels that they should experience serving in the palace.

SPELLING AND VOCABULARY WORDS FROM THE SELECTION

august frivolous

QUOTABLES

"Someone who makes such an effort to be different from others is bound to fall in people's esteem, and I can only think that her future will be a hard one. She is a gifted woman, to be sure. Yet if one gives free rein to one's emotions even under the most inappropriate circumstances, if one has to sample each interesting thing that comes along, people are bound to regard one as frivolous. And how can things turn out well for such a woman?"

—Murasaki Shikibu's comments on Sei Shōnagon

VOCABULARY IN CONTEXT

• Our tour guide warned us that the temple was considered a solemn place, so no frivolous behavior would be tolerated.

Answers to Guided Reading Questions

❶ Women at court do not modestly hide behind fans and screens but are outgoing and meet people face to face.

INTEGRATED SKILLS ACTIVITIES

SPEAKING AND LISTENING

Encourage students to read about feudal Japan in the Unit Introduction, which begins on page 716. You might also send students to the library or to online sources to research further life in feudal Japan. Then encourage students to prepare an extemporaneous speech on the following topic: If you could travel back in time to live as any member of society in feudal Japan, whom would you choose to be—a courtier, a *samurai,* a poet, a painter, a craftsman, or a farmer? Why would you want to experience life from this point of view? What advantages and difficulties do you think you would face as a member of this class? If students need guidelines for preparing an extemporaneous speech, refer them to the Language Arts Survey 3.4, "Public Speaking." A form for assessing students' speeches appears in the Assessment Portfolio 4.11.

▶ Additional practice is provided in the Essential Skills Practice Book: Speaking and Listening 3.4.

❶ *In what ways are women at court different from other women?*

do not spend their time hiding modestly behind fans and screens, but walk about, looking openly at people they chance to meet. Yes, they see everyone face to face, not only ladies-in-waiting like themselves, but even Their Imperial Majesties (whose august names I hardly dare mention), High Court Nobles, senior courtiers, and other gentlemen of high rank. In the presence of such exalted personages the women in the Palace are all equally brazen, whether they be the maids of ladies-in-waiting, or the relations of Court ladies who have come to visit them, or house-keepers, or latrine-cleaners, or women who are of no more value than a roof-tile or a pebble. Small wonder that the young men regard them as immodest! Yet are the gentlemen themselves any less so? They are not exactly bashful when it comes to looking at the great people in the Palace. No, everyone at Court is much the same in this respect.

Women who have served in the Palace, but who later get married and live at home, are called Madam and receive the most respectful treatment. To be sure, people often consider that these women, who have displayed their faces to all and sundry[2] during their years at Court, are lacking in feminine grace. How proud they must be, nevertheless, when they are styled Assistant Attendants, or summoned to the Palace for occasional duty, or ordered to serve as Imperial envoys during the Kamo Festival![3] Even those who stay at home lose nothing by having served at Court. In fact they make very good wives. For example, if they are married to a provincial governor and their daughter is chosen to take part in the Gosechi dances,[4] they do not have to disgrace

2. **all and sundry.** Everyone
3. **Kamo Festival.** Main Shinto festival held in the fourth month of the year
4. **Gosechi dances.** Dances performed by young girls

Words for Everyday Use

au • gust (ô gust´) *adj.,* inspiring awe and reverence

Vocabulary in Context

• Paintings reveal that King Henry VIII of England was an august presence who could easily inspire awe in his subjects.

themselves by acting like provincials and asking other people about procedure. They themselves are well versed in the formalities, which is just as it should be.

HATEFUL THINGS

One is in a hurry to leave, but one's visitor keeps chattering away. If it is someone of no importance, one can get rid of him by saying, "You must tell me all about it next time"; but, should it be the sort of visitor whose presence commands one's best behaviour, the situation is hateful indeed.

One finds that a hair has got caught in the stone on which one is rubbing one's inkstick, or again that gravel is lodged in the inkstick, making a nasty, grating sound.

Someone has suddenly fallen ill and one summons the exorcist.[5] Since he is not at home, one has to send messengers to look for him. After one has had a long fretful wait, the exorcist finally arrives, and with a sigh of relief one asks him to start his incantations. But perhaps he has been exorcising too many evil spirits recently; for hardly has he installed himself and begun praying when his voice becomes drowsy. Oh, how hateful!

A man who has nothing in particular to recommend him discusses all sorts of subjects at random as though he knew everything.

An elderly person warms the palms of his hands over a brazier and stretches out the wrinkles. No young man would dream of behaving in such a fashion; old people can really be quite shameless. I have seen some dreary old creatures actually resting their feet on the brazier and rubbing them against the edge while they speak. These are the kind of people who in visiting someone's house first use their fans to wipe away the dust from the mat and, when they finally sit on it, cannot stay still but are forever spreading out the front of their hunting costume or even tucking it up under their knees. One might suppose that such behaviour was restricted to people of humble station; but I have observed it in quite well-bred people, including a Senior Secretary of the Fifth Rank in the Ministry of Ceremonial and a former Governor of Suruga.

I hate the sight of men in their cups who shout, poke their fingers in their mouths, stroke their beards, and pass on the wine to their neighbours with great cries of "Have some more! Drink Up!" They tremble, shake their heads, twist their faces, and gesticulate like children who are singing, "We're off to see the Governor." I have seen really well-bred people behave like this and I find it most distasteful.

To envy others and to complain about one's own lot: to speak badly about people; to be inquisitive about the most trivial matters and to resent and abuse people for not telling one, or, if one does manage to worm out some facts, to inform everyone in the most detailed fashion as if one had known all from the beginning—oh, how hateful!

One is just about to be told some interesting piece of news when a baby starts crying.

A flight of crows circle about with loud caws.

OXEN SHOULD HAVE VERY SMALL FOREHEADS

Oxen should have very small foreheads with white hair; their underbellies, the ends of their legs, and the tips of their tails should also be white.

I like horses to be chestnut, piebald,[6] dapple-grey, or black roan,[7] with white patches near their shoulders and feet; I also like horses with light chestnut coats and extremely white manes and tails—so white, indeed, that their hair looks like mulberry threads.

I like a cat whose back is black and all the rest white.

---

5. **exorcist.** Person who drives away evil spirits with ritual prayers
6. **piebald.** Covered with black and white patches or spots
7. **roan.** Of a solid color with a thick sprinkling of white hairs

❶ *What are Sei Shōnagon's feelings about rowdy men in public? What is distasteful about the behavior of these men?*

❷ *In what sort of world does Sei Shōnagon live, judging from her use of phrases such as "someone of no importance" and "the sort of visitor whose presence commands one's best behavior"?*

❸ *How does Sei Shōnagon feel about elderly people?*

ANSWERS TO GUIDED READING QUESTIONS

❶ Sei Shōnagon cannot stand men who behave in a rowdy, slovenly manner in public. She finds their lack of self-restraint distasteful.

❷ Sei Shōnagon lives in "high society," a very stratified social world in which social rank and manners are of key importance.

❸ Sei Shōnagon seems to disapprove of the "shameless" manners of the elderly.

CULTURAL/HISTORICAL NOTE

Point out to students that the rosary mentioned on page 774 is a Buddhist rosary, not a Christian one. A number of world religions have made use of prayer beads, including, in addition to Christianity and Buddhism, Hinduism and Islam.

CROSS-CURRICULAR ACTIVITIES

SOCIAL STUDIES

Shinto is a religion indigenous to Japan; nevertheless, this religion remained nameless until Buddhism was introduced in Japan from Korea in either AD 538 or 552 and followers of Shintoism sought to distinguish it from Buddhism. Both Shinto and Buddhist festivals were made parts of the official government during the Yamato and Nara periods, respectively. During the Heian period, in which Sei Shōnagon lived, the emperor cut all ties between Buddhism and the official government, although he encouraged Buddhism as a religion. Interested students might work in small groups to learn more about Shintoism and Buddhism in Japan's history. Students may prepare either written or oral reports.

Answers to Guided Reading Questions

❶ Sei Shōnagon is clearly curious about the business of others. She is observant and enjoys commenting on everything.

❷ Sei Shōnagon says that hearing that something nice has happened to one she loves pleases her more than having something nice happen to herself. Some readers might be surprised by this because in her writing she often does not seem like a generous person.

Selection Check Test with Answers

EX: Who is the speaker in *The Pillow Book*?

The speaker in the *The Pillow Book* is Sei Shōnagon.

1. What time of day does Sei Shōnagon prefer in the spring?

In spring she enjoys the dawn.

2. Where does Sei Shōnagon feel a woman should work?

She feels a woman should work in the palace.

3. For what women does Sei Shōnagon feel disdain?

Sei Shōnagon feels disdain for women who devote their lives to men.

4. For what men does Sei Shōnagon feel disdain?

Sei Shōnagon cannot stand men who behave in a rowdy, slovenly manner in public.

5. What pleases Sei Shōnagon more than having something nice happen to herself?

Sei Shōnagon says that hearing that something nice has happened to one she loves pleases her more than having something nice happen to herself.

ELEGANT THINGS

A white coat worn over a violet waistcoat.
Duck eggs.
Shaved ice mixed with liana syrup[8] and put in a new silver bowl.
A rosary[9] of rock crystal.
Wisteria blossoms. Plum blossoms covered with snow.
A pretty child eating strawberries.

PLEASING THINGS

Finding a large number of tales that one has not read before. Or acquiring the second volume of a tale whose first volume one has enjoyed. But often it is a disappointment.

❶ *Why might someone like Sei Shōnagon enjoy piecing together someone's torn letter?*

Someone has torn up a letter and thrown it away. Picking up the pieces, one finds that many of them can be fitted together.

One has had an upsetting dream and wonders what it can mean. In great anxiety one consults a dream-interpreter, who informs one that it has no special significance.

A person of quality is holding forth about something in the past or about a recent event that is being widely discussed. Several people are gathered round him, but it is oneself that he keeps looking at as he talks.

A person who is very dear to one has fallen ill. One is miserably worried about him even if he lives in the capital and far more so if he is in some remote part of the country. What a pleasure to be told that he has recovered!

❷ *What does Sei Shōnagon say pleases her more than having something nice happen to herself? Is this statement surprising? Why, or why not?*

I am most pleased when I hear someone I love being praised or being mentioned approvingly by an important person.

A poem that someone has composed for a special occasion or written to another person in reply is widely praised and copied by people in their notebooks. Though this is something that has never yet happened to me, I can imagine how pleasing it must be.

A person with whom one is not especially intimate refers to an old poem or story that is unfamiliar. Then one hears it being mentioned by someone else and one has the pleasure of recognizing it. Still later, when one comes across it in a book, one thinks, "Ah, this is it!" and feels delighted with the person who first brought it up.

I feel very pleased when I have acquired some Michinoku paper, or some white, decorated paper, or even plain paper if it is nice and white.

A person in whose company one feels awkward asks one to supply the opening or closing line of a poem. If one happens to recall it, one is very pleased. Yet often on such occasions one completely forgets something that one would normally know.

I look for an object that I need at once, and I find it. Or again, there is a book that I must see immediately; I turn everything upside down, and there it is. What a joy!

When one is competing in an object match (it does not matter what kind), how can one help being pleased at winning?

I greatly enjoy taking in someone who is pleased with himself and who has a self-confident look, especially if he is a man. It is amusing to observe him as he alertly waits for my next repartee; but it is also interesting if he tries to put me off my guard by adopting an air of calm indifference as if there were not a thought in his head.

I realize that it is very sinful of me, but I cannot help being pleased when someone I dislike has a bad experience.

It is a great pleasure when the ornamental comb that one has ordered turns out to be pretty.

I am more pleased when something nice happens to a person I love than when it happens to myself.

Entering the Empress's room and finding that ladies-in-waiting are crowded round her in a tight group, I go next to a pillar which is some distance from where she is sitting. What a delight it is when Her Majesty summons me to her side so that all the others have to make way! ■

8. **liana syrup.** Syrup used for sweetening that comes from the leaves and stems of a vine
9. **rosary.** String of prayer beads

Additional Questions and Activities

In her review, Yumiko discusses the feminist movement in Japan. Invite students to discuss the feminist movement in America. Ask students the following: When did the movement begin and why? What changes have taken place for women and men as a result of the movement? How has the movement affected you and your family? What changes, if any, would you like to see take place?

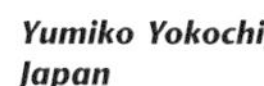

Global Views

Yumiko Yokochi, Japan

Sei Shōnagon's honesty and assertiveness fascinate me. I would not have imagined a person like Sei Shōnagon existed in tenth-century Japan. I like the fact that she was proud of herself and her colleagues, who did not model themselves after ideal women at the time who constantly hid themselves behind fans and screens. I did not know that she was such a feminist! I imagine that it was difficult for her to fit into society. Even now, the feminist movement is not well received in my country. Until the end of World War II, the constitution stated that women must be subjugated to men in general!

I also love when Sei Shōnagon says, "I am more pleased when something nice happens to a person I love than when it happens to myself." I think it shows that she was a loving person who valued the happiness of others more than her own.

Responding to the Selection

What are your reactions to Sei Shōnagon's personality, beliefs, and the world in which she lived? Is she somebody you would like to have known? Why, or why not?

Reviewing the Selection

Recalling	Interpreting
1. What does Sei Shōnagon find most beautiful about each season? What bothers her about winter afternoons?	What is Sei Shōnagon's attitude in most of "In Spring It Is the Dawn"? In what way does her attitude change in the last sentence?
2. For what type of woman does Sei Shōnagon have scorn? What do some men say about women who serve in the palace? Why does she think serving in the palace is a good experience for a woman?	In what way might Sei Shōnagon be overly judgmental and critical? In what way might her criticism of some women's lives be valid? Explain your responses.

Responding to the Selection

In large groups, students might come up with lists of what they perceive as Sei Shōnagon's positive and negative personality traits.

Answers for Reviewing the Selection

RECALLING AND INTERPRETING

1. **Recalling.** In spring she enjoys the dawn, in summer she enjoys the nights, in autumn she enjoys the evenings, and in winter she enjoys the early mornings. She does not like when the fires go out by noon in winter and there is nothing left but white ashes. **Interpreting.** The last line expresses an attitude of annoyance and displeasure, while the rest of the section is enthusiastic in its vivid descriptions of nature.

2. **Recalling.** Sei Shōnagon scorns women who never leave their homes and who live only to serve their husbands. Some men say women who serve in the palace are "frivolous and wicked." Serving in the palace allows a woman to meet people and become independent. It also teaches her social skills that can prove useful in the future. **Interpreting.** Sei Shōnagon harshly criticizes all women who stay at home and do not work in the palace, without recognizing that all people and situations are not the same. Some women would not be happy working in a palace, as she is, and some women might come from families in which they grew up having limited freedom and opportunities. On the other hand, Sei Shōnagon's wish for all women to go out in the world and to have different experiences is admirable. *Responses will vary.*

3. **Recalling.** She describes oxen, horses, and cats. **Interpreting.** Sei Shōnagon holds strong opinions and makes vivid observations about the natural world.

(cont.)

Answers for Reviewing the Selection (cont.)

She is clearly drawn to nature and its beauty.

4. **Recalling.** *Responses will vary.* Sei Shōnagon finds a man who talks too much, as if he knows everything, and an overly talkative visitor particularly hateful. Sei Shōnagon finds hearing praise of someone she loves and talking with a self-confident person particularly pleasing. **Interpreting.** *Responses will vary.* She observes that people are often selfish and that people often speak badly of others. Sei Shōnagon reveals herself to be caring when she states that she loves hearing praise of a person she loves and that she loves hearing that someone is doing well. In general, she has little patience for people who are loud, slovenly, mean-spirited, or unschooled in social graces.

(cont.)

3. What animals does Sei Shōnagon describe in the section "Oxen Should Have Very Small Foreheads"?

▶▶ What might you say about Sei Shōnagon's powers of observation and her interest in the natural world?

4. Name two things that Sei Shōnagon finds particularly hateful. Name two things that Sei Shōnagon finds particularly pleasing.

▶▶ Based on the section called "Hateful Things," name two observations Sei Shōnagon makes about negative aspects of human nature. In "Pleasing Things," name two statements that reveal a sensitive, caring side to Sei Shōnagon. In general, for what behaviors does she have very little patience?

SYNTHESIZING

5. After reading the excerpt from *The Pillow Book*, what can you say about the role of women in Japan's Heian age? What choices were available to women? What is Sei Shōnagon's general attitude toward men and society?

Understanding Literature (Questions for Discussion)

1. **Journal.** A **journal,** like a diary, is a day-to-day record of a person's activities, experiences, thoughts, and feelings. In contrast to *diary*, the word *journal* connotes an outward rather than an inward focus. In what way does Sei Shōnagon's *Pillow Book* share the characteristics of both a journal and a diary? After reading the selections, what insights do you have into Sei Shōnagon's personality? What positive and negative personality traits do the selections reveal? What insights do you have about the world in which Sei Shōnagon lived?

2. **Tone. Tone** is the emotional attitude toward the reader or toward the subject implied by a literary work. Examples of different tones that a work may have include familiar, playful, sad, sarcastic, spiteful, or sincere. Does Sei Shōnagon's tone vary or remain constant throughout the excerpts from *The Pillow Book*? What tone or tones do you find in the excerpts? Explain.

Answers for Reviewing the Selection (cont.)

SYNTHESIZING

Responses will vary. Possible responses are given.

5. Japan's Heian age was restrictive for women in that they could fulfill only certain roles in the home and in the court. An aristocratic woman, such as Sei Shōnagon, needed to be strictly schooled in social graces. Even a highly educated woman was forced to play by strict rules and either serve her husband or an emperor or empress. Sei Shōnagon sharply criticizes the behavior of most men. She is very much a part of society, but she also has many complaints about the ways in which people live and behave.

Answers for Understanding Literature

Responses will vary. Possible responses are given.

1. **Journal.** Students might say that the work is a journal in the way that it captures many of the details of the society in which Sei Shōnagon lives. Students might say that it is also a diary because it reveals Sei Shōnagon's thoughts and feelings. Students might say that her negative traits include impatience, a tendency to be judgmental, and a certain snobbishness. Students might say that her positive traits include her sincere interest in reading and writing to find answers, her displeasure with some mean-spirited behaviors, her appreciation for nature, and her concern for her friends and family. *Responses will vary.*

2. **Tone.** The selections from *The Pillow Book* vary in tone. Many of the diary entries have a sarcastic, biting, or critical tone, and others, the ones in which she reflects on nature or things she enjoys, have a gentle, thoughtful tone.

Responding in Writing

1. **Creative Writing: Pillow Book.** Throughout *The Pillow Book*, Sei Shōnagon organizes her ideas, observations, and opinions into lists with heads such as "Pleasing Things," "Depressing Things," "Features That I Particularly Like," and "Things That Arouse a Fond Memory of the Past." Some of her thoughts on these subjects are humorous and sarcastic, while some are somber. Following this idea, create a "Pillow Book" of your own in which you make at least four lists similar to Sei Shōnagon's lists. You may borrow some of her categories, but you should also try to create some of your own. For example, you might explore topics such as "Annoying Things on Television," or "Things That Frighten Me," or "Interesting Things That Are Colored Blue." As you make your lists, stretch your imagination, and do not censor yourself. Don't be afraid to sound silly or sarcastic or to express your true feelings.

2. **Critical Essay: Character Analysis.** In *The Pillow Book*, Sei Shōnagon reveals a great deal about her own complex personality and character. Write a critical essay in which you analyze the character of Sei Shōnagon, supporting each of your ideas with examples from *The Pillow Book* selections. Examine Sei Shōnagon's opinions, concerns, interests, and tone. Then make concrete judgments about her character. If you wish, you might compare her opinions with those expressed by writers such as Miss Manners or Ann Landers on matters of etiquette and daily living.

Thinking Skills

Making and Testing Hypotheses. As you read, write, and discuss new ideas, it is important to exercise good thinking skills. One important skill is learning how to make a reasonable hypothesis, or educated guess. After formulating a hypothesis, you then look for ways to test whether it is true. For more information about making and testing hypotheses, turn to the Language Arts Survey 4.4, "Making and Testing Hypotheses." Work with other students to brainstorm possible ways in which one might test the following hypotheses:

1. In today's world, preadolescents and adolescents are more likely than adults to take the time to keep journals and diaries.
2. Most people are likely to find the selections from *The Pillow Book*, especially the section titled "Hateful Things," humorous and perceptive.

ANALYTIC SCALES FOR RESPONDING IN WRITING

Assign a score from 1 to 25 for each grading criterion below. (For more detailed evaluation, see the evaluation forms for writing, revising, and proofreading, Assessment Portfolio 4.1–4.9.)

1. Pillow Book

- **Content/Unity.** The "Pillow Book" contains at least four lists of the writer's thoughts on four specific subjects.
- **Organization/Coherence.** Each list refers to an easily recognizable subject, and each list presents details in a sensible order.
- **Language/Style.** The "Pillow Book" uses vivid and precise nouns, verbs, and modifiers.
- **Conventions.** The "Pillow Book" avoids errors in spelling, grammar, usage, mechanics, and manuscript form.

▶ Additional practice is provided in the Essential Skills Practice Book: Writing 1.8.

2. Critical Essay

- **Content/Unity.** The essay presents conclusions the reader has drawn about Sei Shōnagon's character.
- **Organization/Coherence.** The essay begins with an introduction that includes the thesis of the essay. The introduction is followed by supporting paragraphs with clear transitions. The essay ends with a solid conclusion.
- **Language/Style.** The essay uses vivid and precise nouns, verbs, and modifiers.
- **Conventions.** The essay avoids errors in spelling, grammar, usage, mechanics, and manuscript form.

▶ Additional practice is provided in the Essential Skills Practice Book: Writing 1.20.

ANSWERS FOR SKILLS ACTIVITIES

THINKING SKILLS

Students should create lists of possible ways to test each hypothesis. Some possible ways of testing these appear below, but students' responses will vary.

1. Students may suggest surveying groups of adolescents and adults.
2. Students may suggest having a number of readers review the work.

▶ Additional practice is provided in the Essential Skills Practice Book: Study and Research 4.4.

ADDITIONAL RESOURCES

READER'S GUIDE

- Selection Worksheet 9.8

ASSESSMENT PORTFOLIO

- Selection Check Test 2.9.15
- Selection Test 2.9.16

ESSENTIAL SKILLS PRACTICE BOOKS

- Writing 1.8, 1.20
- Study and Research 4.12

PREREADING EXTENSIONS

- Students can research Saudia Arabia and the city of Mecca. Working in small groups, they can choose a focus such as ancient history, modern history, religious significance of Mecca, arts of the region, or another aspect of the country or culture that interests them.
- Have students identify meccas for various groups. For example, what place might be a mecca for art enthusiasts? for jazz lovers? for downhill skiiers? Have students identify other places that may be seen as meccas.

SUPPORT FOR LEP STUDENTS

PRONUNCIATIONS OF PROPER NOUNS AND ADJECTIVES

Ko • ran (kôr an´)
Mec • ca (mek´ə)
Mo • ham • med (mō ham´id)

ADDITIONAL VOCABULARY

bliss—great happiness and contentment
exordium—opening part of a longer work
hurled—thrown
wrath—anger

PREREADING

from the Koran
translated by N. J. Dawood

About the Selection

The Koran (*Qur'an* in Arabic) is the sacred scripture of Islam, the Muslim religion. Muslims, like Christians, believe in one God, called *Allah* in Arabic. Muslims regard the Koran, written by the prophet Mohammed, as God's final revelation to humanity and the ultimate authority on all religious and social issues. According to Islam, the revelations were sent to Mohammed by the angel Gabriel from 610 AD until Mohammed's death in 632. Although many of his followers recorded them, they were gathered into one volume only after his death. The Koran is considered an exact duplicate of an eternal, divine Koran that exists in Heaven, engraved in gold on tablets of marble. Like God, the divine Koran was not created but exists for eternity to guide the earthly activities and faith of Muslims.

The title Koran means "the Recitation," as it is a work intended to be recited. Although the revelations originally came to Mohammed in verses of varying length, these verses were gathered into larger divisions called Suras. The 114 Suras are organized by subject and vary considerably in style. The earliest Suras are short and sound like charms or chants. Later Suras are longer and give practical advice and wise counsel for dealing with everyday matters. Many of the Suras are like sermons written in passionate and poetic language, reminding people to follow God's righteous path. For the most part, the speaker of the Suras is God, although there are some scattered passages in the voices of Mohammed or Gabriel.

Mosque in central city core. Iran

The Koran is considered the finest example of classical Arabic prose. Muslims believe that it was revealed to Mohammed in Arabic so he could provide the Arabs with a holy book in their own language. Its form and content are considered unchangeable, and translations from the Arabic have traditionally been forbidden. Many Muslims throughout the world continue to recite the Koran in Arabic, even if they do not understand the language. Translations are considered mere "paraphrases" that exist only to help people understand the actual sacred scripture. This traditional Islamic belief in the impossibility of truly accurate translation has been confirmed by modern linguists. In translation, something is inevitably lost.

The three Suras you are about to read are The Exordium, The Cataclysm, and Daylight. The Exordium has special meaning to Muslims, who recite it at the beginning of every formal speech, write it on every document, engrave it on every gravestone, and say it before every prayer. The Cataclysm is a forceful Sura that warns Muslims of the Last Judgment, when God will either reward or punish mortals. Daylight is a dialogue between God and Mohammed in which Mohammed's special calling to serve God and God's people on earth is reaffirmed.

CONNECTIONS: Mecca

Mecca, Saudi Arabia, is the most holy city of Islam because it is the birthplace of the prophet Mohammed. Muslims throughout the world face in the direction of Mecca as they pray several times each day. They are also expected to go on a pilgrimage to its shrine at least once in their lives. Non-Muslims are not allowed to enter the gates of the city. The word *mecca* has come to mean any place that people have a strong desire to visit, or a goal that someone wants to achieve.

GOALS/OBJECTIVES

Studying this lesson will enable students to

- enjoy an exploration of a work of classical Arabic prose
- identify the Koran as the scripture of Islam
- define *repetition, tone,* and *image*
- identify repeated elements and images
- recognize varying tones in a literary work
- write a guide to life
- compare and contrast the messages of two literary works
- use search tools for research

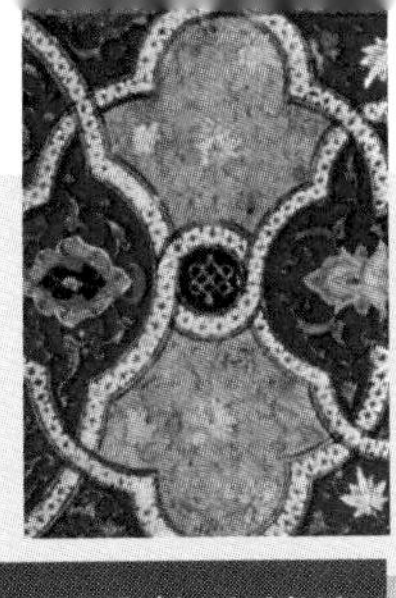

What are some of your beliefs about your role in the universe? What people, books, events, or religious experiences have guided and shaped your beliefs about yourself and this perceived role?

READER'S JOURNAL

FROM THE

Koran

TRANSLATED BY N. J. DAWOOD

THE EXORDIUM

IN THE NAME OF GOD, THE COMPASSIONATE, THE MERCIFUL

Praise be to God, Lord of the Universe,
The Compassionate, the Merciful,
Sovereign of the Day of Judgment!
You alone we worship, and to You alone
we turn for help.
Guide us to the straight path,
The Path of those whom You have favoured,
Not of those who have incurred Your wrath,
Nor of those who have gone astray.

1 What words are used to describe God? Of what is God sovereign?

2 Onto what path do people wish to be guided? What path do they wish to avoid?

THE CATACLYSM

In the Name of God, the
Compassionate, the Merciful

When the sky is rent asunder; when the stars scatter and the oceans roll together; when the graves are hurled about; each soul shall know what it has done and what it has failed to do.

O man! What evil has enticed you from your gracious Lord who created you, gave you an upright form, and proportioned you? In whatever shape He willed He could have moulded you.

Yet you deny the Last Judgment. Surely there are guardians watching over you, noble recorders who know of all your actions.

3 When will each soul "know what it has done and what it has failed to do"?

WORDS FOR EVERYDAY USE

sov • er • eign (säv´rən) *n.,* ruler
in • cur (in kʉr´) *v.,* bring upon oneself
rend (rend) *vt.,* tear, pull, or rip with violence
a • sun • der (ə sun´dər) *adv.,* in pieces

READER'S JOURNAL

As students consider the things that have influenced their lives, ask them if they think that they have a responsibility or duty to teach others to follow a certain way of life. If so, what have they done to teach others or to act as a role model? If not, have them explain why they feel as they do.

ANSWERS TO GUIDED READING QUESTIONS

1 God is described as "Lord of the Universe," "the Compassionate," and "the Merciful." God is "Sovereign of the Day of Judgment."

2 People wish to be guided to the straight path. They wish to avoid the path of those who have incurred God's wrath and gone astray.

3 Each soul will "know what it has done and what it has failed to do" at the Cataclysm, or the day of Last Judgment, when "the sky is rent asunder; when the stars scatter and the oceans roll together; when the graves are hurled about."

SPELLING AND VOCABULARY WORDS FROM THE SELECTION

abhor	incur
asunder	rend
chide	sovereign

VOCABULARY IN CONTEXT

- All decisions in the kingdom are made by the sovereign.
- Gladys incurred Ms. Jyllka's wrath by talking during the lecture.
- Layla feared the two dogs would rend the child's stuffed animal before she could rescue it from their jaws.
- Manny's jacket was torn asunder when his friends played tug-of-war with it.

Answers to Guided Reading Questions

1. On Judgment Day the righteous will "dwell in bliss," and the wicked will suffer.
2. The Day of Judgment is the day when "every soul will stand alone and God will reign supreme."
3. Mohammed should look forward to his life to come, because it "holds a richer prize" than his present life.
4. The Lord found Mohammed as an orphan, and sheltered, guided him, and enriched him. He should proclaim the goodness of the Lord.

Selection Check Test with Answers

EX. In the Koran, of what is God Lord?
God is Lord of the Universe.

1. Onto what path do people wish to be guided?
People wish to be guided onto the path of the righteous.
2. What will every person know at the Cataclysm?
Every person will know what he or she has done and what he or she has failed to do.
3. What is the Day of Judgment?
The Day of Judgment is the day when every soul will stand alone and God will reign supreme.
4. What does "life to come" hold for Mohammed?
Life to come holds a richer prize for him than this present life.
5. What must Mohammed proclaim?
Mohammed must proclaim the goodness of the Lord.

1 *Which people will "dwell in bliss" on Judgment Day? Who will suffer on Judgment Day?*

2 *What is the Day of Judgment?*

The righteous will surely dwell in bliss. But the wicked shall burn in Hell upon the Judgment-day: nor shall they ever escape from it.

Would that you knew what the Day of Judgment is! Oh, would that you knew what the Day of Judgment is! It is the day when every soul will stand alone and God will reign supreme.

DAYLIGHT

In the Name of God, the Compassionate, the Merciful

3 *To what should Mohammed look forward? Why?*

4 *What has the Lord done for Mohammed? What should he proclaim?*

By the light of day, and by the dark of night, your Lord has not forsaken you,[1] nor does He abhor you.

The life to come holds a richer prize for you than this present life. You shall be gratified with what your Lord will give you.

Did He not find you an orphan and give you shelter?

Did He not find you in error and guide you?

Did He not find you poor and enrich you?

Therefore do not wrong the orphan, nor chide away the beggar. But proclaim the goodness of your Lord. ■

1. **you.** Mohammed

Minaret of a mosque. *Kuwait City, Kuwait*

Words for Everyday Use

ab • hor (ab hôr´) *vt.,* hate

chide (chīd) *vt.,* scold

Vocabulary in Context

- Although Yevgene loves summer vacation, she abhors the heat and humidity of summer.
- Lance would chide Vera if she didn't finish her homework before watching television.

Tile inscribed with Arabic letters

ANALYTIC SCALES FOR RESPONDING IN WRITING

Assign a score from 1 to 25 for each grading criterion below. (For more detailed evaluation, see the evaluation forms for writing, revising, and proofreading, Assessment Portfolio 4.1–4.9.)

1. Guide

- **Content/Unity.** The guide consists of the writer's advice about life and each person's role in the world.
- **Organization/Coherence.** The guide presents the writer's ideas in a logical manner.
- **Language/Style.** The guide uses vivid and precise nouns, verbs, and modifiers.
- **Conventions.** The guide avoids errors in spelling, grammar, usage, mechanics, and manuscript form.

► Additional practice is provided in the Essential Skills Practice Book: Writing 1.8.

2. Critical Essay

- **Content/Unity.** The essay compares and contrasts the moral messages of the selections from the Koran and from *The Divine Comedy.*
- **Organization/Coherence.** The essay begins with an introduction that includes a thesis. The introduction is followed by supporting paragraphs with clear transitions. The supporting paragraphs present evidence from both selections. The essay ends with a solid conclusion.
- **Language/Style.** The essay uses vivid and precise nouns, verbs, and modifiers.
- **Conventions.** The essay avoids errors in spelling, grammar, usage, mechanics, and manuscript form.

► Additional practice is provided in the Essential Skills Practice Book: Writing 1.20.

Literary Technique

PARALLELISM

Parallelism is a rhetorical technique in which a writer emphasizes the equal value or weight of two or more ideas by expressing them in the same grammatical form. Have students identify an example of parallelism in Daylight.

ANSWERS

The lines "Did He not find you an orphan and give you shelter? / Did He not find you in error and guide you? / Did He not find you poor and enrich you?" are parallel in structure.

Responding to the Selection

What thoughts and feelings do you associate with the phrase *Judgment Day*? Imagine that you were experiencing Judgment Day as described in this selection. What do you think the results of the judgment would be? Why? Discuss these questions with your classmates.

Reviewing the Selection

RECALLING		INTERPRETING
1. In The Exordium, what do people ask of God? What words are used to describe God and the path on which people wish to walk?	▶▶	What kind of life do speakers of The Exordium wish to lead? What life do they wish to avoid?
2. According to The Cataclysm, what will happen on the Day of Judgment? Which people will "dwell in bliss"? Which people will suffer?	▶▶	What type of person is being addressed in The Cataclysm? Of what is this person being accused? What warning does this type of person receive?
3. The Sura Daylight addresses Mohammed. What does "life to come" hold for Mohammed?	▶▶	According to Daylight, what must Mohammed realize about the Lord's feelings for him, his role on earth, and his future? Why might he have cause to doubt his Lord's love?
4. What has the Lord done to care for Mohammed? What kinds of people must Mohammed therefore help?	▶▶	Why must Mohammed take care of others? To whom must he proclaim the goodness of the Lord?

SYNTHESIZING

5. Describe the relationship between God and his followers as portrayed in the Suras you have read. What does God represent for people devoted to the message of this text? What is Mohammed's role in spreading God's messages?

Understanding Literature (Questions for Discussion)

1. **Repetition. Repetition** is the use, again, of a sound, word, phrase, sentence, or other element. What lines, words, and phrases are repeated in these excerpts from the Koran? Why might these elements be repeated? Does this repetition have a particular effect on the reader? Does it increase the impact of a particular idea? Explain.

RESPONDING TO THE SELECTION

Students might compare the idea of judgment presented in this selection with the ideas about judgment presented in "The Weighing of the Heart of Ani" in Unit 4. Ask students if they worry about being judged and what they might do to prepare for judgment.

ANSWERS FOR REVIEWING THE SELECTION

RECALLING AND INTERPRETING

1. **Recalling.** People ask God for help and for guidance. God is described as "Lord of the Universe," "the Compassionate," and "the Merciful." People wish to walk the "straight" path, and "the Path of those whom You have favoured." **Interpreting.** People wish to live righteous lives and be guided on the straight path. They wish to avoid the path of those who have incurred God's wrath or gone astray from God's wishes.

2. **Recalling.** According to The Cataclysm, on the Day of Judgment every soul will stand alone and God will stand supreme. People will have to answer for all of their actions. Righteous people will "dwell in bliss." Wicked people will suffer. **Interpreting.** A person of wicked ways who has strayed from the teachings of God is being addressed. This person is being accused of turning away from the Lord who created him or her. The person is warned that on the day of the Last Judgment, he or she will stand alone and have to answer for wicked actions.

3. **Recalling.** Mohammed's "life to come" holds a richer prize than his present life. **Interpreting.** Mohammed must realize that the Lord loves him and has chosen him for a special role on earth—that of teacher and aid to the poor. If Mohammed is facing worldly difficulties, he might be unsure of his Lord's love.

4. **Recalling.** The Lord found Mohammed as a orphan and gave him shelter, guided him, and enriched him. Mohammed (cont.)

ANSWERS FOR REVIEWING THE SELECTION (CONT.)

must therefore help other orphans and beggars. **Interpreting.** Mohammed must take care of others in the manner in which God cared for him and proclaim the goodness of the Lord to people on earth because of his own blessings.

SYNTHESIZING

Responses will vary. Possible responses are given.

5. God is Lord of the Universe and Sovereign of the Day of Judgment, but He is also merciful and compassionate. He is willing to guide people onto the straight path, but people must not turn away from Him toward wicked behaviors. This behavior will incur God's wrath. God stands for salvation and an afterlife that holds rewards. God also stands for leadership and compassion, as well as wrath. Mohammed was a teacher, guide, and servant to God.

2. **Tone.** **Tone** is the emotional attitude toward the reader or toward the subject implied by a work. Examples of different tones that a work might have include serious, angry, playful, and gentle. What different tones can be found in these excerpts from the Koran? Is the tone of a particular line or Sura reflective of its message? Explain.

3. **Image.** An **image** is a word or phrase that names something that can be seen, heard, touched, tasted, or smelled. Name some images from these excerpts that you found particularly vivid and striking. Why is one Sura called The Cataclysm? Why is another called Daylight? What images do these words create in your mind? In what way do these images reflect the main ideas of the two Suras?

Responding in Writing

1. **Creative Writing: Guide.** If you were to write your own personal guidebook for life, what ideas would you include in the book? On which of your experiences would you base this guide? Think about the work you did in your Reader's Journal, and spend ten minutes freewriting about this subject. Then, write three or four short paragraphs (or poems, if you would like) that reflect different ideas about life and your role in the world. You might also choose stories, poems, or religious verse that you have read and found inspiring as the subjects of some of your paragraphs.

2. **Critical Essay: Comparing and Contrasting the Koran and *The Divine Comedy*.** Write a short essay comparing and contrasting the moral messages imparted by the Koran and by *The Divine Comedy*. In your essay, answer the following questions: To what activities must people dedicate their lives? When will people be examined and held responsible for their deeds? When this time comes, who will suffer, and who will be rewarded? Support your ideas with concrete details from the excerpts from both texts.

Research Skills

Using a Key Word Search. Review the Language Arts Survey 4.12, "Using Search Tools." Then list possible key words that you could use to find information on each of the following subjects.

1. Islamic Art
2. Prophets of Islam, Judaism, and Christianity
3. Major religious holidays throughout the world
4. Traveling in the Middle East
5. A biography about Mohammed by Michael Cook

Answers for Understanding Literature

Responses will vary. Possible responses are given.

1. Repetition. The line "In the Name of God, the Compassionate, the Merciful," is repeated in each Sura. The idea of proclaiming God as the supreme leader who is good and merciful is repeated. These ideas are important in building the foundation of the religion and guiding the behavior of believers. The repetition reinforces these ideas in the reader's memory.

2. Tone. These excerpts from the Koran include compassionate, harsh and judgmental, exalting, and loving but forceful tones. All of these tones reflect the message of God and the feelings of the people who worship God. The Exordium is full of praise and requests that God have mercy and give guidance; The Cataclysm is a severe and harsh warning about what will happen to those who stray from God; Daylight is a loving but forceful message to Mohammed to proclaim the goodness of God.

3. Image. The images of the Last Judgment—when "the sky is rent asunder; when the stars scatter and the oceans roll together; when the graves are hurled about"—are particularly striking. Students may also point out the images in Daylight of God helping the orphaned Mohammed and asking him to do the same for others. The Cataclysm is about punishment and about forcefully convincing people to follow the word of God; this idea is enforced in the title, which conjures images of violent destruction. Daylight presents a more peaceful, non-threatening image of the duties one has toward God, and its name suggests enlightenment.

Answers for Skills Activity

RESEARCH SKILLS

Responses will vary. Possible responses are given.

1. Islamic Art—art, Islam, Middle Eastern art
2. Prophets of Islam, Judaism, and Christianity—prophets, Islam, Judaism, Christianity
3. Major religious holidays throughout the world—religions, holidays; world religions
4. Traveling in the Middle East—Middle East, travel, specific countries of the Middle East (Iran, Iraq, Saudi Arabia, etc.)
5. A biography about Mohammed by Michael Cook—Cook, Michael; Mohammed; Islam

▶ Additional practice is provided in the Essential Skills Practice Book: Study and Research 4.12.

ADDITIONAL RESOURCES

READER'S GUIDE

- Selection Worksheet 9.9

ASSESSMENT PORTFOLIO

- Selection Check Test 2.9.17
- Selection Test 2.9.18

ESSENTIAL SKILLS PRACTICE BOOKS

- Writing 1.8, 1.20
- Language 2.30–2.35

PREREADING EXTENSIONS

Students may wish to read more of *The Thousand and One Nights.* There are many collections of these stories, ranging from scholarly translations to retellings for children. Some of the most popular stories are the tales of Sinbad, Aladdin, and Ali Baba and the Forty Thieves. Students may also find movies or animated films based on the stories. Students can compare modern adaptations of the stories to other versions. If students are familiar with some of the tales, they might write about or discuss them before reading further. Then students can compare their expectations to their reading.

SUPPORT FOR LEP STUDENTS

PRONUNCIATIONS OF PROPER NOUNS AND ADJECTIVES

A • saf ben Be • ra • khy • a (ə´saf ben bē rə´kē ə)
Shah • ra • zad (shə rə´zad)
Di • nar • zad (dē nər´zad)
Du • ban (do͞o´ban)
Yu • nan (yo͞o´nan)

ADDITIONAL VOCABULARY

consummate—highly expert
interceded—pleaded on behalf of another
parched—dried
retinue—group of followers
wrath—anger

PREREADING

"The Fisherman and the Jinnee" from *The Thousand and One Nights*

Anonymous, translated by N. J. Dawood

About the Selection

"**The Fisherman and the Jinnee**" is one of many stories in a collection of tales called ***The Thousand and One Nights***, or *Arabian Nights Entertainments.* Written in the fourteenth century by an unknown author or authors, *The Thousand and One Nights* is a **frame tale**, or a story that itself provides a vehicle for the telling of other stories. In the frame of *The Thousand and One Nights,* King Shahrayar, distressed by the infidelity of his wife, has her executed and decides to marry a different woman each night and to kill her in the morning before she has a chance to become unfaithful. Having concocted a plan to end the killings, Shahrazad (or Scheharazade), the clever and well-read daughter of the king's advisor, insists on being selected as the next wife. On her wedding night, prompted by her sister Dinarzad, Shahrazad tells her husband a story. As day breaks, she falls quiet. When her sister comments on the strange and wonderful nature of the tale, Shahrazad replies that the story is not nearly as strange or wonderful as the story she will tell the next night. The king is intrigued and decides to keep Shahrazad alive for another night so that he can hear the next story. Shahrazad continues to enthrall the king with stories in this way until he relents and agrees not to kill her.

The collection of stories now known as *The Thousand and One Nights* has Indian, Persian, and Arabic roots. The framework of the story probably had its origins in a collection of Persian fairy tales called the "thousand stories." The terms *thousand* and *thousand and one* were meant to mean "many," but later translators and collectors of stories took these terms literally and added stories to reach the correct number. *The Thousand and One Nights* contains fairy tales, romances, legends, fables, parables, anecdotes, and adventures. This collection was composed and transmitted largely through the oral tradition (see Connections below). Although the stories of *The Thousand and One Nights* have long been popular in the West, they are not regarded as serious literature by many Arabic scholars.

CONNECTIONS: Storytelling and the Oral Tradition

People love to hear and tell stories, and cultures all over the world and in every historical period have told them. Stories help us to explore who we are, who other people are, what our past experiences mean, and what the future might hold. Storytelling is one of the most ancient of human impulses, an impulse from which literature was born. When writing was first invented over five thousand years ago, storytelling was already very, very old. Before stories were written down, they were passed on orally. As different people told a story, it would vary as storytellers forgot bits, added details, or tried to make it more interesting. Many of the stories told in *The Thousand and One Nights* were popular in the oral tradition before they were written down.

GOALS/OBJECTIVES

Studying this lesson will enable students to

- have a positive experience reading a frame tale
- recognize *The Thousand and One Nights* as a famous work of Arabic literature
- define *theme*
- understand the term *frame tale* and be able to identify several frame tales
- work with others to create a literary frame
- write a short tale about a specific theme
- analyze the theme of the selection
- recognize and correct errors in verb usage

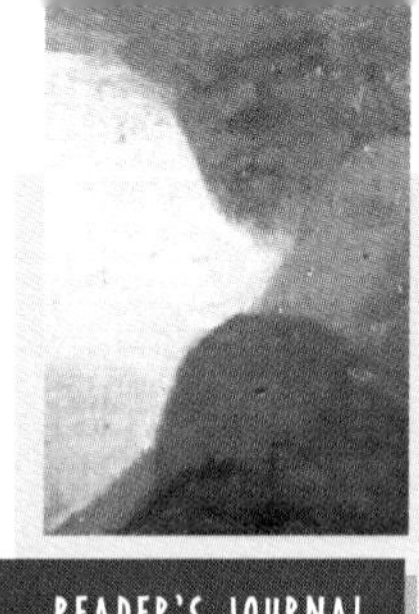

Consider the phrases "Do unto others as you would have them do unto you" and "Life for life,/ Eye for eye, tooth for tooth, hand for hand, foot for foot,/ Burning for burning, wound for wound, stripe for stripe." With which of these ideas do you agree? Which of these mottoes best reflects the way you live? Explain why you prefer one motto to the other.

READER'S JOURNAL

"The Fisherman and the Jinnee"

ANONYMOUS, TRANSLATED BY N. J. DAWOOD

Once upon a time there was a poor fisherman who had a wife and three children to support.

He used to cast his net four times a day. It chanced that one day he went down to the sea at noon and, reaching the shore, set down his basket, rolled up his shirt sleeves, and cast his net far out into the water. After he had waited for it to sink, he pulled on the cords with all his might; but the net was so heavy that he could not draw it in. So he tied the rope ends to a wooden stake on the beach and, putting off his clothes, dived into the water and set to work to bring it up. When he had carried it ashore, however, he found in it a dead donkey.

"By Allah, this is a strange catch!" cried the fisherman, disgusted at the sight. After he had freed the net and wrung it out, he waded into the water and cast it again, invoking Allah's help. But when he tried to draw it in he found it even heavier than before. Thinking that he had caught some enormous fish, he fastened the ropes to the stake and, diving in again, brought up the net. This time he found a large earthen vessel filled with mud and sand.

Angrily the fisherman threw away the vessel, cleaned his net, and cast it for the third time. He waited patiently, and when he felt the net grow heavy he hauled it in, only to find it filled with bones and broken glass. In despair, he lifted his eyes to heaven and cried: "Allah knows that I cast my net only four times a day. I have already cast it for the third time and caught no fish at all. Surely He will not fail me again!"

Why is the fisherman concerned as he casts his net for the fourth time?

With this the fisherman hurled his net far out into the sea and waited for it to sink to the bottom. When at length he brought it to land he found in it a bottle made of yellow copper. The mouth was stopped with lead and bore the seal of our master Solomon, son of David.[1] The fisherman rejoiced and said: "I will sell this in the market of the coppersmiths. It must be worth ten pieces of gold." He shook the bottle and, finding it heavy, thought to himself: "I will first break the seal and find out what is inside."

What did the fisherman catch the first three times he cast his net?

The fisherman removed the lead with his knife and again shook the bottle; but scarcely had he done so when there burst from it a great column of smoke which spread along the shore and rose so high that it almost touched the heavens. Taking shape, the smoke resolved itself into a jinnee of such

1. **Solomon . . . David.** Great kings of Israel, considered by Muslims to be prophets

READER'S JOURNAL

Students can discuss whether they believe in treating others as they would have others treat them, or if they treat others the way others have treated them. Students should explain their reasons for following either course or an alternate course of action.

ANSWERS TO GUIDED READING QUESTIONS

1. He was concerned because he only cast his net four times a day, so this was his last chance to catch some fish.
2. The fisherman caught a dead donkey, an earthenware vessel filled with mud and sand, and bones and broken glass.

SPELLING AND VOCABULARY WORDS FROM THE SELECTION

adjure	rashly
entreaty	regale
munificence	requite
perfidious	sumptuously
perturb	venerable
prodigious	

CROSS-CURRICULAR ACTIVITIES

ARTS AND HUMANITIES

The narrator of *The Thousand and One Nights,* whose name has many spellings (Shahrazad, Scheharazade, Sheherarade) has captured the imagination of many writers, artists, composers, and choreographers. Two works inspired by this fascinating character are Russian composer Nikolai Rimsky-Korsakov's symphonic suite *Sheherazade* (cont.)

CROSS-CURRICULAR ACTIVITIES (CONT.)

(1888) and French composer Maurice Ravel's musical composition Shéhérazade (1903). Ballets have been choreographed to both of these works. Michel Fokine choreographed a ballet to Rimsky-Korsakov's music; this work was first performed in 1910. George Balanchine's ballet to Ravel's music was first performed in 1975.

If possible, play for your students some of one or both of these musical compositions, or show a video of one of the ballets based on these works. Ask students to discuss how the music or dance reflects the mood, theme, or plot of the story.

Interested students can create their own musical or dance numbers to portray the story of Shahrazad.

Answers to Guided Reading Questions

① The fisherman is terrified. He stands quivering, rooted to the ground with his teeth chattering and his eyes staring.

② First the jinnee planned to bestow riches upon the person who freed him from imprisonment. Then the jinnee planned to open up buried treasures of the earth to this person. Still not freed, the jinnee flew into a rage and promised to kill the person who set him free.

③ The fisherman's fear of the jinnee is justified because the jinnee threatens to kill the fisherman.

Literary Note

The word *jinn* is the plural of *jinnee or jinni.* In Arabic mythology, the jinn are spirits that rank below angels and devils. Jinn can be classified into three types: treacherous, form-changing spirits called *Ghūl*, diabolic spirits called *'ifrīt,* and treacherous, nonform-changing spirits called *si'lā*. These spirits of air or fire can take human or animal form and may be found in any inanimate object. Like humans, jinn have needs, such as eating, and they can be killed. They are a vengeful group who enjoy punishing humans for wrongs done to them, whether intentional or accidental. Many accidents and diseases are attributed to jinn. With proper knowledge of magic, a human can control a jinni to his or her benefit. Jinn are popular in the folklore of North Africa, Egypt, Syria, Persia, and Turkey.

prodigious stature that his head reached the clouds, while his feet were planted on the sand. His head was a huge dome and his mouth as wide as a cavern, with teeth ragged like broken rocks. His legs towered like the masts of a ship, his nostrils were two inverted bowls, and his eyes, blazing like torches, made his aspect fierce and menacing.

① *What is the fisherman's reaction when he sees the jinnee?*

The sight of this jinnee struck terror to the fisherman's heart; his limbs quivered, his teeth chattered together, and he stood rooted to the ground with parched tongue and staring eyes.

"There is no god but Allah and Solomon is His Prophet!" cried the jinnee. Then, addressing himself to the fisherman, he said: "I pray you, mighty Prophet, do not kill me! I swear never again to defy your will or violate your laws!"

"Blasphemous giant," cried the fisherman, "do you presume to call Solomon the Prophet of Allah? Solomon has been dead these eighteen hundred years, and we are now approaching the end of time. But what is your history, pray, and how came you to be imprisoned in this bottle?"

② *In what way did the jinnee change the way he planned to treat his rescuer over the years?*

On hearing these words the jinnee replied sarcastically: "Well, then; there is no god but Allah! Fisherman, I bring you good news."

"What news?" asked the old man.

"News of your death, horrible and prompt!" replied the jinnee.

③ *Why are the fisherman's feelings about the jinnee justified?*

"Then may heaven's wrath be upon you, ungrateful wretch!" cried the fisherman. "Why do you wish my death, and what have I done to deserve it? Have I not brought you up from the depths of the sea and released you from your imprisonment?"

But the jinnee answered: "Choose the manner of your death and the way that I shall kill you. Come, waste no time!"

"But what crime have I committed?" cried the fisherman.

"Listen to my story, and you shall know," replied the jinnee.

"Be brief, then, I pray you," said the fisherman, "for you have wrung my soul with terror."

"Know," began the giant, "that I am one of the rebel jinn who, together with Sakhr the Jinnee, mutinied against Solomon, son of David. Solomon sent against me his vizier,[2] Asaf ben Berakhya, who vanquished me despite my supernatural power and led me captive before his master. Invoking the name of Allah, Solomon adjured me to embrace his faith and pledge him absolute obedience. I refused, and he imprisoned me in this bottle, upon which he set a seal of lead bearing the Name of the Most High. Then he sent for several of his faithful jinn, who carried me away and cast me into the middle of the sea. In the ocean depths I vowed; 'I will bestow eternal riches on him who sets me free!' But a hundred years passed away and no one freed me. In the second hundred years of my imprisonment I said: 'For him who frees me I will open up the buried treasures of the earth!' And yet no one freed me. Whereupon I flew into a rage and swore: 'I will kill the man who sets me free, allowing him only to choose the manner of his death!' Now it was you who set me free; therefore prepare to die and choose the way that I shall kill you."

"O wretched luck, that it should have fallen on my lot to free you!" exclaimed the fisherman. "Spare me, mighty jinnee, and Allah will spare you; kill me, and so shall Allah destroy you!"

2. **vizier.** High government officer

Words for Everyday Use

pro • di • gious (prō dij´əs) *adj.,* amazing; enormous

ad • jure (a jo͞or´) *vt.,* command or charge solemnly

Vocabulary in Context

- While Jorge is of normal size for a human being, to the ant, his form is of prodigious proportions.
- Ivana adjured the new recruits to uphold the honor of their company.

"You have freed me," repeated the jinnee. "Therefore you must die."

"Chief of the jinn," cried the fisherman, "will you thus requite good with evil?"

"Enough of this talk!" roared the jinnee. "Kill you I must."

At this point the fisherman thought to himself: "Though I am but a man and he is a jinnee, my cunning may yet overreach his malice." Then, turning to his adversary, he said: "Before you kill me, I beg you in the Name of the Most High engraved on Solomon's seal to answer me one question truthfully."

The jinnee trembled at the mention of the Name, and, when he had promised to answer truthfully, the fisherman asked: "How could this bottle, which is scarcely large enough to hold your hand or foot, ever contain your entire body?"

"Do you dare doubt that?" roared the jinnee indignantly.

"I will never believe it," replied the fisherman, "until I see you enter this bottle with my own eyes!"

Upon this the jinnee trembled from head to foot and dissolved into a column of smoke, which gradually wound itself into the bottle and disappeared inside. At once the fisherman snatched up the leaden stopper and thrust it into the mouth of the bottle. Then he called out to the jinnee: "Choose the manner of your death and the way that I shall kill you! By Allah, I will throw you back into the sea, and keep watch on this shore to warn all men of your treachery!"

When he heard the fisherman's words, the jinnee struggled desperately to escape from the bottle, but was prevented by the magic seal. He now altered his tone and, assuming a submissive air, assured the fisherman that he had been jesting with him and implored him to let him out. But the fisherman paid no heed to the jinnee's entreaties and resolutely carried the bottle down to the sea. "What are you doing with me?" whimpered the jinnee helplessly.

"I am going to throw you back into the sea!" replied the fisherman. "You have lain in the depths eighteen hundred years, and there you shall remain till the Last Judgment! Did I not beg you to spare me so that Allah might spare you? But you took no pity on me, and He has now delivered you into my hands."

"Let me out," cried the jinnee in despair, "and I will give you fabulous riches!"

"Perfidious jinnee," retorted the fisherman, "you justly deserve the fate of the king in the tale of Yunan and the doctor."

"What tale is that?" asked the jinnee.

THE TALE OF KING YUNAN AND DUBAN THE DOCTOR

It is related (began the fisherman) that once upon a time there reigned in the land of Persia a rich and mighty king called Yunan. He commanded great armies and had a numerous retinue of followers and courtiers. But he was afflicted with a leprosy[3] which baffled his physicians and defied all cures.

One day a venerable old doctor named Duban came to the king's capital. He had studied books written in Greek, Persian, Latin, Arabic, and Syriac, and was deeply versed in the wisdom of the ancients. He was master of many sciences, knew the properties of plants and herbs, and was above all skilled in astrology and medicine. When this physician heard of the leprosy with which Allah had plagued the king and of his doctors' vain endeavors to cure him, he put on his finest robes and betook himself to the royal palace. After he had kissed the ground

3. **leprosy.** Progressive infectious disease that attacks the skin, flesh, and nerves

❶ *How does the fisherman's cunning save him from the jinnee?*

❷ *What fate does the fisherman say that the jinnee deserves?*

WORDS FOR EVERYDAY USE

en • treat • y (en trēt´ē) *n.*, earnest request

per • fid • i • ous (pər fid´ē əs) *adj.*, treacherous

ven • er • a • ble (ven´ər ə bəl) *adj.*, worthy of respect due to age, character, or position

ANSWERS TO GUIDED READING QUESTIONS

❶ The fisherman cleverly gets the jinnee to go back into the bottle by questioning how such a large being could fit into such a small bottle and claiming that he would not believe it until he saw it with his own eyes.

❷ The fisherman says that the jinnee deserves the fate of the king in the tale of Yunan and the doctor.

LITERARY NOTE

Discuss with students what it means to be merciful. Ask them if they think that mercy is an important quality. Have them explain their response. As part of your discussion, you may wish to share with students Portia's speech about mercy from William Shakespeare's *The Merchant of Venice,* which appears below.

QUOTABLES

"The quality of mercy is not strained;
It droppeth as the gentle rain from heaven
Upon the place beneath. It is twice blest;
It blesseth him that gives and him that takes.
'Tis mightiest in the mightiest; it becomes
The throned monarch better than his crown.
His sceptre shows the force of temporal power,
The attribute to awe and majesty,
Wherein doth sit the dread and fear of kings;
But mercy is above this scept'red sway;
It is enthroned in the hearts of kings;
It is an attribute to God himself,
And earthly power doth then show likest God's
When mercy seasons justice."

—William Shakespeare
from *The Merchant of Venice*
(act IV, scene i)

VOCABULARY IN CONTEXT

- Zoë begged and pleaded for hours, but her entreaties fell on deaf ears.
- Not until Ryan had been duped did he believe that the seemingly kind stranger was a perfidious con artist.
- The whole town honored the venerable Mrs. Yarovich on her one hundredth birthday.

Answers to Guided Reading Questions

➊ The doctor says that he will cure the king without a potion to drink or an ointment to rub on his body.

➋ The doctor prepares by filling a hollow polo stick with balsams and elixirs. He then tells the king to grasp the stick firmly and to strike with it until his hand and body begin to perspire.

Literary Technique

FRAME TALE

As students will have read on the Prereading page, a **frame tale** is a story that itself provides a vehicle for the telling of other tales. "The Fisherman and the Jinnee" from *The Thousand and One Nights* provides an excellent example of a frame tale because it includes more than one frame. The story of King Shahrayar and Shahrazad is the main frame of *The Thousand and One Nights,* which provides a vehicle for the telling of the story of the fisherman and the jinnee, which in turn acts as a frame for "The Tale of King Yunan and Duban the Doctor." This story acts as a frame for "The Tale of King Sindbad and the Falcon." Point out to students that although each of these stories acts as a frame tale, a frame tale does not have to have a story within a story within a story. Many of the other frame tales they read will not function in this manner. For more information, refer students to Insights: Tales within Tales on page 795.

➊ *What does the doctor say that he will do for the king? What will he not do?*

➋ *How does the doctor prepare to cure the king?*

before the king and called down blessings upon him, he told him who he was and said: "Great king, I have heard about the illness with which you are afflicted and have come to heal you. Yet will I give you no potion to drink, nor any ointment to rub upon your body."

The king was astonished at the doctor's words and asked: "How will you do that? By Allah, if you cure me I will heap riches upon you, and your children's children after you. Anything you wish for shall be yours and you shall be my companion and my friend."

Then the king gave him a robe of honor and other presents and asked: "Is it really true that you can heal me without draught or ointment? When is it to be? What day, what hour?"

"Tomorrow, if the king wishes," he replied.

The doctor took leave of the king, and hastening to the center of the town rented for himself a house, to which he carried his books, his drugs, and his other medicaments. Then he distilled balsams and elixirs,[4] and these he poured into a hollow polo stick.

Next morning he went to the royal palace and, kissing the ground before the king, requested him to ride to the field and play a game of polo with his friends. The king rode out with his viziers and his chamberlains, and when he had entered the playing field the doctor handed him the hollow club and said: "Take this and grasp it firmly. Strike the ball with all your might until the palm of your hand and the rest of your body begin to perspire. The cure will penetrate your palm and course through the veins and arteries of your body. When it has done its work, return to the palace, wash yourself, and go to sleep. Thus shall you be cured; and peace be with you."

The king took hold of the club and, gripping it firmly, struck the ball and galloped after it with the other players. Harder and harder he struck the ball as he dashed up and down the field, until his palm and all his body perspired. When the doctor saw that the cure had begun its work, he ordered the king to return to the palace. The slaves hastened to make ready the royal bath and hurried to prepare the linens and the towels. The king bathed, put on his nightclothes, and went to sleep.

Next morning the physician went to the palace. When he was admitted to the king's presence he kissed the ground before him and wished him peace. The king hastily rose to receive him; he threw his arms around his neck and seated him by his side.

For when the king left the bath the previous evening, he looked upon his body and rejoiced to find no trace of the leprosy. His skin had become as pure as virgin silver.

The king regaled the physician sumptuously all day. He bestowed on him robes of honor and other gifts, and when evening came gave him two thousand pieces of gold and mounted him on his own favorite horse. And so enraptured was the king by the consummate skill of his doctor that he kept repeating to himself: "This wise physician has cured me without draught or ointment. By Allah, I will load him with honors and he shall henceforth be my companion and trusted friend." And that night the king lay down to sleep in perfect bliss, knowing that he was clean in body and rid at last of his disease.

Next morning, as soon as the king sat down upon his throne, with the officers of his court standing before him and his lieutenants and

4. **balsams and elixirs.** Types of potions with healing powers

Words for Everyday Use

re • gale (ri gāl´) *vt.,* entertain by providing a splendid feast

sump • tu • ous • ly (sump´cho͞o əs lē) *adv.,* lavishly; at great expense

Vocabulary in Context

- Mario regaled his guests with a twelve-course meal.
- Mario's guests dined sumptuously and commended him for an excellent feast.

viziers seated on his right and left, he called for the physician, who went up to him and kissed the ground before him. The king rose and seated the doctor by his side. He feasted him all day, gave him a thousand pieces of gold and more robes of honor, and conversed with him till nightfall.

Now among the king's viziers there was a man of repellent aspect, an envious, black-souled villain, full of spite and cunning. When this vizier saw that the king had made the physician his friend and lavished on him high dignities and favors, he became jealous and began to plot the doctor's downfall. Does not the proverb say: "All men envy, the strong openly, the weak in secret?"

So, on the following day, when the king entered the council chamber and was about to call for the physician, the vizier kissed the ground before him and said: "My bounteous master, whose munificence extends to all men, my duty prompts me to forewarn you against an evil which threatens your life; nor would I be anything but a base-born wretch were I to conceal it from you."

Perturbed at these ominous words, the king ordered him to explain his meaning.

"Your majesty," resumed the vizier, "there is an old proverb which says: 'He who does not weigh the consequences of his acts shall never prosper.' Now I have seen the king bestow favors and shower honors upon his enemy, on an assassin who cunningly seeks to destroy him. I fear for the king's safety."

"Who is this man whom you suppose to be my enemy?" asked the king, turning pale.

"If you are asleep, your majesty," replied the vizier, "I beg you to awake. I speak of Duban, the doctor."

"He is my friend," replied the king angrily, "dearer to me than all my courtiers; for he has cured me of my leprosy, an evil which my physicians had failed to remove. Surely there is no other physician like him in the whole world, from East to West. How can you say these monstrous things of him? From this day I will appoint him my personal physician and give him every month a thousand pieces of gold. Were I to bestow on him the half of my kingdom, it would be but a small reward for his service. Your counsel, my vizier, is the prompting of jealousy and envy. Would you have me kill my benefactor and repent of my rashness, as King Sindbad repented after he had killed his falcon?"

THE TALE OF KING SINDBAD
AND THE FALCON

Once upon a time (went on King Yunan) there was a Persian king who was a great lover of riding and hunting. He had a falcon which he himself had trained with loving care and which never left his side for a moment; for even at nighttime he carried it perched upon his fist, and when he went hunting took it with him. Hanging from the bird's neck was a little bowl of gold from which it drank. One day the king ordered his men to make ready for a hunting expedition and, taking with him his falcon, rode out with his courtiers. At length they came to a valley where they laid the hunting nets. Presently a gazelle fell into the snare, and the king said: "I will kill the man who lets her escape!"

They drew the nets closer and closer round the beast. On seeing the king the gazelle stood on her haunches and raised her forelegs to her head as if she wished to salute him. But as he bent forward to lay hold of her, she leaped over his head and fled across the field. Looking round, the king saw his courtiers winking at one another.

❶ *How does the vizier respond to the king's treatment of the doctor?*

❷ *What does the vizier say about the doctor?*

❸ *What is the king's reaction to the vizier's warning?*

WORDS FOR EVERYDAY USE

mu • nif • i • cence (myo͞o nif´ə səns) *n.,* generosity
per • turb (pər turb´) *vt.,* upset, trouble

Answers to Guided Reading Questions

❶ The vizier is jealous of the way the king is treating the doctor.

❷ The vizier says that the doctor is the enemy of the king.

❸ The king becomes angry with the vizier, saying that the doctor is his friend and that he will continue to reward him.

Additional Questions and Activities

When students have finished reading "The Tale of King Sindbad and the Falcon," ask them the following questions:

- What, if anything, is the moral of the story?
- Why does King Yunan tell the story, or what effect does he hope the story will have?

After students have read the story and answered the questions, ask them to write their own stories that present similar morals or lessons.

ANSWERS

The story suggests that it is wrong to accuse or punish those who have helped you in some way. The falcon helps the king. The king is distraught when he realizes that he has killed the creature who saved his life. In King Yunan's story, the doctor plays a similar role to that of the falcon. King Yunan hopes his vizier will see that killing the doctor would be a foolish act.

Vocabulary in Context

- Carla was praised for her munificence after donating one million dollars to the community library.
- Perturbed by the rumors, Loren called a press conference to set the record straight.

Answers to Guided Reading Questions

❶ The king becomes angry because the falcon will not drink. Instead, the falcon knocks over every bowl of water that the king sets before it.

❷ The king strikes the falcon with his sword. He realizes that the water was really the venom of a snake and that the falcon had saved his life.

Art Note

Elihu Vedder (1836–1923) painted *The Fisherman Releasing the Genie* sometime around the year 1861. Vedder was an American Romantic painter and illustrator who drew upon his dreams for many of his works. He studied in Paris from 1856 to 1861. Upon returning to the United States, he made a living by illustrating valentines and calisthenics books and by drawing for the magazine *Vanity Fair.* Vedder moved to Rome in 1866 but continued to visit the United States. His works include "The Lost Mind," "The Lair of the Sea Serpent," an illustrated edition of *The Rubáiyát of Omar Khayyám,* a mural entitled *Rome* for Bowdoin College, and a book *Doubt and Other Things.*

Cross-curricular Activities

Arts and Humanities

Students have probably seen many depictions of genies in illustrated stories, television shows, and films. Ask them to create their own depictions of the genie that comes out of the bottle found by the fisherman. Students may work in any medium to create their interpretations of the genie.

The Fisherman Releasing the Genie. *Elihu Vedder, circa 1861. Courtesy of Museum of Fine Arts, Boston. William Sturgis Bigelow Collection*

❶ *Why does the king become angry?*

❷ *What punishment does the king inflict upon the falcon? What does the king realize about the falcon's actions?*

"Why are they winking?" he asked his vizier.

"Perhaps because you let the beast escape," ventured the other, smiling.

"On my life," cried the king, "I will chase the gazelle and bring her back!"

At once he galloped off in pursuit of the fleeing animal, and when he had caught up with her, his falcon swooped upon the gazelle, blinding her with his beak, and the king struck her down with a blow of his sword. Then dismounting he flayed the animal and hung the carcass on his saddle-bow.

It was a hot day and the king, who by this time had become faint with thirst, went to search for water. Presently, however, he saw a huge tree, down the trunk of which water was trickling in great drops. He took the little bowl from the falcon's neck and, filling it with this water, placed it before the bird. But the falcon knocked the bowl with its beak and toppled it over. The king once again filled the bowl and placed it before the falcon, but the bird knocked it over a second time. Upon this the king became very angry and, filling the bowl a third time, set it down before his horse. But the falcon sprang forward and knocked it over with its wings.

"Allah curse you for a bird of ill omen!" cried the king. "You have prevented yourself from drinking and the horse also."

So saying, he struck the falcon with his sword and cut off both its wings. But the bird lifted its head as if to say: "Look into the tree!" The king raised his eyes and saw in the tree an enormous serpent spitting its venom down the trunk.

The king was deeply grieved at what he had done and, mounting his horse, hurried back to the palace. He threw his kill to the cook, and no sooner had he sat down, with the falcon still perched on his fist, than the bird gave a convulsive gasp and dropped down dead.

The king was stricken with sorrow and remorse for having so rashly killed the bird which had saved his life.

When the vizier heard the tale of King Yunan, he said: "I assure your majesty that my counsel is prompted by no other motive than my devotion to you and my concern for your safety. I beg leave to warn you that, if you put your trust in this physician, it is certain that he will destroy you. Has he not cured you by a device held in the hand? And might he not cause your death by another such device?"

"You have spoken wisely, my faithful vizier," replied the king. "Indeed, it is quite probable that this physician has come to my court as a spy to destroy me. And since he cured my illness by a thing held in the hand, he might as cunningly poison me with the scent of a perfume. What should I do, my vizier?"

"Send for him at once," replied the other, "and when he comes, strike off his head. Only thus shall you be secure from his perfidy."

Thereupon the king sent for the doctor, who hastened to the palace with a joyful heart, not knowing what lay in store for him.

"Do you know why I have sent for you?" asked the king.

"Allah alone knows the unspoken thoughts of men," replied the physician.

"I have brought you here to kill you," said the king.

The physician was thunderstruck at these words and cried: "But why should you wish to kill me? What crime have I committed?"

"It has come to my knowledge," replied the king, "that you are a spy sent here to cause my death. But you shall be the first to die."

Then he called out to the executioner, saying: "Strike off the head of this traitor!"

"Spare me, and Allah will spare you!" cried the unfortunate doctor. "Kill me, and so shall Allah kill you!"

But the king gave no heed to his entreaties. "Never will I have peace again," he cried, "until I see you dead. For if you cured me by a thing held in the hand, you will doubtless kill me by the scent of a perfume or by some other foul device."

"Is it thus that you repay me?" asked the doctor. "Will you thus requite good with evil?"

But the king said: "You must die; nothing can now save you."

When he saw that the king was determined to put him to death, the physician wept and bitterly repented the service he had done him. Then the executioner came forward, blindfolded the doctor and, drawing his sword, held it in readiness for the king's signal. But the doctor continued to wail, crying: "Spare me, and Allah will spare you! Kill me, and so shall Allah kill you!"

Moved by the old man's lamentations, one of the courtiers interceded for him with the king, saying: "Spare the life of this man, I pray you. He has committed no crime against you, but rather has he cured you of an illness which your physicians have failed to remedy."

"If I spare this doctor," replied the king, "he will use his devilish art to kill me. Therefore he must die."

Again the doctor cried: "Spare me, and Allah will spare you! Kill me, and so shall Allah kill you!" But when at last he saw that the king was fixed in his resolve, he said: "Your majesty, if you needs must kill me, I beg you to grant me a day's delay, so that I

❶ *What plea does the doctor make to the king?*

❷ *What effect does the story about the falcon and the king have on the vizier?*

Words for Everyday Use

rash • ly (rash´lē) *adv.*, recklessly; hastily

per • fi • dy (pur´fə dē) *n.*, betrayal of trust; treachery

re • quite (ri kwīt´) *vt.*, reward or retaliate against

Answers to Guided Reading Questions

❶ The doctor begs the king to spare him, saying what the king does to the doctor, Allah will do to the king.

❷ The vizier is unmoved by the king's story and continues to insist that the king should kill the doctor.

Selection Check Test with Answers

EX. Who is the narrator of *The Thousand and One Nights*?
Shahrazad is the narrator.

1. How many times does the fisherman cast his net each day?
The fisherman casts his net four times.

2. What news does the jinnee bring to the fisherman?
The jinnee tells the fisherman of his imminent death.

3. Why does the jinnee go back into its bottle?
The jinnee goes back into its bottle to prove to the fisherman that it can.

4. Why does the king strike the falcon?
The king is angry with the falcon for knocking over the water that the king set out for it.

5. How does the doctor kill the king?
Poison applied to the pages of a book kills the king.

Vocabulary in Context

- In a fit of rage, Uri rashly quit his job.
- After such perfidy, I don't think I can ever trust you again.
- Yesterday somebody helped Avery when he had a flat tire, so today he requited the good deed with one of his own.

Answers to Guided Reading Questions

1 The king has trouble turning the pages. He licks his fingers between each page. In doing so, he ingests the poison the doctor has put on the pages.

2 The king was killed because he failed to be merciful to the doctor. The fisherman is following the example of the doctor and punishing the jinnee for failing to spare his life.

Answers for Understanding Literature

Responses will vary. Possible responses are given.

Theme and Frame Tale. "The Fisherman and the Jinnee," and the story of the doctor contained within it, promote the ideal of mercy and sparing others harsh punishments. This concept of mercy is one that Shahrazad would like the king to adopt. She is telling stories not only for entertainment but also to save her life and the lives of other women who will come after her if she fails.

1 *What happened as the king tried to follow the doctor's instructions about the book?*

2 *In what way is the story of the king and the physician similar to the story of the fisherman and the jinnee?*

may go to my house and wind up my affairs. I wish to say farewell to my family and my neighbors and instruct them to arrange for my burial. I must also give away my books of medicine, of which there is one, a work of unparalleled virtue, which I would offer to you as a parting gift, that you may preserve it among the treasures of your kingdom."

"What may this book be?" asked the king.

"It holds secrets and devices without number, the least of them being this: that if, after you have struck off my head, you turn over three leaves of this book and read the first three lines upon the left-hand page, my severed head will speak and answer any questions you may ask it."

The king was astonished to hear this and at once ordered his guards to escort the physician to his house. That day the doctor put his affairs in order and next morning returned to the king's palace. There had already assembled the viziers, the chamberlains, the nabobs[5] and all the chief officers of the realm, so that with their colored robes the court seemed like a garden full of flowers.

The doctor bowed low before the king; in one hand he had an ancient book and in the other a little bowl filled with a strange powder. Then he sat down and said: "Bring me a platter!" A platter was instantly brought in, and the doctor sprinkled the powder on it, smoothing it over with his fingers. After that he handed the book to the king and said: "Take this book and set it down before you. When my head has been cut off, place it upon the powder to stanch the bleeding. Then open the book."

The king ordered the executioner to behead the physician. He did so. Then the king opened the book, and, finding the pages stuck together, put his finger to his mouth and turned over the first leaf. After much difficulty he turned over the second and the third, moistening his finger with his spittle at every page, and tried to read. But he could find no writing there.

"There is nothing written in this book," cried the king.

"Go on turning," replied the severed head.

The king had not turned six pages when the venom (for the leaves of the book were poisoned) began to work in his body. He fell backward in an agony of pain, crying: "Poisoned! Poisoned!" and in a few moments breathed his last.

"Now, treacherous jinnee," continued the fisherman, "had the king spared the physician, he in turn would have been spared by Allah. But he refused, and Allah brought about the king's destruction. And as for you, if you had been willing to spare me, Allah would have been merciful to you, and I would have spared your life. But you sought to kill me; therefore I will throw you back into the sea and leave you to perish in this bottle!" ■

5. **nabobs.** Rich, important people

Responding to the Selection

Do you agree with the way the fisherman treated the jinnee? What would you have done in his situation? Do you think the jinnee deserved his fate? Explain.

Reviewing the Selection

RECALLING / **INTERPRETING**

1. What does the jinnee threaten to do to the fisherman? What does the fisherman do to trick the jinnee? What story does the fisherman tell the jinnee? ▶▶ Why does the fisherman tell the jinnee this story?
2. What act does King Sindbad regret committing in "The Tale of King Sindbad and the Falcon"? ▶▶ Why does King Yunan tell this story to his vizier? What effect does the story have on the vizier?
3. What does King Yunan decide to do to the doctor? What does he allow the doctor to do? ▶▶ What motivates King Yunan to postpone the doctor's fate?
4. What does the doctor do to King Yunan? ▶▶ In what way are the actions of King Yunan related to the actions of the jinnee?

SYNTHESIZING

5. What reason does each storyteller, the fisherman and King Yunan, have for telling his story? Does either storyteller act upon the moral of the story he tells? Explain.

Understanding Literature (Questions for Discussion)

Theme and Frame Tale. A **theme** is the central idea in a literary work. A **frame tale** is a story that itself provides a vehicle for the telling of other stories. In this selection, each tale serves as a frame for the next. Review the information about the frame of *The Thousand and One Nights* provided in About the Selection on page 784. Then explain how the theme of "The Fisherman and the Jinnee" is related to Shahrazad's situation. Why might she have chosen to tell this story?

RESPONDING TO THE SELECTION

Students might also discuss what might have happened to the fisherman if he had decided to show mercy to the jinnee and set it free rather than returning it in its bottle to the ocean. Would the jinnee have been grateful or would it have been vengeful?

ANSWERS FOR REVIEWING THE SELECTION

RECALLING AND INTERPRETING

1. **Recalling.** The jinnee threatens to kill the fisherman. The fisherman tells the jinnee that he cannot believe the jinnee fits into the bottle unless he sees it with his own eyes. The jinnee goes into the bottle to prove he can do it and the fisherman puts the stopper back on the bottle. The fisherman tells the jinnee the story of King Yunan and Duban the doctor. **Interpreting.** The fisherman tells this story to explain why the jinnee should have shown him mercy.
2. **Recalling.** The king regrets striking his falcon with his sword and killing it. **Interpreting.** The king tells this story to his vizier to explain why he does not wish to kill the doctor. The king believes that the doctor has helped him as the falcon helped the king in his story. The vizier does not take this meaning from the story. It has no effect upon him, and he continues to press for the doctor's death.
3. **Recalling.** The king decides to have the doctor killed. The king allows the doctor to go home and settle his affairs. **Interpreting.** The king postpones killing the doctor for one day because he is greedy or curious and he wants the book the doctor has promised him.
4. **Recalling.** The doctor poisons the king. **Interpreting.** The king decided to be merciless despite the pleas of his victim. The jinnee responded in the same way to the fisherman's pleas.

(cont.)

ANSWERS FOR REVIEWING THE SELECTION (CONT.)

SYNTHESIZING

Responses will vary. Possible responses are given.

5. The fisherman tells his story to support his decision to show no mercy to the jinnee. King Yunan tells his story to explain why he does not want to kill the doctor. The king is originally acting upon the moral of the story of Sindbad and the falcon, but after telling the story, he is swayed by his vizier and disregards the moral of his story. The fisherman follows the actions of the doctor by refusing to show mercy to the jinnee who would not spare his life as the doctor had refused to show mercy to the merciless king. The fisherman, in following the doctor's example, is not following the moral of the story, which would seem to be to show mercy to others that they might show it to you.

ANALYTIC SCALES FOR RESPONDING IN WRITING

Assign a score from 1 to 25 for each grading criterion below. (For more detailed evaluation, see the evaluation forms for writing, revising, and proofreading, Assessment Portfolio 4.1–4.9.)

1. Frame Tale

- **Content/Unity.** The frame of the frame tale should present a reason for the telling of the tales. The stories told within the frame should share a theme.
- **Organization/Coherence.** The frame introduces the telling of the tales. The stories may be told in any order.
- **Language/Style.** The frame tale uses vivid and precise nouns, verbs, and modifiers.
- **Conventions.** The frame tale avoids errors in spelling, grammar, usage, mechanics, and manuscript form.

▶ Additional practice is provided in the Essential Skills Practice Book: Writing 1.8.

2. Critical Essay

- **Content/Unity.** The essay presents analysis of the theme of *The Thousand and One Nights.*
- **Organization/Coherence.** The essay begins with an introduction that includes a thesis. The introduction is followed by supporting paragraphs with clear transitions. The essay ends with a solid conclusion.
- **Language/Style.** The essay uses vivid and precise nouns, verbs, and modifiers.
- **Conventions.** The essay avoids errors in spelling, grammar, usage, mechanics, and manuscript form.

▶ Additional practice is provided in the Essential Skills Practice Book: Writing 1.20.

Responding in Writing

1. **Creative Writing: Frame Tale.** Review the information about frame tales in the Insight on page 795. Work in small groups to create your own frame tales. Each group should brainstorm to come up with an idea for a frame. You may wish to create a frame in which there is one narrator, as in the case of Shahrazad and *The Thousand and One Nights,* or you may wish to create a scenario in which several people decide to tell each other stories for some reason. Choose a broad theme for your tales; a common theme will help tie the stories together. As a group, write the frame for your frame tale based on the decisions that you have made. Then, each member of the group should write a tale that fits into the frame the group has devised. After each person has written his or her tale, compile the tales. You may wish to add dialogue to provide a transition from one tale to another. Share your frame tales by creating a booklet for others to read, or by reading your group's work aloud to your classmates.

2. **Critical Essay: Theme.** Analyze the theme in *The Thousand and One Nights.* Consider Shahrazad's plan and why she might choose to tell stories with a particular theme. Then discuss the theme of "The Fisherman and the Jinnee." In what way is this theme supported or undermined by the message of "The Tale of King Yunan and Duban the Doctor"? In what way is the theme of "The Tale of King Sindbad and the Falcon" related to the themes of the two stories within which it is contained? What overall message does "The Fisherman and the Jinnee" deliver? Would this message be as clear if the other tales were not included within it? Why, or why not? In your thesis statement, introduce your analysis of these themes. Support your thesis with evidence from the text. Resolve your thesis in a concluding paragraph.

Language Lab

Correcting Errors in Verb Usage. Read the Language Arts Survey 2.30–2.35, "Editing for Errors in Verbs." Then, on your own paper, rewrite the following sentences correcting any errors in verb usage.

1. Dina finded a bottle with strange symbols on it.
2. Dina was unable to completely decipher the symbols.
3. When she opens the bottle, a strange, green smoke came out.
4. Dina noted that the green smoke was smelling like spices.
5. The green smoke began to mysteriously materialize into a genie.
6. The genie weared clothing made of the richest and most vibrant silks.
7. Dina expected the genie to kindly offer her three wishes.
8. Instead, the genie asked Dina to quickly smash the bottle.
9. Dina brang the bottle to a rock in the woods and then smashed it down.
10. When the bottle had smashed, the genie disappeared.

ANSWERS FOR LANGUAGE LAB

1. Dina found a bottle with strange symbols on it.
2. Dina was completely unable to decipher the symbols.
3. When she opened the bottle, a strange, green smoke came out.
4. Dina noted that the green smoke smelled like spices.
5. The green smoke mysteriously began to materialize into a genie.
6. The genie wore clothing made of the richest and most vibrant silks.
7. Dina expected the genie kindly to offer her three wishes.
8. Instead, the genie asked Dina to smash the bottle quickly.
9. Dina brought the bottle to a rock in the woods and then smashed it down.
10. When the bottle had been smashed, the genie disappeared.

▶ Additional practice is provided in the Essential Skills Practice Book: Language 2.30–2.35.

Insights

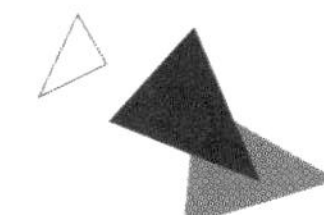

Tales within Tales

A **frame tale** is a story that itself provides a vehicle for the telling of other stories. Popular during the Medieval Period and the Renaissance, the frame tale has been utilized by writers through the present day. *The Thousand and One Nights* is a frame tale because the continuing story of Shahrazad serves to connect many other stories, such as "The Fisherman and the Jinnee," as Shahrazad tells them to her husband.

A frame tale may have one or more narrators. In *The Thousand and One Nights,* some of the stories may seem to have more than one narrator: for example, a fisherman tells "The Tale of King Yunan and Duban the Doctor," and King Yunan tells "The Tale of King Sindbad and the Falcon," but, essentially, Shahrazad is telling all of the tales. In other frame tales, the frame sets up a situation in which several people tell stories. Giovanni Boccaccio's *Decameron* (see page 822) is an example of this type of tale. The frame of the *Decameron* sends ten young people to a country house where they have gone to avoid the plague. There they decide that, to pass the time, each person should tell one story a day, and a topic is chosen for each day. Geoffrey Chaucer also used the idea of a group of people sharing stories in *The Canterbury Tales.* In Chaucer's frame tale, a group of people have gathered at an inn before setting out on a pilgrimage. The innkeeper, or host, suggests that to make the journey less tiresome, the travelers should have a storytelling contest. At the end of the prologue which precedes the tales, the innkeeper says:

> "Each one of you shall help to make things slip
> By telling two stories on the outward trip
> To Canterbury, that's what I intend,
> And, on the homeward journey's end
> Another two, tales from the days of old;
> And then the man whose story is best told,
> That is to say who gives the fullest measure
> Of good morality and general pleasure,
> He shall be given a supper, paid by all,
> Here in the tavern, in this very hall,
> When we come back again from Canterbury."

Thus, the prologue establishes a reason for telling these tales. After the storytelling begins, the pilgrims interrupt each other, argue, and discuss the stories. The interaction between the characters is more natural than the formulaic interchange between Shahrazad and her sister that is interspersed with the stories told in *The Thousand and One Nights.*

Some frame tales are more loosely connected than others. Other frame tales include Marguerite de Navarre's *Heptameron,* a collection of love tales modeled on the frame of Boccaccio's *Decameron*; the *Jataka,* a group of ancient Indian folktales combined under a loosely organized frame of Buddhist teaching; and Henry Wadsworth Longfellow's *Tales of a Wayside Inn,* which includes the famous narrative poem "Paul Revere's Ride." Isabel Allende's *The Stories of Eva Luna,* from which "The Little Heidelberg" is taken (see page 270), is a loosely constructed frame tale. In her contemporary frame tale, Allende refers to the literary tradition upon which she draws by opening her collection with an epigraph from *The Thousand and One Nights*:

> The king ordered the grand vizier to bring him a virgin every night, and when the night was over, he ordered her to be killed. And thus it happened for three years, and in all the city there was no damsel left to withstand the assaults of this rider. But the vizier had a daughter of great beauty named Scheherazade . . . and she was very eloquent, and pleased all who heard her.

This epigraph is followed by an introduction in which Eva Luna's beloved asks her to tell him a story that she has never told anyone before. His request forms the frame from which the stories of the collection spring. Allende closes the collection with reference again to Shahrazad (also spelled Scheherazade):

> And at this moment in her story, Scheherazade saw the first light of dawn, and discreetly fell silent.

Additional Questions and Activities

Have students read one of the frame tales introduced on page 795. Have students answer the following questions about their reading:

- What is the frame of the story—in other words, what situation is introduced to explain the collection of stories?
- Is there a single narrator? If there is more than one narrator, how do they interact?
- Do the stories share one or more themes? If so, what are they?
- Are the stories related in any way to the frame itself? Explain.

ADDITIONAL RESOURCES

Reader's Guide

- Selection Worksheet 9.10

Assessment Portfolio

- Selection Check Test 2.9.19
- Selection Test 2.9.20

Essential Skills Practice Books

- Writing 1.8, 1.20
- Study and Research 4.1

PREREADING EXTENSIONS

In this poem, particularly in stanzas 19 and 20, the speaker describes how nature transforms death into new life. Students may work in small groups to determine to what extent stanzas 19 and 20 describe scientific truths. Students may consult biology texts, do some research in the library, or talk to biology teachers in their school. Each group might present a written paragraph or two on their findings. You might point out that Khayyám would have been more familiar than many people with biological processes because of his work in science and medicine.

SUPPORT FOR LEP STUDENTS

Pronunciations of Proper Nouns and Adjectives

O • mar Khay • yám (ō′mar kī yam′)
Ru • bái • yát (ro͞o′bī yät)

Additional Vocabulary

anon—immediately
bough—branch of a tree
husbanded—cultivated

PREREADING

from *The Rubáiyát of Omar Khayyám*
by Omar Khayyám, translated by Edward FitzGerald

PERSIA

About the Author

Omar Khayyám (AD 1048–1123). Omar Khayyám was born in Nishapur, Persia, on May 18, 1048. The name Khayyám means "tent maker," possibly indicating the profession of Omar's father. Khayyám's primary occupation was as a mathematician and astronomer, and his work on algebra became a standard text. He also mastered the subjects of philosophy, astronomy, law, medicine, and history.

About the Selection

The Rubáiyát is a compilation of roughly five hundred **epigrams,** or short, often witty sayings, presented in quatrains, or *ruba'i,* written throughout Khayyám's life. In his translation, FitzGerald modified the original ordering of the quatrains to increase their thematic coherence. In general, the epigrams, often satiric in tone, express a rebellious dissatisfaction with orthodox belief. Perhaps Khayyám's idea that one should try to get as much pleasure as possible from each passing moment is part of what attracted FitzGerald to the Persian writer's work.

While Khayyám rhymed each of the four lines in a quatrain, FitzGerald rhymed only the first, second, and fourth lines of each quatrain in his translation. The content of FitzGerald's translation mirrors his rhyme scheme, as each third line expressesan idea that is completed in the fourth. This combination defines the "FitzGerald stanza," which other English writers have adopted. The first edition of FitzGerald's *Rubáiyát,* containing only seventy-five quatrains, was published in 1859. The definitive fourth edition (1879) included 101 stanzas.

CONNECTIONS: Carpe Diem

The Rubáiyát of Omar Khayyám brilliantly expresses the *carpe diem,* or "seize the day," theme—a theme that encourages people to enjoy the present moment and make good use of the little time available in life. This theme is found in classical literature as well as in much of English literature. The theme often appears in love poems urging the beloved to follow his or her romantic impulses while there is still time to do so. The sensuality and beauty of Edward FitzGerald's translation of *The Rubáiyát* greatly influenced English poetry in the late nineteenth century.

GOALS/OBJECTIVES

Studying this lesson will enable students to

- appreciate a work of poetry expressing the *carpe diem* theme
- briefly explain the *carpe diem* theme
- define *mood, theme,* and *simile,* and identify moods, themes, and similes in poems they read
- write a creative recipe for happiness
- write a critical essay analyzing the way the *carpe diem* theme is expressed in a literary work
- create a pros and cons chart

Have you ever let an opportunity slip by and regretted it later? Have you ever planned for an important moment only to be disappointed by how it turned out? Write about one such experience and what, if anything, you learned from it.

READER'S JOURNAL

FROM

The Rubáiyát of Omar Khayyám

OMAR KHAYYÁM, TRANSLATED BY EDWARD FITZGERALD

12

A Book of Verses underneath the bough,
A jug of Wine, a Loaf of Bread—and Thou
  Beside me singing in the Wilderness—
Oh, Wilderness were Paradise enow![1]

13

Some for the Glories of This World; and some
Sigh for the Prophet's[2] Paradise to come;
  Ah, take the Cash, and let the Credit go,
Nor heed the rumble of a distant Drum!

14

Look to the blowing Rose about us—"Lo,
Laughing," she says, "into the world I blow,
  At once the silken tassel of my purse
Tear, and its Treasure on the Garden throw."

15

And those who husbanded the Golden Grain,
And those who flung it into the winds like Rain,
  Alike to no such aureate Earth are turned
As, buried once, Men want dug up again.

❶ *What four things would turn a wilderness into a paradise for the speaker of this poem?*

❷ *Does the speaker think we should live for today or for tomorrow?*

❸ *What do lines 13–15 suggest about life?*

1. **enow.** Enough
2. **Prophet's.** Mohammed's

WORDS FOR EVERYDAY USE

au • re • ate (ô´rē it) *adj.*, splendid or brilliant; golden

READER'S JOURNAL

As an alternate activity, you might ask students to write about whether it is better to live for the moment or to plan carefully for the future. Is it possible to do both? How?

ANSWERS TO GUIDED READING QUESTIONS

❶ A book of verses, a jug of wine, a loaf of bread, and "Thou" turn the wilderness to paradise for the speaker.

❷ The speaker believes that people should live for today and for the "Glories of This World."

❸ Lines 13–15 suggest that no matter how one chooses to live life, we all end up buried in the "aureate Earth."

SPELLING AND VOCABULARY WORDS FROM THE SELECTION

aureate sans

VOCABULARY IN CONTEXT

• We were struck with awe watching the aureate sun rise over the surging sea.

Answers to Guided Reading Questions

❶ All people must die. People's hopes are either dashed or they come true and provide only fleeting happiness.

❷ The sleep of the great hunter is actually death. His feats are of little significance, since the animal he once hunted now stamps on his grave.

ANALYTIC SCALES FOR RESPONDING IN WRITING

(SEE PAGE 801.)

Assign a score from 1 to 25 for each grading criterion below. (For more detailed evaluation, see the evaluation forms for writing, revising, and proofreading, Assessment Portfolio 4.1–4.9.)

1. Recipe for Paradise

- **Content/Unity.** The writing presents a recipe for happiness.
- **Organization/Coherence.** The recipe lists details in a sensible order.
- **Language/Style.** The recipe uses vivid and precise nouns, verbs, and modifiers.
- **Conventions.** The recipe avoids errors in spelling, grammar, usage, mechanics, and manuscript form.

▶ Additional practice is provided in the Essential Skills Practice Book: Writing 1.8.

2. Critical Essay

- **Content/Unity.** The essay discusses the way the *carpe diem* theme is presented in the poem.
- **Organization/Coherence.** The essay presents and supports a thesis. The essay has a solid conclusion.
- **Language/Style.** The essay uses vivid and precise nouns, verbs, and modifiers.
- **Conventions.** The essay avoids errors in spelling, grammar, usage, mechanics, and manuscript form.

▶ Additional practice is provided in the Essential Skills Practice Book: Writing 1.20.

Rubáiyát of Omar Khayyám. *Edmund Dulac*

❶ *What is the common fate of all? What happens to people's hopes?*

16

The Worldly Hope men set their Hearts upon
Turns Ashes—or it prospers; and anon,
  Like Snow upon the Desert's dusty Face,
Lighting a little hour or two—is gone.

17

Think, in this battered Caravanserai[3]
Whose Portals are alternate Night and Day,
  How Sultán after Sultán with his pomp
Abode his destined Hour, and went his way.

❷ *Why cannot the great hunter be awakened? Of what significance are his feats now?*

18

They say the Lion and the Lizard keep
The Courts where Jamshyd[4] gloried and drank deep;
  and Bahrám,[5] that great Hunter—the Wild Ass
Stamps o'er his Head, but cannot break his Sleep.

---

3. **Caravanserai.** Inn; here, metaphorically, the world
4. **Jamshyd.** In Persian myth, a king of the fairies who was forced to live a human life because he boasted of his immortality
5. **Bahrám.** A king who was lost while hunting a wild donkey

19

I sometimes think that never blows so red
The Rose as where some buried Caesar bled;
That every Hyacinth[5] the Garden wears
Dropped in her Lap from some once lovely Head.

20

And this reviving Herb whose tender Green
Fledges the River-Lip on which we lean—
Ah, lean upon it lightly! for who knows
From what once lovely Lip it springs unseen!

21

Ah, my Belovéd, fill the cup that clears
TODAY of past Regrets and future Fears:
Tomorrow!—Why, Tomorrow I may be
Myself with Yesterday's sev'n thousand Years.

❶ *What does the speaker want his beloved to do?*

22

For some we loved, the loveliest and the best
That from his Vintage rolling Time hath pressed,
Have drunk their Cup a Round or two before,
And one by one crept silently to rest.

23

And we, that now make merry in the Room
They left, and Summer dresses in new bloom,
Ourselves must we beneath the Couch of Earth
Descend—ourselves to make a Couch—for whom?

24

Ah, make the most of what we yet may spend,
Before we too into the Dust descend;
Dust into Dust, and under Dust to lie,
Sans Wine, sans Song, sans Singer, and—sans End! ■

❷ *What does the speaker think we should do, given that we shall all die?*

5. **Hyacinth.** A plant of the lily family

WORDS FOR EVERYDAY USE

sans (sänz) *prep.*, without

ANSWERS TO GUIDED READING QUESTIONS

❶ The speaker wants his beloved to fill the cup that clears today of regrets and fears.

❷ Since death is inevitable and eternal, we should enjoy the pleasures of this world while we can.

SELECTION CHECK TEST WITH ANSWERS

EX. Who wrote *The Rubáiyát*?
Omar Khayyám wrote *The Rubáiyát*.

1. What is the speaker's recipe for happiness?
Sitting in the wilderness with a book of poetry, food, wine, and his beloved is his recipe for happiness.

2. What, according to the speaker, happens to all people?
All people must die.

3. What, according to the speaker, nourishes plants and flowers?
People who have died nourish plants and flowers.

4. How does the speaker feel about regrets and fears?
The speaker feels that regrets and fears should be cleared away.

5. Of what must people make the most, according to the speaker?
According to the speaker, people must make the most of their time on earth.

VOCABULARY IN CONTEXT

• Louise was annoyed when she ordered her sandwich sans mayonnaise but then received a sandwich dripping with it.

RESPONDING TO THE SELECTION

As an alternate activity, students might discuss the type of person they imagine the speaker of this poem to be. Would they like to meet him? Why, or why not?

ANSWERS FOR REVIEWING THE SELECTION

RECALLING AND INTERPRETING

1. **Recalling.** The speaker's recipe for happiness is a book of verses, a jug of wine, a loaf of bread, and good company, or "Thou." **Interpreting.** Intellectual stimulation, sustenance, and companionship are everything the speaker needs to live a perfectly happy life.

2. **Recalling.** All people, including great sultans, must die. **Interpreting.** Earthly achievements, no matter how important, do not matter in that they do not prevent death. Many of these achievements die when the people who accomplished them die.

3. **Recalling.** According to the speaker, great people who have died nourish hyacinths and herbs. **Interpreting.** The speaker believes that life springs from death—that the flowers in gardens grow from great people who have died. These stanzas reveal the power of the natural world which can create life from death.

4. **Recalling.** People creep silently to rest. **Interpreting.** The speaker is referring to death in stanza 22.

SYNTHESIZING

Responses will vary. Possible responses are given.

5. The speaker tells readers that they should do away with regrets and fears and that they should make the most of time on earth. This advice is related to the speaker's claim that he wants to enjoy the simple things of this world while there is still time. The line in stanza 24, "Ah, make the most of what we yet may spend, / Before we too into the Dust descend," sums up the speaker's advice.

Responding to the Selection

What lines from this selection stand out for you? Why?

Reviewing the Selection

RECALLING / **INTERPRETING**

1. In stanza 12, what does the speaker describe as his recipe for happiness? ▶▶ Why are these things sufficient for the speaker to create a paradise on Earth?
2. What, according to stanzas 17 and 18, happens to all people, including great sultans? ▶▶ What do stanzas 17 and 18 say about the importance of earthly achievements?
3. According to stanzas 19 and 20, what nourishes hyacinths and herbs? ▶▶ In stanzas 19 and 20, what is the speaker's attitude on the cycle of life and death? What do these stanzas say about the natural world?
4. To where do people creep silently after having "drunk their Cup a Round or two before"? ▶▶ To what kind of rest is the speaker referring in stanza 22?

SYNTHESIZING

5. Given the observations made in previous stanzas, what advice does the speaker offer in stanzas 21–24? In what way is this advice related to the speaker's earlier observations? What line in stanza 24 sums up the advice?

Understanding Literature (Questions for Discussion)

1. **Mood. Mood,** or **atmosphere,** is the emotion created in the reader by part or all of a literary work. A writer creates a mood with careful use of concrete details. What is the general mood of the stanzas from *The Rubáiyát* that you have read? Why does the piece have this mood? What words and phrases create this mood?
2. **Theme.** A **theme** is a central idea in a literary work. What is the theme of this excerpt from *The Rubáiyát?* Cite lines and images in the poem that refer directly to this theme.
3. **Simile.** A **simile** is a comparison using *like* or *as*. Find an example of a simile in stanza 16. What two things are being compared? In what way does this comparison support the theme of the poem? Create another simile that expresses this theme.

ANSWERS FOR UNDERSTANDING LITERATURE

Responses will vary. Possible responses are given.

1. **Mood.** Students might say that the mood of the piece is lighthearted, happy, and persuasive. This mood is appropriate because the speaker is trying to convince readers to make the most of life on earth, to do away with regrets and fears, and to seek happiness in simple pleasures. Phrases that describe simple pleasures, the natural world, and doing away with regrets contribute to this mood. For example, "Look to the blowing Rose about us—"Lo, / Laughing," she says, "into the world I blow, / At once the silken tassel of my purse / Tear, and its Treasure on the Garden throw."

2. **Theme.** The theme of this piece is to make the most of time on earth, to seek joy in simple

(cont.)

Responding in Writing

1. **Creative Writing: Recipe for Paradise.** The speaker, in stanza 12, describes "A book of Verses underneath the bough,/A jug of Wine, a Loaf of Bread—and Thou/Beside me singing in the Wilderness—" as paradise. What is your personal recipe for happiness? Write a recipe in which you list the people, places, and things that you would need in order to create a paradise on Earth. Try to write your recipe in the form of a short poem, using vivid language and original details.

2. **Critical Essay: Discussion of the *Carpe Diem* Theme.** What statements, words, and phrases are used to support this poem's central idea of *carpe diem?* Write an essay in which you discuss the *carpe diem* theme as expressed in the poem. In your essay address the following questions: What does the speaker say is inevitable about life? Why should the reader "seize the day"? What examples of what a reader might do to seize the day are present in the poem? Express a thesis in an introductory paragraph. Quote or refer to certain lines or stanzas to support your thesis in following paragraphs, and come to a conclusion in a final paragraph.

Thinking Skills

Problem Solving and Decision Making. Review the Language Arts Survey 4.1, "Problem Solving and Decision Making." Then create a chart in which you weigh the pros and cons of always living for the moment and never worrying about the future. When you have completed your chart, study it and try to come up with a reasonable compromise for your own life. When is planning and thinking for the future important? When might worrying too much about the future stand in the way of enjoying the present moment? When might living too much in the moment cause problems? How might you achieve a balance in your life? Your completed assignment should include a pros and cons chart, as well as statements about what you learned from your chart.

ANSWERS FOR UNDERSTANDING LITERATURE (CONT.)

pleasures, and to do away with regrets and fears. Lines that directly express this idea include stanza 21, "Ah, my Belovéd, fill the cup that clears / TODAY of past Regrets and future Fears" and stanza 24, "Ah, make the most of what we yet may spend."

3. Simile. The speaker compares men's worldly hopes to snow "upon the Desert's dusty Face." Hope and dust are being compared. This line means that men work hard to achieve goals that give them momentary pleasure, but that all of these accomplishments die when people die anyway. The speaker is saying that people should live for the moment because life on earth is so fleeting. *Similes will vary.*

ANSWERS FOR SKILLS ACTIVITIES

THINKING SKILLS

Responses will vary, but students might say that they need to find a balance between achieving goals and seeking the pleasures of the world that are described in *The Rubáiyát.* A chart might look something like this:

Pros of "living for the moment"
—able to enjoy life
—experience less stress
—able to spend time appreciating people and the world
—would not get caught up in worldly greed

Cons of "living for the moment"
—might have trouble making a living
—some accomplishments are worthwhile and lasting
—accomplishments might pave the way for more interesting and broader experiences
—not able to spend time helping others to enjoy life

► Additional practice is provided in the Essential Skills Practice Book: Study and Research 4.1.

ANALYTIC SCALES FOR RESPONDING IN WRITING

Grading scales for Responding in Writing appear on page 798.

Cultural/Historical Note

You may wish to inform students that while FitzGerald's translation of the *Rubáiyát* incited controversy, even more controversy surrounded the first translations of the Bible into English. Before the Protestant Reformation and England's break with the Roman Catholic Church, Bibles were in Latin, as were church services. The Church held untold wealth and power, and the Pope delivered edicts to monarchs. John Wycliffe (1330–1384), the first translator of the Bible into English, believed that members of the Church should give up their worldly possessions to live in evangelical poverty. Known for sympathizing with the poor and uneducated classes, Wycliffe translated the Bible into English sometime in the years 1380 or 1381, hoping to diminish the Church's authority and allow more people to understand the Bible on their own. Wycliffe's unconventional views and his outspokenness led the Church to condemn him as a heretic in 1378. Wycliffe was not punished in England largely because the English monarchy was embroiled in a disagreement with Rome about papal taxes and treasure due the Church. Although Wycliffe continued to write and preach until his death, his followers, known as Lollards, were not so lucky. Once Henry IV was crowned king of England in 1399, a law was passed which called for the burning of heretics, and several of Wycliffe's followers met their deaths in this way.

William Tyndale (1494–1536) believed that the Church should be guided by the Bible alone and that every Christian should be able to read the Bible in his or her own language. Tyndale's translation of the Bible to English was the most beautiful and faithful that had yet appeared, but Tyndale was hounded throughout Europe as he tried to get his translation printed.

(cont.)

Insights

The Art of Translation

We are puppets and the sky is a puppeteer,
From the perspective of reality, not from
the perspective of metaphor . . .
—word-for-word translation of *The Rubáiyát*

We are the playthings and heaven the player,
In a manner that is true in word and deed . . .
—translation of *The Rubáiyát* by Jamal Elias

Impotent pieces of the game he plays
Upon this checkerboard of Nights and Days . . .
—translation of *The Rubáiyát* by Edward FitzGerald

The three excerpts above are different translations of the same lines in *The Rubáiyát*. What do the three excerpts have in common? Why, when the translators were working from the same original poem, do these excerpts have such noticeable language differences?

Translation, or the art of rendering speech or writing into another language, involves more than accurately rewriting each word and phrase of a work in a second language. A translator must transfer meaning from one language to another. This is no simple task, because the words of one language do not always have the same meaning as the words of another language. A translator must understand the subtleties of the language of an original work. The literal, or exact, translation of a particular word in one language might mean or imply something completely different in another language. Because of this problem, a translator must use different words and different sentence structures to capture the spirit, mood, and meaning of an original work. Translators often have different opinions about the true spirit or meaning of an original work, which is why three translations of the same poem can sound so different. Some translators might be more concerned with literal accuracy—translating the poem word-for-word—than others. As a result, the art of translation is controversial.

Rubáiyát of Omar Khayyám. *Edmund Dulac*

Cultural/Historical Note (cont.)

His translation had to be smuggled back into England, and Tyndale himself was imprisoned and executed in 1536. After Henry VIII broke with Rome, Biblical translations were officially approved, and Tyndale's inspired translation became the foundation for the version a group of scholars produced in 1611—the King James Bible, still the best-selling book of all time.

Still Life. *Willem Kalf*

Edward FitzGerald's translation of *The Rubáiyát* has, in fact, inspired a great deal of controversy. Although scholars recognize the poetic beauty of FitzGerald's translation, they argue that he has taken far too many liberties with Omar Khayyám's original work. FitzGerald was more concerned with capturing what he believed was the beauty and spirit of the original piece in a revised English version than with translating the original poem word-for-word. He changed and omitted words and phrases, moved lines, and combined quatrains. A comparison of FitzGerald's translation with more literal translations by others clearly shows the changes in language and structure that he made. In the well-known excerpt below, notice how he chose to combine two quatrains of the original work into one. Why do you think he chose to make these changes?

A Book of Verses underneath the bough,
A jug of Wine, a Loaf of Bread—and Thou
  Beside me singing in the Wilderness—
Oh, Wilderness were Paradise enow!

—translated by Edward FitzGerald

Give me a flagon of red wine, a book of verses, a loaf of bread, and a little idleness. If with such store I might sit by thy dear side in some lonely place, I should deem myself happier than a king in his kingdom.

When the hand possesses a loaf of wheaten bread, two measures of wine, and a piece of flesh, when seated with tulip-cheeks in some lonely spot, behold such joy as is not given to all sultans.

—translated by Justin Huntly McCarthy

I need a jug of wine and a book of poetry,
Half a loaf for a bite to eat,
Then you and I, seated in a deserted spot,
Will have more wealth than a Sultan's realm.

If chance supplied a loaf of white bread,
Two casks of wine and a leg of mutton,
In the corner of a garden with a tulip-cheeked
  girl
There'd be enjoyment no Sultan could outdo.

—translated by Peter Avery and
John Heath-Stubbs

Quotables

"*Traduttori, traditori.*
Translators, traitors."

—Italian proverb

"A translator is to be like his author; it is not his business to excel him."

—Samuel Johnson

"Humour is the first of the gifts to perish in a foreign tongue."

—Virginia Woolf

Additional Questions and Activities

If you have any bilingual students in your classroom, you might encourage them to find and share the original version of a poem or passage in their native or first language and its English translation. Then have them discuss with other students what the work loses in translation.

ADDITIONAL RESOURCES

READER'S GUIDE

- Selection Worksheet 9.11

ASSESSMENT PORTFOLIO

- Selection Check Test 2.9.21
- Selection Test 2.9.22

ESSENTIAL SKILLS PRACTICE BOOKS

- Writing 1.8, 1.20
- Language 2.46–2.53

PREREADING EXTENSIONS

Students can read parables and sermons by Rumi and other Sufis and by writers of different religions. Have them compare the views about the world, the role of human beings, and the abilities or limitations of human beings expressed in stories from various religions. Students may also discuss whether they agree with or follow the ideas presented in the stories they read.

SUPPORT FOR LEP STUDENTS

PRONUNCIATIONS OF PROPER NOUNS AND ADJECTIVES

Az • ra • el (az´rā əl)
Ru • mi (ro͞o´mē)
So • lo • mon (säl´ə mən)

ADDITIONAL VOCABULARY

countenance—face
exile—banished person
wrath—anger

PREREADING

"The Man Who Fled from Azrael"
"The Elephant in the Dark House"
from the *Mathnavi*

PERSIA

by Rumi (Jalāl ad-Dīn ar-Rūmī), translated by Reynold A. Nicholson

About the Author

Rumi (1207–1283). Born in the city of Balkh in what is now northern Afghanistan, Jalāl ad-Dīn ar-Rūmī, commonly called Rumi in the West, is considered by many to be the greatest mystical poet in Persian and Islamic literature. When Rumi was a boy, his father, a theologian and teacher, moved the family out of Balkh to western Anatolia, an area that is now Turkey. This move to the west was most likely the result of Mongol invasions from the East. In 1228, the family settled in Konya, where Rumi's father taught. There, Rumi took up studies in Islamic law and traditions and in Sufism, a variety of Islamic mysticism. After his father died in 1231, Rumi completed his studies and, like his father, became a teacher in the Muslim religious college of Konya. In the last thirty years of Rumi's life, three close spiritual relationships greatly influenced his decision to focus on mystical poetry.

About the Selection

Rumi's works reflect the influence of Sufism, the mystical dimension of Islamic religious belief. Conventional Islamic worship centers on prayer, public worship, fasting, holy pilgrimages, and acts of charity. Sufism, on the other hand, emphasizes deep meditation and withdrawal from the world. Sufism emerged because people were not satisfied with the rituals of traditional Islam and wanted a religion with more emphasis on private inner experience. People who wanted to reform Islam in this way were called Sufis, most likely because of the garments of wool (*Suf* in Arabic) that they wore. The goal of a Sufi is to find divine love and knowledge through direct personal experience with God. Followers of Sufism believe that the world people perceive with their senses is merely an illusion and that this world distracts people from finding true and eternal life. Sufism evolves through three phases: asceticism, or the rejection of worldliness; ecstasy, or desire for union with God; and cognition, or the search for a higher knowledge of the universe than is granted to the average believer.

"The Man Who Fled from Azrael" and **"The Elephant in the Dark House"** are short lesson tales. They are entertaining to read, and they also address certain issues of Sufism. Each story illustrates the limitations of the human world and of human understanding.

CONNECTIONS: Religious Retreat

Most of the world's major religions include teachings that urge followers to retreat from the world to move closer to the meaning of life. In their withdrawal from the world, the Sufis of Islam resemble the monks of the Christian, Hindu, and Buddhist traditions. Vows of poverty and obedience are typical of monastic life.

GOALS/OBJECTIVES

Studying this lesson will enable students to

- enjoy two parables
- recognize Rumi as a notable Persian and Islamic writer
- identify the main tenets of Sufism
- define *irony of situation* and *theme*
- explain examples of irony
- identify a theme
- write a parable
- analyze themes and symbols
- find and correct errors in punctuation

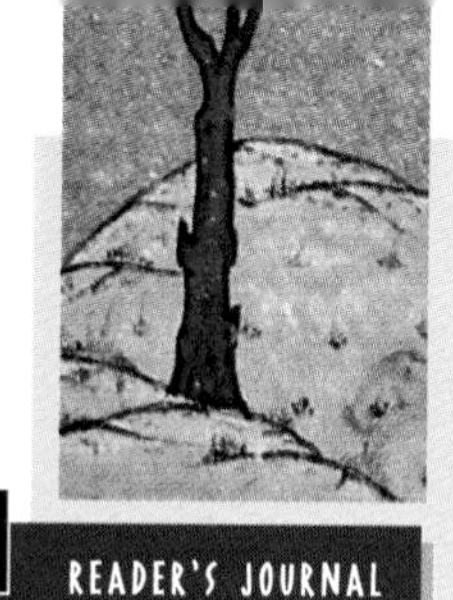

Do you believe there are aspects of the universe that people cannot understand? What do you think are the limits to human knowledge? Why do you think some people try to reach far beyond those limits?

READER'S JOURNAL

"The Man Who Fled from Azrael"

RUMI, TRANSLATED BY R. A. NICHOLSON

One forenoon[1] a freeborn nobleman arrived and ran into Solomon's hall of justice,[2] his countenance pale with anguish and both lips blue. Then Solomon said, "Good sir, what is the matter?"

He replied, "Azrael[3] cast on me such a look, so full of wrath and hate."

"Come," said the king, "what boon[4] do you desire now? Ask!" "O protector of my life," said he, "command the wind to bear me from here to India. Maybe, when thy slave is come thither he will save his life."

Solomon commanded the wind to bear him quickly over the water to the uttermost part of India. Next day, at the time of conference and meeting, Solomon said to Azrael: "Didst thou look with anger on that Moslem in order that he might wander as an exile far from his home?"

Azrael said, "When did I look on him angrily? I saw him as I passed by, and looked at him in astonishment, for God had commanded me, saying, 'Hark, today do thou take his spirit in India.' From wonder I said to myself, 'Even if he has a hundred wings, 'tis a far journey for him to be in India today.'"

➊ *Who runs into Solomon's hall of justice? Why is he upset?*

➋ *What does the nobleman ask of the king? Why does he ask this? Does the king grant him the favor?*

➌ *Why does Azrael look at the man in astonishment rather than with anger?*

1. **forenoon.** Morning
2. **Solomon's hall of justice.** Court of Solomon, a revered leader in both Jewish and Islamic tradition, known for his wisdom
3. **Azrael.** Angel of death in Jewish and Islamic tradition
4. **boon.** Favor

READER'S JOURNAL

Students can discuss the questions about the universe that they do not think humans can answer. Ask students if they think good ever comes from humans trying to reach beyond the limits of their knowledge.

ANSWERS TO GUIDED READING QUESTIONS

➊ A freeborn nobleman runs into Solomon's hall of justice. He is upset because Azrael, the angel of death, casts him a look that is full of wrath and hate.

➋ The nobleman asks the king to command the wind to take him away to India. He hopes to save himself from death. The king does grant him the favor.

➌ Azrael is surprised that the man is able to be in India so quickly.

LITERARY NOTE

The stories by Rumi deal with the limitation of human knowledge. Students can read and discuss the story of the fall of Adam and Eve presented in Genesis. You may also wish to discuss with students the Faust theme. In Western folklore, Faust, or Faustus, sells his soul to the devil to obtain knowledge and power. The story has been widely expressed in literature and in music. Suggest the following works to interested students:

- *The Tragical History of Doctor Faustus,* by Christopher Marlowe
- *Faust,* by Johann Wolfgang von Goethe
- *Doctor Faust,* by Heinrich Heine
- *My Faust,* by Paul Valéry
- *The Damnation of Faust,* by Hector Berlioz

Answers to Guided Reading Questions

1. The elephant is in a dark house. People compare the feel of the elephant to a waterpipe, a fan, a pillar, and a throne.

2. If people had walked into the elephant exhibition with candles, they would have been able to describe the entire elephant, and not just the part they had touched. They must use touch rather than sight and therefore perceive things differently.

Selection Check Test with Answers

EX. To whose hall of justice does the nobleman run?
The nobleman runs to Solomon's hall of justice.

1. Why does the nobleman wish to go to India?
The nobleman wishes to go to India to escape the wrath of Azrael.

2. With what kind of look did Azrael actually look at the nobleman?
Azrael looked at the nobleman with a look of astonishment.

3. What order had God given Azrael?
God had ordered Azrael to take the nobleman's spirit in India.

4. Where was the elephant?
The elephant was in a dark house.

5. What did people have to do, since seeing the elephant with their eyes was impossible?
People had to feel with the the palms of their hands.

"The Elephant in the Dark House"

Rumi, translated by R. A. Nicholson

1 *Where is the elephant? What different things do the people think the elephant is?*

2 *If people walked into the elephant exhibition with candles, in what way would their descriptions of the elephant be different?*

The elephant was in a dark house: some Hindus had brought it for exhibition.

In order to see it, many people were going, every one, into that darkness.

As seeing it with the eye was impossible, each one was feeling it in the dark with the palm of his hand.

The hand of one fell on its trunk: he said, "This creature is like a waterpipe."

The hand of another touched its ear: to him it appeared to be like a fan.

Since another handled its leg, he said, "I found the elephant's shape to be like a pillar."

Another laid his hand on its back: he said, "Truly, this elephant was like a throne."

Similarly, when any one heard a description of the elephant, he understood it only in respect of the part that he had touched. If there had been a candle in each one's hand, the difference would have gone out of their words. ■

The Meeting of the Theologians. *Abd Allah Musawwir, c. 1540–1550. Persian (Bukhara, Uzbek Shaybanid Dynasty). The Nelson-Atkins Museum of Art, Kansas City, MO (Purchase: Nelson Trust)*

Answers for Understanding Literature

Responses will vary. Possible responses are given.

1. **Irony of situation.** Students may say that the story's ending contradicted their expectations by revealing that Azrael was really Solomon's messenger and that Solomon had already commanded Azrael to take the nobleman's life in India. The ending violated the nobleman's expectations because he expected Solomon to protect him from death, not arrange for his death.

Responding to the Selection

Throughout history, people have used stories to teach lessons. Why do you think this is so? In small groups, discuss stories you have been told that taught lessons. Did these stories help you to learn and remember the lessons? Explain why or why not.

Reviewing the Selection

RECALLING		INTERPRETING
1. In "The Man Who Fled from Azrael," for what does the nobleman beg King Solomon? Why?	▶▶	Why would Azrael's angry look frighten the nobleman? What is the nobleman trying to avoid by fleeing?
2. What does King Solomon ask Azrael the next day? What had God ordered Azrael to do? Why did the angel look at the nobleman in astonishment?	▶▶	What, apparently, was inevitable for the nobleman, regardless of where he was? What do you think the writer is trying to say about fate and the power of God over humans?
3. Why is the elephant in a dark house? For what do people mistake the animal?	▶▶	Why can each person understand only a portion of the elephant? What are people unable to understand because of the darkness?
4. Perceptions of the elephant would be different if people were carrying what?	▶▶	What might the darkness represent? What might the elephant represent? What might the candles represent?

SYNTHESIZING

5. In what way do both of these stories address the idea of human limitations? How is the nobleman who sees Azrael limited? How are the people viewing the elephant limited?

Understanding Literature (Questions for Discussion)

1. **Irony of Situation.** In **irony of situation**, an event occurs that violates the expectations of the characters, the reader, or the audience. Explain the irony of situation in "The Man Who Fled from Azrael." In what way did the story's ending contradict your expectations? In what way did it violate the expectations of the characters?

RESPONDING TO THE SELECTION

Students should think about fables, parables, and anecdotes that they have heard or read. You might also use this opportunity to discuss the meaning of *didacticism* with students. Refer them to the Handbook of Literary Terms for a definition.

ANSWERS FOR REVIEWING THE SELECTION

RECALLING AND INTERPRETING

1. **Recalling.** In "The Man Who Fled from Azrael," the nobleman begs King Solomon to command the wind to take him to India. He fears that his life is in danger because he believes the angel of death looked at him with anger. **Interpreting.** Azrael is the angel of death. The nobleman is trying to avoid death.

2. **Recalling.** King Solomon asks Azrael if he did in fact look at the nobleman with anger. God ordered Azrael to take the nobleman's spirit in India. He did not understand how the nobleman could get to India so quickly. **Interpreting.** Death, apparently, was inevitable for the nobleman. The writer is trying to say that people cannot outsmart or hide from God, and if it is God's wish for someone's spirit to be taken, death cannot be avoided.

3. **Recalling.** The elephant is in a dark house for exhibition. People mistake the elephant for a water-pipe, a fan, a pillar, and a throne. **Interpreting.** People do not see the elephant, they only feel parts of it. Because of the darkness, people do not have a complete concept of the elephant.

4. **Recalling.** Perceptions would be different if the people were carrying candles or another source of light. **Interpreting.** The darkness, and the elephant, might represent ignorance, and people

(cont.)

ANSWERS FOR REVIEWING THE SELECTION (CONT.)

searching unsuccessfully for answers in a world that they do not understand. Candles might represent knowledge or divine guidance.

SYNTHESIZING

Responses will vary. Possible responses are given.

5. Humans are limited in that they cannot control their own fates and that they do not always understand the world, particularly the spiritual world. The nobleman is limited by the fact that he is mortal and is unable to outsmart God and live forever. The people in the dark house are limited by being unable to see clearly what is in front of them.

ANSWERS FOR UNDERSTANDING LITERATURE
appear on page 806.

ANALYTIC SCALES FOR RESPONDING IN WRITING

Assign a score from 1 to 25 for each grading criterion below. (For more detailed evaluation, see the evaluation forms for writing, revising, and proofreading, Assessment Portfolio 4.1–4.9.)

1. Parable

- **Content/Unity.** The parable presents a moral in a brief story.
- **Organization/Coherence.** The parable introduces and resolves a conflict. The events of the parable are presented in a logical order.
- **Language/Style.** The parable uses vivid and precise nouns, verbs, and modifiers.
- **Conventions.** The parable avoids errors in spelling, grammar, usage, mechanics, and manuscript form.

▶ Additional practice is provided in the Essential Skills Practice Book: Writing 1.8.

2. Critical Essay

- **Content/Unity.** The essay analyzes the themes and symbols used in the two selections by Rumi.
- **Organization/Coherence.** The essay begins with an introduction that includes a thesis. The introduction is followed by supporting paragraphs that include evidence from the selections. Paragraphs are linked by clear transitions. The essay ends with a solid conclusion.
- **Language/Style.** The essay uses vivid and precise nouns, verbs, and modifiers.
- **Conventions.** The essay avoids errors in spelling, grammar, usage, mechanics, and manuscript form.

▶ Additional practice is provided in the Essential Skills Practice Book: Writing 1.20.

2. **Theme.** A **theme** is a central idea in a literary work. Discuss the themes of the two stories that you just read. In what way do both stories deal with the state of humankind and with human limitations? In what way do these stories illustrate some of the ideas of Sufism discussed on the Prereading page?

Responding in Writing

1. **Creative Writing: Parable.** Parables are very brief stories told to teach moral lessons. The stories you just read by Rumi can be considered parables because they are brief and simple and illustrate moral lessons about the human experience. Try to write your own brief parable. Before you begin, decide what moral lesson you would like to teach your reader. Then freewrite to gather simple story ideas that might illustrate your point. Choose one of these ideas on which to base your parable.

2. **Critical Essay: Theme and Symbol.** Write a short essay in which you discuss the theme of each story by Rumi. Include in your discussion the ways Rumi uses symbols—things that stand for or represent both themselves and something else—to create theme. In what way do symbols such as the nobleman, Azrael, darkness, and the elephant help to illustrate the story's themes? What do each of these stories say about the human experience and human understanding of the universe?

Language Lab

Editing for Errors in Punctuation. Review the Language Arts Survey 2.46–2.53, "Proofreading for Punctuation Errors." Then read the following sentences about a poem by Rumi called "The Soul of Goodness in Things Evil." On your own paper, rewrite the sentences, adding the correct punctuation where it is needed.

EX. Have you heard of the poet Rumi
Have you heard of the poet Rumi?

1. His most famous work is the epic Mathnavi
2. He wrote the poem The Soul of Goodness in Things Evil
3. In the poem Rumi says Fools take false coins because they are like the true
4. My teacher asked if I noticed the poems images of good and evil
5. Yes they were obvious I said
6. He said that if poison and sugar are mixed people will gobble up the poison
7. Rumi exclaims Oh cry not that all creeds are in vain
8. He promises that if people look hard enough they will find truth
9. Do you believe his moral if you seek the truth you will find it is true
10. Well what is truth

ANSWERS FOR LANGUAGE LAB

1. His most famous work is the epic *Mathnavi.*
2. He wrote the poem "The Soul of Goodness in Things Evil."
3. In the poem Rumi says, "Fools take false coins because they are like the true."
4. My teacher asked if I noticed the poem's images of good and evil.
5. "Yes, they were obvious," I said.
6. He said that if poison and sugar are mixed, people will gobble up the poison.
7. Rumi exclaims, "Oh, cry not that all creeds are in vain!"
8. He promises that if people look hard enough, they will find truth.
9. Do you believe his moral, "If you seek the truth, you will find it is true"?
10. Well, what is truth?

SELECTIONS FOR ADDITIONAL READING

FRANCE

from *The Song of Roland*
Anonymous, translated by Frederick Goldin

[Editor's note: The Song of Roland was composed about actual historical events. Charlemagne, Charles of the Franks (in what is now France), was returning from battle in Spain. In the year 778, a portion of his army was conquered by the Basques in the Battle of Roncesvalles, which was fought in a pass in the Pyrenees Mountains between France and Spain. One of the Frenchmen who died in the battle was a nobleman named Lord Roland. Centuries later, around the year 1100, an anonymous poet composed this epic poem about the battle. The poet, however, has elevated the relatively insignificant battle of Roncesvalles to an epic battle between Christians and Muslims, also called Moors, pagans, or Saracens by the medieval Christians. This song about Roland's role in the battle and his tragic death inspired many writers of romance. In this selection, Roland's brigade has been separated from Charlemagne. Roland and his friend Oliver debate whether to sound the call for help.]

104

The battle is fearful and wonderful
and everywhere. Roland never spares himself,
strikes with his lance[1] as long as the wood lasts:
the fifteenth blow he struck, it broke, was lost.
Then he draws Durendal, his good sword, bare,
and spurs his horse, comes on to strike Chernuble,
smashes his helmet, carbuncles[2] shed their light,
cuts through the coif,[3] through the hair on his head,
cut through his eyes, through his face, through that look,
the bright, shining hauberk[4] with its fine rings,
down through the trunk to the fork of his legs,
through the saddle, adorned with beaten gold,
into the horse; and the sword came to rest:
cut through the spine, never felt for the joint;
knocks him down, dead, on the rich grass of the meadow;
then said to him: "You were doomed when you started,
Clown! Nobody! Let Mahum help you now.
No pagan swine will win this field today."

105

Roland the Count comes riding through the field,
holds Durendal, that sword! it carves its way!
and brings terrible slaughter down on the pagans.
To have seen him cast one man dead on another,
the bright red blood pouring out on the ground,
his hauberk, his two arms, running with blood,
his good horse—neck and shoulders running with blood!
And Oliver does not linger, he strikes!
and the Twelve Peers, no man could reproach them;
and the brave French, they fight with lance and sword.
The pagans die, some simply faint away!
Said the Archbishop: "Bless our band of brave men!"
Munjoie! he shouts—the war cry of King Charles.
AOI.[5]

110

The battle is fearful and full of grief.
Oliver and Roland strike like good men,
the Archbishop, more than a thousand blows,
and the Twelve Peers do not hang back, they strike!
the French fight side by side, all as one man.
The pagans die by hundreds, by thousands:
whoever does not flee finds no refuge from death,
like it or not, there he ends all his days.
And there the men of France lose their greatest arms;
they will not see their fathers, their kin again,
or Charlemagne, who looks for them in the passes.
Tremendous torment now comes forth in France,
a mighty whirlwind, tempests of wind and thunder,
rains and hailstones, great and immeasurable,
bolts of lightning hurtling and hurtling down:

1. **lance.** Weapon consisting of a long wooden shaft with a sharp metal spearhead
2. **carbuncles.** Deep red gems
3. **coif.** Skull cap used underneath the helmet of a suit of armor
4. **hauberk.** Medieval coat of armor
5. **AOI.** These letters appear mysteriously at certain points in the text; scholars still debate their significance

The Song of Roland

ABOUT THE SELECTION

The Song of Roland is one of the greatest medieval epics. The poem begins as Charlemagne, who had conquered all of Spain except the city of Saragossa, sends his knight Ganelon to negotiate peace with the Saracen king. Ganelon, Roland's stepfather, is upset with Roland for suggesting him for the difficult and dangerous position. In his anger, Ganelon creates a plan with the Saracens to destroy Roland. Ganelon makes sure that Roland leads the rear guard of the army, which is cut off by a powerful Saracen force in the Roncesvalles pass in the Pyrenees Mountains. When this selection begins, Roland and his force have been separated from Charlemagne's army.

The poem raises Roland to legendary status. His honor and refusal to yield to greater forces are celebrated. This epic presents the personality conflict between the headstrong and courageous Roland and his more level-headed friend, Oliver. Courage, betrayal, and revenge are also themes in the work.

HISTORICAL NOTE

While *The Song of Roland* was based on actual events, the poem differs in some ways from historical records. In the actual battle, the rear guard was led by Eggihard, the count palatine Anselm, and Roland, prefect of the March of Brittany. Legend claims that the attackers were the Moors, but history shows that they were in fact the Basques. Poetic license serves to increase drama and to engage the reader or listener. Changing the Basques to the Moors probably achieved the latter, because at the time, the French were fighting in the Crusades to regain the Holy Lands from the Muslims.

Literary Note

The Song of Roland is an epic, but it is also a *chanson de geste,* or "song of deeds." The term applies to any of several Old French epics that deal with the legend of Charlemagne. The manuscripts for these works generally date from the twelfth to the fifteenth centuries, while the events that they describe occurred mainly in the eighth and ninth centuries.

The *chansons de geste* focus on the struggle between the Christians, under Charlemagne and the Muslims. In many of the chansons, the main players include not only Charlemagne but also his court of Twelve Noble Peers, which includes Roland, Oliver, Ogier the Dane, and Archbishop Turpin.

Scholars generally consider *The Song of Roland* to be the finest example of *chanson de geste,* and it influenced heroic literature throughout Europe. Some of the works that reveal such influence are the Spanish epic *The Song of the Cid* and Italian epics such as Matteo Boiardo's *Orlando Innamorato* and Ludovico Ariosto's *Orlando Furioso* (see page 830).

Cross-curricular Activities

Arts and Humanities and Social Studies

- Have students find a historical map of Europe in the eighth or ninth century. Have them locate the area that Charlemagne won in Spain and the area that he did not control. Have them find the Pyrenees and, if possible, Roncesvalles.
- Have students research the Crusades. Students can research who undertook the Crusades, their routes, and the outcomes and influence of the Crusades. Have students create maps of Crusade routes or illustrated texts showing scenes from one or more Crusades.

it is, in truth, a trembling of the earth.
From Saint Michael-in-Peril to the Saints,
from Besançon to the port of Wissant,
there is no house whose veil of walls does not crumble.
A great darkness at noon falls on the land,
there is no light but when the heavens crack.
No man sees this who is not terrified,
and many say: "The Last Day! Judgment Day!
The end! The end of the world is upon us!"
They do not know, they do not speak the truth:
it is the worldwide grief for the death of Roland.

128

Count Roland sees the great loss of his men,
calls on his companion, on Oliver:
"Lord, Companion, in God's name, what would you do?
All these good men you see stretched on the ground.
We can mourn for sweet France, fair land of France!
a desert now, stripped of such great vassals.
Oh King, and friend, if only you were here!
Oliver, Brother, how shall we manage it?
What shall we do to get word to the King?"
Said Oliver: "I don't see any way.
I would rather die now than hear us shamed." AOI.

129

And Roland said: "I'll sound the olifant,[1]
Charles will hear it, drawing through the passes,
I promise you, the Franks will return at once."
Said Oliver: "That would be a great disgrace,
a dishonor and reproach to all your kin,
the shame of it would last them all their lives.
When I urged it, you would not hear of it;
you will not do it now with my consent.
It is not acting bravely to sound it now—
look at your arms, they are covered with blood."
The Count replies: " I've fought here like a lord." AOI.

132

Turpin the Archbishop hears their bitter words,
digs hard into his horse with golden spurs
and rides to them; begins to set them right:
"You, Lord Roland, and you, Lord Oliver,
I beg you in God's name do not quarrel.
To sound the horn could not help us now, true,
but still it is far better that you do it:
let the King come, he can avenge us then—
these men of Spain must not go home exulting!
Our French will come, they'll get down on their feet,
and find us here—we'll be dead, cut to pieces.
They will lift us into coffins on the backs of mules,
and weep for us, in rage and pain and grief,
and bury us in the courts of churches;
and we will not be eaten by wolves or pigs or dogs."
Roland replies, "Lord, you have spoken well." AOI.

133

Roland has put the olifant to his mouth,
he sets it well, sounds it with all his strength.
The hills are high, and that voice ranges far,
they heard it echo thirty great leagues away.
King Charles heard it, and all his faithful men.
And the King says: "Our men are in a battle."
And Ganelon disputed him and said:
"Had someone else said that, I'd call him liar!" AOI.

134

And now the mighty effort of Roland the Count:
he sounds his olifant; his pain is great,
and from his mouth the bright blood comes leaping out,
and the temple bursts in his forehead.
That horn, in Roland's hands, has a mighty voice:
King Charles hears it drawing through the passes.
Naimon[2] heard it, the Franks listen to it.
And the King said: "I hear Count Roland's horn;
he'd never sound it unless he had a battle."
Says Ganelon: "Now no more talk of battles!
You are old now, your hair is white as snow,
the things you say make you sound like a child.
You know Roland and that wild pride of his—
what a wonder God has suffered it so long!
Remember? he took Noples without your command:
the Saracens rode out, to break the siege;
they fought with him, the great vassal Roland.
Afterwards he used the streams to wash the blood
from the meadows: so that nothing would show.
He blasts his horn all day to catch a rabbit,
he's strutting now before his peers and bragging—
who under heaven would dare meet him on the field?
So now: ride on! Why do you keep on stopping?
The Land of Fathers lies far ahead of us." AOI.

1. **olifant.** Horn
2. **Naimon.** Duke who had convinced the king to send Roland to the rear guard of the army.

152

Before Roland could recover his senses
and come out of his faint, and be aware,
a great disaster had come forth before him:
the French are dead, he has lost every man
except the Archbishop, and Gautier de l'Hum,
who has come back, down from that high mountain:
he has fought well, he fought those men of Spain.
His men are dead, the pagans finished them;
flees now down to these valleys, he has no choice,
and calls on Count Roland to come to his aid:
"My noble Count, my brave lord, where are you?
I never feared whenever you were there.
It is Walter: I conquered Maëlgut,
my uncle is Droün, old and gray: your Walter
and always dear to you for the way I fought;
and I have fought this time: my lance is shattered,
my good shield pierced, my hauberk's meshes broken;
and I am wounded, a lance struck through my body.
I will die soon, but I sold myself dear."
And with that word, Count Roland has heard him,
he spurs his horse, rides spurring to his man. AOI.

153

Roland in pain, maddened with grief and rage:
rushes where they are thickest and strikes again,
strikes twenty men of Spain, strikes twenty dead,
and Walter six, and the Archbishop five.
The pagans say: "Look at those criminals!
Now take care, Lords, they don't get out alive,
only a traitor will not attack them now!
Only a coward will let them save their skins!"
And then they raise their hue and cry[1] once more,
rush in on them, once more, from every side. AOI.

156

Roland the Count fights well and with great skill,
but he is hot, his body soaked with sweat;
has a great wound in his head, and much pain,
his temple broken because he blew the horn.
But he must know whether King Charles will come;
draws out the olifant, sounds it, so feebly.
The Emperor drew to a halt, listened.
"Seigneurs," he said, "it goes badly for us—
My nephew Roland falls from our ranks today.
I hear it in the horn's voice: he hasn't long.
Let every man who wants to be with Roland
ride fast! Sound trumpets! Every trumpet in this host!"
Sixty thousand, on these words, sound, so high
the mountains sound, and the valleys resound.
The pagans hear: it is no joke to them;
cry to each other: "We're getting Charles on us!"

157

The pagans say: "The Emperor is coming, AOI.
listen to their trumpets—it is the French!
If Charles comes back, it's all over for us,
if Roland lives, this war begins again
and we have lost our land, we have lost Spain."
Some four hundred, helmets laced on, assemble,
some of the best, as they think, on that field.
They storm Roland, in one fierce, bitter attack.
And now Count Roland has some work on his hands. AOI.

158

Roland the Count, when he sees them coming,
how strong and fierce and alert he becomes!
He will not yield to them, not while he lives.
He rides the horse they call Veillantif, spurs,
digs into it with his spurs of fine gold,
and rushes at them all where they are thickest,
the Archbishop—that Turpin!—at his side.
Said one man to the other: "Go at it, friend.
The horns we heard were the horns of the French,
King Charles is coming back with all his strength."

168

Now Roland feels that death is very near.
His brain comes spilling out through his two ears;
prays to God for his peers: let them be called;
and for himself, to the angel Gabriel;
took the olifant: there must be no reproach!
took Durendal his sword in his other hand,
and farther than a crossbow's farthest shot
he walks toward Spain, into a fallow land,
and climbs a hill: there beneath two fine trees
stand four great blocks of stone, all are of marble;
and he fell back, to earth, on the green grass,
has fainted there, for death is very near.

169

High are the hills, and high, high are the trees;
there stand four blocks of stone, gleaming of marble.
Count Roland falls fainting on the green grass,
and is watched, all this time, by a Saracen:

1. **hue and cry.** Any loud outcry or clamor

INTEGRATED SKILLS ACTIVITIES

SPEAKING AND LISTENING SKILLS

The Song of Roland was probably composed and passed on orally before it was put into written form. During the Medieval Period, *chansons de geste* were recited or sung to audiences. Ask students to prepare an oral interpretation of part of *The Song of Roland.* The selection contains a great deal of drama that students should present through changes in pace, volume, tone, facial expressions, and gestures. Refer students to the Language Arts Survey 3.5, "Oral Interpretation" for more information about this type of presentation.

► Additional practice is provided in the Essential Skills Practice Book: Speaking and Listening 3.5.

LITERARY TECHNIQUE

HERO

A **hero** is a character whose actions are inspiring and courageous. An **epic hero** represents the ideals of the culture that creates it. What heroic qualities does Roland possess? What ideals does he represent?

ANSWERS

Roland is courageous and determined. He does not spare himself. Roland represents the ideal warrior and the ideal of chivalric loyalty.

"I Sing of a Maiden"

About the Selection

"**I Sing of a Maiden**" (c. 1400) is both a religious poem that celebrates the Virgin Mary and a secular lyric that celebrates the coming of spring. In France, the veneration of Mary developed into the code of courtly love. This code was also influenced by poetry brought from Persia to France. "I Sing of a Maiden" extols Mary's virtues and creates a symbolic comparison between the return of spring and the Virgin Birth.

For another example of a verse with secular and religious significance, refer students to Bieris de Romans's "Lady Maria, your worth and excellence" on page 742. They may wish to compare and contrast the way in which secular and religious themes are combined in the two lyrics.

Literary Note

If necessary, explain to your students that in many Christian belief systems, and in Catholicism in particular, the Virgin Mary is believed to have conceived the infant Jesus by divine intervention. In Catholicism, Mary plays the role of one who intercedes with God on behalf of the prayerful. Traditionally, Mary is the embodiment of gentleness and grace.

Additional Questions and Activities

1. Who is the maiden of the poem? In what way do the two meanings of the word *matchless* apply to her?
2. Who is the maiden's son? To what is his coming compared?
3. To what springtime occurrence does the speaker compare the Virgin Birth? In what way might the two things be similar?

(cont.)

who has feigned death and lies now with the others,
has smeared blood on his face and on his body;
and quickly now gets to his feet and runs—
a handsome man, strong, brave, and so crazed with
pride
that he does something mad and dies for it:
laid hands on Roland, and on the arms of Roland,
and cried: "Conquered! Charles's nephew
conquered!
I'll carry this sword home to Arabia!"
As he draws it, the Count begins to come round.

170

Now Roland feels: *someone taking his sword!*
opened his eyes, and had one word for him:
"I don't know you, you aren't one of ours";
grasps that olifant that he will never lose,
strikes on the helm beset with gems in gold,
shatters the steel, and the head, and the bones,
sent his two eyes flying out of his head,
dumped him over stretched out at his feet dead;
and said: "You nobody! how could you dare
lay hands on me—rightly or wrongly: how?
Who'll hear of this and not call you a fool?
Ah! the bell-mouth of the olifant is smashed,
the crystal and the gold fallen away."

174

Now Roland feels: death coming over him,
death descending from his temples to his heart.
He came running underneath a pine tree
and there stretched out, face down, on the green
grass,
lays beneath him his sword and the olifant.
He turned his head toward the Saracen hosts,
and this is why: with all his heart he wants
King Charles the Great and all his men to say,
he died, that noble Count, a conqueror;
makes confession, beats his breast often, so feebly,
offers his glove, for all his sins, to God. AOI.

175

Now Roland feels that his time has run out;
he lies on a steep hill, his face toward Spain;
and with one of his hands he beat his breast:
"Almighty God, *mea culpa*[1] in thy sight,
forgive my sins, both the great and the small,
sins I committed from the hour I was born
until this day, in which I lie struck down."
And then he held his right glove out to God.
Angels descend from heaven and stand by him. AOI.

176

Count Roland lay stretched out beneath a pine;
he turned his face toward the land of Spain,
began to remember many things now:
how many lands, brave man, he had conquered;
and he remembered: sweet France, the men of his
line,
remembered Charles, his lord, who fostered him:
cannot keep, remembering, from weeping, sighing;
but would not be unmindful of himself:
he confesses his sins, prays God for mercy:
"Loyal Father, you who never failed us,
who resurrected Saint Lazarus from the dead,
and saved your servant Daniel from the lions:
now save the soul of me from every peril
for the sins I committed while I still lived."
Then he held out his right glove to the Lord:
Saint Gabriel took the glove from his hand.
He held his head bowed down upon his arm,
he is gone, his two hands joined, to his end.
The God sent him his angel Cherubin
and Saint Michael, angel of the sea's Peril;
and with these two there came Saint Gabriel:
they bear Count Roland's soul to Paradise. ■

"I Sing of a Maiden"

Anonymous,
translated by Robin Lamb

I sing of a maiden
That is matchless:[1]
King of all kings
As her son she chose.

He came as still
Where his mother was
As dew in April
That falls in the grass.

He came as still
To his mother's bower
As dew in April
That falls on the flower.

1. ***mea culpa.*** My guilt
2. **matchless.** The word is a pun meaning both "unequal" and "without a mate, or match."

Additional Questions and Activities (cont.)

Answers

Responses will vary.

1. The maiden is the Virgin Mary. She is matchless in the sense that she is unequaled by other women and in the sense that she conceived without a mate, or match.
2. The maiden's son is Jesus, the "King of all kings." His coming is compared to the coming of spring.
3. The speaker compares the Virgin Birth to the falling dew. Both occurrences symbolize renewal.

He came as still
Where his mother lay
As dew in April
That falls on the spray.

Mother and maiden
Was never none but she:
Well may such a lady
God's mother be. ■

ITALY

from *The Chronicle of Contemporary Events*

by Dino Compagni, translated by Tatiana Cicuto

Damage and ancient origin of the civil strife in Florence between Guelfs and Ghibellines.[1]

Its citizens[2] must cry, then, over themselves and their children. With their arrogance and malice and ambition they have destroyed a noble city, disgraced its laws, and forfeited the same honor its fathers[3] had acquired over a long time; and they must now wait for Divine Justice to strike them. . . .

After having suffered for many years because of its citizens, the city of Florence was the theater[4] of yet another disagreement. So deeply was this event felt that it caused the citizens of this noble city to splinter into two enemy factions, the Guelfs and the Ghibellines. This was all the doing of a young noble citizen, Buondalmonte de' Buondalmonti, who had promised to take the daughter of Oderigo Giantruffetti for his wife. But one day, while walking by the house of the Donatis, Buondalmonte was noticed by Madonna Aldruda, a noblewoman and the wife of master Forteguerra Donati, who had two very beautiful daughters. Madonna Aldruda, leaning over the balcony of her palace, addressed the young man. The gentlewoman had one of her daughters by her side. She showed her to him and said: "Who have you chosen for a wife? I was saving my daughter for you." He looked at the girl, liked her very much, and replied: "It is too late now. I can't have her anymore." To this Madonna Aldruda declared: "Yes, you can. I will compensate master Oderigo for the damages caused by the breaking of your engagement to his daughter." Buondalmonte, clearly relieved, proclaimed: "And so I want her." And he took her for his wife, leaving behind the one he had first promised to marry. But master Oderigo, stricken with grief and complaining to relatives and friends, decided to avenge his family's honor by hurting and disgracing Buondalmonte. When the noble and powerful family, the Ubertis, received news of these highly shameful circumstances, they decreed that the young man had to die. . . . Orders were given to have him killed the day of his wedding. And so the deed was done, and the citizens of Florence angrily took sides. . . . From it[5] many scandals and murders and civil battles followed.

1. **Guelfs and the Ghibellines.** Opposing political groups in medieval Florence. The Guelfs followed the pope, while the Ghibellines followed the emperor. Compagni was a Guelph, and he personally participated in a great number of the events he described in his work.
2. **citizens.** The citizens of Florence
3. **fathers.** Founding fathers
4. **theater.** Scene
5. **it.** Refers to the death of Buondalmonte and the resulting strife

The Chronicle of Contemporary Events

ABOUT THE AUTHOR

Dino Compagni (c. 1255–1324) lived and worked in Florence and chronicled its history. A member of a wealthy merchant family, Compagni served in the silk guild, in civil administration, and as an official of justice.

ABOUT THE SELECTION

Compagni began writing ***The Chronicle of Contemporary Events*** in 1310. This work, which scholars accept as an accurate history of the period, portrays the events, people, and motivations that shaped the period of conflict between the Guelfs and the Ghibellines and between the Black Guelfs and the White Guelfs in Florence. It was first published in 1726.

Historical Note

In Italy during the Middle Ages, the Guelfs and the Ghibellines were warring factions. The Guelfs supported the papacy, while the Ghibellines supported the Holy Roman emperors. The name *Guelf* comes from the German *Welf,* a family trying to gain control of Italy. The Ghibellines took their name from *Waibligen,* a castle of the Welf's opponents.

During the reign of Frederick I, known as Barbarossa, Italian cities were divided into two camps. As one faction drove out the other, cities began to be associated with either the Guelfs or the Ghibellines. The animosity and fighting between the two groups extended throughout the thirteenth century, and rivalry between city-states increased. The importance of both parties declined in the fourteenth century as the involvement of the emperor diminished and the pope moved from Rome to France. The terms *Guelf* and *Ghibelline* continued to be used to describe local factions.

ADDITIONAL RESOURCES

Assessment Portfolio

- Vocabulary Worksheet 2.9.23
- Study Guide 2.9.24
- Unit Test 2.9.25

Essential Skills Practice Books

WRITING

- Choosing a Purpose: Creative Writing, 1.8
- Writing a Critical Essay, 1.20

LANGUAGE

- Apostrophes, 2.50
- Combining Sentences Using Words and Phrases, 2.21
- Correcting Errors in the Use of Irregular Verbs, 2.31
- Correcting Errors in Verb Agreement I, 2.34
- Correcting Errors in Verb Agreement II, 2.35
- Correcting Errors in Voice and Mood, 2.33
- Correcting Shifts in Verb Tense, 2.30
- Correcting Split Infinitives, 2.32
- Dashes, Hyphens, Parentheses, and Brackets, 2.49
- Ellipses and Quotation of Sources, 2.53
- Other Uses of Quotation Marks, 2.52
- Reducing Wordiness, 2.26
- Semicolons and Colons, 2.48
- Underlining, Italics, and Quotation Marks in Titles, 2.51
- Using Commas, 2.47
- Using End Marks, 2.46

SPEAKING AND LISTENING

- Oral Interpretation, 3.5
- Public Speaking, 3.4

STUDY AND RESEARCH

- Making and Testing Hypotheses, 4.4
- Problem Solving and Decision Making, 4.1
- Using Search Tools, 4.12

UNIT REVIEW

Medieval Literature

VOCABULARY FROM THE SELECTIONS

abhor, 780
abiding, 735
absolve, 760
adjure, 786
admonishment, 725
allurement, 754
amiable, 743
arduous, 749
asunder, 779
assail, 738
attrition, 750
august, 772
aureate, 797
avarice, 750
burgeon, 739
chide, 780
cleft, 723
commemoration, 750
console, 735
covertly, 739
discourse, 753
don, 727
eloquence, 753
enmity, 734
enticement, 754
entreaty, 787
frivolous, 771
gaunt, 750
guile, 735
incur, 779
infatuation, 766
jubilation, 735
lamentation, 751
limpid, 737
mien, 743
munificence, 789
ordain, 725
pang, 735
perfidious, 787
perfidy, 791
perturb, 789
piteous, 749
presumptuous, 766
prodigious, 786
rank, 749
rapaciously, 739
rashly, 791
ratify, 734
ravening, 750
regale, 788
rend, 779
repentance, 755
requite, 791
salutation, 728
sans, 799
sovereign, 779
stipulate, 734
succor, 743
sumptuously, 788
temper, 725
tremulous, 750
truant, 743
uncouth, 726
variance, 737
vassal, 734
venerable, 787
vial, 734

Vocabulary Check Test

Ask students to number their papers from one to ten. Have students complete each sentence with a word from the Vocabulary from the Selections in the Unit Review.

1. The spy operated covertly abroad, and her activities went undetected for decades.
2. In return for his land, the vassal promised to honor and protect his lord.
3. Hester's infatuation with the theater was brief; she soon decided she did not want to become an actress.
4. Carlos was an excellent host who regaled his guests with delicious feasts.
5. Rachel was too kindhearted to chide the disobedient child.
6. Maya rashly decided to attempt the dangerous climb in midwinter.

(cont.)

LITERARY TERMS

allegory, 747
anecdote, 770
apostrophe, 763
atmosphere, 800
canto, 747
catalog, 745
chivalry, 720, 731, 740
courtly love, 721, 740, 746
description, 731
epigram, 796
epitaph, 759
exposition, 769
frame tale, 784, 793, 795
image, 783
imagery, 763
introduction, 769
irony of situation, 807
journal, 776
medieval romance, 732
metaphor, 740
mood, 800
motif, 757
point of view, 763
psychological fiction, 765
Realism, 763
refrain, 763
repetition, 782
simile, 758, 800
symbol, 730
theme, 793, 800, 808
tone, 768, 776, 783

SYNTHESIS: QUESTIONS FOR WRITING, RESEARCH, OR DISCUSSION

GENRE STUDIES

1. In what ways are the selections you have encountered from Medieval Europe, feudal Japan, and Arabia and Persia similar? What "medieval" qualities does this literature share?

2. Define medieval romance. Which selections from this unit are romances? What aspects of romance does each demonstrate? In what way does a medieval romance differ from the contemporary idea of a romance?

THEMATIC STUDIES

3. Moral teachings and codes of behavior were very important during the Medieval Period. Discuss the codes described in the selections in this unit. What morals do other selections teach? Are the morals and codes of different cultures similar or different? Explain.

4. Because life was so uncertain, death emerged as a prominent theme in many medieval works. Which selections from this unit discuss death? What views on death are presented? In what way do contemporary views on life and death differ from medieval views? (You may wish to refer to selections from Unit 4 as well.)

5. Based on the selections from *The Divine Comedy, The Story of the Grail, Tristan,* and *The Song of Roland,* create a description of the ideals expected of a knight both in terms of a code of chivalry and of courtly love. Are chivalry and courtly love ever at odds? Explain.

6. In what way were religious devotion and romantic love often combined in medieval writings? In which selections do these two types of love entwine?

HISTORICAL/BIOGRAPHICAL STUDIES

7. What were the Crusades? In what way did the Crusades affect medieval European literature? How did the literary scholarship of Arabia and Persia affect European scholars?

8. Compare and contrast the courts of medieval Europe to those of Japan. In what way were the lifestyles and attitudes of the aristocracy similar? What attitudes are expressed toward the lower classes by the aristocracy in both cultures?

SPELLING CHECK TEST

Ask students to number their papers from one to ten. Read each word aloud. Then read aloud the sentence containing the word. Repeat the word. Ask students to write the word on their papers, spelling it correctly.

1. **uncouth**
Knights usually scorned members of the peasantry, considering their behavior to be uncouth.

2. **salutation**
The king's cheerful salutation made the knight immediately feel welcome in the hall.

3. **enmity**
Freed of enmity, the opposing sides formed a partnership.

4. **guile**
I would rather work with a straightforward, honest person than one who uses guile to trick me.

5. **burgeons**
It seems that not only flowers but also love burgeons in the spring.

6. **succor**
The good Samaritan stopped to offer succor to the motorist with a flat tire.

7. **frivolous**
Our tour guide warned us that the temple was considered a solemn place, so no frivolous behavior would be tolerated.

8. **sovereign**
All decisions in the kingdom are made by the sovereign.

9. **asunder**
Manny's jacket was torn asunder when his friends played tug-of-war with it.

10. **abhor**
Although Yevgene loves summer vacation, she abhors the heat and humidity of summer.

VOCABULARY CHECK TEST (CONT.)

7. The traitor's perfidy during the war induced even his closest friends to despise him as a treacherous villain.

8. Petina's haughty mien belies her insecure nature.

9. Rhoda wrote a contract to stipulate the terms of the agreement.

10. Gregory's sudden munificence astounded everyone because we had always considered him to be stingy.

UNIT SKILLS OUTLINE

Literary Skills and Concepts

- Allusion, 887
- Character, 859
- Characterization, 881
- Convention, 832
- Couplet, 882
- Courtly Love, 829, 858
- Dramatic Irony, 828, 883
- Enlightenment, 820
- Essay, 860, 866
- Fable, 867, 870
- Frame Tale, 822
- Hyperbole, 832
- Irony, 828, 890
- Irony of Situation, 837
- Medieval Romance, 858
- Meter, 849
- Mock Epic, 852
- Motivation, 825
- Parable, 867
- Parody, 852, 859
- Personification, 870
- Rhyme, 845
- Rhyme Scheme, 845
- Satire, 859, 890
- Simile, 832, 845
- Sonnet, 847, 849
- Stanza, 845
- Symbol, 839
- Tone, 849
- Verbal Irony, 890

Writing Skills and Concepts

- Continuation, 829
- Couplet, 850
- Critical Essay, 829, 846, 850, 859, 866, 871, 882, 891
- Description, 891
- Diatribe, 882
- Fable, 871
- *Ottava Rima,* 846
- Parody, 859
- Personal Essay, 866

Grammar, Usage, and Mechanics Skills and Concepts

- Clichés, 850
- Errors in Modifier Usage, 891
- Other Uses of Quotation Marks, 824, 876
- Personal Pronouns, 846
- Reflexive, Intensive, and Demonstrative Pronouns, 846

Other Language Arts Skills and Concepts

- Active Listening and Interpersonal Communication, 824
- Elements of Verbal and Nonverbal Communication, 875
- Oral Interpretation, 871
- Personal and Business Letters, 829
- Using Dictionaries, 866
- Using Search Tools and Card Catalogs, 859
- Writing Promotional and Public Relations Copy, 882

Unit 10 The Renaissance and the Enlightenment

Mona Lisa. *Leonardo da Vinci, circa 1503–1505*

GOALS/OBJECTIVES

Studying this unit will enable students to

- interpret and appreciate Renaissance and Enlightenment literature
- briefly explain the major characteristics of Renaissance and Enlightenment literature
- briefly explain Petrarch's influence on literature and the ways in which some poets reacted to Petrarchan ideals and conventions
- identify honesty and deception as a major theme in world literature
- write both critically and creatively in response to and in analysis of literature of these periods
- write promotional and public relations copy

"I think, therefore I am."

—René Descartes

817

CROSS-CURRICULAR CONNECTIONS

ARTS AND HUMANITIES
- Censorship, 872
- Contemporary and Modern Views of Labé, 847
- Gustave Doré's Illustrations, 854
- *Man of La Mancha*, 854
- Quixotic Activities, 852
- Researching Neoclassical Artists, 820
- Researching Renaissance Artists, 819

MATHEMATICS AND SCIENCES
- The Psychology of Healing, 825
- Researching the Black Death, 822
- Science during the Renaissance and Enlightenment, 820

SOCIAL STUDIES
- Alexander the Great and Cid Ruy Diaz, 855
- Ariosto and Artillery, 834
- Aristotle, 819
- Biographical Notes on Echoes Authors, 821
- Censorship, 872
- Christian and Islamic Conflict during the Middle Ages, 840
- Corneille and Racine, 877
- Fables as Social Critique, 867
- Gutenberg and the Printing Press, 819
- Joan of Arc, 830
- Mapping Skills, 838
- Nationalism and European Exploration, 818
- Regions of Italy, 823
- Researching the Black Death, 822
- Researching and Debating the Age of Exploration, 860
- Researching Non-European Cultures, 820
- The Seven Years' War, 888
- Women's Education, 831, 886

APPLIED ARTS
- Designing a Typesetting Model, 819

TEACHING THE MULTIPLE INTELLIGENCES

MUSICAL
- *Man of La Mancha*, 854

LOGICAL-MATHEMATICAL
- Censorship, 872
- Christian and Islamic Conflict during the Middle Ages, 840
- Debate, 884
- Researching and Debating the Age of Exploration, 860

(cont.)

TEACHING THE MULTIPLE INTELLIGENCES (CONT.)

SPATIAL
- Designing a Typesetting model, 819
- Gustave Doré's Illustrations, 854
- Mapping Skills, 838
- Nationalism and European Exploration, 818
- Researching Neoclassical Artists, 820
- Researching Renaissance Artists, 819

KINESTHETIC
- Elements of Verbal and Nonverbal Communication, 875
- Oral Interpretation, 871
- Peer Pressure Role Play, 878
- Role Playing Don Quixote's Neighbors, 858

INTERPERSONAL
- Active Listening and Interpersonal Communication, 824

(cont.)

Other Selections Exploring This Period

Empress Nur Jahan
"Your love turned . . . ," page 286

Petrarch
Sonnets 3 and 300, page 251

Edmund Spenser
Sonnet 75, page 286

Princess Zeb-un Nissa
"Though I am Laila . . . ," page 257

Cross-curricular Activities

SOCIAL STUDIES

- Suggest that students research the history of the rise of nationalism in Europe. While we may take for granted the division of the world into nations, the modern nation-state did not develop until feudalism had cleared the way for it. Students might try to determine what the word *nation* meant to people during the transitional time. They might also research the effects of such change on the daily lives of common people. Have students create maps of contemporary Europe and maps of Europe during the Renaissance. Students might also make maps of intervening periods showing how boundaries have changed.
- Students can also research European exploration and its effects on the indigenous peoples of other parts of the world. Suggest that students map the routes of European explorers and the lands that they claimed for Europe.

UNIT 10

Apostle. ***Michelangelo***

Preview:

The Renaissance and the Enlightenment

The Renaissance and the Enlightenment are the designations used to describe the two stages of European history that followed the Medieval Period. Together these periods span European history from the fifteenth century through the early eighteenth century. An interest in the classical works of ancient Greece and Rome helped to shape both the Renaissance and the Enlightenment. Human endeavors in art, literature, science, and philosophy flourished.

The word ***renaissance*** means, literally, a "rebirth." Historians use the word to refer to the period between the fifteenth and early seventeenth centuries, when Europe was influenced by a rebirth of interest in Greek and Latin learning. This renewed focus on classical learning and literature moved Europeans from medieval habits of thought toward a more modern view of the world. During the Medieval Period, people looked for happiness not in this life but in the next. Because they believed that earthly life was brief and of little value, the afterlife became the focus of their hopes and dreams. As a result, medieval literature is dominated by religious subjects and themes. Medieval life was ordered by lines of authority and systems of allegiance: European serfs owed allegiance to a lord, who owed allegiance to a king, who owed allegiance to the Pope of the Roman Catholic Church. In contrast, writers and scholars of classical Greece and Rome believed that individuals must rely on their own consciences rather than on authority figures and systems of allegiance to shape their lives. These classical writers celebrated the arts and other human endeavors with the consequence that their literature embraces this life, not the next.

When scholars, first in Italy and then in the rest of Europe, rediscovered the art, literature, and ideas of the classical world, they spread their enthusiasm, awakening the interest of Renaissance artists and writers in human life on earth. From this shift in thought a new philosophy known as Humanism emerged. Many Humanist philosophers

TEACHING THE MULTIPLE INTELLIGENCES (CONT.)

believed that human beings were created in the image of God and that each person was a little world, or *microcosmos,* complete in himself or herself. They believed that humans, sharing as they did in the divine, could perfect themselves and the institutions of this world. Out of this belief came not only a new emphasis on learning and the arts, but religious and political debates that led to the Protestant Reformation, the decline of feudalism, and the emergence of modern nationalism.

Holy Family. *Titian (Tiziano Vecelli)*

The focus on this world and the growing power and wealth of nations led to an interest in exploring the scope of the earth and acquiring more territory. During the Age of Discovery, Europeans explored the New World and were thereby exposed to cultures previously unknown to them. European writers and scholars like Michel de Montaigne and Jean-Jacques Rousseau were intrigued by the natives of these new lands and began to develop the theory of the "noble savage," the idea that primitive, or "uncivilized," people are naturally good and that any evil they develop stems from the corrupting force of civilization. Explorers, however, were often motivated by greed and simply saw an opportunity to conquer and exploit the native peoples, their lands, and their resources. As a result, entire native civilizations were destroyed during the European exploration that characterized the Age of Discovery.

Geographical discoveries were accompanied by discoveries in other areas. Nicholas Copernicus, a Polish astronomer, published his findings refuting Ptolemy's idea that the earth is the center of the universe. Leonardo da Vinci, one of many great Renaissance artists, was a scientist and inventor as well, expressing the full spirit of the Renaissance. Renaissance interest in human potential sparked a surge in inventive zeal. Johann Gutenberg's invention of the printing press in 1453 was an extremely important development; by this means information spread quickly, and became available even to those who were not wealthy. Such access encouraged independent thought and challenges to authority.

The challenges to authority that arose in the Renaissance led, in the seventeenth and eighteenth centuries, to political and social upheaval in Europe. Among the many notable events of the Enlightenment are the Great Plague of London, the War of Spanish Succession, the Seven Years' War, the American Revolution, and the French Revolution. Amid this chaos, philosophers, writers, and scientists found new ways of looking at and ordering the world. Scientists such as Isaac Newton discovered the

HISTORICAL NOTE

The movable-type printing press was invented by Johannes Gutenberg (c. 1400–1468). During the 1430s and 1440s, Gutenberg worked secretly on his invention. He developed a new kind of printing press, a new metal alloy from which he molded type, a method for casting large quantities of type, and an oil-based ink. Gutenberg's first book, completed around 1455, was the Forty-two Line Bible (also called the Gutenberg Bible). As the name suggests, each column of text consisted of forty-two lines. Like other early books, Gutenberg's Bible had no page numbers. Gutenberg's second work was a collection of psalms for use in church services.

CROSS-CURRICULAR ACTIVITIES

APPLIED ARTS

To gain an appreciation for early bookmaking and the meticulous work it entailed, students can research details of the Gutenberg press or earlier machines and can design their own models for setting type. Other students might use a computer to design and print pages for a book.

ARTS AND HUMANITIES

The Renaissance is often associated with the arts. Have students research one of the following Renaissance artists: Bellini, Botticelli, Donato Bramante, Brunelleschi, Donatello, Leonardo da Vinci, Mantegna, Massaccio, Michelangelo, Piero della Francesca, or Raphael.

BIOGRAPHICAL NOTE

One of the ancient Greek philosophers who had a tremendous influence on Renaissance thought was Aristotle (384–322 BC), who believed that the purpose of human life was to pursue happiness and that the way for an individual to achieve happiness was to exercise intellectual and moral virtues. He further believed that the proper function of a state was to allow its citizens to pursue the good life, although he thought that only a few people in any society were capable of living a truly good and virtuous life. His ideas that human happiness was attainable and that a government should facilitate the happiness of its citizens directly opposed the medieval view of earthly life.

Literary Note

British writer of the Enlightenment Jonathan Swift (1667–1745) wrote biting commentaries and satires. His works include *The Battle of the Books, A Tale of a Tub, Gulliver's Travels,* and "A Modest Proposal." An excerpt from "A Modest Proposal" appears on page 18.

Cross-curricular Activities

ARTS AND HUMANITIES

Have students study some paintings by Neoclassical painters or sculptors. Have them compare the ideals of visual artists of the period with those of writers of the period.

MATHEMATICS AND SCIENCES

Suggest that students research some of the scientific discoveries or theories of the Renaissance and the Enlightenment. Which are still reflected in the thinking of the scientific community today? For ideas that have been replaced, what does current scientific knowledge tell us about our world?

SOCIAL STUDIES

The Enlightenment was a European movement. Have students research cultures in other parts of the world during this period to learn more about government, philosophy, arts and literature, scientific discoveries, and other elements of non-European cultures. Have students present their findings to the class. They might also make a time line to show events from different parts of the world in relation to each other.

Virgin and Child with St. Anne and John the Baptist. *Leonardo da Vinci, circa 1498*

laws of motion and gravitation that govern the movements of the earth and heavenly bodies. These scientists revealed what seemed to be an orderly, clockwork universe regulated by rational principles, and the idea of natural order soon gained many followers. People came to believe that the human intellect could discover natural laws that would solve social, political, and economic problems. Because of this emphasis on intellect, the period is sometimes called the **Enlightenment**, or Age of Reason.

Important philosophers of the Enlightenment included Immanuel Kant, John Locke, and Adam Smith. Kant, a German writer and philosopher, believed that knowledge is a combination of sensation and understanding, that it combines both perception and principles of thought. Locke, a doctor and writer, published *Two Treatises of Government.* This work disputed the divine right of kings and popularized the idea of natural rights—the concept that humans had certain innate moral rights. This concept inspired the Americans who drafted the Declaration of Independence and the Constitution. Smith, a Scottish economist, proposed in his book *The Wealth of Nations* that economies operate by a system of rational, natural law, unless governments and monopolies interfere. Smith's work laid the foundation for capitalism and laissez-faire policy, or the policy that holds that governments should not interfere in business. Kant, Smith, and Locke applied the ideas of rationality and natural law to every sphere of life.

Perhaps because they were surrounded by political and social upheaval, Enlightenment writers looked for order and rationality, not only in the work of contemporary scientists and philosophers, but also in the literature of classical Greece and Rome. Because these writers emulated classical works they are called Neoclassicists. Neoclassical writers used classical allusions and such classic forms as the essay, rhymed couplets, satire, parody, and the epistle, or letter; writers of the period increasingly produced novels as well. These works, promoting the ideals of harmony, tradition, and reason, placed heavy emphasis on wit and on social interactions.

Toward the end of the Enlightenment, many people became disillusioned with the limits of rationality as a guiding principle. Such negative effects of scientific and technological advances as overwork and deteriorating social conditions in cities became apparent, and people began to question the price of progress. Overemphasis on the logical and the rational, along with renewed interest in the power of human emotion, eventually led to the demise of the Neoclassical movement and the rise of Romanticism.

Echoes:

The Renaissance and the Enlightenment

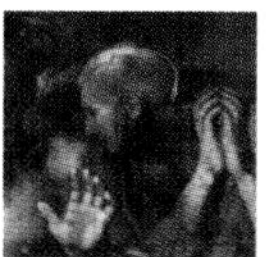

And truly women have excelled indeed
In every art to which they set their hand,
And any who to history pay heed
Their fame will find diffused in every land.
If in some ages they do not succeed,
Their renaissance is not for ever banned.
Envy their merits has perhaps concealed
Or unawareness left them unrevealed.

—Ludovico Ariosto
from *Orlando Furioso*

Not marble, nor the gilded monuments of princes, shall outlive this powerful rhyme.

—William Shakespeare

Beauty is but a flower
Which wrinkles will devour;
Brightness falls from the air;
Queens have died young and fair;
dust hath closèd Helen's eye.
I am sick, I must die.
Lord, have mercy on us!

—Thomas Nashe
from "A Litany in Time of Plague"

The value of life lies not in the length of days but in the use you make of them; he has lived for a long time who has little lived. Whether you have lived enough depends not on the number of your years but on your will.

—Michel de Montaigne

I trained my wits, my body, and my mind with a thousand ingenious works.

—Louise Labé

New opinions are always suspected, and usually opposed, without any other reason but because they are not already common.

—John Locke

During the time men live without a common power [a king] to keep them all in awe . . . the life of man [is] solitary, poor, nasty, brutish, and short.

—Thomas Hobbes
from *Leviathan*

The General ORDER, since the whole began
Is kept in Nature, and is kept in man. . . .
All Nature is but art, unknown to thee;
All chance, direction, which thou canst not see;
All discord, harmony not understood;
All partial evil, universal good:
And, spite of pride, in erring reason's spite,
One truth is clear: Whatever is, is RIGHT.

—Alexander Pope
from "An Essay on Man"

After us the deluge.

—Madame de Pompadour

Biographical Note

Ludovico Ariosto (1474–1533) was an Italian poet and the author of *Orlando Furioso.* A biography of Ariosto appears on page 830.

William Shakespeare (1564–1616) is considered by many the greatest writer of all time. Sonnets by the English dramatist and poet appear on pages 256 and 851.

Thomas Nashe (1567–1601) was an English dramatist and pamphlet writer. He was imprisoned for writing a satire criticizing the government.

Michel de Montaigne (1533–1592) was a French essayist. A biography of Montaigne appears on page 860.

Louise Labé (c. 1524–1566) was a French poet. A biography of Labé appears on page 847.

John Locke (1632–1704), an English philosopher, was one of the initiators of the Enlightenment in England and France. His most important work, *An Essay Concerning Human Understanding,* examines how human beings acquire knowledge through the senses and self-reflection. The United States Constitution was inspired by his political philosophy.

Thomas Hobbes (1588–1679) was an English philosopher. His theories formed the basis of Utilitarianism, a philosophical movement based on the belief that ideas and actions should be judged according to their consequences.

Alexander Pope (1688–1744) was an English poet known for his wit. His couplets are often quoted. An example of his work appears on page 894.

Jeanne-Antoinette Poisson, known as **Madame de Pompadour** (1721–1764) was the influential mistress of Louis XV of France. The phrase *aprés nous le deluge (after us, the deluge)* is attributed to her although it had long been a French saying.

ADDITIONAL RESOURCES

READER'S GUIDE

- Selection Worksheet 10.1

ASSESSMENT PORTFOLIO

- Selection Check Test 2.10.1
- Selection Test 2.10.2

ESSENTIAL SKILLS PRACTICE BOOKS

- Writing 1.8, 1.20
- Language 2.52
- Speaking and Listening, 3.2
- Applied English/Tech Prep 5.1

PREREADING EXTENSIONS

During the fourteenth century, the plague was called the Black Death; the disease claimed one-fourth of the European population (about twenty-five million people). Ask students to research bubonic or pneumatic plague. How was it transmitted? What did people believe about it during the fourteenth century, and what did they do about it? Students can also research recent outbreaks of the plague and discuss their findings in small groups.

SUPPORT FOR LEP STUDENTS

PRONUNCIATIONS OF PROPER NOUNS AND ADJECTIVES

Cam • pi (käm pē´)
Fed • er • i • go (fā dā rē´gō)
Flor • ence (flôr´əns)
Gio • van • ni Boc • cac • cio (jō vän´ nē bōk kät´ chō)
Mes • ser Fi • lip • po Al • ber • i • ghi (mə´ ser fē lēp´pō äl´ber ē´jē)
Mon • na Gio • van • na (mōn´ na jō van´ nə)
Tus • cany (tus´ ke nē)

ADDITIONAL VOCABULARY

merit—worth, value
presumption—forwardness
reproached—blamed and expressed disapproval

PREREADING

"Federigo's Falcon" from the *Decameron*

by Giovanni Boccaccio, translated by Mark Musa and Peter Bondanella

ITALY

About the Author

GIOVANNI BOCCACCIO 1313–1375

Giovanni Boccaccio grew up in Florence, Italy. Despite his interest in literature, his father sent him to Naples to study business. When Boccaccio returned to Florence around 1340, he had already written some poems that would inspire Geoffrey Chaucer decades later. In 1348, the plague claimed many lives in Florence, including that of the woman whom Boccaccio may have loved—Maria d'Aquino. Boccaccio wrote his most influential work, the *Decameron*, between 1348 and 1353.

In 1350, Boccaccio met another great Italian Renaissance writer—Petrarch. Petrarch influenced Boccaccio to turn from writing poetry and prose fiction in Italian to writing scholarly works in Latin. Constantly suffering from poverty, Boccaccio devoted himself to study during his later years and in 1373 began a series of lectures on Dante, whom Boccaccio, unlike Petrarch, admired. Boccaccio died in 1375, just a year after Petrarch.

View from the Campanile, Florence

About the Selection

The ***Decameron*** exerted an enormous influence on European Renaissance literature. This prose work begins with a **frame tale**,—a story that itself provides a vehicle for the telling of other stories—a technique Chaucer later used in his *Canterbury Tales.* In the frame tale, which was based on Boccaccio's experience of witnessing the Black Death in Florence, seven women and three men flee Florence to escape the plague. In a countryside retreat for fourteen days, these young people set aside ten days for exchanging stories. Indeed, the work's title means "Ten Days' Work." Assigning story topics for each day, the young people choose the topic of love that ends happily after difficulty for the day that **"Federigo's Falcon"** is told. Federigo, the main character, perfectly embodies the medieval notion of courtly love.

As a whole, the stories in the *Decameron* are both comic and tragic. By showing people struggling against and sometimes overcoming fate, Boccaccio explores a view of humanity that Renaissance Humanists later embraced.

CONNECTIONS: A Medieval Sport

Falconry is a sport in which falcons and hawks are used to hunt game. This sport was practiced in Assyria as early as the eighth century BC. European crusaders and merchants learned the sport in the east and brought trained falcons back to Europe. Falconry became fashionable among the upper classes of Western Europe during the Medieval Period. Falcons are still used to hunt other birds, such as herons, partridges, pheasants, or quail, and small animals such as rabbits.

GOALS/OBJECTIVES

Studying this lesson will enable students to

- enjoy and appreciate part of a frame tale
- recognize Giovanni Boccaccio as a Renaissance writer
- define *frame tale, irony,* and *courtly love*
- describe the frame of the *Decameron*
- identify an example of dramatic irony in the story
- analyze elements of courtly love in the selection
- write a continuation
- analyze elements of realism in a story
- write a personal letter

What is the most generous thing you have ever done for another person? What prompted you to behave in a generous manner? Write about this experience in your journal.

"Federigo's Falcon"

GIOVANNI BOCCACCIO, TRANSLATED BY MARK MUSA AND PETER BONDANELLA

There was once in Florence a young man named Federigo, the son of Messer Filippo Alberighi, renowned above all other men in Tuscany for his prowess in arms and for his courtliness. As often happens to most gentlemen, he fell in love with a lady named Monna Giovanna, in her day considered to be one of the most beautiful and one of the most charming women that ever there was in Florence; and in order to win her love, he participated in jousts and tournaments, organized and gave feasts, and spent his money without restraint; but she, no less virtuous than beautiful, cared little for these things done on her behalf, nor did she care for him who did them. Now, as Federigo was spending far beyond his means and was taking nothing in, as easily happens he lost his wealth and became poor, with nothing but his little farm to his name (from whose revenues he lived very meagerly) and one falcon which was among the best in the world.

More in love than ever, but knowing that he would never be able to live the way he wished to in the city, he went to live at Campi, where his farm was. There he passed his time hawking whenever he could, asked nothing of anyone, and endured his poverty patiently. Now, during the time that Federigo was reduced to dire need, it happened that the husband of Monna Giovanna fell ill, and realizing death was near, he made his last will: he was very rich, and he made his son, who was growing up, his heir, and, since he had loved Monna Giovanna very much, he made her his heir should his son die without a legitimate heir; and then he died.

Monna Giovanna was now a widow, and as is the custom among our women, she went to the country with her son to spend a year on one of her possessions very close by to Federigo's farm, and it happened that this young boy became friends with Federigo and began to enjoy birds and hunting dogs;

1 *What does Federigo do to win Monna Giovanna's love?*

2 *Who will inherit the husband's money should his son die?*

WORDS FOR EVERYDAY USE

prow • ess (prou´is) *n.*, superior ability, skill

mea • ger • ly (mē´gər lē) *adv.*, inadequately, not fully or richly

READER'S JOURNAL

Ask students to consider the following questions as well: Were they rewarded for their generosity? Did they expect to be? In what way might a reward affect their feelings about what they did? When students have finished writing, have them discuss their responses and come to a consensus on what it means to be generous and what it means to sacrifice.

ANSWERS TO GUIDED READING QUESTIONS

1 Federigo participates in tournaments, gives feasts, and spends his money lavishly in hopes of winning Monna Giovanna's love.

2 Monna Giovanna will inherit her husband's money should their son die.

SPELLING AND VOCABULARY WORDS FROM THE SELECTION

compensate
consolation
meagerly
prowess
prudence

CROSS-CURRICULAR ACTIVITIES

SOCIAL STUDIES

Have students locate on a map the following regions of modern Italy: Abruzzi, Calabria, Campania, Emilia Romagna, Fruili-Venezia-Giulia, Lazio, Liguria, Lombardy, Le Marche, Molise, Piedmont, Puglia, Sardinia, Sicily, Tuscany, Trentino-Alto-Adige, Umbria, Valle d'Aosta, and Veneto.

Students can work in groups to research the differences in climate, terrain, population, economy, and cuisine of these regions.

VOCABULARY IN CONTEXT

- Rahmun's prowess on the course surprised the more experienced golfers.
- There was only one chair and a lamp in the meagerly furnished room.

Answers to Guided Reading Questions

❶ The boy doesn't ask for the falcon because he sees how much Federigo values it.

❷ The falcon is Federigo's only means of support.

Literary Note

If students have not read O. Henry's short story "The Gift of the Magi," have them do so. Then they can compare and contrast the two stories. In what way is Federigo's dilemma similar to the problem Della and Jim face? In what way does Federigo's situation differ?

Integrated Skills Activities

Speaking and Listening

Monna Giovanna and Federigo run into difficulty because they do not speak honestly and clearly to one another. Have students refer to the Language Arts Survey 3.2, "Active Listening and Interpersonal Communication." Then have them work in pairs to role play a situation in which Monna Giovanna and Federigo speak openly and listen to each other.

▶ Additional practice is provided in the Essential Skills Practice Book: Speaking and Listening 3.2.

Language

After students have completed the activity above, have each one write a brief dialogue between Monna Giovanna and Federigo based on their role play. They should pay special attention to the proper use of quotation marks and other punctuation. Refer them to the Language Arts Survey 2.52, "Other Uses of Quotation Marks."

▶ Additional practice is provided in the Essential Skills Practice Book: Language 2.52.

❶ *Why doesn't the boy ask for the falcon? What does the boy ask for once he becomes ill?*

and after he had seen Federigo's falcon fly many times, it pleased him so much that he very much wished it were his own, but he did not dare to ask for it, for he could see how dear it was to Federigo. And during this time, it happened that the young boy took ill, and his mother was much grieved, for he was her only child and she loved him enormously; she would spend the entire day by his side, never ceasing to comfort him, and often asking him if there was anything he desired, begging him to tell her what it might be, for if it were possible to <u>obtain</u> it, she would certainly do everything possible to get it. After the young boy had heard her make this offer many times, he said:

"Mother, if you can arrange for me to have Federigo's falcon, I think I would be well very soon."

When the lady heard this, she was taken aback for a moment, and she began to think what she should do. She knew that Federigo had loved her for a long while, in spite of the fact that he never received a single glance from her, and so, she said to herself:

❷ *What is Federigo's only means of support?*

"How can I send or go and ask for this falcon of his which is, as I have heard tell, the best that ever flew, and besides this, his only means of support? And how can I be so insensitive as to wish to take away from this gentleman the only pleasure which is left to him?"

And involved in these thoughts, knowing that she was certain to have the bird if she asked for it, but not knowing what to say to her son, she stood there without answering him. Finally the love she bore her son persuaded her that she should make him happy, and no matter what the consequences might be, she would not send for the bird, but rather go herself for it and bring it back to him; so she answered her son:

Words for Everyday Use

ob • tain (əb tān´) *vt.,* get through some effort

Vocabulary in Context

• After many hours of driver's ed, Luisa was able to <u>obtain</u> her driver's license.

"My son, take comfort and think only of getting well, for I promise you that the first thing I shall do tomorrow morning is to go for it and bring it back to you."

The child was so happy that he showed some improvement that very day. The following morning, the lady, accompanied by another woman, as if going for a stroll, went to Federigo's modest house and asked for him. Since it was not the season for it, Federigo had not been hawking for some days and was in his orchard, attending to certain tasks; when he heard that Monna Giovanna was asking for him at the door, he was very surprised and happy to run there; as she saw him coming, she greeted him with feminine charm, and once Federigo had welcomed her courteously, she said:

"Greetings, Federigo!" Then she continued: "I have come to compensate you for the harm you have suffered on my account by loving me more than you needed to; and the compensation is this: I, along with this companion of mine, intend to dine with you—a simple meal—this very day."

To this Federigo humbly replied: "Madonna, I never remember having suffered any harm because of you; on the contrary: so much good have I received from you that if ever I have been worth anything, it has been because of your merit and the love I bore for you; and your generous visit is certainly so dear to me that I would spend all over again that which I spent in the past; but you have come to a poor host."

And having said this, he received her into his home humbly, and from there he led her into his garden, and since he had no one there to keep her company, he said:

"My lady, since there is no one else, this good woman here, the wife of this workman, will keep you company while I go to set the table."

Though he was very poor, Federigo, until now, had never before realized to what extent he had wasted his wealth; but this morning, the fact that he found nothing with which he could honor the lady for the love of whom he had once entertained countless men in the past gave him cause to reflect: in great anguish, he cursed himself and his fortune and, like a man beside himself, he started running here and there, but could find neither money nor a pawnable object. The hour was late and his desire to honor the gracious lady was great, but not wishing to turn for help to others (not even to his own workman), he set his eyes upon his good falcon, perched in a small room; and since he had nowhere else to turn, he took the bird, and finding it plump, he decided that it would be a worthy food for such a lady. So, without further thought, he wrung its neck and quickly gave it to his servant girl to pluck, prepare, and place on a spit to be roasted with care; and when he had set the table with the whitest of tablecloths (a few of which he still had left), he returned, with a cheerful face, to the lady in his garden, saying that the meal he was able to prepare for her was ready.

The lady and her companion rose, went to the table together with Federigo, who waited upon them with the greatest devotion, and they ate the good falcon without knowing what it was they were eating. And having left the table and spent some time in pleasant conversation, the lady thought it time now to say what she had come to say, and so she spoke these kind words to Federigo:

"Federigo, if you recall your past life and my virtue, which you perhaps mistook for harshness and cruelty, I do not doubt at all that you will be amazed by my presumption when you hear what my main reason for

❶ *For what is Federigo searching?*

❷ *What does Federigo do? How does he feel about doing this?*

❸ *What compensation does Monna Giovanna offer Federigo?*

❹ *In what way does Federigo's response demonstrate the ideals of courtly love?*

❺ *What does Monna Giovanna say was the cause of her ignoring Federigo?*

Words for Everyday Use

com • pen • sate (käm´pən sāt´) *vt.,* make equivalent or suitable return, recompense; make up for

Answers to Guided Reading Questions

❶ Federigo is searching for something worthy to serve to Monna Giovanna.

❷ Federigo kills his beloved falcon "without further thought" to serve to Monna Giovanna.

❸ She offers to dine with him.

❹ Federigo is honorable and devoted to his beloved lady. All of his trials have resulted from his efforts to earn her respect.

❺ Monna Giovanna says that she ignored Federigo because she is virtuous.

Literary Technique

MOTIVATION

A **motivation** is a force that moves a character to think, feel, or behave in a certain way. What is Monna Giovanna's motivation for asking Federigo for the falcon? What motivates Federigo to kill the falcon and serve it for lunch?

ANSWERS

Monna Giovanna is motivated by love for her son. Federigo is motivated by his love for Monna Giovanna.

Cross-curricular Activities

MATHEMATICS AND SCIENCES

Students may notice that Monna Giovanna's son improves upon hearing that his mother will obtain the coveted falcon for him. Ask students to research psychological stimulus on healing. They can present their findings in a brief written or oral summary.

Vocabulary in Context

• Leland used his allowance to compensate Ms. Petrovich for the window he had broken.

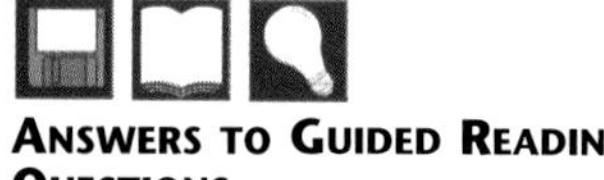

Answers to Guided Reading Questions

1 She says that she is afraid that her son will die unless she brings him the falcon. She says that Federigo should give her the falcon not because of his love but because of his nobility.

2 Federigo weeps because he cannot give Monna Giovanna the falcon.

3 She believes that his action reveals that Federigo possesses a greatness of spirit.

4 The son dies. The narrator suggests that the son may have died of disappointment or that the son would have died anyway.

Selection Check Test with Answers

EX. Whom does Federigo love?
Federigo loves Monna Giovanna.

1. After Federigo spends all his money, what are the two things he has left?
Federigo has a small farm and an excellent falcon.

2. What happens to Monna Giovanna's husband?
Monna Giovanna's husband dies.

3. What does Monna Giovanna's son believe will make him better?
He believes that Federigo's falcon will make him better.

4. What does Federigo serve Monna Giovanna for lunch?
Federigo serves her the falcon for lunch.

5. When her brothers ask her to remarry, who is the only person Monna Giovanna will consider?
Federigo is the only person Monna Giovanna will consider.

coming here is; but if you had children, through whom you might have experienced the power of parental love, it seems certain to me that you would, at least in part, forgive me. But, just as you have no child, I do have one, and I cannot escape the common laws of other mothers; the force of such laws compels me to follow them, against my own will and against good manners and duty, and to ask of you a gift which I know is most precious to you; and it is naturally so, since your extreme condition has left you no other delight, no other pleasure, no other consolation; and this gift is your falcon, which my son is so taken by that if I do not bring it to him, I fear his sickness will grow so much worse that I may lose him. And therefore I beg you, not because of the love that you bear for me, which does not oblige you in the least, but because of your own nobility, which you have shown to be greater than that of all others in practicing courtliness, that you be pleased to give it to me, so that I may say that I have saved the life of my son by means of this gift, and because of it I have placed him in your debt forever."

1 What reason does Monna Giovanna give for requesting the falcon? According to Monna, why should Federigo give her the falcon?

When he heard what the lady requested and knew that he could not oblige her since he had given her the falcon to eat, Federigo began to weep in her presence, for he could not utter a word in reply. The lady, at first, thought his tears were caused more by the sorrow of having to part with the good falcon than by anything else, and she was on the verge of telling him she no longer wished it, but she held back and waited for Federigo's reply after he stopped weeping. And he said:

2 Why does Federigo weep?

"My lady, ever since it pleased God for me to place my love in you, I have felt that Fortune has been hostile to me in many things, and I have complained of her, but all this is nothing compared to what she has just done to me, and I must never be at peace with her again, thinking about how you have come here to my poor home where, while it was rich, you never deigned to come, and you requested a small gift, and Fortune worked to make it impossible for me to give it to you; and why this is so I shall tell you briefly. When I heard that you, out of your kindness, wished to dine with me, I considered it fitting and right, taking into account your excellence and your worthiness, that I should honor you, according to my possibilities, with a more precious food than that which I usually serve to other people; therefore, remembering the falcon that you requested and its value, I judged it a food worthy of you, and this very day you had it roasted and served to you as best I could; but seeing now that you desired it in another way, my sorrow in not being able to serve you is so great that I shall never be able to console myself again."

And after he had said this, he laid the feathers, the feet, and the beak of the bird before her as proof. When the lady heard and saw this, she first reproached him for having killed such a falcon to serve as a meal to a woman; but then to herself she commended the greatness of his spirit, which no poverty was able or would be able to diminish; then, having lost all hope of getting the falcon and, perhaps because of this, of improving the health of her son as well, she thanked Federigo both for the honor paid to her and for his good will, and she left in grief, and returned to her son. To his mother's extreme sorrow, either because of his disappointment that he could not have the falcon, or because his illness must have

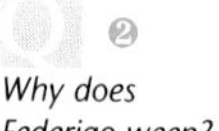

3 How does Monna Giovanna feel about what Federigo has done?

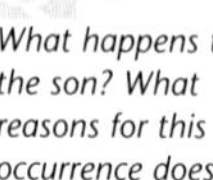

4 What happens to the son? What reasons for this occurrence does the narrator suggest?

Words for Everyday Use

con • so • la • tion (kön´sə lā´shən) *n.,* comfort, solace

Vocabulary in Context

• Although we played well, it was no consolation for losing the championship game.

Still Life with Soup Tureen.
Paul Cézanne

necessarily led to it, the boy passed from this life only a few days later.

After the period of her mourning and bitterness had passed, the lady was repeatedly urged by her brothers to remarry, since she was very rich and was still young; and although she did not wish to do so, they became so insistent that she remembered the merits of Federigo and his last act of generosity—that is, to have killed such a falcon to do her honor—and she said to her brothers:

"I would prefer to remain a widow, if that would please you; but if you wish me to take a husband, you may rest assured that I shall take no man but Federigo degli Alberighi."

In answer to this, making fun of her, her brothers replied:

"You foolish woman, what are you saying? How can you want him; he hasn't a penny to his name?"

To this she replied: "My brothers, I am well aware of what you say, but I would rather have a man who needs money than money that needs a man."

Her brothers, seeing that she was determined and knowing Federigo to be of noble birth, no matter how poor he was, accepted her wishes and gave her in marriage to him with all her riches; when he found himself the husband of such a great lady, whom he had loved so much and who was so wealthy besides, he managed his financial affairs with more prudence than in the past and lived happily the rest of his days. ■

➊ *Who is the only person Monna Giovanna would consider marrying?*

➋ *In what way has Federigo changed?*

WORDS FOR EVERYDAY USE

pru • dence (prōōd´'ns) *n.*, careful management

VOCABULARY IN CONTEXT

• While I admire prudence, there is no need to be stingy.

ANSWERS TO GUIDED READING QUESTIONS

➊ Federigo is the only person Monna Giovanna would consider marrying.

➋ He is more careful with Monna Giovanna's money than he was with his own.

ANALYTIC SCALES FOR RESPONDING IN WRITING

(SEE PAGE 829.)

Assign a score from 1 to 25 for each grading criterion below. (For more detailed evaluation, see the evaluation forms for writing, revising, and proofreading, Assessment Portfolio 4.1–4.9.)

1. Continuation

- **Content/Unity.** The continuation describes the relationship between Monna Giovanna and Federigo.
- **Organization/Coherence.** The continuation is arranged in a logical order.
- **Language/Style.** The continuation uses vivid and precise nouns, verbs, and modifiers.
- **Conventions.** The continuation avoids errors in spelling, grammar, usage, mechanics, and manuscript form.

► Additional practice is provided in the Essential Skills Practice Book: Writing 1.8.

2. Critical Essay

- **Content/Unity.** The essay analyzes elements of realism in the selection.
- **Organization/Coherence.** The essay begins with an introduction that includes a thesis. The introduction is followed by supporting paragraphs with clear transitions. The essay ends with a solid conclusion.
- **Language/Style.** The essay uses vivid and precise language.
- **Conventions.** The essay avoids errors in spelling, grammar, usage, mechanics, and manuscript form.

► Additional practice is provided in the Essential Skills Practice Book: Writing 1.20.

Responding to the Selection

Students might also discuss a time when something they did as a favor or to help somebody else went awry. What was the result of their action? How do they feel about the decision they made?

Answers for Reviewing the Selection

RECALLING AND INTERPRETING

1. **Recalling.** Federigo participates in jousts and tournaments, gives feasts, and spends his money without restraint. Federigo loses his wealth. **Interpreting.** Federigo believed that he could impress Monna Giovanna with his wealth and generosity. Monna Giovanna was already married to someone else and was virtuous. Also, she may not have been impressed by Federigo's lavish display of wealth.
2. **Recalling.** Monna Giovanna's son is so pleased by Federigo's falcon that he wishes it were his own. **Interpreting.** Monna Giovanna's son knows that Federigo highly values and loves his falcon. It shows that the son is not greedy and is sensitive to the feelings of others.
3. **Recalling.** The son believes that owning Federigo's falcon will cure him. Monna Giovanna decides to visit Federigo, dine with him, ask him for the bird, and then bring it back. **Interpreting.** Monna Giovanna knows that the bird is Federigo's source of livelihood and only pleasure; she realizes that it is insensitive to ask for the bird but feels that she must do anything in her power to help her son. Monna Giovanna says that Federigo should give her the falcon not because of his love but because of his noble nature.
4. **Recalling.** Federigo serves her the falcon for lunch. He weeps and says that fortune has been hostile to him. **Interpreting.** Federigo is so in love with (cont.)

Responding to the Selection

If you were in Federigo's position, would you have acted as he does, or would you have acted differently? Explain. If you were in Monna Giovanna's position, would you have acted as she does? Why, or why not? What might you have done differently?

Reviewing the Selection

Recalling		Interpreting
1. At the beginning of the story, what does Federigo do to win the love of Monna Giovanna? What happens to Federigo as a result?	▶▶	Why do you think Federigo believed he could win Monna Giovanna's love in this way? Why do you think Monna Giovanna failed to fall in love with Federigo at that time?
2. What does Monna Giovanna's son think of Federigo's falcon?	▶▶	Why doesn't Monna Giovanna's son ask Federigo for the falcon before his illness? What does this reveal about her son's character?
3. What does the son believe will cure him of his illness? In what way does Monna Giovanna decide to obtain this thing for her son?	▶▶	Why is Monna Giovanna reluctant to ask for this thing? Why does she do so anyway? According to Monna Giovanna, why should Federigo give this thing to her?
4. What does Federigo serve Monna Giovanna for lunch? What is his reaction when he hears her request?	▶▶	Why is Federigo willing to serve this thing for lunch? How does Federigo feel when he discovers the reason for Monna Giovanna's visit?

Synthesizing

5. What does Monna Giovanna expect from Federigo in the name of love? Why does she choose to remain a widow? Why does Monna Giovanna marry Federigo? What qualities matter to her? Which do not? Use examples from the text to support your responses.

Understanding Literature (Questions for Discussion)

1. **Irony. Irony** is a difference between appearance and reality. In **dramatic irony**, something is known by the reader or audience but unknown to the characters. What example of dramatic irony is present in "Federigo's Falcon"? What makes this occurrence ironic? How does irony affect the reader?

Answers for Reviewing the Selection (cont.)

Monna Giovanna that he will make any sacrifice for her. Students may say that although Federigo kills the falcon "without further thought" and goes to the table "with a cheerful face," it must have been difficult for him to sacrifice something he so dearly loved. Federigo feels as if he will never be able to console himself for not being able to serve Monna Giovanna in her request.

SYNTHESIZING

Responses will vary. Possible responses are given.

5. Monna Giovanna expects Federigo to give up the falcon, something that he loves, for the love of her. She asks him to give it to her because of his nobility, but she expects that his love will play a role in convincing him to grant her request. She remains a widow because she does not (cont.)

2. **Courtly Love. Courtly love** is a code of romantic love celebrated in songs and romances of the Medieval Period in France and England. According to this code, a lover knows himself or herself to be truly in love if he or she is overcome by extreme, transforming emotion. The characters in works celebrating courtly love are often one-dimensional. The female lover is often portrayed in ideal and unrealistic terms. She usually requires that the male lover prove his love through a series of tasks. The male lover is led sometimes to depths of despair and sometimes to heights of courtesy and heroism to prove his worth to his lady. In what way is Federigo a perfect representative of the male transformed by courtly love? In what way does Monna Giovanna represent the female courtly lover? Explain, using references to the text.

Responding in Writing

1. **Creative Writing: Continuation.** Ignoring the "happily ever after ending" of the story, write a two- to three-page continuation of the story of Federigo and Monna Giovanna after they are married. Before you begin your continuation, freewrite your responses to the following questions: What would Federigo and Monna be like as a married couple? Would Federigo feel content in the relationship, or would he still feel as if he must constantly prove himself to Monna? Would Monna love Federigo, or would she resent the fact that her brothers urged her to marry? Share your continuations of "Federigo's Falcon" as a class.

2. **Critical Essay: Realism in "Federigo's Falcon."** Write a brief essay analyzing how realistic "Federigo's Falcon" is. Discuss which elements of the story are realistic and which are unrealistic. Remember that this story was written at the beginning of the Italian Renaissance when people often hunted with falcons, when the relationship between men and women was different than it is today, and when people were very concerned with sickness and death because of the plagues that struck Europe. State your thesis in a first paragraph; provide examples of realistic and unrealistic elements of the story in subsequent paragraphs; and come to a conclusion in a final paragraph.

Applied English/Tech Prep Skills

Personal and Business Letters. Read the Language Arts Survey 5.1, "Personal and Business Letters." Then, choose one of the following assignments:

- Imagine that you are Monna Giovanna and that your son has just told you that he believes he will die unless Federigo gives him the falcon. Write a persuasive personal letter to Federigo requesting the falcon. Use proper form for a personal letter.
- Imagine that you are Federigo. Monna has eaten your falcon; her son has died; and she is so angry that she will no longer speak to you. Write a personal letter to Monna explaining why you served her the falcon and asking her to understand and forgive you. Use proper form for a personal letter.

ANSWERS FOR UNDERSTANDING LITERATURE

Responses will vary. Possible responses are given.

1. Irony. When Monna Giovanna goes to Federigo to request that he give her the falcon to save the life of her son and Federigo serves the falcon to her for lunch, this is an example of dramatic irony. This scene is ironic because the reader knows why Monna Giovanna is visiting Federigo before Federigo does, and the reader knows that Monna Giovanna has been served the falcon before she discovers it. Dramatic irony heightens the reader's feeling of suspense.

2. Courtly Love. Students should recognize that Federigo's despair and his extreme generosity are typical of the courtly lover. Students should recognize that while Federigo venerates Monna Giovanna, she is portrayed much more realistically than most idealized women in courtly love literature. The reader sees her inner turmoil and self-doubt, not just her loveliness.

ANALYTIC SCALES FOR RESPONDING IN WRITING

Grading scales for Responding in Writing appear on page 827.

ANSWERS FOR SKILLS ACTIVITIES

APPLIED ENGLISH/TECH PREP

Students should follow the proper form for a personal letter and avoid errors in spelling, grammar, usage, and mechanics. The letter should address the subject chosen in the prompt, and the response should be based on interpretation of the character in the selection.

► Additional practice is provided in the Essential Skills Practice Book: Applied English/Tech Prep 5.1.

ANSWERS FOR REVIEWING THE SELECTION (CONT.)

want to marry again. She marries Federigo because of his noble and generous spirit. Greatness of spirit matters to her, but wealth does not. Monna Giovanna realizes that Federigo is not wealthy. His need to kill his beloved falcon to present her with a proper meal shows his poverty; the fact that he killed it shows his willingness to sacrifice for her and proves his greatness of spirit. That Monna Giovanna chooses to marry Federigo while refusing all others shows that she admires his qualities and overlooks his wealth or lack of it.

ADDITIONAL RESOURCES

Reader's Guide

- Selection Worksheet 10.2

Assessment Portfolio

- Selection Check Test 2.10.3
- Selection Test 2.10.4

Essential Skills Practice Books

- Writing 1.8, 1.10, 1.20
- Language 2.4, 2.5

PREREADING EXTENSIONS

Inform students that while female knights may have been a rarity in medieval and Renaissance Europe, they were not entirely unknown. Ask students to research Joan of Arc (1412–1431), who led the French to victory during the Hundred Years' War. Encourage them to discuss Joan's beliefs, what she accomplished, how and why she died, as well as her significance today. Students might also discuss other famed warrior women of history or legend.

SUPPORT FOR LEP STUDENTS

Pronunciations of Proper Nouns and Adjectives

Bra • da • man • te (brä dä män´tē)
Lu • do • vi • co A • ri • o • sto (lo͞o´də vē´kō ä´rē ô´stō´)
Or • lan • do Fu • ri • o • so (ōr län´ dō für yo´sō)
Ron • ces • val • les (ron sās´vä lās´)
Rug • gier • o (rüd jer´ō)
Sa • cri • pan • te (sä crə pän´tē)

Additional Vocabulary

ado—fuss; trouble
aghast—terrified; horrified

PREREADING

from *Orlando Furioso*
by Ludovico Ariosto, translated by Barbara Reynolds

ITALY

About the Author

LUDOVICO ARIOSTO
1474–1533

Ludovico Ariosto, the eldest son of a courtier who served the noble Este family, was born during the height of the Italian Renaissance. Ariosto enjoyed poetry, but his father compelled him to study law for five years before allowing him to study literature. In 1500, when his father died, Ariosto had to put his literary studies aside. To support his younger siblings, he went to work for the Este family, who dispatched Ariosto to carry out many dangerous diplomatic and military missions. Ariosto preferred a simpler and more scholarly lifestyle, but he did not manage to save enough money to devote himself solely to literary pursuits until 1525. Although Ariosto wrote drama and satire, he is best remembered as the author of *Orlando Furioso,* an epic poem that took about twenty-five years to write. During these years, Ariosto carried the manuscript of the poem about with him, reading it aloud to all who were interested, and allowing his friends to revise his work as they wished.

Painted ceiling, Vatican Museum, Rome, Italy

About the Selection

Orlando Furioso is an epic poem that takes as its focus a popular romantic subject—Charlemagne's defeat by the Basques at Roncesvalles in Spain in 778. According to tradition, Roland, a French hero, died in this battle (see *The Song of Roland,* page 809). Italian romantic writers were also interested in this hero, whom they called Orlando, and Matteo Boiardo, an earlier Italian writer, had written a work about Orlando in love. One of the central story lines in *Orlando Furioso* continues Boiardo's theme, describing what becomes of this hero when he is driven mad by unrequited love. Ariosto transforms Charlemagne's defeat at Roncesvalles into an enormous battle between European Christians and African, Spanish, and Oriental Saracens, or Muslims. *Orlando Furioso* interweaves many story lines, and the author skillfully maintains the reader's interest in many characters and their adventures. Ariosto frequently juxtaposes tragic and comic scenes to entertaining effect. The following selection depicts a female knight, a Christian named Bradamante, who loves Ruggiero, an African knight. Bradamante and Ruggiero are the traditional founders of the House of Este, so Ariosto is complimenting his patrons when he describes the greatness of Bradamante's future offspring.

CONNECTIONS: Ariosto's Renaissance Women: Modernity Meets the Medieval Romance

Ariosto's female characters are as strong, self-determined, and capable as his male characters. In one of his cantos, Ariosto writes verse in praise of women's achievements and suggests that such achievements should be more widely known. Ariosto's strikingly modern attitude may stem from the superior education received by upper-class Italian women during Ariosto's time. Before many other European noblewomen were educated as men were, Italian noblewomen were well-educated and encouraged to develop intellectual pursuits.

GOALS/OBJECTIVES

Studying this lesson will enable students to

- appreciate an excerpt from a work generally considered the greatest Italian romantic epic
- identify Ludovico Ariosto as an Italian Renaissance writer
- define *simile, stanza, rhyme,* and *rhyme scheme,* and identify these elements in an epic poem
- write a stanza in *ottava rima*
- write a critical essay on gender roles
- use personal pronouns correctly

READER'S JOURNAL

In your journal, express your thoughts about gender roles. Before writing, consider the following questions: What do you think a man should be like? What do you think a woman should be like? Is there anything that you believe men or women cannot or should not do because of their gender?

FROM

Orlando Furioso

LUDOVICO ARIOSTO, TRANSLATED BY BARBARA REYNOLDS

FROM CANTO I

[Editor's note: Christians, under the rule of Charlemagne, and Saracens, or Muslims from the East, are engaged in a series of battles for control of Europe. Many of the knights, both Christian and Muslim, who are involved in these battles are in love with Angelica, an Eastern princess and the daughter of the king of Cathay (an old term for China). Angelica, however, is determined to marry none of them. Sacripante, a Saracen king who is wildly in love with Angelica, has encountered her in a grove in the woods, and intends to force her to marry him. Sacripante's plans, however, are interrupted by the arrival of a knight wearing white armor.]

60

Along the forest soon there rides a knight
Who has the semblance of a valiant man.
The armour which he wears is snowy white,
Likewise his plume. The Tartar sovereign,[1]
Being put out by the unwelcome sight
Of one whose coming has thus foiled his plan,
Such interruption of his pleasure brooks[2]
With anger undisguised and stormy looks.

❶ *What words are used to describe the knight?*

❷ *What has the arrival of the knight done to Sacripante's plans?*

1. **Tartar sovereign.** Turkish king, here referring to Sacripante
2. **brooks.** Bears; endures

WORDS FOR EVERYDAY USE

sem • blance (sem´bləns) *n.,* outward form or appearance

READER'S JOURNAL

As an alternate activity, you might ask students to write about a time when their ideas about gender roles were overturned. For example, they might write about learning that women's sports were just as challenging as men's or discovering that many men enjoy cooking, and so on.

ANSWERS TO GUIDED READING QUESTIONS

❶ The knight is described as wearing white armor and as having the outward appearance of a valiant man.

❷ The arrival of the knight has foiled Sacripante's plans to force Angelica to marry him.

SPELLING AND VOCABULARY WORDS FROM THE SELECTION

bemuse	precipitous
credulous	predicament
dismay	procure
elate	progeny
expedition	prostrate
fathom	ravine
guile	semblance
ignominy	stupefaction
immure	terrain
impugn	tribulation
pendulous	winsome
perilous	

CULTURAL/HISTORICAL NOTE

Educational opportunities for women in Ariosto's time were much more limited than those for men (See Connections, page 830). Nevertheless, a few prosperous and educated families, particularly in northern Italy, allowed women to share in the Humanist devotion to scholarship. Among these women were Eleanora of Ferrara, wife of the Ariosto family patron Duke Ercole d'Este, and her daughters Isabella and Beatrice. (cont.)

VOCABULARY IN CONTEXT

- Although the horseman wore the semblance of a chivalrous knight, he was actually a hard-hearted, unmerciful villain.

CULTURAL/HISTORICAL NOTE (CONT.)

For more information on the role of women during the Renaissance, refer to Bonnie S. Anderson and Judith P. Zinsser, *A History of Their Own: Women in Europe from Prehistory to the Present.*

Answers to Guided Reading Questions

❶ The knight in white armor is bigger and stronger.

❷ The two knights' horses collide. The white knight's horse rises, but Sacripante's horse has died, and he is trapped beneath its fallen body.

Literary Technique

SIMILE, HYPERBOLE, AND CONVENTION

A **simile** is a comparison using *like* or *as.* A **hyperbole** is an exaggeration made for rhetorical effect. A **convention** is an unrealistic element in a literary work that is accepted by readers or viewers because the element is traditional. Point out to students that one of the conventions of both epics and romances is that heroes in battle are often compared to animals such as lions, bulls, or rams. (Students will discuss this type of simile further in the first Understanding Literature question.) Another convention is the use of exaggeration or hyperbole in battle descriptions. Ask students to identify an example of hyperbole in the battle described on this page. Why do they think writers and readers came to accept hyperbole as a convention in this type of literature?

ANSWERS

Students should note that "The mountain trembles, as the knights engage, / From its green base to the bare peak it rears," is an example of hyperbole. Students may suggest that hyperbole makes battle scenes seem more dramatic and exciting, so it came to be accepted as a convention.

❶ *Which of the knights is bigger and stronger?*

61

Awaiting his approach, the king defies
The cavalier, thinking to come off best;
But, in comparison of strength and size,
The oncomer, I think, would pass the test.
Cutting the king's boast short, the knight applies
His spurs and quickly puts his lance in rest.
The other, furious, retorts; then both
Full tilt[3] are galloping in all their wrath.

62

No lions run, no bulls advance with rage
In enmity so deadly or so fierce
As these two foemen in the war they wage.
With equal skill each other's shield they pierce.
The mountain trembles, as the knights engage,
From its green base to the bare peak it rears.
And well it is the hauberks[4] stand the test,
Else would each lance be driven through each breast.

❷ *What is the result of the conflict?*

63

The chargers ran unswerving on their course.
Like rams colliding head to head they were.
The pagan's[5] failing to withstand the force
Of impact, fell at once and did not stir
(Although so fine a steed). The other horse
Went down, but rose at once, touched by the spur.
The horse of Sacripante lay prostrate,
Its rider pinned beneath its lifeless weight.

64

The unknown champion, who sat erect,
Seeing the other underneath his steed,
Judged he had done sufficient in respect
Of that encounter, and no further need
Was there to fight; a path which ran direct
Ahead he chose and galloped off at speed.

3. **Full tilt.** At full speed
4. **hauberks.** Coats of armor
5. **The pagan's.** Sacripante's

Words for Everyday Use

pros • trate (präs´ trāt´) *adj.,* thrown or fallen to the ground

Vocabulary in Context

• The servant lay prostrate before the emperor as a sign of humility.

Illustration by Arthur Rackham. Courtesy of Wellesley College Library, Special Collections

Before one from his tangle could unwind him,[6]
The other[7] put a mile or so behind him.

65

As when a ploughman, dazed with stupefaction,
After a thunderbolt has struck, aghast,
Slowly uprights himself where by its action
Beside his lifeless oxen he was cast,
And views, dismayed, the shrivelling contraction
Of pine-trees stripped and withered by the blast,

6. **Before one . . . him.** In other words, before Sacripante could escape from under his lifeless horse
7. **other.** The unknown knight in white armor

Words for Everyday Use

stu • pe • fac • tion (sto͞o´pə fak´shən) *n.,* stunned amazement
dis • may (dis mā´) *vt.,* make afraid or discouraged

Literary Note

Inform students that this excerpt from *Orlando Furioso* skips from canto to canto in following part of Bradamante's story because the work is episodic in nature. In other words, Ariosto strings together a number of different story lines all related to the epic battle taking place between the Christians and the Saracens. One of the reasons why *Orlando Furioso* has long been renowned as the greatest of Italian romantic epic poems is Ariosto's skill in interweaving the many tales he tells. He often juxtaposes sad elements of one story with a comic scene from a different story. He will build a story to a peak of suspense before temporarily abandoning it to turn to other matters. This technique maintains the reader's interest; for hundreds of years, readers have eagerly read on, seeking to discover how an episode concludes. (Students may be familiar with this technique from serial television shows.) This technique is particularly effective because of *Orlando Furioso*'s great length—the poem is longer than most novels. The disadvantage of excerpting any work of *Orlando Furioso*'s length and structure is that it is necessary to focus on one particular strand in the epic, so the reader never sees Ariosto's skill in interweaving tales using cliff-hanging conclusions and interesting juxtapositions, nor does the reader experience Ariosto's talent for telling a wealth of tales.

Vocabulary in Context

- Witnessing firsthand the devastating force of a tornado filled Chris with stupefaction.
- Although the journey was long and arduous, it did not dismay Roland but filled him with confident good cheer.

Answers to Guided Reading Questions

❶ Angelica lifts the dead horse off Sacripante's back. Sacripante is ashamed to have been defeated and in need of help in front of Angelica.

❷ Angelica tells Sacripante that the outcome of the jousting match was his horse's fault. *Responses will vary.* Some students may say that Angelica is insincere because the white knight was obviously a better jouster.

Cultural/Historical Note

On April 11, 1512, Duke Alfonso of Ferrara, who was allied with the French, captured the Italian city of Ravenna from the Pope and Spain during a bloody battle. Ariosto visited the battlefield the next day and was horrified to see dead bodies forming a carpet that covered several miles. This devastation was largely the result of new weaponry: artillery, or large guns, had replaced the swords, lances, and arrows used to fight earlier battles. Ariosto includes artillery in one story in *Orlando Furioso.* (This inclusion is an example of an anachronism, as artillery would not have been in use when the story is set.) Ariosto includes this anachronism to speak out against the use of artillery. Orlando throws the cannons of a king into the sea, condemning them: "Accursed and abominable tool, / In Tartarean depths devised and forged / By that Beelzebub beneath whose rule / The world to its destruction thus is urged." Ariosto was bold to follow his conscience in this way because his condemnation had the potential to offend his patron, Alfonso I of the House of Este, who succeeded upon his father's death. Alfonso is renowned for making the artillery in Ferrara the best in Italy. Ariosto himself found battle without guns, such as that between Sacripante and Brada-mante, far more chivalrous and noble.

So Sacripante rises to his feet,
The damsel having witnessed his defeat.

66

He sighs and groans, but not because a foot
Or arm is broken or is out of place,
But shame alone so makes his colour shoot
That never has he worn so red a face.
Not only has he been defeated, but
Angelica, to add to his disgrace,
Now lifts the heavy burden from his back
And, save for her, all power of speech he'd lack.

❶ *What does Angelica do for Sacripante? How does Sacripante feel about what has happened to him?*

67

'O, pray, my lord,' said she, 'be not dismayed:
Your honour's not impugned because you fell;
But rather should the blame be squarely laid
Upon this hack,[8] which served you none too well,
Its jousting days being over. I'd have said
Yon knight gained little glory and, to tell
The truth, he now the victory should yield,
For he, not you, was first to leave the field.'

❷ *In what way does Angelica comfort Sacripante? Do you think that she is sincere in her consolation? Why, or why not?*

68

And while the damsel thus consoles the king,
They see, with horn and wallet at his side,
An envoy on a nag[9] come galloping.
Weary he seems, and breathless from his ride.
He has, they find, no messages to bring,
But asks the king if he by chance has spied
On horseback in the forest a brave knight
With armour, shield and helmet-plume of white.

69

The pagan answered: 'Here, as you can see,
He has unhorsed me, and not long ago
He left; and who it was thus dealt with me,

8. **hack.** Horse
9. **envoy on a nag.** Messenger on a worn-out horse

Words for Everyday Use

im • pugn (im pōōn´) *vt.,* attack as false or lacking integrity

Vocabulary in Context

- Shara felt that her opponent's claim that she did not spend class revenues wisely might impugn her reputation for honesty.

In case we meet again, I fain[10] would know.'
The envoy said: 'In my capacity
I will inform you without more ado:
You have been felled from horseback by a foeman
Who is a valiant and courageous woman.

70
'She is as beautiful as she is brave;
Nor will I hide her celebrated name:
She at whose hands just now you suffered have
Such ignominy and undying shame
Is Bradamante.' Then the envoy gave
His nag its head. The king, his cheeks aflame,
Knows neither what to say nor what to do
In the dishonoured state he's fallen to;

71
For, having failed to fathom what had come
To pass, he recognizes finally
That by a woman he was overcome. . . .

♦ ♦ ♦

❶ *What does the envoy reveal?*

❷ *How does Sacripante feel about what the envoy has told him?*

FROM CANTO II

[*Editor's note: Bradamante, the female knight who defeated Sacripante, is in love with Ruggiero, a Saracen knight from Africa. After Bradamante leaves Sacripante and Angelica, she comes across a weeping knight and asks him to tell her his story. The knight says that his beloved was stolen by another knight on a winged horse. Searching for his lady, the knight had come upon the steel castle where the lady was held captive. Bradamante's beloved Ruggiero and his companion Gradasso had agreed to help the knight, so they challenged the rider of the winged horse. With the help of a magic shield, the winged knight had captured and imprisoned Ruggiero and Gradasso.*]

10. **fain.** Eagerly; gladly

WORDS FOR EVERYDAY USE

ig • no • min • y (ig´nə min´ē) *n.*, shame and dishonor

fath • om (fath´əm) *vt.*, understand thoroughly

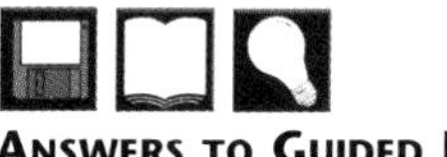

ANSWERS TO GUIDED READING QUESTIONS

❶ The envoy reveals that the knight in white armor who felled Sacripante is a beautiful and brave woman named Bradamante.

❷ Sacripante is both amazed and ashamed.

LITERARY NOTE

Sacripante is not alone in being "overcome" by love for Angelica. Many of the knights in *Orlando Furioso* are driven by love for her, but she spurns them all, playing each against the other and behaving kindly only when she requires their assistance. The title hero Orlando is eventually driven mad by love of her, and even Bradamante's beloved Ruggiero for a time forgets Bradamante when he is overcome with passion for Angelica. Although Angelica never falls in love with these great heroes, she eventually does fall in love with and marry a common soldier named Medoro. Ironically, she falls in love with him after she finds him alone and dying and tends him in his piteous state. In many romances, knights fall in love with fair maidens after rendering them service or aiding them in some way. For Angelica, the reverse is true. Inform students about the many noble knights who pursue Angelica and her eventual choice of a husband. Encourage them to discuss what Ariosto seems to be indicating about love. What is significant about her preference to choose a beloved rather than be chosen? What is significant about her taking the active role in aiding Medoro while he is in a passive state?

VOCABULARY IN CONTEXT

- The basketball player felt he would never live down the ignominy of missing the shot that could have won his team the game.
- No one was able to fathom Philip's reason for behaving so strangely at Sunday brunch.

Answers to Guided Reading Questions

➊ Pinabello is the opposite of a true knight—he is unchivalrous and treacherous.

Literary Note

Although *Orlando Furioso* may be an unfamiliar work to twentieth-century English readers, the work is still renowned and well read in its native Italy. English readers and writers of earlier centuries were as familiar with Ariosto's work as they were with Petrarch's. Christopher Marlowe drew some of the characters in his *Tamburlaine* from *Orlando Furioso*, and Robert Greene wrote a stage adaptation of Ariosto's work. Shakespeare drew some inspiration for *As You Like It* from Ariosto's work. Edmund Spenser was an avowed admirer of Ariosto, and John Milton quotes part of the beginning of *Orlando Furioso* at the beginning of *Paradise Lost.* Other notable admirers of Ariosto and his work include Samuel Johnson, Alexander Pope, Sir Walter Scott, and George Gordon, Lord Byron.

Illustration by Arthur Rackham Courtesy Wellesley College Library, Special Collections

58

The knight resumed his attitude of woe
When he had thus accounted for its cause.
His name and lineage you now must know:
Count Anselm Altaripa's son, he was
Named Pinabel,[11] of all true knights the foe.
Born a Maganzan,[12] he obeyed no laws
Of chivalry, and of that breed accurst
In acts of treachery he was the worst.

➊ *What type of a knight is Pinabello?*

59

With changing looks the Maid[13] in silence heard
The story the Maganzan thus narrated.
The mention of Ruggiero's name had stirred
Great joy, leaving her countenance elated;

11. **Pinabel.** Also known as Pinabello
12. **Maganzan.** Pinabello is a member of the house of Maganza, infamous for treachery
13. **the Maid.** Bradamante is often called by this title.

Words for Everyday Use

e • late (ē lāt´) *vt.,* raise the spirits of; make very happy or proud

Vocabulary in Context

- When Elinor was depressed, a gift of flowers could elate her.

But learning then how her dear love had fared,
When by a magic shield he'd been defeated,
She grew distressed and would not rest content
With one account alone of the event.

60

When she had heard the story through and through,
She said: 'Sir knight, I bid you be of cheer.
This day may yet prove fortunate to you
And serviceable my arrival here.
Let both of us at once press onward to
The robber's den which holds all we hold dear.
Not wasted effort will our journey be
If Fortune treats me not unfavourably.'

61

'Is it your will,' the cavalier replied,
'That I should travel back again across
These rugged mountains, acting as your guide?
To me, thus to retrace my steps will be no loss,
For I have lost my all and more beside.
To you this journey is most perilous;
But if, despite my warning, you see fit
To risk imprisonment, then so be it.'

❶ *What warning does Pinabello give Bradamante? What do you think will happen? Why?*

62

Thus having spoken, turning, he remounts
His steed and guides the Maid along the course
She's chosen for Ruggiero's sake; she counts
As naught[14] the risk of capture or of worse.
As they pursue their journey, all at once
They hear behind them, shouting himself hoarse,
A messenger who calls to them to wait.
It is the envoy we have seen of late.

63

From Narbonne and Montpellier report
He brings that all the standards of Castile

14. **naught.** Nothing

WORDS FOR EVERYDAY USE

per • il • ous (per´ə ləs) *adj.,* dangerous

Answers to Guided Reading Questions

❶ Pinabello warns Bradamante that the journey is dangerous and might end in imprisonment. *Students' predictions will vary.*

Literary Technique

IRONY OF SITUATION

Inform students that **irony** is a difference between appearance and reality. **Irony of situation** is when an event occurs that violates the expectations of the characters, the reader, or the audience. Encourage students to discuss the following questions: Why is Bradamante's setting out to rescue Ruggiero an example of irony of situation in a romance? Why do you think Ariosto chose to include this ironic situation? What does Ariosto seem to be indicating about contemporary views of gender roles?

ANSWERS

It is an example of irony of situation because in romances male knights typically rescue imprisoned females, not the other way around. Ariosto may be questioning whether all women are as helpless as they are made to seem in much of the literature of his day.

Vocabulary in Context

• Few had the courage to undertake the perilous quest.

Answers to Guided Reading Questions

❶ King Charles has given Bradamante governorship of the city of Marseilles because he marvels at her daring deeds.

❷ Bradamante is unsure of what she should do—her duty draws her to protect Marseilles, but her love urges her to rescue Ruggiero. She decides to rescue Ruggiero.

Cross-curricular Activities

SOCIAL STUDIES

Encourage students to work in groups of four of five to create maps of southern Europe, where most of the action in *Orlando Furioso* takes place. Some groups should create maps of the area as it is today, while others should create a map with boundaries as they existed when Ariosto lived. On their maps, students should include pictures or photos that they believe characterize the region during their assigned time period. They should also include the place names mentioned in this selection. Students might then compare and contrast their maps to note how Europe has changed since Ariosto's day.

Have now been raised, with those of Aigues Mortes;
And to the Maid, Marseilles makes an appeal,[15]
In this predicament, for her support,
Giving the envoy orders to reveal
The need they have of her return; and this
The purpose of his expedition is.

64

This city, with the land that lies between
The estuaries[16] of the Var and Rhône,
To Bradamante by King Charles[17] has been
With confidence entrusted as her own,
For, marvelling, the Emperor has seen
How in great deeds of daring she has shone.
Now from Marseilles an envoy, as I said,
Has come to ask assistance of the Maid.

❶ *Why has King Charles given Bradamante governorship of Marseilles?*

65

Suspended between yes and no, she tries
To choose: should she return again that day?
Towards Marseilles the path of duty lies;
The flames of love urge her another way.
She chooses finally the enterprise
Of rescuing Ruggiero; come what may,
If to the task she should unequal prove,
At least she'll be imprisoned with her love.

❷ *Why is Bradamante "suspended between yes and no"? What does she decide to do?*

66

She quietens, by means of an excuse,
The envoy's fears and leaves him satisfied.
Turning her horse, her journey she pursues

15. **From Narbonne . . . an appeal.** The messenger is from Marseilles, in southeastern France. He tells Bradamante that the Muslims from Spain are readying for battle in the south of France, and he asks her for her help in repelling these Spanish invaders. In canto 2, stanza 64, it is revealed that Charlemagne has given Bradamante governorship of Marseilles.
16. **estuaries.** Inlets, or arms, of the sea, especially where a river meets the sea
17. **Charles.** Charlemagne

Words for Everyday Use

pre • dic • a • ment (prē dik´ ə mənt) *n.*, difficult or unpleasant situation

ex • pe • di • tion (eks´pə dish´ən) *n.*, journey, voyage, march for some definite purpose

Vocabulary in Context

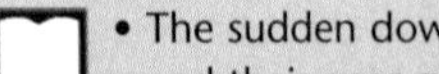

- The sudden downpour caused quite a predicament for the campers because their tents leaked and their gear got soggy.
- Alexander the Great set out from Greece on an expedition to conquer Asia.

With Pinabello, who can scarcely hide
His furious annoyance at the news:
Deep is his hatred of the Clairmont side,[18]
And many <u>tribulations</u> he foresees
If she should once discover who he is.

67

Between the Clairmont and Maganza House
The enmity was ancient and intense.
Many a time they'd split each other's brows;
The toll[19] of blood between them was immense.
And so in his black heart the villain vows
That on the first occasion Fate presents
He will betray the unsuspecting Maid
And leave her unescorted, without aid.

1 *What does Pinabello decide to do? Why?*

68

And, concentrating on his evil scheme,
In hate and fear so deeply did he brood,
That he mistook the way, as in a dream,
And woke to find himself in a dark wood.
There in the very centre, facing him,
Its peak a naked flint, a mountain stood.
And she whose father was the Duke Aymon,[20]
Keeping her guide in sight, still followed on.

69

This is the moment, he now thinks, to try
To rid himself of her who seems a knight.
'Before the sun,' he said, 'has left the sky,
We ought to seek a shelter for the night.
Beyond this mountain, in a vale[21] near by,
A splendid castle stands, if I am right.
Wait here for me, while to the naked rock
I now ascend, and with my own eyes look.'

18. **Deep . . . side.** Pinabello is a member of the house of Maganza, and Bradamante is a descendent of the Clairmont house. These two houses were traditionally in conflict, and all Maganzans were known as traitors.
19. **toll.** Amount taken or extracted
20. **she . . . Aymon.** Bradamante
21. **vale.** Valley

Words for Everyday Use

trib • u • la • tion (trib´yo͞o lā´shən) *n.,* something that causes suffering or distress

Answers to Guided Reading Questions

1 Pinabello decides to betray Bradamante because of the long tradition of enmity between their houses.

Quotables

"In the middle of the journey of our life I came to myself in a dark wood where the straight way was lost."

—Dante Alighieri

"As I walked through the wilderness of this world, I lighted on a certain place where was a Den, and I laid me down in that place to sleep; and, as I slept, I dreamed a dream."

—John Bunyan

Literary Technique

SYMBOL

Read the above quotations to students and inform them that a **symbol** is a thing that stands for or represents both itself and something else. A **conventional symbol** is one with traditional, widely recognized associations. Dark woods and wilderness in literature are often symbols for spiritual or moral confusion. Ask students to discuss the following questions: What might the "dark wood" into which Pinabello leads Bradamante represent? What is he thinking about as he wanders in this place? What might the mountain in the center of the wood represent?

ANSWERS

The "dark wood" may represent Pinabello's immoral, evil, and dark nature. He is planning to betray Bradamante. The mountain represents the "pinnacle" of Pinabello's evil scheme—it is the place where he will betray her.

Vocabulary in Context

- The extremely high tides brought by the hurricane caused as much <u>tribulation</u> as the winds themselves.

Answers to Guided Reading Questions

❶ Pinabello is looking for a good place to hide from Bradamante and abandon her. He finds a deep cavern in the earth.

❷ Pinabello has decided to kill Bradamante or to leave her in the cavern.

❸ Pinabello says he has seen a damsel in distress in the cavern. He has not seen such a damsel.

Cross-curricular Activities

Social Studies

Encourage students to work in groups to research the real-life conflicts that inspired this story about an epic struggle between Christianity and Islam. Some groups might focus on different aspects of the Moorish or Muslim penetration into Europe, while others might focus on aspects of Europe's response—the Crusades into the Near East. Each group should present its findings to the class as an oral report. As a whole, the class might then discuss the conflict between the Christians and the Muslims. What were the costs of this conflict? What harm did it bring? Did it have any positive aspects? If so, what?

70

With this, along the lonely mountain-slope
He pricked his charger to the topmost peak;
And, looking round about him in the hope
Of finding, in that desolate and bleak
Terrain, a corner where there might be scope[22]
To play his cruel game of hide-and-seek,
He came upon a cavern, dark and deep,
For thirty yards descending, sheer and steep.

❶ *For what is Pinabello looking? What does he find?*

71

There was a spacious portal far below
Which to a larger chamber access gave.
From the interior shone forth a glow
As if a torch lit up the mountain cave.
But meanwhile Bradamante was not slow
To follow from afar the scheming knave.
Fearing to lose him if she stayed behind him,
She clambered to the cavern's mouth to find him.

72

And when the traitor knew his first design,
For all his careful plans, would be in vain,
To kill or leave her there, or to combine
Two such betrayals, he began again
To weave a strange new scheme; first, to refine
His treachery, he hastened to explain
That in that deep and dark and hollow place
He glimpsed a damsel with a winsome face.

❷ *What new plan has Pinabello decided upon?*

73

From her fair aspect and her costly gown,
She seemed of noble and of high degree;
But by her attitude of grief she'd shown
That she resided there unwillingly.
When, to learn more about her, he'd begun
The steep descent into the cavity,
Her captor from the inner chamber stepped
And forced her back again, for all she wept.

❸ *What does Pinabello say he has seen in the hollow? Has he really seen this?*

22. **scope.** Room or opportunity for action

Words for Everyday Use

ter • rain (ter rān´) *n.,* geographical area

win • some (win´səm) *adj.,* attractive in a sweet, engaging way

Vocabulary in Context

- The mountainous terrain made the tiny village nestled atop the peak virtually inaccessible.
- Marla baby-sat for a little girl who caused endless mischief, but whenever she flashed Marla her winsome smile, Marla instantly forgave her.

74

Fair Bradamante, who's as credulous
As she is brave, believes his every word.
She longs to be of help, but perilous
She knows descent will be without a cord.
Then on an elm-tree she sees pendulous
A long and leafy branch; with her sharp sword
She quickly cuts it from the parent bole[23]
And lowers it with care into the hole.

75

The severed end she gave to Pinabel
To hold, and, climbing down, herself suspended,
Feet first, into the cavity, until
She dangled at full length, her arms extended.
He, smiling, asked the Maid if she jumped well,
Then flung his hands apart, as he'd intended,
Shouting in triumph: 'Perish all your breed,
And would I might deal thus with all their seed!'

❶ *What does Pinabello do?*

76

The fate of her whom Pinabel thus cursed
Proved other than his traitor's heart had hoped.
Reaching the bottom of the cavern first,
The sturdy branch, though breaking as it dropped,
Softened her fall and saved her from the worst.
Thus his design to kill the Maid was stopped.
Unconscious for a space of time she lay,
And how she later fared I'll later say.

❷ *What saves Bradamante from death?*

23. **bole.** Tree trunk

Words for Everyday Use

cred • u • lous (krej´o͞o ləs) *adj.,* tending to believe too readily

pen • du • lous (pen´dyo͞o ləs) *adj.,* hanging or bending downward

Answers to Guided Reading Questions

❶ Pinabello lets go of the branch so that Bradamante will fall into the cavern.

❷ Her fall is softened because she first falls on the branch of the tree.

Vocabulary in Context

- Because Jeremy never would even consider telling a lie, he was credulous enough to believe what less honest people told him.
- The pendulous branches of the weeping willow formed a green cavern in which the children hid.

Answers to Guided Reading Questions

1 A horse was as important to a knight as his or her sword or armor, and by taking a knight's horse, one was essentially taking a knight's knighthood away.

2 A room that has been constructed as a church lies farther back in the cave.

ANALYTIC SCALES FOR RESPONDING IN WRITING

(SEE PAGE 846.)

Assign a score from 1 to 25 for each grading criterion below. (For more detailed evaluation, see the evaluation forms for writing, revising, and proofreading, Assessment Portfolio 4.1–4.9.)

1. *Ottava Rima*

- **Content/Unity.** The stanza relates a particular part of a plot that a group of students developed.
- **Organization/Coherence.** The stanza contains eight lines using the rhyme scheme *abababcc.* Details in this stanza are presented in a logical order. (Students may or may not choose to experiment with iambic pentameter.)
- **Language/Style.** The stanza uses vivid and precise nouns, verbs, and modifiers.
- **Conventions.** The stanza avoids errors in spelling, grammar, usage, mechanics, and manuscript form.

▶ Additional practice is provided in the Essential Skills Practice Book: Writing 1.8, 1.10.

FROM CANTO III

4

. . . But let us turn to him against whose guile
No shield or breastplate can afford defence.
I speak of Pinabel of Gano's line:
To kill the valiant Maid was his design.

5

The traitor never doubted that the Maid
In the precipitous ravine lay dead.
His countenance a pale and sickly shade,
From the contaminated cave he sped
(By him infected). Where his charger[24] stayed
He soon returned; like one who has been bred
For evil, making matters even worse,
He took away fair Bradamante's horse.

1 *Why might taking away a knight's horse be such a terrible deed?*

6

But let us leave him who, as he thus schemed
Death to another, his own death procured,
And turn to her whom treachery, it seemed,
Both death and burial in one ensured.
Bemused at first and all her senses dimmed
By the fall's impact and the shock endured,
She rose and entered through a door which gave
Into the second and the larger cave:

7

A spacious room, it seemed like a revered
And hallowed church, much sanctified by prayer,
And by the skill of architecture reared
On alabaster[25] columns choice and rare;
And at the very central point appeared
An altar where a lamp burned bright and fair.
So brilliant was the flame with which it glowed,
It shed its light on the entire abode.

2 *What surprising thing does Bradamante find in the cave?*

24. **charger.** Horse
25. **alabaster.** Smooth, white stone

WORDS FOR EVERYDAY USE

guile (gīl) *n.,* slyness and cunning in dealing with others

pre • cip • i • tous (prē sip´ə təs) *adj.,* steep; sheer

ra • vine (rə vēn´) *n.,* long, deep hollow in the earth's surface

pro • cure (prō kyo͞or´) *vt.,* get or bring about by some effort

be • muse (bē myo͞oz´) *vt.,* bewilder, confuse

Vocabulary in Context

- The traitor's guile allowed him to operate unnoticed for several months.
- The Grand Canyon is so precipitous that journeys into it can be made only by foot or on mules.
- Several years ago, an earthquake opened a ravine in the earth.
- Liz promised Phil that she would procure the autographed baseball card he desired.
- When Henry traveled to the city for the first time, he was bemused—there were so many options he didn't know what to do first.

8

Moved by devout humility and awe,
The Maid began, with heart as well as lips,
Soon as the sacred edifice she saw,
To offer prayers to God; kneeling, she keeps
Her head and eyes in reverence held low,
When through a creaking door a lady steps;
Ungirt, unshod,[26] her hair unbound, the Maid
She greeted by her name, then these words said:

9

'O valiant Bradamante, not by chance,
But in fulfilment of a will divine,
You have arrived. I had precognizance[27]
Of your predestined journey to this shrine,
For Merlin[28] said, in a prophetic trance,
Your presence here would coincide with mine.
Thus I have waited to disclose to you
What Heaven has ordained that you must do.

10

'This is the ancient, memorable cave
Which Merlin fashioned, the enchanted seer
Of whom some memory perhaps you have.
The Lady of the Lake betrayed him here.
His sepulchre is yonder in the nave.[29]
Therein his flesh decays. He, without fear,
To please her, with her treachery complied:
Alive he laid him in the tomb—and died.

11

'His spirit with his corpse will ever dwell
Until the trumpet on the Day of Doom
Shall summon it to Heaven or to Hell,
When a dove's form, or raven's, it assume.
Alive, too, is his voice. Clear as a bell
You'll hear it issue from the marble tomb,
For always he has answered questionings
Concerning history and future things. . . .

[*Editor's note: The lady tells Bradamante that she has been waiting for Bradamante's arrival for a month. Bradamante then approaches Merlin's tomb to hear his prophecy.*]

26. **Ungirt, unshod.** Without belt or shoes
27. **had precognizance.** Saw the event before it occurred by means of extrasensory powers
28. **Merlin.** Magician from Arthurian legend
29. **sepulchre . . . nave.** *Sepulchre*—vault for burial, grave; *nave*—part of a church forming the main part of the building

1 *What does Bradamante do in this holy place?*

2 *Who greets Bradamante? In what way did Pinabello speak more truly than he knew?*

3 *Who predicted Bradamante's arrival?*

4 *What has happened to Merlin? What can Merlin do?*

Answers to Guided Reading Questions

1 Bradamante kneels to pray.

2 A lady greets Bradamante. Pinabello told Bradamante that he saw a lady in the cavern to trick her into descending there, but, unknown to Pinabello, there is in fact a lady in the cavern.

3 Merlin predicted Bradamante's arrival.

4 Merlin was betrayed by the Lady of the Lake in this cavern, and now his grave rests there. Merlin's spirit, however, has remained within his body, and he answers questions concerning history and the future.

ANALYTIC SCALES FOR RESPONDING IN WRITING

(SEE PAGE 846.)

Assign a score from 1 to 25 for each grading criterion below. (For more detailed evaluation, see the evaluation forms for writing, revising, and proofreading, Assessment Portfolio 4.1–4.9.)

2. Critical Essay

- **Content/Unity.** The essay explains the way the author portrays the men in the story.
- **Organization/Coherence.** The essay begins with an introduction that includes the thesis of the essay. The introduction is followed by supporting paragraphs with clear transitions. The essay ends with a solid conclusion.
- **Language/Style.** The essay uses vivid and precise nouns, verbs, and modifiers.
- **Conventions.** The essay avoids errors in spelling, grammar, usage, mechanics, and manuscript form.

▶ Additional practice is provided in the Essential Skills Practice Book: Writing 1.20.

Answers to Guided Reading Questions

❶ Merlin says that Bradamante is destined to be the ancestor of descendants who will bring honor to all of Italy. He values her chastity and her nobility.

❷ Merlin says that Bradamante's offspring will restore Italy to the glory it experienced during the height of the Roman empire.

❸ Ruggiero will be rescued. Otherwise he would not be able to marry Bradamante.

Selection Check Test with Answers

ex. With whom is Sacripante in love?
Sacripante is in love with Angelica.

1. Who is the knight who defeats Sacripante?
Bradamante is the knight who defeats Sacripante.

2. Who is the knight who tells Bradamante about Ruggiero's capture?
Pinabello is the knight who tells Bradamante about Ruggiero's capture.

3. From where does the envoy who asks Bradamante for help come?
The envoy comes from Marseilles.

4. What treacherous thing does Pinabello do to Bradamante?
Pinabello lets go of a branch and drops Bradamante into a deep cavern.

5. Who is in the cavern?
Both a lady and the spirit of Merlin are in the cavern.

16

Scarcely has Bradamante passed the doors
That guard the threshold of the secret room
When the still-living spirit of the corse[30]
Speaks thus in dearest accents from the tomb:
'May Fortune favour every wish of yours,
O chaste and noble maiden, in whose womb
The fertile seed predestined is to spring
Which honour to all Italy will bring.

❶ *What does Merlin say about Bradamante? What two of her qualities does he value?*

17

'Since in your veins the ancient blood of Troy
Commingled from two purest strains has been,
From it will bloom the ornament, the joy
Of every lineage the sun has seen
Where Indus, Tagus, Danube, Nile deploy
Their course, or in all lands that lie between
The globe's two poles. Among your progeny
Dukes, marquises and emperors I see.

18

'Thence will come forth the mighty cavaliers
And captains, by whose strategy and sword
The pride and glory of her former years
To valiant Italy will be restored;
Thence princes, whose just rule the world reveres,
As when the wise Octavius[31] was lord,
Or Numa[32] reigned. Beneath the sway they'll hold
Mankind will see renewed the age of gold.

❷ *What does Merlin say Bradamante's offspring will do?*

19

'And that the will of Heaven be effected
Concerning you who as Ruggiero's wife
From earliest beginnings were selected,
Follow courageously your path in life.
By no consideration be deflected
From what you now resolve, for, in your strife
With the vile robber who your love immures,
A speedy victory your fate ensures.' ■

❸ *What will happen to Ruggiero? How do you know?*

30. **corse.** Corpse
31. **Octavius.** Gaius Julius Cæsar Octavianus (63 BC–AD 14), later called Augustus, first Roman emperor
32. **Numa.** Numa Pompilius (715–673 BC), second legendary king of Rome

Words for Everyday Use

prog • e • ny (präj´ə nē) *n.*, children or descendants
im • mure (im myoor´) *vt.*, shut up within walls

Vocabulary in Context

- Queen Elizabeth I never married or left any progeny; therefore James VI of Scotland, a distant relative, was chosen to be the next monarch of England after her death.
- Richard III was so eager to seize the throne that he immured the rightful princes in the notorious Tower of London, where they were later killed.

Responding to the Selection

Explain whether you find Bradamante to be heroic. Are other characters in the selection heroic? Why, or why not?

Reviewing the Selection

RECALLING / **INTERPRETING**

1. What news does the envoy bring Sacripante? What description does the envoy give of Bradamante? ▶▶ How does Sacripante feel when he hears the envoy's news? In what way has Sacripante been overcome by two women?

2. What does Bradamante decide after hearing Pinabello's story? What does the envoy ask Bradamante to do? ▶▶ Of the two conflicting feelings Bradamante experiences, which feeling does Bradamante act upon? Why?

3. What motivates Pinabello to betray Bradamante? What does Pinabello do to entrap Bradamante in the cavern? ▶▶ Is Pinabello a true knight? Why, or why not? How does Pinabello know that his trick will work?

4. Whom does Bradamante meet in the cavern? What prediction does she hear? What will "the mighty cavaliers and captains" do? ▶▶ Why do you think Merlin reveals this prediction to Bradamante?

SYNTHESIZING

5. Which characters respect Bradamante? How can you tell? Which characters do not respect Bradamante? Why? Given Ariosto's portrayal of Bradamante, how would you characterize the author's attitude toward women?

Understanding Literature (Questions for Discussion)

1. **Simile.** A **simile** is a comparison using *like* or *as.* Writers of romances have long used similes to describe battle scenes. What simile does the writer use to describe Sacripante and Bradamante during the jousting match? What simile does the writer use to describe Sacripante after he is defeated?

2. **Stanza, Rhyme, and Rhyme Scheme.** A **stanza** is a recurring pattern of grouped lines in a poem. See the Handbook of Literary Terms for a description of the different types of stanzas. **Rhyme** is the repetition of sounds at the ends of words. A **rhyme scheme** is

RESPONDING TO THE SELECTION

Encourage students to discuss the following characters: Angelica, Sacripante, Pinabello, Ruggiero, and Merlin.

ANSWERS FOR REVIEWING THE SELECTION

RECALLING AND INTERPRETING

1. **Recalling.** The envoy tells Sacripante that the knight who felled him is a woman. The envoy says that Bradamante is beautiful, brave, courageous, and valiant. **Interpreting.** Sacripante is both amazed and ashamed. Sacripante has been overcome by Angelica in love and by Bradamante in war.

2. **Recalling.** Bradamante decides that she and Pinabello will go to the steel tower to rescue Ruggiero and Pinabello's beloved. The envoy asks Bradamante to return to Marseilles to protect the city. **Interpreting.** Bradamante's sense of duty draws her to Marseilles, but her deep love urges her to rescue Ruggiero. She acts upon her love because it is stronger.

3. **Recalling.** Pinabello's family and Bradamante's family have an ancient enmity. Pinabello tells Bradamante that he saw a damsel in distress being held captive in the cavern. **Interpreting.** Pinabello is not a true knight, because he is unchivalrous, treacherous, and dishonest. Pinabello knows that, unlike himself, Bradamante is too kind and bold to refuse help to someone in distress and that she is too honest to believe that others might be dishonest.

4. **Recalling.** Bradamante meets a lady who has been waiting for her, as well as Merlin's spirit. She hears that she will be the founder of a long line of heroes, "the mighty cavaliers and captains," who will restore Italy to its former glory. **Interpreting.** Merlin wants to inspire confidence in Bradamante so she won't be discouraged by Pinabello's treachery.

(cont.)

ANSWERS FOR REVIEWING THE SELECTION (CONT.)

SYNTHESIZING

Responses will vary. Possible responses are given.

5. Sacripante grudgingly respects Bradamante for her military prowess, as shown by his amazement when her identity is revealed. The envoy respects Bradamante for her bravery and courage as revealed by his words of praise. Charlemagne respects Bradamante's daring so much that he makes her the governor of Marseilles. The lady in the cavern shows her respect by waiting for a month to meet Bradamante, and Merlin reveals his respect for her by predicting such an encouraging future for her. Pinabello does not admire Bradamante, perhaps because of jealousy—Bradamante is a better knight than he is, and he may feel threatened by such a powerful female knight. Students may say that Ariosto admired women and held modern notions about what women can accomplish.

Answers for Understanding Literature

Responses will vary. Possible responses are given.

1. **Simile.** The two knights are described as if they were lions or bulls in stanza 62. In stanza 65, the defeated Sacripante is compared to a plowman who discovers that a thunderbolt has killed his oxen.

2. **Stanza, Rhyme, and Rhyme Scheme.** There are eight lines in each stanza of this poem. Such stanzas are called octaves. The rhyme scheme of this poem is *abababcc.*

ANALYTIC SCALES FOR RESPONDING IN WRITING

Grading scales for Responding in Writing appear on pages 842 and 843.

Answers for Language Lab

1. she
2. her
3. his *(that* and *this* are also acceptable)
4. That
5. yourself

▶ Additional practice is provided in the Essential Skills Practice Book: Language 2.4 and 2.5.

indicated using the letters of the alphabet starting with *a*, with rhyming lines being given the same letter. For example the rhyme scheme of

The wayward flocks from field to fold
When rivers rage and rocks grow cold,
and Philomel becometh dumb;
The rest complains of cares to come.

is *aabb,* because *fold* and *cold* rhyme and *dumb* and *come* rhyme. How many lines are in each stanza of *Orlando Furioso*? What are such stanzas called? What is the rhyme scheme of this poem?

Responding in Writing

1. **Creative Writing: *Ottava Rima. Ottava rima*** is a stanza form made up of eight lines of iambic pentameter (see Handbook of Literary Terms), rhyming *abababcc.* Work in groups of four to five students to create a poem composed of four or five stanzas in *ottava rima.* To begin, your group should choose a plot for your poem and assign a part of this plot to each student. You may wish to write your group poem about a typical romantic adventure, or you may wish to satirize such an adventure. Map out your plot on a story map before beginning. Then, write a stanza on your part of the plot in *ottava rima.* If you have difficulty writing in iambic pentameter, try to write an octave, or eight lines with the rhyme scheme *abababcc,* without worrying about meter.

2. **Critical Essay: Gender Roles.** Bradamante is portrayed as a strong and valiant knight. Write an analytical essay in which you explore the way the author portrays the men whom Bradamante encounters. Are they portrayed in the typically masculine roles of medieval romance, or do they seem to take on roles more typical of women in medieval romances? A good way to get started would be by examining Bradamante and Ruggiero's relationship and by comparing and contrasting Bradamante and Pinabello. Write an introduction in which you define your thesis; support this thesis in the following paragraphs; and come to a conclusion in a final paragraph.

Language Lab

Pronouns. Before Ariosto reveals that Bradamante is a woman, he refers to her using personal pronouns such as *he, his,* and *him.* Although this makes the plot more suspenseful, these pronouns are technically incorrect. Read the Language Arts Survey 2.4, "Personal Pronouns," and 2.5, "Reflexive, Intensive, and Demonstrative Pronouns." Then, on your own paper, fill in the blanks in the sentences below with the correct pronoun.

1. Bradamante agreed that ______ had never met a wiser magician than Merlin.
2. Angelica wants to take ______ time before she marries.
3. The envoy gave her ______ message.
4. ______ is why she raced off.
5. You ______ should read *Orlando Furioso.*

PREREADING

Sonnet 23
by Louise Labé, translated by Willis Barnstone

FRANCE

About the Author

Louise Labé (1525–1566). One of the great poets of the Lyons school of Humanist poets, Louise Labé was born Louise Charly in Lyons, France. Her father, Pierre Charly, was a wealthy man called Labé after one of his properties. Louise Labé married an older man and friend of her father named Ennemond Perrin. Her father and her husband were both ropemakers, winning her the name *"La belle Cordière,"* or "The Beautiful Ropemaker." She was also called *"la belle Amazone"* because of her skills on horseback and as an archer. These skills also led to legendary reports that she fought on horseback with Henry II in battles against the Spanish and that she jousted as part of a celebration in honor of his visit to Lyons. Labé fell in love with the poet Olivier de Magny, the subject of many of her poems, when he was passing through Lyons. Although de Magny returned her love, he had to leave Lyons to go to Rome. In his long absence, Labé grew attached to another. De Magny returned and wrote a poem insulting Labé and her husband. Labé moved to the country and died a few years later in Parcieux-en-Dombres after an outbreak of plague. Her death was widely mourned by the people of the city.

About the Selection

A **sonnet** is a fourteen-line poem, usually in iambic pentameter, that follows one of a number of different rhyme schemes. Louise Labé was one of the earliest French writers of the sonnet. She wrote her first sonnet in Italian and twenty-three others in French. She followed the form of the Petrarchan sonnet. The Petrarchan or Italian sonnet is divided into two parts—an octave, or eight-line stanza, and a sestet, or six-line stanza. The rhyme scheme of the octave is *abbaabba*. The rhyme scheme of the sestet can be *cdecde*, *cdcdcd*, or *cdedce*. This translation of the poem uses a slight variation on the traditional rhyme scheme. The subjects of sonnets vary, but many sonnets have been written on the subject of love, often unrequited, and many refer to an idealized woman. Labé's **Sonnet 23** responds to such idealization and presents a portrait of love and separation.

CONNECTIONS: The Woman Warrior

Although the role of the warrior is often considered a man's role, many women, like Louise Labé, have been active in battle. Cleopatra of Egypt, Boadicea of the Iceni of Early Britain, Trung Trac and Trung Nhi of Vietnam, Joan of Arc of France, and Rani of Jhansi of India are all women who led armies into battle. Legendary women warriors also include Athena and the Amazons of Greek mythology and Durga of Hindu myth. In fictional works, women warriors include Britomart in Edmund Spenser's *The Faerie Queene,* Bradamante and Marfisa in Ludovico Ariosto's *Orlando Furioso* (see page 830), and Fu Mu Lan in Maxine Hong Kingston's *The Woman Warrior* (see page 1104).

GOALS/OBJECTIVES

Studying this lesson will enable students to

- empathize with the speaker's feelings toward a former beloved
- define *tone* and identify the tone of a poem
- explain the characteristics of a Petrarchan sonnet
- determine the meter of a poem
- write a couplet on a chosen subject
- write a critical essay about Petrarchan ideals and Labé's rejection of these ideals
- find clichéd phrases and replace these phrases with more original ones

ADDITIONAL RESOURCES

READER'S GUIDE
- Selection Worksheet 10.3

ASSESSMENT PORTFOLIO
- Selection Check Test 2.10.5
- Selection Test 2.10.6

ESSENTIAL SKILLS PRACTICE BOOKS
- Writing 1.8, 1.10, 1.20
- Language 2.72

PREREADING EXTENSIONS

When Labé published her book of verse, she dedicated it to Clémence de Bourges, a noblewoman of good reputation, hoping that this dedication might prevent public censure. Nevertheless, many people were shocked by Labé's poetry and claimed that no decent woman would write so frankly about love and passion. Encourage students to discuss what they think the people who condemned Labé would think of contemporary American society. What would these people think of a modern young woman if they were given the opportunity to meet one? Would students define Labé's attitudes as "modern"? Why, or why not?

SUPPORT FOR LEP STUDENTS

PRONUNCIATIONS OF PROPER NOUNS AND ADJECTIVES

Pi • erre Char • ly (pi (ə)r´ shär lē´)
Lou • ise La • bé (lwēz´ lä bā´)
O • liv • ier de Ma • gny (o lēv´yā də mä gnē´)
En • ne • mond Per • rin (en nā mōn´ pər ən´)

ADDITIONAL VOCABULARY

flare—sudden, bright light
martyrdom—severe, prolonged pain or death, especially when suffered for a noble cause
rave—talk incoherently or wildly, as in a delirious or demented state

READER'S JOURNAL

As an alternative activity, you might ask students to write about how they feel about the conventional standards of beauty they see represented in the media. In what ways do these ideals of beauty affect people?

Answers to Guided Reading Questions

❶ Long ago, the person addressed praised the speaker's golden hair and compared her eyes to the sun.

❷ The speaker accuses her friend of trying to enslave her while telling her that he was serving her.

Selection Check Test with Answers

EX. What is the first thing the speaker says was praised long ago?

The speaker says that her golden hair was praised.

1. To what were the speaker's eyes and beauty compared?

They were compared to the flare of two suns.

2. What binds the love of the speaker's beloved?

Death binds this love.

3. What was the brutal goal of the speaker's friend?

The goal was to make the speaker a slave.

4. What feeling does the speaker express?

The speaker expresses outrage.

5. Of what is the speaker sure?

The speaker is sure that her friend's martyrdom is as hard as her "black dawn," or difficult days.

READER'S JOURNAL

Think about a time when you were separated from somebody for whom you cared very deeply. In your journal, write about the separation and how it made you feel. You may also wish to write about any emotions the other person may have expressed at the time.

Sonnet 23

LOUISE LABÉ, TRANSLATED BY WILLIS BARNSTONE

❶ *What did the person being addressed do long ago?*

❷ *What does the speaker accuse her friend of trying to do to her?*

What good is it to me if long ago
you eloquently praised my golden hair,
compared my eyes and beauty to the flare
of two suns where, you say, love bent the bow,
sending the darts that needled you with grief?
Where are your tears that faded in the ground?
Your death? by which your constant love is bound
in oaths and honor now beyond belief?
Your brutal goal was to make *me* a slave
beneath the ruse of being served by you.
Pardon me, friend, and for once hear me through:
I am outraged with anger and I rave.
Yet I am sure, wherever you have gone,
your martyrdom is hard as my black dawn. ■

WORDS FOR EVERYDAY USE

el • o • quent • ly (el´ə kwənt lē) *adv.,* persuasively and expressively

ruse (ro͞oz) *n.,* trick

Vocabulary in Context

- Ryan eloquently persuaded us to support him in his campaign for student body president.
- One of the most famous ruses in literature is Odysseus's scheme to sneak Achaean soldiers into the city of Troy by hiding them in a wooden horse.

Responding to the Selection

How would you react if the speaker of the poem were addressing you directly? With some of your other classmates, discuss how you might respond to the speaker if this poem addressed you and your actions. You may wish to try to write a response in a verse of your own.

Reviewing the Selection

RECALLING / **INTERPRETING**

1. Which of the speaker's qualities were once praised by the person she addresses? ▶▶ How does the speaker feel about the praise to which she refers?
2. According to lines 6 and 7, what two things is the speaker unable to find? ▶▶ What do the things she asks about represent?
3. How does the speaker define her friend's true goal? ▶▶ What might the friend have done that the speaker considers a ruse?
4. What feelings does the speaker express in lines 12–14? How does she think her friend feels? ▶▶ Why does the speaker use the term *martyrdom?* Why might the speaker be sure that her friend feels this way?

SYNTHESIZING

5. Does this sonnet present an idealized beloved? Does it present an idealized picture of love? Explain your response.

Understanding Literature (Questions for Discussion)

1. **Sonnet.** A **sonnet** is a fourteen-line poem, usually written in iambic pentameter, that follows one of a number of different rhyme schemes. The Petrarchan or Italian sonnet is divided into two parts—an octave, or eight-line stanza, and a sestet, or six-line stanza. What idea is expressed in the octave? What idea is expressed in the sestet? In what way are the octave and the sestet related?
2. **Tone. Tone** is the emotional attitude toward the reader or toward the subject implied by a literary work. A work might have a tone that is familiar, ironic, playful, sarcastic, serious, or sincere. What is the tone of the octave of Sonnet 23? How does the tone change in the sestet? Why do you think the speaker calls the lover "friend" and says "for once hear me through" in line 11? Is the speaker sincere or sarcastic in the final couplet? Use evidence from the sonnet to support your opinion.
3. **Meter.** The **meter** of a poem is its rhythmical pattern. English verse is generally described as being made up of rhythmic units called *feet.* In words such as *insist,* in

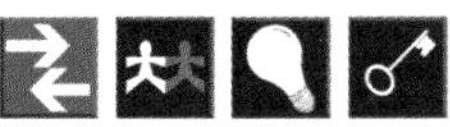

RESPONDING TO THE SELECTION

Some students might prefer to work in pairs to role play a conversation between the speaker and her friend.

ANSWERS FOR REVIEWING THE SELECTION

RECALLING AND INTERPRETING

1. **Recalling.** The speaker says that the person she addresses once praised her golden hair, her beauty, and her eyes. **Interpreting.** The speaker does not think the praise means much.
2. **Recalling.** The speaker has not seen the person's tears or his death. **Interpreting.** The tears and the promise to love her until his death represent the strength of the person's love. That the friend has not shown these two things puts the truth and strength of his love in doubt.
3. **Recalling.** The speaker says her friend's goal was to make her a slave. **Interpreting.** The friend may have treated the speaker kindly until she was willing to do anything for him, whereupon he seems to have abandoned her.
4. **Recalling.** The speaker is outraged and sorrowful. She says she thinks that her friend is suffering. She may think he is not suffering at all. **Interpreting.** The speaker may use the term *martyrdom* to mean that her friend has behaved as though his suffering for love has ennobled him in some way. The speaker says her friend is suffering as she is but she may be speaking ironically. (cont.)

ANSWERS FOR REVIEWING THE SELECTION (CONT.)

SYNTHESIZING

Responses will vary. Possible responses are given.

5. The sonnet does not present an idealized beloved. The speaker of the sonnet rejects her beloved's idealization of her and portrays this person as anything but ideal. He seems to be inconstant and selfish.

ANSWERS FOR UNDERSTANDING LITERATURE

Responses will vary. Possible responses are given.

1. Tone. The tone of the octave is sarcastic. The tone changes in the sestet to one of anger and resignation. The speaker seems to be asking for an opportunity to speak her mind, which her beloved has never granted her. *Responses will vary.*

2. Sonnet. In the octave, the speaker questions the words and actions of her beloved. In the sestet, the speaker accuses her friend and expresses anger directly. The idea brought up in the octave that the beloved was insincere is stated more firmly in the sestet. The feelings expressed in the octave are also expanded upon and resolved in the sestet.

3. Meter. There are ten stresses in each line and five feet. The meter is iambic pentameter with some slight variations.

ANSWERS FOR LANGUAGE LAB

Responses will vary. Possible responses are given.

1. My beloved's hair shimmers like the desert sand.
2. Her eyes gleam like a fortune-teller's crystals.
3. Her disposition is as mild and bland as cream of wheat.
4. The hot flush of her cheeks contrasts with the moonlight glow of her skin.
5. Her voice rings like a bell, and her steps soar like cumulus clouds on a breezy day.

► Additional practice is provided in the Essential Skills Practice Book: Language 2.72.

which the first syllable is weakly stressed and the second syllable is strongly stressed the type of foot is iambic. The stresses in poetry can be marked as follows

⌣ / ⌣ / ⌣ / ⌣ / ⌣ /
What good is it to me if long ago

The ⌣ shows a weak stress and the / shows a heavy stress. Mark the stress patterns in the rest of the lines of Sonnet 23. You may find it helpful to say the lines aloud and refer to the description of meter in the Handbook of Literary Terms. How many stresses are in each line? How many feet? A complete description of the meter of a line includes both the term for the type of foot that predominates and the term for the number of feet in the line. Common types of feet include iambic (⌣ /), trochaic (/ ⌣), anapestic (⌣ ⌣ /), dactylic (/ ⌣ ⌣), and spondaic (/ /). Terms used to describe the number of feet in a line include *monometer* for a one-foot line, *dimeter* for a two-foot line, *trimeter* for a three-foot line, *tetrameter* for a four-foot line, *pentameter* for a five-foot line, *hexameter* or *Alexandrine* for a six-foot line, *heptameter* for a seven-foot line, and *octameter* for an eight-foot line. What is the meter of this poem?

Responding in Writing

1. **Creative Writing: Couplet.** A couplet is a pair of rhyming lines, such as the two that end Louise Labé's Sonnet 23. Many couplets have been written on the theme of love, but a couplet can be about any subject. Choose a subject that is important to you. You may wish to write about love, friendship, the environment, or passion for a sport or other activity. To gather ideas for your couplet, freewrite about your subject. Write out your idea in a long sentence of regular prose. Then experiment with different wordings of the same idea, ones that make use of a regular meter and end rhymes.

2. **Critical Essay: Rejection of Petrarchan Ideals.** Read "Insights: The Petrarchan Ideal" on page 851. Then write a critical essay on Labé's rejection of these ideals. In your first paragraph, briefly define Petrarchan ideals, explain how Labé rejected them, and present reasons why Labé may have done so. Support your reasoning with examples in subsequent paragraphs, and come to a conclusion in a final paragraph. To define Petrarchan ideals, you might use examples from Petrarch's sonnets (see pages 251 and 851).

Language Lab

Clichés. Descriptions used in love poetry can be clichéd. **Clichés** often begin as original phases but become dulled through overuse. Many lines from traditional love poetry, once original and surprising, have since been copied and overused, as in the sentences below. On your own paper, rewrite the sentences, replacing clichés with more original phrases that have the same or similar meaning.

1. My beloved is a golden-haired goddess.
2. Her eyes sparkle brighter than two stars.
3. Her disposition is as mild as a lamb's.
4. Her cheeks are two roses amidst her face of snow.
5. She sings like an angel and walks without touching the ground.

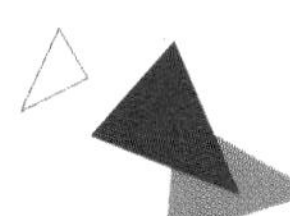

The Petrarchan Ideal

Petrarch (see page 251) had an enormous influence on many writers during the Renaissance and in later years. He is credited with creating the rhyme scheme of the Italian sonnet which is widely recognized and still used today. Of perhaps even greater influence was the way in which he described Laura, the woman he loved. The language that he used to describe her beauty and stunning qualities has been widely borrowed. Petrarch described Laura as having golden hair or hair like golden wires, eyes like the sun or like stars, skin like ivory or snow, cheeks like roses, and movements like a goddess or an angel. Read, for example, Petrarch's Sonnet 90:

She used to let her golden hair fly free
For the wind to toy and tangle and molest;
Her eyes were brighter than the radiant west.
(Seldom they shine so now.) I used to see

Pity look out of those deep eyes on me.
("It was false pity," you would now protest.)
I had love's tinder heaped within my breast;
What wonder that the flame burned furiously?

She did not walk in any mortal way,
But with angelic progress; when she spoke,
Unearthly voices sang in unison.

She seemed divine among the dreary folk
Of earth. You say she is not so today?
Well, though the bow's unbent, the wound
bleeds on.

While many poets chose to use similar comparisons and descriptions, others rejected such ideals. A famous example is William Shakespeare's Sonnet 130.

My mistress' eyes are nothing like the sun;
Coral is far more red than her lips' red;
If snow be white, why then her breasts are dun;
If hair be wires, black wires grow on her head.
I have seen roses damasked, red and white,
But no such roses see I in her cheeks;
And in some perfumes is there more delight
Than in the breath that from my mistress reeks.
I love to hear her speak, yet well I know
That music hath a far more pleasing sound;
I grant I never saw a goddess go;
My mistress, when she walks, treads on the ground.
And yet, by heaven, I think my love as rare
As any she belied with false compare.

Shakespeare does not claim that his beloved has the golden hair, the radiant eyes, the angelic movement, or the divine voice that Petrarch claims for his beloved. Instead, in Shakespeare's sonnet, he claims that the woman he loves is nothing like the idealized, wondrous beauties popularly praised in poetry, yet in the final couplet of this sonnet, he concludes that she is wonderful anyway in her actual, earth-bound form.

Louise Labé, in Sonnet 23, also rejects the Petrarchan ideal, but while Shakespeare shares Petrarch's perspective as a man admiring a beloved, Labé takes the perspective of the woman upon whom such praises have been heaped. Labé's beloved had praised, in Petrarchan fashion, her "golden hair" and "eyes and beauty [like] . . . the flare/of two suns." Now, however, she also dismisses his tears and his proclamations that he would love her until death. Labé, in this sonnet, finds such praise and promises to be empty. Petrarch's writing helped to shape the way in which, even today, people write and talk about love, but many writers have rejected Petrarchan conventions as overly idealistic and unrealistic and have proceeded to create more realistic depictions of love.

Analytic Scales for Responding in Writing

Assign a score from 1 to 25 for each grading criterion below. (For more detailed evaluation, see the evaluation forms for writing, revising, and proofreading, Assessment Portfolio 4.1–4.9.)

1. Couplet

- **Content/Unity.** The couplet is written on a specific theme.
- **Organization/Coherence.** The couplet is a pair of rhyming lines that present ideas in a sensible order.
- **Language/Style.** The couplet uses vivid and precise nouns, verbs, and modifiers.
- **Conventions.** The couplet avoids errors in spelling, grammar, usage, mechanics, and manuscript form.

▶ Additional practice is provided in the Essential Skills Practice Book: Writing 1.8., 1.10.

2. Critical Essay

- **Content/Unity.** The essay explains how and why Labé rejects Petrarchan ideals.
- **Organization/Coherence.** The essay begins with an introduction that includes the thesis of the essay. The introduction is followed by supporting paragraphs with clear transitions. The essay ends with a solid conclusion.
- **Language/Style.** The essay uses vivid and precise nouns, verbs, and modifiers.
- **Conventions.** The essay avoids errors in spelling, grammar, usage, mechanics, and manuscript form.

▶ Additional practice is provided in the Essential Skills Practice Book: Writing 1.20.

ADDITIONAL RESOURCES

READER'S GUIDE

- Selection Worksheet 10.4

ASSESSMENT PORTFOLIO

- Selection Check Test 2.10.7
- Selection Test 2.10.8

ESSENTIAL SKILLS PRACTICE BOOKS

- Writing 1.8, 1.20
- Study and Research 4.12, 4.13, 4.20

    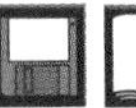 

PREREADING EXTENSIONS

Have students brainstorm a list of actions that might be considered quixotic or be called "tilting at windmills."

Students can also brainstorm other words that have entered the English language through their use in literature—for example, *platonic* from Plato.

SUPPORT FOR LEP STUDENTS

PRONUNCIATIONS OF PROPER NOUNS AND ADJECTIVES

Al • don • za Lor • en • zo (al dōn´ zä lô ren´zō)
Bu • ce • pha • lus (byo͞o sef´ə ləs)
Cid Ruy Di • az (sid rü ē´ dē´äs)
Don Qui • xo • te (dän´kē hōt´ā)
Dul • cin • e • a del To • bo • so (dül´sē nā´ä del tō bō´sō)
Qui • xa • na (kē hä´nä)
Ro • zin • an • te (rō zən än´tā)
San • cho Pan • za (san´chō pan´zə)

ADDITIONAL VOCABULARY

arable—good for growing crops
brace—pair
cleaving—splitting, cutting
cleft—split
conjecture—guess
delusion—fantasy, imagining
domestic—having to do with the home (cont.)

PREREADING

from *The Ingenious Hidalgo Don Quixote de la Mancha*
by Miguel de Cervantes, translated by Walter Starkie

SPAIN

About the Author

MIGUEL DE CERVANTES
1547–1616

Miguel de Cervantes, the most famous of all Spanish authors, was born near Madrid to a family of seven children. Little is known of his early life or education. His father combined the duties of a barber and a surgeon, and his family traveled from town to town. In 1571, Cervantes fought bravely in a sea battle against the Turks and was severely wounded, losing the use of his left hand. In 1575, he was captured and sold into slavery in Algiers. There he remained for five years, until he was ransomed and returned to Spain in 1580. In 1584, he married Ana de Villafranca from the province of La Mancha. The following year, he published his first novel, *La Galatea.* From 1582 to 1587, he wrote numerous plays. As a government officer, he helped raise provisions for the attack of the Spanish Armada on England during the reign of Queen Elizabeth I. The first part of his most famous work, *The Ingenious Hidalgo Don Quixote de la Mancha,* was published in 1605, the second part in 1615.

About the Selection

Don Quixote de la Mancha is a **mock epic** in which a deranged gentleman, having spent too much time reading romances about the adventures of knights in shining armor, decides to become a knight, enlisting as his unwilling companion a servant named Sancho Panza. This **parody** of medieval romance, with its absurd, comic, and tragic hero, has enjoyed enormous popularity throughout the ages and has inspired countless works of literature, music, and art. The novel has also given to the English language the word *quixotic,* meaning "impractical" or "foolishly idealistic," and the phrase *to tilt at windmills,* meaning "to make a ludicrous effort."

CONNECTIONS: *Don Quixote* and Medieval Romance

At the root of medieval romances, such as those read and imitated by the hero of *Don Quixote,* were stories of adventure. These stories dealt with the exploits of knights—with battles, crusades, tournaments, jousts, and the loves that inspired them. Typically, a romance would present a series of loosely connected adventures, each a trial of the knight's virtues—loyalty, honesty, courtesy, skill, and courage. The goal of such quests or trials was to win the favor of a worthy lady. Romances were centered on the idealization of women and on knights' faithful service to them. (See Themes: Chivalry and Courtly Love, page 720.) It is this type of romance that Cervantes parodies in *Don Quixote.*

GOALS/OBJECTIVES

Studying this lesson will enable students to

- have a pleasant experience reading a mock epic
- define *medieval romance, courtly love, character, parody,* and *satire*
- identify elements of medieval romance and courtly love in the selection
- classify a character
- write a parody
- analyze the selection as a parody of medieval romance
- use search tools and card catalogs

Have you ever read a book or seen a movie in which you wanted to take part? Think of a scene from one of these books or movies. Imagine yourself taking part in the scene. What part would you play? What would happen to you? Write about such a scene in your journal.

FROM

The Ingenious Hidalgo Don Quixote de la Mancha

MIGUEL DE CERVANTES, TRANSLATED BY WALTER STARKIE

FROM PART I, BOOK 1

THE QUALITY AND MANNER OF LIFE OF THAT FAMOUS GENTLEMAN DON QUIXOTE OF LA MANCHA

At a village of La Mancha, whose name I do not wish to remember, there lived a little while ago one of those gentlemen who are wont to keep a lance in the rack, an old buckler, a lean horse, and a swift greyhound. His stew had more beef than mutton in it and most nights he ate the remains salted and cold. Lentil soup on Fridays, "tripe and trouble"[1] on Saturdays and an occasional pigeon as an extra delicacy on Sundays, consumed three-quarters of his income. The remainder was spent on a jerkin[2] of fine puce, velvet breeches, and slippers of the same stuff for holidays, and a suit of good, honest homespun for week-days. His family consisted of a housekeeper about forty, a niece not yet twenty, and a lad who served him both in the field and at home and could saddle the horse or use the pruning-knife. Our gentleman was about fifty years of age, of a sturdy constitution, but wizened and gaunt-featured, an early riser and a devotee of the chase.[3] They say that his surname was Quixada or Quesada (for on this point the authors who have written on this subject differ), but we may reasonably conjecture that his name was Quixana. This, however, has very little to do with our story: enough that in its telling we swerve not a jot from the truth. You must know that the above-mentioned gentleman in his leisure moments (which was most of the year) gave himself up with so much delight and gusto to reading books of chivalry that he almost entirely neglected the exercise of the chase and even the management of his domestic affairs: indeed his craze for this kind of literature became so extravagant that he sold many acres of arable land to purchase books of knight-errantry, and he carried off to his house as many as he could possibly find. . . .

1 *What does Quixana like to do in his spare time? What becomes of this interest?*

♦ ♦ ♦

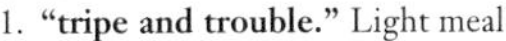

1. **"tripe and trouble."** Light meal
2. **jerkin.** Short, close-fitting jacket or vest
3. **the chase.** Hunting for sport

READER'S JOURNAL

If students say that they have never wanted to be part of a book or a movie, ask them to imagine themselves in the last book they read or the last movie that they watched. Students should explain how they would feel about their role. Have them discuss their responses in small groups.

ANSWERS TO GUIDED READING QUESTIONS

1 In his spare time, Quixana likes to read romances. His interest in romances becomes an obsession which causes him to neglect everything else. He sells his property to buy books about knights.

SPELLING AND VOCABULARY WORDS FROM THE SELECTION

sonorous
caitiff
enmity

SUPPORT FOR LEP STUDENTS (CONT.)

doughty—brave
enchantment—magical spell
enmity—hatred; anger
immersed—completely involved
insolence—disrespect
lance—long, pointed spear
lineage—ancestral line
moldering—growing old
pompous—overly proud
puissant—brave
sallying—rushing forth
stratagem—trick, plan
surname—last name, family name

Art Note

Born in Strassbourg, France, **(Paul) Gustave Doré** (1832–1883) was a prolific printmaker and illustrator. He produced paintings and sculptures as well, but his best works were illustrations. His fantastic, dreamlike scenes were well received by Romantics. Among his famous illustrations are those he made for works by Rabelais and Balzac and for Dante's *Inferno*. Refer students to the illustration on page 856 as well.

Answers to Guided Reading Questions

1 Quixana's thoughts are filled with "a host of fancies he [has] read in his books." He is consumed with the ideas of magic spells, battles, challenges, courtships, and other matters of romances. He begins to think of the fictional worlds as real.

Cross-curricular Activities

ARTS AND HUMANITIES

Have students listen to a recording or view a film of the musical *Man of La Mancha*. Ask students to discuss the similarities and differences between the original version and these adaptations. Refer them to the Connections about the adaptation of literary works to musicals on page 914.

Don Quixote Fighting the Windmill. *Illustrated by Gustave Doré. Courtesy of Wellesley College Library, Special Collections*

1 *What thoughts fill Quixana's imagination? What happens as he mulls over these thoughts?*

In short, he so immersed himself in those romances that he spent whole days and nights over his books; and thus with little sleeping and much reading his brains dried up to such a degree that he lost the use of his reason. His imagination became filled with a host of fancies he had read in his books—enchantments, quarrels, battles, challenges, wounds, courtships, loves, tortures, and many other absurdities. So true did all this phantasmagoria[4] from books appear to him that in his mind he accounted no history in the world more authentic. He would say that the Cid Ruy Diaz was a very gallant knight, but not to be compared with the Knight of the Burning Sword, who with a single thwart blow cleft asunder a brace of hulking blustering giants. He was better pleased with Bernardo del Carpio, because at Roncesvalles he had slain Roland the Enchanted by availing himself of the stratagem Hercules had employed on Antaeus, the son of the Earth, whom he squeezed to death in his arms. He praised the giant Morgante, for he alone was courteous and well-bred among that monstrous brood puffed up with arrogance and insolence. Above all, he admired Rinaldo of Montalvan, especially when he saw him sallying out of his castle to plunder everyone that came his way; and, moreover, when, beyond the seas, he made off with the idol of Mahomet, which, as history says, was of solid gold. But he would have parted with his housekeeper and his niece

4. **phantasmagoria.** Rapidly changing series of imagined figures or events

into the bargain for the pleasure of rib-roasting the traitor Galalon.

At last, having lost his wits completely, he stumbled upon the oddest fancy that ever entered a madman's brain. He believed that it was necessary, both for his own honor and for the service of the state, that he should become knight-errant and roam through the world with his horse and armor in quest of adventures, and practice all that had been performed by the knights-errant of whom he had read. He would follow their life, redressing all manner of wrongs and exposing himself to continual dangers, and at last, after concluding his enterprises, he would win everlasting honor and renown. The poor gentleman saw himself in imagination already crowned Emperor of Trebizond by the valor of his arm. And thus, excited by these agreeable delusions, he hastened to put his plans into operation.

The first thing he did was to furbish some rusty armor which had belonged to his great-grandfather and had lain moldering in a corner. He cleaned it and repaired it as best he could, but he found one great defect: instead of a complete helmet there was just the simple morion.[5] This want he ingeniously remedied by making a kind of visor out of pasteboard, and when it was fitted to the morion it looked like an entire helmet. It is true that, in order to test its strength and see if it was sword-proof, he drew his sword and gave it two strokes, the first of which instantly destroyed the result of a week's labor. It troubled him to see with what ease he had broken the helmet in pieces, so to protect it from such an accident, he remade it and fenced the inside with a few bars of iron in such a manner that he felt assured of its strength, and without making a second trial, he held it to be a most excellent visor. Then he went to see his steed, and although it had more cracks than a Spanish *real* and more faults than Gonela's jade which was all skin and bone, he thought that neither the Bucephalus of Alexander nor the Cid's Babieca could be compared with it. He spent four days deliberating over what name he would give the horse; for (as he said to himself) it was not right that the horse of so famous a knight should remain without a name, and so he endeavored to find one which would express what the animal had been before he had been the mount of a knight-errant, and what he now was. It was indeed reasonable that when the master changed his state, the horse should change his name too, and assume one pompous and high-sounding as suited the new order he was about to profess. So, after having devised, erased and blotted out many other names, he finally determined to call the horse Rozinante—a name, in his opinion, lofty, sonorous and significant, for it explained that he had only been a "rocín" or hack before he had been raised to his present status of first of all the hacks in the world.

Now that he had given his horse a name so much to his satisfaction, he resolved to choose one for himself, and after seriously considering the matter for eight whole days he finally determined to call himself Don Quixote. Wherefore the authors of this most true story have deduced that his name must undoubtedly have been Quixana, and not Quesada, as others would have it. Then remembering that the valiant Amadis had not been content to call himself simply Amadis, but added thereto the name of his kingdom and native country to render it more illustrious, calling himself Amadis of Gaul, so he, like a good knight, also added the name of his province and called himself

❶ *What does Quixana decide that he must do?*

❷ *What name does Quixana give his horse? Explain the significance of this name to Quixana. What makes this name humorous?*

❸ *What name does Quixana choose for himself? Why does he choose this name?*

5. **morion.** Crested helmet without a visor

WORDS FOR EVERYDAY USE

so • no • rous (sə nôr´əs) *adj.,* having an impressive sound

Answers to Guided Reading Questions

❶ He decides that he must become a knight-errant and seek adventures in order to achieve fame.

❷ Quixana names his horse Rozinante. To Quixana the name is significant because it explains that the horse had been only a hack before being raised to its current status. The name is humorous because it points out that Quixana's horse is not a fine creature, yet it sounds lofty, as though the horse were a fancy steed.

❸ Quixana decides to call himself Don Quixote of La Mancha. He chooses Quixote as a variation of Quixana. He adds "of La Mancha" to his name because he remembers that Amadis was called Amadis of Gaul.

Historical Note

The selection makes many allusions to fictional and historical heroes. You may wish to share the following information with your students about two of these historical figures. Both Alexander of Macedonia and Cid Ruy Diaz would make interesting topics for research projects.

- Alexander of Macedonia (356–323 BC), often referred to as Alexander the Great, is legendary for the forceful expansion of his empire, which involved overthrowing the Persian empire. He studied under Aristotle. Bucephalus was his much-beloved horse.
- Cid Ruy Diaz (c. 1040–1099), often referred to as the Cid (or by the Spanish as *El Cid*), was a Castilian leader and hero. He captured Valencia, at the time a kingdom of the Moors. He is the subject of a twelfth-century epic, "The Song of the Cid," and a drama by Pierre Corneille, *Le Cid.*

Vocabulary in Context

- The sonorous sounds of the huge bells made us stop talking and pay attention.

Answers to Guided Reading Questions

❶ Dulcinea is a simple country girl named Aldonza Lorenzo. Quixote calls her Dulcinea because the name sounds like that of a princess or lady of quality and does not vary too much from her original name.

Selection Check Test with Answers

EX. What genre does *Don Quixote* parody?
It parodies medieval romance.

1. What does Quixana most like to do?
He enjoys reading books about chivalry.

2. What does Quixana decide he must become?
He decides he must become a knight-errant.

3. What does Quixana name his horse?
He names it Rozinante.

4. Why does Don Quixote attempt to fight the windmills?
He thinks that the windmills are giants.

5. Who advises Don Quixote not to fight the windmills?
Sancho Panza advises Don Quixote not to fight the windmills.

Don Quixote and Sancho. *Illustrated by Gustave Doré. Courtesy of Wellesley College Library, Special Collections*

Don Quixote of La Mancha. In this way, he openly proclaimed his lineage and country, and at the same time he honored it by taking its name.

Now that his armor was scoured, his morion made into a helmet, his horse and himself new-named, he felt that nothing was wanting but a lady of whom to be enamored; for a knight-errant who was loveless was a tree without leaves and fruit—a body without soul. "If," said he, "for my sins or through my good fortune I encounter some giant—a usual occurrence to knight-errants—and bowling him over at the first onset, or cleaving him in twain, I finally vanquish and force him to surrender, would it not be better to have some lady to whom I may send him as a trophy? so that when he enters into her presence he may throw himself on his knees before her and in accents contrite and humble say: 'Madam, I am the giant Caraculiambro, Lord of the Island of Malindrania, whom the never-adequately-praised Don Quixote of La Mancha has overcome in single combat. He has commanded me to present myself before you, so that your highness may dispose of me as you wish.' " How glad was our knight when he had made these discourses to himself, but chiefly when he had found one whom he might call his lady! It happened that in a neighboring village there lived a good-looking country lass, with whom he had been in love, although it is understood that she never knew or cared a jot. She was called Aldonza Lorenzo, and it was to her that he thought fit to confide the sovereignty of his heart. He sought a name for her which would not vary too much from her own and yet would approach that of a princess or lady of quality: he resolved to call her Dulcinea del Toboso (she was a native of that town), a name in his opinion musical, uncommon and expressive, like the others which he had devised. . . .

Q ❶ *Who is Dulcinea? Why does Don Quixote call her that?*

♦ ♦ ♦

FROM PART I, BOOK 7

THE TERRIFYING AND UNPRECEDENTED ADVENTURE OF THE WINDMILLS, AND THE STUPENDOUS BATTLE BETWEEN THE GALLANT BISCAYAN AND THE PUISSANT MANCHEGAN

Just then they came in sight of thirty or forty windmills which rise from that plain, and as soon as Don Quixote saw them, he said to his squire: "Fortune is guiding our affairs better than we ourselves could have wished. Do you see over yonder, my friend Sancho Panza, thirty or more huge giants? I intend to do battle with them and slay them: with their spoils we shall begin to be rich, for this is a righteous war and the removal of so foul a brood from off the face of the earth is a service God will bless."

"What giants?" said Sancho, amazed.

"Those giants you see over there," replied his master, "with long arms: some of them have them well-nigh two leagues in length."

"Take care, sir," answered Sancho; "those over there are not giants but windmills, and those things which seem to be arms are their sails, which when they are whirled round by the wind turn the millstones."

"It is clear," answered Don Quixote, "that you are not experienced in adventures. Those are giants, and if you are afraid, turn aside and pray whilst I enter into fierce and unequal battle with them."

Uttering those words, he clapped spurs to Rozinante, without heeding the cries of his squire Sancho, who warned him that he was not going to attack giants but windmills. But so convinced was he that they were giants that he neither heard his squire's shouts nor did he notice what they were though he was very near them. Instead, he rushed on, shouting in a loud voice: "Fly not, cowards and vile caitiffs; one knight alone attacks you!" At that moment a slight breeze arose, and the great sails began to move. When Don Quixote saw this he shouted again: "Although ye flourish more arms than the giant Briareus, ye shall pay for your insolence!"

Saying this, and commending himself most devoutly to his Lady Dulcinea, whom he begged to help him in this peril, he covered himself with his buckler,[6] couched his lance, charged at Rozinante's full gallop and rammed the first mill in his way. He ran his lance into the sail, but the wind twisted it with such violence that it shivered the spear to pieces, dragging him and his horse after it and rolling him over and over on the ground, sorely damaged.

1 What foe does Don Quixote intend to fight? What is he really battling?

Sancho Panza rushed up to his assistance as fast as his donkey could gallop, and when he reached the knight he found that he was unable to move, such was the shock that Rozinante had given him in the fall.

"God help us!" said Sancho. "Did I not tell you, sir, to mind what you were doing, for those were only windmills! Nobody could have mistaken them unless he had windmills in his brains."

"Hold your peace, dear Sancho," answered Don Quixote; "for the things of war are, above all others, subject to continual change; especially as I am convinced that the magician Freston—the one who robbed me of my room and books—has changed those giants into windmills to deprive me of the glory of victory: such is the enmity he bears against me. But in the end his evil arts will be of little avail against my doughty sword."

"God settle it his own way," cried Sancho, as he helped his master to rise and remount Rozinante, who was well-nigh disjointed by his fall. ■

6. **buckler.** Small, round shield held by a handle or worn on the arm

WORDS FOR EVERYDAY USE

cai • tiff (kāt´if) *n.,* cowardly person

en • mi • ty (en´mə tē) *n.,* hostility; bitter feelings of an enemy

ANSWERS TO GUIDED READING QUESTIONS

1 Don Quixote intends to fight giants. The "giants" he sees are really windmills.

ANALYTIC SCALES FOR RESPONDING IN WRITING

(SEE PAGE 859.)

Assign a score from 1 to 25 for each grading criterion below. (For more detailed evaluation, see the evaluation forms for writing, revising, and proofreading, Assessment Portfolio 4.1–4.9.)

1. Parody

- **Content/Unity.** The parody satirizes a typical heroic adventure.
- **Organization/Coherence.** The parody is arranged in a logical order, such as chronological order.
- **Language/Style.** The parody uses vivid and precise nouns, verbs, and modifiers.
- **Conventions.** The parody avoids errors in spelling, grammar, usage, mechanics, and manuscript form.

▶ Additional practice is provided in the Essential Skills Practice Book: Writing 1.8.

2. Critical Essay

- **Content/Unity.** The essay describes medieval romance and explains how medieval romances are parodied in *Don Quixote.*
- **Organization/Coherence.** The essay begins with an introduction that includes a thesis. The introduction is followed by supporting paragraphs with clear transitions. The essay ends with a solid conclusion.
- **Language/Style.** The essay uses vivid and precise nouns, verbs, and modifiers.
- **Conventions.** The essay avoids errors in spelling, grammar, usage, mechanics, and manuscript form.

▶ Additional practice is provided in the Essential Skills Practice Book: Writing 1.20.

VOCABULARY IN CONTEXT

- Loren had considered Asha a caitiff until she risked her life to save his.
- Enmity between the two countries continued even after the peace treaty was signed.

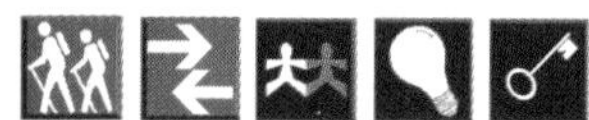

Responding to the Selection

In their role plays, students should present their own views of Don Quixote. Students with both positive and negative perceptions of Don Quixote should work together to discuss his behavior.

Answers for Reviewing the Selection

RECALLING AND INTERPRETING

1. **Recalling.** Quixana decides he must become a knight-errant. In preparation for this life, he gets armor, makes himself a helmet, names his horse Rozinante and himself Don Quixote of La Mancha, and finds a lady to serve. **Interpreting.** His main problem is that the situations in which a knight-errant would take part are imagined. If he were to find true adventure, he would be poorly prepared because his armor and horse are in bad condition.

2. **Recalling.** Don Quixote decides to serve Aldonza Lorenzo, whom he renames Dulcinea del Toboso. **Interpreting.** He imagines her to be a princess. In reality she is a country girl who neither knows nor cares about Quixote's love for her.

3. **Recalling.** He imagines the windmills to be giants. **Interpreting.** *Responses will vary.* Quixote can be seen either as a foolish madman or as a courageous and fanciful believer in the chivalric age. He is made both noble and ludicrous by his faith in the world described in the books of chivalry and by his resulting attempts to make the most common occurrences into adventures.

4. **Recalling.** Quixote, on horseback, charges the windmills, gets his lance caught in one windmill's sail, and is dragged after it, injuring himself. Sancho rushes to Quixote's aid and tries to argue with Quixote about the nature of his adventure. **Interpreting.** Although Sancho Panza realizes

(cont.)

Responding to the Selection

With a small group of your classmates, imagine that you are the neighbors of Don Quixote. Role play a conversation in which you discuss what you think of his quest.

Reviewing the Selection

Recalling		Interpreting
1. After reading many medieval romances, what does Quixana decide that he must do? What preparations does he make for his new life?	▶▶	What problems hinder his plans and preparations?
2. What woman does Don Quixote find to serve?	▶▶	What is the true nature of the relationship that exists between them?
3. What does Don Quixote imagine the windmills to be?	▶▶	Given Quixote's imaginings, what might you say about his character? What makes him both noble and ludicrous?
4. What happens in the battle of the windmills? What does Sancho Panza do to help Don Quixote?	▶▶	Why does Sancho Panza help Quixote to remount for another attack?

Synthesizing

5. Do you know anybody who is quixotic? Can you think of a situation in which somebody you knew was "tilting at windmills," or wasting time trying to do the impossible? Discuss how you reacted or might react to such a person or situation.

Understanding Literature (Questions for Discussion)

1. **Medieval Romance and Courtly Love.** A **medieval romance** is a story from the Middle Ages about the loves and adventures of knights. **Courtly love** is the code of romantic love celebrated in much medieval literature. According to this code, the lover knows himself or herself to be truly in love if he or she is overcome by extreme, transforming emotion. Characters in works celebrating courtly love are often one-dimensional. The female lover is often portrayed in ideal and unrealistic terms. She usually requires that the male lover prove his love through a series of tasks. The male lover is led sometimes to depths of despair and sometimes to heights of courtesy and heroism to prove his worth to his lady. What elements of medieval romance and courtly love are found in these selections from *Don Quixote?*

Answers for Reviewing the Selection (cont.)

that Quixote is not battling giants and although he feels that Quixote's efforts are foolish and dangerous, Sancho adopts the attitude that what will be will be.

SYNTHESIZING

Responses will vary. Possible responses are given.

5. Students might suggest any number of situations in which somebody they knew was trying to do the impossible. They should explain whether their own role was like that of Sancho Panza. Students should explain why they did or did not help the quixotic person.

2. **Character.** A **character** is a person (or sometimes an animal) who figures in the action of a literary work. In literature, a mock hero is a character who burlesques, or imitates derisively and comically, the actions and manner of a traditional hero. Explain whether you consider Don Quixote more a mock hero or more a traditional hero. In what ways is Don Quixote both?

3. **Parody and Satire.** A **parody** is a literary work that imitates another work for humorous, often satirical, purposes. **Satire** is humorous writing or speech intended to point out errors, falsehoods, foibles, or failings. What literary form does Cervantes parody in *Don Quixote?* What elements of this form does Cervantes satirize in these selections from *Don Quixote*?

Responding in Writing

1. **Creative Writing: Parody.** The hero is alive today in popular culture as the superhero of movies, cartoons, and comic strips. Invent your own superhero. Freewrite about the physical appearance, personality traits, heroic qualities, and special powers that your hero possesses. Write a parody of a heroic adventure in which he or she attempts to prove his or her loyalty, honesty, or courage in a rescue scene.

2. **Critical Essay: *Don Quixote*, Cervantes's Parody of Medieval Romance.** Read one or more selections from medieval romances such as Gottfried von Strassburg's *Tristan* (see page 732), Chrétien de Troyes's *Perceval* (see page 722), or one of the many Arthurian romances. Then write an essay in which you describe the medieval romance and discuss how such romances are parodied in *Don Quixote.* Use examples from the romances that you read to support your description of medieval romances. Then explain the ways in which *Don Quixote* imitates such romances as well as the ways in which the imitation is satirical.

Research Skills

Using Search Tools and Card Catalogs. Working in groups of three to four students, create a bibliography of medieval romances and books about the medieval era. Read the Language Arts Survey 4.12, "Using Search Tools" and 4.13, "Using the Card Catalog." Then use either a card or a computerized catalog to find works about medieval subjects. Compile a list of such sources, listing the titles, authors, and publication information.

Answers for Understanding Literature

Responses will vary. Possible responses are given.

1. Medieval Romance and Courtly Love. Quixote practices the values of chivalry, the code of the medieval knight. He is always brave, courteous, and honorable. He follows the code of courtly love by idealizing his lady, loving her from afar, and longing for an adventure in order that he might send his lady a trophy and prove himself a chivalric hero.

2. Character. In many ways Don Quixote is a mock hero. The names he gives his horse, himself, and his beloved can be compared humorously to true heroes of medieval romance. Also, the battle he chooses to fight is not against a living foe but rather against an imagined one. On the other hand, Don Quixote truly believes in the ideals of chivalry and earnestly tries to carry them out.

3. Parody and Satire. Cervantes parodies medieval romance. He satirizes the fantastic giants and monsters, the beautiful but remote princesses, and the incredible exploits of the knights-errant.

Analytic Scales for Responding in Writing

Grading scales for Responding in Writing appear on page 857.

Answers for Skills Activities

RESEARCH SKILLS

Suggest that students also include references to periodicals, audio or video recordings, and online sources about medieval romances or the medieval era. Refer students to the Language Arts Survey 4.20, "Bibliographies and Bibliography Cards" for the correct format for bibliographies.
(cont.)

Answers for Skills Activities (cont.)

As an extension of this activity, students can consult the sources suggested above and provide a brief annotation about the content, style, or suggested use of each source.

► Additional practice is provided in the Essential Skills Practice Book: Study and Research 4.12, 4.13, and 4.20.

ADDITIONAL RESOURCES

Reader's Guide
- Selection Worksheet 10.5

Assessment Portfolio
- Selection Check Test 2.10.9
- Selection Test 2.10.10

Essential Skills Practice Books
- Writing 1.8, 1.10, 1.20
- Study and Research 4.15

PREREADING EXTENSIONS

Encourage students to work in groups to research what happened when Europeans came into contact with the indigenous peoples of the "New World." Some groups may wish to focus on certain European explorers during the Renaissance, while others may choose to focus on the story of a particular native culture, such as the Arawak, the Aztec, or the Inca. Each group should present its findings to the class. Students might then debate the following questions: The age of discovery was undeniably a period of excitement over new lands, new ideas, and new peoples. Was it worth its enormous cost in terms of the suffering inflicted on native peoples? How would the world be different today if this exploration had not taken place? How should explorers have reacted to the peoples they encountered?

SUPPORT FOR LEP STUDENTS

Pronunciations of Proper Nouns and Adjectives

Mi • chel de Mon • taigne (mē shel´ də män ten´yə)

Additional Vocabulary

traffic—buying and selling
successions—acts of taking over an office, estate, or throne

PREREADING

from "Of Cannibals"
by Michel de Montaigne, translated by Donald M. Frame

About the Author

MICHEL DE MONTAIGNE
1533—1592

French essayist **Michel Eyquem de Montaigne** was born near Bordeaux, France. He was educated at an early age by a German tutor who spoke Latin to him. It was not until Montaigne was six years old that he learned to speak French. He studied law in Toulouse. Montaigne married in 1565 and had many children, though only one lived beyond infancy. In 1580, he began a voyage that took him through many countries, including France, Germany, Switzerland, Austria, and Italy. He was still in Italy in 1581 when he received news that he had been elected mayor of Bordeaux, a position his father had held. He served two terms as mayor and helped to ease tensions between Catholics and Protestants. He was imprisoned twice by the Protestant League for supporting Catholic King Henri III. Montaigne spent the end of his life at his chateau.

About the Selection

Montaigne is credited with creating the form of the modern essay. An **essay** is a brief work of nonfiction prose. The original meaning of the term *essay* was "a trial or attempt." Montaigne published three books of essays exploring a variety of subjects.

In 1562, Montaigne met three natives of Brazil who had been brought back to France by explorer Nicolas Durand de Villegagnon. This meeting and his reading of the reports of several travelers to the New World led him to write **"Of Cannibals."** In this essay, Montaigne presents the idea of the noble savage, arguing that the inhabitants of the New World, though often seen as barbarous by Europeans, were more humane, more natural, and, in many ways, superior to Europeans. With a tolerance of other cultures that differed greatly from the views common to his era, Montaigne offers sharp criticism of the horrors that he saw perpetrated by his own culture.

CONNECTIONS: The Age of Discovery and the Noble Savage

Near the end of the fifteenth century, while in search of new trade routes, European explorers "discovered" the Americas. Explorers such as Christopher Columbus, Hernán Cortés, Jacques Cartier, Ferdinand Magellan, and Henry Hudson explored and claimed land in the New World for powers such as England, Portugal, France, and Spain. The age of discovery brought new products to the Americas and to Europe and introduced people to new cultures. During this period, the concept of the noble savage—the idea that primitive human beings are naturally good and that any evil they develop is a result of the corrupting force of civilization—began to emerge, but it was not thoroughly embraced until the Romantic era. Unfortunately, the prevailing European attitude during Montaigne's lifetime was that New World cultures were inferior. Greed and disease carried by Europeans led to the devastation of many of the peoples of the New World.

GOALS/OBJECTIVES

Studying this lesson will enable students to

- enjoy a surprising essay exploring the distinctions between the "civilized" and the "savage" person
- identify Michel Montaigne as the creator of the modern essay
- explain the significance of the age of discovery and the concept of the "noble savage"
- define the characteristics of an essay
- write a personal essay on a chosen topic
- write a critical review
- use dictionaries to find information about words

Have you ever met somebody from a culture or background very different from your own? What aspects of this person's culture seemed especially unusual or interesting to you? What benefits do you see in learning about other cultures? Write about these questions in your journal.

READER'S JOURNAL

FROM

"Of Cannibals"

MICHEL DE MONTAIGNE, TRANSLATED BY DONALD M. FRAME

Now, to return to my subject, I think there is nothing barbarous and savage in that nation, from what I have been told, except that each man calls barbarism whatever is not his own practice; for indeed it seems we have no other test of truth and reason than the example and pattern of the opinions and customs of the country we live in. There is always the perfect religion, the perfect government, the perfect and accomplished manners in all things. Those people are wild, just as we call wild the fruits that Nature has produced by herself and in her normal course; whereas really it is those that we have changed artificially and led astray from the common order, that we should rather call wild. The former retain alive and vigorous their genuine, their most useful and natural, virtues and properties, which we have debased in the latter in adapting them to gratify our corrupted taste. And yet for all that, the savor and delicacy of some uncultivated fruits of those countries is quite as excellent, even to our taste, as that of our own. It is not reasonable that art should win the place of honor over our great and powerful mother Nature. We have so overloaded the beauty and richness of her works by our inventions that we have quite smothered her. Yet wherever her purity shines forth, she wonderfully puts to shame our vain and frivolous attempts:

> Ivy comes readier without our care;
> In lonely caves the arbutus grows more fair;
> No art with artless bird song can compare.
>
> PROPERTIUS

All our efforts cannot even succeed in reproducing the nest of the tiniest little bird, its contexture, its beauty and convenience; or even the web of the puny spider. All things, says Plato, are produced by nature, by fortune, or by art; the greatest and most beautiful by one or the other of the first two, the least and most imperfect by the last.

❶ *What do we call barbarism? What do people think of the place in which they live?*

❷ *What is Montaigne's opinion about art in relation to nature?*

WORDS FOR EVERYDAY USE

de • base (dē bās´) *vt.,* make lower in value, quality, character, or dignity

friv • o • lous (friv´ə ləs) *adj.,* of little value or importance, trivial

con • tex • ture (kən teks´chər) *n.,* structure, composition

READER'S JOURNAL

You might also ask students to consider what fears, thoughts, or anxieties lead people to develop intolerant or prejudiced ideas about other cultures. In what ways does prejudice harm both the group that holds the prejudice and the group that experiences the prejudice?

ANSWERS TO GUIDED READING QUESTIONS

❶ Each person calls barbarism whatever is not his or her own practice. People consider their own country to have perfect religion, government, and manners.

❷ Montaigne believes that we should honor nature more than art.

SPELLING AND VOCABULARY WORDS FROM THE SELECTION

artifice	exhort
contexture	frivolous
debase	temerity
dissimulation	vex

VOCABULARY IN CONTEXT

- We have debased certain qualities in people that other cultures hold most valuable.
- Hans was so devoted to his work that he considered any amusement or entertainment frivolous.
- Through the microscope you could see the contexture of the cell.

Answers to Guided Reading Questions

① These people are ruled by the laws of nature. Montaigne values their "natural" state because he says that they have not yet been "corrupted" by our society.

ANALYTIC SCALES FOR RESPONDING IN WRITING

(SEE PAGE 866.)

Assign a score from 1 to 25 for each grading criterion below. (For more detailed evaluation, see the evaluation forms for writing, revising, and proofreading, Assessment Portfolio 4.1–4.9.)

1. Personal Essay

- **Content/Unity.** The personal essay develops a single idea on any topic.
- **Organization/Coherence.** The personal essay is well structured, following a logical order.
- **Language/Style.** The personal essay uses vivid and precise nouns, verbs, and modifiers.
- **Conventions.** The personal essay avoids errors in spelling, grammar, usage, mechanics, and manuscript form.

► Additional practice is provided in the Essential Skills Practice Book: Writing 1.8, 1.10.

Black Hawk and Son. *Jarvis. 1833*

 ①

What rules the people about whom Montaigne writes? What is Montaigne's opinion of the state of these people?

These nations, then, seem to me barbarous in this sense, that they have been fashioned very little by the human mind, and are still very close to their original naturalness. The laws of nature still rule them, very little corrupted by ours; and they are in such a state of purity that I am sometimes vexed that they were unknown earlier, in the days when there were men able to judge them better than we. I am sorry that Lycurgus and Plato did not know of them; for it seems to me that what we actually see in these nations surpasses not only all the pictures in which poets have idealized the golden age and all their inventions in imagining a happy state of man, but also the conceptions and the very desire of philosophy. They could not imagine a naturalness so pure and simple as we see by experience; nor could they believe that our society could be maintained with so little artifice and human solder.[1] This is a nation, I should say to Plato, in which there is no sort of traffic, no knowledge of letters, no science of numbers, no name for a magistrate or for political superiority, no custom of servitude, no riches or poverty, no contracts, no successions, no partitions, no occupations but leisure ones, no care for any but common kinship, no clothes, no agriculture, no metal, no use of wine or wheat. The very words that signify lying, treachery, dissimulation, avarice, envy, belittling, pardon—unheard of. How far from this perfection would he find the republic that he imagined: *Men fresh sprung from the gods* [Seneca].

These manners nature first ordained.

VIRGIL

For the rest, they live in a country with a very pleasant and temperate climate, so that according to my witnesses it is rare to see a sick man there; and they have assured me that they never saw one palsied,[2] bleary-eyed, toothless, or bent with age. They are settled along the sea and shut in on the land side by great high mountains, with a stretch about a hundred leagues[3] wide in between. They have a great abundance of fish and flesh which bear no resemblance to ours, and they eat them with no other artifice than cooking. The first man who rode a horse there, though he had had dealings with them on several other trips, so horrified them in this posture that they shot him dead with arrows before they could recognize him.

Their buildings are very long, with a capacity of two or three hundred souls; they

1. **solder.** Anything that joins or fuses; bond
2. **palsied.** Having a condition marked by uncontrollable tremors of all or part of the body
3. **leagues.** Units of measurement equal to almost three miles

Words for Everyday Use

vex (veks) *vt.,* annoy, irritate, disturb

ar • ti • fice (ärt´ə fis) *n.,* skill or ingenuity

dis • sim • u • la • tion (di sim´yoo lā´shən) *n.,* state of hiding one's feelings or motives by pretense

Vocabulary in Context

- The endless racket coming from my little brother's room would vex even the most patient person.
- One of Vanessa's artifices was constructing elaborate houses and castles from popsicle sticks.
- The imposter used his utmost skills of dissimulation to hide his true nature and to assume the king's rightful place.

are covered with the bark of great trees, the strips reaching to the ground at one end and supporting and leaning on one another at the top, in the manner of some of our barns, whose covering hangs down to the ground and acts as a side. They have wood so hard that they cut with it and make of it their swords and grills to cook their food. Their beds are of a cotton weave, hung from the roof like those in our ships, each man having his own; for the wives sleep apart from their husbands.

They get up with the sun, and eat immediately upon rising, to last them through the day; for they take no other meal than that one. Like some other Eastern peoples, of whom Suidas tells us, who drank apart from meals, they do not drink then; but they drink several times a day, and to capacity. Their drink is made of some root, and is of the color of our claret wines. They drink it only lukewarm. This beverage keeps only two or three days; it has a slightly sharp taste, is not at all heady, is good for the stomach, and has a laxative effect upon those who are not used to it; it is a very pleasant drink for anyone who is accustomed to it. In place of bread they use a certain white substance like preserved coriander.[4] I have tried it; it tastes sweet and a little flat.

The whole day is spent in dancing. The younger men go to hunt animals with bows. Some of the women busy themselves meanwhile with warming their drink, which is their chief duty. Some one of the old men, in the morning before they begin to eat, preaches to the whole barnful in common, walking from one end to the other, and repeating one single sentence several times until he has completed the circuit (for the buildings are fully a hundred paces long). He recommends to them only two things: valor against the enemy and love for their wives. And they never fail to point out this obligation, as their refrain, that it is their wives who keep their drink warm and seasoned.

There may be seen in several places, including my own house, specimens of their beds, of their ropes, of their wooden swords and the bracelets with which they cover their wrists in combats, and of the big canes, open at one end, by whose sound they keep time in their dances. They are close shaven all over, and shave themselves much more cleanly than we, with nothing but a wooden or stone razor. They believe that souls are immortal, and that those who have deserved well of the gods are lodged in that part of heaven where the sun rises, and the damned in the west.

They have some sort of priests and prophets, but they rarely appear before the people, having their home in the mountains. On their arrival there is a great feast and solemn assembly of several villages—each barn, as I have described it, makes up a village, and they are about one French league from each other. The prophet speaks to them in public, <u>exhorting</u> them to virtue and their duty; but their whole ethical science contains only these two articles: resoluteness in war and affection for their wives. He prophesies to them things to come and the results they are to expect from their undertakings, and urges them to war or holds them back from it; but this is on the condition that when he fails to prophesy correctly, and if things turn out otherwise than he has predicted, he is cut into a thousand pieces if they catch him, and condemned as a false prophet. For this reason, the prophet who has once been mistaken is never seen again.

1 What is the role of the prophet? Why is it important for the prophet to be correct?

4. **coriander.** European herb

WORDS FOR EVERYDAY USE

ex • hort (eg zôrt´) *vi.,* admonish strongly, urge earnestly by advice or warning

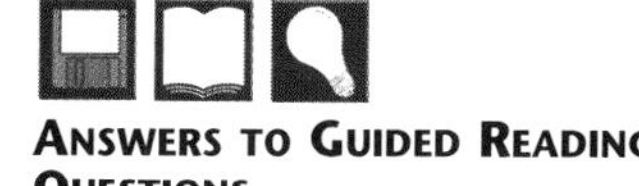

Answers to Guided Reading Questions

1 The prophet urges people to virtue and to duty, telling them to be resolute in war and to love their wives. It is important for the prophet to be correct, because if his prophecy is incorrect, he is condemned and killed.

ANALYTIC SCALES FOR RESPONDING IN WRITING

(SEE PAGE 866.)

Assign a score from 1 to 25 for each grading criterion below. (For more detailed evaluation, see the evaluation forms for writing, revising, and proofreading, Assessment Portfolio 4.1–4.9.)

2. Critical Essay

- **Content/Unity.** The essay reviews Montaigne's "Of Cannibals," explaining whether it is compelling and conclusive.
- **Organization/Coherence.** The essay begins with an introduction that includes the thesis of the essay. The introduction is followed by supporting paragraphs with clear transitions. The essay ends with a solid conclusion.
- **Language/Style.** The essay uses vivid and precise nouns, verbs, and modifiers.
- **Conventions.** The essay avoids errors in spelling, grammar, usage, mechanics, and manuscript form.

▶ Additional practice is provided in the Essential Skills Practice Book: Writing 1.20.

Vocabulary in Context

- The speaker <u>exhorted</u> the audience to recycle and to take an active part in the protection of the environment.

Answers to Guided Reading Questions

❶ Acts of barbarity are noted in others. Europeans are blind to the barbarity of torturing people on the rack, burning them, having them bitten by dogs and swine, and to the fact that Stoic philosophers of Greece advocated cannibalism in times of need.

❷ They treat their prisoners well and hospitably until they kill them with their swords.

❸ From the Portuguese, the native peoples learned to bury their prisoners up to the waist and shoot them full of arrows before hanging them.

Selection Check Test with Answers

EX. What form of literature is Montaigne credited with creating?
He is credited with creating the essay.

1. What does "each man call barbarism"?
Each person calls barbarism whatever is not his or her own practice.

2. What does Montaigne believe people should value more than art?
Montaigne believes that people should value nature more than art.

3. What elements of a "civilized" society do these native people lack?
Students should name at least three of the following: traffic, letters, math, political figures, slavery, riches, poverty, clothes, agriculture, metal, wine, and wheat.

4. What do the priests and prophets of these people preach?
They preach valor in war and love for their wives.

5. In what does Montaigne say Europeans surpass these people?
Montaigne says Europeans surpass them in barbarity.

❶ *What faults are noted in others? According to Montaigne, to what barbarous practices of their own are Europeans blind?*

❷ *What do these people do with their prisoners?*

❸ *What treatment of prisoners did they learn from the Portuguese?*

Divination is a gift of God; that is why its abuse should be punished as imposture. Among the Scythians, when the soothsayers failed to hit the mark, they were laid, chained hand and foot, on carts full of heather and drawn by oxen, on which they were burned. Those who handle matters subject to the control of human capacity are excusable if they do the best they can. But these others who come and trick us with assurances of an extraordinary faculty that is beyond our ken, should they not be punished for not making good their promise, and for the temerity of their imposture?

They have their wars with the nations beyond the mountains, further inland, to which they go quite naked, with no other arms than bows or wooden swords ending in a sharp point, in the manner of the tongues of our boar spears. It is astonishing what firmness they show in their combats, which never end but in slaughter and bloodshed; for as to routs and terror, they know nothing of either.

Each man brings back as his trophy the head of the enemy he has killed, and sets it up at the entrance to his dwelling. After they have treated their prisoners well for a long time with all the hospitality they can think of, each man who has a prisoner calls a great assembly of his acquaintances. He ties a rope to one of the prisoner's arms, by the end of which he holds him, a few steps away, for fear of being hurt, and gives his dearest friend the other arm to hold in the same way; and these two, in the presence of the whole assembly, kill him with their swords. This done, they roast him and eat him in common and send some pieces to their absent friends. This is not, as people think, for nourishment, as of old the Scythians used to do; it is to betoken an extreme revenge. And the proof of this came when they saw the Portuguese, who had joined forces with their adversaries, inflict a different kind of death on them when they took them prisoner, which was to bury them up to the waist, shoot the rest of their body full of arrows, and afterward hang them. They thought that these people from the other world, being men who had sown the knowledge of many vices among their neighbors and were much greater masters than themselves in every sort of wickedness, did not adopt this sort of vengeance without some reason, and that it must be more painful than their own; so they began to give up their old method and to follow this one.

I am not sorry that we notice the barbarous horror of such acts, but I am heartily sorry that, judging their faults rightly, we should be so blind to our own. I think there is more barbarity in eating a man alive than in eating him dead; and in tearing by tortures and the rack a body still full of feeling, in roasting a man bit by bit, in having him bitten and mangled by dogs and swine (as we have not only read but seen within fresh memory, not among ancient enemies, but among neighbors and fellow citizens, and what is worse, on the pretext of piety and religion), than in roasting and eating him after he is dead.

Indeed, Chrysippus and Zeno, heads of the Stoic sect,[5] thought there was nothing wrong in using our carcasses for any purpose in case of need, and getting nourishment from them; just as our ancestors, when besieged by Caesar in the city of Alésia, resolved to relieve their famine by eating old men, women, and other people useless for fighting.

> The Gascons once, 'tis said, their life renewed
> By eating of such food.
>
> JUVENAL

5. **Stoic sect.** Greek school of philosophy that held all things to be governed by natural law and that encouraged people to remain indifferent to the external world

Words for Everyday Use

te • mer • i • ty (tə mer´ə tē) *n.,* foolish or rash boldness, recklessness

Vocabulary in Context

• When Jody dove off the cliff into the shallow water hole below, we were stunned by the temerity of her deed.

And physicians do not fear to use human flesh in all sorts of ways for our health, applying it either inwardly or outwardly. But there never was any opinion so disordered as to excuse treachery, disloyalty, tyranny, and cruelty, which are our ordinary vices.

So we may well call these people barbarians, in respect to the rules of reason, but not in respect to ourselves, who surpass them in every kind of barbarity. ■

Responding to the Selection

Montaigne writes, "Each man calls barbarism whatever is not his own practice; for indeed it seems we have no other test of truth or reason than the example and pattern of the opinions and customs of the country we live in." Do you agree or disagree with this statement? Do you think that customs that differ from your own are strange or bad? Why, or why not?

Reviewing the Selection

Recalling / Interpreting

1. What words are used to describe the native people of Brazil? Does Montaigne agree with these descriptions? Why, or why not? ▶▶ Why might such words have been used by Europeans to describe the natives of Brazil? Were such terms accurate?
2. In what way does Montaigne say that these people seem barbarous? ▶▶ In what way does this meaning of *barbarous* differ from the standard usage of the word?
3. What qualities characterize the natives in war? With what aspects of war are they not familiar? ▶▶ What differences between native Brazilian warfare and European warfare is Montaigne noting?
4. What do the natives of Brazil do with their prisoners of war? What new custom do they learn from the Portuguese? ▶▶ Why do the people of Brazil change their custom? What does this suggest about their opinions of the Portuguese?

Synthesizing

5. Do you think one culture is better or more perfect than another? Of what aspects of your own culture are you particularly proud? What aspects of your own culture would you like to change?

Responding to the Selection

Students might enjoy debating whether Montaigne's views about the values of "nature" and the evils of "civilization" are extreme. Does a "natural" society have problems Montaigne does not address? Does a "civilized" society have benefits he does not discuss?

Answers for Reviewing the Selection

RECALLING AND INTERPRETING

1. **Recalling.** The people are described as wild or barbarous. Montaigne does not agree with these descriptions. He thinks they are applied only because the customs of the people differ from those of the Europeans. **Interpreting.** Europeans may have used such words because the native customs seemed strange and different to them and because the lives of the natives were closer to nature. These terms were not accurate because they reflected European prejudices.

2. **Recalling.** Montaigne says the native people seem barbarous in that they have a less structured, more nature-based way of life. **Interpreting.** This meaning of the word *barbarous* differs from the standard meaning in that it is not negative and carries no connotations of cruelty or inhumanity.

3. **Recalling.** The natives have an astonishing firmness in war. They are not familiar with routs and terror which affect civilian populations in war time. **Interpreting.** Montaigne suggests that the natives are more resolute in war than Europeans, but that they settle their differences on the battlefield rather than extending terror in other ways.

4. **Recalling.** The natives of Brazil treat their captives kindly, then they tie up the captives and kill them quickly with swords. Finally, they eat their captives. From the Portuguese, they learn the custom

(cont.)

Answers for Reviewing the Selection (cont.)

of burying their captives up to the waist and shooting them with arrows before hanging them. **Interpreting.** The people of Brazil have learned many vices from the Portuguese, so they think this must be a more painful and therefore better way to treat their enemies. This imitation of Portuguese customs suggests that they see the Portuguese as more powerful and Portuguese customs as superior in some way to their own.

SYNTHESIZING

Responses will vary. Possible responses are given.

5. Students may suggest that no one culture is better than another but that any given culture has some positive aspects to offer to the world. Students should suggest aspects of their own culture that they see as positive as well as ways in which they would like to see their culture change.

Answers for Understanding Literature

Responses will vary. Possible responses are given.

Essay. Montaigne develops the idea that the natives of Brazil are not the wild barbarians that Europeans make them out to be. He points out that the term *wild,* though it has negative connotations, should suggest a positive trait of the native peoples in their connection with nature. He also points out that the Brazilians learned inhumane behaviors from the Europeans.

ANALYTIC SCALES FOR RESPONDING IN WRITING

Grading scales for Responding in Writing appear on pages 862 and 863.

Answers for Skills Activities

RESEARCH SKILLS

Responses will vary. Possible responses are given.

The words *barbarian* and *barbarous* come from the Latin *barbarus,* from the Greek *barbaros,* meaning "foreign, strange, or ignorant," and from the Indo-European base *barbar–,* used to represent the unintelligible speech of foreigners. *Barbarian* is a noun meaning "foreigner," "member of a group of people who are savage or uncivilized," or "a person who lacks culture." It is also an adjective meaning "uncivilized or crude." *Barbarous* is an adjective meaning "foreign," "characterized by substandard usage in speaking or writing," "lacking in civilization," or "cruel and brutal."

Cannibal comes from the Spanish *caníbal,* meaning "a savage." The term originated with Columbus, who took it form the Arawakan word *Caniba,* a cannibal people. The word is also akin to the Carib word *galibi,* which

(cont.)

Understanding Literature (Questions for Discussion)

Essay. An **essay** is a brief work of prose nonfiction. The original meaning of essay was "a trial or attempt." An essay need not be a complete or exhaustive treatment of a subject but rather a tentative exploration of it. A good essay develops a single idea and is characterized by unity and coherence. What is the single idea that Montaigne develops in this essay? What are the main points he makes to support this idea?

Responding in Writing

1. **Creative Writing: Personal Essay.** An essay is a brief work of prose nonfiction. A good essay develops a single idea and is characterized by unity and coherence. Write an essay on one of the following topics or on any topic about which you feel strongly:
    - the meaning and importance of friendship
    - the necessity of respecting the earth and protecting the environment
    - the pleasures and benefits of reading
    - the importance of cultural diversity

    You might start by making a cluster chart in which you note your ideas about the topic you chose. Then state your main point and support it with the ideas that you have gathered.

2. **Critical Essay: Reviewing "Of Cannibals."** Write a critical review of the excerpt from "Of Cannibals." You may wish to read the rest of the essay and review the essay as a whole. Briefly outline or describe Montaigne's main argument. Then state whether you find Montaigne's essay to be compelling and conclusive, and explain why or why not. Be sure to use examples to support your opinions.

Research Skills

Using Dictionaries. You can use a dictionary to determine the meaning or spelling of a word. Dictionaries also provide information about the etymology of a word, name what part of speech it is, and provide its correct pronunciation, usage, and idiomatic usage. Read the Language Arts Survey 4.15, "Using Dictionaries." Then use a dictionary to find the etymologies, parts of speech, and definitions of the following words:

barbarian

barbarous

cannibal

uncultivated

Answers for Skills Activities (cont.)

means "strong men." *Cannibal* is a noun meaning "a person who eats human flesh, or an animal that eats its own kind." *Cannibal* is also an adjective meaning "of or like a cannibal."

The root word of *uncultivated* is *cultivate,* which comes from the Medieval Latin *cultivatus,* the past participle of *cultivare,* which led to the Late Latin *cultivus,* meaning "tilled," or "(soil) worked for agriculture." This led to the Latin *cultus,* which means "care, cultivation," and comes from the past participle of *colere,* meaning "to till." *Uncultivated* is an adjective meaning "not prepared or used for growing crops; wild, not refined or cultured."

▶ Additional practice is provided in the Essential Skills Practice Book: Study and Research 4.15

PREREADING

from *Fables*
"The Lion and the Rat"
"The Oak and the Reed"
by Jean de La Fontaine, translated by Elizur Wright

FRANCE

About the Author

JEAN DE LA FONTAINE
1621–1695

Jean de La Fontaine grew up in a middle-class French family and married Marie Héricart in 1647. He inherited from his father the position of inspector of forests and waterways, a post he held from 1652 to 1671. During this time he moved to Paris, where he made many contacts and began his writing career. La Fontaine was able to pursue his writing career through the support of many patrons, including minister of finance Nicolas Fouquet; the Duchess of Orléans in Luxembourg; and Mme de La Sabliere, of whose household he was a member. Through his connections with this house, La Fontaine was exposed to many of the great writers, philosophers, and scholars of his day. Although popular with many of the nobility, La Fontaine was unable to win the approval of the king, Louis XIV, who saw him as irreligious and unconventional. Despite the king's opposition, in 1683 La Fontaine was elected to the Académie Française, a noted literary academy founded by Cardinal de Richelieu in 1634 to maintain literary taste. La Fontaine befriended many of the best-known writers of his day, including Molière, Jean Racine, François de La Rochefoucauld, Mme de Sévigné, and Mme de La Fayette. French writers such as François Rabelais and classical writers such as Homer, Virgil, and Ovid influenced La Fontaine's writing.

Sunken garden, Angers, France

About the Selection

La Fontaine wrote stories and poems, but he is most famous for his collection of fables. La Fontaine's ***Fables*** are noted for their author's wit and skillful characterization. Through dialogue and action in such fables as **"The Lion and the Rat"** and **"The Oak and the Reed,"** La Fontaine develops characters with decidedly human traits and derives surprising results from the relationships between these characters. In both of these fables, a mighty being encounters a seemingly weaker creature with unexpected results. In each case, La Fontaine offers keen observations on human nature and presents a moral.

CONNECTIONS: Lesson Tales

According to the ancient Greek philosopher and critic Aristotle, one purpose of literature is to instruct. Stories have been used in many cultures and in many ages to teach moral lessons. Such stories are called **fables** or **parables.** Fables usually contain animal characters, while parables contain human characters. In both literary forms, lessons about vices, social behavior, or other moral issues are taught through brief tales that illustrate a point. Parables can be found in the Bible and in Zen Buddhist teachings. Some of the most famous fables are attributed to the Greek writer Aesop.

GOALS/OBJECTIVES

Studying this lesson will enable students to

- enjoy fables written by a renowned French author
- briefly explain different types of lesson tales found in literature
- define *fable* and *personification*
- write a fable that teaches a particular moral
- write a critical essay comparing and contrasting La Fontaine's work with Ovid's
- prepare an oral interpretation of a fable

ADDITIONAL RESOURCES

READER'S GUIDE
- Selection Worksheet 10.6

ASSESSMENT PORTFOLIO
- Selection Check Test 2.10.11
- Selection Test 2.10.12

ESSENTIAL SKILLS PRACTICE BOOKS
- Writing 1.8, 1.10, 1.20
- Speaking and Listening 3.5

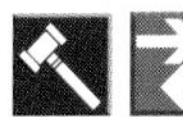   

PREREADING EXTENSIONS

Inform students that La Fontaine sometimes used his fables to critique the court and the social hierarchy of his day. During the time that La Fontaine wrote, Louis XIV was king of France. Louis XIV ruled from 1643 to 1715 and was the perfect symbol of absolutism. In an absolute monarchy, the king holds unlimited powers. Louis was seen as a "visible divinity"— in other words, people believed that, as a ruler, he represented the divine authority of God. He was considered not only the ruler of the people of France but the owner of their property and persons. Ask students to discuss the ways in which "The Lion and the Rat" and "The Oak and the Reed" may critique French society during the reign of Louis XIV. See page 868 if students need additional help.

SUPPORT FOR LEP STUDENTS

PRONUNCIATIONS OF PROPER NOUNS AND ADJECTIVES

Ae • sop (ē säp´)
Jean de La Fon • taine (zhän də lä´ fän tān´)

ADDITIONAL VOCABULARY

behoves—is morally necessary or proper
boon—favor
bower—place enclosed by the boughs of a tree
flits—flutters
sward—grass-covered soil

READER'S JOURNAL

If students have difficulty thinking of aphorisms they have been taught, you might ask them simply to list in their own words different morals or lessons they learned as a child.

Answers to Guided Reading Questions

① The lion spares the rat's life.

② The rat frees the lion from a trap by chewing through the net.

Additional Questions and Activities

If students have difficulty discussing the ways these fables might critique seventeenth-century French society, as suggested in the Prereading Extensions, you might prompt them with the following questions: Lions are often a symbol of kingship or royalty. What aspect of French society might the lion represent? What elements of society might the oak represent? the rat and the reed? If the lion represents the ruling monarch, what qualities does La Fontaine seems to suggest the monarch should develop? What might he be saying about the ways in which monarchs try to accomplish things? What does "The Oak and the Reed" suggest about the type of person who weathers difficulties best?

ANSWERS

Responses will vary.

The lion might represent the king, and the oak, a person of high status. The rat and the reed may represent people of lesser status. La Fontaine suggests that the monarch develop a more kindly attitude toward those who seem to be weaker or of lesser

(cont.)

What morals or lessons were taught to you as a child in the form of aphorisms or short sayings? For example, you may have heard "Where there's a will, there's a way," or "Pride goes before a fall." List as many morals or sayings as you can in your journal. Compare your list with those of your classmates, and discuss the meaning of each saying using concrete examples to illustrate it.

FROM

Fables

JEAN DE LA FONTAINE, TRANSLATED BY ELIZUR WRIGHT

"The Lion and the Rat"

To show to all your kindness, it behoves:
There's none so small but you his aid may need. . . .
From underneath the sward
A rat, quite off his guard,
Popped out between a lion's paws.
The beast of royal bearing
Showed what a lion was
The creature's life by sparing—
A kindness well repaid;
For, little as you would have thought
His majesty would ever need his aid,
It proved full soon
A precious boon.
Forth issuing from his forest glen,
T' explore the haunts of men,
In lion net his majesty was caught,
From which his strength and rage
Served not to disengage.
The rat ran up, with grateful glee,
Gnawed off a rope, and set him free.

By time and toil we sever
What strength and rage could never.

① *What does the lion do for the rat?*

② *In what way does the rat help the lion?*

Additional Questions and Activities (cont.)

status. He may be suggesting that monarchs focus on their strength and power, hoping to accomplish things immediately, rather than on industrious and time-consuming but ultimately successful labor. This fable suggests that the person who assumes a humble attitude and who yields or bends with the times survives best in nature or in society.

"The Oak and the Reed"

The oak, one day, addressed the reed:—
"To you ungenerous indeed
Has nature been, my humble friend,
With weakness aye obliged to bend.
The smallest bird that flits in air
Is quite too much for you to bear;
The slightest wind that wreaths the lake
Your ever-trembling head doth shake.
The while, my towering form
Dares with the mountain top
The solar blaze to stop,
And wrestle with the storm.
What seems to you the blast of death,
To me is but a zephyr's breath.[1]
Beneath my branches had you grown,
That spread far round their friendly bower,
Less suffering would your life have known,
Defended from the tempest's[2] power.
Unhappily, you oftenest show
In open air your slender form.
Along the marshes, wet and low,
That fringe the kingdom of the storm.
To you, declare I must,
Dame Nature seems unjust."
Then modestly replied the reed,
"Your pity, sir, is kind indeed,
But wholly needless for my sake.
The wildest wind that ever blew
Is safe to me, compared with you.
I bend, indeed, but never break." ■

1. **zephyr's breath.** Gentle breeze
2. **tempest's.** Violent storm's

❶ *What does the oak think of the reed?*

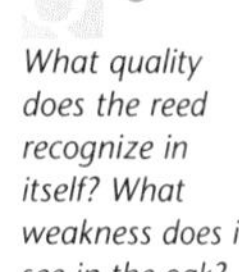

❷ *What quality does the reed recognize in itself? What weakness does it see in the oak?*

Answers to Guided Reading Questions

❶ The oak thinks that the reed is weak.

❷ The reed recognizes that it is flexible and will not break under extreme pressure as the oak will.

Selection Check Test with Answers

EX. What animal's life does the lion spare in "The Lion and the Rat"?

The lion spares the rat's life.

1. What does the rat do to help the lion?

The rat gnaws through a net to free the lion.

2. What enables us to sever that which strength and rage cannot sever?

Through time and toil we can sever that which cannot be severed by strength and rage.

3. What does the oak say about nature in relation to the reed?

The oak says that nature has been unjust to the reed.

4. What does the reed never do?

The reed never breaks.

5. What can the wind do to the oak?

The wind can break the oak.

RESPONDING TO THE SELECTION

As an alternative activity, students may discuss whether they believe that fables are an effective way to teach moral lessons.

ANSWERS FOR REVIEWING THE SELECTION

RECALLING AND INTERPRETING

1. **Recalling.** The lion spares the rat's life. **Interpreting.** By sparing the rat's life, the lion shows its royal bearing and its mercifulness.

2. **Recalling.** The morals are: be kind to everyone, for you may need help someday; and time and effort are more effective than anger and strength. **Interpreting.** The actions of the lion support the first moral because the lion is kind to the rat although he does not expect anything in return. The rat's ability to chew through the net to free the lion who is unable to free himself, despite his strength and effort, supports the second moral.

3. **Recalling.** The oak says that the reed is unable to sustain the weight of the smallest bird and that the slightest wind makes the reed tremble. **Interpreting.** The oak thinks it is mightier than the reed because it is larger and does not bend and bow to the breeze and to the weight of small things.

4. **Recalling.** The reed tells the oak that its pity is uncalled for, because although the reed may bend, it never breaks, whereas a wind might someday fell the mighty oak. **Interpreting.** The oak seems mightier at first, but it can be toppled by the wind. The reed, which seems weak, is mightier because it is able to yield and survive.

SYNTHESIZING

Responses will vary. Possible responses are given.

5. They both address the issue of size and might. In both cases, the smaller being is shown as more powerful than the larger being.

Responding to the Selection

How would you feel at the end of "The Rat and the Lion" if you were the lion? How would you feel at the end of "The Oak and the Reed" if you were the oak? With a partner, role play a situation in which the lion tells the rat what it thinks and how it feels about the rat now or in which the oak shares such information with the reed.

Reviewing the Selection

RECALLING		INTERPRETING
1. What does the lion do for the rat?	▶▶	What does this action demonstrate about the lion?
2. What two morals are given in "The Lion and the Rat"?	▶▶	What actions support each moral?
3. What examples does the oak give to show that the reed is weak?	▶▶	Why does the oak think it is mightier than the reed?
4. What is the reed's response to the oak?	▶▶	Which is mightier, the reed or the oak? Explain.

SYNTHESIZING

5. What similarities do the morals of "The Lion and the Rat" and "The Oak and the Reed" share?

Understanding Literature (Questions for Discussion)

1. **Fable.** A **fable** is a brief story, often with animal characters, told to express a moral. Who are the characters in the fables you have just read? In what way are each of the characters portrayed at the beginning of each fable? In what way do your ideas change about these characters by the fables' ends? Why are the characters in each fable appropriate for expressing its particular moral?

2. **Personification. Personification** is a figure of speech in which an idea, animal, or thing is described as if it were a person. What animals or things are personified in these fables? What human qualities is each animal or thing given?

ANSWERS FOR UNDERSTANDING LITERATURE

Responses will vary. Possible responses are given.

1. **Fable.** The characters in the first fable are a lion and a rat, and in the second, an oak and a reed. The rat and the reed are portrayed as weak, and the lion and the oak are portrayed as mighty. After reading both fables, the reader sees that in certain respects the rat and the reed are more powerful. Oaks and lions represent strength and power well, while rats and reeds seem weak and insignificant but have hidden resources.

2. **Personification.** The lion, the rat, the oak, the reed, and nature are all personified in these fables. The lion is strong, regal, and merciful. The rat is caring and helpful. The oak is condescending. The reed is flexible and astute. The animals or things have the ability to speak.

Responding in Writing

1. **Creative Writing: Fable.** Create your own fable. Begin by choosing a moral you would like to teach, such as "If at first you don't succeed, try and try again," or "Do unto others as you would have done unto you." Brainstorm situations that could demonstrate your moral. Use personified animals or objects as characters in one of these situations. You may wish to illustrate your fable and make a class collection of fables.

2. **Critical Essay: Comparing and Contrasting Ovid and La Fontaine.** La Fontaine was influenced by Ovid. Read or reread the selections from Ovid's *Metamorphoses* on pages 436 and 492. Then write an essay comparing and contrasting the selections by the two writers, focusing on tone, style, and theme. Use a Venn diagram like the one below to gather evidence to support your thesis.

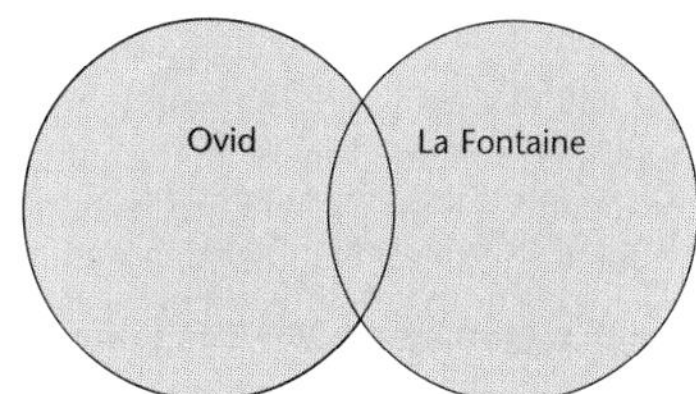

Speaking and Listening Skills

Oral Interpretation. Fables are easily adapted for oral presentation because of their narrative nature and their origins in the oral tradition. Read the Language Arts Survey 3.5, "Oral Interpretation." Then find a collection of fables and choose one that you would like to present orally. You may work with other students to prepare a group presentation. Follow the guidelines given in the Language Arts Survey to prepare your text. Then practice your performance and present it to your class. If possible, arrange to share your performances with a younger audience as well.

ANALYTIC SCALES FOR RESPONDING IN WRITING

Assign a score from 1 to 25 for each grading criterion below. (For more detailed evaluation, see the evaluation forms for writing, revising, and proofreading, Assessment Portfolio 4.1–4.9.)

1. Fable

- **Content/Unity.** The fable presents a moral through a brief story with animal characters.
- **Organization/Coherence.** The fable relates events in a sensible order.
- **Language/Style.** The fable uses vivid and precise nouns, verbs, and modifiers.
- **Conventions.** The fable avoids errors in spelling, grammar, usage, mechanics, and manuscript form.

▶ Additional practice is provided in the Essential Skills Practice Book: Writing 1.8.

2. Critical Essay

- **Content/Unity.** The essay compares and contrasts the tone, style, and theme of Ovid's works and La Fontaine's works.
- **Organization/Coherence.** The essay begins with an introduction that includes the thesis of the essay. The introduction is followed by supporting paragraphs with clear transitions. The essay ends with a solid conclusion.
- **Language/Style.** The essay uses vivid and precise nouns, verbs, and modifiers.
- **Conventions.** The essay avoids errors in spelling, grammar, usage, mechanics, and manuscript form.

▶ Additional practice is provided in the Essential Skills Practice Book: Writing 1.10, 1.20.

ANSWERS FOR SKILLS ACTIVITIES 

SPEAKING AND LISTENING SKILLS

Students should enunciate clearly; use appropriate pace and volume; vary their pitch, volume, and tone; maintain eye contact; and use appropriate body language, gestures, and facial expressions.

▶ Additional practice is provided in the Essential Skills Practice Book: Speaking and Listening 3.5.

PREREADING

from *Tartuffe*
by Molière (Jean-Baptiste Poquelin),
translated by Richard Wilbur

About the Author

MOLIÈRE
1622–1673

Jean-Baptiste Poquelin was born in Paris in 1622. His mother died when he was ten. Educated at the Collège de Clermont, Poquelin began his theater career in 1643 with encouragement from Madeleine Béjert. Soon after, in 1644, he adopted the pen and stage name **Molière**. In 1662, he married Madeleine's sister Armade Béjert with whom he had three children.

Molière's first theatrical success came in 1658, when his troupe performed *The Amorous Doctor* before the king. The king's brother became Molière's patron for seven years. When the king himself began to favor the company, it became known as the King's Troupe. Molière's works often ridicule vices by embodying them in stock characters such as the miser or the hypochondriac. A director of and actor in most of his plays, Molière was playing the role of a hypochondriac in a production of *The Imaginary Invalid* when he collapsed on stage and died at the age of fifty-one.

About the Selection

Tartuffe is one of Molière's most often performed plays, yet soon after the first performance of the play in 1664, it was banned because its ridicule and exposure of religious hypocrisy was viewed, unfairly, as an attack on religion in general. In 1669 permission was finally granted for a third version of the play, the version that now exists, to be performed.

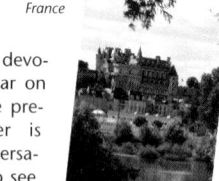

Tartuffe is set in the home of Orgon, a middle-aged, middle-class man who has been taken in by the false piety of Tartuffe, an imposter who flaunts his poverty and prayers as signs of his devotion. Tartuffe does not appear on the stage until act III. In the preceding acts, his character is revealed through the conversations of other characters who see that he is making a fool of Orgon. Orgon refuses to heed the advice of others. Not until Orgon sees Tartuffe's scheme with his own eyes does he believe Tartuffe to be an imposter.

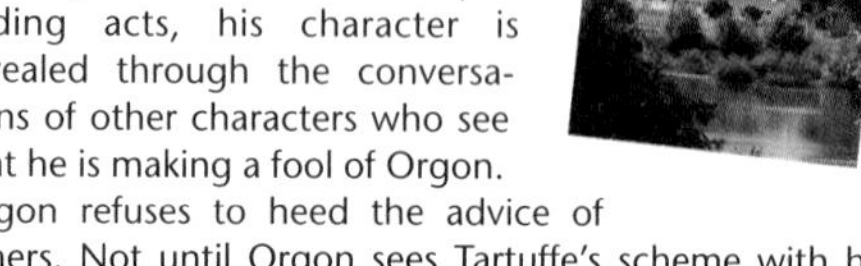
Château Amboise, France

CONNECTIONS: Molière and the Comédie-Française

The Comédie-Française, also known as La Maison de Molière, is the world's oldest established national theater. After Molière's death, his company of actors joined with another theatrical company. This combined group later joined with the company of the Hotel de Bourgogne, becoming in 1680 the only professional troupe in Paris. Membership in this troupe, which later became known as the Comédie-Française, is based on merit. Many of the world's finest actors have belonged to this company, which has had a strong influence on the development of French theater.

ADDITIONAL RESOURCES

READER'S GUIDE
- Selection Worksheet 10.7

ASSESSMENT PORTFOLIO
- Selection Check Test 2.10.13
- Selection Test 2.10.14

ESSENTIAL SKILLS PRACTICE BOOKS
- Writing 1.8, 1.20
- Language 2.52
- Speaking and Listening 3.1
- Applied English/Tech Prep 5.6

PREREADING EXTENSIONS

Molière faced a number of problems with the censorship of *Tartuffe.* Have students debate the issue of censorship. The following list provides possible topics for the debate: banning books in school or public libraries, censoring on the Internet, freedom of the press and of school newspapers. Students should research their subject, be prepared to present and support their opinion, and to counter opposing arguments.

SUPPORT FOR LEP STUDENTS

PRONUNCIATIONS OF PROPER NOUNS AND ADJECTIVES

Clé • ante (clā änt´)
Da • mis (dä mē´)
Do • rine (dō rēn´)
El • mire (el mēr´)
Ma • ri • ane (mä´rē än)
Mo • lière (mōl yer´)
Or • gon (ôr gōn´)
Tar • tuffe (tär toof´)

ADDITIONAL VOCABULARY

disbursed—given out
importunate—annoyingly persistent
loathe—hate, despise
perish—die
rectitude—righteousness

GOALS/OBJECTIVES

Studying this lesson will enable students to

- enjoy and appreciate a comedy
- recognize Molière as a French dramatist
- identify the three main methods of characterization
- describe a character
- define *couplet*
- identify couplets
- write a diatribe
- analyze the comedy of the selection
- write public relations copy

READER'S JOURNAL

Think of a time when someone deceived you. What did the person do to deceive you? How did you learn of the deception? How did you feel when the deception was revealed? Write about these questions in your journal.

FROM

Tartuffe

MOLIÈRE, TRANSLATED BY RICHARD WILBUR

Characters in *Tartuffe*

Orgon	**Elmire** Orgon's wife
Mariane Orgon's daughter	**Dorine** Mariane's maid
Cléante Orgon's brother-in-law	**Tartuffe** Imposter living in the home of Orgon

[Editor's note: In act III, scene iii, Tartuffe professes his desire for Elmire. He is overheard by Damis, Orgon's son, who is more than eager to expose Tartuffe to his father. Orgon fails to believe the claims Damis and Elmire make and encourages Tartuffe to spend as much time as possible with Elmire. He also disinherits Damis, giving all he owns to Tartuffe, and announces that he will give his daughter Mariane to Tartuffe in marriage. At the beginning of this selection, Elmire, Mariane, Cléante (who recognizes Tartuffe for the hypocrite he is), and Dorine (who is also untrusting of Tartuffe) are assembled. Orgon arrives and announces the news of Mariane's engagement.]

ACT IV

SCENE III

ORGON. Hah! Glad to find you all assembled here. (*To* MARIANE)
This contract, child, contains your happiness,
And what it says I think your heart can guess.

MARIANE. (*Falling to her knee.*) Sir, by that Heaven which sees me here distressed,
And by whatever else can move your breast,
Do not employ a father's power, I pray you,
To crush my heart and force it to obey you,
Nor by your harsh commands oppress me so

READER'S JOURNAL

Students might also write about a time when they deceived someone else. Why did they do it? How did they feel about their actions? How was their deception revealed? What happened when the deception was revealed?

QUOTABLES

"Oh, what a tangled web we weave,
When first we practice to deceive!"

—Sir Walter Scott

ADDITIONAL QUESTIONS AND ACTIVITIES

Share the preceding quotation by Sir Walter Scott with students. Ask them to discuss the idea it presents. In what way does deception become a web? How does one lie beget another? Students might share their own experiences or those about which they have read to illustrate their responses.

SPELLING AND VOCABULARY WORDS FROM THE SELECTION

acquiesce	judicious
assuage	merit
contemptible	palpable
feign	partial
intervene	

Answers to Guided Reading Questions

1. Mariane is horrified by the idea of marrying Tartuffe. She abhors him.

2. Orgon does not believe Elmire because he believes that she is only going along with the story to support Damis, to whom Orgon says she is partial. Also, he does not believe that she is acting as she would if she were telling the truth.

3. Orgon tells Mariane that it will be ennobling to marry Tartuffe and that doing so will mortify her flesh.

Literary Note

Although Orgon in *Tartuffe* is a comic character and Oedipus in *Oedipus the King* (see page 618) is a tragic character, they both suffer from blindness to the truth. If students have read Oedipus, have them compare and contrast the two characters, their blindness to the truth and their reactions to advice or counsel. Students might respond in small group discussions or in a comparison-and-contrast essay.

---

1 *How does Mariane feel about marrying Tartuffe? What is her opinion of Tartuffe?*

2 *Why doesn't Orgon believe what Elmire and Damis have told him about Tartuffe?*

3 *What reason does Orgon give Mariane for going through with the marriage?*

That I'll begrudge the duty which I owe—
And do not so embitter and enslave me
That I shall hate the very life you gave me.
If my sweet hopes must perish, if you refuse
To give me to the one I've dared to choose,
Spare me at least—I beg you, I implore—
The pain of wedding one whom I abhor;
And do not, by a heartless use of force,
Drive me to contemplate some desperate course.

ORGON. (*Feeling himself touched by her*) Be firm, my soul. No human weakness, now.

MARIANE. I don't resent your love for him. Allow
Your heart free rein, Sir; give him your property,
And if that's not enough, take mine from me;
He's welcome to my money; take it, do,
But don't, I pray, include my person too.
Spare me, I beg you; and let me end the tale
Of my sad days behind a convent veil.

ORGON. A convent! Hah! When crossed in their amours,
All lovesick girls have the same thought as yours.
Get up! The more you loathe the man, and dread him,
The more ennobling it will be to wed him.
Marry Tartuffe, and mortify your flesh!
Enough; don't start that whimpering afresh.

DORINE. But why . . . ?

ORGON. Be still, there. Speak when you're spoken to.
Not one more bit of impudence out of you.

CLÉANTE. If I may offer a word of counsel here . . .

ORGON. Brother, in counseling you have no peer;
All your advice is forceful, sound, and clever;
I don't propose to follow it, however.

ELMIRE. (*To* ORGON) I am amazed, and don't know what to say;
Your blindness simply takes my breath away.
You are indeed bewitched, to take no warning
From our account of what occurred this morning.[1]

ORGON. Madam, I know a few plain facts, and one
Is that you're partial to my rascal son;
Hence, when he sought to make Tartuffe the victim
Of a base lie, you dared not contradict him.
Ah, but you underplayed your part, my pet;
You should have looked more angry, more upset.

ELMIRE. When men make overtures, must we reply
With righteous anger and a battle-cry?
Must we turn back their amorous advances
With sharp reproaches and with fiery glances?
Myself, I find such offers merely amusing,
And make no scenes and fusses in refusing;
My taste is for good-natured rectitude,
And I dislike the savage sort of prude
Who guards her virtue with her teeth and claws,
And tears men's eyes out for the slightest cause:
The Lord preserve me from such honor as that,
Which bites and scratches like an alley-cat!
I've found that a polite and cool rebuff
Discourages a lover quite enough.

ORGON. I know the facts, and I shall not be shaken.

1. **what occurred this morning.** Elmire refers to Tartuffe's profession of his desire for her.

Words for Everyday Use

par • tial (pär´shəl) *adj.*, favoring one person or thing more than another; prejudiced

Vocabulary in Context

- Monica thinks that *Tartuffe* is Molière's best play, but Juanita is partial to *The Miser.*

ELMIRE. I marvel at your power to be mistaken.
Would it, I wonder, carry weight with you
If I could *show* you that our tale was true?

ORGON. Show me?

ELMIRE. Yes.

ORGON. Rot.

ELMIRE. Come, what if I found a way
To make you see the facts as plain as day?

ORGON. Nonsense.

ELMIRE. Do answer me; don't be absurd.
I'm not now asking you to trust our word.
Suppose that from some hiding-place in here
You learned the whole sad truth by eye and ear—
What would you say of your good friend, after that?

ORGON. Why, I'd say . . . nothing, by Jehoshaphat!
It can't be true.

ELMIRE. You've been too long deceived,
And I'm quite tired of being disbelieved.
Come now: let's put my statements to the test,
And you shall see the truth made manifest.

ORGON. I'll take that challenge. Now do your uttermost.
We'll see how you make good your empty boast.

ELMIRE. (*To* DORINE) Send him to me.

DORINE. He's crafty; it may be hard
To catch the cunning scoundrel off his guard.

ELMIRE. No, amorous men are gullible. Their conceit
So blinds them that they're never hard to cheat.
Have him come down (*To* CLÉANTE *and* MARIANE) Please leave us, for a bit.

SCENE IV

ELMIRE. Pull up this table, and get under it.

Photo: Richard Feldman. Huntington Theatre Company

ORGON. What?

ELMIRE. It's essential that you be well-hidden.

ORGON. Why there?

ELMIRE. Oh, Heavens! Just do as you are bidden.
I have my plans; we'll soon see how they fare.
Under the table, now; and once you're there,
Take care that you are neither seen nor heard.

ORGON. Well, I'll indulge you, since I gave my word
To see you through this infantile charade.

ELMIRE. Once it is over, you'll be glad we played.
(*To her husband, who is now under the table*)

INTEGRATED SKILLS ACTIVITIES

SPEAKING AND LISTENING

Orgon claims that one of the reasons he does not believe Elmire is that her reaction was not appropriate. He claims that she should have "looked more angry, more upset." Although people react in different ways in different situations—for example, some people weep when faced with death, others may be saddened but do not show their emotions openly—facial expression, gestures, and body language relay a great deal of information about a speaker or listener. Refer students to the Language Arts Survey 3.1, "Elements of Verbal and Nonverbal Communication." Then have them use elements of nonverbal communication to convey an emotional reaction to the following events:

- winning an award
- arriving at a surprise party
- losing a game
- saying goodbye to a friend who is moving to another state
- listening to something that bores them

Students might work in groups and try to guess what emotion a student is trying to convey. They can then identify what elements of nonverbal communication in each portrayal might have been misread.

▶ Additional practice is provided in the Essential Skills Practice Book: Speaking and Listening 3.1.

Answers to Guided Reading Questions

➊ Elmire explains that her actions may seem odd to Orgon because she is going to act as though she is submitting to Tartuffe's desires in order to trick him. She does not want him to think that she is actually encouraging Tartuffe.

INTEGRATED SKILLS ACTIVITIES

LANGUAGE

Students will recognize that drama consists mainly of dialogue, but that it does not have tag lines. Have students rewrite a passage of *Tartuffe* as though it were a work of prose. Remind them that they should start a new paragraph for each new speaker. For advice on using quotation marks correctly, refer them to the Language Arts Survey 2.52, "Other Uses of Quotation Marks." Suggest that students paraphrase the work rather than working it in couplets.

► Additional practice is provided in the Essential Skills Practice Book: Language 2.52.

 ➊

What explanation does Elmire make to Orgon when he has hidden under the table? Why does she tell him this?

I'm going to act quite strangely, now, and you
Must not be shocked at anything I do.
Whatever I may say, you must excuse
As part of that deceit I'm forced to use.
I shall employ sweet speeches in the task
Of making that imposter drop his mask;
I'll give encouragement to his bold desires,
And furnish fuel to his amorous fires.
Since it's for your sake, and for his destruction,
That I shall seem to yield to his seduction,
I'll gladly stop whenever you decide
That all your doubts are fully satisfied.
I'll count on you, as soon as you have seen
What sort of man he is, to intervene,
And not expose me to his odious lust
One moment longer than you feel you must.
Remember: you're to save me from my plight
Whenever . . . He's coming! Hush! Keep out of sight!

SCENE V

TARTUFFE. You wish to have a word with me, I'm told.

ELMIRE. Yes. I've a little secret to unfold.
Before I speak, however, it would be wise
To close that door, and look about for spies.
(*Tartuffe goes to the door, closes it, and returns.*)
The very last thing that must happen now
Is a repetition of this morning's row.
I've never been so badly caught off guard.
Oh, how I feared for you! You saw how hard
I tried to make that troublesome Damis
Control his dreadful temper, and hold his peace.
In my confusion, I didn't have the sense
Simply to contradict his evidence;
But as it happened, that was for the best,
And all has worked out in our interest.
This storm has only bettered your position;
My husband doesn't have the least suspicion,
And now, in mockery of those who do,
He bids me be continually with you.
And that is why, quite fearless of reproof,
I now can be alone with my Tartuffe,
And why my heart—perhaps too quick to yield—
Feels free to let its passion be revealed.

TARTUFFE. Madam, your words confuse me. Not long ago,
You spoke in quite a different style, you know.

ELMIRE. Ah, Sir, if that refusal made you smart,
It's little that you know of woman's heart,
Or what that heart is trying to convey
When it resists in such a feeble way!
Always, at first, our modesty prevents
The frank avowal of tender sentiments;
However high the passion which inflames us,
Still, to confess its power somehow shames us.
Thus we reluct, at first, yet in a tone
Which tells you that our heart is overthrown,
That what our lips deny, our pulse confesses,
And that, in time, all noes will turn to yesses.
I fear my words are all too frank and free,
And a poor proof of woman's modesty;
But since I'm started, tell me, if you will—
Would I have tried to make Damis be still,
Would I have listened, calm and unoffended,
Until your lengthy offer of love was ended,
And been so very mild in my reaction,
Had your sweet words not given me satisfaction?

WORDS FOR EVERYDAY USE

in • ter • vene (in´tər vēn´) *vi.,* come between to settle an argument or to disrupt an action

Vocabulary in Context

• Mario and Lucia bickered for an hour before Constantine intervened.

Photo: Richard Feldman. Huntington Theatre Company

And when I tried to force you to undo
The marriage-plans my husband has in view,
What did my urgent pleading signify
If not that I admired you, and that I
Deplored the thought that someone else might own
Part of a heart I wished for mine alone?

Tartuffe. Madam, no happiness is so complete
As when, from lips we love, come words so sweet;
Their nectar floods my every sense, and drains
In honeyed rivulets through all my veins.
To please you is my joy, my only goal;
Your love is the restorer of my soul;
And yet I must beg leave, now, to confess
Some lingering doubts as to my happiness.
Might this not be a trick? Might not the catch
Be that you wish me to break off the match
With Mariane, and so have feigned to love me?
I shan't quite trust your fond opinion of me
Until the feelings you've expressed so sweetly
Are demonstrated somewhat more concretely,
And you have shown, by certain kind concessions,
That I may put my faith in your professions.

Elmire. (*She coughs, to warn her husband.*)
Why be in such a hurry? Must my heart
Exhaust its bounty at the very start?
To make that sweet admission cost me dear,
But you'll not be content, it would appear,
Unless my store of favors is disbursed

❶ *Does Tartuffe believe Elmire's confession? What would make him more willing to believe her?*

Words for Everyday Use

feign (fān) *vt.*, pretend

Answers to Guided Reading Questions

❶ Tartuffe says he is not quite convinced by Elmire's confession, but that concrete signs of her affection would convince him.

Biographical Note

Molière is often considered the master of French comedy, and the two great tragedians of his time were Pierre Corneille and Jean Racine.

Pierre Corneille (1601–1684) is credited with creating French classical tragedy. His most famous works include *Le Cid,* based on the Spanish hero El Cid; *Horace,* based on an account by Livy (see page 683); *Cinna,* which tells of a conspiracy against Roman emperor Augustus; and *Polyeucte,* which critics often consider Corneille's finest work. Although he is best known for his tragedies, Corneille had an impact on comedy in French theaters, influencing Molière and others.

To become a dramatist, **Jean Racine** (1639–1699) broke with his family who condemned theatrical life. His best-known works are *Britannicus, Bérénice, Bajazet,* and *Phèdre.* A conflict developed between the two tragedians at the staging of Racine's *Britannicus,* when Corneille was rude and hostile to Racine. Racine retired suddenly, less than a year after *Phèdre* premiered in 1677.

Vocabulary in Context

• Dmitri feigned surprise when his friends jumped out of their hiding places, but he had known about the party for weeks.

Answers to Guided Reading Questions

❶ Tartuffe says that we do not believe that we will receive the things that will make us happy or that dreams will come true until it actually happens. He is hoping to convince Elmire to demonstrate her affection to him.

❷ Elmire suggests that Heaven, which demands virtue, is an obstacle to their love. Tartuffe makes light of the obstacle and says that they won't be punished for their sins as long as their intentions are pure. He reveals that he is not the pious, virtuous man he pretends to be.

Additional Questions and Activities

In this scene Tartuffe is trying to convince Elmire to do something that she does not want to do and does not think is right. Students may often face similar situations in the form of peer pressure. Ask students to discuss situations in which they have been pressured to do something that they did not want to do and how they dealt with the situation. Students can brainstorm a list of situations and role play to develop ideas for reacting to such pressure.

To the last farthing, and at the very first.

Tartuffe. The less we merit, the less we dare to hope,
And with our doubts, mere words can never cope.
We trust no promised bliss till we receive it;
Not till a joy is ours can we believe it.
I, who so little merit your esteem,
Can't credit this fulfillment of my dream,
And shan't believe it, Madam, until I savor
Some palpable assurance of your favor.

❶ *What opinion does Tartuffe express about joy and dreams? What purpose lies behind this statement?*

Elmire. My, how tyrannical your love can be,
And how it flusters and perplexes me!
How furiously you take one's heart in hand,
And make your every wish a fierce command!
Come, must you hound and harry me to death?
Will you not give me time to catch my breath?
Can it be right to press me with such force,
Give me no quarter, show me no remorse,
And take advantage, by your stern insistence,
Of the fond feelings which weaken my resistance?

Tartuffe. Well, if you look with favor upon my love,
Why, then, begrudge me some clear proof thereof?

Elmire. But how can I consent without offense
To Heaven, toward which you feel such reverence?

❷ *What does Elmire suggest is an obstacle to their love? What does Tartuffe think of the obstacle that Elmire presents? What does he reveal about himself in these lines?*

Tartuffe. If Heaven is all that holds you back, don't worry.
I can remove that hindrance in a hurry.
Nothing of that sort need obstruct our path.

Elmire. Must one not be afraid of Heaven's wrath?

Tartuffe. Madam, forget such fears, and be my pupil,
And I shall teach you how to conquer scruple.
Some joys, it's true, are wrong in Heaven's eyes;
Yet Heaven is not averse to compromise;
There is a science, lately formulated,
Whereby one's conscience may be liberated,
And any wrongful act you care to mention
May be redeemed by purity of intention.
I'll teach you, Madam, the secrets of that science;
Meanwhile, just place on me your full reliance.
Assuage my keen desires, and feel no dread:
The sin, if any, shall be on my head.
(Elmira *coughs, this time more loudly.*)
You've a bad cough.

Elmire. Yes, yes. It's bad indeed.

Tartuffe. (*Producing a little paper bag*)
A bit of licorice may be what you need.

Elmire. No, I've a stubborn cold, it seems. I'm sure it
Will take much more than licorice to cure it.

Tartuffe. How aggravating.

Elmire. Oh, more than I can say.

Tartuffe. If you're still troubled, think of things this way:
No one shall know our joys, save us alone,
And there's no evil till the act is known;
It's scandal, Madam, which makes it an offense,
And it's no sin to sin in confidence.

Elmire. (*Having coughed once more*)
Well, clearly I must do as you require,
And yield to your importunate desire.
It is apparent, now, that nothing less
Will satisfy you, and so I acquiesce.

Words for Everyday Use

mer • it (mer´it) *vt.,* deserve, be worthy of

pal • pa • ble (pal´pə bəl) *adj.,* that can be touched or felt

as • suage (ə swāj´) *vt.,* lessen or satisfy a need; relieve

ac • qui • esce (ak´wē es´) *vi.,* agree without protest but also without enthusiasm

Vocabulary in Context

- "The unusual circumstances merit an extension," Mr. Kirobe decided after hearing Lani's case.
- Jolene squeezed my hand in a palpable sign of reassurance.
- Use aloe vera to assuage the pain of your sunburn.
- Refusing to acquiesce to the unjust decision, Lavinia joined the protesters at the demonstration.

Photo: Richard Feldman. Huntington Theatre Company

To go so far is much against my will;
I'm vexed that it should come to this; but still,
Since you are so determined on it, since you
Will not allow mere language to convince you,
And since you ask for concrete evidence, I
See nothing for it, now, but to comply.
If this is sinful, if I'm wrong to do it,
So much the worse for him who drove me to it.
The fault can surely not be charged to me.

TARTUFFE. Madam, the fault is mine, if fault there be,
And . . .

ELMIRE. Open the door a little, and peek out;
I wouldn't want my husband poking about.

TARTUFFE. Why worry about the man? Each day he grows
More gullible; one can lead him by the nose.
To find us here would fill him with delight,
And if he saw the worst, he'd doubt his sight.

ELMIRE. Nevertheless, do step out for a minute
Into the hall, and see that no one's in it.

SCENE VI

ORGON. (*Coming out from under the table*)
That man's a perfect monster, I must admit!
I'm simply stunned. I can't get over it.

ELMIRE. What, coming out so soon? How premature!

❶ *What is Tartuffe's opinion of Orgon? What might Orgon be thinking when he hears Tartuffe talk about him in this way?*

Answers to Guided Reading Questions

❶ Tartuffe thinks that Orgon is a fool and easily manipulated. Orgon is likely outraged that Tartuffe is speaking of him in this way. Orgon is also likely to be a bit embarrassed that he was taken in by Tartuffe.

Additional Questions and Activities

Ask students to write a journal entry describing a time when they overheard somebody talking about them. Was what they heard positive or negative? How did hearing this about themselves make them feel? Have they ever been caught talking about somebody behind his or her back? With what results? How did they feel when they learned they had been overheard?

Answers to Guided Reading Questions

❶ Orgon has given Tartuffe the deed to his house, so efforts to remove Tartuffe from the house will be impeded. It is Orgon who will be forced to leave.

Selection Check Test with Answers

EX. To what does Orgon refer when he says he has the contract that contains Mariane's happiness?
He refers to her marriage to Tartuffe.

1. Why does Orgon fail to believe Elmire about the morning's events?
He does not believe her because she did not seem very angry or upset.

2. Where does Elmire have Orgon hide?
She has him hide under the table.

3. What does Tartuffe require to ensure that Elmire is speaking truthfully?
He demands palpable proof of what she feels.

4. What obstacle does Elmire present, only to have Tartuffe brush it off?
Elmire suggests that they will offend Heaven.

5. When Orgon emerges from under the table, what does he demand of Tartuffe?
He demands that Tartuffe leave his house immediately.

Get back in hiding, and wait until you're sure.
Stay till the end, and be convinced completely;
We mustn't stop till things are proved concretely.

ORGON. Hell never harbored anything so vicious!

ELMIRE. Tut, don't be hasty. Try to be judicious.
Wait, and be certain that there's no mistake.
No jumping to conclusions, for Heaven's sake!
(*She places* ORGON *behind her, as* TARTUFFE *reenters.*)

SCENE VII

TARTUFFE. (*Not seeing* ORGON) Madam, all things have worked out to perfection;
I've given the neighboring rooms a full inspection;
No one's about; and now I may at last . . .

ORGON. (*Intercepting him*) Hold on, my passionate fellow, not so fast!
I should advise a little more restraint.
Well, so you thought you'd fool me, my dear saint!
How soon you wearied of the saintly life—
Wedding my daughter, and coveting my wife!
I've long suspected you, and had a feeling
That soon I'd catch you at your double-dealing.
Just now, you've given me evidence galore;
It's quite enough; I have no wish for more.

ELMIRE. (*To* TARTUFFE) I'm sorry to have treated you so slyly,
But circumstances forced me to be wily.

TARTUFFE. Brother, you can't think . . .

ORGON. No more talk from you;
Just leave this household, without more ado.

TARTUFFE. What I intended . . .

ORGON. That seems fairly clear.
Spare me your falsehoods and get out of here.

TARTUFFE. No, I'm the master, and you're the one to go!
This house belongs to me, I'll have you know,
And I shall show you that you can't hurt me
By this contemptible conspiracy,
That those who cross me know not what they do,
And that I've means to expose and punish you,
Avenge offended Heaven, and make you grieve
That ever you dared order me to leave. ■

 ❶ *What problem has Orgon's blindness to Tartuffe's character caused?*

Words for Everyday Use

ju • di • cious (jo͞o dish´əs) *adj.*, wise and careful

con • tempt • i • ble (kən temp´tə bəl) *adj.*, deserving scorn; worthless

Vocabulary in Context

- Although Yuri often makes unsound decisions, he was very judicious when deciding which college to attend.
- Cheaters are contemptible people.

Responding to the Selection

At the end of this selection do you feel sympathetic toward Orgon? Why, or why not? What are your feelings toward Tartuffe? Elmire? Do you think her anger toward her husband is justified?

Reviewing the Selection

RECALLING		INTERPRETING
1. What two reasons does Orgon give for not believing what Elmire has told him about the morning's events involving Tartuffe?	▶▶	What do you know about Orgon's opinion of Tartuffe based on his reaction to the morning's events?
2. When Orgon is under the table, what does Elmire say about her actions?	▶▶	Why does she make this explanation?
3. What obstacle does Elmire present to consenting to Tartuffe's demands? What responses does Tartuffe offer to her concerns?	▶▶	What does Tartuffe reveal about his character in this passage?
4. According to Tartuffe, why is there no need to fear Orgon catching them?	▶▶	How might Orgon feel upon hearing what Tartuffe says about him? Is what Tartuffe says true? Explain.

SYNTHESIZING

5. Deception is used throughout this selection. Identify two people who are deceptive. Whom does each person deceive? Why is each person deceptive? In what ways do the two forms of deception differ?

Understanding Literature (Questions for Discussion)

1. **Characterization. Characterization** is the use of literary techniques to create a character. Writers use three major techniques to create characters: direct description, portrayal of characters' behavior, and representations of characters' internal states. For explanations of these techniques, refer to the entry on characterization in the Handbook of Literary Terms. Which methods are used to characterize Tartuffe? Give examples of the methods, and explain what you learn about Tartuffe from each example.

RESPONDING TO THE SELECTION

Ask students to put themselves in Orgon's place. How would they fell about Tartuffe? about Elmire? If they were in Elmire's place, how would they feel toward Orgon? toward Tartuffe? If they were Tartuffe, how would they feel about being caught? about Orgon? about Elmire? Students might also like to discuss their reactions to being deceived in their own lives.

ANSWERS FOR REVIEWING THE SELECTION

RECALLING AND INTERPRETING

1. **Recalling.** Orgon says that he does not believe Elmire because she is partial to Damis and would lie for him and because she did not seem upset enough considering what she claimed had happened. **Interpreting.** Orgon thinks that Tartuffe can do no wrong. He looks more highly on Tartuffe than he does on members of his family.

2. **Recalling.** Elmire explains that her actions may seem strange to Orgon because she is going to act in such a way as to encourage Tartuffe's advances. **Interpreting.** Elmire does not want Orgon to think that she means what she says or to discredit what he learns about Tartuffe because of her actions.

3. **Recalling.** Elmire suggests that their actions might offend Heaven or God, toward whom Tartuffe has made a great show of being devoted. Tartuffe tells her that he can remove such obstacles and show her how to avoid guilt by acting with purity of intention. **Interpreting.** Tartuffe reveals that his religious fervor and piety is a hoax.

4. **Recalling.** Tartuffe says they do not need to fear Orgon because he is a fool and because he would be delighted to find them together.

(cont.)

ANSWERS FOR REVIEWING THE SELECTION (CONT.)

Interpreting. Orgon would probably be outraged that Tartuffe would speak of him in this way, after everything Orgon has done for Tartuffe. He might also be embarrassed to learn of his folly in trusting Tartuffe. Tartuffe's words are true. Orgon has been a fool and has been blind to Tartuffe's deception.

SYNTHESIZING

Responses will vary. Possible responses are given.

5. Tartuffe and Elmire are both deceptive in this selection. Tartuffe deceives Orgon and tries to deceive the other members of Orgon's household to gain control of Orgon's money, house, and family. Elmire deceives Tartuffe by pretending to submit to his advances. Her deceit is designed to reveal Tartuffe's deceit to Orgon.

Answers for Understanding Literature

Responses will vary. Possible responses are given.

1. **Characterization.** Direct description and portrayal of characters' behavior is used to characterize Tartuffe. Dorine says that Tartuffe is "crafty" and a "cunning scoundrel," revealing that Tartuffe is clever, dishonest, and distrusted by some of the other characters. When Tartuffe insists that Elmire display her affection for him and tells her that "it's no sin to sin in confidence," he reveals that he is persistent, demanding, and unscrupulous. He shows that many of the values and qualities that he pretended to possess were merely a facade used to cover his desires.
2. **Couplet.** Students may choose any couplets from the selection. Three examples are the following: "He's welcome to my money; take it, do / But don't, I pray, include my person too," "Come, what if I found a way / To make you see the facts as plain as day?" and "I've long suspected you, and had a feeling / That soon I'd catch you at your double-dealing."

Answers for Skills Activities

APPLIED ENGLISH/TECH PREP

Before writing the press release or ad copy, students may wish to gather additional information about the play by reading the complete play, reading reviews of other performances of the play, or viewing a video of the play.

As an alternate activity, students may wish to create promotional copy for an event that is actually taking place in their school or community.

▶ Additional practice is provided in the Essential Skills Practice Book: Applied English/Tech Prep 5.6.

2. **Couplet.** A **couplet** is two lines of verse that usually rhyme. Couplets such as the following by Alexander Pope were a popular literary form during the Enlightenment:

   One science only will one genius fit;
   So vast is art, so narrow human wit.

   Identify several couplets from Tartuffe.

Responding in Writing

1. **Creative Writing: Diatribe.** A diatribe is a bitter or abusive criticism of something or someone. Throughout most of the play, Orgon has only praises for Tartuffe. By the end of act IV, scene vii, Orgon's eyes have been opened to Tartuffe's deception, and his attitude toward Tartuffe has changed drastically. Write a diatribe about Tartuffe from Orgon's point of view.
2. **Critical Essay: The Comic Genius of Molière.** Molière has been called by many the greatest French writer of comedy. Analyze this selection for elements of comedy. Consider that comedies often present less-than-exalted characters who display all-too-human limitations, foibles, faults, and misunderstandings, and that stock elements of comedy include mistaken identities, word play, satire, and exaggerated characters and events. Write a one- to two-page essay in which you analyze a comic character or situation from *Tartuffe*.

Applied English/Tech Prep Skills

Writing Promotional and Public Relations Copy. Read the Language Arts Survey 5.6, "Writing Promotional and Public Relations Copy." Then imagine that the drama club at your school is performing Molière's *Tartuffe.* Write a press release or a radio advertisement to promote the performance. Remember that your goal is to capture the interest of your audience and to convey, concisely, all the necessary information about the upcoming performance.

Additional Questions and Activities

You may wish to have students read some of the stories mentioned in Themes: Honesty and Deception on page 883. Have them discuss the ways in which the methods of deception, reasons for deception, and effects of deception are similar or different in the works they have read.

Use the following questions to stimulate discussion about honesty and deception: Is it ever acceptable to lie, or is honesty always the best policy? Is telling only part of the truth the same as lying? Can anything positive come of deception? Students should explain their responses.

Themes

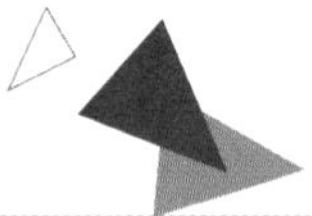

Honesty and Deception

Deception is a recurrent theme in world literature and is found in the earliest literature from the oral tradition, including trickster tales and fables. Fables featuring tricksters, such as the Anansi Spider stories of the Ashanti peoples and the Coyote stories of many Native American peoples of the Southwest, often deal with heroes who win because of their imagination or inventiveness rather than their brawn or bravery. Trickery or deception is also used in fables to teach moral lessons, as in Aesop's "The Boy Who Cried 'Wolf,'" which warns, "Tell the truth; be not too clever, for fooled once is warned forever," and "The Wolf in Sheep's Clothing," which admonishes, "Beware of those who look too fine; remember how the wolf did dine." Perhaps one of the most famous stories of trickery is found in Homer's epic poems the *Iliad* and the *Odyssey,* in which the people of Troy fall prey to a trick devised by Odysseus. The Trojans unwittingly allow the Achaeans, their enemies, into their city hidden inside a great wooden horse.

Deception often involves **dramatic irony** in which something is known by the reader or audience but unknown to one or more of the characters. The reader or audience is often aware of the deception at work, although the characters remain ignorant of the deceit. In *Tartuffe,* subtitled *The Imposter,* the dramatic irony of deception has a comic effect. Tartuffe convinces Orgon that he is a humble, pious man, while in reality he is a scheming charlatan with corrupt morals. Tartuffe's deception is especially effective because the character he purports to be is an honest, highly moral one. The dramatic irony of the situation creates humor throughout the play, and the scene in which Tartuffe's true nature is revealed is especially comic. In *Tartuffe,* the deceiver is ultimately undone by another's deception, when Elmire pretends to fall prey to Tartuffe's charm. Elmire warns Orgon:

> Whatever I may say, you must excuse
> As part of that deceit I'm forced to use.
> I shall employ sweet speeches in the task
> Of making the imposter drop his mask.

Elmire refers to Tartuffe's deceptiveness as an imposter's mask. The mask or disguise is a common contrivance for deception in the theater.

A double, one who takes the place of another character, is another common means of deception. In *Cyrano de Bergerac* (see page 958), Cyrano and Christian combine the strengths of each man—Cyrano's romantic ideals and language and Christian's beauty—to create Roxane's ideal suitor. This deception is perhaps best portrayed in the balcony scene in which Cyrano, hidden from view, whispers lines for Christian to speak to Roxane until, carried away, he begins speaking to her himself; Roxane literally falls in love with Cyrano's words. Christian is unable to woo Roxane in his own words; when left to his own devices, he fails to capture her interest. Cyrano, on the other hand, is unable to interest Roxane because of his unattractive appearance, despite the words and sentiments that delight her.

Tricksters, doubles, and unscrupulous swindlers are some of the deceptive characters you will encounter in your reading. You will find that deception has many faces and that the use of deception as a theme can achieve entertaining and enlightening results.

ANALYTIC SCALES FOR RESPONDING IN WRITING

Assign a score from 1 to 25 for each grading criterion below. (For more detailed evaluation, see the evaluation forms for writing, revising, and proofreading, Assessment Portfolio 4.1–4.9.)

1. Diatribe

- **Content/Unity.** The diatribe criticizes Tartuffe from Orgon's point of view. The tone is bitter or angry.
- **Organization/Coherence.** The diatribe may be arranged in a logical order such as part-by-part order or it may reflect a flow of stream of consciousness.
- **Language/Style.** The diatribe uses vivid and precise nouns, verbs, and modifiers.
- **Conventions.** The diatribe avoids errors in spelling, grammar, usage, mechanics, and manuscript form.

► Additional practice is provided in the Essential Skills Practice Book: Writing 1.8.

2. Critical Essay

- **Content/Unity.** The essay presents and supports analysis of the elements of comedy in the selection.
- **Organization/Coherence.** The essay catches the reader's attention and presents a thesis in the introduction. The introduction is followed by supporting paragraphs with clear transitions. The essay ends with a solid conclusion.
- **Language/Style.** The essay uses vivid and precise nouns, verbs, and modifiers.
- **Conventions.** The essay avoids errors in spelling, grammar, usage, mechanics, and manuscript form.

► Additional practice is provided in the Essential Skills Practice Book: Writing 1.20.

ADDITIONAL RESOURCES

READER'S GUIDE

- Selection Worksheet 10.8

ASSESSMENT PORTFOLIO

- Selection Check Test 2.10.15
- Selection Test 2.10.16

ESSENTIAL SKILLS PRACTICE BOOKS

- Writing 1.8, 1.10, 1.20
- Language 2.41–2.42

PREREADING EXTENSIONS

Students can hold a debate on the idea that "this is the best of all possible worlds." Students should work in separate teams of three or four, and each team should develop logical arguments in agreement or disagreement with the idea.

SUPPORT FOR LEP STUDENTS

PRONUNCIATIONS OF PROPER NOUNS AND ADJECTIVES

Fran • çois Ma • rie A • rou • et (frän swå´ mä rē´ a roo ā´)
Can • dide (can dēd´)
Gott • fried Leib • niz (got´frēt līp´nits)
Vol • taire (vōl tayr´)

ADDITIONAL VOCABULARY

accordance—agreement
consternation—fear or shock that makes one helpless
genealogy—a line of descent
ignominious—shameful, dishonorable

PREREADING

from *Candide*
by Voltaire (François Marie Arouet)

FRANCE

About the Author

VOLTAIRE
1694–1778

Born in Paris, **François Marie Arouet** was educated at a Jesuit school where he had an active social life and gained an appreciation for literature and drama. He began to study law, but in his early twenties, he chose the world of literature instead, adopting the pseudonym **Voltaire**. As a young writer, Voltaire won acclaim for his dramatic works. Nevertheless, he enraged certain French nobles and was imprisoned twice in the Bastille. In his mid-thirties, he was exiled to England, where Jonathan Swift, Alexander Pope, and other leading writers and thinkers befriended him. Impressed by the relative freedom of thought in England, Voltaire wrote his *Philosophical Letters on the English.* After returning to France and publishing this work, a satirical attack on the French church and state, he was forced into exile again. He sought refuge with Mme du Châtelet, whose interest in and study of science and metaphysics greatly influenced his work. For most of the rest of his life, Voltaire moved often between Belgium, Cirey, and Paris. He also paid a long visit to Frederick the Great, king of Prussia. During the later years of his life, he published the widely read *Philosophic Dictionary* and wrote satirical tales such as *Zadig* in 1747 and *Candide* in 1759. Despite the many genres in which Voltaire wrote, including tragedy, epic, history, philosophy, and fiction, most of his works treat similar themes—religious tolerance and the need to respect human rights by abolishing torture and unnecessary punishments.

About the Selection

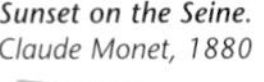
Sunset on the Seine.
Claude Monet, 1880

Candide is a satirical attack on philosophical optimists such as Gottfried Leibniz, whose philosophy is reduced in *Candide* to "everything is for the best in this, the best of all worlds." Candide, a simple, naive character, faces a number of horrible experiences, including war, disease, and natural disaster. In spite of this suffering, Candide's tutor Pangloss continues to maintain that everything is for the best. Voltaire satirizes this idea, renouncing Pangloss's blind, shallow optimism because it does not take into account human experience and suffering.

CONNECTIONS: Innocence and Social Critique

Candide is an innocent character who often seems unaware of the import of events that occur around him. Another such character, Chance, appears in *Being There* (see page 1078). Chance is often swept into situations in which he has a very different perception from others. Such innocent characters allow authors to critique society by showing it from a naive point of view. Such critiques are usually ironic, as the audience's awareness of an event is something quite different from what the character perceives.

GOALS/OBJECTIVES

Studying this lesson will enable students to

- appreciate and interpret humor and criticism in a work of satire
- explain the philosophical view that Voltaire attacks in *Candide*
- define *satire a*nd identify its effects in literature
- define *irony* and identify and interpret its effects as they encounter it in their reading
- write a description of a utopia
- write a critical essay critiquing a philosophy
- edit sentences for errors in modifier usage

Are you an optimist or a pessimist? What is the difference between blind optimism and clear-sighted optimism? Do you agree or disagree with the statement that "This is the best of all possible worlds"? Explain your response in your journal.

READER'S JOURNAL

As an alternate activity, encourage students to list both the benefits and drawbacks of optimism and pessimism.

ANSWERS TO GUIDED READING QUESTIONS

➊ Candide's name reflects his simple-mindedness and his honesty. Voltaire may have chosen such a name to symbolize the optimism he wished to satirize.

FROM

Candide

VOLTAIRE

CHAPTER I

HOW CANDIDE WAS BROUGHT UP IN A NOBLE CASTLE AND HOW HE WAS EXPELLED FROM THE SAME

In the castle of Baron Thunder-ten-tronckh in Westphalia[1] there lived a youth, endowed by Nature with the most gentle character. His face was the expression of his soul. His judgment was quite honest and he was extremely simple-minded; and this was the reason, I think, that he was named Candide.[2] Old servants in the house suspected that he was the son of the Baron's sister and a decent honest gentleman of the neighbourhood, whom this young lady would never marry because he could only prove seventy-one quarterings,[3] and the rest of his genealogical tree was lost, owing to the injuries of time. The Baron was one of the most powerful lords in Westphalia, for his castle possessed a door and windows. His Great Hall was even decorated with a piece of tapestry. The dogs in his stable-yards formed a pack of hounds when necessary; his grooms were his huntsmen; the village curate was his Grand Almoner.[4] They all called him "My Lord," and laughed heartily at his stories. The Baroness weighed about three hundred and fifty pounds, was therefore greatly respected, and did the honours of the house with a dignity which rendered her still more respectable. Her daughter Cunegonde, aged seventeen, was rosy-cheeked, fresh, plump and tempting. The Baron's son appeared in every respect worthy of his father. The tutor Pangloss[5] was the oracle of the house, and

➊ *What makes Candide's name fitting? Why might Voltaire have chosen such a name?*

1. **Westphalia.** Region in northwestern Germany
2. **Candide.** The word *candid* means "frank" or "honest."
3. **quarterings.** Divisions of a coat of arms showing degrees of nobility
4. **Grand Almoner.** Distributor of alms or charity
5. **Pangloss.** The name in Greek means "all tongue."

SPELLING AND VOCABULARY WORDS FROM THE SELECTION

blackguard	oracle
clemency	prodigy
furrow	regiment
metaphysician	vivacity

QUOTABLES

"I disapprove of what you say, but I will defend to the death your right to say it."

—Voltaire

WORDS FOR EVERYDAY USE

or • a • cle (ôr´ə kəl) *n.,* person in communication with the gods; person of great knowledge or wisdom

VOCABULARY IN CONTEXT

• People in ancient Greece would seek answers from the oracle at Delphi, who was believed to communicate with Apollo.

Answers to Guided Reading Questions

❶ Pangloss taught Candide that there is no effect without a cause and that this is the best of all possible worlds.

❷ Candide considers the four greatest happinesses to be being Baron Thunder-ten-tronckh, being Mademoiselle Cunegonde, seeing Mademoiselle Cunegonde every day, and listening to Doctor Pangloss.

Cultural/Historical Note

Point out that Pangloss taught only Candide and not the baron's daughter, Mademoiselle Cunegonde. Boys and girls born to aristocratic families were usually educated at home; however, a girl's education focused more on social refinements than on intellectual pursuits. While this was generally the case, there were some aristocratic families in certain times and places who believed that boys and girls should be taught the same subjects. (For example, several aristocratic Italian families during the Renaissance encouraged young female family members to pursue their studies.) Nevertheless, the notion of equal education for men and women remained more an aberration than the norm. In fact, by the year 1786, only 27 percent of French women were literate.

❶ *What philosophical views did Pangloss teach Candide?*

❷ *What does Candide consider to be the four greatest happinesses?*

little Candide followed his lessons with all the candour of his age and character. Pangloss taught metaphysico-theologo-cosmol-onigology. He proved admirably that there is no effect without a cause and that in this best of all possible worlds,[6] My Lord the Baron's castle was the best of castles and his wife the best of all possible Baronesses. "'Tis demonstrated," said he, "that things cannot be otherwise; for, since everything is made for an end, everything is necessarily for the best end. Observe that noses were made to wear spectacles; and so we have spectacles. Legs were visibly instituted to be breeched, and we have breeches. Stones were formed to be quarried and to build castles; and My Lord has a very noble castle; the greatest Baron in the province should have the best house; and as pigs were made to be eaten, we eat pork all the year round; consequently, those who have asserted that all is well talk nonsense; they ought to have said that all is for the best." Candide listened attentively and believed innocently; for he thought Mademoiselle Cunegonde extremely beautiful, although he was never bold enough to tell her so. He decided that after the happiness of being born Baron of Thunder-ten-tronckh, the second degree of happiness was to be Mademoiselle Cunegonde; the third, to see her every day; and the fourth to listen to Doctor Pangloss, the greatest philosopher of the province and therefore of the whole world. . . .

◆ ◆ ◆

Next day, when they left the table after dinner, Cunegonde and Candide found themselves behind a screen; Cunegonde dropped her handkerchief, Candide picked it up; she innocently held his hand; the young man innocently kissed the young lady's hand with remarkable vivacity, tenderness and grace; their lips met, their eyes sparkled, their knees trembled, their hands wandered. Baron Thunder-ten-tronckh passed near the screen, and, observing this cause and effect, expelled Candide from the castle by kicking him in the backside frequently and hard. Cunegonde swooned; when she recovered her senses, the Baroness slapped her in the face; and all was in consternation in the noblest and most agreeable of all possible castles.

CHAPTER II

WHAT HAPPENED TO CANDIDE AMONG THE BULGARIANS

Candide, expelled from the earthly paradise, wandered for a long time without knowing where he was going, turning up his eyes to Heaven, gazing back frequently at the noblest of castles which held the most beautiful of young Baronesses; he lay down to sleep supperless between two furrows in the open fields; it snowed heavily in large flakes. The next morning the shivering Candide, penniless, dying of cold and exhaustion, dragged himself towards the neighbouring town, which was called Waldberghoff-trarbk-dikdorff. He halted sadly at the door of an inn. Two men dressed in blue noticed him. "Comrade," said one, "there's a well-built young man of the right height." They went up to Candide and very civilly invited him to dinner. "Gentlemen," said Candide with charming modesty, "you do me a great honour, but I have no money to pay my share." "Ah, sir,"

6. **best of all possible worlds.** Voltaire is satirizing the beliefs of the German philosopher Leibniz.

Words for Everyday Use

vi • vac • i • ty (vī vas´ə tē) *n.,* liveliness

fur • row (fʉr´ō) *n.,* groove made in the earth by a plow

Vocabulary in Context

- Exhausted by a long day of traveling, the entertainer lacked her usual vivacity.
- The planter followed the plow, dropping seeds into the furrow.

Bridge at Argenteuil. *Claude Monet, 1874*

said one of the men in blue, "persons of your figure and merit never pay anything; are you not five feet five tall?" "Yes, gentlemen," said he, bowing, "that is my height." "Ah, sir, come to table; we will not only pay your expenses, we will never allow a man like you to be short of money; men were only made to help each other." "You are in the right," said Candide, "that is what Doctor Pangloss was always telling me, and I see that everything is for the best." They begged him to accept a few crowns, he took them and wished to give them an IOU; they refused to take it and all sat down to table. "Do you not love tenderly . . ." "Oh, yes," said he. "I love Mademoiselle Cunegonde tenderly." "No," said one of the gentlemen. "We were asking if you do not tenderly love the King of the Bulgarians." "Not a bit," said he, "for I have never seen him." "What! He is the most charming of Kings, and you must drink his health." "Oh, gladly, gentlemen." And he drank. "That is sufficient," he was told. "You are now the support, the aid, the defender, the hero of the Bulgarians; your fortune is made and your glory assured." They immediately put irons on his legs and took him to a regiment. He was made to turn to the right and left, to raise the ramrod[7] and return the ramrod, to take aim, to fire, to double up, and he was given thirty strokes with a stick; the next day he drilled not quite so badly, and received only twenty strokes; the day after, he only had ten and was looked on as a prodigy by his comrades. Candide was completely mystified and could not make out how he was a hero. One fine spring day he thought he would take a walk, going straight ahead, in the belief that to use his legs as he pleased was a privilege of the human species as well

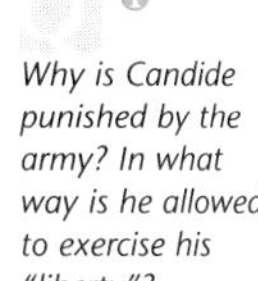

1

Why is Candide punished by the army? In what way is he allowed to exercise his "liberty"?

7. **ramrod.** Poker used for loading a muzzle-loaded rifle

WORDS FOR EVERYDAY USE

reg • i • ment (rej´ə ment) *n.,* unit of soldiers

prod • i • gy (präd´ə jē) *n.,* child or other person with talent or genius

ANSWERS TO GUIDED READING QUESTIONS

1 Candide is punished for drilling badly and for taking a walk. He is allowed to exercise his "liberty" by deciding which of two terrible punishments he prefers.

LITERARY TECHNIQUE

ALLUSION

Inform students that an **allusion** is a rhetorical technique in which reference is made to a person, event, object, or work from history or literature. Then ask students the following questions: On page 886, Candide's expulsion from the castle is described as an expulsion from an "earthly paradise." To what does this description allude? For what sin is Candide expelled from this paradise? In what way is this sin similar to or different from the sin for which Adam and Eve were thrust from the Garden of Eden?

ANSWERS

This is an allusion to the expulsion of Adam and Eve from the Garden of Eden in the Book of Genesis. Candide is expelled for the sin of kissing Cunegonde. Both sins mark a fall from innocence.

VOCABULARY IN CONTEXT

- The general stationed the regiment of soldiers in the run-down barracks.
- Mozart was a child prodigy who performed for royal audiences at age six.

Answers to Guided Reading Questions

① Candide expects that he will be well treated in Holland.

Cultural/Historical Note

Point out that Voltaire published *Candide* in the midst of a conflict known as the Seven Years' War (1756–1763). Although the war was primarily a struggle between Great Britain and France for worldwide colonial control, other nations, including France, Austria, Saxony, Sweden, and Russia, entered the conflict with their own agendas. In 1775, Frederick II of Prussia, also known as Frederick the Great, signed the Treaty of Westminster with George II of England, hoping to gain complete control of Germany. By the end of the war, Great Britain emerged as the world's chief colonial empire, and Prussia had become a major European power. Voltaire comments on the bloody conflicts between the Prussians and the French in his bitterly satiric description of the battle between the Bulgarians and the Abares.

as of animals. He had not gone two leagues when four other heroes, each six feet tall, fell upon him, bound him and dragged him back to a cell. He was asked by his judges whether he would rather be thrashed thirty-six times by the whole regiment or receive a dozen lead bullets at once in his brain. Although he protested that men's wills are free and that he wanted neither one nor the other, he had to make a choice; by virtue of that gift of God which is called *liberty*, he determined to run the gauntlet[8] thirty-six times and actually did so twice. There were two thousand men in the regiment. That made four thousand strokes which laid bare the muscles and nerves from his neck to his backside. As they were about to proceed to a third turn, Candide, utterly exhausted, begged as a favor that they would be so kind as to smash his head; he obtained this favor; they bound his eyes and he was made to kneel down. At that moment the King of the Bulgarians came by and inquired the victim's crime; and as this King was possessed of a vast genius, he perceived from what he learned about Candide that he was a young metaphysician very ignorant in worldly matters, and therefore pardoned him with a clemency which will be praised in all newspapers and all ages. An honest surgeon healed Candide in three weeks with the ointments recommended by Dioscorides. He had already regained a little skin and could walk when the King of the Bulgarians went to war with the King of the Abares.[9]

① What does Candide expect will happen in Holland?

CHAPTER III

HOW CANDIDE ESCAPED FROM THE BULGARIANS AND WHAT BECAME OF HIM

Nothing could be smarter, more splendid, more brilliant, better drawn up than the two armies. Trumpets, fifes, hautboys,[10] drums, cannons, formed a harmony such as has never been heard even in hell. The cannons first of all laid flat about six thousand men on each side; then the musketry removed from the best of worlds some nine or ten thousand blackguards who infested its surface. The bayonet also was the sufficient reason for the death of some thousands of men. The whole might amount to thirty thousand souls. Candide, who trembled like a philosopher, hid himself as well as he could during this heroic butchery. At last, while the two Kings each commanded a Te Deum[11] in his camp, Candide decided to go elsewhere to reason about effects and causes. He clambered over heaps of dead and dying men and reached a neighbouring village, which was in ashes; it was an Abare village which the Bulgarians had burned in accordance with international law. . . .

◆ ◆ ◆

Candide fled to another village as fast as he could; it belonged to the Bulgarians, and Abarian heroes had treated it in the same way. Candide, stumbling over quivering limbs or across ruins, at last escaped from the theatre of war, carrying a little food in his knapsack, and never forgetting Mademoiselle Cunegonde. His provisions were all gone when he reached Holland;

8. **to run the gauntlet.** To face an ordeal, in this case passing by soldiers, each of whom will strike him
9. **Bulgarians . . . Abares.** Voltaire's Bulgarians and Abarians represent, respectively, the Prussians under Frederick the Great and the French.
10. **fifes, hautboys.** Fife—small flute; hautboy—early name for an oboe
11. **Te Deum.** Hymn of thanksgiving beginning with the Latin words *Te Deum laudamus* ("We praise thee, O God")

Words for Everyday Use

met • a • phy • si • cian (met´ə fə zish´ən) *n.,* one who studies metaphysics, that branch of philosophy that deals with ultimate realities and the nature of being

clem • en • cy (klem´ən sē) *n.,* leniency, mercy

black • guard (blag´ərd) *n.,* scoundrel, villain, low person

Vocabulary in Context

- Metaphysicians from many countries participated in the panel discussion on the limits of knowledge.
- The governor showed clemency by granting a stay of execution to the prisoner.
- In the movies of the silent era, the blackguard rarely wins, and the hero triumphs in the end.

but, having heard that everyone in that country was rich and a Christian, he had no doubt at all but that he would be as well treated as he had been in the Baron's castle before he had been expelled on account of Mademoiselle Cunegonde's pretty eyes. He asked an alms of several grave persons, who all replied that if he continued in that way he would be shut up in a house of correction to teach him how to live. He then addressed himself to a man who had been discoursing on charity in a large assembly for an hour on end. This orator, glancing at him askance, said: "What are you doing here? Are you for the good cause?" "There is no effect without a cause," said Candide modestly. "Everything is necessarily linked up and arranged for the best. It was necessary that I should be expelled from the company of Mademoiselle Cunegonde, that I ran the gauntlet, and that I beg my bread until I can earn it; all this could not have happened differently." "My friend," said the orator, "do you believe that the Pope is Anti-Christ?" "I had never heard so before," said Candide, "but whether he is or isn't, I am starving." "You don't deserve to eat," said the other. "Hence, rascal; hence, you wretch; and never come near me again." The orator's wife thrust her head out of the window and seeing a man who did not believe that the Pope was Anti-Christ, she poured on his head a full . . . O Heavens! To what excess religious zeal is carried by ladies! A man who had not been baptized, an honest Anabaptist[11] named Jacques, saw the cruel and ignominious treatment of one of his brothers, a featherless two-legged creature with a soul; he took him home, cleaned him up, gave him bread and beer, presented him with two florins,[12] and even offered to teach him to work at the manufacture of Persian stuffs which are made in Holland. Candide threw himself at the man's feet, exclaiming: "Doctor Pangloss was right in telling me that all is for the best in this world, for I am vastly more touched by your extreme generosity than by the harshness of the gentleman in the black cloak and his good lady." The next day when he walked out he met a beggar covered with sores, dull-eyed, with the end of his nose fallen away, his mouth awry, his teeth black, who talked huskily, was tormented with a violent cough and spat out a tooth at every cough.

❶ *How does the "charity" orator respond to Candide's request for alms? How do his preachings correspond to his own actions?*

CHAPTER IV

HOW CANDIDE MET HIS OLD MASTER IN PHILOSOPHY, DOCTOR PANGLOSS, AND WHAT HAPPENED

❷ *What state is Pangloss in when Candide meets him again? Can Pangloss's current condition be explained by his own philosophy?*

Candide, moved even more by compassion than by horror, gave this horrible beggar the two florins he had received from the honest Anabaptist, Jacques. The phantom gazed fixedly at him, shed tears and threw its arms round his neck. Candide recoiled in terror. "Alas!" said the wretch to the other wretch, "don't you recognise your dear Pangloss?" ■

11. **Anabaptist.** Member of a radical Protestant sect that opposed infant baptism

12. **florins.** Coins

ANSWERS TO GUIDED READING QUESTIONS

❶ The charity orator asks Candide if he is for the "good cause". When Candide does not agree with the orator that the "Pope is Anti-Christ," but instead shows no interest in the issue, the orator states that Candide does not deserve to eat. His actions do not correspond to what he preaches.

❷ Pangloss is a dull-eyed beggar covered with sores and afflicted with illness. Pangloss's condition does not seem to fit in the best of all worlds, but most likely Pangloss can present what he believes to be a reasonable chain of causes and effects that have led to his current condition.

SELECTION CHECK TEST WITH ANSWERS

EX. What German philosopher is satirized in *Candide*?

Gottfried Leibniz is satirized in *Candide*.

1. Who is Pangloss?

Pangloss is a philosopher and Candide's tutor.

2. What is Pangloss's opinion of the world in which he lives?

Pangloss believes that this is the best of all possible worlds.

3. In what way is Candide punished while in the army?

He is forced to run the gauntlet.

4. What is the topic of the orator from whom Candide begs food?

The orator is speaking of charity.

5. At the end of the selection, whom does Candide encounter on the street?

Candide runs into Pangloss.

Responding to the Selection

As an alternate activity, you might encourage students to discuss whether this selection seemed realistic or exaggerated to them, explaining the reasons for their opinions.

Answers for Reviewing the Selection

RECALLING AND INTERPRETING

1. **Recalling.** Pangloss teaches Candide that there is no effect without a cause and that this is the best of all possible worlds. **Interpreting.** *Responses will vary.* Students may say Candide's life outside of the castle seems dismal and certainly not the best of all worlds.

2. **Recalling.** The description of the scene before the battle is regal and splendid. The armies are described as smart, splendid, brilliant and well drawn up. During the battle, many people are senselessly killed. **Interpreting.** An attitude of contempt for the idea that war is glorious is expressed.

3. **Recalling.** The anti-Catholic speaker discourses on charity. He tells Candide that he is not worthy of help. **Interpreting.** The scene displays the hypocrisy of those who preach the importance of helping others but who are too busy preaching to give any help themselves.

4. **Recalling.** Pangloss is a dull-eyed beggar afflicted with sores and illness. **Interpreting.** Pangloss might explain that his condition is for the best because of many possible chains of causes and effects. He must disregard his own condition to hold this view.

SYNTHESIZING

Responses will vary. Possible responses are given.

5. Candide's expulsion from his home in the Baron's castle, the horrors of war, Candide's hunger, and Pangloss's decline all suggest that this is not the best of all possible worlds.

Responding to the Selection

How would you feel upon meeting Pangloss again if you were Candide? Would you agree with Pangloss's assessment that this is the best of all possible worlds and that everything that happens is for the best possible end? Why, or why not?

Reviewing the Selection

RECALLING	INTERPRETING
1. What philosophy does Pangloss teach Candide?	Does this philosophy seem to apply to Candide's situation after being expelled from the castle of the baron? Explain.
2. What description is given of the battle scene before the battle? What happens during the battle itself?	What attitude is expressed toward war?
3. What is the topic of the anti-Catholic speaker? How does he react to Candide's request for help?	What hypocrisy is displayed in this scene?
4. Describe Pangloss's condition when Candide finds him again.	How might Pangloss explain his condition according to his philosophy that all is for the best in this world? What must Pangloss disregard or ignore to maintain his view?

SYNTHESIZING

5. What evidence is offered in this selection to contradict the idea that all things are connected in a series of causes and effects to create the "best of all possible worlds"?

Understanding Literature (Questions for Discussion)

1. **Satire. Satire** is humorous writing or speech intended to point out errors, falsehoods, foibles, or failings. It is written for the purpose of reforming human behavior or human institutions. What absurdities and injustices are satirized in this selection from *Candide*? What aspects of society do you think Voltaire wants to improve?

2. **Irony. Irony** is a difference between appearance and reality. **Verbal irony** is irony in which a statement made implies its opposite. What examples of human folly, or lack of reason, are revealed through verbal irony in the selection from *Candide*?

Answers for Understanding Literature

Responses will vary. Possible responses are given.

1. **Satire.** The self-serving nature of rulers and governments is ridiculed in the actions of the Bulgarian king, whose pardon of Candide "will be praised in all newspapers and all ages." The absurd war between the Bulgarian and Abarian kings who both give thanks for the day of death and destruction is satirized. Groups that preach charity but fail to act upon their words are satirized as well. The philosophy of Leibniz that Pangloss teaches to Candide is satirized throughout the selection.

2. **Irony.** Pangloss's statement of his philosophy as he sits begging on the street is ironic. The reference to the "gift of liberty" is ironic because Candide is not really free to choose what he would like.

Responding in Writing

1. **Creative Writing: Description.** A utopia is an imaginary, idealized world. In this selection from *Candide,* Pangloss states his philosophy that this is the best of all possible worlds. In fact, there are many things about this world that do not make it the best. Think about what a perfect world would be like. Write a description of an idealized, perfect world, or utopia. You might begin by considering the problems in this world that would not exist in a perfect world. Make a cluster chart like the one below to identify problems in this world. Address these issues as you create your utopia.

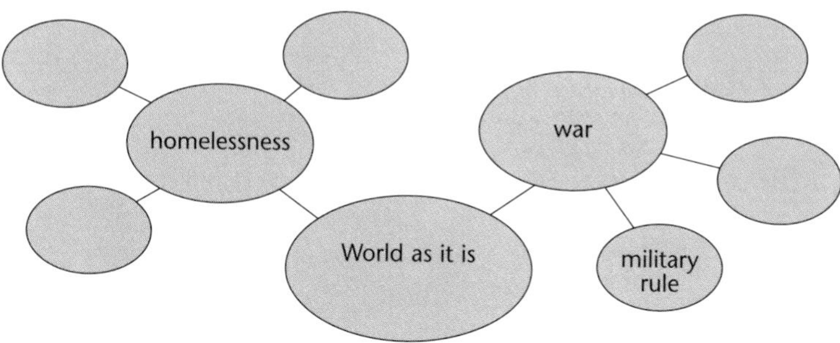

2. **Critical Essay: Critiquing Pangloss's Philosophy.** Pangloss teaches Candide that this is the best of all possible worlds, yet the events experienced by both Pangloss and Candide refute this idea. Write a critical essay in which you first explain Pangloss's philosophy, and then explain why this philosophy cannot be applied to every situation. Use examples from *Candide* and from your own life to support your opinion of this philosophy.

Language Lab

Errors in Modifier Usage. Read the Language Arts Survey 2.41–2.42, "Errors in Modifier Usage I and II." Then, on your own paper, rewrite the sentences below, correcting any errors in modifier usage.

1. When Candide meets his old teacher, Pangloss is not looking good.
2. In fact, Candide has never seen his teacher looking worst.
3. Pangloss, however, still contends that that is the best of all worlds.
4. Candide felt badly for Pangloss, but Pangloss explained the causes and effects that had led to his condition.
5. Candide can't hardly argue with Pangloss's explanation; he believes in them ideas expressed by Pangloss as well.

ANALYTIC SCALES FOR RESPONDING IN WRITING

Assign a score from 1 to 25 for each grading criterion below. (For more detailed evaluation, see the evaluation forms for writing, revising, and proofreading, Assessment Portfolio 4.1–4.9.)

1. Description

- **Content/Unity.** The description presents a vision of a utopia.
- **Organization/Coherence.** The description presents aspects of the utopia in a sensible order.
- **Language/Style.** The description uses vivid and precise nouns, verbs, and modifiers.
- **Conventions.** The description avoids errors in spelling, grammar, usage, mechanics, and manuscript form.

▶ Additional practice is provided in the Essential Skills Practice Book: Writing 1.8, 1.10.

2. Critical Essay

- **Content/Unity.** The essay critiques philosophical optimism.
- **Organization/Coherence.** The essay should begin with an introduction that includes the thesis of the essay. The introduction should be followed by supporting paragraphs with clear transitions. The essay should end with a solid conclusion.
- **Language/Style.** The essay uses vivid and precise nouns, verbs, and modifiers.
- **Conventions.** The essay avoids errors in spelling, grammar, usage, mechanics, and manuscript form.

▶ Additional practice is provided in the Essential Skills Practice Book: Writing 1.20.

ANSWERS FOR LANGUAGE LAB

1. When Candide meets his old teacher, Pangloss is not looking well.
2. In fact, Candide has never seen his teacher looking worse.
3. Pangloss, however, still contends that this is the best of all worlds.
4. Candide felt bad for Pangloss, but Pangloss explained the causes and effects that had led to his condition.
5. Candide can hardly argue with Pangloss's explanation; he believes in the ideas expressed by Pangloss as well.

▶ Additional practice is provided in the Essential Skills Practice Book: Language 2.41–2.42.

FROM *THE PRINCE*

ABOUT THE AUTHOR

Niccolo Machiavelli (1469–1527) was a political theorist and writer born in Florence, the son of noble but poor parents. He later became a statesman in the Florentine Republic, which had recently ousted a powerful family of rulers named the Medici. Political life in Florence was difficult at this time—Italy was made up of a number of small states in which the archrivals France and Spain often struggled for power. In 1512, with the aid of Spain, the Medici overthrew the Republic and reestablished their rule. The Medici believed that Machiavelli had taken part in a plot against them, so they had him imprisoned and tortured, but he maintained his innocence. After he was released, he lived in abject poverty but wrote two works that brought him lasting fame, *The Prince* and *Discourses on the First Ten Books of Livy.* Machiavelli finally regained the favor of the Medici family and served as a minor government official until his death.

ABOUT THE SELECTION

The Prince is the work that, perhaps unjustly, won Machiavelli a reputation as an amoral cynic who advocates expedience and duplicity above all else in rulers. This politically theoretical work was inspired by Machiavelli's longing for an ideal prince who would expel foreign powers from Italy and return the country to its former glory. Machiavelli believed that his pessimistic view of human nature was more realistic than the views of his contemporaries who discussed how rulers should be rather than what actual rulers were like. He longed for an ideal state but found that human nature would not support one, so he simply described the existing political world as he saw it.

SELECTIONS FOR ADDITIONAL READING

ITALY

from *The Prince*
by Niccolo Machiavelli,
translated by Allan H. Gilbert

ON THE THINGS FOR WHICH MEN, AND ESPECIALLY PRINCES, ARE PRAISED OR CENSURED

. . . Because I know that many have written on this topic, I fear that when I too write I shall be thought presumptuous, because, in discussing it, I break away completely from the principles laid down by my predecessors. But since it is my purpose to write something useful to an attentive reader, I think it more effective to go back to the practical truth of the subject than to depend on my fancies about it. And many have imagined republics and principalities that never have been seen or known to exist in reality. For there is such a difference between the way men live and the way they ought to live, that anybody who abandons what is for what ought to be will learn something that will ruin rather than preserve him, because anyone who determines to act in all circumstances the part of a good man must come to ruin among so many who are not good. Hence, if a prince wishes to maintain himself, he must learn how to be not good, and to use that ability or not as is required.

Leaving out of account, then, things about an imaginary prince, and considering things that are true, I say that all men, when they are spoken of, and especially princes, because they are set higher, are marked with some of the qualities that bring them either blame or praise. To wit, one man is thought liberal, another stingy (using a Tuscan word, because *avaricious* in our language is still applied to one who desires to get things through violence, but *stingy* we apply to him who refrains too much from using his own property); one is thought open-handed, another grasping; one cruel, the other compassionate; one is a breaker of faith, the other reliable; one is effeminate and cowardly, the other vigorous and spirited; one is philanthropic, the other egotistic; one is lascivious, the other chaste; one is straight-forward, the other crafty; one hard, the other easy to deal with; one is firm, the other unsettled; one is religious, the other unbelieving and so on.

And I know that everybody will admit that it would be very praiseworthy for a prince to possess all of the above-mentioned qualities that are considered good. But since he is not able to have them or to observe them completely, because human conditions do not allow him to, it is necessary that he be prudent enough to understand how to avoid getting a bad name because he is given to those vices that will deprive him of his position. He should also, if he can, guard himself from those vices that will not take his place away from him, but if he cannot do it, he can with less anxiety let them go. Moreover, he should not be troubled if he gets a bad name because of vices without which it will be difficult for him to preserve his position. I say this because, if everything is considered, it will be seen that some things seem to be virtuous, but if they are put into practice will be ruinous to him; other things seem to be vices, yet if put into practice will bring the prince security and well-being

ON LIBERALITY AND PARSIMONY[1]

Beginning, then, with the first of the above-mentioned qualities, I assert that it is good to be thought liberal. Yet liberality, practiced in such a way that you get a reputation for it, is damaging to you, for the following reasons: If you use it wisely and as it ought to be used, it will not become known, and you will not escape being censured for the opposite vice. Hence, if you wish to have men call you liberal, it is necessary not to omit any sort of lavishness. A prince who does this will always be obliged to use up all his property in lavish actions; he will then, if he wishes to keep the name of liberal, be forced to lay heavy taxes on his people and exact money from them, and do everything he can to raise money. This will begin to make his subjects hate him, and as he grows poor he will be little esteemed by anybody. So it comes about that because of this liberality of his, with which he has damaged a large number and been of advantage to but a few, he is affected by every petty annoyance and is in peril from every slight danger. If he recognizes this and wishes to draw back, he quickly gets a bad name for stinginess.

Since, then, a prince cannot without harming himself practice this virtue of liberality to such an extent that it will be recognized, he will, if he is prudent, not care about being called stingy. As time goes on he will be thought more and more liberal, for the people will see that because of his economy his income is enough for him, that he can defend himself from those who make war against him, and that he can enter upon undertakings without burdening his people.

1. **parsimony.** Stinginess, a tendency to be over-careful in spending

Such a prince is in the end liberal to all those from whom he takes nothing, and they are numerous; he is stingy to those to whom he does not give, and they are few. In our times we have seen big things done only by those who have been looked on as stingy; the others have utterly failed. Pope Julius II, though he made use of a reputation for liberality to attain the papacy, did not then try to maintain it, because he wished to be able to make war. The present King of France has carried on great wars without laying unusually heavy taxes on his people, merely because his long economy has made provision for heavy expenditures. The present King of Spain, if he had continued liberal, would not have carried on or completed so many undertakings.

Therefore a prince ought to care little about getting called stingy, if as a result he does not have to rob his subjects, is able to defend himself, does not become poor and contemptible, and is not obliged to become grasping. For this vice of stinginess is one of those that enables him to rule. Somebody may say: Cæsar, by means of his liberality became emperor, and many others have come to high positions because they have been liberal and have been thought so. I answer: Either you are already prince, or you are on the way to become one. In the first case liberality is dangerous; in the second it is very necessary to be thought liberal. Cæsar was one of those who wished to attain dominion over Rome. But if, when he had attained it, he had lived for a long time and had not moderated his expenses, he would have destroyed his authority. Somebody may answer: Many who have been thought very liberal have been princes and done great things with their armies. I answer: The prince spends either his own property and that of his subjects or that of others. In the first case he ought to be frugal; in the second he ought to abstain from no sort of liberality. When he marches with his army and lives on plunder, loot, and ransom, a prince controls the property of others. To him liberality is essential, for without it his soldiers would not follow him. You can be a free giver of what does not belong to you or your subjects, as were Cyrus, Cæsar, and Alexander, because to spend the money of others does not decrease your reputation but adds to it. It is only the spending of your own money that hurts you.

There is nothing that eats itself up as fast as does liberality, for when you practice it you lose the power to practice it, and become poor and contemptible, or else to escape poverty you become rapacious[1] and therefore are hated. And of all the things against which a prince must guard himself, the first is being an object of contempt and hatred. Liberality leads you to both of these. Hence there is more wisdom in keeping a name for stinginess, which produces a bad reputation without hatred, than in striving for the name of liberal, only to be forced to get the name of rapacious, which brings forth both bad reputation and hatred. ■

FRANCE

"When You Are Very Old"

by Pierre Ronsard, translated by Sara Hyry

When you are very old, by evening's candlelight,
You'll sit in the fire's glow where you'll wind and spin
You'll sing my lines with wonder and marvel again;
Ronsard praised me when I was a beautiful sight.

And at that time the maid who hears your lulling voice,
Although before she may have half-succumbed to sleep,
Will, at the sound of my name, wake herself and leap
To bless your immortal name, to praise and rejoice.

I will be under the ground, a phantom formless,
By the solemn myrtles I take my final rest;
Squatting by the fire you will be an ancient wife,

Regretting my love and also your prideful scorn.
Live, if you remember me, wait not for the morn;
Enjoy and gather today, the roses of life. ■

FRANCE

from *Pensées*

by Blaise Pascal, translated by William F. Trotter

. . . Let us then examine this point, and say, "God is, or He is not." But to which side shall we incline? Reason can decide nothing here. There is an infinite chaos which separated us. A game is being played at the extremity of this infinite distance where heads or tails will turn up. What will you wager? According to reason, you can do neither the one thing nor the other; according to reason, you can defend neither of the propositions.

Do not then reprove for error those who have made a choice; for you know nothing about it. "No, but I blame them for having made, not this choice, but a choice; for again both he who chooses heads and he who chooses tails are equally at fault, they are both in the wrong. The true course is not to wager at all."

Yes; but you must wager. It is not optional. You are embarked. Which will you choose then? Let us see. Since you must choose, let us see which interests you least. You have two things to lose, the true and the good; and two things to stake, your reason and your will, your knowledge

1. **rapacious.** Greedy or grasping

"When You Are Very Old"

About the Author

Pierre Ronsard (1524–1585) was a French poet. As a young man, he was interested in diplomacy, but illness left him partially deaf, and he turned to the study of literature, reading widely in ancient Greek, Latin, and Italian. With other lovers of poetry he formed a group called the Pléiade, who sought to equal the achievement of a group of ancient Greek poets from Alexandria. His work was renowned throughout France, winning him the title "the Prince of Poets."

About the Selection

"When You Are Very Old" is a lyric poem in which a speaker addresses his beloved, who has rejected him. This poem plays upon the *carpe diem* theme.

From *Pensées*

About the Author

Blaise Pascal (1623–1662) was a French mathematician, physicist, and religious writer. He is as renowned for his scientific discoveries as he is for the two works that won him literary fame, *Les Provinciales* and the posthumously published *Pensées.*

About the Selection

Pensées is composed of different notes and fragments written as a defense of Christianity. Pascal was devoted to a Roman Catholic movement called Jansenism. Jansenists and Jesuits were engaged in a power struggle in France during Pascal's life.

FROM *AN ESSAY ON CRITICISM*

ABOUT THE AUTHOR

Alexander Pope (1688–1744) is one of the most frequently quoted authors in the English language. As a young boy, Pope was educated primarily at home by Catholic priests. An extremely bright child, he learned Greek, Latin, French, and Italian. At the age of twelve he produced some of his first poetry, imitating the style of poets he was reading. By young adulthood, Pope's extensive output of literary work had begun. This output included numerous volumes of verse and complete translations of Homer's *Iliad* and *Odyssey.*

ABOUT THE SELECTION

Pope wrote ***An Essay on Criticism*** when he was only twenty-one years old. The poem presents critical precepts derived from Greek and Latin authorities. It is written in heroic couplets, or pairs of rhymed lines that make use of Pope's favorite meter, iambic pentameter. Many of these lines and couplets have gained the status of proverbs used commonly by English speakers around the globe, such as "To err is human, to forgive, divine."

and your happiness; and your nature has two things to shun, error and misery. Your reason is no more shocked in choosing one rather than the other, since you must of necessity choose. This is one point settled. But your happiness? Let us weigh the gain and the loss in wagering that God is. Let us estimate these two chances. If you gain, you gain all; if you lose, you lose nothing. Wager, then, without hesitation that He is. ■

GREAT BRITAIN

from *An Essay on Criticism*
by Alexander Pope

'Tis hard to say, if greater want of skill
Appear in writing or in judging ill;
But of the two less dangerous is the offense
To tire our patience than mislead our sense.
Some few in that, but numbers err in this,
Ten censure wrong for one who writes amiss;
A fool might once himself alone expose,
Now one in verse makes many more in prose.
'Tis with our judgments as our watches, none
Go just alike, yet each believes his own.
In poets as true genius is but rare,
True taste as seldom is the critic's share;
Both must alike from Heaven derive their light,
These born to judge, as well as those to write.
Let such teach others who themselves excel,
And censure freely who have written well.
Authors are partial to their wit, 'tis true,
But are critics to their judgment too?
Yet if we look more closely, we shall find
Most have the seeds of judgment in their mind:
Nature affords at least a glimmering light;
The lines, though touched but faintly, are drawn right.
But as the slightest sketch, if justly traced,
Is by ill coloring but the more disgraced,
So by false learning is good sense defaced:
Some are bewildered in the maze of schools,
And some made coxcombs[1] Nature meant but fools.
In search of wit these lose their common sense,
And then turn critics in their own defense:
Each burns alike, who can, or cannot write,
Or with a rival's or an eunuch's spite.
All fools have still an itching to deride,
And fain would be upon the laughing side.
If Maevius[2] scribble in Apollo's spite,
There are who judge still worse than he can write.
Some have at first for wits, then poets passed,
Turned critics next, and proved plain fools at last.
Some neither can for wits nor critics pass,
As heavy mules are neither horse nor ass.
Those half-learn'd witlings, numerous in our isle,
As half-formed insects on the banks of Nile;
Unfinished things, one knows not what to call,
Their generation's so equivocal:
To tell[3] them would a hundred tongues require,
Or one vain wit's, that might a hundred tire.
But you who seek to give and merit fame,
And justly bear a critic's noble name,
Be sure yourself and your own reach to know,
How far your genius, taste, and learning go;
Launch not beyond your depth, but be discreet,
And mark that point where sense and dullness meet.
Nature to all things fixed the limits fit,
And wisely curbed proud man's pretending wit.
As on the land while here the ocean gains,
In other parts it leaves wide sandy plains;
Thus in the soul while memory prevails,
The solid power of understanding fails;
Where beams of warm imagination play,
The memory's soft figures melt away.
One science only will one genius fit,
So vast is art, so narrow human wit.
Not only bounded to peculiar arts,
But oft in those confined to single parts.
Like kings we lose the conquests gained before,
By vain ambition still to make them more;
Each might his several province well command,
Would all but stoop to what they understand.
First follow Nature, and your judgment frame
By her just standard, which is still the same;
Unerring Nature, still divinely bright,
One clear, unchanged, and universal light,
Life, force, and beauty must to all impart,
At once the source, and end, and test of art.
Art from that fund each just supply provides,
Works without show, and without pomp presides.
In some fair body thus the informing soul
With spirits feeds, with vigor fills the whole,
Each motion guides, and every nerve sustains;
Itself unseen, but in the effects remains.
Some, to whom Heaven in wit has been profuse,
Want as much more to turn it to its use;
For wit and judgment often are at strife,
Though meant each other's aid, like man and wife.

1. **coxcombs.** Silly, vain, foppish fellows
2. **Maevius.** Silly poet alluded to by Virgil and Horace
3. **tell.** Count

'Tis more to guide than spur the Muse's steed,
Restrain his fury than provoke his speed;
The wingèd courser,[1] like a generous horse,
Shows most true mettle when you check his course.
Those rules of old discovered, not devised,
Are Nature still, but Nature methodized;
Nature, like liberty, is but restrained
By the same laws which first herself ordained. ■

from *Natural Theology*
by William Paley

In crossing a heath,[2] suppose I pitched my foot against a *stone* and were asked how the stone came to be there, I might possibly answer that for anything I knew to the contrary it had lain there forever; nor would it, perhaps, be very easy to show the absurdity of this answer. But suppose I had found a *watch* upon the ground, and it should be inquired how the watch happened to be in that place, I should hardly think of the answer which I had before given, that for anything I knew the watch might have always been there. Yet why should not this answer serve for the watch as well as the stone; why is it not as admissible in the second case as in the first? For this reason, and for no other, namely, that when we come to inspect the watch, we perceive—what we could not discover in the stone—that its several parts are framed and put together for a purpose, e.g., that they are so formed and adjusted as to produce motion, and that motion so regulated as to point out the hour of the day; that if the different parts had been differently shaped from what they are, or placed after any other manner or in any other order than that in which they are placed, either no motion at all would have been carried on in the machine, or none which would have answered the use that is now served by it. To reckon up a few of the plainest of these parts and of their offices, all tending to one result: we see a cylindrical box containing a coiled elastic spring, which, by its endeavor to relax itself, turns round the box. We next observe a flexible chain—artificially wrought[3] for the sake of flexure—communicating the action of the spring from the box to the fusee. We then find a series of wheels, the teeth of which catch in and apply to each other, conducting the motion from the fusee to the balance and from the balance to the pointer, and at the same time, by the size and shape of those wheels, so regulating that motion as to terminate in causing an index, by an equable and measured progression, to pass over a given space in a given time. We take notice that the wheels are made of brass, in order to keep them from rust; the springs of steel, no other metal being so elastic; that over the face of the watch there is placed a glass, a material employed in no other part of the work, but in the room of which, if there had been any other than a transparent substance, the hour could not be seen without opening the case. This mechanism being observed—it requires indeed an examination of the instrument, and perhaps some previous knowledge of the subject, to perceive and understand it; but being once, as we have said, observed and understood—the inference we think is inevitable, that the watch must have had a maker—that there must have existed, at some time and at some place or other, an artificer or artificers who formed it for the purpose which we find it actually to answer, who completely comprehended its construction and designed its use. ■

1. **Muse's steed . . . wingèd courser.** Refers to Pegasus, the winged horse associated with the Muses and inspiration
2. **heath.** Barren land
2. **wrought.** Made

FROM *NATURAL THEOLOGY*

ABOUT THE AUTHOR

Priest and philosopher **William Paley** (1743–1805) was born in Peterborough, England. Paley was educated at Giggleswick School and graduated from Christ's College, Cambridge. Upon graduation he became a fellow and tutor of the school. He served the villages of Musgrave, Dalston, and Appleby as a rector, and in 1782 he was made archdeacon of Carlisle. Paley supported the abolition of slavery. Because Paley was considered liberal and progressive by many, he did not achieve the success he might have through his diligent study and conscientious work. However, his writings were well received. His first book, *The Principles of Moral and Political Philosophy*, became a standard text at Cambridge for many years. Other works include *Horae Paulinae* and *View of the Evidences of Christianity.* He is best known for his last book, *Natural Theology*, which was published three years before his death. In this work, he argues that there must be a divine creator based on empirical evidence of design in nature.

ABOUT THE SELECTION

In ***Natural Theology***, William Paley presents an argument for the existence of God, the creator, based on design, or the complex construction of the natural world and its elements. Paley supports his argument by making an analogy, or comparison, to a watch. The argument of design presented by Paley was not a new one when *Natural Theology* was published, nor was the analogy of the watch original. The argument had been made in works such as *The Wisdom of God Manifested in the Works of the Creation*, by John Ray; *Physico-Theology*, by William Durham; and the writings of Dutch philosopher Bernard Nieuwentyt, from whom Paley borrowed the analogy of the watch. Paley is known for this argument because he expressed it so well.

UNIT REVIEW

The Renaissance and the Enlightenment

VOCABULARY FROM THE SELECTIONS

acquiesce, 879	fathom, 835	predicament, 838
artifice, 862	feign, 877	procure, 842
assuage, 878	frivolous, 861	prodigy, 887
bemuse, 842	furrow, 886	progeny, 844
blackguard, 888	guile, 842	prostrate, 832
caitiff, 857	ignominy, 835	prowess, 823
clemency, 888	immure, 844	prudence, 827
compensate, 825	impugn, 834	ravine, 842
consolation, 826	intervene, 876	regiment, 887
contemptible, 880	judicious, 880	ruse, 848
contexture, 861	meagerly, 823	semblance, 831
credulous, 841	merit, 878	sonorous, 855
debase, 861	metaphysician, 888	stupefaction, 833
dismay, 833	oracle, 885	temerity, 864
dissimulation, 862	obtain, 824	terrain, 840
elate, 836	palpable, 878	tribulation, 839
eloquently, 848	partial, 874	vex, 862
enmity, 857	pendulous, 841	vivacity, 886
exhort, 863	perilous, 837	winsome, 840
expedition, 838	precipitous, 842	

LITERARY TERMS

character, 859	irony, 828, 890	rhyme, 845
characterization, 881	medieval romance, 858	rhyme scheme, 845
couplet, 882	meter, 849	satire, 859, 890
courtly love, 829, 858	mock epic, 852	simile, 845
dramatic irony, 828, 883	*ottava rima,* 846	sonnet, 847, 849
Enlightenment, 820	parable, 867	stanza, 845
essay, 860, 866	parody, 852, 859	tone, 849
fable, 867, 870	personification, 870	verbal irony, 890
frame tale, 822	Renaissance, 818	

ADDITIONAL RESOURCES

ASSESSMENT PORTFOLIO

- Vocabulary Worksheet 2.10.17
- Study Guide 2.10.18
- Unit Test 2.10.19

ESSENTIAL SKILLS PRACTICE BOOKS

WRITING
- Choosing a Purpose: Creative Writing, 1.8
- Gathering Ideas, 1.10
- Writing a Critical Essay, 1.20

LANGUAGE
- Clichés and Euphemisms, 2.72
- Errors in Modifier Usage I, 2.41
- Errors in Modifier Usage II, 2.42
- Other Uses of Quotation Marks, 2.52
- Personal Pronouns, 2.4
- Reflexive, Intensive, and Demonstrative Pronouns, 2.5

SPEAKING AND LISTENING
- Active Listening and Interpersonal Communication, 3.2
- Elements of Verbal and Nonverbal Communication, 3.1
- Oral Interpretation, 3.5

STUDY AND RESEARCH
- Bibliographies and Bibliography Cards, 4.20
- Distinguishing Fact and Opinion, 4.5
- Using the Card Catalog, 4.13
- Using Dictionaries, 4.15
- Using Search Tools, 4.12

APPLIED ENGLISH/TECH PREP
- Personal and Business Letters, 5.1

VOCABULARY CHECK TEST

Ask students to number their papers from one to ten. Have students complete each sentence with a word from the Vocabulary from the Selections in the Unit Review.

1. The journey down that river is perilous because there are several miles of white water.
2. Although my father gives the semblance of being stern, he actually is very kindhearted and forgiving.
3. After a long hike, we stopped for sandwiches to assuage our hunger. (cont.)

VOCABULARY CHECK TEST (CONT.)

4. To impugn his opponent's reputation, the candidate claimed that the current governor obtained campaign funds illegally.
5. If you feign illness too often, you may find that people don't believe you when you really are ill.
6. The sonorous peal of trumpets indicated that the king was about to issue a decree.
7. Through a great act of dissimulation, Ariana was able to hide her true motivations and feelings.
8. While Harriet is suspicious of people's words and actions, her brother is far more credulous.
9. The painting depicted a winsome scene of a mother cradling her child on a hillside full of flowers.
10. Raoul prepared a speech to exhort his audience to donate to the charity.

SYNTHESIS: QUESTIONS FOR WRITING, RESEARCH, OR DISCUSSION

GENRE STUDIES

1. What is satire? What do the authors of *Don Quixote* and *Candide* satirize? What makes these satires effective?

2. Describe the characteristics of a medieval romance. (If you need help, refer to the Handbook of Literary Terms or the Unit 9 introduction.) Miguel de Cervantes' *Don Quixote* and Ludovico Ariosto's *Orlando Furioso* are reactions to medieval romance. Compare and contrast the way in which these two selections treat medieval romance.

THEMATIC STUDIES

3. Compare and contrast the way in which love is portrayed in Louise Labé's Sonnet 23 and Giovanni Boccaccio's "Federigo's Falcon." Discuss each author's attitude toward courtly love and/or Petrarchan ideals.

4. Which selections in this unit criticize society? What problems do they point out? What techniques do the authors of these selections use to present their criticisms?

5. In many selections in this unit, characters' expectations of others are shown to be incorrect. Identify characters who outdo the expectations of others. What makes their actions surprising?

6. Many selections in this unit deal with the themes of honesty and deception. Compare and contrast the reasons for and the outcomes of Monna's deception of Federigo and Federigo's deception of Monna in "Federigo's Falcon" and Tartuffe's deception of Orgon in the selection from *Tartuffe.*

HISTORICAL/BIOGRAPHICAL STUDIES

7. The Renaissance saw the emergence of a new emphasis on the individual and on the value of life on earth, in sharp contrast to the emphasis in medieval literature on society and on the afterlife. Which selections in this unit exalt the individual? Which selections focus on enjoying the present world?

8. What are the characteristics of Neoclassical writing? What qualities in people or in the world around them did writers of this period seem to value? Use examples from selections in this unit to support your answers.

Spelling Check Test

Ask students to number their papers from one to ten. Read each word aloud. Then read aloud the sentence containing the word. Repeat the word. Ask students to write the word on their papers, spelling it correctly.

1. **meagerly**

There was only one chair and a lamp in the meagerly furnished room.

2. **consolation**

Although we played well, it was no consolation for losing the championship game.

3. **stupefaction**

Witnessing firsthand the devastating force of a tornado filled Chris with stupefaction.

4. **ignominy**

The basketball player felt he would never live down the ignominy of missing the shot that could have won his team the game.

5. **eloquently**

Ryan eloquently persuaded us to support him in his campaign for student body president.

6. **caitiff**

Loren had considered Asha a caitiff until she risked her life to save his.

7. **temerity**

When Jody decided to dive off the cliff into the shallow water hole below, we were stunned by the temerity of her deed.

8. **dissimulation**

The imposter used his utmost skills of dissimulation to hide his true nature and to assume the king's rightful place.

9. **partial**

Monica thinks that *Tartuffe* is Molière's best play, but Juanita is partial to *The Miser.*

10. **vivacity**

Exhausted by a long day of traveling, the entertainer lacked her usual vivacity.

UNIT SKILLS OUTLINE

Literary Skills and Concepts

- Antihero, 991
- Apostrophe, 929
- Characterization, 948, 949
- Dialogue, 963
- Dramatic Irony, 982
- Flashback, 949, 1009
- Foreshadowing, 948
- Hyperbole, 949
- Internal Monologue, 991
- Irony, 941, 947, 967, 982
- Irony of Situation, 947
- Metaphor, 940, 971
- Mood, 912
- Motivation, 957
- Naturalism, 902, 924, 930, 939, 984
- One-Dimensional Character, 924
- Paradox, 906
- Parallelism, 906
- Personification, 929, 940
- Psychological Fiction, 991
- Realism, 901, 924
- Romanticism, 900, 924
- Setting, 912, 940
- Simile, 940, 957
- Symbol, 995
- Theme, 982
- Three-Dimensional Character, 924
- Tone, 929

Writing Skills and Concepts

- Critical Essay, 907, 913, 924, 929, 940, 948, 957, 983, 991
- Dramatic Continuation, 983
- Interview, 957
- Observation and Description, 948
- Paradoxes, 907
- Personal Letter, 924
- Personal Philosophy, 991
- Personification, 929
- Social Critique, 940
- Song, 913

Grammar, Usage, and Mechanics Skills and Concepts

- Pronoun Reference and Agreement, 907
- Proofreading for Errors in Capitalization, 992
- Using Commas, 969

Other Language Arts Skills and Concepts

- Discussion, 957
- Identifying Faulty Arguments and Propaganda, 913
- Research Skills, 948
- Writing Promotional and Public Relations Copy, 924

Unit 11 Romanticism, Realism, and Naturalism

Still Life. *Caravaggio*

GOALS/OBJECTIVES

Studying this unit will enable students to

- interpret and appreciate Romantic, Realist, and Naturalist literature
- explain the major characteristics and goals of Romanticism, Realism, and Naturalism
- recognize some major writers of each movement
- briefly explain reactions to Neoclassicism
- write critically and creatively in response to and in analysis of Romantic, Realist, and Naturalist literature

"It was the best of times, it was the worst of times."

—Charles Dickens

Cross-Curricular Connections

Arts and Humanities

- Children's Picture Book of Hyperbole, 949
- Comparing "The False Gems" with "The Necklace," 941
- Dante Gabriel Rossetti, 900
- Hippolyte Adolphe Taine, 935
- Honoré Daumier, 901
- Improvisation, 983
- Jack London, 902
- Mining in Films, 932
- Musicals, 914
- Music for the Lute, 960
- Nobel Prizes, 984
- Popularity of *Cyrano de Bergerac,* 958
- Practicing Naturalist Writing, 930
- Preface to *Lyrical Ballads,* 904
- Researching Portugal, 925
- Revolution and Romanticism, 901
- Writing in the Style of Cyrano and Christian, 968

Mathematics and Sciences

- Exchange Rates, 916
- History of Mining, 933
- Isaac Newton Projects, 908
- Mining Research, 932
- Nature Walk, 929
- Nobel Prizes, 984

Social Studies

- Biographical Notes on Echoes Authors, 903
- Carthage, 1009
- Catholic and Protestant Conflicts, 964
- Crime and Punishment, 917
- Diogenes, 977
- Fencing, 974
- History of Mining, 933
- Jack London, 902
- Mapping Sardinia, 985
- Nobel Prizes, 984
- Pages, 971
- Prussian History, 909
- Researching Labor Laws, 940
- Researching Portugal, 925
- Revolution and Romanticism, 901
- Russian History and Gogol's Work, 1001
- The Thirty Years' War, 964

Applied Arts

- Children's Picture Book of Hyperbole, 949
- Isaac Newton Projects, 908
- Nature Walk, 929
- Writing Promotional and Public Relations Copy, 924

Teaching the Multiple Intelligences

Musical

- Musicals, 914
- Music for the Lute, 960

Logical-Mathematical

- Additional Reading, 901
- Comparing "The False Gems" with "The Necklace," 941
- Exchange Rates, 916
- Identifying Faulty Arguments and Propaganda, 913
- Mining Research, 932
- Nature Walk, 929
- Religion in France, 921
- Researching French History or Society, 948
- Researching Portugal, 925
- Revolution and Romanticism, 901
- Russian History and Gogol's Work, 1001

Spatial

- Balcony Scene, 976
- Children's Picture Book of Hyperbole, 949
- Dante Gabriel Rossetti, 900
- Honoré Daumier, 901
- Mapping Sardinia, 985
- Mining Research, 932
- Nature Walk, 929
- Researching Portugal, 925

(cont.)

OTHER SELECTIONS EXPLORING THIS THEME

Robert Burns
"Song Composed in August," page 384

Henrik Ibsen
A Doll's House, page 110

Leo Tolstoy
from *The Death of Iván Ilyich*, page 314

ART NOTE

Dante Gabriel Rossetti (1828–1882), a British poet and painter born in London, England, was part of a talented, Anglo-Italian family. The son of an exiled Italian poet and politician, Rossetti enjoyed a childhood home that was often a gathering place for Italian exiles who discussed politics, art, and literature. He, his brother William, and his sister Christina wrote poetry and painted from childhood.

At twenty, Rossetti helped to found a group of writers, artists, and critics known as the Pre-Raphaelite Brotherhood, whose goals of simplicity, naturalness, and expressiveness in art and literature was modeled on the artwork produced in Italy before the Renaissance.

Rossetti's paintings are known for bright, glowing color and mystical beauty, and his poetry for its rich and unique imagery.

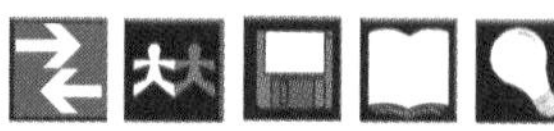

ADDITIONAL QUESTIONS AND ACTIVITIES

Ask students if they approve of or agree with the ideals of Romanticism as they understand them. As students discuss these ideals, encourage them to explain their responses.

UNIT 11

Preview:
Romanticism, Realism, and Naturalism

Beata Beatrix. *Dante Gabriel Rossetti*

The period from the late eighteenth century through the nineteenth century was a time of great change, particularly in many European nations. During this period, artists, writers, and philosophers tended to break with ideas of the past and search for new ways of defining people and nature.

Romanticism, a movement of the late eighteenth and early nineteenth centuries, was an artistic, literary, and philosophical rebellion against the rational, orderly forms of Neoclassicism and the Enlightenment. Romantic thinkers valued emotion over reason, nature over industry, and ordinary people over aristocrats. Romantics also focused on the private feelings and inevitable isolation of the individual, believing that reason deals with truths that can be understood and shared by many, but private feelings and insights are intensely personal and, thus, tend to isolate people from one another. Romantic art and literature celebrated the inherent beauty of the individual as well as that of nature. In fact, the exaltation of nature was key to Romantic thought. Romantics viewed the purity and beauty of nature as the opposite of the filth and ugliness of industrial civilization. Romantics saw nature not as something to be manipulated, but as something to be cherished and experienced. The era defined by Romantic ideals encompassed the early years of American independence, major civil and political reforms in England, and the French Revolution. In fact, the libertarian ideals behind the French Revolution had a great deal to do with the Romantic movement and its influence on European thought. This Revolution, which started in 1789 when civilians attacked the royal prison, was a demand for individual rights and power for common people.

The ideas of French philosopher and writer Jean-Jacques Rousseau, a leading figure of the Enlightenment, became central to Romanticism. Other French Romantic writers include Victor Hugo, François René de Chateaubriand, and George Sand. Influential English Romantic writers

TEACHING THE MULTIPLE INTELLIGENCES (CONT.)

KINESTHETIC
- Balcony Scene, 976
- Improvisation, 983
- Music for the Lute, 960
- Nature Walk, 929

INTERPERSONAL
- Additional Reading, 901
- Balcony Scene, 976
- Catholic and Protestant Conflicts, 964
- Children's Picture Book of Hyperbole, 949
- Comparing "The False Gems" with "The Necklace," 941
- Discussing Capital Punishment, 957
- Grammar Game, 961
- Improvisation, 983
- Mining Research, 932
- Musicals, 914
- Popularity of *Cyrano de Bergerac,* 958
- Religion in France, 921
- Researching French History or Society, 948
- Researching Labor Laws, 940
- Revolution and Romanticism, 901
- Russian History and Gogol's Work, 1001
- Writing in the Style of Cyrano and Christian, 968
- Writing Promotional and Public Relations Copy, 924

Print Collector. *Honoré Daumier*

include poets William Wordsworth, Samuel Taylor Coleridge, Percy Bysshe Shelley, Lord Byron, and John Keats; essayists Charles Lamb and William Hazlitt; and novelists Mary Shelley and Sir Walter Scott. Associated with German Romanticism are Friedrich von Schiller, Johann Wolfgang von Goethe, Heinrich Heine, and the brothers Grimm. Writers contributing to the Romantic movement in other European countries include Russian poet Alexander Pushkin and Italian poet Giacomo Leopardi. American Romantic writers include James Fenimore Cooper, Edgar Allan Poe, and Transcendentalist writers such as Henry David Thoreau and Ralph Waldo Emerson.

In part a reaction to the idealistic characteristics of Romantic art and literature and in part a reaction to the social ills brought on by industrialization and the growth of cities in Europe, **Realism** is an attempt to render in art or literature an accurate portrayal of reality. Although the development of the novel in the eighteenth century, with its detailed descriptions of characters and settings, could be considered an example of Realism, literary historians usually apply the term to works of the late nineteenth century that dealt with the harsher details of ordinary lives.

As literacy became more common among the middle class in Europe, the novel became increasingly popular. Realistic, detailed descriptions of everyday life, and especially of its darker aspects, appealed to many

Art Note

Honoré Daumier (1808–1879) was a French caricaturist, painter, and sculptor who was considered the greatest social satirist of his day. His cartoons and drawings focused on nineteenth-century French politics and society.

Daumier was born in Marseilles, France, to parents who were both unsuccessful artists. When Daumier was still a young boy, his parents arranged for him to study with Alexander Lenoir, a fairly well-known artist of the time.

Daumier began to work at the age of thirteen, first as a bailiff's messenger in the courts, then as a bookstore clerk at the Palais-Royal, the center of commerce in Paris. When he was nineteen, he decided to pursue an artistic career. Daumier quickly learned that he could not earn a living by painting and sculpting alone, so he began to take commissions for portraits and cartoons. In his cartoons, he satirized a variety of people—lawyers, businessmen, physicians, professors, and royalty. Daumier was thrown into prison for six months in 1832 for two unflattering caricatures of King Louis-Philippe.

After working as a lithographer, cartoonist, and sculptor from 1830 to 1847, Daumier tried his hand at impressionist painting. As there was little demand for this type of work, he did not create many paintings. Daumier's reputation as an artist was built on his unforgettable cartoons and lithographs.

Additional Questions and Activities

Invite each student to read the work of one of the Romantic or Realist writers named in this introduction but not included in the textbook. Students can compare the work to that of a writer represented in this text.

Cross-curricular Activities

Invite students to form small groups and research different aspects of the American Revolution, the French Revolution, or some of the major civil and political reforms in England.

Students should share their findings with one another, and discuss the following questions:

- What similarities do they find in the political changes in each country?
- In what ways are these changes related to the ideals of the Romantic movement?

Additional Questions and Activities

Encourage students who are interested in Naturalism to read some of the works of Jack London, Stephen Crane, Frank Norris, and Theodore Dreiser.

Students can use the library or online resources to find works by these authors and autobiographical information about them. You might ask students to give book reports to the rest of the class.

Literary Note

Jack London (1876–1916), whose most famous works include *The Call of the Wild* and *White Fang,* was often inspired by his experiences during the Klondike Gold Rush in the Yukon Territory of northwest Canada. Like many other Klondike gold-seekers, London was attracted to the area's promise of wealth and its setting for testing courage, adaptability, and endurance. London was also attracted to the Yukon Territory because of his personal philosophy, which was based on the theory of Social Darwinism. He embraced the idea that human societies are or should be managed according to the principle of "survival of the fittest." This idea seemed to be fulfilled in the wild and harsh Yukon Territory, where laws and law enforcement were virtually nonexistent. In *The Call of the Wild,* London combined Social Darwinism with Naturalism.

Avenue De Clichy. *Louis Anquetin, 1887*

readers who were disillusioned by the "progress" going on around them. Common subjects in Realist writing included families, religion, and social reform. Early literary Realists included French writers Honoré de Balzac and Gustave Flaubert; British writers Charles Dickens, George Eliot, and Thomas Hardy; Norwegian writer Henrik Ibsen; and Russian writer Anton Chekhov.

Naturalism, another form of Realism, is based on the philosophical theory that actions and events result not from human intentions but from largely uncontrollable external forces. Naturalist writers, like Realists, chose subjects and themes common to the lower and middle classes. They were also attentive to details, striving for accuracy and authenticity in their descriptions. Naturalism, which flourished in the nineteenth century, had its greatest influence in France, where it is closely associated with writers Émile Zola and Guy de Maupassant, and in the United States as practiced by writers Stephen Crane, Frank Norris, Theodore Dreiser, and Jack London.

In this unit you have the opportunity to sample works by authors representing each of the important literary movements of the eighteenth and nineteenth centuries—Romanticism, Realism, and Naturalism.

Echoes:

Romanticism, Realism, and Naturalism

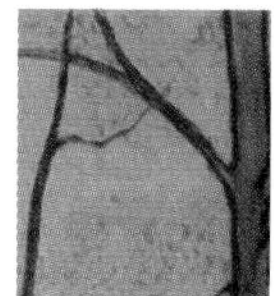

Liberty, equality, fraternity.

—Rallying cry of the French Revolution, 1789

The road of excess leads to the palace of wisdom.

—William Blake
The Marriage of Heaven and Hell

Dismissing then those pretty feminine phrases, which the men condescendingly use to soften our slavish dependence, and despising that weak elegancy of mind, exquisite sensibility, and sweet docility of manners, supposed to be the sexual characteristics of the weaker vessel, I wish to show that elegance is inferior to virtue, that the first object of laudable ambition is to obtain a character as a human being, regardless of the distinction of sex.

—Mary Wollstonecraft
A Vindication of the Rights of Woman

A stand can be made against invasion by an army; no stand can be made against invasion by an idea.

—Victor Hugo

Truth is on the march and nothing can stop it.

—Émile Zola
J'Accuse

I sit on a man's back, choking him and making him carry me, and yet assure myself and others that I am very sorry for him and wish to ease his lot by all possible means—except by getting off his back.

—Leo Tolstoy
What Then Must We Do?

The true security is to be found in social solidarity rather than in isolated individual effort.

—Feodor Dostoevsky

Nature never deceives us; it is always we who deceive ourselves.

—Jean-Jacques Rousseau
Émile, ou De L'Education

Everything there is simply order and beauty, luxury, peace and sensual indulgence.

—Charles Baudelaire
L'Invitation au Voyage

Biographical Notes

William Blake (1757–1827) was a late eighteenth- and early nineteenth-century author and artist. Blake was an early leader of the Romantic movement and is best known for his collections of poems *Songs of Innocence* and *Songs of Experience.* Blake himself illustrated, printed, and distributed all of his books.

Mary Wollstonecraft (1759–1797) is recognized as one of the first great feminist writers and thinkers. Her masterpiece *A Vindication of the Rights of Woman* (1792) examines the lack of opportunities and education for women in Wollstonecraft's day.

Victor Hugo (1802–1885) was a politically active French writer who has been called "the most powerful mind of the Romantic movement." For more information about Hugo, see page 914.

Émile Zola (1840–1902) was a French writer and the founder of Naturalism. For more information about Zola, see page 930.

Leo Tolstoy (1828–1910), a Russian writer and philosopher, is considered to be one of the world's greatest novelists. For more information about Tolstoy, see page 314.

Feodor Dostoevsky (1821–1881) was a nineteenth-century Russian author who, along with Tolstoy, is considered one of the world's great novelists. His novels include *Crime and Punishment* and *The Brothers Karamazov.*

Jean-Jacques Rousseau (1712–1778) was an eighteenth-century French philosopher and one of the leading figures of the Enlightenment. His ideas about people and nature became central to Romanticism.

Charles Baudelaire (1821–1867) was a French poet and essayist of the mid-nineteenth century. His most famous collection of poems is called *Les Fleurs du mal* (*Flowers of Evil*).

Additional Questions and Activities

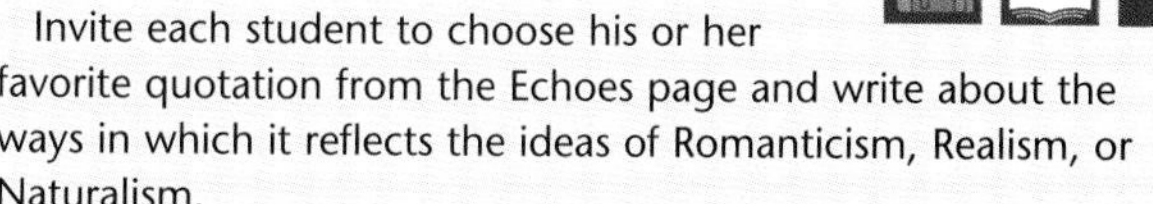

Invite each student to choose his or her favorite quotation from the Echoes page and write about the ways in which it reflects the ideas of Romanticism, Realism, or Naturalism.

When students have finished writing, ask them to form pairs to discuss their ideas. Be sure that students in each pair have chosen different quotations.

ADDITIONAL RESOURCES

READER'S GUIDE

- Selection Worksheet 11.1

ASSESSMENT PORTFOLIO

- Selection Check Test 2.11.1
- Selection Test 2.11.2

ESSENTIAL SKILLS PRACTICE BOOKS

- Writing 1.8, 1.20
- Language 2.40

PREREADING EXTENSIONS

You might want to share with students all or part of the following excerpt from Wordsworth's preface to *Lyrical Ballads*:

The principal object, then, which I myself proposed in these poems was to choose incidents and situations from common life, and to relate or describe them, throughout, as far as possible in a selection of language really used by men; and, at the same time to throw over them a certain coloring of imagination, whereby ordinary things should be presented to the mind in an unusual way; . . . Humble and rustic life was generally chosen, because in that condition, the essential passions of the heart find a better soil in which they can attain their maturity, are less under restraint, and speak a plainer and more emphatic language; because in that condition of life our elementary feelings coexist in a state of greater simplicity, and, consequently, may be more accurately contemplated, and more forcibly communicated.

SUPPORT FOR LEP STUDENTS

ADDITIONAL VOCABULARY

behold—hold in view; notice; look at

bound—attached

PREREADING

"My Heart Leaps Up When I Behold"
by William Wordsworth

About the Author

WILLIAM WORDSWORTH 1770–1850

William Wordsworth, often considered to be the founder of the Romantic movement in England, was born in the English Lake District, a countryside that inspired his profound love of nature. He attended Cambridge but did not enjoy academic life. After leaving school in 1791, he lived for a year in France, where he became an enthusiastic supporter of the democratic ideals of the French Revolution before returning to his own country. When the revolution in France degenerated into the Reign of Terror, Wordsworth became disillusioned and despondent. This period of suffering was made bearable by his sister, Dorothy, and by his friendship with fellow poet Samuel Taylor Coleridge.

Coleridge and Wordsworth co-authored *Lyrical Ballads* (1798), a collection of poems that expressed their radical new ideas about poetry. From 1797 to 1807, Wordsworth created his finest poems, most of which deal with the elevation of the soul through communion with nature. Thereafter, Wordsworth's poetic powers declined as his political conservatism, spawned in bitterness over the failures of the French Revolution, grew. This conservative attitude earned him the scorn of younger, more radical poets, including Percy Bysshe Shelley, John Keats, and Robert Browning.

In 1843, Wordsworth accepted the position of poet laureate of England with the provision that he not be required to write occasional or official verse. In his later years, he cared patiently and devotedly for his sister. Upon his death, Wordsworth was buried in Grasmere Church-yard in the Lake District that he had immortalized in his work.

About the Selection

Wordsworth was inspired to write "**My Heart Leaps Up When I Behold**" as he was inspired to write many of his poems—by observing nature, in this case a rainbow. For Wordsworth, observing nature was an intense, spiritual experience that led him outside of himself to contemplate the mysteries of life and the spiritual world. He considered himself to be "a trusting child of nature." In the poem that you are about to read, Wordsworth expresses his hope that he will always retain his youthful exuberance in the presence of nature.

CONNECTIONS: Wordsworth's Beliefs about Poetry

In the controversial preface to *Lyrical Ballads*, Wordsworth argued, in keeping with his revolutionary, democratic principles, that poetry should be written not in flowery, formal language but rather in the voice of the common person. The verse in *Lyrical Ballads* contains portraits of nature and of ordinary but noble people. It rejects artificial, mechanical devices of style in favor of "a selection of the language actually used by men" and records moments of spontaneous emotional transport over which has been thrown "a certain coloring of the imagination."

GOALS/OBJECTIVES

Studying this lesson will enable students to

- enjoy a poem that expresses a speaker's exuberance in the presence of nature
- discuss the life and work of William Wordsworth
- discuss reactions to Neoclassicism
- define the terms *paradox* and *parallelism*
- write original paradoxes
- write a critical essay about the work of Wordsworth and the ideals of Romanticism
- practice pronoun reference and agreement

How do you feel when you observe a beautiful scene in the natural world? If such a scene has ever moved you, describe it along with the thoughts and feelings that it evoked. If you have never been moved by nature, explain why natural scenes do not evoke strong emotional reactions in you, and state what type of scene does inspire such a reaction in you.

READER'S JOURNAL

"My Heart Leaps Up When I Behold"

WILLIAM WORDSWORTH

My heart leaps up when I behold
A rainbow in the sky:
So was it when my life began;
So is it now I am a man;
So be it when I shall grow old,
Or let me die!
The Child is father of the Man;
And I could wish my days to be
Bound each to each by natural piety. ■

❶ *What emotion does the speaker experience when he sees a rainbow?*

❷ *By what does the speaker wish all his days to be bound?*

WORDS FOR EVERYDAY USE

pi • e • ty (pī´ə tē) *n.,* devotion to religious or family duties and practice

READER'S JOURNAL

Encourage students to take time to freewrite for several moments, writing down the first thoughts that come into their minds when they think about a particular scene.

ANSWERS TO GUIDED READING QUESTIONS

❶ The speaker experiences joy.

❷ The speaker wishes that all his days were bound "each to each by natural piety."

SELECTION CHECK TEST WITH ANSWERS

EX. In what country did the author of this poem live most of his life?
The author of this poem lived most of his life in Great Britain.

1. When does the speaker's heart "leap up"?
The speaker's heart leaps up when he beholds a rainbow in the sky.

2. When was the first time the speaker's heart leaped in this way?
The first time was when his life began.

3. What does the speaker hope will happen if "it" is not so when he grows old?
He hopes that he will die.

4. Who is the father of the Man?
The Child is the father of the Man.

5. By what does the speaker want his days bound?
The speaker wants his days bound by "natural piety."

VOCABULARY IN CONTEXT

• My grandfather's religious piety earns him respect among the most devout believers at the synagogue he attends.

RESPONDING TO THE SELECTION

Students might also discuss whether or not the attitude of the speaker toward nature reflects the attitudes of most people today toward nature.

ANSWERS FOR REVIEWING THE SELECTION

RECALLING AND INTERPRETING

1. **Recalling.** The speaker's heart "leaps up" when he beholds a rainbow. **Interpreting.** The speaker of this selection feels joy in the presence of natural beauty.

2. **Recalling.** The speaker first had this reaction when his "life began," or in his youth. The speaker hopes that he will die if he doesn't experience extreme joy when viewing nature in his old age. **Interpreting.** The speaker longs to retain his youthful exuberance in nature throughout his life. The speaker sees his joy in nature as an essential part of himself.

3. **Recalling.** The speaker says that the "Child is father of the Man." **Interpreting.** Students may say that a child instructs adults in how to play and enjoy themselves, how to delight in the natural world, and how to look at the world with innocent wonder rather than with jaded cynicism.

4. **Recalling.** The speaker wishes for his days to be bound together by "natural piety." **Interpreting.** Students may say that the speaker wants his reverence for nature to be the connecting theme of his life. Students may say that natural piety means revering and worshipping nature.

SYNTHESIZING

Responses will vary. Possible responses are given.

5. The speaker admires children for the way in which they experience pure joy and wonder when they encounter nature. The speaker has sought to retain this sense of wonder in his adult life.

Responding to the Selection

If you were about to take a long walk through a beautiful rural setting, would you want the speaker of this selection to come along? Explain why or why not.

Reviewing the Selection

RECALLING		INTERPRETING
1. What happens when the speaker beholds a rainbow?	▶▶	What emotions does the speaker of this selection feel in the presence of natural beauty?
2. When did the speaker first have this reaction to the natural spectacle of a rainbow? What does he hope will happen if he does not have this reaction to nature when he is "old"?	▶▶	What does the speaker long to retain throughout his life? Why does he wish to retain this thing?
3. What surprising relationship does the speaker see between "Child" and "Man"?	▶▶	In what ways might a child instruct an adult?
4. By what does the speaker wish his days to be bound?	▶▶	What do you think the speaker means by the final two lines? How would you define *natural piety?*

SYNTHESIZING

5. Explain how the speaker's feelings about youth and childhood are related to his feelings about nature.

Understanding Literature (Questions for Discussion)

1. **Paradox.** A **paradox** is a seemingly contradictory statement, idea, or event. "The Child is father of the Man" is a famous example of paradox. Explain what is contradictory about the line. Explain what the speaker means by *father.* In what way can this apparent contradiction be resolved, and the thought be understood as logical?

2. **Parallelism. Parallelism** is a rhetorical technique in which a writer emphasizes the equal value or weight of two or more ideas by expressing them in the same grammatical form. What example of parallelism can you find in this poem? What point does the author make through the use of parallelism?

ANSWERS FOR UNDERSTANDING LITERATURE

Responses will vary. Possible responses are given.

1. **Paradox.** The idea that a child could be the father of a grown man is contradictory because men are the fathers of children. The speaker may mean teacher, instructor, leader, or creative inspiration. Students may say that the idea that grown men can learn much from a child's thought processes and reactions is noncontradictory. Students may also say that because the adult grows out of the child, every child is the parent or creator of his or her own adult self.

2. **Parallelism.** Students should point out lines 3–5 as an example of parallelism. Students may say that the author points out that an appreciation for nature is an essential part of all the stages of life.

Responding in Writing

1. **Creative Writing: Paradoxes.** Writers make use of paradox because this technique causes the reader to pause and reflect. Try to write at least five of your own paradoxes to save and use in future creative writing assignments. For example, you might write, "He heard the soundless roar of the crowd," and later use this paradox in a lyric poem about loneliness. Begin by making a list of contradictory things such as sound and noise, and light and dark. Refer to this list when writing your paradoxes.

2. **Critical Essay: Wordsworth and Romanticism.** Write an essay explaining why Wordsworth's poem is a good example of Romantic poetry. Review the description of Romanticism that appears in the introduction to this unit, paying close attention to the descriptions of what Romantics valued and what they were rebelling against. Then examine "My Heart Leaps Up When I Behold" closely. Which of these values does it express? Against what does it seem to rebel? Use a chart like the one below to organize your ideas. State your thesis clearly in an introductory paragraph, support it with evidence and quotations from the unit introduction and from the poem itself, and come to a conclusion in a final paragraph.

Elements of Romanticism	"My Heart Leaps Up..."
Values or celebrates nature	

Language Lab

Pronoun Reference and Agreement. In the poem you have just read, you may have been confused by the pronoun *it* in lines 3–5 because the pronoun refers to the response to a natural event implied in lines 1–2, rather than to a clear antecedent. Review the rules for making sure that pronouns refer correctly to antecedents in the Language Arts Survey 2.40, "Pronoun Reference and Agreement." Then, reword the sentences below so that pronouns agree in number, person, and gender with their antecedents; pronouns refer clearly to their antecedents; and there are no indefinite or general references.

1. Just before the French Revolution, William Wordsworth met and fell in love with a French woman named Annette Vallon. It was not to last.
2. They say that Annette and William had a child together.
3. Wordsworth, however, was experiencing financial difficulties and there were tensions between England and France, which led to Wordsworth's departure from France.
4. Although he never forgot Annette, Wordsworth later married a woman named Mary Hutchinson with whom she had five children.
5. Each woman gave their love to the great poet.

ANALYTIC SCALES FOR RESPONDING IN WRITING

Assign a score from 1 to 25 for each grading criterion below. (For more detailed evaluation, see the evaluation forms for writing, revising, and proofreading, Assessment Portfolio 4.1–4.9.)

1. Paradoxes

- **Content/Unity.** The paradoxes are striking and cause a reader to pause and reflect on an idea.
- **Organization/Coherence.** The paradoxes focus on contradictory things.
- **Language/Style.** The paradoxes use vivid and precise nouns, verbs, and modifiers.
- **Conventions.** The paradoxes avoid errors in spelling, grammar, usage, mechanics, and manuscript form.

▶ Additional practice is provided in the Essential Skills Practice Book: Writing 1.8.

2. Critical Essay

- **Content/Unity.** The essay explains why Wordsworth's poem "My Heart Leaps Up When I Behold" is a good example of Romantic poetry.
- **Organization/Coherence.** The essay begins with an introduction that includes the thesis of the essay. The introduction is followed by supporting paragraphs with clear transitions. The essay ends with a solid conclusion.
- **Language/Style.** The essay uses vivid and precise nouns, verbs, and modifiers.
- **Conventions.** The essay avoids errors in spelling, grammar, usage, mechanics, and manuscript form.

▶ Additional practice is provided in the Essential Skills Practice Book: Writing 1.20.

ANSWERS FOR LANGUAGE LAB

1. Just before the French Revolution, William Wordsworth met and fell in love with a French woman named Annette Vallon. Their relationship was not to last.
2. Annette and William had a child together.
3. Wordsworth, however, was experiencing financial difficulties and there were tensions between England and France; these problems led to Wordsworth's departure from France.
4. Although he never forgot Annette, Wordsworth later married a woman named Mary Hutchinson with whom he had five children.
5. Each woman gave her love to the great poet.

▶ Additional practice is provided in the Essential Skills Practice Book: Language 2.40.

Additional Questions and Activities

Ask students to answer the following questions about Blake's poem "Mock On, Mock On, Voltaire, Rousseau" in a class discussion:

What, according to the speaker, do Voltaire and Rousseau throw against the wind? What happens as a result? What do you think the speaker means in the first stanza? What does the sand signify?

ANSWERS

According to the speaker, Voltaire and Rousseau throw sands against the wind. *Responses will vary.*

Cross-curricular Activities

MATHEMATICS AND SCIENCES AND APPLIED ARTS

You might share the following information with students and then ask them to complete one of the activities that follows:

Isaac Newton was a seventeenth- and early eighteenth-century English scientist and mathematician. Newton's work contributed greatly to scientific understanding of light, motion, and gravity, the force that draws all things in the earth's sphere toward the center of the earth. Newton also invented calculus, a branch of mathematics that is used in most modern sciences.

- Research to learn more about the work of Isaac Newton. Share your findings with the rest of the class by writing a paper or preparing a presentation.
- Research to learn more about other scientists whose work during the Enlightenment helped to form the foundation for modern science.
- Write an essay that examines both the positive and negative aspects of scientific research and discoveries.

Insights

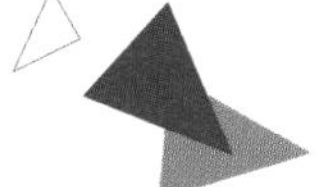

Reactions to Neoclassicism

Illustration by William Blake. Courtesy of Wellesley College Library, Special Collections

During the Enlightenment, also known as the Age of Reason, Neoclassical writers sought rationality and order. In the years following the Enlightenment, from roughly 1785 to 1832, writers, thinkers, and artists rebelled against the Neoclassical focus and began to praise emotion rather than reason, nature rather than human artifice, the individual rather than society, common people rather than royalty, and spontaneity and abandon rather than decorum and control. One of the first writers to express the sensibilities that later became known as Romantic was the artist, writer, and mystic William Blake. William Blake was an intensely religious but unconventional person who saw visions of God looking in at him through a window and who developed his own rather complex mythology in his literary works. Much of Blake's deceptively simple writing is an attack on the complacent rationality and orderliness of the Enlightenment. While Blake condemns rationality, he celebrates energy, creative vitality, and the imagination as the means to perceive God. In the following poem, Blake critiques writers such as François-Marie Arouet de Voltaire (see page 884) and Jean-Jacques Rousseau (see page 993) who, in their quest for rationality, opposed the kind of personal religion that Blake practiced. He also critiques Democritus, the Greek philosopher who first proposed that all substances are composed of particles of atoms, and Isaac Newton. This poem emphasizes the celebration of emotion and nature that became hallmarks of later Romantic writers:

Mock on, Mock on, Voltaire, Rousseau:
Mock on, Mock on; 'tis all in vain!
You throw the sands against the wind,
And the wind blows it back again.

And every sand becomes a Gem
Reflected in the beams divine;
Blown back they blind the mocking Eye,
But still in Israel's paths they shine.

The Atoms of Democritus
And Newton's Particles of light
Are sands upon the Red sea shore,
Where Israel's tents do shine so bright.

Although Blake himself was not enamored of Wordsworth's writing, annotating "My Heart Leaps Up When I Behold" with the words "There is no such Thing as Natural Piety Because The Natural Man is at Enmity with God," he did share the younger writer's love of innocence. While Wordsworth saw spirituality in nature itself, Blake admired the innocence and beauty in nature as the work of a divine creator. This is the theme expressed in the following lines from "Auguries of Innocence."

To see a World in a Grain of Sand
And a Heaven in a Wild Flower,
Hold Infinity in the palm of your hand
And Eternity in an hour.

Additional Questions and Activities

You might have students complete one of the following activities:

- Go to the library and choose one poem by William Wordsworth and one poem by William Blake. Read each poem carefully and then write a short paper comparing and contrasting the styles of the two poems.
- Write an essay comparing and contrasting Neoclassicism with Romanticism. Try to use examples from the works of writers representing each period. (Review the introductions for Units 10 and 11 to find the names of writers representing each period.)

PREREADING

"Loreley"
by Heinrich Heine, translated by Ernst Feise

About the Author

HEINRICH HEINE
1797–1856

Born in Dusseldorf, Prussia, **Heinrich Heine** established himself as a writer with *The Book of Songs*, published in 1827. His successful writing career followed unsuccessful attempts at banking and business. His uncle financed his education at the universities of Bonn, Berlin, and Gottingen, and Heine earned a degree in law. Barred as a Jew from work in civil service, Heine unwillingly converted to Protestantism but never practiced law. During his university years, he fell in love with two of his cousins, both of whom scorned him, probably because of his bleak financial prospects. In 1831, Heine moved to Paris where he spent the rest of his life. His later years were troubled by struggles for his inheritance from his uncle, which he finally got only by agreeing to censor parts of his memoirs. After suffering from health problems, he died in France and was buried at Montmartre Cemetery.

Heine wrote poetry, travelogues, newspaper articles, and cultural and philosophical studies. His satires and critiques angered the German government, which tried to suppress many of his publications. After his death, the popularity of his works demanded their inclusion in Nazi songbooks, but the author was listed as unknown. Heine's fame outlasted the Nazi regime, and his name is equally renowned outside of Germany.

About the Selection

Like many of the poems included in *The Book of Songs,* **"Loreley,"** written in the meter and rhyme scheme of a traditional folk song, is a highly musical lyric poem. In fact, it has been set to music by more than twenty-five composers and has become a very popular German song.

According to myth, the Loreley was once a woman whose beloved was unfaithful. She threw herself into the Rhine and became a creature whose song lures sailors to destruction. The subject and imagery of the poem reflect the importance of nature and imagination to the Romantics. Desire for the unobtainable and an ensuing cynical vision of love are central themes of the poem.

CONNECTIONS: Sirens

The Sirens are creatures of Greek mythology, half-bird and half-woman, who, like the Loreley, use song to lure sailors to destruction. According to Homer, Odysseus had to pass these creatures on his journey home. Warned by Circe of the danger, he had his sailors plug their ears with wax so they could not hear the song, and he had himself tied to the mast of his ship so that he could hear their song but could not change the course of the ship. Another Greek myth claims that the Argonauts—adventurers on a quest with the hero Jason—were able to successfully pass the Sirens because Orpheus sang so beautifully that the sailors ignored the Sirens' song.

ADDITIONAL RESOURCES

READER'S GUIDE
- Selection Worksheet 11.2

ASSESSMENT PORTFOLIO
- Selection Check Test 2.11.3
- Selection Test 2.11.4

ESSENTIAL SKILLS PRACTICE BOOKS
- Writing 1.8, 1.20
- Study and Research 4.6

PREREADING EXTENSIONS

Explain to students that Prussia, the place of Heine's birth, was a former state in northern Germany.

Prussia was originally part of Poland, but established its independence in the eighteenth century. Prussia went on to build up its army and conquer many areas in northern Europe. By the nineteenth century, Prussia was leading an economic and political unification of German states and it became the largest and most influential state in the German Empire. At its most powerful, Prussia occupied more than half of present-day Germany.

Prussia was abolished as a state in 1947 after Germany's defeat in World War II. Its land was divided among East Germany, West Germany, Poland, and the Soviet Union.

SUPPORT FOR LEP STUDENTS

PRONUNCIATIONS OF PROPER NOUNS AND ADJECTIVES

Hein • rich Heine (hīn´rik hī´nə)
Lor • el • ey (lôr´ə lī)

ADDITIONAL VOCABULARY

confounds—confuses
turbulent—rough; stormy
twilight—sunset or sunrise

GOALS/OBJECTIVES

Studying this lesson will enable students to

- enjoy a poem with a mythical subject and the rhyme scheme and meter of a traditional folk song
- discuss the life and work of Heinrich Heine
- define the terms *setting* and *mood*
- write a song based on "Loreley"
- write a critical essay which analyzes the tone of a poem
- identify faulty arguments and propaganda

READER'S JOURNAL

Students might also write about specific contemporary temptations that have attracted them or people they know. Why might people find these things appealing? What dangers do they present? How might one avoid these temptations?

ANSWERS TO GUIDED READING QUESTIONS

❶ The speaker refers to the story of the Loreley, which saddens, haunts, and confounds him.

❷ The story takes place in the evening.

❸ The lovely maiden combs her hair and sings.

SPELLING AND VOCABULARY WORDS FROM THE SELECTION

allay	skiff

READER'S JOURNAL

Think about a temptation you may have experienced to do something dangerous. Write about that situation. What was intriguing or appealing to you about the temptation? Did you think about the risks involved before you acted? What happened as a result of your actions? If you have not been in such a situation, or if you do not wish to write about such a situation, write about the effects temptation might have on a person's judgment.

"Loreley"

HEINRICH HEINE, TRANSLATED BY ERNST FEISE

❶ *To what story does the speaker refer? What effect does the story have on the speaker?*

❷ *At what time of day does the action of the poem take place?*

❸ *What does the lovely maiden do?*

I do not know what haunts me,
What saddened my mind all day;
An age-old tale confounds me,
A spell I cannot allay.

The air is cool and in twilight
The Rhine's[1] dark waters flow;
The peak of the mountain in highlight
Reflects the evening glow.

There sits a lovely maiden
Above, so wondrous fair,
With shining jewels laden,
She combs her golden hair.

It falls through her comb in a shower,
And over the valley rings
A song of mysterious power
That lovely maiden sings.

1. **Rhine.** River in western Europe, flowing north from Switzerland through Germany

WORDS FOR EVERYDAY USE

al • lay (a lā´) *vt.,* put to rest; quiet, calm

VOCABULARY IN CONTEXT

• The police officers are trying to allay the public's fears surrounding the recent string of burglaries.

Rocks at Belle-Isle. *Claude Monet, 1886*

The boatman in his small <u>skiff</u> is
Seized by turbulent love,
No longer he marks where the cliff is,
He looks to the mountain above.

I think the waves must fling him
Against the reefs nearby,
And that did with her singing
The lovely Loreley. ■

❶ *What effect does the song of the Loreley have on the sailor?*

Words for Everyday Use

skiff (skif) *n.*, small, open boat propelled by oars or sail

Answers to Guided Reading Questions

❶ The boatman is seized by love and forgets to watch for the dangerous cliff. He is killed on the reefs.

Selection Check Test with Answers

EX. What confounds the speaker?
An "age-old tale" confounds the speaker.

1. To what time of day does the speaker refer?
The speaker refers to evening.

2. What is the lovely maiden doing?
She is combing her golden hair and singing.

3. Who is seized by turbulent love?
A boatman is seized by turbulent love.

4. What does this person stop doing?
He stops paying attention to the cliff.

5. What happens to this person as a result of the song of the Loreley?
He is flung against the reefs.

Quotables

"It must require an inordinate share of vanity and presumption, too, after enjoying so much that is good and beautiful on earth, to ask the Lord for immortality in addition to it all."

—Heinrich Heine
City of Lucca

Vocabulary in Context

- The small, red <u>skiff</u> bobbed on the lake's tiny waves.

RESPONDING TO THE SELECTION

You might give students time to freewrite about what the poem means to them before they begin discussions.

ANSWERS FOR REVIEWING THE SELECTION

RECALLING AND INTERPRETING

1. **Recalling.** The story haunts the speaker and makes him or her sad and confused. **Interpreting.** The story of the Loreley has as profound an effect upon the speaker as the song of the Loreley has upon the sailor.
2. **Recalling.** The Loreley is lovely, fair, and bedecked with jewels. She combs her golden hair and sings. **Interpreting.** The actions of the Loreley seem innocent and calm. The word *mysterious* makes the actions seem more threatening.
3. **Recalling.** The boatman is overcome by turbulent love. His emotion makes him ignore the dangerous cliffs. **Interpreting.** Stanza 5 suggests that love can make one blind or ignorant of danger and that it can cause one to act irrationally.
4. **Recalling.** The speaker thinks that the sailor must have been flung upon the reefs by the waves. **Interpreting.** The speaker thinks the Loreley is dangerous, but he is intrigued by her as well.

SYNTHESIZING

Responses will vary. Possible responses are given.

5. The Loreley's song may be prompted by a wish for others to experience the destruction to which she was led by love.

Responding to the Selection

Has there ever been in your life a Loreley, or something that seemed wonderful but actually drove you to danger? How might you avoid the call of the Loreley? Discuss these questions with your classmates.

Reviewing the Selection

RECALLING		INTERPRETING
1. What effect does the story of the Loreley have on the speaker?	▶▶	In what way is the story about the Loreley like the song of the Loreley?
2. Describe the Loreley. What is she doing?	▶▶	How might you classify such actions if you were unaware of the story of the Loreley? What word in stanza 4 changes the reader's perception of these actions? What effect does this word have?
3. What emotion overcomes the boatman? What effect does this emotion have on him?	▶▶	What message about love does stanza 5 convey?
4. What does the speaker think must have happened to the sailor?	▶▶	What attitude does the speaker have toward the Loreley? How can you tell?

SYNTHESIZING

5. Consider the origin of the Loreley. How might the circumstances that led to the creation of the Loreley be related to her actions?

Understanding Literature (Questions for Discussion)

Setting and Mood. The **setting** of a literary work is the time and place in which it occurs, together with all the details used to create a sense of a particular time and place. Describe the setting of the poem. **Mood,** or **atmosphere,** is the emotion created in the reader by part or all of a literary work. What mood is created through the description of the setting in stanza 2? To what does the mood change in later stanzas? What details contribute to the later mood?

ANSWERS FOR UNDERSTANDING LITERATURE

Responses will vary. Possible responses are given.

Setting and Mood. The poem is set on the Rhine in the evening. The air is cool, the water is dark, and there is the slight glow of twilight. The mood is peaceful. The shining of the Loreley contrasts with the dim, calm glow of the evening. The mysteriousness of the Loreley's song changes the mood to eerie and slightly menacing. The words *seized, turbulent,* and *fling* are dramatic and powerful and contribute to the menacing mood.

Responding in Writing

1. **Creative Writing: Song.** The Loreley's song is haunting and powerful. What might a modern version of the Loreley's song sound like? Write the lyrics to such a song. Before you begin, think about what things might tempt somebody to destruction. Freewrite about the following questions: What might you say to them to grab your listeners' attention? How might you appeal to their sense of pride, honor, loneliness, or love? What emotions might the song evoke? What words or images might create such emotions in the listener? Choose the ideas that you think are most compelling and try to arrange them into verses. If you wish, you may set the lyrics to a tune you know or to one of your own creation.

2. **Critical Essay: Analyzing Tone.** Tone is the emotional attitude toward the reader or toward the subject implied by a literary work. Examples of the different tones that a work may have include familiar, ironic, playful, sarcastic, serious, and sincere. In a brief essay, analyze the tone of "Loreley." Consider language that shows the speaker's mood, the setting and time of day, the appearance and behavior of the Loreley, the effect of the Loreley's song on the sailor, and the effect of the tale of the Loreley on the speaker. Write a thesis statement identifying the tone. Then, support your thesis statement using references to the text of the poem.

Thinking Skills

Identifying Faulty Arguments and Propaganda. Sometimes emotions can affect decision making. Propaganda is misleading language that attempts to lead a reader or listener to an illogical conclusion by appealing to his or her emotions. Read the Language Arts Survey 4.6, "Identifying Faulty Arguments and Propaganda." Then identify which type of propaganda is used in each sentence below.

1. President Imara reads everything by Heinrich Heine that she can get her hands on. He's such a great writer.
2. Heine's work was printed in Nazi songbooks.
3. Don't bother reading Heine's love poems; he loved, but he was a loser.
4. Everyone is lining up to buy The Sirens' new release *Waves of Destruction.* Have you gotten your copy yet?
5. Freaks and bums will riot in the streets if The Sirens are allowed to play in Rocky Shore Park.

ANALYTIC SCALES FOR RESPONDING IN WRITING

Assign a score from 1 to 25 for each grading criterion below. (For more detailed evaluation, see the evaluation forms for writing, revising, and proofreading, Assessment Portfolio 4.1–4.9.)

1. Song

- **Content/Unity.** The song is a modern version of the Loreley's song.
- **Organization/Coherence.** The song grabs the reader's attention; appeals to a sense of pride, loneliness, or love; and uses images that evoke emotions.
- **Language/Style.** The song uses vivid and precise nouns, verbs, and modifiers.
- **Conventions.** The song avoids errors in spelling, grammar, usage, mechanics, and manuscript form.

▸ Additional practice is provided in the Essential Skills Practice Book: Writing 1.8.

2. Critical Essay

- **Content/Unity.** The essay identifies and analyzes the tone of "Loreley."
- **Organization/Coherence.** The essay begins with an introduction that includes the thesis of the essay. The introduction is followed by supporting paragraphs with clear transitions. The essay ends with a solid conclusion.
- **Language/Style.** The essay uses vivid and precise nouns, verbs, and modifiers.
- **Conventions.** The essay avoids errors in spelling, grammar, usage, mechanics, and manuscript form.

▸ Additional practice is provided in the Essential Skills Practice Book: Writing 1.20.

ANSWERS FOR THINKING SKILLS

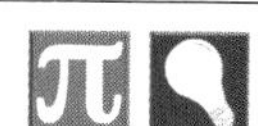

1. False testimonial
2. Transfer
3. Character assassination
4. Bandwagon
5. Loaded words

▸ Additional practice is provided in the Essential Skills Practice Book: Study and Research 4.6.

ADDITIONAL RESOURCES

READER'S GUIDE
- Selection Worksheet 11.3

ASSESSMENT PORTFOLIO
- Selection Check Test 2.11.5
- Selection Test 2.11.6

ESSENTIAL SKILLS PRACTICE BOOKS
- Writing 1.8, 1.20
- Applied English/Tech Prep 5.6

PREREADING EXTENSIONS

Ask students to read portions of *Old Possum's Book of Practical Cats, Pygmalion, The Tragedy of Romeo and Juliet, Don Quixote*, or *The Secret Garden* and then listen to the soundtracks from the musical adaptations of each work. Some of the musicals, including *My Fair Lady* and *West Side Story*, have been made into movies that are available on video. After students have listened to the soundtracks or viewed the film versions of the musicals, ask them to share and discuss their opinions about the music. What other works would they like to see as musicals? Why?

SUPPORT FOR LEP STUDENTS

PRONUNCIATIONS OF PROPER NOUNS AND ADJECTIVES

Jean Val • jean (zhän´ val zhän´)
Ma • dame Mag • loire (mə dam´ mäg lə wär´)
Mon • seign • eur Bi • en • ve • nu (män sēn yōr´ bē än´vä no͞o)

ADDITIONAL VOCABULARY

apparition—ghost
expel—force out
gendarme—French soldier serving as a police officer
liberated—given freedom
profoundly—extremely, deeply
tranquil—calm
traversed—walked across

PREREADING

from *Les Misérables*
by Victor Hugo

FRANCE

About the Author

VICTOR HUGO
1802–1885

In his day, **Victor Hugo** was called "the most powerful mind of the Romantic movement." A national hero to the French people, Hugo shared in this admiration of himself, once suggesting that Paris be renamed Hugo in his honor. Hugo's father was a general in Napoleon Bonaparte's army, so Hugo's early life involved a great deal of travel. Uprooted from one city to another, including Naples, Italy and Madrid, Spain, Hugo considered Paris to be his true home and called the city the birthplace of his soul. Displaying his talent for writing while still a teenager, Hugo soon became one of the most prolific writers of all time, producing at least one hundred lines of verse or twenty pages of prose every morning. He explored many different literary forms, including lyric and epic poetry, essays, novels, and verse dramas. One of Hugo's early dramas, *Hernani*, was so unconventional that it provoked a battle between Classicists and Romantics that solidified the prominence of Romanticism in French drama for the first half of the nineteenth century.

Hugo was also active politically. Because he opposed the ascension of Napoleon III as emperor in 1851, Hugo feared for his life and fled from France, living for a time in Brussels and then on the islands of Jersey and Guernsey. While in exile, Hugo wrote abundantly. Although this exile was imposed at first, it later became a source of pride to Hugo, who refused to return to his beloved Paris until Napoleon III fell from power and the Third Republic was established in 1870. Hugo's return was a triumph. He lived as a literary celebrity in France until 1885, when he died and was given an elaborate national funeral, which was attended by more than a million mourners.

About the Selection

Hugo began writing ***Les Misérables*** in 1843, a time of overwhelming grief in his life, as his daughter and her husband had drowned. Hugo resumed work on this novel while in exile. *Les Misérables* is a detective story, a stirring social commentary, and an epic of the people of Paris. The following selection reveals how the novel's hero, a former convict named Jean Valjean, becomes a changed man under the influence of a kindhearted bishop, Monseigneur Bienvenu.

CONNECTIONS: Literary Musicals and Popular Culture

Les Misérables has been adapted as a popular musical, which opened at London's Palace Theater in 1985. Many other literary works have been adapted as musicals. For example, the poet T. S. Eliot's *Old Possum's Book of Practical Cats* graced the stage as the enormously popular musical *Cats*. George Bernard Shaw's *Pygmalion* was made into a musical hit of the 1950s, *My Fair Lady*. Shakespeare's classic story of tragic love *The Tragedy of Romeo and Juliet* was adapted as the 1960s musical *West Side Story*, and Miguel de Cervantes's *Don Quixote* was adapted as *Man of La Mancha*.

GOALS/OBJECTIVES

Studying this lesson will enable students to

- empathize with a character who is challenged to change his lifestyle
- describe the life and work of Victor Hugo
- identify one-dimensional and three-dimensional characters
- write a fictional personal letter
- write a critical essay that describes the elements of Romanticism, Realism, and Naturalism in this excerpt from *Les Misérables*
- write promotional and public relations copy

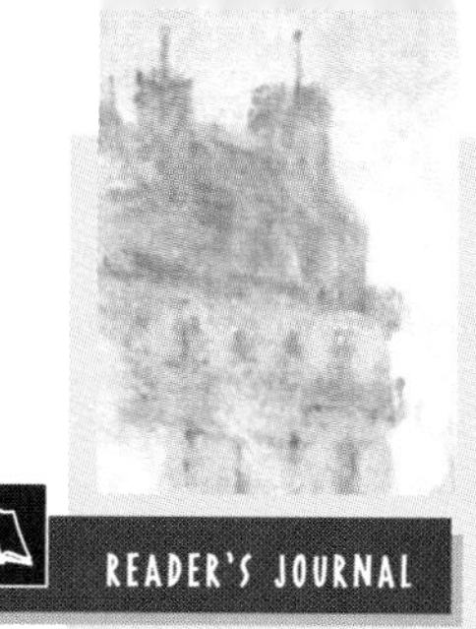

Have you ever known someone who, having been mistreated, returned kindness to the one who mistreated him or her? If so, describe the situation, and speculate about why this person was able to return kindness for cruelty. If you have not come across such a situation, speculate what might motivate a person to "turn the other cheek," or to be kind to someone who injured him or her.

READER'S JOURNAL

FROM

Les Misérables

VICTOR HUGO

CHAPTER III

The door opened.

It opened wide with a rapid movement, as though some one had given it an energetic and resolute push.

A man entered.

We already know the man. It was the wayfarer[1] whom we have seen wandering about in search of shelter.

He entered, advanced a step, and halted, leaving the door open behind him. He had his knapsack on his shoulders, his cudgel in his hand, a rough, audacious, weary, and violent expression in his eyes. The fire on the hearth lighted him up. He was hideous. It was a sinister apparition.

Madame Magloire had not even the strength to utter a cry. She trembled, and stood with her mouth wide open.

Mademoiselle Baptistine turned round, beheld the man entering, and half started up in terror; then, turning her head by degrees towards the fireplace again, she began to observe her brother,[2] and her face became once more profoundly calm and serene.

The Bishop fixed a tranquil eye on the man.

As he opened his mouth, doubtless to ask the newcomer what he desired, the man rested both hands on his staff, directed his gaze at the old man and the two women, and without waiting for the Bishop to speak, he said, in a loud voice:—

"See here. My name is Jean Valjean. I am a convict from the galleys.[3] I have passed nineteen years in the galleys. I was liberated four days ago, and am on my way to Pontarlier, which is my destination. I have been walking

1. **wayfarer.** Person who travels from place to place, especially on foot

2. **her brother.** Mademoiselle Baptistine's brother is the bishop Monseigneur Bienvenu.

3. **galley.** Long, low, single-decked ship upon which convicted felons were forced to work

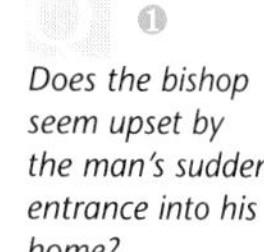

1 *Does the bishop seem upset by the man's sudden entrance into his home?*

2 *What has the man who enters the room been doing?*

3 *Why might Madame Magloire be frightened by the man?*

WORDS FOR EVERYDAY USE

cudg • el (kuj´əl) *n.,* short, thick stick or club

au • da • cious (ô dā´shəs) *adj.,* bold or daring

READER'S JOURNAL

Students might also freewrite about different ways in which they can show kindness and understanding to their classmates or family members.

ANSWERS TO GUIDED READING QUESTIONS

1 No, the bishop remains tranquil.

2 The man has been wandering about, searching for shelter.

3 Madame Magloire might be frightened by the man because of his rough and sinister appearance and because of the "violent expression in his eyes."

SPELLING AND VOCABULARY WORDS FROM THE SELECTION

abyss	ignominy
audacious	inarticulate
avidity	ostentation
consternation	perdition
cudgel	physiognomy
disconcert	stupefaction

VOCABULARY IN CONTEXT

- We couldn't find a hammer, so we pounded the nails with a cudgel.
- She was an audacious mountain climber—always challenging herself to climb taller mountains.

Answers to Guided Reading Questions

1. Jean Valjean suddenly understands that the bishop is allowing him to stay for the night. Jean is overjoyed. He told the bishop the worst about himself because he expected the bishop to expel him.

2. The woman probably knew of the bishop's kindness toward strangers and knew that the bishop would take Jean Valjean in for the night.

3. Jean Valjean stops the bishop because he doesn't think that the bishop understands that he is a former convict.

Cross-curricular Activities

Mathematics and Sciences

Jean Valjean says that he has "one hundred and nine francs fifteen sous" that he saved over the course of nineteen years. Some students might be interested in looking up how much money this would be in dollars and cents today. Students might also want to research the concept of exchange rates, and the current exchange rates between the United States and other countries in addition to France.

1 *What does Jean Valjean suddenly understand? How does he feel about this situation? Why did he tell the bishop at once the worst about himself? What did he expect the bishop to do?*

2 *Why do you think the woman directed Jean to the bishop's house?*

3 *Why does Jean Valjean stop the bishop after he orders that a place at the table be set for Jean?*

for four days since I left Toulon. I have traveled a dozen leagues[4] today on foot. This evening, when I arrived in these parts, I went to an inn, and they turned me out, because of my yellow passport,[5] which I had shown at the townhall. I had to do it. I went to an inn. They said to me, 'Be off,' at both places. No one would take me. I went to the prison; the jailer would not admit me. I went into a dog's kennel; the dog bit me and chased me off, as though he had been a man. One would have said that he knew who I was. I went into the fields, intending to sleep in the open air, beneath the stars. There were no stars. I thought it was going to rain, and I re-entered the town, to seek the recess of a doorway. Yonder, in the square, I meant to sleep on a stone bench. A good woman pointed out your house to me, and said to me, 'Knock there!' I have knocked. What is this place? Do you keep an inn? I have money—savings. One hundred and nine francs fifteen sous, which I earned in the galleys by my labor, in the course of nineteen years. I will pay. What is that to me? I have money. I am very weary; twelve leagues on foot; I am very hungry. Are you willing that I should remain?"

"Madame Magloire," said the Bishop, "you will set another place."

The man advanced three paces, and approached the lamp which was on the table. "Stop," he resumed, as though he had not quite understood; "that's not it. Did you hear? I am a galley-slave; a convict. I come from the galleys." He drew from his pocket a large sheet of yellow paper, which he unfolded. "Here's my passport. Yellow, as you see. This serves to expel me from every place where I go. Will you read it? I know how to read. I learned in the galleys. There is a school there for those who choose to learn. Hold, this is what they put on this passport: 'Jean Valjean, discharged convict, native of'—that is nothing to you—'has been nineteen years in the galleys: five years for house-breaking and burglary; fourteen years for having attempted to escape on four occasions. He is a very dangerous man.' There! Every one has cast me out. Are you willing to receive me? Is this an inn? Will you give me something to eat and a bed? Have you a stable?"

"Madame Magloire," said the Bishop, "you will put white sheets on the bed in the alcove." We have already explained the character of the two women's obedience.

Madame Magloire retired to execute these orders.

The Bishop turned to the man.

"Sit down, sir, and warm yourself. We are going to sup in a few moments, and your bed will be prepared while you are supping."

At this point the man suddenly comprehended. The expression of his face, up to that time somber and harsh, bore the imprint of stupefaction, of doubt, of joy, and became extraordinary. He began stammering like a crazy man:—

"Really? What! You will keep me? You do not drive me forth? A convict! You call me *sir*! You do not address me as *thou*?[6] 'Get out of here, you dog!' is what people always say to me. I felt sure that you would expel me, so I told you at once who I am. Oh, what a good woman that was who directed me hither! I am going to sup! A bed with a mattress and sheets, like the rest of the world! a bed! It is nineteen years since I have slept in a bed! You actually do not want me to go! You are good people. Besides, I have money. I will pay well. Pardon me, monsieur the

4. **dozen leagues.** Roughly thirty-six miles
5. **yellow passport.** Papers marking Jean Valjean as a former convict
6. **thou.** Familiar form, used to address inferior persons

Words for Everyday Use

stu • pe • fac • tion (stoo͞´ pə fak´ shən) *n.,* stunned amazement

Vocabulary in Context

- The children stared at the athlete in stupefaction when he told them how many hours he spends training.

The Pont de l'Europe. Claude Monet, 1887

inn-keeper, but what is your name? I will pay anything you ask. You are a fine man. You are an inn-keeper, are you not?"

"I am," replied the Bishop, "a priest who lives here."

"A priest!" said the man. "Oh, what a fine priest! Then you are not going to demand any money of me? You are the curé,[7] are you not? the curé of this big church? Well! I am a fool, truly! I had not perceived your skull-cap."

As he spoke, he deposited his knapsack and his cudgel in a corner, replaced his passport in his pocket, and seated himself.

Mademoiselle Baptistine gazed mildly at him. He continued:

"You are humane, Monsieur le Curé; you have not scorned me. A good priest is a very good thing. Then you do not require me to pay?"

"No," said the Bishop; "keep your money. How much have you? Did you not tell me one hundred and nine francs?"

"And fifteen sous," added the man.

"One hundred and nine francs fifteen sous. And how long did it take you to earn that?"

"Nineteen years."

"Nineteen years!"

The Bishop sighed deeply.

The man continued: "I have still the whole of my money. In four days I have spent only twenty-five sous, which I earned by helping unload some wagons at Grasse. Since you are an abbé,[8] I will tell you that we had a chaplain in the galleys. And one day I saw a bishop there. Monseigneur is what they call

7. **curé.** In France, a parish priest

8. **abbé.** French title of respect, given to a priest or minister

❶ *How long did Jean work to earn this money? How do you think the bishop feels about the fact that Jean had to labor so long for so little?*

Answers to Guided Reading Questions

❶ Jean worked for nineteen years to earn this money. The bishop seems saddened and sorry for Jean.

Additional Questions and Activities

Ask students to answer the following questions on paper or in a class discussion:

1. If Jean Valjean came to your door, would you welcome him as the bishop is welcoming him, or would you be suspicious? Explain your response.
2. What is the bishop's reaction when he hears that Jean Valjean worked so long for so little? Do you feel as sympathetic as the bishop does toward Jean Valjean? Explain.

Historical Note

Explain to students that the ways in which people deal with crime and punishment have changed in many countries throughout the world since the days of Jean Valjean. Many countries, although not all, have adopted standards designed to make sure that people are given fair trials and punishments appropriate for the crimes committed. Many countries have also adopted prison standards designed to protect people from torture or unsanitary conditions.

Countries that have adopted such standards recognize that convicted criminals who are punished appropriately for their crimes, but who are treated at the same time as human beings capable of change, are more likely to return to society as reformed, productive individuals.

Answers to Guided Reading Questions

➊ The bishop let Jean in so readily because he says that all who have suffered are welcome to "the house of Jesus Christ."

➋ The bishop didn't need to know Jean Valjean's name because he already considered him a brother as a fellow human being.

➌ Jean feels gratitude and joy when the bishop calls him *sir.* The narrator compares the value of a title of respect to a convict to a glass of water to the shipwrecked.

➍ The priest says that heaven rejoices more in a single repentant sinner than in one hundred just men.

Additional Questions and Activities

Ask students to discuss the following topics:

- Do you know of any people in your personal life or in the world at large who are as forgiving and loving as the bishop? Who are these people? Why are they forgiving rather than bitter and cynical?
- Do you think, in the long run, that it is healthier to be bitter and cynical or understanding and forgiving? How does it feel inside when you are angry? How does it feel when you are kind, or when you attempt to understand someone?

➊ *Why did the bishop let Jean in so readily? According to the bishop, to whom does his home really belong?*

➋ *Why didn't the bishop need to know Jean Valjean's name?*

➌ *How does Jean feel when the bishop calls him sir? To what does the narrator compare the worth of a title of respect to a convict?*

➍ *According to the priest, in what does heaven rejoice?*

him. He was the Bishop of Majore at Marseilles. He is the curé who rules over the other curés, you understand. Pardon me, I say that very badly; but it is such a far-off thing to me! You understand what we are! He said mass in the middle of the galleys, on an altar. He had a pointed thing, made of gold, on his head; it glittered in the bright light of midday. We were all ranged in lines on the three sides, with cannons with lighted matches facing us. One could not see very well. He spoke; but he was too far off, and we did not hear. That is what a bishop is like."

While he was speaking, the Bishop had gone and shut the door, which had remained wide open.

Madame Magloire returned. She brought a silver fork and spoon, which she placed on the table.

"Madame Magloire," said the Bishop, "place those things as near the fire as possible." And turning to his guest: "The night wind is harsh on the Alps. You must be cold, sir."

Each time that he uttered the word *sir*, in his voice which was so gently grave and polished, the man's face lighted up. *Monsieur* to a convict is like a glass of water to one of the shipwrecked of the *Medusa*. Ignominy thirsts for consideration.

"This lamp gives a very bad light," said the Bishop.

Madame Magloire understood him, and went to get the two silver candlesticks from the chimney-piece in Monseigneur's bedchamber, and placed them, lighted, on the table.

"Monsieur le Curé," said the man, "you are good; you do not despise me. You receive me into your house. You light your candles for me. Yet I have not concealed from you whence I come and that I am an unfortunate man."

The Bishop, who was sitting close to him, gently touched his hand. "You could not help telling me who you were. This is not my house; it is the house of Jesus Christ. This door does not demand of him who enters whether he has a name, but whether he has a grief. You suffer, you are hungry and thirsty; you are welcome. And do not thank me; do not say that I receive you in my house. No one is at home here, except the man who needs a refuge. I say to you, who are passing by, that you are much more at home here than I am myself. Everything here is yours. What need have I to know your name? Besides, before you told me, you had one which I knew."

The man opened his eyes in astonishment.

"Really? You knew what I was called?"

"Yes," replied the Bishop, "you are called my brother."

"Stop, Monsieur le Curé," exclaimed the man. "I was very hungry when I entered here; but you are so good, that I no longer know what has happened to me."

The Bishop looked at him, and said,—

"You have suffered much?"

"Oh, the red coat, the ball on the ankle, a plank to sleep on, heat, cold, toil, the convicts, the thrashings, the double chain for nothing, the cell for one word; even sick and in bed still the chain! Dogs, dogs are happier! Nineteen years! I am forty-six. Now, there is the yellow passport. That is what it is like."

"Yes," resumed the Bishop, "you have come from a very sad place. Listen. There will be more joy in heaven over the tear-bathed face of a repentant sinner than over the white robes of a hundred just men. If you emerge from that sad place with thoughts of

Words for Everyday Use

ig • no • min • y (igˊnə minˊē) *n.,* shame and dishonor

Vocabulary in Context

- The ignominy of going to prison encouraged the young man to change his ways.

hatred and of wrath against mankind, you are deserving of pity; if you emerge with thoughts of goodwill and of peace, you are more worthy than any one of us."

In the meantime, Madame Magloire had served supper: soup made with water, oil, bread, and salt; a little bacon, a bit of mutton, figs, a fresh cheese, and a large loaf of rye bread. She had, of her own accord, added to the Bishop's ordinary fare a bottle of his old Mauves wine.

The Bishop's face at once assumed that expression of gayety which is peculiar to hospitable natures. "To table!" he cried vivaciously. As was his custom when a stranger supped with him, he made the man sit on his right. Mademoiselle Baptistine, perfectly peaceable and natural, took her seat at his left.

The Bishop asked a blessing; then helped the soup himself, according to his custom. The man began to eat with avidity. All at once the Bishop said: "It strikes me there is something missing on this table."

Madame Magloire had, in fact, only placed the three sets of forks and spoons which were absolutely necessary. Now, it was the usage of the house, when the Bishop had any one to supper, to lay out the whole six sets of silver on the tablecloth—an innocent ostentation. This graceful semblance of luxury was a kind of child's play, which was full of charm in that gentle and severe household, which raised poverty into dignity.

Madame Magloire understood the remark, went out without saying a word, and a moment later the three sets of silver forks and spoons demanded by the Bishop were glittering upon the cloth, symmetrically arranged before the three persons seated at the table.

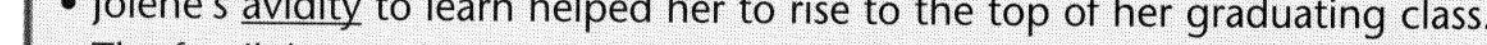

FROM CHAPTER XI

[Editor's note: Later that night, Jean Valjean watches the Bishop sleeping and contemplates whether to steal the Bishop's silver.]

His eye never quitted the old man. The only thing which was clearly to be inferred from his attitude and his physiognomy was a strange indecision. One would have said that he was hesitating between the two abysses,—the one in which one loses one's self and that in which one saves one's self. He seemed prepared to crush that skull or to kiss that hand.

At the expiration of a few minutes his left arm rose slowly towards his brow, and he took off his cap; then his arm fell back with the same deliberation, and Jean Valjean fell to meditating once more, his cap in his left hand, his club in his right hand, his hair bristling all over his savage head.

The Bishop continued to sleep in profound peace beneath that terrifying gaze.

The gleam of the moon rendered confusedly visible the crucifix over the chimney-piece, which seemed to be extending its arms to both of them, with a benediction for one and pardon for the other.

Suddenly Jean Valjean replaced his cap on his brow; then stepped rapidly past the bed, without glancing at the Bishop, straight to the cupboard, which he saw near the head; he raised his iron candlestick as though to force the lock; the key was there; he opened it; the first thing which presented itself to him was the basket of silverware; he seized it, traversed the chamber with long strides, without taking any precautions and without troubling himself about the noise, gained the door, re-entered the oratory,[9] opened the window, seized his cudgel, bestrode the windowsill of the ground floor, put the silver into his knap-

9. **oratory.** Private place of prayer

1 *What are the two abysses between which Jean is hesitating?*

2 *What does the bishop note is missing? What is the bishop trying to show Jean Valjean?*

3 *What does the crucifix seem to be doing in the moonlight?*

4 *What does Jean decide not to do? What does he decide to do?*

Words for Everyday Use

a • vid • i • ty (ə vid´ə tē) *n.*, eagerness

os • ten • ta • tion (äs´ tən tā´shən) *n.*, showy display, as of wealth

phys • i • og • no • my (fiz´ē äg´ nə mē) *n.*, facial features as they expose character

a • byss (ə bis´) *n.*, bottomless gulf

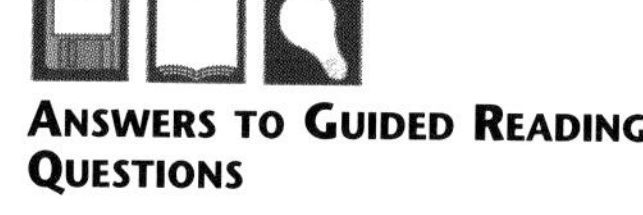

Answers to Guided Reading Questions

1 He is hesitating between crushing the bishop's skull and stealing his silver and kissing the bishop's hand and renouncing a life of crime.

2 The bishop notes that the rest of the set of silver is missing. He is trying to show Jean Valjean that he trusts him even though he is a former thief.

3 The crucifix seems to be offering benediction to the bishop and pardon to Jean.

4 Jean decides not to injure or kill the sleeping bishop, but he does decide to steal the silver.

Additional Questions and Activities

Ask students to answer the following questions, either on paper or in a discussion:

1. Why do students feel that Jean Valjean stole? Why was it hard for him to ignore the urge he had to steal?

2. How do you feel about Jean Valjean after he steals from the bishop?

Vocabulary in Context

- Jolene's avidity to learn helped her to rise to the top of her graduating class.
- The family's mansion, yacht, and expensive cars are examples of ostentation.
- Her manner and her physiognomy revealed a desire to be helpful.
- The deep abyss in the ocean floor was home to many mysterious sea creatures.

Answers to Guided Reading Questions

① The bishop says that the silver rightfully belonged to the poor, and, since a poor man took it, no real crime was committed.

② The bishop seems indifferent to what may have happened to the silver. Madame Magloire is upset about the missing silver and doesn't understand why he is calm.

③ She thinks it was a bad idea to let Jean in and that they are lucky he only stole the silver and did not injure anyone.

ANALYTIC SCALES FOR RESPONDING IN WRITING

(SEE PAGE 924.)

Assign a score from 1 to 25 for each grading criterion below. (For more detailed evaluation, see the evaluation forms for writing, revising, and proofreading, Assessment Portfolio 4.1–4.9.)

1. Personal Letter

- **Content/Unity.** The personal letter is written creatively from the point of view of Jean Valjean.
- **Organization/Coherence.** The personal letter follows standard personal letter format and, in the character of Jean Valjean, describes what he has done with his life since leaving the bishop and why the bishop's lesson was successful or unsuccessful.
- **Language/Style.** The personal letter uses vivid and precise nouns, verbs, and modifiers.
- **Conventions.** The personal letter avoids errors in spelling, grammar, usage, mechanics, and manuscript form.

► Additional practice is provided in the Essential Skills Practice Book: Writing 1.8.

sack, threw away the basket, crossed the garden, leaped over the wall like a tiger, and fled.

CHAPTER XII

① *Why doesn't the bishop mind that the silver is missing?*

The next morning at sunrise Monseigneur Bienvenu was strolling in his garden. Madame Magloire ran up to him in utter consternation.

② *What is the bishop's attitude toward the missing silver? What does Madame Magloire think of his reaction?*

"Monseigneur, Monseigneur!" she exclaimed, "does your Grace know where the basket of silver is?"

"Yes," replied the Bishop.

"Jesus the Lord be blessed!" she resumed; "I did not know what had become of it."

The Bishop had just picked up the basket in a flower-bed.

He presented it to Madame Magloire.

"Here it is."

"Well!" said she. "Nothing in it! And the silver?"

"Ah," returned the Bishop, "so it is the silver which troubles you? I don't know where it is."

"Great, good God! It is stolen! That man who was here last night has stolen it."

In a twinkling, with all the vivacity of an alert old woman, Madame Magloire had rushed to the oratory, entered the alcove, and returned to the Bishop. The Bishop had just bent down, and was sighing as he examined a plant of cochlearia des Guillons, which the basket had broken as it fell across the bed. He rose up at Madame Magloire's cry.

"Monseigneur, the man is gone! The silver has been stolen!"

③ *What does Madame Magloire think of the bishop's attitude toward Jean Valjean?*

As she uttered this exclamation, her eyes fell upon a corner of the garden, where traces of the wall having been scaled were visible. The coping[10] of the wall had been torn away.

"Stay! yonder is the way he went. He jumped over into Cochefilet Lane. Ah, the abomination! He has stolen our silver!"

The Bishop remained silent for a moment; then he raised his grave eyes, and said gently to Madame Magloire:—

"And, in the first place, was that silver ours?"

Madame Magloire was speechless. Another silence ensued; then the Bishop went on:—

"Madame Magloire, I have for a long time detained that silver wrongfully. It belonged to the poor. Who was that man? A poor man, evidently."

"Alas! Jesus!" returned Madame Magloire. "It is not for my sake nor for Mademoiselle's. It makes no difference to us. But it is for the sake of Monseigneur. What is Monseigneur to eat with now?"

The Bishop gazed at her with an air of amazement.

"Ah, come! Are there no such things as pewter forks and spoons?"

Madame Magloire shrugged her shoulders.

"Pewter has an odor."

"Iron forks and spoons, then."

Madame Magloire made an expressive grimace.

"Iron has a taste."

'Very well," said the Bishop, "wooden ones then."

A few moments later he was breakfasting at the very table at which Jean Valjean had sat on the previous evening. As he ate his breakfast, Monseigneur remarked gaily to his sister, who said nothing, and to Madame Magloire, who was grumbling under her breath, that one really does not need either fork or spoon, even of wood, in order to dip a bit of bread in a cup of milk.

"A pretty idea, truly," said Madame Magloire to herself, as she went and came, "to take in a man like that! and to lodge him close to one's self! And how fortunate that he did

10. **coping.** Top layer of masonry on a wall

Words for Everyday Use

con • ster • na • tion (kän′ stər nā shən) *n.,* fear or shock which makes one feel helpless

Vocabulary in Context

- The firefighters and the crowd were in a state of consternation when the fire spread to the next city block.

Route de Louveciennes. *Camille Pissarro*

nothing but steal! Ah, mon Dieu! it makes one shudder to think of it!"

As the brother and sister were about to rise from the table, there came a knock at the door.

"Come in," said the Bishop.

The door opened. A singular and violent group made its appearance on the threshold. Three men were holding a fourth man by the collar. The three men were gendarmes;[11] the other was Jean Valjean.

A brigadier of gendarmes, who seemed to be in command of the group, was standing near the door. He entered and advanced to the Bishop, making a military salute.

"Monseigneur—" said he.

At this word, Jean Valjean, who was dejected and seemed overwhelmed, raised his head with an air of stupefaction.

"Monseigneur!" he murmured. "So he is not the curé?"

"Silence!" said the gendarme. "He is Monseigneur the Bishop."

In the meantime, Monseigneur Bienvenu had advanced as quickly as his great age permitted.

"Ah! here you are!" he exclaimed, looking at Jean Valjean. "I am glad to see you. Well, but how is this? I gave you the candlesticks too, which are of silver like the rest, and for which you can certainly get two hundred francs. Why did you not carry them away with your forks and spoons?"

Jean Valjean opened his eyes wide, and stared at the venerable Bishop with an expression which no human tongue can render any account of.

"Monseigneur," said the brigadier of gendarmes, "so what this man said is true, then? We came across him. He was walking like a man who is running away. We stopped him to look into the matter. He had this silver—"

1 *What is the bishop's surprising response to the captured thief?*

2 *What does Jean Valjean finally realize about the man who sheltered him?*

11. **gendarmes.** French police officers

Answers to Guided Reading Questions

1 The bishop asks Jean why he didn't take the candlesticks he was given, along with the forks and spoons.

2 Jean finally realizes that the man who sheltered him is a bishop, not a simple parish priest.

ANALYTIC SCALES FOR RESPONDING IN WRITING

(SEE PAGE 924.)

2. Critical Essay

- **Content/Unity.** The essay examines the ways in which the selection from *Les Misérables* is an example of Romanticism, Realism, and Naturalism.
- **Organization/Coherence.** The essay begins with an introduction that includes the thesis of the essay. The introduction is followed by supporting paragraphs with clear transitions. The essay ends with a solid conclusion.
- **Language/Style.** The essay uses vivid and precise nouns, verbs, and modifiers.
- **Conventions.** The essay avoids errors in spelling, grammar, usage, mechanics, and manuscript form.

► Additional practice is provided in the Essential Skills Practice Book: Writing 1.20.

Additional Questions and Activities

On page 922, Gabrielle says that "unlike today in France, religion [in the nineteenth century] was very influential." Share with students the following information: Since the 1970s there has been a decline in the number of practicing Catholics in France, and 40 percent of Catholic infants are not baptized. Only 12 percent of Catholics regularly attend church, with women being the majority of this group. According to a recent survey, 80 percent of native French people said they are Catholic, 15 percent claimed no religion, 2 percent are Protestant, 1 percent are Muslim, and less than 1 percent are Jewish. Invite students to speculate on why religion might be less important today in France than in the nineteenth century. You might extend the discussion to the importance of religion in America today versus when the country was founded.

Answers to Guided Reading Questions

❶ Jean is shocked almost to inarticulateness.

❷ The bishop gives Jean the candlesticks.

❸ The bishop says that Jean has promised to use the money to become an honest man. The bishop has "bought" Jean's soul from him. The bishop says that he withdraws Jean's soul from evil and gives it to God.

Selection Check Test with Answers

EX. Where did Jean Valjean spend nineteen years of his life?
He spent nineteen years as a convict in the galleys.

1. What does the bishop invite Jean Valjean to do?
The bishop invites Jean Valjean to eat and to spend the night.

2. What does Jean take from the bishop?
Jean takes silver from the bishop.

3. What does the bishop say to the gendarmes when they return Jean and the silver?
The bishop tells the gendarmes that he gave the silver to Jean as a gift.

4. What does the bishop give Jean?
The bishop gives Jean the silver candlesticks.

5. What does the bishop believe he has bought from Jean?
The bishop believes he has bought Jean's soul.

"And he told you," interposed the Bishop with a smile, "that it had been given to him by a kind old fellow of a priest with whom he had passed the night? I see how the matter stands. And you have brought him back here? It is a mistake."

"In that case," replied the brigadier, "we can let him go?"

"Certainly," replied the Bishop.

The gendarmes released Jean Valjean, who recoiled.

"Is it true that I am to be released?" he said, in an almost <u>inarticulate</u> voice, and as though he were talking in his sleep.

❶ *What is Jean's reaction to the bishop's surprising words?*

"Yes, thou art released; dost thou not understand?" said one of the gendarmes.

"My friend," resumed the Bishop, "before you go, here are your candlesticks. Take them."

❷ *What does the bishop give to Jean?*

He stepped to the chimney piece, took the two silver candlesticks, and brought them to Jean Valjean. The two women looked on without uttering a word, without a gesture, without a look which could <u>disconcert</u> the Bishop.

Jean Valjean was trembling in every limb. He took the two candlesticks mechanically, and with a bewildered air.

"Now," said the Bishop, "go in peace. By the way, when you return, my friend, it is not necessary to pass through the garden. You can always enter and depart through the street door. It is never fastened with anything but a latch, either by day or by night."

Then, turning to the gendarmes:—

"You may retire, gentlemen."

The gendarmes retired.

Jean Valjean was like a man on the point of fainting.

The Bishop drew near to him, and said in a low voice:—

"Do not forget, never forget, that you have promised to use this money in becoming an honest man."

❸ *What does the bishop say that Jean must use the money from the silver to do? What has the bishop "bought" from Jean? What does he plan to do with this thing?*

Jean Valjean, who had no recollection of ever having promised anything, remained speechless. The Bishop had emphasized the words when he uttered them. He resumed with solemnity:—

"Jean Valjean, my brother, you no longer belong to evil, but to good. It is your soul that I buy from you; I withdraw it from black thoughts and the spirit of <u>perdition</u>, and I give it to God." ■

Gabrielle Riemer, France

Victor Hugo is probably France's most famous writer. He is also one of my favorite authors because of the realistic way he portrays the social injustice in nineteenth-century France. Unlike today in France, religion at that time was very influential, and the clergy was powerful and respected. Hugo, who had strong religious convictions, wanted to show how the often remote, elitist clergy could take an active role in improving society. He made Monseigneur Bienvenu a good person and gave him a name which means "welcome" in French. Everyone else rejects Jean Valjean as a criminal, but Bienvenu treats him as an honored guest. When Valjean mistakenly calls the bishop "curé," which means parish priest, Bienvenu does not correct him. Rather than show off his social rank, he considers himself on the same level as his guest.

Words for Everyday Use

in • ar • tic • u • late (in´är tik´ yo͞o lit) *adj.*, not able to speak understandably, as because of strong emotion

dis • con • cert (dis´kən surt´) *vt.*, frustrate the plans of; upset the composure of

per • di • tion (pər dish´ən) *n.*, loss of the soul; damnation

Vocabulary in Context

- The man was overcome with emotion and nearly <u>inarticulate</u> as he accepted his award.
- The noisy audience members seemed to <u>disconcert</u> the performers on stage.
- The religious leaders hoped that they were leading people away from <u>perdition</u> and toward salvation.

Responding to the Selection

What do you think of Jean Valjean? In small groups, discuss your opinion of Jean Valjean's behavior. Do you think that he will take the bishop's advice to heart and try to become an "honest man"?

Reviewing the Selection

RECALLING		INTERPRETING
1. What has happened to Jean during his attempt to find lodging for the night? What does he tell the bishop about himself?	▶▶	Does Jean expect the bishop to offer him lodging? Why do you think Jean keeps asking the bishop if he understands who he is and what he has done? In what way have his earlier experiences shaped his attitude toward his potential host?
2. What does the bishop offer Jean? How does Jean feel about the bishop's actions? What reason does the bishop provide for his actions?	▶▶	What do the bishop's actions reveal about his character? Why might a simple act of kindness mean more to Jean than it would to most people?
3. What does the bishop do to show that he trusts Jean? that he respects him? What does Jean do to violate this trust and respect?	▶▶	Why are trust and respect "like a glass of water to one of the shipwrecked" for Jean? Why do you think Jean violates the bishop's trust and respect? Do you think the bishop is surprised by Jean's violation? Why, or why not?
4. What does the bishop do when the police return Jean, accusing him of thievery? What is Jean's reaction to the bishop's words and actions?	▶▶	What do you think Jean expected the bishop to do? Why might this have been a reasonable expectation? Were you surprised by the bishop's actions at the end of the selection? Why, or why not?

SYNTHESIZING

5. What elements of society is the author critiquing in this selection from *Les Misérables*? What elements is he affirming? How do you know?

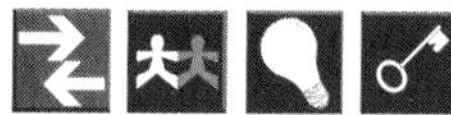

RESPONDING TO THE SELECTION

Invite students to discuss their ideas about Jean Valjean in pairs or in small groups.

ANSWERS FOR REVIEWING THE SELECTION

RECALLING AND INTERPRETING

1. **Recalling.** Jean has been told to go away by innkeepers, a jailer has refused to admit him to prison, and a dog has bitten him. Jean tells the bishop that he is a former convict and considered a dangerous man. **Interpreting.** Jean expects the bishop to expel him. Jean can't believe that anyone would take him in, so he expects to be thrown out. His earlier experiences have made it difficult for him to believe that anyone would treat him kindly.

2. **Recalling.** The bishop offers Jean a meal, a place to stay, and a bed. Jean is overwhelmed by the bishop's kindness and by his own good luck in finding him. The bishop says that he aids Jean because he is a fellow human, hence his brother, and because all who have suffered are welcome to Jesus' house. **Interpreting.** The bishop's actions reveal that he takes his role as a servant of God very seriously and that he is a kindhearted and generous individual. Jean has not received kind treatment and expects none, so the bishop's simple act of kindness stuns and overwhelms Jean.

3. **Recalling.** The bishop has his good silver candlesticks and silverware brought out and he does not lock these valuable items away. The bishop addresses Jean as *sir* and *Monsieur.* Jean steals the bishop's silver and flees. **Interpreting.** Trust and respect are as rare and as valuable to the convict as water is to the shipwrecked, and trust and respect restore Jean's self-esteem, just as water restores life. Jean is overcome by greed. *Responses will vary.*

(cont.)

ANSWERS FOR REVIEWING THE SELECTION (CONT.)

4. **Recalling.** The bishop pretends that he has given Jean the silverware and asks him why he did not remember to take the candlesticks he had given him as well. Jean is stunned and speechless. **Interpreting.** Jean probably expected the bishop to condemn him as a thief. This is a reasonable expectation because the bishop has shown him nothing but kindness and yet Jean had robbed him anyway. *Responses will vary.*

SYNTHESIZING

Responses will vary. Possible responses are given.

5. Students may say that the author is critiquing an unduly harsh penal system that "hardens" the criminal and criticizing as well those people who do not believe in offering others a second chance.

ANSWERS FOR UNDERSTANDING LITERATURE

Responses will vary. Possible responses are given.

1. One-Dimesional and Three-Dimensional Characters. Students may say that the bishop is a one-dimensional character because he consistently exhibits goodness and forgiveness. Students may say that Jean Valjean is a three-dimensional character because he exhibits a wider variety of traits and emotions.

ANALYTIC SCALES FOR RESPONDING IN WRITING

Grading scales for Responding in Writing appear on pages 920 and 921.

ANSWERS FOR SKILLS ACTIVITIES

APPLIED ENGLISH/TECH PREP

You might encourage students to use their imaginations to work out the details of the show on paper before they begin composing their radio advertisement. They need to decide on such essential information as when the show will take place, its location, and the price of tickets. Students might also choose names for people in the cast.

Remind students that a good advertisement requires thorough planning and should be persuasive and convincing. As they write, students should think about how the ad will sound to listeners. You might invite students to read their completed advertisements aloud.

Understanding Literature (Questions for Discussion)

One-Dimensional and Three-Dimensional Characters. A **one-dimensional character, flat character**, or **caricature** is one who exhibits a single dominant quality, or character trait. A **three-dimensional, full,** or **rounded character** is one who exhibits the full complexity of traits associated with actual human beings. Would you classify the bishop as a one-dimensional or as a three-dimensional character? Provide reasons for classifying him as you do. Would you classify Jean Valjean as a one-dimensional or as a three-dimensional character? Provide reasons for classifying him as you do.

Responding in Writing

1. **Creative Writing: Personal Letter.** Imagine that you are Jean Valjean. What happens next in your life after you leave the bishop? Do you take his advice to heart, or do you scorn it? Write a letter to the bishop in which you let him know what is happening in your life and what you have done with the money he has given you. You may choose to thank him for turning your life around, or you may wish to point out why his lesson proved unsuccessful. You can be as imaginative as you like when considering what may happen to Jean after leaving the bishop.

2. **Critical Essay: Romanticism, Realism, and Naturalism.** Romanticism was a literary movement of the eighteenth and nineteenth centuries that placed value on emotion and imagination over reason, of the individual over society, nature over human works, the countryside over the town, common people over aristocrats, and freedom over authority. Realism is the attempt to render in art an accurate portrayal of life. Naturalism was a literary movement of the late nineteenth and early twentieth centuries whose proponents saw actions and events as resulting inevitably from biological or natural forces or from forces in the environment. Although Hugo is considered a Romantic, this selection can serve as an example of the writing of each of these three movements. Write an essay in which you explain why this selection from *Les Misérables* represents Romanticism, Realism, and Naturalism. Be sure to use examples and quotations from the selection to support your opinion. For more information on these three literary movements, see the Handbook of Literary Terms or the introduction to this unit.

Applied English/Tech Prep Skills

Writing Promotional and Public Relations Copy. Imagine that your school is planning to stage a production of the musical *Les Misérables* and that you are responsible for writing a radio advertisement promoting the show. First, review the Language Arts Survey 5.6, "Writing Promotional and Public Relations Copy." Then, write a radio advertisement that encourages your audience to attend the show. Your ad should be persuasive, but it should also include essential information, such as the date(s) and time(s) of the show, its location, and the price of the tickets.

PREREADING

"They say that plants don't talk . . ."
by Rosalia de Castro, translated by John Frederick Nims

SPAIN

About the Author

ROSALIA DE CASTRO
1837–1885

Born in Santiago de Compostela, **Rosalia de Castro** was influenced to become a writer by a good private education and an influential family servant. This servant, La Choina, taught de Castro folk songs in her native Galician, the dialect of northwest Spain. Galician has a rich tradition of song, and de Castro went on to write her own songs in the dialect, although she wrote in Spanish as well.

De Castro married a Galician historian and gave birth to five children. After separating from her husband, she fell into a life of loneliness and poverty. She died of cancer at a young age. All of de Castro's writing has been compiled in *Collected Works* (1944).

About the Selection

De Castro is known for poetry filled with detailed images of nature that reflect her own feelings. Although her work may seem sentimental to contemporary sensibilities, it reflects the style of the period in which she wrote. At the same time, her work can be dark and self-critical. **"They say that plants don't talk . . ."** reflects all of these descriptions. The poet uses vivid nature imagery to reflect her feelings about life and her future. Often sentimental in her observations of nature and in her thoughts about life, she also acknowledges some dark realities about herself and about the world around her. As you read, notice the rich language and the way in which de Castro helps nature to come to life for her reader. In this vital poem a speaker explains her dreams and describes how they help her to survive in a fleeting world.

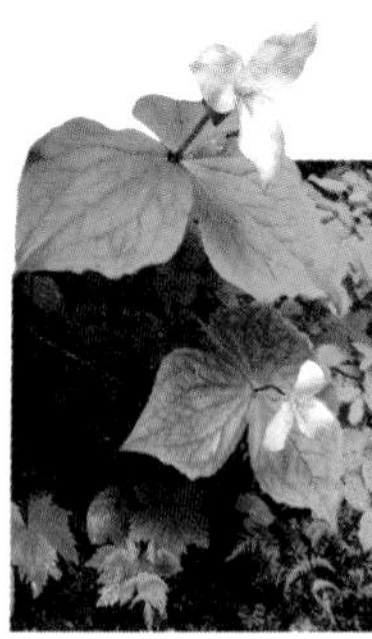

CONNECTIONS: Spain and Portugal

The Galician dialect is directly related to Portuguese. Portugal, a relatively small republic in southwestern Europe bordered by Spain to the north and east, is famous for its explorers of the fifteenth and sixteenth centuries who colonized many parts of the world. By the middle of the sixteenth century, Portugal controlled a large overseas empire, most notably Brazil in South America. Beginning in the late sixteenth century, Portugal endured sixty years under Spanish rule. Aside from this period, Portugal has been independent since the twelfth century when Christians regained control from the Muslims, and it became a kingdom.

ADDITIONAL RESOURCES

READER'S GUIDE
- Selection Worksheet 11.4

ASSESSMENT PORTFOLIO
- Selection Check Test 2.11.7
- Selection Test 2.11.8

ESSENTIAL SKILLS PRACTICE BOOKS
- Writing 1.8, 1.20

PREREADING EXTENSIONS

Students might want to gather more information about the country of Portugal. Encourage students to locate the country on a map and research aspects of life in Portugal, such as the people, religion, arts, music, economy, education, and language.

Students can form small groups to research these different areas and then share their findings with one another.

SUPPORT FOR LEP STUDENTS

ADDITIONAL VOCABULARY

receding—leaving, becoming less

GOALS/OBJECTIVES

Studying this lesson will enable students to

- enjoy a poem that uses nature imagery to reflect the speaker's feelings about the world
- discuss the life and work of Rosalia de Castro
- define the literary terms *apostrophe, personification,* and *tone*
- practice using the technique of personification
- write a critical essay that examines the relationship between the speaker of the poem and nature
- plan a nature walk for young children

READER'S JOURNAL

Give students several minutes to focus on and freewrite about the natural images they choose.

Answers to Guided Reading Questions

❶ People say that these elements of nature do not talk, but the speaker hears them whisper and yell.

❷ The speaker calls herself a poor, incurable sleepwalker. She dreams about "life's endless spring," and "the perennial freshness of fields and souls."

Selection Check Test with Answers

EX. What do plants not do?
Plants don't talk.

1. Who or what does the speaker hear yelling at her?
The speaker hears plants, brooks, birds, waves, and stars.

2. What covers the speaker's head and what is in the meadow?
There are gray hairs on the speaker's head and there is frost in the meadow.

3. What does the speaker spend much of her time doing?
The speaker spends much of her time dreaming.

4. About what does the speaker say stars, brooks, and flowers should not gossip?
Stars, brooks, and flowers should not gossip about her dreams.

5. What could the speaker not do without her dreams?
She could not admire nature or live.

READER'S JOURNAL

Choose two or three natural images. Describe these images in detail. In what ways do these images "speak" to you? In other words, in what way do these aspects of nature affect you?

"They say that plants don't talk . . ."

ROSALIA DE CASTRO, TRANSLATED BY JOHN FREDERICK NIMS

❶ *What do people say about plants, brooks, birds, waves, and stars? Why doesn't the speaker agree?*

They say that plants don't talk, nor do
    brooks or birds,
nor the wave with its chatter, nor stars
    with their shine.
They say it but it's not true, for whenever
    I walk by
they whisper and yell about me
                    "There goes the crazy woman dreaming
of life's endless spring and of fields
and soon, very soon, her hair
    will be gray.
She sees the shaking, terrified frost
    cover the meadow."
There are gray hairs in my head; there is frost
    on the meadows,
but I go on dreaming—a poor, incurable
    sleepwalker—
of life's endless spring that is receding
and the perennial freshness of fields
    and souls,

❷ *What does the speaker call herself? About what does she dream?*

WORDS FOR EVERYDAY USE

per • en • ni • al (pər en´ē əl) *adj.,* lasting or continuing for a long time

Vocabulary in Context

• The perennial beauty of the towering trees in the park always impresses people in the community.

Cactus. *Charles Sheeler, 1931. Philadelphia Museum of Art: The Louise and Walter Arensburg Collection*

although fields dry and souls burn up.
Stars and brooks and flowers! Don't gossip about my dreams:
without them how could I admire you? How could I live? ■

 ❶

Why must nature stop gossiping about the speaker's dreams?

ANSWERS TO GUIDED READING QUESTIONS

❶ Nature must stop gossiping about the speaker's dreams because they are important to her—without them she could not admire nature or live.

ANALYTIC SCALES FOR RESPONDING IN WRITING
(SEE PAGE 929.)

Assign a score from 1 to 25 for each grading criterion below. (For more detailed evaluation, see the evaluation forms for writing, revising, and proofreading, Assessment Portfolio 4.1–4.9.)

1. Personification

- **Content/Unity.** In the paragraph or poem, an element of nature is imaginatively described as if it were a person.
- **Organization/Coherence.** The paragraph or poem focuses on one human-like quality in a particular element of nature.
- **Language/Style.** The paragraph or poem uses vivid and precise nouns, verbs, and modifiers.
- **Conventions.** The paragraph or poem avoids errors in spelling, grammar, usage, mechanics, and manuscript form.

►Additional practice is provided in the Essential Skills Practice Book: Writing 1.8.

2. Critical Essay

- **Content/Unity.** The essay describes the relationship between the speaker of the poem and nature.
- **Organization/Coherence.** The essay answers the following questions: What does nature mean to the speaker? In what way does the speaker communicate with nature? In what way does she relate the qualities of nature to her own life?
- **Language/Style.** The essay uses vivid and precise nouns, verbs, and modifiers.
- **Conventions.** The essay avoids errors in spelling, grammar, usage, mechanics, and manuscript form.

►Additional practice is provided in the Essential Skills Practice Book: Writing 1.20.

RESPONDING TO THE SELECTION

Students might either respond to these questions in writing or meet in pairs to discuss their responses.

ANSWERS FOR REVIEWING THE SELECTION

RECALLING AND INTERPRETING

1. **Recalling.** They call her a crazy woman who is dreaming of "life's endless spring and of fields." **Interpreting.** Nature "whispers and yells" to the speaker. Nature says that the speaker dreams of perennial spring when all of nature cycles through periods of spring and frost.

2. **Recalling.** Both say that her hair will be gray and that frost will cover the meadow. She claims that she goes on dreaming. **Interpreting.** Both stand for change and the end of a stage of life. The arrival of both forecast death and represent the fleeting nature of life.

3. **Recalling.** The speaker dreams of "life's endless spring" and the "perennial freshness of fields and souls." **Interpreting.** Particular elements of nature make the speaker dream because they are full of life, beauty, and constancy. These elements stand for life and beauty.

4. **Recalling.** The speaker realizes that fields dry and souls burn up. Despite these facts, the speaker must have her dreams because without them she could not live. **Interpreting.** The speaker understands that nothing lasts forever, and that every living thing is temporary. The speaker needs her dreams in order to live with this knowledge. (cont.)

Responding to the Selection

If you were a friend of the speaker of this poem and happened to meet her after one of her walks through the woods, what might she tell you about the importance that nature has for her? What might she say to describe her feelings about life?

Reviewing the Selection

RECALLING		INTERPRETING
1. What do plants, brooks, birds, waves, and stars say to the speaker?	▶▶	In what manner does nature "speak" to the speaker? What is the meaning of the message nature shares with her? In what way do they feel she idealizes things too much?
2. What is said by both nature and the speaker about gray hairs and frost? What does she claim to go on doing despite gray hairs and frost?	▶▶	What do gray hairs and frost have in common? What does the arrival of both mean in this poem?
3. About what does the speaker dream?	▶▶	Why do particular elements of nature make the speaker dream? What do these elements mean to her?
4. What unfortunate facts does the speaker realize about fields and souls? Despite these facts, why must the speaker keep her dreams?	▶▶	What does the plight of fields and souls mean to the speaker? Why are her dreams so important to her?

SYNTHESIZING

5. Compare and contrast the feelings about nature experienced by the speaker of "They say that plants don't talk . . ." with those experienced by the speaker of "My Heart Leaps Up When I Behold."

ANSWERS FOR REVIEWING THE SELECTION (CONT.)

SYNTHESIZING

Responses will vary. Possible responses are given.

5. In both "They say that plants don't talk . . ." and "My Heart Leaps Up When I Behold," the speakers find a great deal of solace and comfort in nature. Wordsworth, in "My Heart Leaps Up When I Behold," expresses the hope that he will always retain his youthful fascination with and appreciation of nature. The speaker in "They say that plants don't talk . . ." recognizes that her youth and the beauty of nature are fleeting—that death and change affect everything. She knows, however, that in order to survive she must not dwell on this knowledge. She must hold onto her youthful dreams. Both speakers recognize a need for innocence and youthful exuberance.

Understanding Literature (Questions for Discussion)

1. **Apostrophe. An apostrophe** is a rhetorical technique in which an object or person is directly addressed. What is being directly addressed in lines 22–25? What request does the speaker make in this apostrophe? Through this request, what does the speaker show about her values?

2. **Personification. Personification** is a figure of speech in which an idea, animal, or thing is described as if it were a person. Give two examples of personification in "They say that plants don't talk . . ." Why is this technique so important to the poem?

3. **Tone. Tone** is the emotional attitude toward the reader or toward the subject implied by a literary work. Describe the tone of this piece. What words and phrases shape its tone?

Responding in Writing

1. **Creative Writing: Personification.** Write a short paragraph or poem in which you practice using the technique of personification. Choose one element of nature—wind, wave, thunder, sunbeam, falling leaf—and write about it in your paragraph or poem as if it were a person. What human qualities might this element appear to have on first glance or first hearing? To begin, brainstorm a list of interesting elements of nature. Then focus on the item on your list that you find most interesting and "human-like." Does thunder sound like a snoring sky? Do sunbeams appear to be reaching out to you? Does a falling leaf seem to dance to jazz music? Use your imagination as you describe your element of nature.

2. **Critical Essay: Relationship with Nature.** Write a short essay in which you describe the relationship the speaker of "They say that plants don't talk . . ." has with nature. As you write, think about the following questions: What does nature mean to the speaker? In what way does she communicate with nature? In what way does she relate elements of nature with aspects of her own life?

Project

Nature Walk. Plan a nature walk for young children. First select a site for your walk. Notice the kinds of plants, insects, and other wildlife in this area and do some research to learn about the different aspects of the area, living and nonliving. Plan short explanations of various aspects of the site and prepare questions to ask the children. Try out your nature walk with young children.

Answers for Understanding Literature

Responses will vary. Possible responses are given.

1. Apostrophe. Specific elements of nature are being addressed in this poem. The speaker asks these elements of nature not to gossip about her dreams. The speaker, through this request, reveals that nature and her own dreams are important for her survival in the world. The speak is obviously connected with nature.

2. Personification. Students might name the phrase "shaking, terrified frost," or the idea of stars, brooks, and flowers gossiping. The poet uses this technique to illustrate the ways in which nature seems to be communicating with the speaker of the poem, and to show how nature comes alive for her.

3. Tone. Students might say that the tone of this piece is contemplative, thoughtful, insistent, pleading, sad, and desperate for understanding. Students might name words and phrases like "dreaming," "endless," "fields dry and souls burn up," and "How could I live?"

Analytic Scales for Responding in Writing

Grading scales for Responding in Writing appear on page 927.

Project Notes

See the evaluation form for projects, Assessment Portfolio 4.12.

Nature Walk. Students can complete this project as a class, individually, or in pairs or small groups. You might try to invite young children who attend local elementary schools. Help students to research the places in your community that would be safe and suitable for a nature walk.

Encourage students to take the walk themselves before they bring along young children. On their preliminary walk, they can identify the most interesting areas and prepare short explanations of the plants, insects, and other wildlife in the area.

ADDITIONAL RESOURCES

READER'S GUIDE

- Selection Worksheet 11.5

ASSESSMENT PORTFOLIO

- Selection Check Test 2.11.9
- Selection Test 2.11.10

ESSENTIAL SKILLS PRACTICE BOOKS

- Writing 1.8, 1.20

PREREADING EXTENSIONS

Naturalist writers wanted their work to be completely realistic, so they usually researched their subjects in order to portray them accurately. For example, Zola did extensive research to portray accurately the lives of coal mining families in Montsou in *Germinal*. You might have students research a particular time and place, and then write a short descriptive passage, dialogue, or character sketch based on what they've learned about this time and place.

SUPPORT FOR LEP STUDENTS

PRONUNCIATIONS OF PROPER NOUNS AND ADJECTIVES

Bonne • mort (bôn môr)
É • ti • enne Lan • ti • er (ā tyen´ län´ tyā)
Mont • sou (mōn´ sʉ)
Vor • eux (vôr´ ə)

ADDITIONAL VOCABULARY

benumbed—made numb, as by cold
excavated—unearthed; dug into
gesture—movement of the hand or body, as to emphasize or make a point
immense—extremely large
keen—sharp, extreme
melancholy—sad
parcel—package
settlement—area in which people have set up homes

PREREADING

from *Germinal*
by Émile Zola, translated by Havelock Ellis

FRANCE

About the Author

ÉMILE ZOLA
1840–1902

Émile Zola was born in Paris but moved with his family to Aix-en-Provence in 1842. After his father's unexpected death in 1847, Zola and his mother moved back to Paris. Zola studied at the Lycée Saint-Louis but failed the final examination for the bachelor of arts degree. He spent the next two years searching for work and suffering from poverty. According to rumor, his situation was so bleak he lived on sparrows caught outside his window and stayed in bed because he had to pawn his trousers. During this period, Zola experimented with poetry and eventually found work in a publishing house. After publishing a collection of short stories and an autobiographical novel, Zola left his job to write full time. Zola successfully realized his ambition to complete a cycle of twenty novels called the *Rougon-Macquart* that were connected loosely by their focus on two French families, the Rougons and the Macquarts. These novels, among them *Germinal*, won Zola a reputation as France's greatest living writer, although conservatives frequently denounced his work. Scandal (see Connections below) led Zola to flee to England in 1898, where he remained for almost a year. In 1902, Zola and his wife were poisoned by carbon monoxide from a fire left burning in the fireplace in their closed bedroom. While Zola's wife recovered, Zola died before help could arrive.

About the Selection

Zola is known as the founder of **Naturalism** in literature. Naturalists saw actions and events as resulting inevitably from biological or natural forces or forces in the environment. Influenced by the scientific determinism of his day, Zola believed that human nature is completely determined by heredity, and that one individual passes on his or her virtues or vices to the next generation. ***Germinal***, which focuses on the residents of a mining town called Montsou, serves both as an excellent example of Zola's Naturalist beliefs and as a social commentary on the brutal lives of the wretchedly poor. Naturalists tended to research their subjects exhaustively in order to portray them accurately. Zola portrays, in minute detail, the lives of the coal mining families of Montsou who struggle to survive while the owners of the mines grow wealthy.

CONNECTIONS: The Dreyfus Affair

In 1894, Alfred Dreyfus, a Jewish officer in the French army, was accused and convicted of selling military secrets to Germany. Anti-Semites welcomed the verdict but others began to question the irregular nature of his trial and the authenticity of the evidence. Army officials struggled to cover their actions with forgeries, rumors, and by stirring up anti-Semitic feelings. Émile Zola, however, supported Dreyfus. On January 13, 1898, his letter "J'Accuse" was published on the front page of a prominent paper. Zola accused the army of trying to cover up its wrongful conviction of Dreyfus. Zola's letter caused an uproar and he was tried and found guilty of libel. Dreyfus was pardoned in 1899, and in 1904, a court of appeals reversed his conviction.

GOALS/OBJECTIVES

Studying this lesson will enable students to

- appreciate a classic French novel that is an example of Naturalism and social commentary on the lives of the poor
- discuss the life and work of Émile Zola
- define the literary terms *metaphor, Naturalism, personification, setting,* and *simile*
- write a social critique and a critical essay exploring Naturalism
- work in small groups to research the impact of labor laws on working people

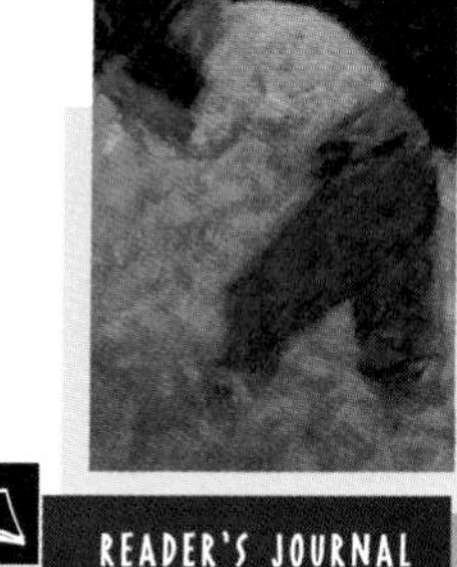

READER'S JOURNAL

Imagine that you are an adult and that you suddenly lose your job. Times are hard, and you have difficulty finding new work right away. If you were in this position, what fears and concerns would you have? What would you do to get back on your feet again? Write about these questions in your journal.

FROM

Germinal

ÉMILE ZOLA

CHAPTER 1

Over the open plain, beneath a starless sky as dark and thick as ink, a man walked alone along the highway from Marchiennes to Montsou, a straight paved road ten kilometres in length, intersecting the beetroot-fields. He could not even see the black soil before him, and only felt the immense flat horizon by the gusts of March wind, squalls as strong as on the sea, and frozen from sweeping leagues of marsh and naked earth. No tree could be seen against the sky, and the road unrolled as straight as a pier in the midst of the blinding spray of darkness.

The man had set out from Marchiennes about two o'clock. He walked with long strides, shivering beneath his worn cotton jacket and corduroy breeches. A small parcel tied in a check handkerchief troubled him much, and he pressed it against his side, sometimes with one elbow, sometimes with the other, so that he could slip to the bottom of his pockets both the benumbed hands that bled beneath the lashes of the wind. A single idea occupied his head—the empty head of a workman without work and without lodging—the hope that the cold would be less keen after sunrise. For an hour he went on thus, when on the left, two kilometres from Montsou, he saw red flames, three fires burning in the open air and apparently suspended. At first he hesitated, half afraid. Then he could not resist the painful need to warm his hands for a moment.

The steep road led downwards, and everything disappeared. The man saw on his right a paling, a wall of coarse planks shutting in a line of rails, while a grassy slope rose on the left surmounted by confused gables, a vision of a village with low uniform roofs. He went on some two hundred paces. Suddenly, at a bend in the road, the fires reappeared close to him, though he could not understand how they burnt so high in the dead sky, like smoky moons. But on the level soil another sight had struck him. It was a heavy mass, a low pile of buildings from which rose the silhouette of a factory chimney; occasional gleams appeared

1 *At what time of day and in what weather conditions is the man journeying?*

2 *What single thought occupies the man? What does he see that might fulfill his needs? Is this a long term solution to his problem?*

WORDS FOR EVERYDAY USE

squall (skwôl) *n.,* brief, violent windstorm, usually with rain or snow

sil • hou • ette (sil´o͞o et´) *n.,* outline drawing, filled in with a solid color, usually black

READER'S JOURNAL

As an alternative activity, ask students to describe the importance of having options and being able to make positive choices in their own lives. Ask them how it might feel to be trapped in an unpleasant job or place and what might cause people to feel trapped in jobs or places?

ANSWERS TO GUIDED READING QUESTIONS

1 The man is journeying at night in a cold windstorm.

2 The man only hopes that it will be less cold after sunrise. The man sees three fires burning outside and decides to approach them. The fires will probably not provide a long-term solution to his problem, but he admits that he needs desperately to warm his hands.

SPELLING AND VOCABULARY WORDS FROM THE SELECTION

apparition	profound
gluttonous	sated
grimace	silhouette
immobility	squall
invalid	tabernacle
obliquely	vain
pension	venture

VOCABULARY IN CONTEXT

- Violent snow squalls throughout the day made driving treacherous.
- We liked the simplicity of the portrait, which featured a silhouette of the child's profile.

Answers to Guided Reading Questions

➊ The carman tells Étienne that there is no work to be found. The carman stops to spit up something black.

➋ He sees a factory with chimneys and a coal pit. His despair returns because he believes that there will be no work at this place.

➌ The man addresses an old carman who is leading a horse that is drawing trams.

➍ He is Étienne Lantier, an engine-man. Étienne seeks work. He is about twenty-one years old, dark, strong, and handsome.

Cross-curricular Activities

Mathematics and Sciences

Ask students to work in pairs to research different aspects of mining. Some suggestions for research topics include: health risks, methods of mining, treatment of miners throughout history and in different parts of the world, and types of materials mined. Some students might want to draw diagrams of typical coal mines of different periods.

Arts and Humanities

You may wish to show your students all or part of a film depicting mining so they may better visualize the activities going on at the Voreux. *Germinal* has been adapted into a French film with English subtitles. Another possible choice is *Matewan*, a film that depicts life in the West Virginia coal mines. After students have seen all or parts of these films, have them freewrite their responses about conditions in mines.

➊ *What does the carman tell Étienne? What strange thing interrupts their conversation?*

➋ *What does the man see when he approaches the fires? Why does his despair return?*

➌ *Whom does the man address? What is this person doing?*

➍ *Who is the man who addresses the old carman? What does he do for a living? What is he seeking? What is his physical appearance?*

from dirty windows, five or six melancholy lanterns were hung outside to frames of blackened wood, which vaguely outlined the profiles of gigantic stages; and from this fantastic apparition, drowned in night and smoke, a single voice arose, the thick, long breathing of a steam escapement that could not be seen.

Then the man recognized a pit.[1] His despair returned. What was the good? There would be no work. Instead of turning towards the buildings he decided at last to ascend the pit bank, on which burnt in iron baskets the three coal fires which gave light and warmth for work. The labourers in the cutting must have been working late; they were still throwing out the useless rubbish. Now he heard the landers push the wagons on the stages. He could distinguish living shadows tipping over the trams[2] or tubs near each fire.

'Good day,' he said, approaching one of the baskets.

Turning his back to the fire, the carman stood upright. He was an old man, dressed in knitted violet wool with a rabbit-skin cap on his head; while his horse, a great yellow horse, waited with the immobility of stone while they emptied the six trams he drew. The workman employed at the tipping-cradle, a red-haired lean fellow, did not hurry himself; he pressed on the lever with a sleepy hand. And above, the wind grew stronger—an icy north wind—and its great, regular breaths passed by like the strokes of a scythe.[3]

'Good day,' replied the old man. There was silence. The man, who felt that he was being looked at suspiciously, at once told his name.

'I am called Étienne Lantier. I am an engine-man.[4] Any work here?'

The flames lit him up. He might be about twenty-one years of age, a very dark, handsome man, who looked strong in spite of his thin limbs.

The carman, thus reassured, shook his head.

'Work for an engine-man? No, no! There were two came yesterday. There's nothing.'

A gust cut short their speech. Then Étienne asked, pointing to the sombre pile of buildings at the foot of the platform:

'A pit, isn't it?'

The old man this time could not reply: he was strangled by a violent cough. At last he expectorated,[5] and his expectoration left a black patch on the purple soil.

'Yes, a pit. The Voreux. There! The settlement is quite near.'

In his turn, and with extended arm, he pointed out in the night the village of which the young man had vaguely seen the roofs. But the six trams were empty, and he followed them without cracking his whip, his legs stiffened by rheumatism;[6] while the great yellow horse went on of itself, pulling heavily between the rails beneath a new gust which bristled its coat.

The Voreux was now emerging from the gloom. Étienne, who forgot himself before the stove, warming his poor bleeding hands, looked round and could see each part of the pit: the shed tarred with siftings, the pit-

1. **pit.** Pit where coal is mined
2. **trams.** Open railway car for carrying loads in mines
3. **scythe.** Tool with a long, single-edged blade set at an angle on a long curved handle, used for cutting grass, grain, etc.
4. **engine-man.** Person who supervises or operates a railroad locomotive or other mechanical device
5. **expectorated.** Spat
6. **rheumatism.** Any of various painful conditions of the joints and muscles, characterized by stiffness, inflammation, etc.

Words for Everyday Use

ap • pa • ri • tion (ap´ə rish´ən) *n.,* anything that appears unexpectedly or in an extraordinary way

im • mo • bil • i • ty (im´mō bil´ə tē) *n.,* quality of being unmovable or unchanging

Vocabulary in Context

- Everybody stared at the tornado, which was an amazing apparition.
- We needed to cross the street, but the immobility of the crowd made that impossible.

The Stone Breaker. Georges Seurat

frame, the vast chamber of the winding machine, the square turret of the exhaustion pump. This pit, piled up in the bottom of a hollow, with its squat brick buildings, raising its chimney like a threatening horn, seemed to him to have the evil air of a gluttonous beast crouching there to devour the earth. While examining it, he thought of himself, of his vagabond existence these eight days he had been seeking work. He saw himself again at his workshop at the railway, delivering a blow at his foreman, driven from Lille, driven from everywhere. On Saturday he had arrived at Marchiennes, where they said that work was to be had at the Forges, and there was nothing, neither at the Forges nor at Sonneville's. He had been obliged to pass the Sunday hidden beneath the wood of a cartwright's yard, from which the watchman had just turned him out at two o'clock in the morning. He had nothing, not a penny, not even a crust; what should he do, wandering along the roads without aim, not knowing where to shelter himself from the wind? Yes, it was certainly a pit; the occasional lanterns lighted up the square; a door, suddenly

❶ *To what does Étienne compare the coal pit?*

❷ *How long has Étienne been out of work? Why was he fired from his last job?*

Words for Everyday Use

glut • ton • ous (glut´'n əs) *adj.,* inclined to eat too much

Answers to Guided Reading Questions

❶ He compares the coal pit to a beast that greedily devours the earth.

❷ Étienne has been out of work for eight days. He was fired for striking a foreman at his place of work.

Historical Note

People have mined the earth for minerals, stone, and metal for thousands of years. Coal mining became an important industry in the late Middle Ages. Early miners worked from the earth's surface to acquire coal, but by the end of the Middle Ages many surface deposits of coal were exhausted. Shafts, or deep vertical openings, were then dug into the earth.

Drainage has been a problem in deep mines because of underground bodies of water. Miners have used horizontal tunnels, buckets and chains, windmill-powered pumps, and engine-driven pumps to drain coal mines. Until the latter half of the twentieth century, many coal mines operated much as they had in the eighteenth century: men and women scraped at the coal with pickaxes, and people, horses, or mules dragged the coal up steep slopes to the surface.

Vocabulary in Context

- At Thanksgiving dinner, everyone reached for food in a gluttonous manner.

Answers to Guided Reading Questions

❶ Montsou's once prosperous factories have been closing and workmen have been fired due to straitened economic times.

❷ They complain about the high rate of unemployment and the difficulty of affording even the most meager food.

Additional Questions and Activities

Ask students to answer the following questions:

1. Do France's political leaders or factory owners seem to have any concern for the working poor who have been displaced? How do you know?

2. Do you think society today is kinder to the poor or unemployed? Explain your response.

ANSWERS

Responses will vary.

1. Students should recognize that leaders and factory owners do not seem to care, as people are starving to death.

2. Students might say that society today has unemployment compensation and other funds designed to help people experiencing hardship.

opened, had enabled him to catch sight of the furnaces in a clear light. He could explain even the escapement of the pump, that thick, long breathing that went on without ceasing, and which seemed to be the monster's congested respiration.

The workman, expanding his back at the tipping-cradle, had not even lifted his eyes on Étienne, and the latter was about to pick up his little bundle, which had fallen to the earth, when a spasm of coughing announced the carman's return. Slowly he emerged from the darkness, followed by the yellow horse drawing six more laden trams.

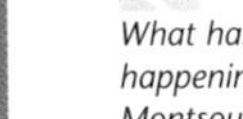

❶ *What has been happening in Montsou?*

'Are there factories at Montsou?' asked the young man.

The old man expectorated, then replied in the wind:

'Oh, it isn't factories that are lacking. Should have seen it three or four years ago. Everything was roaring then. There were not men enough; there never were such wages. And now they are tightening their bellies again. Nothing but misery in the country; every one is being sent away; workshops closing one after the other. It is not the emperor's fault, perhaps; but why should he go and fight in America? without counting that the beasts are dying from cholera,[7] like the people.'

Then, in short sentences and with broken breath, the two continued to complain. Étienne narrated his <u>vain</u> wanderings of the past week: must one, then, die of hunger? Soon the roads would be full of beggars.

'Yes,' said the old man, 'this will turn out badly, for God does not allow so many Christians to be thrown on the street.'

❷ *About what issues do the men complain?*

'We don't have meat every day.'

'But if one had bread!'

'True, if one only had bread.'

Their voices were lost, gusts of wind carrying away the words in a melancholy howl.

'Here!' began the carman again very loudly, turning towards the south. 'Montsou is over there.'

And stretching out his hand again he pointed out invisible spots in the darkness as he named them. Below, at Montsou, the Fauvelle sugar works were still going, but the Hoton sugar works had just been dismissing hands; there were only the Dutilleul flour mill and the Bleuze rope walk for mine-cables which kept up. Then, with a large gesture he indicated the north half of the horizon: the Sonneville workshops had not received two-thirds of their usual orders; only two of the three blast furnaces of the Marchiennes Forges were alight; finally, at the Gagebois glass works a strike was threatening, for there was talk of a reduction of wages.

'I know, I know,' replied the young man at each indication. 'I have been there.'

'With us here things are going on at present,' added the carman; 'but the pits have lowered their output. And see opposite, at the Victoire, there are also only two batteries of coke furnaces[8] alight.'

He expectorated, and set out behind his sleepy horse, after harnessing it to the empty trams.

Now Étienne could oversee the entire country. The darkness remained <u>profound</u>, but the old man's hand had, as it were, filled it with great miseries, which the young man unconsciously felt at this moment around him everywhere in the limitless tract. Was it not a cry of famine that the March wind rolled up across this naked plain? The squalls were furious: they seemed to bring

7. **cholera.** Any of several intestinal diseases

8. **coke furnaces.** Place where gas is removed from coal by heating

Words for Everyday Use

vain (vān) *adj.*, worthless; unprofitable

pro • found (prō found´) *adj.*, unbroken; deeply or intensely felt

Vocabulary in Context

- I gave up my <u>vain</u> attempts to sell knives door-to-door and looked for a new job.
- We had a <u>profound</u> admiration for Ms. Chan, our science teacher.

the death of labour, a famine which would kill many men. And with wandering eyes he tried to pierce shades, tormented at once by the desire and by the fear of seeing. Everything was hidden in the unknown depths of the gloomy night. He only perceived, very far off, the blast furnaces and the coke ovens. The latter, with their hundreds of chimneys, planted obliquely, made lines of red flame; while the two towers, more to the left, burnt blue against the blank sky, like giant torches. It resembled a melancholy conflagration.[9] No other stars rose on the threatening horizon except these nocturnal fires in a land of coal and iron.

'You belong to Belgium, perhaps?' began again the carman, who had returned behind Étienne.

This time he only brought three trams. Those at least could be tipped over; an accident which had happened to the cage, a broken screw nut, would stop work for a good quarter of an hour. At the bottom of the pit bank there was silence; the landers no longer shook the stages with a prolonged vibration. One only heard from the pit the distant sound of a hammer tapping on an iron plate.

'No, I come from the South,' replied the young man.

The workman, after having emptied the trams, had seated himself on the earth, glad of the accident, maintaining his savage silence; he had simply lifted his large, dim eyes to the carman, as if annoyed by so many words. The latter, indeed, did not usually talk at such length. The unknown man's face must have pleased him that he should have been taken by one of these itchings for confidence which sometimes make old people talk aloud even when alone.

'I belong to Montsou,' he said, 'I am called Bonnemort.'[10]

'Is it a nickname?' asked Étienne, astonished.

The old man made a grimace of satisfaction and pointed to the Voreux:

'Yes, yes; they have pulled me three times out of that, torn to pieces, once with all my hair scorched, once with my gizzard full of earth, and another time with my belly swollen with water, like a frog. And then, when they saw that nothing would kill me, they called me Bonnemort for a joke.'

His cheerfulness increased, like the creaking of an ill-greased pulley, and ended by degenerating into a terrible spasm of coughing. The fire basket now clearly lit up his large head, with its scanty white hair and flat, livid face, spotted with bluish patches. He was short, with an enormous neck, projecting calves and heels, and long arms, with massive hands falling to his knees. For the rest, like his horse, which stood immovable, without suffering from the wind, he seemed to be made of stone; he had no appearance of feeling either the cold or the gusts that whistled at his ears. When he coughed his throat was torn by a deep rasping; he spat at the foot of the basket and the earth was blackened. Étienne looked at him and at the ground which he had thus stained.

'Have you been working long at the mine?'

Bonnemort flung open both arms.

'Long? I should think so. I was not eight when I went down into the Voreux and I am now fifty-eight. Reckon that up! I have been everything down there; at first trammer, then putter, when I had the strength to wheel, then pikeman for eighteen years. Then, because of my cursed legs, they put me into the earth cutting, to bank up and

9. **conflagration.** Big, destructive fire
10. **Bonnemort.** French for good death

❶ *How long has Bonnemort worked at the mines? When did he start?*

❷ *What is the old carman called? Why did others give him this nickname?*

Words for Everyday Use

ob • lique • ly (ə blek´lē) *adv.,* in a slanted way; not level

gri • mace (grim´is) *n.,* twisting of the face expressing pain, contempt, or disgust, or a wry look as in seeking to amuse

Answers to Guided Reading Questions

❶ Bonnemort has worked in the mines for fifty years. He started when he was eight.

❷ The old carman is called Bonnemort because he has survived three disasters in the mine, and Bonnemort in French means "good death."

Literary Note

Zola was influenced by French critic and historian Hippolyte Adolphe Taine (1828–1893), whose theories formed the basis of Naturalism. Taine's writings influenced philosophy, aesthetics, literary criticism, and the social sciences. His works include *On Intelligence* (1870) and *The Origins of Contemporary France* (1876).

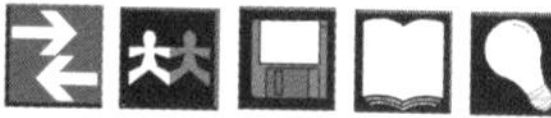

Additional Questions and Activities

You might ask students to describe Bonnemort and what they know of his life. What descriptive words and phrases used by Zola to describe Bonnemort and his situation particularly stand out to students?

Vocabulary in Context

- The child's clubhouse leaned obliquely; it looked as though it might collapse.
- Most faces in the crowd began to grimace at the sound of the terrible music.

Answers to Guided Reading Questions

➊ They want Bonnemort to rest or to retire. Bonnemort won't do this because he would lose the pension he will earn in another two years.

ANALYTIC SCALES FOR RESPONDING IN WRITING

(SEE PAGE 940.)

Assign a score from 1 to 25 for each grading criterion below. (For more detailed evaluation, see the evaluation forms for writing, revising, and proofreading, Assessment Portfolio 4.1–4.9.)

1. Social Critique

- **Content/Unity.** The critique focuses on a social problem that the writer finds appalling.
- **Organization/Coherence.** The piece is an essay, editorial, or political cartoon, and it clearly describes or shows a social problem and the writer's or illustrator's feelings about the problem.
- **Language/Style.** The critique uses vivid and precise nouns, verbs, and modifiers.
- **Conventions.** The critique avoids errors in spelling, grammar, usage, mechanics, and manuscript form.

▶ Additional practice is provided in the Essential Skills Practice Book: Writing 1.8.

Smash. *Edward Hopper, 1918*

patch, until they had to bring me up, because the doctor said I should stay there for good. Then, after five years of that, they made me carman. Eh? that's fine—fifty years at the mine, forty-five down below.'

While he was speaking, fragments of burning coal, which now and then fell from the basket, lit up his pale face with their red reflection.

 ➊ *What do the people who manage the mine want Bonnemort to do? Why won't he do this?*

'They tell me to rest,' he went on, 'but I'm not going to; I'm not such a fool. I can get on for two years longer, to my sixtieth, so as to get the pension of one hundred and eighty francs. If I wished them good evening to-day they would give me a hundred and fifty at once. They are cunning, the beggars. Besides, I am sound, except my legs. You see, it's the water which has got under my skin through being always wet in the cuttings. There are days when I can't move a paw without screaming.'

A spasm of coughing interrupted him again.

'And that makes you cough so,' said Étienne.

But he vigorously shook his head. Then, when he could speak:

'No, no! I caught cold a month ago. I never used to cough; now I can't get rid of it. And the queer thing is that I spit, that I spit—'

The rasping was again heard in his throat, followed by the black expectoration.

'Is it blood?' asked Étienne, at last venturing to question him.

Words for Everyday Use

pen • sion (pen´shən) *n.,* payment, not wages, made regularly to a person who has fulfilled certain conditions of service or reached a certain age

ven • ture (ven´chər) *vt.,* express at the risk of criticism, objection, denial, etc.

Vocabulary in Context

- My grandmother receives a generous pension from the company at which she worked for thirty years.
- I will venture to ask my brother if he is responsible for the broken lamp.

Bonnemort slowly wiped his mouth with the back of his hand.

'It's coal. I've got enough in my carcass to warm me till I die. And it's five years since I put a foot down below. I stored it up, it seems, without knowing it; it keeps you alive!'

There was silence. The distant hammer struck regular blows in the pit, and the wind passed by with its moan, like a cry of hunger and weariness coming out of the depths of the night. Before the flames which grew low, the old man went on in lower tones, chewing over again his old recollections. Ah, certainly: it was not yesterday that he and his began hammering at the seam.[11] The family had worked for the Montsou Mining Company since it started, and that was long ago, a hundred and six years already. His grandfather, Guillaume Maheu, an urchin of fifteen then, had found the rich coal at Requillart, the Company's first pit, an old abandoned pit today down below near the Fauvelle sugar works. All the country knew it, and as a proof, the discovered seam was called the Guillaume, after his grandfather. He had not known him—a big fellow, it was said, very strong, who died of old age at sixty. Then his father, Nicolas Maheu, called Le Rouge, when hardly forty years of age had died in the pit, which was being excavated at that time: a land-slip, a complete slide, and the rock drank his blood and swallowed his bones. Two of his uncles and his three brothers, later on, also left their skins there. He, Vincent Maheu, who had come out almost whole, except that his legs were rather shaky, was looked upon as a knowing fellow. But what could one do? One must work; one worked here from father to son, as one would work at anything else. His son, Toussaint Maheu, was being worked to death there now, and his grandsons, and all his people, who lived opposite in the settlement. A hundred and six years of mining, the youngsters after the old ones, for the same master. Eh? there were many bourgeois[12] that could not give their history so well!

'Anyhow, when one has got enough to eat!' murmured Étienne again.

'That is what I say. As long as one has bread to eat one can live.'

Bonnemort was silent; and his eyes turned towards the settlement, where lights were appearing one by one. Four o'clock struck in the Montsou tower and the cold became keener.

'And is your company rich?' asked Étienne.

The old man shrugged his shoulders, and then let them fall as if overwhelmed beneath an avalanche of gold.

'Ah, yes! Ah, yes! Not perhaps so rich as its neighbour, the Anzin Company. But millions and millions all the same. They can't count it. Nineteen pits, thirteen at work, the Voreux, the Victoire, Crèvecoeur, Mirou, St. Thomas, Madeleine, Feutry-Cantel, and still more, and six for pumping[13] or ventilation, like Réquillart. Ten thousand workers, concessions reaching over sixty-seven communes, an output of five thousand tons a day, a railway joining all the pits, and workshops, and factories! Ah, yes! ah, yes! there's money there!'

The rolling of trams on the stages made the big yellow horse prick his ears. The cage was evidently repaired below, and the landers had got to work again. While he was harnessing his beast to re-descend, the carman added gently, addressing himself to the horse:

'Won't do to chatter, lazy good-for-nothing! If Monsieur Hennebeau knew how you waste your time!'

Étienne looked thoughtfully into the night. He asked:

'Then Monsieur Hennebeau owns the mine?'

'No,' explained the old man, 'Monsieur Hennebeau is only the general manager; he is paid just the same as us.'

With a gesture the young man pointed into the darkness.

11. **seam.** Thin layer of coal in the rock

12. **bourgeois.** Person of the middle-class

13. **pumping.** Pumping water from the ground so that the mines will not flood

❶ *What does Bonnemort cough up?*

❷ *In what way does the financial state of the mining company contrast with the financial state of its workers?*

❸ *What happened to Bonnemort's father, uncles, and brothers in the mine? Why does Bonnemort's family continue to work there?*

Answers to Guided Reading Questions

❶ Bonnemort coughs up the coal that has lodged in his lungs over the years.

❷ The company has acquired millions, while the workers struggle to survive.

❸ Bonnemort's father, two uncles, and three brothers died in the mines. Bonnemort's family continues to work there because they need the work desperately and because they are experienced in this type of work.

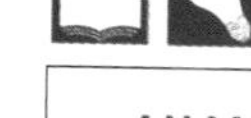

ANALYTIC SCALES FOR RESPONDING IN WRITING
(SEE PAGE 940.)

2. Critical Essay

- **Content/Unity.** The essay explores themes typical of Naturalism that can be found in the first chapter of *Germinal*.
- **Organization/Coherence.** The essay includes an introduction with a clear thesis statement, a body providing evidence that supports the thesis, and a conclusion.
- **Language/Style.** The essay uses vivid and precise nouns, verbs, and modifiers.
- **Conventions.** The essay avoids errors in spelling, grammar, usage, mechanics, and manuscript form.

▶ Additional practice is provided in the Essential Skills Practice Book: Writing 1.20.

① What does Étienne resolve? What doubt troubles him?

② To what does the narrator compare Bonnemort's attitude toward the mine's owners?

③ What does the mine appear to be doing to the miners who are descending into it?

'Who does it all belong to, then?'

But Bonnemort was for a moment so suffocated by a new and violent spasm that he could not get his breath. Then, when he had expectorated and wiped the black froth from his lips, he replied in the rising wind:

'Eh? all that belongs to? Nobody knows. To people.'

And with his hand he pointed in the darkness to a vague spot, an unknown and remote place, inhabited by those people for whom the Maheus had been hammering at the seam for more than a century. His voice assumed a tone of religious awe; it was as if he were speaking of an inaccessible tabernacle containing a sated and crouching god to whom they had given all their flesh and whom they had never seen.

'At all events, if one can get enough bread to eat,' repeated Étienne, for the third time, without any apparent transition.

'Indeed, yes; if we could always get bread, it would be too good.'

The horse had started, the carman, in his turn, disappeared, with the trailing step of an invalid. Near the tipping-cradle the workman had not stirred, gathered up in a ball, burying his chin between his knees, with his great dim eyes fixed on emptiness.

When he had picked up his bundle, Étienne still remained at the same spot. He felt the gusts freezing his back, while his chest was burning before the large fire. Perhaps, all the same, it would be as well to inquire at the pit, the old man might not know. Then he resigned himself, he would accept any work. Where should he go, and what was to become of him in this country famished for lack of work? Must he leave his carcass behind a wall, like a strayed dog? But one doubt troubled him, a fear of the Voreux in the middle of this flat plain, drowned in so thick a night. At every gust the wind seemed to rise as if it blew from an ever-broadening horizon. No dawn whitened the dead sky. The blast furnaces alone flamed, and the coke ovens, making the darkness redder without illuminating the unknown. And the Voreux, at the bottom of its hole, with its posture as of an evil beast, continued to crunch, breathing with a heavier and slower respiration, troubled by its painful digestion of human flesh. ■

Responding to the Selection

If you were in Étienne's position, would you take a job at the Voreaux? Explain what factors would influence your decision.

Words for Everyday Use

tab • er • nac • le (tab´ər nak´əl) *n.* place of worship
sat • ed (sāt´əd) *adj.,* satisfied completely
in • va • lid (in´və lid) *n.,* weak, sickly person

ANSWERS TO GUIDED READING QUESTIONS

① Étienne resolves to ask about jobs in the mine and to accept any job offered. He is troubled by his fear of the Voreux mine.

② The narrator compares Bonnemort's attitude to the awe with which one might regard a god who lives in an inaccessible tabernacle and demands flesh.

③ The mine appears to be eating the miners.

RESPONDING TO THE SELECTION

Students might get together to discuss Étienne's options or lack of options. Ask them to discuss why he might take the job and then why he should avoid the job.

SELECTION CHECK TEST WITH ANSWERS

EX. In what weather conditions does the man journey?
The man journeys in stormy weather.

1. What single thought occupies the man as he travels?
He wants to warm himself.

2. What does the man feel when he sees a coal pit?
He feels despair.

3. Why does Bonnemort continue to work at the mine?
He continues to work at the mine because he feels he has no other options.

4. What is the financial state of the mining company in comparison with the financial state of its workers?
The mining company has made millions and the workers are desperately poor.

5. What does the mine seem to be doing to the miners descending into it?
The mine appears to be eating and digesting miners.

VOCABULARY IN CONTEXT

- Worshippers kneeled at the front of their tabernacle.
- The sated dogs lay down by the fireplace after their large meal.
- After her car accident, Margie could not get used to being an invalid for an entire month.

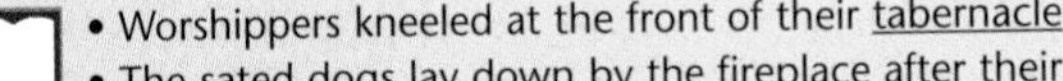

Reviewing the Selection

RECALLING / **INTERPRETING**

1. What is Étienne's situation? What is his single hope? What attracts his attention? How does he feel when he sees the pit? ▶▶ Why does Étienne despair that there will be no work before he speaks to anyone at the mine? Characterize his mental state.

2. What has Étienne's job search been like? What does the old carman say to Étienne about finding work at the mine? What does the old carman say has happened to the factories in Montsou? ▶▶ From Étienne's and the carman's conversation, what can you tell about the economic situation in France during the time when this story is set? What does "the March wind" signify to Étienne?

3. What is the old carman called? Why was he given this nickname? How long has he worked at the mine? What does the carman keep doing? Why doesn't the carman want to retire? What happened to the carman's family members in the mine? ▶▶ What effects has working in the mine had on the carman and his family? Why do you think they have all continued to work there?

4. Whom does Bonnemort say owns the mines? What tone does his voice assume when speaking of the owners? What does Étienne resolve to do? ▶▶ Compare and contrast the mine workers' situations with that of the mines' owners. Why do you think Bonnemort assumes this tone of voice? Is Étienne firm in this resolution? Explain.

SYNTHESIZING

5. This excerpt is the first chapter of *Germinal.* What do you learn from this chapter about the novel's setting? about the lives of its characters? What seems to dominate the lives of all people living in Montsou? Based on this selection, do you think Étienne will work in the mines? Explain. Predict some other issues, subjects, or plot elements that you think the author will raise in following chapters. Explain your responses.

Understanding Literature (Questions for Discussion)

1. **Naturalism. Naturalism** was a literary movement of the late nineteenth and early twentieth centuries that saw actions and events as resulting inevitably from biological or natural forces or from forces in the environment. In what way do the characters in this chapter make decisions that are determined by external forces beyond their control? Why does Étienne come to Montsou? Why does he resolve to seek work there even though he seems to detest and fear the mine? Why do Bonnemort and his family continue to work in the mine despite the adverse effect that working there has had upon them? Why don't they leave and seek work elsewhere?

Answers for Reviewing the Selection

RECALLING AND INTERPRETING

1. **Recalling.** Étienne is wandering at night in an icy wind. He is out of work and has no place to stay. He hopes that it will be less chilly after sunrise. The fires at a coal mine attract his attention. He feels despair when he sees the pit. **Interpreting.** Étienne believes there will be no work, both because he knows work is scarce and because he feels hopeless. He is depressed and dejected.

2. **Recalling.** Étienne has been wandering from town to town, seeking work for eight days without any food or a place to stay. The old carman says that there is no work to be found at the mine, and that the factories are firing their workers and closing. **Interpreting.** Industry seems to be dying, leaving many people out of work. Étienne hears "a cry of famine" in the March wind, believing that it brings a lack of labor and death to many people.

3. **Recalling.** The old carman is called Bonnemort because he has survived three accidents in the mine. He has worked at the mine for fifty years. The carman keeps spitting up black coal. The carman's father, two uncles, and three brothers have all died in the mine. **Interpreting.** The mine has had a very adverse effect on the lives and health of Bonnemort's family. The family probably did not have other career options.

4. **Recalling.** Bonnemort does not know who owns the mines. He assumes a tone of religious awe. Étienne resolves to take any work at the mine that he can find. **Interpreting.** The mine workers lead miserable lives, while the owners have earned millions from the workers' labor. Bonnemort assumes this tone of voice because he is awed by the wealth and position the owners of the mine possess. Étienne seems to be unresolved because he fears the Voreux, which swallows up the humanity of its workers.

(cont.)

Answers for Reviewing the Selection (cont.)

SYNTHESIZING

Responses will vary. Possible responses are given.

5. Students may say that many people in France are in dire economic circumstances when this story takes place, that it takes place in a mine and in a mining town, and that many of the main characters are struggling to keep themselves and their families from starving. The mine seems to dominate the characters' lives. Students may say that Étienne's need will drive him to work in the mine and that there may be a struggle between the impoverished workers and the wealthy owners.

2. **Simile, Metaphor, and Personification.** A **simile** is a comparison using *like* or *as.* A **metaphor** is a figure of speech in which one thing is spoken or written about as if it were another. **Personification** is a figure of speech in which an idea, animal, or thing is described as if it were a person. Identify the similes and metaphors the author uses to describe the mine and its owners. To what does the author compare the mine and its owners? To what are the workers in the mine compared? What human qualities does the author attribute to the mine?

3. **Setting.** The **setting** of a literary work is the time and place in which it occurs, together with all the details used to create a sense of a particular time and place. In what way is this story's setting, particularly the weather, appropriate given its subject matter? What interpretation does Étienne make of the environmental forces around him?

Responding in Writing

1. **Creative Writing: Social Critique.** In the time period in which this story is set, there were few labor laws to protect workers. Children often left school and began to work at very young ages to help support their families; workers labored many more hours than workers typically do today; and working conditions were dangerous and unhealthy. Zola's novel serves as a social critique of such conditions. Think of a social condition that you find appalling. Using the form of an essay, an editorial, or a political cartoon, express your feelings about this issue.

2. **Critical Essay: Exploring Naturalism.** Write a two-page essay exploring the themes typical of Naturalism that Zola expresses in this first chapter from *Germinal.* Focus on the degree to which characters act and make choices as determined by forces beyond their control rather than by their own free will. What social and economic conditions determine a person's fate in this story? To begin, think about your responses to the first Understanding Literature question. Formulate a thesis and review the selection to find the evidence you need to support this thesis. Be sure to include an introduction, clearly stating your thesis; a body, providing evidence to support your thesis; and a conclusion.

Project

Researching Labor Laws. Working in small groups, research the impact that labor laws have made on the lives of working people. At least one group should research the labor conditions that existed in Europe and the United States before labor laws were introduced. At what age did people typically start working in factories, mills, and mines? How long was a workday? a workweek? What were the condition in the factories, mills, and mines? What dangers existed there? Other groups should research various labor laws, the intent of those who enacted these laws, and how, when, and why they were passed. In what way did these labor laws affect the lives of working people?

Answers for Understanding Literature

Responses will vary. Possible responses are given.

1. Naturalism. The characters' fates and decisions about where to work and how to live are determined by their adverse economic situation. To live they need to work themselves to death in the mines. Étienne comes to Montsou because he needs work to survive. He has no other options. Bonnemort and his family also are driven by their need for food and the economy seems to have fixed their position in life as workers in the mine. To survive, they start working in the mine at young ages and are unable to receive the education necessary to better their positions. They cannot leave, because they need the money from their jobs and have no other skills.

2. Simile, Metaphor, and Personification. Students should note the following similes and metaphors: "The pit . . . seemed to have the evil air of a gluttonous beast crouching there to devour the earth," "as if he were speaking of an inaccessible tabernacle containing a sated and crouching god to whom they had given all their flesh and whom they had never seen," "And the Voreux . . . with its posture as of an evil beast, continued to crunch, breathing with a heavier and slower respiration, troubled by its painful digestion of human flesh." The mine and its owners are compared to a terrible beast that greedily devours workers. The workers are compared to food. To the mine are attributed characteristics of hunger and evil.

3. Setting. The weather is as cold and bleak as the characters' lives. Étienne believes that the wind is blowing in famine and death.

Analytic Scales for Responding in Writing

Grading scales for Responding in Writing appear on pages 936 and 937.

Project Notes

See the evaluation form for projects, Assessment Portfolio 4.12.

Researching Labor Laws. You might also ask students to examine how labor laws established years ago continue to affect workers and their employers. What labor laws are particularly important to today's workers? What does a worker need to do when he or she is experiencing a problem at work?

Encourage students to add to their research by interviewing employees, employers, and people at a local employment office to find answers to their questions.

PREREADING

"The False Gems"
by Guy de Maupassant, translated by M. Walter Dunne

FRANCE

About the Author

GUY DE MAUPASSANT
1850–1893

Born in Normandy, France, **Guy de Maupassant** was a nineteenth-century French Realist (see Connections, below) considered to be a master of the short story. Maupassant was tutored by his mother until the age of thirteen. He then spent three years at a seminary but was expelled and went on to graduate from public school. After joining the French army and fighting in the Franco-Prussian War (1870–1871), Maupassant moved to Paris, where he met many famous writers, including Gustave Flaubert. Maupassant studied under Flaubert and was greatly influenced by his style and techniques. Maupassant's "Boule de suif" ("Ball of Tallow"), a story about the Franco-Prussian war published in 1880, established his reputation as a writer. From 1880 to 1890, Maupassant wrote six novels and more than three hundred short stories.

About the Selection

The subjects of Maupassant's short stories were drawn from his own experiences and observations. He selected subjects from peasant life in Normandy, the behavior of the French middle class, and the fashionable high society of Paris.

In **"The False Gems,"** as in many of his stories, Maupassant creates a sense of the incongruity and complexity of experience through the use of **irony**, or the contrast of the difference between appearance and reality. Maupassant often told his stories with detachment, showing no compassion for his main characters and their flaws. This detached tone is another interesting feature of "The False Gems." As you read this story about a man who makes a shocking discovery about his late wife and her collection of false gems, take note of Maupassant's distinct literary style.

CONNECTIONS: The Influence of Flaubert and Zola

Novelist Gustave Flaubert was an old friend of Guy de Maupassant's mother, and while in Paris, Maupassant went to literary gatherings at Flaubert's house. For ten years Flaubert tutored Maupassant in the art of writing, passing on his realistic style, which required Maupassant to be a careful observer of the details of ordinary life. This style led Maupassant to admire the work of Émile Zola (see page 930), who was a leader of the new Naturalistic school of fiction writing. Detached narration, careful detail, and accurate historical background are three of the characteristics that distinguished the work of Maupassant and other Naturalist writers. Naturalists sought to portray people and society as truthfully as possible. For more on Realism and Naturalism, turn to the Unit 11 introduction (page 900).

GOALS/OBJECTIVES

Studying this lesson will enable students to

- enjoy a short story that explores the difference between appearance and reality in a relationship
- discuss the life and work of Guy de Maupassant
- define *characterization, foreshadowing,* and *irony*
- write a descriptive paragraph based on personal observations
- write an essay comparing the work of Maupassant and Flaubert
- research an aspect of French history that influenced Maupassant's writing

ADDITIONAL RESOURCES

READER'S GUIDE

- Selection Worksheet 11.6

ASSESSMENT PORTFOLIO

- Selection Check Test 2.11.11
- Selection Test 2.11.12

ESSENTIAL SKILLS PRACTICE BOOKS

- Writing 1.8, 1.20
- Study and Research 4.11–4.17, 4.19–4.24

PREREADING EXTENSIONS

Another well-known Maupassant story that is similar to "The False Gems" in its use of irony is "The Necklace." You might have students read this story and then, in a short essay or in a class discussion, compare its premise and outcome to that of "The False Gems."

SUPPORT FOR LEP STUDENTS

PRONUNCIATIONS OF PROPER NOUNS AND ADJECTIVES

Bo • he • mi • an (bō hē´mē ən)
Lan • tin (län tăn´)

ADDITIONAL VOCABULARY

droll—humorous in a quirky way
heartrending—extremely sad
imperceptible—slight, not easily seen
incurred—acquired
infinite—unending
matrimony—marriage
paste—material used to make a false gem, or itself a false gem
rhinestone—artificial gem made of glass, often cut like a diamond
tête-á-tête—private conversation between two people

READER'S JOURNAL

As an alternate activity, you might ask students to write about the relationships in their lives. Do they feel they know most people well?

Answers to Guided Reading Questions

❶ The young woman's mother had hoped to make "a favorable marriage for her daughter." The speaker describes the family as poor, honest, quiet, and unaffected.

❷ The speaker blames his wife for her love of the theater and her taste for false jewelry.

❸ People never tire of saying how happy the man who marries the young woman will be. M. Lantin asks her to marry him.

SPELLING AND VOCABULARY WORDS FROM THE SELECTION

adorn	procure
assuage	rancor
contemptuous	remonstrate

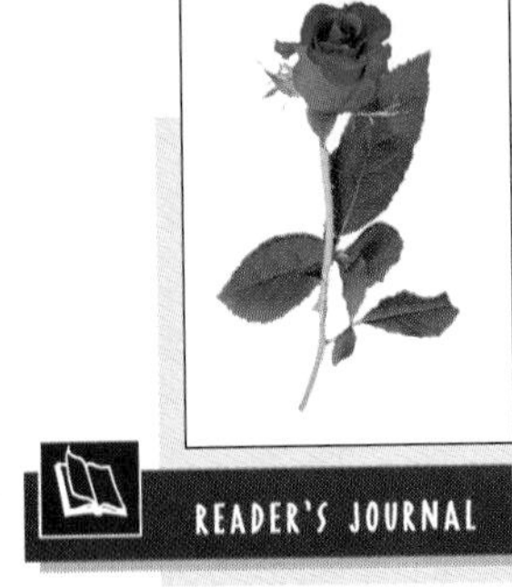

Describe a time when something happened to change completely your image of a person or a situation. What image had been in your mind? What happened to change this image? How did the image change? How did you feel when this happened? Was it a positive or negative experience? Why?

READER'S JOURNAL

"The False Gems"

GUY DE MAUPASSANT, TRANSLATED BY M. WALTER DUNNE

M. Lantin[1] had met the young woman at a *soirée*,[2] at the home of the assistant chief of his bureau, and at first sight had fallen madly in love with her.

She was the daughter of a country physician who had died some months previously. She had come to live in Paris, with her mother, who visited much among her acquaintances, in the hope of making a favorable marriage for her daughter. They were poor and honest, quiet and unaffected.

The young girl was a perfect type of the virtuous woman whom every sensible young man dreams of one day winning for life. Her simple beauty had the charm of angelic modesty, and the imperceptible smile which constantly hovered about her lips seemed to be the reflection of a pure and lovely soul. Her praises resounded on every side. People never tired of saying: "Happy the man who wins her love! He could not find a better wife."

Now M. Lantin enjoyed a snug little income of $700, and, thinking he could safely assume the responsibilities of matrimony, proposed to this model young girl and was accepted.

He was unspeakably happy with her; she governed his household so cleverly and economically that they seemed to live in luxury. She lavished the most delicate attentions on her husband, coaxed and fondled him, and the charm of her presence was so great that six years after their marriage M. Lantin discovered that he loved his wife even more than during the first days of their honeymoon.

He only felt inclined to blame her for two things: her love of the theater, and a taste for false jewelry. Her friends (she was acquainted with some officers' wives) frequently procured for her a box at the theater, often for the first representations of the new plays; and her husband was obliged to accompany her, whether he willed or not, to these amusements, though they bored him excessively after a day's labor at the office.

❶ *What had the young woman's mother hoped to do? What words does the speaker use to describe the young woman's family?*

❷ *For what two things does the speaker blame his wife?*

❸ *What do people never tire of saying about the young woman? What does M. Lantin do?*

1. **M. Lantin.** Monsieur, or Mister, Lantin
2. ***soirée.*** Party

WORDS FOR EVERYDAY USE

pro • cure (prō kyoor´) *vt.,* obtain through some effort

Vocabulary in Context

• We had to wait in line for hours in order to procure tickets to that concert.

After a time, M. Lantin begged his wife to get some lady of her acquaintance to accompany her. She was at first opposed to such an arrangement; but, after much persuasion on his part, she finally consented—to the infinite delight of her husband.

Now, with her love for the theater came also the desire to adorn her person. True, her costumes remained as before, simple, and in the most correct taste; but she soon began to ornament her ears with huge rhinestones which glittered and sparkled like real diamonds. Around her neck she wore strings of false pearls, and on her arms bracelets of imitation gold.

Her husband frequently remonstrated with her, saying:

"My dear, as you cannot afford to buy real diamonds, you ought to appear adorned with your beauty and modesty alone, which are the rarest ornaments of your sex."

But she would smile sweetly, and say:

"What can I do? I am so fond of jewelry. It is my only weakness. We cannot change our natures."

Then she would roll the pearl necklaces around her fingers, and hold up the bright gems for her husband's admiration, gently coaxing him:

"Look! are they not lovely? One would swear they were real."

M. Lantin would then answer, smilingly:

"You have Bohemian tastes, my dear."

Often of an evening, when they were enjoying a tête-à-tête by the fireside, she would place on the tea table the leather box containing the "trash," as M. Lantin called it. She would examine the false gems with a passionate attention as though they were in some way connected with a deep and secret joy, and she often insisted on passing a necklace around her husband's neck, and laughing heartily would exclaim: "How droll you look!" Then she would throw herself into his arms and kiss him affectionately.

One evening in the winter she attended the opera, and on her return was chilled through and through. The next morning she coughed, and eight days later she died of inflammation of the lungs.

M. Lantin's despair was so great that his hair became white in one month. He wept unceasingly; his heart was torn with grief, and his mind was haunted by the remembrance, the smile, the voice—by every charm of his beautiful, dead wife.

Time, the healer, did not assuage his grief. Often during office hours, while his colleagues were discussing the topics of the day, his eyes would suddenly fill with tears, and he would give vent to his grief in heartrending sobs. Everything in his wife's room remained as before her decease; and here he was wont to seclude himself daily and think of her who had been his treasure—the joy of his existence.

But life soon became a struggle. His income, which in the hands of his wife had covered all household expenses, was now no longer sufficient for his own immediate wants; and he wondered how she could have managed to buy such excellent wines, and such rare delicacies, things which he could no longer procure with his modest resources.

He incurred some debts and was soon reduced to absolute poverty. One morning, finding himself without a cent in his pocket, he resolved to sell something, and, immediately, the thought occurred to him of disposing of his wife's paste jewels. He cherished in

1 *What does M. Lantin beg his wife to do? What is her response to this request?*

2 *What happens to M. Lantin's wife?*

3 *What happens to M. Lantin's financial situation after his wife's death? What does he wonder about his wife's ability to handle financial matters? What does desperation drive him to do?*

4 *In what way does the young woman look at her gems?*

WORDS FOR EVERYDAY USE

a • dorn (ə dôrn´) *vt.,* be an ornament to; add beauty

re • mon • strate (ri män´strāt) *vt.,* say or plead in protest, objection, complaint

as • suage (ə swāj´) *vt.,* lessen, relieve

Answers to Guided Reading Questions

1 M. Lantin begs his wife to get one of her friends to go with her to the opera so that he doesn't have to go. She finally agrees to do this.

2 M. Lantin's wife dies after attending the opera on a chilly day in winter.

3 He becomes quite poor. He wonders how his wife had been able to handle financial matters so well, buying rare and expensive wines and food, while he cannot afford these things now. He decides to try to sell her false jewelry.

4 The young woman looks at her gems with "passionate attention" as though they are connected with a deep and secret joy.

ANALYTIC SCALES FOR RESPONDING IN WRITING

(SEE PAGE 948.)

Assign a score from 1 to 25 for each grading criterion below. (For more detailed evaluation, see the evaluation forms for writing, revising, and proofreading, Assessment Portfolio 4.1–4.9.)

1. Observation and Description

- **Content/Unity.** The descriptive paragraph focuses on a specific photo or illustration.
- **Organization/Coherence.** The descriptive paragraph is based on the writer's observation of a particular photo or illustration and uses accurate details.
- **Language/Style.** The paragraph uses vivid and precise nouns, verbs, and modifiers.
- **Conventions.** The paragraph avoids errors in spelling, grammar, usage, mechanics, and manuscript form.

► Additional practice is provided in the Essential Skills Practice Book: Writing 1.8.

Vocabulary in Context

- For the dance, Helena decided to adorn the refreshment table with fresh flowers.
- Members of the community plan to remonstrate with authorities the closing of the library.
- I'm hoping that this warm cloth on my forehead will assuage my headache.

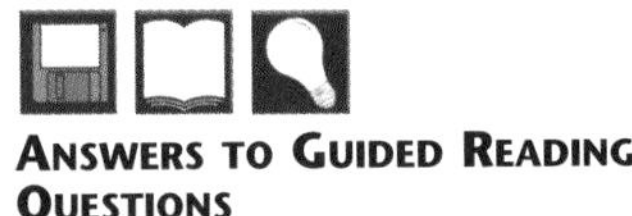

Answers to Guided Reading Questions

1 M. Lantin hates the false gems. The sight of the gems spoils his memory of his wife.

ANALYTIC SCALES FOR RESPONDING IN WRITING

(SEE PAGE 948.)

2. Critical Essay

- **Content/Unity.** The essay focuses on the similarities between the styles of Maupassant and works by Flaubert.
- **Organization/Coherence.** The essay begins with an introduction containing a thesis statement about similarities in works by Maupassant and Flaubert. The introduction is followed by supporting paragraphs and a concluding paragraph.
- **Language/Style.** The essay uses vivid and precise nouns, verbs, and modifiers.
- **Conventions.** The essay avoids errors in spelling, grammar, usage, mechanics, and manuscript form.

▶ Additional practice is provided in the Essential Skills Practice Book: Writing 1.20.

The New Necklace. *William McGregor Paxton, 1910. Zoë Oliver Sherman Collection. Courtesy Museum of Fine Arts, Boston*

1 *How does M. Lantin feel about the false gems? What effect does the sight of them have on him?*

his heart a sort of rancor against the false gems. They had always irritated him in the past, and the very sight of them spoiled somewhat the memory of his lost darling.

To the last days of her life, she had continued to make purchases; bringing home new gems almost every evening. He decided to sell the heavy necklace which she seemed to prefer, and which, he thought, ought to be worth about six or seven francs; for although paste it was, nevertheless, of very fine workmanship.

He put it in his pocket and started out in search of a jeweler's shop. He entered the first one he saw; feeling a little ashamed to expose his misery, and also to offer such a worthless article for sale.

"Sir," said he to the merchant, "I would like to know what this is worth."

The man took the necklace, examined it, called his clerk and made some remarks in an undertone; then he put the ornament back on the counter, and looked at it from a distance to judge of the effect.

Words for Everyday Use

ran • cor (raŋ′kər) *n.,* continuing and bitter hate or ill will

Vocabulary in Context

- Just the thought of the person who burglarized her grandparents' store fills Angela with rancor.

M. Lantin was annoyed by all this detail and was on the point of saying: "Oh! I know well enough it is not worth anything," when the jeweler said: "Sir, that necklace is worth from twelve to fifteen thousand francs; but I could not buy it unless you tell me now whence it comes."

The widower opened his eyes wide and remained gaping, not comprehending the merchant's meaning. Finally he stammered: "You say—are you sure?" The other replied dryly: "You can search elsewhere and see if anyone will offer you more. I consider it worth fifteen thousand at the most. Come back here if you cannot do better."

M. Lantin, beside himself with astonishment, took up the necklace and left the store. He wished time for reflection.

Once outside, he felt inclined to laugh, and said to himself: "The fool! Had I only taken him at his word! That jeweler cannot distinguish real diamonds from paste."

A few minutes after, he entered another store in the Rue de la Paix. As soon as the proprietor glanced at the necklace, he cried out:

"Ah, *parbleu!* I know it well; it was bought here."

M. Lantin was disturbed, and asked:

"How much is it worth?"

"Well, I sold it for twenty thousand francs. I am willing to take it back for eighteen thousand when you inform me, according to our legal formality, how it comes to be in your possession."

This time M. Lantin was dumbfounded. He replied:

"But—but—examine it well. Until this moment I was under the impression that it was paste."

Said the jeweler:

"What is your name, sir?"

"Lantin—I am in the employ of the Minister of the Interior. I live at No. 16 Rue des Martyrs."

The merchant looked through his books, found the entry, and said: "That necklace was sent to Mme. Lantin's address, 16 Rue des Martyrs, July 20, 1876."

The two men looked into each other's eyes—the widower speechless with astonishment, the jeweler scenting a thief. The latter broke the silence by saying:

"Will you leave this necklace here for twenty-four hours? I will give you a receipt."

"Certainly," answered M. Lantin, hastily. Then, putting the ticket in his pocket, he left the store.

He wandered aimlessly through the streets, his mind in a state of dreadful confusion. He tried to reason, to understand. His wife could not afford to purchase such a costly ornament. Certainly not. But, then, it must have been a present!—a present!—a present from whom? Why was it given her?

He stopped and remained standing in the middle of the street. A horrible doubt entered his mind—she? Then all the other gems must have been presents, too! The earth seemed to tremble beneath him—the tree before him was falling—throwing up his arms, he fell to the ground, unconscious. He recovered his senses in a pharmacy into which the passers-by had taken him, and was then taken to his home. When he arrived he shut himself up in his room and wept until nightfall. Finally, overcome with fatigue, he threw himself on the bed, where he passed an uneasy, restless night.

The following morning he arose and prepared to go to the office. It was hard to work after such a shock. He sent a letter to his employer requesting to be excused. Then he remembered that he had to return to the jeweler's. He did not like the idea; but he could not leave the necklace with that man. So he dressed and went out.

It was a lovely day; a clear blue sky smiled on the busy city below, and men of leisure were strolling about with their hands in their pockets.

Observing them, M. Lantin said to himself: "The rich, indeed, are happy. With money it is possible to forget even the deepest sorrow.

❶ *What kind of person does the second jeweler believe M. Lantin to be?*

❷ *What does M. Lantin realize about the necklace and all the other jewels in his wife's possession? What question is in his mind?*

❸ *How has learning his wife's secret made him feel?*

❹ *What does M. Lantin decide as he observes the men of leisure?*

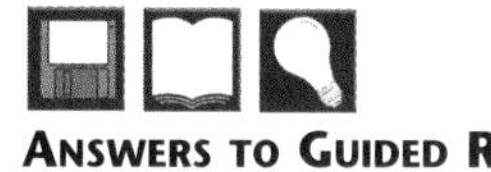

ANSWERS TO GUIDED READING QUESTIONS

❶ The second jeweler believes M. Lantin might be a thief.

❷ M. Lantin realizes that the necklace and all the other jewels in his wife's possession must have been gifts from someone, as she couldn't possibly have afforded to buy them herself. He wonders who gave them to her.

❸ Learning his wife's secret has made M. Lantin uneasy and restless.

❹ M. Lantin decides that if he were rich he would feel better about his life and get over his grief.

QUOTABLES

"The human understanding is like a false mirror, which receiving rays irregularly distorts and discolors the nature of things by mingling its own nature with it."

—Francis Bacon
Novum Organum

ADDITIONAL QUESTIONS AND ACTIVITIES

Ask students to answer the following questions:

Why do you think M. Lantin is in a "state of dreadful confusion" when he learns the truth about the gems? How might you feel if you were M. Lantin? What does he believe about his wife?

ANSWERS

Responses will vary.

He feels she must have kept secrets from him, and that there was more to her life than met the eye. He feels deceived. He believes she must have had an admirer who bought her the gems.

Answers to Guided Reading Questions

❶ He decides to try to sell them as well, and learns that they too are worth a great deal of money.

❷ He enjoys his life of wealth and leisure, eating well and going to the theater. He eventually marries a woman of virtue who has a violent temper.

Additional Questions and Activities

Ask students to use their imaginations to describe M. Lantin's second wife and the circumstances of their meeting. What about her probably attracted him? Students can create a scene that features dialogue between the two, or they can create a descriptive piece.

Selection Check Test with Answers

EX. Why did M. Lantin's wife originally come to Paris?
Her mother wanted her to get married.

1. For what two interests does M. Lantin "blame" his wife?
He blames her for her interest in theater and in false gems.

2. With what does M. Lantin struggle after the death of his wife?
M. Lantin struggles with his finances.

3. What shocking secret does M. Lantin learn about his wife's "false gems"?
He learns that the gems are genuine.

4. In what manner does M. Lantin live after selling the gems?
He lives as a wealthy man.

5. How is M. Lantin's second wife described?
She has a violent temper and causes him much sorrow.

❶ *After receiving money for the necklace, what does M. Lantin decide to do with the other gems? What does he learn about them?*

One can go where one pleases, and in travel find that distraction which is the surest cure for grief. Oh! if I were only rich!"

He began to feel hungry, but his pocket was empty. He again remembered the necklace. Eighteen thousand francs! Eighteen thousand francs! What a sum!

He soon arrived in the Rue de la Paix, opposite the jeweler's. Eighteen thousand francs! Twenty times he resolved to go in, but shame kept him back. He was hungry, however—very hungry, and had not a cent in his pocket. He decided quickly, ran across the street in order not to have time for reflection, and entered the store.

The proprietor immediately came forward and politely offered him a chair; the clerks glanced at him knowingly.

"I have made inquiries, M. Lantin," said the jeweler, "and if you are still resolved to dispose of the gems, I am ready to pay you the price I offered."

"Certainly, sir," stammered M. Lantin.

Whereupon the proprietor took from a drawer eighteen large bills, counted and handed them to M. Lantin, who signed a receipt and with a trembling hand put the money into his pocket.

As he was about to leave the store, he turned toward the merchant, who still wore the same knowing smile, and lowering his eyes, said:

❷ *In what way does M. Lantin's life change when he first inherits his fortune? What does he do to change his situation? What kind of person does he marry?*

"I have—I have other gems which I have received from the same source. Will you buy them also?"

The merchant bowed: "Certainly, sir."

M. Lantin said gravely: "I will bring them to you." An hour later he returned with the gems.

The large diamond earrings were worth twenty thousand francs; the bracelets thirty-five thousand; the rings, sixteen thousand; a set of emeralds and sapphires, fourteen thousand; a gold chain with solitaire pendant, forty thousand—making the sum of one hundred and forty-three thousand francs.

The jeweler remarked, jokingly:

"There was a person who invested all her earnings in precious stones."

M. Lantin replied, seriously:

"It is only another way of investing one's money."

That day he lunched at Voisin's and drank wine worth twenty francs a bottle. Then he hired a carriage and made a tour of the Bois, and as he scanned the various turn-outs with a contemptuous air he could hardly refrain from crying out to the occupants:

"I, too, am rich!—I am worth two hundred thousand francs."

Suddenly he thought of his employer. He drove up to the office, and entered gaily, saying:

"Sir, I have come to resign my position. I have just inherited three hundred thousand francs."

He shook hands with his former colleagues and confided to them some of his projects for the future; then he went off to dine at the Café Anglais.

He seated himself beside a gentleman of aristocratic bearing, and during the meal informed the latter confidentially that he had just inherited a fortune of four hundred thousand francs.

For the first time in his life he was not bored at the theater, and spent the remainder of the night in a gay frolic.

Six months afterward he married again. His second wife was a very virtuous woman, with a violent temper. She caused him much sorrow. ■

Words for Everyday Use

con • temp • tu • ous (kən temp´cho͞o əs) *adj.*, scornful; disdainful

Vocabulary in Context

• The star of the play treated the actors with minor roles in a contemptuous manner.

Responding to the Selection

Imagine that you are M. Lantin. How would you feel after finding out the secret of the "false gems"? What questions might be in your own mind?

Reviewing the Selection

Recalling / **Interpreting**

1. Why had the young woman with whom M. Lantin falls in love come to Paris? What does M. Lantin know about her family? According to other people, what kind of person is the young woman? ▶▶ Why does M. Lantin want to marry the young woman? What about her personality does he, and other people, find most appealing and why? Do you think his love for her runs deep?
2. What is M. Lantin's opinion about his wife's interest in theater and her love of false jewelry? What specific comments and suggestions does he make concerning the theater and the jewelry? ▶▶ How might you describe the young woman's attachment to her jewelry? Why do you think she continues to wear it, despite her husband's opinion? Do you think M. Lantin knows his wife well? Explain.
3. After his wife's death, why does M. Lantin decide to sell her necklace? What does he learn about the necklace when he visits the jeweler? ▶▶ What feelings begin to overtake M. Lantin's feelings of grief? How does he respond when he learns the truth about his wife's gems? How did she acquire the jewels?
4. What does M. Lantin do after he sells the jewelry? What does he tell his employer? ▶▶ How does M. Lantin react to being a wealthy man? Is he comfortable with the idea? Explain.

Synthesizing

5. Why do you think M. Lantin's wife is given no name in the story? How might you describe their relationship? Why do you think M. Lantin's second marriage is unhappy?

Understanding Literature (Questions for Discussion)

1. **Irony. Irony** is a difference between appearance and reality. In **irony of situation**, an event occurs that violates the expectations of the characters. What instances of irony of situation can you find in this story?

Responding to the Selection

You might also ask students if they feel any sympathy for M. Lantin. What relationship advice might they want to give him?

Answers for Reviewing the Selection

RECALLING AND INTERPRETING

1. **Recalling.** Her mother had hoped to make her a suitable marriage. M. Lantin knows that she is poor, honest, quiet, and unaffected. People believe that the woman is beautiful and angelic. **Interpreting.** The speaker wants to marry the young woman because she is angelic and beautiful. He, like others, thinks she is the ideal wife because of her beauty and her virtue. *Responses will vary.* Students might say that the man seems attracted to the woman's beauty and to the fact that she comes from a good family, which shows that his love might not run deep.

2. **Recalling.** He strongly dislikes the theater and his wife's false jewelry. He would like a female acquaintance to accompany his wife to the theater, as he does not wish to attend. He feels that if his wife cannot buy genuine jewels, she should not wear jewelry at all. **Interpreting.** The young woman loves her jewelry, which seems to have special meaning for her. M. Lantin does not seem to understand her feelings or her interests.

3. **Recalling.** M. Lantin decides to sell her necklace because he is suffering financially. He discovers that the necklace is worth a great deal of money. **Interpreting.** Financial concerns begin to overtake M. Lantin's feelings of grief. He feels shocked and uneasy when he learns that someone must have given his wife the jewels. (cont.)

Answers for Reviewing the Selection (cont.)

4. **Recalling.** M. Lantin enjoys his wealth by eating well and going to the theater. He tells his employer that he no longer wishes to work. **Interpreting.** M. Lantin enjoys being a wealthy man. He becomes so comfortable that he even quits his job, and pursues leisure and pleasure.

SYNTHESIZING

Responses will vary. Possible responses are given.

5. M. Lantin's wife is not named in the story because she is mysterious and unknown to her husband. She played a role as his wife, but he was not aware of the intricacies of her life or personality. He falls in a similar way into a second marriage that is unhappy because he is unable to look beneath superficial levels to the personality of the second wife.

Answers for Understanding Literature

Responses will vary. Possible responses are given.

1. Irony. Students should cite the fact that M. Lantin's wife is said to be so simple and virtuous, yet she carries on a complex, immoral inner life. Students might also cite the fact that M. Lantin admires his wife and her family for being simple, poor, and unaffected, yet he falls easily into a wealthy lifestyle. The very gems he hated bring him this new life, which includes the pastime he begrudged his wife. There is also irony in the story's ending—when M. Lantin has everything he needs, he marries a woman who causes him sorrow.

2. Foreshadowing. Students should point out the strange attachment and love the wife seems to have for her jewelry. The author describes at length the way she looks at her jewels. Students might also have been suspicious in the beginning of the story, which focused so strongly on the innocence, simplicity, and angelic qualities of the woman.

3. Characterization. M. Lantin is characterized primarily by his actions, his interactions with other people, and his thoughts. His wife is characterized primarily by his opinions and the opinions of the community about her, by her tastes and her attachment to her jewels, and finally by the enormous secret she carried. M. Lantin seems to be a static character.

Analytic Scales for Responding in Writing

Grading scales for Responding in Writing appear on pages 943 and 944.

2. **Foreshadowing. Foreshadowing** is the act of presenting materials that hint at events to come later in the story. M. Lantin's realization about his wife's jewelry comes as a complete surprise to him, but to the reader, the fact that the jewelry was worth more than it seemed was foreshadowed. What clues appear earlier in the story?

3. **Characterization. Characterization** is the use of literary techniques to create a character. Three techniques—direct description, portrayal of behavior, and representation of internal states—are used by authors to create characters. How is M. Lantin characterized? How is his wife characterized? A *static character* is one who does not change during the course of the action. A *dynamic character* is one who does change. Which type of character is M. Lantin? Explain.

Responding in Writing

1. **Creative Writing: Observation and Description.** Maupassant was a careful observer of the world around him and always strove to present an accurate picture of people, places, and situations. Bring to class two or three detailed photos or illustrations from magazines and books, particularly pictures of people and places. Display your pictures alongside those chosen by your classmates. Then carefully observe the pictures. Pick one picture without letting anyone else know which you have chosen, and write a descriptive paragraph about it, using accurate details. Take turns reading your paragraphs aloud and trying to determine which picture each describes.

2. **Critical Essay: Maupassant and Flaubert.** You have learned that Flaubert was a teacher and mentor to Maupassant, and that the two share similar styles. Write a short essay in which you discuss the similarities you find in the "The False Gems" and in the excerpt from *Madame Bovary* (found in Selections for Additional Reading, page 1006.) As you write, think about the following questions: What similarities can you see in the descriptive language used in these two pieces? What similarities can you see in the ways in which the authors develop and reveal character? Be sure to back up your ideas with details from each story.

Research Skills

Research Skills. Review the Language Arts Survey 4.11–4.17 and 4.19–4.24, which deal with use of source materials, documenting sources, and taking notes. Then, with a partner, research and write a short paper or do a small project. Take as your subject one aspect of French history or society that influenced Maupassant's writing. Before you begin, you might want to discuss as a class possible subjects for research. Each pair should focus on a different topic, and present its paper or project to the rest of the class. You might try finding topics within the following subject areas: the Franco-Prussian War, peasant life in Normandy, lives of the French middle class, or the fashionable life of Paris.

Answers for Skills Activities

RESEARCH SKILLS

You might allow students to visit the library and then hold a class brainstorming session about potential topics before separating into pairs to work on papers or projects.

Students should be evaluated on the quality of their research and the creativity and meaningfulness of their papers and projects. Give each pair time to share its work. Students should also have the opportunity to evaluate the work of others.

▶ Additional practice is provided in the Essential Skills Practice Book: Study and Research 4.11–4.17 and 4.19–4.24.

PREREADING

"The Bet"
by Anton Chekhov, translated by Ronald Hingley

About the Author

ANTON CHEKHOV
1860–1904

Playwright and short story writer **Anton Chekhov** is one of the most notable Russian Realists. He was born in Taganrog, Russia, in 1860. His grandfather was a serf who bought his freedom; his father was a struggling grocer. After the business failed, the family moved to Moscow. Chekhov, however, remained in Taganrog to finish his high school education. Soon after joining his family in Moscow in 1879, he enrolled in the university medical program and became a doctor in 1884. His medical work as well as his writing were crucial to his family's support. In 1890, he took a long and arduous journey across Siberia to the island of Sakhalin, the site of a Russian penal colony. Chekhov published a research thesis, *The Island of Sakhalin,* based on his journey and his studies on the island. After returning from this trip, he bought an estate in Melikhovo, where he lived for six years with his parents and sister, Mariya. His writings during this time include "Ward Number Six," "My Life," and *The Seagull.* Complications of tuberculosis caused Chekhov to move to the coastal resort of Yalta where he wrote many dramas including *Three Sisters* and *The Cherry Orchard.* In 1901, he married Olga Knipper, an actress. Three years later, he died of tuberculosis.

About the Selection

In **"The Bet,"** a hasty and ill-considered wager between a banker and a lawyer provides the reader with an opportunity to examine the effects of greed on two characters. The story begins with a **flashback** (that is, it presents an event that occurred earlier than the current time in the story) to a party at which the bet was made. Over the course of the fifteen years that the story spans, the bet has a powerful impact on both characters. Chekhov uses the three main types of **characterization**—direct description, portrayal of characters' behavior, and representations of characters' internal states—to develop these two characters.

Red Square. *Moscow, Russia*

CONNECTIONS: Hyperbole

A **hyperbole** is an exaggeration made for effect. Many commonly used expressions are examples of hyperbole, such as "I'm so hungry I could eat a horse," or "I'm so happy I could die." Such exaggeration is meant to emphasize a point and is not meant to be taken literally. In "The Bet," a statement that in most cases would be interpreted as hyperbole is taken literally, and a man bets that he can exist in solitary confinement for fifteen years, for which he will receive two million rubles.

GOALS/OBJECTIVES

Studying this lesson will enable students to

- enjoy a story about an unusual bet between a banker and a lawyer
- discuss the life and work of Anton Chekhov
- define the literary terms *motivation and simile*
- write a fictional interview with a main character in the story
- write a critical essay that examines the character of the lawyer in the story
- explore with classmates the legal issue of capital punishment

ADDITIONAL RESOURCES

Reader's Guide
- Selection Worksheet 11.7

Assessment Portfolio
- Selection Check Test 2.11.13
- Selection Test 2.11.14

Essential Skills Practice Books
- Writing 1.8, 1.20
- Speaking and Listening 3.2, 3.3

PREREADING EXTENSIONS

Ask students to work in pairs to put together a children's picture book of hyperbole. Each pair can write a funny story filled with examples of hyperbole or make a children's dictionary of well-known hyperboles such as "I'm so hungry I could eat a horse." Tell students that hyperboles such as these would work well with humorous illustrations.

Encourage students to share their books with children they know or give them to a local library.

SUPPORT FOR LEP STUDENTS

Pronunciations of Proper Nouns and Adjectives

Chek • hov (chek´ ôf)

Additional Vocabulary

academics—teachers or students at a college or university
contempt—disdain
forestall—anticipate and then delay something
nodule—small knot or lump
obsession—an idea that takes over one's thoughts
reel—become overwhelmed or confused
sequel—something that follows something else
zealously—enthusiastically

READER'S JOURNAL

As an alternative activity, you might ask students to imagine and write about either the ultimate policeman or the master criminal.

Answers to Guided Reading Questions

❶ The banker remembers discussing capital punishment. He felt that capital punishment was more humane than imprisonment since life imprisonment is really a slow, torturous death.

❷ The lawyer thinks that any kind of life is better than no life. The banker bets two million rubles that the lawyer could not last five years in solitary confinement.

SPELLING AND VOCABULARY WORDS FROM THE SELECTION

absolve	obscure
canvass	posterity
compulsory	procure
contempt	renunciation
emaciated	sallow
ethereal	scorn
futile	transcendental
impetuosity	

Quotables

“Love, friendship, respect do not unite people as much as a common hatred for something.”

—Anton Chekhov
Notebooks

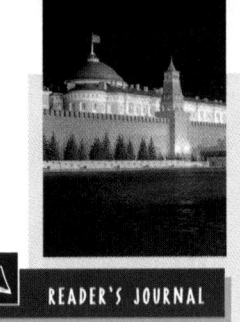

READER'S JOURNAL

Imagine that you were placed in solitary confinement for five years. You are allowed to read, to write, to play or listen to music, and you are provided with whatever food you wish. How would you spend your time? What might you think about? What would you miss most? Write your responses to these questions in your journal. You might write several entries that show your feelings during different periods of your confinement.

"The Bet"

ANTON CHEKHOV, TRANSLATED BY RONALD HINGLEY

I

One dark autumn night an elderly banker was pacing up and down his study and recalling the party that he had given on an autumn evening fifteen years earlier. It had been attended by a good few clever people, and fascinating discussions had taken place, one of the topics being capital punishment. The guests, including numerous academics and journalists, had been largely opposed to it, considering the death penalty out of date, immoral and unsuitable for Christian states. Several of them felt that it should be replaced everywhere by life imprisonment.

❶ *What topic does the banker remember discussing fifteen years earlier? What opinion on the issue had the banker expressed?*

'I disagree,' said their host the banker. 'I've never sampled the death penalty or life imprisonment myself. Still, to judge *a priori,*[1] I find capital punishment more moral and humane than imprisonment. Execution kills you at once, whereas life imprisonment does it slowly. Now, which executioner is more humane? He who kills you in a few minutes, or he who drags the life out of you over a period of several years?'

❷ *What opinion does the young lawyer express? What wager does the banker offer? What do you think of the lawyer's decision to accept the bet?*

A guest remarked that both were equally immoral. 'Both have the same object—the taking of life. The state isn't God, and it has no right to take what it can't restore if it wishes.'

Among the guests was a young lawyer of about twenty-five. 'The death sentence and the life sentence are equally immoral,' said he when his opinion was canvassed. 'But, if I had to choose between them, I'd certainly choose the second. Any kind of life is better than no life at all.'

A lively argument had ensued. The banker, younger and more excitable in those days, had suddenly got carried away and struck the table with his fist. 'It's not true!' he shouted at the young man. 'I bet you two million you wouldn't last five years in solitary confinement.'

1. ***a priori.*** Based on theory instead of experience

WORDS FOR EVERYDAY USE

can • vass (kan´vəs) *vt.,* solicit opinions, votes, etc.

Vocabulary in Context

• We will canvass the neighborhood to gather opinions about the building of a new park.

'I'll take you on if you mean it,' was the reply. 'And I won't just do a five-year stretch, I'll do fifteen.'

'Fifteen? Done!' cried the banker. 'Gentlemen, I put up two million.'

'Accepted! You stake your millions and I stake my freedom,' said the young man.

And so the outrageous, futile wager was made. The banker, then a spoilt and frivolous person, with more millions than he could count, was delighted, and he made fun of the lawyer over supper. 'Think better of it while there's still time,' said he. 'Two million is nothing to me, young man, but you risk losing three or four of the best years of your life, I say three or four because you won't hang on longer. And don't forget, my unfortunate friend, that confinement is far harder when it's voluntary than when it's compulsory. The thought that you can go free at any moment will poison your whole existence in prison. I'm sorry for you.'

Pacing to and fro, the banker now recalled all this. 'What was the good of that wager?' he wondered. 'What's the use of the man losing fifteen years of his life? Or of my throwing away two million? Does it prove that the death penalty is better or worse than life imprisonment? Certainly not! Stuff and nonsense! On my part it was a spoilt man's whim, and on his side it was simply greed for money.'

Then he recalled the sequel to that evening. It had been decided that the young man should serve his term under the strictest supervision in one of the lodges in the banker's garden. For fifteen years he was to be forbidden to cross the threshold, to see human beings, to hear the human voice, to receive letters and newspapers. He was allowed a musical instrument, and books to read. He could write letters, drink wine, smoke. It was stipulated that his communications with the outside world could not be in spoken form, but must take place through a little window built specially for the purpose. Anything he needed—books, music, wine and so on—he could receive by sending a note, and in any quantity he liked, but only through the window. The contract covered all the details and minutiae that would make his confinement strictly solitary, and compel him to serve precisely fifteen years from twelve o'clock on the fourteenth of November 1870 until twelve o'clock on the fourteenth of November 1885. The slightest attempt to break the conditions, even two minutes before the end, absolved the banker from all obligation to pay the two million.

So far as could be judged from the prisoner's brief notes, he suffered greatly from loneliness and depression in his first year of incarceration. The sound of his piano could be heard continually, day and night, from the lodge. He refused strong drink and tobacco. Wine stimulates desires, wrote he, and desires are a prisoner's worst enemy. Besides, is there anything drearier than drinking good wine and seeing nobody? And tobacco spoilt the air of his room. The books that he had sent during the first year were mostly light reading—novels with a complex love plot, thrillers, fantasies, comedies and so on.

In the second year there was no more music from the lodge, and the prisoner's notes demanded only literary classics. In the fifth year music was heard again, and the captive asked for wine. Those who watched him through the window said that he spent all that year just eating, drinking and lying on his bed, often yawning and talking angrily to himself. He read no books. Sometimes he would sit and write at night. He would spend hours writing, but would tear up everything

❶ *How have the banker's feelings about the bet changed in the fifteen years since it was made? What do you think caused this change of feeling?*

❷ *With what activities does the prisoner fill his first year? What does he do differently the second year? In what way has his attitude changed?*

❸ *Explain the conditions of the contract. What will the lawyer be allowed to do? What will he not be allowed to do?*

Words for Everyday Use

fu • tile (fyo͞ot´ l) *adj.*, useless, vain

com • pul • so • ry (kəm pul´sər ē) *adj.*, required, obligatory, that must be done

ab • solve (ab zälv´) *vt.*, free from a duty or promise

Answers to Guided Reading Questions

❶ The banker had been arrogant and delighted by the bet when he first made it. Fifteen years later, he looks at it as a waste of a life and sees himself as a spoiled man for having suggested the bet in the first place.

❷ During the first year, the prisoner suffered from loneliness and depression. He played the piano and did a great deal of light reading. During the second year, he stopped playing the piano and he began reading the classics. He seems to have become more resigned to his situation, but he also seems to be more serious about his pursuits.

❸ The lawyer must stay in the lodge from twelve o'clock on November 14, 1870 to twelve o'clock on November 14, 1885. He must make no effort to leave even two minutes before the chosen hour. He will be supplied with musical instruments, books, and food as he desires. His requests must be made in writing and delivered through a window. He cannot receive letters or newspapers, see human beings, hear human voices, or cross the threshold.

Additional Questions and Activities

- Ask students to predict the outcome of the unusual bet, based on what they have read so far.
- You might have students write a fictional letter to the lawyer, giving him their own personal tips for survival.

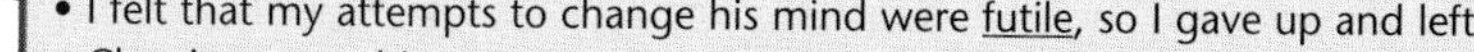

Vocabulary in Context

- I felt that my attempts to change his mind were futile, so I gave up and left.
- Cleaning our cabins was a compulsory chore at the summer camp we attended.
- If you return your library books this month, we agree to absolve you of any fines.

Answers to Guided Reading Questions

① The prisoner begins studying languages, philosophy, and history. He asks his jailer to show his work to experts and to fire a shot in the garden if his work has been successful. He has a high opinion of humankind and the achievements of humankind.

Additional Questions and Activities

• Ask students if they believe they would survive living in captivity, as the lawyer is doing. What activities would they want to have available to them? What foods would they want? What would they miss the most about the outside world?

• Ask students to discuss why writing the lines in six languages and then receiving recognition meant so much to the lawyer.

Bedroom in Ainmillerstrasse. *Vassily Kandinsky, 1909*

he had written by dawn. More than once he was heard weeping.

① *What does the prisoner do during his sixth year of confinement? What request does he make of his jailer? What is his opinion of humankind based on his studies of philosophy and history?*

In the second half of the sixth year the captive eagerly embraced the study of languages, philosophy and history. So zealously did he tackle these subjects that the banker could hardly keep up with his book orders—in four years some six hundred volumes were procured at his demand. During the period of this obsession the banker incidentally received the following letter from the prisoner.

'My dearest Gaoler,[2]

'I write these lines in six languages. Show them to those who know about these things. Let them read them. If they can't find any mistakes I beg you to have a shot fired in the garden—it will show me that my efforts have not been wasted. The geniuses of all ages and countries speak different languages, but the same flame burns in them all. Oh, did you but know what a transcendental happiness my soul now experiences from my ability to understand them!'

The captive's wish was granted—the banker had two shots fired in the garden.

After the tenth year the lawyer sat stock-still at the table, reading only the Gospels.[3]

2. **Gaoler.** Jailer
3. **Gospels.** First four books of the New Testament

Words for Everyday Use

pro • cure (prō ko͞orʹ) *vt.,* obtain, secure

tran • scen • den • tal (tranʹsen dentʹ 'l) *adj.,* extraordinary; surpassing the ordinary

Vocabulary in Context

• I would like to procure tickets to the opera for my father.
• The teacher had a transcendental concern for each of her students.

The banker marvelled that one who had mastered six hundred obscure tomes in four years should spend some twelve months reading a single slim, easily comprehensible volume. Theology and histories of religion followed the Gospels.

In the last two years of his imprisonment the captive read an enormous amount quite indiscriminately. Now it was the natural sciences, now he wanted Byron or Shakespeare. There were notes in which he would simultaneously demand a work on chemistry, a medical textbook, a novel and a philosophical or theological treatise. His reading suggested someone swimming in the sea surrounded by the wreckage of his ship, and trying to save his life by eagerly grasping first one spar[4] and then another.

II

'He regains his freedom at twelve o'clock tomorrow,' thought the old banker as he remembered all this. 'And I should pay him two million by agreement. But if I do pay up I'm done for—I'll be utterly ruined.'

Fifteen years earlier he had had more millions than he could count, but now he feared to ask which were greater, his assets or his debts. Gambling on the stock exchange, wild speculation, the impetuosity that he had never managed to curb, even in old age—these things had gradually brought his fortunes low, and the proud, fearless, self-confident millionaire had become just another run-of-the-mill banker trembling at every rise and fall in his holdings.

'Damn this bet!' muttered the old man, clutching his head in despair. 'Why couldn't the fellow die? He's only forty now. He'll take my last penny, he'll marry, he'll enjoy life, he'll gamble on the Exchange, while I look on enviously, like a pauper, and hear him saying the same thing day in day out: "I owe you all my happiness in life, so let me help you." No, it's too much! My only refuge from bankruptcy and disgrace is that man's death.'

Three o'clock struck and the banker cocked an ear. Everyone in the house was asleep, and nothing was heard but the wind rustling the frozen trees outside. Trying not to make a noise, he took from his fireproof safe the key of the door that had not been opened for fifteen years, put his overcoat on, and went out.

It was dark and cold outside, and rain was falling. A keen, damp wind swooped howling round the whole garden, giving the trees no rest. Straining his eyes, the banker could not see the ground, the white statues, the lodge or the trees. He approached the area of the lodge, and twice called his watchman, but there was no answer. The man was obviously sheltering from the weather, and was asleep somewhere in the kitchen or the greenhouse.

'If I have the courage to carry out my intention the main suspicion will fall on the watchman,' the old man thought.

He found the steps to the lodge and the door by feeling in the dark, entered the hall, groped his way into a small passage, and lit a match. There was no one there—just a bedstead without bedding on it, and the dark hulk of a cast-iron stove in the corner. The seals on the door leading to the captive's room were intact. When the match went out the old man peered through the small window, trembling with excitement.

In the prisoner's room a candle dimly burned. He was sitting near the table, and all that could be seen of him were his back, the hair on his head and his hands. On the table, on two armchairs, and on the carpet near the table, lay open books.

4. **spar.** Pole that supports the sail of a ship

1 *What does the banker see as his only hope? What does he intend to do?*

2 *Describe the prisoner's reading habits during the last two years of his confinement. To what does the narrator compare the prisoner's reading? What does this comparison suggest about the prisoner's state of mind during the last two years?*

3 *On the day before the terms of the bet will be completed, what is troubling the banker? What change in circumstances has he undergone during the last fifteen years?*

WORDS FOR EVERYDAY USE

ob • scure (əb skyoor´) *adj.,* not well-known, not famous

im • pet • u • os • i • ty (im pech´oo äs´i tē) *n.,* quality of being rash or impulsive

ANSWERS TO GUIDED READING QUESTIONS

1 The banker sees the lawyer's death as his only hope. He plans to kill the man.

2 The prisoner's reading habits are haphazard. The narrator compares the prisoner to a drowning person, trying to save himself by grasping at one bit of wreckage and then the next. This comparison suggests that the prisoner is looking for answers, that he is unhappy or floundering in his life.

3 The banker will be ruined if he has to pay off the bet. He has had some bad luck and been reckless with his money. Now, instead of being excessively rich, he worries constantly about money.

ANALYTIC SCALES FOR RESPONDING IN WRITING

(SEE PAGE 957.)

Assign a score from 1 to 25 for each grading criterion below. (For more detailed evaluation, see the evaluation forms for writing, revising, and proofreading, Assessment Portfolio 4.1–4.9.)

1. Interview

- **Content/Unity.** The interview questions the lawyer in "The Bet," about his years in solitary confinement.
- **Organization/Coherence.** The interview consists of questions and the fictional responses of the lawyer.
- **Language/Style.** The interview uses vivid and precise nouns, verbs, and modifiers and is written in conversational language.
- **Conventions.** The interview avoids errors in spelling, grammar, usage, mechanics, and manuscript form.

▶ Additional practice is provided in the Essential Skills Practice Book: Writing 1.8.

VOCABULARY IN CONTEXT

- The obscure comedian did not draw much of a crowd, but we enjoyed his act.
- Because of their impetuosity, I felt that I could not rely on them.

Answers to Guided Reading Questions

❶ The lawyer has aged prematurely. He is gaunt and weak. He is pale and sickly from lack of sun, and his hair is unkempt and turning gray.

❷ The man no longer values life on earth as he did fifteen years earlier. Before his imprisonment, he felt that "any kind of life is better than no life at all." Now he despises all earthly things and claims they are worthless since death will wipe them away. His studies during his early years of confinement had made him exultant about the achievements and spirit of humankind. He now looks on these achievements with scorn.

Analytic Scales for Responding in Writing

(See page 957.)

2. Critical Essay

- **Content/Unity.** The essay uses details from the story either to defend the lawyer in "The Bet" as a sympathetic character or to condemn him as unworthy of sympathy.
- **Organization/Coherence.** The essay begins with an introduction that includes the thesis of the essay. This introduction is followed by supporting paragraphs with clear transitions. The essay ends with a solid conclusion.
- **Language/Style.** The essay uses vivid and precise nouns, verbs, and modifiers.
- **Conventions.** The essay avoids errors in spelling, grammar, usage, mechanics, and manuscript form.

► Additional practice is provided in the Essential Skills Practice Book: Writing 1.20.

Five minutes passed without the prisoner once stirring—fifteen years of confinement had taught him to sit still. The banker tapped the window with a finger, but the captive made no answering movement. Then the banker cautiously broke the seals on the door, and put the key in the keyhole. The rusty lock grated and the door creaked. The banker expected to hear an immediate shout of surprise and footsteps, but three minutes passed and it was as quiet as ever in there. He decided to enter.

❶ *What effect has confinement had on the lawyer physically?*

At the table a man unlike ordinary men sat motionless. He was all skin and bones, he had long tresses like a woman's, and a shaggy beard. The complexion was sallow with an earthy tinge, the cheeks were hollow, the back was long and narrow, and the hand propping the shaggy head was so thin and emaciated that it was painful to look at. His hair was already streaked with silver, and no one looking at his worn, old-man's face would have believed that he was only forty. He was asleep, and on the table in front of his bowed head lay a sheet of paper with something written on it in small letters.

'How pathetic!' thought the banker. 'He's asleep, and is probably dreaming of his millions. All I have to do is to take this semi-corpse, throw it on the bed, smother it a bit with a pillow, and the keenest investigation will find no signs of death by violence. But let us first read what he has written.'

❷ *How has the man's opinion of the world changed from his opinion before his confinement? from the opinion he held during his early years of confinement?*

Taking the page from the table, the banker read as follows.

'At twelve o'clock tomorrow I regain my freedom and the right to associate with others. But I think fit, before I leave this room for the sunlight, to address a few words to you. With a clear conscience, and as God is my witness, I declare that I despise freedom, life, health and all that your books call the blessings of this world.

'I have spent fifteen years intently studying life on earth. True, I have not set eyes on the earth or its peoples, but in your books I have drunk fragrant wine, sung songs, hunted stags and wild boars in the forests, loved women. Created by the magic of your inspired poets, beautiful girls, ethereal as clouds, have visited me at night, and whispered in my ears magical tales that have made my head reel. In your books I have climbed the peaks of Elbrus and Mont Blanc, whence I have watched the sun rising in the morning, and flooding the sky, the ocean and the mountain peaks with crimson gold in the evening. From there I have watched lightnings flash and cleave the storm clouds above me. I have seen green forests, fields, rivers, lakes, cities. I have heard the singing of the sirens and the strains of shepherds' pipes. I have touched the wings of beautiful devils who flew to me to converse of God. In your books I have plunged into the bottomless pit, performed miracles, murdered, burnt towns, preached new religions, conquered whole kingdoms.

'Your books have given me wisdom. All that man's tireless brain has created over the centuries has been compressed into a small nodule inside my head. I know I'm cleverer than you all.

'I despise your books, I despise all the blessings and the wisdom of this world. Everything is worthless, fleeting, ghostly, illusory as a mirage. Proud, wise and handsome though you be, death will wipe you from the face of the earth along with the mice burrowing under the floor. Your posterity, your history, your deathless geniuses—all will freeze or burn with the terrestrial globe.

Words for Everyday Use

sal • low (sal´ō) *adj.*, sickly, pale yellow in hue

e • ma • ci • a • ted (ē mā´shē āt´əd) *adj.*, abnormally lean or thin as if through disease

e • the • re • al (ē thir'ē əl) *adj.*, very light, airy, delicate

pos • ter • i • ty (päs ter' ə tē) *n.*, descendants; all succeeding generations

Vocabulary in Context

- Spending the summer sick in bed left her with a sallow complexion.
- When the doctor removed the cast, Jaime noticed that his leg was emaciated.
- The angel food cake, made with egg whites, was sweet and ethereal.
- Grandmother saved a trunk full of family photographs and letters for posterity.

'You have lost your senses and are on the wrong path. You take lies for truth, and ugliness for beauty. You would be surprised if apple and orange trees somehow sprouted with frogs and lizards instead of fruit, or if roses smelt like a sweating horse. No less surprised am I at you who have exchanged heaven for earth. I do not want to understand you.

'To give you a practical demonstration of my contempt for what you live by, I hereby renounce the two million that I once yearned for as one might for paradise, but which I now scorn. To disqualify myself from receiving it I shall leave here five hours before the time fixed, thus breaking the contract.'

After reading this the banker laid the paper on the table, kissed the strange man on the head and left the lodge in tears. At no other time— not even after losing heavily on the stock exchange—had he felt such contempt for himself. Returning to his house, he went to bed, but excitement and tears kept him awake for hours.

Next morning the watchmen ran up, white-faced, and told the banker that they had seen the man from the lodge climb out of his window into the garden, go to the gate and vanish. The banker went over at once with his servants and made sure that the captive had indeed fled. To forestall unnecessary argument he took the document of renunciation from the table, went back to the house and locked it in his fireproof safe. ■

❶ *After reading the letter, how does the banker feel about himself? about his situation?*

Words for Everyday Use

scorn (skôrn) *vt.,* refuse or reject as wrong or disgraceful

con • tempt (kən tempt´) *n.,* feeling or attitude of one who looks down on somebody or something as being low, mean, or unworthy

re • nun • ci • a • tion (ri nun´ sē ā´ shən) *n.,* surrender, formally or voluntarily, of a right

Answers to Guided Reading Questions

❶ The banker feels contempt for himself, but he is excited and happy that he will not be ruined, nor will he have to kill the lawyer.

Selection Check Test with Answers

EX. For how many years does the lawyer agree to be confined?
He agrees to be confined for fifteen years.

1. What does the lawyer read during his second year in confinement?
He reads the classics.

2. What signal does the lawyer request during his sixth year?
He requests that a shot be fired if his language and philosophy studies have been successful.

3. What does the lawyer spend twelve months reading?
He spends twelve months reading the Gospels.

4. Why is the banker worried as the time period agreed upon for the bet draws to a close?
He will be ruined if he has to pay the lawyer.

5. Why does the banker not pay the lawyer?
The lawyer willfully breaks the contract by leaving five hours early.

Vocabulary in Context

- Members of the community will scorn products from Company X in protest of its plans to lay off thousands of workers.
- It often feels better to treat people with kindness than with contempt.
- Jeff, much to everyone's surprise, announced his renunciation of his club membership.

RESPONDING TO THE SELECTION

You might also ask students to imagine that they have just emerged from a fifteen-year confinement. What would they want to do first? Would they continue their life as they had left off or would they pursue a different type of life?

ANSWERS FOR REVIEWING THE SELECTION

RECALLING AND INTERPRETING

1. **Recalling.** The banker remembers discussing capital punishment. He thinks that the death penalty is more humane because it kills quickly, whereas life in prison kills a person slowly and gradually. The lawyer finds both equally immoral, but prefers life imprisonment because, as he put it "any kind of life is better than no life at all." The banker bets two million that the lawyer could not last five years in solitary confinement. **Interpreting.** The banker makes the bet because he is impulsive. The lawyer accepts it because of greed. At the time the bet is made, both men take life and freedom lightly while they place importance on money.

2. **Recalling.** The lawyer is allowed to read and write, play music, and have whatever food and drink he wants. He is not allowed to see people, to speak to others, or to cross the threshold of his lodge. During his first year, he plays the piano and does light reading. During his second year he turns to reading classics. During the fifth year, he turns again to music, sleeps, lays idle, talks to himself, or writes, though he destroys his writings. He does not read. **Interpreting.** During the first year, the lawyer goes through an initial depression and tries to fill his time with light activities. The second year, he seems to need more stimulation and perhaps tries to find solace in great literature. During the fifth year, he searches for new solace in music. The lack of communication seems to be affecting him. (cont.)

Responding to the Selection

What kind of life do you think the lawyer will lead, now that he has left his confinement? What is his attitude toward life? How might this attitude affect his relationships with others? Are you sympathetic toward this character? Why, or why not? Discuss these questions with a small group of your classmates.

Reviewing the Selection

RECALLING	INTERPRETING
1. When the banker thinks back upon the party, what issue does he remember discussing? What was his opinion on the issue? What was the lawyer's opinion? What does the banker bet?	What character traits led the banker to make the bet? What traits led the lawyer to accept it? What does the bet reveal about the values of both men?
2. What was the lawyer allowed to do during his solitary confinement? What experiences was he denied? What does the lawyer do during his first year of confinement? during the second year? during the fifth year?	What does the lawyer's change of activities suggest about his emotions and attitudes during the first five years?
3. What does the lawyer do during the sixth year? What request does he make of the banker?	Why does the lawyer make this request? What is his opinion of humanity at this point?
4. Why is the banker unhappy about having to pay the bet? What does he intend to do? What stops him from committing this act?	What is the banker's attitude toward the lawyer when he goes to the lodge? What is his attitude when he leaves the lodge? What accounts for this change of attitude?

SYNTHESIZING

5. At the beginning of the story, the banker says that the death penalty is more humane than life imprisonment. The lawyer disagrees, saying that any life is better than no life. At the end of the story, does either man agree with the opinion he expressed at the beginning of the story? Explain.

ANSWERS FOR REVIEWING THE SELECTION (CONT.)

3. **Recalling.** The lawyer studies languages, religion, and history. He gives his jailer a note written in six languages and asks him to have it reviewed by experts. He requests that a shot be fired in the garden if his efforts are successful. **Interpreting.** The lawyer is searching connection with the outside world. He has a positive attitude toward humanity.

4. **Recalling.** The banker will be ruined financially if he has to pay the bet. He plans to kill the lawyer but does not do so because he discovers that the lawyer plans to break their contract. **Interpreting.** The banker feels hatred toward the lawyer when he enters the lodge. After reading the note, he is grateful to the lawyer because he will not be ruined. He now feels contempt for himself as he recognizes how petty and materialistic he is. He feels shame for having been willing to kill the lawyer to protect (cont.)

Understanding Literature (Questions for Discussion)

1. **Simile.** A **simile** is a comparison using *like* or *as.* What simile is used to describe the lawyer's reading habits during the last two years of his confinement? What does this simile reveal about his state of mind at the end of his confinement?
2. **Motivation.** A **motivation** is a force that moves a character to think, feel, or behave in a certain way. What motivation causes the banker to make the bet and go through with it? What is the lawyer's motivation for accepting the bet? Are the actions that result from these motivations what the characters expect? What motivates the lawyer to end the bet as he does?

Responding in Writing

1. **Creative Writing: Interview.** Imagine that you are a reporter who has been granted an exclusive interview with the lawyer after he leaves his solitary confinement. What would you want to know about the bet, about his confinement, and about his future plans? Create a series of questions that you would ask the ex-prisoner. Then write the lawyer's responses. When deciding how the lawyer would answer the questions, consider aspects of his character and his attitudes as they are revealed in the story and how these things would affect his thoughts and actions. After you have written responses to the questions, you may wish to reorder some of the questions, or add transitions between the questions to make the interview more fluid.
2. **Critical Essay: Reactions to a Character.** Is the lawyer in "The Bet" a sympathetic character? What is your opinion of him at the beginning of the story? What is your opinion of him at the end of the story? What accounts for your responses? Write a persuasive essay in which you defend the lawyer as a sympathetic character or condemn him as unworthy of sympathy. In either case, present your position in a thesis statement, support it with references to the story, and come to a conclusion in a final paragraph.

Speaking and Listening Skills

Discussion. The bet the banker makes arises from a discussion of capital punishment. Take time to explore and research this moral and legal issue. Consider responses to such questions as these: Should the death penalty be used? If so, when? If not, what alternatives should be used? Then, in small groups, discuss the issue of capital punishment. Be respectful of the opinions of others, and listen actively when you are not speaking. Before you begin, review the Language Arts Survey 3.2, "Active Listening and Interpersonal Communication," and 3.3, "Collaborative Learning and Discussion."

ANSWERS FOR UNDERSTANDING LITERATURE

Responses will vary. Possible responses are given.

1. Simile. The lawyer's reading habits are compared to the actions of a drowning person grasping at first one bit of wreckage and then another in an attempt to save himself or herself. The simile suggests that the lawyer is floundering in his beliefs and understandings. He is searching for answers or direction.

2. Motivation. The banker is motivated by impulsiveness and pride. The lawyer is motivated by greed. The banker did not expect his rash wager to fail, nor did he expect the the payoff to undo him. The lawyer expects to put aside fifteen years of his life, but to have a great deal of money with which to enjoy himself afterward. When he makes the bet he does not expect to come to terms with his greed, nor does he expect to find failings in humanity. He loses the innocence and optimism that he has about life at the beginning of the story.

ANALYTIC SCALES FOR RESPONDING IN WRITING

Grading scales for Responding in Writing appear on pages 953 and 954.

ANSWERS FOR SKILLS ACTIVITIES

SPEAKING AND LISTENING SKILLS

Evaluate the ways in which students present their opinions and listen actively to one another. On the chalkboard keep track of interesting points made by students.

▶ Additional practice is provided in the Essential Skills Practice Book: Speaking and Listening 3.2 and 3.3.

ANSWERS FOR REVIEWING THE SELECTION (CONT.)

his own material wealth.

SYNTHESIZING

Responses will vary. Possible responses are given.

The banker, seeing the pitiable state of the lawyer at the end of the story, may still agree with his earlier opinion that the death penalty is more humane than imprisonment. The lawyer, who once expressed the opinion that any life is better than no life, seems contemptuous of life and human endeavors. While the banker may prefer the death penalty because he feels the effects of life imprisonment are inhumane, the lawyer may now prefer the death penalty because he sees life as useless and futile.

ADDITIONAL RESOURCES

READER'S GUIDE

- Selection Worksheet 11.8

ASSESSMENT PORTFOLIO

- Selection Check Test 2.11.15
- Selection Test 2.11.16

ESSENTIAL SKILLS PRACTICE BOOKS

- Writing 1.8, 1.20

PREREADING EXTENSIONS

Students might be interested to know that when *Cyrano de Bergerac* made its first appearance on stage, it was presented for five hundred consecutive performances and quickly became the most popular play of the era. There has hardly ever been a time when it is not being performed, in some form, somewhere in the world.

As they read, students should think about why the themes presented in this play are so timeless and so popular.

SUPPORT FOR LEP STUDENTS

PRONUNCIATIONS OF PROPER NOUNS AND ADJECTIVES

Cyr • an • o de Ber • ge • rac (sir´ə nō de bʉr´zhə rak)
The Du • en • na (do͞o en´ ə)
De Guiche (də gēsh´)
Ra • gue • neau (rä gə nō´)
Rox • ane (räks än´)

ADDITIONAL VOCABULARY

besiege—attack
lunacy—craziness
minuet—type of ballroom music and dance
Musketeer—soldier armed with a musket, which is a type of gun
serenade—musical performance outdoors at night, often given beneath the window of one's sweetheart
wager—bet

PREREADING

from *Cyrano de Bergerac*
by Edmond Rostand, translated by Brian Hooker

About the Author

EDMOND ROSTAND
1868–1918

Born in Marseilles, France, **Edmond Rostand** showed an interest in poetry and theater at an early age, but, encouraged by his father, he studied law. Although he earned a legal degree and was admitted to the bar, as an adult Rostand devoted himself to his early passion—writing. His first play was produced in 1888, and a collection of his poetry was published in 1890. His greatest play, *Cyrano de Bergerac,* a romantic five-act drama in verse, was produced in 1898, drawing crowds first in France and then throughout Europe and the United States. Many of the finest actors of Rostand's day, including Sarah Bernhardt and Constant Coquelin, appeared in his plays. Rostand's last work for the theater, *The Last Night of Don Juan,* was produced in 1922, four years after his death.

About the Selection

Cyrano de Bergerac is a very late example of French Romantic drama. Audiences of Rostand's day were used to seeing bleak and serious works, so Rostand's exuberant return to Romanticism excited audiences—the play was emotionally charged and featured a passionate and struggling hero. Since its debut, theatergoers have considered *Cyrano de Bergerac* one of the greatest love stories ever written. The play achieves a remarkable balance between comic and tragic moments as it examines the relationship between love and physical beauty.

Set in France in 1640, the drama centers around Cyrano, a poet and a soldier, a man who is equally agile with the pen and the sword. Although Cyrano's skills make him attractive, he has a problem—a nose so enormous it can be considered a deformity. In the selection that you are about to read, you will discover Cyrano's deep love for the beautiful Roxane, who is being courted by a handsome fool named Christian. Cyrano, believing that his looks would prevent him from winning Roxane's love, agrees to assist Christian in his courtship, supplying him with the poetic words with which to win her heart. Cyrano experiences the pleasure of knowing that his words spark Roxane's love but the pain of seeing Roxane's heart won by another man.

CONNECTIONS: Notable Noses

Both Cyrano and the main character in Ryunosuke's "The Nose" (see page 92) are concerned with the size of their noses. Cyrano believes his nose to be so unsightly that he lets it stand in the way of expressing his love for Roxane. Not everyone has expressed such a negative attitude toward large noses. For example, Napoleon Bonaparte said, "Give me a man with a good allowance of nose . . . When I want any good headwork done, I always choose a man, if suitable otherwise, with a long nose." Cyrano himself at one point remarks, "A big nose is the mark of a man affable, good, courteous, witty, liberal, brave, such as I am."

GOALS/OBJECTIVES

Studying this lesson will enable students to

- appreciate a famous French Romantic drama
- discuss the life and work of Edmond Rostand
- define the literary terms *irony, dramatic irony,* and *theme*
- write an original dramatic continuation of *Cyrano de Bergerac*
- write a critical essay that analyzes an important speech in *Cyrano de Bergerac*
- practice the art of improvisation

READER'S JOURNAL

Imagine that two people are in love with you. The first person is not physically beautiful but is very entertaining, intelligent, and imaginative. The second person is outwardly beautiful but foolish and boring. Whom would you choose? Explain why.

FROM

Cyrano de Bergerac

EDMOND ROSTAND, TRANSLATED BY BRIAN HOOKER

Characters in *Cyrano de Bergerac*

The Duenna Roxane's chaperone
Ragueneau a poet and a pastry chef
Roxane woman loved by Cyrano, Christian, and De Guiche
Cyrano main character
Pages
De Guiche Colonel in love with Roxane
Christian beautiful but foolish suitor of Roxane
Capuchin a priest

ACT III
ROXANE'S KISS

A little square in the old Marais: old houses, and a glimpse of narrow streets. On the right, the House of ROXANE *and her garden wall, overhung with tall shrubbery. Over the door of the house a balcony and a tall window; to one side of the door, a bench.*

Ivy clings to the wall; jasmine[1] *embraces the balcony, trembles, and falls away.*

By the bench and the jutting stonework of the wall one might easily climb up to the balcony.

➊ *What might one easily do?*

Opposite, an ancient house of the like character, brick and stone, whose front door forms an entrance. The knocker on this door is tied up in linen like an injured thumb.

At the Curtain Rise the DUENNA *is seated on the bench beside the door. The window is wide open on* ROXANE*'s balcony; a light within suggests that it is early evening. By the* DUENNA *stands* RAGUENEAU *dressed in what might be the livery*[2] *of one attached to the household. He is by way of telling her something, and wiping his eyes meanwhile.*

RAGUENEAU: —And so she ran off with a Musketeer!
I was ruined—I was alone—Remained
Nothing for me to do but hang myself,
So I did that. Presently along comes
Monsieur de Bergerac, and cuts me down,

1. **jasmine.** Plant with fragrant, colorful flowers
2. **livery.** Identifying uniform; characteristic dress or appearance

READER'S JOURNAL

As an alternate activity, you might ask students to discuss in their journals why it is not wise to place too much importance on popular standards of physical beauty.

ANSWERS TO GUIDED READING QUESTIONS

➊ One might easily climb up to Roxane's balcony.

SPELLING AND VOCABULARY WORDS FROM THE SELECTION

forlorn
gaudy
languidly
reverie
rhapsodize

QUOTABLES

"The perception of beauty is a moral test."

—Henry David Thoreau
Journal

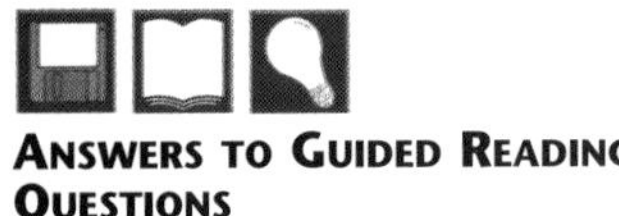

Answers to Guided Reading Questions

➊ They are planning to attend a formal discussion about love.

Cross-curricular Activities

ARTS AND HUMANITIES

Explain to students that the theorbos, the seventeenth-century stringed instrument with two necks played by Cyrano, is a type of lute. The lute was at the height of its popularity in western Europe throughout the sixteenth century and in the early seventeenth century. During this time, a great deal of music was composed and published for the lute. There were many amateur lute players, and professional players were associated with all the great courts and houses.

- Students who are interested in music might like to go to a library or music store to locate recordings of chamber music or other types of music written for the lute and related instruments of the same era. Listen to these recordings in class. You might have students freewrite as they listen.
- Students who are musically inclined might want to play or dance to some of the music of this period.

And makes me steward to his cousin.

The Duenna: Ruined?—
I thought your pastry was a great success!

Ragueneau: (*Shakes his head.*) Lise loved the soldiers, and I loved the poets—
Mars ate up all the cakes Apollo left;
It did not take long. . .

The Duenna: (*Calls up to window.*) Roxane! Are you ready?
We are late!

Voice of Roxane: (*Within.*) Putting on my cape—

➊ *What are the duenna and Roxane planning to attend?*

The Duenna: (*To* Ragueneau, *indicating the house opposite.*) Clomire
Across the way receives on Thursday nights—
We are to have a psycho-colloquy
Upon the Tender Passion.[3]

Ragueneau: Ah—the Tender . . .

The Duenna: (*Sighs.*) —Passion! . . .
(*Calls up to window.*) Roxane!—Hurry, dear—we shall miss
The Tender Passion!

Roxane: Coming!—

(*Music of stringed instruments off-stage approaching.*)

The Voice of Cyrano: (*Singing.*) La, la, la!—

The Duenna: A serenade?—How pleasant—

Cyrano: No, no, no!—
F natural,[4] you natural born fool!

(*Enters, followed by two* Pages, *carrying theorbos.*[5])

First Page: (*Ironically.*) No doubt your honor knows F natural
When he hears—

Cyrano: I am a musician, infant!—
A pupil of Gassendi.

The Page: (*Plays and sings.*) La, la,—

Cyrano: Here—
Give me that— (*He snatches the instrument from the* Page *and continues the tune.*)
La, la, la—

Roxane: (*Appears on the balcony.*) Is that you,
Cyrano?

Cyrano: (*Singing.*) I, who praise your lilies fair,
But long to love your ro . . . ses!

---

3. **psycho-colloquy . . . Passion.** Formal discussion on the subject of love
4. **F natural.** Musical term referring to the key of the music
5. **theorbos.** Large, seventeenth-century stringed instruments with two necks and two sets of strings

Photo: Gerry Goodstein. Huntington Theatre Company

ROXANE: I'll be down—
Wait!— (*Goes in through window.*)

THE DUENNA: Did you train these virtuosi?[6]

CYRANO: No—
I won them on a bet from D'Assoucy.
We were debating a fine point of grammar
When, pointing out these two young nightingales
Dressed up like peacocks, with their instruments,
He cries: "No, but I know! I'll wager you
A day of music." Well, of course he lost;
And so until to-morrow they are mine,
My private orchestra. Pleasant at first,
But they become a trifle— (*To the* PAGES.)
Here! Go play
A minuet to Montfleury—and tell him
I sent you!

(*The* PAGES *go up to the exit.* CYRANO *turns to the* DUENNA.)

How did Cyrano acquire the pair of musicians?

6. **virtuosi.** People displaying great technical skill in some fine art, especially in the performance of music

ANSWERS TO GUIDED READING QUESTIONS

1 Cyrano acquired them from a man named D'Assoucy in a bet about a point of grammar.

QUOTABLES

"Music, the greatest good that mortals know,
And all of heaven that we have below."

—Joseph Addison, "Song for St. Cecilia's Day"

"If music be the food of love, play on;
Give me excess of it, that, surfeiting,
The appetite may sicken, and so die."

—William Shakespeare, *Twelfth Night*

ADDITIONAL QUESTIONS AND ACTIVITIES

In this selection, Cyrano says that he won the services of two musicians because he correctly answered a question about proper grammar. As a class, form two teams. Each team should make a list of questions about proper grammar, using the Language Arts Survey as a reference. Each team should then pose its questions to the other. The team that answers the most questions correctly can request that the losing team sing whatever song the winning team desires.

Answers to Guided Reading Questions

❶ Cyrano has come to ask Roxane about their friend.

❷ Roxane loves the fact that Christian is beautiful, but she seems more impressed with the things he says and writes.

❸ Roxane accuses Cyrano of being jealous of Christian's poetry.

Additional Questions and Activities

The music discussed in this selection is reflective of the period in which the play is set and the class of people featured in the play. Ask students to discuss contemporary music. If they were to write a play about life set in their high school, what types of music, art, clothing, and other examples of popular culture would be featured to characterize different types of students in their high school and to familiarize audiences with their era?

❶ *Why has Cyrano come?*

I came here as usual
To inquire after our friend—

(*To* PAGES.)

Play out of tune.
And keep on playing!

(*The* PAGES *go out. He turns to the* DUENNA.)

Our friend with the great soul.

❷ *What does Roxane love about Christian?*

ROXANE: (*Enters in time to hear the last words.*) He is beautiful and brilliant—and I love him!

CYRANO: Do you find Christian . . . intellectual?

ROXANE: More so than you, even.

CYRANO: I am glad.

ROXANE: No man
Ever so beautifully said those things—
Those pretty nothings that are everything.
Sometimes he falls into a reverie;
His inspiration fails—then all at once,
He will say something absolutely . . . Oh! . . .

CYRANO: Really!

ROXANE: How like a man! You think a man
Who has a handsome face must be a fool.

CYRANO: He talks well about . . . matters of the heart?

ROXANE: He does not *talk*; he rhapsodizes . . . dreams . . .

CYRANO: (*Twisting his moustache.*) He . . . writes well?

ROXANE: Wonderfully. Listen now:
(*Reciting as from memory.*)
"Take my heart; I shall have it all the more;
Plucking the flowers, we keep the plant in bloom—"
Well?

CYRANO: Pooh!

ROXANE: And this:
"Knowing you have in store
More heart to give than I to find heart-room—"

CYRANO: First he has too much, then too little; just
How much heart does he need?

❸ *Of what does Roxane accuse Cyrano?*

ROXANE: (*Tapping her foot.*) You are teasing me!
You are jealous!

WORDS FOR EVERYDAY USE

rev • er • ie (rev´ər ē) *n.,* dreamy thinking or imagining; daydreaming

rhap • so • dize (rap´sə dīz´) *vi.,* speak or write in an extravagantly enthusiastic manner

Vocabulary in Context

- Jean's reverie in class kept him from hearing the full lesson.
- Josh was so impressed with the beauty of the opera singer's voice that he rhapsodized about it for hours.

CYRANO: (*Startled.*) Jealous?

ROXANE: Of his poetry—
You poets are like that . . .
And these last lines
Are they not the last word in tenderness?—
"There is no more to say: only believe
That unto you my whole heart gives one cry,
And writing, writes down more than you receive;
Sending you kisses through my finger-tips—
Lady, O read my letter with your lips!"

CYRANO: H'm, yes— those last lines . . . but he overwrites!

ROXANE: Listen to this—

CYRANO: You know them all by heart?

ROXANE: Every one!

CYRANO: (*Twisting his moustache.*) I may call that flattering . . .

ROXANE: He is a master!

CYRANO: Oh—come!

ROXANE: Yes—a master!

CYRANO: (*Bowing.*) A master—if you will!

THE DUENNA: (*Comes down stage quickly.*) Monsieur de Guiche!—
(*To* CYRANO, *pushing him toward the house.*)
Go inside—If he does not find you here,
It may be just as well. He may suspect—

ROXANE: —My secret! Yes; he is in love with me
And he is powerful. Let him not know—
One look would frost my roses before bloom.

CYRANO: (*Going into house.*) Very well, very well!

ROXANE: (*To* DE GUICHE, *as he enters.*) We were just going—

DE GUICHE: I came only to say farewell.

ROXANE: You leave
Paris?

DE GUICHE: Yes—for the front.

ROXANE: Ah!

DE GUICHE: And to-night!

ROXANE: Ah!

DE GUICHE: We have orders to besiege Arras.[7]

ROXANE: Arras?

DE GUICHE: Yes. My departure leaves you . . . cold?

ROXANE: (*Politely.*) Oh! Not that.

DE GUICHE: It has left me desolate—

7. **Arras.** City in France

❶ *What does Cyrano say about the writing in general? What does he say when he learns that Roxane has memorized the lines?*

❷ *How does Roxane feel about De Guiche's love for her?*

❸ *How does Roxane feel about the thought of De Guiche leaving to go to war?*

ANSWERS TO GUIDED READING QUESTIONS

❶ Cyrano says that it is overwritten. When he learns that Roxane has memorized the lines he says, "I may call that flattering."

❷ Roxane does not return De Guiche's love, but she does not want him to know that she loves another.

❸ Roxane is indifferent.

LITERARY TECHNIQUE

DIALOGUE

Explain to students that dialogue is conversation involving two or more people or characters, and that plays are made up of dialogue and stage directions. Tell them that when reading a play, it is important to pay close attention to both dialogue and stage directions in order to learn about the characters and their relationships.

Ask students to look closely at the dialogue between Roxane and Cyrano on this page. As Roxane talks freely and innocently about her love for Christian and his beautiful verse, the reader can sense the hidden meaning in Cyrano's responses and questions. Naturally, he is curious to hear her opinion of Christian's writing, which is really his writing, but he cannot raise suspicion by acting too curious or by praising Christian's work.

ANSWERS TO GUIDED READING QUESTIONS

1 Roxane is overcome with anxiety. De Guiche believes that Roxane is concerned because he is going off to war.

HISTORICAL NOTE

Explain to students that the war under discussion in *Cyrano de Bergerac* is the Thirty Years' War, a series of early seventeenth-century political and religious wars. The wars began in Germany and were rooted in conflicts between German Catholics and German Protestants. Eventually the European countries of France, Spain, Sweden, Denmark, and Austria became involved.

The Peace of Westphalia ended the war in 1648, but there were no definite winners or losers. The treaty did state, however, that German rulers could decide if their individual states were to be Catholic or Protestant.

CROSS-CURRICULAR ACTIVITIES

SOCIAL STUDIES

Some students might want to research conflicts between Catholics and Protestants throughout history and then present their findings to the rest of the class.

When shall I see you? Ever? Did you know
I was made Colonel?

ROXANE: (*Indifferent.*) Bravo.

DE GUICHE: Regiment
Of the Guards.

ROXANE: (*Catching her breath.*) Of the Guards?—

DE GUICHE: *His* regiment
Your cousin,[8] the mighty man of words!—
(*Grimly.*) Down there
We may have an accounting!

ROXANE: (*Suffocating.*) Are you sure
The Guards are ordered?

DE GUICHE: Under my command!

1 *How does Roxane feel when she learns that Christian is also going off to war? How does De Guiche interpret her reaction?*

ROXANE: (*Sinks down, breathless, on the bench; aside.*)
Christian![9]—

DE GUICHE: What is it?

ROXANE: (*Losing control of herself.*) To the war—perhaps
Never again to—When a woman cares,
Is that nothing?

DE GUICHE: (*Surprised and delighted.*) You say this now—to me—
Now, at the very moment?—

ROXANE: (*Recovers—changes her tone.*) Tell me something:
My cousin—You say you mean to be revenged
On him. Do you mean that?

DE GUICHE: (*Smiles.*) Why? Would you care?

ROXANE: Not for him.

DE GUICHE: Do you see him?

ROXANE: Now and then.

DE GUICHE: He goes about everywhere nowadays
With one of the Cadets—de Neuve—Neuville—
Neuvillers[10]—

ROXANE: (*Coolly.*) A tall man?—

DE GUICHE: Blond—

ROXANE: Rosy cheeks?—

DE GUICHE: Handsome!—

ROXANE: Pooh!—

DE GUICHE: And a fool.

---

8. **cousin.** Cyrano is Roxane's cousin. It was not uncommon for cousins to marry.
9. **Christian.** Both Christian and Cyrano are members of the Regiment of the Guards who have been ordered to besiege the French city of Arras.
10. **Cadets . . . Neuvillers.** De Guiche is referring to Christian

ROXANE: (*Languidly.*) So he appears . . .
(*Animated.*) But Cyrano? What will you do to him?
Order him into danger? He loves that!
I know what *I* should do.

DE GUICHE: What?

ROXANE: Leave him here
With his Cadets, while all the regiment
Goes on to glory! That would torture him—
To sit all through the war with folded arms—
I know his nature. If you hate that man,
Strike at his self-esteem.

DE GUICHE: Oh woman—woman!
Who but a woman would have thought of this?

ROXANE: He'll eat his heart out, while his Gascon[11] friends
Bite their nails all day long in Paris here.
And you will be avenged!

DE GUICHE: You love me then,
A little? . . .
(*She smiles.*) Making my enemies your own,
Hating them—I should like to see in that
A sign of love, Roxane.

ROXANE: Perhaps it is one . . .

DE GUICHE: (*Shows a number of folded despatches.*) Here are the orders—for each company—
Ready to send . . .
(*Selects one.*) So—This is for the Guards—
I'll keep that. Aha, Cyrano!
(*To* ROXANE.) You too,
You play your little games, do you?

ROXANE: (*Watching him.*) Sometimes . . .

DE GUICHE: (*Close to her, speaking hurriedly.*) And you!—Oh, I am mad over you!—Listen—
I leave to-night—but—let you through my hands
Now, when I feel you trembling?—Listen—Close by,
In the Rue d'Orléans, the Capuchins[12]

❶ *What does Roxane try to convince De Guiche to do? Why does she do this?*

❷ *In what way does De Guiche interpret Roxane's plan?*

11. **Gascon.** Refers to Cyrano's regiment
12. **Capuchins.** Members of a branch of the Roman Catholic Franciscan order, founded by St. Frances of Assisi in 1209

WORDS FOR EVERYDAY USE

lan • guid • ly (laŋ´gwid lē) *adv.,* without vigor or vitality; listlessly, indifferently

ANSWERS TO GUIDED READING QUESTIONS

❶ Roxane tries to convince De Guiche that the best way to revenge himself upon Cyrano would be to prevent him from going off to battle with the regiment. She is trying to protect Christian, who is in Cyrano's group of cadets.

❷ De Guiche believes that Roxane is really trying to injure Cyrano, so he sees her actions as a sign of her love for him.

ADDITIONAL QUESTIONS AND ACTIVITIES

Ask students the the following questions to make sure that they understand the subtle exchange between De Guiche and Roxane:

1. Who is De Guiche? What is his job?
2. Why is Roxane suddenly interested in what De Guiche has to say?

ANSWERS

Responses will vary.

1. De Guiche is the colonel of the regiment of the guards, the regiment to which Cyrano and Christian belong.
2. Roxane is upset when she hears from De Guiche that Christian will be going to war, and wants to use De Guiche's power to stop this from happening.

VOCABULARY IN CONTEXT

• On the hot afternoon, the children rested languidly in the hammock.

Answers to Guided Reading Questions

1 By pretending to side with De Guiche, she has prevented Christian from being sent to war.

2 She pretends to love De Guiche so that he will go off to war and leave Cyrano, and hence Christian, behind.

3 Roxane thinks that Cyrano would be very angry if he discovered she prevented him from going off to war.

Additional Questions and Activities

Ask students to answer the following question:

What can you tell about the character of Roxane, based on what she values in Christian and on the way she is able to manipulate De Guiche?

ANSWERS

Responses will vary.

Students might say that Roxane is smart, romantic, clever, and hard to please. She seems smart and romantic because she values Christian's poetic skills as well as his good looks. She seems demanding and hard to please because Cyrano is not able to win her love for him because of his outlandish nose. Roxane's cleverness shows when she easily manipulates De Guiche to get what she wants.

Have their new convent. By their law, no layman[13]
May pass inside those walls. I'll see to that—
Their sleeves are wide enough to cover me—
The servants of my Uncle-Cardinal
Will fear his nephew. So—I'll come to you
Masked, after everyone knows I have gone—
Oh, let me wait one day!—

ROXANE: If this be known,
Your honor—

DE GUICHE: Bah!

ROXANE: The war—your duty—

DE GUICHE: (*Blows away an imaginary feather.*) Phoo!—
Only say yes!

ROXANE: No!

DE GUICHE: Whisper. . .

ROXANE: (*Tenderly.*) I ought not
To let you . . .

DE GUICHE: Ah! . . .

1 *What has Roxane accomplished by pretending to side with De Guiche in his dispute with Cyrano?*

ROXANE: (*Pretends to break down.*) Ah, go!
(*Aside.*) —Christian remains—
(*Aloud—heroically.*) I must have you a hero—Antoine . . .

DE GUICHE: Heaven! . . .
So you can love—

2 *Why does Roxane pretend to love De Guiche?*

ROXANE: One for whose sake I fear.

DE GUICHE: (*Triumphant.*) I go! Will that content you? (*Kisses her hand.*)

ROXANE: Yes—my friend!

He goes out.

THE DUENNA: (*As* DE GUICHE *disappears, making a deep curtsey behind his back, and imitating Roxane's intense tone.*) Yes—my friend!

3 *How does Roxane think Cyrano would feel if he knew what she has done?*

ROXANE: (*Quickly, close to her.*) Not a word to Cyrano—
He would never forgive me if he knew
I stole his war!
(*She calls toward the house.*) Cousin!

(CYRANO *comes out of the house; she turns to him, indicating the house opposite.*)

We are going over—
Alcandre speaks to-night—and Lysimon.

THE DUENNA: (*Puts finger in her ear.*) My little finger says we shall not hear
Everything.

CYRANO: Never mind me—

13. **layman.** Person who is not a member of the clergy

THE DUENNA: (*Across the street.*) Look—Oh, look!
The knocker tied up in a napkin—Yes,
They muzzled you because you bark too loud
And interrupt the lecture—little beast!

ROXANE: (*As the door opens.*) Enter . . .
(*To* CYRANO.) If Christian comes, tell him to wait.

CYRANO: Oh—
Roxane returns.
When he comes, what will you talk about?
You always know beforehand.

ROXANE: About . . .

CYRANO: Well?

ROXANE: You will not tell him, will you?

CYRANO: I am dumb.

ROXANE: About nothing! Or about everything—
I shall say: "Speak of love in your own words—
Improvise! Rhapsodize! Be eloquent!"

CYRANO: (*Smiling.*) Good!

ROXANE: Sh!—

CYRANO: Sh!—

ROXANE: Not a word!
She goes in; the door closes.

CYRANO: (*Bowing.*) Thank you so much—

ROXANE: (*Opens door and puts out her head.*)
He must be unprepared—

CYRANO: Of course!

ROXANE: Sh!—
Goes in again.

CYRANO: (*Calls.*) Christian!
(CHRISTIAN *enters.*) I have your theme—bring on your memory!—
Here is your chance now to surpass yourself,
No time to lose—Come! Look intelligent—
Come home and learn your lines.

1 What does Cyrano tell Christian to do?

CHRISTIAN: No.

CYRANO: What?

CHRISTIAN: I'll wait
Here for Roxane.

CYRANO: What lunacy is this?
Come quickly!

CHRISTIAN: No, I say! I have had enough—
Taking my words, my letters, all from you—

ANSWERS TO GUIDED READING QUESTIONS

1 Cyrano tells Christian to memorize his lines to say to Roxane and to look "intelligent."

LITERARY TECHNIQUE

IRONY

Tell students that **irony** is the difference between appearance and reality, and that **dramatic irony** occurs when something is known by the reader or audience but is unknown by a character or characters.

Point out to students the subtle irony in Roxanne's statement about Christian on this page:

"I shall say (to Christian) 'Speak of love in your own words—Improvise! Rhapsodize! Be eloquent!'"

She does not know that her request is impossible because when he speaks to her in verse, he is not using his own words.

Answers to Guided Reading Questions

❶ Christian does not want to use Cyrano's words to woo Roxane anymore. He does not want to do this because Roxane has come to love him and their relationship is on the verge of becoming more serious.

❷ Christian decides that he would like Cyrano to stay and help him. Cyrano leaves, telling Christian to speak for himself, probably because he is jealous of Christian and it is painful to watch them together.

❸ Roxane is unhappy with the way Christian speaks of love. She wants him to be more eloquent.

Additional Questions and Activities

Ask students to answer the following questions:

1. What kind of a person is Christian? What does the fact that he no longer believes he needs Cyrano tell you about his character?

2. How might Christian be feeling as he hears Roxane's reaction to his personal words of love?

ANSWERS

Responses will vary.

1. Christian seems to be a simple, perhaps overly confident person. When he realizes that Roxane has strong feelings of love for him, he no longer wants to use Cyrano's poetry to impress her.

2. Students might imagine that Christian probably feels frustration and disappointment when Roxane reject his own words.

❶ *What doesn't Christian want to do anymore? Why doesn't he want to do this?*

Making our love a little comedy!
It was a game at first; but now—she cares . . .
Thanks to you. I am not afraid. I'll speak
For myself now.

CYRANO: Undoubtedly!

CHRISTIAN: I will!
Why not? I am no such fool—you shall see!
Besides—my dear friend—you have taught me much.
I ought to know something . . . By God, I know
Enough to take a woman in my arms!

❷ *What does Christian decide once he sees Roxane? What does Cyrano do? Why?*

ROXANE *appears is the doorway, opposite.*
There she is now . . . Cyrano, wait! Stay here!

CYRANO: (*Bows.*) Speak for yourself, my friend! *He goes out.*

ROXANE: (*Taking leave of the company.*) —Barthénoide!
Alcandre! . . . Grémione! . . .

THE DUENNA: I told you so—
We missed the Tender Passion! *She goes into* ROXANE'S *house.*

ROXANE: Urimédonte!—
Adieu![14]
(*As the guest disappear down the street, she turns to* CHRISTIAN.)
Is that you, Christian? Let us stay
Here, in the twilight. They are gone. The air
Is fragrant. We shall be alone. Sit down
There—so . . .
(*They sit on the bench.*) Now tell me things.

CHRISTIAN: (*After a silence.*) I love you.

ROXANE: (*Closes her eyes.*) Yes,
Speak to me about love . . .

❸ *How does Roxane react to Christian's words of love when he speaks without Cyrano's help?*

CHRISTIAN: I love you.

ROXANE: Now
Be eloquent!. . .

CHRISTIAN: I love—

ROXANE: (*Opens her eyes.*) You have your theme—
Improvise! Rhapsodize!

CHRISTIAN: I love you so!

ROXANE: Of course. And then? . . .

CHRISTIAN: And then . . . Oh, I should be
So happy if you loved me too! Roxane,
Say that you love me too!

ROXANE: (*Making a face.*) I ask for cream
You give me milk and water. Tell me first
A little, how you love me.

14. **Adieu.** French word meaning "good-bye"

Cross-curricular Activities

ARTS AND HUMANITIES

Ask students to work in pairs to write two poems or personal letters, one in the style of Cyrano and one in the style of Christian.

Before the students in each pair begin writing, they should discuss for a moment what they know of each character's style. In the early pages of the selection, Roxane discusses what she loves about the poetry of Christian, which is actually the poetry of Cyrano. On this page, students begin to hear Christian's attempts at verse after he decides to speak without Cyrano's help.

Students can complete this activity by writing a brief poem or heartfelt personal letter to Roxane in the style of each character. Students may exaggerate each character's style to add humor to their pieces.

Photo: Gerry Goodstein. Huntington Theatre Company

CHRISTIAN: Very much.

ROXANE: Oh—tell me how you *feel*!

CHRISTIAN: (*Coming nearer, and devouring her with his eyes.*) Your throat . . . If only
I might . . . kiss it—

ROXANE: Christian!

CHRISTIAN: I love you so!

ROXANE: (*Makes as if to rise.*) Again?

CHRISTIAN: (*Desperately, restraining her.*) No, not again—I do not love you—

ROXANE: (*Settles back.*) That is better. . . .

CHRISTIAN: I adore you!

ROXANE: Oh!— (*Rises and moves away.*)

CHRISTIAN: I know;

INTEGRATED SKILLS ACTIVITIES

LANGUAGE

Read the following sentences aloud to students, or write them on the chalkboard. Then ask students to rewrite the sentences, adding commas where they are necessary. If students want to review comma usage before they begin the exercise, they can review the Language Arts Survey 2.47, "Using Commas."

1. Christian was to be called to war but Roxane did her best to try to stop him from leaving.

2. Cyrano the poet behind Christian's verses of love likes to hear Roxane's praises of his work.

3. She unfortunately does not know that Cyrano is the true poet.

4. Most people wonder "Would Roxane be angry if she discovered the deception?"

5. It is clear that the men do not trick Roxane as a joke and they do not wish to hurt her.

ANSWERS

1. Christian was to be called to war, but Roxane did her best to try to stop him from leaving.

2. Cyrano, the poet behind Christian's verses of love, likes to hear Roxane's praises of his work.

3. She unfortunately does not know that Cyrano is the true poet.

4. Most people wonder, "Would Roxane be angry if she discovered the deception?"

5. It is clear that the men do not trick Roxane as a joke, and they do not wish to hurt her.

► Additional practice is provided in the Essential Skills Practice Book: Language 2.47.

Answers to Guided Reading Questions

❶ Christian's lack of eloquence is as disgusting to her as ugliness.

❷ Roxane shuts the door in Christian's face because he is unable to speak eloquently of his love for her. He turns to Cyrano for help.

Additional Questions and Activities

Ask students to discuss the following questions:

1. Why is Roxane so upset?
2. Do you think she is being fair to Christian? Why, or why not?
3. If you were Christian, what would you do next?

Answers

Responses will vary.

1. Students might say that Roxane is so upset because she does not understand why Christian refuses to speak to her in the verse she loves so much. She might feel that he is teasing her or that he no longer loves her.
2. Students may say that Roxane is expecting Christian to speak or behave as he has done in the past. Students might suggest that by deceiving Roxane, Christian is being unfair.
3. Christian might reveal his deceit and explain why he did it. He might ask the musicians to play for Roxane. He might try to rhapsodize until Roxane gives up on him.

❶ *To what does Roxane compare Christian's lack of eloquence?*

❷ *Why does Roxane shut the door in Christian's face? To whom does Christian turn for help?*

I grow absurd.

Roxane: (*Coldly.*) And that displeases me
As much as if you had grown ugly.

Christian: I—

Roxane: Gather your dreams together into words!

Christian: I love—

Roxane: I know; you love me. Adieu. *She goes to the house.*

Christian: No,
But wait—please—let me—I was going to say—

Roxane: (*Pushes the door open.*) That you adore me. Yes; I know that too.
No! . . . Go away! . . . *She goes in and shuts the door in his face.*

Christian: I . . . I . . .

Cyrano *enters.*

Cyrano: A great success!

Christian: Help me!

Cyrano: Not I.

Christian: I cannot live unless
She loves me—now, this moment!

Cyrano: How the devil
Am I to teach you now—this moment?

Christian: (*Catches him by the arm.*) —Wait!—
Look! Up there!—Quick— (*The light shows in* Roxane*'s window.*)

Cyrano: Her window—

Christian: (*Wailing.*) I shall die!—

Cyrano: Less noise!

Christian: Oh, I—

Cyrano: It does seem fairly dark—

Christian: (*Excitedly.*) Well?—Well?—Well?—

Cyrano: Let us try what can be done;
It is more than you deserve—stand over there,
Idiot—there!— before the balcony—
Let me stand underneath. I'll whisper you
What to say.

Christian: She may hear—she may—

Cyrano: Less noise!

The Pages *appear up stage.*

First Page: Hep!—

Cyrano: (*Finger to lips.*) Sh!—

First Page: (*Low voice.*) We serenaded Montfleury!—
What next?

CYRANO: Down to the corner of the street—
One this way—and the other over there—
If anybody passes, play a tune!

PAGE: What tune, O musical Philosopher?

CYRANO: Sad for a man, or merry for a woman—
Now go! *The* PAGES *disappear, one toward each corner of the street.*

CYRANO: (*To* CHRISTIAN) Call her!

CHRISTIAN: Roxane!

CYRANO: Wait . . .
(*Gathers up a handful of pebbles.*)
Gravel . . .
(*Throws it at the window.*) There!—

ROXANE: (*Opens the window.*) Who is calling?

CHRISTIAN: I—

ROXANE: Who?

CHRISTIAN: Christian.

ROXANE: You again?

CHRISTIAN: I had to tell you—

CYRANO: (*Under the balcony.*) Good—Keep your voice down.

ROXANE: No. Go away. You tell me nothing.

CHRISTIAN: Please!—

ROXANE: You do not love me any more—

CHRISTIAN: (*To whom* CYRANO *whispers his words*) No—no—
Not any more—I love you . . . evermore . . .
And ever . . . more and more!

ROXANE: (*About to close the window—pauses.*) A little better . . .

CHRISTIAN: (*Same business.*) Love grows and struggles like . . . an angry child . . .
Breaking my heart . . . his cradle . . .

ROXANE: (*Coming out on the balcony.*) Better still—
But . . . such a babe is dangerous; why not
Have smothered it new-born?

CHRISTIAN: (*Same business.*) And so I do . . .
And yet he lives . . . I found . . . as you shall find . . .
This new-born babe . . . an infant . . . Hercules![15]

ROXANE: (*Further forward.*) Good!—

CHRISTIAN: (*Same business.*) Strong enough . . . at birth . . . to strangle those
Two serpents—Doubt and . . . Pride.

ROXANE: (*Leans over balcony.*) Why, very well!

15. **Hercules.** In Greek and Roman mythology, Hercules, the son of the god Zeus and the mortal Alcmene, was renowned for his strength.

❶ *For what purpose does Cyrano use the musicians?*

❷ *Why does Roxane believe that Christian does not love her anymore?*

❸ *How does Christian know what to say to woo Roxane?*

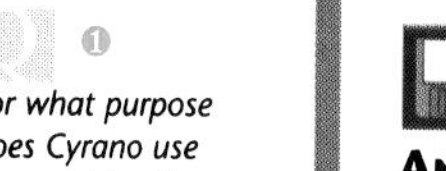

ANSWERS TO GUIDED READING QUESTIONS

❶ He uses them to warn him of the approach of others.

❷ Roxane believes that Christian does not love her anymore because he no longer expresses his love eloquently.

❸ Cyrano whispers the right words to Christian.

CULTURAL/HISTORICAL NOTE

Pages, like those who appear in *Cyrano de Bergerac,* were servants, usually young boys, who worked for people of high rank.

The word *page* as we use it today comes from these early pages. A page today is any person who runs errands or delivers messages, for example, in a government office or hotel. We also use the word *page* as a verb meaning to signal or summon.

LITERARY TECHNIQUE

METAPHOR

Metaphor is a figure of speech in which one thing is spoken or written about as if it were another.

Ask students to reread the following bit of verse that Cyrano secretly recites to Christian as he stands below Roxane's window:

Love grows and struggles like an angry child
Breaking my heart . . . his cradle,

(Roxane asks why he does not smother the dangerous babe, or feeling of love.)

And so I do . . . And yet he lives.
I found as you shall find
This new-born babe an infant Hercules!

Ask students to identify the metaphor in this verse—which compares Christian's feelings of love to a newborn baby of unconquerable strength.

Answers to Guided Reading Questions

❶ Roxane notices that Christian is speaking haltingly. Christian is speaking haltingly because he does not know what to say until Cyrano whispers his line.

❷ Cyrano decides to speak to Roxane himself, imitating Christian's low tone of voice.

❸ Cyrano says that this is his one chance to speak unseen to Roxane. Responses will vary, but students may say that Roxane would be surprised to see Cyrano speaking in Christian's place or that she would be angry to learn how she had been deceived.

Additional Questions and Activities

Ask students to answer the following questions:

Why is Roxane at first still unsatisfied with what she hears from Christian? What does Cyrano say to explain the hesitation in poetic terms?

ANSWERS

She is unsatisfied because he seems to be hesitating. Cyrano says that his words must "grope in darkness to find her" and that they are "heavy with honey."

 ❶

What does Roxane notice? What is the real reason for this?

❷

What does Cyrano decide to do?

Tell me now why you speak so haltingly—
Has your imagination gone lame?

CYRANO: (*Thrusts* CHRISTIAN *under the balcony, and stands in his place.*)
Here—
This grows too difficult!

ROXANE: Your words to-night
Hesitate. Why?

CYRANO: (*In a low tone, imitating* CHRISTIAN.)
Through the warm summer gloom
They grope in darkness toward the light of you.

ROXANE: My words, well aimed, find you more readily.

CYRANO: My heart is open wide and waits for them—
Too large a mark to miss! My words fly home,
Heavy with honey like returning bees,
To your small secret ear. Moreover—yours
Fall to me swiftly. Mine more slowly rise.

ROXANE: Yet not so slowly as they did at first.

CYRANO: They have learned the way, and you have welcomed them.

ROXANE: (*Softly.*) Am I so far above you now?

CYRANO: So far—
If you let fall upon me one hard word,
Out of that height—you crush me!

ROXANE: (*Turns.*) I'll come down—

CYRANO: (*Quickly.*) No!

ROXANE: (*Points out the bench under the balcony.*) Stand you on the bench.
Come nearer!

CYRANO: (*Recoils into the shadow.*) No!—

ROXANE: And why—so great a *No?*

❸

What explanation does Cyrano provide for his hesitation to come closer? What do you think Roxane's reaction would be if Cyrano did allow himself to be seen?

CYRANO: (*More and more overcome by emotion.*) Let me enjoy
The one moment I ever—my one chance
To speak to you . . . unseen!

ROXANE: Unseen?

CYRANO: Yes!—yes . . .
Night, making all things dimly beautiful,
One veil over us both—You only see
The darkness of a long cloak in the gloom,
And I the whiteness of a summer gown—
You are all light—I am all shadow! . . . How
Can you know what this moment means to me?
If I was ever eloquent—

ROXANE: You were
Eloquent—

CYRANO: —You have never heard till now
My own heart speaking!

ROXANE: Why not?

CYRANO: Until now,
I spoke through . . .

ROXANE: Yes?—

CYRANO: —through that sweet drunkenness
You pour into the world out of your eyes!
But to-night . . . but to-night, I indeed speak
For the first time!

ROXANE: For the first time—Your voice,
Even, is not the same.

CYRANO: *(Passionately; moves nearer.)*
How should it be?
I have another voice—my own,
Myself, daring—
(He stops, confused; then tries to recover himself.) Where was I? . . . I forget! . . .
Forgive me. This is all sweet like a dream . . .
Strange—like a dream . . .

ROXANE: How, strange?

CYRANO: Is it not so
To be myself to you, and have no fear
Of moving you to laughter?

ROXANE: Laughter—why?

CYRANO: *(Struggling for an explanation.)* Because . . . What am I . . . What is any man,
That he dare ask for you? Therefore my heart
Hides behind phrases. There's a modesty
In these things too—I come here to pluck down
Out of the sky the evening star—then smile,
And stoop to gather little flowers.

ROXANE: Are they
Not sweet, those little flowers?

CYRANO: Not enough sweet
For you and me, to-night!

ROXANE: *(Breathless.)* You never spoke
To me like this . . .

CYRANO: Little things, pretty things—
Arrows and hearts and torches—roses red,
And violets blue—are these all? Come away,
And breathe fresh air! Must we keep on and on
Sipping stale honey out of tiny cups
Decorated with golden tracery,
Drop by drop, all day long? We are alive;

➊ *What does Cyrano almost admit?*

ANSWERS TO GUIDED READING QUESTIONS

➊ Cyrano almost reveals his identity, his love for Roxane, and the fact that he has been proclaiming his love through Christian.

QUOTABLES

"Oh, what a tangled web we weave,

When first we practice to deceive!"

—Sir Walter Scott
Marmion

"Everything that deceives may be said to enchant."

—Plato
The Republic

ADDITIONAL QUESTIONS AND ACTIVITIES

Ask students to discuss how they feel, at this point in the play, about the deception of Roxane. Do they feel sympathy for her? Why, or why not? Do they feel that Christian should have stopped pretending as soon as he began to notice Roxane's strong feelings of love? Do they understand why Christian does not stop using Cyrano's poetic verses? Do students feel that Cyrano is to blame? What could Cyrano do to correct the situation at this point?

Answers to Guided Reading Questions

① Cyrano says that poetry is a "game of words" that fences or toys with life. He says that Roxane should be able to appreciate the beauty in life for what it is instead of needing it dressed up in romantic words.

Cultural/Historical Note

On this page, Cyrano uses fencing as a metaphor. You might want to give students the following information about fencing:

Fencing, or sword-fighting, is a skill that has been practiced throughout the world for centuries. People used different types of swords in battle or, more commonly, in one-on-one combat known as a duel. After duels were forbidden by law in many places, fencing became a nonfatal sport that remains popular today.

The weapons and rules of modern fencing come from combat fencing of the past. The foil, a light, flexible weapon with a blunted point, was originally used for practice. The epee, or dueling sword, is a straight, narrow weapon without cutting edges. The saber has a flexible, triangular blade with cutting edges.

Fencing matches may be individual, as in a duel, or between teams. Points are made by touching the opponent. Modern fencers wear protective clothing, including heavy canvas jackets, wire-mesh masks, and gloves. Fencing was first developed as a sport by the Germans in the fourteenth century. It was one of the original events in the first modern Olympic games in 1896.

We thirst—Come away, plunge, and drink, and drown
In the great river flowing to the sea!

Roxane: But . . . Poetry?

Cyrano: I have made rimes[16] for you—
Not now—Shall we insult Nature, this night,
These flowers, this moment—shall we set all these
To phrases from a letter by Voiture?
Look once at the high stars that shine in heaven,
And put off artificiality!
Have you not seen great gaudy hothouse flowers,
Barren, without fragrance?—Souls are like that:
Forced to show all, they soon become all show—
The means to Nature's end ends meaningless!

Roxane: But . . . Poetry?

① *According to Cyrano, why should Roxane be more concerned with enjoying love in her life than with hearing it expressed in poetry?*

Cyrano: Love hates that game of words!
It is a crime to fence with life—I tell you,
There comes one moment, once—and God help those
Who pass that moment by!—when Beauty stands
Looking into the soul with grave, sweet eyes
That sicken at pretty words!

Roxane: If that be true—
And when that moment comes to you and me—
What words will you? . . .

Cyrano: All those, all those, all those
That blossom in my heart, I'll fling to you—
Armfuls of loose bloom! Love, I love beyond
Breath, beyond reason, beyond love's own power
Of loving! Your name is like a golden bell
Hung in my heart; and when I think of you,
I tremble, and the bell swings and rings—
"Roxane!" . . .
"Roxane!" . . . along my veins, "Roxane!" . . .
I know
All small forgotten things that once meant You—
I remember last year, the First of May,
A little before noon, you had your hair
Drawn low, that one time only. Is that strange?
You know how, after looking at the sun,

16. **rimes.** Rhymes

Words for Everyday Use

gaud • y (gôd´ē) *adj.,* cheaply brilliant and ornate; bright and showy but lacking in good taste

Vocabulary in Context

• For the costume party, we decorated ourselves with gaudy, fake jewelry.

Photo: Gerry Goodstein. Huntington Theatre Company

One sees red suns everywhere—so, for hours
After the flood of sunshine that you are,
My eyes are blinded by your burning hair!

ROXANE: (*Very low.*) Yes . . . that is . . . Love—

CYRANO: Yes, that is Love—that wind
Of terrible and jealous beauty, blowing
Over me—that dark fire, that music . . .
Yet
Love seeketh not his own! Dear, you may take
My happiness to make you happier,
Even though you never know I gave it you—
Only let me hear sometimes, all alone,
The distant laughter of your joy! . . .
I never
Look at you, but there's some new virtue born
In me, some new courage. Do you begin
To understand, a little? Can you feel
My soul, there in the darkness, breathe on you?
—Oh, but to-night, now, I dare say these things—

1 *What does Cyrano say he is giving Roxane? What does he want in return? Is Cyrano speaking for Christian or for himself?*

Answers to Guided Reading Questions

1 Cyrano says that he is giving Roxane all his happiness to make her happier and only asks to be allowed to hear her laughter in the distance in return. Cyrano is speaking for himself, revealing how he feels about Roxane.

Quotables

"Poetry is the spontaneous overflow of powerful feelings: it takes its origin from emotion recollected in tranquility"

—William Wordsworth, *Lyrical Ballads*

Additional Questions and Activities

Cyrano shares his ideas about poetry with Roxane. A famous quotation by Wordsworth on poetry appears on this page. Invite students to discuss their own ideas about poetry. In their discussion, they might answer the following questions:

What kinds of poetry do you enjoy most? Would you want someone to express his or her feelings of love for you in the form of poetry? Why, or why not?

Literary Note

Cyrano's words, "Love seeketh not his own!" may be an allusion to "The Clod and the Pebble," by William Blake:

Love seeketh not Itself to please,
Nor for itself hath any care;
But for another gives its ease,
And builds a Heaven in Hell's despair.

Answers to Guided Reading Questions

❶ The knowledge that his voice has filled Roxane with love and passion is enough to make him die satisfied.

❷ Christian interrupts Cyrano to ask Roxane for a kiss. Christian says that he wants to take advantage of Roxane's impassioned state.

Additional Questions and Activities

Ask students to discuss the following questions:

What are some of the most vivid images of nature Cyrano uses in the verse at the top of the page? Do you like his romantic verses? Why, or why not?

ANSWERS

Cyrano compares Roxane on her balcony in the dark to a blossom trembling among the leaves. Students will have differing opinions of Cyrano's verses, but they should give reasons for their opinions.

❶ *What makes Cyrano happy enough to die satisfied?*

I . . . to you . . . and you hear them! . . . It is too much!
In my most sweet unreasonable dreams,
I have not hoped for this! Now let me die,
Having lived. It is my voice, mine, my own,
That makes you tremble there in the green gloom
Above me—for you do tremble, as a blossom
Among the leaves—You tremble, and I can feel,
All the way down along these jasmine branches,
Whether you will or no, the passion of you
Trembling . . . (*He kisses wildly the end of a drooping spray of jasmine.*)

ROXANE: Yes, I do tremble . . . and I weep . . .
And I love you . . . and I am yours . . . and you
Have made me thus!

CYRANO: (*After a pause; quietly.*) What is death like, I wonder?
I know everything else now . . .
I have done
This, to you—I, myself . . .
Only let me
Ask one thing more—

❷ *Why does Christian interrupt Cyrano? What reason does he provide for his actions?*

CHRISTIAN: (*Under the balcony.*) One kiss!

ROXANE: (*Startled.*) One?—

CYRANO: (*To* CHRISTIAN.) You! . . .

ROXANE: You ask me
For—

CYRANO: I . . . Yes, but—I mean—
(*To* CHRISTIAN.) You go too far!

CHRISTIAN: She is willing!—Why not make the most of it?

CYRANO: (*To* ROXANE.) I did ask . . . but I know I ask too much . . .

ROXANE: Only one—Is that all?

CYRANO: All!—How much more
Than all!—I know—I frighten you—I ask . . .
I ask you to refuse—

CHRISTIAN: (*To* CYRANO.) But why? Why? Why?

CYRANO: Christian, be quiet!

ROXANE: (*Leaning over.*) What is that you say
To yourself?

CYRANO: I am angry with myself
Because I go too far, and so I say
To myself: "Christian, be quiet!"—
(*The theorbos begin to play.*) Hark—someone
Is coming—

(ROXANE *closes her window.* CYRANO *listens to the theorbos, one of which plays a gay melody, the other a mournful one.*)

Cross-curricular Activities

Some students, working in small groups, might want to rehearse and present parts of the balcony scene involving Christian, Cyrano, and Roxane.

Allow each group to be creative in the way it stages the scene. Tell students that their productions can be as simple or elaborate as they choose. They might want to arrange to have costumes, music, and scenery. Each group might want to feature one student as a narrator. If the class is small enough, you might want to divide the scene among a few groups, so that each group can perform a different part of the scene for the other members of the class.

If you have a large class, you might choose to have the class perform the entire play.

A sad tune, a merry tune—
Man, woman—what do they mean?—
(*A* CAPUCHIN *enters; he carries a lantern, and goes from house to house, looking at the doors.*)
Aha!—a priest!
(*To the* CAPUCHIN.) What is this new game of Diogenes?

THE CAPUCHIN: I am looking for the house of Madame—

CHRISTIAN: (*Impatient.*) Bah!—

THE CAPUCHIN: Madeleine Robin—

CHRISTIAN: What does he want?

CYRANO: (*To the* CAPUCHIN; *points out a street.*) This way—
To the right—keep to the right—

THE CAPUCHIN: I thank you, sir!—
I'll say my beads for you to the last grain.

CYRANO: Good fortune, father, and my service to you!

The CAPUCHIN *goes out.*

CHRISTIAN: Win me that kiss!

CYRANO: No.

CHRISTIAN: Sooner or later—

CYRANO: True . . .
That is true . . . Soon or late, it will be so
Because you are young and she is beautiful—
(*To himself.*) Since it must be, I had rather be myself
(*The window re-opens.* CHRISTIAN *hides under the balcony.*) The cause of . . . what must be.

1 *What is Cyrano's real reason for refusing to win Christian a kiss?*

2 *What reason does Cyrano provide for all his aid to Christian in his pursuit of Roxane?*

ROXANE: (*Out on the balcony.*) Are you still there?
We were speaking of—

CYRANO: A kiss. The word is sweet—
What will the deed be? Are your lips afraid
Even of its burning name? Not much afraid—
Not too much! Have you not unwittingly
Laid aside laughter, slipping beyond speech
Insensibly, already, without fear,
From words to smiles . . . from smiles to sighs . . . from sighing,
Even to tears? One step more—only one—
From a tear to a kiss—one step, one thrill!

ROXANE: Hush—

CYRANO: And what is a kiss, when all is done?
A promise given under seal—a vow
Taken before the shrine of memory—
A signature acknowledged—a rosy dot
Over the i of Loving—a secret whispered
To listening lips apart—a moment made

ANSWERS TO GUIDED READING QUESTIONS

1 Cyrano loves Roxane and seeing Christian kiss her would wound him.

2 Cyrano believes that Christian and Roxane are destined to be together because they are young and beautiful. Since Cyrano could never hope to win her love and feels he can do nothing to stop them from being together, he chooses to win some small comfort in being the inspiration of Roxane's love.

HISTORICAL NOTE

On this page Cyrano asks the Capuchin, "What is this new game of Diogenes?" Tell students that Diogenes (c. 412–323 BC) was a Greek philosopher who taught that a virtuous life is a simple life. He condemned corruption in his society and supposedly went about the streets with a lantern seeking an honest man. Cyrano is comparing the Capuchin with his lantern to Diogenes. This comparison is supposed to be humorous and ironic because of Cyrano's duplicity and the priest's foolishness.

Answers to Guided Reading Questions

➊ Cyrano probably feels dejected and heartbroken.

ANALYTIC SCALES FOR RESPONDING IN WRITING

(SEE PAGE 983.)

Assign a score from 1 to 25 for each grading criterion below. (For more detailed evaluation, see the evaluation forms for writing, revising, and proofreading, Assessment Portfolio 4.1–4.9.)

1. Dramatic Continuation

- **Content/Unity.** The piece is an original, believable final scene for *Cyrano de Bergerac.*
- **Organization/Coherence.** The final scene continues the storyline of *Cyrano de Bergerac* and is in keeping with the personalities Rostand created.
- **Language/Style.** The dramatic continuation uses vivid and precise nouns, verbs, and modifiers and imitates the style of Rostand.
- **Conventions.** The dramatic continuation avoids errors in spelling, grammar, usage, mechanics, and manuscript form.

▶ Additional practice is provided in the Essential Skills Practice Book: Writing 1.8.

Immortal, with a rush of wings unseen—
A sacrament of blossoms, a new song
Sung by two hearts to an old simple tune—
The ring of one horizon around two souls
Together, all alone!

ROXANE: Hush! . . .

CYRANO: Why, what shame?—
There was a Queen of France, not long ago,
And a great lord of England—a queen's gift,
A crown jewel!

ROXANE: Indeed!

CYRANO: Indeed, like him,
I have my sorrows and my silences;
Like her, you are the queen I dare adore;
Like him I am faithful and forlorn—

ROXANE: Like him,
Beautiful—

CYRANO: (*Aside.*) So I am—I forgot that!

ROXANE: Then—Come; . . . Gather your sacred blossom . . .

CYRANO: (*To* CHRISTIAN.) Go!—

ROXANE: Your crown jewel . . .

CYRANO: Go on!—

ROXANE: Your old new song . . .

➊ *How do you think that Cyrano feels about Christian claiming a kiss from Roxane?*

CYRANO: Climb!—

CHRISTIAN: (*Hesitates.*) No—Would you?—not yet—

ROXANE: Your moment made
Immortal . . .

CYRANO: (*Pushing him.*) Climb up, animal!

(CHRISTIAN *springs on the bench, and climbs by the pillars, the branches, the vines, until he bestrides the balcony railing.*)

CHRISTIAN: Roxane! . . .
(*He takes her in his arms and bends over her.*)

CYRANO: (*Very low.*) Ah!. . . Roxane! . . .
I have won what I have won—
The feast of love—and I am Lazarus![17]

17. **Lazarus.** Diseased beggar who is eventually rewarded in Jesus' parable of the rich man and the beggar (Luke 16:19–31)

Words for Everyday Use
for • lorn (fôr lôrn´) *adj.,* abandoned or deserted

Vocabulary in Context

- We fed the forlorn stray dog and gave him a place to sleep.

Yet . . . I have something here that is mine now
And was not mine before I spoke the words
That won her—not for me! . . . Kissing my words
My words, upon your lips!
(*The theorbos begin to play.*) A merry tune—
A sad tune—So! The Capuchin!
(*He pretends to be running, as if he had arrived from a distance; then calls up to the balcony.*) Hola!

ROXANE: Who is it?

CYRANO: I. Is Christian there with you?

CHRISTIAN: (*Astonished.*) Cyrano!

ROXANE: Good morrow, Cousin!

CYRANO: Cousin, . . . good morrow!

ROXANE: I am coming down. *She disappears into the house.*

The CAPUCHIN *enters up stage.*

CHRISTIAN: (*Sees him.*) Oh—again!

THE CAPUCHIN: (*To* CYRANO.) She lives *here*, Madeleine Robin!

CYRANO: You said RO-LIN.

THE CAPUCHIN: No—
R-O-B-I-N

ROXANE: (*Appears on the threshold of the house, followed by* RAGUENEAU *with a lantern, and by* CHRISTIAN.) What is it?

THE CAPUCHIN: A letter.

CHRISTIAN: Oh! . . .

THE CAPUCHIN: (*To* ROXANE.) Some matter profitable to the soul—
A very noble lord gave it to me!

ROXANE: (*To* CHRISTIAN.) De Guiche!

CHRISTIAN: He dares?—

ROXANE: It will not be for long;
When he learns that I love you . . .
(*By the light of the lantern which* RAGUENEAU *holds, she reads the letter in a low tone, as if to herself.*) "Mademoiselle
The drums are beating, and the regiment
Arms for the march. Secretly I remain
Here, in the Convent. I have disobeyed;
I shall be with you soon. I send this first
By an old monk, as simple as a sheep,
Who understands nothing of this. Your smile
Is more than I can bear, and seek no more.
Be alone to-night, waiting for one who dares
To hope you will forgive . . . —" etcetera—
(*To the* CAPUCHIN.) Father, this letter concerns you . . .

❶ *What does Cyrano say that Christian is doing by kissing Roxane?*

❷ *Why has De Guiche written a letter to Roxane?*

ANSWERS TO GUIDED READING QUESTIONS

❶ Cyrano says that Christian is kissing his words upon Roxane's lips.

❷ De Guiche has written Roxane a letter to tell her that he is sending his regiment to war but that he is remaining behind for one night to meet Roxane secretly.

ANALYTIC SCALES FOR RESPONDING IN WRITING

(SEE PAGE 983.)

2. Critical Essay

- **Content/Unity.** The essay examines Cyrano's speech which begins "Yes, that is Love—that wind."
- **Organization/Coherence.** The essay begins with a thesis statement that describes what Cyrano's speech reveals about his situation and feelings. The introduction is followed by supporting paragraphs that cite lines from the speech. The essay has a solid conclusion.
- **Language/Style.** The essay uses vivid and precise nouns, verbs, and modifiers.
- **Conventions.** The essay avoids errors in spelling, grammar, usage, mechanics, and manuscript form.

► Additional practice is provided in the Essential Skills Practice Book: Writing 1.20.

Answers to Guided Reading Questions

❶ Roxane says that the letter instructs the Capuchin to marry Roxane to Christian on the orders of the Cardinal, whether Roxane wants to do so or not.

Literary Note

Some students might be curious about the ending of *Cyrano de Bergerac*. You might direct them to read the rest of the play on their own, or share with them the following synopsis:

Roxane pretends that the letter from de Guiche tells the monk to marry her to Christian right away. The monk agrees to marry the two while Cyrano keeps De Guiche from discovering them.

While Christian is away in battle, Cyrano writes and sends letters to Roxane, supposedly from Christian. Roxane falls more deeply in love, and Christian feels too guilty to continue deceiving her. He tells Cyrano to break the news of the deception to Roxane. Cyrano agrees to do so, but before he has a chance, Christian is killed in battle.

Fifteen years go by, and Roxane is still in mourning, living in a convent. She carries Christian's last letter close to her heart. Cyrano visits her weekly to share local gossip. One day, on the way to visit Roxane, Cyrano is mortally injured by one of his enemies. He still manages to visit Roxane, but this time he asks to read Christian's last letter. As he reads, she realizes that it is too dark for him to actually see the words of the letter and that it was his voice that she had heard beneath her balcony. Cyrano dies, and Roxane feels that she has lost the love of her life, not once but twice.

Photo: Gerry Goodstein. Huntington Theatre Company

(*To* Christian.) —and you.
Listen: (*The others gather around her. She pretends to read from the letter, aloud.*)
"Mademoiselle:
The Cardinal
Will have his way, although against your will;
That is why I am sending this to you
By a most holy man, intelligent,
Discreet. You will communicate to him
Our order to perform, here and at once
The rite of . . .
(*Turns the page.*) —Holy Matrimony. You
And Christian will be married privately
In your house. I have sent him to you. I know
You hesitate. Be resigned, nevertheless
To the Cardinal's command, who sends herewith
His blessing. Be assured also of my own
Respect and high consideration—*signed*,
Your very humble and— etcetera—"

❶ *What does Roxane say the purpose of the letter is?*

The Capuchin: A noble lord! I said so—never fear—

A worthy lord!—a very worthy lord!—

ROXANE: (*To* CHRISTIAN.) Am I a good reader of letters?

CHRISTIAN: (*Motions toward the* CAPUCHIN.) Careful!—

ROXANE: (*In a tragic tone.*) Oh, this is terrible!

THE CAPUCHIN: (*Turns the light of his lantern on* CYRANO.) You are to be—

CHRISTIAN: *I* am the bridegroom!

THE CAPUCHIN: (*Turns his lantern upon* CHRISTIAN; *then, as if some suspicion crossed his mind, upon seeing the young man so handsome.*)
Oh—why, *you* . . .

ROXANE: (*Quickly.*) Look here—
"Postscript: Give to the Convent in my name
One hundred and twenty pistoles"[18]—

THE CAPUCHIN: Think of it!
A worthy lord—a worthy lord! . . .
(*To* ROXANE, *solemnly.*) Daughter, resign yourself!

ROXANE: (*With an air of martyrdom.*) I am resigned . . .

(*While* RAGUENEAU *opens the door for the* CAPUCHIN *and* CHRISTIAN *invites him to enter, she turns to* CYRANO.)

De Guiche may come. Keep him out here with you
Do not let him—

CYRANO: I understand!
(*To the* CAPUCHIN.) How long
Will you be?—

THE CAPUCHIN: Oh, a quarter of an hour.

CYRANO: (*Hurrying them into the house.*) Hurry—I'll wait here—

ROXANE: (*To* CHRISTIAN.) Come!

They go into the house. ■

18. **pistoles.** Gold coins

Responding to the Selection

Imagine that you are Roxane. What would your reaction be to the proclamation of love Cyrano delivers for Christian? How would you feel toward Cyrano if you knew that the words were his own? How would you feel toward Christian? Discuss these questions in small groups.

RESPONDING TO THE SELECTION

Ask students if they would be angry with Cyrano for his actions or if they would understand why he acted as he did, given his circumstances.

SELECTION CHECK TEST WITH ANSWERS

EX. Whom does Cyrano love?
Cyrano loves Roxane.

1. Why does Roxane love Christian?
She loves Christian because of his love poetry and his beauty.

2. Who has actually written the poetry that Christian reads to Roxane?
Cyrano has written the poetry.

3. Why does Cyrano feel that Roxane would never love him?
He feels that she would never love him because of his nose.

4. What happens when Christian tries to speak to Roxane on his own?
She is annoyed by the fact that he no longer speaks to her in beautiful verse.

5. What do Cyrano and Christian decide to do when Roxane notices that Christian speaks haltingly?
Cyrano speaks, pretending to be Christian.

Reviewing the Selection

RECALLING

INTERPRETING

1. What does Roxane tell Cyrano she loves about Christian? What does she recite to Cyrano from memory? ▶▶ How does Roxane feel about the words she recites? How do you think Cyrano feels when Roxane recites? Why does he feel this way?

2. What plan does Roxane come up with to put off De Guiche as a suitor? to remain close to Christian? ▶▶ What do these plans reveal about Roxane's character?

3. What does Christian say he wishes to do on his own? What does Roxane say about Christian's words when he speaks for himself? ▶▶ What quality do you think Roxane values more, physical beauty or poetic ability and intelligent eloquence? How do you think she would react if Cyrano revealed his love for her?

4. What does Roxane notice about Christian's speech during the balcony scene? What does Cyrano do to remedy the situation? What does he say that almost reveals the true situation? What does Christian climb up the balcony to claim from Roxane? ▶▶ Why do you think Cyrano almost lets the role he is playing slip to reveal his true identity? When did you first realize that he was speaking from his heart, not just playing a role? Why might the scene that follows Cyrano's declaration of love be particularly difficult for Cyrano?

SYNTHESIZING

5. What motivates Cyrano to help Christian win Roxane? What makes the situation in which Cyrano has put himself unfair to him? to Roxane? to Christian? If you could advise Cyrano on this situation, what would you tell him? Explain.

Understanding Literature (Questions for Discussion)

1. **Irony and Dramatic Irony. Irony** is a difference between appearance and reality. In **dramatic irony,** something is known by the reader or audience but unknown to the characters. Examine the passage in which Roxane accuses Cyrano of being jealous of Christian's poetic ability. Explain the way in which this scene is ironic. In what way is Roxane speaking more truly than she realizes? What does the reader know that Roxane does not?

2. **Theme.** A **theme** is a central idea in a literary work. What does this play reveal about love? Which character is more worthy of Roxane's love, Cyrano or Christian? What does the play say about the importance of respecting and believing in yourself despite shortcomings that you cannot change?

Answers for Reviewing the Selection

RECALLING AND INTERPRETING

1. **Recalling.** Roxane says that she loves Christian because he is "beautiful and brilliant." She recites some of "Christian's" love poetry from memory. **Interpreting.** Roxane is very impressed by the verse she recites. Cyrano probably feels a mixture of self-consciousness, joy, and frustration because the words Roxane loves are really his.

2. **Recalling.** Roxane gets rid of De Guiche by telling him to go off to war and become a hero. At the same time, she tells him to shame Cyrano by keeping him and his cadets out of the war as a ploy to keep Christian close by and safe. Then, when she receives the letter from De Guiche offering to meet her that night, she tells the Capuchin that the letter contains orders that she and Christian be married as soon as possible. **Interpreting.** These plans reveal that Roxane is more than an empty-headed beauty. Like Cyrano, she is quick-witted, clever, and determined.

3. **Recalling.** He wishes to speak to Roxane on his own. Roxane says that Christian's absurd words displease her as much as his appearance would if he were ugly. **Interpreting.** Roxane seems to value both beauty and intelligence. Because she respects poetry, she may be able to look past Cyrano's looks to love his poetic soul.

4. **Recalling.** Roxane notices that Christian is speaking haltingly. Cyrano speaks on his own, pretending to be Christian. He starts to say that Roxane has never heard his heart speaking until now because he was always speaking through someone, but he stops himself mid-sentence. Christian claims a kiss from Roxane. **Interpreting.** Cyrano is so excited finally to be expressing his love for Roxane that he almost forgets that he is supposed to be speaking for Christian. Cyrano has just expressed his undying love and devotion only to see Christian kiss Roxane and claim her as his bride.

(cont.)

Answers for Reviewing the Selection (cont.)

SYNTHESIZING

Responses will vary. Possible responses are given.

5. Cyrano's love for Roxane might be motivating him to help Christian win Roxane—he wants to see if his words of love could move her. The situation is unfair to Cyrano because he is never able to admit his love for Roxane except while pretending to be Christian, and because he has to witness the growth of Roxane's love for another. The situation is unfair to Roxane because it is deceptive—Roxane never really knows either the true Christian or the true Cyrano. She is never given the opportunity to decide if she loves either man as he truly is. The situation is unfair to Christian because Christian is forced to pretend to be what he is not—a poetic person—and so can never speak to Roxane using his own words.

Responding in Writing

1. **Creative Writing: Dramatic Continuation.** How would you like this play to end? Do you want Roxane to learn of Cyrano's love for her and fall in love with him? Do you think Roxane should uncover the way that Cyrano and Christian have deceived her and reject them both as suitors? Do you think De Guiche should discover the way Roxane has tricked him and come to stop her marriage to Christian? Do you think Roxane should discover on her own the kind of person Christian really is? For at least fifteen minutes, freewrite about how you think the play would best end. Then write a short (not more than two or three pages) final scene for the play. Try to make sure that your characters' lines are in keeping with their personalities as Rostand created them. Share your endings for *Cyrano de Bergerac* as a class. You may wish to go to the library to find a copy of *Cyrano de Bergerac* to compare and contrast your endings to Rostand's.

2. **Critical Essay: A Close Reading.** Although Cyrano purports to be speaking for Christian, in actuality he reveals the truth about his situation and his own feelings in the balcony scene. Look closely at Cyrano's speech that begins, "Yes, that is Love—that wind." Write an essay analyzing what this speech reveals about Cyrano's situation and feelings. To begin, you might go through this speech line by line, applying each line to what you know about Cyrano's life and feelings. You should analyze how Cyrano uses the many figures of speech he uses in this passage. For help with figures of speech, see the Handbook of Literary terms.

PROJECT

Improvisation. Improvisation is the art of acting with very little preparation. The key to good improvisation is to take on a character and act and speak in ways appropriate to that character. With other students in your class, improvise the following scenes involving the characters from *Cyrano de Bergerac:*

- A scene in which a friend tells Roxane the truth about Christian and Cyrano
- A scene in which Cyrano comes to Roxane and confesses the truth to her
- A scene in which Christian, having had a quarrel with Roxane, begs Cyrano to write a letter of apology for him

Answers for Understanding Literature

Responses will vary. Possible responses are given.

1. **Irony and Dramatic Irony.** The passage is ironic because Cyrano *is* jealous of Christian—not because of his poetry, but because he enjoys Roxane's love. The passage is also ironic because Cyrano is the author of the poetry Roxane accuses him of envying.

2. **Theme.** The play reveals the conflict in romantic love between physical attraction and the finding of a soul mate. Students may say that Cyrano is more worthy of Roxane's love because, in the long run, he would make her a better companion. He also seems more interested in talking to Roxane and sharing his feelings, whereas Christian seems more interested in getting kisses. The play reveals that if you do not respect yourself and accept your shortcomings, you may limit your own opportunities in life.

Analytic Scales for Responding in Writing

Grading scales for Responding in Writing appear on pages 978 and 979.

PROJECT NOTES

See the evaluation form for projects, Assessment Portfolio 4.12.

Improvisation. You might want to break the class into small groups for the improvisations. As they perform, informally evaluate students according to the following criteria:

- Do they speak clearly and with expression?
- Do they speak and act in ways appropriate to their characters?
- Do they work to make their scene creative and interesting?

ADDITIONAL RESOURCES

READER'S GUIDE

- Selection Worksheet 11.9

ASSESSMENT PORTFOLIO

- Selection Check Test 2.11.17
- Selection Test 2.11.18

ESSENTIAL SKILLS PRACTICE BOOKS

- Writing 1.8, 1.20
- Language 2.54–2.61

PREREADING EXTENSIONS

Tell students that the Nobel Prize for literature, which Deledda won in 1926, is an award given annually for outstanding literary achievement. Nobel Prizes are also given for excellence in the areas of physics, chemistry, literature, economics, medicine, physiology, and working for peace.

Prizewinners are called Nobel laureates and they receive their prizes in ceremonies in Stockholm, Sweden. The one exception is the Peace Prize, which is presented in Oslo, Norway.

SUPPORT FOR LEP STUDENTS

PRONUNCIATIONS OF PROPER NOUNS AND ADJECTIVES

El • i • a Car • ái (ā´ lyä kə rī´)
Graz • i • a Del • e •dda (grät´ syä dā lād´ dä)
Aug • o • stin • o (ou gō stē´ nō)

ADDITIONAL VOCABULARY

emeritus—retired but holding onto one's high rank
enchantment—a charm or great pleasure
milestone—a significant moment in history or in one's life
provisions—supplies
tormenting—painful, torturing

PREREADING

"The Shoes"
by Grazia Deledda, translated by Althea Graham

ITALY

About the Author

Grazia Deledda (1875–1936). Grazia Deledda was born in Sardinia, Italy. Although she married young and moved to Rome, she frequently returned to visit Sardinia. Indeed, the bulk of her work is about life on this island. With little formal schooling, she demonstrated her adeptness in storytelling, beginning to write when she was seventeen. Many of her early stories are based on themes from folklore, and her later works focus on the effects of temptation and sin. Of her nearly fifty novels, the most important works are *After the Divorce, Elias Portolu,* and *The Mother.* In 1926, Deledda received the Nobel Prize for literature. An autobiographical novel, *Cosima,* was published after her death in 1936.

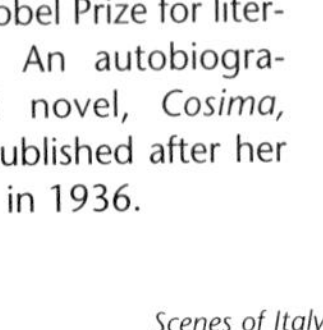

Scenes of Italy

About the Selection

Grazia Deledda was a prominent writer of the *verismo* movement, which emerged after the unification of Italy. *Verismo* writers used literature to document social conditions, and, in this way, the *verismo* movement was similar to **Naturalism**, a literary movement of the late nineteenth and early twentieth centuries that saw actions and events as resulting inevitably from biological or natural forces or from forces in the natural and economic environment. Naturalist writers, like Realists, focus on the everyday life of the middle and lower classes. **"The Shoes"** can be classified as *verismo* or as Naturalistic writing. Like most of Deledda's works, it shows a detailed view of Sardinian life. The main character, Elia Carái, poor and living in troubling economic times, dreams of gaining an inheritance that will solve his financial problems. Following the tenets of Naturalism, Elia's actions grow out of his economic situation.

CONNECTIONS: Sardinia

Sardinia is an island and a region of Italy, located in the Mediterranean, off the west coast of Italy and south of Corsica. Sardinia had been ruled by the Romans, the Vandals, the Byzantines, and the Arabs before Pisa and Genoa, two warring Italian states, struggled for control of the island during the eleventh century. It was ruled by the Spanish from 1326 until 1708, when the Austrians took control. In 1720, Sardinia became part of the Piedmont, today a region of Italy, but annexed by France at that time. In 1861, when Victor Emmanuel II became king of Italy, Sardinia became part of that nation. While the official language of the island is Italian, many dialects of Sardinian, a Romance language closely linked to Latin, are also spoken. The region is notable for its rich tradition of folklore, which influenced Deledda's early writing.

GOALS/OBJECTIVES

Studying this lesson will enable students to

- enjoy a story by a prominent Italian writer that reflects the ideas of Naturalism and the *verismo* movement
- discuss the life and work of Grazia Deledda
- define the terms *antihero, internal monologue,* and *psychological fiction*
- write a detailed personal philosophy
- write a critical essay about Naturalism and "The Shoes"
- proofread for errors in capitalization

READER'S JOURNAL

Do you think you have control over your life, or do you think of it as controlled by outside forces? Think about a time when something bad happened or when you were dissatisfied with your life. How did you react? Did you blame yourself or forces outside your control? Respond to these questions in your journal.

"The Shoes"

GRAZIA DELEDDA, TRANSLATED BY ALTHEA GRAHAM

It often happened now that Elia Carái had nothing to do; for times were bad, folk hesitated about going to law, and even people like famous barristers[1] and emeritus professors and retired government officials had to work as simple attorneys. But even when he had no cases, Elia used to go to the Law Courts all the same, settle down in the waiting-room, and there, leaning his note-book on his knee or on the wall, he would write poems in dialect to his wife. The storm raged around him. The crowd surged hither and thither; poor women, who had come about a matter of a few pence shouted abuse at each other, as solemn and tragic as if they had the whole world to divide; swindlers, perfectly ready to swear they owed nothing to their own creditors, went by with their heads in the air and their chests thrust forward proudly; the solicitors, poorer than their own clients, went round from one to the other wondering how they could manage to get hold of a sheet of stamped paper.[2] Elia took it all very calmly. He wrote, in his old-fashioned verse, which he dedicated to his wife:

Su mundu lu connosco e donzi cosa
Chi succedit succedere deviat.

"I know what the world is like, and I know that everything that happens was destined to happen. I am a poet and a philosopher; nothing ever surprises me in this world. Life is a see-saw, one day up and the next day down, and the next day up again. Do not despair, my golden lily. Perhaps Uncle Agostino, who has driven his wife out of the house and disinherited her, will remember us one day. Then we will go to the seaside together, we will watch the boats in the distance, and hold hands like a honeymoon couple. And, after all, we too are happy now; peace and love reign in our dwellings, and thou, Cedar of Lebanon, *Venus hermosa*, art my riches and my queen. . . ."

One winter morning, a carter[3] slapped Elia heavily on the shoulder with a hand that felt like stone.

"Run, man! I've just been to Terranova with a load of rubbish, and I saw the carrier, your Uncle Agostino. He's dangerously ill. . . ."

Elia stood up calmly and smoothed his grey hair with his hand as a sign of grief.

"I will go and tell my wife the sad news at once."

His wife did not seem much disturbed by the sad news; she did not even get up from the doorstep where she was sitting, trying to get warm in the sun. She was respectably dressed,

1. **barristers.** Members of the legal profession who present and plead cases in court
2. **stamped paper.** Special government-issue paper for official use
3. **carter.** Person who transports goods

❶ *What is Elia Carái's profession? How is business lately? What does he do when he does not have any cases?*

❷ *What does Elia know about the world? What does he hope will happen? Describe his philosophy of life.*

READER'S JOURNAL

Ask students if they are more comfortable with the idea of their lives being controlled by themselves or by the idea of their lives being controlled by outside forces. Ask them to explain their responses. Students may have mixed feelings. Ask them to explain what causes these feelings.

ANSWERS TO GUIDED READING QUESTIONS

❶ Elia Carái is an attorney. Business has been slow. When he does not have cases he goes to the law courts anyway and writes poems to his wife.

❷ Elia knows what the world is like and believes that everything that happens was destined to happen.

SPELLING AND VOCABULARY WORDS FROM THE SELECTION

anemic	sheepishly
degradation	skein
inert	unshod
moor	wayfarer

CROSS-CURRICULAR ACTIVITIES

SOCIAL STUDIES

You might have students locate Sardinia, Italy on a map and then research one or two facts about the region. Students can also create their own maps of the region, highlighting Sardinia and its neighboring areas.

Answers to Guided Reading Questions

1 Elia's wife is inert and indifferent. Her actions are similar to Elia's actions in court. Their actions suggest that Elia and his wife are not very aggressive people. They do not have goals or strong opinions.

2 Elia's shoes give way. Elia gets upset, rather than taking the situation with his usual philosophical calm. The problem is troubling because he cannot get somebody to mend the shoes, nor can he borrow a new pair, and he finds it degrading to appear at his uncle's house looking like a beggar.

ANALYTIC SCALES FOR RESPONDING IN WRITING

(SEE PAGE 991.)

Assign a score from 1 to 25 for each grading criterion below. (For more detailed evaluation, see the evaluation forms for writing, revising, and proofreading, Assessment Portfolio 4.1–4.9.)

1. Personal Philosophy

- **Content/Unity.** The personal philosophy explains the writer's ideas about life and outlines a set of instructions for living.
- **Organization/Coherence.** The writer's instructions for living are categorized under clear headings such as Facing Adversity or Following Dreams.
- **Language/Style.** The personal philosophy uses vivid and precise nouns, verbs, and modifiers.
- **Conventions.** The personal philosophy avoids errors in spelling, grammar, usage, mechanics, and manuscript form.

▶ Additional practice is provided in the Essential Skills Practice Book: Writing 1.8.

wore shoes, and had her hair done in the latest fashion; but her worn, frayed frock, her old shoes, and thin hair framing her dead-white, anemic face like a halo, only served to show off her poverty more clearly. Her great eyes, which had once seemed so dark, were now a kind of golden hazel-colour, and indifferent and staring, like the eyes of a hare.

From inside the house, where the two occupied one little ground-floor room giving on to the yard, came a noise like the noise of the Law Courts. It was the owners of the house quarreling, while in the public-house that belonged to them, men were playing *morra*[4] and laughing.

Elia's wife behaved like her husband in the Law Courts—inert, and indifferent to what went on around her. He loved her and wanted her just like that.

1 *How does Elia's wife act? In what way are her actions similar to his? What does this type of behavior suggest about Elia and his wife?*

"Do you know what I'm going to do?" he asked, stroking her hair and looking up at the sky. "I'm going."

"Where?"

"Where? But haven't you been listening? To Uncle Agostino's, of course. It's fine today," he added, without saying all that he was thinking; but his wife must have guessed because she looked down at his shoes, which were worn and full of holes, and asked:

"What about money for the journey?"

"I've got enough. Never you mind about me, don't worry. In this world everything is bound to go all right in the end, if only you take things calmly and sensibly; the only thing that really matters is being fond of people and treating them kindly. I was just thinking about that sort of thing this morning; here . . . would you like to read it?"

He tore the sheet on his pad, and blushed as he shyly let it drop into her lap. It was all he left her in the way of provisions while he was away.

He set off on foot. He had only three lire in the world, and he was much too wise to lose time by trying to borrow money for the journey.

He was, however, used to this sort of thing; he never expected anything to help him apart from his philosophic calm and his Uncle Agostino's will. He was an excellent walker, and thought far more about his shoes than about his feet; if matters went as well as he expected, then everything would be mended in due course.

Matters went well as far as Orosei. The road was downhill all the way, smooth and straight, accompanied, preceded, and followed by the most beautiful scenery; the very sight of it made one forget all earthly cares and troubles. It was like travelling in an enchanted land; the sun, like a great diamond, shed its cold, pure lustre around; the rocks and the grass were glistening. Then, as he went farther down, Elia felt the sun grow warmer and more golden, and at last, on the marble background of hills towards the sea, he saw, as in spring, pink almond-blossom in flower.

2 *Why do matters take a turn for the worse? How does Elia accept this turn of events? Why is this problem troubling to him?*

But the sun went down with cruel suddenness; after a short spell of twilight, the cold night fell, and Elia felt his feet were getting wet. His shoes had given way. This was obviously one of the things that were destined to happen, but all the same he did not accept it with his usual philosophical calm. He could not possibly mend them or get someone to lend him a pair now. It was very uncomfortable walking with holes in one's shoes, and dreadfully lacking in dignity, moreover, to appear at one's uncle's house looking like a beggar. For the sake of the future, for his wife's health and well-being, he must get hold of a pair of shoes at all costs. The

4. ***morra.*** Popular hand game in Italy similar to the game of rock, paper, scissors

Words for Everyday Use

a • ne • mic (ə nē´mēk) *adj.,* lacking vigor or vitality; lifeless

in • ert (in ʉrt´) *adj.,* physically or mentally inactive; dull; slow

Vocabulary in Context

- After having the flu for two weeks, she appeared thin and anemic.
- We sat in the humid classroom, fanning ourselves with books and feeling inert.

Clogs. Vincent van Gogh, 1884

question was, how? Elia had not the slightest idea. And, meanwhile, he reached the village.

The streets were dark and swept by sea-wind; not a soul was astir. Only, on the piazza,[5] a tiny inn shed a hospitable light. Elia went in and asked for a night's lodging; he paid in advance and was given a bed in a dirty-looking room where two other wayfarers were asleep. One of them was snoring like Pluto.[6] Elia lay down with his clothes on, but he could not get to sleep; he saw endless rows of shoes along all the streets in the world, among houses, and out in the fields; whenever there was a man, there was a pair of shoes. A great many pairs were hidden away in drawers and cupboards and all sorts of odd corners; others stood at the end of their master's bed, watching over his sleep; others were waiting outside doors, and there were still others, like his own, that shared the poverty and despair of their wearers. . . .

The roaring of the wind outside, and the snoring of the man beside him, made an accompaniment to his obsession. The hours went by, a star rose in the heavens, delicately blue as if steeped in the waters of the sea, and stopped outside the rattling window-panes. Elia thought of his wife, and the poems he wrote for her, and the easy life they would both lead if only Uncle Agostino left them all his belongings. . . .

He got up and bent over, trembling, to take the snoring man's shoes. They were heavy; their worn nails felt cold against his hot fingers. He put them down, and groped

5. **piazza.** Open, public square surrounded by buildings
6. **Pluto.** In Greek and Roman mythology, the god who ruled over the lower world, known as Hades, Dis, or Orcus

❶ *What does Elia imagine as he tries to sleep? Why is he so preoccupied with these things?*

Words for Everyday Use

way • far • er (wā fer´ər) *n.*, person who travels from place to place, especially on foot

Answers to Guided Reading Questions

❶ Elia imagines rows and rows of shoes in streets, fields, drawers, cupboards, and corners. He is preoccupied by shoes because his problem is the damage to his own shoes and his need for a new pair.

ANALYTIC SCALES FOR RESPONDING IN WRITING

(SEE PAGE 991.)

2. Critical Essay

- **Content/Unity.** The essay defines Naturalism and then explains why "The Shoes" is or is not an example of Naturalism.
- **Organization/Coherence.** The essay begins with an introductory paragraph containing a thesis statement. Supporting paragraphs refer to the text of the story to support the writer's thesis statement. The essay has a strong conclusion.
- **Language/Style.** The essay uses vivid and precise nouns, verbs, and modifiers.
- **Conventions.** The essay avoids errors in spelling, grammar, usage, mechanics, and manuscript form.

▶ Additional practice is provided in the Essential Skills Practice Book: Writing 1.20.

Vocabulary in Context

- When I put on my hiking boots, hat, and heavy backpack, I looked like a seasoned wayfarer.

Answers to Guided Reading Questions

❶ Elia is on the floor because he is stealing a pair of shoes. He feels degraded and depressed when he hears a noise and thinks that he might be discovered.

❷ Elia has trouble walking quickly in the shoes and thinks that he hears people following him.

❸ Elia notices that everything in both man and nature has a tendency to fall. He has fallen from dignity.

❹ The landscape looks different because Elia's mindset is different. He is tortured, so the landscape looks tortured. The sounds of mocking voices in the distance are imaginary.

Additional Questions and Activities

Tell students that, like Elia, the character of Pangloss in Voltaire's *Candide* (see page 884) has strong philosophical views about life. Pangloss says that "there is no effect without a cause," that the world is "the best of all possible worlds," and that "since everything is made for an end, everything is necessary for the best end." Ask students to compare this philosophy with that of Elia, who says, on page 985, "I know what the world is like, and I know that everything that happens was destined to happen. . . . Life is a see-saw, one day up and the next day down, and the next day up again."

about on the floor to find the other man's shoes, but he found nothing.

❶ *Why is Elia on the floor? How does he feel when he hears a noise and fears he might be discovered?*

Then he heard a vague noise in the corridor, like the steps of unshod feet. He stopped there motionless, crouching down with his hands on the floors and trembling like a frightened animal. He realized to the full the extent of his degradation; an instinctive sadness, like the sorrow of a heart in danger, weighed heavily upon him. But as soon as the noise had stopped, he went out to the door to see there was no one there, and by the light of a tiny lamp at the end of the passage he saw a cat rubbing itself against the wall with its tail in the air, and a pair of elastic-sided shoes by the door beside it, throwing a shadow on the floor like two great hooks.

❷ *Describe the effect the shoes have on Elia. Why might he have this reaction to the shoes?*

He took them, hid them under his cloak, and went downstairs. A man was sleeping on a mat in the yard so as to watch over people's horses; the big gates were just closed with a latch. Elia managed to get away quietly, and found himself on the sea front, by the grey sea under the twinkling stars that seemed to wish to fall down from the sky, lower and lower. . . .

❸ *What observation does Elia make as he leaves the inn? In what way is this observation related to his own situation?*

"It's odd, how everything in man and nature has a tendency to fall," mused Elia, walking quickly with the wind across the dark, hollow land, the dark mountains and the grey sea.

After walking half an hour or so, he decided it was the moment to put on the stolen shoes. He sat down on a milestone, put on the shoes, and felt them critically. He was delighted; they were soft and roomy, but as he bent down over them he felt the sense of degradation suddenly overwhelm him again. . . .

❹ *Why do you think the landscape now appears differently to Elia?*

"What if they follow me? A pretty figure I'll cut then. . . . Whatever will my wife say! 'While you're about it, Elia Carái, you might just as well steal a million lire as a pair of shoes!'"

Then: "A million lire! The question is where to find them, then I'd take them at once," he added, laughing at himself, stretching out his feet, and wriggling his toes about inside his shoes. It was an odd thing; but his feet burned and throbbed, and seemed to have a violent objection to being inside those shoes.

When he started walking back, with his own shoes under his arm so that he could put them on quickly and throw away the other pair if by any chance he was being followed, he found he could not walk anything like as quickly as before. His legs shook, and he stopped every now and then, seeming to hear steps coming up behind him.

Dawn rose from the pale sea behind a veil of mist, and terrified him, like a ghost. Now the people he had met on the road to Crosei could see him quite well, and when they reached the village and heard the story of the stolen shoes, they would be able to say: "Yes, I met a man who looked rather a suspicious character; he had a sort of parcel thing under his cloak."

As a matter of fact he did meet a peasant, walking quiet and dark through the dawn, with a knapsack and a stick; and Elia imagined he turned round to look at him and smiled.

Day was breaking, sad and grey; the clouds, like great, black, tangled skeins, ran from mountain to sea, from sea to mountain, clinging to cliffs and rocks that unravelled them a little. And the crows cawed as they passed over the windswept moorlands.

The quiet landscape of the day before seemed to have disappeared; now everything looked tortured and diabolical, and Elia thought he could hear voices in the distance, the voices of people following and mocking him.

Words for Everyday Use

un • shod (un shäd') *adj.*, without shoes

deg • ra • da • tion (deg´rə dā´shən) *n.*, lowering or being lowered in rank or status

skein (skān) *n.*, quantity of thread or yarn wound in a coil

Vocabulary in Context

- Don't walk in the workshed with unshod feet—you might step on a nail.
- The actor's feelings of degradation after losing the part in the movie nearly drove him to a new profession.
- I bought some knitting needles and a skein of red yarn.

At last he put on his old shoes again and left the others by the roadside; but still he found no peace. Fantastic happenings went on in his mind; one of the two poor travellers he had slept with was on the same road and picked up the shoes; then this man was followed and found out and pronounced guilty and let in for goodness knows how many awful punishments. . . . Or else the people he imagined were after him found the stolen shoes and went on tormenting him and tormenting him until finally in great shame he confessed what he had done. What would his wife say? The idea grew in his childish mind, excited by exhaustion, cold, and hunger, and spread like the great clouds in the stormy winter sky. He wished he had never set out at all, and had not forsaken his usual peace and quiet merely to run after a shadow. His uncle's legacy would probably involve endless worries and complications; and meanwhile, he had completely disgraced himself.

He turned back, found the shoes where he had left them, and stood a long while looking at them sheepishly. He wondered what he had better do. If he hid them or buried them, it did not alter the fact that they had been stolen. He had stolen them; and the thought of that moment when he was on all fours on the floor, trembling like a frightened animal, would cast its shadow over his whole existence.

He hid the stolen shoes under his cloak again and went back to the village, lingering on the way so as not to get there before evening. He had eaten nothing for twenty-four hours, and felt so weak that the wind made him sway like a blade of grass. He arrived at the inn in a dream, ready to confess what he had done; but everything was quiet, no one mentioned the theft or bothered about him or his cloak in the least. He had supper and asked for a bed; he was given the same one as on the previous night. He put back the shoes where he had found them and then went to sleep. His sleep was heavy as death; he had to be woken up and told it was twelve o'clock. He bought a loaf of bread with the penny he had left, and went on his way again.

The weather was fine again now, and the moors, shut in between the dark mountains and the blue sea, had all the sorrowful enchantment of a primitive landscape; everything was green and strong, but, just as you see in certain human lives, it seemed as if no flowers could ever bloom there.

Elia was walking well, in spite of his old shoes; and because of them, he enjoyed the privilege of being treated everywhere as a tramp, and given milk and bread to eat.

When he arrived, he found his uncle had died a few hours previously. The maid looked at Elia rather suspiciously, and asked:

"Are you really his nephew? Then why didn't you come sooner?" Elia did not answer.

"The master was expecting you. He sent a wire to you three days ago. He always used to say you were his only relative, but that you'd forgotten all about him. So this morning, when he saw you hadn't come, he decided to leave everything to the sailors' orphans."

Elia went home and found his wife sitting there in the sun, pale and indifferent to everything.

"Why on earth didn't you say I'd already gone, when the telegram came, my good woman?"

"But surely you'd have got there anyhow, wouldn't you? Why did you take such a long time?"

Elia did not answer. ■

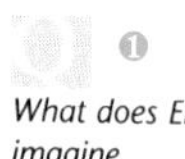

❶ *What does Elia imagine happening? What do these imaginings suggest about his state of mind?*

❷ *What does Elia learn when he arrives at his uncle's house? How do you think Elia feels?*

❸ *What decision does Elia make? Do you think his decision is wise? Explain.*

Words for Everyday Use

sheep • ish • ly (shēp′ ish lē) *adv.*, in an awkwardly shy or bashful manner

moor (mo͞or) *n.*, tract of open, rolling wasteland

Answers to Guided Reading Questions

❶ Elia imagines that one of the travelers who shared his room in the inn was accused and found guilty of stealing the shoes. He also imagines that he will be found and harassed until he confesses what he has done. These imaginings suggest a tormented state of mind and a deep sense of guilt.

❷ Elia learns that his uncle has already died, and, since Elia had not arrived, had given all his money to the sailors' orphans. Elia is probably filled with chagrin. He probably wishes that he had traveled with his own shoes despite their worn state.

❸ Elia goes back to the inn to return the shoes. *Responses will vary.*

Selection Check Test with Answers

EX. What is Elia Carái's profession?
He is a lawyer.

1. What is Elia's financial situation?
His business is not doing well and his financial situation looks grim.

2. What news does the carter bring Elia?
The carter tells him that his uncle is dying.

3. What does Elia steal from the people at the inn?
He steals shoes.

4. What does Elia decide to do when guilt gets the better of him?
He decides to return the shoes.

5. What disappointing news is Elia given when he gets to his uncle's house?
His uncle had died assuming that Elia had forgotten all about him. He has given away the inheritance that was supposed to go to Elia.

Vocabulary in Context

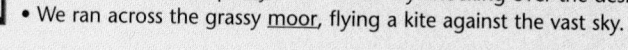

- Marissa smiled sheepishly after accidently knocking over the desk chair.
- We ran across the grassy moor, flying a kite against the vast sky.

Responding to the Selection

Ask students to form pairs to discuss the situation of Elia and his wife and to think about what they might say to the couple and why.

Answers for Reviewing the Selection

RECALLING AND INTERPRETING

1. **Recalling.** Elia's financial situation is grim at the beginning of the selection. When he does not have a case, he sits in the law courts and writes poems to his wife. He is hopeful that his uncle will leave him money when he dies. **Interpreting.** Elia is indifferent to his situation. He hopes for more money, but he does not seem to care very strongly one way or the other. He does not do anything to change his life, because he believes that life has its ups and downs and that everything that happens is destined to be.
2. **Recalling.** The carter tells Elia that his uncle is dying. The beginning of Elia's journey goes well. Things change when his shoes give out. **Interpreting.** Elia's reaction shows that he takes both the good and bad in life with little disturbance. He is not upset by the news that his uncle is near death, nor is he excited by the possibility of his dreamed-of inheritance.
3. **Recalling.** Elia is ashamed and degraded. He thinks he hears somebody following him and imagines that one of the other travelers will be accused and found guilty of stealing the shoes or that he will be found and harassed until he confesses. **Interpreting.** Elia decides to take an active role in influencing his own fate. He reacts to his problem by choosing to steal the shoes.

(cont.)

Responding to the Selection

What do you think the rest of life will be like for Elia and his wife? What advice would you give them about their situation?

Reviewing the Selection

Recalling		Interpreting
1. Describe Elia's financial situation. What does he do when he does not have a case? What does he hope will happen?	▶▶	How does Elia feel about his situation? Why doesn't he do anything to change his life?
2. What news does the carter bring Elia? How does the beginning of Elia's journey go? What problem does he encounter?	▶▶	What do Elia's reaction to the news and his feelings about his journey tell you about his outlook on life?
3. How does Elia feel when he finds himself crouched on the floor stealing shoes? What does he imagine as he travels along the road?	▶▶	In what way is Elia's decision to steal shoes different from his usual reaction to difficulties?
4. What news does Elia receives upon arriving at his uncle's house? How does Elia react to this news? Why didn't Elia's wife say anything when she received the telegram?	▶▶	In what way are Elia's reaction and his wife's reaction similar? Do you think they are upset by the news? Why, or why not?

Synthesizing

5. Do you agree with Elia's philosophy of life? Do you think it served him well? Explain.

Answers for Reviewing the Selection (cont.)

4. **Recalling.** Elia learns that his uncle has died and left his money to the sailors' orphans. Elia does not say anything. His wife had not said anything when she received the telegram because she expected that Elia would have arrived already. **Interpreting.** They both seem to accept that they were not meant to have this money. In fact, if they had acted differently they might have had it.

SYNTHESIZING

Responses will vary. Possible responses are given.

5. Students may say that Elia's philosophy has not served him well, since he lost his inheritance. Some students may note that Elia's departure from his philosophy led to his loss of the inheritance. Others may say that Elia's philosophy of life allows him to accept the situation without being greatly disappointed.

Understanding Literature (Questions for Discussion)

1. **Antihero.** An **antihero** is a central character who lacks many of the qualities traditionally associated with heroes. What characteristics do you think define a hero? Which of these characteristics is Elia lacking?

2. **Internal Monologue.** An **internal monologue** presents the private sensations, thoughts, and emotions of a character. The reader is allowed to step inside the character's mind and overhear what is going on in there. Reread Elia's internal monologue after he has stolen the shoes and left the inn. What does he think as he watches the stars that seem to fall? In what way is this observation related to his own situation? What fear does he have? What effect does guilt have on Elia?

3. **Psychological Fiction.** **Psychological fiction** is fiction that emphasizes the interior, subjective experiences of its characters, and especially such fiction when it deals with emotional or mental disturbance or anguish. Does "The Shoes" serve as an example of psychological fiction? Why, or why not? Upon whose interior, subjective experiences does the story focus? In what way would you describe these interior experiences?

Responding in Writing

1. **Creative Writing: Personal Philosophy.** Elia says, "In this world everything is bound to go all right in the end, if only you take things calmly and sensibly; the only thing that really matters is being fond of people and treating them kindly." Do you agree with his ideas on life? How do you deal with problems and difficulties? What advice have you been given about how to live your life? What decisions have you made about what is important? What advice would you like to give others? You may wish to discuss these questions with a partner to clarify your ideas before you begin writing. Then, write a set of instructions for living. Categorize each piece of advice under such topics as Facing Adversity, Interacting with Others, Following Dreams, and others you devise.

2. **Critical Essay: Naturalism.** Review the information about Naturalism in the About the Selection material, and see the entry *Naturalism* in the Handbook of Literary Terms. Is "The Shoes" an example of Naturalism? Write a critical essay in which you address this question. In your essay, define Naturalism. Then explain why the story is or is not an example of Naturalism. Use references to the text to support your opinion. You may wish to consider Elia's financial state, his attitude or philosophy of life, the actions he takes, and the events that spark these actions.

Answers for Understanding Literature

Responses will vary. Possible responses are given.

1. **Antihero.** Responses will vary. Students may say that a hero is wise, strong, honest, dignified, and active. One of the most marked differences between Elia and a hero is Elia's lack of action. A hero is often noted for the deeds that he or she performs. Elia is noted for his lack of action. Elia also shows a lack of honesty and dignity when he steals the shoes.

2. **Internal Monologue.** Elia notes that everything in nature and in man seems destined to fall. His observation suggests that he realizes how low he has sunk. He fears that he will be caught. His fear makes him imagine that he is being followed and that people are mocking him. He also imagines what might happen to him or to another accused of stealing the shoes.

3. **Psychological Fiction.** The story is an example of psychological fiction because it focuses on the interior emotions of Elia, especially on his anguish over his decision to steal a newer pair of shoes.

Analytic Scales for Responding in Writing

Grading scales for Responding in Writing appear on page 986 and 987.

Answers for Language Lab

1. Grazia Deledda won the Nobel Prize for literature in 1926.
2. The prize was established in 1901 by Alfred Bernhard Nobel.
3. In his will, Nobel indicated five fields for which awards should be given—physics, chemistry, physiology or medicine, literature, and working for peace.
4. To fulfill Nobel's wishes, an institution, the Nobel Foundation, was established.
5. The selection process begins in early autumn and the winners are chosen by November 15.
6. All of the prizes are awarded in Stockholm, Sweden, with the exception of the prize for peace which is awarded in Oslo, Norway.
7. Any of the prizes can be withheld if there is not a worthy candidate or if a world situation, such as World War I or World War II, makes the selection process impossible.
8. The first recipients of the prize for peace were Jean Henri Dunant of Switzerland and Frédéric Passy of France.
9. The Peace Prize, unlike the other prizes, can be awarded to an institution, such as the 1917 winner, the International Red Cross Committee.
10. In 1969, a sixth prize was created to honor accomplishment in economic science.

▶ Additional practice is provided in the Essential Skills Practice Book: Writing 2.54–2.61.

Language Lab

Proofreading for Errors in Capitalization. Read the Language Arts Survey 2.54–2.61, "Proofreading for Errors in Capitalization." Then, on your own paper, rewrite the following sentences, correcting any errors in capitalization.

1. Grazia Deledda won the nobel prize for literature in 1926.
2. The Prize was established in 1901 by Alfred bernhard nobel.
3. in his will, Nobel indicated five fields for which awards should be given—Physics, Chemistry, Physiology or medicine, Literature, and Peace.
4. To fulfill Nobel's wishes, an institution, the Nobel foundation, was established.
5. The selection process begins in early Autumn and the winners are chosen by november 15.
6. All of the prizes are awarded in stockholm, Sweden, with the exception of the prize for peace which is awarded in Oslo, norway.
7. Any of the prizes can be withheld if there is not a worthy candidate or if a world situation, such as world war I or world war II, makes the selection process impossible.
8. The first recipients of the prize for peace were Jean henri dunant of switzerland and Frédéric Passy of france.
9. The peace prize, unlike the other prizes, can be awarded to an institution, such as the 1917 winner, the international red cross committee.
10. In 1969, a sixth prize was created to honor accomplishment in Economic Science.

SELECTIONS FOR ADDITIONAL READING

FRANCE

from *The Confessions*
by Jean-Jacques Rousseau,
translated by J. M. Cohen

1712–1719. I have resolved on an enterprise which has no precedent, and which, once complete, will have no imitator. My purpose is to display to my kind a portrait in every way true to nature, and the man I shall portray will be myself.

Simply myself. I know my own heart and understand my fellow man. But I am made unlike any one I have ever met; I will even venture to say that I am like no one in the whole world, I may be no better, but at least I am different. Whether Nature did well or ill in breaking the mould in which she formed me, is a question which can only be resolved after the reading of my book.

Let the last trump sound when it will, I shall come forward with this work in my hand, to present myself before my Sovereign Judge, and proclaim aloud: 'Here is what I have done, and if by chance I have used some immaterial embellishment it has been only to fill a void due to a defect of memory. I may have taken for fact what was no more than probability, but I have never put down as true what I knew to be false. I have displayed myself as I was, as vile and despicable when my behaviour was such, as good, generous, and noble when I was so. I have bared my secret soul as Thou thyself hast seen it, Eternal Being! So let the numberless legion of my fellow men gather around me, and hear my confessions. Let them groan at my depravities, and blush for my misdeeds. But let each one of them reveal his heart at the foot of Thy throne with equal sincerity, and may any man who dares, say "I was a better man than he."' ■

RUSSIA

"The Overcoat"
by Nikolai Gogol,
translated by Isabel F. Hapgood

IN THE DEPARTMENT OF . . . but it is better not to name the department. There is nothing more irritable than all kinds of departments, regiments, courts of justice and, in a word, every branch of public service. Each separate man nowadays thinks all society insulted in his person. They say that, quite recently, a complaint was received from a justice of the peace, in which he plainly demonstrated that all the imperial institutions were going to the dogs, and that his sacred name was being taken in vain; and in proof he appended to the complaint a huge volume of some romantic composition, in which the justice of the peace appears about once in every ten lines, sometimes in a drunken condition. Therefore, in order to avoid all unpleasantness, it will be better for us to designate the department in question as *a certain department.*

So, *in a certain department* serves *a certain official*—not a very prominent official, it must be allowed—short of stature, somewhat pockmarked, rather red-haired, rather blind, judging from appearances, with a small bald spot on his forehead, with wrinkles on his cheeks, with a complexion of the sort called sanguine. . . . How could he help it? The Petersburg[1] climate was responsible for that. As for his rank—for with us the rank must be stated first of all—he was what is called a perpetual titular councillor, over which, as is well known, some writers make merry and crack their jokes, as they have the praiseworthy custom of attacking those who cannot bite back.

His family name was Bashmachkin. It is evident from the name, that it originated in *bashmak* (shoe); but when, at what time, and in what manner, is not known. His father and grandfather, and even his brother-in-law, and all the Bashmachkins, always wore boots, and only had new heels two or three times a year. His name was Akakii Akakievich. It may strike the reader as rather singular and far-fetched; but he may feel assured that it was by no means far-fetched, and that the circumstances were such

1. **Petersburg.** Seaport in northwest Russia; later named Petrograd, then Leningrad, now St. Petersburg

FROM *THE CONFESSIONS*

ABOUT THE AUTHOR

Jean-Jacques Rousseau (1712–1778) was an eighteenth-century French philosopher and one of the leading figures of the Enlightenment. Rousseau believed that in their natural state, people are good and that social institutions corrupt them. His ideas about people and nature became central to Romanticism.

Rousseau was born in Geneva, Switzerland, and by the age of sixteen became a vagabond, wandering through Switzerland, Italy, and France. He supported himself during this time by working as a tutor, music instructor, and secretary.

As an adult, Rousseau influenced society in several different ways. He wrote a book called *The Social Contract*, which stated that no laws should be binding unless they are agreed upon by the people governed by them. This idea affected French thinking, and it became one of the forces that brought on the French Revolution of 1789. Rousseau also helped to change the education of children. In his novel *Emile*, he urged people to give children more freedom to play and to enjoy nature. He argued that children's learning should be scheduled to coincide with specific periods in their development. Rousseau also inspired a change in literature, encouraging writers to include more images of nature in their work.

ABOUT THE SELECTION

Rousseau's autobiography ***The Confessions*** is considered a landmark work. It made popular a new, extremely personal and revealing style of autobiography.

In this selection, Rousseau expresses ideas about himself and his life's work.

ADDITIONAL QUESTIONS AND ACTIVITIES

Encourage students to write their thoughts about the ideas of Rousseau and the attitude he expresses in this excerpt from *The Confessions*. As they write, they might refer back to the biography provided on this page and keep the following questions in mind:

- Do you agree with Rousseau's ideas about laws and the rights of the people? Explain.
- Do you agree that social institutions can be corrupting? Explain.
- Do you agree that children should raised with a great deal of freedom? Explain.
- Do you believe that images of nature have a place in great literature? Explain.

"The Overcoat"

About the Author

Nikolai Gogol (1809–1852) is often referred to as the father of modern Russian Realism. He was one of the first Russian authors both to criticize the government in his country and to write about the common people of Russia.

Gogol was born on March 31, 1809, in Mirgorod, a village in Ukraine. His parents were small landowners, and he was the third of twelve children. When Gogol was nineteen, he went to St. Petersburg and worked as a civil service clerk and as a history teacher while writing in his free time.

In 1832, the publication of *Evenings on a Farm Near Dikanka*, a two-volume collection of stories, made Gogol famous. From that point on he wrote many more stories and plays. The idea of saving the people of Russia from moral indifference was important to him, and this theme is reflected in many of his writings.

About the Selection

"The Overcoat," which first appeared in 1842, is Gogol's most well-known story. This story focuses on the main character Akakii Akakievich and the ways in which his life changes after he acquires an overcoat that becomes strangely significant to him.

that it would have been impossible to give him any other name; and this was how it came about.

Akakii Akakievich was born, if my memory fails me not, towards night on the 23rd of March. His late mother, the wife of an official, and a very fine woman, made all due arrangements for having the child baptized. His mother was lying on the bed opposite the door: on her right stood the godfather, a most estimable man, Ivan Ivanovich Eroshkin, who served as presiding officer of the senate; and the godmother, the wife of an officer of the quarter, a woman of rare virtues, Anna Semenovna Byelobrushkova. They offered the mother her choice of three names—Mokiya, Sossiya or that the child should be called after the martyr Khozdazat. "No," pronounced the blessed woman, "all those names are poor." In order to please her, they opened the calendar at another place: three more names appeared—Triphilii, Dula and Varakhasii. "This is a judgment," said the old woman. "What names! I truly never heard the like. Varadat or Varukh might have been borne, but not Triphilii and Varakhasii!" They turned another page—Pavsikakhii and Vakhtisii. "Now I see," said the old woman, "that it is plainly fate. And if that's the case, it will be better to name him after his father. His father's name was Akakii, so let his son's be also Akakii." In this manner he became Akakii Akakievich.

They christened the child, whereat he wept, and made a grimace, as though he foresaw that he was to be a titular councillor. In this manner did it all come about. We have mentioned it, in order that the reader might see for himself that it happened quite as a case of necessity, and that it was utterly impossible to give him any other name. When and how he entered the department, and who appointed him, no one could remember. However much the directors and chiefs of all kinds were changed, he was always to be seen in the same place, the same attitude, the same occupation—the same official for letters; so that afterwards it was affirmed that he had been born in undress uniform with a bald spot on his head.

No respect was shown him in the department. The janitor not only did not rise from his seat when he passed, but never even glanced at him, as if only a fly had flown through the reception-room. His superiors treated him in a coolly despotic manner. Some assistant chief would thrust a paper under his nose without so much as saying, "Copy," or, "Here's a nice, interesting matter," or any thing else agreeable, as is customary in well-bred service. And he took it, looking only at the paper, and not observing who handed it to him, or whether he had the right to do so: he simply took it, and set about copying it.

The young officials laughed at and made fun of him, so far as their official wit permitted; recounted there in his presence various stories concocted about him, and about his landlady, an old woman of seventy; they said that she beat him; asked when the wedding was to be; and strewed bits of paper over his head, calling them snow. But Akakii Akakievich answered not a word, as though there had been no one before him. It even had no effect upon his employment: amid all these molestations he never made a single mistake in a letter.

But if the joking became utterly intolerable, as when they jogged his hand, and prevented his attending to his work, he would exclaim, "Leave me alone! Why do you insult me?" And there was something strange in the words and the voice in which they were uttered. There was in it something which moved to pity; so that one young man, lately entered, who, taking pattern by the others, had permitted himself to make sport of him, suddenly stopped short, as though all had undergone a transformation before him, and presented itself in a different aspect. Some unseen force repelled him from the comrades whose acquaintance he had made, on the supposition that they were well-bred and polite men. And long afterwards, in his gayest moments, there came to his mind the little official with the bald forehead, with the heart-rending words, "Leave me alone! Why do you insult me?" And in these penetrating words, other words resounded—"I am thy brother." And the poor young man covered his face with his hand; and many a time afterwards, in the course of his life, he shuddered at seeing how much inhumanity there is in man, how much savage coarseness is concealed in delicate, refined worldliness and, O God! even in that man whom the world acknowledges as honorable and noble.

It would be difficult to find another man who lived so entirely for his duties. It is saying but little to say that he served with zeal: no, he served with love. In that copying, he saw a varied and agreeable world. Enjoyment was written on his face: some letters were favorites with him, and when he encountered them, he became unlike himself, he smiled and winked, and assisted with his lips, so that it seemed as though each letter might be read in his face, as his pen traced it. If his pay had been in proportion to his zeal, he would, perhaps, to his own surprise, have been made even a councillor of state. But he served, as his companions, the wits, put it, like a buckle in a button-hole.

Moreover, it is impossible to say that no attention was paid to him. One director being a kindly man, and desirous of rewarding him for his long service, ordered him to be given something more important than mere copying; namely, he was ordered to make a report of an already concluded affair, to another court: the matter consisted simply in changing the heading, and altering a few words from the first to the third person. This caused him so much toil, that he was all in a perspiration, rubbed his forehead, and finally said, "No, give me rather something to copy." After that they let him copy on forever.

Outside this copying, it appeared that nothing existed for him. He thought not at all of his clothes: his undress uniform was not green, but a sort of rusty-meal color. The collar was narrow, low, so that his neck, in spite of the fact that it was not long, seemed inordinately long as it emerged from that collar, like the necks of plaster cats which wag their heads, and are carried about upon the heads of scores of Russian foreigners. And something was always sticking to his uniform—either a piece of hay or some trifle. Moreover, he had a peculiar knack, as he walked in the street, of arriving beneath a window when all sorts of rubbish was being flung out of it: hence he always bore about on his hat melon and watermelon rinds, and other such stuff.

Never once in his life did he give heed to what was going on every day in the street; while it is well known that his young brother official, extending the range of his bold glance, gets so that he can see when anyone's trouser-straps drop down upon the opposite sidewalk, which always calls forth a malicious smile upon his face. But Akakii Akakievich, if he looked at anything, saw in all things the clean, even strokes of his written lines, and only when a horse thrust his muzzle, from some unknown quarter, over his shoulder, and sent a whole gust of wind down his neck from his nostrils, did he observe that he was not in the middle of a line, but in the middle of the street.

On arriving at home, he sat down at once at the table, supped his cabbage-soup quickly and ate a bit of beef with onions, never noticing their taste, ate it all with flies and anything else which the Lord sent at the moment. On observing that his stomach began to puff out, he rose from the table, took out a little vial with ink and copied papers which he had brought home. If there happened to be none, he took copies for himself, for his own gratification, especially if the paper was noteworthy, not on account of its beautiful style, but of its being addressed to some new or distinguished person.

Even at the hour when the gray Petersburg sky had quite disappeared, and all the world of officials had eaten or dined, each as he could, in accordance with the salary he received, and his own fancy; when all were resting from the departmental jar of pens, running to and fro, their own and other people's indispensable occupations and all the work that an uneasy man makes willingly for himself, rather than what is necessary; when officials hasten to dedicate to pleasure the time that is left to them—one bolder than the rest goes to the theater; another, into the streets, devoting it to the inspection of some bonnets; one wastes his evening in compliments to some pretty girl, the star of a small official circle; one—and this is the most common case of all—goes to his comrades on the fourth or third floor, to two small rooms with an ante-room or kitchen, and some pretensions to fashion, a lamp or some other trifle which has cost many a sacrifice of dinner or excursion—in a word, even at the hour when all officials disperse among the contracted quarters of their friends, to play at whist[1], as they sip their tea from glasses with a kopek's worth of sugar, draw smoke through long pipes, relating at times some bits of gossip which a Russian man can never, under any circumstances, refrain from, or even when there is nothing to say, recounting everlasting anecdotes about the commandant whom they had sent to inform that the tail of the horse on the Falconet Monument[2] had been cut off—in a word, even when all strive to divert themselves, Akakii Akakievich yielded to no diversion.

No one could ever say that he had seen him at any sort of an evening party. Having written to his heart's content, he lay down to sleep, smiling at the thought of the coming day—of what God might send to copy on the morrow. Thus flowed on the peaceful life of the man, who, with a salary of four hundred rubles,[3] understood how to be content with his fate and thus it would have continued to flow on, perhaps, to extreme old age, were there not various ills sown among the path of life for titular councillors as well as for private, actual, court and every other species of councillor, even for those who never give any advice or take any themselves.

There exists in Petersburg a powerful foe of all who receive four hundred rubles salary a year, or thereabouts. This foe is no other than our Northern cold, although it is said to be very wholesome. At nine o'clock in the morning, at the very hour when the streets are filled with men bound for the departments, it begins to bestow such powerful and piercing nips on all noses impartially that the poor officials really do not know what to do with them. At the hour when the foreheads of even those who occupy exalted positions ache with the cold, and tears start to their eyes, the poor titular councillors are sometimes unprotected. Their only salvation lies in traversing as quickly as possible, in their thin little overcoats, five or six streets, and then warming their feet well in the porter's room and so thawing all their talents and qualifications for official service, which had become frozen on the way.

1. **whist.** Card game
2. **Falconet Monument.** Famous statue of Peter the Great, czar of Russia from 1682 to 1725, on a horse
3. **rubles.** Monetary unit of Russia

Literary Technique

SYMBOL

A **symbol** is a thing that stands for or represents both itself and something else.

Ask students to make notes about the overcoat as a symbol as they read this short story. Ask them to look closely at the thoughts and feelings of Akakii toward the overcoat, as well as the ways in which the coat affects his treatment by others.

The overcoat in Gogol's story gains significance as the story progresses. You might want to ask students to keep a chart like the one below in which they can record their thoughts about the overcoat and its effect on Akakii's life. Under *Scene* they might briefly explain the overcoat's role in a particular scene of the story. Under *Significance,* they should express their thoughts about the overcoat's possible symbolism in this same scene.

OVERCOAT
Scene: Significance:
Scene: Significance:

Additional Questions and Activities

Ask students to write about one of the following prompts in their journals:

- Do you view yourself differently at different times depending on who you are with, what you are doing, or what you might be wearing at the time?
- Why do you think, in this society, our clothing and possessions can at times influence the way we feel about ourselves?

Akakii Akakievich had felt for some time that his back and shoulders suffered with peculiar poignancy, in spite of the fact that he tried to traverse the legal distance with all possible speed. He finally wondered whether the fault did not lie in his overcoat. He examined it thoroughly at home, and discovered that in two places, namely, on the back and shoulders, it had become thin as mosquito-netting: the cloth was worn to such a degree that he could see through it, and the lining had fallen into pieces.

You must know that Akakii Akakievich's overcoat served as an object of ridicule to the officials: they even deprived it of the noble name of overcoat, and called it a kapota.[1] In fact, it was of singular make: its collar diminished year by year, but served to patch its other parts. The patching did not exhibit great skill on the part of the tailor, and turned out, in fact, baggy and ugly. Seeing how the matter stood, Akakii Akakievich decided that it would be necessary to take the overcoat to Petrovich, the tailor, who lived somewhere on the fourth floor up a dark staircase, and who, in spite of his having but one eye, and pock-marks all over his face, busied himself with considerable success in repairing the trousers and coats of officials and others; that is to say, when he was sober, and not nursing some other scheme in his head.

It is not necessary to say much about this tailor: but, as it is the custom to have the character of each personage in a novel clearly defined, there is nothing to be done; so here is Petrovich the tailor. At first he was called only Grigorii, and was some gentleman's serf;[2] he began to call himself Petrovich from the time when he received his free papers, and began to drink heavily on all holidays, at first on the great ones, and then on all church festivals without discrimination, wherever a cross stood in the calendar. On this point he was faithful to ancestral custom; and, quarreling with his wife, he called her a low female and a German.

As we have stumbled upon his wife, it will be necessary to say a word or two about her; but, unfortunately, little is known of her beyond the fact that Petrovich has a wife, who wears a cap and a dress; but she cannot lay claim to beauty, it seems—at least, no one but the soldiers of the guard, as they pulled their mustaches, and uttered some peculiar sound, even looked under her cap when they met her.

Ascending the staircase which led to Petrovich—which, to do it justice, was all soaked in water (dishwater), and penetrated with the smell of spirits which affects the eyes, and is an inevitable adjunct to all dark stairways in Petersburg houses—ascending the stairs, Akakii Akakievich pondered how much Petrovich would ask, and mentally resolved not to give more than two rubles. The door was open; for the mistress, in cooking some fish, had raised such a smoke in the kitchen that not even the beetles were visible.

Akakii Akakievich passed through the kitchen unperceived, even by the housewife, and at length reached a room where he beheld Petrovich seated on a large, unpainted table, with his legs tucked under him like a Turkish pasha.[3] His feet were bare, after the fashion of tailors as they sit at work; and the first thing which arrested the eye was his thumb, very well known to Akakii Akakievich, with a deformed nail thick and strong as a turtle's shell. On Petrovich's neck hung a skein of silk and thread, and upon his knees lay some old garment. He had been trying for three minutes to thread his needle, unsuccessfully, and so was very angry with the darkness, and even with the thread, growling in a low voice, "It won't go through, the barbarian! you pricked me, you rascal!"

Akakii Akakievich was displeased at arriving at the precise moment when Petrovich was angry: he liked to order something of Petrovich when the latter was a little downhearted, or, as his wife expressed it, "when he had settled himself with brandy, the one-eyed devil!" Under such circumstances, Petrovich generally came down in his price very readily, and came to an understanding, and even bowed and returned thanks. Afterwards, to be sure, his wife came, complaining that her husband was drunk, and so had set the price too low; but, if only a ten-kopek[4] piece were added, then the matter was settled. But now it appeared that Petrovich was in a sober condition, and therefore rough, taciturn, and inclined to demand, Satan only knows what price. Akakii Akakievich felt this, and would gladly have beat a retreat, as the saying goes; but he was in for it. Petrovich screwed up his one eye very intently at him; and Akakii Akakievich involuntarily said, "How do you do, Petrovich!"

"I wish you a good-morning, sir," said Petrovich, and squinted at Akakii Akakievich's hands, wishing to see what sort of booty he had brought.

"Ah! I . . . to you, Petrovich, this"—It must be known that Akakii Akakievich expressed himself chiefly by prepositions, adverbs, and by such scraps of phrases as had no meaning whatever. But if the matter was a very difficult one, then he had a habit of never completing his sentences; so that quite frequently, having begun his phrase with the words, "This, in fact, is quite" . . . there was no more of it, and he forgot himself, thinking that he had already finished it.

"What is it?" asked Petrovich, and with his one eye scanned his whole uniform, beginning with the collar down

1. **kapota**. Woman's cloak
2. **serf**. Slave
3. **Turkish pasha**. High official in the Ottoman Empire
4. **kopek.** Monetary unit equal to 1/100 of a ruble

to the cuffs, the back, the tails and button-holes, all of which were very well known to him, because they were his own handiwork. Such is the habit of tailors: it is the first thing they do on meeting one.

"But I, here, this, Petrovich, . . . an overcoat, cloth . . . here you see, everywhere, in different places, it is quite strong . . . it is a little dusty, and looks old, but it is new, only here in one place it is a little . . . on the back, and here on one of the shoulders, it is a little worn, yes, here on this shoulder it is a little . . . do you see? this is all. And a little work . . ."

Petrovich took the overcoat, spread it out, to begin with, on the table, looked long at it, shook his head, put out his hand to the window-sill after his snuff-box, adorned with the portrait of some general—just what general is unknown, for the place where the face belonged had been rubbed through by the finger, and a square bit of paper had been pasted on. Having taken a pinch of snuff, Petrovich spread the overcoat out on his hands, and inspected it against the light, and again shook his head; then he turned it, lining upwards, and shook his head once more; again he removed the general-adorned cover with its bit of pasted paper, and, having stuffed his nose with snuff, covered and put away the snuff-box, and said finally, "No, it is impossible to mend it: it's a miserable garment!"

Akakii Akakievich's heart sank at these words.

"Why is it impossible, Petrovich?" he said, almost in the pleading voice of a child: "all that ails it is that it is worn on the shoulders. You must have some pieces. . . ."

"Yes, patches could be found, patches are easily found," said Petrovich, "but there's nothing to sew them to. The thing is completely rotten: if you touch a needle to it—see, it will give way."

"Let it give way, and you can put on another patch at once."

"But there is nothing to put the patches on; there's no use in strengthening it; it is very far gone. It's lucky that it's cloth, for, if the wind were to blow, it would fly away."

"Well, strengthen it again. How this, in fact . . ."

"No," said Petrovich decisively, "there is nothing to be done with it. It's a thoroughly bad job. You'd better, when the cold winter weather comes on, make yourself some foot-bandages out of it, because stockings are not warm. The Germans invented them in order to make more money. (Petrovich loved, on occasion, to give a fling at the Germans.) But it is plain that you must have a new overcoat."

At the word *new*, all grew dark before Akakii Akakievich's eyes, and everything in the room began to whirl round. The only thing he saw clearly was the general with the paper face on Petrovich's snuff-box cover. "How a new one?" said he, as if still in a dream: "Why, I have no money for that."

"Yes, a new one," said Petrovich, with barbarous composure.

"Well, if it came to a new one, how, it . . ."

"You mean how much would it cost?"

"Yes."

"Well, you would have to lay out a hundred and fifty or more," said Petrovich, and pursed up his lips significantly. He greatly liked powerful effects, liked to stun utterly and suddenly, and then to glance sideways to see what face the stunned person would put on the matter.

"A hundred and fifty rubles for an overcoat!" shrieked poor Akakii Akakievich—shrieked perhaps for the first time in his life, for his voice had always been distinguished for its softness.

"Yes, sir," said Petrovich, "for any sort of an overcoat. If you have marten fur on the collar, or a silk-lined hood, it will mount up to two hundred."

"Petrovich, please," said Akakii Akakievich in a beseeching tone, not hearing, and not trying to hear, Petrovich's words, and all his "effects," "some repairs, in order that it may wear yet a little longer."

"No, then, it would be a waste of labor and money," said Petrovich; and Akakii Akakievich went away after these words, utterly discouraged. But Petrovich stood long after his departure, with significantly compressed lips, and not betaking himself to his work, satisfied that he would not be dropped, and an artistic tailor employed.

Akakii Akakievich went out into the street as if in a dream. "Such an affair!" he said to himself: "I did not think it had come to" . . . and then after a pause, he added, "Well, so it is! see what it has come to at last! and I never imagined that it was so!" Then followed a long silence, after which he exclaimed, "Well, so it is! see what already exactly, nothing unexpected that . . . it would be nothing . . . what a circumstance!" So saying, instead of going home, he went in exactly the opposite direction without himself suspecting it.

On the way, a chimney-sweep brought his dirty side up against him, and blackened his whole shoulder: a whole hatful of rubbish landed on him from the top of a house which was building. He observed it not; and afterwards, when he ran into a sentry, who, having planted his halberd[1] beside him, was shaking some snuff from his box into his horny hand—only then did he recover himself a little, and that because the sentry said, "Why are you thrusting yourself into a man's very face? Haven't you the sidewalk?" This caused him to look about him, and turn towards home.

1. **halberd.** Combination spear and battle ax

Additional Questions and Activities

Ask students to answer the following questions in writing or in a class discussion:

In what way does the overcoat cause people to look at the main character differently? Why do people seem to look at him differently?

There only, he finally began to collect his thoughts, and to survey his position in its clear and actual light, and to argue with himself, not brokenly, but sensibly and frankly, as with a reasonable friend, with whom one can discuss very private and personal matters. "No," said Akakii Akakievich, "it is impossible to reason with Petrovich now: he is that . . . evidently, his wife has been beating him. I'd better go to him Sunday morning: after Saturday night he will be a little cross-eyed and sleepy, for he will have to get drunk, and his wife won't give him any money; and at such a time, a ten-kopek piece in his hand will—he will become more fit to reason with, and then the overcoat, and that . . ."

Thus argued Akakii Akakievich with himself, regained his courage and waited until the first Sunday, when, seeing from afar that Petrovich's wife had gone out of the house, he went straight to him. Petrovich's eye was very much askew, in fact, after Saturday: his head drooped, and he was very sleepy; but for all that, as soon as he knew what the question was, it seemed as though Satan jogged his memory. "Impossible," said he: "please to order a new one." Thereupon Akakii Akakievich handed over the ten-kopek piece. "Thank you, sir; I will drink your good health," said Petrovich: "but as for the overcoat, don't trouble yourself about it; it is good for nothing. I will make you a new coat famously, so let us settle about it now."

Akakii Akakievich was still for mending it, but Petrovich would not hear of it, and said, "I shall certainly make you a new one, and please depend upon it that I shall do my best. It may even be, as the fashion goes, that the collar can be fastened by silver hooks under a flap."

Then Akakii Akakievich saw that it was impossible to get along without a new overcoat, and his spirit sank utterly. How, in fact, was it to be accomplished? Where was the money to come from? He might, to be sure, depend, in part, upon his present at Christmas; but that money had long been doled out and allotted beforehand. He must have some new trousers, and pay a debt of long standing to the shoemaker for putting new tops to his old boots, and he must order three shirts from the seamstress and a couple of pieces of linen which it is impolite to mention in print— in a word, all his money must be spent; and even if the director should be so kind as to order forty-five rubles instead of forty, or even fifty, it would be a mere nothing, and a mere drop in the ocean towards the capital necessary for an overcoat: although he knew that Petrovich was wrongheaded enough to blurt out some outrageous price, Satan only knows what, so that his own wife could not refrain from exclaiming, "Have you lost your senses, you fool?"

At one time he would not work at any price, and now it was quite likely that he had asked a price which it was not worth. Although he knew that Petrovich would undertake to make it for eighty rubles, still, where was he to get the eighty rubles? He might possibly manage half; yes, a half of that might be procured: but where was the other half to come from? But the reader must first be told where the first half came from. Akakii Akakievich had a habit of putting, for every ruble he spent, a groschen[1] into a small box, fastened with lock and key, and with a hole in the top for the reception of money. At the end of each half-year, he counted over the heap of coppers, and changed it into small silver coins. This he continued for a long time; and thus, in the course of some years, the sum proved to amount to over forty rubles.

Thus he had one half on hand; but where to get the other half? where to get another forty rubles? Akakii Akakievich thought and thought, and decided that it would be necessary to curtail his ordinary expenses, for the space of one year at least—to dispense with tea in the evening, to burn no candles, and, if there was anything which he must do, to go into his landlady's room, and work by her light; when he went into the street he must walk as lightly as possible, and as cautiously, upon the stones and flagging, almost upon tiptoe, in order not to wear out his heels in too short a time; he must give the laundress as little to wash as possible; and in order not to wear out his clothes, he must take them off as soon as he got home, and wear only his cotton dressing-gown, which had been long and carefully saved.

To tell the truth, it was a little hard for him at first to accustom himself to these deprivations, but he got used to them at length, after a fashion and all went smoothly—he even got used to being hungry in the evening; but he made up for it by treating himself in spirit, bearing ever in mind the thought of his future coat. From that time forth, his existence seemed to become, in some way, fuller, as if he were married, as if some other man lived in him, as if he were not alone, and some charming friend had consented to go along life's path with him—and the friend was no other than that overcoat, with thick wadding and a strong lining incapable of wearing out. He became more lively, and his character even became firmer, like that of a man who has made up his mind, and set himself a goal. From his face and gait, doubt and indecision—in short all hesitating and wavering traits—disappeared of themselves.

Fire gleamed in his eyes: occasionally, the boldest and most daring ideas flitted through his mind; why not, in fact, have marten fur on the collar? The thought of this nearly made him absent-minded. Once, in copying a letter, he nearly made a mistake, so that he exclaimed almost aloud, "Ugh!" and crossed himself. Once in the course of each month, he had a conference with Petrovich on the subject

1. **groschen.** Coin of little value

of the coat—where it would be better to buy the cloth, and the color, and the price—and he always returned home satisfied, though troubled, reflecting that the time would come at last when it could all be bought, and then the overcoat could be made.

The matter progressed more briskly than he had expected. Far beyond all his hopes, the director appointed neither forty nor forty-five rubles for Akakii Akakievich's share, but sixty. Did he suspect that Akakii Akakievich needed an overcoat? or did it merely happen so? at all events, twenty extra rubles were by this means provided. This circumstance hastened matters. Only two or three months more of hunger—and Akakii Akakievich had accumulated about eighty rubles. His heart, generally so quiet, began to beat.

On the first possible day, he visited the shops in company with Petrovich. They purchased some very good cloth—and reasonably, for they had been considering the matter for six months, and rarely did a month pass without their visiting the shops to inquire prices; and Petrovich said himself, that no better cloth could be had. For lining, they selected a cotton stuff, but so firm and thick, that Petrovich declared it to be better than silk, and even prettier and more glossy. They did not buy the marten fur, because it was dear, in fact; but in its stead, they picked out the very best of cat-skin which could be found in the shop, and which might be taken for marten at a distance.

Petrovich worked at the coat two whole weeks, for there was a great deal of quilting: otherwise it would have been done sooner. Petrovich charged twelve rubles for his work—it could not possibly be done for less: it was all sewed with silk, in small, double seams; and Petrovich went over each seam afterwards with his own teeth, stamping in various patterns.

It was—it is difficult to say precisely on what day, but it was probably the most glorious day in Akakii Akakievich's life, when Petrovich at length brought home the coat. He brought it in the morning, before the hour when it was necessary to go to the department. Never did a coat arrive so exactly in the nick of time; for the severe cold had set in, and it seemed to threaten increase. Petrovich presented himself with the coat as befits a good tailor. On his countenance was a significant expression, such as Akakii Akakievich had never beheld there. He seemed sensible to the fullest extent that he had done no small deed, and that a gulf had suddenly appeared, separating tailors who only put in linings, and make repairs, from those who make new things.

He took the coat out of the large pocket-handkerchief in which he had brought it. (The handkerchief was fresh from the laundress: he now removed it, and put it in his pocket for use.) Taking out the coat, he gazed proudly at it, held it with both hands, and flung it very skillfully over the shoulders of Akakii Akakievich; then he pulled it and fitted it down behind with his hand, then he draped it around Akakii Akakievich without buttoning it. Akakii Akakievich, as a man advanced in life, wished to try the sleeves. Petrovich helped him on with them, and it turned out that the sleeves were satisfactory also. In short, the coat appeared to be perfect, and just in season.

Petrovich did not neglect this opportunity to observe that it was only because he lived in a narrow street, and had no signboard, and because he had known Akakii Akakievich so long, that he had made it so cheaply; but, if he had been on the Nevsky Prospect, he would have charged seventy-five rubles for the making alone. Akakii Akakievich did not care to argue this point with Petrovich, and he was afraid of the large sums with which Petrovich was fond of raising the dust. He paid him, thanked him, and set out at once in his new coat for the department. Petrovich followed him, and, pausing in the street, gazed long at the coat in the distance, and went to one side expressly to run through a crooked alley, and emerge again into the street to gaze once more upon the coat from another point, namely, directly in front.

Meantime Akakii Akakievich went on with every sense in holiday mood. He was conscious every second of the time, that he had a new overcoat on his shoulders; and several times he laughed with internal satisfaction. In fact, there were two advantages—one was its warmth; the other, its beauty. He saw nothing of the road, and suddenly found himself at the department. He threw off his coat in the ante-room, looked it over well, and confided it to the especial care of the janitor. It is impossible to say just how every one in the department knew at once that Akakii Akakievich had a new coat, and that the "mantle" no longer existed. All rushed at the same moment into the ante-room, to inspect Akakii Akakievich's new coat. They began to congratulate him, and to say pleasant things to him, so that he began at first to smile, and then he grew ashamed.

When all surrounded him, and began to say that the new coat must be "christened," and that he must give a whole evening at least to it, Akakii Akakievich lost his head completely, knew not where he stood, what to answer, and how to get out of it. He stood blushing all over for several minutes, and was on the point of assuring them with great simplicity that it was not a new coat, that it was so and so, that it was the old coat. At length one of the officials, some assistant chief probably, in order to show that he was not at all proud, and on good terms with his inferiors, said "So be it: I will give the party instead of Akakii Akakievich; I invite you all to tea with me to-night; it happens quite *apropos*, as it is my name-day."[1]

1. **name-day.** Feast of the saint after whom one is named

Additional Questions and Activities

Ask students to answer the following questions in a discussion:

In ways does Akakii start to see himself differently? What details does he begin to notice about the world around him?

The officials naturally at once offered the assistant chief their congratulations, and accepted the invitation with pleasure. Akakii Akakievich would have declined; but all declared that it was discourteous, that it was simply a sin and a shame, and that he could not possibly refuse. Besides, the idea became pleasant to him when he recollected that he should thereby have a chance to wear his new coat in the evening also.

That whole day was truly a most triumphant festival day for Akakii Akakievich. He returned home in the most happy frame of mind, threw off his coat, and hung it carefully on the wall, admiring afresh the cloth and the lining; and then he brought out his old, worn-out coat, for comparison. He looked at it, and laughed, so vast was the difference. And long after dinner he laughed again when the condition of the "mantle" recurred to his mind. He dined gaily, and after dinner wrote nothing, no papers even, but took his ease for a while on the bed, until it got dark. Then he dressed himself leisurely, put on his coat, and stepped out into the street.

Where the host lived, unfortunately we cannot say: our memory begins to fail us badly; and everything in St. Petersburg, all the houses and streets, have run together, and become so mixed up in our head, that it is very difficult to produce anything thence in proper form. At all events, this much is certain, that the official lived in the best part of the city; and therefore it must have been anything but near to Akakii Akakievich.

Akakii Akakievich was first obliged to traverse a sort of wilderness of deserted, dimly lighted streets; but in proportion as he approached the official's quarter of the city, the streets became more lively, more populous, and more brilliantly illuminated. Pedestrians began to appear; handsomely dressed ladies were more frequently encountered; the men had otter collars; peasant wagoners, with their grate-like sledges stuck full of gilt nails, became rarer; on the other hand, more and more coachmen in red velvet caps, with lacquered sleighs and bear-skin robes, began to appear; carriages with decorated coach-boxes flew swiftly through the streets, their wheels scrunching the snow.

Akakii Akakievich gazed upon all this as upon a novelty. He had not been in the streets during the evening for years. He halted out of curiosity before the lighted window of a shop, to look at a picture representing a handsome woman, who had thrown off her shoe, thereby baring her whole foot in a very pretty way; and behind her the head of a man with side-whiskers and a handsome mustache peeped from the door of another room. Akakii Akakievich shook his head, and laughed, and then went on his way. Why did he laugh? Because he had met with a thing utterly unknown, but for which every one cherishes, nevertheless, some sort of feeling; or else he thought, like many officials, as follows: "Well, those French! What is to be said? If they like anything of that sort, then, in fact, that" . . . But possibly he did not think that. For it is impossible to enter a man's mind, and know all that he thinks.

At length he reached the house in which the assistant chief lodged. The assistant chief lived in fine style: on the staircase burned a lantern; his apartment was on the second floor. On entering the vestibule, Akakii Akakievich beheld a whole row of overshoes on the floor. Amid them, in the center of the room, stood a samovar,[1] humming, and emitting clouds of steam. On the walls hung all sorts of coats and cloaks, among which there were even some with beaver collars or velvet facings. Beyond the wall the buzz of conversation was audible, which became clear and loud when the servant came out with a trayful of empty glasses, cream-jugs, and sugar-bowls. It was evident that the officials had arrived long before, and had already finished their first glass of tea.

Akakii Akakievich, having hung up his own coat, entered the room; and before him all at once appeared lights, officials, pipes, card-tables; and he was surprised by a sound of rapid conversation rising from all the tables, and the noise of moving chairs. He halted very awkwardly in the middle of the room, wondering, and trying to decide, what he ought to do. But they had seen him: they received him with a shout, and all went out at once into the ante-room, and took another look at his coat. Akakii Akakievich, although somewhat confused, was open-hearted, and could not refrain from rejoicing when he saw how they praised his coat. Then, of course, they all dropped him and his coat, and returned, as was proper, to the tables set out for whist. All this—the noise, talk, and throng of people—was rather wonderful to Akakii Akakievich. He simply did not know where he stood, or where to put his hands, his feet, and his whole body. Finally he sat down by the players, looked at the cards, gazed at the face of one and another, and after a while began to gape, and to feel that it was wearisome—the more so, as the hour was already long past when he usually went to bed. He wanted to take leave of the host; but they would not let him go, saying that he must drink a glass of champagne, in honor of his new garment, without fail.

In the course of an hour, supper was served, consisting of vegetable salad, cold veal, pastry, confectioner's pies, and champagne. They made Akakii Akakievich drink two glasses of champagne, after which he felt that the room grew livelier: still, he could not forget that it was twelve

1. **samovar.** Metal urn used for tea

o'clock, and that he should have been at home long ago. In order that the host might not think of some excuse for detaining him, he went out of the room quietly, sought out, in the ante-room, his overcoat, which, to his sorrow, he found lying on the floor, brushed it, picked off every speck, put it on his shoulders, and descended the stairs to the street.

In the street all was still bright. Some petty shops, those permanent clubs of servants and all sorts of people, were open: others were shut, but, nevertheless, showed a streak of light the whole length of the door-crack indicating that they were not yet free of company, and that probably domestics, both male and female, were finishing their stories and conversations, leaving their masters in complete ignorance as to their whereabouts.

Akakii Akakievich went on in a happy frame of mind: he even started to run, without knowing why, after some lady, who flew past like a flash of lightning, and whose whole body was endowed with an extraordinary amount of movement. But he stopped short, and went on very quietly as before, wondering whence he had got that gait. Soon there spread before him those deserted streets, which are not cheerful in the daytime, not to mention the evening. Now they were even more dim and lonely: the lanterns began to grow rarer—oil, evidently, had been less liberally supplied, then came wooden houses and fences: not a soul anywhere; only the snow sparkled in the streets, and mournfully darkled the low-roofed cabins with their closed shutters. He approached the place where the street crossed an endless square with barely visible houses on its farther side, and which seemed a fearful desert.

Afar, God knows where, a tiny spark glimmered from some sentry box, which seemed to stand on the edge of the world. Akakii Akakievich's cheerfulness diminished at this point in a marked degree. He entered the square, not without an involuntary sensation of fear, as though his heart warned him of some evil. He glanced back and on both sides—it was like a sea about him. "No, it is better not to look," he thought, and went on, closing his eyes; and when he opened them, to see whether he was near the end of the square, he suddenly beheld, standing just before his very nose, some bearded individuals—of just what sort, he could not make out. All grew dark before his eyes, and his breast throbbed.

"But of course the coat is mine!" said one of them in a loud voice, seizing hold of the collar. Akakii Akakievich was about to shout for the watch, when the second man thrust a fist into his mouth, about the size of an official's head, muttering, "Now scream!"

Akakii Akakievich felt them take off his coat, and give him a push with a knee: he fell headlong upon the snow, and felt no more. In a few minutes he recovered consciousness, and rose to his feet; but no one was there. He felt that it was cold in the square, and that his coat was gone: he began to shout, but his voice did not appear to reach to the outskirts of the square. In despair, but without ceasing to shout, he started on a run through the square, straight towards the sentry-box, beside which stood the watchman, leaning on his halberd, and apparently curious to know what devil of a man was running towards him from afar, and shouting. Akakii Akskievich ran up to him, and began in a sobbing voice to shout that he was asleep, and attended to nothing, and did not see when a man was robbed. The watchman replied that he had seen no one; that he had seen two men stop him in the middle of the square, and supposed that they were friends of his; and that, instead of scolding in vain, he had better go to the captain on the morrow, so that the captain might investigate as to who had stolen the coat.

Akakii Akakievich ran home in complete disorder: his hair, which grew very thinly upon his temples and the back of his head, was entirely disarranged; his side and breast, and all his trousers, were covered with snow. The old woman, mistress of his lodgings, hearing a terrible knocking, sprang hastily from her bed, and, with a shoe on one foot only, ran to open the door, pressing the sleeve of her chemise to her bosom out of modesty; but when she had opened it, she fell back on beholding Akakii Akakievich in such a state.

When he told the matter, she clasped her hands, and said that he must go straight to the superintendent, for the captain would turn up his nose, promise well, and drop the matter there: the very best thing to do, would be to go to the superintendent; that he knew her, because Finnish Anna, her former cook, was now nurse at the superintendent's; that she often saw him passing the house; and that he was at church every Sunday, praying but at the same time gazing cheerfully at everybody; and that he must be a good man, judging from all appearances.

Having listened to this opinion, Akakii Akakievich betook himself sadly to his chamber; and how he spent the night there, anyone can imagine who can put himself in another's place. Early in the morning, he presented himself at the superintendent's, but they told him that he was asleep. He went again at ten—and was again informed that he was asleep. He went at eleven o'clock, and they said, "The superintendent is not at home." At dinner-time, the clerks in the ante-room would not admit him on any terms, and insisted upon knowing his business, and what brought him, and how it had come about—so that at last, for once in his life Akakii Akakievich felt an inclination to show some spirit, and said curtly that he must see the superintendent in person; that they should not presume to refuse him entrance; that

Cross-curricular Activities

SOCIAL STUDIES

Ask students to go to the library and research Russia in the mid-1800s, when "The Overcoat" was first published. After they have completed their research, ask them to identify, in small group discussions, the ways in which real events might have influenced Gogol as he wrote the story.

he came from the department of justice, and, when he complained of them, they would see.

The clerks dared make no reply to this, and one of them went to call the superintendent. The superintendent listened to the extremely strange story of the theft of the coat. Instead of directing his attention to the principal points of the matter, he began to question Akakii Akakievich. Why did he return so late? Was he in the habit of going, or had he been, to any disorderly house? So that Akakii Akakievich got thoroughly confused, and left him without knowing whether the affair of his overcoat was in proper train, or not.

All that day he never went near the court (for the first time in his life). The next day he made his appearance, very pale, and in his old "mantle," which had become even more shabby. The news of the robbery of the coat touched many; although there were officials present who never omitted an opportunity, even the present, to ridicule Akakii Akakievich. They decided to take up a collection for him on the spot, but it turned out a mere trifle; for the officials had already spent a great deal in subscribing for the director's portrait, and for some book, at the suggestion of the head of that division, who was a friend of the author: and so the sum was trifling.

One, moved by pity, resolved to help Akakii Akakievich with some good advice at least, and told him that he ought not to go to the captain, for although it might happen that the police-captain, wishing to win the approval of his superior officers, might hunt up the coat by some means, still, the coat would remain in the possession of the police if he did not offer legal proof that it belonged to him: the best thing for him would be to apply to a certain *prominent personage*; that this *prominent personage*, by entering into relations with the proper persons, could greatly expedite the matter.

As there was nothing else to be done, Akakii Akakievich decided to go to the *prominent personage*. What was the official position of the *prominent personage*, remains unknown to this day. The reader must know that the *prominent personage* had but recently become a prominent personage, but up to that time he had been an insignificant person.

Moreover, his present position was not considered prominent in comparison with others more prominent. But there is always a circle of people to whom what is insignificant in the eyes of others, is always important enough. Moreover, he strove to increase his importance by many devices; namely, he managed to have the inferior officials meet him on the staircase when he entered upon his service: no one was to presume to come directly to him, but the strictest etiquette must be observed; the "Collegiate Recorder" must announce to the government secretary, the government secretary to the titular councillor, or whatever other man was proper, and the business came before him in this manner. In holy Russia, all is thus contaminated with the love of imitation: each man imitates and copies his superior. They even say that a certain titular councillor, when promoted to the head of some little separate courtroom, immediately partitioned off a private room for himself, called it the *Audience Chamber*, and posted at the door a lackey with red collar and braid, who grasped the handle of the door, and opened to all comers; though the audience chamber would hardly hold an ordinary writing-table.

The manners and customs of the *prominent personage* were grand and imposing, but rather exaggerated. The main foundation of his system was strictness. "Strictness, strictness, and always strictness!" he generally said, and at the last word he looked significantly into the face of the person to whom he spoke. But there was no necessity for this, for the half score of officials who formed the entire force of the mechanism of the office were properly afraid without it: on catching sight of him afar off, they left their work, and waited, drawn up in line, until their chief had passed through the room. His ordinary converse with his inferiors smacked of sternness, and consisted chiefly of three phrases: "How dare you?" "Do you know to whom you are talking?" "Do you realize who stands before you?"

Otherwise he was a very kind-hearted man, good to his comrades, and ready to oblige, but the rank of general threw him completely off his balance. On receiving that rank, he became confused, as it were, lost his way, and never knew what to do. If he chanced to be with his equals, he was still a very nice kind of man—a very good fellow in many respects and not stupid: but just the moment that he happened to be in the society of people but one rank lower than himself, he was simply incomprehensible; he became silent; and his situation aroused sympathy, the more so as he felt himself that he might have made an incomparably better use of the time. In his eyes, there was sometimes visible a desire to join some interesting conversation and circle; but he was held back by the thought, Would it not be a very great condescension on his part? Would it not be familiar? and would he not thereby lose his importance? And in consequence of such reflections, he remained ever in the same dumb state uttering only occasionally a few monosyllabic sounds, and thereby earning the name of the most tiresome of men.

To this *prominent personage*, our Akakii Akakievich presented himself, and that at the most unfavorable time, very inopportune for himself, though opportune for the *prominent personage*. The prominent personage was in his cabinet, conversing very, very gaily with a recently arrived old acquaintance and companion of his childhood, whom he had not seen for several years. At such a time it was announced to him that a person named Bashmachkin had come. He asked abruptly, "Who is he?" "Some official," they told him. "Ah, he can wait! this is no time," said the important man. It must be remarked here, that the important man lied outrageously: he had said all he had to say to his friend long before, and the conversation had been interspersed for some time with very long pauses, during which they merely slapped each other on the leg, and said, "You think so, Ivan Abramovich!" "Just so, Stepan Varlamovich!" Nevertheless, he ordered that the official should wait, in order to show his friend—a man who had not been in the service for a long time, but had lived at home in the country—how long officials had to wait in his ante-room.

At length, having talked himself completely out, and more than that, having had his fill of pauses, and smoked a cigar in a very comfortable arm-chair with reclining back, he suddenly seemed to recollect, and told the secretary, who stood by the door with papers of reports, "Yes, it seems, indeed, that there is an official standing there. Tell him that he may come in." On perceiving Akakii Akakievich's modest mien, and his worn undress uniform, he turned abruptly to him, and said, "What do you want?" in a curt, hard voice, which he had practiced in his room in private, and before the looking-glass, for a whole week before receiving his present rank.

Akakii Akakievich, who already felt betimes the proper amount of fear, became somewhat confused: and as well as he could, as well as his tongue would permit, he explained, with a rather more frequent addition than usual of the word that, that his overcoat was quite new, and had been stolen in the most inhuman manner; that he had applied to him, in order that he might, in some way, by his intermediation, that . . . he might enter into correspondence with the chief superintendent of police, and find the coat.

For some inexplicable reason, this conduct seemed familiar to the general. "What, my dear sir!" he said abruptly, "don't you know etiquette? Where have you come to? Don't you know how matters are managed? You should first have entered a complaint about this at the court: it would have gone to the head of the department, to the chief of the division, then it would have been handed over to the secretary, and the secretary would have given it to me. . . ."

"But, your excellency," said Akakii Akakievich, trying to collect his small handful of wits, and conscious at the same time that he was perspiring terribly, "I, your excellency, presumed to trouble you because secretaries that . . . are an untrustworthy race. . . ."

"What, what, what!" said the *important personage*. "Where did you get such courage? Where did you get such ideas? What impudence towards their chiefs and superiors has spread among the young generation!" The prominent personage apparently had not observed that Akakii Akakievich was already in the neighborhood of fifty. If he could be called a young man, then it must have been in comparison with some one who was seventy. "Do you know to whom you speak? Do you realize who stands before you? Do you realize it? do you realize it? I ask you!" Then he stamped his foot, and raised his voice to such a pitch that it would have frightened even a different man from Akakii Akakievich.

Akakii Akakievich's senses failed him; he staggered, trembled in every limb, and could not stand; if the porters had not run in to support him he would have fallen to the floor. They carried him out insensible. But the prominent personage, gratified that the effect should have surpassed his expectations, and quite intoxicated with the thought that his word could even deprive a man of his senses, glanced sideways at his friend in order to see how he looked upon this, and perceived, not without satisfaction, that his friend was in a most undecided frame of mind, and even beginning, on his side, to feel a trifle frightened.

Akakii Akakievich could not remember how he descended the stairs and stepped into the street. He felt neither his hands nor feet. Never in his life had he been so rated by any general, let alone a strange one. He went on through the snow-storm, which was howling through the streets, with his mouth wide open, slipping off the sidewalk: the wind, in Petersburg fashion, flew upon him from all quarters, and through every cross-street. In a twinkling it had blown a quinsy into his throat, and he reached home unable to utter a word: his throat was all swollen, and he lay down on his bed. So powerful is sometimes a good scolding!

The next day a violent fever made its appearance. Thanks to the generous assistance of the Petersburg climate, his malady progressed more rapidly than could have been expected: and when the doctor arrived, he found, on feeling his pulse, that there was nothing to be done, except to prescribe a fomentation, merely that the sick man might not be left without the beneficent aid of medicine; but at the same time, he predicted his end in another thirty-six hours. After this, he turned to the landlady, and said, "And as for you, my dear, don't waste your time on him: order his pine coffin now, for an oak one will be too expensive for him."

Did Akakii Akakievich hear these fatal words? and, if he heard them, did they produce any overwhelming effect upon him? Did he lament the bitterness of his life?—We know not, for he continued in a raving, parching

ADDITIONAL QUESTIONS AND ACTIVITIES

Ask students to answer the following questions in a class discussion:

1. What are the many things the overcoat begins to represent to Akakii?

2. What do you think is the story's theme, or central message?

condition. Visions incessantly appeared to him, each stranger than the other: now he saw Petrovich, and ordered him to make a coat, with some traps for robbers, who seemed to him to be always under the bed; and he cried, every moment, to the landlady to pull one robber from under his coverlet: then he inquired why his old "mantle" hung before him when he had a new overcoat, then he fancied that he was standing before the general, listening to a thorough setting-down, and saying "Forgive, your excellency!" but at last he began to curse, uttering the most horrible words, so that his aged landlady crossed herself, never in her life having heard anything of the kind from him—the more so, as those words followed directly after the words *your excellency*. Later he talked utter nonsense, of which nothing could be understood: all that was evident, was that his incoherent words and thoughts hovered ever about one thing—his coat.

At last poor Akakii Akakievich breathed his last. They sealed up neither his room nor his effects, because, in the first place, there were no heirs, and, in the second, there was very little inheritance, namely, a bunch of goose-quills, a quire[1] of white official paper, three pairs of socks, two or three buttons which had burst off his trousers, and the "mantle" already known to the reader. To whom all this fell, God knows. I confess that the person who told this tale took no interest in the matter. They carried Akakii Akakievich out, and buried him. And Petersburg was left without Akakii Akakievich, as though he had never lived there. A being disappeared, and was hidden, who was protected by none, dear to none, interesting to none, who never even attracted to himself the attention of an observer of nature, who omits no opportunity of thrusting a pin through a common fly, and examining it under the microscope—a being who bore meekly the jibes of the department, and went to his grave without having done one unusual deed, but to whom, nevertheless, at the close of his life, appeared a bright visitant in the form of a coat, which momentarily cheered his poor life, and upon whom, thereafter, an intolerable misfortune descended, just as it descends upon the heads of the mighty of this world! . . .

Several days after his death, the porter was sent from the department to his lodgings, with an order for him to present himself immediately ("The chief commands it!"). But the porter had to return unsuccessful, with the answer that he could not come; and to the question, Why? he explained in the words, "Well, because: he is already dead! He was buried four days ago." In this manner did they hear of Akakii Akakievich's death at the department; and the next day a new and much larger official sat in his place, forming his letters by no means upright, but more inclined and slantwise.

But who could have imagined that this was not the end of Akakii Akakievich—that he was destined to raise a commotion after death, as if in compensation for his utterly insignificant life? But so it happened, and our poor story unexpectedly gains a fantastic ending.

A rumor suddenly spread throughout Petersburg that a dead man had taken to appearing on the Kalinkin Bridge, and far beyond, at night, in the form of an official seeking a stolen coat, and that, under the pretext of its being the stolen coat, he dragged every one's coat from his shoulders without regard to rank or calling—cat-skin, beaver, wadded, fox, bear, raccoon coats; in a word, every sort of fur and skin which men adopted for their covering. One of the department employees saw the dead man with his own eyes, and immediately recognized in him Akakii Akakievich: nevertheless, this inspired him with such terror, that he started to run with all his might, and therefore could not examine thoroughly, and only saw how the latter threatened him from afar with his finger.

Constant complaints poured in from all quarters, that the backs and shoulders, not only of titular but even of court councillors, were entirely exposed to the danger of a cold, on account of the frequent dragging off of their coats. Arrangements were made by the police to catch the corpse, at any cost, alive or dead, and punish him as an example to others, in the most severe manner: and in this they nearly succeeded, for a policeman, on guard in Kirushkin Alley, caught the corpse by the collar on the very scene of his evil deeds, for attempting to pull off the frieze coat of some retired musician who had blown the flute in his day.

Having seized him by the collar, he summoned, with a shout, two of his comrades, whom he enjoined to hold him fast, while he himself felt for a moment in his boot, in order to draw thence his snuff-box, to refresh his six times forever frozen nose; but the snuff was of a sort which even a corpse could not endure. The policeman had no sooner succeeded, having closed his right nostril with his finger, in holding half a handful up to the left, than the corpse sneezed so violently that he completely filled the eyes of all three. While they raised their fists to wipe them, the dead man vanished utterly, so that they positively did not know whether they had actually had him in their hands at all. Thereafter the watchmen conceived such a terror of dead men, that they were afraid even to seize the living, and only screamed from a distance, "Hey, there! go your way!" and the dead official began to appear, even beyond the Kalinkin Bridge, causing no little terror to all timid people.

But we have totally neglected that *certain prominent personage*, who may really be considered as the cause of

1. **quire.** Twenty-four or twenty-five sheets

the fantastic turn taken by this true history. First of all, justice compels us to say, that after the departure of poor, thoroughly annihilated Akakii Akakievich, he felt something like remorse. Suffering was unpleasant to him: his heart was accessible to many good impulses, in spite of the fact that his rank very often prevented his showing his true self. As soon as his friend had left his cabinet he began to think about poor Akakii Akakievich. And from that day forth, poor Akakii Akakievich, who could not bear up under an official reprimand, recurred to his mind almost every day. The thought of the latter troubled him to such an extent, that a week later he even resolved to send an official to him, to learn whether he really could assist him, and when it was reported to him that Akakii Akakievich had died suddenly of fever, he was startled, listened to the reproaches of his conscience, and was out of sorts for the whole day.

Wishing to divert his mind in some way, and forget the disagreeable impression, he set out that evening for one of his friends' houses, where he found quite a large party assembled; and, what was better, nearly every one was of the same rank, so that he need not feel in the least constrained. This had a marvelous effect upon his mental state. He expanded, made himself agreeable in conversation, charming: in short, he passed a delightful evening. After supper he drank a couple of glasses of champagne—not a bad recipe for cheerfulness, as every one knows. The champagne inclined him to various out-of-the-way adventures; and, in particular, he determined not to go home, but to go to see a certain well-known lady, Karolina Ivanovna, a lady, it appears, of German extraction, with whom he felt on a very friendly footing.

It must be mentioned that the prominent personage was no longer a young man, but a good husband, and respected father of a family. Two sons, one of whom was already in the service, and a good-looking sixteen-year-old daughter, with a rather *retroussé*[1] but pretty little nose, came every morning to kiss his hand, and say, "*Bonjour, papa.*" His wife, a still fresh and good-looking woman, first gave him her hand to kiss, and then, reversing the procedure, kissed his. But the prominent personage though perfectly satisfied in his domestic relations, considered it stylish to have a friend in another quarter of the city. This friend was hardly prettier or younger than his wife; but there are such puzzles in the world, and it is not our place to judge them.

So the important personage descended the stairs, stepped into his sleigh, and said to the coachman, "To Karolina Ivanovna's," and, wrapping himself luxuriously in his warm coat, found himself in that delightful position than which a Russian can conceive nothing better, which is, when you think of nothing yourself, yet the thoughts creep into your mind of their own accord, each more agreeable than the other, giving you no trouble to drive them away, or seek them. Fully satisfied, he slightly recalled all the gay points of the evening just passed, and all the *mots*[2] which had made the small circle laugh. Many of them he repeated in a low voice, and found them quite as funny as before; and therefore it is not surprising that he should laugh heartily at them.

Occasionally, however, he was hindered by gusts of wind, which, coming suddenly, God knows whence or why, cut his face, flinging in it lumps of snow, filling out his coat-collar like a sail, or suddenly blowing it over his head with supernatural force, and thus causing him constant trouble to disentangle himself. Suddenly the important personage felt someone clutch him very firmly by the collar. Turning round, he perceived a man of short stature, in an old, worn uniform, and recognized, not without terror, Akakii Akakievich. The official's face was white as snow, and looked just like a corpse's. But the horror of the important personage transcended all bounds when he saw the dead man's mouth open, and, with a terrible odor of the grave, utter the following remarks:

"Ah, here you are at last! I have you, that . . . by the collar! I need your coat. You took no trouble about mine, but reprimanded me; now give up your own." The pallid prominent personage almost died. Brave as he was in the office and in the presence of inferiors generally, and although, at the sight of his manly form and appearance, everyone said, "Ugh! how much character he has!" yet at this crisis, he, like many possessed of an heroic exterior, experienced such terror, that, not without cause, he began to fear an attack of illness.

He flung his coat hastily from his shoulders, and shouted to his coachman in an unnatural voice, "Home, at full speed!" The coachman, hearing the tone which is generally employed at critical moments, and even accompanied by something much more tangible, drew his head down between his shoulders in case of an emergency, flourished his knout,[3] and flew on like an arrow. In a little more than six minutes the prominent personage was at the entrance of his own house.

Pale, thoroughly scared, and coatless, he went home instead of to Karolina Ivanovna's, got to his chamber after some fashion, and passed the night in the direst distress; so that the next morning over their tea, his daughter said plainly, "You are very pale today, papa." But papa remained silent, and said not a word to anyone of what had happened to him, where he had been, or where he had intended to go.

This occurrence made a deep impression upon him. He even began to say less frequently to the under-officials,

1. ***retroussé.*** Turned up at the tip
2. ***mots.*** Witticisms
3. **knout**. Leather whip

Additional Questions and Activities

Ask students to choose an everyday item, like the overcoat in Gogol's story, and describe it in great detail. They should then plan an original lesson tale around this item. In what way might their item represent an idea, belief, feeling, or political view and teach readers a lesson?

You might choose to have students complete this activity working in pairs.

FROM *MADAME BOVARY*

ABOUT THE AUTHOR

Gustave Flaubert (1821–1880) was born December 12, 1821, in Rouen, France. Flaubert showed an interest in literature, particularly the work of Romantic novelists, at an early age. To satisfy his father's wishes, Flaubert went to Paris to study law in 1841. He later left to devote his life to literature. He received a large inheritance that allowed him to retire to his family's estate and write. In 1875 he lost his fortune trying to help his niece and her husband financially. Flaubert was a meticulous writer who would sometimes spend days trying to find the precise word or formulate a flawless sentence. He spent five years writing his best-known work, *Madame Bovary*. His other works include *L'Education Sentimentale* and *La Tentation de St. Antoine*.

ABOUT THE SELECTION

Madame Bovary, Flaubert's masterpiece, is a novel about a young married woman who, stirred by romantic ideals and dissatisfaction with her marriage, rebels against her middle-class lifestyle by having love affairs and trying to live an extravagant lifestyle.

When *Madame Bovary* was first published as a magazine serial in 1856, the public was shocked by its subject matter. In fact, Flaubert was bought to trial for publishing a work that was morally offensive. He defended himself against a conservative and judgmental public by saying that, far from making adultery look attractive, the tragic results of Emma Bovary's extravagance and romantic encounters serve as a lesson in using good moral judgment. Flaubert was acquitted in 1857, and the story came out in book form that same year.

The selection you are about to read is chapter 8 of *Madame Bovary*. Emma Bovary, the title character, and her husband Charles have just arrived at Vaubyessard, a chateau owned by the Marquis

(cont.)

"How dare you? do you realize who stands before you?" and, if he did utter the words, it was after first having learned the bearings of the matter. But the most noteworthy point was, that from that day the apparition of the dead official quite ceased to be seen; evidently the general's overcoat just fitted his shoulders; at all events, no more instances of his dragging coats from people's shoulders were heard of.

But many active and apprehensive persons could by no means reassure themselves, and asserted that the dead official still showed himself in distant parts of the city. And, in fact, one watchman in Kolomna saw with his own eyes the apparition come from behind a house, but being rather weak of body—so much so, that once upon a time an ordinary full-grown pig running out of a private house knocked him off his legs, to the great amusement of the surrounding public coachmen, from whom he demanded a groschen apiece for snuff, as damages—being weak, he dared not arrest him, but followed him in the dark, until, at length, the apparition looked round, paused, and inquired, "What do you want?" and showed such a fist as you never see on living men. The watchman said, "It's of no consequence," and turned back instantly. But the apparition was much too tall, wore huge mustaches, and, directing its steps apparently towards the Obukhoff Bridge, disappeared in the darkness of the night. ■

FRANCE

from *Madame Bovary*
by Gustave Flaubert,
translated by Marx Aveling

The château, a modern building in Italian style, with two projecting wings and three flights of steps, lay at the foot of an immense greensward, on which some cows were grazing among groups of large trees set out at regular intervals, while large beds of arbutus, rhododendron, syringas, and guelder roses bulged out their irregular clusters of green along the curve of the gravel path. A river flowed under a bridge; through the mist one could distinguish buildings with thatched roofs scattered over the field bordered by two gently sloping well-timbered hillocks, and in the background amid the trees rose in two parallel lines the coach houses and stables, all that was left of the ruined old château.

Charles's dogcart pulled up before the middle flight of steps; servants appeared; the Marquis came forward, and offering his arm to the doctor's wife, conducted her to the vestibule.

It was paved with marble slabs, was very lofty, and the sound of footsteps and that of voices reechoed through it as in a church. Opposite rose a straight staircase, and on the left a gallery overlooking the garden led to the billiard room, through whose door one could hear the click of the ivory balls. As she crossed it to go to the drawing room, Emma saw standing around the table men with grave faces, their chins resting on high cravats.[1] They all wore orders, and smiled silently as they made their strokes. On the dark wainscoting of the walls large gold frames bore at the bottom names written in black letters. She read: "Jean-Antoine d'Andervilliers d'Yverbonville, Count de la Vaubyessard and Baron de la Fresnaye, killed at the battle of Coutras on the 20th of October 1587." And on another: "Jean-Antoine-Henri-Guy d'Andervilliers de la Vaubyessard, Admiral of France and Chevalier of the Order of St. Michael, wounded at the battle of the Hougue-Saint-Vaast on the 29th of May 1692; died at Vaubyessard on the 23rd of January 1693." One could hardly make out those that followed, for the light of the lamps lowered over the green cloth threw a dim shadow around the room. Burnishing the horizontal pictures, it broke up against these in delicate lines where there were cracks in the varnish and from all these great black squares framed in with gold stood out here and there some lighter portion of the painting—a pale brow, two eyes that looked at you, perukes[2] flowing over and powdering red-coated shoulders, or the buckle of a garter above a well-rounded calf.

The Marquis opened the drawing-room door; one of the ladies, the Marchioness herself, came to meet Emma. She made her sit down by her on an ottoman, and began talking to her as amicably as if she had known her a long time. She was a woman of about forty, with fine shoulders, a hook nose, a drawling voice, and on this evening she wore over her brown hair a simple guipure fichu[3] that fell in a point at the back. A fair young woman was by her side in a high-backed chair, and gentlemen with flowers in their buttonholes were talking to ladies around the fire.

At seven dinner was served. The men, who were in the majority, sat down at the first table in the vestibule; the ladies at the second in the dining room with the Marquis and Marchioness.

Emma, on entering, felt herself wrapped around by the warm air, a blending of the perfume of flowers and of the fine linen, of the fumes of the viands, and the odor of the truffles. The silver dish covers reflected the lighted wax candles in the candelabra, the cut crystal covered with light steam reflected from one to the other pale rays; bouquets were placed in a row the whole length of the table; and in the large bordered plates each napkin, arranged after the

1. **cravats.** Neckerchiefs or scarves; neckties
2. **perukes.** Powdered wigs worn by men in the seventeenth and eighteenth centuries
3. **guipure fichu.** Lace cape worn with the ends crossed or fastened in front

ABOUT THE SELECTION (CONT.)

d'Andervilliers. They have received an invitation to an elegant ball at the chateau, and Emma, who feels trapped in her marriage and in her middle-class life, is looking forward to escaping for the evening into a world she sees as romantic and exciting.

fashion of a bishop's miter,[1] held between its two gaping folds a small oval-shaped roll. The red claws of lobsters hung over the dishes; rich fruit in open baskets was piled up on moss; there were quails in their plumage; smoke was rising; and in silk stockings, knee breeches, white cravat, and frilled shirt, the steward, grave as a judge, offering ready carved dishes between the shoulders of the guests, with a touch of the spoon gave you the piece chosen. On the large stove of porcelain inlaid with copper baguettes the statue of a woman, draped to the chin, gazed motionless on the room full of life.

Madame Bovary noticed that many ladies had not put their gloves in their glasses.

But at the upper end of the table, alone among all these women, bent over his full plate, and his napkin tied around his neck like a child, an old man sat eating, letting drops of gravy drip from his mouth. His eyes were bloodshot, and he wore a little queue[2] tied with a black ribbon. He was the Marquis's father-in-law, the old Duke de Laverdière, once on a time favorite of the Count d'Artois, in the days of the Vaudreuil hunting parties at the Marquis de Conflans', and had been, it was said, the lover of Queen Marie Antoinette, between Monsieur de Coigny and Monsieur de Lauzun. He had lived a life of noisy debauch, full of duels, bets, elopements; he had squandered his fortune and frightened all his family. A servant behind his chair named aloud to him in his ear the dishes that he pointed to stammering, and constantly Emma's eyes turned involuntarily to this old man with hanging lips, as to something extraordinary. He had lived at court and slept in the bed of queens!

Iced champagne was poured out. Emma shivered all over as she felt it cold in her mouth. She had never seen pomegranates nor tasted pineapples. The powdered sugar even seemed to her whiter and finer than elsewhere.

The ladies afterwards went to their rooms to prepare for the ball.

Emma made her toilet with the fastidious care of an actress on her début. She did her hair according to the directions of the hairdresser, and put on the barège dress spread out upon the bed. Charles's trousers were tight across the belly.

"My trouser-straps will be rather awkward for dancing," he said.

"Dancing?" repeated Emma.

"Yes!"

"Why, you must be mad! They would make fun of you; keep your place. Besides, it is more becoming for a doctor," she added.

Charles was silent. He walked up and down waiting for Emma to finish dressing.

He saw her from behind in the glass between two lights. Her black eyes seemed blacker than ever. Her hair, undulating towards the ears, shone with a blue luster; a rose in her chignon[3] trembled on its mobile stalk, with artificial dewdrops on the tip of the leaves. She wore a gown of pale saffron trimmed with three bouquets of pompon roses mixed with green.

Charles came and kissed her on her shoulder.

"Let me alone!" she said; "you are tumbling me."

One could hear the flourish of the violin and the notes of a horn. She went downstairs restraining herself from running.

Dancing had begun. Guests were arriving. There was some crushing. She sat down on a form near the door.

The quadrille[4] over, the floor was occupied by groups of men standing up and talking and servants in livery bearing large trays. Along the line of seated women painted fans were fluttering, bouquets half hid smiling faces, and gold stoppered scent bottles were turned in partly closed hands, whose white gloves outlined the nails and tightened on the flesh at the wrists. Lace trimmings, diamond brooches, medallion bracelets trembled on bodices, gleamed on breasts, clinked on bare arms. The hair, well smoothed over the temples and knotted at the nape, bore crowns, or bunches, or sprays of myosotis, jasmine, pomegranate blossoms, ears of corn, and cornflowers. Calmly seated in their places, mothers with forbidding countenances were wearing red turbans.

Emma's heart beat rather faster when, her partner holding her by the tips of the fingers, she took her place in a line with the dancers, and waited for the first note to start. But her emotion soon vanished, and, swaying to the rhythm of the orchestra. she glided forward with slight movements of the neck. A smile rose to her lips at certain delicate phrases of the violin, that sometimes played alone while the other instruments were silent; one could hear the clear clink of the louis d'or that were being thrown down upon the card tables in the next room; then all struck in again, the cornet-a-piston uttered its sonorous note, feet marked time, skirts swelled and rustled, hands touched and parted; the same eyes falling before you met yours again.

A few men (some fifteen or so) of twenty-five to forty, scattered here and there among the dancers or talking at the doorways, distinguished themselves from the crowd by a certain air of breeding, whatever their differences in age, dress or face.

Their clothes, better made, seemed of finer cloth, and their hair, brought forward in curls towards the temples, glossy with more delicate pomades.[5] They had the

1. **miter.** Headdress; tall ornamental cap with peaks in front and back
2. **queue.** Braid of hair at the back of the head
3. **chignon.** Knot or coil of hair worn at the back of the neck
4. **quadrille.** Dance performed by four couples
5. **pomades.** Perfumed ointments for the hair

Additional Questions and Activities

Ask students to answer the following questions about the selection:

1. What is life like at Vaubyessard, where Emma and Charles visit? During the dinner scene, what details are used to describe the Marquis's father-in-law? What does Emma see when she looks at him?

2. How does Emma feel about visiting Vaubyessard and attending the ball? Why is Emma's perception of the Marquis's father-in-law so different from the actual description of him? What clouds her perception?

3. As they dress for the ball, how does Emma respond to Charles's questions and his kiss on her shoulder? At the ball, what does Emma notice about some of the men who "distinguished themselves from the crowd"? How does Emma feel after her first waltz?

4. What does Emma's treatment of Charles say about her feelings for him? Why is Emma so taken with the Viscount and the other men like him? How do you know that the scene at the ball is rather foreign to Emma?

ANSWERS

1. Life at Vaubyessard is luxurious and elegant. The Marquis's father-in-law is described as having a napkin tied around his neck like a child, drops of gravy falling from his mouth, and bloodshot eyes. He has lived a wild life, frightening his family and squandering his money. Emma thinks only about the fact that he has lived in court and mingled with queens.

2. Emma is thrilled to visit Vaubyessard and attend the ball. Emma is so impressed with the man's social status that she cannot see his true nature. Her romantic illusions cloud her perception of the man.

(cont.)

Additional Questions and Activities (cont.)

3. Emma responds to Charles's questions and his kiss on her shoulder with disdain. At the ball, Emma notices that the men who "distinguished themselves from the crowd" seem to have better clothing, more delicate hair, and wealthier-looking complexions. Emma feels tired and defeated after her first waltz.

4. Emma is annoyed with her life with Charles and the fact that he is not part of this elegant world. Emma idealizes the men because they are wealthy and stylish. She tastes things for the first time at dinner, and she waltzes for the first time. Also, the fact that she idealizes Vaubyessard shows that she is looking in at this particular social world from its outskirts.

Additional Questions and Activities

Ask students to answer the following questions about the selection:

1. What is Charles doing just before the ball ends? What is the first thing he does when he returns to the room? What is the first thing Emma does when she returns to the room?

2. What do the reactions of Charles and Emma at the end of the dance reveal about their individual perspectives on their lives and their relationship?

3. What does Charles find on the ground as he and Emma leave Vaubyessard? What happens between Emma and the maid, Natasie, when Charles and Emma arrive home? What might be the reason behind Emma's hostility?

ANSWERS

Responses will vary.

1. Charles is sleeping, standing up, by the card tables. He takes his boots off and prepares for sleep. Emma leans out of the window and breathes in the night air, not wanting the elegant night to end.

2. They are both satisfied with different things—Charles is happy being a middle-class doctor and living an average life. Emma wants to be part of the elegant world of Vaubyessard. They do not agree on this major point, and they do not seem to communicate well or understand each other.

3. Charles finds cigars on the ground as he and Emma leave Vaubyessard. Emma gets mad at Natasie because dinner is late, Natasie answers rudely, and Emma fires her. Emma is hostile because she does not live in the luxurious world that she just left and feels powerless to get out of her own world, in which she is bored and unhappy.

complexion of wealth—that clear complexion that is heightened by the pallor of porcelain, the shimmer of satin, the veneer of old furniture, and that an ordered regimen of exquisite nurture maintains at its best. Their necks moved easily in their low cravats, their long whiskers fell over their turned-down collars, they wiped their lips upon handkerchiefs with embroidered initials that gave forth a subtle perfume. Those who were beginning to grow old had an air of youth, while there was something mature in the faces of the young. In their unconcerned looks was the calm of passions daily satiated, and through all their gentleness of manner pierced that peculiar brutality, the result of a command of half easy things, in which force is exercised and vanity amused—the management of thoroughbred horses and the society of loose women.

A few steps from Emma a gentleman in a blue coat was talking of Italy with a pale young woman wearing a parure of pearls.

They were praising the breadth of the columns of St. Peter's, Tivoli, Vesuvius, Castellamare, and Cassines, the roses of Genoa, the Coliseum by moonlight. With her other ear Emma was listening to a conversation full of words she did not understand. A circle gathered round a very young man who the week before had beaten "Miss Arabella" and "Romolus," and won two thousand louis jumping a ditch in England. One complained that his race horses were growing fat; another of the printers' errors that had disfigured the name of his horse.

The atmosphere of the ball was heavy; the lamps were growing dim. Guests were flocking to the billiard room. A servant got upon a chair and broke the window panes. At the crash of the glass Madame Bovary turned her head and saw in the garden the faces of peasants pressed against the window looking in at them. Then the memory of the Bertaux came back to her. She saw the farm again, the muddy pond, her father in a blouse under the apple trees, and she saw herself again as formerly, skimming with her finger the cream off the milk pans in the dairy. But in the refulgence of the present hour her past life, so distinct until then, faded away completely, and she almost doubted having lived it. She was there; beyond the ball was only shadow overspreading all the rest. . . .

After supper, where were plenty of Spanish and Rhine wines, soups *à la bisque* and *au lait d'amandes,* puddings *à la Trafalgar,* and all sorts of cold meats with jellies that trembled in the dishes, the carriages one after the other began to drive off. Raising the corners of the muslin[1] curtain, one could see the light of their lanterns glimmering through the darkness. The seats began to empty, some card players were still left; the musicians were cooling the tips of their fingers on their tongues. Charles was half asleep, his back propped against a door.

At three o'clock the cotillion began. Emma did not know how to waltz. Everyone was waltzing, Mademoiselle d'Andervilliers herself and the Marquis; only the guests staying at the castle were still there, about a dozen persons.

One of the waltzers, however, who was familiarly called Viscount, and whose low cut waistcoat seemed molded to his chest, came a second time to ask Madame Bovary to dance, assuring her that he would guide her, and that she would get through it very well.

They began slowly, then went more rapidly. They turned; all around them was turning—the lamps, the furniture, the wainscoting, the floor, like a disc on a pivot. On passing near the doors the bottom of Emma's dress caught against his trousers. Their legs commingled; he looked down at her; she raised her eyes to his. A torpor seized her; she stopped. They started again, and with a more rapid movement; the Viscount, dragging her along, disappeared with her to the end of the gallery, where, panting, she almost fell, and for a moment rested her head upon his breast. And then, still turning, but more slowly, he guided her back to her seat. She leaned back against the wall and covered her eyes with her hands.

When she opened them again, in the middle of the drawing-room three waltzers were kneeling before a lady sitting on a stool. She chose the Viscount, and the violin struck up once more.

Everyone looked at them. They passed and repassed, she with rigid body, her chin bent downward, and he always in the same pose, his figure curved, his elbow rounded, his chin thrown forward. That woman knew how to waltz! They kept up a long time, and tired out all the others.

Then they talked a few moments longer, and after the good nights, or rather good mornings, the guests of the château retired to bed.

Charles dragged himself up by the balusters. His "knees were going up into his body." He had spent five consecutive hours standing bolt upright at the card tables, watching them play whist, without understanding anything about it, and it was with a deep sigh of relief that he pulled off his boots.

Emma threw a shawl over her shoulders, opened the window, and leaned out.

The night was dark; some drops of rain were falling. She breathed in the damp wind that refreshed her eyelids. The music of the ball was still murmuring in her ears, and she tried to keep herself awake in order to prolong the illusion of this luxurious life that she would soon have to give up.

1. **muslin.** Strong and sheer cotton cloth of plain weave

Day began to break. She looked long at the windows of the château, trying to guess which were the rooms of all those she had noticed the evening before. She would fain have known their lives, have penetrated, blended with them. But she was shivering with cold. She undressed, and cowered down between the sheets against Charles, who was asleep.

There were a great many people to luncheon. The repast lasted ten minutes; no liquors were served, which astonished the doctor. Next, Mademoiselle d'Andervilliers collected some pieces of roll in a small basket to take them to the swans on the ornamental waters, and they went to walk in the hot houses, where strange plants, bristling with hairs, rose in pyramids under hanging vases, where, as from overfilled nests of serpents, fell long green cords interlacing. The orangery, which was at the other end, led by a covered way to the outhouses of the château. The Marquis, to amuse the young woman, took her to see the stables. Above the basketshaped racks porcelain slabs bore the names of the horses in black letters. Each animal in its stall whisked its tail when anyone went near and said "Tchk! tchk!" The boards of the harness room shone like the flooring of a drawing-room. . . .

Charles, meanwhile, went to ask a groom to put his horse to. The dogcart was brought to the foot of the steps, and all the parcels being crammed in, the Bovarys paid their respects to the Marquis and Marchioness and set out again for Tostes.

Emma watched the turning wheels in silence. Charles, on the extreme edge of the seat, held the reins with his two arms wide apart, and the little horse ambled along in the shafts that were too big for him. The loose reins hanging over his crupper[1] were wet with foam, and the box fastened on behind the chaise gave great regular bumps against it.

They were on the heights of Thibourville when suddenly some horsemen with cigars between their lips passed laughing. Emma thought she recognized the Viscount, turned back, and caught on the horizon only the movement of the heads rising or falling with the unequal cadence of the trot or gallop.

A mile farther on they had to stop to mend with some string the traces that had broken.

But Charles, giving a last look to the harness, saw something on the ground between his horse's legs, and he picked up a cigar case with a green silk border and emblazoned in the center like the door of a carriage.

"There are even two cigars in it," said he; "they'll do for this evening after dinner."

"Why, do you smoke?" she asked.

"Sometimes, when I get a chance."

He put his find in his pocket and whipped up the nag.

When they reached home the dinner was not ready. Madame lost her temper. Natasie answered rudely.

"Leave the room!" said Emma. "You are forgetting yourself. I give you warning."

For dinner there was onion soup and a piece of veal with sorrel. Charles, seated opposite Emma, rubbed his hands gleefully.

"How good it is to be at home again!"

Natasie could be heard crying. He was rather fond of the poor girl. She had formerly, during the wearisome time of his widowhood, kept him company many an evening. She had been his first patient, his oldest acquaintance in the place.

"Have you given her warning for good?" he asked at last.

"Yes. Who is to prevent me?" she replied.

Then they warmed themselves in the kitchen while their room was being made ready. Charles began to smoke. He smoked with lips protruding, spitting every moment, recoiling at every puff.

"You'll make yourself ill," she said scornfully.

He put down his cigar and ran to swallow a glass of cold water at the pump. Emma seizing hold of the cigar case threw it quickly to the back of the cupboard.

The next day was a long one. She walked about her little garden, up and down the same walks, stopping before the beds, before the espalier,[2] before the plaster curate, looking with amazement at all these things of once-on-a-time that she knew so well. How far off the ball seemed already! What was it that thus set so far asunder the morning of the day before yesterday and the evening of to-day? Her journey to Vaubyessard had made a hole in her life, like one of those great crevasses that a storm will sometimes make in one night in mountains. Still she was resigned. She devoutly put away in her drawers her beautiful dress, down to the satin shoes whose soles were yellowed with the slippery wax of the dancing floor. Her heart was like these. In its friction against wealth something had come over it that could not be effaced.

The memory of this ball, then, became an occupation for Emma. Whenever the Wednesday came round she said to herself as she awoke, "Ah! I was there a week—a fortnight— three weeks ago." And little by little the faces grew confused in her remembrance. She forgot the tune of the quadrilles; she no longer saw the liveries and appointments so distinctly; some details escaped her, but the regret remained with her. ■

1. **crupper.** Part of a padded leather saddle-strap passed around the base of a horse's tail to keep the saddle from moving forward

2. **espalier.** Lattice or trellis on which shrubs are trained to grow flat

LITERARY TECHNIQUE

FLASHBACK

A **flashback** is a section of a literary work that presents an event or series of events that occurred earlier than the current time in the work. Point out to students that in the text on page 1008 Emma has a flashback to her childhood on a farm. She sees a muddy pond, her father, some apple trees, and herself. She remembers skimming cream from milk pans with her finger. This scene shows that Emma has grown up on a farm and is not familiar with the elegant world of the people at the ball.

ADDITIONAL QUESTIONS AND ACTIVITIES

Ask students if they understand the feelings of Emma Bovary. Why, or why not? If they were her friends, what might they say to her about her life or about her behavior?

You might also ask students if they have ever wished they had a life different from their own. Has this wish ever kept them from appreciating the special things in their own lives?

HISTORICAL NOTE

Flaubert's novel *Salammbo*, published in 1862, is about a heroine named Salammbo who is the daughter of a general in Carthage. Carthage was an ancient city in north Africa established by Phoenician traders. It was a rival of Rome, and the Romans destroyed Carthage at the end of the Punic Wars. In Virgil's *Aeneid*, the character Queen Dido is the queen of Carthage.

ADDITIONAL QUESTIONS AND ACTIVITIES

Ask students to think about a favorite character from a book or movie and imagine this character at the elegant ball that Emma attended. They should then write a one-page descriptive piece in which they describe this character in these surroundings. Tell students to keep the following questions in mind: Does your character feel comfortable? If not, where would your character rather be? Does your character like the people at the ball? If not, what people does he or she prefer?

ADDITIONAL RESOURCES

Assessment Portfolio

- Vocabulary Worksheet 2.11.19
- Study Guide 2.11.20
- Unit Test 2.11.21

Essential Skills Practice Books

WRITING

- Choosing a Purpose, 1.8
- Writing a Critical Essay, 1.20

LANGUAGE

- Astronomical Terms, Time, Days, Months, Years, Holiday, Events, and Periods, 2.54
- Directions, Regions, Place Names, Organizations, Institutions, Brand and Trade Names, Buildings, Structures, and Vehicles, 2.56
- First Words, Interjections, and the Pronoun *I*, 2.57
- Names, Titles of Persons, Occupations, and Family Relationships, 2.55
- Poetry, Outlines, and Letters, 2.60
- Pronoun Reference and Agreement, 2.40
- Quotations and Sacred Names, 2.59
- School Subjects, Classes, Grades, and Awards, 2.61
- Titles of Works of Art, Literature, and Music, 2.58

SPEAKING AND LISTENING

- Active Listening and Interpersonal Communication, 3.2
- Collaborative Learning and Discussion, 3.3

STUDY AND RESEARCH

- Bibliographies and Bibliography Cards, 4.20
- The Classification of Library Materials, 4.11
- Computer-assisted Research, 4.17
- Documenting Sources in a Report, 4.23
- Evaluating Sources, 4.19
- Footnotes and Endnotes, 4.24
- Informal and Formal Note-Taking, 4.22
- Paraphrasing and Summarizing, 4.21
- Using the Card Catalog, 4.13
- Using Dictionaries, 4.15
- Using Reference Works, 4.14
- Using Search Tools, 4.12
- Using Thesauruses, 4.16

APPLIED ENGLISH/TECH PREP

- Writing Promotional and Public Relations Copy, 5.6

UNIT REVIEW

Romanticism, Realism, and Naturalism

VOCABULARY FROM THE SELECTIONS

absolve, 951	disconcert, 922	obliquely, 935	sallow, 954
abyss, 919	emaciated, 954	obscure, 953	sated, 938
adorn, 943	ethereal, 954	ostentation, 919	scorn, 955
allay, 910	forlorn, 978	pension, 936	sheepishly, 989
anemic, 986	futile, 951	perdition, 922	silhouette, 931
apparition, 932	gaudy, 974	perennial, 926	skein, 988
assuage, 943	gluttonous, 933	physiognomy, 919	skiff, 911
audacious, 915	grimace, 935	piety, 905	squall, 931
avidity, 919	ignominy, 918	posterity, 954	stupefaction, 916
canvass, 950	immobility, 932	procure, 942, 952	tabernacle, 938
compulsory, 951	impetuosity, 953	profound, 934	transcendental, 952
consternation, 920	inarticulate, 922	rancor, 944	unshod, 988
contempt, 955	inert, 986	remonstrate, 943	vain, 934
contemptuous, 946	invalid, 938	renunciation, 955	venture, 936
cudgel, 915	languidly, 965	reverie, 962	wayfarer, 987
degradation, 988	moor, 989	rhapsodize, 962	

LITERARY TERMS

antihero, 991	metaphor, 940	psychological fiction, 991
apostrophe, 929	mood, 912	Realism, 901, 924
characterization, 948, 949	motivation, 957	Romanticism, 900, 924
dramatic irony, 982	Naturalism, 902, 924, 930, 939, 984	setting, 912, 940
flashback, 949	one-dimensional character, 924	simile, 940, 957
foreshadowing, 948	paradox, 906	theme, 982
hyperbole, 949	parallelism, 906	three-dimensional character, 924
internal monologue, 991	personification, 929, 940	tone, 929
irony, 941, 947, 982		
irony of situation, 947		

Vocabulary Check Test

Ask students to number their papers from one to ten. Have students complete each sentence with a word from the Vocabulary from the Selections in the Unit Review.

1. Because of her broken leg, Sky was forced to remain in her bed for several weeks; she did not enjoy feeling like an invalid.
2. Parents of students in the school district went to the town meeting to remonstrate proposed cuts in the school budget.
3. We stared in stupefaction at the comet blazing through the night sky.
4. Anna stunned the class by winning the election for student council president and then offering her renunciation of the prestigious position.
5. The criminal confessed to her crime to (cont.)

SYNTHESIS: QUESTIONS FOR WRITING, RESEARCH, OR DISCUSSION

GENRE STUDIES

1. Compare and contrast the poems in this unit. In what way does each poem deal with ideas of Romanticism? How are the poems similar? How are they different?

2. Analyze the selections from the novels *Les Misérables* and *Madame Bovary*. In what ways are their themes, tones, moods, and points of view similar? In what ways do these aspects of the selections differ?

3. Define *short story*. Then compare and contrast "The False Gems," "The Bet," and "The Shoes." What are their similarities? What are their differences? How is irony used effectively in each story?

THEMATIC STUDIES

4. Define *Romanticism* and *Realism*. Contrast these literary movements using passages from the selections in this unit to support your ideas.

5. Discuss the theme of illusion versus reality as it appears in "The Loreley," the selection from *Madame Bovary*, and "The False Gems." Which characters are deluded by romantic ideals? What do they imagine? What seems to be the reality of their situations? How do their delusions interfere with their ability to live happy lives? Support your ideas using concrete details.

6. Discuss the nature imagery that appears in selections in this unit. How is nature portrayed? In what way does this portrayal reflect the themes of Romanticism?

HISTORICAL/BIOGRAPHICAL STUDIES

7. Examine the Romantic selections in this unit. Against what ideas were Romantic thinkers rebelling? In what way did their ideas speak to the status of the individual?

8. Define *Realism* and *Naturalism*. What led to the emergence of these movements? What changes in the world did they reflect?

SPELLING CHECK TEST

Ask students to number their papers from one to ten. Read each word aloud. Then read aloud the sentence containing the word. Repeat the word. Ask students to write the word on their papers, spelling it correctly.

1. **piety**
My grandfather's religious piety earns him respect among the most devout believers at the synagogue he attends.

2. **allay**
The police officers are trying to allay the public's fears surrounding the recent string of burglaries.

3. **audacious**
She was an audacious mountain climber—always challenging herself to climb taller mountains.

4. **ignominy**
The ignominy of going to prison encouraged the young man to change his ways.

5. **consternation**
The firefighters and the crowd were in a state of consternation when the fire spread to the next city block.

6. **inarticulate**
The man was overcome with emotion and nearly inarticulate as he accepted his award.

7. **gluttonous**
At Thanksgiving dinner, everyone reached for food in a gluttonous manner.

8. **contemptuous**
The star of the play treated the actors with minor roles in a contemptuous manner.

9. **scorn**
Members of the community will scorn products from Company X in protest of its plans to lay off thousands of workers.

10. **forlorn**
We fed the forlorn stray dog and gave him a place to sleep.

VOCABULARY CHECK TEST (CONT.)

assuage her feelings of guilt.

6. I was required to take so many compulsory courses this year, I was unable to fit any electives into my schedule.

7. Robin took in the stray cat because it was emaciated and in desperate need of food and care.

8. People cited Patrick's purchase of a new sixty-foot yacht as an example of ostentation.

9. Taking a walk outside felt great after spending so many hours sitting inert in the car.

10. Rex was too modest to accept compliments gracefully—he would only smile sheepishly when praised.

UNIT SKILLS OUTLINE

Literary Skills and Concepts
- Alliteration, 1042, 1063, 1070
- Allusion, 1051
- Anecdote, 1044
- Antihero, 1078, 1085
- Aphorism, 1111
- Archetype, 1102
- Assonance, 1072
- Atmosphere, 1025, 1092
- Autobiography, 1111
- Biography, 1026, 1033
- Character, 1058
- Cliché, 1068
- Courtly Love, 1020
- Dramatic Irony, 1033, 1085
- Existentialism, 1058
- Extended Metaphor, 1084
- Fantasy, 1077
- Figure of Speech, 1044
- Free Verse, 1038
- Image, 1024, 1042, 1102
- Imagery, 1024, 1042, 1102
- Internal Monologue, 1033
- Irony, 1033, 1051
- Irony of Situation, 1033, 1051
- Metaphor, 10, 721111
- Metonymy, 1044, 1051
- Mood, 1025, 1092, 1097
- Negritude Movement, 1040
- Parody, 1075
- Point of View, 1092, 1099
- Realism, 1099
- Repetition, 1038
- Rhyme, 1063
- Romance, 1020
- Satire, 1033, 1075, 1115
- Science Fiction, 1065, 1077
- Setting, 1097
- Stream-of-Consciousness Writing, 1033
- Symbol, 1038, 1115
- Synaesthesia, 1033
- Tone, 1047, 1063
- Verbal Irony, 1033

Writing Skills and Concepts
- Anecdote, 1051
- Autobiographical Sketch, 1111
- Biography, 1034
- Childhood Memory, 1025
- Critical Essay, 1025, 1034, 1039, 1043, 1051, 1058, 1063, 1076, 1085, 1093, 1102, 1111, 1115
- Free-Verse Poem, 1039
- News Story, 1085
- Occasional Poem or Speech, 1043
- Personal Memoir, 1102
- Poem or Fable with an Unusual Point of View, 1115
- Reinventing a Traditional Character, 1058
- Science Fiction Description, 1076
- Snapshots of an Event, 1092
- Tribute, 1063

Grammar, Usage, and Mechanics Skills and Concepts
- Connotation and Denotation, 1111
- Correcting Sentence Strings, 1115
- Semicolons and Colons, 1034
- Underlining, Italics, and Quotation Marks in Titles, 1064
- Uses of Quotation Marks, 1115

Other Language Arts Skills and Concepts
- Active Listening and Interpersonal Communication, 1055
- Collaborative Learning and Discussion, 1025, 1055
- Research Skills, 1039
- Taking Essay Tests, 1059
- Technical Writing, 1076
- Television and Film, 1081
- Using Reference Works, 1096

Unit 12 Modern and Contemporary Literature

Eiffel Tower. Robert Delaunay, 1924–1926. Hirshhorn Museum and Sculpture Garden, Smithsonian Institution, Gift of Joseph H. Hirshhorn Foundation, 1972

GOALS/OBJECTIVES

Studying this unit will enable students to

- have a positive experience reading modern and contemporary literature
- recognize and discuss trends and movements of modern and contemporary literature
- understand the historical events that affected the changes in literature during the twentieth century
- discuss the use of literature as a means of social criticism
- write creatively in response to literature
- write critically about literature

"And in today already walks tomorrow."

—Samuel Taylor Coleridge

1013

Cross-Curricular Connections

Arts and Humanities
- African Arts, 1043
- America the Violent?, 1116
- Analyzing Nonsense Verse, 1069
- *Cante Jondo*, 1035
- Camus's Novels, 1052
- Ceremonies, 1093
- Chinese History and Literature, 1104
- Creative Writing about Science and Technology, 1077
- Depicting Scenes in *Orlando*, 1028
- Expressions of Emotion in Different Cultures, 1116
- Figure of Speech Collage, 1051
- History and Culture of Australia, 1060
- Latin American Women Writers, 1044
- Modern and Contemporary Art, 1015
- Oral History Project, 1040
- Persian Bazaars, 1018
- Researching Twentieth-Century Spain, 1039
- Science Fiction, 1065

Mathematics and Sciences
- Creative Writing about Science and Technology, 1077
- Eastern Approaches in Western Medicine, 1117
- Gardening, 1085
- Science and Technology Fair, 1070
- Seasons and World Climate, 1096

Social Studies
- African Arts, 1043
- Algeria, 1054
- America the Violent?, 1116
- Biographical Notes on Echoes Authors, 1016
- Botswana, 1088
- Catalog of Children's Games, 1103
- Ceremonies, 1093
- Chinese History and Literature, 1104
- Cultural Losses and Gains, 1117
- Eastern Approaches in Western Medicine, 1117
- Expressions of Emotion in Different Cultures, 1116
- History and Culture of Australia, 1060
- The Internet and the Global Village, 1117
- Meeting the President, 1078
- Modern Greek History, 1112
- Oral History Project, 1040
- Race Relations in South Africa, 1086
- Researching Botswana, 1089
- Researching James I of England, 1026
- Researching Twentieth-Century Events, 1015
- Researching Twentieth-Century Spain, 1039
- Seasons and World Climate, 1096
- Theory of the Cat, 1116

Applied Arts
- Catalog of Children's Games, 1103
- Gardening, 1085
- History of Technology, 1067
- The Internet and the Global Village, 1117
- Persian Bazaars, 1018
- Science and Technology Fair, 1070
- Technological Advances, 1015

Teaching the Multiple Intelligences

Musical
- African Arts, 1043
- *Cante Jondo*, 1035
- Ceremonies, 1093
- Themes in Echoes, Movies, and Song, 1017

Logical-Mathematical
- Analyzing Nonsense Verse, 1069
- Catalog of Children's Games, 1103
- Chinese History and Literature, 1104
- Comparing "Araby" and "Games at Twilight," 1094

(cont.)

Teaching the Multiple Intelligences (cont.)

- Comparing and Contrasting Love Stories, 1047
- Connotation and Denotation, 1111
- Creative Writing about Science and Technology, 1077
- Cultural Losses and Gains, 1117
- Debating Capital Punishment, 1055
- Defining Poetry, 1071
- Eastern Approaches in Western Medicine, 1117
- Echoes Themes and Meanings, 1017
- Figure of Speech Collage, 1051
- Formal Discussion, 1025
- Latin American Women Writers, 1044
- Love Survey, 1027
- Meeting the President, 1078
- Persian Bazaars, 1018
- Researching Botswana, 1089
- Researching James I of England, 1026
- Researching Twentieth-Century Events, 1015
- Science and Technology Fair, 1070
- Seasons and World Climate, 1096
- Television and Film Habits, 1081
- Theory of the Cat, 1116

Spatial
- African Arts, 1043
- Catalog of Children's Games, 1103
- Ceremonies, 1093
- Depicting Scenes in *Orlando*, 1028
- Figure of Speech Collage, 1051
- Gardening, 1085
- History and Culture of Australia, 1060
- Modern and Contemporary Art, 1015
- Persian Bazaars, 1018
- Science and Technology Fair, 1070

(cont.)

OTHER SELECTIONS EXPLORING THIS PERIOD

(cont.)

UNIT 12

Preview: Modern and Contemporary Literature

Blue Cinema. *René Magritte, 1926*

Modern and contemporary literature is characterized by a revolt against older literary forms and traditions and by the sense that we are living in a sometimes confusing or troubling era. Of course, people of every age have considered themselves to be living in a "modern" age, and writers working in many literary movements, from Renaissance writers to the Romantics, have broken with previously established literary traditions. Perhaps what distinguishes the literature of the twentieth century from the works of earlier centuries is diversity—the variety of styles, forms, and movements that have arisen in the twentieth century is remarkable. This century has been a tumultuous period, marked by enormous technological advances, warfare, revolutions, changing forms of government, the overthrow of colonialism, and the founding of many new nations. Twentieth-century literature reflects these violent changes. So many different literary and artistic movements have emerged that this century has been called a "century of isms."

The first important "ism" of the twentieth century was Modernism. This movement arose in response to World War I. The "War to End All Wars" involved almost all of Europe as well as the United States and parts of Asia. The first "modern" war, fought with new weaponry such as machine guns and chemical weapons such as mustard gas, claimed the lives of more than ten million soldiers and one million civilians. In many ways, this war also claimed the innocence of a generation. Stripped of their illusions, people began questioning traditional beliefs and values. Modernist writers sought to express the uncertainty of the modern individual who had lost connections to the beliefs and values of preceding generations. Much of Modernist writing is elliptical or fragmented, and the themes are often left ambiguous, creating a sense of uncertainty.

Certain Modernist writers were influenced by Sigmund Freud's explorations of the subconscious mind; writers such as James Joyce and Virginia Woolf developed a new type of writing called stream-of-consciousness

OTHER SELECTIONS EXPLORING THIS PERIOD (CONT.)

that attempted to render the flow of feelings, thoughts, and impressions in the minds (conscious and subconscious) of their characters. Other Modernist writers such as Ezra Pound practiced Imagism, an attempt to free poetry of the poet's explicit comments about feeling or meaning. A typical Imagist poem presents a single, clear snapshot of a moment of perception. It does not tell the reader how to feel about the picture or image but relies on the image itself to create emotion in the reader. Another type of Modernist writing is Surrealism. Surrealists rejected middle-class values, believing that these values led to the devastation of World War I. Surrealist painters such as René Magritte and Salvador Dalí strove to heighten awareness of the human mind, both conscious and unconscious, by juxtaposing seemingly unrelated images. The viewer had to seek possible connections. Surrealist literature also made use of seeming contradictions and startling images. The Modernist poet Federico García Lorca owed much of his poetic style to both the Imagist and the Surrealist movements.

The "War to End All Wars" did not deserve its designation. Rather, World War I sowed the seeds for another colossal conflict—World War II. From 1939 to 1945 the Axis powers—Germany, Italy, and Japan—fought against the Allies—Great Britain, France, the Soviet Union, and the United States. This war was played out across the globe, claiming the lives of more than twelve million soldiers and more than twenty million civilians. Nazi Germany initiated a horrific plan to slaughter systematically all those who did not live up to their Aryan ideal. The Nazis' victims included millions of Jews as well as Gypsies, the disabled, dissenters, and homosexuals. World War II also spelled the gradual death of Imperialism—boundaries of older nations were redefined, and new nations in Africa and Asia claimed their independence from the colonial powers that had once ruled them.

World War II and its aftermath shaped contemporary literature in a number of important ways. Just as writers such as Wilfred Owen, Ernest Hemingway, and Erich Maria Remarque portrayed the horrors of World War I, survivors of the Holocaust such as Elie Wiesel depicted the atrocities of World War II in starkly realistic narratives. Another writer who survived World War II, and who later produced grim semi-autobiographical novels about his experience, was the Polish-born writer Jerzy Kosinski.

Other writers coped with the tragedy of World War II by struggling to find meaning in a seemingly absurd universe. These writers, known as Absurdists and Existentialists, believed that humans exist only by chance and that choice and action are ultimately meaningless in an indifferent universe; humans are free to make choices but one choice is as good, or as meaningless, as another. Playwrights such as Samuel Beckett and Eugene Ionesco portrayed the senselessness of existence and the lack of meaningful connections between people. Prose writers such as Franz Kafka and Albert Camus embraced Existentialism and explored its view of the individual in their writing.

World War II made it increasingly clear to many that, for better or for worse, technology would profoundly shape human life. Writers such as

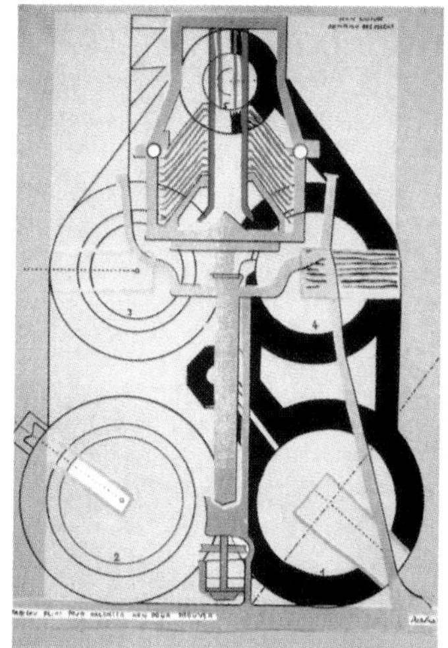

Little Solitude. *Francis Picabia, 1919*

Cross-curricular Activities

ARTS AND HUMANITIES

Ask students to study Surrealism or another movement in modern or contemporary art. Have students locate three examples of the type of art that they choose and explain why each piece reflects the ideals of the movement that created it. Students might then try to create a work in the style they have chosen.

SOCIAL STUDIES

Assign students to research one of the following topics that have had a major impact on the twentieth century.

- Battles of World War I
- Battles of World War II
- Emerging warfare technology
- The Holocaust
- New nations and the fall of colonial powers
- The Russian Revolution
- Space exploration
- Women's suffrage

Because these topics are broad, students may wish to focus their research on one aspect of the topic, or they may wish to work in groups to explore several aspects of the topic. Students might also choose a topic from current events that interests them. Students should share their findings with the class.

APPLIED ARTS

Technological advances during the modern period have had enormous impact on the world. Ask students to choose one new technology to research. Have students describe, in an oral or written report, the impact, both positive and negative, that this new technology has had, or continues to have, on the world and human experience.

TEACHING THE MULTIPLE INTELLIGENCES (CONT.)

Biographical Note

Sigmund Freud (1856–1939) founded psychoanalysis and the Freudian theory of psychology. It was during his work with patients diagnosed as hysterics that Freud began to believe in the concept of mental disorders with purely psychological causes. His works include *Studies in Hysteria, The Interpretation of Dreams, Three Essays on the Theory of Sexuality, Totem and Taboo,* and *Civilization and Its Discontents.*

Simone de Beauvoir (1908–1986) was a French writer, Existentialist, and feminist. Her best-known work is *The Second Sex,* which became a classic of feminist literature in the 1960s. Her novels, including *She Came to Stay* and *The Mandarins,* are largely Existentialist. De Beauvoir also wrote books of philosophy, travel, autobiography, and essays. Many of her works present a view of the French intellectual scene during her lifetime.

Elena Poniatowska (1933–) was born in France but moved to Mexico when she was eight. Her adopted country and her perceptions and experiences there play a large role in her writing. Poniatowska is both a prize-winning journalist and a novelist.

William Butler Yeats (1865–1939) is one of the greatest poets of the twentieth century. Much of his early poetry draws heavily on Irish folk tales and legends. His unrequited love for Maud Gonne surfaces in many of his finest poems. With Lady Augusta Gregory, Yeats founded the Irish National Theater (later named the Abbey Theater), for which he wrote plays based on Irish themes.

American writer **Henry Miller** (1891–1980) was born in Brooklyn. His childhood experiences are reflected in his book *Black Spring.* His experiences in New York also appear in *Tropic of Capricorn.* After a move to

(cont.)

Bodegon De Limon. *Ponce De Leon, 1936*

Stanislaw Lem observed the positive and negative effects of technology on human life and critiqued society through science fiction, highly imaginative writing which includes fantastic elements based on scientific principles and discoveries.

Many of the world's contemporary writers have seen their cultures in conflict. Wars or revolutions have taken place in many nations. Other nations, many of them countries that have newly won independence from former colonial powers, have experienced a more subtle type of conflict—between older, more traditional ways of life and the modern or "Western" way of life. Writers who explore the clash between traditional and Western ways of life include Chinua Achebe of Nigeria; Anita Desai, Rabindranath Tagore, and Santha Rama Rau of India; Bessie Head of South Africa and Botswana; Léopold Sédar Senghor of Senegal; and Maxine Hong Kingston, American-born child of Chinese immigrants. Movements such as Aimé Césaire's and Senghor's Negritude movement promoted the richness of traditional African cultures.

Like citizens of new nations, women have had to struggle for equality and independence. In most nations, including the United States, women were not granted the right to vote until the twentieth century. In many nations and cultures, women still struggle for a level playing field—for opportunity to step outside traditional roles, to vote, for equal employment opportunities and compensation, and to be perceived as competent and intelligent equals. This struggle has inspired an increase in feminist writing and work that examines the role of women. Examples of such writing include the novels and essays of Virginia Woolf, Judith Wright's "Request to a Year," Margaret Atwood's "Simmering," and Maxine Hong Kingston's *The Woman Warrior.*

Latin America is a hotbed of contemporary literature, producing such writers as Laura Esquivel, Pablo Neruda, Isabel Allende, Gabriel García Márquez, Gabriela Mistral, Clarice Lispector, and, in this unit, Rachel de Queiroz and Jorge Luis Borges. Many of these writers, led by García Márquez, have experimented with magical realism, fiction which is for the most part realistic but contains elements of fantasy. Like stream-of-consciousness and Surrealistic writers before them, Magical Realists explore the subconscious mind in their writing.

A large number of literary movements have emerged since the end of World War II in 1945, and many writers have produced works of outstanding quality. It is impossible to do more than guess which works and movements will be remembered. Future generations will determine what literature will become "classic" and may classify twentieth-century literature in ways we cannot predict.

Biographical Note (cont.)

France in 1930, Miller wrote about his difficulties in Depression-era Paris in *Tropic of Cancer.* His other works include a trilogy entitled *Rosy Crucifixion,* which includes the works *Sexus, Plexus,* and *Nexus,* and two collections of essays: *The Cosmological Eye* and *The Wisdom of the Heart.*

Albert Camus (1913–1960) was a French Existentialist writer. For a biography of Camus see page 1052.

Hannah Arendt (1906–1975) was a German-born American political scientist and philosopher. After the Nazis came to power in Germany, she fled to Paris. A few years later she fled the Nazis again, this time moving to the United States. Her writing focuses on Jewish affairs and totalitarianism. Her works include *Eichmann in Jerusalem,*

(cont.)

Echoes:

Modern and Contemporary Literature

I am actually not at all a man of science, not an observer, not an experimenter, not a thinker. I am by temperament nothing but a conquistador—an adventurer.

—Sigmund Freud

How is it that this world has always belonged to the men . . . ?

—Simone de Beauvoir

To this day, if I ask so many questions, it is because I don't have a single answer. I believe I will die like this, still searching, with a question mark engraved on my eyelids.

—Elena Poniatowska

Things fall apart; the center cannot hold;
Mere anarchy is loosed upon the world.

—William Butler Yeats
"The Second Coming"

The new always carries with it the sense of violation, of sacrilege. What is dead is sacred; what is new, that is, *different,* is evil, dangerous, or subversive.

—Henry Miller

Each generation doubtless feels called upon to reform the world. Mine knows that it will not reform it, but its task is perhaps even greater. It consists in preventing the world from destroying itself.

—Albert Camus
from his Nobel Prize acceptance speech

With the loss of tradition we have lost the thread which safely guided us through the vast realms of the past, but this thread was also the chain fettering each successive generation to a predetermined aspect of the past.

—Hannah Arendt

Time is change; we must measure its passage by how much things alter.

—Nadine Gordimer

The classics can console. But not enough.

—Derek Walcott

War is only a cowardly escape from the problems of peace.

—Thomas Mann

We tell our children that the bombs cannot kill everyone, that they must not be afraid. . . . We know our sacrifice is necessary. If the bombs do not fall on you, they fall on friends. We accept fate. We are calm. It is useless to be a pessimist. Some day we will win a beautiful life, if not for ourselves, then for our children.

—Nguyen Thi Binh

ESTRAGON: I can't go on like this.
VLADIMIR: That's what you think.

—Samuel Beckett
Waiting for Godot

BIOGRAPHICAL NOTE (CONT.)

The Human Condition, Between Past and Future, and *On Violence.*

South African writer **Nadine Gordimer** (1923–) won the 1991 Nobel Prize for literature. The prize committee commended her for her "continued involvement on behalf of literature and free speech in a police state where censorship and persecution of books and people exist." She has fought throughout her career to expose South Africa's apartheid system. From 1958 to 1991, her books were banned in her own country. Her novels include *A Guest of Honour, Burger's Daughter, July's People,* and *My Son's Story.*

Derek Walcott (1930–) won the Nobel Prize for literature in 1992. Born in St. Lucia in the Caribbean, Walcott attended the University of the West Indies in Jamaica. He began a career as a painter, then became a writer and a teacher. His work combines the English tradition of lyric poetry with the scenery, attitudes, and sounds of the Caribbean and urban America. For more information on Derek Walcott, see page 279.

Thomas Mann (1875–1955) wrote both novels and essays. He is considered the greatest German novelist of the twentieth century. His novels include *Buddenbrooks, Death in Venice,* and *The Magic Mountain.* He wrote essays on such notable figures as Leo Tolstoy, Sigmund Freud, and Friedrich Nietzsche. Mann won the Nobel Prize for literature in 1929.

Nguyen Thi Binh (1930–) is a Vietnamese politician. She has served as the foreign minister of the South Vietnamese National Liberation Front.

Samuel Beckett (1906–1989), winner of the Nobel Prize for literature in 1969, was a novelist and a playwright. He lived in Ireland and France and wrote in both English and French. He is best known for his plays, including *Waiting for Godot* and *Endgame.*

ADDITIONAL QUESTIONS AND ACTIVITIES

- Ask students to identify some main themes that two or more of these quotations share. Have students identify other quotations from modern or contemporary writers or from movies or songs that share such themes.
- Have students choose one of the quotations on this page. In a personal essay, each student should reflect on the meaning of the quotation and its applicability to the world in the twentieth century, and especially to the student's own experiences.
- Many of the quotations on this page are by highly respected writers of this period. Ask students to read and review one work by one of these writers.

ADDITIONAL RESOURCES

READER'S GUIDE

- Selection Worksheet 12.1

ASSESSMENT PORTFOLIO

- Selection Check Test 2.12.1
- Selection Test 2.12.2

ESSENTIAL SKILLS PRACTICE BOOKS

- Writing 1.8, 1.20
- Speaking and Listening 3.3

PREREADING EXTENSIONS

You might encourage students to research the bazaars of Persia (modern Iran and Turkey) or North Africa. Students may wish to find pictures of bazaars or to interview friends or family members who have visited one. Students might then work together to create a model of Araby or paintings or drawings depicting scenes from this bazaar. Some groups may wish to represent what Araby may have looked like while busy during the day, while others may wish to show Araby deserted at night, as the narrator encounters it.

SUPPORT FOR LEP STUDENTS

PRONUNCIATIONS OF PROPER NOUNS AND ADJECTIVES

Dub • lin (dub´ lən)
James Joyce (jāmz jois´)

ADDITIONAL VOCABULARY

career—swift course
converged—came together
diverged—went off in different directions
luxuriated—took great pleasure
resignedly—in a yielding and uncomplaining manner

PREREADING

"Araby" from *Dubliners* by James Joyce

IRELAND

About the Author

JAMES JOYCE (1882–1941)

James Joyce was born in Dublin, Ireland, and educated at Jesuit schools and at University College, Dublin. In 1902, rebelling against Catholicism, Irish nationalism, and his family, Joyce left Dublin. He spent the rest of his life in self-imposed exile, living in Paris, Trieste, Rome, and Zurich, returning to Ireland only for a brief visit. Nora Barnacle, an uneducated Dublin chambermaid, accompanied him to Trieste in 1904, and the two later married. Supported by Joyce's meager earnings as a clerk and as a teacher of languages, the couple wandered about Europe, eventually with two children. In 1914 Joyce published *Dubliners,* and in 1916 he published his largely autobiographical novel, *A Portrait of the Artist as a Young Man.* Because of deteriorating eyesight, Joyce relied on his memory and on the secretarial help of friends in his work. A perfectionist, Joyce wrote and repeatedly revised his novel *Ulysses* for seven years, from 1914 to 1921. A second large, experimental novel, *Finnegans Wake,* took seventeen years to complete. Both novels incited controversy and were denounced as obscure, nonsensical, and sometimes even obscene, until critics explained Joyce's innovative methods and other writers began imitating his experimental techniques. Joyce is now regarded as one of the twentieth century's greatest writers, known for his revolutionary innovations in prose style.

About the Selection

Dubliners, the first of James Joyce's masterpieces, is a collection of fifteen stories set in Dublin at the turn of the century. The stories, linked by their focus on the poor of Dublin, deal with different stages of life—childhood, young adulthood, maturity, old age, and death.

The story you are about to read, **"Araby,"** is the last of three childhood stories. In this piece, a boy wishes to attend the Araby Bazaar, held in Dublin in 1894, so that he might purchase something for a young woman he loves. This type of bazaar—a market of shops and stalls in which various goods are sold—is a Middle Eastern tradition. During the nineteenth century, the British Isles were becoming more exposed to Eastern cultures through increased trade and Eastern literature such as the *Rubáiyát of Omar Khayyám* (see page 796) and *The Thousand and One Nights* (see page 785). Many westerners were fascinated by Eastern cultures and traditions, which they saw as exotic and magical. In this story, a young boy pins his hopes on bringing back a prize from the bazaar to impress the person he idolizes.

CONNECTIONS: *Joyce's Dublin*

Today Dublin is the Republic of Ireland's most important commercial and cultural center. In the nineteenth and early twentieth centuries, the city became a center for nationalist activity, and attempts to free Ireland from British control led to violence and bloodshed. Dublin at this time was also experiencing renewed interest in Irish language and literature. Writers of this movement include not only James Joyce, but Lady Augusta Gregory, Sean O'Faolain, and William Butler Yeats as well.

GOALS/OBJECTIVES

Studying this lesson will enable students to

- enjoy one of James Joyce's short stories
- define *image,* recognize images in a literary work, and explain their significance
- define *mood* and identify moods in a literary work
- write about a childhood memory from the first-person point of view
- write a critical essay analyzing how mood and plot are related in a short story
- use collaborative learning and discussion skills to hold a group discussion on a literary work

Describe a time when you experienced strong feelings, such as love, anger, or frustration, toward a person. Why did you have these feelings? How did these feelings affect your behavior, or your opinion about yourself?

"Araby"

JAMES JOYCE

North Richmond Street, being blind,[1] was a quiet street except at the hour when the Christian Brothers' School set the boys free. An uninhabited house of two storeys stood at the blind end, detached from its neighbours in a square ground. The other houses of the street, conscious of decent lives within them, gazed at one another with brown imperturbable faces.

The former tenant of our house, a priest, had died in the back drawing-room. Air, musty from having been long enclosed, hung in all the rooms, and the waste room behind the kitchen was littered with old useless papers. Among these I found a few paper-covered books, the pages of which were curled and damp: *The Abbot*, by Walter Scott, *The Devout Communicant* and *The Memoirs of Vidocq*. I liked the last best because its leaves were yellow. The wild garden behind the house contained a central apple-tree and a few straggling bushes under one of which I found the late tenant's rusty bicycle-pump. He had been a very charitable priest; in his will he had left all his money to institutions and the furniture of his house to his sister.

When the short days of winter came dusk fell before we had well eaten our dinners. When we met in the street the houses had grown sombre. The space of sky above us was the colour of ever-changing violet and towards it the lamps of the street lifted their feeble lanterns. The cold air stung us and we played till our bodies glowed. Our shouts echoed in the silent street. The career of our play brought us through the dark muddy lanes behind the houses where we ran the gantlet[2] of the rough tribes from the cottages, to the back doors of the dark dripping gardens where odours arose from the ash-pits, to the dark odorous stables where a coachman smoothed and combed the horse or shook music from the buckled harness. When we returned to the street light from the kitchen windows had filled the areas. If

1. **blind.** A dead end
2. **ran the gantlet.** Ran while under attack from both sides

❶ *What season does the narrator describe? What activities filled the narrator's afternoons?*

❷ *Who had been a former tenant in the narrator's house? What was the air like in the narrator's home?*

WORDS FOR EVERYDAY USE

im • per • turb • a • ble (im´pər tʉr´bə bəl) *adj.*, unable to be disturbed

READER'S JOURNAL

As an alternate activity, you might encourage students to write about a time when they wanted to do something or go somewhere and either they never did or were disappointed when they did. What made this experience so disappointing?

ANSWERS TO GUIDED READING QUESTIONS

❶ The narrator describes winter. The narrator spends his afternoons playing with his friends until evening.

❷ A priest had been a former tenant at the house. The air was musty, from having been enclosed.

SPELLING AND VOCABULARY WORDS FROM THE SELECTION

amiability	innumerable
annihilate	intervening
chafe	litany
discreetly	pious
garrulous	sodden
imperturbable	veil
incessant	

QUOTABLES

"Around us fear, descending
Darkness of fear above
And in my heart how deep unending
Ache of love!"

—James Joyce

VOCABULARY IN CONTEXT

• Nothing frustrates my little brother more than when I remain imperturbable no matter what he does to upset or annoy me.

Answers to Guided Reading Questions

❶ The narrator imagines carrying a chalice safely through a group of enemies. He may be hoping to perform some action that would prove his worth to Mangan's sister and to win her love.

❷ The narrator watches Mangan's sister until she comes to the doorstep, when he runs to the hall, grabs his books, and follows her. He does this because her name was "like a summons to all my foolish blood."

❸ The narrator has romantic feelings and feelings of adoration for Mangan's sister. He murmurs "O love! O love!"

❹ Mangan's sister speaks to the narrator for the first time when she asks him if he is going to Araby.

Literary Technique

ROMANCE AND COURTLY LOVE

A **romance** is a medieval story about the adventures and loves of knights. **Courtly love** is a code of romantic love celebrated in songs and romances of the Medieval Period. According to this code, the lover knows himself or herself to be truly in love if he or she is overcome by extreme, transforming emotion. Characters in works celebrating courtly love are often one-dimensional. The female lover is often portrayed in ideal and unrealistic terms. She usually requires that the male lover prove his love through a series of tasks. The male lover is led sometimes to the depths of despair and sometimes to heights of courtesy and heroism to prove his worth to his lady. Encourage students to discuss the ways in which this work resembles a romance. In what ways is the narrator's love for Mangan's sister courtly? What task does he imagine himself performing, and where may he have gotten this idea? Explain whether Joyce's short story ultimately celebrates the code of courtly love or critiques it as unrealistic.

(cont.)

❶ *What does the narrator imagine? How might this be related to his feelings for Mangan's sister?*

❷ *What does the narrator do each morning, when he sees his friend Mangan's sister? Why does he do this?*

❸ *What feelings does the narrator have for Mangan's sister? What does he murmur to himself?*

❹ *What were Mangan's sister's first words to the narrator?*

my uncle was seen turning the corner we hid in the shadow until we had seen him safely housed. Or if Mangan's sister came out on the doorstep to call her brother in to his tea we watched her from our shadow peer up and down the street. We waited to see whether she would remain or go in and, if she remained, we left our shadow and walked up to Mangan's steps resignedly. She was waiting for us, her figure defined by the light from the half-opened door. Her brother always teased her before he obeyed and I stood by the railings looking at her. Her dress swung as she moved her body and the soft rope of her hair tossed from side to side.

Every morning I lay on the floor in the front parlour watching her door. The blind was pulled down to within an inch of the sash so that I could not be seen. When she came out on the doorstep my heart leaped. I ran to the hall, seized my books and followed her. I kept her brown figure always in my eye and, when we came near the point at which our ways diverged, I quickened my pace and passed her. This happened morning after morning. I had never spoken to her, except for a few casual words, and yet her name was like a summons to all my foolish blood.

Her image accompanied me even in places the most hostile to romance. On Saturday evenings when my aunt went marketing I had to go to carry some of the parcels. We walked through the flaring streets, jostled by drunken men and bargaining women, amid the curses of labourers, the shrill <u>litanies</u> of shopboys who stood on guard by the barrels of pigs' cheeks, the nasal chanting of street-singers, who sang a come-all-you about O'Donovan Rossa, or a ballad about the troubles in our native land. These noises converged in a single sensation of life for me: I imagined that I bore my chalice[3] safely through a throng of foes. Her name sprang to my lips at moments in strange prayers and praises which I myself did not understand. My eyes were often full of tears (I could not tell why) and at times a flood from my heart seemed to pour itself out into my bosom. I thought little of the future. I did not know whether I would ever speak to her or not or, if I spoke to her, how I could tell her of my confused adoration. But my body was like a harp and her words and gestures were like fingers running upon the wires.

One evening I went into the back drawing-room in which the priest had died. It was a dark rainy evening and there was no sound in the house. Through one of the broken panes I heard the rain impinge upon the earth, the fine <u>incessant</u> needles of water playing in the <u>sodden</u> beds. Some distant lamp or lighted window gleamed below me. I was thankful that I could see so little. All my senses seemed to desire to <u>veil</u> themselves and, feeling that I was about to slip from them, I pressed the palms of my hands together until they trembled, murmuring: *O love! O love!* many times.

At last she spoke to me. When she addressed the first words to me I was so confused that I did not know what to answer. She asked me was I going to *Araby.* I forgot whether I answered yes or no. It would be a splendid bazaar, she said; she would love to go.

—And why can't you? I asked.

While she spoke she turned a silver bracelet round and round her wrist. She could not go, she said, because there would be a retreat that week in her convent. Her brother and two other boys were fighting for

3. **chalice.** Cup; goblet

Words for Everyday Use

lit • a • ny (lit´'n ē) *n.,* repetitive recitation
in • ces • sant (in ses´ənt) *adj.,* never ceasing
sod • den (säd´'n) *adj.,* filled with moisture; soaked through
veil (vāl) *vt.,* conceal, hide, disguise

Vocabulary in Context

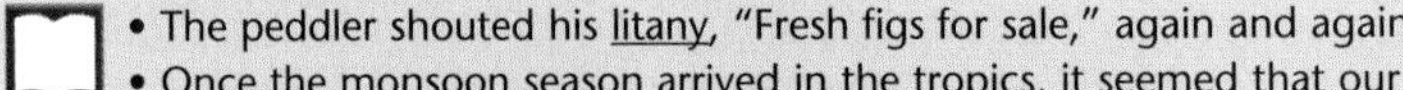

- The peddler shouted his <u>litany</u>, "Fresh figs for sale," again and again.
- Once the monsoon season arrived in the tropics, it seemed that our days were filled with <u>incessant</u> rainstorms.
- Carl's boots were so old that every rainstorm, snowstorm, or puddle left him with <u>sodden</u> socks.
- Our cat likes to keep out of sight; she <u>veils</u> herself behind one of the curtains or wedges herself beneath the couch.

Two Girls.
Pierre Auguste Renoir, 1881

their caps and I was alone at the railings. She held one of the spikes, bowing her head towards me. The light from the lamp opposite our door caught the white curve of her neck, lit up her hair that rested there and, falling, lit up the hand upon the railing. It fell over one side of her dress and caught the white border of a petticoat, just visible as she stood at ease.

—It's well for you, she said.

—If I go, I said, I will bring you something.

What innumerable follies laid waste my waking and sleeping thoughts after that evening! I wished to annihilate the tedious intervening days. I chafed against the work of school. At night in my bedroom and by day in the classroom her image came between me and the page I strove to read. The syllables of the word *Araby* were called to me through the silence in which my soul luxuriated and cast an Eastern enchantment over me. I asked for leave to go to the bazaar on Saturday night. My aunt was surprised and hoped it was not some Freemason affair. I answered few questions in class. I watched my master's face pass from amiability to sternness; he hoped I was not beginning to

❶ *What does the narrator promise to do for Mangan's sister?*

WORDS FOR EVERYDAY USE

in • nu • mer • a • ble (in nōō´mər ə bəl) *adj.*, too numerous to be counted
an • ni • hi • late (ə nī´ə lāt´) *vt.*, destroy completely
in • ter • ven • ing (in´tər vēn´iŋ) *adj.*, being or lying between
chafe (chāf) *vt.*, become irritated or impatient
a • mi • a • bil • i • ty (ā´mē ə bil´ə tē) *n.*, friendliness; good will

Vocabulary in Context

- In spring the whole hillside turned gold with the countless bursts of yellow of innumerable buttercups.
- Hannah hoped to annihilate illiteracy completely in her town by starting a number of free reading programs for children and adults.
- The school children kept careful track of the intervening days before summer vacation.
- Lana considered herself to be such a perfect bowler that she chafed when anyone tried to give her a few pointers or offer her constructive criticism.
- That breed of dog is known for its amiability; it is not a good watchdog because it loves all people.

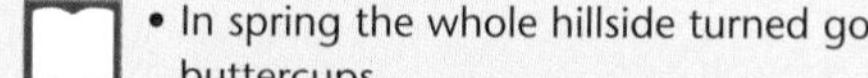

Answers to Guided Reading Questions

❶ The narrator promises to bring Mangan's sister something from Araby.

ANALYTIC SCALES FOR RESPONDING IN WRITING

(SEE PAGE 1025.)

Assign a score from 1 to 25 for each grading criterion below. (For more detailed evaluation, see the evaluation forms for writing, revising, and proofreading, Assessment Portfolio 4.1–4.9.)

1. Childhood Memory

- **Content/Unity.** The writing retells a childhood memory from the first-person point of view.
- **Organization/Coherence.** The childhood memory is retold in a sensible order.
- **Language/Style.** The childhood memory uses vivid and precise nouns, verbs, and modifiers.
- **Conventions.** The childhood memory avoids errors in spelling, grammar, usage, mechanics, and manuscript form.

▶ Additional practice is provided in the Essential Skills Practice Book: Writing 1.8.

Literary Technique (cont.)

ANSWERS

The narrator sees Mangan's sister in an idealized manner, as touched with light (see this page). She is never made a three-dimensional character to the reader. Like a traditional courtly lover, the narrator hopes to prove himself to win her love. He may have gotten the daydream of carrying a chalice through a throng of foes from medieval literature, particularly stories about the Grail. Joyce critiques the code of courtly love by pointing out that real life is not a heroic struggle—people often fail, and love is often futile or frustrated.

Answers to Guided Reading Questions

❶ The speaker reminds his uncle that he wishes to go to the bazaar in the evening. The uncle responds to him curtly.

❷ The narrator might have to miss the bazaar because his uncle is late, and he needs to get money from his uncle to attend.

❸ The narrator rides a train to the bazaar. He arrives at ten minutes to ten.

Analytic Scales for Responding in Writing

(See page 1025.)

2. Critical Essay

- **Content/Unity.** The essay explains how changes in the mood in "Araby" are related to its plot.
- **Organization/Coherence.** The essay begins with an introduction that includes the thesis of the essay. The introduction is followed by supporting paragraphs with clear transitions. The essay ends with a solid conclusion.
- **Language/Style.** The essay uses vivid and precise nouns, verbs, and modifiers.
- **Conventions.** The essay avoids errors in spelling, grammar, usage, mechanics, and manuscript form.

▶ Additional practice is provided in the Essential Skills Practice Book: Writing 1.20.

idle. I could not call my wandering thoughts together. I had hardly any patience with the serious work of life which, now that it stood between me and my desire, seemed to me child's play, ugly monotonous child's play.

❶ *Of what does the speaker remind his uncle? In what tone of voice does the uncle respond?*

On Saturday morning I reminded my uncle that I wished to go to the bazaar in the evening. He was fussing at the hallstand, looking for the hat brush, and answered me curtly:

—Yes, boy, I know.

❷ *Why might the narrator have to miss the bazaar?*

As he was in the hall I could not go into the front parlour and lie at the window. I left the house in bad humour and walked slowly towards the school. The air was pitilessly raw and already my heart misgave me.

When I came home to dinner my uncle had not yet been home. Still it was early. I sat staring at the clock for some time and, when its ticking began to irritate me, I left the room. I mounted the staircase and gained the upper part of the house. The high cold empty gloomy rooms liberated me and I went from room to room singing. From the front window I saw my companions playing below in the street. Their cries reached me weakened and indistinct and, leaning my forehead against the cool glass, I looked over at the dark house where she lived. I may have stood there for an hour, seeing nothing but the brown-clad figure cast by my imagination, touched discreetly by the lamplight at the curved neck, at the hand upon the railings and at the border below the dress.

When I came downstairs again I found Mrs Mercer sitting at the fire. She was an old garrulous woman, a pawnbroker's widow, who collected used stamps for some pious purpose. I had to endure the gossip of the tea-table. The meal was prolonged beyond an hour and still my uncle did not come. Mrs Mercer stood up to go: she was sorry she couldn't wait any longer, but it was after eight o'clock and she did not like to be out late, as the night air was bad for her. When she had gone I began to walk up and down the room, clenching my fists. My aunt said:

—I'm afraid you may put off your bazaar for this night of Our Lord.

At nine o'clock I heard my uncle's latchkey in the hall-door. I heard him talking to himself and heard the hallstand rocking when it had received the weight of his overcoat. I could interpret these signs. When he was midway through his dinner I asked him to give me the money to go to the bazaar. He had forgotten.

—The people are in bed and after their first sleep now, he said.

I did not smile. My aunt said to him energetically:

—Can't you give him the money and let him go? You've kept him late enough as it is.

My uncle said he was very sorry he had forgotten. He said he believed in the old saying: *All work and no play makes Jack a dull boy.* He asked me where I was going and, when I had told him a second time he asked me did I know *The Arab's Farewell to his Steed.* When I left the kitchen he was about to recite the opening lines of the piece to my aunt.

❸ *How does the narrator get to the bazaar? At what time does he arrive?*

I held a florin[4] tightly in my hand as I strode down Buckingham Street towards the station. The sight of the streets thronged with buyers and glaring with gas recalled to me the purpose of my journey. I took my seat in a third-class carriage of a deserted train. After an intolerable delay the train moved out of the station slowly. It crept onward among ruinous houses and over the twinkling river. At Westland Row Station a crowd of people pressed to the carriage doors; but the porters moved them back,

4. **florin.** British coin

Words for Everyday Use

dis • creet • ly (di skrēt´lē) *adv.*, carefully, in a manner maintaining privacy

gar • ru • lous (gar´ə ləs) *adj.*, talking too much, especially about unimportant things; loquacious

pi • ous (pī´əs) *adj.*, having or showing religious devotion

Vocabulary in Context

- The reporter followed his leads discreetly, so his story would not attract undue attention before its publication.
- We were amazed at how garrulous Shelley was; she talked on the phone about nothing at all for hours at a time.
- The school was run by a sisterhood of pious, good-hearted nuns.

saying that it was a special train for the bazaar. I remained alone in the bare carriage. In a few minutes the train drew up beside an improvised wooden platform. I passed out on to the road and saw by the lighted dial of a clock that it was ten minutes to ten. In front of me was a large building which displayed the magical name.

I could not find any sixpenny[5] entrance and, fearing that the bazaar would be closed, I passed in quickly through a turnstile, handing a shilling to a weary-looking man. I found myself in a big hall girdled at half its height by a gallery. Nearly all the stalls were closed and the greater part of the hall was in darkness. I recognized a silence like that which pervades a church after a service. I walked into the centre of the bazaar timidly. A few people were gathered about the stalls which were still open. Before a curtain, over which the words *Café Chantant* were written in coloured lamps, two men were counting money on a salver.[6] I listened to the fall of the coins.

Remembering with difficulty why I had come I went over to one of the stalls and examined porcelain vases and flowered teasets. At the door of the stall a young lady was talking and laughing with two young gentlemen. I remarked their English accents and listened vaguely to their conversation.

—O, I never said such a thing!

—O, but you did!

—O, but I didn't!

—Didn't she say that?

—Yes. I heard her.

—O, there's a . . . fib!

Observing me the young lady came over and asked me did I wish to buy anything. The tone of her voice was not encouraging; she seemed to have spoken to me out of a sense of duty. I looked humbly at the great jars that stood like eastern guards at either side of the dark entrance to the stall and murmured:

—No, thank you.

The young lady changed the position of one of the vases and went back to the two young men. They began to talk of the same subject. Once or twice the young lady glanced at me over her shoulder.

I lingered before her stall, though I knew my stay was useless, to make my interest in her wares seem the more real. Then I turned away slowly and walked down the middle of the bazaar. I allowed the two pennies to fall against the sixpence in my pocket. I heard a voice call from one end of the gallery that the light was out. The upper part of the hall was now completely dark.

Gazing up into the darkness I saw myself as a creature driven and derided by vanity; and my eyes burned with anguish and anger. ■

5. **sixpenny.** Cheap

6. **salver.** Tray on which refreshments, letters, visiting cards, and so on are placed

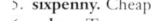

❶ *What does the young lady ask the narrator? What does the narrator sense about the way she speaks to him?*

❷ *When the narrator finally gets to the bazaar, how does he know that it is almost over?*

❸ *What does a voice call out? How does the narrator feel as he gazes into the darkness?*

Responding to the Selection

Imagine that you are on the train with the narrator of this story, both as he travels to the bazaar and then as he travels home. What might he say about his expectations as he travels to the bazaar? On the way home, what might he say about his brief experience?

Answers to Guided Reading Questions

❶ The young lady asks the narrator if he wishes to buy anything. The narrator senses that the woman doesn't really care if he buys anything or not—she speaks to him out of duty.

❷ Many of the stalls are closed, and the greater part of the hall is in darkness. There is also a silence, similar to the silence that is in a church after a service has ended.

❸ The voice calls that the light is out. The narrator feels that he is a creature driven by vanity. He feels anguish and anger.

Selection Check Test with Answers

EX: Who was a former tenant in the home of the narrator?

A priest was a former tenant in the home of the narrator.

1. Why does the narrator wait for Mangan's sister each morning?

He waits for her because he loves her and wishes to follow her.

2. What is Araby?

Araby is a type of bazaar and open-air market.

3. When Mangan's sister speaks to the narrator for the first time, what does she ask him?

She asks him if he is going to Araby.

4. What promise does the narrator make to Mangan's sister?

He promises to bring her something from Araby.

5. Why is the narrator late for the bazaar?

His uncle is late getting home and makes the narrator late.

Responding to the Selection

Students might also wish to work in pairs to role play a conversation with the narrator on the narrator's way to the bazaar and again on his way home. What advice might they give the narrator?

ANSWERS FOR REVIEWING THE SELECTION

RECALLING AND INTERPRETING

1. **Recalling.** The narrator spends his days playing with his friends. The children hide until the narrator's uncle is in the house. **Interpreting.** The writer uses words and phrases such as "When the short days of winter came dusk fell before we had well eaten our dinners"; and "The cold air stung us and we played till our bodies glowed." The narrator seems afraid of his uncle. He is not anxious to greet him when he comes home.

2. **Recalling.** The narrator watches Mangan's sister's front door until he sees her leave, then follows her and passes her. The narrator compares his body to a harp and the words and gestures of Mangan's sister to fingers "running upon the wires." **Interpreting.** The narrator is experiencing strong romantic feelings toward Mangan's sister. Like a harp in the hands of a musician, the narrator feels controlled and manipulated by his strong feelings for Mangan's sister. She has the power to affect him and fill him with a type of music.

3. **Recalling.** He imagines that he is carrying a chalice "safely through a throng of foes." The first words Mangan's sister addresses to the narrator are to ask him if he will be going to Araby. He tells her that he will bring her something from Araby. **Interpreting.** Going to Araby becomes important to him because it is a taste of independence and, most importantly, a way for him to impress and delight Mangan's sister. He has imagined carrying a chalice to Mangan's sister and now sees an opportunity to perform such a noble deed by bearing something from Araby to her.

4. **Recalling.** The narrator's uncle is late. When the narrator finally arrives, everything is closing. There is silence and darkness. A young woman asks him if he is going to buy anything. She is busy talking to two young gentlemen.

(cont.)

Reviewing the Selection

RECALLING / **INTERPRETING**

1. What activities fill the narrator's days? What do the children do when they see the narrator's uncle? ▶▶ What vivid words and phrases are used to give the reader the sense of a crisp winter night? What is the narrator's attitude toward his uncle?

2. What does the narrator do each morning? To what does the narrator compare his body and the words and gestures of Mangan's sister? ▶▶ What feelings is the narrator experiencing toward Mangan's sister? Explain the comparison the narrator makes concerning himself and the words and gestures of Mangan's sister. Why is this a vivid expression of how he is feeling?

3. What does the narrator imagine when he goes shopping with his aunt? What are the first words Mangan's sister addresses to the narrator? What does he tell her he will do? ▶▶ Why does going to Araby become so important to the narrator? In what way is his promise to Mangan's sister related to his earlier imaginings? Why does the bazaar consume his thoughts?

4. Why is the narrator's trip to Araby delayed? When he finally arrives, what is happening at the bazaar? What does the young woman at the stall say to him? What is the young woman busy doing? ▶▶ In what manner does the narrator approach the bazaar? What effect does the young woman's tone of voice have on the narrator? Why is the narrator unable to accomplish what he desires at the bazaar?

SYNTHESIZING

5. Why do you believe the narrator feels such "anguish and anger" at the end of the story? In what way has the narrator been "derided by vanity"?

Understanding Literature (Questions for Discussion)

1. **Image.** An **image** is a word or phrase that names something that can be seen, heard, touched, tasted, or smelled. The images in a literary work are referred to, collectively, as the work's **imagery**. The young narrator in "Araby" is familiar with religious imagery. Look through the story and find examples of religious imagery. In what way does the narrator associate these familiar images with the new emotion of love he feels for Mangan's sister? What role do images of light and dark play in this story?

ANSWERS FOR REVIEWING THE SELECTION (CONT.)

Interpreting. The narrator approaches the bazaar nervously and timidly. The cool tone of the young woman's voice makes him feel out of place and unwelcome. The bazaar is closing, and the narrator becomes too embarrassed and disappointed to buy anything.

SYNTHESIZING

Responses will vary. Possible responses are given.

5. The narrator has built up the bazaar in his mind to something of great importance, and he leaves feeling as though he has failed. He had many hopes and expectations pinned on his night at Araby, and none of his expectations have been met. He will return home empty-handed, his dreams of impressing Mangan's sister crushed.

2. **Mood. Mood**, or **atmosphere**, is the emotion created in the reader by part or all of a literary work. What is the mood at the beginning of the story, as the narrator describes his games with his friends? How does this mood change as he devotes more time to thoughts of Mangan's sister? as he prepares to go to Araby? What is the mood at the end of the story?

Responding in Writing

1. **Creative Writing: Childhood Memory.** As you read on the Prereading page, "Araby" is one of three stories in *Dubliners* about childhood experiences. It can be interesting to look back on meaningful moments in your childhood and try to see them again through the eyes of a child. Visualize an incident or event that was important to you—perhaps an annual town parade, the time your dog was missing for two days, or a first day of school. Then retell the event from the first-person point of view, trying to capture your emotions during the experience. If you chose a childhood memory for the Reader's Journal activity, refer to the thoughts you recorded earlier.

2. **Critical Essay: Mood and Plot.** In a short essay, describe the different moods in "Araby," and explain how the changes in mood are related to the action of the plot of the story. As you organize your essay, you might want to keep the following questions in mind: What is the mood in the opening paragraphs of the piece? When does this mood begin to change? What is the mood at the end of the story? Make a plot pyramid like the one below. Next to each plot element, identify a related event from "Araby" and note the mood.

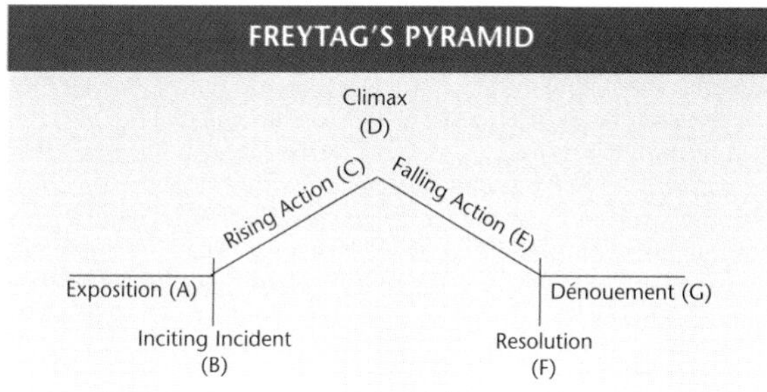

Speaking and Listening Skills

Collaborative Learning and Discussion. Review the Language Arts Survey 3.3, "Collaborative Learning and Discussion." Then form small groups of three or four. As a group, choose a story, play, or group of poems from one of the Irish authors noted in the Connections on page 1018 to read and discuss. Read the literature you have chosen, and as you read, take notes. Then come back to your group for discussion. Each person should be prepared to present to the group three ideas for discussion.

Answers for Understanding Literature

Responses will vary. Possible responses are given.

1. Image. As examples of religious imagery, students might refer to the priest who used to live in the narrator's house, the phrase "I bore my chalice safely through a throng of foes," the narrator's prayers, and the description of the silence in the bazaar as "that which pervades a church after a service." The narrator's mind turns to religious rituals and images because these are familiar to him as new, transporting feelings take hold of him. Images of light describe Mangan's sister and the narrator's hopes of winning her love; images of darkness reflect the disappointment of his hopes at the bazaar.

2. Mood. The mood at the beginning of the story is lighthearted and innocent. The narrator is a child playing a child's games. The narrator, and consequently the mood of the story, becomes increasingly serious and intense as his feelings for Mangan's sister take hold of him. After she speaks to him, he can think of nothing else but her and the bazaar. The mood at the end of the story is one of anger, disappointment, and sadness.

Analytic Scales for Responding in Writing

Grading scales for Responding in Writing appear on pages 1021 and 1022.

Answers for Skills Activities

SPEAKING AND LISTENING SKILLS

You may wish to evaluate students' efforts in group discussions by monitoring the discussions and filling out a Collaborative Learning Evaluation Form for each student. This form appears in the Assessment Portfolio 4.10.

► Additional practice is provided in the Essential Skills Practice Book: Speaking and Listening 3.3.

ADDITIONAL RESOURCES

READER'S GUIDE

- Selection Worksheet 12.2

ASSESSMENT PORTFOLIO

- Selection Check Test 2.12.3
- Selection Test 2.12.4

ESSENTIAL SKILLS PRACTICE BOOKS

- Writing 1.8, 1.20
- Language 2.48

PREREADING EXTENSIONS

Share with students the following information about James I, or have them research this king and England under his rule.

The death of Elizabeth I in 1603 brought to the throne the first of the Stuart kings, James VI of Scotland, who became James I of England. James was a Protestant, but he had Catholic sympathies. He released Catholics from prison and tried to force all English people to adopt the rituals of the Protestant high church. These actions brought him into conflict with the House of Commons, which was dominated by Puritans, and led, after his death, to a revolution against the monarchy.

SUPPORT FOR LEP STUDENTS

PRONUNCIATIONS OF PROPER NOUNS AND ADJECTIVES

George Vil • liers (jöərj vil´arz)
Green • wich (gren´ich)

ADDITIONAL VOCABULARY

coronation—crowning of a monarch
discomposed—disturbed
gaiety—joyfulness, merriment
mortality—death rate

PREREADING

from *Orlando*
by Virginia Woolf

About the Author

VIRGINIA WOOLF
1882–1941

Virginia Woolf was born in London, England. Educated at home by her father, she made good use of his extensive library and met many of the outstanding literary and intellectual figures of her time. In 1912, Virginia married Leonard Woolf, a political writer and economist. Five years later, the couple established the Hogarth Press, which became a successful publishing house, printing works by Katherine Mansfield, E. M. Forster, and T. S. Eliot, as well as Virginia Woolf's own work. After Woolf's first two novels, *The Voyage Out* and *Night and Day,* were written, she began to experiment with elements of fiction such as interior monologues and stream-of-consciousness writing. Her novels include *Jacob's Room, Mrs. Dalloway, To the Lighthouse,* and *The Waves.* Her short stories were published in the collections *Monday or Tuesday* and *A Haunted House.* One of the most distinguished critics of her time, Woolf published numerous essays and works of literary criticism, including *Mr. Bennet and Mrs. Brown, The Common Reader, A Room of One's Own, Flush, Three Guineas, Roger Fry,* and *The Death of the Moth.* In 1953, Leonard Woolf edited and published *A Writer's Diary,* extracts from Woolf's writing diary.

About the Selection

Orlando is a fictional biography. A **biography** is the story of a person's life, told by someone other than that person. Although *Orlando* is fictional and was written to satirize biographical writing, the story was inspired in part by the life of Woolf's close friend, Victoria Mary Sackville-West. Sackville-West was a poet and novelist who traveled widely with her diplomat husband. *Orlando* is a fantastic tale, spanning the centuries from the reign of Queen Elizabeth I to 1928. Within the course of these centuries, Orlando becomes an ambassador, travels the world, meets great literary figures, writes a poem titled "The Oak Tree," and falls in love several times. Woolf also changes her title character's sex partway through the book to examine more effectively the role gender has played throughout history. As the story begins, Orlando is a young nobleman in Renaissance England. This selection from the novel begins soon after Elizabeth I's death as James I is about to be crowned king. In her guise as "biographer," Woolf tells the story of a Great Frost that has devastating effects upon both England and Orlando—much of England is frozen solid, and Orlando meets the Russian princess who will break his heart.

CONNECTIONS: The Bloomsbury Group

After their father's death, Virginia Woolf and her sister, Vanessa, continued to live in Gordon Square in the Bloomsbury section of London. There they hosted gatherings of writers and artists, a circle of Cambridge-educated friends that came to be known as the Bloomsbury Group. Other noted writers and thinkers active in the group were John Maynard Keynes, a renowned economist and a patron of the arts; Lytton Strachey, a biographer and essayist; and novelist E. M. Forster, known for works such as *A Room with a View, Howards End,* and *A Passage to India.*

GOALS/OBJECTIVES

Studying this lesson will enable students to

- appreciate a mock biography
- identify Virginia Woolf as modern British writer
- define *biography, satire, irony, internal monologue, stream-of-consciousness writing,* and *synaesthesia*
- explain ironic and satiric elements
- identify an internal monologue
- identify examples of synaesthesia
- analyze elements of fantasy and realism in a literary work
- use colons and semicolons correctly

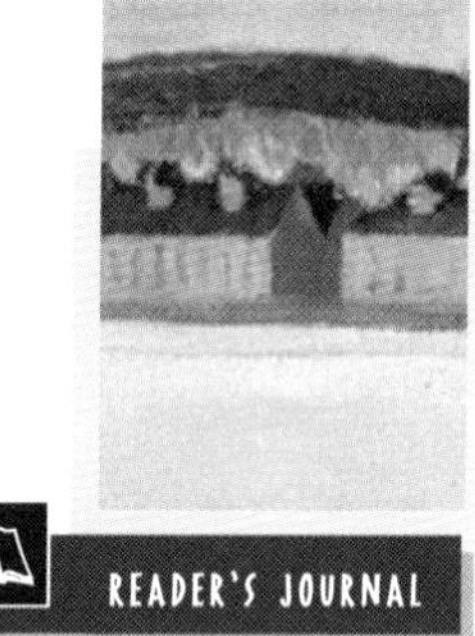

READER'S JOURNAL

Do you believe in love at first sight? Based on your own experiences and what you have seen in movies, television, books, and popular song, explain in your journal whether you believe love at first sight is possible. In what way might a relationship based on love at first sight be different from a relationship developed more slowly out of friendship or shared experiences and values?

FROM

Orlando

VIRGINIA WOOLF

The Great Frost was, historians tell us, the most severe that has ever visited these islands. Birds froze in mid-air and fell like stones to the ground. At Norwich[1] a young countrywoman started to cross the road in her usual robust health and was seen by the onlookers to turn visibly to powder and be blown in a puff of dust over the roofs as the icy blast struck her at the street corner. The mortality among sheep and cattle was enormous. Corpses froze and could not be drawn from the sheets. It was no uncommon sight to come upon a whole herd of swine frozen immovable upon the road. The fields were full of shepherds, ploughmen, teams of horses, and little bird-scaring boys[2] all struck stark in the act of the moment, one with his hand to his nose, another with the bottle to his lips, a third with a stone raised to throw at the raven who sat, as if stuffed, upon the hedge within a yard of him. The severity of the frost was so extraordinary that a kind of petrifaction sometimes ensued; and it was commonly supposed that the great increase of rocks in some parts of Derbyshire[3] was due to no eruption, for there was none, but to the solidification of unfortunate wayfarers who had been turned literally to stone where they stood. The Church could give little help in the matter, and though some landowners had these relics blessed, the most part preferred to use them either as landmarks, scratching posts for sheep, or, when the form of the stone allowed, drinking troughs for cattle, which purposes they serve, admirably for the most part, to this day.

But while the country people suffered the extremity of want, and the trade of the country was at a standstill, London enjoyed a carnival of the utmost brilliancy. The Court was at Greenwich, and the new King[4] seized the opportunity that his coronation gave him to curry favour with the citizens. He directed

1. **Norwich.** County seat of Norfolk in eastern England
2. **bird-scaring boys.** Boys who scared birds away from crops
3. **Derbyshire.** County in central England
4. **new King.** James I, king of England from 1603–1625

1 *What do historians tell us? What happens during this period? Do these events seem more like history or fantasy?*

2 *What is the time of the Great Frost like for country people? What is the king's response to this disaster?*

3 *What happens to some of the people who have been frozen stiff? To what uses do the English people put these unfortunate victims' remains?*

WORDS FOR EVERYDAY USE

ro • bust (rō bust´) *adj.,* strong and healthy; hardy

pet • ri • fac • tion (pe´tri fak´shən) *n.,* state in which objects have been made rigid or hard

en • sue (en so͞o´) *vi.,* come afterward, follow immediately

ex • trem • i • ty (ek strem´ə tē) *n.,* the greatest degree

READER'S JOURNAL

To explore this idea further, students can conduct a survey to find out whether other people believe in love at first sight, how many have fallen in love at first sight, and how many feel that they have had a successful relationship with somebody with whom they fell in love at first sight. Students should also devise other questions that are related to this subject. Students may wish to analyze the results by sex, by age, or by other groupings. Have students graph the results of their survey.

ANSWERS TO GUIDED READING QUESTIONS

1 Historians tell us that the Great Frost was the most severe frost ever to visit Great Britain. Birds freeze in midair, and a countrywoman is turned into powder and blown away by the wind. These events seem more like fantasy than history.

2 The Great Frost creates terrible difficulties for the poor country people, but the king uses this freak natural occurrence as an opportunity to create a carnival on the frozen river for the people of London.

3 They are petrified and become like stone. While some landowners have the unfortunate victims' remains blessed, others use them as scratching posts for sheep, landmarks, or drinking troughs for cattle.

SPELLING AND VOCABULARY WORDS FROM THE SELECTION

drollery
ensue
extremity
insipid
predictable
petrifaction
robust

VOCABULARY IN CONTEXT

- Two weeks after her illness, Nika had lost her frail, wan look and had returned to her usual robust appearance.
- In the cold, petrifaction causes the flexible plastic pieces to become rigid.
- Wild cheering ensued when Ms. Vicuña announced that our class had won the prize.
- Gladys attempted the climb although she was aware of the extremity of the danger.

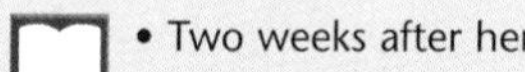

Answers to Guided Reading Questions

❶ The ice is perfectly clear but as hard as steel, and fire does not melt it.

❷ Philosophers wonder whether the fish are dead or in a state of suspended animation and will revive when the ice thaws.

❸ King James especially likes to see a woman who had been bringing her apples to market when she froze solid.

Cross-curricular Activities

Arts and Humanities

The scenes depicted in this selection from *Orlando* are quite vivid. Ask students to imagine the carnival on the ice and the images of creatures captured by the ice. Have students create their own visual depictions of these scenes. Students might paint or draw one or more of the scenes, create a model or diorama of the scene, or make a video in which they use props and costumes to depict the scene. Students can share their creations with the class.

Biographical Note

Orlando was inspired in part by Woolf's friend **Victoria Mary Sackville-West** (1892–1962), often simpified as V. Sackville-West, or Vita. Sackville-West was an English novelist and poet. She spent most of her life in the Kentish countryside, a locale that figured prominently in her writing. Her best-known works are the long poem *The Land* and her novels *The Edwardians* and *All Passion Spent.*

that the river, which was frozen to a depth of twenty feet and more for six or seven miles on either side, should be swept, decorated and given all the semblance of a park or pleasure ground, with arbours,[5] mazes, alleys, drinking booths, etc., at his expense. For himself and all the courtiers, he reserved a certain space immediately opposite the Palace gates; which, railed off from the public only by a silken rope, became at once the center of the most brilliant society in England. Great statesmen, in their beards and ruffs, despatched affairs of state under the crimson awning of the Royal Pagoda. Soldiers planned the conquest of the Moor and the downfall of the Turk in striped arbours surmounted by plumes of ostrich feathers. Admirals strode up and down the narrow pathways, glass[6] in hand, sweeping the horizon and telling stories of the north-west passage[7] and the Spanish Armada.[8] Lovers dallied upon divans spread with sables. Frozen roses fell in showers when the Queen[9] and her ladies walked abroad. Coloured balloons hovered motionless in the air. Here and there burnt vast bonfires of cedar and oak wood, lavishly salted, so that the flames were of green, orange, and purple fire. But however fiercely they burnt, the heat was not enough to melt the ice which, though of singular transparency, was yet of the hardness of steel. So clear indeed was it that there could be seen, congealed at a depth of several feet, here a porpoise, there a flounder. Shoals[10] of eels lay motionless in a trance, but whether their state was one of death or merely of suspended animation which the warmth would revive puzzled the philosophers. Near London Bridge, where the river had frozen to a depth of some twenty fathoms,[11] a wrecked wherry boat[12] was plainly visible, lying on the bed of the river where it had sunk last autumn, overladen with apples. The old bumboat[13] woman, who was carrying her fruit to market on the Surrey side, sat there in her plaids and farthingales[14] with her lap full of apples, for all the world as if she were about to serve a customer, though a certain blueness about the lips hinted the truth. 'Twas a sight King James specially liked to look upon, and he would bring a troupe of courtiers to gaze with him. In short, nothing could exceed the brilliancy and gaiety of the scene by day. But it was at night that the carnival was at its merriest. For the frost continued unbroken; the nights were of perfect stillness; the moon and stars blazed with the hard fixity of diamonds, and to the fine music of flute and trumpet the courtiers danced.

❶ *What is unusual about the ice in the river?*

❷ *What do philosophers wonder about the frozen fish?*

❸ *What does King James especially enjoy about the frost?*

Orlando, it is true, was none of those who tread lightly the coranto and lavolta;[15] he was clumsy; and a little absent-minded. He much preferred the plain dances of his own country, which he had danced as a child to these fantastic foreign measures. He had indeed just brought his feet together about six in the evening of the seventh of January at the finish of some such quadrille or minuet when he beheld, coming from the pavilion of the Muscovite Embassy, a figure, which, whether boy's or woman's, for the loose tunic and trousers of the Russian fashion served to disguise the sex, filled him with the highest curiosity. The person, whatever the name or sex, was about middle height, very slenderly fashioned, and dressed entirely in oyster-coloured velvet, trimmed with some unfamiliar greenish-coloured fur. But these details were obscured by the extraordinary

5. **arbours.** Places shaded by trees or by vines on a latticework
6. **glass.** Binoculars
7. **north-west passage.** Water route from the Atlantic to the Pacific that Renaissance explorers eagerly sought, hoping to find a new route to the wealth of Asia
8. **Spanish Armada.** Fleet of warships, destroyed by English troops, that Spain sent to attack England in 1588
9. **Queen.** Anne of Denmark married James in 1589; she was known for her extravagance and love of court entertainments.
10. **Shoals.** Large schools or groups
11. **twenty fathoms.** 120 feet
12. **wherry boat.** Large, broad, but light barge, used for moving freight
13. **bumboat.** Small boat used in a port to peddle goods to ships' crews
14. **farthingales.** Hoop or frame worn under the skirt by European women in the sixteenth and seventeenth centuries
15. **coranto and lavolta.** Types of dances

Additional Questions and Activities

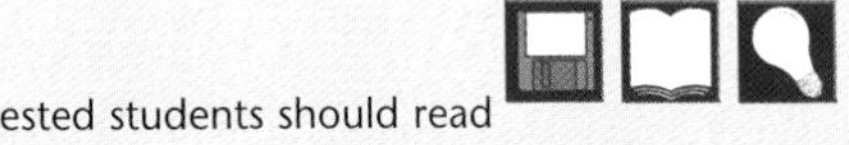

Ask students to discuss the two quotations on page 1029 from *A Room of One's Own,* Woolf's long essay on the status of women and the difficulties of being a woman artist. In discussing the role of women in society and as writers and artists, you may wish to refer students to Insights: Women—Rights and Writers on page 167.

Interested students should read *A Room of One's Own* or Woolf's published diaries. Students can write a personal essay about their response to the ideas and issues Woolf addresses in her writing.

Five A.M. Edward Hopper, 1937

seductiveness which issued from the whole person. Images, metaphors of the most extreme and extravagant twined and twisted in his mind. He called her a melon, a pineapple, an olive tree, an emerald, and a fox in the snow all in the space of three seconds; he did not know whether he had heard her, tasted her, seen her, or all three together. (For though we must pause not a moment in the narrative we may here hastily note that all his images at this time were simple in the extreme to match his senses and were mostly taken from things he had liked the taste of as a boy. But if his senses were simple they were at the same time extremely strong. To pause therefore and seek the reasons of things is out of the question.) . . . A melon, an emerald, a fox in the snow—so he raved, so he called her.

1 *What comes to Orlando's mind when he sees the mysterious person?*

♦ ♦ ♦

The stranger's name, he found, was the Princess Marousha Stanilovska Dagmar Natasha Iliana Romanovitch, and she had come in the train of the Muscovite Ambassador, who was her uncle perhaps, or perhaps her father, to attend the coronation. Very little was known of the Muscovites. In their great beards and furred hats they sat almost silent; drinking some black liquid which they spat out now and then upon the

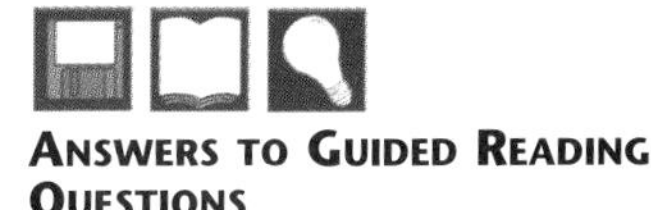

Answers to Guided Reading Questions

1 He produces a variety of images and metaphors, calling her "a melon, a pineapple, an olive tree, an emerald, and a fox in the snow."

Additional Questions and Activities

Ask students to note the difficulty that the English court has communicating with Princess Marousha Stanilovska Dagmar Natasha Iliana Romanovitch. Then have students discuss the benefits of learning more than one language. Ask students if they think that learning multiple languages is worth the time and effort it takes. Students should use examples both general and from their own lives to support their responses.

Quotables

"Women have served all these centuries as looking-glasses possessing the magic and delicious power of reflecting the figure of a man at twice its natural size."

"I would venture to guess that Anon, who wrote so many poems without signing them, was often a woman."

—Virginia Woolf
A Room of One's Own

Answers to Guided Reading Questions

❶ The English cannot communicate with the Muscovites because the English can't speak Russian or French and the Muscovites can't speak English.

❷ The English lords are in a predicament because they cannot understand a word of French.

❸ Orlando is composing an impassioned sonnet. The princess interrupts him by asking him to pass the salt.

❹ The narrator is implying that Orlando's ability to speak French may lead to a romance with the princess that will break Orlando's heart.

❺ One lord offers her horseradish, and the other has his dog beg for a bone. She laughs at them.

❻ Orlando feels that he didn't really know what love was until he met the princess.

Selection Check Test with Answers

EX. What event does the selection describe?
The selection describes the Great Frost.

1. What does the king do to curry favor with his citizens?
He has a carnival on the frozen river.

2. What sight does King James especially like?
He likes to look on the frozen woman who was carrying apples to market.

3. Who is the stranger who enchants Orlando?
The stranger is a Muscovite princess.

4. What language does the stranger speak?
She speaks French and Russian.

5. What question interrupts Orlando's sonnet?
The princess asks him to pass the salt.

---

❶ *Why can't the English communicate with the Muscovites?*

❷ *Why does the Muscovite princess put the English lords in a "predicament"?*

❸ *What is Orlando doing mentally while gazing at the princess? What interrupts his thoughts?*

❹ *Why do you think the narrator says that it would have been better for Orlando never to have learned French?*

❺ *What do the English lords do in response to the princess's attempts to make conversation? What is her response?*

❻ *How does Orlando feel about his former loves now?*

ice. None spoke English, and French with which some at least were familiar was then little spoken at the English Court.

It was through this accident that Orlando and the Princess became acquainted. They were seated opposite each other at the great table spread under a huge awning for the entertainment of the notables. The Princess was placed between two young Lords, one Lord Francis Vere and the other the young Earl of Moray. It was laughable to see the predicament she soon had them in, for though both were fine lads in their way, the babe unborn had as much knowledge of the French tongue as they had. When at the beginning of dinner the Princess turned to the Earl and said, with a grace which ravished his heart, "Je crois avoir fait la connaissance d'un gentilhomme qui vous etais apparanté en Pologne l'été dernier," or "La beauté des dames de la cour d'Angleterre me met dans le ravissement. On ne peut voir une dame plus gracieuse que votre reine, ni une coiffure plus belle que la sienne,"[16] both Lord Francis and the Earl showed the highest embarrassment. The one helped her largely to horse-radish sauce, the other whistled to his dog and made him beg for a marrow bone. At this the Princess could no longer contain her laughter, and Orlando, catching her eyes across the boars' heads and stuffed peacocks, laughed too. He laughed, but the laugh on his lips froze in wonder. Whom had he loved, what had he loved, he asked himself in a tumult of emotion, until now? An old woman,[17] he answered, all skin and bone. Red-cheeked trulls too many to mention. A puling[18] nun. A hard-bitten cruel-mouthed adventuress. A nodding mass of lace and ceremony.[19] Love had meant to him nothing but sawdust and cinders. The joys he had had of it tasted insipid in the extreme. He marvelled how he could have gone through with it without yawning. For as he looked the thickness of his blood melted; the ice turned to wine in his veins; he heard the waters flowing and the birds singing; spring broke over the hard wintry landscape; his manhood woke; he grasped a sword in his hand; he charged a more daring foe than Pole or Moor; he dived in deep water; he saw the flower of danger growing in a crevice; he stretched his hand—in fact he was rattling off one of his most impassioned sonnets when the Princess addressed him, "Would you have the goodness to pass the salt?"

He blushed deeply.

"With all the pleasure in the world, Madame," he replied, speaking French with a perfect accent. For, heaven be praised, he spoke the tongue as his own; his mother's maid had taught him. Yet perhaps it would have been better for him had he never learnt that tongue; never answered that voice; never followed the light of those eyes. . . .

The Princess continued. Who were those bumpkins[20] she asked him, who sat beside her with the manners of stablemen? What was the nauseating mixture they had poured

16. **"Je crois . . . la sienne."** French for "I believe I made the acquaintance of a gentleman related to you in Poland last summer," and "The beauty of the ladies of the court of England puts me in rapture. One cannot see a lady more gracious than your queen, nor a hairstyle more beautiful than hers."
17. **old woman.** Orlando is talking about Queen Elizabeth whom he met and admired as a youth.
18. **puling.** Whimpering and whining
19. **Red-cheeked . . . ceremony.** Orlando is negatively characterizing his former love interests, whom he despises now that he has met the Russian princess.
20. **bumpkins.** Awkward or simple people from the country

Words for Everyday Use

pre • dic • a • ment (prē dik´ə mənt) *n.*, unpleasant, embarrassing, or comical situation

in • sip • id (in sip´id) *adj.*, without flavor; dull

Vocabulary in Context

- Embarrassed by the predicament, the committee was forced to announce that they had ordered dinners for only half of the guests.
- Gianna yawned at the insipid conversation and tried to enliven the discussion by bringing up a controversial topic.

on her plate? Did the dogs eat at the same table with the men in England? Was that figure of fun at the end of the table with her hair rigged up like a Maypole (une grande perche mal fagotée[21]) really the Queen? And did the King always slobber like that? And which of those popinjays[22] was George Villiers?[23] Though these questions rather discomposed Orlando at first, they were put with such archness and drollery that he could not help but laugh; and as he saw from the blank faces of the company that nobody understood a word, he answered her as freely as she asked him, speaking, as she did, in perfect French. ■

What does the princess really think of the English court?

21. **(une . . . fagotée).** "A tall pole badly put together"; beehive-type hairstyle
22. **popinjays.** Talkative, conceited persons
23. **George Villiers.** English statesman (1592–1628), also known as the Duke of Buckingham

WORDS FOR EVERYDAY USE

droll • er • y (drol´ə rē) *n.,* quaint or wry humor

VOCABULARY IN CONTEXT

- Spencer's skit was wryly amusing, and we all smiled at the drollery.

ANSWERS TO GUIDED READING QUESTIONS

The princess is really appalled by the manners, fashion, and food of the English court.

ANALYTIC SCALES FOR RESPONDING IN WRITING

(SEE PAGE 1034.)

Assign a score from 1 to 25 for each grading criterion below. (For more detailed evaluation, see the evaluation forms for writing, revising, and proofreading, Assessment Portfolio 4.1–4.9.)

1. Biography

- **Content/Unity.** The biography tells a part of a person's life and may include anecdotes, description, or dialogue.
- **Organization/Coherence.** The biography is arranged in a logical order, such as chronological order.
- **Language/Style.** The biography uses vivid and precise nouns, verbs, and modifiers.
- **Conventions.** The biography avoids errors in spelling, grammar, usage, mechanics, and manuscript form.

► Additional practice is provided in the Essential Skills Practice Book: Writing 1.8.

2. Critical Essay

- **Content/Unity.** The essay analyzes the use of fantasy and realism in the selection.
- **Organization/Coherence.** The essay presents a clear thesis. The body of the essay supports the thesis. The body of the essay is followed by a strong conclusion.
- **Language/Style.** The essay uses vivid and precise nouns, verbs, and modifiers.
- **Conventions.** The essay avoids errors in spelling, grammar, usage, mechanics, and manuscript form.

► Additional practice is provided in the Essential Skills Practice Book: Writing 1.20.

RESPONDING TO THE SELECTION

Suggest that student think of ways in which they have seen local, national, or world leaders deal with catastrophe and compare this to King James's reaction to the Great Frost.

ANSWERS FOR REVIEWING THE SELECTION

RECALLING AND INTERPRETING

1. **Recalling.** The narrator says that historians have provided us with information about the Great Frost. The Great Frost is devastating to the countryside and its people, as both people and animals are frozen solid. King James throws a carnival on the frozen river to curry favor with the citizens of London. **Interpreting.** The author may cite historians to satirize the nonfictional and unbiased air most biographers assume and to play with the reader's sense of reality and fantasy. Students may expect a ruler to aid the people of his country during a time of hardship and say that the monarch was far removed from the everyday lives of the common people; he was more concerned with entertaining his courtiers lavishly than with helping the common people.

2. **Recalling.** The ice is as hard as steel and cannot be melted by fire, yet it is perfectly transparent. King James and his courtiers especially like to look upon a woman who had been bringing apples to market when she became frozen. **Interpreting.** King James is unfeeling and insensitive. Students may suggest that the author chooses to have a Great Frost descend upon England to reveal that King James was a cold, icy, and unrelenting personality.

3. **Recalling.** Orlando falls in love with the Muscovite princess. Orlando mentally compares her to a melon, a pineapple, an olive tree, an emerald, and a fox in the snow. Orlando rattles off a sonnet. **Interpreting.** Orlando is an (cont.)

Responding to the Selection

What do you think of King James's winter carnival? If you were the leader in charge of England, what would your reaction to the Great Frost have been? What do you think of the English nobility as they are characterized in this selection from *Orlando*?

Reviewing the Selection

RECALLING / **INTERPRETING**

1. According to the narrator, who has provided us with information about the Great Frost? What is the effect of the Great Frost on the English countryside and its people? What does King James do in response to the Great Frost? ▶▶ What purpose do you think the author has for citing historians? What does James's reaction to the Great Frost reveal about the monarch's relation to and attitude toward the common people?
2. What is unusual about the ice that forms on the river? Upon what do King James and his courtiers especially like to look? ▶▶ What might the author be saying about King James's character and his reign by telling of the Great Frost and the ice? What does the fact that King James enjoys looking upon this scene reveal about him?
3. Who is the person with whom Orlando falls in love at first sight? What images come into Orlando's mind when he first sees this person? At the dinner table, what does Orlando "rattle off" when near this person? ▶▶ What does Orlando's reaction to love reveal about his character?
4. Why can't most of the English court speak with the Muscovite princess? What does the princess say in French to the English lords about the ladies of the English court? ▶▶ What does the princess really think about the English court? How does Orlando feel about her opinions? Why does language play an essential role in the relationship that begins between Orlando and the princess?

SYNTHESIZING

5. Virginia Woolf described this novel as "an escapade, half-laughing, half-serious; with great splashes of exaggeration." Discuss what "splashes of exaggeration" appear in this selection from the novel. What are some of its humorous elements? What more serious issues are raised?

ANSWERS FOR REVIEWING THE SELECTION (CONT.)

emotional and sensitive person who is overwhelmed and transfigured by love. He has a poetic nature.

4. **Recalling.** Most of the English court cannot converse with her, because the English speak neither Russian nor French—the princess's two languages. The princess says that the women of the English court are beautiful and that she greatly admires the English queen's hairstyle.

Interpreting. The princess really feels that the queen looks ridiculous, the English lords have no manners, the food is disgusting, and the king slobbers. Orlando is troubled at first but comes to find her opinions charming and amusing. Because Orlando is the only one who can understand and communicate with the princess, an intimacy springs up between them, along with a sense of their being (cont.)

Understanding Literature (Questions for Discussion)

1. **Biography and Satire.** A **biography** is the story of a person's life, told by someone other than that person. **Satire** is humorous writing or speech intended to point out errors, falsehoods, foibles, or failings. *Orlando* is a mock biography; in other words, Woolf humorously imitates the form and style of the biography to satirize both biographies and biographers. For example, after Orlando first sees the princess, the narrator, Orlando's presumed "biographer," interrupts, "For though we must pause not a moment in the narrative we may here hastily note. . . ." The narrator then explains something about Orlando's sensations and concludes, "To pause therefore and seek the reason of things is out of the question." What makes this interruption humorous or ironic? What do you think Woolf is pointing out about many biographers?
2. **Irony. Irony** is a difference between appearance and reality. Types of irony include **dramatic irony**, in which something is known by the reader or audience but unknown to the characters; **verbal irony**, in which a statement is made that implies its opposite; and **irony of situation**, in which an event occurs that violates the expectations of the characters, the reader, or the audience. Explain why the following scenes from the selection are ironic:
   - King James throws a carnival during the devastating Great Frost, which has created hardship for common people and killed many of them and their animals.
   - The Muscovite ambassador comes to England. The Muscovites speak no English, only Russian and French. The English speak no Russian and only a very few people, such as Orlando, speak French.
   - When Orlando is "rattling off one of his most impassioned sonnets," the princess interrupts, asking him to pass the salt.
3. **Internal Monologue, Stream-of-Consciousness Writing, and Synaesthesia.** An **internal monologue** presents the private sensations, thoughts, and emotions of a character. **Stream-of-consciousness writing** is literature that attempts to render the flow of feelings, thoughts, and impressions within the minds of characters. **Synaesthesia** is a figure of speech that combines in a single expression images related to two or more different senses. Modernist writers are known for employing internal monologues and stream-of-consciousness writing to portray vividly their characters' inner thoughts and desires. Virginia Woolf is considered a master of this type of writing. Identify two passages from this selection in which the reader is allowed to see the flow of feelings, thoughts, and impressions within Orlando. What do these passages allow you to understand about Orlando? What role does synaesthesia play in these passages?

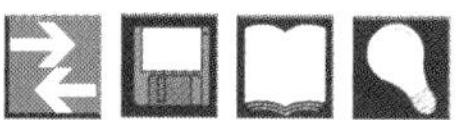

ANSWERS FOR UNDERSTANDING LITERATURE

Responses will vary. Possible responses are given.

1. **Biography and Satire.** This interruption is humorous or ironic because the narrator interrupts the flow of Orlando's thoughts to say that one should not pause in the narrative, thereby effectively pausing in the narrative. Woolf is pointing out that biographers cannot be absent from their work, and thereby affect the truth of what is told.

2. **Irony.**
- This situation is ironic because although the Great Frost is a time of terrible hardship, the king sees it as an opportunity for merriment.
- This situation is ironic because an ambassador's job is to communicate with representatives of other nations, but the English and the Muscovite ambassador are unable to understand each other.
- Orlando is ecstatically creating poetry about the princess, but the princess interrupts his reverie with a very mundane question, thereby violating Orlando's expectations.

3. **Internal Monologue, Stream-of-Consciousness Writing, and Synaesthesia.** *Responses will vary.* Students may point to the passage when Orlando first sees and falls in love with the princess and the passage in which Orlando is sitting with the princess at dinner and contemplating whether he had ever truly loved before. In both passages, senses are intermingled. For example in the first passage, "He called her a melon, a pineapple, an olive tree, an emerald, and a fox in the snow all in the space of three seconds; he did not know whether he had heard her, tasted her, seen her, or all three together."

ANSWERS FOR REVIEWING THE SELECTION (CONT.)

together in a separate world.

SYNTHESIZING

Responses will vary. Possible responses are given.

5. The Great Frost itself, as well as the king's response to it, are exaggerated. Humorous elements include the princess's true feelings about the English, the country woman turning to powder, and the frozen wayfarers being used as troughs and scratching posts. The following are some of the serious issues raised: the degree to which a biography can be completely true to life and unbiased, whether rulers pay enough attention to the needs and suffering of common people, whether courtly manners are ridiculous and too extravagant, and whether love at first sight can mature into a good relationship.

ANALYTIC SCALES FOR RESPONDING IN WRITING

Grading scales for Responding in Writing appear on page 1031.

ANSWERS FOR LANGUAGE LAB

1. Virginia Woolf's first two novels, *The Voyage Out* and *Night and Day*, are realistic; however, Woolf soon stopped writing conventional novels to focus on exploring her characters' internal states and impressions using a fluid style of writing that came to be known as stream-of-consciousness.
2. The novels that ensured Woolf's reputation as a great Modernist writer were these: *Mrs. Dalloway, To the Lighthouse,* and *The Waves.*
3. In *To the Lighthouse,* Woolf describes a family on holiday in the Hebrides; Woolf's portrayal of this place is based on her own family vacations in Cornwall.
4. The central characters in the novel are Mrs. Ramsay, the gracious hostess; Mr. Ramsay, her self-involved and philosophical husband; Augustus Carmichael, an elderly poet; and Lily Briscoe, a painter.
5. The novel is broken into three distinct sections: "The Window," "Time Passes," and "The Lighthouse."

▶ Additional practice is provided in the Essential Skills Practice Book: Language 2.48.

Responding in Writing

1. **Creative Writing: Biography.** *Orlando* is a fictional biography, but most biographies are nonfiction works that tell about the lives of real people. Choose a person you know, such as a family member, friend, or teacher. Write a short excerpt from this person's biography, focusing on any part or aspect of this person's life. You might gather information by interviewing your subject or by interviewing other people who know him or her. (See the Language Arts Survey 1.10, "Gathering Information," for more information on interviewing.) To make the subject of your biography more vivid to your reader, you might use description, dialogue, or anecdotes.

2. **Critical Essay: Realism and Fantasy.** Realism is the attempt to render in art an accurate portrayal of reality. A fantasy is a literary work that contains highly unrealistic elements. In *Orlando,* Woolf combines elements of realistic writing with elements of fantastic writing. Write an essay evaluating the elements of realism and fantasy in the selection. What is the effect of combining realism with fantasy in this way? Your thesis should pose a possible explanation for Woolf's blend of the real and the fantastic. In the following paragraphs, support your thesis with evidence and quotations from the selection, and come to a conclusion in a final paragraph.

Language Lab

Semicolons and Colons. You may have noticed that many of Woolf's sentences are quite long. These sentences, however, are grammatically correct because clauses, long statements, and lists are linked, often using the semicolon or the colon as punctuation. Review the Language Arts Survey 2.48, "Semicolons and Colons." Then read the sentences below. These sentences lack semicolons and colons in the proper places. On your own paper, rewrite the sentences below, punctuating them correctly.

1. Virginia Woolf's first two novels, *The Voyage Out* and *Night and Day,* are realistic however, Woolf soon stopped writing conventional novels to focus on exploring her characters' internal states and impressions, using a fluid style of writing that came to be known as stream-of-consciousness.
2. The novels that ensured Woolf's reputation as a great Modernist writer were these *Mrs. Dalloway, To the Lighthouse,* and *The Waves.*
3. In *To the Lighthouse*, Woolf describes a family on holiday in the Hebrides Woolf's portrayal of this place is based on her own family's vacations in Cornwall.
4. The central characters in the novel are Mrs. Ramsay, the gracious hostess, Mr. Ramsay, her self-involved and philosophical husband, Augustus Carmichael, an elderly poet, and Lily Briscoe, a painter.
5. The novel is broken into three distinct sections "The Window," "Time Passes," and "The Lighthouse."

PREREADING

"The Guitar"
by Federico García Lorca, translated by Elizabeth du Gué Trapier

About the Author

FEDERICO GARCÍA LORCA
1898–1936

Federico García Lorca, a poet and playwright, was Spain's best-known modern writer. He grew up in a rural area outside the city of Grenada and attended the University of Madrid where he met Salvador Dalí, a painter whose surrealistic technique profoundly influenced García Lorca's work. García Lorca was also inspired by music, particularly by the *cante jondo*, or "deep song," of the Spanish gypsies; he became a talented pianist after befriending the composer Manuel de Falla.

García Lorca did not intend for his poetry to be viewed as political; however, because modern themes—life, death, and compassion for those suffering from lost hope and inhumanity—run through García Lorca's work, the new Nationalist government in Spain found García Lorca's work offensive and labeled him an "undesirable." On July 19, 1936, Nationalists kidnapped García Lorca just before he was supposed to meet his friend and fellow poet Pablo Neruda. The kidnappers forced him to dig his own grave and then shot him. García Lorca died in a cemetery in his beloved Grenada.

About the Selection

"The Guitar" is based on Federico García Lorca's views on life and humanity during the time of the Fascist Nationalist Movement in Spain. In the poem, García Lorca expresses sorrow using *cante jondo* or "deep song" as a source of inspiration. The music of the Flamenco dancers and Spanish gypsies, *cante jondo* is deeply emotional, evoking passion about both life and death. Inspired by this passion, García Lorca uses the image of a weeping guitar and its music to express feelings of longing and sorrow. Like many modern poets, García Lorca relied on images to create emotions and mental associations in the reader.

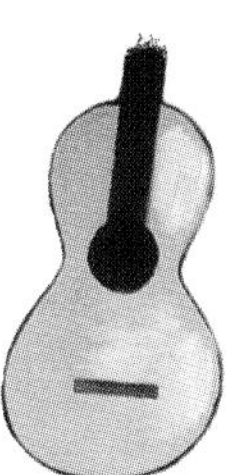

CONNECTIONS: The Nationalist Movement in Spain

In 1936, the rise of Fascism was a major conflict for the people of Spain. The Nationalist Movement, widely supported in large, influential towns, provinces, and food-producing areas, favored a system of government characterized by a rigid one-party dictatorship, forcible suppression of opposition, private economic enterprise under centralized governmental control, belligerent nationalism, racism, and militarism. Opposing forces clashed in the Spanish Civil War (1936–1939). The Republicans were aided by the Soviet Union, France, and Mexico, while Nationalists drew aid from Germany and Italy. Resistors were not powerful enough to prevent the ascension of the Nationalists, and a dictatorship ruled Spain for almost forty years.

ADDITIONAL RESOURCES

READER'S GUIDE
- Selection Worksheet 12.3

ASSESSMENT PORTFOLIO
- Selection Check Test 2.12.5
- Selection Test 2.12.6

ESSENTIAL SKILLS PRACTICE BOOKS
- Writing 1.8, 1.20
- Study and Research 4.12–4.18

PREREADING EXTENSIONS

Students may have a better understanding of the poem if they listen to the music that inspired García Lorca—*cante jondo*. Play some of this music for students, or if you have musically inclined students in your class, ask them to play a sample for other students to hear. Then discuss with students the emotions or mood the music evokes.

SUPPORT FOR LEP STUDENTS

PRONUNCIATIONS OF PROPER NOUNS AND ADJECTIVES

Fe • de • ri • co Gar • cia Lor • ca (fā thā rē´kō gär thē´ä lôr´kä)

ADDITIONAL VOCABULARY

monotonously—in a dull, repetitive way
vaults—any arches, including the sky

GOALS/OBJECTIVES

Studying this lesson will enable students to
- appreciate and enjoy a modern poem
- recognize Federico García Lorca as a great modern Spanish poet
- define *symbol, free verse,* and *repetition*
- identify repetition and symbols
- write a free-verse poem
- write an analysis of the mood of a poem
- use the library and online sources to research a topic
- present a group oral report

READER'S JOURNAL

Suggest that students might respond to the prompt through another medium such as painting, sculpture, dance, or music. The works should demonstrate the students' feelings about the events that hurt them in some way.

Answers to Guided Reading Questions

❶ The crying of the guitar begins at the beginning of each day.

❷ Besides the guitar, the water and wind weep.

❸ The guitar cries for distant things such as warm southern sands that desire white camellias. It cries for the arrow without a target, the evening without morning, the first bird dead upon a branch, and a wounded heart.

❹ The heart is wounded by five swords.

Selection Check Test with Answers

EX. What begins now?
The cry of the guitar begins now.

1. What does the cry of the guitar break?
The cry breaks the vaults of dawn.

2. What is it useless and impossible to do?
It is useless and impossible to still the crying of the guitar.

3. What word is used to describe the way the guitar weeps?
The guitar weeps monotonously.

4. Which arrow does the guitar mourn?
The guitar mourns the arrow without a target.

5. What have wounded the heart?
Five swords have wounded the heart.

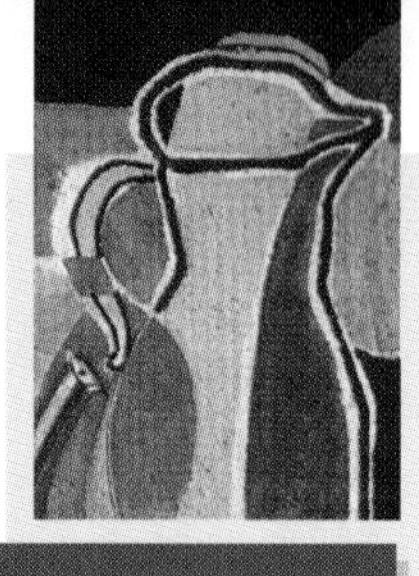

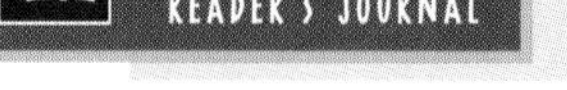

When was the last time that you felt really sad or hurt? What caused your sadness? Did a person or the outcome of an event disappoint you? How did you deal with your feelings of sadness? In your journal, describe the experience.

"The Guitar"

Federico García Lorca, translated by Elizabeth du Gué Trapier

❶ *When does the crying of the guitar begin?*

❷ *What other things besides the guitar weep?*

❸ *Why does the guitar cry?*

❹ *How is the heart wounded?*

Now begins the cry
Of the guitar,
Breaking the vaults
Of dawn.
Now begins the cry
Of the guitar.
Useless
To still it.
Impossible
To still it.
It weeps monotonously
As weeps the water,
As weeps the wind
Over snow.
Impossible
To still it.
It weeps
For distant things,
Warm southern sands
Desiring white camellias.[1]
It mourns the arrow without a target,
The evening without morning.
And the first bird dead
Upon a branch.
O guitar!
A wounded heart,
Wounded by five swords. ■

1. **camellias.** Evergreen trees and shrubs of the tea family, with glossy leaves and waxy, rose-like flowers

Still Life—"Le Jour." Georges Braque, 1929. National Gallery of Art, Washington, D.C., Chester Dale Collection.

Responding to the Selection

What sort of music inspires strong feelings of sadness in you? In small groups, share pieces of music that express sadness. Compare and contrast this music to the music described in the poem and the emotional effect the poem has on you.

Responding to the Selection

Students may bring samples of the music that makes them sad to class to share with the people in their group. Ask students to distinguish between songs with sad lyrics and music that is sad.

ANALYTIC SCALES FOR RESPONDING IN WRITING

(SEE PAGE 1039.)

Assign a score from 1 to 25 for each grading criterion below. (For more detailed evaluation, see the evaluation forms for writing, revising, and proofreading, Assessment Portfolio 4.1–4.9.)

1. Free-Verse Poem

- **Content/Unity.** The poem uses a symbol to express an emotion.
- **Organization/Coherence.** The poem does not use regular rhythm, stanzas, line breaks, or rhyme.
- **Language/Style.** The poem uses vivid and precise nouns, verbs, and modifiers.
- **Conventions.** The poem avoids errors in spelling, grammar, usage, mechanics, and manuscript form.

► Additional practice is provided in the Essential Skills Practice Book: Writing 1.8.

2. Critical Essay

- **Content/Unity.** The essay analyzes the mood of the poem.
- **Organization/Coherence.** The essay presents and supports a thesis.
- **Language/Style.** The essay uses vivid and precise nouns, verbs, and modifiers.
- **Conventions.** The essay avoids errors in spelling, grammar, usage, mechanics, and manuscript form.

► Additional practice is provided in the Essential Skills Practice Book: Writing 1.20.

Reviewing the Selection

Recalling

1. According to the speaker, what is it useless and impossible to do?

Interpreting

What other things in life are useless and impossible to try to stop? In other words, to what might the speaker be comparing the sound of the guitar?

2. For what things does the guitar weep? What does it mourn? How many "swords" wound the heart of the guitar?

▶▶ What do lines 17–24 reveal about human desires and sorrows? Why might the speaker call these things distant? What might this image of swords wounding a heart represent?

Synthesizing

3. This poem can be interpreted as a work about death. What words, phrases, and images in this poem contribute to this interpretation? Do you find this to be a reasonable interpretation of this work? Explain.

Understanding Literature (Questions for Discussion)

1. **Symbol.** A **symbol** is a thing that stands for or represents both itself and something else. Writers use two types of symbols—conventional, and personal or idiosyncratic. A conventional symbol is one with traditional, widely recognized associations. Such symbols include doves for peace, laurel wreaths for heroism or victory, the color green for jealousy, and so forth. A personal or idiosyncratic symbol is one that assumes its secondary meaning because of the special way a writer uses it. What personal symbol is used in García Lorca's poem? What does it represent? What does the action of the symbol represent?

2. **Free Verse. Free verse** is poetry that avoids use of regular rhyme, rhythm, meter, or division into stanzas. In the twentieth century, many poets have broken away from traditional poetic forms to experiment with free verse. In what way would this poem be different if it had regular rhyme and rhythm? Would it change the mood of the poem? If you had to break the poem into stanzas, where would you do so? What effect would this change have on the poem?

3. **Repetition. Repetition** is the use, again, of a sound, word, phrase, sentence, or other element. Find a few examples of repetition in this poem. This poem was inspired by the *cante jondo*, or "deep song" of the gypsies. Explain how the use of repetition gives the poem a musical quality.

Answers for Reviewing the Selection

RECALLING AND INTERPRETING

1. **Recalling.** It is useless and impossible to still the crying of the guitar. **Interpreting.** The speaker may be saying that is impossible to stop sadness and death, that the guitar expresses the pain that all humans feel. It seems impossible to stop the ills of society, social and political injustice, and a loss of humanity. The speaker might be comparing the sound of the guitar to a cry from a human heart.

2. **Recalling.** The guitar weeps for "distant things," "warm southern sands," "white camellias," "the arrow without a target," "the evening without morning," and the first dead bird on a branch. The heart is wounded by five swords. **Interpreting.** Lines 17–24 reveal that people often want what they cannot have, they are disturbed by lack of direction or order. People have expectations about how the world should be; sorrow arises, in part, because these expectations are not met. These things may be called distant because they are longed for and are not part of daily life. These things might also be called distant because people are detached from them and long to be emotionally connected to nature, to order, and be able to accept their own mortality. The five swords may, in the imagery of the guitar, represent the five fingers strumming the guitar. The fingers create the heart-breaking sound of the guitar that signifies pain and death that people face.

SYNTHESIZING

Responses will vary. Possible responses are given.

3. The mourning and crying reflects people's reactions to death. The fact that it is useless and impossible to stop the weeping of the guitar suggests that it is useless and impossible to try to stop death. The "arrow without a target" suggests unfinished

(cont.)

Answers for Reviewing the Selection (cont.)

business, and the "evening without morning" suggests somebody who never awoke. The poem also mentions death in "the first bird dead," and injury in "A wounded heart, / Wounded by five swords." Based on the examples of death and mourning imagery presented, students are likely to find the analysis of "The Guitar" as a death poem to be reasonable. Also, the information that students have about García Lorca's life and influences support such an analysis.

Responding in Writing

1. **Creative Writing: Free-Verse Poem.** García Lorca's free-verse poem expresses a definite emotion using the symbol and music of the guitar as a medium. Think back to a time in your life when you were overcome by an emotion, such as anger, joy, sadness, jealousy, or love. Then choose a symbol that you might use to express this emotion. For example, if you have chosen to write about anger, you might use a tornado as a symbol of that emotion. Then, using the symbol you have chosen, write a free-verse poem in which the symbol's actions or description portrays the emotion you remember.

2. **Critical Essay: Analyzing Mood.** Mood, or atmosphere, is the emotion created in the reader by part or all of a literary work. Write a three-paragraph essay in which you analyze the mood of "The Guitar." Questions to consider include the following: Does the poem create one consistent mood, or does the mood change throughout the poem? If the mood changes, where does it change, and why? What words and phrases help to create this mood? State your opinion about the mood of this poem in your first paragraph; support your opinion by referring to and quoting from the text of the poem in your second paragraph; and come to a conclusion in the third.

Research Skills

Researching Twentieth-Century Spain. Review the Language Arts Survey 4.12–4.18, "Research Skills." Then, working in small groups, use the library and the Internet to find more information on Spanish arts and history in the twentieth century. Choose one of the topics below or another topic that interests your group. Present your findings to the class using visual aids such as maps, charts, graphs, photographs, or reproductions of artwork.

Possible topics:

- Spanish Civil War
- Basque and Catalan regionalism
- Spain under Franco
- Spanish literature (Vicente Aleixandre, Juan Ramón Jiménez)
- Spanish painting (Pablo Picasso, Jean Miró, Salvador Dalí)
- Spanish architecture (Alejandro de la Sota, José Rafael Corrales, Antonio Gaudí)
- Spanish sculpture (Eduardo Chillida, Pablo Gargallo, Julio González)

ANALYTIC SCALES FOR RESPONDING IN WRITING

Grading scales for Responding in Writing appear on page 1037.

Answers for Understanding Literature

Responses will vary. Possible responses are given.

1. **Symbol.** García Lorca uses the guitar as a personal symbol. The sound of the guitar signifies weeping and death. The ceaseless sound is impossible to stop, representing the inevitability of death.

2. **Free Verse.** The poem reflects the irregularity of life and the suddenness of death through the poem's use of irregular rhyme, rhythm, and stanza breaks. If the poem were more structured, the mood of the poem might be less intense. Students may choose to break the poem anywhere, but they should explain why they chose certain places to break it.

3. **Repetition.** The lines "Now begins the cry / Of the guitar" is repeated. The phrase "to still it" is repeated after "Useless" and "Impossible." The lines "Impossible / To still it" are repeated. The repetitions connect various parts of the poem. They act almost as a refrain within the poem, giving it a musical quality.

Answers for Skills Activities

RESEARCH SKILLS

Students may choose another topic related to Spain in the twentieth century. The names listed for literature, painting, architecture, and sculpture represent a starting point for research. There are many other talented Spanish artists whose work students should explore.

Suggest that each group begin by choosing a topic and making a plan for research. For example, one student might research Picasso, while another researches Miró, or one student might search on the Internet, while another student finds books on the subject.

ADDITIONAL RESOURCES

Reader's Guide

- Selection Worksheet 12.4

Assessment Portfolio

- Selection Check Test 2.12.7
- Selection Test 2.12.8

Essential Skills Practice Books

- Writing 1.8, 1.20

PREREADING EXTENSIONS

Senghor believed that one of the traditional values of Africa that is necessary in the contemporary world is connection to one's ancestors. Ask students to complete an oral history project in which they talk to an elderly relative or another person from their cultural heritage. Students should use this opportunity to learn more about their family or cultural history. Ask students to transcribe and comment on their discussions with their source.

SUPPORT FOR LEP STUDENTS

Pronunciations of Proper Nouns and Adjectives

Lé • o • pold Sé • dar Sen • ghor (lā ô pôld´ sā där´ sän gôr´)
Gui • nea (gin´ ē)
Su • dan • ese (so͞o´də nēz´)

Additional Vocabulary

primordial—primitive; original
serene—peaceful
somber—dark and gloomy

PREREADING

"And We Shall Be Steeped"
by Léopold Sédar Senghor, translated by John Reed and Clive Wake

SENEGAL

About the Author

LÉOPOLD SÉDAR SENGHOR 1906–

Léopold Sédar Senghor is notable in the world of literature and in the sphere of politics. Senghor was born in the fishing village of Joal in Senegal. As a child, Senghor learned traditional culture from his uncle. This traditional culture and the power of language, which struck the boy as he listened to recitations of traditional poetry, had a powerful impact on Senghor's life. As Senegal was then a colony of France, Senghor was educated in French. He studied in a nearby village and later in Dakar, the capital of Senegal. Abandoning thoughts of becoming a priest, Senghor continued his education and won a scholarship to study in France. Living in France destroyed Senghor's idealized impression of Europe and strengthened his belief in the cultural mark that Africa had made, and had the potential to make, on world culture. Senghor taught in France from 1935 to 1940, when he was forced into a Nazi concentration camp. After his release in 1942, he began his political career. An ardent advocate for Africa as deputy of Senegal for the French Constituent Assembly and through his writing, Senghor has published an African cultural journal and an anthology of works by French-speaking black Africans. Senegal became a republic in 1960, and Senghor was elected president, a post he held until 1980.

About the Selection

Léopold Senghor, with poet Aimé Césaire, was one of the founders of the **Negritude** movement, a literary movement that flourished from the 1930s through the 1950s. In reaction to colonialism, African and Caribbean writers redefined and promoted the richness of African culture, noting that traditional values such as mysticism, closeness to nature, and connection to one's ancestors are necessary in the modern world. An excellent example of Negritude ideals, **"And We Shall Be Steeped"** celebrates the cultural and historical wonders of Africa. To evoke the richness of this heritage, Senghor uses vivid imagery.

CONNECTIONS: Senegalese Art

Senghor recognized the influence of African art around the world. This art, including sculpture, music, and dance, retains many traditional aspects. Senegalese sculpture relies on abstraction. Dance and music are highly improvised and dependent upon rhythm. Despite the impact of Senghor and other writers, a large part of Senegalese literature is still passed on orally. Museums, theaters, and the craft village of Soumbedioune in Dakar preserve and support the continuation of African art.

GOALS/OBJECTIVES

Studying this lesson will enable students to

- enjoy and appreciate a lyric poem
- identify Léopold Sédar Senghor as a contemporary Senegalese writer
- define *imagery* and *alliteration*
- identify images
- write an occasional poem or speech
- analyze the poem in light of the ideals of the Negritude movement
- use a variety of resources to research a topic
- prepare a group presentation on African arts

Do you think cultural traditions are important, or do you think they are outdated? In your journal, write your opinions about your cultural heritage and the role it plays in your life. You might also write about the attitudes you perceive others have about your heritage.

READER'S JOURNAL

"And We Shall Be Steeped"

LÉOPOLD SÉDAR SENGHOR, TRANSLATED BY JOHN REED AND CLIVE WAKE

For Khalam[1]
And we shall be steeped my dear in the presence of Africa.
Furniture from Guinea and Congo,[2] heavy and polished, somber and serene.
On the walls, pure primordial masks distant and yet present.
Stools of honor for hereditary guests, for the Princes of the High Lands.
Wild perfumes, thick mats of silence
Cushions of shade and leisure, the noise of a wellspring of peace.
Classic words. In a distance, antiphonal[3] singing like Sudanese[4] cloths
And then, friendly lamp, your kindness to soothe this obsessive presence
White black and red, oh red as the African soil. ■

❶ In what will the speaker be steeped? How do you think the speaker feels about this presence?

❷ What symbols of the past are mentioned? What is the speaker's attitude toward the past?

❸ According to the speaker, what will the lamp do?

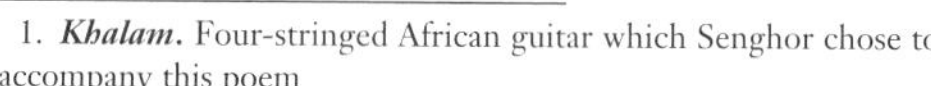

1. ***Khalam.*** Four-stringed African guitar which Senghor chose to accompany this poem
2. **Guinea and Congo.** Two present-day African nations that were also powerful states in earlier African history
3. **antiphonal.** Alternately sung or chanted
4. **Sudanese.** From the Sudan, a present-day nation and a region that stretches across Africa south of the Sahara

WORDS FOR EVERYDAY USE

steep (stēp) *vt.,* immerse, saturate

READER'S JOURNAL

Students might also comment on aspects of other cultures that intrigue or interest them. Suggest that students consider how their culture is adapting to our changing world.

ANSWERS TO GUIDED READING QUESTIONS

❶ The speaker will be steeped in the presence of Africa. The speaker admires Africa.

❷ Masks and stools of honor for hereditary guests are mentioned. The past is revered.

❸ The lamp will bring kindness to soothe the obsessive presence of Africa.

SELECTION CHECK TEST WITH ANSWERS

EX. About what continent does Senghor write?
He writes about Africa.

1. Where is the furniture from?
The furniture is from Guinea and Congo.

2. What are "distant and yet present"?
The primordial masks are "distant and yet present."

3. For whom are the stools of honor prepared?
The stools of honor are prepared for the hereditary guests and the Princes of the High Lands.

4. To what is the antiphonal singing compared?
The antiphonal singing is compared to Sudanese cloth.

5. What colors are mentioned in the last line? Which is the color of the African soil?
Black, white, and red are mentioned. Red is the color of the soil.

VOCABULARY IN CONTEXT

- While writing her dissertation on the oral traditions of Senegal, Birungi was steeped in the folklore of that country.

Responding to the Selection

As an additional or alternate activity, students may compare and contrast their feelings about their culture to the speaker's feelings about his culture.

Answers for Reviewing the Selection

RECALLING AND INTERPRETING

1. **Recalling.** The speaker will be steeped in the presence of Africa. **Interpreting.** The speaker finds being so steeped to be an agreeable or admirable experience.

2. **Recalling.** The masks are pure and primordial, distant, and yet present. **Interpreting.** The masks represent the past and tradition to the speaker. They are distant because they represent the past. They are present because they are physically on the wall, bringing the past within the speaker's reach.

3. **Recalling.** The stools of honor are prepared for the hereditary guests and the Princes of High Lands. **Interpreting.** This detail suggests that in the speaker's culture, ancestors and legends of the past are important.

4. **Recalling.** Senghor evokes the image of white, black, and red. **Interpreting.** This image might represent the racial conflict between blacks and whites in Senegal. The red, the color of the African soil, might also represent the blood that has been shed.

SYNTHESIZING

Responses will vary. Possible responses are given.

5. The poem as a form of literature reflects Senghor's activity in the world of writing. The subject matter—the culture and history of Senegal, including the conflict between Africans and colonists—reflects his activity in political life.

Responding to the Selection

What attitudes toward, or impressions of, Africa do you have after reading this poem? With your classmates, discuss your answers to this question.

Reviewing the Selection

RECALLING		INTERPRETING
1. In what will the speaker be steeped?	▶▶	What is the speaker's attitude toward being steeped in this thing?
2. What words describe the masks on the walls?	▶▶	What do the masks represent to the speaker? Why are they both distant and present?
3. For whom are the stools of honor prepared?	▶▶	What does this detail suggest about the values of the speaker's culture?
4. What image does Senghor evoke in the last line?	▶▶	In what way might this image reflect Senegalese history?

SYNTHESIZING

5. Senghor was active in both the political and the literary worlds of Senegal. In what way does "And We Shall Be Steeped" reflect Senghor's interest in both of these worlds?

Understanding Literature (Questions for Discussion)

1. **Imagery. Imagery** is the collective images in a literary work. An **image** is a word or phrase that names something that can be seen, heard, touched, tasted, or smelled. On your own paper, make a sensory detail chart like the one below. Fill in the chart with images used in the poem.

AFRICA				
Sight	Sound	Touch	Taste	Smell

Answers for Understanding Literature

Responses will vary. Possible responses are given.

1. **Imagery.** Under "Sight" students might include furniture, primordial masks, stools of honor, lamplight, black, white, and red. Under "Sound" students might include mats of silence, noise of a wellspring of peace, antiphonal singing like Sudanese cloths. Under "Touch" students might include cushions of shade and leisure, kindness soothing. Under "Smell" students might include wild perfumes.

2. **Alliteration.** The *p* sound recurs throughout the poem in *presence, polished, pure primordial distant yet present, Princes, perfumes, peace, presence.* The *s* sound is also alliterated in *shall be steeped, somber and serene, stools, silence, shade, singing like Sudanese, soothe, soil.*

2. **Alliteration. Alliteration** is the repetition of initial consonant sounds. Identify examples of alliteration throughout the poem.

Responding in Writing

1. **Creative Writing: Occasional Poem or Speech.** "And We Shall Be Steeped" praises the history and culture of Africa. Think of a place that is important to you. Imagine that this place is celebrating a milestone in its history, such as a centennial or other anniversary, and that you have been chosen to give a speech or to read a poem for the occasion. To gather ideas for your speech or poem, make a cluster chart (see Language Arts Survey 1.10, "Gathering Ideas") about the place you have chosen. You might include information about the history of this place, the importance of this place in the world, why this place might appeal to others, and why this place is special to you. Make a rough outline to organize the ideas you have gathered. Then put these ideas together in a cohesive speech or poem that uses vivid images to make clear the appeal of this place to your audience.

2. **Critical Essay: Senghor and the Negritude Movement.** Senghor was one of the founders of the Negritude movement. Write a critical essay in which you examine "And We Shall Be Steeped" in light of the purpose of this movement. Before you begin writing, review the information about Negritude on the Prereading page of this selection, or consult an encyclopedia or a biography of Senghor. Make a rough outline that shows the major aims or characteristics of the movement, and reread the poem, keeping in mind the points you have outlined. Then write a thesis that discusses whether "And We Shall Be Steeped" supports and embodies the goals of the Negritude movement. Support your thesis with analysis of these goals and with references to the text of the poem.

Project

African Arts. Work in small groups to research African arts. Each group should cover a geographic section of Africa—North Africa, Southern Africa, East Africa, West Africa, and Central Africa. Use libraries, museums, the Internet, or people in your community as sources of information on African sculpture, masks, textiles, metal work, dance, and music. Each group should share its findings with the class. Enliven your presentation with examples, reproductions, or photographs of works or with recordings or performances of music or dance from the region that you are representing. You may wish to work as a class to plan an African Arts Celebration, based on your presentations. Invite other classes from your school or people from your community to share in your celebration.

ANALYTIC SCALES FOR RESPONDING IN WRITING

Assign a score from 1 to 25 for each grading criterion below. (For more detailed evaluation, see the evaluation forms for writing, revising, and proofreading, Assessment Portfolio 4.1–4.9.)

1. Occasional Poem or Speech

- **Content/Unity.** The poem or speech presents information and the speaker's feelings about a place.
- **Organization/Coherence.** The poem or speech presents the speakers feelings in a logical, cohesive fashion.
- **Language/Style.** The poem or speech uses vivid and precise nouns, verbs, and modifiers.
- **Conventions.** The poem or speech avoids errors in spelling, grammar, usage, mechanics, and manuscript form.

▶ Additional practice is provided in the Essential Skills Practice Book: Writing 1.8.

2. Critical Essay

- **Content/Unity.** The essay presents analysis of the poem in light of the goals of the Negritude movement.
- **Organization/Coherence.** The essay presents a thesis. The thesis is supported by analysis of the goals of the movement and by reference to the poem. The essay has a strong conclusion.
- **Language/Style.** The essay uses vivid and precise nouns, verbs, and modifiers.
- **Conventions.** The essay avoids errors in spelling, grammar, usage, mechanics, and manuscript form.

▶ Additional practice is provided in the Essential Skills Practice Book: Writing 1.20.

PROJECT NOTES

See the evaluation form for projects, Assessment Portfolio 4.12.

African Arts. Literature may also be added to the list of types of arts students research. Students should seek ancient works of art and literature, types of traditional arts that are still practiced, and contemporary art from the area that they are researching.

Students may also wish to examine the influence of African arts on arts in other places or the popularity of African arts in areas other than Africa.

ADDITIONAL RESOURCES

READER'S GUIDE

- Selection Worksheet 12.5

ASSESSMENT PORTFOLIO

- Selection Check Test 2.12.9
- Selection Test 2.12.10

ESSENTIAL SKILLS PRACTICE BOOKS

- Writing 1.8, 1.20

PREREADING EXTENSIONS

Suggest that students read a story or novel by one of the writers listed in Connections: Latin American Women Writers. If students have not already read the selections by these writers in this textbook, that would be a good place to start. If students have already read these selections, ask them to find another work by one of these writers. Have them write a review of the work, discussing its themes, plot, characters, and use of literary techniques.

SUPPORT FOR LEP STUDENTS

PRONUNCIATIONS OF PROPER NOUNS AND ADJECTIVES

Fran • ces • ca (frän ches´kä)
I • sol • de (i sōl´də)
Ma • tos Peix • o • to (mä´tōs pā shō´tü)
Pa • o • lo (pä ō´lō)
Ra • chel de Quei • roz (rā´chəl dā kē ros´)
Tris • tan (tris´tən)

ADDITIONAL VOCABULARY

embellish—improve upon; adorn
gross—twelve dozen
hoax—trick or fraud
revive—bring back to life
saturated—soaked through

PREREADING

"Metonymy, or The Husband's Revenge"
by Rachel de Queiroz, translated by William L. Grossman

About the Author

RACHEL DE QUEIROZ
1910–

A member of the Northeastern school, a group of authors who set many of their novels and works of social criticism in northeastern Brazil, **Rachel de Queiroz** is recognized as an outstanding novelist, dramatist, and translator. Queiroz grew up on a ranch in northeastern Brazil. Her works reflect issues of her homeland, dealing with drought, forgotten people of the backlands, and bandits. Queiroz also explores issues of women's independence and education in *Rocky Road* and *The Three Marias.* Having mastered the form of the journalistic essay, Queiroz gained a large audience for her general interest pieces. She also generated interest in short prose forms. In recognition of her literary accomplishments, Queiroz was elected to the Brazilian Academy of Letters in 1977, the first woman to receive this honor. In addition to her literary work, Queiroz served as Brazil's representative to the United Nations in 1964.

Self Portrait.
Frida Kahlo, 1930

About the Selection

A **figure of speech** is an expression that has more than a literal meaning. One type of figure of speech is **metonymy,** or the naming of an object associated with a thing in place of the name of the thing itself. For example, a writer or speaker might use metonymy by referring to the White House when he or she means the executive branch of the United States government. Queiroz's short story, **"Metonymy, or The Husband's Revenge,"** suggests a surprising extension or application of this technique. The narrator begins by presenting two **anecdotes,** brief stories with a specific point or moral, that reflect the use of metonymy, one in a literary sense and one in the context of daily life. These anecdotes introduce a more fully developed example of the application of metonymy, one with tragic results.

CONNECTIONS: Latin American Women Writers

Exploring the theme of the role of women in Brazil, Rachel de Queiroz challenges traditional roles and attacks inadequate and unequal education for women. Her writing brings these issues to light and has made Queiroz a well-known and respected literary figure. Other notable women writers of Latin America include Laura Esquivel (see page 9) and Elena Poniatowska of Mexico; Luisa Valenzuela (see page 214) of Argentina; Isabel Allende (see page 270), Gabriela Mistral (see page 395), and Maria Luisa Bombal of Chile; and Clarice Lispector (see page 474) and Lydia Fagundes Telles of Brazil.

GOALS/OBJECTIVES

Studying this lesson will enable students to

- interpret and enjoy a story about an extended figure of speech
- identify Rachel de Queiroz as a contemporary Latin American writer
- define *metonymy, irony,* and *allusion*
- identify examples of metonymy and allusion
- write an anecdote
- analyze irony and foreshadowing in a story
- think creatively about figures of speech
- work in a group to prepare a collage

READER'S JOURNAL

Have you ever blamed somebody, not because of what he or she has done, but because this person is associated with something that makes you unhappy or angry? For example, have you ever been angry at a family member who gave you some bad news or been annoyed with a slow driver or people in a long line because you are running late? Think about one such situation, and write about it in your journal. Describe your reaction to the situation and to the person involved.

"Metonymy, or The Husband's Revenge"

RACHEL DE QUEIROZ, TRANSLATED BY WILLIAM L. GROSSMAN

Metonymy. I learned the word in 1930 and shall never forget it. I had just published my first novel. A literary critic had scolded me because my hero went out into the night "chest unbuttoned."

"What deplorable nonsense!" wrote this eminently sensible gentleman. "Why does she not say what she means? Obviously, it was his shirt that was unbuttoned, not his chest."

I accepted his rebuke with humility, indeed with shame. But my illustrious Latin professor, Dr. Matos Peixoto came to my rescue. He said that what I had written was perfectly correct; that I had used a respectable figure of speech known as metonymy; and that this figure consisted in the use of one word for another word associated with it—for example, a word representing a cause instead of the effect, or representing the container when the content is intended. The classic instance, he told me, is "the sparkling cup"; in reality, not the cup but the wine in it is sparkling.

The professor and I wrote a letter, which was published in the newspaper where the review had appeared. It put my unjust critic in his place. I hope he learned a lesson. I know I did. Ever since, I have been using metonymy—my only bond with classical rhetoric.

Moreover, I have devoted some thought to it, and I have concluded that metonymy may be more than a figure of speech. There is, I believe, such a thing as practical or applied metonymy. Let me give a crude example, drawn from my own experience. A certain lady of my acquaintance suddenly moved out of the boardinghouse where she had been living for years and became a mortal enemy of the woman who owned it. I asked her why. We both knew that the woman was a kindly soul; she had given my friend injections when she needed them,[1] had often loaned her a hot water bottle, and had always waited on her when she had her little heart attacks.

1. **injections . . . needed them**. The speaker's friend has diabetes and so must receive insulin injections.

❶ *What word does the narrator say she learned in 1930? What example of this figure of speech had she used?*

❷ *In the first example of applied metonymy given by the narrator, why does the woman leave the boardinghouse?*

❸ *What is metonymy? What classic example of this figure of speech does the narrator's professor provide?*

WORDS FOR EVERYDAY USE

em • i • nent • ly (em´ə nənt lē) *adv.*, standing high in comparison with others

re • buke (ri byo͞ok´) *n.*, sharp reprimand

rhet • o • ric (ret´ər ik) *n.*, art of using words effectively in speaking or writing

READER'S JOURNAL

Ask students to discuss why they transferred emotions in the situation they wrote about in their journals. Students might work in small groups to brainstorm ways of diffusing such negative feelings.

ANSWERS TO GUIDED READING QUESTIONS

❶ The speaker says she learned about metonymy. She had written that her hero went out "chest unbuttoned."

❷ The woman leaves because she associates the telephone problems with the owner of the telephone who runs the boarding house.

❸ Metonymy is a figure of speech in which one word is used for another word with which it is associated. The classic example is "the sparkling cup."

SPELLING AND VOCABULARY WORDS FROM THE SELECTION

emaciated	rhetoric
eminently	row
illicit	scrutinize
ingratiating	tepid
rebuke	

VOCABULARY IN CONTEXT

- Devon is eminently serious; even while others are chuckling, he never cracks a grin.
- Taking the rebuke about her sloppy work seriously, Colandra became more careful and precise.
- Dana's heartfelt impromptu speech was more effective than the carefully planned rhetoric he usually spouted.

Answers to Guided Reading Questions

❶ The man was sickly and spent. He was able to find a woman who would marry him because he was rich.

❷ The woman was pale and sickly looking. The easier life and better nutrition the woman experiences after her marriage give her a healthy look, and the beauty that was masked by hunger and poverty is revealed. The woman begins to resent her husband. She finds him a burden and a bore.

Additional Questions and Activities

1. What details does the narrator refuse to name?
2. Why does she keep these details secret?
3. What effect does the narrator's comments about the secret details have?
4. What does the sergeant look like?
5. Why may the sergeant be especially appealing to the woman?

Answers

1. The narrator refuses to name the city in which the events took place and the names of the parties involved. She also refuses to say what branch of the military the sergeant was part of.
2. The narrator does not want the story revived.
3. The narrator's comments make the story seem realistic.
4. The sergeant is muscular, young, manly, and looks gloriously martial in his uniform.
5. The sergeant may be especially appealing to the woman because her husband is sickly and takes little interest in her or anything else.

My friend replied: "It's the telephone in the hall. I hate her for it. Half the time when I answered it, the call was a hoax or joke of some sort."

"But the owner of the boardinghouse didn't perpetrate these hoaxes. She wasn't responsible for them."

"No. But whose telephone was it?"

I know another case of applied metonymy, a more disastrous one, for it involved a crime. It happened in a city of the interior, which I shall not name for fear that someone may recognize the parties and revive the scandal. I shall narrate the crime but conceal the criminal.

❶ *Why might the man have had trouble finding a wife? Why was he able to find a woman to marry?*

Well, in this city of the interior there lived a man. He was not old, but he was spent, which is worse than being old. In his youth he had suffered from beriberi.[2] His legs were weak, his chest was tired and asthmatic, his skin was yellowish, and his eyes were rheumy.[3] He was, however, a man of property; he owned the house in which he lived and the one next to it, in which he had set up a grocery store. Therefore, although so unattractive personally, he was able to find himself a wife. In all justice to him, he did not tempt fate by marrying a beauty. Instead, he married a poor, emaciated girl who worked in a men's clothing factory. By her face one would have thought that she had consumption.[4] So our friend felt safe. He did not foresee the effects of good nutrition and a healthful life on a woman's appearance. The girl no longer spent eight hours a day at a sewing table. She was the mistress of her house. She ate well: fresh meat, cucumber salad, pork fat with beans and manioc[5] mush, all kinds of sweets, and oranges, which her husband bought by the gross for his customers. The effects were like magic. Her body filled out, especially in the best places. She even seemed to grow taller. And her face—what a change! I may have forgotten to mention that her features, in themselves, were good to begin with. Moreover, money enabled her to embellish her natural advantages with art; she began to wear make-up, to wave her hair, and to dress well.

❷ *What did the woman whom the shopkeeper married look like? What effect did her change of lifestyle have? How did she feel about her husband as her appearance changed?*

Lovely, attractive, she now found her sickly, prematurely old husband a burden and a bore. Each evening, as soon as the store was closed, he dined, mostly on milk (he could not stomach meat), took his newspaper, and rested on his chaise longue until time to go to bed. He did not care for movies or for soccer or for radio. He did not even show much interest in love. Just a sort of tepid, tasteless cohabitation.

And then Fate intervened: it produced a sergeant.

Granted, it was unjust for a young wife, after being reconditioned at her husband's expense, to employ her charms against the aforesaid husband. Unjust; but, then, this world thrives on injustice, doesn't it? The sergeant—I shall not say whether he was in the army, the air force, the marines, or the fusiliers,[6] for I still mean to conceal the identities of the parties—the sergeant was muscular, young, ingratiating, with a manly, commanding voice and a healthy spring in his walk. He looked gloriously martial in his high-buttoned uniform.

2. **beriberi.** Disease caused by lack of vitamin B and characterized by nerve disorders
3. **rheumy.** Watery, mucus-filled
4. **consumption.** Disease that causes the wasting away of the body; especially tuberculosis
5. **manioc.** Root or starch extracted from any of several tropical American plants, used in making breads and tapioca
6. **fusiliers.** Regiment of armed soldiers

Words for Everyday Use

e • ma • ci • at • ed (ē mā´shē āt ed´) *adj.,* abnormally lean

tep • id (tep´id) *adj.,* lukewarm; lacking warmth of feeling or enthusiasm

in • gra • ti • at • ing (in grā´shē āt ŋ) *adj.,* trying to be acceptable; trying to bring oneself into another's good graces

Vocabulary in Context

- We wondered if Laila had been eating properly when we saw her emaciated figure.
- After the crowd's tepid response to the new song, the group decided that it still needed work.
- Instead of being impressed with Hildegarde's attitude and actions, her new boss found her ingratiating efforts annoying.

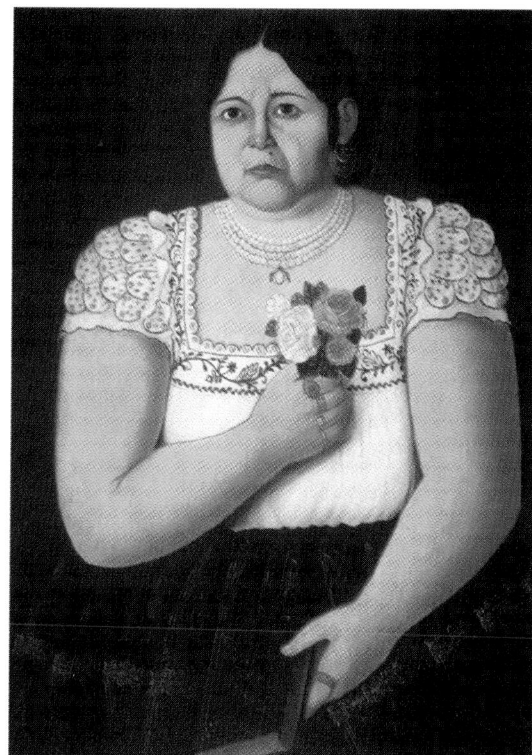

Girl with Roses.
Anonymous, 1880

One day, when the lady was in charge of the counter (while her husband lunched), the sergeant came in. Exactly what happened and what did not happen is hard to say. It seems that the sergeant asked for a pack of cigarettes. Then he wanted a little vermouth. Finally he asked permission to listen to the sports broadcast on the radio next to the counter. Maybe it was just an excuse to remain there awhile. In any case, the girl said it would be all right. It is hard to refuse a favor to a sergeant, especially a sergeant like this one. It appears that the sergeant asked nothing more that day. At most, he and the girl exchanged expressive glances and a few agreeable words, murmured so softly that the customers, always alert for something to gossip about, could not hear them.

Three times more the husband lunched while his wife chatted with the sergeant in the store. The flirtation progressed. Then the husband fell ill with a grippe,[7] and the two others went far beyond flirtation. How and where they met, no one was able to discover. The important thing is that they were lovers and that they loved with a forbidden love, like Tristan and Isolde or Paolo and Francesca.[8]

❶ *To what is the love of the shopkeeper's wife and the sergeant compared?*

7. **grippe.** Influenza (the flu)

8. **Tristan . . . Francesca.** Legendary adulterous pairs; the forbidden love between Tristan and Isolde was celebrated in several medieval romances, although there is no historical evidence of either character's existence. The tragic and adulterous love affair of Paolo Malatesta and Francesca da Rimini, two actual historical figures of the thirteenth century, was referred to in Dante's *Inferno* and inspired several plays and operas.

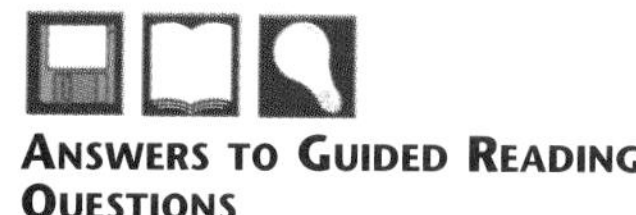

Answers to Guided Reading Questions

❶ Their love is compared to that of Tristan and Isolde or Paolo and Francesca, two legendary pairs of lovers.

Additional Questions and Activities

Ask students to read about the legendary lovers Tristan and Isolde and Paolo and Francesca. The beginning of the love affair between Tristan and Isolde appears on page 732.

Have students compare the role of fate in the stories of these lovers with the role of fate in the story of the shopkeeper's wife and the sergeant. Students can also compare the relationships in the three stories. Students can write a comparison and contrast essay about two of the three stories.

Literary Technique

TONE

Tone is the emotional attitude toward the reader or toward the subject implied by a literary work. Examples of the different tones that a work may have include familiar, ironic, playful, sarcastic, serious, and sincere. Ask students to identify the narrator's tone toward the shopkeeper's wife and the sergeant. Have students find examples of specific passages that reflect or contribute to this theme.

Answers to Guided Reading Questions

❶ Fate does not like illicit love. The sergeant is transferred.

❷ The man begins to suspect his wife after the sergeant has left. His wife's unhappiness makes him suspicious.

❸ The woman keeps her love letters in a box given to her by her husband as a wedding gift in which he told her to keep her secrets.

Selection Check Test with Answers

EX. What word did the narrator learn in 1930?
She learned the word *metonymy.*

1. What phrase did the critic find objectionable?
The critic objected to the phrase "chest unbuttoned."

2. Why did the acquaintance of the narrator become the enemy of the owner of her boardinghouse?
She blamed the owner for the prank phone calls because the owner of the boardinghouse owned the phone.

3. To what pairs of lovers does the narrator compare the shopkeeper's wife and the sergeant?
She compares them to Tristan and Isolde or Paolo and Francesca.

4. Where did the woman keep her love letters from the sergeant?
She kept them in a chest her husband had given her to store her secrets.

5. Whom does the shopkeeper kill?
The shopkeeper kills the mailman who delivered the love letters.

How does Fate feel about illicit love? What happens to the sergeant?

When does the shopkeeper begin to suspect his wife's affair? Why does he become suspicious?

Where does the wife keep her love letters? What had her husband told her about this place?

Then Fate, which does not like illicit love and generally punishes those who engage in it, transferred the sergeant to another part of the country.

It is said that only those who love can really know the pain of separation. The girl cried so much that her eyes grew red and swollen. She lost her appetite. Beneath her rouge could be seen the consumptive complexion of earlier times. And these symptoms aroused her husband's suspicion, although, curiously, he had never suspected anything when the love affair was flourishing and everything was wine and roses.

He began to observe her carefully. He scrutinized her in her periods of silence. He listened to her sighs and to the things she murmured in her sleep. He snooped around and found a postcard and a book, both with a man's name in the same handwriting. He found the insignia of the sergeant's regiment and concluded that the object of his wife's murmurs, sighs, and silences was not only a man but a soldier. Finally he made the supreme discovery: that they had indeed betrayed him. For he discovered the love letters, bearing airmail stamps, a distant postmark, and the sergeant's name. They left no reasonable doubt.

For five months the poor fellow twisted the poisoned dagger of jealousy inside his own thin, sickly chest. Like a boy who discovers a bird's nest and, hiding nearby, watches the eggs increasing in number every day, so the husband, using a duplicate key to the wood chest where his wife put her valuables, watched the increase in the number of letters concealed there. He had given her the chest during their honeymoon, saying, "Keep your secrets here." And the ungrateful girl had obeyed him.

Every day at the fateful hour of lunch, she replaced her husband at the counter. But he was not interested in eating. He ran to her room, pulled out a drawer in her bureau, removed the chest from under a lot of panties, slips, and such, took the little key out of his pocket, opened the chest, and anxiously read the new letter. If there was no new letter, he reread the one dated August 21; it was so full of realism that it sounded like dialogue from a French movie. Then he put everything away and hurried to the kitchen, where he swallowed a few spoonfuls of broth and gnawed at a piece of bread. It was almost impossible to swallow with the passion of those two thieves sticking in his throat.

When the poor man's heart had become utterly saturated with jealousy and hatred, he took a revolver and a box of bullets from the counter drawer; they had been left, years before, by a customer as security for a debt which had never been paid. He loaded the revolver.

One bright morning at exactly ten o'clock, when the store was full of customers, he excused himself and went through the doorway that connected the store with his home. In a few seconds the customers heard the noise of a row, a woman's scream, and three shots. On the sidewalk in front of the shopkeeper's house they saw his wife on her knees, still screaming, and him, with the revolver in his trembling hand, trying to raise her. The front door of the house was open. Through it, they saw a man's legs, wearing khaki trousers and boots. He was lying face down, with his head and torso in the parlor, not visible from the street.

The husband was the first to speak. Raising his eyes from his wife, he looked at the terror-

Words for Everyday Use

il • lic • it (il lis´ it) *adj.,* not allowed by law or custom; unauthorized

scru • ti • nize (skroot´'n īz´) *vt.,* examine closely

row (rou) *n.,* noisy quarrel, dispute, or disturbance

Vocabulary in Context

- Morgan was severely chastised for his illicit actions.
- The detective scrutinizes the scene of the crime, looking for clues.
- Mikhail and Prianjiali are still not speaking after the row they had last week.

stricken people and spotted among them his favorite customer. He took a few steps, stood in the doorway, and said:

"You may call the police."

At the police station he explained that he was a deceived husband. The police chief remarked, "Isn't this a little unusual? Ordinarily you kill your wives. They're weaker than their lovers."

The man was deeply offended.

"No," he protested. "I would be utterly incapable of killing my wife. She is all that I have in the world. She is refined, pretty, and hardworking. She helps me in the store, she understands bookkeeping, she writes the letters to the wholesalers. She is the only person who knows how to prepare my food. Why should I want to kill my wife?"

"I see," said the chief of police. "So you killed her lover."

The man shook his head.

"Wrong again. The sergeant—her lover—was transferred to a place far from here. I discovered the affair only after he had gone. By reading his letters. They tell the whole story. I know one of them by heart, the worst of them. . . ."

The police chief did not understand. He said nothing and waited for the husband to continue, which he presently did:

Portrait Lady. *Diego Rivera, 1928*

"Those letters! If they were alive, I would kill them, one by one. They were shameful to read—almost like a book. I thought of taking an airplane trip. I thought of killing some other sergeant here, so that they would all learn a lesson not to fool around with another man's wife. But I was afraid of the rest of the regiment; you know how these military men stick together. Still, I had to do something. Otherwise I would have gone crazy. I couldn't get those letters out of my head. Even on days when none arrived, I felt terrible, worse than my wife. I had to put an end to it, didn't I? So today, at last, I did it. I waited till the regular time and, when I saw the wretch appear on the other side of the street, I went into the house, hid behind a door, and lay there waiting for him."

"The lover?" asked the police chief stupidly.

"No, of course not. I told you I didn't kill her lover. It was those letters. The sergeant sent them—but he delivered them. Almost every day, there he was at the door, smiling, with the vile envelope in his hand. I pointed the revolver and fired three times. He didn't say a word; he just fell. No, Chief, it wasn't her lover. It was the mailman." ■

❶ *What reasons does the shopkeeper give for his inability to kill his wife?*

❷ *Whom does the police chief think the shopkeeper has killed? Whom has he killed? Why did he kill this person?*

Answers to Guided Reading Questions

❶ The man says that his wife is all that he has, that she is pretty, refined, and hardworking. Also, his wife does many things for him.

❷ The police chief thinks the man has killed his wife's lover. The man killed the mailman because he was the one who delivered the love letters.

ANALYTIC SCALES FOR RESPONDING IN WRITING

(SEE PAGE 1051.)

Assign a score from 1 to 25 for each grading criterion below. (For more detailed evaluation, see the evaluation forms for writing, revising, and proofreading, Assessment Portfolio 4.1–4.9.)

1. Anecdote

- **Content/Unity.** The anecdote illustrates the idea of applied metonymy.
- **Organization/Coherence.** The anecdote describes the details of an event in a logical order.
- **Language/Style.** The anecdote uses vivid and precise nouns, verbs, and modifiers.
- **Conventions.** The anecdote avoids errors in spelling, grammar, usage, mechanics, and manuscript form.

▶ Additional practice is provided in the Essential Skills Practice Book: Writing 1.8.

2. Critical Essay

- **Content/Unity.** The essay analyzes the irony and foreshadowing in the story.
- **Organization/Coherence.** The essay presents and supports a clearly stated thesis.
- **Language/Style.** The essay uses vivid and precise language.
- **Conventions.** The essay avoids errors in spelling, grammar, usage, mechanics, and manuscript form.

▶ Additional practice is provided in the Essential Skills Practice Book: Writing 1.20.

Responding to the Selection

Ask students to review their responses to the Reader's Journal activity. Ask them to discuss, in light of the story they have just read, how they feel about their transfer of emotion.

Answers for Reviewing the Selection

RECALLING AND INTERPRETING

1. **Recalling.** The narrator learns the word *metonymy*. Metonymy is a figure of speech in which one word is substituted for another word with which the first word is associated. **Interpreting.** The narrator's friend associated the owner of the telephone with the telephone that caused her so much vexation. To vent her anger, she substituted the boardinghouse owner for the perpetrator of the prank calls.

2. **Recalling.** The shopkeeper is weak, spent, and asthmatic. He has yellow skin and rheumy eyes. **Interpreting.** The sergeant is strong, healthy, and commanding, attributes that are accentuated in contrast with the weakness and sickness of the spent man.

3. **Recalling.** The woman cries until her eyes grew red and swollen, losing her healthy appearance. Her husband begins to suspect that she was having an affair. The man reads his wife's love letters. **Interpreting.** The man is hurt and angered by the letters. He keeps reading them because he has a terrible fascination with his wife's affair, and he does not know how to deal with the matter.

4. **Recalling.** Witnesses heard a fight, a woman's scream, and three shots. They saw the shopkeeper's wife on her knees, the shopkeeper with the revolver in his hand, and a man's legs in khaki trousers and boots. The man said that he could never kill his

(cont.)

Responding to the Selection

Were you surprised by the end of the story? In small groups discuss the ending of the story. If you were surprised by the ending, discuss what you thought would happen and why you thought this event would occur. If you were not surprised, identify your reasons for expecting the ending.

Reviewing the Selection

Recalling		Interpreting
1. What word does the narrator learn in 1930? Define this word.	▶▶	Explain why the decision by the narrator's friend to leave her boardinghouse is an example of applied metonymy.
2. Describe the shopkeeper.	▶▶	In what ways do the sergeant's appearance and demeanor contrast with those of the shopkeeper? How does the shopkeeper's treatment of his wife differ from the sergeant's treatment of her?
3. What is the wife's reaction to the transfer of the sergeant? What does her husband begin to suspect? What does the shopkeeper do during his lunch time?	▶▶	How does the shopkeeper feel when he reads his wife's letters? Why do you think he continues to read them?
4. Describe events as the customers witness them on the day the shopkeeper's heart became saturated with jealousy and hatred. What reasons does the shopkeeper give when asked why he did not kill his wife?	▶▶	How does the shopkeeper feel about his wife?

Synthesizing

5. Based on this story, give an example of metonymy. Then define extended or applied metonymy. Read about transfer in the Language Arts Survey 4.6, "Identifying Faulty Arguments and Propaganda." Why might a contemporary advertisement that uses the transfer technique be considered a type of extended metonymy? Find three examples of advertisements to support your claims.

Answers for Reviewing the Selection (cont.)

wife because she is all that he has and that she is pretty, refined, and hardworking. Also, his wife does many things for him. **Interpreting.** The man sees his wife as a possession and as somebody who can do things for him. He may think that he loves her, but he really uses her.

SYNTHESIZING

Responses will vary. Possible responses are given.

5. In a case of applied metonymy, a person or thing is treated as though it were another person or thing with which it is associated. The feelings toward the one person or thing are transferred to the other. This is similar to the propaganda technique of transfer in which the positive or negative aspects of one thing are transferred to another thing or person. *Examples will vary.*

Understanding Literature (Questions for Discussion)

1. **Metonymy. Metonymy** is the naming of an object associated with a thing in place of the name of the thing itself. The narrator offers the story of the jealous man as an example of applied metonymy. Identify two examples from the story of this figure of speech in its standard use.
2. **Irony. Irony** is a difference between appearance and reality. In **irony of situation**, an event occurs that violates the expectations of the characters, the reader, or the audience. Whom does the shopkeeper kill? Whom might the reader expect him to kill? Why is the ending of the story ironic?
3. **Allusion.** An **allusion** is a rhetorical technique in which reference is made to a person, event, object, or work from history or literature. What literary allusion does Queiroz make in this story?

Responding in Writing

1. **Creative Writing: Anecdote.** Write an anecdote, or a brief story with a specific point or moral, based on your own experience that illustrates the idea of applied metonymy. Think of a person, thing, or experience that you associate with a particular experience. For example, you might associate running late in the morning with hitting the snooze button on your alarm too often, so you might blame your lateness on the clock. You might feel affection for an object belonging to a person as an extension of your feeling for the person. You may wish to refer to your response to the Reader's Journal activity for ideas. Freewrite about the experience, trying to note many concrete details that you can use in relating your anecdote. In your anecdote, describe the event in detail, and use your example of applied metonymy to show your reaction to the situation.
2. **Critical Essay: Irony and Foreshadowing.** What expectations did you have as you approached the end of the story? In what way did the end of the story meet or fail to meet your expectations? What clues earlier in the story led you toward these expectations? What effect did foreshadowing, or the presentation of materials that hint at events to occur later in a story, have on the irony of the ending of the story? Write a brief critical essay in which you address these questions.

Project

Figure of Speech Collage. Figures of speech are expressions that have more than literal meanings. Metonymy is one type of figure of speech. Others include hyperbole, metaphor, simile, personification, synaesthesia, and synecdoche. If you need more information about any of these terms, see the entry for that word in the Handbook of Literary Terms. As a class, brainstorm a list of examples for each of these types of figures of speech. Then make a humorous collage in which you illustrate each figure of speech according to its literal meaning. Work in small groups with each group responsible for one type of figure of speech.

Answers for Understanding Literature

Responses will vary. Possible responses are given.

1. Metonymy. The sparkling cup is an example of metonymy because it is the wine in the cup that sparkles. The unbuttoned chest is an example of metonymy because it is the shirt, not the chest, that is unbuttoned.

2. Irony. The man kills the mailman. The reader might expect the man to kill his wife or the sergeant. The ending is ironic because it counters this expectation.

3. Allusion. Queiroz alludes to other pairs of lovers, Tristan and Isolde and Paolo and Francesca, to make a comparison to the relationship between the shopkeeper's wife and the sergeant.

Analytic Scales for Responding in Writing

Grading scales for Responding in Writing appear on page 1049.

Project Notes

See the evaluation form for projects, Assessment Portfolio 4.12.

Figure of Speech Collage. Before students begin the project, you may wish to review as a class the figures of speech listed. Suggest that students try to find an example of each figure of speech in a piece of literature they have read and use these along with the examples they brainstorm on their own.

As an alternate activity, students may create a game in which players try to guess what figure of speech is being represented by a picture. Students should use their imagination in creating such a game.

ADDITIONAL RESOURCES

READER'S GUIDE

- Selection Worksheet 12.6

ASSESSMENT PORTFOLIO

- Selection Check Test 2.12.11
- Selection Test 2.12.12

ESSENTIAL SKILLS PRACTICE BOOKS

- Writing 1.8, 1.20
- Speaking and Listening 3.2, 3.3
- Study and Research 4.27

PREREADING EXTENSIONS

You may wish to excerpt sections from some of Camus's fictional works and share these with students, so students can see how Camus applied the beliefs described on this page and revealed in "The Myth of Sisyphus" in his novels. Students might enjoy excerpts from *The Stranger,* a novel about a clerk in Algeria who shoots an Arab and is tried for murder; *The Plague,* a novel about an outburst of plague and the resulting quarantine of a city in Algeria (Camus used the idea of a plague to symbolize the spread of death and evil during World War II); or *The Guest,* which explores postcolonial conflicts between Algerians and the French in Algeria.

SUPPORT FOR LEP STUDENTS

PRONUNCIATIONS OF PROPER NOUNS AND ADJECTIVES

Al • bert Ca • mus (al ber ka mo͞o´)
Si • sy • phus (sis´ə fəs)

ADDITIONAL VOCABULARY

constitute—make up; form
contrary—in opposition
rashly—recklessly; too hastily

PREREADING

"The Myth of Sisyphus"
by Albert Camus, translated by Justin O'Brien

About the Author

ALBERT CAMUS (1913–1960)

Albert Camus was born in Mondovi, Algeria. Camus's family was quite poor, and less than a year after his birth, his father was killed in World War I. Camus later studied philosophy at the University of Algeria while supporting himself with odd jobs, but he was forced to leave when he developed tuberculosis.

Camus's first published works were collections of essays about life in Algeria. He also wrote and acted for the Workers' Theater, a theater dedicated to producing plays for working-class audiences. Camus eventually moved to France and began working as an investigative reporter. During World War II he supported the French Resistance movement against the Germans by editing the illegal Resistance newspaper *Combat.*

Camus's strong moral principles come through in his writing. His best known works are the novels *The Stranger* (1942), *The Plague* (1947), and *The Fall* (1956) and the essay "The Myth of Sisyphus" (1942). Camus won the Nobel Prize for literature in 1957, just three years before he was killed in a car accident in France.

About the Selection

"**The Myth of Sisyphus**" examines Camus's personal philosophy—Existentialism combined with a belief in traditional human values such as truth, justice, and compassion. Camus's philosophy was shaped by the senseless violence, cruelty, and desperate conditions that existed in Europe during the World War II era. Like all Existentialists, Camus believed in the absurdity of the human condition: humans exist only by chance and human beliefs and choices are ultimately meaningless in an indifferent universe. At the same time, Camus also believed that individual humans could choose to behave morally, creating values even though there are no "right" choices. This selection reveals what Camus saw as the key to happiness—accepting the absurdity of one's fate, recognizing that one's own life is the culmination of one's actions and choices, and enjoying "the wholly human origin of all that is human."

CONNECTIONS: Literature of the Absurd

The Existentialist philosophy of Albert Camus and Jean-Paul Sartre helped to shape a form of literature known as literature of the absurd. This type of literature emphasizes the meaninglessness of life and the isolation, or alienation, of individuals. Much of the literature of the absurd is filled with horrors, anguish, and random, illogical, or improbable events. Modern writers of the literature of the absurd include novelists Franz Kafka (see page 454), Thomas Pynchon, and Kurt Vonnegut, Jr., as well as playwrights Eugene Ionesco (see page 46), Samuel Beckett, Edward Albee, and Harold Pinter.

GOALS/OBJECTIVES

Studying this lesson will enable students to

- appreciate a work of existentialist prose
- explain why Camus believes that Sisyphus must be imagined as happy
- briefly explain Existentialism
- explain the difference between one-dimensional and three-dimensional characters
- write a creative description "reinventing" a traditional character
- write a critical essay comparing Sisyphus to the average working person
- take an essay test

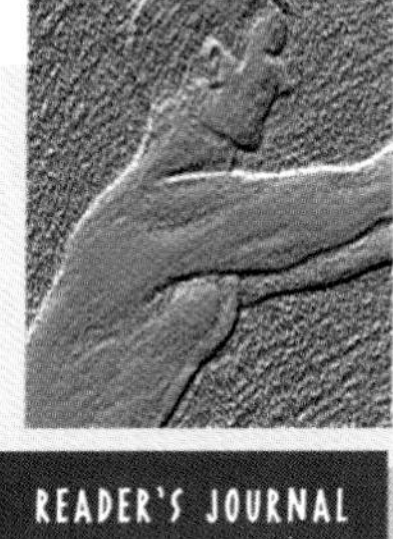

READER'S JOURNAL

What activity or task in your life do you find most boring or meaningless? In your journal, write your thoughts about performing this activity. What would your response be to someone who claimed that you should find joy in this task?

"The Myth of Sisyphus"

ALBERT CAMUS, TRANSLATED BY JUSTIN O'BRIEN

The gods had condemned Sisyphus to ceaselessly rolling a rock to the top of a mountain, whence the stone would fall back of its own weight. They had thought with some reason that there is no more dreadful punishment than futile and hopeless labor.

If one believes Homer, Sisyphus was the wisest and most prudent of mortals. According to another tradition, however, he was disposed to practice the profession of highwayman.[1] I see no contradiction in this. Opinions differ as to the reasons why he became the futile laborer of the underworld. To begin with, he is accused of a certain levity in regard to the gods. He stole their secrets. Ægina, the daughter of Æsopus, was carried off by Jupiter.[2] The father was shocked by that disappearance and complained to Sisyphus. He, who knew of the abduction, offered to tell about it on condition that Æsopus would give water to the citadel of Corinth.[3] To the celestial thunderbolts he preferred the benediction of water. He was punished for this in the underworld. Homer tells us also that Sisyphus had put Death in chains. Pluto[4] could not endure the sight of his deserted, silent empire. He dispatched the god of war, who liberated Death from the hands of her conqueror.

It is said also that Sisyphus, being near to death, rashly wanted to test his wife's love. He ordered her to cast his unburied body into the middle of the public square. Sisyphus woke up in the underworld. And there, annoyed by an obedience so contrary to human love, he obtained from Pluto permission to return to earth in order to chastise his wife. But when he had seen again the face of this world, enjoyed water and sun, warm stones and the sea, he no longer wanted to go back to the infernal darkness. Recalls, signs of anger, warnings were of no avail. Many years more he lived facing the curve of the gulf, the sparkling sea, and the

1. **highwayman.** Thief, usually on horseback, who robs travelers on the road
2. **Jupiter.** Chief Roman deity, god of thunder and the skies
3. **citadel of Corinth.** Ancient fortified city at the head of the Gulf of Corinth
4. **Pluto.** Roman god of the underworld

❶ *Why do the gods think that repeatedly rolling a rock to the top of a mountain, only to watch it roll back down again, is a suitable punishment for Sisyphus?*

❷ *Why does Sisyphus leave the underworld and return to earth? What happens when he gets there?*

❸ *What secret does Sisyphus give away? What deal does he make with Æsopus?*

WORDS FOR EVERYDAY USE

cease • less • ly (sēs´lis lē) *adv.*, continually
fu • tile (fyo͞ot´'l) *adj.*, useless, vain
lev • i • ty (lev´i tē) *n.*, lack of seriousness
ce • les • tial (sə les´chəl) *adj.*, of the sky or heaven
ben • e • dic • tion (ben´ə dik´shən) *n.*, blessing

READER'S JOURNAL

You might also ask students to write about what future plans, goals, or thoughts motivate them to complete successfully tasks they dislike.

ANSWERS TO GUIDED READING QUESTIONS

❶ The gods feel that there is no more dreadful punishment than futile and hopeless labor.

❷ Sisyphus leaves the underworld to chastise his wife, who had, at his request, thrown his body into the middle of the public square. When he had made this request, he was only testing his wife and was "annoyed by an obedience so contrary to human love." When he returns to earth, he doesn't want to leave and go back to the underworld.

❸ Sisyphus tells Æsopus that Jupiter has carried off his daughter. Sisyphus agrees to give Æsopus this information in return for water for Corinth, his city.

SPELLING AND VOCABULARY WORDS FROM THE SELECTION

benediction	lucidity
ceaselessly	melancholy
celestial	myriad
decree	negate
fidelity	proletarian
futile	sterile
impudent	surmount
levity	

VOCABULARY IN CONTEXT

- Snow ceaselessly accumulates on the peaks of the world's highest mountains.
- Ivan felt that it was futile to wrestle someone who outweighed him by so much, but he gave the match his best anyway.
- The mood of levity that the partygoers shared came to an abrupt halt when Rolanda announced the news that a close friend was seriously ill.
- We identified the celestial body in the evening sky as the planet Venus.
- After the religious service was over, the priest gave us his benediction, or blessing.

Answers to Guided Reading Questions

❶ He is returned to the underworld and is forced to roll the rock up the mountain.

❷ Sisyphus's "scorn of the gods, his hatred of death, and his passion for life" win him the unspeakable penalty in which his whole being is exerted toward accomplishing nothing.

Cross-curricular Activities

SOCIAL STUDIES

Encourage students to work in small groups to research and prepare reports on the country where Camus was born and that inspired much of his writing—Algeria. Point out to students that when Camus was born, Algeria was a French colony. The French entered Algeria in 1830 under the pretext of quelling the Barbary pirates who were preying on Mediterranean trading ships and selling Europeans into slavery. By 1884, the French had subdued most of Algeria. Algeria did not gain its independence from France until 1962. Possible topics for student research include the land itself and the different peoples living in Algeria, the activities of the Barbary pirates, French struggles to establish a colony in Algeria, other French colonies in North Africa, the Nationalist movement, the Algerian Reformist Ulama, the Algerian War, and Algerian struggles with France since independence. Each group should present its findings to the class.

❶ *What happens when Mercury snatches Sisyphus away from earth?*

❷ *What "unspeakable penalty" does Sisyphus's "scorn of the gods, his hatred of death, and his passion for life" win him?*

smiles of earth. A decree of the gods was necessary. Mercury[5] came and seized the impudent man by the collar and, snatching him from his joys, led him forcibly back to the underworld, where his rock was ready for him.

You have already grasped that Sisyphus is the absurd hero. He *is*, as much through his passions as through his torture. His scorn of the gods, his hatred of death, and his passion for life won him that unspeakable penalty in which the whole being is exerted toward accomplishing nothing. This is the price that must be paid for the passions of this earth. Nothing is told us about Sisyphus in the underworld. Myths are made for the imagination to breathe life into them. As for this myth, one sees merely the whole effort of a body straining to raise the huge stone, to roll it and push it up a slope a hundred times over; one sees the face screwed up, the cheek tight against the stone, the shoulder bracing the clay-covered mass, the foot wedging it, the fresh start with arms outstretched, the wholly human security of two earth-clotted hands. At the very end of his long effort

5. **Mercury.** Messenger of the gods

Words for Everyday Use

de • cree (dē krē´) *n.*, order, edict, decision
im • pu • dent (im´pyo͞o dənt) *adj.*, bold or disrespectful

Vocabulary in Context

- King George's decree to increase taxes in the American colonies prompted Americans to revolt against British rule.
- Tommy's impudent expression reveals his tendency to come up with mischievous schemes.

measured by skyless space and time without depth, the purpose is achieved. Then Sisyphus watches the stone rush down in a few moments toward that lower world whence he will have to push it up again toward the summit. He goes back down to the plain.

It is during that return, that pause, that Sisyphus interests me. A face that toils so close to stones is already stone itself! I see that man going back down with a heavy yet measured step toward the torment of which he will never know the end. That hour like a breathing space which returns as surely as his suffering, that is the hour of consciousness. At each of those moments when he leaves the heights and gradually sinks toward the lairs of the gods, he is superior to his fate. He is stronger than his rock.

If this myth is tragic, that is because its hero is conscious. Where would his torture be, indeed, if at every step the hope of succeeding upheld him? The workman of today works every day in his life at the same tasks, and this fate is no less absurd. But it is tragic only at the rare moments when it becomes conscious. Sisyphus, proletarian of the gods, powerless and rebellious, knows the whole extent of his wretched condition: it is what he thinks of during his descent. The lucidity that was to constitute his torture at the same time crowns his victory. There is no fate that cannot be surmounted by scorn.

♦ ♦ ♦

If the descent is thus sometimes performed in sorrow, it can also take place in joy. This word is not too much. Again I fancy Sisyphus returning toward his rock, and the sorrow was in the beginning. When the images of earth cling too tightly to memory, when the call of happiness becomes too insistent, it happens that melancholy rises in man's heart: this is the rock's victory, this is the rock itself. The boundless grief is too heavy to bear. These are our nights of Gethsemane.[6] But crushing truths perish from being acknowledged. Thus, Oedipus[7] at the outset obeys fate without knowing it. But from the moment he knows, his tragedy begins. Yet at the same moment, blind and desperate, he realizes that the only bond linking him to the world is the cool hand of a girl. Then a tremendous remark rings out: "Despite so many ordeals, my advanced age and the nobility of my soul make me conclude that all is well." Sophocles' Oedipus, like Dostoevsky's Kirilov,[8] thus gives the recipe for the absurd victory. Ancient wisdom confirms modern heroism.

One does not discover the absurd without being tempted to write a manual of happiness. "What! by such narrow ways—?" There is but one world, however. Happiness and the absurd are two sons of the same earth. They are inseparable. It would be a mistake to say that happiness necessarily springs from the absurd discovery. It happens as well that the feeling of the absurd springs from happiness. "I conclude that all is well," says Oedipus, and that remark is sacred. It echoes in the wild and limited universe of man. It teaches that all is not, has not been, exhausted. It drives out of this world a god who had come into it with dissatisfaction and a preference for futile sufferings. It makes of fate a human matter, which must be settled among men.

6. **Gethsemane.** Scene of the agony, betrayal, and arrest of Jesus

7. **Oedipus.** Tragic Greek hero who unwittingly killed his father and married his mother

8. **Kirilov.** Character in Feodor Dostoevsky's novel *The Possessed*

❶ *What thoughts and images make Sisyphus's task more melancholy? How, on the other hand, might "crushing truths" be made to perish?*

❷ *For what does Oedipus, with his remark, give a recipe? What does his ancient wisdom confirm?*

❸ *Why is the myth of Sisyphus tragic? In what way is the average working person's fate just as absurd as the fate of Sisyphus? Why, at the same time, is the fate of the average working person far less tragic?*

❹ *According to the speaker, why is the remark of Oedipus sacred? What does it make of fate?*

Words for Everyday Use

pro • le • tar • i • an (prō´lə ter´ē ən) *n.*, member of the working class

lu • cid • i • ty (lo͞o cid´i tē) *n.*, clarity of thought; comprehension

sur • mount (sər mount´) *vi.*, overcome; surpass, exceed

mel • an • chol • y (mel´ən käl´ē) *n.*, sadness and depression of spirits

Answers to Guided Reading Questions

❶ Thoughts and images of earth and happier times make Sisyphus's task more melancholy. "Crushing truths" might be made to feel less burdensome if they are acknowledged.

❷ Oedipus, with his remark, gives a recipe for absurd victory—"Despite so many ordeals, my advanced age and the nobility of my soul make me conclude that all is well." This ancient wisdom confirms modern heroism.

❸ The myth is tragic because its hero is conscious. The average working person goes to work each day at the same meaningless tasks. His or her fate is far less tragic because, unlike Sisyphus, he or she is often less conscious of the tragedy.

❹ The remark of Oedipus is sacred because it teaches that "all is not, has not been, exhausted." It makes of fate a human matter.

Quotables

"Capital punishment . . . is irreconcilable with humanism."

"Let us call it by the name which, for lack of any other nobility, will at least give the nobility of truth, and let us recognize it for what it essentially is: a revenge."

—Albert Camus

Integrated Skills Activities

Speaking and Listening

Camus's anti-capital punishment stance is revealed in many of his literary works. Encourage students to hold a debate on capital punishment. Be sure to have them read the Language Arts Survey 3.2, "Active Listening and Interpersonal Communication," and 3.3, "Collaborative Learning and Discussion." Remind students to listen carefully to others' points of view and to keep their emotions under control even if they disagree with another student's opinion.

▶ Additional practice is provided in the Essential Skills Practice Book: Speaking and Listening 3.2 and 3.3.

Vocabulary in Context

- The political party hoped to win the proletarian vote by claiming it would help the average worker.
- I'm always astounded by my great-grandmother's lucidity; she's ninety-nine years old, but her wit is as sharp as ever.
- Mona is known for energetically tackling any crisis or setback; she is confident that she can surmount any problem that arises.
- Reading about gloomy forests matched Marissa's melancholy mood.

Answers to Guided Reading Questions

❶ Sisyphus can find joy in his fate by deciding that "his rock is his thing" and that his fate belongs to him. The average working person can find joy in an "absurd" existence by contemplating and saying yes to it.
❷ The "struggle itself" toward the heights is enough to fill a person's heart. One must imagine Sisyphus happy.
❸ A person will see, in glancing backward over life on earth, a series of his or her unrelated actions that become his or her fate. This action helps a person to know that his or her actions have meaning in that they are truly his own—human in origin.

Selection Check Test with Answers

EX: Who has punished Sisyphus?
The gods have punished Sisyphus.

1. In one story, what does Sisyphus do to Death?
He puts Death in chains.

2. In one story, why does Sisyphus return to earth from the underworld?
Sisyphus leaves the underworld to chastise his wife, who had, at his request, thrown his body into the middle of the public square.

3. What is Sisyphus's punishment?
Sisyphus's punishment is that for eternity he must roll a rock up the side of a mountain, only to watch it roll back down again.

4. According to Camus, why is the fate of Sisyphus worse than the fate of the common man?
According to Camus, the fate of Sisyphus is worse because he is fully aware of his fate.

5. According to Camus, in what way must people imagine Sisyphus?
People must imagine Sisyphus happy.

❶ *Why can Sisyphus find joy in his fate? Why, then, can the average person find joy in an "absurd" existence?*

❷ *What is enough to fill a person's heart? How must one imagine Sisyphus?*

❸ *According to the speaker, what can a person see when glancing backward over his or her life on earth? What does this action help a person to do?*

All Sisyphus' silent joy is contained therein. His fate belongs to him. His rock is his thing. Likewise, the absurd man, when he contemplates his torment, silences all the idols. In the universe suddenly restored to its silence, the <u>myriad</u> wondering little voices of the earth rise up. Unconscious, secret calls, invitations from all the faces, they are the necessary reverse and price of victory. There is no sun without shadow, and it is essential to know the night. The absurd man says yes and his effort will henceforth be unceasing. If there is a personal fate, there is no higher destiny, or at least there is but one which he concludes is inevitable and despicable. For the rest, he knows himself to be the master of his days. At that subtle moment when man glances backward over his life, Sisyphus returning toward his rock, in that slight pivoting he contemplates that series of unrelated actions which becomes his fate, created by him, combined under his memory's eye and soon sealed by his death. Thus, convinced of the wholly human origin of all that is human, a blind man eager to see who knows that the night has no end, he is still on the go. The rock is still rolling.

I leave Sisyphus at the foot of the mountain! One always finds one's burden again. But Sisyphus teaches the higher <u>fidelity</u> that <u>negates</u> the gods and raises rocks. He too concludes that all is well. This universe henceforth without a master seems to him neither <u>sterile</u> nor futile. Each atom of that stone, each mineral flake of that night-filled mountain, in itself forms a world. The struggle itself toward the heights is enough to fill a man's heart. One must imagine Sisyphus happy. ■

Words for Everyday Use

myr • i • ad (mir´ē əd) *n.,* large number of persons or things
fi • del • i • ty (fə del´ə tē) *n.,* loyalty, faithfulness
ne • gate (ni gāt´) *vt.,* deny existence or truth of; make ineffective
ster • ile (stər´əl) *adj.,* barren; lacking interest or vitality

Vocabulary in Context

- Marlene felt that with such a <u>myriad</u> of careers in today's job market, she would never be able to decide which one to pursue.
- Hortense's <u>fidelity</u> to that club is unshakable; she would never even consider joining a rival organization.
- Simon was disappointed to discover something in lab that <u>negated</u> the hypothesis he had formed.
- To an inexperienced eye, the desert landscape seems <u>sterile</u>, but a wealth of hardy life forms survive in this forbidding ecosystem.

Responding to the Selection

Reread the following quote by Oedipus: "Despite so many ordeals . . . [I] conclude that all is well." What does this mean to you? Can you say this about your own life? Why, or why not?

Reviewing the Selection

Recalling / Interpreting

1. What is the final punishment that Sisyphus must endure? What are the various stories about Sisyphus and how he earned this fate? ▶▶ What do the different stories reveal about the character of Sisyphus? Why is it reasonable to say that "futile and hopeless" labor is a dreadful form of punishment?

2. What part of Sisyphus's task particularly interests Camus? Why, according to Camus, is this myth tragic? ▶▶ Why is each trip Sisyphus makes down the mountain an "hour of consciousness"? If a proletarian is a member of the lowest working class, in what way is Sisyphus the "proletarian of the gods"? Why does consciousness make Sisyphus's situation different from that of the average worker?

3. What feeling besides grief might Sisyphus have as he descends the mountain? According to Camus, what causes crushing truths to perish? ▶▶ According to Camus, why must one accept or acknowledge one's fate no matter how terrible or absurd? How does the story of Oedipus illustrate his point?

4. What remark made by Oedipus does Camus consider sacred? ▶▶ What does Oedipus's remark make of fate? At what point can Sisyphus and other human beings find satisfaction or joy in their absurd fate? Why might accepting one's fate allow a person to struggle on with "unceasing" effort?

Synthesizing

5. Why, according to Camus, must one imagine Sisyphus happy? What does this essay say about the importance of putting forth effort and holding onto human values, even in an absurd, or meaningless, world?

RESPONDING TO THE SELECTION

Inform students that Camus considers the story of Oedipus to be uplifting and inspiring. Encourage students to discuss stories from literature or life from which they have drawn or can draw inspiration.

ANSWERS FOR REVIEWING THE SELECTION

RECALLING AND INTERPRETING

1. **Recalling.** Sisyphus must roll a rock up a mountain, only to watch it roll back down, for an eternity. According to one story, Sisyphus tells Æsopus that Jupiter has carried off his daughter. Sisyphus agrees to give Æsopus this information in return for water for Corinth, his city. This angers the gods, and Sisyphus is sent to the underworld, where he puts Death in chains. Because of this, Pluto dispatches the god of war to free Death. Sisyphus is punished. Another story says that Sisyphus leaves the underworld to chastise his wife, who had, at his request, thrown his body into the middle of the public square. When he made this request, he was only testing his wife and was "annoyed by an obedience so contrary to human love." When he returns to earth, he doesn't want to leave and return to the underworld. The gods are angered, and Mercury is sent after him. Sisyphus is taken back to the underworld, where his rock waits for him. **Interpreting.** Sisyphus is a bold character who wants to experience life and who acts according to his own interests. Having to complete "futile and hopeless" labor is a dreadful form of punishment because it can make a person feel useless and it can drive a person mad.

2. **Recalling.** It is the pause, during which Sisyphus watches the stone roll back down the mountain, that interests Camus. (cont.)

ANSWERS FOR REVIEWING THE SELECTION (CONT.)

According to Camus, this myth is tragic because the hero is conscious. **Interpreting.** Sisyphus's trip down the mountain is the "hour of consciousness" because it is when he has time to think about his task. Sisyphus is the "proletarian of the gods" because he spends his days working at a meaningless task. Consciousness makes his situation different from that of the average worker because he knows his efforts to be futile. The average worker does not always see the larger picture and is not conscious that his or her work is meaningless.

3. **Recalling.** Sisyphus might choose to complete the task in joy, and not feel grief as he descends the mountain. According to Camus, crushing truths perish when they are acknowledged.

(cont.)

Understanding Literature (Questions for Discussion)

1. **Existentialism. Existentialism** is a twentieth-century philosophical school that assumes the essential absurdity and meaninglessness of life. How does Camus, in this essay, turn Sisyphus into an existential character? What does Camus say about humans and their need to find meaning, despite their "absurd" existence? What inescapable burden does he believe humans have, and what is their only hope in dealing with this burden?

2. **Character.** A **character** is a person who figures in the action of a literary work. Often characters in myths are one-dimensional, meaning they exhibit a single dominant quality, or character trait. Usually this one-dimensional character is meant simply to be a vehicle for the main idea or lesson of a particular myth. For his essay, Camus changes Sisyphus from a one-dimensional character to a three-dimensional character, or one who exhibits the complexity of traits associated with actual human beings. Give examples from the essay that show Sisyphus to be a three-dimensional character. What feelings does he experience? Why does he have these feelings? What part of the myth of Sisyphus does Camus examine most closely, and why?

Responding in Writing

1. **Creative Writing: Reinventing a Traditional Character.** Reread the paragraph in the essay "The Myth of Sisyphus" that describes in detail how Sisyphus rolls the boulder up the mountain, watches it roll back down, and then walks back down the mountain. Here, Camus takes a common myth and expands on it, giving the reader a closer look at the experience of one character. Choose a character who appears in a myth, fairy tale, or folk tale from any culture or era. Focus on the character and write a one-page detailed description of a scene or moment in the story, using your imagination to "breathe life" into it. Decide how your character really feels at this moment in the story. To begin, first make a list of possible myths, folk tales, or fairy tales. You might be able to think of several immediately, or you might want to make a trip to the library to find a tale that engages you. Then rewrite the portion of the story on which you would like to focus, including vivid, original details and observations of your character.

2. **Critical Essay: Comparison and Contrast.** Think about Camus's Existentialist views concerning the absurdity of the world and the fate of humankind. Then write an essay in which you compare and contrast the plight of Sisyphus to the plight of the average working person. You may wish to base your view of the working person on family members or friends with full-time jobs, or you may wish to use your own experiences in the working world in part-time or summer jobs. Support your ideas with statements Camus makes in his essay. Allow the following questions to guide you as you organize your essay: What does Camus believe is tragic in both situations? In what way is the plight of Sisyphus more tragic? What is the one thing both Sisyphus and the average modern-day working person can do to make their lives less tragic?

Answers for Reviewing the Selection (cont.)

Interpreting. According to Camus, a person must acknowledge his or her fate so that he or she can start to find his or her own joy and meaning in it. The story of Oedipus illustrates his point because it is a story of fate and the positive way in which Oedipus deals with fate.

4. **Recalling.** Camus considers the following remark by Oedipus sacred: "Despite so many ordeals, my advanced age and the nobility of my soul make me conclude that all is well." **Interpreting.** The sentiment expressed by Oedipus makes of fate a "human matter," and people can find joy in whatever fate is their own. Sisyphus can find joy in his fate by understanding that the struggle is his and by trying to find his own meaning in his fate. People can find joy in an "absurd" existence by making their own meaning from it. Accepting one's fate as the result of one's own actions might allow a person to see a struggle as something important to one's identity.

SYNTHESIZING

Responses will vary. Possible responses are given.

5. One must imagine that Sisyphus is making the most of his existence and that he has decided to care about his task. His task is no more futile than any other human task, so if Sisyphus can be happy, everyone can be happy. This essay says that people need to find their own meaning in their lives. They must learn to make the best of their existence by holding onto human values.

Answers for Understanding Literature

Responses will vary. Possible responses are given.

1. **Existentialism.** Camus makes Sisyphus an existentialist character by describing his task of rolling the rock up that mountain as meaningless and reflective of the fate of all. Camus says that human beings, like Sisyphus, must hold onto human values and find meaning in their everyday existences. Camus believes that humans beings have (cont.)

Answers for Understanding Literature (cont.)

the inescapable burden of living meaningless existences. Their only hope in dealing with this burden is to find joy in their everyday actions.

2. **Character.** Sisyphus is shown as a complex character in the conflicting stories that show him as a highwayman, bartering for water for Corinth, putting Death in chains, testing his wife's love, and wanting to return to earth. Sisyphus is shown wanting desperately to live even though the gods have sent him to the underworld; feeling strain as he pushes the rock up the mountain; and feeling torment as he watches it roll back down. Camus then suggests that Sisyphus might be trying to feel joy in his task. Camus focuses on Sisyphus's struggle with the rock because it epitomizes the meaning a person [with all his or her complexities] must make of an otherwise meaningless existence.

Study and Research Skills

Taking Essay Tests. Review the Language Arts Survey 4.27, "Taking Essay Tests." Read the following essay question and analyze it, writing down and attempting to define terms that are challenging. Then, prepare an outline for a response to the essay question, and write the introductory paragraph of that response. Your outline should include as main heads the major points you wish to address in each paragraph of your essay; the outline should also include as subheads the details you will use to support your major points. Your introductory paragraph should include a thesis statement in which you explain the position you will take in your essay.

> Many people think of Existentialists as having a cynical and bleak outlook on the universe, yet Camus writes, "Happiness and the absurd are two sons of the same earth. They are inseparable." Think about Camus's statement, and then take a position on it. Do you agree that happiness and an Existentialist outlook are linked, or do you fail to see any possibilities for happiness within the Existentialist's "absurd" universe?

Edge of the Pond.
Paul Gauguin, 1885

ANALYTIC SCALES FOR RESPONDING IN WRITING

Assign a score from 1 to 25 for each grading criterion below. (For more detailed evaluation, see the evaluation forms for writing, revising, and proofreading, Assessment Portfolio 4.1–4.9.)

1. Reinventing a Traditional Character

- **Content/Unity.** The writing describes in detail a scene from the life of a traditional character.
- **Organization/Coherence.** The writing presents details about this event or moment in a sensible order, most likely chronological.
- **Language/Style.** The writing uses vivid and precise nouns, verbs, and modifiers.
- **Conventions.** The writing avoids errors in spelling, grammar, usage, mechanics, and manuscript form.

► Additional practice is provided in the Essential Skills Practice Book: Writing 1.8.

2. Critical Essay

- **Content/Unity.** The essay compares and contrasts Sisyphus's plight to that of an average working person.
- **Organization/Coherence.** The essay begins with an introduction that includes the thesis of the essay. The introduction is followed by supporting paragraphs with clear transitions. The essay ends with a solid conclusion.
- **Language/Style.** The essay uses vivid and precise nouns, verbs, and modifiers.
- **Conventions.** The essay avoids errors in spelling, grammar, usage, mechanics, and manuscript form.

► Additional practice is provided in the Essential Skills Practice Book: Writing 1.20.

ANSWERS FOR SKILLS ACTIVITIES

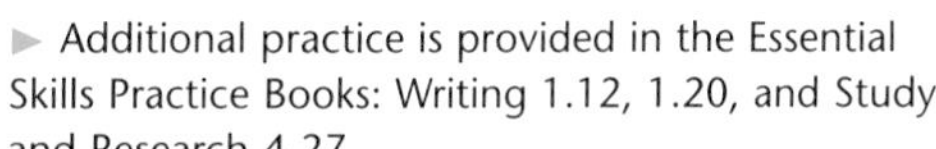

STUDY AND RESEARCH SKILLS

If students need help in preparing outlines, refer them to the Language Arts Survey 1.12, "Outlining." You might also encourage them to review the Language Arts Survey 1.20, "Writing a Critical Essay," for further instruction.

► Additional practice is provided in the Essential Skills Practice Books: Writing 1.12, 1.20, and Study and Research 4.27.

ADDITIONAL RESOURCES

READER'S GUIDE

- Selection Worksheet 12.7

ASSESSMENT PORTFOLIO

- Selection Check Test 2.12.13
- Selection Test 2.12.14

ESSENTIAL SKILLS PRACTICE BOOKS

- Writing 1.8, 1.20
- Language 2.51

PREREADING EXTENSIONS

Ask students to work in groups to research the history and culture of Australia. The following list suggests some possible topics for research:

- Aborigines
- Arts, literature, and music
- Geography and its effects on settlement and economy
- Penal colony origins and British colonialism
- Tourism
- Women's rights

Students should create a class booklet or display about Australia to share with others. Each student should contribute to the final product.

SUPPORT FOR LEP STUDENTS

PRONUNCIATIONS OF PROPER NOUNS AND ADJECTIVES

Ju • dith Wright (jūd´əth rīt)

ADDITIONAL VOCABULARY

devotee—person who is highly dedicated to something

petticoats—underskirt

PREREADING

"Request to a Year"
by Judith Wright

About the Author

JUDITH WRIGHT 1915–

Judith Wright was born in Armidale, Australia. After graduating from the University of Sydney, Wright worked in an advertising agency. Later she was employed as a secretary for the University of Sydney, as a clerk in Brisbane, and as a statistician. In 1946, Wright published her first volume of poetry, *The Moving Image.* Three years later, Wright began lecturing part-time at various universities in Australia and published her second volume of poetry, *Woman to Man.* Her first two volumes of poetry were followed by *The Gateway; The Two Fires; City Sunrise;* a collection of short stories, *The Nature of Love; Collected Poems 1942–1970;* and *The Double Tree,* an updated selection of Wright's poetry. In addition to poetry, she has written literary criticism, children's books, a biography of the Australian poet Charles Harpur, a book on the Australian short story writer Charles Lawson, and a book on her pioneering grandparents' settlement in Australia.

About the Selection

Judith Wright is known for insightful poetry that explores the dynamics and mysteries of human relationships. In **"Request to a Year,"** a speaker examines a moment in the life of her great-great-grandmother, who combined the difficult job of mothering eight children with a love of the arts. To do this, the speaker focuses on one frightening incident that her great-great-grandmother handles in an unusual and memorable manner. As you read, notice Wright's skillful use of rhyme and vivid imagery.

The Cliff Walk. Claude Monet

CONNECTIONS: Early Australian Literature

The Aborigines of Australia, a native hunting and gathering people, have lived on the continent for 20,000 years. Many Australians today, however, are descendants of the British who colonized Australia in the early 1800s. In its earliest colonial days, Australia was a penal colony for British convicts. Criminals were regularly transported to the continent, and by 1830 they made up half of the immigrant population. In time this practice changed, and free British settlers began to populate the area. Australian writing of the colonial period often consists of settlers' impressions of the faraway continent, written to satisfy the curiosity of people at home in Great Britain. Out of this early period came journals, ballads, and convict songs and stories. The first works of fiction were guidebook-like novels, written to encourage British immigration. The first important Australian poet was Charles Harpur (1813–1868), who wrote lyric poetry in the manner of William Wordsworth (see page 904).

GOALS/OBJECTIVES

Studying this lesson will enable students to

- enjoy a lyric poem
- identify Judith Wright as a contemporary Australian poet
- define *tone, rhyme,* and *alliteration*
- identify the tone of the poem
- find examples of rhyme and alliteration
- write a tribute to somebody they admire
- analyze the theme of the poem and relate the title to the theme
- correctly punctuate titles

READER'S JOURNAL

If you were to borrow one talent or character trait from an older relative, friend, or mentor, what would it be? In what way would this talent or character trait help you in your own life?

"Request to a Year"

JUDITH WRIGHT

If the year is meditating a suitable gift,
I should like it to be the attitude
of my great-great-grandmother,
legendary devotee of the arts,

who, having had eight children
and little opportunity for painting pictures,
sat one day on a high rock
beside a river in Switzerland

and from a difficult distance viewed
her second son, balanced on a small ice-floe,
drift down the current towards a waterfall
that struck rock-bottom eighty feet below,

while her second daughter, impeded,
no doubt, by the petticoats of the day,
stretched out a last-hope alpenstock[1]
(which luckily later caught him on his way).

1 *What gift would the speaker like to have?*

2 *What does the speaker's great-great-grandmother view from a difficult distance?*

3 *What does the second daughter do to help her brother?*

1. **alpenstock.** Strong, iron-pointed staff used by mountain climbers

WORDS FOR EVERYDAY USE

im • pede (im pēd´) *vt.,* obstruct or delay; hinder the progress of

VOCABULARY IN CONTEXT

• Deep, heavy snow and treacherous patches of ice could impede our progress to the top of the mountain.

READER'S JOURNAL

Suggest that students also write about a way in which the older relative, friend, or mentor has displayed or used this quality or trait.

ANSWERS TO GUIDED READING QUESTIONS

1 The speaker would like to have her great-great-grandmother's attitude.

2 The speaker's great-great-grandmother views one of her sons in a dangerous situation—he is drifting on an ice floe toward a waterfall.

3 The second daughter stretches out a walking stick for him to grab.

SELECTION CHECK TEST WITH ANSWERS

EX. About whom is "Request to a Year"?
"Request to a Year" is about the speaker's great-great-grandmother.

1. What gift would the speaker like to have?
The speaker would like to have her great-great-grandmother's attitude.

2. To what was the speaker's great-great-grandmother devoted?
She was devoted to the arts.

3. What does the speaker's great-great-grandmother view from a difficult distance?
She sees one of her sons in a dangerous situation—he is drifting toward a waterfall.

4. What does the second daughter do to help her brother?
She stretches out a walking stick for him to grab.

5. What does the great-great-grandmother do as the incident unfolds?
She sketches the scene.

Answers to Guided Reading Questions

➊ The great-great-grandmother sketches the scene.

Responding to the Selection

Students might also describe a person whom they admire in a manner similar to the way in which the speaker admires her great-great-grandmother.

Answers for Reviewing the Selection

RECALLING AND INTERPRETING

1. **Recalling.** The speaker would like the attitude of her great-great-grandmother, who was devoted to the arts. **Interpreting.** The speaker greatly admires her great-great-grandmother.
2. **Recalling.** The speaker's great-great-grandmother views one of her sons in a dangerous situation—he is drifting on an ice floe toward a waterfall. The second daughter tries to save him by holding out a walking stick for him to grab. **Interpreting.** The second son could have gone over the waterfall and been killed or seriously hurt. By referring to the children by birth order, the speaker shows that there were many children under her great-great-grandmother's care.
3. **Recalling.** The woman is too far away to help her son. She sketches the scene as it unfolds. Her sketch survives to prove the story. **Interpreting.** The artist isolates the scene from her personal feelings of panic and distress and sketches it with objectivity.
4. **Recalling.** The speaker addresses the year in the final lines. The speaker wishes for the firmness of her great-great-grandmother's hand. **Interpreting.** The "firmness of . . . hand" is the ability to hold oneself together and

(cont.)

What does the great-great-grandmother do as the incident unfolds?

Nothing, it was evident, could be done;
and with the artist's isolating eye
my great-great-grandmother hastily sketched the scene.
The sketch survives to prove the story by.

Year, if you have no Mother's Day present planned,
reach back and bring me the firmness of her hand.

Responding to the Selection

What do you think of the speaker's request? Do you share her feelings of admiration for her great-great grandmother? Why, or why not?

Reviewing the Selection

Recalling | **Interpreting**

1. What "gift" would the speaker find most suitable? To what was the speaker's great-great-grandmother devoted? ▶▶ After reading the first two stanzas, what can you say about the speaker's feelings toward her great-great grandmother?
2. What does the speaker's great-great-grandmother view from a difficult distance? What does the second daughter try to do? ▶▶ What could have happened to the second son? Why might the speaker refer to the children by their birth order, rather than by name?
3. Why is the great-great-grandmother helpless as she watches her son? What does she do as the dramatic scene involving her son and daughter unfolds? What survives to prove the story? ▶▶ The speaker says that her great-great grandmother looks at the situation "with the artist's isolating eye." Explain this phrase.
4. Who or what does the speaker address in the final two lines of the poem? For what does the speaker wish? ▶▶ What is the "firmness of . . . hand" to which the speaker refers? How has the great-great-grandmother demonstrated this firmness of hand?

Answers for Reviewing the Selection (cont.)

be objective even under the most stressful circumstances and to know what one can and cannot control. The great-great-grandmother has demonstrated this firmness of hand by sketching the picture during a stressful situation.

SYNTHESIZING

Responses will vary. Possible responses are given.

5. The speaker notes that her great-great-grandmother did not have many opportunities to paint pictures and that her second daughter was impeded by her clothing. She notes that the women in her family have not succumbed to these restrictions but rather have overcome them. The speaker wants to share the strength and perseverance of the women of her family.

SYNTHESIZING

5. What limitations on women does the speaker note? How does she feel about the way the women in her family have reacted to these restrictions? In what way are these feelings related to the speaker's request?

Understanding Literature (Questions for Discussion)

1. **Tone. Tone** is the emotional attitude toward the reader or toward the subject implied by a literary work. Examples of different tones that a work may have include familiar, ironic, playful, sarcastic, serious, and sincere. What is the tone of "Request to a Year"? Is it different than one would expect, considering the seriousness of the story that the poem shares? In what way does this tone reflect the great-great-grandmother's attitude toward the events of the poem? Explain your response.

2. **Rhyme and Alliteration. Rhyme** is the repetition of sounds at the ends of words. **Alliteration** is the repetition of initial consonant sounds. Cite some examples of rhyme in this poem. Cite some examples of alliteration. In what way do these repetitions of sound affect the tone of the poem?

Responding in Writing

1. **Creative Writing: Tribute.** Imagine that you have been asked to take part in honoring an old friend, a member of your family, or a mentor at a special dinner or awards ceremony. Write a tribute in the form of a speech, song, or poem to this person. As part of your tribute, share an anecdote, which is a brief story that usually has a specific point or moral, about this person. To begin, freewrite about the person you have chosen, keeping the following questions in mind: Why is this person admirable? What character traits or actions make this person stand out? What one anecdote would demonstrate this person's character to your audience?

2. **Critical Essay: Title and Theme.** Write a short essay in which you discuss the theme, or the central idea, of "Request to a Year," and explore how the title of the poem relates to the theme. As you organize your essay, think about the following questions: What is the speaker's request? Why is the speaker making this request? Back up your statements with concrete details from the poem.

ANALYTIC SCALES FOR RESPONDING IN WRITING

Assign a score from 1 to 25 for each grading criterion below. (For more detailed evaluation, see the evaluation forms for writing, revising, and proofreading, Assessment Portfolio 4.1–4.9.)

1. Tribute

- **Content/Unity.** The tribute honors someone known to the writer and includes an anecdote that reveals something about the character of the subject of the tribute.
- **Organization/Coherence.** The tribute introduces the subject and presents information about him or her in a logical manner.
- **Language/Style.** The tribute uses vivid and precise nouns, verbs, and modifiers.
- **Conventions.** The tribute avoids errors in spelling, grammar, usage, mechanics, and manuscript form.

► Additional practice is provided in the Essential Skills Practice Book: Writing 1.8.

2. Critical Essay

- **Content/Unity.** The essay analyzes the theme of the poem and relates the title to the theme.
- **Organization/Coherence.** The essay presents a thesis in the opening paragraph. The following paragraphs present analysis and references to the text to support the thesis. The essay has a solid conclusion.
- **Language/Style.** The essay uses vivid and precise nouns, verbs, and modifiers.
- **Conventions.** The essay avoids errors in spelling, grammar, usage, mechanics, and manuscript form.

► Additional practice is provided in the Essential Skills Practice Book: Writing 1.20.

ANSWERS FOR UNDERSTANDING LITERATURE

Responses will vary. Possible responses are given.

1. Tone. The tone of the poem is one of distance and detachment. This tone is reflective of the great-great-grandmother's attitude toward the situation as it unfolds. She is looking at the scene, not through the eyes of a mother but through the eyes of an artist.

2. Rhyme and Alliteration. Examples of rhyme include the words *day* and *way* in lines 14 and 16, the words *eye* and *by* in lines 18 and 20, and the words *planned* and *hand* in lines 21 and 22. Examples of alliteration include **d**ifficult **d**istance in line 9; **s**econd, **s**on, and **s**mall in line 10; **d**rift and **d**own in line 11; **b**ottom and **b**elow in line 12; and **s**ketched, **s**cene, **s**ketch, **s**urvives, and **s**tory in lines 18 and 19.

Answers for Language Lab

1. In the late nineteenth century, Australians were influenced by a controversial magazine called The Bulletin, which encouraged them to shed their British heritage.
2. This literary and political magazine influenced such writers and balladeers as A. B. Paterson, who wrote the words for a song called "Waltzing Matilda."
3. Many poems memorized by Australian schoolchildren, including "My Country" by Dorothea Mackellar, came from this period.
4. My Brilliant Career was a popular film version of a book by Miles Franklin, an Australian writer who wrote in the early 1900s.
5. In 1973, Patrick White became the first Australian to win the Nobel Prize; his novels include The Tree of Man and The Eye of the Storm.
6. *Correct*
7. Today, the main literary journals of Australia include Southerly, Quadrant, and Scripsi.
8. In class on Friday, the students read a magazine article called "Australia: Land of Immigrants," because, like the United States, Australia is a land of immigrants.
9. Our neighbor's grandmother is from Australia, and she wrote a play about her childhood there entitled A Child's Life in Armidale, Australia.
10. I would like to read the autobiography The Road from Coorain by Jill Ker Conway, who is from Australia.

▶ Additional practice is provided in the Essential Skills Practice Book: Language 2.51.

Language Lab

Underlining, Italics, and Quotation Marks in Titles. Review the Language Arts Survey 2.51, "Underlining, Italics, and Quotation Marks in Titles." Then, on your own paper, rewrite the following sentences, adding underlines, italics, and quotation marks as necessary. If a sentence is correct as written, write *Correct* next to the number on your paper. (Note: Underlining is used instead of italics in handwritten documents.)

EXAMPLE Request to a Year is a wonderful poem by Judith Wright.
"Request to a Year" is a wonderful poem by Judith Wright.

1. In the late nineteenth century, Australians were influenced by a controversial magazine called The Bulletin, which encouraged them to shed their British heritage.
2. This literary and political magazine influenced such writers and balladeers as A. B. Paterson, who wrote the words for a song called Waltzing Matilda.
3. Many poems memorized by Australian schoolchildren, including My Country by Dorothea Mackellar, came from this period.
4. My Brilliant Career was a popular film version of a book by Miles Franklin, an Australian writer who wrote in the early 1900s.
5. In 1973, Patrick White became the first Australian to win the Nobel Prize; his novels include The Tree of Man and The Eye of the Storm.
6. After the 1950s and 1960s, Aboriginal authors, such as poet Oodgeroo Noonuccal and novelist Mudrooroo Narogin, began writing and contributing to the literature of Australia.
7. Today, the main literary journals of Australia include Southerly, Quadrant, and Scripsi.
8. In class on Friday, the students read a magazine article called Australia: Land of Immigrants, because, like the United States, Australia is a land of immigrants.
9. Our neighbor's grandmother is from Australia, and she wrote a play about her childhood there entitled A Child's Life in Armidale, Australia.
10. I would like to read the autobiography The Road from Coorain by Jill Ker Conway, who is from Australia.

PREREADING

"The First Sally (A) or Trurl's Electronic Bard"
by Stanislaw Lem, translated by Michael Kandel

 POLAND

About the Author

STANISLAW LEM
1921–

Stanislaw Lem, imaginative even as a young child, grew up in Lvov, Poland. Lem's sense of happiness and safety as a youth came to an abrupt end during the Nazi occupation of Poland during World War II. Lem, whose family was Jewish, was forced to change his name and withdraw from his medical studies at the university. He took a job at a garage, where he would often sabotage German vehicles as he pretended to make repairs. He also regularly put his life at great risk to transport messages for Polish Resistance fighters.

By the end of the war, Lem's family had lost all of their possessions and had moved to Kraków, Poland, which was controlled by the Soviet Union. Lem returned to medical school and began to write to earn money. His first two books, *The Astronauts* (1951) and *The Magellan Nebula* (1955), sold well in the Soviet Union. Lem eventually left medical school because he disagreed with some of the theories he was being taught and was discouraged by the new Soviet government's restrictions on what was taught and studied. He devoted himself to his science fiction writing and his study of cybernetics (see Connections below). Lem's other works include *Memoirs of a Space Traveler* (1957), *Solaris* (1961), *The Invincible* (1973), *The Cyberiad* (1974), and *The Futurological Congress* (1983).

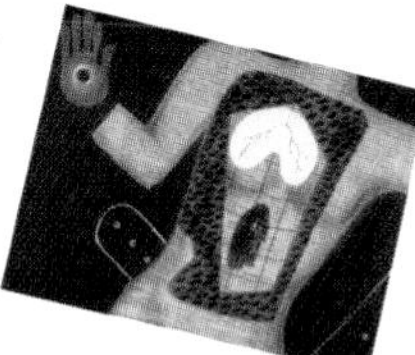

About the Selection

The following selection by Stanislaw Lem is a science fiction story from his book *The Cyberiad.* **Science fiction** is highly imaginative fiction based on scientific principles, discoveries, or laws. Like many science fiction writers, Lem uses futuristic stories about space and extraterrestrials to comment on aspects of his own society that he finds humorous, strange, or even disturbing. "**The First Sally (A) or Trurl's Electronic Bard**" highlights Lem's sense of humor and his aptitude for satire, as it tells the story of a scientist who sets out to build an electronic bard, or poet. Featured in the story are offbeat parodies of Virgil's *Aeneid* and a classic poem by Christopher Marlowe.

CONNECTIONS: Lem and Cybernetics

The Cyberiad, the title of Stanislaw Lem's collection of short stories, is based on the word *cybernetics,* coined in 1948 by Norbert Wiener, an American mathematician and pioneer in this field. Lem has pursued studies in this field, which is a comparative study of control and communications systems in natural organisms and machines. Cybernetics utilizes a mathematical analysis of these systems.

GOALS/OBJECTIVES

Studying this lesson will enable students to

- enjoy a science fiction story
- identify Stanislaw Lem as a contemporary Polish science fiction writer
- identify elements of science fiction
- define *satire* and *parody*
- explain satiric and parodic elements of a work
- write a description using elements of science fiction
- analyze the use of elements of science fiction for satirical purposes
- use technical writing skills to produce directions

ADDITIONAL RESOURCES

READER'S GUIDE

- Selection Worksheet 12.8

ASSESSMENT PORTFOLIO

- Selection Check Test 2.12.15
- Selection Test 2.12.16

ESSENTIAL SKILLS PRACTICE BOOKS

- Writing 1.8, 1.20
- Applied English/Tech Prep 5.5

PREREADING EXTENSIONS

Ask students to jot down their feelings about science fiction and the ideas they have about its subjects, themes, and purposes. After they have read the story, ask them to look at their notes. Have them write again, answering the following questions: Have your feelings about science fiction changed? Explain. Did the story meet or contradict your expectations? Explain.

SUPPORT FOR LEP STUDENTS

PRONUNCIATIONS OF PROPER NOUNS AND ADJECTIVES

Kla • pau • cius (klä pô´shus)
Stan • is • law Lem (stan´ is lô´ lem´)

ADDITIONAL VOCABULARY

auxiliary—additional
chagrin—feeling of embarrassment and annoyance
chaos—lack of order or organization
injunction—court order prohibiting something
punitive—concerning punishment
septillion—number represented by one followed by twenty-four zeros

► Point out to students that Lem made up many of the terms of technical jargon.

READER'S JOURNAL

Have students use specific examples of the positive and negative results they have seen come from emerging technology. After students have responded in their journals, they can break into groups to debate this issue.

Answers to Guided Reading Questions

❶ The narrator says that Trurl's sally did not involve Trurl leaving his house (except for a few trips to the hospital and a trip to an asteroid). It was a journey that almost took Trurl "beyond the realm of possibility."

❷ Trurl decides to build a machine that can write poetry. He reads eight hundred and twenty tons of books on cybernetics and twelve thousand tons of the finest poetry.

❸ Building a poetry machine is complicated because the program found in the head of the average human poet was written by the poet's understanding and interpretation of his or her own civilization, which in turn is programmed by everything that has happened since the beginning of time. Trurl needs to "repeat the entire Universe from the beginning."

Spelling and Vocabulary Words from the Selection

ambiguous
anomaly
apropos
cajole
colossus
daunt
decimate
eddy
elegist
ensue
epigram
intrepid
pantomime
primordial
repertoire
semantic
unscathed

Do you believe that computers can take the place of humans in all areas? Why, or why not? Are you excited by advances in computer technology, or do such advances ever worry or bother you? Explain.

READER'S JOURNAL

"The First Sally (A) or Trurl's Electronic Bard"

STANISLAW LEM, TRANSLATED BY MICHAEL KANDEL

❶ *What does the narrator say about Trurl's "sally"? Why should it be considered a far journey even though Trurl didn't go anywhere?*

❷ *What does Trurl decide to build? Why does he decide to build this thing? What books does he read to begin his work?*

❸ *Why is building a poetry machine so complicated? What does Trurl need to do in order to match what is in the head of the average poet?*

First of all, to avoid any possible misunderstanding, we should state that this was, strictly speaking, a sally[1] to nowhere. In fact, Trurl never left his house throughout it—except for a few trips to the hospital and an unimportant excursion to some asteroid. Yet in a deeper and/or higher sense this was one of the farthest sallies ever undertaken by the famed constructor, for it very nearly took him beyond the realm of possibility.

Trurl had once had the misfortune to build an enormous calculating machine that was capable of only one operation, namely the addition of two and two, and that it did incorrectly. As is related earlier in this volume, the machine also proved to be extremely stubborn, and the quarrel that <u>ensued</u> between it and its creator almost cost the latter his life. From that time on Klapaucius teased Trurl unmercifully, making comments at every opportunity, until Trurl decided to silence him once and for all by building a machine that could write poetry. First Trurl collected eight hundred and twenty tons of books on cybernetics[2] and twelve thousand tons of the finest poetry, then sat down to read it all. Whenever he felt he just couldn't take another chart or equation, he would switch over to verse, and vice versa. After a while it became clear to him that the construction of the machine itself was child's play in comparison with the writing of the program. The program found in the head of an average poet, after all, was written by the poet's civilization, and that civilization was in turn programmed by the civilization that preceded it, and so on to the very Dawn of Time, when those bits of information that concerned the poet-to-be were still swirling about in the <u>primordial</u> chaos of

1. **sally.** Excursion or trip; witty retort
2. **cybernetics.** Comparative study of the human brain and nervous system with complex electronic systems

Words for Everyday Use

en • sue (en so͞o´) *vi.,* immediately follow as a result of some occurrence

pri • mor • di • al (prī môr´dē əl) *adj.,* existing at the beginning; first in time

Vocabulary in Context

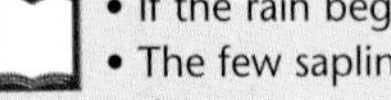

- If the rain begins suddenly, a mad dash for cover will <u>ensue</u>.
- The few saplings that were recently planted cannot replace the splendor of the <u>primordial</u> forest that once stood on this ground.

the cosmic deep. Hence in order to program a poetry machine, one would first have to repeat the entire Universe from the beginning—or at least a good piece of it.

Anyone else in Trurl's place would have given up then and there, but our intrepid constructor was nothing daunted. He built a machine and fashioned a digital model of the Void, an Electrostatic Spirit to move upon the face of the electrolytic waters,[3] and he introduced the parameters[4] of light, a protogalactic cloud or two, and by degrees worked his way up to the first ice age—Trurl could move at this rate because his machine was able, in one five-billionth of a second, to simulate one hundred septillion events at forty octillion different locations simultaneously. And if anyone questions these figures, let him work it out for himself.

Next Trurl began to model Civilization, the striking of fires with flints and the tanning of hides, and he provided for dinosaurs and floods, bipedality[5] and taillessness, then made the paleo-paleface (*Albuminidis sapientia*), which begat the paleface, which begat the gadget, and so it went, from eon to millennium, in the endless hum of electrical currents and eddies. Often the machine turned out to be too small for the computer simulation of a new epoch, and Trurl would have to tack on an auxiliary unit—until he ended up, at last, with a veritable metropolis of tubes and terminals, circuits and shunts,[6] all so tangled and involved that the devil himself couldn't have made head or tail of it. But Trurl managed somehow, he only had to go back twice—once, almost to the beginning, when he discovered that Abel had murdered Cain[7] and not Cain Abel (the result, apparently, of a defective fuse), and once, only three hundred million years back to the middle of the Mesozoic, when after going from fish to amphibian to reptile to mammal, something odd took place among the primates and instead of great apes he came out with gray drapes. A fly, it seems, had gotten into the machine and shorted out the polyphase step-down directional widget.[8] Otherwise everything went like a dream. Antiquity and the Middle Ages were recreated, then the period of revolutions and reforms which gave the machine a few nasty jolts—and then civilization progressed in such leaps and bounds that Trurl had to hose down the coils and cores repeatedly to keep them from overheating.

Toward the end of the twentieth century the machine began to tremble, first sideways, then lengthwise—for no apparent reason. This alarmed Trurl; he brought out cement and grappling irons just in case. But fortunately these weren't needed; instead of jumping its moorings, the machine settled down and soon had left the twentieth century far behind. Civilizations came and went thereafter in fifty-thousand-year intervals: these were the fully intelligent beings from whom Trurl himself stemmed. Spool upon spool of computerized history was filled and ejected into storage bins; soon there were so many spools, that even if you stood at the top of the machine with high-power binoculars, you wouldn't see the end of them. And all to construct some versifier![9] But then,

3. **Void . . . waters.** Plays on Genesis 1:2: "And the Earth was without form and void . . . and the Spirit of God moved upon the face of the waters."
4. **parameters.** Boundaries or limits
5. **bipedality.** Ability to walk on two legs
6. **shunts.** Conductors that connect two points in a circuit
7. **Abel . . . Cain.** Refers to the biblical account in Genesis of Cain's murder of his brother, Abel
8. **polyphase . . . widget.** Author's imaginary technological jargon
9. **versifier.** Poet

❶ *Why is Trurl able to repeat historical events at a fast rate? What challenge does the narrator present to the reader?*

❷ *What happens to the machine at the end of the twentieth century? When does this story take place?*

❸ *What are the only two problems that occur? Why do they occur?*

Words for Everyday Use

in • trep • id (in trep´id) *adj.*, fearless, bold

daunt (dônt) *vt.*, make afraid or discouraged; intimidate; dishearten

ed • dy (ed´ē) *n.*, current moving in a whirling motion

Answers to Guided Reading Questions

❶ Trurl is able to repeat historical events at a fast rate because his machine was able to simulate "one hundred septillion events" at "forty octillion" different locations simultaneously in one five-billionth of a second.

❷ At the end of the twentieth century, the machine begins to tremble for no apparent reason. The story goes well into the twenty-first century.

❸ Trurl discovers that for some reason Abel murders Cain instead of Cain murdering Abel, and then he discovers that when going from reptile to mammal he comes out with gray drapes instead of great apes. This happens because a fly had gotten into the machine and shorted out something.

Cross-curricular Activities

APPLIED ARTS

Ask students to research how technology has grown and changed through the years. Encourage them to answer the following questions: What were some of the earliest machines? When did the world really begin to be technologically advanced? Have students demonstrate some of the latest machines and technology that they use frequently. Have them explain the impact that such technology has on their lives.

Vocabulary in Context

- The intrepid explorer set off fearlessly into the uncharted territory.
- Hakeem was daunted by the stack of work he was given upon returning from vacation.
- The toy boat was caught up in an eddy and twirled about merrily as it hastened downstream.

Answers to Guided Reading Questions

❶ Trurl adds devices he calls "self-regulating egocentripetal narcissistors" to the machine. These machines make the machine vain and self-absorbed.

❷ Trurl bypassed half the logic circuits and "made the emotive more electromotive." This made the machine extrasensitive and depressed. Trurl then made the semantic fields more intense and attached a strength of character component. Trurl also installed a "philosophical throttle."

❸ Trurl is not happy with the first poem. He is forced to install six cliché filters.

Literary Technique

Cliché

A **cliché** is a tired or hackneyed expression such as *quiet as a mouse* or *couch potato.* Most clichés originate as vivid, colorful expressions but soon become uninteresting because of overuse. Careful writers and speakers avoid clichés, which are dull and signify lack of originality.

Trurl recognizes the weakness of writing that includes clichés. He recognizes that doggerel is filled with trite expressions and tries to rid his machine of such phrases by adding cliché filters made of corundum steel.

Ask students to become cliché filters for themselves and for their peers. Each student should write a brief poem or paragraph, purposely including several clichés. Then have students trade papers, find the clichés, and replace them with original words or phrases.

such is the way of scientific fanaticism. At last the programs were ready; all that remained was to pick out the most applicable—else the electropoet's education would take several million years at the very least.

During the next two weeks Trurl fed general instructions into his future electropoet, then set up all the necessary logic circuits, emotive elements, semantic centers. He was about to invite Klapaucius to attend a trial run, but thought better of it and started the machine himself. It immediately proceeded to deliver a lecture on the grinding of crystallographical surfaces as an introduction to the study of submolecular magnetic anomalies. Trurl bypassed half the logic circuits and made the emotive more electromotive; the machine sobbed, went into hysterics, then finally said, blubbering terribly, what a cruel, cruel world this was. Trurl intensified the semantic fields and attached a strength of character component; the machine informed him that from now on he would carry out its every wish and to begin with add six floors to the nine it already had, so it could better meditate upon the meaning of existence. Trurl installed a philosophical throttle instead; the machine fell silent and sulked. Only after endless pleading and cajoling was he able to get it to recite something: "I had a little froggy." That appeared to exhaust its repertoire. Trurl adjusted, modulated, expostulated, disconnected, ran checks, reconnected, reset, did everything he could think of, and the machine presented him with a poem that made him thank heaven Klapaucius wasn't there to laugh—imagine, simulating the whole Universe from scratch, not to mention Civilization in every particular, and to end up with such dreadful doggerel![10] Trurl put in six cliché filters, but they snapped like matches; he had to make them out of pure corundum steel. This seemed to work, so he jacked the semanticity up all the way, plugged in an alternating rhyme generator—which nearly ruined everything, since the machine resolved to become a missionary among destitute tribes on far-flung planets. But at the very last minute, just as he was ready to give up and take a hammer to it, Trurl was struck by an inspiration; tossing out all the logic circuits, he replaced them with self-regulating egocentripetal narcissistors.[11] The machine simpered a little, whimpered a little, laughed bitterly, complained of an awful pain on its third floor, said that in general it was fed up, through, life was beautiful but men were such beasts and how sorry they'd all be when it was dead and gone. Then it asked for pen and paper. Trurl sighed with relief, switched it off and went to bed. The next morning he went to see Klapaucius. Klapaucius, hearing that he was invited to attend the debut of Trurl's electronic bard, dropped everything and followed—so eager was he to be an eyewitness to his friend's humiliation.

Trurl let the machine warm up first, kept the power low, ran up the metal stairs several times to take readings (the machine was like the engine of a giant steamer, galleried, with rows of rivets, dials and valves on every tier)—till finally, satisfied all the decimal places were where they ought to be, he said yes, it was ready now, and why not start with something simple. Later, of course, when the machine had gotten the feel of it, Klapaucius could ask it to produce poetry on absolutely whatever topic he liked.

❶ *What electronic devices does Trurl add to the machine? What do these devices do to the machine's personality? What is the machine finally ready to do?*

❷ *What alterations does Trurl make to the machine? Describe how each of these adjustments affects the machine as a "character."*

❸ *What does Trurl think of the machine's first poem? What is he forced to install?*

10. **doggerel.** Bad poetry

11. **self-regulating . . . narcissistors.** Imaginary gadgets with names suggesting self-involvement and vanity

Words for Everyday Use

se • man • tic (si man´ tik) *adj.*, pertaining to the meaning of words or symbols

a • nom • a • ly (ə nom´ə lē) *n.*, deviation from the expected; abnormality

ca • jole (kə jōl´) *vt.*, coax or persuade by flattery

rep • er • toire (rep´ər twär´) *n.*, stock of material available for performance

Vocabulary in Context

- Interested in the meanings of words and symbols, Gustave studied semantics.
- The heart-shaped pancake was an anomaly; usually pancakes are round.
- Uncharacteristically complimenting his older sister, Blair tried to cajole her into taking him to the mall.
- Imogene's repertoire for the variety show includes tap dancing, magic tricks, and a stand-up comedy routine.

Now the potentiometers indicated the machine's lyrical capacitance was charged to maximum, and Trurl, so nervous his hands were shaking, threw the master switch. A voice, slightly husky but remarkably vibrant and bewitching, said:

"Phlogisticosh. Rhomothriglyph. Floof."

"Is that it?" inquired Klapaucius after a pause, extremely polite. Trurl only bit his lip, gave the machine a few kicks of current, and tried again. This time the voice came through much more clearly; it was a thrilling baritone, solemn yet intriguingly sensual:

Pev't o' tay merlong gumin gots,
Untle yun furly päzzen ye,
Confre an' ayzor, azor ots,
Bither de furloss bochre blee!

"Am I missing something?" said Klapaucius, calmly watching a panic-stricken Trurl struggling at the controls. Finally Trurl waved his arms in despair, dashed clattering several flights up the metal stairs, got down on all fours and crawled into the machine through a trapdoor; he hammered away inside, swearing like a maniac, tightened something, pried at something, crawled out again and ran frantically to another tier. At long last he let out a cry of triumph, threw a burnt tube over his shoulder—it bounced off the railing and fell to the floor, shattering at the feet of Klapaucius. But Trurl didn't bother to apologize; he quickly put in a new tube, wiped his hands on a chammy cloth and hollered down for Klapaucius to try it now. The following words rang out:

Mockles! Fent on silpen tree,
Blockards three a-feening
Mockles, what silps came to thee
In thy pantry dreaming?

"Well, that's an improvement!" shouted Trurl, not entirely convinced. "The last line particularly, did you notice?"

"If this is all you have to show me . . ." said Klapaucius, the very soul of politeness.

"Damn!" said Trurl and again disappeared inside the machine. There was a fierce banging and clanging, the sputtering of shorted wires and the muttering of an even shorter temper, then Trurl stuck his head out of a trapdoor on the third story and yelled, "*Now* try it!"

Klapaucius complied. The electronic bard shuddered from stem to stern and began:

Oft, in that wickless chalet all begorn,
Where whilom soughed the mossy sappertort
And you were wont to bong—

Trurl yanked out a few cables in a fury, something rattled and wheezed, the machine fell silent. Klapaucius laughed so hard he had to sit on the floor. Then suddenly, as Trurl was rushing back and forth, there was a crackle, a clack, and the machine with perfect poise said:

The Petty and the Small
Are overcome with gall
When Genius, having faltered, fails to fall.

Klapaucius too, I ween,
Will turn the deepest green
To hear such flawless verse from Trurl's machine.

"There you are, an epigram! And wonderfully apropos!" laughed Trurl, racing down the metal stairs and flinging himself

1 What does the machine's voice sound like? What is wrong with the poetry?

2 What does Trurl find that he believes is causing the problem?

WORDS FOR EVERYDAY USE

ep • i • gram (ep´ə gram´) *n.,* short poem with a witty or satirical point

ap • ro • pos (ap´rə pō´) *adj.,* apt; fitting the occasion

ANSWERS TO GUIDED READING QUESTIONS

1 The machine's voice is baritone, solemn, yet sensual. The poetry does not make sense. The machine does not appear to be using any real language.

2 Trurl finds a burnt tube that appears to be the problem.

QUOTABLES

"Twas brillig, and the slithy toves
Did gyre and gimble in the wabe;
All mimsy were the borogoves,
And the mome raths outgrabe."

—Lewis Carroll

LITERARY NOTE

The lines above are from Lewis Carroll's apparent nonsense poem "Jabberwocky." **Nonsense verse** is a kind of light verse that contains elements that are silly, absurd, or meaningless. Sometimes, as is the case with "Jabberwocky," the apparent nonsense of the verse makes sense upon closer analysis. Carroll's poem turns out not to be nonsense at all but rather an ingenious retelling, in a mock heroic ballad, of a stock folktale story—that of a young person who sets off on a quest, slays a terrible beast, and returns home victorious.

Have students read "Jabberwocky" and identify nonsensical elements. Then have them trace the story told in the poem. Finally, have them compare the nonsense written by Trurl's electronic bard to Carroll's work.

VOCABULARY IN CONTEXT

- "We think our fathers fools, so wise we grow; our wiser sons, no doubt, will think us so," is an epigram by Alexander Pope.
- Helmer always knows what to say in any situation; his comments are always apropos.

Answers to Guided Reading Questions

❶ Klapaucius is not impressed with the machine's poetry. He says that the machine's poem is nothing and accuses Trurl of setting it all up beforehand.

❷ Klapaucius asks the machine to compose a poem about a haircut in a lofty, heroic style. He also insists that the poem be rhymed and have only words beginning with the letter *s*. Trurl is angered by the request—he feels that it's idiotic. The machine is able to produce a poem to Klapaucius's specifications.

Cross-curricular Activities

Mathematics and Sciences and Applied Arts

Hold a science and technology fair. Each student should create an experiment or invention that demonstrates or uses some aspect of science or technology. At the fair, each student should present his or her project. Students might present their project through an annotated display, an oral presentation, or an interactive demonstration. Students may wish to invite other classes or members of the community to visit their science and technology fair.

Literary Technique

Alliteration

Remind students that when Klapaucius asks the machine to begin every word with the letter *s*, he is asking for an extreme example of alliteration. **Alliteration** is the repetition of initial consonant sounds.

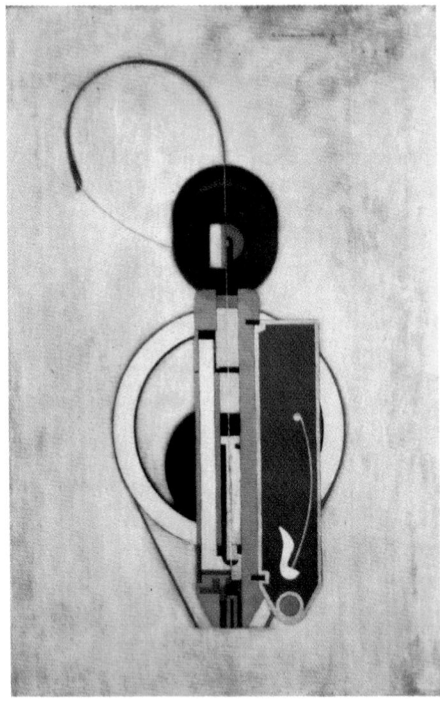

Mechanical Abstraction. *Morton Schamberg, 1916. Philadelphia Museum of Art. Louise and Walter Arensberg Collection*

❶ *Is Klapaucius impressed with the machine's poetry? What does he say about it?*

❷ *What kind of poem does Klapaucius ask the machine to compose? What is Trurl's reaction to this request? Is the machine able to do it?*

delightedly into his colleague's arms. Klapaucius, quite taken aback, was no longer laughing.

"What, *that?*" he said. "That's nothing. Besides, you had it all set up beforehand."

"Set up?!"

"Oh, it's quite obvious . . . the ill-disguised hostility, the poverty of thought, the crudeness of execution."

"All right, then ask it something else! Whatever you like! Go on! What are you waiting for? Afraid?!"

"Just a minute," said Klapaucius, annoyed. He was trying to think of a request as difficult as possible, aware that any argument on the quality of the verse the machine might be able to produce would be hard if not impossible to settle either way. Suddenly he brightened and said:

"Have it compose a poem—a poem about a haircut! But lofty, noble, tragic, timeless, full of love, treachery, retribution, quiet heroism in the face of certain doom! Six lines, cleverly rhymed, and every word beginning with the letter *s*!!"

"And why not throw in a full exposition of the general theory of nonlinear automata while you're at it?" growled Trurl. "You can't give it such idiotic—"

But he didn't finish. A melodious voice filled the hall with the following:

Seduced, shaggy Samson snored.
She scissored short. Sorely shorn,
Soon shackled slave, Samson sighed,
Silently scheming,
Sightlessly seeking
Some savage, spectacular suicide.[12]

12. ***Seduced . . . suicide.*** The poem refers to the biblical story of Samson and Delilah.

Additional Questions and Activities

Have students create their own difficult assignments for the electronic bard. Suggest that students review the different meters and stanza types before listing their specifications.

Then ask them to try to write a poem that meets their specifications. Students need not worry about creating a piece of fine literature. Instead they should have fun mixing forms, meters, tones, and subjects that would not seem to go together. For example, students might write a haughty haiku about halitosis, or they might write a tragic ode about garbage in which every line rhymes.

"Well, what do you say to that?" asked Trurl, his arms folded proudly. But Klapaucius was already shouting:

"Now all in *g*! A sonnet, trochaic hexameter, about an old cyclotron who kept sixteen artificial mistresses, blue and radioactive, had four wings, three purple pavilions, two lacquered chests, each containing exactly one thousand medallions bearing the likeness of Czar Murdicog the Headless . . ."

"Grinding gleeful gears, Gerontogyron grabbed / Giggling gynecobalt-60 golems," began the machine, but Trurl leaped to the console, shut off the power and turned, defending the machine with his body.

"Enough!" he said, hoarse with indignation. "How dare you waste a great talent on such drivel? Either give it decent poems to write or I call the whole thing off!"

"What, those aren't decent poems?" protested Klapaucius.

"Certainly not! I didn't build a machine to solve ridiculous crossword puzzles! That's hack work, not Great Art! Just give it a topic, any topic, as difficult as you like . . ."

Klapaucius thought, and thought some more. Finally he nodded and said:

"Very well. Let's have a love poem, lyrical, pastoral, and expressed in the language of pure mathematics. Tensor algebra mainly, with a little topology[13] and higher calculus, if need be. But with feeling, you understand, and in the cybernetic spirit."

"Love and tensor algebra? Have you taken leave of your senses?" Trurl began, but stopped, for his electronic bard was already declaiming:

Come let us hasten to a higher plane,
Where dyads tread the fairy fields of Venn,
Their indices bedecked from one to n,
Commingled in an endless Markov chain!

Come, every frustum longs to be a cone,
And every vector dreams of matrices.
Hark to the gentle gradient of the breeze:
It whispers of a more ergodic zone.

In Riemann, Hilbert or in Banach space
Let superscripts and subscripts to their ways.
Our asymptotes no longer out of phase,
We shall encounter, counting, face to face.

I'll grant thee random access to my heart,
Thou'lt tell me all the constants of thy love;
And so we two shall all love's lemmas prove,
And in our bound partition never part.

For what did Cauchy know, or Christoffel,
Or Fourier, or any Boole or Euler,
Wielding their compasses, their pens and rulers,
Of thy supernal sinusoidal spell?

Cancel me not—for what then shall remain?
Abscissas, some mantissas, modules, modes,
A root or two, a torus and a node:
The inverse of my verse, a null domain.

Ellipse of bliss, converge. O lips divine!
The product of our scalars is defined!
Cyberiad draws nigh, and the skew mind
Cuts capers like a happy haversine.

I see the eigenvalue in thine eye,
I hear the tender tensor in thy sigh.
Bernoulli would have been content to die,
Had he but known such $a^2 \cos 2\varphi$*!*[14]

This concluded the poetic competition, since Klapaucius suddenly had to leave, saying he would return shortly with more topics for the machine; but he never did, afraid that in so doing, he might give Trurl more cause to boast. Trurl of course let it be known that Klapaucius had fled in order to hide his envy and chagrin. Klapaucius meanwhile spread the word that Trurl had more than one screw loose on the subject of that so-called mechanical versifier.

Not much time went by before the news of Trurl's computer laureate reached the genuine—that is, the ordinary—poets. Deeply offended, they resolved to ignore the machine's existence. A few, however, were

❶ *Why does Trurl become annoyed with Klapaucius? What does he want Klapaucius to ask the machine?*

❷ *What kind of love poem does Klapaucius demand?*

❸ *Why does Klapaucius leave? How does Trurl explain his departure? What does Klapaucius tell people about Trurl?*

13. **topology.** Study of the properties of geometric figures
14. **Come, let us . . . cos 2 ø!** Plays on Christopher Marlowe's "The Passionate Shepherd to His Love," a lyric poem; its famous first stanza begins, "Come live with me and be my love. . ."

Answers to Guided Reading Questions

❶ Trurl becomes annoyed with Klapaucius because he wants the machine to compose decent poems—not what he considers drivel or hack work. He wants Klapaucius to ask the machine to compose a poem based on a difficult topic.

❷ Klapaucius asks for a lyrical, pastoral poem, expressed in the language of mathematics such as algebra, topology, or higher calculus. He also wants it to have feeling and be in the "cybernetic" spirit.

❸ Klapaucius leaves to gather more topics for the machine. Trurl decides that Klapaucius left because he could no longer hide his envy and chagrin over what Trurl has accomplished. Klapaucius tells people that Trurl has a "screw loose."

Quotables

"Poetry is emotion recollected in tranquility."

—William Wordsworth

"Poetry is the record of the best and happiest moments of the happiest and best minds."

—Percy Bysshe Shelley

"Poetry is speech framed . . . to be heard for its own sake and interest even over and above its interest of meaning."

—Gerard Manley Hopkins

"Poetry is the best words in the best order."

—Samuel Taylor Coleridge

"Poetry is not an assertion of truth, but the making of the truth more fully real to us."

—T. S. Eliot

"Poetry is the language of a state of crisis."

—Stéphane Mallarmé

Additional Questions and Activities

Share with students the quotations about poetry in the Quotables box. Ask them to discuss the different definitions of poetry. Ask the following questions: Which definitions do you think are appropriate? Why? Why can more than one of these definitions be applicable?

Then ask students to try to come up with a definition of their own. Suggest that students first identify the elements that they think are essential to good poetry. You might at this point want to discuss the difference between good poetry and doggerel, using examples of each.

After the class has created a definition, ask each student to critique any poem as either good poetry or doggerel based on the class's definition.

Answers to Guided Reading Questions

1. The avant-garde poets make fun of the machine because it writes only in the traditional manner. The machine's program is based only on the classics.
2. True poets are devastated by the machine's success.
3. Editors love Trurl's machine because it had a high-quality poem to fit every occasion and length. Readers were enraptured, bemused, and deeply moved by the poetry.
4. The third-rate poets do not know good poetry from bad poetry, so they are not even aware that they are being outdone by a machine.

Literary Technique

Readers are moved by the poetry of Trurl's bard. Two of the literary techniques used by the bard are metaphor and assonance. Review these terms with your students. Then ask them to find examples of each technique in poetry from their textbook.

METAPHOR

A **metaphor** is a figure of speech in which one thing is spoken or written about as if it were another. This figure of speech invites the reader to make a comparison between the two things. The two things involved are the writer's actual subject, the tenor of the metaphor, and another thing to which the subject is likened, the vehicle of the metaphor.

ASSONANCE

Assonance is the repetition of vowel sound in stressed syllables that end with different consonant sounds.

1 *Why do the avant-garde poets make fun of Trurl's machine? What is the machine's poetic background?*

2 *How do true poets react to the electronic bard?*

3 *What do magazine editors and readers like about Trurl's machine?*

4 *Why do the third-rate poets remain unaffected by the machine?*

curious enough to visit Trurl's electronic bard in secret. It received them courteously, in a hall piled high with closely written paper (for it worked day and night without pause). Now these poets were all avant-garde,[15] and Trurl's machine wrote only in the traditional manner; Trurl, no connoisseur of poetry, had relied heavily on the classics in setting up its program. The machine's guests jeered and left in triumph. The machine was self-programming, however, and in addition had a special ambition-amplifying mechanism with glory-seeking circuits, and very soon a great change took place. Its poems became difficult, ambiguous, so intricate and charged with meaning that they were totally incomprehensible. When the next group of poets came to mock and laugh, the machine replied with an improvisation that was so modern, it took their breath away, and the second poem seriously weakened a certain sonneteer who had two State awards to his name, not to mention a statue in the city park. After that, no poet could resist the fatal urge to cross lyrical swords with Trurl's electronic bard. They came from far and wide, carrying trunks and suitcases full of manuscripts. The machine would let each challenger recite, instantly grasp the algorithms[16] of his verse, and use it to compose an answer in exactly the same style, only two hundred and twenty to three hundred and forty-seven times better.

The machine quickly grew so adept at this, that it could cut down a first-class rhapsodist with no more than one or two quatrains.[17] But the worst of it was, all the third-rate poets emerged unscathed; being third-rate, they didn't know good poetry from bad and consequently had no inkling of their crushing defeat. One of them, true, broke his leg when, on the way out, he tripped over an epic poem the machine had just completed, a prodigious work beginning with the words:

Arms, and machines I sing, that forced by fate,
And haughty Homo's unrelenting hate,
Expell'd and exiled, left the Terran shore . . .[18]

The true poets, on the other hand, were decimated by Trurl's electronic bard, though it never laid a finger on them. First an aged elegist, then two modernists committed suicide, leaping off a cliff that unfortunately happened to lie hard by the road leading from Trurl's place to the nearest train station.

There were many poet protests staged, demonstrations, demands that the machine be served an injunction to cease and desist. But no one else appeared to care. In fact, magazine editors generally approved: Trurl's electronic bard, writing under several thousand different pseudonyms at once, had a poem for every occasion, to fit whatever length might be required, and of such high quality that the magazine would be torn from hand to hand by eager readers. On the street one could see enraptured faces, bemused smiles, sometimes even hear a quiet sob. Everyone knew the poems of Trurl's electronic bard, the air rang with its delightful rhymes. Not infrequently, those citizens of a greater sensitivity, struck by a particularly marvelous metaphor or assonance, would actually fall into a faint. But this colossus of inspiration was prepared even for that eventuality; it would immediately supply the necessary number of restorative rondelets.[19]

Trurl himself had no little trouble in connection with his invention. The classicists,

15. **avant-garde.** New and unconventional
16. **algorithms.** Systematic methods of solving certain kinds of problem
17. **quatrains.** Four-line stanzas or poems
18. ***Arms, and machines. . . shore.*** Parody of the *Aeneid,* Virgil's epic which begins, "I sing of arms and the man"
19. **rondelets.** French verse form with five to seven lines

Words for Everyday Use

am • big • u • ous (am big´yo͞o əs) *adj.,* having two or more possible meanings

un • scathed (un skāthd) *adj.,* unharmed

dec • i • mate (des´ə māt´) *vt.,* destroy or kill a large part of

el • e • gist (el´ə jist) *n.,* poet who writes poems of lament

co • los • sus (kə läs´əs) *n.,* giant

Vocabulary in Context

- Norbert claims there is one obvious answer, but I think the question is ambiguous.
- Kayla emerged unscathed from the debate in which the other candidate tried to tarnish her reputation.
- The drought decimated the crops in the field.
- Although Reva is mainly an elegist, she has produced a few successful lighthearted poems.
- Next to an ant, even the smallest child is a colossus.

generally elderly, were fairly harmless; they confined themselves to throwing stones through his windows and smearing the sides of his house with an unmentionable substance. But it was much worse with the younger poets. One, for example, as powerful in body as his verse was in imagery, beat Trurl to a pulp. And while the constructor lay in the hospital, events marched on. Not a day passed without a suicide or a funeral; picket lines formed around the hospital; one could hear gunfire in the distance—instead of manuscripts in their suitcases, more and more poets were bringing rifles to defeat Trurl's electronic bard. But the bullets merely bounced off its calm exterior. After his return from the hospital, Trurl, weak and desperate, finally decided one night to dismantle the homeostatic[20] Homer he had created.

But when he approached the machine, limping slightly, it noticed the pliers in his hand and the grim glitter in his eye, and delivered such an eloquent, impassioned plea for mercy, that the constructor burst into tears, threw down his tools and hurried back to his room, wading through new works of genius, an ocean of paper that filled the hall chest-high from end to end and rustled incessantly.

The following month Trurl received a bill for the electricity consumed by the machine and almost fell off his chair. If only he could have consulted his old friend Klapaucius! But Klapaucius was nowhere to be found. So Trurl had to come up with something by himself. One dark night he unplugged the machine, took it apart, loaded it onto a ship, flew to a certain small asteroid, and there assembled it again, giving it an atomic pile for its source of creative energy.

Then he sneaked home. But that wasn't the end of it. The electronic bard, deprived now of the possibility of having its masterpieces published, began to broadcast them on all wavelengths, which soon sent the passengers and crews of passing rockets into states of stanzaic stupefaction, and those more delicate souls were seized with severe attacks of esthetic ecstasy besides. Having determined the cause of this disturbance, the Cosmic Fleet Command issued Trurl an official request for the immediate termination of his device, which was seriously impairing the health and well-being of all travelers.

At that point Trurl went into hiding, so they dropped a team of technicians on the asteroid to gag the machine's output unit. It overwhelmed them with a few ballads, however, and the mission had to be abandoned. Deaf technicians were sent next, but the machine employed pantomime. After that, there began to be talk of an eventual punitive expedition, of bombing the electropoet into submission. But just then some ruler from a neighboring star system came, bought the machine and hauled it off, asteroid and all, to his kingdom.

20. **homeostatic.** Maintaining internal stability; self-regulating

❶ *What does the machine do from the asteroid? What is Trurl ordered to do?*

❷ *What happens when Trurl tries to dismantle the machine?*

❸ *How is the problem of getting rid of the bard finally solved?*

Words for Everyday Use

pan • to • mime (pan´tə mīm) *n.,* dramatic presentation using only actions and gestures, not speech

Answers to Guided Reading Questions

❶ The machine broadcasts its poetry from the asteroid on all wavelengths, interfering with the activities of rockets. Trurl is ordered to terminate his device.

❷ When Trurl tries to dismantle the machine, the machine lets out an eloquent plea for mercy that makes Trurl cry.

❸ A ruler from a neighboring star system buys the machine and hauls it off to his kingdom.

Selection Check Test with Answers

EX. What was Trurl's first invention?
Trurl invented a calculating machine.

1. What does Trurl decide to create next?
Trurl decides to create a machine that writes poetry.

2. What process must Trurl duplicate to program his machine?
He must repeat the entire history of the universe from the beginning.

3. What is wrong with the first verses from the machine?
The first verses are full of clichés.

4. Whom does Trurl's machine anger, after it has achieved some success?
The machine angers poets.

5. Who finally buys Trurl's machine?
The leader of a neighboring star system buys the machine.

Vocabulary in Context

- After losing his voice, Yves resorted to pantomime to express himself.

Quotables

"Science is for those who learn; poetry, for those who know."

—Joseph Roux

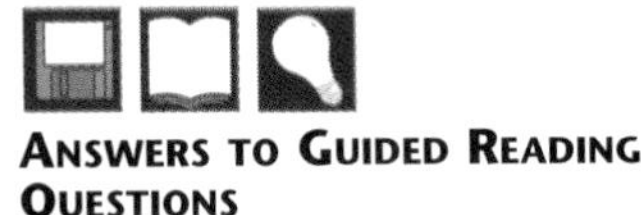

ANSWERS TO GUIDED READING QUESTIONS

➊ Trurl vows never again to make a cybernetic model of the Muse.

RESPONDING TO THE SELECTION

As an extension of this activity, ask students to discuss the limitations they think exist in the ability of machines and computers to perform what are usually human functions. Students should say whether they think these limitations will ever be overcome and explain their answer.

ANSWERS FOR REVIEWING THE SELECTION

RECALLING AND INTERPRETING

1. **Recalling.** Trurl decides to build a machine capable of writing poetry because he had at one time built a calculating machine that did not work properly, and one of his colleagues teased him about it. Trurl wanted to silence him once and for all. In an attempt to build a poet's brain, he reconstructs history from its earliest beginnings. **Interpreting.** The poetry machine has to engage in complex thought, while the calculating machine needed only to add numbers together. The poetry machine needs to have a certain depth of character and experience, sensitivity, and a specific type of personality. The section on the building of the machine's personality is humorous because Trurl treats it as though it has a specific formula—as if the personality of a poet starts with a particular recipe. He also bases this recipe on certain humorous stereotypes concerning the artistic temperament.

2. **Recalling.** Trurl sets up all the necessary "emotive elements [and] semantic centers." In doing this he first bypasses logic circuits and makes the "emotive more electro- (cont.)

Now Trurl could appear in public again and breathe easy. True, lately there had been supernovae[21] exploding on the southern horizon, the like of which no one had ever seen before, and there were rumors that this had something to do with poetry. According to one report, that same ruler, moved by some strange whim, had ordered his astro-engineers to connect the electronic bard to a constellation of white supergiants,[22] thereby transforming each line of verse into a stupendous solar prominence; thus the Greatest Poet in the Universe was able to transmit its thermonuclear creations to all the illimitable reaches of space at once. But even if there were any truth to this, it was all too far away to bother Trurl, who vowed by everything that was ever held sacred never, never again to make a cybernetic model of the Muse. ■

➊ *What is Trurl's vow?*

21. **supernovae.** Stars which increase in brightness and magnitude over a short period
22. **supergiants.** Immense and vividly bright stars

Responding to the Selection

What do you think of the "electronic bard"? Is it likely that one could really be invented? Why, or why not?

Reviewing the Selection

RECALLING

1. Why does Trurl decide to build a machine capable of writing poetry? What does he do in an attempt to build a poet's brain?

INTERPRETING

▶▶ How does the poetry machine differ from the calculating machine? What makes it more complicated? What makes Trurl's technical approach to building the mind of a poet unusual or humorous?

RECALLING

2. What steps does Trurl take to mold his machine's personality and temperament?

INTERPRETING

▶▶ Why does the machine's first lecture after Trurl's trial run alert Trurl that there is a problem? What personality traits does Trurl associate with poets? Why does the speech the machine gives after Trurl replaces the logic circuits with "egocentripetal narcissistors" please Trurl?

RECALLING

3. What does the machine do when it is first run for Klapaucius? Is Klapaucius impressed when he hears the first intelligible bit of verse? What does Trurl then invite him to do?

INTERPRETING

▶▶ Describe the relationship and interactions between Trurl and Klapaucius. What kind of tension exists between the two scientists? Why do you think there is tension between them?

ANSWERS FOR REVIEWING THE SELECTION (CONT.)

motive." He then intensifies the semantic fields, attaches strength of character components, and installs a philosophical throttle. He also installs something called a "self-regulating egocentripetal narcissistors." **Interpreting.** The speech is dry and scientific. Trurl associates vanity, egocentrism, sensitivity, depression, intelligence, thoughtfulness, and a lack of logic with poets. The speech pleases Trurl because the machine displays in its speech the qualities Trurl associates with poets.

3. **Recalling.** The machine first spouts nonsense. It slowly begins to make more sense. It finally creates an apropos epigram. Klapaucius is not impressed. Trurl invites him to test the machine. **Interpreting.** Trurl and Klapaucius are rivals. They are constantly trying to outdo each other. *Responses will vary.*

(cont.)

4. What happens when news of the electronic bard reaches poets? How do magazine editors feel about the electronic bard? When does Trurl decide to dismantle the machine, and why is he unable to do it?

Why might human poets be "deeply offended" by a machine designed to write poetry? In what way does the machine's existence belittle their creative efforts?

SYNTHESIZING

5. Do you think Lem believes that it is possible to control and perfect the creative process? Why, or why not? What ideas make this story humorous? At what two personality types does Lem's story poke fun?

Understanding Literature (Questions for Discussion)

1. **Satire. Satire** is humorous writing or speech intended to point out errors, falsehoods, foibles, or failings. Describe how Lem uses satire to mock poets as being overly emotional and vain. Which particular groups of poets does Lem mock? Describe how Lem uses satire to make fun of the overly rational tendencies of scientists. What language does he use to mock the technical thought processes of scientists and to lampoon their stereotypical contempt for anything that cannot be explained by logic and mathematics?

2. **Parody.** A **parody** is a literary work that imitates another work for humorous, often satirical, purposes. Lem parodies both Virgil's *Aeneid* and Christopher Marlowe's lyric poem "The Passionate Shepherd to His Love." Read the following stanzas from Marlowe's original poem. Then reread Lem's more "scientific" parody of the poem. What makes the Lem version of the poem humorous? At what is Lem poking fun?

> Come live with me and be my love,
> And we will all the pleasures prove
> That valleys, groves, hills, and fields,
> Woods, or steepy mountain yields.
>
> And we will sit upon the rocks,
> Seeing the shepherds feed their flocks,
> By shallow rivers to whose falls
> Melodious birds sing madrigals. . . .
>
> The shepherds' swains shall dance and sing
> For thy delight each May morning:
> If these delights thy mind may move,
> Then live with me and be my love.

Answers for Reviewing the Selection (cont.)

4. **Recalling.** Other poets are at first skeptical. Then they hear that the machine is writing good poetry, and they rush to hear the bard for themselves. After a while, poets begin to get hostile. Magazine editors love the electronic bard, and its work becomes popular with readers. Trurl decides to dismantle the machine when he realizes how much electricity it requires. He is later ordered to do so by the government. He is unable to dismantle the machine because it gives a stirring speech on its own behalf. **Interpreting.** The poets might feel that the machine's existence belittles their creative efforts because its creation suggests that great poetry is the result of a particular equation. The poets believe that the creation of great poetry is the result of talent and creativity.

SYNTHESIZING

Responses will vary. Possible responses are given.

5. Students may say that Lem does not believe that the creative process can be replicated as shown by his satiric treatment of a machine designed to do just that. Other students may say Lem shows that given advanced technology, the creative process can be reproduced. The story is humorous because of the matter-of-fact manner in which Trurl tries to build a personality and duplicate the creative process. It makes fun of both poets and scientists.

Answers for Understanding Literature

Responses will vary. Possible responses are given.

1. **Satire.** Lem is using satire to mock the stereotypical personalities of poets in the way that he builds the machine's personality. The imaginary devices that reflect personality traits such as vanity, self-indulgence, and lack of logic (cont.)

Answers for Understanding Literature (cont.)

are part of this satire. Lem makes fun of modern, avant-garde poets; classical poets; and third-rate poets. The building of the poet's personality and the replicating of the creative process with a particular formula and certain devices mocks the supposed analytical and overly rational natures of scientists. The writer shows Trurl thinking and speaking using highly technical language.

2. **Parody.** The machine's poem makes fun of the pastoral style in Marlowe's poem, as well as the way in which Marlowe pleads with his beloved to come live with him and tries to convince her with elaborate promises. The machine's version of the poem is humorous in that instead of using pastoral images of the beauty of nature, the machine uses images of mathematics.

ANALYTIC SCALES FOR RESPONDING IN WRITING

Assign a score from 1 to 25 for each grading criterion below. (For more detailed evaluation, see the evaluation forms for writing, revising, and proofreading, Assessment Portfolio 4.1–4.9.)

1. Science Fiction Description

- **Content/Unity.** The description uses elements of science fiction to identify an imaginative invention.
- **Organization/Coherence.** The science fiction description is arranged in a logical order such as part-by-part order.
- **Language/Style.** The science fiction description uses vivid and precise nouns, verbs, and modifiers.
- **Conventions.** The science fiction description avoids errors in spelling, grammar, usage, mechanics, and manuscript form.

► Additional practice is provided in the Essential Skills Practice Book: Writing 1.8.

2. Critical Essay

- **Content/Unity.** The essay analyzes the use of science fiction to satirize society.
- **Organization/Coherence.** The essay presents a clear thesis in an introductory paragraph. The following paragraphs of the essay present analysis and evidence from the selection to support the thesis. The essay has a solid conclusion.
- **Language/Style.** The essay uses vivid and precise nouns, verbs, and modifiers.
- **Conventions.** The essay avoids errors in spelling, grammar, usage, mechanics, and manuscript form.

► Additional practice is provided in the Essential Skills Practice Book: Writing 1.20.

Responding in Writing

1. **Creative Writing: Science Fiction Description.** Write a one-page description that features elements of science fiction. To begin, imagine that you are a scientist driven to create something that you hope will make life easier for people in your society. Freewrite possible ideas for such an invention. When you have settled on one idea, describe it using vivid details. What is your invention? How might it help people? How did you create it? If you would like, you might even write a scene featuring characters interacting with your invention, using dialogue to dramatize the scene.

2. **Critical Essay: Satire and Science Fiction.** In a short essay, describe the way in which Lem uses elements of science fiction to criticize, or satirize, aspects of society. To begin, describe the details that fit "The First Sally (A) or Trurl's Electronic Bard" into the category of science fiction. Then describe what aspects of society the story holds up to scrutiny. Refer to your responses to question 1 of Understanding Literature as a starting place when formulating your thesis.

Applied English/Tech Prep Skills

Technical Writing. Imagine that Trurl had been encouraged by his experiences with his invention, the electronic bard. If so, he may have wanted to produce more electronic bards, or to sell his idea to companies so that other versions might be manufactured. In any case, Trurl would need to have strong technical writing skills in order to explain how versions of his machine might be built and used correctly.

Developing good technical writing skills is important. Nearly every worker, regardless of his or her profession, will eventually be in the position of having to explain in writing a procedure or complex process. Review the Language Arts Survey 5.5, "Technical Writing." Then, following the guidelines for documenting technical procedures, document a procedure with which you are familiar. You may choose a topic from the following list or one of your own.

- tuning or replacing strings in a guitar
- making papier-mâché or some other craft project
- dancing a particular line dance
- setting up and playing a favorite game
- using a computer application
- planting a garden

ANSWERS FOR SKILLS ACTIVITIES

APPLIED ENGLISH/TECH PREP SKILLS

Students should choose a procedure with which they are very familiar. The documentation they produce should follow these guidelines:

- Alert the user of any danger.
- List tools or materials needed.
- Use the second-person imperative.
- Use language appropriate for the audience.
- Use short, simple steps.
- Arrange the steps in the order in which they should be completed.
- Include all necessary steps and exclude unnecessary steps or information.

► Additional practice is provided in the Essential Skills Practice Book: Applied English/Tech Prep 5.5.

Themes

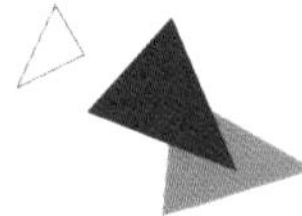

Science Fiction and Social Criticism

Science fiction—highly imaginative fiction containing fantastic elements based on scientific principles, discoveries, or laws—has been fueling the imagination, and fear, of readers for many years. Stories of this genre, which are similar to fantasy but with a scientific basis, often play on people's fascination with and concerns about technology, change, and explorations into the unknown. Often science fiction deals with speculations about the future, the distant past, or with worlds other than our own, such as distant planets, parallel universes, and worlds under the ground or sea. Over the years, science fiction has also become a vehicle for social criticism in which writers create imaginary worlds that reflect the worst in their own worlds or that express pessimism about human nature.

Elements of science fiction appear in literature as early as the eighteenth century. Earlier advances in astronomy and physics produced new telescopes that enabled people to look closely for the first time into the sky and wonder about the possibility of alien civilizations in distant galaxies. In 1726, English writer Jonathan Swift published *Gulliver's Travels,* a novel which features strange creatures, and French writer Voltaire's work *Micromegas,* published in 1752, features an imaginary trip to the moon. Works such as these were influenced by the new technology of the time.

Mary Shelley's *Frankenstein,* written in 1817, is one of the first true precursors of modern science fiction. Shelley based Dr. Frankenstein's creation of artificial life on nineteenth-century experiments with so-called animal magnetism, or the electrical energy believed to motivate living things and distinguish them from nonliving things. Shelley took what was at the time scientific theory and imagined what would happen if a scientist overstepped the boundaries between the human and the divine by trying to create life.

Modern science fiction as we know it first appeared in the late nineteenth century work of writers Jules Verne and H. G. Wells. Verne, a French writer, wrote adventure stories that were often set in the future. His classic science fiction novels include *Journey to the Center of the Earth* (1864) and *Twenty Thousand Leagues Under the Sea* (1870). These stories of future possibilities and the marvels of technology greatly influenced the early work of English writer H. G. Wells, whose books were published between 1895 and 1908. Wells is considered an important figure who laid the foundation for science fiction that is being written today. Wells's first novels, including *The Time Machine, War of the Worlds,* and *The First Men on the Moon,* display his fascination with technology and feature his speculations about the future. His later books, including *The Food of the Gods* and *When the Sleeper Awakes,* deal with social and political reform. Since Wells's time, writers have used science fiction as a useful and effective tool for criticizing the faults and excesses of humans and their institutions. Much of the work of Stanislaw Lem falls into this double category of science fiction and social criticism, as he often used his futuristic stories to criticize the Communist government and policies in his native Poland. Other science fiction writers who incorporate social criticism into their work are Aldous Huxley, author of *Brave New World;* Arthur C. Clarke, whose work includes *Childhood's End;* George Orwell, author of the well-known dystopia *1984;* Ursula K. Le Guin, whose work includes *The Dispossessed;* and Kurt Vonnegut, Jr., author of *Slaughterhouse Five.*

The Secret Player. *René Magritte, 1927*

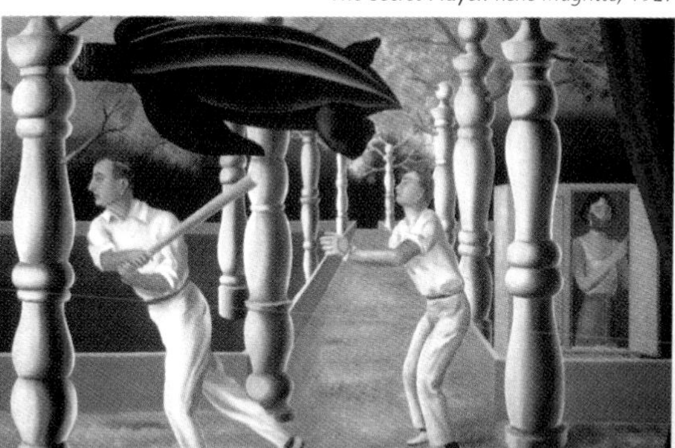

Additional Questions and Activities

Have students read one of the science fiction works listed on page 1077 or one of their own choosing. Students might also choose to view a science fiction movie. Students can then write a brief essay explaining what elements of science fiction are used in the work and what the work reveals about our society.

Literary Note

Discuss with students the similarities and differences between science fiction and fantasy. Share the following definition of *fantasy* with your class: A **fantasy** is a literary work that contains highly unrealistic elements. Fantasy differs from science fiction in that there is no scientific or pseudoscientific basis given for the unrealistic elements in fantasy. Fantasy, like science fiction, is often used to illuminate problems with our society by creating interesting alternatives.

Cross-curricular Activities

Mathematics and Sciences and Arts and Humanities

First, have students do some research about recent scientific and technological advances or discoveries. Students can discuss these advances or discoveries and their possible impacts on people or on the world.

Then, ask students to assume that this scientific idea is taken to the next level or exaggerated in some way. Ask them to imagine what the world would be like. Have them write a short story about the world they imagine.

ADDITIONAL RESOURCES

READER'S GUIDE

- Selection Worksheet 12.9

ASSESSMENT PORTFOLIO

- Selection Check Test 2.12.17
- Selection Test 2.12.18

ESSENTIAL SKILLS PRACTICE BOOKS

- Writing 1.8, 1.20
- Speaking and Listening 3.6

PREREADING EXTENSIONS

You might encourage students to write an essay about what they would do if they were told they would be given an opportunity to meet the president. What preparations would they make? What questions or issues would they want to discuss with the president? How would they feel immediately before meeting the president?

After students have read this excerpt, have them discuss the ways in which their thoughts and concerns about meeting the president compare and contrast with Chance's.

SUPPORT FOR LEP STUDENTS

PRONUNCIATIONS OF PROPER NOUNS AND ADJECTIVES

Jer • zy Ko • sin • ski (jer zē´ kō zin´skē)

ADDITIONAL VOCABULARY

briskly—in a quick or busy manner
glistened—shined
mere—nothing more or other than
proximity—state or quality of being near
reprimand—rebuke or scold

PREREADING

from *Being There*
by Jerzy Kosinski

About the Author

JERZY KOSINSKI
1933–1991

Jerzy Kosinski was born in Poland in 1933. His childhood was shattered in 1939 when Nazi Germany invaded his country. As Kosinski's parents were Jews, they went into hiding and entrusted him to the care of a rural woman who died two months after his arrival. Until the end of World War II, Kosinski wandered from one peasant village to another, seeking shelter in a countryside transfigured by war, intolerance, and suspicion. Although he was reunited with his parents after the war, Kosinski's horrific experiences rendered him mute for a time. In 1957, he escaped Communist Poland and emigrated to the United States.

Although he began his life in America with neither money nor friends, Kosinski soon achieved success. He earned a master's degree in history and political science through his studies at The New School for Social Research and at Columbia University. His first novel, *The Painted Bird,* a semi-autobiographical work about his experiences during the war, was published in 1965 and won *Le Prix du Meilleur Livre Etranger* (the best foreign book award) in France. In 1968, he published another novel, *Steps,* which won the 1969 National Book Award in Fiction. The American Academy of Arts and Letters honored him for his creative work in literature in 1970. Kosinski gave a critically acclaimed performance in the 1981 Warren Beatty film *Reds*.

About the Selection

Published in 1970, Jerzy Kosinski's novel ***Being There*** features an antihero named Chance. An **antihero** is a central character who lacks many of the qualities associated with heroes, such as beauty, courage, grace, intelligence, or moral scruples. As the novel opens, Chance lives with an elderly man and tends the man's garden. Chance has never lived anywhere else, knows no other life, and has no experience with the outside world, except through television. When his employer dies, Chance is forced out of the house and away from the garden that he loves. As he is leaving, he is accidentally hit by a car. The owner of the car insists upon bringing him to her house and tending to his injuries. When Chance states his name and says that he is a gardener, EE Rand, the woman in the car, mistakenly believes him to be a businessman named Chauncey Gardiner. He is welcomed into the Rand home and treated as a prominent guest. His frame of reference is limited to the two things with which he has experience—his garden and television.

CONNECTIONS: *Gardens as Literary Symbols*

Gardens are symbols of regeneration and life and are also associated with the Garden of Eden described in Genesis. Adam and Eve were expelled from this paradise for disobeying God. The expulsion from the garden symbolizes the archetypal fall from a state of grace and innocence into one of experience. In *Being There,* Chance is also expelled from a garden, but he does not lose his innocence when he is thrust into the world.

GOALS/OBJECTIVES

Studying this lesson will enable students to

- enjoy a humorous excerpt from a contemporary novel
- define *extended metaphor* and recognize this technique in a literary work
- define *antihero* and identify a character as such
- define and recognize *dramatic irony*
- write a new story
- write a critical essay comparing and contrasting Voltaire's Candide and Kosinski's Chance
- experiment with gardening

Think about a time when you did not know the answer to a question you were asked or when you did not understand a conversation in which you were expected to take part. How did you handle the situation? Did you ask questions or admit your lack of knowledge? Did you try to pretend that you understood? Did you change the subject or leave the conversation? Write about the conversation, how you participated, and how you felt about the situation.

READER'S JOURNAL

FROM

Being There

JERZY KOSINSKI

On Wednesday, as Chance was dressing, the phone rang. He heard the voice of Rand: "Good morning, Chauncey. Mrs. Rand wanted me to wish you good morning for her too, since she won't be at home today. She had to fly to Denver. But there's another reason I called. The President will address the annual meeting of the Financial Institute today; he is flying to New York and has just telephoned me from his plane. He knows I am ill and that, as the chairman, I won't be able to preside over the meeting as scheduled. But as I am feeling somewhat better today, the President has graciously decided to visit me before the luncheon. It's nice of him, don't you think? Well, he's going to land at Kennedy and then come over to Manhattan by helicopter. We can expect him here in about an hour." He stopped; Chance could hear his labored breathing. "I want you to meet him, Chauncey. You'll enjoy it. The President is quite a man, quite a man, and I know that he'll like and appreciate you. Now listen: the Secret Service people will be here before long to look over the place. It's strictly routine, something they have to do, no matter what, no matter where. If you don't mind, my secretary will notify you when they arrive."

"All right, Benjamin, thank you."

"Oh, yes, one more thing, Chauncey. I hope you won't mind . . . but they will have to search you personally as well. Nowadays, no one in close proximity to the President is allowed to have any sharp objects on his person—so don't show them your mind, Chauncey, they may take it away from you! See you soon, my friend!" He hung up.

There must be no sharp objects. Chance quickly removed his tie clip and put his comb on the table. But what had Rand meant when he said "your mind"? Chance looked at himself in the mirror. He liked what he saw: his hair glistened, his skin was ruddy, his freshly pressed dark suit fitted his body as bark covers a tree. Pleased, he turned on the TV.

After a while, Rand's secretary called to say that the President's men were ready to come up. Four men entered the room, talking and smiling easily, and began to go through it with an assortment of complicated instruments.

Chance sat at the desk, watching TV. Changing channels, he suddenly saw a huge helicopter descending in a field in Central Park. The announcer explained that at that very moment the President of the United States was landing in the heart of New York City.

1 *What does Rand warn Chance that the Secret Service people will do? What does he tell Chance not to show them? What does Chance make of Rand's remarks?*

2 *Who is going to visit Rand? Why is this person making this visit? What does Rand want Chance to do?*

READER'S JOURNAL

As an alternate activity, you might encourage students to write on one of the following topics:

- What do you think a completely innocent and naive person would think of contemporary American society? To what extent would he or she be able to understand it?
- What do you think are the effects of watching too much television? How might too much television affect a person's sense of what is and what is not real?

ANSWERS TO GUIDED READING QUESTIONS

1 He warns Chance that the Secret Service will search him for sharp objects. He tells Chance not to show them his mind. Chance removes his tie clip and comb, but he is puzzled by the remark about his mind.

2 The president is going to visit Rand. The president is making this visit because he is going to address the annual meeting of the Financial Institute, of which Rand is chairman. Since Rand is too sick to attend, the president has decided to visit him personally. Rand wants Chance to meet the president.

SPELLING AND VOCABULARY WORDS FROM THE SELECTION

imminent
oblivion
pallid

Answers to Guided Reading Questions

❶ Chance stammers and is uncertain about what he should do. He is not comfortable in this situation.

❷ Chance remember seeing the president before on television when the president attended a military parade. He remembers an image of the president waving his hand, his eyes "veiled with distant thought."

Additional Questions and Activities

Draw students' attention to the passages in which television is mentioned before Chance meets the president, such as the last paragraph on page 1079, the last full paragraph on page 1080, and the paragraph that spans pages 1080–1081. Ask students to discuss whether Chance seems to understand that the events he sees and remembers seeing on television are related in any way to what is about to happen to him—meeting the president. Does Chance make a distinction between television and life? Does television seem like real life to him, or does real life seem like television?

ANSWERS

Responses will vary.

Students might say that Chance does not seem to understand that seeing the president arriving on television and his memories of what the president is like on television are connected in any way to the man he is about to meet. Chance makes no distinction between television and life. Real life seems unreal—like television—to him.

❶ *How does Chance react to the president's arrival? Is he comfortable in this situation?*

❷ *Where does Chance remember seeing the president before? What image does Chance have of the president?*

The Secret Service men stopped working to watch too. "Well, the Boss has arrived," one of them said. "We better hurry with the other rooms." Chance was alone when Rand's secretary called to announce the President's imminent arrival.

"Thank you," he said. "I guess I'd better go down right now, don't you think?" He stammered a bit.

"I think it is time, sir."

Chance walked downstairs. The Secret Service men were quietly moving around the corridors, the front hall and the elevator entrance. Some stood near the windows of the study; others were in the dining room, the living room, and in front of the library. Chance was searched by an agent, who quickly apologized and then opened the door to the library for him.

Rand approached and patted Chance's shoulder. "I'm so glad that you'll have the opportunity to meet the Chief Executive. He's a fine man, with a sense of justice nicely contained by the law and an excellent judgment of both the pulse and purse of the electorate. I must say, it's very thoughtful of him to come to visit me now. Don't you agree?"

Chance agreed.

"What a pity EE isn't here," Rand declared. "She's a great fan of the President and finds him very attractive. She telephoned from Denver, you know."

Chance said that he knew about EE's call.

"And you didn't talk to her? Well, she'll call again; she'll want to know your impressions of the President and of how things went. . . . If I should be asleep, Chauncey, you will speak to her, won't you, and tell her all about the meeting?"

"I'll be glad to. I hope you're feeling well, sir. You do look better."

Rand moved uneasily in his chair. "It's all makeup, Chauncey—all make-up. The nurse was here all night and through the morning, and I asked her to fix me up so the President won't feel I'm going to die during our talk. No one likes a dying man, Chauncey, because few know what death is. All we know is the terror of it. You're an exception, Chauncey, I can tell. I know that you're not afraid. That's what EE and I admire in you: your marvelous balance. You don't stagger back and forth between fear and hope; you're a truly peaceful man! Don't disagree; I'm old enough to be your father. I've lived a lot, trembled a lot, was surrounded by little men who forgot that we enter naked and exit naked and that no accountant can audit life in our favor."

Rand looked pallid. He reached for a pill, swallowed it, and sipped some water from a glass. A phone rang. He picked up the receiver and said briskly: "Mr. Gardiner and I are ready. Show the President into the library." He replaced the receiver and then removed the glass of water from the desk top, placing it behind him on a bookshelf. "The President is here, Chauncey. He's on the way."

Chance remembered seeing the President on a recent television program. In the sunshine of a cloudless day, a military parade had been in progress. The President stood on a raised platform, surrounded by military men in uniforms covered with glittering medals, and by civilians in dark glasses. Below, in the open field, never-ending columns of soldiers marched, their faces riveted upon their leader, who waved his hand. The President's eyes were veiled with distant thought.

He watched the thousands in their ranks, who were reduced by the TV screen to mere

Words for Everyday Use

im • mi • nent (im´ə nənt) *adj.,* likely to happen without delay; impending

pal • lid (pal´id) *adj.,* faint in color; pale

Vocabulary in Context

- The thick, black clouds and the sudden chill in the air convinced us that rain was imminent.
- The movie frightened Ariana so much that her normally rosy cheeks turned pallid.

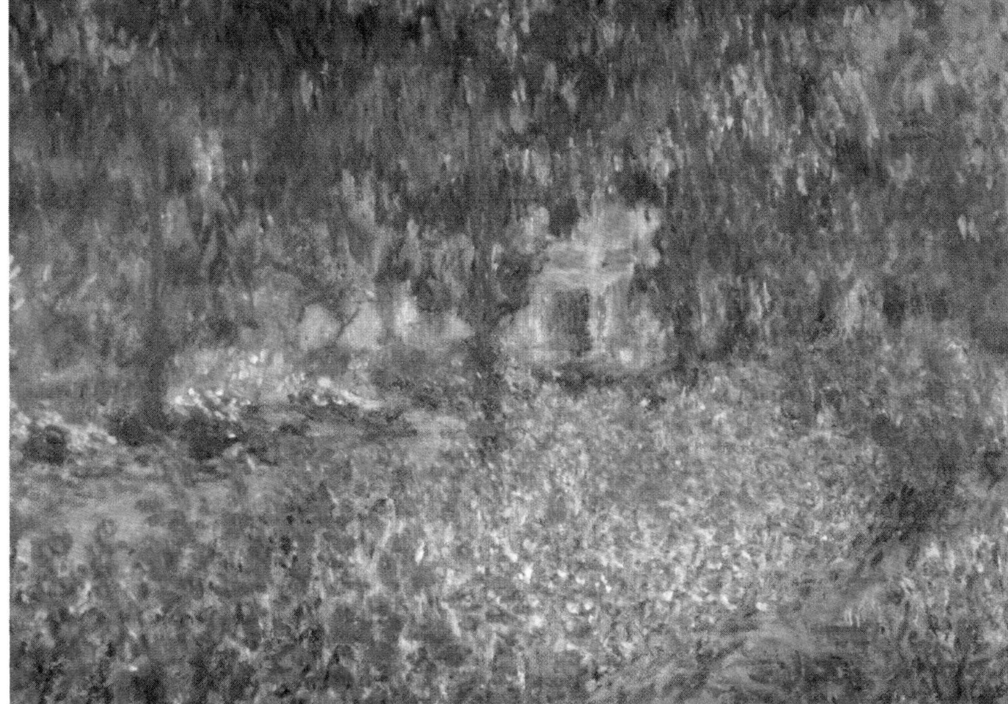

Monet's Garden. *Claude Monet, 1900*

mounds of lifeless leaves swept forward by a driving wind. Suddenly, down from the skies, jets swooped in tight, faultless formations. The military observers and the civilians on the reviewing stand barely had time to raise their heads when, like bolts of lightning, the planes streaked past the President, hurling down thunderous booms. The President's head once more pervaded the screen. He gazed up at the disappearing planes; a fleeting smile softened his face.

◆ ◆ ◆

"It's good to see you, Mr. President," Rand said, rising from his chair to greet a man of medium height who entered the room smiling. "How thoughtful of you to come all this way to look in on a dying man."

The President embraced him and led him to a chair. "Nonsense, Benjamin. Do sit down, now, and let me see you." The President seated himself on a sofa and turned to Chance.

"Mr. President," Rand said, "I want to introduce my dear friend, Mr. Chauncey Gardiner. Mr. Gardiner—the President of the United States of America." Rand sank into a chair, while the President extended his hand, a wide smile on his face. Remembering that during his TV press conferences, the President always looked straight at the viewers, Chance stared directly into the President's eyes.

"I'm delighted to meet you, Mr. Gardiner," the President said, leaning back on a sofa. "I've heard so much about you."

Chance wondered how the President could have heard anything about him. "Please do sit down, Mr. Gardiner," the President said. "Together, let's reprimand our friend Benjamin for the way he shuts himself up at home. Ben . . ." he leaned toward the old man—"this country needs

1 *What does Chance remember about the president? What does he do as a result of this memory? What might this action suggest to the president about Chance?*

Answers to Guided Reading Questions

1 Chance remembers that on TV the president always looks directly at the viewer. Chance looks directly into the president's eyes. This might suggest to the president that Chance is a straightforward, piercing, or perceptive individual.

Literary Note

Being There makes many allusions to the Biblical story of Adam and Eve in Genesis (see page 518). It may be worth having students read the chapters of *Being There* that precede this excerpt, so you can discuss the way Kosinski reworks certain details of the Biblical story to create a unique and entertaining tale. You might, for example, point out that Chance was raised to tend a garden, just like Adam and Eve, and this garden is all he knows of the world, just like Adam and Eve before their expulsion. Just as God makes life possible for Adam and Eve in the Garden of Eden, a mysterious and remote father-figure establishes Chance in his position as gardener. Just as Adam and Eve live in a state of bliss in Eden, Chance's life in the garden is free from the cares of the outside world. Kosinski's tale differs, however, in that while Adam and Eve are expelled from the garden for a sin—tasting the fruit from the Tree of Knowledge, which makes them lose their innocence—Chance is expelled for a much more prosaic reason—the owner of the house in which he lives dies. Unlike Adam and Eve, Chance is expelled into a much more confusing world with his innocence intact. Kosinski's story results from exploring the humorous results of what happens when a perfectly innocent character encounters modern America.

Integrated Skills Activities

SPEAKING AND LISTENING SKILLS

Chance spends a lot of time watching television. Ask students to assess their own television watching habits. Students might consider, as well, the types of movies they view. Have students read the Language Arts Survey 3.6, "Film and Television." Then ask them to develop a concrete plan to adjust their television and movie watching for one week.

▶ Additional practice is provided in the Essential Skills Practice Book: Speaking and Listening 3.6

Answers to Guided Reading Questions

❶ The president is impressed by Chance's comments. He thinks Chance is speaking metaphorically, suggesting that periods of cutting back or loss are necessary for regrowth in financial matters as they are in the natural world.

❷ Chance does not participate because he does not understand the conversation. He thinks Rand and the president are speaking in another language for security reasons.

❸ Chance's thoughts are compared to roots being yanked out of the ground. Chance speaks of the seasons in a garden.

Literary Note

You might encourage students to discuss the significance of Chance's name. Prompt students with the following questions: To what extent are the events described in this chapter more a result of chance or fortune than any action Chance takes? Is the success of Chance's meeting with the president the result of his wit and his words themselves or of luck? Explain. Why do you think that Kosinski chose this name for his main character? What was he trying to indicate about Chance?

❶ *What is the president's opinion of Chance's comments? How does the president interpret Chance's remarks?*

❷ *Why doesn't Chance take part in the conversation? What does he think Rand and the president are doing?*

❸ *To what are Chance's thoughts compared? What does Chance say when asked about the "bad season on The Street"?*

you, and I, as your Chief Executive, haven't authorized you to retire."

"I am ready for oblivion, Mr. President," said Rand mildly, "and, what's more, I'm not complaining; the world parts with Rand, and Rand parts with the world: a fair trade, don't you agree? Security, tranquillity, a well-deserved rest: all the aims I have pursued will soon be realized."

"Now be serious, Ben!" The President waved his hand. "I have known you to be a philosopher, but above all you're a strong, active businessman! Let's talk about life!" He paused to light a cigarette. "What's this I hear about your not addressing the meeting of the Financial Institute today?"

"I can't, Mr. President," said Rand. "Doctor's orders. And what's more," he added, "I obey pain."

"Well . . . yes . . . after all, it's just another meeting. And even if you're not there in person, you'll be there in spirit. The Institute remains your creation; your life's stamp is on all its proceedings."

The men began a long conversation. Chance understood almost nothing of what they were saying, even though they often looked in his direction, as if to invite his participation. Chance thought that they purposely spoke in another language for reasons of secrecy, when suddenly the President addressed him: "And you, Mr. Gardiner? What do you think about the bad season on The Street?"[1]

Chance shrank. He felt that the roots of his thoughts had been suddenly yanked out of their wet earth and thrust, tangled, into the unfriendly air. He stared at the carpet. Finally, he spoke: "In a garden," he said, "growth has its season. There are spring and summer, but there are also fall and winter. And then spring and summer again. As long as the roots are not severed, all is well and all will be well." He raised his eyes. Rand was looking at him, nodding. The President seemed quite pleased.

"I must admit, Mr. Gardiner," the President said, "that what you've just said is one of the most refreshing and optimistic statements I've heard in a very, very long time." He rose and stood erect, with his back to the fireplace. "Many of us forget that nature and society are one! Yes, though we have tried to cut ourselves off from nature, we are still part of it. Like nature, our economic system remains, in the long run, stable and rational, and that's why we must not fear to be at its mercy." The President hesitated for a moment, then turned to Rand. "We welcome the inevitable seasons of nature, yet we are upset by the seasons of our economy! How foolish of us!" He smiled at Chance. "I envy Mr. Gardiner his good solid sense. This is just what we lack on Capitol Hill." The President glanced at his watch, then lifted a hand to prevent Rand from rising. "No, no, Ben—you rest. I do hope to see you again soon. When you're feeling better, you and EE must come to visit us in Washington. And you, Mr. Gardiner . . . You will also honor me and my family with a visit, won't you? We'll all look forward to that!" He embraced Rand, shook hands swiftly with Chance, and strode out the door.

Rand hastily retrieved his glass of water, gulped down another pill, and slumped in his chair. "He is a decent fellow, the President, isn't he?" he asked Chance.

"Yes," said Chance, "though he looks taller on television."

"Oh, he certainly does!" Rand exclaimed. "But remember that he is a political being, who diplomatically waters with kindness

1. **The Street.** Wall Street, meaning the stock market

Words for Everyday Use

ob • liv • i • on (ə bliv´ ē ən) *n.,* condition of forgetting and being forgotten

Vocabulary in Context

• Andy longed to be famous so that many years from now, after he died, his name would not sink into oblivion.

every plant on his way, no matter what he really thinks. I do like him! By the way, Chauncey, did you agree with my position on credit and tight money as I presented it to the President?"

"I'm not sure I understood it. That's why I kept quiet."

"You said a lot, my dear Chauncey, quite a lot, and it is what you said and how you said it that pleased the President so much. He hears my sort of analysis from everyone, but, yours, unfortunately . . . seldom if ever at all."

The phone rang. Rand answered it and then informed Chance that the President and the Secret Service men had departed and that the nurse was waiting with an injection. He embraced Chance and excused himself. Chance went upstairs. When he turned the TV on, he saw the presidential motorcade moving along Fifth Avenue. Small crowds gathered on the sidewalks; the President's hand waved from the limousine's window. Chance did not know if he had actually shaken that hand only moments before. ■

❶ *What does Chance do after the president leaves? What does he see? What is his reaction to this sight?*

Responding to the Selection

What do you think of Chance? If the president asked for your opinion about making Chance an advisor, what would you say? Discuss with you classmates reasons for or against giving Chance such a position.

Answers to Guided Reading Questions

❶ Chance watches the president's departure on the television. He sees the president wave. He wonders if the hand that he sees is the one that he has just shaken.

Selection Check Test with Answers

EX. What does Rand call Chance?
He calls him Chauncey Gardiner.

1. To whom is Chance introduced?
He is introduced to the president.

2. What sharp object does Rand tell Chance to hide?
Rand tells Chance to hide his sharp mind.

3. What question causes Chance to shrink?
The president asks Chance what he thinks about "the bad season on The Street."

4. What does the visitor say about Chance's response?
He says that Chance's response is refreshing and optimistic.

5. What does Chance do after the visitor leaves?
He watches TV.

Responding to the Selection

As an alternate activity, you might encourage students to discuss whether they found this selection humorous. Was there a serious message as well? If so, what was it? Did the humor distract from this message or make it more clear?

Answers for Reviewing the Selection

RECALLING AND INTERPRETING

1. **Recalling.** Rand wants Chance to meet the president. He says the Secret Service will search him. He warns Chance not to show them his sharp mind or they might take it away. Chance is confused by this joke. **Interpreting.** Rand thinks Chance is intelligent and quick-witted. Chance is actually rather simple, contrary to Rand's opinion, which is also rather naive.

2. **Recalling.** Chance has learned from the TV. He remembers that the president looks straight at the viewers. **Interpreting.** Chance might have expected a man who looks directly at people and who appears thoughtful and larger than life because of camera angles.

3. **Recalling.** Chance does not participate because he does not understand the matters being discussed. He says that in a garden there are seasons of growth, but that there are also periods of fall and winter, and that as long as roots are not severed, all will be well. **Interpreting.** The president thinks that Chance is referring to periods of financial growth, stagnation, and decay. Students might suggest that Chance did not understand the question but only said what he knew about bad seasons in gardens and that his response was meant quite literally.

4. **Recalling.** Rand says that the president does not receive analysis like Chance's very often. After the president leaves, Chance watches him depart on TV. **Interpreting.** Chance is nonplussed by this event. He does not understand the effect that his words had on the president. His response to seeing the president on TV suggests that he does not have a firm grasp on reality.

SYNTHESIZING

Responses will vary. Possible responses are given.

5. Responses will vary, but students should provide reasons for their opinions.

Reviewing the Selection

RECALLING / **INTERPRETING**

1. Whom does Rand want Chance to meet? What does he say the Secret Service will do? What warning does he give Chance? Does Chance understand Rand's joke? ▶▶ What does Rand think of Chance's intelligence? What do Chance's thoughts and actions reveal about Rand's opinion?

2. From what source has Chance learned about the president? What does he remember when he is introduced to the president? ▶▶ In what ways might Chance's meeting with the president have conformed to or differed from his expectations?

3. Why does Chance refrain from participating in the discussion between the president and Rand, even though he notices inviting looks from them? What does he say when the president asks him about the bad season on The Street? ▶▶ Why is the president concerned about the economic situation? What does the president think that Chance means? What do you think Chance means?

4. What does Rand say about Chance's analysis? What does Chance do after the president leaves? ▶▶ How does Chance feel about this event? What does his reaction to this event suggest about his sense of reality?

SYNTHESIZING

5. Do you think that Chance's observations are as astute as the president and Rand think they are? Has he accurately assessed the situation? Explain. Is Chance's response an appropriate analogy for modern life? Why, or why not?

Understanding Literature (Questions for Discussion)

1. **Extended Metaphor.** An **extended metaphor** is a point-by-point presentation of one thing as though it were another. The description is meant as an implied comparison, inviting the reader to associate the thing being described with something that is quite different from it. When asked about the bad season on The Street, Chance replies by describing seasons in a garden. Explain why Rand or the president might have interpreted these remarks as an extended metaphor. Find other passages from this selection in which the reader is invited to compare something to garden imagery. What does the use of garden imagery as an extended metaphor throughout this selection reveal about Chance?

Answers for Understanding Literature

Responses will vary. Possible responses are given.

1. **Extended Metaphor.** Rand or the president might have felt that Chance was saying that in the financial world there is a time for growth and prosperity, but that there is also a time of cutting back and no improvement. Chance compares a television crowd to "mounds of lifeless leaves" and his thoughts to "roots" yanked into open air. Chance is so naive that he can only think about the world in relation to what he does understand—gardening.

2. **Antihero and Dramatic Irony.** Chance lacks the intelligence often associated with a hero. The reader recognizes that Chance is not being metaphorical in his speech. His lack of understanding is lost on the other characters, so the reader sees Chance as an antihero, while the other characters might see him as a hero.

2. **Antihero and Dramatic Irony.** An **antihero** is a central character who lacks many of the qualities traditionally associated with heroes, such as courage, beauty, grace, or intelligence. What qualities of a hero does Chance lack? What heroic qualities does he possess? Why do you think the author has chosen a character like Chance to serve as his main character? What is intriguing about him? **Dramatic irony** occurs when something is known by the reader or audience but unknown to the characters. Why is Chance an ironic antihero?

Responding in Writing

1. **Creative Writing: News Story.** Imagine that you are a reporter who was able to sit in on the meeting between Chance and the president. Write a news story in which you describe the meeting and the conversation, and explain Chance's theories and the president's reaction. You may wish to imagine and "report" what the president might say, after this discussion, about Chance's ideas or to speculate on what might happen as a result of this discussion. In your news story, answer the classic questions of journalism: who, what, when, where, how, and why. Give your story a catchy headline.

2. **Critical Essay: Naive Characters and Social Critique.** Chance in *Being There*, like the title character of *Candide* (see page 884), is a simple character, inexperienced in the ways of the world into which he has been thrust from an earthly "paradise." Compare and contrast the ways in which Kosinski and Voltaire use simple characters for effect. When planning your essay, consider the following questions: What can seeing the world through the eyes of simple or naive characters tell us about the world? Why might such characters be used for social criticism? What does the name of each character suggest? What difficulties or misunderstandings occur when the naive character interacts with others? Are these characters similar or do their experiences differ greatly? Use examples from both selections to support your response.

Project

Gardening. Chance is an expert on gardening. As a class, try your hands at gardening on some scale. If there is a place near your school or in your community where you can plant flowers or vegetables, try to get permission to tend this land. If there is no place to plant a garden, try a window box garden of flowers or herbs. Before you begin, you will need to assess the growing conditions in your garden space and consider appropriate plants. Consult gardening books or magazines, or talk to people with gardening experience, such as people who work in a greenhouse or members of a local gardening club. Use this information to plan and plant your garden. Make and carry out a care plan for your garden including watering, feeding, weeding, mulching, cutting, and anything else that needs to be done to tend to your plants. You might keep a log to record changes in your plants over time.

ANALYTIC SCALES FOR RESPONDING IN WRITING

Assign a score from 1 to 25 for each grading criterion below. (For more detailed evaluation, see the evaluation forms for writing, revising, and proofreading, Assessment Portfolio 4.1–4.9.)

1. News Story

- **Content/Unity.** The news story reports what occurred during Chance's meeting with the president.
- **Organization/Coherence.** The news report presents details in a logical order, most likely chronological.
- **Language/Style.** The news report uses vivid and precise nouns, verbs, and modifiers.
- **Conventions.** The news report avoids errors in spelling, grammar, usage, mechanics, and manuscript form.

▶ Additional practice is provided in the Essential Skills Practice Book: Writing 1.8.

2. Critical Essay

- **Content/Unity.** The essay compares and contrasts Voltaire's character Candide with Kosinski's character Chance.
- **Organization/Coherence.** The essay begins with an introduction that includes the thesis of the essay. The introduction is followed by supporting paragraphs with clear transitions. The essay ends with a solid conclusion.
- **Language/Style.** The essay uses vivid and precise nouns, verbs, and modifiers.
- **Conventions.** The essay avoids errors in spelling, grammar, usage, mechanics, and manuscript form.

▶ Additional practice is provided in the Essential Skills Practice Book: Writing 1.20.

PROJECT NOTES

See the evaluation form for projects, Assessment Portfolio 4.12.

Gardening. You may wish to locate an experienced gardener to come to your classroom and advise and work with students to ensure this project's success. Students might share some of the vegetables or flowers they grow with others. You might encourage them to bring flowers to a children's wing in a hospital or to a nursing home or their produce to a local food bank or soup kitchen.

ADDITIONAL RESOURCES

READER'S GUIDE

- Selection Worksheet 12.10

ASSESSMENT PORTFOLIO

- Selection Check Test 2.12.19
- Selection Test 2.12.20

ESSENTIAL SKILLS PRACTICE BOOKS

- Writing 1.8, 1.20

PREREADING EXTENSIONS

You might point out that as a person of mixed heritage, Bessie Head experienced firsthand the discrimination of apartheid in South Africa. Bessie Head's mother was white and her father was African. Relationships between races were illegal in South Africa during this period, so the relationship between Head's parents was viewed as scandalous. Head's mother was locked in a mental asylum while pregnant with Bessie, and Head's father disappeared not long after the relationship was discovered. Head was raised by foster parents for a time before being sent to an orphanage school. You might encourage students to read more about apartheid in Insights: Apartheid on page 203.

SUPPORT FOR LEP STUDENTS

PRONUNCIATIONS OF PROPER NOUNS AND ADJECTIVES

Ke • go • le • ti • le (kē gō lē tē´lē)
Ma • tha • ta (mä thä´tä)
Mma Klau • du (mä ko͞o´do͞o)
Ne • o (nē´ō)

ADDITIONAL VOCABULARY

ascertain—make certain

PREREADING

"Snapshots of a Wedding"
by Bessie Head

About the Author

BESSIE HEAD
1937–1986

Bessie Head, a writer whose three novels and two historical chronicles gained her international recognition, was born in Pietermaritzburg, South Africa. Trained as a teacher, she taught elementary school for several years before working as a reporter in Johannesburg and Cape Town, two of South Africa's largest cities. Head later decided to leave South Africa because she could no longer tolerate the racism of the South African government. She moved to Botswana, a country north of South Africa that was formerly a British territory known as Bechuanaland. Most of Head's writing is inspired by life in Botswana. Her work explores political oppression, injustice, racism, and personal freedom. Her three novels are titled *When Rain Clouds Gather* (1969); *Maru* (1971); and *A Question of Power* (1973). Head also published a collection of interviews with residents of her own village in Botswana called *Serowe: Village of the Rain Wind* (1981).

About the Selection

"Snapshots of a Wedding" is one of the short stories in Bessie Head's collection entitled *The Collector of Tales*. Several of the stories in this collection describe life in Botswana, both before and after it gained full independence from Great Britain in 1966. By telling the story of one family preparing for a wedding, Head shows the tension that results when traditional ways of life meet with the modern world, and when people with different value systems try to coexist peacefully.

CONNECTIONS: Marriage Customs

Marriage of some kind has existed for many thousands of years in most cultures, and people have developed a variety of elaborate rituals to surround it. Marriage customs change according to the laws, beliefs, and attitudes of specific cultures and specific periods in history, but they have many elements in common. In almost every society a main function of marriage is the raising of children for the continuation of the tribe, clan, or society. Thus, many marriage rituals relate to fertility. Other rituals, such as the joining of hands, an exchange of rings, or the tying of garments, relate to the idea of marriage as a sacred union. The offering of gifts to the bride and bridegroom is another ritual common to many cultures and symbolizes a wish for good fortune for the couple. In some cultures, marriage is seen as a free choice and is associated with love. In many other societies, marriage is not a matter of choice. Parents or the community decide who will marry whom.

GOALS/OBJECTIVES

Studying this lesson will enable students to

- have a positive experience reading a story about the effects of European influences in a traditional society
- explain how point of view can affect a story
- identify changes in mood within a literary work
- write "snapshots" of an important event in someone's life
- write a critical essay explaining how the story reveals a clash between cultures
- research the ceremonies of different cultures

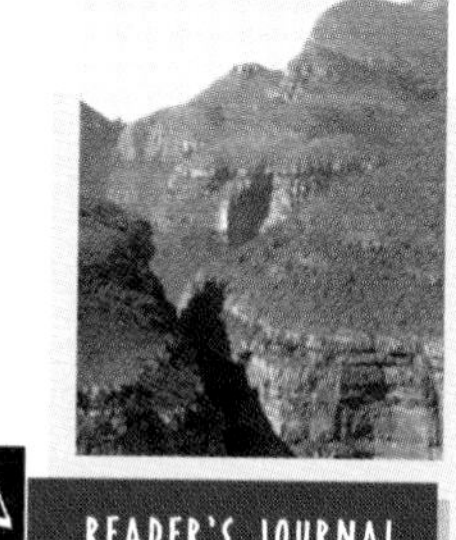

Why do people sometimes feel threatened by others whose values and ideas are different from their own? Have you ever witnessed such a clash of values and ideas? Have you ever had a conflict or a discussion with someone whose system of values and ideas was vastly different from yours? Write about this situation in your journal.

READER'S JOURNAL

"Snapshots of a Wedding"

BESSIE HEAD

Wedding days always started at the haunting, magical hour of early dawn when there was only a pale crack of light on the horizon. For those who were awake, it took the earth hours to adjust to daylight. The cool and damp of the night slowly arose in shimmering waves like water and even the forms of the people who bestirred themselves at this unearthly hour were distorted in the haze; they appeared to be dancers in slow motion, with fluid, watery forms. In the dim light, four men, the relatives of the bridegroom, Kegoletile, slowly herded an ox before them towards the yard of MmaKhudu, where the bride, Neo, lived. People were already astir in MmaKhudu's yard, yet for a while they all came and peered closely at the distorted fluid forms that approached, to ascertain if it were indeed the relatives of the bridegroom. Then the ox, who was a rather stupid fellow and unaware of his sudden and impending end as meat for the wedding feast, bellowed casually his early morning yawn. At this the beautiful ulululating of the women rose and swelled over the air like water bubbling rapidly and melodiously over the stones of a clear, sparkling stream. In between ululating all the while, the women began to weave about the yard in the wedding dance; now and then they bent over and shook their buttocks in the air. As they handed over the ox, one of the bridegroom's relatives joked:

'This is going to be a modern wedding.' He meant that a lot of the traditional courtesies had been left out of the planning for the wedding day; no one had been awake all night preparing diphiri[1] or the traditional wedding breakfast of pounded meat and samp;[2] the bridegroom said he had no church and did not care about such things; the bride was six months pregnant and showing it, so there was just going to be a quick marriage ceremony at the police camp.

'Oh, we all have our own ways,' one of the bride's relatives joked back. 'If the times are

1. **diphiri.** Cereal-like dish
2. **samp.** Coarse meal of Indian corn

❶ *When do wedding days begin? What do relatives of the bridegroom bring to the bride? Why?*

❷ *What kind of wedding is taking place? Why is it described in this way?*

WORDS FOR EVERYDAY USE

ul • u • late (yo͞ol´ yo͞o lāt´) *vi.,* howl or hoot

READER'S JOURNAL

You might choose to have students write specifically about how they see other cultures or values impacting or changing their own beliefs and values.

ANSWERS TO GUIDED READING QUESTIONS

❶ Wedding days always began in the early dawn. Relatives of the bridegroom bring an ox, who will end up being part of the wedding feast.

❷ A modern wedding is taking place. It is described as being modern because a lot of tradition has been left out, at the request of the bridegroom.

SPELLING AND VOCABULARY WORDS FROM THE SELECTION

`ululate

VOCABULARY IN CONTEXT

• In certain cultures, funerals are attended by hired mourners who loudly ululate to grieve over the death.

Answers to Guided Reading Questions

❶ The bride's family thinks the bride is rude and arrogant, and they are anxious to be rid of her. Neo, the bride, has an education, and her family feels that because of this, she thinks she is better than everyone else. They keep their feelings secret; Neo does not know about them.

❷ Neo's relatives feel Kegoletile has chosen her as his bride because she can earn a good income and perhaps help them to be wealthy.

❸ Kegoletile is torn, even after he makes the decision to marry Neo, between Neo and Mathata.

❹ Neo is educated and will most likely have many opportunities in her life. Mathata is uneducated and will most likely be a housemaid.

Cultural/Historical Note

Inform students that Botswana, the country to which Head moved and the setting for many of her literary works, is a landlocked country in Southern Africa. Much of it is covered by the Kalahari Desert. The country was a British protectorate named Bechuanaland until 1966. Botswana is named after one of its largest ethnic groups, the Tswana. The Tswana live in large villages and raise cattle, which are often grazed in lands distant from the village. Each village has a communal cattle enclosure, called a *kraal,* and a *kgotla,* or public meeting place near both the chief's house and the kraal. Each village comprises its own small democracy, with disputes being settled in the kgotla. Extended families live together in the same compound in the village, and traditional duties for males involve tending cattle. Traditional duties for females, as mentioned in this selection, involve carrying water. Life in Botswana is still strongly centered on traditional activities.

changing, we keep up with them.' And she weaved away ululating joyously.

❶ *How does the bride's family feel about the bride? Why do they feel this way? Does Neo know about these feelings?*

❷ *According to Neo's relatives, why has Kegoletile chosen Neo as his bride?*

Whenever there was a wedding the talk and gossip that preceded it were appalling, except that this time the relatives of the bride, Neo, kept their talk a strict secret among themselves. They were anxious to be rid of her; she was an impossible girl with haughty, arrogant ways. Of all her family and relatives, she was the only one who had completed her 'O' levels[3] and she never failed to rub in this fact. She walked around with her nose in the air; illiterate relatives were beneath her greeting—it was done in a clever way, she just turned her head to one side and smiled to herself or when she greeted it was like an insult; she stretched her hand out, palm outspread, swung it down laughing with a gesture that plainly said: 'Oh, that's you!' Only her mother seemed bemused by her education. At her own home Neo was waited on hand and foot. Outside her home nasty remarks were passed. People bitterly disliked conceit and pride.

'That girl has no manners!' the relatives would remark. 'What's the good of education if it goes to someone's head so badly they have no respect for the people? Oh, she is not a person.'

❸ *What secret conflict does Kegoletile experience?*

❹ *What is the difference between Neo and Mathata?*

Then they would nod their heads in that fatal way, with predictions that one day life would bring her down. Actually, life had treated Neo rather nicely. Two months after completing her 'O' levels she became pregnant by Kegoletile with their first child. It soon became known that another girl, Mathata, was also pregnant by Kegoletile. The difference between the two girls was that Mathata was completely uneducated; the only work she would ever do was that of a housemaid, while Neo had endless opportunities before her—typist, bookkeeper, or secretary. So Neo merely smiled; Mathata was no rival. It was as though the decision had been worked out by circumstance because when the families converged on Kegoletile at the birth of the children—he was rich in cattle and they wanted to see what they could get—he of course immediately proposed marriage to Neo; and for Mathata, he agreed to a court order to pay a maintenance of R10.00[4] a month until the child was twenty years old. Mathata merely smiled too. Girls like her offered no resistance to the approaches of men; when they lost them, they just let things ride.

'He is of course just running after the education and not the manners,' Neo's relatives commented, to show they were not fooled by human nature. 'He thinks that since she is as educated as he is they will both get good jobs and be rich in no time. . .'

Educated as he was, Kegoletile seemed to go through a secret conflict during the year he prepared a yard for his future married life with Neo. He spent most of his free time in the yard of Mathata. His behaviour there wasn't too alarming but he showered Mathata with gifts of all kinds—food, fancy dresses, shoes and underwear. Each time he came, he brought a gift and each time Mathata would burst out laughing and comment: 'Ow, Kegoletile, how can I wear all these dresses? It's just a waste of money! Besides, I manage quite well with the R10.00 you give every month for the child . . .'

She was a very pretty girl with black eyes like stars; she was always smiling and happy; immediately and always her own natural self. He knew what he was marrying—something quite the opposite, a new kind of girl with false postures and acquired, grand-madame ways. And yet, it didn't pay a man these days to look too closely into his heart. They all wanted as wives, women who were big money-earners and they were so ruthless about it! And yet it was as though the society itself stamped each of its individuals with its own particular brand of wealth and Kegoletile had not yet escaped it; he had about him an engaging humility and eagerness to help and please that made him loved

3. **'O' levels.** Examination for college
4. **R10.00.** Ten rands; a rand is a monetary unit in South Africa

South African landscape

and respected by all who knew him. During those times he sat in Mathata's yard, he communicated nothing of the conflict he felt but he would sit on a chair with his arms spread out across its back, turn his head sideways and stare at what seemed to be an empty space beside him. Then he would smile, stand up and walk away. Nothing dramatic. During the year he prepared the huts in his new yard, he frequently slept at the home of Neo.

Relatives on both sides watched this division of interest between the two yards and one day when Neo walked patronisingly into the yard of an aunt, the aunt decided to frighten her a little.

'Well aunt,' she said, with the familiar careless disrespect which went with her so-called, educated, status. 'Will you make me some tea? And how's things?'

The aunt spoke very quietly.

'You may not know it, my girl, but you are hated by everyone around here. The debate we have going is whether a nice young man like Kegoletile should marry bad-mannered rubbish like you. He would be far better off if he married a girl like Mathata, who though uneducated, still treats people with respect.'

The shock the silly girl received made her stare for a terrified moment at her aunt. Then she stood up and ran out of the house. It wiped the superior smile off her face and brought her down a little. She developed an anxiety to greet people and also an anxiety about securing Kegoletile as a husband—that was why she became pregnant six months before the marriage could take place. In spite of this, her own relatives still disliked her and right up to the day of the wedding they were still debating whether Neo was a suitable wife for any man. No one would have guessed it though with all the dancing, ululating and happiness expressed in the yard and streams of guests gaily ululated themselves along the pathways with wedding gifts precariously balanced on their heads. Neo's maternal aunts, all sedately decked up in shawls, sat in a select group by themselves in a corner of the yard. They sat on the bare ground with their legs stretched out before them but they were served like

❶ *Why would it be hard to know the true feelings of the family on the day of the wedding?*

❷ *What does an aunt say to Neo to shock her? What effect do her words have on Neo?*

Answers to Guided Reading Questions

❶ Neo's family is dancing and celebrating even though they are not fond of Neo.

❷ The aunt tells Neo that she is hated by everyone and that Kegoletile would be better off if he married Mathata. The aunt's words shock Neo, fill her with anxiety, and humble her a bit.

Cross-curricular Activities

SOCIAL STUDIES

You might encourage students to work in groups to prepare oral reports on Botswana. Interesting topics for them to consider are the following:

- Botswana received a large influx in population early in the nineteenth century due to the activities of the leader of the Zulu Empire, Shaka. Who was Shaka? How did he form the Zulu Empire? How extensive was this empire, and why did it collapse?
- Botswana was one of the many regions involved in the Boer War. What other nations were involved in the Boer War? When and why did it take place? What were the results of this war for the people in the involved nations? for Botswana?

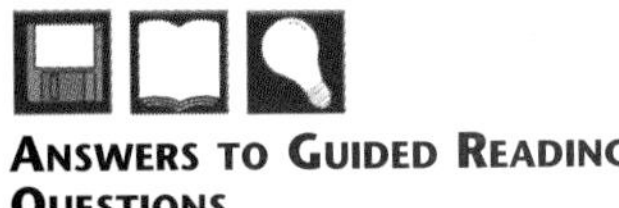

Answers to Guided Reading Questions

❶ It is supposed to symbolize plowing the land, and Neo will most likely not do that kind of work. She already has a well-paid job in an office.

❷ The request for water signifies the tradition of the bride carrying water to her in-law's home. Kegoletile is told that he must plow and supply his maternal aunts with corn each year. Neo is told that she must obey her husband and carry water for him.

❸ She says loudly "Be a good wife!"

Selection Check Test with Answers

EX. When do wedding days begin?

Wedding days always begin in the early dawn.

1. What do relatives of the bridegroom bring to the bride?

Relatives of the bridegroom bring an ox, which will end up being part of the wedding feast.

2. What kind of wedding does the bridegroom's relative say is taking place?

He says a modern wedding is taking place.

3. How does the bride's family feel about the bride?

The bride's family thinks of the bride as rude and arrogant, and they are anxious to be rid of her.

4. What is the difference between Neo and Mathata?

Neo is educated and will most likely have many opportunities in her life. Mathata is uneducated and will most likely be a housemaid.

5. What does the aunt who had scolded Neo say to Neo on the wedding day?

She says loudly, "Be a good wife!"

---

❶ *Why is the chopping at the ground with a hoe only a formality?*

❷ *What does the request for water stand for? What are Neo and Kegoletile told they must do to honor tradition and their marriage vows?*

❸ *What does the aunt who had scolded Neo say to Neo on the wedding day?*

queens the whole day long. Trays of tea, dry white bread, plates of meat, rice, and salad were constantly placed before them. Their important task was to formally hand over the bride to Kegoletile's maternal aunts when they approached the yard at sunset. So they sat the whole day with still, expressionless faces, waiting to fulfil this ancient rite.

Equally still and expressionless were the faces of the long column of women, Kegoletile's maternal aunts, who appeared outside the yard just as the sun sank low. They walked slowly into the yard indifferent to the ululating that greeted them and seated themselves in a group opposite Neo's maternal aunts. The yard became very silent while each group made its report. Kegoletile had provided all the food for the wedding feast and a maternal aunt from his side first asked:

'Is there any complaint? Has all gone well?'

'We have no complaint,' the opposite party replied.

'We have come to ask for water,' Kegoletile's side said, meaning that from times past the bride was supposed to carry water in her in-law's home.

'It is agreed to,' the opposite party replied.

Neo's maternal aunts then turned to the bridegroom and counselled him: 'Son, you must plough and supply us with corn each year.'

Then Kegoletile's maternal aunts turned to the bride and counselled her: 'Daughter, you must carry water for your husband. Beware, that at all times, he is the owner of the house and must be obeyed. Do not mind if he stops now and then and talks to other ladies. Let him feel free to come and go as he likes . . .'

The formalities over, it was now time for Kegoletile's maternal aunts to get up, ululate and weave and dance about the yard. Then, still dancing and ululating, accompanied by the bride and groom they slowly wound their way to the yard of Kegoletile where another feast had been prepared. As they approached his yard, an old woman suddenly dashed out and chopped at the ground with a hoe. It was all only a formality. Neo would never be the kind of wife who went to the lands to plow. She already had a well-paid job in an office as a secretary. Following on this another old woman took the bride by the hand and led her to a smeared and decorated courtyard wherein had been placed a traditional animal-skin Tswana mat. She was made to sit on the mat and a shawl and kerchief were placed before her. The shawl was ceremonially wrapped around her shoulders; the kerchief tied around her head—the symbols that she was now a married woman.

Guests quietly moved forward to greet the bride. Then two girls started to ululate and dance in front of the bride. As they both turned and bent over to shake their buttocks in the air, they bumped into each other and toppled over. The wedding guests roared with laughter. Neo, who had all this time been stiff, immobile, and rigid, bent forward and her shoulders shook with laughter.

The hoe, the mat, the shawl, the kerchief, the beautiful flute-like ululating of the women seemed in itself a blessing on the marriage but all the guests were deeply moved when out of the crowd, a woman of majestic, regal bearing slowly approached the bride. It was the aunt who had scolded Neo for her bad manners and modern ways. She dropped to her knees before the bride, clenched her fists together and pounded the ground hard with each clenched fist on either side of the bride's legs. As she pounded her fists she said loudly:

'Be a good wife! Be a good wife!' ■

Responding to the Selection

For which character or characters do you feel the most understanding? What qualities does this character possess with which you can identify? Are there any characters whom you are unable to understand? Why?

Reviewing the Selection

RECALLING / INTERPRETING

1. When does the wedding day begin? What traditions are described in the story's first paragraph? ▶▶ What does the first paragraph reveal about the values of the people holding the wedding?

2. What does Neo's family say about her? When does Neo learn how people feel about her? How do the aunt's words affect Neo? ▶▶ Why might the older relatives feel so much hostility toward Neo and her education? Do you think that Neo seems as arrogant as people say she is?

3. What are the differences between Neo's personality and background and Mathata's personality and background? ▶▶ How does Kegoletile feel about his decision concerning whom he will marry? Why does he make the decision he makes? Provide evidence from the story to support your responses.

4. What accident occurs as two women dance in front of the bride? What is Neo's reaction to this accident? What does the aunt do and say after she moves out of the crowd? ▶▶ Explain why the "snapshot" of the dancing accident is placed near the "snapshot" of the majestic aunt who represents the old ways? How might the aunt's ideas about being a good wife differ from Neo's ideas?

SYNTHESIZING

5. Why are the brief scenes in this story described as "snapshots"? What serious conflict do these "snapshots" reveal?

RESPONDING TO THE SELECTION

Students may wish to discuss the attitudes toward women revealed in this society and their reactions to these attitudes.

ANSWERS FOR REVIEWING THE SELECTION

RECALLING AND INTERPRETING

1. **Recalling.** The wedding day begins at dawn. In the first paragraph, women are dancing as men deliver an ox to the home of the bride. **Interpreting.** A reader can tell from the first paragraph that the people described value traditions.

2. **Recalling.** Neo's family says that she is rude, arrogant, and haughty. Neo learns about how her family feels from an aunt. The aunt's words shock Neo and fill her with anxiety. She becomes nervous around people, even Kegoletile. **Interpreting.** The older relatives might feel hostility because education represents a way of life with which they are not familiar. They feel education has made Neo arrogant and rude and that she might have been better off without it. Students are likely to say that Neo does not seem arrogant at this point—she seems to have had no idea that people had such strong feelings about her.

3. **Recalling.** Neo is educated, has numerous opportunities, and walks around with more confidence and self-assurance. Mathata is uneducated, not forceful about her own needs, and appears to be always smiling and happy. (cont.)

ANSWERS FOR REVIEWING THE SELECTION (CONT.)

Interpreting. Kegoletile is filled with conflict about his decision. His decision to marry Neo is influenced by the fact that she can earn high wages. It is the trend for men to marry such women, but he is still drawn to Mathata.

4. **Recalling.** The women bump into each other. Neo laughs. The aunt clenches her fists, pounds the earth, and tells Neo in a loud voice to be a good wife. **Interpreting.** The accident and the crowd's reaction to the accident represent the changing times and the fall of tradition, and the "majestic" aunt represents the old ways and the old ideas about marriage. The aunt's idea of a good wife is someone like Mathata, while Neo is drawn to a new way of life and to taking a more modern role in her marriage.

(cont.)

ANSWERS FOR REVIEWING THE SELECTION (CONT.)

SYNTHESIZING

Responses will vary. Possible responses are given.

5. They are brief scenes filled with dialogue and activity. Each scene provides the reader with a different picture of the events leading up to the wedding. The conflict is between old ways and new ways, traditional life and modern life.

ANSWERS FOR UNDERSTANDING LITERATURE

Responses will vary. Possible responses are given.

1. Point of View. Head wants to give the reader the feeling that he or she is looking at a collection of snapshots. She also wants people to be able to look at the events of the wedding objectively. If the story were told strictly from the point of view of one character, the reader would be more inclined to see the events only from the perspective of that character and not have any understanding of other characters' perspectives. *Responses will vary.*

2. Mood. The mood is solemn and respectful as the sacred day is described. Descriptions of people carefully following traditions are told with a certain amount of distance—at this point nothing is known about individual characters. The line "This is going to be a modern wedding" jars the reader and prepares the reader for new information about what is actually going on "behind the scenes" of this wedding, which seems traditional only on the surface. The mood of the final paragraphs is different in that the reader has more information about characters and has a much clearer picture of family tensions and the conflicts that exist between the characters.

Understanding Literature (Questions for Discussion)

1. **Point of View. Point of view** is the vantage point from which a story is told. In "Snapshots of a Wedding," Bessie Head tells her story not from the perspective of one of the main characters, but in the third person, from the point of view of a bystander who is familiar with the issues surrounding the wedding. Why might Head have chosen to tell the story in this way? How might the story have been different if it had been told by Neo, Mathata, Kegoletile, or one of the relatives?

2. **Mood. Mood**, or **atmosphere**, is the emotion created in the reader by part or all of a literary work. What is the mood in the opening paragraph of the story? In what way does this mood change with the line from one of the bridegroom's relatives, "This is going to be a modern wedding"? In what way is the mood of the closing description of the wedding different from the mood of the opening paragraph? Why has the mood changed?

Responding in Writing

1. **Creative Writing: Snapshots of an Event.** Bessie Head tells the story of an important event in the life of one African community in snapshots—brief and vivid scenes that give important bits of information about characters and relationships. Write your own descriptive "snapshots" of an important time in your life or the life of someone close to you. You might describe the events leading to a wedding, graduation, birth, or adventure in your own family. Feel free to write about any event, day, or incident that has affected you in some way. First decide what you want your snapshots to convey to your reader. Then make a chart like the one below in which you organize vivid details about actions, dialogue, and characters. Sort out which details are important and which are not as important. From your chart, write three or four descriptive snapshots of your event.

Possible Snapshots	Characters Involved	Actions	Dialogue

2. **Critical Essay: Analyzing Theme: Cultural Change.** "Snapshots of a Wedding" presents pictures of cultural change. Bessie Head focuses on a wedding to show how the realities of a modern world can clash with customs and beliefs of the past. Write a short essay in which you discuss how this theme is treated in the story. You might want to address the following questions: What parts of the story show the contrast between the old world and the modern world of which Neo is a part? In what way does the author use the characters of Mathata and Neo to illustrate this contrast? How does the conflict between old and new values affect Kegoletile? Form a thesis based on one or more of these questions or on another aspect of the theme of the story. Use examples from the story to support your thesis.

PROJECT

Ceremonies. It is interesting to explore the traditional ceremonies of different times and cultures. Break into groups of two, three, or four. Each group should be in charge of researching an important ceremony from a particular time and place. In your initial research, try to discover interesting ceremonies surrounding marriage, birth, death, or other life-changing events. Once you have decided on a particular ceremony, plan a presentation for your classmates on one aspect of the ceremony. For example, you might learn a traditional song or dance; put together, paint, or draw pictures of traditional costumes; or prepare an authentic meal traditional to your ceremony. Try to give your classmates an idea of the importance of the ceremony and the meaning behind the aspect of the ceremony that you are presenting. After each group has had a chance to give its presentation, have a class discussion about ceremonies and rituals. Discuss the following topics:

- Why are ceremonies and rituals so important in peoples' lives?
- As the world changes, do ceremonies and rituals change? Are there fewer of them? Give examples.

ANALYTIC SCALES FOR RESPONDING IN WRITING

Assign a score from 1 to 25 for each grading criterion below. (For more detailed evaluation, see the evaluation forms for writing, revising, and proofreading, Assessment Portfolio 4.1–4.9.)

1. Snapshots of an Event

- **Content/Unity.** The writing presents "snapshots," or brief and vivid scenes, of an important event in a person's life.
- **Organization/Coherence.** Each scene is written in a sensible order, and the scenes themselves are ordered logically.
- **Language/Style.** The writing uses vivid and precise nouns, verbs, and modifiers.
- **Conventions.** The writing avoids errors in spelling, grammar, usage, mechanics, and manuscript form.

► Additional practice is provided in the Essential Skills Practice Book: Writing 1.8.

2. Critical Essay

- **Content/Unity.** The essay explains how "Snapshots of a Wedding" depicts cultures in conflict and cultural change.
- **Organization/Coherence.** The essay begins with an introduction that includes the thesis of the essay. The introduction is followed by supporting paragraphs with clear transitions. The essay ends with a solid conclusion.
- **Language/Style.** The essay uses vivid and precise nouns, verbs, and modifiers.
- **Conventions.** The essay avoids errors in spelling, grammar, usage, mechanics, and manuscript form.

► Additional practice is provided in the Essential Skills Practice Book: Writing 1.20.

PROJECT NOTES

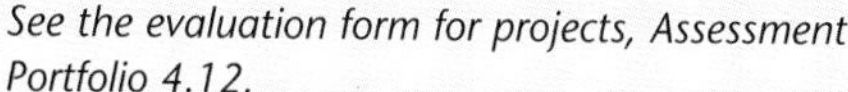

See the evaluation form for projects, Assessment Portfolio 4.12.

Ceremonies. If students have difficulty coming up with topics, share with them the following possible ceremonies and rituals to research: the coming of age ceremony in Japan, Hindu wedding customs, Chinese ceremonies for the birth of a male infant, modern American Christian wedding traditions, Jewish wedding ceremonies, or Muslim funeral ceremonies.

ADDITIONAL RESOURCES

READER'S GUIDE

- Selection Worksheet 12.11

ASSESSMENT PORTFOLIO

- Selection Check Test 2.12.21
- Selection Test 2.12.22

ESSENTIAL SKILLS PRACTICE BOOKS

- Writing 1.8, 1.10, 1.20
- Study and Research 4.14
- Applied English/Tech Prep 5.5

PREREADING EXTENSIONS

If students have not yet read James Joyce's "Araby," you might encourage them to do so before reading the selection. Tell them that even though the main character in Desai's story is much younger than the narrator of "Araby," both suffer a disappointment that makes them lose some of their innocence, and both express negative feelings about their new realizations. After students have read both works, encourage them to discuss the similarities and differences in the two characters' experiences.

SUPPORT FOR LEP STUDENTS

PRONUNCIATIONS OF PROPER NOUNS AND ADJECTIVES

A • ni • ta De • sai (ä nē´tä də sī´)
Ra • ghu (rä gū´)
Ra • vi (rä vē´)

ADDITIONAL VOCABULARY

arid—dry and barren
dogged—stubborn; not giving in readily
fray—noisy quarrel or fight
milling—slowly circling
seethed—was violently agitated or disturbed
sidled—move sideways in a shy or stealthy manner

PREREADING

"Games at Twilight"
by Anita Desai

About the Author

ANITA DESAI
1937–

Critics consider **Anita Desai** to be one of the most gifted contemporary Indian writers. She was born in Mussoorie, India, a popular resort area for residents of Delhi. Her father was a Bengali, or native of the northeastern region of India, and her mother was German. Three languages were spoken in Desai's home—English, German, and Hindi. Desai attended a school in Old Delhi run by English missionaries, so she learned English before mastering Hindi. Desai also chose English as her "literary language" and displayed an interest in writing at a very early age, contributing to children's magazines before she was ten. Desai graduated from Delhi University, married, and had four children. She has taught creative writing in England at Girton College, and in the United States at Mount Holyoke and Smith College. Desai's novels include *Fire on the Mountain, Clear Light of Day,* and *Baumgartner's Bombay,* among many others. Her short stories have appeared in numerous magazines, as well as in the collection *Games at Twilight and Other Stories.*

About the Selection

Desai's fiction focuses upon her native land. Although she portrays bustling urban life in India, she focuses on characters who are "outsiders," those who feel lost among or alienated from the crowd. Desai often depicts modern family life as chaotic and, sometimes, as violent. **"Games at Twilight,"** the title story from Desai's first collection of short stories, depicts the experiences of a young boy named Ravi, a member of a large, wealthy Indian family. The story also explores an archetypal theme in literature—the fall from a state of innocence to a state of experience. This theme has been explored in such diverse works as the story of Adam and Eve in Genesis (see page 518), *The Epic of Gilgamesh* (see page 502), and Jerzy Kosinski's *Being There* (see page 1078). For Ravi, this fall comes in the course of a rather common activity—playing hide-and-seek with his brothers, sisters, and cousins. After the game, Ravi looks at his family, himself, and his place in the world much differently.

CONNECTIONS: The Impact of British Rule on Indian Society

As you may have already read on the Prereading page of "By Any Other Name" (see page 204), the British ruled India from early in the nineteenth century until 1947. British values and ways of life made a lasting mark on Indian culture. Many wealthy Indian families still model their lives after the British pattern, and many English words have infiltrated India's languages. Even children's games have been affected by this long period of British rule. For example, in the selection you are about to read, Indian children play such common Western games as hide-and-seek and a variation of "Eeny, Meeny, Miney, Mo" or "One Potato, Two Potato."

GOALS/OBJECTIVES

Studying this lesson will enable students to

- appreciate a contemporary short story that explores the loss of innocence theme
- define *archetype* and recognize archetypes in literature
- define *image* and *imagery,* and recognize imagery in a literary work
- write a personal memoir
- write a critical essay comparing and contrasting the story to either Genesis or *Gilgamesh*
- create a catalog of children's games

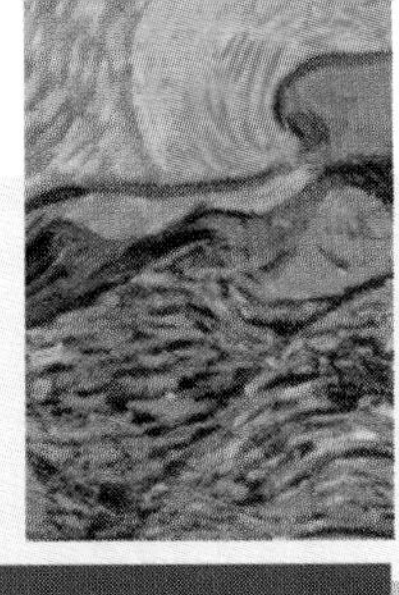

Think back to your childhood and describe a time when you felt left out, forgotten, or disillusioned by something. What happened to make you feel this way? How did you feel about being left out or disillusioned? Angry? resentful? frightened? saddened? What did you do about the situation? Write your responses to these questions in your journal.

READER'S JOURNAL

"Games at Twilight"

ANITA DESAI

It was still too hot to play outdoors. They had had their tea, they had been washed and had their hair brushed, and after the long day of confinement in the house that was not cool but at least a protection from the sun, the children strained to get out. Their faces were red and bloated with the effort, but their mother would not open the door; everything was still curtained and shuttered in a way that stifled the children, made them feel that their lungs were stuffed with cotton wool and their noses with dust and if they didn't burst out into the light and see the sun and feel the air, they would choke.

"Please, Ma, please," they begged. "We'll play in the veranda[1] and porch—we won't go a step out of the porch."

"You will, I know you will, and then—"

"No—we won't, we won't," they wailed so horrendously that she actually let down the bolt of the front door, so that they burst out like seeds from a crackling, overripe pod into the veranda with such wild, maniacal yells that she retreated to her bath and the shower of talcum powder and the fresh sari[2] that were to help her face the summer evening.

They faced the afternoon. It was too hot. Too bright. The white walls of the veranda glared stridently in the sun. The bougainvillea[3] hung about it, purple and magenta, in livid balloons. The garden outside was like a tray made of beaten brass, flattened out on the red gravel and the stony soil in all shades of metal—aluminum, tin, copper and brass. No life stirred at this arid time of day—the birds still drooped, like dead fruit, in the papery tents of the trees; some squirrels lay limp on the wet earth under the garden tap. The outdoor dog lay stretched as if dead on the veranda mat, his paws and ears and tail all reaching out like dying travellers in search of

1 *What is it like outside? In what terms are the animals described?*

2 *What do the children want to do? Why do they wish to do this so badly?*

1. **veranda.** Open porch, usually roofed, along the outside of a house
2. **sari.** Garment worn by Hindu women, consisting of a long piece of cloth that is draped across one shoulder and forms an ankle-length skirt
3. **bougainvillea.** Flowering tropical vines

WORDS FOR EVERYDAY USE

ma • ni • a • cal (mə nī´ə kəl) *adj.*, characterized by excessive or persistent enthusiasm

stri • dent • ly (strī´dənt lē) *adv.*, in a harsh-sounding, shrill, or grating manner

liv • id (liv´id) *adj.*, brightly discolored as by a bruise; black and blue

READER'S JOURNAL

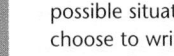

Students might list a number of possible situations first and then choose to write about the one that evokes the strongest memories and reactions in them.

ANSWERS TO GUIDED READING QUESTIONS

1 It is very hot and bright outside, and the garden is dry and metallic-colored. The animals are described as limp and lifeless.

2 The children want to go outside because they feel stifled being confined in the curtained and shuttered house.

SPELLING AND VOCABULARY WORDS FROM THE SELECTION

defunct	seethe
hirsute	sepulchral
ignominy	slake
livid	stridently
lugubrious	superciliously
maniacal	temerity
mortuary	

VOCABULARY IN CONTEXT

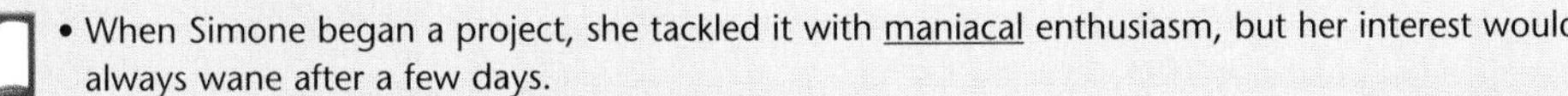

- When Simone began a project, she tackled it with maniacal enthusiasm, but her interest would always wane after a few days.
- It was impossible to sleep during the storm; the wind howled, and the crows outside shrieked stridently, upset by the strong gusts and the rain.
- When Tanya examined her knee after falling, she found it to be swollen and livid with bruises.

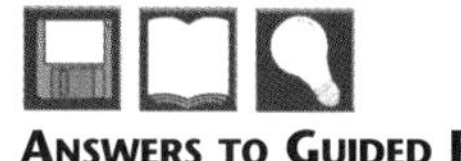

Answers to Guided Reading Questions

① The "business" of the children is play. They decide to play hide-and-seek.

② Raghu lets out a "blood-curdling yell" and chases after Manu, who falls down and begins to cry. Students may describe Raghu as a bully. The hiding children are compared to his prey.

③ The children play a clapping game in which children who are "safe" leave the circle until only the person who is It remains. Students may describe such rhymes and games as "Eeny, Meeny, Miny, Mo."

Cross-curricular Activities

MATHEMATICS AND SCIENCE AND SOCIAL STUDIES

You may point out to students that India, like many other nations, experiences a cool season, a hot season, and a monsoon season. This story takes place in the hot season, which lasts from early April to mid-June in India. Temperatures, however, in the northern elevated regions are much cooler than in the south. Encourage students to work in small groups to research the climate in a country of their choosing. Each group should then create a poster, divided into as many sections as the country has seasons. Each section should depict the weather conditions in the majority of the country during that season with accompanying text.

Other students may wish to research Earth's climactic conditions in the distant past, focusing on important warming and cooling trends. These groups should prepare oral presentations, explaining what the world's climate was like in this period and how it affected plant and animal life. Refer students to the Language Arts Survey 4.14, "Using Reference Works," before they begin to research.

▶ Additional practice is provided in the Essential Skills Practice Book: Study and Research 4.14.

water. He rolled his eyes at the children—two white marbles rolling in the purple sockets, begging for sympathy—and attempted to lift his tail in a wag but could not. It only twitched and lay still.

Then, perhaps roused by the shrieks of the children, a band of parrots suddenly fell out of the eucalyptus tree, tumbled frantically in the still, sizzling air, then sorted themselves out into battle formation and streaked away across the white sky.

Q ① *What is the "business" of the children? What do they decide to do?*

The children, too, felt released. They too began tumbling, shoving, pushing against each other, frantic to start. Start what? Start their business. The business of the children's day which is—play.

"Let's play hide-and-seek."

"Who'll be It?"

"You be It."

"Why should I? You be—"

"You're the eldest—"

"That doesn't mean—"

Q ② *What happens when Raghu sees Manu? How would you describe Raghu? To what are the children who hide from him compared?*

The shoves became harder. Some kicked out. The motherly Mira intervened. She pulled the boys roughly apart. There was a tearing sound of cloth, but it was lost in the heavy panting and angry grumbling, and no one paid attention to the small sleeve hanging loosely off a shoulder.

"Make a circle, make a circle!" she shouted, firmly pulling and pushing till a kind of vague circle was formed. "Now clap!" she roared, and clapping, they all chanted in melancholy unison "Dip, dip, dip—my blue ship—" and every now and then one or the other saw he was safe by the way his hands fell at the crucial moment—palm on palm, or back of hand on palm—and dropped out of the circle with a yell and a jump of relief and jubilation.

Q ③ *How do the children decide who will be It? Is there a game you used to play to determine who would be It? If so, describe it.*

Raghu was It. He started to protest, to cry, "You cheated—Mira cheated—Anu cheated—" but it was too late; the others had all already streaked away. There was no one to hear when he called out, "Only in the veranda—the porch—Ma said—Ma *said* to stay in the porch!" No one had stopped to listen; all he saw was their brown legs flashing through the dusty shrubs, scrambling up brick walls, leaping over compost heaps and hedges; and then the porch stood empty in the purple shade of the bougainvillea and the garden was as empty as before; even the limp squirrels had whisked away, leaving everything gleaming, brassy and bare.

Only small Manu suddenly reappeared, as if he had dropped out of an invisible cloud or from a bird's claws, and stood for a moment in the center of the yellow lawn, chewing his finger and near to tears as he heard Raghu shouting, with his head pressed against the veranda wall, "Eighty-three, eighty-five, eighty-nine, ninety . . ." and then made off in a panic, half of him wanting to fly north, the other half counseling south. Raghu turned just in time to see the flash of his white shorts and the uncertain skittering of his red sandals and charged after him with such a blood-curdling yell that Manu stumbled over the hose pipe, fell into its rubber coils and lay there weeping, "I won't be It—you have to find them all—all—All!"

"I know I have to, idiot," Raghu said, superciliously kicking him with his toe. "You're dead," he said with satisfaction, licking the beads of perspiration off his upper lip, and then stalked off in search of worthier prey, whistling spiritedly so that the hiders should hear and tremble.

Ravi heard the whistling and picked his nose in a panic, trying to find comfort by burrowing the finger deep—deep into that soft tunnel. He felt himself too exposed,

Words for Everyday Use

su • per • cil • i • ous • ly (sōō´pər sil´ē əs lē) *adv.*, in a haughty, scornful, or disdainful manner

Vocabulary in Context

• The sultan was renowned for his haughty manner; he spoke superciliously to everyone, inclu[ding] his own family members.

Rising Moon. *Vincent van Gogh, 1889*

sitting on an upturned flower pot behind the garage. Where could he burrow? He could run around the garage if he heard Raghu come—around and around and around—but he hadn't much faith in his short legs when matched against Raghu's long, hefty, hairy footballer legs. Ravi had a frightening glimpse of them as Raghu combed the hedge of crotons and hibiscus,[4] trampling delicate ferns underfoot as he did so. Ravi looked about him desperately, swallowing a small ball of snot in his fear.

The garage was locked with a great, heavy lock to which the driver had the key in his room, hanging from a nail on the wall under his work shirt. Ravi had peeped in and seen him still sprawling on his string cot in his vest and striped underpants, the hair on his chest and the hair in his nose shaking with the vibrations of his phlegm-obstructed snores. Ravi had wished he were tall enough, big enough to reach the key on the nail, but it was impossible, beyond his reach for years to come. He had sidled away and sat dejectedly on the flower pot. That at least was cut to his own size.

But next to the garage was another shed with a big green door. Also locked. No one even knew who had the key to the lock. That shed wasn't opened more than once a year, when Ma turned out all the old broken bits of furniture and rolls of matting and leaking buckets, and the white ant hills were broken and swept away and Flit sprayed into the spider webs and rat holes so that the whole

4. **crotons and hibiscus.** Crotons are tropical shrubs with ornamental, leathery leaves; hibiscus are plants and shrubs with large, colorful flowers.

1

What two incidents make Ravi wish he were bigger?

Answers to Guided Reading Questions

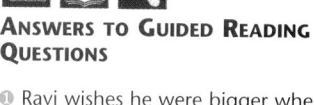

1 Ravi wishes he were bigger when he notes how much bigger and stronger Raghu is and when he wishes he could reach the key to the garage hung on the nail in the driver's room.

Literary Technique

Setting and Mood

The **setting** of a literary work is the time and place in which it occurs, together with all the details used to create a sense of a particular time and place. **Mood,** or **atmosphere,** is the emotion created in the reader by part or all of a literary work. Encourage students to discuss the following questions about the setting and mood established at the opening of this story: Where is the action of this story set? What is the weather like in this place? What is the effect of this setting on the children? What mood does the setting help to create? Is this mood consistent with the action at this point in the story—children's games? In what ways do the mood and the setting hint at the later action in the story?

Answers

The story is set in an arid garden in the afternoon. The sun is scorching, and it is intensely hot outside, so hot that the world seems lifeless. The weather seems to make the children agitated and irritable, as they bicker a lot. Students may say that the mood created is oppressive, troubled, and almost foreboding. The mood is not consistent with lighthearted and carefree children's games, but it is consistent with the arguments and scuffling that accompany this particular group of children's games. The death imagery in the setting hints at the death imagery in the story's close, and the troubled mood hints at Ravi's disillusionment at the story's end.

Answers to Guided Reading Questions

❶ The cleaning of the shed is compared to "the looting of a poor, ruined and conquered city."

❷ Ravi doesn't want to enter the shed because it reminds him of a mortuary and because it is filled with "alarming animal life."

❸ Ravi feels very proud of himself, but he is also afraid. The smell of the shed is compared to the smell of graves. Ravi was once locked in the linen cupboard for half an hour. The linen cupboard wasn't too frightening because it was familiar and because it smelled of clean laundry and his mother. The shed is more alarming because it is unfamiliar and smells of rats, ant hills, and spider webs.

Quotables

"[I write] to dispel the notion that fiction is untruth and lies, because I believe literature and art really contain the essence of life and the world, uncover its innermost secrets, and present those truths that one might ordinarily miss or ignore."

—Anita Desai

Additional Questions and Activities

Ask students to discuss Desai's views about literature and writing revealed in the above quotation. Do they agree or disagree with Desai's views? Is literature untruth and lies? Is it true? Is it a combination of the two? Is Desai talking about something other than the literal truth? Point out to students that "Games at Twilight" is a work of fiction—its characters and their situations are made up. In what ways, if any, is the story true?

To what is the annual cleaning of the shed compared?

Why doesn't Ravi want to enter the shed?

operation was like the looting of a poor, ruined and conquered city. The green leaves of the door sagged. They were nearly off their rusty hinges. The hinges were large and made a small gap between the door and the walls—only just large enough for rats, dogs and, possibly, Ravi to slip through.

Ravi had never cared to enter such a dark and depressing mortuary of defunct household goods seething with such unspeakable and alarming animal life, but, as Raghu's whistling grew angrier and sharper and his crashing and storming in the hedge wilder, Ravi suddenly slipped off the flower pot and through the crack and was gone. He chuckled aloud with astonishment at his own temerity so that Raghu came out of the hedge, stood silent with his hands on his hips, listening, and finally shouted, "I heard you! I'm coming! Got you—" and came charging round the garage only to find the upturned flower pot, the yellow dust, the crawling of white ants in a mud hill against the closed shed door—nothing. Snarling, he bent to pick up a stick and went off, whacking it against the garage and shed walls as if to beat out his prey.

❸ *How does Ravi feel once inside the shed? To what is the smell of the shed compared? What similar experience has Ravi had? What makes his current situation different?*

Ravi shook, then shivered with delight, with self-congratulation. Also with fear. It was dark, spooky in the shed. It had a muffled smell, as of graves. Ravi had once got locked into the linen cupboard and sat there weeping for half an hour before he was rescued. But at least that had been a familiar place and even smelt pleasantly of starch, laundry and, reassuringly, his mother. But the shed smelt of rats, ant hills, dust and spider webs. Also of less definable, less recognizable horrors. And it was dark. Except for the white-hot cracks along the door, there was no light. The roof was very low. Although Ravi was small, he felt as if he could reach up and touch it with his fingertips. But he didn't stretch. He hunched himself into a ball so as not to bump into anything, touch or feel anything. What might there not be to touch him and feel him as he stood there, trying to see in the dark? Something cold or slimy—like a snake. Snakes! He leapt up as Raghu whacked the wall with his stick—then quickly realizing what it was, felt almost relieved to hear Raghu, hear his stick. It made him feel protected.

But Raghu soon moved away. There wasn't a sound once his footsteps had gone around the garage and disappeared. Ravi stood frozen inside the shed. Then he shivered all over. Something had tickled the back of his neck. It took him a while to pick up the courage to lift his hand and explore. It was an insect—perhaps a spider—exploring him. He squashed it and wondered how many more creatures were watching him, waiting to reach out and touch him, the stranger.

There was nothing now. After standing in that position—his hand still on his neck, feeling the wet splodge of the squashed spider gradually dry—for minutes, hours, his legs began to tremble with the effort, the inaction. By now he could see enough in the dark to make out the large, solid shapes of old wardrobes, broken buckets and bedsteads piled on top of each other around him. He recognized an old bathtub—patches of enamel glimmered at him, and at last he lowered himself onto its edge.

He contemplated slipping out of the shed and into the fray. He wondered if it would not be better to be captured by Raghu and returned to the milling crowd as long as he could be in the sun, the light, the free spaces of the garden and the familiarity of his brothers, sisters and cousins. It would

Words for Everyday Use

mor • tu • ar • y (môr´to͞o er ē) *n.* place where dead bodies are kept before burial or cremation

de • funct (dē fuŋkt´) *adj.*, dead

seethe (sēth) *vt.*, boil; be violently agitated or disturbed

te • mer • i • ty (tə mer´ə tē) *n.*, foolish or rash boldness

Vocabulary in Context

- Egyptians spent months lavishly preparing their dead for entombment in mortuaries.
- The computer company hoped that their new model would make all other computers defunct.
- If you travel to Yellowstone, you can see a geyser begin to seethe faithfully every hour, churning up steam and vapors from its depths.
- When James dove off that cliff into the sea, we admired his temerity, but we did not want to take such a foolish risk ourselves.

be evening soon. Their games would become legitimate. The parents would sit out on the lawn on cane basket chairs and watch them as they tore around the garden or gathered in knots to share a loot of mulberries or black, teeth-splitting *jamun*[5] from the garden trees. The gardener would fix the hose pipe to the water tap, and water would fall lavishly through the air to the ground, soaking the dry, yellow grass and the red gravel and arousing the sweet, the intoxicating, scent of water on dry earth—that loveliest scent in the world. Ravi sniffed for a whiff of it. He half rose from the bathtub, then heard the despairing scream of one of the girls as Raghu bore down upon her. There was the sound of a crash and of rolling about in the bushes, the shrubs, then screams and accusing sobs of "I touched the den—" "You did not—" "I did—" "You liar, you did not," and then a fading away and silence again.

Ravi sat back on the harsh edge of the tub, deciding to hold out a bit longer. What fun if they were all found and caught—he alone left unconquered! He had never known that sensation. Nothing more wonderful had ever happened to him than being taken out by an uncle and bought a whole slab of chocolate all to himself, or being flung into the soda man's pony cart and driven up to the gate by the friendly driver with the red beard and pointed ears. To defeat Raghu—that hirsute, hoarse-voiced football champion—and to be the winner in a circle of older, bigger, luckier children—that would be thrilling beyond imagination. He hugged his knees together and smiled to himself almost shyly at the thought of so much victory, such laurels.

There he sat smiling, knocking his heels against the bathtub, now and then getting up and going to the door to put his ear to the broad crack and listening for sounds of the game, the pursuer and the pursued, and then returning to his seat with the dogged determination of the true winner, a breaker of records, a champion.

It grew darker in the shed as the light at the door grew softer, fuzzier, turned to a kind of crumbling yellow pollen that turned to yellow fur, blue fur, gray fur. Evening. Twilight. The sound of water gushing, falling. The scent of earth receiving water, slaking its thirst in great gulps and releasing that green scent of freshness, coolness. Through the crack Ravi saw the long purple shadows of the shed and the garage lying still across the yard. Beyond that, the white walls of the house. The bougainvillea had lost its lividity, hung in dark bundles that quaked and twittered and seethed with masses of homing sparrows. The lawn was shut off from his view. Could he hear the children's voices? It seemed to him that he could. It seemed to him that he could hear them chanting, singing, laughing. But what about the game? What had happened? Could it be over? How could it when he was still not found?

It then occurred to him that he could have slipped out long ago, dashed across the yard to the veranda and touched the "den." It was necessary to do that to win. He had forgotten. He had only remembered the part of hiding and trying to elude the seeker. He had done that so successfully, his success had occupied him so wholly, that he had quite forgotten that success had to be clinched by that final dash to victory and the ringing cry of "Den!"

With a whimper he burst through the crack, fell on his knees, got up and stumbled

❶ *What is happening outside the shed?*

❷ *Why does Ravi "hold out a bit longer"? What does he long to do? What would be so exciting about defeating Raghu?*

❸ *What has Ravi forgotten?*

5. ***jamun.*** Type of plum

Words for Everyday Use

hir • sute (hʉr´sōōt´) *adj.,* hairy; shaggy; bristly

slake (slāk) *vt.,* satisfy

Vocabulary in Context

- Our dog has a hirsute coat, resembling a wolf's bristly fur.
- After a long hike, we were happy to slake our thirst at an old water pump.

Answers to Guided Reading Questions

❶ The sun is setting, and the day is fading into twilight and evening.

❷ Ravi decides to hold out a bit longer so that he can be the only one left unfound and experience victory over Raghu. He longs to defeat Raghu and to be included as a winner among the older and bigger children. It would be exciting for Ravi to defeat Raghu because Raghu is older, bigger, and a football champion.

❸ Ravi has forgotten that the winner of hide-and-seek must run to the "den" and touch it.

Literary Technique

REALISM AND POINT OF VIEW

Inform students that **Realism** is the attempt to render in art an accurate portrayal of reality. **Point of view** is the vantage point from which a story is told. Have students review the information on first-person, third-person, limited, and omniscient points of view under the entry for *point of view* in the Handbook of Literary Terms. Then ask them the following questions: From what point of view is the story told? Does this story have a narrator who stands outside the action of the story? Is the narrator limited or omniscient? How realistically does the author portray Ravi's point of view? In other words, do Ravi's emotions and experiences seem convincing to you? Explain whether Desai's portrayal of childhood is an example of Realism.

ANSWERS

The story is told from the third-person point of view. There is a narrator who is limited to revealing the inner thoughts of Ravi. Students may say that Desai portrays both Ravi's point of view and childhood itself realistically. She does not idealize childhood but reveals its confusion and its difficult lessons.

Answers to Guided Reading Questions

❶ Ravi cries as he runs to the pillar, or "den." His voice breaks with rage and pity at his own disgrace. The other children stare at Ravi in amazement.

❷ The children have been too busy playing to notice that Ravi was missing.

❸ Ravi's passion and his "wild animal howling" surprise the other children.

❹ Ravi is upset because the game is so melancholy and mournful.

❺ Ravi wanted victory and triumph. Instead he got a funeral. He refuses to join in the game when he had been forgotten and left out previously.

Selection Check Test with Answers

EX. What is the afternoon weather like in this story?

It is hot and sunny.

1. What game do the children decide to play that afternoon?

They decide to play hide-and-seek.

2. Where does Ravi finally decide to hide?

He decides to hide in the shed behind the garage.

3. What does Ravi feel exploring him?

He feels a spider exploring him.

4. What does Ravi forget?

He forgets that you have to reach the "den" to win the game.

5. What does Ravi do when the children continue playing their game after he finally comes out?

Ravi charges into their midst, crying, "I won, I won."

❶ *What does Ravi do as he dashes to the pillar? What makes his voice break? How do the other children react to his appearance?*

❷ *What have the children been too busy playing to do?*

❸ *What about Ravi surprises the other children?*

❹ *What upsets Ravi about the children's new game?*

❺ *What did Ravi want? What does he get instead? What does he refuse to do?*

on stiff, benumbed legs across the shadowy yard, crying heartily by the time he reached the veranda so that when he flung himself at the white pillar and bawled, "Den! Den! Den!" his voice broke with rage and pity at the disgrace of it all, and he felt himself flooded with tears and misery.

Out on the lawn, the children stopped chanting. They all turned to stare at him in amazement. Their faces were pale and triangular in the dusk. The trees and bushes around them stood inky and sepulchral, spilling long shadows across them. They stared, wondering at his reappearance, his passion, his wild animal howling. Their mother rose from her basket chair and came toward him, worried, annoyed, saying, "Stop it, stop it, Ravi. Don't be a baby. Have you hurt yourself?" Seeing him attended to, the children went back to clasping their hands and chanting, "The grass is green, the rose is red. . . ."

But Ravi would not let them. He tore himself out of his mother's grasp and pounded across the lawn into their midst, charging at them with his head lowered so that they scattered in surprise. "I won, I won, I won," he bawled, shaking his head so that the big tears flew. "Raghu didn't find me. I won, I won—"

It took them a minute to grasp what he was saying, even who he was. They had quite forgotten him. Raghu had found all the others long ago. There had been a fight about who was to be It next. It had been so fierce that their mother had emerged from her bath and made them change to another game. Then they had played another and another. Broken mulberries from the tree and eaten them. Helped the driver wash the car when their father returned from work. Helped the gardener water the beds till he roared at them and swore he would complain to their parents. The parents had come out, taken up their positions on the cane chairs. They had begun to play again, sing and chant. All this time no one had remembered Ravi. Having disappeared from the scene, he had disappeared from their minds. Clean.

"Don't be a fool," Raghu said roughly, pushing him aside, and even Mira said, "Stop howling, Ravi. If you want to play, you can stand at the end of the line," and she put him there very firmly.

The game proceeded. Two pairs of arms reached up and met in an arc. The children trooped under it again and again in a lugubrious circle, ducking their heads and intoning

"The grass is green,
The rose is red;
Remember me
When I am dead, dead, dead, dead . . ."

And the arc of thin arms trembled in the twilight, and the heads were bowed so sadly, and their feet tramped to that melancholy refrain so mournfully, so helplessly, that Ravi could not bear it. He would not follow them: he would not be included in this funereal game. He had wanted victory and triumph—not a funeral. But he had been forgotten, left out and he would not join them now. The ignominy of being forgotten—how could he face it? He felt his heart go heavy and ache inside him unbearably. He lay down full length on the damp grass, crushing his face into it, no longer crying, silenced by a terrible sense of his insignificance. ■

Words for Everyday Use

se • pul • chral (sə pul´krəl) *adj.,* dismal, gloomy; suggestive of the grave or burial

lu • gu • bri • ous (lə go͞o´brē əs) *adj.,* very sad or mournful, especially in a way that seems exaggerated or ridiculous

ig • no • min • y (ig´nə min´ē) *n.,* shame and dishonor

Vocabulary in Context

- The close, stuffy, tomblike air in the old, abandoned house gave it a sepulchral character that discouraged even the boldest adventurers from entering.
- The hero's death scene in the play was enacted in such a lugubrious manner that the ridiculously mournful expressions of the actors made the audience laugh rather than cry.
- The soldier felt that he could never outlive the ignominy of having been defeated in battle.

Responding to the Selection

If you were younger and in Ravi's position, how would you react to his situation? Would you react as he does or in some other way?

Reviewing the Selection

Recalling

1. What is it like outside in the afternoon? What do the children decide to play once they are outside? What does Raghu do when he sees Manu?

Interpreting

Why doesn't the children's mother want to let them outside? Describe the way in which the children interact. What type of person does Raghu seem to be?

2. What does Ravi plan to do if Raghu catches him sitting on the flower pot? Why won't this plan work? Where does Ravi decide to hide?

How does Ravi feel about Raghu? Why is Ravi afraid of his new hiding place? How does he feel once he enters it? Why does he feel this way?

3. About what favorite time of day does Ravi daydream? What sound startles Ravi out of his daydream? What does he decide to do? What are the most wonderful things that have ever happened to Ravi? For what does he long?

In what way does the sound that startles Ravi out of his daydream contrast with his mental image of the special time of day? What feelings motivate Ravi to make his decision? What do the experiences that Ravi considers wonderful reveal about him?

4. What has Ravi forgotten? What does he do as he runs? What does he do to interrupt the children's new game? In what way does his family react to his reappearance? What have they done? What does Ravi refuse to do?

Why does Ravi feel "rage and pity at the disgrace of it all" as he runs? Why doesn't his family understand his emotional reaction? Why does Ravi refuse to join in the children's game?

Synthesizing

5. Both Ravi and the other children cry throughout this story. Why doesn't Ravi cry at the story's end? In what way is he less innocent and more experienced than he was at the beginning of the story? What knowledge has Ravi gained?

RESPONDING TO THE SELECTION

You might encourage students to discuss things that were important to them when they were younger but that seem less important now. Why have their feelings changed?

ANSWERS FOR REVIEWING THE SELECTION

RECALLING AND INTERPRETING

1. **Recalling.** It is so hot and bright out before twilight that scarcely any life stirs outside. The children decide to play hide-and-seek. Raghu chases Manu, speaks superciliously to him, kicks him with his toe, and tells him, "You're dead." **Interpreting.** The children's mother probably worries that they might suffer from sunstroke or exhaustion in the heat. The children seem overexcited and interact roughly, pushing and shoving each other and fighting. Raghu, one of the older children, seems to be a bully.

2. **Recalling.** Ravi plans to run around and around the garage. This plan won't work because Ravi is younger and weaker than Raghu. Ravi decides to hide in the shed next to the garage. **Interpreting.** Ravi is afraid of the shed because it is like a "mortuary of defunct household goods," and because it is filled with creepy creatures, such as rats, spiders, and ants. Ravi is both afraid of the shed and proud for doing something so brave.

3. **Recalling.** Ravi daydreams about evening, or twilight, when it is deliciously cool and the parents watch the children playing their games. The sound of Raghu chasing down one of the girls and the ensuing sobs and fight startles Raghu out of his daydream. Ravi decides to stay in the shed until everyone is caught so that he can win the game. Ravi's uncle once took him out and bought him a chocolate bar "all to himself," and

(cont.)

ANSWERS FOR REVIEWING THE SELECTION (CONT.)

the soda man drove him to the gate in his pony cart. He longs to be "the winner in a circle of older, bigger, luckier children." **Interpreting.** Ravi's daydream about twilight is peaceful and pleasant, while the actual dynamics among the children are chaotic and violent. Ravi wants to be the victor and defeat the older and dreaded Raghu. He longs to be accepted by the older children. The experiences that Ravi considers wonderful reveal that he longs to be singled out as special, to be somehow distinguished from all the other children in his family.

4. **Recalling.** Ravi has forgotten that it is necessary to run to the "den" to win hide-and-seek. He cries as he runs to the pillar marking the "den." He runs into the children's midst, bawling, "Raghu didn't find me. I won, I won." His family stares at him in

(cont.)

Understanding Literature (Questions for Discussion)

1. **Archetype.** An **archetype** is an inherited, often unconscious ancestral memory or motif that recurs throughout history or literature. One theme that is treated throughout world literature is a character's fall from a state of innocence to a state of experience. Usually, the character gains some knowledge that the world is not perfect and that evil, death, and suffering exist. Describe in your own words Ravi's fall from a state of innocence to a state of experience. What "innocence" does he lose? What "experience" does he gain? In what way is Ravi different at the end of the story than he was at its beginning?

2. **Image and Imagery.** An **image** is a word or phrase that names something that can be seen, heard, touched, tasted, or smelled. The images in a literary work are referred to, collectively, as the work's **imagery.** "Games at Twilight" is filled with death imagery. For example, the birds outside in the trees are referred to as "dead fruit," and the shed is called a "mortuary of defunct household goods." Twilight or evening is a time of day that is also associated with the end of life. Name some other examples of death imagery that appear in this selection. What is the purpose of this death imagery? What does this death imagery indicate about Ravi's fall from a state of innocence to a state of experience?

Responding in Writing

1. **Creative Writing: Personal Memoir.** A memoir is a biographical sketch. Write a personal memoir about an incident from your own life in which you felt left out or forgotten. Imagine that you will someday show this personal memoir to a child or grandchild of your own who also feels forgotten, to make him or her feel better about the situation. Before writing your memoir, review your responses to the Reader's Journal activity. Then create a sensory detail chart, like the one shown in the Language Arts Survey 1.10, "Gathering Ideas." Fill in this chart with the sight, sounds, smells, feelings, and tastes that you associate with your experience of being left out or forgotten. Refer to your Reader's Journal and sensory detail chart when writing your memoir. Try to make your writing as vivid as possible to convince this future child that you understand what he or she is experiencing. You should include an explanation of how you overcame or dealt with the negative sensation of your experience.

2. **Critical Essay: Comparing and Contrasting Treatments of Archetypal Themes.** Write an essay in which you compare and contrast the way Desai treats the theme of the loss of innocence to the way this theme is treated in either the Book of Genesis or *The Epic of Gilgamesh* in Unit 7. After you have chosen the work to which you would like to compare and contrast "Games at Twilight," review both works. Then do a focused freewrite on one of the following prompts. For more information on focused freewriting, see the Language Arts Survey 1.10, "Gathering Ideas."

ANSWERS FOR REVIEWING THE SELECTION (CONT.)

surprise; they do not know what he is talking about. They have forgotten him and have not noticed that he has been missing. Ravi refuses to join the children's melancholy game. **Interpreting.** Ravi probably realizes that he will not achieve the victory he so desires and that he has made a fool of himself by staying in the shed for so long. His family forgets him because they are busy with new games and the day's activities and because there are so many children in the family. His family doesn't understand his reaction because they don't know why he stayed in the shed so long or why winning the game of hide-and-seek meant so much to him. Ravi refuses to join in the game because the funereal game contradicts his hopes and expectations of a victorious celebration.

SYNTHESIZING

Responses will vary. Possible responses are given.

5. Ravi doesn't cry at the end of the story because he feels so insignificant that crying would be an empty gesture. Ravi has realized that his dreams of being hailed as a victor and crowned in laurels are hollow. He senses that as a mortal he is only a small, insignificant part of a troubling, enormous world.

ANSWERS FOR UNDERSTANDING LITERATURE

Responses will vary. Possible responses are given.

1. **Archetype.** Students may say that Ravi loses his innocent belief that he is special and should be singled out as a winner or victor. He gains knowledge of mortality and the fact that he will only occupy an insignificant place briefly in a large, busy, and confusing world.

(cont.)

ANSWERS FOR UNDERSTANDING LITERATURE (CONT.)

2. **Image and Imagery.** Students may cite the description of the limp squirrels, the "dead" outdoor dog, Raghu telling Manu that he is "dead," the smell of "graves" emanating from the shed, the "inky and sepulchral" foliage behind the children, the children's song about being remembered after death, and the "funereal game." This death imagery not only contrasts with Ravi's dreams of victory but also illustrates that Ravi has had his first glimpse of his own mortality and insignificance within the universe.

• In what way is Ravi's fall from a state of innocence to a state of experience similar to and different from the fall of Adam and Eve? In what way are the gardens in each selection similar or different? In what way is each garden related to its inhabitants' fall from a state of innocence? Compare and contrast the degree to which Ravi and Adam and Eve are responsible for their fall. In what different ways do the characters react to the fall? What are the consequences of the fall for Adam? for Eve? for Ravi?

• In what way is Ravi's fall from a state of innocence to a state of experience similar to or different from Gilgamesh's fall? In what way is Ravi's journey into the shed similar to and different from Gilgamesh's journey to seek eternal life? What similarity exists between the shed and the land that lies beyond the pass in the Mashu mountains? What do both characters learn about death? about their roles in the universe?

After you have written your responses to one set of these questions, organize the similarities and differences between the two works into a Venn diagram. For more information on Venn diagrams, see the Language Arts Survey 1.10, "Gathering Ideas." Refer to both your freewriting and your Venn diagram when writing your essay. Remember that your essay should have an introductory paragraph in which you state your thesis, explaining the major ways in which the two works are similar or different. Include supporting paragraphs that refer to or quote from the texts of both works, and end your essay with a concluding paragraph.

Project

A Catalog of Children's Games. What games do you remember playing when you were younger? Work with your classmates to make a catalog of children's games. As a class, brainstorm a list of games. Then, do some research to discover other interesting childhood games from around the world. Everyone should then choose a game, either one with which he or she is familiar or one that he or she has researched. Write instructions for playing your chosen game. For information on how to write clear, easy-to-follow instructions, see the Language Arts Survey 5.5, "Technical Writing." Add illustrations where appropriate to enhance your instruction.

Once you have completed your game instructions, gather your game and those of your classmates into a catalog. Two or three people should create a cover with the title "Games from Around the World," with pictures representing this theme—pictures of children from many different cultures, a map of the world, or a picture of children playing. Clearly label the games to show the part of the world where the game originated and explain whether it is a unique game played only in your home town, a game played throughout the United States, or a game played in a different part of the world. When your catalog is finished, you may wish to "test" some of the games with which you are least familiar by playing them. Finally, you might donate your catalog to a classroom of young children for their enjoyment.

ANALYTIC SCALES FOR RESPONDING IN WRITING

Assign a score from 1 to 25 for each grading criterion below. (For more detailed evaluation, see the evaluation forms for writing, revising, and proofreading, Assessment Portfolio 4.1–4.9.)

1. Personal Memoir

- **Content/Unity.** The personal memoir describes an incident in which the writer felt left out or forgotten.
- **Organization/Coherence.** The personal memoir recounts details in a sensible order, most likely chronological.
- **Language/Style.** The personal memoir uses vivid and precise nouns, verbs, and modifiers.
- **Conventions.** The personal memoir avoids errors in spelling, grammar, usage, mechanics, and manuscript form.

▶ Additional practice is provided in the Essential Skills Practice Book: Writing 1.8, 1.10.

2. Critical Essay

- **Content/Unity.** The essay compares and contrasts Desai's treatment of the loss of innocence theme with the way that theme is treated either in Genesis or *The Epic of Gilgamesh.*
- **Organization/Coherence.** The essay begins with an introduction that includes the thesis of the essay. The introduction is followed by supporting paragraphs with clear transitions. The essay ends with a solid conclusion.
- **Language/Style.** The essay uses vivid and precise nouns, verbs, and modifiers.
- **Conventions.** The essay avoids errors in spelling, grammar, usage, mechanics, and manuscript form.

▶ Additional practice is provided in the Essential Skills Practice Book: Writing 1.10, 1.20.

PROJECT NOTES

See the evaluation form for projects, Assessment Portfolio 4.12.

A Catalog of Children's Games. Encourage students to include a good mix of games in their catalog—common American games, more obscure American games, and games from around the world. Point out that students should include how several people can play and suggested age levels in their instructions. Tell them to bear in mind that younger people will be following their instructions, so they must take extra care in writing them to ensure that they are simple and easy to follow.

▶ Additional practice is provided in the Essential Skills Practice Book: Applied English/Tech Prep 5.5.

ADDITIONAL RESOURCES

READER'S GUIDE

- Selection Worksheet 12.12

ASSESSMENT PORTFOLIO

- Selection Check Test 2.12.23
- Selection Test 2.12.24

ESSENTIAL SKILLS PRACTICE BOOKS

- Writing 1.8, 1.20
- Language 2.73

PREREADING EXTENSIONS

Students should use the library, the Internet, museums, and knowledgeable acquaintances to research one of the following topics:

- the history of Chinese immigration to the United States, including laws enacted and social reactions and prejudices toward immigrants
- legends and myths from the Chinese literary tradition

Students should discuss their findings in small groups before reading the selection.

SUPPORT FOR LEP STUDENTS

PRONUNCIATIONS OF PROPER NOUNS AND ADJECTIVES

Max • ine Hong King • ston (mak sēn´ hông kiŋz´tən)
Fu Mu Lan (fä mo͞o län´)
Shao-lin (shau´lin)
Con • fu • cius (kən fyo͞o´shəs)

ADDITIONAL VOCABULARY

avenger—person who seeks vengeance or retribution
cowering—huddling and trembling in fear
mercenary—motivated by money
sway—influence
vouch—affirm, guarantee

PREREADING

from *The Woman Warrior*
by Maxine Hong Kingston

About the Author

MAXINE HONG KINGSTON 1940–

Maxine Hong Kingston was born in Stockton, California, in 1940. Her father was a scholar and her mother a midwife before they emigrated from China, working in a laundry and in a casino in the United States. Kingston graduated from the University of California, Berkeley in 1962 and earned a teaching certificate in 1965. She taught at several high schools in Hawaii between 1965 and 1977 and later at the University of Hawaii, Honolulu.

In her writing, Kingston blends history, myth, memory, and fantasy. She received the National Book Critics Circle Award for general nonfiction in 1976 and the American Book Award for general nonfiction in 1981. Kingston's books include *The Woman Warrior, China Men, Hawaii One Summer,* and *Tripmaster Monkey: His Fake Book.*

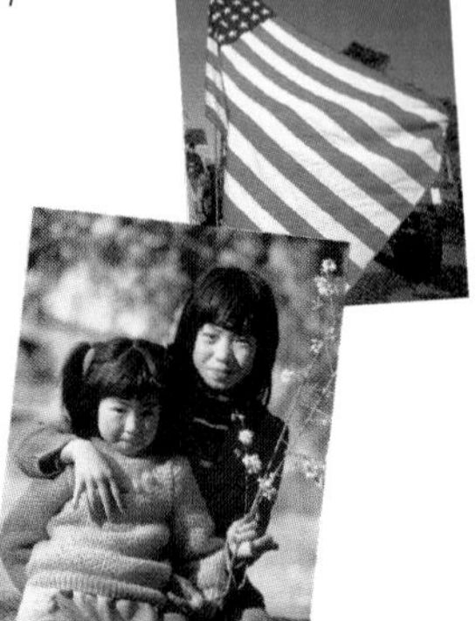

About the Selection

Considered a work of nonfiction, ***The Woman Warrior*** is based on Kingston's experiences as a Chinese American and on the experiences of other women in her family, but it also draws heavily on mythical elements and traditional stories that Kingston has embellished and adapted. Throughout *The Woman Warrior,* Kingston recognizes the power of words and of memory. In this selection, she is reminded of the woman warrior Fa Mu Lan whose story she learned as a child from her mother who "talked-story." Kingston explores the harsh, negative attitudes expressed openly toward girls in Chinese culture and the subversive, conflicting message that legends, such as that of Fa Mu Lan, taught to girls.

CONNECTIONS: Chinese Mythology

Scholars have not been able to piece together much of the earliest Chinese mythology. Only fragments of the myths of the earliest Chinese dynasties exist. Material from the Han dynasty (206 BC–AD 220) is plentiful but must be analyzed with caution since many of the writings from this period made major changes to earlier works. With the introduction of Buddhism to China (c. AD 100), new gods replaced older gods who gradually became forgotten. Over time, popular historical figures were mythologized and became part of the legendary tradition. By including mythical elements in her writing, Kingston takes part in the continuing evolution of Chinese mythology.

GOALS/OBJECTIVES

Studying this lesson will enable students to

- appreciate and interpret an autobiographical selection
- recognize Maxine Hong Kingston as a contemporary American writer
- define *autobiography, aphorism,* and *metaphor*
- explain the purpose of aphorisms and metaphors
- write an autobiographical sketch
- compare and contrast the attitudes presented in literary works with their own attitudes
- understand the connotations of words

Do you think your parents and other adults respect you? What expectations do you think they have for your future? Do you share these expectations, or do you have different plans for your future? Write your responses to these questions in your journal.

READER'S JOURNAL

FROM

The Woman Warrior

MAXINE HONG KINGSTON

When we Chinese girls listened to the adults talk-story, we learned that we failed if we grew up to be but wives or slaves. We could be heroines, swordswomen. Even if she had to rage across all China, a swordswoman got even with anybody who hurt her family. Perhaps women were once so dangerous that they had to have their feet bound.[1] It was a woman who invented white crane boxing only two hundred years ago. She was already an expert pole fighter, daughter of a teacher trained at the Shao-lin temple, where there lived an order of fighting monks. She was combing her hair one morning when a white crane alighted outside her window. She teased it with her pole, which it pushed aside with a soft brush of its wing. Amazed, she dashed outside and tried to knock the crane off its perch. It snapped her pole in two. Recognizing the presence of great power, she asked the spirit of the white crane if it would teach her to fight. It answered with a cry that white crane boxers imitate today. Later the bird returned as an old man, and he guided her boxing for many years. Thus she gave the world a new martial art.

This was one of the tamer, more modern stories, mere introduction. My mother told others that followed swordswomen through woods and palaces for years. Night after night my mother would talk-story until we fell asleep. I couldn't tell where the stories left off and the dreams began, her voice the voice of the heroines in my sleep. And on Sundays, from noon to midnight, we went to the movies at the Confucius Church. We saw swordswomen jump over houses from a standstill; they didn't even need a running start.

At last I saw that I too had been in the presence of great power, my mother talking-story. After I grew up, I heard the chant of Fa Mu Lan, the girl who took her father's place in battle. Instantly I remembered that as a child I had followed my mother about the house, the two of us singing about how Fa Mu Lan fought gloriously and returned alive from war to settle in the village. I had forgotten this chant that was once mine, given me by my mother, who may not have known its power to remind. She said I would grow up a wife and a slave, but she taught me the song of the warrior woman, Fa Mu Lan. I would have to grow up a warrior woman.

◆ ◆ ◆

1. **feet bound.** Chinese custom, from the T'ang dynasty to the early twentieth century, of binding, from early childhood, women's feet; this practice resulted in small, deformed feet that were considered aesthetically pleasing, but that made walking difficult and painful.

❶ *What did Chinese girls learn from listening to adults talk-story? What does the narrator suppose about the custom of feet-binding?*

❷ *What power does the narrator come to recognize?*

❸ *What does the narrator hear as a grown-up? What does she remember? What conclusion does she reach?*

READER'S JOURNAL

Students might write about plans for their education, career, family, and where they will live.

As an alternate activity, students might write about a time when they felt compelled to do something because it was expected of them although it may have conflicted with their own dreams or plans.

ANSWERS TO GUIDED READING QUESTIONS

❶ Chinese girls learned that they could be heroines or swordswomen. The narrator suggests that perhaps the practice of binding feet began because women were once so powerful and dangerous.

❷ The narrator comes to recognize the powerful presence of her mother talking-story.

❸ The narrator hears the chant of Fa Mu Lan. She remembers singing with her mother of Fa Mu Lan's glorious victory. She concludes that she would have to grow up a woman warrior.

SPELLING AND VOCABULARY WORDS FROM THE SELECTION

exorcize
grievance
reprieve

Answers to Guided Reading Questions

❶ The warrior has to fight the baron who drafted her brother and committed crimes against her village people.

❷ The warrior wants the life of the baron in payment for his crimes against the villagers.

❸ The baron tries to be charming. He quotes the sayings that the warrior hates: "Girls are maggots in the rice," and "It is more profitable to raise geese than daughters." The narrator is angry and vengeful toward the baron.

Quotables

"Some of my characters are trapped by history and by oppressive mores; others somehow break free. Women who were born and raised in slavery have been able to become feminists and to invent new roles and identities. They were able to do this by finding liberating myths, such as that of the woman warrior, by discovering heroines and role models, and by seeing through injustices that society takes for granted, and thus being strong enough to work hard to change the world."

—Maxine Hong Kingston

Additional Questions and Activities

- Share with students the quotation from Kingston. Discuss with students the power of myths and other stories from the oral tradition. Ask students to identify some myths, legends, and fairy tales, and describe the roles of women and men these stories project.
- Have students research women who have changed the world and create posters about the women and their accomplishments and the impact of their contributions.

[Editor's note: The story of the woman warrior—receiving the call, being trained, and beginning to fight—is told in one of the mother's mythical stories, stories that blur into the narrator's dreams. In this story, a girl follows a bird up a mountain where she meets an old man and an old woman who become her teachers. She lives with them for fifteen years, learning strength and survival techniques and gaining wisdom and insight about the world. The ancient couple show her scenes of her village being ravaged by a baron. Seven years later, when she has been fully trained, she returns to her village to take her father's place in the army. Before she leaves for battle, her parents carve names and oaths of revenge on her back. She gathers an army and sets out for vengeance. The army battles, defeats and kills the emperor, and makes a peasant the new ruler.]

❶ *What is the last battle that the warrior has to fight?*

Carrying the news about the new emperor, I went home, where one more battle awaited me. The baron who had drafted my brother would still be bearing sway over our village. Having dropped my soldiers off at crossroads and bridges, I attacked the baron's stronghold alone. I jumped over the double walls and landed with swords drawn and knees bent, ready to spring. When no one accosted me, I sheathed the swords and walked about like a guest until I found the baron. He was counting his money, his fat ringed fingers playing over the abacus.[2]

"Who are you? What do you want?" he said, encircling his profits with his arms. He sat square and fat like a god.

❷ *What is the goal of the warrior?*

"I want your life in payment for your crimes against the villagers."

"I haven't done anything to you. All this is mine. I earned it. I didn't steal it from you. I've never seen you before in my life. Who are you?"

❸ *How does the baron treat the warrior? What does he quote? How does the warrior feel about the baron?*

"I am a female avenger."

Then—heaven help him—he tried to be charming, to appeal to me man to man. "Oh, come now. Everyone takes the girls when he can. The families are glad to be rid of them. 'Girls are maggots in the rice.' 'It is more profitable to raise geese than daughters.'" He quoted to me the sayings I hated.

"Regret what you've done before I kill you," I said.

"I haven't done anything other men—even you—wouldn't have done in my place."

"You took away my brother."

"I free my apprentices."

"He was not an apprentice."

"China needs soldiers in wartime."

"You took away my childhood."

"I don't know what you're talking about. We've never met before. I've done nothing to you."

"You've done this," I said, and ripped off my shirt to show him my back. "You are responsible for this." When I saw his startled eyes at my breasts, I slashed him across the face and on the second stroke cut off his head. I pulled my shirt back on and opened the house to the villagers. The baron's family and servants hid in closets and under beds. The villagers dragged them out into the courtyard, where they tried them next to the beheading machine. "Did you take my harvest so that my children had to eat grass?" a weeping farmer asked.

"I saw him steal seed grain," another testified.

"My family was hiding under the thatch on the roof when the bandits robbed our house, and we saw this one take off his mask." They spared those who proved they could be reformed. They beheaded the others. Their necks were collared in the beheading machine, which slowly clamped shut. There was one last-minute reprieve of a bodyguard

2. **abacus.** Frame of wire-strung beads used for calculations

Words for Everyday Use

re • prieve (ri prēv´) *n.,* relief or postponement of punishment

Vocabulary in Context

- Moira was granted a reprieve when she learned that the final exam for which she had not studied had been postponed.

when a witness shouted testimony just as the vise was pinching blood. The guard had but recently joined the household in exchange for a child hostage. A slow killing gives a criminal time to regret his crimes and think of the right words to prove he can change.

I searched the house, hunting out people for trial. I came upon a locked room. When I broke down the door, I found women, cowering, whimpering women. I heard shrill insect noises and scurrying. They blinked weakly at me like pheasants that have been raised in the dark for soft meat. The servants who walked the ladies had abandoned them, and they could not escape on their little bound feet. Some crawled away from me, using their elbows to pull themselves along. These women would not be good for anything. I called the villagers to come identify any daughters they wanted to take home, but no one claimed any. I gave each woman a bagful of rice, which they sat on. They rolled the bags to the road. They wandered away like ghosts. Later, it would be said, they turned into the band of swordswomen who were a mercenary army. They did not wear men's clothes like me, but rode as women in black and red dresses. They bought up girl babies so that many poor families welcomed their visitations. When slave girls and daughters-in-law ran away, people would say they joined these witch amazons.[3] They killed men and boys. I myself never encountered such women and could not vouch for their reality.

After the trials we tore down the ancestral tablets. "We'll use this great hall for village meetings," I announced. "Here we'll put on operas; we'll sing together and talk-story." We washed the courtyard; we exorcised the house with smoke and red paper. "This is a new year," I told the people, "the year one."

I went home to my parents-in-law and husband and son. My son stared, very impressed by the general he had seen in the parade, but his father said, "It's your mother. Go to your mother." My son was delighted that the shiny general was his mother too. She gave him her helmet to wear and her swords to hold.

Wearing my black embroidered wedding coat, I knelt at my parents-in-law's feet, as I would have done as a bride. "Now my public duties are finished," I said. "I will stay with you, doing farmwork and housework, and giving you more sons."

"Go visit your mother and father first," my mother-in-law said, a generous woman. "They want to welcome you."

My mother and father and the entire clan would be living happily on the money I had sent them. My parents had bought their coffins. They would sacrifice a pig to the gods that I had returned. From the words on

3. **amazons.** Women warriors

1 *Whom does the warrior find when she breaks into the locked room? What happens to these people?*

2 *What does the warrior do after finishing her business with the baron?*

3 *In what way will the warrior's accomplishments be celebrated?*

Words for Everyday Use

ex • or • cise (eks´ôr sīz´) *vt.,* drive out evil through ritual or prayer

Vocabulary in Context

• Lucinda used burning sage to exorcise the negative energy from the room.

Answers to Guided Reading Questions

1 The warrior finds cowering, whimpering women who are unable to walk on their bound feet. According to legend, these women turn into a roving, mercenary army.

2 The woman performs her duty as a wife and resigns herself to private work.

3 The warrior's family will roast a pig, and the village would make a legend about her filiality.

ANALYTIC SCALES FOR RESPONDING IN WRITING

(SEE PAGE 1111.)

Assign a score from 1 to 25 for each grading criterion below. (For more detailed evaluation, see the evaluation forms for writing, revising, and proofreading, Assessment Portfolio 4.1–4.9.)

1. Autobiographical Sketch

- **Content/Unity.** The sketch describes an event and explains its meaning in the student's life.
- **Organization/Coherence.** The sketch is organized logically.
- **Language/Style.** The sketch uses vivid and precise language.
- **Conventions.** The sketch avoids errors in spelling, grammar, usage, mechanics, and form.

► Additional practice is provided in the Essential Skills Practice Book: Writing 1.8.

2. Critical Essay

- **Content/Unity.** The essay compares and contrast attitudes toward the role of women.
- **Organization/Coherence.** The essay presents and supports a clear thesis.
- **Language/Style.** The essay uses vivid and precise language.
- **Conventions.** The essay avoids errors in spelling, grammar, usage, mechanics, and manuscript form.

► Additional practice is provided in the Essential Skills Practice Book: Writing 1.20.

Answers to Guided Reading Questions

❶ The narrator's mother is not impressed by her daughter's accomplishments. She tells her daughter about a girl who saved her village. The narrator feels worthless.

❷ The narrator no longer heard people say disparagingly, "All girls." The negative attitude toward girls was reiterated as she watched the special treatment given to boys that girls did not receive.

❸ The narrator's parents and other villagers say: "Feeding girls is feeding cowbirds," "There's no profit in raising girls," "Better to raise geese than girls," "No use wasting all that discipline on a girl," "When you raise girls, you're raising children for strangers." The attitude is that girls are worthless.

❹ The outward tendency refers to the Chinese tradition that girls or women leave, or desert, their families. The narrator intends to prove that she does not have an outward tendency by never marrying.

Selection Check Test with Answers

EX. Who does the narrator sing about with her mother?
They sing about Fa Mu Lan.

1. What does the woman warrior want of the baron?
She wants his life in payment for his crimes against the villagers.

2. What does the warrior find in the locked room?
She finds cowering women who could not escape on bound feet.

3. What does the woman do after fulfilling her last duty as a warrior?
She devotes herself to being a wife and daughter-in-law.

4. What word does the narrator use to describe her American life?
Her life is a disappointment.

5. What will the narrator do to prove that girls do not have an outward tendency?
She will never marry.

❶ *How does the narrator's mother react to her accomplishments? How does this make the narrator feel?*

❷ *What good came of the birth of the narrator's brothers? In what way did the birth of her brothers renew the message the narrator had been receiving about girls?*

❸ *What sayings do the narrator's parents and the other villagers repeat about girls? What is the general attitude toward girls?*

❹ *What does the "outward tendency in females" mean? What does the narrator intend to prove? How will she prove it?*

my back, and how they were fulfilled, the villagers would make a legend about my perfect filiality.[4]

My American life has been such a disappointment.

"I got straight A's, Mama."

"Let me tell you a true story about a girl who saved her village."

I could not figure out what was my village. And it was important that I do something big and fine, or else my parents would sell me when we made our way back to China. In China there were solutions for what to do with little girls who ate up food and threw tantrums. You can't eat straight A's.

When one of my parents or the emigrant villagers said, "'Feeding girls is feeding cowbirds,'" I would thrash on the floor and scream so hard I couldn't talk. I couldn't stop.

"What's the matter with her?"

"I don't know. Bad, I guess. You know how girls are. 'There's no profit in raising girls. Better to raise geese than girls.'"

"I would hit her if she were mine. But then there's no use wasting all that discipline on a girl. 'When you raise girls, you're raising children for strangers.'"

"Stop that crying!" my mother would yell. "I'm going to hit you if you don't stop. Bad girl! Stop!" I'm going to remember never to hit or to scold my children for crying, I thought, because then they will only cry more.

"I'm not a bad girl," I would scream. "I'm not a bad girl. I'm not a bad girl." I might as well have said, "I'm not a girl."

"When you were little, all you had to say was 'I'm not a bad girl,' and you could make yourself cry," my mother says, talking-story about my childhood.

I minded that the emigrant villagers shook their heads at my sister and me. "One girl—and another girl," they said, and made our parents ashamed to take us out together. The good part about my brothers being born was that people stopped saying, "All girls," but I learned new <u>grievances</u>. "Did you roll an egg[5] on *my* face like that when I was born?" "Did you have a full-month party for *me*?" "Did you turn on all the lights?" "Did you send *my* picture to Grandmother?" "Why not? Because I'm a girl? Is that why not?" "Why didn't you teach me English?" "You like having me beaten up at school, don't you?"

"She is very mean, isn't she?" the emigrant villagers would say.

"Come, children. Hurry. Hurry. Who wants to go out with Great-Uncle?" On Saturday mornings my great-uncle, the ex-river pirate, did the shopping. "Get your coats, whoever's coming."

"I'm coming. I'm coming. Wait for me."

When he heard girls' voices, he turned on us and roared, "No girls!" and left my sisters and me hanging our coats back up, not looking at one another. The boys came back with candy and new toys. When they walked through Chinatown, the people must have said, "A boy—and another boy—and another boy!" At my great-uncle's funeral I secretly tested out feeling glad that he was dead—the six-foot bearish masculinity of him.

I went away to college—Berkeley in the sixties—and I studied, and I marched to change the world, but I did not turn into a boy. I would have liked to bring myself back as a boy for my parents to welcome with chickens and pigs. That was for my brother, who returned alive from Vietnam.

If I went to Vietnam, I would not come back; females desert families. It was said,

4. **filiality.** Devotion of a daughter or son to parents
5. **roll an egg.** Part of a Chinese custom performed for baby boys

Words for Everyday Use

griev • ance (grēv´əns) *n.*, complaint or resentment

Vocabulary in Context

• Reshma filed a <u>grievance</u> with the Better Business Bureau against Mickey's Mail Mall because it did not send her order, nor did they respond to her calls and letters.

"There is an outward tendency in females," which meant that I was getting straight A's for the good of my future husband's family, not my own. I did not plan ever to have a husband. I would show my mother and father and the nosey emigrant villagers that girls have no outward tendency. I stopped getting straight A's.

And all the time I was having to turn myself American-feminine, or no dates.

There is a Chinese word for the female *I*—which is "slave." Break the women with their own tongues!

I refused to cook. When I had to wash dishes, I would crack one or two. "Bad girl," my mother yelled, and sometimes that made me gloat rather than cry. Isn't a bad girl almost a boy?

"What do you want to be when you grow up, little girl?"

"A lumberjack in Oregon."

Even now, unless I'm happy, I burn the food when I cook. I do not feed people. I let the dirty dishes rot. I eat at other people's tables but won't invite them to mine, where the dishes are rotting.

If I could not-eat, perhaps I could make myself a warrior like the swordswoman who drives me. I will—I must—rise and plow the fields as soon as the baby comes out.

Once I get outside the house, what bird might call me; on what horse could I ride away? Marriage and childbirth strengthen the swordswoman, who is not a maid like Joan of Arc. Do the women's work; then do more work, which will become ours too. No husband of mine will say, "I could have been a drummer, but I had to think about the wife and kids. You know how it is." Nobody supports me at the expense of his own adventure. Then I get bitter: no one supports me; I am not loved enough to be supported. That I am not a burden has to compensate for the sad envy when I look at women loved enough to be supported. Even now China wraps double binds around my feet. ■

❶ *What does one of the words for the female I mean? What does the narrator recognize about language?*

❷ *Why does the narrator become bitter? In what way has China wrapped double binds on her feet?*

Responding to the Selection

At the end of this selection, the narrator says, "Even now China wraps double binds around my feet." Have you been restricted by cultural or societal beliefs or traditions? How do you react to such restrictions?

Reviewing the Selection

RECALLING

1. What two legendary women does the narrator discuss? Who tells her about these women?
2. What news does the woman warrior carry home? What does she still have to do? What sayings does the baron quote?

INTERPRETING

- In what way is the narrator's mother "talking-story" a great power? In what way does Kingston share this power?
- Why must the woman warrior complete this last task? How does she feel about these sayings? Do her actions reflect these sayings? Explain.

ANSWERS TO GUIDED READING QUESTIONS

❶ One of the Chinese words for the female *I* means "slave." The narrator sees that this word will "break the women with their own tongues." She recognizes that language has the power to influence our ideas about ourselves and others.

❷ The narrator becomes bitter because nobody supports her. She equates not being supported with not being loved. She is bound by duty and by her desire to break with tradition. In fulfilling either expectation she is left unsatisfied.

RESPONDING TO THE SELECTION

If students do not feel that they have been restricted by cultural or societal beliefs or traditions, ask them to discuss restrictions they have seen placed on others or the ways in which their freedom from such restrictions differs from the experiences of past generations. Students may also wish to discuss ways in which cultural or societal traditions have supported them or helped them.

ANSWERS FOR REVIEWING THE SELECTION

RECALLING AND INTERPRETING

1. **Recalling.** The narrator discusses Fa Mu Lan, a woman warrior, and the woman who invented white crane boxing. She learns about these women from her mother. **Interpreting.** Through talking-story, the narrator's mother creates other worlds, passes on values, history, and traditions. She enchants and engages her listener with language. Kingston uses the power of language and her power as a storyteller for similar ends, but she uses a written form rather than the oral form used by her mother.

(cont.)

ANSWERS FOR REVIEWING THE SELECTION (CONT.)

2. **Recalling.** The woman warrior carries news of the defeat of the emperor. She still has to avenge her family and her village by slaying the baron who has been bearing sway over, or dominating, their village and who has drafted her brother. The baron quotes the sayings that the warrior hates: "Girls are maggots in the rice" and "It is more profitable to raise geese than daughters." **Interpreting.** The woman warrior is bound by duty to avenge her family and her village. She is angered and hateful toward these sayings the baron quotes. Her actions do not reflect the sayings. She is certainly more useful to her village and to her family than a goose. She is not a maggot or an insignificant or destructive being. Instead, she shows that girls and women can be vital parts of their communities.

(cont.)

ANSWERS FOR REVIEWING THE SELECTION (CONT.)

RECALLING AND INTERPRETING

3. **Recalling.** The warrior finds women who are unable to walk on their bound feet without help. The women wander off and supposedly become a group of roving mercenaries or amazons. After fulfilling her duty, the woman returns to her village and takes on the role of a dutiful wife and daughter-in-law. Her return is celebrated by her parents. **Interpreting.** Both the swordswomen and the woman warrior are avengers. The woman warrior works with male soldiers, while the band of swordswomen takes on only new female warriors. They do not dress the same. The woman warrior was an avenger for her village, while the swordswomen were avengers for girls and women. The woman warrior's return to her family and work at home are based on duty as were her battle tasks. In both roles, the woman warrior is concerned with fulfilling her duty toward her family.

4. **Recalling.** The narrator gets all *A*s. The narrator's mother is not impressed and tells her about a girl who saved her village. The narrator's mother's reaction reflects the community's ideas that girls are of little worth, although her story suggests that girls can accomplish great things. The narrator dreams of becoming a swordswoman. **Interpreting.** The narrator wishes that she could be strong like the woman warrior, that she could be recognized for her accomplishments and seek vengeance on those who have belittled her.

SYNTHESIZING

Responses will vary. Possible responses are given.

5. Some injustices and wrongs a modern warrior might fight are racism, sexism, homelessness, or environmental destruction. The warrior might become an avenger, helping individuals who have been wronged, fight via demonstrations or hunger strikes, or use the media in his or her fight.

3. Whom does the warrior find as she is searching the house? What happens to these people? What does the woman do when she has fulfilled her duty as a warrior? What kind of reception does she receive from her parents? ▶▶ In what ways are the purposes of the woman warrior and the band of swordswomen similar? different? In what way is the woman warrior's action when she completes her battle tasks similar to her work as a warrior? What does this similarity suggest?

4. What is the narrator's accomplishment? What is her mother's reaction? In what way does the mother's reaction reflect the reaction of her community? What does the narrator dream of becoming? ▶▶ In what ways are the narrator's hopes and disappointments related to the story of the woman warrior?

SYNTHESIZING

5. The woman warrior avenged her family and village by fighting the injustice of the emperor and the evil baron. What injustices might a modern warrior fight? In what way might he or she do battle?

Understanding Literature (Questions for Discussion)

1. **Autobiography.** An **autobiography** is the story of a person's life, written by that person. An autobiography, or memoir, is a work of nonfiction—writing about real events. Maxine Hong Kingston, like many writers of the twentieth century, has blurred the line between fiction and nonfiction. Her autobiography of her childhood has elements of both fiction and nonfiction. Identify some elements of this selection that seem fictional. In what way do these fictional elements relate to the life of the writer?

2. **Aphorism.** An **aphorism** is a short saying or pointed statement. "Haste makes waste" is an example of an aphorism. Identify four aphorisms about girls in this selection. What do these aphorisms tell you about the role of females in Chinese society?

3. **Metaphor.** A **metaphor** is a figure of speech in which one thing is written or spoken about as if it were another. This figure of speech invites the reader to make a comparison between the two things. When the narrator says, "Even now China wraps double binds around my feet," she is speaking metaphorically. What effect did feet-binding have on the women found by the warrior in the locked room? In what way do cultural expectations create a similar effect on the narrator?

Responding in Writing

1. **Creative Writing: Autobiographical Sketch.** Choose one event from your life to write about in a short autobiographical sketch. Freewrite about your life or read through your journal for topic ideas. When you have chosen an event, do a focused freewrite for each of the following prompts:
   - Where did this event take place? Describe this place in detail.
   - Who else participated in this event? What were their reactions? Write a brief dialogue between the people involved.
   - What sights, sounds, smells, tastes, or objects do you associate with this event?
   - What effect did this event have on you at the time? Why is this event significant now?

   After you have completed these prewriting activities, begin to write your sketch. You may organize the events in chronological order, or you might begin by discussing a recent image or event that triggers a memory and flashes back to the event you are discussing. Whatever method of organization you choose, your sketch should not only describe the event, but also show its significance.

2. **Critical Essay: Women's Roles.** Write a critical essay in which you compare and contrast the attitudes toward the roles of women as portrayed in the selection from Maxine Hong Kingston's *The Woman Warrior* and in Judith Wright's "Request to a Year" with your own view of the roles and treatment of women. Both Kingston and Wright refer to physical constraints that relate to or symbolize emotional or spiritual constraints. Your thesis statement should identify these constraints, and state whether you think women face such constraints in our society today. In your essay, identify the images Kingston and Wright use and explain their symbolic message. What conflicting message does each selection reveal? Use examples from your own life and from the two selections to support the claims that you make. In a final paragraph, come to some conclusions about restrictions on and expectations of women in today's society.

Language Lab

Connotation and Denotation. Kingston writes, "There is a Chinese word for the female *I*—which is 'slave.' Break the women with their own tongues!" Kingston recognizes that a single word can be of enormous importance. Words have basic meanings, or denotations, but a word often has emotional associations or connotations as well. The words you choose when you speak or write should be chosen carefully to reflect your meaning. For example, "My mother rambled on about ancient people's unrealistic stories" has a very different connotation from "My mother tirelessly shared the mythical stories of our ancestors." In small groups, discuss the differences in connotation of the pairs of words below. Then choose one pair of words and enact the difference for your small group or the entire class.

1. cocky confident
2. pushy assertive
3. thrifty stingy
4. determined stubborn
5. sneaky discreet

Answers for Understanding Literature

Responses will vary. Possible responses are given.

1. **Autobiography.** Students may say that the use of dialogue, flashbacks, and legends seems fictional. The legend reflects the dichotomy the narrator feels between the desire and ability to be free and do great things and the sense of duty that tradition places on her. The use of the legend and the mystical tone of part of the selection suggest the power of stories and of "talking-story" to the narrator.

2. **Aphorism.** Examples of aphorisms include: "Girls are maggots in the rice," "It is more profitable to raise geese than daughters," "Feeding girls is feeding cowbirds," and "When you raise girls, you're raising children for strangers." These aphorisms show the lack of respect for females. These sayings show that girls and women are seen as worthless and burdensome.

3. **Metaphor.** Because their feet had been bound, the women had a difficult time moving without help. They were dependent upon others. The narrator is confined by cultural traditions and expectations that tell her she is worthless and that she should be dutiful and submissive. Not being dutiful and submissive makes her feel unworthy of love for which she yearns. It is this double bind that confines the narrator.

Analytic Scales for Responding in Writing

Grading scales for Responding in Writing appear on page 1107.

Answers for Language Lab

Responses will vary. Possible responses are given.

Students should note the positive connotations of *confident, assertive, thrifty, determined,* and *discreet,* and the negative connotations of *cocky, pushy, stingy, stubborn,* and *sneaky.* Students can use examples to illustrate the difference between the two words in each pair.

Students may wish to work in pairs to enact scenes showing the difference between the connotations of each pair of words. Students' actions should reflect a clear understanding of the difference in connotations.

▶ Additional practice is provided in the Essential Skills Practice Book: Language 2.73.

ADDITIONAL RESOURCES

READER'S GUIDE

- Selection Worksheet 12.13

ASSESSMENT PORTFOLIO

- Selection Check Test 2.12.25
- Selection Test 2.12.26

ESSENTIAL SKILLS PRACTICE BOOKS

- Writing 1.8, 1.20
- Language 2.27, 2.52

PREREADING EXTENSIONS

Inform students that the twentieth century has been a turbulent one for modern Greece. Encourage students to work in small groups to prepare oral reports on Greece's history during the twentieth century. Possible topics to research include internal conflicts in Greece during World War I; the war with Turkey after World War I; Greece's refusal to join the Axis powers and the occupation of Greece during World War II; the Greek Civil War; the struggles among Britain, Greece, and Turkey over Cyprus; the period of the military junta; and the restoration of parliamentary government.

SUPPORT FOR LEP STUDENTS

PRONUNCIATIONS OF PROPER NOUNS AND ADJECTIVES

Jen • ny Mas • to • ra • ki (jen´ nē mas tô rä´kē)

ADDITIONAL VOCABULARY

press—journalists; people who write for newspapers and magazines

PREREADING

"The Wooden Horse then said"
by Jenny Mastoraki, translated by Nikos Germanakos

About the Author

Jenny Mastoraki (1949–). Although there are contemporary Greek poets who are better known to American audiences, Jenny Mastoraki's terse, satirical poems make her one of modern Greece's most powerful poets. Mastoraki was born in Athens and later studied philosophy at the University of Athens. Mastoraki actively resisted the Greek junta, or group of military leaders who established an oppressive government that ruled Greece from 1967 to 1974. In 1973, she took part in a student protest at the Polytechnic Institute. The students were beaten severely by the police, and Mastoraki received life-threatening injuries. Mastoraki's first collection of poetry, *Right of Passage,* was written in protest of the period of military government in Greece. Her later collections of poetry include *The Vandals* and *Prometheus.*

About the Selection

The Acropolis, Athens

Like many modern Greek writers, such as Constantine Cavafy (see page 37), Odysseus Elytis, and Yannis Ritsos (see page 266), Jenny Mastoraki draws upon the great literary and cultural history of Greece in her writing. In **"The Wooden Horse then said,"** she refers to an ancient Greek story about the Trojan War. According to tradition, the Achaeans, or Greeks, won the war against the Trojans by employing a ruse developed by the hero Odysseus. The Achaeans left a large wooden horse filled with Achaean soldiers outside Troy's walls, apparently as tribute, and pretended to sail away. The Trojans brought the horse into their city, fearful of offending the gods and thankful that the long war was over and that their city was spared. That night the hidden Achaean soldiers crept out of the wooden horse to unlock the gates of Troy, letting the Achaean army into the city. As a result of this deception, the great city of Troy was razed, many of its people were murdered, and the survivors were driven out of the city.

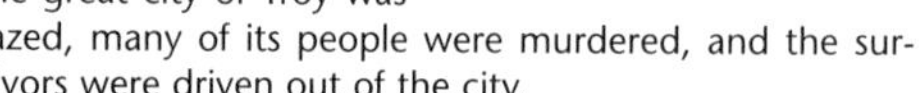

Mastoraki's poem, however, does not refer only to Greece's distant past. "The Wooden Horse then said" also serves as commentary on Greece's recent past—the period of military government, whose oppression Mastoraki experienced firsthand.

CONNECTIONS: Military Rule in Greece: 1967–1974

A coup d'état is a sudden, forcible overthrow of a ruler or government. Such a coup occurred in Greece on April 21, 1967, when the junta seized power, creating a military state. Many Greeks, both prominent figures and average citizens, were arrested, democracy was dismantled, trial by jury was abolished, and the media was strictly censored. The Greek junta fell toward the end of 1973, and in 1974, the restoration of democracy, a form of government that had its birthplace in Greece, began.

GOALS/OBJECTIVES

Studying this lesson will enable students to

- enjoy a satirical poem
- briefly explain the story of the Trojan horse
- define *symbol* and identify what symbols in literary works represent
- define *satire* and recognize elements of satire in a literary work
- write a poem or fable with an unusual point of view
- write a critical essay analyzing tone
- correct sentence strings and use quotation marks

Think about a time in your life when you asked someone a difficult or controversial question and this person changed the subject to avoid talking about the issue. Why do you think he or she tried to talk about something else? Was it an effective tactic in the short-term? in the long-term? In your journal, write your opinion of changing the subject to avoid controversy.

READER'S JOURNAL

"The Wooden Horse then said"

JENNY MASTORAKI, TRANSLATED BY NIKOS GERMANAKOS

The Wooden Horse then said
no I refuse to see the press
and they said why not and he said
he knew nothing about the killing,
and anyway he himself always ate
lightly in the evenings
and once in his younger days
he'd worked as a pony on a merry-go-round. ■

❶ *What does the wooden horse refuse to do?*

❷ *What does the wooden horse claim?*

❸ *What does the wooden horse say he did in his "younger days"?*

READER'S JOURNAL

Students might also write about a time when they themselves were asked such a question and changed the subject to avoid talking about the issue.

ANSWERS TO GUIDED READING QUESTIONS

❶ The wooden horse refuses to see the press.

❷ The wooden horse says he knew nothing about the killing.

❸ The wooden horse says he worked in his younger days as one of the ponies on a merry-go-round.

SELECTION CHECK TEST WITH ANSWERS

EX. Who speaks in this poem?
The wooden horse is speaking.

1. What does the wooden horse refuse to do?
The wooden horse refuses to see the press.

2. What does the press want to know?
The press wants to know why the wooden horse refuses to see them.

3. About what does the wooden horse say he knows nothing?
The wooden horse says that he knows nothing about the killing.

4. What does the wooden horse do in the evenings?
The wooden horse eats lightly in the evenings.

5. What did the wooden horse do in his "younger days"?
The wooden horse worked as a pony on a merry-go-round.

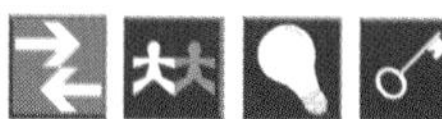

Responding to the Selection

Students might wish to work in pairs to role play an interview between a member of the press and the wooden horse.

Answers for Reviewing the Selection

RECALLING AND INTERPRETING

1. **Recalling.** The wooden horse refuses to see the press. He says that he knows nothing about the killing. **Interpreting.** Students may say that the wooden horse is trying to avoid being blamed for his role in the "killing." Students may say that the horse is lying, as the Trojan horse would have witnessed the killing of the Trojans.

2. **Recalling.** The wooden horse says that he always eats lightly in the evenings. He says that he used to work as a pony on a merry-go-round. **Interpreting.** Students may say that the wooden horse says these seemingly unrelated things in an attempt to portray his innocence in the killings that have occurred. The wooden horse is trying to portray himself as gentle and as someone who can't possible be associated with violence and death.

SYNTHESIZING

Responses will vary. Possible responses are given.

3. Students may say that both events involved surprise and a sudden burst of violence. "The Wooden Horse then said" may use the subject of how the Trojans were overthrown as a vehicle for critiquing the military government, which had recently overthrown the Greek republic.

Responding to the Selection

Imagine that you are the member of the press who asked the question that prompted the wooden horse's response. What did you ask? What are you trying to discover? How do you feel about the wooden horse's response?

Reviewing the Selection

RECALLING / **INTERPRETING**

1. What does the wooden horse refuse to do? About what does he say he knows nothing? ▶▶ What do you think is the wooden horse's reason for refusing? Do you think the wooden horse really knows nothing as he claims?

2. What does the wooden horse say about his habits? about his younger days? ▶▶ Why do you think the wooden horse says these things? What would the wooden horse like others to think of him?

SYNTHESIZING

3. Compare and contrast what you know about the rise to power of the junta in modern Greece with what you know about the Achaeans' defeat of Troy during the Trojan War. In what way might "The Wooden Horse then said" reflect both events?

Understanding Literature (Questions for Discussion)

1. **Symbol.** A **symbol** is a thing that stands for or represents both itself and something else. Of what might the wooden horse be a symbol? In other words, what do you think the wooden horse represents?

2. **Satire. Satire** is humorous writing or speech intended to point out errors, falsehoods, foibles, or failings. It is written for the purpose of reforming human behavior or human institutions. What elements in this poem do you find humorous? What makes these elements humorous? What errors, falsehoods, or failings of human nature do you think the author of this selection is trying to point out?

Answers for Understanding Literature

Responses will vary. Possible responses are given.

1. **Symbol.** Students may say that the wooden horse represents deception, subversiveness, or trickery.

2. **Satire.** Students may say that they find the idea of the wooden horse working as a pony on a merry-go-round humorous because of the contrast between the Trojan horse's role in helping the Achaeans win the Trojan War and the idea of him delighting children at a fairground or circus. This image is humorous because of the contrast. Students may say that the author is pointing out that sometimes certain groups try to control the press in order to distort the truth.

Responding in Writing

1. **Creative Writing: Poem or Fable with an Unusual Point of View.** What flaws or failings do you see in today's society or in your community? Write a poem in the style of "The Wooden Horse then said" or a fable that exposes these shortcomings. (A fable is a brief story, often with animal characters, told to express a moral.) Choose an unusual point of view from which to tell your poem or fable, just as Mastoraki has explored the point of view of the Trojan horse. Begin by making a list of problems in human behavior or institutions that you would like to see corrected. For example, you might wish to address the need to conserve more beautiful natural settings by establishing more national parks. Then choose an unusual point of view from which to explore this issue, such as that of a river threatened by pollution. After you have revised several drafts of your poem or fable, you may wish to read it to the class as part of an "Examining Society through Literature Day" in your classroom.

2. **Critical Essay: Analyzing Tone. Tone** is the emotional attitude toward the reader or toward the subject implied by a literary work. A few examples of the different tones that a work may have include familiar, ironic, playful, sarcastic, and sincere. Write a brief three- or four-paragraph essay analyzing the tone of "The Wooden Horse then said." In your first paragraph, clearly state your ideas about the tone of this poem. In your following paragraph or paragraphs, support your analysis of the tone by referring to and quoting from the text of the poem. Come to a conclusion—perhaps suggesting why the author may have chosen this particular tone—in a final paragraph.

Language Lab

Correcting Sentence Strings and Uses of Quotation Marks. Poets, particularly modern and contemporary poets, sometimes avoid following traditional grammatical rules as part of their poetic style. For example, Mastoraki's "The Wooden Horse then said" is composed of sentence strings. Sentence strings are formed of several sentences strung together with conjunctions. Imagine that "The Wooden Horse then said" was not a poem but part of a conversation reported in a newspaper article. Edit the text by breaking up the sentence strings into separate sentences and using quotation marks correctly. Remember that when you break up sentence strings and add quotation marks, you will also have to pay close attention to capitalization. After you have "corrected" the text with your classmates, you may wish to discuss why the poet chose to use sentence strings in her poem and why she did not use quotation marks. Which way is the poem more effective? Why?

ANALYTIC SCALES FOR RESPONDING IN WRITING

Assign a score from 1 to 25 for each grading criterion below. (For more detailed evaluation, see the evaluation forms for writing, revising, and proofreading, Assessment Portfolio 4.1–4.9.)

1. Poem or Fable

- **Content/Unity.** The poem or fable is told from an unusual point of view and points out flaws or failures in human behavior or institutions.
- **Organization/Coherence.** The poem or fable is written in a sensible order.
- **Language/Style.** The poem or fable uses vivid and precise nouns, verbs, and modifiers.
- **Conventions.** The poem or fable avoids errors in spelling, grammar, usage, mechanics, and manuscript form.

► Additional practice is provided in the Essential Skills Practice Book: Writing 1.8.

2. Critical Essay

- **Content/Unity.** The essay analyzes the tone of "The Wooden Horse then said."
- **Organization/Coherence.** The essay begins with an introduction that includes the thesis of the essay. The introduction is followed by supporting paragraphs with clear transitions. The essay ends with a solid conclusion.
- **Language/Style.** The essay uses vivid and precise nouns, verbs, and modifiers.
- **Conventions.** The essay avoids errors in spelling, grammar, usage, mechanics, and manuscript form.

► Additional practice is provided in the Essential Skills Practice Book: Writing 1.20.

ANSWERS FOR LANGUAGE LAB

The Wooden Horse then said, "No, I refuse to see the press."

They said, "Why not?"

He said that he knew nothing about the killing and that anyway he always ate lightly in the evenings. He added that once in his younger days he'd worked as a pony on a merry-go-round.

► Additional practice is provided in the Essential Skills Practice Book: Language 2.27, 2.52.

Cross-curricular Activities

ARTS AND HUMANITIES AND SOCIAL STUDIES

- In addition to her comments in the discussion, Sarah says that Greece provides other cultures with an example of a refreshing emotional attitude. "In Greece, people are forceful about their emotions, whether they are sad or happy," she says. "If a father is angry about something his son has done, he will speak out strongly about it and maybe even pound the table. If you're from another background, you might react to this kind of behavior in a bad way, but Greeks think it's healthy. They get it out of their system." Yumiko, on the other hand, notes on page 91 that Japanese culture values silence so much that a popular Japanese saying is, "By your mouth you shall perish." Help students to explore these cultural differences by asking which approach they find closer to their own. Students might role play situations in which someone from an emotionally expressive culture encounters someone more reticent.
- In addition to his comments in the discussion, Denis notes that "after watching many American movies, Russians think the most valuable things for Americans are power and money; they think America is as violent as the movies." Have students list five recent American movies they have seen. Then have them analyze the types of messages these movies convey about American culture. Ask the following: Do these movies portray America accurately? Why, or why not? What positive and negative images of American culture might people from another culture gain from these movies?

SOCIAL STUDIES

In the discussion, Jiannong says that China has become a major player in the world economy. In his opinion, China's economic prosperity is due, in part, to ideas borrowed from other economic systems in the world. "In China,"

(cont.)

Global Voices

A MULTICULTURAL CONVERSATION

Discussing the "Global Village"

Students were asked to discuss the influence their culture has had on the rest of the world and the ways in which their culture has been influenced by other cultures.

Elio: Mexican culture has greatly influenced the United States because we share a border; Mexican food and the Spanish language are changing the United States. We're rich in natural resources and export just about everything in great amounts. At the same time, Mexicans see a lot of things from the United States on TV and consider anything American good. Older people in the rural areas resent this because as the younger generation leans toward the new things that are coming, they leave the old ways behind.

Jiannong: A long time ago China was a closed country. The Chinese considered themselves the greatest civilization and the rest of the world barbarians who were not worthy trading partners. Now we are a major player in the world economy. Almost all of the cheap commodities in the United States are made in China. Besides exporting goods, China has influenced Asian countries such as Japan, Korea, Singapore, and Malaysia. Others have also influenced China. For example, Buddhism came to China from India about five hundred years ago. Now it's our main religion.

Yumiko: In Japan, our written characters, Buddhism, and much of our art are from China; rice is from Korea. But because it is surrounded by the sea and far away from other continents, Japan has had room to modify these outside influences; it modified Buddhism with aspects of Shintoism, our indigenous religion, for example. It was not until after World War II that Japan started feeling a Western influence. This is why Japan might seem so different to Americans.

Gabrielle: French people want to keep their identity and are scared to lose their culture. France is an old country with a strong past and the French don't want outside influences to change their culture. A few years ago, a law was passed saying that no one could use English words officially—in newspapers, TV shows, or speeches. So words like hamburger and weekend are translated into French. During the French Open [tennis tournament], the umpires make the calls only in French, while in other countries the umpires do it in both English and the language of the host country.

Sarah: Greeks have always embraced the foreigner and foreign things; they like to adapt and learn from them. At the same time, Greeks feel they've contributed in a huge way, in terms of mythology, literature, and the beginnings of Western civilization.

Avik: India is basically a land of invaders, beginning with the Aryans, then Alexander, the Mughals, and finally the British. India assimilated aspects of its culture from all of them. Indian folklore is rich in stories about Sikander—the Indian name for Alexander. Our cuisine is adorned with delicacies such as *Biryani,* courtesy of the Mughals. Our government structure is similar to that of the British. There is, however, a darker side to this assimilation. Foreign values, when adopted without analysis, can cause problems.

Cross-curricular Activities (cont.)

he says, "we have a saying that comes from [former leader] Deng Xiaoping: 'Whether the cat is black or white, the one that can catch the mouse is the good cat.' We call this the theory of the cat. It's a realistic philosophy that allows us to choose whatever is useful to us, whatever will improve people's lives. The government can change its plan and incorporate some Western ideas if that works best for China."

Discuss the theory of the cat with students. In what ways does it make sense? How have other countries adapted foreign ideas and systems to fit their own needs, according to the views expressed in this Global Voices discussion? What has our country borrowed from others?

Ebere: There is a culture clash going on between traditional values and Western values in Nigeria. The younger generation is preoccupied with Western tastes and values. This isn't bad necessarily, but it is changing our identity. At the same time, there's a growing awareness among educated people that it's important to identify with traditions. People in other parts of the world now want to relate to their "homeland." This is common among African Americans, for example, who fix their hair, dress, and makeup in traditional African style.

Yumiko: Our values, especially for beauty, are rooted in Western values. Japanese people sometimes think Western people are more beautiful than we are. If you look at TV commercials and magazines, you see a lot of Western people. The Western influence comes mainly from America, but there is also British influence. Many Japanese people are very brand conscious. One theory is that most Japanese can't afford to buy a big house, so for the economy to grow, we're encouraged to spend a lot of money on things like bags and clothes.

Denis: When you enter the Russian equivalent of a shopping mall, 70 percent of store names are in English, with goods from the West. We have more American movies than Russian ones and lots of American TV shows.

Ebere: The influence of other countries can be a good thing because it is easier to understand people if you know a little about their culture, but it is also important that we do not lose our own identity.

Yumiko: I personally think being influenced by other cultures is good. I think it's a growing process for everyone.

Sarah: I agree. There are a lot of influences from other countries, but Greece has such a long history and so many traditions that they would be difficult to lose.

Denis: It's good to have influence from other countries as long as Russia has its own traditions. If there is too much influence, Russia will become another America; it wouldn't be interesting. Now, we have a balance.

Avik: I think that the influence of other countries is inevitable. What can be judged to be good or bad is the manner in which a society interprets and accepts these influences. A good outcome is when foreign influence prompts self-reflection and strengthens one's sense of identity.

Elio: It's impossible for cultures to stay isolated. I once heard Carlos Fuentes speak and he said something to the effect that "Cultures perish in isolation." I think Mexico will acquire new influences from other countries, but so will the rest of the world. ■

Cross-curricular Activities

MATHEMATICS AND SCIENCES AND SOCIAL STUDIES

In addition to the insights he shares in the discussion, Avik notes that many traditions, such as the practice of yoga and ayurveda (an ancient form of medicine), are vanishing in India. At the same time, Western medicine has begun to look to Eastern methods of meditation for relaxation and pain management. Have students research these practices and others that originated in the East. Bill Moyers's *Healing and the Mind* might provide a good starting point. After their research, ask students how, based on what they have learned, they could use these alternate approaches to medicine in their own lives. You might want to arrange to have a practitioner of one of these approaches come to class and answer questions or demonstrate a medical approach.

SOCIAL STUDIES

After students have read the Global Voices conversation, lead a discussion on the losses and gains each culture has experienced because of influences from other cultures. Which changes do students see as beneficial? as harmful? Sarah and Denis stress the importance of maintaining cultural traditions in their countries, and Gabrielle notes that the French government has passed laws restricting English words from entering the French language. To what lengths should a culture go to retain its identity? To what extent should it welcome outside influences?

SOCIAL STUDIES AND APPLIED ARTS

What does the idea of a global village or international community mean to students in your class? For this activity, students will need access to the Internet and at least an hour of access time. You might assign this activity for students to do individually or in small groups if computer resources in your school are limited.

(cont.)

Cross-curricular Activities (cont.)

Have students seek international perspectives on topics that interest them. They might look for information about books, sports, issues, or hobbies. They might also correspond with international students by doing a search with the key phrase "pen pals." Then have them discuss their experience and the international perspectives they have gained about their topic. You can extend this activity by having students compile a directory of hot Internet sites, organizing it by country or topic, and displaying it in the school library for others to use. Students might also design their own home page that provides links to these sites and information about topics that students would like to share with others around the world.

"The Book of Sand"

ABOUT THE AUTHOR

Jorge Luis Borges (1899–1986) was born in Buenos Aires, Argentina. Borges's family folklore claims that when Jorge was six years old, he announced to his father, an author, that he too wanted to be a writer. Borges studied in Geneva, Switzerland, where he learned French and German. After World War I, Borges moved to Spain, where he was influenced by the avant-garde literary movement. He returned to Argentina in 1923 and published his first book of poems, *Passion for B.A.* After the overthrow of the Perón government, he was appointed director of the National Library. By the age of seventy, Borges was almost totally blind; to continue writing, he relied upon dictation. Among Borges's internationally acclaimed works are *Ficciones, Labyrinths, Six Problems for Don Isidro Parodi, The Conspirators,* and *Dr. Brodie's Report.*

ABOUT THE SELECTION

"The Book of Sand" reveals Borges's influential role in modern fiction. He was one of the first modern writers to reject the strictly Realistic or Naturalistic approach to writing and to introduce elements of fantasy into otherwise realistic narratives. The narrator of this short story is, like Borges, a former librarian and an avid lover of books. His meeting with a Bible seller is strictly realistic until Borges introduces the fantastic item he sells—a book with an infinite number of pages.

SELECTIONS FOR ADDITIONAL READING

ARGENTINA

"The Book of Sand"
by Jorge Luis Borges

The line is made up of an infinite number of points; the plane of an infinite number of lines; the volume of an infinite number of planes; the hypervolume of an infinite number of volumes. . . . No, unquestionably this is not—*more geometrico*[1]—the best way of beginning my story. To claim that it is true is nowadays the convention of every made-up story. Mine, however, *is* true.

I live alone in a fourth-floor apartment on Belgrano Street, in Buenos Aires. Late one evening, a few months back, I heard a knock at my door. I opened it and a stranger stood there. He was a tall man, with nondescript features—or perhaps it was my myopia[2] that made them seem that way. Dressed in gray and carrying a gray suitcase in his hand, he had an unassuming look about him. I saw at once that he was a foreigner. At first, he struck me as old; only later did I realize that I had been misled by his thin blond hair, which was, in a Scandinavian sort of way, almost white. During the course of our conversation, which was not to last an hour, I found out that he came from the Orkneys.[3]

I invited him in, pointing to a chair. He paused awhile before speaking. A kind of gloom emanated from him—as it does now from me.

"I sell Bibles," he said.

Somewhat pedantically,[4] I replied, "In this house are several English Bibles, including the first—John Wiclif's. I also have Cipriano de Valera's, Luther's—which, from a literary viewpoint, is the worst—and a Latin copy of the Vulgate. As you see, it's not exactly Bibles I stand in need of."

After a few moments of silence, he said, "I don't only sell Bibles. I can show you a holy book I came across on the outskirts of Bikaner.[5] It may interest you."

He opened the suitcase and laid the book on a table. It was an octavo[6] volume, bound in cloth. There was no doubt that it had passed through many hands. Examining it, I was surprised by its unusual weight. On the spine were the words "Holy Writ" and, below them, "Bombay."

"Nineteenth century, probably," I remarked.

"I don't know," he said. "I've never found out."

I opened the book at random. The script was strange to me. The pages, which were worn and typographically poor, were laid out in double columns, as in a Bible. The text was closely printed, and it was ordered in versicles.[7] In the upper corners of the pages were Arabic numbers. I noticed that one left-hand page bore the number (let us say) 40,514 and the facing right-hand page 999. I turned the leaf; it was numbered with eight digits. It also bore a small illustration, like the kind used in dictionaries—an anchor drawn with pen and ink, as if by a schoolboy's clumsy hand.

It was at this point that the stranger said, "Look at the illustration closely. You'll never see it again."

I noted my place and closed the book. At once, I reopened it. Page by page, in vain, I looked for the illustration of the anchor. "It seems to be a version of Scriptures[8] in some Indian language, is it not?" I said to hide my dismay.

"No," he replied. Then, as if confiding a secret, he lowered his voice. "I acquired the book in a town out on the plain in exchange for a handful of rupees and a Bible. Its owner did not know how to read. I suspect that he saw the Book of Books as a talisman.[9] He was of the lowest caste; nobody but other untouchables[10] could tread his shadow without contamination. He told me his book was called the Book of Sand, because neither the book nor the sand has any beginning or end."

The stranger asked me to find the first page.

I laid my left hand on the cover and, trying to put my thumb on the flyleaf, I opened the book. It was useless. Every time I tried, a number of pages came between the cover and my thumb. It was as if they kept growing from the book.

"Now find the last page."

1. ***more geometrico.*** Latin phrase meaning "geometrical delay"
2. **myopia.** Nearsightedness
3. **Orkneys.** Group of islands north of Scotland
4. **pedantically.** With undue stress on obscure points of scholarship
5. **Bikaner.** City in northwest India
6. **octavo.** Book measuring 6 by 9 inches
7. **versicles.** Short verses or verse parts, usually referring to Psalms
8. **Scriptures.** The Bible
9. **talisman.** Charm; object engraved with magic symbols
10. **caste . . . untouchables.** Untouchables are members of the lowest caste, or hereditary social class, in India. Touching such a person is traditionally believed to cause defilement.

Again I failed. In a voice that was not mine, I barely managed to stammer, "This can't be."

Still speaking in a low voice, the stranger said, "It can't be, but it *is*." The number of pages in this book is no more or less than infinite. None is the first page, none the last. I don't know why they're numbered in this arbitrary way. Perhaps to suggest that the terms of an infinite series admit any number."

Then, as if he were thinking aloud, he said, "If space is infinite, we may be at any point in space. If time is infinite, we may be at any point in time."

His speculations irritated me. "You are religious, no doubt?" I asked him.

"Yes, I'm a Presbyterian. My conscience is clear. I am reasonably sure of not having cheated the native when I gave him the Word of God in exchange for his devilish book."

I assured him that he had nothing to reproach himself for, and I asked if he were just passing through this part of the world. He replied that he planned to return to his country in a few days. It was then that I learned that he was a Scot from the Orkney Islands. I told him I had a great personal affection for Scotland, through my love of Stevenson and Hume.[1]

"You mean Stevenson and Robbie Burns,[2]" he corrected.

While we spoke, I kept exploring the infinite book.

With feigned indifference, I asked, "Do you intend to offer this curiosity to the British Museum?"

"No. I'm offering it to you," he said, and he stipulated[3] a rather high sum for the book.

I answered, in all truthfulness, that such a sum was out of my reach, and I began thinking. After a minute or two, I came up with a scheme.

"I propose a swap," I said. "You got this book for a handful of rupees and a copy of the Bible. I'll offer you the amount of my pension check, which I've just collected, and my black-letter Wiclif Bible. I inherited it from my ancestors."

"A black-letter Wiclif!" he murmured.

I went to my bedroom and brought him the money and the book. He turned the leaves and studied the title page with all the fervor of a true bibliophile.[4]

"It's a deal," he said.

It amazed me that he did not haggle. Only later was I to realize that he had entered my house with his mind made up to sell the book. Without counting the money, he put it away.

We talked about India, about Orkney, and about the Norwegian jarls[5] who once ruled it. It was night when the man left. I have not seen him again, nor do I know his name.

I thought of keeping the Book of Sand in the space left on the shelf by the Wiclif, but in the end I decided to hide it behind the volumes of a broken set of The Thousand and One Nights. I went to bed and did not sleep. At three or four in the morning, I turned on the light. I got down the impossible book and leafed through its pages. On one of them I saw engraved a mask. The upper corner of the page carried a number, which I no longer recall, elevated to the ninth power.

I showed no one my treasure. To the luck of owning it was added the fear of having it stolen, and then the misgiving that it might not truly be infinite. These twin preoccupations intensified my old misanthropy.[6] I had only a few friends left; I now stopped seeing even them. A prisoner of the book, I almost never went out anymore. After studying its frayed spine and covers with a magnifying glass, I rejected the possibility of a contrivance[7] of any sort. The small illustrations, I verified, came two thousand pages apart. I set about listing them alphabetically in a notebook, which I was not long in filling up. Never once was an illustration repeated. At night, in the meager intervals my insomnia granted, I dreamed of the book.

Summer came and went, and I realized that the book was monstrous. What good did it do me to think that I who looked upon the volume with my eyes, who held it in my hands, was any less monstrous? I felt that the book was a nightmarish object, an obscene thing that affronted and tainted reality itself.

I thought of fire, but I feared that the burning of an infinite book might likewise prove infinite and suffocate the planet with smoke. Somewhere I recalled reading that the best place to hide a leaf is in a forest. Before retirement, I worked on Mexico Street, at the Argentine National Library, which contains nine hundred thousand volumes. I knew that to the right of the entrance a curved staircase leads down into the basement, where books and maps and periodicals are kept. One day I went there and, slipping past a member of the staff and trying not to notice at what height or distance from the door, I lost the Book of Sand on one of the basement's musty shelves. ■

1. **Stevenson and Hume.** Refers to Robert Louis Stevenson (1850–1894), a Scottish novelist and poet, and Daniel Hume (1711–1776), a Scottish philosopher
2. **Robbie Burns.** Robert Burns (1759–1796) was a Scottish poet who wrote in the Scottish dialect.
3. **stipulated.** Made part of a bargain
4. **bibliophile.** Collector and lover of books
5. **jarls.** Scandinavian chieftains or noblemen
6. **misanthropy.** Hatred or distrust of all people
7. **contrivance.** Trick

Additional Questions and Activities

Encourage students to discuss the following questions:

1. The narrator says that the way he begins this story is not the best way. In what way *is* this beginning directly related to the tale he tells? What does this beginning reveal about the story that follows.
2. The Bible salesman describes the book as "devilish." Does the narrator's own experiences with the book confirm or deny his description? Explain.
3. What do you think the author is implying about the concept of infinity?
4. Why is what the narrator chooses to do with the book appropriate given its nature?

ANSWERS

Responses will vary.

1. The beginning sentences discuss infinity in mathematics, which is directly related to the narrator's later quest to discover how a book can have a seemingly infinite number of pages.
2. Students may say that the book is indeed devilish both because of its unrealistic nature and the fact that it immediately obsesses the narrator, almost driving him to the brink of madness.
3. Students may say that the author is implying that it is impossible for humans to comprehend the infinite.
4. Students may say that the narrator chooses to lose an infinite book within the seemingly infinite (but actually quite finite) number of books in a national library's collection.

"A Song on the End of the World"

About the Author

Czeslaw Milosz (1911–) is a poet, essayist, and novelist. He knew from an early age that he wanted to be a writer, but in school he studied law to gain a deeper understanding of society.

Soon after World War II began, Milosz moved to Warsaw. During the four years he lived there, he took part in the underground activities that defied the Nazi regime. After the war, he served as a Polish diplomat in Washington, DC. In the 1960s he became a professor of Slavic literature at the University of California at Berkeley. In 1980, he was awarded the Nobel Prize for literature.

About the Selection

After the Nazis and the Soviets invaded Poland in September 1939, Warsaw ended up controlled by the Germans. All Poles faced terrible treatment, including dangerous forced labor, torture, and death, at the hands of the Nazis. Milosz doubted that he would survive the war. **"A Song on the End of the World,"** which was written during the time Milosz was living in Warsaw, deals ironically with the sense of doom that pervaded Poland. At the same time, it creates a picture of a world that, unlike Warsaw in 1944, had not fallen apart and was in fact operating very peacefully.

Additional Questions and Activities

Ask students the following questions about Milosz's poem.

1. What do people do on the day the world ends?
2. Who is disappointed? Why?
3. What is ironic about the end of the world as Milosz describes it?
4. Find examples of parallelism and repetition. What ideas are emphasized by the use of these techniques?

(cont.)

POLAND

"A Song on the End of the World"

by Czeslaw Milosz, translated by Anthony Milosz

On the day the world ends
A bee circles a clover,
A fisherman mends a glimmering net.
Happy porpoises jump in the sea,
By the rainspout young sparrows are playing
And the snake is gold-skinned as it should always
be.

On the day the World ends
Women walk through the fields under their
umbrellas,
A drunkard grows sleepy at the edge of a lawn,
Vegetable peddlers shout in the street
And a yellow-sailed boat comes nearer the island,
The voice of a violin lasts in the air
And leads into a starry night.

And those who expected lightning and thunder
Are disappointed.
And those who expected signs and archangels'
trumps
Do not believe it is happening now.
As long as the sun and the moon are above,
As long as the bumblebee visits a rose,
As long as rosy infants are born
No one believes it is happening now.

Only a white-haired old man, who should be a
prophet
Yet is not a prophet, for he's much too busy,
Repeats while he binds his tomatoes:
There will be no other end of the world,
There will be no other end of the world.

Warsaw, 1944. ■

CANADA

"Simmering"

by Margaret Atwood

It started in the backyards. At first the men concentrated on heat and smoke, and on dangerous thrusts with long forks. Their wives gave them aprons in railroad stripes, with slogans on the front—*Hot Stuff, The Boss*—to spur them on. Then it began to get all mixed up with who should do the dishes, and you can't fall back on paper plates forever, and around that time the wives got tired of making butterscotch brownies and jello salads with grated carrots and baby marshmallows in them and wanted to make money instead, and one thing led to another. The wives said that there were only twenty-four hours in a day; and the men, who in that century were still priding themselves on their rationality, had to agree that this was so.

For a while they worked it out that the men were in charge of the more masculine kinds of food: roasts, chops, steaks, dead chickens and ducks, gizzards, hearts, anything that had obviously been killed, that had visibly bled. The wives did the other things, the glazed parsnips and the prune whip, anything that flowered or fruited or was soft and gooey in the middle. That was all right for about a decade. Everyone praised the men to keep them going, and the wives, sneaking out of the houses in the mornings with their squeaky new briefcases, clutching their bus tickets because the men needed the station wagons to bring home the carcasses, felt they had got away with something.

But time is not static, and the men refused to stay put. They could not be kept isolated in their individual kitchens, kitchens into which the wives were allowed less and less frequently because, the men said, they did not sharpen the knives properly, if at all. The men began to acquire kitchen machines which they would spend the weekends taking apart and oiling. There were a few accidents at first, a few lost fingers and ends of noses, but the men soon got the hang of it and branched out into other areas: automatic nutmeg graters, electric gadgets for taking the lids off jars. At cocktail parties they would gather in groups at one end of the room, exchanging private recipes and cooking yarns, tales of soufflés daringly saved at the last minute, pears flambées which had gone out of control and had to be fought to a standstill. Some of these stories had risqué phrases in them, such as *chicken breasts*. Indeed, sexual metaphor was changing: bowls and forks became prominent, and *eggbeater*, *pressure cooker* and *turkey baster* became words which only the most daring young women, the kind who thought it was a kick to butter their own toast, would venture to pronounce in mixed company. Men who could not cook very well hung about the edges of these groups, afraid to say much, admiring the older and more experienced ones, wishing they could be like them.

Soon after that, the men resigned from their jobs in large numbers so they could spend more time in the kitchen. The magazines said it was a modern trend. The

1. **misanthropy.** Hatred or distrust of all people
2. **contrivance.** Trick

Additional Questions and Activities (cont.)

Answers

1. Fishermen mend nets, women walk through fields, a drunkard grows sleepy, peddlers sell their wares. People go about as though it were any other day.
2. The people "who expect the world to end in lightning and thunder" are disappointed because there are no such signs of apocalypse.
3. The end of the world seems as if it should be a momentous, tumultuous event. Such expectations are broken by the ordinary, calm day described.
4. The lines "On the day the world ends," and "There will be no other end of the world" are repeated, emphasizing that the world is ending, although it may not seem to be so, and that the world will no longer exist and therefore can have

(cont.)

wives were all driven off to work, whether they wanted to or not: someone had to make the money, and of course they did not want their husbands' masculinity to be threatened. A man's status in the community was now displayed by the length of his carving knives, by how many of them he had and how sharp he kept them, and by whether they were plain or ornamented with gold and precious jewels.

Exclusive clubs and secret societies sprang up. Men meeting for the first time would now exchange special handshakes—the Béchamel[1] twist, the chocolate mousse double grip—to show that they had been initiated. It was pointed out to the women, who by this time did not go into the kitchens at all on pain of being thought unfeminine, that *chef* after all means *chief* and that Mixmasters were common but no one had ever heard of a Mixmistress. Psychological articles began to appear in the magazines on the origin of women's kitchen envy and how it could be cured. Amputation of the tip of the tongue was recommended, and, as you know, became a widespread practice in the more advanced nations. If Nature had meant women to cook, it was said, God would have made carving knives round and with holes in them.

This is history. But it is not a history familiar to many people. It exists only in the few archival collections that have not yet been destroyed, and in manuscripts like this one, passed from woman to woman, usually at night, copied out by hand or memorized. It is subversive of me even to write these words. I am doing so, at the risk of my own personal freedom, because now, after so many centuries of stagnation,[2] there are signs that hope and therefore change have once more become possible.

The women in their pinstripe suits, exiled to the livingrooms where they dutifully sip the glasses of port brought out to them by the men, used to sit uneasily, silently, listening to the loud bursts of male and somehow derisive laughter from behind the closed kitchen doors. But they have begun whispering to each other. When they are with those they trust, they tell of a time long ago, lost in the fogs of legend, hinted at in packets of letters found in attic trunks and in the cryptic frescoes[3] on abandoned temple walls, when women too were allowed to participate in the ritual which now embodies the deepest religious convictions of our society: the transformation of the consecrated[4] flour into the holy bread. At night they dream, long clandestine[5] dreams, confused and obscured by shadows. They dream of plunging their hands into the earth, which is red as blood and soft, which is milky and warm. They dream that the earth gathers itself under their hands, swells, changes its form, flowers into a thousand shapes, for them too, for them once more. They dream of apples; they dream of the creation of the world; they dream of freedom. ■

---

1. **Béchamel.** Basic white sauce of milk, butter, and flour
2. **stagnation.** State of unchanging stillness
3. **frescoes.** Paintings on walls
4. **consecrated.** Set apart as holy
5. **clandestine.** Secret; hidden

"Simmering"

About the Author

Canadian writer **Margaret Atwood** (1939–) first became famous as a poet and is now well known for her intense, ironic, and sometimes disturbing novels and stories. She grew up in Ottawa and Toronto, Ontario, but came to know the Canadian wilderness during summers spent in northern Quebec. She graduated from the University of Toronto and received a master's degree at Radcliffe in Cambridge, Massachusetts.

Her first book of poetry, *The Circle Game,* won a Governor General's Award in 1966, and she has won many other awards since. Atwood's writing probes varied subjects, including male-female relationships, the Canadian pioneer spirit, the influence of myth, and international human rights. Atwood is also an editor and critic.

About the Selection

"Simmering," like many of Atwood's works, uses terse language and is filled with sharp, witty observations. Atwood comments on gender roles in this humorous piece.

This selection can be classified as a short short, or flash fiction. A **short short** is an extremely brief short story. Short shorts sometimes take the form of anecdotes, or retellings of single incidents. Alternatively, they may attempt to develop an entire plot within the compass of a few paragraphs. Many short shorts are highly poetic and may be considered prose poems.

Bibliographic Note

Atwood's works include the following:

POETRY
- *Animals in That Country*
- *Double Persephone*
- *Good Bones and Simple Murders*
- *Murder in the Dark*

(cont.)

Additional Questions and Activities (cont.)

no other ending. Lines 14 and 16 are parallel, emphasizing that people who expect any kind of sign of the end will not understand that the world is ending for there will be no such signs. Lines 19 and 20 are parallel. The bumble bee landing on a rose and infants being born are both life-affirming activities that suggest beginnings rather than ends. Such things will continue to happen even as the world ends.

Bibliographic Note (cont.)

- *Procedures for Underground*
- *Selected Poems*
- *You Are Happy*

FICTION
- *Alias Grace*
- *Bodily Harm*
- *Cat's Eye*
- *The Edible Woman*
- *The Handmaid's Tale*
- *Lady Oracle*
- *Life Before Man*
- *The Robber Bride*
- *Surfacing*
- *Wilderness Tips*

ADDITIONAL RESOURCES

Assessment Portfolio

- Vocabulary Worksheet 2.12.27
- Study Guide 2.12.28
- Unit Test 2.12.29

Essential Skills Practice Books

WRITING

- Choosing a Purpose, 1.8
- Outlining, 1.12
- Writing a Critical Essay, 1.20

LANGUAGE

- Connotation and Denotation, 2.73
- Correcting Sentence Fragments, Run-ons, and Sentence Strings, 2.27
- Other Uses of Quotation Marks, 2.52
- Semicolons and Colons, 2.48
- Underlining, Italics, and Quotation Marks in Titles, 2.51

SPEAKING AND LISTENING

- Active Listening and Interpersonal Communication, 3.2
- Collaborative Learning and Discussion, 3.3
- Television and Film, 3.6

STUDY AND RESEARCH

- Computer-assisted Research, 4.17
- Other Sources of Information, 4.18
- Taking Essay Tests, 4.27
- Using Dictionaries, 4.15
- Using Reference Works, 4.14
- Using Search Tools, 4.12
- Using the Card Catalog, 4.13
- Using Thesauruses, 4.16

APPLIED ENGLISH/TECH PREP

- Technical Writing, 5.5

UNIT REVIEW

Modern and Contemporary Literature

VOCABULARY FROM THE SELECTIONS

ambiguous, 1072
amiability, 1021
annihilate, 1021
anomaly, 1068
apropos, 1069
benediction, 1053
cajole, 1068
ceaselessly, 1053
celestial, 1053
chafe, 1021
colossus, 1072
daunt, 1067
decimate, 1072
decree, 1054
defunct, 1098
discreetly, 1022
drollery, 1031
eddy, 1067
elegist, 1072
emaciated, 1046
eminently, 1045
ensue, 1027, 1066
epigram, 1069
exorcise, 1108
extremity, 1027
fidelity, 1056
futile, 1053
garrulous, 1022
grievance, 1108
hirsute, 1099
illicit, 1048
ignominy, 1100
imminent, 1080
impede, 1061
imperturbable, 1019
impudent, 1054
incessant, 1020
ingratiating, 1046
innumerable, 1021
insipid, 1030
intervening, 1021
intrepid, 1067
levity, 1053
litany, 1020
livid, 1095
lucidity, 1055
lugubrious, 1100
maniacal, 1095
melancholy, 1055
mortuary, 1098
myriad, 1056
negate, 1056
oblivion, 1082
pallid, 1080
pantomime, 1073
petrifaction, 1027
pious, 1022
predicament, 1030
primordial, 1066
proletarian, 1055
rebuke, 1045
repertoire, 1068
reprieve, 1106
rhetoric, 1045
robust, 1027
row, 1048
scrutinize, 1048
seethe, 1098
semantic, 1068
sepulchral, 1100
slake, 1099
sodden, 1020
steep, 1041
sterile, 1056
stridently, 1095
superciliously, 1096
surmount, 1055
temerity, 1098
tepid, 1046
ululate, 1087
unscathed, 1072
veil, 1020

LITERARY TERMS

alliteration, 1042, 1063
allusion, 1051
anecdote, 1044
antihero, 1078, 1085
aphorism, 1111
archetype, 1102
atmosphere, 1025, 1092
autobiography, 1111
biography, 1026, 1033
character, 1058
dramatic irony, 1033, 1085
Existentialism, 1058
extended metaphor, 1084
figure of speech, 1044
free verse, 1038
image, 1024, 1042, 1102
imagery, 1024, 1042, 1102
internal monologue, 1033
irony, 1033, 1051
irony of situation, 1033, 1051
metaphor, 1111
metonymy, 1044, 1051
mood, 1025, 1092
Negritude movement, 1040
parody, 1075
point of view, 1092
repetition, 1038
rhyme, 1063
satire, 1033, 1075, 1115
science fiction, 1065, 1077
stream-of-consciousness writing, 1033
symbol, 1038, 1115
synaesthesia, 1033
tone, 1063
verbal irony, 1033

Vocabulary Check Test

Ask students to number their papers from one to ten. Have students complete each sentence with a word from the Vocabulary from the Selections in the Unit Review.

1. The stormy waters will impede the progress of the rescue team.
2. When Uri had laryngitis, he had to communicate through pantomime.

(cont.)

Vocabulary Check Test (cont.)

3. The food was pallid to both the eye and the palate, and Leona longed for a spicy, colorful meal.
4. The sound of lugubrious hymns filled the air as the funeral procession made its way toward the graveyard.
5. Luis was annoyed every time Marc called stridently to him.
6. Riding in an inner tube, we twirled about in the eddies on the river.
7. The mayor will decree July 12 as Summerfest, a yearly holiday.
8. Uma expected an enthusiastic welcome, but she received a tepid reception.
9. A great commotion will ensue when school is let out for the summer.
10. Although the interviewer tried to rattle him, Nathan was imperturbable.

SYNTHESIS: QUESTIONS FOR WRITING, RESEARCH, OR DISCUSSION

GENRE STUDIES

1. Define *autobiography* and *biography.* Virginia Woolf's *Orlando* is a mock biography, and Maxine Hong Kingston's *The Woman Warrior* is an unusual autobiography. Discuss elements of the selections from these two works that reflect conventions of biographies and autobiographies. What fictional or unrealistic elements are used in each selection?

2. Modernist writers often favored particular forms of writing, such as free verse, stream-of-consciousness writing, and internal monologue. Define each of these terms and give examples of each form from the modernist selections in this unit.

THEMATIC STUDIES

3. Cultural conflict may arise when two cultures are thrown together as happens in cases of colonization or emigration. Consider the attitudes expressed toward traditional culture and cultural change or assimilation in the following works: Bessie Head's "Snapshots of a Wedding," Léopold Senghor's "And We Shall Be Steeped," and the selection from Maxine Hong Kingston's *The Woman Warrior.* Compare and contrast the attitudes expressed in these selections and draw some conclusions about the values of cultural traditions and their role in the contemporary world.

4. Identify examples of death imagery used in Federico García Lorca's "The Guitar" and Anita Desai's "Games at Twilight." What is the effect of the imagery in each selection?

5. Judith Wright in "Request to a Year," Maxine Hong Kingston in *The Woman Warrior,* and Margaret Atwood in "Simmering" explore changing gender roles. Compare and contrast the ideas each writer expresses. What tone does each author use? What is the effect of each tone? Do the three selections have a similar purpose? Explain.

6. The fall from innocence to experience is an archetypal theme. What events lead the innocent characters in Anita Desai's "Games at Twilight" and in James Joyce's "Araby" to knowledge and understanding? In what way does the innocent character in Jerzy Kosinski's novel *Being There* differ from these characters? What is the attitude of the other characters in these works toward the innocent characters?

7. In what way do both Jenny Mastoraki and Stanislaw Lem use personified objects to present social criticism? Why might they use these objects rather than people to present these criticisms?

HISTORICAL/BIOGRAPHICAL STUDIES

8. Research the social conditions that led to the creation of the philosophical school of Existentialism and the Negritude literary movement. In what way do the lives of Albert Camus and Léopold Senghor reflect the movements in which they were respectively involved?

SPELLING CHECK TEST

Ask students to number their papers from one to ten. Read each word aloud. Then read aloud the sentence containing the word. Repeat the word. Ask students to write the word on their papers, spelling it correctly.

1. **sodden**

Carl's boots were so old that every rainstorm, snowstorm, or puddle left him with sodden socks.

2. **amiability**

That breed of dog is known for its amiability; it is not a good watchdog because it loves all people.

3. **primordial**

The few saplings that were recently planted cannot replace the splendor of the primordial forest that once stood on this ground.

4. **melancholy**

Reading about gloomy forests matched Marissa's melancholy mood.

5. **celestial**

We identified the celestial body in the evening sky as the planet Venus.

6. **scrutinizes**

The detective scrutinizes the scene of the crime, looking for clues.

7. **rebuke**

Taking the rebuke about her sloppy work seriously, Colandra became more careful and precise.

8. **steeped**

While writing her dissertation on the oral traditions of Senegal, Birungi was steeped in the folklore of that country.

9. **robust**

Two weeks after her illness, Nika had lost her frail, wan look and had returned to her usual robust appearance.

10. **predicament**

Embarrassed by the predicament, the committee was forced to announce that they had ordered dinners for only half of the guests.

LANGUAGE ARTS SURVEY

1. *Essential Skills: Writing*
    - Introduction to Writing
    - Understanding the Writing Process
2. *Essential Skills: Language*
    - Grammar Handbook
        - Introduction to Grammar
        - The Parts of Speech
        - Building Sentences
        - Expanding and Combining Sentences
        - Editing for Errors in Pronoun Usage
        - Editing for Errors in Modifier Usage
    - Usage Handbook
    - Mechanics Handbook
        - Proofreading for Punctuation Errors
        - Proofreading for Errors in Capitalization
    - Spelling Handbook
    - Vocabulary Handbook
    - Varieties of English
3. *Essential Skills: Speaking and Listening*
4. *Essential Skills: Study and Research*
    - Thinking Skills
    - Reading Skills
    - Research Skills
    - Test-taking Skills
5. *Essential Skills: Applied English/Tech Prep*
    - Personal and Professional Communication
    - Writing and Researching to Enter the Job Market
    - Writing on the Job

Essential Skills: *Writing*

INTRODUCTION TO WRITING

1.1 The Writing Process

From the interpersonal level to the international level, success in our world depends on good communication. Whether you are trying to resolve a problem with a friend or negotiate world peace, you need to be able to communicate well. In our information-driven society, which depends so heavily on the written word, the most important action you can take to ensure your future success is to learn how to write clearly and effectively.

Writing is not a mysterious skill for which some people have talent and others do not. You can learn to write well through practice and by learning each step involved in the **writing process.** The chart below breaks down the writing process into its component parts. This portion of the Language Arts Survey will teach you how to perform each step so you can create an effective piece of writing.

SIX STAGES IN THE PROCESS OF WRITING	
1. Prewriting	In the prewriting stage, you **plan** your writing: choose a topic, audience, purpose, and form; gather ideas; and arrange them logically.
2. Drafting	In this stage, you **jot** your ideas down on paper without worrying about getting everything just right.
3. Peer and Self-Evaluation	To evaluate is to **judge** something. In the evaluation stage, your writing is judged and studied to see how it might be improved. When a classmate judges your writing, that is called **peer evaluation.** When you judge your own writing, that is called **self-evaluation.**
4. Revising	In the revising stage, you work to **improve** content, organization, and style, or the way you express your ideas.
5. Proofreading	In the proofreading stage, you **check** your writing for errors in spelling, grammar, usage, capitalization, and punctuation. After correcting these errors, you make a final copy of your paper and proofread it again.
6. Publishing and Presenting	In the publishing and presenting stage, you **share** your work with an audience.

1.2 Keeping a Journal

In his autobiography, Benjamin Franklin asserts that "The next thing most like living one's life over again seems to be a recollection of that life." He recommends that a person "make that recollection as durable as possible by putting it down in writing." A **journal** is a written recollection of your experiences, ideas, wishes, and dreams. Keeping such a record enables you to look at your life and see where you have been and where you are going. Although you can't live your life over—or even live one day again—as you reexamine your life, you can learn from your mistakes and make tomorrow different from yesterday.

A journal can be kept in a composition book, a spiral notebook, a looseleaf binder, or a bound book with blank pages. Some people even keep electronic journals on computers. Choose whatever format you like, try to write something every day, and be sure to save your old journals. Reading old journals can be entertaining as well as enlightening—and maybe someday your journals will be published or will prove a valuable source to a future biographer or historian!

Journal entries can be classified according to purpose. Study the chart below to learn about different types of journals and their contents.

TYPES OF JOURNAL ENTRIES	
A Diary, or Day-to-day Record of Your Life	August 30, 1999. Summer is over. Now we're on our way home from our family reunion. Sometimes I wonder why we go. The six of us pile into the car, drive for twelve hours, spend two days with 50-odd (and I do mean odd) relatives, turn around and drive for another twelve hours to get home, and then start school the next day. It's crazy. Vanessa and Mark have been bickering for hours, and I hardly have any room to write in this cramped backseat. Why do we drive halfway across the continent to be with these people just because they happen to be family? Some of them are really weird. But there must be something to this business of being family. I only see my second cousins once a year, but we pick up right where we left off the year before.
A Reader Response Journal	Today I read Gabriel García Márquez's story "Tuesday Siesta." It was hard to understand at first; I had to reread it a couple of times before I knew what was going on. I wonder what was going through the mother's mind as she was on her way to her son's grave. I wonder why she didn't cry, and why she didn't want her daughter to cry. I wonder what the son was really like. What did the priest mean when he said, "God's will is inscrutable"?
A Commonplace Book, or Book of Quotations	"Pale death, with impartial step, knocks at the hut of the poor and the towers of kings." —Horace "Love bears all things, believes all things, hopes all things, endures all things." —1 Corinthians
A Writer's Lab, or Collection of Ideas for Writing	Science Fiction Story Idea: What if I could relive one day in my life? Which one would it be? What would I do differently? What would I make happen, or prevent from happening? How would it change the days to follow?

CONTINUED

A Learning Log, or Record of What You Have Learned	Science: Today we were talking about the battle medical science is waging against infectious diseases. In some ways we are losing the battle—there are more germs and stronger ones than ever. But at least there is one true success story. Many people used to die from the smallpox virus, but then a vaccine was developed. People in my parents' generation had to get vaccinated against the virus, but even the vaccination could be dangerous; when my aunt was a baby she reacted against the vaccine and was very sick. Now, thanks to medical science and to a worldwide effort to protect people, the disease has been eliminated from the planet. History: I wonder how the Native Americans felt when the Europeans arrived in their country—maybe like we would feel if aliens landed on our planet and tried to impose their "superior" culture upon us. Today we learned about one of the many shameful episodes in the U. S. government's dealings with Native Americans—the "Trail of Tears," when 16,000 Cherokees were forced to march from their eastern homeland to "Indian Territory" (Oklahoma). At least 2,000 died along the way. What would we do if aliens drove us from our homes?
A Record of Questions	How is the nose able to smell? When and where did the Renaissance begin? If I wanted to spend the summer fighting forest fires, what would I need to do?
A Daily Organizer	Things to do tomorrow: • Go to library and check out book(s) on Greek mythology • Go to dentist appointment after school • Call Verena about buying her guitar • Write rough draft of English paper

1.3 Your Writing Portfolio

A **writing portfolio** is a collection of your writing. A portfolio may be a simple file folder with your name on it and your writing in it, or you may design or buy a fancy portfolio. You can even keep an electronic portfolio on a computer. Your teacher may ask you to keep a **complete portfolio**, one that includes all the pieces that you write. Another possibility is that your teacher will ask you to keep a **selected portfolio**, one that contains only your very best pieces of writing.

When you put a piece of writing in your portfolio, make sure that your name and the date are on it. Attach any notes or earlier drafts of the writing that you have. You should also include any completed evaluation forms that your teacher requests of you. If you are keeping a selected portfolio, do not throw away pieces of writing you do not include in your portfolio. Save them so that you or your teacher can refer to them.

From time to time, you and your teacher will **evaluate,** or examine, your portfolio. You will meet in a **student-teacher conference** and talk about your pieces of writing. Your teacher will help you to find strengths and weaknesses in your writing. He or she will help you to make plans for improving your writing in the future.

Keeping a writing portfolio can be exciting. In very little time, you can build a collection of your work. Looking over this work, you can take pride in your past accomplishments. You can also see how you are growing as a writer from month to month.

1.4 Using Computers for Writing

Computers are not essential to good writing. After all, Shakespeare did just fine without one; in fact, the vast majority of great writing has been done without computers. Nevertheless, using a personal computer can make many parts of the writing process simpler.

Computer Hardware

Hardware is the actual machinery of a computer. The heart of this machinery is the **central processing unit**, or **CPU**, which carries out the instructions given by the computer user. Connected to the CPU, or sometimes in the same case with it, are various **peripherals**—devices for storing, inputting, and outputting information, or **data**.

COMMON COMPUTER PERIPHERALS	
Storage Devices	• **Floppy diskettes**, or **floppies**, are small, flat media used to store and to transport limited amounts of data, such as individual computer files and programs. • **Hard drives** store large amounts of data on revolving disks. A hard drive can be **internal** (located inside the case with the CPU) or **external** (housed in a separate case and connected to the CPU by a cable). • **Removable media**, like hard drives, store large amounts of data. However, unlike hard drives, they can be inserted and ejected, like floppy disks. Common removable media include CD-ROMs, optical disks, and DAT tapes.
Input Devices	• **Keyboards**, the most common of all input devices, allow you to type numbers, alphabetic characters, and special computer commands. • **Mice** and **trackballs** are devices that are used to point to and select items on a computer monitor. • **Digitizing tablets** allow you to write in longhand and to draw directly onto the computer screen. • **Scanners** allow you to turn pictures or words into computer files that can then be edited or otherwise manipulated. • **Voice recognition devices** allow you to speak commands to the computer. Some will even transcribe, or write, your speech into a computer file that can then be edited.
Output Devices	• **Monitors** are the most common output devices. A monitor is a screen, similar to the one on a television, that shows you the work that you are doing on the computer. • **Printers** are machines that create **hard copies**, or printed versions, of the work that you have done on the computer. • **Modems** are devices for communicating, over telephone lines, with other computers.

Computer Software

Software is the set of instructions for making a computer do specific tasks. A particular piece of software is called a **program.** The people who create programs are called **programmers.** The chart below describes common programs used by writers.

SOFTWARE FOR WRITERS	
Operating System	An **operating system,** or **OS,** is a program that tells the computer how to do general tasks—how to create, save, and store files; what to do when specific commands are given; how to print files, and so on.
Application Software	An **application program** enables the user to accomplish a particular kind of task. Common application programs include the following: • **Word-processing programs** allow you to key in words. Most such programs also allow you to revise your writing, to check its spelling, to add special formatting such as boldface or italic letters, and to save and print your work. Many of these programs also allow you to consult a built-in dictionary and/or thesaurus and to check your grammar, usage, capitalization, and punctuation. • **Page-layout programs** allow you to put your writing into columns and boxes and to add graphic elements such as lines, borders, photographs, and illustrations. Such programs are used to produce newsletters, posters, flyers, newspapers, magazines, and books. • **Graphics programs** allow you to create illustrations and to edit photographs. • **Telecommunications programs** allow you to use a **modem** to connect over telephone lines to other computers, to **online information services,** or to **computer networks** such as the **Internet** and the **World Wide Web.** Other types of applications often used by writers allow you to create outlines, graphs, charts, indexes, and bibliographies.

Applications of Computers to Writing

Obviously, a computer can be useful simply as a means for getting words onto a page. However, any typewriter can do that. A typewriter also allows you to save separate drafts of your writing as hard copy, giving you a record of the development of your writing. Nonetheless, computers offer some advantages that typewriters do not:

- the ability to revise, or edit, your writing easily, simply by moving words, sentences, or paragraphs around on the monitor or disk without having to rekey everything;
- the ability to format your writing in special ways (by adding bold or italic formatting; by specifying the sets of letters, or fonts, to be used; by automating functions such as paragraph, page, and line breaks, and so on);
- the ability to look up definitions, synonyms, and antonyms and to perform, automatically, such editing functions as checking your spelling, grammar, usage, and mechanics;

- the ability to print multiple copies of your work;
- the ability to add photographs and illustrations to your work;
- the ability to use computer-accessed information sources, such as online information services and reference materials such as encyclopedias on CD-ROM

Despite these advantages, many writers still prefer to work in longhand or to use typewriters. Like most aspects of writing, the choice of writing instrument is up to you. It depends, of course, not only on your personal preferences, but also on the availability of machines and of instruction on how to use them. Many schools have **writing labs** with computers available to students, and computers are sometimes available in school or public libraries. If you do not have access to a personal computer, check with your teachers and librarians about computers and computer training available to students in your area.

UNDERSTANDING THE WRITING PROCESS

1.5 Making a Writing Plan

The first step in undertaking any venture is to make a plan. In the **prewriting stage** of the writing process, you formulate a plan. You decide on a topic, audience, purpose, and form. You also gather ideas and organize them.

THE PARTS OF A WRITING PLAN	
Topic	A **topic** is simply something to write about. For example, you might write about a sports hero or about a cultural event in your community.
Audience	An **audience** is the person or group of people intended to read what you write. For example, you might write for yourself, for a friend, for a relative, or for your classmates.
Purpose	A **purpose**, or **aim**, is the goal that you want your writing to accomplish. For example, you might write to express your feelings, to provide information, to persuade, or to entertain.
Form	A **form** is a kind of writing. For example, you might write a paragraph, an essay, a short story, a poem, or a newspaper article.

1.6 Choosing a Topic

Finding a Topic

Have you ever found yourself staring out the window, trying to come up with a good topic for a paper? It is usually fruitless to wait for a topic just to pop into your mind. The following table provides some concrete steps you can take to help you find interesting topics.

WAYS TO FIND A WRITING TOPIC	
Check Your Journal	Search through your journal for ideas that you jotted down in the past. Many professional writers get their ideas from their journals.
Think about Your Experiences	Think about people, places, or events that affected you strongly. Recall experiences that taught you important lessons or that created strong feelings in you.
Look at Reference Works	Reference works include dictionaries, atlases, almanacs, and encyclopedias. Many reference works are available in print and on computer.
Browse in a Library	Libraries are treasure houses of information and ideas. Simply looking around in the stacks of a library can suggest lots of good writing ideas.
Use the Mass Media	Mass media include newspapers, magazines, radio, television, and films. All can suggest good writing topics. For example, a glance at listings for public television programs might suggest topics related to the arts, to history, or to nature.
Talk to People	Friends, relatives, teachers, and other people you know make great sources for writing topics.
Do Some Freewriting	Simply put your pen or pencil down on a piece of paper and write about whatever pops into your mind. Write for two to five minutes without pausing to worry about whether your writing is perfect. Then look back over what you have written to see if you can find any good topics there.
Ask "What If" Questions	Ask questions beginning with "What if" to come up with topics for creative writing. For example, you might ask, "What if I could become part of any work of art? Which one would I choose? What would I do once inside?"
Make a Cluster Chart	Write the name of a general subject, such as music or sports, in the middle of a circle in the center of a piece of paper. Then, around it, write other ideas that come into your mind as you think about the subject. Circle these ideas, surround them with new ideas, and indicate connections between ideas with connecting lines.

Student Model: Renée needed to come up with a topic for a creative writing assignment in English. She decided to ask herself some "What if" questions to spark her imagination.

> What if my parents wanted another child but couldn't have one? What if cloning humans were possible? What if I could be cloned? What if another me could be grown in a test tube? How would I feel toward this younger but identical version of myself? How would she see me? How would we relate to each other? How would my parents treat her? What would I try to teach her about growing up?

Renée decided to write a story about having a clone-sister.

Focusing a Topic

Sometimes a topic is too broad to be treated in a short piece of writing. When you have a topic that is too broad, you must **focus,** or limit, the topic.

WAYS TO FOCUS A WRITING TOPIC	
Analyze the Topic	Break the topic down into its parts. Then think about how the parts relate to one another.
Do a Tree Diagram	Write the topic at the top of a page. Then break it into parts, and break those parts into parts.
Ask Questions about the Topic	Begin your questions with the words *who, what, where, when, why,* and *how.* Decide which answers to these questions are most important to answer in your piece.
Do Some Free-writing or Make a Cluster Chart	For information on these techniques, see the Language Arts Survey 1.10, "Gathering Ideas."

Student Model: Elizabeth decided to write a paper about the Middle Ages but realized that the topic was much too large for a short paper. Therefore, she wrote some questions about that topic:

What was the structure of society in the Middle Ages?
What roles did women play in medieval society?
What wars took place during the Middle Ages?
What religious beliefs prevailed during the Middle Ages?
Why were the Crusades undertaken?

She decided to write about the crusades to regain Jerusalem during the Middle Ages.

1.7 Choosing an Audience

Your writing will be most effective if you write with a specific audience in mind. Knowing the audience you are targeting will help you to make important decisions about your work with respect to the details, examples, or arguments you include; the focus of your writing; what information to include or to leave out; and how formal or informal and how complex or simple your language should be. For example, if you are writing for young children, you will use simple words and ideas that they will understand. Keep the following questions in mind when choosing and thinking about your audience.

THINKING ABOUT YOUR AUDIENCE

- What people would most appreciate the kind of writing that I am doing or be most interested in my topic?
- How much does the audience that I am considering already know about the topic? How much background information do I need to provide?
- What words, phrases, or concepts in my writing will my audience not understand? For which ones will I have to provide clear explanations?
- What can I do in my opening sentences to capture my audience's attention?

1.8 Choosing a Purpose

Writing to Express Yourself

The novelist E. M. Forster once said that he could not possibly know what he really thought about something until he wrote it down. Writing is the best way to clarify your thoughts and feelings and to come to understand yourself better. Getting your own thoughts and feelings on paper is called **expressive writing.** Expressive writing often makes interesting reading, but it is done primarily for oneself, not for another reader.

To write expressively, you need to look into yourself and draw out what you find there. As Sir Philip Sidney wrote in one of his sonnets, his Muse advised him, "Look in thy heart, and write." Expressive writing can take many different forms, but its most common form is the journal or diary entry. For more information about journal writing, see the Language Arts Survey 1.2, "Keeping a Journal." Certain types of poetry can also be considered expressive writing. For example, Pablo Neruda's "Tonight I Can Write" expresses his feelings about the end of a relationship with a woman he had loved deeply.

Writing to Inform

Often people write to convey information to someone else. Such communication of facts is called **informative writing.** Important types of informative writing include news reports, memoranda, scientific and technical reports, directions, recipes, encyclopedia articles, and many of the essays and research papers that you write for classes in school.

Whether you are taking a telephone message or writing a magazine article, your communication needs to be clear and accurate. When writing informatively, you should usually avoid statements of opinion. When you do include opinions, you should support them with facts. For more information on fact and opinion, see the Language Arts Survey 4.5, "Distinguishing Fact and Opinion." An example of writing that is primarily informative is "Insights: Apartheid" (see page 203).

Writing to Persuade

The purpose of **persuasive writing** is to convince others to believe something or to do something. When writing persuasively, you attempt to get your readers to adopt your views and/or to take some action. Common types of persuasive writing include editorials, sales letters, advertising copy, and political speeches. Great literature may also be persuasive in nature; Elie Wiesel wrote *Night* (see page 181) to make sure that the world did not forget—or repeat—the Holocaust.

To write convincingly, you must back up your opinions with reasons. Your reasons should include solid facts and also an appeal to your readers' feelings—perhaps your readers' sympathy or their sense of justice. Remember, however, that people can sense when they are being manipulated, so try to be persuasive without being manipulative.

Creative Writing

Creative writing attempts to amuse, entertain, thrill, delight, anger, or scare the readers. It can take many forms, including stories, poems, novels, plays, cartoons, and letters. Most of the selections in this textbook are examples of creative writing.

To write creatively, let your imagination take you down different paths until you hit upon ideas you would like to pursue. Use the techniques described in the Language Arts Survey 1.10, "Gathering Ideas."

1.9 Choosing a Form

Another important decision that a writer needs to make is what form his or her writing will take. The following chart lists some types of writing that you might want to consider.

FORMS OF WRITING		
Abstract	Concrete poem	Found poem
Acceptance speech	Constitution	Free verse
Ad copy	Constructive speech	Gothic tale
Address to a jury	Consumer report	Graduation speech
Adventure	Contract	Grant application
Advice column	Court decision	Greeting card
Afterword	Credo	Haiku
Agenda	Critical analysis	Headline
Allegory	Curriculum	History
Annals	Daydream	Horoscope
Annotation	Debate	Human interest story
Annual report	Detective story	Informative essay
Apology	Dialogue	Instructions
Appeal	Diary	Insult
Autobiography	Diatribe	Interview questions
Ballad	Dictionary entry	Introduction
Bibliography	Directions	Invitation
Billboard	Docudrama	Itinerary
Biography	Dramatic narrative	Jingle
Birth announcement	Dream analysis	Joke
Blank verse	Dream report	Journal entry
Book review	Editorial	Keynote address
Brief	Elegy	Lament
Brochure	Encyclopedia article	Law (statute)
Bulletin board	Epic	Learning log
Business letter	Epic poem	Letter of complaint
Business proposal	Epigram	Letter to the editor
Bylaws	Epilogue	Libretto
Campaign speech	Epistolary fiction	Limerick
Captions	Epitaph	Love letter
Cartoon	Essay	Lyric poem
Cause-and-effect essay	Eulogy	Magazine article
Chant	Experiment	Manifesto
Character sketch	Explication	Manual
Charter	Exposé	Memoir
Cheer	Fable	Memorandum
Children's story	Fabliau	Memorial plaque
Cinquain	Family history	Menu
Classified ad	Fantasy	Minutes
Comeback speech	Filmstrip	Monologue
Comedy	Flyer	Monument inscription
Comic strip	Foreword	Movie review
Community calendar	Fortune cookie insert	Mystery

CONTINUED

Myth
Narrative poem
Nature guide
News story
Nomination speech
Nonsense rhyme
Novel
Novella
Nursery rhyme
Obituary
Ode
One-act play
Oracle
Ottava rima
Packaging copy
Parable
Paragraph
Paraphrase
Parody
Party platform
Pastoral
Personal letter
Persuasive essay
Petition
Play
Police/Accident Report
Political advertisement
Prediction
Preface
Press release
Proclamation
Profile
Prologue
Proposal
Prose poem
Protocol
Public service announcement
Quatrain
Radio play
Radio spot
Rap
Reader's theater production
Rebuttal
Recipes
Recommendation
Referendum question
Research report
Resignation
Restaurant review
Resume
Riddle
Roast
Romance
Sales letter
Schedule
Science fiction
Screenplay
Sermon
Short short story
Short story
Sign
Situation comedy
Slide show
Slogan
Song lyric
Sonnet (Petrarchan, Elizabethan, or Spenserian)
Specifications
Spell
Sports story
Storyboard
Stream-of-consciousness fiction
Summary
Summation
Survey
Sutra
Tall tale
Tanka
Technical writing
Terza rima
Test
Thank-you note
Theater review
Toast
Tour guide
Tragedy
Translation
Treaty
TV spot
Villanelle
Vows
Want ad
Wanted poster
Warrant
Wish list

1.10 Gathering Ideas

Once you have chosen a topic for writing, the next step is to gather ideas. This section of the Language Arts Survey will introduce you to some of the most productive ways to come up with ideas and to begin to put them together.

Freewriting

Your own mind is a rich source of ideas; the trick is to be able to pull out those ideas when you need them. **Freewriting** is a way to get the ideas flowing by simply taking a pen and paper and writing whatever comes into your consciousness. Try to write for several minutes without stopping and without worrying about spelling, grammar, usage, or mechanics. If you get stuck, just repeat the last few words until something new pops into your mind.

To gather ideas about a specific topic, you might want to try **focused freewriting.** In a focused freewrite, you still write nonstop for a few minutes, but you stick with one topic and write whatever comes to mind as you think about that topic.

Student Model: Ramon's English teacher has the class practice freewriting for a few minutes each day. Here is an example from Ramon's first freewriting session:

> I'm supposed to be concentrating on writing, but I can't help looking out at the snow. . . . the snow . . . the snow . . . It's the first real snow of the season. The flakes are so huge they look like feathers. It looks like a billion chickens being plucked—or a colossal pillow fight. Seeing the snow makes me think of those mountain climbers who were trapped on Mount Everest. One of the survivors was interviewed on TV. His face was all black from frostbite. But he was one of the lucky ones—seven of his companions didn't make it. I wonder what it would be like to be caught in a life-or-death situation.

Clustering

Another good way to tap what you already know is to make a **cluster chart.** To make a cluster chart, draw a circle in the center of your paper. In this circle write a topic you would like to explore. Draw more circles branching out from your center circle, and fill them with subtopics related to your main topic.

Student Model: Leo needed to write a paper for science class. He thought he might want to write about something related to astronomy, so he made a cluster chart.

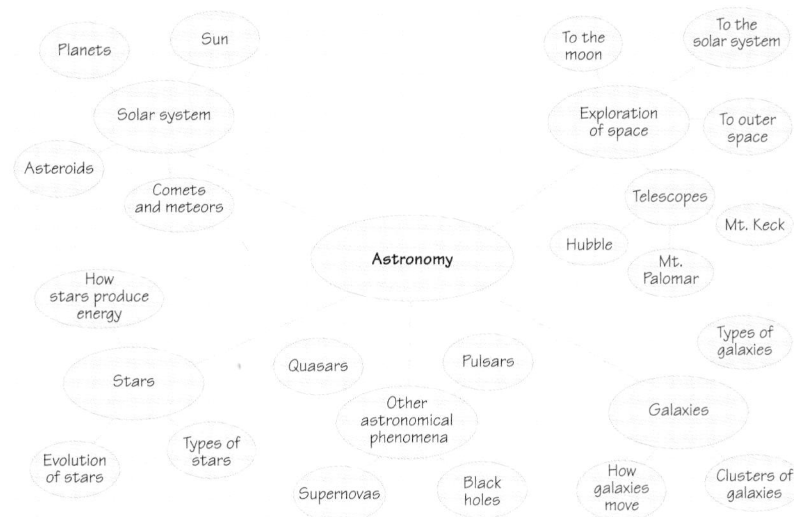

Leo decided to research the Hubble telescope and write about the latest discoveries in space.

ESSENTIAL SKILLS: WRITING

Questioning

Another excellent technique for gathering ideas is **questioning.** Writers often find that they can generate good ideas by asking **reporting questions** that begin with the words *who, what, where, when, why,* and *how.* This approach is especially useful for gathering information about an event or for planning a story.

If you are doing expressive or creative writing, also try asking questions that begin with the words *what if.* "What if" questions can spark your imagination and lead you down unexpected and interesting paths. Here are some examples:

EXAMPLES What if I could trade places with someone? How would I react in totally foreign surroundings?

What if a large meteorite were to collide with the earth, causing global damage? How would the nations of the world respond?

What if someone decided to pave his or her entire yard with cement and this idea caught on, becoming a fad all over the world?

Analyzing

To **analyze** is to break something down into its parts and then think about how the parts are related. The technique of analysis can be used to study an object, a process, a phenomenon, or a piece of writing. An **analysis chart** can help you to list the parts and to describe how each part is related to the whole.

Student Model: Wallace decided to write a critical essay about Sonnet 18 by William Shakespeare on page 256. Wallace created the following chart to analyze the four parts of this poem.

ANALYSIS OF SONNET 18		
PART	DESCRIPTION	RELATION OF PART TO WHOLE
Quatrain 1	Speaker questions whether he should compare his beloved to a summer day, decides to do so, and finds his beloved more lovely because summer is brief and windy.	Speaker sets up the comparison between the beauty of his beloved and a summer day.
Quatrain 2	Speaker points out that the summer sun is changeable—too hot or too dim.	Speaker faults beauty of summer for being too extreme and too inconstant.
Quatrain 3	Speaker claims that his beloved's beauty will not fade nor shall she die as long as she lives in verse.	Speaker finds his beloved's beauty more lasting than summer's.
Couplet	Speaker reinforces the idea that the sonnet has immortalized his beloved.	Speaker explains that it is poetry that gives his beloved her eternal beauty.

Sensory Detail Charts

We receive information about the world through five major pathways: sight, sound, touch, taste, and smell. The more of these **senses** you use to observe something, the more information you will collect. A **sensory detail chart** can help you employ all your senses to gather data about something so you can describe it thoroughly.

To make a sensory detail chart, begin by writing the name of your subject at the top of the page. Make a box with a column for each of the five senses. In the column under each heading, list the details about the subject that you learn through that sense.

Student Model: Elise wanted to write an article for the community newspaper about the Fourth of July celebration at the town park. She made a sensory detail chart to record her observations.

FOURTH OF JULY CELEBRATION				
SIGHT	SOUND	TOUCH	TASTE	SMELL
hundreds of people in colorful dress flags flying uniformed soldiers marching	band playing patriotic songs crowd cheering excited children shouting	heat from sun jostling from crowds sticky cotton candy	hamburger with relish lemonade blueberry pie	smoke from barbecue trampled grass

Time Lines

A **time line** can be useful when you are planning to write a story or a historical account. A time line gives you an overview of the sequence of events during a particular time period. To make a time line, draw a line on a piece of paper and divide it into equal parts. Label each part with a date or a time. Then add key events at the right places along the time line. Here is a sample time line showing major events in medieval history and culture:

Major Events in Medieval History and Culture

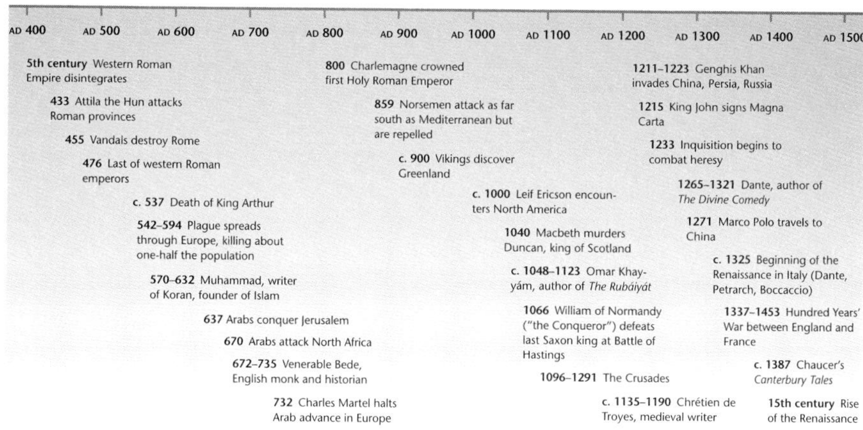
AD 400 AD 500 AD 600 AD 700 AD 800 AD 900 AD 1000 AD 1100 AD 1200 AD 1300 AD 1400 AD 1500
5th century Western Roman Empire disintegrates
433 Attila the Hun attacks Roman provinces
455 Vandals destroy Rome
476 Last of western Roman emperors
c. 537 Death of King Arthur
542–594 Plague spreads through Europe, killing about one-half the population
570–632 Muhammad, writer of Koran, founder of Islam
637 Arabs conquer Jerusalem
670 Arabs attack North Africa
672–735 Venerable Bede, English monk and historian
732 Charles Martel halts Arab advance in Europe
800 Charlemagne crowned first Holy Roman Emperor
859 Norsemen attack as far south as Mediterranean but are repelled
c. 900 Vikings discover Greenland
c. 1000 Leif Ericson encounters North America
1040 Macbeth murders Duncan, king of Scotland
c. 1048–1123 Omar Khayyám, author of The Rubáiyát
1066 William of Normandy ("the Conqueror") defeats last Saxon king at Battle of Hastings
1096–1291 The Crusades
c. 1135–1190 Chrétien de Troyes, medieval writer
1211–1223 Genghis Khan invades China, Persia, Russia
1215 King John signs Magna Carta
1233 Inquisition begins to combat heresy
1265–1321 Dante, author of The Divine Comedy
1271 Marco Polo travels to China
c. 1325 Beginning of the Renaissance in Italy (Dante, Petrarch, Boccaccio)
1337–1453 Hundred Years' War between England and France
c. 1387 Chaucer's Canterbury Tales
15th century Rise of the Renaissance

Story Maps

A **story map** is a chart that shows the various parts of a fable, myth, tall tale, legend, short story, or other fictional work. Most story maps include the elements listed in the following chart:

ELEMENT	DESCRIPTION
Setting	The time and place in which the story occurs
Characters	The people (or sometimes animals) who figure in the action of a story
Plot	The series of events taking place in the story. A typical plot involves the introduction of a conflict, its development, and its eventual resolution. Terms used to describe elements of plot include the following: • The **inciting incident** is the event that introduces the central conflict. • The **climax** is the high point of interest or suspense in the plot. • The **resolution** is the point at which the central conflict is ended, or resolved.
Conflict	A struggle between two forces in the story
Mood	The emotion created in the reader by the story
Theme	The central idea of the story

Student Model: Pablo made a story map of Boccaccio's story "Federigo's Falcon":

"Federigo's Falcon"

Setting and Mood

Time *fourteenth century*

Place *Florence, Italy*

Mood *disappointment, grief, anguish, hope, joy*

Major characters

Federigo

Monna Giovanna

Conflict internal ✓ external

Federigo tries to win Monna Giovanna's love.

Conflict ✓ internal external

Monna Giovanna struggles over whether to request Federigo's falcon.

Conflict ✓ internal external

Federigo desires to please the lady and is unable to oblige her.

Plot

Inciting incident *Monna Giovanna's son falls ill and asks for Federigo's prized falcon.*

Climax *Not knowing that the lady has come to request his falcon for her son, Federigo kills the falcon to prepare a meal for her.*

Resolution *Monna Giovanna is so impressed by Federigo's nobility that she resolves to marry him.*

Themes *courtly love, motherly love, loss, patience, nobility, virtue*

Venn Diagrams

A **Venn diagram** is useful for showing the similarities and differences between two things. It is especially effective for planning comparison-and-contrast writing. To create such a diagram, draw two intersecting circles and label each with the name of one of your subjects.

Then write similarities between the two subjects in the intersection of the two circles. Write differences outside the intersection of the two circles.

Sample Venn Diagram

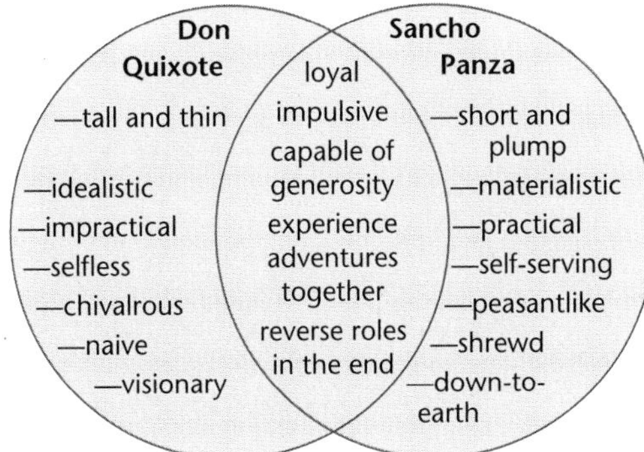

Imagining

Imagination is the ability to form mental images or pictures of things that are non-existent or not present to the senses. **Imagining** is the process of thinking of things not as they are but as they might be. It is this faculty that enables writers to create new settings, themes, characters, and plots.

In ancient days, imagining was considered a mysterious, spiritual process. The ancient Greeks believed that the **Muses,** the daughters of Zeus and the goddess Memory, provided inspiration for both learning and the arts.

Creativity remains today a mysterious process. There is much that we still do not understand about it. However, it is possible to use a few simple techniques, known as **heuristics,** to trigger our imaginations to come up with new, creative ideas for writing.

HEURISTICS FOR IMAGINING

1. Ask questions beginning with the words *what if.* (Example: What if President Kennedy had not been assassinated? How would the world be different?)
2. Combine previously existing things in a new way. (Example: Create a new character by giving a street child from Brazil the mind of Einstein.)
3. Magnify something, making it bigger or more consequential than it is now. (Example: Imagine a society in which a person's status is determined by the size of his or her ears.)
4 Simplify something to make it more manageable to write about. (Example: Let a minor character in your story have a one-dimensional personality rather than a fully developed one. She might have a knack for putting her foot in her mouth as her single defining quality.)
5. Project a trend into the future. (Example: Write an essay about a future society in which scientists have learned how to manipulate genes so as to program the characteristics of babies to be born.)

CONTINUED

6. Start with something as it is and change it systematically. (Example: Write a story about a community that is like your own except that the adults are being attacked by a strange virus that causes them to regress to childish behavior. Adolescents have to take over running their families, the schools, the police department, and so on.)
7. Work against type. (Example: Write a children's story about a friendly, tender-hearted, fire-breathing dragon.)
8. Make a drawing, sketch, or diagram. (Example: Draw a sketch of a castle as the setting for a drama.)

Role Playing

Role playing is acting out a situation. Typically, you work with others, choose a situation or a setting, and take on the roles of certain characters. You can use role playing to help you develop characters or explore controversial issues. When you actually take on a character, you may find yourself better able to articulate that person's thoughts and feelings. You may wish to tape record or videotape your role-playing sessions so you can consider them more closely later on. Another possibility is to have someone watch your role playing and take notes on it.

Brainstorming

When you **brainstorm,** you think of as many different ideas as you can, as quickly as you can, without pausing to evaluate or criticize the ideas. Brainstorming is to writing what improvisation is to acting—anything goes. Sometimes even silly-sounding ideas can lead to productive ones. When you brainstorm in a group, often one person's idea will stimulate another person to build on that concept. It is a good way to come up with creative, new ideas and innovative solutions to problems. Remember that no idea should be rejected in the brainstorming stage; receive all ideas with an encouraging response such as, "Great! Any other ideas?" Be sure to record all ideas so they can be considered and judged later.

Discussion

Discussion, like brainstorming, is a way of getting ideas flowing by sharing them with others. Members of a discussion group can play different roles. The **group leader** presents the topic, asks questions, elicits responses, mediates between group members, and tries to keep the discussion focused on the topic. The **participants** in the discussion share their thoughts. Participants should listen attentively to others, respond to others' comments, and add their own contributions, speaking calmly and politely. Often groups choose a **secretary** to record the ideas presented in the discussion.

Pro and Con Charts

A **pro and con chart** shows arguments for and against a particular position on some issue. This technique can be useful when you need to think through a decision or take sides on an issue. To create a pro and con chart, begin by writing a **proposition** at the top of a piece of paper. A proposition is an idea to be considered, a statement to be proved, or a policy to be debated. Under the proposition, make two columns, one labeled *Pro* and the other labeled *Con.* In the *Pro* column, list arguments in favor of the proposition. In the *Con* column, list arguments against the proposition.

Student Model: Hannah had to write a persuasive essay about whether the minimum driving age should be raised to eighteen. To determine where she stood on the issue and to find arguments to support her position (as well as arguments she would have to disprove), she created the following pro and con chart:

Pro and Con Chart

Proposition: The minimum driving age should be raised to 18

Pro	Con
—young, inexperienced drivers have a high accident rate	—all drivers have to pass the same skill test
—teenagers tend to be more reckless than other drivers	—many teens are very responsible and they would be penalized by such a law
—having many young drivers on the road drives up insurance rates for everyone	—many have jobs that require transportation
	—it would place an extra burden on parents who already do a lot of chauffeuring

Interviewing

In an **interview**, you ask someone questions. Interviewing experts is an excellent way to gain information about a particular topic. For example, if you are interested in understanding how the court system works, you might interview a judge or a lawyer.

When planning an interview, you should put some forethought into the questions you plan to ask. Write out a list of questions, including some about the person's background as well as about your topic. Other questions might occur to you as the interview proceeds. For guidelines on being a good listener, read the Language Arts Survey 3.2, "Active Listening and Interpersonal Communication." Here are some more tips for conducting an interview:

- If possible, tape-record the interview. Then you can review what was said at your leisure.
- If you do not have access to a tape recorder, take notes on a notepad. Write down the main points and some key words to help you remember details. Record the person's most important statements word for word.
- Be sure to get the correct spelling of the person's name and to ask permission to print his or her statements.

Using Reference Works

No matter what subject you wish to explore, you can probably find information about it in a **reference work.** Reference works include encyclopedias, dictionaries, almanacs, atlases, indexes, and more. Many reference works are available in print and on the computer. See a librarian in your school or community library for more information on the reference works available for your use. For additional information about reference materials and how to find them, see the Language Arts Survey 4.14, "Using Reference Works."

Whenever you use someone else's writing to help you in your own writing, you need to take good notes. You should have a system for recording information about your subject. You should also keep track of where you find your information. For tips about taking notes, see the Language Arts Survey 4.22, "Informal and Formal Note-taking."

1.11 Organizing Ideas

After you have gathered your ideas for a piece of writing, the next step is to organize these ideas in a sensible and interesting way. If you are writing a story, whether it is fiction or nonfiction, you will probably want to organize your ideas in **chronological order** (that is, in the order in which events occur). Other types of writing may follow different formats.

Writing a Thesis Statement

If you are writing an essay, the first step is to identify the major idea that you want to communicate. Present this idea in a sentence called your **thesis statement.** For more information, see the Language Arts Survey 1.20, "Writing a Critical Essay."

Main Ideas and Supporting Details

Next you must select, from the details that you have gathered, several **main ideas** related to your thesis statement. Review your notes and pick out several main ideas you would like to present. For each main idea, list several **supporting details**—statements, facts, and examples that more fully explain or illustrate your main idea. Here is an example of concepts organized according to thesis statement, main ideas, and supporting details:

"*A Doll's House:* Torvald's Role in Causing Nora to Slam the Door"

Thesis statement: In Henrik Ibsen's play *A Doll's House,* Torvald's condescending attitude toward Nora leads her to deceptive behavior, dissatisfaction with her marriage, and eventual rebellion against an unequal relationship.

Main idea: Torvald treats Nora in a condescending way.

—Supporting idea: He calls her by childish names such as "my skylark twittering," "my squirrel rustling," "my little squanderbird," "my little sweet tooth," "little silly," and "my poor helpless little darling."

—Supporting idea: He tries to control even what she eats (limits her sweets).

—Supporting idea: Torvald thinks Nora is incapable of handling money; he manages their finances and does not want her to know their state of affairs.

Main idea: Because of Torvald's patronizing attitude, Nora deceives him.

—Supporting idea: In eight years of marriage, Nora and Torvald have never really communicated honestly, so the stage is set for deception.

—Supporting idea: Nora knows that Torvald would never let her borrow money or run financial affairs, so she feels she must take matters into her own hands.

—Supporting idea: Nora's deception and the ensuing events simply reveal the relationship for what it is.

Main idea: Nora finds that Torvald's attitude is demeaning to her and she finally seeks her independence from an unsatisfactory marriage.

—Supporting idea: Torvald believes that by forgiving Nora he makes her "become his property in a double sense."

—Supporting idea: Nora feels that Torvald has done her a great wrong; he has not loved her but simply made her his toy.

—Supporting idea: Nora concludes that she is "first and foremost a human being" and must discover truth for herself.

Another way to organize your writing is to choose an overall, guiding organizational principle. The following chart describes some common ways in which writers organize ideas:

METHOD	DESCRIPTION
Chronological Order	Give events in the order in which they happen or should be done; connect events by using transition words such as *first, second, next, then,* and *finally.* Chronological organization would be a good method for giving a recipe, writing a how-to article on building a bird-feeder, or to describe a process, such as what happens when a volcano erupts.
Spatial Order	Describe parts in order of their location in space, for example, from back to front, left to right, or top to bottom; connect your descriptions with transition words or phrases such as *next to, beside, above, below, beyond,* and *around.* Spatial order would be a useful form for an article describing a kitchen renovation, or a descriptive passage in a science fiction story set in a space station.
Order of Importance	List details from least important to most important or from most important to least important; connect your details with transition phrases such as *more important, less important, most important,* and *least important.* A speech telling voters why they should elect you class president could be organized from the least important reason and build to the most important reason.
Comparison-and-Contrast Order	Details of two subjects are presented in one of two ways. In the first method, the characteristics of one subject are presented, followed by the characteristics of the second subject. This method would be useful to organize an essay that compares and contrasts two fast-food chains. You could use this method to say why one is superior to another. "BurgerWorld has the most restaurants. They broil their hamburgers, and offer a line of low-fat meals. Ma's Burgers has far fewer restaurants, fries their hamburgers, and offers no low-fat choices." In the second method, both subjects are compared and contrasted with regard to one characteristic, then with regard to a second characteristic, and so on. An essay organized according to this method could compare the platforms of two political parties, issue by issue: the environment, the economy, and so on. Ideas are connected by transitional words and phrases that indicate similarities or differences, such as *likewise, similarly, in contrast, a different kind,* and *another difference.*
Cause-and-Effect Order	One or more causes are presented followed by one or more effects, or one or more effects are presented followed by one or more causes. A public health announcement warning children about the dangers of playing with fire would be usefully organized by cause-and-effect. An essay discussing the outbreak of World War I and the events that led up to it could be organized by effect and causes. Ideas are connected by transitional words and phrases that indicate cause and effect, such as *one cause, another effect, as a result, consequently,* and *therefore.*
Part-by-Part Order	Ideas are presented according to no *overall* organizational pattern. However, each idea is connected logically to the one that precedes it and/or to the one that follows it. A letter to a friend might be organized part by part. One paragraph might discuss a party the writer just attended and the next could focus on the writer's feelings about a person he or she met there. After chronological order, this is the most common method for organizing ideas in writing. Ideas are connected by any transitional word or phrase that indicates the relationship or connection between the ideas.

1.12 Outlining

An excellent way to organize a piece of writing is to make an **outline.** An outline is a framework for highlighting main ideas and related ideas. There are two main types of outlines commonly used by writers.

Rough Outlines

To start giving order to your ideas, make a **rough**, or **informal**, **outline.** To create a rough outline, simply list your main ideas in some logical order. Under each main idea, list the supporting details set off by dashes or bullets.

Student Model: Miguel was fascinated by the Nazca lines in Peru and wanted to find out more about them. He used the reporting questions as the basis for a rough outline for a research paper:

The Nazca Lines

What are the Nazca lines?
—hundreds of giant drawings etched on the desert floor
—images of animals (including killer whales, a monkey, and a spider), birds, and geometric figures
—up to 1000 feet in size
—discovered in 1939 by a scientist flying over the region

When and where were the Nazca lines made?
—made over a period of several hundred years early in the common era
—located in a 30-mile range between Nazca and Palpa in southern Peru

Who made the Nazca lines?
—ancient Nazca Indians, a pre-Inca civilization
—some writers have proposed that the markings were made by visitors from outer space

How were the Nazca lines made?
—surface soil brushed away to reveal lighter colored soil beneath
—preserved for about 2,000 years owing to complete lack of rain

Why were the Nazca lines made?
—an astronomical calendar?
—linked to mountain worship and fertility?
—lines made to be seen by the gods so they would help the people?
—part of extraterrestrial landing strip?

Formal Outlines

A **formal outline** has headings and subheadings identified by Roman numerals, letters, and numbers. One type of formal outline is the **topic outline.** Entries in such an outline are written as words or phrases rather than complete sentences. In a **sentence outline,** the entries are complete sentences. For information about capitalization in a formal outline, see the Language Arts Survey 2.60, "Poetry, Outlines, and Letters."

Student Model: Cecilia wanted to learn more about the heart and how it works. She made this formal outline for a paper about the heart:

The Heart

I. Facts about the heart
  A. Function
    1. To pump blood all over the body
    2. To send life-giving nutrients and chemicals to every cell
  B. Statistics
    1. Size of fist
    2. Five quarts of blood in circulatory system
    3. 60,000 miles of blood vessels
    4. Three billion beats in average lifetime
II. Structure of the heart
  A. Chambers
    1. Atria
    2. Ventricles
  B. Valves
  C. Veins and arteries
III. How the heart works
  A. Energy source: electricity
  B. Action of muscles and nerves
  C. Action of valves and blood vessels
IV. How to keep the heart healthy
  A. Diet
  B. Exercise
  C. Avoid smoking
V. How to repair the heart and arteries
  A. Surgery
    1. Angioplasty
    2. Bypass
    3. Transplant
  B. Medicines

1.13 Drafting

After you have gathered your information and organized it, the next step in writing is to produce a **draft.** A draft is simply an early attempt at writing a paper. When working on a draft, keep in mind that you do not have to get everything just right the first time through. The beauty of a draft is that you can rework it many times until you are happy with the final product.

There are two basic approaches to drafting, either of which can produce great writing. Some writers prefer to work slowly and carefully, perfecting each part as they go. Producing such a **careful draft** can be rewarding, because you get to see a finished, polished piece emerging part by part. Other writers find that perfecting each part of their writing, sentence by sentence, bogs down the process. These writers prefer to write a **discovery draft,** getting all their ideas down on paper in rough form, and then go back over the paper to polish it. When writing a discovery draft, you need not worry about details of spelling, grammar, usage, and mechanics. You can take care of those matters during revision.

1.14 Evaluating

When you **evaluate** something, you examine it carefully to find its strengths and weaknesses. After producing a rough draft of a piece of writing, the next step is to evaluate that draft to find out what you need to improve.

Self-evaluation

Evaluating your own writing is called **self-evaluation.** A good self-evaluation practice is to read through the piece of writing three times:

- Check for content. Make sure that you have said all that you want to say, that you have not left out important details, and that you have not included unimportant or unrelated details.
- Check for organization. Make sure that your ideas are presented in a reasonable order.
- Check style and language. Make sure that your language is appropriately formal or informal, that your tone is appropriate to your message, and that you have defined any key or unfamiliar terms.

As you check your writing, make notes about what you need to revise, or change. For further information on what to look for as you evaluate your writing, see the Revision Checklist in the Language Arts Survey 1.15, "Revising."

Peer Evaluation

A **peer evaluation** is an evaluation of a piece of writing done by a classmate, or peer. The following are some guidelines for doing a peer evaluation:

For the Writer

- Mention to your evaluator any aspects of the writing that particularly concern you. For example, if you are wondering whether something you have said is clear, ask the evaluator if he or she understands that part of what you have written.
- Feel free to ask questions to clarify comments that your evaluator makes.
- Accept your evaluator's comments graciously. Try not to personalize the process. Remember that criticism can help you to identify weaknesses and thus produce a better piece through revision.

For the Evaluator

- Be focused. Concentrate on content, organization, and style. Refer to the Revision Checklist in the Language Arts Survey 1.15, "Revising." Do not concentrate at this point on proofreading matters such as spelling and punctuation; they can be fixed later.
- Be positive. Let the writer know what he or she has done right. Show how the paper could be improved by making the changes that you are suggesting.
- Be specific. Give the writer concrete ideas for improving his or her work. For example, if you think that a particular portion of the writing is weak, suggest a way that it might be strengthened.
- Be tactful. Consider the other person's feelings, and use a pleasant tone of voice. Do not criticize the writer. Instead, focus on the writing itself.

1.15 Revising

After identifying weaknesses in a draft through self-evaluation and peer evaluation, the next step is to revise the draft. Here are four basic techniques that you can use when revising:

Adding

Sometimes a piece of writing can be improved by adding details, examples, or transitions to connect ideas. Added adjectives, for example, can make a piece of writing clearer or more vivid.

UNREVISED SENTENCE	We saw a hill through the windowpane.
REVISED SENTENCE	We saw a rolling, snow-covered hill through the frosty windowpane.

Cutting

In *The Elements of Style* (1918), William Strunk, Jr. advised, "Omit unnecessary words. Vigorous writing is concise." Pieces of writing can often be improved by cutting unnecessary or unrelated material.

UNREVISED SENTENCE	Many ancient civilizations or cultures created explanatory stories or myths about the creation of all the people in the world.
REVISED SENTENCE	Many ancient civilizations developed myths about the creation of people.

Replacing

Sometimes weak parts of a piece of writing can be replaced with parts that are stronger, more concrete, more vivid, or more precise. Notice that the revised sentence below is more descriptive and striking.

UNREVISED SENTENCE	To express his gratitude, the captain gave my father a gift.
REVISED SENTENCE	To express his gratitude, the captain gave my father a chest of gold doubloons he had hidden from the pirates who plundered the vessels of the Spanish Main.

Moving

Often you can improve the organization of a piece of writing by moving part of it so that related ideas appear near one another.

UNREVISED SENTENCES	Chris characterized her father for us. He died without having made peace with his relatives. He was a stern, unforgiving person.
REVISED SENTENCES	Chris characterized her father as stern and unforgiving. He died without having made peace with his relatives.

When you mark a piece of writing for revisions, use the standard proofreading symbols. The symbols for adding, cutting, replacing, and moving are the first four symbols in the chart 1165.

The following chart lists some questions to ask yourself whenever you are revising a piece of writing. If you cannot answer *yes* to any of these questions, then you need to revise your work. Continue revising until you can answer *yes* to all of these questions.

REVISION CHECKLIST	
Content	• Does the writing achieve its purpose? • Are the main ideas clearly stated and supported by details?
Organization	• Are the ideas arranged in a sensible order? • Are the ideas within paragraphs and between paragraphs connected to one another?
Style	• Is the language appropriate to the audience and purpose? • Is the mood appropriate to the purpose of the writing?

1.16 Proofreading

Like many students, you may think that using correct spelling, grammar, and punctuation in your writing is relatively unimportant. "The main thing is to get my thoughts across," goes the reasoning. However, poor mechanics distracts from good ideas. The power of your ideas will be diminished if the reader has to stumble through faulty spelling, grammar, capitalization, and punctuation. Furthermore, your credibility may be called into question; the reader may think subconsciously, "If this person doesn't know how to check his or her spelling, maybe he or she doesn't know what he or she is talking about either."

Therefore, it is extremely important to **proofread** your writing—to read it through, look for errors, and mark corrections. After you have revised your draft, make a clean copy of it and proofread it for errors in spelling, grammar, capitalization, and punctuation using the following proofreading checklist. Refer to the chart of proofreading symbols to mark your corrections.

PROOFREADING CHECKLIST	
Spelling	• Are all words, including names, spelled correctly?
Grammar	• Does each verb agree with its subject? • Are verb tenses consistent and correct? • Are irregular verbs formed correctly? • Are there any sentence fragments or run-ons? • Have double negatives been avoided? • Have frequently confused words, such as *affect* and *effect*, been used correctly?
Capitalization	• Do all proper nouns and proper adjectives begin with capital letters?
Punctuation	• Does every sentence end with an end mark? • Are commas, semicolons, hyphens, and dashes used correctly?

When you mark corrections to your writing, use the standard proofreading symbols. With just a little practice you'll find them very easy and convenient.

PROOFREADER'S SYMBOLS	
Symbol and Example	**Meaning of Symbol**
The very first time	Delete (cut) this material.
cat cradle	Insert (add) something that is missing.
George	Replace this letter or word.
All the horses king's	Move this word to where the arrow points.
french toast	Capitalize this letter.
the vice-President	Lowercase this letter.
housse	Take out this letter and close up space.
book keeper	Close up space.
gebril	Change the order of these letters.
end. "Watch out," she yelled.	Begin a new paragraph.
Love conquers all	Put a period here.
Welcome friends.	Put a comma here.
Getthe stopwatch	Put a space here.
Dear Madam	Put a colon here.
She walked he rode.	Put a semicolon here.
name brand products	Put a hyphen here.
cats meow	Put an apostrophe here.
cat's cradle stet	Let it stand. (Leave as it is.)

1.17 Proper Manuscript Form

After proofreading your draft, you will want to prepare your final manuscript. Follow the guidelines given by your teacher or, if your teacher tells you to do so, the guidelines given here:

GUIDELINES FOR PREPARING A MANUSCRIPT

1. Keyboard your manuscript using a typewriter or word processor, or write it out neatly using blue or black ink.
2. Double-space your paper. Leave one blank line between every line of text.
3. Use one side of the paper.
4. Leave one-inch margins on all sides of the text.
5. Indent the first line of each paragraph.

CONTINUED

6. In the upper right-hand corner of the first page, put your name, class, and date. On every page after the first, include the page number in this heading, as follows:
   Mallory Grisham
   English 12
   April 6, 1999
   p. 6
7. Make a cover sheet listing the title of the work, your name, the date, and the class.

After preparing a final manuscript according to these guidelines, proofread it one last time for errors.

1.18 Publishing or Presenting Your Work

Some writing is done just for one's self. Journal writing usually falls into that category. Most writing, however, is meant to be shared with others. There are many ways in which to share your work. Here are several ways in which you can publish your writing or present it to others:

- Find a local publication that will accept such work. (A school literary magazine, a school newspaper, or a community newspaper are possibilities.)
- Submit the work to a regional or national publication. Check a reference work such as *Writer's Market* to find information on types of manuscripts accepted, manuscript form, methods and amounts of payment, and so on.
- Enter the work in a contest. Your teacher may be able to tell you about writing contests for students. You can also find out about such contests by looking for announcements in writers' magazines and literary magazines.
- Read your work aloud to classmates, friends, or family members.
- Obtain permission to read your work aloud over the school's public address system.
- Work with other students to prepare a publication—a brochure, literary magazine, anthology, or newspaper.
- Prepare a poster or bulletin board, perhaps in collaboration with other students, to display your writing.
- Make your own book by typing or word processing the pages and binding them together in some way. Another possibility is to copy your work into a blank book.
- Hold a recital of student writing as a class or schoolwide project.
- Share your writing with other students in a small writers' group that meets periodically to discuss students' recent work. (Members of the group should receive the work to be discussed beforehand, so they can read it and make notes on it.)
- If the work is dramatic in nature, work with other students to present a performance of it. If the work is poetry, fiction, or nonfiction, work with others to present it as an oral interpretation. Oral interpretation is the reading or recital of a piece of writing with careful attention to expression of the ideas, tone, and rhythms of the work. Students might form pairs, exchange pieces, and coach one another in oral interpretations.

1.19 Writing an Essay

An **essay** is a brief piece of nonfiction writing that explores a single topic or main idea in several paragraphs. An essay differs from a longer nonfiction work—from a book-length history or biography, for example—in that it does not present an exhaustive or comprehensive treatment of its subject. Instead, a writer of essays explores some part of a subject, often in a tentative or speculative way.

Types of Essays

Essays can be divided into two main categories—ones written from the **first-person point of view,** in which the author refers to himself or herself using pronouns such as *I* and *we*, and ones written from the **third-person point of view,** in which the author does not refer to himself or herself directly.

The **first-person,** or **personal, essay** treats a subject in a highly individual way, describing the author's own experiences, reflections, and attitudes in relation to that subject. Personal essays tend to be informal in style, using language that one might use in ordinary conversation. They are also subjective, giving the reader the impression that the author is sharing his or her innermost feelings. An examination of the concept of loyalty, with examples drawn from the author's own life, or a description of an author's experiences adjusting to life in a new country are examples of personal essays. You may be asked to write personal essays for classes or as part of college applications.

There are many different types of **formal, third-person essay,** in which the focus is not on the author but on the subject. In such essays, the author does not mention himself or herself and does not share subjective feelings but rather presents information or opinions objectively, backing up what he or she claims with evidence and rational argument.

FORMAL, THIRD PERSON ESSAYS

An **informative essay** provides information about one or more subjects. Types of informative essays include

- the **how-to essay,** which explains how to do something, such as how to plan for a vacation or how to silkscreen
- the **process essay,** which describes an activity or event that takes place over time, such as an essay on how the solar system developed or what happens to people as they age
- the **comparison-contrast essay,** which explains the similarities and differences between two or more subjects, such as an essay that compares the capability of the human brain to that of a computer, or one that examines types of running shoes and makes recommendations about which are the best buys
- the **definition essay,** which defines one or more terms and gives examples, such as an essay describing the characteristics and content of a certain type of music, or an essay on the meaning of courage, with examples from the lives of famous people

CONTINUED

- the **analysis essay,** which breaks a subject into its parts, describes the parts, and shows how they relate to one another or function together, such as an essay on the parts and functions of the federal government in the United States or an essay on the electric guitar and how it functions
- the **classification essay,** which organizes a group of things into classes, or categories, based on specific criteria, such as an essay on different kinds of friends (best friends, "fun" friends, close friends, partners, acquaintances, and so on) or an essay on types of frozen dessert confections (ice cream, frozen yogurt, sorbet, sherbet, and so on)

A **persuasive essay** attempts to move an audience to change in some way—to take some action or to adopt some attitude, opinion, or belief. In a persuasive essay, the author presents arguments and evidence to convince his or her readers to make this change. A persuasive essay differs from a personal opinion essay by focusing on the audience rather than on the author. In a persuasive essay, the author does not refer to himself or herself directly but rather concentrates on appeals to readers. A persuasive essay is also more formal in language than is a personal opinion essay. An essay that presents reasons for keeping high schools open year-round and one that attempts to convince readers of the importance of recycling are examples of the persuasive essay.

A **critical essay** analyzes some aspect of one or more literary works and offers an interpretation based on that analysis. A critical essay is informative in that it presents information about literary works and concepts. It is also persuasive, in that it attempts to convince the reader to adopt the author's interpretation. Some critical essays will also require you to compare and contrast, to define, and/or to classify elements of a literary work or works. For more information on critical essays, see the next section of this Language Arts Survey.

Form of the Essay

Essays vary widely in length and in structure. Most, however, consist of three parts: the introduction, the body, and the conclusion.

The **introduction,** often a single paragraph, captures the reader's attention and presents the subject of the essay. In most formal essays, the introduction also presents the author's **main idea,** or **thesis.**

The **body** of the essay develops the main idea, or thesis, in several paragraphs. Usually, each paragraph presents a single idea that supports the thesis.

The **conclusion,** often a single paragraph, sums up the ideas presented in the essay and gives the reader a satisfactory sense of resolution.

A common structure for essays is the **five-paragraph essay** form. In a five-paragraph essay, the first paragraph is the introduction, paragraphs two through four are the body, and the fifth paragraph is the conclusion. You may be asked to write five-paragraph essays in classes or in essay tests. For more information about essay tests, see the Language Arts Survey 4.27, "Taking Essay Tests."

1.20 Writing a Critical Essay

You will probably be asked to write critical essays in many of your English classes and in the classes you may take in college. While writing a critical essay might seem difficult at first, remember that this type of writing is like any other skill—it gets easier with practice. Just as there is no "correct" way to produce a piece of creative writing, there is also no single "correct" interpretation of a literary work. Because almost every literary work can be interpreted in more than one way, the success of any critical essay lies in how well you support your ideas about that work. A skillful writer considers other possible interpretations, and if these interpretations oppose his or her own view, he or she will sometimes comment upon these interpretations to point out flaws and to support more effectively his or her ideas about the literary work. Critical essays should have all of the parts of an essay described in 1.19, "Writing an Essay," so be sure to include an introduction, a body, and a conclusion. The following sections will tell you how to find a topic for such an essay as well as how to develop its three essential parts.

Finding a Topic

Often, your English teacher will give you a topic or a choice of topics about which to write. For example, each selection in your textbook features a topic for a critical essay. If you are choosing your own topic for an essay about literature, begin with a specific work that interests you. The stronger your feelings about the work, the more likely it is that you will be able to sustain your interest as you research, plan, and write your essay. You might choose to write about one of the following aspects of the work:

IDEAS FOR CRITICAL ESSAYS

1. **Literary Technique.** Choose a literary technique, such as metaphor or symbolism; define it; and give examples of the technique from one or more literary works.
2. **Structure of a Literary Work.** Choose a literary structure, or form, such as the sonnet or the epic; describe the form; then show how a specific literary work follows that form.
3. **Literary Movement.** Choose a literary, artistic, or philosophical movement such as Romanticism, Naturalism, or Expressionism; describe the environment of the movement and its main characteristics, giving examples from one or more literary works.
4. **Theme.** Choose a literary work and explain how its elements follow a theme, or main idea.
5. **Character Analysis.** Choose a character from a literary work and describe the character's main traits and how the character is revealed or changes in the course of the work.
6. **Biographical Influences of a Literary Work.** Show how a literary work relates to events or circumstances in the author's life.
7. **Historical Influences on a Literary Work.** Show how a literary work is related to the times in which the author lived.
8. **Comparing and Contrasting Characters.** Choose two characters from the same literary work, or from different works, and compare and contrast them.

CONTINUED

9. **Setting and Mood.** Define setting and mood; then show how elements of the setting of a literary work create its mood.
10. **Treatment of a Moral Issue or Dilemma in a Literary Work.** Pose a question about a moral issue or dilemma; then show how that question is explored in or answered by one or more literary works.
11. **Gender Roles and Relations in a Literary Work.** Analyze the male and female characters in a literary work to show what view of gender roles and relations the work reveals.
12. **Relations between Individuals from Different Cultures or Social Classes in a Literary Work.** Analyze the relationships between characters from different cultures, heritages, or social classes to determine what view of such factors is presented in the literary work.
13. **Religious or Philosophical Implications of a Literary Work.** Explain what philosophical or religious view is expressed by a literary work and show how the work supports this view.

One student's approach to finding a topic, developing this idea, and writing a critical essay appears in the Student Model sections that follow.

Student Model: Marika really enjoyed Olive Senior's story "Love Orange," on page 287. She read the story several times. She noticed that the orange and the doll both had symbolic meaning and thought that she might like to write about this symbolism. She also noticed that the narrator experienced a fall from innocence into experience, a theme that she was familiar with from other works she had read. She decided that the connection between this archetype and the symbols she had noticed would make an interesting writing topic.

Writing a Thesis Statement

After you have chosen a topic or have been assigned a topic, identify the main idea that you wish to express in your essay. The main idea should reflect a specific issue related to your topic and present a position you support throughout your paper. This idea will be expressed as a **thesis statement** in your introduction. A thesis statement is simply a sentence that presents the main idea or the position you will take in your essay. A thesis statement should be based on your reading of the literary work, any relevant biographical or historical material about the author and his or her times, and any other background or critical writing about the work that you use as sources. You will support the thesis statement in the body of your essay.

Student Model: Marika put her main idea into a sentence called a thesis statement:

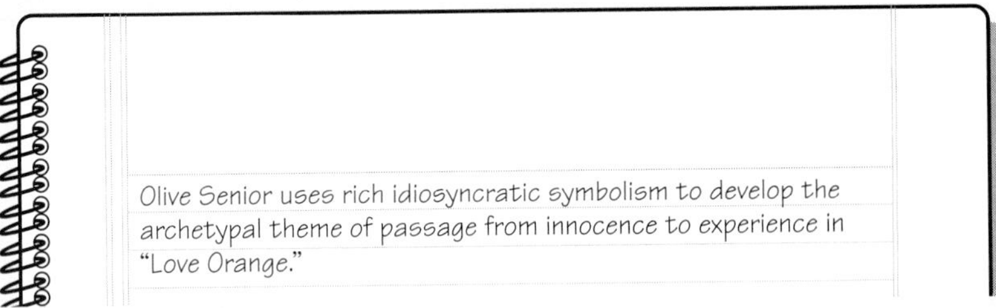
Olive Senior uses rich idiosyncratic symbolism to develop the archetypal theme of passage from innocence to experience in "Love Orange."

Gathering and Organizing Ideas

Once you have a thesis statement, the next step is to gather ideas to support your topic. If you are writing about works in this textbook, you may wish to refer to the Prereading page for the selection or selections about which you are writing. Unit introductions, Insights or Theme features, and the Handbook of Literary Terms may also prove to be useful sources. You might also wish to refer to other critical sources or reference works. Most importantly, gather evidence from the literary work itself. To do so, read the work closely, bearing your thesis statement in mind and examining all the elements of the literary work. Record your ideas and evidence on notecards or on notebook paper, making sure to note the source of any material that you take from a published work so that you can document your sources in the final version of the paper. (For more information on taking notes and on documenting sources, see the Language Arts Survey 4.22–4.23.)

After gathering ideas for your paper, organize these ideas to form the introduction and body of your essay. Make a rough outline for your essay. Begin by writing your thesis at the top of a piece of paper. Then list the main points you will use to support your thesis. Under each main point, list evidence that backs up the supporting idea.

Student Model: Marika took notes and then organized her ideas in a rough outline. The following is Marika's outline for her essay:

Thesis: Olive Senior uses rich idiosyncratic symbolism to develop the archetypal theme of passage from innocence to experience in "Love Orange."

—"Our worlds wait outside"/Hiding under grandfather's bed
- —Talisman phrase against fears
- —Set out to see world, happy to come back to safety
- —Outside world can wait

—Doll as symbol of loss of innocence
- —Imperfection/hopes dashed
- —Associations with death
    - —Buried doll
    - —Rises up as people die

—Orange as symbol of love
- —Definite amount of love to be given
- —Serves as talisman as well
- —Wants to protect love by giving to Miss Aggie
- —Tries to use orange to save grandmother
- —Recognizes that love is not omnipotent

Drafting

After outlining your essay, write a rough draft. Keep the following directions in mind when writing a draft of the three essential parts of your essay.

Drafting an Introduction

The purpose of the introduction is to capture the attention of the reader and to present the subject of the essay. It should culminate in your thesis. You might find that you need to adjust your thesis slightly to fit the context of your introduction, but you should not change its meaning, unless you discover that you need to rework the focus of your essay. Some writers follow their thesis with a statement of how the thesis will be supported in the body of the essay; others simply move on to the first paragraph of the body of the essay.

Drafting the Body of an Essay

For the body of your essay, refer to your outline. Each heading in your outline will become the main idea of one of your paragraphs. You may use transitional words or phrases to connect your paragraphs, or you may use connections between the subjects of the two paragraphs to provide transition. As you draft, include evidence from the literary work or from other sources to support the ideas that you present. This evidence can be paraphrased, summarized, or quoted directly. Be sure to cite anything you quote directly or any ideas that you borrow. (For information on documenting sources, see the Language Arts Survey 4.23, "Documenting Sources in a Report.")

In a critical essay, you will often find it useful to quote directly from literary works or from critical sources. While quotations serve as examples or illuminate points to support your thesis, the overuse of quotations will make your paper weak. Choose your quotations carefully. Each quotation should have a purpose. Introduce your quote by explaining your purpose in quoting the material, by setting a scene for the quote you will use, or by indicating the person you are quoting. After the quotation, comment upon it by tying it to the main idea in the paragraph or by offering a differing opinion which you should then support. The quoted material should flow seamlessly with the rest of your essay.

Use the proper form for quotations: When quoting directly from a source, put quotation marks around quotations that are less than four lines long and run the quotation in with the rest of your writing. If the quotation is four lines or longer, indent from the left margin and single space the quotation but do not use quotation marks.

Drafting a Conclusion

In the conclusion, bring together the various elements you have introduced in the body of your essay and create a sense of closure to the issue you raised in your thesis. There is no single right way to conclude an essay. Some possibilities include making a generalization, restating the thesis and the major supporting ideas in different words, summarizing the points made in the rest of the essay, drawing a lesson or moral from what has been presented in the rest of the essay, calling on the reader to adopt some viewpoint or to take some action, and expanding on your thesis by connecting it to the reader's immediate interests or to some larger issue or concern.

Evaluating, Revising, and Proofing

Once your rough draft is complete, evaluate it. Make sure that the organization of the draft is logical and that you have used evidence to support your ideas. Also make sure that any quotations that you have used are correct. Revise your draft. Proofread for errors in spelling, grammar, usage, capitalization, and punctuation. Then make a clean, final copy. If your teacher does not have a preferred format, follow the guidelines given in the Language Arts Survey 1.17, "Proper Manuscript Form." Proofread the final copy one last time.

Student Model: Here is the final draft of Marika's essay.

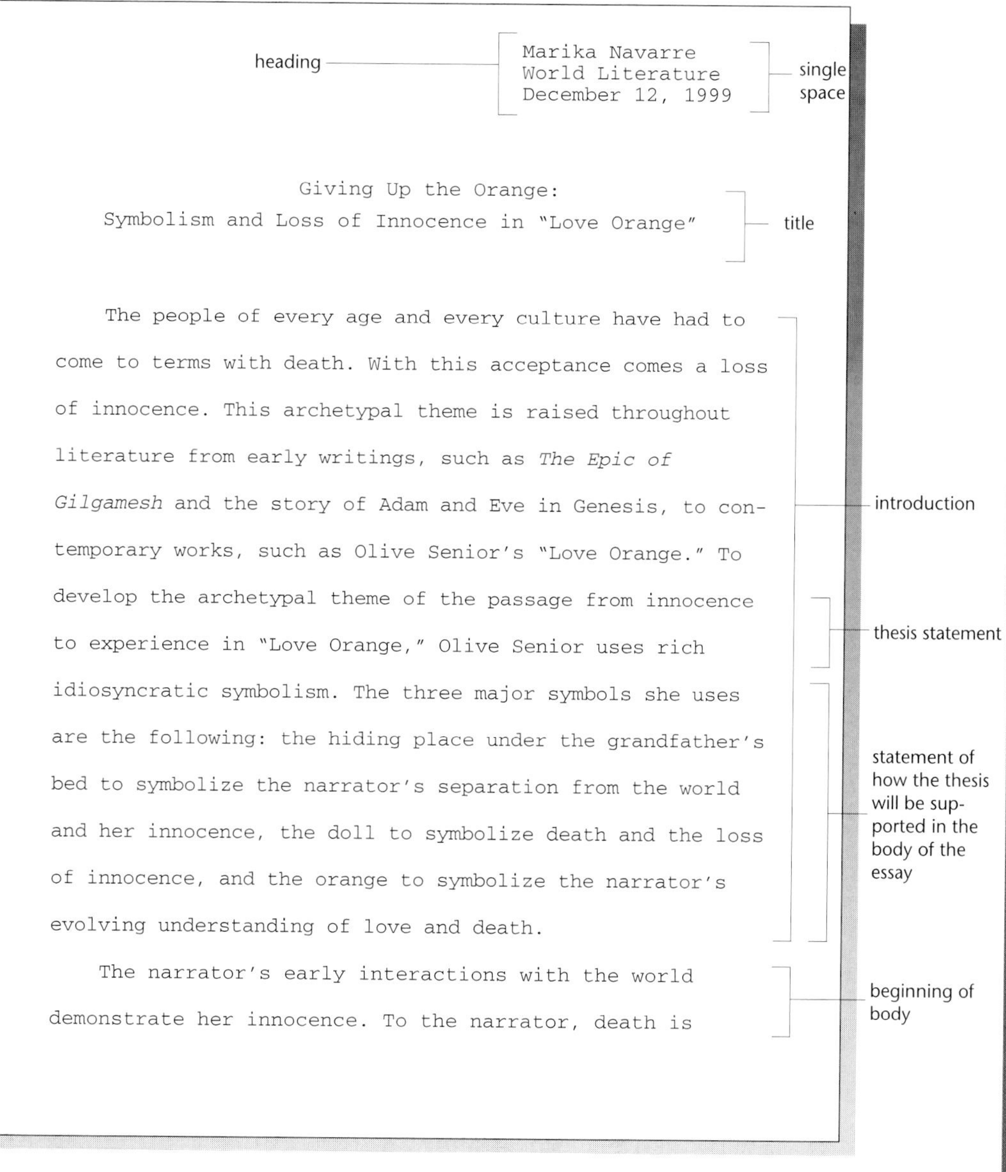
heading
Marika Navarre
World Literature
December 12, 1999
single space
Giving Up the Orange:
Symbolism and Loss of Innocence in "Love Orange"
title
The people of every age and every culture have had to come to terms with death. With this acceptance comes a loss of innocence. This archetypal theme is raised throughout literature from early writings, such as *The Epic of Gilgamesh* and the story of Adam and Eve in Genesis, to contemporary works, such as Olive Senior's "Love Orange." To develop the archetypal theme of the passage from innocence to experience in "Love Orange," Olive Senior uses rich idiosyncratic symbolism. The three major symbols she uses are the following: the hiding place under the grandfather's bed to symbolize the narrator's separation from the world and her innocence, the doll to symbolize death and the loss of innocence, and the orange to symbolize the narrator's evolving understanding of love and death.
The narrator's early interactions with the world demonstrate her innocence. To the narrator, death is
introduction
thesis statement
statement of how the thesis will be supported in the body of the essay
beginning of body

heading with page number

Marika Navarre
World Literature
December 12, 1999
p. 2

setting the scene for a quote

short quotation

in-text citation

citation for quotation from previously cited source

something she only dreams of and love is an orange—a palpable but limited amount of emotional attachment. When any new threatening situation arises, the narrator hides under her grandfather's bed and uses the talisman phrase "our worlds wait outside" to ward away negative thoughts and feelings (Senior, 288). This action and this phrase suggest that the narrator is isolated from the realities of the world. When she does venture out into the world, she is happy to be found and brought back to the safety of her grandparents' home. Her belief that "experience can wait . . . death too" shows that she does not, at this point, understand death (288).

The narrator's loss of innocence and the beginning of her acceptance of death are closely related to a doll that she was given for Christmas. The broken face and missing eye and finger of the doll symbolize the broken dreams of the narrator who longed for and expected a beautiful, whole doll for Christmas. When the narrator buries the doll, she buries some of her hope and part of her innocence as well. The doll remains in her memory, however, and the thought of the broken face often makes her feel ill. As the narrator begins to experience the loss to death of people she knows, the negative associations the doll brings to mind extend to become inextricably linked

Marika Navarre
World Literature
December 12,1999
p.3

to these losses. For example, the box that holds the cremated remains of the deceased son of a neighbor reminds her of the shoe box in which she buried the doll. She hopes that when this box is buried, the doll will no longer haunt her; in effect she is hoping that this death will free her from facing others. She clings to the innocence she has left.

evidence

The narrator's loss of innocence is most closely tied to her ideas about love, which she compares to an orange. Because she believes that the amount of love she has to give is limited, the narrator holds greedily to her love-orange. This object serves as a talisman as well. When the narrator is afraid or upset, she imagines squeezing the rough roundness of the orange between her hands and is comforted. The narrator's beliefs about this symbol of love and security are naive and reveal that she is not yet ready to experience love and the sense of loss that love can sometimes bring. The meaning of the love-orange begins to evolve when the narrator associates it with a string of deaths. When the narrator attends a funeral for the first time, she does not understand the implications of death. Placing a rubber ball, which stands for the orange, in the hands of the dead woman, she hopes to preserve and protect her love by hiding it in death.

Marika Navarre
World Literature
December 12, 1999
p. 4

Later, when the narrator's grandmother is dying, the narrator makes an enormous sacrifice. For the first time, she reveals her secret and in doing so learns the truth about the symbol of love that she had held for so long:

longer, indented quotation

> "Grandma," I said quickly, searching for something to say, something that would save her, "Grandma, you can have my whole orange," and I placed it in the bed beside her hand. But she kept on dying and I knew then that the orange had no potency, that love could not create miracles (289).

The narrator realizes that love is not omnipotent, that this powerful emotion cannot conquer death. Her innocence is lost. When the narrator breaks her hand in the car door, she feels nothing—the familiar love-orange she once held is gone. The magical talismans of her innocence no longer exist to help her through her loss.

end of body

conclusion

By the end of the story, the narrator has undergone a dramatic change, and her relationship to the objects that symbolized her innocence has changed. While the narrator might physically return to the safe haven under her grandfather's bed, her knowledge of the world has destroyed the place as a refuge. The doll the narrator dreads may finally stay buried, for the narrator's eyes are now open to the mortality of all people. In giving away the orange, a symbol of both love and innocence, the narrator surrenders a talisman that once protected her from the outside world. These three symbols gained their personal meaning to the

Marika Navarre
World Literature
December 12, 1999
p. 5

narrator in her state of innocence; the lack of meaning they hold for the narrator at the end of the story demonstrates her fall from innocence into experience. The world no longer waits outside for her—she enters that world along with her painful, hard-won knowledge of love and death.

conclusion

Notes

Senior, Olive. "Love Orange." Literature and the Language Arts: World Literature. St. Paul: EMC, 1998. 287-289.

source citation

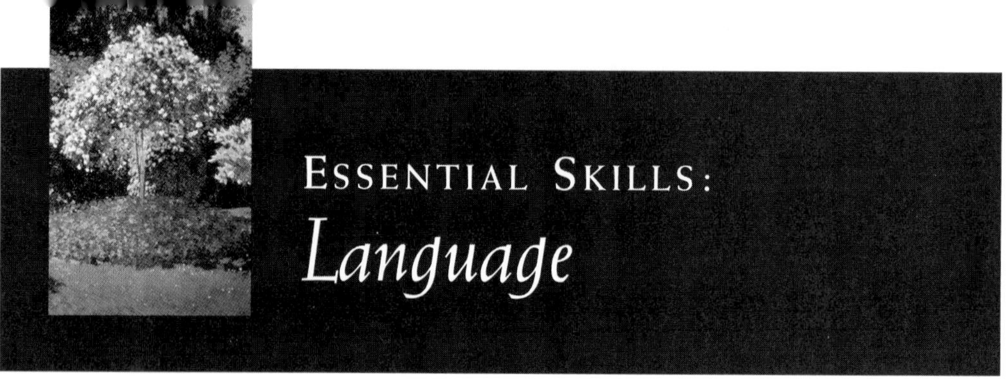

ESSENTIAL SKILLS: *Language*

GRAMMAR HANDBOOK

INTRODUCTION TO GRAMMAR

2.1 The Grammar You Already Know

Grammar is something you know, even if you have never studied it. Inside the head of every person is a sophisticated device that works, all by itself, to learn how to put words and phrases together grammatically. Even if you don't know an adverb from an aardvark, you know, if you are a speaker of English, that

the daring young diver

is grammatical and that

the diver daring young

is not. You can tell that one string of words is grammatical and the other isn't because you have learned, unconsciously, many thousands of rules governing how words can be put together and how they can't.

When you study a grammar textbook, therefore, what you are really learning is not the grammar of the language—for the most part, that's something you already know. What you are learning is terminology for describing what you know so that you can use that terminology when discussing language. Incidentally, as you study textbook grammar, you will also learn a few rules that you never quite learned unconsciously. Remember, however, that most of the grammar is already inside your head. Learning to describe that grammar can therefore be viewed as learning more about yourself and your amazing unconscious abilities.

2.2 The Uses of Grammar

Why study grammar? After all, no amount of grammar study can match the value of hands-on reading and writing. Grammar is useful, however. It gives you a way to speak about and understand your own writing and that of others. Contrast the following examples:

At last, having lost his wits completely, he stumbled upon the oddest fancy that ever entered a madman's brain. He believed that it was necessary, both for his own honor and for the service of the state, that he should become knight-errant and roam through the world with his horse and armor in quest of adventures, and practice all that had been performed by the knights-errant of whom he had read. He would follow their life, redressing all manner of wrongs and exposing himself to continual dangers, and at last, after concluding his enterprises, he would win everlasting honor and renown.

—Miguel de Cervantes Saavedra, *Don Quixote de La Mancha*

The door opened.

It opened wide with a rapid movement, as though some one had given it an energetic and resolute push.

A man entered.

We already know the man. It was the wayfarer whom we have seen wandering about in search of shelter.

He entered, advanced a step, and halted, leaving the door open behind him. He had his knapsack on his shoulders, his cudgel in his hand, a rough, audacious, weary, and violent expression in his eyes. The fire on the hearth lighted him up. He was hideous. It was a sinister apparition. —Victor Hugo, *Les Misérables*

If you had to describe the difference between these two passages, you would find it useful to have precise grammatical terms at your command. The paragraph from *Don Quixote* contains long, compound-complex sentences with many participial phrases and prepositional phrases. The passage from *Les Misérables* has short, crisp simple sentences, consisting mostly of simple subjects, verbs, and predicates. Vivid adjectives make it a powerful description. You may *sense* the differences in these two styles of writing instinctively, but grammar gives you a way to *understand* and *communicate* those differences.

THE PARTS OF SPEECH

2.3 TYPES OF NOUNS

A **noun** is a word used to refer to a person, place, thing, or idea.

NOUNS Nicholas, Japan, butterfly, humor

A **common noun** is a name that belongs to (is *common* to) all the persons, places, or things in a group. A **proper noun** refers to a *particular* person, place, or thing and begins with a capital letter.

COMMON NOUNS athlete, city, holiday
PROPER NOUNS Jesse Owens, Paris, Halloween

A **concrete noun** refers to an object that you can perceive by hearing, seeing, smelling, tasting, or touching. An **abstract noun** names a quality, characteristic, or idea.

CONCRETE NOUNS bell, dragon, coffee, broccoli, heat
ABSTRACT NOUNS loyalty, fear, compassion, subtlety, Easter
"The **future** belongs to those who believe in the **beauty** of their **dreams.**"

A **compound noun** is made up of two or more words used together as a single noun. A **collective noun** refers to a group of similar things.

COMPOUND NOUNS	babysitter, grocery store, framework, mother-of-pearl
COLLECTIVE NOUNS	herd, troop, litter, gang, choir, Senate, Syracuse Symphony Orchestra

2.4 Personal Pronouns

A **pronoun** is a word used as a substitute for a noun. The word a pronoun stands for is called an **antecedent** or **referent.** In the following example, *Parthenon* is the antecedent of the pronoun *it.*

PRONOUN AND ANTECEDENT	The **Parthenon** is in Athens. **It** served as a model for much of Greek architecture.

A **personal pronoun** is a pronoun that substitutes for the name of a person or thing. The personal pronouns are *I, me, my, mine, we, us, our, ours, you, your, yours, he, him, his, she, her, hers, it, its, they, them, their,* and *theirs.*

PERSONAL PRONOUNS	**We** spent the summer in Italy.
	The police chief gave **him** a commendation for courage.

2.5 Reflexive, Intensive, and Demonstrative Pronouns

A **reflexive pronoun** is a pronoun used to show that an action is done to or reflects upon someone or something. An **intensive pronoun** is a pronoun used to emphasize a noun or pronoun already given. The reflexive and intensive pronouns are *myself, ourselves, yourself, yourselves, himself, herself, itself,* and *themselves.* A **demonstrative pronoun** is a pronoun used to point out a particular person, place, or thing. The demonstrative pronouns are *this, that, these,* and *those.*

REFLEXIVE PRONOUNS	The candle finally burned **itself** out.
	Allow **yourselves** plenty of time to complete your projects.
INTENSIVE PRONOUNS	Vivian **herself** admitted that it was a bad idea.
	The band members **themselves** raised the money to go on tour.
DEMONSTRATIVE PRONOUNS	**This** is my final offer.
	Those are the most striking portraits I have ever seen.

2.6 Indefinite, Interrogative, and Relative Pronouns

An **indefinite** pronoun is a pronoun that points out a person, place, or thing, but not a particular one. Some of the most common indefinite pronouns are *some, someone, somebody, something, any, anyone, anybody, anything, everyone, everybody, everything, other, another, either, neither, all, many, few, each, both, one, none, nobody,* and *nothing.* An **interrogative pronoun** is a pronoun used in asking a question. The interrogative pronouns are *who, whose, what, whom,* and *which.* A **relative pronoun** is a pronoun that connects a group of words with an antecedent. The relative pronouns are *that, which, who, whom,* and *whose.*

INDEFINITE PRONOUNS	A **few** of the Senators opposed the bill, but **most** supported it.
	Someone left this gym bag in the locker room.
INTERROGATIVE PRONOUNS	To **whom** is the package addressed?
	What are your symptoms?
RELATIVE PRONOUNS	Travis is the young cellist **whose** brilliant performance brought a standing ovation.
	The event **that** sparked World War I was the assassination of an Austrian archduke.

2.7 Types of Verbs

A **verb** is a word that expresses action or a state of being. An **action verb** expresses physical or mental activity. A **linking verb** connects a noun with another noun, pronoun, or adjective that describes it or identifies it. Most linking verbs are forms of the verb *to be.* They include *am, are, is, was,* and *been.* Other words that can be used as linking verbs include *seem, sound, look, stay, feel, remain* and *become.* An **auxiliary verb** is a verb that helps to make some form of another verb. Common auxiliary verbs are *can, could, may, might, must, shall, should, will, would,* and forms of the verbs *to be, to have,* and *to do.*

ACTION VERBS	Alyssa **ran** with the bulls in Pamplona.
	Pecola **longs** for blue eyes.
LINKING VERBS	Gandhi **became** the leader of India's movement for independence.
	Emil **seems** especially chipper today.
AUXILIARY VERBS	You **should** be a stand-up comedian.
	Phoebe **can** hit the target every time.

2.8 Transitive and Intransitive Verbs

The **direct object** of a verb is a noun or pronoun that names the person or thing upon which the verb acts. Verbs that must have direct objects are **transitive verbs**. Verbs that do not need direct objects are **intransitive verbs**. Some verbs are both transitive and intransitive.

TRANSITIVE VERB	The young wife **wore** ornate jewelry.
INTRANSITIVE VERB	Her husband **wept** unceasingly after her death.

2.9 Verbals

A **participle** is a form of a verb that can be used as an adjective. A participle may end in *–ing* or *–ed.* A **gerund** is a form of a verb ending in *–ing* that is used as a noun. Be careful not to confuse gerunds with participles. An **infinitive** is a form of a verb that can be used as a noun, an adjective, or an adverb. Most infinitives begin with *to.* (See 2.10 for more information about adjectives and adverbs.)

PARTICIPLES **Feeling** full of confidence, Don Quixote set out to right the wrongs in the world.
The circus dogs leaped through the **flaming** hoops.
A faint smile appeared on the old woman's **wrinkled** face.

GERUNDS **Beachcombing** can be fun and may yield real treasures.
The burglar was afraid of **triggering** an alarm.
He remembered **climbing** the tree but not **falling** from it.

INFINITIVES The moral of "The Fable of the Lion and the Rat" is: "**To show** to all your kindness, it behoves."
Never hesitate **to ask** questions when you don't understand.
Please help me **carry** in the grocery bags.

2.10 Adjectives and Articles

An **adjective** is a word used to modify a noun or pronoun. *To modify* means to change the meaning of something. Adjectives change the meaning of nouns or pronouns by answering the questions *What kind? Which one?* or *How many?*

ADJECTIVES **juicy** strawberry, **youngest** daughter, **forty** thieves

A **proper adjective** is an adjective formed from a proper noun.

PROPER ADJECTIVES **Persian** carpet, **Buddhist** temple, **Petrarchan** ideal, **Socratic** wisdom

The adjectives *a, an,* and *the* are called **articles.** *A* and *an* are **indefinite articles** because they refer indefinitely to any one of a group. *The* is the **definite article** because it refers to a definite person, place, thing, or idea.

ARTICLES **a** sword, **an** avalanche, **the** mirror

Every sentence is made up of two parts, a **subject** and a **predicate.** The subject is what or whom the sentence is about. The predicate tells something about the subject's actions or condition.

SUBJECT **Achilles** was nearly invincible.
PREDICATE His mother **had dipped him in the River Styx.**

A **predicate adjective** is an adjective that follows a linking verb and modifies the subject of a verb.

PREDICATE ADJECTIVES Ravi felt **insignificant** when the other children forgot about him.
Samuel was usually **shy** and **withdrawn**, but when it came to playing chess, he was **ferocious.**

2.11 Adverbs

An **adverb** is a word used to modify a verb, an adjective, or another adverb.

ADVERBS MODIFYING VERBS Elia believed that the only thing that **really** matters is treating people **kindly.**
ADVERB MODIFYING ADJECTIVE Eva was **mildly** annoyed by her brother's incessant questions.
ADVERB MODIFYING ADVERB François accepted the challenge **more** enthusiastically than anyone else.

If you know a word is either an adjective or adverb but are not sure which it is, look at the word it modifies. Adjectives modify nouns and pronouns. Adverbs modify verbs, adjectives, and adverbs.

ADJECTIVES **radiant** smile, **furtive** glance, **steadfast** friend, **forward** pass, **early** riser
ADVERBS tremble **uncontrollably, mysteriously** strange encounter, crying **almost** hysterically

Many, but not all words with *–ly* endings are adverbs. Generally speaking, if you take the *–ly* ending off a word and are left with a noun, the *–ly* word is an adjective. If you are left with an adjective, the *–ly* word is an adverb.

ADJECTIVES timely, ghostly, manly, brotherly, heavenly
ADVERBS hopefully, falsely, intently, overly, remotely

2.12 Prepositions and Prepositional Phrases

A **preposition** is used to show how a noun or a pronoun, its **object,** is related to some other word in the sentence. Common prepositions are *after, among, at, behind, beside, off, through, until, upon,* and *with.* A preposition introduces a **prepositional phrase**. The following examples show prepositional phrases in sentences.

PREPOSITIONAL PHRASES The shivering commuters huddled **beneath the shelter** as the rain pelted **around them.**
Rosalía de Castro was secretly raised **by a peasant woman,** then "adopted" **by her biological mother.**

ESSENTIAL SKILLS: LANGUAGE

2.13 Conjunctions and Interjections

A **conjunction** is a word used to join words or groups of words. A **coordinating conjunction** connects words or groups of words that are used in the same way—nouns with nouns, verbs with verbs, and so on. Thus a coordinating conjunction *coordinates*, or orders the relationship between two words or groups of words. The main coordinating conjunctions are *and, but, for, nor, or, so,* and *yet.*

COORDINATING CONJUNCTIONS Anna Akhmatova **and** Leo Tolstoy were Russian writers.
Pedro loved Tita, **but** he agreed to marry Rosaura.
Bernard has been there many times, **so** he knows the way.
Do you prefer jazz **or** folk music?

A **correlative conjunction** is a pair of conjunctions that joins words or groups of words that are used in the same way. Some common correlative conjunctions are *both . . . and; either . . . or; neither . . . nor; not only . . . but also;* and *whether . . . or.*

CORRELATIVE CONJUNCTIONS Claude is **both** an accomplished musician **and** an outstanding football player.
Luisa faced a wrenching dilemma: she would **either** lose her friend **or** lose her honor.

A **clause** is a group of words with its own subject and verb.

CLAUSES **A river flowed through the cave.**
As the poison took effect, numbness spread from Socrates' feet up through his body.
Meletis is the boy **whose quick thinking saved the life of the little girl.**

A **subordinate clause** is a clause that cannot stand by itself as a complete sentence. It depends on another clause and adds information about that clause. A **subordinating conjunction** connects a subordinate clause to another clause. Some common subordinating conjunctions are *after, as, as well as, because, if, in order that, provided, since, so that, than, that, though, unless, when,* and *why.*

SUBORDINATING CONJUNCTIONS The little man claimed **that** he could spin straw into gold.
Unless anyone can offer a better suggestion, let's try Rolf's idea.

An **interjection** is a word used to express emotion. It stands apart from the rest of a sentence. Common interjections are *ah, oh, say, well,* and *wow.*

INTERJECTIONS **Well,** I guess it wouldn't hurt to try.
Hey! Watch where you're going!

2.14 Conjunctive Adverbs

A **conjunctive adverb** is a conjunction that both introduces and modifies a clause. Some conjunctive adverbs are *accordingly, furthermore,* and *moreover.*

CONJUNCTIVE ADVERBS Federigo was earning nothing and living beyond his means; **therefore,** he soon squandered all his wealth and became poor.
Sisyphus labored to roll the stone up the hill; **however,** each time he reached the top, the stone rolled back down.

2.15 Using Vivid Nouns, Verbs, and Modifiers

When you are writing, choose nouns that tell your reader precisely what you mean. If you use precise nouns, rather than nouns with a vague or general meaning, your writing will sparkle. Avoid using an adjective and a noun, as in *stingy person,* when using a single, precise noun, such as *miser,* will do.

VAGUE The **people** marched around the **building.**
PRECISE The **athletes** marched around the **coliseum.**

Note the precise nouns in this passage from "Song Composed in August," by Robert Burns:

PRECISE NOUNS The **partridge** loves the fruitful **fells;**
The **plover** loves the **mountains;**
The **woodcock** haunts the lonely **dells**
The soaring **hern** the **fountains.**

Like precise nouns, vivid verbs create a picture in the reader's mind. Instead of using a vague, general verb like *look (at),* a writer can produce a concrete picture by using a vivid verb such as *contemplate, eye, explore, gape, gawk, gaze, glance, glimpse, inspect, ogle, peek, peep, peer, peruse, regard, scan, scrutinize, search, stare,* or *survey.* Instead of using an adverb and a verb, as in *looked sternly,* a writer can use a single, precise verb such as *glared.*

DULL The children **ate** the rice pudding.
VIVID The children **gobbled** the rice pudding.

Note the vivid verbs used by Heinrich Heine in the poem "Loreley":

VIVID VERBS I do not know what **haunts** me,
What **saddened** my mind all day;
An age old tale **confounds** me,
A spell I cannot **allay.**

A **modifier** is a word that modifies—that is, changes or explains—the meaning of another word. Adjectives and adverbs are modifiers. Rather than use trite or vague modifiers in your writing, search out adjectives and adverbs that add freshness and meaning. Consider the modifiers in these lines from Ludovico Ariosto's *Orlando Furioso:*

COLORFUL MODIFIERS As when a ploughman, **dazed** with stupefaction,
After a thunderbolt has struck, **aghast** . . .
Views, **dismayed**, the **shrivelling** contraction
Of pine-trees **stripped** and **withered** by the blast . . .

By using precise nouns, vivid action verbs, and colorful modifiers, you can turn bland prose into dynamic reading. Note the difference between the dull sentence below and the actual opening sentence of Bessie Head's "Snapshots of a Wedding":

DULL Wedding days always started first thing in the morning when the sun was just coming up.

COLORFUL "Wedding days always started at the haunting, magical hour of early dawn when there was only a pale crack of light on the horizon."

BUILDING SENTENCES

2.16 The Functions of Sentences

Sentences are classified according to their functions. They may be **declarative, imperative, interrogative**, or **exclamatory.** A **declarative sentence** makes a statement and is followed by a period.

DECLARATIVE SENTENCES The President will give his State of the Union address at eight o'clock tonight.
Camus believed that Sisyphus was an absurd hero.

An **imperative sentence** gives a command or makes a request. It usually ends with a period but may end with an exclamation point.

IMPERATIVE SENTENCES Take this basket of goodies to Grandmama.
Don't tell me that you've never heard of King Arthur!

An **interrogative sentence** asks a question. It ends with a question mark.

INTERROGATIVE SENTENCES In Greek mythology, who is the god of the sea?
How did Solomon solve that knotty problem?

An **exclamatory sentence** expresses a strong feeling about something. It ends with an exclamation point.

EXCLAMATORY SENTENCES On my word of honor, I never laid eyes on her before!
The old hermit left an estate worth six million dollars!
Quick! Hide the evidence!

2.17 Simple Sentences

The most basic sentence is one that combines a **substantive** and a verb in the form SUB + V. A substantive is anything used as a noun—a noun, pronoun, gerund, infinitive, or noun clause.

NOUN **Power** corrupts.
PRONOUN **She** speaks.
GERUND **Gesturing** clarifies.
NOUN CLAUSE **That you don't trust me** hurts.

You can build the next kind of basic sentence by adding another substantive as the direct object of an action verb, producing a sentence with the form SUB + AV + SUB. In the following examples, the direct object is boldfaced.

EXAMPLES Haste makes **waste.**
Lions eat **meat.**
Vincent helped **them.**
Petrarch loved **Laura.**

Imagine you had a linking verb in your simple sentence instead of an action verb. Your sentence would then follow the pattern SUB + LV + SUB. The second substantive would be a **predicate nominative**, which is a word or group of words that follows a linking verb and refers to the same person or thing as the subject of the verb. In the following examples, the predicate nominative is boldfaced.

EXAMPLES Honesty is **the best policy.**
What is **sushi?**
Winning isn't **everything.**
Her goal is **to swim the English Channel.**

Now imagine you made the element after the verb a predicate adjective. (See 2.10 for the definition of a predicate adjective.) Then the sentence pattern would be SUB + LV + ADJ. In the following examples, the predicate adjective is boldfaced.

EXAMPLES The sea was **tranquil.**
Silence is **golden.**
Parasailing can be **dangerous.**
To succeed is **satisfying.**

Another type of simple sentence can be formed by following the pattern substantive + action verb + substantive + substantive (SUB + AV + SUB + SUB). One of the substantives after the action verb will be a direct object. The other may be an **indirect object**. An indirect object is a noun or pronoun that comes between an action verb and a direct object. It shows *to whom* or *to what* or *for whom* or *for what* the action of the verb is done. In the following examples, the indirect object is boldfaced.

EXAMPLES King Midas's greed caused **him** untold grief.
Texas Instruments offered **her** an excellent position.
The storyteller told **the enraptured children** an enchanting tale.
Seeking revenge will cost **you** everything.

Instead of an indirect object, however, one of the elements may be an objective complement. An **objective complement** is a word or group of words that helps complete the meaning of an action verb by identifying or modifying the direct object. The words *to be* may be inferred as appearing before the objective complement. In the following examples, the objective complement is boldfaced.

EXAMPLES The sixth grade voted Andrés **class clown.** (The class voted Andrés [to be] class clown.)
David considered Jonathan **his most loyal friend.** (David considered Jonathan [to be] his most loyal friend.)

2.18 Independent and Dependent Clauses

A **clause** is a group of words with its own subject and verb. An **independent clause** expresses a complete thought and can stand by itself as a sentence. All the examples in 2.17 are also examples of independent clauses. A **dependent** (or **subordinate**) **clause** has its own subject and verb but cannot stand by itself as a complete sentence. It depends on another clause and adds information about that clause.

INDEPENDENT CLAUSES Mrs. Linde's mother had passed away, and her sons did not need her anymore either.
The firemen fought valiantly to save the old factory.

DEPENDENT CLAUSES Mrs. Linde felt inexpressibly empty **because her mother had passed away and her sons did not need her anymore either.**
Although the firemen fought valiantly to save the factory, the old building finally gave way to the ravaging flames.

2.19 Sentences Containing Clauses

You can expand on a sentence that has only one independent clause by adding another independent clause. You will then have a **compound sentence**—one formed of two or more independent clauses but no subordinate clauses. (See 2.18 for the definition of a subordinate clause.) Related independent clauses can be joined by a semicolon; by a coordinating conjunction such as *and, or, for, nor, but, so,* or *yet* and a comma; or by a semicolon followed by a conjunctive adverb such as *however* or *therefore* and a comma.

COMPOUND SENTENCES Four times the fisherman cast his net into the sea; the fourth time, he hauled in a bottle made of yellow copper.
Klaus dreamed of running the marathon in the Olympics, so he trained diligently, no matter what the weather.
Augusto called every day; however, Olenka was not interested in him.

You can also expand a sentence that has only one independent clause by adding a subordinate clause. You will then have a **complex sentence**—one formed of an independent clause and at least one subordinate clause. In the following examples the subordinate clauses are boldfaced.

COMPLEX SENTENCES	These are the times **that try men's souls.**
	When Lekisha speaks, people listen.
	Albert Einstein was a physicist **who developed the theories of relativity.**

If you combine a compound sentence and a complex sentence, you will have a **compound-complex** sentence. This kind of sentence must have two or more independent clauses and at least one subordinate clause. In the following examples the subordinate clauses are boldfaced.

COMPOUND-COMPLEX SENTENCES	"Thus my consciousness was awakened to the pervasiveness of 'petty apartheid,' and **everywhere I went in the white world,** I was met by visible and invisible guards of racial segregation." —Mark Mathabane
	Whenever the alarm sounded, the station came to life, and the firefighters sprang into action.

EXPANDING AND COMBINING SENTENCES

2.20 Expanding Sentences

Simple, compound, complex, and compound-complex sentences can be expanded by adding modifiers such as adjectives and adverbs.

BASIC SENTENCE	The steaks sizzled.
SENTENCE WITH ADDED MODIFIERS	The **juicy** steaks sizzled **temptingly.**
BASIC SENTENCE	The airliner shuddered and began to plummet.
SENTENCE WITH ADDED MODIFIERS	The **crippled** airliner shuddered **hideously** and began to plummet **wildly.**
BASIC SENTENCE	The gymnast performed her routine, which was exceedingly difficult.
SENTENCE WITH ADDED MODIFIERS	The **spunky** gymnast **flawlessly** performed her routine, which was exceedingly difficult.

Adding a prepositional phrase is another way to expand sentences. The prepositional phrase you add can be an adjectival phrase or an adverbial phrase. An **adjectival phrase** modifies a noun or pronoun. An **adverbial phrase** modifies a verb, an adjective, or an adverb. In the following examples, the prepositional phrases are boldfaced.

SENTENCES WITH ADDED PREPOSITIONAL PHRASES	The juicy steaks sizzled temptingly **on the grill.**
	After the blast, the crippled airliner shuddered hideously and began to plummet wildly **into the black abyss.**
	With her ankle heavily taped, the spunky gymnast **from the underdog team** flawlessly performed her routine, which was exceedingly difficult, **on the beam, before a crowd of zealous fans.**

Note that expanding sentences can cause problems instead of adding interest and variety. The third sentence, above, is bloated and should be trimmed down.

Still another way to expand sentences is to add an **appositive** or an **appositive phrase.** An appositive is a noun or pronoun placed beside another noun or pronoun to identify or explain it. An appositive phrase is made up of the appositive and its modifiers. The modifiers can be adjectives or adverbs.

BASIC SENTENCE	Benjamin Franklin was a key figure in early American history.
WITH APPOSITIVES	Benjamin Franklin, a **writer, inventor,** and **diplomat,** was a key figure in early American history.
WITH APPOSITIVE PHRASES	Benjamin Franklin, an **erudite writer, clever inventor,** and **level-headed diplomat,** was a key figure in early American history.

A **predicate** is a main verb and any auxiliary verbs, together with any words, phrases, or clauses that modify or complement the verb. You can expand sentences by adding predicates.

BASIC SENTENCE	Odysseus had many perilous adventures.
WITH ADDED PREDICATE	Odysseus had many perilous adventures but **eventually returned home to his wife, Penelope.**

Subordinate clauses may also be used to expand the meaning of a sentence.

BASIC SENTENCE	The stolen shoes were soft and comfortable, but Elia's feet seemed to object violently to being in those shoes.
WITH SUBORDINATE CLAUSES	The stolen shoes were soft and comfortable, but Elia's feet seemed to object violently to being in those shoes, **which reminded him of his degradation with every step.**

2.21 Combining Sentences Using Words and Phrases

Often you can combine two sentences that deal with the same topic to make your writing briefer and more effective. Rather than repeat information, you take the vital information from one sentence and insert it in the other, either in its original form or slightly altered.

GIVEN SENTENCES	Lot's wife wanted one last look at Sodom. It was her native town.
COMBINED SENTENCE	Lot's wife wanted one last look at her **native** Sodom.
GIVEN SENTENCES	The wounded bear was attacking his rival. He was vicious.
COMBINED SENTENCE	The wounded bear was **viciously** attacking his rival.
GIVEN SENTENCES	The magazine carried several articles about the scandal. They were hard-hitting.
COMBINED SENTENCE	The magazine carried several **hard-hitting** articles about the scandal.

A second way to combine two sentences that deal with the same topic is to take a prepositional phrase or a participial phrase from one sentence and move it into the other.

GIVEN SENTENCES	He decided to hide the Book of Sand. He decided to hide it in the library.
COMBINED SENTENCE	He decided to hide the Book of Sand **in the library.**
GIVEN SENTENCES	Enkidu died in shame. He was suffering greatly in body and in mind.
COMBINED SENTENCE	Enkidu, **suffering greatly in body and in mind,** died in shame.

Sometimes you may need to change a part of the sentence into a prepositional phrase, or change a verb into a participle, before you can insert the idea into another sentence.

GIVEN SENTENCES	Kamala Das has written many poems. Many of her poems deal with the longing to be loved.
COMBINED SENTENCE	Kamala Das has written many poems **about the longing to be loved.**
GIVEN SENTENCES	She cradled the shivering kitten in her arms. She tenderly stroked its wet fur.
COMBINED SENTENCE	**Cradling the shivering kitten in her arms,** she tenderly stroked its wet fur.

2.22 Combining Sentences Using Clauses

A third way to combine two sentences that have the same topic is to make one the independent clause and the other the subordinate clause in a combined sentence.

GIVEN SENTENCES	Arvid has a brilliant mind. He doesn't have much common sense.
COMBINED SENTENCE	**Although Arvid has a brilliant mind,** he doesn't have much common sense.
GIVEN SENTENCES	The Wise Men returned home a different way. They had been warned in a dream not to go back to Herod.
COMBINED SENTENCE	The Wise Men returned home a different way, **because they had been warned in a dream not to go back to Herod.**

ESSENTIAL SKILLS: LANGUAGE

EDITING SENTENCES

2.23 Varying Sentence Openings, Length, and Structure

Many of the examples in this handbook begin with a subject for the sake of simplicity. When you are writing, however, you will find that *always* beginning with a subject makes for a dull style. You can make your writing more varied and interesting by beginning sentences with adjectives, adverbs, participles—just about any part of speech—as well as with phrases and clauses. You may have to reword your sentences slightly as you vary the sentence openings.

GIVEN SENTENCE The werewolves emerge at exactly midnight.
EDITED SENTENCE **At exactly midnight**, the werewolves emerge.

GIVEN SENTENCE The blind woman reached the summit, defying all odds.
EDITED SENTENCE **Defying all odds,** the blind woman reached the summit.

GIVEN SENTENCE She sat looking in the mirror for long hours and tried to discover the secret of her ugliness.
EDITED SENTENCE **Long hours she sat looking in the mirror,** trying to discover the secret of her ugliness.

Repeated sentences of the same length and structure soon become monotonous. Use a variety of simple, compound, complex, and compound-complex sentences in your writing. Notice that the first passage below, composed of simple sentences of similar length, soon becomes tedious. The second, an actual passage from Cervantes's *Don Quixote,* employs a variety of sentence structures and is far more interesting.

PASSAGE WITH SIMPLE SENTENCES

He uttered those words. He clapped spurs to Rozinante. He did not heed the cries of his squire, Sancho. Sancho warned him. He was not going to attack giants but windmills. He was convinced that they were giants. He did not hear his squire's shouts. He did not notice what they were. He was very near them. Instead, he rushed on. . . . He commended himself most devoutly to his Lady Dulcinea. He begged her to help him in this peril. He covered himself with his buckler. He couched his lance. He charged at Rozinante's full gallop. He rammed the first mill in his way. He ran his lance into the sail. The wind twisted it violently. It shivered the spear to pieces. It dragged him and his horse after it. It rolled him over and over on the ground. He was sorely damaged.

PASSAGE WITH VARIED SENTENCE LENGTH AND STRUCTURE

Uttering those words, he clapped spurs to Rozinante, without heeding the cries of his squire Sancho, who warned him that he was not going to attack giants but windmills. But so convinced was he that they were giants that he neither heard his squire's shouts nor did he notice what they were though he was very near them. Instead, he rushed on. . . . Commending himself most devoutly to his Lady Dulcinea, whom he begged to help him in this peril, he covered himself with his buckler, couched his lance, charged at Rozinante's full gallop and rammed the first mill in his way. He ran his lance into the sail, but the wind twisted it with such violence that it shivered the spear to pieces, dragging him and his horse after it and rolling him over and over on the ground, sorely damaged.

—Miguel de Cervantes Saavedra, *Don Quixote de la Mancha*

2.24 Using the Active Voice

A verb is in the **active voice** when the subject of the verb performs the action. It is in the **passive voice** when the subject of the verb receives the action.

ACTIVE Anna Akhmatova memorized her poem *Requiem* as she wrote it.
PASSIVE The poem *Requiem* was memorized by Anna Akhmatova.

A common characteristic of poor writing is overuse of the passive voice. Keep your verbs in the active voice unless you have a good reason for using the passive voice. In the examples that follow, note how the active verbs make the writing more natural, interesting, and concise.

WITH PASSIVE VERBS The European discovery of America **may have been made** by the Vikings more than five hundred years before Columbus arrived. According to ancient Norse writings, America **was reached** by Leif the Lucky in AD 985. The Atlantic **was crossed** by the Vikings in wooden longboats. The sailors **were guided** on their journey by the sun, stars, and movements of sea birds.

WITH ACTIVE VERBS The Vikings **may have made** the European discovery of America more than five hundred years before Columbus arrived. According to ancient Norse writings, Leif the Lucky **reached** America in AD 985. The Vikings **crossed** the Atlantic in wooden longboats. The sun, stars, and movements of sea birds **guided** the sailors on their journey.

2.25 Achieving Parallelism

A sentence has **parallelism** when it uses the same grammatical forms to express ideas of equal, or parallel, importance. When you edit your sentences during revision, check to be sure that your parallelism is not faulty.

FAULTY Lloyd is afraid of **taking risks** and **to be in unfamiliar situations.**
PARALLEL Lloyd is afraid of **taking risks** and **being in unfamiliar situations.**

FAULTY **Having something worth saying** and **to communicate it well** are both essential elements of speech-making.

PARALLEL **To have something worth saying** and **to communicate it well** are both essential elements of speech-making.

FAULTY The dishonest woodcutter claimed **the golden ax is mine** and **that he had dropped it in the water.**

PARALLEL The dishonest woodcutter claimed **that the golden ax was his** and **that he had dropped it in the water.**

2.26 Reducing Wordiness

When you edit your writing, check carefully for repeated or unnecessary ideas. Remove any words that do not contribute to your meaning.

REPETITION Marilda glided out **on the stage** and danced with utter abandon **on the stage.**

CORRECTED SENTENCE Marilda glided out on the stage and danced with utter abandon.

UNNECESSARY IDEA The setting sun, **which was setting in the west,** cast long shadows over the somber assembly.

CORRECTED SENTENCE The setting sun cast long shadows over the somber assembly.

When you write, use only as many words as you need to express your meaning. While editing, replace complicated or unclear words and phrases with ones that are simple and clear.

WORDY His idea that he thought up seems to me as I think about it to be absurd and preposterous.

DIRECT His idea seems absurd to me.

WORDY The jinnee implored and begged the fisherman to let him come back out of the bottle again and promised and swore that he would give him fabulous riches if he would let him come back out again.

DIRECT The jinnee begged the fisherman to let him back out of the bottle and promised to give him fabulous riches.

Look for ways to reduce the length of your sentences by replacing a clause with a phrase that conveys the same meaning. In some cases, you can even replace a lengthy phrase with a single word.

WORDY Elie Wiesel, **who was a concentration camp survivor,** wrote *Night,* **which is a book about the Holocaust.**

DIRECT Elie Wiesel, **a concentration camp survivor,** wrote *Night,* **a book about the Holocaust.**

WORDY **The kind of quality of your character** is more important than **the amount of wealth you have.**

DIRECT **Your character** is more important than **your wealth.**

2.27 Correcting Sentence Fragments, Run-ons, and Sentence Strings

A **sentence** should express a complete thought and contain both a subject and a verb. A **sentence fragment** is a phrase or clause that does not express a complete thought but has been punctuated as though it did. You can correct a sentence fragment by changing its punctuation or structure so that it expresses a complete thought.

FRAGMENTED Nora was terrified. That Torvald would read the letter from Krogstad.

CORRECTED Nora was terrified that Torvald would read the letter from Krogstad.

In sentences in which the subject will be understood by the reader, the subject can be left unexpressed. Such sentences are not sentence fragments.

SENTENCE WITH IMPLIED, UNEXPRESSED SUBJECT [You] Take good care of my sweater.

A **run-on** is formed of two or more sentences that have been run together as if they were one complete thought. Edit a run-on by making it into two sentences, by adding a comma and a coordinating conjunction, or by adding a semicolon.

RUN-ON	Socrates was a leading Athenian philosopher his most famous student was Plato who in turn became the teacher of Aristotle.
TWO SENTENCES	Socrates was a leading Athenian philosopher. His most famous student was Plato, who in turn became the teacher of Aristotle.
COORDINATED CLAUSES	Socrates was a leading Athenian philosopher, and his most famous student was Plato, who in turn became the teacher of Aristotle.
CLAUSES WITH SEMICOLON	Socrates was a leading Athenian philosopher; his most famous student was Plato, who in turn became the teacher of Aristotle.

Sentence strings are formed of several sentences strung together with conjunctions. Edit sentence strings by breaking them up into separate sentences and subordinate clauses. In the example that follows, the first passage is a sentence string; the second is a passage broken up into separate sentences and clauses.

STRINGY He was, however, used to this sort of thing, and he never expected anything to help him apart from his philosophic calm and his Uncle Agostino's will, and he was an excellent walker, and he thought far more about his shoes than about his feet, and if matters went as well as he expected, then everything would be mended in due course.

REVISED He was, however, used to this sort of thing; he never expected anything to help him apart from his philosophic calm and his Uncle Agostino's will. He was an excellent walker, and thought far more about his shoes than about his feet; if matters went as well as he expected, then everything would be mended in due course.

—Grazia Deledda, "The Shoes"

2.28 Correcting Dangling or Misplaced Modifiers

A **dangling modifier** is a modifying phrase or clause that seems to modify a word it is not intended to modify. Sometimes this error occurs because the modifier is too far from the word it is supposed to modify. It is then called a **misplaced modifier**. You can edit dangling and misplaced modifiers by adding a word for the phrase or clause to modify or by rewording the sentence.

DANGLING	Valerie drove to the airport while reading my book.
WORDS ADDED	Valerie drove to the airport while **I was** reading my book.
MISPLACED	Aleksei played a solo on the cello wearing a white tuxedo.
REWORDED	**Wearing a white tuxedo**, Aleksei played a solo on the cello.

2.29 Inverting Sentences for Emphasis

When editing your writing, look for opportunities to add emphasis and clarify your meaning. One way to add emphasis is to **invert** a sentence—to change the usual order of its parts.

REGULAR ORDER	He seems weary and breathless from his ride.
INVERTED ORDER	Weary he seems, and breathless from his ride.
REGULAR ORDER	He is not an orator.
INVERTED ORDER	An orator he is not.

EDITING FOR ERRORS IN VERBS

2.30 Correcting Shifts in Verb Tense

When the verbs in a sentence or group of sentences shift from past to present or from present to past without reason, the reader may not be able to follow the intended meaning. Correct the shift by using consistent tenses for all verbs.

WITH TENSE SHIFT Henrik Ibsen was a nineteenth century Norwegian author who writes powerful plays on social and political themes.

CORRECTED Henrik Ibsen was a nineteenth century Norwegian author who wrote powerful plays on social and political themes.

2.31 Correcting Errors in the Use of Irregular Verbs

Every verb has four **principle parts:** the **base form**, the **present participle**, the **past**, and the **past participle.** All the other verb forms can be made from these parts. As you can see from the table below, the present participle is formed by adding *–ing* to the base form (sometimes dropping an *e*), and the past and past participle are formed by adding *–d* or *–ed* (or sometimes *–t*) to the base form.

BASE FORM	PRESENT PARTICIPLE	PAST	PAST PARTICIPLE
enter	[is] entering	entered	[has] entered
hope	[is] hoping	hoped	[has] hoped
learn	[is] learning	learned	[has] learned

Some verbs, however, form the past and past participle in some way other than by adding *–d* or *–ed* (or sometimes *–t*) to the base form. These verbs are called *irregular verbs.* English has dozens of them. The table below shows just a few examples. If you are in doubt about whether a verb is irregular, look it up in the dictionary; if it is irregular, you will find its principle parts listed.

BASE FORM	PRESENT PARTICIPLE	PAST	PAST PARTICIPLE
begin	[is] beginning	began	[has] begun
choose	[is] choosing	chose	[has] chosen
fling	[is] flinging	flung	[has] flung
hide	[is] hiding	hid	[has] hidden
speak	[is] speaking	spoke	[has] spoken

When using irregular verbs in the so-called perfect tenses (with *has* or *have*), make sure you do not use the past form instead of the past participle.

NONSTANDARD PARTICIPLE Her majesty **has spoke.**
STANDARD PARTICIPLE Her majesty **has spoken.**

Another error to watch for is using the past participle form without a helping verb or mistaking the past participle for the past.

NONSTANDARD You **been** caught in the act!
STANDARD You **have been** caught in the act!

NONSTANDARD The child **drunk** a glass of milk to neutralize the poison he had swallowed.
STANDARD The child **drank** a glass of milk to neutralize the poison he had swallowed.

Finally, do not add *–d* or *–ed* or *–t* to the present or past form of an irregular verb.

NONSTANDARD The escaped convict **rided** eighty miles in a boxcar.
STANDARD The escaped convict **rode** eighty miles in a boxcar.

2.32 Correcting Split Infinitives

In English, the infinitive often takes the form of two words, *to* and the base. In their discussion of this form, the first English grammarians—influenced by their knowledge of Latin, in which the infinitive is a single word—decreed that the infinitive should never be "split" in English. Under this rule, adverbs and other sentence components should not stand between *to* and the base form. However, the normal sentence rhythms of English, and the demands of sense, often call for an infinitive to be split.

STRAINED WORD ORDER The paramedic told me **to straighten out gently** my friend's twisted leg.
NATURAL WORD ORDER The paramedic told me **to gently straighten out** my friend's twisted leg.
STRAINED WORD ORDER After the accident, Wynne resolved **to urge strongly** his grandfather to surrender his driver's license.
NATURAL WORD ORDER After the accident, Wynne resolved **to strongly urge** his grandfather to surrender his driver's license.

In using the infinitive, keep *to* and the base form together where possible, but do not hesitate to separate them where the rhythm or sense of the sentence requires it. (Note that a phrase such as *to be fully informed* is not a split infinitive; it is an infinitive of the verb *to be* followed by a predicate nominative modified by an adverb.)

EXAMPLES **To safely detonate** the explosives requires great expertise.
You ought **to at least try** to talk some sense into her.
I need **to be fully informed** about every development in this case.

Although the rule that infinitives should not be split was based on Latin rather than English, it has been widely accepted. You should be aware that some people may find fault with the use of a split infinitive, even in cases where such a use is required by sound and sense.

2.33 Correcting Errors in Voice and Mood

Shifts in **voice** from active to passive can be as confusing as shifts in tense. Check your sentences to be sure voice is consistent. Rewrite and change subjects as necessary.

WITH VOICE SHIFT Santha went out one night to watch the moonrise, and finally the ghost was caught sight of by her.

CORRECTED **Santha went out** one night to watch the moonrise and finally **caught sight** of the ghost.

In addition to watching for voice shifts, check to be sure your verbs are in the appropriate **mood.** Mood is a characteristic that shows the way in which a verb is used. Each verb has three moods: **indicative, imperative,** and **subjunctive.**

Use a verb in the *indicative mood* to express a fact, an opinion, or a question.

INDICATIVE MOOD The Greek historian Herodotus **wrote** the first narrative of Western history.
It **is** better to have loved and lost than never to have loved at all.
Have you **heard** of the Peruvian band Inca Son?

Use the *imperative mood* to express a direct command or request.

IMPERATIVE MOOD **Give** the devil his due.
"**Speak** of love in your own words—**Improvise! Rhapsodize! Be** eloquent."

Use the *subjunctive mood* in the present to express a suggestion or a necessity.

SUBJUNCTIVE MOOD It is crucial that the figures **be** accurate.
I recommend that he **have** the tests done as soon as possible.

Use the *past subjunctive* to express a wish or a condition that is not true (contrary to fact).

PAST SUBJUNCTIVE If I **were** in your shoes, I'd feel the same way.
We all wish he **were** here with us.

Notice that the singular of most verbs in the subjunctive looks like a plural of a verb in the indicative.

INDICATIVE PLURAL The children **were** not aware that Ravi had been hiding so long.
SUBJUNCTIVE SINGULAR If Harlan **were** honest with himself, he would see the futility of it.

2.34 Correcting Errors in Verb Agreement I

A word that refers to one person or thing is said to be **singular in number.** A word that refers to more than one person or thing is said to be **plural in number.** Most nouns that end in *–s* are plural, but most verbs that refer to the present and end in *–s* are singular.

SINGULAR NOUNS	shadow, dolphin, product
PLURAL NOUNS	shadow**s**, dolphin**s**, product**s**
SINGULAR VERBS	wobble**s**, happen**s**, believe**s**
PLURAL VERBS	wobble, happen, believe

Each verb in a sentence should be singular if its subject is singular and plural if its subject is plural. In other words, a verb must **agree in number** with its subject.

EXAMPLES The **orchestra plays** both classical and contemporary pieces.
The **lungs transfer** oxygen into the blood and **remove** carbon dioxide.

The pronouns *I* and *you,* though singular, almost always take forms that look plural. The only exceptions are the forms *I am* and *I was.*

EXAMPLES **I tremble** when **I think** of facing her.
You **expect** too much of yourself.

A **compound subject** is formed of two or more nouns or pronouns that are joined by a conjunction and have the same verb. A compound subject joined by the conjunction *and* usually takes a plural verb.

EXAMPLE **Mishmash, Mushrush, and Clapsaddle** work in the electronics division.

A compound subject takes a singular verb if the compound subject really names only one person or thing.

EXAMPLE My dear **friend** and **mentor is** Mrs. Walters.

A compound subject formed of two singular subjects joined by the conjunctions *or* or *nor* takes a singular verb.

EXAMPLES Either **Schroeder** or **Harrington is** responsible for leaking the information.
Neither **Chinese food** nor **pizza sounds** too appealing to me right now.

A compound subject formed of a singular subject and a plural subject, joined by the conjunctions *or* or *nor,* takes a verb that agrees in number with the subject nearer the verb.

EXAMPLES Neither **Elise** nor the **twins have had** chicken pox.
Neither the **twins** nor **Elise has had** chicken pox.

These indefinite pronouns are singular and take a singular verb: *anybody, anyone, anything, each, either, everybody, everyone, everything, neither, nobody, no one, nothing, one, somebody, someone,* and *something.*

EXAMPLES **Neither** of the players **has** a strong serve.
Something is dreadfully wrong with Kyle.

These indefinite pronouns are plural and take a plural verb: *both, few, many,* and *several.*

EXAMPLES When Premila and Santha went to the Anglo-Indian school, **both were** given English names.
Few of the students **understand** Dr. Duchardt's discourses.

The following indefinite pronouns can be singular or plural: *all, any, most, none,* and *some.*

EXAMPLES **All** of the furniture **is** old and dilapidated.
All of the chairs **are** old and dilapidated.
Most of the snow **has** melted.
Most of the icicles **have** melted.

When you invert sentences for emphasis, make sure you maintain agreement in number between subject and verb.

EXAMPLES Seventy miles **he commutes** to work every day.
One load of bread **they were** able to buy.

The contraction *doesn't* (from *does not*) is third-person singular and should be used only with a third-person singular subject. The contraction *don't* (from *do not*) should be used with all other subjects.

EXAMPLES **Gunther doesn't** speak any English.
Obstacles **don't** deter Denise from her goal.

2.35 Correcting Errors in Verb Agreement II

When a sentence begins with *here, there, when,* or *where,* often the subject follows the verb. In editing your writing, use extra care to check that the subject and verb of such sentences agree in number. Remember that the contractions *here's, there's, when's,* and *where's* contain a singular verb (*is*) and should only be used with a singular subject.

EXAMPLES Here**'s** the information you requested.
There **are** nine Muses in classical mythology.
When**'s** the next train?
Where **are** the screwdriver and the wrench?

Also check to be sure a verb in a sentence with a predicate nominative agrees in number with the subject and not with the predicate nominative. (See 2.17 for the definition of a predicate nominative.)

EXAMPLES **Brussels sprouts are** my favorite vegetable.
My favorite **vegetable is** Brussels sprouts.

A collective noun takes a singular verb when the noun refers to the group as a unit, and it takes a plural verb when it refers to the members of the group as individuals.

AS SINGULAR The entire **faculty is** dedicated and caring.
AS PLURAL All **faculty have earned** at least a master's degree.

While editing your work, check for nouns that are plural in form but singular in meaning. They should take singular verbs.

EXAMPLES measles, gymnastics, cryogenics, gallows

The title of a creative work such as a book or song takes a singular verb, as does a group of words used as a unit.

EXAMPLES Ovid's ***Metamorphoses* is** a long poem with many accounts of miraculous transformations.
Chicken and dumplings is our family's favorite chicken dish.

An expression stating an amount is singular and takes a singular verb when the amount is considered as one unit. It is plural and takes a plural verb when the amount is considered as something with many parts.

AS SINGULAR **Ten days seems** like forever to wait for the test results.
AS PLURAL **Ten days have** elapsed since our dog disappeared.

A fraction or a percentage is singular when it refers to a singular word and plural when it refers to a plural word.

AS SINGULAR Over **half** the **population** in that country **suffers** from malnutrition.
AS PLURAL Over **half** the **people** in that country **suffer** from malnutrition.
AS SINGULAR **Twenty percent** of their **budget is** spent on overhead.
AS PLURAL **Twenty percent** of their **funds are** spent on overhead.

Expressions of measurement, such as area, length, volume, and weight, are usually singular.

EXAMPLE **Four units is** a dangerous amount of blood to lose.
Ninety pounds is too much for a child of his height to weigh.

EDITING FOR ERRORS IN PRONOUN USAGE

2.36 Pronoun Case

Case is the form that a noun or a pronoun takes to indicate its use in a sentence. English nouns and pronouns have three cases: nominative, objective, and possessive. The **nominative case** is used for the subject of a verb or for a predicate nominative. The **objective case** is used for a direct object, an indirect object, or the object of a preposition. The **possessive case** is used to show possession. The form of the nominative and objective cases of nouns is the same, and most nouns form possessives by adding an apostrophe and an *s* to the singular and an apostrophe only to the plural. But many pronouns have different forms to show nominative, objective, and possessive cases.

PERSONAL PRONOUNS		
SINGULAR		
Nominative Case (for subjects or predicate nominatives)	**Objective Case** (for direct objects, indirect objects, and objects of prepositions)	**Possessive Case** (to show possession)
I	me	my, mine
you	you	your, yours
he, she, it	him, her, it	his, her, hers, its
PLURAL		
we	us	our, ours
you	you	your, yours
they	them	their, theirs

To determine which form of the pronoun to use when writing a sentence, first decide whether the pronoun is used as a subject, predicate nominative, as some kind of object, or as a possessive. Doing so will tell you in what case the pronoun should be.

SUBJECT	**She** felt an overpowering chill upon hearing the news.
PREDICATE NOMINATIVE	It was **he** who drove his spear into Hector's neck.
DIRECT OBJECT	William the Conqueror defeated **them** in the Battle of Hastings.
INDIRECT OBJECT	The salesperson offered **us** a free cutting board with the knife set.
OBJECT OF PREPOSITION	Great-uncle Wilfred bequeathed his coin collection to **you** and **me.**

Remember that in standard English, prepositions *always* take an object in the objective case. The phrase *between you and I,* for example, is nonstandard English.

Use the possessive pronouns *mine, yours, his, hers, its, ours, yours,* and *theirs* just as you use the pronouns in the nominative and objective cases.

AS SUBJECT	My paintings and **his** are hanging in the gallery.
AS PREDICATE NOMINATIVE	The Mitsubishi is **hers.**
DIRECT OBJECT	After Dale received his award, I went up to get **mine.**
INDIRECT OBJECT	Mr. Garrison gave our project an A and **theirs** a B.
OBJECT OF PREPOSITION	This package is for our family and the other one is for **yours.**

Use the possessive pronouns *my, your, his, her, its, our,* and *their* as adjectives before nouns.

EXAMPLES When Alfonso was confronted, **his** first response was to deny everything.
"It is not only the inscriptions on **their** graves that mark them out; . . . in people's hearts, **their** memory abides and grows."

As you edit your writing, check the case of nouns and pronouns before a gerund. They should always be in the possessive case.

WITH GERUND **Their singing** sounds more like screeching to me.

Do not confuse the gerund and the present participle (see 2.9). Compare the example above with the following example, in which no possessive is required before the participle:

WITH PARTICIPLE We heard them **singing** as they scrubbed the floor.

2.37 *Who* and *Whom*

The pronoun *who* is referred to as an **interrogative pronoun** when it is used to form a question. When it is used to introduce a **subordinate clause,** it is referred to as a **relative pronoun.** In both cases, the nominative is *who,* the objective is *whom,* and the possessive is *whose.* As you edit your writing, check these pronouns to see if the form of the pronoun you have used is appropriate for its use in the sentence or subordinate clause in which it appears.

SUBJECT	**Who** cut Samson's hair?
SUBJECT	The intrepid inventor **who** built the poetry machine was Trurl.
DIRECT OBJECT	**Whom** did Brutus assassinate?
DIRECT OBJECT	The woman **whom** you saw was Mrs. King.
OBJECT OF PREPOSITION	**From whom** did he steal the shoes?
OBJECT OF PREPOSITION	I don't remember **to whom** I lent the lawnmower.

In spoken English, *whom* is gradually being replaced by *who.* In some formal speech, however, and in all writing of standard English except dialogue, the form *whom* should still be used where grammatically correct.

2.38 Pronouns in Appositive Constructions

When a pronoun is used with an appositive, its form matches its use in the sentence. (See 2.20 for the definition of an appositive.)

SUBJECT	**We, the undersigned,** endorse the candidacy of Walter Wright.
PREDICATE NOMINATIVE	The culprit is **I, Harriet Dunbar.**
DIRECT OBJECT	The Rams defeated **us Lancers** in the championship.
INDIRECT OBJECT	You can tell **me, your trusted confidante,** the secret.
OBJECT OF PREPOSITION	The beast was killed by **him, the hero Sunjata.**

When a pronoun is itself used as an appositive, it should be in the same case as the word to which it refers.

PRONOUN IN APPOSITION TO SUBJECT	Two of the least athletic girls in history, Emma and **I,** actually enjoyed the hike.
PRONOUN IN APPOSITION TO THE OBJECT OF A PREPOSITION	Awards were presented to the leading vocalists, Victoria and **him.**

2.39 Pronouns in Comparison

The ends of sentences that compare people or things are often left unexpressed. Pronouns in such sentences should be in the same case as they would have been if the sentence had been completed.

EXAMPLES Dickens is more widely read than **they** [are].
The prospect of going down into that cave was more daunting to me than [it was] to **him.**

2.40 Pronoun Reference and Agreement

Check the pronouns in your writing to be sure they agree in **number, person,** and **gender** with their antecedents. (For a discussion of number, see 2.34.) Person is the form a word takes to indicate the person speaking (the *first person,* corresponding to *I* or *we*), the person spoken to (the *second person,* corresponding to *you*), or the person spoken of or about (the *third person,* corresponding to *he, she, it,* or *they*). Gender is the form a word takes to indicate whether it is *masculine, feminine,* or *neuter* (neither masculine nor feminine).

INCORRECT NUMBER	Confucius believed that a **man** should be trustworthy in words and that **they** should make close friends only with those of benevolence.
CORRECT NUMBER	Confucius believed that a **man** should be trustworthy in words and that **he** should make close friends only with those of benevolence.
INCORRECT GENDER	The bridegroom approached the altar with trepidation but carried **herself** with poise and confidence.
CORRECT GENDER	The bridegroom approached the altar with trepidation but carried **himself** with poise and confidence.

As you edit, check each pronoun to be sure that it refers clearly to its antecedent.

CLEAR REFERENCE **Gilgamesh** went on a quest for everlasting life because **he** was afraid of death.

CLEAR REFERENCES **Zenchi** was ashamed of his huge nose; **he** tried a variety of measures to shorten it.

Weak reference occurs when a pronoun refers to an antecedent that has not been expressed. If you find a weak reference while editing your writing, either change the pronoun into a noun or give the pronoun a clear antecedent.

WEAK REFERENCE Making sausages was a real ritual in which **they** all had to participate.

PRONOUN CHANGED TO NOUN PHRASE Making sausages was a real ritual in which **all the women in the family** had to participate.

WEAK REFERENCE Richard ironed all the **clothing** and then proceeded to put on one of **them.**

PRONOUN GIVEN CLEAR ANTECEDENT Richard ironed all the **shirts** and then proceeded to put on one of **them.**

Ambiguous reference occurs when a pronoun can refer to either of two antecedents. Clarify ambiguous references by rewording the sentence or by replacing the pronouns with a noun.

AMBIGUOUS When the explorer finally found the long-lost missionary, **he** allegedly said, "Doctor Livingstone, I presume."

CLEAR When the explorer finally found the long-lost missionary, the **explorer** allegedly said, "Doctor Livingstone, I presume."

An **indefinite reference** occurs when the pronouns *you, it,* or *they* have no reference to a specific person or thing. Edit out an indefinite reference by rewording the sentence to explain to whom or what the pronoun refers, or by eliminating the pronoun altogether.

INDEFINITE REFERENCE The fallen king was mortified to learn that **it** had been done by a woman.

PRONOUN ELIMINATED The fallen king was mortified to learn that **he had been felled** by a woman.

INDEFINITE REFERENCE In the manual **it** explained how to change the oil.

PRONOUN ELIMINATED The manual explained how to change the oil.

INDEFINITE REFERENCE **They** say that laughter helps heal the human body.

PRONOUN REPLACED **Researchers** say that laughter helps heal the human body.

A **general reference** occurs when a pronoun refers to a general idea implied in the previous clause, rather than to a specific antecedent. Edit general references by replacing the pronoun with a noun or by rewording the sentence.

GENERAL REFERENCE	Project Mercury was a United States space program designed to put a man in orbit around the earth, **which** ran from 1961 to 1963.
SENTENCE REWORDED	Project Mercury, **which** ran from 1961 to 1963, was a United States space program designed to put a man in orbit around the earth.
GENERAL REFERENCE	For forty days and nights, rain fell on the land and many people drowned. **This** caused severe flooding.
PRONOUN REPLACED AND SENTENCES REWORDED	For forty days and nights, rain fell on the land, causing severe flooding. Many people drowned.

EDITING FOR ERRORS IN MODIFIER USAGE

2.41 ERRORS IN MODIFIER USAGE I

When you wish to modify the subject of a linking verb, use an adjective. When you wish to modify an action verb, use an adverb.

LINKING VERB AND ADJECTIVES	My great-grandmother's hair **was luminous** and **pink** in the light of the setting sun.
ACTION VERB AND ADVERB	The stars **flickered weakly** against the vast, black curtain of the sky.

Check whether your use of an adjective or adverb is correct by temporarily replacing the verb you have written with the verb *seem.* If the sentence still makes some kind of sense, the original verb is a linking verb and should take an adjective. If the substitution of *seem* produces nonsense, the original verb is an action verb and should take an adverb. You can see how this works by substituting *seem* in each of the examples given above.

SUBSTITUTION MAKES SENSE	My great-grandmother's hair **seemed luminous** and **pink** in the light of the setting sun.
SUBSTITUTION MAKES NO SENSE	The stars **seemed weakly** against the vast, black curtain of the sky.

Comparison refers to the change in the form of a modifier to show an increase or a decrease in the quality expressed by the modifier. Each modifier has three forms of comparison: **positive, comparative,** and **superlative**. Most one-syllable modifiers and some two-syllable modifiers form the comparative and superlative degrees by adding *-er* and *-est.* Other two-syllable modifiers, and all modifiers of more than two syllables, use *more* and *most* to form these degrees.

	POSITIVE	COMPARATIVE	SUPERLATIVE
ADJECTIVES	clear	clearer	clearest
	hungry	hungrier	hungriest
	daring	more daring	most daring
	beneficial	more beneficial	most beneficial
ADVERBS	late	later	latest
	seldom	more seldom	most seldom
	fully	more fully	most fully
	pretentiously	more pretentiously	most pretentiously

To show a decrease in the quality of any modifier, form the comparative and superlative degrees by using *less* and *least.*

EXAMPLES dense, less dense, least dense
skeptically, less skeptically, least skeptically

Some modifiers form their comparative and superlative degrees irregularly. Check the dictionary if you are unsure about the comparison of a modifier.

EXAMPLES good, better, best well, better, best bad, worse, worst

Use the comparative degree when comparing two things. Use the superlative degree when comparing more than two things.

COMPARATIVE Santha was the **more easily** intimidated of the two sisters.
SUPERLATIVE The skin is the **largest** organ of the human body.

As you edit your writing, check sentences for **illogical comparison.** Such comparison occurs when one member of a group is compared with the group of which it is a part. Clarify illogical comparison by including the word *other* or *else* in the sentence.

ILLOGICAL Hydrogen is more abundant than any element in the universe.
LOGICAL Hydrogen is more abundant than any **other** element in the universe.

Another problem to check for is **double comparison.** This occurs when two comparative forms or two superlative forms are used to modify the same word. Correct double comparison by editing out one of the comparative or superlative forms.

DOUBLE COMPARISON The chandeliers were **more fancier** than any I had ever seen.
SINGLE COMPARISON The chandeliers were **fancier** than any I had ever seen.

In English a **double negative** is a nonstandard construction in which two negative words are used instead of one. Check your writing to be sure you have not used a negative word such as *no, none, not* (and its contraction, *–n't*), *nothing, barely, hardly,* or *scarcely* with any other negative word. If you find a double negative, change it by deleting one of the negative words.

DOUBLE NEGATIVE She was so shocked she **couldn't scarcely** speak.
SINGLE NEGATIVE She was so shocked she **couldn't** speak.
SINGLE NEGATIVE She was so shocked she **could scarcely** speak.

DOUBLE NEGATIVE The Book of Sand **didn't** have **no** beginning or end.
SINGLE NEGATIVE The Book of Sand had **no** beginning or end.

2.42 Errors in Modifier Usage II

The demonstrative pronouns *this* and *these* are used to refer to things near the speaker. The pronouns *that* and *those* refer to objects at some distance. Thus you might say, "This apple in my hand is poisonous" if you were referring to an apple you were actually holding, but if you were pointing at an apple in a picture of yourself, you might say, "That apple in my hand is poisonous." The two pairs of pronouns are often used to distinguish between objects or sets of objects.

EXAMPLE **These** papers are to be filed and **those** are to be shredded.

Check your writing to see that your use of *this* and *these,* and *that* and *those* makes sense.

NONSENSICAL **That** sofa here in the living room should go next to **this** old piano downstairs in the family room.
SENSIBLE **This** sofa here in the living room should go next to **that** old piano downstairs in the family room.

The pronoun *them* is a personal pronoun in standard English and should not be substituted for the demonstrative pronoun *those.*

NONSTANDARD One would swear **them** gems were genuine.
STANDARD One would swear **those** gems were genuine.

Modifiers that often give writers trouble are *bad* and *badly.* Check instances of these words in your writing to make sure you have used *bad* as an adjective and *badly* as an adverb. Only the adjective should follow a linking verb such as *feel, sound, look, smell,* or *taste.*

NONSTANDARD Samantha felt **badly** about her inadvertent breach of confidence.
STANDARD Samantha felt **bad** about her inadvertent breach of confidence.

Similarly distinguish between *good* and *well. Good* is an adjective and should not be used to modify an action verb. *Well,* however, can be used either as an adverb meaning "capably" or "in a satisfactory way," or as an adjective meaning "healthy" or "of a satisfactory condition."

NONSTANDARD Cheri paints landscapes good.
STANDARD Cheri paints good landscapes.
STANDARD Cheri paints landscapes **well.**
STANDARD However, she does not sculpt **well.**
STANDARD Yesterday she did not feel **good**, but today she is looking **well.**

ESSENTIAL SKILLS: LANGUAGE

USAGE HANDBOOK

2.43 Usage Problems I

The following sections (2.43–2.45) explain some common problems to watch for as you edit your writing.

adapt, adopt. *Adapt* means "to make [something] fit a specific use or situation by modifying"; *adopt* means to "take something and make it in some sense one's own."

EXAMPLES Mrs. Sandburg was devastated to have to leave the home she had grown up in, but she gradually **adapted** to living in the nursing home.
The compassionate couple **adopted** eleven handicapped children.

affect, effect. If you wish to use a verb meaning "have an effect on," use *affect.* If you wish to use a noun meaning "the result of an action," use *effect.*

VERB The book about the Red Cross **affected** her so deeply that she resolved to become a nurse herself.
NOUN One of the **effects** of the earthquake was the creation of huge tsunamis that pounded coastlines hundreds of miles from the epicenter.

As a verb, *effect* means to bring something about despite obstacles.

EXAMPLES The Westport basketball team **effected** a major upset against Jamesville in the semi-finals.
The defeat **affected** the Jamesville fans so much that all sat in stunned silence after the final buzzer.

2.44 Usage Problems II

imply, infer. Most writers accept the following meanings for these words: *imply* means "to express indirectly rather than openly"; *infer* means "to arrive at a conclusion by reasoning from evidence." Although this distinction between *imply* and *infer* has not always been observed, it is a useful one.

EXAMPLES Daniel's guilty grin **implied** that he had taken the brownie.
Daniel's mother **inferred** from his guilty grin that he had taken the brownie.

like, as, as if. Although *like* is frequently used to introduce subordinate clauses in informal English, it is considered a preposition, not a conjunction. Do not use it in place of *as* or *as if* in your writing.

INFORMAL I feel **like** I'm being taken for granted.
FORMAL I feel **as if** I'm being taken for granted.
FORMAL I feel **like** an idiot.

literally. Most writers limit their use of *literally* to the sense "actually," and avoid using it in the sense "not actually, but in effect, or for all practical purposes." This distinction, though sometimes ignored, is worth observing.

CLEAR The sewing machine repair man **literally** had no fingers on his right hand.
CONFUSING Dad **literally** raised the roof when he heard that I had smashed the car.

2.45 Usage Problems III

of. The preposition *of* should not be used in place of *have* after verbs such as *could, should, would, might, must,* and *ought.*

NONSTANDARD You must **of** taken my keys by mistake.
STANDARD You must **have** taken my keys by mistake.
STANDARD You must'**ve** taken my keys by mistake.

Avoid *off of.*

NONSTANDARD The parachutists jumped **off of** the Seattle Space Needle.
STANDARD The parachutists jumped **off** the Seattle Space Needle.

then, than. Use *than* as a conjunction in comparisons. Use *then* as an adverb that tells when something occurred.

EXAMPLES Iván Ilyich was more concerned about his illness **than** anyone else seemed to be.
First get your chores done, **then** we'll discuss going to the movies.

PROOFREADING FOR PUNCTUATION ERRORS

2.46 Using End Marks

An **end mark** signals the end of a sentence. It also shows the purpose of the sentence.

A declarative sentence ends with a **period.** If a declarative sentence already has a period at the end because an abbreviation occurs there, no other end mark is needed. If a declarative sentence ends with a quotation, place the period inside the quotation marks.

DECLARATIVE	Chinua Achebe is considered by many to be the greatest living African novelist**.**
WITH ABBREVIATION AT END	Minerva finds inspiration in the words of Martin Luther King, Jr**.**
WITH QUOTATION AT END	God said, "Let there be light**.**"

A question ends with a **question mark.** Indirect questions, however, do not require a question mark. If a question ends with an abbreviation, add a question mark after the final period. If a question is quoted, the question mark appears inside the closing quotation marks; if a question contains a quotation, the question mark appears outside the closing quotation marks. Polite questions often end with a period instead of a question mark.

DIRECT QUESTION	Who was Omar Khayyám**?**
ENDING IN ABBREVIATION	What were you doing outside at 3 A.M.**?**
INDIRECT QUESTION	Sylvia asked me what I was making**.**
QUOTED QUESTION	Vasilios asked, "What is the meaning of life**?**"
QUESTION INCLUDING QUOTATION	Did Nick actually say, "I liked the opera"**?**
POLITE QUESTION	Will you please tell me where to find Haddonfield Drive**.**

An exclamation ends with an **exclamation point.** If an exclamation is quoted, the exclamation point appears inside the closing quotation marks; if an exclamation contains a quotation, the exclamation point appears outside the closing quotation marks. An imperative sentence may end with a period instead of an exclamation point.

EXCLAMATION	Flash**!** Apollo 13 has landed safely**!**
QUOTED EXCLAMATION	"Stop**!**" Ian yelled, "You're getting too close to the edge**!**"
EXCLAMATION CONTAINING QUOTE	I can't believe Aaron said, "You're not bad—for a girl"**!**
IMPERATIVE SENTENCE	Let's take the scenic route.

2.47 Using Commas

As you proofread your writing, check to see that you have used commas after certain introductory elements. Such elements include mild exclamations such as *yes, no, oh,* and *well;* participial phrases; prepositional phrases; and adverb clauses.

MILD EXCLAMATION **Well,** we have nothing to lose.

PARTICIPIAL PHRASE **Having been expelled from the castle,** Candide wandered for a long time, not knowing where he was going.

TWO PREPOSITIONAL PHRASES **For the rest of his life,** William carried a burden of guilt for what he had done.

ADVERB CLAUSE **When Tartuffe expressed his true intentions,** Orgon saw him for the monster he was.

A comma is also used to set off an element that interrupts a sentence, such as a parenthetical expression or a word used in direct address.

PARENTHETICAL EXPRESSION She tormented herself, **however,** wondering if she had done the right thing.

DIRECT ADDRESS **Papa,** I am going to marry with a great love for Tita that will never die.

A **serial comma** is a comma used to separate items in a series, whether the items are words, phrases, or clauses. Some writers omit the last comma when *and, or,* or *nor* joins the last two items in a series, but this construction sometimes makes a sentence unclear.

WORDS At the ceremony of induction into the knighthood, a knight was given armor, a horse, a helmet, and a lance.

PHRASES Camus said that Sisyphus's scorn of the gods, his hatred of death, and his passion for life won him the unspeakable penalty of exerting the whole being toward accomplishing nothing.

CLAUSES "Time flies, death urges, knells call, heaven invites,/Hell threatens."

—Edward Young

Some paired words may be considered a single item.

PAIRED WORDS Items on the menu include chicken a la king, **liver and onions**, and beef stew.

If all the items in a series are joined by *and, or,* or *nor,* do not separate them with commas.

EXAMPLE The raven ate and flew around and cawed and did not return to the boat.

Two or more adjectives preceding a noun are separated by commas.

EXAMPLE Montaigne wrote of a country in which it was rare to see a sick, palsied, bleary-eyed, or toothless man.

Use a comma before *and, but, for, nor, or, so,* and *yet* when they join two independent clauses. The comma may be omitted before *and, but, nor,* and *or* if the clauses are very short and the resulting sentence is still clear in meaning.

LONG CLAUSE The magpies of New South Wales have a song-like call, while the call of the kookaburra resembles demonic laughter.

SHORT CLAUSE The pit bull growled and Clarice backed out of his range.

Do not use a comma between two parts of a compound verb or compound predicate.

A **nonrestrictive** participial phrase or clause is one that does not restrict or limit the meaning of the substantive to which it refers. You can test a phrase or clause when proofreading your writing by seeing if the main meaning of the sentence is lost if you omit the phrase or clause. If the phrase or clause is indeed nonrestrictive, make sure it is set off by commas.

RESTRICTIVE The wedding dress **that Mary Ellen found in the chest** belonged to her great-grandmother.

NONRESTRICTIVE Mary Ellen's great-grandmother, **who came over from Greece when she was fifteen,** married a butcher when she was seventeen.

Appositives and appositive phrases can be either restrictive or nonrestrictive.

RESTRICTIVE The Polish astronomer Nicholas Copernicus refuted the notion that the earth is the center of the universe.

NONRESTRICTIVE Nicholas Copernicus, **a Polish astronomer,** refuted the notion that the earth is the center of the universe.

2.48 Semicolons and Colons

A **semicolon** is used as punctuation between clauses in several situations. Use a semicolon between closely related independent clauses that are not joined by *and, but, for, nor, or, so,* or *yet.*

EXAMPLE The children wanted to know why their mother did not return**;** they did not understand that she was dead.

Use a semicolon between independent clauses joined by a conjunctive adverb or transitional expression that is followed by a comma.

EXAMPLE Nelson was hopelessly behind after falling; however, he picked up his bike and finished the race.

Use a semicolon between linked independent clauses or items in a list if the clauses or items already contain commas.

INDEPENDENT CLAUSES "Be upright in their presence, and they will hold you in respect; be filial and benevolent, and they will be loyal to you; use the righteous and instruct the unqualified, and they will try their best in service." —Confucius

LIST OF ITEMS WITH COMMAS Important philosophers of the Enlightenment included Immanuel Kant, who wrote critiques investigating the limits of human reasoning; John Locke, who disputed the divine right of kings; and Adam Smith, whose ideas about economics led to the growth of capitalism.

A **colon** introduces a long statement or quotation or a list of items.

QUOTATION Tartuffe gave Elmire the oldest line in the book: "Well, if you look with favor upon my love,/Why, then, begrudge me some clear proof thereof?"

LIST According to the Mayan Book of the Dawn of Life, these are the names of the first people: Jaguar Quitze, Jaguar Night, Mahucutah, and True Jaguar.

2.49 Dashes, Hyphens, Parentheses, and Brackets

A **dash** is used to show an abrupt break in thought.

EXAMPLE living and speaking like barbarians,
excluded—what a catastrophe!—from the Hellenic way of life. — Cavafy

Sometimes the dash serves in place of such expressions as *in other words, that is,* or *namely.*

EXAMPLE The main character in Chinua Achebe's "Marriage is a Private Affair" acts on a shocking notion—that marriages should be based on love.

A **hyphen** is used to link words in a compound adjective, adverb, or noun.

EXAMPLES forest-dwelling creatures, ninth-inning grand slam, well-rounded student, first-rate product, strong-willed woman, three-year-old brat, half-heartedly, even-handedly, self-confidently, good-naturedly, go-ahead, set-up, rock-bottom, lady-in-waiting

If you have questions about whether you should hyphenate a particular compound word, look it up in the dictionary. If the dictionary offers no information, consider whether the hyphen is needed to make the meaning of the sentence clear.

UNCLEAR The **thick skinned** girl was not perturbed by their criticisms.

CLEAR The **thick-skinned** girl was not perturbed by their criticisms.

Parentheses are used to enclose an aside or information that is less important than the main information offered in a sentence.

ASIDE Dominic Mazzini **(I think you know his brother)** played a brilliant violin solo.

LESS IMPORTANT Turn left at the blue house **(the one with the picket fence)** and go to the top of the hill.

Brackets are used to enclose a writer's corrections or comments in someone else's quoted material, and as parentheses within parentheses.

QUOTED MATERIAL "The best-laid schemes o' mice an' men
Gang aft a-gley **[often go astray]**." —Robert Burns

PARENTHESES WITHIN PARENTHESES The article about Gibraltar ("Britain's Precarious Stronghold" **[*National Geographic,* November 1996, page 62]**) tells of an exciting cave sixty feet high and more than a hundred feet deep.

2.50 Apostrophes

An **apostrophe** is used to form the possessive of nouns and some—but not all—pronouns. To form the possessive of a singular noun, add an apostrophe and an *s.* If the noun already ends in an *s* sound, has two or more syllables, and would be hard to pronounce with an additional *s,* add only an apostrophe. These rules apply also to hyphenated words, names of organizations, and indefinite pronouns.

WITH ADDED *S* boss**'s** office, Pandora**'s** box, everyone else**'s** opinion, *Pilgrim's Progress,* Dickens**'s** *Oliver Twist,* mother-in-law**'s** wig

WITHOUT ADDED *S* Moses' staff, righteousness' sake, Jesus' teachings

To form the possessive of a plural noun, add only an apostrophe if the plural form ends in *s.* If the plural form ends in some other letter, add an apostrophe and an *s.*

ENDING WITH *S* four days' journey, ten years' imprisonment, two weeks' pay

ENDING WITHOUT *S* people**'s** choice, oxen**'s** lowing, dice**'s** spots, geese**'s** formation

While proofreading, check to see that you have not used an apostrophe to form the plural of a noun. Note also that the possessive pronouns, including *yours, ours, hers,* and *its,* do not have an apostrophe.

INCORRECT PLURAL It took six rescuer's to dig out the man buried by the avalanche.

CORRECT PLURAL It took six **rescuers** to dig out the man buried by the avalanche.

INCORRECT POSSESSIVE By 3 A.M. the game was losing it's appeal.

CORRECT POSSESSIVE By 3 A.M. the game was losing **its** appeal.

To show joint possession by all people in a group, add *'s* (or an apostrophe only) to the last word. To show individual possession of similar items by each member of a group, add *'s* (or an apostrophe only) to each noun in the group.

JOINT POSSESSION Fred and Lynn**'s** car is covered with snow and ice.

INDIVIDUAL POSSESSION Fred**'s** and Lynn**'s** cars are covered with snow and ice.

ESSENTIAL SKILLS: LANGUAGE

Use an apostrophe to form the possessive of words that refer to time or that indicate amounts in dollars or cents.

EXAMPLES a day's wages, a moment's notice, ten dollars' worth of rice

2.51 UNDERLINING, ITALICS, AND QUOTATION MARKS IN TITLES

Italics are a type of slanted printing used to show emphasis. (**Underlining** is used instead of italics in handwritten documents or in forms of printing in which italics are not available.) The following examples show the categories of words that should receive italics (underlining) for emphasis.

WORKS OF ART	Wyeth's *Christina's World,* Raphael's *The School of Athens,* Michelangelo's *Pietà*
BOOKS, PLAYS	Pasternak's *Doctor Zhivago,* Ibsen's *Hedda Gabler*
FILMS, TELEVISION PROGRAMS	*Casablanca, I Love Lucy*
PERIODICALS	*Herald-American, The Saturday Evening Post*
AIRCRAFT, SHIPS, SPACECRAFT, TRAINS	*Gossamer Albatross, Andrea Doria, Columbia, Tom Thumb*

Italicize the titles of long musical compositions unless they are merely the names of musical forms such as *fantasy, symphony, concerto, sonata,* and *nocturne.* The titles of short pieces such as songs should be placed in quotation marks.

SHORT MUSICAL COMPOSITION	Irving Berlin's "White Christmas"
LONG MUSICAL COMPOSITION	Beethoven's *Moonlight Sonata,* Tchaikovsky's Piano Concerto No. 2

As you proof your writing, check for words used as words, letters used as letters, and words from foreign languages. These should all be in italics (or underlined).

EXAMPLES The word *zing* is an example of onomatopoeia.
Pelicans fly in single file, while ducks and geese fly in a *V.*
The selling of our house is a *fait accompli*—something that has already been done.

Quotation marks are used to enclose titles of short works.

PARTS OF BOOKS	Part One: "The Solar System"
SONGS	"Auld Lang Syne"
SHORT POEMS	"Penelope's Despair"
STORIES	"The Bet"
ESSAYS, ARTICLES	"The Myth of Sisyphus"

2.52 Other Uses of Quotation Marks

Quotation marks are used to enclose a **direct quotation,** or a person's exact words. They are not used to enclose an **indirect quotation,** which is a reworded version of a person's words. Commas and periods that follow a quotation should be placed inside closing quotation marks; colons and semicolons should be placed outside. Do not, however, use a period to separate a direct quotation from the rest of a sentence.

DIRECT "I must stand on my own feet if I am to find out the truth about myself and about life."

DIRECT WITH PERIOD The book of Proverbs says that a good name is "more desirable than great riches."

DIRECT WITH COMMA "Tis held that sorrow makes us wise," affirmed Alfred, Lord Tennyson.

DIRECT WITH SEMICOLON Achilles burst out in despair, "Let me die at once"; his own death seemed preferable to living with his grief.

INDIRECT Yevgeny Yevtushenko said that his descendants would remember with bitter shame those times when people referred to simple honesty as fearlessness.

When writing **dialogue,** a conversation between speakers, begin a new paragraph each time the speaker changes, and enclose each speaker's words in quotation marks. When an indication of the speaker, such as *she said,* divides a sentence into two parts, the second part begins with a small letter.

EXAMPLES Said the jinnee sarcastically, "Fisherman, I bring you good news."

"What news?" asked the old man.

"News of your death, horrible and prompt!" replied the jinnee. . . .

"Be brief, then, I pray you," said the fisherman, "for you have wrung my soul with terror."

—from *The Thousand and One Nights*

Single quotation marks are used to enclose a quotation within a quotation.

EXAMPLE Francesca admitted, "I was thinking only of myself, but then I remembered Confucius' admonition that we should not worry 'about being misunderstood but about understanding others.'"

2.53 Ellipsis in Quotations

Ellipsis points are used to indicate an **ellipsis,** or omission, in quoted material. Use three ellipsis points (with a space before the first point) if the quoted material that precedes the omission is not a complete sentence; if it is a complete sentence, keep the end mark and add the ellipsis points.

COMPLETE SENTENCE BEFORE OMISSION "Fourscore and seven years ago our fathers brought forth on this continent a new nation. . . . Now we are engaged in a great civil war."

INCOMPLETE SENTENCE BEFORE OMISSION "[W]e here highly resolve . . . that this nation, under God, shall have a new birth of freedom."

Ellipsis points are also used in much the same way to show a pause in a written passage.

EXAMPLE "Help me carry . . . oh, never mind, I can do it."

PROOFREADING FOR ERRORS IN CAPITALIZATION

2.54 Astronomical Terms, Time, Days, Months, Years, Holidays, Events, and Periods

Capitalize the names of astronomical bodies such as planets, stars, and constellations.

EXAMPLES Mercury, Saturn, Sirius, Vega, Cassiopeia, Orion, Andromeda, Large Magellanic Cloud

Do not capitalize units of time such as the words *second, minute, hour, day, year, decade, century,* or the names of the seasons.

EXAMPLES In the second year of King Darius, on the first day of the sixth month, the prophet Haggai spoke to the people of Israel.
Miranda looks best in autumn colors, while Shari comes alive in winter colors.

Capitalize the names of days, months, and holidays.

EXAMPLES Wednesday, Friday, January, August, Independence Day, Thanksgiving

Do not capitalize references to decades or centuries.

EXAMPLES the twenties, the fifth century

Capitalize historical events, special events, and recognized periods of time.

HISTORICAL EVENTS Peloponnesian Wars, Spanish Inquisition, American Revolution
SPECIAL EVENTS Stanley Cup, Earth Day, World Series
HISTORICAL PERIODS Mesozoic Era, Renaissance, Industrial Age

2.55 Names, Titles of Persons, Occupations, and Family Relationships

Capitalize the names of persons and titles of address such as *Mr., Mrs., Ms., Miss, Madame,* or *Monsieur* when used in addressing a person or before a name.

EXAMPLES Laura Unsworth, Ms. Hughes, Franz Kafka, Dr. Jenner

Check a reference book if you are unsure about the capitalization of *de la, du, van, von,* and other parts of names. Sometimes the part of a name that follows *Mc–* or *Mac–* is capitalized and sometimes it is not.

EXAMPLES Vasco da Gama, Cecil B. De Mille, Robert De Niro, Fiorello La Guardia, Louis L'Amour, John le Carré, Douglas MacArthur, Harold Macmillan, Paul McCartney, James Van Allen, Vincent van Gogh, Wernher von Braun

Capitalize official titles of persons when they immediately precede a person's name or when they are used instead of a name in direct address.

EXAMPLES King George, President Hoover, General Grant, Pope Pius
O King, grant us mercy!

Do not capitalize references to occupations.

EXAMPLES the dentist, the editor, the engineer, the professor, the banker, the painter

Capitalize the names of family relationships used as titles unless they are preceded by a modifier.

MODIFIED your sister, my dad, Yvonne's aunt
NOT MODIFIED We painted Grandma's house last weekend.

If the name of a family relationship precedes a proper name, capitalize it even if it is modified.

EXAMPLES Aunt Madeline, old Uncle Alf

2.56 Directions, Regions, Place Names, Organizations, Institutions, Brand and Trade Names, Buildings, Structures, and Vehicles

Capitalize the names of commonly recognized geographical regions.

EXAMPLES North Pole, Pacific Basin, Southeast Asia, Arctic

ESSENTIAL SKILLS: LANGUAGE

Do not capitalize words such as *east, west, north,* and *south* when they are used only to indicate direction.

EXAMPLES Poughkeepsie is **n**orth of New York City on the Hudson River.
The **S**outh suffered great devastation in the American Civil War.

The adjectives *eastern, western, northern,* and *southern* are not capitalized when they are used as temporary designations.

TEMPORARY **e**astern Australia, **s**outhern India, **w**estern Pennsylvania
STANDARD **N**orthern Ireland, **W**estern Europe, **S**outhern California

Capitalize the names of places. Capitalize any term such as *lake, mountain, river,* or *valley* if it is used as part of a name.

BODIES OF WATER	**R**io **G**rande, **L**ake **L**ouise, **A**rctic **O**cean
CITIES AND TOWNS	**A**thens, **M**exico **C**ity, **K**igali
COUNTIES	**M**arin **C**ounty, **C**ayuga **C**ounty, **M**iddlesex **C**ounty
COUNTRIES	**M**alaysia, **E**cuador, **R**epublic of the **S**udan
ISLANDS	**J**ava, **H**onshu, **I**sle of **W**ight
MOUNTAINS	**M**ount **H**uascarán, **P**ike's **P**eak, **P**indus **M**ountains
STATES	**M**ontana, **D**elaware, **O**klahoma
STREETS AND HIGHWAYS	**N**ew **J**ersey **T**urnpike, **E**rie **B**oulevard, **P**ennsylvania **A**venue

Do not capitalize generic terms for places without specific modifiers.

EXAMPLES There was a multi-vehicle collision on the **t**urnpike.
The still **l**ake perfectly mirrored the snow-capped **m**ountains.

Capitalize the names of organizations and institutions, whether they are public, private, athletic, business, or government bodies.

PUBLIC	**S**mithsonian **I**nstitution, **O**hio **S**tate **U**niversity, **N**iagara **M**ohawk **P**ower
PRIVATE	**S**ociety of **I**ndustrial and **A**pplied **M**athematics, **N**ational **W**ildlife **F**ederation
ATHLETIC	**M**iami **H**eat, **N**ew **Y**ork **R**angers, **L**os **A**ngeles **D**odgers
BUSINESS	**G**eneral **E**lectric, **E**astman **K**odak, **M**etropolitan **L**ife
GOVERNMENT	**P**arliament, **N**ational **A**eronautics and **S**pace **A**dministration, **D**epartment of **E**ducation

Capitalize the brand names and trademarks of products made by businesses. The dictionary may indicate if a name is trademarked. Do not capitalize the noun following a trade name that indicates what type of product it is.

EXAMPLES **G**ap jeans, **C**heerios, **C**oleman stove

Capitalize the names of important or widely recognized buildings and other structures or monuments. Capitalize the noun following a building, structure, or monument name that indicates its type.

EXAMPLES Chesapeake Bay Bridge, Fort Sumter, Parthenon, Alhambra, St. Paul's Cathedral, Bunker Hill Monument, Eiffel Tower, Chrysler Building, Taj Mahal

Contrast the absence of capitalization in the following example of a building that is not widely known:

EXAMPLE The **c**athedral has massive stained-glass windows, flying buttresses, and grotesque gargoyles.

Capitalize the names of vehicles only if they are trade names.

EXAMPLES **O**ldsmobile, **S**aturn, **M**iata, **A**strovan, **m**inivan, **s**tation **w**agon, **c**ablecar

2.57 First Words, Interjections, and the Pronoun *I*

Capitalize the first word in a sentence.

EXAMPLES "**T**he great masses of the people will more easily fall victims to a big lie than to a small one." —Adolf Hitler
"**I**f winter comes, can spring be far behind?" —Percy Bysshe Shelley

Do not capitalize the interjection *oh* unless it begins a sentence or stands alone. Do, however, capitalize the word *O*, which is technically not an interjection but a **vocative**—a word used to call someone.

EXAMPLES **O**h! How I wish it were true.
Oh, no! My camera fell in the water!
I have . . . **o**h, about sixteen hours of homework tonight.
"There, there I would go, **O** my beloved, with thee!" —Johann von Goethe

Capitalize the pronoun *I* wherever it appears, except in quoted material where the pronoun is lowercased in the original.

EXAMPLES "**I** leave this rule for others when **I**'m dead,
Be always sure you're right—then go ahead." —Davy Crockett
"**i** do excuse me, love, to Death and Time" —e. e. cummings

2.58 Titles of Works of Art, Literature, and Music

Apply **title capitalization** to titles of works of art. In title capitalization, the following are capitalized: the first word, the last word, all nouns, pronouns, adjectives, verbs, adverbs, and subordinating conjunctions. Articles *(a, an, the)* are written lowercased unless they are the first or last word. Some writers also capitalize any preposition over five letters long.

EXAMPLES Botticelli's *The **B**irth of **V**enus,* Rembrandt's ***S**upper at **E**mmaus,* Winslow Homer's *The **C**oming of the **G**ale*

Apply title capitalization to titles of literary works.

EXAMPLES Thomas's "**A** **R**efusal to **M**ourn the **D**eath by **F**ire of a **C**hild in **L**ondon," Verne's *Around the **W**orld in **E**ighty **D**ays,* Dostoyevsky's *Crime and **P**unishment*

Apply title capitalization to titles of musical works.

EXAMPLES "Take **M**e **O**ut to the **B**all **G**ame," Stravinsky's *The **R**ite of **S**pring,* Gilbert and Sullivan's *The **P**irates of **P**enzance*

2.59 Quotations and Sacred Names

Capitalize the first word of a sentence in a direct quotation even if it begins within the sentence where it is quoted.

EXAMPLE Margaret Thatcher remarked, "**I**n politics, if you want anything said, ask a man; if you want anything done, ask a woman."

Do not capitalize a quoted fragment that completes the sense of part of the sentence outside the quotation marks.

EXAMPLE In 1604, King James I of England wrote that smoking was "**a** custom loathsome to the eye, harmful to the brain, [and] dangerous to the lungs."

Capitalize references to sacred beings or persons, including God, gods, prophets, apostles, and saints. Some adjectives traditionally linked to such beings and persons are sometimes capitalized as well.

EXAMPLES **J**ehovah, **M**essiah, **K**ing of **K**ings, **H**oly **M**ary, **A**hura **M**azda, **D**alai **L**ama, **V**ishnu

Capitalize the names of sacred writings and parts of such writings.

EXAMPLES **P**salms, **S**eptuagint, **N**ew **T**estament, **B**ook of **M**ormon, **U**panishad, **K**oran

2.60 Poetry, Outlines, and Letters

The first word in each line of a poem was capitalized in English until recent times.

EXAMPLE Now waving grain, wide o'er the plain,
 Delights the weary farmer;
And the moon shines bright, when I rove at night,
 To muse upon my charmer. —Robert Burns

Most writers in this century, however, have broken with this tradition.

EXAMPLE The time will come
when, with elation,
you will greet yourself arriving
at your own door, in your own mirror
and each will smile at the other's welcome. —Derek Walcott

Capitalize the first word of each entry in an outline. Most of the index letters that identify parts of the outline are also capitalized. The following example is an outline for a report on the Amazon River; observe that lowercase letters are used as index letters after the Arabic numeral level.

The Amazing Amazon

I. **D**escription of the Amazon
  A. **L**ocation
    1. **S**ource
      a. **P**rincipal source
      b. **T**ributaries
    2. **C**ourse
    3. **M**outh
  B. **S**ize
    1. **L**ength and volume
    2. **W**idth and depth
II. **E**xploration of the Amazon
  A. **E**arly exploration
    1. **F**rancisco de Orellana
    2. **A**lexander von Humboldt
  B. **T**wentieth-century exploration
    1. **T**heodore Roosevelt
    2. **N**ational Geographic Society
III. **P**eople of the Amazon
  A. **F**irst people of Amazonia
  B. **E**xploitation of people
  C. **P**opulation of Amazonia today
IV. **R**iches of the Amazon
  A. **W**ildlife
  B. **P**lants
  C. **N**atural resources

Capitalize letters used as grades, as musical tones, or as a designation for a person, thing, or location.

EXAMPLES Getting a **C** on my term paper brought my average down to **B**+.
That piece in **B** minor has an eerie sound.
Going from point **A** to point **B** is not as simple as it looks on the map.

ESSENTIAL SKILLS: LANGUAGE

2.61 School Subjects, Classes, Grades, and Awards

Capitalize a school subject when it is also the name of a language or when it is followed by a number indicating that it is the name of a specific course.

EXAMPLES German, Sociology 101, science, social studies, algebra

Expressions such as *tenth grade, twelfth grade, sophomore, junior,* or expressions such as *freshman year, junior year,* are not capitalized unless they are part of the title of an official program.

EXAMPLES sophomore English, Senior Seminar

Capitalize the names of awards and prizes. Some words that go with prize names are not capitalized, however.

EXAMPLES Nobel Prize in chemistry, National Book Award, Life Achievement Award, Grammy Award, Templeton Prize, Presidential Medal of Freedom

SPELLING HANDBOOK

2.62 Proofreading for Spelling Errors

After you have checked your writing for other problems, read it through with an eye open for spelling errors. Even if you have confidence in your spelling, you may make a mistake in keyboarding your work or writing it out by hand. Of course, the difficulty in detecting errors is that you will tend to see the words as you meant to write them, rather than as they really stand on the page. Professional proofreaders have a helpful technique: they read the text backwards word by word. If you come across a word that causes the slightest doubt, check it in the dictionary.

2.63 Using Spelling Rules

Many spelling problems arise from a common operation: forming plurals. Form the plurals of most nouns by simply adding *s.* Some nouns ending in *o* preceded by a consonant have plurals ending in *es,* as do nouns ending in *s, x, z, ch,* or *sh.*

EXAMPLES signs, decisions, gardens, trumpets, principles
heroes, potatoes, vetoes
dresses, taxes, adzes, branches, flashes

The plurals of words ending in *o* preceded by a vowel are formed by adding *s.* The plurals of most musical terms ending in *o* are also formed by adding *s.*

EXAMPLES radios, studios, rodeos
oratorios, trios, altos, cellos, arpeggios

Form the plurals of nouns ending in *y* preceded by a vowel by adding *s.* (The **vowels** are the letters *a, e, i, o, u.* Sometimes the letter *y* also represents a vowel sound.)

EXAMPLES **rays,** don**keys,** bu**oys,** gu**ys**

Form the plurals of nouns ending in *y* preceded by a consonant by changing the *y* to *i* and adding *es.* (The **consonants** are all the letters that are not vowels.)

EXAMPLES authorit**ies,** countr**ies,** sp**ies,** centur**ies**

The plurals of some nouns are irregular.

EXAMPLES mouse—**mice,** goose—**geese,** woman—**women,** phenomenon—**phenomena**

Form the plural of a compound noun consisting of a noun and a modifier by making the main noun component plural.

EXAMPLES lad**ies**-in-waiting, sister**s**-in-law, maid**s** of honor, Secretar**ies** of State

Another operation that causes spelling errors is adding **prefixes** or **suffixes** to a word. A prefix is a letter or a group of letters added to the beginning of a word to change its meaning. When adding a prefix to a word, do not change the word itself.

EXAMPLES extra + curricular = **extra**curricular super + natural = **super**natural

A **suffix** is a letter or group of letters added to the end of a word to change its meaning. The spelling of most words is not changed when the suffix *–ness* or *–ly* is added.

EXAMPLES author + ship = author**ship** help + ful = help**ful**

In the case of many words of more than one syllable ending in *y,* however, change the *y* to *i* before adding *–ly* or *ness.*

EXAMPLES silly + ness = sill**iness** happy + ly = happ**ily**

In most cases of words ending in a final silent *e,* drop the *e* when adding a suffix beginning with a vowel, and keep the *e* when adding a suffix beginning with a consonant.

EXAMPLES like + able = lik**able** care + ful = care**ful**
serve + ant = serv**ant** shame + less = shame**less**

ESSENTIAL SKILLS: LANGUAGE

You can increase your **vocabulary**—the words you have at your command that empower you in communicating with others—by taking a few simple steps. When you encounter a new word, whether in reading, in speaking with others, in class, or outside school altogether, write it down in a list in your journal. Check the meaning in a dictionary and jot that down, too. Then review your vocabulary list from time to time. This procedure will vastly increase the chances that you will recall the new words you encounter.

2.64 Using Context Clues

Although a dictionary is the best resource to check when you encounter a new word, sometimes a dictionary is not at hand. Even if a dictionary is available, you may prefer not to break the stream of your thought by consulting it. At times like these, you can often deduce the meaning of a word from context clues.

One type of context clue to look for is **restatement.** The author may tell you the meaning of a word you do not know by using different words to express the same idea in another sentence. Consider the following example.

EXAMPLE Andrew's analysis of the poem reveals a striking **perspicacity;** he has a **solid grasp** of the writer's allegorical meanings and **keen insight** into the themes of the poem.

An alert reader will guess from the restatement (printed here in boldface) that *perspicacity* means "keenness of mental perception; discernment."

A second and related type of context clue is **apposition.** Look for a word or phrase that is specifically intended to clarify or modify the word you do not know.

EXAMPLE Mr. Clayton is a **paradigm, or model,** of the old Southern aristocrat.

A third related type of context clue is the use of **examples.**

EXAMPLE Some notable **misanthropes** in literature are Ebenezer Scrooge, Silas Marner, and the Grinch.

The examples suggest that *misanthrope* means "one who dislikes or distrusts people."

Another context clue is the use of **comparison.** Imagine a reader does not know the meaning of the word *raze.* The comparison in the following sentence will allow him or her to deduce the meaning from the context.

EXAMPLE The demolition crew tore down the crumbling landmark building and also **razed**

A comparison of the parallel phrases in the predicate indicates that *raze* means "tear down, demolish."

Contrast is a similar type of context clue.

EXAMPLE When confronted about plagiarizing their term papers, Aaron was above board and readily admitted his guilt, but Carlton **prevaricated.**

Contrast suggests that *prevaricate* means "to deviate from the truth."

2.65 Base Words, Prefixes, and Suffixes

Building vocabulary is easier if you know the building blocks of words. Many words are formed by adding **prefixes** to a **base.** For example, imagine you come across the word *counterrevolution* and are unfamiliar with it. You do, however, recognize the **base word,** *revolution.* And you know from words such as *counterclockwise* and *countermeasure* that the prefix *counter–* means "against" or "contrary to." You can then quickly deduce that a counterrevolution is a movement in opposition to a revolution. The following table gives further examples.

PREFIX	MEANING	EXAMPLE	MEANING
pseudo–	"false"	pseudoheroic	falsely heroic
ultra–	"extremely"	ultraorganized	highly organized
semi–	"half, partly"	semiopaque	partly opaque
meta–	"more comprehensive"	metalanguage	language used to talk about language

Like prefixes, **suffixes** can provide valuable clues to words you do not know. The following table lists a few examples.

SUFFIX	MEANING	EXAMPLE	MEANING
–able	"capable of"	tunable	able to be tuned
–fold	"multiplied by"	fourfold	four times as much
–ful	"amount capable of filling"	planetful	amount capable of filling a planet
–less	"not having"	witless	having no wits
–logy	"science of"	zoology	science of living things

ESSENTIAL SKILLS: LANGUAGE

2.66 Greek and Latin Roots

Although English is primarily a Germanic language, its vocabulary is in large part based on ancient Greek and Latin. Some Greek and Latin words came to English by way of other languages such as French; others were borrowed directly from Greek and Latin sources by scientists, researchers, and writers, who have always looked to Greek and Latin for components to build new words. The word *telephone,* for instance, comes from the Greek root *tele–*, meaning "far away," and *phone,* meaning "voice."

The following table shows some words with **Greek and Latin roots.** Notice that the words formed from Latin roots are more common, though the words formed from Greek roots are nearly identical in meaning.

FROM GREEK	FROM LATIN	MEANING OF GREEK AND LATIN ROOTS
dys • trophy	mal • nutrition	"bad-nourishment"
hypo • thesis	sup • position	"under-put"
peri • phrasis	circum • locution	"around-say"
sym • pathy	com • passion	"with-feel"
dia • phanous	trans • parent	"through-show"
mono • morphic	uni • form	"one-form"
poly • glottal	multi • lingual	"many-tongued"

2.67 Word Origins

Knowing how speakers of English form words can help you recognize new words when you see them. **Names of people and places** are a common source of new words. The following table gives several examples.

WORD	ORIGIN
brobdingnagian	From Brobdingnag, the land of giants in Jonathan Swift's *Gulliver's Travels.* The word means "giant" or "huge."
panacea	From the daughter of the Greek god of medicine. Panacea could cure any ailment, and her name has come to mean a cure-all, a remedy for any problem.
chauvinism	From the name of a French war hero, Nicolas Chauvin, who became an almost idolatrous worshipper of Napoleon. The French word *chauvinisme* became synonymous with fanatical patriotism, and the English word *chauvinism* came to include the idea of prejudice against those of a different sex, class, nationality, etc.
maverick	From a Texas lawyer turned rancher who failed to brand his calves. The name *maverick* soon meant any unbranded stock, and later any person who holds himself apart from the herd, a nonconformist.

Another source of new words is **acronyms**, or words formed from the first letter or letters of each of the major parts of a compound term.

EXAMPLES quasar, from "**qua**si-stell**ar** object; pixel, from "**pic**ture **el**ement"; VISTA from "**V**olunteers **i**n **S**ervice **t**o **A**merica"; ZIP code, from **Z**one **I**mprovement **P**lan

Many words are simply **borrowed** from other languages.

EXAMPLES **boomerang** (Aboriginal), **kow-tow** (Chinese), **bureau** (French), **protein** (German), **anthology** (Greek), **jubilee** (Hebrew), **pajama** (Hindu), **miniature** (Italian), **siesta** (Spanish), **chutzpah** (Yiddish)

New words are also formed by shortening longer words. The word *phone,* short for *telephone,* is one such **clipped form.**

EXAMPLES **flu** (from *influenza*), **cello** (from *violincello*), **memo** (from *memorandum*), **fan** (from *fanatic*), **stereo** (from *stereophonic receiver*)

New words are often **coined**, or deliberately created to fill a need.

EXAMPLES **meltdown,** a condition in which the reactor core of a nuclear power plant burns through or melts into the ground, releasing dangerous radiation
sit-in, a term coined to refer to a method of protesting the policy of a government or business. Demonstrators sit in, and refuse to leave, a public place, thus disrupting operations.
red tape, from the red ribbons used by government officials to tie their papers together. The term refers to excessive bureaucracy or rigid adherence to rules and regulations.

Brand names are often taken into the language, even though their owners may struggle to protect their exclusive status. Such names may be altered slightly as they enter public use.

EXAMPLES Scotch tape, Dixie cup, Jell-O or jello

As you study other subjects besides English, be alert for colorful words with extended meanings that might be of use in your writing. Keep a list of these words in your journal. The table on the next page gives some examples of words from other curricular areas, as well as sample sentences showing how these words might be used in your writing.

SUBJECT	WORDS
Arts and Humanities	I found myself in a **Catch-22** situation; no matter what I chose to do, there was an inherent impossibility in each alternative. This poem has exquisite **harmony** in its structure and interweaving of themes. Will's holy **grail** was getting into Harvard; all through high school he remained focused on this one dream. "The depressing nature of his surroundings seemed, by **counterpoint,** to enhance his sunny mood." —S. Brett
Mathematics	Although only a small **fraction** of the ancient poet's writings remain, we are able to get a glimpse into his world and his thought. The author has created a **one-dimensional** character with a narrow **range** of emotions and little **depth** of personality. Reading Mark Mathabane's *Kaffir Boy* enabled the students to see the problem of apartheid from a new **angle.** Making the decision was extremely complex because there were so many **variables,** all intertwined with each other.
Social Studies	Jasmine persistently **lobbied** her parents for permission to go on the ski weekend. Many of Charles Dickens's works express sympathy for the **disenfranchised** poor of nineteenth-century England. Velma tended to **monopolize** conversations, causing others to avoid discussions with her. Many young people of the '60s climbed on the **bandwagon** to protest the war in Vietnam.
Science	The **budding** gymnast's skill took a **quantum** leap forward under the tutelage of the former Olympic coach. When she arrives home after a stressful day at work, my mom needs some time to **decompress** before fixing dinner. The **acid test** of Socrates' philosophy and self-discipline came when he looked death in the face. Emily read the essay carefully and **distilled** it down to one concise paragraph.
Technical Preparatory	After the game we watch video clips of key plays and the coach gave us **feedback** on our performance. Mrs. McWhinney stood guard at the hors d'oeuvres table, her **antenna** poised to catch the latest gossip. If a large meteorite collided with the Earth, as many scientists believe happened in the Yucatan Peninsula 65 million years ago, human civilization would have to **reboot** completely. After their son was diagnosed with leukemia, the Cormiers found support by **networking** with other families who had children with life-threatening illnesses.

VARIETIES OF ENGLISH

2.68 Formal and Informal English

Writers use **formal English** to write papers, some magazine articles, nonfiction books, and some literary works. It is spoken at public ceremonies and in official speeches. We use **informal English** to write personal notes and letters, in most newspaper and magazine articles, some nonfiction and fiction books, and some short stories and plays. We speak informal English in everyday conversation.

How do you decide whether to use formal or informal English? You will naturally tend to use informal English, so all you need to bear in mind are those situations (just described) in which formal English may be expected instead.

How do you distinguish formal from informal English? First, informal English allows grammatical constructions that would not be acceptable in formal English. Many of these constructions are described in the Grammar Handbook (where they are labeled "nonstandard"). Second, informal English is enlivened by **colloquialisms.** These are the words and phrases that speakers of a language use naturally in conversation.

EXAMPLES Whenever Jeremy gets tired of a girlfriend, he **ditches** [abandons] her.
I'll tell you the plan, but keep it **under your hat** [confidential].

Third, informal English is often salted with **slang,** a form of speech made up of coined words, words whose meaning has been changed for no known reason, and words used facetiously.

EXAMPLES It **blew his mind** [caused him great shock and mental excitement] to find out that his uncle was a spy.
Franklin's gym socks are totally **grody** [disgusting].

Informal grammatical constructions, colloquialisms, and slang sometimes have a place even in writing that is otherwise formal. Literary works, for example, may rely on these devices to make dialogue colorful and realistic.

2.69 Register, Tone, and Voice

To understand the concept of **register,** imagine that all the different kinds of usage in a language—both formal and informal—form one large set. A register is a subset of language usage specific to a particular relationship between people. In talking to a friend, for example, you speak in a register that is casual, warm, and open. In speaking to a little child, you speak in a register that is nonthreatening and simple to understand. In speaking to an official such as a police officer or a government clerk, you speak in a register that is polite but firm—the same register they should use with you. The words you choose, the grammar you employ to say those words, and your tone of voice will change depending on the register in which you are speaking.

Another way to understand register is to examine its meaning as a musical term. In music, *register* means the range of notes a singer or instrument is capable of producing. Your speaking and writing, however, are not limited to one range of usage. You can call on any part of a broad scale of usage, ranging from a grunt to a complex and formal declaration of your thought.

One hallmark of people who adapt to society is their ability to choose and use the appropriate register for whatever situation they are in. They do not offend strangers by being too familiar or puzzle their friends by being too formal. The same is true of written language. When you write, use language that is appropriate for the context and for your intended reader. Your personal journal will be in a different register from a term paper, and a story you write for a child will be in a different register from a short story you write for your English class.

Tone is the quality of a work that shows the attitude of the person writing or supposedly writing it. In the opening octave of Louise Labé's Sonnet 23, the tone of the speaker is sarcastic. The questions the speaker poses to her beloved such as "Where are your tears that faded in the ground?/Your death? by which your constant love is bound in oaths and honor now beyond belief?" are sneering and caustic. The speaker does not say, "You no longer cry for me, and you have given up your impassioned oaths to love me until death parts us," because this would be a sincere, more detached tone.

In any writing you do, you can adopt a tone appropriate for the message you wish to convey. Your **diction**, or choice of words, determines much of your tone. For instance, when writing a letter to a government official protesting a new regulation, do you want to say, "Your new regulation is utterly unacceptable to the honest citizens of this state," or "The new regulation is unpopular among many of your constituents"? The tone you convey will depend upon your choice.

Voice is the quality of a work that tells you that one person in particular wrote it—not several, and not just anyone. Voice is one feature that makes a work unique. The voice of a work can be difficult to define; it may have to do with the way a writer views people, events, objects, ideas, the passage of time, even life itself. If this treatment of the subject is consistent throughout, despite variations in tone, register, point of view, and so forth, then the writer has **established a voice,** a sense of individuality, in the work.

In your own writing, you should strive to develop your own voice, not to imitate the voices of others. What that voice is, and how it compares to others, are matters no one can decide for you. "To thine own self be true," says Polonius in Shakespeare's *Hamlet,* "and thou canst not then be false to any man." He might well have been speaking about literary voice. Be true to your own voice, and your experience will speak directly to the experience of others.

2.70 Dialects of English

Dialects are varieties of a language. Dialects fall into one of two main classes: dialects based on **social differences** (for example, upper class, middle class, and lower class) and dialects based on **regional differences** (in the United States the major regional dialects are northern, southern, midland, and western).

All dialects are equally capable of expressing thought, which is what language is for. Therefore, no dialect is *better* than any other dialect. Some dialects are accepted by social classes that hold power; their dialect is generally considered the **standard** form of a language, and other dialects are considered **nonstandard.** But *standard* does not mean "correct" or "better than others." Knowledge of the standard dialect is useful because it is widely understood, and because in many situations, speaking or writing in the standard dialect will ensure that people focus on *what* you say rather than *how* you say it. They will understand your meaning, without being distracted by your use of an unfamiliar dialect.

Knowledge of nonstandard dialects is also useful to writers. Consider Robert Burns's use of the Scots dialect in "Song Composed in August" to make his dialogue more lively and authentic.

2.71 Jargon and Gobbledygook

Jargon is the specialized vocabulary used by members of a profession. It tends to be incomprehensible to people outside the profession. A plumber may speak of a "hubless fitting" or a "street elbow" (kinds of pipe). A computer programmer may talk of "ram cache" (part of computer memory) or a "shell" (a type of operating software for computers).

Jargon is useful to writers who want to lend authenticity to their description of situations in which jargon would naturally be used. For instance, a novel about fighter pilots on an aircraft carrier would probably be full of aviation jargon. A scriptwriter developing a science fiction film would be sure to work in futuristic jargon about warps in space, energy shields, and tractor beams.

Gobbledygook is unclear, wordy jargon used by bureaucrats or government officials. For instance, the failure of a program might be called an "incomplete success." A bureaucrat might say, "We are engaged in conducting a study with a view to ascertaining which employees might be assigned to the mobility pool and how we might create revenue enhancement" when he means "We are planning lay-offs and tax increases."

2.72 Clichés and Euphemisms

A **cliché** is an expression that has been used so often it has become colorless and uninteresting.

The use of clichés instantaneously makes writing dull.

EXAMPLES
quick as a wink
hungry as an ox
keep up with the Joneses
pretty as a picture

A **euphemism** (from the Greek verb meaning "to speak with good words") is an inoffensive term that substitutes for one considered offensive.

EXAMPLES
aerial mishap (for "airplane crash")
powder room (for "toilets")
environmentally handicapped people (for "homeless people")
building engineer (for "janitor")
euthanize (for "kill")

ESSENTIAL SKILLS: LANGUAGE

2.73 Connotation and Denotation

A **denotation** of a word is its dictionary definition. A **connotation** of a word is all the associations that it has in addition to its literal meaning. For example, the words *cheap* and *economical* both denote "inexpensive," but *cheap* connotes shoddy and inferior while *economical* connotes a good value for the money. Contrast the denotations and connotations of the following examples.

EXAMPLES inquisitive, curious, nosy, snoopy, prying
self-esteem, assertiveness, self-confidence, pride, arrogance, haughtiness
vocation, calling, career, job, work, labor, toil, travail, drudgery, grind

Writers should be aware of the connotations as well as the denotations of the words they use. You would be remiss to say, "The honcho jabbered for eons about his pet proposition," when what you meant was, "The president spoke for a long time about the proposal he favored."

ESSENTIAL SKILLS: *Speaking and Listening*

3.1 Elements of Verbal and Nonverbal Communication

Communication can be verbal or nonverbal. **Verbal communication** is made by means of words and other sounds uttered by speakers. **Nonverbal communication** is made through body movements. Face-to-face communication has one major advantage over writing and over speaking on the telephone: it enables the communicator to send nonverbal as well as verbal messages. The following charts list the major elements of verbal and nonverbal communication and provide guidelines for using them:

ELEMENTS OF VERBAL COMMUNICATION

ELEMENT	DESCRIPTION	GUIDELINES FOR SPEAKERS
Volume	The loudness or softness of the voice	Speak loudly enough to be heard, but not so loudly as to make your audience uncomfortable.
Pitch, or Intonation	The highness or lowness of the voice	Vary your pitch to give your expressions a musical quality and to communicate meaning (for example, a rising pitch at the end of a sentence indicates a question). Avoid using a single pitch, or **monotone.**
Enunciation	The clearness with which syllables are spoken	Slightly exaggerate the clearness of your syllables to ensure that you are understood. Do not drop or clip the ends of words or sentences.
Pace	The speed with which something is said	Do not speak too slowly or too quickly.
Stress	The emphasis given to syllables, words, or phrases	Use stress to emphasize important ideas. Vary stress along with pitch to avoid monotony.
Tone	The emotional quality of the speech	Suit the tone to the message. Vary the tone appropriately throughout the communication.

ELEMENTS OF NONVERBAL COMMUNICATION		
ELEMENT	**DESCRIPTION**	**GUIDELINES FOR SPEAKERS**
Eye contact	Looking your listeners in the eye	Maintain eye contact to keep your listeners engaged in what you are saying.
Facial expressions	Displays of emotion using the face (e.g., smiles, scowls, frowns, etc.)	Match your facial expressions to your message.
Body language	Positions of the body that have meaning to listeners	Match your body language to your message. Maintain good posture.
Gestures	Meaningful motions of the hands and arms	Use gestures sparingly to emphasize points. Match gestures to your message.
Proximity	Distance from listeners	Maintain a comfortable distance, not too close for comfort, but not so far away as to hamper communication.

Elements of verbal and nonverbal communication are valuable to public speakers as well. In general, when speaking to an audience, follow these guidelines:

USING ELEMENTS OF COMMUNICATION IN PUBLIC SPEAKING

1. Make sure that you can be heard and understood by using an appropriate volume and pace.
2. Suit your volume, pitch, pace, stress, and tone to your message.
3. Vary all the verbal elements of your speech to make the presentation more lively, colorful, and interesting.
4. Slightly heighten or exaggerate each of the verbal elements of your speech above the level that you would use in ordinary conversation.
5. Make eye contact with your audience. Reading from a prepared speech makes it difficult to maintain eye contact; instead memorize your speech, or rehearse it and refer to notes.
6. Use appropriate gestures, facial expressions, and body language to engage your audience and to emphasize your message.

For more information about public speaking, refer to the Language Arts Survey 3.4, "Public Speaking."

3.2 Active Listening And Interpersonal Communication

Listening is not a spectator sport. For complete communication to occur, the listener has to participate fully and actively in the process and respond to what he or she is hearing. Here are some ways you can **listen** actively:

- **Mental Activity.** Listen for main ideas and supporting details. Summarize, predict, question, and interpret as you listen.
- **Note-taking.** If you are listening to a lecture or to a long monologue, you may want to take notes in rough outline form. List major ideas and related details, as follows:

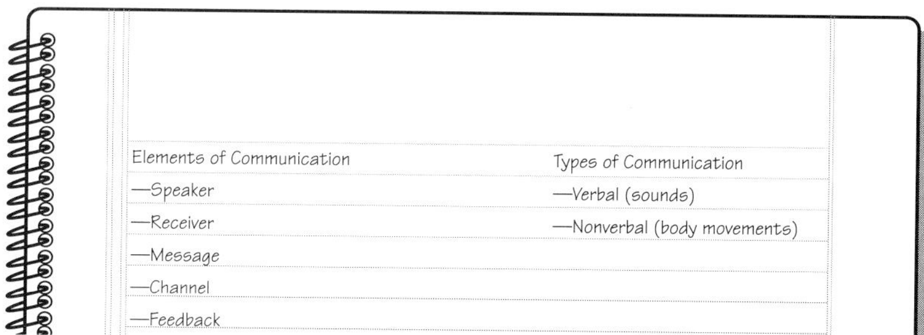

Elements of Communication
—Speaker
—Receiver
—Message
—Channel
—Feedback
Types of Communication
—Verbal (sounds)
—Nonverbal (body movements)

Refer to the Language Arts Survey 1.12, "Outlining" or 4.22, "Formal and Informal Notetaking" for additional information.

- **Questioning and Other Feedback.** As you listen, maintain eye contact. Provide feedback to the speaker by means of gestures, facial expressions, body language, and proximity. In conversation, encourage the speaker and show that you understand him or her by making statements like "yes" and "uh-huh" and "I see." If you think that you may have misunderstood something or if the communication is highly emotional, pause and rephrase what the speaker has said as a means of checking your own understanding. When the speaker has finished a thought and there is a pause in the flow of speech, you can ask questions or make comments to clarify or to expand upon what the speaker has said.

Active listening is an important element of effective **interpersonal communication.** Interpersonal communication, or communication between individuals, serves a number of important functions:

- Transmission of information
- Establishment of relationships
- Maintenance of relationships
- Personal validation

Here are some ways to use verbal and nonverbal techniques to improve your interpersonal communication:

- Make eye contact and keep your body stance relaxed and open.
- Give feedback by asking questions and by reiterating what was said.

- Think before you speak.
- If you find yourself feeling negative emotions, pause, take a deep breath, and get your emotions under control before continuing the communication. If you cannot get your emotions under control, ask to continue the communication at a later time.

3.3 Collaborative Learning and Discussion

Collaborative learning, or learning with others, is a useful way to discover and enjoy many subjects. Types of collaborative learning include group projects, brainstorming, group debates, small group discussions, and peer evaluations. For information on brainstorming and peer evaluation, see the Language Arts Survey 1.10, "Gathering Ideas," and 1.14, "Evaluating." Collaborative learning benefits the participants because each person brings different knowledge, strengths, talents, and skills to the group. Working effectively with others is important in school and in the workplace. Personality conflicts, misunderstandings, poor communication, and lack of direction can cause difficulty in group efforts. The following guidelines will also help you to avoid some of these problems and to successfully complete group projects.

Guidelines for Projects

- Choose a group leader to conduct the meetings of your project group.
- Set a goal for the group—some specific outcome or set of outcomes that you want to bring about.
- Make a list of tasks that need to be performed.
- Make a schedule for completing the tasks, including dates and times for completion of each task.
- Make an assignment sheet. Assign particular tasks to particular group members. Be fair in distributing the work to be done.
- Set times for future meetings. You might want to schedule some meetings to evaluate your progress toward your goal as well as meetings to actually carry out specific tasks.
- When the project is completed, meet to evaluate your overall success and the individual contributions of group members.

Discussion, one of the many forms of collaborative learning, is a means for sharing ideas and information among several people at once. Many of the activities in this text will ask you to discuss you opinions about various issues and your responses to the literature you have read. Discussions vary from highly informal chats among friends to highly formal, rule-governed interactions in parliamentary bodies. The following chart describes the roles of group members and important elements of the process in a semiformal discussion.

DISCUSSION	
Roles	• **Group leader or chairperson.** Presents the subject, or discussion question, and keeps the discussion on track when people begin to digress or veer away from the subject, asks questions when the discussion starts to flag, makes sure everyone participates • **Secretary.** Takes notes or records what is said and later prepares a description (**minutes**) of the discussion • **Participants.** Take part in the discussion, listen attentively to others, provide feedback
Process	• **Discussion question.** States the subject of the discussion and is usually put forward by the group leader. In a formal discussion, the discussion question is called a **proposition**. • **Agenda.** A step-by-step plan for the discussion, usually written and distributed at the beginning of the discussion by the group leader or secretary

3.4 Public Speaking

If you are afraid of speaking in public, you are not alone. Polls consistently show that most people feel extremely anxious when called upon to speak in public. However, by preparing carefully, you can increase your level of comfort about speaking. You may even be able to harness your anxiety and turn it into positive energy that will move your audience.

Types of Speeches

There are three main types of speech.

- **impromptu speech**—one given without any preparation
- **memorized speech**—one that is written out entirely beforehand, committed to memory, and recited to the audience
- **extemporaneous speech**, in which the speaker prompts himself or herself from carefully prepared note cards

While impromptu speeches may suffer from having not been prepared in advance, memorized speeches tend to sound over-prepared and stilted. That is why most professional speakers prefer the the extemporaneous speech which combines the spontaneity of the impromptu speech with the preparedness of the memorized speech.

Writing a Speech

When writing a speech, just as when writing a paper, you should make sure that it has a beginning, a middle, and an end. The beginning, or introduction, should capture the attention of the audience and present your main topic or idea. The middle, or body, should develop the main idea. The end, or conclusion, should be memorable and should give the audience a satisfying sense of an ending.

Preparing an Extemporaneous Speech

The following chart describes steps to take when preparing an extemporaneous speech.

STEPS IN PREPARING AN EXTEMPORANEOUS SPEECH
1. Begin by prewriting (see Language Arts Survey 1.10, "Gathering Ideas").
2. Research your topic.
3. Write your speech. Prepare note cards, capturing important facts, points, and prompts in easy-to-read notes; place them in order.
4. Make a plan for using verbal and nonverbal elements of communication in your speech.
5. Rehearse with your note cards, using a tape recorder, a video recorder, a mirror, or a practice audience.
6. Deliver your speech, attending to both verbal and nonverbal elements of the delivery.

3.5 Oral Interpretation

Oral interpretation is the process of presenting a dramatic reading of a literary work or group of works. The presentation should be sufficiently dramatic to convey to the audience a sense of the particular qualities of the work. Here are the steps you need to follow to prepare an oral interpretation:

1. **Choose a cutting.** The cutting may be a single piece; a selection from a single piece; or, most commonly, several short, related pieces on a single topic or theme.
2. **Write the introduction and any necessary transitions**. The introduction should mention the name of the piece, the author, and, if appropriate, the translator. It should also present the overall topic or theme of the interpretation. Transitions should introduce and connect the parts of the interpretation.
3. **Rehearse, using appropriate variations in volume, pitch, pace, stress, tone, gestures, facial expressions, and body language.** However, avoid movement—that's for drama. If your cutting contains different voices (a narrative voice and characters' voices, for example), distinguish them. Try to make your verbal and nonverbal expression mirror what the piece is saying. Practice in front of an audience or a mirror or use a video camera or tape recorder.

3.6 Film and Television

Films

We watch movies for a multitude of reasons, but perhaps the most common is that a movie allows us to escape our own realities for a couple of hours. It lets us visit new places, see and try exciting new things, and experience life in someone else's shoes. A great film gives us insight into the lives of others and so expands our understanding and our sympathies. Some films, however, are created solely for the purpose of making money through exploitation of sensational elements or gimmicks. Although you cannot control the types of movies Hollywood decides to make, you can control the types of movies you choose to watch. The following guidelines will enable you to become a more discriminating consumer of films.

1. **Plan ahead**. Decide in advance which films you would like to see. Don't settle for just any movie that happens to be playing at your local theater or on television.
2. **Listen, watch, and read what the critics have to say.** Take what the critics have to say into consideration to help you decide which movies to see. Once you have seen the movie, decide for yourself whether you agree or disagree with a particular critic. Consider what elements of the movie you liked or disliked, and what could have been altered to make it better. If, after a while, you find one particular critic with whom you tend to agree on a regular basis, use his or her opinion to help you choose which movies to see.
3. **Be a critic yourself.** Be critical of dialogue and story lines. Many films recycle conventional story lines and dialogue. Many contain sensational scenes that provoke audiences but forfeit quality in story line, dialogue, and content. When you see a film, ask yourself questions such as the following:
   - Does each scene move the story forward?
   - Do the characters' actions fit their motives? Is their dialogue believable?
   - Are the themes raised in the film fully developed?
4. **Be aware of previews and coming attractions**. These are designed with the help of the production company's marketing and sales departments to motivate you to see their film. Previews can make a film seem more humorous, exciting, and powerful than it really is by showing only the best dialogue and action.
5. **Try something new!** Try viewing a film that is much different from the type and genre that you usually see. Keep an open mind; you might just surprise yourself and enjoy it.
6. **Never substitute.** Never see a film adaptation of a literary work as a substitute for reading the work itself. While seeing such an adaptation can be a good introduction to a literary work, do not rely on it to capture all the richness of the original.

Television

Television is another medium of communication. You may not be able to respond directly to the broadcaster, but you can still control the broadcast message. Follow the guidelines below to effectively control television output:

1. **Plan your television time.** Rather than accepting whatever program happens to be on, look at the television guide and choose programs that are of interest to you.
2. **Be a critic.** Question what you see and hear. What criticisms do you have about a program: its quality, its message, its originality, the depth and reliability of its coverage?
3. **Remember that advertisers pay for most broadcast programs.** They also control the content of the programs they sponsor and pay for your attention because they want to sell you something. Listen to and watch these advertisements and programs critically. Read the Language Arts Survey 4.5, "Distinguishing Fact and Opinion," and 4.6, "Identifying Faulty Arguments and Propaganda" for tips on evaluating information critically.

Essential Skills: *Study and Research*

THINKING SKILLS

All human beings have a great number of thinking skills and perform astonishing feats of thinking every day, but often people get set in thinking habits and patterns that aren't very efficient. Learning a few simple thinking strategies can dramatically improve anyone's ability to learn, to solve problems, and to make decisions.

4.1 Problem Solving and Decision Making

All problem solving involves four steps.

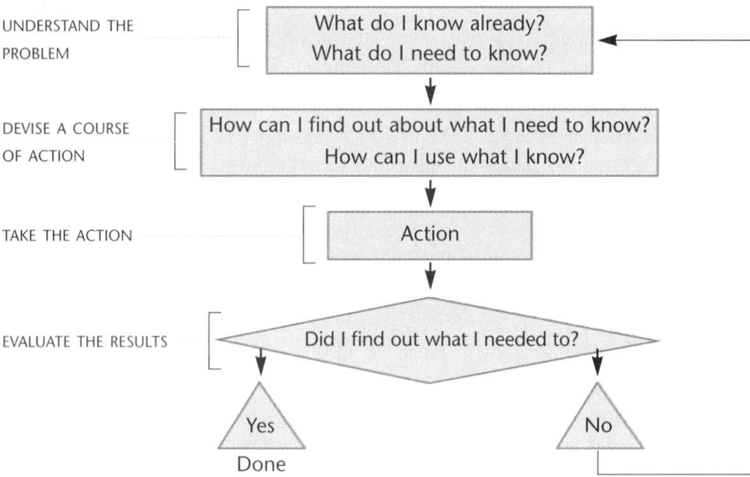
UNDERSTAND THE PROBLEM
What do I know already?
What do I need to know?
DEVISE A COURSE OF ACTION
How can I find out about what I need to know?
How can I use what I know?
TAKE THE ACTION
Action
EVALUATE THE RESULTS
Did I find out what I needed to?
Yes
Done
No

Within this **general problem-solving framework,** there are many particular strategies you can use. A guaranteed strategy for solving a problem is called an **algorithm.** A less than surefire strategy is called a **heuristic** or, if the strategy is very simple and straightforward, a **rule of thumb.** For any complex problem you will almost certainly need to use more than one strategy. Using a good strategy does not guarantee that you will solve a given problem; try to be creative and flexible.

Trial and error. This is the simplest of all problem-solving strategies: make a guess and see if it works. Trial and error is useful when only a few possible solutions seem likely. It can also be useful when there are a great many possibilities and you need to accustom yourself to the problem in order to find a more systematic strategy. As a rule, though, you should not spend very much time using the trial-and-error method.

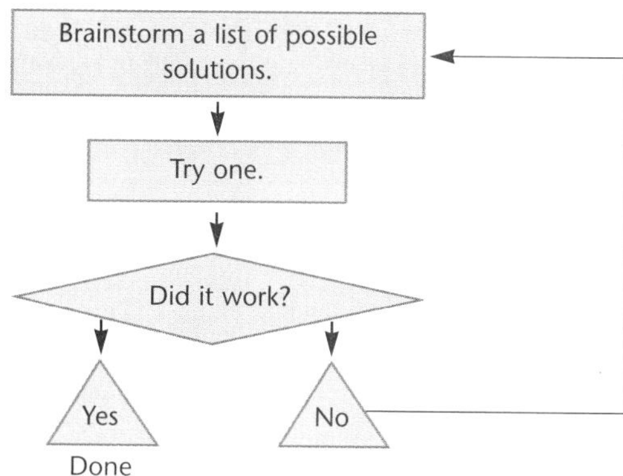

Represent the situation. When you face a problem that is complex or confusing, it can be especially useful to make a visual or physical **representation** of the problem. You might draw a diagram or a picture, or you might construct a model. This technique often helps you to see more clearly important relationships among the parts of the problem.

Means-end analysis. An **end** is a goal, and **means** are the tools and methods used to achieve the goal. To use this strategy, compare what you know about the current situation and about the situation that will exist when the goal has been reached. Then think of ways to reduce the differences between the two situations.

Divide and conquer. Sometimes it is best to divide the problem into parts and then solve each of the parts separately, one step at a time. If a part is still too difficult to solve immediately, you can apply the same strategy to it. You can work on the parts in a logical sequence.

PROBLEM You are writing a story. You have already decided that at the beginning of the story, the main character is a well-respected emergency room physician, married to her work. At the end of the story, the main character has left her work and is hiding away in the south of France. How can you get the character to make this change?

SOLUTION STRATEGY Break the goal into parts: by the end of the story, the main character must (1) have an experience that causes her to go into hiding; (2) leave her work; and (3) go to the south of France. Then solve each part separately: (1a) What happens to this physician to alter her life? (1b) Why must she go into hiding? (2) Why does she leave her work? (3) How does she end up in the south of France?

Work backward. Describe in detail the situation that would exist after you solved the problem. Then think about what would have to happen for that situation to come about. Continue working backward until you get to a situation that you know how to bring about.

Pros and cons. Make a list of your options. For each option, list the reasons for choosing it (the **pros**) and the drawbacks of choosing it (the **cons**). Then compare the lists.

PROS AND CONS: POSSIBLE VACATION PLANS

	Visit Cousins in Colorado	Visit Cousins in Chicago	Washington, D.C.
Pros	favorite cousins walk in woods mountain climbing skiing	movies comedy shows great museums restaurants	visit president (?) White House, Capitol monuments Smithsonian Museum
Cons	long bus ride expensive travel might be snow haven't been invited	nobody my age there long bus ride expensive travel expensive city	nearby no friends there expensive hotels

Criteria analysis. Make a chart. Down the left side of your chart, list the results you want to achieve. Across the top, list your options. Then, assign points from 1 to 5 to each option, according to how well it will achieve the results you have listed. Add up the points and choose the option with the highest total.

CRITERIA ANALYSIS: ORGANIZATION SYSTEMS

	Desktop Filing Box	File Cabinet	Boxes under Bed
1. Convenience	5	4	2
2. Small size	5	1	5
3. Low cost	3	1	5
4. No spare papers, cards, letters	3	3	5
	2	4	3
	18	13	20

4.2 Types of Thinking

Classifying. To **classify** is to put into classes or categories. Items belong in the same category because they share one or more characteristics. You might use classifying to divide extracurricular activities into those that interest you and those in which you have little interest. William Wordsworth's poem "My Heart Leaps Up When I Behold" and Heinrich Heine's poem "Loreley" are classified as Romantic poetry because they have features that characterize

Romantic poetry (e.g., importance of the self and individual experience, a sense of nature and the transcendental).

You should have precise definitions of your categories or concepts before you use them for classifying. When you classify, be sure to base your decisions on the particular characteristics that define the class. If you were classifying essays as either persuasive or expository, for example, you would determine for each essay whether its purpose was to explain or to convince, and you would ignore all other features, such as tone or style.

You may find that some of the things you are classifying fit in more than one of your categories. When this occurs, it may be because the categories are imprecisely defined, or because the categories are not parallel. This book, *Literature and the Language Arts,* presents models of several genres of literature, including poetry, drama, and nonfiction; but sometimes poetry is drama, as, for instance, Rostand's *Cyrano de Bergerac;* and sometimes drama is nonfiction, as, for instance, Shakespeare's *The Life of Henry the Fifth.* The categories poetry, drama, and nonfiction are not parallel, for they fail to refer to parallel features of literary works. Writing is classed as poetry because of its content and language—its special attention to sound and images. Writing is classed as drama because of its form—it includes stage directions and dialogue, for instance. As *The Tempest* shows, writing can have poetic content and language yet be dramatic in form.

The key step in classifying is choosing appropriate categories. Your purposes and needs will partly determine what categories are suitable. For example, if you wanted to compare how Molière's *Tartuffe* and Austen's *Pride and Prejudice* treat the theme of pride, you might classify the two works according to literary form—*Tartuffe* as drama, *Pride and Prejudice* as novel—and then explain how the works' different treatments of this theme reflect the differences between plays and novels. If you instead wanted to compare how the two works use irony, you might classify the points of your discussion in terms of narrative elements such as characterization, dialogue, plot, and language. As you can see, a classification scheme can provide a natural way of organizing a piece of informative or persuasive writing (see 1.11, "Organizing Ideas").

Comparing and Contrasting. To **compare** and **contrast** A with B is to examine A and B in order to describe their similarities and differences. To **compare** A to B is to describe the similarities between A and B. To **contrast** A with B is to describe the differences between A and B. You are using comparing and contrasting skills when you examine two different pairs of rollerblades before deciding which pair to buy or when you choose to take one elective rather than another. When you compare people or things, you place them in the same category: for instance, Oedipus and Sunjata are comparable characters—they are similar—insofar as they are both legendary heroes. When you contrast people or things, you place them in separate and incompatible categories: for instance, Oedipus and Sunjata are contrasting characters—they are different—in that Oedipus is a tragic hero and Sunjata is a warrior hero.

When comparing and contrasting, most often you will want to contrast items that are similar in important respects. In the above example, Oedipus and Sunjata are both heroes, but they are different types of heroes. They share a feature that places them in the category "hero," but they share that feature differently and belong in different subcategories. Whenever you compare people or objects, examine carefully the ways in which they exhibit shared features; the ways in which they exhibit these features are likely to differ, and these differences are probably interesting.

The method of comparing and contrasting is a tool that can help you to explain, to define, or to evaluate. In your literature class, you can expect to be asked to compare and contrast periods, authors, works, techniques and devices, or aspects of works. Remember to discuss *both* points of similarity *and* points of difference. (For tips on organizing a comparison-and-contrast essay, see 1.11, "Organizing Ideas.")

Estimating and Quantifying. To support your points in an argument or in a persuasive essay, you need to provide facts, and often the facts you need are numbers or **quantities.** If you claim, for instance, that too many persons are without health insurance, you ought to **quantify** your claim by stating how many. The numbers you need may be available in reference works (see 4.14, "Using Reference Works"). If not, a combination of research, general knowledge, and common-sense reasoning can help you **estimate**, or find the approximate quantity. Sometimes you will have only enough knowledge to estimate a **range** within which the actual number probably falls.

Analyzing. To **analyze** a thing is to break or divide it in your imagination into its parts and examine the parts and their relations. You can analyze anything in many, many different ways, depending on how you understand its "parts." Suppose, for instance, you were to analyze an automobile. You might analyze it in terms of systems: fuel system, power system, electrical system, cooling system, suspension system, and so on. You might analyze it in terms of places: engine compartment, passenger compartment, underside. You might analyze it in terms of individual parts: brake shoes, brake pads, brake lines, brake fluid, fenders, paint, windows, and so on. You might analyze it in terms of materials: glass, steel, aluminum, plastic, rubber, petroleum, and so on. You might analyze it in terms of how it affects people: costs to individuals, benefits to individuals, costs to society, benefits to society.

To analyze a work of literature, you might look at such parts as words, metaphors, sentence structure, plot, characters, theme, tone, arguments, supporting details, genre, or purpose.

Generalizing and Deducing. To **generalize** is to make a general or universal claim based on some particular observations. Generalizations are often false because they make claims that are broader than what is strictly justified by the information available. For instance, Chiara has seen swans in parks and zoos and on television, and they have all been white. She could truthfully say, "All the swans I have ever seen are white." This claim is only about what she has actually experienced. She also may be tempted to generalize that "All swans are white," but she would be mistaken to do so; in fact, there are also black swans, even though Chiara has not experienced them.

On the other hand, a generalization is liable to be true when it is based on something more than just observations. Chiara knows that if she drops an egg from the bell tower atop the town hall onto the sidewalk, the egg will break. She knows this even though she has never seen an egg dropped from a bell tower. She knows more than merely what she has observed: she knows *why* eggs break. Forming a general rule based on reasoning—rather than on mere observation—is called **induction.**

Deducing or **inferring** is coming to a logical conclusion based on some facts, called **premises.** Suppose you know that the Renaissance occurred in Europe from the early 1400s to the late 1600s (first premise). Later you learn that Ludovico Ariosto, the Italian writer, was born in 1564 (second premise). You can deduce that Ariosto was a Renaissance writer (conclusion). A deduction is valid if the conclusion follows from or is forced by the premises; otherwise it is invalid. Valid deductions have the important property of preserving truth, which is to say that if you start with true premises and you make valid deductions, then your conclusions will always be true.

EXAMPLE 1. If a person can write in Italian, that person must be able to read Italian. 2. Ludovico Ariosto wrote in Italian. 3. Therefore, he must have been able to read Italian.

Most commonly, a deduction is based on a conditional or "If . . . then . . ." statement (although often this statement is tacit). A conditional says that *if* something is true, *then* something else must be true.

In a conditional statement, the part following the *if* is called the **antecedent** (the prefix *ante–* means "before") and the part following the *then* is called the **consequent** (compare *consequence,* meaning "result"). In the example, "a person is able to play an instrument" is the antecedent, and "that person must be able to read music" is the consequent.

A conditional statement also implies that, if the consequent is false, the antecedent must be false:

EXAMPLE 1. If a person can write in Italian, that person must be able to read Italian. 2. Cory cannot read Italian. 3. Therefore, Cory must not be able to write in Italian.

INFERENCES FROM CONDITIONALS

Facts	Implications
Antecedent: true	Consequent: true
Consequent: false	Antecedent: false
Antecedent: false	none*
Consequent: true	none*

*See "Fallacies of Affirming the Antecedent and of Denying the Consequent" in the Language Arts Survey 4.6, "Identifying Faulty Arguments and Propaganda."

4.3 Using Mnemonic Techniques

Remembering involves two steps. First, you have to save the information in your mind, and then you have to find it when you need it. If you had a contract or a letter you wanted to save, you probably wouldn't just toss it into a large filing cabinet with thousands of other pieces of paper: you'd never be able to find it when you needed it. If you spend a little time thinking about why you are saving it, you can save it in a way that makes it easy to find later. For instance, if the letter was from your grandmother, you might put it in a folder labeled "Letters: Personal," or "Letters from Grandma," or "Grandma: Letters," and then file the folder in alphabetical order. Your mind works in somewhat the same way. The better you understand some idea or piece of information, the easier you can find and then retrieve it from your mental filing system.

Mnemonics. A **mnemonic** is an association that aids memorizing. To use a mnemonic, you put together information that you need to remember with information that you can remember easily or that you already know well. The easy-to-remember information helps you remember the information that you pair it with. For instance, you probably learned the alphabet by associating it with an easy-to-remember melody. Mnemonics can use either images or words.

MNEMONICS			
Name of Strategy	**Strategy**	**Information to be Learned**	**Information Easy to Remember**
Embellished Letter	Form an acronym using the first letters of the information to be remembered.	Items in a series, e.g. the colors of the spectrum (red, orange, yellow, green, blue, indigo, violet)	Roy G. Biv
Method of Loci	Imagine a place you know well (e.g., your home). Form an image of each object to be remembered in a particular spot or room in that place.	Items in a series, e.g., the first ten presidents (Washington, Adams, Jefferson, Adams, Madison, Monroe, Jackson, Van Buren, Harrison, Tyler)	Washington is pitcher, Adams is catcher, Jefferson at first base, and so on.
Key Word	Form an image of the items doing something to or with each other.	Associations, e.g., a server at a restaurant must remember that the man in the blue shirt ordered chicken with baked potato.	Bizarre images, e.g., a man is terrified (chicken) of a potato.

Repetition. Merely repeating information over and over is generally a poor way to remember it. If you want to remember something, you should try to become familiar with it and to know it in a variety of ways. However, repetition is an important *part* of memorizing. The more you use or work with some idea or information, the more likely you are to remember how to use it. For instance, you probably know your close friend's phone number without thinking about it, but you probably cannot recall the phone number of a movie theater that you have called only once.

Remembering and Visualizing. Think of a friend with whom you like to spend time. Can you picture him or her in your mind? Take a moment and try.

Often you will want to visualize a person, scene, or object so you can write about it and describe it accurately and vividly. When trying to remember and visualize, you may find it helpful to use reasoning to remind yourself of details. For instance, when you tried to visualize your friend, you may have thought about articles of clothing that he or she typically wears, places where the two of you have gone together, activities that the two of you have done together, or characteristic facial or verbal expressions that he or she uses.

Observing. Think about how differently the following people would observe ancient Mayan ruins: a geologist, an astronomer, a sculptor, a watercolorist, a graphic designer, a structural engineer, a short-story writer, or a high school English teacher. In any situation there is an infinite amount of information; therefore, before you make your observations, you must decide what you will look for. If you have a hypothesis you are testing, decide what evidence might be relevant to proving or disproving it. If you want some material on which to base a character sketch, decide beforehand what types of characters you are interested in. If you are looking for evidence, however, you need to avoid making prejudgments. Be careful that you do not bias your observations by having strong expectations of what you will see.

Usually, you will find it helpful to prepare a chart on which to record your observations.

OBSERVATIONS OF PEOPLE WAITING AT A BUS STOP

Subject	Appearance, Dress	Expressions	Actions	Interactions with Others
Tardy business-person	navy suit, carry-ing briefcase	grimace, glares at others	looks at watch, taps foot impatiently	tells musician to be quiet
Student	casual, baseball cap, wearing backpack	glazed look, sneers, smiles at musician	cracks gum, flips through book	tells business-person to lighten up
Musician	jeans, batik t-shirt, short red hair	smiles at crowd, pained expression during song	takes out guitar, plays, and sings	tries to get crowd's attention, ignores criticism

4.4 Making and Testing Hypotheses

A **hypothesis** is an educated guess about a cause or an effect. When you make a prediction based on a theory, your prediction is a hypothesis. Also, when you observe something and suggest a possible explanation, your explanation is a hypothesis. A hypothesis always needs to be tested against experience. You can test hypotheses by conducting actual experiments, by examining many relevant examples, or by conducting a thought experiment, asking "What if" questions (see 1.10, "Gathering Ideas: Questioning").

Notice that a hypothesis can be disproved by only one counterinstance. However, a hypothesis cannot be proved merely by gathering examples. (see 4.2, "Types of Thinking: Generalizing"). Theories and hypothesis always remain subject to modification in the light of future discoveries.

4.5 Distinguishing Fact and Opinion

It can often prove difficult to distinguish fact from opinion. When evaluating a fact, ask yourself whether it can be proved through direct observation or by checking a reliable source, such as a reference work or an unbiased expert. An opinion is as good as the facts that support it. Some opinions are well supported by facts and can be trusted. Others are not supported by facts and cannot be trusted. The opinion that Mandarin Chinese is the greatest language on Earth is supported by such facts as the number of speakers that it has. However, some might argue that English is the greater language because it is spoken more widely around the globe. Of course, no list of facts would conclusively prove or disprove either opinion.

When you write and speak, express opinions sparingly. Usually, you can make a stronger case by substituting related facts for opinions. For example, instead of saying, "This was a wonderful day," you could say something like, "Today the sun was shining, it was seventy-four degrees outside, I got an *A* on my math test," and so on. When you express an opinion, especially in writing, include facts to back up or support that opinion.

When reading or listening, be critical about the statements that you encounter. Ask yourself, "Is this a fact or an opinion?" If it is a statement of fact, consider whether it can be proved or seems likely. If it is an opinion, consider whether it is supported by facts.

4.6 Identifying Faulty Arguments and Propaganda

A **logical fallacy** is a logical mistake. You commit a fallacy when you make an invalid inference, one that is not warranted by the facts at hand.

It is important to recognize that although statements based on fallacies are groundless, they still can be true, just as wild guesses can sometimes be correct. Also, not every mistake involves a logical fallacy: errors also result from faulty information, lack of information, carelessness, or other problems. In practice, it can be hard to tell when a mistake is a result of faulty logic and when it is a result of something else.

False analogy. An argument by analogy begins by claiming that two things are alike in some way and concludes that they are alike in another way. This type of argument can begin an interesting discussion, but it is not a valid proof. To see why it is fallacious, consider that by using this strategy you could "prove" that everything is identical to everything else.

EXAMPLE "This vacuum cleaner is a red machine, powered by electricity, that picks up dirt. This hair dryer is a red machine, powered by electricity. Therefore, it picks up dirt."

ANALYSIS The similarities between the two objects do not guarantee similarity in function.

Circularity. A circular argument is one that assumes the truth of the proposition that it is intended to prove. This type of argument is also called **begging the question.** A common type of circular argument merely restates an assumption in different words. Circular arguments can "prove" anything at all, and so are obviously fallacious.

EXAMPLE "I liked seeing this movie a lot because I really enjoyed it and thought it was entertaining."

ANALYSIS The two "reasons" the speaker gives for liking the movie are just different ways of saying that the speaker liked the movie.

Post hoc (ergo) propter hoc. If one event causes another, the cause always comes before the effect. The *post hoc* fallacy is to assume, simply because one event occurred *after* another, that the first event *caused* the second. This fallacy confuses consequence with sequence, causation with correlation.

EXAMPLE "As the cost of higher education increases, school library resources have decreased. Let's cut the cost of education and get our school libraries up to par."

ANALYSIS The author confuses correlation with causation. No reasoning has been offered to explain why the resources of the school libraries have diminished. It may or may not have to do with the increasing cost of higher education. In either case, no explanation is offered as to why cuts in the costs of higher education will result in increased library resources.

Fallacies of affirming the antecedent and of denying the consequent. A **conditional** or "If . . . then . . ." statement says that *if* something—the **antecedent**—is true *then* something else—the **consequent**—must be true. See 4.2, "Types of Thinking: Deducing." As the chart there shows, if the consequent is true, nothing is implied about the antecedent.

EXAMPLE The more time and effort a person spends learning to ski, the more skilled a skier that person will be. What can you conclude about the practice habits of someone who skis poorly?

ANALYSIS Not much. There are many elements involved in mastering a skill, and practice is only one of them. To infer that a person does not ski well because that person does not practice often would be fallacious.

As the chart also shows, if the antecedent is false, nothing is implied about the consequent.

EXAMPLE The more time and effort a person spends learning to ski, the more skilled a skier that person will be. What can you conclude about the performance of someone who does not spend much time or effort learning to ski?

ANALYSIS Again, not much. You can conclude that that person could do better. However, you cannot conclude that that person skis poorly. Again, there are many factors involved in performance. Perhaps the person skis well without working hard at it because he or she has a natural ability to ski or is very gifted in sports involving balance.

Fallacies of composition and decomposition. If a whole has a certain quality, it does not follow that each part of that whole has that quality on its own. To assume that it does is to commit the fallacy of decomposition.

EXAMPLE "My sister is on our debate team; our team was voted worst in the state during the state school competition, so my sister is one of the worst student debaters in the state."

ANALYSIS The team might be poor because of the sister, or it may be bad because of the other debaters. Perhaps they are all average debaters led by a poor coach. The sister may even be one of the best debaters in the state.

Likewise, it is fallacious to argue that because some parts have a certain quality, whatever they are parts of must also have that quality. This is the fallacy of composition.

EXAMPLE "Each line in my poem is perfect. Therefore, my poem is perfect."

ANALYSIS A good poem is more than just a number of good lines. The lines must be organized and related in certain ways. Poems have **holistic** properties—properties that pertain to the whole.

Non sequitur. A ***non sequitur*** is a conclusion that simply does not follow from the reasons given and may have nothing to do with them.

EXAMPLE Stephen King is obviously the best fiction writer because he uses the most believable characters and actual locations.

ANALYSIS To say that some person (or thing) is the best is to say that it is better than all of his or her (or its) competitors. In the example, no competitors are mentioned; therefore, the conclusion does not follow.

Ad hominem. An argument that attacks or defends a person instead of the point at issue is known as an ***argumentum ad hominem*** (literally, "argument to the person"). Whether Tanya Hernandez is a good or bad or a smart or dull person, whether she is a liberal or a conservative or a Communist, or even whether she is honest or dishonest, does not determine the truth of what she says. To see this, consider that since everybody is imperfect in some way, you could use *ad hominem* arguments to "prove" that everything ever said must be false; but since everybody has some good quality, you could also "prove" that everything ever said must be true.

EXAMPLE "My soccer coach was dismissed from her last position. Her opinions on the performance of the team are misguided and untrue."

ANALYSIS Nothing that is said here has any bearing on whether the coach's opinions are sound. The coach's opinions have not been attacked directly, let alone disproved.

False dichotomy. To set up a **false dichotomy** is to assume that there are only two sides to an issue. This type of argument is also called an "either/or" argument. An argument from false dichotomy becomes propagandistic when it takes a form such as "Anyone who's not for me is against me."

EXAMPLE "Either you like spinach or you don't."

ANALYSIS This is a false dichotomy. It assumes that there are only two possibilities, which is false. You may like spinach in certain dishes but dislike it plain.

As always, showing that an argument is faulty shows that the "conclusion" is not proven, but it does not prove that the conclusion is false.

Hasty generalization. To **generalize** is to make a general or universal claim based on some particular observations (see 4.2, "Types of Thinking: Generalizing"). Generalizations based on too few examples are illegitimate.

EXAMPLE "I saw a musical once. They're boring."

ANALYSIS Musicals differ greatly from one another. One cannot make a conclusion about all musicals based on seeing just one of them.

Equivocation. An **equivocation** is a statement that is meant to be ambiguous and to mislead because of its ambiguity. Equivocation creates the appearance of a logical connection between the reasons and the conclusion where there is no logical connection; therefore, an argument that equivocates is a *non sequitur.*

EXAMPLE "The business of government is business."

ANALYSIS This clever phrase may appear self-evident, but the appearance belies an equivocation. The term *business* is used in the first instance with the meaning "proper responsibility or concern" and in the second instance with the meaning "industry and commerce."

Vague terms. Most of the time people do not speak as precisely as they could. In particular, people use terms of approval and disapproval in a vague fashion. Very rarely do people specify exactly what they mean by *good, wrong, desirable, harmful,* and so on. This practice allows people to agree on practical issues and decisions without first agreeing on every basic issue of politics, morality, and taste. It also affords opportunity for misunderstandings.

EXAMPLE "I meant no wrong. I regret giving my brother the high-paying job for which he was underqualified, and he has resigned."

ANALYSIS Both *meant* and *regret* are vague terms in this example. Is the speaker saying that what she did was not wrong; or that she did not know it was wrong; or that, although she may have known it was wrong, she was not thinking about whether it was wrong at the time she acted? Does the speaker regret the action because she thinks it was morally wrong; or because it was illegal; or because, having been discovered, the action has jeopardized her political career?

Propaganda Techniques. You already know that you cannot believe everything you read. How can you decide what is believable? You must rely on your knowledge and your critical-thinking abilities. Propaganda is misleading language that tries to lead the reader or listener into a logical mistake by appealing to the emotions. It may work on you if you are not careful to avoid logical fallacies. You can spot the propagandists if you are on your toes *and* if you know what to look for.

Bandwagon. Often, people do not want to feel different from others: they want to feel "hip" and up-to-date; and they don't want to miss out on anything. Propaganda that tries to make people worry about being unique or that appeals to the desire to be part of the crowd is known as **bandwagon appeal.**

EXAMPLE "Everybody's lining up to go to the spectacular year-end sale. Get down here soon, or you'll miss the greatest shopping opportunity of the year."

ANALYSIS Ask yourself, "If I didn't go, would I be missing anything important? If it were important, could I get it somewhere else or at a different time? Won't somebody make more of it if it's so popular? Is is worth it to me to stand in that line behind 'everybody'?" Then tell yourself, "I'm somebody, and I'm not there. I have worthwhile things to do, so it doesn't matter if I never find out what these people are doing."

Transfer. Transfer relies on guilt or honor by association. A television commercial shows a famous athlete using a camera. A billboard shows a famous fashion model wearing a pair of jeans with a prominent label. A newspaper photograph shows a political candidate shaking hands and laughing with a movie star. In each instance, the image has been set up in the hope that your good feeling about someone—the athlete, the model, or the movie star—will **transfer** to or rub off on someone or something else—the camera, the jeans, or the politician. No reasons are even offered: your rationality is bypassed.

False testimonial. A **testimonial** is a statement endorsing a person, object, or idea. Advertisers and politicians often solicit and pay celebrities to endorse them or their products. When experts offer testimonials without compensation, it is wise to listen.

EXAMPLE "Joyce Musman endorses this environmental legislation. It's good for our community."

ANALYSIS Joyce Musman may be a famous actor, director, or a renowned writer. However, none of this provides a reason to follow her opinion on environmental legislation. If you knew that she was also an environmental biologist, you would have reason to give her opinion some thought.

Loaded words. Depending on word choice, descriptions of the same person, thing, or event can be laden with either positive, negative, or neutral associations. (See the entries *connotation* and *denotation* in the Handbook of Literary Terms.) A word may have strongly positive, strongly negative, or relatively neutral connotations. Using words with strong connotations can be a way to sway opinion without offering reasons.

EXAMPLE 1 "Field's program directs tax dollars to provide food and medical care for the needy."

EXAMPLE 2 "Field's program is socialism: it takes from hard-working taxpayers and gives to freeloaders and bums."

ANALYSIS The word *socialism* has strongly negative connotations for many Americans. *Socialism* is a loaded word. The expressions the *needy, hard-working taxpayers, freeloaders,* and *bums* are loaded words also. The first two expressions seem to suggest that these people deserve sympathy, while the second two expressions seem to suggest that these people deserve scorn.

Character assassination. This is a form of *ad hominem* argument that tries to persuade by attacking the opponent's character.

EXAMPLE "Ms. Feaps is a staunchy, old, indecisive tyrant. Don't believe her when she says there aren't any funds for medical supplies."

ANALYSIS There may or may not be funds for medical supplies. Their existence or absence is independent of Ms. Feaps's character.

Bias charges. Another form of *ad hominem* argument attacks a speaker's neutrality. Of course, any person who has a personal stake in an issue has a motive to lie or distort the facts in his or her favor. This does not mean that every such person is guilty of distortion. Furthermore, a person who has no personal stake in an issue is not likely to be involved in an argument about it. That a person may be biased is a good reason for scrutinizing what that person says but is not a sufficient reason for assuming it to be false.

EXAMPLE "Ignore Representative Dugan. He opposes this campaign reform law only because this reform would cut back funds for future campaigns."

ANALYSIS The argument does not give a reason to support the proposed law, nor does it address Dugan's arguments against the law. The argument is not to the point.

READING SKILLS

4.7 Reading Rates

Depending on your purposes in reading, you may choose among three techniques.

READING RATES		
Technique	**Purpose**	**Tips**
Scanning	Finding specific information quickly	Look for key words; look at chapter and part headings.
Skimming	Getting a general idea of the content of a piece	Ask questions; look at introductions; look at chapter and part headings.
Slow and Careful Reading	Learning and enjoyment	Read actively.

Scanning

Scanning is very quickly looking through a piece of writing to find some particular information that you want. On Monday morning you might scan the newspaper to find out how the Cardinals did on Sunday. You would first scan for the box scores, ignoring the headlines, articles, and advertisements. Once you found the box scores, you would scan for the score you want, ignoring all the other scores.

Scanning is used locate information you want. You will probably want to scan reference and other works when you are researching a paper or project. You will also probably scan reading selections to find answers for written exercises or to find quotations or other support for your opinions.

To scan, pick out a few key words to look for. Capitalized words, such as names, are good words to scan for, because capital letters are easily noticed on a page. Glance quickly down each page, one page at a time, looking for those key words. When you find a key word, stop scanning and begin reading carefully to gather the information.

Skimming

Skimming is glancing quickly through a piece of writing to get a general idea of it. Many people use skimming when they have insufficient time to do their work. A prudent person will avoid procrastinating and poor planning, but sometimes there is more work than time to do it. When you do research, you will use skimming efficiently to examine books or articles to determine whether they are of potential use or interest to you. You might also use skimming as a technique in previewing your reading (see 4.18, "Previewing Your Reading") or in reviewing your reading before taking a test or planning an essay.

QUESTIONS FOR SKIMMING

- What is this piece of writing about?
- What does the author say about it?
- What evidence or support is given?

You will skim more effectively if you hold in mind the few questions above.

To skim, first find and read the title of the piece and any chapter and section titles until you settle on an answer to the first question. Start reading from the beginning of the piece until you find a general answer to the second question. Then glance at any other headings or other material in distinguishing type to fill out your idea of the author's views and to get an answer to the third question. Last, look rather closely at the first few and the last few paragraphs of each section.

Slow and Careful Reading

When you are reading carefully, you will go more slowly because you will be more thorough. If you come across words you do not know, you will look them up in a dictionary. You will think about the reasons the author gives and the quality of her or his evidence. You will try to imagine what it would be like to know the characters or to be them. You will think of related issues and consider what the author would think about them. You will try to apply the author's ideas to other situations, perhaps situations in your own life. You will ask questions and expect the author to answer them. You will, as some have said, engage in a conversation with the author.

4.8 Previewing Your Reading

Thinking about what you will read before you begin can help you read more productively. You may ask, "How can I think about what I am going to read if I haven't read it yet?" There are a number of helpful **previewing** activities that will help you once you begin reading *per se.*

PREVIEWING ACTIVITIES	
1. **Read** the title.	**Ask:** What is the piece about? What seems to be the author's attitude toward it?
2. **Skim** the first paragraph(s).	**Ask:** What is the main point of the piece?
3. **Skim** the last paragraph(s) (but not if the piece to be read is a work of literature).	**Ask:** What is the author's conclusion?
4. **Read** the headings.	**Ask:** What are the main points?
5. **Ask:** Do all the parts seem to fit together? Do I have any unresolved questions?	

4.9 Reading Actively

Reading actively does not mean reading fast, nor does it mean fidgeting in your chair or pacing while you read. Reading actively means thinking about what you are reading. Reading actively is a way to increase reading interest and comprehension.

Responding to Your Reading

Keep your journal next to you as you read, and make notes of your initial reactions to what you are reading. Ask yourself these questions after each paragraph or section:

- "In what I've just read, what in particular do I find convincing or unconvincing?"
- "How does what I've just read make me feel? What about it in particular makes me feel that way?"

Freely explore your feelings. You may want to wait until after you have finished reading to analyze and evaluate these feelings.

Questioning

Asking yourself questions as you read keeps your mind more active and helps you process what you are reading. You can ask questions based on the 5*W*s and *H*: Who, what, where, when, why, and how.

When you are reading this book, you can use the Guided Reading questions and the Responding to the Selection questions in addition to your own questions.

TYPES OF READER RESPONSE QUESTIONS	
Who?	• Questions about characters or persons in the text • Questions about the author
What?	• Questions about objects and events
Where?	• Questions about location
When?	• Questions about sequence • Questions about time period
Why?	• Questions about motivation • Questions about reasoning and evidence
How?	• Questions about possibilities • Questions about actions

Predicting

As you read, try to guess what will come next. Ask yourself why you think this.

Summarizing

Summarizing is simplifying a statement into a briefer statement of the main points. Summarizing helps you understand what you have read by forcing you to think about which points are important and which are not. Summarizing in your own words also helps you to remember. Be careful to state only the main points and not to inject your own opinions into your summary.

Identifying Main Ideas

In the simplest nonfiction writing, there is one main idea, which is stated clearly in the introduction in a thesis statement and restated in the conclusion. Likewise, the main idea of a paragraph is often stated in a topic sentence. Perhaps most of the writing you see, including some of the most excellent writing, will not be like this. Very often, as in much irony and satire, a main idea is not directly stated at all and must be inferred by the reader.

Identifying Relationships

You can understand better what you are reading if you can discover the writer's plan. Passages that show the writer's ordering scheme—e.g., chronological order or comparison-and-contrast order—provide important clues to interpreting the writer's meaning. More generally, you should pay special attention to any passages that indicate relationships between people, things, or ideas. Make notes of these relationships.

Making Inferences

Making inferences is drawing conclusions and finding implications by putting together facts to figure out something that is not explicitly stated. Making inferences is an important part of understanding what you read. In nonfiction works, an author will often leave her or his conclusion unstated, so it is up to you to infer (and evaluate, of course) the author's intended conclusion. Furthermore, you can only discover that an author's argument is flawed if you can make an inference that the author overlooked.

Making inferences is also important in reading works of fiction. You often need to make inferences from descriptions and context in order to understand the characters' actions and motivations. For instance, if one character says something that contradicts something said earlier by a different character, you need to make inferences to determine what's going on: Is one of them lying, or merely mistaken? Which one? (On drawing conclusions, see 4.2, "Types of Thinking: Deducing.")

4.10 Reading Charts and Graphs

Writers use charts and graphs to present ideas and information visually and compactly. The information necessary for reading the chart or graph is given in the title, headings, and other labels surrounding the graphic.

Pie charts. A **pie chart** is used primarily to depict relative proportions or shares in relation to a whole. It shows how different amounts **compare** to each other.

The whole pie represents all of something. In the following example, the pie represents an American football team's total gained yardage: 6,222 yards. Each piece of the pie represents a portion of that whole. In this example, the portions compare the yardage gained from passing and the yardage gained from running. The size of the piece represents its share. In this example, running has a two-thirds share, twice as much as passing. The pie chart visually shows this relationship.

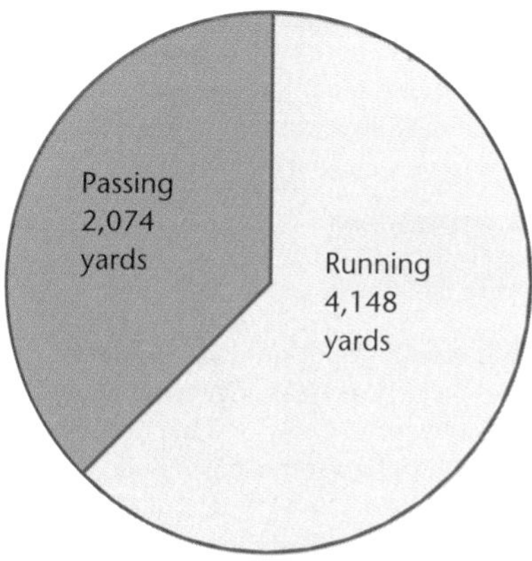

Bar graphs. The length of each bar in a **bar graph** represents an absolute quantity of something. In the following graph, each bar represents the number of syntactical errors of a specific type made by a student on a diagnostic test. Each student's scores are grouped, making it obvious right away how well each student did in relation to every other. Bar graphs show relative quantities, but unlike pie charts they do not depict relation to a whole.

Designers sometimes distort bar graphs in various ways to make them more visually interesting. You should be aware that these design changes often make the graphs' appearance misleading. Read and think carefully before coming to any conclusions.

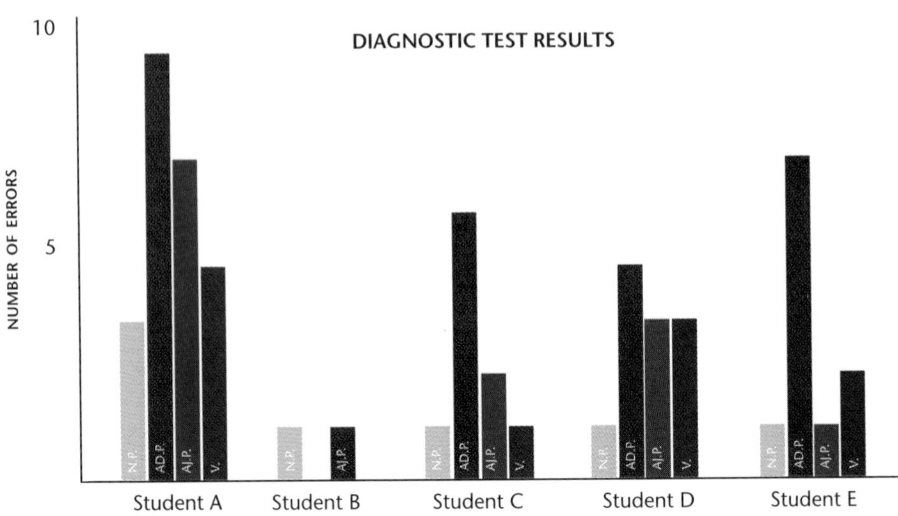

Key N.P. = noun phrase; AD.P. = adverb phrase; AJ.P. = adjective phrase; V. = verbals

Line graphs. A **line graph** is little more than a bar graph with the bars removed and their top points connected. The line shows a continuous pattern or trend. A line chart could be used to show the number of errors a given student made over time in a series of tests.

RESEARCH SKILLS

Conducting **research** means looking for ideas and information. Research is a combination of detective work, puzzle solving, and learning. When you research, you start with a more-or-less vague idea of what you want to know or a hypothesis you want to prove. This starts you on a trail. You follow the trail to find some information and then use this information to find other information, and so on.

You probably already know that a library is essentially a storehouse of sources of ideas and information. All this information and all these ideas are linked in a number of different ways. The following sections will teach you some tricks and tools that you can use to navigate these linkages and find the trail to the ideas and information you want.

4.11 The Classification of Library Materials

Each book in a library is assigned a unique number, called a **call number.** The call number is printed on the **spine** (edge) of each book. The numbers serve to classify books as well as to help the library keep track of them.

Libraries commonly use one of two systems for classifying books. Most school and public libraries use the **Dewey Decimal System**. Most college libraries use the **Library of Congress Classification System** (known as the LC system).

THE DEWEY DECIMAL SYSTEM

Call Numbers	Subjects[1]
000–099	Reference and General Works
100–199	Philosophy, Psychology
200–299	Religion
300–399	Social Studies
400–499	Language
500–599	Science, Mathematics
600–699	Technology
700–799	Arts
800–899	Literature
900–999	History, Geography, Biography[2]

1. The Dewey system does not number fiction. Works of fiction are arranged alphabetically by author.
2. Biographies (920s) are arranged alphabetically by subject.

THE LIBRARY OF CONGRESS SYSTEM

Call Letters	Subjects
A	Reference and General Works
B–BJ	Philosophy, Psychology
BK–BX	Religion
C–DF	History
G	Geography, Autobiography, Recreation
H	Social Sciences
J	Political Science
K	Law
L	Education
M	Music
N	Fine Arts
P	Language, Literature
Q	Science, Mathematics
R	Medicine
S	Agriculture
T	Technology
U	Military Science
V	Naval Science
Z	Bibliography, Library Science

In both systems, the first part of the call number is used to categorize books by subject. Since the call number begins with the subject code, and since books are placed on the shelves in call number order, this means that books on similar subjects can be found next to each other on the shelf. How convenient!

You can see that only general subjects are listed in the charts. Each system has a way to specify further a book's subject. In one Dewey system library, for instance, A. W. Marlow's *The Early American Furnituremaker's Manual* is 684.1 / M. The numbers 600–699 span technology. Within that class, 684 identifies books on furniture making. The subject can be further specified by adding numbers after the decimal point.

In another example, in the LC system, BJ identifies the more specific area of ethics and etiquette within the general area of philosophy, psychology, and religion (B). Further, BJ 1012 identifies the precise topic within that area (here, philosophical ethical theory). There may even be an additional identifying number, beginning with a decimal point, that further narrows the subject.

The second part of the call number is used to distinguish and identify individual books on the same subject. In the Dewey system, the first one to three letters of the author's last name can be added on the line below the subject identifier, as with the *M* in the furniture book. In the LC system, the call numbers for two books might be BJ 1012/.C95/1990 and BJ 1012/.P24/1992, for example. The letter after the decimal is the author's last initial, and the following two digits uniquely identify the author. The last four numbers identify the year of publication.

Locating materials in the library. Besides books, libraries house many types of publications, including magazines, academic and professional journals, newspapers, audio and video recordings, microfiche and microfilm, and government documents. Commonly, each of these types of materials is stored in a distinct place in the library and has its own classification system. For instance, government documents have their own numbering system and their own catalog (see 4.12 and 4.13, "Using Search Tools" and "Using the Card Catalog"). Recordings also usually have a separate catalog. Many libraries have viewing and listening equipment available for use in the library, and some will allow you to borrow the equipment with your library card.

If you know the call number of the book you want, or if you know the subject classification number (Dewey or LC), you can go to the bookshelves, or **stacks,** and get the book or browse through books nearby. At a large library, look for a sign or notice that lists the locations of the various call numbers. There may be a "map" of the library with the call numbers located on it. These signs are usually posted in the card catalog area, near the circulation (check-out and check-in) desk, or on the doors to the stacks.

At some libraries, the public is not permitted into the stacks. If you want to look at a book, you must ask a librarian to get it for you by writing its call number on a request slip.

4.12 Using Search Tools

All the books in a library are listed in the library's **catalog.** If your library has one of the many types of computerized catalogs, you will need to learn how to use the particular system it has. At most libraries, signs or flyers explain how to use the system, and the computer keys are labeled. There is also usually a "help" button. Following is an example of what you will find on the screen when using the computerized catalog system:

Author info.	Giere, Mark A., 1899-1974
Title	On Writing and Reading Literature
Date of pub.	1970
Publisher	Harper Ferry
LC Call no.	LC PE3412.K95 1970
ISBN no.	ISBN 0465286480
No. of pages	xvi, 241 p.
Page size, cover material	22 cm., pap
Copyright info.	c1963 Mark Giere, c1970 Jamison Giere
Index page nos.	Index p.238-241
Supplementary sections	Hist. Note, App., List of Authors Quoted
Subject	Writing and Reading Literature and Language Skills

Generally, you are given a choice of searching by author, title, subject, or key words. See the chart below for tips on searching.

When you search by subject on computer, using the correct subject head is crucial. Each library chooses the names of the subjects it uses from a special list. Many libraries use the list of subjects published by the Library of Congress, but others use different lists. If you can find nothing on your subject, the library probably uses a different word or phrase than you did to identify your subject. For instance, you will not find any books if you look up "history of marriage" because the library calls that subject "marriage: history." Before you look for books on a subject, check the list to see what wording your library uses. The list will help you find what you want by providing **cross-references.** In the example above, when you looked under "history of marriage" in the subject list, you may have found a note saying: "history of marriage. *See* marriage: history."

When typing your entry, double check your spelling since the computer cannot compensate for spelling errors (however, capitalization does not matter).

Once you get a list of books, you have the choice of getting more ideas and information about specific books in the list, narrowing the list with another search, scrolling up or down to see other titles, or starting over. Use the results of your search to help you search better. For example, if you turn up a book that seems to be just what you are looking for, check its key words and subjects, and use those in new searches.

Write down the call numbers of each book you want and head for the shelves (see 4.11, "The Classification of Library Materials").

COMPUTERIZED CATALOG SEARCHES

Search by . . .	Example	
author	gould, stephen j	(the) mismeasure of man

continued

ESSENTIAL SKILLS: STUDY AND RESEARCH

COMPUTERIZED CATALOG SEARCHES (CONT.)		
Search by . . .	**Example**	**Hints**
title	(the) mismeasure of man	Omit articles such as *a, an,* or *the* at the beginning of titles.
subject	intelligence tests; ability-testing	Use the list of subjects provided by the library.
keywords	darwin; intelligence; craniology	Use related topics if you can't find anything in your subject.

Interlibrary Loan. Your borrowing privileges at your local library may allow you to obtain books and articles from other libraries through an interlibrary loan. In many libraries, the computerized catalog covers the collections of several libraries that participate in a local library network or consortium. The catalog will tell you which library holds the book you want. If your book is in a different library, you will need to fill out a request slip and give it to your librarian. You may wait from one day up to a few weeks for your request to be filled.

4.13 Using the Card Catalog

The library's catalog contains basic information about each book in the library. If the library uses a **card catalog**, the information is typed on paper cards. The cards are arranged alphabetically in drawers. For each book there is a **title card**, one **author card** for each author, and at least one **subject card.** All of these cards give the book's title, author, and call number. Hence, you have a variety of ways to find each book; you can search by author, title, or subject (see the Language Arts Survey 4.12, "Using Search Tools," for tips on how to search).

AN AUTHOR CARD

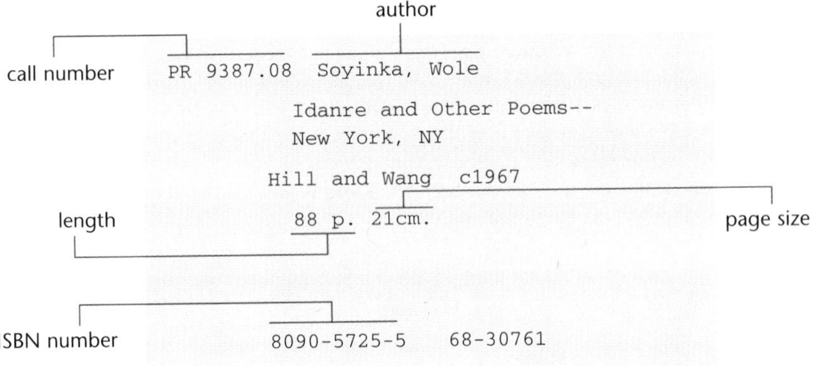

A TITLE CARD

```
PR      Idanre and Other Poems
9387.9  Soyinka, Wole
         Idanre and Other Poems--New York,
         NY
       Hill and Wang. c1967
         88 p.  :21cm.

        8090-5725-5  68-30761
```

A SUBJECT CARD

```
                LITERATURE
PR      Soyinka, Wole
9387.9
         Idanre and Other Poems--New York,
         NY
       Hill and Wang. c1967
         88 p.  :21cm.

        8090-5725-5  68-30761
```

If you cannot find what you want in the catalog, ask the librarian whether your library can get books from other libraries through an interlibrary loan. Otherwise, write down the call numbers of each book you want, and head for the shelves.

Many libraries are in the process of changing, or have completed the change, from paper card catalogs to computerized catalogs. Often you may need to search in *both* the computer system—for new books—*and* the card catalog—for older books—to find everything the library has on your topic (see 4.12, "Using Search Tools").

4.14 Using Reference Works

No matter what your interest, the chances are excellent that somebody has written about it. Human beings have been collecting and sharing knowledge for thousands of years. Probably, most of what you want to know can be found in one or more **reference works,** works in which knowledge is compiled and organized for easy access. Some reference works, such as the library catalog and indexes, are designed to help you find other works that contain the ideas and information you want. Other reference works contain the ideas and information themselves. For the most part, current reference works cannot be checked out of the library.

Almanacs and **Yearbooks.** An almanac contains statistics and lists of all sorts, such as lists and biographies of important inventors, authors, artists, celebrities, etc.; lists of and statistics about wars, battles, and political figures and events; sports records and achievements; lists of award-winners (e.g., Nobel prize, Pulitzer prize, Oscars); lists of major colleges, museums, and libraries; and statistics and other information about weather and the fifty states. To find information in an almanac, use the index.

Most almanacs also contain a summary of major events that occurred in the previous year. This information is available in more detail in a yearbook, which is published separately, as your high school yearbook is. Some yearbooks are published by encyclopedia publishers and are shelved with the encyclopedias.

Atlases. An atlas is primarily a collection of maps, but each atlas has its own special focus and contains information in addition to maps. Depending on the focus of the atlas, the maps may show natural features (e.g., mountains, rivers, natural resources), developed features (e.g., roads, bridges, airports), political features (e.g., counties, cities), or other geographic information (e.g., land use, weather, population). A **historical atlas** contains maps depicting places as they used to be and enables you to trace various historical developments. A key feature of many atlases is the gazetteer, which is an index listing every item located on the maps.

Encyclopedias. An encyclopedia is meant to provide a survey of knowledge. General encyclopedias, such as *World Book, Compton's,* or *Britannica,* contain information on almost every topic imaginable. Specialized encyclopedias, such as *The Oxford Companion to English Literature* or *Benet's Readers' Encyclopedia,* contain information on more narrowly defined subjects. Different topics are treated in articles, which are arranged alphabetically by topic.

On your first try, you may find nothing on your topic. Don't worry. Most likely, the editors have used a different word or phrase to identify your subject. Use the index to find out which articles cover the information you want. Using the index also ensures that you do not overlook ideas and information when your topic is treated in more than one article. The index of a multivolume encyclopedia is found in one or two separate volumes.

Encyclopedias are excellent first sources, because they provide an outline and overview of just about anything you could want to know about. Since an encyclopedia article is a survey article, you are liable to want more information than it provides. Most encyclopedias supply a list of additional sources of information at the end of each article.

Indexes. An index is an alphabetical directory to published information and ideas. Each index covers a limited range of publications. Many individual periodicals also publish their own indexes from time to time. *The Readers' Guide to Periodical Literature* is a comprehensive index to nearly all of the popular weekly, monthly, and quarterly publications. Many libraries subscribe to the *New York Times Index* because the *New York Times* newspaper covers national and world news. It has been published nearly continuously since 1851 and is available on microfilm. The *Short Story Index* and the *Play Index* list short stories and plays, respectively, that have been published in collected volumes.

Periodicals. Magazines, daily newspapers, specialized newspapers, trade journals, and professional journals are among the publications received by libraries on a regular and periodic basis. Because they are published frequently and quickly, periodicals are excellent sources for the latest news and information. On the other hand, information in periodicals is less likely to have been evaluated carefully by experts.

Current issues are usually available in a reading room in the library. Recent issues may be stored beneath or behind the current issue. If the library retains older issues, these are either bound and stored in the stacks or copied onto microfilm or microfiche.

Other reference works. In addition to the sources already mentioned, the reference section of your library probably has collections of quotations (e.g., *Bartlett's Familiar Quotations*), biographies (e.g., *Contemporary Authors, Dictionary of American Biography, Who's Who*), book reviews (e.g., *Book Review Digest*), state and local laws, telephone directories, business directories, guidebooks and manuals, catalogs and admissions information from colleges and universities, and many other materials.

4.15 Using Dictionaries

Dictionaries provide much more information about words than just their spellings and definitions.

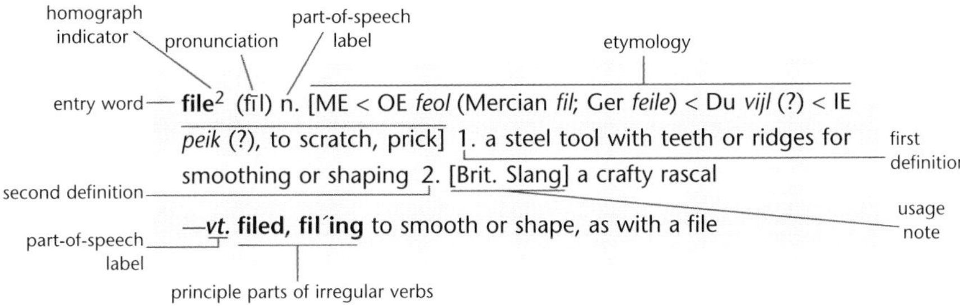

Immediately following the entry word is the **pronunciation,** usually in parentheses, as in the example here. You can find a complete key to pronunciation symbols by looking in the dictionary table of contents. In some dictionaries, a simplified key for quick reference is at the bottom of each page.

A word's part-of-speech label tells the ways in which a word can be used. In the example, the letter *n.* following the pronunciation shows that the word is used as a noun. Later in the entry, the dash followed by *vt.* shows that the word can also be used as a transitive verb. If you glance through a dictionary, you will notice that many words can be used in more than one way.

An etymology is a word's history. In most cases, the etymology is summarized in the entry. (When a word is a compound or is a variation on another word, a cross-reference is provided to the entry containing the etymology). In the example, *file* comes from a Middle English (ME) word *file*, which came from an Old English (OE) word *feol*, which may have come from a Dutch (Du) word *vijl*, which may have come from an Indo-European (IE) word, *peik*, meaning "to scratch or prick."

The definitions tell the different meanings the word can take. When a word can be used with more than one meaning, the different definitions are numbered. (There are two definitions for *file* in the sample entry.) When a word can be used as different parts of speech, the definitions follow each part-of-speech label. (A definition for *file* used as a transitive verb is provided in the sample.) However, when two words are homographs—i.e., have the same spelling but different etymologies and meanings, such as *can* (verb) and *can* (noun)—the words are listed as separate entries. In the sample entry, the superscript *2* after the entry word shows that *file* is a homograph.

Usage notes—such as "slang," "colloquial," or "technical"—describe any nonstandard usages. In the sample, *file* used with the second definition is primarily a British slang word.

If the word were common in any idiomatic phrases, these phrases would be defined at the end of the entry. Here, too, would be listed other forms based on the word (none are listed for *file*).

4.16 Using Thesauruses

A thesaurus is a reference book that groups words with similar meanings. A thesaurus can help you find exact synonyms, related words, and antonyms. It can be useful when you have a word that means almost but not quite what you want, or when you have used a word so many times that it is becoming noticeable and tiresome. You might also enjoy browsing in a thesaurus and contemplating the subtle differences among words in an entry.

There are two types of thesaurus. A dictionary-type thesaurus is organized alphabetically. If the word you look up is an entry word, related words will be listed beneath it. If it is not an entry word, you should find a cross-reference to an entry word (or else the thesaurus does not recognize your word). Subheadings beneath each entry word identify different meanings or word forms. At the end of the entry is a list of antonyms.

Roget's Thesaurus is organized by idea rather than alphabetically. Pierre Roget tried to devise a system to categorize all existence and ideas. He used his categories as headings, such as *Thought* or *Measurement,* under which he grouped words with similar or related meanings. To this he added an index. To use *Roget's Thesaurus,* look up your word in the index in the back part of the book. Beneath it you will find a number of related words. Choose the related word whose meaning is closest to what you want. (Of course, if the related word *is* the word you want, you're done.) Note that the numbers listed in this section are not page numbers; they refer to a section and subsection in the first part of the book.

Roget's Thesaurus may appear complicated at first, but it is an interesting and useful tool once you get used to it.

4.17 Computer-Assisted Research

Online Research

With a computer and a modem you can connect to a variety of sources of information. If you, your school, or your library subscribes to an online service, you probably have access to current news, online encyclopedias, abstracts of periodicals and government documents, homework and studying assistance, online courses, and research services. You may also be able to use the service to connect to the Library of Congress, other libraries and museums, and the Internet, which allows you to connect to universities, libraries, businesses, individuals, and government agencies all around the world. Your school may also be connected to a special education network, such as TENET (Texas Education Network). Find out from your school or public librarian if you can use these services.

CD-ROM and Other Computer Media

A CD-ROM database works just like an online database. The difference is that you retrieve the information directly from a CD instead of working through a network. Your library may have a collection of CDs that you, or in some cases the librarian only, can insert into the computer.

The Internet

The Internet is a valuable way to connect and communicate with a variety of resources around the globe. Most businesses, schools, and organizations have an Internet address through which people can inquire about information, communicate about projects, and pose questions regarding that business or organization. Web sites are also becoming more popular among businesses and organizations as well as among individual computer users. Web sites are specific areas containing information about a particular subject, business, or organization. There are a number of different tools or applications that have been designed to help you navigate to different sites. Most of these tools allow you to search by subject and by key word. For example, if you were to type in the subject "college admissions," you might get a listing of the Web sites of admissions offices at colleges and universities all over the world. Furthermore, you might also get a listing of the Web sites created by individuals much like yourself, who want to share insights on getting into a college or university, choosing a school, or some matter pertaining to admissions.

4.18 Other Sources of Information

Vertical files. Besides books and periodicals, libraries collect other sources of information, such as pamphlets, brochures, maps, clippings, photographs, and posters. These items are not cataloged. They are stored in folders in filing cabinets. You can look through the files to see if they include anything on your topic.

Organizations and associations. Local businesses, business groups, religious organizations, environmental groups, political parties and organizations, lobbying groups, charities, volunteer and service organizations, and professional societies are groups of people and/or companies who share interests and concerns. Most are anxious to provide information on topics of concern to them. Since many of these groups strongly advocate a particular point of view, their information is liable to be incomplete, one-sided, or even misleading.

Community institutions such as museums, art galleries, historical societies, orchestras and symphonies, dance troupes, other performing arts groups, and colleges can be good sources of ideas and information on certain topics.

Information about many of these groups is available in the *Encyclopedia of Associations*. You can find names and addresses of local groups in your local telephone listings.

Experts. In your community or in nearby communities, someone may have extensive knowledge of your topic. Someone may have explored your topic through work or recreation and may have learned a great deal about it. Also consider that professionals such as lawyers, doctors, engineers, and college professors have spent several years beyond college studying their specialized subject. Many of these people are glad to have an opportunity to share their knowledge and experience with students and others.

If you don't know anyone who knows about your topic, you can look in the phone book. Better still, ask your teachers, parents, friends, and relatives if they know someone who might help you. Ask your contact if he or she can arrange an interview, or arrange an interview yourself by calling the person directly (see 1.10, "Gathering Ideas: Interviewing").

Before you contact someone for assistance, remind yourself that you are requesting a favor. Prepare before approaching people so they do not feel that you are wasting their time. Be as specific as possible about what your project is and what you would like them to do for you. Don't take advantage of others' generosity by asking for too much. You can find out a great deal in fifteen to twenty minutes. Remember to thank the person.

4.19 Evaluating Sources

As you conduct your research, you will soon realize that you cannot read everything that has been written on your topic. You should also remind yourself that you cannot simply believe everything you read. To conduct your research efficiently, you need to evaluate your sources and set priorities among them. Ideally, a source will be . . .

- **Unbiased.** All authors take a personal interest in their subject. However, when an author has a personal stake in what people think about a subject, that author may withhold or distort information. Investigate the author's background to see if she or he is liable to be biased. Using loaded language and overlooking obvious counter-arguments are signs that an author is biased.
- **Authoritative.** An authoritative source is one that is reliable and trustworthy. An author's reputation, especially her or his reputation among others who conduct research in the same field, is a sign of authoritativeness. Likewise, periodicals and publishers acquire reputations for careful and responsible editing and research, or for shoddiness.
- **Timely.** In some subjects the state of knowledge is expanding and changing very rapidly. An astronomy text published last year may already be out of date. In other fields—for instance, algebra—older texts may be perfectly adequate. If your interest is historical, you will want to seek out old and dated works. Consult with your teacher and your librarian to decide how current your sources must be.
- **Available.** Having access to materials across the country and all over the world sounds wonderful. However, when you have an approaching deadline, you may be frustrated to find that the nearest circulating copy of the book you need is two thousand miles away. (In this case, the advantage of getting an early start on your research project becomes starkly clear.) Borrowing through interlibrary loan, tracing a book that is missing, or recalling a book that has been checked out to another person takes time that you may not have. Ask your librarian how long you can expect to wait.
- **At the appropriate level.** You want sources that present useful information in a way you can understand. Materials written for children or "young people" may be so simple as to be uninformative or even misleading. Books written for experts may presume knowledge that you do not have. Struggling with an extremely difficult text is often worth the effort, but if you do so, monitor your time and be sure to keep to your schedule.

4.20 Bibliographies and Bibliography Cards

Bibliographies. A **bibliography** is a list of sources on some given topic. If you are writing a research paper, your teacher will ask you to include one of the following types of bibliography.

TYPES OF BIBLIOGRAPHY	
Complete Bibliography	A comprehensive list of works on your topic
Works Cited ***or*** **References**	A list of all the works referred to or quoted in your paper
Works Consulted	A list of every work you learned from in your research, even if you did not directly use or cite these works in your paper

Bibliography cards. For each source that you work with, prepare a 3" × 5" index card listing complete bibliographical information. Prepare a card for each potential source you find.

You will need the information on your bibliography cards to document your sources for your bibliography, and in case you need to find the source again. Follow the proper form for the type of material, as shown in the chart on the following pages, when preparing your cards. Doing so will make preparing the final bibliography easy, and you can be certain that you will not be missing any needed bibliographic information.

INFORMATION TO INCLUDE ON A BIBLIOGRAPHY CARD FOR A BOOK OR PERIODICAL	
Author(s)	Write the complete name(s) of all author(s), editor(s), and translator(s).
Title	Write the complete title, including any subtitle and any series title. If the piece is an article or chapter in a periodical or book, write • the title of the particular piece; • the beginning and ending page numbers; and • the title of the larger work.
Edition	Note "2nd edition," "revised edition," etc.
Publisher	Write exactly as it appears on the title page.
Place and date of publication	For periodicals, write the date as well as the issue and volume numbers. For republished works, write both the original publication date and the date of your edition.
Location and call number	Note where you found the book. If it is in a library collection, write the call number.
Card number	Give each bibliography card that you prepare a number. Write that number in the top right-hand corner of the card and circle it. When you take notes from the source, include this number on each note card so that you will be able to identify the source of the note later on.

SAMPLE BIBLIOGRAPHY CARD

①

```
Soyinka, Wole. Idanre and Other Poems
        First American Edition.
        New York: Hill and Wang, 1968,
        c. 1967
PR      Peabody Institute Library
9387.9
S6
I3
1968
3
```

Other information may be necessary for other types of sources such as film, CD-ROM, or the Internet. See the following chart for the form and information needed for such sources.

To prepare your bibliography, first arrange your bibliography cards in alphabetical order. Type or copy the information from each card onto your paper. Follow the form for entries as given in the chart. Set up your pages and type the bibliography as described in the following chart.

FORMS FOR BIBLIOGRAPHY ENTRIES

A. A book with one author

Piercy, Marge. Braided Lives. New York: Summit, 1982.

B. A book with two authors

Note that only the first author's name is inverted.

Woodward, Bob, and Scott Armstrong. The Brethren: Inside the Supreme Court. New York: Simon, 1979.

C. A book with three authors

Note that only the first author's name is inverted.

Kinzer, Charles, Robert Sherwood, and John Bransford. Computer Strategies for Education. Columbus, OH: Merrill: 1986.

D. A book with four or more authors

The abbreviation *et al.* means "and others." Use *et al.* (and others) instead of listing all the authors.

Dewey, John, et al. Creative Intelligence. New York: Holt, 1917.

E. A book with no author given

Literary Market Place: The Directory of the American Book Publishing Industry. 1995 ed. New York: Bowker, 1994.

F. A book with an editor, but no single author

Yeats, W. B., ed. The Oxford Book of Modern Verse. New York: Oxford UP, 1937.

G. A book with two or three editors

Bly, Robert, James Hillman, and Michael Meade, eds. The Rag and Bone Shop of the Heart: Poems for Men. New York: HarperCollins, 1992.

H. A book with four or more editors

The abbreviation *et al.* means "and others." Use *et al.* instead of listing all the editors.

McFarlan, Donald, et al., eds. The Guinness Book of Records 1992. New York: Facts on File, 1991.

I. A book with an author and a translator

Alighieri, Dante. The Divine Comedy. Trans. Henry Wadsworth Longfellow. Boston and New York: Houghton, 1895.

J. A second, or later, edition of a book

Copi, Irving M. Introduction to Logic. 5th ed. New York: Macmillan, 1978.

K. A book or monograph that is part of a series

Ermarth, Elizabeth Deeds. George Eliot. Twayne's English Authors ser. Boston: Twayne, 1985.

L. A multivolume work

If you use only one volume of a multivolume work, cite only that volume; otherwise cite only the entire work.

The Works of Aphra Behn. Ed. Montagne Summers, 1915. Vol. 4. New York: Blom, 1967.

The Works of Aphra Behn. Ed. Montagne Summers. 1915. 6 Vols. New York: Blom, 1967.

M. A volume with its own title that is part of a multivolume work with a different title

Durant, Will, and Ariel Durant. The Age of Voltaire: A History of Civilization in Western Europe from 1715 to 1756, with Special Emphasis on the Conflict between Religion and Philosophy. New York: Simon, 1965. Vol. 9 of The Story of Civilization. 11 vols. 1935–75.

N. A republished book or literary work available in several editions

Give the original publication date after the title. Then give complete information for the edition that you have used.

Twain, Mark [Samuel Clemens]. The Adventures of Tom Sawyer. 1876. New York: Dodd, 1958.

O. A government publication

United States. U.S. Govt. Printing Office. United States Government Printing Office Style Manual. Washington: GPO, 1984.

Parts of Books

A. A poem, short story, essay, or chapter in a collection of works by one author

Vidal, Gore. "The Second American Revolution." United States: Essays: 1952-1992. New York: Random, 1993. 956-79.

B. A poem, short story, essay, or chapter in a collection of works by several authors

Eberle, Nancy. "Dream Houses." Reinventing Home. By Laurie Abraham et al. New York: Plume, 1991. 54-58.

C. A novel or play in a collection under one cover

Lorca, Federico García. The House of Bernarda Alba. Three Tragedies. New York: New Directions, 1955. 155-211.

D. An introduction, preface, foreword, or afterword written by the author(s) of a work

Nabokov, Vladimir. Foreword. The Gift. New York: Putnam's, 1963.

E. An introduction, preface, foreword, or afterword written by someone other than the author(s) of a work

Toth, Emily. Introduction. A Vocation and a Voice. By Kate Chopin. New York: Penguin, 1991. vii-xxvi.

F. A reprint of a previously published article or essay

Give complete information for the original publication, followed by "Rpt. in" and complete information for the collection.

Sontag, Susan. "Resnais' Muriel." Film Quarterly 17 (1964): 23-27. Rpt. in Against Interpretation. New York: Dell, 1966. 232-241.

Magazines, Encyclopedias, Reports, Newspapers, and Newsletters

A. An article in a quarterly or monthly magazine

Lutz, John. "Beyond Good and Evil." The Writer December 1994: 9-12.

B. An article in a weekly magazine

Horowitz, Craig. "The Bronx is Up." New York 21 Nov. 1994: 54-59.

C. A magazine article with no author given

"Beowulf Bests Dragons in Cyberspace." National Geographic December 1994: N. pag.

D. An article in a daily newspaper

Savage, David G. "Ruling Boosts Frequent Fliers." Boston Globe 19 Jan. 1995: 33+.

E. An editorial in a newspaper

"From Parade to Charade." Editorial. Boston Globe 19 Jan. 1995: 10.

F. **An article or story in a journal**
Give the volume number, the year, and the page number(s) after the title of the journal.
Addison, Catherine. "Once Upon a Time: A Reader-Response to Prosody." <u>College English</u> 56.6 (1994): 655–78.

G. **An article in an encyclopedia, dictionary, or other alphabetically organized reference work**
Give the title of the article, the title of the work, and the year.
"Hieroglyphics." <u>Dictionary of Literary Themes and Motifs</u>. Ed. Jean-Charles Deigneuret. New York: Greenwood, 1988.

H. **A review**
Blount, Roy, Jr. "Rustily Vigilant." <u>Rev. of For Keeps: Thirty Years at the Movies</u>. By Pauline Kael. New York: Dutton, 1994. <u>Atlantic Monthly</u> Dec. 1994: 131–43.

I. **A report or a pamphlet**
Same as for a book.

Media and Other Sources

A. **An interview that you have conducted**
Sawyer, Dianne. Personal interview. 21 November 1994.

B. **A letter that you have received**
Bush, Barbara. Letter to the author. 11 June 1992.

C. **A fax or e-mail communication**
Same as for a letter.

D. **A thesis or dissertation**
Whitherspoon, Penelope. "Socio-Economical Forces in Victorian England: The Commercial Object in Dickens's Works." Diss., Whitehead U, 1945.

E. **A film**
<u>The Big Heat</u>. Dir. Fritz Lang. With Glenn Ford and Gloria Grahame. Writ. Sidney Boehm. Based on the novel of the same title by William P. McGiven. 90 min. Columbia, 1953.

F. **A work of visual art**
Blake, William. <u>The Ancient Days</u>. British Museum, London.

G. **A television or radio program**
Give the episode name; the names of the episode's writer, director, producer, or actors; the series or program title; and any information that you wish to include about the series's writer, director, or producer. Then give the network, station call letters, city, and date.
"A Desert Blooming." Writ. Marshall Riggan. <u>Living Wild</u>. Dir. Harry L. Gordon. Prod. Peter Argentine. PBS. WTTW, Chicago. 29 Apr. 1984.

H. A musical composition

Stravinsky, Igor. Le Sacre du Printemps.

I. An audio recording (LP, compact disc, audiocassette)

Davis, Miles. "So What." Kind of Blue. LP. Columbia, PC 8163, Nd.

J. A lecture, speech, or address

Give the name of the speaker and the name of the speech. If there is no title, give the kind of speech—e.g. lecture, introduction, address. Then give the event, place, and date.

Jackson, Philip. Address. Semi-annual convention. Easton, PA, 2 Jan. 177.

K. Material from a periodically published CD-ROM with printed analogue

Give the information as you would for the printed analogue, followed by the publication medium (CD-ROM), vender if applicable, and the electronic publication date.

L. Material from a periodically published CD-ROM without a printed analogue

Cite the author, title of material, date of material, title of database, publication medium, name of vendor, and electronic publication date.

United States. Dept. of State. "Industrial Outlook for Petroleum and Natural Gas." 1992. National Trade Data Bank. CD-ROM. US Dept. of Commerce. Dec. 1993.

M. Material from a nonperiodical CD-ROM

Provide the information as you would for a book and add the type of medium.

Brontë, Emily. "Fall, Leaves." The EMC Masterpiece Series, Literature and the Language Arts, Electronic Library. CD-ROM. St. Paul: EMC, 1998.

N. Material from a computer service with a printed analogue

Give the name of the author, publication information for the printed source, title of the database, publication medium, name of service, and date of access.

Stempel, Carl William. "Towards a Historical Sociology of Sport in the United States, 1825-1875." DAI 53 (1993): 3374A. U of Oregon, 1992. Dissertation Abstracts Online. Online. OCLC Epic. 3 Dec. 1993.

O. Material from a service without a printed analogue

Give the name of the author, title of material accessed, date of material, title of the database, publication medium, name of service, and date of access.

Glicken, Morley D. "A Five-Step Plan to Renew Your Creativity." National Business Employment Weekly. Online. Dow Jones News Retrieval. 10 Nov. 1992.

P. Material accessed through a computer network

If the information is from an online journal or newsletter, use the format for a printed journal, followed by the publication medium, the computer network, and the date of access.

Alston, Robin. "The Battle of the Books." Humanist 7.0176 (10 Sept. 1993): 10 pp. Online. Internet. 10 Oct. 1993.

MANUSCRIPT FORM FOR BIBLIOGRAPHIES

1. Begin on a new page.
2. Indent one inch from both side margins, one and one-half inches on the left side and one inch on the right side if the report is to be bound.
3. Place your last name and the page number, flush right, one-half inch from the top of the paper.
4. Drop down another one-half inch and insert the title "Works Consulted" or "Works Cited." Use uppercase and lowercase letters, and do not underscore.
5. Begin each entry at the left margin. Single space within each entry. Indent run-over lines five spaces from the left margin.
6. Double space between the title and the first entry and between each entry.

4.21 Paraphrasing and Summarizing

Quoting. Words that are **quoted**—borrowed exactly from someone else—should be placed inside quotation marks (for punctuation with quotations, see 2.51 and 2.52; for capitalization with quotations, see 2.59). Use a quotation when you need to prove that someone said something in particular. Avoid quotation for other purposes. In particular, do not quote for the purpose of showing that some esteemed author shares your views.

When you do quote, be sure to provide proper documentation (see 4.23, "Documenting Sources in a Report").

Paraphrasing. Paraphrasing is restating someone else's ideas in your own words. When taking notes, quote directly rather than paraphrase. When you use your note cards to write your paper, you can be sure that you have not inadvertently paraphrased a source if you have the exact quotations to look at.

Paraphrasing does not relieve you of the obligation to give credit when you use the words or ideas of others (see 4.23, "Documenting Sources in a Report"). Although you do not borrow the words of another when you paraphrase, you do borrow another's ideas, and that borrowing must be acknowledged.

Summarizing. To summarize a piece of writing is to simplify it by making a brief statement of its main points, condensing someone else's ideas into fewer words of your own. When you summarize, you leave out details, even important details.

A summary should tell what the author said. Be careful not to inject your own opinions into your summary. A summary should state only the main points of a piece of writing. Do not include minor or trivial points. Your purposes will determine how much supporting detail to include in your summary and how much to omit.

EXAMPLE

Summary: *The Awakening*

A married, middle-aged mother goes against the norms of a conservative society during the late 1800s, trying to build and to sustain a life all her own.

Outlining. An excellent way to summarize nonfiction reading is to outline what you read (see 1.12 and 1.13). Paraphrase the title and headings (if any) in the piece you are summarizing to use as the title and headings of your outline. After each heading, note the main point or points made in the section.

4.22 Informal and Formal Note-taking

Informal Note-taking. Take informal notes when you want information for your own use only, and when you will not need to quote or document your sources. You would take informal notes when preparing materials to use in studying, for instance, as you watch a film or listen to a lecture.

Informal note-taking is much like outlining (see 1.12, "Outlining: Rough Outlines"). Use important ideas as headings, and write relevant details below. You will not be able to copy every word, nor is there any need to. Write phrases instead of sentences.

QUOTATION "Jerzy Kosinski came to the United States in 1957, and in 1958 he was awarded a Ford Foundation fellowship."

NOTE Jerzy Kosinski
—came to US 1957
—Ford Foundation fellowship 1958

You will also want to record information about the event or performance, including the date, time, place, speaker, and title, as applicable.

After you are done taking notes, read them over to ensure that they are legible and meaningful. If you have used idiosyncratic shorthand or abbreviations that you may not later recall, write out your notes more fully.

Formal Note-taking. Take formal notes when you may need to quote or document your sources. When you are keeping formal notes for a project—for instance, for a debate or a research paper—you should use 4" × 6" index cards.

PREPARING NOTE CARDS

1. Identify the source at the top right corner of the card. (Use the source numbers from your bibliography cards.)
2. Identify the subject or topic of the note on the top line of the card. (This will make it easier to organize the cards later.)
3. Use a separate card for each fact or quotation. (This will make it easier to organize the cards later.)
4. Write the pertinent source page number or numbers after the note.

SAMPLE NOTE CARD

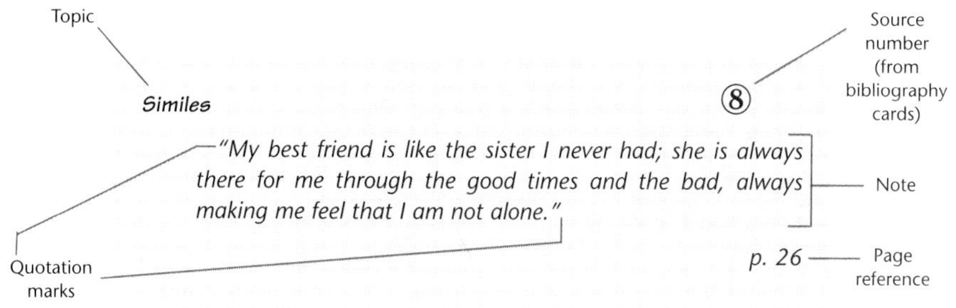

Topic

Similes ⑧

Source number (from bibliography cards)

"My best friend is like the sister I never had; she is always there for me through the good times and the bad, always making me feel that I am not alone." — Note

Quotation marks

p. 26 — Page reference

Your notes will consist of quotations, paraphrases, and summaries.

FORMAL NOTE-TAKING		
Type of Note	**When to Use**	**What to Watch for**
Quotation	When the exact wording of a primary source is important to your topic; or When you are providing a definition; or When the wording of a secondary source is particularly elegant, pithy, concise, amusing, etc.	Be sure you exactly copy spelling, capitalization, punctuation, and numbers. Place quotation marks around all direct quotations. Record, when appropriate, explanatory background information about the speaker or the context of a quotation.
Paraphrase	Most of the time	Bear in mind your main purpose, and note only points that are related to your topic. Place quotation marks around any quoted words or phrases.
Summary	When the point in which you are interested does not require the detail of a paraphrase	Reread the source after writing your summary to be sure that you have not altered the meaning.

4.23 Documenting Sources in a Report

Documentation. In your writing, you must indicate to your reader when you are using the words or ideas of others. This is called **documentation.** A note that tells from whom an idea comes is called a **citation** or a **reference.**

Presenting the words or ideas of others as if they were your own is called plagiarism. If you use someone else's words or ideas and do not give that person credit, you are guilty of plagiarism—even if you weren't trying to plagiarize.

In most schools, plagiarism is punishable by severe penalties, including a failing grade for the project or for the course and possibly even expulsion. Outside of school, plagiarism constitutes a violation of copyright and can result in a lawsuit and great financial expense.

In addition to protecting you from plagiarizing, documenting your sources is an important part of writing. Whether your aim as a writer is to explain or to persuade, your job is to convince your readers. Wouldn't you be more likely to be convinced by an author who can document research thoroughly and who tells you exactly where he or she obtained his or her facts? Documenting your sources enables your reader to judge the reliability and accuracy of your facts and arguments.

Documentation is a helpful courtesy as well. It enables your reader to investigate points you discuss. Finally, documentation is honest. It shows that you recognize and appreciate the contributions to human knowledge made by those who have gone before you.

Parenthetical documentation. Parenthetical documentation is currently the most widely used form of documentation. To use this method to document the source of a quotation or an idea, you place a brief note identifying the source in parentheses immediately after the borrowed material. This type of note is called a **parenthetical citation,** and the act of placing such a note is called **citing a source.**

The first part of a parenthetical citation refers the reader to a source in your List of Works Cited or Works Consulted. For the reader's ease in finding the source in your bibliography, you must cite the work according to how it is listed in the bibliography. The reference to the source should also be as brief as possible. If the source is clearly identified in the text, omit it from the citation and give only the page number.

The second part of the citation refers the reader to a specific page or place within the source. If you are referring to a whole work, do not cite the page numbers since they are already given in the bibliography.

SAMPLE PARENTHETICAL CITATIONS

A. For works listed by title, use an abbreviated title.

Sample bibliographic entry

"History." Encyclopedia Britannica: Macropædia. 1992 ed.

Sample citation

Historians go through three stages in textual criticism ("History" 615).

B. For works listed by author or editor, use the author's or editor's last name.

Sample bibliographic entry

Brown, Dee. Bury My Heart at Wounded Knee: An Indian History of the American West. New York: Holt, 1970.

Sample citation

"Big Eyes Schurz agreed to the arrest" (Brown 364).

C. When the listed name or title is stated in the text, cite only the page number.

Brown avers that Big Eyes Schurz agreed to it (364).

CONTINUED

D. For works of multiple volumes, use a colon after the volume number.

Sample bibliographic entry

Pepys, Samuel. *The Diary of Samuel Pepys*. Ed. Robert Latham and William Matthews. 10 vols. Berkeley: University of California Press, 1972.

Sample citation

On the last day of 1665, Pepys took the occasion of the new year to reflect, but not to celebrate (6: 341-2).

E. For works quoted in secondary sources, use the abbreviation "qtd. in."

Sample citation

According to R. Bentley, "reason and the facts outweigh a hundred manuscripts" (qtd. in "History" 615).

F. For classic works that are available in various editions, give the page number from the edition you are using, followed by a semicolon; then identify the section of the work to help people with other editions find the reference.

4.24 Footnotes and Endnotes

The method of documentation described in Section 4.23 is the most common of many accepted systems. Footnoting and endnoting are two other accepted methods.

Footnotes. Instead of putting citations in parentheses within the text, you can place them at the bottom or foot of the page; hence the term **footnote**. In this system, a number or symbol is placed in the text at the location where the parenthetical citation would otherwise be, and a matching number or symbol, at the bottom of the page, identifies the citation. Footnotes are also used to supply information useful but extraneous to the immediate purposes of the work. For example, *Literature and the Language Arts* uses numbered footnotes in the literature selections to define obscure words and to provide background information.

Endnotes. Because typists and publishers find it difficult to place notes at the bottom of pages, and because many readers find these notes distracting, many books use **endnotes** instead of footnotes. Endnotes are exactly like footnotes in that a number or symbol is placed within the text, but the matching citations and extraneous material are compiled at the end of the book, chapter, or article rather than at the foot of the page.

Footnote and endnote entries begin with the author's (or editor's) name in its usual order (first, then last) and include publication information and a page reference.

SAMPLE FOOTNOTE OR ENDNOTE CITATIONS	
A BOOK WITH ONE AUTHOR	[1]Jean Paul-Sartre, *Being and Nothingness* (New York: The Citadel Press, 1966) 149-151.
A BOOK WITH ONE EDITOR AND NO SINGLE AUTHOR	[2]Shannon Ravenel, ed., *New Stories from the South: The Year's Best, 1992* (Chapel Hill, NC: Algonquin Books, 1992) 305.
A MAGAZINE ARTICLE	[3]Andrew Gore, "Road Test: The Apple Powerbook," *MacUser* December 1996: 72.

TEST TAKING SKILLS

4.25 Taking Objective Tests

Your teacher's job is to help you learn. Your teacher may test you periodically to determine how well you have been learning what she or he has taught. Teachers also give tests as additional encouragement to students to learn. All teachers want their students—including you—to do well on their tests, because that shows that they have done their job well.

The way to do well on a classroom test is to study and work with the materials presented to you by your teacher. If you have a text, read it carefully. If your teacher gives lectures or leads discussions, take thorough notes of what is said.

STRATEGIES FOR TAKING OBJECTIVE TESTS

Before the Test

- Get ample sleep the night before the test.
- Eat a nutritious breakfast.
- Study over as long a period of time as possible.
- Review frequently.
- Try to predict questions that may be on the test, and make sure you can answer them.
- Bring extra pencils, erasers, and any other required materials.

During the Test

- Determine how much time is allowed for each question. If a question takes too long, guess and/or come back to it if you have time.
- *Read each question carefully.*
- Work quickly but do not rush.
- Write legibly.
- Review all your work before submitting it.

Whenever you are taking a test, skip a question that seems too difficult and go on to the next one. Make a note to return to the unanswered question(s) if you have extra time at the end of the test period. The following are types of questions that commonly appear on objective tests.

True/False Questions

A true/false question gives you a statement and asks you to decide whether the statement is true or false. If you do not know the answer right away, try to guess.

You probably will not see many true/false tests because scores are too easily influenced by guessing. If you are given a true-false test, watch out for these potential traps:

Negatives and double negatives. The word *not* completely changes the meaning of a sentence. To evaluate a sentence with a negative, see if its opposite makes sense or is plausible. If so, the original must be false.

Quantifiers and qualifiers. Look for words such as *all, sometimes, never,* etc. These words control what a sentence really says.

Excess information. The more information a sentence contains, the more liable it is to be false. Be sure to evaluate all the claims a sentence makes before you judge it.

Multiple-choice Questions

Multiple-choice questions are perhaps the most widely used type of test question. A multiple-choice test item asks a question and then gives you a few possible answers from which to choose. Only one is correct; the others are called distracters. You must choose the best answer, even if none appears to you to be exactly correct.

If you know the answer from reading the question, look for it. However, some multiple-choice items can be answered only by evaluating all of the choices.

EXAMPLE In Chinua Achebe's "Marriage Is a Private Affair," why doesn't Nnaemeka wish to marry Ugoye?

(A) because Nnaemeka's father wishes for him to marry her
(B) because she doesn't work outside the home
(C) because he doesn't like her
(D) because she is uneducated
(E) none of the above

Short-answer Questions

Short-answer questions are common on quizzes and in class discussions. Not surprisingly, a short-answer question calls for a short answer—a word, a phrase, or a sentence.

Most teachers require that all responses to short-answer questions be complete sentences. Your teacher will tell you whether you must provide complete sentences.

EXAMPLE In the selection from Émile Zola's *Germinal,* where do most of the people of the town work?

Most of the townspeople work in a coal mine.

4.26 Taking Standardized Tests

The most familiar standardized tests are created by private companies and used by colleges and other organizations to evaluate students as part of the process of granting admissions and scholarships. Standardized tests are also used by states and school districts to assess achievement.

SOME STANDARDIZED TESTS

Common Abbreviation	Test
PSAT/NMSQT	Pre-Scholastic Aptitude Test/National Merit Scholarship Qualifying Test
ACT	American College Testing Program
MAT	Miller Analogies Test
SAT	Scholastic Aptitude Test
ACH	College Board Achievement Tests

These tests are all multiple-choice tests. Items are answered on special sheets that can be read and graded by a computer. You choose your answer by filling in or blackening a bubble. If you take one of these tests, be sure to use the type of pencil or pen specified by the test monitor. Also be sure to fill in bubbles *completely* and *neatly.*

If you do not know the answer, you can at least try to rule out some wrong choices and increase your chances of finding the correct answer.

If a question seems too difficult, remember that your best strategy is to skip it and go on to the next one. You can come back to it if you have extra time at the end of the test period. Blank spaces on your answer sheet will indicate which questions you have not answered. Make certain you place the marks in the correct answer block after skipping a question. Note that while you can go back to questions within a section, most tests do not allow you to go back to a previous section. Always obey the instructions given to you by the test monitor.

Analogy Questions

Analogy questions ask you to select a pair of words that bear a particular relationship to each other. Instead of telling you explicitly what relationship you are to form, the test gives you another pair of words as an example. Analogy questions are set up as if they read "*A* is related to *B* as ___ is related to ___.

EXAMPLE CHAIR : LEG::

(A) pilot : plane
(B) cork : bottle
(C) jar : lid
(D) wheel : car
(E) tree : branch

You can only answer analogy questions by examining *all* the answers. More than one answer may seem correct. Choose the *best* answer.

Do not be misled by irrelevant relationships between the words in the example and words in the choices. Focus on the *relationship between the two words* in the example.

Sentence-Completion Questions

Sentence-completion questions present you with a sentence that has two words missing. You must select the pair of words that best completes the sentence.

EXAMPLE The expansion of Cedar Hospital was largely ________ by the citizens of Minor county, even though it was a major ________ for the taxpayers.

(A) needed. . . contribution
(B) cheered. . . burden
(C) criticized. . . expense
(D) welcomed. . . dilemma
(E) scrutinized. . . anxiety

Sentence-completion questions require that you try all the choices to see which words work best in the sentence. You often can eliminate one or two answers right away because they do not fit syntactically or because they make no sense at all. When you come to try the correct answer, you may see a relationship that was not apparent before.

Grammar, Usage, and Mechanics Questions

There are at least three common types of grammar, usage, and mechanics questions. Each of them presents a sentence or paragraph containing underlined and labeled passages.

Error identification questions ask you to identify the passage that contains an error. You do not have to tell what type of error it is or correct the error. **Error correction questions** ask you to correct the error by choosing a passage to replace it.

Sample Error Identification Question

Choose the letter that corresponds to an error in the sentence.

Rita Wongo began her law career as a (A) court stenographer at the (B) Warley District Court in Billerica. Ms. Wongo, presently a (C) tax attorney, is employee (D) at The Boston Mutual Funds and Safe Bank No error (E).

(A) (B) (C) (D) (E)

Sample Error Correction Question

Select the letter of the word or words that should replace the underlined word.

Eurlenko has performed (1) in many plays since he began his acting career.

1. (A) No change (B) perform (C) performs (D) had performed (E) was performing

ANSWERING ERROR IDENTIFICATION AND ERROR CORRECTION QUESTIONS

1. Ignore the underlining and proofread the sentence or paragraph carefully.
   - Proofread for errors in grammar, usage, and mechanics.
   - Look especially for agreement—in tense, person, number, and mood.
2. If you do not find the error, look specifically at the underlined passages.
3. Read the whole sentence through before settling on your answer.

Construction shift questions give you a sentence and ask you to revise it in some specified way.

Sample Construction Shift Question

> Rewrite the following sentence according to the instruction. Then, from the choices provided, select the phrase that best fits in the revised sentence.
>
> Without a doubt, the most famous and symbolic scene in Kate Chopin's novel, The Awakening, is the water scene at the end.
>
> Begin with *the water scene at the end*
>
> (A) doubt, famous
> (B) without a question
> (C) is Kate Chopin's novel
> (D) symbolic scene.
> (E) famous or well-known

ANSWERING CONSTRUCTION SHIFT QUESTIONS

- Try to revise the whole sentence as directed.
- Make all necessary changes to avoid errors in grammar and usage.
- Make as few as possible changes in wording.
- Watch for word order and placement of modifiers.

There are usually a few ways in which to revise the sentence. You must find the word or word group that would be in the best possible sentence.

You can practice for all grammar, usage, and mechanics questions by studying the lessons in 2.1–2.73 of this Language Arts Survey, doing the Language Lab activities that follow the selections in this textbook, doing the activities in the *Essential Skills Practice Book: Language,* and completing your reading and writing assignments conscientiously.

Reading Comprehension Questions

Reading comprehension questions precede or follow a short piece of writing. The questions address the content of the passage. Many questions will ask you to go beyond the text by making an inference or an interpretation.

STEPS IN ANSWERING READING COMPREHENSION QUESTIONS

1. Read all the questions quickly.
2. Read the passage.
3. Reread the first question carefully.
4. Reread the passage while bearing in mind the first question.
5. Answer the first question.
6. Continue with each subsequent question in the same manner.

To select the correct answer, you will have to try all the choices and select the best available. Be sure that you base your answers only on the passage and not on your own opinions.

Synonym and Antonym Questions

Synonym and antonym questions give you a word and ask you to select the word that means the same or that means the opposite, respectively. You must select the *best* answer, even if none is exactly correct.

EXAMPLE Write the letter of the word that is most nearly *opposite* in meaning to the word in capital letters.
1. CHOICE
(A) restriction (B) instinct (C) decision (D) selection

Synonym and antonym questions require that you try all the choices to see which works best. The choices almost always include both synonyms and antonyms, so make sure that you remember whether you are working on a synonym or an antonym question.

Don't select an answer just because (1) it is similar to the given word in appearance or sound; (2) it shares with the given word a root, prefix, or suffix; or (3) it is a long or unfamiliar-sounding word.

4.27 Taking Essay Tests

It would appear obvious that you cannot do well on an essay test if you do not understand the essay question. Yet, worried about finishing on time, many students don't make the effort to make sure they do understand before they begin writing.

After reading the *whole* question carefully, look for key words in the question that indicate what is expected. Underline or circle these words if you are permitted; otherwise, write them on your own note paper. Many questions ask for more than one type of response. Be careful to answer *all* parts of the question.

UNDERSTANDING AN ESSAY QUESTION

Type of Essay Question	Tasks of Essay
analyze	break into parts and describe the parts and their relationships
compare; compare and contrast	identify and describe similarities and differences
describe; explain	tell the steps in a process; identify causes and effects
define; describe; identify	classify and tell the features of
interpret	tell the meaning and significance of
summarize	retell very briefly, stating only the main points
argue; prove; show	tell and evaluate reasons for believing a statement

In most testing situations, you do not have time to go through the entire writing process. Part of your planning must include allocating your time. Allow time for planning, drafting, and reviewing. If you plan and pace yourself, you will have no reason to worry about running out of time.

Perhaps the most important thing you can do is to plan your essay before you begin writing. The organization of your essay can show your insight, understanding, and originality, even if you do not have time to complete your plan. Make an outline and add notes about points you will make and details, examples, or quotations you can use. Later, if you find yourself running out of time, you would do better to complete the essay by making your main points briefly and without elaboration than to end the essay without a conclusion.

Work hard to write a clear introduction. Your introduction should state your main point or points and present your plan for the essay. As you write each paragraph or section of your essay, check the introduction to see that you are still on track. Follow your introduction using strong paragraphs that include evidence to support the points you are making. As in any essay you should end with a conclusion. While your conclusion may be brief it should give your essay a sense of completion, tie up any loose ends, and reiterate the main point of your essay.

You can revise your writing as you go, but watch that you do not use all your time editing an incomplete essay.

Before you submit your completed essay, take as much time as you can to review and polish it.

QUESTIONS FOR REVIEWING AN ANSWER TO AN ESSAY QUESTION

- Does the essay answer all parts of the question?
- Does the introduction state clearly the main point of the essay?
- Is the conclusion consistent with the main point?
- Does the essay cover all the points in your outline?
- Are there any points that could be made more strongly or clearly?
- Is every word in the essay easily legible?
- Is the essay free of errors in grammar, usage, and mechanics?

Essential Skills: *Applied English/Tech Prep*

Long after you have written your last high-school essay or college term paper, you will be applying your writing skills in a variety of day-to-day situations. Whether you're corresponding with a loan officer at the bank, writing to a friend across the country, communicating via electronic mail with a co-worker, or preparing a news release about your theater group's upcoming performance, you will want to take care to ensure that your writing reflects your intentions precisely, conveying your thoughts, feelings, and any pertinent information.

Familiarizing yourself with the conventions of practical writing can help you achieve a positive outcome, particularly when addressing individuals or groups who do not know you personally.

PERSONAL AND PROFESSIONAL COMMUNICATION

5.1 Personal and Business Letters

Personal Letters

If you check your home mailbox today, you may find it stuffed with bills, magazines, catalogs, and miscellaneous junk mail. Imagine, though, your response if you were to discover a cache of personal letters, cards, and invitations, all addressed to you. A few decades ago, when society relied more heavily on the postal service and less on telecommunications, such a discovery might not have been unusual.

Although we still enjoy receiving personal correspondence, most of us now reach for the telephone or for a personal computer to send e-mail—rather than a pen or typewriter—when we want to communicate with friends or distant family members. When, however, you sit down to compose a letter, you allow yourself time to develop your thoughts more carefully and express them more deliberately than you would in conversation. Furthermore, written communications, which can be saved and savored time and again, tend to carry more weight than spontaneous comments.

A personal letter may be relatively informal, depending on the writer's relationship with the intended recipient. It will typically include the following:

1. a **return address**, including the writer's address and the date the letter was composed
2. a **salutation**, or greeting, followed by a comma
3. the **body**, or text, of the letter
4. an appropriate **closing**, followed by a comma
5. a **signature**
6. an optional **postscript**, preceded by the abbreviation "P.S."

Following is a sample thank-you letter.

1227 Madison Road
Boston, MA 02147
July 7, 1998

Dear Aunt Sophie,

Thank you so much for taking me to the photography exhibit last weekend. I really enjoyed it. Maybe someday you'll see my work on display.

I've been taking a lot of pictures and spending a lot of time in the darkroom lately. I've sent you one of my favorite shots. I thought you'd enjoy it because I know how much you like birds.

Thanks again for going to the exhibit with me and for all your encouragement.

Your shutterbug niece,

Alicia

P.S. We should take in another exhibit soon.

Business Letters

The first rule when writing a business letter is to take nothing for granted. Because your business letters will typically be addressed to strangers or business acquaintances, you cannot assume that the individuals receiving them will respond positively to them, or to you, the writer. It's up to you to make a good impression. When composing a business letter, it makes sense to be conservative. If you adhere to widely accepted business conventions, your letter is more likely to be well received.

Like a typical personal letter, a business letter includes a **return address, salutation, body, closing**, and **signature**. It will occasionally include a **postscript.** In addition, it includes one more component, called the **inside address**. The inside address, located below the heading and above the salutation, will include the name and title of the person to whom you are writing (or a department name, if you are not writing to a specific individual), the name of the company or organization, and its address.

It is important that the salutation and closing of a business letter be respectful and formal. The salutation, which is separated from the inside address by a double space, typically begins with the word "Dear," followed by the courtesy or professional title used in the inside address. "Ms.," "Mr.," "Dr.," "Miss," or "Mrs." are among the appropriate choices. If you aren't writing to a specific person, you can use a salutation such as "Dear Sir or Madam" or "Ladies and Gentlemen." The salutation is followed by a colon.

In a business letter, it isn't advisable to use a creative closing. Acceptable closings include "Very truly yours," "Sincerely," "Sincerely yours," and "Respectfully yours." Note that only the first word of the closing is capitalized.

Sign your name, in either blue or black ink, below the closing. Your full name should be typed below your signature.

Business letters are usually structured in either **block form** or **modified block form.** In **block**

form, each of the letter's components—the heading, inside address, salutation, body, closing, and signature—begin at the left margin. Paragraphs are not indented but are separated by a double space. In **modified block form**, the return address and closing are aligned along an imaginary line located a bit to the right of the center of the page. Paragraphs are indented, typically five spaces from the left margin. (See the sample personal letter on page 1276 for an example of modified block form.)

Throughout your letter, try to maintain a courteous, formal tone. Use standard English and avoid slang expressions and contractions. Outline your main points before you begin to compose the letter, organizing your thoughts so that your letter will be clear, easy to read, and as brief as possible. Remember to review your grammar, punctuation, and spelling. Your reader will form an impression of you based on what he or she sees on the page.

Guidelines for Writing a Business Letter

- Outline your letter's main points before you begin the writing process.
- Type your letter, if at all possible, and use clean 8½" × 11" white or off-white paper. Type on one side of the paper only.
- Select a standard business-letter format, either block form or modified block form.
- Use single-spacing, leaving a blank line between paragraphs.
- Avoid abbreviations in the date and in the street address in both the return address and the inside address. Use standard postal abbreviations for states.
- Select a standard salutation and closing.
- Stick to the subject, keeping the letter brief and informative.
- Maintain a formal tone, avoiding slang and contractions.
- Be neat. A sloppy appearance may make your letter less effective.
- Check your grammar, usage, punctuation, capitalization, and spelling.
- Reread your letter. Have you conveyed your main points clearly and effectively? Don't make your reader guess at your intentions.

You will come across many opportunities for composing business correspondence. For example, you may want to obtain a schedule of evening classes from a local community college, commend your local fire fighters for their prompt response to an emergency, or inform the telephone company of an error on your bill.

In any of these cases, you might consider making a phone call instead of sending a letter, but a phone call may be less effective. People are often more attentive to written requests than to verbal requests. Moreover, when you write a letter, you can save a copy of your correspondence either electronically (if you've keyed your letter on a computer) or by making a photocopy. Your copy of the letter will then serve as a record of your contact with the individual or group in question.

Letters of commendation are especially welcome. A pat on the back or a verbal "thank you" is nice, but people appreciate it when you go to the extra effort of expressing your thanks in a letter. On the following page is an example of a typical business letter in block form.

13 Maple Avenue
Wheatland, TN
May 5, 1998

Purchasing Manager
The Art Mart
75 Molding Avenue
Archus, TX 90067

Dear Sir or Madam:

I am preparing to work on a clay coil pot. I am familiar with working with red earthenware clay and gray clay; however, someone suggested to me that I try self-hardening clay for this project.

I was in your shop a week ago, hoping to find this self-hardening clay. I was very disappointed to learn that you do not carry it. I inquired with a member of your staff and he was not familiar with the product.

May I respectfully request that you consider purchasing self-hardening clay for your art store? I have checked with other art stores in the area, and they do not carry it either. I would be very interested in purchasing it from your store, as you have been the primary source of the art supplies I have purchased.

Sincerely yours,

Misato Lam

Misato Lam

WRITING AND RESEARCHING TO ENTER THE JOB MARKET

Finding the right career for you and getting hired are two important areas where you will put your writing and research skills to work.

5.2 Finding Career Information

Deciding what field to pursue after high school or college is not an easy task. For many, choosing a career can be stressful as people worry about what they will do after graduation, whether they will find a job they enjoy, and whether they will be able to succeed in this field. Choosing a career, however, can be a very rewarding experience. As you consider your career options, ask yourself these questions:

- What do I like to do?
- What skills do I possess? (For example: Do I work well with other people? Am I organized? Am I a leader?) How can my skills be of use to others?
- In what kind of an environment would I like to work? (For example, would I prefer to work in an office, outdoors, in a retail setting?)

- Do I like to work independently or do I prefer interaction with others?
- What rewards would I like to get from my career?

Many people find that the career they start out wanting to enter and the career in which they actually end up working are two very different things. Whatever you decide to do, keep in mind that every new experience should be looked upon as an opportunity for growth and enrichment. Remember that if you decide that the career you have chosen is not the right one for you, you should keep exploring other options until you find your own niche in the working world. Below is a list of valuable resources and guidelines for discovering and exploring career options:

- *The College Guide to Jobs and Career Planning* by Joyce Slayton Mitchel
- *Peterson's Guide to Internships* (get the latest edition)
- *Peterson's Summer Opportunities* (get the latest edition)
- *What Color is Your Parachute?* by Richard Nelson
- *Job Hunter's Sourcebook* edited by Michelle LeCompte
- *National Business Employment Weekly* published by *The Wall Street Journal*

These are just a few of the published resources available at your local library or bookstore. Local libraries and colleges also have information on working and studying abroad, interviewing techniques, and books on specific careers ranging from correction officer to casting director. In addition, you might try the following methods of locating career information:

- **Informational Interviews.** Write a business letter (using the guidelines found in section 5.1) to a business or company in which you are interested, requesting an informational interview. In a week or so, make a follow-up call.
- **People You Know.** Do you know anyone in the field you are interested in? If so, find out how he or she got started. Most people are flattered when others take an interest in their work. Prepare a list of questions to ask in advance. For example: Is your acquaintance happy with what he or she is doing? What skills or education is needed to succeed in the field? Did your acquaintance's career meet his or her expectations?
- **On-line Help.** Do you have access to it? If so, there's a whole world of information only a few keystrokes away. The Internet carries information from career counseling and personality tests to specific employment ads and resume and cover letter samples.

5.3 Writing Resumes and Cover Letters

Perhaps the most important letters you will ever write will be those you address to potential employers. The care you take in preparing these letters will help determine the jobs you will be hired to fill, and thus the course of your career.

When applying for a job, you commonly submit both a **resume** and a letter of application, or **cover letter**. Together, these documents should present a brief history of your education, skills, and work experience, highlighting your assets and suggesting how your unique mix of skills and abilities might benefit the organization you hope to join.

The information presented in your resume and cover letter must be honest and accurate, but you should never minimize or discount the value of your experience. Design your resume and cover letter in a way that makes the most of what you have to offer, presenting yourself to the reader in a positive light.

While your resume should be relatively detailed, you will probably want to write it so that it won't require substantial editing each time you apply for a job. The cover letter accompanying your resume, on the other hand, should address the specific needs of the particular organization to which you are applying.

Resumes

The information you include in your resume may be organized in many different ways. Your guidance counselor or librarian may have a file of sample resumes for you to review. Select a style that looks neat and businesslike. Most resumes list the applicant's **objective** or career goal, **work experience, education, extracurricular activities, skills** (particularly computer skills in today's marketplace), and **references.**

Try to limit your resume to a single page. It should be typed and printed on high-quality paper, preferably the same paper stock used for your cover letter. Check the quality of the print to make sure it's easy to read. The following is just one example of a resume.

Edward T. Stolarz
10 Madelaine Avenue
Clearview, NJ 87263
(376) 555-6226

Objective

To obtain an entry-level camp counselor position that will enable me to gain experience in the organization of youth clubs and activities.

Work Experience

10/97–present *Karen's Play School, Clearview, NJ*
Child Care Assistant: Assist child care teachers with the planning and coordination of activities at a small, private early childhood development and daycare center.

6/96–10/97 *Riverton Children's Hospital, Riverton, NJ*
Volunteer: Provided part-time assistance and support to hospital staff.

Education

9/95–present *Clearview Memorial High School, Clearview, NJ*
Class of 1999. College Preparatory program
Academic Achievements: Debate Club Award for Leadership; Honor Roll
Grade-point average: 3.1

Skills

Familiarity with word processing
Proficiency in French
Organized
Flexible
Team player

Extracurricular Activities

French Tutor, Debate Team, Soccer Team

Interests

Soccer, Aerobics, Cooking, Dancing

References Available upon request

Cover Letters

Guidelines for composing a cover letter:

- Limit your cover letter to a single page.
- State your interest in obtaining a position within the organization, indicating the type of position (or specific job opening) for which you would like to be considered.
- If you are applying for a specific position, describe how you learned of the job's availability.
- Briefly describe your qualifications.
- Refer to your resume, enclosed with your letter.
- Mention your interest in scheduling an interview and where and when you may be reached (typically by telephone) to make arrangements.
- Thank the reader for considering your application.

Following is an example of a typical cover letter. (The letter uses modified block form.)

10 Madelaine Avenue
Clearview, NJ 87263
March 3, 1999

Elaina Rolli
Camp Director
Oak Grove Camp Fire Kids
3372 Wyoming Boulevard
Daring, NJ 87276

Dear Ms. Rolli:

I was pleased to learn from your ad in *The Village Examiner* that you are interested in hiring summer camp counselors at Oak Grove Camp Fire Kids. I would very much like to be considered for the position and have enclosed my resume as requested.

As you will see from my resume, I have had significant experience working with children. It is my goal to gain experience working with young children and youths of all ages and in a variety of settings so that I may pursue a career in child psychology.

I am very interested in meeting with you regarding the position. Please contact me if you have any questions. I can usually be reached after 3 P.M. any weekday.

Sincerely,

Edward T. Stolarz

Edward T. Stolarz

Enclosure

WRITING ON THE JOB

In the course of your working life, regardless of whether you choose to become a professional writer, you will have many opportunities to write.

A common complaint heard from employers today is that many employees can not write well enough to communicate with one another or with the clients with whom they interact. Without question, learning to organize your thoughts on paper will serve you well on the job. Sometimes it isn't what you know but how you communicate your knowledge to others that makes the difference.

5.4 Writing a Memorandum

When employees of an organization need to communicate with one another, they often do so via interoffice **memoranda**, or **memos**. A memo may be forwarded from one employee to another or circulated throughout an entire organization, and it can be used to communicate information and ideas on a wide variety of topics. A manager may, for example, write a memo to schedule a meeting, to announce changes in an office policy or procedure, or to delegate an assignment.

Today's employees typically compose and type their memos at their computer workstations, forwarding them to one another over a computer network via electronic mail, called "e-mail" for short. Small companies, or those that don't make extensive use of computers, may provide their employees with standard memo forms.

Memos are usually brief but can be used to circulate lengthy reports. Of course, even a short memo must be clear and to the point. Reviewing the memo and proofreading it, before photocopying and distributing it or striking that e-mail "send" button, can prevent embarrassing errors.

The tone of a memo will depend largely on the memo's topic and the writer's relationship to the person receiving the memo.

Although memos typically communicate work-related information, they also serve a social function. A memo may be circulated regarding an upcoming party for a departing coworker, for example, or serve as an invitation to lunch. Following is a sample memo.

MEMORANDUM

TO: Ms. Blaney
FR: Hilde Aaro **C:** Sean McDougherty
DT: January 3, 1999
RE: Holiday Party

On behalf of the International Student Association, I would like to thank you for all of your help and support in the coordination of the holiday party. I'm not sure we would have pulled it off so smoothly without all your help and expertise.

Merci! Gracias! Thank you! Grazie!

Note the "**C**" line on the sample form. On the "**C**" line, the author includes the name of anyone who will receive a copy of the memo.

5.5 Technical Writing

If you peruse the Help Wanted section in your Sunday newspaper, you are likely to see many advertisements announcing job openings for technical writers. These ads are typically placed by companies looking for individuals who can write **documentation** to accompany complex products that would be difficult to use without proper explanation and instruction.

The manuals and user guides that technical writers produce help consumers, medical personnel, automobile and aircraft mechanics, and others working with sophisticated equipment. For example, a technical writer may produce documentation to help consumers use a word processing package designed to run on a personal computer or write a manual explaining how to use an electronic data collector to survey a parcel of land.

Nearly every worker, regardless of his or her profession, will eventually be in the position of having to explain a procedure or complex process in writing. A future employer may one day ask you to write a training manual for new employees or to document a procedure that you are familiar with so that others may learn it as well.

If you find yourself in a similar situation, you will benefit by incorporating the basics of good technical writing. Poor documentation can lead to costly, embarrassing, or dangerous mistakes.

Guidelines for documenting technical procedures

- First, make sure you are very familiar with the procedure you will be documenting.
- Warn the reader of any potentially hazardous steps or materials.
- List any tools or equipment needed to complete the process.
- Break the task into a series of short, simple steps.
- List each step in the proper sequence.
- Use the second person imperative. Write "Press the enter key," not "The user should press the enter key."
- Keep your vocabulary simple, avoiding unexplained technical jargon.
- If appropriate, incorporate pictures and diagrams.
- Don't leave out any steps or include unnecessary steps.
- Proofread your instructions to make sure they are easy to follow and unambiguous.
- Ask someone who isn't familiar with the operation to follow the directions you have written. If necessary, adjust your instructions based on his or her experience.

Writing documentation can test just how careful a writer you are and indicate how well you understand the material you are trying to explain. Indeed, you may find that you understand a process better after you have written about it. You won't know how well you have succeeded, though, until your readers try to follow your instructions and you learn whether they have achieved satisfactory results. Following is an example of typical technical writing.

Making a Clay Coil Pot

Materials needed:

Self-hardening clay, water, sponge, work board or tray, sculpting knife (optional), spatula

Steps:

Warning: If you fold clay during any part of this process, it must be "wedged" out immediately afterwards to avoid air bubbles.

1. Wedge clay out by slamming it down on your work board or tray. This process should be done for approximately five minutes. Do not fold when wedging.
2. Begin by separating your pieces of clay into long strips, approximately ten to twelve inches long, depending on the intended size of the bowl. Note: To avoid drying out clay, keep the pieces you are not currently using under a damp paper towel.
3. Create a flat base for your pot by smoothing out a circle of clay with the wet sponge.
4. Roll your strips into long snake-like pieces and begin coiling them around the circumference of your base. Join the end of one "snake" to the next with wet clay. Build up the sides of the pot with the "snakes" until you reach the desired depth.
5. If you wish, you may smooth out the coil effect with the sponge or enhance it with a sculpting knife or equivalent tool.
6. Repeat steps four and five as many times as desired to achieve the desired look.
7. If you do not finish your coil pot in one sitting, remember to wet it down with wet paper towels and cover it before you put it away (a large piece of plastic over the whole tray works well).
8. When finished, carefully pry the bowl off the tray with the spatula to keep it from sticking as it dries. Allow the bowl to dry on the tray overnight.

5.6 Writing Promotional and Public Relations Copy

Writers of promotional and public relations, or PR, copy are practitioners of a delicate art. They must learn to capture a reader's attention and gain his or her sympathy, with the goal of persuading the reader to purchase a product or accept a particular viewpoint. Their task requires proficiency in the craft of writing; an in-depth understanding of their product, organization, or cause; and an ability to empathize with readers and predict their responses.

Promotional and public relations writers are responsible for a host of materials, including press releases; radio, television, and newspaper ads; direct mail copy; speeches; news and feature articles; scripts for films, tapes, and slide shows; letters to newspaper and magazine editors; and annual reports. They may work in the service of big corporations or small, nonprofit organizations, persuading their audiences to spend their money, make donations, or modify their behavior. They may write fast-food jingles, draft political speeches, or pen slogans for an antismoking campaign.

Writing a good promotional or public relations piece requires research and planning. If the writer's copy isn't grounded in reality, reflecting a product or organization's real merits, it may ultimately fail and spark a negative backlash.

Although you may never work in PR, studying the basic principles of good promotional writing can help make your writing more effective. Like a good promotional writer, you should make a habit of asking yourself one important question: How will my reader react? Below is an example of a sample press release:

For immediate release
Contact person: David Danielpou

Admissions Department
(495) 555-4312

Barwood College's Division of Continuing Education in Tempur now offers a program leading to a Bachelor's Degree in Health Care Administration. This program was developed with the help of the National Board of Medical Assistance to meet the demanding need for management and business administration skills within the health care industry. The program is designed to enhance the skills of health care professionals presently working in the industry and to introduce new students to a challenging and growing field.

According to Sylvia Guerrero, coordinator of the Health Care Administration program at Barwood, "We have developed this program to ensure that graduating students will be proficient in all aspects of health care administration; they will be able to go into a medical setting in any area of the industry and perform the administrative duties that are necessary for it to run efficiently."

Barwood offers small, individualized classes that foster thorough and productive learning. Students may pursue their degree during evening or weekend study. Financial assistance is available to those who qualify. Barwood also provides career counseling and job placement assistance.

Barwood College is fully accredited by the Northeastern Board of Education, and offers more than seventy-three majors in a variety of disciplines. For more information on any of our certificate, associate, or bachelor's degree programs, please call our Admissions Office at (495) 555-4312.

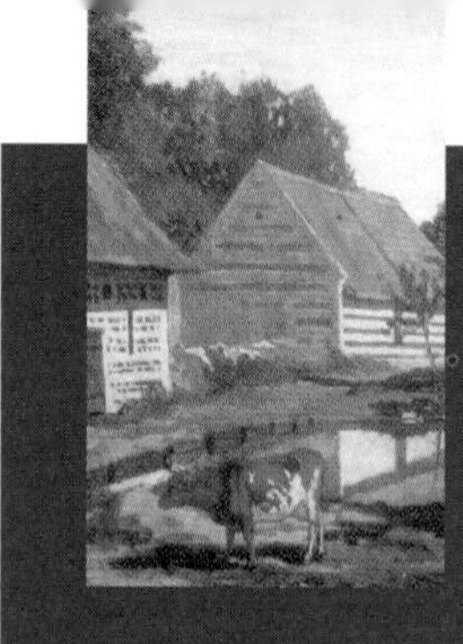

HANDBOOK OF *Literary Terms*

abridgment An **abridgment** is a shortened version of a work. When doing an abridgment, an editor attempts to preserve the most significant elements of the original. Elie Wiesel abridged *Night,* cutting it from eight hundred pages of Yiddish to one hundred pages in French. See also *abstract, bowdlerize,* and *paraphrase.*

abstract **1.** *n.* An **abstract,** ***précis,*** or **summary** is a brief account of the main ideas or arguments presented in a work. A well-made abstract presents those ideas or arguments in the same order as in the original. Writing an abstract is an excellent way to commit to memory the major ideas of a nonfiction work such as an essay or a chapter in a textbook. See *paraphrase.* **2.** *adj.* An **abstract** word or phrase is one that refers to something that cannot be directly perceived by the senses. *Freedom, love, integrity, honesty,* and *loyalty* are examples of abstract terms. The opposite of *abstract* in this sense is *concrete.* See *concrete.*

absurd See *literature of the absurd.*

accent See *stress.*

acronym An **acronym** is a word created from the first, or initial, letters of a series of words. Examples of acronyms include *scuba,* from the words *self-contained underwater breathing apparatus,* and *radar,* from *radio detecting and ranging.*

acrostic An **acrostic** is a poem organized so that the first or last letters of each line form a word, a phrase, or a regular sequence of letters of the alphabet.

act An **act** is a major division of a drama. The first dramas were not divided into acts, but rather into scenes in which the actors performed and scenes in which the chorus spoke. The dramas of ancient Rome were generally divided into five acts, as were the plays of the Renaissance and the Enlightenment. In modern times, plays are most often divided into three acts, and short plays called "one-acts" are common.

action The **action** is the sequence of events that actually occur in a literary work, as opposed to those that occur off-scene or that precede or follow the events in the work itself. A common literary technique, inherited from the classical *epic,* is to begin a work *in medias res,* in the middle of the action, and to fill in the background details later through flashbacks. See *flashback.*

actor An **actor** is one who performs the role of a character in a play. The term is now used both for male and female performers.

adage See *proverb.*

adaptation An **adaptation** is a rewriting of a literary work in another form. In modern times, adaptations for film are often made of successful novels, musicals, and plays. A film adaptation was made of Laura Esquivel's novel *Like Water for Chocolate.* Richard Wagner's opera *Tristan und Isolde* is an adaptation of Gottfried von Strassburg's *Tristan.* Claude Schoneberg, Alain Boubil, and Herbert Kretezmer's musical *Les Misérables* is an adaptation of Victor Hugo's novel.

aesthetics **Aesthetics** is the philosophical study of beauty. *Aesthetic principles* are guidelines established for the making and judging of works of art. From age to age, accepted aesthetic principles have differed, and these differences have dramatically influenced the nature of works of art produced in those ages. For example, the ancient Greek philosopher Aristotle propounded an aesthetic of *mimesis,* or *imitation,* believing that the proper function of art was to provide an accurate portrayal of life, an idea perhaps best expressed in Shakespeare's description of dramatic art as "a mirror held up to nature." In sharp contrast to such an aesthetic is the idea, derived from the Greek philosopher Plato, that the function of art is to rise above ordinary nature and to embody ideal, or *sublime,* forms of a kind not found in this material world of the ordinary and transient.

In Europe and the United States, the dominant aesthetics have been the Neoclassical, dating from the eighteenth century; the Romantic, dating from the nineteenth century; and the Realistic and Naturalistic, dating from the late nineteenth and early twentieth centuries.

The Neoclassical aesthetic values order, rationality, and artifice. The Romantic aesthetic values wildness, emotion, imagination, and nature. The Realist aesthetic harkens back to Aristotle and values imitation, but imitation of a modern kind—of the depths as well as the heights of human experience. The Naturalistic aesthetic, like the Realistic, views the purpose of art as the accurate imitation of life, but it also attempts to show how all things, including human actions, thoughts, and feelings, are caused, or determined, by circumstances.

The critic I. A. Richards claimed that a radical shift away from an aesthetic based on beauty to one based on interest occurred in the twentieth century. While beauty, however defined, remains the guiding principle of artistic judgment in low-brow circles—as for example, in popular judgments made about sentimental novels and verses—interest, both intellectual and emotional, has emerged as the primary standard by which professional critics today judge works of art. See *Naturalism, Neoclassicism, Realism,* and *Romanticism.*

affective fallacy The **affective fallacy** is the evaluation of works of art based not on their artistic merit but rather on their emotional effects on the reader, viewer, or listener. A person who holds a didactic or utilitarian view of the function of art would not consider this approach a fallacy. See *didacticism.*

afterword An **afterword** is a statement made at the end of a work, often an analysis, a summary, or a celebration of the preceding work. See *epilogue.*

Age of Reason See *Enlightenment* and *Neoclassicism.*

aim A writer's **aim** is the primary purpose that his or her work is meant to achieve. One commonly used method of classifying writing by aim, proposed by James Kinneavey in *A Theory of Discourse,* describes four major aims: to express oneself (expressive writing), to persuade (persuasive writing), to inform (informative writing), and to create a work of literary art (literary writing).

Alexandrine An **Alexandrine**, or **iambic hexameter,** is a verse with six iambic feet.

allegory An **allegory** is a work in which each element *symbolizes,* or represents, something else. In *naive allegory*, characters, objects, places, and actions are personifications of abstractions. In more sophisticated allegories, such as Dante's *The Divine Comedy,* the elements of the work make an *extended metaphor* in which the literal elements are described but their part-by-part interpretation is left to the reader. In one sense, all literature can be viewed as allegorical in that individual characters, objects, places, and actions are types representing others of their kind. See *concrete universal* and *extended metaphor.*

alliteration **Alliteration** is the repetition of initial consonant sounds. Some writers use the term as well to describe repeated initial vowel sounds. The following line from Leopold Senghor's "And We Shall Be Steeped" contains an example of alliteration.

> On the walls, **p**ure **p**rimordial masks distant
> and yet **p**resent.

allusion An **allusion** is a rhetorical technique in which reference is made to a person, event, object, or work from history or literature. Yannis Ritsos's poem "Penelope's Despair" alludes, or refers, to the return of Odysseus as told in Homer's *Odyssey.*

ambiguity An **ambiguity** is a statement that has a double meaning or a meaning that cannot be clearly resolved. In English, the word *cleave* is oddly ambiguous, for it can mean either "to cling together" or "to cut apart." Many literary *figures of speech,* including *metaphors, similes, personifications,* and *symbols*, are examples of intentional ambiguity, speaking of one thing when another is intended.

amplification See *elaboration.*

anachronism An **anachronism** is a reference to something that did not exist at the time being described. Thus a reference to a watch in a modern retelling of an Arthurian romance would be an anachronism because watches had not been invented in the time of King Arthur.

anagram An **anagram** is a word or a phrase created by rearranging the letters of another word or phrase. The title of Samuel Butler's novel *Erewhon* is an anagram for *nowhere*. See *palindrome.*

analects **Analects** are collections of passages from the works of one or more authors. A famous example of such a collection is *The Analects* of the Chinese philosopher Confucius.

analogy An **analogy** is a comparison of two things that are alike in some respects but different in others. In an analogy, the comparison is direct, not implied. A *simile* is a type of analogy. See *simile.*

analysis **Analysis** is a thinking strategy in which one divides a subject into parts and then examines the relationships among the parts and between individual parts and the whole. An analysis of a short story, for example, might consist of a division of the work into such parts as the exposition, the rising action, the climax, the resolution, and the dénouement, along with an examination of the role played by each of these parts in advancing the plot. An analysis of a line of poetry might consist of a careful examination of its rhythm, its figures of speech, its images, and its meaning or meanings.

anapest An **anapest** is a poetic foot containing two weakly stressed syllables followed by one strongly stressed syllable, as in the words *unimpressed* and *correlate.* A line of poetry made up of anapests is said to be *anapestic.*

anaphora An **anaphora**, as that term is used by linguists, is any word or phrase that repeats or refers to something that precedes or follows it. Consider, for example, these lines from Virgil's *Aeneid*:

> The riddling words of seers in ancient days,
> Foreboding sayings, made her thrill with fear.

In these lines, the phrase *Foreboding sayings* is an example of anaphora because it refers back to, or renames, the riddling words of seers.

anecdote An **anecdote** is a brief story, usually with a specific point or moral.

Anglo-Norman literature **Anglo-Norman literature** is the literature written in French by the Norman conquerors of England. Anglo-Norman literature, along with literature written in Latin, dominated English literary life for two centuries following the Norman Conquest in 1066. Examples of this literature are the *lays,* or songs, of Marie de France. See *Breton lay.*

antagonist See *character.*

antihero An **antihero** is a central character who lacks many of the qualities traditionally associated with heroes. An antihero may be lacking in beauty, courage, grace, intelligence, or moral scruples. Antiheroes are common figures in modern fiction and drama. See *hero.*

antithesis **Antithesis** is a rhetorical technique in which words, phrases, or ideas are strongly contrasted, often by means of a repetition of grammatical structure. An example is Alexander Pope's description of the ideal critic in "An Essay on Criticism," who is "Still pleased to praise, yet not afraid to blame."

aphorism An **aphorism** is a short saying or pointed statement. Examples of aphorisms include Alfred, Lord Tennyson's "'Tis Better to have loved and lost/Than never to have loved at all" and William Shakespeare's "All the world's a stage." An aphorism that gains currency and is passed from generation to generation is called a *proverb* or *adage.* See *proverb.*

apocrypha **Apocrypha** are works that are doubtful in their origin or authorship. The term was first used to describe works from Biblical times not considered to be divinely inspired. It is now sometimes used to describe works of doubtful authorship.

apology An **apology** is a literary defense. A famous example is Plato's *Apology,* which defends Socrates against the charges of impiety brought against him.

apostrophe An **apostrophe** is a rhetorical technique in which an object or person is directly addressed. Examples include Judith Wright's request posed directly to the year at the end of "Request to a Year" and Yehuda Amichai's address to Jerusalem in "If I Forget Thee, Jerusalem."

apposition An **apposition** is a grammatical form in which a thing is renamed in a different word, phrase, or clause. An example of apposition appears in Psalm 18:

> The Lord is my rock, and my fortress, and
> my deliverer; my God, my strength, in
> whom I will trust; my buckler, and the horn
> of my salvation, and my high tower.

archaic language **Archaic language** consists of old or obsolete words or phrases such as *smote* for *hit*. Edmund Spenser uses intentionally archaic language in Sonnet 75 to transport his readers back to the days of chivalry and romance.

archetype An **archetype** is an inherited, often unconscious, ancestral memory or motif that recurs throughout history and literature. The notion of the archetype derives from the psychology of Carl Jung, who described archetypes as symbols from humanity's "collective unconscious." The term is often used, more generally, to refer to any element that recurs throughout the literature of the world. Thus the story of the journey, in which someone sets out on a path, experiences adventures, and emerges wiser, may be considered archetypal, for it is found in all cultures and in all times. See *motif.*

argument **1.** An **argument** is a summary, in prose, of the plot or meaning of a poem or drama. **2.** In nonfiction writing, an **argument** is the case for accepting or rejecting a proposition or course of action.

argumentation **Argumentation,** one of the modes of writing, presents reasons or arguments for accepting a position or for adopting a course of action. See *mode.*

Arthurian romance **Arthurian romances** are stories of the exploits of the legendary King Arthur and his knights of the Round Table. See the selection from Chrétien de Troyes's *The Story of the Grail* and the Prereading page for this selection.

article An **article** is a brief work of nonfiction on a specific topic. The term *article* is typically used of encyclopedia entries and short nonfiction works that appear in newspapers and popular magazines. The term is sometimes used as a synonym of *essay,* though the latter term often connotes a more serious, important, or lasting work. See *essay.*

aside An **aside** is a statement made by a character in a play, intended to be heard by the audience but not by other characters on the stage.

assonance **Assonance** is the repetition of vowel sounds in stressed syllables that end with different consonant sounds. An example is the repetition of the long *e* and *i* sounds in:

> I arise from dreams of thee
> In the first sweet sleep of night
> —Percy Bysshe Shelley

atmosphere See *mood.*

autobiography An **autobiography** is the story of a person's life, written by that person. Some editors and critics distinguish between autobiographies, which focus on personal experiences, and *memoirs,* which focus on public events, though the terms are often used interchangeably. *Kaffir Boy* is the autobiography of Mark Mathabane.

background information See *flashback, plot,* and *setting.*

ballad A **ballad** is a simple narrative poem in four-line stanzas, usually meant to be sung and usually rhyming *abcb. Folk ballads,* composed orally and passed by word of mouth from generation to generation, have enjoyed enormous popularity from the Middle Ages to the present. *Literary ballads,* written in imitation of folk ballads, have also been very popular. An example of the literary ballad is Robert Burns's "Song Composed in August." The folk ballad stanza usually alternates between lines of four and three feet. Common techniques used in ballads include repeated lines, or *refrains,* and *incremental repetition,* the repetition of lines with slight, often cumulative, changes throughout the poem. See *refrain.*

bibliography A **bibliography** is a list of works on a given subject or of works consulted by an author. See *List of Works Cited.*

Bildungsroman A ***Bildungsroman*** is a novel that tells the story of the growth or development of a person from youth to adulthood. The first example of this type of work is Johann Wolfgang von Goethe's *Wilhelm Meister's Apprenticeship.*

biographical criticism See *criticism.*

biography A **biography** is the story of a person's life, told by someone other than that person. Plutarch's *The Parallel Lives of the Noble Grecians and Romans* contains many classical biographies.

blank verse **Blank verse** is unrhymed poetry written in iambic pentameter. An *iambic pentameter* line consists of five *feet,* each containing two syllables, the first weakly stressed and the second strongly stressed. Blank verse was introduced into English in Surrey's translation of Virgil's *Aeneid.*

blend A **blend,** or **portmanteau,** is a word created by joining together two previously existing words, such as *smoke* and *fog* for *smog* or *whale* and *horse* for *walrus.* In his poem "Jabberwocky," Lewis Carroll coined *slithy* by joining together, or blending, *lithe* and *slimy*.

Bloomsbury Group The **Bloomsbury Group** was a circle of English writers and thinkers of the 1920s and 1930s that included Virginia Woolf, John Maynard Keynes, Lytton Strachey, and E. M. Forster.

bowdlerize To **bowdlerize** a piece of writing is to censor it by deleting material considered offensive. The term comes from the name of Thomas Bowdler, who published a "bowdlerized" edition of Shakespeare's works in the early nineteenth century.

Breton lay A **Breton lay** is a brief medieval romance of the kind produced in Brittany and later in England in imitation of such works. Breton lays dealt with conventional romance themes such as courtly love. An example of such works is Marie de France's "Lay of the Werewolf."

cacophony **Cacophony** is harsh or unpleasant sound. Writers sometimes intentionally use cacophony for effect.

cæsura A **cæsura** is a major pause in a line of poetry, as in the following line from William Shakespeare's Sonnet 130:

> I love to hear her speak, || yet well I know

canon A **canon** is a group of literary works considered to be authentic or worthy. The term was originally used for Biblical books believed to be divinely inspired. It was later adapted to describe works that can be definitely assigned to a given author (as in *the canonical works of Geoffrey Chaucer*). The term is also used to describe those works in a given literary tradition considered to be classics and thus worthy of inclusion in textbooks, in anthologies, and on the reading lists of courses in schools and universities. In the eighteenth century, there was much debate in France and England concerning whether the canon should include primarily modern or ancient works. In the twentieth century, debates over the canon centered on the inattention given works by non-male, non-European writers. Feminist critics, in particular, noted the tendency of male editors and anthologists to include in their collections works by male writers and to exclude works by female writers. See *feminist criticism* under the entry for *criticism.*

canto A **canto** is a section or part of a long poem. The sections of such long poems as Dante's *The Divine Comedy* and Ludovico Ariosto's *Orlando Furioso* are called cantos. The word comes from the Latin *cantus,* meaning "song."

caricature In literature, a **caricature** is a piece of writing that exaggerates certain qualities of a character in order to satirize or ridicule that character or type. See *satire.*

carpe diem ***Carpe diem*** is a Latin term meaning "seize the day." The *carpe diem* theme, telling people not to waste time but rather to enjoy themselves while they have a chance, was common in Renaissance English poetry. The following stanza by Robert Herrick is one of the most famous expression of this theme in English:

> Gather ye rosebuds while ye may,
> Old Time is still a-flying;
> And this same flower that smiles today,
> Tomorrow will be dying.

catalog A **catalog** is a list of people or things. Sei Shonogon's *The Pillow Book* contains many catalogs.

catastrophe The **catastrophe** is a conclusion of a work, particularly of a tragedy, marked by the fall of the central character. In the catastrophe, the central conflict of the play is ended, or resolved. See *plot.*

catharsis The ancient Greek philosopher Aristotle described tragedy as bringing about a **catharsis,** or purging, of the emotions of fear and pity. Some critics take Aristotle's words to mean that viewing a tragedy causes the audience to feel emotions of fear and pity, which are then released at the end of the play, leaving the viewer calm, wiser, and perhaps more thoughtful. The idea that catharsis calms an audience has been contradicted by recent psychological studies that suggest that people tend to imitate enacted feelings and behaviors that they witness.

Celtic **Celtic** is a term used to refer to the art and culture of the Celts, a people who inhabited ancient Britain and much of Europe. It is also used to refer to the art and culture of descendants of the Celts, including modern Welsh, Cornish, Breton, Irish, Manx, and Scottish peoples. The late nineteenth and early twentieth centuries saw in Ireland a Celtic Revival or Celtic Renaissance, characterized by the renewed use of the Gaelic language and by an explosion of literary productions based on Irish themes by authors such as William Butler Yeats, Lady Augusta Gregory, and James Joyce.

censorship **Censorship** is the act of examining works to see if they meet predetermined standards of political, social, or moral acceptability. Official censorship is aimed at works that will undermine authority or morals and has often in the past resulted in the suppression of works considered dangerous or licentious. See *bowdlerize.*

central conflict A **central conflict** is the primary struggle dealt with in the plot of a story or drama. See *conflict* and *plot.*

character A **character** is a person (or sometimes an animal) who figures in the action of a literary work. A *protagonist,* or *main character,* is the central figure in a literary work. An *antagonist* is a character who is pitted against a protagonist. *Major characters* are those who play significant roles in a work. *Minor characters* are those who play lesser roles. A *one-dimensional character, flat character,* or *caricature* is one who exhibits a single dominant quality, or *character trait.* A *three-dimensional, full,* or *rounded character* is one who exhibits the complexity of traits associated with actual human beings. A *static character* is one who does not change during the course of the action. A *dynamic character* is one who does change. A *stock character* is one found again and again in different literary works. An example of a stock character is the mad scientist of nineteenth- and twentieth-century science fiction.

characterization **Characterization** is the use of literary techniques to create a character. Writers use three major techniques to create characters: direct description, portrayal of characters' behavior, and representations of characters' internal states. When using direct description, the writer, through a speaker, a narrator, or another character, simply comments on the character, telling the reader about such matters as the character's appearance, habits, dress, background, personality, motivations, and so on. In portrayal of a character's behavior, the writer presents the actions and speech of the character, allowing the reader to draw his or her own conclusions from what the character says or does. When using representations of internal states, the writer reveals directly the character's private thoughts and emotions, often by means of what is known as the *internal monologue.* See *character* and *internal monologue.*

chiasmus A **chiasmus** is a rhetorical technique in which the order of occurrence of words or phrases is reversed, as in the line "We can weather changes, but we can't change the weather."

chivalry **Chivalry** was the code of conduct of the medieval knight. The word derives from the French *cheval,* for "horse," indicating the importance of this animal to the knight, who typically traveled and fought on horseback. According to the code of chivalry, a knight was to be a loyal servant to his lord or lady and a perfect exemplar of such virtues as bravery, courage, courtesy, honesty, faith, and gentleness. Medieval romance literature, such as Chrétien de Troyes's *The Story of the Grail,* typically presents a series of tests (trials or quests) of these knightly virtues. See *romance.*

chronological order **Chronological order** is the arrangement of details in order of their occurrence. It is the primary method of organization used in narrative writing. It is also common in nonfiction writing that describes processes, events, and cause-and-effect relationships.

classic A **classic** is a work of literature that is widely held to be one of the greatest creations within a given literary tradition. The question of what works are to be considered classic, and thus the question of what constitutes the *canon,* is a much-debated one. See *canon.*

Classical Era The **Classical Era** is the period in European history that saw the flowering of the ancient Greek and Roman cultures. Classical literature is the literature of ancient Greece and Rome from the time of Homer and Hesiod to the fall of the Roman Empire in AD 410.

Classicism **Classicism** is a collection of ideas about literature and about art in general derived from study of works by Greeks and Romans of the *Classical Era.* Definitions of what constitutes the Classical style differ, but most would agree that the Classical aesthetic emphasizes authority, austerity, clarity, conservatism, decorum, imitation, moderation, order, reason, restraint, self-control, simplicity, tradition, and unity. Classicism is most often contrasted with *Romanticism.* See *Classical Era* and *Neoclassicism.*

cliché A **cliché** is a tired or hackneyed expression such as *quiet as a mouse* or *couch potato.* Most clichés originate as vivid, colorful expressions but soon lose their interest because of overuse. Careful writers and speakers avoid clichés, which are dull and signify lack of originality.

climax The **climax** is the point of highest interest and suspense in a literary work. The term also is sometimes used to describe the *turning point* of the action in a story or play, the point at which the rising action ends and the falling action begins. See *crisis* and *plot*.

closed couplet See *couplet*.

closet drama A **closet drama** is one that is meant to be read rather than acted. Examples of the form include Milton's *Samson Agonistes,* Percy Bysshe Shelley's *The Cenci,* and Robert Browning's *Pippa Passes*.

coherence **Coherence** is the logical arrangement and progression of ideas in a speech or piece of writing. Writers achieve coherence by presenting their ideas in a logical sequence and by using transitions to show how their ideas are connected to one another. See *transition*.

coined words **Coined words** are those that are intentionally created, often from the raw materials provided by already existing words and word parts. Examples of recently coined words include *spacewalk* and *quark,* the latter taken from James Joyce's *Finnegans Wake*.

colloquialism **Colloquialism** is the use of informal language. Much modern poetry is characterized by its use of colloquialism, the language of ordinary speech first championed by William Wordsworth in the Preface to *Lyrical Ballads*.

comedy Originally a literary work with a happy ending, a **comedy** is any lighthearted or humorous work, especially one prepared for the stage or the screen. Comedy is often contrasted with tragedy, in which the hero meets an unhappy fate. (It is perhaps only a slight exaggeration to say that comedies end with wedding bells and tragedies with funeral bells.) Comedies typically present less-than-exalted characters who display human limitations, faults, and misunderstandings. The typical progression of the action in a comedy is from initial order to a humorous misunderstanding or confusion and back to order again. Stock elements of comedy include mistaken identities, word play, satire, and exaggerated characters and events. See *tragedy*.

comedy of manners The **comedy of manners** is a type of satirical comedy that originated in the late seventeenth century and that deals with the conventions and manners of a highly artificial and sophisticated society. Typical subjects dealt with in the comedy of manners include amorous intrigue, fakery, pomposity, and flattery. Examples of the genre include Jean-Baptiste de Moliere's *Tartuffe* and François-Marie Arouet de Voltaire's *Candide*.

comic relief Writers sometimes insert into a serious work of fiction or drama a humorous scene that is said to provide **comic relief,** because it relieves the seriousness or emotional intensity felt by the audience. Paradoxically, a scene introduced for comic relief can sometimes, because of the contrast it provides, increase the perceived intensity or seriousness of the action around it.

commonplace book A **commonplace book** is a collection of quotations gleaned from various sources.

comparative literature **Comparative literature** is the study of relationships among works of literature written at different times, in different places, or in different languages. A study that showed influences of French revolutionary writing on English *Romanticism* would be an example, as would a study that dealt with the motif of the foundling left in a basket floating upon the waters. The latter motif is found in such widely separated stories as the Mesopotamian *Epic of Gilgamesh,* the story of Moses in the Hebrew Scriptures, and the story of Romulus and Remus from Roman mythology.

complaint A **complaint** is a lyric poem that deals with loss, regret, unrequited love, or some other negative state experienced by the speaker of the poem. The poems of Catullus are examples of complaints.

complication The **complication** is the part of a plot in which the conflict is developed or built to its high point of intensity. See *plot*.

concrete A **concrete** word or phrase is one that names or describes something that can be directly perceived by one or more of the five senses. *Rainbow, lark, scorpion,* and *field* are examples of concrete terms. See *abstract* and *concrete universal*.

concrete poem A **concrete poem,** or shape poem, is one printed or written in a shape that suggests its subject matter.

concrete universal A **concrete universal** is a particular object, person, action, or event that provides an instance or example of a general type. So, for example, Percival is a concrete example of an innocent or foolish character. During the Neoclassical Age, writers tended to disparage concrete particulars and to write, instead, in abstract terms. As a result, modern readers sometimes find Neoclassical literature not to their taste. In our times, literary tastes tend toward the particular. See *abstract, concrete, Neoclassicism,* and *objective correlative*.

confessional poetry **Confessional poetry** is verse that describes, sometimes with painful explicitness, the private or personal affairs of the writer. Contemporary confessional poets include Allen Ginsberg, Sylvia Plath, Anne Sexton, and Robert Lowell.

conflict A **conflict** is a struggle between two forces in a literary work. A *plot* involves the introduction, development, and eventual resolution of a conflict. One side of the *central conflict* in a story or drama is usually taken by the *main character.* That character may struggle against another character, against the forces of nature, against society or social norms, against fate, or against some element within himself or herself. A struggle that takes place between a character and some outside force is called an *external conflict.* A struggle that takes place within a character is called an *internal conflict.* In the *Aeneid,* there is an external conflict between Dido and Aeneas, but Aeneas also experiences an internal conflict between his feelings for Dido and his feelings of duty toward his country and his god. See *central conflict* and *plot.*

connotation A **connotation** is an emotional association or implication attached to an expression. For example, the word *inexpensive* has positive emotional associations, whereas the word *cheap* has negative ones, even though the two words both *denote*, or refer to, low cost. Good writers choose their words carefully in order to express appropriate connotations. See *denotation.*

consonance **Consonance** is the use in stressed syllables of identical final consonants preceded by vowels with different sounds. The following lines from Robert Burns's "Song Composed in August" provide an example:

Thus ev'ry kind their pleasure find
The Savage and the **tender;**
Some social join, and leagues combine
Some solitary **wander;**

convention A **convention** is an unrealistic element in a literary work that is accepted by readers or viewers because the element is traditional. One of the conventions of fiction, for example, is that it uses the past tense to describe current or present action. Rhyme schemes and organization into stanzas are among the many commonly employed conventions of poetry. Violation of accepted conventions is one of the hallmarks of *avant garde* or *Modernist* literature. See *dramatic convention.*

conventional symbol See *symbol.*

couplet A **couplet** is two lines of verse that usually rhyme. These lines from Jean de La Fontaine's fable "The Lion and the Rat" provide an example:

Through time and toil we sever
What strength and rage could never.

A closed couplet is a pair of rhyming lines that present a complete statement.

True wit is Nature to advantage dressed,
What oft was thought, but ne'er so well
expressed.
—Alexander Pope, *An Essay on Criticism*

A pair of rhyming iambic pentameter lines is called a *heroic couplet.* Couplets were a very poplular form in the eighteenth century.

courtly love **Courtly love** is a code of romantic love celebrated in songs and romances of the Medieval Period. According to this code, the lover knows himself or herself to be truly in love if he or she is overcome by extreme, transforming emotion. Characters in works celebrating courtly love are often one-dimensional. The female lover is often portrayed in ideal and unrealistic terms. She usually requires that the male lover prove his love through a series of tasks. The male lover is led sometimes to the depths of despair and sometimes to heights of courtesy and heroism to prove his worth to his lady. Courtly love was one of the primary themes of medieval *romance* literature. See *romance.*

crisis In the plot of a story or a drama, the **crisis** is that point in the development of the conflict at which a decisive event occurs that causes the main character's situation to become better or worse. See *plot.*

critic A literary **critic** is a person who evaluates or interprets a work of literature. See *criticism.*

critical essay A **critical essay** is a type of informative or persuasive writing that presents an argument in support of a particular interpretation or evaluation of a work of literature. A well-constructed critical essay presents a clear *thesis*, or main idea, supported by ample evidence from the work or works being considered.

criticism **Criticism** is the act of evaluating or interpreting a work of art or the act of developing general guidelines or principles for such evaluation or interpretation. Over the centuries, many schools, or philosophies, of criticism have been developed. However, most readers and teachers are eclectic critics, drawing consciously or unconsciously upon various schools of critical thought. Common schools of criticism include the following:

Biographical criticism attempts to account for elements of literary works by relating them to events in the lives of their authors. Neruda's "Tonight I can write" read as a reflection of his own failed love would be an example of biographical criticism.

Deconstructionist criticism calls into question the very idea of the meaning or interpretation of a literary work by inviting the reader to reverse the binary, or two-part, relations that structure meaning in the work. For example, a deconstructionist analysis might invite the reader to consider again the conflict between Nora and Torvald in *A Doll's House.* It might claim that Torvald is controlling for a reason and that Nora's rebellion is an example, not of her maturity, but rather of the permanence of her childish nature. Such a reading deconstructs the conventional reading of the play, which insists that Ibsen intended to encourage women to see their role in the world in a new light. See *structuralist criticism.*

Didactic criticism evaluates works of art in terms of the moral, ethical, or political messages that they convey. Dismissal of a book as dangerous or obscene would be an example of didactic criticism.

Feminist criticism evaluates and interprets works of art with regard to their portrayal of or influence upon gender roles. Many feminist critics and scholars have been particularly concerned to rescue women writers from the obscurity that male critics, editors, scholars, and teachers may have forced upon them. Other feminist critics point out gender bias in literary works by analyzing variations in literary depictions of males and females, and by analyzing the effects of literary works, activities, and movements on cultural norms related to gender. An example of feminist criticism would analyze how women in medieval courtly love and romance literature are idealized and point out consequences of that idealization on later Western ideas about femininity and relations between the sexes.

Formal criticism analyzes a work of literature in terms of its genre or type. An explanation of those characteristics of *Sunjata* that make it an epic would be an example of formal criticism.

Freudian criticism draws upon the works of the founder of psychoanalysis, Sigmund Freud, and generally views literary works or the parts thereof as expressions of unconscious desires, as wish fulfillment, or as neurotic sublimations of unresolved conflicts from childhood. An example of Freudian criticism would be the interpretation of the ancient Greek Oedipus myth, in which Oedipus unwittingly marries his mother, as an expression of the young male child's competition with his father for his mother's affection.

Historical criticism views the work of art as a product of the period in which it was produced. Examples of historical criticism would be a description of the influence of the French and American revolutions on the development of *Romanticism* in England or an analysis of the effects of the plague on the writings of Boccaccio.

Jungian criticism explores the presence in works of art of archetypes—unconscious images, symbols, associations, or concepts presumed to be a common inheritance of all human beings. An analysis of symbols of rebirth in a number of myths or folk tales would be an example of Jungian criticism.

Marxist criticism, based upon the work of the German-born political philosopher Karl Marx, evaluates and interprets works of art with regard to the material, economic forces that shape them or with regard to their origins in or depictions of struggle between the social classes. An example of Marxist criticism would be an explanation of the "The Myth of Sisyphus" as propaganda intended to create harmony and to prevent oppressed workers from rebelling against their menial and repetitive labor.

Mimetic criticism, which derives from the teachings of Aristotle, views works of art as imitations of nature or of the real world and evaluates them according to the accuracy of those portrayals. Insisting that a character is poorly drawn because he or she is unrealistic is an example of mimetic criticism.

The ***New Criticism,*** championed in the early- to mid-twentieth century by such critics as I. A. Richards and Cleanth Brooks, insists upon the interpretation and evaluation of literary works based on details found in the works themselves rather than on information gathered from outside the works. It disregards such matters as the life of the author, the period in which the work was written, the literary movement that led to its production, and the emotional effect of the work upon the reader. The New Critics insisted on the importance of close analysis of literary texts and the irreducibility of those texts to generalizations or paraphrases.

Pragmatic or ***rhetorical criticism*** interprets or evaluates a work of art in terms of its effects on an audience. Critics have claimed that Jorge Luis Borges intended his readers to identify with the narrator in "The Book of Sand," so, as they ponder the concept of infinity and the questions raised by the story, readers can experience the same feelings of frustration as the narrator. This is an example of rhetorical criticism.

Reader-response criticism views the meaning of a text as resulting from a relationship between the text itself and the subjective experiences or consciousness of a reader. According to reader-response theory, a literary text has no meaning *per se.* It is, instead, an occasion for a participatory experience that the reader has. That experience may be meaningful or significant to the reader, but its meaning and significance will depend, in part, on what the reader brings to the text.

Romantic or ***expressivist criticism*** views a work of art as primarily an expression of the spirit, ideas, beliefs, values, or emotions of its creator. A reading of "My Heart Leaps Up When I Behold" as expressive of the moral posture adopted by William Wordsworth would be an example of expressivist criticism.

Structuralist criticism analyzes works of literature and art in terms of binary, or two-part, relationships or structures. A structuralist analysis of Ibsen's *A Doll's House,* for example, might view Nora's final act as a resolution of her quest for adulthood in conflict with Torvald's treatment of her as a child.

Textual criticism analyzes the various existing manuscript and printed versions of a work in order to construct an original or definitive text for use by readers.

dactyl A **dactyl** is a poetic foot made up of a strongly stressed syllable followed by two weakly stressed syllables, as in the word *feverish.* A line of poetry made up of dactyls is said to be *dactylic.*

dead metaphor A **dead metaphor** is one that is so familiar that its original metaphorical meaning is rarely thought of when the expression is used. An example is the word *nightfall,* which describes the coming of darkness as a falling object.

deconstructionist criticism See *criticism.*

definition A **definition** is an explanation of the meaning of a word or phrase. A dictionary definition typically consists of two parts: the *genus,* or class to which the thing belongs, and the *differentia,* or differences between the thing and other things of its class. Consider, for example, Oscar Wilde's tongue-in-cheek definition of *cynic:* "A man who knows the price of everything and the value of nothing." In this definition, "man" is the genus. The rest of the definition presents the differentia.

denotation The **denotation** is the basic meaning or reference of an expression, excluding its emotional associations, or *connotations.* For example, the words *dirt* and *soil* share a single common denotation. However, *dirt* has negative connotations of uncleanliness, whereas *soil* does not. See *connotation.*

dénouement See *plot.*

description A **description,** one of the modes of writing, portrays a character, an object, or a scene. Descriptions make use of *sensory details*—words and phrases that describe how things look, sound, smell, taste, or feel. See *mode.*

dialect A **dialect** is a version of a language spoken by the people of a particular place, time, or social group. Writers often use dialect, as Robert Burns does in "Song Composed in August," to give their works a realistic flavor. In this poem, Burns represents a dialect of English known as Scots. A *regional dialect* is one spoken in a particular place. A *social dialect* is one spoken by members of a particular social group or class.

dialogue **1. Dialogue** is conversation involving two or more people or characters. Plays are made up of dialogue and stage directions. Fictional works are made up of dialogue, narration, and description. **2. Dialogue** is also used to describe a type of literary composition in which characters debate or discuss an idea. Many of Plato's philosophical works were presented in the form of dialogues. Dialogues between abstractions such as the body and the soul, or virtue and vice, were common in the poetry of the Middle Ages.

diary A **diary** is a day-to-day record of a person's activities, experiences, thoughts, and feelings. The diary first gained popularity during the Renaissance and has remained popular to this day. See *journal.*

diction **Diction,** when applied to writing, refers to word choice. Much of a writer's style is determined by his or her diction, the types of words that he or she chooses. Diction can be formal or informal, simple or complex, contemporary or archaic, ordinary or unusual, foreign or native, standard or dialectical, euphemistic or blunt. See *style*.

didactic criticism See *criticism*.

didacticism **Didacticism** is the use of works of art to convey moral, social, educational, or political messages. A didactic work is one in which the artistic values of the work are subordinated to the message or meaning. Didacticism was a common element of literature in the Middle Ages and of the proletarian art and literature produced in Communist countries in the twentieth century.

dimeter See *meter*.

dirge A **dirge** is a funeral song or a poem written in imitation thereof.

dominant impression See *effect*.

drama A **drama** is a story told through characters played by actors. The script of a drama typically consists of characters' names, dialogue spoken by the characters, and stage directions. Because it is meant to be performed before an audience, drama can be distinguished from other forms of non-performance-based literary works by the central role played in it by the spectacle—the sensory presentation to the audience, which includes such elements as lighting, costumes, make-up, properties, set pieces, music, sound effects, and the movements and expressions of actors. Another important distinguishing feature of drama is that it is collaborative. The interpretation of the work depends not only upon the author and his or her audience, but also upon the director, the actors, and others involved in mounting a production. Two major types of drama are comedy and tragedy. Jean-Baptiste Poquelin Moliere's *Tartuffe* is an example of the former; Sophocles's *Oedipus the King,* of the latter. See *comedy, dialogue, spectacle, stage directions,* and *tragedy*.

dramatic convention A **dramatic convention** is an unreal element in a drama that is accepted as realistic by the audience because it is traditional. Such conventions include the impersonation of characters by actors, the use of a curtain to open or close an act or a scene, the revelation of a character's thoughts through *asides* and *soliloquies*, and the removal of the so-called *fourth wall* at the front of the stage that allows the audience to see action taking place in an imagined interior. See *convention* and *suspension of disbelief.*

dramatic irony See *irony*.

dramatic monologue A **dramatic monologue** is a poem that presents the speech of a single character in a dramatic situation. The speech is one side of an imagined conversation. Robert Browning is often credited with the creation of the dramatic monologue. He popularized the form in such poems as "My Last Duchess" and "Andrea del Sarto." See *soliloquy*.

dramatic poem A **dramatic poem** is a verse that relies heavily on dramatic elements such as monologue or dialogue. Types of dramatic poetry include the *dramatic monologue* and the *soliloquy*.

dramatis personae ***Dramatis personae*** are the characters in a literary work. The term is most often used for the characters in a drama.

dream record A **dream record** is a diary or journal in which a writer records his or her dreams. See *diary* and *journal*.

dynamic character See *character*.

dystopia A **dystopia** is an imaginary, horrible world, the opposite of a utopia. Dystopias are common in science fiction. Famous examples of dystopias include the societies described in Aldous Huxley's *Brave New World,* H. G. Wells's *The Time Machine,* and George Orwell's *Nineteen Eighty-Four*. See *utopia*.

eclogue An **eclogue** is a pastoral poem written in imitation of Greek works by Theocritus and Virgil. See *pastoral poem*.

editorial An **editorial** is a short, persuasive piece that appears in a newspaper, magazine, or other periodical.

effect The **effect** of a literary work is the general impression or emotional impact that it achieves. Some writers and critics, notably Edgar Allan Poe, have insisted that a successful short story or poem is one in which each detail contributes to the overall effect, or dominant impression, produced by the piece.

elaboration **Elaboration,** or **amplification,** is a writing technique in which a subject is introduced and then expanded upon by means of repetition with slight changes, the addition of details, or similar devices.

elegiac lyric An **elegiac lyric** is a poem that expresses a speaker's feelings of loss. Chilean poet Pablo Neruda's "Tonight I can write" is an example.

elegy An **elegy** is a long, formal poem about death or loss.

Elizabethan sonnet See *sonnet.*

emphasis **Emphasis** is importance placed on an element in a literary work. Writers achieve emphasis by various means, including repetition, elaboration, stress, restatement in other words, and placement in a strategic position at the beginning or end of a line or a sentence.

end rhyme **End rhyme** is rhyme that occurs at the ends of lines of verse. See *rhyme.*

end-stopped line An **end-stopped line** is a line of verse in which both the sense and the grammar are complete at the end of the line. The opposite of an end-stopped line is a run-on line. The following lines are end-stopped:

> Oh, oh, you will be sorry for that word!
> Give back my book and take my kiss
> instead.
> —Edna St. Vincent Millay

Excessive use of end-stopped lines gives verse an unnatural, halting quality. See run-on line.

English sonnet See *sonnet.*

enjambment See *run-on line.*

Enlightenment The **Enlightenment** was an eighteenth-century philosophical movement characterized by belief in reason, the scientific method, and the perfectibility of people and society. Thinkers of the Enlightenment Era, or Age of Reason, believed that the universe was governed by discoverable, rational principles like the laws of physics discovered by Sir Isaac Newton. By extension, they believed that people could, through application of reason, discover truths relating to the conduct of life or of society. Leading thinkers of the Enlightenment included Denis Diderot; Benjamin Franklin; Edward Gibbon; David Hume; Thomas Jefferson; Immanuel Kant; John Locke; Charles-Louis de Secondat, baron de La Brède et de Montesquieu; Alexander Pope; Adam Smith; Jonathan Swift, and François-Marie Arouet de Voltaire. See *Neoclassicism.*

epic An **epic** is a long story, often told in verse, involving heroes and gods. Grand in length and scope, an epic provides a portrait of an entire culture, of the legends, beliefs, values, laws, arts, and ways of life of a people. Famous epic poems include *The Epic of Gilgamesh* from ancient Mesopotamia, the *Ramayana* of India, the *Popol Vuh* of the Quiché Maya, Homer's *Iliad* and *Odyssey,* Virgil's *Aeneid,* Dante's *The Divine Comedy,* and the anonymous Mali epic, the *Sunjata.*

epic hero See *hero.*

epigram An **epigram** is a short, often witty, saying. Voltaire's "We can not always oblige, but we can always speak obligingly," is an example.

epigraph An **epigraph** is a quotation or motto used at the beginning of the whole or part of a literary work to help establish the work's theme. Jorge Luis Borges's "The Book of Sand" begins with an epigraph.

epilogue An **epilogue** is a concluding section or statement, often one that comments on or draws conclusions from the work as a whole.

epiphany When applied to literature, the term ***epiphany*** refers to a moment of sudden insight in which the essence, or nature, of a person, thing, or situation is revealed. The use of the term in this sense was introduced by James Joyce.

episode An **episode** is a complete action within a literary work.

episodic structure **Episodic structure** is the stringing together of loosely related incidents, or episodes. Many medieval romances have an episodic structure. They tell about the loosely related adventures of a knight or group of knights.

epistle An **epistle** is a letter, especially one that is highly formal. Letters in verse are sometimes called epistles.

epistolary fiction **Epistolary fiction** is imaginative prose that tells a story through letters, or epistles. Famous epistolary novels include Samuel Richardson's *Pamela* and his *Clarissa,* written in the mid-1700s.

epitaph An **epitaph** is an inscription or verse written to be used on a tomb or written in commemoration of someone who has died. The epitaph on the grave of the Spartan heroes who bravely fought the Persians at the battle of Thermopylae reads, "Go tell the Spartans, thou that passest by/That here, obedient to their laws, we lie."

epithet An **epithet** is a word or phrase used to describe a characteristic of a person, place, or thing. Homer's description of dawn as "rosy-fingered" is an example.

eponym An **eponym** is a person or character from whose name a word or title is derived, or a name that has become synonymous with some general characteristic or idea. Julius Cæsar is the eponym of the medical term *Cæsarean section.* The greek actor Thespis is the eponym of the word *thespian*, another term for actor. A reference to Helen of Troy, used in place of the more general term *beauty,* or a reference to an Einstein, in place of a more general term such as *a smart person,* would be an eponym.

essay An **essay** is a brief work of prose nonfiction. The original meaning of essay was "a trial or attempt," and the word retains some of this original force. An essay need not be a complete or exhaustive treatment of a subject but rather a tentative exploration of it. A good essay develops a single idea and is characterized by *unity* and *coherence*. See *coherence* and *unity.*

euphemism A **euphemism** is an indirect word or phrase used in place of a direct statement that might be considered too offensive. The phrase *passed away,* used instead of *died,* is a euphemism.

euphony **Euphony** is pleasing sound. Writers achieve euphony by various means, including repetitions of vowel and consonant sounds, rhyme, and parallelism. See *cacophony.*

Existentialism **Existentialism** is a twentieth-century philosophical school that assumes the essential absurdity and meaninglessness of life. Existentialist philosophers such as Albert Camus and Jean-Paul Sartre argued that existence, or being, emerges out of nothingness without any essential, or defining, nature. A human being simply finds himself or herself alive and aware without having any essential, defining direction. Any choices that a person makes in order to define himself or herself are made freely and therefore absurdly—one may as well make one choice as another. Freedom of the will is therefore seen by the Existentialist as a terrific burden, one causing anguish to people, who long for meaningfulness, not absurd choices. Another significant aspect of Existentialism is its insistence on the essential isolation of each individual consciousness and the consequent anguish of people looking for meaningful connection to others. Though many of the essential tenets of Existentialism have been discredited by contemporary philosophers, the school nonetheless exerted tremendous influence on mid-twentieth-century literature in Europe, Great Britain, and the United States. See *literature of the absurd* and *theater of the absurd.*

exposition **1. Exposition,** one of the modes of writing, presents factual information. See *mode.* **2.** In a plot, the **exposition** is that part of a narrative that provides background information, often about the characters, setting, or conflict. See *plot.*

Expressionism **Expressionism** is the name given to a twentieth-century movement in literature and art that reacted against *Realism* in favor of an exaggeration of the elements of the artistic medium itself, in an attempt to express ideas or feelings. The use in a play of characters named, simply, Person, Mother, and Character 1 is an example of Expressionism. Modern Expressionist dramatists include Karel Capek, Luigi Pirandello, Elmer Rice, and Edward Albee.

extended metaphor An **extended metaphor** is a point-by-point presentation of one thing as though it were another. The description is meant as an implied comparison, inviting the reader to associate the thing being described with something that is quite different from it. Sir Thomas Wyatt's "Whoso List to Hunt" is an example. In the poem, a woman is described as a deer, the pursuit of the woman as poaching, and the woman's mate as Cæsar, the owner of the property on which the poaching might be done.

external conflict See *conflict.*

eye rhyme See *sight rhyme.*

fable A **fable** is a brief story, often with animal characters, told to express a moral. Famous fables include those of Aesop and La Fontaine.

fabliau A **fabliau** is a brief, humorous tale, often ribald. The form was extremely popular during the Middle Ages.

fairy tale A **fairy tale** is a story that deals with mischievous spirits and other supernatural occurrences, often in medieval settings. The name is generally applied to stories of the kinds collected by Charles Perrault in France and the Brothers Grimm in Germany or told by Hans Christian Andersen of Denmark. "Cinderella," "The White Snake," and "The Little Mermaid" are famous examples.

falling action See *plot.*

fantasy A **fantasy** is a literary work that contains highly unrealistic elements. Magical realist stories such as "The Little Heidelberg" contain elements of fantasy. Fantasy is often contrasted with *science fiction*, in which the unreal elements are given a scientific or pseudo-scientific basis.

See *magical realism* and *science fiction.*

farce A **farce** is a type of comedy that depends heavily on so-called low humor and on improbable, exaggerated, extreme situations or characters.

feminist criticism See *criticism.*

fiction **Fiction** is prose writing about imagined events or characters. The primary forms of fiction are the novel and the short story.

figurative language **Figurative language** is language that suggests something more than the literal meanings of the words might be taken to suggest. See *figures of speech.*

figure of speech **A figure of speech,** or **trope,** is an expression that has more than a literal meaning. Hyperbole, metaphor, metonymy, personification, simile, synaesthesia, synecdoche, and understatement are all figures of speech. See *hyperbole, metaphor, metonymy, personification, simile, synaesthesia, synecdoche,* and *understatement.*

first-person point of view See *point of view.*

flashback A **flashback** is a section of a literary work that presents an event or series of events that occurred earlier than the current time in the work. Writers use flashbacks for many purposes, but most notably to provide background information, or exposition. In popular melodramatic works, including modern romance fiction and detective stories, flashbacks are often used to end suspense by revealing key elements of the plot such as a character's true identity or the actual perpetrator of a crime. One common technique is to begin a work with a final event and then to tell the rest of the story as a flashback that explains how that event came about. Another common technique is to begin a story *in medias res* (in the middle of the action) and then to use a flashback to fill in the events that occurred before the opening of the story.

flash fiction See *short short.*

flat character See *character.*

foil A **foil** is a character whose attributes, or characteristics, contrast with, and therefore throw into relief, the attributes of another character. In Ibsen's *A Doll's House,* for example, Christine Linde, a character who has had to support herself and struggle, provides a foil for Nora, who has been taken care of her entire life, first by her father and then by Torvald.

folk ballad See *ballad.*

folk song A **folk song** is an anonymous song that is transmitted orally. Examples include the ballad "Bonny Barbara Allan," the sea chantey "Blow the Man Down," the children's song "Row, Row, Row Your Boat," the spiritual "Go Down, Moses," the railroad song "Casey Jones," and the cowboy song "The Streets of Laredo." The term *folk song* is sometimes used for works composed in imitation of true folk songs. Modern composers of songs in the folk tradition include Bob Dylan, Paul Simon, Joan Baez, and the Indigo Girls. See *ballad.*

folk tale A **folk tale** is a brief story passed by word of mouth from generation to generation. Writers often make use of materials from folk tales. Heinrich Heine's "The Loreley," for example, retells a traditional folk tale. Famous collections of folk tales include the German *Märchen,* or fairy tales, collected by the Brothers Grimm; Yeats's collection of Irish stories, *Mythologies;* and Zora Neale Hurston's collection of African-American folk tales and other folklore materials, *Of Mules and Men.* See *fairy tale, folklore,* and *oral tradition.*

folklore **Folklore** is a body of orally transmitted beliefs, customs, rituals, traditions, songs, verses, or stories. Folk tales, fables, fairy tales, tall tales, nursery rhymes, proverbs, legends, myths, parables, riddles, charms, spells, and ballads are all common kinds of folklore, though each of these can be found, as well, in literary forms made in imitation of works from the oral tradition.

foot In a poem, a **foot** is a unit of rhythm consisting of strongly and weakly stressed syllables. See *meter* and *scansion.* Also see the specific types of feet: *anapest, dactyl, iamb, spondee,* and *trochee.*

foreshadowing **Foreshadowing** is the act of presenting materials that hint at events to occur later in a story. In Sophocles's *Oedipus the King,* Oedipus taunts the blind seer Teiresias, who warns Oedipus, "You have your eyes but see not where you are/in sin, nor where you live, nor whom you live with,/ . . . A deadly footed, double striking curse,/from father and mother both, shall drive you forth/out of this land, with darkness on your eyes." Teiresias's words foreshadow the revelation that Oedipus has indeed killed his father and married his mother and will blind himself and be exiled from Thebes.

foreword See *preface.*

HANDBOOK OF LITERARY TERMS

formal criticism See *criticism.*

fourteener See *meter.*

fourth wall See *dramatic convention.*

frame tale A **frame tale** is a story that itself provides a vehicle for the telling of other stories. The *Thousand and One Nights,* Boccaccio's *Decameron,* and Chaucer's *The Canterbury Tales* are frame tales.

free verse **Free verse,** or ***vers libre,*** is poetry that avoids use of regular rhyme, rhythm, meter, or division into stanzas. Ferderico García Lorca's "The Guitar" and Czeslaw Milosz's "A Song on the End of the World" are examples. Much of the poetry written in the twentieth century is in free verse.

Freudian criticism See *criticism.*

full character See *character.*

genre A **genre** (zhän´rə) is one of the types or categories into which literary works are divided. Some terms used to name literary genres include *autobiography, biography, comedy, drama, epic, essay, lyric, narrative, novel, pastoral, poetry, short story,* and *tragedy.* Literary works are sometimes classified into genres based on subject matter. Such a classification might describe detective stories, mysteries, adventure stories, romances, westerns, and science fiction as different genres of fiction.

Gothic novel A **Gothic novel,** or **Gothic romance,** is a long story containing elements of horror, suspense, mystery, and magic. Gothic novels often contain dark, brooding descriptions of settings and characters. Emily Brontë's *Wuthering Heights* contains many Gothic elements. Toni Morrison is a contemporary writer who occasionally includes Gothic elements in her writing, most notably in her Pulitzer Prize-winning novel *Beloved.*

Gothic romance See *Gothic novel.*

haiku A **haiku** is a traditional Japanese three-line poem containing five syllables in the first line, seven in the second, and five again in the third. A haiku presents a picture, or image, in order to arouse in the reader a specific emotional and/or spiritual state.

half rhyme See *slant rhyme.*

heptameter See *meter.*

hero A **hero** is a character whose actions are inspiring and courageous. An **epic hero** represents the ideals of the culture that creates it. In early literature, a hero is often part divine and has remarkable abilities, such as magical power, superhuman strength, or great courage. A **tragic hero** is a character of high status who possesses noble qualities but who also has a tragic flaw, or personal weakness. In much contemporary literature, the term *hero* often refers to any main character. See *antihero* and *tragic flaw.*

heroic couplet See *couplet.*

heroic epic A **heroic epic** is an epic that has a main purpose of telling the life story of a great hero. Examples of the heroic epic include *The Epic of Gilgamesh,* the *Ramayana,* the *Sunjata,* Homer's *Iliad* and *Odyssey,* and Virgil's *Aeneid.* See epic.

hexameter See *meter.*

high style See *style.*

historical criticism See *criticism.*

hymn A **hymn** is a song or verse of praise, often religious. Akhenaten's "Hymn to the Sun" and the Indian "Creation Hymn" are two ancient examples of hymns.

hyperbole A **hyperbole** (hī pur´bə lē) is an exaggeration made for rhetorical effect. Empress Nur Jahan uses hyperbole in "Your love turned . . ." when she writes,

> Your love turned my body
> into water.

iamb An **iamb** is a poetic foot containing one weakly stressed syllable followed by one strongly stressed syllable, as in the words *afraid* and *release.* A line of poetry made up of iambs is said to be iambic.

iambic See *iamb.*

idyll An **idyll** is a short poem or work of prose that describes a peaceful, rural scene. See *pastoral poem.*

image An **image** is a word or phrase that names something that can be seen, heard, touched, tasted, or smelled. The images in a literary work are referred to, collectively, as the work's imagery.

imagery See *image.*

in medias res See *action* and *flashback.*

inciting incident See *plot.*

incremental repetition See *ballad.*

internal conflict See *conflict.*

internal monologue An **internal monologue** presents the private sensations, thoughts, and emotions of a character. The reader is allowed to step inside the character's mind and overhear what is going on in there. Which characters' internal states can be revealed in a work of fiction depends on the *point of view* from which the work is told. See *point of view.*

introduction See *preface.*

inversion An **inversion** is a poetic technique in which the normal order of words in an utterance is altered. Wole Soyinka's "Now, garnerers we," is an inversion of the usual order of expression: "Now, we garnerers."

irony **Irony** is a difference between appearance and reality. Types of irony include the following: *dramatic irony,* in which something is known by the reader or audience but unknown to the characters; *verbal irony,* in which a statement is made that implies its opposite; and *irony of situation,* in which an event occurs that violates the expectations of the characters, the reader, or the audience.

irony of situation See *irony.*

journal A **journal,** like a *diary,* is a day-to-day record of a person's activities, experiences, thoughts, and feelings. In contrast to *diary,* the word *journal* connotes an outward rather than an inward focus. However, the two terms are often used interchangeably. See *diary.*

Jungian criticism See *criticism.*

limited point of view See *narrator* and *point of view.*

List of Works Cited A **List of Works Cited** is a type of bibliography that lists works used or referred to by an author. A standard feature of a research paper, the List of Works Cited appears at the end of the paper and is arranged in alphabetical order.

literary ballad See *ballad.*

literature of the absurd **Literature of the absurd** is literature influenced by Existentialist philosophy, which represents human life as meaningless or absurd because of the supposed lack of essential connection between human beings and the world around them. In brief, the Existentialist philosophers, such as Albert Camus and Jean-Paul Sartre, believed that a person's conscious existence precedes any essential self-definition and that self-definition can occur only as a result of making an absurd, completely free choice to act, think, or believe in certain ways. The literature of the absurd emphasizes the meaninglessness of life and the isolation, or alienation, of individuals. Much of the literature of the absurd is filled with horrors, anguish, random events, and illogical or improbable occurrences. Modern practitioners of the literature of the absurd include the novelists Franz Kafka, Thomas Pynchon, and Kurt Vonnegut, Jr., and the playwrights Eugene Ionesco, Samuel Beckett, Edward Albee, and Harold Pinter. See *Existentialism* and *theater of the absurd.*

low style See *style.*

lyric poem A **lyric poem** is a highly musical verse that expresses the emotions of a speaker. Judith Wright's "Request to a Year" and Yannis Ritsos's "Penelope's Despair" are examples. Lyric poems are often contrasted with narrative poems, which have storytelling as their main purpose.

magical realism **Magical realism** is a kind of fiction that is for the most part realistic but that contains elements of fantasy. Isabel Allende's "The Little Heidelberg" is an example of magical realism.

main character See *character.*

major character See *character.*

Marxist criticism See *criticism.*

metaphor A **metaphor** is a figure of speech in which one thing is spoken or written about as if it were another. This figure of speech invites the reader to make a comparison between the two things. The two "things" involved are the writer's actual subject, the tenor of the metaphor, and another thing to which the subject is likened, the vehicle of the metaphor. When, in "Though I am Laila of the Persian romance," Princess Zeb-un-Nissa writes that "Modesty is chains on my feet," she is using a metaphor:

TENOR	VEHICLE
modesty	chains on feet

Personification and similes are types of metaphor. See *dead metaphor, mixed metaphor, personification,* and *simile.*

meter The **meter** of a poem is its rhythmical pattern. English verse is generally described as being made up of rhythmical units called *feet,* as follows:

TYPE OF FOOT	STRESS PATTERN	EXAMPLE
iambic	⌣ /	insist
trochaic	/ ⌣	freedom
anapestic	⌣ ⌣ /	unimpressed
dactylic	/ ⌣ ⌣	feverish
spondaic	/ /	baseball

Some scholars also use the term *pyrrhic* to describe a foot with two weak stresses. Using this term, the word *unbelievable* might be described as consisting of two feet, an anapest followed by a pyrrhic:

⌣ ⌣ / | ⌣ ⌣
un be liev | a ble

Terms used to describe the number of feet in a line include the following:

monometer for a one-foot line
dimeter for a two-foot line
trimeter for a three-foot line
tetrameter for a four-foot line
pentameter for a five-foot line
hexameter, or *Alexandrine*, for a six-foot line
heptameter for a seven-foot line
octameter for an eight-foot line

A seven-foot line of iambic feet is called a *fourteener.*

A complete description of the meter of a line includes both the term for the type of foot that predominates in the line and the term for the number of feet in the line. The most common English meters are iambic tetrameter and iambic pentameter. The following are examples of each:

IAMBIC TETRAMETER:
⌣ / ⌣ / ⌣ / ⌣ /
O slow | ly, slow | ly rose | she up

IAMBIC PENTAMETER:
⌣ / ⌣ / ⌣ / ⌣ /
The cur | few tolls | the knell | of part |

⌣ /
ing day,

metonymy **Metonymy** is the naming of an object associated with a thing in place of the name of the thing itself. Speaking of *the White House* when one means *the administrative or executive branch of the United States government* is an example of metonymy. Rachel de Queiroz's "Metonymy, or the Husband's Revenge" explores this literary technique.

middle style See *style.*

mimetic criticism See *criticism.*

minor character See *character.*

mixed metaphor A **mixed metaphor** is an expression or passage that garbles together two or more metaphors. An example of mixed metaphor would be the sentence "The chariot of the sun screamed across the sky," in which the sun is described, inconsistently, as both a chariot and as something that screams. See *metaphor.*

mode A **mode** is a form of writing. One common classification system, based on content, divides types of writing into four modes: argumentation, description, exposition, and narration. See *argumentation, description, exposition,* and *narration.*

monometer See *meter.*

mood **Mood,** or **atmosphere,** is the emotion created in the reader by part or all of a literary work. A writer creates a mood through judicious use of concrete details.

motif A **motif** is any element that recurs in one or more works of literature or art. Examples of common folk tale motifs found in oral traditions throughout the world include grateful animals or the grateful dead, three wishes, the trial or quest, and the magical metamorphosis, or transformation of one thing into another. "Cinderella," "The Ugly Duckling," and the Arthurian "Sword in the Stone" are examples of the transformation motif, in which persons or creatures of humble station are revealed to be exceptional. Much can be revealed about a literary work by studying the motifs within it. In Anita Desai's "Games at Twilight," for example, death is a recurring motif.

motivation A **motivation** is a force that moves a character to think, feel, or behave in a certain way. Greed motivates the lawyer to make the bet with the banker in Anton Chekhov's "The Bet."

Muse In ancient Greek and Roman myth, the **Muses**—the nine daughters of Zeus and Mnemosyne, or Memory—were believed to provide the inspiration for the arts and sciences. Calliope was the Muse of epic poetry; Clio, the Muse of history; Erato, the Muse of lyrical poetry; Euterpe, the Muse of music; Melpomene, the Muse of tragedy; Polyhymnia, the Muse of sacred choral poetry; Terpischore, the Muse of choral dance and song; Thalia, the Muse of comedy; and Urania, the Muse of astronomy. The idea of the Muse has often been used by later writers to explain the vagaries and mysteries of literary inspiration. In the opening of the *Iliad,* the poet calls upon a Muse. The connection of the Muses with entertainments and the arts survives in our English words *amusing* and *amusement.*

myth A **myth** is a story that explains objects or events in the natural world as resulting from the action of some supernatural force or entity, most often a god. Every early culture around the globe has produced its own myths. A typical example is the Greek myth of the origin of the Narcissus flower. Narcissus was a vain boy who liked to look at his own reflection in pools of water. The punishment for his vanity was to be turned into a flower that grows near water. There he can look at his own reflection for as long as the world lasts. European literature often alludes to or makes use of materials from Greek, Roman, Germanic, and Celtic myths. Modern and contemporary African and Asian writers often draw upon the myths of their cultures in their writing.

narration **Narration,** one of the modes of writing, tells a story. The story is made up of occurrences, or events. See *mode.*

narrative poem A **narrative poem** is a verse that tells a story. "The Passion of Queen Dido" is part of an epic, but it is also considered narrative verse because it tells a story.

narrator A **narrator** is one who tells a story. In a drama, the narrator may be a character who introduces, concludes, or comments upon the action of the play. However, dramas typically do not have narrators. Works of fiction, on the other hand, always do, unless they consist entirely of dialogue without tag lines, in which case they cease to be fictions and become closet dramas, drama meant to be read but not performed. The narrator in a work of fiction may be a central or minor character or simply someone who witnessed or heard about the events being related. Writers achieve a wide variety of ends by varying the characteristics of the narrator chosen for a particular work. Of primary importance is the choice of the narrator's point of view. Will the narrator be omniscient, knowing all things, including the internal workings of the minds of the characters in the story, or will the narrator be limited in his or her knowledge? Will the narrator participate in the action of the story or stand outside that action and comment on it? Will the narrator be reliable or unreliable? That is, will the reader be able to trust the narrator's statements? These are all questions that a writer must answer when developing a narrator. See *point of view* and *speaker.*

Naturalism **Naturalism** was a literary movement of the late nineteenth and early twentieth centuries that saw actions and events as resulting inevitably from biological or natural forces or from forces in the environment. Often these forces were beyond the comprehension or control of the characters subjected to them. Taken to its extreme, Naturalism views all events as mechanically determined by external forces, including the decisions made by people. Much of modern fiction, with its emphasis on social conditions leading to particular consequences for characters, is naturalistic in this sense. Nobel Prize-winner Grazia Deledda's "The Shoes" shows how one man's fate is determined by economic forces beyond his control. Great writers of fiction informed by the philosophy of Naturalism include Émile Zola, Stephen Crane, Jack London, and Theodore Dreiser.

near rhyme See *slant rhyme.*

Negritude Negritude was a literary movement that flourished from the 1930s through the 1950s. As a reaction to colonialism, African and Caribbean writers redefined and promoted the richness of African culture, noting that traditional values such as mysticism, closeness to nature, and connection with ancestors are necessary in the modern world, though there is tension between the traditional and the modern. Negritude writers chose African subjects and tried to inspire the desire for political freedom. Important writers of the Negritude movement were founders Léopold Sédar Senghor and Aimé Césaire; poets Birago Diop, David Diop, Tchicaya U Tam'si; and novelists Mongo Beti and Ferdinand Oyono.

Neoclassicism **Neoclassicism** is the term used to describe the revival during the European Enlightenment of ideals of art and literature derived from the Greek and Roman classics. These ideals included respect for authority and tradition, austerity, clarity, conservatism, decorum, economy, grace, imitation of the natural order, harmony, moderation, proportion, reason, restraint, self-control, simplicity, tradition, wit, and unity. Neoclassical literature was witty and socially astute but tended toward excessive didacticism and an excessive distrust of invention and imagination. Popular forms of Neoclassical writing included the essay, the epistle, the satire, the parody, poems in rhymed couplets, and the earliest novels. Neoclassical writers wrote primarily about social life and social interactions. Great Neoclassical writers include Daniel Defoe, John Dryden, Henry Fielding, Jean de La Fontaine, Jean-Baptiste Poquelin Moliere, Montesquieu, Blaise Pascal, Alexander Pope, Samuel Richardson, Tobias Smollet, and François-Marie Arouet de Voltaire. *Romanticism* can be seen as a reaction against Neoclassical restraint. See *Classicism, didacticism,* and *Romanticism.*

New Criticism See *criticism.*

nonfiction **Nonfiction** is writing about real events. Essays, autobiographies, biographies, and news stories are all types of nonfiction. See *prose.*

nonsense verse A **nonsense verse** is a kind of light verse that contains elements that are silly, absurd, or meaningless. Sometimes, as is the case with Lewis Carroll's "Jabberwocky," the apparent nonsense of the verse gives way to sense upon closer analysis. Carroll's poem turns out not to be nonsense at all, but rather an ingenious retelling, in a mock heroic ballad, of a stock folk tale story—that of a young person who sets off on a quest, slays a terrible beast, and returns home victorious. Stanislaw Lem includes nonsense verse in his science fiction story "The First Sally (A) or Trurl's Electronic Bard":

> Mockles! Fent on silpen tree,
> Blockards three a-feening
> Mockles, what silps came to thee
> In the pantry dreaming!

novel A **novel** is a long work of prose fiction. Often novels have involved plots; many characters, both major and minor; and numerous settings. One of the first extended works of prose fiction was Lady Murasaki Shikibu's *Tale of Genji,* written in the eleventh century AD. In Europe, the novel arose as a literary form soon after the publication of Miguel de Cervantes's *Don Quixote* in 1605. Novels soon gained lasting popularity throughout Europe. European Imperialism spread European literary forms throughout the world. For example, despite Lady Murasaki Shikibu's success in Japan and her numerous imitators, other literary forms remained more popular than the novel until Japanese writers became acquainted with modern European writing. In the twentieth century, novels have enjoyed popularity throughout the world, not only in Europe and Japan but in places from Nigeria to India, from Latin America to the Far East.

novella A **novella** is a short novel.

nursery rhyme A **nursery rhyme** is a children's verse. Famous English writers of nursery rhymes include Rudyard Kipling and Edward Lear.

objective correlative An **objective correlative** is a group of images that together create a particular emotion in the reader. The term was coined by T. S. Eliot. See *image.*

occasional verse An **occasional verse** is one written to celebrate or commemorate some particular event. Maya Angelou wrote a poem called "On the Pulse of Morning" to celebrate the inauguration of President Clinton in 1993.

octameter See *meter.*

octave An **octave** is an eight-line stanza. A Petrarchan sonnet begins with an octave. See *meter* and *sonnet.*

ode An **ode** is a lofty lyric poem on a serious theme. It may employ alternating stanza patterns, developed from the choral ode of Greek dramatic poetry. These stanza patterns are called the *strophe*, the *antistrophe*, and the *epode*. However, not all odes follow this pattern.

off rhyme See *slant rhyme.*

omniscient point of view See *narrator* and *point of view.*

one-act See *act.*

one-dimensional character See *character.*

onomatopoeia **Onomatopoeia** is the use of words or phrases that sound like the things to which they refer. Examples of onomatopoeia include words such as *buzz*, *click*, and *pop*. Poets and other writers often make use of onomatopoeia.

oral tradition An **oral tradition** is a work, a motif, an idea, or a custom that is passed by word of mouth from generation to generation. Materials transmitted orally may be simplified in the retelling. They also may be sensationalized because of the tendency of retellers to add to or elaborate upon the materials that come down to them. Often, works in an oral tradition contain miraculous or magical elements. Common works found in the oral traditions of peoples around the world include folk tales, fables, fairy tales, tall tales, nursery rhymes, proverbs, legends, myths, parables, riddles, charms, spells, and ballads. See *folklore.*

ottava rima ***Ottava rima*** is a stanza form made

up of eight iambic pentameter lines rhyming *abababcc.* Ludovico Ariosto used *ottava rima* in *Orlando Furioso.* For an example see *rhyme scheme.*

oxymoron An **oxymoron** is a statement that contradicts itself. Words like *bittersweet, tragicomedy,* and *pianoforte* (literally, "soft-loud") are oxymorons that develop a complex meaning from two seemingly contradictory elements. Describing Teiresias in *Oedipus the King* as a blind seer is an example of an oxymoron.

palindrome A **palindrome** is a word, a phrase, or a sentence that reads the same backward as forward. Examples include the word *radar* and the phrase *A man, a plan, a canal—Panama.*

parable A **parable** is a very brief story told to teach a moral lesson. The most famous parables are those, such as the parable of the prodigal son, told by Jesus in the Bible. The medieval *exemplum* was a kind of parable.

paradox A **paradox** is a seemingly contradictory statement, idea, or event. All forms of irony involve paradox. An oxymoron is a paradoxical statement. William Wordsworth's statement that "The Child is father of the Man" is an example of a paradox that can be resolved, on analysis, into a coherent, noncontradictory idea. Some paradoxes, however, present unresolvable contradictory ideas. An example of such a paradox is the statement, "This sentence is a lie." If the sentence is true, then it is false; if it is false, then it is true. See *irony* and *oxymoron.*

parallelism **Parallelism** is a rhetorical technique in which a writer emphasizes the equal value or weight of two or more ideas by expressing them in the same grammatical form. An example of parallelism appears in Psalm 27:

> The Lord is my light and my salvation;
> whom shall I fear?
> The Lord is the strength of my life; of
> whom shall I be afraid?

paraphrase A **paraphrase** is a rewriting of a passage in different words. A paraphrase is often distinguished from an abstract or summary as follows: a summary is shorter than the original, whereas a paraphrase may be as long as or longer than the original. One of the central ideas of the so-called New Criticism was that it is impossible to paraphrase a literary work precisely. Much of the content or meaning of a literary work lies in how it is expressed. Changing the expression therefore inevitably changes the meaning. See *abstract.*

parody A **parody** is a literary work that imitates another work for humorous, often satirical, purposes. In *The Bluest Eye,* Toni Morrison parodies children's literature in the following lines:

> Run, Jip, run. Jip runs, Alice runs. Alice has
> blue eyes.
> Jerry has blue eyes. Jerry runs. Alice runs.
> They run
> with their blue eyes. Four blue eyes. Four
> pretty
> blue eyes. Blue-sky eyes. Blue—like Mrs.
> Forrest's
> blue blouse eyes. Morning-glory-blue-eyes.
> Alice-and-Jerry-blue-storybook-eyes.

pastoral poem A **pastoral poem,** from the Latin *pastor,* meaning "shepherd," is a verse that deals with idealized rural life. Examples of pastoral poems include Psalm 23 which begins "The Lord is my shepherd" and T'ao Ch'ien's "I Built My Cottage among the Habitations of Men." In China, Taoist religion encouraged people to turn away from bustling city life to contemplate nature, thus sparking a surge in the popularity of pastoral verse, first in China, then in Japan. In Europe, pastoral verse, based on the *Idylls* of Theocritus and the *Eclogues* of Virgil, enjoyed great popularity during the Renaissance.

pathetic fallacy The **pathetic fallacy** is the tendency to attribute human emotions to nonhuman things, particularly to things in the natural world. The term was coined by the Victorian critic John Ruskin and has often been used to describe the excesses of sentimental verse.

pentameter See *meter.*

periodical A **periodical** is a newspaper, magazine, journal, newsletter, or other publication that is produced on a regular basis.

persona A **persona** consists of the qualities of a person or character that are shown through speech or actions.

personal essay A **personal essay** is a short work of nonfictional prose on a single topic related to the life or interests of the writer. Personal essays are characterized by an intimate and informal style and tone. They are often, but not always, written in the first person. See *essay.*

personal symbol See *symbol.*

personification **Personification** is a figure of speech in which an idea, animal, or thing is described as if it were a person. La Fontaine personifies both an oak and a reed in his fable "The Oak and the Reed."

Petrarchan sonnet See *sonnet.*

plagiarism **Plagiarism** is the act of using material gathered from another person or work without crediting the source of the material.

plot A **plot** is a series of events related to a central *conflict*, or struggle. A typical plot involves the introduction of a conflict, its development, and its eventual resolution. Terms used to describe elements of plot include the following:

- The **exposition**, or **introduction**, sets the tone or mood, introduces the characters and the setting, and provides necessary background information.
- The **inciting incident** is the event that introduces the central conflict.
- The **rising action**, or **complication**, develops the conflict to a high point of intensity.
- The **climax** is the high point of interest or suspense in the plot.
- The **crisis**, or **turning point**, often the same event as the climax, is the point in the plot where something decisive happens to determine the future course of events and the eventual working out of the conflict.
- The **falling action** is all of the events that follow the climax.
- The **resolution** is the point at which the central conflict is ended, or resolved.
- The **dénouement** is any material that follows the resolution and that ties up loose ends.
- The **catastrophe**, in tragedy, is the event that marks the ultimate tragic fall of the central character. Often this event is the character's death.

Plots rarely contain all these elements in precisely this order. Elements of exposition may be introduced at any time in the course of a work. A work may begin with a catastrophe and then use flashback to explain it. The exposition or dénouement or even the resolution may be missing. The inciting incident may occur before the beginning of the action actually described in the work. These are but a few of the many possible variations that plots can exhibit. See *conflict.*

poetic license **Poetic license** is the right, claimed by writers, to change elements of reality to suit the purposes of particular works that they create. François Villon's use in "Ballade" of hanged characters who talk even though they are dead is an example of poetic license. Such things do not happen in reality, but they are accepted by readers willing to suspend disbelief in order to have imaginary experiences. See *suspension of disbelief.*

point of view **Point of view** is the vantage point from which a story is told. Stories are typically written from a first-person point of view, in which the narrator uses words such as *I* and *we,* or from a third-person point of view, in which the narrator uses words such as *he, she, it,* and *they* and avoids the use of *I* and *we.* In stories written from a first-person point of view, the narrator may be a participant or witness of the action. In stories told from a third-person point of view, the narrator generally stands outside the action. In some stories, the narrator's point of view is limited. In such stories, the narrator can reveal the private, internal thoughts of himself or herself or of a single character. In other stories, the narrator's point of view is omniscient. In such stories the narrator can reveal the private, internal thoughts of any character.

portmanteau See *blend.*

pragmatic criticism See *criticism.*

précis See *abstract.*

preface A **preface** is a statement made at the beginning of a literary work, often by way of introduction. The terms *foreword, preface,* and *introduction* are often used interchangeably.

prologue A **prologue** is an introduction to a literary work, often one that sets the scene and introduces the conflict or the main characters.

proscenium stage See *stage.*

prose **Prose** is the broad term used to describe all writing that is not drama or poetry, including fiction and nonfiction. Types of prose writing include novels, short stories, essays, and news stories. Most biographies, autobiographies, and letters are written in prose. See *fiction.*

prose poem A **prose poem** is a work of prose, usually a short work, that makes such extensive use of poetic language, such as figures of speech and words that echo their sense, that the line between prose and poetry becomes blurred. An example of a prose poem is Margaret Atwood's "Simmering."

prosody **Prosody,** or **versification,** is the study of the structure of poetry. In particular, prosodists study meter, rhyme, rhythm, and stanza form. See *meter, rhyme, rhythm,* and *stanza.*

protagonist See *character.*

proverb A **proverb,** or **adage,** is a traditional saying, such as "You can lead a horse to water, but you can't make it drink" or the title of Shakespeare's play *All's Well That Ends Well.*

psalm A **psalm** is a lyrical hymn of praise, supplication, or thanksgiving. The Biblical hymn, attributed to David, that begins with the line "The Lord is my shepherd," is an example.

pseudonym A **pseudonym** is a name assumed by a writer. Examples of pseudonyms include Gabriela Mistral, the pseudonym of Lucila Godoy Alcayaga, and Madhavikutty, the pseudonym of Kamala Das.

psychological fiction **Psychological fiction** is fiction that emphasizes the interior, subjective experiences of its characters, and especially such fiction when it deals with emotional or mental disturbance or anguish. Grazia Deledda's "The Shoes" can be considered an example of psychological fiction.

pun A **pun** is a play on words, one that wittily exploits a double meaning.

purpose See *aim.*

pyrrhic See *meter.*

quatrain A **quatrain** is a stanza containing four lines.

quintain A **quintain,** or **quintet,** is a stanza containing five lines.

quintet See *quintain.*

rap **Rap** is improvised, rhymed verse that is chanted or sung, often to a musical accompaniment.

reader-response criticism See *criticism.*

Realism **Realism** is the attempt to render in art an accurate portrayal of reality. The theory that the purpose of art is to imitate life is at least as old as Aristotle. The eighteenth-century development of the novel, with its attention to details of character, setting, and social life, can be thought of as a step toward increased Realism in writing. However, the term *Realism* is generally applied to literature of the late nineteenth century, written in reaction to *Romanticism* and emphasizing details of ordinary life.

redundancy **Redundancy** is needless repetition. The phrase *firmly determined* is redundant because the word *determined* already implies firmness.

refrain A **refrain** is a line or group of lines repeated in a poem or song. Many ballads contain refrains.

regional dialect See *dialect.*

Renaissance The **Renaissance** was the period from the fourteenth to the early seventeenth century when Europe was making the transition from the medieval to the modern world. The word *renaissance* means "rebirth." The term refers to the rebirth of interest in ancient Greek and Latin writing that occurred during the period, a rebirth that is known as Humanism. The Renaissance was characterized by a lessening of reliance on authority, by a decline in feudalism and in the universal authority of the church, by increased nationalism, by increasingly active university and city life, by increased opportunities for individual economic attainment and freedom, and by increased belief in the value of this life (as opposed to the afterlife), in and of itself.

repetition **Repetition** is the use, again, of a sound, word, phrase, sentence, or other element.

requiem A **requiem** is a song or service for the dead. Anna Akhmatova's poem *Requiem* was inspired by fears that her son would die and honors those who did die during Joseph Stalin's Great Purge.

resolution See *plot.*

reversal A **reversal** is a dramatic change in the direction of events in a drama or narrative, especially a change in the fortunes of the protagonist. See *plot.*

review A **review** is a written evaluation of a work of art, a performance, or a literary work, especially one that appears in a periodical or on a broadcast news program. Common subjects of reviews include books, films, art exhibitions, restaurants, and performances of all kinds, from rock concerts to ballets.

rhetoric **Rhetoric** is the study of ways in which speech and writing affect or influence audiences.

rhetorical criticism See *criticism.*

rhetorical question A **rhetorical question** is one asked for effect but not meant to be answered because the answer is clear from context. "The

HANDBOOK OF LITERARY TERMS

Creation Hymn" from the Rig Veda poses a number of rhetorical questions.

rhetorical technique A **rhetorical technique** is an extraordinary but literal use of language to achieve a particular effect on an audience. Common rhetorical techniques include *antithesis, apostrophe, catalog, chiasmus, parallelism, repetition,* and *the rhetorical question.*

rhyme **Rhyme** is the repetition of sounds at the ends of words. Types of rhyme include *end rhyme* (the use of rhyming words at the ends of lines), *internal rhyme* (the use of rhyming words within lines), *exact rhyme* (in which the rhyming words end with the same sound or sounds), and *slant rhyme* (in which the rhyming sounds are similar but not identical). An example of exact rhyme is the word pair *moon/June*. Examples of slant rhyme are the word pairs *rave/rove* and *rot/rock.* See *slant rhyme* and *rhyme scheme.*

rhyme scheme A **rhyme scheme** is a pattern of end rhymes, or rhymes at the ends of lines of verse. The rhyme scheme of a poem is designated by letters, with matching letters signifying matching sounds. Take, for example, the following lines from *Orlando Furioso.*

> No lions run, no bulls advance with rage
> In enmity so deadly or so fierce
> As these two foemen in the war they wage.
> With equal skill each other's shield they pierce.
> The mountain trembles, as the knights engage,
> From its green base to the bare peak it rears.
> And well it is the hauberks stand the test,
> Else would each lance be driven through each
> breast.

The rhyme scheme for this stanza is *abababcc* because lines 1, 3, and 5 rhyme; lines 2, 4, and 6 rhyme; and lines 7 and 8 rhyme.

rhythm **Rhythm** is the pattern of beats or stresses in a line of verse or prose. See *meter.*

riddle A **riddle** is a word game in which something is described in an unusual way and the reader or listener must figure out what that something is. Riddles are common in folklore and myth throughout the world. Oedipus solves the riddle of the Sphinx, saving the people of Thebes.

rising action See *plot.*

romance **Romance** is a term used to refer to four types of literature: **1.** medieval stories about the adventures and loves of knights; **2.** novels and other fictions involving exotic locales and extraordinary or mysterious events and characters; **3.** nonrealistic fictions in general; and **4.** in popular, modern usage, love stories of all kinds. The term originated in the Middle Ages. It was first used to describe stories believed to be based upon Latin originals (stories told by the Romans). It came to be used in Europe and England for stories in prose or poetry about knightly exploits, including those told about such characters as Alexander the Great, Roland, Percival, Tristan and Isolde, and King Arthur and his knights of the Round Table. Because the later medieval romances were, for the most part, told in prose, the term came to be applied to prose fictions in general, and especially to those that were highly imaginative. In the nineteenth century, the term was commonly used to describe fictional works, such as the novels of Sir Walter Scott, that dealt with adventure in exotic locales. It was used by Nathaniel Hawthorne to describe such stories as his *Blithedale Romance* and *House of the Seven Gables* because of their deviations from *Realism*. Today, the term is quite widely used to refer to love stories, especially popular, sentimental stories.

Romantic criticism See *criticism.*

Romanticism **Romanticism** was a literary and artistic movement of the eighteenth and nineteenth centuries that placed value on emotion or imagination over reason, the individual over society, nature and wildness over human works, the country over the town, common people over aristocrats, and freedom over control or authority. Major writers of the Romantic Era included William Blake, William Wordsworth, Victor Hugo, George Sand, Frederich von Schiller, Johann Wolfgang von Goethe, Heinrich Heine, Alexander Pushkin, Giacamo Leopardi.

rounded character See *character.*

run-on line A **run-on line** is a line of verse in which the sense or the grammatical structure does not end with the end of the line but rather is continued on one or more subsequent lines. The following lines from Heine's "The Loreley" form a single sentence:

> I think the waves must fling him
> Against the reefs nearby,
> And that did with her singing
> The lovely Loreley.

The act of continuing a statement beyond the end of a line is called *enjambment*. See *end-stopped line.*

satire **Satire** is humorous writing or speech intended to point out errors, falsehoods, foibles, or failings. It is written for the purpose of reforming human behavior or human institutions. Voltaire's *Candide*, for example, satirizes political and social institutions.

scansion **Scansion** is the art of analyzing poetry to determine its meter. See *meter*.

scene A **scene** is a short section of a literary work that presents action that occurs in a single place or at a single time. Long divisions of dramas are often divided into scenes.

science fiction **Science fiction** is highly imaginative fiction containing fantastic elements based on scientific principles, discoveries, or laws. It is similar to fantasy in that it deals with imaginary worlds but differs from fantasy in having a scientific basis. Mary Shelley's *Frankenstein* was an early precursor of modern science fiction. She based her idea of the creation of artificial life on nineteenth-century experiments with so-called animal magnetism, the electrical charge believed by some people in those days to be the force motivating living things and distinguishing them from nonliving things. Stanislaw Lem's short story "The First Sally (A) or Trurl's Electronic Bard," which is set in the distant future, is an example of science fiction. Often science fiction deals with the future, the distant past, or with worlds other than our own, such as other planets, parallel universes, and worlds under the ground or the sea. The genre allows writers to suspend or alter certain elements of reality in order to create fascinating and sometimes instructive alternatives. Important writers of science fiction include H. G. Wells, Jules Verne, Ray Bradbury, Arthur C. Clarke, Isaac Asimov, Ursula K. Le Guin, Robert Heinlein, and Kurt Vonnegut, Jr. See *fantasy*.

sensory detail See *description*.

sentimentality **Sentimentality** is an excessive expression of emotion. Much popular literature of the nineteenth and twentieth centuries is characterized by sentimentality.

septet A **septet** is a stanza with seven lines.

sestet A **sestet** is a stanza with six lines, such as the second part of a Petrarchan sonnet. See *meter* and *sonnet*.

set A **set** is a collection of objects on a stage arranged in such a way as to create a scene.

setting The **setting** of a literary work is the time and place in which it occurs, together with all the details used to create a sense of a particular time and place. Writers create setting by various means. In drama, the setting is often revealed by the stage set and the costumes, though it may be revealed through what the characters say about their environs. In fiction, setting is most often revealed by means of description of such elements as landscape, scenery, buildings, furniture, clothing, the weather, and the season. It can also be revealed by how characters talk and behave. In its widest sense, setting includes the general social, political, moral, and psychological conditions in which characters find themselves. See *set*.

Shakespearean sonnet See *sonnet*.

shape poem See *concrete poem*.

short short A **short short**, or **flash fiction**, is an extremely brief short story. This recently recognized genre of the short story is currently enjoying considerable popularity among readers of literary magazines and short story collections published in the United States. Short shorts sometimes take the form of anecdotes, or retellings of single incidents. Alternatively, they may attempt to develop an entire plot within the compass of a few paragraphs. Many short shorts are highly poetic and may be considered prose poems. An example of the genre is Margaret Atwood's "Simmering." See *anecdote* and *prose poem*.

short story A **short story** is a form of short prose fiction that relates a narrative. Short stories are typically crafted carefully to develop a plot, a conflict, characters, a setting, a mood, and a theme, all within relatively few pages. This form of literature gained popularity in the nineteenth century. Anton Chekhov's "The Bet" and Guy de Maupassant's "The False Gems" are examples of the short story. See *conflict*, *character*, *mood*, *plot*, *setting*, and *theme*.

sight rhyme A **sight rhyme**, or **eye rhyme**, is a pair of words, generally at the ends of lines of verse, that are spelled similarly but pronounced differently. The words *lost* and *ghost* and *give* and *thrive* are examples.

simile A **simile** is a comparison using *like* or *as*. Anita Desai's "Games at Twilight" makes use of the following simile: "The garden outside was like a tray made of beaten brass." A simile is a type of *metaphor*, and like any other metaphor, can be divided into two parts, the tenor (or subject being described), and the vehicle (or object being used in the description). In the simile "your locks are like the snow," the tenor is locks of hair and the vehicle is snow. They can be compared because they share some quality, in this case, whiteness. See *metaphor.*

slang **Slang** is extremely colloquial speech not suitable for formal occasions and usually associated with a particular group of people. An example of slang current among young people in the United States in the 1920s is "the bee's knees," for something uniquely attractive or wonderful. Among young people in the northeastern United States, the word *wicked* is now sometimes used as a slang term meaning "extremely," as in "That song is *wicked* good." Writers sometimes use slang in an attempt to render characters and setting vividly.

slant rhyme A **slant rhyme, half rhyme, near rhyme,** or **off rhyme** is substitution of assonance or consonance for true rhyme. The pairs *world/boiled* and *bear/bore* are examples. See *assonance, consonance,* and *rhyme.*

social dialect See *dialect.*

soliloquy A **soliloquy** is a speech delivered by a lone character that reveals the speaker's thoughts and feelings.

sonnet A **sonnet** is a fourteen-line poem, usually in iambic pentameter, that follows one of a number of different rhyme schemes. The *English, Elizabethan,* or *Shakespearean sonnet* is divided into four parts: three *quatrains* and a final *couplet.* The rhyme scheme of such a sonnet is *abab cdcd efef gg.* The sonnets by Shakespeare in this book are examples. The *Italian* or *Petrarchan sonnet* is divided into two parts: an *octave* and a *sestet.* The rhyme scheme of the octave is *abbaabba.* The rhyme scheme of the sestet can be *cdecde, cdcdcd,* or *cdedce.* Sir Thomas Wyatt's "Whoso List to Hunt" is an example of the Petrarchan sonnet.

sonnet cycle See *sonnet sequence.*

sonnet sequence A **sonnet sequence** is a group of related sonnets. Famous sonnet sequences in English include the sonnets of Petrarch, William Shakespeare, Sir Philip Sidney's *Astrophel and Stella,* and Edmund Spenser's *Amoretti.* See *sonnet.*

source A **source** is a work from which an author takes his or her materials. For example, William Shakespeare used Plutarch's *Lives* as a source.

speaker The **speaker** is the character who speaks in, or narrates, a poem—the voice assumed by the writer. The speaker and the writer of a poem are not necessarily the same person. The speaker of Yannis Ritsos's "Penelope's Despair," for example, is Odysseus's estranged wife Penelope.

spectacle In drama, the **spectacle** is all the elements that are presented to the senses of the audience, including the lights, setting, costumes, make-up, music, sound effects, and movements of the actors.

spondee A **spondee** is a poetic foot containing two strongly stressed syllables, as in the words *compound* and *roughhouse.* Such a foot is said to be *spondaic.*

stage A **stage** is any arena on which the action of a drama is performed. For a description of Greek stages, see Insights: Understanding Greek Drama. In the Middle Ages, stages often consisted of the beds of wagons, which were wheeled from place to place for performances. From the use of such wagons in inn yards, the *thrust stage* developed. This was a platform that extended out into the audience and that was closed at the back. In front of the platform in the first English theaters, such as Shakespeare's Globe Theatre, was an open area, the pit, where common people stood. Around the pit were balconies in imitation of the balconies of inns. The modern *proscenium stage* typically is closed on three sides and open at the front, as though the fourth wall had been removed. Sometimes contemporary plays are performed as *theater in the round,* with the audience seated on all sides of the playing area.

stage directions **Stage directions** are notes included in a play, in addition to the dialogue, for the purpose of describing how something should be performed on stage. Stage directions describe setting, lighting, music, sound effects, entrances and exits, properties, and the movements of characters. They are usually printed in italics and enclosed in brackets or parentheses.

stanza A **stanza** is a recurring pattern of grouped lines in a poem. The following are some types of stanza:

two-line stanza	couplet
three-line stanza	tercet or triplet
four-line stanza	quatrain
five-line stanza	quintain
six-line stanza	sestet
seven-line stanza	heptastich
eight-line stanza	octave

static character See *character.*

stereotype A **stereotype** is an uncritically accepted, fixed or conventional idea, particularly such an idea held about whole groups of people. A stereotypical, or stock, character is one who does not deviate from conventional expectations of such a character. Examples of stereotypical characters include the merciless villain, the mad scientist, and the hard-boiled private eye. See *character.*

stock character See *character* and *stereotype.*

story A **story,** or **narrative,** is writing or speech that relates a series of events. When these events are causally connected and related to a conflict, they make up a plot. See *plot.*

stream-of-consciousness writing **Stream-of-consciousness writing** is literary work that attempts to render the flow of feelings, thoughts, and impressions within the minds of characters. Modern masters of stream-of-consciousness writing include Virginia Woolf, James Joyce, and William Faulkner. An example of stream-of-consciousness writing appears in the selection from Virginia Woolf's *Orlando.*

stress **Stress,** or **accent,** is the level of emphasis given to a syllable. In English metrics, the art of rhythm in written and spoken expression, syllables are generally described as being strongly or weakly stressed, in other words, accented or unaccented. A strongly stressed or accented syllable receives a strong emphasis. A weakly stressed or unaccented syllable receives a weak one. In the following line on the beauty of Helen of Troy, the strongly stressed or accented syllables are marked with a slash mark (/).

/ / / / /
Is this the face that launched a thousand ships?

—Christopher Marlowe,
The Tragical History of Doctor Faustus

structuralist criticism See *criticism.*

style **Style** is the manner in which something is said or written. Traditionally, critics and scholars have referred to three levels of style: high style, for formal occasions or lofty subjects; middle style, for ordinary occasions or subjects; and low style, for extremely informal occasions or subjects. A writer's style depends upon many things, including his or her *diction* (the words that the writer chooses), selection of grammatical structures (simple versus complex sentences, for example), and preference for abstract or concrete words. Any recurring feature that distinguishes one writer's work from another can be said to be part of that writer's style. See *abstract* and *fiction.*

subplot A **subplot** is a subordinate story told in addition to the major story in a work of fiction. Often a subplot mirrors or provides a foil for the primary plot. See *plot* and *story.*

summary See *abstract.*

suspense **Suspense** is a feeling of expectation, anxiousness, or curiosity created by questions raised in the mind of a reader or viewer.

suspension of disbelief **Suspension of disbelief** is the phrase used by Coleridge in his *Biographia Literaria* to describe the act by which the reader willingly sets aside his or her skepticism in order to participate imaginatively in the work being read. A modern adult reader of the *Sunjata,* for example, will most likely not believe in shape-shifting. However, he or she may suspend disbelief in shape-shifters and imagine, while reading, what the world would be like if such creatures did exist. The willingness to suspend disbelief, to participate imaginatively in a story being read, is the most important attribute, beyond literacy, that a person can bring to the act of reading.

symbol A **symbol** is a thing that stands for or represents both itself and something else. Writers use two types of symbols—conventional, and personal or idiosyncratic. A *conventional symbol* is one with traditional, widely recognized associations. Such symbols include doves for peace; laurel wreaths for heroism or poetic excellence; the color green for jealousy; the color purple for royalty; the color red for anger; morning or spring for youth; winter, evening, or night for old age; wind for change or inspiration; rainbows for hope; roses for beauty; the moon for fickleness or inconstancy; roads or paths for the journey through life; woods or darkness for moral or spiritual confusion; thorns for troubles or pain; stars for unchangeableness or constancy; mirrors for vanity or introspection; snakes for evil or duplicity; and owls for wisdom. A *personal* or *idiosyncratic symbol* is one that assumes its secondary meaning because of the special use to which it is put by a writer. Thus in Olive Senior's story "Love Orange," the narrator's imaginary orange becomes a symbol of love.

synaesthesia **Synaesthesia** is a figure of speech that combines in a single expression images related to two or more different senses. Virginia

Woolf describes Orlando's thoughts when he first sees the princess in the following manner: "He called her a melon, a pineapple, an olive tree, an emerald, and a fox in the snow." Orlando's thoughts are an example of synaesthesia involving the senses of sight, taste, smell, and touch.

synecdoche A **synecdoche** is a figure of speech in which the name of part of something is used in place of the name of the whole or *vice versa.* In the command *"All hands on deck!" hands* is a synecdoche in which a part (hands) is used to refer to a whole (people, sailors). Addressing a representative of the country of France as *France* would be a synecdoche in which a whole (France) is used to refer to a part (one French person).

syntax **Syntax** is the pattern of arrangement of words in a statement. Poets often vary the syntax of ordinary speech or experiment with unusual syntactic arrangements. For example, in "A Refusal to Mourn the Death by Fire of a Child in London," Dylan Thomas begins with a long series of adjectives, delaying until the third line the appearance of the noun that is modified:

> Never until the mankind making,
> Bird, beast, and flower-fathering,
> And all-humbling darkness . . .

See *inversion.*

tag line A **tag line** is an expression in a work of fiction that indicates who is speaking and sometimes indicates the manner of speaking. Examples include the familiar *she said* as well as more elaborate expressions such as *Raoul retorted angrily.*

tanka A **tanka** is a traditional Japanese five-line poem containing five syllables in the first line, seven in the second, five in the third, seven in the fourth, and seven in the fifth. Ki no Tsurayuki's "In the lingering wake" is an example of a tanka.

tall tale A **tall tale** is a story, often light-hearted or humorous, that contains highly exaggerated, unrealistic elements.

tenor See *metaphor.*

tercet See *triplet.*

terza rima ***Terza rima*** is a three-line stanza of the kind used in Dante's *Divine Comedy,* rhyming *aba, bcb, cdc, ded,* and so on.

tetrameter See *meter.*

textual criticism See *criticism.*

theater (playing area) See *stage.*

theater in the round See *stage.*

theater of the absurd The **theater of the absurd** is a kind of twentieth-century drama that presents illogical, absurd, or unrealistic scenes, characters, events, or juxtapositions in an attempt to convey the essential meaninglessness of human life, although playwrights have often used the form to convey significant moral messages. Practitioners of the theater of the absurd, which grew out of the philosophy of *Existentialism,* include Eugene Ionesco, Samuel Beckett, Edward Albee, and Harold Pinter. See *Existentialism* and *literature of the absurd.*

theme A **theme** is a central idea in a literary work. One reading of Wordsworth's "My Heart Leaps Up When I Behold," for example, might say that the poem's theme is the great spiritual or emotional cost of our modern alienation from the natural world.

thesis A **thesis** is a main idea that is supported in a work of nonfictional prose.

third-person point of view See *point of view.*

three-dimensional character See *character.*

thrust stage See *stage.*

tone **Tone** is the emotional attitude toward the reader or toward the subject implied by a literary work. Examples of the different tones that a work may have include familiar, ironic, playful, sarcastic, serious, and sincere.

tragedy A **tragedy** is a drama (or by extension any work of literature) that tells the story of the fall of a person of high status. It celebrates the courage and dignity of a tragic hero in the face of inevitable doom. Sometimes that doom is made inevitable by a tragic flaw in the hero, such as the hubris that brings about the fall of Sophocles's Oedipus. In the twentieth century, writers have extended the definition of *tragedy* to cover works that deal with the fall of any sympathetic character, despite his or her status.

tragic flaw A **tragic flaw** is a personal weakness that brings about the fall of a character in a tragedy. See *tragedy.*

tragic hero See *hero* and *tragedy.*

transition A **transition** is a word, phrase, sentence, or paragraph used to connect ideas and to show relationships between them. *However, therefore, in addition,* and *in contrast* are common transitions. Repeated nouns, synonyms, and pronouns can also serve as transitions.

translation **Translation** is the art of rendering speech or writing into another language. See Insights: The Art of Translation.

trimeter See *meter.*

triplet A **triplet**, or **tercet**, is a stanza of three lines.

trochee A **trochee** is a poetic foot consisting of a strongly stressed syllable followed by a weakly stressed syllable, as in the word *winter.* A line of poetry made up of trochees is said to be *trochaic.*

trope See *figure of speech.*

turning point See *plot.*

understatement An **understatement** is an ironic expression in which something of importance is emphasized by being spoken of as though it were not important, as in "He's sort of dead, I think."

unity A work has **unity** when its various parts all contribute to creating an integrated whole. An essay with unity, for example, is one in which all the parts help to support the thesis statement, or main idea. See *essay.*

unreliable narrator An **unreliable narrator** is one whom the reader cannot trust. See *narrator.*

utopia A **utopia** is an imaginary, idealized world. The term comes from the title of Sir Thomas More's *Utopia,* which described what More believed to be an ideal society. More took the word from the Greek roots meaning "no-place." See *dystopia.*

vehicle See *metaphor.*

verbal irony See *irony.*

vernacular The **vernacular** is the speech of the common people. During the Middle Ages, much writing throughout Europe was done in Latin, the official language of the church. Only gradually, during the late Middle Ages and the Renaissance Era, did the vernacular languages of Europe replace Latin for scholarly purposes. The term *vernacular* is often used loosely today to refer to dialogue or to writing in general that uses colloquial, dialectical, or slang expressions.

versification See *prosody.*

vers libre See *free verse.*

villanelle A **villanelle** is a complex and intricate nineteen-line French verse form. The rhyme scheme is *aba aba aba aba abaa.* The first line is repeated as lines 6, 12, and 18. The third line is repeated as lines 9, 15, and 19. The first and third lines appear as a rhymed couplet at the end of the poem.

Glossary

OF WORDS FOR EVERYDAY USE

Pronunciation Key

Vowel Sounds

a	**h**a**t**	i	**s**i**t**	o͞o	**bl**ue, **st**ew	ə	**extr**a
ā	**pl**ay	ī	**m**y	oi	**b**oy		**und**e**r**
ä	**st**a**r**	ō	**g**o	ou	**w**ow		**civ**i**l**
e	**th**e**n**	ô	**p**aw, **b**o**rn**	u	up		**hon**o**r**
ē	**m**e	o͝o	**b**oo**k**, **p**u**t**	ʉ	**b**u**rn**		**bog**u**s**

Consonant Sounds

b	**b**ut	j	**j**ump	p	**p**op	v	**v**alley
ch	wa**tch**	k	bri**ck**	r	**r**od	w	**w**ork
d	**d**o	l	**l**ip	s	**s**ee	y	**y**ell
f	**f**udge	m	**m**oney	sh	**sh**e	z	plea**s**ure
g	**g**o	n	o**n**	t	si**t**		
h	**h**ot	ŋ	so**ng**, si**nk**	th	wi**th**		

a • base (ə bās´) *vt.*, humble, humiliate

a • bate (ə bāt´) *vi.*, make less in amount

ab • hor (ab hôr´) *vt.*, hate

a • bid • ing (ə bid´iŋ) *adj.*, continuing without change; enduring; lasting

a • bom • i • na • ble (ə bäm´ə nə bəl) *adj.*, extremely disagreeable

a • bom • i • na • tion (ə bäm´ə nā´shən) *n.*, anything hateful and disgusting

a • brupt • ly (ə brupt´lē) *adv.*, suddenly, unexpectedly

ab • solve (ab zälv´) *vt.*, pronounce free from guilt or blame; free from a duty or promise

a • byss (ə bis´) *n.*, bottomless gulf or pit

ac • cord • ance (ə kôrd´ ’ns) *n.*, agreement

ac • o • lyte (ak´ə līt´) *n.*, young religious apprentice

ac • qui • esce (ak´wē es´) *vi.*, agree without protest but also without enthusiasm

ad • journ (ə jʉrn´) *vt.*, put off or suspend until a future time

ad • jure (a jo͞or´) *vt.*, command or charge solemnly

ad • mon • ish (ad män´ish) *vt.*, caution against or scold mildly

ad • mon • ish • ment (ad män´ish mənt) *n.*, warning

ad • mo • ni • tion (ad´mə nish´ən) *n.*, warning; reprimand

a • dorn (ə dôrn´) *vt.*, be an ornament to; add beauty

a • droit • ness (ə droit´nəs) *n.*, clever skill; resourcefulness

aes • thet • i • cal • ly (es thet´i kal ē) *adv.*, relating to beauty

af • firm (ə furm´) *vt.*, say positively

af • fray (ə frā´) *n.*, attack; alarm

a • las (ə las´) *interj.*, exclamation of worry or sorrow

al • ien (āl´ yən) *adj.*, foreign, strange

al • lay (a lā´) *vt.*, put to rest; quiet, calm

al • le • vi • ate (ə lē´vē āt´) *vt.*, reduce or decrease

al • lot (ə lät´) *vt.*, give or assign as one's share

al • lure • ment (ə lo͞or´mənt) *n.*, something tempting or fascinating

a • loof (ə lo͞of´) *adv.*, at a distance, removed

al • tru • is • tic (al´tro͞o is´tik) *adj.*, unselfish

am • big • u • ous (am big´yo͞o əs) *adj.*, having two or more possible meanings

a • men • i • ty (ə men´ə tē) *n.*, pleasant quality, attractiveness

a • mi • a • bil • i • ty (ā´mē ə bil´ə tē) *n.*, friendliness; good will

a • mi • a • ble (ā´mē ə bəl) *adj.*, good-natured

a • mi • a • bly (ā´mē ə blē) *adv.*, in a friendly manner; agreeably

am • i • ca • bly (am´i kə blē) *adv.*, with friendliness or good will

am • ple (am´pəl) *adj.*, more than enough; abundant

a • ne • mic (ə nē´mēk) *adj.*, lacking vigor or vitality; lifeless

an • ni • hi • late (ə nī´ə lāt´) *vt.,* destroy completely

a • nom • a • ly (ə nom´ə lē) *n.,* deviation from the expected; abnormality

ap • pa • ri • tion (ap´ə rish´ən) *n.,* anything that appears unexpectedly or in an extraordinary way

ap • pease (ə pēz´) *vt.,* satisfy by giving into the demands of

ap • pend • age (ə pen´dij) *n.,* branch or limb of a plant or animal

ap • ro • pos (ap´rə pō´) *adj.,* apt; fitting the occasion

ar • bi • trar • y (är´bə trer´ē) *adj.,* not fixed by rules, but left to one's judgment or choice

ar • du • ous (är´jo͞o´əs) *adj.,* difficult, burdensome

ar • ti • fice (ärt´ə fis) *n.,* skill or ingenuity

a • skew (ə skyo͞o) *adv.,* to one side, crooked

as • sail (ə sāl´) *vi.,* attack physically, assault

as • ser • tion (a sʉr´shən) *n.,* positive statement

as • sid • u • ous (ə sij´o͞o əs) *adj.,* constant and careful; diligent

as • suage (ə swāj´) *vt.,* lessen or satisfy a need; relieve

a • sun • der (ə sun´dər) *adv.,* in pieces

a • tone • ment (ə tōn´mənt) *n.,* satisfactory payment for an offense or injury

at • trib • ute (ə trib´yo͞ot) *vt.,* recognize as the cause of

at • tri • tion (ə trish´ən) *n.,* act or process of wearing away or weakening

au • da • cious (ô dā´shəs) *adj.,* bold or daring

au • gu • ry (ô´gyo͞o rē) *n.,* divination from omens

au • gust (ô gust´) *adj.,* inspiring awe and reverence

au • re • ate (ô´rē it) *adj.,* splendid or brilliant; golden

av • a • rice (av´ə ris) *n.,* greed

a • vert (ə vʉrt´) *vt.,* turn away from

a • vi • ar • y (ā´vē er´ē) *n.,* large cage or building for keeping birds

a • vid • i • ty (ə vid´ə tē) *n.,* greedy desire or craving

a • vow • al (ə vou´ əl) *n.,* open acknowledgment or declaration

az • ure (azh´ər) *adj.,* blue

ba • bel (bab´əl) *n.,* confusion of sounds or voices

balk (bôk´) *vi.,* obstinately refuse to move or act

be • guile (bē gīl´) *vt.,* deceive; mislead by cheating or tricking

be • muse (bē myo͞oz´) *vt.,* bewilder, confuse

ben • e • dic • tion (ben´ə dik´shən) *n.,* blessing

be • nev • o • lent (bə nev´ə lənt) *adj.,* good, charitable

black • guard (blag´ərd) *n.,* scoundrel, villain, low person

boon (bo͞on) *n.,* favor granted, gift, or request

brand (brand) *vt.,* mark with disgrace; stigmatize

bran • dish (bran´dish) *vt.,* wave, shake, or exhibit in a menacing or challenging way

brusque (brusk) *adj.,* abrupt

bu • col • ic (byo͞o käl´ik) *adj.,* pastoral; of country life or farms; rustic

buf • fet (buf´it) *vt.,* hit, strike

bur • den (bʉrd´'n) *n.,* anything which is carried; load

bur • geon (bʉr´jən) *vi.,* put forth buds; sprout; flourish

cai • tiff (kāt´if) *n.,* cowardly person

ca • jole (kə jōl´) *vt.,* coax or persuade by flattery

ca • lum • ny (kal´əm nē) *n.,* false and malicious statement meant to hurt someone's reputation

can • vass (kan´vəs) *vt.,* solicit opinions, votes, etc.

ca • price (kə prēs´) *n.,* sudden, impulsive change in the way one thinks or acts; whim

ca • pri • cious (kə prish´ əs) *adj.,* erratic, flighty, tending to change abruptly

ca • reer (kər rir´) *vi.,* rush

cas • sock (kas'ək) *n.,* long, close-fitting vestment, generally black, worn by clergy

cas • ti • gate (kas´ti gāt´) *vt.,* punish or rebuke severely

ca • tas • tro • phe (kə tas´ trə fē) *n.,* disastrous end, bringing overthrow or ruin

cease • less • ly (sēs´lis lē) *adv.,* continually

ce • les • tial (sə les´chəl) *adj.,* of the sky or heaven

cen • ser (sen´sər) *n.,* container in which incense is burned

chafe (chāf) *vt.,* become irritated or impatient

chide (chīd) *vt.,* scold

clam • or (klam´ər) *n.,* loud outcry; uproar (*clamour* is the British spelling of this word)

clan • des • tine (klan des´tin) *adj.,* kept secret or hidden; furtive

cleft (kleft) *n.,* crack, crevice

clem • en • cy (klem´ən sē) *n.,* leniency, mercy

co • in • ci • dence (kō in´sə dəns) *n.,* accidental and remarkable occurrence of events or ideas at the same time

co • los • sus (kə läs´əs) *n.,* giant

com • mem • o • ra • tion (kə mem´ə rā´shən) *n.,* celebration in remembrance

com • mis • er • ate (kə miz´ər āt) *vt.,* feel pity for

com • pass (kum´ pəs) *vt.,* go around, make a circuit; reach successfully

com • pen • sate (köm´pən sāt´) *vt.,* make equivalent or suitable return, recompense; make up for

comp • en • sa • tion (käm´pən sā´ shən) *n.,* something given to make up for a loss of something else

com • pe • tent (käm´pə tənt) *adj.,* capable

com • pla • cen • cy (käm plā´sən sē) *n.,* being too self-satisfied or smug

com • ple • ment (käm´plə mənt´) *vt.,* differ but balance and complete

com • po • sure (kəm pō´zher) *n.,* calmness of mind or manner

com • pul • sion (kəm pul´shən) *n.,* compelling, driving force

com • pul • so • ry (kəm pul´sər ē) *adj.,* required, obligatory, that must be done

con • fis • cate (kän´fis kāt´) *vt.,* seize or take away by authority

con • fla • gra • tion (kän´flə grā´shən) *n.,* great and destructive fire

con • jec • ture (kən jec´chər) *n.,* guess; prediction made with incomplete evidence

con • sign (kən sīn´) *vt.,* hand over; give up or deliver

con • so • la • tion (kön´sə lā´shən) *n.,* comfort, solace

con • sole (kən sōl´) *vt.,* help to feel less sad or disappointed

con • spic • u • ous (kən spik´yo͞o es) *adj.,* attracting attention; noticeable

con • ster • na • tion (kän´ stər nā shən) *n.,* fear or shock which makes one feel helpless

con • sum • ma • tion (kän´sə mā shen) *n.,* completeness; fulfillment

con • tempt (kən tempt´) *n.,* feeling or attitude of one who looks down on somebody or something as being low, mean, or unworthy

con • tempt • i • ble (kən temp´tə bəl) *adj.,* deserving scorn; worthless

con • temp • tu • ous (kən temp´cho͞o əs) *adj.,* scornful; disdainful

con • tex • ture (kən teks´chər) *n.,* structure, composition

con • trite • ly (kən trīt´lē) *adv.,* apologetically

con • tri • vance (kən tri´vəns) *n.,* act of devising, scheming, or planning

con • vic • tion (kən vik´shən) *n.,* strong belief

con • vul • sion (kən vul´shən) *n.,* violent spasm

cor • don (kôr´ dən) *n.,* line or circle of police stationed around an area to guard it

cor • ru • gat • ed (kôr´ə gāt id) *adj.,* shaped into ridges for added strength

cos • mo • pol • i • tan (käz´mə päl´ə tən) *adj.,* representative of many parts of the world

coun • te • nance (koun´tə nəns) *n.,* facial expression

co • vert • ly (kuv´ərt lē) *adv.,* secretly

cov • et (kuv´it) *vi.,* long for with envy

crag (krag) *n.,* steep, rugged rock that rises above other rocks

cra • ven (krā´vən) *adj.,* cowardly, afraid

cred • u • lous (krej´o͞o ləs) *adj.,* tending to believe too readily

crest • fall • en (krest´fôl´ən) *adj.,* sad; humbled

cudg • el (kuj´əl) *n.,* short, thick stick or club

cu • ne • i • form (kyo͞o nē´ə fôrm´) *n.,* wedge-shaped characters from ancient Middle Eastern inscriptions

curt (kurt) *adj.,* short; brief to the point of rudeness

cus • tom • ar • y (kus´tə mer´ē) *adj.,* usual

daunt (dônt) *vt.,* make afraid or discouraged; intimidate; dishearten

de • base (dē bās´) *vt.,* make lower in value, quality, character, or dignity

de • bunk (dē buŋk´) *vt.,* expose false or exaggerated claims or pretensions

dec • i • mate (des´ə māt´) *vt.,* destroy or kill a large part of

de • cor • um (di kō´rəm) *n.,* propriety and good taste in behavior

de • cree (dē krē´) *n.,* order, edict, decision

def • er • ence (def´ər əns) *n.,* courteous regard or respect

def • er • en • tial (def´ ər ən´ shəl) *adj.,* very respectful

de • fi • cient (dē fish´ənt) *adj.,* lacking or inadequate

de • funct (dē fuŋkt´) *adj.,* dead

deg • ra • da • tion (deg´rə dā´shən) *n.,* lowering or being lowered in rank or status

del • uge (del´yo͞oj´) *n.,* great flood; overwhelming abundance

de • nun • ci • a • tion (dē nun´sē ā´shən) *n.,* public accusation

de • praved (dē prāvd´) *adj.,* morally bad, corrupt, perverted

de • sist (di sist´) *v.,* stop

de • spised (di spīz´d) *adj.,* looked down on; hated

de • spond • ent (di spän´dənt) *adj.,* dejected, without courage or hope

des • pot • ic (des pät´ik) *adj.,* autocratic; tyrannical; absolute

de • vi • a • tion (dē´vē ā´shən) *n.,* sharp divergence from normal behavior

dex • ter • ous (deks´tər əs) *adj.,* having or showing skill in use of hands or body

di • a • bol • i • cal (dī´ə bäl´i kəl) *adj.,* wicked or cruel

di • a • dem (di´ə dem´) *n.,* crown

di • gres • sion (dī gresh´ən) *n.,* departure from main path, subject, or idea

dil • i • gent • ly (dil´ə jənt lē) *adv.,* carefully and steadily

di • min • u • tive (də min´ yo͞o tiv) *adj.,* much smaller than ordinary or average

dirge (durj) *n.,* slow, sad song or poem expressing grief or mourning

dis • cern • i • ble (di zurn´ə bəl) *adj.,* recognizable

dis • ci • ple (di sī´pəl) *n.,* pupil or follower of any teacher or school of religion, learning, or art

dis • com • fi • ture (dis kum´fi chər) *n.,* frustration

dis • con • cert (dis´kən surt´) *vt.,* frustrate the plans of; upset the composure of

dis • con • cert • ing • ly (dis´kən surt´iŋ lē) *adv.,* in a manner that upsets or confuses

dis • con • so • late • ly (dis kän´ sə lit lē) *adv.,* so unhappily that nothing will comfort; cheerlessly

dis • course (dis´kôrś) *n.,* communication of ideas and information

dis • creet • ly (di skrēt´lē) *adv.,* carefully, in a manner maintaining privacy

dis • em • bark (dis´im bärk´) *vi.,* leave a means of transportation

di • shev • eled (di shev´əld) *adj.,* disarranged and untidy, tousled, rumpled

dis • may (dis mā´) *vt.,* make afraid or discouraged

dis • sem • ble (di sem´bəl) *vt.,* disguise, conceal under false appearance

dis • sim • u • la • tion (di sim´yo͞o lā´shən) *n.,* state of hiding one's feelings or motives by pretense

dis • so • lu • tion (dis´ə lo͞o´ shən) *n.,* dissolving or being dissolved; death

dis • sua • sion (di swā´zhən) *n.,* persuasion against something
di • vine (də vīn´) *vt.,* to guess by intuition
do • min • ion (də min´yən) *n.,* rule or power to rule; sovereign authority
don (dän) *vt.,* put on
dor • mant (dôr´mənt) *adj.,* inoperative; inactive
dow • ry (dou´rē) *n.,* property that a woman brings to her husband on marriage, provided by the bride's family
droll • er • y (drol´ə rē) *n.,* quaint or wry humor
du • ress (do͞o res´) *n.,* compulsion; use of force or threats
ebb (eb) *vi.,* flow back out, recede
ech • e • lon (esh´ə län´) *n.,* level of responsibility or importance in an organization
ed • dy (ed´ē) *n.,* current moving in a whirling motion
e • go • cen • tric (ē´gō sen´ trik) *adj.,* self-centered
e • late (ē lāt´) *vt.,* raise the spirits of; make very happy or proud
e • la • tion (ē lā´shən) *n.,* feeling of joy or pride, high spirits
el • e • gist (el´ə jist) *n.,* poet who writes poems of lament
e • lix • ir (ē liks´ir) *n.,* supposed remedy for all ailments
el • o • quence (el´ə kwəns) *n.,* speech or writing that is vivid, forceful, and persuasive
el • o • quent • ly (el´ə kwənt lē) *adv.,* persuasively and expressively
e • ma • ci • a • ted (ē mā´shē āt´əd) *adj.,* abnormally lean or thin as if through disease
em • bel • lish (em bel´ish) *vt.,* decorate or adorn
em • blem (em´bləm) *n.,* visible symbol
em • i • nent • ly (em´ə nənt lē) *adv.,* standing high in comparison with others
en • dow (en dou´) *vt.,* provide with some talent or quality
en • dur • a • ble (en do͞or´ə bəl) *adj.,* bearable
en • mi • ty (en´mə tē) *n.,* bitter attitude toward an enemy; hostility
en • sue (en so͞o´) *vi.,* come afterward, follow immediately
en • tice • ment (en tīs´mənt) *n.,* something that attracts by offering hope, reward, or pleasure
en • treat • y (en trēt´ē) *n.,* earnest request or plea
ep • i • gram (ep´ə gram´) *n.,* short poem with a witty or satirical point
e • qui • lib • ri • um (ē´kwə lib´rē əm) *n.,* proper steadiness, balance of the body
e • the • re • al (ē thir´ē əl) *adj.,* not earthly; heavenly
eu • phor • ic (yo͞o fôr´ik) *adj.,* happy; in high spirits
ex • as • per • a • tion (eg zas' pər ā´ shən) *n.,* great irritation or annoyance
ex • hort (eg zôrt´) *vi.,* admonish strongly, urge earnestly by advice or warning
ex • or • bi • tant (eg zor´bi tənt) *adj.,* going beyond what is reasonable, just, proper, or usual
ex • or • cise (eks´ôr sīz´) *vt.,* drive out evil through ritual or prayer
ex • pe • di • tion (eks´pə dish´ən) *n.,* journey, voyage, march for some definite purpose
ex • pi • a • tion (eks´pē ā´shən) *n.,* act of atonement or reconciliation
ex • trem • i • ty (ek strem´ə tē) *n.,* the greatest degree
fath • om (fath´əm) *vt.,* understand thoroughly
fawn (fôn) *vi.,* act servilely; cringe
feign (fān) *vt.,* pretend
fer • vent • ly (fʉr'vənt lē) *adv.,* passionately, with intensity
fes • toon (fes to͞on´) *vt.,* adorn or hang with a wreath or garland of flowers
fet • tered (fet´ərd) *adj.,* shackled or chained by the feet
fi • del • i • ty (fə del´ə tē) *n.,* loyalty, faithfulness
fil • i • al (fil´ē əl) *adj.,* showing respect to a parent or superior
fir • ma • ment (fʉrm´ə mənt) *n.,* sky, viewed poetically as a solid arch or vault
flux (fluks) *n.,* continuous movement or change
for • lorn (fôr lôrn´) *adj.,* abandoned or deserted
friv • o • lous (friv´ə ləs) *adj.,* of little value or importance, trivial
fru • i • tion (fro͞o ish´ən) *n.,* realization; a coming to fulfillment
fur • row (fʉr´ō) *n.,* groove made in the earth by a plow
fur • tive • ly (fʉr´tiv lē) *adv.,* in a sneaky or stealthy manner
fu • sil • lade (fyo͞o´sə läd´) *n.,* rapid fire or attack
fu • tile (fyo͞o t´ l) *adj.,* useless; vain; hopeless
gai • ly (gā´ lē) *adv.,* happily, merrily
gar • ru • lous (gar´ə ləs) *adj.,* talking too much, especially about unimportant things; loquacious
gaud • y (gôd´ē) *adj.,* cheaply brilliant and ornate; bright and showy but lacking in good taste
gaunt (gônt) *adj.,* thin and bony, haggard
gin • ger • ly (jin´jər´lē) *adv.,* carefully or cautiously
glut • ton • ous (glut´'n əs) *adj.,* inclined to eat too much
goad (gōd) *vt.,* prod into action; urge on
gra • tu • i • tous (grə to͞o´i təs) *adj.,* without cause or justification
griev • ance (grēv´əns) *n.,* complaint or resentment
gri • mace (grim´is) *n.,* twisting of the face expressing pain, contempt, or disgust, or a wry look as in seeking to amuse
grov • el (gruv´əl) *vi.,* lie prone or crawl in a prostrate position; behave humbly or abjectly, as before authority
guile (gīl) *n.,* slyness and cunning in dealing with others
har • mon • ize (här´mə nīz´) *vi.,* work together in an orderly way
heed • less (hēd´lis) *adj.,* careless; unmindful
herb • al • ist (hʉr´bəl ist) *n.,* person who deals in medicinal herbs
hir • sute (hʉr´so͞ot´) *adj.,* hairy; shaggy; bristly
hom • i • ly (häm´ə lē) *n.,* sermon
hone (hōn´) *vi.,* focus
hoo • li • gan (ho͞o´li gən) *n.,* hoodlum or lawless person, especially a young one

i • dle (īd´'l) *vi.*, move aimlessly, waste time

ig • no • min • y (ig´nə min´ē) *n.*, shame and dishonor

il • lic • it (il lis´it) *adj.*, not allowed by law or custom; unauthorized

il • lu • mined (i lo͞o ´mənd) *adj.*, lighted up

im • mense (im mens´) *adj.*, limitless; very large

im • mi • nent (im´ə nənt) *adj.*, likely to happen; impending

im • mo • bil • i • ty (im´mō bil´ə tē) *n.*, quality of being unmovable or unchanging

im • mure (im myoor´) *vt.*, shut up within walls

im • pas • sive (im pas´iv) *adj.*, not feeling or showing emotion; placid; calm

im • pede (im pēd´) *vt.*, bar or hinder the progress of

im • pend • ing (im pend´iŋ) *adj.*, threatening; about to happen

im • per • ti • nent • ly (im purt´'n ənt lē) *adv.*, insolently, impudently, not showing the proper respect

im • per • turb • a • ble (im´pər tur´bə bəl) *adj.*, unable to be disturbed

im • pet • u • os • i • ty (im pech´o͞o äs'i tē) *n.*, quality of being rash or impulsive

im • pet • u • ous (im pech´o͞o əs) *adj.*, moving with great force

im • plic • it (im plis´it) *adj.*, complete

im • plic • it • ly (im plis´ it lē) *adv.*, without reservation or doubt, absolutely

im • plore (im plôr´) *vt.*, beg

im • por • tu • ni • ty (im´pôr to͞on´ i tē) *n.*, persistence in requesting or demanding

im • pre • ca • tion (im´pri kā´shən) *n.*, act of invoking evil or cursing

im • pu • dent (im´pyo͞o dənt) *adj.*, bold or disrespectful

im • pugn (impo͞on´) *vt.*, attack as false or lacking integrity

in • an • i • mate (in an´ ə mit) *adj.*, not living

in • ar • tic • u • late (in´är tik´yo͞o lit) *adj.*, not able to speak understandably, as because of strong emotion

in • aus • pi • cious (in ôs´pish es´) *adj.*, ill-omened; unlucky

in • ca • pac • i • tate (in´kə pas´ə tāt´) *vt.*, make incapable of normal activity

in • car • na • tion (in kär nā´ shen) *n.*, any person or animal serving as the embodiment of a god or spirit

in • ces • sant (in ses´ənt) *adj.*, never ceasing, constant

in • com • pre • hen • si • ble (in´ käm´prē hen´sə bəl) *adj.*, not understandable

in • cred • u • lous (in krej´oo ləs) *adj.*, unwilling or unable to believe

in • cred • u • lous • ly (in krej´oo ləs lē) *adv.*, with disbelief; skeptically

in • cur (in kur´) *v.*, bring upon oneself

in • di • gence (in´di jəns) *n.*, condition of being poor or in poverty

in • dis • cre • tion (in´di skresh´ən) *n.*, unwise or immoral act or remark

in • duce (in do͞os´) *vt.*, persuade; lead on to some action, condition, or belief

in • dul • gent • ly (in dul´ jent lē) *adv.*, leniently, with an attempt to gratify or humor

in • ert (in urt´) *adj.*, physically or mentally inactive; dull; slow

in • fal • li • ble (in fal´ə bəl) *adj.*, reliable, not likely to fail, sure

in • fa • mous • ly (in´fə məs lē) *adv.*, notoriously; disgracefully; scandalously

in • fa • my (in´fə mē) *n.*, disgraceful or dishonorable act

in • fat • u • a • tion (in fach´o͞o ā´shən) *n.*, love

in • fes • ta • tion (in´fes ta´tion) *n.*, swarm of harmful or bothersome things

in • ge • nu • i • ty (in´jə no͞o´ə tē) *n.*, cleverness, originality, skill

in • gra • ti • at • ing (in grā´shē āt iŋ) *adj.*, trying to be acceptable; trying to bring oneself into another's good graces

in • junc • tion (in juŋk´shən) *n.*, command

in • nate (in´nāt´) *adj.*, existing naturally rather than acquired

in • nu • mer • a • ble (in no͞o´mər ə bəl) *adj.*, too numerous to be counted

in • scru • ta • ble (in skro͞ot'ə bəl) *adj.*, not easily understood

in • sip • id (in sip´id) *adj.*, without flavor; dull

in • so • lence (in´sə ləns) *n.*, impudence; bold disrespect

in • su • lar (in´sə lər) *adj.*, isolated

in • teg • ri • ty (in teg´rə tē) *n.*, quality or state of being honest or sincere

in • ter • mi • na • ble (in tur'mi nə bəl) *adj.*, without end, lasting forever

in • ter • vene (in´tər vēn´) *vi.*, come between to settle an argument or to disrupt an action

in • ter • ven • ing (in´tər vēn´iŋ) *adj.*, being or lying between

in • ti • mate (in´ tə māt´) *vt.*, announce, make known

in • tim • i • date (in tim´ə dāt´) *vt.*, make afraid

in • trep • id (in trep´id) *adj.*, not afraid, bold, fearless

in • va • lid (in´və lid) *n.*, weak, sickly person

in • vid • i • ous (in vid´ē əs) *adj.*, giving offense; exciting envy

in • voke (in vōk´) *vt.*, call on; summon

ir • rel • e • vant • ly (ir rel´ə vənt´lē) *adv.*, without importance

i • tin • er • ar • y (ī tin´ər er´ē) *n.*, record of a journey

joc • u • lar • i • ty (jäk´ yo͞o lar´ə tē) *n.*, state of being full of jokes and fun

ju • bi • la • tion (jo͞o´bə lā´shən) *n.*, happy celebration

ju • di • cious (jo͞o dish´əs) *adj.*, wise and careful

junc • ture (juŋk´chər) *n.*, particular or critical moment in the development of events

knave (nāv) *n.*, dishonest or deceitful person

lad • en (lād´'n) *adj.*, densely loaded; full

la • ment (lə ment´) *n.*, mourning, wailing

lam • en • ta • tion (lam´ən tā´shən) *n.*, expression of grief or sorrow, especially through weeping or wailing

lan • guid • ly (laŋ´gwid lē) *adv.*, without vigor or vitality; listlessly, indifferently

lav • ish • ly (lav´ish lē) *adv.,* extravagantly; in a generous, abundant, or liberal manner

lay • man (lā´mən) *n.,* person who does not belong to the clergy

lev • el (lev´əl) *vt.,* knock to the ground, demolish, lay low

lev • i • ty (lev´i tē) *n.,* lack of seriousness

li • ba • tion (lī bā´shən) *n.,* ritual of pouring wine or oil as a sacrifice to a god

lim • pid (lim´pid) *adj.,* perfectly clear; transparent

lin • e • age (lin´ē ij) *n.,* ancestry, family line

lit • a • ny (lit´'n ē) *n.,* repetitive recitation

liv • id (liv´id) *adj.,* brightly discolored as by a bruise; black and blue

lu • cid • i • ty (lo͞o cid´i tē) *n.,* clarity of thought; comprehension

lu • gu • bri • ous (lə go͞o´brē əs) *adj.,* very sad or mournful, especially in a way that seems exaggerated or ridiculous

lu • mi • nous (lo͞o´mə nəs) *adj.,* bright, shining, giving off light

lux • u • ri • ate (lug zho͞or´ē āt´) *vi.,* take great pleasure

mal • ice (mal´is) *n.,* active ill will

ma • lin • ger • er (mə ling´gər ər) *n.,* one who pretends to be ill to evade work

ma • ni • a • cal (mə nī´ə kəl) *adj.,* characterized by excessive or persistent enthusiasm

man • i • fes • ta • tion (man´ə fes tā´shən) *n.,* concrete form in which something reveals itself

man • tle (man´təl) *n.,* anything that cloaks or covers

mar (mär) *vt.,* injure or damage so as to make imperfect

mea • ger • ly (mē´gʉr lē) *adv.,* inadequately, not fully or richly

mel • an • chol • y (mel´ən käl´ē) *n.,* sadness and depression of spirits

mer • it (mer´it) *vt.,* deserve, be worthy of

met • a • phy • si • cian (met´ə fə zish´ən) *n.,* one who studies metaphysics, that branch of philosophy that deals with ultimate realities and the nature of being

me • tic • u • lous (mə tik´yoo ləs) *adj.,* extremely or excessively careful about details

mien (mēn) *n.,* manner, bearing

min • ion (min´yən) *n.,* favorite; servile follower

mirth (mʉrth) *n.,* pleasure, joy

mod • u • lat• ed (mäj´ə lāt´ əd) *adj.,* varied in pitch or intensity, often to a lower degree

moor (mo͞or) *n.,* tract of open, rolling wasteland

mor • tu • ar • y (môr´to͞o er ē) *n.,* place where dead bodies are kept before burial or cremation

mum • mi • fy (mum´ə fī´) *vt.,* turn into a mummy

mu • nif • i • cence (myo͞o nif´ə səns) *n.,* generosity

mu • ti • lat • ed (myo͞ot´'lāt´ad) *adj.,* damaged, especially by having a part removed

myr • i • ad (mir´ē əd) *n.,* large number of persons or things

ne • gate (ni gāt´) *vt.,* deny existence or truth of; make ineffective

nes • tle (nes´əl) *vi.,* settle down comfortably and snugly

non • cha • lance (nän´shə läns´) *n.,* state or attitude of being unconcerned

nought (nôt) *n.,* nothing

ob • lique • ly (ə blek´lē) *adv.,* in a slanted way; not level

ob • liv • i • on (ə bliv´ē ən) *n.,* condition of forgetting and being forgotten

ob • liv • i • ous (ə bliv´ē əs) *adj.,* forgetful or unmindful

ob • lo • quy (äb´lə kwē) *n.,* ill repute; disgrace

ob • scure (əb skyoor´) *adj.,* not well-known, not famous

ob • se • qui • ous • ness (əb sē´kwē əs nes) *n.,* overwillingness to please others

ob • sti • na • cy (äb´stə nə sē) *n.,* stubbornness; unreasonable determination to have one's way

ob • sti • nate (äb´stə nət) *adj.,* stubborn; not yielding to reason or plea

ob • struc • tion (əb struk´shən) *n.,* anything that blocks, hinders, or keeps something from being seen

ob • tain (köm´pən sāt´) *vt.,* get or procure through some effort

o • ra • tion (ō rā´shən) *n.,* formal public speech

or • dain (ôr dān´) *vt.,* predetermine; establish

os • ten • ta • tion (äs´ tən tā´shən) *n.,* showy display, as of wealth

os • ten • ta • tious (äs´tən tā´shəs) *adj.,* pretentious; showy

page (pāj) *n.,* boy servant to a person of high rank

pal • lid (pal´id) *adj.,* faint in color; pale

pal • pa • ble (pal´pə bəl) *adj.,* that can be touched or felt

pal • pi • tate (pal´pə tāt´) *vi.,* beat rapidly, flutter

pang (paŋ) *n.,* sudden pain, sharp and brief

pan • to • mime (pan´tə mīm) *n.,* dramatic presentation using only actions and gestures, not speech

par • a • sol (par´ə sol´) *n.,* lightweight umbrella used to provide shade from the sun

parch • ing (pärch´iŋ) *adj.,* hot and drying

par • tial (pär´shəl) *adj.,* favoring one person or thing more than another; prejudiced

pate (pāt) *n.,* head

pa • ter • nal • is • tic (pə tʉr´nəl is´tik) *adj.,* fatherly in a condescending manner

pa • tron • ize (pa´trən īz´) *vt.,* be kind or helpful, but in a snobby manner, as if dealing with an inferior

pa • vil • ion (pə vil´yən) *n.,* large tent or building, partly open, once used by royalty and now typically used at fairs and other outdoor entertainments

peal (pēl) *n.,* loud, prolonged sound

pee • vish • ness (pēv´ish nəs) *n.,* impatience; crossness

pen • du • lous (pen´dyo͞o ləs) *adj.,* hanging or bending downward

pen • i • tent (pen´i tənt) *n.,* person who is truly sorry for having sinned or done wrong

pen • sion (pen´shən) *n.,* payment, not wages, made regularly to a person who has fulfilled certain conditions of service or reached a certain age

per • di • tion (pər dish´ən) *n.*, loss of the soul; damnation

per • en • ni • al (pər en´ē əl) *adj.*, lasting or continuing for a long time

per • fid • i • ous (pər fid´ē əs) *adj.*, treacherous

per • fi • dy (pʉr´fə dē) *n.*, betrayal of trust; treachery

per • func • to • ri • ly (pər funk´tə rə lē) *adv.*, carelessly, indifferently

per • il • ous (per´ə ləs) *adj.*, dangerous

per • me • ate (pʉr´mē āt') *vt.*, penetrate or spread through

per • pet • u • al (pər pech´o͞o əl) *adj.*, lasting forever

per • plex (pər pleks´) *vt.*, confuse

per • turb (pər tʉrb´) *vt.*, upset, trouble

per • va • sive • ness (pər vā´siv nəs) *n.*, penetration throughout

pes • ti • lence (pes´tə ləns) *n.*, any deadly infectious disease

pet • ri • fac • tion (pe´tri fak´shən) *n.*, state in which objects have been made rigid or hard

pet • u • lant (pech´ə lənt) *adj.*, impatient or irritable

phys • i • og • no • my (fiz´ē äg´ nə mē) *n.*, facial features as they expose character

pi • e • ty (pī´ə tē) *n.*, devotion to religious or family duties and practice

pil • lage (pil´ij) *vt.*, rob violently; plunder

pin • na • cle (pin´ə kəl) *n.*, small turret or spire

pi • ous (pī´əs) *adj.*, having or showing religious devotion

pit • e • ous (pit´ē əs) *adj.*, arousing or deserving pity or compassion

plain • tive (plān´tiv) *adj.*, mournful; sad

plau • si • ble (plô´zə bəl) *adj.*, believable, acceptable

pluck (pluk) *n.*, courage; strength to bear misfortune or pain

pos • ter • i • ty (päs ter' ə tē) *n.*, descendants; all succeeding generations

prac • ti • ca • ble (prak´ti kə bəl) *adj.*, possible

pre • car • i • ous (prē ker´ē əs) *adj.*, uncertain, insecure

pre • cinct (prē´ siŋkt´) *n.*, any limited area; boundary

pre • cip • i • tous (prē sip´ə təs) *adj.*, steep; sheer

pre • cur • sor (prē kûr´sər) *n.*, that which comes before; harbinger

pre • dic • a • ment (prē dik´ə mənt) *n.*, unpleasant, embarrassing, or comical situation

pre • sen • ti • ment (prē zent´ə mənt) *n.*, a sense that something unfortunate is about to happen

pre • sump • tu • ous (prē zump´cho͞o əs) *adj.*, too bold or forward; showing overconfidence

pre • tense (prē tens´) *n.*, false claim or show

pre • ter • nat • u • ral (prēt´ər nach´ər əl) *adj.*, abnormal; supernatural

pre • vail (prē vāl´) *vi.*, gain the advantage or mastery, become stronger

pri • mor • di • al (pri môr´dē əl) *adj.*, existing at the beginning; first in time

pro • cure (prō ko͝or´) *vt.*, obtain, secure

pro • di • gious (prō dij´əs) *adj.*, amazing; enormous

prod • i • gy (präd´ə jē) *n.*, child or other person with talent or genius

pro • found (prō found´) *adj.*, unbroken; deeply or intensely felt

prog • e • ny (präj´ə nē) *n.*, offspring; descendants

pro • le • tar • i • an (prō´lə ter´ē ən) *n.*, member of the working class

pro • lif • er • ate (prō lif´ər āt´) *vi.*, multiply rapidly; increase profusely

pro • pi • tious (prō pi´shəs) *adj.*, favorable

pros • trate (präs´trāt´) *adj.*, thrown or fallen to the ground

pro • té • gé (prōt´ə zhā) *n.*, person guided or helped by another

pro • vin • cial (prō vin´ shəl) *adj.*, having the ways, speech, attitudes of a certain province, especially a rural one; countrified; rustic

pro • vi • sion (prō vizh´ən) *n.*, stock of food or supplies

prow • ess (prou´is) *n.*, superior ability, skill

pru • dence (pro͞od´'ns) *n.*, careful management

pru • dent (pro͞od´ 'nt) *adj.*, cautiously wise

punc • tu • al • ly (puŋk´ cho͞o əl lē) *adv.*, promptly, on time

purge (pərj) *vt.*, cleanse of guilt, sin, or ceremonial defilement

pyre (pīr) *n.*, pile, especially of wood, on which a dead body is burned in a funeral rite

quick (kwik) *adj.*, living, alive

rail • ler • y (rāl´ər ē) *n.*, good-natured ridicule

ran • cor (raŋ'kər) *n.*, continuing and bitter hate or ill will

rank (raŋk) *adj.*, growing vigorously and coarsely

ran • kle (raŋ´kəl) *vt.*, cause to have long-lasting anger, rancor, or resentment

ra • pa • cious • ly (rə pā´shəs lē) *adv.*, greedily

rash • ly (rash´lē) *adv.*, recklessly; hastily

rasp (räsp) *n.*, rough, grating sound

rat • i • fy (rat´ə fī´) *vt.*, approve or confirm

rav • age (rav´ij) *vt.*, destroy violently; ruin

rav • en • ing (rav´ən iŋ) *adj.*, greedily searching

ra • vine (rə vēn´) *n.*, long, deep hollow in the earth's surface

re • buke (ri byo͞ok´) *n.*, sharp reprimand

re • course (rē´kôrs´) *n.*, something to which one turns for safety or help

re • gale (ri gāl´) *vt.*, entertain by providing a splendid feast

reg • i • ment (rej´ə ment) *n.*, unit of soldiers

rem • nant (rem´nənt) *n.*, what is left over; small, remaining part

re • mon • strate (ri män´strāt) *vt.*, say or plead in protest, objection, complaint

rend (rend) *vt.*, tear, pull, or rip with violence

re • nun • ci • a • tion (ri nun´ sē ā´ shən) *n.*, surrender, formally or voluntarily, of a right

re • pent • ance (ri pen´təns) *n.*, feeling of sorrow for wrongdoing, remorse

rep • er • toire (rep´ər twär´) *n.,* stock of material available for performance

re • plen • ish (ri plen´ish) *vt.,* make full or complete again; repeople

re • pose (ri pōz´) *n.,* rest or sleep

re • prieve (ri prēv´) *n.,* relief or postponement of punishment

re • proach (ri prōch´) *v.,* severely criticize; blame

re • quite (ri kwīt´) *vt.,* reward or retaliate against

res • o • nant (rez´ə nənt) *adj.,* full of echoing sound

ret • i • na (ret´'n ə) *n.,* innermost coat lining the interior of the eyeball

ret • i • nue (ret´ 'n yo͞o´) *n.,* body of assistants, followers, or servants attending a person of rank or importance

re • tort (ri tôrt´) *vi.,* reply or respond rudely or insultingly

re • ver • be • ra • tion (ri vʉr´bə rā´shən) *n.,* echo and re-echo; multiple reflections of sound waves

rev • er • ence (rev´ər əns) *vt.,* treat with great respect, love, and awe, as for something sacred

rev • er • ie (rev´ər ē) *n.,* dreamy thinking or imagining; day-dreaming

rhap • so • dize (rap´sə dīz´) *vi.,* speak or write in an extravagantly enthusiastic manner

rhet • o • ric (ret´ər ik) *n.,* art of using words effectively in speaking or writing

rig • id (rij´id) *adj.,* stiff and hard

riv • u • let (riv´yo͞o lit) *n.,* little stream, brook

ro • bust (rō bust´) *adj.,* strong and healthy; hardy

row (rou) *n.,* noisy quarrel, dispute, or disturbance

ru • di • men • ta • ry (ro͞o´də men´tər ē) *adj.,* incompletely or imperfectly developed; basic

ruse (ro͞oz) *n.,* trick

saf • fron (saf´rən) *adj.,* orange-yellow

sage (sāj) *n.,* wise teacher; experienced person, respected for having good judgment

sal • low (sal´ō) *adj.,* sickly, pale yellow in hue

sal • u • ta • tion (sal´yo͞o tā´shən) *n.,* act of greeting or welcoming

san • guine (saŋ´ gwin) *adj.,* reddish, ruddy

sans (sänz) *prep.,* without

sash (sash) *n.,* frame holding glass of a window

sat • ed (sāt´əd) *adj.,* satisfied completely

sa • voir • faire (sav´wär fer´) *n.,* ready knowledge of what to do or say

sa • vor • y (sā´vər ē) *adj.,* pleasing to the taste or smell

scorn (skôrn) *vt.,* refuse or reject as wrong or disgraceful

scorn • ful • ly (skôrn´ fəl lē) *adv.,* with disdain or contempt

scourge (skʉrj) *n.,* means of inflicting severe punishment, suffering, or vengeance

scru • ti • nize (skro͞ot´'n īz´) *vt.,* examine closely

scul • ler • y (skul´ər ē) *n.,* room adjoining the kitchen

se • date • ly (si dāt´lē) *adv.,* calmly; quietly

seethe (sēth) *vt.,* boil; be violently agitated or disturbed

seg • re • ga • tion (seg´rə gā´shən) *n.,* policy of compelling people of different racial groups to live separately from each other

se • man • tic (si man´ tik) *adj.,* pertaining to the meaning of words or symbols

sem • blance (sem´bləns) *n.,* outward form or appearance

se • pul • chral (sə pul´krəl) *adj.,* dismal, gloomy; suggestive of the grave or burial

sheep • ish • ly (shēp' ish lē) *adv.,* in an awkwardly shy or bashful manner

si • es • ta (sē es´tə) *n.,* brief nap or rest taken after the noon meal

sil • hou • ette (sil´o͞o et´) *n.,* outline drawing, filled in with a solid color, usually black

skein (skān) *n.,* quantity of thread or yarn wound in a coil

skiff (skif) *n.,* small, open boat propelled by oars or sail

slake (slāk) *vt.,* satisfy or make less intense

sod • den (säd´'n) *adj.,* filled with moisture; soaked through

sol • emn (säl´əm) *adj.,* serious, quiet

som • nam • bu • lant (säm nam´byo͞o lant) *adj.,* sleepwalking, in a trance

so • no • rous (sə nôr´əs) *adj.,* having an impressive sound

sooth • say • er (so͞oth´sā ər) *n.,* person who professes to foretell the future

sor • did (sôr´did) *adj.,* dirty; ignoble

sov • er • eign (säv´rən) *n.,* ruler

spec • tral (spek´trəl) *adj.,* ghostlike

spliced (splīsd´) *adj.,* joined or united by weaving together

squal • id (skwäl´id) *adj.,* foul or unclean

squall (skwôl) *n.,* brief, violent windstorm, usually with rain or snow

squeam • ish • ly (skwēm´ish lē) *adv.,* in a prudish, excessively fastidious, oversensitive, or dainty manner

steep (stēp) *vt.,* immerse, saturate

ster • ile (stər´əl) *adj.,* barren; lacking interest or vitality

stip • u • late (stip´yo͞o lāt´) *vt.,* include specifically in the terms of an agreement

straits (strātz) *n.,* difficulty, distress

stri • dent • ly (strī´dənt lē) *adv.,* in a harsh-sounding, shrill, or grating manner

strive (strīv) *vi.,* make great efforts; try very hard

stu • pe • fac • tion (sto͞o´ pə fak´shən) *n.,* stunned amazement

stu • por (sto͞o´pər) *n.,* state in which the mind and senses are dulled, as from shock

sub • orn (sə bôrn´) *vt.,* induce or instigate to do something illegal, especially to commit perjury

suc • cor (suk´ər) *n.,* help, aid, relief

suc • cumb (sə kum´) *vi.,* give way to, yield

suf • fice (sə fis´) *vi.,* be enough; be sufficient or adequate

sum • mit (sum´it) *n.,* the top, as of a mountain

sump • tu • ous • ly (sump´cho͞o əs lē) *adv.,* lavishly; at great expense

sun • dries (sun´ drēz) *n.*, minor items

su • per • cil • i • ous • ly (so͞o´pər sil´ē əs lē) *adv.*, in a haughty, scornful, or disdainful manner

su • per • flu • ous (so͞o´pûr´ flo͞o əs) *adj.*, unnecessary

su • per • nal (sə purn´əl) *adj.*, divine

sup • ple (sup´əl) *adj.*, easily bent or twisted; flexible

sup • pli • cate (sup´lə kāt´) *vt.*, ask for humbly and earnestly

sup • pli • ca • tion (sup´lə kā´shən) *n.*, humble request or prayer

sup • po • si • tion (sup´ə zish´ən) *n.*, something supposed; assumption

sur • feit (surʹfit) *n.*, excess; too great an amount or supply

surge (surj) *vi.*, have a heavy, violent swelling motion

sur • mount (sər mount´) *vi.*, overcome; surpass, exceed

sur • rep • ti • tious • ly (sur´əp tish´əs lē) *adv.*, secretly

tab • er • nac • le (tab´ər nak´əl) *n.*, place of worship

tar • ry (tar´ē) *vi.*, delay, linger, be tardy

teem (tēm) *vi.*, be full; abound; swarm

te • mer • i • ty (tə mer´ə tē) *n.*, foolish or rash boldness, recklessness

tem • per (tem´pər) *vt.*, bring to proper texture, consistency, or hardness

tem • per • ed (tem´pərd) *adj.*, brought to proper texture, hardness, and strength

tem • pes • tu • ous (tem pes´cho͞o əs) *adj.*, violent, stormy

tep • id (tep´id) *adj.*, lukewarm; lacking warmth of feeling or enthusiasm

ter • rain (ter rān´) *n.*, geographical area

the • o • log • i • cal (thē ə läj´i kəl) *adj.*, based on religious doctrines

thith • er (thith´ər) *adv.*, to or toward that place

thresh • old (thresh´ōld´) *n.*, entrance

throng (thrôŋ) *n.*, crowd; great number of people

ti • rade (tī´rād´) *n.*, long speech, especially one that is critical or angry

toil (toil) *n.*, labor; hard work

to • ken (tō´kən) *n.*, symbol

tran • scen • den • tal (tran´sen dent´'l) *adj.*, extraordinary; surpassing the ordinary

trem • u • lous (trem´yo͞o ləs) *adj.*, trembling, quivering; fearful, timid

trib • u • la • tion (trib´ yo͞o lā´shən) *n.*, great misery or distress

tri • pod (trī´päd) *n.*, three-legged caldron, or large kettle

tru • ant (tro͞o´ənt) *adj.*, straying

ul • u • late (yo͞ol´yo͞o lāt´) *vi.*, howl or hoot

un • as • sail • a • ble (un´ə sāl´ə bəl) *adj.*, that which cannot be attacked

un • con • scion • a • ble (un kän´shən ə bəl) *adj.*, not fair or just

un • couth (un ko͞oth´) *adj.*, uncultured, crude

un • re • mit • ting (un ri mit´iŋ) *adj.*, persistent

un • scathed (un skāthd) *adj.*, unharmed

un • shod (un shäd') *adj.*, without shoes

ut • ter (ut´ər) *vt.*, produce, speak, or express audibly

vag • a • bond (vag´ə band´) *n.*, person who wanders from place to place

vain (vān) *adj.*, worthless; unprofitable

val • id (val´id) *adj.*, binding under law

var • i • ance (ver´ē əns) *n.*, disagreement; quarrel

vas • sal (vas´əl) *n.*, person who held land and owed loyalty and military service to a lord

vault (vôlt) *n.*, arched space

ve • he • ment • ly (vē´ə mənt lē) *adv.*, passionately, fervently

ve • ran • da (və ran´ də) *n.*, open porch, usually roofed, along the outside of a building

veil (vāl) *vt.*, conceal, hide, disguise

ven • er • a • ble (ven´ər ə bəl) *adj.*, worthy of respect due to age, character, or position

ven • ture (ven´chər) *vt.*, express at the risk of criticism, objection, denial, etc.

ver • nal (vurn´əl) *adj.*, of the spring

ver • sa • til • i • ty (vur´sə til´ə tē) *n.*, competence or skill in many things

ves • sel (ves´əl) *n.*, container such as a vase, bowl, or pot

ves • tige (ves´tij) *n.*, trace; mark or sign of something that once existed but now has passed away

vex (veks) *vt.*, annoy, irritate, disturb

vex • a • tion (veks ā´shən) *n.*, state of disturbance, annoyance, irritation

vi • al (vī´əl) *n.*, small vessel or bottle, usually of glass, for containing liquids

vig • or • ous • ly (vig´ ər əs lē) *adv.*, with energy and force

vile • ly (vil´lē) *adv.*, sinfully, wickedly

vis • age (viz´ ij) *n.*, face

vi • vac • i • ty (vī vas´ə tē) *n.*, liveliness

wave • let (wāv´lit) *n.*, little wave, ripple

way • far • er (wā´fer´ər) *n.*, person who travels, especially on foot

whet • ted (hwet´əd) *adj.*, sharpened

win • some (win´səm) *adj.*, attractive in a sweet, engaging way

wiz • ened (wiz´ənd) *adj.*, dried up, shriveled

wrought (rôt) *adj.*, shaped and designed

Index of Titles and Authors

Index of Special Features

Index of Skills

Reading and Literature

Writing Skills

Language Skills

Speaking and Listening Skills

Study and Research Skills

Applied English/Tech Prep

Index of Fine Art

Art Acknowledgments

The Bohemian. Adolphe-William Bouguereau, 1890, The Minneapolis Institute of Arts, **cover**; Indian Barbers—Saharanpore. Edwin Lord Weeks, Josyln Art Museum, Omaha, NB, **71**; The River Bridge at Uji. The Nelson-Atkins Museum of Art, Kansas City, MO, **95**; La Jeune Bonne. Amedeo Modigliani, 1981, Albright-Knox Art Gallery, Buffalo, NY, **174**; Gwendolyn. John Sloan, 1918, National Museum of American Art, Smithsonian Institution, NY, **192**; Saying Farewell at Hsü, (Hsun-yang sung-pieh). Ch'iu Ying, Ming Dynasty, 1364-1644, The Nelson-Atkins Museum of Art, Kansas City, MO (Purchase: Nelson: Trust), **247**; Villa Malta, Rome. Sanford Robinson Gifford, 1879, National Museum of American Art, Washington, DC/Art Resource, NY, **253**; Flower Garden and Bungalow, Bermuda. Winslow Homer, 1899, The Metropolitan Museum of Art, NY, **281**; The Death of Socrates. Jacques-Louis David, 1787, The Metropolitan Museum of Art, **305**; Mount Fuji in Clear Weather. (Art from Edo Japan), Musées Royaux D'art et D'histoire, **326**; The Kirifuri Waterfall at Mount Kurokami. Shimozuke Province, Katsushika Hokusa, circa 1831, **360**; Painted Stele of Lady Taperet: Taperet before Re-Harakhte. Lower Egypt (Lybia), 22nd dynasty, 950-730 BC, Louvre, Paris, France, Giraudon/Art Resource, NY, **367**; Valle de México. José Maria Velasco, Smithsonian Institution Traveling Exhibition Service, Washington, DC, **398**; Un chat couche, allongé de gauche à droit. Théophile Alexandre Steinlen, Museum of Fine Art, Boston, MA, **409**; Precious Paisley. Susan Y. West, **412**; The Wounded Stag. Ralph Albert Blakelock, circa 1880, The Hirshhorn Museum and Sculpture Garden, Smithsonian Institute, **439**; Baby Dolls. Marianne Ashurst, **484**; Gilgamesh in Combat with a Lion and Enkidu with a Bull. Museum of Fine Arts, Boston, MA, **505**; Don Quixote. Gustave Doré, Wellesley College Library, Special Collections, **516**; Elohim Creating Adam. William Blake, Tate Gallery, London, Great Britain, Art Resource, NY, **521**; The Body of Abel Found by Adam and Eve. William Blake, Tate Gallery, London, Great Britain, Art Resource, NY, **525**; Confucius, (c.551-479 B.C.). Ink rubbing from a Chinese Stele, 1734, the Grainger Collection, NY, **552**; Ravana. Freer Gallery of Art, Smithsonian Institute, Washington, D.C., **564**; Death of Ravana. Freer Gallery of Art, Smithsonian Institute, Washington, D.C., **569**; Bust of Homer. SEF/Art Resource, NY, **592**; Fresco of the Iliad. Sabatelli, Scala/Art Resource, NY, **601**; Achilles Dragging Hector. Museum of Fine Arts, Boston, MA, **604**; Oedipus and the Sphinx. Scala/Art Resource, NY, **619**; Destiny. J. William Waterhouse, 1900, Towneley Hall Art Gallery and Museum, Manchester, Great Britain, Bridgeman Art Library/Art Resource, NY, **736**; The Fisherman Releasing the Genie. Elihu Vedder, Museum of Fine Arts, Boston, MA, **790**; The Meeting of the Theologians. Allah Musawwir, circa. 1540-50, The Nelson-Atkins Museum of Art, Kansas City, MO, **806**; Illustration by Arthur Rackham. Wellesley College Library, Special Collections, **833**; Illustration by Arthur Rackham. Wellesley College Library, Special Collections, **836**; Don Quixote Fighting the Windmill. Gustave Doré, Wellesley College Library, Special Collections, **854**; Don Quixote and Sancho. Gustave Doré, Wellesley College Library, Special Collections, ***xxii*, 856**; Eiffel Tower. Robert Delaunay, Hirshhorn Museum of Art and Sculpture Garden, Smithsonian Institution, **1012**; Still Life—"Le Jour." Georges Braque, National Gallery of Art, Washington, D.C., Chester Dale Collection, **1037**; Mechanical Abstraction. Morton Schamberg, Philadelphia Museum of Art, **1070**

Courtesy of Planet Art: 2, 5, 6, 7, 20, 21, 22, 27, 29, 31, 43, 49, 60, 63, 90, 91, 92, 98, 104, 108, 115, 127, 130, 132, 135, 139, 143, 147, 153, 157, 171, 218, 220, 222, 231, 261, 263, 274, 278, 292, 294, 299, 307, 314, 319, 333, 341, 362, 364, 376, 377, 378, 386, 387, 422, 432, 452, 498, 578, 579, 580, 586, 593, 677, 714, 716, 717, 718, 720, 721, 772, 781, 784, 796, 805, 851, 862, 884, 887, 987, 1014, 1015, 1016, 1021, 1029, 1035, 1040, 1044, 1047, 1049, 1052, 1060, 1065, 1073, 1077, 1081, 1097
Courtesy of Corel: *xxiii, xxiv,* 5, 6, 7, 8, 20, 21, 22, 23, 33, 34, 35, 36, 37, 41, 42, 43, 44, 45, 54, 55, 56, 57, 65, 66, 67, 68, 69, 76, 77, 78, 79, 80, 83, 88, 89, 90, 91, 92, 98, 119, 168, 204, 226, 234, 239, 242, 251, 257, 266, 269, 270, 279, 302, 303, 310, 323, 339, 347, 353, 371, 372, 379, 381, 384, 390, 395, 406, 417, 436, 470, 500, 515, 517, 518, 531, 532, 535, 537, 538, 540, 541, 544, 547, 555, 560, 571, 572, 575, 588, 589, 590, 616, 671, 627, 649, 651, 674, 691, 693, 742, 744, 759, 765, 770, 778, 780, 803, 816, 818, 819, 820, 822, 827, 830, 867, 872, 984, 1086, 1089, 1104, 1107, 1112
Courtesy of Archive Photo: 180, 181, 184, 186, 199, 203, 424
Courtesy of the Library of Congress: 167, 189
Courtesy of Digital Stock Corp: 421
Courtesy of Silvio Fiore/Superstock: 595
Courtesy of Photo Disc: 1056

Additional Photo and Illustration Credits
Courtesy of the Lyric Stage Company: Oedipus and Jocasta, 567; Oedipus and Tieresias, 633; Oedipus and Jocasta, 643; Oedipus Threatening the Herdsman, 663
Photos: Charles Bent: 852; **Richard Feldman.** Huntington Theatre Company: 875, 877, 879; **Gerry Goodstein.** Huntington Theatre Company: 961, 969, 975, 980;
John Hruska: 4, 20, 33, 42, 46, 54, 55, 65, 76, 79, 88, 91, 177, 213, 247, 285, 344, 355, 419, 425, 426, 491, 572, 671, 775, 922, 1117
Illustrations: **Laura DaSilva:** 444; **Sara Day:** 824, 868, 883; **David Ferarra:** 208, 350, 462, 465, 466; **Rick Hudson:** 13, 14; **Peter Pasquerello**, 447; **Janet Stebbings:** 476, 1054; **David Stowell:** 489; **Andy White:** 392

Literary Acknowledgments *(continued from copyright page)*

This page constitutes an extension of the copyright page. We have made every effort to trace the ownership of all copyrighted material and to secure permission from copyright holders. In the event of any question arising as to the use of any material, we will be pleased to make the necessary corrections in future printings. Thanks are due to the following authors, publishers, and agents for permission to use the material indicated.

Aliki Barnstone and Willis Barnstone

"They say that plants don't talk . . ." by Rosalia de Castro, translated by Aliki Barnstone and Willis Barnstone.

Alison M. Bond, Ltd.

Selected poems "My life, my love, you say our love will last forever," "My woman says that she would rather wear the wedding-veil for me," "I hate and love," " You are the cause of this destruction, Lesbia," from the *Poems of Catullus*, copyright © 1956 by the Estate of Horace Gregory. Used by permission of the Estate.

Aunte Lute Books

"The Youngest Doll," by Rosario Ferré, from *Reclaiming Medusa: Short Stories by Comtemporary Puerto Rican Women*, edited and translated by Diana Velez. Copyright © 1988 by Diana Velez. Reprinted by permission of Aunte Lute Books.

B. O. Foster

Excerpts from *Livy* translated by B. O. Foster, Ph.D., first published in 1919. Harvard University Press London.

Bantam Doubleday Dell

Excerpt from *Like Water for Chocolate*, by Laura Esquivel. Copyright Translation © 1992 by Doubleday, a div. of Bantam Doubleday Dell Publishing Group, Inc. Used by permission of Doubleday, a division of Bantam Doubleday Dell Publishing Group, Inc.

Excerpt "Marriage Is a Private Affair," from *Girls at War and Other Stories* by Chinua Achebe. Copyright © 1972, 1973 by Chinua Achebe. Used by permission of Doubleday, a division of Bantam Doubleday Dell Publishing Group, Inc.

"Simmering" from *Good Bones and Simple Murders*, by Margaret Atwood. Copyright © 1983, 1992, 1994 O. W. Toad Ltd. A Nan A. Talese Book. Used by permission of Doubleday, a division of Bantam Doubleday Dell Publishing Group.

Carcanet Press

"Great Is My Envy of You," by Francis Petrarch, from *Collected Poems*, translated by Edwin Morgan. Repinted by permission of Carcanet Press.

"The Fifth Story," from *The Foreign Legion* by Clarice Lispector. Copyright © 1964, 1986 by Clarice Lispector. English translated © 1986 by Giovanni Pontiero. Reprinted by permission of Carcanet Press.

Carol Publishing Group

Excerpt "The Weighing of the Heart of Ani," from *The Book of the Dead*, translated by E. A. Wallis Budge. Copyright © 1960, 1988 by University Book, a division of Carol Publishing Group.

Columbia University Press

Excerpt from *The Complete Works of Chuang Tzu*, by Chuang Chou, translated by Burton Watson.

"Four Noble Truths," *Sources of Indian Tradition* by William Theodore de Bary. Copyright © 1988 Columbia University Press. Reprinted by permission of the publisher.

"The Rules of Courtly Love" by Andreas Capelianus, from *The Art of Courtly Love*. Copyright © 1990 by Columbia University Press. Reprinted by permission of the publisher.

Excerpts "In Spring It Is the Dawn," "When I Make Myself Imagine," "Hateful Things," "Oxen Should Have Very Small Foreheads," "Elegant Things," "Pleasing Thing" from *The Pillow Book of Sei Shōnagon*, by Ivan Morris. Copyright © 1991 by Columbia University Press. Reprinted by permission of the publisher.

Continuum Publishing Group

"The First Sally (A) or Trurl's Electronic Bard" by Stanislaw Lem, translated by Michael Kandel from *The Cyberiad: Fables for the Cybernetic Age* by Stanislaw Lem. Copyright © 1974 by The Continuum Publishing Company. Reprinted by permission.

David Higham Associates, Ltd.

Excerpts from *Orlando Furioso*, by Ludovico Ariosto, translated by Barbara Reynolds. Copyright © 1975 by Barbara Reynolds. Reprinted by permission of David Higham Associates, Ltd., London.

"Life is Sweet at Kumansenu," from *Married Woman and Other Stories*, by Abioseh Nicol. Copyright © 1965 by Oxford University Press, London. Reprinted by permission of David Higham Associates Ltd., London.

Dial Press, NY

"Poseidonians," from *Passion and Ancient Days*, by Constantine Cavafy, translated by Edmund Keeley and George Savidis. Copyright © 1963, 1968 by Kyveli A. Singopoulo. Copyright © 1971 by Edmund Keeley and George Savidis. Dial Press, NY.

Duke University Press

"The Wooden Horse then said," by Jenny Mastoraki, translated by Nikos Germanakos from *boundary 2*, Vol. 2, (Winter 1973). Copyright © 1973. Reprinted by permission of Duke University Press.

Edna St. Vincent Millay Society

"Oh, oh, you will be sorry for that word," by Edna St. Vincent Millay. From *Collected Poems*, HarperCollins. Copyright © 1923, 1951 by Edna St. Vincent Millay and Norma Millay Ellis. All rights reserved. Reprinted by permission Elizabeth Barnett, literary executor.

Ehsan Yarshater

"Lament for His Son" from *The Epic of the Kings*, translated by Reuben Levy. Reprinted by permission of Ehsan Yarshater, Columbia University.

ETT Imprint

"Request to a Year" from *A Human Pattern: Selected Poems by Judith Wright*. (ETT Imprint, Watsons Bay, Australia, 1996.) Reprinted by permission.

Everymans Library

"The Lay of the Werewolf," from *Lays of Marie de France and Other French Legends*, translated by Eugene Mason. Reprinted by permission of Everymans Library, London.

Excerpt from *Germinal* by Emile Zola, translation by Havelock Ellis. Everymans Library, 1933, revised 1946 edition. Reprinted by permission of Everymans Library, London.

Farrar, Straus & Giroux, Inc.

Excerpts reprinted by permission of Hill & Wang, a division of Farrar, Straus & Giroux Inc. from *Night*, by Elie Wiesel. Copyright © 1960 by MacGibbon & Kee. Copyright renewed © 1988 by The Collins Publishing Group.

"Love after Love," Reprinted by permission of Farrar, Straus & Giroux, Inc. from Derek Walcott, *Collected Poems* 1948–1984. Copyright © 1986 by Derek Walcott.

"Season," Reprinted by permission of Hill and Wang, a division of Farrar, Straus & Giroux, Inc. from *Idanre & Other Poems* by Wole Soyinka. Copyright © 1967 by Wole Soyinka.

Garland Publishing, Inc.

"Lady Maria, your worth and excellence," Bieris de Romans, from *The Writings of Medieval Women*, translated by Marcelle Thiebaux. Copyright © 1994 by Marcelle Thiebaux. Reprinted by permission of Garland Publishing, Inc.

Grove/Atlantic, Inc.

"The Bald Soprano," from *The Bald Soprano and Other Plays*, by Eugene Ionesco, translated by Donald Allen. Copyright © 1958 by Grove Press, Inc. Used by permission of Grove/Atlantic, Inc.

Harcourt Brace and Company

"The Street-Sweeping Show," from *Chrysanthemum and Other Stories*, by Feng Jicai, translated by Susan Wilf Chen, copyright © 1985 by Susan Wilf Chen, reprinted by permission of Harcourt Brace and Company.

"Lot's Wife," [by Anna Akhmatova]: from *Walking to Sleep: New Poems and Translations*, copyright © 1969 by Richard Wilbur, printed by permission Harcourt Brace & Company.

Scenes 3-7, Act 4, from *Tartuffe* by Moliere, English translation copyright © 1963, 1962, 1961 and renewed 1991, 1990, 1989 by Richard Wilbur, reprinted by permission of Harcourt Brace & Company. Caution: Professionals and amateurs are hereby warned that this translation, being fully protected under the copyright laws of the United States of America, the British Empire, including the Dominion of Canada, and all other countries which are signatories to the Universal Copyright Convention and the International Copyright Union is subject to royalty. All rights, including professional, amateur, motion picture, recitation, lecturing, public reading, radio broadcasting, and television, are strictly reserved. Particular emphasis is placed on the question of readings, permission for which must be secured in writing. Inquiries on professional rights should be addressed to Mr. Gilbert Parker, Curtis Brown Ltd., 10 Astor Place, New York, NY 10003. Inquiries on translation rights should be addressed to Harcourt Brace & Company, Permissions Dept., Orlando, FL 32887-6777. The amateur acting rights of *Tartuffe* are controlled exclusively by the Dramatists Play Service, Inc., 440 Park Ave. South, New York, NY. No amateur performance of the play may be given without obtaining in advance the written permission of the Dramatists Play Services, Inc. and paying of requisite fee.

Excerpt from *Being There*, copyright © 1970 by Jerzy Kosinski, reprinted by permission of Harcourt Brace & Company.

"The Garden of Stubborn Cats," from *Marcovaldo Or The Seasons in the City*, by Italo Calvino, copyright © 1963 by Giulio Einaudi editore, s.p.a., Torino, English translation copyright © 1983 by Harcourt Brace & Company, and Martin Secker and Warburg Ltd. Reprinted by permission of Harcourt Brace & Company.

Excerpt from *Orlando*, copyright 1928 by Virginia Woolf, copyright © renewed 1956 by Leonard Woolf, reprinted by permission of Harcourt Brace & Company.

Harold Ober Associates, Inc.

"A Doll's House," by Henrik Ibsen, from *The Plays of Ibsen, Volume I*, translated by Michael Meyer. Reprinted by permission of Harold Ober Associates, Inc. Copyright © 1965, 1974, 1980 by Michael Meyer.

HarperCollins Ltd

"The Man Who Fled from Azrael," and "The Elephant in the Dark House" from *Rumi Poet and Mystic* by Rumi, translated by Reynold A. Nicholson. HarperCollins Publishers Ltd.

HarperCollins Publishers, Inc.

All pages from "By Any Other Name," from *Gifts of Passage*, by Santha Rama Rau. Copyright © 1951 by Vasanthi Rama Rau Bowers. Reprinted by permission of HarperCollins Publishers, Inc. "By Any Other Name" originally appeared in *The New Yorker*.

"Tuesday Siesta," [all pages] from the *No One Writes to the Colonel* by Gabriel García Márquez. Copyright © 1968 in the English translation by Harper & Row, Publishers, Inc. Reprinted by permission of HarperCollins Publishers, Inc.

"Games at Twilight" from *Games at Twilight* by Anita Desai. Copyright © 1978 by Anita Desai. Reprinted by permission of HarperCollins Publishers, Inc.

Hendricks House

Excerpt from *The Prince and Other Works* by Niccolo Machiavelli, translated by Allan H. Gilbert. Reprinted by permission of Hendricks House.

Henry Holt & Co.

The Third Act from *Cyrano de Bergerac* by Edmund Rostand, translated by Brian Hooker. Copyright © 1923 by Henry Holt and Company, and © 1951 by Doris C. Hooker. Reprinted by permission of Henry Holt & Co.

The Hispanic Society of America, Inc.

"The Guitar" by Federico Garcia Lorca, from *Translations from Hispanic Poets*, ed. by Elizabeth du Gue Trapier. Reprinted by permission of The Hispanic Society of America.

Houghton Mifflin Company

"Ballade" from *The Poems of Francois Villon*, translated by Galway Kinnell. Copyright © 1965, 1977 by Galway Kinnell. Reprinted by permission of Houghton Mifflin Company. All rights reserved.

Indiana University Press

"I Built My Cottage Among the Habitations of Men," by T'ao Ch'ien [translated by Liu Wu-chi], from *An Introduction to Chinese Literature* by Liu Wu-chi, p. 64. Copyright © 1966 by Liu Wu-chi. Reprinted by permission of Indiana University Press.

"The Story of Actaeon," from *Metamorphoses* by Ovid, pp. 61–64, translated by Rolfe Humphries. Copyright © 1955 Indiana University Press. Reprinted by permission.

"Apollo and Daphne," from *Metamorphoses* by Ovid, pp. 16–21, translated by Rolfe Humphries. Copyright © 1955 by Indiana University Press. Reprinted by permission.

International Creative Management, Inc.

Excerpt from *The Bluest Eye*, by Toni Morrison. Copyright © 1970 by Henry Holt & Co. Reprinted by permission of International Creative Management, Inc.

Joan Daves Agency

"The Flower of Air," copyright © 1961 by Doris Dana. Reprinted by arrangement with Doris Dana, c/o Joan Daves Agency as agent for the proprietor.

John Johnson Ltd

"Snapshots of a Wedding" from *The Collector of Treasures*, by Bessie Head. Published by Heinemann in their African Writers Series. Copyright © The Estate of Bessie Head, 1977. Used by permission of John Johnson Ltd., London.

John Reed and Clive Wake

"And We Shall Be Steeped" from *Nocturnes*, by Leopold Senghor, translated by John Reed and Clive Wake. Copyright © 1971 by John Reed and Clive Wake.

Kamala Markandaya

Excerpt from *Nectar in a Sieve*, by Kamala Markandaya.

Liveright Publishing Corporation

"The Nose," from *Japanese Short Stories*, by Ryunosuke Akutagawa, translated by Takashi Kojima. Translation copyright © 1961 by Liveright Publishing Corporation. Reprinted by permission of Liveright Publishing Corporation.

Louise Maude and Aylmer Maude

Excerpt from "The Death of Iván Ilyich," by Leo Tolstoy, translated by Louise Maude and Aylmer Maude, from *The Norton Anthology of World Masterpieces, Vol II.*

Luisa Valenzuela

"The Censors," by Luisa Valenzuela, from *Short Stories*, edited by Irving Howe and Hana Howe, translated by David Unger. Copyright by Luisa Valenzuela.

Macmillan London

Excerpts from *Don Quixote de La Mancha*, by Miguel de Cervantes Saavedra, translated by Walter Starkie. Macmillan London, 1957. Reprinted by permission of the publisher.

Macmillan NY

Excerpt "The Little Heidelberg," reprinted with the permission of Scribner, a division of Simon & Schuster from *The Stories of Eva Luna*, by Isabel Allende, translated by Margaret Sayers Peden. Copyright © 1989 by Isabel Allende. English translation © 1991 by Macmillan Publishing Company.

Madhavikutty (Kamala Das)

Excerpt "Rice Pudding," by Madhavikutty (Kamala Das), from Susie Tharu and K. Lalita, (Eds.), *Women Writing in India 600 B.C. to the Present, Vol II*, pp. 395–397. Reprinted by permission of the author.

Marx Aveling

Excerpt from *Madame Bovary* by Gustave Flaubert, translated by Marx Aveling. Harper & Brothers, 1950.

Morris Bishop

Sonnet 90 "The Eyes That Drew from Me," by Francis Petrarch, translated by Morris Bishop from *The Norton Anthology of World Masterpieces, Vol 1*.

National Textbook Company

"The Five Worlds and Their Suns" [anonymous], from *World Mythology, 2nd*, ed. by Donna Rosenberg. Copyright © 1994, 1986 by NTC Publishing Group. Reprinted by permission.

Excerpt from the "Sunjata" from *World Mythology, 2nd*, ed. by Donna Rosenberg. Copyright © 1994, 1986 by NTC Publishing Group. Reprinted by permission.

New Directions Publishing Corp.

"The River-Merchant's Wife: A Letter," [Li Po] by Ezra Pound, from *Personsae*. Copyright © 1926 by Ezra Pound. Reprinted by permission of New Directions Publishing Corp.

"A Refusal to Mourn the Death by Fire of a Child in London," by Dylan Thomas from *The Collected Poems of Dylan Thomas*. Copyright © 1945 by The Trustees for the Copyrights of Dylan Thomas. Reprinted by permission of New Directions Publishing Corp.

New Hungarian Quarterly

"Crazed Man in Concentration Camp," by Ágnes Gergeley, translated by Edwin Morgan. © Edwin Morgan and *New Hungarian Quarterly*. Reprinted by permission of Hungarian News Agency/*New Hungarian Quarterly*.

Oxford University Press UK

"The Bet" Copyright © 1980 by Ronald Hingley. Reprinted from *The Oxford Chekhov, Vol 4, Stories from 1888–1889*, translated by Ronald Hingley (1980) by permission of Oxford University Press, London.

Pantheon Books / Schocken Books

"Though I am Laila of the Persian romance," by Princess Zeb-un-Nissa [1638–1702]: From *A Book of Women Poets from Antiquity to Now*, by Aliki Barnstone and Willis Barnstone, editors. Copyright © 1980, 1992 by Schocken Books. Reprinted by permission of Schocken Books, distributed by Pantheon Books, a division of Random House, Inc.

"Your love turned . . . ," by Empress Nur Jahan [?–1646]: From *A Book of Women Poets from Antiquity to Now*, by Aliki Barnstone and Willis Barnstone, editors. Copyright © 1980, 1992 by Schocken Books. Reprinted by permission of Schocken Books, distributed by Pantheon Books, a division of Random House, Inc.

"Of Autumn," by Veronica Porumbacu: *From A Book of Women Poets from Antiquity to Now*, by Aliki Barnstone and Willis Barnstone, editors. Copyright © 1980, 1992 by Schocken Books. Reprinted by permission of Schocken Books, distributed by Pantheon Books, a division of Random House, Inc.

"The Metamorphosis," from *Franz Kafka 1883–1924 The Complete Stories*, edited by Nahum N. Glatzer. Copyright © 1946, 1947, 1948, 1949, 1954, 1958, 1971 by Schocken Books, Inc. Reprinted by permission of Schocken Books, distributed by Pantheon Books, a division of Random House, Inc.

Sonnet 23 by Louise Labé: From *A Book of Women Poets from Antiquity to Now*, by Aliki Barnstone and Willis Barnstone, editors. Copyright © 1980, 1992 by Schocken Books. Reprinted by permission of Schocken Books, distributed by Pantheon Books, a division of Random House, Inc.

Penguin Books Ltd. Penguin UK

"Pericles' Funeral Oration," from *History of the Peloponnesian War*, by Thucydides, translated by Rex Warner (Penguin Classics 1954). Translation copyright © 1954 by Rex Warner. Reproduced by permission of Penguin Books Ltd.

Excerpt from *The Epic of Gilgamesh*, [anonymous] English version by N. K. Sandars (Penguin Classics 1960, Second revised edition 1972). Copyright © 1960, 1964, 1972 by N. K. Sandars. Reproduced by permission of Penguin Books Ltd.

"Creation Hymn" from *The Rig Veda*, translated by Wendy Doniger O'Flaherty (Penguin Classics 1981). Copyright © 1981 by Wendy Doniger O'Flaherty. Reproduced by permission of Penguin Books Ltd.

"The Death of Socrates" from the *The Last Days of Socrates* by Plato, translation by Hugh Tredennick, revised by Harold Tarrant (Penguin Classics 1954, revised translation 1993) copyright © Hugh Tredennick, 1954, 1959, 1969 and revised by Harold Tarrant copyright © 1993. Reproduced by permission of Penguin Books Ltd.

Excerpt from *Herodotus The Histories*, translated by Aubrey de Selincourt revised by A. R. Burn (Penguin Classics 1954, revised edition 1972) copyright © the Estate of Aubrey de Selincourt, 1954, copyright © 1972 A. R. Burn. Reproduced by permission of Penguin Books Ltd.

Excerpt from "The Story of the Grail-Perceval" in *Arthurian Romances* by Chrétien de Troyes, translated by William W. Kibler (Penguin Classics, 1991). Translation copyright © 1991 by William W. Kibler. Reproduced by permission of Penguin Books, Ltd.

Excerpt "The Love Potion," from *Tristan* by Gottfried von Strassburg, translated by A. T. Hatto (Penguin Classics 1960, revised edition 1967) copyright © A. T. Hatto, 1960. Reproduced by permission of Penguin Books, Ltd.

Excerpts "The Exordium," "The Cataclysm," "Daylight" from *The Koran*, translated by N. A. Dawood (Penguin Classics 1956, Fifth revised edition 1990) copyright © 1956, 1959, 1966, 1968, 1974, 1990 by N. A. Dawood. Reproduced by permission of Penguin Books, Ltd.

"The Fisherman and the Jinnee," from *Tales From the Thousand and One Nights*, translated by N. J. Dawood (Penguin Classics 1954, revised edition 1973). Translation copyright © 1954, 1973 by N. J. Dawood. Penguin Classics, 1955. Reproduced by permission of Penguin Books, Ltd.

Excerpt "I have resolved on . . . ," from *The Confessions of Jean-Jacques Rousseau*, translated by J. M. Cohen (Penguin Classics 1953) copyright © 1954 by J. M. Cohen. Reproduced by permission of Penguin Books, Ltd.

Penguin USA

"Conversation with an American Writer," from *Yevtushenko Poems*, by Yevgeny Yevtushenko, translated by Herbert Marshall. Translation copyright © 1966 by E. P. Dutton. Used by permission of Dutton Signet, a division of Penguin Books USA, Inc.

Excerpt from the *Iliad*, by Homer, translation by Robert Fagles. Translation copyright © 1990 Robert Fagles. Used by permission of Viking Penguin Books, a division of Penguin Books USA, Inc.

"At Last," "But Not Everyone Wants Love," "I Think of Achilles," "It Gives Me Joy to Think," "Let's Not Pretend," "Life Slips By," "Many Have Been Cheated by Oblivion," "Love Songs" from *Love Songs of Sappho*, by Paul Roche, translator. Translated by Paul Roche, Translation copyright © 1966, 1991 by Paul Roche. Used by permission of Dutton Signet, a division of Penguin Books USA, Inc.

"The Book of Sand" from *The Book of Sand* by Jorges Luis Borges, translated by Norman Thomas di Giovanni. Translation copyright © 1971, 1975, 1976, 1977 by Emece Editores, S.A. and Norman Thomas di Giovanni. Used by permission of Dutton Signet, a division of Penguin Books USA, Inc.

"Araby" from *Dubliners* by James Joyce. Copyright 1916 by B. W. Heubach. Definitive text Copyright © 1967 by the Estate of James Joyce. Used by permission of Viking Penguin, a division of Penguin Books USA, Inc.

"Tonight I Can Write" from *Twenty Love Poems and A Song of Despair* by Pablo Neruda, translated by W. S. Merwin. Translation copyright © 1969 by W. S. Merwin. Used by permission of Penguin Books USA, Inc.

Random House, Inc.

Excerpt "The Passion of Queen Dido," from *The Aeneid*, [by Publius Vergilius Maro (Virgil)]. Translated by Robert Fitzgerald. Translation copyright © 1980, 1982, 1983 by Robert Fitzgerald. Reprinted by permission of Random House, Inc.

Sonnet 3: "It Was the Morning," from *Petrarch's Sonnets* by Francis Petrarch, translated by Joseph Auslander. Copyright © 1931 by Longmans, Green & Co. Reprinted by permission of Random House, Inc.

"The Iguana" from *Out of Africa*, by Isak Dinesen. Copyright © 1937 by Random House, Inc. Copyright renewed 1965 by Rungstedlundfonden. Reprinted by permission of Random House, Inc.

"Julius Caesar" and "Mark Antony" from *The Lives of the Noble Grecians and Romans* (Plutarch). The Dryden translation, revised by Arthur Hugh Clough. Modern Library, a division of Random House. Reprinted by permission of Random House, Inc.

Excerpts from "White Tigers" from *The Woman Warrior: Memoirs of a Girlhood Among Ghosts*, by Maxine Hong Kingston. Copyright © 1975, 1976 by Maxine Hong Kingston. Reprinted by permission of Random House, Inc.

Simon & Schuster

Excerpt reprinted with the permission of Simon & Schuster from *Popol Vuh* [anonymous], by Dennis Tedlock, translator. Copyright © 1985 by Dennis Tedlock.

Excerpt from *Kaffir Boy*: Reprinted with the permission of Simon &

Schuster from *Kaffir Boy* by Mark Mathabane. Copyright © 1986 by Mark Mathabane.

"The Gardener," XXXVIII: Reprinted with the permission of Simon & Schuster from *The Gardener* by Rabindranath Tagore. Copyright © 1913 by Macmillan Publishing Company, renewed 1941 by Rabindranth Tagore.

"The Shoes" by Grazia Deledda, translated by Althea Graham: Reprinted with the permission of Simon & Schuster from *The Copeland Translations*, edited by Charles Townsend Copeland. Copyright © 1934 by Charles Townsend Copeland. Copyright renewed © 1962 by Charles F. Dunbar.

Sinolingua

Excerpts from *Analects of Confucius*. Copyright © 1994 by Sinolingua, Beijing, China. Reprinted by permission.

Stanford University Press

"In the lingering wake": Reprinted from *Kokin Wakashu: The First Imperial Anthology of Japanese Poetry*. Translated and annotated by Helen Craig McCullough, with permission of the publishers, Stanford University Press. Copyright © 1985 by the Board of Trustees of the Leland Stanford Junior University.

"the old pond," "the sound of the water jar," and "the first snow": Reprinted from *Bashō and His Interpreters: Selected Hokku With Commentary*, by Makoto Ueda with permission of the publishers, Stanford University Press. Copyright © 1992 by the Board of Trustees of the Leland Stanford Junior University.

"Of Cannibals": Reprinted from *The Complete Essays of Montaigne*, translated by Donald M. Frame, with permission of the publishers, Stanford University Press. Copyright © 1958 by the Board of Trustees of the Leland Stanford Junior University.

The Ecco Press

"Penelope's Despair" from *Exile & Return: Selected Poems (1967–1974)* by Yannis Ritsos, translated by Edmund Keeley. Copyright © 1985 by Edmund Keeley. Reprinted by permission of The Ecco Press.

"the snow is melting" and "in the summer rain," from *The Essential Haiku*, edited and translations by Robert Hass. Copyright © 1994 by Robert Hass. Reprinted by permission of The Ecco Press.

"A Song on the End of the World" from *The Collected Poems 1931–1987* by Czeslaw Milosz, translated by Antony Milosz. Copyright © 1988 by Czeslaw Milosz Royalties, Inc. Reprinted by permission of The Ecco Press.

University of California Press

Excerpts from *Ramayana*, by William Buck. Copyright © 1976 by The Regents of the University of California. Reprinted by permission of the University of California Press.

University of Chicago Press

Excerpts from *Oedipus the King* by Sophocles, translated by David Grene, from D. Grene and R. Lattimore (Eds.) *Complete Greek Tragedies*. Copyright © 1954 by The University of Chicago. Reprinted by permission of the University of Chicago Press.

University of Oklahoma Press

"Hymn to the Sun," [Akhenaten], from *Echoes of Egyptian Voices*, translated by John L. Foster. Copyright © 1992 by John L. Foster. University of Oklahoma Press. Reprinted by permission of the publisher.

University of Pittsburgh Press

"Loreley" from *Heinrich Heine: Lyric Poems and Ballads*, translated by Ernst Feise. Copyright © 1961, 1989 by University of Pittsburgh Press. Reprinted by permission of University of Pittsburgh Press.

Victor Hugo

Excerpt from *Les Misérables*, by Victor Hugo. The Century Company, 1908.

W. W. Norton & Company, Inc.

"Canto 1 of The Inferno" by Dante Alighieri, from *The Divine Comedy*, translated by John Ciardi. Translation copyright © 1954, 1957, 1959, 1960, 1961, 1965, 1967, 1970 by the Ciardi Family Publishing Trust. Reprinted by permission of W. W. Norton & Company, Inc.

Stanzas 104, 105, 110, 128–29, 132–34, 152–53, 156–58, 168–70, 174–76 from *The Song of Roland*, by Frederick Goldin, translator. Copyright © 1978 by W. W. Norton & Company, Inc. Reprinted by permission of W. W. Norton & Company, Inc.

To "Free-Spirited Fisherman" [Li Ch'ing Chao] from *An Anthology of Chinese Literature, Beginnings to 1911* by Stephen Owen, ed. and translator. Copyright © 1996 by Stephen Owen and The Council for Cultural Planning and Development of the Executive Yuan of the Republic of China, by W. W. Norton & Company, Inc. Reprinted by permission of W. W. Norton & Company, Inc.

"Federigo's Falcon," from *The Decameron*, by Giovanni Boccaccio, translated by Mark Musa and Peter Bondanella. Reprinted by permission of W. W. Norton & Company. Copyright © 1982 by Mark Musa and Peter Bondanella.

William L. Grossman

"Metonymy, or the Husband's Revenge," by Rachel de Queiroz from *Modern Brazilian Short Stories*, translated by William L. Grossman, University of California Press.

Yale University Press

"Inanna and Ishkur," adapted by Willis and Aliki Barnstone from the translation by William W. Hallo and J. J. A. van Dijk in *The Exaltation of Inanna*. Copyright © 1968 by Yale University. Reprinted by permission of Yale University Press.

Yehuda Amichai

"If I Forget Thee, Jerusalem," by Yehuda Amichai, translated by Assis Gutmann.

Zephyr Press

"Requiem," from *The Complete Poems of Anna Akhmatova*, translated by Judith Hemschemeyer. Copyright © 1989 by Judith Hemschemeyer. Reprinted by permission of Zephyr Press.